MW00861580

JONES & BARTLETT LEARNING
CDX Automotive

We support ASE
program certification
through
ASE NATEF
Improving Programs
Through Certification

FUNDAMENTALS OF

Automotive Maintenance and Light Repair

Kirk T. VanGelder
ASE Certified Master Automotive Technician & L1
NATEF Evaluation Team Leader
Certified Automotive Service Instructor
Vancouver, Washington, USA

Ian W. Andrew
I Eng, CMILT, MSAE, MIAME, MIRTE, MSOE
Brisbane, Queensland, Australia

JONES & BARTLETT
LEARNING

World Headquarters
Jones & Bartlett Learning
5 Wall Street
Burlington, MA 01803
978-443-5000
info@jblearning.com
www.jblearning.com

Jones & Bartlett Learning books and products are available through most bookstores and online booksellers. To contact Jones & Bartlett Learning directly, call 800-832-0034, fax 978-443-8000, or visit our website, www.jblearning.com.

Substantial discounts on bulk quantities of Jones & Bartlett Learning publications are available to corporations, professional associations, and other qualified organizations. For details and specific discount information, contact the special sales department at Jones & Bartlett Learning via the above contact information or send an email to specialsales@jblearning.com.

Production Credits
Chief Executive Officer: Ty Field
President: James Homer
Chief Product Officer: Eduardo Moura
Executive Publisher—CDX and Electrical: Vernon Anthony
Acquisitions Editor—CDX: Ian Andrew
Editorial Management: B-Books, Ltd. Developmental Editor: Jamie Bryant
Production Manager: Susan P. Beckett
Senior Marketing Manager: Brian Rooney
V.P., Manufacturing and Inventory Control: Therese Connell
Composition: B-books, Ltd.
Cover Design: Kristin E. Parker
Cover Image: © Mikhail Bakunovich/Shutterstock, Inc.
Rights & Photo Research Manager: Lauren Miller
Printing and Binding: Courier Companies
Cover Printing: Courier Companies

Photo Credits
Chapter 1: 1.1 © Universal History Arc/age fotostock; 1.2 © Courtesy Everett Col/age fotostock; 1.3 © Rainer Plendl/ShutterStock, Inc.; 1.4 Courtesy of Shoreline Community College, Seattle, Washington. *Chapter 2:* 2.CO © GlowImages/Alamy Images; 2.1A © William Attard McCarthy/ShutterStock, Inc.; 2.1B © Rob Wilson/ShutterStock, Inc.; 2.2 © Maksim Toome/ShutterStock, Inc.; 2.3 © Rob Wilson/ShutterStock, Inc.; 2.4 © Maksim Toome/ShutterStock, Inc.; 2.5 © Michael Shake/ShutterStock, Inc.; 2.6 © Maksim Toome/ShutterStock, Inc.; 2.7 © Transtock Inc./Alamy Images; 2.8 © Brad Sauter/ShutterStock, Inc.; 2.9 © Alvey & Towers Picture Library/Alamy Images; 2.10 © Maksim Toome/ShutterStock, Inc.; 2.21A © Gordan Milic/ShutterStock, Inc. *Chapter 3:* 3.12 © Guy Croft SciTech/Alamy Images; 3.13 Courtesy of CRC Industries. *Chapter 4:* 4.16 © Picsfive/ShutterStock, Inc.; *Chapter 7:* 7.2 Courtesy of Rob Schnepp. *Chapter 12:* 12.4 © Vasily Smirnov/ShutterStock, Inc. *Chapter 17:* 17.1 © Bettmann/Corbis/AP Photos; 17.2 © National Motor Museum/age fotostock; 17.13 © Kosarev; Alexander/ShutterStock, Inc.; 17.14 © sydeen/ShutterStock, Inc.; 17.19 © William Ju/ShutterStock, Inc. *Chapter 18:* 18.13C © Engine Photos/ShutterStock, Inc. *Chapter 33:* 33.12 © 2003-2012 Snap-on Incorporated; All rights reserved. *Chapter 35:* 35.1 © Radoslaw Lecyk/Shutterstock.com. *Chapter 41:* 41.1 Image courtesy of the U.S. Department of Energy

Unless otherwise indicated, all photographs and illustrations are under copyright of Jones & Bartlett Learning, courtesy of Snap-on, Incorporated, or have been provided by the authors.

Copyright © 2015 by Jones & Bartlett Learning, LLC, an Ascend Learning Company

All rights reserved. No part of the material protected by this copyright may be reproduced or utilized in any form, electronic or mechanical, including photocopying, recording, or by any information storage and retrieval system, without written permission from the copyright owner.

Fundamentals of Automotive Maintenance and Light Repair is an independent publication and has not been authorized, sponsored, or otherwise approved by the owners of the trademarks or service marks referenced in this product.

Some images in this book feature models. These models do not necessarily endorse, represent, or participate in the activities represented in the images.

The procedures and protocols in this book are based on the most current recommendations of responsible sources. The publisher, however, makes no guarantee as to, and assumes no responsibility for, the correctness, sufficiency, or completeness of such information or recommendations. Other or additional safety measures may be required under particular circumstances.

For every task, the following safety requirements must be strictly enforced: Comply with personal and environmental safety practices associated with clothing and eye protection; hand tools; power equipment; proper ventilation; and the handling, storage, and disposal of chemicals/materials in accordance with local, state, and federal safety and environmental regulations.

ISBN: 978-1-284-05673-0

Library of Congress Cataloging-in-Publication Data Unavailable at Time of Printing

6048

Printed in the United States of America
17 16 15 14   10 9 8 7 6 5 4 3 2 1

BRIEF CONTENTS

CONTENTS

SECTION 2 Engine Repair

SECTION 3 Automatic Transmission

SECTION 6 Brakes

SECTION 7 Electrical

SECTION 8 Heating and Air Conditioning

SECTION 9 Engine Performance

CHAPTER 39 Induction and Exhaust 1098
Introduction 1100
The Intake System 1100
The Exhaust System 1111
Diagnosis and Testing 1116

ACKNOWLEDGMENTS

CDX Automotive would like to thank the following individuals and organizations for their contributions to this textbook.

Editorial Board

Bob Rodriguez
Bob Rodriguez and Associates, LLC
Round Hill, Virginia

Keith Santini
Addison Trail High School
Addison, Illinois

Kevin Jesser
Lake MacDonald, Queensland
Australia

Merle Saunders
Nyssa, Oregon

Tim Dunn
Sydney, New South Wales
Australia

Contributors

Aims Community College
Greeley, Colorado

Addison Trail High School
Addison, Illinois

Larry Baker
Aims Community College
Greeley, Colorado

Ron Beaumont
Brisbane, Queensland
Australia

Roy Belding
King Limousine Service
King of Prussia, Pennsylvania

Michael Broud
Heritage High School
Palm Bay, Florida

Walter Brueggeman
Tidewater Community College
Chesapeake, Virginia

Casey's Independent Auto Repair
Vancouver, Washington

Kent Chambers
Northwest Technical Institute
Lowell, Arkansas

Sean Chesney
Vancouver, Washington

CJC Auto Parts
Lombard, Illinois

Clark College
Vancouver, Washington

Clark County Skills Center
Vancouver, Washington

Roger Duvall
Grayson County Technology Center
Leitchfield, Kentucky

John Frala
Rio Hondo Community College
Whittier, California

Fraser Automotive
Plainfield, Illinois

Brandon Fryman
Denver, Colorado

Tony Gumushian
Prairie State High School
Chicago, Illinois

Haggerty Automotive Group
Glen Ellyn, Illinois

Kaz Harris
Brisbane, Queensland
Australia

Ed Heim
Battleground High School
Yacolt, Washington

Kelly Herbert
WarrenTech
Arvada, Colorado

Nancy Hoffman
Dover, New Hampshire

Jim Hunnicutt
F. H. Peterson Academies of Technology
Jacksonville, Florida

Matthew Lamperd
Brisbane, Queensland
Australia

Les Schwab Tire Centers
Battle Ground, Washington
Orchards, Washington

McCord's Vancouver Toyota
Vancouver, Washington

Tom Millard
WarrenTech
Arvada, Colorado

Jennifer Miller
Port St. Lucie, Florida

Jesse Mitchell
Stark State College
North Canton, Ohio

Joe Moore
Southern Maine Community College
Portland, Maine

Kevin Murphy
Stark State College
North Canton, Ohio

Jeffrey Rehkhopf
Florida State College
Jacksonville, Florida

Ron's Automotive
Vancouver, Washington

David Sitchler
Burlington County Institute of Technology
Westampton, New Jersey

Emma Spencer
Brisbane, Queensland
Australia

Russ Strayline
Abington, Pennsylvania

Warren Tech
Lakewood, Colorado

Reviewers

Michael A. Broud
Heritage High School
Palm Bay, Florida

Timothy Campbell
Wenatchee Valley Technical Center
Wenatchee, Washington

Matt Carpenter
Southern Alberta Institute of Technology
Calgary, Alberta
Canada

Frederick Cole
Tidewater Community College
Chesapeake, Virginia

Brett Colston
Oconee Fall Line Technical College
Dublin, Georgia

Al Cox
Metropolitan Community College
Omaha, Nebraska

Joe Cruz
Tennessee Department of Education/CTE
Nashville, Tennessee

Seth DeArmond
Indianapolis Public Schools Career Technology Magnet
Indianapolis, Indiana

Ken Dunn
Liverpool Community College
Everton, Liverpool
United Kingdom

Robert William Evans
Yankton Senior High School
Yankton, South Dakota

Hervey Forward
OCM BOCES, McEvoy Campus
Cortland, New York

Jerry Friesen
Brooks Composite High School
Brooks, Alberta
Canada

Joshua E. George
The Billings Career Center
Billings, Montana

Joe Glassford
Vested, LLC
Sunriver, Oregon

Curtis J. Goodwin
Northwest Kansas Technical College
Goodland, Kansas

Alan Grant
Westlake High School
Westlake Village, California

Allan Haberman
Blue Streak-Hygrade Motor Products
Winnipeg, Manitoba
Canada

Ben Haggeman
Southern Alberta Institute of Technology
Calgary, Alberta
Canada

Wade Hansma
West Central High School
Rocky Mountain House, Alberta
Canada

Kaz Harris
Brisbane, Queensland
Australia

Chance Henderson
Dauphin Regional Comprehensive Secondary School
Dauphin, Manitoba
Canada

Reginald Hildebrand
Assiniboine Community College
Brandon, Manitoba
Canada

Todd Hills
Northeast Iowa Community College
Calmar, Iowa

Robert Holm
Walla Walla University
College Place, Washington

David Howell
Tidewater Community College Regional
Chesapeake, Virginia

Kevin Human
Tennessee Technology Center at Harriman
Harriman, Tennessee

Tim Isaac
Foothills Composite High School
Okotoks, Alberta
Canada

Robert Jackson
Copper Mountain College
Joshua Tree, California

Shawn Klemm
Iowa Lakes Community College
Algona, Iowa
Algona High School
Algona, Iowa

Mark P. Lammers
Ivy Tech Community College
Evansville, Indiana

Harry Lewis
Niagara College
Niagara Falls, Ontario
Canada

Robbie Lindhorst
Southeastern Illinois College
Harrisburg, Illinois

Katherine Luhman
Montana State University
Billings College of Technology
Billings, Montana

David Macholz
Suffolk County Community College
Eastern Suffolk BOCES, Edward J. Milliken Technical Center
Oakdale, New York

Andy Murray
Motherwell College
Motherwell, United Kingdom

Michael Myrowich
Red River College
Winnipeg, Manitoba
Canada

Larry Nobles
Tidewater Community College
Portsmouth, Virginia

Raymond H. Oviyach
Consultant, Automotive Vocational & Technical Education
Kingwood, Texas

Joseph Palazzolo
GKN Driveline
Commerce Township, Michigan

Katherine Pfau
Montana State University
Billings, Montana

Jeffrey Rehkopf
Florida State College
Jacksonville, Florida

Mark Ridgeway
Gates Corporation
Denver, Colorado

Jon Severson
Sioux Falls Career and Technical Education Academy
Sioux Falls, South Dakota

Matthew Shanahan
College of DuPage
Bartlett, Illinois

Mark Spisak
Central Piedmont Community College
Joe Hendrick Center for Automotive Excellence
Charlotte, North Carolina

Jim Stafford
Tennessee Technology Center at Newbern
Newbern, Tennessee

Don Sykora
Morton College
Cicero, Illinois

Shane Taplin
Wellington Institute of Technology
Lower Hutt, Wellington
New Zealand

Donald Thompson
Florida State College
Jacksonville, Florida

Rob Thompson
South-Western Career Academy
Grove City, Ohio

Joe Wash
Clifton High School
Clifton, New Jersey
Lincoln Technical Institute
Union, New Jersey

Bill Weber
Seminole State College of Florida
Sanford, Florida

David W. Wharf
Thompson Rivers University
Kamloops, British Columbia
Canada

Kenneth Wurster
SUNY Canton
Canton, New York

Peter Zifovich
Campbelltown, New South Wales
Australia

Marty Zuzens
Assiniboine Community College
Brandon, Manitoba
Canada

DELL
DELL

SECTION I

Safety and Foundation

CHAPTER 1

KNOW
SEE
DO
PROVE

NATEF Tasks

There are no NATEF tasks for this chapter.

KNOW
SEE
DO
PROVE

Knowledge Objectives

After reading this chapter, you will be able to:

1. Outline the history of motor vehicles and their maintenance requirements. (pp 6–7)
2. Describe the roles and responsibilities of a:
   - lube technician (p 8)
   - light line technician (p 8)
   - heavy line technician (p 8)
   - chassis and brake technician (pp 8–10)
   - electrical technician (p 10)
   - drivability technician (p 11)
   - transmission specialist (p 11)
   - shop foreman (p 11)
   - service consultant (p 11)
   - service manager (p 12)
3. Describe the types of repair facilities. (pp 12–13)
4. Describe ASE certification and NATEF accreditation. (pp 13–14)

Careers in Automotive Technology

Know
See
Do
Prove

Skills Objectives

There are no skills objectives for this chapter.

Introduction

Early vehicles were very basic machines with engines that were started by manually operating a crank handle. The maintenance requirements of these early vehicles were vastly different from the highly technical requirements of modern vehicles. As vehicle technology has developed over time, the maintenance requirements have changed. Although the basic systems on the early vehicles and today's vehicles are the same—ignition, cooling, engine, drive train, suspension, and lubrication—the systems on modern vehicles are much more sophisticated and reliable. Modern vehicles travel much greater distances between maintenance appointments than their predecessors. For example, it is not unusual for a vehicle manufacturer to require maintenance at 7500- to 10,000-mile (12,000- to 16,000-km) intervals. And there is a push to extend maintenance intervals even further as new oils are being developed. In fact, some manufacturers are predicting maintenance intervals of 25,000 miles (40,000 km) in the near future; in comparison, some earlier vehicles required maintenance every 1000 miles (1600 km).

TECHNICIAN TIP

Service or maintenance intervals will also be influenced by the severity of operating conditions; the more severe the conditions, the more frequent the required maintenance. Most service information gives both a normal-duty and a severe-duty maintenance schedule.

A Brief History of the Automobile

In the late 1800s, several engineers were working on the concept and design of the automobile. Karl Benz is generally acknowledged to have invented the modern automobile around 1885 **FIGURE 1-1**. In those early days, the concept of the automobile continued to develop, with many inventors producing various models. The early versions of the automobile were little more than horse carriages converted into automobiles with engines. These early automobiles tended to be unreliable and expensive and were considered a novelty that only the wealthy could afford.

FIGURE 1-1 Karl Benz is generally acknowledged to have invented the modern automobile around 1885.

You Are the Automotive Technician

A customer brings her 2012 V6 Dodge Minivan to the dealership for its 15,000 mile oil change. After pulling the vehicle into the bay, you set the vehicle safely on the hydraulic hoist. Next, you reference the computer to check the service history and any technical service bulletins (TSBs) or recalls for the vehicle. All previous service has been performed according to the schedule and there are no TSBs or recalls for the vehicle. You then verify the manufacturer's scheduled maintenance recommendations for the mileage on the vehicle and find that the tires also need to be rotated and the air filter inspected. After you complete the tire rotation, you use the hydraulic hoist to raise the vehicle and then proceed to perform the oil and filter change. First, you drain and dispose of the old oil, remove and replace the filter, and then you add 4.5 quarts of new oil. When finished, you check all of the fluids, belts, hoses, and air filter and find them to be in good condition. You reset the oil life monitor on the vehicle, clean your area, return tools to the proper location, and process the customer's invoice with notes from your inspection, tire rotation, and oil change. You then review all work and the invoice with the customer. You thank the customer for her business and provide her with a reminder sticker to return at the next scheduled maintenance date and mileage.

1. If you had noticed a worn belt or hose during the oil change, which type of technician would you have asked to look at the vehicle?
2. In your shop, who is responsible for keeping track of the work that is performed on customer vehicles?

In the early 1900s, the advent of mass production made automobiles available to a wider community FIGURE 1-2. Henry Ford applied two concepts that helped make the Model T affordable for the masses. The first was the concept of "interchangeability," which meant parts did not have to be custom built to match a particular car. Each part was made to the same specification so it would fit properly with its related parts. Thus, parts did not have to be produced where the vehicle was being assembled; they could be stockpiled, ready for later use. The second concept was the assembly line. Instead of the workers moving to the car as it was being assembled, the assembly line brought the car to the worker. This approach made assembly much more efficient, increasing the number of vehicles that could be built in a shift and thereby lowering production costs. Developments over the ensuing years produced more powerful and reliable automobiles, and with the further development of larger, more reliable gasoline engines, they became the predominant mode of personal transportation.

Vehicle Manufacturing

Vehicle manufacturing developed from small independent makers in the late 1800s, which relied on large amounts of labor and limited automation, to the present methods, which use large-scale production lines and extensive automation. The globalization of the automotive industry has seen manufacturers sharing models and making vehicles that are sold across the world. Modern assembly lines require large-scale investments, so manufacturers must be sure that a new vehicle model will succeed in the market before they will invest billions of dollars in production line retooling FIGURE 1-3.

Today's vehicles are assembled on high-volume production lines, with robots used for many of the assembly processes, including welding seams. Assemblers continue to work up and down the assembly line doing tasks that are still far too complicated for robotic assembly. Often, various parts of the vehicle are made by large-scale parts manufacturers who supply the parts to the specific vehicle manufacturer's specifications. Vehicle manufacturing is a high-volume business, so everything needs to work in the correct timing and sequence, from the supply of parts required to build a vehicle, right down to the speed at which the production line runs. Modern vehicle plants use sophisticated technology to mass produce a product that is high quality and affordable.

Technology in Vehicles

Technology in vehicles continues to adapt and change as new research and development reach the production line. The automotive sector is very competitive and has been influenced over the years by competition between manufacturers, consumer expectations for increased technology, and, in more recent times, the need to reduce the impact on the environment. The modern vehicle contains complex electrical, electronic, and mechanical systems designed to improve efficiency, reduce emissions, and provide safety to vehicle passengers. The use of technology will continue to increase in the future as the automotive industry responds to the current pressures of climate change and the ever-decreasing availability and increasing cost of crude oil–based products like oil, gas, and diesel.

FIGURE 1-2 The assembly line was essential in the mass production of vehicles.

FIGURE 1-3 Modern assembly lines require large-scale investments in high-tech equipment.

Careers in the Automotive Sector

The automotive sector provides for numerous career choices within the service, retail, and manufacturing industries. The automotive manufacturing sector provides a number of career choices, from factory workers and assemblers to design engineers and senior administrators FIGURE 1-4. In the service and retail sector, occupations range from maintenance/service technicians, light vehicle technicians, and heavy vehicle technicians to service advisors and service managers. As technical complexity has grown in modern vehicles, so has the need for more specialized job roles. For example, there is now a need for hybrid technicians, who service the systems on hybrid vehicles.

Lube Technician

Lube technicians carry out all aspects of manufacturer-scheduled maintenance activities on a range of vehicle components, such as the lubrication system FIGURE 1-5. Lube technicians change oil and filters and carry out lubrication, fluid inspection, fluid service, and tire rotations. While performing these duties, lube technicians also perform a visual inspection of the vehicle, looking for any other service needs such as worn belts, hoses, and suspension system parts. When servicing vehicles, lube technicians are required to raise vehicles using hydraulic hoists or jacks and to use hand tools.

In addition, lube technicians may have to complete time cards or scheduled maintenance paperwork. They may be required to assist other types of technicians with dismantling or removing engine assemblies, transmissions, steering mechanisms, and other components; repairing or replacing worn or defective parts; and reassembling mechanical components. Finally, lube technicians are responsible for keeping their workspace, tools, and equipment clean and organized.

FIGURE 1-5 Lube technicians are responsible for carrying out all aspects of the standard manufacturer's scheduled maintenance.

Light Line Technician

Light line technicians diagnose and replace the mechanical and electrical components of motor vehicles, such as gaskets, belts, hoses, timing belts, water pumps, radiators, alternators, and starters. In doing their job, light line technicians may be required to discuss problems with vehicle owners, operate special test equipment, and test-drive vehicles to identify faults. They need to be able to research service information, interpret wiring diagrams, and use this information to diagnose and make repairs. Sometimes they may be required to use oxyacetylene and electric welders to make repairs.

In addition, light line technicians reassemble, test, clean, and adjust repaired or replaced parts or assemblies using various instruments to make sure the parts are working properly. They also test and repair electrical systems such as lighting, instrumentation, vehicle sensors, and engine management systems. Finally, light line technicians inspect vehicles and may issue state safety certificates or list the work required before a certificate can be issued.

Heavy Line Technician

Heavy line technicians undertake major engine, transmission, and differential overhaul and repair. They may diagnose, overhaul, repair, or replace parts and assemblies. They must be able to research service information and use the information to help determine the cause of the problem and make the appropriate repairs. They also reassemble, test, clean, and adjust repaired or replaced parts or assemblies, using various test and measuring instruments and tools to make sure the parts are working properly. Some heavy line technicians are more generalized and work on a broad range of vehicles, while others specialize in particular areas by working on specific brand makes and models. Heavy line technicians may also specialize in particular vehicle systems, such as engines, transmissions, or final drives.

Chassis and Brake Technician

Chassis and brake technicians specialize and work only on the chassis and brakes of vehicles, which include steering and suspension. A chassis and brake technician may service the vehicle braking, steering, and suspension systems. A chassis and brake technician may also inspect and

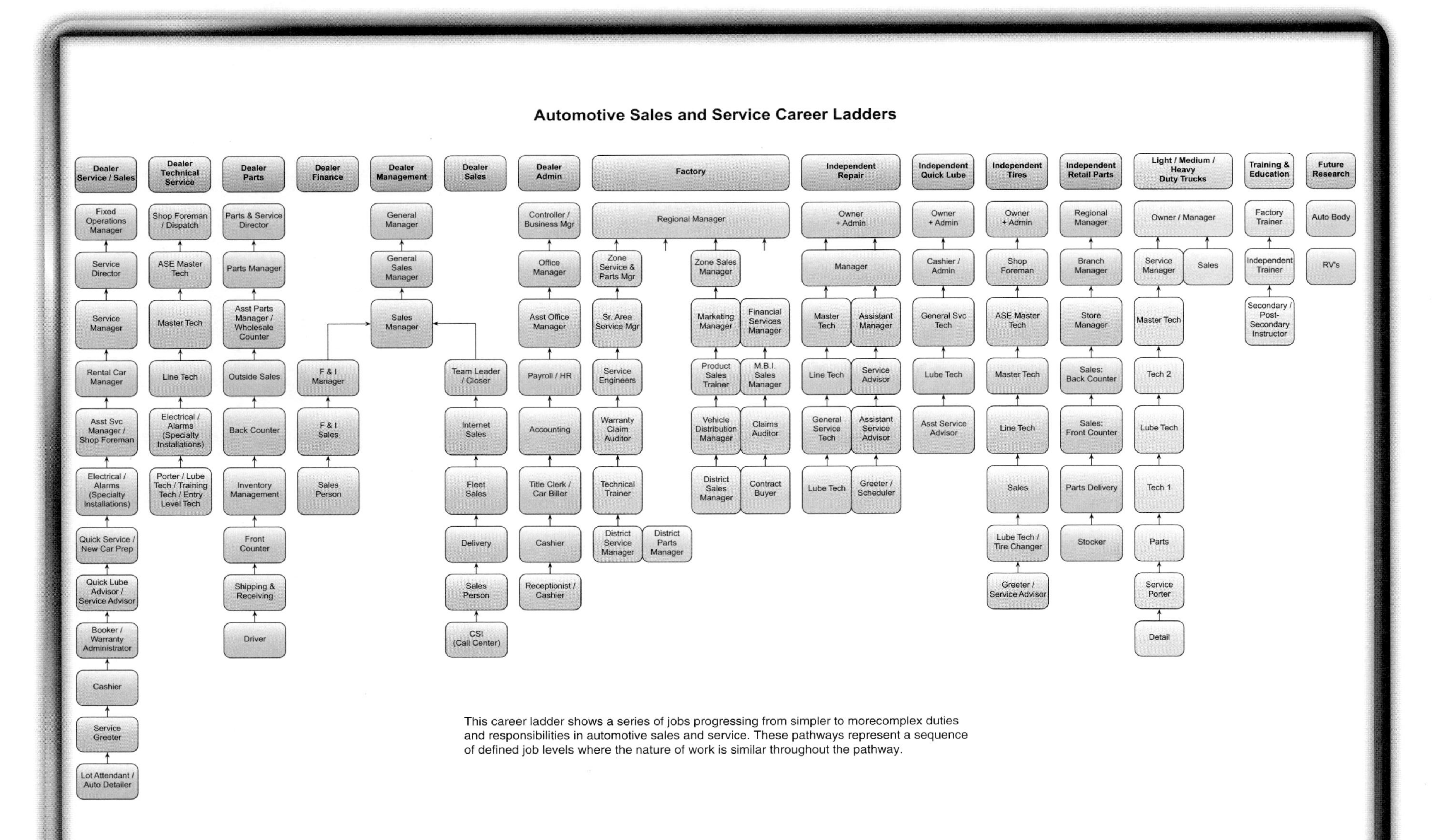
Automotive Sales and Service Career Ladders
Dealer Service / Sales
Fixed Operations Manager
Service Director
Service Manager
Rental Car Manager
Asst Svc Manager / Shop Foreman
Electrical / Alarms (Specialty Installations)
Quick Service / New Car Prep
Quick Lube Advisor / Service Advisor
Booker / Warranty Administrator
Cashier
Service Greeter
Lot Attendant / Auto Detailer
Dealer Technical Service
Shop Foreman / Dispatch
ASE Master Tech
Master Tech
Line Tech
Electrical / Alarms (Specialty Installations)
Porter / Lube Tech / Training Tech / Entry Level Tech
Dealer Parts
Parts & Service Director
Parts Manager
Asst Parts Manager / Wholesale Counter
Outside Sales
Back Counter
Inventory Management
Front Counter
Shipping & Receiving
Driver
Dealer Finance
F & I Manager
F & I Sales
Sales Person
Dealer Management
General Manager
General Sales Manager
Sales Manager
Dealer Sales
Team Leader / Closer
Internet Sales
Fleet Sales
Delivery
Sales Person
CSI (Call Center)
Dealer Admin
Controller / Business Mgr
Office Manager
Asst Office Manager
Payroll / HR
Accounting
Title Clerk / Car Biller
Cashier
Receptionist / Cashier
Factory
Regional Manager
Zone Service & Parts Mgr
Sr. Area Service Mgr
Service Engineers
Warranty Claim Auditor
Technical Trainer
District Service Manager
District Parts Manager
Zone Sales Manager
Marketing Manager
Financial Services Manager
Product Sales Trainer
M.B.I. Sales Manager
Vehicle Distribution Manager
Claims Auditor
District Sales Manager
Contract Buyer
Independent Repair
Owner + Admin
Manager
Master Tech
Assistant Manager
Line Tech
Service Advisor
General Service Tech
Assistant Service Advisor
Lube Tech
Greeter / Scheduler
Independent Quick Lube
Owner + Admin
Cashier / Admin
General Svc Tech
Lube Tech
Asst Service Advisor
Independent Tires
Owner + Admin
Shop Foreman
ASE Master Tech
Master Tech
Line Tech
Sales
Lube Tech / Tire Changer
Greeter / Service Advisor
Independent Retail Parts
Regional Manager
Branch Manager
Store Manager
Sales: Back Counter
Sales: Front Counter
Parts Delivery
Stocker
Light / Medium / Heavy Duty Trucks
Owner / Manager
Service Manager
Sales
Master Tech
Tech 2
Lube Tech
Tech 1
Parts
Service Porter
Detail
Training & Education
Factory Trainer
Independent Trainer
Secondary / Post-Secondary Instructor
Future Research
Auto Body
RV's
This career ladder shows a series of jobs progressing from simpler to morecomplex duties and responsibilities in automotive sales and service. These pathways represent a sequence of defined job levels where the nature of work is similar throughout the pathway.

FIGURE 1-4 The opportunities for challenging and rewarding careers are endless in the automotive field.

diagnose the steering, brakes, and suspension systems before performing repairs.

There are also separate brake technicians and chassis technicians. Chassis technicians diagnose, repair, and service steering system components and suspension systems on all types of vehicles. They diagnose faults in steering and suspension systems by speaking with the vehicle owner and test-driving the vehicle, noting its performance and comparing that to their knowledge of how the components and systems function. Chassis technicians also perform wheel alignments and wheel balancing, and they diagnose and replace faulty components. This work could include replacing bushings, servicing wheel bearings, or checking and replacing shock absorbers or steering joints and knuckles.

Brake technicians diagnose and repair faults, replace or overhaul brake systems, and test the components of disc, drum, and power brake systems used on all types of vehicles FIGURE 1-6. They diagnose faults in brake systems by speaking with the vehicle's owner and driving the vehicle and noting its performance, or by reading data from the vehicle's computer control system. This information is used along with the technician's knowledge to properly diagnose and service the vehicle. Brake technicians also can visually inspect brake units for wear, damage, or possible failure, and repair or replace the components as required. Brake technicians can measure brake drums and disc rotors to the nearest 0.0001" (0.00254 mm) to determine if the wear or finished size meets specifications. Often, they will replace leaky brake cylinders, machine rotors, and drums when necessary and ensure that brake systems are filled with the correct brake fluid, are bled or flushed, and are functioning properly.

Electrical/Drivability Technician

The roles of the electrical and drivability technician may be performed by a single person or by technicians who specialize in more than one area. For example, in larger shops, roles could be assigned to separate electrical and drivability technicians, whereas in smaller shops, one technician could perform both roles. Often, roles cross over. For example, an electrical technician needs to understand drivability, and a drivability technician needs to understand electrical systems.

Electrical Technician

Electrical technicians diagnose, replace, maintain, identify faults with, and repair electrical wiring and computer-based equipment in vehicles FIGURE 1-7. They work with computer-controlled engine management systems to service, identify, and repair faults on electronically controlled vehicle systems such as fuel injection, ignition, anti-lock braking, cruise control, and automatic transmissions. They also install electrical components such as alternators and starter motors, accessories such as radios, air conditioners, driving lamps, and anti-theft systems.

Often, electrical technicians use meters, oscilloscopes, test instruments, and circuit wiring diagrams to diagnose electrical faults. They test and replace faulty charging system components, starter motors, and related items such as batteries. They also repair or replace faulty ignition components, electrical wiring, fuses, and lamps and switches, often using solder equipment when repairing electrical components.

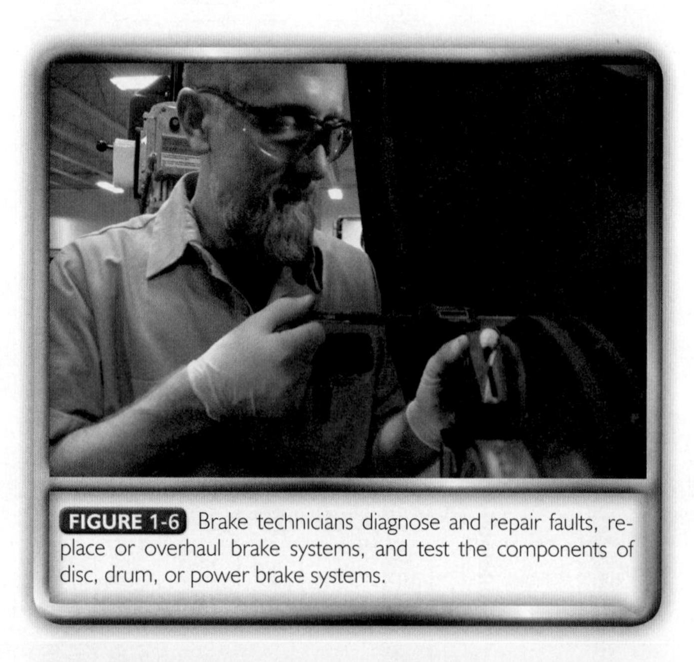

FIGURE 1-6 Brake technicians diagnose and repair faults, replace or overhaul brake systems, and test the components of disc, drum, or power brake systems.

FIGURE 1-7 Electrical technicians install, maintain, identify faults with, and repair electrical wiring and computer-based equipment in vehicles.

Drivability Technician

Drivability technicians diagnose and identify mechanical and electrical faults that affect the performance and emissions of vehicles. They carry out maintenance activities, replace parts, and repair both electrical wiring and computer-based equipment in vehicles. They work with computer-controlled engine management systems to service, identify, and repair faults on electronically controlled vehicle systems such as fuel injection, ignition, and automatic transmissions.

Often, drivability technicians use electronic test equipment, scan tools, pressure transducers, exhaust gas analyzers, lab scopes, meters, and circuit wiring diagrams to locate electrical, fuel, and emission systems faults. They may be required to program or reprogram (reflash) engine control units using computerized equipment on a wide variety of vehicles; in doing so, they use updates supplied by the manufacturer to ensure that vehicles run at peak performance and within acceptable emissions limits.

Transmission Specialist

With the increasing complexity of modern transmissions and the requirement for even more specialized service equipment to repair them, comes the need for transmission specialists. **Transmission specialists** diagnose, overhaul, and repair transmission units FIGURE 1-8. They work on various types of manual and automatic transmissions. Transmission specialists may work on both light vehicle and heavy vehicle transmissions or may specialize in either light vehicle or heavy truck transmissions, earthmoving transmissions, or automatic transmissions.

Transmission specialists may also work on the other components of the drivetrain, including the drive shafts and differentials. They test-drive vehicles and listen to customer concerns. They use many of the hand tools that heavy vehicle technicians use and also use specialized equipment to measure tolerances, check electrical circuits, and check hydraulic pressures.

Shop Foreman

A **shop foreman** is the supervisor in a shop. Shop foremen oversee the work of all types of technicians and staff, communicate with customers and external suppliers, and handle the various administrative duties involved with operating a business. Many shop foremen are responsible for hiring and training new workers and provide regular performance reviews. They oversee technicians' work to ensure that customers receive quality repair work. The shop foreman may own a small shop and provide services to the general public, work in a large commercial repair shop for light vehicles, or work in a shop that specializes in maintaining trucks. Finally, the shop foreman is responsible for enforcing safety procedures at all times to avoid accidental injuries to technicians or damage to vehicles.

Service Consultant

Service consultants (advisors) work with both customers and technicians FIGURE 1-9. They are the first point of contact for the customer and provide advice and assistance to customers concerning their vehicles. Service consultants will book customer work into the shop, fill out repair orders, price repairs, invoice, keep track of work being performed on customer vehicles, and build customer relations in order to provide a high level of customer support. They are the interface between the technician and the customer, so good communication and administration skills are essential. A service consultant can progress to become a service manager.

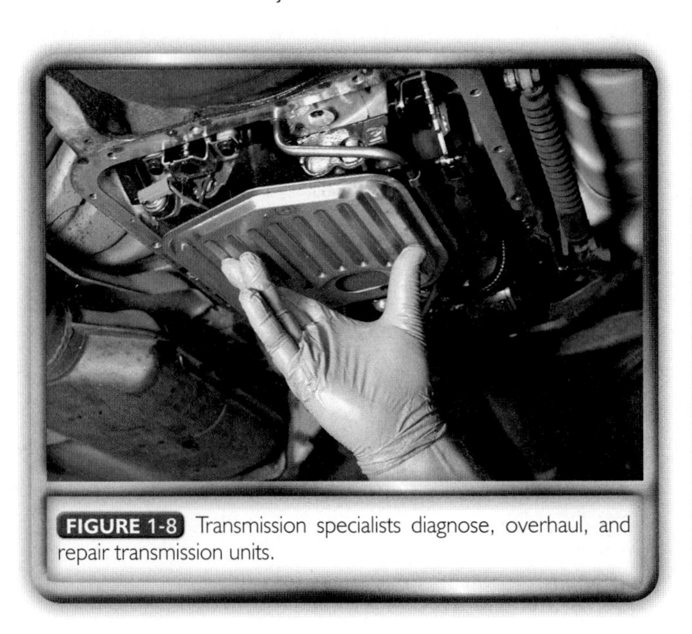

FIGURE 1-8 Transmission specialists diagnose, overhaul, and repair transmission units.

FIGURE 1-9 Service consultants work with both customers and technicians.

Service Manager

The role of a service manager is very demanding and challenging. **Service managers** are responsible for the functioning of the service department. This career requires well-established skills in communicating, motivating, and creating positive work environments. The service manager often supervises many people, has to deal with customer complaints, and is accountable for the overall performance of the shop.

This job requires a high level of personal commitment and focus, exceptional people skills, and excellent leadership qualities. Service managers may have worked their way up through the various roles within a shop. For example, the service manager may have once been a light vehicle technician on the floor, or a service consultant at the counter. Others may enter the field with backgrounds and college degrees in business management.

Types of Shops

There are many facilities that cater to specific customer needs. The types of repair facilities can generally be broken down into the following categories:

- Dealership
- Independent shop
- Specialty shop
- Franchise/retailer
- Fleet shop

Each type of shop caters to a particular segment of the industry. For example, dealerships are affiliated with a specific vehicle manufacturer. The dealership sells new and used vehicles. Dealership technicians perform maintenance, service, and warranty repairs on vehicles sold by that manufacturer **FIGURE 1-10**. In many cases, customers bring their new vehicles back to the dealership for maintenance and repair work while the vehicle is in warranty, and then seek out other shops after that.

Because dealership technicians are working on the latest vehicles, they are right at the cutting edge of technology. Most dealerships send their technicians to manufacturer training regularly so that they will know how to maintain, diagnose, and repair their vehicles. Because the dealership is affiliated with the manufacturer, dealership technicians generally have instant access to the manufacturer's service information as well as the manufacturer's service representatives when they encounter a difficult diagnostic situation.

Independent shops are not affiliated with vehicle manufacturers, making it harder for independent technicians to access training on new vehicle technology **FIGURE 1-11**. In many cases, they service a broad range of vehicles. Because vehicles are becoming more and more specialized and complex, it is common that they limit their clientele to European, Asian, or domestic vehicles. Some independent shops may limit their work and specialize in a particular system of the vehicle, such as brakes and alignment. In many cases, independent technicians work on vehicles that are out of warranty and are not the latest technology.

Specialty shops are usually independent shops that focus on one type of service, such as transmission service, electrical system repair, or emission system diagnosis. Since these shops offer limited services, they usually work on a variety of vehicles from a variety of manufacturers. A shop that specializes in one area such as air-conditioning (AC) may experience a slow period during certain times of the year.

FIGURE 1-10 Dealership technicians perform maintenance, service, and warranty repairs on vehicles sold by a particular manufacturer.

INDEPENDENT
AUTO REPAIR
INDEPENDENT
AUTO REPAIR

FIGURE 1-11 Independent shops are not affiliated with vehicle manufacturers.

Franchises are similar to specialty shops, but they are connected to a larger parent organization that can help with marketing and provide a mechanism for warranty claims that are honored at related franchise shops across the country. Some examples include Goodyear Tire Company, AAMCO Transmissions, and Jiffy Lube.

A fleet shop is usually connected with either a business that runs multiple vehicles or with equipment that is maintained and repaired in house, or it could be a government agency such as a city or county would have for maintenance and repair of its vehicles and equipment. Since fleet shops maintain and repair vehicles for the company or agency, it is more likely that the vehicles will be serviced on a regular basis.

Automotive Industry Certification

The automotive service industry in the United States is generally not subject to licensure requirements. This means that a technician does not have to pass a licensure test in order to receive a license to work in the industry. At the same time, to promote professionalism and demonstrate a level of competence, many technicians become **Automotive Service Excellence (ASE)** certified FIGURE 1-12. ASE is an independent, nonprofit organization dedicated to the improvement of vehicle repair through the testing and certification of automotive professionals. A few localities require technicians to be ASE certified, and many shops require it of technicians they hire. But overall it is a voluntary certification.

To earn ASE certification, technicians are required to pass one or more ASE certification tests and have 2 years of qualifying work experience as a technician. ASE certification needs to be renewed every 5 years by taking and passing recertification tests. There are currently approximately 275,000 certified ASE technicians in the United States.

A relatively new option open to automotive students is to earn ASE Student Certification. This certification is designed to evaluate and certify students who are near the end of their studies. Passing one or more of the tests is the beginning step in becoming a fully certified ASE technician. Because there is no work experience required for this certification, students can leave their training program with their first ASE recognized certification, which is valid for two years. In 2013, ASE added a Maintenance and Light Repair (MLR) Certification test, which goes along with the new NATEF MLR standards.

The **National Automotive Technicians Education Foundation (NATEF)** is an accrediting body for secondary and post-secondary automotive training programs FIGURE 1-13. NATEF is an independent, nonprofit organization under the umbrella of the ASE. In order for programs to be accredited by NATEF, they have to demonstrate their compliance to a rigorous list of standards developed by the automotive industry. Program instructors must also maintain ASE certification in the areas they teach, as well as receive a minimum of 20 hours of technical update training each year. NATEF accreditation is valid for 5 years, and then the program must go through a reaccreditation process.

The **Automotive Youth Educational Systems (AYES)** is an independent, nonprofit organization that is a partnership between automotive manufacturers, their dealerships, and affiliated secondary automotive programs FIGURE 1-14. Because of the partnership, AYES programs receive access to new vehicle technology as well as manufacturer service information to help prepare students for working on today's vehicles and technology.

ASE
WE SUPPORT
PROFESSIONAL CERTIFICATION
THROUGH THE
National Institute for
AUTOMOTIVE
SERVICE
EXCELLENCE

FIGURE 1-12 ASE logo.

We Support
ASE
NATEF
Improving Programs
Through Certification

FIGURE 1-13 NATEF logo.

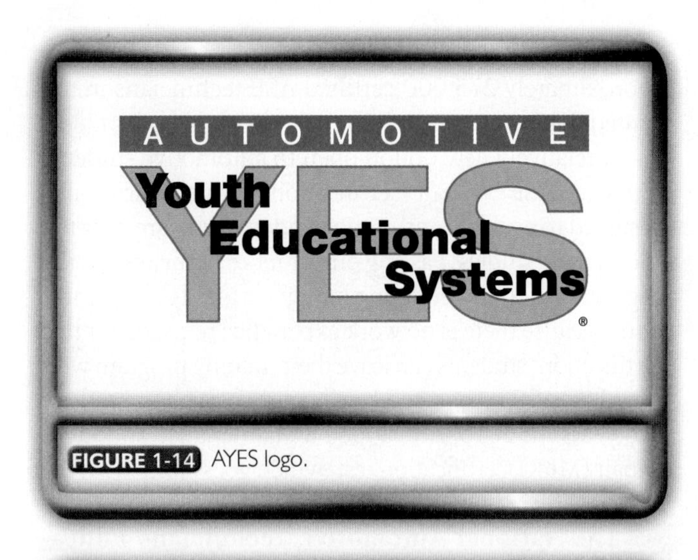
AUTOMOTIVE
Youth
Educational
Systems
YES

FIGURE 1-14 AYES logo.

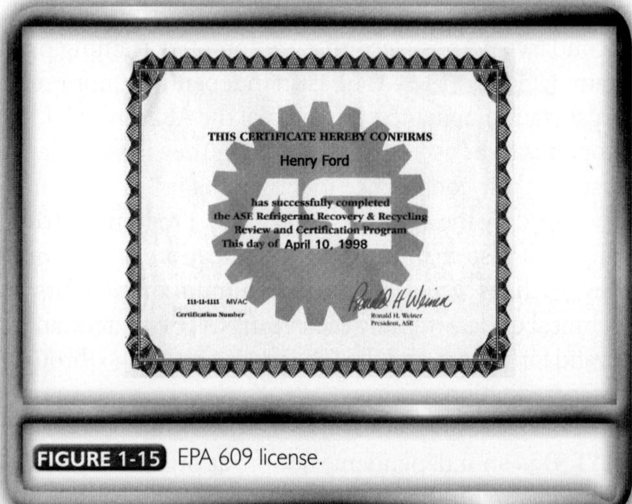
THIS CERTIFICATE HEREBY CONFIRMS
Henry Ford
has successfully completed
the ASE Refrigerant Recovery & Recycling
Review and Certification Program
This day of April 10, 1998
111-11-1111 MVAC
Certification Number
Ronald H. Weiner
President, ASE

FIGURE 1-15 EPA 609 license.

Students receive the opportunity to intern at participating dealerships working alongside a mentor technician. This is a great way for the students to put into practice what they are learning in the training program. The dealers and manufacturers benefit from gaining access to highly motivated students who are preparing to go to work for them. To become an AYES program, the school has to be NATEF certified and then be evaluated by AYES against another set of standards related to the commitments of carrying out the AYES training model.

Special Certification

The automotive industry has two special certification requirements for certain automotive technician specialists. To diagnose and repair emission failures on vehicles in some localities, technicians must be certified by the appropriate agency. In many cases, the technician must have ASE Advanced Engine Performance certification or have taken and passed a course specifically for emission specialists, as administered by the agency.

The second special certification required is for technicians who handle refrigerants or work on AC systems. They are required to be Environmental Protection Agency (EPA) Section 609 certified FIGURE 1-15. This requires taking a training course and passing the 609 exam. Once certified, technicians are legally able to handle refrigerants and repair AC systems. It is advisable that all students obtain their 609 certification during their training program to show prospective employers when they graduate.

Wrap-up

Ready for Review

- Modern vehicles are more sophisticated with longer maintenance intervals than early vehicles.
- Karl Benz is considered the inventor of the modern automobile (in 1885).
- Application of interchangeability and the assembly line made cars more affordable for the masses.
- Today's production lines are high-volume, high-technology plants.
- Lube technicians carry out standard maintenance services.
- Light line technicians are responsible for maintenance and repair of mechanical and electrical components.
- Heavy line technicians diagnose and repair major engine or transmission problems and perform differential overhaul.
- Chassis and brake technicians repair the vehicle's chassis and brakes (respectively, or in combination), including steering and suspension.
- Electrical technicians diagnose and repair the vehicle's electrical wiring and computer-based equipment.
- Drivability technicians are responsible for inspecting the mechanical and electrical faults that can affect the performance and emissions of vehicles.
- Transmission specialists diagnose and repair transmission units (manual and automatic).
- The shop foreman is responsible for administrative duties, supervising technicians, and ensuring customer satisfaction.
- Service consultants work to ensure that customers are satisfied with their experience at the shop.
- Service managers run the service department and must create a positive work environment.
- Types of repair facilities are dealerships, independent shops, specialty shops, franchises/retailers, and fleet shops.
- Automotive technicians may become ASE certified; training programs may be NATEF accredited; school programs may be AYES authorized; and technicians may choose to receive certification in emission failures and/or air-conditioning systems.
- Automotive students can earn ASE Student Certification near the end of their studies.

Key Terms

Automotive Service Excellence (ASE) An independent, nonprofit organization dedicated to the improvement of vehicle repair through the testing and certification of automotive professionals.

Automotive Youth Educational Systems (AYES) An independent, nonprofit organization that is a partnership between automotive manufacturers, their dealerships, and affiliated secondary automotive programs.

brake technician A technician who specializes in working on vehicle brake systems.

chassis technician A technician who specializes in working on vehicle suspension and steering systems.

drivability technician A technician who diagnoses and identifies mechanical and electrical faults that affect vehicle performance and emissions.

electrical technician A technician who diagnoses, replaces, maintains, identifies fault with, and repairs electrical wiring and computer-based equipment in vehicles.

heavy line technician A technician who undertakes major engine, transmission, and differential overhaul and repair.

light line technician A technician who diagnoses and replaces the mechanical and electrical components of motor vehicles.

lube technician A technician who carries out scheduled maintenance activities on a range of mechanical and related vehicle components.

National Automotive Technicians Education Foundation (NATEF) An accrediting body for secondary and post-secondary automotive training programs; an independent, nonprofit organization under the umbrella of the ASE.

service consultant/advisor A service worker who works with both customers and technicians; the first point of contact for customers seeking vehicle repairs.

service manager The shop supervisor who is responsible for the management of the service department.

shop foreman The supervisor in a shop who oversees the work of technicians and staff and communicates with customers and external suppliers.

transmission specialist A technician who diagnoses, overhauls, and repairs transmissions.

ASE-Type Questions

1. Tech A says that newer vehicles require less maintenance compared to older vehicles. Tech B says that service intervals for an older vehicle can be extended if new oils are used. Who is correct?
   a. Tech A
   b. Tech B
   c. Both A and B
   d. Neither A nor B
2. Tech A says that Henry Ford is credited with the invention of the automobile. Tech B says that Carl Benz is credited with the invention of the automobile. Who is correct?
   a. Tech A
   b. Tech B
   c. Both A and B
   d. Neither A nor B
3. Tech A says that the production of vehicles today requires a mix of robotic and human assembly to be profitable. Tech B says that most parts on a car are preassembled before they reach the assembly line for higher assembly numbers per day. Who is correct?
   a. Tech A
   b. Tech B
   c. Both A and B
   d. Neither A nor B
4. Tech A says that the automotive industry is highly technical and only a certain few people will find jobs. Tech B says the automotive industry is wide open with job opportunities for almost every level of skill. Who is correct?
   a. Tech A
   b. Tech B
   c. Both A and B
   d. Neither A nor B
5. Tech A says that a technician can specialize in different areas based on his or her interest and ability. Tech B says that when a technician specializes in a certain area, he or she will only work on certain vehicle models. Who is correct?
   a. Tech A
   b. Tech B
   c. Both A and B
   d. Neither A nor B
6. Tech A says that the foreman is the frontline contact for customer relations. Tech B says that the service consultant is the frontline contact for customer relations. Who is correct?
   a. Tech A
   b. Tech B
   c. Both A and B
   d. Neither A nor B
7. Tech A says that dealership technicians generally have access to manufacturers training to help prepare them as technicians. Tech B says that an independent shop works on a wide variety of equipment that requires a broad skill level in technicians. Who is correct?
   a. Tech A
   b. Tech B
   c. Both A and B
   d. Neither A nor B
8. Tech A says that AYES certifies technicians. Tech B says that ASE certifications can help get you a job. Who is correct?
   a. Tech A
   b. Tech B
   c. Both A and B
   d. Neither A nor B
9. Tech A says that the maintenance requirements of a vehicle have not changed since the creation of the automobile. Tech B says that manufacturers are predicting 25,000-mile (40,000-km) intervals. Who is correct?
   a. Tech A
   b. Tech B
   c. Both A and B
   d. Neither A nor B
10. Tech A says that a technician can progress to different jobs within the industry. Tech B says that carriers in the automotive industry include new car assembly lines. Who is correct?
    a. Tech A
    b. Tech B
    c. Both A and B
    d. Neither A nor B

CHAPTER 2

Know
See
Do
Prove

NATEF Tasks

There are no NATEF tasks for this chapter.

Know
See
Do
Prove

Knowledge Objectives

After reading this chapter, you will be able to:

1. Identify vehicle body types and their characteristics. (pp 20–23)
2. Describe vehicle chassis designs. (pp 23–24)
3. Describe how a vehicle operates in general terms. (pp 24–26)
4. Describe various drive train layouts. (pp 26–27)
5. Identify various engine configurations. (pp 27–29)
6. Describe live and dead axles. (pp 29–30)
7. Describe live axle locations. (pp 30–31)
8. Describe two applications of torque in automotives. (p 31)
9. Describe transmissions and final drives. (pp 31–32)
10. Describe four-wheel drive and all-wheel drive systems. (p 32)

Introduction to Automotive Technology

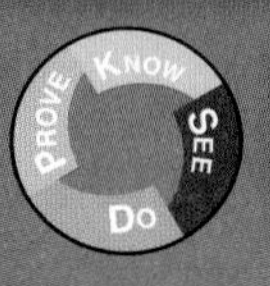
KNOW
SEE
DO
PROVE

Skills Objectives

There are no skills objectives for this chapter.

Introduction

As you prepare to work in the automotive repair industry, you will need to learn a whole new vocabulary. Terms like hygroscopic, asymmetrical, reciprocating motion, and volumetric efficiency are only a few examples of the new vocabulary you will need to master. Healthcare professionals need to know how each of the body's systems function, the organs that make up the system, and how to diagnose an issue. Automotive technicians need to have the same level of understanding about vehicles. The good news is that automotive names aren't in Latin; however, you will need to master the metric system.

Knowing the correct automotive terminology and concepts will help you fit into your new work environment as well as accurately communicate with customers, suppliers, and fellow employees. You will also be able to properly complete repair orders, parts requisitions, and warranty paperwork as you maintain, diagnose, and repair vehicles. This chapter will help you start the process of learning automotive terminology as it relates to vehicle types, drive train layouts, engine configurations, and axle arrangements.

Body Designs

Vehicle bodies come in a variety of designs primarily depending on the intended function of the vehicle. But they also are designed to accommodate style, aesthetics, and, most importantly, safety. Vehicle body design continues to evolve to accommodate the owners' lifestyles and personal tastes, such as the Scion XB or the M-Benz Smart Fortwo FIGURE 2-1. Vehicle body design is also used as a strong marketing tool by manufacturers to entice buyers to purchase their particular vehicles.

Common types of body design cater to both passenger and light commercial use. Terms to describe various body designs have become part of common automotive language, although names describing the same body design type can vary from country to country. For example, a vehicle described as a sedan in the United States is called a saloon in the United Kingdom. Other types of body designs include station wagons, hatchbacks, convertibles, coupes, vans, minivans, pick-ups, crossover utility vehicles (CUVs), and sport utility vehicles (SUVs).

Sedan

A **sedan** has an enclosed body, with a maximum of four doors to allow access to the passenger compartment FIGURE 2-2. The sedan design also allows for storage of luggage or other items in a trunk located in the rear of the vehicle and accessible from a trunk lid. A sedan traditionally has a fixed roof; however, there are soft-top versions of sedans, which have only two doors.

Coupe

A **coupe** has only two doors. Reducing the number of doors to the passenger compartment makes the vehicle structure more rigid. Traditionally, a coupe has two

You Are the Automotive Technician

The sales manager asks you to provide training for her new vehicle sales associates in your recently expanded dealership. The first training lesson takes place in the dealership showroom where several styles of vehicles are on display. You explain the concept of the unibody design and compare it to the full frame design. You also show examples of various drivetrain layouts and their pros and cons. The second lesson is in the shop area, designated for engine repair. You show them the various engine classifications and configurations.

1. What are the common vehicle body types and their characteristics?
2. What are the benefits of the unibody design? How does it differ from the full-frame vehicle?
3. What are the various engine configurations, and how do they differ?

FIGURE 2-1 Vehicle body design continues to evolve to accommodate the owners' lifestyles and personal tastes. **A.** Car from the 1950s. **B.** Car from the 2000s.

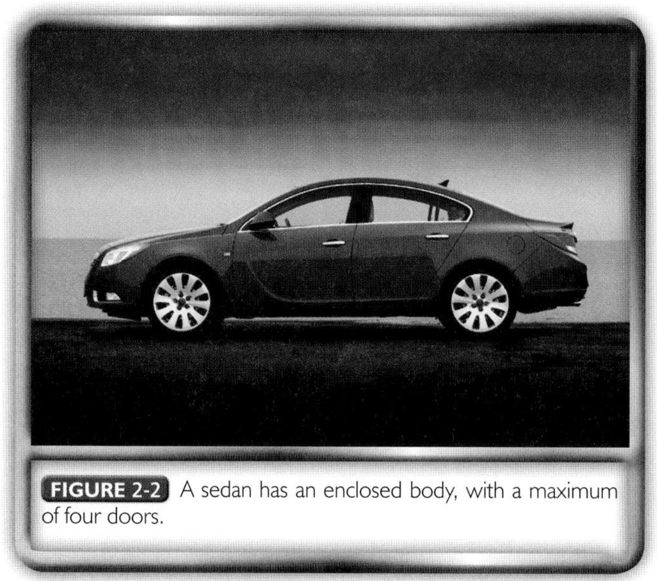

FIGURE 2-2 A sedan has an enclosed body, with a maximum of four doors.

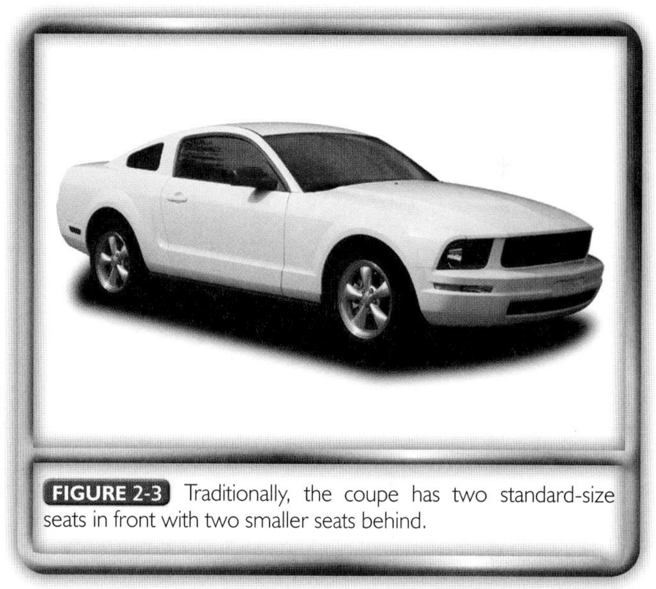

FIGURE 2-3 Traditionally, the coupe has two standard-size seats in front with two smaller seats behind.

standard-size seats in front and possibly two smaller seats behind FIGURE 2-3. Coupes are available in both fixed-roof and convertible style. They also are equipped with a trunk for storage purposes, although they can sometimes be on the small side.

Hatchback

Hatchbacks are available in three-door and five-door designs, with the odd-numbered door being a hatch that lifts up at the rear of the vehicle. This gives access to the luggage area. The rear seats usually fold down to increase the luggage area FIGURE 2-4. Often the rear seat will be split, which provides more flexibility because only one side needs to be folded down if the other seat is required for a passenger. Hatchbacks are versatile vehicles, combining some of the benefits of both sedans and station wagons.

FIGURE 2-4 Rear seats in hatchbacks usually fold down to increase the luggage area.

Convertible

A **convertible** is an automobile that can convert from having an enclosed top to having an open top by means of a roof that can be removed, retracted, or folded away FIGURE 2-5. The roofing material is most often a flexible fabric such as canvas or vinyl, and most convertibles have a mechanism driven by electric motors that retracts or raises the roof cover. In some vehicles, known as hardtop convertibles, the roof can be a series of folding steel or fiberglass panels. When in place, the hard roof makes such vehicles look more like conventional fixed-roof coupe vehicles FIGURE 2-6. In other vehicles, only a smaller section of the roof area is convertible. Traditionally, the term roadster was applied to a vehicle with no permanent roof covering or side windows, but today that name is most often used to describe any convertible sports car.

FIGURE 2-5 A convertible is an automobile that can convert from having an enclosed top to having an open top by means of a roof that can be removed, retracted, or folded away.

FIGURE 2-6 Hardtop convertibles have a hard roof that makes the vehicle look more like a conventional fixed-roof vehicle.

TECHNICIAN TIP

A convertible is commonly known as a cabriolet in Europe.

Station Wagon

A **station wagon** has an extended roof that goes all the way to the rear of the vehicle. It is similar to a van but not as tall. The extra length in the roof increases the luggage capacity. In some cases, the passenger capacity is increased with extra seats in the very rear of the vehicle. Station wagons have a large rear door for easy access, and the rear seats can usually be folded to increase storage capacity even further FIGURE 2-7. Station wagons usually have fixed roofs.

Pick-up

The **pick-up**, or **truck**, carries and tows cargo. Usually it has heavier-duty chassis components and suspension than a passenger car to support greater loads. Traditionally, pick-ups had only a single cab with two doors, which limited the number of passengers they could carry. Today's pick-ups have options for extended cabs or four-door versions to carry more passengers FIGURE 2-8. In some cases, the four-door pick-up has a reduced cargo-carrying space to accommodate the extra seating in the passenger cab.

Vans

Vans come in many sizes and configurations, from minivans to full-size vans and sprinters. **Minivans** are generally lighter-duty vehicles with suspension

FIGURE 2-7 A station wagon has increased luggage capacity and a large rear door for access.

FIGURE 2-8 More recent versions of pick-ups have options for extended cabs or four-door versions to carry more passengers.

systems more like passenger cars than full-size vans, which use heavy-duty pick-up truck–type suspension systems. Minivans can be configured to maximize the number of seats for passengers or redesigned so that maximum cargo space is available FIGURE 2-9. Also, since they are lighter duty, the fuel economy of minivans is substantially better than that of full-size vans.

Vans also come in full-size vehicles as well. They are usually much heavier duty and built on truck chassis. Full-size vans can be configured to carry passengers, cargo, or both. Full-size passenger vans typically have side windows, while cargo vans usually don't. Conventional full-size vans generally come in standard length and can seat up to 12 passengers. Extended vans are longer and can seat up to 15 passengers.

Sprinter vans are an increasingly popular type of full-size van. They are taller than conventional full-size vans, making them ideal for both cargo and passengers. When sprinter vans are equipped with a diesel engine, their fuel economy makes them a good choice for commercial applications.

Sport Utility Vehicle

Sport utility vehicles (SUVs) are popular in the United States since they can easily be used to carry out functions that would otherwise require several different vehicles FIGURE 2-10. They act like both a full-size van and a pick-up in that they have a heavier-duty chassis so they can carry heavier loads. This load can be in the form of passengers, luggage, or cargo. They can also tow moderately heavy loads, making them a great vehicle for family outings, since they can pull a trailer while still carrying a number of passengers and luggage.

Crossover Utility Vehicles

Crossover utility vehicles, also called **CUVs**, get their name from being a cross between an SUV and a passenger vehicle. CUVs typically have a lighter-duty chassis, similar to a passenger vehicle, but the body design of an SUV. Their taller interiors make crossover utility vehicles ideally suited for passengers interior, but because of their lighter-duty chassis, they can't haul the heavier loads that a typical SUV can haul. Most CUVs are front-wheel drive, although some come in rear-wheel drive or all-wheel drive. Regardless, CUVs are not built to withstand much off-road driving.

Vehicle Chassis

A **chassis** is an underlying supporting structure for vehicles—similar to the skeleton of a human—on which additional components are mounted. In a vehicle, a traditional chassis gives the vehicle structural strength

FIGURE 2-9 Minivans can be based on common interior sedan designs or redesigned so that maximum cargo space is available.

CAPTIVA

FIGURE 2-10 Sport utility vehicles (SUVs) are designed for flexible use while being heavier duty than minivans.

as well as a platform on which to mount the engine, the wheels, the transmission, and all the other mechanical components. Also bolted onto this frame is the body. Originally made of wood, vehicle chassis were soon changed to an open steel ladder-frame structure, which is easier to manufacture and is longer lasting FIGURE 2-11.

Body-on-frame is the term used when a vehicle body is mounted on a rigid frame or chassis. It was the preferred way of building passenger vehicles because it allowed manufacturers to release new models of vehicles with different body styles without having to retool most of the mechanical and structural components. However, by the 1960s, most manufacturers switched to vehicle designs that either partially or wholly integrated the bodywork into a single unit with the chassis so that the vehicle body became part of the vehicle structure rather than just an external skin. This is the **unibody design**, or single shell design FIGURE 2-12. The unibody design is constructed of a large number of steel sheet metal panels that are precisely formed in presses and spot-welded together into a structural unit.

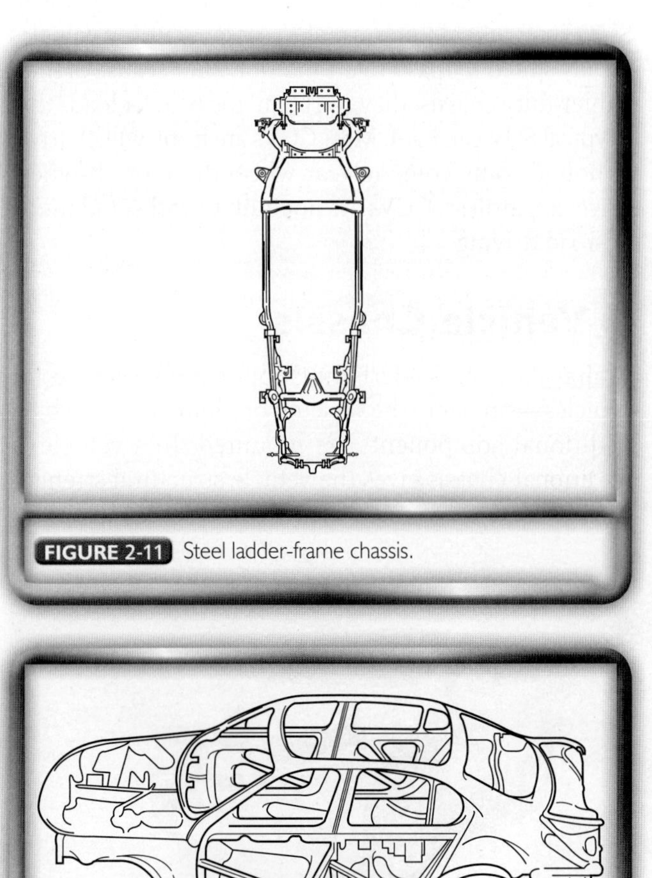

FIGURE 2-11 Steel ladder-frame chassis.

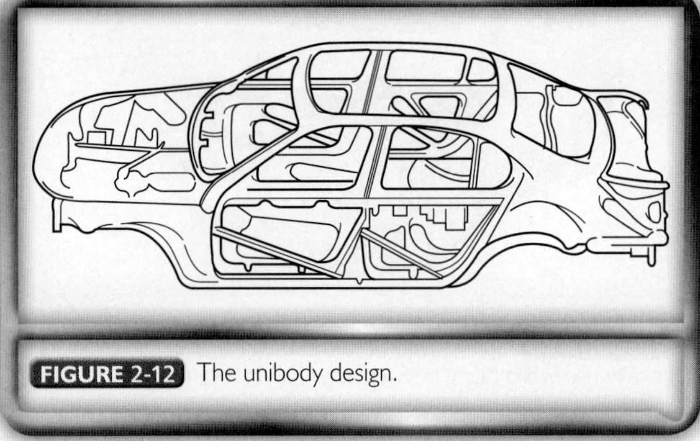

FIGURE 2-12 The unibody design.

> **TECHNICIAN TIP**
>
> Some high-performance racing cars today have no chassis at all. Their structural strength comes from their light, stiff, and stable body shells molded from newer lightweight materials such as carbon fiber–reinforced plastics.

The unibody design was first used in aircraft and then spread to automobiles. It became popular with vehicle manufacturers because with less of a chassis component, it was quicker to manufacture and lighter in weight. The lighter weight meant less cost in both material and labor. Another benefit of being lighter was that the vehicles became more fuel efficient.

Vehicle Closure Designs

A vehicle body contains many openings apart from the vehicle doors. They include the engine compartment hood, hatch and tailgate openings, the fuel door, and in some cases, a battery access cover. All of these openings have to be secured and may require a remote switch or lever to be activated. In some cases, the access door is opened mechanically by the driver pulling a lever, which moves a cable and releases a latch. Other doors may use electric- or vacuum-operated solenoids to release the latch. In this case, the driver pushes a switch that sends an electric or vacuum signal to the release mechanism, which releases the door. Some rear hatch doors have a hinged window incorporated; this window offers the owner easy access to the storage space without opening the entire back door.

Engine compartment hoods on today's vehicles usually have a remote release lever to prevent unauthorized access to the engine compartment for security reasons. The release lever is usually located inside the passenger compartment: under the dash, in the glove compartment, or on a doorjamb FIGURE 2-13. Once the hood is open, it is held in the open position by one of three methods: large springs on the hinges, pressurized gas strut assemblies, or a prop rod.

Vehicle Operation Overview

For a vehicle to operate, it requires a means of converting stored energy into a form of energy that can turn the wheels. In the majority of vehicles, the stored energy is in the chemical form of gasoline or diesel fuel, but newer vehicles are using natural gas, alcohol, biodiesel, hydrogen, and battery acid as their stored chemical energy source. Chemical energy can be converted into mechanical energy in two primary ways: through the operation of an internal combustion engine or through the operation of an electric motor FIGURE 2-14. Both of these methods take energy in chemical form and convert it to mechanical energy by causing a shaft to rotate—the crankshaft in an internal combustion engine and the armature in an electric motor. The shaft then provides mechanical energy to move the vehicle as well as power all of the other accessories on the vehicle.

The vehicle's combustion engine converts the energy from the fuel supply by combining the fuel with the air to create a combustible mixture, which is compressed by the pistons and ignited by a spark plug in the engine cylinders. When the driver initiates the starting process by turning the ignition key to run (or using a smart key), power is supplied from the battery to various vehicle circuits and the fuel pump pressurizes the fuel system in preparation for the engine to start. When the key is moved to the crank position (or the start button is pressed), the starter motor is energized and cranks over the engine. As soon as the engine has started and is running, the ignition key is released from the start position and the engine continues to run while the ignition key is in the run position. Depressing the accelerator increases the amount of fuel and air entering the engine and increases the engine speed and power.

FIGURE 2-13 The engine compartment release may be located inside the passenger compartment under the dash, in the glove compartment, or on a doorjamb.

> **TECHNICIAN TIP**
>
> Some high-end sports car manufacturers are no longer fitting an engine compartment release to their vehicles. The hood can only be released by the manufacturer's scan tool or by a service key fitted into a secluded opening on the vehicle body (usually behind a manufacturer's badge).

As the engine cranks, the engine management system monitors the engine sensors and makes decisions about such matters as the correct timing to fire the spark plugs and injecting and metering the proper amount of fuel. The fuel mixture is ignited by the ignition system, which causes the hot gases to expand. This expansion pushes each piston down into the cylinder, which in turn causes the crankshaft to rotate.

As the pistons continue moving up and down, they rotate the crankshaft, turning the **flywheel** or flex plate, which is bolted to the engine crankshaft. For a manual transmission, the flywheel transmits the engine output to the transmission through a clutch; for an automatic transmission, the flex plate transmits the engine output through a torque convertor.

HYBRID
SYNERGY
DRIVE

FIGURE 2-14 Stored chemical energy is converted to mechanical energy to propel the vehicle down the road. **A.** Internal combustion engine. **B.** Hybrid engine with internal combustion engine and electric motor.

The vehicle's transmission allows for a number of different gear ratios, which match the engine's speed and power output to the desired road speed. The transmission allows the vehicle to start at low speeds with high torque to the wheels to get the vehicle moving, and as gear ratios are changed, the vehicle attains higher road speed with lower engine speed. The vehicle's driveshaft connects the output from the transmission to the wheels via **axles** through a final drive assembly that divides up the drive to the powered wheels.

> **TECHNICIAN TIP**
>
> The unibody design is the predominant vehicle construction technology used today.

Vehicle brakes are fitted to the wheels to provide a means of slowing down or stopping the vehicle and operate on the principle of hydraulic pressure. They are fitted to each wheel and are operated by a brake pedal next to the accelerator pedal. The brake pedal is connected to a master brake cylinder fitted under the hood. The master brake cylinder has a power booster fitted to it that amplifies the hydraulic pressure to the wheel brake units. The wheel brake units apply brake friction pads to metal discs or drums connected to the wheels, creating friction, which slows the wheels' rotation. The harder the driver pushes on the brake pedal, the harder the brakes are applied.

The vehicle suspension system connects the wheels to the chassis or vehicle body through various linkages, shock absorbers, and springs. The suspension system evens out the road shocks caused by the irregular road surface. The suspension system provides the passengers with a comfortable ride and safely keeps the tires in contact with the road surfaces. The steering system makes the connection between the steering wheel and the road wheels so the driver can point the vehicle in the intended direction of travel. Power steering systems provide assistance to the driver to turn the vehicle's wheels and use either an engine-driven or an electric-driven pump to power the system.

The electrical system is interconnected to all of the other systems. It includes the battery, which stores a supply of electricity for the purpose of starting the vehicle and operating the electrical accessories such as lights, windshield wipers, and heater system when the engine is not operating. The battery is continually recharged, and the electrical accessories are operated by the charging system whenever the engine is running. The electrical system also includes the power train control system, the lighting system, accessory systems, safety systems, passenger comfort systems, and entertainment systems.

Drive Train Layouts

The **drive train** encompasses the major assemblies that power the vehicle down the road, including the engine, transmission/transaxle, differential, axles, and wheels FIGURE 2-15. Drive trains are designed in different layouts based on the vehicle application and manufacturer's preferences. For example, the drive train layout is different in a pick-up used for driving up muddy mountain roads than in a high-performance sports car that runs around a smooth asphalt track. Differences in configuration between each of the drive train's major assemblies define the drive train layout.

The drive train layout includes three main engine mounting positions: front, mid, and rear FIGURE 2-16. The front engine design is the most common in everyday vehicles and has the engine mounted between the front wheels. Mid-engine vehicles have the engine mounted in front of the rear wheels and provide a more equal weight distribution between the front and rear wheels. Rear-engine vehicles have the engine mounted between or behind the rear wheels. Mid- and rear-engine designs are usually reserved for performance-type vehicles, although there have been some exceptions, such as the Volkswagen Beetle. Manufacturers also mount engines in one of two orientations, **longitudinal** (front to back) and **transverse** (side to side), depending on which design best fits the vehicle and the rest of the drive train.

FIGURE 2-15 The drive train encompasses the engine, transmission, differential, axles, and wheels.

The engine does not necessarily drive all four wheels. Drive train layouts accommodate four common drive wheel arrangements. **Front-wheel drive (FWD)** is very common in modern vehicles; in this arrangement, only the front wheels are driven by the engine. **Rear-wheel drive (RWD)** is when the engine drives only the rear wheels. Both of these arrangements are called two-wheel drive vehicles. Becoming increasingly popular is **all-wheel drive (AWD)**, with all four wheels driven by the engine all the time. The final arrangement is **four-wheel drive (4WD)**, which is slightly different from all-wheel drive. In a 4WD vehicle, the driver can select between two-wheel drive and four-wheel drive.

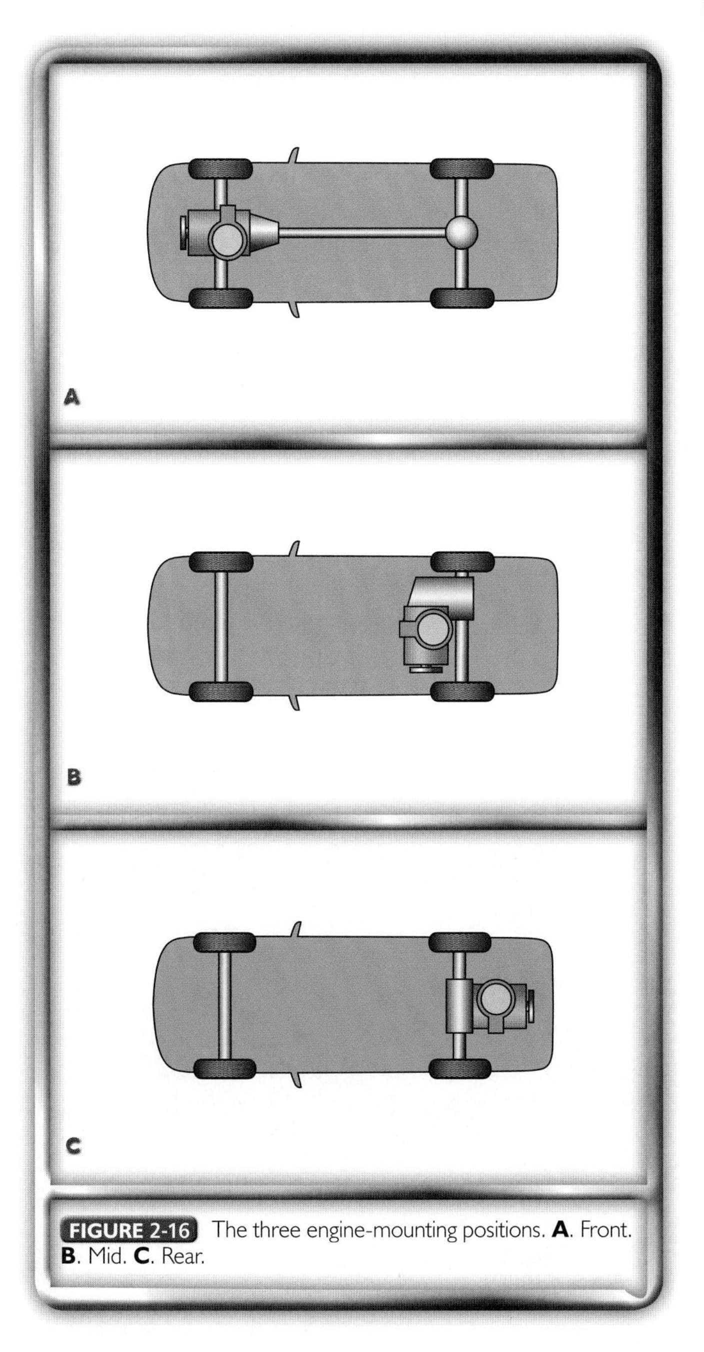
A
B
C

FIGURE 2-16 The three engine-mounting positions. **A**. Front. **B**. Mid. **C**. Rear.

The combination of engine position, engine orientation, and type of drive defines the drive train layout. For example, using the different variations can give the following drive train layouts:

- Front-engine, front-wheel drive
- Front-engine, rear-wheel drive
- Front-engine, all-wheel drive/4WD
- Rear-engine, rear-wheel drive
- Rear-engine, all-wheel drive
- Mid-engine, rear-wheel drive
- Mid-engine, all-wheel drive

Classifying Engines

Engines are classified by type, cylinder arrangement, number of cylinders/rotors, and total engine displacement in cubic inches or liters. Two common types of engines are piston and rotary. The piston engine uses cylindrical pistons that move up and down in cylinder bores, while the rotary engine uses a triangular rotor that turns inside of an oval chamber. The vast majority of automotive engines are of the piston type rather than the less common rotary type because they have a longer life and produce fewer emissions.

Piston Engines

In a **piston engine**, the way engine cylinders are arranged is called the **engine configuration**. Multi-cylinder internal combustion automotive engines are produced in four common configurations:

- In-line: The pistons are all in one bank on one side of a common crankshaft.
- Horizontally opposed: The pistons are in two banks on both sides of a common crankshaft.
- V: The pistons are in two banks on opposite sides, forming a deep V with a common crankshaft at the base of the V.
- VR and W: In a VR engine, the pistons are in one bank but form a shallow V within the bank. The W engine consists of two VR banks in a deep V configuration with each other.

TECHNICIAN TIP

In-line, horizontally opposed, and V configurations are the most common engine configurations. Recent additions are the VR and W arrangements.

Engineers design engines with tilted cylinder banks to reduce engine height. This can reduce the height of the hood as well, which allows a more streamlined hood line FIGURE 2-17. Tilting can be carried to an extreme by designing the engine to lie completely on its side in the case of a horizontally opposed engine, also called a flat engine. This greatly reduces the engine height.

As the number of cylinders increases, the length of the engine block and the crankshaft can become a problem structurally and space-wise. One way to avoid this problem is by having more than one row of cylinders, as in a horizontally opposed, V, or W configuration. These designs make the engine block and the crankshaft shorter and more rigid. In vehicle applications, the number of cylinders can vary, usually up to 12. Some examples are:

- In-line 4: Compact, fairly inexpensive, easier to work on, and better fuel economy than other types.
- V8: Approximately twice as powerful as the in-line 4, but less than twice the space. Good power for its size and not overly complicated.
- Flat 6: Low-profile engine that fits well in vehicles with very low hood lines.
- W12: Most powerful compared to its overall dimensions, but more complicated and expensive than the other engines.

Common angles between the banks of cylinders are 180 degrees, 90 degrees, 60 degrees, and 15 degrees. Angles vary due to the number of cylinders and the manufacturer's design considerations.

In-line

Cylinders arranged side by side in a single row identify the **in-line engine** and can be found in 3-, 4-, 5-, and 6-cylinder configurations FIGURE 2-18. There have been in-line 8-cylinder engines, but they are too long to fit into the engine bay of a conventional modern car. In-line engines can be mounted longitudinally (lengthwise) or transversely (sideways) in the engine bay. In-line engines are generally less complicated to design and manufacture since they do not have to share components with a second bank of cylinders. This lack of shared components can mean extra working room in the engine compartment when performing maintenance and repairs. As a general rule of thumb, in-line engines are easier to work on than the other cylinder arrangements.

FIGURE 2-18 Cylinders arranged side by side in a single row identify the in-line engine.

Horizontally Opposed

Horizontally opposed engines are sometimes referred to as "flat" engines and are commonly found in 4- and 6-cylinder configurations FIGURE 2-19. They are shorter

FIGURE 2-17 Tilting cylinder banks can reduce both engine height and hood height, which allows a more streamlined hood line.

FIGURE 2-19 Horizontally opposed engines are commonly found in 4- and 6-cylinder configurations.

lengthwise than a comparable in-line engine but wider than a V type. Horizontally opposed engines have two banks of cylinders, 180 degrees apart, on opposite sides of the crankshaft. It is a useful design when little vertical space is available. A horizontally opposed engine is only fitted longitudinally.

V

V engines have two banks of cylinders sitting side by side in a V arrangement sharing a common crankshaft FIGURE 2-20. This compact design allows for about twice the power output from a V engine as an in-line engine of the same length. In automotive applications, V engines can typically be found in 6-, 8-, 10-, and 12-cylinder configurations. A V6 will have two banks of 3 cylinders, a V8 two banks of 4 cylinders, etc. The angle of the V tends to vary according to the number of cylinders and can be found by dividing 720 degrees (two rotations of the crankshaft, which equals one complete cycle) by the number of cylinders. The natural angle for a V8 is 90 degrees. The natural angle for a V6 is 120 degrees, for a V10 is 72 degrees, and for a V12 is 60 degrees. Designing the engine around the natural angle means the engine can have a shorter length because each crankshaft throw can be shared between two cylinders. Some manufacturers vary their angles from those natural angles and use 90 degrees for a V6 and 15 degrees for a VR6 due to convenience or design requirements. Varying away from the natural angle means that the crankshaft must have one cylinder per crank throw, making the engine slightly longer.

VR and W

The **VR engine** uses a single bank of cylinders, but the cylinders are staggered at a shallow 15-degree V within the bank. This design not only allows the engine to be shorter than an in-line engine, but also makes it narrower than a typical V engine . The **W engine** consists of two VR cylinder banks in a deeper V arrangement to each other. This gives a very compact, yet powerful engine design.

FIGURE 2-20 V engines are shorter than in-line engines of equivalent capacity.

Rotary Engines

Rotary engines are very powerful for their size, but they do not use conventional pistons that slide back and forth inside a straight cylinder. Instead, a rotary engine uses a triangular rotor that turns inside an oval-shaped housing. The rotary engine has three combustion events for each rotation of the rotor. As the rotor turns, it carries the air/fuel mixture around the chambers, which are created between the tips of the rotor and the chamber wall. The rotor compresses the air/fuel mixture, and spark plugs ignite the mixture just like a conventional engine. The rotary engine does not have intake and exhaust valves like a traditional piston engine; instead it has exhaust and intake ports that are covered and uncovered by the rotating rotor in the chamber. This design reduces the number of parts and makes it less complicated than a piston engine. Rotary engines generally have more than one rotor, with two being most common. The design of the rotary engine provides a very compact power unit.

Transmission and Axle Configurations

In most vehicles, the engine is bolted firmly to either a transmission or a transaxle FIGURE 2-21. A transmission transmits engine power to a drive shaft, final drive and differential gears, and driving axles. Transmissions are usually used in front-engine, rear-wheel drive vehicles. Alternatively, a transaxle is a self-contained unit with the transmission, final drive gears, and differential located in one casing. It is usually used on front-engine, front-wheel drive vehicles or rear-engine, rear-wheel drive vehicles. It can also be used on some sports cars with front-engine, rear-wheel drive, with the transaxle connected to the engine by a drive shaft.

Live and Dead Axles

Vehicles can be described by the number of axles and driven wheels. Each axle typically has one wheel on each end of the axle. Axles come in two configurations: live axle and dead axle. Live axles use the engine's torque to turn the wheels (drive the vehicle) and at the same time support the weight of the vehicle. The wheels and axles on a live axle are also called drive wheels and drive axles since they propel the vehicle. Dead axles support the weight of the vehicle only while allowing the wheels to

A

FIGURE 2-21 **A.** Transmission. **B.** Transaxle.

rotate freely on the axle. The wheels on dead axles are not considered drive wheels since they support the vehicle's weight. Most light vehicles have only two axles: one live axle and one dead axle FIGURE 2-22. On commercial vehicles, the load carried on a single axle is limited by law, so vehicles with extra axles are common. A heavy vehicle may have six wheels (three axles) to support the vehicle, but only four wheels (two axles) actually drive it. The extra axle at the rear is used only to support the weight of the vehicle and is sometimes called a lazy axle. This vehicle is called a 6 × 2 (expressed as "6-by-2") vehicle. If the lazy axle is changed to a drive axle, this becomes a 6 × 4 vehicle. Some heavy transport vehicles have an extra steering axle, which allows even more weight to be carried.

Location of Live Axles

The location of the live axle determines whether the vehicle is classified as rear-wheel drive, front-wheel drive, four-wheel drive, or all-wheel drive. If the live axle is at the front of the vehicle, it is considered a front-wheel drive vehicle. Front-wheel drive vehicles use the front wheels to pull the vehicle along. In light passenger vehicles, a live front axle in the front of the vehicle gives it lighter body weight and increased interior room. The engine and transaxle are at the front and can be mounted transversely, with the engine parallel to the front axle, or longitudinally where the engine is in line with the centerline of the vehicle. This gives good traction on the front wheels but less traction on the rear wheels, especially when braking or making evasive maneuvers.

If the live axle is at the rear of the vehicle, it is considered a rear-wheel drive vehicle and pushes the vehicle along. With the engine in front, this spreads out the weight of the drive train assemblies throughout the vehicle, putting more of the weight on the rear wheels. Some rear-wheel drive vehicles have the engine at the rear, driving the wheels through a transaxle. Moving the

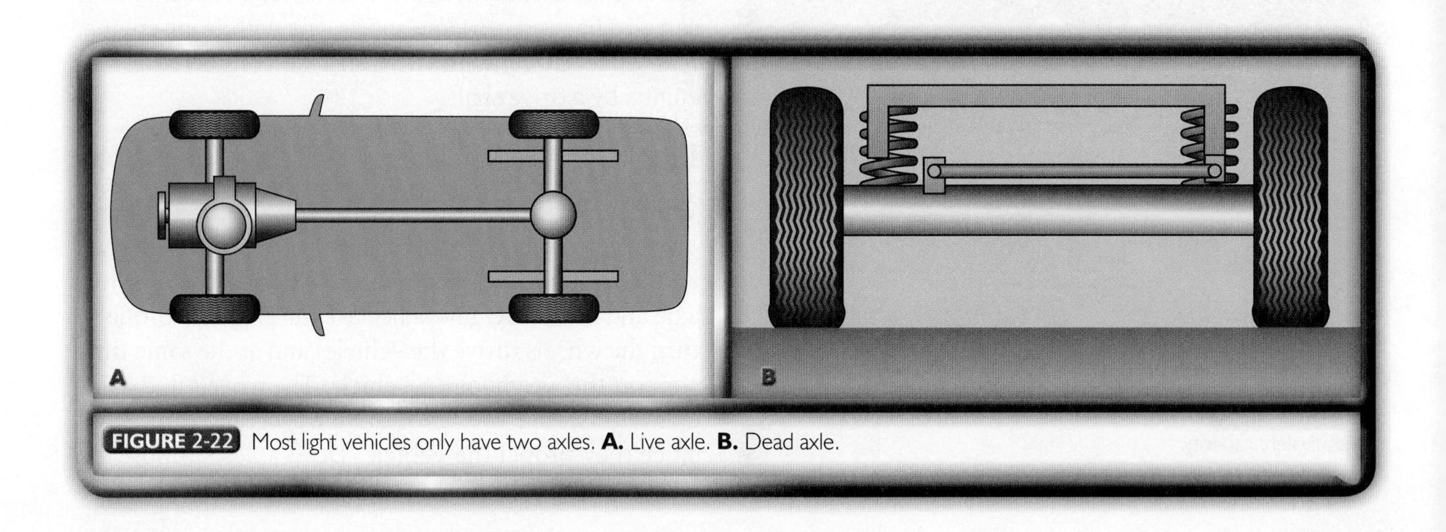
A
B

FIGURE 2-22 Most light vehicles only have two axles. **A.** Live axle. **B.** Dead axle.

engine to the rear allows a lower hood line, which may improve aerodynamics. The increase in weight over the rear wheels can improve their traction, but at the expense of less traction on the front wheels.

A vehicle in which the engine is located behind the driver but in front of the rear drive axle is called a mid-engine, rear-wheel drive vehicle. A mid-engine design locates the weight of the engine near the center of the vehicle. This allows for a low hood profile, balanced distribution of weight, and good handling. This layout is commonly used in sports cars.

The previous examples would be called two-wheel drive vehicles, or 4 × 2. This means that there are four wheels, but only two drive wheels. On all-wheel drive vehicles, both axles are live and all four wheels drive (4 × 4) the vehicle. Driving all four wheels requires additional components and complexity, which add weight and cost. Most 4 × 4 vehicles are more expensive and less fuel efficient than similar 4 × 2 vehicles.

Torque

Torque is the twisting force applied to a shaft. In a vehicle, torque is used to drive the vehicle down the road. Torque is developed in the engine when combustion of the air/fuel mixture causes high pressure to push the piston down the cylinder and apply a twisting force to the crankshaft. The torque in the crankshaft is then used to twist the gears in the transmission, which is then used to twist the gears in the final drive assembly, which is then used to twist the axles, which is then used to twist the wheels and tires, which drive the vehicle down the road.

Torque is also used by technicians when tightening bolts and nuts. Most of the bolts and nuts on the vehicle have a torque specified by the manufacturer that they must be tightened to. This is accomplished by using a special wrench that has the ability to measure torque. Thus, torque is an important concept for technicians to understand. Torque in the Imperial system is measured by the foot-pound (ft-lb) and inch-pound (in-lb), and in the metric system it is measured by the Newton meter (Nm). TABLE 2-1 lists standard torque conversions.

TABLE 2-1: Torque Conversions

12 in-lb	1 ft-lb
1 in-lb	0.08 ft-lb
1 Nm	0.74 ft-lb
1 Nm	8.8 in-lb

Torque Designations

The measure of torque is based on the equivalent twisting force exerted by an amount of weight (mass) applied to a perpendicular lever of a given length. The following designations are used in measuring torque:

- A foot-pound (ft-lb) is the twisting force applied to a shaft by a lever 1 foot long with a 1 pound mass on the end.
- An inch-pound (in-lb) is the twisting force applied to a shaft by a lever 1 inch long with a 1 pound mass on the end.
- A Newton meter (Nm) is the twisting force applied to a shaft by a lever 1 meter long with a force of 1 Newton applied to the end of the lever. (1 N is equivalent to the force applied by a mass of 102 grams, or .102 kg.)

Transmissions and Final Drives

A vehicle with a manual transmission uses a clutch to engage and disengage the engine from the transmission FIGURE 2-23. Engine torque is transmitted through the clutch to the transmission or transaxle. The transmission or transaxle contains sets of gears that increase or decrease the torque, which allows the vehicle to have more pulling power in low gears and higher road speed in higher gears. Drive from the transmission is then transmitted to the rest of the drive train. The lower the gear ratio selected, the higher the torque transmitted. A vehicle starting from rest needs a lot of torque, but once it is moving, it can maintain speed with only a relatively small amount of torque. A higher gear ratio can then be selected and engine speed reduced.

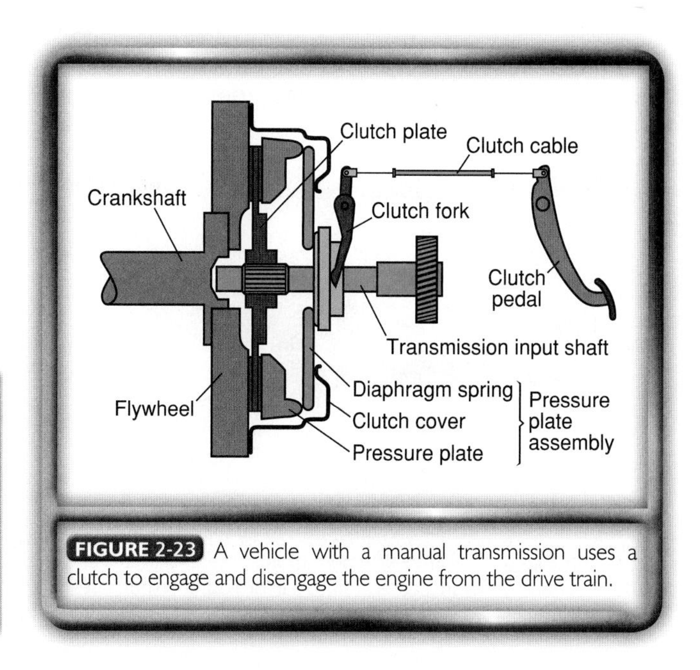
Clutch plate
Clutch cable
Crankshaft
Clutch fork
Clutch pedal
Transmission input shaft
Flywheel
Diaphragm spring
Clutch cover
Pressure plate
Pressure plate assembly

FIGURE 2-23 A vehicle with a manual transmission uses a clutch to engage and disengage the engine from the drive train.

A conventional vehicle with the engine at the front and driving wheels at the rear uses a **drive shaft** to transmit torque from the transmission to the final drive. The **final drive** provides a final gear reduction to multiply the torque before applying it to the drive axles FIGURE 2-24. On front-engine, rear-wheel drive vehicles, the drive shaft is fitted down the centerline of the vehicle, and the final drive at the rear of the vehicle changes the direction of the drive by 90 degrees from the center of the vehicle out to the wheels via the axles. Inside the final drive, a **differential gear set** divides the torque to the axles and allows for the difference in speed of each wheel when cornering.

Axles transmit the torque to the driving wheels. In a rear-wheel drive vehicle, the axles can be solid or contain joints to allow for movement of the suspension. For a transaxle-equipped vehicle, each drive shaft has movable joints to allow for suspension and steering movement.

An automatic transmission or transaxle performs similar functions to a manual transmission or transaxle, except that gear selection is automatically controlled either hydraulically or electronically. The automatic transmission uses a **torque converter** (instead of a clutch), which acts as a hydraulic coupling to transfer the drive from the engine to the transmission. Automatic transmissions are covered in more depth in the Automatic Transmission section.

Four-Wheel Drive

A four-wheel drive (4WD) vehicle can drive all four wheels so it has a drive shaft, a final drive and differential gears, and axles for both the front and rear axle assemblies. A transfer case is attached to the transmission. The transfer case controls the drive to the front and rear axles. It has a selector lever to select two- or four-wheel drive. Some transfer cases also allow for selection of high and low range, which changes the gear ratios to the wheels.

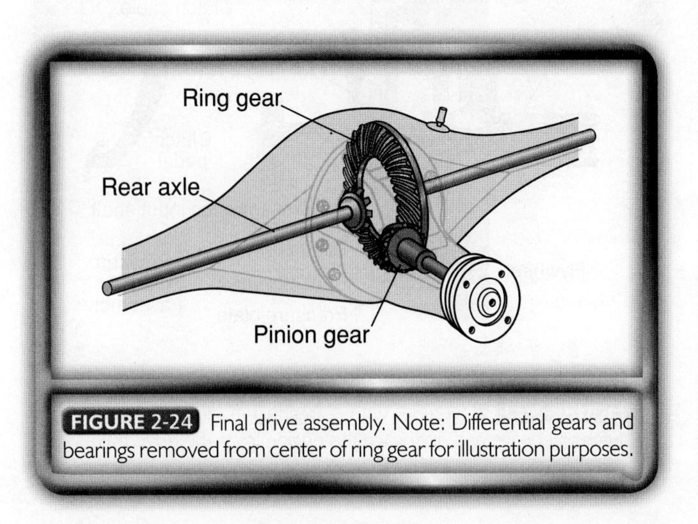
Ring gear
Rear axle
Pinion gear

FIGURE 2-24 Final drive assembly. Note: Differential gears and bearings removed from center of ring gear for illustration purposes.

This is helpful when driving in rough off-road conditions where vehicle speed is very slow.

Part-time 4WD means the vehicle is usually driven in two-wheel drive and switched to full-time when needed by engaging the transfer case. The transfer case locks the drive shafts together and directs torque through them to both axles. When disengaged, the vehicle transfer case is coupled to one drive shaft only. When 4WD is disengaged, most part-time 4WD vehicles drive the rear wheels. Constant 4WD, also called all-wheel drive, uses a third differential in the transfer case to allow for the difference in speed between the front and rear wheels during cornering.

All-Wheel Drive

All-wheel drive vehicles provide drive to all four wheels of the vehicle. All-wheel drive systems should not be confused with part-time four-wheel drive vehicles. The all-wheel drive cannot normally be disconnected or deselected. The all-wheel drive vehicle can be used on hard pavement with drive to all wheels because the transfer case employs a center differential unit that allows the front and rear axles to rotate at slightly different speeds. There are various methods of splitting the drive between the front and rear wheels. Some transfer cases use an electronically controlled multiplate clutch, while others use a **viscous coupling**. Both of these devices allow a small difference in speed between the front and rear axles when the vehicle is turning but do not allow any great difference in speed such as when one or more of the wheels lose traction. The driver can still temporarily lock the front and rear axles together by moving a separate lever as in a conventional 4WD or by moving the main gear selector. This is called a differential lock.

Some full-time 4WD sedans use a front engine and transaxle, with a drive shaft connected to drive the rear wheels. These cars are lighter and less rugged than conventional off-road types and usually operate at higher speeds. The drive to all four wheels provides better balanced handling and traction for cornering in slippery conditions.

Regardless of the type of system fitted, the aim is the same—to provide drive to all four wheels constantly while the vehicle is in motion. The power is not necessarily split 50/50 between the front and rear wheels; torque is usually split 60% to front wheels and 40% to rear wheels. Some vehicles incorporate sophisticated traction and torque control systems to the vehicle to maintain effective traction of the wheels to the road under all driving conditions. These systems vary the torque split between the front and rear wheels.

Wrap-up

Ready for Review

- Learning automotive terminology is essential to becoming an automotive technician.
- Vehicle body design types include sedan, station wagon, hatchback, convertible, coupe, van, minivan, pickup, crossover utility vehicle (CUV), and sport utility vehicle (SUV).
- Sedans have enclosed bodies with a maximum of four doors, while coupes only have two doors; either design can be fixed roof or convertible.
- The hatch of a hatchback lifts up at the rear of the vehicle to provide luggage area access.
- Convertibles can convert from enclosed top to open top via a retractable roof.
- Station wagons have increased luggage capacity due to an extended roof.
- Pickup trucks are designed to support greater loads than passenger cars.
- Minivans are lighter duty versions of full-size vans.
- SUVs can carry and/or tow moderately heavy loads.
- A vehicle chassis is the steel structure that supports the engine, wheels, and transmission.
- The unibody vehicle design replaced the body-on-frame design, allowing for lighter-weight cars that could be manufactured more quickly.
- Vehicle openings include: engine compartment hood, hatch and tailgate openings, fuel door, and battery access covers.
- Engine compartment hoods have remote release levers to prevent unauthorized access.
- Vehicles must convert stored chemical energy into active mechanical energy.
- Stored energy sources include: gasoline, diesel fuel, natural gas, alcohol, bio-diesel, hydrogen, and battery acid.
- Conversion of chemical energy occurs via an internal combustion engine or operation of an electric motor.
- The transmission changes gear ratios to match engine speed and output to desired road speed.
- The suspension system uses shock absorbers, linkages, and springs to connect the wheels to the chassis.
- The electrical system includes the battery, powertrain control system, lighting system, accessory systems, safety systems, passenger comfort systems, and entertainment systems.
- The drive train consists of the engine, transmission/transaxle, differential, axles, and wheels.
- Drive train layout can have a front-, mid-, or rear-mounted engine, which can be oriented longitudinally or transversely.
- The four common drive wheel arrangements are: front-wheel drive, rear-wheel drive, all-wheel drive, and four-wheel drive.
- Engines are classified according to type, cylinder arrangement, number of cylinders/rotors, and total engine displacement.
- The two types of engine are piston (most common) and rotary.
- Piston engines are configured in one of four ways: in-line, horizontally opposed, V, or VR/W.
- Multicylinder engines vary in the number of cylinders; examples include in-line 4, V8, Flat 6, W12.
- In-line engines have a single row of side-by-side cylinders.
- Horizontally opposed engines separate two banks of cylinders by 180 degrees, on either side of the crankshaft.
- V engines have two rows of side-by-side cylinders that share a crankshaft.
- VR/W engines are narrower and shorter than other engines.
- Rotary engines use one or more triangular rotors.
- Axles can be live and use engine torque to turn the wheels or dead and just support the weight of the vehicle.
- Axle location determines the drive wheel arrangement.
- Torque is a twisting force that is applied to the crankshaft by movement of the pistons or to nuts and bolts by a technician's wrench.
- Manual transmissions require a clutch to transmit torque and engage/disengage the engine from the transmission.
- A conventional vehicle uses a drive shaft to transmit torque from the transmission to the final drive.
- Automatic transmissions use a torque converter instead of a clutch.
- Four-wheel drive vehicles can switch from two-wheel to four-wheel drive by engaging the transfer case attached to the transmission.
- All-wheel drive vehicles cannot be switched to two-wheel drive.
- All-wheel drive vehicles provide constant drive to all four wheels, with only a small difference in speed between front and rear axles when the vehicle is turning.

Key Terms

all-wheel drive (AWD) A drive train arrangement in which all of the wheels drive the vehicle.

axle A shaft connected to wheels that transmits the driving torque to the wheels.

chassis The main support frame in a vehicle. It includes the running gear, such as suspension, the engine, and the drive train.

convertible A vehicle that converts from having an enclosed top to having an open top by a roof that can be removed, retracted, or folded away.

coupe A two-door vehicle that has seating for two people and may have a small rear seat.

crossover utility vehicle (CUV) A vehicle that is a cross between an SUV and a passenger vehicle.

differential gear set The arrangement of gears between two axles that allows each axle to spin at its own speed when the vehicle is going around a corner.

drive shaft The shaft or tube fitted with universal couplings that is connected between the transmission and other drive train components to transmit torque and rotation.

drive train A term used to identify the engine, transmission/transaxle, differential, axles, and wheels.

engine configuration The way engine cylinders are arranged—for example, V, flat, or in-line.

final drive A component that provides a final gear reduction and allows for the difference in speed of each wheel when cornering.

flywheel The heavy disc bolted to the rear of the crankshaft that smooths out the power pulses and stores energy from the power stroke for use in keeping the crankshaft rotating through the other three strokes.

four-wheel drive (4WD) A drive train layout in which the engine drive has either two wheels or four wheels depending on which mode is selected by the driver.

front-wheel drive (FWD) A drive train layout in which the engine drives the front wheels.

hatchback A vehicle that has a shared passenger and cargo area; it typically is available in three- and five-door arrangements.

horizontally opposed engine An engine with two banks of cylinders, 180 degrees apart, on opposite sides of the crankshaft. It is also called a flat engine or a boxer engine.

in-line engine An engine in which the cylinders are arranged side by side in a single row.

longitudinal A term used to describe the front-to-back engine orientation when mounted in the engine compartment.

minivan A lighter-duty van used for carrying six to eight occupants or light cargo.

pick-up A vehicle that carries cargo; it has stronger chassis components and suspension than a sedan.

piston engine An internal combustion engine that uses cylindrical pistons moving back and forth in a cylinder to extract mechanical energy from chemical energy.

rear-wheel drive (RWD) A drive train layout in which the engine drives the rear wheels.

rotary engine An engine that uses a triangular rotor turning in a housing instead of conventional pistons.

sedan A vehicle configuration that has an enclosed body, with a maximum of four doors to allow access to the passenger compartment.

sport utility vehicle (SUV) A passenger vehicle built on a light-truck chassis; it is usually equipped with four-wheel drive and capable of hauling heavier loads than typical passenger vehicles.

station wagon A vehicle configuration with four doors with a roof line that continues into the rear cargo area and a rear door for access.

torque Twisting force.

torque converter A device that is turned by the crankshaft and transmits torque to the input shaft of an automatic transmission.

transverse A term used to describe the side-to-side engine orientation when mounted in the engine compartment.

truck A large heavy vehicle for carrying cargo.

unibody design A vehicle design that does not use a rigid frame to support the body. The body panels are designed to provide the strength for the vehicle.

V engine A term used to describe an engine configuration that uses a single bank of cylinders staggered at a shallow 15-degree V.

viscous coupling A device that acts like a limited slip clutch.

VR engine An engine in which the pistons are in one bank but form a shallow V within the bank.

W engine A term used to describe an engine configuration consisting of two VR cylinder banks in a deep V arrangement.

ASE-Type Questions

1. Tech A says that most vehicles today are built with a ladder frame. Tech B says that most vehicles today do not have a frame. Who is correct?
   a. Tech A
   b. Tech B
   c. Both A and B
   d. Neither A nor B
2. Tech A says that a roadster is a coupe. Tech B says that a station wagon and a hatchback are the same. Who is correct?
   a. Tech A
   b. Tech B
   c. Both A and B
   d. Neither A nor B
3. Tech A says that gasoline is energy in chemical form. Tech B says that chemical energy is converted to mechanical energy in the combustion process of an engine. Who is correct?
   a. Tech A
   b. Tech B
   c. Both A and B
   d. Neither A nor B
4. Tech A says that a live axle is an axle that can be steered. Tech B says that a dead axle supports the weight of the vehicle, but doesn't power it. Who is correct?
   a. Tech A
   b. Tech B
   c. Both A and B
   d. Neither A nor B
5. Tech A says that the gear ratio in the transmission helps the vehicle gain speed. Tech B says that the gear ratio of the final drive can be selected with a gearshift lever. Who is correct?
   a. Tech A
   b. Tech B
   c. Both A and B
   d. Neither A nor B
6. Tech A says that pushing on the brake pedal stops the vehicle by converting chemical energy into thermal energy. Tech B says that brake pedal pressure is transmitted to the brakes hydraulically. Who is correct?
   a. Tech A
   b. Tech B
   c. Both A and B
   d. Neither A nor B
7. Tech A says that one advantage of a mid-engine design is better weight distribution. Tech B says that the rear-engine design is commonly used in 4-wheel drive vehicles. Who is correct?
   a. Tech A
   b. Tech B
   c. Both A and B
   d. Neither A nor B
8. Tech A says that the purpose of the battery is to charge the vehicle. Tech B says that in-line engines are generally easier to work on than V engines. Who is correct?
   a. Tech A
   b. Tech B
   c. Both A and B
   d. Neither A nor B
9. Tech A says that the natural angle of a V6 is 90 degrees. Tech B says that the natural angle of a V10 is 60 degrees. Who is correct?
   a. Tech A
   b. Tech B
   c. Both A and B
   d. Neither A nor B
10. Tech A says that the definition of torque is how far the crankshaft twists. Tech B says that torque can relate to tightness of bolts. Who is correct?
    a. Tech A
    b. Tech B
    c. Both A and B
    d. Neither A nor B

INSTRUCTIONS:
1. PULL PIN. HOLD UPRIGHT.
2. START BACK 10 FEET (3 m), AIM AT BASE OF FIRE.
3. DEPRESS PUSH LEVER, SWEEP SIDE TO SIDE.
SimplexGrinnell

CHAPTER 3

KNOW
SEE
DO
PROVE

NATEF Tasks

Required Supplemental Tasks
Shop and Personal Safety

	Page
■ Identify general shop safety rules and procedures.	38–60
■ Identify the location of the posted evacuation routes.	39
■ Identify marked safety areas.	42–43
■ Identify the location and the types of fire extinguishers and other fire safety equipment; demonstrate knowledge of the procedures for using fire extinguishers and other fire safety equipment.	47–49
■ Identify the location and use of eye wash stations.	49
■ Locate and demonstrate knowledge of safety data sheets (SDS).	49–58

Introduction to Automotive Safety

Know
See
Do
Prove

Knowledge Objectives

After reading this chapter, you will be able to:

1. Describe how to follow safe practices in the workplace. (pp 38–42)
2. Describe how the Occupational Safety and Health Administration (OSHA) and the Environmental Protection Agency (EPA) impact the workplace. (p 40)
3. Describe the difference between a shop policy and a shop procedure. (pp 40–41)
4. Explain how shop policies, procedures, and safety inspections make the workplace safer. (pp 41, 59)
5. Describe how to identify hazardous environments and the safety precautions that should be undertaken in hazardous environments. (pp 42–43)
6. Identify workplace safety signs and their meanings. (pp 42–43)
7. Describe the standard safety equipment that should be in the workplace. (p 44)
8. Describe how to maintain a safe level of air quality in the workplace. (pp 44–45)
9. Describe the safety precautions to be taken when working with electrical tools and equipment. (pp 45–46)
10. Explain how the shop layout contributes to efficiency and safety. (pp 46–47)
11. Describe how to reduce the risk of fires in the shop. (p 47)
12. Describe how to use firefighting equipment. (pp 47–49)
13. Explain how to use an SDS. (pp 49–58)
14. Describe how to manage toxic dust. (pp 50–52)
15. Manage engine oil and fluids (p. 59)

Know
See
Do
Prove

Skills Objectives

After reading this chapter, you will be able to:

1. Identify hazardous environments and apply appropriate risk prevention strategies. (p 42)
2. Locate information on an SDS and apply appropriate safety measures. (pp 49–58)
3. Safely clean and dispose of brake dust. (p 51)

Introduction

Occupational safety and health is very important to ensure that everyone can work without being injured. Governments will normally have legislation in place with significant penalties for those who do not follow safe practices in the workplace. Potential hazards are in most workplaces, especially automotive shops. It is important to learn about hazards so you can identify them and take action to protect yourself and your coworkers. Some hazards are obvious, such as vehicles falling from hoists or jacks or tires exploding during inflation. Other hazards are less obvious, such as the long-term effects of fumes from solvents. There are many things to learn about safety in the automotive shop, but it is impossible to cover every situation you will encounter. One of the most important skills to learn is the ability to recognize unsafe practices or equipment and put in place measures to prevent injuries from happening.

Occupational safety and health is everyone's responsibility. You have a responsibility to ensure that you work safely and take care not to put others at risk by acting in an unsafe manner. Your employer also has a responsibility to provide a safe working environment. To ensure the safety of yourself and others, make sure you are aware of the correct safety procedures at your workplace. This means listening very carefully to safety information provided by your employer and asking for clarification, help, or instructions if you are unsure how to perform a task safely. Always think about how you are performing shop tasks, be on the lookout for unsafe equipment and work practices, and wear the correct **personal protective equipment (PPE)**. PPE refers to items of safety equipment like safety footwear, gloves, clothing, protective eyewear, and hearing protection FIGURE 3-1.

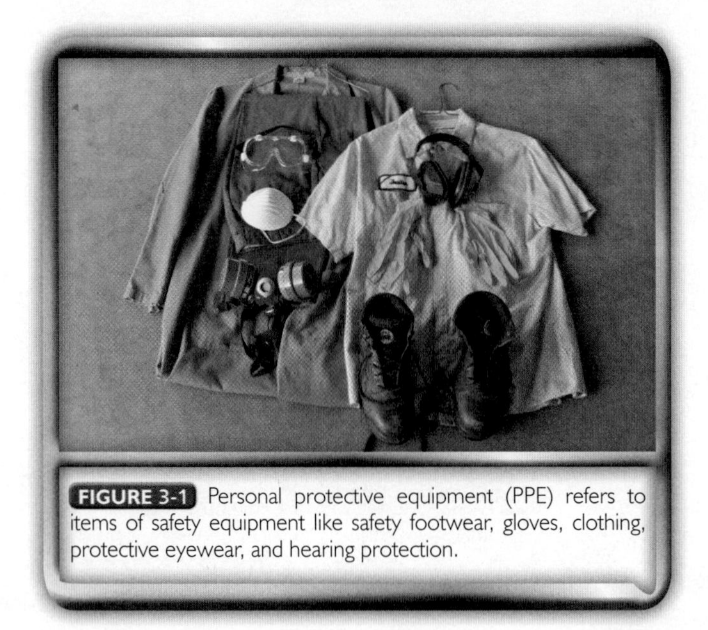

FIGURE 3-1 Personal protective equipment (PPE) refers to items of safety equipment like safety footwear, gloves, clothing, protective eyewear, and hearing protection.

Safety Overview

Motor vehicle servicing is one of the most common vocations worldwide. Hundreds of thousands of shops service millions of vehicles every day. That means many people are conducting automotive servicing and there is a great potential for things to go wrong. It is up to you and your workplace to make sure work activities are conducted safely. Accidents are not caused by properly maintained tools; accidents are caused by people.

You Are the Automotive Technician

You are changing the oil on a new type of vehicle for the first time. The oil pan has the drain plug on the side of the oil pan, instead of the bottom of the pan. You place the drain pain directly under the drain plug like you normally do. Unfortunately, when the plug comes out, the oil shoots sideways right over the side of the drain pan. You reposition it quickly, but not before a large puddle is on the floor.

1. Why is it important to review the SDS before cleaning up a spill?
2. What is the minimum PPE that should be worn to manage this spill?
3. What are some of the health hazards of coming into frequent or prolonged contact with used engine oil?

Don't Underestimate the Dangers

Because vehicle servicing and repair are so commonplace, it is easy to overlook the many potential risks relating to this field. Think carefully about what you are doing and how you are doing it. Think through the steps, trying to anticipate things that may go wrong and taking steps to prevent them. Also be wary of taking shortcuts. In most cases, the time saved by taking a shortcut is nothing compared to the time spent recovering from an accident.

Accidents and Injuries Can Happen at Any Time

There is the possibility of an accident occurring whenever work is undertaken. For example, fires and explosions are a constant hazard wherever there are flammable fuels. Electricity can kill quickly, as well as cause painful shocks and burns. Heavy equipment and machinery can easily cause broken bones or crush fingers and toes. Hazardous solvents and other chemicals can burn or blind as well as contribute to many kinds of illness. Trips and falls can be caused by things such as oil spills and tools left lying around. Poor lifting and handling techniques can cause chronic strain injuries, particularly to your back **FIGURE 3-2**.

Accidents and Injuries are Avoidable

Almost all accidents are avoidable or preventable by taking a few precautions. Think of nearly every accident you have witnessed or heard about. In most cases someone made a mistake. Whether involved in horse play or neglecting maintenance on tools or equipment, these instances lead to injury. Most of these accidents can be prevented if people follow policies and develop a "safety first" attitude.

By following regulations and safety procedures, you can make your workplace safe. Learn and follow all of the correct safety procedures for your workplace. Always wear the right PPE and stay alert and aware of what is happening around you. Think about what you are doing, how you are doing it, and its effect on others. You will also need to know what to do in case of an emergency. Document and report all accidents and injuries whenever they happen, and take the proper steps to make sure they never happen again.

Evacuation Routes

Evacuation routes are a safe way of escaping danger and gathering in a safe place where everyone can be accounted for in the event of an emergency. It is important to have more than one evacuation route in case any single route is blocked during the emergency. Your shop may have an evacuation procedure that clearly identifies the evacuation routes **FIGURE 3-3**.

Often the evacuation routes will be marked with colored lines painted on the floors. Exits should be highlighted with signs that may be illuminated. Always make sure you are familiar with the evacuation routes for the shop. Before conducting any task, identify which route you will take if an emergency occurs.

Work Environment

The work environment can be described as anywhere you work. The condition of the work environment plays an important role in making the workplace safer. A safe work environment goes a long way toward preventing

FIGURE 3-2 Poor lifting and handling techniques can cause chronic strain injuries, particularly to your back.

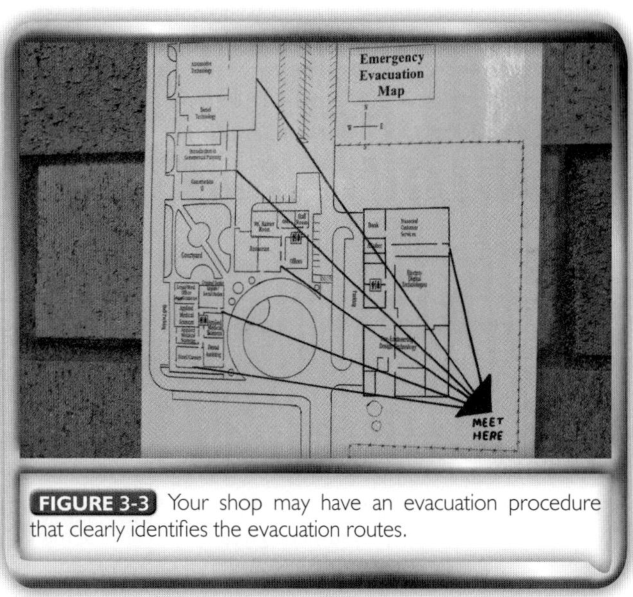
Emergency
Evacuation
Map
MEET
HERE

FIGURE 3-3 Your shop may have an evacuation procedure that clearly identifies the evacuation routes.

accidents, injuries, and illnesses. There are many ways to describe a safe work environment, but generally it would contain a well-organized shop layout, use of shop policies and procedures, safe equipment, safety equipment, safety training, employees who work safely, a workplace orientation, good supervision, and a workplace culture that supports safe work practices.

OSHA and EPA

OSHA stands for the **Occupational Safety and Health Administration (OSHA)**. It is a U.S. government agency that was created to provide national leadership in occupational safety and health. It finds the most effective ways to help prevent worker fatalities and workplace injuries and illnesses. It has the authority to conduct workplace inspections and, if required, fine employers and workplaces if they violate OSHA regulations and procedures. For example, a fine may be imposed on the employer or workplace if a worker is electrocuted by a piece of faulty machinery that has not been regularly tested and maintained.

EPA stands for the **Environmental Protection Agency**. This federal government agency deals with issues related to environmental safety. The EPA conducts research and monitoring, sets standards, and can hold employees and companies legally accountable in order to keep the environment protected. Shop activities will need to comply with EPA laws and regulations by ensuring that waste products are disposed of in an environmentally responsible way, chemicals and fluids are correctly stored, and work practices do not contribute to damaging the environment.

> **TECHNICIAN TIP**
>
> Never place anything in the way of evacuation routes, including equipment, tools, parts, or vehicles.

Shop Policies and Procedures

Shop policies and procedures are a set of documents that outline how tasks and activities in the shop are to be conducted and managed. They also ensure that the shop operates according to OSHA and EPA laws and regulations. A **policy** is a guiding principle that sets the shop direction, while a **procedure** is a list of the steps required to get the same result each time a task or activity is performed. An example of a policy would be an OSHA document for the shop that describes how the shop complies with legislation.

Applied Science

AS-2: Environmental Issues: The technician develops and maintains an understanding of all federal, state, and local rules and regulations regarding environmental issues related to the work of the automobile technician.

You need to keep up to date with local laws and regulations regarding environmental issues. There are large fines associated with disregarded environmental regulations. To remain informed, you can log on to local state websites to check the latest laws and regulations. The US Environmental Protection Agency (EPA) website also has up-to-date information on environmental regulations (www.epa.gov/lawsregs/). More information can be found on the specific regulations for the automotive industry at www.epa.gov/lawsregs/sectors/automotive.html. This site has a full listing of laws and regulations, compliance measures, and enforcement tactics. For additional laws that are enforced by your local state environmental agencies, go to www.epa.gov/epahome/state.htm.

AS-3: Environmental Issues: The technician uses such things as government impact statements, media information, and general knowledge of pollution and waste management to correctly use and dispose of products that result from the performance of a repair task.

When you complete a job, you must be able to identify what to do with any waste products created from the repair task. This could be as simple as knowing where and how to recycle cardboard boxes or as complex as knowing what to do with brake components that may contain asbestos. Normally there will be a table posted in the garage that details the correct measures for disposing of and storing waste material. A sample table follows:

Component	Material/Parts	Removal and Safety Information	Recommended Storage
Air-conditioning gases (refrigerant)	R12, R134a	Use approved evacuation and collection equipment required. **NOTE:** Requires A/C license.	Use approved storage containers—reused or recycled.
Batteries	Plastic, rubber, lead, sulfuric acid	Avoid contact between sulfuric acid and your skin, clothing, or eyes.	Store off the ground in a covered area for collection by recycler.
Brake fluid	Diethylene and polyethylene glycol-monoalkyl ethers	Corrosive and highly toxic to the environment. Drain into pan or tray.	Store in a drum in a covered area for collection by a licensed operator.

(continues)

(continues)

Component	Material/Parts	Removal and Safety Information	Recommended Storage
Brake shoes and pads pre-2004	Asbestos	Fibers are dangerous if inhaled.	Put in a plastic bag in a sealed container for collection by contractor.
Coolant	Phosphoric acid, hydrazine ethylene glycol, alcohols	Radiator coolant can be toxic to the environment.	Store in sealed drums in a covered area for recycling or collection by a licensed operator.
Coverings for plastic parts, and plastic bags and containers for parts shipping	Plastic-made components	Plastic components that can be recycled will bear a recycling symbol: This symbol will have a number inside telling the recycling company what the product is made of. 1	If the plastic container has a recycle code on the product, then put it in the recycle bin. If it does not, then put in general waste. Plastic oil containers cannot be recycled.
Fuel	Unleaded, diesel	Avoid fumes. Fire hazard; keep well away from ignition sources. Siphon from tank to avoid spillage.	Store in a drum in a covered area.
Metal	Brake discs, housings made of metal (gearbox/ engine case and components), metal cuttings	Some metal products can be heavy, so lift with care.	All metal components can be recycled; keep waste metal in a separate recycle bin for sale or disposal.
Oil	Engine, transmission, and differential oils	Fire hazard; keep well away from ignition sources.	Store in a drum/container in a covered area for collection by a licensed operator.
Oil filters	Steel paper fiber	—	Drain filter then crush and store in a leak-proof drum for collection.
Parts boxes and paperwork	Paper, cardboard	—	Store in a recycling bin to be taken away for recycling.
Tires	Rubber, steel, fabric	Keep away from ignition sources.	Store in a fenced area for collection by recycler.
Trim, plastic fittings, and seats	Plastic, metal, cloth	—	Store racked or binned for reuse, sale, or recycling.
Tubes and rubber components	Rubber hoses, mounts, etc.	Keep away from ignition sources.	Store in a collection bin, to be collected and recycled.
Undeployed airbags	Plastics, metals, igniters, explosives	Recommended specific training on airbags before attempting removal. Handle with care; accidental deployment can cause serious harm. If unit is to be scrapped, ensure that it is safely deployed first.	Store faceup in a secure area.

A procedure would be a document that describes the steps required to safely use the vehicle hoist.

Each shop will have its own set of policies and procedures and a system in place to make sure the policies and procedures are regularly reviewed and updated. Regular reviews ensure that new policies and procedures are developed and old ones are modified in case something has changed. For example, if the shop moves to a new building, then a review of policies and procedures will ensure sure that they relate to the new shop, its layout, and equipment. In general, the policies and procedures are written to guide shop practice; help ensure compliance with laws, statutes, and regulations; and reduce the risk of injury. Always follow your shop policies and procedures to reduce the risk of injury to your coworkers and yourself and to prevent damage to property.

It is everyone's responsibility to know and follow the rules. Locate the general shop rules and procedures for your workplace. Look through the contents or index pages to familiarize yourself with the contents. Discuss the policy and the shop rules and procedures with your supervisor. Ask questions to ensure that you understand how the rules and procedures should be applied and your role in making sure they are followed.

Identifying Hazardous Environments

A **hazardous environment** is a place where hazards exist. A **hazard** is anything that could hurt you or someone else, and most workplaces have them. It is almost impossible to remove all hazards, but it is important to identify hazards and work to reduce their potential for causing harm by putting specific measures in place. For example, operating a bench grinder poses a number of hazards. While it is not possible to eliminate the hazards of using the bench grinder, by putting specific measures in place, the risk of those hazards can be reduced.

A risk analysis of a bench grinder would identify the following hazards and risks: a high-velocity particle that could damage your eyesight or that of someone working nearby; the grinding wheel breaking apart, damaging eyesight or causing cuts and abrasion; electrocution if electrical parts are faulty; a risk to your hands from heat or high-velocity particles; a risk to your hearing due to excessive noise; and a risk of entrapment of clothing or body parts through rotating machinery. To reduce the risk of these hazards, the following measures are taken: position the bench grinder in a safe area away from where others work; make sure electrical items are regularly checked for electrical and mechanical safety; when operating the equipment, wear PPE such as protective eyewear, gloves, hearing protection, hairnets, or caps; and do not wear loose clothing that can be caught in the bench grinder.

Note that special work areas in hazardous environments are defined by painted lines. These lines show the hazardous zone around certain machines and areas. If you are not working on the machines, you should stay outside the marked area. In addition to recognizing hazardous areas, you should understand all the warning signs around your shop, including the meaning of the signal word, the colors, the text, and the symbols or pictures on each sign. Ask your supervisor if you do not fully understand any part of the sign.

To identify hazardous environments, follow the steps in SKILL DRILL 3-1.

Standard Safety Measures

Signs

Always remember that a shop is a hazardous environment. To make people more aware of specific shop hazards, legislative bodies have developed a series of safety signs. These signs are designed to give adequate warning of an unsafe situation. Each sign has four components:

- **Signal word:** There are three signal words—danger, warning, and caution. *Danger* indicates an immediately hazardous situation, which, if not avoided, will result in death or serious injury. Danger is usually indicated by white text with a red background. *Warning* indicates a potentially hazardous situation, which, if not avoided, could result in death or serious injury. The sign is usually in black text with a yellow background. *Caution* indicates a potentially hazardous situation, which, if not avoided, may result in minor or moderate injury. It may also be used to alert against unsafe practices. This sign is usually in black text with a yellow background FIGURE 3-4.

DANGER
EYE PROTECTION REQUIRED IN THIS AREA
WARNING
Units can tip or strike you.
• Do not open more than one loaded drawer at a time.
• Keep children away.
• Close lid and lock drawers and doors before moving.
• Apply brakes on locking casters when not moving unit.
• Do not step in or on drawers.
• Secure units together with fasteners.
• Read Instruction Manual.
Tipping of storage unit or unit striking you can cause injury.
Units' edges can cut or pinch.
• Do not pull; push to move.
• Wear gloves when lifting by edges.
• Keep feet and fingers clear of edges when stacking, hanging, or moving units.
Units' edges can cause injury.
P/N 8-24062A
B
CAUTION
WATCH YOUR STEP
C

FIGURE 3-4 Signs. **A.** Danger is usually indicated by white text on a red background. **B.** Warning is usually in black text with an orange background. **C.** Caution is usually in black text with a yellow background.

- **Background color:** The choice of background color also draws attention to potential hazards and is used to provide contrast so the letters or images stand out. For example, a red background identifies a definite hazard; yellow indicates caution for a potential hazard. A green background is used for emergency-type signs, such as for first aid, fire protection, and emergency equipment. A blue background is used for general information signs.
- **Text:** The sign will sometimes include explanatory text intended to provide additional safety information. Some signs are designed to convey a personal safety message.
- **Pictorial message:** In symbol signs, a pictorial message appears alone or is combined with explanatory text. This type of sign allows the safety message to be conveyed to people who are illiterate or who do not speak the local language.

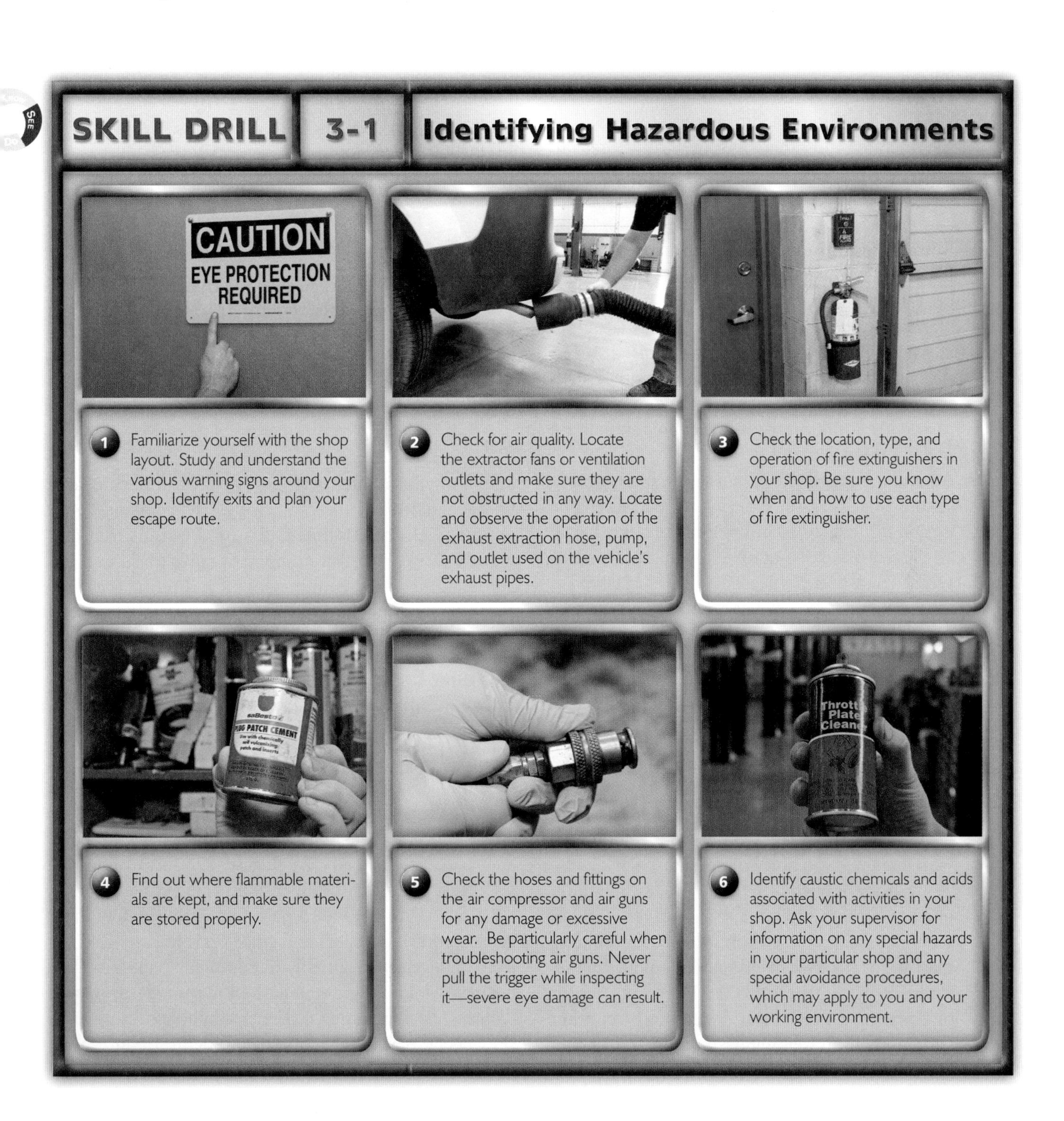
SKILL DRILL 3-1 Identifying Hazardous Environments
CAUTION
EYE PROTECTION REQUIRED
1 Familiarize yourself with the shop layout. Study and understand the various warning signs around your shop. Identify exits and plan your escape route.
2 Check for air quality. Locate the extractor fans or ventilation outlets and make sure they are not obstructed in any way. Locate and observe the operation of the exhaust extraction hose, pump, and outlet used on the vehicle's exhaust pipes.
3 Check the location, type, and operation of fire extinguishers in your shop. Be sure you know when and how to use each type of fire extinguisher.
PLUG PATCH CEMENT
4 Find out where flammable materials are kept, and make sure they are stored properly.
5 Check the hoses and fittings on the air compressor and air guns for any damage or excessive wear. Be particularly careful when troubleshooting air guns. Never pull the trigger while inspecting it—severe eye damage can result.
6 Identify caustic chemicals and acids associated with activities in your shop. Ask your supervisor for information on any special hazards in your particular shop and any special avoidance procedures, which may apply to you and your working environment.

Safety Equipment

Shop safety equipment includes items such as:

- **Handrails:** Handrails are used to separate walkways and pedestrian traffic from work areas. They provide a physical barrier that directs pedestrian traffic and also provide protection from vehicle movements.
- **Machinery guards:** Machinery guards and yellow lines prevent people from accidentally walking into the operating equipment or indicate that a safe distance should be kept from the equipment.
- **Painted lines:** Large, fixed machinery such as lathes and milling machines present a hazard to the operator and others working in the area. To prevent accidents, a machinery guard or a yellow painted line on the floor usually borders this equipment.
- **Soundproof rooms:** Soundproof rooms are usually used when a lot of noise is made by operating equipment. An example is the use of a chassis dynamometer. A vehicle operating on a dynamometer produces a lot of noise from its tires, exhaust, and engine. To protect other shop users from the noise, the dynamometer is usually placed in a soundproof room, keeping shop noise to a minimum.
- **Adequate ventilation:** Exhaust gases in shops are a serious health hazard. Whenever a vehicle's engine is running, toxic gases are emitted from its exhaust. To prevent an excess of toxic gas buildup, a well-ventilated work area is needed as well as a method of directly venting the vehicle's exhaust to the outside.
- **Gas extraction hoses:** The best way to get rid of these gases is with a suction hose that fits over the vehicle's exhaust pipe. The hose is attached to an extraction pump that vents the gas to the outside.
- **Doors and gates:** Doors and gates are used for the same reason as machinery guards and painted lines. A doorway is a physical barrier that can be locked and sealed to separate a hazardous environment from the rest of the shop or a general work area from an office or specialist work area.
- **Temporary barriers:** In the day-to-day operation of a shop, there is often a reason to temporarily separate one work bay from others. If a welding machine or an oxyacetylene cutting torch is in use, it may be necessary to place a temporary screen or barrier around the work area to protect other shop users from welding flash or injury.

TECHNICIAN TIP

Stay alert for hazards or anything that might be dangerous. If you see, hear, or smell anything odd, take steps to fix it or tell your supervisor about the problem.

TECHNICIAN TIP

Whenever you perform a task in the shop, you must use personal protective clothing and equipment that are appropriate for the task and that conform to your local safety regulations and policies. Among other items, these may include:

- Work clothing, such as coveralls and steel-capped footwear
- Eye protection, such as safety glasses and face masks
- Ear protection, such as earmuffs and earplugs
- Hand protection, such as gloves and barrier cream
- Respiratory equipment, such as face masks and valved respirators

If you are not certain what is appropriate or required, ask your supervisor.

Air Quality

Managing air quality in shops helps protect you from potential harm and also protects the environment. There are many shop activities and stored liquids that can reduce the quality of air in shops. Some of these are dangerous fumes from running engines, welding (gas and electric), painting, liquid storage areas, air-conditioning servicing, and dust particles from brake servicing.

Running Engines

Running engines produce dangerous exhaust gases including carbon monoxide and carbon dioxide. Carbon monoxide in small concentrations can kill or cause serious injuries. Carbon dioxide is a greenhouse gas, and vehicles are a major source of carbon dioxide in the atmosphere. Exhaust gases also contain hydrocarbons and oxides of nitrogen. These gases can form smog and also cause breathing problems for some people.

Carbon monoxide in particular is extremely dangerous, as it is odorless and colorless and can build up to toxic levels very quickly in confined spaces. In fact, it doesn't take very much carbon monoxide to pose a danger. The maximum OSHA permissible exposure limit (PEL) is 50 parts per million (ppm) of air for an 8-hour period. The National Institute for Occupational Safety and Health has established a recommended exposure limit of 35 ppm for an 8-hour period. The reason the PEL is so low is because carbon monoxide attaches itself to red blood cells much more easily than oxygen does, and it never leaves the blood cell. This prevents the blood cells from carrying as much oxygen, and if enough carbon monoxide has been inhaled, it effectively asphyxiates the person. Always follow the correct safety precautions when running engines indoors or in a confined space, including over service pits since gases can accumulate there.

The best solution when running engines in an enclosed space is to directly couple the vehicle's exhaust pipe to an exhaust extraction system hose that will ventilate the fumes away from the enclosed space to the outside air. The extraction hose should be vented to where the fumes will not be drawn back indoors, to a place well away from other people and other premises FIGURE 3-5.

Do not assume that an engine fitted with a catalytic converter can be run safely indoors; it cannot. Catalytic converters are fitted into the exhaust system in a similar way as mufflers and have a ceramic core with a catalyst that when in operation controls exhaust emissions through chemical reaction. They require high temperatures to operate efficiently and are less effective when the exhaust gases are relatively cool, such as when the engine is only idling or being run intermittently. A catalytic convertor can never substitute for adequate ventilation or exhaust extraction equipment. In fact, even if the catalytic converter were working at 100% efficiency, the exhaust would contain large amounts of carbon dioxide and very low amounts of oxygen, neither of which conditions can sustain life.

Electrical Safety

Many people are injured by electricity in shops. Poor electrical safety practices can cause shocks and burns, as well as fires and explosions. Make sure you know where the electrical panels for your shop are located. All circuit breakers and fuses should be clearly labeled so that you know which circuits and functions they control FIGURE 3-6. In the case of an emergency, you may need to know how to shut off the electricity supply to a work area or to your entire shop.

Keep the circuit breaker and/or electrical panel covers closed to keep them in good condition, prevent unauthorized access, and prevent accidental contact with the electricity supply. It is important that you do not block or obstruct access to this electrical panel; keep equipment and tools well away so emergency access is not hindered. In some localities, 3 feet (0.91 m) of unobstructed space must be maintained around the panel at all times.

There should be a sufficient number of electrical receptacles in your work area for all your needs. Do not connect multiple appliances to a single receptacle with a simple double adapter. If necessary, use a multi-outlet safety strip that has a built-in overload cutout feature. Electric receptacles should be at least 3 feet (0.91 m) above floor level to reduce the risk of igniting spilled fuel vapors or other flammable liquids.

Portable Electrical Equipment

If you need to use an extension cord, make sure it is made of flexible wiring—not the stiffer type of house wiring—and that it is fitted with a ground wire. The cord should be neoprene-covered, as this material resists oil damage

FIGURE 3-5 Extraction hoses should be vented so that the fumes will not be drawn back indoors.

FIGURE 3-6 All electrical switches and fuses should be clearly labeled so that you know which circuits and functions they control.

FIGURE 3-7. Always check it for cuts, abrasions, or other damage. Be careful how you place the extension cord so it does not cause a tripping hazard. Also avoid rolling equipment or vehicles over it, as doing so can damage the cord. Never use an extension cord in wet conditions or around flammable liquids.

Portable electric tools that operate at 240 volts are often sources of serious shock and burn accidents. Be particularly careful when using these items. Always inspect the cord for damage and check the security of the attached plug before connecting the item to the power supply. Use 110-volt or lower voltage tools if they are available.

All electric tools must be equipped with a ground prong or double-insulated. If they are not, do *not* use them. Never use any high-voltage tool in a wet environment. Air-operated tools cannot give you an electric shock, because they operate on air pressure instead of electricity; so they are safer to use in a wet environment.

Portable Shop Lights

Portable shop lights/droplights can be very useful tools to add light to a particular area or spot on the vehicle you are working on. Always make sure you follow the safety directions when using shop lights. Shop lights should have protective covers fitted to them to prevent accidentally breaking the lamp. If a lamp breaks, it can be an electrical hazard, particularly if a metal object comes in contact with exposed live electricity. For this reason, often low-voltage lamps or lamps with safety switches fitted are used to prevent accidental electrocution. Some shop lights are now cordless, particularly those with LEDs fitted as the light source. Cordless lights are a very safe option because they isolate you from the high voltage.

Electric droplights are a common source of shocks, especially if they are the wrong type for the purpose or if they are poorly constructed or maintained. All droplights should be designed in such a way that the electrical parts can never come into contact with the outer casing of the device. Such lights are called **double-insulated**. The bulb should be completely enclosed in a transparent insulating case or protected within a robust insulating cage FIGURE 3-8.

The bulbs used in electric droplights are very vulnerable to impact and must not be used without insulating cage protection. Incandescent bulbs present an extreme fire hazard if broken in the presence of flammable vapors or liquids and should not be used in repair shops. LED and fluorescent bulbs, while still hazardous, are much safer.

> **TECHNICIAN TIP**
>
> Always inspect the wiring for damage and check the security of the attached plug before connecting a droplight to the power supply. Always switch off and unplug a droplight before changing the bulb.

Shop Layout

The shop should have a layout that is efficient and safe with clearly defined working areas and walkways. Customers should not be allowed to wander through work areas unescorted. A good shop layout can be achieved by thinking about how the work is to be done, how equipment is used, and what traffic movements, both pedestrian and vehicular, occur within the shop. A well-planned shop should have clearly defined areas for

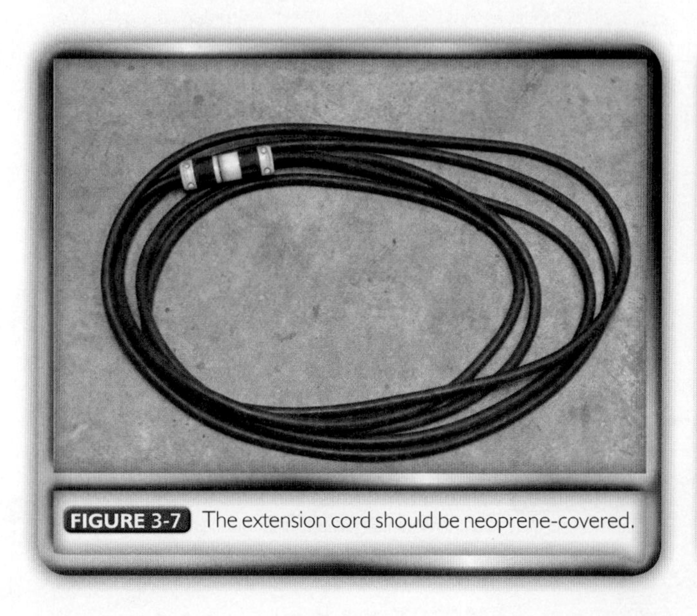

FIGURE 3-7 The extension cord should be neoprene-covered.

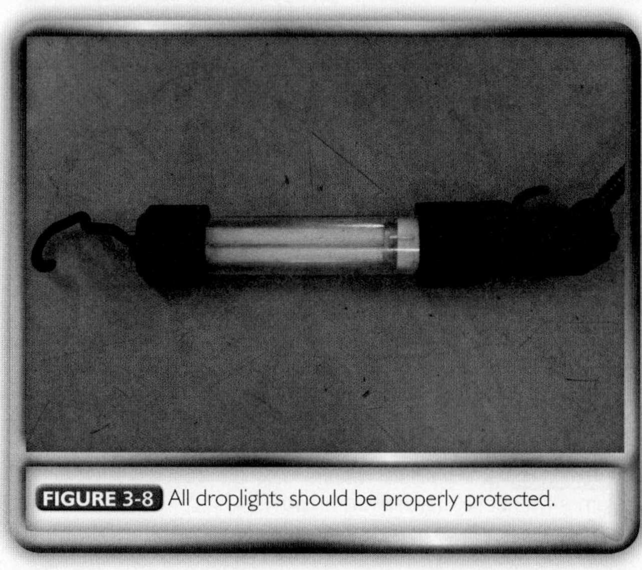

FIGURE 3-8 All droplights should be properly protected.

various activities, like parts cleaning, parts storage, tool storage, flammable liquid storage, jacking or lifting, tire fitting, and painting. All flammable items should be kept in an approved fireproof storage container or cabinet, with firefighting equipment close at hand.

TECHNICIAN TIP

The danger of a fire is always present in shops, particularly because of the amount of flammable liquids and materials used in shops and vehicles. Always be aware of the potential for a fire, and plan ahead by thinking through the task you are about to undertake. Know where firefighting equipment is kept and how it works.

Preventing Fires

The danger of a gasoline fire is always present in an automotive shop. Most automobiles carry a fuel tank, often with large quantities of fuel on board, which is more than sufficient to cause a large, very destructive, and potentially explosive fire. Take precautions to make sure you have the correct type and size of extinguishers on hand for a potential fuel fire. Make sure you clean up spills immediately and avoid ignition sources, like sparks, in the presence of flammable liquids or gases.

Fuel Vapor

Liquid fuel vaporizes rapidly, especially when spilled, and the vapor is extremely easy to ignite. Because fuel vapor is invisible and heavier than air, it can spread unseen across a wide area, and a source of ignition can be quite some distance from the original spill. Fuel can even vaporize from the cloths or rags used to wipe up liquid spills. These materials should be allowed to dry in the open air, not held in front of a heater element. Any spark or naked flame, even a lit cigarette, can start an explosive fire.

Spillage Risks

Spills frequently occur when technicians remove and replace fuel filters. They also occur during removal of a fuel tank sender unit, which can be located on the side of the fuel tank, without first emptying the tank safely. Spills also can occur when fuel lines are damaged and are being replaced, when fuel systems are being checked, or when fuel is being drained into unsuitable containers. Avoid spills by following the manufacturer's specified procedure when removing fuel system components. Also, keep a spill response kit nearby to deal with any spills quickly. Spill kits should contain absorbent material and barrier dams to contain moderate-sized spills.

Draining Fuel

If there is a possibility of fuel spillage while working on a vehicle, then you should first remove the fuel safely. Do this only in a well-ventilated, level space, preferably outside in the open air. Make sure all potential sources of ignition have been removed from the area, and disconnect the battery on the vehicle. Do not drain fuel from a vehicle over an inspection pit. Make sure the container you are draining into is an approved fuel storage container (fuel retriever) and that it is large enough to contain all of the fuel in the system being drained.

Using a Fuel Retriever

Always use a fuel retriever, preferably removing the fuel through the filler neck. A fuel retriever will minimize the chance of sudden large spills occurring **FIGURE 3-9**. You may need to use narrow-diameter hoses or adapters to drain fuel lines or to bypass anti-spillage devices. Check the service manual for details on how best to drain the fuel from the vehicle you are working on.

Safety

Never weld anywhere near a gas tank or any kind of fuel line. Welding work on a tank is a job for specialists. An empty fuel tank can still contain vapor and therefore can be even more dangerous than one full of liquid fuel. Do not attempt to repair a tank yourself.

UNLEADED
GASOLINE

FIGURE 3-9 Always use a fuel retriever; this tool will minimize the chance of sudden large spills occurring.

Extinguishing Fires

Three elements must be present at the same time for a fire to occur: fuel, oxygen, and heat. The secret of firefighting involves the removal of at least one of these elements, usually the oxygen or the heat, to extinguish the fire. For example, a fire blanket when applied correctly removes the oxygen, while a water extinguisher removes heat from the fire. In the shop, fire extinguishers are used to extinguish the majority of small fires. Never hesitate to call the fire department if you cannot extinguish a fire safely.

Fire Classifications

In the United States, there are five classes of fire:

- Class A fires involve ordinary combustibles such as wood, paper, or cloth.
- Class B fires involve flammable liquids or gaseous fuels.
- Class C fires involve electrical equipment.
- Class D fires involve combustible metals such as sodium, titanium, and magnesium.
- Class K fires involve cooking oil or fat.

Fire Extinguisher Types

Fire extinguishers are marked with pictograms depicting the types of fires that the extinguisher is approved to fight **FIGURE 3-10**:

- Class A: Green triangle
- Class B: Red square
- Class C: Blue circle
- Class D: Yellow pentagram
- Class K: Black hexagon

Fire Extinguisher Operation

Always sound the alarm before attempting to fight a fire. If you cannot fight the fire safely, leave the area while you wait for backup. You will need to size up the fire before you make the decision to fight it with a fire extinguisher by identifying what sort of material is burning, the extent of the fire, and the likelihood of it spreading.

To operate a fire extinguisher, follow the acronym for fire extinguisher use: PASS (Pull, Aim, Squeeze, Sweep). *Pull* out the pin that locks the handle at the top of the fire extinguisher to prevent accidental use. Carry the fire extinguisher in one hand, and use your other hand to *aim* the nozzle at the base of the fire. Stand about 8–12' (2.4–3.7 m) away from the fire and *squeeze* the handle to discharge the fire extinguisher. Remember that if you release the handle on the fire extinguisher, it will stop discharging. *Sweep* the nozzle from side to side at the base of the fire **FIGURE 3-11**. Continue to watch the fire. Although it may appear to be extinguished, it may suddenly reignite.

If the fire is indoors, you should be standing between the fire and the nearest safe exit. If the fire is outside, you should stand facing the fire with the wind on your back, so that the smoke and heat are being blown away from you. If possible, get an assistant to guide you and inform you of the fire's progress. Again, make sure you have a means of escape, should the fire get out of control. When you are certain that the fire is out, report it to your supervisor. Also report what actions you took to put out the fire. Once the circumstances of the fire have been investigated, and your supervisor or the fire department has given you the all clear, clean up the debris and submit the used fire extinguisher for inspection.

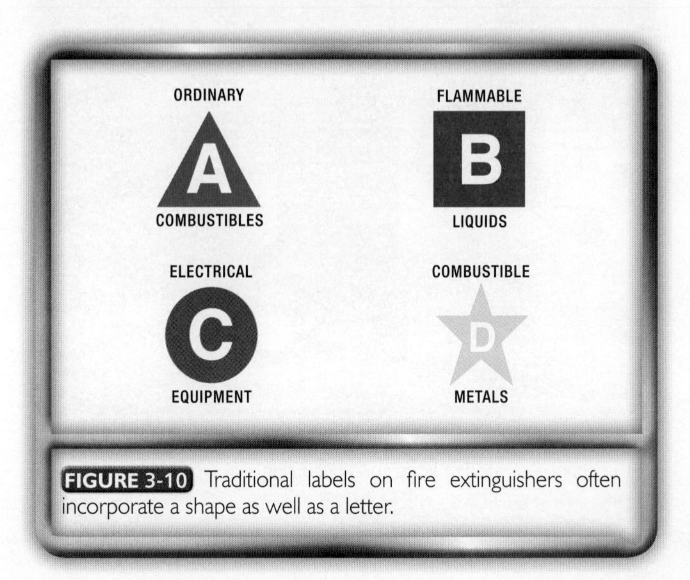
ORDINARY
A
COMBUSTIBLES
FLAMMABLE
B
LIQUIDS
ELECTRICAL
C
EQUIPMENT
COMBUSTIBLE
D
METALS

FIGURE 3-10 Traditional labels on fire extinguishers often incorporate a shape as well as a letter.

Fire Blankets

Fire blankets are designed to smother a small fire and are very useful in putting out a fire on a person. They are also used in situations where a fire extinguisher could cause damage. For example, if there is a small fire under the hood of a vehicle, a fire blanket might be able to smother the fire without running the risk of getting fire extinguisher powder down the intake system. Obtain a fire blanket and study the how-to-use instructions on the packaging. If instructions are not provided, research how to use a fire blanket or ask your supervisor. You may require instruction from an authorized person in using the fire blanket. If you do use a fire blanket, make sure you return the blanket for use or, if necessary, replace it with a new one.

Eyewash Stations and Emergency Showers

Hopefully you will never need to use an eye wash station or emergency shower. The best treatment is prevention, so make sure you wear all the PPE required for each

FIGURE 3-11 To operate a fire extinguisher, follow PASS. **A.** Pull. **B.** Aim. **C.** Squeeze. **D.** Sweep.

specific task to avoid injury. Eye wash stations are used to flush the eye with clean water or sterile liquid in the event that you get foreign liquid or particles in your eye. There are different types of eye washers; the main ones are disposable eye wash packs and eye wash stations. Some emergency or deluge showers also have an eye wash station built in FIGURE 3-12.

When individuals get chemicals in their eyes, they typically need assistance in reaching the eye wash station. Take their arm and lead them to it. They may not want to open their eyes even in the water, so encourage them to use their fingers to pull their eyelids open. If a chemical splashed in their eyes, encourage them to rinse their eyes for 15 minutes. While they are rinsing their eyes, call for medical assistance.

Hazardous Materials Safety

A **hazardous material** is any material that poses an unreasonable risk of damage or injury to persons, property, or the environment if it is not properly controlled during handling, storage, manufacture, processing, packaging, use and disposal, or transportation. These materials can be solids, liquids, or gases. Most shops use hazardous materials daily, such as cleaning solvents, gasket cement, brake fluid, and coolant. Hazardous materials must be properly handled, labeled, and stored in the shop.

EYE WASH

FIGURE 3-12 The main types of eye washers include disposable eye wash packs and eye wash stations. Some emergency showers have an eye wash station built in.

Safety Data Sheets

Hazardous materials are used daily and may make you very sick if they are not used properly. **Safety data sheets (SDS)** contain detailed information about hazardous materials to help you understand how they should be safely used, any health effects relating to them, how to treat a person who has been exposed to them, and how to deal with them in a fire situation. SDS can be obtained from the manufacturer of the material. The shop should have an SDS for each hazardous substance or dangerous product. In the United States it is required that workplaces have an SDS for every chemical that is on site.

Safety Data Sheets (SDS) were formerly called Material Safety Data Sheets (MSDS). In 2012, OSHA changed the requirements for the Hazards Communication System (HCS) to conform to the United Nations Globally Harmonized System of Classification and Labeling of Chemicals (GHS). The MSDS needed to change its name and its format to fit the new standards. Whereas the original MSDS had 8 sections, Safety Data Sheets are required to have 16 sections that provide additional details and make it easier to find specific data when needed. In addition, GHS requires all employers to train their employees in the new chemical labeling requirements and the new format for the Safety Data Sheets.

Whenever you deal with a potentially hazardous product, you should consult the SDS to learn how to use that product safely. If you are using more than one product, make sure you consult all the SDS for those products. Be aware that certain combinations of products can be more dangerous than any of them separately.

SDS are usually kept in a clearly marked binder and should be regularly updated as chemicals come into the workplace. Generally the SDS must contain at least the following information FIGURE 3-13:

- Revision date
- Material and manufacturer ID
- Hazardous ingredients
- Health hazard data
- Fire and explosion data
- Details about the material mixing or reacting with other materials
- Special precautions

SAFETY DATA SHEET

Section 1: Product & Company Identification

Product Name: **Brakleen® Brake Parts Cleaner** (aerosol)

Product Number (s): **05089, 05089-6, 05089T, 75089, 85089, 85089AZ**

Product Use: Brake parts cleaner

Manufactured / Supplier Contact Information:

In United States:	In Canada:	In Mexico:
CRC Industries, Inc.	CRC Canada Co.	CRC Industries Mexico
885 Louis Drive	2-1246 Lorimar Drive	Av. Benito Juárez 4055 G
Warminster, PA 18974	Mississauga, Ontario L5S 1R2	Colonia Orquídea
www.crcindustries.com	www.crc-canada.ca	San Luís Potosí, SLP CP 78394
1-215-674-4300(General)	1-905-670-2291	www.crc-mexico.com
(800) 521-3168 (Technical)		52-444-824-1666
(800) 272-4620 (Customer Service)		

24-Hr Emergency – CHEMTREC: (800) 424-9300 or (703) 527-3887

FIGURE 3-13 An example of an SDS.

(Continues)

Product Name: Brakleen® Brake Parts Cleaner (aerosol)
Product Number (s): 05089,05089-6, 05089T, 75089, 85089, 85089AZ

Section 2: Hazards Identification

Emergency Overview

DANGER: Vapor Harmful. Contents Under Pressure.
As defined by OSHA's Hazard Communication Standard, this product is hazardous.
Appearance & Odor: Colorless liquid, irritating odor at high concentrations

Potential Health Effects:

ACUTE EFFECTS:

EYE: May cause slight temporary eye irritation. Vapors may irritate the eyes at concentrations of 100 ppm.

SKIN: Short single exposures may cause skin irritation. Prolonged exposure may cause severe skin irritation, even a burn. A single prolonged exposure is not likely to result in the material being absorbed through skin in harmful amounts.

INHALATION: Dizziness may occur at concentrations of 200 ppm. Progressively higher levels may also cause nasal irritation, nausea, incoordination, and drunkenness. Very high levels or prolonged exposure could lead to unconsciousness and death.

INGESTION: Single dose oral toxicity is considered to be extremely low. Swallowing large amounts may cause injury if aspirated into the lungs. This may be rapidly absorbed through the lungs and result in injury to other body systems.

CHRONIC EFFECTS: Repeated contact with skin may cause drying or flaking of skin. Excessive or long term exposure to vapors may increase sensitivity to epinephrine and increase myocardial irritability.

TARGET ORGANS: Central nervous system. Possibly liver and kidney.

Medical Conditions Aggravated by Exposure: None known.

See Section 11 for toxicology and carcinogenicity information on product ingredients.

Section 3: Composition/Information and Ingredients

COMPONENT	CAS NUMBER	% by Wt.
Tetrachloroethylene (PERC)	127-18-4	> 95
Carbon Dioxide	124-38-9	< 5

Section 4: First Aid Measures

Eye Contact: Immediately flush with plenty of water for 15 minutes. Call a physician if irritation persists.

Skin Contact: Remove contaminated clothing and wash affected area with soap and water. Call a physician if irritation persists. Wash contaminated clothing prior to re-use.

Inhalation: Remove person to fresh air. Keep person calm. If not breathing, give artificial respiration. If breathing is difficult give oxygen. Call a physician.

Ingestion: Do NOT induce vomiting. Call a physician immediately.

Note to Physicians: Because rapid absorption may occur through lungs if aspirated and cause systemic effects, the decision of whether to induce vomiting or not should be made by a physician. If lavage is performed, suggest endotracheal and/or esophageal control. If burn is present, treat as any thermal burn, after decontamination. Exposure may increase myocardial irritability. Do not administer sympathomimetic drugs unless absolutely necessary. No specific antidote.

(Continues)

Product Name: Brakleen® Brake Parts Cleaner (aerosol)
Product Number (s): 05089,05089-6, 05089T, 75089, 85089, 85089AZ

Section 5: Fire-Fighting Measures

Flammable Properties: This product is nonflammable in accordance with aerosol flammability definitions. (See 16 CFR 1500.3(c)(6))

Flash Point: None (TCC) Upper Explosive Limit: None
Autoignition Temperature: None Lower Explosive Limit: None

Fire and Explosion Data:

Suitable Extinguishing Media: This material does not burn. Use extinguishing agent suitable for surrounding fire.

Products of Combustion: Hydrogen chloride, trace amounts of phosgene and chlorine

Explosion Hazards: Aerosol containers, when exposed to heat from fire, may build pressure and explode.

Protection of Fire-Fighters: Firefighters should wear self-contained, NIOSH-approved breathing apparatus for protection against suffocation and possible toxic decomposition products. Proper eye and skin protection should be provided. Use water spray to keep fire-exposed containers cool and to knock down vapors which may result from product decomposition.

Section 6: Accidental Release Measures

Personal Precautions: Use personal protection recommended in Section 8. Do not breathe vapors.

Environmental Precautions: Take precautions to prevent contamination of ground and surface waters. Do not flush into sewers or storm drains.

Methods for Containment & Clean-up: Dike area to contain spill. Ventilate the area with fresh air. If in confined space or limited air circulation area, clean-up workers should wear appropriate respiratory protection. Recover or absorb spilled material using an absorbent designed for chemical spills. Place used absorbents into proper waste containers.

Section 7: Handling and Storage

Handling Procedures: Vapors of this product are heavier than air and will collect in low areas. Make sure ventilation removes vapors from low areas. Do not eat, drink or smoke while using this product. Use caution around energized equipment. The metal container will conduct electricity if it contacts a live source. This may result in injury to the user from electrical shock and/or flash fire. For product use instructions, please see the product label.

Storage Procedures: Store in a cool dry area out of direct sunlight. Aerosol cans must be maintained below 120 F to prevent cans from rupturing.

Aerosol Storage Level: I

Section 8: Exposure Controls/Personal Protection

Exposure Guidelines:

	OSHA		ACGIH		OTHER		
COMPONENT	TWA	STEL	TWA	STEL	TWA	SOURCE	UNIT
Tetrachloroethylene	100	N.E.	25	100	N.E.		ppm
Carbon dioxide	5000	30000 v	5000	30,000	N.E.		ppm

N.E. – Not Established (c) – ceiling (s) – skin (v) – vacated

(Continues)

Product Name: Brakleen® Brake Parts Cleaner (aerosol)
Product Number (s): 05089,05089-6, 05089T, 75089, 85089, 85089AZ

Controls and Protection:

Engineering Controls: Area should have ventilation to provide fresh air. Local exhaust ventilation is generally preferred because it can control the emissions of the contaminant at the source, preventing dispersion into the general work area. Use mechanical means if necessary to maintain vapor levels below the exposure guidelines. If working in a confined space, follow applicable OSHA regulations.

Respiratory Protection: None required for normal work where adequate ventilation is provided. If engineering controls are not feasible or if exposure exceeds the applicable exposure limits, use a NIOSH-approved cartridge respirator with organic vapor cartridge. Air monitoring is needed to determine actual employee exposure levels. Use a self-contained breathing apparatus in confined spaces and for emergencies.

Eye/face Protection: For normal conditions, wear safety glasses. Where there is reasonable probability of liquid contact, wear splash-proof goggles.

Skin Protection: Use protective gloves such as PVA, Teflon, or Viton. Also, use full protective clothing if there is prolonged or repeated contact of liquid with skin.

Section 9: Pysical and Chemical Properties

Physical State: liquid
Color: colorless
Odor: irritating odor
Odor Threshold: 50 ppm
Specific Gravity: 1.619
Initial Boiling Point: 250 F
Freezing Point: ND
Vapor Pressure: 13 mmHg @ 68 F
Vapor Density: 5.76 (air = 1)
Evaporation Rate: very fast
Solubility: 0.015 g/ 100 g @ 77 F in water
Coefficient of water/oil distribution (log P_{ow}): 2.88
pH: NA
Volatile Organic Compounds: wt %: 0 g/L: 0 lbs./gal: 0

Section 10: Stability and Reactivity

Stability: Stable

Conditions to Avoid: Avoid direct sunlight or ultraviolet sources. Avoid open flames, welding arcs, and other high temperature sources which induce thermal decomposition.

Incompatible Materials: Avoid contact with metals such as: aluminum powders, magnesium powders, potassium, sodium, and zinc powder. Avoid unintended contact with amines. Avoid contact with strong bases and strong oxidizers.

Hazardous Decomposition Products: Hydrogen chloride, trace amounts of chlorine and phosgene

Possibility of Hazardous Reactions: No

Section 11: Toxicological Information

Long-term toxicological studies have not been conducted for this product. The following information is available for components of this product.

(Continues)

Product Name: Brakleen® Brake Parts Cleaner (aerosol)
Product Number (s): 05089,05089-6, 05089T, 75089, 85089, 85089AZ

Acute Toxicity:

Component	Oral LD50 (rat)	Dermal LD50 (rabbit)	Inhalation LC50 (rat)
Tetrachloroethylene	2629 mg/kg	> 10 g/kg	5200 mg/kg/4H
Carbon dioxide	No data	No data	470,000 ppm/30M

Chronic Toxicity:

Component	OSHA Carcinogen	IARC Carcinogen	NTP Carcinogen	Irritant	Sensitizer
Tetrachloroethylene	No	Group 2A	Reasonably Anticipated to be a Carcinogen	E (mild) / S (severe)	No
Carbon dioxide	No	No	No	None	No

E – Eye S – Skin R - Respiratory

Reproductive Toxicity: No information available
Teratogenicity: No information available
Mutagenicity: Tetrachloroethylene: in vitro studies were negative
animal studies were negative
Synergistic Effects: No information available

Section 12: Ecological Information

Ecological studies have not been conducted for this product. The following information is available for components of this product.

Ecotoxicity: Tetrachloroethylene -- 96 Hr LC50 Rainbow Trout: 5.28 mg/L (static)
96 Hr LC50 Fathead minnow: 13.4 mg/L (flow-through)

Persistence / Degradability: Biodegradation under aerobic conditions is below detectable limits. Biodegradation may occur under anaerobic conditions. Biodegradation rate may increase in soil and/or water with acclimation.

Bioaccumulation / Accumulation: Bioconcentration potential is low (BCF less than 100).

Mobility in Environment: Potential for mobility in soil is medium.

Section 13: Disposal considerations

Waste Classification: The dispensed liquid product is a RCRA hazardous waste for toxicity with the following potential waste codes: U210, F001, F002, D039. Pressurized containers are a D003 reactive waste. (See 40 CFR Part 261.20 – 261.33)
Empty aerosol containers may be recycled. Any liquid product should be managed as a hazardous waste.

All disposal activities must comply with federal, state, provincial and local regulations. Local regulations may be more stringent than state, provincial or national requirements.

Section 14: Transport Information

US DOT (ground): Consumer Commodity, ORM-D

ICAO/IATA (air): Consumer Commodity, ID8000, 9

IMO/IMDG (water): Aerosols, UN1950, 2.2, Limited Quantity

Special Provisions: None

(Continues)

Product Name: Brakleen® Brake Parts Cleaner (aerosol)
Product Number (s): 05089,05089-6, 05089T, 75089, 85089, 85089AZ

Section 15: Regulatory Information

U.S. Federal Regulations:

Toxic Substances Control Act (TSCA):
All ingredients are either listed on the TSCA inventory or are exempt.

Comprehensive Environmental Response, Compensation and Liability Act (CERCLA):
Reportable Quantities (RQ's) exist for the following ingredients: Tetrachloroethylene (100 lbs)

Spills or releases resulting in the loss of any ingredient at or above its RQ require immediate notification to the National Response Center (800-424-8802) and to your Local Emergency Planning Committee.

Superfund Amendments Reauthorization Act (SARA) Title III:
Section 302 Extremely Hazardous Substances (EHS): None

Section 311/312 Hazard Categories:

Fire Hazard	No
Reactive Hazard	No
Release of Pressure	Yes
Acute Health Hazard	Yes
Chronic Health Hazard	Yes

Section 313 Toxic Chemicals: This product contains the following substances subject to the reporting requirements of Section 313 of Title III of the Superfund Amendments and Reauthorization Act of 1986 and 40 CFR Part 372:

Tetrachloroethylene (97.7%)

Clean Air Act:
Section 112 Hazardous Air Pollutants (HAPs): | Tetrachloroethylene

U.S. State Regulations:

California Safe Drinking Water and Toxic Enforcement Act (Prop 65):
This product may contain the following chemicals known to the state of California to cause cancer, birth defects or other reproductive harm: Tetrachloroethylene

Consumer Products VOC Regulations: This product cannot be sold for use in California and New Jersey. In other states with Consumer Products VOC regulations, this product is compliant as a Brake Cleaner.

State Right to Know:

New Jersey:	127-18-4, 124-38-9
Pennsylvania:	127-18-4, 124-38-9
Massachusetts:	127-18-4, 124-38-9
Rhode Island :	127-18-4, 124-38-9

Canadian Regulations:

Canadian DSL Inventory: All ingredients are either listed on the DSL Inventory or are exempt.

WHMIS Hazard Class: A, D1B, D2A, D2B

European Union Regulations:

RoHS Compliance: This product is compliant with Directive 2002/95/EC of the European Parliament and of the Council of 27 January 2003. This product does not contain any of the restricted substances as listed in Article 4(1) of the RoHS Directive.

Additional Regulatory Information: None

(Continues)

Product Name: Brakleen® Brake Parts Cleaner (aerosol)
Product Number (s): 05089,05089-6, 05089T, 75089, 85089, 85089AZ

Section 16: Other Information

HMIS® (II)	
Health:	2
Flammability:	0
Reactivity:	0
PPE:	B

Ratings range from 0 (no hazard) to 4 (severe hazard)

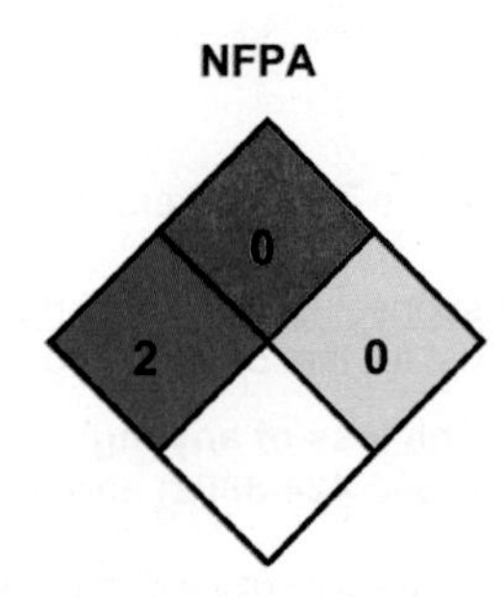
NFPA
0
2
0

Prepared By: Michelle Rudnick
CRC #: 491G
Revision Date: 01/25/2010

Changes since last revision: SDS reformatted to meet the requirements of the Canadian Controlled Products Regulations.

The information contained in this document applies to this specific material as supplied. It may not be valid for this material if it is used in combination with any other materials. This information is accurate to the best of CRC Industries' knowledge or obtained from sources believed by CRC to be accurate. Before using any product, read all warnings and directions on the label. For further clarification of any information contained on this SDS consult your supervisor, a health & safety professional, or CRC Industries.

ACGIH: American Conference of Governmental Industrial Hygienists
CAS: Chemical Abstract Service
CFR: Code of Federal Regulations
DOT: Department of Transportation
DSL: Domestic Substance List
g/L: grams per Liter
HMIS: Hazardous Materials Identification System
IARC: International Agency for Research on Cancer
IATA: International Air Transport Association
ICAO: International Civil Aviation Organization
IMDG: International Maritime Dangerous Goods
IMO: International Maritime Organization
lbs./gal: pounds per gallon
LC: Lethal Concentration
LD: Lethal Dose
NA: Not Applicable
ND: Not Determined
NIOSH: National Institute of Occupational Safety & Health
NFPA: National Fire Protection Association
NTP: National Toxicology Program
OSHA: Occupational Safety and Health Administration
PMCC: Pensky-Martens Closed Cup
PPE: Personal Protection Equipment
ppm: Parts per Million
RoHS: Restriction of Hazardous Substances
STEL: Short Term Exposure Limit
TCC: Tag Closed Cup
TWA: Time Weighted Average
WHMIS: Workplace Hazardous Materials Information System

To identify information found on an SDS, follow the steps in SKILL DRILL 3-2:

1. Once you have studied the information on the container label, find the SDS for that particular material. Always check the revision date to ensure that you are reading the most recent update.
2. Note the chemical and trade names for the material, its manufacturer, and the emergency telephone number to call.
3. Find out why this material is potentially hazardous. It may be flammable, it may explode, or it may be poisonous if inhaled or touched with your bare skin. Check the **threshold limit values (TLVs)**. The concentration of this material in the air you breathe in your shop must not exceed these figures. There could be physical symptoms associated with breathing harmful chemicals. Find out what will happen to you if you suffer overexposure to the

material, either through breathing it or by coming into physical contact with it. This will help you take safety precautions, such as eye, face, or skin protection, wearing a mask or respirator while using the material, or washing your skin afterwards.

4 Note the flash point for this material so that you know at what temperature it may catch fire. Also note what kind of fire extinguisher you would use to fight a fire involving this material. The wrong fire extinguisher could make the emergency even worse.

5 Study the reactivity for this material to identify the physical conditions or other materials that you should avoid when using this material. It could be heat, moisture, or some other chemical.

6 Find out what special precautions you should take when working with this material. This will include personal protection for your skin, eyes, or lungs and storage and use of the material.

7 Be sure to refresh your knowledge of your SDS from time to time. Be confident that you know how to handle and use the material and what action to take in an emergency, should one occur.

Cleaning Toxic Dust Safely

Toxic dust is any dust that may contain fine particles that could be harmful to humans or the environment. If you are unsure as to the toxicity of dust, then you should always treat it as toxic and take the precautions identified in the SDS or shop procedures. Brake and clutch dust are potential toxic dusts that automotive shops must manage. The dust is made up of very fine particles that can easily spread and contaminate an area. One of the more common sources of toxic dust is inside drum brakes and manual transmission bell housings.

It is a good idea to avoid all dust if possible, whether it is classified as toxic or not. If you do have to work with dust, never use compressed air to blow it from components or parts and always use PPE such as face masks, eye protection, and gloves. If you are cleaning up your area after a repair, do not dry sweep dust; instead, use a low-pressure wet cleaning method. Such methods include a soap and water solution used in a dedicated portable wash station, a low-pressure aerosol brake cleaning solution, or a pump spray bottle filled with water. You may also use a HEPA vacuum cleaner to collect dust and clean equipment. HEPA stands for high-efficiency particulate absorbing. HEPA filters can trap very small particles and prevent them from being redistributed into the surrounding air.

After completing a servicing or repair task on a vehicle, there is often dirt left behind. The chemicals present in this dirt usually contain toxic chemicals that can build up and cause health problems. To keep the levels of dirt to a minimum, clean up dirt immediately after the task is complete. The vigorous action of sweeping causes the dirt to rise; therefore, when sweeping the floor, use a soft broom that pushes, rather than flicks, the dirt forward. Create smaller dirt piles and dispose of them frequently. Another successful way of cleaning shop dirt is to use a water hose. The waste water must be caught in a settling pit and not run into a storm water drain.

Various tools have been developed to clean toxic dust from vehicle components. The most common one is the brake wash station. It uses an aqueous solution to wet down and wash the dust into a collection basin. The basin needs periodic maintenance to properly dispose of the accumulated sludge. This tool is probably the simplest way to effectively deal with hazardous dust because it is easy to set up, use, and store.

Another such tool uses a vacuum cleaner that has a large cone attachment at the nozzle end. The base of the cone is open so the brake assembly can fit into the cone. A compressed air nozzle, which is also attached to the inside of the cone, is used to loosen dirt particles. The particles are drawn into the cleaner via a very fine filter. Domestic vacuum cleaners are not suitable for this

TECHNICIAN TIP

- Some vehicle components, including brake and clutch linings, contain asbestos, which, despite having very good heat properties, is toxic. Asbestos dust causes lung cancer. Complications from breathing the dust may not show until decades after exposure.
- Airborne dust in the shop can also cause breathing problems such as asthma and throat infections.
- Never cause dust from vehicle components to be blown into the air. It can stay floating for many hours, meaning that other people will breathe the dust unknowingly.
- Wear protective gloves whenever using solvents.
- If you are unfamiliar with a solvent or a cleaner, refer to the SDS for information about its correct use and applicable hazards.
- Always wash your hands thoroughly with soap and water after performing repair tasks on brake and clutch components.
- Always wash work clothes separately from other clothes so that toxic dust does not transfer from one garment to another.
- Always wear protective clothing and the appropriate safety equipment.

application because their filters are not fine enough to capture very small dust particles.

To safely clean brake dust, follow the steps in SKILL DRILL 3-3.

> **TECHNICIAN TIP**
>
> Whenever using an atomizer with solvents and cleaners, make sure there is adequate exhaust ventilation. Wear appropriate breathing apparatus and eye protection.

Used Engine Oil and Fluids

Used engine oil and fluids are liquids that have been drained from the vehicle, usually during servicing operations. Used oil and fluids will often contain dangerous chemicals and impurities and need to be safely recycled or disposed of in an environmentally friendly way FIGURE 3-14. There are laws and regulations that control the way in which they are to be handled and disposed. The shop will have policies and procedures that describe how you should handle and dispose of used engine oil and fluids. Be careful not to mix incompatible fluids such

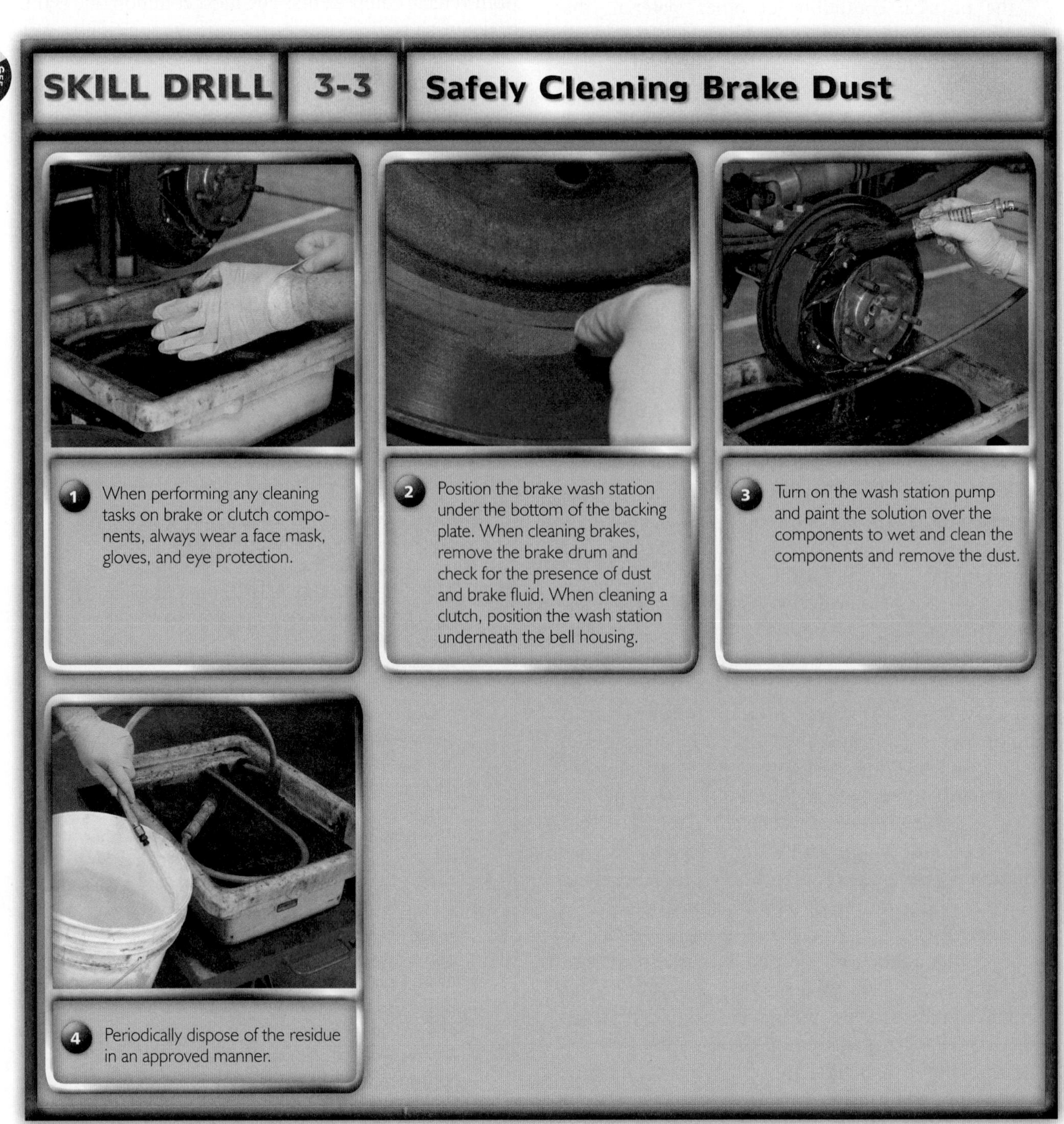
PROVE KNOW SEE DO

SKILL DRILL 3-3 Safely Cleaning Brake Dust

1. When performing any cleaning tasks on brake or clutch components, always wear a face mask, gloves, and eye protection.
2. Position the brake wash station under the bottom of the backing plate. When cleaning brakes, remove the brake drum and check for the presence of dust and brake fluid. When cleaning a clutch, position the wash station underneath the bell housing.
3. Turn on the wash station pump and paint the solution over the components to wet and clean the components and remove the dust.
4. Periodically dispose of the residue in an approved manner.

USED OIL
USED OIL ONLY

FIGURE 3-14 Used oil and fluids will often contain dangerous chemicals and need to be safely recycled or disposed of in an environmentally friendly way.

as used engine oil and used coolant. Generally speaking, petroleum products can be mixed together. Follow your local, state, and federal regulations when disposing of waste fluids.

Used engine oil is a hazardous material containing many impurities that can damage your skin. Coming into frequent or prolonged contact with used engine oil can cause dermatitis and other skin disorders, including some forms of cancer. Avoid direct contact as much as possible by always using gloves and other protective clothing, which should be cleaned or replaced regularly. Using a barrier-type hand lotion will also help protect your hands as well as make cleaning them much easier. Also follow safe work practices, which minimize the possibility of accidental spills. Keeping a high standard of personal hygiene and cleanliness is important so that you get into the habit of washing off harmful materials as soon as possible after contact. If you have been in contact with used engine oil, you should regularly inspect your skin for signs of damage or deterioration. If you have any concerns, see your doctor.

Shop Safety Inspections

Shop safety inspections are valuable ways of identifying unsafe equipment, materials, or activities so they can be corrected to prevent accidents or injuries. The inspection can be formalized by using inspection sheets to check specific items, or they can be general walk-arounds where you consciously look for problems that can be corrected. Some of the commons things to look for would be items blocking emergency exits or walkways, poor safety signage, unsafe storage of flammable goods, tripping hazards, faulty or unsafe equipment or tools, missing fire extinguishers, clutter, spills, unsafe shop practices, and people not wearing the correct PPE. Formal and informal safety inspections should be held regularly. For example, an inspection sheet might be used weekly or monthly to formally evaluate the shop, while informal inspections might be held daily to catch issues that are of a more immediate nature.

Applied Science

AS-4: Waste Management: The technician identifies the waste products resulting from a repair task.

The most important part of identifying waste is first to determine what products are waste and what can be reused or recycled. The second is to identify what type of material the waste is and then determine what type of disposal needs to take place with the waste material.

If you replace a set of front disc brake rotors and pads, then you will have to determine where to put the waste material from this job. You will have to refer to the waste disposal table posted in the garage to determine where each item of waste should go. Most plastic bags cannot be recycled, so these items will be put in the standard waste bin. The disc brake rotors will be put in the metal scrap bin for recycling. The disc brake pads may also be put in the metal bin for recycling unless they were manufactured before 2004. If so, they may contain asbestos and need to be put in a plastic airtight bag for removal by a licensed contractor.

AS-5: Waste Management: The technician handles the disposal of materials such as automotive lubricants in accordance with applicable federal, state, and local rules and regulations.

When you carry out a major service, you may have to replace the engine oil and oil filter, coolant, and automatic transmission oil. You will have to determine where to put the waste material from this job by consulting the waste disposal guidelines posted in the garage. For example, if you refer to the sample waste disposal table shown in a previous Applied Science box, you can see that engine oil and transmission oil need to be collected and stored in a container for removal by a licensed contractor. The oil filter needs to be drained and then crushed and kept in a leak-proof container to be collected by a licensed contractor. The coolant needs to be kept in a separate container and collected to be recycled by a licensed operator. Cardboard boxes that oil or air filters may come in can be put in the recycling bin for recycling.

Wrap-up

Ready for Review

- Your employer is responsible for maintaining a safe work environment; you are responsible for working safely.
- Always wear the correct personal protective equipment, such as gloves or hearing protection.
- Accidents and injuries can be avoided by safe work practices.
- Every shop should mark evacuation routes; always know the evacuation route for your shop.
- OSHA is a federal agency that oversees safe workplace environments and practices.
- The EPA monitors and enforces issues related to environmental safety.
- Shop policies and procedures are designed to ensure compliance with laws and regulations, create a safe working environment, and guide shop practice.
- Identify hazards and hazardous materials in your work environment.
- Safety signs include a signal word, background color, text, and a pictorial message.
- Shop safety equipment includes handrails, machinery guards, painted lines, soundproof rooms, adequate ventilation, gas extraction hoses, doors and gates, and temporary barriers.
- Air quality is an important safety concern.
- Carbon monoxide and carbon dioxide from running engines can create a hazardous work environment.
- Electrical safety in a shop is important to prevent shocks, burns, fires, and explosions.
- Portable electrical equipment should be the proper voltage and should always be inspected for damage.
- Use caution when plugging in or using a portable shop light.
- Shop layouts should be well planned to maximize safety.
- Fuels and fuel vapors are potential fire hazards.
- Use fuel retrievers when draining fuel and have a spill response kit nearby.
- Fuel, oxygen, and heat must all be present for fire to occur.
- Types of fires are classified as A, B, C, D, or K, and fire extinguishers match them accordingly.
- Do not fight a fire unless you can do so safely.
- Operating a fire extinguisher involves the PASS method: pull, aim, squeeze, and sweep.
- Eyewash stations and emergency showers allow flushing of chemicals or other irritants.
- Safety data sheets contain important information on each hazardous material in the shop.
- Vacuuming and using water are the safest methods of cleaning dust or dirt that may be toxic.
- Used engine oil and fluids must be handled and disposed of properly.
- Shop safety inspections ensure that safety policies and procedures are being followed.

Key Terms

double-insulated Tools or appliances that are designed in such a way that no single failure can result in a dangerous voltage coming into contact with the outer casing of the device.

Environmental Protection Agency (EPA) Federal government agency that deals with issues related to environmental safety.

hazard Anything that could hurt you or someone else.

hazardous environment A place where hazards exist.

hazardous material Any material that poses an unreasonable risk of damage or injury to persons, property, or the environment if it is not properly controlled during handling, storage, manufacture, processing, packaging, use and disposal, or transportation.

Occupational Safety and Health Administration (OSHA) Government agency created to provide national leadership in occupational safety and health.

personal protective equipment (PPE) Safety equipment designed to protect the technician, such as safety boots, gloves, clothing, protective eyewear, and hearing protection.

policy A guiding principle that sets the shop direction.

procedure A list of the steps required to get the same result each time a task or activity is performed.

safety data sheet (SDS) A sheet that provides information about handling, use, and storage of a material that may be hazardous.

threshold limit value (TLV) The maximum allowable concentration of a given material in the surrounding air.

toxic dust Any dust that may contain fine particles that could be harmful to humans or the environment.

PROVE
KNOW
SEE
DO

ASE-Type Questions

1. Tech A says that exposure to solvents may have long-term effects. Tech B says that accidents are almost always avoidable. Who is correct?
   a. Tech A
   b. Tech B
   c. Both A and B
   d. Neither A nor B
2. Tech A says that after an accident you should take measures to avoid it in the future. Tech B says that it is OK to block an exit for a shop. Who is correct?
   a. Tech A
   b. Tech B
   c. Both A and B
   d. Neither A nor B
3. Tech A says that both OSHA and the EPA can inspect facilities for violations. Tech B says that a shop safety rule does not have to be reviewed once put in place. Who is correct?
   a. Tech A
   b. Tech B
   c. Both A and B
   d. Neither A nor B
4. Tech A says that all hazards can be removed from a shop. Tech B says that it is a good practice to disconnect an air gun when inspecting it. Who is correct?
   a. Tech A
   b. Tech B
   c. Both A and B
   d. Neither A nor B
5. Tech A says that both caution and danger indicate a potentially hazardous situation. Tech B says that an exhaust extraction hose is not needed if the vehicle is only going to run for a few minutes. Who is correct?
   a. Tech A
   b. Tech B
   c. Both A and B
   d. Neither A nor B
6. Tech A says that if you are unsure of what personal protective equipment (PPE) to use to perform a job, you should just use what is nearby. Tech B says that air tools are less likely to shock you than electrically powered tools. Who is correct?
   a. Tech A
   b. Tech B
   c. Both A and B
   d. Neither A nor B
7. Tech A says that firefighting equipment includes safety glasses. Tech B says that a class A fire extinguisher can be used to fight an electrical fire only. Who is correct?
   a. Tech A
   b. Tech B
   c. Both A and B
   d. Neither A nor B
8. Tech A says that a safety data sheet (SDS) contains information on procedures to repair a vehicle. Tech B says that you only need an SDS if your safety may be in danger. Who is correct?
   a. Tech A
   b. Tech B
   c. Both A and B
   d. Neither A nor B
9. Tech A says that a good way to clean dust off brakes is with compressed air. Tech B says that asbestos may be in current auto parts. Who is correct?
   a. Tech A
   b. Tech B
   c. Both A and B
   d. Neither A nor B
10. Tech A says that when cleaning brake and clutch components, the wash station should be placed directly under the component. Tech B says that you should follow state and local regulations when disposing of used oil. Who is correct?
    a. Tech A
    b. Tech B
    c. Both A and B
    d. Neither A nor B

CHAPTER 4

Know
See
Do
Prove

NATEF Tasks

Required Supplemental Tasks
Shop and Personal Safety

	Page
■ Comply with the required use of safety glasses, ear protection, gloves and shoes during lab/shop activities.	64–70
■ Identify and wear appropriate clothing for lab/shop activities.	64–70
■ Secure hair and jewelry for lab/shop activities.	70
■ Utilize proper ventilation procedures for working within the lab/shop area.	70–71

Know
See
Do
Prove

Knowledge Objectives

After reading this chapter, you will be able to:

1. Identify the standard items of personal protective equipment that should be worn in the shop. (pp 64–70)
2. Describe how to use personal protective equipment to reduce the risk of injury in the workplace. (pp 64–70)
3. Explain how to apply injury protection practices. (pp 70–71)

Personal Safety

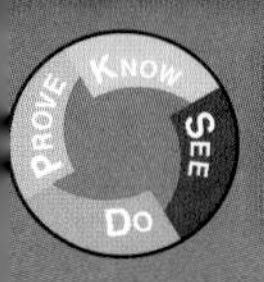
Know
See
Do
Prove

Skills Objectives

There are no skills objectives for this chapter.

Introduction

Personal protective equipment (PPE) is equipment used to block the entry of hazardous materials into the body or to protect the body from injury. PPE includes clothing, shoes, safety glasses, hearing protection, masks, and respirators FIGURE 4-1. Before you undertake any activity, think about all potential hazards and select the correct PPE based on the risk associated with the activity. For example, if you are going to change hydraulic brake fluid, put on some gloves to protect your skin from chemicals.

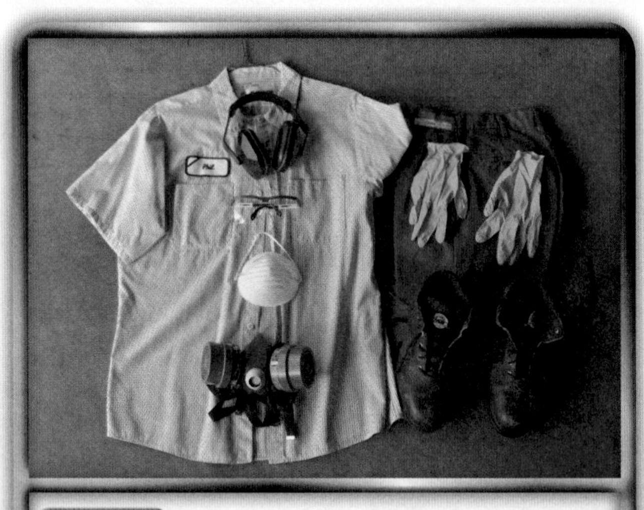

FIGURE 4-1 Personal protective equipment (PPE) includes clothing, shoes, safety glasses, hearing protection, masks, and respirators.

As you go through this chapter, you will learn how to identify the correct PPE for a given activity and how to wear it safely. It is important that the PPE you use fits correctly and is appropriate for the task you are undertaking. For example, if the task requires you to wear eye protection and specifies that you should use a full face shield, do not try to cut corners and only wear safety glasses. You also need to make sure the PPE you are using is worn correctly. For example, a hairnet that does not capture all of your hair is not protecting you adequately.

Personal Protective Equipment

Protective Clothing

Protective clothing includes items like shirts, pants, shoes, and gloves. These items are your first line of defense against injuries and accidents and must be worn when performing any work. Always make sure protective clothing is kept clean and in good condition. You should replace any clothing that is not in good condition, since it is no longer able to fully protect you.

> **TECHNICIAN TIP**
>
> Each shop activity will require specific clothing depending on its nature. Research and identify what specific type of clothing is required for every activity you undertake. Wear appropriate clothing for various activities according to the shop's policy and procedures.

You Are the Automotive Technician

It's your first day on the job and you are asked to report to the main office where your new supervisor gives you your personal protective equipment (PPE). Before you can begin working on the shop floor, you are given training on the proper use of personal protective equipment.

1. Which type of gloves should be worn when handling solvents and cleaners?
2. Why must safety glasses be worn at all times in the shop?
3. Why should rings, watches and jewelry never be worn in the shop?
4. When should hearing protection be worn?
5. What types of tasks should a face shield be worn?
6. Why must hair be tied up or restrained in the shop?
7. Which type of eye protection should be worn when using or assisting a person using an oxyacetylene welder?

Work Clothing

Always wear appropriate work clothing. Whether this is a one-piece coverall/overall or a separate shirt and pants, the clothes you work in should be comfortable enough to allow you to move, without being loose enough to catch on machinery. The material must be flame retardant and strong enough that it cannot be easily torn. A flap must cover buttons or snaps. If you wear a long sleeve shirt, the cuffs must be close fitting, without being tight. Pants should not have cuffs, so that hot debris cannot become trapped in the fabric.

Care of Clothing

Always wash your work clothes separately from your other clothes. Start a new working day with clean work clothes and change out of contaminated clothing as soon as possible. It is a good idea to keep a spare set of work clothes in the workshop in case a toxic or corrosive fluid is spilled on the clothes you are wearing.

Footwear

The proper footwear provides protection against items falling on your feet, chemicals, cuts, abrasions, and slips. The soles of your shoes must be acid and slip resistant, and the uppers must be made from a puncture-proof material such as leather. Some shops and technicians prefer safety shoes with a steel cap to protect the toes FIGURE 4-2. Always wear shoes that comply with your local shop standards.

Headgear

Headgear includes items like hairnets, caps, and hard hats. They help protect you from getting your hair caught in rotating machinery and protect your head from knocks or bumps. For example, your hard hat can protect you from bumping your head on a vehicle when the vehicle is raised on a hoist. It is also good practice to wear a cap to hold longer hair in place and to keep it clean when working under a vehicle. Some caps are designed specifically with additional padding on the top to provide extra protection against bumps.

Hand Protection

Hands are a very complex and sensitive part of the body with many nerves, tendons, and blood vessels. They are susceptible to injury and damage. Nearly every activity performed on vehicles requires the use of your hands, which provides many opportunities for injury. Whenever possible, wear gloves to protect your hands. There are many types of gloves available and their applications vary greatly. It is important to wear the correct type of glove for the various activities you perform.

Chemical Gloves

Heavy-duty and impenetrable chemical gloves should always be worn when using solvents and cleaners. They should also be worn when working on batteries. Chemical gloves should extend to the middle of your forearm to reduce the risk of chemicals splashing onto your skin FIGURE 4-3. Always inspect chemical gloves for holes or cracks before using them, and replace them when they become worn.

Some chemical gloves are also slightly heat resistant. This type of chemical glove is suitable for use when removing radiator caps and mixing coolant.

FIGURE 4-2 The proper footwear provides protection against items falling on your feet, chemicals, cuts, abrasions, and slips.

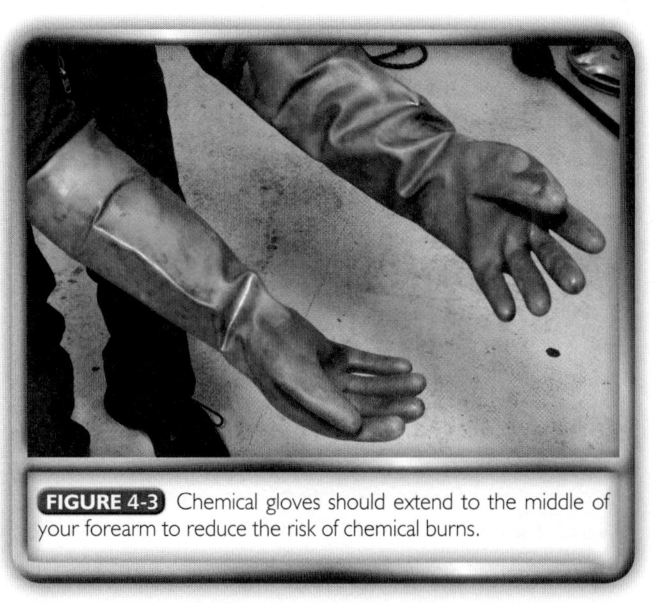

FIGURE 4-3 Chemical gloves should extend to the middle of your forearm to reduce the risk of chemical burns.

Leather Gloves

Leather gloves will protect your hands from burns when welding or handling hot components FIGURE 4-4. You should also use them when removing steel from a storage rack and when handling sharp objects. When using leather gloves for handling hot components, be aware of the potential for **heat buildup**. Heat buildup occurs when the leather glove can no longer absorb or reflect heat, and heat is transferred to the inside of the leather glove. At this point, the leather gloves' ability to protect you from the heat is reduced and you will need to stop work, remove the leather gloves, and allow them to cool down before continuing to work. Also, avoid picking up very hot metal with leather gloves because it causes the leather to harden, making it less flexible during use. If very hot metal must be moved, it would be better to use an appropriate pair of pliers.

Light-Duty Gloves

Light-duty gloves should be used to protect your hands from exposure to greases and oils FIGURE 4-5. Light-duty gloves are typically disposable and can be made from a few different materials, such as nitrile, latex, and even plastic. Some people have allergies to these materials. If you have an allergic reaction when wearing these gloves, try using a glove made from a different material.

General-Purpose Cloth Gloves

Cloth gloves are designed to be worn in cold temperatures, particularly during winter, so that cold tools do not stick to your skin FIGURE 4-6. Over time, cloth gloves will accumulate dirt and grime so you will need to wash them regularly. Regularly inspect cloth gloves for damage and wear, and replace them when required. Cloth gloves are not an effective barrier against chemicals or oils, so never use them for that purpose.

Barrier Cream

Barrier cream looks and feels like a moisturizing cream, but it has a specific formula to provide extra protection from chemicals and oils. Barrier cream prevents chemicals from being absorbed into your skin and should be applied to your hands before you begin work FIGURE 4-7. Even the slightest exposure to certain chemicals can lead to dermatitis, a painful skin irritation. Never use a standard moisturizer as a replacement for proper barrier cream. Barrier cream also makes it easier to clean your hands because it can prevent fine particles from adhering to your skin.

Cleaning Your Hands

When cleaning your hands, use only specialized hand cleaners, which protect your skin FIGURE 4-8. Your hands are porous and easily absorb liquids on contact. Never use solvents such as gasoline or kerosene to clean your hands,

FIGURE 4-5 Light-duty gloves should be used to protect your hands from exposure to greases and oils.

FIGURE 4-4 Leather gloves will protect your hands from burns when welding or handling hot components.

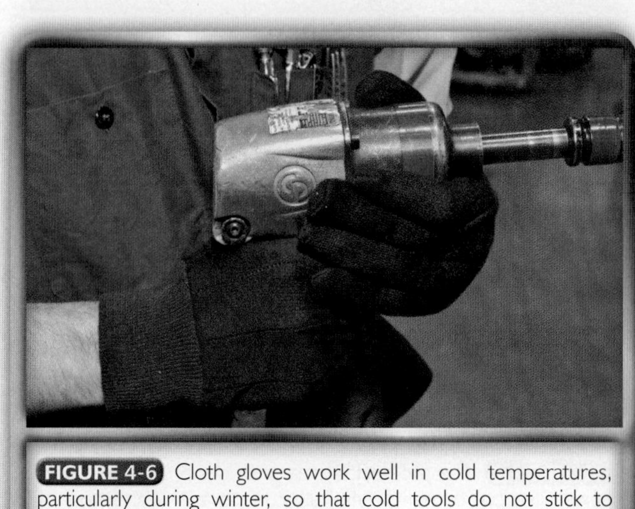

FIGURE 4-6 Cloth gloves work well in cold temperatures, particularly during winter, so that cold tools do not stick to your skin.

because they can be absorbed into the bloodstream and remove the skin's natural protective oils.

Ear Protection

Ear protection should be worn when sound levels exceed 85 decibels, when you are working around operating machinery for any period of time, or when the equipment you are using produces loud noise. If you have to raise your voice to be heard by a person who is 2' away from you, then the sound level is about 85 decibels or more. Ear protection comes in two forms: One type covers the entire outer ear, and the other is fitted into the ear canal FIGURE 4-9. Generally speaking, the in-the-ear style has higher noise-reduction ratings. If the noise is not excessively loud, either type of protection will work. If you are in an extremely loud environment, you will want to verify that the option you choose is rated high enough.

Breathing Devices

Dust and chemicals from your workspace can be absorbed into the body when you breathe. When working in an environment where dust is present or where the task you are performing will produce dust, you should always wear some form of breathing device. There are two types of breathing devices: disposable dust masks and respirators.

Disposable Dust Mask

A disposable dust mask is made from paper with a wire-reinforced edge that is held to your face with an elastic strip. It covers your mouth and nose and is disposed of at the completion of the task FIGURE 4-10. This type of mask should only be used as a dust mask and should not be used if chemicals, such as paint solvents, are present in the atmosphere.

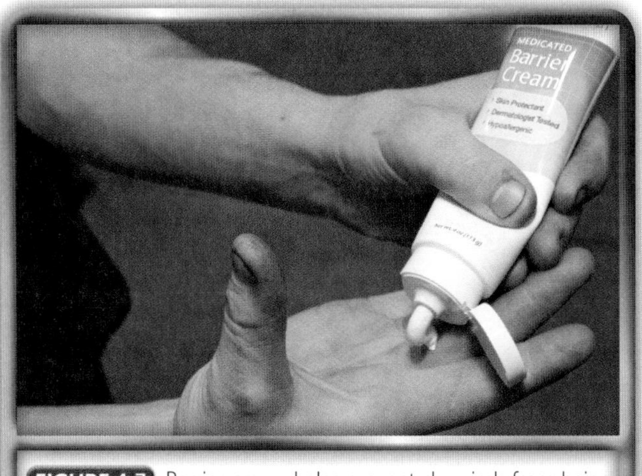
MEDICATED
Barrier
Cream
FIGURE 4-7 Barrier cream helps prevent chemicals from being absorbed into your skin and should be applied to your hands before you begin work.

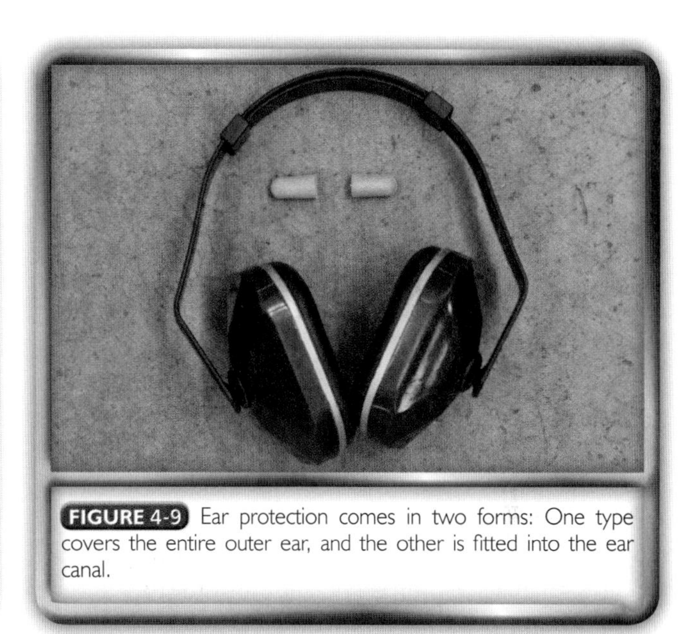
FIGURE 4-9 Ear protection comes in two forms: One type covers the entire outer ear, and the other is fitted into the ear canal.

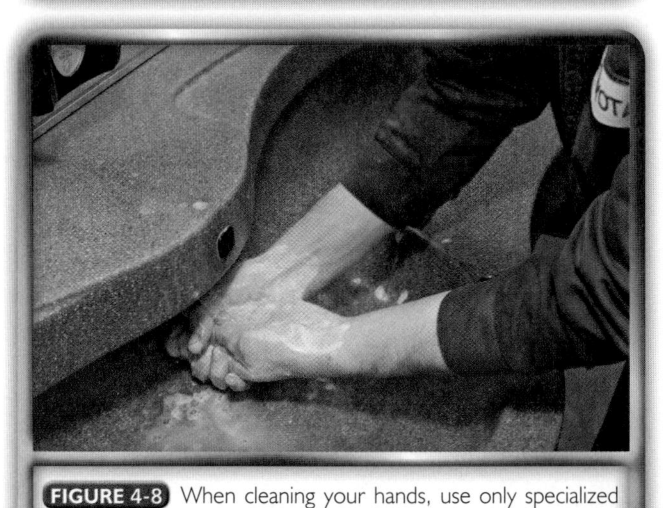
FIGURE 4-8 When cleaning your hands, use only specialized hand cleaners, which protect your skin.

FIGURE 4-10 A disposable dust mask covers your mouth and nose and is disposed of at the completion of the task.

Respirator

The **respirator** has removable cartridges that can be changed according to the type of contaminant being filtered. Always make sure the cartridge is the correct type for the contaminant in the atmosphere. For example, when chemicals are present, use the appropriate chemical filter in your respirator. The cartridges should be replaced according to the manufacturer's recommendation to ensure their effectiveness. To be completely effective, the respirator mask must make a good seal onto your face FIGURE 4-11.

FIGURE 4-11 To be completely effective, the respirator mask must make a good seal onto your face.

Eye Protection

Eyes are very sensitive organs and they need to be protected against damage and injury. There are many things in the workshop environment that can damage or injure eyes, such as high-velocity particles coming from a grinder or high-intensity light coming from a welder. In fact, the American National Standards Institute (ANSI) reports that 2000 workers per day suffer on-the-job eye injuries. Always select the appropriate eye protection for the work you are undertaking. Sometimes this may mean that more than one type of protection is required. For example, when grinding, you should wear a pair of safety glasses underneath your face shield for added protection.

Safety Glasses

The most common type of eye protection is a pair of safety glasses, which must be marked with "Z87" on the lens and frame. Safety glasses have built-in side shields to help protect your eyes from the side. Approved safety glasses should be worn whenever you are in a workshop. They are designed to help protect your eyes from direct impact or debris damage FIGURE 4-12. The only time they should be removed is when you are using other eye protection equipment. Prescription and tinted safety glasses are also available. Tinted safety glasses are designed to be worn outside in bright sunlight conditions. Never wear them indoors or in low light conditions because they reduce your ability to see.

FIGURE 4-12 Safety glasses are designed to protect your eyes from direct impact or debris damage.

Welding Helmet

Wear a **welding helmet** when using or assisting a person using an electric welder. The light from a welding arc is very bright and contains high levels of ultraviolet radiation. The lens on a welding helmet has heavily tinted glass to reduce the intensity of the light from the welding tip, allowing you to see the task you are performing more clearly FIGURE 4-13. Lenses come in a variety of ratings depending on the type of welding you are doing; always make sure you are using a properly rated lens.

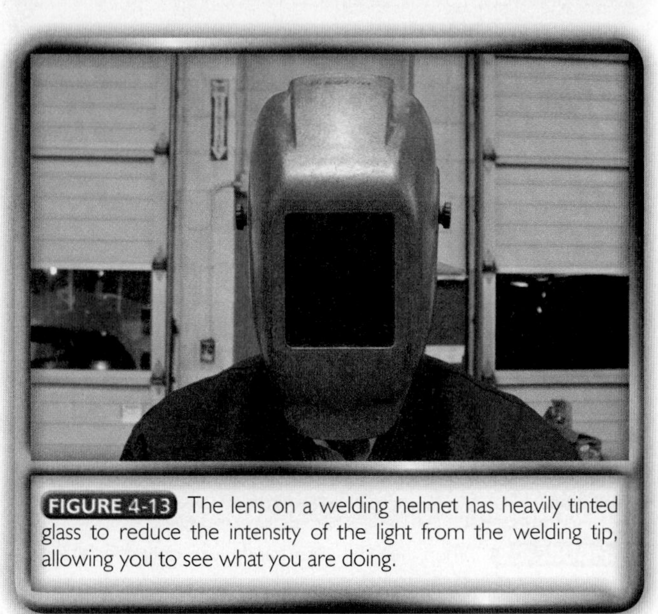

FIGURE 4-13 The lens on a welding helmet has heavily tinted glass to reduce the intensity of the light from the welding tip, allowing you to see what you are doing.

The remainder of the helmet is made from a durable material that blocks any other light from reaching your face. Welding helmets that tint automatically when an arc is struck are also available. Their big advantage is that you do not have to lift and lower the lens by hand.

Safety

Be aware that the ultraviolet radiation can burn your skin like a sunburn, so wear the appropriate welding apparel to protect yourself from this hazard.

Gas Welding Goggles

Gas welding goggles can be worn instead of a welding mask when using or assisting a person using an oxyacetylene welder FIGURE 4-14. The eyepieces are available in heavily tinted versions, but not as tinted as those used in an electric welding helmet. There is no ultraviolet radiation from an oxyacetylene flame, so the welding helmet is not required. However, the flame is bright enough to damage your eyes, so always use goggles of the correct rating.

Full Face Shield

It is necessary to use a full face shield when using solvents and cleaners, epoxies, and resins or when working on a battery FIGURE 4-15. The clear mask of the face shield allows you to see all that you are doing, but will protect your entire face from chemical burns should there be any splashes or battery explosions. It is also recommended that you use a full face shield combined with safety goggles when using a bench or angle grinder.

Safety Goggles

Safety goggles provide much the same eye protection as safety glasses but with added protection against harmful chemicals that may splash up behind the lenses of glasses FIGURE 4-16. Goggles also provide additional protection from foreign particles. Safety goggles must be worn when servicing air-conditioning systems or any other system that contains pressurized gas. Goggles can sometimes fog up when in use; if this occurs, use one of the special anti-fog cleaning fluids or cloths to clean them.

TECHNICIAN TIP

Each lab/shop activity will require at least the safe use of safety glasses, clothing, and shoes depending on its nature. Research and identify whether any additional safety devices are required for every activity you undertake.

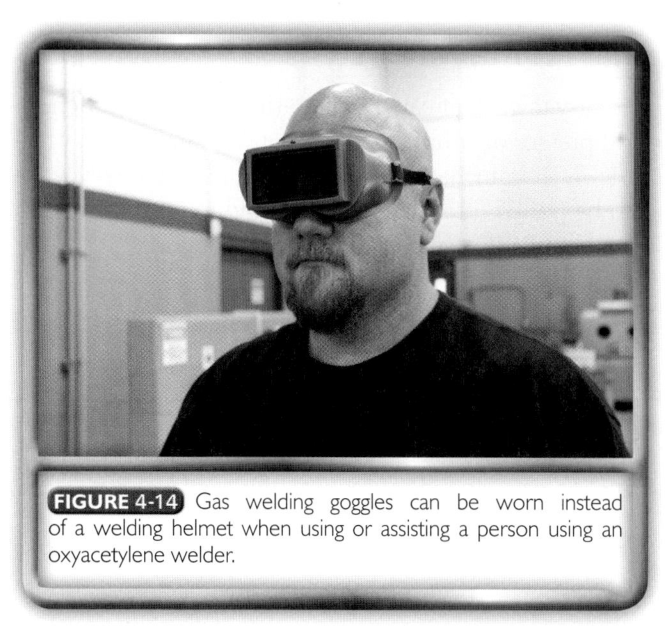

FIGURE 4-14 Gas welding goggles can be worn instead of a welding helmet when using or assisting a person using an oxyacetylene welder.

FIGURE 4-15 It is necessary to use a full face shield when using a grinder, solvents and cleaners, epoxies, and resins or when working on a battery.

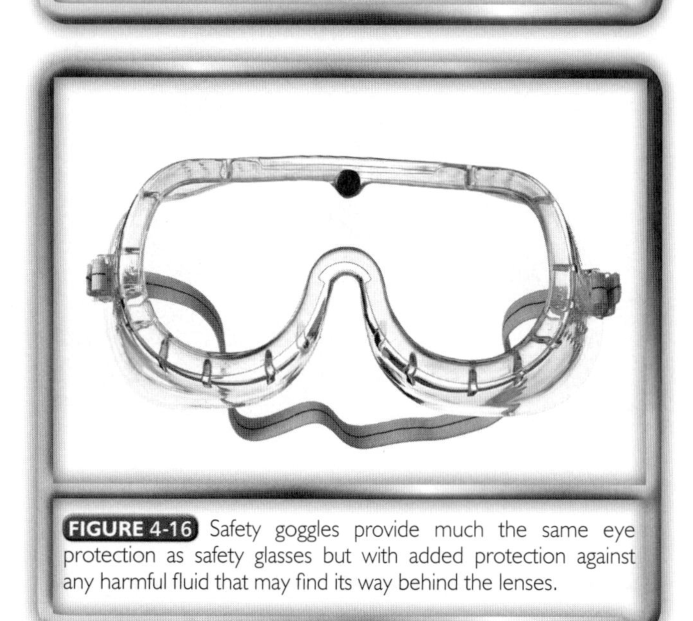

FIGURE 4-16 Safety goggles provide much the same eye protection as safety glasses but with added protection against any harmful fluid that may find its way behind the lenses.

Hair Containment

It is easy to get hair caught in rotating machinery, such as drill presses or running engines, and it can happen very quickly. If your hair gets caught in the machinery, you can be pulled into the machinery and injured or killed. Hair should always be tied back and contained within a hairnet or cap.

Your workshop will have policies and procedures relating to appropriate hairstyles for shop activities. Research the policy and procedures to determine appropriate hairstyles for activities. Always wear your hair according to the policy and procedures. Use hairnets, caps, or elastic bands as required for each activity.

Watches and Jewelry

When in a workshop environment, watches, rings, and jewelry present a number of hazards. They can get caught in rotating machinery, and because they are mainly constructed from metal, they can conduct electricity. Imagine leaning over a running engine with a dangling necklace; it could get caught in the fan belt and be ripped from your neck; not only will it get destroyed, but it could seriously injure you. A ring or watch could inadvertently short out an electrical circuit, heat up quickly and severely burn you, or cause a spark that may make the battery explode. A ring can also get caught on moving parts, breaking the finger bone or even ripping the finger out of the hand FIGURE 4-17. To be safe, always remove watches, rings, and jewelry before starting work. Not only is it safer to remove these items, but your valuables will not get damaged or lost.

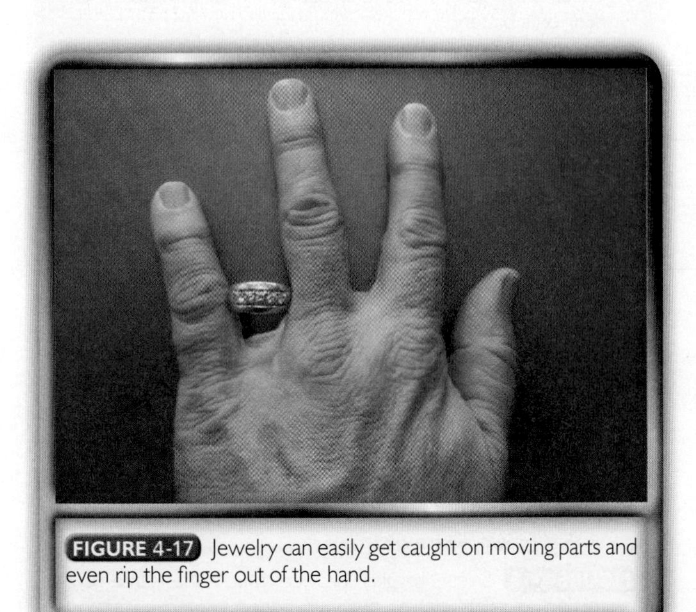

FIGURE 4-17 Jewelry can easily get caught on moving parts and even rip the finger out of the hand.

Applied Science

AS-1: Safety: The technician follows all safety regulations and applicable procedures while performing the task. Using a bench grinder to grind down a steel component is a simple everyday activity in shops. In terms of its potential safety implications, it carries significant risk of injury. Before beginning the task, you must ensure that the machinery is safe and ready to use. Inspect and/or adjust the guards/shields, grinding wheels, electrical cord, etc. From a personal perspective, you must make sure your clothing is suitable and safe for the task. Clothing cannot be loose, as it may get caught in the grinder; it must be made of flame-retardant material, due to the risk of ignition from sparks. Long hair must be tied back or contained within a hairnet or cap due to the risk of it getting caught in rotating machinery.

Various items of PPE are required to safely carry out this task: safety goggles to protect against foreign objects entering the eyes, ear protection to guard against hearing damage due to excessive noise, steel-capped boots to prevent injury from falling heavy objects, and heavy-duty gloves to protect against skin contact with grinding wheels or burns due to heat buildup in the metal component.

Injury Protection Practices

Safe Attitude

Develop a safe attitude toward your work. You should always think "safety first" and then act safely. Think ahead about what you are doing, and put in place specific measures to protect yourself and those around you. For example, you could ask yourself the following questions:

- What could go wrong?
- What measures can I take to ensure that nothing goes wrong?
- What PPE should I use?
- Have I been trained to use this piece of equipment?
- Is the equipment I'm using safe?

Answering these questions and taking appropriate action before you begin will help you work safely.

Proper Ventilation

Proper ventilation is required for working in the shop area. The key to proper ventilation is to ensure that any task or procedure that may produce dangerous or toxic fumes is recognized so that measures can be put in place to provide adequate ventilation. Ventilation can be provided by natural means, such as by opening doors and windows to provide air flow for low-exposure situations. However, in high-exposure situations, such as vehicles running in the shop, a mechanical means of ventilation is required; an example is an exhaust extraction system.

Parts cleaning areas or areas where solvents and chemicals are used should also have good general ventilation, and if required, additional exhaust hoods or fans should be installed to remove dangerous fumes. In some cases, such as when spraying paint, it may be necessary to use a personal respirator in addition to proper ventilation.

> **TECHNICIAN TIP**
>
> Before beginning a task, research the proper ventilation procedure for working within the shop area. Use the correct ventilation equipment and procedures for the activities you are working on within the shop area.

Lifting

Whenever you lift something, there is always the possibility of injury; however, by lifting correctly, you reduce the chance of something going wrong. Before lifting anything, you can reduce the risk of injury by breaking down the load into smaller quantities, asking for assistance if required, or possibly using a mechanical device to assist the lift. If you have to bend down to lift something, you should bend your knees to lower your body; do not bend over with straight legs because this can damage your back **FIGURE 4-18**. Place your feet about shoulder width apart and lift the item by straightening your legs while keeping your back as straight as possible.

Housekeeping and Orderliness

Good housekeeping is about always making sure the shop and your work surroundings are neat and kept in good order. Trash and liquid spills should be quickly cleaned up, tools need to be cleaned and put away after use, spare parts need to be stored correctly, and generally everything needs to have a safe place to be kept. You should carry out good housekeeping practices while working, not just after a job is completed. For example, get rid of trash as it accumulates, clean up spills when they happen, and put tools away when you are finished working with them. It is also good practice to periodically perform a deep clean of the shop so that any neglected areas are taken care of.

> **Safety**
>
> Never lift anything that is too heavy for you to comfortably lift, and always seek assistance if you need help.

FIGURE 4-18 Prevent back injuries when lifting heavy objects by crouching with your legs slightly apart, standing close to the object, and positioning yourself so that the center of gravity is between your feet.

Slip, Trip, and Fall Hazards

Slip, trip, and fall hazards are ever present in the shop, and they can be caused by trash, tools and equipment, or liquid spills being left lying around. Always be on the lookout for hazards that can cause slips, trips, or falls. Floors and steps can become slippery so they should be kept clean and have anti-slip coatings applied to them. High-visibility strips with anti-slip coatings can be applied to the edge of step treads to reduce the hazard.

Clean up liquid spills immediately and mark the area with wet floor signs until the floor is dry. Make sure the workshop has good lighting so hazards are easy to spot, and keep walkways clear from obstruction. Think about what you are doing and make sure the work area is free of slip, trip, and fall hazards as you work.

Wrap-up

Ready for Review

- Personal protective equipment (PPE) protects the body from injury but must fit correctly and be task-appropriate.
- Work clothing should be clean, loose enough for movement, and flame-retardant.
- Footwear should be acid- and slip-resistant and made of puncture-proof material.
- Headgear can protect your head from bumps and should hold long hair in place.
- Hand protection includes chemical gloves, leather gloves, light-duty gloves, general-purpose cloth gloves, and barrier cream.
- Hazardous chemicals and oils can be absorbed into your skin.
- Wear ear protection if the sound level is 85 decibels or above.
- Breathing devices include disposable dust masks and respirators.
- Forms of eye protection are safety glasses, welding helmet, gas welding goggles, full face shield, and safety goggles.
- You may need two types of eye protection for some tasks.
- Before starting work, remove all jewelry and watches, and make sure your hair is contained.
- Thinking "safety first" will lead to acting safety.
- All shops require proper ventilation.
- Lifting correctly or seeking assistance will prevent back injuries.
- Safety includes keeping a clean shop with everything put where it belongs and all spills cleaned up.

Key Terms

barrier cream A cream that looks and feels like a moisturizing cream but has a specific formula to provide extra protection from chemicals and oils.

ear protection Protective gear worn when the sound levels exceed 85 decibels, when working around operating machinery for any period of time, or when the equipment you are using produces loud noise.

gas welding goggles Protective gear designed for gas welding; they provide protection against foreign particles entering the eye and are tinted to reduce the glare of the welding flame.

headgear Protective gear that includes items like hairnets, caps, or hard hats.

heat buildup A dangerous condition that occurs when the glove can no longer absorb or reflect heat and heat is transferred to the inside of the glove.

personal protective equipment (PPE) Equipment used to block the entry of hazardous materials into the body or to protect the body from injury.

respirator Protective gear used to protect the wearer from inhaling harmful dusts or gases. Respirators range from single-use disposable masks to types that have replaceable cartridges. The correct types of cartridge must be used for the type of contaminant encountered.

welding helmet Protective gear designed for arc welding; it provides protection against foreign particles entering the eye, and the lens is tinted to reduce the glare of the welding arc.

ASE-Type Questions

1. Tech A says that personal protective equipment (PPE) does not include clothing. Tech B says that the PPE used should be based on the task you are performing. Who is correct?
   a. Tech A
   b. Tech B
   c. Both A and B
   d. Neither A nor B
2. Tech A says that protective clothing that is not in good condition should be replaced. Tech B says that safety glasses are adequate to protect your eyes regardless of the activity. Who is correct?
   a. Tech A
   b. Tech B
   c. Both A and B
   d. Neither A nor B
3. Tech A says that appropriate work clothes include loose-fitting clothing. Tech B says that you should always wear cuffed pants when working in a shop. Who is correct?
   a. Tech A
   b. Tech B
   c. Both A and B
   d. Neither A nor B
4. Tech A says that proper footwear may include both leather and steel-toed shoes. Tech B says that leather-soled shoes provide slip resistance. Who is correct?
   a. Tech A
   b. Tech B
   c. Both A and B
   d. Neither A nor B
5. Tech A says that a hat can help keep your hair clean when working on a vehicle. Tech B says that chemical gloves may be used when working with solvent. Who is correct?
   a. Tech A
   b. Tech B
   c. Both A and B
   d. Neither A nor B
6. Tech A says that you should only wear gloves when it is absolutely necessary. Tech B says that leather gloves are used to pick up very hot pieces of metal. Who is correct?
   a. Tech A
   b. Tech B
   c. Both A and B
   d. Neither A nor B
7. Tech A says that barrier creams are used to make cleaning your hands easier. Tech B says that hearing protection only needs to be worn by people operating loud equipment. Who is correct?
   a. Tech A
   b. Tech B
   c. Both A and B
   d. Neither A nor B
8. Tech A says that dust masks should be used when painting. Tech B says that a respirator should be used when the TLV for a chemical is exceeded. Who is correct?
   a. Tech A
   b. Tech B
   c. Both A and B
   d. Neither A nor B
9. Tech A says that tinted safety glasses can be worn when working outside. Tech B says that welding can cause a sunburn. Who is correct?
   a. Tech A
   b. Tech B
   c. Both A and B
   d. Neither A nor B
10. Tech A says that you should put tools away when done using them. Tech B says that there's always a risk of injury whenever you lift something. Who is correct?
    a. Tech A
    b. Tech B
    c. Both A and B
    d. Neither A nor B

CAMRY
REPAIR MANUAL
REPAIR MANUAL
CAMRY
REPAIR MANUAL
AVALON
REPAIR MANUAL
VOL. 2

CHAPTER 5

KNOW
SEE
DO
PROVE

NATEF Tasks

Required Supplemental Tasks

Preparing Vehicle for Service	Page
■ Identify information needed and the service requested on a repair order.	84–85
■ Complete work order to include customer information, vehicle identifying information, customer concern, related service history, cause, and correction.	84–85
■ Review vehicle service history.	86
■ Demonstrate use of the three Cs (concern, cause, and correction).	90

KNOW
SEE
DO
PROVE

Knowledge Objectives

After reading this chapter, you will be able to:

1. Describe the purpose and use of owner's manuals and shop manuals/service information. (pp 76–81)
2. Explain how TSBs, service campaigns, and recall information are used. (pp 81–82)
3. Describe the purpose and use of labor guides. (pp 82–84)
4. Identify the purpose and use of a parts program. (pp 83–84)
5. Describe the information and its use within a repair/work order. (pp 84–85)
6. Describe the purpose and use of service history. (p 86)
7. Explain the purpose and application of VINs. (pp 87–88)
8. Explain how the 3 Cs are applied in repairing and servicing vehicles. (p 90)

Vehicle, Customer, and Service Information

Know
See
Do
Prove

Skills Objectives

After reading this chapter, you will be able to:

1. Use an owner's manual to obtain vehicle information. (p 77)
2. Use a shop/repair manual while conducting a service or repair. (pp 78–79)
3. Use a service information program while conducting a service or repair. (pp 80–81)
4. Use a labor guide to estimate the cost or charge of conducting a service or repair. (p 83)
5. Use a parts program to identify and order the correct replacement parts for a service or repair. (p 84)
6. Use a repair/work order to identify the information needed and the service requested. (p 85)
7. Use service history in the repair and service of vehicles. (p 86)
8. Use VINs when repairing and servicing vehicles. (pp 87–88)
9. Decode a North American VIN. (p 88)
10. Apply the 3 Cs when repairing and servicing vehicles. (p 90)

Introduction

Over the last 100 years, motor vehicles have become increasingly comfortable and reliable through the application of technology and improved manufacturing processes. For example, the modern motor vehicle has complex computer-controlled electrical systems where older vehicles had very basic wiring with no electronic components. The increased complexity and expanded range of makes and models have created a need for timely access to relevant, complete, and accurate information to perform maintenance and repair activities.

Vehicle and customer information from various sources provides the fundamental knowledge required to conduct repairs and servicing. Today, the ability to properly perform maintenance and repair activities is increasingly dependent on the technician's ability to research and apply technical information. Vehicle information can come from a number of sources, including vehicle identification plates, owner's manuals, shop manuals, repair orders, service and parts programs, and technical service bulletins. The various sources of information can be published in books or manuals or made available through software packages or the Internet. It is important that you know how to research and apply this information correctly so you can properly repair and service vehicles.

Owner's Manual

Manufacturers supply a vehicle owner's manual, which comes with every new vehicle purchased. The owner's manual is usually kept in the vehicle's glove compartment. Secondhand vehicles may or may not have the owner's manual in the glove compartment. The **owner's manual** contains information about the vehicle and is a valuable source of information for both the owner and the technician.

The information contained in the owner's manual will vary for each manufacturer. In general, it contains basic information on the safe operation and specifications of the vehicle. A typical owner's manual includes an overview of the controls and features of the vehicle; the proper operation, care, and maintenance of the vehicle; owner service procedures; and specifications or technical data **FIGURE 5-1**. The owner's manual also details such elements

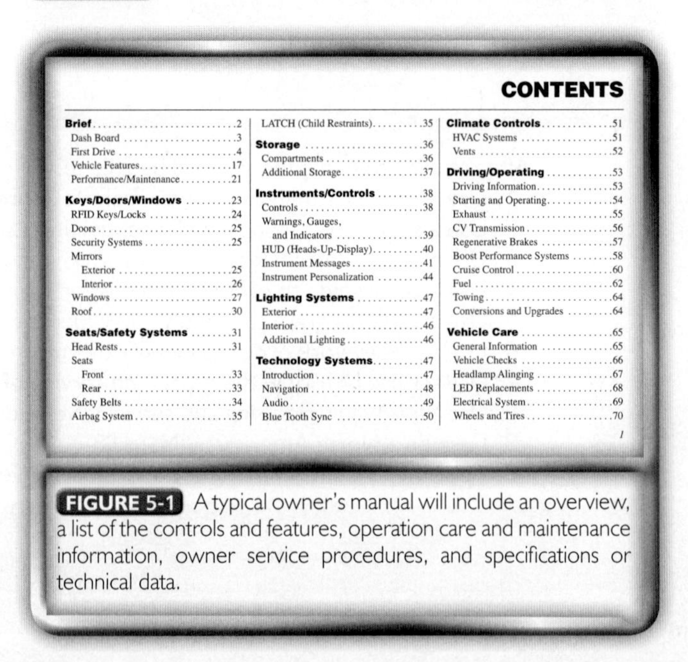

CONTENTS

Brief 2
Dash Board 3
First Drive 4
Vehicle Features 17
Performance/Maintenance 21

Keys/Doors/Windows 23
RFID Keys/Locks 24
Doors 25
Security Systems 25
Mirrors
Exterior 25
Interior 26
Windows 27
Roof 30

Seats/Safety Systems 31
Head Rests 31
Seats
Front 33
Rear 33
Safety Belts 34
Airbag System 35
LATCH (Child Restraints) 35

Storage 36
Compartments 36
Additional Storage 37

Instruments/Controls 38
Controls 38
Warnings, Gauges, and Indicators 39
HUD (Heads-Up-Display) 40
Instrument Messages 41
Instrument Personalization 44

Lighting Systems 47
Exterior 47
Interior 46
Additional Lighting 46

Technology Systems 47
Introduction 47
Navigation 48
Audio 49
Blue Tooth Sync 50

Climate Controls 51
HVAC Systems 51
Vents 52

Driving/Operating 53
Driving Information 53
Starting and Operating 54
Exhaust 55
CV Transmission 56
Regenerative Brakes 57
Boost Performance Systems 58
Cruise Control 60
Fuel 62
Towing 64
Conversions and Upgrades 64

Vehicle Care 65
General Information 65
Vehicle Checks 66
Headlamp Alinging 67
LED Replacements 68
Electrical System 69
Wheels and Tires 70

1

FIGURE 5-1 A typical owner's manual will include an overview, a list of the controls and features, operation care and maintenance information, owner service procedures, and specifications or technical data.

You Are the Automotive Technician

A well-known foreign vehicle manufacturer has recalled over 400,000 of their vehicles for a brake issue. The issue is can be repaired with a software update that will reprogram the vehicles PCM to overcome the problem. But not all of the suspect vehicles will need the software update. The technical service bulletin describes the steps needed to verify if the vehicle has the fault. The manufacturer has notified their customers of a product recall through both mail and email. The dealership that you work for has been receiving many calls from customers to set up recall appointments. Today, you are working on the first vehicle for this recall.

1. Where would you locate the Technical Service Bulletins (TSB), service campaigns, and recalls in the dealership?
2. Why is it important to verify if the TSB has been issued for that particular vehicle?
3. What sources would you use to look up the scheduled maintenance chart for the vehicle?

as vehicle security PIN codes; warranty and service information; fuel, lubricant, and coolant capacities; tire changing specifications; jacking and towing information; and a list of service facilities. The layout and amount of detail in an owner's manual will vary according to the manufacturer and age of the vehicle.

Using an Owner's Manual

To locate the specifications for servicing a vehicle, follow the steps in SKILL DRILL 5-1:

1. Decide what information you need to know about the job and about the vehicle. For example, if your job is to change the engine oil, make sure you know the make, model, and year of manufacture of the vehicle and the type and size of the engine. In order to change the oil, you need to know the engine oil specifications, how much oil to put in, and what grade of oil to use.
2. Locate the appropriate manual. This kind of information is most readily found in the vehicle's owner's manual, which is usually kept in the glove compartment. Open the owner's manual to the first page, which is usually a table of contents to help you quickly find the information you need. Find the correct page and turn to it.
3. Locate the vehicle specifications and identify the correct grade of motor oil for this vehicle. The table of contents lists a page number for the fuel and lubricant capacities and another page number for the refill capacities. First turn to the page listing all of the vehicle's lubricant specifications. Find the correct specifications for the engine crankcase oil and make a note. Next turn to the page listing the refill capacities FIGURE 5-2. You find that this eight-cylinder engine requires 5 quarts (4.7 liters) of oil.
4. Another way of finding information is to refer to the index at the back of the owner's manual FIGURE 5-3. For example, look under *E* for engine, and find "Engine Oil," or look under *L* for lubricants or *O* for oil. Each item should refer you to the same page.
5. Once you have the specific requirements of the vehicle, you are ready to begin servicing the vehicle.

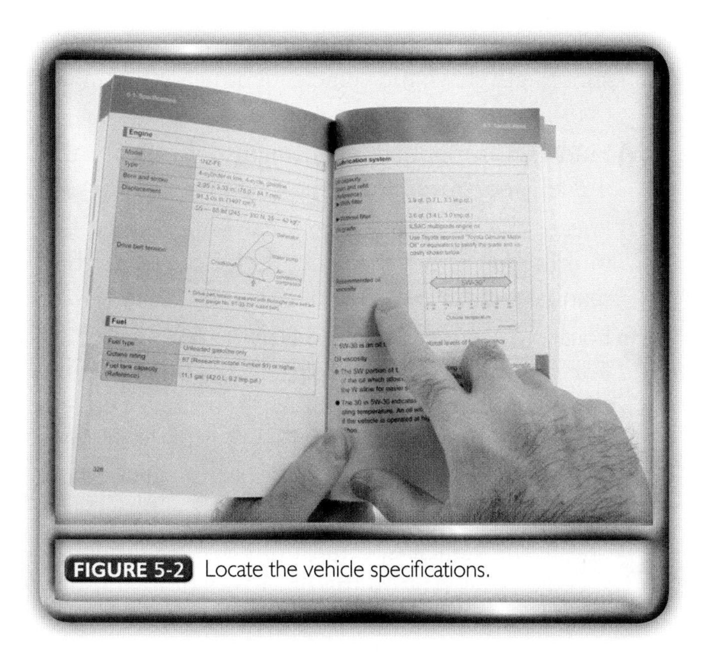

FIGURE 5-2 Locate the vehicle specifications.

FIGURE 5-3 Another way of finding information is to refer to the index at the back of the owner's manual.

Shop Manual

Shop or service manuals are available for just about every make and model of every vehicle made. Service manuals come in two types—factory and after-market. Factory manuals are produced by vehicle manufacturers and specify the procedures to maintain, repair, and diagnose their vehicles. Usually a factory service manual is specific to one year and make of vehicle, such as a 2012 Ford Expedition.

After-market service manuals are published by independent companies for the same purpose. Usually, after-market manuals are not as detailed as factory manuals; they may not cover topics such as trim, entertainment systems, and so on. They are arranged in one of two ways: They either cover a range of years for a particular vehicle, such as 2005 to 2010 Ford Mustangs, or they cover a range of vehicles for a single year, such as 2011 General Motors vehicles.

Paper shop manuals have become less common over the years as less expensive electronic versions that can be installed on a computer have become available.

> **TECHNICIAN TIP**
>
> While factory manuals are usually more complete, it can be very costly to maintain a library of individual manuals for each of the vehicles serviced by a shop. After-market manuals help make the cost of service information more affordable. The modern vehicle is becoming very complex with all the technology now fitted to it, and this means shop manuals have also grown in complexity and size, resulting in significant expense and storage requirements.

> **TECHNICIAN TIP**
>
> Here is an example of how much more a technician of today needs to know versus 65 years ago. In 1947, MOTOR, an organization devoted to supplying automotive data, produced a repair manual that covered the repair procedures and specifications for all of the vehicles produced by more than 20 manufacturers from 1935 to 1946. This reference was only about 1100 pages long. Today it takes MOTOR two to three 1100-page books to cover the same information for one manufacturer for one year. Technicians rely on service information more now than ever before.

In addition, most manufacturers and providers of shop manuals have made the information available online. These services are usually provided through a daily, monthly, or yearly subscription. Electronic versions are becoming very popular because they allow shops to access the information they need without having to pay for and store large numbers of shop manuals. Also, it is easier for the publisher to update information as changes or corrections are needed, so the information is generally more accurate than printed materials, which require supplemental printed updates on a periodic basis.

Typical shop manuals will be broken into a number of sections that relate to systems within the vehicle—for example, engine, transmission, drivetrain, suspension, and electrical. The sections of the shop manuals will be further divided into topics or subject areas; for example, in the engine section, topics could be general description, engine diagnosis, and on-vehicle service. A typical shop manual page will have a task description broken into steps and diagrams or pictures to aid the technician **FIGURE 5-4**. It is important to know that all service manuals arrange the content in their own way, so using a variety of different manuals will help you become familiar with finding the information you are looking for.

MAINTENANCE/SPECIFICATIONS

CHANGING YOUR WIPERS

The wiper arms can be manually moved when the ignition is disabled. This allows for ease of blade replacement and cleaning under the blades.

1. Disable the ignition before removing the blade.
2. Pull the arm away from the glass.
3. Left leading edge retaining block to release the blade. Swing the blade, away from with the arm, to remove it.
4. Swing the new blade toward the arm and snap it into place. Replace the retaining block at the leading edge of the wiper arm. Lower the wiper arm back to the windshield. The wiper arms will automatically return to their normal position the next time the ignition is enabled.

Refresh wiper blades at least twice a year for premium performance.

Poor preforming wipers quality can be improved by cleaning the blades and the windshield. See *Windows and wiper blades* in the *Cleaning* chapter.

To extend the life of wiper blades, scrape off the ice on the windshield BEFORE turning on the wipers. The ice has many sharp edges and will damage and shread the cleaning edge of your wiper blade.

6

FIGURE 5-4 A typical shop manual page will have a task description broken into steps and diagrams or pictures to aid the technician.

Using a Shop Manual

Shop manuals are developed by manufacturers or after-market publishers to provide you with correct information on performing all service and repair tasks on the vehicles produced. The information found in shop manuals provides a systematic procedure and identifies special tools, safety precautions, and specifications relevant to the task. Shop manuals are organized according to vehicle systems and have indexes for quick referencing. Knowing that a water pump is part of the cooling system and that the cooling system is part of the engine system (or in some cases the HVAC system) will help you locate the specific information you need.

To identify correct service procedures using a shop manual, follow the steps in **SKILL DRILL 5-2**:

1. Decide what information you need to know about the job and about the vehicle. Make sure you know the make, model, and year of manufacture of the vehicle, and the type and size of the engine. You should also have the vehicle identification number (VIN) handy.
2. Find the appropriate shop manual for the make, model, and year of the vehicle you are working on.
3. Locate the correct section that will contain the information you need. The first page of the shop manual is usually a table of contents.
4. Locate the service procedures in the proper section. For example, if you were performing brake repairs, you would turn to the "Brakes" section. The text and the pictures describe how to properly perform a procedure and tell you the tools to use and how to use them.
5. Locate the vehicle specifications by consulting the specifications page in the proper section. You may need to know the type of engine of the vehicle to

Applied Science

AS-7: Maps/Charts/Tables/Graphs: The technician uses the information in service manual charts, tables, or graphs to determine the manufacturer's specifications for system(s) operation(s).

AS-8: Maps/Charts/Tables/Graphs: The technician uses the information in service manual charts, tables, or graphs to determine the appropriate repair/replacement procedure and/or part.

Most service manuals will have a chart that you will need to consult before performing preventative maintenance. The chart lists what needs to be performed according to the vehicle's mileage. As you can see, there is a big difference between a 43,000 mile (minor) service to a 52,000 mile (major) service. On the 52,000 mile service, far more items are inspected and or replaced. If the vehicle came into the workshop for a 43,000 mile service, you easily read from the service chart what needs to be done.

Mileage	43,000 Miles	52,000 Miles
Maintenance Items	I: Drive belts. R: Engine oil. R: Engine oil filter. I: Battery. I: Engine air cleaner filter. I: Brake pedal and parking brake. I: Brake pads and discs. I: Brake fluid. I: Clutch fluid. I: Brake pipes and hose. I: Power steering fluid I: Steering wheel I: Drive shaft boots. I: Suspension ball joint and dust covers I: Tires and psi. I: Rotate wheels. I: Seatbelt, webbing condition, buckle and retractor mechanism operation C: Air conditioner filter I: Refrigerant amount of air conditioner I: Valve clearance	I: Drive belts R: Engine oil R: Engine oil filter I: Cooling and heater system I: Engine Coolant I: Exhaust pipe and mountings I: Battery R: Engine air cleaner filter I: Brake pedal and parking brake I: Parking brake linings and drums I: Brake pads and discs R: Brake fluid I: Brake pipes and hoses I: Power steering fluid I: Steering wheel and linkage I : Front and rear suspension I: Lights, horns, wipers and washers I: Seatbelt, webbing condition, buckle and retractor mechanism operation C: Air conditioner filter

Note: T = Tighten, R = Replace, I = Inspect, A= Adjust, L = Lubricate, and C= Clean.

find the correct specifications for the vehicle you are working on.

Using a Service Information Program

Service information programs are computer applications used to provide technical information for the repair and maintenance of vehicles **FIGURE 5-5**. The software can be installed on the computer, accessed via the Internet using a browser, or run from a CD or DVD.

To use a service information program, you need to have a basic understanding of how to start and use a computer. Usernames and passwords may be required to log in to the computer and the service information program, so make sure you have these available before you start. A printer is also helpful to print copies of the information so that you can use it when conducting service and repairs; alternatively, you may need to take notes.

FIGURE 5-5 Computer databases provide information on procedures, parts, and service problems.

To obtain the correct information, you will need vehicle identification information, such as the date of manufacture, model, engine and VIN numbers, and an understanding of the type of repair or scheduled service that is being performed. The repair order may provide you with this information, or you may have to research vehicle identification information from the vehicle. You may need to perform some initial diagnosis of the fault to further continue the search for information.

Information can usually be obtained by searching for the vehicle and then selecting from the list of systems such as brakes or maintenance, followed by subsystems such as disc brakes or fluid capacities. A keyword search may also be available; for example, use the keyword "service interval" to obtain a list of scheduled service intervals. Using a generic word like "engine" may return a very large list. If this occurs, the search can be narrowed further by entering more specific criteria such as "engine oil," "water pump," or "camshaft."

The information will be displayed on pages that will have a mixture of text and diagrams with explanations. Some of the diagrams may have detailed views so you can see how parts fit together, while links may be provided to other relevant information such as a schematic diagram. Most systems will contain help menus or training guides with examples to assist you in using the software, if required.

To use a service information program, follow the steps in SKILL DRILL 5-3:

1. If necessary, start the computer and select the service information program.
2. Log in to the application using the appropriate username and password.
3. Enter the vehicle identification information into the system in the appropriate places: year, make, model, engine, and possibly VIN.
4. Search for the information you require to perform the service or repair.
5. The search engine will provide a list of possible matches for you to select from. If the initial search does not produce what you are looking for, try changing the search criteria. Keep searching until you find the information.
6. Finally, once the general details for the item are displayed, gather the specific information on the

Applied Science

AS-11 Information Processing: The technician can use computer databases to input and retrieve customer information for billing, warranty work, and other record-keeping purposes.

Dealership service departments have access to databases run by manufacturers for the purposes of accessing warranty information, tracking vehicle servicing and warranty repair history, and logging warranty repair jobs for payment by the manufacturer. When a customer presents their vehicle for a warranty repair, the customer service department staff begin by consulting the database to confirm that the vehicle is within its warranty period, and that the warranty has not been invalidated for any reason. Once it is confirmed that the vehicle is still under valid warranty, the repair order will be passed to the workshop for diagnosis and repair. Any parts required for the warranty repair must be labeled by the technician and stored for possible recall by the manufacturer.

For example, a young man comes in complaining that his vehicle is "running rough." The customer service staff will confirm that the vehicle is nine months old only has 14,500 miles, confirming that the vehicle is within the manufacturer's 3 year/100,000 mile warranty period. They check the manufacturer's database to confirm that the vehicle's warranty has not been invalidated before handing the repair order onto the workshop. Then a technician diagnoses the fault as a defective ignition coil and fills out a warranty parts form.

Once the repair has been completed and the parts labeled, the warranty parts form and any repair order papaerwork is passed back to administrative staff for processing. Processing will include billing the manufacturer for the correct, pre-approved amount of time, logging the repair on the database for payment, and ensuring that all documentation is correct for auditing purposes.

WARRANTY PARTS Form

Customer complaint:	*Vehicle running rough*	VEHICLE INFORMATION.	
Cause:	*# 6 ignition coil open circuit on primary winding.*	VIN:	*1G112345678910111*
Correction:	*Replaced #6 ignition coil*	RO Number:	*123456*
Parts description:	*# 6 ignition coil*	Date of repair:	*10/04/2011*

specifications or repairs. You may need more than one piece of information.

7. Print out or write down the information needed. Put this on a clipboard and take it with you to perform the service or repair.

Technical Service Bulletins

Technical service bulletins (TSBs) are issued by manufacturers to provide information to technicians on unexpected problems, updated parts, or changes to repair procedures that may occur with a particular vehicle system, part, or component FIGURE 5-6. The typical TSB contains step-by-step procedures and diagrams on how to identify if there is a fault and perform an effective repair.

At the time of production, manufacturers prepare service and technical information and attempt to anticipate the information the technicians will require to undertake service and repairs. Once the vehicle is in use, situations can arise when particular components or repair procedures may need either additional information or changes. This is where TSBs are most useful. For example, suppose there is a change to the procedure that bleeds air from the cooling system. In this situation, the manufacturer would issue a service bulletin explaining the problem and the changes to the current procedure performed to bleed air from the cooling system.

Using TSBs

To use a TSB, follow these guidelines. Locate where the TSBs are kept in your shop or look them up with your electronic service information system. Prior to performing repairs, look through the TSBs and get to know the type of information contained in them. Before working on a vehicle, it is good practice to check if a TSB has been issued for that vehicle and type of fault or repair. This can save a lot of wasted time.

Compare the information contained in the TSB to that found in the shop manual. Note the differences, and if necessary, copy the TSB and take it with you to perform the repair. Perform the repair following the TSB where appropriate while also referring to the shop manual. If required in your shop policy, note the details of the service bulletin in the appropriate area on the repair order.

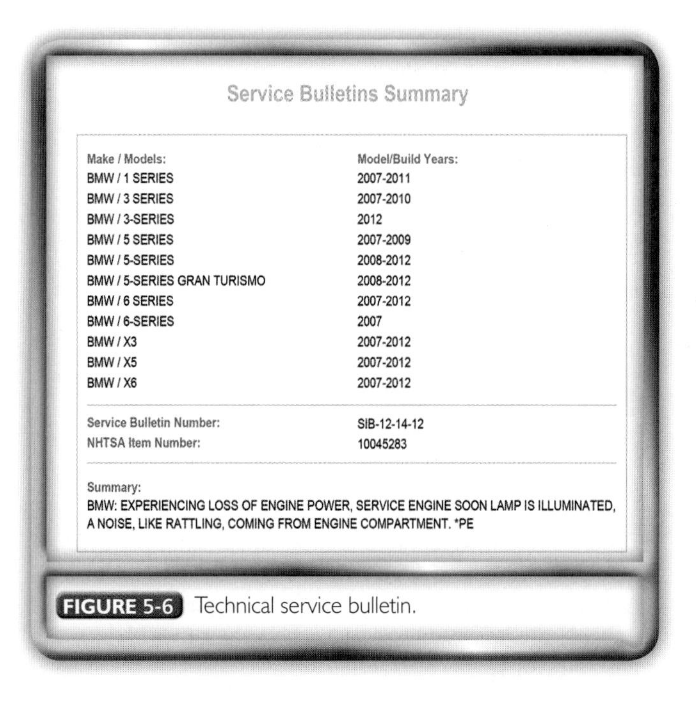

Service Bulletins Summary

Make / Models:	Model/Build Years:
BMW / 1 SERIES	2007-2011
BMW / 3 SERIES	2007-2010
BMW / 3-SERIES	2012
BMW / 5 SERIES	2007-2009
BMW / 5-SERIES	2008-2012
BMW / 5-SERIES GRAN TURISMO	2008-2012
BMW / 6 SERIES	2007-2012
BMW / 6-SERIES	2007
BMW / X3	2007-2012
BMW / X5	2007-2012
BMW / X6	2007-2012

Service Bulletin Number: SIB-12-14-12
NHTSA Item Number: 10045283

Summary:
BMW: EXPERIENCING LOSS OF ENGINE POWER, SERVICE ENGINE SOON LAMP IS ILLUMINATED, A NOISE, LIKE RATTLING, COMING FROM ENGINE COMPARTMENT. *PE

FIGURE 5-6 Technical service bulletin.

Service Campaigns and Recalls

Service campaigns and recalls are usually conducted by manufacturers when a safety issue is discovered with a particular vehicle. Recalls are costly to manufacturers because they can require the repair of an entire model or production run of vehicles. Potentially, this could involve many thousands of vehicles. Depending on the nature of the problem, recalls can be mandatory and enforced by law, or manufacturers may choose to voluntarily conduct a recall to ensure the safe operation of the vehicle or minimize damage to their business and product image.

Safety

Each country has specific laws regarding product recalls. Find out the laws in your jurisdiction.

An example of a mandatory recall is a fault within the airbag system of a vehicle that results in the airbag not deploying or deploying when it should not. In this case, the manufacturer would need to identify the problem, its cause, the vehicles affected, and the recertification requirements. A recall would then be issued and advertised in popular media. Letters would be sent from the manufacturer to known owners of the particular vehicle indicating that the vehicles should be returned for repair. Usually all costs associated with the recall are paid by the manufacturer.

Using Service Campaign Information

To utilize service campaigns or recall information, follow these guidelines. Locate where the special service messages, service campaigns/recalls, vehicle/service warranty applications, and service interval recommendations can be accessed in your shop. Look through the TSBs, service recalls, service warranty applications, and service interval recommendations, and get to know the type of information that is contained in them. Identify how they could be used in your daily tasks.

When working on vehicles, check to see if a TSB has been issued for that vehicle and type of repair. Perform service and repairs following the special service messages, service campaigns/recalls, vehicle/service warranty applications, and service interval recommendations. Fill in the required documentation as required in your shop policies. Note the details of the special service messages, service campaigns/recalls, vehicle/service warranty applications, and service interval recommendations in the appropriate area on the repair order.

Caring for the Customer

Customer satisfaction ratings are very important to dealerships and shops. One way to impress customers is to check for recalls on every vehicle that comes in for service and inform the customer if you find anything. Some manufacturers will flag a vehicle for any outstanding recalls when the VIN is entered into the dealership's computerized repair system when the vehicle is brought in for service.

Labor Guide

Labor guides list how much time will be involved in performing a standard or warranty-related service or repair. They are regularly updated as new models are released into the market and provide a basis for making job estimates and standard charges for the customer. Flat rate servicing costs are usually derived from a labor guide. For example, if a customer wants to know how much it will cost to replace a leaking intake manifold gasket on a particular vehicle, then a technician can look up this procedure in a labor guide and find the information on the time and parts required for that particular repair on the specific vehicle.

With the advent of technology and the Internet, many providers of labor guides have started making them available online as well as in print. The online versions are paid for by subscription, which is usually a monthly or annual fee to access the information. Having access to online labor guides means the shop does not have to wait for a new version of the print publication to become available. Online versions of labor guides also can be updated as new models of vehicles are released or updates are made by the manufacturer.

Using a Labor Guide

The labor guide indicates how quickly an average technician can complete the task. Experienced technicians who have performed the task many times and who are working efficiently can usually perform the job quicker than the labor guide specifies. But since each task and vehicle has its small differences, the time is not always completely accurate. The information contained within a labor guide is referenced in a similar manner as a repair manual or online service information system.

To use a labor guide, follow the steps in SKILL DRILL 5-4.

Parts Program

Parts programs are the modern-day version of parts manuals. They are essentially an electronic version of a parts manual. Parts programs may be available via a CD/DVD, a computer network, or the Internet. Technicians and **parts specialists**, the individuals working at the parts counter, use these programs to identify parts and find order numbers.

Parts manuals are produced for all makes and models of vehicles and are essentially a catalogue of all the parts that make up a vehicle. The parts are catalogued by systems—for example, brake, engine, and transmission. Diagrams of each part are shown along with a part number, which is a unique identifying number for that particular part.

Using a Parts Program

A parts program is a computer application that is used to identify part numbers for vehicle components. Part numbers need to be identified so that correct replacement components can be ordered to replace faulty parts. The software can be installed on the computer, accessed via the Internet using a browser, or run from a CD or DVD.

To use a parts program, you need to have a basic understanding of how to start and use a computer. Usernames and passwords may be required to log in to the computer and the parts program, so make sure you have those available before you start. A printer is also

TECHNICIAN TIP

Dealership technicians have one advantage over most independent technicians: They have an onsite parts department that stocks many of the parts needed for repairs. Many independent shops maintain a relatively small inventory of high-demand parts such as filters, belts, and light bulbs and use a local parts house to supply the less common parts. This can result in delays waiting for parts to arrive.

SKILL DRILL 5-4 Using a Labor Guide

ALLDATA
REPAIR
Library and Educational Version

ENTER

System Requirements

1. Log in to the labor estimating system.

YEAR	MAKE	MODEL
2014	Acura	Fiesta
2013	Acura Truck	Focus
2012	Audi	Fusion AWD
2011	BMW	Fusion FWD
2010	Buick	Fusion FWD Energi
2009	Buick Truck	Fusion FWD Hybrid
2008	Cadillac	Mustang
2007	Cadillac Truck	
2006	Chevrolet	
2005	Chevy Truck	**ENGINE**
2004	Chrysler	V6-3.7L
2003	Chrysler Truck	V8-5.0L VIN F
2002	Dodge	V8-5.0L VIN U
2001	Dodge or Ram Truck	V8-5.8L SC
2000	Fiat	
1999	Ford	
1998	Ford Truck	

2. Enter the vehicle information into the system.

Maintenance
Technical Service Bulletins
Specifications

A L L Diagnostic Trouble Codes DTC)
Accessories and Optional Equipment
Body and Frame
Brakes and Traction Control
Cruise Control
Engine, Cooling and Exhaust
Heating and Air Conditioning
Hybrid Drive Systems
Instrument Panel, Gauges and Warning Indicators

3. Find the labor operation either by working your way through the menu tree or by typing a keyword into the search bar.

Labor Information	Skill Level	Mfg. Warranty	Standard
Hydraulic Control Assembly - Antilock Brakes			
Replace			
Modulator Valve	B	1.5	2.0

4. The next screen tracks time in two columns. "Warranty time" is the amount of time the manufacturer would pay the shop for the operation under a customer warranty. "Customer pay" time is the amount of time a customer would be billed for and is usually 20–40% longer than warranty time. Time is tracked in tenths of an hour, so every increment of 0.1 hour equals 6 minutes (e.g., 0.6 hours equals 36 minutes).

Labor Information	Skill Level	Mfg. Warranty	Standard
Spark Plug			
Replace	C	1.4	1.8

Labor Information	Skill Level	Mfg. Warranty	Standard
Compression Check			
Diagnose/Test			
Compression, Test *Includes: R&I Spark Plugs.*	B	0.0	2.1

5. Identify "combination" jobs. Combined tasks often save a lot of time over performing individual tasks because the customer is already being charged for part of the job in the first task. For example, replacing the spark plugs is easier to do when performing a compression test, since the spark plugs would already be removed.

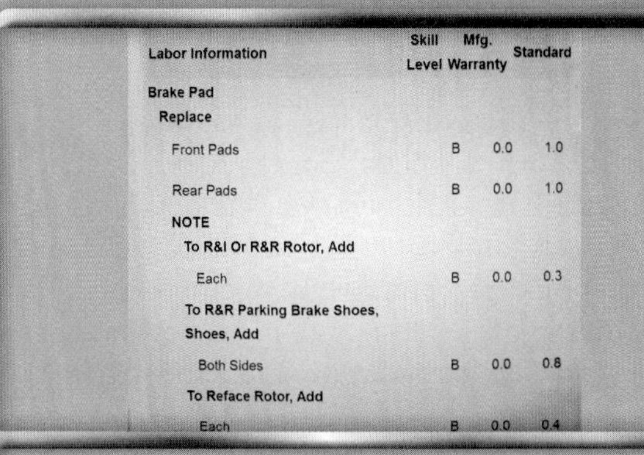

Labor Information	Skill Level	Mfg. Warranty	Standard
Brake Pad			
Replace			
Front Pads	B	0.0	1.0
Rear Pads	B	0.0	1.0
NOTE			
To R&I Or R&R Rotor, Add			
Each	B	0.0	0.3
To R&R Parking Brake Shoes, Shoes, Add			
Both Sides	B	0.0	0.8
To Reface Rotor, Add			
Each	B	0.0	0.4

6. Identify "additional time"—extra time needed to handle relatively common situations, for example to account for differences in vehicle-installed options. For example, when replacing brake pads on a vehicle with wheel locks, the customer should be charged the time needed to find the lock key and remove and install the wheel locks. Extra time should be added to the base operation.

> **TECHNICIAN TIP**
>
> Follow these guidelines when using a technical service bulleting (TSB):
>
> - Locate where the TSBs are kept in your shop or look them up with your electronic service information system.
> - Prior to performing repairs, look through the TSBs and become familiar with the type of information contained in them.
> - Before working on a vehicle, check whether a TSB has been issued for that vehicle and the type of fault or repair.
> - Compare the information contained in the TSB to the shop manual information and note the differences. You may copy the TSB and take it with you to perform the repair.
> - Perform the repair following the TSB where appropriate while also referring to the shop manual.
> - If required by your shop policy, note the details of the service bulletin in the appropriate area on the repair order.

helpful to print out copies of the information so that you can use it when ordering parts; alternatively, you may need to take notes.

To identify the correct part, you will need to know where on the vehicle the part is installed, what system or subsystem it comes from, and vehicle identification information, such as date of manufacture, model, and engine and VIN numbers. Make sure you have this information on hand before you use the system. Searches can be conducted by keywords. If the part is for the brake system, in the search criteria box, enter "brake." Using a generic word like "brake" may return a very large list. If this occurs, the search can be narrowed further by entering more specific criteria such as "disc brake."

The parts will be displayed in diagrams that are labeled and show individual parts in exploded view, making it easier to identify parts. The diagrams may number the parts and have a key on the page for reference to part numbers, or arrows may point to listed part numbers on the page. Most systems will contain help menus or training guides with examples to assist you in using the software, if required.

To locate parts information on the computer, follow the steps in SKILL DRILL 5-5:

1. Log in to the application using the appropriate username and password.
2. Enter the year, make, model, and engine and VIN number information into the system in the appropriate places.
3. Search for the parts you require to conduct the service or repair.
4. The search engine will provide a list of possible matches for you to select from. If the initial search does not produce what you are looking for, try changing the search criteria. Keep searching until you find the information.
5. Gather information on the identified parts, including part numbers, location, availability, and cost.
6. Print, write down, or directly place an order for the desired parts.

Repair Order Information

A **repair order**, or work order, is a form used by shops to collect information regarding a vehicle coming in for repair FIGURE 5-7. Initial information for the repair order includes customer and vehicle details, along with a brief description of the customer's complaint(s). The repair order is used by the technician to guide him or her to the problem, and by the customer service staff to create the invoice when the work is completed.

Detailed information that will be on the repair order includes customer details such as name and address; the vehicle make, model, and year; the odometer reading; the date; customer concern information; the cause of the problem(s); the correction for the problem(s); the hours of labor; and the parts used for the repair. The repair order should always include all of the information pertaining to the customer, vehicle, and cost of repair. Repair orders are legal documents that can be used as evidence in the event of a lawsuit. Make sure the

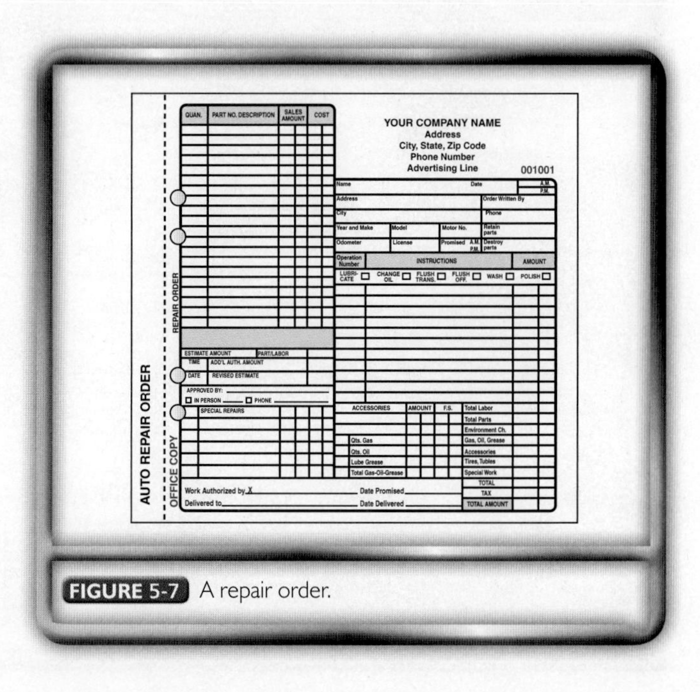

AUTO REPAIR ORDER
OFFICE COPY
REPAIR ORDER

YOUR COMPANY NAME
Address
City, State, Zip Code
Phone Number
Advertising Line
001001

QUAN. | PART NO. DESCRIPTION | SALES AMOUNT | COST

Name | Date | A.M. P.M.
Address | Order Written By
City | Phone
Year and Make | Model | Motor No. | Retain parts
Odometer | License | Promised A.M. P.M. | Destroy parts
Operation Number | INSTRUCTIONS | AMOUNT
LUBRICATE ☐ CHANGE OIL ☐ FLUSH TRANS. ☐ FLUSH OFF. ☐ WASH ☐ POLISH ☐

ESTIMATE AMOUNT | PART/LABOR
TIME | ADD'L AUTH. AMOUNT
DATE | REVISED ESTIMATE
APPROVED BY:
☐ IN PERSON ☐ PHONE
SPECIAL REPAIRS

ACCESSORIES | AMOUNT | F.S.
Qts. Gas
Qts. Oil
Lube Grease
Total Gas-Oil-Grease

Total Labor
Total Parts
Environment Ch.
Gas, Oil, Grease
Accessories
Tires, Tubes
Special Work
TOTAL
TAX
TOTAL AMOUNT

Work Authorized by X
Date Promised
Delivered to
Date Delivered

FIGURE 5-7 A repair order.

> **TECHNICIAN TIP**
>
> Repair orders are used also to inform the customer of needed repairs or service. This usually results in the customer agreeing to the needed repair, in which case all is well. But if he or she does not agree to the repair and the vehicle is involved in an accident because of the faulty components, having the customer's initials on the repair order signifying that he or she understands the safety issues can help prevent the shop from being held liable for the accident.

information is complete and accurate whenever filling out a repair order, and store it in an organized safe place, such as in a file cabinet or electronically on a secure computer network.

To identify the information needed and the service requested on a repair order, follow the steps in SKILL DRILL 5-6:

1. Locate a repair order used in your shop.
2. Familiarize yourself with the repair order, and identify the following information on the repair order:
   a. Date
   b. Customer details: name and address, daytime phone number
   c. Vehicle details: year, make, model, color, odometer reading, VIN
   d. Customer concern details

   Note any additional information that is required on your shop's repair order.
3. Following the shop procedures, determine the workflow for the tasks that are listed.
4. Use the repair order to carry out the requested service or repair. Fill in the repair order with details of the cause of the customer concern(s) and the correction(s) conducted.

Applied Communications

AC-23: Repair Orders: The technician writes a repair order containing customer vehicle information, customer complaints, parts and materials used (including prices), services performed, labor hours, and suggested repairs/maintenance.

A repair order is a key document used to communicate with both your customers and co-workers. It is a legal contract between the service provider and the customer. It contains details of the services to be provided by you and the authorization from the customer. To make sure everyone understands clearly what is involved, a repair order should contain information about:

- Your company or service providers: The service provider section contains the company name, address, and contact details; the name of a service advisor who is overseeing the job; and the amount of time the service technician will have to service the vehicle.
- The customer: The customer section contains the customer's name, address, and contact phone numbers.
- The customer's vehicle: The vehicle section includes details about the vehicle to be serviced. Check the vehicle's license plate before starting work. The license plate numbers are usually unique within a country. You should also record information about the vehicle's make, model, and color. This information will make it easier for you to locate the vehicle on the parking lot. You need to know the manufacture date of the vehicle to be able to order the right parts. The odometer reading and the date will help keep track of how much distance the vehicle travels and the time period between each visit to the shop. The VIN is designed to be unique worldwide and contains specific information about the vehicle. Many shops do a "walk-around" with the customer to note any previous damage to the vehicle and to look for any obvious faults such as worn tires, rusted-out exhaust pipes, or torn wiper blades.
- The service operations: This section contains the details of the service operations and parts.
  - The first part is the service operation details. For example, the vehicle is in for a 150,000-mile (240,000-km) service, which can be done in 3 hours resulting in approximately a $300 of labor cost. The information about the chargeable labor time to complete a specific task can be found in a labor guide manual. In some workplaces, this information is built into the computer system and will be automatically displayed.
  - The second part of this section is the details of parts used in the service including the descriptions, quantities, codes, and prices. The codes for each service and part are normally abbreviations that are used for easy reference in the shop. Some shops may have their own reference code system.
  - As you do the vehicle inspection, you may discover other things that need replaced or repaired. These additional services can be recorded in another section. It is essential that you check with your customers and obtain their approval before carrying out any additional services.
- The parts requirements: This section lists the parts required to perform the repair.

Some repair orders also contain accounting information so they can be used as invoices.

Accounting

The accounting section contains information about the methods of payment, which can be cash, credit card, or account. An account system can be set up to handle all payments related to a customer or to a company that uses your service for a number of vehicles. When a vehicle on an account system comes in, you need to record both the account number and the order number. To work out the total cost of the service, you need to know:

- The labor cost
- The cost of parts
- The tax amounts
- The cost of gas and consumables you used to service the vehicle

You also need to have the customer's authorization to carry out the service. Remember, before making any changes to this service invoice or work order after the authorization, you will need to receive the customer's approval.

> **TECHNICIAN TIP**
>
> Always obtain the customer's authorization before servicing his or her vehicle, and also make sure you have the customer's approval before making any changes to the service invoice or the work order.

> **TECHNICIAN TIP**
>
> A vehicle's service history is valuable for several reasons:
>
> - It can provide helpful information to the technician when performing repairs.
> - It allows potential new owners of the vehicle to know how well the vehicle and its systems were maintained.
> - Manufacturers use the history to evaluate warranty claims.

Service History

Service history is a complete list of all the servicing and repairs that have been performed on a vehicle **FIGURE 5-8**. The scheduled service history is often recorded in a service booklet or owner's manual that is kept in the glove compartment. The service history can provide valuable information to technicians when conducting repairs. It also can provide potential new owners of used vehicles

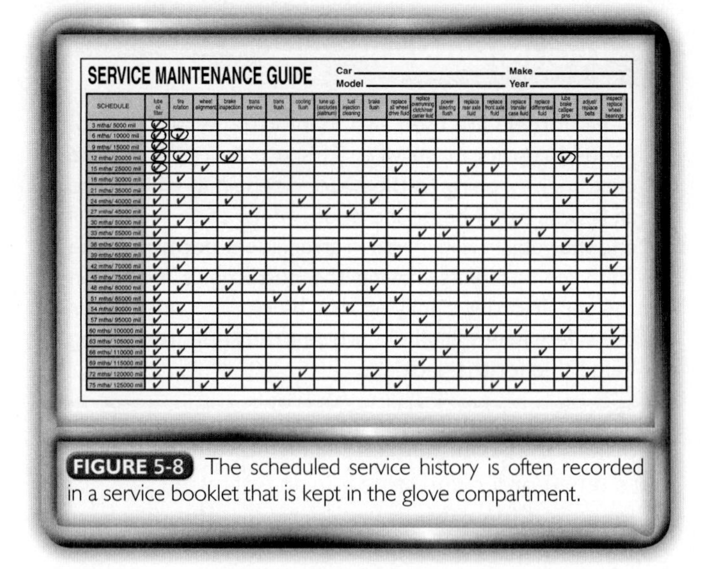

SERVICE MAINTENANCE GUIDE

Car ______ Make ______
Model ______ Year ______

SCHEDULE	lube oil filter	tire rotation	wheel/ alignment	brake inspection	trans service	trans flush	cooling flush	tune up (excludes platinum)	fuel injection cleaning	brake flush	replace all wheel drive fluid	replace overrunning clutch/rear carrier fluid	power steering flush	replace rear axle fluid	replace front axle fluid	replace transfer case fluid	replace differential fluid	lube brake calliper pins	adjust/ replace belts	inspect/ replace wheel bearings
3 mths/ 5000 mil	✓																			
6 mths/ 10000 mil	✓	✓																		
9 mths/ 15000 mil	✓																			
12 mths/ 20000 mil	✓	✓		✓														✓		
15 mths/ 25000 mil	✓		✓								✓			✓	✓					
18 mths/ 30000 mil	✓	✓																	✓	
21 mths/ 35000 mil	✓											✓								✓
24 mths/ 40000 mil	✓	✓		✓			✓			✓								✓		
27 mths/ 45000 mil	✓				✓			✓	✓		✓									
30 mths/ 50000 mil	✓	✓	✓											✓	✓	✓				
33 mths/ 55000 mil	✓											✓	✓				✓			
36 mths/ 60000 mil	✓	✓		✓						✓								✓	✓	
39 mths/ 65000 mil	✓										✓									
42 mths/ 70000 mil	✓	✓																		✓
45 mths/ 75000 mil	✓		✓		✓							✓		✓	✓					
48 mths/ 80000 mil	✓	✓		✓			✓			✓								✓		
51 mths/ 85000 mil	✓					✓					✓									
54 mths/ 90000 mil	✓	✓						✓	✓										✓	
57 mths/ 95000 mil	✓											✓								
60 mths/ 100000 mil	✓	✓	✓	✓						✓				✓	✓	✓		✓		✓
63 mths/ 105000 mil	✓										✓									✓
66 mths/ 110000 mil	✓	✓											✓				✓			
69 mths/ 115000 mil	✓											✓								
72 mths/ 120000 mil	✓	✓		✓			✓			✓								✓	✓	
75 mths/ 125000 mil	✓		✓			✓					✓				✓	✓				

FIGURE 5-8 The scheduled service history is often recorded in a service booklet that is kept in the glove compartment.

an indication of how well the vehicle was maintained. A vehicle with a regular service history is a good indication that all of the vehicle's systems have been well maintained and the vehicle will often be worth more during resale. Most manufacturers store all service history performed in their dealerships (based on the VIN) on a corporate server that is accessible from any of their dealerships. They will also use this vehicle service history when it comes to evaluating warranty claims. A vehicle that does not have a complete service history may not be eligible for warranty claims. Independent shops generally keep records of the repairs they perform. However, if a vehicle is repaired at multiple shops, repair history is much more difficult to track and, again, may result in a denial of warranty claims.

To review the vehicle service history, follow the steps in **SKILL DRILL 5-7**:

1. Locate the service history for the vehicle. This may be in shop records or in the service history booklet within the vehicle glove compartment. Some shops may keep the vehicle's service history on a computer.
2. Familiarize yourself with the service history of the vehicle.
   a. On what date was the vehicle first serviced?
   b. On what date was the vehicle last serviced?
   c. What was the most major service performed?
   d. Was the vehicle ever serviced for the same problem more than once?
3. Compare the vehicle service history to the manufacturer's scheduled maintenance requirements and list any discrepancies.
   a. Have all the services been performed?
   b. Have all the items been checked?
   c. Are there any outstanding items?

VIN and Production Date Code, and Vehicle Information Labels

Large numbers of vehicles with many variations of makes and models with different equipment levels are produced every day across the world. Vehicle information labels have become very important because they help to uniquely identify the vehicle.

VIN stands for **vehicle identification number** and is a unique serial number that is assigned to each vehicle produced. This means that no two vehicles have the same VIN FIGURE 5-9. Since 1981, the VIN has been made up of 17 characters. It is usually located on the front left corner of the windshield and is also inscribed on various vehicle parts. VINs can be used to check the service history of a vehicle and also are used to identify the vehicle for ordering components. Labeling the vehicle and vehicle parts with VINs also deters auto theft because it provides an easy way of uniquely identifying and tracing the vehicle and its major parts.

Production date codes and vehicle information labels also add to the identification information available on vehicles. The production date is the date of manufacture by year and month. Other information labels are fitted to the vehicle to provide ready access to information—for example, tire inflation pressures, vehicle weight, and load-carrying capacity. All of these information labels are used regularly by technicians to identify vehicles, order parts, and check service history.

Locating the VIN and Production Date Code

In order to locate a VIN and production date code, it is important to understand the principles of VINs and correctly identify the components that make up a vehicle identification number. The VIN is a 17-character identification composed of letters and digits. The VIN is designed to identify motor vehicles of all kinds: cars, trucks, buses, motorcycles, etc. It was originally defined in the International Standards Organization (ISO) Standard 3779 in 1977 and was revised in 1983.

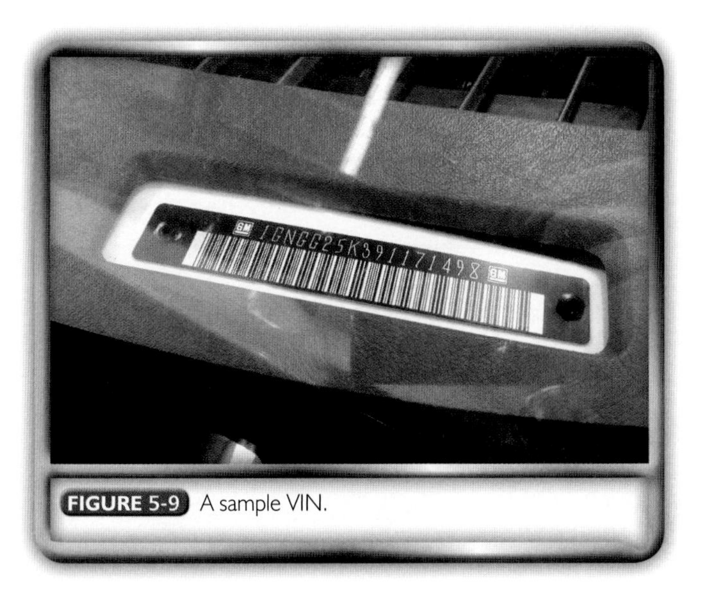
GM
1GNGG25K391171498
GM
FIGURE 5-9 A sample VIN.

The VIN is usually located on the front left corner of the windshield and is also inscribed on the engine, the transmission, both front guards, the hood, the doors, both bumpers, both rear quarter panels, and the trunk or hatchback. The VIN is unique worldwide, identifying the country of manufacture, manufacturer's name, division name, model, and other important information. Since 1981, all worldwide vehicle manufacturers use this numbering system. By learning to interpret the system, the identity of a vehicle or a component can be determined and verified.

Whenever a vehicle is registered or a registered vehicle is sold, a record of the VIN is kept. From this registry, information about the vehicle can be accessed, including the **title history**, which can tell you who has owned the vehicle. The registry may reveal a **salvage title**, which tells you that the vehicle has been wrecked and suffered irreparable damage. It also can tell you if a **lemon law buyback** has occurred. Lemon laws exist in some states to protect consumers from purchasing vehicles that have undergone several unsuccessful attempts to repair the same fault or from purchasing vehicles in which repair of the defects has caused the vehicle to be out of service for an extended time. The registry can also indicate if the vehicle has had an odometer rollback (mileage reduction), which is evidence of odometer tampering.

To locate the VIN and production date code, follow the steps in SKILL DRILL 5-8:

1. Locate the make of the vehicle from the body nameplate, which is usually found on the front or rear of the vehicle. Now locate the model from the body trim. The model may be a name, number, letter, or combination of these elements.
2. Next locate the VIN, usually found on a plate in the upper left dashboard and often visible through the windshield. In some instances, the plate may be mounted in a different location. If the plate is not visible through the windshield, check under the hood to see if it is mounted in the engine bay area. Note each letter and number exactly as it appears on the plate.
3. Decode the VIN and note the information. Each manufacturer provides a VIN decoding chart for its

vehicles in its shop service information. This chart is normally found in the "general information" section of the manual or electronic service information system. Using the VIN decoding chart, write down the information or print it for later use when locating specifications or parts.

Decoding a VIN

There are two different, but essentially compatible, 17-character VIN standards: the North American VIN system and the ISO Standard 3779, which is used in most of the rest of the world. FIGURE 5-10 shows how the numbers are structured.

To decode a North American VIN, follow the steps in SKILL DRILL 5-9:

1. The VIN is 1G1YN3DE-A5100001. The first character is the country of origin. This number or letter tells you where the vehicle was manufactured. For instance, a "1" means that the vehicle was made in the United States, a "2" is for Canada, a "J" means Japan, and so on.
2. The second character is usually a letter; it tells you the name of the manufacturer.
3. The third character tells you the division that made the vehicle. It could be a Pontiac, an Oldsmobile, or a GMC truck, for example.
4. The fourth and fifth characters give you the model, or series, of the vehicle. You will need a decoding chart for the details. Here we have a Corvette ZR1 Custom 3ZR Manual.
5. The sixth character describes the body type: two-door, four-door, coupe, sedan, and so on. Here we have a two-door convertible.
6. The seventh character tells you the type of seat restraints fitted to the vehicle. In this case it is active manual seat belts, airbags front (driver and passenger) and front seat side.
7. The eighth character is the engine code, which provides details of the engine type, size, or displacement, and where the engine was made. Here we have a 7.0 L, LS&, gas, eight-cylinder, SFI, aluminum, GM.
8. The ninth character is the check character. It is used internally by the manufacturer.
9. The tenth character tells you the year of manufacture. You can decode this character according to a model year identification chart, which in this example shows us that the vehicle was assembled for the 2010 model year.
10. The eleventh character tells you the assembly plant or factory where the vehicle was put together.
11. The final six numbers make up the sequential number of the vehicle as it comes off the assembly line, starting at a base number, which is usually one hundred thousand (100000). So the first vehicle to be produced will usually, but not always, have the number 100001. In our example, the vehicle was the first to come off the assembly line in that year.

Using Other Vehicle Information Labels

Vehicle Emission Control Information (VECI) Label

The **Vehicle Emission Control Information (VECI) label** is used by technicians to identify engine and

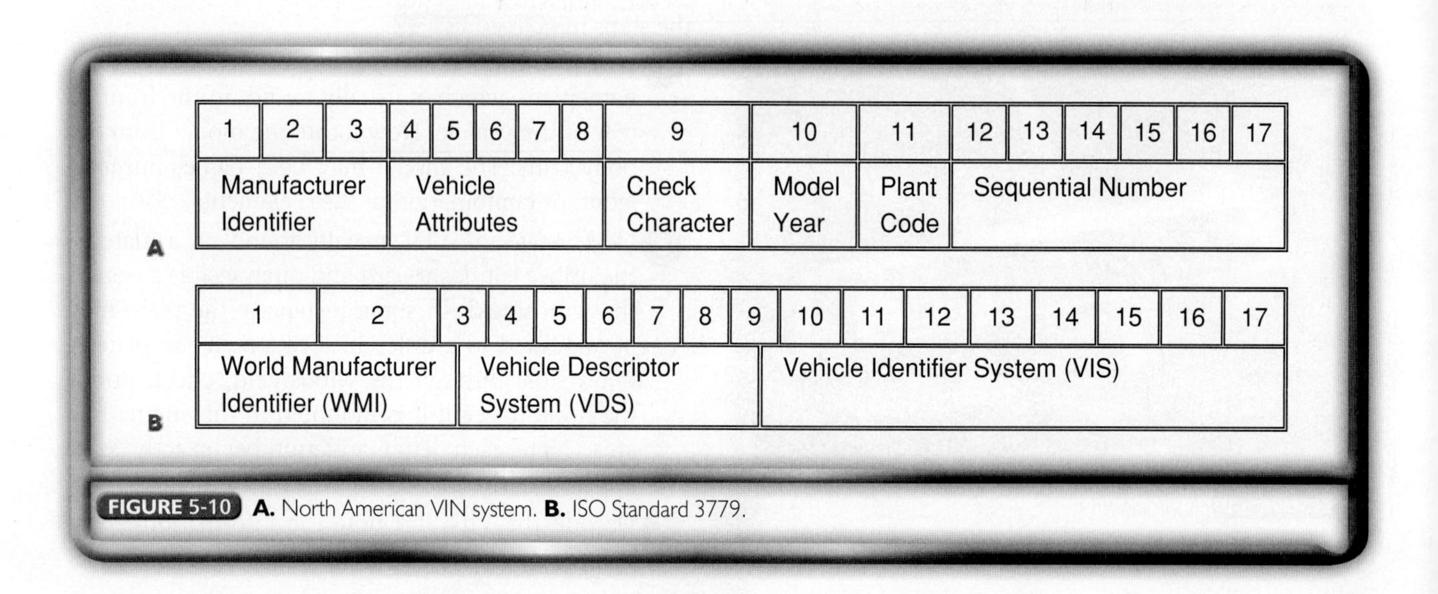
A
1 2 3 4 5 6 7 8 9 10 11 12 13 14 15 16 17
Manufacturer Identifier
Vehicle Attributes
Check Character
Model Year
Plant Code
Sequential Number
B
1 2 3 4 5 6 7 8 9 10 11 12 13 14 15 16 17
World Manufacturer Identifier (WMI)
Vehicle Descriptor System (VDS)
Vehicle Identifier System (VIS)

FIGURE 5-10 **A.** North American VIN system. **B.** ISO Standard 3779.

emission control information for the vehicle FIGURE 5-11. It is usually located in the engine compartment on either the hood, strut tower, or radiator support. It typically includes the following information:

- Engine family and displacement
- Model year the vehicle conforms to
- Spark plug part number and gap
- Evaporative emission system family
- Emission control system schematic
- Certification application

Vehicle Safety Certification (VSC) Label

The **Vehicle Safety Certification (VSC) label** certifies that the vehicle meets the Federal Motor Vehicle Safety, Bumper, and Theft Prevention Standards in effect at the time of manufacture FIGURE 5-12. It is used by technicians to identify some basic types of information about the vehicle such as month and year of manufacture, Gross Vehicle Weight Rating (GVWR), and tire information. It is usually affixed to the driver's side door pillar or on the side of the door next to the pillar. It typically includes the following information:

- Month and year of manufacture
- GVWR and Gross Axle Weight Rating (GAWR)
- VIN
- Recommended tire sizes
- Recommended tire inflation pressures
- Paint and trim codes

Other Labels

Other labels include the refrigerant label, the coolant label, and the belt routing label. The **refrigerant label** lists the type and total capacity of refrigerant that is installed in the A/C system FIGURE 5-13. The **coolant label** lists the type of coolant installed in the cooling system FIGURE 5-14.

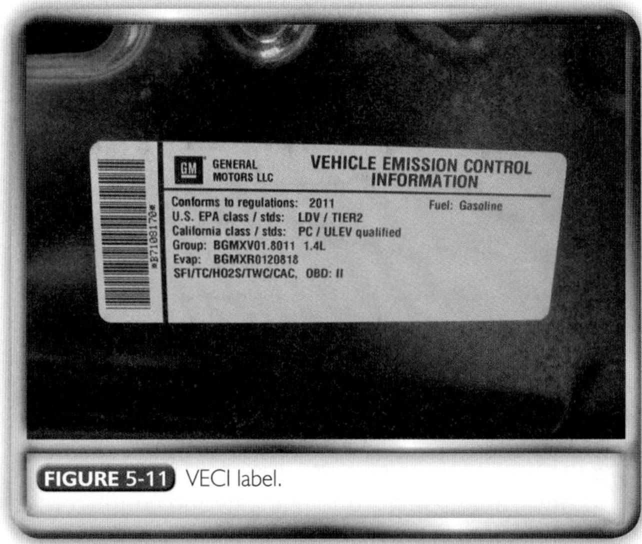
GM
GENERAL MOTORS LLC
VEHICLE EMISSION CONTROL INFORMATION
Conforms to regulations: 2011
Fuel: Gasoline
U.S. EPA class / stds: LDV / TIER2
California class / stds: PC / ULEV qualified
Group: BGMXV01.8011 1.4L
Evap: BGMXR0120818
SFI/TC/HO2S/TWC/CAC, OBD: II
B7108170

FIGURE 5-11 VECI label.

AIR CONDITIONING SYSTEM
HFC134a USE ONLY
OIL ND-OIL 8
REFRIGERANT 500±30g
M50

FIGURE 5-13 Refrigerant label.

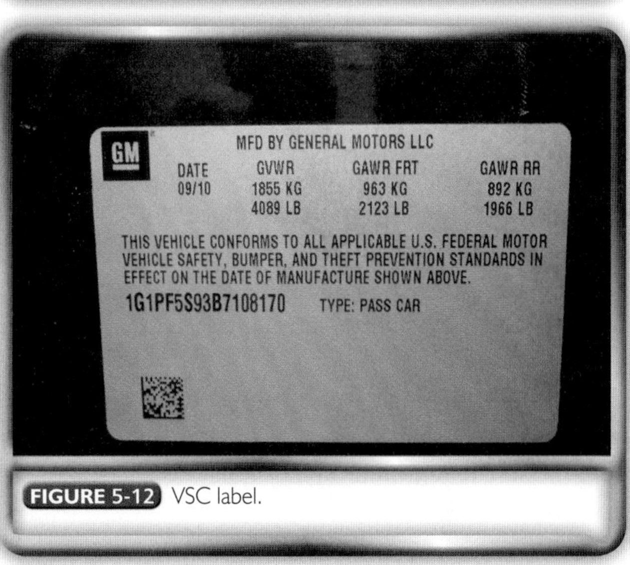
GM
MFD BY GENERAL MOTORS LLC
DATE 09/10
GVWR 1855 KG 4089 LB
GAWR FRT 963 KG 2123 LB
GAWR RR 892 KG 1966 LB
THIS VEHICLE CONFORMS TO ALL APPLICABLE U.S. FEDERAL MOTOR VEHICLE SAFETY, BUMPER, AND THEFT PREVENTION STANDARDS IN EFFECT ON THE DATE OF MANUFACTURE SHOWN ABOVE.
1G1PF5S93B7108170
TYPE: PASS CAR

FIGURE 5-12 VSC label.

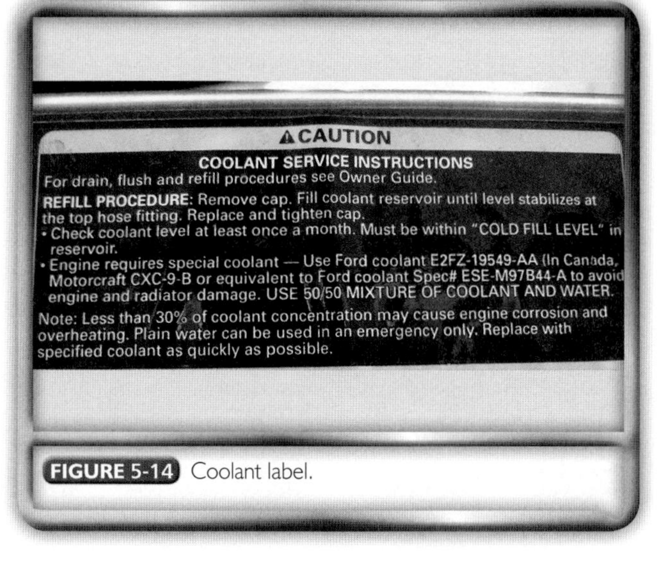
CAUTION
COOLANT SERVICE INSTRUCTIONS
For drain, flush and refill procedures see Owner Guide.
REFILL PROCEDURE: Remove cap. Fill coolant reservoir until level stabilizes at the top hose fitting. Replace and tighten cap.
• Check coolant level at least once a month. Must be within "COLD FILL LEVEL" in reservoir.
• Engine requires special coolant — Use Ford coolant E2FZ-19549-AA (In Canada, Motorcraft CXC-9-B or equivalent to Ford coolant Spec# ESE-M97B44-A to avoid engine and radiator damage. USE 50/50 MIXTURE OF COOLANT AND WATER.
Note: Less than 30% of coolant concentration may cause engine corrosion and overheating. Plain water can be used in an emergency only. Replace with specified coolant as quickly as possible.

FIGURE 5-14 Coolant label.

The **belt routing label** lists a diagram of the serpentine belt routing for the engine accessories FIGURE 5-15.

3 Cs

The 3 Cs are an easy way to learn the fundamental steps in conducting repairs. They stand for **c**oncern, **c**ause, and **c**orrection. *Concern* stands for the customer's understanding of the vehicle problem. Customers experience an issue with their vehicle and attempt to communicate that to the service advisor, who helps the customer put the concern into words that make sense. For example, a customer has trouble starting his car. He may initially communicate that the engine won't crank over. With some questioning and answers, the service advisor helps the customer identify that the engine is cranking over, but not starting. So the actual concern is: "engine cranks, but won't start." That is a vastly different situation than "engine will not crank." By understanding the actual concern, you can plan your approach to diagnosing the vehicle by testing systems and components. This will require you to take the time to fully understand the concern, read the repair order, and talk to the customer to gather further information if needed. Think through the problem and develop a strategy to attack it. Then you will know what tests you need to conduct and the order in which to conduct them.

Cause stands for understanding the reason that there is a fault. Understanding the cause and effect of the fault enables the technician to conduct a repair that is effective. This step may require you to conduct tests or inspect various components to narrow down exactly where the fault lies, what is wrong, and what components may be faulty.

It is important that you determine the root cause of the fault. This means you must distinguish between the cause and the effect and determine the ultimate cause of the fault. For example, if the brake lights are not working, you might find the brake fuse blown. That is definitely the cause of the brake lights not working (effect). But what caused the brake fuse to blow? Maybe it was a chaffed wire in the trunk that intermittently short-circuits to ground (root cause). If you only replace the fuse, the problem will likely reoccur. The root cause in this case is an intermittent short circuit due to an improperly routed or protected brake light wire.

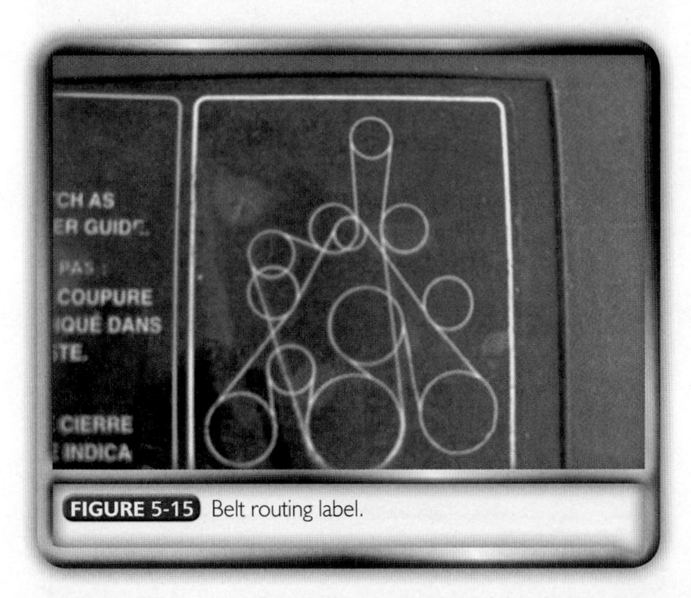
COUPURE
CIERRE
INDICA

FIGURE 5-15 Belt routing label.

Correction stands for the procedure and parts that will be used to fix the problem. In the preceding situation, the correction would be: "Repair the brake light wire and reroute it so it doesn't chaff and short-circuit again." This step occurs once the problem and faults are fully understood and the damage assessed so the correct parts can be fitted to complete a successful repair. Don't forget that to ensure a successful repair, the system should be thoroughly checked to confirm that everything is working as it should before returning the vehicle to the customer.

To apply the 3 Cs, follow the steps in SKILL DRILL 5-10:

1. Using the 3 Cs, document the repair process required for a repair order.
2. Identify and document the concern. This should be on the repair order. Obtain as much information as possible, as this will help you to understand the problem. Identify what the problem is and what vehicle systems are involved. Gather information on any recent repairs or servicing. Ask questions like, How long has the problem been occurring? or, Does it occur at any particular time or temperature? All of this information will help to identify the problem.
3. Identify and document the root cause of the concern. Research shop manuals and conduct tests to identify the cause of the problem. This may require a number of tests across multiple systems.
4. Review the information you collect from the tests. To review effectively, you need to understand how the systems work and interact.
5. Always work safely and use the proper tools and correct personal protective equipment (PPE).
6. Identify and document the correction required, including work activities and parts required or used. Make repairs or replace parts to complete the repair.
7. Retest the vehicle to be sure the fault has been corrected.
8. Fill in the required repair order with details of the work conducted.

Wrap-up

Ready for Review

- The owner's manual, usually kept in the glove compartment, provides information on how to operate the vehicle and basic maintenance to be performed.
- Manufacturers provide shop (or service) manuals for each make and model of car; these manuals provide vehicle-specific instructions on service and repair.
- Service information programs allow users to access maintenance and repair information via computer.
- After-market repair manuals are not produced by manufacturers and provide less detailed information for specific makes and models.
- Manufacturers provide technical service bulletins (TSBs) as updates to shop manuals when new problems or maintenance concerns arise for certain vehicle makes or models.
- If a safety issue is discovered on a certain make of vehicle, the manufacturer may issue a service campaign or recall.
- Labor guides provide up-to-date information on service repair times and cost estimates.
- Parts programs are electronic catalogues of vehicle parts.
- Repair or work orders detail customer concern information to guide the service technician, as well as information on services as they are performed.
- Account systems track repair costs and customer methods of payment.
- A vehicle's service history consists of records of all maintenance and repairs performed on the vehicle.
- Vehicle information numbers (VINs) are unique identifiers for each vehicle produced.
- VINs are made up of 17 characters and are usually located on the front left corner of the windshield and on the engine, transmission, and other vehicle parts.
- VINs assist customers and technicians in tracking title history and reveal whether the vehicle has been wrecked or had repeated unsuccessful repairs for a particular fault.
- The two worldwide VIN systems are the North American VIN system and ISO Standard 3779.
- The VIN contains information on country of origin, manufacturer, make and model, body type, seat restraints, engine type, year of manufacture, assembly plant, and the order the vehicle came off the assembly line.
- Manufacturers also provide vehicle information labels to provide further specifications for each model of vehicle.
- The 3 Cs of vehicle repair are concern, cause, and correction.

Key Terms

belt routing label A label that lists a diagram of the serpentine belt routing for the engine accessories.

coolant label A label that lists the type of coolant installed in the cooling system.

labor guide A guide that provides information to make estimates for repairs.

lemon law buyback A consumer protection law used in some states to identify a new vehicle that has undergone several unsuccessful attempts to repair the same fault.

owner's manual An informational guide supplied by the manufacturer; it contains basic vehicle operating information.

parts program A computer software program for identifying and ordering replacement vehicle parts.

parts specialist The person who serves customers at the parts counters.

refrigerant label A label that lists the type and total capacity of refrigerant that is installed in the A/C system.

repair order A form used by shops to collect information regarding a vehicle coming in for repair, also referred to as a work order.

salvage title Also called a branded title; a record that a vehicle has been severely damaged or deemed a total loss by an insurance company.

service campaign and recall A corrective measure conducted by manufacturers when a safety issue is discovered with a particular vehicle.

service history A complete list of all the servicing and repairs that have been performed on a vehicle.

shop or service manual Manufacturer's or after-market information on the repair and service of vehicles.

technical service bulletin (TSB) Information issued by manufacturers to alert technicians of unexpected problems or changes to repair procedures.

vehicle emission control information (VECI) label A label used by technicians to identify engine and emission control information for the vehicle.

title history A detailed account of a vehicle's past.

vehicle identification number (VIN) A unique serial number that is assigned to each vehicle produced.

vehicle safety certification (VSC) label A label certifying that the vehicle meets the Federal Motor Vehicle Safety, Bumper, and Theft Prevention Standards in effect at the time of manufacture.

ASE-Type Questions

1. Tech A says that the owner's manual will have the oil pan drain plug torque information. Tech B says that oil pan capacity information for that specific vehicle will be in the owner's manual. Who is correct?
   a. Tech A
   b. Tech B
   c. Both A and B
   d. Neither A nor B
2. Tech A says that vehicle security PIN codes can be found in the service manual. Tech B says that vehicle security PIN codes can be found in the owner's manual. Who is correct?
   a. Tech A
   b. Tech B
   c. Both A and B
   d. Neither A nor B
3. Tech A says that paper service manuals are gone and electronic versions of the service manual are now available. Tech B says that online manuals are more current, as they can be updated periodically. Who is correct?
   a. Tech A
   b. Tech B
   c. Both A and B
   d. Neither A nor B
4. Tech A says that service information programs are extremely helpful, as the technician can use a laptop at the repair for quick access to the procedure to perform a repair. Tech B says that service information programs allow a technician to know the labor guide and, with the support of the program, perform the task in the time allowed. Who is correct?
   a. Tech A
   b. Tech B
   c. Both A and B
   d. Neither A nor B
5. Tech A says that TSBs are updates to the owner's manual. Tech B says that TSBs are generally updated information on model changes that do not affect the technician. Who is correct?
   a. Tech A
   b. Tech B
   c. Both A and B
   d. Neither A nor B
6. Tech A says that labor guides are necessary for the service writer to quote prices for a customer on the repair bill. Tech B says that labor guides are what the customer pays and that warranty pays more for labor using a different labor guide. Who is correct?
   a. Tech A
   b. Tech B
   c. Both A and B
   d. Neither A nor B
7. Tech A says that locating the part number the technician needs requires computer knowledge and mechanical knowledge. Tech B says that anybody can be a parts person. Who is correct?
   a. Tech A
   b. Tech B
   c. Both A and B
   d. Neither A nor B
8. Tech A says that the repair order is just a piece of paper telling the technician what to do. Tech B says that the repair order is a legal and binding contract between the customer and the repair facility. Who is correct?
   a. Tech A
   b. Tech B
   c. Both A and B
   d. Neither A nor B
9. Tech A says that customer authorization for a change in the repair order after initial authorization is the responsibility of the service writer or foreman. Tech B says that changes to the repair order can be dealt with after the repair is complete, as the customer will be satisfied if more repairs are completed. Who is correct?
   a. Tech A
   b. Tech B
   c. Both A and B
   d. Neither A nor B
10. Tech A says that the VIN number on a vehicle can help identify which engine is installed in the chassis. Tech B says that most digits in the VIN number can be an identifier for information pertinent to that vehicle. Who is correct?
    a. Tech A
    b. Tech B
    c. Both A and B
    d. Neither A nor B

CHAPTER 6

NATEF Tasks

Required Supplemental Tasks Shop and Personal Safety		Page
■ Utilize safe procedures for handling of tools and equipment.		97–100
Tools and Equipment		
■ Identify tools and their usage in automotive applications.		97–164
■ Demonstrate safe handling and use of appropriate tools.		97–164
■ Identify standard and metric designation.		100
■ Demonstrate proper use of precision measuring tools (i.e., micrometer, dial-indicator, dial-caliper).		129–136
■ Demonstrate proper cleaning, storage, and maintenance of tools and equipment.		162, 164
Engine Repair **General**		
■ Perform common fastener and thread repair, to include: remove broken bolt, restore internal and external threads, and repair internal threads with thread insert.	 	151–153

Knowledge Objectives

After reading this chapter, you will be able to:

1. Describe the safety procedures to take when handling and using tools. (pp 97–100)
2. Describe the common air tools that a technician may use in the shop. (pp 100–102)
3. Describe the common fasteners used in the shop. (pp 106–110)
4. Describe how fasteners are used in the application of torque specifications. (pp 106–110)
5. Describe the common types of wrenches and when they are utilized in the shop. (pp 110–113)
6. Describe the common types of sockets and when they are utilized in the shop. (pp 113–114)
7. Describe the common types of pliers and when they are utilized in the shop. (pp 114–115)
8. Describe the common types of cutting tools and when they are utilized in the shop. (pp 115–116)
9. Describe the common types of screwdrivers and when they are utilized in the shop. (pp 116–117)

Tools and Equipment

Knowledge Objectives, continued

10. Describe the common types of hammers and when they are utilized in the shop. (pp 117–118)
11. Describe the common types of chisels and when they are utilized in the shop. (pp 118–119)
12. Describe the common types of punches and when they are utilized in the shop. (p 118)
13. Describe the common types of clamps and when they are utilized in the shop. (pp 121–122)
14. Describe the common types of taps and dies and when they are utilized in the shop. (pp 122–123)
15. Describe the common types of flaring tools and when they are utilized in the shop. (pp 124–126)
16. Describe the common types of riveting tools and when they are utilized in the shop. (pp 125–128)
17. Describe the applications of a soldering tool. (pp 128–129)
18. Describe the common types of measuring tools and when they are utilized in the shop. (pp 129–136)
19. Describe the common types of power tools and when they are utilized in the shop. (pp 136–144)
20. Describe the common types of cleaning tools and when they are utilized in the shop. (pp 143–152)
21. Describe when thread repair is performed in the shop. (pp 151–153)
22. Describe the common types of welding and cutting equipment and when they are utilized in the shop. (pp 154–163)

Know
See
Do
Prove

Skills Objectives

After reading this chapter, you will be able to:

1. Safely handle and use tools. (pp 97–98)
2. Use safe procedures for handling tools and equipment. (pp 98–99)
3. Charge a battery. (p 104)
4. Jump-start a vehicle. (pp 105–106)
5. Use a torque angle gauge in conjunction with a torque wrench. (pp 110–111)
6. Use a gear puller. (pp 123–124)
7. Use a flaring tool. (pp 125–126)
8. Use riveting tools. (pp 127–128)
9. Use soldering tools. (pp 129–130)
10. Use a micrometer. (p 133)
11. Use vernier calipers. (pp 133–134)
12. Use a dial indicator. (pp 134–135)
13. Use feeler gauges. (pp 136–137)
14. Use a bench grinder. (pp 138–139)
15. Use an angle grinder. (pp 140–141)
16. Use an air nozzle. (pp 142–143)
17. Use an air impact wrench. (pp 142–144)
18. Use an air drill. (pp 143–145)
19. Use an air hammer. (pp 144–145)

Skills Objectives, continued

20. Use a pressure washer. (pp 146–147)
21. Use a spray wash cabinet. (p 148)
22. Use a solvent tank. (pp 148–149)
23. Use a brake washer. (pp 148–150)
24. Use a sand or bead blaster. (pp 150–152)
25. Perform thread repair. (pp 151–153)
26. Purge an oxyacetylene torch. (pp 154–155)
27. Set up an oxyacetylene torch. (p 156)
28. Use an oxyacetylene torch for heating. (p 157)
29. Use a welding tip for welding. (pp 157–158)
30. Use a welding tip for brazing. (p 159)
31. Use a cutting tip. (pp 159–160)
32. Use a plasma cutter. (pp 160–161)
33. Use a wire feed welder. (pp 161–163)
34. Clean tools and equipment. (pp 162, 164)

Introduction

In this chapter, we will be exploring a variety of tool and equipment topics that are fundamental to your success as an automotive technician. Tools and equipment are very important to an efficient and effective shop operation. They provide the means for work to be undertaken on vehicles, from lifting to diagnosing, removing, installing, cleaning, and inspecting. Nearly all shop tasks involve the use of some sort of tool or piece of equipment. This makes their purchase, use, and maintenance very important to the overall performance of the shop. Always use tools and equipment in the way they are designed to be used. It is important to think about the task at hand, identify the most effective tools to do the task, inspect the tool before using it, use it correctly, clean and inspect it after you use it, and store it in the correct location.

General Guidelines

While it is important to be trained on the safe use of tools and equipment, it is even more critical to have a safe attitude. A safe attitude will help you avoid being involved in an accident. Students who think they will never be involved in an accident will not be as aware of unsafe situations as they should be. And that can lead to accidents. So while we are covering the various tools and equipment you will encounter in the shop, pay close attention to the safety and operation procedures. Tools are a technician's best friend, but if used improperly, they can injure or kill.

Work Safe and Stay Safe

Whenever using tools, always think safety first. There is nothing more important than your personal safety. If tools (both hand and power) are used incorrectly, you can potentially injure yourself and others. Always follow equipment and shop instructions, including the use of recommended personal protective equipment (PPE). Accidents only take a moment to occur but can take a lifetime to recover from. You are ultimately responsible for your safety, so remember to work safe and stay safe.

Safe Handling and Use of Tools

Tools must be safely handled and used to prevent injury and damage. Always inspect tools prior to use and never use damaged tools. Check the manufacturer and the shop procedures or ask your supervisor if you are uncertain about how to use tools. Inspect and clean tools when you are finished using them. Always return tools to their correct storage location.

To safely handle and use appropriate tools, follow the steps in **SKILL DRILL 6-1**.

You Are the Automotive Technician

After finishing work on the last vehicle of the day, you are required to return your workstation back to order. You clean, inspect, and return tools and equipment to their designated place. You wipe up any spills according to the shop procedure and clear the floor of any debris to avoid slips and falls. During your workspace inspection, you determine that the insulation on the drop light cord is frayed, there are some tools that need to be cleaned, and air-powered tools to be put away.

1. What needs to happen with the drop light?
2. What should you do to air tools before using them each day?
3. What are the steps you take in cleaning electric power tools?

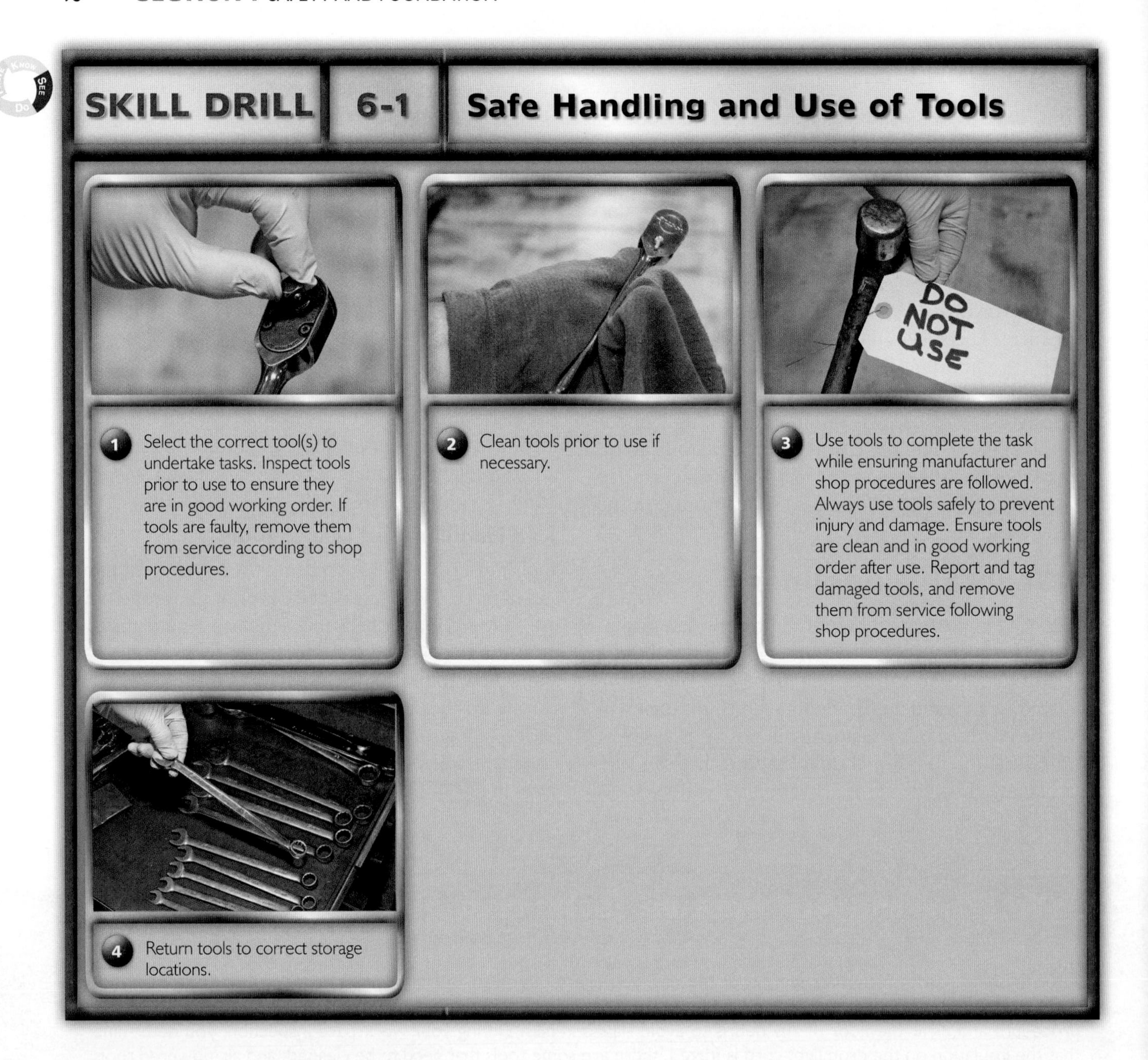
SKILL DRILL 6-1 Safe Handling and Use of Tools
DO NOT USE
1 Select the correct tool(s) to undertake tasks. Inspect tools prior to use to ensure they are in good working order. If tools are faulty, remove them from service according to shop procedures.
2 Clean tools prior to use if necessary.
3 Use tools to complete the task while ensuring manufacturer and shop procedures are followed. Always use tools safely to prevent injury and damage. Ensure tools are clean and in good working order after use. Report and tag damaged tools, and remove them from service following shop procedures.
4 Return tools to correct storage locations.

Safe Procedures for Handling Tools and Equipment

Some tools are heavy or awkward to use, so seek assistance if required and use correct manual handling techniques when using tools. To utilize safe procedures for handling tools and equipment, follow the steps in SKILL DRILL 6-2.

Tool Usage

Tools extend our abilities to perform many tasks; for example, jacks, stands, and hoists extend our ability to lift and hold heavy objects. Hand tools extend our ability to perform fundamental tasks like gripping, turning, tightening, measuring, and cutting. Electrical meters enable us to measure things we cannot see, feel, or hear, while power and air tools multiply our strength by performing tasks quickly and efficiently. As you are working, always think about what tool can make the job easier, safer, or more efficient. As you become familiar with more tools, your productivity, quality, and effectiveness will improve.

Every tool is designed to be used in a certain way to do the job safely. It is critical to use a tool in the way it is designed to be used and to do so safely. For example, a screwdriver is designed to tighten and loosen screws, not to be used as a chisel. Ratchets are designed to turn sockets, not to be used as a hammer. Think about the task you are undertaking, select the correct tools for the task, and use each tool as it was designed.

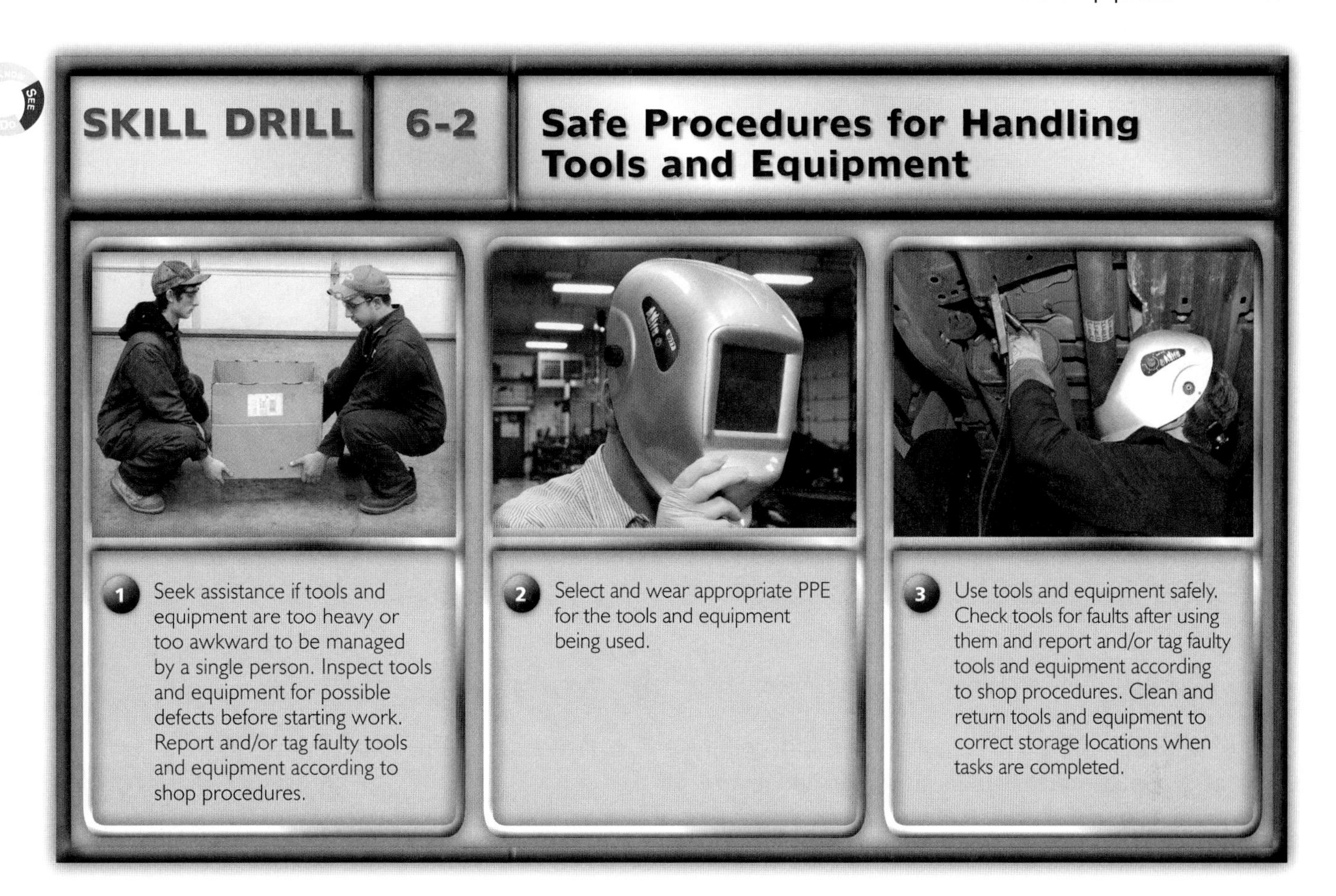
SKILL DRILL 6-2
Safe Procedures for Handling Tools and Equipment
1 Seek assistance if tools and equipment are too heavy or too awkward to be managed by a single person. Inspect tools and equipment for possible defects before starting work. Report and/or tag faulty tools and equipment according to shop procedures.
2 Select and wear appropriate PPE for the tools and equipment being used.
3 Use tools and equipment safely. Check tools for faults after using them and report and/or tag faulty tools and equipment according to shop procedures. Clean and return tools and equipment to correct storage locations when tasks are completed.

TECHNICIAN TIP

Using tools can make you much more efficient and effective in performing your job. Without tools, it would be very difficult to carry out vehicle repairs and servicing. It is also the reason that many technicians invest well over $20,000 in their personal tools. If purchased wisely, tools can help you perform more work in a shorter amount of time, thereby making you more money. So think of your tools as an investment that pays for itself over time.

Lockout/Tagout

<u>Lockout/tagout</u> is an umbrella term that describes a set of safety practices and procedures that are intended to reduce the risk of technicians inadvertently using tools, equipment, or materials that have been determined to be unsafe or potentially unsafe or that are in the process of being serviced. An example of lockout would be physically securing a broken, unsafe, or out-of-service tool so that it cannot be used by a technician. In many cases, the item is also tagged out so it is not inadvertently placed back into service or operated. An example of tagout would be affixing a clear and unavoidable label to a piece of equipment that describes the fault found, the name of the person who found the fault, the date that the fault was found, and that warns not to use the equipment FIGURE 6-1.

Safety

Standardized lockout/tagout procedures are a mandatory part of workplace safety regulations in most countries. Familiarize yourself with your local legislation and with the specific lockout/tagout practices that apply in your workplace.

Tool Location

The shop will usually have a selection of tools available for use, and these tools will be located in a number of areas. They include specialized manufacturer tools, high-cost tools, and tools that are not portable, such as hoists and compressors. Technicians will have a selection of their own tools, which will include various hand tools and electrical meters. Often they will add to their toolbox over time.

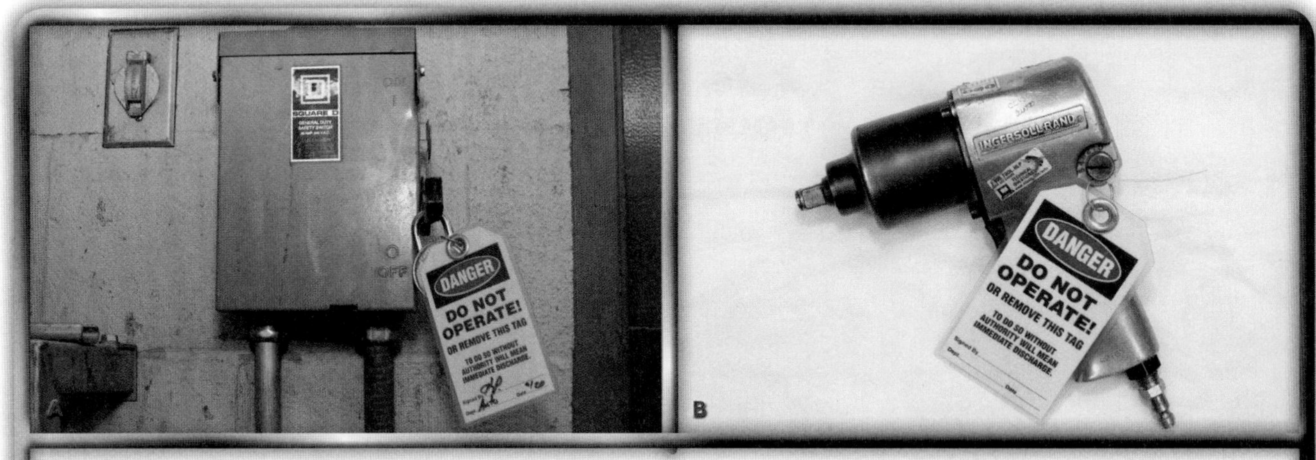
DANGER
DO NOT OPERATE!
OR REMOVE THIS TAG
INGERSOLL RAND
DANGER
DO NOT OPERATE!
OR REMOVE THIS TAG
B

FIGURE 6-1 **A.** An example of lockout would be physically locking out a tool or piece of equipment so that it cannot be accessed and used by someone who may be unaware of the potential danger of doing so. **B.** An example of tagout would be affixing a clear and unavoidable label to a piece of equipment that describes the fault found and that warns not to use it.

To identify tools and their usage in automotive application, follow these steps:

1. Create a list of tools in your tool chest and identify their application for automotive repair and service.
2. Look through the shop's tool storage areas and create a list of the tools found in each storage area; identify their application for automotive repair and service.

Standard and Metric Designations

Many tools, measuring instruments, and fasteners come in United States customary system (USCS) sizes, more commonly referred to as "standard," or in metric sizes. Tools and measuring instruments can be identified as standard or metric by markings identifying their size on tools or the increments on a measuring tool. Fasteners bought new will have their designation identified on the packaging. Other fasteners may have to be measured by a ruler or **vernier caliper** to identify their designation. Manufacturer's charts showing thread and fastener sizing will assist in identifying standard or metric sizing.

To identify standard and metric designation, follow these steps:

1. Examine the component, tool, or fastener to see if any marking identifies it as standard or metric. Manufacturer specifications and shop manuals can be referred to and may identify components as standard or metric.
2. If no markings are available, use measuring devices to gauge the size of the item and compare thread and fastener charts to identify the sizing. Inch-to-metric conversion charts will assist in identifying component designation.

Air Tools

Compressed Air Equipment

The term **compressed air equipment** covers a wide range of tools and equipment required in a compressed air system. Tools that use compressed air include drills, grinders, pumps, grease guns, jacks, and impact wrenches FIGURE 6-2. The compressed air system is made up of a compressor, a pressure regulator, air hose or fixed piping, and the actual tool or item that is powered by the compressed air. The air compressor has a storage tank and is driven by an electric motor or, for more portability, a gasoline engine. In many shops, the air compressor is housed in a separate room to help isolate the noise.

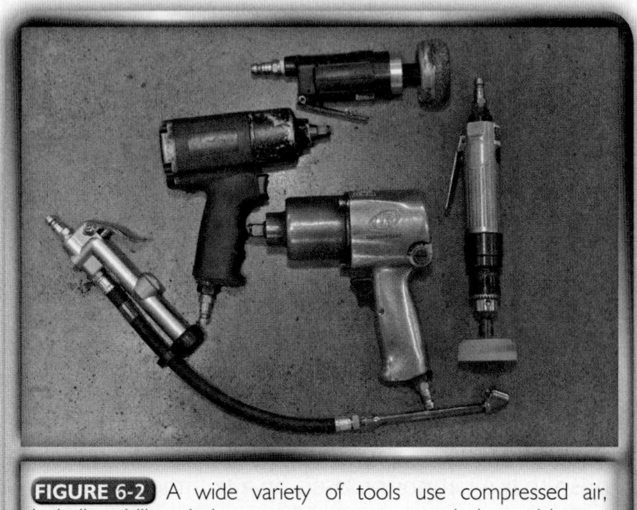

FIGURE 6-2 A wide variety of tools use compressed air, including drills, grinders, pumps, grease guns, jacks, and impact wrenches.

Standard compressors have been, and still are, based on piston-type compressors, which operate similar to a piston engine where each piston compresses the air on the compression stroke. But in the case of a compressor, the piston forces the air out of the cylinder and into a storage tank under pressure. Many newer air compressors are of the scroll compressor type, which uses a pair of rotating scrolls to compress the air and is much quieter and more efficient. With either type of compressor, a pressure regulator controls the air pressure being supplied to the distribution system while the air hose or lines transport the compressed air from the compressor to the tool.

Safety

Always respect compressed air: Wear appropriate PPE, and never use compressed air inappropriately.

Compressed Air Safety

Serious, sometimes fatal, injuries can be caused by compressed air being injected into the body through the skin or into a body opening, such as your mouth or ear. Do not play with air equipment, such as blowing air at another person or yourself. Internal human blood vessels and organs will rupture at much lower pressures than those found in compressed air lines. So always handle air equipment carefully and with respect. Be extra careful when working with air equipment in a confined or awkward space, such as under a vehicle, and when clearing or cleaning the equipment.

Safety

If air, grease, or any other substance is injected into someone's body, it is not always easy to tell how much damage has been done. Always provide initial first aid and then seek medical advice if any kind of penetration injury occurs.

Air Driers and Automatic Oilers

Air driers are fitted to compressed air systems to remove the moisture or water from the compressed air that is condensed as a result of compressing air from the atmosphere, which contains water in the form of humidity. If water gets into the air lines, it may damage air tools. Air driers can be a stand-alone device fitted to the compressed air system or incorporated into a filter/regulator system. The combination filter/regulator system removes water from the air, filters any debris that may come from the compressor tank, and regulates the line pressure from the tank.

An air drier can be a simple water trap that catches condensed water as hot air cools down slowly and the water condenses FIGURE 6-3. This type of air drier usually needs to be drained manually on a periodic basis. However, some devices drain automatically.

Another type of air drier is a chiller unit, which uses the principles of air conditioning to chill the hot compressed air and force condensation to occur at a higher rate. This system is much more expensive but does a good job of removing all traces of water. You may find this system in a body shop, where virtually all traces of water in the compressed air must be removed so that it cannot mix with the paint as it is being sprayed onto the surface of the vehicle.

Compressed air tools and equipment require a regular application of a lubricating oil to reduce wear and tear. Automatic oilers are designed to regularly oil

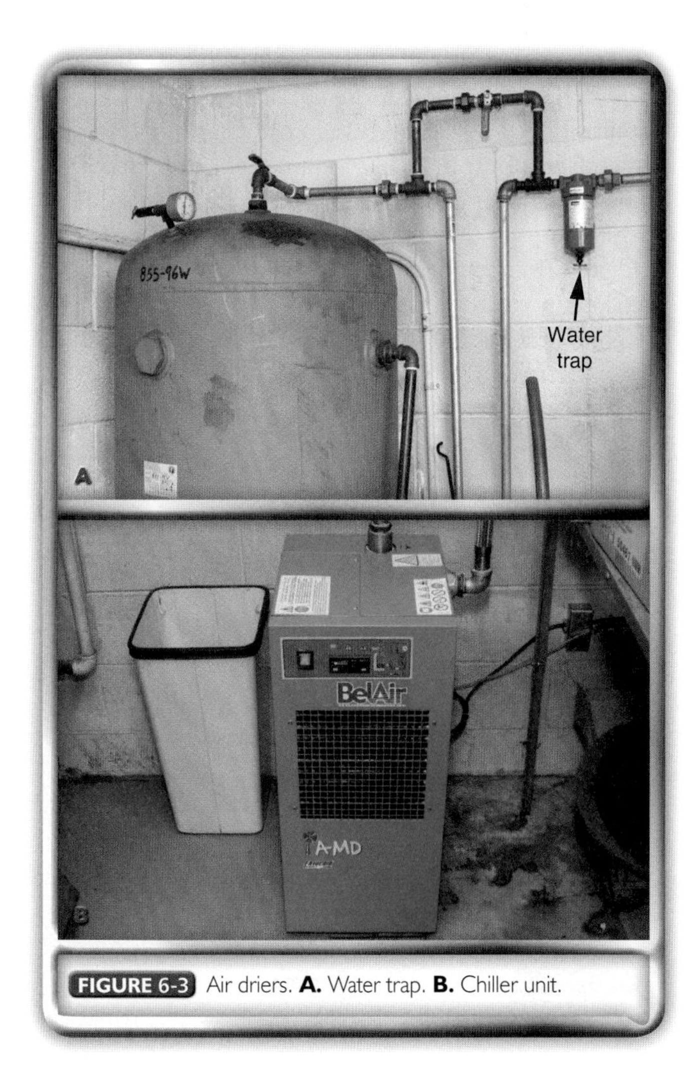
855-96W
Water trap
A
BelAir
A-MD
B

FIGURE 6-3 Air driers. **A.** Water trap. **B.** Chiller unit.

an air tool or air equipment so it does not have to be done manually, before or during its use FIGURE 6-4. Automatic oilers are usually fitted near the air tool or equipment and regularly supply small amounts of oil into the stream of compressed air, which is then transported along with air to the tool or equipment. Automatic oilers need periodic inspection to make sure they deliver the correct amount of oil. The built-in oil reservoir also needs to be refilled with air tool oil on a regular schedule.

Batteries and Chargers

Batteries are common in shops and are used in vehicles and rechargeable tools. Extreme caution should be taken when working around or with batteries, whether or not they are being charged. Batteries can produce dangerous and explosive hydrogen gases, so sparks and short circuits across the battery terminals should be avoided. Always wear appropriate PPE such as goggles, gloves, and protective clothing when working around or with batteries. Also, some regulatory agencies require that an eyewash station be located near a battery charging station in the case of a battery explosion. Check with your local authorities to determine any distance requirements.

There are many different types of **battery chargers**, and each is designed for a particular purpose and application. Battery chargers can be **fast chargers**, with high current output to charge a battery quickly. **Slow chargers** take longer to charge a battery and have lower current outputs; they put less stress on the battery, which is ideal if time is not a consideration. **Smart chargers** incorporate microprocessors to monitor and control the charge rate so the battery receives the correct amount of charge depending on its state of charge. These types of chargers are becoming more popular and ensure that the battery receives the optimal charge, promoting longer battery life.

Even though typically a motor vehicle battery is 12 volts, it stores a lot of energy. The high current supply from a battery can be very dangerous. Remember, they have to deliver enough power to crank over a cold engine. They also produce enough power to melt a metal rod resting across the terminals. High-voltage battery packs, like those fitted to hybrid vehicles, are even more dangerous because of the potential for high voltage and current, so special precautions for dealing with high-voltage systems must be taken FIGURE 6-5. Always treat batteries with care and respect.

FIGURE 6-4 Compressed air automatic oiler.

TECHNICIAN TIP

Vehicle batteries are usually lead acid types, often in a 12-volt configuration. If a vehicle requires 24 volts, then either one 24-volt battery or two 12-volt batteries can be connected in series (by connecting the positive of one battery to the negative of the other battery) to provide 24 volts.

Technology changes in vehicles have increased the need for more electrical power, and in the future this will drive the need for higher-voltage battery systems. Hybrid vehicles are an example of this. Their operating voltages are typically 200–600 volts. Generally, the higher the system voltage, the more efficient the system is because the electrical current can be lower for a given amount of power. And since wire size is determined by current, the wires can be smaller. However, higher voltages also create a greater shock hazard, so bear this in mind when working around and with batteries.

Safety

High voltages used in a hybrid vehicle are extremely dangerous. The voltage and current flow is several times greater than that needed to kill a person. Most hybrid manufacturers require technicians to undergo special factory training before they will allow them to service a hybrid vehicle. Also, they usually allow only very experienced technicians to undergo the training, not novices. In fact, one of the tools that Toyota requires of their shops for working on a hybrid vehicle is a non-conductive shepherd's hook. This can be used to drag a technician away from high voltage if the technician is electrocuted while working on the vehicle.

FIGURE 6-5 High-voltage battery packs, like those fitted to hybrid vehicles, are extremely dangerous because of the potential for high voltage and current. Take special precautions for dealing with high-voltage systems.

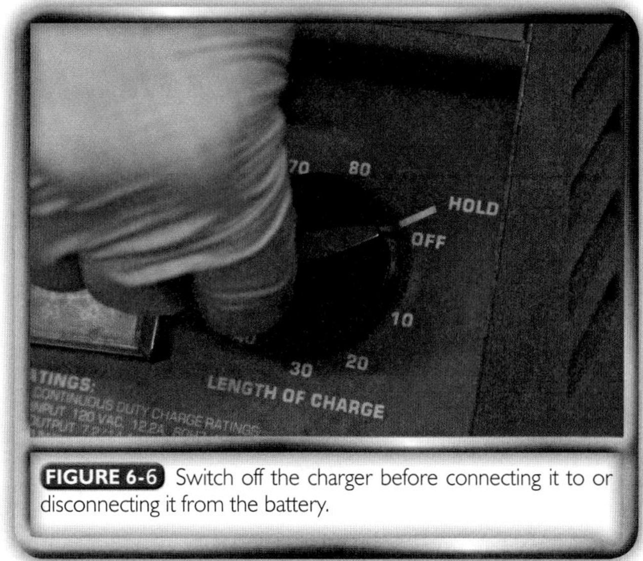
70
80
HOLD
OFF
10
20
30
LENGTH OF CHARGE

FIGURE 6-6 Switch off the charger before connecting it to or disconnecting it from the battery.

Safety

Batteries give off hydrogen gas while they are being charged and for some time afterward. Hydrogen is a light and highly explosive gas that is easily ignited by a simple spark. Batteries are filled with **sulphuric acid**, so if the hydrogen does explode, the battery case can then rupture and spray everything and everyone nearby with this dangerous and corrosive liquid.

Be very careful not to create a spark when you are connecting or disconnecting battery cables or hooking up a charger to the battery terminals. Switch off the charger before connecting and disconnecting them from the battery FIGURE 6-6.

Do not try to charge a battery faster than the battery manufacturer recommends, and never use a battery load tester immediately after charging a battery. This is because both charging and rapidly discharging a battery generate heat and hydrogen. If you load-test a battery after charging it without waiting for it to cool down, you will increase the risk of distorting the plates inside the battery, as well as increase the risk of explosion.

Safety

Always remove your hand, wrist, and neck jewelry before working with batteries and electrical systems. If it comes into contact with the battery terminals or power wire, it can cause a short circuit. You will receive painful skin burns from the very rapid heating of the metal you are wearing, or even flash burns from an arcing current. A wristwatch or ring is much harder to take off when it is red- or white-hot and burned onto your skin!

How to Charge Batteries

Batteries go dead for a variety of reasons. A common cause is the driver forgetting to turn off the headlights when exiting the vehicle. Or maybe the owner went on vacation for a month and the battery discharged slowly over that time. Since the battery only stores electricity, anything that stays on when the vehicle is not running drains the battery.

Slow charging a battery is less stressful on a battery than fast charging, so if possible, slow charge a battery instead of fast charging it. Removing the negative battery terminal while changing a battery reduces the risk of burning up any electronic devices on the vehicle, especially with today's electronically intensive cars. However, disconnecting the vehicle's battery risks losing information such as radio presets and other learned data. Use a **memory saver (memory minder)**, which provides backup power to retain electronic memory settings in the vehicle's computer systems.

Manufacturers install multiple batteries in some vehicles to provide additional battery power when needed, such as in diesel pick-up trucks and SUVs. Knowing how the batteries are connected together will determine how you connect a battery charger properly. Batteries can be connected in series (connected in line with each other, with the positive of one connected to the negative of the other) or parallel (connected side by side, with positive connected to positive and negative to negative). Two 12-volt batteries connected in series will have the positive terminal of one battery connected to the negative terminal of the second battery. The output voltage will be equal to the sum of the voltages of the individual batteries and is taken from the negative terminal of one battery and the positive terminal of the other battery. For example, two 12-volt batteries connected in series will have a nominal output voltage of 24 volts across the most negative and most positive battery terminals. If you have a 24-volt battery charger, you can charge both batteries at once by connecting the battery charger to these same terminals. If you only have a 12-volt charger, you will have to either charge one battery at a time, or reconnect them so they are connected in parallel. Just make sure you charge both batteries fully, which could take more than 12 hours each, if slow charging.

Batteries connected in parallel have the negative terminals of both batteries connected to each other and the positive terminals of each battery connected to each other. The output voltage will be equal to the voltage of one battery and is taken from the positive and negative posts of either battery. For example, two 12-volt batteries connected in parallel have an output voltage of 12 volts. In this situation, a 12-volt charger can be used to charge both batteries at the same time while the batteries are connected together. But it is likely to take about twice as long as it would if only charging one battery.

After charging and reinstalling the battery, it is good practice to clean the battery terminals and posts. To correctly charge a battery using battery charging equipment, follow the steps in SKILL DRILL 6-3. Note that you should

SKILL DRILL 6-3 Charging Batteries
ACDelco
LENGTH OF CHARGE
RATINGS
CRANKING ASSIST
1 Determine the voltage of the system that needs charging. If you are charging a 12-volt battery, use the 12-volt setting on the charger. If you are charging a 24-volt battery, or two 12-volt batteries connected in series, use the 24-volt setting on the charger, if it has one. Identify the positive and negative terminals. Inspect the battery to ensure there are no cracks, holes, or damage to the casing.
2 Verify that the charger is unplugged from the wall and turned off. Connect the red lead from the charger to the positive battery terminal. Connect the black lead from the charger to the negative battery terminal.
3 Check the settings on the charger and verify that they are correct for what you are charging. Turn the charger on and select the automatic setting, if equipped. Select the rate of charge. Verify that the voltage and amperage the charger is putting out is proper.
4 Once the battery is charged, turn the charger off. Disconnect the black lead from the negative battery terminal and the red lead from the positive battery terminal.
5 Allow the battery to stand for at least 5 minutes before testing the battery. Using a capacitance tester, load tester, or hydrometer, test the charged state of the battery.

never simply use the color of the cables to determine the positive or negative terminals; use the + and – or the Pos and Neg marks.

Jump-Starting Vehicles

Jump-starting a vehicle is the process of using one vehicle with a charged battery to provide electrical energy to start another vehicle that has a discharged or dead battery. Since starting a vehicle requires a high amount of electrical energy, jump-starting a vehicle can put stresses on both vehicles. When the discharged vehicle is being cranked, the battery voltage tends to fall very low because the battery is already discharged. This causes the alternator on the running vehicle to put out its maximum current, putting it under heavy load. But as soon as the jumped vehicle stops cranking, the voltage shoots up quickly, potentially high enough to damage electronic components in either vehicle. The same voltage spike can happen when the battery cables are being disconnected.

TECHNICIAN TIP

Alternators are not generally designed to charge a dead battery while running several accessories. If a battery must be jump-started, it is always best to recharge the battery using a battery charger. That way, the alternator will not have to work so hard. Some technicians say it takes only 15 minutes to burn up an alternator when charging a dead battery.

Safety

Make sure the hood is secured with a hood prop before going under it; otherwise it could fall and injure someone or short out the jumper cables causing a spark, which could result in the battery blowing up.

Safety

When connecting jumper cables, a spark will almost always occur on the last connection you make. That is why it is critical that you make the last connection on the engine block away from the battery and any other flammables. A spark also occurs when you disconnect the first jumper cable connection, so that also needs to be the connection at the engine block.

Some vehicle manufacturers are now recommending that their vehicles should not be jump-started and that instead the battery be charged or replaced. In the same way, some towing companies have policies stating that they will not jump-start certain vehicles and that they will only replace the battery or tow the vehicle to a shop to be recharged. If you do decide to jump-start a vehicle, *always* read the owner's manual for both vehicles and follow their jump-starting guidelines. And never attempt to jump-start a frozen battery.

Safety

- Keep your face and body as far back as you can while connecting jumper leads.
- Do not connect the negative cable to the discharged battery because the spark may blow up the battery.
- Use only specially designed heavy-duty jumper cables to start a vehicle with a dead battery. Do not try to connect the batteries with any other type of cable.
- Always make sure you wear the appropriate PPE before starting the job. Remember, batteries contain sulfuric acid and it is very easy to injure yourself.
- Always follow any manufacturer's personal safety instructions to prevent damage to the vehicle you are servicing.

It is usually best to let the running vehicle charge the battery on the other vehicle for 5 to 10 minutes before trying to start the vehicle. Once the dead vehicle's engine has started, let both vehicles come to an idle for a moment. Do not turn off the vehicle with the discharged battery; it needs an extended amount of time to recharge. Before you disconnect the service battery from the discharged battery, it is good practice to place a load on the charged battery by turning on an accessory. Turning on the headlights will help absorb any sudden rise in voltage that may occur as the load on the alternator is suddenly decreased. In most modern vehicles there are many sensitive electronic devices. These devices are very susceptible to voltage surges. One method of reducing the risk of damage to such devices is by using jumper leads that have a built-in or auxiliary **surge protector**.

To start a vehicle with a discharged battery using jumper leads and a second vehicle or battery, follow the steps in **SKILL DRILL 6-4**.

SKILL DRILL 6-4 Jump-Starting Vehicles

1. Position the charged battery close enough to the discharged battery that it is within comfortable range of your jumper cables. If the charged battery is in another vehicle, make sure the two vehicles are not touching. Always connect the leads in this order: First, connect the red jumper lead to the positive terminal (+) of the discharged battery. Next, connect the other end of this lead to the positive terminal of the charged battery. Connect the black jumper lead to the negative terminal (–) of the charged battery. Connect the other end of the negative lead to a good ground on the engine block of the vehicle with the discharged battery, and as far away as possible from the battery. Do NOT connect the lead to the negative terminal of the discharged battery itself; doing so may cause a dangerous spark. Also, do not connect the negative lead to the body or chassis, as the ground wire from the body back to the negative battery terminal is usually too small to carry current needed for jump-starting the vehicle.

2. Try to start the vehicle with the discharged battery. If the booster battery does not have enough charge or the jumper cables are too small of diameter to do this, start the engine in the booster vehicle and allow it to partially charge the discharged battery for several minutes. Try starting the first vehicle again with the booster vehicle's engine running. Turn on the head lights on the booster vehicle to reduce the possibility of a voltage spike damaging electronic equipment.

3. Disconnect the leads in the reverse order of connecting them. Remove the negative lead from the ground away from the battery. Then disconnect the negative from the booster battery. Next remove the positive lead from the booster battery, and lastly, disconnect the other positive end from the battery in the vehicle you have just started. If the charging system is working correctly and the battery is in good condition, the battery will be recharged while the engine is running, although it could end up overheating and damaging the alternator.

Fasteners and Torque

Fasteners are designed to secure parts that are under various tension and sheer stresses. The nature of the stresses placed on parts and fasteners depends on their use and location. For example, head bolts withstand tension stresses by clamping the head gasket between the cylinder head and the block. The bolts must withstand the very high combustion pressures trying to push the head off of the engine block in order to leak past the head gasket. An example of fasteners withstanding sheer stresses is lug studs and lug nuts. They clamp the wheel assembly to the suspension system, and the weight of the vehicle tries to sheer the lug studs. If this were to happen, the wheel would fall off the vehicle, leading to an accident.

To accomplish their job, fasteners come in a variety of diameters and hardnesses, which are defined in grades. Fasteners with screw threads are designed to be tightened to a specific rating depending on the job at hand, the grade or hardness of the material they are made from, their size, and the thread type. If a fastener is overtightened, it could become damaged or could break. If it is undertightened, it could work loose over time. **Torque** is a way of defining how much a fastener should be tightened.

Bolts, Studs, and Nuts

Bolts, studs, and nuts are fasteners designed for heavier jobs than screws and tend to be made of metal or metal alloys FIGURE 6-7. **Bolts** are a cylindrical piece of metal with a hexagonal head on one end and a thread cut into the shaft at the other end. The thread acts as an inclined plane; as the bolt is turned, it is drawn into or out of the matching thread. Hexagonal **nuts** thread onto the bolt thread. The hexagonal heads for the bolt and nut are designed to fit tools such as combination wrenches and sockets.

A **stud** does not have a fixed hexagonal head; rather, it has a thread cut on each end. It is threaded into one part where it stays. The mating part is then slipped over it and a nut is threaded onto the end of the stud to secure the part. Studs are commonly used to attach a throttle body to the intake manifold. Studs can have different threads on each end. On one end, there is a thread that is best for gripping the hole in the intake manifold and to locate the throttle body, and on the other end, there is a thread for pulling everything together tightly with a steel nut.

Bolts, nuts, and studs can have either standard or metric threads. They are designated by their thread diameter, thread pitch, length, and grade. The diameter is measured across the outside of the threads; it is measured in fractions of an inch for standard-type fasteners, and millimeters for metric-type fasteners. So a 3/8″ (9.5 mm) bolt has a thread diameter of 3/8″ (9.5 mm), not the size of the bolt head.

The coarseness of any thread is called its **thread pitch** FIGURE 6-8. In the standard system, bolts, studs, and nuts are measured in threads per inch (tpi). To determine the tpi, simply count the number of threads there are in 1 inch. Each bolt diameter in the standard system can have one of two thread pitches, **coarse (UNC)** or **fine (UNF)**. For example, a 3/8 – 16 is coarse, while a 3/8 – 24 is fine. In the metric system, the thread pitch is measured by the distance between the peaks of the threads in millimeters. Each bolt diameter in the metric system can have up to four thread pitches. See a metric thread pitch chart since there is no clear pattern of thread pitches for metric fasteners. These charts can be found in tap and die sets or on the Internet.

The length of a bolt is fairly straightforward. It is measured from the end of the bolt to the bottom of the head and is listed in inches or millimeters. The grade of a fastener relates to its strength. The higher the grade number, the higher the **tensile strength**, which refers to how much tension it can withstand before it breaks. Tensile strength for fasteners is generally listed in pounds per square inch of bolt shaft area.

The Society of Automotive Engineers (SAE) is one certifying body that certifies fasteners. Their rating scale is from grade 1 to grade 8 for typical fasteners. Most general-purpose bolts used in automotive are grade 5. Bolts under higher stresses, such as connecting rod bolts, are a higher grade. In any critical component, you must replace an original bolt with a bolt of the same grade; use

FIGURE 6-7 Bolts, studs, and nuts.

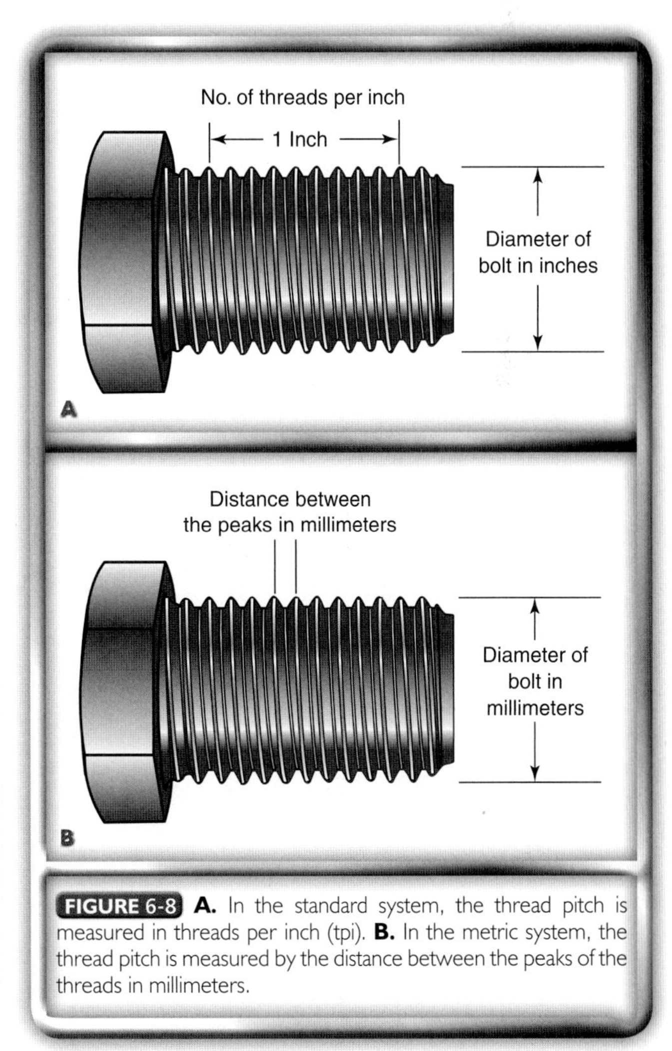
No. of threads per inch
1 Inch
Diameter of bolt in inches
A
Distance between the peaks in millimeters
Diameter of bolt in millimeters
B

FIGURE 6-8 **A.** In the standard system, the thread pitch is measured in threads per inch (tpi). **B.** In the metric system, the thread pitch is measured by the distance between the peaks of the threads in millimeters.

> **TECHNICIAN TIP**
>
> Threads are cut on screws, bolts, nuts, and studs and inside holes to allow components to be attached and assembled. There was a time when there were many different thread designs used throughout the world. Modern vehicles still use a range of thread patterns, but due to standardization it is getting much simpler. Nearly all the nuts, bolts, screws, and studs on a vehicle have a V-thread cut into them. A screw jack or a clamp has **square threads** cut into it. The square thread is more difficult to machine and is mainly used in situations where rotational movement needs to be transferred into lateral movement—for example, the screw in a vice where the rotary movement of turning the handle is translated into the lateral movement of the jaws closing.

neither a lower grade nor a higher grade, as each could cause a failure if it is not designed for the task.

Many automotive bolts and nuts need to be tightened to a specified level—tight enough to hold components together but not so tight that the component or the fastener could fail. This level of tightness is called the **torque specification**. Bolts and nuts are often marked with grades to tell you their strength, which determines how much torque can be safely applied to them. For example, a grade 8 bolt is stronger and can be tightened to a higher torque than a grade 5 bolt. Once bolts are tightened, the challenge is to ensure they stay tight. There are several different ways for this to be accomplished. For example, a locking washer, a locking chemical compound, or a nylon locking device built into the nut may be used.

Torque Charts

Torque specifications for bolts and nuts in vehicles will usually be contained within shop manuals. Bolt, nut, and stud manufacturers also produce torque charts, which contain all the information you need to determine the maximum torque of bolts or nuts. For example, most charts include the bolt diameter, threads per inch, grade, and maximum torque setting for both dry and lubricated bolts and nuts. A lubricated bolt and nut will reach maximum torque value at a lower setting. In practice, most torque specifications call for the nuts and bolts to have dry threads prior to tightening. There are some exceptions, so close examination of the torque specification chart is critical TABLE 6-1.

TABLE 6-1: Torque Specification Chart

Bolt Dia.	Thread per inch	Hex Head					
		Grade 5		Grade 7		Grade 8	
		Dry	Oiled	Dry	Oiled	Dry	Oiled
1/4	20	8	6	10	8	12	9
1/4	28	10	7	12	9	14	10
5/16	18	17	13	21	16	25	18
5/16	24	19	14	24	18	29	20
3/8	16	30	23	40	20	45	35
3/8	24	35	25	45	35	50	40
7/16	14	50	35	60	45	70	55
7/16	20	55	40	70	50	80	60
1/2	13	75	55	95	70	110	80
1/2	20	90	65	100	80	120	90
9/16	12	110	80	135	100	150	110
3/8	18	120	90	150	110	170	130
5/8	11	150	110	140	190	220	170
5/8	18	180	130	210	160	240	180
3/4	10	260	200	320	240	380	280
3/4	16	300	220	360	280	420	320
7/8	9	430	320	520	400	600	460
7/8	14	470	360	580	440	660	500
1	8	640	480	800	600	900	680
1	12	710	530	860	666	990	740

Torque Wrenches

A **torque wrench** is also known as a tension wrench FIGURE 6-9. It is used to tighten fasteners to a predetermined torque. It is designed to tighten bolts and nuts using the drive on the end, which fits with any socket and accessory of the same drive size, found in an ordinary socket set. While manufacturers do not specify torque settings for every nut and bolt, when they do, it is important to follow the specifications. For example, manufacturers specify a torque for head bolts. The torque specified will ensure that the bolt provides the proper clamping pressure and will not come loose, but will not be so tight as to risk breaking the bolt or stripping the threads.

The torque value will be specified in foot-pounds (lb-ft), inch-pounds (in-lb), or newton meters (Nm). The torque value is the amount of twisting force applied to a fastener by the torque wrench. A foot-pound is described as the amount of twisting force applied to a shaft by a perpendicular lever 1 foot long with a weight of 1 pound placed on the outer end. A torque value of 100 lb-ft will be the same as a 100-lb weight placed at the end of a 1-foot-long lever. A torque value of an inch-pound will be 1 pound placed at the end of a 1-inch-long lever. Also note that 1 lb-ft equals 12 in-lb. A newton meter is described as the amount of twisting force applied to a shaft by a perpendicular lever 1 meter long with a force of 1 newton applied to the outer end. A torque value of 100 Nm will be the same as applying a 100-newton force to the end of a 1-meter-long lever. One lb-ft is equal to 1.35 Nm.

Torque wrenches come in various types: beam style, clicker, dial, and electronic. The simplest and least expensive is the beam-style torque wrench. It uses a spring steel beam that flexes under tension. A smaller fixed rod then indicates the amount of torque on a scale mounted to the bar. The amount of deflection of the bar coincides with the amount of torque on the scale. One drawback of this design is that you have to be positioned directly above the scale so you can read it accurately. That can be a problem when working under the hood of a vehicle.

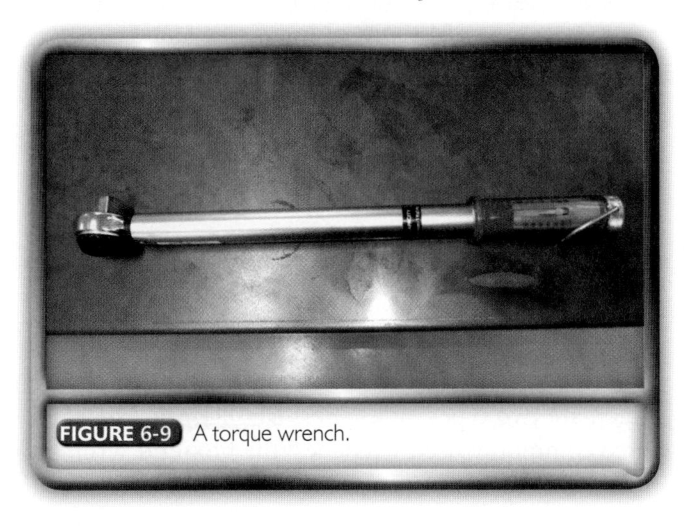

FIGURE 6-9 A torque wrench.

The clicker-style torque wrench uses an adjustable clutch inside that slips (clicks) when the preset torque is reached. You can set it for a particular torque on the handle. As the bolt is tightened, once the preset torque is reached, the torque wrench will click. The higher the torque, the louder the click; the lower the torque, the quieter the click. Be careful when using this style of torque wrench, especially at lower torque settings. It is easy to miss the click and overtighten, break, or strip the bolt. Once the torque wrench clicks, stop turning it, as it will continue to tighten the fastener if you turn it past the click point.

The dial torque wrench turns a dial that indicates the torque based on the torque being applied. Like the beam-style torque wrench, you have to be able to see the dial to know how much torque is being applied. Many dial torque wrenches have a movable indicator that is moved by the dial and stays at the highest reading. That way you can double-check the torque achieved once the torque wrench is released. Once the proper torque is reached, the indicator can be moved back to zero for the next fastener being torqued.

The digital torque wrench usually uses a spring steel bar with an electronic strain gauge to measure the amount of torque being applied. The torque wrench can be preset to the desired torque. It will then display the torque as the fastener is being tightened. When it reaches the preset torque, it will usually give an audible signal, such as a beep. This makes it useful in situations where a scale or dial cannot be read.

Torque wrenches fall out of calibration over time or if they are not used properly, so they should be checked and calibrated on a periodic basis. This can be performed in the shop if the proper calibration equipment is available, or the torque wrench can be sent to a qualified service center. Most quality torque wrench manufacturers provide a recalibration service for their customers.

Using Torque Wrenches

The torque wrench is used to apply a specified amount of torque to a fastener. There are various methods used by torque wrenches to indicate that the correct torque has been reached. Some will give an audible signal such as a click or a beep, while others will give a visual signal such as a light or a pin moving or clicking out. Some must be observed while you are torquing the fastener. To help ensure that the proper amount of torque gets from the torque wrench to the bolt, support the head of the torque wrench with one hand. When using a torque wrench, it is best to not use extensions. Extensions make it harder to support the head, which can end up absorbing some of the torque. If possible, use a deep socket instead.

> **Safety**
>
> - Refer to the manufacturer's specifications when tightening fasteners.
> - Return the torque wrench to its lowest setting when finished.
> - If replacing a fastener, make sure it has the correct tensile value for the task it will perform.

Torque-to-Yield and Torque Angle

Torque is not always the best method of ensuring that a bolt is tightened enough as to give the proper amount of clamping force. If the threads are rusty, rough, or damaged in any way, the amount of twisting force required to tighten the fastener increases. Tightening the rusty fastener to a particular torque will not provide as much clamping force as a smooth fastener torqued the same amount. All threads must be clean before tightening the fastener to a specified torque. This also brings up the question of whether threads should be lubricated. In most automotive cases, the torque values specified are for dry, non-lubricated threads. But always check the manufacturer's specifications.

When bolts are tightened, they are also stretched. As long as they are not tightened too much, they will return to their original length when loosened. This is called **elasticity**. If they continue to be tightened and stretch beyond their point of elasticity, they will not return to their original length when loosened. This is called the **yield point**. **Torque-to-yield** means that a fastener is torqued to, or just beyond, its yield point.

With the changes in engine metallurgy that manufacturers are using in today's vehicles, bolt technology had to change also. To help prevent bolts from loosening over time and to maintain an adequate clamping force when the engine is both cold and hot, manufacturers have adopted **torque-to-yield (TTY) bolts**. TTY bolts are designed to provide a consistent clamping force when torqued to their yield point or just beyond. The challenge is that the torque does not increase very much, or at all, once yield is reached. So using a torque wrench by itself will not indicate the point at which the manufacturer wants the bolt tightened. So TTY bolts generally require a new torquing procedure called torque angle. Also, it is important to note that in virtually all cases, TTY bolts cannot be reused because they have been stretched into their yield zone and would very likely fail if retorqued.

Torque angle is considered a more precise method to tighten TTY bolts and is essentially a multistep process. Bolts are first torqued in the required pattern using a standard torque wrench to a required moderate torque setting. They are then further tightened an additional specified angle (torque angle) using an angle gauge, thus providing further tightening, which tightens the bolt to, or beyond, its yield point. In some cases, after torquing, the manufacturer first wants all of the bolts to be turned to an initial angle, and then turned an additional angle. And in other cases, the manufacturer wants all of the bolts torqued in a particular sequence, then detorqued in a particular sequence, then retorqued once again in a particular sequence, and finally tightened an additional specified angle. So always check the manufacturer's specifications and procedure before torquing TTY bolts.

To use a torque angle gauge in conjunction with a torque wrench, follow the steps in SKILL DRILL 6-5.

Basic Hand Tools

Like all tools, hand tools extend our ability to do work. Hand tools come in a variety of shapes, sizes, and functions. A large percentage of your personal tools will be hand tools. Over the years, manufacturers have introduced new fasteners, wire harness terminals, quick-connect fittings for fuel and other lines, and additional technologies that require their own different types of hand tools. This means that technicians need to add tools to their toolbox all of the time.

> **TECHNICIAN TIP**
>
> Invest in quality tools. Since tools extend your abilities, poor-quality tools will affect the quality and quantity of your work. Price is not always the best indicator of quality, but it plays a role. As you learn the purpose and function of the tools in this chapter, you should be able to identify high-quality tools versus poor-quality tools by looking at them, handling them, and putting them to work.

Wrenches

Wrenches are used to tighten and loosen nuts and bolts, which are two types of fasteners FIGURE 6-10. There are three commonly used wrenches: the **box-end wrench**, the **open-end wrench**, and the **combination wrench**.

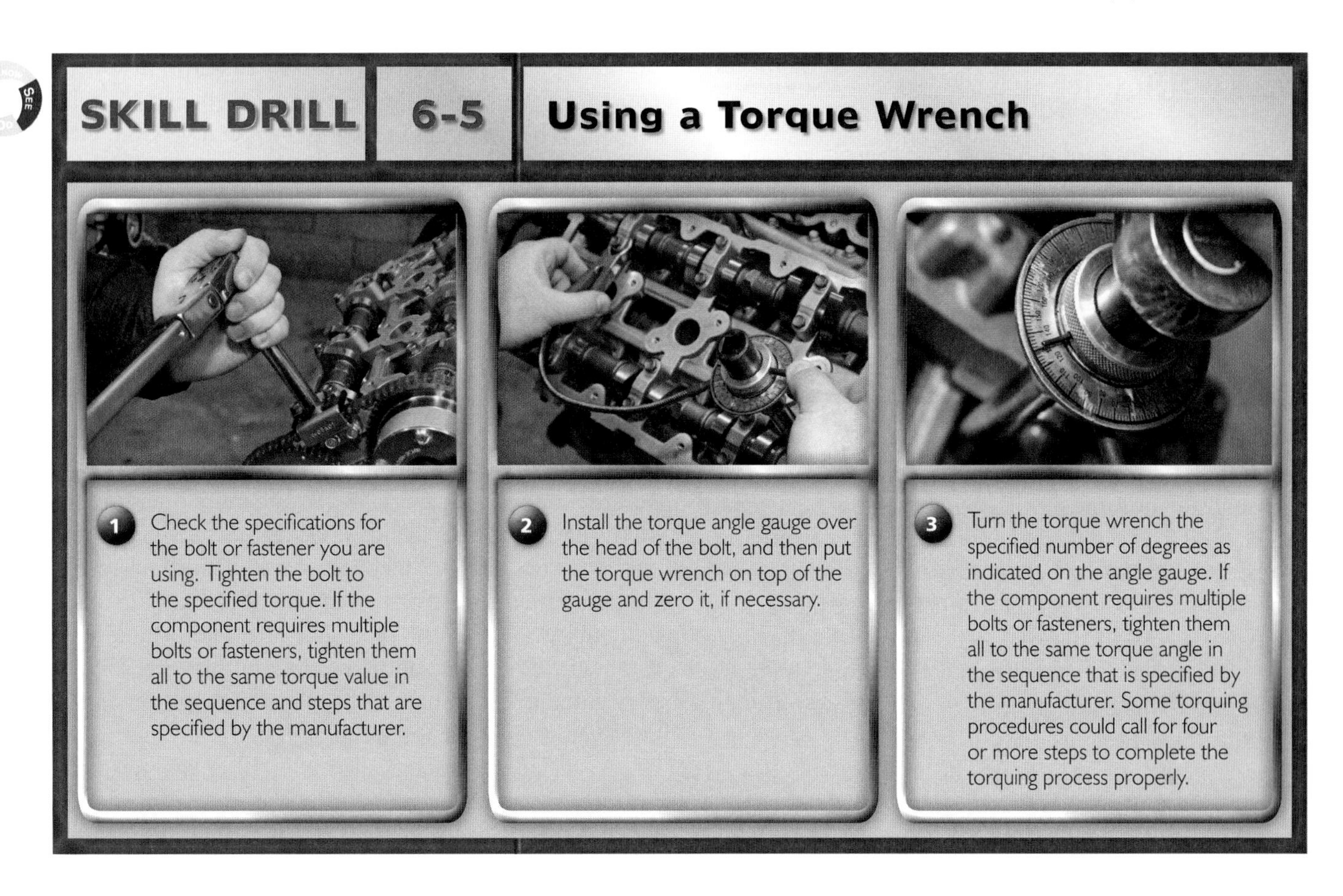

SKILL DRILL 6-5 Using a Torque Wrench

1. Check the specifications for the bolt or fastener you are using. Tighten the bolt to the specified torque. If the component requires multiple bolts or fasteners, tighten them all to the same torque value in the sequence and steps that are specified by the manufacturer.
2. Install the torque angle gauge over the head of the bolt, and then put the torque wrench on top of the gauge and zero it, if necessary.
3. Turn the torque wrench the specified number of degrees as indicated on the angle gauge. If the component requires multiple bolts or fasteners, tighten them all to the same torque angle in the sequence that is specified by the manufacturer. Some torquing procedures could call for four or more steps to complete the torquing process properly.

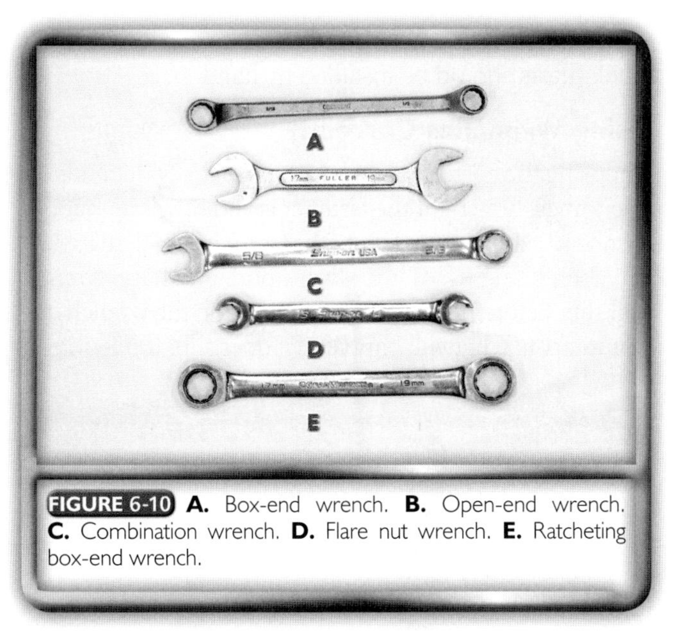
A
B
C
D
E

FIGURE 6-10 **A.** Box-end wrench. **B.** Open-end wrench. **C.** Combination wrench. **D.** Flare nut wrench. **E.** Ratcheting box-end wrench.

The box-end wrench fits fully around the head of the bolt or nut and grips each of the six points at the corners just like a socket. This is just the sort of grip needed if a nut or bolt is very tight and makes it less likely to round off the points on the head of the bolt than the open-end wrench. This grip gives you a better chance at loosening very tight fasteners. The ends of box-end wrenches are bent or offset so they are easier to grip and have different-sized heads at each end. One disadvantage of the box-end wrench is that it can be awkward to use once the nut or bolt has been loosened a bit because you have to lift it off the head of the fastener and move it to each new position.

The open-end wrench is open on the end and the two parallel flats only grip two points of the fastener. Open-end wrenches usually either have different-sized heads on each end of the wrench, or they have the same size, but with different angles. The head is at an angle to the handle and is not bent or offset, so it can be flipped over and used on both sides. This is a good wrench to use in very tight spaces as you can flip it over and get a new angle so the head can catch new points on the fastener. While an open-end wrench often gives the best access to a fastener, if the fastener is extremely tight, the open-end should not be used, as this type of wrench only grips two points. If the jaws flex slightly or the flats don't fit tightly around them, the wrench can suddenly slip when force is applied. This slippage can round off the points of the fastener. The best way to approach the situation with a tight fastener is to use a box-end wrench to break the bolt or nut free, then use the open-end wrench to finish the job. The open-end wrench should only be used on fasteners that are no more than firmly tightened.

The combination wrench has an open-end head on one end and a box-end head on the other end. Both ends

> **TECHNICIAN TIP**
>
> Wrenches (which are also known as spanners in some countries) will only do a job properly if they are the right size for the given nut or the bolt head. The size used to describe a wrench is the distance across the flats of the nut or bolt. There are two systems in common use—standard (in inches) and metric (in millimeters). Each system provides a range of sizes, which are identified by either a fraction, which indicates fractions of an inch for the standard system, or a number, which indicates millimeters for the metric system.

are usually of the same size. That way the box-end wrench can be used to break the bolt loose and the open end can be used for turning the bolt. Because of its versatility, this is probably the most popular wrench for technicians.

A variation on the open-end wrench is the **flare nut wrench**, also called a flare tubing wrench. It gives a better grip than the open-end wrench because it grabs all six points of the fastener, not two. However, since it is open on the end, it is not as strong as a box-end wrench. The partially open sixth side lets the wrench be placed over tubing or pipes so the wrench can be used to turn the tube fittings. Do not use the flare nut wrench on extremely tight fasteners as the jaws may spread, damaging the nut.

One other open-end wrench is the open-end adjustable wrench or crescent wrench. This wrench has a movable jaw that can be adjusted by turning an adjusting screw to fit any fastener within its range. It should only be used if other wrenches are not available because it is not as strong as a fixed wrench, so it can slip off of and damage the head of tight bolts or nuts. Still, it is a handy tool to have since it can be adjusted to fit most any fastener size.

A **ratcheting box-end wrench** is a useful tool in some applications because it does not require removal of the tool to reposition it. It has an inner piece that fits over and grabs the fastener points and is able to rotate within the outer housing. A ratcheting mechanism lets it rotate in one direction and lock in the other direction. In some cases, the wrench just needs to be flipped over to be used in the opposite direction. In other cases, it has a lever that changes the direction from clockwise to counterclockwise. Just be careful to not overstress this tool by using it to tighten or loosen very tight fasteners, as the outer housing is not very strong.

There is also a ratcheting open-end wrench, but it uses no moving parts. One of the sides is partially removed so that only the bottom one-third remains to catch a point on the bolt. When it is used, the normal side works just like a standard open-end wrench. The shorter side of the open-end wrench catches the point on the fastener so it can be turned. When moving the wrench to get a new bite, the wrench is pulled slightly outward, disengaging the short side while leaving the long side to slide along the faces of the bolt. The wrench is then rotated to the new position and pushed back in so the short side engages the next point. This wrench, like other open-end wrenches, is not designed to tighten or loosen tight fasteners, but it does work well in blind places where a socket or ratcheting box-end wrench cannot be used.

Specialized wrenches such as the **pipe wrench**, grips pipes and can exert a lot of force to turn them FIGURE 6-11. Because the handle pivots slightly, the more pressure put on the handle to turn the wrench, the more the grip tightens. The jaws are hardened and serrated, and increasing the pressure also increases the risk of marking or even gouging metal from the pipe. The jaw is adjustable so it can be threaded in or out to fit different pipe sizes. Also, they come in different lengths, allowing you to increase the leverage applied to the pipe.

A specialized wrench called an **oil filter wrench** grabs the filter and gives you extra leverage to remove an oil filter when it is tight. They are available in various designs and sizes. Some oil filter wrenches are adjustable to fit many filter sizes. Also note that an oil filter wrench should be used *only* to remove an oil filter, never to install it. Almost all oil filters should be installed by hand.

Using Wrenches Correctly

Choosing the correct wrench for a job usually depends on two things: how tight the fastener is and how much room there is to get the wrench onto the fastener, and then to turn it. When being used, it is always possible that a wrench will slip. Before putting a lot of tension on the wrench, try to anticipate what will happen if it does slip. If possible, it

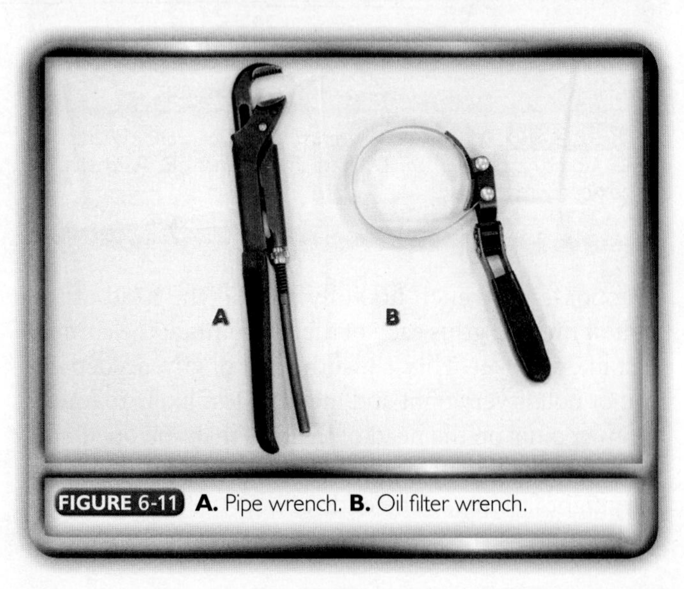
A
B

FIGURE 6-11 **A.** Pipe wrench. **B.** Oil filter wrench.

is usually better to pull a wrench toward you than to push it away. If you have to push, use an open palm to push so your knuckles won't get crushed if the wrench slips.

Sockets

Sockets are very popular because of their adaptability and ease of use FIGURE 6-12. Sockets are a good choice where the top of the fastener is reasonably accessible. The **socket** fits onto the fastener snugly and grips it on all six corners, providing the type of grip needed on any nut or bolt that is extremely tight. They come in a variety of configurations, and technicians usually have a lot of sockets so they can get in a multitude of tight places. Individual sockets fit a particular size nut or bolt, so they are usually purchased in sets.

Sockets are classified by the following characteristics:

- Standard or metric
- Size of drive used to turn them: ½″, ⅜″, and ¼″ are most common; 1″ and ¾″ are less common.
- Number of points: 6 and 12 are most common; 4 and 8 are less common.
- Depth of socket: Standard and deep are most common; shallow is less common.
- Thickness of wall: Standard and impact are most common; thin wall is less common.

> **TECHNICIAN TIP**
>
> Since sockets are usually purchased in sets, with each set providing a slightly different capability, you can see why technicians could easily have several hundred sockets in their toolbox.

Sockets are built with a recessed square drive that fits over the square drive of the ratchet or other driver FIGURE 6-13. The size of the drive determines how much twisting force can be applied to the socket. The larger the drive, the larger the twisting force. Small fasteners usually only need a small torque, so having too large of a drive may make it so the socket cannot gain access to the bolt. For fasteners that are really tight, an impact wrench exerts a lot more torque on a socket than turning it by hand. Impact sockets are usually thicker walled than standard wall sockets and have six points so they can withstand the forces generated by the impact wrench as well as grip the fastener securely.

Six- and 12-point sockets fit the heads of hexagonal-shaped fasteners. Four- and 8-point sockets fit the heads of square-shaped fasteners. Since 6-point and 4-point sockets fit the exact shape of the fastener, they have the strongest grip on the fastener, but they only can fit on the fastener in half as many positions as a 12-point or 8-point socket.

Another factor in accessing a fastener is the depth of the socket. If a nut is threaded quite a ways down a stud, then a standard length socket will not fit far enough over the stud to reach the nut. In this case, a deep socket will usually reach the nut.

Turning a socket requires a handle. The most common socket handle, the **ratchet**, makes easy work of tightening or loosening a nut where not a lot of pressure is involved. It can be set to turn in either direction and does not need much room to swing. It is built to be convenient, not super strong, so too much pressure could damage it. For heavier tightening or loosening, a breaker bar gives the most leverage. When that is not available, a **sliding T-handle** may be more useful. With this tool, both hands

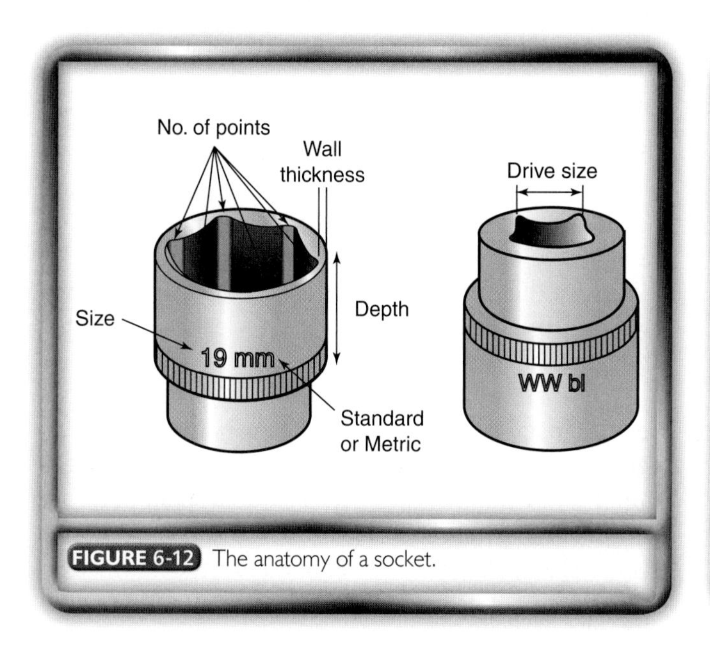
No. of points
Wall thickness
Drive size
Size
Depth
19 mm
WW bl
Standard or Metric

FIGURE 6-12 The anatomy of a socket.

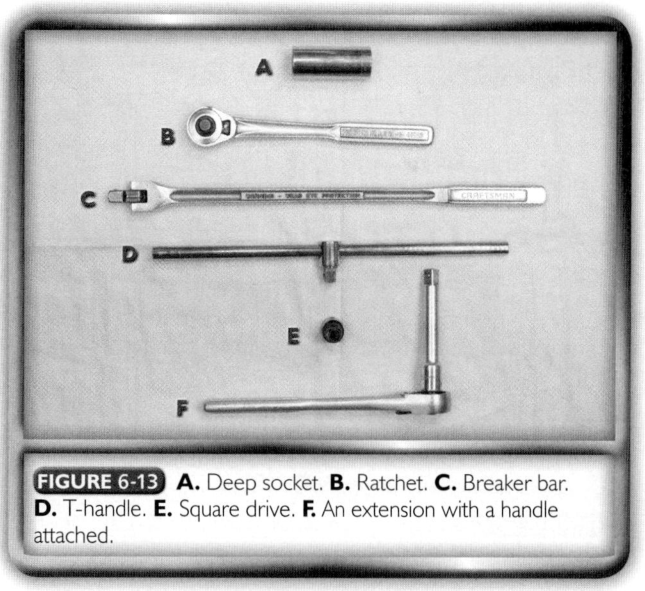
A
B
C
D
E
F

FIGURE 6-13 **A.** Deep socket. **B.** Ratchet. **C.** Breaker bar. **D.** T-handle. **E.** Square drive. **F.** An extension with a handle attached.

can be used, and the position of the tee piece is adjustable to clear any obstructions when turning it.

The connection between the socket and the accessory is made by a square drive. The larger the drive, the heavier and bulkier the socket will be. The 1/4″ drive is for small work in difficult areas. The 3/4″ drive accessories handle a lot of general work where torque requirements are not too high. The 1/2″ drive is required for all-around service. The 3/4″ and 1″ drives are required for large work with high-torque settings. Many fasteners are located in positions where access can be difficult. There are many different lengths of extensions available to allow the socket to be on the fastener while extending the drive point out to where a handle can be attached **FIGURE 6-14**.

A **speed brace** or speeder handle is the fastest way to spin a fastener on or off a thread by hand, but it cannot apply much torque to the fastener; therefore, it is mainly used to remove a fastener that has already been loosened, or to run the fastener onto the thread until it begins to tighten. A universal joint can take the turning force that needs to be applied to the socket through an angle.

A **lug wrench** has special-sized lug nut sockets permanently attached to it. One common model, the lug wrench, has four different-sized sockets, one on each arm. Never hit or jump on a lug wrench when loosening lug nuts. If the lug wrench will not remove them, you should use an impact wrench. The impact wrench provides a hammering effect in conjunction with rotation to help loosen tight fasteners. *Never* use an impact tool to tighten lug fasteners. Torque all lug fasteners to the proper torque with a properly calibrated torque wrench.

Pliers

Pliers are a hand tool designed to hold, cut, or compress materials **FIGURE 6-15**. They are usually made out of two pieces of strong steel joined at a fulcrum point with jaws and cutting surfaces at one end and handles designed to provide leverage at the other. There are many types of pliers, including slip-joint, combination, arc joint, needle-nosed, and flat-nosed **FIGURE 6-16**.

FIGURE 6-15 Pliers are used for grasping and cutting.

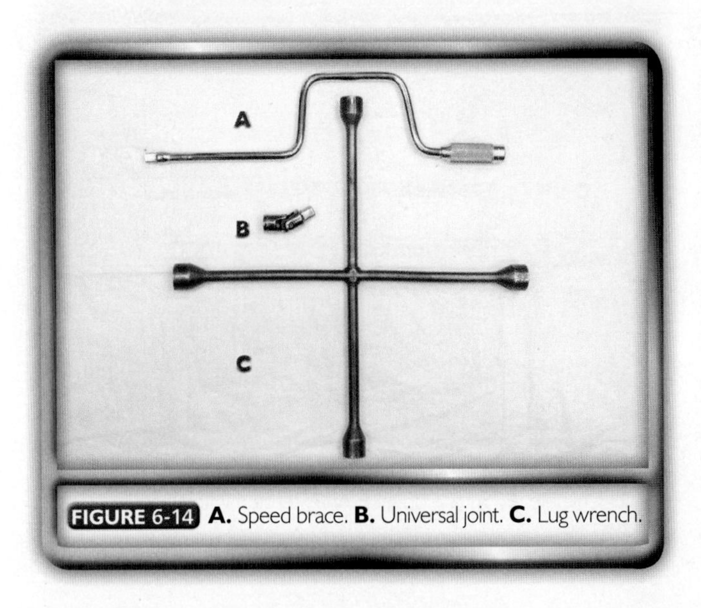
A
B
C

FIGURE 6-14 **A.** Speed brace. **B.** Universal joint. **C.** Lug wrench.

Quality **combination pliers** are the most commonly used pliers in a shop. They are made from two pieces of high carbon or alloy steel. They pivot together so that any force applied to the handles is multiplied in the strong jaws. Some pliers provide a powerful grip on objects, while others are designed to cut. Combination pliers can do both, which is why they are the most common type of pliers.

Combination pliers offer two surfaces, one for gripping flat surfaces and one for gripping rounded objects, and two pairs of cutters. The cutters in the jaws should be used for softer materials that will not damage the blades. The cutters next to the pivot can shear through hard, thin materials, like steel wire or pins.

Most pliers are limited by their size in what they can grip. Beyond a certain point, the handles are spread too wide, or the jaws cannot open wide enough, but **arc joint pliers** overcome that limitation with a moveable pivot. Often, these are called Channellocks™ after the company that first made them. These pliers have parallel jaws that allow you to increase or decrease the size of the jaws by selecting a different set of channels. They are useful for a wider grip and a tighter squeeze on parts too big for conventional pliers.

There are a few specialized pliers in most shops. **Needle-nosed pliers**, which have long pointed jaws, can reach tight spots or hold small items that other pliers cannot. For example, they can pick up a small bolt that has fallen into a tight spot. **Flat-nosed pliers** have an end or nose that is flat and square; in contrast, combination pliers have a rounded end. A flat nose makes it possible

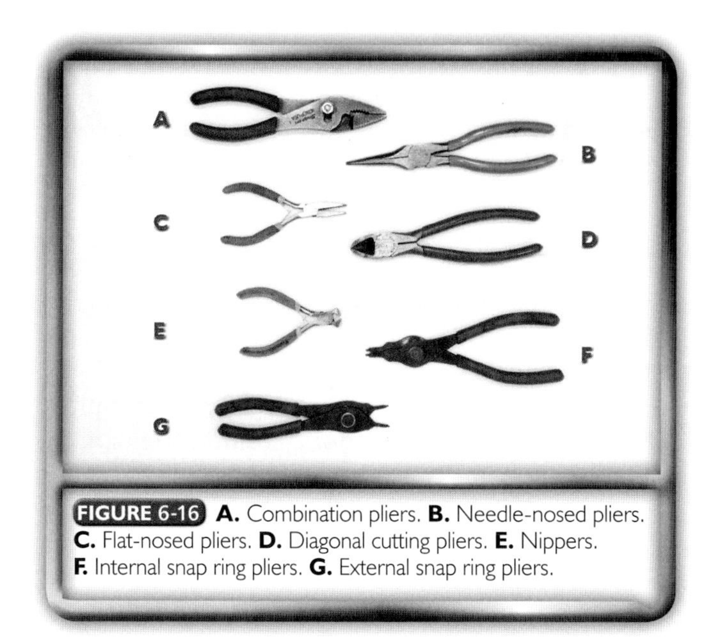
A
B
C
D
E
F
G

FIGURE 6-16 **A.** Combination pliers. **B.** Needle-nosed pliers. **C.** Flat-nosed pliers. **D.** Diagonal cutting pliers. **E.** Nippers. **F.** Internal snap ring pliers. **G.** External snap ring pliers.

to bend wire or even a thin piece of sheet steel accurately along a straight edge. **Diagonal cutting pliers** are used for cutting wire or cotter pins. Diagonal cutters are the most common cutters in the toolbox, but they should not be used on hard or heavy-gauge materials because the cutting surfaces will be damaged. End cutting pliers, also called **nippers**, have a cutting edge at right angles to their length. They are designed to cut through soft metal objects sticking out from a surface.

Snap ring pliers have metal pins that fit in the holes of a snap ring. Snap rings can be of the internal or external type. If internal, then internal snap ring pliers compress the snap ring so it can be removed from and installed in its internal groove. If external, then external snap ring pliers are used to remove and install the snap ring in its external groove. Always wear safety glasses when working with snap rings, as the rings can easily slip off the snap ring pliers and fly off at tremendous speeds, possibly causing severe eye injuries.

Safety

When applying pressure to pliers, make sure your hands are not greasy or they might slip. Select the right type and size of pliers for the job. As with most tools, if you have to exert almost all your strength to get something done, then you are using either the wrong tool or the wrong technique. If the pliers slip, you will get hurt. At the very least, you will damage the tool and what you are working on. Pliers get a lot of hard use in the shop, so they do get worn and damaged. If they are worn or damaged, they will be inefficient and can be dangerous. Always check the condition of all shop tools on a regular basis.

Locking pliers, also called vice grips, are general-purpose pliers used to clamp and hold one or more objects FIGURE 6-17. Locking pliers are helpful by freeing up one or more of your hands when working because they can clamp something and lock themselves in place to hold it. They are also adjustable so they can be used for a variety of tasks. To clamp an object with locking pliers, put the object between the jaws, turn the screw until the handles are almost closed, then squeeze them together to lock them shut. You can increase or decrease the gripping force with the adjustment screw. To release them, squeeze the release lever and they should open right up.

Cutting Tools

Bolt cutters cut heavy wire, non-hardened rods, and bolts FIGURE 6-18. Their compound joints and long handles give the leverage and cutting pressure that is needed

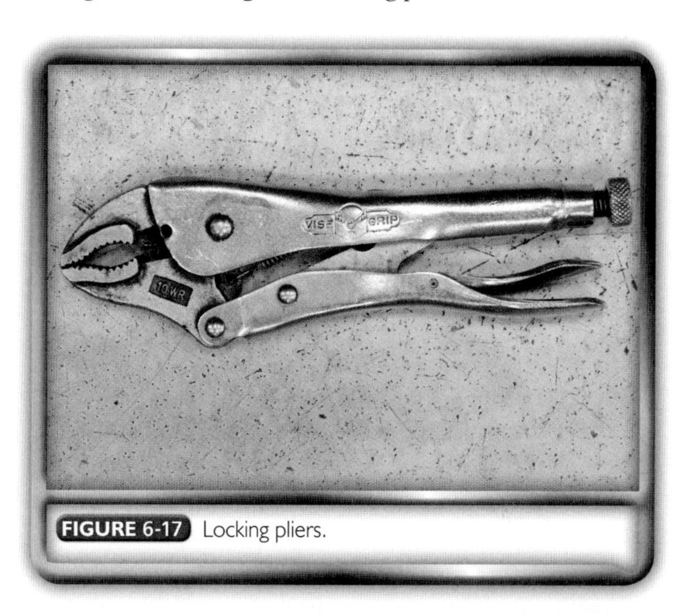
VISE GRIP
10WR

FIGURE 6-17 Locking pliers.

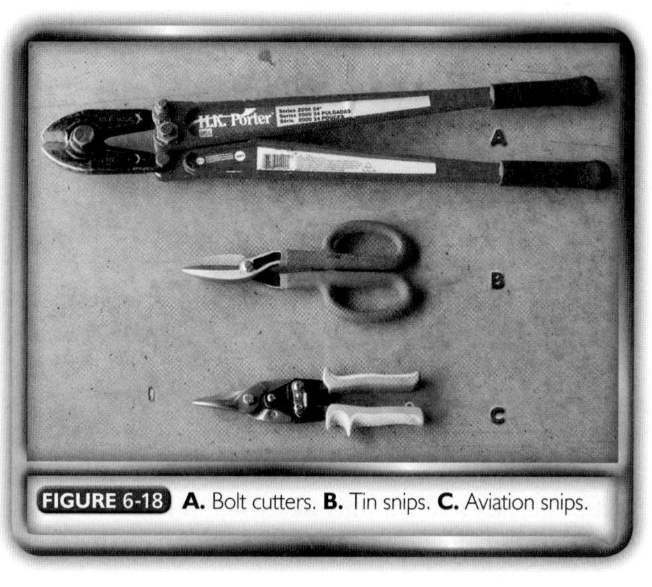
H.K. Porter
A
B
C

FIGURE 6-18 **A.** Bolt cutters. **B.** Tin snips. **C.** Aviation snips.

for heavy gauge materials. **Tin snips** are the nearest thing in the toolbox to a pair of scissors. They can cut thin sheet metal, and lighter versions make it easy to follow the outline of gaskets. Most snips come with straight blades but if there is an unusual shape to cut, there is a pair with left or right hand curved blades. **Aviation snips** are designed to cut soft metals. They are easy to use because the handles are spring loaded open and double pivoted for extra leverage.

Allen Wrenches

Allen wrenches, sometimes called Allen or hex keys, are tools designed to tighten and loosen fasteners with Allen heads FIGURE 6-19. The Allen head has an internal hexagonal recess that the Allen wrench fits in. Allen wrenches come in sets, and there is a correct wrench size for every Allen head. They give the best grip on a screw or bolt of all the drivers, and their shape makes them good at getting into tight spots. Care must be utilized to make sure the correct size of Allen key is used or the key and/or socket head will be rounded off. The traditional Allen wrench is a hexagonal bar with a right angle bend at one end. They are made in various sizes in both metric and standard. As their popularity has increased, so too has the number of tool variations. Now Allen sockets are available, as are T-handle Allen keys.

Screwdrivers

The correct screwdriver to use depends on the type of slot or recess in the head of the screw or bolt, and how accessible it is FIGURE 6-20. Most screwdrivers cannot grip as securely as wrenches, so it is very important to match the tip of the screwdriver exactly with the slot or recess in the head of a fastener. Otherwise the tool might slip, damaging the fastener or the tool and possibly injuring you. When using a screwdriver, always check where the screwdriver blade can end up if it slips off the head of the screw. Many technicians who have not taken this precaution have stabbed a screwdriver into or through their hand.

The most common screwdriver has a flat tip, or blade, which gives it the name **flat blade screwdriver**. The blade should be almost as wide and thick as the slot in the fastener so that twisting force applied to the screwdriver is transferred right out to the edges of the head where it has most effect. The blade should be a snug fit in the slot of the screw head. Then the twisting force is applied evenly along the sides of the slot. This will guard against the screwdriver suddenly chewing a piece out of the slot and slipping just when the most force is being exerted. Flat blade screwdrivers come in a variety of sizes and lengths, so find the right one for the job.

If viewed from the side, the blade should taper slightly until the very end where the tip fits into the slot. If the tip of the blade is not clean and square, it should be reshaped or replaced.

When you use a flat blade screwdriver, support the shaft with your free hand as you turn it (but keep it behind the tip). This helps keep the blade square on the slot and centered. Screwdrivers that slip are a common source of damage and injury in shops.

A screw or bolt with a cross-shaped recess requires a **Phillips head screwdriver** or a Pozidriv screwdriver. The cross-shaped slot holds the tip of the screwdriver securely on the head. The Phillips tip fits a tapered recess while the Pozidriv fits into slots with parallel sides in the head of the screw. Both a Phillips and a Pozidriv screwdriver are less likely to slip sideways because the point is centered in the screw, but again the screwdriver must be the right size. The fitting process is simplified with these two types of screwdrivers because four sizes are enough to fit almost all fasteners with this sort of screw head.

FIGURE 6-19 Allen wrench.

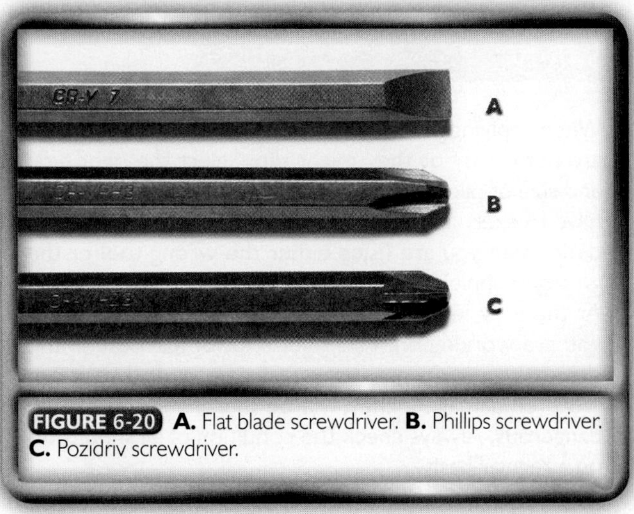
A
B
C

FIGURE 6-20 **A.** Flat blade screwdriver. **B.** Phillips screwdriver. **C.** Pozidriv screwdriver.

The offset screwdriver fits into spaces where a straight screwdriver cannot and is useful where there is not much room to turn it FIGURE 6-21. The two tips look identical, but one is set at 90 degrees to the other. This is because sometimes there is only room to make a quarter turn of the driver. Thus the driver has two blades on opposite ends so that offset ends of the screwdriver can be used alternately.

The ratcheting screwdriver is a popular screwdriver handle that usually comes with a selection of flat and Phillips tips. It has a ratchet inside the handle that turns the blade in only one direction depending on how the slider is set. When set for loosening, a screw can be undone without removing the tip of the blade from the head of the screw. When set for tightening, a screw can be inserted just as easily.

An impact driver is used when a screw or a bolt is rusted/corroded in place or overtightened and needs a tool that can apply more force than the other members of this family. Screw slots can easily be stripped with the use of a standard screwdriver. The force of the hammer pushing the bit into the screw and at the same time turning it makes it more likely the screw will break loose. The impact driver accepts a variety of special, impact tips. Choose the right one for the screw head, fit the tip in place, and then tension it in the direction it has to turn. A sharp blow with the hammer breaks the screw free, and then it can be unscrewed.

Magnetic Pickup Tools and Mechanical Fingers

Magnetic pickup tools and mechanical fingers are very useful for grabbing items in tight spaces FIGURE 6-22. A magnetic pickup tool typically is a telescoping stick that has a magnet attached to the end on a swivel joint. The magnet is strong enough to pick up screws, bolts, and sockets. For example, if a screw is dropped into a tight crevice where your fingers cannot reach, a magnetic pickup tool can be used to extract it.

Mechanical fingers are also designed to extract or insert objects in tight spaces. Because they actually grab the object, they can pick up non-magnetic objects, which makes them handy for picking up rubber or plastic parts. They use a flexible body and come in different lengths but typically are about 12–18" (305–457 mm) long. They have expanding grappling fingers on one end to grab items while the other end has a push mechanism to expand the fingers and a retracting spring to contract the fingers.

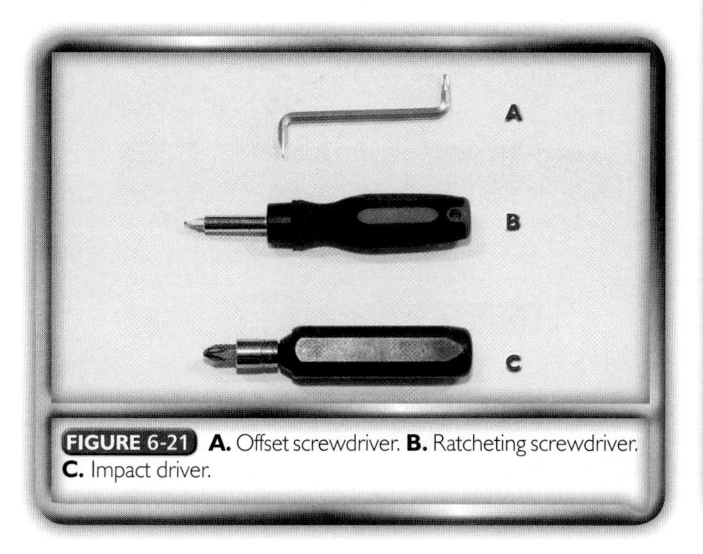
A
B
C

FIGURE 6-21 **A.** Offset screwdriver. **B.** Ratcheting screwdriver. **C.** Impact driver.

Hammers

Hammers are a vital part of the shop tool collection, and a variety are commonly used FIGURE 6-23. The most common hammer in an automotive shop is the

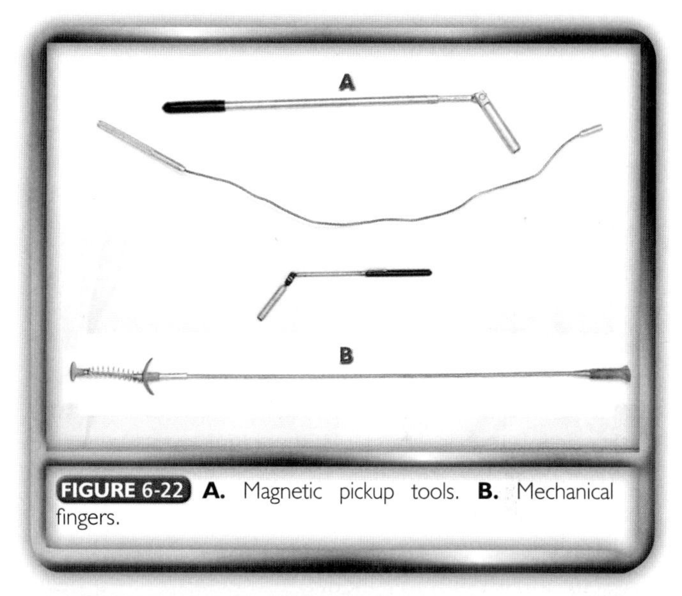
A
B

FIGURE 6-22 **A.** Magnetic pickup tools. **B.** Mechanical fingers.

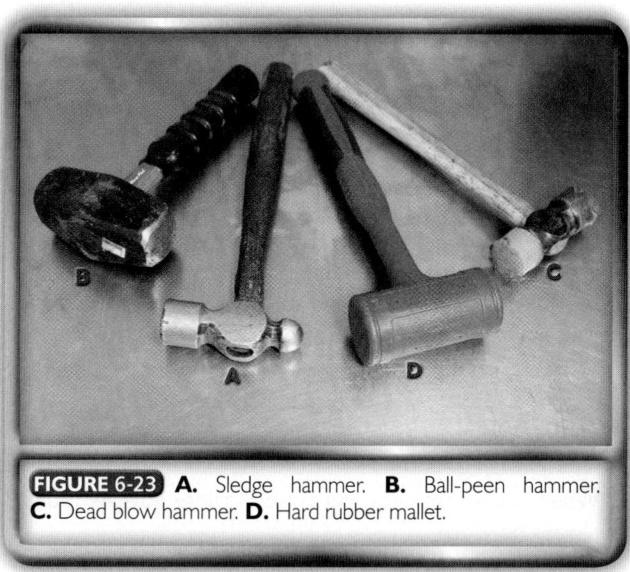
B
A
D
C

FIGURE 6-23 **A.** Sledge hammer. **B.** Ball-peen hammer. **C.** Dead blow hammer. **D.** Hard rubber mallet.

TECHNICIAN TIP

It may be challenging getting the magnet down inside some areas because the magnet wants to keep sticking to other objects. One trick in this situation is to roll up a piece of paper so that a tube is created. Stick that down into the area of the dropped part, then slide the magnet down the tube, which will help it get past magnetic objects. Once the magnet is down, you may want to remove the roll of paper. Just remember two things: First, patience is important when using this tool, and second, don't drop anything in the first place!

ball-peen (engineer's) hammer. Like most hammers, its head is hardened steel. A punch or a chisel can be driven with the flat face. Its name comes from the ball peen or rounded face. It is usually used for flattening or **peening** a rivet. The hammer should always match the size of the job, and it is usually better to use one that is too big than too small.

Hitting chisels with a **steel hammer** is fine, but sometimes you only need to tap a component to position it. A steel hammer might mark or damage the part, especially if it is made of a softer metal, such as aluminum. In such cases, a soft-faced hammer should normally be used for the job. Soft-faced hammers range from very soft with rubber or plastic heads to slightly harder with brass or copper.

When a large chisel needs a really strong blow, it is time to use a **sledge hammer**. The sledge hammer is like a small mallet, with two square faces made of high carbon steel. It is the heaviest type of hammer that can be used one-handed. The sledge hammer would be used in conjunction with a chisel to cut off a bolt where corrosion has made it impossible to remove the nut.

The most common mallet in the shop has a head made of hard rubber. A **hard rubber mallet** is a special-purpose tool and is often used for moving things into place where it is important not to damage the item being moved. For example, it can be used to tap a crankshaft, to measure end play, or to break a gasket seal on an aluminum casing.

A **dead blow hammer** is designed not to bounce back when it hits something. A rebounding hammer can be dangerous or destructive. A dead blow hammer can be made with a lead head or more commonly a hollow polyurethane head filled with lead shot or sand. The head absorbs the blow when the hammer makes contact, reducing any bounce-back or rebounding. This hammer can be used when working on the vehicle chassis or when dislodging stuck parts.

Safety

The hammer you use depends on the part you are striking. Hammers with a metal face should almost always be harder than the part you are hammering. Never strike two hardened tools together, as this can cause the hardened parts to shatter.

Safety

When using hammers and chisels, safety goggles must always be worn.

Safety

Chisels and punches are designed with a softer striking end than hammers. Over time, this softer metal "mushrooms" and small fragments are prone to breaking off when hammered. These fragments can cause eye or other penetrative injuries to people in the area. Always inspect chisels and punches for mushrooming and dress them on a grinder when necessary.

Chisels

The most common kind of chisel is a **cold chisel** FIGURE 6-24. It gets its name from the fact it is used to cut cold metals, rather than heated metals. It has a flat blade made of high-quality steel and a cutting angle of approximately 70 degrees. The cutting end is tempered and hardened because it has to be harder than the metals that need to be cut. The head of the chisel needs to be softer so it will not chip when it is hit with a hammer. Technicians sometimes use a cold chisel to remove bolts whose heads have rounded off.

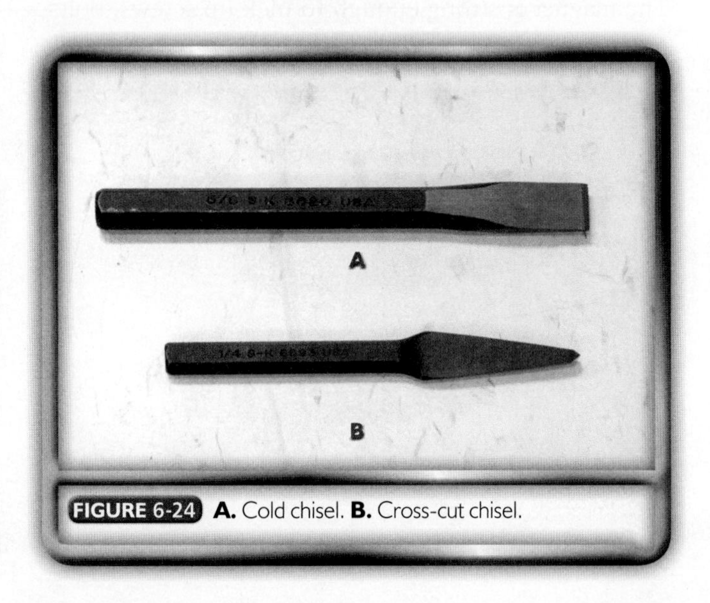
A
B

FIGURE 6-24 **A.** Cold chisel. **B.** Cross-cut chisel.

A **cross-cut chisel** is so named because the sharpened edge is across the blade width. This chisel narrows down along the stock, so it is good for getting in grooves. It is used for cleaning out or even making key ways. The flying chips of metal should always be directed away from the user.

Punches

Punches are used when the head of the hammer is too large to strike the object being hit without causing damage to adjacent parts FIGURE 6-25. A punch transmits the hammer's striking power from the soft upper end down to the tip that is made of hardened high carbon steel. A punch transmits an accurate blow from the hammer at exactly one point, something that cannot be guaranteed using a hammer on its own.

When marks need to be drawn on an object like a steel plate to help locate a hole to be drilled, a **prick punch** can be used to mark the points so they will not rub off. They can also be used to scribe intersecting lines between given points. The prick punch's point is very sharp, so a gentle tap leaves a clear indentation. The **center punch** is not as sharp as a prick punch and is usually bigger. It makes a bigger indentation that centers a drill bit at the point where a hole is required to be drilled.

A **drift punch** is also named a starter punch because you should always use it first to get a pin moving. It has a tapered shank and the tip is slightly hollow so it does not spread the end of a pin and make it an even tighter fit. Once the starter drift has gotten the pin moving, a suitable pin punch will drive the pin out or in. A drift punch also works well for aligning holes on two mating objects, such as a valve cover and cylinder head. Forcing the drift punch in the hole will align both components for easier installation of the remaining bolts.

Pin punches are available in various diameters. A pin punch has a long slender shaft that has straight sides. It is used to drive out rivets or pins FIGURE 6-26. A lot of components are either held together or accurately located by pins. Pins can be pretty tight and a group of pin punches is specially designed to deal with them.

Special punches with hollow ends are called **wad punches** or **hollow punches**. They are the most efficient tool to make a hole in soft sheet material like shim steel, plastic, and leather, or, most commonly, in a gasket. When being used, there should always be a soft surface under the work, ideally the end grain of a wooden block. If a hollow punch loses its sharpness or has nicks around its edge, it will make a mess instead of a hole.

Numbers and letters, like the engine numbers on some cylinder blocks, are usually made with number and letter punches that come in boxed sets. The rules for using a number or letter punch set are the same as for all punches. The punch must be square with the surface being worked on, not on an angle, and the hammer must hit the top squarely.

Pry Bars

Pry bars are tools composed of a strong metal that are used as a lever to move, adjust, or pry FIGURE 6-27. Pry bars come in a variety of shapes and sizes. Many have a

Safety

Hands should always be kept away from the surface of the file and the metal that is being worked on. Filing can produce small slivers of metal that can be difficult to remove from a finger or hand. Clean hands will help avoid slipping and lessen the corrosion caused by acids and moisture from the skin.

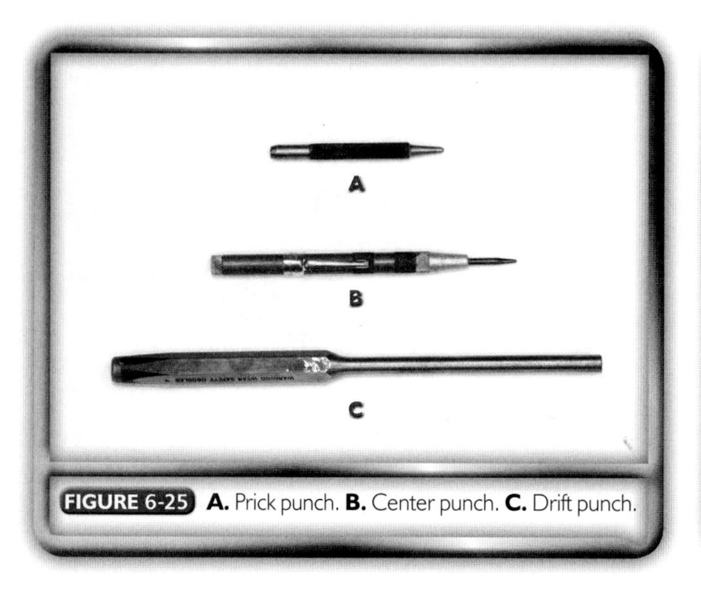
A
B
C

FIGURE 6-25 **A.** Prick punch. **B.** Center punch. **C.** Drift punch.

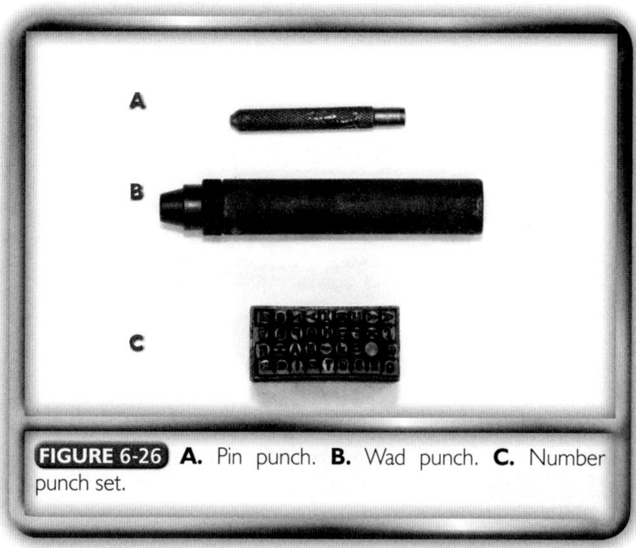
A
B
C

FIGURE 6-26 **A.** Pin punch. **B.** Wad punch. **C.** Number punch set.

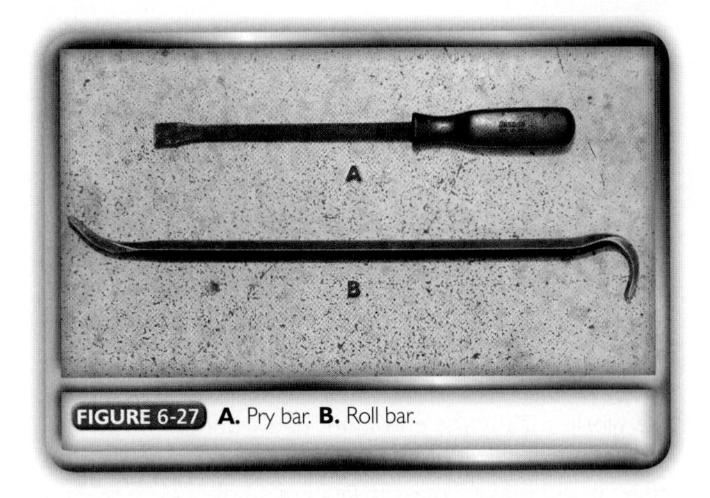
A
B
FIGURE 6-27 **A.** Pry bar. **B.** Roll bar.

> **TECHNICIAN TIP**
>
> Many engine components are made of aluminum. Since aluminum is quite soft, it is critical that you use the gasket scraper very carefully so as not to damage the surface. This can be accomplished by keeping the gasket scraper at a fairly flat angle to the surface. Also, the gasket scraper should only be used by hand, not with a hammer. Some manufacturers specify using plastic gasket scrapers only on certain aluminum components such as cylinder heads and blocks.

tapered end that is slightly bent, with a plastic handle on the other end. This design works well for applying force to tension belts or for moving parts into alignment. Another type of pry bar is the **roll bar**. One end is sharply curved and tapered, which is used for prying. The other end is tapered to a dull point and is used to align larger holes such as transmission bell housings or engine motor mounts. Because pry bars are made of hardened steel, care should be taken when using them on softer materials to avoid any damage.

Gasket Scrapers

A **gasket scraper** has a hardened, sharpened blade. It is designed to remove a gasket without damaging the sealing face of the component when used properly FIGURE 6-28. On one end, it has a comfortable handle to grip like a screwdriver handle; on the other end, a blade is fitted with a sharp edge to assist in the removal of gaskets. The gasket scraper should be kept sharp to make it easy to remove all traces of the old gasket and sealing compound. The blades come in different sizes, with a typical size being 1″ (25 mm) wide. Whenever you use a gasket scraper, be very careful not to nick or damage the surface being cleaned.

Files

Files are hand tools designed to remove small amounts of material from the surface of a workpiece. Files come in a variety of shapes, sizes, and coarseness depending on the material being worked and the size of the job. Files have a pointed tang on one end that is fitted to a handle. Files are often sold without handles, but they should not be used until a handle of the right size has been fitted. A correctly sized handle will fit snugly without working loose while using the file. Always check the handle before using the file. If the handle is loose, give it a sharp rap to tighten it up, or if it is the threaded type, screw it on tighter. If it fails to fit snugly, you must use a different size handle.

What makes one file different from another is not just the shape but how much material it is designed to remove with each stroke. The teeth on the file determine how much material will be removed FIGURE 6-29. Since the teeth face one direction only, the file cuts in one direction only. Dragging the file backward over the surface of the metal only dulls the teeth and wears them out quickly.

Teeth on a coarse-grade file are longer, with a greater space between them. A coarse-grade file working on a piece of mild steel will remove a lot of material with each stroke, but it leaves a rough finish. A smooth-grade file

FIGURE 6-28 A gasket scraper.

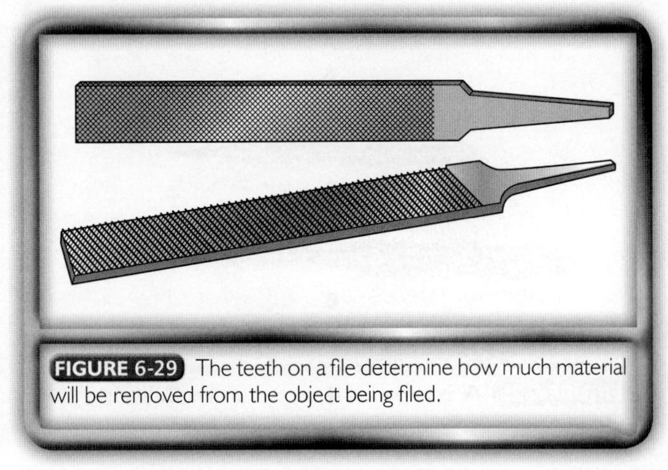
FIGURE 6-29 The teeth on a file determine how much material will be removed from the object being filed.

has shorter teeth cut more closely together. It removes much less material on each stroke, and the finish is much smoother. On a job, the coarse file is used first to remove material quickly, then a smoother file gently removes the last of it and leaves a clean finish to the work.

The full list of grades in flat files, from rough to smooth, follows:

- Rough files have the coarsest teeth, with approximately 20 teeth per inch. They are used when a lot of material must be removed quickly. They leave a very rough finish and will have to be followed by the use of finer files to produce a smooth final finish.
- Coarse bastard files are still a coarse file, with approximately 30 teeth per inch, but they are not as course as the rough file. They are also used to rough out or remove material quickly from the job.
- Second cut files have approximately 40 teeth per inch and provide a smoother finish than the rough or coarse bastard file. They are good all-round intermediary files and leave a reasonably smooth finish.
- Smooth files have approximately 60 teeth per inch and are a finishing file used to provide a smooth final finish.
- Dead smooth files have 100 teeth per inch or more and are used where a very fine finish is required.

Some flat files are available with one smooth edge, called safe edge files. They allow filing up to an edge without damaging it. Flat files are fine on straightforward jobs, but files must be able to work in some awkward spots as well. A **warding file** is thinner than other files and comes to a point; it is used for working in narrow slots FIGURE 6-30. A **square file** has teeth on all four sides, so you can use it in a square or rectangular hole. A square file can make the right shape for a squared metal key to fit in a slot. A **triangular file** has three sides. It is triangular, so it can get into internal corners. It is able to cut right into a corner without removing material from the sides.

Curved files are either half-round or round. A half-round file has a shallow convex surface that can file in a concave hollow or in an acute internal corner FIGURE 6-31. The fully round file, sometimes called a rat-tail file, can make holes bigger. It can also file inside a concave surface with a tight radius.

The **thread file** cleans clogged or distorted threads on bolts and studs. Thread files come in either standard or metric configurations, so make sure you use the correct file. Each file has eight different surfaces that match different thread dimensions, so the right face must be used.

Files should be cleaned after each use. If they are clogged, they can be cleaned by using a file card, or file

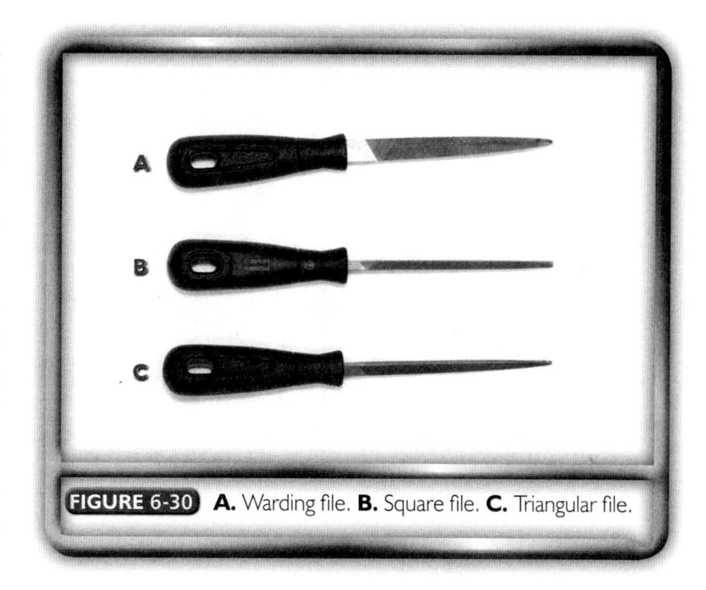
A
B
C

FIGURE 6-30 **A.** Warding file. **B.** Square file. **C.** Triangular file.

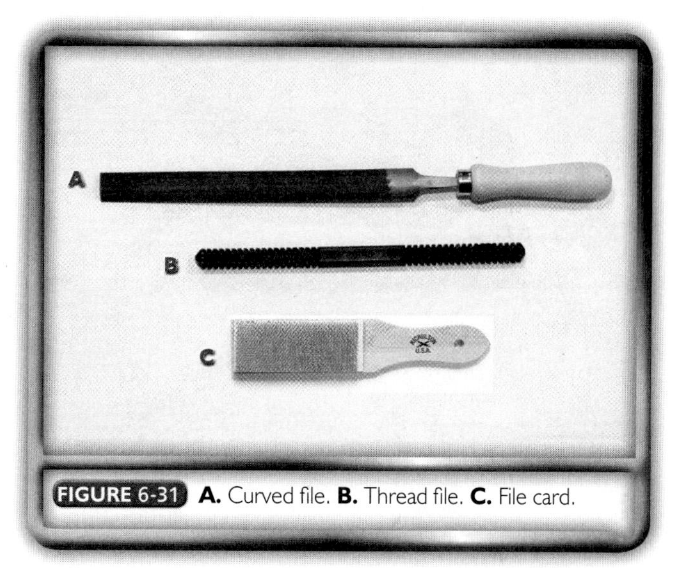
A
B
C

FIGURE 6-31 **A.** Curved file. **B.** Thread file. **C.** File card.

brush. This tool has short steel bristles that clean out the small particles that clog the teeth of the file. Rubbing a piece of chalk over the surface of the file prior to filing will make it easier to clean.

Clamps

There are many types of vices or clamps available FIGURE 6-32. The **bench vice** is a useful tool for holding anything that can fit into its jaws. Some common uses include sawing, filing, or chiseling. The jaws are serrated to give extra grip. They are also very hard, which means that when the vice is tightened, the jaws can mar whatever they are gripping. To prevent this, a pair of soft jaws can be fitted whenever the danger of damage arises. They are usually made of aluminum or some other soft metal or can have a rubber-type surface applied to them.

When materials are too awkward to grip vertically in a plain vice, it may be easier to use an **offset vice**. The offset

A
B
C

FIGURE 6-32 **A.** Bench vice. **B.** Drill vice. **C.** C-clamp.

vice has its jaws set to one side to allow long components to be held vertically. For example, a long threaded bar can be held vertically in an offset vice to cut a thread with a die.

A **drill vice** is designed to hold material on a drill worktable. The drill worktable has slots cut into to it to allow the vice to bolted down on the table to hold material securely. To hold something firmly and drill it accurately, the object must be secured in the jaws of the vice. The vice can be moved on the bed until the precise drilling point is located and then tightened down by bolts to hold the drill vice in place during drilling.

The name for the **C-clamp** comes from its shape. It can hold parts together while they are being assembled, drilled, or welded. It can reach around awkwardly shaped pieces that will not fit in a vice. It is also commonly used to retract disc brake caliper pistons. This clamp is portable, so it can be taken to the work.

Taps and Dies

Taps cut threads inside holes or nuts FIGURE 6-33. They normally come in three different types. The first is known as a **taper tap**. It narrows at the tip to give it a good start in the hole where the thread is to be cut. The diameter of the hole is determined by a tap drill chart, which can be obtained from engineering suppliers. This chart shows what hole size has to be drilled and what tap size is needed to cut the right thread for any given bolt size. Just remember that if you are drilling a .250″ (6 mm) or larger hole, use a smaller pilot drill first. Once the properly sized hole has been drilled, the taper tap can tap a thread right through a piece of steel to enable a bolt to be screwed into it.

The second type of tap is an **intermediate tap**, also known as a plug tap, and the third is a **bottoming tap**. They are used to tap a thread into a hole that does not come out the other side of the material, called a blind hole. A taper tap is used to start the thread in the hole and then the intermediate tap is used, followed by a bottoming tap to take the thread right to the bottom of the blind hole.

A **tap handle** has a right-angled jaw that matches the squared end that all taps have. The jaws are designed to hold the tap securely, while the handles provide the

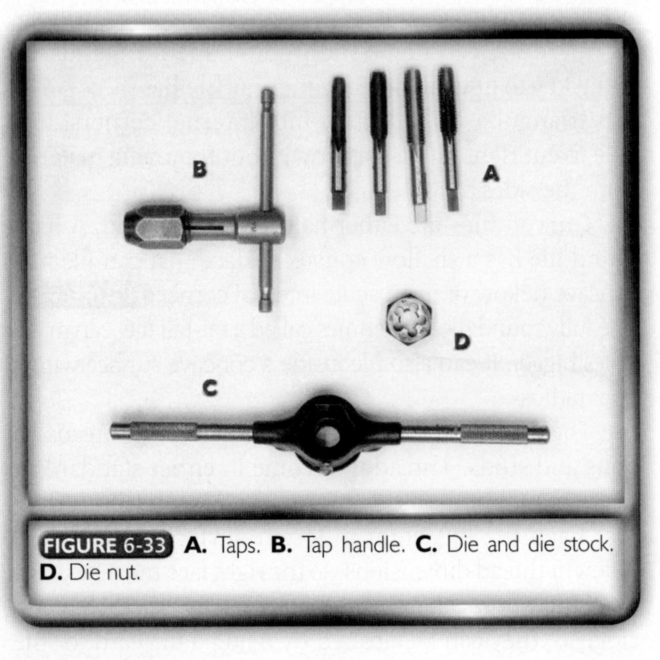
A
B
C
D

FIGURE 6-33 **A.** Taps. **B.** Tap handle. **C.** Die and die stock. **D.** Die nut.

leverage for the operator to comfortably rotate the tap to cut the thread. To cut a thread in an awkward space, a T-shaped tap handle is very convenient. Its handles are not as long, so it fits into tighter spaces; however, it is harder to turn and to guide accurately.

To cut a brand new thread on a blank rod or shaft, a die held in a **die stock** is used. The die may be split so that it can be adjusted more tightly onto the work with each pass of the die as the thread is cut deeper and deeper, until the nut fits properly. The die nut is also common in the shop. It is hexagonal shaped to fit a wrench, and it is commonly used to clean up threads that are rusty or have been damaged.

Screw extractors are devices designed to remove screws, studs, or bolts that have broken off in threaded holes. A common type of extractor uses a course left-hand tapered thread formed on its hardened body. Normally, a hole is drilled in the center of the broken screw and then the extractor is screwed into the hole. The left-hand thread grips the broken part of the bolt and unscrews it. The extractor is marked with the sizes of the screw it is designed to remove and the hole that needs to be drilled. It is important to carefully drill the hole in the center of the bolt or stud in the case you end up having to drill the bolt out. If you drill the hole off center, you will not be able to drill it out all the way to the inside diameter of the threads and removal will be nearly impossible.

Pullers

Pullers are a very common universal tool that can be used for removing bearings, bushings, pulleys, and gears FIGURE 6-34. Specialized pullers are also available for specific tasks where a standard puller is not as effective. The most common pullers have two or three legs that grip the part to be removed. A center bolt, called a forcing screw or jacking bolt, is then screwed in, producing a jacking or pulling action, which extracts the part.

Gear pullers come in a range of sizes and shapes, all designed for particular applications. They consist of three main parts: jaws, a cross-arm, and a forcing screw. There are normally two or three jaws on a puller. They are designed to work either externally around a pulley or internally. The **forcing screw** is a long, fine-threaded bolt that is applied to the center of the cross-arm. When the forcing screw is turned, it applies many tons of force through the component you are removing. The cross-arm attaches the jaws to the forcing screw. There may be two, three, or four arms. If the **cross-arm** has four arms, three of the arms will be spaced 120 degrees apart. The fourth arm will be positioned 180 degrees apart from one arm. This allows the cross-arm to be used as either a two- or a three-arm puller.

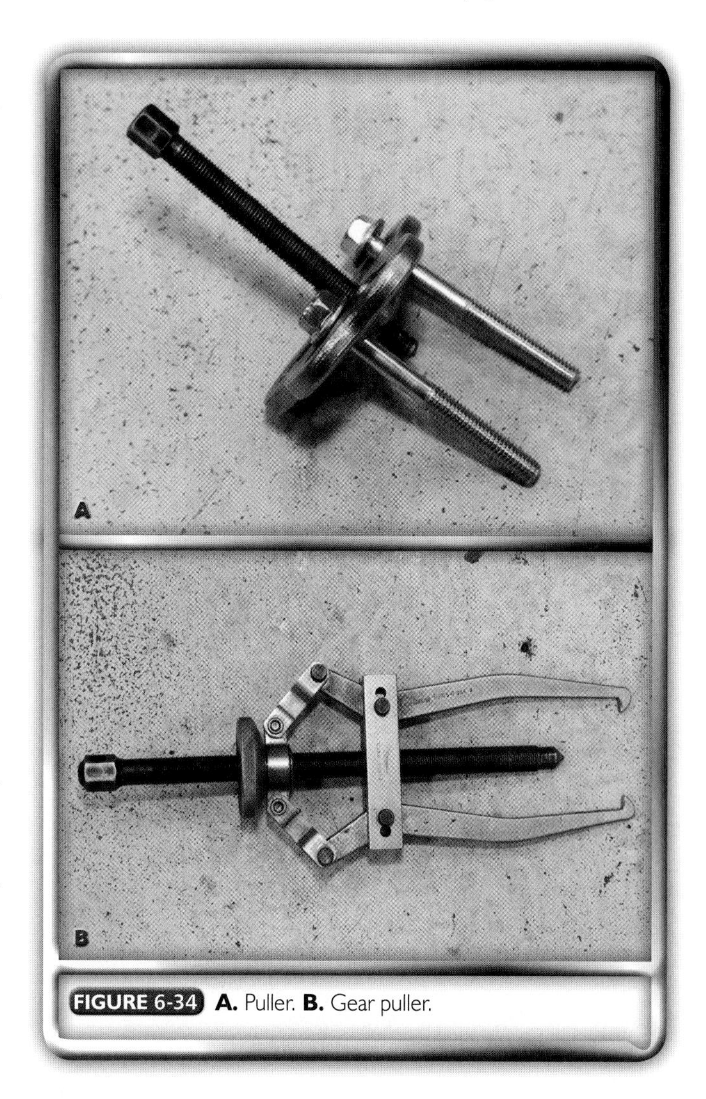
A
B

FIGURE 6-34 **A.** Puller. **B.** Gear puller.

Safety

- Always wear eye protection when using a gear puller.
- Make sure the puller is located correctly on the workpiece. If the jaws cannot be fitted correctly on the part, then select a more appropriate puller. Do not use a puller that does not fit the job.

Using Gear Pullers

Gear and bearing pullers are designed for hundreds of applications. Their main purpose is to remove a component, such as a gear, pulley, or bearing from a shaft, or to remove a shaft from inside a hole. Normally these components will have been pressed onto that shaft or into the hole, so removing them will require considerable force.

To select, install, and use a gear puller to remove a pulley, follow the steps in SKILL DRILL 6-6.

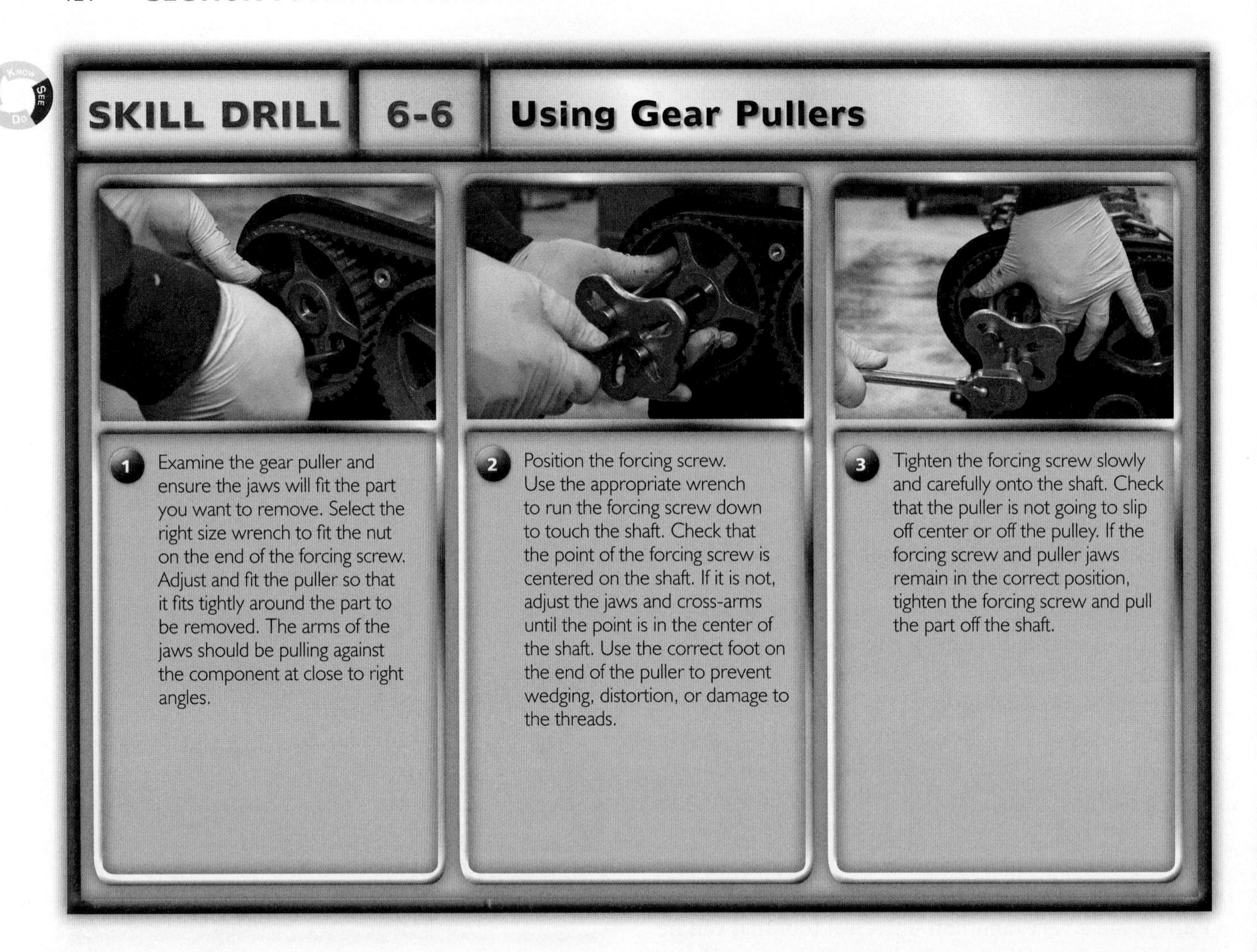

SKILL DRILL 6-6 Using Gear Pullers
1 Examine the gear puller and ensure the jaws will fit the part you want to remove. Select the right size wrench to fit the nut on the end of the forcing screw. Adjust and fit the puller so that it fits tightly around the part to be removed. The arms of the jaws should be pulling against the component at close to right angles.
2 Position the forcing screw. Use the appropriate wrench to run the forcing screw down to touch the shaft. Check that the point of the forcing screw is centered on the shaft. If it is not, adjust the jaws and cross-arms until the point is in the center of the shaft. Use the correct foot on the end of the puller to prevent wedging, distortion, or damage to the threads.
3 Tighten the forcing screw slowly and carefully onto the shaft. Check that the puller is not going to slip off center or off the pulley. If the forcing screw and puller jaws remain in the correct position, tighten the forcing screw and pull the part off the shaft.

Flaring Tools

A **tube flaring tool** is used to flare the end of a tube so it can be connected to another tube or component. One example of this is where the brake line screws into a wheel cylinder. The flared end is compressed between two threaded parts such that it will seal the joint and withstand high pressures. The three most common shapes of flares are the **single flare**, for tubing carrying low pressures like a fuel line; the **double flare**, for higher pressures such as in a brake system; and the ISO flare (sometimes called a bubble flare), which is the metric version used in brake systems **FIGURE 6-35**.

Flaring tools have two parts, a set of bars with holes that match the diameter of the tube end that is being shaped, and a yoke that drives a cone into the mouth of the tube. To make a single flare, the end of the tube is placed level with the surface of the top of the flaring bars. With the clamp screw firmly tightened, the feed screw flares the end of the tube.

Making a double flare is similar, but an extra step is added and more of the tube is exposed to allow for the folding over into a double flare. A double flaring button is placed into the end of the tube, and when it is removed after tightening, the pipe looks like a bubble. Placing the cone and yoke over the bubble allows you to turn the feed screw and force the bubble to fold in on itself, forming the double flare.

An ISO flare uses a flaring tool made specifically for that type of flare. It is similar to the double-flare process but stops with the use of the button. It does not get doubled back on itself. It should resemble a bubble shape when you are finished.

A **tubing cutter** is more convenient and neater than a saw when cutting pipes and metal tubing. The sharpened wheel does the cutting. As the tool turns around the pipe, the screw increases the pressure, driving the wheel deeper and deeper through the pipe until it finally cuts through. There is a larger version that is used for cutting exhaust pipes.

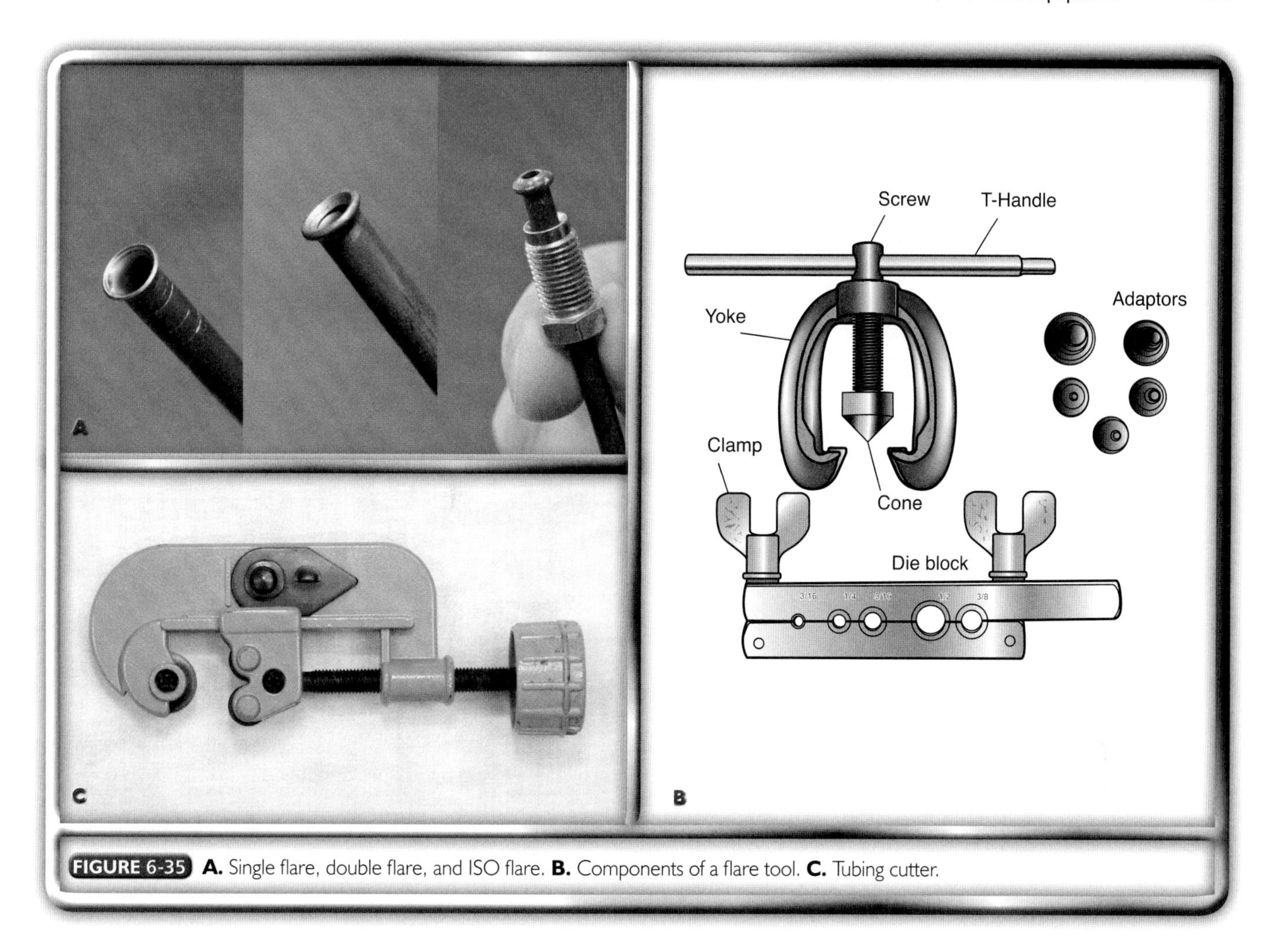
Screw
T-Handle
Yoke
Adaptors
Clamp
Cone
Die block
A
B
C

FIGURE 6-35 **A.** Single flare, double flare, and ISO flare. **B.** Components of a flare tool. **C.** Tubing cutter.

Safety

A flaring tool is used to produce a pressure seal for sealing brake lines and fuel system tubing. Make sure you test the flared joint for leaks before completing the repair; otherwise the brakes could fail or the fuel could catch on fire.

Using Flaring Tools

To make a successful flare, it is important to have the correct amount of tube protruding through the tool before clamping. Otherwise, too much of the end will fold over too far and leave too small of a hole for fluid to pass through. Too little and there won't be enough tube to fold over properly and the joint won't have full surface contact. If you are making a double flare or ISO flare, make sure you use the correctly sized button for the tubing size. The button is also used to measure the amount of tube required to protrude from the tool prior to forming it. To prevent the tool from slipping on the tube and ruining the flare, make sure the tool is sufficiently tight around the tube before starting to create the flare.

Safety

Always wear eye protection when using a flaring tool. Make sure the tool is clean and in good condition and is suitable for the type of material you are going to flare.

To use a flaring tool to make a flare in a piece of tubing, follow the steps in SKILL DRILL 6-7.

Riveting Tools

There are many applications for blind rivets, and various rivet types and tools may be used to do the riveting. **Pop rivet guns** are convenient for occasional riveting of light materials FIGURE 6-36. A typical pop or **blind rivet** has a body, which will form the **finished rivet**, and a mandrel, which is discarded when the riveting is completed FIGURE 6-37. It is called a blind rivet because there is no

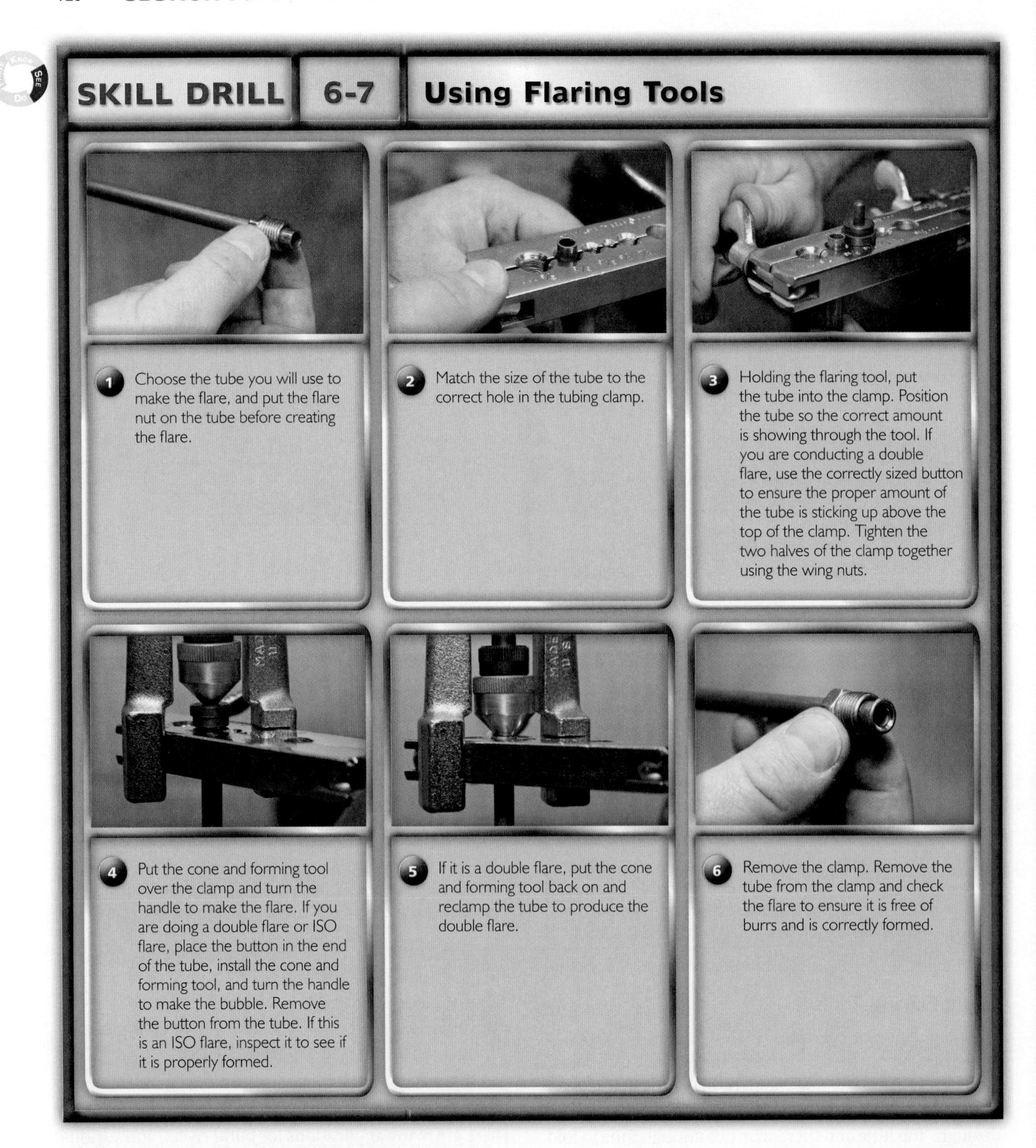
SKILL DRILL 6-7 Using Flaring Tools

1 Choose the tube you will use to make the flare, and put the flare nut on the tube before creating the flare.

2 Match the size of the tube to the correct hole in the tubing clamp.

3 Holding the flaring tool, put the tube into the clamp. Position the tube so the correct amount is showing through the tool. If you are conducting a double flare, use the correctly sized button to ensure the proper amount of the tube is sticking up above the top of the clamp. Tighten the two halves of the clamp together using the wing nuts.

4 Put the cone and forming tool over the clamp and turn the handle to make the flare. If you are doing a double flare or ISO flare, place the button in the end of the tube, install the cone and forming tool, and turn the handle to make the bubble. Remove the button from the tube. If this is an ISO flare, inspect it to see if it is properly formed.

5 If it is a double flare, put the cone and forming tool back on and reclamp the tube to produce the double flare.

6 Remove the clamp. Remove the tube from the clamp and check the flare to ensure it is free of burrs and is correctly formed.

need to see or reach the other side of the hole in which the rivet goes to do the work. In some types, the rivet is plugged shut so that it is waterproof or pressure-proof.

The rivet is inserted into the riveting tool, which, when squeezed, pulls the end of the **mandrel** back through the body of the rivet. Because the **mandrel head** is bigger than the hole through the body, it swells out as it comes through the body. Finally, the mandrel head will snap off under the pressure and fall out, leaving the rivet body gripping the two sheets of material together.

FIGURE 6-36 Pop rivet guns.

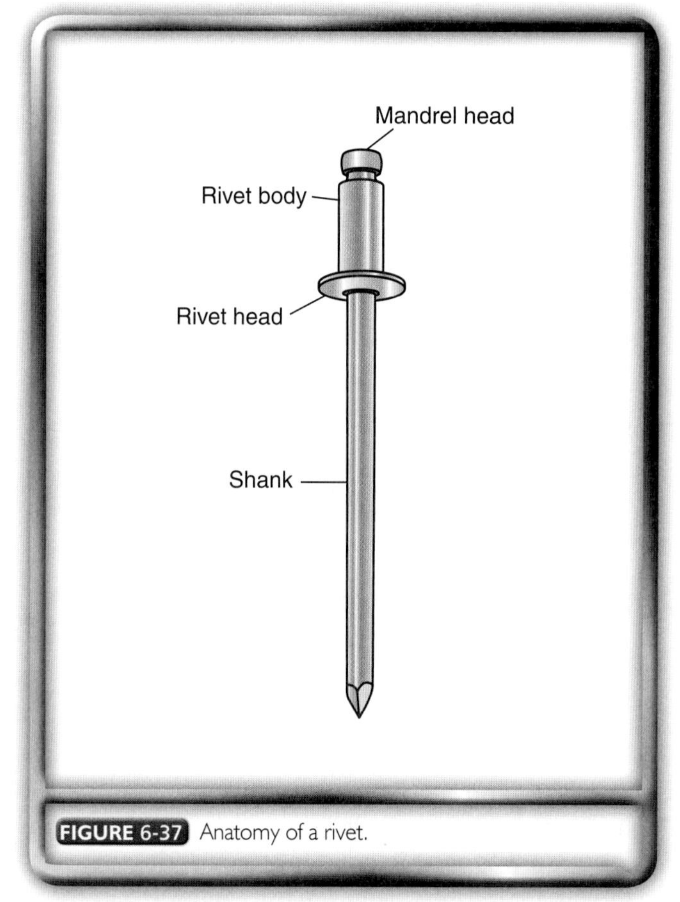
Mandrel head
Rivet body
Rivet head
Shank

FIGURE 6-37 Anatomy of a rivet.

Safety

When compressing the rivet handles, be careful not to place your fingers in the mechanism.

Using Riveting Tools

Rivet tools are used to join two pieces of metal together—for example, when sheet metal needs to be attached to a frame. To perform a riveting operation, you will need a rivet gun, rivets, a drill, the properly sized drill bit, and the materials to be riveted.

Rivets come in various diameters and lengths for different sizes of jobs and are made of various types of metals to suit the job at hand. When selecting rivets to suit the job, consider the diameter, length, and rivet material. Wider diameter rivets should be used for jobs that require more strength. The rivet length should be sufficient to protrude past the thickness of the materials being riveted by about 1.6 times the diameter of the rivet stem. Always select rivets that are made from the same material as that being riveted. For example, stainless steel rivets should be used for riveting stainless steel, and aluminum rivets should be used to rivet aluminum.

Pilot holes will need to be drilled through the metal to be riveted. Ensure that the hole is just large enough for the rivet to comfortably pass through it, but do not make it too large. If the hole is too large, the rivet will be loose and will not hold the materials securely together. When drilling holes for rivets, provide clearance from the material's edge to ensure that the rivets do not break through the edge of the materials being riveted. A good rule of thumb is to allow at least twice the diameter of the rivet stem as clearance from any edge.

The rivet tool is capable of riveting various sizes of rivets and has a number of nosepiece sizes to work with different sizes of rivets. Make sure you select the correct nosepiece size for the rivet you are using.

To use a riveting tool to rivet two pieces of material together, follow the steps in SKILL DRILL 6-8.

TECHNICIAN TIP

A rivet is a one-time use fastener. Unlike a nut and bolt, which can normally be disassembled and reused, a rivet cannot. The metal shell that makes up a pop rivet is crushed into place so that it holds the parts firmly together. If it ever needs to be removed, it must be drilled out.

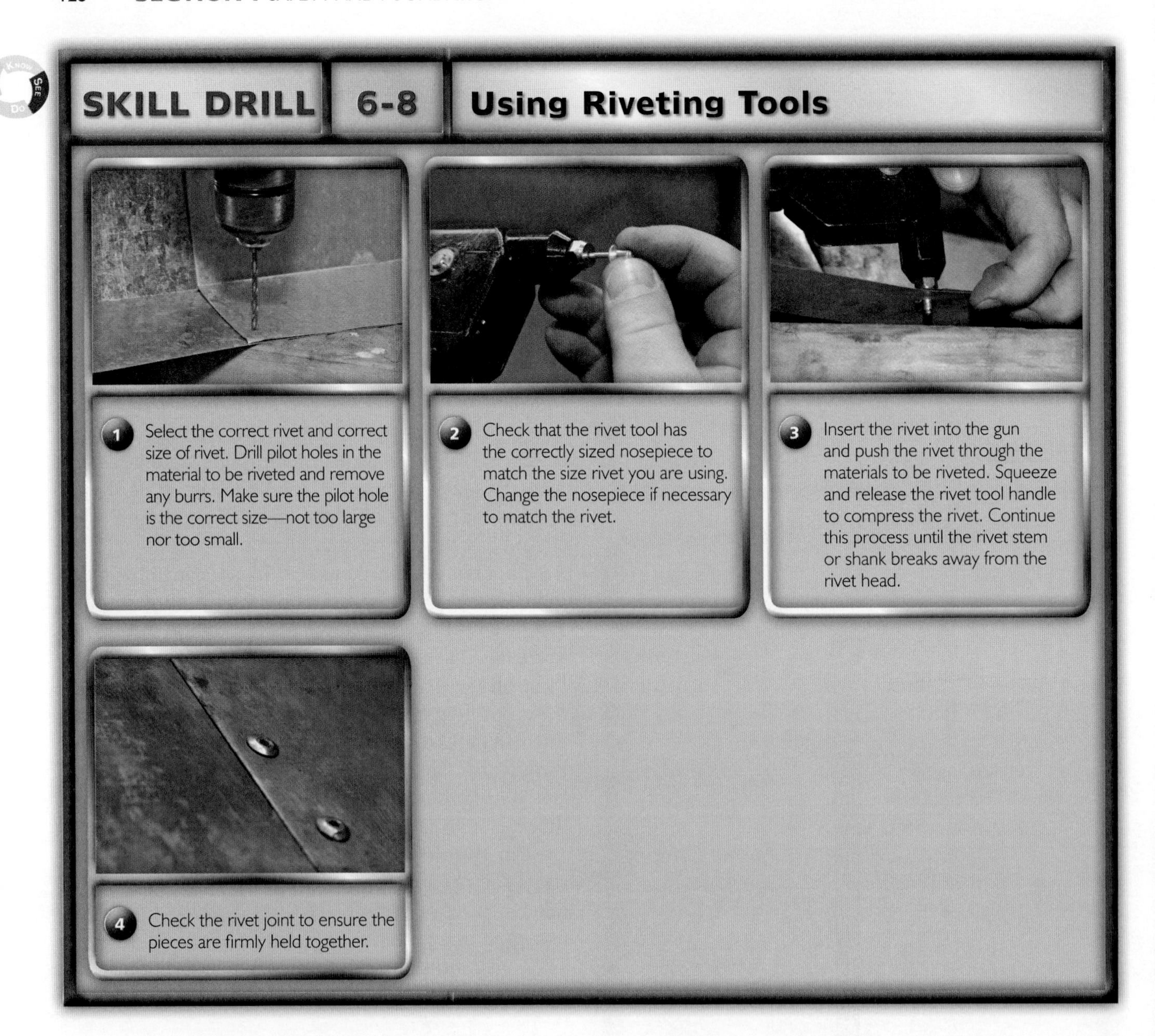
SKILL DRILL 6-8 Using Riveting Tools
1 Select the correct rivet and correct size of rivet. Drill pilot holes in the material to be riveted and remove any burrs. Make sure the pilot hole is the correct size—not too large nor too small.
2 Check that the rivet tool has the correctly sized nosepiece to match the size rivet you are using. Change the nosepiece if necessary to match the rivet.
3 Insert the rivet into the gun and push the rivet through the materials to be riveted. Squeeze and release the rivet tool handle to compress the rivet. Continue this process until the rivet stem or shank breaks away from the rivet head.
4 Check the rivet joint to ensure the pieces are firmly held together.

Soldering Tools

Solder is a mixture of metals with low melting points and is used to join metals together. Tin/lead solder has been used for soldering wires and other metals together for decades. Tin/lead solder for automotive applications consists of approximately 60% tin and 40% lead, and melts at approximately 370°F (188°C). With the environmental hazards of lead becoming an issue over the past 30 years, lead-free solder was introduced in the past decade. Lead-free solder is made up of tin and copper, or of tin, copper, and silver, and usually has a melting point about 20–30°F higher than tin/lead solder. Because solder is a relatively soft compound, it is not used to make joints in situations where high stresses are involved.

In automotive applications, solder generally comes in the form of a wire. It can be solid, requiring an external **flux** cleaning agent of **rosin** if soldering electrical connections or acid if soldering non-electrical connections. The solder can also be hollow, with the rosin or acid in the core. In this case, it would be referred to as rosin-core solder or acid-core solder. Make sure you use rosin with electrical connections and acid with all other connections.

The process of soldering involves heating the metals (wires) hot enough so that the solder melts and fills the spaces between the metals. When the solder cools, the solder holds the parts together and transmits electricity, if used in electrical circuits. The temperature of the soldering operation is critical. If it is not hot enough, the solder does not flow very well and does not make good contact

Safety

- Always wear eye and hand protection when soldering.
- Always wipe excess solder from the iron; never flick the iron to remove excess solder.
- Make sure the tool is clean and in good condition and is suitable for the type of material you are going to solder.
- Check electrical leads and plugs for damage prior to use.

with the metal surfaces and tends to glob up. This makes for a weak joint and poor electrical conductivity. If it is too hot, the solder tends to run off the joint and overheat the components being soldered. In the case of electronic components, overheating can make them inoperative. Only heat the components enough to melt the solder and cause it to flow.

The heat is provided by a **soldering iron** or gun. The heat in soldering irons is usually generated from electricity or gas. A typical soldering iron has a handle that is thermally insulated. The soldering tip is heated and the heat is transferred by metal-to-metal contact from the tip into the metal to be soldered.

Basic soldering irons are heated manually by a gas flame while more sophisticated soldering irons are electrically operated and have thermal tips that are controlled by thermostats to maintain more accurate tip temperatures. Soldering irons can either have fixed tip sizes or tips can be interchanged with different sizes for different sizes of jobs.

Using Soldering Tools

Apply flux to the joint if **cored solder** is not used. Always remove any excess flux when finished. Ensure that the joint is held steady during and after the solder is applied. A dull solder surface indicates a cold and high-resistance joint and should be resoldered. Select the correct tip size to heat the joint and solder within a few seconds. Overheating a joint or using too small of a tip will produce a poor solder joint.

To use a soldering iron to solder two pieces of wire or metal together, follow the steps in SKILL DRILL 6-9.

Precision Measuring Tools

Technicians are required to perform a variety of measurements while carrying out their job. This requires knowledge of what tools are available and how to use them. Measuring tools can generally be classified according to what type of measurements they can make FIGURE 6-38. A measuring tape is useful for measuring longer distances and is accurate to a millimeter or fraction of an inch. A steel rule is capable of accurate measurements on shorter lengths, down to a millimeter or a fraction of an inch. Precision measuring tools are accurate to much smaller dimensions, such as a micrometer, which in some cases can accurately measure down to $^1/_{10,000}$ of an inch (0.0001″), or $^1/_{1000}$ of a millimeter (0.001 mm).

Measuring Tapes

Measuring tapes are a flexible type of ruler and are a common measuring tool. The most common type found in shops is a thin metal strip about 0.5″ to 1″ (13 to

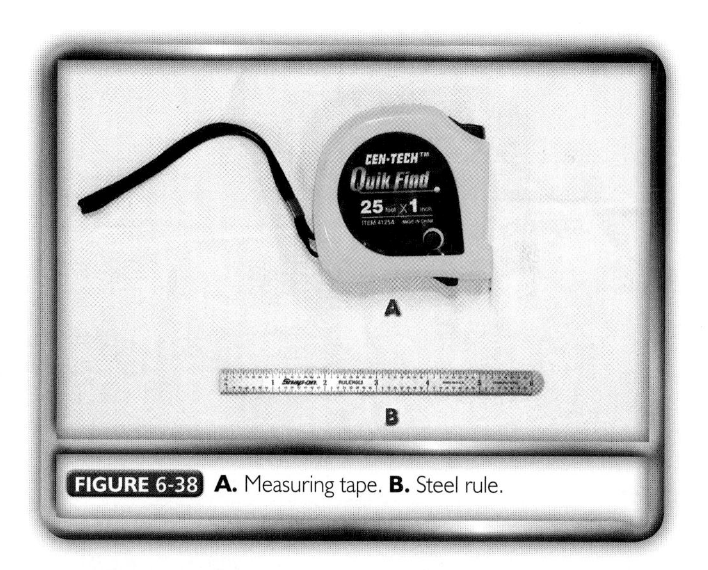
CEN-TECH™
Quik Find
25 x 1
A
B

FIGURE 6-38 **A.** Measuring tape. **B.** Steel rule.

TECHNICIAN TIP

The United States customary system (USCS), also called the standard system, and the metric system are two sets of standards for quantifying weights and measurements. Each system has defined units. For example, the standard system uses inches, feet, and yards while the metric system uses millimeters, centimeters, and meters. Conversions can be undertaken from one system to the other. For example, 1 inch is equal to 25.4 millimeters, while 1 foot is equal to 304.8 millimeters.

Tools that make use of a measuring system, such as wrenches, sockets, drill bits, micrometers, rulers, and many others, come in both standard and metric measurements. To work on modern vehicles, an understanding of both systems and their conversion is required. Conversion tables can be used to convert from one system to the other. The more you work with both systems, the easier it will be to understand how they relate to each other.

SKILL DRILL 6-9 Using Soldering Tools

1. Prepare the materials to be soldered. Strip wires or clean metal parts before soldering.
2. Prepare the soldering iron by ensuring the correctly sized tip is fitted and is clean. Tin the soldering iron tip by melting some solder to it and wiping any excess from the tip.
3. Apply flux to the wires or metal to be soldered. This may not be necessary if you are using cored solder.
4. Apply the hot solder iron tip to heat the joint, then apply solder to the joint (not the iron). If the solder does not melt within a few seconds, remove it and allow the joint to heat further before reapplying.
5. Once the solder has been applied, ensure the joint does not move until the solder has cooled sufficiently to set. Once cooled, inspect the joint; it should be shiny and firm.
6. Clean any excess flux from the joint.

25 mm) wide that is rolled up inside a housing with a spring return mechanism. Measuring tapes can be of various lengths, with 16' or 25' (5 or 8 m) being very common. The measuring tape is pulled from the housing to measure items, and a spring return winds it back into the housing. The housing will usually have a built-in locking mechanism to hold the extended measuring tape against the spring return mechanism.

> **TECHNICIAN TIP**
>
> Micrometers are precision measuring instruments and must be handled and stored with care. They should always be stored with a gap between the spindle and anvil so metal expansion does not interfere with their calibration.

Steel Rulers

As the name suggests, a **steel rule** is a ruler that is made from steel. Steel rules commonly come in 12″, 24″, and 36″ lengths. They are used like any ruler to measure and mark out items. They are a very strong ruler, have precise markings, and resist damage. When using a steel rule, you can rest it on its edge so the markings are closer to the material being measured, which helps to mark the work precisely. Always protect the steel rule from damage by storing it carefully; a damaged ruler will not give an accurate measurement. Never take measurements from the very end of a damaged steel rule, as damaged ends may affect the accuracy of your measurements.

Outside, Inside, and Depth Micrometers

Micrometers are precise measuring tools designed to measure small distances and are available in both inch and millimeter (mm) calibrations. Typically they can measure down to a resolution of $^1\!/_{1000}$ of an inch (0.001″) for a standard micrometer or $^1\!/_{100}$ of a millimeter (0.01 mm) for a metric micrometer. Vernier micrometers equipped with the addition of a vernier scale can measure down to $^1\!/_{10,000}$ of an inch (0.0001″) or $^1\!/_{1000}$ of a millimeter (0.001 mm).

The most common types of micrometers are the outside, inside, and depth micrometers **FIGURE 6-39**. As the name suggests, an **outside micrometer** measures the outside dimensions of an item. For example, it could measure the diameter of a valve stem. The **inside micrometer** measures inside dimensions. For example, the inside micrometer could measure an engine cylinder bore. **Depth micrometers** measure the depth of an item such as how far a piston is below the surface of the block.

The most common micrometer is an outside micrometer. The horseshoe-shaped part is the frame. It is built to make sure the micrometer holds its shape. Some frames have plastic finger pads so that body heat is not transferred to the metal frame as easily, as heat can cause the metal to expand slightly and affect the reading. On one end of the frame is the anvil, which contacts one side of the part being measured. The other contact point is the spindle. The micrometer measures the distance between the anvil and spindle, so that is where the part being measured fits.

The measurement is read on the sleeve/barrel and thimble. The sleeve/barrel is stationary and has the linear markings on it. The thimble fits over the sleeve and has the graduated marking on it. The thimble is connected directly to the spindle, and both turn as a unit. Since the spindle and sleeve/barrel have matching threads, the thimble rotates the spindle inside of the sleeve/barrel and the thread moves the spindle inward and outward. The thimble usually incorporates either a ratchet or a clutch mechanism, which prevents overtightening of the micrometer thimble when taking a reading. A lock nut, lock ring, or lock screw is used on most micrometers and locks the thimble in place while you read the micrometer.

Standard micrometers use a specific thread of 40 tpi on the spindle and sleeve. This means that the thimble will rotate exactly 40 turns in 1 inch. Every complete rotation moves the spindle a 40th of an inch, or 0.025″ ($1 \div 40 = 0.025$). In four rotations, the spindle moves 0.100″ ($0.025 \times 4 = 0.100$). The linear markings on the sleeve show each of the 0.100″ marks between 0 and 1 inch as well as each of the 0.025″ marks. Since the thimble has graduated marks from 0 to 24 (each mark representing 0.001″), every complete turn of the thimble will uncover another one of the 0.025″ marks on the sleeve. If the thimble

> **TECHNICIAN TIP**
>
> If the end of a rule is damaged, you may be able to measure from the 1" mark and subtract an inch from the measurement.

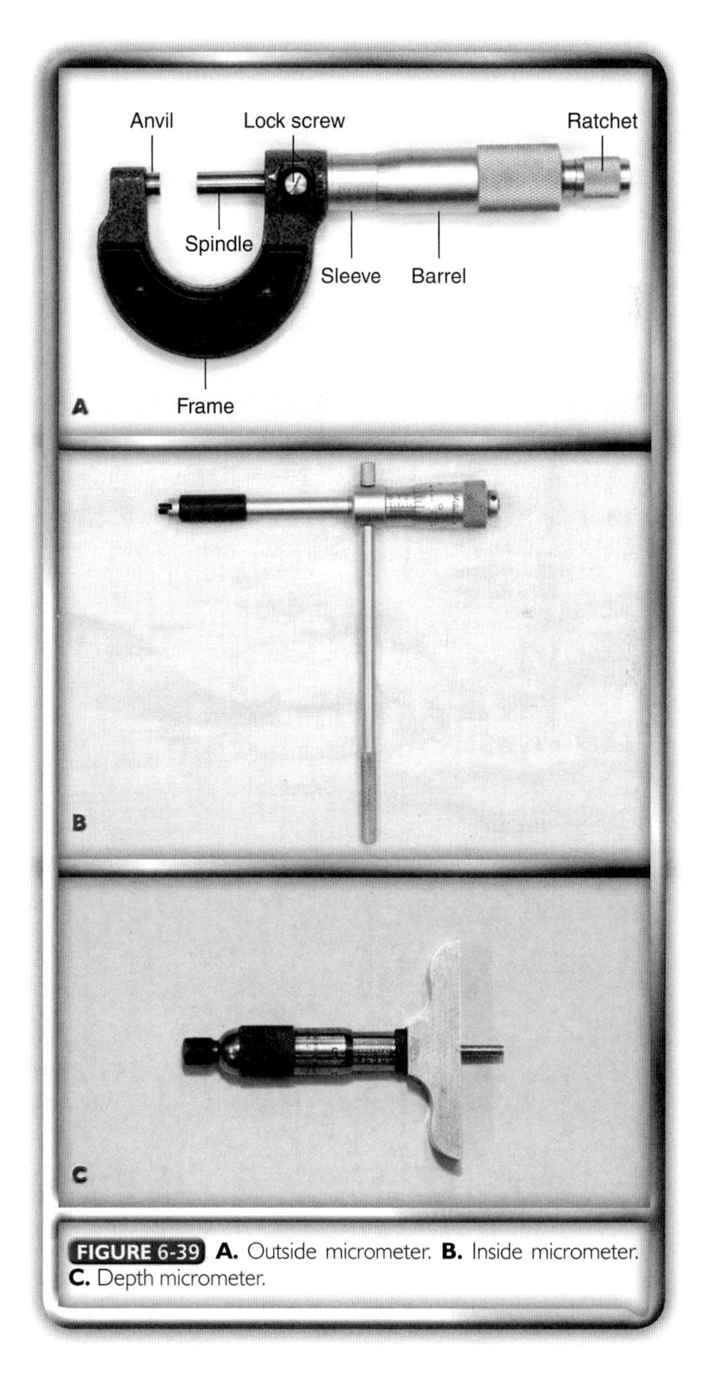
Anvil
Lock screw
Ratchet
Spindle
Sleeve
Barrel
Frame
A
B
C

FIGURE 6-39 **A.** Outside micrometer. **B.** Inside micrometer. **C.** Depth micrometer.

stops short of any complete turn, it will indicate the exact number of 0.001″ marks past the zero line on the sleeve.

To read a standard micrometer, perform the following steps **FIGURE 6-40**:

1. Verify that the micrometer is properly calibrated.
2. Verify what size of micrometer you are using. If it is a 0–1″ micrometer, start with 0.000. If it is a 1–2″ micrometer, start with 1.000″. A 2–3″ micrometer would start with 2.000″, and so on. (To give an example, let's say it is 2.000″.)
3. Read how many 0.100″ marks the thimble has uncovered. (example: 0.300″)
4. Read how many 0.025″ marks the thimble has uncovered past the 0.100″ mark in step 3. (example: 2 × 0.025 = 0.050″)
5. Read the number on the thimble that lines up with the zero line on the sleeve. (example: 13 × 0.001 = 0.013″)
6. Lastly, total all of the individual readings. (example: 2.000 + 0.300 + 0.050 + 0.013 = 2.363″)

A metric micrometer uses the same components as the standard micrometer. However, it uses a different thread pitch on the spindle and sleeve. It uses a 0.5-mm thread pitch (2.0 threads per millimeter) and opens up approximately 25 mm. Each rotation of the thimble moves the spindle 0.5 mm, and it therefore takes 50 rotations of the thimble to move the full 25-mm distance. The sleeve/barrel is labeled with individual millimeter marks and half-millimeter marks from the starting millimeter to the ending millimeter, 25 mm away. The thimble has graduated marks from 0 to 49.

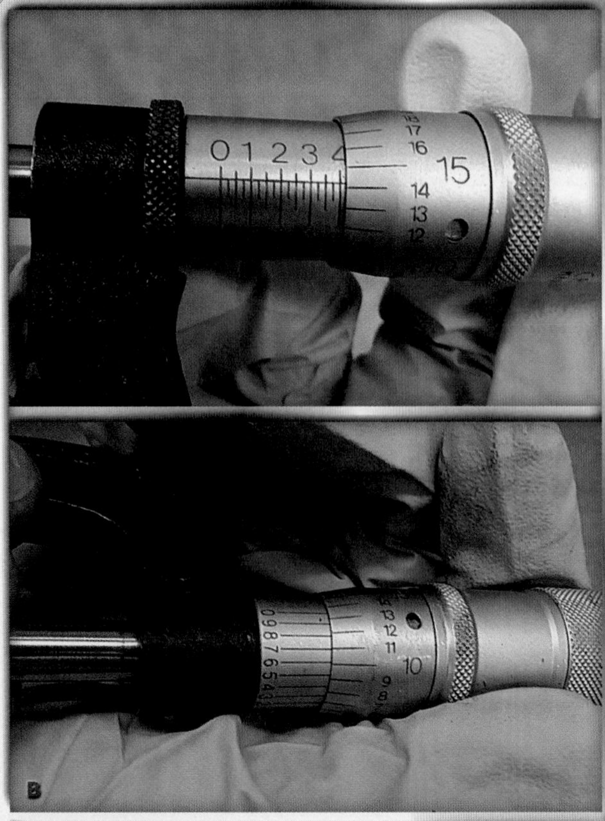

Reading a metric micrometer involves the following steps:

1. Read the number of full millimeters the thimble has passed. (To give an example, let's say it is 23.00 mm.)
2. Check to see if it passed the 0.5-mm mark. (example: 0.50 mm)
3. Check to see which mark on the thimble lines up with or is just passed. (example: 37 × 0.01 mm = 0.37 mm)
4. Total all of the numbers (example: 23.00 mm + 0.50 mm + 0.37 mm = 23.87 mm)

If the micrometer is equipped with a vernier gauge, meaning it can read down to $\frac{1}{10,000}$ of an inch (0.0001″) or $\frac{1}{1000}$ of a millimeter (0.001 mm), you need to complete one more step. Identify which of the vernier lines is closest to one of the lines on the thimble. Sometimes it is hard to determine which is the closest, so decide which three are the closest and then use the center line. At the frame side of the sleeve will be a number that corresponds to the vernier line. It will be numbered 1-0. Take the vernier number and add it to the end of your reading. For example: 2.363 + 0.0007 = 2.3637″, and 23.77 + 0.007 = 23.777 mm.

For inside measurements, the inside micrometer works on the same principles as the outside micrometer and so does the depth micrometer. The only difference is that the scale on the sleeve of the depth micrometer is backward, so be careful when reading it.

FIGURE 6-40 **A.** Read how many 0.100" marks the thimble has uncovered. **B.** Read the number on the thimble that lines up with the zero line on the sleeve.

TECHNICIAN TIP

All micrometers need to be checked for calibration (also called "zeroing") before each use. A 0–1" or 0–25 mm outside micrometer can be lightly closed all of the way. If the anvil and spindle are clean, the micrometer should read 0.000, indicating the micrometer is calibrated correctly. If the micrometer is bigger than 1" or 25 mm, then a "standard" is used to verify the calibration. A standard is a hardened machined rod of a precise length, such as 2" or 50 mm. When inserted in the same-sized micrometer, the reading should be exactly the same as listed on the standard. If a micrometer is not properly calibrated, it should not be used until it is recalibrated. See the tool's instruction manual for the calibration procedure.

Using Micrometers

To maintain accuracy of measurements, it is important that both the micrometer and the items to be measured are clean and free of any dirt or debris. Also make sure the micrometer is zeroed before taking any measurements. Never overtighten a micrometer or store it with its measuring surfaces touching, as this may damage the tool and affect its accuracy. When measuring, make sure the item can pass through the micrometer surfaces snugly and squarely. This is best accomplished by using the ratchet to tighten the micrometer. Always take the measurement a number of times and compare results to ensure you have measured accurately.

To correctly measure using an outside micrometer, follow the steps in **SKILL DRILL 6-10**.

Vernier Calipers

Vernier calipers are a precision instrument used for measuring outside dimensions, inside dimensions, and depth measurements, all in one tool. They have a graduated bar with markings like a ruler. On the bar, a sliding sleeve with jaws is mounted for taking inside or outside measurements. Measurements on older versions of vernier calipers are taken by reading the graduated bar scales, while fractional measurements are read by comparing the scales between the sliding sleeve and the graduated bar. Technicians will often use vernier calipers to measure length and diameters of bolts and pins or the depth of blind holes in housings.

Newer versions of vernier calipers have dial and digital scales. The dial vernier has the main scale on the

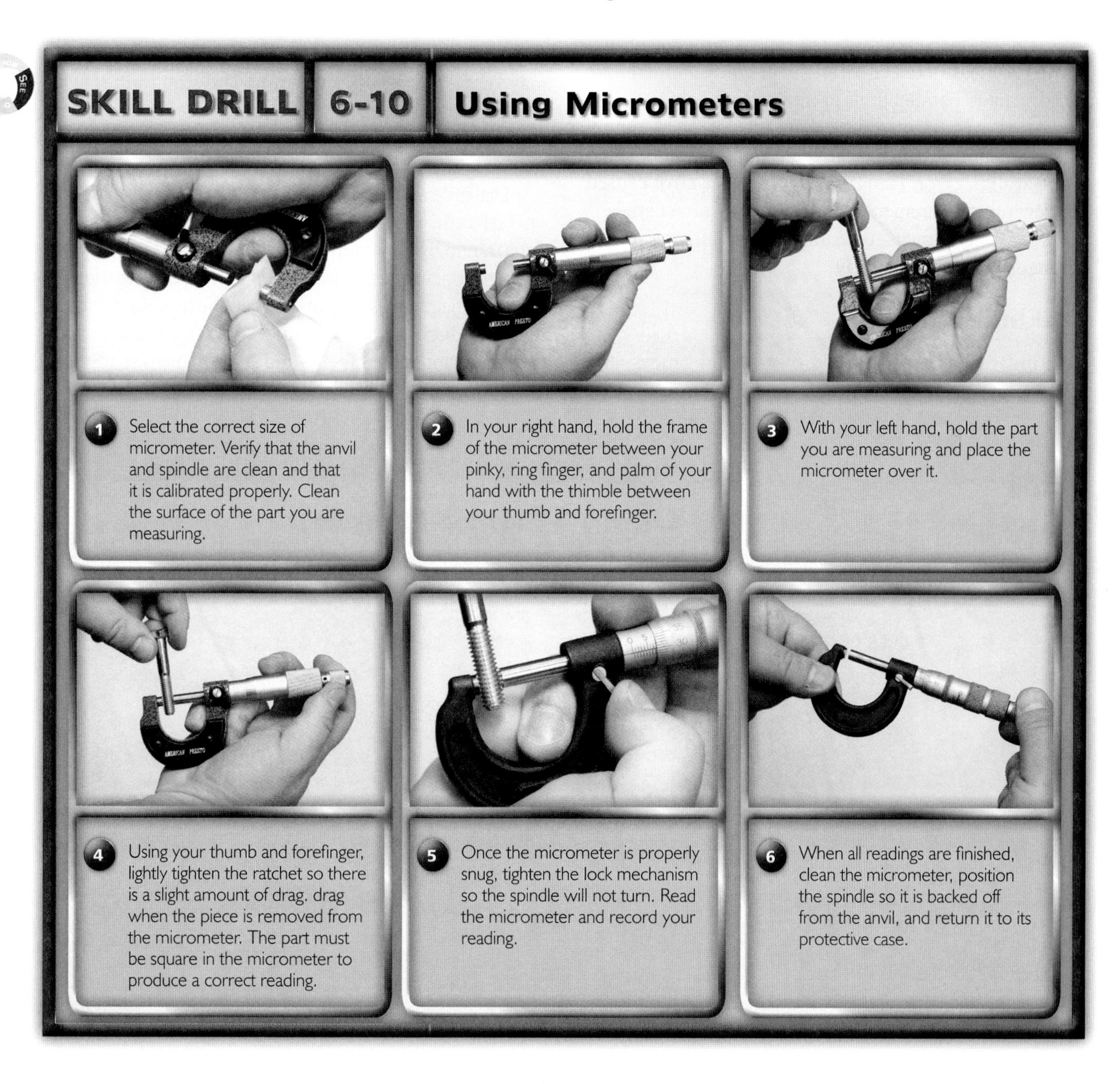
SKILL DRILL 6-10 Using Micrometers
1 Select the correct size of micrometer. Verify that the anvil and spindle are clean and that it is calibrated properly. Clean the surface of the part you are measuring.
2 In your right hand, hold the frame of the micrometer between your pinky, ring finger, and palm of your hand with the thimble between your thumb and forefinger.
3 With your left hand, hold the part you are measuring and place the micrometer over it.
4 Using your thumb and forefinger, lightly tighten the ratchet so there is a slight amount of drag. drag when the piece is removed from the micrometer. The part must be square in the micrometer to produce a correct reading.
5 Once the micrometer is properly snug, tighten the lock mechanism so the spindle will not turn. Read the micrometer and record your reading.
6 When all readings are finished, clean the micrometer, position the spindle so it is backed off from the anvil, and return it to its protective case.

graduated bar, while fractional measurements are taken from a dial with a rotating needle. These tend to be easier to read than the older versions. More recently, digital scales on vernier calipers have become commonplace. The principle of their use is the same as any vernier caliper; however, they have a digital scale that reads the measurement directly.

Using Vernier Calipers

Always store vernier calipers in a storage box to protect them and ensure the measuring surfaces are kept clean for accurate measurement. If making an internal or external measurement, make sure the caliper is at right angles to the surfaces to be measured. You should always repeat the measurement a number of times and compare results to ensure you have measured accurately. Note that internal and external readings are normally made with the vernier caliper positioned at 90 degrees to the face of the component to be measured. Length and depth measurements are usually made parallel to or in line with the object being measured. Always read the dial or face of a non-digital caliper straight on. A view from the side can give a considerable **parallax error**. Parallax error is a visual error caused by viewing measurement markers at an incorrect angle.

To correctly measure using vernier calipers, follow the steps in SKILL DRILL 6-11.

Dial Indicators

Dial indicators can also be known as dial gauges, and as the name suggests, they have a dial and needle where measurements are read. They have a measuring plunger with a pointed contact end that is spring-loaded and connected via the housing to the dial needle. The dial accurately measures movement of its plunger in and out as it rests against an object. For example, they can be used to measure the trueness of a rotating disc brake rotor.

A dial indicator can also measure how round something is. A **crankshaft** can be rotated in a set of **V blocks**. If the crankshaft is bent, it will show as movement on the dial indicator as the crankshaft is rotated. The dial indicator senses slight movement at its tip and magnifies it into a measurable swing on the dial.

Dial indicators normally have either one or two indicator needles. The large needle indicates the fine reading of thousandths of an inch. If it has a second needle, it will be smaller and indicates the coarse reading of tenths of an inch. The large needle is able to move numerous times around the outer scale. One full turn may represent 0.100″ or 1 mm. The small inner scale indicates how many times the outer needle has moved around its scale. In this way, the dial indicator is able to read movement of up to 1″ or 2 cm.

Dial indicators can measure with an accuracy of 0.001″ or 0.01 mm. The type of dial indicator you use will be determined by the amount of movement you expect from the component you are measuring. The indicator must be set up so that there is no gap between the dial indicator and the component to be measured. Most dial indicator sets contain various attachments and support arms so they can be configured specifically for the measuring task.

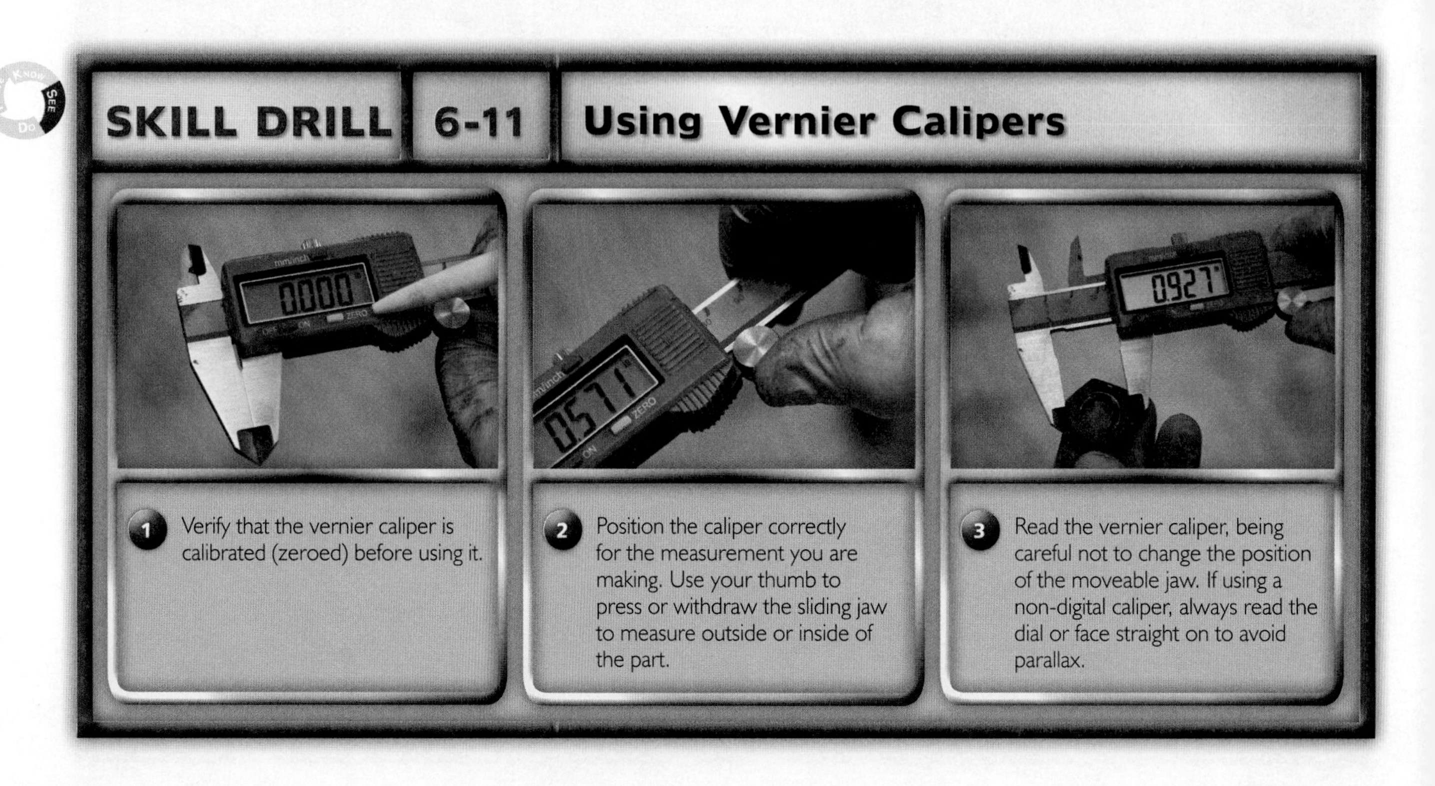
KNOW
SEE
DO
PROVE
0.000
ZERO
0.571
ZERO
0.927

SKILL DRILL 6-11 Using Vernier Calipers

1. Verify that the vernier caliper is calibrated (zeroed) before using it.
2. Position the caliper correctly for the measurement you are making. Use your thumb to press or withdraw the sliding jaw to measure outside or inside of the part.
3. Read the vernier caliper, being careful not to change the position of the moveable jaw. If using a non-digital caliper, always read the dial or face straight on to avoid parallax.

Using Dial Indicators

Dial indicators are used in many types of service jobs. They are particularly useful in determining runout on rotating shafts and surfaces. Runout is the side-to-side variation of movement when a component is turned.

When attaching a dial indicator, keep support arms as short as possible. Make sure all attachments are tightened to prevent unnecessary movement between the indicator and the component. Make sure the dial indicator plunger is positioned at 90 degrees to the face of the component to be measured. Always read the dial face straight on, as a view from the side can give a considerable parallax error. The outer face of the dial indicator is designed so it can be rotated so that the zero mark can be positioned directly over the pointer. This is how a dial indicator is zeroed.

To correctly measure using a dial indicator, follow the steps in SKILL DRILL 6-12.

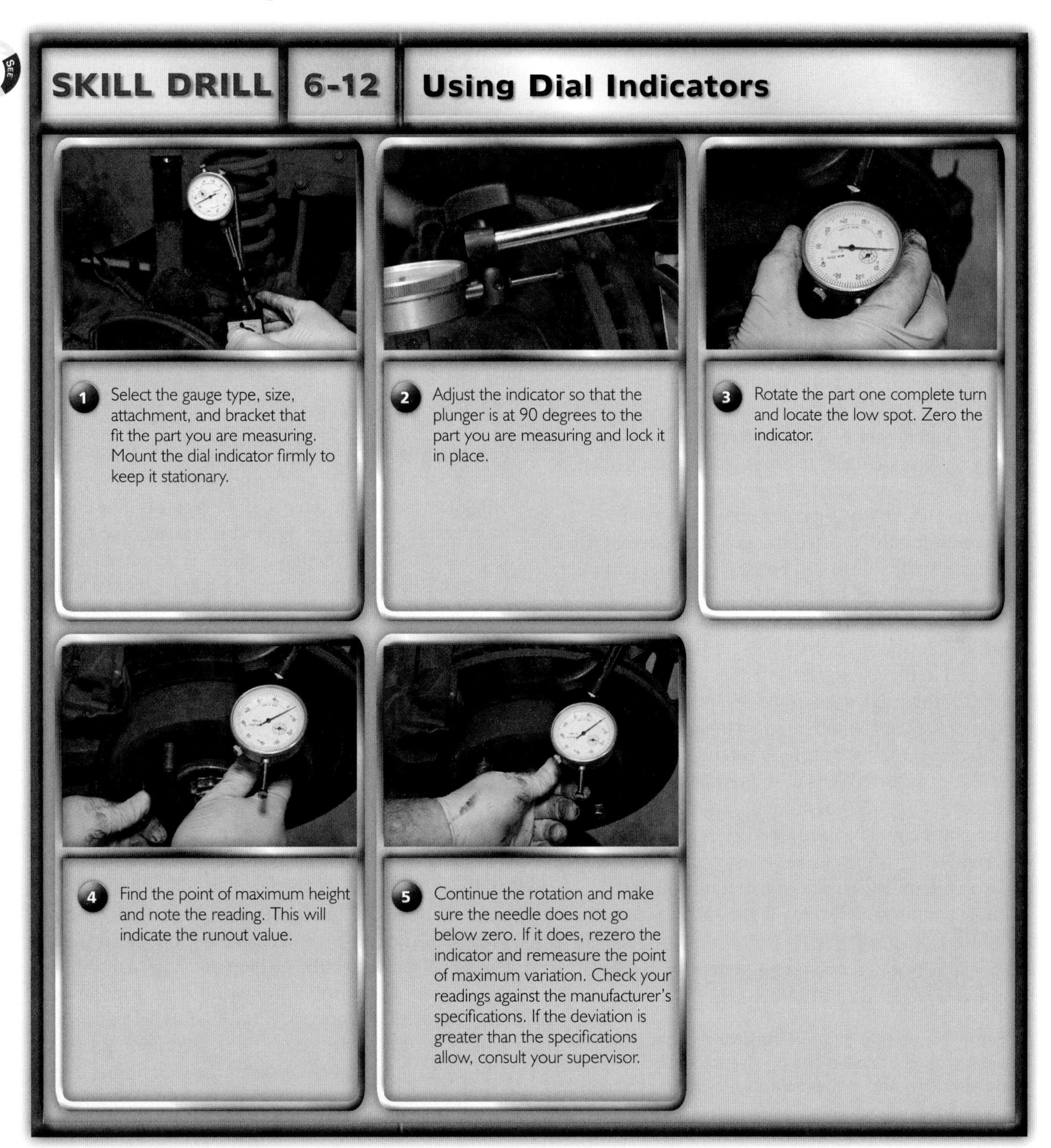
SKILL DRILL 6-12 Using Dial Indicators
1 Select the gauge type, size, attachment, and bracket that fit the part you are measuring. Mount the dial indicator firmly to keep it stationary.
2 Adjust the indicator so that the plunger is at 90 degrees to the part you are measuring and lock it in place.
3 Rotate the part one complete turn and locate the low spot. Zero the indicator.
4 Find the point of maximum height and note the reading. This will indicate the runout value.
5 Continue the rotation and make sure the needle does not go below zero. If it does, rezero the indicator and remeasure the point of maximum variation. Check your readings against the manufacturer's specifications. If the deviation is greater than the specifications allow, consult your supervisor.

Straight Edges

Straight edges are usually made from hardened steel and are machined so that the edge is perfectly straight. A straight edge is used to check the flatness of a surface. It is placed on its edge against the surface to be checked. The gap between the straight edge and the surface can be measured by using feeler gauges. Sometimes the gap can be seen easily if light is shone from behind the surface being checked. Straight edges are often used to measure the amount of warpage the surface of a cylinder head has.

Feeler Gauges

Feeler gauges (also called feeler blades) are used to measure the width of gaps, such as the clearance between valves and rocker arms. Feeler gauges are flat metal strips of varying thicknesses. The thickness of each feeler gauge is clearly marked on each one. They are sized from fractions of an inch or fractions of a millimeter. They usually come in sets with different sizes and are available in standard and metric measurements. Some sets contain feeler gauges made of brass. These are used to take measurements between components that are magnetic. If steel gauges were used, the drag caused by the magnetism would mimic the drag of a proper clearance. Brass gauges are not subject to magnetism, so they work well in that situation.

Some feeler gauges come in a bent arrangement to be more easily inserted in cramped spaces. Others come in a stepped version. For example, the end might be 0.010″ thick while the rest of the gauges is 0.012″ thick. This works well for adjusting valve clearance. If the specification is 0.010″, then the 0.010 section can be placed in the gap. If the 0.012 section slides into the gap, then the valve needs to be readjusted. If it stops at the lip of the 0.012″ section, then the gap is correct.

Two or more feeler gauges can be stacked together to make up a desired thickness. For example, to measure a thickness of 0.029 of an inch, a 0.017 and a 0.012 feeler gauge could be used together to make up the size. Alternatively, if you want to measure an unknown gap, you can interchange feeler gauges until you find the one or more that fits snugly into the gap and total their thickness to measure the gap. In conjunction with a straight edge, they can be used to measure surface irregularities in a cylinder head.

Safety

Feeler gauges are strips of hardened metal that have been ground or rolled to a precise thickness. They can be very thin and will cut through skin if not handled correctly.

Using Feeler Gauges

If the feeler gauge feels too loose when measuring a gap, select the next size larger and measure the gap again. Repeat this procedure until the feeler gauge has a slight drag between both parts. If the feeler gauge is too tight, select a smaller size until the feeler gauge fits properly. When measuring a spark plug gap, feeler gauges should not be used because the surfaces are not perfectly parallel, so it is preferable to use wire feeler gauges. Wire feeler gauges use accurately machined pieces of wire instead of metal strips.

To select and use feeler gauge sets, follow the steps in SKILL DRILL 6-13.

Safety

Never use feeler gauges on operating machinery.

Power Tools

Power tools are typically powered by an electricity or compressed air. They can also be powered by burning of propellant, such as in a nail gun, or by a gasoline engine, such as in a portable compressor. A power tool can be stationary, such as a bench grinder, or portable, such as a portable electric drill. There are many different power tools designed to perform specific tasks. Some are corded and have to be plugged in, while others are cordless and have batteries. Power tools make many tasks quicker and easier to perform, and they can save many hours of work when used and maintained correctly.

Drills and Drill Bits

Many components make up a drill set FIGURE 6-41. A portable drill can be corded or cordless. A corded drill has a cord that you have to plug into an electrical supply. The operating voltage of a drill will depend on the country's supply. Corded drills are a good choice when moderate power is needed or if extended drilling is required. Cordless drills use their own internal batteries. When you cannot bring the work to the drill, you can take the drill to the work. But don't expect a cordless drill to be able to drill large holes through hard metal. Although they are very versatile, they are limited to the amount of work they can do by their power rating. The biggest drill bit that will fit into the chuck of these drills

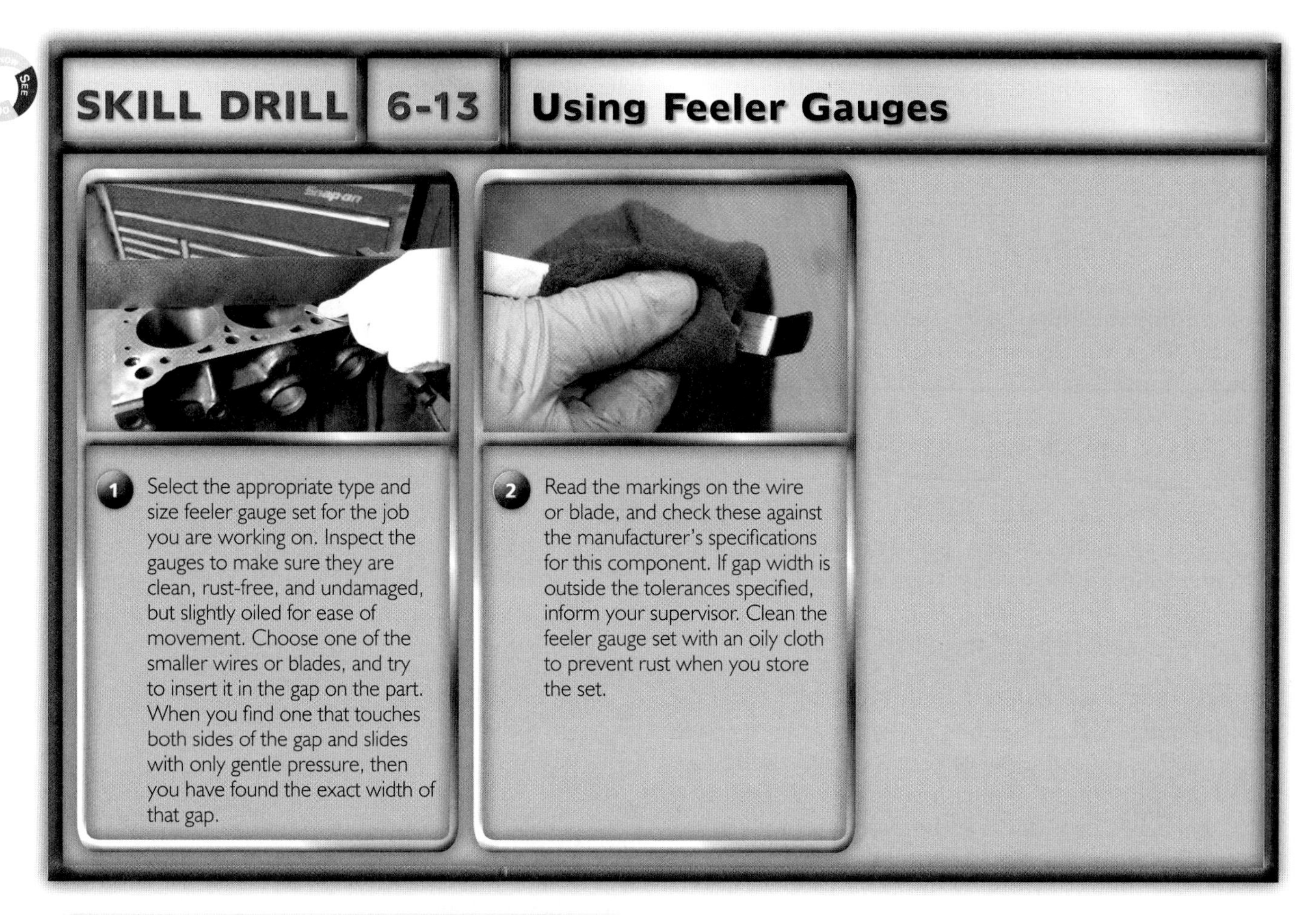

SKILL DRILL 6-13 Using Feeler Gauges

1. Select the appropriate type and size feeler gauge set for the job you are working on. Inspect the gauges to make sure they are clean, rust-free, and undamaged, but slightly oiled for ease of movement. Choose one of the smaller wires or blades, and try to insert it in the gap on the part. When you find one that touches both sides of the gap and slides with only gentle pressure, then you have found the exact width of that gap.

2. Read the markings on the wire or blade, and check these against the manufacturer's specifications for this component. If gap width is outside the tolerances specified, inform your supervisor. Clean the feeler gauge set with an oily cloth to prevent rust when you store the set.

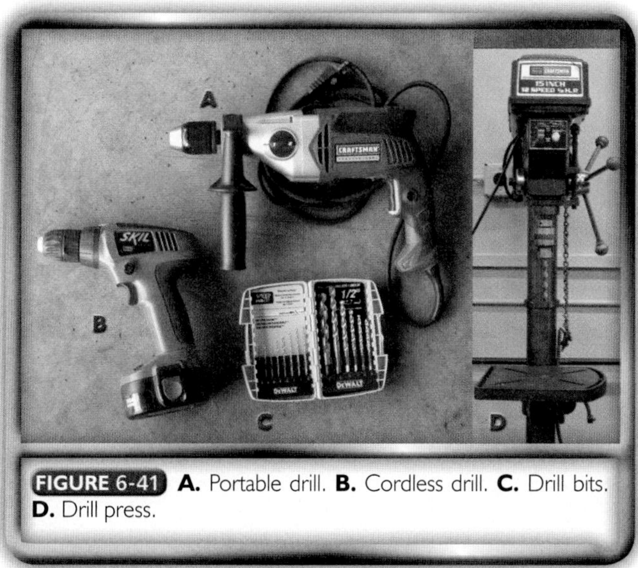
A
B
C
D

FIGURE 6-41 **A.** Portable drill. **B.** Cordless drill. **C.** Drill bits. **D.** Drill press.

is usually marked on the body of the drill or chuck, along with the speeds at which it will turn. Some portable drills have two operating speeds, but most portable drills have a variable speed rating that is determined by how much pressure is placed on the trigger and can be set to any speed within the drill's range.

Drill bits come in many closely spaced sizes and types. The most common is the **twist drill** bit. It has a point with cutting flutes that form a common angle of 118 degrees. Its body, which usually has two spiral grooves, and its shank are gripped in the jaws of the **drill chuck**. A drill chuck is a device for securely gripping drill bits in a drill. The twist drill bit is a good all-purpose bit for drilling metals.

A **drill press** allows for accurate drilling with more control than is offered by a portable drill, which although convenient, can be difficult to guide accurately. A mounted drill can feed the drill bit at a controlled rate, and the worktable on the drill typically has a vice to secure the job at a constant angle to the drill bit. Also, this drill can be set to run at different drilling speeds. Most drill presses have a drill chuck that takes bits up to 0.5″ (13 mm) or more in diameter.

Morse taper is a system for securing drill bits to drills. The Morse taper size changes according to drill size. The shank of the drill bit is tapered and looks like the tang of a file. It fits snugly into the drill spindle, which

> **TECHNICIAN TIP**
>
> Drills are also used to drive other accessories such as rotary files, screwdriver bits, and sockets.

has a similar taper on its inside. The tang on the drill bit is located in the spindle, and it drives the drill. It is a quick way to change drills without constantly adjusting the chuck.

When there is already a hole drilled in sheet metal that needs enlarging, a multi-fluted tapered hole drill will do the job in practically the same time it takes to say the name of this tool. A drilling speed chart is usually supplied with the drill press and should be kept nearby for handy reference. It compares drill sizes and metals to show the proper speed. For example, to drill a 0.375″ (10-mm) hole through a piece of aluminum, the drill speed should be 1800 rpm. Drilling metals is also best performed with the aid of a lubricant. The lubricant helps cool the cutting edges of the drill bit as well as lubricate it. Each metal requires its own type of lubricant, so check a drilling guide for the metal you are working on.

Bench and Angle Grinders

Power grinders come in different ranges of sizes and speeds **FIGURE 6-42**. The size of a power grinder is normally determined by the diameter of the largest grinding wheel or disc that can be fitted to it. Some grinders are fixed to a bench or pedestal and the work is brought to the grinder; others are portable devices that can be taken to the work. Bench or pedestal grinders tend to be powered by electricity, while portable ones can be electric or air powered.

Grinding wheels and discs usually have a maximum safe operating speed printed on them. This maximum speed must never be exceeded or the wheel or disc could disintegrate. Every well-equipped shop has a solidly mounted grinder, either on a pedestal bolted to the shop floor or securely attached to the workbench. Appropriate eye protection must be worn when grinders are being used, and the wheel guards and shields must be correctly and firmly in place.

A **bench grinder (pedestal grinder)** normally has a rating with the size of the grinding wheel it can take. Do not try to attempt to install a grinding wheel larger or smaller than it is rated for. Grinding wheels come in grades from coarse to very fine, depending on the size of the abrasive grains that are bonded together to make the wheel. They also range in hardness, depending on the abrasive used and the material that bonds the particles together. If a particular grinding application is required, a check should be done to find out the most suitable grinding wheel for it.

An **angle grinder** is usually needed when the bench grinder is not appropriate. The angle grinder uses discs rather than wheels. During grinding, the face of the disc is used instead of the edge. An angle grinder can throw sparks many feet, so direct the sparks in a safe direction or set up a guard to catch them. Also use hearing protection whenever grinding, as it is very noisy and can damage your ears.

While not as common in an automotive shop, the **straight grinder** takes conventional grinding wheels, just like the stationery grinders. However, the grinding wheel diameter is limited to about 4.75″ (126 mm). In many cases, the grinder has a long shaft that moves the grinding wheel away from the motor. This makes it handy to get into recessed areas.

Hand-held cut-off wheels can be powered by electricity or air. They use a special thin grinding disk to enable them

Safety

Ask your supervisor to demonstrate the differences between grinding wheels for soft and hard materials and wire brush wheels. As the abrasive wheel wears down, the gap between the wheel and the tool rest will increase. This creates a dangerous situation. As the gap enlarges, the metal you are grinding could get pulled into it and be thrown back out with great force.

A
Milwaukee
B

FIGURE 6-42 **A.** Bench grinder. **B.** Angle grinder.

to cut. They use the edge of the wheel for cutting and are useful for jobs that cannot be reached with a hacksaw.

Using Bench Grinders

When grinding metal, it must not be allowed to overheat, because this will adversely affect its hardness. If the metal becomes too hot and is allowed to cool slowly, it may become soft. If it is cooled quickly (quenched), it may become brittle. As you grind the metal, stop and dip it regularly into the water pot attached to the base of the grinder, which will prevent the metal from getting too hot. Some bench grinders are not supplied with a water pot. If this is the case, you will need to have a water can located near the grinder so that you can cool the piece you are grinding.

> **TECHNICIAN TIP**
>
> When using a bench grinder, the face of the abrasive wheel must be kept square. This is done with a dressing tool, which removes some of the abrasive compound. If the abrasive wheel is not square, use a dressing tool. Then readjust the tool rest to the proper clearance.

To set up, adjust, and use a bench grinder, follow the steps in SKILL DRILL 6-14. If you need help or are unsure how to adjust the grinder, ask your supervisor.

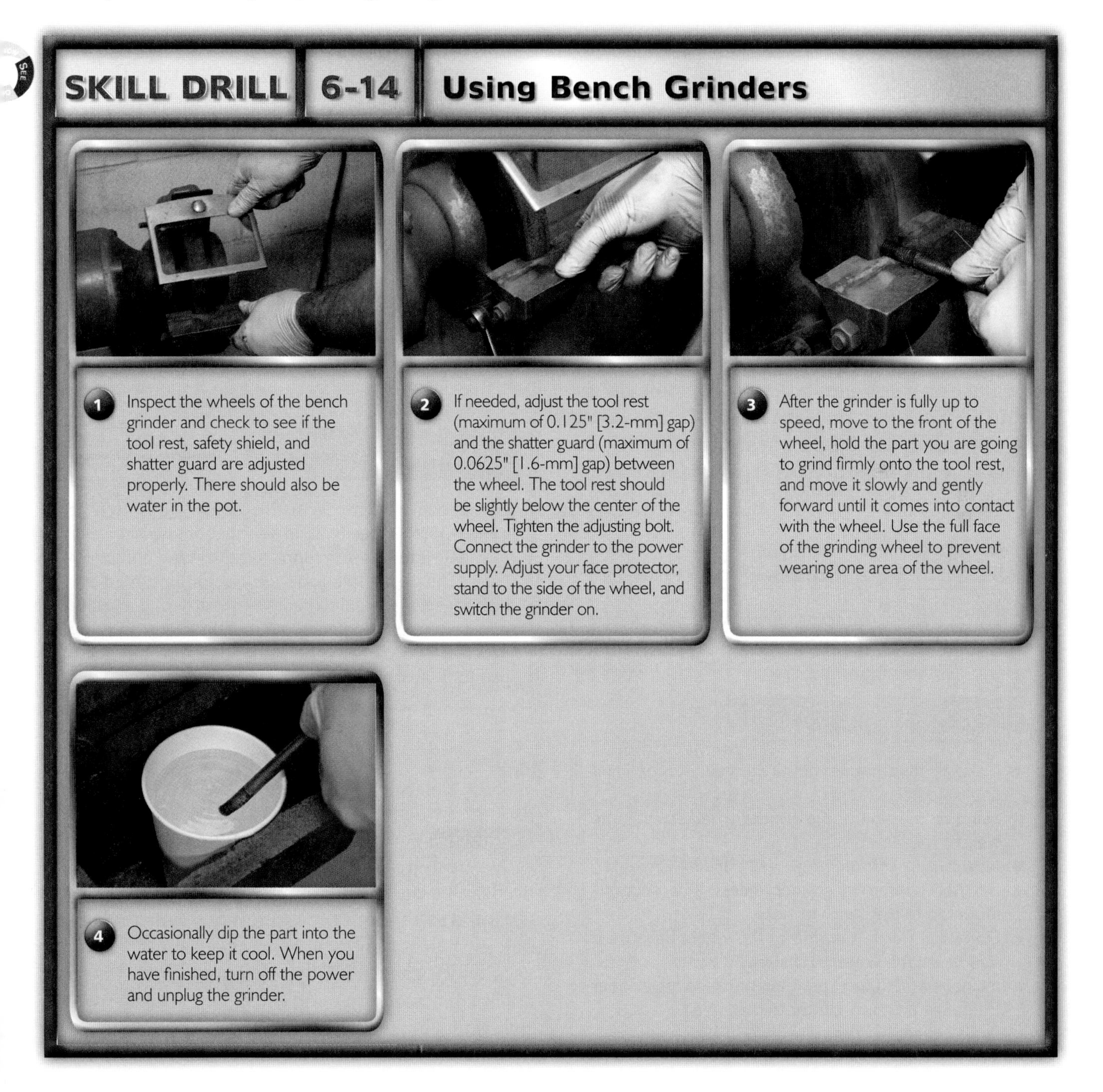

SKILL DRILL 6-14 Using Bench Grinders

1. Inspect the wheels of the bench grinder and check to see if the tool rest, safety shield, and shatter guard are adjusted properly. There should also be water in the pot.
2. If needed, adjust the tool rest (maximum of 0.125" [3.2-mm] gap) and the shatter guard (maximum of 0.0625" [1.6-mm] gap) between the wheel. The tool rest should be slightly below the center of the wheel. Tighten the adjusting bolt. Connect the grinder to the power supply. Adjust your face protector, stand to the side of the wheel, and switch the grinder on.
3. After the grinder is fully up to speed, move to the front of the wheel, hold the part you are going to grind firmly onto the tool rest, and move it slowly and gently forward until it comes into contact with the wheel. Use the full face of the grinding wheel to prevent wearing one area of the wheel.
4. Occasionally dip the part into the water to keep it cool. When you have finished, turn off the power and unplug the grinder.

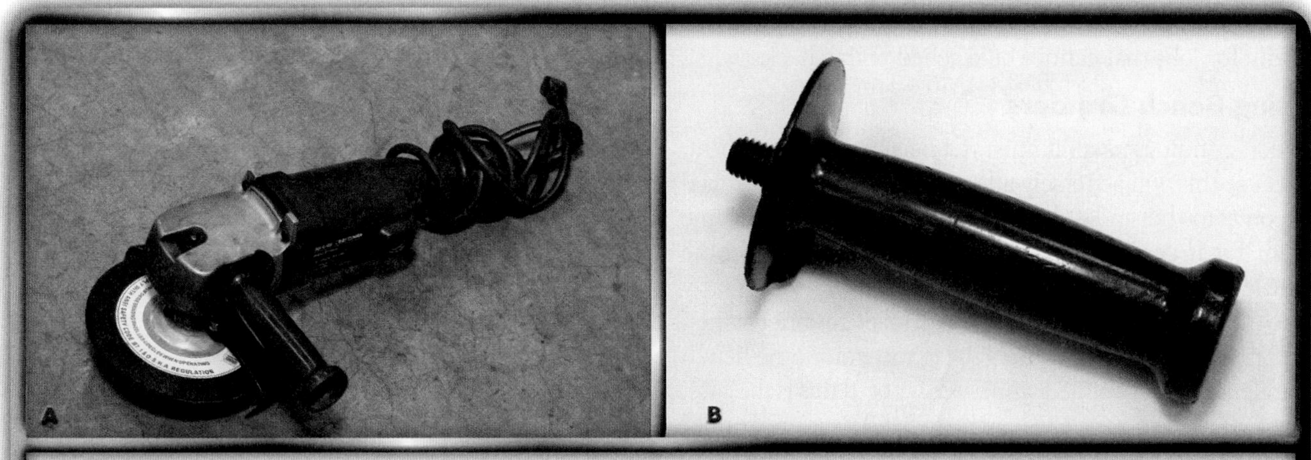

FIGURE 6-43 A. The angle grinder uses an electric motor to drive an abrasive disc at a high speed. B. An extra handle is provided that can be attached to the grinder head.

Using Angle Grinders

The angle grinder uses an electric motor to drive an abrasive disc at a high speed FIGURE 6-43. The grinder disc is turned at speeds that range from 5000 to 12,000 rpm. The turning disc is used to grind or cut metal. The grinder size relates to the diameter of the cutting disc, which can range from 4″ to 9″ (102 mm to 229 mm). The size of grinder you use depends on the type of job you are doing. The smaller the grinder, the higher the speed it turns. Sanding discs and wire wheels can be fitted on the grinder, making it a versatile electric tool. An extra handle is provided that can be attached to the grinder head. This handle can be fitted to either the left, right, or top of the head to make it easy to use for left-handed as well as right-handed people.

Safety

Be very careful when grinding thin metal pieces, as they are more easily grabbed by the wheel.

Safety

- Make all adjustments with the grinder stopped and unplugged.
- Stand to the side of the grinder when starting the electric motor.
- Never use a cracked or gouged grinding wheel.
- Do not operate a grinder unless it is securely mounted to the bench or floor.
- Do not grind on the side of the wheel because it may cause the wheel to shatter.
- Maintain a 2" (0.6-m) perimeter around the grinder free of flammables, clutter, and people.

The **abrasive disc**, or **cutting wheel**, is attached to the grinder by a flange and nut. The nut is specially designed to fit in a recess in the center of the pad or wheel. It is tightened by a tool that is provided with the grinder when purchased. Do not lose this wrench because it is the only tool that can tighten the nut properly. When using the grinder with cutting discs, you should always use the edge of the disc rather than the face.

To correctly use an angle grinder, follow the steps in SKILL DRILL 6-15.

TECHNICIAN TIP

Do not confuse a grinder with a **sander/polisher**. The sander/polisher turns at lower speeds, typically 600 to 3000 rpm. It is commonly used to sand and polish paint. The pads these tools use cannot be turned at a high speed. If the polish pad were attached to an angle grinder, the higher rotational speed would cause the polishing pad to burn the paint and cause the polish pad to fly apart.

Air Tools

Air tools use compressed air at high pressure to operate FIGURE 6-44. Air compressors in automotive shops typically run at greater than 90 psi (621 kPa), so caution needs to be exercised around them. Compressed air is transported through pipes and hoses. Air tools have quick-connect fittings so that various air tools can be used on the same air hose. There are several styles of quick-connect fittings, and a shop will usually use one style throughout the entire shop.

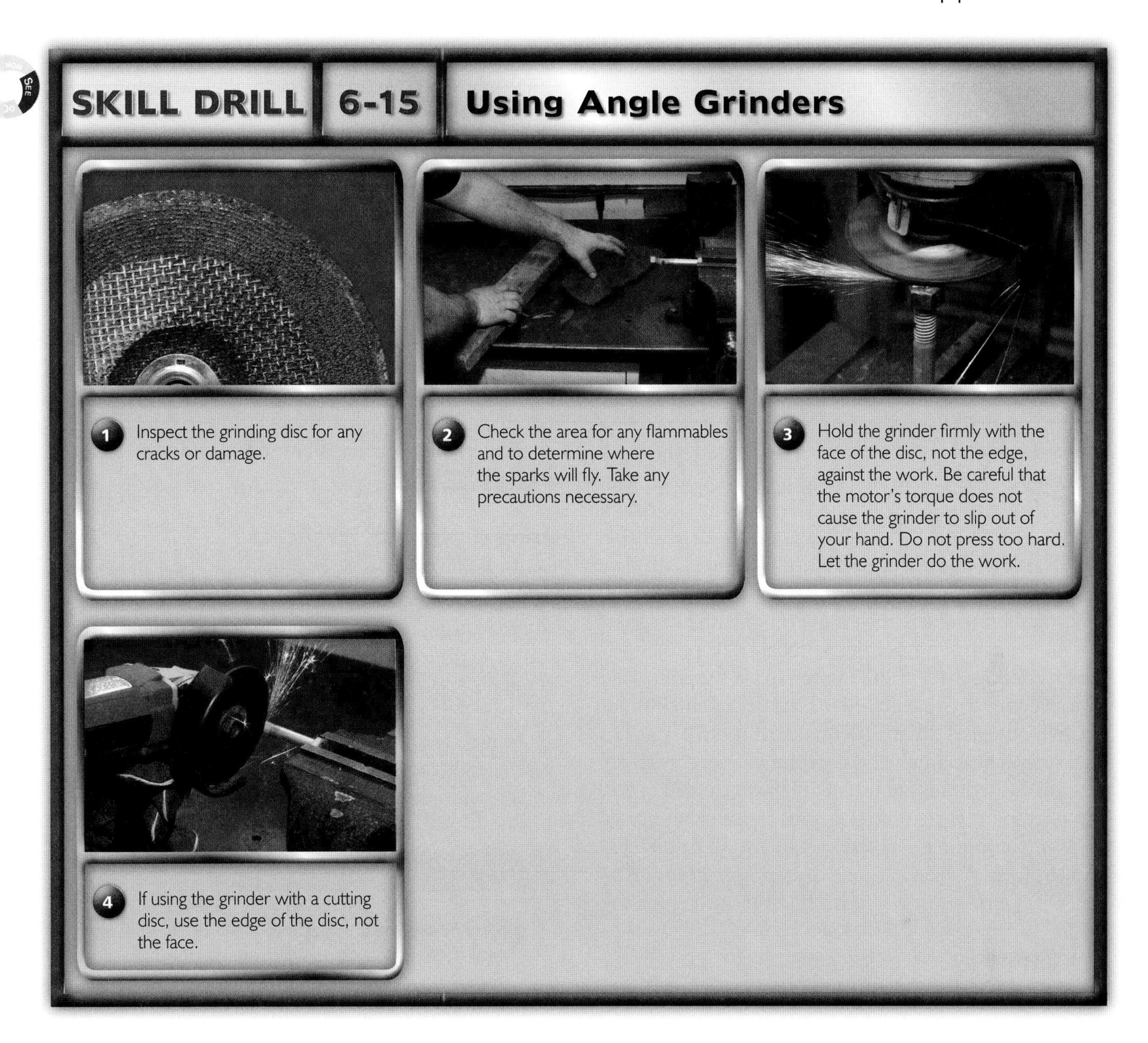
SKILL DRILL 6-15 Using Angle Grinders
1 Inspect the grinding disc for any cracks or damage.
2 Check the area for any flammables and to determine where the sparks will fly. Take any precautions necessary.
3 Hold the grinder firmly with the face of the disc, not the edge, against the work. Be careful that the motor's torque does not cause the grinder to slip out of your hand. Do not press too hard. Let the grinder do the work.
4 If using the grinder with a cutting disc, use the edge of the disc, not the face.

The most common air tool in an automotive shop is the **air impact wrench**. It is sometimes called an impact gun or **rattle gun**, and it is easy to understand why when you hear one. Taking the wheels off a car to replace the tires is a typical application for this air tool. Removing lug nuts often requires a lot of torque to twist the nuts free, and air impact wrenches work well for that.

The air impact wrench can be set to spin in either direction, and a valve roughly controls how much torque it applies. It should never be used for final tightening of wheel nuts. There is a danger in overtightening the wheel nuts, as it can cause the bolts to fail and the wheel to separate from the vehicle while it is moving. Another rule with the air impact wrench is that you have to use special hardened impact sockets, extensions, and joints. The sockets are special heavy-duty, six-point types, and

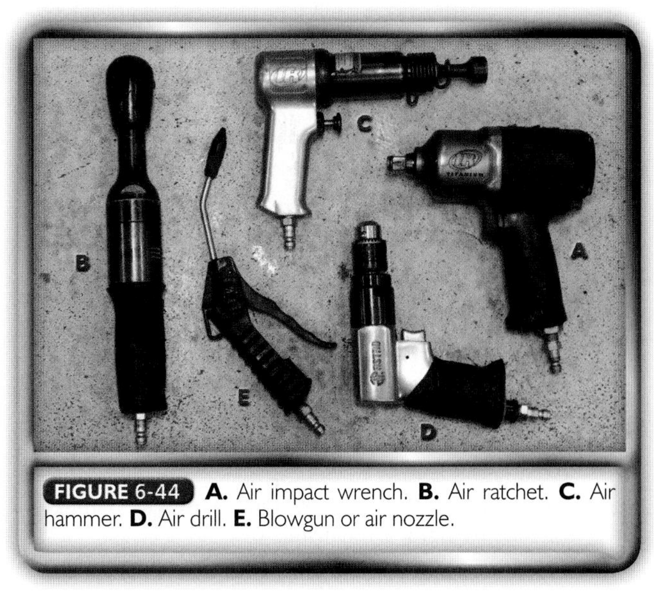
C
A
B
E
D

FIGURE 6-44 **A.** Air impact wrench. **B.** Air ratchet. **C.** Air hammer. **D.** Air drill. **E.** Blowgun or air nozzle.

the flats can withstand the hammering force that the impact wrench subjects them to.

An **air ratchet** uses the force of compressed air to turn a ratchet drive. It is used on smaller nuts and bolts. Once the nut is loosened, the air ratchet spins it off in a fraction of the time it would take by hand. It also works well where there isn't much room to swing a ratchet handle.

An **air hammer**, sometimes called an air chisel, is useful for driving and cutting. The extra force that is generated by the compressed air makes it more efficient than a hand chisel and hammer. Just as there are many chisels, there are many bits that fit into the air hammer, depending on the job at hand.

An **air drill** has some important advantages over the more common electric power drill. With the right attachment, it can drill holes, grind, polish, and clean parts. Unlike the electric drill, it does not run the risk of producing sparks, which is important around flammable liquids or gasoline tanks. An air drill does not trail a live electric cable behind it that could be cut, possibly causing shock and burns. It also does not get hot with heavy use.

A blowgun, or **air nozzle**, is probably the simplest air tool. It controls the flow of compressed air. It is controlled by a lever or valve that is used to blast debris and dirt out of confined spaces. Blasting debris and dirt can be dangerous, so eye protection must be worn whenever this tool is used. Noise levels are usually high, so ear protection should also be worn. It is dangerous to use an air nozzle to clean yourself off. Its blast should always be directed away from the user and anyone else working nearby. Also note that OSHA-approved nozzles lower the tip pressure by venting some of the air for safety reasons. Only use OSHA-approved nozzles for general blowing purposes.

Safety

- Always wear impact-resistant protective glasses, ear protection, and a full-face shield when using an angle grinder.
- Wear safety shoes, leather gloves, and an apron to protect your body from flying metal chips. Make sure the blade guard is firmly secured.
- Use the correct type of disc.
- Make sure the guard handles are secure.
- Use the correct flange or spindle nut for the type of disc being used. If you do not, the disc can shatter at high speeds and injure you.
- Angle grinders, like all portable grinding tools, need to be equipped with safety guards to protect you from flying fragments in case the disc breaks apart.
- Always follow the manufacturer's recommendations to make sure the spindle wheel does not exceed the abrasive wheel specifications.
- Make sure there are no obvious defects or damage to the disc before you install it.

Using Air Nozzles

An air nozzle can be a handy tool for blowing dirt and debris out of holes such as around spark plugs prior to removing them. It is helpful to activate the air nozzle away from the area you intend to blow off before doing it; this way you can get a feel for how the valve operates. To operate an air nozzle, pull the trigger gently and modulate the flow of air through the nozzle. If too much air is allowed through, you may blow dirt particles back at you, so always wear your safety glasses. Also keep your mouth closed, as it helps prevent eating a bunch of dirt!

To correctly operate an air nozzle, follow the steps in SKILL DRILL 6-16.

Using Air Impact Wrenches

The amount of torque an air impact wrench can produce will be determined by the tool and the pressure in the air system feeding it. Because this pressure will vary, there is no way of determining how much torque an impact wrench is applying to a fastener, so it is easy to over- or undertighten fasteners. An air impact wrench can generally be used to take up the looseness in a nut or stud, but the final tightening must be performed by using a torque wrench set to the manufacturer's specifications.

Safety

- Do not use the air nozzle to clean brake dust from brake components. It will disperse the hazardous dust.
- Do not use a high-pressure air nozzle to disperse liquid solvents or fuels. A low-pressure blowing action can help these volatile materials to evaporate more quickly, but a high-pressure air jet could atomize the liquid, allowing it to form a flammable mixture.
- Do not point the air nozzle at other people.
- Never use the air nozzle to blow air over yourself or other people.
- Always wear eye protection when using air tools.
- Do not drive over the air hoses.
- Make sure the hoses are in good condition before using.

Safety

- Air tools generally produce more noise than electric tools, so wear ear protection when using air tools.
- Always use impact sockets with impact guns.

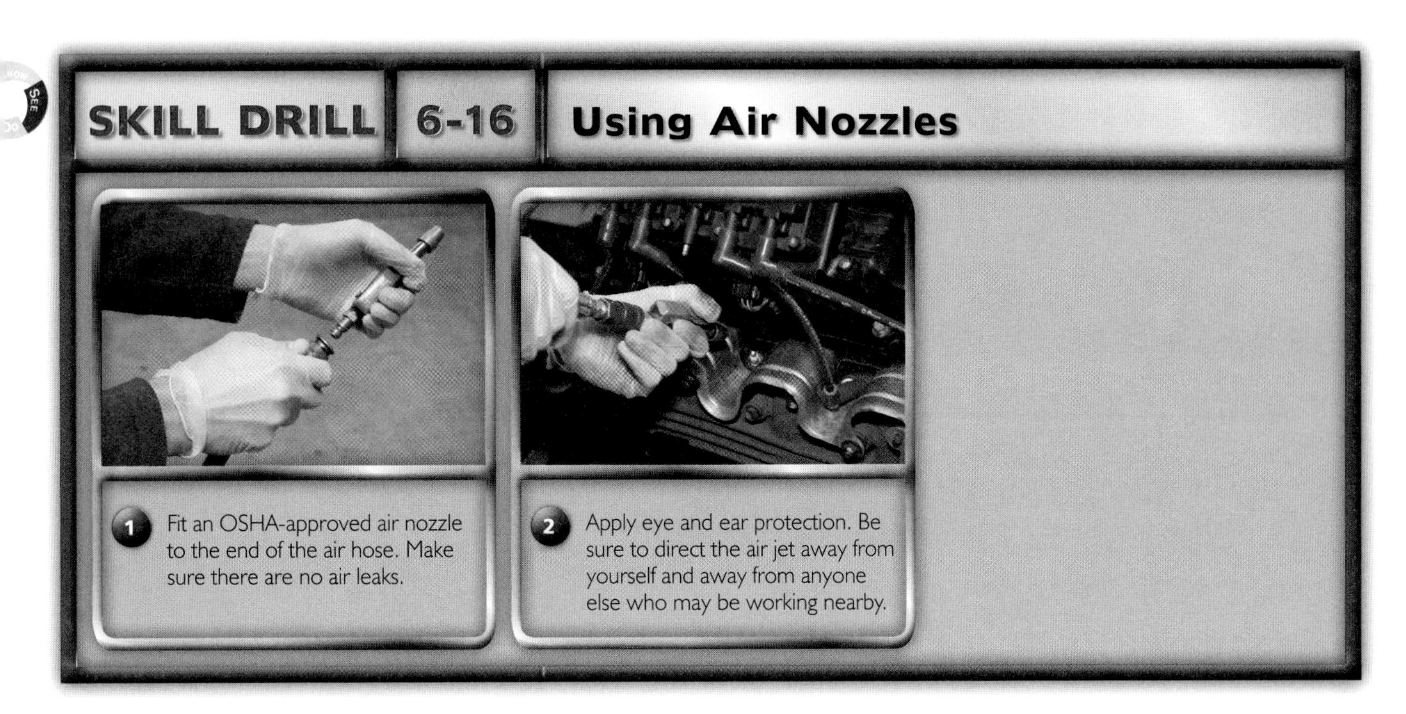
SKILL DRILL 6-16 Using Air Nozzles
1 Fit an OSHA-approved air nozzle to the end of the air hose. Make sure there are no air leaks.
2 Apply eye and ear protection. Be sure to direct the air jet away from yourself and away from anyone else who may be working nearby.

Every impact wrench will have a control mechanism that allows it to be driven in either direction. Always use six-point impact sockets when using an air impact wrench; these sockets are manufactured from a different blend of materials and have thicker walls than a standard socket.

To correctly operate an air impact wrench, follow the steps in SKILL DRILL 6-17.

Using Air Drills

Air drills are another tool operated by compressed air. Since they are powered by air and not electricity, they are safer to use in an environment where flammable materials are present. The amount of torque an air drill can produce will be determined by the pressure in the air system feeding it. Air drills are smaller and turn at slower speeds than electric drills. Air drills operate similarly to their electric counterparts and are equipped with the same type of drill chuck, which clamps onto the drill bit using a special key. Most air drills are of the 90-degree angle style and fit in places a typical electric drill might not.

To correctly operate an air drill, follow the steps in SKILL DRILL 6-18.

Using Air Hammers

Air hammers act in a manner similar to a jackhammer; however, their size makes their cycling rate faster. There are a variety of attachments, so use the correct attachment for the task you are performing. This could be a chisel for cutting a bolt or a punch for driving out a broken lug stud. The attachment is held in place by a coil spring that tends to break over time, so inspect it and never use the air hammer if it is broken. Place the tool bit against the workpiece and hold it firmly before you pull the trigger, as it is likely to want to jump around.

To use an air hammer, follow the steps in SKILL DRILL 6-19.

Safety

An air hammer's operation produces a noise level that exceeds the maximum exposure level for human ears. Always wear ear protection when using an air hammer.

Cleaning Tools

Pressure Washers and Cleaners

Pressure washers and cleaners are valuable tools for cleaning vehicles, engine compartments, and components. They can be powered by an electric motor or a gasoline engine fitted to a high-pressure pump. The pressure washer takes water at normal pressure and boosts it through the high-pressure pump to exit through a cleaning gun, which has a control trigger. The **cleaning gun** has a high-pressure nozzle that focuses high-pressure water (possibly over 2000 psi [13790 kPa]) to quickly clean accumulated dirt and grease from components. Some pressure washers have a provision for detergent to be injected into the high-pressure output to more effectively clean. Others have the ability to heat the water, in some cases hot enough to turn it to steam. Hot water and steam help loosen oil and grease buildup.

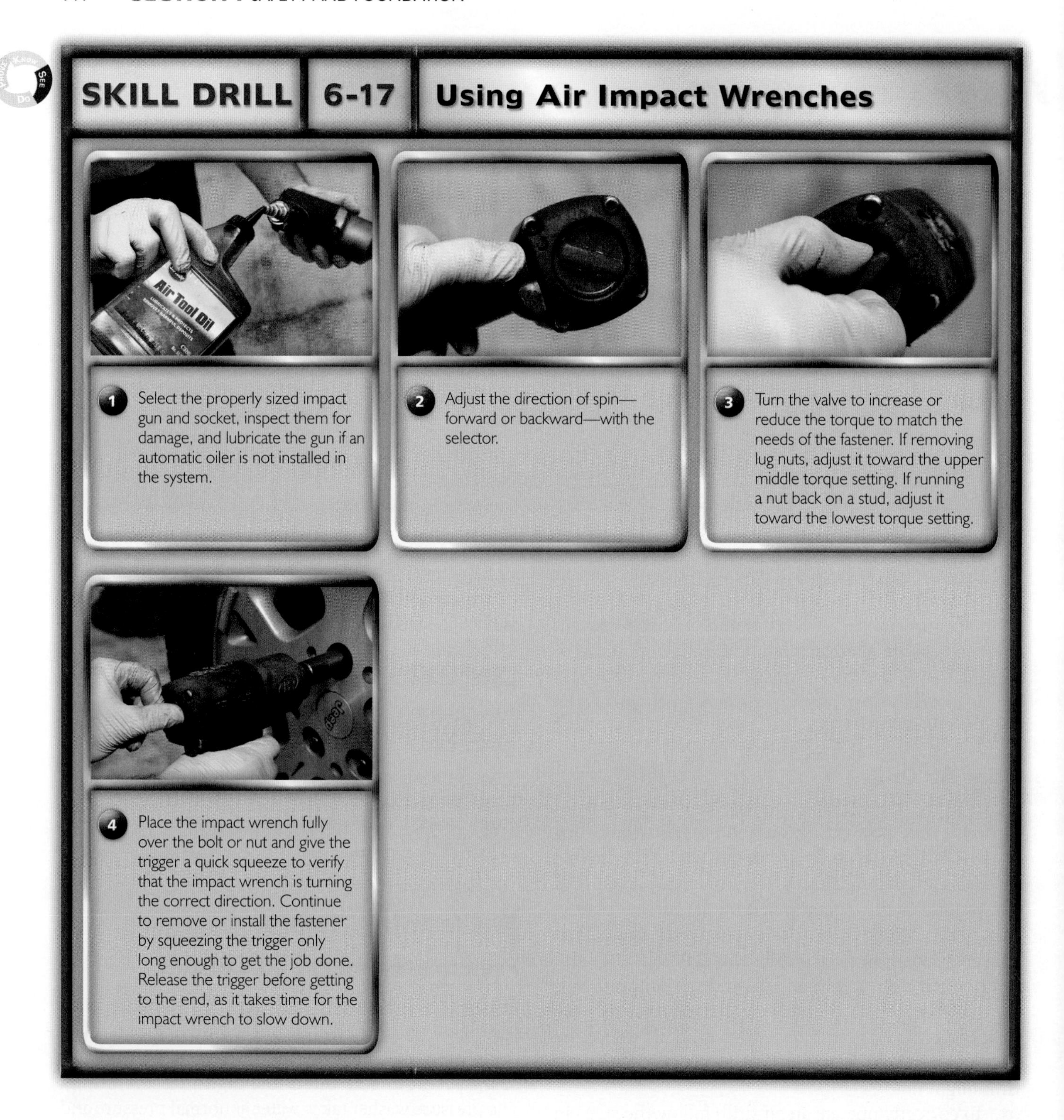
Air Tool Oil

SKILL DRILL 6-17 Using Air Impact Wrenches

1. Select the properly sized impact gun and socket, inspect them for damage, and lubricate the gun if an automatic oiler is not installed in the system.
2. Adjust the direction of spin—forward or backward—with the selector.
3. Turn the valve to increase or reduce the torque to match the needs of the fastener. If removing lug nuts, adjust it toward the upper middle torque setting. If running a nut back on a stud, adjust it toward the lowest torque setting.
4. Place the impact wrench fully over the bolt or nut and give the trigger a quick squeeze to verify that the impact wrench is turning the correct direction. Continue to remove or install the fastener by squeezing the trigger only long enough to get the job done. Release the trigger before getting to the end, as it takes time for the impact wrench to slow down.

Pressure washers are dangerous because of their high pressure and possibly high temperature. Always wear appropriate PPE when working with pressure cleaners—for example, goggles or face shield, protective gloves, close-fitting clothes with long sleeves and full-length pants, and leather-type boots or shoes.

Using Pressure Washers

Pressure washers and cleaners used in automotive applications are available in a range of makes and types depending on the application. There are fixed washers for cleaning components and mobile pressure washers that can be used to wash vehicle systems and engine compartments. Familiarize yourself with the equipment prior to use; incorrect handling can result in damage to the washer or to the vehicle or components you are cleaning, in addition to health risks to yourself and your coworkers.

The biggest advantage of using fluid to clean vehicles, components, and spaces is that it wets the dirt or contaminants, so no dust is created. However, the waste products

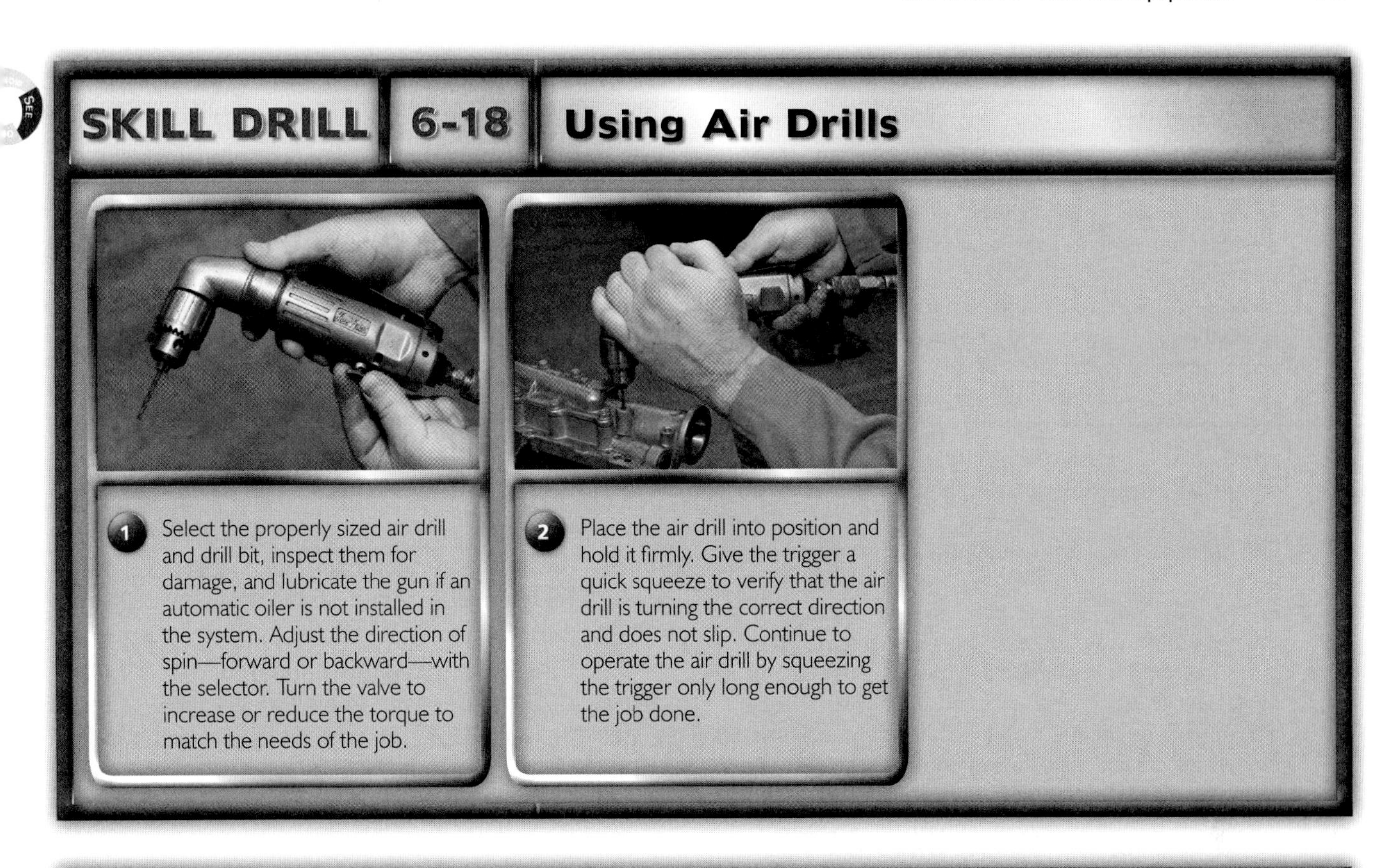
SKILL DRILL 6-18 Using Air Drills
1 Select the properly sized air drill and drill bit, inspect them for damage, and lubricate the gun if an automatic oiler is not installed in the system. Adjust the direction of spin—forward or backward—with the selector. Turn the valve to increase or reduce the torque to match the needs of the job.
2 Place the air drill into position and hold it firmly. Give the trigger a quick squeeze to verify that the air drill is turning the correct direction and does not slip. Continue to operate the air drill by squeezing the trigger only long enough to get the job done.

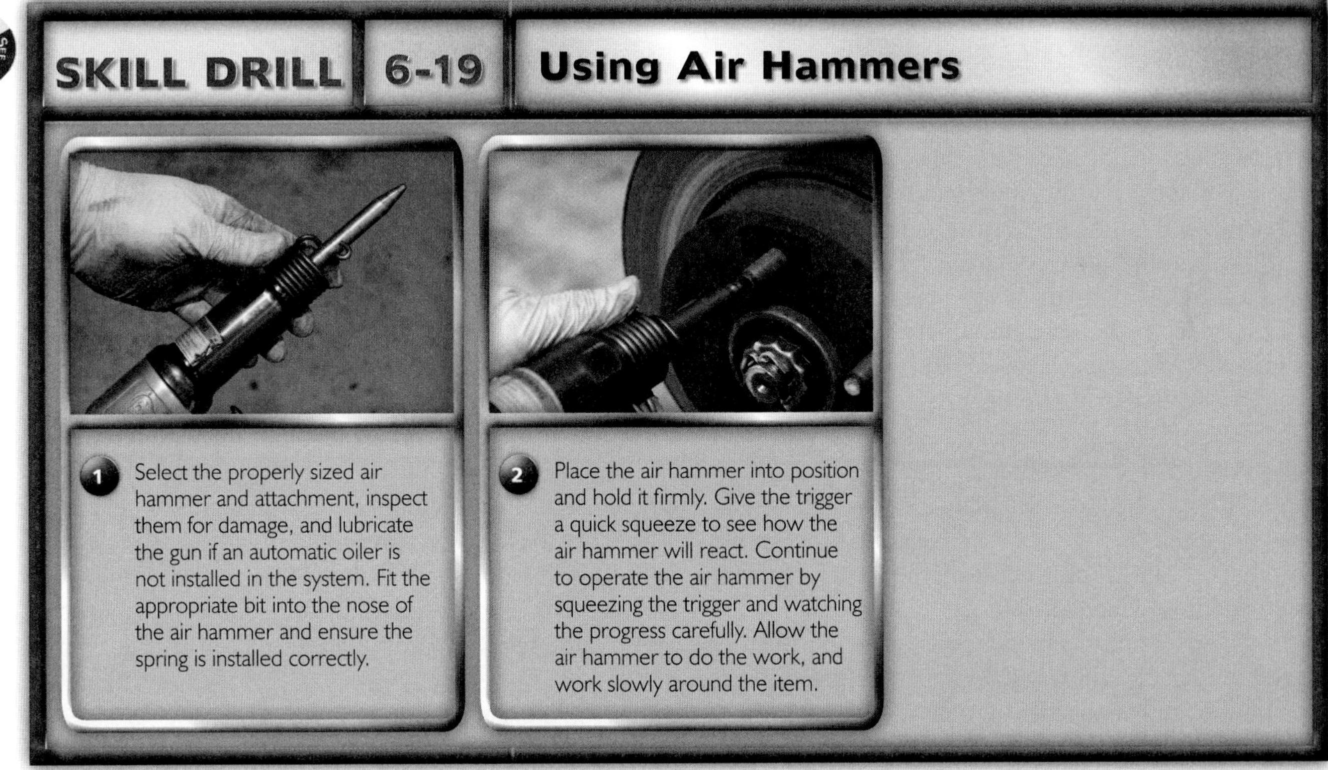
SKILL DRILL 6-19 Using Air Hammers
1 Select the properly sized air hammer and attachment, inspect them for damage, and lubricate the gun if an automatic oiler is not installed in the system. Fit the appropriate bit into the nose of the air hammer and ensure the spring is installed correctly.
2 Place the air hammer into position and hold it firmly. Give the trigger a quick squeeze to see how the air hammer will react. Continue to operate the air hammer by squeezing the trigger and watching the progress carefully. Allow the air hammer to do the work, and work slowly around the item.

must be caught and disposed of properly in either a catch basin or a waste water settling system. The waste materials must not be released into a storm water drain.

It is imperative that you read the instructions beforehand and be familiar with the operation of the pressure washer. When cleaning exterior paintwork, extreme care must be taken to ensure that the pressure does not damage or remove paint. If in doubt, clean the area manually using a clean sponge and clean water. It is very important to note the type of solvent being used in

Safety

- Always wear a face shield and gloves when using cleaning and washing equipment.
- Always wear safety shoes when using any washing equipment to prevent slips on slippery surfaces.
- Always be aware of the location of safety switches located on equipment and of eyewash and first aid stations should an accident occur.
- Do not place your hand or any other part of your body in the stream of water from the high-pressure wand. Many pressure washers generate enough pressure to instantly cut skin and muscle to the bone.
- Do not aim the high-pressure wand at another person.
- Always test the temperature of the wand and the hose before you pick it up. The handle of the pressure wand is insulated to protect the user from heat, but the wand extension and the hose are not.
- If the pressure cleaner uses a heating element, turn the heater off and allow water to flow through the wand until is has cooled before you turn the unit off.
- If you are unfamiliar with a solvent or a cleaning agent, refer to the material safety data sheet (MSDS) for information about its correct use and applicable hazards.

a pressure washer, as some vehicle components can be damaged by some solvents and should only be cleaned in wash tanks containing the correct cleaning fluid.

When using high-pressure washers, it is always important not to spray in areas where water and water-based solvents can have a detrimental effect on electrical equipment such as fuse boxes, relays, and control units. If you are required to use a pressure washer in those areas of the vehicle, take precautionary measures to protect the units from high-pressure water damage by covering them with sturdy plastic bags. The damage may not become apparent for some time after the cleaning process, but it can have a catastrophic effect on the vehicle, causing system failures, which are difficult to diagnose.

If the washer results in the wheel brake units getting wet, ensure that the vehicle is driven for a short distance with the brakes slightly applied. This will remove any residual water from the brake shoes or pads through heat transfer and subsequent evaporation of the water. Depending on the outside temperature, it usually only takes several seconds to return the brakes to their proper operation.

On completion of the job, the correct disposal of contaminated materials is a top priority. Operators of cleaning equipment may be subject to prosecution for the incorrect disposal of waste materials. So always know the regulations and follow all policies and guidelines for the jurisdiction you are in.

Before using a pressure washer, identify the location of the eyewash and first-aid stations; put on a face shield, work apron, and gloves; and identify the location of safety switches on the washer itself. As with any piece of equipment, always refer to the manufacturer's manual for specific operating instructions. To safely use pressure washers, follow the steps in SKILL DRILL 6-20.

Spray Wash Cabinets

Spray wash cabinets spray high-temperature, high-pressure cleaning solutions onto parts inside a sealed cabinet. They are automated and act like a dishwasher for parts. This significantly reduces the labor required to clean parts because once the door is closed and the unit is turned on, the technician is free to move onto other tasks. They are available in a variety of sizes to cater to different-sized parts and provide a high level of cleaning performance. The cleaning solution is designed to effectively clean without leaving residue on the parts, and most spray cabinets are fitted with a filtering system to reduce the frequency of cleaning solution changes.

Using Spray Wash Cabinets

Spray wash cabinets used in automotive applications are available in a range of makes and types depending on the application. It is imperative that you read the instructions beforehand and be familiar with the operation of the spray wash cabinet. Incorrect handling can result in damage to the components that you are cleaning in addition to health risks to yourself and your coworkers.

Spray wash cabinets must either incorporate a built-in waste recovery system or be used only where the contaminated washer fluids can be captured to enable disposal in an environmentally friendly manner. Always follow recommended safety procedures. Spray wash cabinets use potentially dangerous chemicals at very high pressure to clean away the contaminants.

It is very important to note the type of cleaning agent being used, as some vehicle components can be damaged by some agents. On completion of the job, the correct

Safety

- Do not operate the spray wash cabinet without the door securely closed.
- The spray wash cabinet uses high-pressure, high-temperature cleaning fluid, and parts will be hot after being in the spray cabinet.

SKILL DRILL 6-20 Using Pressure Washers
1 Locate the position of safety switches and put on a face shield, work apron, and gloves. Note the location of the eyewash and first aid stations. If not permanently connected, follow the manufacturer's instructions and connect the pressure washer hose to the water supply, and the electrical plug to a power outlet protected by a ground fault circuit interrupter (GFCI). Protect adjacent areas from water spray.
2 If necessary, apply a degreasing agent with a spray bottle and hand brush to penetrate and soften excess dirt.
3 Turn on the water supply but not the power switch. Water should flow freely but not at high pressure. Turn the power on and you will hear the motor engage. Point the wand toward the ground and test that the water is flowing at high pressure.
4 Pull the trigger and using either a circular or a sweeping motion, direct the high-pressure water onto the area to be cleaned.
5 When the contaminants have been removed, release the trigger and remove the wand from the cleaning area. Turn the electrical power off, then turn the water supply off.
6 Use an air nozzle to disperse any residual water from electrical components that have come into contact with the cleaning fluids. Start the vehicle and let it run for a few moments to dry, and then remove any residual water in the engine compartment area. Clean up any residual material and place it in a bin or an environmental waste container.

disposal of any contaminated materials is a top priority. Operators of this equipment may be subject to prosecution for the incorrect disposal of waste materials.

Before using a spray cabinet, identify the location of the eyewash and first-aid stations, put on a face shield and gloves, and identify the location of safety switches on the cabinet itself. As with any piece of equipment, always refer to the manufacturer's manual for specific operating instructions. To use a spray wash cabinet to clean components, follow the steps in **SKILL DRILL 6-21**.

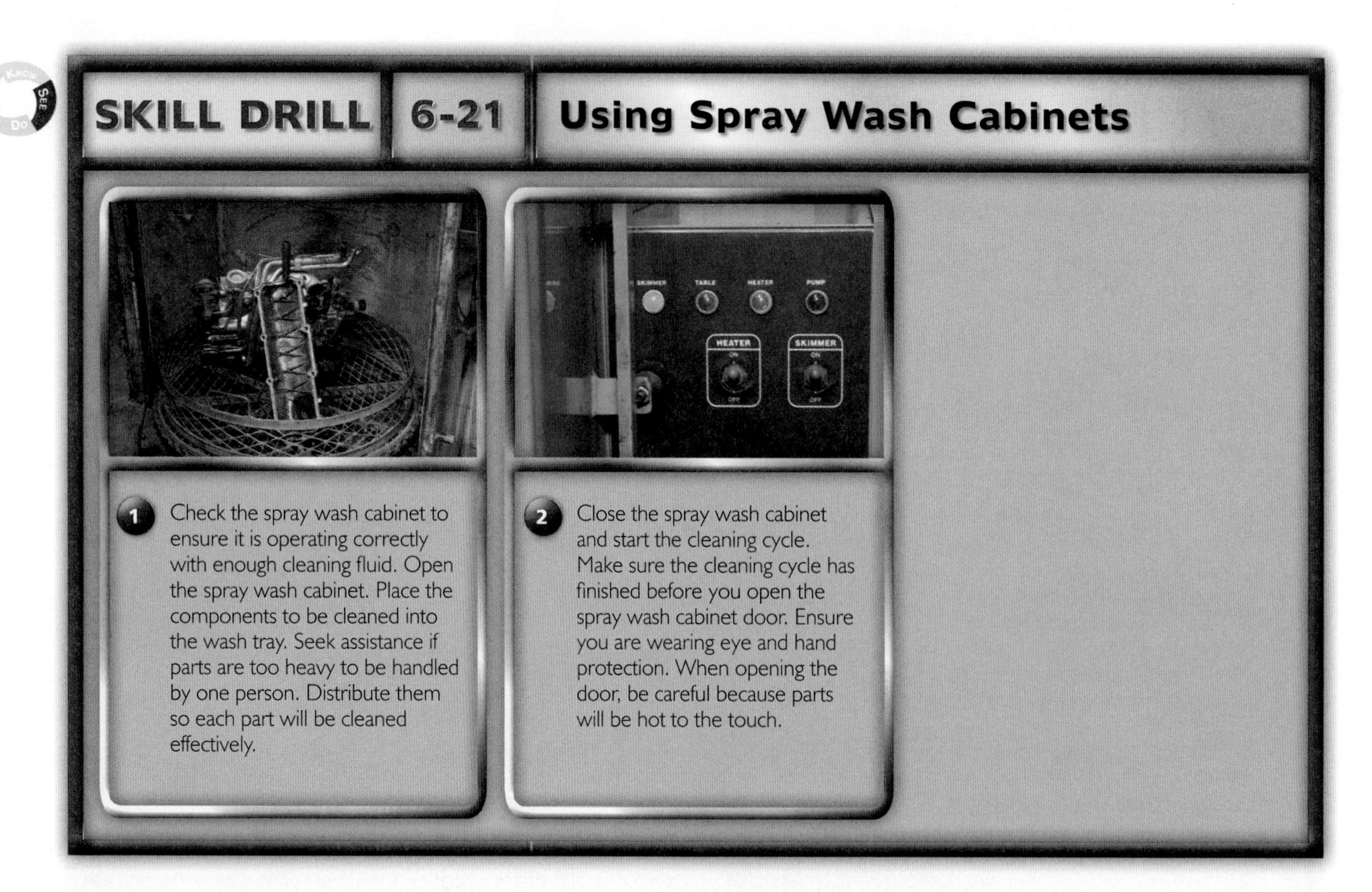
SKILL DRILL 6-21 Using Spray Wash Cabinets
1 Check the spray wash cabinet to ensure it is operating correctly with enough cleaning fluid. Open the spray wash cabinet. Place the components to be cleaned into the wash tray. Seek assistance if parts are too heavy to be handled by one person. Distribute them so each part will be cleaned effectively.
2 Close the spray wash cabinet and start the cleaning cycle. Make sure the cleaning cycle has finished before you open the spray wash cabinet door. Ensure you are wearing eye and hand protection. When opening the door, be careful because parts will be hot to the touch.

Solvent Tanks

A **solvent tank** is a cleaning tank that is filled with a suitable solvent to clean parts by removing oil, grease, dirt, and grime. Solvent tanks are available in different sizes. Many solvent tanks have a pump that pushes solvent out a nozzle into a sink where it can be directed to the parts being cleaned. A brush either on the nozzle or separate from it can be used to loosen the grease and grime. The solvent falls back into the bottom of the solvent tank where the heavier residue can settle to the bottom. Other solvent tanks are designed so that parts can be immersed into the tank on racks or suspended on pieces of wire, and slowly lowered and soaked in the tank for a period of time. Some solvent tanks may have an agitation system or use a heated cleaning fluid to speed up the process. They may also have a circulation system and filters to remove debris and residue in the solvent to extend its life between changes.

Safety

Whenever using a tank-type cleaner with solvents, make sure there is adequate exhaust ventilation and wear appropriate breathing apparatus and eye protection.

Using Solvent Tanks

Familiarize yourself with the equipment prior to use; incorrect handling can result in damage to components that you are cleaning in addition to health risks to yourself and your coworkers. Solvent tanks may use potentially poisonous and/or flammable chemicals to clean parts. It is very important to note the type of solvent being used and to take all necessary precautions as listed on the MSDS. Also, some vehicle components can be damaged by some solvents, so ask your supervisor about what can be safely washed and what cannot. On completion of the job, the correct disposal of contaminated materials is a top priority. Operators of this equipment may be subject to prosecution for the incorrect disposal of waste materials.

Before using a solvent tank, identify the location of

Safety

- If equipped, keep lids closed as much as possible, since many solvents are flammable and evaporate.
- The cleaning solution may be hot.
- Make sure there is adequate exhaust ventilation.
- Wear appropriate eye and hand protection, and if necessary appropriate breathing apparatus.

the eyewash and first-aid stations, put on a face shield and gloves, and identify the location of safety switches on the cabinet itself. As with any piece of equipment, always refer to the manufacturer's manual for specific operating instructions. To use a solvent tank to clean components, follow the steps in SKILL DRILL 6-22.

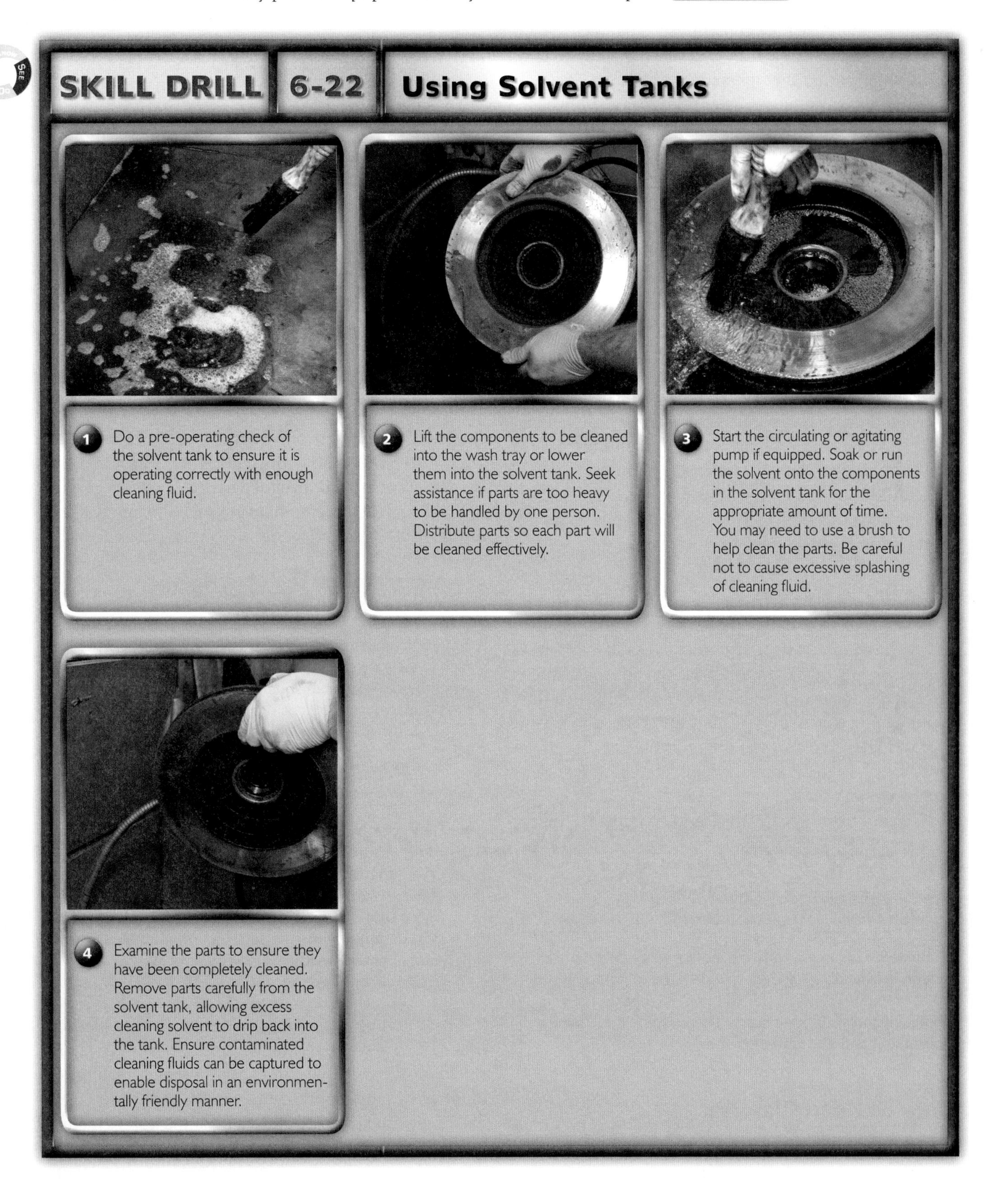

SKILL DRILL 6-22 Using Solvent Tanks

1. Do a pre-operating check of the solvent tank to ensure it is operating correctly with enough cleaning fluid.
2. Lift the components to be cleaned into the wash tray or lower them into the solvent tank. Seek assistance if parts are too heavy to be handled by one person. Distribute parts so each part will be cleaned effectively.
3. Start the circulating or agitating pump if equipped. Soak or run the solvent onto the components in the solvent tank for the appropriate amount of time. You may need to use a brush to help clean the parts. Be careful not to cause excessive splashing of cleaning fluid.
4. Examine the parts to ensure they have been completely cleaned. Remove parts carefully from the solvent tank, allowing excess cleaning solvent to drip back into the tank. Ensure contaminated cleaning fluids can be captured to enable disposal in an environmentally friendly manner.

Brake Washers

Brake washers are used to wash brake dust from wheel brake units and their components. Since it is possible that the brake dust may contain asbestos, which is a cancer-causing agent, and dust in general is a lung irritant, brake washers are designed to capture the brake dust before it enters the shop environment. It does so by wetting down the dust on the brake parts and then washing it into the cleaning tray. Brake washers incorporate a built-in waste recovery system where the contaminated washer fluids can be captured to enable disposal in an environmentally friendly manner.

Brake washers are normally designed to operate at low pressure and use a range of cleaning agents. The most popular agent is an aqueous solution made up of water and a water-soluble detergent. A low-pressure air blower may be provided to remove the fluid from the component into the tray area and then back to the tank by gravity.

Avoid using solvent when cleaning brake components, as it contaminates friction materials and may cause seals to swell. Never use kerosene as a general cleaning agent to clean brake components, as it does not clean away brake fluid, can be absorbed into lining materials, and can cause seals to swell. Soapy water is a good cleaning agent for brake components.

Using Brake Washers

Brake washers are a handy piece of shop equipment to deal with hazardous dust in a quick and relatively easy manner, especially if the washer uses an aqueous (water and detergent) cleaning solution. The one thing that this solution is not suited for is cleaning greasy residue. If you need to remove grease, you might be able to first use a paper towel or grease rag to wipe it off, and then clean the brake dust with the brake washer.

To use a brake washer to clean components, follow the steps in SKILL DRILL 6-23.

Safety

Familiarize yourself with the equipment prior to use; incorrect handling can result in damage to components that you are cleaning in addition to health risks to yourself and your coworkers. The waste products must be caught and disposed of properly.

Sand or Bead Blasters

Sand or bead blasters use high pressure to blast small abrasive particles to clean the surface of parts. The most common method of propelling the sand or glass beads is with compressed air. Sand or bead blasting can occur in a specially designed cabinet or there are portable models that are available for use in open-air situations. The cabinets contain the blasting operation in a controlled safe environment and are best for smaller parts that can fit into the cabinet. Portable systems that do not operate within a cabinet can blast larger parts but do require more protection for the operator and surrounding environment.

The sand or bead blaster cabinet is fitted with a hand-operated blasting nozzle, a viewing port, and an on/off switch (often this may be a foot-operated switch), and it has openings with tough rubber gloves sealed into them to allow a technician's hands to be inside the cabinet while being protected from the abrasive sand or beads. Wet sand or bead blasters are also available and have the added advantage of reducing the amount of dust and providing additional cleaning to the part being cleaned.

Using Sand or Bead Blasters

Technicians use sand or bead blasters to clean paint, corrosion, or dirt from metal parts. Since the sand or beads are abrasive, they can remove metal from the surface of the components, so be careful what you use it on. Sand or bead blasters used in automotive applications are available in a range of makes and models, depending on application.

Safety

Sand or bead blasters use potentially very fine particles at high pressure to clean away the contaminants. Also, silica from the sand particles should not be inhaled; it can cause lung damage, called silicosis, over a long period of time.

Safety

- Do not operate the sand/bead blaster without the door securely closed.
- Wear appropriate breathing apparatus or a dust mask.
- Always wear eye protection to prevent injury from flying particles or escaping compressed air.
- On completion of the job, the correct disposal of contaminated materials is a top priority.

Before using a sand or bead blaster, identify the location of the eyewash and first-aid stations; put on a face shield, dust mask, and gloves; and identify the location of safety switches on the cabinet itself. As with any piece of equipment, always refer to the manufacturer's manual for specific operating instructions.

To use a sand or bead blaster to clean components, follow the steps in SKILL DRILL 6-24.

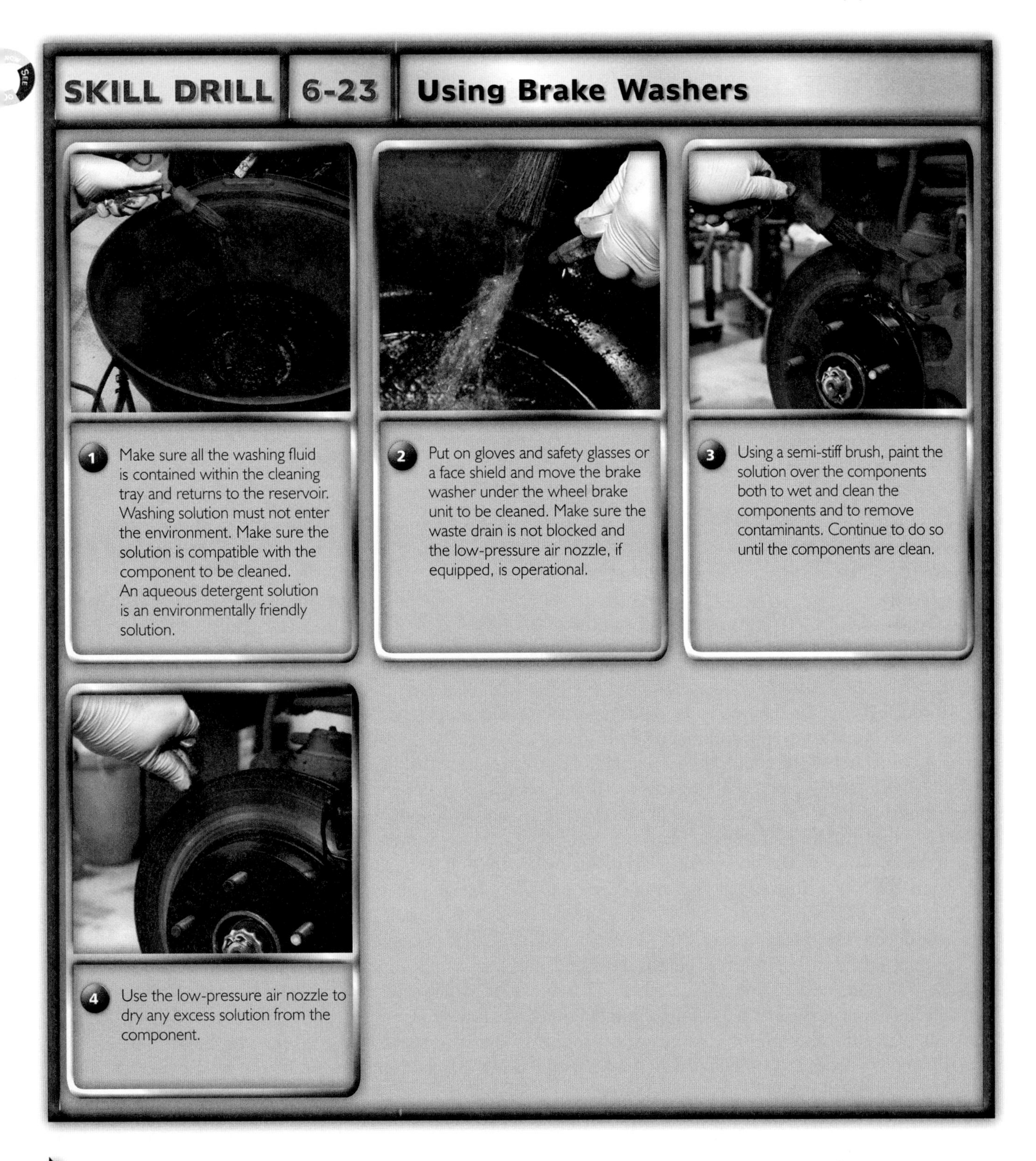
SKILL DRILL 6-23 Using Brake Washers
1 Make sure all the washing fluid is contained within the cleaning tray and returns to the reservoir. Washing solution must not enter the environment. Make sure the solution is compatible with the component to be cleaned. An aqueous detergent solution is an environmentally friendly solution.
2 Put on gloves and safety glasses or a face shield and move the brake washer under the wheel brake unit to be cleaned. Make sure the waste drain is not blocked and the low-pressure air nozzle, if equipped, is operational.
3 Using a semi-stiff brush, paint the solution over the components both to wet and clean the components and to remove contaminants. Continue to do so until the components are clean.
4 Use the low-pressure air nozzle to dry any excess solution from the component.

Thread Repair

Thread repair is used in situations where it is not possible to replace a damaged component. This may be because the thread is located in a large expensive component, such as the engine block or cylinder head of a vehicle, or because parts are not available. The aim of thread repair is to restore the thread to a condition that restores the fastening integrity. It can be performed on internal threads, such as in a housing, engine block, or cylinder head, or on external threads, such as on a bolt.

Types of Thread Repair

Many different tools and methods can be used to repair a thread. The least invasive method is to reshape the

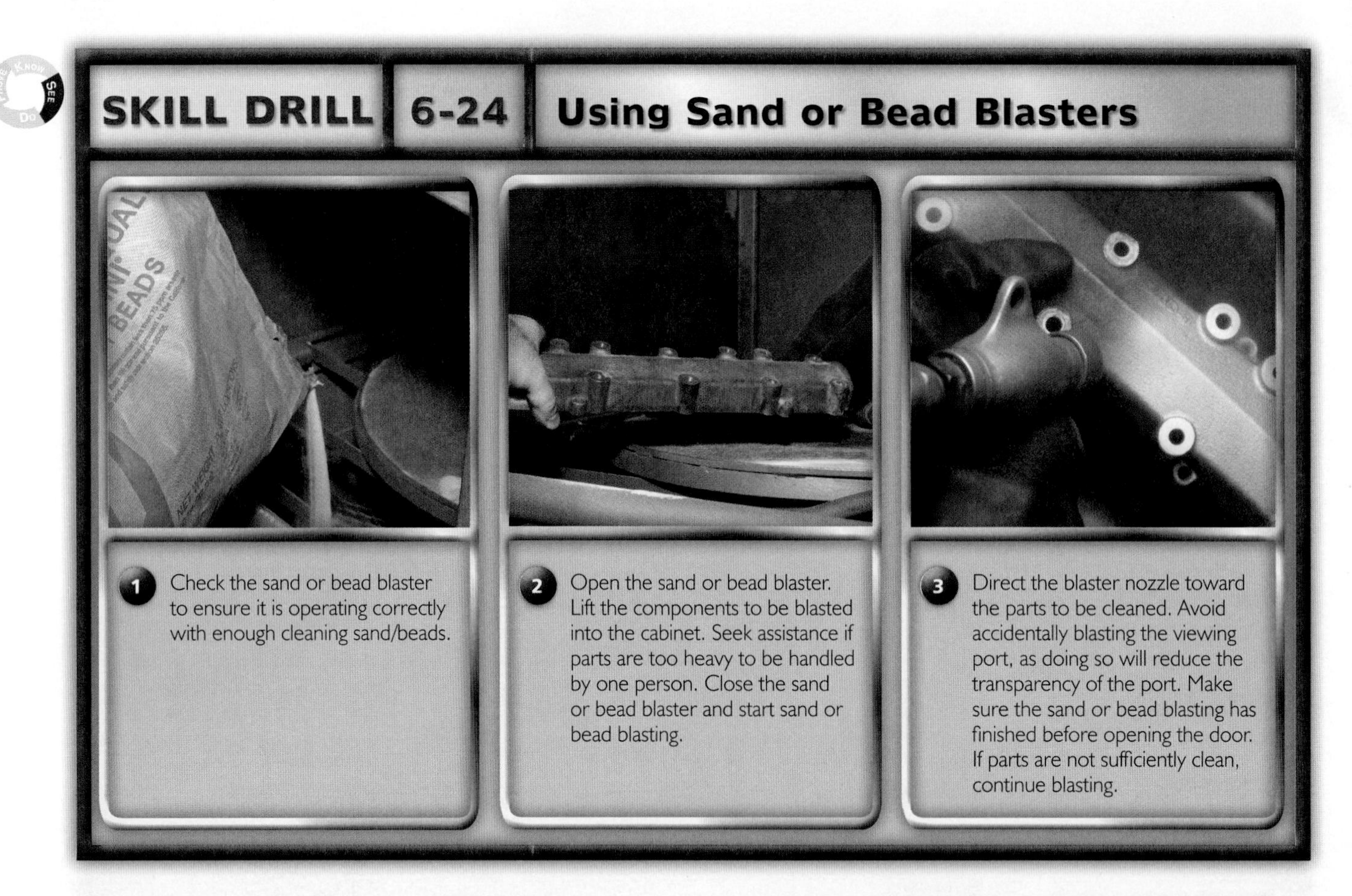
SKILL DRILL 6-24 Using Sand or Bead Blasters
1 Check the sand or bead blaster to ensure it is operating correctly with enough cleaning sand/beads.
2 Open the sand or bead blaster. Lift the components to be blasted into the cabinet. Seek assistance if parts are too heavy to be handled by one person. Close the sand or bead blaster and start sand or bead blasting.
3 Direct the blaster nozzle toward the parts to be cleaned. Avoid accidentally blasting the viewing port, as doing so will reduce the transparency of the port. Make sure the sand or bead blasting has finished before opening the door. If parts are not sufficiently clean, continue blasting.

threads. If the threads are not too badly damaged, such as the outer thread is slightly damaged from being started crooked (cross-threaded), then a thread file can be used to clean them up or a restoring tool can be used to reshape them. Each thread file has eight different sets of file teeth that match various thread pitches. Select the set that matches the bolt you are working on and file the bolt in line with the threads. The file will remove any distorted metal from the threads. Only file until the bad spot is reshaped. The thread-restoring tool looks like an ordinary tap and die set, but instead of cutting the threads, it reshapes the damaged portion of the thread.

Threads that have substantial damage require other methods of repair. A common method for repairing damaged internal threads is a thread insert. A number of manufacturers make thread inserts, and they all work in a similar fashion. The thread insert is a sleeve that has both internal and external threads. The internal thread on the insert matches the original damaged thread size. The hole with the damaged thread is made larger and a fresh larger-diameter thread is cut. This thread matches the external thread on the insert. The thread insert can then be screwed and secured into the prepared hole. The insert provides a brand new internal thread that matches the original size.

You should always make sure the tools are clean and in good condition and are suitable for the thread repair. Determine the type and size of the thread to be repaired. Thread pitch gauges and vernier calipers may be used to measure the thread. Thread repair can include removal of a broken bolt, restoration of internal and external threads, and the use of a thread insert to repair an internal thread.

To remove a broken bolt, inspect the site. If enough of the bolt is sticking out of the surface, then a pair of pliers or locking pliers may be enough to turn and remove the bolt. If the bolt is broken off flush with the surface, then a screw or bolt extraction tool will be needed. Select the correct size of extractor, and drill the designated hole size in the center of the broken bolt to accommodate the extractor. Use a center punch to mark the bolt to assist in centering the hole to drill. Once the hole is drilled, insert the extractor and turn it counterclockwise. The flutes on the extractor should grab the inside of the bolt and hopefully back out. Be careful not to exert too much force on the extractor if the bolt is extremely stuck in place. If the extractor breaks, it is almost impossible to remove it since it is made of hardened metal that cannot be cut by most drill bits. Once the broken bolt is removed, run a lubricated tap or thread-restoring tool of the correct size and thread pitch through the hole to clean up any rust or damage.

To conduct thread repair, follow the steps in SKILL DRILL 6-25.

SKILL DRILL 6-25 Thread Repair

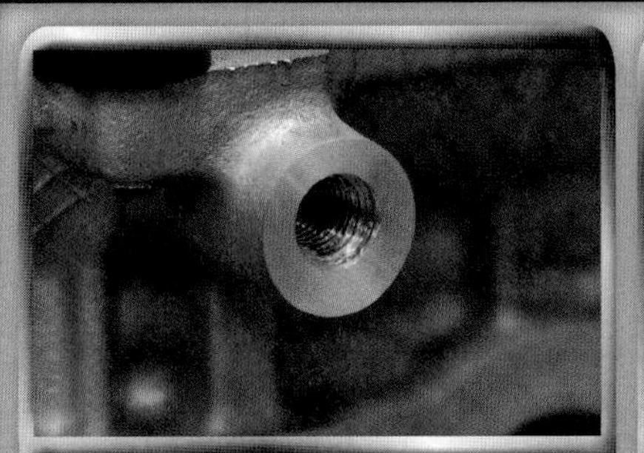

1. Inspect the condition of the threads and determine the repair method.

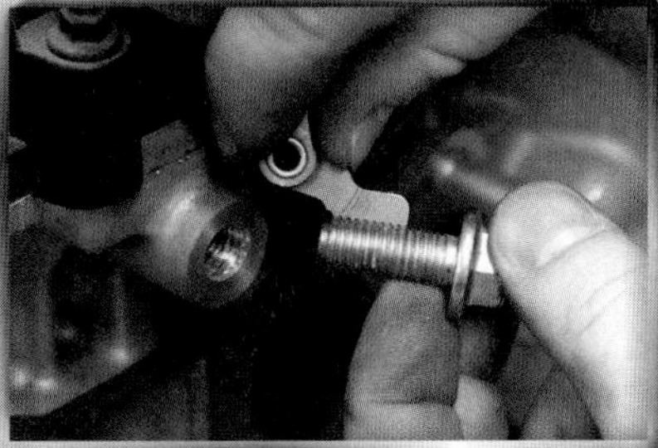

2. Determine the type and size of the thread to be repaired. Thread pitch gauges and vernier calipers may be used to measure the thread.

3. Prepare materials for conducting the repair: dies and taps or a drill bit and drill, cutting oil, if required, and inserts. Select the correctly sized tap or die if conducting a minor repair. Run the die or tap through or over the thread; be sure to use cutting lubricant.

4. If using inserts, select the correctly sized insert. Drill the damaged hole, ensuring the drill is in perfect alignment with the hole.

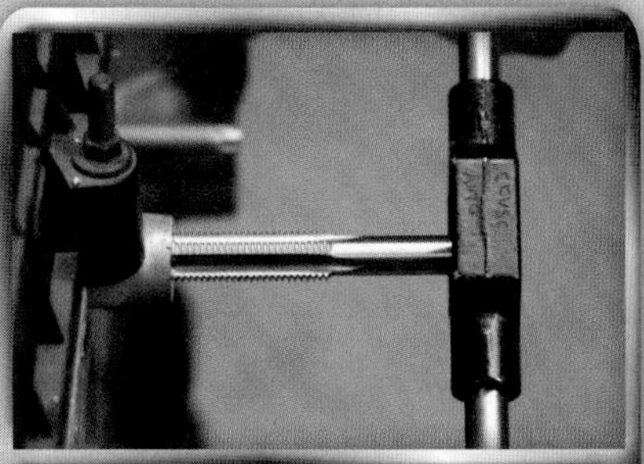

5. Cut the new thread to hold the insert using the appropriate tap. Make sure you use cutting lubricant if required.

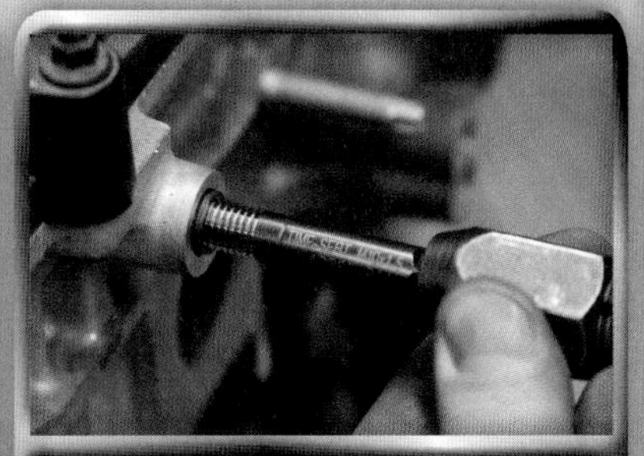

6. Using the insert-installing tool, install the insert by screwing it into the newly cut threads. Make sure the insert is secure or locked into the hole using the method specified by the manufacturer.

7. Test the insert to ensure it is secure and the bolt will screw all the way in.

Welding and Cutting Equipment

Oxyacetylene

Oxyacetylene torches are occasionally used by technicians to heat, braze, weld, and cut metal. Acetylene is a highly combustible gas, and when combined with oxygen, it produces a very hot temperature of 6300°F to 6800°F (3480°C to 3760°C). Heating is used to loosen rusted fasteners to help remove them. Brazing uses brass filler rod, which is melted by the torch to join or patch metals. Welding is the process of joining metals by melting the metals together, usually along with a filler rod, which provides extra material to fill any gaps. Cutting involves heating metals until they are so hot that when given an extra shot of oxygen, the metal burns.

The torch consists of an acetylene cylinder, an oxygen cylinder, a pressure regulator for each cylinder, hoses, a flashback arrestor for each hose, the torch handle, and the tip. The cylinders hold the gases. Each pressure regulator has two pressure gauges. One gauge shows how much pressure is in the cylinder, and the other gauge shows how much pressure is in the line. The line (hose) pressure is adjusted on the pressure regulator by the operator. The hoses run from each regulator to the flashback arrestors on the torch handle. The acetylene hose is red, and the oxygen hose is green. The **flashback arrestors** are spring-loaded check valves that allow flow through the hoses in one direction only—from the cylinders to the torch handle. They prevent flame from traveling back up the hose in the case of a flashback, which is when the oxygen and acetylene ignite inside the torch handle. Flashback happens if the torch valves are set lower than they should be for a particular tip, which produces low gas flow out of the tip; if a welding spark jumps up into the tip; or if the torch is set with too much oxygen flowing. The torch handle may have the flashback arrestors screwed into it or they may be built directly into the handle. The gas flow valves are near the base of the handle. The top of the handle is threaded so that different tips can be installed.

Different tip sizes are available depending on the size and thickness of the metal to be heated, welded, or cut FIGURE 6-45. Larger tips allow more gas (oxygen and acetylene) mixture to flow out of the hole in the tip, which produces a larger flame. Welding tips usually have a single hole in the tip—a small hole for thin metals or a larger hole for thicker metals. Larger heating tips, usually called "rose buds," have multiple holes, typically five or more in a circle toward the outside tip face. The multiple holes allow the rose bud to create the same amount of heat as a much larger single-hole tip but with a lower chance of flashback. The cutting torch tip uses multiple holes in a circle similar to a rose bud, but it also has a central hole for pure oxygen inside the circle of holes.

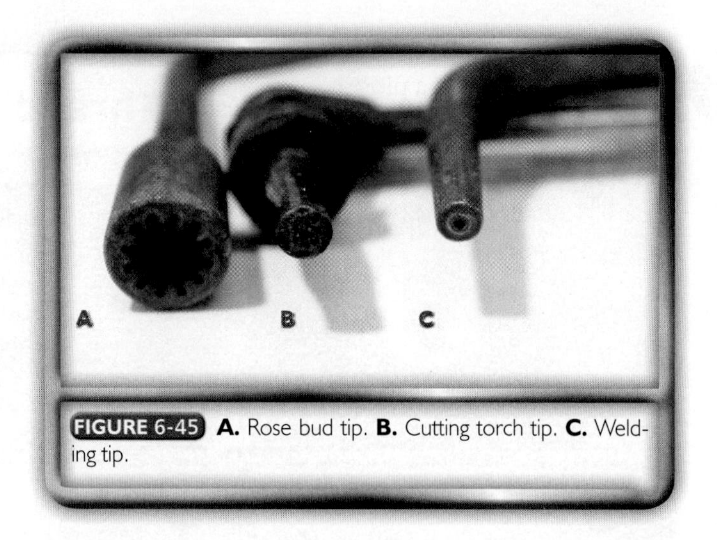
A
B
C

FIGURE 6-45 **A.** Rose bud tip. **B.** Cutting torch tip. **C.** Welding tip.

When oxyacetylene is used to cut steel, a cutting torch is fitted in place of the welding tip. The outer circle of holes provides the oxygen and acetylene for heating the metal. The center hole injects a stream of pure oxygen into the red-hot metal and causes it to burn, thereby cutting the metal. The oxygen flow is controlled by a spring-loaded lever and activated by the technician.

Oxyacetylene Torch Safety

Safety needs to be first and foremost when working with an oxyacetylene torch. Oxyacetylene cylinders carry very high pressures. The acetylene pressure in a full cylinder is approximately 250 psi (1724 kPa), and the oxygen cylinder is approximately 2200 psi (15,168 kPa). If an oxygen cylinder falls over and breaks the main valve off, the cylinder will become a missile and can even go through concrete block walls, so always secure the cylinders properly to the wall or an approved welding cart.

Wear a leather apron or similar protective clothing and welding gloves when using an oxyacetylene torch. T-shirts, nylon, and polyester blend clothing will not provide enough protection because ultraviolet light and sparks of hot metal will pass through them. Always use proper welding goggles. Do not use sunglasses because they do not filter the extreme ultraviolet light as effectively and the plastic used in the lenses of sunglasses will not protect your eyes from sparks.

Never point the lighted flame toward another person or any flammable material. Always light the oxyacetylene torch with the striker. A cigarette lighter could explode, and a match would put your hand too close to the igniting tip. Wherever possible, use a heat shield behind the component you are heating. This will prevent nearby objects from becoming hot. After heating a piece of metal, label it as "HOT" with a piece of chalk so that others will not attempt to pick it up.

Purging Oxyacetylene Torches

Purging the oxyacetylene system is the process of venting all of the gas in the system from the cylinder valve to the torch handle tip and setting the valves so nothing can enter the system. Purging the system is required when you are finished with the torch for the day, if you are not sure if the torch was shut down properly the last time it was used, or if you are making repairs to the system.

To properly purge an oxyacetylene system, follow the steps in SKILL DRILL 6-26.

Safety

- Oxygen and acetylene cylinders must be securely stored in an upright position.
- Listen and look for leaks.
- An oxyacetylene torch can produce a large amount of heat. Be aware that any objects you direct the flame toward will become hot.
- Always have a suitable fire extinguisher near your work area.
- Do not use an oxyacetylene torch near any flammable materials.

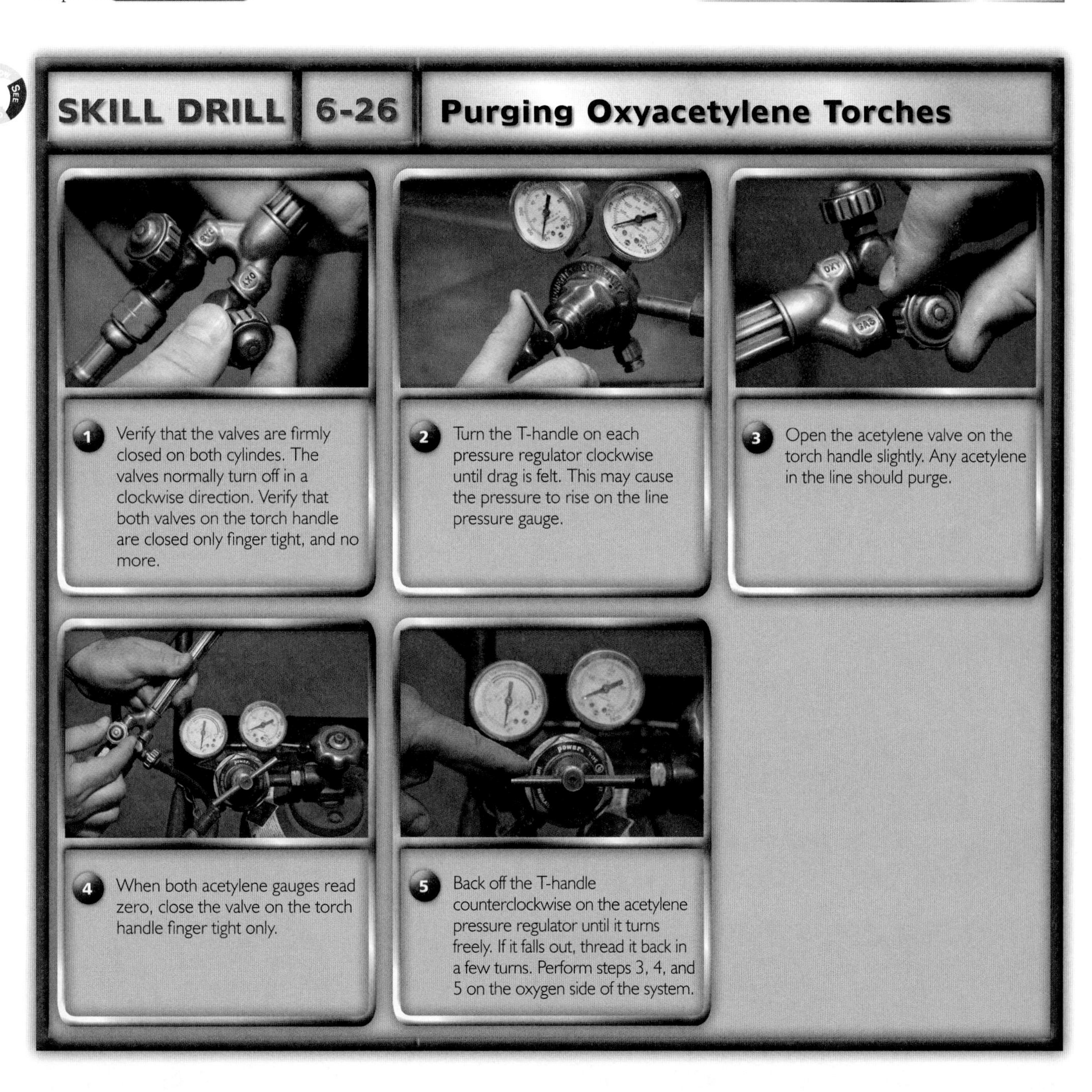
SKILL DRILL 6-26 Purging Oxyacetylene Torches
1 Verify that the valves are firmly closed on both cylinders. The valves normally turn off in a clockwise direction. Verify that both valves on the torch handle are closed only finger tight, and no more.
2 Turn the T-handle on each pressure regulator clockwise until drag is felt. This may cause the pressure to rise on the line pressure gauge.
3 Open the acetylene valve on the torch handle slightly. Any acetylene in the line should purge.
4 When both acetylene gauges read zero, close the valve on the torch handle finger tight only.
5 Back off the T-handle counterclockwise on the acetylene pressure regulator until it turns freely. If it falls out, thread it back in a few turns. Perform steps 3, 4, and 5 on the oxygen side of the system.

Setting up Oxyacetylene Torches

Setting up an oxyacetylene torch means getting it ready to use. There are precise steps that need to be followed for the sake of safety. Each of these steps are used no matter what kind of torch work you are performing. If in doubt, always refer the torch manufacturer's instructions.

To set up an oxyacetylene torch for heating, follow the steps in SKILL DRILL 6-27.

SKILL DRILL 6-27 Setting up Oxyacetylene Torches

1. Verify that the two cylinders are secured in an upright position. Verify that the valves on each of the cylinders are completely and firmly turned off. If both gauges on each cylinder do not read zero, you must purge the system of any gas on each cylinder following the steps in the previous skill drill. Verify that the T-handles on the pressure regulators are backed off and turn freely.

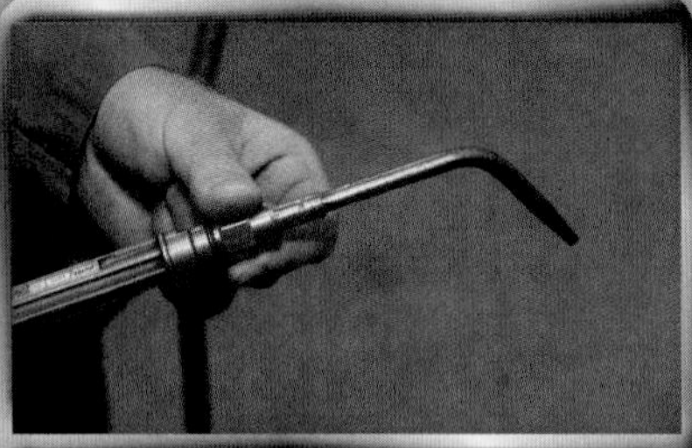

2. Select the tip you will be using and thread it onto the torch handle by hand. Position the tip so that it faces away from you. Tighten it only moderately hand tight., as it normally uses O-rings to seal the joint.

3. Standing off to the side of the pressure gauges, very slowly open the valve on the top of the oxygen cylinder. When pressure stabilizes, continue to open it all the way until it stops. While still standing off to the side of the pressure gauges, slowly open the valve on the top of the acetylene cylinder ¼ to ½ turn only so it can be quickly shut off if needed.

4. Open the acetylene valve on the torch handle about ⅛ turn and then turn the T-handle on the acetylene pressure regulator (clockwise) until the low-pressure gauge reads 5 psi. (Never exceed 15 psi line pressure on acetylene.) Lightly turn off the valve on the torch handle. Open the oxygen valve on the torch handle about ⅛ turn and then turn the T-handle on the oxygen pressure regulator (clockwise) until the low-pressure gauge reads 10 psi (if welding or heating) or 20–25 psi (if cutting). Lightly turn off the valve on the torch handle.

5. Before you light the torch, check the area you are working in to make sure there are no flammable materials, fluids, or people nearby. Wear the right safety gear: gloves and tinted goggles or welding helmet. Turn the acetylene valve on the torch handle slightly counterclockwise. You should hear the gas hissing. Hold the striker against the tip of the torch with the lighter cup pointing away from you. Flick the striker to create the spark that will ignite the gas at the tip of the torch. Open the acetylene valve slowly until the sooty smoke produced by the torch disappears. Then slowly open the oxygen valve on the torch handle.

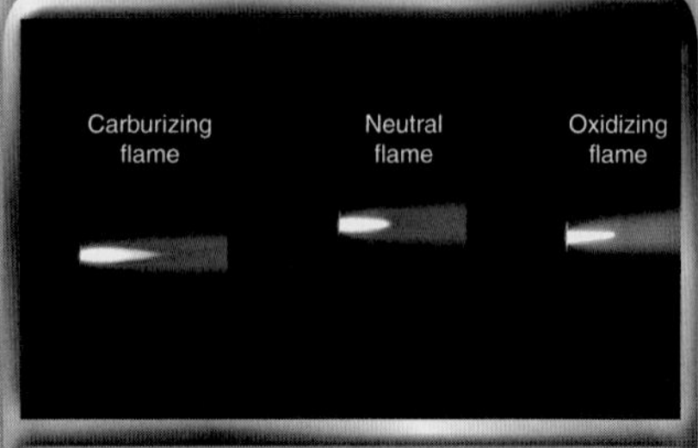
Carburizing flame
Neutral flame
Oxidizing flame

6. As you open the oxygen valve, you will see the color of the flame change. Continue to open the oxygen valve slowly until you can observe a single small, sharp blue cone in the center of the torch flame. This is the neutral flame you need for general heating and welding. If you want more heat, open the acetylene valve a bit further, then open the oxygen valve to bring the flame back to neutral. To create less heat, close the oxygen valve slightly, then close the acetylene valve until a neutral flame is obtained. When you are ready to shut down the torch, quickly close the oxygen valve finger tight on the torch handle, followed by closing the acetylene valve finger tight on the handle. Purge the system.

Using Oxyacetylene Torches for Heating

Technicians use an oxyacetylene torch to heat a variety of objects such as rusted bolts or brake drums that will not break loose. A torch might also be used to heat a container of water to test a thermostat in. Being able to safely use a torch is a valuable skill in a shop.

To use an oxyacetylene torch for heating, follow the steps in SKILL DRILL 6-28.

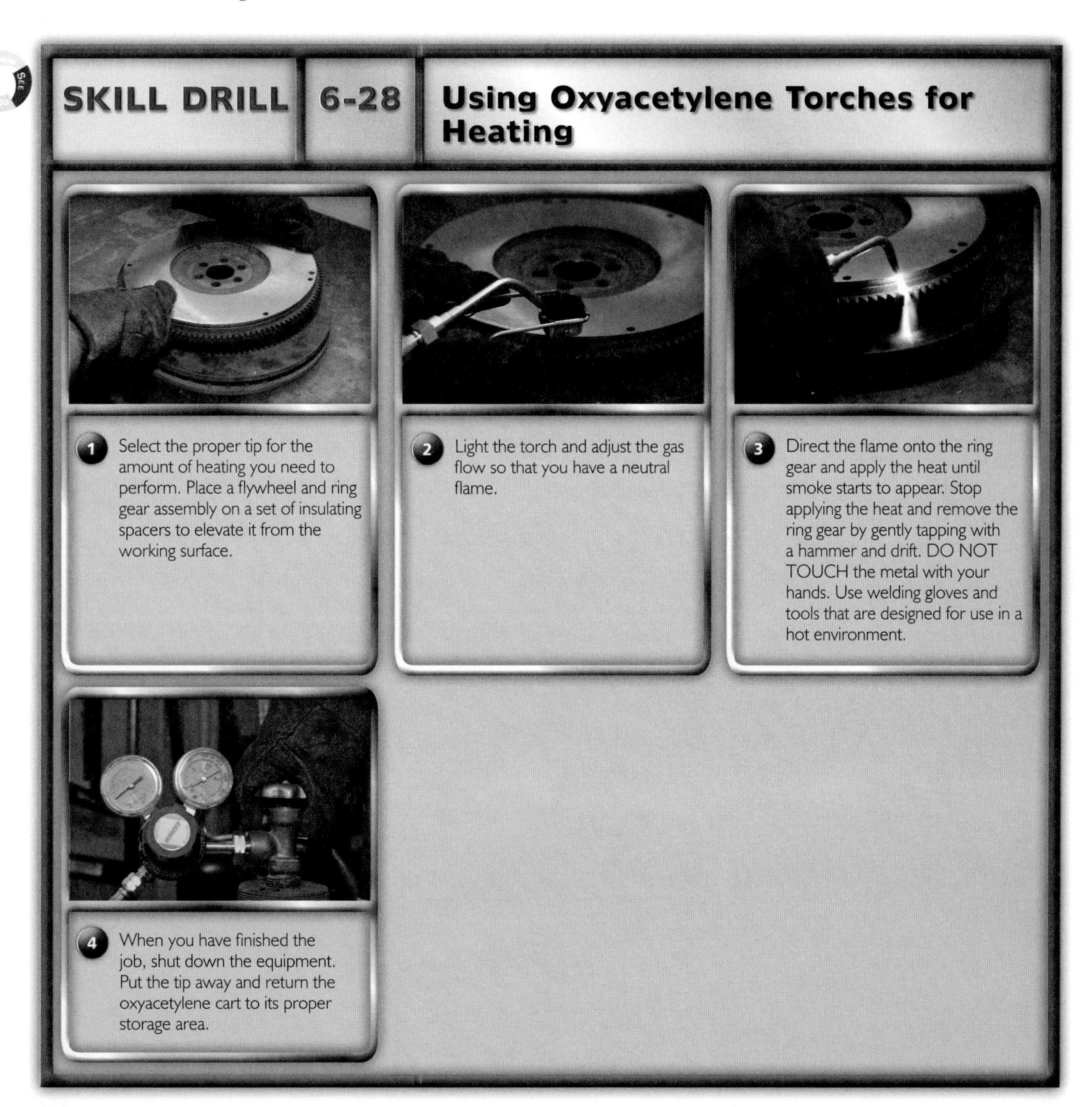

SKILL DRILL 6-28 Using Oxyacetylene Torches for Heating

1. Select the proper tip for the amount of heating you need to perform. Place a flywheel and ring gear assembly on a set of insulating spacers to elevate it from the working surface.
2. Light the torch and adjust the gas flow so that you have a neutral flame.
3. Direct the flame onto the ring gear and apply the heat until smoke starts to appear. Stop applying the heat and remove the ring gear by gently tapping with a hammer and drift. DO NOT TOUCH the metal with your hands. Use welding gloves and tools that are designed for use in a hot environment.
4. When you have finished the job, shut down the equipment. Put the tip away and return the oxyacetylene cart to its proper storage area.

Using Welding Tips for Welding

Welding is a handy skill for technicians to have. Sometimes tools need to be modified so they will work in particular situations, or a bracket breaks and needs to be welded back together. Being able to weld gives you another option in your quest to fix and repair vehicles.

To use an oxyacetylene torch for welding, follow the steps in SKILL DRILL 6-29.

SKILL DRILL 6-29 Using Welding Tips for Welding

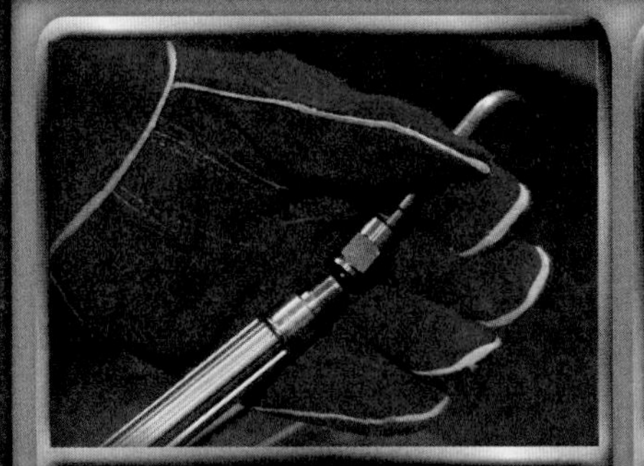

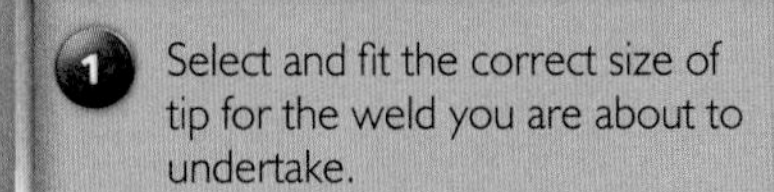

1. Select and fit the correct size of tip for the weld you are about to undertake.

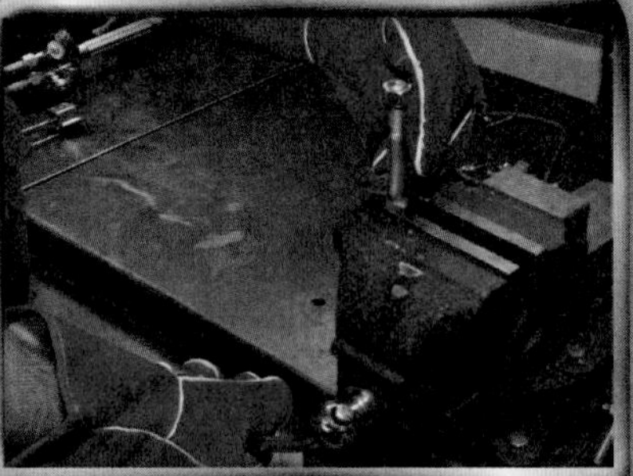

2. Make sure you have assembled all the materials you need to undertake the weld, including safety equipment, a fire extinguisher close at hand, welding filler rod, and the items to be welded. Position the items to be welded and secure them with clamps if necessary.

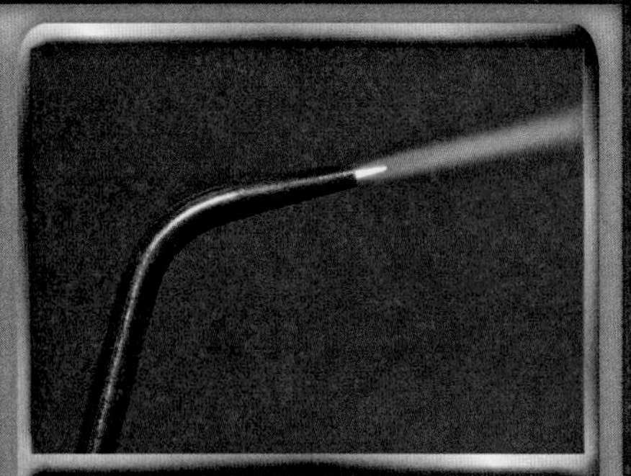

3. Light the torch and adjust the gas flow so that you have a neutral flame.

4. Direct the flame into the area to be welded and apply the heat until the metal just starts to melt a small pool of metal. Do not overheat the metals. Slowly add the welding rod into the molten pool of metal. If welding rod sticks to the metal, twist it with your thumb and forefinger to break loose.

5. Move the torch along the weld joint, continuously adding filler rod until the weld is complete. Avoid overheating the joint and try to confine the heated area just to the spot you are welding.

6. When the weld is complete, stop applying the heat. DO NOT TOUCH the metal with your hands. Use welding gloves and tools that are designed for use in a hot environment. When you have finished the job, properly shut down the equipment.

Using Welding Tips for Brazing

Brazing allows a technician to join metals in a similar manner to soldering, but at higher temperatures of about 850°F (454°C), but not as hot as welding. Brazing typically uses brass filler rod, which melts at higher temperatures and is stronger than solder. Brazing works well when joining a heavier metal part to a thinner metal part such as a brass fitting to a thin sheet metal oil pan. It also bonds tighter to the metals, so it is more permanent than soldering.

To use an oxyacetylene torch for brazing, follow the steps in **SKILL DRILL 6-30**.

Using Cutting Torches

Technicians use a cutting torch for various reasons. They may need to cut fasteners that cannot be disassembled due to rust and corrosion, such as exhaust pipe clamps that are frozen in place. Or they may need to cut a wrench to shorten it so it will fit into a tight space. Technicians who are very skilled with a torch can even cut out a broken-off bolt from its threaded hole. However, don't try this unless you are *very* skilled with a cutting torch.

To use an oxyacetylene torch for cutting, follow the steps in **SKILL DRILL 6-31**.

Plasma Cutters

A **plasma cutter** is a tool for cutting various thicknesses of metal. Plasma cutters work by applying a pressurized gas such as air, oxygen, nitrogen, or argon through a nozzle located in the center of a hand piece with an electrode. When power is applied to the electrode and a return electrical path is established through the metal that needs to be cut, a powerful spark is created. The spark heats the gas, changing it to plasma, a fourth state of matter. The plasma is very hot—approximately 30,000°F (16,600°C)—and moving very fast. The plasma heats the metal very quickly and blows the molten metal out to produce a clean cut through the metal.

Plasma cutters have been around for quite a long time, but in the past they have been expensive, large machines reserved for large-scale manufacturing. More recently, shop-sized machines have been developed and are relatively inexpensive. This has made them very accessible and an alternative to using oxyacetylene as a cutting tool for metal.

SKILL DRILL 6-30 Using Welding Tips for Brazing

1. Select and fit the correct size tip for the braze you are about to undertake. Make sure you have assembled all the materials you need to undertake the braze, including safety equipment, a fire extinguisher close at hand, brazing filler rod, appropriate flux, and the items to be brazed. Position the items to be brazed and secure them with clamps if necessary. Light the torch and adjust the gas flow so that you have a slightly carburizing flame.

2. Direct the flame into the area to be brazed and apply the heat until the metal is cherry red. Be careful to not overheat the metals. Slowly add the brazing rod with flux into the space to be brazed. Some filler rods come with a flux coating attached; others require the addition of flux. This is achieved by slightly heating the filler rod with the welding torch and dipping the heated brazing rod into the flux.

3. Move the torch along the weld joint, continuously adding filler rod until the braze is complete. Avoid overheating the joint and try to confine the heated area to only the spot you are brazing. When the braze is complete, stop applying the heat. DO NOT TOUCH the metal with your hands. Use welding gloves and tools that are designed for use in a hot environment. When you have finished the job, you will need to properly shut down the equipment.

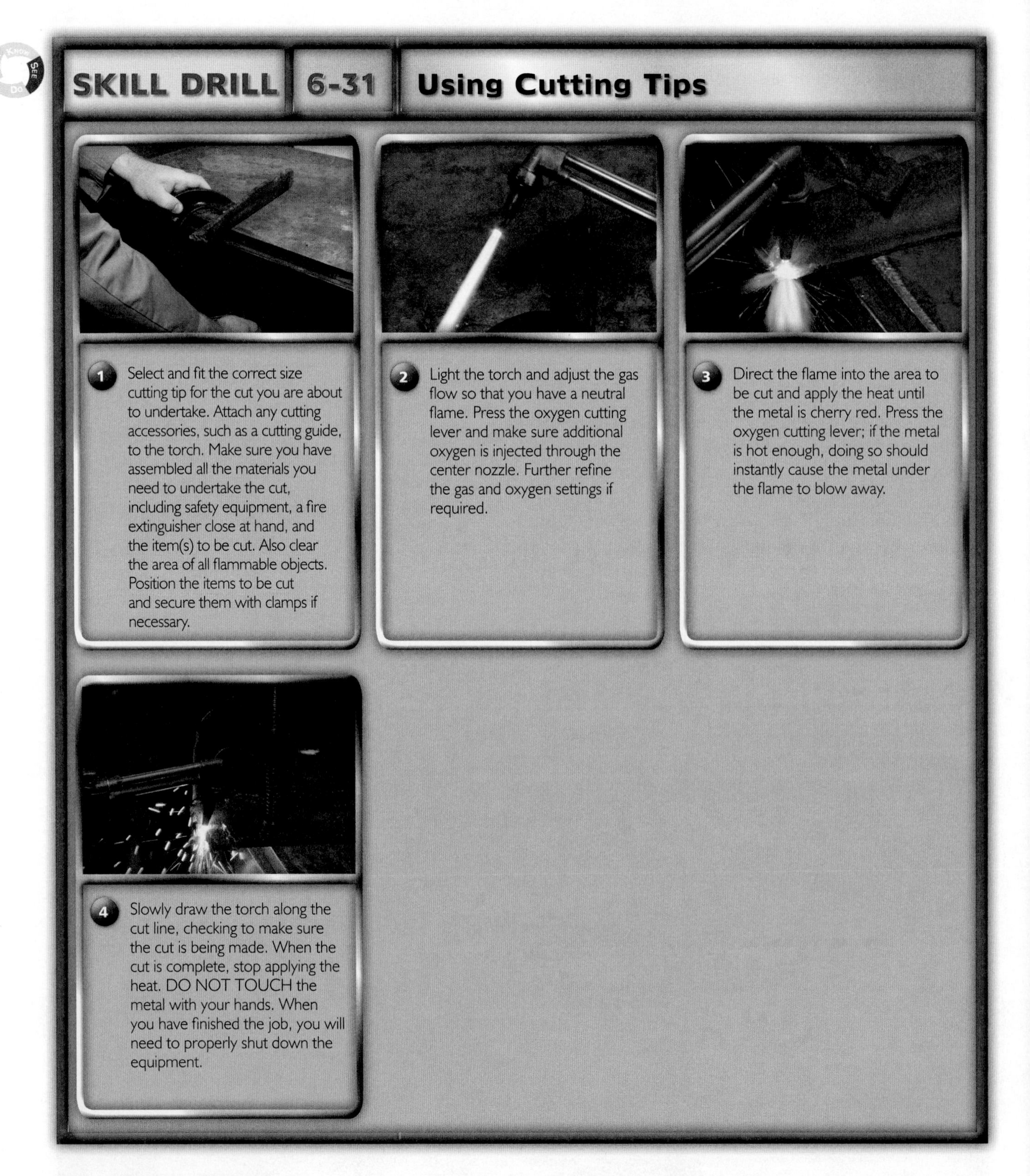
SKILL DRILL 6-31 Using Cutting Tips
1 Select and fit the correct size cutting tip for the cut you are about to undertake. Attach any cutting accessories, such as a cutting guide, to the torch. Make sure you have assembled all the materials you need to undertake the cut, including safety equipment, a fire extinguisher close at hand, and the item(s) to be cut. Also clear the area of all flammable objects. Position the items to be cut and secure them with clamps if necessary.
2 Light the torch and adjust the gas flow so that you have a neutral flame. Press the oxygen cutting lever and make sure additional oxygen is injected through the center nozzle. Further refine the gas and oxygen settings if required.
3 Direct the flame into the area to be cut and apply the heat until the metal is cherry red. Press the oxygen cutting lever; if the metal is hot enough, doing so should instantly cause the metal under the flame to blow away.
4 Slowly draw the torch along the cut line, checking to make sure the cut is being made. When the cut is complete, stop applying the heat. DO NOT TOUCH the metal with your hands. When you have finished the job, you will need to properly shut down the equipment.

Using Plasma Cutters

If using the plasma cutter on a vehicle, make sure the battery is disconnected.

Wherever possible, use a heat shield behind the component you are heating. This will prevent nearby objects from becoming hot. After cutting a piece of metal, label it as "HOT" with a piece of chalk so that others will not attempt to pick it up.

Before using a plasma cutter, identify the location of the eyewash and first-aid stations, and put on a welding helmet and gloves. As with any piece of equipment, always refer to the manufacturer's manual for specific operating instructions. To use a plasma cutter for cutting, follow the steps in SKILL DRILL 6-32.

Wire Feed Welders

Wire feed welders are a type of welder that has the filler rod automatically feeding into the welding joint via the hand piece. They are becoming commonplace in shops. The wire feed is controlled by a trigger on the hand piece, and its rate of feed can be adjusted on the welder to accommodate the size of weld being conducted. The welder has controls for amperage, like on a traditional arc welder, and this is adjusted depending on the thickness of metal to be welded.

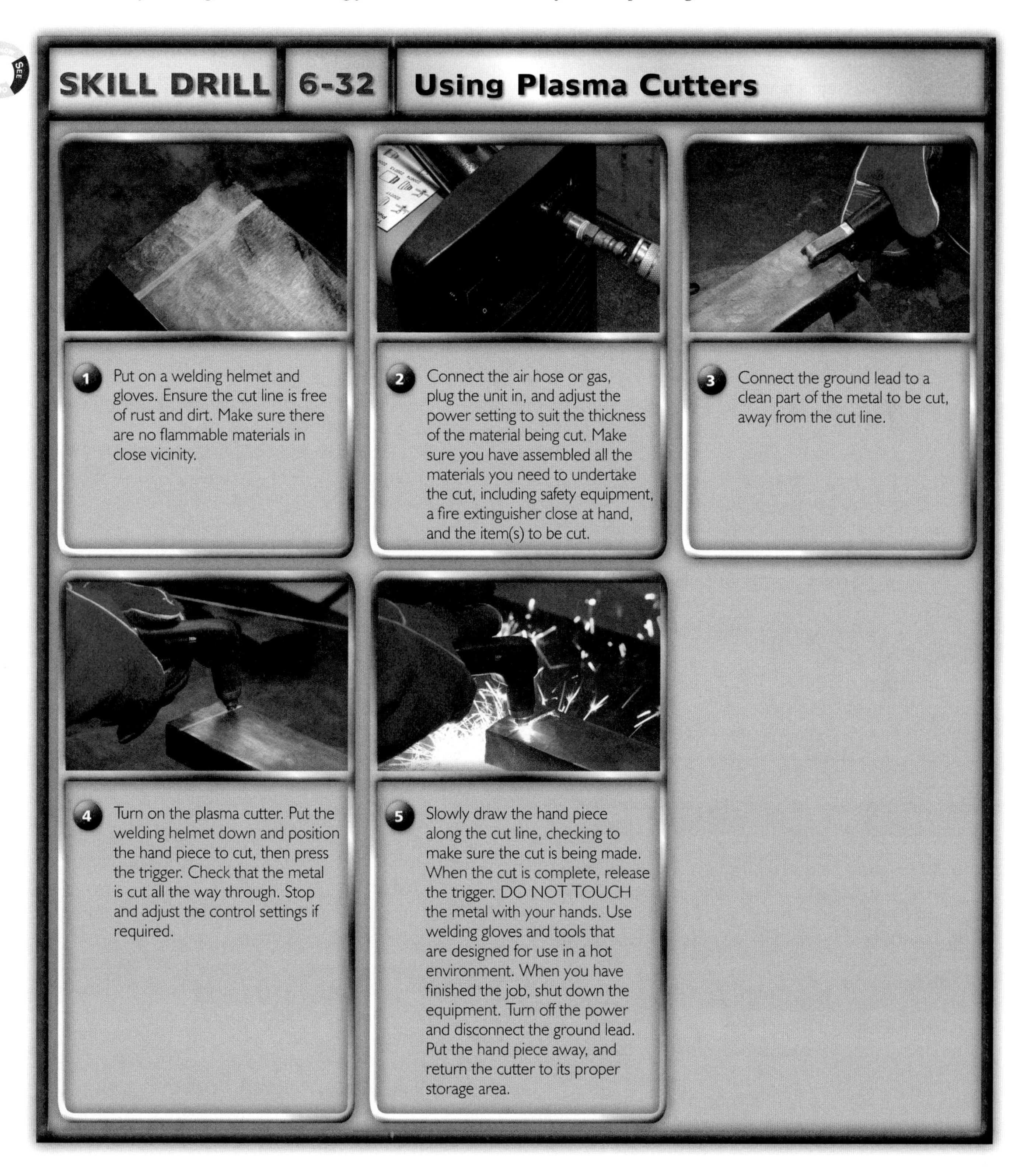

SKILL DRILL 6-32 Using Plasma Cutters

1. Put on a welding helmet and gloves. Ensure the cut line is free of rust and dirt. Make sure there are no flammable materials in close vicinity.
2. Connect the air hose or gas, plug the unit in, and adjust the power setting to suit the thickness of the material being cut. Make sure you have assembled all the materials you need to undertake the cut, including safety equipment, a fire extinguisher close at hand, and the item(s) to be cut.
3. Connect the ground lead to a clean part of the metal to be cut, away from the cut line.
4. Turn on the plasma cutter. Put the welding helmet down and position the hand piece to cut, then press the trigger. Check that the metal is cut all the way through. Stop and adjust the control settings if required.
5. Slowly draw the hand piece along the cut line, checking to make sure the cut is being made. When the cut is complete, release the trigger. DO NOT TOUCH the metal with your hands. Use welding gloves and tools that are designed for use in a hot environment. When you have finished the job, shut down the equipment. Turn off the power and disconnect the ground lead. Put the hand piece away, and return the cutter to its proper storage area.

Like any electric welder, the weld requires a flux or inert gas shield to prevent the oxidization of the weld. In a standard arc welder, this is provided by a coating on the filler stick. For wire feed welders, this can be provided either by an inert gas that is supplied through a nozzle to the welding tip or by a flux core in the center of the filler wire that evaporates as it is heated by the arc. This method shields the weld from oxidization. Wire feed welders are usually classified as gas or gasless. The gas wire feed welder has a provision for an inert gas bottle to be fitted to the welder to supply the shield gas to the welding tip. Gasless welders rely on the flux being in the core of the filler wire. Many wire feed welders can accommodate both gas and gasless operation.

Using Wire Feed Welders

Wear a leather apron or similar protective clothing and welding gloves when using a plasma cutter. T-shirts, nylon, and polyester blend clothing will not provide enough protection. Ultraviolet light and sparks of hot metal will pass through them. Always use appropriate eye protection and a welding helmet. Do not use sunglasses because they do not filter the extreme ultraviolet light as effectively. The plastic used in the lenses of sunglasses will not protect your eyes from sparks.

If using the wire feed welder on a vehicle, make sure the battery is disconnected. Wherever possible, use a heat shield behind the component you are welding. This will prevent nearby objects from becoming hot. After welding a piece of metal, label it as "HOT" with a piece of chalk so that others will not attempt to pick it up.

Before using a wire feed welder, identify the location of the eyewash and first-aid stations, and put on a welding helmet and gloves. As with any piece of equipment, always refer to the manufacturer's manual for specific operating instructions. To use a wire feed welder, follow the steps in SKILL DRILL 6-33.

Safety

- Wire feed welders require high amperage. Make sure you plug the welder into an appropriately sized outlet.
- A wire feed welder can produce a large amount of heat. Be aware that any objects you weld will become hot.
- Always have a suitable fire extinguisher near your work area.
- Do not use a wire feed welder near any flammable materials.

Safety

Do not use flammable cleaners or water on electrical equipment.

Cleaning Tools and Equipment

Clean tools and equipment work more safely and efficiently. At the end of each working day, clean the tools and equipment you used and check them for any damage. If you note any damage, tag the tool as faulty and organize a repair or replacement. Electrical current can travel over oily or greasy surfaces. Be sure to keep electrical power tools clean.

All shop equipment should have a maintenance schedule. Always complete the tasks described on the schedule at the required time. This will help to keep the equipment in safe working order.

Store commonly used tools in an easy-to-reach location. If a tool or piece of equipment is too difficult to return, then it will likely be left on a workbench or on the floor where it will become a safety hazard. Keep your work area tidy. This will help you work more efficiently and safely.

Keep a trash can close to your work area and place any waste in it as soon as possible. Dispose of liquid and solid waste, such as oils, coolant, and worn components, in the correct manner. Local authorities provide guidelines for waste disposal with fines for noncompliance. When cleaning products lose their effectiveness, they will need to be replaced. Refer to the supplier's recommendations for collection or disposal. Do not pour solvents or other chemicals into the sewage system. This is both environmentally damaging and illegal.

Always use chemical gloves when using any cleaning material because excessive exposure to cleaning materials can damage skin. Also, absorbing some chemicals through the skin over time can cause permanent harm to your body. Some solvents are flammable; never use cleaning materials near an open flame or cigarette. The fumes from cleaning chemicals can be toxic, so wear appropriate respirator and eye protection wherever you are using these products.

To keep work areas and equipment clean and operational, follow the steps in SKILL DRILL 6-34.

SKILL DRILL 6-33 Using Wire Feed Welders

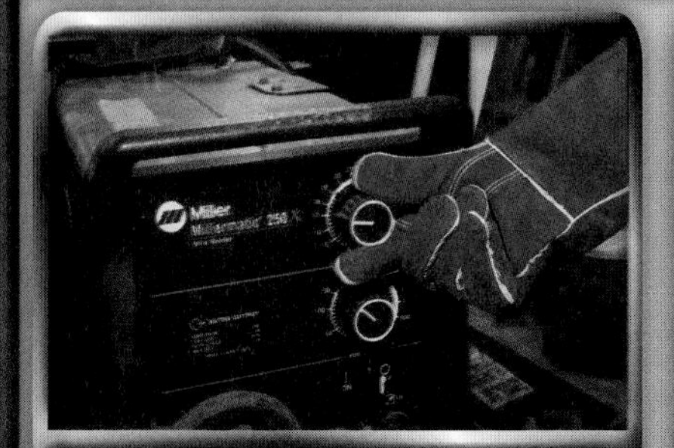

1. Prepare the area to be welded. Ensure the material is free of rust and dirt. Make sure there are no flammable materials in close vicinity. Prepare the wire feed welder. Ensure enough wire is in the reel, set up the gas if using gas operation, plug the unit in and adjust the power setting and wire feed speed to suit the material thickness being welded. Make sure you have assembled all the materials you need to undertake the weld, including safety equipment, a fire extinguisher close at hand, and the item(s) to be welded.

2. Connect the ground lead to a clean part of the metal to be welded, as close as possible to the weld but away from the welding line.

3. Position the items to be welded and secure them with clamps if necessary.

4. Turn on the welder. Put on the welding helmet, position the hand piece to weld, and press the trigger. Direct the weld into the joint at about a 15-degree angle. Don't let the welding wire protrude more than about half an inch from the gun. Check that the weld is satisfactory. Stop and adjust the control settings if required.

5. Slowly draw the hand piece along the line to be welded, checking to make sure the weld is being made. When the weld is complete, release the trigger. DO NOT TOUCH the metal with your hands. When you have finished the job, you will need to shut down the equipment. Turn off the power and disconnect the ground lead. Put the hand piece away, and return the welder to its proper storage area.

SKILL DRILL 6-34 Cleaning Tools and Equipment

1. Clean hand tools. Keep your hand tools in good, clean condition with two sets of rags. One rag should be lint-free to clean or handle precision instruments or components. The other should be oily to prevent rust and corrosion.

2. Clean floor jacks. Wipe off any oil or grease on the floor jack and check for fluid leaks. If you find any, remove the jack from use and have it repaired or replaced. Occasionally, apply a few drops of lubricating oil to the wheels and a few drops to the posts of threaded jack stands.

3. Clean electrical power tools. Brush off any dust and wipe off excess oil or grease with a clean rag. Inspect any electrical cables for dirt, oil, or grease, and for any chafing or exposed wires. With drills, inspect the chuck and lubricate it occasionally with machine oil.

Air Tool Oil
LUBRICATES & PROTECTS
REMOVES HARMFUL DEPOSITS

4. Clean air-powered tools. Apply a few drops of oil into the inlet of your air tools every day. Although these tools have no electrical motor, they do need regular lubrication of the internal parts to prevent wear.

5. Clean hoists and heavy machinery. Locate the checklist or maintenance record for each hoist or other major piece of equipment before carrying out cleaning activities. You should clean equipment operating mechanisms and attachments of excess oil or grease.

Wrap-up

Ready for Review

- Tools and equipment should be used only for the task they were designed to do.
- Always have a safe attitude when using tools and equipment.
- Do not use damaged tools; inspect before using, then clean and inspect again before putting them away.
- Lockouts and tagouts are meant to prevent technicians from using tools and equipment that are potentially unsafe.
- Many tools and measuring instruments have USCS or metric system markings to identify their size.
- Compressed air systems are comprised of a compressor, a pressure regulator, an air hose or fixed piping, and the tool to be powered.
- Standard compressors use a piston to force air into a storage tank, while scroll compressors use rotating scrolls to compress air.
- Always use caution: Compressed air injuries can be fatal.
- Many compressed air systems use air driers to remove all traces of moisture from the compressed air.
- Automatic oilers provide a regular application of lubricating oil to the stream of compressed air which then lubricates air tools and equipment.
- Threaded fasteners include bolts, studs, and nuts, and are designed to secure vehicle parts under stress.
- Torque defines how much a fastener should be tightened.
- Bolts, nuts, and studs use threads to secure each part; these threads can be in standard or metric measures.
- Thread pitch refers to the coarseness of the thread; USCS bolts, nuts, and studs are measured in threads per inch (tpi), classified as coarse (UNC) or fine (UNF).
- Fasteners are graded by tensile strength (how much tension can be withstood before breakage).
- The SAE rates fasteners from grade 1 to grade 8; always replace a nut or bolt with one of the same grade.
- Torque specification indicates the level of tightness each bolt or nut should be tightened to; torque charts list torque specifications for nuts and bolts.
- Torque (or tension) wrenches tighten fasteners to the correct torque specification.
- Torque value—the amount of twisting force applied to a fastener by the torque wrench—is specified in foot-pounds, inch-pounds, or newton meters.
- Torque wrench styles are beam (simplest and least expensive), clicker, dial, and electronic. Each gives an indication of when proper torque is achieved.
- Bolts that are tightened beyond their yield point do not return to their original length when loosened.
- Torque-to-yield (TTY) bolts can be torqued just beyond their yield point, but should not be reused.
- Torque angle can be used to tighten TTY bolts and requires both a torque wrench and an angle gauge.
- Common wrenches include box end, open end, combination (most popular), flare nut (or flare tubing), open-end adjustable, and ratcheting box end.
- Box-end wrenches can loosen very tight fasteners, but open-end wrenches usually work better once the fastner has been broken loose.
- Use the correct wrench for the situation, so as not to damage the bolt or nut.
- Sockets grip fasteners tightly on all six corners and are purchased in sets.
- Sockets are classified as follows: standard or metric, size of drive used to turn them, number of points, depth of socket, and thickness of wall.
- The most common socket handle is a ratchet; a breaker bar gives more leverage, or a sliding T-handle may be used.
- Fasteners can be spun off or on (but not tightened) by a speed brace or speeder handle.
- Pliers hold, cut, or compress materials; types include slip-joint, combination, arc joint, needle nose, flat, diagonal cutting, snap ring, and locking.
- Always use the correct type of pliers for the job.
- Cutting tools include bolt cutters, tin snips, and aviation snips.
- Allen wrenches are designed to fit into fasteners with recessed hexagonal heads.
- Screwdriver types include flat blade (most common), Phillips, Pozidriv, offset, ratcheting, and impact.
- The tip of the screwdriver must be matched exactly to the slot or recess on the head of a fastener.
- Magnetic pickup tools and mechanical fingers allow for the extraction and insertion of objects in tight places.

- Types of hammers include ball peen (most common), sledge, mallet, and dead blow.
- Chisels are used to cut metals when hit with a hammer.
- Punches are used to mark metals when hit with a hammer and come in different diameters and different points for different tasks; types of punches include prick, center, drift, pin, ward, and hollow.
- Pry bars can be used to move, adjust, or pry parts.
- Gasket scrapers are designed to remove gaskets without damaging surrounding materials.
- Files are used to remove material from the surface of an automotive part.
- Flat files come in different grades to indicate how rough they are; grades are rough, coarse bastard, second cut, smooth, and dead smooth.
- Types of files include flat, warding, square, triangular, curved, and thread.
- Bench vices, offset vices, drill vices, and C-clamps all hold materials in place while they are worked on.
- Taps are designed to cut threads in holes or nuts; types include taper, intermediate, and bottoming.
- A die is used to cut a new thread on a blank rod or shaft.
- Gear and bearing pullers are designed to remove components from a shaft when considerable force is needed.
- Flaring tools create flares at the end of tubes to connect them to other components; types include single, double, and ISO.
- Rivet tools join together two pieces of metal; each rivet can be used only once.
- Solder is a mixture of metals, often in the form of a wire, that is melted with a soldering gun or iron to join metals together.
- Measuring tapes and steel rules are commonly used measuring tools; more precise measuring tools include micrometers, gauges, calipers, dial indicators, and straight edges.
- Micrometers can be outside, inside, or depth.
- Learn to read micrometer measurements on the sleeve/barrel and thimble; always verify the micrometer is properly calibrated before use.
- Vernier calipers measure outside, inside, and depth dimensions; newer versions have dial and digital scales.
- Dial indicators are used to measure movement.
- A straight edge is designed to assess the flatness of a surface.
- Feeler blades are flat metal strips that are used to measure the width of gaps.
- Power tools can be stationary or portable, corded or cordless, and are powered by electricity, batteries, compressed air, a propellant, or a gasoline engine.
- Drills are designed to drive a drill bit into metal (or other material) to create a hole; check drilling speed charts for proper drilling speed.
- Portable grinders are designed to grind down metals, but can also be fitted with a cutting disc to cut sheets of metal.
- Air tools use compressed, pressurized air for power; types include the air impact wrench, air ratchet, air hammer, air drill, and blowgun/air nozzle.
- Always wear eye and ear protection when using air tools; never use air nozzles on yourself or other people.
- Pressure washers/cleaners use focused, pressurized water to clean accumulated dirt and grease from vehicle components; water must be directed properly so as not to damage other parts.
- Familiarize yourself with pressure washer operating instructions and waste water disposal regulations.
- Spray wash cabinets are designed to clean automotive parts in a sealed cabinet, much like a dishwasher.
- Solvent tanks are designed for immersion of vehicle parts to remove oil, dirt, grease, and grime; always note the type of solvent being used and take necessary precautions.
- Brake washers are designed to remove brake dust from wheel brake units and their components.
- Sand or bead blasters are designed to clean paint, corrosion, or dirt from metal parts by blasting small abrasive particles onto the surface.
- Thread repair is performed to restore fastening integrity to a damaged fastener.
- Threads can be reshaped with a file, or a thread insert may be used.
- Oxyacetylene torches are designed to heat, braze, weld, and cut metal by combining acetylene with oxygen at a high temperature.
- Flashback arrestors prevent flames from traveling back up the hose in the event the oxygen and acetylene ignite inside the torch handle (flashback).
- Wear protective clothing and gear when using an oxyacetylene torch and follow all related safety precautions.
- Plasma cutters are designed to cut various thicknesses of metal and are an alternative to oxyacetylene torches.
- A wire feed welder has a filler rod automatically feeding into the welding joint at an adjustable rate.

- Battery chargers can be fast or slow, depending on current output; smart chargers calculate and provide the correct amount of charge needed for the battery.
- Vehicle batteries can be dangerous due to their high voltage; hybrid vehicle batteries have extremely high voltage and current flows.
- Batteries should be charged slowly, if possible.
- Jump-starting a vehicle places a stress on both vehicles; the current can damage electrical components in both vehicles.
- Keep work area, tools, and equipment clean and organized.

Key Terms

abrasive discs (cutting wheels) Abrasive wheels or flat discs fitted to bench, pedestal, and portable grinders.

air drier A device fitted to compressed air lines to remove moisture.

air drill A compressed air–powered drill.

air hammer A tool powered by compressed air with various hammer, cutting, punching, or chisel attachments. Also called an air chisel.

air impact wrench An impact tool powered by compressed air designed to undo tight fasteners.

air nozzle A compressed air device that emits a fine stream of compressed air for drying or cleaning parts.

air ratchet A ratchet tool for use with sockets powered by compressed air.

Allen wrench A type of hexagonal drive mechanism for fasteners.

angle grinder A portable grinder for grinding or cutting metal.

arc joint pliers Pliers with parallel slip jaws that can increase in size. Also called Channellocks.

automatic oiler A device fitted to compressed air systems to oil air tools.

aviation snips A scissor-like tool for cutting sheet metal.

ball-peen (engineer's) hammer A hammer that has a head that is rounded on one end and flat on the other; designed to work with metal items.

battery A device that converts and stores electrical energy through chemical reactions.

battery charger A device that charges a battery, reversing the discharge process.

bench grinder (pedestal grinder) A grinder that is fixed to a bench or pedestal.

bench vice A device that securely holds material in jaws while it is being worked on.

blind rivet A rivet that can be installed from its insertion side.

bolt A type of threaded fastener with a thread on one end and a hexagonal head on the other.

bolt cutters Strong cutters available in different sizes, designed to cut through non-hardened bolts and other small-stock material.

bottoming tap A thread-cutting tap designed to cut threads to the bottom of a blind hole.

box-end wrench A wrench or spanner with a closed or ring end to grip bolts and nuts.

C-clamp A clamp shaped like the letter C; it comes in various sizes and can clamp various items.

center punch Less sharp than a prick punch, the center punch makes a bigger indentation that centers a drill bit at the point where a hole is required to be drilled.

cleaning gun A device with a nozzle controlled by a trigger fitted to the outlet of pressure cleaners.

coarse (UNC) Used to describe thread pitch; stands for Unified National Coarse.

cold chisel The most common type of chisel, used to cut cold metals. The cutting end is tempered and hardened so that it is harder than the metals that need to be cut.

combination pliers A type of pliers for cutting, gripping, and bending.

combination wrench A type of wrench that has an open end on one end and a box-end wrench on the other.

compressed air equipment Tool or machinery that operates on compressed air.

cored solder Solder that is in the form of a hollow wire. The center is filled with flux, which is used as a cleaning agent while the solder is being applied to the metal surfaces.

crankshaft A vehicle engine component that transfers the reciprocating movement of pistons into rotary motion.

cross-arm A description for an arm that is set at right angles or 90 degrees to another component.

cross-cut chisel A type of chisel for metal work that cleans out or cuts key ways.

curved file A type of file that has a curved surface for filing holes.

dead blow hammer A type of hammer that has a cushioned head to reduce the amount of head bounce.

depth micrometer A measuring device that accurately measures the depth of a hole.

dial indicator An accurate measuring device where measurements are read from a dial and needle.

diagonal cutting pliers Cutting pliers for small wire or cable.

die stock A handle for securely holding dies to cut threads.

double flare A seal that is made at the end of metal tubing or pipe.

drift punch A type of punch used to start pushing roll pins to prevent them from spreading.

drill chuck A device for securely gripping drill bits in a drill.

drill press A device that incorporates a fixed drill with multiple speeds and an adjustable worktable. It can be free-standing or fixed to a bench.

drill vice A tool with jaws that can be attached to a drill press table for holding material that is to be drilled.

elasticity The amount of stretch or give a material has.

fast chargers A type of battery charger that charges batteries quickly.

fasteners Devices that securely hold items together, such as screws, cotter pins, rivets, and bolts.

feeler gauge A thin blade device for measuring space between two objects.

finished rivet A rivet after the completion of the riveting process.

fine (UNF) Used to describe thread pitch; it stands for Unified National Fine.

flare nut wrench A type of box-end wrench that has a slot in the box section to allow the wrench to slip through a tube or pipe. Also called a flare tubing wrench.

flashback arrestor A spring-loaded valve installed on oxyacetylene torches as a safety device to prevent flame from entering the torch hoses.

flat blade screwdriver A type of screwdriver that fits a straight slot in screws.

flat-nosed pliers Pliers that are flat and square at the end of the nose.

flux A liquid or paste that protects a soldering or welding joint from oxidization.

forcing screw The center screw on a gear, bearing, or pulley puller. Also called a jacking screw.

gasket scraper A broad sharp flat blade to assist in removing gaskets and glue.

gear pullers A tool with two or more legs and a cross bar with a center forcing screw to remove gears.

grinding wheels and discs Abrasive wheels or flat discs fitted to bench, pedestal, and portable grinders.

hard rubber mallet A special-purpose tool with a head made of hard rubber; often used for moving things into place where it is important not to damage the item being moved.

hollow punch A punch with a center hollow for cutting circles in thin materials such as gaskets.

impact driver A tool that is struck with a hammer to provide an impact turning force to remove tight fasteners.

inside micrometer A micrometer designed to measure internal diameters.

intermediate tap One of a series of taps designed to cut an internal thread. Also called a plug tap.

locking pliers A type of plier where the jaws can be set and locked into position.

lockout/tagout A safety tag system to ensure that faulty equipment or equipment in the middle of repair is not used.

lug wrench A tool designed to remove wheel lugs nuts and commonly shaped like a cross.

magnetic pickup tools An extending shaft, often flexible, with a magnet fitted to the end for picking up metal objects.

mandrel The shaft of a pop rivet.

mandrel head The head of the pop rivet that connects to the shaft and causes the rivet body to flare.

measuring tape A thin measuring blade that rolls up and is contained in a spring-loaded dispenser.

mechanical fingers Spring-loaded fingers at the end of a flexible shaft that pick up items in tight spaces.

memory saver (memory minder) Battery backup device for vehicle computer systems.

micrometer An accurate measuring device for internal and external dimensions. Commonly abbreviated mic.

Morse taper A tapered mounting shaft for drill bits and chucks in larger drills and lathes.

needle-nosed pliers Pliers with long tapered jaws for gripping small items and getting into tight spaces.

nippers (pincer pliers) Pliers designed to cut protruding items level with the surface.

nut A fastener with a hexagonal head and internal threads for screwing on bolts.

offset screwdriver A screwdriver with a 90-degree bend in the shaft for working in tight spaces.

offset vice A vice that allows long objects to be gripped vertically.

oil filter wrench A specialized wrench that allows extra leverage to remove an oil filter when it is tight.

open-end wrench A wrench with open jaws to allow side entry to a nut or bolt.

outside micrometer A micrometer designed to measure the external dimensions of items.

oxyacetylene torch A gas welding system that combines oxygen and acetylene.

parallax error A visual error caused by viewing measurement markers at an incorrect angle.

peening A term used to describe the action of flattening a rivet through a hammering action.

Phillips head screwdriver A type of screwdriver that fits a head shaped like a cross in screws.

pin punch A type of punch in various sizes with a straight or parallel shaft.

pipe wrench A wrench that grips pipes and can exert a lot of force to turn them. Because the handle pivots slightly, the more pressure put on the handle to turn the wrench, the more the grip tightens.

plasma cutter A tool that uses electricity and compressed gas to produce a stream of high-temperature gas to cut metal.

pliers A hand tool with gripping jaws.

pop rivet gun A hand tool for installing pop rivets.

power tools Tools powered by electricity or compressed air.

pressure washer/cleaner A cleaning machine that boosts low-pressure tap water to a high-pressure output.

prick punch A pinch with a sharp point for accurately marking a point on metal.

pry bar A high-strength carbon steel rod with offsets for levering and prying.

pullers A generic term to describe hand tools that mechanically assist the removal of bearings, gears, pulleys, and other parts.

punches A generic term to describe a high-strength carbon steel shaft with a blunt point for driving. Center and prick punches are exceptions and have a sharp point for marking or making an indentation.

ratchet A generic term to describe a handle for sockets that allows the user to select direction of rotation. It can turn sockets in restricted areas without the user having to remove the socket from the fastener.

ratcheting box-end wrench A wrench with an inner piece that is able to rotate within the outer housing, allowing it to be repositioned without being removed.

ratcheting screwdriver A screwdriver with a selectable ratchet mechanism built into the handle that allows the screwdriver tip to ratchet as it is being used.

rattle gun A term used describe an air impact wrench based on the noise it makes.

roll bar Another type of pry bar, with one end used for prying and the other end for aligning larger holes, such as engine motor mounts.

rosin A type of liquid or paste (flux) used to prevent oxidization that is in solid form contained within the solder.

sand or bead blasters A cleaning system that uses high-pressure fine particles of glass bead or sand.

sander/polisher A power tool with a rotating disc or head to which polishing or sanding discs can be attached.

screw extractor A tool for removing broken screws or bolts.

single flare A sealing system made on the end of metal tubing.

sledge hammer A heavy hammer, usually with two flat faces, that provides a strong blow.

sliding T-handle A handle fitted at 90 degrees to the main body that can be slid from side to side.

slow charger A battery charger that charges at low current.

smart charger A battery charger with microprocessor-controlled charging rates and times.

snap ring pliers A pair of pliers for installing and removing snap rings or circlips.

socket An enclosed metal tube commonly with 6 or 12 points to remove and install bolts and nuts.

solder A mixture of lead and tin with a low melting point for connecting wires.

soldering irons A heating tool to heat solder and wires to produce a low-resistance joint.

solvent tank A tank containing solvents to clean vehicle parts.

speed brace A U-shaped socket wrench that allows high-speed operation. Also called a speeder handle.

spray wash cabinet A cleaning cabinet that sprays cleaning solution under pressure to clean vehicle parts.

square file A type of file with a square cross section.

square thread A thread type with square shoulders used to translate rotational to lateral movement.

steel hammer A hammer with a head made of hardened steel.

steel rule An accurate measuring ruler made of steel.

straight edge A measuring device generally made of steel to check how flat a surface is.

straight grinder A powered grinder with the wheel set at 90 degrees to the shaft.

stud A type of threaded fastener with a thread cut on each end rather than having a bolt head on one end.

sulphuric acid A type of acid that when mixed with pure water forms the basis of battery acid or electrolyte.

surge protector An electrical protection device for preventing electrical surges.

tap A term used to generically describe an internal thread-cutting tool.

taper tap A tap with a tapper; it is usually the first of three taps used when cutting internal threads.

tap handle A tool designed to securely hold taps for cutting internal threads.

tensile strength In reference to fasteners, the amount of force it takes before a fastener breaks.

thread file A type of file that cleans clogged or distorted threads on bolts and studs.

thread pitch The coarseness or fineness of a thread as measured by either the threads per inch or the distance from the peak of one thread to the next. Metric fasteners are measured in millimeters.

thread repair A generic term to describe a number of processes that can be used to repair threads.

tin snips Cutting device for sheet metal, works in a similar fashion to scissors.

torque Twisting force applied to a shaft that may or may not result in motion.

torque angle A method of tightening bolts or nuts based on angles of rotation.

torque specifications Supplied by manufacturers and describes the amount of twisting force allowable for a fastener or a specification showing the twisting force from an engine crankshaft.

torque-to-yield A method of tightening bolts close to their yield point or the point at which they will not return to their original length.

torque-to-yield (TTY) bolts Bolts that are tightened using the torque-to-yield method.

torque wrench A tool used to measure the rotational or twisting force applied to fasteners.

triangular file A type of file with three sides so it can get into internal corners.

tubing cutter A hand tool for cutting pipe or tubing squarely.

tube flaring tool A tool that makes a sealing flare on the end of metal tubing.

twist drill A hardened steel drill bit for making holes in metals, plastics, and wood.

V blocks Metal blocks with a V-shaped cutout for holding shafts while working on them. Also referred to as vee blocks.

vernier calipers An accurate measuring device for internal, external, and depth measurements that incorporates fixed and adjustable jaws.

wad punch A type of punch that is hollow for cutting circular shapes in soft materials such as gaskets.

warding file A type of thin, flat file with a tapered end.

wire feed welder A welding machine that automatically feeds the filler wire by operating a trigger mechanism on a welding gun.

wrenches A generic term to describe tools that tighten and loosen fasteners with hexagonal heads.

yield point The point at which a bolt is stretched so hard that it will not return to its original length when loosened; it is measured in pounds per square inch of bolt cross section.

ASE-Type Questions

1. Tech A says that knowing how to use tools correctly creates a safe working environment. Tech B says that a flare nut wrench is used to loosen very tight bolts and nuts. Who is correct?
   a. Tech A
   b. Tech B
   c. Both A and B
   d. Neither A nor B
2. Tech A says that lockout/tagout is a safety procedure for a safe working environment. Tech B says that a soldering iron is used to weld, cut, and braze steel components. Who is correct?
   a. Tech A
   b. Tech B
   c. Both A and B
   d. Neither A nor B
3. Tech A says that torque wrenches need to be calibrated periodically to ensure proper torque values. Tech B says that when a bolt is torqued the bolt stretches beyond its yield point and the bolt has to be replaced when removed. Who is correct?
   a. Tech A
   b. Tech B
   c. Both A and B
   d. Neither A nor B
4. Tech A says that head bolts are tightened past their yield point. Tech B says that head bolts are torqued then tightened to their yield point. Who is correct?
   a. Tech A
   b. Tech B
   c. Both A and B
   d. Neither A nor B
5. Tech A says that a box-end wrench is more likely to round the head of a bolt than an open-end wrench. Tech B says that 6-point sockets and wrenches have more surface area on the bolt and will hold more firmly when removing and tightening. Who is correct?
   a. Tech A
   b. Tech B
   c. Both A and B
   d. Neither A nor B
6. Tech A says that it is usually better to pull a wrench to tighten or loosen a bolt. Tech B says that pushing a wrench will protect your knuckles if the wrench slips. Who is correct?
   a. Tech A
   b. Tech B
   c. Both A and B
   d. Neither A nor B
7. Tech A says that when jump starting a vehicle, a spark typically occurs when making the last jumper cable connection. Tech B says that all four of the jumper cable connections should be made at the battery terminals. Who is correct?
   a. Tech A
   b. Tech B
   c. Both A and B
   d. Neither A nor B
8. Tech A says that a dead blow hammer reduces rebound of the hammer. Tech B says that a dead blow hammer should be used to cut the head of a bolt off with a chisel. Who is correct?
   a. Tech A
   b. Tech B
   c. Both A and B
   d. Neither A nor B
9. Tech A says that gaskets can be removed quickly and safely with a portable grinder as long as the grinding wheel isn't too coarse. Tech B says that extreme care must be used when removing a gasket on an aluminum surface. Who is correct?
   a. Tech A
   b. Tech B
   c. Both A and B
   d. Neither A nor B
10. Tech A says that when using a file, apply pressure to file in the direction of the cut and no pressure when pulling the file back. Tech B says that file cards are used to file uneven surfaces. Who is correct?
   a. Tech A
   b. Tech B
   c. Both A and B
   d. Neither A nor B

ROTARY
LIFT

CHAPTER 7

KNOW
SEE
DO
PROVE

NATEF Tasks

Required Supplemental Tasks Shop and Personal Safety	Page
■ Identify and use proper procedures for safe lift operation.	178–187
■ Identify and use proper placement of floor jacks and jack stands.	178–184
Preparing Vehicle for Service	
■ Identify purpose and demonstrate proper use of fender covers, mats.	175, 177
Preparing Vehicle for Customer	
■ Ensure vehicle is prepared to return to customer per school/company policy (floor mat, steering wheel cover, etc.)	184, 186

KNOW
SEE
DO
PROVE

Knowledge Objectives

After reading this chapter, you will be able to:

1. Explain the precautions and procedures to prevent vehicle damage while conducting repairs. (pp 174–177)
2. Describe the application and purpose of lifting equipment. (p 178)
3. Describe the safe use of lifting equipment. (pp 178–184)
4. Explain how to prepare a vehicle for customer pickup. (pp 184, 186)

Vehicle Protection and Jack and Lift Safety

Know
See
Do
Prove

Skills Objectives

After reading this chapter, you will be able to:

1. Use fender covers and floor mats. (p 177)
2. Lift and secure a vehicle with a floor jack and jack stands. (p 183)
3. Lift a vehicle using a two-post hoist. (p 185)
4. Lift a vehicle using a four-post hoist. (p 186)
5. Prepare a vehicle for customer pickup. (p 186)

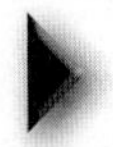

Introduction

Whenever a shop conducts repairs, its professionalism is on display. Customers expect their vehicle to be repaired and returned clean and free of any additional damage. A professional shop always takes precautions to guarantee that the customer's vehicle is treated with respect by ensuring that all work is conducted safely and efficiently. Before you undertake a task, pause for a moment to identify good work practices that will help prevent accidental damage to a customer's vehicle. For example, before starting work, install protective covers to ensure that interiors, steering wheels, and fenders are protected from accidental spills and scratches.

For your personal safety, it is important that lifting equipment such as vehicle lifts, jacks, jack stands, engine hoists, slings, and chains are inspected before each use and are well maintained. Some states require annual certification inspections of vehicle lifts and hydraulic jacks to help ensure their safety.

Preventing Vehicle Damage

Customers expect their vehicles to be treated with care and respect while in your shop. To accomplish this, you need to protect the vehicle from damage, keep it clean, and ensure that all property is returned in satisfactory condition to its owner. This can be achieved by taking the appropriate actions to protect the vehicle from further damage while conducting repairs. For example, you should use vehicle protective covers as a barrier for the fender, floor, seat, and steering wheel.

Customer Property

To avoid customer dissatisfaction, it is good practice for the service advisor to perform a vehicle walk-around with the customer. During this time, any existing damage or missing components on the vehicle should be noted on the check-in sheet or repair order and discussed with the customer. This helps prevent the customer from coming back to the shop and complaining that his or her vehicle was damaged in the shop. You should also check the customer's vehicle before starting

Caring for the Customer

The preservice vehicle walk-around with the customer can be very valuable. Occasionally, a customer will be unaware of damage to his or her vehicle that was sustained before dropping the vehicle off at the shop for service. For example, maybe the customer stopped by the store to pick up a couple of things before dropping the vehicle off at the shop. While in the store, another car sideswiped the passenger side of the vehicle. Since it was on the passenger side, the driver never saw it. However, when the customer picks up the car from the shop and looks it over to make sure nothing is damaged, she sees that the passenger side has been sideswiped. The customer immediately blames the shop, saying, "My car wasn't that way when I dropped it off." A good preservice walk-around can prevent this kind of misunderstanding.

You Are the Automotive Technician

A customer brings her 2009 BMW 325i into the auto dealership for routine service. During the vehicle walk-around, you determine that the rear tires are worn and need replacement. Using a tread-depth indicator, you demonstrate to the customer that the tires are worn below the legal amount. After determining the best tires for the customer, you escort her to customer service to purchase new tires and wait for her vehicle. Before moving the vehicle for service, you install seat covers, a steering wheel cover, and floor mats.

1. What type of hoist is best for rotating and changing vehicle tires?
2. Why is it important to check safe working load (SWL) of the lifting equipment before using it?
3. A vehicle is about to be removed from the vehicle inspection pit; what are some safety precautions you must perform before it can be removed?
4. What are some steps you need to take before returning the vehicle to the customer?

to work on it. If there are any valuables in the vehicle or if it has damage, note this on your repair order and notify your supervisor.

Always use seat and steering wheel covers, floor mats, and fender covers when working on a vehicle to protect it from grease or corrosive materials. Clean any oil and grease off the vehicle when you have completed the job. If a vehicle has been damaged in the course of its repair, immediately notify your supervisor.

Fender, Seat, Carpet, and Steering Wheel Covers

Working on vehicles requires the use of tools, equipment, and chemicals and the physical process of testing and replacing parts. All of these activities have the potential to damage the vehicle if the proper precautions are not taken. For example, a dropped screwdriver or wrench may scratch the paint if fender covers are not used.

The vehicle and its components tend to be more prone to accidental damage in areas that have higher levels of service activity such as the engine bay and passenger compartment. The engine bay is the center of activity where many tools are used, batteries serviced, and oil changed. The chance of an accident in the engine bay is high if caution and care are not applied.

Protective equipment for vehicles is used to prevent damage to sensitive areas while conducting repairs and servicing **FIGURE 7-1**. Fender covers are a protective layer used to cover the fenders when work is conducted around the engine bay. They are usually made from either a durable fabric blanket or a flexible energy-absorbing foam compound about a quarter of an inch thick. They are designed to fit across the top and down the side of the fender, providing protection to those areas vulnerable to accidental damage.

FIGURE 7-1 Always use seat and steering wheel covers, floor mats, and fender covers when working on a vehicle.

Seats, carpets, and steering wheels are made from materials that are sensitive to marks and damage from grease, oil, and dirt. Protectors for these areas are made from materials that provide a barrier to oil, grease, and dirt and are designed to prevent accidental damage to the delicate materials. For example, waxed or plastic laminated carpet protectors, plastic or fabric seat protectors, and plastic steering wheel covers can be used to prevent damage and stains.

> **TECHNICIAN TIP**
>
> Many of today's vehicles use very thin sheet metal in their fenders, making them easily dented if you lean against them or put your body weight against them. Fender covers *cannot* protect the vehicle from this kind of damage.

> **Caring for the Customer**
>
> Always use the appropriate protection to prevent accidental damage to vehicles. Fender, carpet, seat, and steering wheels covers should be the first thing on and the last thing removed when working on vehicles.

> **TECHNICIAN TIP**
>
> Never place tools in your back pocket. If you were to put a screwdriver in your back pocket and then sit in the driver's seat, the screwdriver would likely poke a hole in the seat upholstery, even if you used a seat cover.

Corrosives and Greases

Corrosives, such as battery acids and greases, such as wheel bearing grease, have the potential to cause damage. Use proper precautions when handling these substances. Special containers are designed to hold specific substances; for example, corrosives are stored in a special type of plastic container **FIGURE 7-2**. Greases are stored in a container designed to hold grease, often made from plastic or tin. Incorrectly storing materials in the improper containers may lead to a spill. Do not reuse containers or store products in them that the container was not designed to handle.

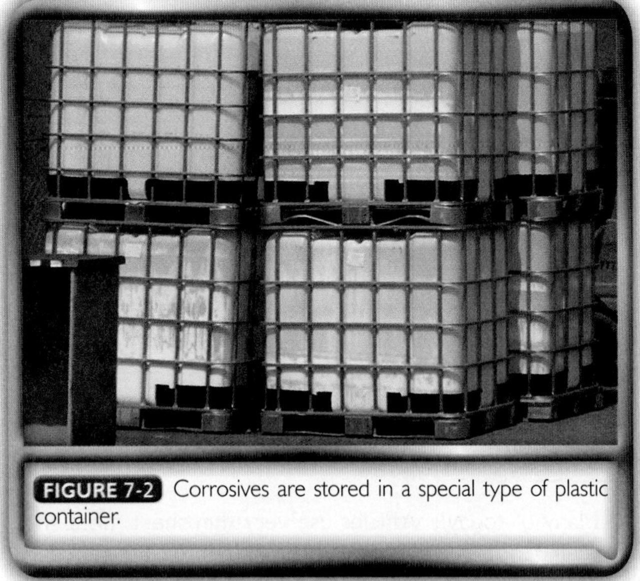

FIGURE 7-2 Corrosives are stored in a special type of plastic container.

FIGURE 7-3 Special absorbent materials in granular form can be used to absorb some liquid spills, such as engine oil.

If spills do occur, be sure to clean them up thoroughly using appropriate methods, which can usually be found in the material safety data sheets (MSDS) for each material. Damage caused by corrosive agents may not be immediately visible and may lead to other problems, such as rust or corrosion, if the corrosive agents are not cleaned up and neutralized immediately. If you are handling corrosive materials and believe they have spilled, take precautions, clean the area immediately, and use a neutralizer. For example, a battery electrolyte contains acid. This material can be cleaned up by neutralizing it with an alkaline such as common baking soda and flushing the area with fresh water. Special absorbent materials in granular form can also be used to absorb some liquid spills such as engine oil FIGURE 7-3. Once the engine oil is absorbed, the granules can be swept up for disposal in an environmentally safe way.

Greases and liquids can cause stains at any time, so be sure to work as cleanly as possible and use protective covers to prevent damage. If a liquid spill does occur, clean up any excess with an absorbent material. Then use a cleaner suitable for the type of spill and the material being cleaned. For example, use upholstery cleaner for spills on vehicle seats or carpet cleaner for carpets.

Mechanical Damage

The possibility for accidental mechanical damage is always present when a vehicle is in the shop. It can occur easily; for example, an incorrectly jacked vehicle may damage the suspension or body. The best way to minimize accidental mechanical damage is to think carefully about the task or work you are performing, plan what you intend to do, follow shop and manufacturer procedures, use tools and equipment correctly, and seek advice if you are not sure. For example, if you have to rotate a vehicle's tires, you would use the proper jacking or hoisting equipment to ensure easy and safe access to the wheels and tires.

Moving and Road Testing Vehicles

Vehicles often need to be road tested or simply moved from one place to another in the shop. Accidents can occur at this time, especially if the driver involved is inexperienced or unqualified. Only authorized, fully trained, and licensed drivers should be given the responsibility to move vehicles. Only the most skilled and experienced drivers available should be allowed to test-drive higher performance vehicles.

Have someone outside the vehicle supervise and guide any vehicle movement inside the shop, especially in restricted spaces, when reversing, and when nearing blind corners. Often hand signals will be used by someone directing you to maneuver the vehicle. Make sure you understand what the hand signals mean by discussing them before moving the vehicle. If you are the person guiding the driver, use large hand signals and make sure you stand where the driver can clearly see you, but not directly in front of or behind the vehicle FIGURE 7-4.

Using Protective Covers

Proper Use of Fender Covers and Floor Mats

Since the purpose of fender covers and floor mats is to protect the vehicle, you should always inspect them for

FIGURE 7-4 If you are the person guiding the driver, use large hand signals and make sure you stand where the driver can clearly see you.

Safety

Vehicles do not always run properly when they are brought in for service, which can lead to an accident. For example, a car with a hesitation problem will not move until the throttle is pressed down farther than normal. When the car does move, it lurches forward. In the tight spaces of a shop, this could cause the vehicle to run into something or someone. You have two options in this situation. The safest option is to push the vehicle instead of driving it. The second is a bit controversial—two-footing the pedals. Two-footing means that you put your left foot on the brake pedal, ready to apply the brakes, and your right foot on the gas pedal. Thus, as you are driving, you can use the brakes to keep the speed of the vehicle very slow. This method takes practice and goes against most driver's training. But when the engine is not running properly, the standard method puts the vehicle at risk of an accident.

damage prior to use. Ensure that fender covers and floor mats are clean on both sides and do not have any metal or hard objects stuck to them. Ensure that they fit securely and provide adequate protection.

To properly apply fender covers and floor mats, follow the steps in **SKILL DRILL 7-1**.

TECHNICIAN TIP

Make sure customers and visiting drivers are aware of your rules for moving cars. Keep the keys for all vehicles secure and away from the vehicles when not in use.

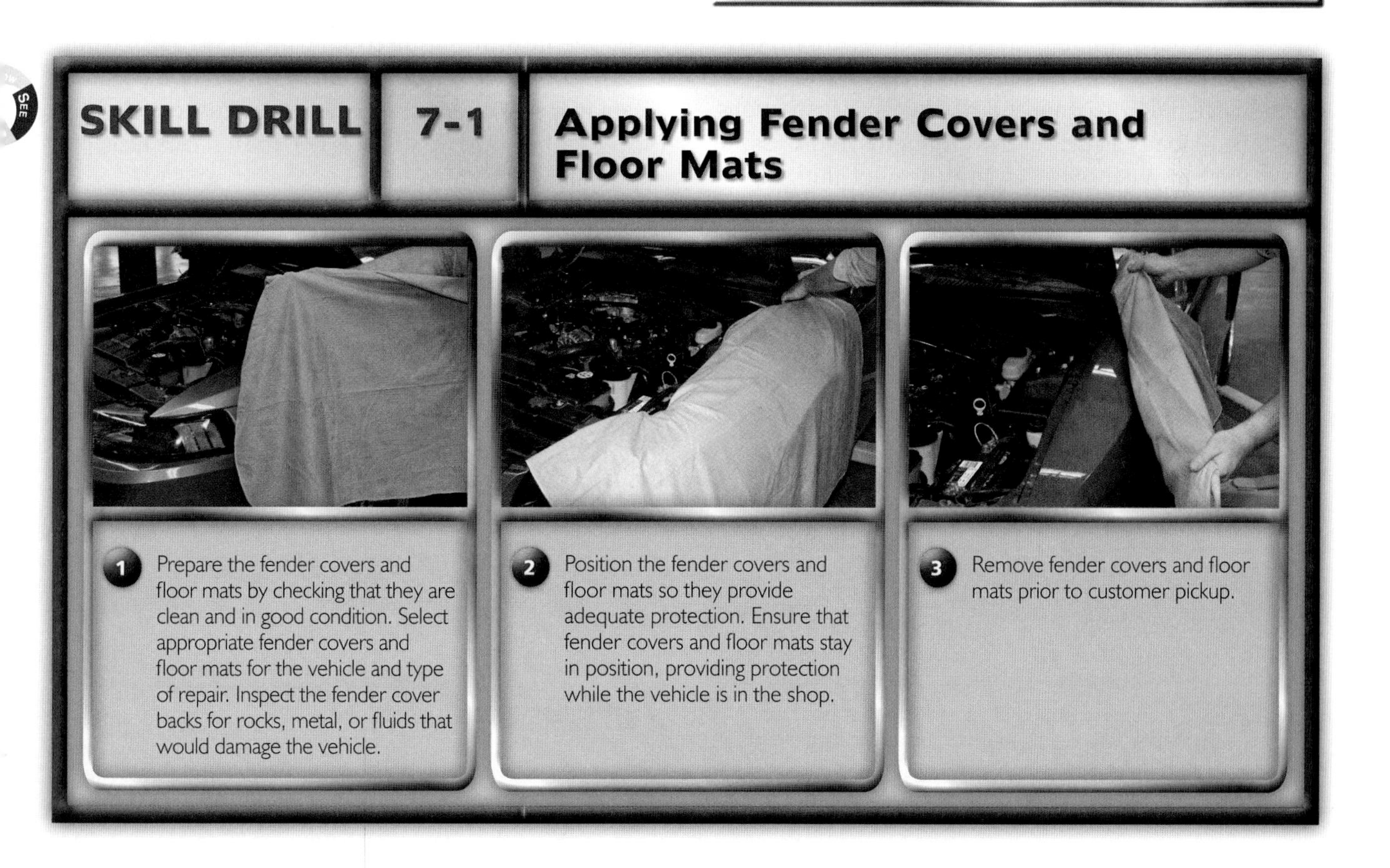

SKILL DRILL 7-1 Applying Fender Covers and Floor Mats

1. Prepare the fender covers and floor mats by checking that they are clean and in good condition. Select appropriate fender covers and floor mats for the vehicle and type of repair. Inspect the fender cover backs for rocks, metal, or fluids that would damage the vehicle.
2. Position the fender covers and floor mats so they provide adequate protection. Ensure that fender covers and floor mats stay in position, providing protection while the vehicle is in the shop.
3. Remove fender covers and floor mats prior to customer pickup.

Lifting Equipment

Many different types of lifting equipment may be used in a shop. Some examples include vehicle hoists, floor jacks, jack stands, engine and component hoists, chains, slings, and shackles **FIGURE 7-5**. Lifting equipment is designed to lift and securely hold loads. Each piece of lifting equipment is designed for a specific purpose and has an operating capacity. The operating capacity is usually expressed as the **safe working load (SWL)**. For example, if the SWL is 1 ton, the equipment can safely lift up to 1 ton, or 2,000 lb (907 kg). When using lifting equipment, never exceed its capacity and always maintain some reserve capacity as an extra safety margin.

Each piece of lifting equipment should only be used for the purpose for which it is designed. For example, a vehicle hoist should only be used to lift vehicles within its capacity. Using lifting equipment incorrectly may lead to equipment failure that can cause serious injury and damage.

TECHNICIAN TIP

Some fender covers are made with a magnetic strip in them, which is designed to help hold the fender cover in place. Unfortunately, the magnet attracts metal particles, which can be held between the cover and the fender and scratch the paint. Always check these types of covers very thoroughly for metal particles.

TECHNICIAN TIP

When multiple pieces of lifting equipment are used, the SWL is limited to the lowest rated piece of equipment. For example, if a chain with an SWL of 2 tons is used with a 5-ton SWL shackle and a 3-ton SWL engine hoist, then the maximum amount of weight that can be lifted is 2 tons.

Testing of Lifting Equipment

Lifting equipment should be periodically checked and tested to make sure it is safe. The testing should be recorded for each piece of lifting equipment in accordance with local legislation or shop procedures and the equipment tagged with its inspection date and SWL. Inspections should identify any damage, such as cracks, dents, marks, cuts, and abrasions, that may prevent the lifting equipment from performing as it is designed. Refer to the manufacturer's manual to find out how often they recommend maintenance inspections. The time frame is usually every 12 months in the case of hoists and lifts, but may be longer for items of lifting equipment such as chains and slings. Always check local regulations to determine the requirements for periodic testing of lifting equipment.

Check the Test Certificate

In some countries, lifting equipment is subject to statutory testing and certification. If this is the case where you work, the **test certificate** should be attached to or displayed near the lifting equipment **FIGURE 7-6**. Before using a piece of lifting equipment, make sure the most recent inspection recorded on the test certificate is within the prescribed time limit. If it is not, the test certificate has expired and you should notify your supervisor.

FIGURE 7-5 Some examples of lifting equipment are vehicle hoists, floor jacks, jack stands, engine and component hoists, chains, slings, and shackles.

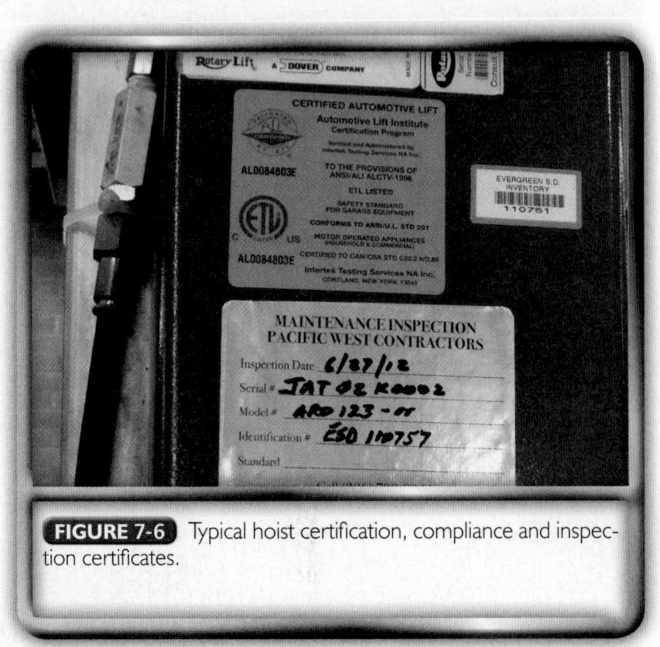
RotaryLift
A DOVER COMPANY
CERTIFIED AUTOMOTIVE LIFT
Automotive Lift Institute
Certification Program
ETL LISTED
MAINTENANCE INSPECTION
PACIFIC WEST CONTRACTORS
Inspection Date
Serial #
Model #
Identification #
Standard

FIGURE 7-6 Typical hoist certification, compliance and inspection certificates.

> **TECHNICIAN TIP**
>
> Manufacturers supply operating information for lifting equipment, including the equipment's SWL. Check the SWL of the lifting equipment and never exceed the SWL.

Jacks and Jack Stands

Jacks

A **vehicle jack** is a lifting tool used to raise part of a vehicle from the ground prior to removing or replacing components or to raise heavy components into position. The vehicle's emergency jack can be used to raise and support the vehicle while changing a wheel on the side of the road. Vehicle jacks must not be used to support the weight of the vehicle during any task that requires you to get underneath any part of the vehicle. For those shop tasks, a vehicle jack should be used only to raise the vehicle so that it can then be lowered onto suitably rated and carefully positioned stable jack stands FIGURE 7-7.

There are three main types of mechanisms that provide the lifting action for vehicle jacks: **hydraulic jacks**, **pneumatic jacks**, and **mechanical jacks**. Hydraulic and pneumatic jacks are the most common types of vehicle jacks. They can be mounted on slides or on a wheeled trolley. In hydraulic jacks, pressurized oil acts on a piston to provide the lifting action; in pneumatic jacks, compressed air lifts the vehicle. In mechanical jacks, a screw or gears provide the mechanical leverage required for lifting.

FIGURE 7-7 A vehicle jack should be used only to raise the vehicle so that it can then be lowered onto suitably rated and carefully positioned stable jack stands.

Different jacks are available for different purposes, including FIGURE 7-8:

- Floor jacks are a common type of hydraulic jack that is mounted on four wheels, two of which swivel to provide a steering mechanism. The floor jack has a long handle that is used both to operate the jacking mechanism and to move and position the jack. Floor jacks have a low profile, making them suitable to position under vehicles.

A
NAPA
LIFTING EQUIPMENT
B
C

FIGURE 7-8 Jacks. **A.** Floor jacks. **B.** High-lift (or farm) jacks. **C.** Transmission jack.

- High-lift (or farm) jacks are a versatile type of jack designed to lift, winch, clamp, pull, and push. They have a mechanical mechanism and are designed to provide high lift capability—for example, 36 inches (0.91 m) or more. Because of their high lift capability, they are often used on farms or on four-wheel drive vehicles.
- Bottle jacks are a portable jack that usually has either a mechanical screw or a hydraulic ram mechanism that rises vertically from the center of the jack as the handle is operated. They are relatively inexpensive and may be provided with vehicles for the purpose of changing flat tires.
- Air jacks use compressed air to either operate a large ram or inflate an expandable air bag to lift the vehicle. Often the air jack is fitted to a moveable platform with a long handle. Air jacks are used to lift vehicles as an alternative to floor jacks. Because a compressed air supply is required, air jacks are usually used in the shop and not for mobile operations.
- Scissor jacks are one of the most common types of jacks provided as part of the vehicle tool kit. They are used to jack a vehicle one wheel at a time. They employ a scissor action that is controlled by turning a long horizontal screw that acts on levers to raise or lower the scissor jack.
- Sliding bridge jacks are usually fitted in pairs to four-post hoists as an accessory to allow the vehicle to be lifted off the drive-on hoist runways. Operated by a hydraulic mechanism or compressed air, they use a platform mounted to a scissor-action jack to lift the vehicle along the length of the runway, thus making it more convenient to work on wheels and brakes.
- Transmission jacks are specialized jacks for lifting and lowering transmissions during removal and installation. Transmission jacks are usually mounted on a trolley with wheels and have a large flat plate area on which the transmission rests securely. They are usually operated by a hydraulic mechanism but can also be powered by compressed air.

> **TECHNICIAN TIP**
>
> Make sure you always use the correct type of jack with the correct load capacity for your task.

> **Safety**
>
> All vehicle jacks must always be used in accordance with the manufacturer's instructions and should be inspected on a regular basis to ensure that they are in safe working order.

Jack Stands

Jack stands (axle stands) are adjustable supports that are used with vehicle jacks and are designed to support the weight of the vehicle after the vehicle has been raised by a vehicle jack. Jack stands are mechanical devices, meaning they mechanically lock in place at the height selected. This makes them very dependable if they are rated strong enough for the load they are holding and if they are used properly.

Always grip jack stands by the sides to move them. Never grip them by the top or the bottom to move them, as they can slip and pinch or injure you. Check that the base of the stand is flat on the ground before lowering the vehicle onto it; otherwise the stand might tip over, causing the vehicle to slip off. When positioned correctly, the vehicle can be lowered onto the jack stands and the vehicle jack can be moved out of the way.

Jack stands provide a stable support for a raised vehicle that is safer than the jack because the vehicle cannot be accidentally lowered while the jack stands are in place. To lower a vehicle that is on jack stands, it first has to be raised again so that the jack stands can be removed.

Lifting devices are also lowering devices, so it is unsafe to work underneath a vehicle that is supported only by a vehicle jack because it could give way or be accidentally lowered. Jack stands should never be used for a job for which they are not recommended. They normally come in matched pairs and should always be used as a pair FIGURE 7-9. Jack stands are load rated and should

FIGURE 7-9 Jack stands normally come in matched pairs and should always be used as a pair.

only be used for loads less than the rating indicated on the jack stand.

Some shops have tall jack stands that are used along with a vehicle hoist; they are much taller than standard jack stands. Tall jack stands are used to stabilize a vehicle up on a hoist that is having a heavy component, such as a transaxle, removed or installed. Do not try to lower the vehicle with the tall jack stands still in place; doing so can cause the vehicle to slip off of the hoist.

Vehicle Hoists

Vehicle hoists raise whole vehicles off the ground so that a technician can easily work on the underside of the vehicle. The vehicle hoist is also useful for raising the vehicle to a height that removes the need for the technician to bend down. For example, when changing tires the vehicle can be raised to waist height to avoid excessive bending.

There are a number of different designs of vehicle hoists, and they come in a range of sizes and configurations to meet the particular needs of the shop. For instance, there are vehicle hoists that are mobile and vehicle hoists that are designed for use where the ceiling height is limited. Some vehicle hoists can be linked together electronically so they can be used on longer vehicles such as trucks and buses.

The most common types of vehicle hoists in general use are single-post, two-post, and four-post hoists. Other types of hoists include: scissor lifts, parallelogram lifts, and mobile or specialty lifts. A **single-post hoist** raises the vehicle on a platform supported by a single solid shaft located centrally under the vehicle. This type of hoist is very compact in the workshop and leaves the perimeter of the vehicle easily accessible, but the central post obscures part of the underside of the vehicle, making jobs such as transmission removal difficult or impossible.

TECHNICIAN TIP

Some vehicles are equipped with an automatic leveling system, which must be disabled before lifting the vehicle. Always check the service information to see if this applies to the vehicle you are lifting.

Safety

Never use a hoist to lift any weight greater than the lifting capacity of the hoist, sling, chains, or bolts.

Four-Post Hoist

A **four-post hoist** is very easy to use with most vehicles. The vehicle is driven between the four posts so that the wheels rest on two long, narrow platforms, one on each side of the vehicle FIGURE 7-10. The platforms are then raised, taking the vehicle with them. The underside of the vehicle is accessible to the technician. Since the vehicle rests on its wheels on the four-post hoist, the wheels cannot be removed, unless the hoist is fitted with sliding bridge jacks.

Two-Post Hoist

Two-post hoists come in two configurations—symmetrical and asymmetrical. Symmetrical two-post hoists have arms that are of approximately equal length so that the vehicle is roughly centered lengthwise between the posts. This positioning creates a challenge because the posts of the hoist are usually right in the way of the vehicle's front doors, making it harder to get into and out of the vehicle. Asymmetrical hoists have shorter arms in front of the posts than in the rear of the posts. This allows the vehicle to be positioned farther back on the hoist, allowing better access to the doors on the vehicle. Both types of two-post hoists leave the underside of the vehicle easily accessible and also allow a technician to remove the wheels while the vehicle is raised.

Two-post hoists and single-post hoists require careful positioning of the hoist arms so that they are under the appropriate lifting points, two on each side of the vehicle FIGURE 7-11. The service information for the vehicle will detail where those lifting points are so that the vehicle can be raised without causing structural damage.

FIGURE 7-10 A four-post hoist.

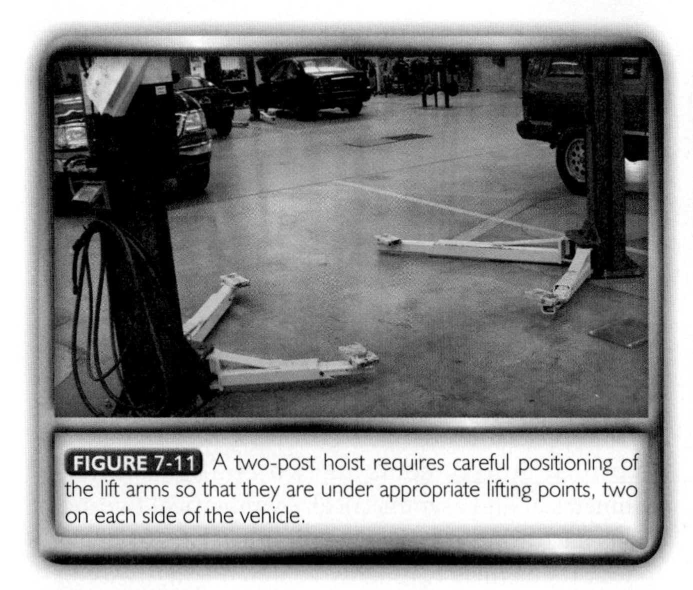

FIGURE 7-11 A two-post hoist requires careful positioning of the lift arms so that they are under appropriate lifting points, two on each side of the vehicle.

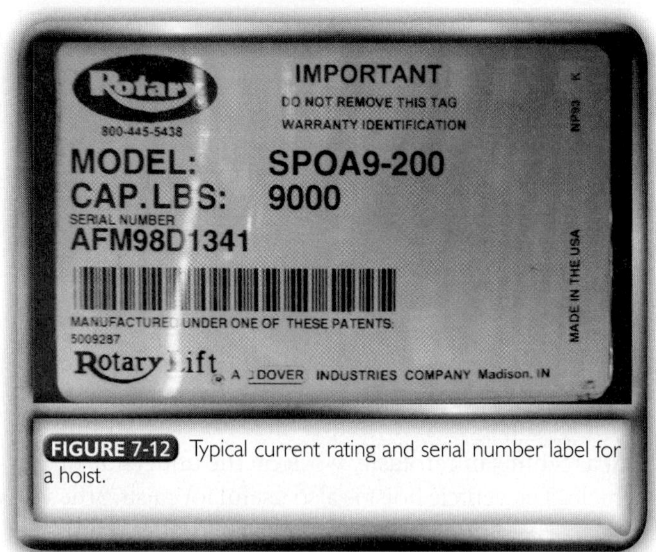
Rotary
800-445-5438
IMPORTANT
DO NOT REMOVE THIS TAG
WARRANTY IDENTIFICATION
MODEL: SPOA9-200
CAP.LBS: 9000
SERIAL NUMBER
AFM98D1341
MANUFACTURED UNDER ONE OF THESE PATENTS:
5009287
Rotary Lift A DOVER INDUSTRIES COMPANY Madison, IN
MADE IN THE USA

FIGURE 7-12 Typical current rating and serial number label for a hoist.

Safety Locks

Every vehicle hoist in the shop must have a built-in mechanical locking device so that the vehicle hoist can be secured at the chosen height after the vehicle is raised. This locking device prevents the vehicle from being accidentally lowered and holds the vehicle in place, even if the lifting mechanism fails. You should never physically go under a raised vehicle for any reason unless the safety locking mechanism has been activated.

Ratings and Inspections

All vehicle hoists are rated for a particular weight and/or type of vehicle and should never be used for any task other than that recommended by the manufacturer. In particular, a vehicle hoist should never be used to lift a vehicle that is heavier than its rated limit. In most countries, there are regulations that require hoists to be periodically inspected, typically annually, and certified as fit for use. Before you use a vehicle hoist, check the identification plate for its rating, and make sure it has a current registration or certification label FIGURE 7-12.

Using Lifting Equipment

Using Vehicle Jacks and Stands

The size of vehicle jack you use will be determined by the weight of the vehicle you want to lift. Most workshops will have a vehicle jack that has a lifting capacity of about 2.5 tons. If the end of the vehicle is heavier than that, or if the vehicle is loaded, you will need to use a vehicle jack with a larger lifting capacity.

Make sure the jack stands are in good condition before you use them to support the vehicle. If they are cracked or bent, they will not support the vehicle safely. Always use matched pairs of jack stands.

Never support a vehicle on anything other than jack stands. Do not use wood or steel blocks to support the vehicle; they may slide or split under the weight of the vehicle. Do not use bricks or concrete blocks to support the vehicle; they will crumble under the weight of the vehicle.

Before you try to use the jack, check for leaks in the hydraulic system. Check the pad, or saddle, and the wheels of the jack. They should rotate freely and show no signs of damage. Also check the manufacturer's label on the vehicle jack. The specifications will tell you the maximum load (weight) it will bear; it must suit the vehicle you want to raise. Finally, always refer to the owner's manual to find out where you can safely place the vehicle jack. This is usually a major point on the chassis, a cross member, or an axle unit.

To lift and secure a vehicle with a floor jack and jack stands, follow the steps in SKILL DRILL 7-2.

Safety

Some independent suspension components are not strong enough to support the weight of the vehicle. Make sure you always use the specified lift points to lift the vehicle.

Using Two-Post Hoists

Before lifting any vehicle, make sure the frame is structurally sound. If you see rust or signs of major repair, lifting the vehicle with a vehicle hoist may cause damage to the vehicle or may be dangerous to you. Make sure you know exactly how to operate the vehicle hoist. Take particular care that you know exactly where the stop control is so that you can use it quickly in an emergency. Refer to the operations manual for the correct procedure.

SKILL DRILL 7-2 Lifting and Securing a Vehicle with a Vehicle Jack and Jack Stands

1. Position the vehicle on a flat, solid surface. Put the vehicle into neutral or park and set the parking brake. Place wheel chocks in front of and behind the wheels that are not going to be raised off the ground.

2. Select two jack stands of the same type, suitable for the weight of the vehicle. Place one jack stand on each side of the vehicle at the same point, and adjust them so that they are both the same height.

3. Roll the vehicle jack under the vehicle, and position the lifting pad correctly under the frame or cross member. Turn the jack handle clockwise, and begin pumping the handle up and down until the lifting pad touches and begins to lift the vehicle.

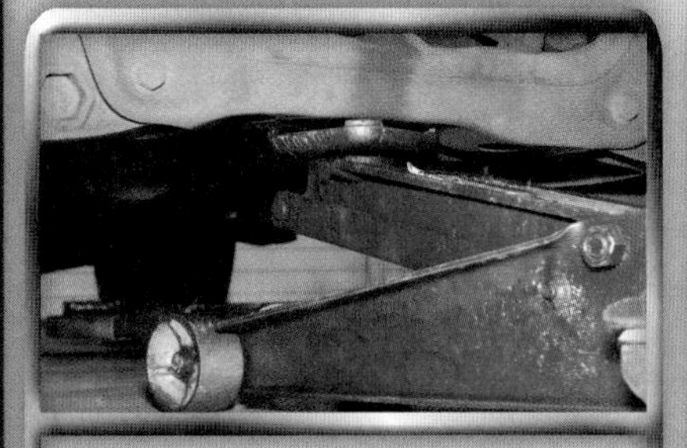

4. Once the wheels lift off the floor, stop and check the placement of the lifting pad under the vehicle to make sure there is no danger of slipping. Double-check the position of the wheel chocks to make sure they have not moved. If the vehicle is stable, continue lifting it until it is at the height at which you can safely work under it.

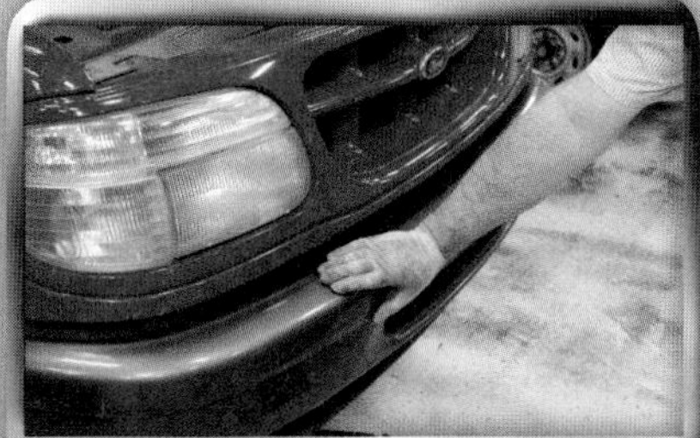

5. Slide the two jack stands underneath the vehicle and position them to support the vehicle's weight. Slowly turn the jack handle counterclockwise to open the release valve and gently lower the vehicle onto the jack stands. When the vehicle has settled onto the jack stands, lower the vehicle jack completely and remove it from under the vehicle. Gently push the vehicle sideways to make sure it is secure. Repeat this process to lift the other end of the vehicle.

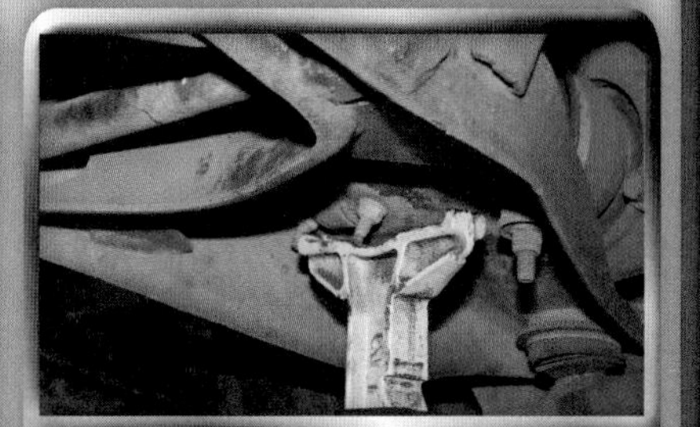

6. When the repairs are complete, use the jack to raise the vehicle off the jack stands. Slide the jack stands from under the vehicle. Make sure no one goes under the vehicle or puts any body parts under the vehicle since the jack could fail or slip.

7. Slowly turn the jack handle counterclockwise to gently lower the vehicle to the ground. Return the jack, jack stands, and wheel chocks to their storage area before you continue working on the vehicle.

Check the amount of clearance under the vehicle. If any of the lifting mechanism is designed so that the vehicle is driven over it, verify that the vehicle has enough clearance. Driving a low-slung vehicle over the lifting mechanism may result in damage to the underside of the vehicle. These vehicles may require shallow ramps that raise the vehicle's wheels so it can go onto the hoist.

The lifting points on a vehicle are typically located at the same place as the jacking points. Check the vehicle's service manual if you are not sure where the lift points are. The lifting arms must be positioned under the center of the lift points so that the weight of the vehicle is distributed evenly. Check whether the vehicle requires rubber pads to protect the undercoating. If the vehicle is equipped with running boards, verify that the hoist arms will not contact the running boards before contacting the lift points. You may be able to set the hoist pads to a higher setting so that the running boards clear the hoist arms.

Make sure there will be adequate headroom above the vehicle once it is raised. Taller vehicles, especially those fitted with roof racks, may need more headroom than you think. Ask your supervisor if there is the least bit of doubt!

The vehicle hoist should be raised so you can comfortably work under it. Lock the lift in place before moving underneath or working on the vehicle. To lift a vehicle using a two-post hoist, follow the steps in SKILL DRILL 7-3. Read and follow the safety instructions that are provided with the two-post hoist. They should be displayed near the lift operating controls. Check the hydraulic system for leaks. Make sure there are no oil spills around or under the two-post hoist.

Using Four-Post Hoists

Four-post hoists are often used to lift a vehicle for wheel alignment services and brake repairs. Make sure you know how to operate the four-post hoist, taking particular care to know where the stop control is so that you can use it quickly in an emergency. Always refer to the operations manual for the correct procedure for stopping the four-post hoist.

Before using a four-post hoist, read and follow the safety instructions that are provided with the four-post hoist. They should be displayed near the lift operating controls. Also check the hydraulic system for any leaks and the steel cables for any sign of damage. Make sure there are no oil spills around or under the hoist.

The four-post hoist should be completely down before you attempt to drive the vehicle onto it. The platform may have built-in wheel restraints or attachments for wheel alignment equipment. A set of bars is normally mounted at the front of each ramp to prevent the vehicle from being driven off the front of the four-post hoist. At the back there will be ramps that allow the vehicle to be driven onto the four-post hoist. These ramps will pivot upward when the hoist is raised and prevent the vehicle from rolling off the back. To lift a vehicle using a four-post hoist, follow the steps in SKILL DRILL 7-4.

Preparation for Customer Pickup

Make sure all vehicle protection is removed prior to releasing the vehicle to the customer. After removing the vehicle protection, such as fender covers, floor mats, and steering and seat covers, ensure that no damage to the vehicle has been sustained during repair. Check the vehicle for cleanliness by ensuring that all trash has been removed and no oil or grease marks are on the vehicle prior to returning it to the customer. Check that all of the windows are crystal clear, that the dashboard, knobs, steering wheel, and center console are spotless and clean, that floor mats have no dirt, and that there are no fingerprints on the door latches, fenders, or the backs of the mirrors FIGURE 7-13. Now go back through the vehicle and look for tools. Wear appropriate personal protective gear such as safety glasses and gloves when working with cleaning materials.

FIGURE 7-13 Preparing a vehicle for a customer.

SKILL DRILL 7-3 Lifting a Vehicle Using a Two-Post Hoist

1. Prepare to use the two-post hoist. Check the hoist and check the vehicle clearance. Carefully drive the vehicle so that it is centered between the two posts, left and right. Also ensure that it is positioned properly, front to back, for the type of hoist and vehicle you are using. Leave the vehicle in neutral and apply the emergency brake.

2. Position the lifting pads under the vehicle lifting points. Make sure the lifting pads are adjusted to the same height for both sides of the vehicle. Move to the operating controls and raise the two-post hoist just far enough to come into contact with the vehicle.

3. Make sure no one is near the vehicle and then raise the vehicle just until the wheels are a couple of inches off the floor. Check the position of the lifting pads, and shake the vehicle gently to confirm that it is stable. Lift the vehicle to slightly above working height, and then lower it onto the locks or safety device.

4. Before the two-post hoist is lowered, remove all tools and equipment from the area and wipe up any spilled fluids. Raise the hoist to unlock the lift before lowering it. Make sure no one is near the vehicle before lowering it. Once the vehicle is on the ground, remove the lifting arms and drive it away.

PROVE
KNOW
SEE
DO

SKILL DRILL 7-4 Using Four-Post Hoists to Lift a Vehicle

1. Prepare to safely use the vehicle hoist. With the aid of an assistant guiding the driver, or a large mirror in front of the hoist, drive the vehicle slowly and carefully onto the four-post hoist and position it centrally. If the vehicle has front wheel restraints, drive the vehicle forward until the wheels lock into the brackets.

2. Get out of the vehicle and check that it is correctly positioned on the platform. If it is, apply the emergency brake and select first gear for a manual transmission or park for an automatic.

3. Make sure the four-post hoist area is clear. Move to the controls and lift the vehicle until it reaches the appropriate work height. If the four-post hoist has a manual safety mechanism, lock it in place to engage whatever safety device is used.

PUSH TO RELEASE LATCHES
EXIT

4. Before the four-post hoist is lowered, remove all tools and equipment from the area and wipe up any spilled fluids. Remove the safety device or unlock the lift before lowering it. Make sure no one is near the area. Once the four-post hoist is fully lowered, with the help of a guide, you can carefully back the vehicle off the hoist.

To ensure that the vehicle is prepared to return to the customer per school/company policy, follow the steps in SKILL DRILL 7-5:

1. Identify shop policy or procedures for returning a customer's vehicle.
2. Check the vehicle for cleanliness.
3. Clean the vehicle according to shop policy.
4. Remove all vehicle protection prior to customer pickup.
5. Dispose of any waste products in an environmentally safe manner, and clean and return fender covers, seat covers, and floor mats to the appropriate storage area.

Wrap-up

Ready for Review

- Vehicles under repair must be protected from further damage occurring while in the shop.
- A preservice vehicle walk-around will ensure that the shop and customer are in agreement about existing damage to the car.
- Use protective equipment, such as seat covers, floor mats, and fender covers, to prevent damage and to protect vehicles against grease, oil, and dirt.
- Use specified containers for corrosives and grease; clean up spills thoroughly.
- Carefully use tools and jacking or hoisting equipment to prevent mechanical damage to a customer's car.
- Only experienced, licensed drivers should test-drive high-performance vehicles.
- Moving cars in and out of the shop is another opportunity for damage to occur.
- Inspect protective covers (fender covers and floor mats) for existing damage prior to use.
- The safe working load indicates the operating capacity for lifting equipment.
- Lifting equipment includes vehicle hoists, floor jacks, jack stands, engine and component hoists, chains, slings, and shackles.
- Periodically check and test lifting equipment; consult the test certificate if available.
- Vehicle jacks can be classified by the type of lifting mechanism they use: hydraulic, pneumatic, or mechanical.
- Jack types include floor jacks, high-lift (farm) jacks, bottle jacks, air jacks, scissor jacks, sliding bridge jacks, and transmission jacks.
- Jack stands support a vehicle's weight when it has been raised; always use jack stands in pairs.
- Vehicle hoists raise the vehicle to allow technicians underside access.
- Vehicle hoists are most commonly single-post, four-post, or two-post.
- Never use a vehicle hoist without activating the safety lock or for lifting a vehicle heavier than the rated limit.
- Cover or fence inspection pits when not in use to prevent others from falling in.
- Choose vehicle jacks according to size and lifting capacity.
- Do not use a vehicle hoist if the vehicle's frame is not structurally sound.
- Make sure a vehicle has enough clearance over the lifting mechanism.
- Clean the vehicle and remove tools and vehicle protection before returning it to the customer.

Key Terms

four-post hoist A type of hoist that the vehicle is driven onto that uses two long, narrow platforms to lift the vehicle.

hydraulic jack A type of vehicle jack that uses oil under pressure to lift vehicles.

jack stands Metal stands with adjustable height to hold a vehicle once it has been jacked up.

mechanical jack A type of vehicle jack that uses mechanical leverage to lift a vehicle.

pneumatic jack A type of vehicle jack that uses compressed gas or air to lift a vehicle.

safe working load (SWL) The maximum safe lifting load for lifting equipment.

single-post hoist A type of vehicle hoist that uses a single central platform to lift a vehicle.

test certificate A certificate issued when lifting equipment has been checked and deemed safe.

two-post hoist A type of vehicle hoist that uses two parts (one on each side of vehicle) and four arms to lift the vehicle.

vehicle hoist A type of vehicle lifting tool designed to lift the entire vehicle.

vehicle jack A tool for lifting a vehicle.

ASE-Type Questions

1. Tech A says that you should always deal with the customer's valuables according to company policy. Tech B says that you should protect a customer's vehicle by washing it when you are finished with it. Who is correct?
   a. Tech A
   b. Tech B
   c. Both A and B
   d. Neither A nor B
2. Tech A says that it is a good practice to perform a walk-around inspection of the vehicle with the customer. Tech B says that fender covers will protect the fenders from dents when working on the engine. Who is correct?
   a. Tech A
   b. Tech B
   c. Both A and B
   d. Neither A nor B
3. Tech A says that a vehicle jack can be used to support the vehicle while working under it. Tech B says that a jack stand automatically adjusts to the vehicle's height. Who is correct?
   a. Tech A
   b. Tech B
   c. Both A and B
   d. Neither A nor B
4. Tech A says that hoists should be inspected and certified perodically. Tech B says that safety locks do not need to be applied before working under the vehicle, unless you will be working for more than 10 minutes. Who is correct?
   a. Tech A
   b. Tech B
   c. Both A and B
   d. Neither A nor B
5. Tech A says that an engine hoist can lift more weight when the legs and arm are extended. Tech B says that the bolts used to mount an engine to a stand should complete at least six turns. Who is correct?
   a. Tech A
   b. Tech B
   c. Both A and B
   d. Neither A nor B
6. Tech A says that gasoline vapors are lighter than air, so inspection pits do not have a fire hazard like above ground hoists. Tech B says that you should never lift a fully loaded vehicle off the ground. Who is correct?
   a. Tech A
   b. Tech B
   c. Both A and B
   d. Neither A nor B
7. Tech A says that you should always ensure that the vehicle has enough ground clearance before driving on a lift. Tech B says that you should center the vehicle on the lift before raising it. Who is correct?
   a. Tech A
   b. Tech B
   c. Both A and B
   d. Neither A nor B
8. Tech A says that you should always inspect a lifting device for leaks and operation before using it. Tech B says that all mechanical safety locks on a hoist should be in place before getting under the vehicle. Who is correct?
   a. Tech A
   b. Tech B
   c. Both A and B
   d. Neither A nor B
9. Tech A says that if you damage a customer's vehicle, insist the damage was there before you started working on it. Tech B says that you should always use seat and steering wheel covers, floor mats, and fender covers whenever a vehicle is being worked on. Who is correct?
   a. Tech A
   b. Tech B
   c. Both A and B
   d. Neither A nor B
10. Tech A says that a person outside the vehicle should be used to supervise and guide a vehicle while it is being driven in the shop. Tech B says that as long as you are a student in the Auto Tech program you can drive any of the vehicles. Who is correct?
    a. Tech A
    b. Tech B
    c. Both A and B
    d. Neither A nor B

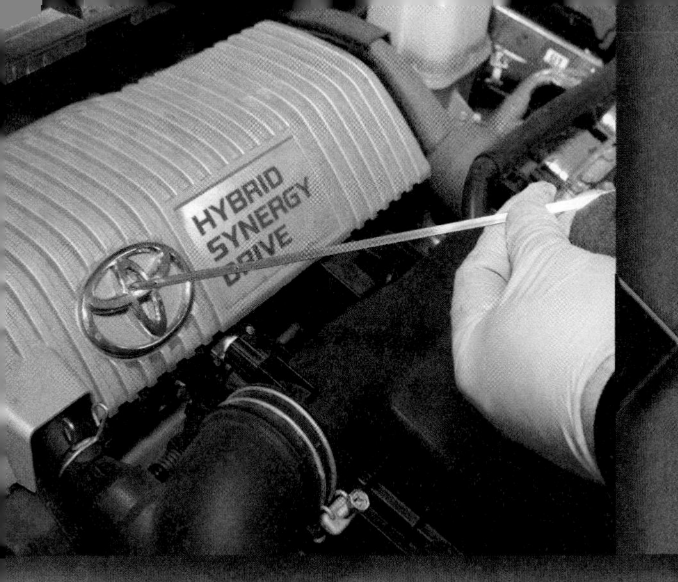
HYBRID
SYNERGY
DRIVE

CHAPTER 8

KNOW
SEE
DO
PROVE

NATEF Tasks

Engine Repair General			Page
■ Verify operation of the instrument panel engine warning indicators.	MLR	AST	207–208
Engine Performance **Ignition System**			
■ Check and refill diesel exhaust fluid (DEF).	MLR	AST	196
■ Inspect, service, or replace air filters, filter housings, and intake duct work.	MLR	AST	199–201
■ Inspect condition of exhaust system hangers, brackets, clamps, and heat shields; repair or replace as needed.	MLR	AST	208–211

KNOW
SEE
DO
PROVE

Knowledge Objectives

After reading this chapter, you will be able to:

1. Describe what fluids are used in the typical modern automobile. (pp 192–197)
2. Explain the systems to be inspected when performing an underhood inspection. (pp 192–200)
3. Describe possible faults found on engine drive belts. (pp 197–198)
4. Explain why the belts and hoses need to be inspected on a regular basis. (pp 197–198)
5. Explain how to tell whether the vehicle air filter needs replacement. (pp 199–201)
6. Describe what to check when performing a vehicle exterior inspection. (pp 200–206)
7. Explain the procedure for checking interior and exterior lighting. (pp 203–205)
8. Describe what is checked during an in-vehicle inspection. (pp 206–208)
9. List the areas that are to be inspected during an under-vehicle inspection. (pp 208–211)
10. Describe the characteristics of different types of leaking fluids. (pp 209, 211)

Vehicle Maintenance Inspection

Know
See
Do
Prove

Skills Objectives

After reading this chapter, you will be able to:

1. Check and refill windshield washer fluid. (pp 196–197)
2. Change the air filter. (pp 199–200)
3. Perform a visual inspection. (p 201)
4. Check and replace the windshield wiper blades. (pp 202–203)
5. Inspect the windshield. (pp 203–204)
6. Inspect the interior lights.(pp 203–204)
7. Inspect the exterior lights. (pp 203–205)
8. Check instrument panel warning lamps. (pp 207–208)
9. Perform a horn check. (pp 208–209)
10. Perform an under-vehicle components inspection. (pp 208–211)

Introduction

A regular inspection of the many systems and components of a vehicle helps to ensure the safe and reliable operation of the vehicle. These inspections include an underhood inspection, an exterior inspection, certain in-vehicle inspections, and an under-vehicle inspection. Vehicle fluid levels, lighting systems, tires, suspension, belts, and hoses will all be checked. Any faults or concerns should be noted for service or repair. This chapter will explain what to look for and how to perform these important services.

Underhood Inspection

A check under the hood is important to the life and operation of the vehicle **FIGURE 8-1**. The inspection should be performed at the manufacturer's recommended intervals and also prior to any long driving trip. Component damage or failure is often caused by a lack of service or low fluid level in the related system. For example, low oil level in the engine can cause major damage to the engine bearings and crankshaft. Future problems also can be prevented by a thorough inspection of the underhood systems, where the discovery of a torn belt or a low fluid level may help to avoid a breakdown on the highway.

FIGURE 8-1 A check under the hood is vital to the life and operation of the vehicle.

Fluids

Some of the fluids used in a vehicle, such as engine oil, are needed to keep the mechanical systems lubricated and functioning correctly. Other fluids may be safety related, such as windshield washer fluid and brake fluid. Always use the manufacturer's recommended type and amount of fluid when checking these items.

For the engine, the lubrication oil and engine coolant levels must be checked. The brake, hydraulic clutch, and anti-lock brake systems all depend on the proper level of brake fluid. Power steering fluid and transmission fluid need to be at the recommended level for these systems to operate properly. The windshield washer is an important safety feature and the fluid level should be checked as needed.

Just as the level of the fluid is important, so too is the quality of the fluid. Nearly all of the fluids in a vehicle, except some automatic transmission/transaxle fluids, get old and wear out, requiring replacement; therefore, whenever you check the level of any fluid, check the quality of the fluid, too. You might notice a change in color, a change in consistency, a mix of fluids, or a change in smell, such as burnt transmission/transaxle fluid. Each

You Are the Automotive Technician

You work for a car rental company that maintains their vehicles in house. Your main task today is to perform preventive maintenance on a vehicle in the fleet that is scheduled for its next service. To perform a routine maintenance check, you follow a procedural checklist that includes changing the oil and filter; rotating the tires and inspecting brake, steering, and suspension systems; and checking/inspecting other important parts. During the inspection, you notice that the brake fluid level is low, the wiper blades smear badly, and the left rear brake light isn't working, which requires a bulb replacement.

1. What two conditions can low brake fluid level indicate?
2. How do you determine what engine oil to use?
3. What must be done after an oil change to remind the customer of the next change?
4. What is used to check the oil level after it has been changed?

fluid shows its age differently, so become familiar with how to identify both good and bad fluids.

Engine Oil

The level of the oil in the engine's lubrication system is critical to the engine's operation FIGURE 8-2. The engine oil is picked up by the oil pump, filtered through the oil filter, and then sent under pressure to the crankshaft and camshaft bearings. If the level is too low, the oil pump will starve for oil. If the level is too high, the oil will be struck by the crankshaft, churning it into foam. The bearings require a steady flow of oil for lubrication, not air. If the oil is too low or too high, the engine bearings can be damaged.

The engine oil level should be checked periodically, usually at every fuel stop or two, as part of a preventive maintenance plan. Always check the oil level when the vehicle is on a level surface, not on a hill or slope. The oil can be checked with the dipstick, which is usually marked "oil" or brightly colored. Always check engine oil with the engine off. Wipe off the dipstick, identify the marks on the dipstick, and reinsert it fully in the tube. Then pull it out and hold it horizontally to read it. The marks on the oil dipstick usually have lines that indicate "full" and "add," or "min" and "max." The difference in quantity between the add and full marks on an engine oil dipstick is typically 1 quart (0.9 liters), but can be as much as 2 quarts (1.9 liters). Refer to the manufacturer's recommendations as noted in the vehicle owner's manual or the manufacturer's published service information.

When checking the oil level, also consider checking whether it is time for an oil change. The manufacturer will specify that the vehicle's oil-life monitoring (OLM) system be referenced to determine the amount of oil life remaining, or the manufacturer will specify when the oil should be changed depending on the miles traveled or period of time since the last oil change. If the vehicle is due for an oil change, the level should still be checked first. A low reading on the dipstick could indicate that a seal or gasket is leaking or that the engine is using oil. Either of these situations requires further investigation.

> **LINK**
>
> Refer to the Engine Lubrication chapter for information on selecting the correct oil for the vehicle being serviced and for skill drills on how to change the oil in the engine lubrication system.

Engine Coolant

The engine **coolant** level and condition should be checked whenever the oil level is checked. The engine cooling system depends on the coolant to transfer excessive heat from the engine to the radiator. The engine temperature must be controlled to prevent overheating and to maintain proper exhaust emission levels. Some vehicles will have a transparent reservoir or surge tank marked with "hot" and "cold," which allows checking the coolant without removing the cap FIGURE 8-3. Some also may have an overflow tank with a tube leading from the radiator cap filler neck to a transparent overflow tank. The level can usually be seen through the side of the tank and compared to the marks.

> **Safety**
>
> Do not remove the pressure cap (radiator cap) when the engine is warm or hot. The system is under pressure, and removing the cap could allow the coolant to immediately boil and spray out, causing severe burns. Always allow the system to cool before removing the cap.

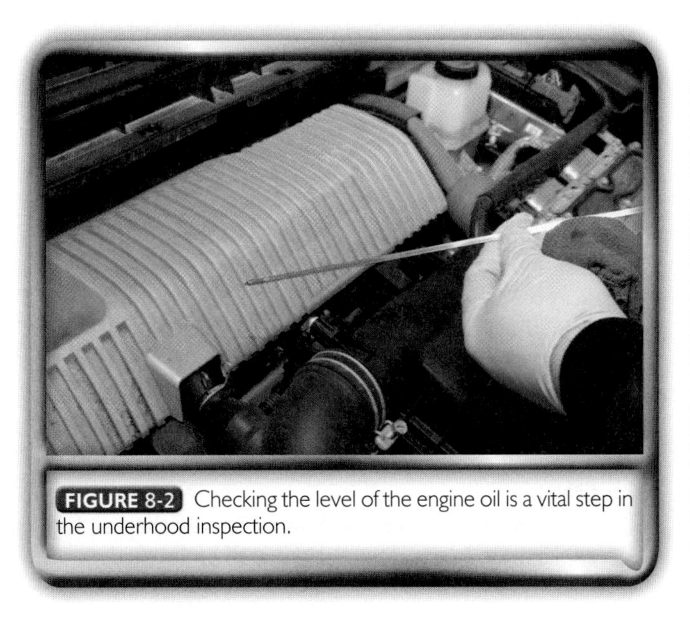

FIGURE 8-2 Checking the level of the engine oil is a vital step in the underhood inspection.

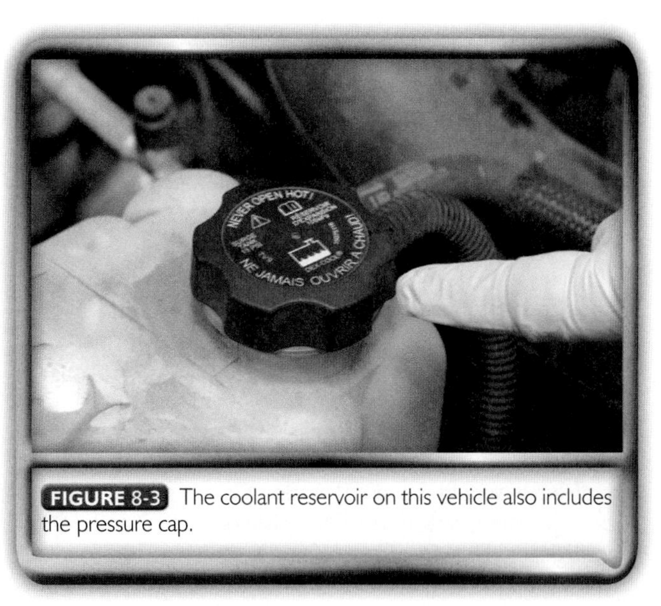
NEVER OPEN HOT!
NE JAMAIS OUVRIR A CHAUD!

FIGURE 8-3 The coolant reservoir on this vehicle also includes the pressure cap.

Older vehicles, which do not have an overflow tank, usually have a radiator cap located on top of the radiator that must be removed when checking the coolant level. If there is no overflow tank, then the coolant level in the radiator should be about 1.5" (38 mm) below the filler neck.

Low coolant levels can cause engine overheating, which will lead to damaged cylinder head gaskets or piston rings. The technician should note at each maintenance inspection if any coolant needs to be added and if so, how much. Coolant levels that are consistently low indicate a coolant leak that will need to be diagnosed and repaired.

Since the coolant also provides freeze protection, the coolant freezing point also should be checked during the underhood inspection. An insufficient amount of anti-freeze could allow the coolant to freeze during temperatures below freezing. Since water expands when frozen, freezing of the coolant could crack the engine block, cylinder head, radiator, or other engine components. The anti-freeze protection level can be checked with an anti-freeze **hydrometer**. Select a hydrometer that is designed to be used with the type of anti-freeze being tested. Draw enough coolant into the hydrometer to bring it up to the "fill" line. Hold the hydrometer vertically and read the freeze protection level.

A refractometer also can be used to measure the freeze protection level of coolant. A drop or two of coolant is placed on a sample plate. A cover plate is then lowered onto the sample and the reading is taken. If held roughly level with a light source directly above the refractometer, you can look into the eyepiece and see a sharp line between a dark section and a light section. The sharp line indicates the reading. In many cases, there will be several scales that you can check, such as battery acid, ethylene glycol, and propylene glycol. Make sure you are reading the proper scale.

Applied Math

AM-36: Ratios/Percentages: The technician can convert test readings in decimal or fractional form to a ratio or percentage form for comparison with the manufacturer's specifications and vice versa.

A technician is servicing the cooling system of a vehicle with a 12-quart capacity per service information. Because of the cold climate of the location, the shop supervisor informed the technician to fill the cooling system with a 60/40 mix of antifreeze and distilled water. Considering that the total capacity of the system is 12 quarts, the technician will need to convert the percentages to a fractional form.

This can be done by multiplying the total quantity by each percentage. So 12 quarts × 60% is 12 × 0.60, which equals 7.2 quarts of antifreeze. And, 2 quarts × 40% is 12 × 0.40, which equals 4.8 quarts of distilled water. Most climates require a 50/50 mix of antifreeze and water. This can be converted to a ratio or percentage form. Six quarts of distilled water and 6 quarts of antifreeze would be a 1:1 ratio. Concerning the percentage form, we have 50% distilled water and 50% antifreeze. This is often referred to as a 50/50 mix.

▸ LINK

Refer to the Engine Cooling chapter for a detailed discussion on the proper type and amount of coolant for the vehicle and how to check and fill the engine cooling system.

Brake and Clutch Fluid

A hydraulic braking system depends on a special fluid called brake fluid. The brake fluid is stored in a reservoir attached to or near to the brake system master cylinder FIGURE 8-4. If the brake fluid level gets too low, air can be pulled into the hydraulic system, which will cause the brake pedal to be soft or too low. This will cause the brakes to work poorly or not at all. The brake fluid should be checked whenever the oil level is checked or at least monthly. Also check the color of the brake fluid. Most brake fluid is very clear. If it is getting dark, it is most likely becoming oxidized or contaminated and will need to be changed. Most brake fluids are **hygroscopic**, meaning they absorb water from the atmosphere. Because of this, most manufacturers recommend changing brake fluid every 2 to 4 years. However, the best process is to check the condition of the brake fluid with either a brake fluid tester or brake fluid test strips. Check service information or the vehicle owner's manual for specific recommendations.

Vehicles with a manual transmission may have a hydraulic clutch system that uses both a master cylinder and brake fluid. Depending on the vehicle, the brake fluid reservoir also may supply the clutch master cylinder, or the clutch may have a separate fluid reservoir FIGURE 8-5. Be sure to check both of these reservoirs for the proper fluid level.

TECHNICIAN TIP

Low master cylinder brake fluid levels usually indicate an issue with the system. Either there is a brake fluid leak in the system or, on vehicles equipped with disc brakes, the brake pads are worn. If the brake fluid level is low, inform your supervisor; a brake lining inspection may be necessary.

▸ LINK

Refer to the Hydraulics and Power Brakes chapter for an explanation of the different types of brake fluid.

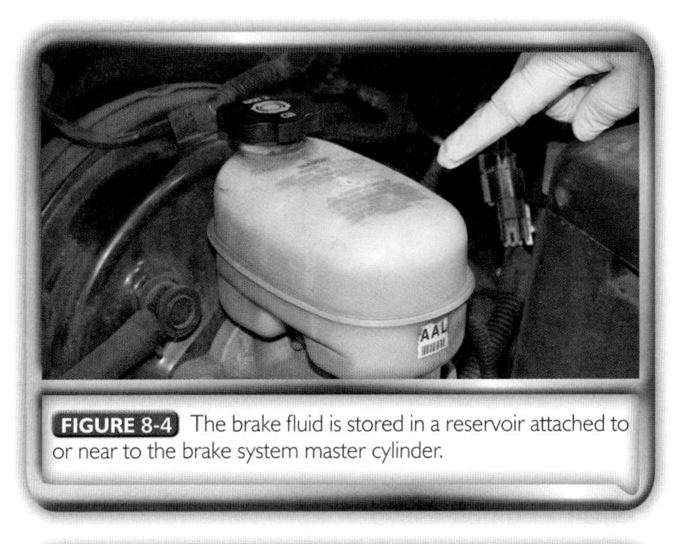

FIGURE 8-4 The brake fluid is stored in a reservoir attached to or near to the brake system master cylinder.

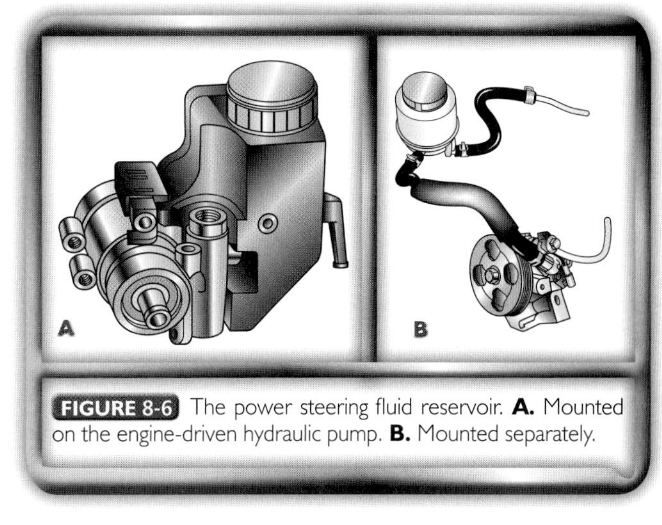
A
B

FIGURE 8-6 The power steering fluid reservoir. **A.** Mounted on the engine-driven hydraulic pump. **B.** Mounted separately.

FIGURE 8-5 Check both the brake fluid reservoir and the clutch fluid reservoir in vehicles with manual transmissions.

Power Steering Fluid

Most vehicles are equipped with power-assisted steering systems. The power for the system usually comes from an engine-driven hydraulic pump. Some vehicles, typically hybrid-electric vehicles, use an electrically driven pump. The pump delivers fluid under pressure to the power unit at the steering box, or rack-and-pinion, through connecting hoses and pipes. The fluid reservoir can be mounted as part of the engine-driven hydraulic pump, or it can be a separate container FIGURE 8-6. The power steering fluid level must be at the proper level to avoid drawing air into the hydraulic system and to prevent fluid overflow when the engine is hot.

In most cases, the power steering fluid level can be checked with a dipstick connected to the filler cap. The engine should be idling and the fluid hot. In many cases, the dipstick lists both a "cold" and a "hot" level, or a "safe" level. When checking the level, you also should check the appearance of the fluid. Dark or black fluid usually means the fluid is old and needs to be changed. The power steering fluid level should be checked as a normal part of the underhood inspection.

> **LINK**
> Refer to the Servicing Steering Systems chapter for more information on power steering fluid types and how to check them.

Automatic Transmission/Transaxle Fluid

The correct automatic transmission/transaxle fluid level (referred to as automatic transmission fluid from here on) is critical to the effective and efficient operation of the transmission. If the level is too low, slipping and shift timing faults can result. Since reverse gear usually requires a larger volume of fluid, a shift into reverse could be delayed. If the fluid level is too high, the transmission fluid will churn and aerate, which can lead to low pressures, resulting in slipping clutches. Always make sure the transmission fluid level is correct.

Automatic transmission fluid level is usually checked with a dipstick located under the hood, usually toward the back of the engine compartment. Some automatic transmissions do not have a dipstick; they are checked using a fill plug or level plug on the side of the transmission FIGURE 8-7. If the transmission does use a dipstick, the fluid level is usually checked with the engine running, the transmission warmed up fully, and the gear selector in park or neutral, depending on the vehicle. When checking transmission fluid, wipe off the dipstick, observe the markings, and reinsert the dipstick into the tube briefly. Remove the dipstick and hold it horizontally to read it.

If adding transmission fluid, make sure you select the correct fluid, as there are a number of different transmission fluids specified for various vehicles. Fluid is added through the dipstick tube, so use a funnel. The lines between "full" and "add" are usually only about 1 pint (0.5 liters), so add only a small amount of fluid and then recheck the fluid level.

In a manual transmission/transaxle, fluid splashing up from the lower gear sets lubricates the bearings. Early bearing failure is the result of driving with the transmission fluid level too low. In most cases, transmission fluid level on manual transmissions/transaxles can only be checked from under the vehicle. The vehicle must be level. The level is usually accessed through a fill plug on the side of the transmission/transaxle. If fluid comes out of the fill hole when the plug is removed, allow any extra to drain out, then reinsert the fill plug. If no fluid comes out of the fill hole, carefully stick a finger in the hole and bend your finger down to feel the level of the fluid.

If the level is within a quarter inch of the bottom of the fill hole, the level is OK and the fill plug can be reinserted. If the fluid level is lower than that, the proper fluid will need to be added until the level is even with the bottom of the fill hole. Always check the manufacturer's specifications to identify the proper fluid for the vehicle you are working on.

Safety

Do not rotate the wheels or engine with your finger in the hole, as transmission parts could pinch or sever your finger.

LINK

Refer to the Servicing the Automatic Transmission chapter for more details about fluid types and checking fluid levels.

TECHNICIAN TIP

Many newer vehicles—typically European models and some Asian imports—do not have a specified method of checking the transmission fluid level. The transmissions are considered sealed and lubricated for the life of the vehicle. The manufacturers have determined that the transmission fluid will not be low as long as there are no leaks; any leak will require that the transmission be repaired.

Diesel Exhaust Fluid

Some late-model diesel-powered vehicles use a fluid called **diesel exhaust fluid (DEF)**, or AdBlue™ DEF is injected into the exhaust stream to reduce oxides of Nitrogen during certain driving conditions. Since the DEF is consumed over time, it needs to be replenished periodically, ideally during oil changes. The DEF fluid filler cap is often located under the hood and may be colored blue FIGURE 8-8. *Do not* make the expensive mistake of putting washer fluid (or any other fluid) in the DEF tank.

Windshield Washer Fluid

The windshield washer system on any vehicle is an important safety feature. Driving in muddy conditions, light mist, fog, or any other condition that causes the windshield to be obstructed requires that the washer system be ready to work when needed. The washer fluid reservoir is normally located under the hood of the vehicle FIGURE 8-9. Some vehicles also may have a separate washer reservoir for the rear wiper, located somewhere in

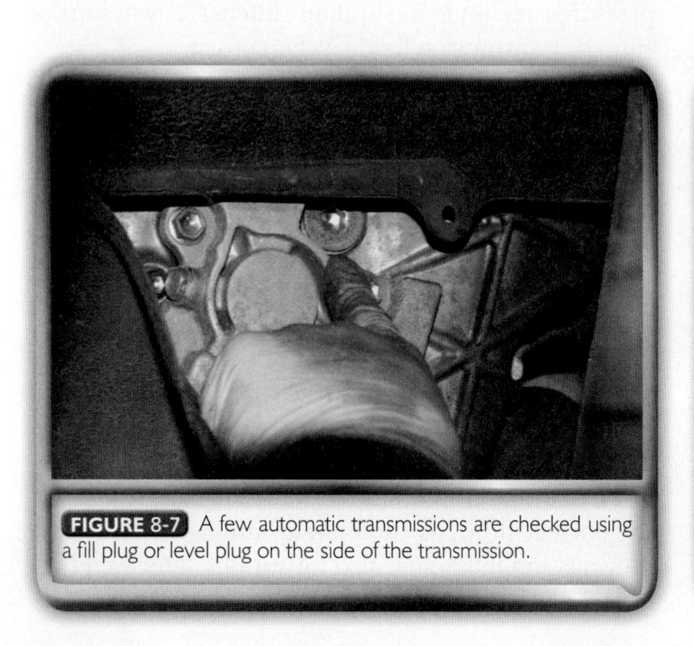

FIGURE 8-7 A few automatic transmissions are checked using a fill plug or level plug on the side of the transmission.

DEF ONLY

FIGURE 8-8 DEF fluid reservoir.

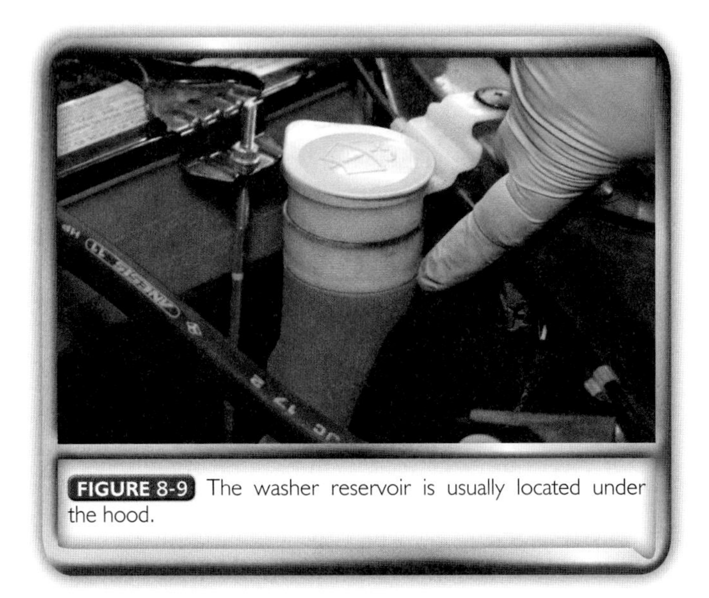

FIGURE 8-9 The washer reservoir is usually located under the hood.

the rear hatch or trunk area. Refer to the owner's manual or service information to locate the filler cap.

The windshield washer fluid should be checked whenever the oil is changed or at each vehicle service. Driving in dusty or wet conditions may require that the windshield washer fluid be checked more often. It is important to use properly formulated and mixed washer fluid, especially in freezing weather. The fluid is normally purchased premixed in the proper ratio that protects against freezing.

To check and add to the windshield washer fluid, follow the steps in **SKILL DRILL 8-1**.

> **TECHNICIAN TIP**
>
> Never use laundry or dishwashing detergent to top off the reservoir, as the chemicals in the detergent can damage the vehicle's paint.

Belts and Hoses

The engine drive belts and coolant hoses are maintenance items that should be inspected and replaced according to the manufacturer's service schedule. They do not last the life of the vehicle. Whenever the vehicle is being serviced, the belts and hoses should be checked. On most vehicles, the failure of a belt or hose when driving will result in overheating of the engine, causing extensive damage to the engine.

Engine Drive Belts

Engine drive belts are used to operate the various accessories on the engine, such as the water pump, power steering pump, air conditioner compressor, and alternator. As the vehicle ages, these belts will wear, along with their associated idler and tensioner pulleys. Some manufacturers recommend that the belts be replaced at about 5 years of age, as part of a preventive maintenance program.

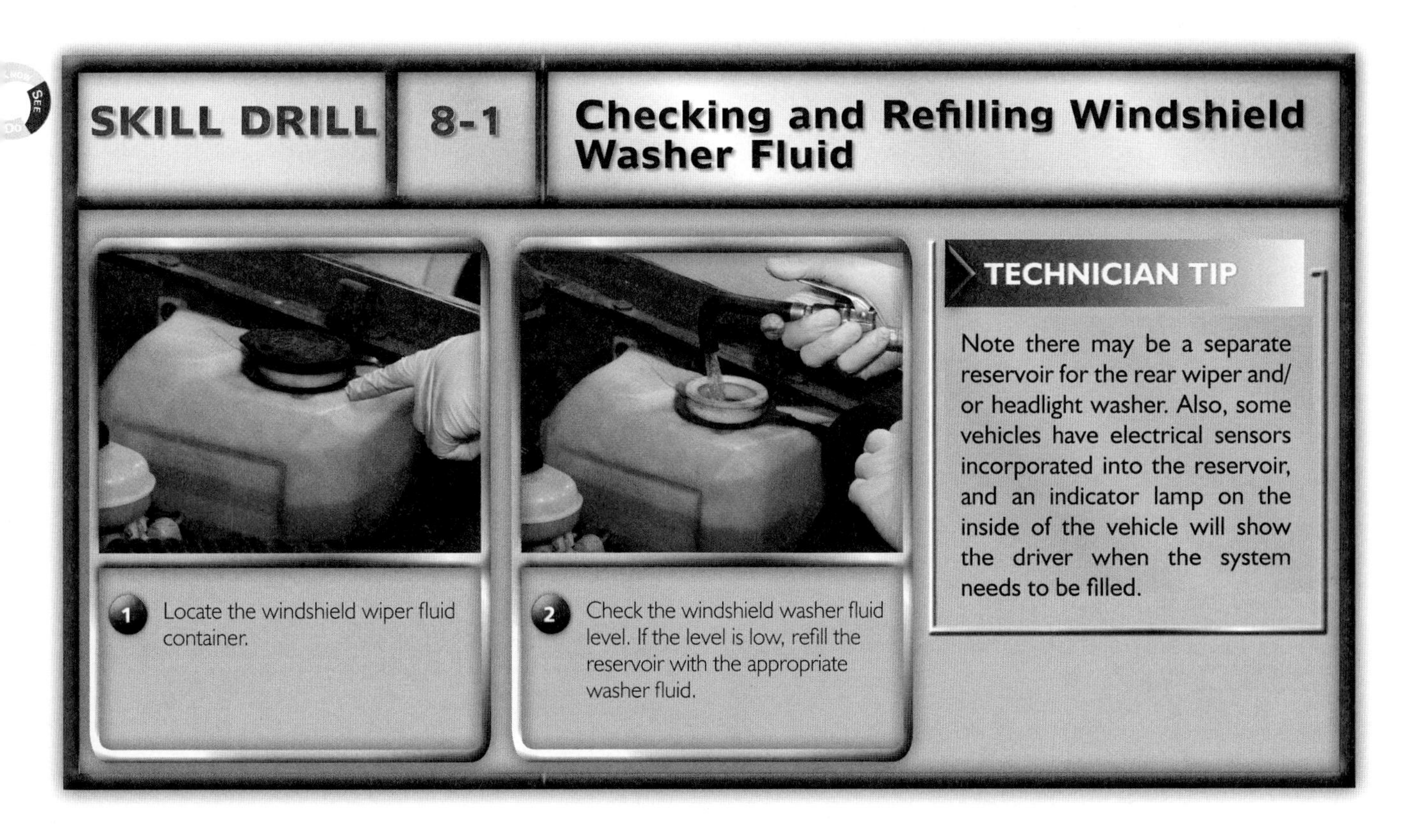

SKILL DRILL 8-1 Checking and Refilling Windshield Washer Fluid

1. Locate the windshield wiper fluid container.
2. Check the windshield washer fluid level. If the level is low, refill the reservoir with the appropriate washer fluid.

> **TECHNICIAN TIP**
>
> Note there may be a separate reservoir for the rear wiper and/or headlight washer. Also, some vehicles have electrical sensors incorporated into the reservoir, and an indicator lamp on the inside of the vehicle will show the driver when the system needs to be filled.

There are two types of drive belts: the V-type and the serpentine type. A V-type belt sits inside a deep V-shaped groove in the pulley. The sides of the V-belt contact and wedge in the sides of the V in the pulley. Serpentine-type belts have a flat profile with a number of grooves running lengthwise along the belt. These grooves are the exact reverse of the grooves in the outer diameter of the pulleys; they increase the contact surface area and prevent the belt from slipping off the drive pulley as it rotates FIGURE 8-10.

Check the drive belts whenever the hood is opened for service. The water pump is the most important component driven by the belt, and the engine will quickly overheat if the belt breaks or comes off. If the belts are more than 5 to 6 years old, check the manufacturer's replacement schedule in the service information. Most vehicles using a serpentine belt also have a spring-operated tensioner and pulley. This tensioner may have a built-in damper that reduces noise and vibration. Some manufacturers recommend that the tensioner be replaced along with the belt. Some belts, called stretchy belts or Stretch Fit™ belts, do not use a method for tensioning the belt. Their stretchiness applies an appropriate amount of tension to the belt over its useful life, which some vehicle manufacturers claim can be up to 150,000 miles.

A
V-Belt
V-Belt
B

FIGURE 8-10 Drive belts. **A.** A V-type belt fits into the V of the drive pulley. **B.** Serpentine-type belts have a flat profile with a number of grooves running lengthwise along the belt.

The belts should be checked for the following:

- Cracks: Cracks that exceed a certain number per inch in a belt indicate that the belt may soon fail and should be replaced FIGURE 8-11.
- Oil soaking: A belt that has been soaked in oil will not grip properly on the pulleys and will slip. If the oil contamination is severe enough for this to happen, replace the belt.
- Glazing: Glazing is shininess on the surface of the belt, which comes in contact with the pulley. If the belt is very worn, the glazing could be due to the belt bottoming out, and it should be replaced. If it is not old and worn, glazing could indicate that the belt is not tight enough. Tightening the belt may be all that is necessary, depending on how bad the glazing is.
- Tears: Torn or split belts are unserviceable and should be replaced.
- Bottoming out: When a V-type belt or serpentine belt becomes very worn, the bottom of the V may contact the bottom of the groove in the pulley, preventing the sides of the belt from making good contact with the sides of the pulley grooves. This reduced friction causes slippage. A belt worn enough to bottom out should be replaced FIGURE 8-12.

Hoses

The vehicle will usually have at least two large radiator hoses and some smaller heater hoses. At the radiator, there will be a large upper radiator hose (near the top

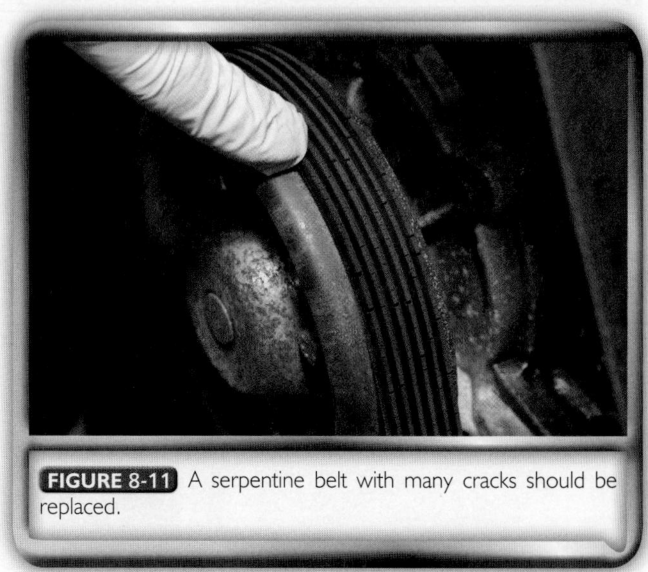

FIGURE 8-11 A serpentine belt with many cracks should be replaced.

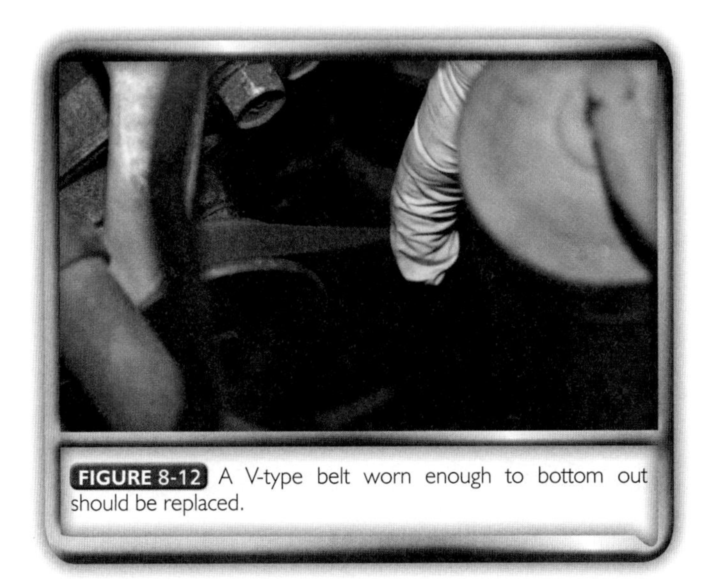

FIGURE 8-12 A V-type belt worn enough to bottom out should be replaced.

of the radiator) and a large lower radiator hose (near the bottom of the radiator). The smaller heater hoses (usually two) run from the engine block, manifold, or water pump to connections at the heater assembly (near the firewall). The engine should be cool when inspecting the hoses. A hot engine will have pressure in the cooling system that may make a soft hose feel stiff, when it really may need to be replaced. If the engine is hot, look for bulging in the hoses.

If you find one defective hose, chances are that the other hose(s) may be deteriorating in the same way and will soon need to be replaced. For this reason, most technicians will generally recommend replacing all of the coolant hoses at once as a sensible precaution. This will include the upper and lower radiator hoses and both heater hoses. Also check for any small hoses that may connect components, such as between the water pump and the engine block.

Applied Math

AM-50: Deductive Reasoning: The technician can identify the specific cause of the problem by generating conclusions based on known symptoms related to the problem.

Drive belt squeal is typically a high-pitched squealing noise caused by the V or serpentine belt slipping against the pulleys. This frequently occurs only when a load is applied to the belt, so may be noticed only when turning with power steering or when air conditioning is turned on. Common causes include worn or age-hardened belts, incorrect belt adjustment, incorrect length or pitch belt fitted, oil contamination of the belt, or the belt pulleys being worn or incorrectly aligned.

A practical example may be a car that emits a loud squealing noise occurring only when the steering wheel is turned. A technician can easily reproduce the noise in the shop and can hear that the noise is coming from the drive belt area. A visual inspection will determine the condition and adjustment of the belt. If the belt is replaced with a new, correct part, and the noise returns, the technician can reason that the fault is related to the belt tensioner or pulley, and can inspect them for condition and alignment.

TECHNICIAN TIP

In most cases, hoses need to be felt to determine their condition. They should be neither too hard nor too soft. Also, the relative stiffness should be consistent over the length of the hose. If you feel differences in stiffness, the hose should be replaced.

Changing the Air Filter

The engine needs a free flow of clean air in order to operate correctly and with low emissions. Dust and grit in the air can be very abrasive and will shorten the life of the engine if not filtered out. If the filter element is not fitted correctly and does not seal properly, air can bypass the filter and enter the engine without being filtered.

The location of the air filter will vary, depending on the type of fuel system on the vehicle, so check the vehicle service information or owner's manual for the exact procedure. Some air filters are mounted to the top of the engine, usually found on older vehicles using a carburetor or throttle body fuel injection. The air cleaner on a multiport fuel-injected vehicle is typically located in a rectangular box within the air induction system. While inspecting the air filter, take a look at the air cleaner housing and duct work for cracks or holes, which would allow unfiltered air to enter the engine.

To change the air filter, follow the steps in SKILL DRILL 8-2.

TECHNICIAN TIP

The paper filter element actually becomes more efficient at filtering dirt particles as it is used. This is because the passageways become smaller as dirt is caught in them, so smaller and smaller dirt particles are caught over time. However, if the filter becomes too clogged, it will restrict air, which reduces engine power output. If it is left too long, the filter can become deformed from the excess vacuum caused by the restricted air filter.

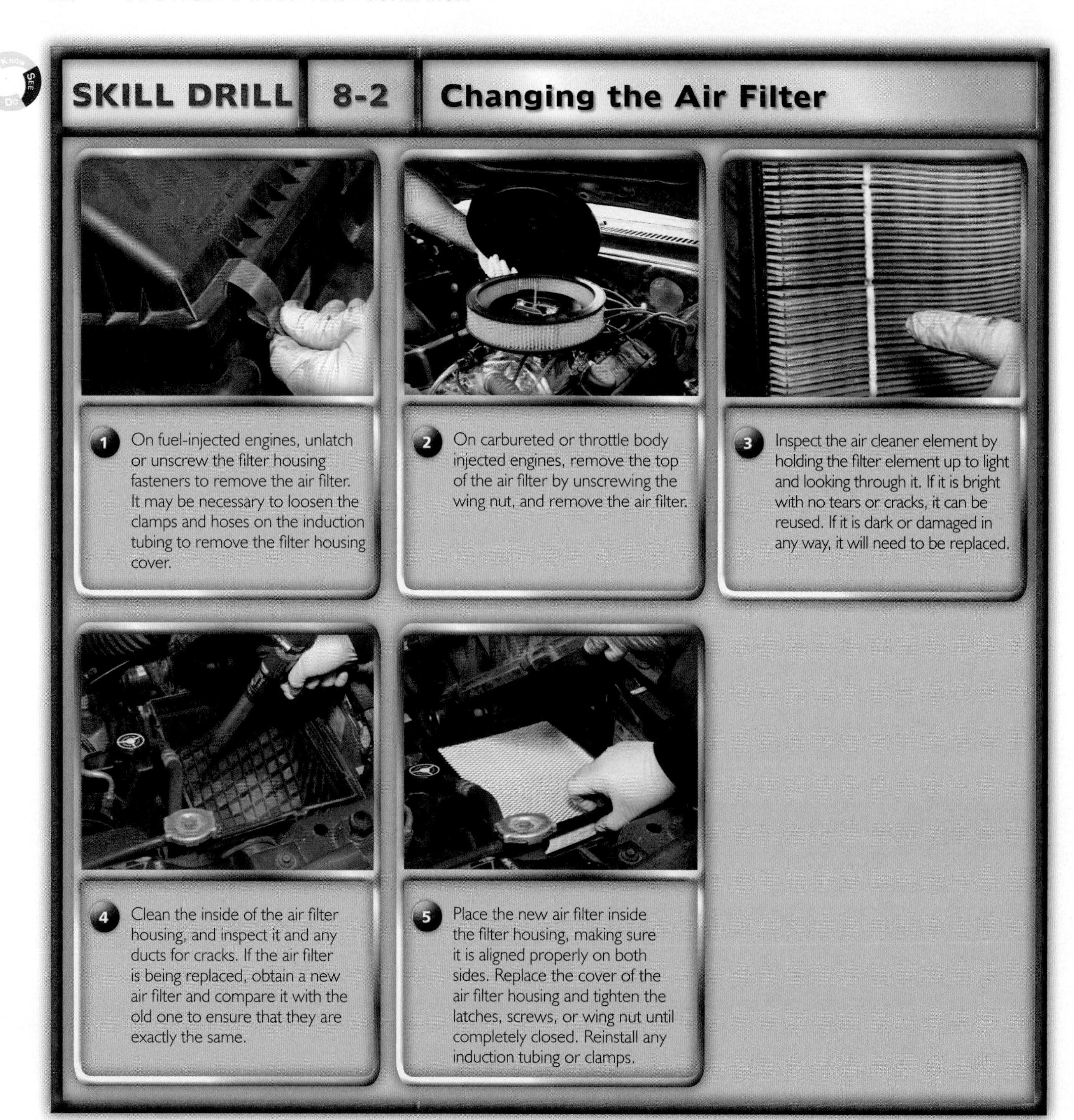

See
SKILL DRILL 8-2 Changing the Air Filter
1 On fuel-injected engines, unlatch or unscrew the filter housing fasteners to remove the air filter. It may be necessary to loosen the clamps and hoses on the induction tubing to remove the filter housing cover.
2 On carbureted or throttle body injected engines, remove the top of the air filter by unscrewing the wing nut, and remove the air filter.
3 Inspect the air cleaner element by holding the filter element up to light and looking through it. If it is bright with no tears or cracks, it can be reused. If it is dark or damaged in any way, it will need to be replaced.
4 Clean the inside of the air filter housing, and inspect it and any ducts for cracks. If the air filter is being replaced, obtain a new air filter and compare it with the old one to ensure that they are exactly the same.
5 Place the new air filter inside the filter housing, making sure it is aligned properly on both sides. Replace the cover of the air filter housing and tighten the latches, screws, or wing nut until completely closed. Reinstall any induction tubing or clamps.

Cabin Air Filters

Many manufacturers have added cabin air filters to the inlet side of the heating/air-conditioning box where fresh air enters the cabin. This filter is designed to catch dust and outside contaminates so they do not get blown into the cabin. Many are paper just like the air filter for the engine. As such, they should be checked regularly and replaced when they begin to clog. Otherwise, they will cause the system to be inefficient due to poor airflow FIGURE 8-13. Some manufacturers are using activated charcoal cabin filters to trap odors and airborne pollutants such as carbon monoxide and oxides of nitrogen. Cabin air filters should usually be replaced once a year or between 12,000 and 15,000 miles. Check the service information to verify the vehicle has a cabin air filter, its location, and the procedure to service it.

Exterior Vehicle Inspections

A periodic inspection of the vehicle's exterior can prevent troubles that may cause safety or operational concerns. It is much better to discover a worn tire or broken taillight lens during an inspection than when broken down on the side of the road or pulled over by the police. A small percentage of owners check their own vehicle for problems, but most depend on the service technician to do it for them. Any maintenance procedure should include this inspection.

FIGURE 8-13 Cabin filters. **A.** Clean. **B.** Dirty.

Performing a Visual Inspection

Once a month or prior to any long trip, a vehicle should be checked for overall roadworthiness. Although the vehicle owner may perform this inspection, the service technician more often does it during periodic maintenance of the vehicle. The inspection also should be made any time the vehicle is serviced at the dealer or repair shop. While doing this inspection, the technician should be sure to work in a systematic manner. Using an inspection sheet and inspecting each vehicle the same way will ensure that a faulty bulb or other component is not missed.

To perform a visual inspection, follow the steps in SKILL DRILL 8-3.

> **Caring for the Customer**
>
> The customer or owner of the vehicle can perform an inspection while washing the vehicle. Bad wiper blades, loose trim, and other items may be noticed that are otherwise not seen.

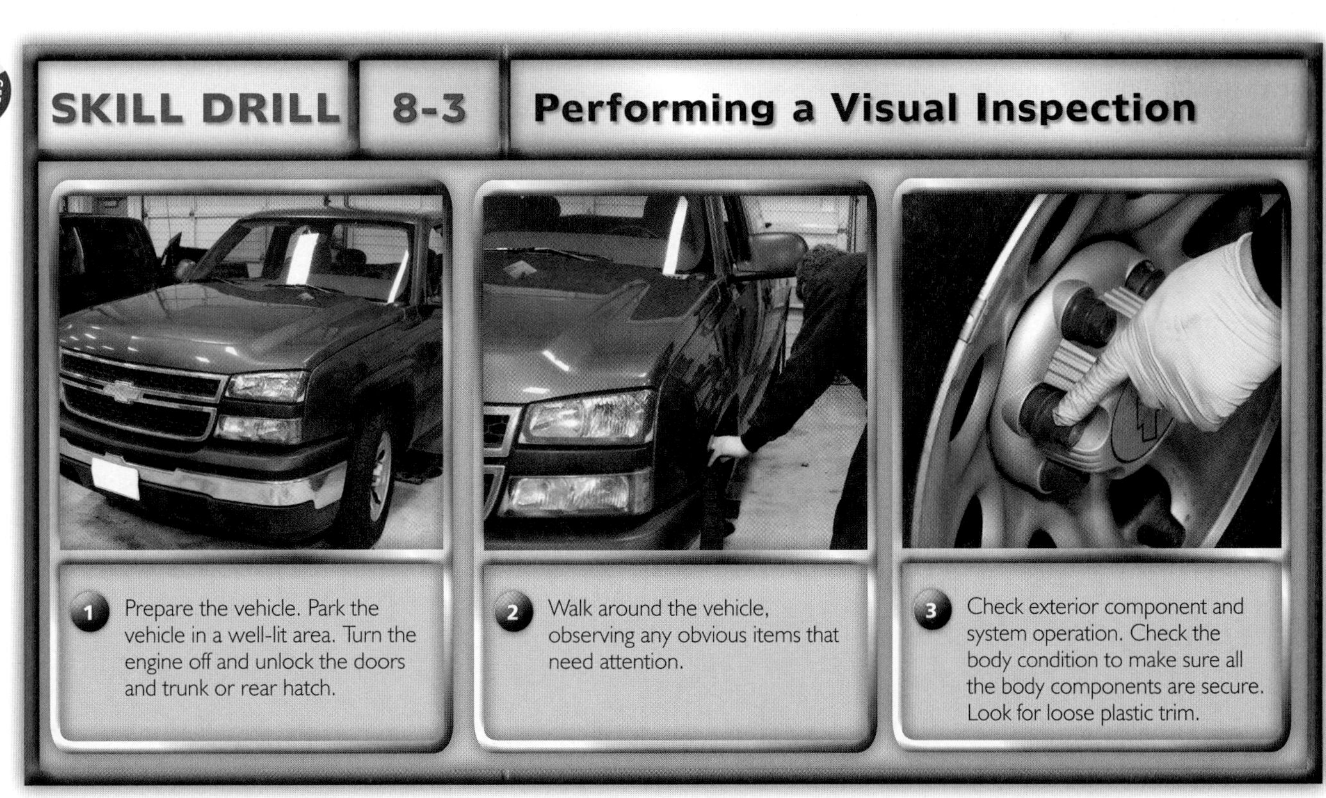

SKILL DRILL 8-3 Performing a Visual Inspection

1. Prepare the vehicle. Park the vehicle in a well-lit area. Turn the engine off and unlock the doors and trunk or rear hatch.
2. Walk around the vehicle, observing any obvious items that need attention.
3. Check exterior component and system operation. Check the body condition to make sure all the body components are secure. Look for loose plastic trim.

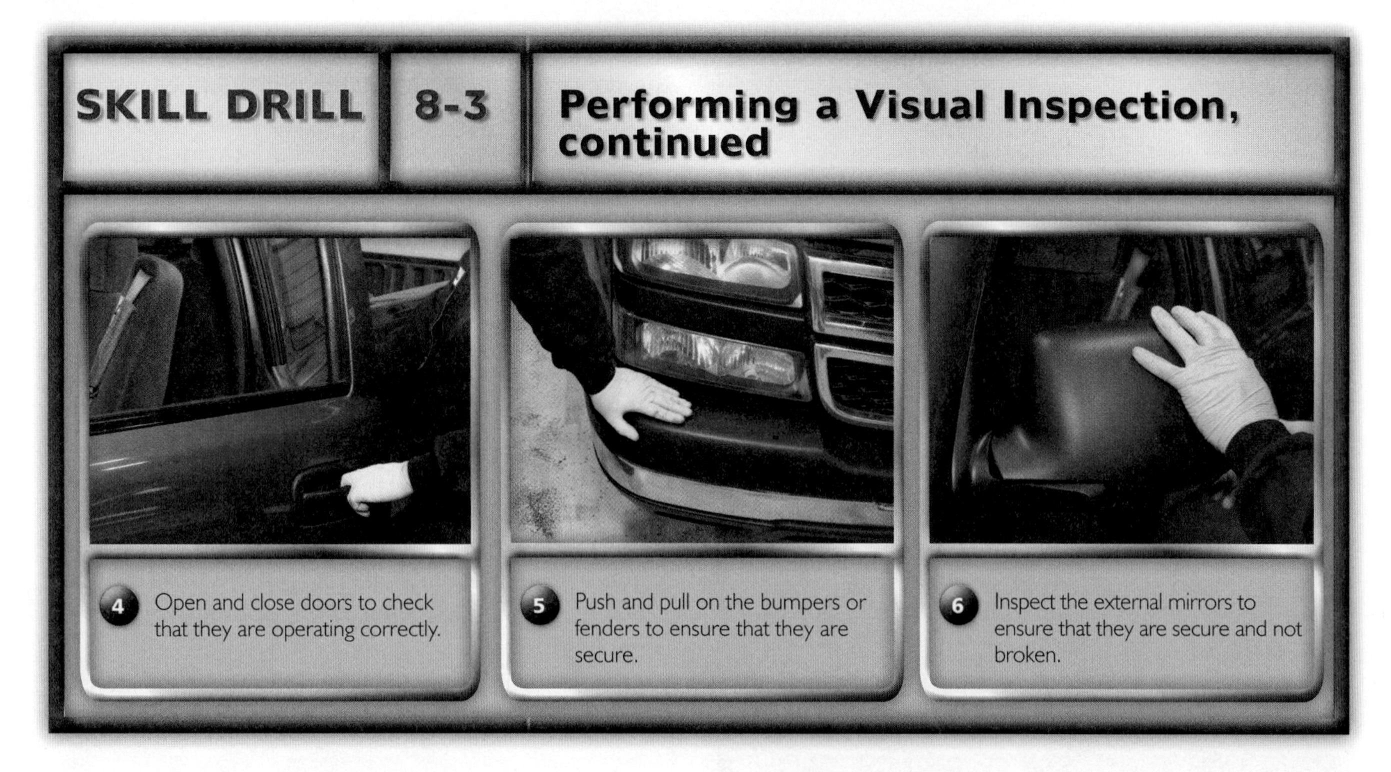
SKILL DRILL
8-3
Performing a Visual Inspection, continued
4 Open and close doors to check that they are operating correctly.
5 Push and pull on the bumpers or fenders to ensure that they are secure.
6 Inspect the external mirrors to ensure that they are secure and not broken.

Checking the Wiper Blades

The windshield wiper blades and arms are an important safety system on every vehicle. Many states with a vehicle inspection program will fail a vehicle if the wiper blades are missing, torn, or worn out. The blades, along with the washer system, help the driver to see clearly under all driving conditions.

The wiper blades should be checked as part of the exterior inspection. Usually any wiper blade that is more than a year old will be ready for replacement, especially if the vehicle is parked outside. Both the blade and the wiper arm should be checked. The wiper blade should be flexible and not torn. The wiper arm should flex at the hinge and be held firmly against the windshield by the wiper arm spring. The rear wiper blade and arm are checked in the same way.

Never operate the wipers when they are dry because this may damage the blades or scratch the surface of the windshield. Never bend the arms to make better contact with the windshield. The arms are pre-tensioned by the manufacturer, and damage could result. If the arms seem to have lost their spring tension, obtain a suitable replacement.

To check and replace windshield wiper blades, follow the steps in SKILL DRILL 8-4.

Inspecting the Windshield

The windshield should be inspected during the wiper blade inspection process. Scratched, scored, or pitted glass will not wipe clean, even with new blades. Windshields may become etched or pitted, causing the wipers to function poorly. This is a safety hazard and should be repaired. The glass in some cases may be polished to repair the condition or it may have to be replaced. Some small chips or cracks can be repaired with special resins and tools. These services can be performed by an automotive glass repair service or at some collision repair shops. Large chips or cracks longer than 3" (76 mm) may be reasons to replace the windshield.

To inspect the windshield, follow the steps in SKILL DRILL 8-5.

> **TECHNICIAN TIP**
>
> Many a windshield has been broken while inspecting or replacing windshield wiper blades. The spring holds the wiper arm firmly against the windshield. If you drop the wiper arm while holding it away from the windshield, the spring will snap it against the windshield with enough force to potentially break the windshield, especially if the wiper blade is removed from the arm. You can prevent a broken windshield by making sure the arm is never allowed to slip or by placing a fender cover on the windshield where the wiper blade would hit.

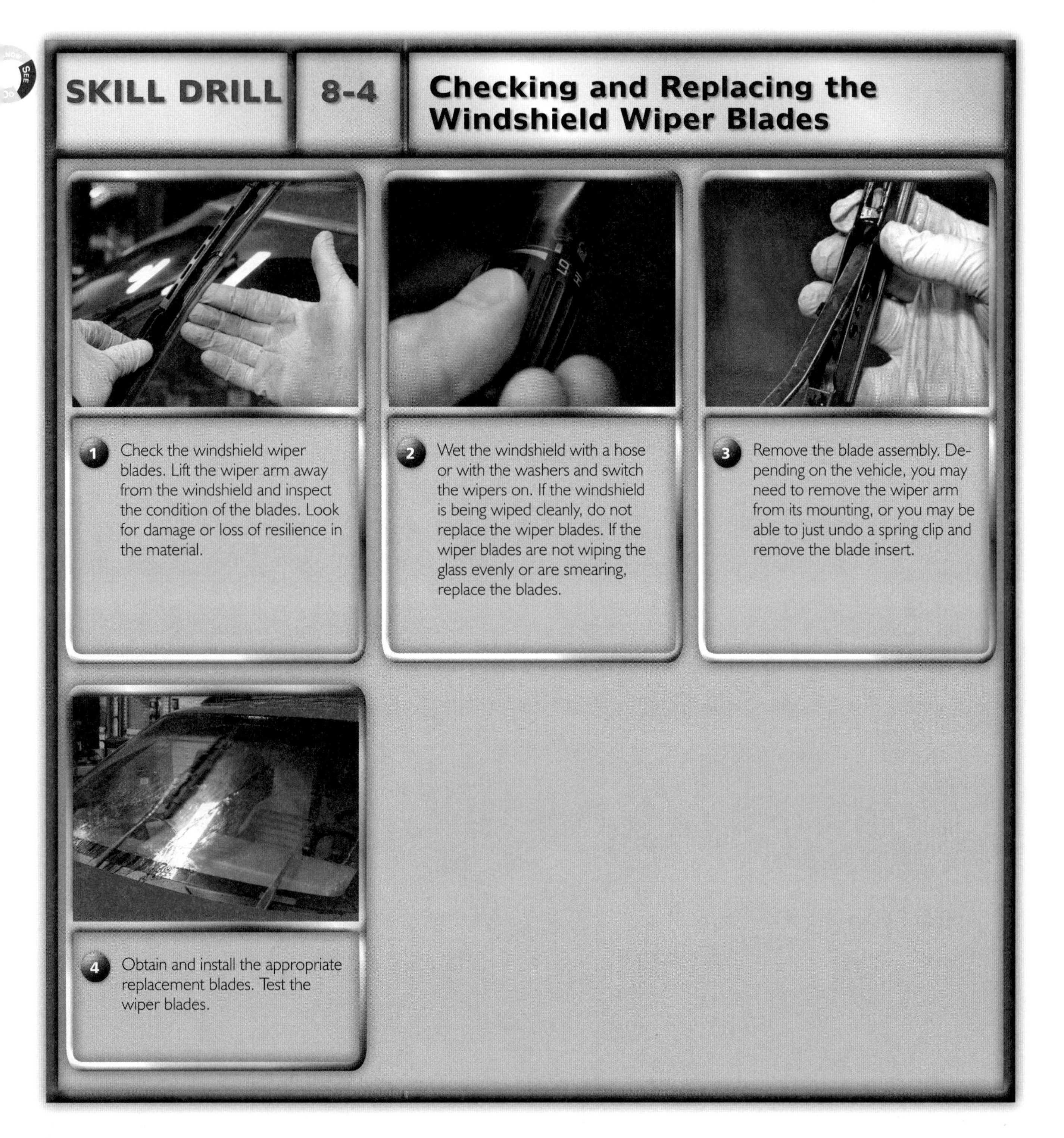
SKILL DRILL 8-4 Checking and Replacing the Windshield Wiper Blades
1 Check the windshield wiper blades. Lift the wiper arm away from the windshield and inspect the condition of the blades. Look for damage or loss of resilience in the material.
2 Wet the windshield with a hose or with the washers and switch the wipers on. If the windshield is being wiped cleanly, do not replace the wiper blades. If the wiper blades are not wiping the glass evenly or are smearing, replace the blades.
3 Remove the blade assembly. Depending on the vehicle, you may need to remove the wiper arm from its mounting, or you may be able to just undo a spring clip and remove the blade insert.
4 Obtain and install the appropriate replacement blades. Test the wiper blades.

Inspecting the Interior and Exterior Lights

The lighting system allows the driver to see the road and sides of the road when driving at night or in poor-visibility conditions and to signal to other drivers. Interior lights include the courtesy lights, dome lights, and map lights.

To inspect the interior lights, follow the steps in **SKILL DRILL 8-6**.

The exterior lighting system includes the headlights, taillights, turn signals, side markers, brake lights, license plate lights, and backing lights. Some vehicles may have cornering lights, driving lights, or fog lights. Note that the rear lights may have three or more bulbs per side; be sure to check that they all are working.

To inspect the exterior lights, follow the steps in **SKILL DRILL 8-7**.

Prove
Know
See
Do

SKILL DRILL 8-5 Inspecting the Windshield

1 Prepare the windshield. First, use glass cleaner to clean the windshield thoroughly.

2 Inspect the glass. Look closely at the surface of the glass. It may help to use a flashlight or trouble light at an angle while inspecting.

> **TECHNICIAN TIP**
>
> Look for fine paint particles, chips, scratches, or etching that does not wash off. Look at the edges and corners of the windshield for cracks or signs of delamination.

Prove
Know
See
Do

SKILL DRILL 8-6 Inspecting the Interior Lights

1 Park the vehicle inside or in a shaded area. Using the remote key fob or door key, unlock the doors. On most vehicles, unlocking the doors will cause the interior lights to come on. Check that each light works as intended. On some vehicles, the lights will not come on until the door is actually opened. Check each door on the vehicle.

2 Enter tthe vehicle and close the door. Many vehicles have a dimming feature that will cause the lights to stay on for 10 to 15 seconds after the door is closed. Wait to see that the lights go off after a time. Repeat this check with each door on the vehicle.

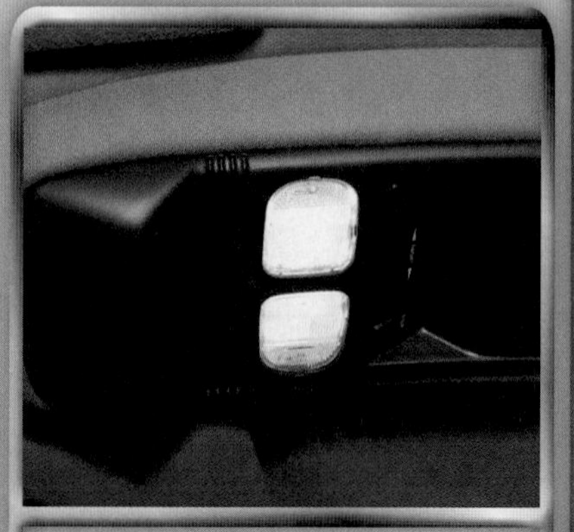

3 Operate the courtesy lights from any other switches. Check the map lights. Some vehicles have map lights in addition to the courtesy lights. Usually a manual switch is pushed to turn them on and off. Check the owner's manual if you are not sure how to operate them.

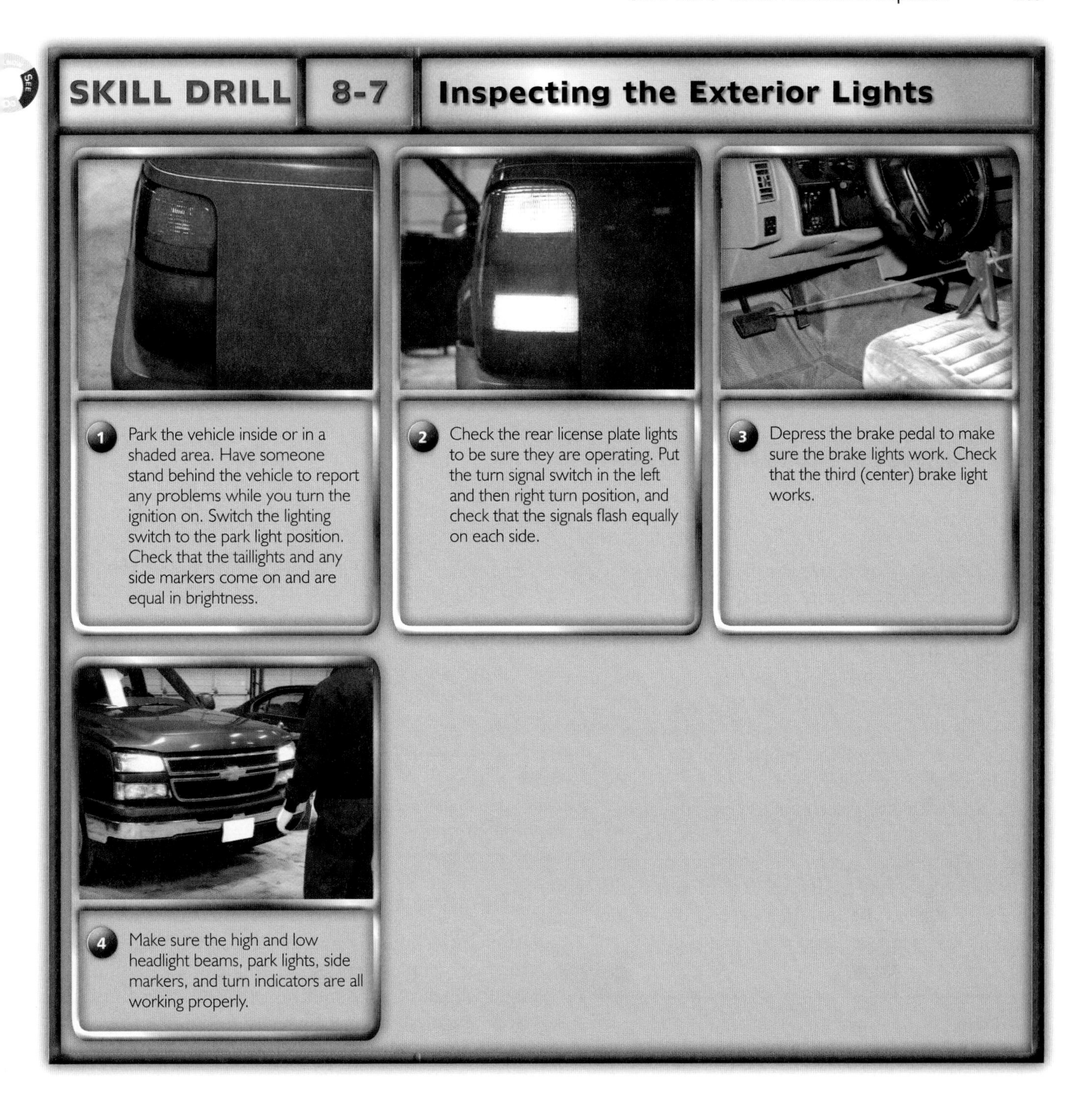

SKILL DRILL 8-7 Inspecting the Exterior Lights

1. Park the vehicle inside or in a shaded area. Have someone stand behind the vehicle to report any problems while you turn the ignition on. Switch the lighting switch to the park light position. Check that the taillights and any side markers come on and are equal in brightness.
2. Check the rear license plate lights to be sure they are operating. Put the turn signal switch in the left and then right turn position, and check that the signals flash equally on each side.
3. Depress the brake pedal to make sure the brake lights work. Check that the third (center) brake light works.
4. Make sure the high and low headlight beams, park lights, side markers, and turn indicators are all working properly.

Inspecting the Tires

Tires should be inspected as part of the vehicle inspection process. They are checked for pressure, wear patterns, cuts, and tread depth FIGURE 8-14. The tires and their condition are one of the most important safety considerations on the vehicle. A tire worn to a minimum tread depth may work fine on dry pavement but be dangerous in wet weather. Keep this in mind as you inspect the tires.

Tires are inflated using pressurized air or nitrogen to support the weight of the vehicle. Nitrogen-filled tires can be identified by a green cap on the valve stem. Nitrogen-filled tires should normally only be topped up with nitrogen. Normal tire pressures will vary from vehicle to vehicle, according to the vehicle's use and driver preference. Recommended tire pressures for the vehicle are located on the vehicle manufacturer's tire placard, typically placed on the driver's side door pillar. Tire pressures should be checked and adjusted when the tire is cold. If the tire is hot, the pressure may be higher than the pressure listed on the tire placard, and shouldn't be adjusted down to the recommended cold pressure. The maximum

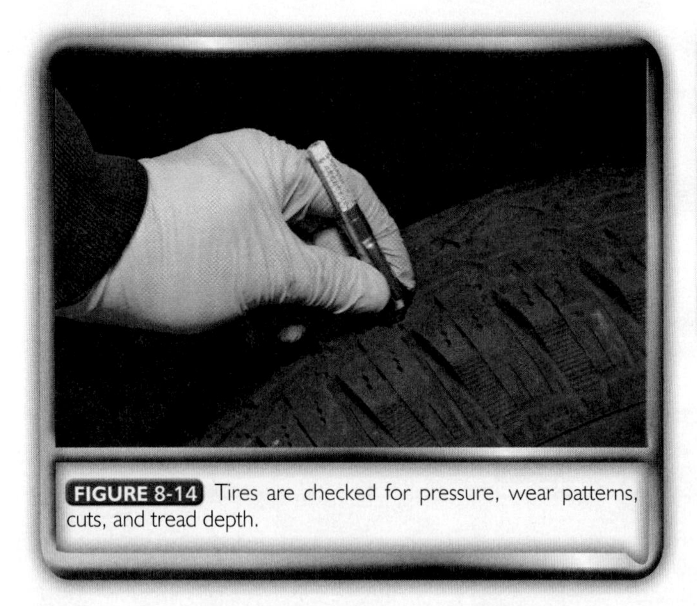

FIGURE 8-14 Tires are checked for pressure, wear patterns, cuts, and tread depth.

tire pressure, located on the tire sidewall, is the maximum pressure for that tire, not the pressure for the vehicle. Never inflate the tire above the manufacturer's recommended maximum pressure, as the tire may explode.

Many newer vehicles are equipped with a Tire Pressure Monitoring System (TPMS). Technicians need to be aware of these systems when servicing wheels and tires. For example, if one or more tires are under-inflated or over-inflated beyond the set point of the system, a warning light or message will be displayed on the dash. If the warning is displayed, you will need to verify the pressure in the tires with a very accurate tire pressure gauge, and adjust the pressure accordingly. If you are rotating the tires from one corner of the vehicle to another, you may need to reprogram the TPMS sensors in their new positions. Check the service information for correct procedure for the vehicle you are working on.

LINK

Refer to the Servicing Wheels chapter for more information on tires, checking the tire pressure, and inspecting the tire tread.

In-Vehicle Inspections

Certain in-vehicle inspections and checks should be made as the vehicle is driven into the service bay. Pay attention to the instrument cluster and warning lights. Note how the pedals feel and how the vehicle sounds when first started. Report anything unusual to the shop foreman or supervisor. These checks can be done quickly when the vehicle is first started and then completed as the vehicle is positioned in the stall.

Caring for the Customer

There may be concerns with the brake pedal feel or instrument panel warning lights that the customer is unaware of. The customer is used to the way the vehicle drives and feels; the technician can detect a fault when the customer may think the fault is a normal condition.

Checking the Brake Pedal

The brake pedal acts as a lever to increase the force applied to the brake assemblies by the driver. Changes to how far the pedal travels or to its resistance—if it feels harder or softer than normal—can be an indicator of problems such as low fluid levels or even a leak in the hydraulic system. You should always check the brake pedal feel and travel before driving a vehicle into or out of the shop. Also listen for unusual brake noises when driving the vehicle into the shop. High-pitched scraping noises or heavy grinding noises could indicate a worn brake lining. The owner of the vehicle may be used to the feel of a low pedal or the sound of noisy brakes, while you will recognize it as an indication of a problem.

LINK

See the Hydraulics and Power Brakes chapter for more information on checking the brake pedal.

Checking the Parking Brake

All vehicles must be manufactured with a foot brake (service brake) system and a parking brake system. Most light vehicles use a foot brake that operates through a hydraulic system on all wheels, and a hand-operated parking brake that acts mechanically on the rear wheels only. The parking brake is used to hold the vehicle in

TECHNICIAN TIP

If the vehicle does not have a hand- or foot-operated parking brake, check for a "P" button on the console or dash. The vehicle may be equipped with an electronically controlled parking brake.

LINK

See the Disc Brake System chapter for more information on checking the parking brake.

position when parked. The parking brake should be checked as part of a routine safety or vehicle inspection. On vehicles with automatic transmissions, the parking brake may not work at all and the owner would not know until it is needed. In climates with below-freezing temperatures, the parking brake cable can freeze in the applied position, making it so the parking brake will not release. In this situation, it is probably best not to test the parking brake operation.

Checking the Instrument Panel Warning Lamps

The many instrument panel warning lamps can indicate faults with various systems on the vehicle TABLE 8-1. They also can indicate proper operation of the system. The warning lamps perform a self-check each time the ignition is switched on or the engine cranked. You should observe the action of the lights when operating

TABLE 8-1: Warning Lights

Warning Light	Color	What It Means When Illuminated	Response
Oil pressure light/display	Red	Illuminates when the oil pressure falls below a pre-determined minimum	If the oil pressure light comes on, the engine should be shut off as soon as it is safe to do so, typically within seconds if driven lightly.
Temperature light/display	Red	Illuminates when the engine reaches an unsafe temperature.	If the temperature light comes on, the engine should be shut off as soon as it is safe to do so, typically within a minute or two if driven lightly.
Charge light/display	Red	Illuminates when the charging system is not functioning. This could be due to a charging system fault, or a broken accessory drive belt.	In either case it is best to turn off as many electrical accessories as you can safely. You should be able to drive the vehicle a several miles (unless it overheats due to a broken belt, at which point the engine will need to be shut down like above).
Malfunction Indicator Light	Yellow	Illuminates when the vehicle's PCM finds a fault in the system.	If the light is on steady, you can typically drive it safely to a repair facility. If the light is blinking, the PCM has found a catalytic converter destroying fault. The engine should be shut down within a minute or two, if driven lightly.
Brake Warning light (!)(P) BRAKE	Red	Illuminates during one of the following situations: 1. Parking brake is applied. 2. Brake fluid level is low in the reservoir. 3. A brake fluid leak in the brake system.	1. Release parking brake. 2. Check fluid level—if low, check for brake fluid leaks or worn brake pads. 3. Inspect brake system for leaks.
ABS Warning light (ABS)	Yellow	Illuminates when a fault is present in the ABS system.	When the ABS light is on, the service brakes will work, but not with anti-lock function, making it less safe to drive.
Low tire pressure light/display	Yellow	Illuminates when one or more tires are not within the safe tire pressure range.	If the light is steady, the vehicle can typically be driven to a service facility if the pressure isn't too low. If the light is flashing, one or more tires has a severe leak and the vehicle needs to be driven to the side of the road as soon as it is safe to do so.

the vehicle to determine whether any additional service may be required. For example, the amber anti-lock brake system (ABS) warning lamp will come on, then stay on for a few seconds, and then go off, indicating that the ABS control module has successfully completed a preliminary self-check.

To check instrument panel warning lamps, follow the steps in SKILL DRILL 8-8.

Checking the Horn

The vehicle horn is usually operated by a relay or by the vehicle **body control module (BCM)**. There may be a single horn or a pair of horns, depending on the vehicle. With two horns, one will sound at a lower pitch than the other. The horns are located at the front of the vehicle, behind the grill or bumper. The horn can easily be checked before driving the vehicle into the shop.

To perform a horn check, follow the steps in SKILL DRILL 8-9.

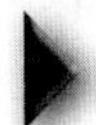

Under-Vehicle Inspection

The under-vehicle inspection is a systematic visual inspection of all major vehicle systems. Be prepared to write down any faults to discuss later with your supervisor. With the vehicle safely lifted on a hoist, an under-body inspection is a good way to get a feel for the overall condition of the vehicle. Additional areas of concern will often be found during the inspection, saving the customer an extra trip to the shop for repairs.

The under-vehicle inspection includes:

- The steering area: The steering area inspection includes the tie-rods and tie-rod ends, idler and pitman arm, steering rack, wheel bearings, and tires and wheels. Suspension bushings, shock absorbers, and brake hoses and lines are also inspected.
- The front-wheel drive axles: This inspection includes the constant velocity joints (**CV joints**) and dust boots. Look for cracked, torn, or leaking boots.
- The engine area: Check for coolant, oil, and fuel leaks. Look for torn or cracked motor mounts, coolant hoses, and belts.
- The transmission area: This inspection includes the transmission case, clutch housing, external linkages, and wiring connectors. In the transmission area, check for fluid leaks, loose mounting bolts, and faults or looseness in the clutch mechanism or shift linkage.
- The exhaust system: Clamps and bolts may need tightening on the exhaust system or on the exhaust system-to-manifold bolts or gaskets. Check for signs of exhaust leaks, corrosion, or deterioration, including the exhaust hanger hardware. Check the condition of any heat shields.

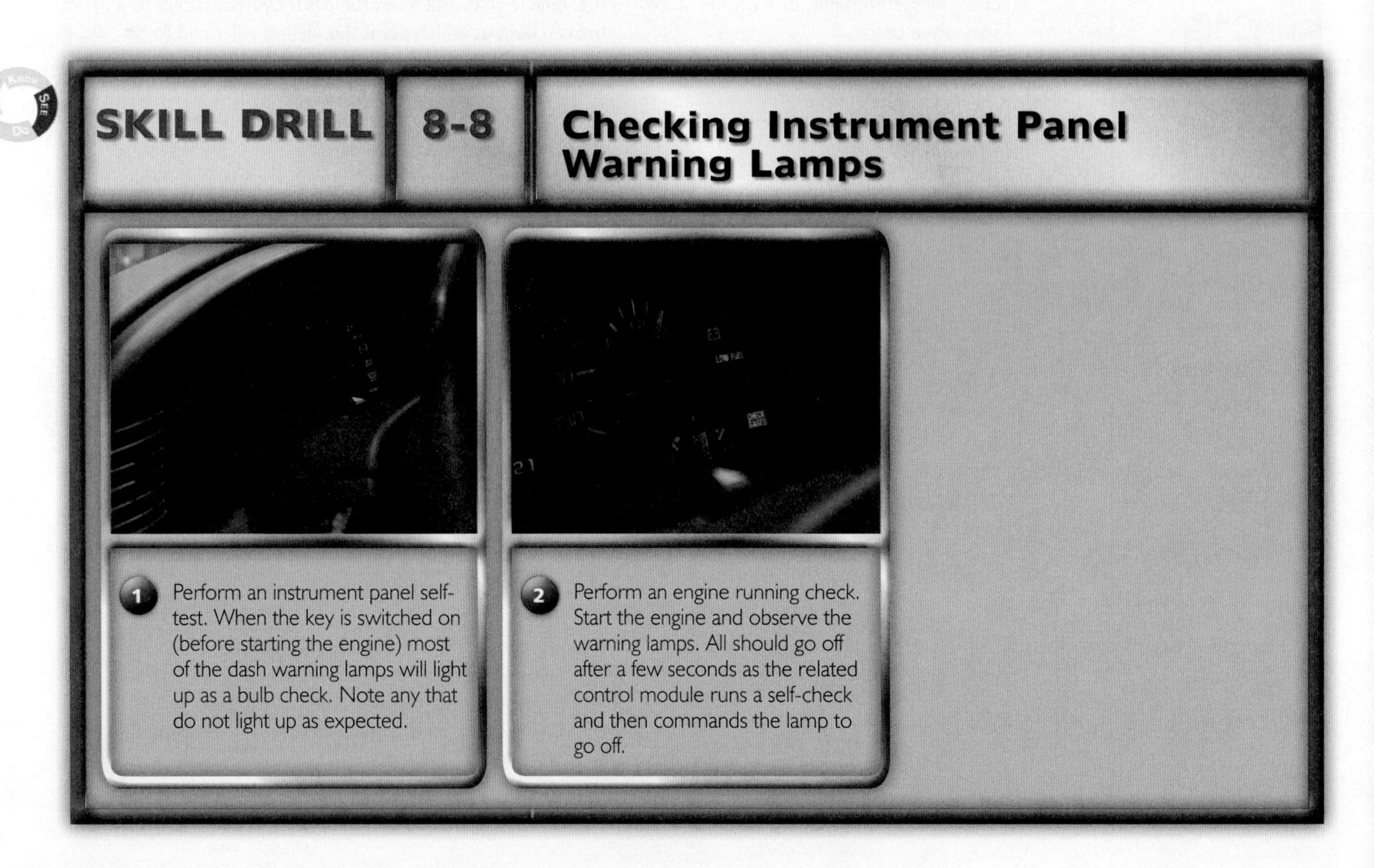
SEE
KNOW
DO
SKILL DRILL 8-8 Checking Instrument Panel Warning Lamps
LOW FUEL
CHECK GAGES
1 Perform an instrument panel self-test. When the key is switched on (before starting the engine) most of the dash warning lamps will light up as a bulb check. Note any that do not light up as expected.
2 Perform an engine running check. Start the engine and observe the warning lamps. All should go off after a few seconds as the related control module runs a self-check and then commands the lamp to go off.

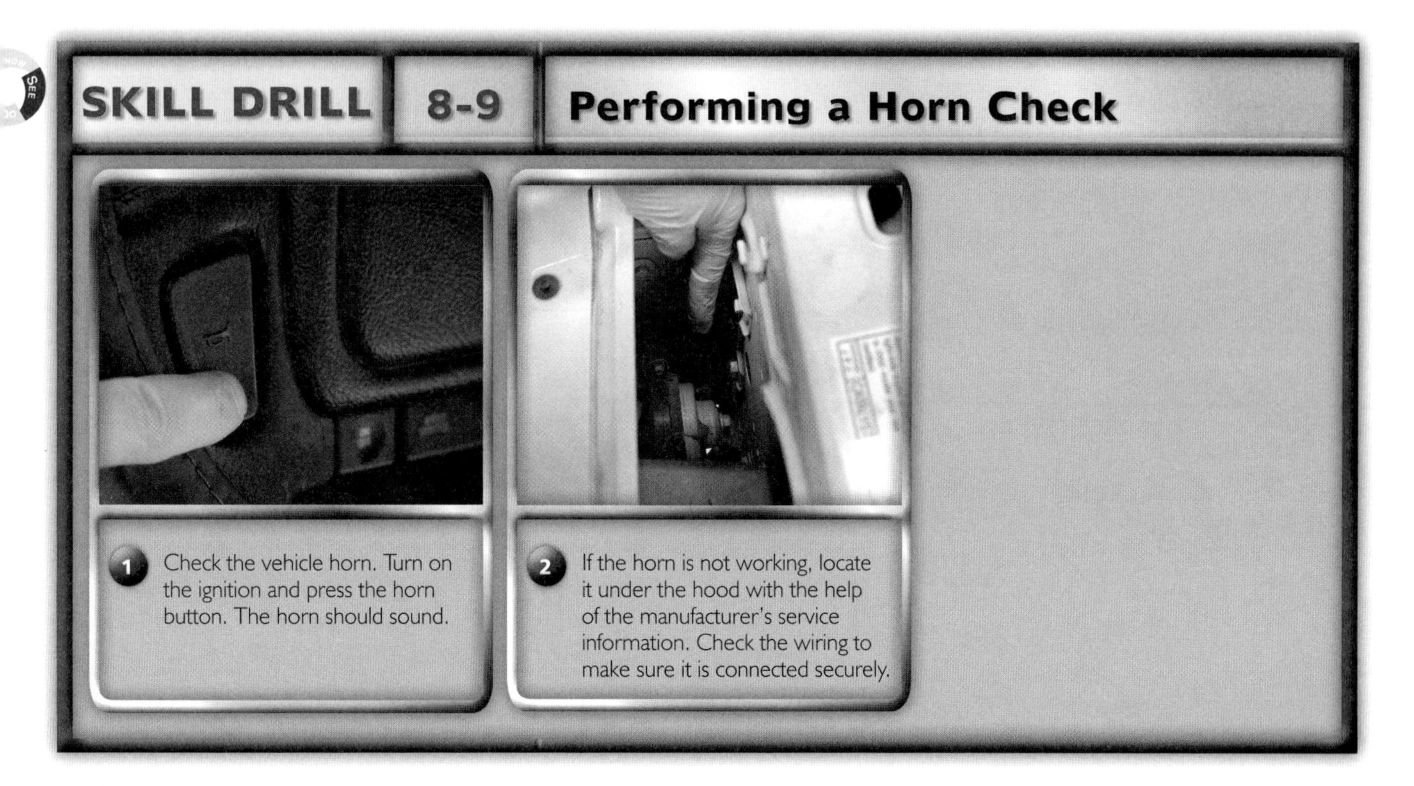
SKILL DRILL 8-9 Performing a Horn Check

1 Check the vehicle horn. Turn on the ignition and press the horn button. The horn should sound.

2 If the horn is not working, locate it under the hood with the help of the manufacturer's service information. Check the wiring to make sure it is connected securely.

- The parking brake cables: The cables are encased in a housing that attaches the parking brake lever or pedal to the rear brakes. Check for rusted, frozen, broken, or crushed cables.
- The driveshaft: The driveshaft transmits power from the transmission to the rear axle on rear-wheel drive vehicles. Check for any excess movement in driveshaft universal joints. Look for any dents or bending of the shaft.
- The differential, rear axle, and rear suspension area: The rear axle includes the differential and axle shafts. Look for leaks around the differential, and check the rear shock absorbers, leaf springs, brake hoses, and lines. Inspect the **pinion shaft** oil seal for any obvious signs of leakage.
- The fuel tank: The fuel tank is metal or plastic, depending on the vehicle. Inspection should include the filler tube and hose, the vent and fuel delivery lines, and the fuel tank straps and protective shields. The fuel tank must be secure and fuel lines inspected for damage or abrasion.

> **TECHNICIAN TIP**
>
> When checking the fuel tank, any odor of gasoline indicates a leak. Keep checking until you find it. It is not normal for today's vehicles to have any odor of gasoline.

To perform an under-vehicle components inspection, follow the steps in **SKILL DRILL 8-10**.

Checking for Fluid Leaks

The service bay should be clean and dry before driving the vehicle into the shop. This will help you to locate any fluid leaks that may be present on the vehicle. Active leaks will leave telltale drips or puddles on the clean floor, making it easier to identify what may be leaking. Fluids that may be leaking include brake fluid, transmission fluid, power steering fluid, coolant, fuel, and engine oil. Some fluids come in a variety of colors, such as red, which can be used for automatic transmission fluid or anti-freeze. Become familiar with each fluid's distinctive colors, feel, or smell:

- Brake fluid: May be clear or light amber looking for DOT 3 and DOT 4, while DOT 5 is usually purple; slightly slippery; has an unpleasant, slightly acid-type smell.
- Automatic transmission fluid and some manual transmission fluid: Normally reddish in color, although some manufacturers may use a clear or amber color; very slippery and oily; has an oily smell.
- Power steering fluid: Has similar characteristics as automatic transmission fluid.
- Coolant: Normally green, orange, or yellow in color; some manufacturers (e.g., General Motors) use a coolant that is red or light red; slippery; has a sweet smell, like syrup.

Prove
Know
See
Do

SKILL DRILL 8-10 Performing an Under-Vehicle Components Inspection

1. Safely raise the vehicle to a comfortable working height. Be ready to record any faults found, and begin the inspection at either end of the vehicle. Whichever end you choose, work systematically in one direction. Note any problems you find and discuss them with your supervisor. Pay particular attention to any fluid leaks, which will probably be the easiest problems to spot.

2. Check the steering area. Locate the tie-rods and twist, push, and pull on them. Grasp the front and rear of the tire and wheel assembly and pivot it to detect lateral movement in the tie-rod end. Grasp the tire at the top and bottom and pivot it to detect movement in the wheel bearings or ball joint. Look for missing or torn rubber boots around the tie-rod ends and steering rack. Check the security of the steering box or rack mountings. Inspect rubber suspension bushings, and check shock absorbers for signs of damage or leaks. Inspect any wiring harness that is accessible for damage. Check the brake hoses and lines for signs of cracking or abrasions.

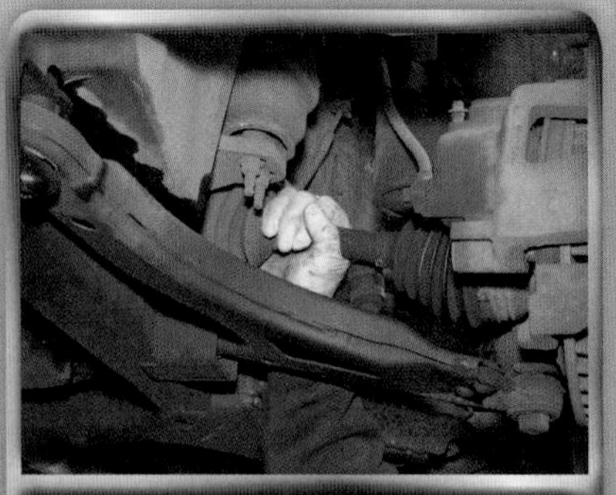

3. Check the front-wheel drive axles. On vehicles with front-wheel drive, check the drive axles for up-and-down looseness. Examine the inner and outer boots for cracks or tears. Check the fuel delivery lines and the vent lines for leaks.

4. Check the transmission area. Look for loose mounting or cover bolts. Trace and record the source of fluid leaks. With a manual transmission, check the clutch operating mechanism for damage. For an automatic transmission, check the shift linkage for any damage. If the transmission is electronically controlled, check the wiring for damage.

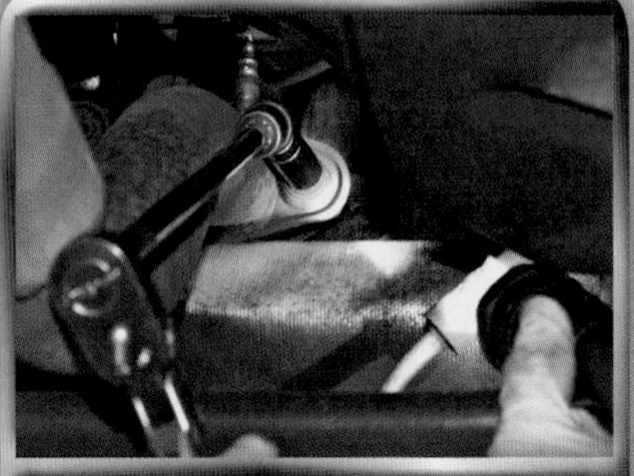

5. Check the exhaust system. Check the tightness of the flange bolts on the engine manifold pipe. Examine the catalytic converter, muffler, and resonator for signs of corrosion or deterioration. Inspect the heat shields. Check the tailpipe for corrosion, and check for looseness in the mounting brackets or hangers.

6. Check the parking brake cables. Inspect the hand brake cable to make sure it is not frayed, damaged, or binding. Look for rusted or swollen cable housings. Pull on the cables and check that the parking brake applies.

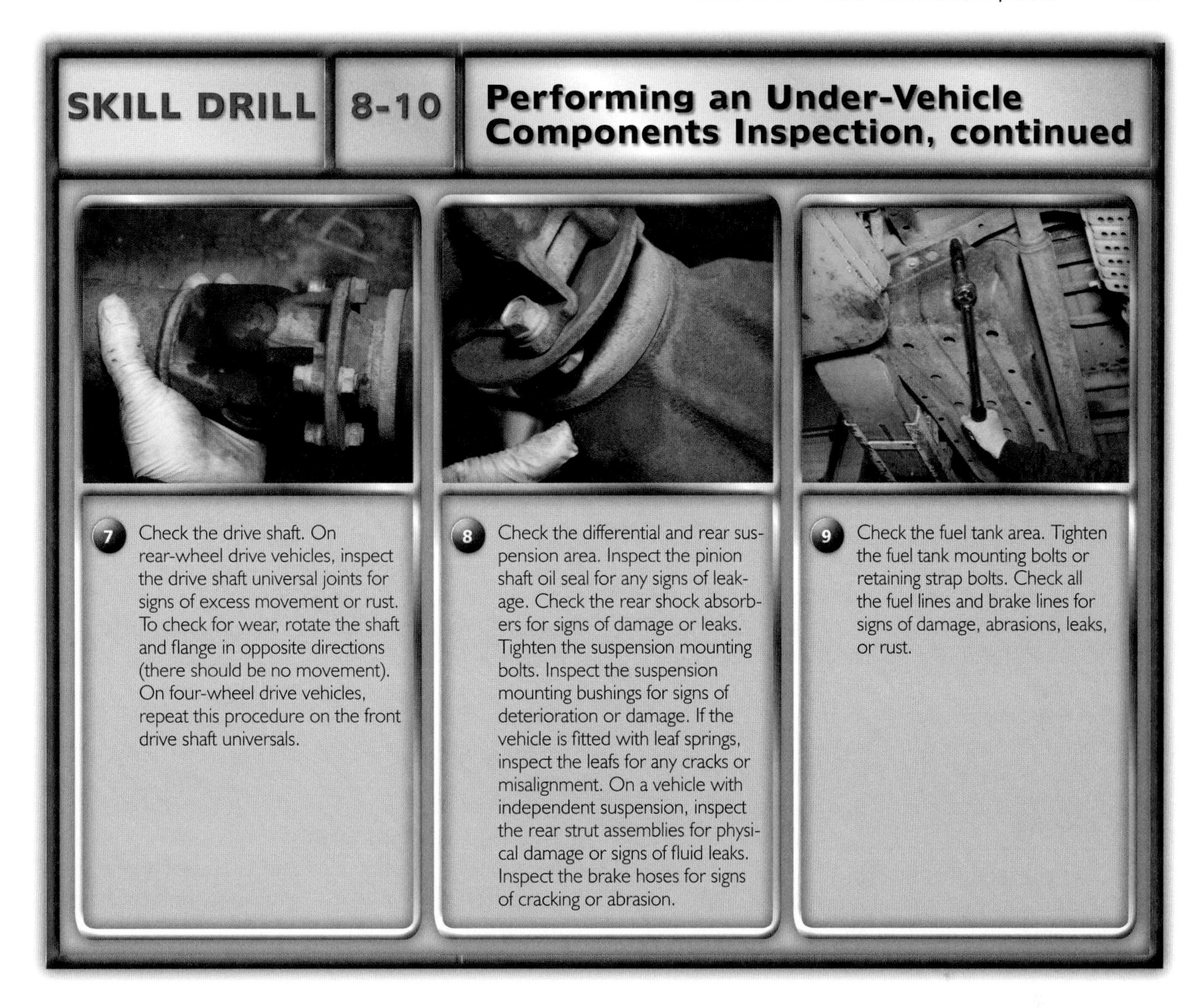

SKILL DRILL 8-10 Performing an Under-Vehicle Components Inspection, continued

7. Check the drive shaft. On rear-wheel drive vehicles, inspect the drive shaft universal joints for signs of excess movement or rust. To check for wear, rotate the shaft and flange in opposite directions (there should be no movement). On four-wheel drive vehicles, repeat this procedure on the front drive shaft universals.

8. Check the differential and rear suspension area. Inspect the pinion shaft oil seal for any signs of leakage. Check the rear shock absorbers for signs of damage or leaks. Tighten the suspension mounting bolts. Inspect the suspension mounting bushings for signs of deterioration or damage. If the vehicle is fitted with leaf springs, inspect the leafs for any cracks or misalignment. On a vehicle with independent suspension, inspect the rear strut assemblies for physical damage or signs of fluid leaks. Inspect the brake hoses for signs of cracking or abrasion.

9. Check the fuel tank area. Tighten the fuel tank mounting bolts or retaining strap bolts. Check all the fuel lines and brake lines for signs of damage, abrasions, leaks, or rust.

- Engine oil: Brown or black in color; very slippery and a bit thick; has an oily smell.
- Manual transmission fluid: Light brown in color; very slippery and thick, like syrup; has an oily smell.
- Gasoline: Clear in color; evaporates easily; has a distinctive gas odor.
- Diesel: Dirty clear in color; thin; has an oily smell.

Checking for leaks can be done as part of the under-vehicle inspection or with a light on a clean floor. The leaks will normally be more visible on a warmed-up vehicle, although some coolant leaks only appear when the engine is cold. Discuss with the customer whether there are any unusual smells in the morning when the vehicle is first started.

To check for leaks, drive the vehicle into a clean, well-lit work stall. Ideally, the stall will also have a lift so that the vehicle can be further inspected if a leak is suspected. Use a flashlight or trouble light to inspect the underside of the vehicle for any drips or wet areas. With the engine running, wait a few minutes to see if any leaks appear. Turn the engine off and wait for a time to see if anything drips on the floor. Try to identify the type of fluid that is leaking and the area from which it is leaking. Remember that gravity will tend to pull any leaking fluids down, so always look toward the top of the wet area to help determine the source of the leak. If fluid leaks onto a moving part, it can be thrown a good distance, so check for a common source. Lastly, a leak under pressure such as coolant can be sprayed a good distance from a small hole, so always use a good light to help identify the location of the leak. Finding the leak's source will tell you which component on the vehicle to inspect more closely.

Safety

If a fuel leak is discovered or suspected, the vehicle is unsafe to drive. Inform your supervisor if a fuel leak is found.

Wrap-up

Ready for Review

- A check under the hood is important to the life and operation of the vehicle.
- The correct type and amount of fluid is important for reliable and safe operation of the vehicle.
- The engine drive belts and coolant hoses are maintenance items that should be inspected and replaced according to the manufacturer's service schedule.
- The engine needs a free flow of clean air from the air filter in order to operate correctly.
- A periodic inspection of the vehicle's exterior can prevent troubles that may cause safety or operational concerns.
- Once a month or prior to any long trip, a vehicle should be visually checked for overall roadworthiness.
- The windshield wiper blades and arms are an important safety system on every vehicle.
- The windshield should be inspected during the wiper blade inspection process.
- The lighting system allows the driver to see when driving at night or in poor-visibility conditions and to signal to other drivers.
- The tires and their condition are one of the most important safety considerations on the vehicle.
- Certain in-vehicle inspections and checks should be made as the vehicle is driven into the service bay.
- The technician should always check the brake pedal feel and travel before driving a vehicle into or out of the shop.
- The parking brake should be checked as part of a routine safety or vehicle inspection.
- The many instrument panel warning lamps can indicate faults with various systems on the vehicle.
- The horn can easily be checked before driving the vehicle into the shop.
- With the vehicle safely lifted on a hoist, an underbody inspection is a good way to get a feel for the overall condition of the vehicle.

Key Terms

body control module (BCM) An onboard computer that controls many vehicle functions including the vehicle interior and exterior lighting, horn, door locks, power seats, and windows.

coolant When anti-freeze concentrate is mixed with water, the resulting mixture is called engine coolant. Most manufacturers recommend a 50/50 mixture.

CV joint CV is an abbreviation for constant velocity, a type of universal joint used on the drive axles or half-shafts of a vehicle. Usually refers to front-wheel drive vehicles.

diesel exhaust fluid (DEF) A mixture of urea and water that is injected into the exhaust system of a late-model diesel-powered vehicle to reduce exhaust nitrogen oxide emissions.

hydrometer A tool that measures the specific gravity of a liquid.

hygroscopic A property of a substance or liquid that causes it to absorb moisture (water), as a sponge absorbs water. Brake fluid will absorb water out of the air; thus it is hygroscopic.

pinion shaft On a drive axle using a ring-and-pinion gear assembly, the input component that drives the ring gear.

ASE-Type Questions

1. Tech A says that during an exterior inspection of a vehicle you should open and close doors to check that they are operating correctly. Tech B says you should never pull on bumpers or fenders. Who is correct?
   a. Tech A
   b. Tech B
   c. Both A and B
   d. Neither A nor B
2. Tech A says wiper blade condition cannot cause a vehicle to fail a safety inspection in some states. Tech B says check wiper blades for wear and tear. Who is correct?
   a. Tech A
   b. Tech B
   c. Both A and B
   d. Neither A nor B
3. Tech A says that a low oil level is bad for the engine but that it is OK for the level to be too high. Tech B says that overfilling the engine oil is bad for the engine. Who is correct?
   a. Tech A
   b. Tech B
   c. Both A and B
   d. Neither A nor B
4. Tech A says that improper handling of a windshield wiper can lead to a broken windshield. Tech B says you should place a fender cover on the windshield to prevent damage while working on windshield wipers. Who is correct?
   a. Tech A
   b. Tech B
   c. Both A and B
   d. Neither A nor B
5. While servicing an automatic transaxle–equipped vehicle, the transaxle dipstick cannot be found. Tech A says that some of these vehicles do not have a transaxle dipstick. Tech B says that the dipstick may have fallen off, since all vehicles have a transaxle dipstick. Who is correct?
   a. Tech A
   b. Tech B
   c. Both A and B
   d. Neither A nor B
6. Tech A says to test new wiper blades against a dry windshield to ensure they seat properly. Tech B says to wet the windshield and operate the wipers to check their performance. Who is correct?
   a. Tech A
   b. Tech B
   c. Both Tech A and Tech B
   d. Neither Tech A nor Tech B
7. An engine serpentine belt has broken and come off of the pulleys. Tech A says that it is OK to drive the vehicle without the belt. Tech B says that the belt only runs the charging system, so it is OK to drive a short distance without the belt. Who is correct?
   a. Tech A
   b. Tech B
   c. Both A and B
   d. Neither A nor B
8. Tech A says to clean a windshield first, and then inspect the windshield for chips, scratches, or etching. Tech B says to always clean a windshield first and then inspect the windshield for cracks or signs of delamination. Who is correct?
   a. Tech A
   b. Tech B
   c. Both A and B
   d. Neither A nor B
9. Tech A says that unlocking doors on most vehicles turns on the interior lights. Tech B says on some vehicles the interior light will not turn on until a door is actually opened. Who is correct?
   a. Tech A
   b. Tech B
   c. Both A and B
   d. Neither A nor B
10. Tech A says you should test the rear lights with the help of an assistant. Tech B says some shops have a mirror mounted in the service bay so the technician can check rear lights. Who is correct?
    a. Tech A
    b. Tech B
    c. Both A and B
    d. Neither A nor B

CHAPTER 9

KNOW
SEE
DO
PROVE

NATEF Tasks

There are no NATEF tasks for this chapter.

KNOW
SEE
DO
PROVE

Knowledge Objectives

After reading this chapter, you will be able to:

1. Describe the barriers to effective listening. (pp 216–217)
2. Describe the components of active listening. (pp 216–218)
3. Explain the elements of effective speaking, including asking constructive questions and proper phone etiquette. (pp 218–222)
4. Explain the purpose of people skills and self-presentation, including appearance, body language, and tone of voice. (p 222)
5. Describe the elements of good customer service. (pp 223–224)
6. Explain effective reading and researching techniques. (pp 224–227)
7. Describe effective writing or documentation techniques. (pp 227–231)

Communication

Know
See
Do

Skills Objectives

After reading this chapter, you will be able to:

1. Use effective strategies for listening. (pp 216–218)
2. Use effective strategies for speaking. (pp 218–222)
3. Use effective strategies for reading. (pp 224–227)
4. Use effective strategies for writing, including completing a repair order, a shop or equipment inspection sheet, an accident report, and a vehicle inspection form. (pp 227–230)
5. Properly identify faulty equipment. (pp 230–231)

Introduction

Although we've been communicating all of our lives, most of us aren't aware of the listening, reading, writing, and speaking skills needed to be a good communicator. It doesn't require any extra effort to communicate well, once you know the principles behind each communication skill. Learning and applying good communication skills will save you time and help you avoid or get through tricky situations. These skills will build over time, and you will find that you learn something new every day when you encounter new situations or meet new people. It's a lifelong learning process to perfect your communication skills.

Since communication is an essential workplace skill needed to function successfully in the automotive service facility, this entire chapter is dedicated to communication. This chapter describes the steps to becoming an effective communicator, offers tips on how to be a good listener—the first step in good communication—and explains how to speak to both customers and your coworkers. Along the way, we will discuss the requirement for writing and preparing documentation used in the workplace.

Note: The majority of NATEF's Applied Academic Skills for Communication are covered in the context of this chapter. While the applied science and math boxes found in other chapters provide examples of how to apply concepts to everyday activities in the shop, this chapter provides examples of how to apply the concepts of good communication in everyday life.

Active Listening

Applied Communication

AC-15: Listening/Reading/Speaking/Writing: The technician identifies and uses effective strategies for listening, reading, speaking, and writing when dealing with customers, coworkers, and supervisors.

AC-34: Listening: The technician adapts a listening strategy that will obtain the information required for solving the problem.

Active listening is an essential skill. We may hear what someone is saying, but are we truly understanding what the person is trying to communicate? The listening process can be difficult to perfect but is one of the most important skills to possess when gathering information from a customer or any other person. The active listener focuses all of his or her attention on the speaker, including verbal and nonverbal messages. When appropriate, the active listener encourages the speaker to further communicate details that may have otherwise been left out.

The Listening Process

To be a good listener, we need to be aware of barriers that can disrupt the listening process. These barriers can be mental and physical.

Mental barriers are thoughts and feelings that interfere with our listening, such as our own assumptions,

You Are the Automotive Technician

During your second week on the job, your supervisor has pulled you off the shop floor and into the service department office. You will be shadowing the service manager, Bob, to gain firsthand experience communicating effectively with customers in person. The first customer has an appointment with the service department for a safety recall issue. Bob asks questions to gather all the necessary information from the customer while making eye contact with him. As a new service technician, you will practice writing up your own work orders for Bob to critique after the customer has been taken care of. After the customer has answered all the questions, Bob reviews and reiterates to the customer his understanding of the concern to be sure it is accurate. Bob writes up a work order, reviews the concern and agreed upon course of action with the customer, and then guides the customer to the service department lounge to wait for his vehicle.

1. What are the three types of "right questions" to ask when gathering information?
2. What are the three Cs all work orders should contain?
3. Explain why empathy is an important skill to have when dealing with upset customers.

emotions, and prejudices. To fully absorb what someone is telling us, we need to learn to set these feelings aside. It takes effort and isn't always easy, but it is important to keep an open mind throughout the listening process. For example, when listening to a customer who is describing his or her vehicle concern, it is good practice to allow the customer to fully complete what he or she is saying, even if you believe you have all the information you need. Keeping an open mind is also an important first step in practicing empathy, discussed later.

As a listener and active participant, we can encourage the flow of communication by welcoming the speaker, letting him or her know that we care enough to want to understand the message, and acknowledging the speaker's feelings and concerns. To accomplish that, give the speaker your undivided attention by focusing on him or her. This means removing as many distractions as possible. Stop what you are doing, clear your mind of distractions, and look the speaker in the eye.

As the person is speaking, you will also need to provide listening feedback, which indicates to the speaker that you are engaged in what he or she is saying. Feedback can be nonverbal (e.g., facial expressions, body posture) and verbal. Nonverbal language, such as nodding while listening and gesturing while speaking, is used to reinforce or add emphasis. If, while speaking, you send a conflicting message, such as looking annoyed while stating that you value the customer's opinion, the person may tend to believe the nonverbal message over the verbal one, even though it is only half of the total message. For example, a customer has his car, which will not start, towed in to your shop. He tells you that the cause is a bad headlight. You may be tempted to roll your eyes at this assertion, but regardless of your personal opinion, you must, as a professional, maintain a sincere and attentive attitude toward the customer. Because nonverbal communication is perceived to be more spontaneous and less conscious, most people tend to believe the nonverbal message more than the actual words expressed. In this case, rolling your eyes would likely override any amount of "correct" words that you might say.

Caring for the Customer

In many situations, nonverbal communication can be more important than the verbal message itself.

Empathy

Empathy can help us to avoid selective hearing. To empathize with someone is to attempt to see the situation from his or her point of view. It requires good listening skills, which include an effective use of verbal and nonverbal listening feedback, in order to take in and consider the message without applying our own biases. True empathy means breaking down or putting aside existing mental barriers. For example, when a customer brings a vehicle in with a fault requiring an expensive repair that is not in his or her budget, we can come across as uncaring with a take it or leave it attitude. Expressing your understanding of the customer's situation and seeking to explore valid options to resolve the issue will go a long way in building trust with the customer. Remember, we can empathize with people even if we do not agree with them. Also, we don't have to take responsibility for their problem. But we can at least attempt to help them find the best possible solution that will work for them. You will know that you have demonstrated empathy when no valid options were found but the customer thanks you deeply for your assistance.

Empathy not only helps you understand the message better, but also helps you to be less reactive in a negative way as you realize you could feel the same way in that person's position. It may also help to motivate you to find a better resolution of the situation, knowing that it could be you in the very same situation.

Nonverbal Feedback

Applied Communication

AC-35: Nonverbal and Verbal Cues: **The technician uses verbal and nonverbal cues in discussion to help identify, verify, and solve problems.**

Nonverbal feedback can be a very useful tool when listening. Your body position, eye contact, and facial expression can all set the direction of a conversation.

We use body language to help emphasize our message, and when listening, we can use it to provide listening feedback. When listening to a speaker, try to sit or stand upright, while making eye contact. Try to avoid folding your arms, as this can be perceived as either an aggressive stance or defensive. At the same time, do not act too casual, such as standing with your hands in your pockets. It may seem harmless, but a customer or supervisor would likely see such a posture as a sign of disrespect or disinterest. Imagine that you are talking to a service manager during a job interview and the manager leans back and puts his or her feet up on the desk. That one gesture would send you a message about the manager's level of professionalism and his or her respect for you and overall interest in the conversation, and in turn would have an effect on the way you viewed the meeting.

Maintaining some eye contact during the conversation, and not looking down at something or someone else, will also let your speaker know you are paying attention. If you are taking notes, be sure to look up periodically and make eye contact with the person.

Just as our own facial expressions are being noted by the speaker, remember to pay attention to the speaker's facial expressions to get a clearer sense of his or her message. If, for example, a customer scrunches up her face while talking about the squealing noise the brakes are making, you can probably assume the customer would be happy if you could make that noise go away.

Verbal Feedback

Verbal feedback includes very simple signals that can enhance the conversation and let the person know you comprehend. Some examples are the use of validating statements and supporting statements.

A **validating statement** shows common interest in the topic being discussed. A phrase such as "I see" or "Tell me more" indicates that you are paying attention. A validating statement also helps show empathy for the person speaking and can be a simple "I understand" or "That must be frustrating for you."

A **supporting statement** can urge the speaker to elaborate on a particular topic. Statements like "Go on" and "Give me an example" let the speaker know you would like more detail because you are genuinely interested in finding a solution. This is a necessary part of communication when you are gathering information from the customer—by asking for more details, you are likely to obtain more thorough information, giving you a better starting point for solving the problem. For example, imagine you are talking with a customer about a noise his car made while going over a bump. If you were to say "Tell me more," the customer would know that you understood but wanted a little more information.

As an example, a customer brings in a car as a "no start," meaning it will not crank over. Technician A speaks with this customer and gets enough information to fill out the work order, but does not ask any clarifying questions, so doesn't gather any further details. Technician B gathers the same information as technician A, but also uses supporting statements to gather further details that will assist in diagnosis. What is the end result for the two technicians? Technician B was able to find out that the customer had recently gotten a new key cut for the vehicle. This led the technician to check to see if the key had been programed to the security system, causing the no start, which is exactly what was wrong. Technician A and technician B were both able to diagnose the fault, but technician B was able to come to a conclusion much quicker than technician A because of the extra information acquired using supporting statements.

The Art of Speaking

Applied Communication

AC-28: Speaking: The technician employs communication strategies for customers, supervisors, and coworkers that will yield high-quality information for use in problem solving.
AC-29: Information–Oral: The technician evaluates the usefulness of oral information provided by customers and coworkers when analyzing a problem.
AC-30: Information–Oral: The technician makes logical inferences and recommends solutions to problems based on discussions with customers, coworkers, and supervisors.
AC-31: Information–Oral: The technician comprehends information gathered during discussions with customers, supervisors, and coworkers regarding problem symptoms and possible solutions.
AC-32: Information–Oral/Written: The technician analyzes information based on discussions, notes, observations, personal experiences, and data searches that will assist in solving the problem.
AC-33: Information Supplying: The technician clarifies information to customers, associates, parts suppliers, and supervisors.

Speaking is often referred to as an art. That is because there are so many facets to effectively communicate and/or information gather. Whether you are asking a customer about a vehicle or your boss for a raise, knowing how to "artfully speak" will benefit you.

Speaking is a three-step process:

1. *Think* about the message.
2. Accurately *present* the message.
3. *Check* whether the message is correctly understood. If it's not, we have to respond by rethinking and re-presenting the message and rechecking with our listener. This process continues until we are satisfied that the listener correctly understands our message.

Think before you speak is easier said than done, but it's not impossible. In some situations, we have time to think and plan beforehand. Others require us to think on our feet. Thinking on your feet simply means you may be called upon to answer or handle a difficult situation quickly. Having to get things right in a fast-paced setting can result in rash decisions, but there are a few tactics you can use to make these situations easier:

1. *Relax.* It is not easy to do in an urgent situation, but attempting to remain calm is extremely beneficial,

keeping your mind clear and helping you to embody the confidence needed in such a situation.

2. *Listen*: If the situation requires you to answer a tough question, make sure you fully understand the question before answering. You can always ask the questioner to repeat or, better yet, rephrase the question. This gives you more time to think about your answer and also another chance to read into the intent of the question. Remember that if someone is asking a question of you, then he or she is showing interest. Interest is a good thing!
3. *Pause*. Silence is golden—when used properly. Most people are uncomfortable with silence, but it is perfectly acceptable to take slight pauses before speaking to organize your thoughts. This will also give you the advantage of controlling the pace of the conversation. If a situation that you have been put in charge of is slipping out of control, regain control with slight pauses and thoughtful answers. It may be beneficial to say something like, "Let me think about that for a second." Or you may take a few seconds to restate your understanding of the problem and the person's question. Doing so can help the other person understand that you are devoting effort to the question while giving you a bit of time to decide on an answer.

Before speaking, take a moment to consider that your tone of voice reveals a lot about your feelings and adds significant meaning to your message. The tone of voice includes how high or low the pitch of our voice is, how fast or slow we speak, how soft or loud, and most importantly, what our voice characteristics or emotional indications are.

Even if you disagree with what is being asserted, try to first use empathizing statements, such as "I understand" or "I can imagine how frustrating that would be" before offering a solution. For example, a regular customer had brought his vehicle in last week for a malfunction indicator lamp (MIL). The vehicle was fixed and the codes were erased. Now the same customer is back with the MIL on again and furious that he had to return. Regardless if the MIL is on for the same cause or not, you still have an upset customer to deal with. Most times, people who are angry will respond well to a statement like, "I can imagine how frustrating it is for you to have to return." When you say this, remember to keep a calm and steady tone of voice. Ultimately, the goal is to de-escalate the customer's anger. Try not to argue with the customer but rather support the customer and offer a solution that will work for both of you. In the same situation, you could say, "I can imagine how frustrating that is for you. Let's bring it in and see if it is the same problem as before or something different. If it is the same problem, our one-year warranty will cover it. Can I get you a cup of coffee in our waiting room while we look into it?" So, when encountering an upset customer, the goal is to de-escalate the anger, guide the situation back to rational communication, and come to an agreement about how the problem will be resolved. Always empathize, de-escalate, do not argue, and focus the discussion on finding a mutually agreeable solution, if possible.

After thinking about what we want to say, and how to say it, we can then use the second step of the process by presenting a message using verbal and nonverbal language. Remember that when we say verbal language, we mean the actual words that are being spoken. Nonverbal language includes how we speak those words—our tone of voice, body language, and appearance—and takes into consideration the environment. Imagine you are with a friend in a quiet café, drinking coffee, and she is telling you how much she values your opinion. Now imagine that she is clenching her fists, scowling, and screaming those same words to you. It would change the message a little, wouldn't it?

The last step of the speaking process is to make sure our message is correctly understood by the listener. Look to see that the listener is making eye contact with you. If you perceive a lack of understanding or confusion, be prepared to repeat yourself while trying to explain it in another way or by using an example. Make sure you suppress any outward irritation you may feel at needing to do so. In stressful situations, the parties involved are often not as open minded as in calmer moments and are therefore not as receptive to your words. This can also end with misunderstandings and expectations that go unmet. So take the extra step and ask clarifying questions or summarize the message.

Caring for the Customer

A calm and happy customer or coworker is normally easy to communicate with. Most people struggle with how to handle the angry one. In almost all cases, keeping a calm and steady tone of voice and overall demeanor is the best bet. Never lose your temper; doing so will only escalate the situation and lead to an unwanted outcome.

Asking Questions

Questioning is an important speaking skill that helps keep us out of a lot of trouble. We speak to deliver a message, but many times we need more information or we need to confirm the details of an agreement. Asking questions to gather more information can provide us with enough information to make good decisions. Or once we come to an agreement with another person, we can use questions to confirm those details. In either of these situations, we have avoided trouble. In the first case, we gathered enough information to avoid a bad decision. And in the second, we confirmed the expectations that each person had regarding the agreement, helping to avoid disappointment and loss of trust.

To use questions effectively, we need to know how to ask the right questions. We can ask three types of questions:

- Open questions
- Closed questions
- Yes or no questions

Each type of question is beneficial when used appropriately. Good communicators know when and how to use the appropriate type. If you have mastered each of these types of questions, you can keep a conversation going while speaking very little. These questions can be used in all types of situations, from casual conversations with new acquaintances to detailed conversations with customers. In dealing with customers, we usually start with open questions to gather general information about the issue. Then we use closed questions to find out specific details. We use yes/no questions to further check or confirm the listener's responses or to gain the customer's agreement to authorize a repair or diagnostic procedure.

Open Questions

An open question encourages people to speak freely so we can gather facts, insights, and opinions from them. It's a good way to start a conversation with a new acquaintance or even a customer. Open questions usually begin with the words:

- What
- How
- Why
- Could you tell me

For example, if you were questioning a customer about her visit to a repair facility, you could ask, "What type of service did you receive from XYZ Automotive?" This question opens the topic up for discussion and allows the customer to give details about her visit.

Closed Questions

If we want to know more information, we can use closed questions to establish facts and details. Closed questions usually begin with the words:

- When
- Where
- Which
- Who
- How many
- How much

This type of question requires a specific answer, and there is usually only one answer. For example, you could ask a customer, "How many times have you visited XYZ Automotive?" or, "When did you start going to them?" These closed questions allow for only one answer, without much room for discussion. These questions help you to narrow the topic and guide the discussion in the direction you would like it to go, which is helpful when talking with a customer.

Yes/No Questions

Yes/no questions allow individuals to answer with a simple yes or no. This type of question is useful for checking or confirming a person's responses. For example, "Would you recommend them?" gets to the point and helps clarify information. We should generally not start out with yes/no questions because they discourage further explanation or discussion. However, ending with yes/no questions is a good way to get confirmation. For example, after explaining the need for replacing the customer's water pump and answering the customer's questions about the job, it would be very appropriate to ask, "Can we go ahead and replace that leaky water pump for you?"

Telephone Skills

We've learned about the important aspects of the speaking process. A phone conversation presents some different challenges. Since we can't see each other, we can rely only upon verbal messages and some nonverbal cues, such as the tone of voice. Other nonverbal cues that we miss are body language, appearance, and the environment.

On the phone, we are limited in how we present our messages, so we need to think about our words and tone more carefully perhaps than in person. It is a good idea to plan and even write down each of the points you want to say before even picking up the phone.

Phone communication consists of three parts: greeting, exchanging messages, and finishing the call.

We should always answer a phone call by first saying hello, identifying ourselves, and identifying our place of business, succinctly and clearly. An example could be, "Hello, this is John with XYZ Automotive. How may I help you?" Try to keep your greeting friendly and short.

The second part of the phone conversation is exchanging messages. This requires concise, clear communication followed by clarifying questions and summarizing any main points. At all times, we should be polite and considerate, and remember that the most important nonverbal clue we send out over the phone is our tone of voice, since it reveals a lot about our feelings. Here are a few tips to create a good impression:

- Do not sound bored. Try to keep some inflection in your voice; do not speak in a monotone.
- Sound calm and in control, even if you were caught at a busy moment.
- No matter what, never lose your temper or patience.
- If there is a need to keep someone on hold for an extended time, offer to call him or her back, and do it.

Finish a call by confirming actions both you and the caller will take to ensure that the messages on both sides were accurately received, and end with a pleasant and friendly goodbye **FIGURE 9-1**. Remember to thank all customers for their business, and invite them to come back. When taking a phone message for someone else, make sure you have the caller's name and organization, contact details, the date and time of the call, and a summary of the caller's message.

When making a phone call, use these same skills and always have necessary information available to give to the person you are calling. For example, if you need to order parts, relevant vehicle information should be shared with your parts supplier. You usually need to have vehicle make, model, year, engine size, and transmission type, and many times you will need the vehicle identification number (VIN).

FIGURE 9-1 Always end calls with a friendly goodbye.

Giving and Receiving Instructions

Applied Communication

AC-14: Directions/Task: The technician follows all written and oral directions that relate to the applicable task or system.

A critical aspect of an efficient and well-run workshop is the ability to give clear, logical instructions and to receive instructions. Usually, instructions should contain information about who, what, when, where, and why, and direction on how a task should be completed. What is the job that needs to be done? Who should do it? When should the job be done? Apart from knowing what information we should include in our instructions, we should also know how to present them.

When receiving instructions, we should make sure we can understand and follow the instructions successfully. For example, the instruction "Use the tire machine to mount a set of four tires" indicates what to do. Asking follow-up questions such as, "White lettering or sidewalls out?" "Install new valve stems?" or "Install them back on the vehicle once mounted?" helps ensure we understood correctly. Such questions may not be needed every time an instruction is given, but by clarifying, the quality of work will be closer to the person's expectations and will save time in the long run.

Communication in a Team

Being part of a team can make working an enjoyable experience or a horrible experience, depending on the team. In large part, the ability of each team member to communicate effectively will determine the success of the team. A high-performing team can accomplish much. As the saying goes, the sum is greater than its parts. We can achieve more when we effectively work together. Being part of a team allows us to:

- Learn new things from other team members
- Share ideas, knowledge, and resources
- Complement each other's strengths and weaknesses
- Feel a sense of belonging

A poorly functioning team spends a lot of time and energy bickering and blaming, and not enough time and energy being productive. Transitioning from a poorly functioning team to a high-performing team requires commitment to the team along with self-discipline. When all team members are committed to a set of common goals, they can contribute in positive ways to the success of the team.

Developing such a team requires good leadership skills as well as good followership skills. Good leadership skills involve setting a clear vision of the goals, empowering each team member to contribute his or her best efforts, and recognizing each team member's strengths and weaknesses. Good leadership also provides training or mentoring to address any weaknesses in the team. Followership is just as important as leadership. Not much would get done if everyone were a leader. Good followership skills involve being fully engaged in the team and its goals, stepping in and performing the work that needs to be done, participating fully in all decision making, and giving honest feedback.

We need to be committed to the team and team goals to make teamwork successful. Each team member should have a defined role and responsibilities that go with that role. Each member is then able to rely on the others to do their part. Think of a team as a chain; one broken link can break the whole chain. A good team player is someone who commits to being a part of that team and contributes to its success by fulfilling his or her role.

> **TECHNICIAN TIP**
>
> To be able to fulfill the team commitment, we need to know what our roles and responsibilities are and what is expected of us. Leaders help facilitate that. Good communication is then required for the team to come together and work efficiently.

Appearance and Environment

Our appearance is the image we present of ourselves to the public. All aspects of our physical appearance, including our clothes, jewelry, hairstyle, posture, and outward demeanor, culminate to create the first impression made in any encounter. That first impression often informs the judgment others make about us, which in turn affects the level of respect and trust you achieve. It is much harder to convey your message effectively if your audience is distracted by some aspect of your appearance or does not take you seriously. When working in a professional environment, always do your best to look professional. Remember that while you are at work, you embody the image of your company. Shorts, improper footwear, or untucked or filthy clothes can all send negative signals to a customer. A customer will be much more willing to have his or her vehicle serviced by someone who looks well put together than someone who does not **FIGURE 9-2**.

FIGURE 9-2 When working in a professional environment, always do your best to look professional.

The surrounding environment is also worth consideration, as it can affect the outcome of our communication. A disorganized, cluttered, and dirty area leaves a negative impression with most customers, leading them to believe that you don't care about appearances or quality. Look around you and evaluate the housekeeping. Is it clean, organized, and inviting? Or is it neglected, dirty, and gross? A little housekeeping goes a long way toward making customers feel comfortable. You will also want to avoid distractions such as excessive background noise, a blaring radio, or inappropriate coworker conversations. Interruptions by both coworkers and phone calls can hinder communication. Whenever it is in your power to do so, work to keep these distractions at a minimum.

Be aware of dangers around you as well. While most insurance policies prohibit customers in the work area, there may be occasional times when they need to see a particular issue. If you have to take customers into the shop, always escort them, and be sure to keep them safe. Do they need safety glasses on? Escort them back out of the shop as soon as possible and continue the conversation in the customer write-up area.

Time and Space

We know that in the work environment, time is money. This is especially true in most repair shop environments, where every minute is costing somebody something—the customer, the shop owner, and/or the technician. Punctuality is an important nonverbal message in a business environment. When you are punctual, you demonstrate a good work attitude and professionalism. Punctual means showing up on time (typically 5–10 minutes early to get ready to start work at the appointed time). If you have an unexpected delay, such as finding a flat tire when you get into your car to go to work, make sure you call your supervisor and let him or her know what happened and when you will be in. The same applies if you need to call in sick; do so as soon as you can so that other arrangements can be made.

Punctuality also means you will complete the job when you say you will. If you tell a customer his vehicle will be finished at 3:00, you should plan on finishing it prior to that just in case something goes wrong. Occasionally there will be unforeseen events that keep you from completing a job on time, but those should be rare exceptions. If there is a delay, then you need to communicate that to your customers as quickly as possible so that they can make other arrangements.

Lastly, you should be giving a full measure of work for the time you are being paid. Routinely texting your friends or taking personal calls during work hours is stealing from your employer. Use your work time efficiently, just as you would want your own employees to do.

When we say that space is a part of nonverbal language, we are referring to the physical space between ourselves and the people with whom we are communicating, commonly known as "personal space" (generally 3 feet). How we use personal space depends on how we feel about others; it is also a consideration for another person's comfort level. Familiarity, gender, status, and culture will determine the use of our personal space. Be aware of space as a nonverbal message and adjust accordingly.

Customer Service

Good customer service is vital in today's competitive business environment. The quality of our customer service influences people to choose us over our competitors; good service makes people feel good about continuing to buy our products or services, which is how the business gets the money to pay your wages. So customer service has a direct impact on the ability of employers to hire employees, provide wages, and offer promotions. In fact, vehicle manufacturers place great importance on the customer satisfaction index (CSI) rating at their dealerships. The CSI rating is gathered from virtually all of the customers who have service work completed. The CSI rating is reported each month and used to evaluate individual technicians and the entire service facility. If the CSI rating is high, bonuses can be paid to everyone who contributed to that success. If the CSI rating slips, bonuses can be withheld, and new processes can be implemented to help restore the CSI rating.

To be able to provide good customer service, we must first understand who our customers are and then identify their needs. Internal customers, such as parts suppliers, are as important as external customers. By helping our coworkers with their jobs, it will ultimately help our external customers and our organization. It is helpful to remember that it is almost always external customers who bring resources into your organization when they trade their money for your service or product.

Being focused on customer service means you are fully engaged in providing the highest level of service that you can. This includes clear, friendly communication to help prevent misunderstandings and helping to establish achievable expectations **FIGURE 9-3**. It also means simple things like not getting grease on the vehicle's steering wheel, upholstery, or paint. And it means taking extra steps such as washing the vehicle when the work is completed or vacuuming it out so it is cleaner than when you started working on it. Keep in mind, one of the most important parts of customer service is repairing the vehicle correctly the first time. This goes a long way toward maintaining customer satisfaction.

Identifying Our Customers' Needs

Applied Communication

AC-25: Notes: The technician makes notes regarding symptoms, possible causes, and other data that will aid in diagnosing and solving the problem.
AC-36: Information Requests: The technician requests specific symptom information from the customer and discusses solutions with supervisors and associates.

Different customers have different needs. The same customer may have different needs at different times.

FIGURE 9-3 Focus on customer service and communicate clearly.

In most cases, we can divide our customers into three categories: those who are more concerned about getting things right; those who want to get things done; and those who just want to get along with people. Each of these customers is motivated by different factors. The person who wants the job done right will usually not be interested in lesser quality parts and will want you to take the time to make sure the job isn't rushed. If the diagnosis was rushed and was incorrect, this person will likely not be happy. People who are most interested getting things done will probably be very keen to have the repairs finished on schedule. If the vehicle is not finished on schedule, this person will likely not be happy. For the person who just wants to get along with people, it will be important that a level of trust is maintained. If trust is broken, it will be hard to regain. We have to identify what our customers' needs are, so we can serve them properly.

If you are the one in charge of questioning the customer about symptoms, be sure to get specific information from the customer about what happens, when it happens, and how often it happens. Take notes that will help to diagnose the problem. Then be sure that when relaying this information to someone else, the other person understands the symptoms with the same detail in which you do. For example, a customer is concerned about a particular noise in his vehicle. If the noise doesn't happen all the time, then we would ask when the noise happens or under what conditions the noise happens. We may need to prompt the customer with follow-up questions like, "Does it happen when it is cold or hot, or when going around a corner or over bumps, or when braking or accelerating?" We may need to ask where he thinks the noise is coming from. Of course, if the noise can be reproduced, we may need to drive or ride with the customer so that he can identify the noise for us.

Effective Reading

Every day we are faced with interpreting service information, emails, voicemails, and work orders with customer concerns. Understanding these messages without the verbal and nonverbal clues that come with face-to-face communication can be more difficult.

Reading Comprehension

Technicians are required to read a lot of information, including repair orders, service information, technical service bulletins (TSBs), and training materials. Many of these reading materials can be written at high grade levels. For example, many service manuals and TSBs are written at grade level 14 and higher. Technicians need to be proficient readers to be able to comprehend this information. Before we start reading, we need to know the purpose of the particular material and what we intend to do with the information once we understand it. In reading, the objective may be to:

- Access information quickly, such as a particular specification
- Understand the information, such as how to perform a particular series of tests on a system you are diagnosing
- Remember the information, such as learning about new technology that a manufacturer is introducing to its vehicles, how it works, and what kind of tests are used during diagnosis

Once we know our reading purpose, we can choose the suitable reading method, which can be selective, comprehending, or absorbing. *Selective* reading is reading only the parts we need to know. This method is useful when looking for a particular piece of information. The quickest way to use selective reading is to read through the table of contents, introduction, conclusion, headings, and index until we find what we are looking for. When we use *comprehending* reading, we need to interpret and understand the information. Understanding what is being communicated requires careful attention to the structure of the sentences and paragraphs. To use an *absorbing* reading method, we need to:

- Interpret and understand the information
- Absorb it into our memory
- Review the information regularly

When we talk about reading, we are not concerned only about how fast we can read but also how well we

Applied Communication

AC-1: Reading: The technician adapts a reading strategy for all written materials (e.g., customer's notes, service information, and computer/data readouts) to help identify the solution to the problem.

AC-3: Abbreviations/Acronyms: The technician identifies and uses written abbreviations and acronyms in diagnosing and solving problems.

AC-6: Charts/Tables/Graphs: The technician consults charts, tables, and graphs to determine the manufacturer's specifications to identify out-of-tolerance system components.

AC-7: Sequence: The technician consults service information to determine the appropriate sequence of procedures required for solving a specific problem.

AC-13: Skimming/Scanning: The technician reviews service information to identify problems and applies that information to appropriate repair procedures.

understand and retain what we have read. Unfortunately, the faster we try to read, the less we are likely to concentrate on the meaning, so these two objectives (speed and comprehension) work against each other. Reading is about practice, and the more we practice, the faster, more efficiently, and more accurately we can read.

All of these reading strategies can be used when researching a particular problem with a vehicle. For example, if you have a vehicle that is hard to start only when it is cold outside, you might first check the service information to see if there are any related TSBs. A TSB is released when there are many of the same vehicles having the same symptoms and causes, so you can quickly skim through hundreds of TSBs looking for specific symptoms. When one is found, read it and interpret the information. Then if the TSB addressing the fault is found, absorb the information presented, including the symptoms, cause, test procedures, and corrective actions, into your memory.

> **TECHNICIAN TIP**
>
> Charts, tables, and graphs help you to find information in a timely manner. An example would be torque specifications listed in an easy-to-use format. This information is usually presented as a chart showing the component and the required torque, usually listed in newton-meters (Nm) as well as foot-pounds (ft-lb).

> **TECHNICIAN TIP**
>
> The Society of Automotive Engineers (SAE) has a well-known list of J1930 terms, which are abbreviations used by the automotive manufacturers. In addition, each manufacturer may have additional abbreviations that differ from the SAE terms. For example, the term GEN (generator) is used by the SAE, and the term ALT (alternator) is used by several automotive manufacturers.

Researching and Using Information Sources

Technicians spend a lot of time researching information FIGURE 9-4. This could be looking for a specification needed to perform a specific step in a task, or it could be researching how a manufacturer designed the system to operate in order to determine if it is operating correctly or not. In some cases, research is needed to see what work has been performed on the vehicle in previous shop visits so you will know what has and hasn't been performed previously.

FIGURE 9-4 Research is like conducting an investigation.

Applied Communication

AC-8: Dictionary: The technician refers to a dictionary to check spelling and define unfamiliar terms.
AC-9: Text Resources: The technician uses glossaries, indexes, database menus, and tables of contents to gather the information needed for diagnosis and repair.
AC-10: Database: The technician uses databases to obtain service information.
AC-11: Operator's Manual: The technician comprehends and applies information from accompanying manuals in order to use and maintain automotive tools and equipment.
AC-12: Service (Shop) Manual: The technician uses service information in both database and print formats to identify potential malfunctions.
AC-16: Study Habits/Methods: The technician uses proven research methods when consulting the manufacturer's service information (e.g., shop manuals, service bulletins, and computer databases).
AC-17: Prior Knowledge: The technician uses prior knowledge of similar problems to determine the specific cause(s) of problems.
AC-18: Cause/Effect Relationships: The technician comprehends and uses cause-and-effect relationships presented in service information problem-solving trees.
AC-19: Definitions: The technician applies industry definitions to solve problems in automotive components and systems.

Researching is like conducting an investigation. It can be done in three steps. When we first come across a problem, we have to define what the real issue is; that requires us to know how the system or part is meant to work. Then, we look for information or clues that can help us solve the problem. Finally, we put the pieces together to determine the best solution.

If using a book for reference, start at the table of contents to help find the section you are looking for. If you come across a word you do not understand, look up the definition. Most books will have a dictionary or glossary of terms toward the rear of the text. When using an online resource or database, try to familiarize yourself with the site's/database's navigation first. Take note of all drop-down menus, shortcut options, and search features.

While using these types of resources, you can use the skimming technique discussed earlier to find information quickly. Try skimming for key words. For example, if you are looking for information on oil specifications for a particular vehicle, you could just skim through the resource's text looking for the words *oil*, *lubrication*, or *specifications*. Charts, tables, and graphs, if included in the reference material, are usually easy to scan.

Most automotive resources will include diagnostic trouble charts. These provide a great way to narrow down faults without missing any steps in the procedure. Trouble trees also use the cause-and-effect approach to diagnosis. For example, if a fuse is blown, you can use the trouble tree to help you, step by step, find the cause of what made the fuse blow, rather than simply replace the fuse. As you gather symptoms and perform the diagnostic tests, you should take notes on your results to aid you in diagnosing and solving the problem as well as to complete the repair order when finished.

Always save the manuals for shop equipment and tools, and organize them in one place for future reference. Refer to these documents to maintain the equipment and tools. For example, most air tools require a drop or two of hydraulic oil every day, along with the use of a water separator in the air line.

When encountering problems with a new or unique system, it is often helpful to look up a definition or description of that system. This information can typically be found in either the front or the back of a book, or you may be able to search for it on computer-based information systems.

As you gain experience in the automotive industry, you will find that many vehicles have similar faults. Don't hesitate to use your prior knowledge to assist you in a new diagnostic situation. Just don't assume that all similar problems are caused by the same fault. You will want to test and verify your assumptions before suggesting a course of action to the customer.

Defining the Problem

Before you spend much time researching information, it is important that you define the problem. As you are defining the problem, make sure you narrow it down as accurately as possible. For example, if the car won't start, does it not crank over at all, or does it crank over but not start? Narrowing the problem down in this way will help you to filter out irrelevant information. If the problem is very broad, it is better to break it into smaller chunks and conduct a separate research activity on each one. Once the research is complete, you will have a better idea of how to proceed with determining the cause of the problem.

The next step is to look for the information that may help solve the problem. There is plenty of information readily available, but to determine how useful and reliable the information is, we need to know the sources of that information. We can obtain information from two sources: primary and secondary. The primary sources of information are people who have direct experience with the same or a similar problem. We can obtain information by interviewing those primary sources directly. However, information from primary sources can be subjective. Therefore, it is not always reliable. Information from secondary sources, or secondhand information, is compiled from a variety of sources. It is usually more reliable since it is more generic and objective.

This secondhand information is available in various formats, including print, audiovisual, and computerized **FIGURE 9-5**. We can divide this information into different content categories, including:

- Vehicle service information
- Automotive educational sources
- Troubleshooting

Vehicle Information

The first place to look for information about a vehicle is in the shop. Computer databases, shop manuals, aftermarket

FIGURE 9-5 Compile primary and secondary information to define the problem.

manuals, and owner manuals are good resources for basic service information, including vehicle systems and how to operate them, the locations of major components and lifting points, and vehicle care and maintenance information.

Manufacturers usually provide training videos covering specific information about a vehicle of a particular make and model. Similarly, aftermarket and components suppliers will provide specific information about their products. This information is also available from their DVDs and websites.

The manufacturer's service information will guide the technician in the correct sequence of procedures to correct a given problem. The basic idea is to check the simple things first. In most cases, this will involve a visual inspection for obvious issues such as a vacuum line or electrical connector that is loose or disconnected. If no problem is found, then the technician will go to the next step in the service procedure, which will likely involve test equipment. The service information will continue to guide the technician in other steps as necessary.

Educational Sources

Publishers provide extensive materials covering the basic theory of operation of automotive systems and components. These materials come in a variety of forms. Textbooks and workbooks come as paper-based materials. Then there are computer-based materials, which provide more options for interactivity and visual engagement of the student. While there is free information available, most of these sources require a subscription to enroll in their courses.

Technical Assistance Services

For troubleshooting, there is help available on the phone and on the Internet. To use either resource, you must subscribe as a member, which normally involves paying a fee. Technical assistance hotlines put you in contact with professionals who can assist you in diagnosing a particularly difficult problem over the phone. The technical assistant has access to a variety of technical service information. Some of this information is gathered while helping other technicians with their issues. Thus, a large database of information can be accumulated, which can save a technician a lot of time.

For free information, there are chat rooms and bulletin boards where questions can be posted to other technicians online, although there is no guarantee of the accuracy and availability of the resources. The websites of automotive hobbyists, enthusiasts, and car clubs are often good resources as well.

One very good online reference that is available only to professional automotive technicians is the International Automotive Technicians Network (www.iatn.net). This organization consists of over 75,000 active members, with more than 1.7 million years of combined experience, who share their knowledge with each other on over a dozen forums. They recently have begun granting free student accounts to students of member instructors. These free student accounts allow students to monitor the forums and learn from them, while not allowing the students to interact with the technicians.

TECHNICIAN TIP

If you are ever working on a vehicle and seem to have hit a dead end in diagnosis, don't be afraid to discuss the symptoms with other technicians or supervisors around you. Sometimes others have seen the same issue or have a bit more experience and will be able to help. Or maybe they will look at the problem from a slightly different perspective, which can give you something new to try.

Effective Writing

Technicians need to document their findings, conclusions, and any repairs on the repair order. This requires an accurate, short, but complete summary of the work you completed. In fact, the shop and ultimately the technicians get paid based on the quality of the write-up of the repair order. If there is ever a problem in the future, such as a customer filing a lawsuit against the shop over the repair, the repair order becomes a legal document that will be used by the court to determine if the shop has any liability in the situation. Thus, if the repair order is poorly written, incomplete, or inaccurate, the shop will be much more likely to lose the court case, putting it at risk of having to pay thousands of dollars—or more in the case of an injury accident. So writing is one of the most important tasks a technician does on a daily basis.

Writing Business Correspondence

Writing for technicians generally involves completing a write-up of diagnosis and repair conclusions on repair orders and filling out parts requests. However, they may sometimes need to undertake a more formal business correspondence using complete paragraphs. As with any type of writing, first think about what you want to say and draft your message, then refine and finalize your message. Just as it is important to think before we speak, we also

Applied Communication

AC-2: Information–Written: The technician can comprehend and apply the available written information needed to diagnose, analyze, and solve a problem.
AC-4: Information–Written: The technician evaluates the usefulness of available written information clearly and thoroughly when analyzing a problem.
AC-5: Information–Written: The technician makes logical inferences and recommendations based on information provided on the repair order.
AC-20: Summaries: The technician uses appropriate grammar and sentence structures when summarizing problems in reports.
AC-21: Sentences: The technician uses conventional sentence structure, spelling, capitalization, and punctuation when composing sentences for warranty reports.
AC-22: Writing: The technician adapts a writing strategy that is most appropriate for the intended audience (e.g., customers, supervisor, and fellow employees) when documenting repairs.
AC-24: Purpose: The technician adapts speaking and/or writing styles that are consistent with the purpose of the communication.
AC-26: Paragraphs: The technician composes complete paragraphs, with appropriate details, presenting accurate information regarding symptoms, diagnosis, and results when preparing warranty claims and work orders.
AC-27: Diction/Structure: The technician adapts diction and structure to the context of all verbal and written communication based on the audience, purpose, and specific situation.

need to think about what we want to say, and what we want to achieve, before we compose our written message. Using your notes, sketch out a short outline of major topics; this is a great place to start when writing. Then use the outline to assist you in the writing. Use complete sentences. Remember to carefully proofread your writing so that you catch and fix any spelling or grammatical errors. You should use spell-check, but don't rely on it to catch everything; spell-checkers can't tell you when you have used "two" and "to" incorrectly, or "there" and "their," or when you meant to use "they" and only typed "the"—to mention a few examples. Once you have completed the draft, it may be necessary to create a final version of the write-up.

When writing a business letter, after creating an outline of the main points, you must then organize and put them together. Here are a few tips:

- Structure your letter logically so readers can follow your flow of thoughts; check the content by reading it out loud.
- Use plain English when addressing a customer, avoiding complicated words or technical jargon. On the other hand, when addressing a manufacturer or warranty clerk, be very specific.
- Check your spelling and punctuation. This is easily done using spell-check or by looking up the term(s). Be aware that spell-check can misinterpret your words, so you need to double-check spelling corrections.
- Be courteous and empathize with the readers, especially when writing a complaint letter or delivering bad news.
- Be precise, direct, and to the point. Repetition or unnecessary words waste time and can confuse readers.

There is a simple but necessary format to follow when creating a business letter. The letter should have your company name and address at the top. Most business letterheads have these details preprinted. Next include the date, followed by the recipient's name and address. Usually, you should start a letter with a greeting like "Dear Sir or Madam," or when we know the receiver's name, "Dear Mr. Mortenson." "Re:" or "Reference" is followed by the subject or purpose of the letter. The next part is the content that you composed in your outline. A business letter usually concludes with a complimentary closing, such as "Sincerely." Finally, a letter needs to be signed and followed by the sender's typewritten name and position.

Completing a Repair Order

If you are writing up your findings, conclusions, and repairs performed on a repair order, one thing to remember is that the information needs to be concise, yet complete. This is a difficult skill to develop, but will improve with practice.

A work order should contain:

- The customer's concern: Describe the concern and how you verified the concern and any related issues found.
- The cause of the concern: Describe what specifically is the root cause of the concern.
- The action taken, or needed to be taken, to correct the concern: Describe specifically how the concern was, or could be, resolved.

These elements constitute what is called the three "Cs": Concern, Cause, and Correction. Remember that each of these sections needs to be written up as concisely yet completely as possible. For example:

Concern: The vehicle overheats within about 10 minutes of vehicle operation from a cold start, no matter whether it is hot or cold outside. Coolant is full and protected to −30°F. Started vehicle, monitored engine temperature with temp gun. Temperature exceeded specified 195°F thermostat opening temperature, and still not open at 205°F.

Cause: Thermostat faulty, not opening at specified temperature. Removed, no external damage noted.

Correction: Replaced thermostat with new OE thermostat. Retested, thermostat starts to open at 193°F, which is within specifications.

While in school, you will document tasks performed in the shop on forms referred to as job sheets or tasksheets. You can use these forms to develop your ability to accurately complete the 3 Cs. Doing so will prepare you for the repair orders you will complete when working out in the industry.

A repair order should also contain the customer's contact information, vehicle information (e.g., make/model/VIN), parts, prices, labor time, taxes, and any recommended service that is found while repairing the vehicle.

Completing a Shop Safety Inspection Form

Most shops should have a safety inspection form that needs to be completed on a regular basis, typically weekly or monthly, although some tasks may need to be performed daily. This form will guide you to visually inspect critical items in the shop such as automotive lifts, overhead doors, hydraulic equipment, pneumatic equipment, hoses and cords, fire extinguishers, and emergency exits. The importance of these inspections should not be taken lightly, as neglect of these items can cause safety issues and cause premature product failure. These pieces of equipment are used often and will require frequent inspection.

Safety inspection forms are also a way of keeping up on routine maintenance tasks, such as changing the oil or replacing the belt of an air compressor, refilling the tire machine automatic oiler, and draining any water traps in the compressed air system. If you are the person completing the inspection, make sure you are trained to evaluate the safety and condition of the items you are inspecting. Inspect the items carefully and thoroughly so you don't miss any issues.

Completing a Defective Equipment Report

One way to help ensure safety in the workshop is to inspect equipment regularly and arrange for repair or replacement whenever it does not meet safety standards. Keeping equipment well maintained will help avoid equipment downtime to provide a safer work environment.

Whenever you come across any defective equipment, you should do the following:

- Tag the defective items and either place them in a secured area or secure them so no one else can use them by mistake.
- Complete a defective equipment report.
- Notify your supervisor.

Your immediate actions can help protect coworkers from accidents and injuries. If there is an accident resulting from defective equipment, you will need to complete both an accident report and a defective equipment report.

On the report, you will record the date when the defect was detected, the location of the defective equipment, the name of the equipment, the serial number (if possible), and a description of the defect and the action you have taken. Then sign your name as the reporter. Finally, notify your supervisor.

Completing an Accident Report

Safety is the most important issue in the workplace. We must make a conscious decision to work safely and act responsibly to protect others and ourselves. Unfortunately, accidents do happen. When one occurs, an accident report should be completed by those involved, both the victim and witnesses, if possible. The information in the report is used to protect both employees and employers. It protects the employer and employee against false claims. And it protects future employees by calling attention to a situation that caused an accident, so hopefully measures can be taken to prevent it in the future. To ensure that the information is accurate, the accident report should be completed as soon as practically possible while the facts of the accident are still fresh in everyone's memory.

A typical accident report includes the date and time when the accident happened, the location where the accident happened, the name of the person who was injured, the name of any witnesses, the details of the accident, any first aid treatment provided, and any medical assistance rendered. It is also important to note if the accident will be subject to, or covered by, any insurance claims. Finally, the form needs to be signed by the person reporting the accident and turned in to the supervisor.

Completing a Vehicle Inspection Form

We provide customers with a very beneficial service when we perform a thorough inspection of their vehicles. When performing an inspection, we need to check that all major components and systems are operational, secured, and safe in accordance with the vehicle manufacturer's recommendations. This means testing the operation of the electrical and mechanical systems, such as lights and brakes, and visual inspections of the components such as tires and glass.

An inspection form is a useful guide when conducting a vehicle inspection. By following the checklist, a technician can test all the components in a systematic way and ensure that they are operational or serviceable. It also becomes a record for the shop to bring a customer's attention to needed service, or in the event that a customer declines repairs, shows that the shop made the customer aware of them. Many shops use their own inspection form that lists every item tested, which are known as points. Depending on the number of points covered, the inspection may be called a 30-point inspection, a 72-point inspection, and so forth.

To complete the inspection form, you must inspect all the components and systems on the checklist, including:

- Fluids, belts, and hoses
- Steering and suspension system
- Brakes
- Drive line
- Fuel system
- Exhaust system
- Tires
- Lighting system
- Electrical system
- Visibility
- Seat belts
- General components

Once the inspection is completed, the results should be presented to the customer so he or she can decide if any repairs are to be made. This is where verbal communication comes back into play, as it is important to accurately communicate with the customer so he or she has a good understanding of what the vehicle needs, why it is important to have it repaired, and the consequences of not repairing it. All of this conversation should be based on trust and the relationship you have built with the customer during his or her experience with you and the shop. And as you can see, successful communication includes good verbal, nonverbal, listening, clarifying, writing, and presentation skills.

Lockout/Tagout

There are many dangers in the automotive repair facility that may need to be properly documented and tagged. One example could be a defective automotive lift. If a problem is noticed with a piece of equipment, the lockout/tagout procedure should be followed. Lockout/tagout procedures have been developed to prevent avoidable and unnecessary workshop accidents. These procedures have many functions:

- The tag notifies other users that the tool or component is dangerous to use. Any equipment that is found to be faulty needs to be identified so that other users are not put at risk. Write the fault, the date, and your name on the tag. Attach the tag to the tool. Smaller equipment should also be tagged and placed in a location where it is not forgotten. Notify your supervisor so that repairs or a replacement can be arranged.
- If a machine is faulty, the lockout procedure is used. Most large workshop equipment is permanently wired to the electrical supply and usually will have an isolation switch that will disconnect the electrical power. A lockout tag should be placed on the isolation switch as well as the equipment. Turn the machine off at the power and master switches, attaching the lockout tag in a manner that prevents the switches from being turned on. Once again, notify your supervisor so repairs can be arranged.
- The lockout/tagout procedure is also used to notify other technicians that a vehicle is not drivable.

Your workshop will have a procedure for vehicle lockout/tagout. It may involve the technician filling out a "defective vehicle" label listing the nature of the defect, name of the technician, and date and time of the defect.

If you remove the vehicle keys, do not keep them in your pocket or on your workbench. Attach a label or tag to the keys that identify the vehicle they belong to and store them in a secure key organizer.

If a vehicle is going through a relearn process (i.e., the vehicle's computer communicating with another computer), it may be necessary to leave the ignition on for many hours. In this case, tag the vehicle with instructions to leave the ignition on; otherwise a passing technician may turn it off in an effort to be helpful. If a vital component has been removed for service, it may not be obvious to a casual observer, so it is necessary to tag the vehicle. The best place to tag the vehicle is in on the steering wheel or driver's window where others trying to operate the vehicle will see it. Also, remove the ignition key and store it in a safe place.

Ask your supervisor to demonstrate the lockout/tagout process used in your workshop and to show you the location of the key organizer.

To properly identify faulty equipment, follow the steps in **SKILL DRILL 9-1**.

In conclusion, communication is a critical component of a successful business and an efficient workplace. Often overlooked in our current digital world, where face-to-face contact is getting less and less common, it is increasingly important to familiarize yourself with a wide variety of communication skills. From listening to simply filling out an inspection report, using and practicing these skills can be a big determining factor in how far you can go and how much money you make in the automotive industry. And the good news is that it doesn't even require expensive tools!

SKILL DRILL 9-1 Identifying Faulty Equipment

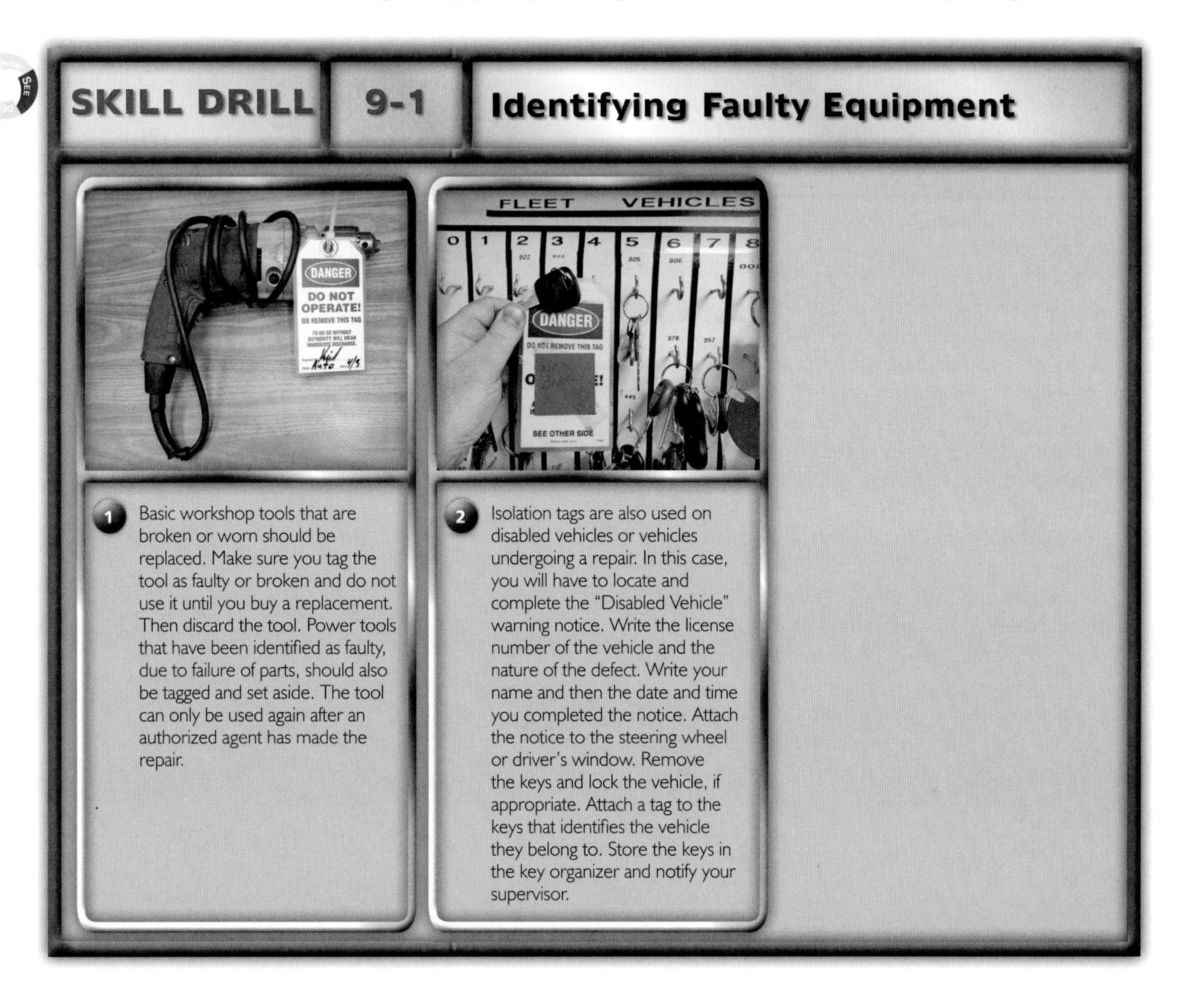
DANGER
DO NOT
OPERATE!
OR REMOVE THIS TAG
FLEET VEHICLES
0 1 2 3 4 5 6 7 8
DANGER
DO NOT REMOVE THIS TAG
SEE OTHER SIDE

1. Basic workshop tools that are broken or worn should be replaced. Make sure you tag the tool as faulty or broken and do not use it until you buy a replacement. Then discard the tool. Power tools that have been identified as faulty, due to failure of parts, should also be tagged and set aside. The tool can only be used again after an authorized agent has made the repair.

2. Isolation tags are also used on disabled vehicles or vehicles undergoing a repair. In this case, you will have to locate and complete the "Disabled Vehicle" warning notice. Write the license number of the vehicle and the nature of the defect. Write your name and then the date and time you completed the notice. Attach the notice to the steering wheel or driver's window. Remove the keys and lock the vehicle, if appropriate. Attach a tag to the keys that identifies the vehicle they belong to. Store the keys in the key organizer and notify your supervisor.

Wrap-up

Ready for Review

- Communication includes listening, reading, writing, and speaking skills—soft skills that every good automotive technician needs to master over time.
- To empathize with someone is to attempt to see the situation from his or her point of view.
- Nonverbal feedback helps to emphasize our message. When listening, we can use it to provide listening feedback.
- Verbal feedback includes very simple signals that can enhance the conversation and let the person know you comprehend.
- A supporting statement can urge the speaker to elaborate on a particular topic.
- Speaking is often referred to as an art because there are so many facets involved in effectively communicating and/or information gathering.
- Speaking is a three-step process: think about the message, present it, and check that it was understood.
- When encountering an upset customer, empathize, de-escalate, do not argue, and stay calm.
- There are three types of questions: open, closed, and yes/no.
- A critical aspect of an efficient and well-run workshop is the ability to give clear, logical instruction and to receive instruction.
- Your appearance makes the first impression and informs others' judgment of who you are.
- In the work environment, time is money. Always strive to be on time, ready to do your part by being present, both physically and mentally.
- Good customer service is vital in today's competitive business environment.
- Every day we are faced with interpreting service information, emails, voicemails, and work orders with customer concerns.
- Researching is an important part of troubleshooting a vehicle. First define the problem, then gather clues, and then put all the pieces together to get the conclusion.
- When a technician is writing a repair order, the three Cs need to be included: concern, cause, and correction. The customer and vehicle information should also be included.

Key Terms

supporting statement A statement that urges the speaker to elaborate on a particular topic.

validating statement A statement that shows common interest in the topic being discussed.

ASE-Type Questions

1. Tech A says that repair orders are legal documents so they need to be filled out accurately and carefully. Tech B says that ensuring the repair order is well written, clear, and concise promotes a professional reputation. Who is correct?
   a. Tech A
   b. Tech B
   c. Both A and B
   d. Neither A nor B
2. Tech A says that you shouldn't waste time inspecting a vehicle in for a repair unless the customer requests it. Tech B says that performing an inspection in addition to a repair can lead to discovery of additional concerns. Who is correct?
   a. Tech A
   b. Tech B
   c. Both A and B
   d. Neither A nor B
3. Tech A says that the proper way to listen to a customer is to maintain eye contact with the customer in between taking notes. Tech B says that eye contact distracts you from taking good notes. Who is correct?
   a. Tech A
   b. Tech B
   c. Both A and B
   d. Neither A nor B
4. Tech A says it is best to quietly listen to the customer and refrain from asking questions as much as possible. Tech B says it is constructive to ask questions throughout the conversation to obtain more details. Who is correct?
   a. Tech A
   b. Tech B
   c. Both A and B
   d. Neither A nor B
5. Tech A says that maintaining an appearance of neatness is important as it conveys to the customer the idea of careful, professional technicians. Tech B says that a dirty and cluttered shop indicates that the shop gets a lot of quality work done. Who is correct?
   a. Tech A
   b. Tech B
   c. Both A and B
   d. Neither A nor B
6. Tech A says researching the service information is a waste of time. Tech B says that researching the service information saves time. Who is correct?
   a. Tech A
   b. Tech B
   c. Both A and B
   d. Neither A nor B
7. Tech A says that an example of an open question is: "What are the conditions like when your A/C is not working?" Tech B says that an example of an open question is: "Does your A/C work at all?" Who is correct?
   a. Tech A
   b. Tech B
   c. Both A and B
   d. Neither A nor B
8. Tech A says that one customer who has a bad experience stemming from miscommunication and a misdiagnosed repair due to a technician's failure to listen has more of an effect on the repair shop than several good and happy customers. Tech B says that it is only one customer, and since the happy ones paid their bills, all is well. Who is correct?
   a. Tech A
   b. Tech B
   c. Both A and B
   d. Neither A nor B
9. Tech A says that it is primarily the job of the service writer to be customer-oriented and learn listening skills. Tech B says that customer service is the responsibility of all service employees to achieve the goal of customer satisfaction. Who is correct?
   a. Tech A
   b. Tech B
   c. Both A and B
   d. Neither A nor B
10. Tech A says that the 3 Cs are the "customer, complaint, and concern." Tech B says that the 3 Cs are "concern, cause, and correction." Who is correct?
    a. Tech A
    b. Tech B
    c. Both A and B
    d. Neither A nor B

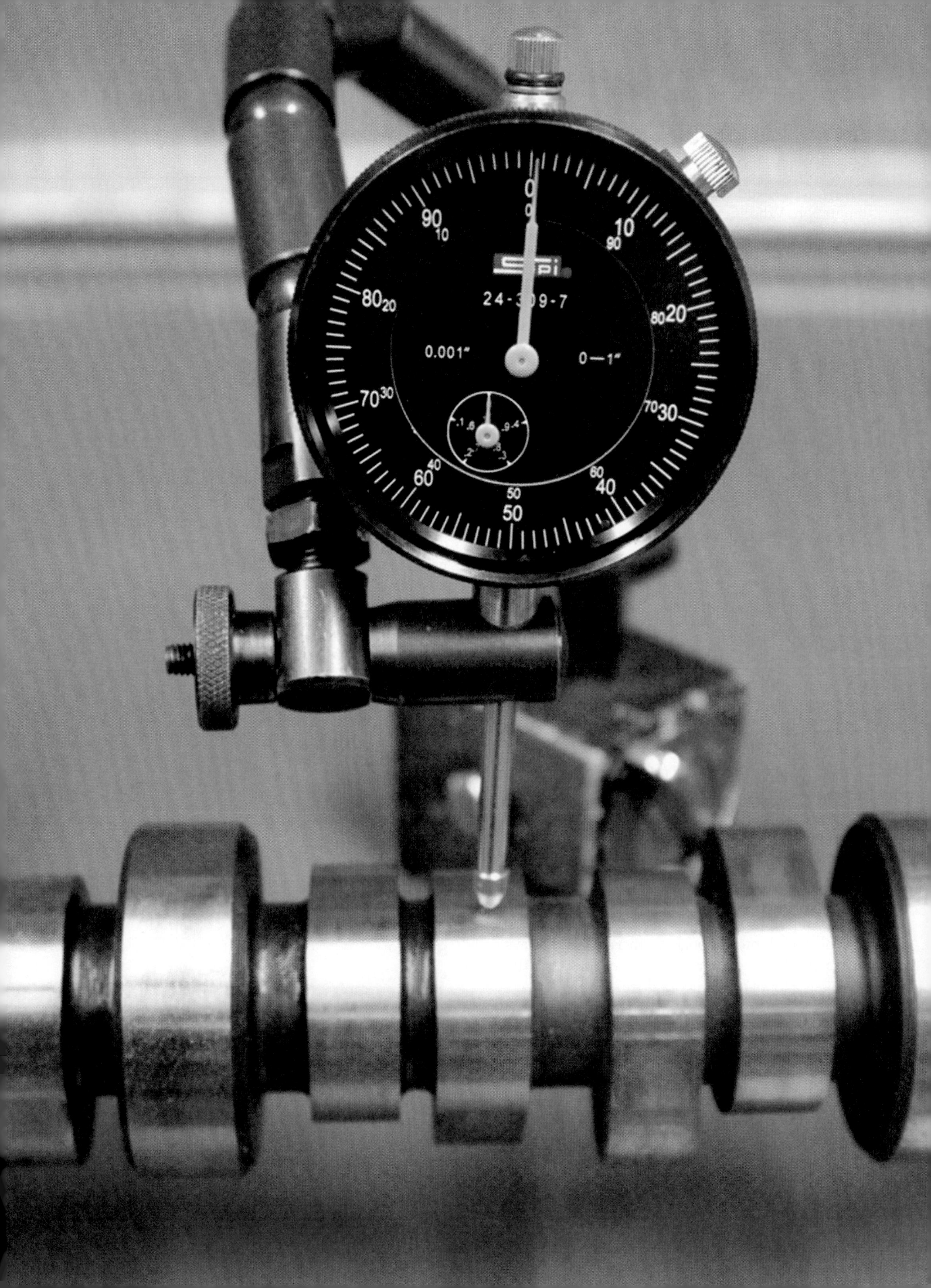
0.001"
0—1"

SECTION II

Engine Repair

CHAPTER 10

KNOW
SEE
DO
PROVE

NATEF Tasks

There are no NATEF tasks for this chapter.

KNOW
SEE
DO
PROVE

Knowledge Objectives

After reading this chapter, you will be able to:

1. Explain the difference between external combustion engines and internal combustion engines. (pp 238–239)
2. Explain the relationships between pressure, temperature, and volume. (pp 240–242)
3. Explain force, work, and power. (p 242)
4. Describe reciprocating and rotary motion. (pp 243, 258–259)
5. Explain the five events common to all internal combustion engines. (pp 245–246)
6. Describe the functions of the cylinder head. (p 254)
7. Describe the difference between a cam-in-block engine and an overhead cam (OHC) engine. (pp 252–253)
8. Describe how the camshaft works. (pp 253–254)
9. Describe how the valve train functions. (pp 254–257)
10. Describe intake and exhaust manifold. (p 257)

Motive Power Types—Spark-Ignition (SI) Engines

Know
See
Do
Prove

Skills Objectives

There are no skills objectives for this chapter.

Introduction

The internal combustion engine is an irreplaceable part of modern society. We rely on it to haul food and water, deliver passengers to their destinations, and even save lives. Over time the internal combustion engine has seen many changes; however, the basics have remained similar. In this chapter, we will cover the types of spark-ignition engines that are available, identify the components that make up the engine, and describe how these components operate together.

Principles of Thermodynamic Internal Combustion Engines

Thermodynamics is generally defined as the branch of physical science that deals with heat and its relation to other forms of energy such as mechanical energy. In this chapter, we will discuss how heat energy is used in the internal combustion engine to produce power and make work happen.

In automotive applications, the useful effect is to move a vehicle down the road as well as provide motive (moving) power for all of the onboard systems. Engines used for motive power may be classified as external combustion or internal combustion engines. External combustion means that the fuel is being burned outside of the engine, while internal combustion means the fuel is burned inside of the engine. Two examples of the **external combustion engine** are the steam engine and the Stirling engine FIGURE 10-1.

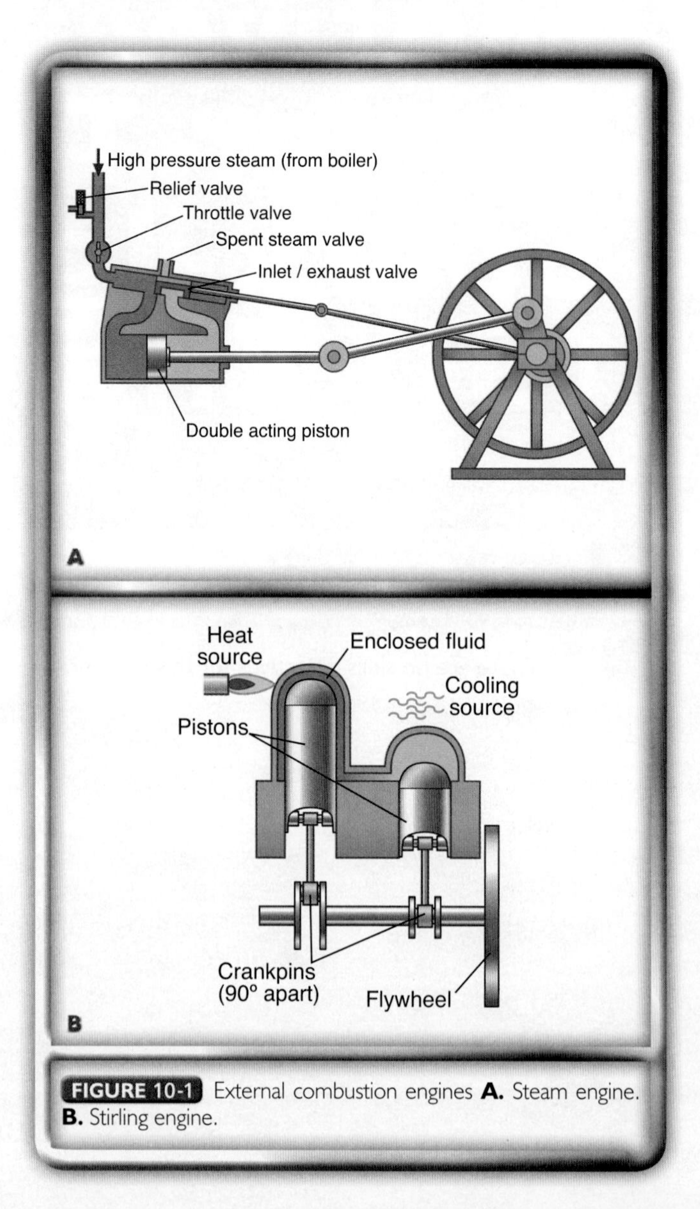
High pressure steam (from boiler)
Relief valve
Throttle valve
Spent steam valve
Inlet / exhaust valve
Double acting piston
A
Heat source
Enclosed fluid
Cooling source
Pistons
Crankpins (90° apart)
Flywheel
B

FIGURE 10-1 External combustion engines **A.** Steam engine. **B.** Stirling engine.

You Are the Automotive Technician

You are working in the back shop when a salesman from the new car sales department asks if you could answer some questions for a customer. The customer's previous car was totaled in a parking lot accident, and he is very interested in a couple of cars on the lot. He has some technical questions that need to be answered, and the service manager selected you to answer the questions. You greet the customer, and he asks you the following questions:

1. "I see a nice diesel pick-up truck that I could use on the farm. How does a compression ignition engine operate differently than a spark ignition engine?"
2. "My son would like me to buy that RX8. How does a rotary engine operate differently from a piston engine?"
3. "As I am looking at specifications on the vehicles, what is the difference between horsepower and torque?"
4. "What is meant by camshaft lift and duration specifications?"

At one time, external combustion engines, such as steam engines, were used to power almost all equipment. Steam engines are the best example of external engines powering equipment such as farm tractors, railroad trains, automobiles, boats and ships, and more. Even a steam-powered airplane was produced, although it never became popular.

In a steam engine, steam is created in an external boiler (external combustion) and used to push a piston back and forth in a cylinder. Most steam engines applied steam alternately to each side of the piston, so the piston was powered in both directions. One problem with steam engines is that they take a relatively long time to generate steam pressure, so you could not just hop in a steam-powered car and take off. The boilers also presented an explosion hazard if they generated too much pressure or if the boiler weakened due to rust.

The Stirling engine is also an external combustion engine. It holds promise as an alternative source of power but has not become popular for transportation since its output cannot be easily varied. Solar-powered Stirling engines are gaining popularity as home power sources because they are environmentally friendly. Since solar energy is used to provide the heat for the engine, so there are no by-products of combustion to worry about. Stirling engines can run almost silently and therefore can be used near people without disturbing them.

The **internal combustion engine** has almost completely replaced the external combustion engine and has been around for well over a century. It is still the favored mode of power for the transportation industry, whether for on-road applications (cars, trucks, buses, etc.) or for non-road applications (tractors, trains, ships, etc.). This chapter focuses on spark-ignition internal combustion engines, since they are the most widely used engines in modern automobiles.

Gasoline (spark ignition) and diesel (compression ignition) engines are prime examples of internal combustion engines. Fuel is burned *inside* the internal combustion engine. According to Charles's law, when a gas is heated, it expands. Since fuel contains energy in chemical form, when it is burned in a sealed combustion chamber, it creates high pressure that pushes on a moveable piston. The moving piston produces power to do work.

▸ LINK
Refer to the Alternative Fuel Systems chapter for more information on hybrid vehicles, flex-fuel vehicles, "pure" battery-electric vehicles (BEVs), fuel cell vehicles (FCVs), and other alternative-fueled vehicles.

The internal combustion engine (ICE) can be classified in two ways: as a reciprocating piston engine or as a rotary engine. The gasoline **piston engine** uses a crankshaft to convert the reciprocating movement of the pistons in their cylinder bores into rotary motion at the crankshaft. The piston engine may be of the **two-stroke** or **four-stroke** design. The **rotary engine** uses a rotating motion rather than reciprocating motion. It uses ports rather than valves to control intake and exhaust flow. Both the piston and the rotary engine will be described in greater detail later in this chapter.

Piston engines are either **spark ignition (SI) engines** or **compression-ignition (CI) engines**. In SI engines, liquid fuels such as gasoline, ethanol, methanol, or butenol are compressed and ignited by an electrical spark, which jumps across the air gap of a spark plug in the combustion chamber. Timing of combustion is totally reliant on when the spark jumps across the electrodes of the spark plug **FIGURE 10-2**. In diesel engines, air in the sealed combustion chamber is compressed so tightly that it becomes hot enough to ignite the fuel as soon as it is injected into the combustion chamber. Timing of the combustion process is reliant on when the fuel is injected; therefore, CI engines do not use spark plugs **FIGURE 10-3**.

▸ LINK
Refer to the Compression-Ignition Engine chapter for a more complete description of diesel engines.

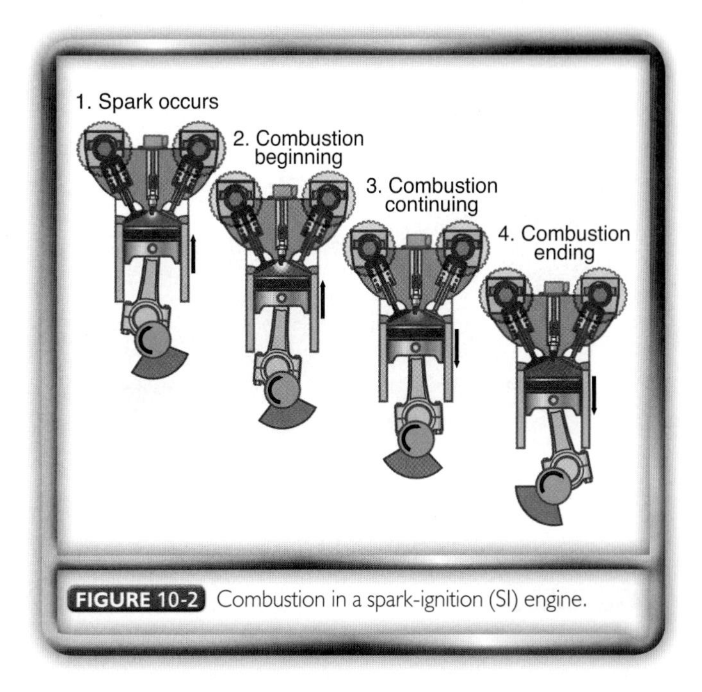
1. Spark occurs
2. Combustion beginning
3. Combustion continuing
4. Combustion ending

FIGURE 10-2 Combustion in a spark-ignition (SI) engine.

Principles of Engine Operation

Engines operate according to the unchanging laws of physics and thermodynamics. Understanding the physics and science involved with an engine will help you to diagnose engine problems. For example, knowing that pressure rises when the volume of a sealed container is reduced will help you to understand the need for sealing the chamber for maximum power.

Realize, too, that when molecules are tightly packed together, they produce far more expansion pressure during combustion than when they are not. Valves and ports in the engine's cylinder head(s) provide a means of sealing the combustion chamber. If the valves leak, the pressure in the cylinder will not rise as it should during the compression stroke of the piston. If there is too little pressure squeezing the air/fuel mixture together in the cylinder, the mixture will not get packed tightly enough, and less engine power will be developed when it is ignited.

A good example of the importance of compression would be the burning of black powder in open air; it will produce fire and smoke but no explosion. If the same powder is wrapped tightly, it becomes a fire cracker (or even a stick of dynamite)—exploding the wrapping and producing the bang. More power is produced when air and fuel are compressed into a tightly packed space.

Pressure and Temperature

Recall that according to Charles's law, in a sealed chamber, the pressure and temperature of a gas are directly related to each other. As pressure rises, so does temperature; as pressure decreases, so does temperature. For example, think of a portable propane bottle used when boiling water on a camp stove. The bottle has a fixed amount of gas inside of it. As the propane is used, the metal propane bottle gets ice cold and frosts over due to the pressure being released.

In contrast, think of a cylinder with a moveable plunger at one end FIGURE 10-4. This plunger seals tightly in the cylinder so that no air can escape past the plunger. Installed on the other end of the cylinder are a pressure gauge and a thermometer. As we push the plunger in, the air pressure rises in the sealed cylinder as the air molecules are squeezed together. As the air molecules are squeezed together more tightly, the pressure and the temperature rise as a result of friction between the air molecules as they bounce off each other with greater force. The air in the cylinder heats up as this happens, so we see not only the pressure rise on the pressure gauge but also the temperature rise on the thermometer. The same amount of heat is in the cylinder as when uncompressed, but when it is compressed, the heat is concentrated; thus, the temperature rises.

A diesel engine uses this principle to ignite the fuel injected into an engine cylinder. The air is compressed so tightly that it becomes hot enough to ignite the fuel when it arrives; this is why diesel engines are called compression-ignition engines. Again using our plunger in a cylinder example, what happens when the plunger is pulled outward? Pulling out the plunger reduces gas pressure and gives the molecules more room to move; they

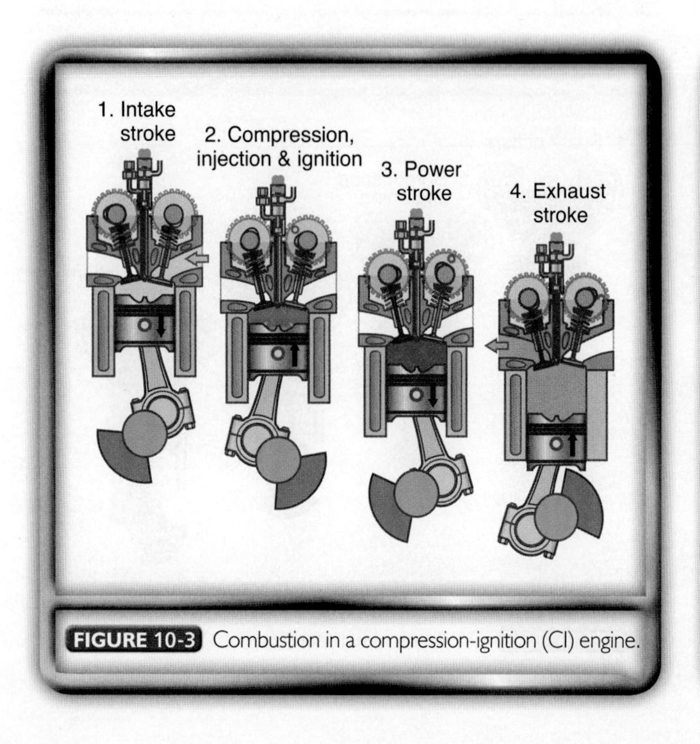
1. Intake stroke
2. Compression, injection & ignition
3. Power stroke
4. Exhaust stroke

FIGURE 10-3 Combustion in a compression-ignition (CI) engine.

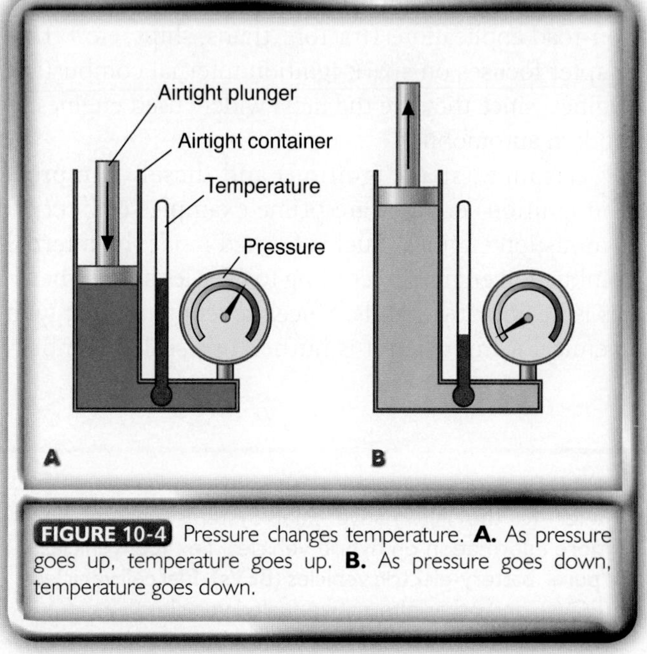
Airtight plunger
Airtight container
Temperature
Pressure
A
B

FIGURE 10-4 Pressure changes temperature. **A.** As pressure goes up, temperature goes up. **B.** As pressure goes down, temperature goes down.

affect each other less and temperature decreases. Thus, a drop in pressure produces a lower temperature because even though the same amount of heat is contained in the cylinder, the heat is more spread out.

Looking at a related scenario, what happens to pressure when the gas *temperature* changes? When a gas is heated, its molecules start to move more quickly and want more space. Heating a gas in a sealed container will increase the pressure in the container (thermal expansion) **FIGURE 10-5**. Cooling a gas has the opposite effect. As the molecules slow down, they demand less space. As a result of cooling a gas in a sealed container, the pressure will drop.

Temperature and Energy

The temperature of a gas is one measure of how much energy it has. The more energy a gas has, the more work it can do. The heating of gas particles makes them move faster, which produces more pressure. This pressure exerts more force on the container in which the gas is located, which is how an ICE functions. Pressure is first raised through compression and then through combustion of the air/fuel mixture. Burning the air/fuel mixture increases the heat temperature inside the container tremendously, which creates the necessary pressure to produce work. The more energy the air/fuel mixture has, the more force it exerts on the piston and the more work the piston can do **FIGURE 10-6**. This principle takes place during the power stroke and pushes the piston down the sealed container.

Latent (stored) heat energy exists in various kinds of fuels; it is released to do work when the fuel is ignited and burned. Types of fuels that contain latent heat energy include liquid fuels such as gasoline, diesel, and ethanol; gaseous fuels such as natural gas, propane, and hydrogen; and solid fuels such as gunpowder, wood, and coal. Latent heat energy is often measured and expressed as British thermal units, abbreviated Btu.

One Btu equals the heat required to raise the temperature of 1 pound (lb) of water by 1°F. Gasoline has a comparatively high Btu per gallon rating of around 14,000 Btu. Diesel fuel is even more energy dense, however, at around 25,000 Btu per gallon. Coal has a much lower Btu rating, which is one reason why both the home heating and the transportation (rail) industries have moved from coal to petroleum (i.e., home heating oil and diesel fuel) for better energy efficiency (transport and storage of a liquid fuel is also lots easier).

Pressure and Volume

Pressure and volume are inversely related; as one rises, the other falls. A cylinder with a pressure gauge and movable piston is a good example. It contains air, and as the piston is pushed in, the inside air is forced into a smaller volume. At the same time, the pressure gauge shows an increase in pressure. It is this increase in pressure that allows the pump to do its work. When the piston is pulled out, the volume occupied by the gas grows larger, and the pressure drops. A larger volume will have less gas pressure, and when the volume is reduced, the gas pressure will rise. Keep in mind that larger pressures

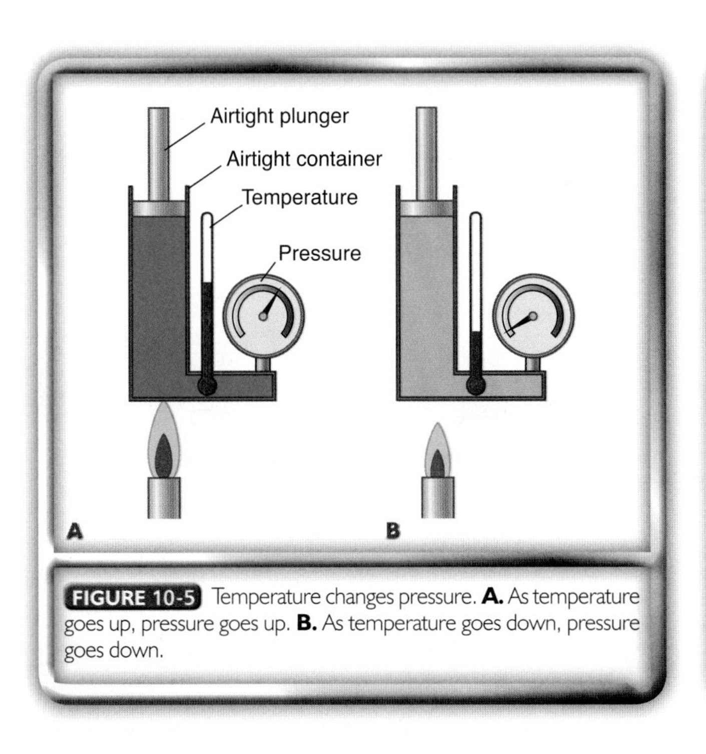
Airtight plunger
Airtight container
Temperature
Pressure
A
B

FIGURE 10-5 Temperature changes pressure. **A.** As temperature goes up, pressure goes up. **B.** As temperature goes down, pressure goes down.

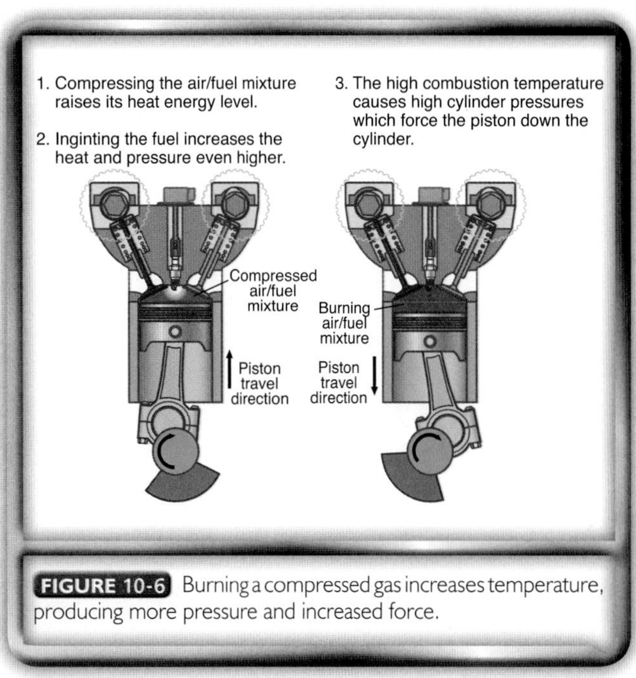
1. Compressing the air/fuel mixture raises its heat energy level.
2. Inginting the fuel increases the heat and pressure even higher.
3. The high combustion temperature causes high cylinder pressures which force the piston down the cylinder.
Compressed air/fuel mixture
Burning air/fuel mixture
Piston travel direction
Piston travel direction

FIGURE 10-6 Burning a compressed gas increases temperature, producing more pressure and increased force.

are desirable to increase the amount of work done in an engine FIGURE 10-7.

Force, Work, and Power

Effort to produce a push or pull action is referred to as **force**. A compressed spring applies force to cause, or resist, movement. A tensioned lifting cable applies force to cause lifting movement. Force is measured in pounds, kilograms, or newtons. When force causes movement, **work** is done FIGURE 10-8.

For example, when the compressed spring or the tensioned lifting cable causes movement, work is performed. Without movement, work cannot be performed even if force is applied. *Work is equal to distance moved times force applied*. If the lifting cable of a hoist lifts a 250-lb engine 4′ in the air, the amount of work done is equal to 4′ times 250 lb, or 1000 foot-pounds of work. Work is measured in foot-pounds (ft-lb), watts, or joules. Work can only be accomplished when something is moved.

> **TECHNICIAN TIP**
>
> Holding a heavy starter motor in place while trying to get the bolts started is not technically work; it is force. Although it seems like you are working hard, your arm muscles twitching as you stand under the vehicle and hold the part in place, you are not performing work in the true physics sense. It takes movement, along with force, to qualify as work. So lifting the starter from the ground to its position on the engine is work, but holding it there is not work. Understanding the difference between these two terms will give you a good foundation for understanding power.

The rate or speed at which work is performed is called **power** FIGURE 10-9. The more power that can be produced, the more work can be performed in a given amount of time. Power is measured in ft-lb per second or ft-lb per minute. If an electric motor can lift a 600-lb weight 20′ in 10 seconds, power used would be equal to

$$20 \text{ (feet)} \times 600 \text{ (lb)} \div 10 \text{ (seconds)} = 1200 \text{ ft-lb per second.}$$

One horsepower equals 550 ft-lb per second, or 33,000 ft-lb per minute. So 1200 ft-lb per second equals 2.18 horsepower. The watt or kilowatt (1000 watts) is the metric unit of measurement for power, where 746 watts equals 1 horsepower. So the electric motor in the example would be developing 2.18 (horsepower) times 746 (watts), which equals 1627 watts, or 1.627 kilowatts, of power.

Work = distance moved × force applied
= 4 ft × 150 lb
= 600 ft-lb
4 feet
150 pounds

FIGURE 10-8 Work.

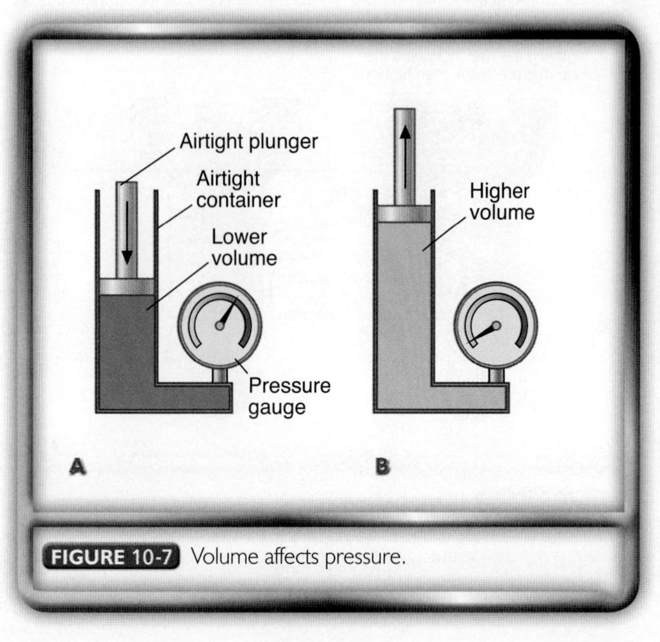
Airtight plunger
Airtight container
Lower volume
Pressure gauge
Higher volume
A
B

FIGURE 10-7 Volume affects pressure.

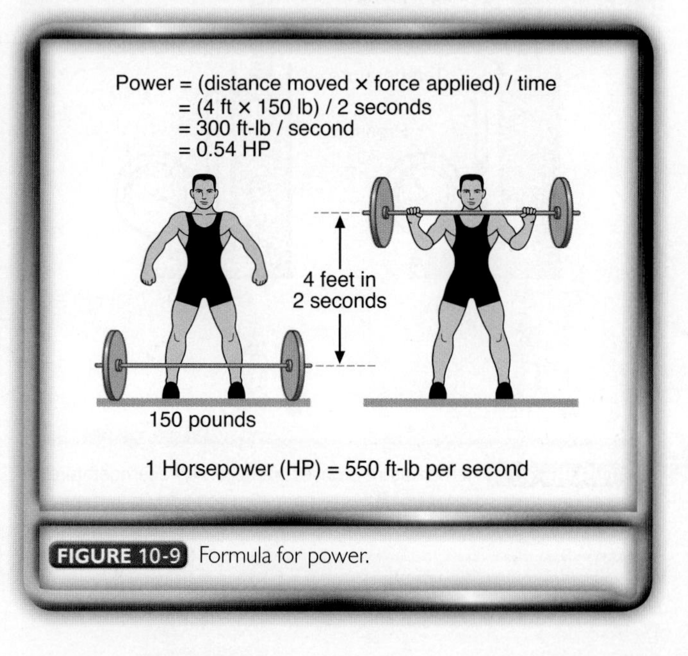
Power = (distance moved × force applied) / time
= (4 ft × 150 lb) / 2 seconds
= 300 ft-lb / second
= 0.54 HP
4 feet in 2 seconds
150 pounds
1 Horsepower (HP) = 550 ft-lb per second

FIGURE 10-9 Formula for power.

Power and Torque

Torque is described as a twisting force. Movement does not have to occur to have torque. Torque is applied before or during movement. When a twist cap on a water bottle is removed, maximum torque is applied just before the cap starts to turn. When the same cap is tightened, maximum torque is applied once the cap starts to get tight. The concept of "twisting force" should always come to mind when the term torque is used. When a piston is pushed down a cylinder during the power stroke, it applies force to a connecting rod linking the piston and crankshaft, causing the crankshaft to rotate. The rotational force applied to the crankshaft is called torque.

The unit of measurement for torque in the imperial system is ft-lb; in the metric system it is newton meters. If a force of 100 lb is applied to the end of a 1′ long wrench (lever) attached to a bolt, the resulting torque applied to the wrench will be 100 ft-lb.

The measurement of engine power is calculated from the amount of torque at the crankshaft and the speed at which it is turning in rpm. The formula for engine horsepower is:

$$\text{Horsepower} = \text{rpm} \times \text{ft-lb} \div 5252.$$

For example, if an engine creates 500 ft-lb of torque at 4000 rpm, then the amount of horsepower is:

$$500 \times 4000 \div 5252, \text{ or } 380 \text{ horsepower at } 4000 \text{ rpm.}$$

Because horsepower would change with rpm, it is necessary to express not only the power value but to include the engine speed, in rpm, at which it occurs. Power can also be measured in kilowatts. A kilowatt (1,000 watts) is equivalent to 1000 newtons per meter per second.

The formula for computing an engine's horsepower might seem confusing since we said earlier that 1 horsepower equals 33,000 ft-lb per minute; yet we divide the product of torque × rpm by 5252. Why do we use 5252 instead of 33,000? The reason is a bit complicated, having to do with the definition of ft-lb. When relating to *work*, ft-lb means force times distance moved. That works well in a lifting situation but not so well in a twisting (torque) situation. In a *torque* situation, ft-lb means a twisting force applied to a shaft—that is, applied force times lever distance of the applied force. Thus, it is possible for torque to result in no movement, only an applied force. And we label that force in ft-lb even though for work or power to happen, movement must take place.

To calculate the twisting power of a shaft, we need a way to add *distance moved* and *time* to the equation so that power can be represented; we can't just say that 33,000 ft-lb = 1 horsepower when talking about torque. That is why rpm is included in the formula. Because rpm refers to a certain number of revolutions per minute, it includes both time and distance. But how much distance is 1 rpm? The answer relates to radians. A radian describes how many radius distances there are in the circumference of a circle FIGURE 10-10. Since there are 3.14 diameters in the circumference of a circle, there are twice as many, or 6.28, radius distances (radians) in the circumference of any circle. The larger the circle, the longer the radians, but still only 6.28 of them fit within the total circumference. And that is where we get our distance. Since torque relates to an equivalent amount of force a certain distance from the rotational center (radius), and there are 6.28 radians in the circumference of a circle, every revolution equals a distance of 6.28 radians.

To convert torque ft-lb to work ft-lb, there has to be movement. We can either multiply the rpm by 6.28 and use the 33,000 (ft-lb per horsepower) factor, or divide the 33,000 ft-lb by 6.28 (distance around a circle in radians) and come up with a new factor, which is 5252, that we can use with the original "torque × rpm" numbers for calculating engine horsepower. To keep the numbers more manageable, most people go with the 5252 factor. Thus, if we multiply the ft-lb of torque × rpm and divide that number by 5252, we will have calculated the engine's horsepower at that particular rpm.

Torque Versus Horsepower

As torque is a twisting or turning force, **horsepower** is the rate (in time and distance) at which that force (torque) is produced. Torque alone does not mean work has been accomplished. It takes movement and time to accomplish a given amount of work in a given amount of time (horsepower). At the same time, for an engine to produce torque, it has to be running. So the rotation of

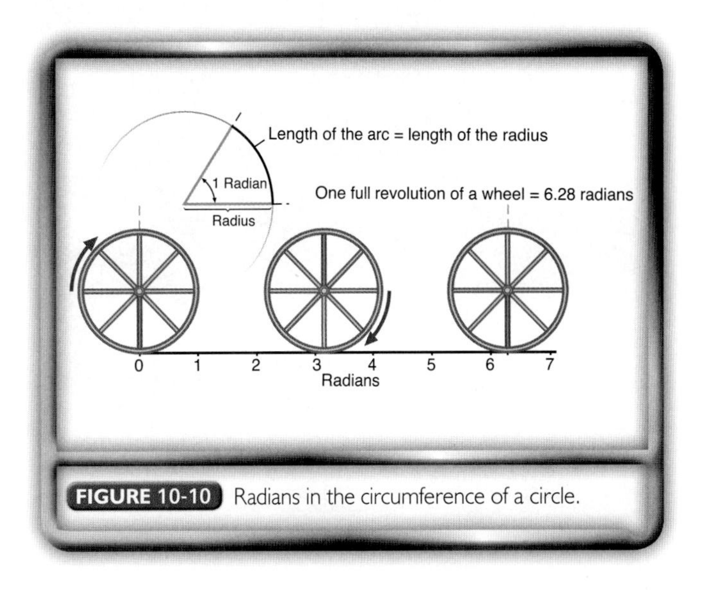
Length of the arc = length of the radius
1 Radian
One full revolution of a wheel = 6.28 radians
Radius
0
1
2
3
4
5
6
7
Radians

FIGURE 10-10 Radians in the circumference of a circle.

the crankshaft (torque × distance) in a running engine means that work and power are occurring since torque × rpm gives us power FIGURE 10-11. Also, an engine will put out varying amounts of torque and power as it is operating. Thus, if it is producing torque, it is producing power. Factors that affect an engine's torque output include engine **volumetric efficiency** (the rate of air intake and exhaust) at various crankshaft speeds and internal component friction (**parasitic losses**). In a naturally aspirated engine (nonpressurized intake system), torque peaks at the rpm where the engine's cylinders fill the most with air. Torque starts to drop as engine speed increases past peak torque rpm.

Actually, in a naturally aspirated (naturally breathing, nonpressurized) engine, air never completely fills the combustion chamber while the engine is running. Peak engine torque rpm occurs at the peak volumetric efficiency (somewhere around 85% in an unmodified engine). Peak torque usually occurs at some low- to mid-rpm engine speed, depending on bore and stroke of the engine, as well as intake and exhaust port size and valve timing.

Since engine rpm tends to rise faster than torque falls off (above peak volumetric efficiency), an engine's maximum horsepower occurs at a higher rpm than the peak torque rpm. At some point in the rpm range, the torque on the crankshaft drops so low that the crankshaft can no longer do additional work and the horsepower actually starts to decrease. Remember, it is horsepower that does the work, but torque makes it happen. Engine torque (and therefore horsepower) increases can be achieved through any engine modifications that improve volumetric efficiency FIGURE 10-12. In fact, a turbocharger or supercharger will increase an engine's volumetric efficiency well above 100%. For example, a 1.6-liter Volkswagen diesel engine when turbocharged to its rated 11 lb of boost would be theoretically equivalent, horsepower-wise, to a naturally aspirated 2.8-liter engine.

Applied Science

AS-97: Torque: The technician can demonstrate an understanding of how torque relates to force and angular acceleration.

Newton's second Law of Motion states that the change in speed of an object over a given time is proportional to the force exerted on it. We know that a train is much slower to accelerate than a car, and once it is moving the train is far more difficult to stop. This is the basis for our understanding of the concept of torque relating to force and angular acceleration.

Physics can tell us a lot about how engines react to forces. Consider a flywheel attached to the crankshaft of an engine, which is an example of rotational motion. The torque necessary for the assembly to rotate is the product of force multiplied times distance.

In physics, torque can be thought of as a rotational force that causes a change in rotary motion. The term "twisting force" is used by most automotive technicians. To determine angular acceleration, which is measured in radians per second squared, we need to know several other items of information. We would need to know the initial and final angular velocities and time. Angular velocity describes the speed of rotation of an object that is following a specific axis. Angular acceleration is the rate of change of angular velocity with time and is measured in radians per second squared. The angular acceleration is caused by the torque, which produces the force to make it happen. This process is proportional as stated in Newton's second Law of Motion.

FIGURE 10-11 An automotive chassis dynamometer measures output of the engine at the wheels of the vehicle.

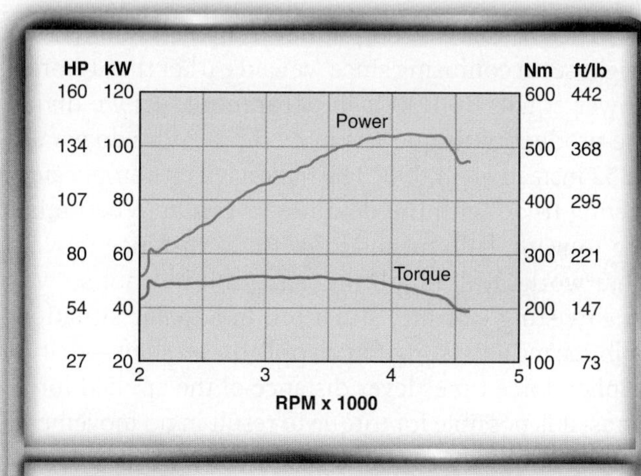
HP kW
160 120
134 100
107 80
80 60
54 40
27 20
Nm ft/lb
600 442
500 368
400 295
300 221
200 147
100 73
Power
Torque
2
3
4
5
RPM x 1000

FIGURE 10-12 The relationship between torque and horsepower.

Applied Science

AS-50: Work: The technician can explain the relationship between torque and horsepower.

Two technicians are discussing the relationship between torque and horsepower during their break time at work. Al believes that torque is the turning force at the engine's crankshaft. Bob says that horsepower is the rate at which force is produced. Both technicians are correct as they discuss the unique relationship of torque and horsepower. One cannot exist without the other.

When we compare a race car to a bulldozer, we can see two different applications of torque and horsepower. A bulldozer has lots of torque but the engine may be operating at 2,000 RPM. A race car may be operating at 8,000 RPM with a lower amount of torque. Low-speed torque is needed in some situations and high-rpm horsepower is needed in others. (Additional information on the relationship between torque and horsepower is described in this chapter.)

Four-Stroke Spark-Ignition Engines

The SI engine used in today's vehicles operates on the four-stroke cycle principle: It takes four strokes of the piston to complete one cycle. When the piston in a cylinder is at the position farthest away from the crankshaft, it is at **top dead center (TDC)**. When the piston in the cylinder is at a position closest to the crankshaft, it is said to be at **bottom dead center (BDC)**. When the piston moves from TDC to BDC or from BDC to TDC, one **stroke** has occurred FIGURE 10-13. Two or more strokes are called **reciprocating motion**, meaning an up-and-down motion within the cylinder. Piston engines are therefore referred to as reciprocating engines.

Piston engines can be simple, single-piston engines such as those on lawn mowers, or they can be much more complicated, multipiston engines, such as those in automobiles, trucks, and heavy equipment. Multicylinder engines come in various cylinder arrangements. Some automotive engines have cylinders arranged in a line (in-line engine), with pistons one behind each other. Some automobile engines are flat, with opposed cylinders lying horizontally. This style of engine is called a boxer engine. Other automobile engines have cylinders at an angle (a V-type engine), with the pistons forming a V configuration.

Basic Four-Stroke Operation

In a single four-stroke cycle, only one stroke out of four delivers new energy to turn the crankshaft. The four strokes must include the five key events common to all ICEs: intake, compression, ignition, power, and exhaust FIGURE 10-14. The **intake stroke** starts with the exhaust valve closed, the intake valve(s) opening, and the piston moving from TDC to BDC. As the piston moves down, the volume above the top of the piston increases. This makes pressure inside the cylinder lower than the pressure outside the cylinder. Higher outside air pressure forces the air (usually with fuel) into the cylinder. As the piston reaches BDC, the intake valve(s) closes, and the intake stroke ends.

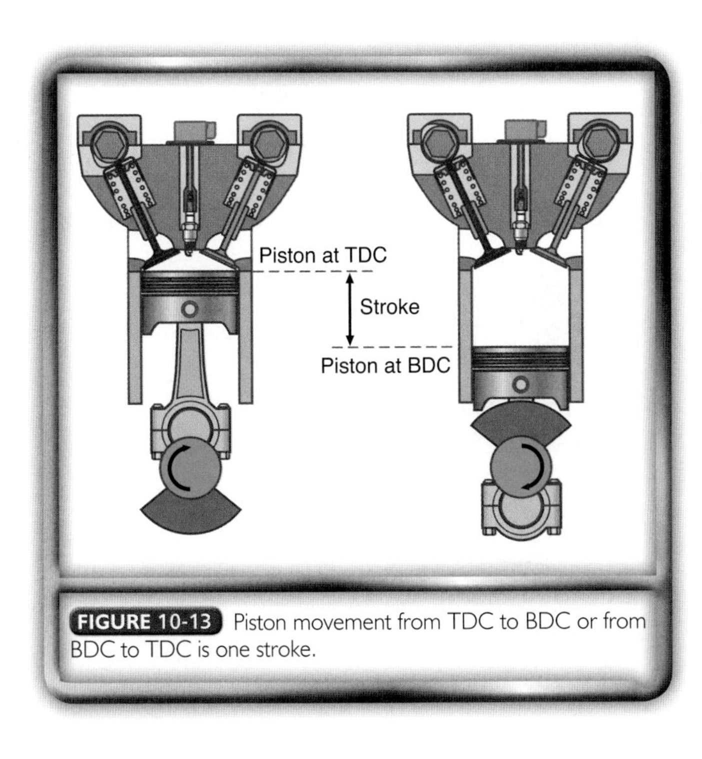
Piston at TDC
Stroke
Piston at BDC

FIGURE 10-13 Piston movement from TDC to BDC or from BDC to TDC is one stroke.

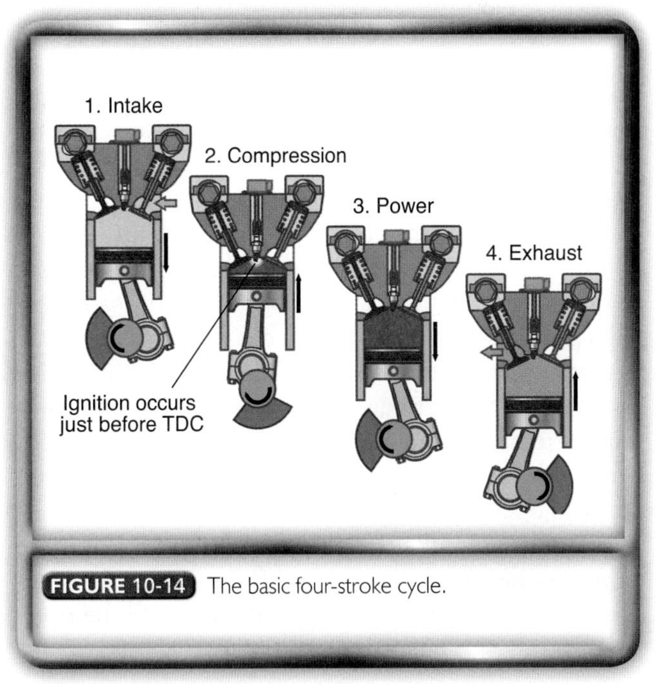
1. Intake
2. Compression
3. Power
4. Exhaust
Ignition occurs just before TDC

FIGURE 10-14 The basic four-stroke cycle.

Applied Science

AS-99: Rotational: The technician can explain how rotational motion can be converted to linear motion and why balance is important in rotating systems.

When working in an automotive repair facility, it is important that the technician understand basic engine operation. The text has explained much regarding each component of the engine block assembly and cylinder head. The technician should know that reciprocating motion is an up and down motion such as the pistons in a cylinder. The crankshaft converts this linear motion into rotational motion.

It is also important to know that the camshaft lobe converts rotary motion into linear motion. As described in the text, the lobe is the raised portion on a camshaft used to lift the lifter and open the valve. Opening the valve requires linear motion on overhead cam engines as well as cam in block engines. The text describes a cam as an egg-shaped piece (lobe) mounted on the camshaft. The egg shape of the cam lobe is designed to lift the valve open, hold it open, and let it close. This is the operation that converts rotating motion into linear motion.

Balance is extremely important in a rotating system for a number of reasons. In order to have a smooth running engine, balance is necessary. In order to have long engine life and dependability, balance is also necessary. On the crankshaft, we have a vibration damper or harmonic balancer as described in the text. This important component is carefully engineered to meet the needs of a specific engine regarding proper balance.

The **compression stroke** starts near BDC when the intake valve(s) closes. The piston moves from BDC to TDC. As the piston moves up, the air–fuel mixture is compressed into a smaller and smaller volume. Compression of air caused by the moving piston causes the air/fuel charge temperature to rise, making ignition easier and the combustion (burning of fuel) more complete and efficient.

As the piston reaches TDC of the compression stroke, the next event occurs: **ignition**. The air/fuel mixture is ignited and burns rapidly, at up to about 4500°F (2482°C). The heat of combustion causes burning gases to expand greatly (thermal expansion), which creates very high pressure in the combustion chamber. This pressure is also applied to the top of the piston, which is free to move down the cylinder. The **power stroke** occurs as this extreme force moves the piston from TDC to BDC with both valves remaining closed. The exhaust valve(s) starts to open near BDC.

At the end of the power stroke, the **exhaust stroke** occurs as the piston moves from BDC to TDC and pushes the burned gases out of the cylinder through the open exhaust valve(s). When the piston nears TDC, the exhaust valve(s) starts to close and the intake valve(s) starts to open, and the four-stroke cycle starts over from the beginning. Note that the crankshaft has completed two full rotations during the four-stroke cycle. Thus, four complete strokes make one complete cycle.

Engine Measurement—Size

ICEs are designated by the amount of space (volume) their pistons displace as they move from TDC to BDC, which is called **engine displacement**. So, a 5.4-liter V8 engine has 8 cylinders that displace a total volume of 5.4 liters. Displacement can be listed in cubic centimeters, liters, or cubic inches. To find an engine's displacement, you need to know the bore, stroke, and number of cylinders for a particular engine.

The diameter of the engine cylinder is the **cylinder bore**. The bore is measured across the cylinder, parallel with the **block deck**, which is the machined surface of the block farthest from the crankshaft. Automotive cylinder bores can vary in size from less than 3″ to more than 4″.

The distance the piston travels from TDC to BDC, or from BDC to TDC, is called the **piston stroke**. Piston stroke is determined by the offset portion of the crankshaft called the **throw**. The crankshaft will be described in greater detail later in this chapter. Piston stroke also varies from less than 3″ to more than 4″. Generally, the longer the stroke, the greater the engine torque produced. A shorter stroke lets the engine run at higher rpm to create greater horsepower. Engine specifications typically list the bore size first and the stroke length second (bore vs. stroke).

The volume that a piston displaces from BDC to TDC is **piston displacement**. Increasing the diameter of the bore or increasing the length of the stroke will produce a larger piston displacement. The formula for calculating piston displacement is FIGURE 10-15:

cylinder bore squared × 0.785 × the piston stroke.

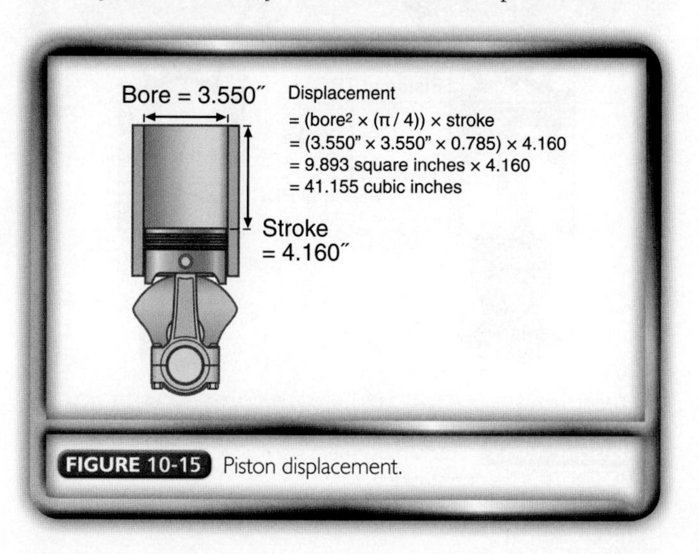
Bore = 3.550″
Displacement
= (bore^2 × (π / 4)) × stroke
= (3.550" × 3.550" × 0.785) × 4.160
= 9.893 square inches × 4.160
= 41.155 cubic inches
Stroke
= 4.160″

FIGURE 10-15 Piston displacement.

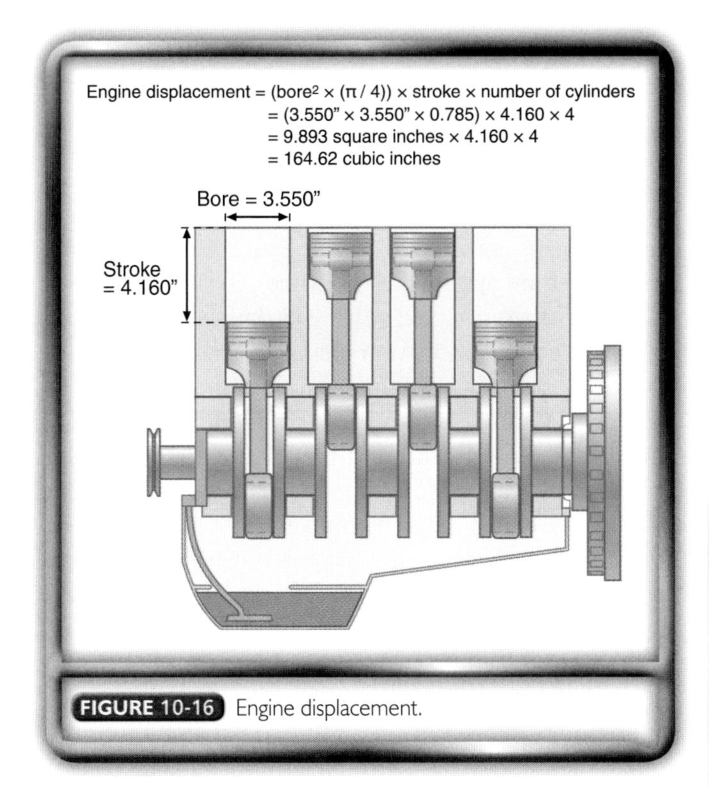

Engine displacement = (bore2 × (π / 4)) × stroke × number of cylinders
= (3.550" × 3.550" × 0.785) × 4.160 × 4
= 9.893 square inches × 4.160 × 4
= 164.62 cubic inches
Bore = 3.550"
Stroke = 4.160"

FIGURE 10-16 Engine displacement.

This formula works for calculating both the standard displacement in cubic inches, or the metric displacement in cubic centimeters (ccs) or liters.

For example, a 5.4-liter (329-cubic inch) V8 truck engine has a 3.55″ bore, a 4.16″ stroke, and 8 cylinders. Using the formula for displacement:

$$3.55 \times 3.55\ (\text{bore}^2) = 12.6025 \times 0.785\ (\text{constant}) = 9.893 \times 4.16\ (\text{stroke}) = 41.155\text{-cubic inch piston displacement.}$$

Once you know the piston displacement, the next step to finding engine displacement is to multiply piston displacement times the number of cylinders in the engine FIGURE 10-16. Continuing from the previous example:

$$41.155\text{-cubic inch piston displacement} \times 8\ (\text{number of cylinders}) = 329.24\text{-cubic inch engine displacement.}$$

The displacement of an engine (also called engine size) can be altered by changing cylinder bore (diameter), piston stroke (length), or the number of cylinders.

Compression ratio (CR) compares cylinder volumes with the piston at BDC and at TDC FIGURE 10-17 . Maximum cylinder volume will be at BDC, and minimum cylinder volume will be at TDC. The ratio is given as two numbers. A compression ratio listed as 8:1 (8 to 1) means that the maximum cylinder volume is eight times larger than the minimum cylinder volume. Compression ratio is affected by changing the size and shape of the top of the piston, changing the size of the combustion chamber, or altering valve timing. The higher the compression ratio, the higher the compression pressures within the combustion chamber and therefore the higher the thermal expansion during combustion, making the engine more fuel efficient. But too high of a compression ratio can cause the air–fuel mixture to be ignited by the high compression temperature before the correct time, which is when the spark occurs. This early ignition can cause damage to the engine bearings and piston; therefore, manufacturers design their engines with an optimum compression ratio.

> **TECHNICIAN TIP**
>
> An engine with the same size bore and stroke is referred to as a square engine. An engine with a larger bore than stroke is called an oversquare engine (short-stroke engine). An engine with a bore smaller than the stroke is called an undersquare engine (long-stroke engine). Oversquare engines tend to make their power at higher rpm, while undersquare engines tend to make their power at lower rpm.

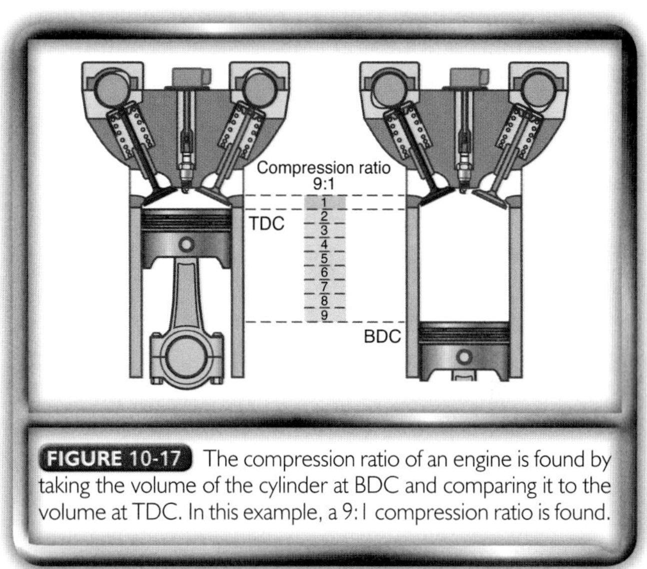

Compression ratio
9:1
TDC
1
2
3
4
5
6
7
8
9
BDC

FIGURE 10-17 The compression ratio of an engine is found by taking the volume of the cylinder at BDC and comparing it to the volume at TDC. In this example, a 9:1 compression ratio is found.

Atkinson and Miller Cycle Engines

The **Miller cycle** engine and the **Atkinson cycle** engine are both variations on the traditional four-stroke SI engine. These engines operate more efficiently but produce lower power outputs for the same displacement. In a conventional four-stroke cycle, the compression and the power (expansion) strokes are the same length. Increasing engine efficiency by increasing the stroke and raising the expansion ratio also raises the compression ratio. There is a limit to how high the compression ratio can be because raising it too much results in high enough temperatures to ignite the air–fuel mixture prematurely, before the ignition spark occurs. The Miller and the Atkinson cycles overcome this by using valve timing variations to make the effective compression stroke shorter than the expansion stroke. The effective compression stroke is shortened by delaying the closing of the intake valve at the beginning of the compression stroke. This shortens the distance that the piston has to compress the air–fuel mixture. The combustion chamber is slightly smaller so that the engine will still have a normal compression ratio. Thus, the compression pressure at ignition is still typically the same as that of a conventional four-stroke engine. The effective expansion stroke is lengthened by delaying the opening of the exhaust valve until closer to BDC, so more of the pressure created by the expansion of the burning gases can act on the piston longer, applying pressure to the crankshaft for a longer time and increasing efficiency.

Because some of the intake gases are pushed back from the cylinder into the intake manifold, Miller and Atkinson engines can use a larger throttle opening for a given amount of power. This design results in lower manifold vacuum, reduced pumping (parasitic drag) losses, and increased fuel efficiency. The Miller cycle engine adds an engine-driven supercharger to increase volumetric efficiency and boost power output when required. When the engine is operating at low load and speed, the supercharger is not needed. A clutch disengages the drive so there is no unnecessary drag on the engine. When extra power is required, the clutch is engaged and the supercharger boosts the amount of air drawn into the engine, supercharging the cylinder.

The Atkinson cycle engine is efficient within a specific operating range (the so-called engine "sweet spot" of peak torque rpm), typically between 2000 and 4500 rpm, but its overall power output and torque are lower than a conventional ICE. This type of engine is less useful as a primary power source, but it is ideal in applications such as a series-parallel hybrid vehicle where it can work in tandem with a battery-driven electric motor as well as charge the high-voltage battery.

Also, the lower maximum operating rpm allows engine components to be of lighter construction and weight as compared to a conventional ICE. Lighter and smaller components reduce friction and increase engine efficiency. In addition, the crankshaft is mounted slightly off-center from the cylinder bores. This position reduces the thrust load on the piston, thereby reducing power loss due to friction.

Scavenging

Scavenging is the process of using a column of moving air to create a low-pressure area behind it to assist in removing any remaining burned gases from the combustion chamber and replacing these gases with a new charge. As the exhaust stroke ends and the intake stroke begins, both valves are open for a short time. The time that both valves are open is called **valve overlap**. As the exhaust gases leave the combustion chamber, the flow tends to continue, creating a low pressure behind it that helps to draw the intake air and fuel charge in. At the same time, the flow of the air and fuel charge being pushed (by atmospheric pressure) into the combustion chamber also helps to push the remaining exhaust gases out. The flow effect during this valve overlap is called scavenging. Valve overlap has a desirable effect during high power/high rpm demand as more air and fuel are able to be pulled into the engine; however, during engine idling, valve overlap produces a rougher idle as exhaust gases are moving slowly and tend to be drawn back into the intake manifold, diluting the incoming air. The rpm at which the most efficient scavenging occurs contributes to peak volumetric efficiency and engine peak torque. Better exhaust scavenging and induction system (intake) breathing work together to improve volumetric efficiency. This is achieved by smoothing intake and exhaust passages, using tuned intake and exhaust runners (to maximize ram effect and scavenging), and using a low back-pressure exhaust.

Components of the Spark-Ignition Engine

The SI engine is the most widely used engine to power passenger vehicles in the United States. It is the vehicle's main power plant, providing power to drive the vehicle down the road and operate the many accessories that drivers have come to expect, such as power steering, air conditioning, entertainment systems, and other features. SI engines have evolved over their 125-year life, but the fundamental principles are still the same: an air/fuel mixture is brought into the cylinder, it is compressed to increase its energy, it is ignited by a high-voltage spark, the mixture burns rapidly causing the thermal expansion needed to push the piston down, and the exhaust gases are pushed out of the cylinder. Modern materials, machining processes, and lubricants have made these engines longer-lasting, more powerful, and more environmentally friendly than ever.

Manufacturers have made incredible gains in the manufacturing of engines and engine components. Many of these gains are due to new technologies that have found their way into the automotive field. Engine blocks and cylinder heads are commonly manufactured from lightweight aluminum, valve covers and intake manifolds are being made of durable plastic materials, pistons are made of newer aluminum alloys, and in some cases connecting rods are manufactured from powdered metals.

The engine can be divided into a couple of main assemblies: the bottom end and the top end. The engine's so-called "bottom end" is the crankcase where the crankshaft, bearings, and connecting rod "big ends" reside. They also make up what is called the rotating assembly. The so-called "top end" is where the cylinder heads and combustion chambers reside. The engine block contains the pistons and connecting rods, crankshaft, and flywheel; if of the cam-in-block configuration, it also contains the camshaft. The cylinder head(s) contains the overhead valves and valve train; if of the cam-in-head configuration (overhead cam), it also contains the camshaft. Each of these assemblies and components will be explored further.

Short Block and Long Block

If a rebuilt engine is needed, an engine subassembly may be purchased. A short block replacement includes the engine block from below the head gasket to above the oil pan. A cam-in-block engine also includes the camshaft and timing gears. An overhead-cam short block does not include the camshaft or timing gears. A long block replacement engine includes the short block, plus the cylinder head(s), new or reconditioned valve train, camshaft and timing chain, and/or gears (or timing belt) FIGURE 10-18. A long block engine replacement still requires swapping parts from the original engine to the long block, including the intake and exhaust manifolds, fuel injection system, the starter, alternator, power steering pump, and air-conditioning compressor.

Cylinder Block, Crankshaft, and Flywheel

The cylinder block is the single largest part of the engine. The block can be made of cast iron or aluminum, which is much lighter. The block casting includes the cylinder bore openings, also known as cylinders, which are machined into the block to allow for the fitting of pistons FIGURE 10-19. The block deck is the top of the block and is machined flat. The cylinder head bolts to the block deck. Passages for the flow of coolant and lubrication are machined or cast into the block. Holes machined into the bottom of the block called main bearing bores have

FIGURE 10-18 The engine contains many parts that work together to power the vehicle.

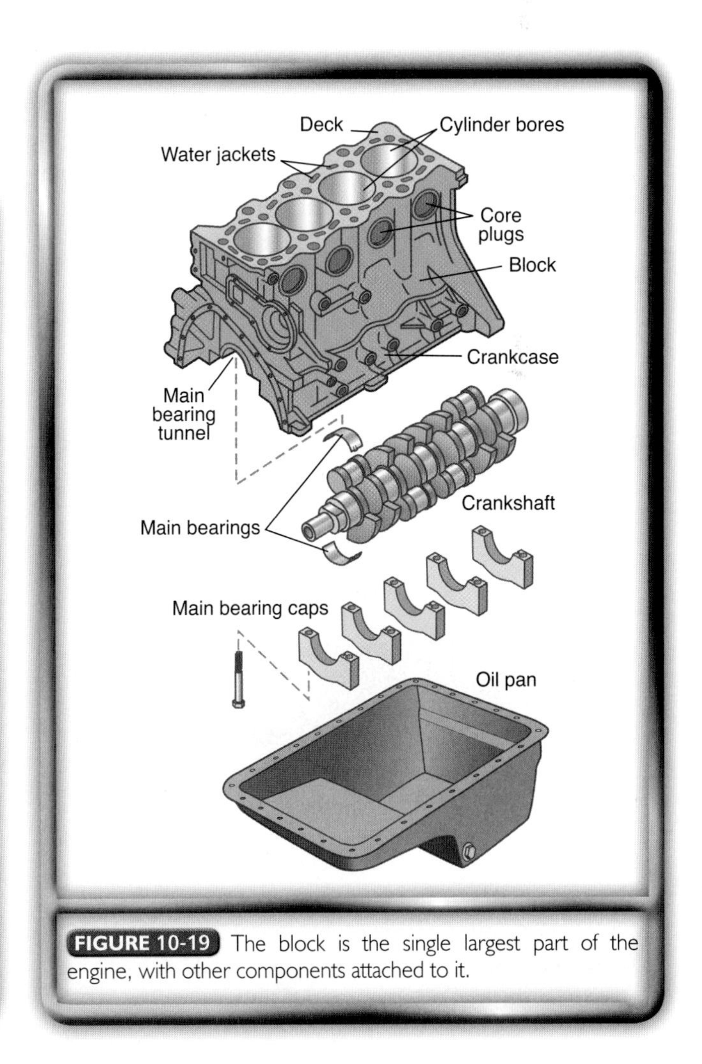
Deck
Cylinder bores
Water jackets
Core plugs
Block
Crankcase
Main bearing tunnel
Crankshaft
Main bearings
Main bearing caps
Oil pan

FIGURE 10-19 The block is the single largest part of the engine, with other components attached to it.

removable main caps and are used to hold the crankshaft in place. Each cap is held in place with two or more bolts. Reinforcements for strength and attachment points for related parts are also machined into the block. The lowest portion of the block is called the crankcase because it houses the crankshaft.

The oil pan completes the crankcase. On most modern engines, the main bearing caps are now a part of the engine girdle, also called a bed plate. The use of a girdle provides an even stronger design as all main bearing caps are connected and reinforce each other.

The crankshaft can be made of cast iron or forged steel, or can be machined out of a solid piece of steel. The crankshaft converts the reciprocating motion of the pistons into rotary motion at the crankshaft. The rotary motion is transferred to the engine flywheel and transmission to ultimately (in a conventional vehicle) drive the wheels. The crankshaft is machined for main bearing support and for the connecting rods **FIGURE 10-20**. The crankshaft is supported by Babbitt-lined main bearing inserts, which fit in the main bearing saddles of the block. End movement of the crankshaft is limited by a thrust bearing at one end of the main bearings.

The crankshaft has main journals that are machined and polished to fit into the block's main bearings. Offset from the crankshaft centerline are the rod journals, also called throws. They are essentially the levers of the crankshaft. The longer the throw of the crankshaft, the longer the stroke of the piston and the more torque that can be produced from the engine. The rod journals are also machined and polished. As the crankshaft turns, the rod journals' "big ends" circle around the centerline of the crankshaft. To prevent vibration, counterweights are formed on the crankshaft. The counterweights balance the weight of the piston assembly, connecting rods, and rod journals. At the front of the crankshaft is a "snout" that provides a mount for a vibration damper (harmonic balancer) and drive gears, sprockets, or pulleys. The back of the crankshaft has a flange where the flywheel is connected by bolts or studs. A **flywheel** is a weighted assembly that stores kinetic energy from each power stroke and helps keep the crankshaft turning through nonpower strokes. Vehicles with manual transmissions have a clutch assembly attached to the flywheel. Vehicles with automatic transmissions use a flex plate and torque converter assembly. The effect on the crankshaft is the same with either assembly—that of storing energy and keeping the crankshaft rotating smoothly.

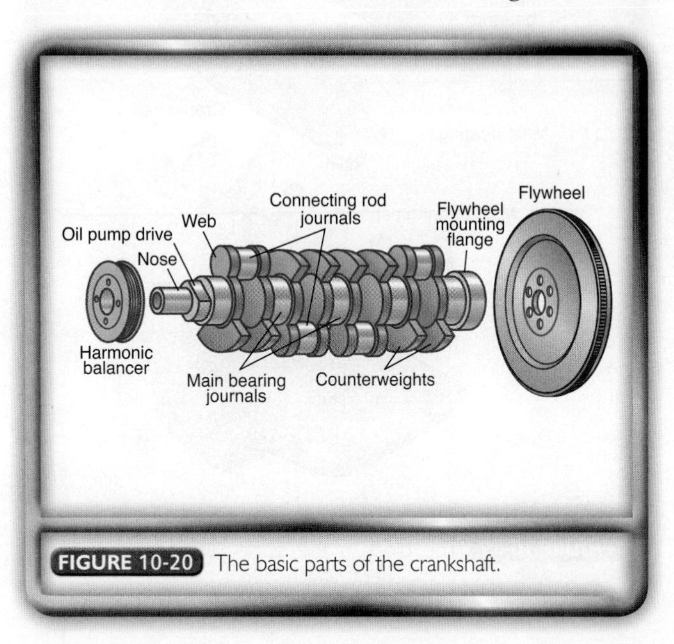
Connecting rod journals
Web
Oil pump drive
Nose
Flywheel
Flywheel mounting flange
Harmonic balancer
Main bearing journals
Counterweights

FIGURE 10-20 The basic parts of the crankshaft.

Connecting Rod and Piston

A connecting rod is made of cast iron or steel in most engines, although some race cars and exotic sports cars use aluminum or titanium connecting rods to make the engine rev quicker and higher, producing more power. The connecting rod connects the piston to the crankshaft and transfers piston movement and combustion pressure to the crankshaft rod journals. The piston end (small end) of the connecting rod follows the reciprocal movement of the piston, pivoting on a piston pin or "wrist pin" attachment. The wrist pin attaches the piston to the connecting rod and fits into a one-piece bushing in the small end of the rod. The other end (large end) of the connecting rod attaches to the crankshaft throw or rod journal through the use of a removable rod cap that bolts to the end of the connecting rod body. The connecting rod and cap are machined to allow the fit of the connecting rod bearing.

The connecting rod causes piston movement during the intake, compression, and exhaust strokes, which are nonpower strokes. The connecting rod needs to be strong for its size to prevent twisting or bending under the pressure of compression and combustion. A cross section of the connecting rod would reveal an I-beam shape; this shape provides for high strength and light weight. The connecting rod receives lubricating oil from the crankshaft to lubricate the wrist pin, either by spraying oil from a hole in the connecting rod or by carrying it through a hole drilled in the connecting rod to the small wrist pin journal.

The piston is typically made of lightweight aluminum and possibly synthetic material and transfers combustion pressures to the crankshaft through the connecting rod. Pistons change direction multiple times a second **FIGURE 10-21**. Consider that with an engine idling at 750 rpm, the piston changes direction 25 times each second. We can imagine that piston movement would

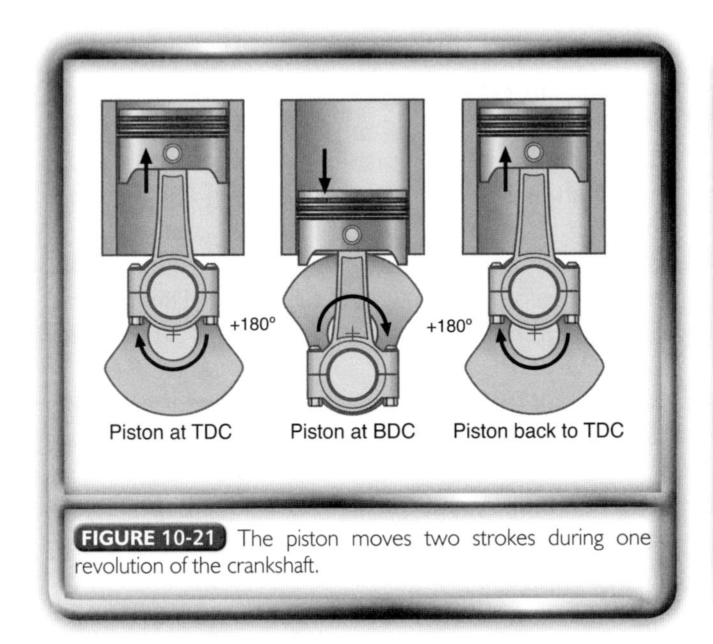
+180°
+180°
Piston at TDC
Piston at BDC
Piston back to TDC

FIGURE 10-21 The piston moves two strokes during one revolution of the crankshaft.

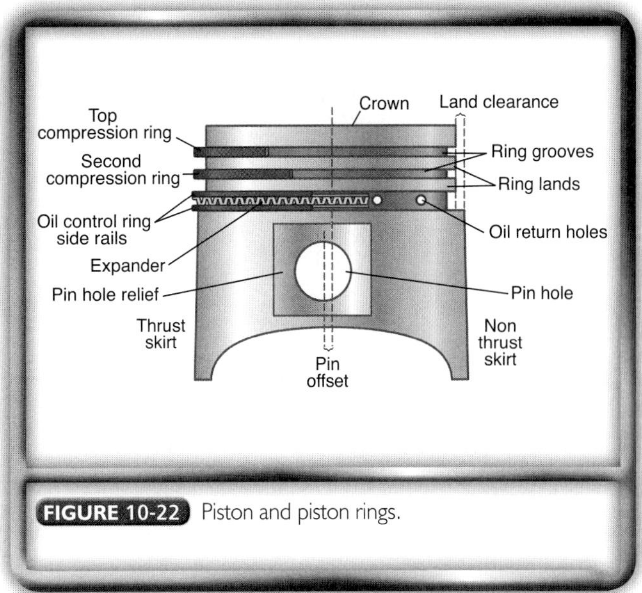
Top compression ring
Second compression ring
Oil control ring side rails
Expander
Pin hole relief
Thrust skirt
Crown
Land clearance
Ring grooves
Ring lands
Oil return holes
Pin hole
Non thrust skirt
Pin offset

FIGURE 10-22 Piston and piston rings.

be hard to see even at idle, but at a redline (maximum allowed) speed of 6000 rpm, can you imagine the stress placed on engine parts as each piston comes to a stop at TDC and at BDC of each stroke? At 6000 rpm, the pistons and rods change direction 200 times per second. What's more, a 12,000-rpm redline sports car or motorcycle engine would experience *400* piston reversals per second!

The top of the piston, called the piston head, is exposed to extremes of heat and pressure during combustion. Below the piston head are grooves machined into the piston that hold circular piston sealing rings. The piston rings provide a seal between the outside of the piston and the inside of the cylinder wall as the piston moves in its stroke FIGURE 10-22. Usually, a total of three rings are used. The upper two rings are compression rings, which prevent combustion pressure, called **blowby gas**, from leaking past the pistons into the crankcase. The lower piston ring is an oil control ring that keeps lubricating oil on the cylinder wall and out of the combustion chamber. The oil control ring is typically two thin rings with an expander that keeps the rings expanded outward against the cylinder wall. The lower ring groove has oil holes that allow collected oil to flow through the side of the piston and drain back to the crankcase.

The **ring lands** are the areas between the ring grooves that support the rings as the piston moves. The side of the piston below the ring groove area is called the **piston skirt**. The piston skirt prevents the piston from rocking and jamming in the cylinder bore. The piston body has a piston pinhole machined through a reinforced area called the **piston pin boss**. This area is reinforced to withstand the load of combustion pressure. The space between the sides of the piston and the cylinder wall is called **piston clearance**. This clearance allows for oil lubrication between the piston and the cylinder wall to reduce friction. The clearance also allows for piston expansion due to the heat of combustion.

Pistons are made of aluminum alloy for weight savings. An **alloy** is a combination of materials that has properties that are different from the original materials. Aluminum by itself is too soft and expands too rapidly to stand up to the heat and pressure of combustion. If aluminum is mixed with other materials, such as silicon, aluminum alloys are produced that are strong and lightweight and that can withstand the heat and pressures of combustion and resist expansion. If expansion can be kept low, then the piston clearance can be tighter, helping to reduce blowby.

Pistons can come in many styles of crowns, such as dished, domed, or flat top, depending on the compression ratio desired by the engine designer. Manufacturers today are using ceramic coatings on the pistons to provide better lubrication qualities and reduced heat absorption.

The Oil Pan

The oil pan seals off the bottom of the crankcase and holds oil for the engine lubrication system FIGURE 10-23. It radiates oil heat to the outside ambient air and may include cooling fins (heat sinks) to effectively transfer heat to the airstream flowing below the vehicle. The oil pan bolts onto the bottom of the engine block and has undergone many changes since the first engine design. The oil pan was originally designed as part of the engine block in cast iron but was later changed to lighter stamped steel. Most are now designed of lightweight aluminum or thermoplastic. The oil pan has become more of a structural part of the engine and helps to reinforce the engine block.

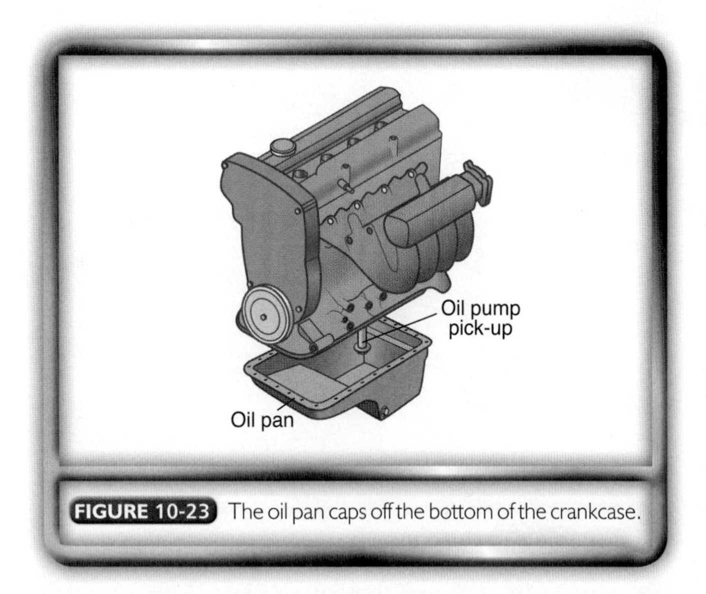
Oil pump
pick-up
Oil pan

FIGURE 10-23 The oil pan caps off the bottom of the crankcase.

On many engines, the oil pan houses the oil pump, which is the heart of the engine in that it supplies critical lubrication and cooling for the internal moving parts of the engine. In some engines, the oil pump is located on the front of the block surrounding the crankshaft. The oil pump is typically driven by either the crankshaft or the camshaft, so it supplies oil to the engine components whenever the engine is running. The screened oil pump pickup lies near the bottom of the oil pan and is used to screen out any larger particles that may contaminate the oil.

The Cylinder Head

The cylinder head is constructed of cast iron or aluminum. Most engines are now constructed using an aluminum cylinder head, which reduces the weight of the engine. The cylinder head contains the valves and valve train (valve actuating components) of the engine. The head also includes intake and exhaust ports to which intake and exhaust manifolds are attached. The head forms the top of the cylinder and is sealed in place with the use of a head gasket. The cylinder head has a combustion chamber either cast or machined into it. Combustion chambers in the cylinder head come in several different designs, such as the wedge or the hemispherical combustion chamber, a variation that is used in most engines now FIGURE 10-24.

Engine Cam and Camshaft

The ICE uses so-called "poppet" valves. These are somewhat mushroom-shaped parts that slide up and down in the valve guides. When not actuated (closed), the valves, under pressure from the valve springs, rest on seats of hardened material such as Stellite. Valves need a system to make them open and close. Control of the valves is accomplished through the use of cams on a common shaft. A **cam** is an egg-shaped piece (lobe) mounted on the **camshaft** FIGURE 10-25. The egg shape of the cam lobe is designed to lift the valve open, hold it open, and let it close. The camshaft is timed to the rotation of the crankshaft to ensure that the valves open at the correct position of the piston. Timing the valve opening to the piston position is critical to ensure proper power output and low-emissions operation of the engine. The camshaft is turned either by gears, a toothed belt, or a chain that is driven by sprockets.

Up until the 1950s, many engines had their valves installed in the engine block. Such engines are called **flat-head engines**. Some manufacturers still place the camshaft in the center of the block, but the valves are installed in the cylinder head(s). So-called **cam-in-block engines** use **pushrods** to transfer the camshaft's lifting motion to the valves by way of **rocker arms** on top of the cylinder head. **Tappets**, or "lifters," ride on the camshaft **lobes** to actuate the pushrods, rocker arms, and valves.

FIGURE 10-24 Combustion chambers can be designed in several configurations (wedge combustion chamber shown).

FIGURE 10-25 Cam lobes on a camshaft.

In most automotive engines today, however, the camshaft is mounted on top of the cylinder head. These engines are called overhead cam (OHC) engines FIGURE 10-26. Intake and exhaust valves may all be actuated by a single camshaft, or there may be two camshafts per head, called dual overhead cam (DOHC) engines. One camshaft may be used to actuate all of the intake valves and another to actuate all of the exhaust valves. When separate intake and exhaust camshafts are used, there is no need for rocker arms. Most manufacturers use a lifter called a "bucket lifter" placed right on top of the valve and valve spring to actuate the valve directly from the camshaft.

Camshaft lobes are designed, as described previously, to open the valve, hold it, and allow it to close. The opening, holding, and closing of the valves are critical to ensure that the engine operates correctly. In designing the cam lobe, engineers seek a proper compromise for the application of the engine. If the engine is designed to operate at one engine rpm, then the camshaft can be designed to provide optimal power, economy, and emissions. Automotive engines do not operate at one rpm, however, so a camshaft must be designed to provide the best balance of all requirements. High-performance engines built for racing use camshafts designed for high rpm power but would not work well for use on the street where engines rarely stay above 3000 rpm. Newer engine designs have overcome some of these limitations by using variable valve timing, which is discussed further in the Cylinder Head Components chapter.

FIGURE 10-26 **A.** Cam-in-block engine. **B.** Overhead cam (OHC) engine.

Camshaft Specifications

The base circle of the cam lobe is the rounded bottom part of the egg shape; this is where the lifters rest when the valves are closed FIGURE 10-27. The shape of the camshaft lobes themselves affects the power range of the engine. One specification of the cam lobe is the lift of the cam lobe. Lift is the amount the valve train moves with the cam. The more the valve is lifted off its seat, the more air that can enter the engine. However, more lift creates more pressure on the valve train components due to pushing the valve further and compressing the valve spring further. Too much lift can create coil bind in the valve springs. Coil bind occurs when the coils of the spring touch each other. This will cause the spring or the camshaft and lifter to wear or break. Another problem with too much valve lift is too little valve-to-piston clearance. Too much valve lift can cause the valve to hit the piston and ruin the engine.

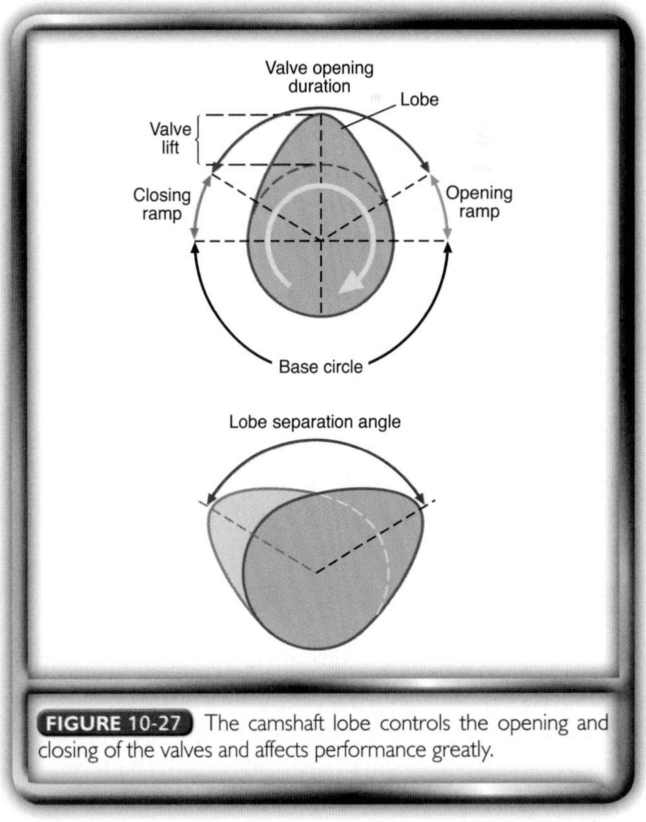

Valve opening duration
Lobe
Valve lift
Closing ramp
Opening ramp
Base circle
Lobe separation angle

FIGURE 10-27 The camshaft lobe controls the opening and closing of the valves and affects performance greatly.

Valve duration is another specification engineers use when designing a cam lobe. Duration is the amount of time the valve stays open, given in degrees of *crankshaft* rotation (not camshaft rotation). The longer the valve is kept open, the more air will be able to move into and out of the engine. **Cam lobe centerline** is where the cam lobe is located in relation to TDC of the engine in degrees. Changing the mechanical timing of the engine can change this setting. Cam centerline and duration can be used to determine when the valves will open in degrees of crankshaft rotation. **Cam lobe separation** is the number of degrees between the centerline of the intake lobe and the centerline of the exhaust lobe; it determines the amount of valve overlap. The smaller the number of degrees of lobe separation, the more valve overlap there is. Valve overlap simply means that the intake and exhaust valves are open at the same time. The **cam lobe ramp** is where the rise of the cam lobe starts from the base circle to the top of the lobe. The ramp is where the valve starts to lift and is on the opposite side from where it starts to close. The degree of rotation the valve remains open and the degree of cam lobe separation are specifications measured in camshaft degrees, not in crankshaft degrees. Valve lift, duration, and overlap are features determined by the grind (profile) of the camshaft.

High-performance engines have more degrees of valve overlap than street engines because of longer cam duration. Increased valve overlap and lift increase top-end rpm power due to **column inertia** (ram effect) but reduce low-speed power and idle quality, again due to a loss of column inertia. Valve overlap specifications will not be given if you have a DOHC engine since the exhaust and intake lobes run on separate shafts. So-called street cams, three-quarter race, and full race cams have progressively more lift and duration, all tailored to meet the operating conditions of the engine. For street engines, too much lift or duration may not be beneficial because the lower intake manifold vacuum caused be greater valve overlap will cause the engine to idle roughly.

When comparing cam specifications, it is important to know that there are two listings for specifications: advertised specifications and specifications at 0.050″ lift FIGURE 10-28. Advertised specifications measure the duration from where the valve first starts to open. Specifications at 0.050″ lift measure the duration starting when the valve hits 0.050″ and ending when it returns to 0.050″. The advertised lift is a better indicator of the camshaft's profile, and how it will affect the operation of the engine.

Specifications for a 2000- to 5000-rpm street camshaft:

	Intake		Exhaust
Lift	0.440		0.440
Duration at 0.050″	222°		222°
Cam lobe centerline	109° atdc		116° btdc
Lobe separation angle (camshaft degrees)		113° between lobe Centerlines	
Degree valve opens at 0.050″	2° btdc		48° bbdc
Degree valve closes at 0.050″	40° abdc		–6° atdc

Specifications for the same camshaft to be used up to 6500 rpm:

	Intake		Exhaust
Lift	0.500		0.515
Duration at 0.050″	256°		270°
Cam lobe centerline	108° atdc		116° btdc
Lobe separation angle (camshaft degrees)		112° between lobe Centerlines	
Degree valve opens at 0.050″	20° btdc		71° bbdc
Degree valve closes at 0.050″	56° abdc		19° atdc

FIGURE 10-28 An aftermarket performance camshaft will include a specifications card that is used during engine assembly to ensure correct timing. The top chart shows the specifications of a street camshaft and the bottom chart a higher performance camshaft. Notice the differences in valve lift and duration.

Valves

A valve is used to open and close a port in a cylinder head. The intake controls the flow of air and/or fuel into the combustion chamber. The exhaust valve controls the flow of exhaust gases out of the combustion chamber and cylinder. The exposed intake port area usually must be larger than the exhaust port area to make it easier for the piston to pull air into the engine on the intake stroke. Engine vacuum created by the piston on the intake stroke is not as effective at moving air into the engine as the pressure created by the piston on the exhaust stroke is at pushing exhaust gases from the engine. The exposed port area can be increased by making the intake valve larger than the exhaust valve, or the manufacturer can use multiple intake valves. In the case of a three-valve engine, there would be two intake valves and one exhaust valve, but the intake valves would be smaller than the exhaust valve in this case.

The valve head is disc shaped, and the top of the valve head faces the combustion chamber. A machined surface on the back of the valve head is the **valve face** FIGURE 10-29. The valve face seals on a hardened valve seat in the cylinder head. Located between the valve head and the valve face is a flat surface on the outer edge of the valve head called the **valve margin**. The margin helps to prevent the valve head from melting under the heat and pressure of combustion. A shaft attached to the valve head is the **valve stem**. The stem operates in a **valve guide** in the cylinder head. The valve stem and guide work together to maintain valve alignment as the valve slides open and closed. The opposite end of the stem has grooves machined into its end to receive locking pieces, sometimes referred to as valve **keepers**, that retain a valve spring retainer and spring on the valve. Keepers hold the retainer, preventing it from coming loose while under tension from the valve spring, and preventing the parts from coming loose under normal use. Engines may have two to five valves per cylinder.

Intake and Exhaust Valves

Intake and exhaust valves, in conjunction with the camshaft(s), are the controlling mechanism of the ICE. If the valves do not open and seal at the proper times, combustion will be irregular, weak, or nonexistent. The valves are an incredibly important part of the four-stroke ICE. The intake valve tends to run much cooler than the exhaust since it is always passing cool air and fuel past it when it lifts off its seat. The exhaust valve, in contrast, runs very hot since when it lifts off its seat it is surrounded by extremely hot exhaust gases. Because the exhaust valve runs hotter than the intake valve, some manufacturers use sodium-filled valves, which transfer heat away from the head of the valve more quickly. The valve face may also be coated in a material called Stellite, which is a mixture of chromium and cobalt that can hold up to higher heat. The problem with getting the exhaust valve too hot is that it can either melt or it will deform the sealing surface of the face as it slams closed. The need for new, stronger materials will persist as engines are pushed for maximum power and minimum fuel consumption.

Mechanical and Hydraulic Valve Train

The valve train is the combination of parts that work together to open and close the valves of the engine. The valve train operates off of the camshaft, and the part that rides against the cam lobe is the **valve lifter**. The lifter transfers motion from the cam lobe to a pushrod, or may directly act on the valve and spring, depending on if the cam is in the engine block or on the cylinder head. The valve lifter works as a mechanical spacer, providing a hardened bearing surface that slides across the cam lobe. If the lifter is a mechanically solid piece, it is said to be a mechanical lifter, and therefore the engine is said to have a mechanical valve train. If the lifter has a hydraulic plunger in its center, it is a hydraulic lifter, and the engine is said to have a hydraulic valve train. The hydraulic plunger allows for the expansion and contraction of components during engine warm-up and cool down.

With a hydraulic valve train, valve adjustment is made by the hydraulic lifter, which takes up any clearance automatically. If a mechanical valve train is used, valve adjustments will be necessary at periodic intervals to ensure proper clearance is maintained as parts in the valve train wear.

Valve Clearance

Valve clearance is the amount of slack between the rocker arm or cam follower and the valve stem, or the cam and the lifter if it is a bucket-style OHC engine **FIGURE 10-30**. If valve clearance is too large, the valves will tick and

FIGURE 10-29 The parts of a valve.

FIGURE 10-30 Valve adjustments. **A.** Rocker arm screw and locknut. **B.** Rocker arm center bolt.

make enough noise to irritate the operator and increase wear of the valve train. If valve clearance is too small, the valve can be held open longer than it should be. As the cylinder head and valve train parts heat, they expand, so adequate clearance is needed to allow for this expansion. Insufficient valve clearance could result in burned valves. Some valves are adjustable through the use of adjusting screws, nuts, or metal shims. Other valves are nonadjustable and the rocker arm simply bolts to the head, or the valve lifter is a preset dimension before it is installed under the camshaft if it is a bucket setup. Bucket lifters contain solid metal discs (shims) of different thicknesses. These shims are used to preset the proper valve clearance during cylinder head assembly or during a major tune-up.

Valve Train Drives

The valve train is driven by the camshaft, which in turn is driven by a chain or belt (depending on the engine design) driven by the crankshaft **FIGURE 10-31**. In older engine designs, the camshaft was driven by a gear-to-gear arrangement like that found in small lawnmower engines. The trouble with a gear-to-gear design is that it tends to be a bit noisy compared to a chain or belt and the camshaft needs to be relatively close to the crankshaft. In any four-cycle engine design, the camshaft must rotate at half of crankshaft speed. This may be accomplished by using a camshaft gear or pulley that has twice the number of teeth as the crankshaft gear. The ratio of the crank to cam gear is 2:1; thus it takes two turns of the crankshaft to turn the camshaft one turn.

FIGURE 10-31 Cam drives. **A.** Belt-driven OHC. **B.** Chain-driven OHC.

The timing chain drive is louder than a belt, but the belt will not last as long as the timing chain and if exposed to fluids or dirt will wear out more quickly. The timing chain must have a constant supply of engine oil to lubricate the chain to keep it from wearing out quickly. Timing gears rarely jump time, but if the timing chain or belt breaks, serious engine damage could result, depending on if it is a freewheeling engine or an interference engine. A freewheeling engine will not be damaged, but in an interference engine, the valves will be tap-dancing on the piston crowns, bending the valves, with the valves possibly punching holes in the pistons.

The **freewheeling engine** has enough clearance between the pistons and the valves so that in the event the timing belt breaks any valve that is hanging all the way open will not contact the piston, thus preventing engine damage. A broken timing belt will be an inconvenience to the customer. The engine dies and will not restart; the good news is that no mechanical engine damage occurs. By contrast, the **interference engine** has minimal clearance between the valves and pistons during normal operation. When the timing belt breaks, the pistons keep moving and hit the remaining open valves. A broken timing belt on an interference engine means a huge repair expense and in some cases the entire engine will need to be replaced. The manufacturer's service information will normally tell you if the engine is an interference engine.

The timing chain camshaft drive used in a cam-in-block engine is very different from that used in the OHC engine. The pushrod engine typically uses a chain behind a timing chain cover located on the front of the engine. This type of timing chain is fairly short since the camshaft is close to the crankshaft. Some pushrod engines use a timing chain tensioner to ensure that the correct timing chain tension is maintained; however, most designs do not use a tensioner. The timing chain tensioner applies pressure against the chain; as the chain wears and gets longer, the tensioner takes up play in the chain. As the timing chain stretches, cam timing may become retarded. Slack of the chain affects the positioning of the cam gear in relation to the crank gear. Retarded cam timing in this case can create undesirable engine performance problems.

The OHC engine requires a longer timing chain or belt, and in this design one or more tensioners are required. The timing chain in an OHC engine typically has hard plastic-type guides for the chain to slide on and assist the tensioner(s) with correct tracking and tension of the timing chain. The OHC timing chain must run in oil to ensure that the chain is lubricated. Without oil the chain would wear out rapidly.

A belt system uses a toothed or cogged belt to turn toothed or cogged pulleys on the camshaft. The belt is a scheduled maintenance replacement item and needs to be replaced at the mileage or time recommended by the manufacturer (e.g., 60,000 miles [100,000 kilometers] or 5 years, whichever occurs first).

Intake Manifold

The intake manifold is part of the air intake (induction) system of the engine package. It sits between the throttle body and the cylinder head(s). On a V-type engine, it usually is located between the cylinder heads. For an inline engine, it bolts to the side of the head. Intake manifolds deliver air (air with fuel on carbureted or throttle body–injected engines) to the cylinder head.

Intake manifold designs have seen many changes since the first engines. Once rectangular and boxy in shape, they are now sleek. The materials from which they are made has also changed. Intake manifolds were first manufactured in cast iron, and later in lightweight aluminum. Now, most manufacturers are using even lighter thermoplastic materials for intake manifolds. Lighter engines usually equate to better fuel economy, so manufacturers are always looking for new lighter materials to make their vehicles more fuel efficient. How smooth the inside of the intake manifold is, its inside diameter, and its length all affect how an intake manifold will contribute to engine performance. Some sportier vehicles use variable-length "tuned" intake runners, which switch between a shorter or longer path for the air to flow, depending on engine rpm. Intake manifold design can greatly affect engine performance; this topic is discussed further in the Induction and Exhaust chapter.

Exhaust Manifold

The exhaust manifold is the output side of the engine's breathing apparatus. With a crossflow head, the exhaust manifold bolts to the cylinder head across from the intake manifold and is designed to carry exhaust gases out of the engine and deliver them to the exhaust system. As with intake manifolds, exhaust manifold design can have a great impact on the performance of the engine due to scavenging. So-called "tuned headers," for example, direct exhaust gases from each individual cylinder using equal-length tubes (runners) to scavenge (extract) the exhaust from neighboring cylinders.

> **LINK**
> Refer to the Induction and Exhaust chapter for more information about the exhaust system.

Two-Stroke Spark-Ignition Engines

Two-stroke engines are notable in their ability to produce a large power to weight ratio. The power capabilities of this engine come from the fact that every other stroke (TDC to BDC) is a power stroke. However, there are drawbacks to this engine design—namely that it is a high-emissions engine. Almost all car manufacturers have moved away from two-stroke production.

The two-stroke SI engine is different from the four-stroke SI engine. In a two-stroke engine, the inlet and exhaust ports are opened and closed by the movement of the piston; there are no poppet valves like those used in the four-stroke cycle engine. The two-stroke engine is still an ICE and shares the five events common to all SI engines. What is different is the method of air induction and scavenging used:

- *Intake* occurs in two parts. First, the air–fuel mixture is drawn into the crankcase as the piston moves up. It is then transferred from the crankcase to above the piston when the piston moves down.
- During *compression*, the mixture is forced into a small volume as the piston moves up.
- During *ignition*, the spark from the spark plug ignites the mixture and it burns.
- During the *power stroke*, energy released by combustion generates the force that pushes the piston down and turns the crankshaft.
- During *exhaust*, leftover gases are expelled from the cylinder when the piston is near BDC.

As in all ICEs, expanding gases drive the piston down and turn the crankshaft and flywheel, which pushes the piston back up to TDC in the cylinder.

With the two-stroke cycle engine, the crankshaft makes one revolution (two strokes) for every complete cycle. In one revolution of the crankshaft, two piston strokes occur: one down and one up. Each downward stroke of the piston is a power stroke and turns the crankshaft.

The two-stroke cycle engine differs from the four-stroke cycle engine because the upward piston movement creates suction in the crankcase to pull the air–fuel mixture into it as the piston moves from BDC to TDC. The air and fuel sit in the crankcase until the piston begins to move down, which then creates a small pressure in the crankcase, referred to as crankcase compression. As the piston moves downward with the power stroke, it uncovers a transfer port and the fuel and air rush into the cylinder from the crankcase FIGURE 10-32.

The piston begins moving up toward TDC, creating another draw of air and fuel into the crankcase. The air and fuel above the piston get squeezed in the combustion chamber and the spark plug ignites the mixture. As the piston moves down, it also uncovers the exhaust port, and exhaust gases exit the exhaust system. As the piston moves farther down, it uncovers the transfer port again, and crankcase compression pushes the air and fuel into the cylinder once again.

To summarize, with upward movement of the piston, compression of the air–fuel mixture is happening in the cylinder above the piston, and intake of new air and fuel is happening in the crankcase below the piston. When the piston moves down, power is being applied to the crankshaft, exhaust is happening, and crankcase compression is building to push air and fuel through the transfer port into the cylinder. The placement of the ports makes all these processes possible and eliminates the use of valves to let fuel and air in and exhaust out.

Rotary Combustion Spark-Ignition Engine

As we have seen from the two-stroke engine, the fewer parts that are used, the better the power production and the smaller the engine can be. The rotary engine fits into the same category of using fewer parts to produce power. The rotary combustion (RC) engine has found its way into automobiles, planes, helicopters, boats,

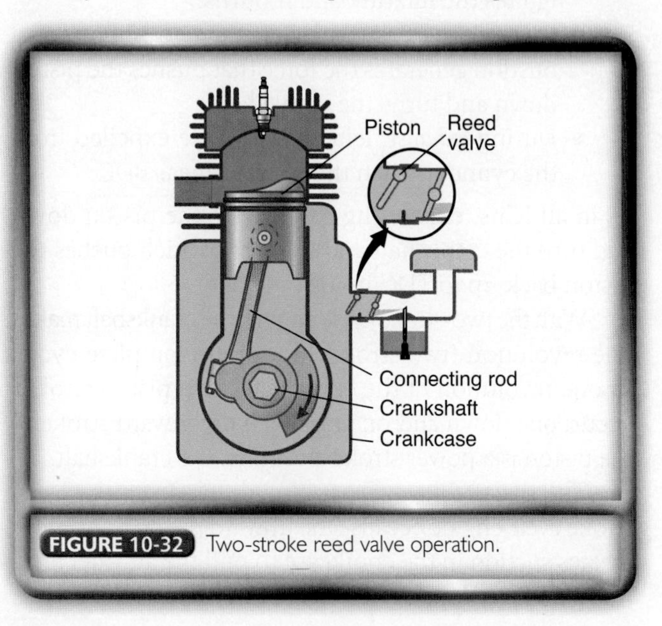
Piston
Reed valve
Connecting rod
Crankshaft
Crankcase

FIGURE 10-32 Two-stroke reed valve operation.

motorcycles, lawn mowers, and other applications. Displacement has varied from tiny air-cooled models to much larger liquid-cooled, multirotor units.

The rotary engine is also called the "Wankle" engine because it was improved upon by Felix Wankle for automotive use in the 1940s. The RC engine was commercially released in 1964 in the NSU Wankel Spider and in 1967 with a two-rotor engine in the NSU RO80. Under license from NSU, Mazda successfully used the rotary engine in several vehicles from the late 1960s all the way through the RX series. The engines were a redefining period for engine development, but were never really a success for a number of other companies.

Althogh rotary engine (aka, Wankle engine) is not as common as the four-stroke or two-stroke cycle engines, its basic principle is well accepted. The rotary engine layout is vastly different from that of a reciprocating engine. The piston engine is called a reciprocating engine because the pistons move back and forth over the same path. This reciprocating motion is converted to rotary motion at the crankshaft.

By contrast, a rotary engine does not use a piston that reciprocates; rather, it has a rotor that—you guessed it—rotates. The rotary engine does not need to convert inefficient reciprocating motion to rotary motion since the rotor functions as the piston in the engine. In the reciprocating engine, the piston assembly must stop at BDC and move back up to TDC, then back down to BDC, and so on, many times a second. The stopping and starting of the piston assembly puts tremendous pressure on the connecting rod and rod bolts. Due to inertia, the piston tries to move out of the top of the cylinder bore and through the bottom of the oil pan. The rotary engine does not have to stop–start its "piston" as it rotates. The rotor is roughly triangular in shape and turns inside of a housing. The housing works on a geometric principle called an epitrochoid curve. An **epitrochoid curve** is the circular movement around the perimeter of another circle. The rotor moves in a unique pattern to ensure that the rotor ends follow the oblong shape of the housing FIGURE 10-33.

Because the rotor spins, rather than moving up and down, engine operation is relatively smooth and vibration free. Each rotor and housing is akin to that of a three-cylinder two-stroke engine because of the rotor's three-sided shape. The rotor has three working chambers; thus, for each rotation of the rotor, we get three power pulses. Low-end torque is improved to the point that (while not recommended) a four-speed transmission rotary vehicle can be driven and accelerated from a standstill in fourth gear without excessive lugging. Rotary engines can be made with one, two, or even three or more rotor housings stacked side to side.

FIGURE 10-33 Cutaway of a rotary engine.

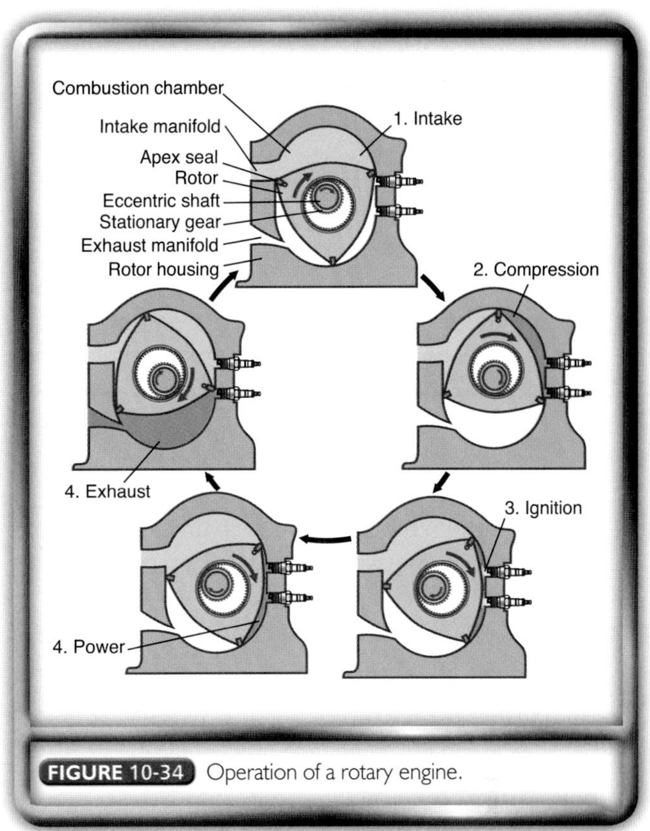
Combustion chamber
Intake manifold
Apex seal
Rotor
Eccentric shaft
Stationary gear
Exhaust manifold
Rotor housing
1. Intake
2. Compression
3. Ignition
4. Power
4. Exhaust

FIGURE 10-34 Operation of a rotary engine.

Let's look at the basic principles of a rotary engine. While it appears different, the rotary engine is still an ICE. Recall the five events common to all ICEs: intake, compression, ignition, power, and exhaust.

The rotary engine's intake cycle occurs when one face of the rotor passes the intake port and draws the air/fuel mixture into the working chamber through the inlet port FIGURE 10-34. The turning rotor then carries it around to the spark plugs. Along the way, the volume of the working chamber decreases and compresses the mixture. The mixture is ignited and combustion occurs. Expanding gases produce a power pulse, driving the rotor farther around. When the exhaust port is uncovered, exhaust occurs as the rotor sweeps burned gases out of the housing. Each face of the rotor is a separate working chamber, so three combustion events occur for each single revolution of the rotor.

Wrap-up

Ready for Review

- Most modern vehicles use internal combustion engines.
- Internal combustion engines are typically either piston (spark ignition, using reciprocating motion of pistons) or rotary (spark ignition, using planetary motion).
- Piston engines can be spark ignition (passenger vehicles; uses a spark plug) or compression ignition (diesel vehicles; no spark plug).
- Pressure and temperature have a direct relationship in that when pressure rises so does temperature, and vice versa.
- Internal combustion engines work by heating a gas, which increases pressure (thermal expansion), creating force to push the piston down the cylinder.
- Pressure and volume have an inverse relationship: when one increases, the other decreases.
- Force (effort) tends to cause movement, which creates work; the speed at which this happens is known as power.
- Work = distance moved × force applied.
- Power = distance × force / time in minutes.
- Engine power is measured by the amount of torque (turning effort) applied to the crankshaft, times the RPM at which it is turning divided by 5252.
- Torque and power produced by an engine are called engine output.
- Horsepower refers to the speed at which torque is produced.
- Load factor refers to the period of time a vehicle can operate at maximum speed and power.
- Piston stroke refers to the distance traveled from top dead center (TDC) to bottom dead center (BDC) (or BDC to TDC).
- Internal combustion engines have either a two-stroke or four-stroke cycle.
- In a four-stroke cycle, five events must occur: intake, compression, ignition, power, and exhaust.
- The compression ratio of an engine is based on cylinder volume at BDC compared to cylinder volume at TDC, and can be affected by changes in piston stroke, piston head shape, head gasket thickness, and combustion chamber size.
- Piston displacement (the volume of movement from BDC to TCD) is calculated as: bore squared × 3.14 × stroke / 4.
- Engine displacement is calculated as piston displacement × number of engine cylinders.
- Two variations on the typical four-stroke spark ignition engine are the Miller cycle engine and the Atkinson cycle engine, both of which use valve timing variations to create unequal compression and expansion strokes.
- The Miller cycle engine has an engine-driven compressor that functions at high load and speed to boost power output.
- The Atkinson cycle engine is ideal for hybrid vehicles, as it has a lower power output and torque than conventional engines.
- Valve overlap refers to the short time that both intake and exhaust valves are open, allowing more air and fuel into the engine during high power high rpm.
- Major components of an internal combustion engine include: cylinder block, crankshaft, flywheel, connecting rod and piston, intake manifold, oil pan, oil pump, exhaust manifold, cylinder head, valve train, and engine camshaft.
- The cylinder block, the largest engine component, includes cylinder bores, coolant and lubrication passages, and the crankcase.
- The function of the crankshaft is to convert the piston's reciprocating motion into rotary (turning) motion.
- The flywheel stores energy from each piston's power stroke to smooth out the power strokes.
- The connecting rod connects the piston to the crankshaft and causes piston movement (via the crankshaft) during non-power strokes.
- Components that make up and support the piston are: piston head, piston rings (compression and oil control), ring grooves, ring lands, piston skirt, pin hole, and pin boss.
- Compression and combustion gases can leak past piston rings and enter the crankcase; this is known as blowby.
- The purpose of an intake manifold is to deliver air or air and fuel to the cylinder head.
- Oil for the engine lubrication system is stored in the oil pan.
- The camshaft opens the valves and allows them to close at the right time, which ensures correct engine operation.
- Parts of the camshaft lobe include: base circle, nose, cam lobe centerline, and cam lobe ramps.
- Engineers designing camshaft lobes must consider the issues of lift and duration, as well as the cam centerline and separation.

- Parts of an intake valve include: head, face, margin, and stem.
- The intake valve is typically larger and tends to run cooler than the exhaust valve.
- Exhaust valves are typically smaller, allow exhaust to exit the cylinder, and tends to be run hotter than intake valves.
- Valve clearance must be accurate, so as not to create noise (meaning clearance is too high) or a loss of compression past the valve (clearance is too low).
- The engine control module (ECM) controls variable cam timing using the following inputs: mass airflow sensor or manifold absolute pressure sensor, throttle position sensor, intake air temperature sensor, engine coolant temperature sensor, and crankshaft position sensor.
- Engine design—freewheeling or interference—determines the amount of damage that will result if the timing belt breaks.
- Two-stroke engines use the piston to open and close intake and exhaust ports allowing air-fuel to enter the cylinder.
- All events of an internal combustion engine are accomplished by a two-stroke engine within one up and one down stroke of the piston.
- Rotary, or Wankel, engines use a rotor in place of a piston and move it in an epitrochoid curve to create a nearly vibration-free engine operation.
- Rotary engines have two spark plugs—leading and trailing—per rotor to enable complete combustion.
- The rotor moves along the curved surface of its housing and pushes on an eccentric shaft to produce power.
- A rotary engine cycle has four phases: intake, compression, power, and exhaust.
- Each of the three faces of the rotor act as a combustion chamber, and have a power pulse every revolution of the rotor.

Key Terms

after top dead center (ATDC) The position of the piston once it has moved beyond top dead center.

alloy The mixture of materials to make a substance that has properties different from the original materials. Aluminum alloy has silica added to make it perform better than pure aluminum.

Atkinson cycle An engine cycle that uses a longer effective exhaust stroke than intake stroke to reduce exhaust emissions. This type of engine is widely used in hybrid-electric vehicles.

base circle The rounded bottom part of the camshaft (off the lobe) where the valves remain closed or at rest.

block deck The "top" of the engine block and cylinder bore where the cylinder head is bolted on.

before top dead center (BTDC) The position of the piston when it has not yet reached top dead center.

blowby gas The result of combustion gases leaking past the compression rings and getting into the crankcase.

bottom dead center (BDC) The position of the piston at the end of its stroke when it is closest to the crankshaft.

cam The egg-shaped lobe machined to a shaft used to cause opening and closing of the valves of a four-stroke cycle engine.

cam-in-block engine An engine in which the camshaft is located in the engine block rather than on the cylinder head.

cam lobe centerline The location of the cam lobe in relation to top dead center of the engine in degrees.

cam lobe ramp The rise of the lobe from the base circle to the top of the lobe, which is where the valve starts to lift, on the side opposite of where it starts to close.

cam lobe separation The number of degrees between the centerline of the intake lobe and the centerline of the exhaust lobe; this with cam duration determines the amount of valve overlap.

camshaft The part of the engine that activates the valve train by using lobes riding against lifters.

coil bind A result of excessive valve lift. When the coils of the spring touch each other, the spring breaks, flattening the cam lobe and bending the pushrod.

column inertia The principle that as a column of air flows, it creates inertia, which keeps air flowing until its inertia energy is spent; sometimes referred to as a "ram effect" when using tuned intake or exhaust systems.

compression-ignition (CI) engine An internal combustion engine that uses the heat of compression to ignite the compressed air-fuel mixture.

compression ratio (CR) The volume of the cylinder with the piston at bottom dead center as compared to the volume of the cylinder at top dead center, given in a ratio such as 9:1 CR.

compression stroke The stroke of the piston during which air and fuel is being compressed into a small area prior to ignition.

cylinder bore The hole in the engine block that the piston fits into.

dual overhead cam (DOHC) A design that, in a V-engine, includes four cams; also called a twin cam engine.

duration The amount of time the valve stays open, given in degrees of rotation of the crankshaft.

engine displacement The size of the engine given in cubic inches, cubic centimeters, and liters. It is found by multiplying the piston displacement by the number of cylinders the engine has. Sometimes called "swept volume."

epitrochoid curve The circular movement around the perimeter of another circle. This is the movement that the rotary engine uses to ensure that the rotor stays in contact with the housing.

exhaust stroke The stroke of piston during which the exhaust valve is open and the piston is moving from bottom dead center to top dead center to push exhaust gas out of the cylinder.

external combustion engine An engine that runs on heat applied externally to the cylinder. For example: the steam engine.

flathead engine An L-head engine with valves in the block.

flywheel The heavy, circular flat plate that keeps the engine rotating when power is not produced, such as on the exhaust, intake, and compression strokes.

force The effort to produce a push or pull action.

four-stroke engine An engine that uses four strokes—intake, compression, power, and exhaust—to complete its cycle.

freewheeling engine An engine that has enough clearance between the piston and the valves so that in the event the timing belt or chain breaks, the valves that are hanging all the way open will not contact the piston, thus preventing engine damage.

horsepower An amount of work performed in a given time.

ignition The lighting of the fuel and air mixture in the combustion chamber.

intake stroke The stroke of the piston from top dead center to bottom dead center during which the intake valve is open and air is pulled into the cylinder.

interference engine An engine that has minimum clearance between the valves and the pistons during normal operation; in the event that the timing belt or chain breaks, the open valves will be contacted by the piston and bend the valves, possibly breaking the piston.

internal combustion engine An engine that burns a fuel internally and creates movement due to thermal expansion of gases.

keepers Locking devices that keep the valve retained by the valve spring seat.

lift The amount the valve will open. The more the valve lifts off its seat, the more air can get into and out of the engine.

lobe The raised portion on a camshaft; used to lift the lifter and open the valve.

Miller cycle An engine cycle that uses a longer exhaust stroke than intake stroke through delayed closing of the intake valve. This engine uses a supercharger to pressurize air into the cylinder when needed.

overhead cam (OHC) engine An I-head engine with the camshaft located on top of the cylinder head rather than in the block.

parasitic loss A loss of engine efficiency caused by internal friction, inefficient breathing, etc.

piston clearance The clearance between the piston and the cylinder wall that allows for lubricating oil to reduce friction.

piston displacement The volume of air that is moved by the piston from bottom dead center to top dead center.

piston engine An engine that uses pistons that move when expanding gases from combustion press against them.

piston pin boss The reinforced area of the piston where the piston wrist pin attaches the piston to the connecting rod.

piston skirt The area below the ring groove area of the piston that prevents the piston from cocking and becoming jammed in the cylinder bore.

piston stroke The up or down motion the piston makes from one limiting position to the other.

power The rate or speed at which work is done.

power stroke The stroke during which combustion is pushing the piston from top dead center to bottom dead center in the cylinder. This stroke is where power is produced.

pushrod A tubular rod that stands between the tappet and the rocker arm in an overhead valve engine; the pushrod transfers cam motion to the rocker arm.

reciprocating motion An up-and-down motion within the cylinder.

ring lands The metal between the ring grooves that supports the rings as the piston moves.

rocker arm The fulcrum that transfers pushrod endwise motion to the valve stem.

rotary engine A nonreciprocating engine with a rotor and housing instead of pistons.

scavenging The process of removing burned gases from the cylinder through the use of moving airflow pulling or extracting the gases out.

spark ignition (SI) engine An engine that relies on an electrical spark to ignite the air and fuel mixture.

stroke The movement of an object in a straight line. The piston sees four strokes during one combustion cycle in a four-stroke cycle engine, meaning it moves up and down twice each during a cycle.

tappet Another name for a valve lifter. Tappets may be flat or have rollers to ride on the cam lobes.

throw The offset area of the crankshaft where the connecting rod bolts on.

top dead center (TDC) The position of the piston when it is farthest from the crankshaft.

torque The amount of twisting force applied in a turning application, usually measured in foot-pounds.

two-stroke engine An engine that uses only two strokes to complete its running cycle.

valve face A machined surface on the back of the valve head; this area seals onto the valve seat in the cylinder head.

valve guide An insert in the cylinder head through which the valve stem passes and moves.

valve lifter A device that transfers motion from the cam lobe to a pushrod or directly acts on the valve and spring, depending on if the cam is in the engine block or the cylinder head; sometimes called a tappet.

valve margin The flat surface on the outer edge of the valve head between the valve head and the valve face.

valve overlap The time, usually expressed in degrees of crankshaft rotation, during which both the intake valve and the exhaust valve are open at the same time.

valve stem The shaft that is attached to the valve head and provides the sliding surface for the valve in its guide as it opens and closes.

volumetric efficiency A ratio, given as a percentage, of the amount of air actually inducted at a given engine speed at full throttle compared to the internal engine displacement. For a normally aspirated engine (without supercharging or turbocharging), an engine's volumetric efficiency may peak at around 85%. Peak engine torque is developed at peak volumetric efficiency.

work The result of force creating movement.

PROVE
KNOW
SEE
DO

ASE-Type Questions

1. Tech A says that engines using compression ignition control timing by regulating when fuel is injected into the cylinder. Tech B says that engines using spark ignition control timing by regulating when fuel is injected into the cylinder. Who is correct?
   a. Tech A
   b. Tech B
   c. Both A and B
   d. Neither A nor B
2. Tech B says that horsepower is a measurement of the amount of work being performed. Tech B says that horsepower can be calculated by multiplying torque by rpm and dividing by 5252. Who is correct?
   a. Tech A
   b. Tech B
   c. Both A and B
   d. Neither A nor B
3. Tech B says that in a four-stroke engine, the piston is at TDC four times to complete the cycle. Tech B says that the air/fuel mixture is ignited once every two strokes. Who is correct?
   a. Tech A
   b. Tech B
   c. Both A and B
   d. Neither A nor B
4. Tech A says that spark ignition typically occurs before TDC. Tech B says that spark ignition typically occurs after TDC. Who is correct?
   a. Tech A
   b. Tech B
   c. Both A and B
   d. Neither A nor B
5. Tech A says that valve overlap occurs between the exhaust stroke and the intake stroke. Tech B says that valve overlap occurs to assist in scavenging the cylinder. Who is correct?
   a. Tech A
   b. Tech B
   c. Both A and B
   d. Neither A nor B
6. Tech A says that compression ratio is the comparison of the volume above the piston at BDC to the volume above the piston at TDC. Tech B says that scavenging of the exhaust gases occurs once the exhaust valve closes. Who is correct?
   a. Tech A
   b. Tech B
   c. Both A and B
   d. Neither A nor B
7. Tech A says that the weight of the flywheel smooths out the engine's power pulses. Tech B says that the flex plate and torque converter perform the same function as the flywheel. Who is correct?
   a. Tech A
   b. Tech B
   c. Both A and B
   d. Neither A nor B
8. Tech A says that an interference engine is designed such that the pistons may hit the valves if the timing belt breaks. Tech B says that the shape of the cam lobe determines how long and far the valves are held open. Who is correct?
   a. Tech A
   b. Tech B
   c. Both A and B
   d. Neither A nor B
9. Tech A says that blowby gases occur when compression and combustion gases leak past the piston rings. Tech B says that a rotary engine uses one or two intake valves to control the flow of air and fuel into the cylinder. Who is correct?
   a. Tech A
   b. Tech B
   c. Both A and B
   d. Neither A nor B
10. Tech A says that the principle of thermal expansion is what pushes the piston down the cylinder on the power stroke. Tech B says that the piston is pulled down the cylinder on the intake stroke. Who is correct?
    a. Tech A
    b. Tech B
    c. Both A and B
    d. Neither A nor B

Snap-on
EEPV309A00

CHAPTER 11

Know
See
Do
Prove

NATEF Tasks

Engine Repair General			Page
■ Complete work order to include customer information, vehicle identifying information, customer concern, related service history, cause, and concern.		AST	268
■ Research applicable vehicle and service information, such as internal engine operation, vehicle service history, service precautions, and technical service bulletins.	MLR	AST	268
■ Inspect engine assembly for fuel, oil, coolant, and other leaks; determine necessary action.	MLR	AST	272–274
Engine Performance General			
■ Perform engine absolute (vacuum/boost) manifold pressure tests; determine necessary action.	MLR	AST	273–275
■ Perform cylinder power balance tests; determine necessary action.	MLR	AST	275–277
■ Perform cylinder cranking and running compression tests; determine necessary action.	MLR	AST	277–280
■ Perform cylinder leakage tests; determine necessary action.	MLR	AST	280–282
■ Diagnose abnormal engine noises or vibration concerns; determine necessary action.		AST	281–283

Engine Mechanical Testing

KNOW
SEE
DO

Knowledge Objectives

After reading this chapter, you will be able to:

1. Explain the basic principles of engine mechanical testing. (pp 268–270)
2. List the tools required for engine testing. (pp 268–270)
3. Describe the various types and causes of fluid leaks in engines. (pp 270–272)
4. List the factors involved in a cranking sound diagnosis. (pp 271–273)
5. Explain how vacuum testing can be used to determine the engine's general condition. (pp 273–276)
6. Describe a cylinder power balance test. (pp 275–277)
7. List the factors involved in cranking and running compression tests. (pp 277–280)
8. Describe the principles of the cranking compression test. (pp 277–278)
9. Describe the principles of the running compression test. (pp 278–280)
10. Explain the factors involved in a cylinder leakage test. (pp 280–282)
11. Describe the variety of noises and vibrations that a running engine creates. (pp 281–283)
12. Describe how consumption of oil or coolant not located due to visual leaks may be determined by the color of the exhaust. (p 283)

KNOW
SEE
DO

Skills Objectives

After reading this chapter, you will be able to:

1. Perform a fluid leak inspection by looking under the hood. (pp 271–272)
2. Perform a fluid leak inspection by looking under the vehicle. (pp 271–272)
3. Perform a cranking sound diagnosis. (p 273)
4. Test engine vacuum using a vacuum gauge. (p 275)
5. Test engine vacuum using a pressure transducer and lab scope. (pp 275–276)
6. Perform a cylinder power balance test. (p 277)
7. Perform a cranking compression test. (p 279)
8. Perform a running compression test. (p 280)
9. Perform a cylinder leakage test. (pp 281–282)
10. Inspect and replace the camshaft and drive belt/chain. (pp 285–286)

Introduction

For an engine to operate efficiently and effectively, the mechanical condition of the engine must be in good working order. The pistons, piston rings, cylinder walls, head gasket, and valves must seal properly. If they do not, then the engine will not operate correctly and all of the tuning in the world will not be able to fix it. So assessing the condition of the engine is a critical step in the diagnostic process before tune-up parts are replaced. There are few things more dreaded than having to tell a customer that the $300 tune-up you just performed did not resolve the vehicle's misfiring problem caused by a burned valve and that the vehicle really needs a $1500 valve job, or a $4000 engine replacement. First, the customer will not be happy that the vehicle is not fixed. Second, the repair will now cost substantially more money than the customer expected. Third, the customer now has very good reason to doubt your competence and wonder if you are correct now, when you were wrong earlier. This is a no-win situation, but it can be avoided by always diagnosing the problem instead of throwing parts at it.

Engine mechanical testing is also performed to diagnose more accurately what major engine work is needed, such as replacing a head gasket, rebuilding of the cylinder heads, or performing a full engine replacement. Understanding exactly what is wrong will allow you to better advise the customer on the appropriate repairs. It will also help you build credibility with your customers by fully understanding the situation and clearly communicating it to the customers in a professional manner. This chapter will help you learn the skills and procedures for performing engine mechanical tests.

Engine Mechanical Testing

Engine mechanical testing uses a series of tests to assess the mechanical condition of the engine. The tests start off broad and narrow down as each test is performed. This process will first help you to identify the location of the fault and then the cause of the fault. Having a good understanding of engine theory will help you evaluate the results of each test and provide you the information needed to know what path to follow after each step.

Mechanical testing starts with a good visual inspection. A visual inspection of the engine assembly for leaks will affirm the ability of the seals and gaskets to contain each of the engine's fluids. Starting the engine and listening to its operation can indicate a host of problems, from loose belts to worn main bearings. It can also reveal if the engine is misfiring and how steady the misfire is. After a good inspection, it is time to pull out the tools and equipment to take a deeper look at the mechanical condition of the engine.

Testing Tools

Although some seasoned mechanics have been known to use bubble gum and a bubble gum wrapper to diagnose a burned valve (see the Technician Tip on page 272), a

You Are the Automotive Technician

A customer comes into the dealership complaining that her vehicle is not running as smoothly as before and the check engine light is flashing, which indicates a potentially catalyst damaging fault. As an experienced, certified technician, you explain to the customer that she did the right thing by bringing in the vehicle for diagnosis. First, you locate the customer's vehicle history and write up a repair order including the customers concerns. Second, you use a scan tool to retrieve the DTCs and find a P0304-cylinder 4 misfire detected code. Third, you hold the throttle to the floor with the ignition switch in the off position; and then crank the engine over. The engine exhibits an uneven cranking sound indicating a compression related fault. Next, you research the technical service bulletins (TSBs) and find one that relates to this code and low compression condition. The TSB indicates possible soft camshaft lobes, which can wear down and not open the valve/s fully. To verify whether this is the case, the TSB directs you to perform a cranking compression test along with a running compression test on any misfiring cylinders. The TSB then lists the acceptable minimum pressures for each test.

1. Why did the engine have an uneven cranking sound?
2. What does the running compression test indicate?
3. How would you determine which cylinder is misfiring if the engine computer doesn't have that capability?

variety of tools and equipment are available today that allow technicians to fully assess the mechanical condition of modern engines. Each of the tools introduced here has a specific function and will be further described in the Skill Drills later in this chapter:

- Compression tester: A **compression tester** is used when a technician suspects a cylinder may have low compression. The compression tester measures the amount of compression pressure a cylinder can generate **FIGURE 11-1**.
- Vacuum gauge: The **vacuum gauge** measures the amount of vacuum an engine can generate during various operating conditions **FIGURE 11-2**.
- Pressure transducer and lab scope: The **pressure transducer** measures engine vacuum or pressure and displays it graphically on a lab scope. Because it is very accurate, it creates a detailed trace on the lab scope, which can be compared to a known good trace and used to determine mechanical issues in the engine **FIGURE 11-3**.
- Cylinder leakage tester: A **cylinder leakage tester** pumps air into the cylinder and measures the percentage of air that is leaking from the cylinder. The technician can determine where the pressurized air is leaking from the cylinder by looking, listening, or feeling **FIGURE 11-4**.
- Scan tool: The scan tool communicates to the vehicle's computers through the **data link connector (DLC)**. It displays the readings from the various sensors; retrieves trouble codes, freeze-frame data, and system monitor data; and on some vehicles performs output tests such as a cylinder

FIGURE 11-1 A compression tester.

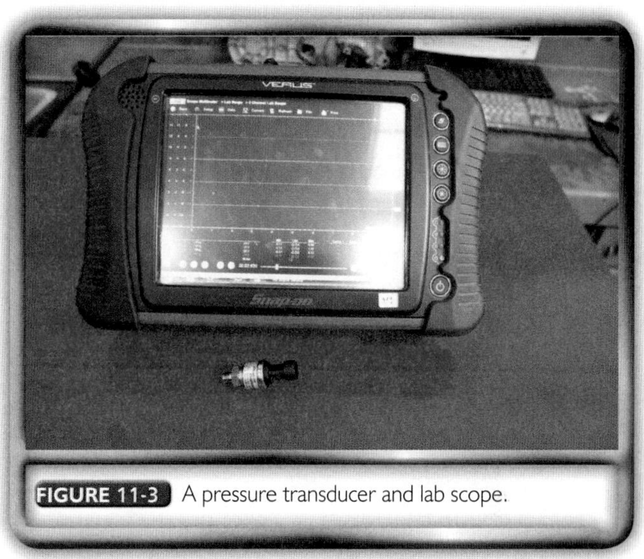
VERUS
Snap-on

FIGURE 11-3 A pressure transducer and lab scope.

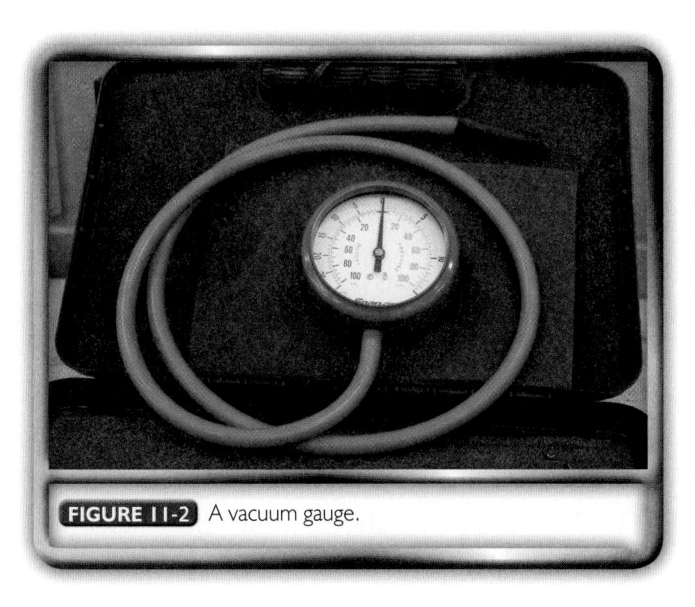

FIGURE 11-2 A vacuum gauge.

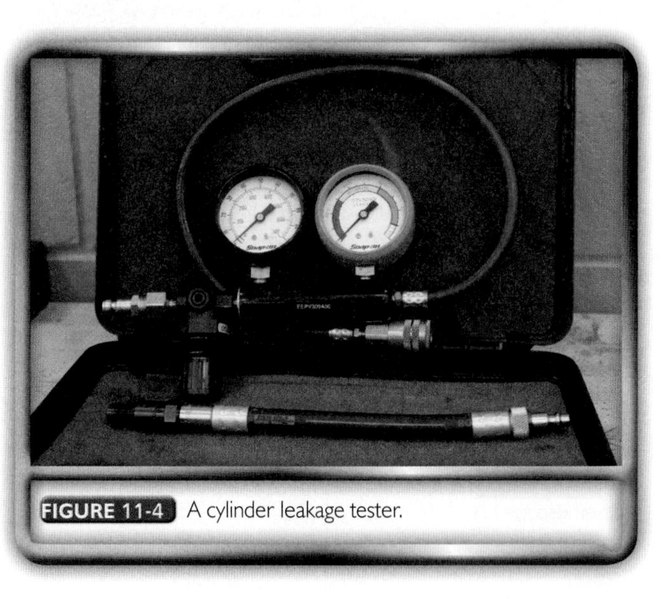

FIGURE 11-4 A cylinder leakage tester.

power balance test, or commands other output devices to operate FIGURE 11-5.

- Stethoscope—standard and electronic: A stethoscope is used by technicians to listen to unusual noises in the vehicle. Stethoscopes come in both standard and electronic FIGURE 11-6.

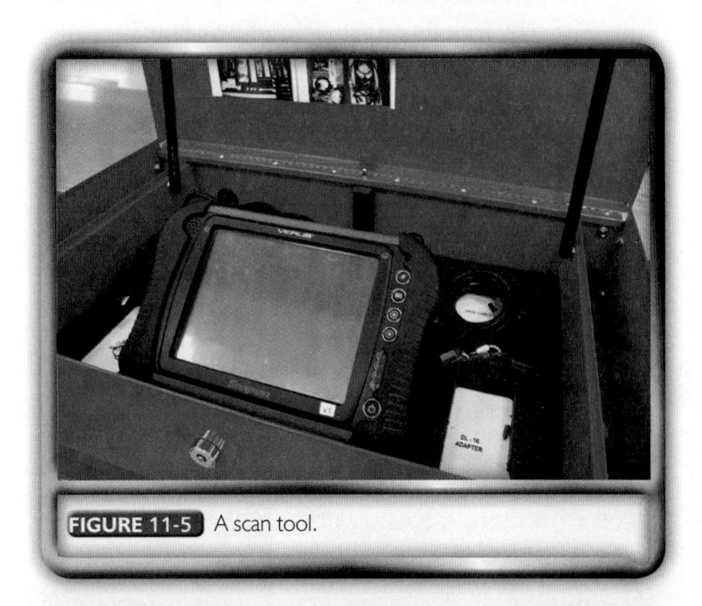

FIGURE 11-5 A scan tool.

Blue-Point
Wireless ChassisEAR
CHANNEL SELECT
1
2
3
4

FIGURE 11-6 A standard stethoscope and an electronic stethoscope.

TECHNICIAN TIP

So how is it that a mechanic could diagnose a burned valve with just a piece of bubble gum and its wrapper? Knowing that each power pulse pushes exhaust gases out of the exhaust pipe, there should be steady pressure pulses if all of the cylinders are operating correctly. Besides listening to the engine and hearing a misfire, the technician used the gum to attach the wrapper to the end of the exhaust pipe. Each pulse pushed the wrapper away from the opening of the pipe, and each misfire tended to pull it back. If the engine had a burnt exhaust valve, the negative pressure pulse was stronger than just a misfire because some of the exhaust gases were pulled back into the cylinder through the burned exhaust valve, creating more of a vacuum in the exhaust pipe. The wrapper was pulled into the exhaust pipe during the misfire in this case and blown back out during the next power pulse, resulting in a wrapper that was slapping the exhaust pipe.

Suspecting that the exhaust valve was burned, the mechanic would shut off the engine, disable the ignition system, crank the engine over, and hear the telltale uneven cranking sound of a cylinder with low compression. Taking the results of both tests, the mechanic would conclude that the engine had a burnt exhaust valve. Pulling the spark plug wires off one at a time with the engine running resulted in one cylinder not contributing to the engine idle revolutions per minute (rpm), so the mechanic knew the burnt valve was located in this cylinder.

The process is similar today but involves tools and equipment that measure the results and display them numerically or graphically to more accurately assess the mechanical condition of the engine.

Fluid Leaks

Inspecting the engine assembly for fluid leaks is a common task that technicians perform during any kind of routine maintenance or service. It is also common to inspect the vehicle for leaks when the customer complains about fluid spots left on his or her driveway or if the fluid levels need to be topped off more frequently than is considered normal. It is a good practice to inspect the engine assembly for leaks before performing any engine repairs so that leaks can be taken care of at the same time.

The color of the leaking fluid can give you a clue as to the source. Black fluid could be engine oil or gear lube, reddish-orange or green fluid could be anti-freeze, and red could be transmission or power steering fluid. The smell of the fluid can also provide a clue; fuel and brake fluid have very different scents. Remember that gravity will cause fluid to be pulled downward, so be sure to inspect all the way up to a place where there is no more fluid present. Also, be aware that air from the fan or wind created by the speed of the vehicle can push the fluid in the direction of the airflow.

There are several processes you may need to undertake to discover the origin of the fluid leak. The vehicle might need to be pressure washed or cleaned and reinspected for leaks. Sometimes adding a special fluorescent dye to the fluid will help locate the leak; the fluid becomes fluorescent when using a black light and can then be more easily located. If a coolant leak is suspected, it will be easier to locate the leak if you pressure test the cooling system using a cooling system pressure tester.

Inspecting the Engine Assembly for Fuel, Oil, Coolant, and Other Leaks

Most leaks can be identified and located by means of a thorough visual inspection. Use of a good light and mirror will help you pinpoint the source of the leak. Sometimes, leaks can be seen from the top of the engine under the hood; others can be seen only from under the vehicle. And in some cases, covers or heat shields will need to be removed so that you can see the area that needs inspection. If you identify the source of the leak with the engine off, you may need to start the vehicle and perform the visual inspection with the engine running. If you do so, be extremely careful around the moving parts. Sometimes seals leak only when the engine is running. Sometimes seals leak only when the engine is off. You may have to try it both ways.

If you cannot locate the source of the leak visually, you may need to use a fluorescent dye. If this is the case, add a compatible dye to the fluid you suspect is leaking, then operate the vehicle for the time recommended by the dye manufacturer to circulate the dye through the system. If it is a small leak, you may need to have the customer drive the vehicle for a few days to help make the leak show up. Once the dye has had a chance to circulate, inspect the engine assembly for leaks using the recommended light for the dye you are using. In some cases, you are required to wear special glasses to enhance the fluorescence of the dye.

To perform a fluid leak inspection by looking under the hood, follow the steps in SKILL DRILL 11-1.

To perform a fluid leak inspection by looking under the vehicle, follow the steps in SKILL DRILL 11-2.

Cranking Sound Diagnosis Overview

Engine noises can give a technician valuable insight into the condition of the engine. As you have learned, compression is one of the five critical requirements for each cylinder to operate properly. If the compression in one or more cylinders is too low, then the affected cylinders will not create as much power as cylinders with the proper amount of compression. If one or more cylinders have low compression, the engine will run rough, in many cases misleading the customer to request a "tune-up." Yet, performing a tune-up by replacing spark plugs and any

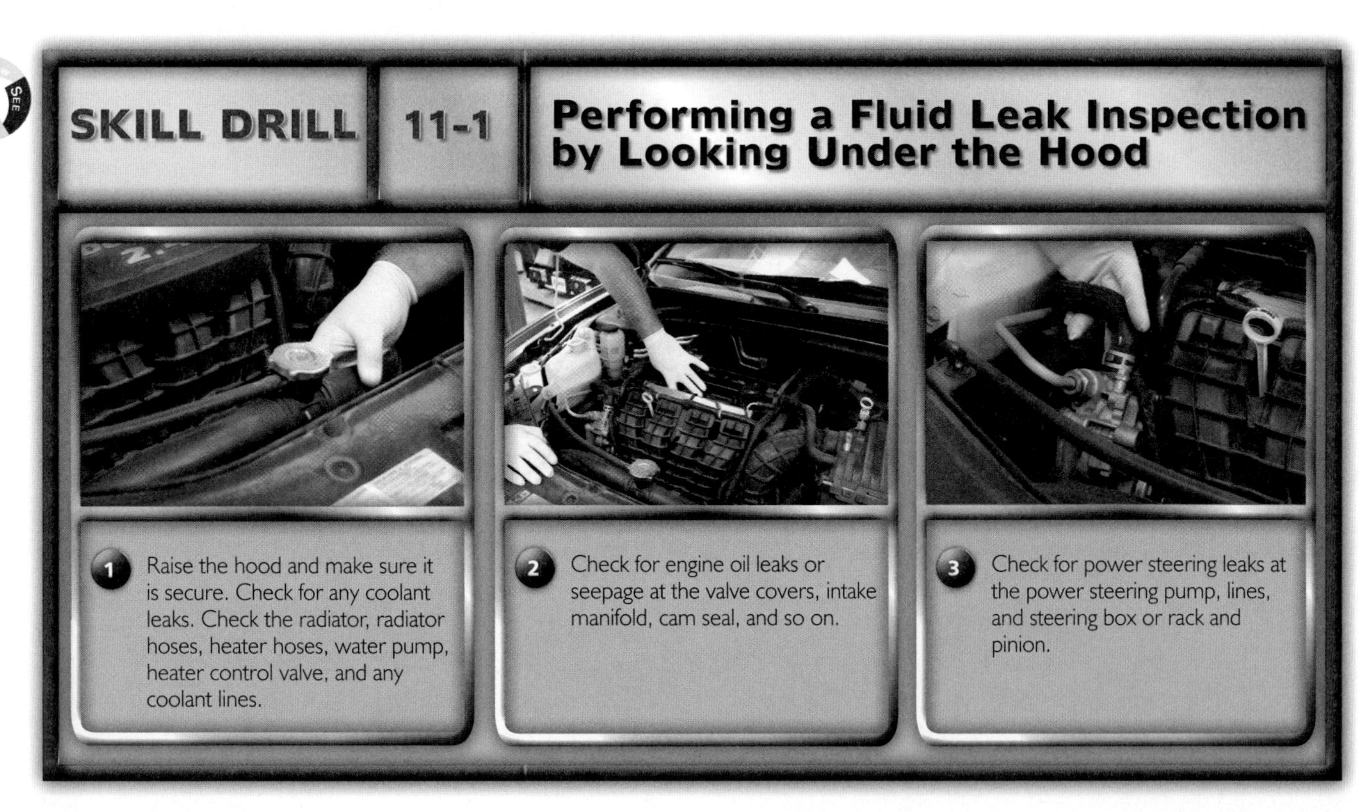

SKILL DRILL 11-1 Performing a Fluid Leak Inspection by Looking Under the Hood

1. Raise the hood and make sure it is secure. Check for any coolant leaks. Check the radiator, radiator hoses, heater hoses, water pump, heater control valve, and any coolant lines.
2. Check for engine oil leaks or seepage at the valve covers, intake manifold, cam seal, and so on.
3. Check for power steering leaks at the power steering pump, lines, and steering box or rack and pinion.

SKILL DRILL 11-1 Performing a Fluid Leak Inspection by Looking Under the Hood, continued

4 Check the master cylinder brake lines. Check the rear seal of the brake master cylinder, looking for signs of seepage between the master cylinder and the vacuum booster.

SKILL DRILL 11-2 Performing a Fluid Leak Inspection by Looking Under the Vehicle

1 Raise the vehicle using a hoist, making sure the vehicle is being lifted on the proper lift points. Check for any coolant seepage or leakage on each side of the block around the soft plugs.

2 Inspect for engine oil leaks around the front main seal, oil pan, oil filter, oil pressure switch, and rear main seal.

3 Inspect for transmission and transaxle leaks.

4 Inspect the front and rear differentials if equipped.

other related tune-up items will not fix the low compression issue, causing the engine to still run poorly after the tune-up. This results in an unhappy customer as well as technician. To help avoid that situation, a cranking sound diagnosis can identify whether the compression is similar across all of the cylinders. If compression is not similar across all cylinders, a tune-up will not fix the problem. If compression is similar across all cylinders, then compression is not likely causing the engine to run rough.

When you perform a cranking sound diagnosis, you should disable the engine so that it will not start. Then crank the engine over using the key and listen to the cranking sounds. It might take a few times to isolate any noises. The noise could be from a misaligned starter, the clunk of a spun crankshaft bearing noise, an uneven cranking sound that a low-compression cylinder gives, or a fast cranking sound from a no-compression condition that is due to bent valves caused by a broken timing belt. Each of these noises can give you a clue as to where the problem may lie.

Diagnosing Cranking Sound

During engine cranking, the engine will make a rhythmic cranking sound if the compression is similar across the cylinders. As each piston comes up on compression, it loads down the starter motor and slows the cranking speed. If the compression of the engine is not the same at each cylinder, the engine will make an uneven sound. To train your ear to pick up the different compression sounds, take a vehicle with known good compression and disable the engine so that it will not start. To disable the engine, disable the fuel pump by pulling the fuel pump fuse or relay. You can also disable the ignition system (see service manual for proper procedure) so that it will crank but not start. You can then crank the engine and listen to the sounds it makes. Next perform the same task on a vehicle with known bad compression and listen to the difference in cranking sounds.

To perform a cranking sound diagnosis, follow the steps in SKILL DRILL 11-3:

1. Raise the hood and make sure it is secure.
2. Disable the engine by disabling the fuel pump or the ignition system. Refer to the service manual for proper procedures, or use the "clear flood" mode described above.
3. Crank the engine over using the key, and listen to the sound the engine makes while cranking. Determine any necessary actions.

Applied Science

AS-34: Ultraviolet: The technician can demonstrate an understanding of why dyes are added to lubricants fluoresce in ultraviolet light.

An ultraviolet dye leak detection kit can be one of the technician's most valuable tools for locating the source of a fluid leak. In the case of an engine oil leak, a special dye will be added to the engine oil. The engine will be started in order to circulate the dye. An ultraviolet light will be used to search for the source of the leak as evidenced by a fluorescent yellow dye. In some cases, the detection kit may contain a special pair of glasses to assist the operator in finding the leak.

The basic scientific principle of how this works is based upon the electromagnetic spectrum. Light travels in waves called electromagnetic waves. The electromagnetic spectrum covers a wide range of components such as gamma rays, X-rays, visible light, ultraviolet light, infrared rays and radio waves. Visible light is generally considered to be in the middle of the electromagnetic spectrum. There are many different types of electromagnetic waves that cannot be seen with the human eye. By the use of an ultraviolet light, we are able to see another part of the electromagnetic spectrum. The use of special dyes enhances our ability to find fluid leaks under the ultraviolet light source. The ultraviolet dye leak detection kit is an excellent tool for troubleshooting difficult to find leaks.

Vacuum Testing

A vacuum gauge is used to determine the engine's general condition. The vacuum gauge reading shows the difference between outside atmospheric pressure and the amount of vacuum (manifold pressure) in the

Applied Science

AS-35: Ultraviolet: The technician can demonstrate a process for determining the source of leakage using ultraviolet light.

A vehicle is in the shop due to an engine oil leak. This is the third repair attempt to solve the customer's concern. On two previous occasions, a technician had replaced the oil pan gasket. The technician was convinced that the engine oil pan gasket was the source of the leak; however, after a short period of time, the owner brought the vehicle back to the shop.

On this third repair attempt, the service manager suggested the use of an ultraviolet dye leak detection kit be used. A special dye was added to the engine lubricating oil. After running the engine for 10 minutes, the technician used an ultraviolet light to search for the leak.

After checking the engine over carefully with the ultraviolet light, the technician discovered that a slight crack in the oil pressure sending unit was the actual source of the leak. The oil was running down the block and collecting on the lip of the oil pan. The exact source of the leak was easily found as the dye showed up with a fluorescent yellow color under the ultraviolet light.

Applied Science

AS-6: Operational: The technician can relate scientific terms to automotive system diagnosis, service, and repair.

The use of pressure gauges is a common procedure in most automotive repair facilities. When assigned to perform engine mechanical testing, the technician will work with pounds per square inch (psi) as related to engine compression gauge readings and cylinder leakage tests. A vehicle with low compression will produce a number of drivability problems including a rough idle condition. For a smooth running engine, cylinder compression should be as uniform as possible between cylinders. Psi refers to the primary units of measure for pressure in the United States. The metric unit is the Kilopascal or kPa. 10 psi is equal to approximately 68.95 kPa. Most manufacturers will supply both units as technical information. If necessary, the technician can consult conversion charts to obtain the U.S. standard or metric unit that is needed.

TECHNICIAN TIP

Many newer vehicles are programmed with a "clear flood" capability. This effectively shuts off the fuel injectors as long as the throttle is held to the floor before the ignition key is turned to the run or crank position. When the key is turned to crank (with the throttle still held down), the vehicle's power train control module (PCM) will shut off the fuel injectors. This allows the engine to crank without starting. If the engine starts, it means either that the vehicle is not equipped with clear flood mode or that fuel has leaked into the intake manifold and will need to be diagnosed. Using the clear flood mode is a quick way of performing a cranking sound diagnosis on these vehicles.

TECHNICIAN TIP

Atkinson and Miller cycle engines are designed to reduce pumping losses at idle by operating at a substantially lower intake manifold vacuum (higher manifold pressure) at idle than a standard engine. Make sure you look up the specifications for the engine you are working on when interpreting vacuum readings.

engine. The vacuum gauge is installed in a vacuum port on the intake manifold. Always select the largest and most centrally located vacuum port. This may require using a vacuum tee so that the vacuum gauge can be connected and, at the same time, vacuum can still be supplied to the existing component. The typical vacuum reading for a properly running engine at idle is a steady 17" to 21" of vacuum (57.6 to 71.1 kPa) TABLE 11-1. A low reading could relate to a problem with ignition or valve timing. A sharp oscillation back and forth in the needle or a dip in the gauge reading could relate to a problem such as a bad valve. A low reading at a constant 2500 rpm could indicate a restricted exhaust system.

TABLE 11-1: Chart of Vacuum Readings—Vacuum Gauge

Reading	Indication
17" to 21", steady needle at idle.	Good reading
Needle oscillates back and forth about 4" to 8".	Burned or constantly leaking valve
A low and steady reading.	Possible late valve timing or late ignition timing
Snap acceleration needle drops to zero and then only reads 20" to 23" of vacuum; should be much higher, around 27".	Possible worn rings
Good reading at idle. As engine speeds up to a steady 2500 rpm, the needle slowly goes down and may continue to drop.	Possible restricted exhaust system

With the advent of lab scope diagnostics, many technicians are using a pressure transducer to measure the engine's manifold pressure and display it graphically on a lab scope. The pressure transducer is a very accurate measuring tool; when attached to a vacuum port and hooked up to a lab scope, it gives a pressure trace that shows the low pressure created by each piston's intake stroke FIGURE 11-7. If the ignition pattern for cylinder 1 is monitored on a separate trace, the vacuum pulses can be tied to specific cylinders. Technicians can view these traces and see how well each cylinder is functioning at producing and maintaining a vacuum.

Testing Engine Vacuum Using a Vacuum Gauge

During an engine vacuum test, all vacuum gauges are calibrated at sea level and all instructions and readings are referenced to sea level. When testing above sea level, you will need to compensate. For instance, if the gauge reads 18" of vacuum at sea level, it would drop to 17" at 1000' above sea level.

The vacuum gauge reading shows the difference between outside atmospheric pressure and the amount of vacuum in the engine in a non-turbo or non-supercharged engine. The average inches of vacuum for a good running

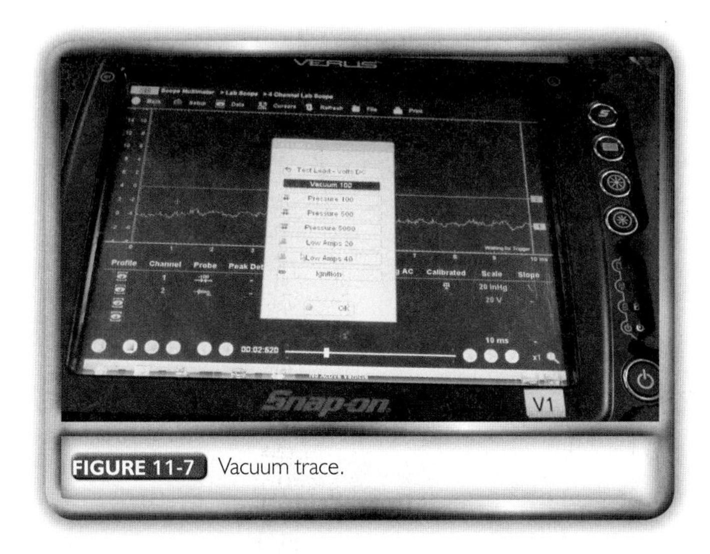
VERUS
Snap-on
V1

FIGURE 11-7 Vacuum trace.

> **TECHNICIAN TIP**
>
> A pressure transducer can be adapted to fit in the spark plug hole to create a pressure trace of running and cranking compression. It can also be used in the exhaust system to measure the exhaust pulses. Pressure transducers are used more and more commonly when diagnosing engine problems.

engine at idle is a steady 17" to 21" of vacuum. The average inches of vacuum at idle for a performance camshaft with a high lift and large overlap duration is around 15". The amount of vacuum an engine creates relies on the piston rings, valves, ignition timing, and fuel.

To test engine vacuum using a vacuum gauge, follow the steps in SKILL DRILL 11-4:

1. Connect the vacuum gauge to the intake manifold. You might have to use a vacuum tee.
2. Make sure the engine is at operating temperature. Start the engine, take a reading at idle, and record the reading.
3. Snap accelerate the engine by quickly opening and closing the throttle; record the highest vacuum reading attained.
4. Hold the throttle steady at 2500 rpm and record your reading.

Testing Engine Vacuum Using a Pressure Transducer

Using a pressure transducer and lab scope is a similar process to using a vacuum gauge, except it is much more accurate and allows you to look at the vacuum graphically. When paired with a second trace consisting of the ignition pattern for cylinder 1, any issues with the vacuum trace can be tied to a specific cylinder. By using a pressure transducer on a variety of vehicles with various issues, you will become familiar with the patterns of common faults.

To use a pressure transducer and lab scope for testing engine vacuum, follow the steps in SKILL DRILL 11-5.

Cylinder Power Balance Test Overview

A cylinder power balance test (also called a power balance test for short) is used for two purposes. First, it identifies which cylinder(s) are not operating properly when the vacuum test indicates a mechanical issue or when the engine is not running smoothly. Second, it is used as a general indication of each cylinder's overall health. Every cylinder in the engine should contribute equally to the engine's power output. When a mechanical, electrical, or fuel problem occurs within an engine, the affected cylinders will not produce as much, if any, power when compared to the other cylinders. We can test to see how much each cylinder is contributing to the engine's output by disabling one cylinder at a time and measuring the rpm drop. Disabling a cylinder that is not operating correctly will not produce much, if any, rpm drop. Disabling a cylinder that is working properly, however, will produce a much larger rpm drop. The greater the difference in rpm drop, the greater the difference between each cylinder's ability to produce its share of the engine's power.

Many newer vehicles control the idle speed electronically through the PCM. In these vehicles if something loads the engine down, such as the air-conditioning compressor turning on, the PCM will allow more air and fuel into the engine so that the idle speed stays relatively the same. In the case of a manual power balance test, disabling one of the cylinders will not produce a drop in rpm because the PCM will compensate for it. In these cases, use the PCM's built-in power balance feature, if equipped. Alternatively, in some vehicles you can disconnect the electrical connector on the idle speed control system to prevent the PCM from changing the idle speed. Unfortunately, in some vehicles if you disconnect the connector on the idle speed control system, the engine will die. On these vehicles, you can usually perform the power balance test slightly above idle, since the PCM only controls engine speed at idle. Raising the rpm can be accomplished by wedging an appropriate tool between the throttle body and the throttle linkage or by having an assistant hold the throttle steady while you perform the test.

The purpose of the power balance test is to see whether the cylinders are creating equal amounts of power and, if not, to isolate the problem to a particular cylinder or cylinders. Once the problem is isolated, we

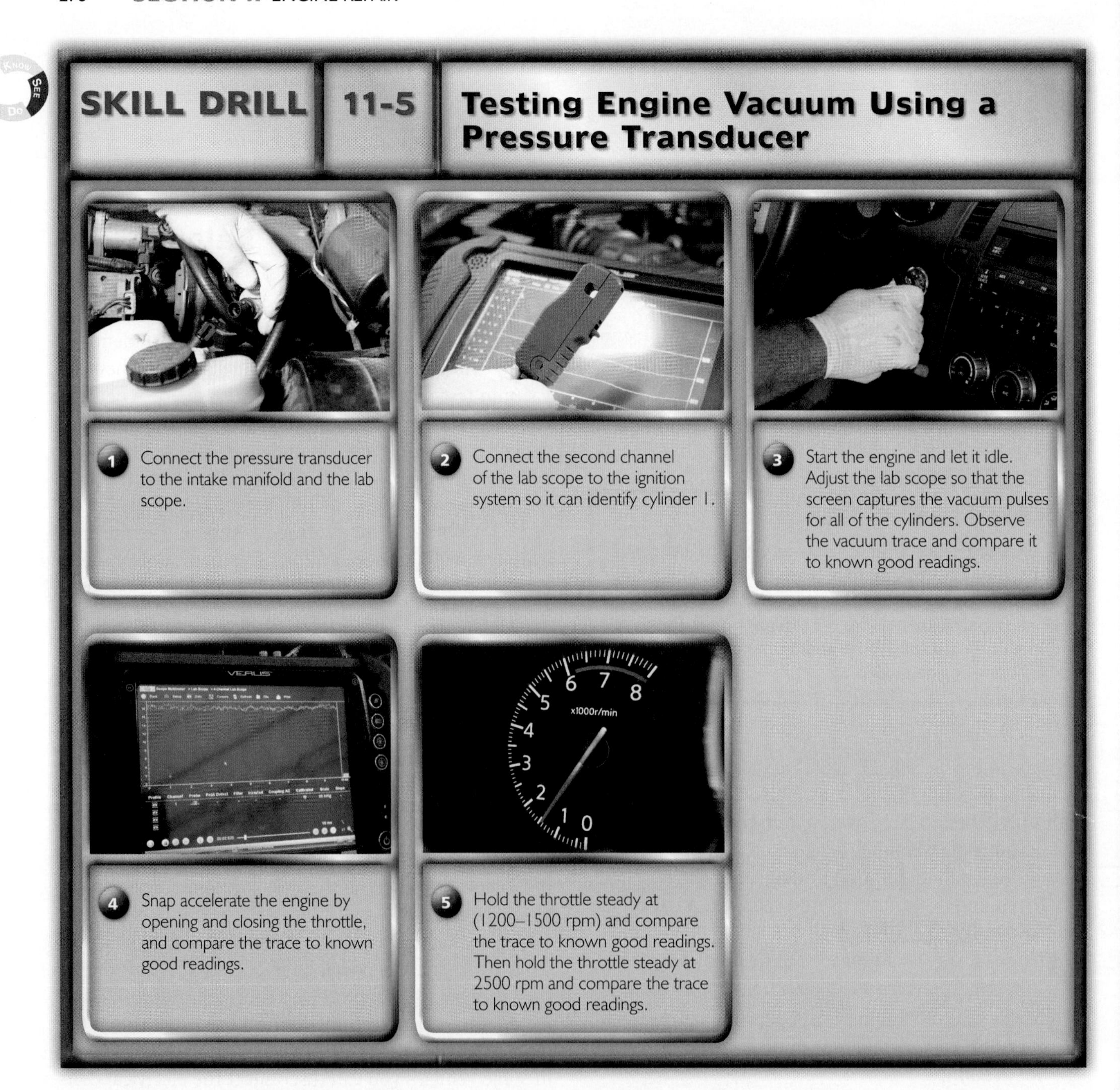
SKILL DRILL 11-5 Testing Engine Vacuum Using a Pressure Transducer
1 Connect the pressure transducer to the intake manifold and the lab scope.
2 Connect the second channel of the lab scope to the ignition system so it can identify cylinder 1.
3 Start the engine and let it idle. Adjust the lab scope so that the screen captures the vacuum pulses for all of the cylinders. Observe the vacuum trace and compare it to known good readings.
4 Snap accelerate the engine by opening and closing the throttle, and compare the trace to known good readings.
5 Hold the throttle steady at (1200–1500 rpm) and compare the trace to known good readings. Then hold the throttle steady at 2500 rpm and compare the trace to known good readings.

can take the next step, which is to determine whether it is a mechanical issue related to compression or an ignition- or fuel-related issue.

Performing a Cylinder Power Balance Test

There are several ways that a power balance test can be performed. Knowing each of the options will allow you to choose the easiest one for the vehicle you are diagnosing. Which is easiest is determined by the capabilities of the PCM, the ease of accessing the required components, and the tools available. For many OBDII vehicles, you can identify which cylinders are misfiring by using a scan tool to access stored diagnostic trouble codes (DTCs) in the PCM. Or you can access mode 6 data, which will give you information on how prevalent misfires are on each cylinder. In some cases, you can also use the scan tool to command the PCM to perform an automatic power balance test and report the results right on the scan tool. On most newer vehicles, using the scan tool is by far the best method of performing a power balance test.

If the system is not set up to perform the test automatically, you will have to do it manually. You will need to determine whether to disable the ignition or the fuel to each individual cylinder. If the engine has port fuel injectors that are accessible, disconnecting the electrical connector from each injector one at a time will shut off the fuel to the cylinder. Shutting off the fuel to the cylinder is the preferred method since it stops injecting fuel in the cylinder. If the ignition system is disabled for a cylinder, the fuel will still be delivered but will not be burned in the cylinder. However, it will burn in the catalytic converter, which can cause it to overheat and possibly be damaged. Therefore, shutting down the fuel is preferable if it is an option on the engine you are working on.

If the engine has individual ignition coils on each spark plug, you can disconnect the primary electrical connector, which will shut off the spark to the spark plug. If the vehicle has coils that share cylinders (waste spark system), then you can place a 1" (25-mm) section of vacuum hose between each coil tower and spark plug wire. Then connect the alligator clip from a nonpowered test light to a good engine ground and touch the tip of the test light to each length of vacuum hose to short out each spark plug one at a time. If the vehicle is equipped with a distributor, disconnect one spark plug at a time from the distributor cap (it is good to use a test lead to ground the spark at the distributor cap terminal to prevent the spark from damaging the ignition module in the distributor), which shuts down the spark for the cylinder being tested.

To perform a cylinder power balance test, follow the steps in **SKILL DRILL 11-6**.

Cranking and Running Compression Tests

In a cranking or a running compression test, a high-pressure hose is hand-threaded in the spark plug hole of the cylinder to be tested and then connected to the compression gauge. The engine needs to be cranked over or started, depending on the test that is being performed. The compression gauge reads the amount of pressure that the piston is producing by compressing the air in the cylinder. You should always check factory specifications before performing the test so that you know what the results should be.

Performing a Cranking Compression Test

During a cranking compression test, the engine is cranked over but is not started by the starter. As the piston moves up, it compresses the air in the cylinder. The engine should crank until at least five compression pulses are observed on the compression gauge to get an accurate reading. If the final reading is low, there could be a problem with the valves, rings, pistons, or head gasket.

The cranking compression test is performed when indications show a misfiring or dead cylinder that is not caused by an ignition or fuel problem. A compression test measures the air pressure as it is compressed in the cylinder. The cylinders should all measure within 10% to 15% of each other.

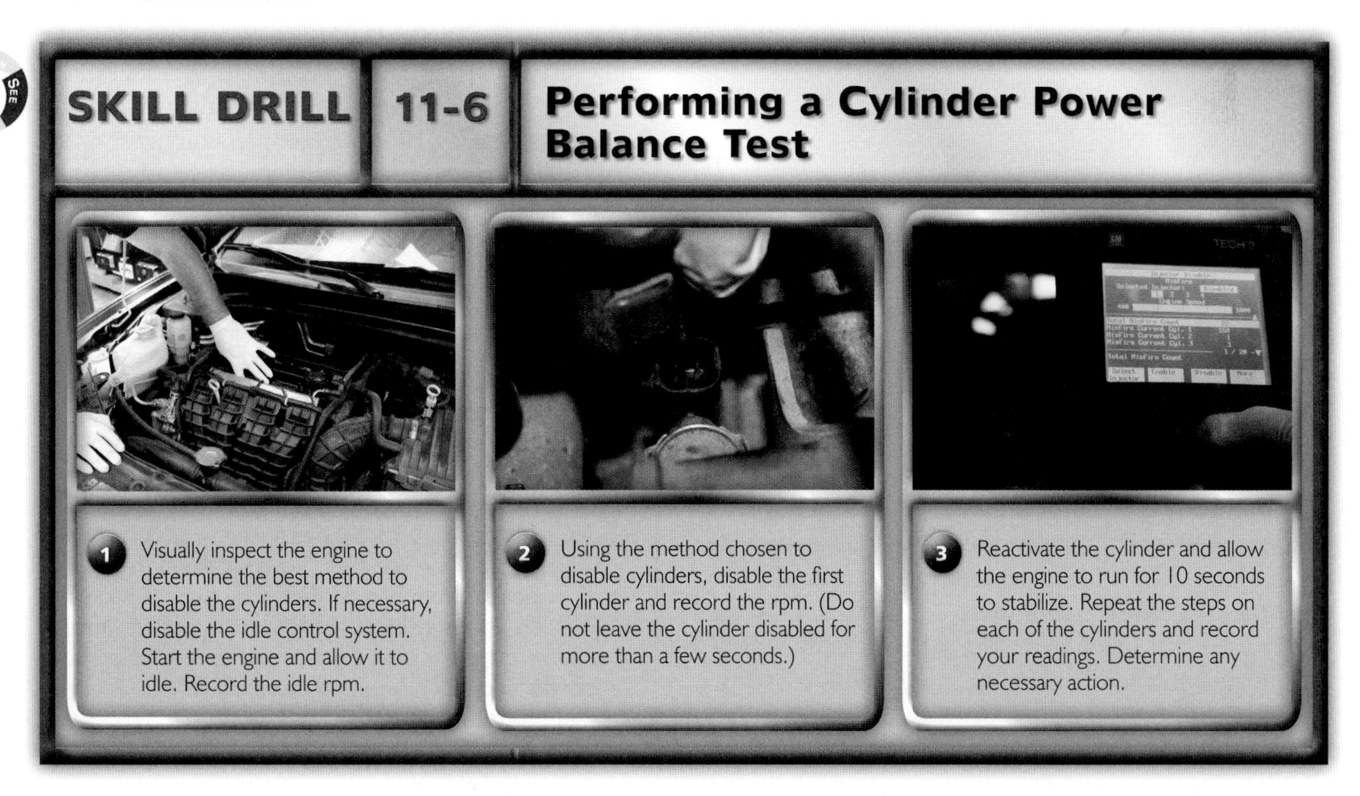
SKILL DRILL 11-6 Performing a Cylinder Power Balance Test
1 Visually inspect the engine to determine the best method to disable the cylinders. If necessary, disable the idle control system. Start the engine and allow it to idle. Record the idle rpm.
2 Using the method chosen to disable cylinders, disable the first cylinder and record the rpm. (Do not leave the cylinder disabled for more than a few seconds.)
3 Reactivate the cylinder and allow the engine to run for 10 seconds to stabilize. Repeat the steps on each of the cylinders and record your readings. Determine any necessary action.

For the compression test to be completely accurate, it is recommended that the engine be at operating temperature, all of the spark plugs be removed, the battery be fully charged, the throttle be held wide open, and at least five compression pulses be made on each cylinder (the same number of pulses for each cylinder). All of these conditions will help the engine create maximum compression and accurate readings. At the same time, if a technician suspects that only one or two cylinders have excessively low compression (due to failing the power balance test), then only the suspect spark plugs will be removed and a compression test made. If the compression is substantially low on that cylinder, then the engine has a compression problem and further testing of the cylinder will be required. If the compression is reasonably close to the specifications, then the compression is not causing the issue and there is likely a fuel or ignition fault causing the problem.

To perform a cranking compression test, follow the steps in SKILL DRILL 11-7.

Performing a Running Compression Test

In a running compression test, the engine is running during the compression test. Unlike the cranking compression test, which checks the sealing capability of the cylinder, the running compression test checks the engine's ability to move air into and out of the cylinder. This is referred to as the engine's ability to breathe. For example, if a camshaft lobe is badly worn, less air will be entering or exiting the cylinder, depending on which valve is affected. The running compression test helps a technician to evaluate this process.

The test is performed in two parts, idle and snap throttle. During idle, since the engine is running and the throttle is relatively closed, the compression pressure will be approximately half of the cranking compression pressure. The second part of the test is a snap throttle test. With the engine idling, the throttle is snapped open and then closed fairly quickly, which allows a big rush of air into the intake manifold. The idea is to not make the rpm change very much during the test. If the intake and exhaust system are operating correctly, then the compression tester needle will jump to about 80% of the cranking compression pressure. If the intake side of the system is restricted, then the reading will be lower than the 80% threshold. If there is a restriction on the exhaust side of the system, then the pressure will be substantially higher than the 80% threshold.

The running compression test is performed by leaving all of the spark plugs in the engine except for the one in the cylinder that you are testing. Most technicians leave the Schrader valve in the compression tester to hold pressure in the tester while performing the running compression test, although it can be hard on the Schrader valves. Always have a couple of spares handy. Also know that compression tester Schrader valves use lighter-weight springs than tire Schrader valves, so do not interchange them. The compression tester needs to be installed in the cylinder to be tested and then the engine can be started. This test can detect flat cam lobes,

Applied Math

AM-16: Charts/Tables/Graphs: The technician can construct a chart, table, or graph that depicts and compares a range of performance characteristics of various system operational conditions.

A typical diagnostic test would be checking the compression of an engine. In this scenario, we have a four cylinder engine that has the customer's concern of running rough at idle. A visual inspection did not reveal any problems that could easily be identified. A compression gauge will be used to measure the compression on each cylinder. The technician will record the information as the readings are taken from each cylinder and the results could be recorded on the following chart. By consulting the manufacturer's specifications, the technician will be able to determine if the compression is satisfactory or not.

Cylinder	Cranking Compression in PSI	Running Compression in PSI
Cylinder 1		
Cylinder 2		
Cylinder 3		
Cylinder 4		

TECHNICIAN TIP

Another way to measure compression is with a relative compression test. This test uses an inductive ammeter connected to a lab scope to measure the current flow for the starter as the engine is being cranked. As each cylinder comes up on the compression stroke, the engine is harder to turn, so the starter works harder and the current flow is higher. If every cylinder has the same relative compression, then the current spikes will be similar. If a cylinder has low compression, then that current spike will be lower than the rest. This is a quick way of checking to see if there is a compression-related problem.

SKILL DRILL 11-7 Performing a Cranking Compression Test

1. Remove any spark plug wires or ignition coils connected directly to the spark plugs.

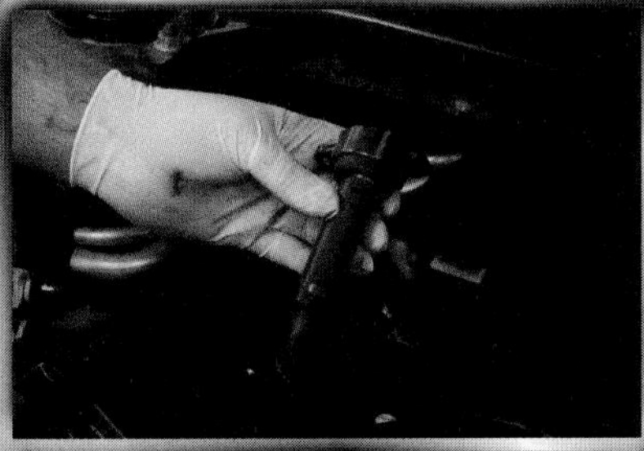

2. Disable the ignition system by grounding the coil wire(s) or disconnecting the coil primary circuit(s).

3. Disable the injectors or remove the fuel pump fuse or relay.

4. Remove all spark plugs.

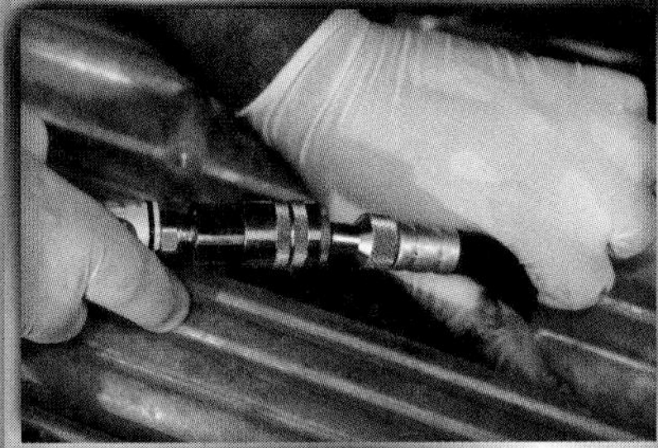

5. Connect the compression tester to the spark plug hole to be tested. Check the thread length and diameter for the proper fitting. If separate, connect the hose to the compression tester.

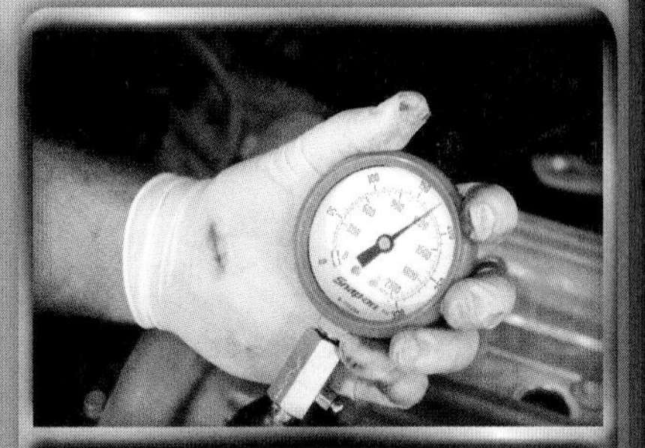

6. Hold the throttle down and crank the engine over so that the compression tester needle jumps at least five times. Record the first and last needle readings. Repeat this procedure on the other cylinders.

7. Perform a wet test on any cylinders with low compression. Determine any necessary action.

TECHNICIAN TIP

To perform a wet test, place a couple of squirts of clean engine oil in the low cylinder, and retest the compression. If the compression pressure increases substantially, the piston rings are worn. If the compression doesn't change much, a valve, the head gasket, or top of the piston has a leak.

> **TECHNICIAN TIP**
>
> When performing a compression test, the final reading is not the only thing to observe. If the piston rings are sealing well, then the first compression pulse on the gauge should be at least half as much pressure as the final reading.
>
> When a low-compression cylinder is found, you should put a couple squirts of oil (about a tablespoon) into the spark plug hole, crank the engine a few turns, and recheck the compression. If the compression rises significantly, the problem is typically worn piston rings in that cylinder, as indicated by the higher compression due to the short-term sealing ability of the added oil. Worn piston rings are a substantial problem that typically requires rebuilding or replacement of the engine. If the oil did not make the compression rise, then the problem is likely to be either a leaky valve or head gasket or a hole in the piston. A cylinder leakage test can determine which.

broken valve springs or rocker arms, carboned-up valves, or restricted intake and exhaust passageways in general. To confirm your diagnosis, do a visual inspection of the suspect components.

To perform a running compression test, follow the steps in **SKILL DRILL 11-8**.

Cylinder Leakage Test Overview

The cylinder leakage test is performed on a cylinder with low compression to determine the severity of the compression leak and where the leak is located. Compressed air is applied to the cylinder through a tester that is calibrated to show the amount of cylinder leakage as a percent of air entering the cylinder. An ideal reading is close to 0%. But since piston rings have a small gap between their ends to allow for expansion as the engine heats up, a cylinder will not be sealed 100%. There will almost always be at least a small amount of leakage past the piston ring gaps. Typically manufacturers will consider up to 20% cylinder leakage past the piston rings acceptable, but the smaller the leakage, the better. Although it is OK to have a small amount of leakage past the piston rings, it is not OK to have *any* leakage past one of the valves or the head gasket. Leaks at these places mean the engine likely has a major mechanical engine issue.

The point of this test is to measure how much air is leaking as well as to determine where it is leaking from. The gauge tells you the percentage of air leaking from the cylinder, so that is straightforward. Determining where the air is leaking from is a bit more challenging. Because there is always some air leaking past the piston rings, you

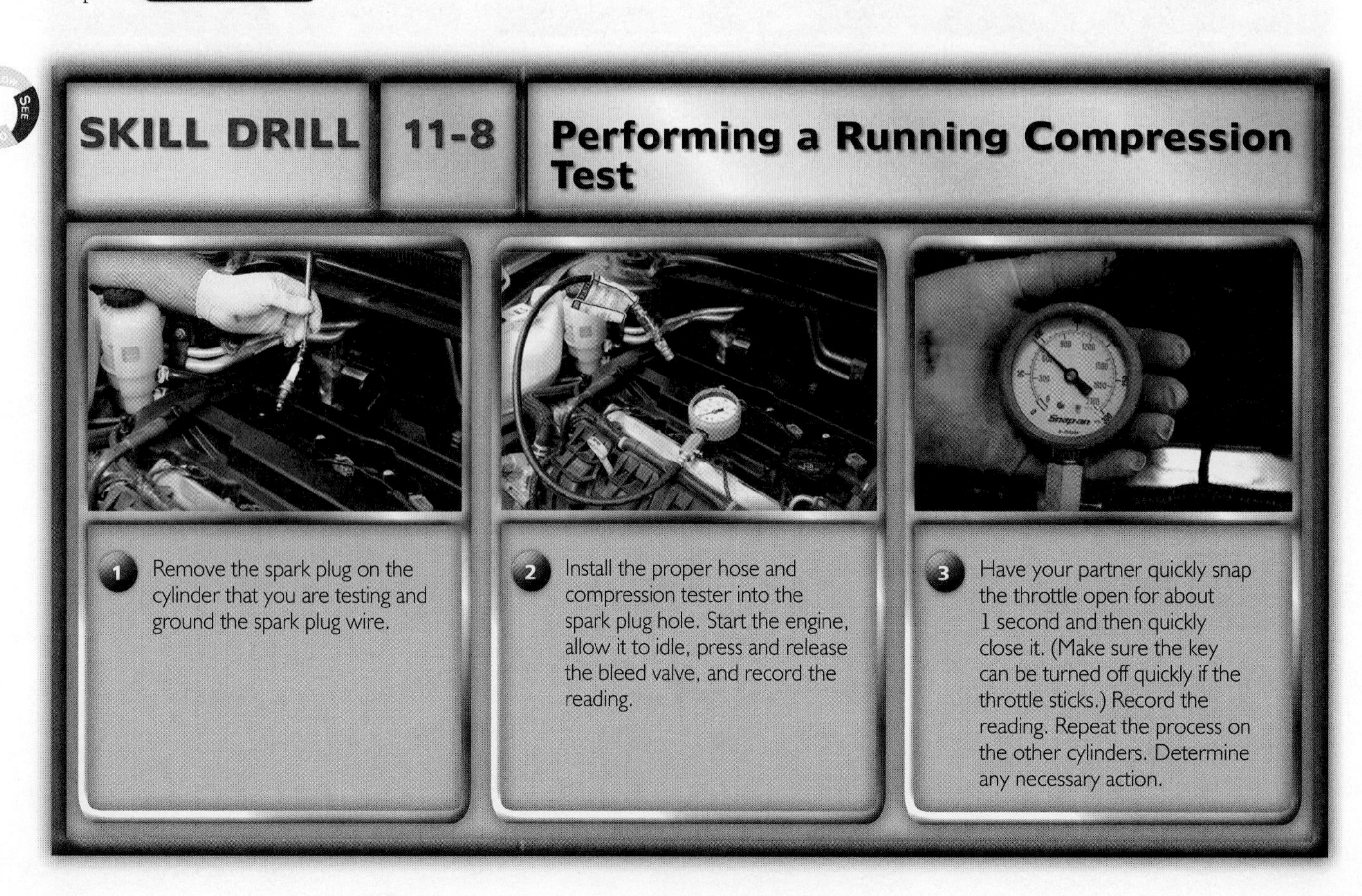

SKILL DRILL 11-8 Performing a Running Compression Test

1. Remove the spark plug on the cylinder that you are testing and ground the spark plug wire.
2. Install the proper hose and compression tester into the spark plug hole. Start the engine, allow it to idle, press and release the bleed valve, and record the reading.
3. Have your partner quickly snap the throttle open for about 1 second and then quickly close it. (Make sure the key can be turned off quickly if the throttle sticks.) Record the reading. Repeat the process on the other cylinders. Determine any necessary action.

will be able to hear some air leaking out of the oil fill hole when the oil fill cap is removed. If that is the only leak that you end up diagnosing, then the gauge will indicate if the leakage past the piston rings is excessive.

If an exhaust valve is burnt or warped, then you will hear leakage out of the exhaust pipe. If the intake valve is burnt or warped, then you will hear leakage out the air intake system. There should be no leakage past either of the valves, so any leak in the exhaust or intake is a bad leak. If the head gasket is blown, then you will either hear air coming out of an adjacent spark plug hole or see bubbles in the coolant when the radiator cap is removed.

Performing a Cylinder Leakage Test

There are a couple of critical steps needed to make sure the cylinder leakage test is accurate. First, the engine should be near operating temperature, which will ensure that oil has been circulated to the piston rings to help them seal. Next, it is helpful to loosen each of the spark plugs about one turn for the cylinders you will be testing and then run the engine at 1500 rpm for 10 to 15 seconds. This process helps blow out any chunks of carbon that were straddling the spark plug to cylinder head gap that break off when the spark plugs are removed. If you do not do this, it is possible for one of these chunks of carbon to get stuck between a valve and valve seat, holding the valve open slightly and producing a false reading.

Since the cylinder leakage test is usually only performed on a cylinder with low compression, you must remove only the spark plug for the cylinder you are testing and the spark plug for each of the cylinders next to that one. If the suspect cylinder is in the middle of the bank, then you will need to remove the spark plug on either side. If the suspect cylinder is at the end of the bank, then you will need to remove only the nearest spark plug. It also helps to remove the air cleaner assembly and radiator cap for listening purposes during the test.

Cylinder leakage is measured when the piston is on top dead center on the compression stroke. This means that you will have to turn the crankshaft to position each piston in this position before pressurizing the system. The challenge is that the piston, connecting rod, and crankshaft throw must be in near perfect alignment; otherwise the pressure on the piston from the cylinder leakage tester will push the piston down, which turns the crankshaft. If this happens, then the intake or exhaust valve will open, depending on which way the piston ends up turning the crankshaft.

The hardest part is getting the piston exactly on top dead center. There are two primary ways to do so. One is to screw the cylinder leakage tester into the spark plug hole and then slowly turn the engine over by hand while lightly floating your thumb over the end of the hose to feel pressure and vacuum. When you feel the transition from pressure to vacuum, turn the engine in the opposite direction slightly and stop right as the pressure stops and before the vacuum begins. It takes experience to get the feel for this. The second way is to use a plastic straw that fits down the spark plug hole and that can be pushed up by the piston without damaging the cylinder or piston. Rotate the engine by hand until the piston is as high as it will go, as indicated by the plastic straw. While the piston is on top dead center, you will not know if it is on the top of the compression stroke or the exhaust stroke until you pressurize the cylinder (unless the engine is equipped with a distributor and you can see where the rotor is pointing). If it is wrong, turn the engine one complete revolution and try it again.

To perform a cylinder leakage test, follow the steps in **SKILL DRILL 11-9**.

> **TECHNICIAN TIP**
>
> There are a couple of ways that a technician can get in trouble when interpreting the results of a cylinder leakage test. First, if a valve is being held open due to a piece of carbon, or not enough valve lash, then the problem could be misdiagnosed. To verify a leaky valve, remove the valve cover and verify that the valve has the proper valve lash. Also try tapping the valve open with a soft hammer while watching the cylinder leakage gauge. If tapping on the valve stops the leakage, there was likely some carbon holding the valve slightly open. If the valve is being held open by the valve train, try adjusting the valve and retest the valve for leakage. You should know that a valve that had too little valve lash is likely to be burnt. The longer it was operated with too little clearance, the more likely it is burnt.

Diagnosing Engine Noise and Vibrations

Running engines are fairly quiet considering all of the mechanical activity that happens within them. But if something starts to go wrong, noises can be one of the first indicators. Noise issues can indicate something as simple to fix as a worn accessory belt or as complicated as a spun connecting rod bearing, which would generally require rebuilding the entire engine. Understanding the engine's theory of operation and how the individual components of an engine work will give you a good foundation to start from.

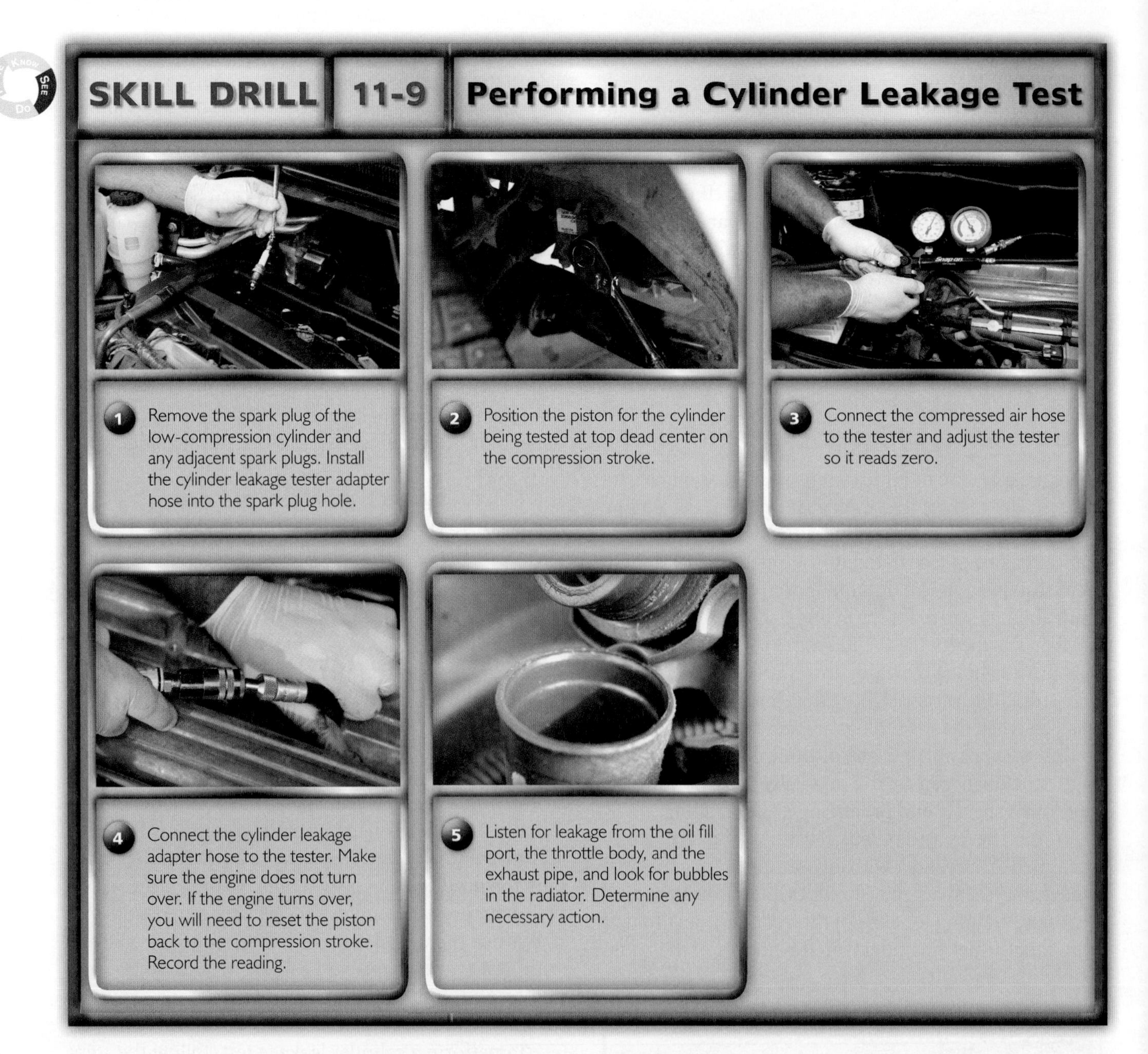
SKILL DRILL 11-9 Performing a Cylinder Leakage Test
1 Remove the spark plug of the low-compression cylinder and any adjacent spark plugs. Install the cylinder leakage tester adapter hose into the spark plug hole.
2 Position the piston for the cylinder being tested at top dead center on the compression stroke.
3 Connect the compressed air hose to the tester and adjust the tester so it reads zero.
4 Connect the cylinder leakage adapter hose to the tester. Make sure the engine does not turn over. If the engine turns over, you will need to reset the piston back to the compression stroke. Record the reading.
5 Listen for leakage from the oil fill port, the throttle body, and the exhaust pipe, and look for bubbles in the radiator. Determine any necessary action.

Many sounds can be pinpointed through an experienced technician's previous knowledge, so investigate unusual noises and build your experience. A loud knocking noise could be from a bad main bearing or connecting rod bearing due to a worn or spun bearing. A main bearing noise is generally deeper sounding than a rod bearing. Also, a main bearing makes an evenly spaced single knock while a rod bearing generally makes a double knock. A light ticking noise could be a valve lifter problem, which can be heard near the camshaft area. Or you might hear a light knocking noise that comes under slight rocking of the throttle that is caused by a collapsed piston skirt. A whirring noise can be caused by worn bearings in alternators, water pumps, and belt tensioners. One way to help locate any type of engine noise is to use a mechanic's stethoscope. Mechanical stethoscopes are the most common, but many electronic stethoscopes have settings that enhance selected sound frequencies, while filtering out others, making them very handy. Place the stethoscope against engine components in a variety of positions around the engine and listen to the noises. Generally, the louder the noise, the closer you are to its source.

Depending on the noise, a stethoscope may not be appropriate. In the case of a squeaky belt, spraying water on one belt at a time will make the noise go away temporarily when you spray the one that is squeaking. Squeaks and creaks that come from linkage and joints can sometimes be sprayed one at a time with a lubricant and operated until the offending joint is found.

Vibrations can be difficult to pinpoint. Vibrations can come from the engine or the drive train. The best clue is to determine if the vibration occurs only when the vehicle is being driven or if it occurs with the engine running irrespective of vehicle movement. If the vibration occurs only when the vehicle is moving, suspect a component within the drive train or drive line, the U-joints, or even the tire balance. A good way to isolate the drive train is to drive the vehicle up to the speed at which the vibration is noticeable. Then place the transmission in neutral and allow the engine to idle. If the vibration is still there, then the issue is probably associated with the wheels, tires, or axles. If the vibration goes away, then raise the engine rpm while still in neutral. If the vibration reoccurs, then the issue is most likely with the engine. If there is no vibration, reengage the appropriate drive gear and accelerate moderately. If the vibration reappears, then the issue is likely with the driveshaft, U-joints, or CV joints.

Diagnosing Oil Consumption, Coolant Consumption, and Exhaust Color

While coolant should have no consumption if the cooling system is working properly, engine oil can have a small amount of consumption and still be considered normal. Most manufacturers will specify the maximum allowable consumption. In many cases, this is stated as no more than 1 quart in a certain number of miles. As long as the consumption is less than that specified, no action is necessary, unless it is related to a particular customer concern. If the consumption is greater than specified, a visual inspection as described in Skill Drills 11-1 and 11-2 at the beginning of this chapter is the first order of business. Consumption of oil or coolant that cannot be located with a visual inspection may in some cases be diagnosed by the color of the exhaust. If the color has a bluish tint, it indicates that engine oil is burning. If the blue color is constant while the engine is running, it is likely that the rings are not sealing due to worn rings or cylinder walls. If the blue color is present only when you start the engine, it is likely to be a valve stem seal or valve guide issue. Black exhaust indicates an excessively rich fuel mixture. White exhaust after the engine is warmed up is an indication that coolant is leaking into the exhaust, which could mean a blown head gasket, blown intake gasket, cracked cylinder head, or leaky exhaust gas recirculation cooler on some vehicles. When coolant leaks into the exhaust, it also gives off a sweet anti-freeze odor. This is the same smell as when the heater core is leaking.

Inspecting and Replacing Camshaft and Drive Belt/Chain

The camshaft and drive belt/chain assembly make up an important system for the internal combustion engine. They link the valve train system to the crankshaft and determine the right time in the engine cycle for the valves to open and close. Due to operational wear, these areas need to be serviced to make sure the engine continues to operate correctly. The system is first inspected through a visual inspection of the parts to check for wear or worn parts that can be seen. Through visual inspection, it can be determined which parts are in need of replacement by following the manufacturers recommendations in the service information.

Since OHC engines use a tensioner to keep the belt or chain properly tensioned, this design can make it harder to get the timing correct during replacement. The tensioner pulls all of the slack to one side of the belt or chain, which causes the cam to rotate slightly. Thus, the cam timing can be out of specifications. There are many different timing set configurations for these engines. It is essential that the correct service information be used when setting the cam-to-crankshaft timing on these types of engines.

OHC chain drives typically are of the roller chain style, which looks a lot like a bicycle chain. Roller chain has a long life, usually lasting the life of the engine as long as the engine oil is maintained properly. Chains need lubrication to operate, so engine oil is usually sprayed onto the chain from the front of the block. The timing chain area of the engine is sealed from the outside. OHC engines using timing chains have guides and chain tensioners to keep the chain in place, in addition to two or more sprockets. Refer to the service information for timing mark locations and the specific instructions for installing these.

Chain tensioners are installed with the tensioner in the collapsed position **FIGURE 11-8**. When installing the chain, you might be directed to count the chain links between the mark on the crank sprocket and the mark on the cam sprocket to get the right timing. Usually the timing links are a different color to make alignment easier. Align the links to the chain gear pip marks on both the crank and the cam sprockets **FIGURE 11-9**. Install any chain guides and then release the chain tensioner to take up the slack in the chain. Before rotating the engine,

> **TECHNICIAN TIP**
>
> On dual overhead cam (DOHC) engines, it is important to install the correct cam gear on each camshaft. Failure to do so will cause the cam timing to be off, which could lead to valve and piston damage, as well as an engine that will not run. The same thing can happen if the camshafts are installed in the wrong place.

recheck the timing marks to be sure they are still lined up after the tensioner is released. Always refer to the manufacturer's installation procedures and diagrams.

Belt-driving timing sets use a flexible belt to transmit drive from the crankshaft to the camshaft. The belt runs more quietly than a chain and does not require lubrication. But timing belts do wear out and need to be changed periodically, typically between 50,000 and 100,000 miles (80,000 to 160,000km), depending on the vehicle manufacturer. Since they do not need to be lubricated, they are generally behind a timing belt cover that is not sealed to the front of the engine. The cover acts more as a belt guard and to protect it from dirt and debris.

As with the timing chain type of engine, always refer to current service information for timing mark locations. Install the cogged gears onto the camshaft if not already installed, being sure not to forget the keys, if equipped. They should have already been aligned when the cylinder head was on the bench, but it is best to double-check for the proper alignment of the timing marks. Be careful not to move the camshaft very much, as the valves could have an interference fit to the pistons. If the camshaft does need to move substantially, turn the crankshaft so it is approximately 20 to 30 degrees before or after TDC. This will pull all of the pistons down from the top of the cylinder so that the valves will not hit the pistons when the cam is turned. With the timing marks aligned FIGURE 11-10, install the timing belt with as much of the slack as possible on the tensioner side of the belt, and then install the belt tensioner FIGURE 11-11. Verify that all timing marks are aligned. Always refer to the manufacturer's installation procedures on timing belts and belt tension.

To inspect and replace the camshaft and drive belt/chain, follow the steps in SKILL DRILL 11-10.

FIGURE 11-8 Chain tensioner in collapsed position.

Timing mark lined
up with head surface
FIGURE 11-10 Timing marks aligned.

FIGURE 11-9 Chain links in position on the timing sprocket marks.

FIGURE 11-11 Timing belt tensioner installed.

SKILL DRILL 11-10 Inspecting and Replacing the Camshaft and Drive Belt/Chain

1. Determine all the specifications for timing chain or belt tension assembly according to the manufacturer of the engine assembly being serviced. Remove all fluids from systems as indicated by the manufacturer's service procedures Remove all components that cover the timing chain/belt assembly, such as the harmonic balancer, water pump, alternators, and power steering pump.

2. Remove the camshaft timing chain/belt cover. Inspect the cover for wear marks, and replace if worn. Look for causes for the worn cover.

Timing mark lined
up with head surface

3. With the timing chain/belt cover off and the timing gears and belts/chains in full view, turn the engine over manually to line up the timing marks of the crankshaft and camshaft sprockets with the appropriate marks on the block and head.

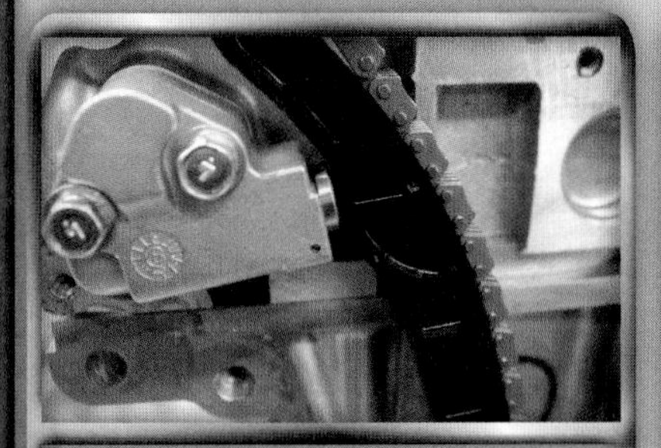

4. Inspect the belt/chain and measure for wear, and replace if not within specifications. Measure the clearance between tensioners, if applicable, and replace if not within specifications.

5. Remove the chain or belt following the specified procedure. Use the proper cam holding tool, if specified, to prevent damage to valves.

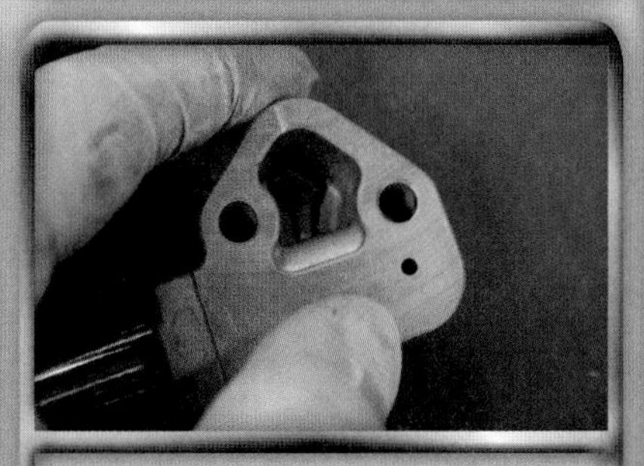

6. If the tensioner is oil operated, check the oil passages to the tensioner for clogs or buildup of dirt sludge, and clean or replace according to recommendations.

SKILL DRILL 11-10 Inspecting and Replacing the Camshaft and Drive Belt/Chain, continued

7. Inspect any guide pulleys for smooth rotation on their bearings, and replace if damaged. With the chain/belt removed, inspect the cam sprockets visually for wear, cracking, and damage. Inspect sprockets for backlash and end play, if applicable, on the vehicle.

8. On engines with any type of variable valve timing, check components for worn and damaged parts on the gears, inspect any oil control devices for leaks, and perform other tests on components according to the manufacturer's recommendations.

9. Reinstall new parts according to the manufacturer's recommendations. Reassemble the timing chain/belt assembly. Turn the crankshaft two complete revolutions by hand, and recheck the timing marks and belt/chain tension. Reassemble components following the specified procedure.

Wrap-up

Ready for Review

- Appropriate service information is needed to make an accurate diagnosis.
- The best source for vehicle service information is the vehicle manufacturer.
- Major vehicle components often have identification numbers.
- A systematic mechanical testing and verification process is needed to diagnose and repair an engine problem.
- Engine mechanical testing tools include a compression gauge, vacuum gauge, cylinder leakage tester, and scan tool.
- The color of a leaking fluid can assist in identifying the source of a leak.
- During engine cranking, the engine will make an even cranking sound if the compression is even between the cylinders.
- A vacuum gauge is used to determine the general condition of an engine.
- A cylinder power balance test is used to determine whether all of the engine cylinders are working properly.
- A cranking compression test measures the compressed air pressure in the cylinder.
- A running compression test checks the engine's breathing ability.
- A cylinder leakage test is performed on a cylinder with low compression.
- A stethoscope can be used to isolate an engine noise.
- Exhaust smoke can indicate the source of an engine problem.
- An odor can help diagnose an engine problem.
- Engine tests must be properly interpreted to correct an engine problem.

Key Terms

compression tester A device used to measure the amount of compression pressure a cylinder can generate.

cylinder leakage tester A device that pumps air into the cylinder and measures the percentage of air that is leaking out of the cylinder.

data link connector (DLC) The connector through which the scan tool communicates to the vehicle's computers; it will display the readings from the various sensors and can retrieve trouble codes, freeze-frame data, and system monitor data.

pressure transducer A device used to measure engine vacuum and display it graphically on a lab scope.

vacuum gauge A device used to measure the amount of vacuum an engine can generate during various operating conditions.

ASE-Type Questions

1. Tech A says that a cranking sound diagnosis can be used to diagnose problems in the ignition system. Tech B says that a cranking sound diagnosis can indicate differences in compression. Who is correct?
   a. Tech A
   b. Tech B
   c. Both A and B
   d. Neither A nor B
2. Tech A says that a power balance test is a good way to narrow a misfire down to a particular cylinder or cylinders. Tech B says that a cylinder power balance test measures the volumetric efficiency of the cylinder being tested. Who is correct?
   a. Tech A
   b. Tech B
   c. Both A and B
   d. Neither A nor B
3. Tech A says that a cranking compression wet test can indicate if the cylinder has worn piston rings. Tech B says that the throttle should be held wide open during a cranking compression check. Who is correct?
   a. Tech A
   b. Tech B
   c. Both A and B
   d. Neither A nor B
4. Tech A says that low compression on a single cylinder will cause an engine not to start. Tech B says that low compression on a single cylinder will affect the engine's cranking sound. Who is correct?
   a. Tech A
   b. Tech B
   c. Both A and B
   d. Neither A nor B
5. Tech A says that a cylinder leakage test is performed on a cylinder with low compression to determine the severity of the leak and where it is located. Tech B says that manufacturers will consider up to 50% cylinder leakage past the piston rings acceptable. Who is correct?
   a. Tech A
   b. Tech B
   c. Both A and B
   d. Neither A nor B
6. Tech A says that a scan tool connected to the data link connector (DLC) will perform a cylinder power balance test and report cylinder pressures. Tech B says that a scan tool will perform a cylinder power balance test and report whether the rings or valves have failed. Who is correct?
   a. Tech A
   b. Tech B
   c. Both A and B
   d. Neither A nor B
7. Tech A says that researching related service information for a vehicle repair will assist the technician. Tech B says that research should be done only when the technician needs direction. Who is correct?
   a. Tech A
   b. Tech B
   c. Both A and B
   d. Neither A nor B
8. Tech A says that a vacuum gauge needle that dips 4–8 inches rhythmically can indicate a burned valve. Tech B says that a stethoscope can be used to determine the source of unusual engine noises. Who is correct?
   a. Tech A
   b. Tech B
   c. Both A and B
   d. Neither A nor B
9. Tech A says that a vacuum test can determine exhaust restriction. Tech B says that when performing a cylinder power balance test, results should be 5% or less. Who is correct?
   a. Tech A
   b. Tech B
   c. Both A and B
   d. Neither A nor B
10. Tech A says that a bad cam lobe or broken valve spring will show up during a running compression test. Tech B says that when performing a cylinder leakage test the engine must be running to get proper results. Who is correct?
    a. Tech A
    b. Tech B
    c. Both A and B
    d. Neither A nor B

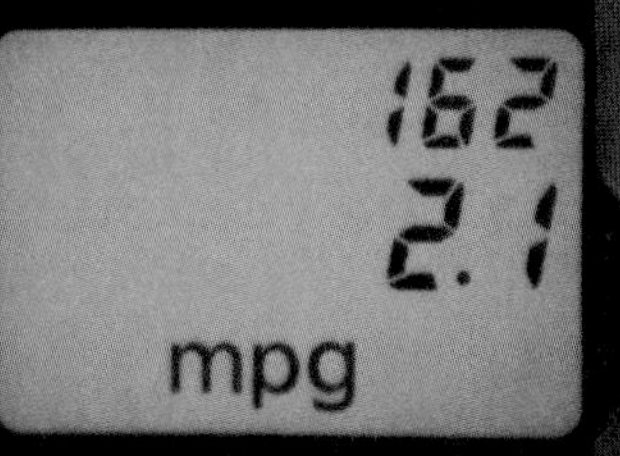

162
2.1
mpg

CHAPTER 12

KNOW
SEE
DO
PROVE

NATEF Tasks

Engine Repair
Lubrication and Cooling Systems

		Page
■ Perform oil and filter change.	MLR AST	307–313

KNOW
SEE
DO
PROVE

Knowledge Objectives

After reading this chapter, you will be able to:

1. Describe the components of lubricating oil. (p 292)
2. Describe the functions of lubricating oil. (p 293)
3. Describe the types of common additives added to lubricating oil. (p 294)
4. Describe the three types of oil. (pp 297–298)
5. Identify the components of the lubrication system. (pp 298–304)
6. Describe the operation of the lubrication system. (pp 304–305)
7. Describe the types of lubrication systems and how they operate. (pp 305–306)

Engine Lubrication

Know
See
Do
Prove

Skills Objectives

After reading this chapter, you will be able to:

1. Check the engine oil. (pp 307–308)
2. Drain the engine oil. (pp 309–310)
3. Replace a spin-on filter. (pp 311–312)
4. Replace a cartridge filter (replaceable element). (p 312)
5. Refill the engine oil. (p 313)

Introduction

Machinery, like our automobiles, relies on lubrication to keep the moving parts from wearing out quickly. Lubricating oil is processed from crude oil in a refinery with gasoline and diesel, along with many other beneficial and useful products. Oil is much more than simply crude oil dumped into our engine's crankcase; it is heavily processed to remove impurities, and many additives are put into the processed oil by scientists in a lab to enhance its lubricating qualities.

Each moving part in the engine needs lubricating oil. The system that moves the oil through the engine is called the lubrication system. This chapter will cover the theory of lubrication systems and the methods and specialized tools involved to ensure that you can properly diagnose and correct common problems associated with this system.

Oil

Oil originates from the ground as **crude oil** FIGURE 12-1. Crude oil varies in color from a dirty yellow to dark brown to black. It can be thin like gasoline or a thick oil- or tarlike substance. Crude oil is pumped from the ground and processed into many products such as fuel for use in diesel and gasoline vehicles. Crude oil is also broken down into other products, which are used in plastics manufacturing as well as in kerosene, aviation fuel, asphalt, cosmetics, pharmaceuticals, and many other products. Many of the products refined from crude oil are used in the transportation industry. For example, **lubricating oil** is distilled from the crude oil and used as a base stock. Additives are added to the base stock to make the lubricating oil useful in engines. Other additives, such as thickening agents, are added to the base stocks and used as lubricating grease in bearings. The additives that are added to the base stock perform a variety of tasks such as keeping acids from forming, cutting down on oxidation, and maintaining the correct viscosity over a broader temperature range.

FIGURE 12-1 Crude oil straight from the ground.

You Are the Automotive Technician

A customer brings his 5-year-old vehicle into your shop for an oil and filter change. The vehicle is right at the recommended 7,500 mile interval. He said he has noticed some oil spots on his garage floor, and the oil level was a bit below the "add" mark this morning when he checked it. He is concerned that he has an oil leak, and he would like to know why the oil pressure light on the dash didn't indicate that his oil level was low. You pull the vehicle onto the hoist. The oil light comes on when the key is turned to "run" and goes off once the engine starts, proving that the oil pressure warning light circuit is working. With the engine running, you find a that a drop of oil forms every so often on the end of the oil pressure switch, indicating it is leaking and needs to be replaced. None of the engine seals and gaskets show any signs of leakage.

1. What are the functions that oil performs inside an engine?
2. Why didn't the oil pressure light indicate that the oil was below the "add" line?
3. How often should the oil and filter be changed?

> **TECHNICIAN TIP**
>
> Lubricating oil has been used since the invention of machinery. When metal moves on another piece of metal, the parts wear quickly without lubrication. Lubricating oil also helps to quiet the moving parts and remove heat from metal surfaces.

Functions of Lubricating Oil

Lubricating oil performs five main functions: lubricates, cushions, cools, cleans, and seals. Lubrication involves reducing friction, protecting against corrosion, and preventing metal-to-metal contact between the moving surfaces. Friction occurs between all surfaces that come into contact with each other. When moving surfaces come together, friction tends to slow them down. Friction can be useful, as in a brake system. In the moving parts of engines, friction is a bad thing and will lead to serious damage. Friction can make metal parts so hot they melt and fuse together. When this happens, an engine is said to have seized.

Lubrication reduces unwanted friction and reduces wear on moving parts. Clearances, such as those between the crankshaft journal and crankshaft bearing, fill with lubricating oil so that engine parts move or float on layers of oil instead of directly on each other **FIGURE 12-2**. By reducing friction, less power is needed to move these components and more of the engine's power can be used to turn the crankshaft instead of wasted as heat; the result is increased power to move the vehicle and better fuel economy.

How long an engine lasts depends mostly on how well it is lubricated, especially at the points of extreme loading, or high-wear areas, such as between the cam lobe and cam follower. At the same time, the connecting rod and crankshaft bearings take large amounts of stress as the piston tries to drive through the crankshaft each time the cylinder fires. A power stroke can put as much as 2 tons of force on the main bearings. The lubricating oil between the surfaces helps to cushion these shock loads, similar to the way a shock absorber absorbs a bump in the road.

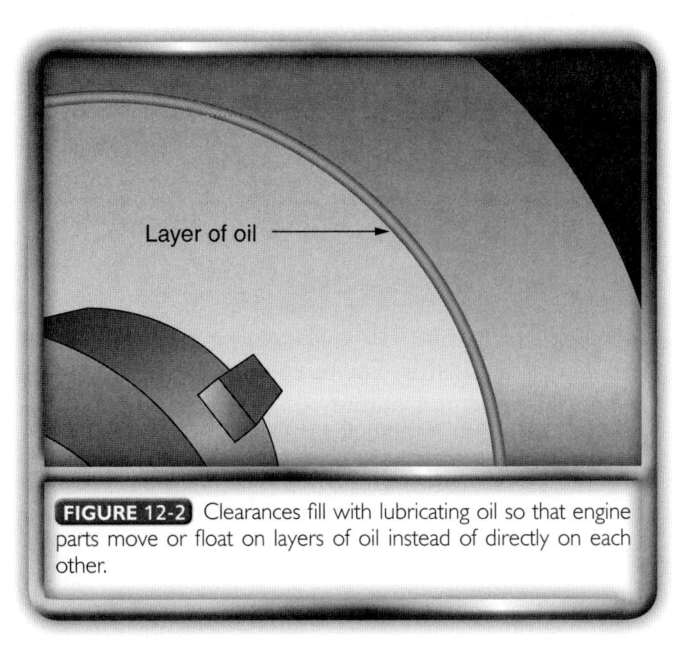
Layer of oil

FIGURE 12-2 Clearances fill with lubricating oil so that engine parts move or float on layers of oil instead of directly on each other.

Lubricating oil also helps cool an engine. The lubricating oil collects heat from the engine's components and then returns to the sump, where it cools. The heat from the lubricating oil is picked up by the air moving over the oil sump. Many heavy-duty and high-performance vehicles have cooling fins on their oil pan or even a separate oil cooler to help the oil do its job of cooling critical engine components.

Lubricating oil also works as a cleaning agent. There are additives in the lubricating oil that allow it to collect particles of metal and carbon and carry them back to the oil sump. Larger pieces fall to the bottom of the oil sump, while smaller pieces are suspended in the oil and are removed when the oil moves through the oil filter. When oil is changed, most of the particles are removed with the oil filter and old oil.

The last function of oil is that it seals. It plays a key role in sealing the piston rings to the cylinder walls. Without a small film of oil between the rings and cylinder walls, blow-by gases would be much higher, resulting in diluted oil, lower compression, lower power, and lower fuel economy.

Corrosion Protection

Acids build up in the engine due to the accumulation of combustion by-products and moisture. Blow-by gases contain chemicals that are trapped in the oil. The chemicals react and form acids. When the engine is turned off, it begins to cool. The cooling process creates moisture that then condenses into droplets that fall into the oil and form acids. The acids attack the internal components causing unnecessary damage. The oil contains anticorrosion additives that coat the engine surfaces, helping to protect them from the effects of the acid.

Viscosity

For oil to do all of the work that is expected of it, it must have special properties. Its viscosity is crucial. **Viscosity** is a measure of how easily a liquid flows. Low-viscosity liquid is thin and flows easily. High-viscosity liquid is thick and flows slowly. Lubricating oil must be thin enough to circulate easily between moving parts, but not so thin that it will be squeezed out easily. If it is too viscous, it moves too slowly to protect the moving parts, especially in a cold engine. As engine machining and metal technology have become more advanced, the clearances between lubricated parts have decreased. As a result, engine manufacturers have specified thinner oils for their engines so that oil can flow into the smaller clearances. The thinner oil also flows more easily, which increases fuel economy.

Applied Science

AS-25 Inhibitors: The technician can explain the need for additives in automobile lubricants.

Automotive lubricants are composed of base stock plus an additive package. In addition to engine oil, additives are used in lubricants for manual and automatic transmissions, as well as differentials.

Oil additives are a very necessary part of modern lubricants. The improvements in modern automotive lubricants are one of the factors that enable vehicles to last longer than ever before. Oil additives consist of chemical compounds that have many beneficial functions.

Detergents are additives that help keep the oil clean. Corrosion (or rust) inhibiting additives work to prevent oxidation of engine parts. According to Wikipedia, a corrosion inhibitor is a chemical compound that, when added to a liquid or gas, decreases the corrosion rates of a material, typically a metal or an alloy.

Oil Additives

Special chemicals called additives are added to the base oil by the oil companies. Different combinations of these additives allow the oil to do different jobs in an engine. A description of common additives follows:

- **Extreme-pressure additives** coat parts with a protective layer so that the oil resists being forced out under heavy load.
- **Oxidation inhibitors** stop very hot oil from combining with oxygen in the air to produce a sticky tarlike material, which coats parts and clogs the oil **galleries** and drain-back passages. Oil galleries are the passageways that carry oil through the engine. They are either cast or drilled into the engine block and head(s).
- **Corrosion inhibitors** help stop acids from forming that cause corrosion, especially on bearing surfaces. Corrosion due to acid etches into bearing surfaces and causes premature wear of the bearings.
- **Antifoaming agents** reduce the effect of oil churning in the crankcase and minimize foaming. Foaming allows air bubbles to form in the engine oil, reducing the lubrication quality of oil and contributing to breakdown of the oil due to oxidation. Since air is compressible, oil with foam reduces the ability of the oil to keep the moving parts separated, causing more wear and friction. The antifoaming additives keep these conditions from occurring.
- **Detergents** reduce carbon deposits on parts such as piston rings and valves.
- **Dispersants** collect particles that can block the system, separate them from each other, and keep them moving. They will be removed when the oil is changed.
- **Pour point depressants** keep oil from forming wax particles under cold temperature operation. When wax crystals form, they result in the **gelling** of the oil and keep oil from flowing during cold start-up conditions. Gelling is the thickening of oil to a point that it will not flow through the engine; it becomes close to a solid in extreme cold temperatures.
- Base stock derived from crude oil will not retain its viscosity if the temperature gets cold enough, so viscosity improvers are added to the stock. A **viscosity index improver** is an additive that helps to reduce the change in viscosity as the temperature of the oil changes. Viscosity index improvers also keep the engine oil from becoming too thin during hot operation.

TECHNICIAN TIP

Before multiviscosity oils, it was a normal practice for engines to need one grade of lubricating oil for summer and another for winter.

Oil Rating Standards

There are several certifying bodies for engine oil, each with its own standards. The three most common are the American Petroleum Institute (API), the American Society of Automotive Engineers (SAE), and the International Lubricant Standardization and Approval Committee (ILSAC). However, there are three others that technicians must be aware of: the Japanese Automotive Standards

Organization (JASO), the Association des Constructeurs Européens d'Automobiles (ACEA), also called the European Automobile Manufacturers Association, and the vehicle manufacturers' (OEM) own standards. Let's look at them one at a time.

American Petroleum Institute (API)

The API sets minimum performance standards for lubricants including engine oils. The API has a two-part classification: service class and service standard. The API service class has two general classifications: S for spark ignition engines and C for compression ignition engines, also referred to as "commercial." Engine oil that meets the API standards may display the API Service Symbol, which is also known as the API "donut." This protocol is important to understand because oil rated S only cannot be used in compression ignition engines unless they also carry the C rating and vice versa. Be careful that the wrong oil is not used in a particular engine.

The API service standard (SA) was used in engines up to 1930, which means pure mineral oil without any additives. As engine manufacturers improved engine technology—or as government regulations changed, such as requiring reduced amounts of phosphorus—engine oil with new qualities was required, and the API would introduce a new rating level. The API SN level was added in October 2010 for 2011 gasoline vehicles. API CJ-4 was added in 2010 to meet four-stroke diesel engine requirements.

The API symbol is the donut symbol located on the back of the oil bottle FIGURE 12-3. In the top half of the symbol is the service class—S or C—and the service standard that the oil meets. The center part carries the SAE viscosity rating for the oil. The API symbol may also carry an energy saving designation if it is a fuel-saving oil. Be sure to use oil that has a correct API rating and also an energy-conserving designation in all North American vehicles.

> **TECHNICIAN TIP**
>
> In most cases, higher rated engine oils are backward compatible. This means you can use SM oil in a vehicle that requires SL. But there is one exception that some technicians have found. SN-rated oil has very low levels of phosphorus and zinc, which aids in flat tappet camshaft lubrication. So if you are working on an older engine that uses flat tappets, you probably do not want to use SN-rated oil, but SM instead.

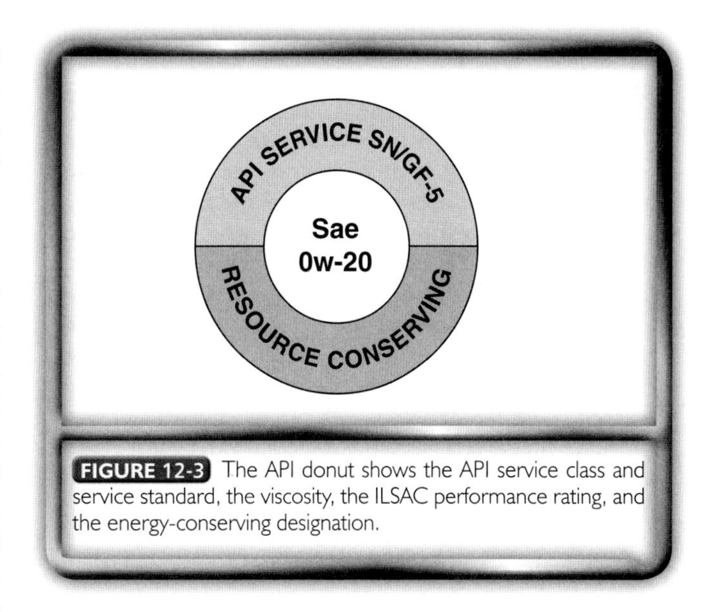
API SERVICE SN/GF-5
Sae
Ow-20
RESOURCE CONSERVING

FIGURE 12-3 The API donut shows the API service class and service standard, the viscosity, the ILSAC performance rating, and the energy-conserving designation.

American Society of Automotive Engineers (SAE)

Engine oil producers must also meet the SAE viscosity rating for each particular oil. Engine oil with an SAE number of 50 has a higher viscosity, or is thicker, than an SAE 20 oil. Oils with low viscosity ratings, such as SAE 0W, 5W, and 10W (the "W" stands for winter viscosity), are tested at a low temperature—around 0°F (–17.8°C). These ratings indicate how the oil will flow when started cold in cold climate conditions. Oils with high viscosity ratings, such as SAE 20, 30, 40, and 50, are tested at a high temperature—around 210°F (98.9°C). These ratings indicate how the oil will flow when the engine is being used under loaded conditions in hotter conditions.

Modern oils are blends of oils that combine these properties. The oils are blended with viscosity index improvers to form multigrade, or multiviscosity, oils. They provide better lubrication over a wider range of climatic conditions than monograde oils. These oils are classified by a two-part designation, such as SAE 0W-20. In this example, when the oil was tested at 0°F (–17.8°C), it met the specifications for a viscosity of 0W weight oil, and when the same oil was tested at 210°F (98.9°C), it met the viscosity specifications for 20 weight oil. Multiviscosity oils flow easily during cold engine start-up but do not thin out as much as the engine and oil come up to operating temperature. These properties allow the oil to get to the components quicker during start-up while maintaining its ability to cushion components when it is hot. While multiviscosity oils extend the operating temperature range of the engine, always refer to the vehicle's service information to determine the correct oil viscosity to use for the climate the engine will be operated in.

Applied Science

AS-103: Viscosity: The technician can demonstrate an understanding of fluid viscosity as a measurement and explain how it impacts engine performance.

Viscosity is the measurement of a liquid's resistance to flow. This concept is often best understood by example. Imagine you have a small funnel that you fill with honey. You will find that the funnel drains quite slowly. If you filled the funnel with water, it would drain almost instantly. The difference is because honey has a higher viscosity than water.

Late-model engines are assembled with tighter clearances between moving parts to maximize efficiency and minimize mechanical noise. High-viscosity oil, as used in older vehicles, will not move quickly enough to protect crucial parts in late-model engines, especially on a cold start. Low-viscosity oils, used in older engines, will flow too rapidly past components with large clearances and will provide insufficient lubrication and insufficient oil pressure. The result in both cases is excessive mechanical noise and premature failure with continued operation.

International Lubricant Standardization and Approval Committee (ILSAC)

ILSAC works in conjunction with the API in creating new specifications for gasoline engine oil. However, ILSAC requires that the oil provide increased fuel economy over a base lubricant. These oils should reduce vehicle owners' fuel costs a small amount compared to an oil that does not meet the ILSAC standard. Like the API standard, ILSAC issues sequentially higher rating levels each time the standards are changed. ILSAC GF-5 replaced GF-4 and became the standard in September 2011. Engine oils that meet the GF-4 and GF-5 standard can display the API starburst symbol, which the API created to verify that the oil meets the highest ILSAC standard.

Association des Constructeurs Européens d'Automobiles (ACEA)

The ACEA classifications formulated for engine oils used in European vehicles are much more stringent than the API and ILSAC standards. Some of the characteristics the ACEA-rated oil must score high on are soot thickening, water, sludge, piston deposits, oxidative thickening, fuel economy, and after-treatment compatibility. While some of these may be tested by the API and ILSAC, the standards are set high to achieve ACEA certification ratings. This means that the engine oil provides additional protection or characteristics that API- or ILSAC-rated oils may not match. If you are servicing a European vehicle, it is advised that you do not go by any API recommendations; instead, make sure the oil meets the recommended ACEA rating specified by the manufacturer or the manufacturer's own specification rating.

Japanese Automotive Standards Organization (JASO)

The JASO standards set the classification for motorcycle engines, both two-stroke and four-stroke, as well as Japanese automotive diesel engines. For four-cycle motorcycle engines, the JASO T 903:2011 came into effect in October 2011 and designates different ratings for wet clutch (MA) and dry clutch (MB). For two-stroke motorcycles, JASO M 34:2003 came into effect in October 2003. And for automotive diesel engines, JASO M355:2008 came into effect in August 2008.

OEM-Specific Standards

As engine manufacturers continued to design new features or longer drain intervals into their engines, faster than some of the oil rating organizations could (or would) change their standards, engine manufacturers came up with their own standards. These standards are specific to individual manufacturers or even individual engines of a particular manufacturer. A few examples follow: Oil meeting Volkswagon's VW 506.00 standard are suitable for use on diesel engines (not with single injector pump) with an extended service interval of up to 31,000 miles or 2 years. Oil meeting General Motor's Dexos1™ is specified for use in all 2011 GM vehicles except those equipped with Duramax diesel engines and is backward compatible in all older GM vehicles. Its viscosity is SAE 5W-30 and meets the ACEA A3/B3 standard. It has a service interval of up to 18,600 miles. Oil meeting BMW's Longlife-04 standard is approved for fully synthetic long-life oil and is usually required for BMWs equipped with a diesel particulate filter.

As you can see, it is important to understand the oil requirements for the vehicle you are working on and only use the specified oil. Using the wrong oil can result in severe damage to the engine. Furthermore, using the wrong oil can void the customer's warranty, leaving the customer, or your shop, responsible for repairs. Long gone are the days of grabbing five bottles of any 10W-30 oil off the shelf and putting it into any car that rolls through the door.

TECHNICIAN TIP

Be sure to check the owner's manual or service manual of the vehicle to ensure that you are using the correct oil rating and viscosity for the engine. Do not use just any oil that is sitting on the parts shelf.

American Petroleum Institute Classifications

The API classifies oils into five groups:

1. Group 1 oils are produced by simple distillation of crude oil, which separates the components of the oil by their boiling point, and by the use of solvents to extract sulfur, nitrogen, and oxygen compounds. This method was the only commercial refinement process until the early 1970s, and the bulk of commercial oil products on the market are still produced by this process, such as conventional engine oils.
2. Group 2 and group 3 oils are refined with hydrogen at much higher temperatures and pressures, in a process known as **hydro-cracking**. This process results in a base mineral oil with many of the higher performance characteristics of synthetic oils.
3. The more heavily hydro-cracked group 3 oils have a very high viscosity index (above 120) and many, but not all, of the higher performance characteristics of a full polyalphaolefin (PAO) synthetic oil. Although not fully synthetic, these oils can be sold as synthetic oil in North America.
4. Group 4 oils are all of the full synthetic PAO group (most common true synthetic).
5. Group 5 includes all other types of synthetic oil.

> **TECHNICIAN TIP**
>
> Over time, lubricating oil breaks down by reacting with dissolved atmospheric oxygen. In most refineries, impurities are removed by using solvent. **Hydrogenating** is a newer process that is more effective at removing impurities. Hydrogenation is the use of hydrogen during refining to assist with removing impurities. By hydrogenating the oil, and with the use of oxidation-inhibiting additives, this deterioration rate can be slowed by more than a hundredfold. Hydrogenating also reduces the presence of aromatic hydrocarbons, thereby giving more effective oxidation inhibitor action, minimizing sludge and varnish deposits, and generally avoiding other related machinery problems.

Types of Oil

There are three types of oils sold by oil manufacturers: conventional, synthetic, and synthetic blend. **Conventional oil** is processed from petroleum and uses additives to help the oil work properly in today's high-tech engines. **Synthetic oil** can be man-made or highly processed petroleum. Synthetic oil has fewer impurities since it either is made in a lab, rather than pumped from the ground, or, if it is pumped from the ground, is more highly refined and processed. Synthetic blends are used because they are cheaper to purchase and give the benefit of half synthetic. Manufacturers publish the required oil for each vehicle in the owner's manual.

Conventional Oil

Conventional oil is processed from crude oil pumped from the ground FIGURE 12-4. The crude oil contains many impurities that are removed during the refining process. One of the impurities found in all crude oil is wax. This wax is removed during refining and is used for candle wax; it also serves as an additive in some food and candy. Wax is not a good thing in oil since it creates a thickening effect when it gets cold, becoming too thick to flow through the engine. Crude is broken down into mineral oil, which is then combined with additives to enhance the lubricating qualities. Without the additives, conventional oil would not work well. It would foam easily, break down quickly, and corrode the engine parts after being in the engine for a short time.

FIGURE 12-4 Conventional oil is processed from crude oil pumped from the ground.

Synthetic Oil

There are two main categories of synthetic lubricating oils: type 3, which is not a true synthetic, and type 4 (PAO), which is a true synthetic. Both types of synthetics are more costly to manufacture, since the base stocks are more highly refined or are developed in a lab, and are therefore more costly to the customer. Synthetic lubricants have a number of advantages over conventional oils. They offer better protection against engine wear and can operate at the higher temperatures needed by performance engines. Synthetic oils have better low temperature viscosity, which allows the oil to be circulated through the engine more quickly during low temperature engine start-ups. Synthetics have fewer wax impurities that coagulate at low temperatures, they are chemically more stable, and they are generally thinner so they allow for closer tolerances in engine components without loss of lubrication. Modern high-performance engines run much tighter tolerances, so the need for a thinner oil that is able to hold up under higher temperatures is desirable. Some synthetics also last considerably longer, extending oil change intervals to 20,000 miles (30,000 kilometers [km]) or more, which benefits the environment by reducing the used oil stream and reducing the need for finding new sources of oil.

True synthetic oils are based on man-made hydrocarbons, commonly **polyalphaolefin (PAO)** oil, which is a man-made oil base stock—meaning it is not refined from crude oil. Synthetic oils were developed in Germany during World War II due to the lack of crude oil. Synthetic oil was used primarily in jet engines due to the high heat demands of these engines. Normal conventional oil would create heavy carbon deposits on bearings due to the extreme heat, which led to failures. Amsoil was the first synthetic to be approved by the API in 1972. Many companies now offer synthetic oils. Very few synthetic oils on the market are full PAO oils. Many of the oils allowed to be labeled as synthetic are in fact blends of processed **mineral oil** (highly refined base stock refined from crude oil) and PAO, or even just highly refined base stock, that possess lubrication qualities similar to PAOs.

Synthetic Blends

Synthetic blends give some of the benefit of the full synthetic with the cost effectiveness of conventional oil. These oils are a mix of conventional high-quality oil and full synthetic oil. They need to be changed sooner than a full synthetic but less frequently than conventional oil. The more pure the base stock is after the refinement process, the longer the oil will last in the engine. Some manufacturers are now recommending synthetic blend oil over conventional oil due to the better protection and performance of these types of oils. Because it is half synthetic, half conventional, the full benefit of the thinner, higher performance pure synthetic is diluted, but in turn the conventional half is improved by adding oil that has no impurities. If the vehicle will be used hard, such as for hauling or towing, synthetic blends will perform better than conventional oil because of the ability of the synthetic oil to stand up to the higher heat and heavier load placed on the engine.

> **TECHNICIAN TIP**
>
> Be sure to use at least the minimum recommended oil by the manufacturer. Manufacturers of engines spend a lot of money and time designing engines that are efficient and long lasting. Always follow the manufacturer's recommendations.

Lubrication Systems

The **lubrication system** is a series of engine components that work together to keep the moving parts inside an engine lubricated FIGURE 12-5. Proper lubrication ensures that the engine runs cooler, produces maximum power, and gets maximum fuel efficiency. Lubrication also ensures that the engine will last for a long time. The lubrication system has many components that work together to deliver the oil to the correct locations in the engine. A typical lubrication system consists of an **oil sump**, an oil pump strainer (also called a pickup tube), an **oil pump**, a pressure regulator, **oil galleries**, an oil filter, and a low pressure warning system.

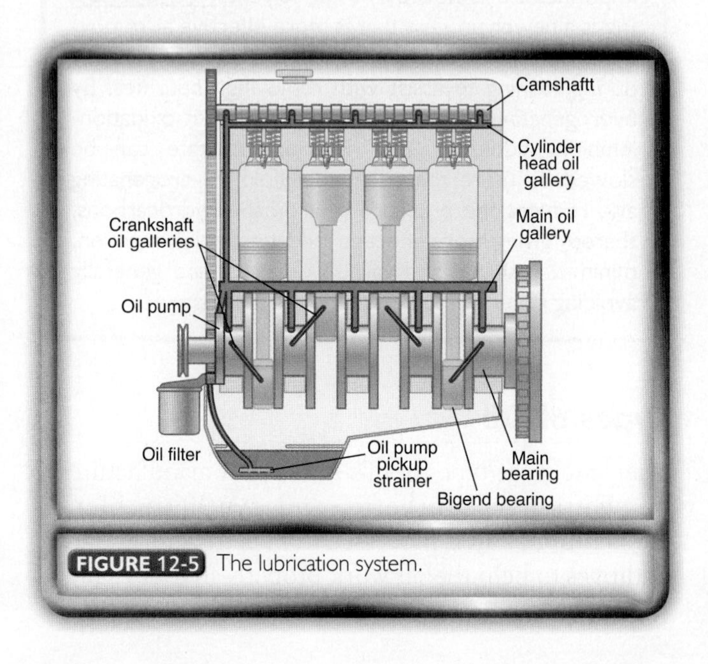
Camshaftt
Cylinder head oil gallery
Main oil gallery
Crankshaft oil galleries
Oil pump
Oil filter
Oil pump pickup strainer
Main bearing
Bigend bearing

FIGURE 12-5 The lubrication system.

The oil is stored in the oil sump. Oil is drawn through the oil pump strainer from the oil sump by an oil pump. The oil travels from the oil pump to the oil filter, which removes particles of dirt from the oil. Oil moves from the filter to the oil galleries. Oil galleries are small passages in the cylinder block and head(s) that direct oil to the moving parts. Oil that has been pumped to the crankshaft main bearings travels through oil-ways to the connecting rods. Oil may also be splashed from the connecting rods onto the cylinder walls, and the circulation of the oil assists with the cooling of the internal parts.

Oil Pan

The **oil pan** is located at the bottom of the engine FIGURE 12-6. On a wet sump lubricating system, the oil pan holds the entire volume of the oil required to lubricate the engine. The lowest point of the oil pan is the oil sump. This is where the **oil pump strainer** is located. The deep point in the oil pan ensures that there should never be a shortage of oil for the oil pump to pick up if the correct amount of oil is in the engine. The oil pan is sealed to the engine with silicone or an oil pan gasket. The sump is equipped with a drain plug that allows the oil to be drained from the engine during oil changes FIGURE 12-7.

Pickup Tube

Between the oil sump and oil pump is a **pickup tube** with a flat cup and a wire mesh strainer immersed in the oil. The pickup tube pulls oil from the oil sump by suction of the oil pump and atmospheric pressure. A strainer on the pickup tube stops large particles of debris from entering the oil pump and damaging it. The pickup tube leads to the inlet of the oil pump, on the low-pressure side of the oil pump. The pickup tube fits tightly into the oil pump and is usually bolted in place by a bracket to ensure that it does not fall out due to vibration. If the pickup tube were to fall out, the engine would not receive oil, since the pump would not reach down into the sump from which oil is drawn.

FIGURE 12-6 The oil pan.

FIGURE 12-7 A drain plug allows oil to be drained during oil changes.

Oil Pump

Oil pumps move oil from one side of the pump to the other. Most oil pumps are of the positive displacement type. This means that they move a given amount of oil from the inlet to the outlet each revolution. The faster the pump turns, the more oil that is pumped. Oil pressure is determined by two factors: (1) the size of the leaks in the system, which in the case of an engine means the amount of clearance between the bearings and the journals and the diameter of any spurt holes, and (2) the amount of oil flowing in the system. As you can imagine, an engine has a fairly consistent set of leaks. When the engine is new, the leaks are fairly small. When the engine has acquired many miles, the leaks are larger. This is why engine oil pressure falls over the life of the engine. In fact, low oil pressure can mean one of three things (other than a bad oil pressure gauge). Either the oil leaks inside the engine have gotten excessive (e.g., worn bearings), the oil pump is worn out and not creating as much flow as it needs to, or the oil is thinner than it should be (e.g., saturated with gasoline from a leaky fuel injector), which causes it to drain from the leaks faster than it should.

Oil pumps may be driven from the camshaft or the crankshaft. In a **rotor-type oil pump**, an inner rotor drives an outer one; as they turn, the volume between them increases FIGURE 12-8A. The larger volume created between the rotors lowers the pressure at the pump inlet, creating a vacuum. Outside atmospheric pressure, which is higher, forces oil into the pump, and the oil fills the spaces between the **rotor lobes**. As the lobes of the inner rotor move into the spaces in the outer rotor, oil is squeezed out through the outlet. In other words, oil is drawn into the spaces between the lobes on the inlet side and travels around with the lobes. The oil cannot get back to the inlet side because the lobes come together, and it is therefore forced out of the pump outlet.

The **crescent pump** uses a similar principle FIGURE 12-8B. It is usually mounted on the front of the cylinder block and straddles the front of the crankshaft.

Applied Math

AM-29: Volume: The technician can use various measurement techniques to determine the volume as applicable.

Two technicians are examining an engine oil pan as it is being cleaned. It is a standard automotive pan from a V6 engine and has a rectangular shape. Randy says that the volume of the pan could be calculated by multiplying the area of the base times the height. Tom agrees with this and adds that in the U.S. system of measurement the result would be in cubic inches which can be converted into quarts.

At break time, they decide to measure the pan and calculate its volume in quarts. The pan measures 6 inches wide, 9 inches long, and 5.35 inches deep. The area of the base is 6×9, which is 54 square inches. Next, they multiply times the height of 5.35 inches for 288.9 square inches. This is approximately 5 quarts (considering one quart is equal to 57.750 cubic inches).

To calculate the example in metric units the process would be very similar except that we would be using metric units. Centimeters would be used for the linear units to determine the base $\times$ height. There would be cubic centimeters to convert to liters.

The inner gear is then driven by the crankshaft directly. An external toothed gear meshes with the inner one. Some gear teeth are meshed but others are separated by the crescent-shaped part of the pump housing. The increasing volume between gear teeth causes pressure to fall, creating a vacuum, and atmospheric pressure pushes oil into the pump. Oil is then carried around between the gears and crescent before being discharged to the outlet port.

In a **geared oil pump**, the driving gear meshes with a second gear FIGURE 12-8C. As both gears turn, their teeth separate, creating a low-pressure area. Higher atmospheric pressure outside forces the oil up into the inlet, which fills the spaces between the gear teeth. As the gears rotate, they carry oil around the chamber. As the teeth mesh again, oil is forced from the outlet into the oil gallery and toward the oil filter where it is filtered of any particles.

Oil Pressure Relief Valve

A normal oil pump is capable of delivering more oil than an engine needs. Extra volume provides a safety measure to ensure the engine is never starved for oil. As the oil pump rotates, and engine speed increases, the volume of oil delivered also increases. The fixed clearances between the moving parts of the engine slow the escaping of oil back to the oil sump, and pressure builds up in the lubrication system. An **oil pressure relief valve** stops excess pressure from developing. It is like a controlled leak, releasing just enough oil back to the oil sump to regulate the pressure in the whole system. The oil pressure relief valve contains a spring that is calibrated to a specific pressure. When the pressure is

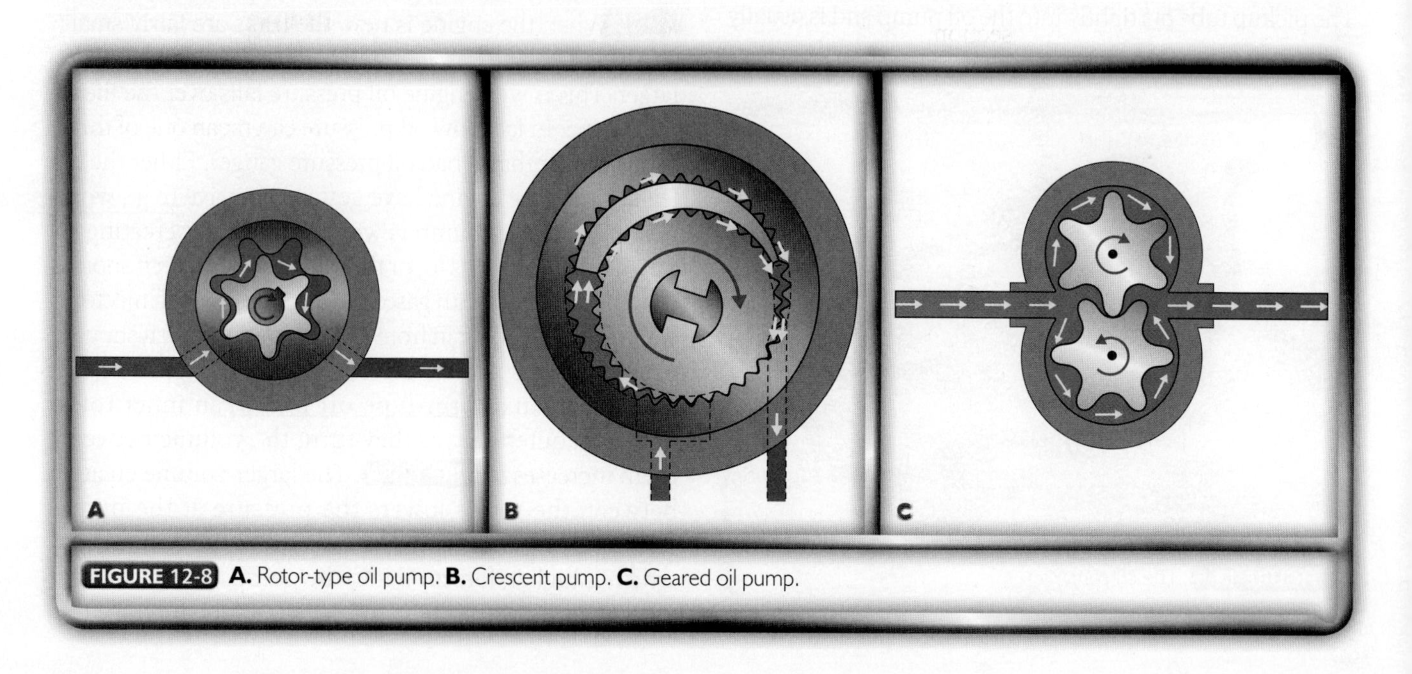
A
B
C

FIGURE 12-8 **A.** Rotor-type oil pump. **B.** Crescent pump. **C.** Geared oil pump.

reached, the oil pressure relief valve slides open just enough to bleed sufficient oil back to the pan to maintain the preset maximum relief pressure. If the engine speed and oil flow increase, the pressure relief valve will open farther and allow more oil to escape back to the sump. If the engine speed and oil flow decrease, the pressure relief valve will close an appropriate amount.

TECHNICIAN TIP

So what is the difference between a high-pressure oil pump and a high-volume oil pump? A high-pressure pump has a stiffer pressure relief spring, which allows the pump to create higher oil pressure. A high-volume pump has greater volume between the rotor or gear teeth, usually accomplished by making both the rotor/gear and the oil pump housing deeper. This design causes more oil to be drawn into the pump during each revolution, and therefore more oil is forced out of the pump each revolution. Generally speaking, a high-volume pump is more beneficial; because it can pump more oil, the pressure will not fall as quickly as the engine experiences wear and tear.

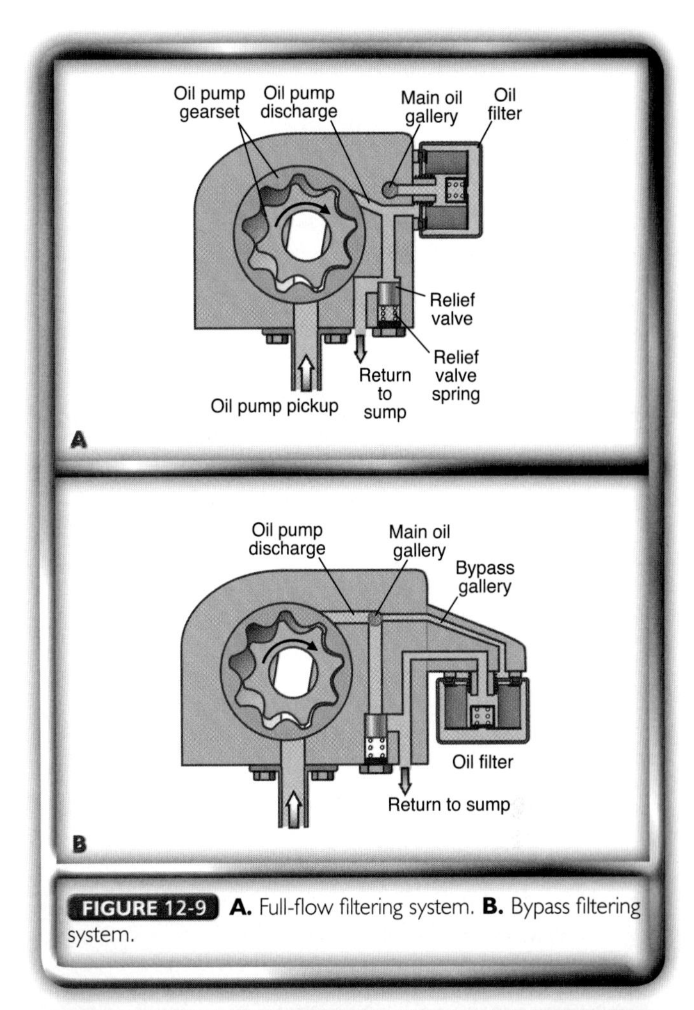
Oil pump gearset
Oil pump discharge
Main oil gallery
Oil filter
Relief valve
Relief valve spring
Return to sump
Oil pump pickup
A
Oil pump discharge
Main oil gallery
Bypass gallery
Oil filter
Return to sump
B

FIGURE 12-9 **A.** Full-flow filtering system. **B.** Bypass filtering system.

Oil Filters

There are two basic oil-filtering systems: full-flow and bypass FIGURE 12-9. The most common, **full-flow filters**, are designed to filter all of the oil before delivering it to the engine. The location of the filter right after the oil pump ensures that all of the oil is filtered before it is sent to the lubricated components. The bypass filtering system is more common on diesel engines and is used in conjunction with a full-flow filtering system. The **bypass filter** is discussed later in this section.

Oil filters use a pleated filter paper for the filtering medium FIGURE 12-10. Oil flows through the paper and as it does so, it filters out particles in the oil. Most full-flow oil filters will catch particles down to 30 microns. A micron is 0.000039" (0.001 mm)—a very small particle. A human hair's thickness can be as small as 50 microns, for example. As the oil filter catches these fine particles, the paper filter element will begin to clog, making it harder for the oil to flow through. As the engine is initially started cold for a few seconds, or if the filter becomes clogged, the bypass valve will open to let unfiltered oil flow to the lubricated components. The manufacturers believe it is better to have unfiltered oil flow to components than no oil at all. To prevent excessive engine wear, it is critical to change the oil filter at the manufacturer's recommended interval.

FIGURE 12-10 Pleated oil filter paper.

There are two common types of oil filters: spin-on and cartridge FIGURE 12-11. The spin-on type is the most common. It uses a one-piece filter assembly with a crimped housing and threaded base. The pleated paper filter element is formed into the inside of the crimped housing. This kind of filter spins off with the use of an oil filter wrench and tightens by hand force only. A square-cut rubber O-ring fits into a groove in the base of the filter

HASTINGS
PREMIUM FILTERS

FIGURE 12-11 **A.** Spin-on filter and O-ring. **B.** Cartridge paper filter, housing, and bolt.

Applied Math

AM-30: Volume: The technician can determine if the existing volume is within the manufacturer's recommended tolerance.

A technician was instructed to change the engine oil and filter on a late model automobile. In addition to this, he was also to change the automatic transmission fluid and filter. The technician has access to manufacturer's service information, which he consulted before starting the tasks. The service information stated that 5.5 quarts of oil would be needed for an engine oil change with filter replacement. Concerning the automatic transmission fluid and filter change, the manual stated 9.5 quarts are needed for this service.

The technician begins working by draining the engine oil and filter. As he puts the new oil into the engine, the technician counts the number of quart containers. He discovers that after the engine was started, to fill the oil filter and shut off, it takes a total of 5.5 quarts to bring the oil level to the exact full mark on the dipstick. By this method, the technician was able to determine that the existing volume is within the manufacturer's tolerance.

At this point, the technician goes on to the transmission fluid and filter change. He drains the fluid and changes the filter. As before, the technician counts the number of quart containers necessary for filling the system properly. He pours in one quart at a time, in order to take an accurate count. The technician observes that it takes 9.5 quarts to fill the system to the full line on the dipstick, with the engine running in park. By this method, the technician is able to verify that the existing volume is within the manufacturer's tolerance.

and seals the base of the filter to the engine block. A new O-ring comes with the filter, so it gets replaced with the filter. Be aware, though, that the old O-ring may stick to the filter adapter on the engine block. If you do not notice this and leave the old O-ring on along with the new O-ring, the old one will not be able to stay in place because it is not in any groove. As a result, it will get pushed out of place when the engine is started and most, if not all, of the engine oil will be pumped out onto the ground. Always check for the old O-ring when removing the oil filter.

The cartridge style of oil filter uses a separate reuseable metal or plastic housing and a replaceable filter cartridge. It is typically held together in one of two ways: threaded center bolt or screw-on housing. If it uses a center bolt, it will have a sealing washer between the bolt and the housing to prevent oil from leaking out. There is also a seal that fits either between the cylindrical housing and the filter adapter on the block or between the cylindrical housing and the end cap, depending on the design. Cartridge filters must be disassembled, the housing cleaned, and the paper filter element and any O-rings or seals replaced with new ones.

Most oil filters on diesel engines are larger than those on similar gasoline engines, and some diesel engines

TECHNICIAN TIP

Magnets are also used as a type of filter. They attract ferrous metal particles and hold them in place until they can be cleaned off. Some manufacturers use magnetic drain plugs, which then need to be inspected and cleaned off as part of an oil change. Others place a magnet to the inside or outside of the oil pan. Although this style cannot readily be cleaned, it does hold the magnetic particles in place so they cannot travel freely.

have two oil filters. Diesel engines produce more carbon particles than gasoline engines, so the oil filter can have a full-flow element to trap larger impurities and a bypass element to collect sludge and carbon soot. In a bypass system, the bypass element filters only some of the oil from the oil pump by tapping an oil line into the oil gallery. It collects finer particles than a full-flow filter. After this oil is filtered, it is returned to the oil sump. If the bypass filter were to clog and stop oil flow, the flow of oil lubricating the engine components would not be affected.

Spurt Holes and Galleries

Pistons, rings, and pins are lubricated by oil thrown onto the cylinder walls from the connecting rod bearings. Some connecting rods have **oil spurt holes** that are positioned to receive oil from similar holes in the crankshaft FIGURE 12-12. Oil can then spurt out at the point in the engine cycle when the largest area of cylinder wall is exposed. This oil sprays from the connecting rod holes and lubricates the cylinder walls and piston wrist pin, and may help cool the underside of the piston.

Oil is fed to the cylinder head through oil galleries and on to the camshaft bearings and valve train. When oil reaches the top of the cylinder head and lubricates the valve train, it has completed its pressurized journey. The oil drains back to the oil sump through oil drain-back holes located in the cylinder head and engine block.

> **TECHNICIAN TIP**
>
> In many cases, the ends of the oil galleries are plugged with a threaded pipe plug or a small soft plug. During an engine rebuild, these plugs are normally removed and the galleries cleaned with stiff wire brushes. It is very important to make sure the plugs have been reinstalled with a sealer and tightened properly so that they do not leak. Many a technician has started up a newly rebuilt engine and had oil pour out of the bell housing, all because one or more of the oil gallery plugs were missing.

FIGURE 12-12 Some connecting rods have oil spurt holes, which are positioned to receive oil from similar holes in the crankshaft.

Oil Indicators

A lubrication system failure can be catastrophic to the engine. Because of the damage that would happen if the lubrication system failed, a warning system is installed to let the driver know the system has failed. If oil pressure falls too low, a pressure sensor threaded into a gallery can activate a low oil pressure warning light, register pressure on a gauge, or turn on a low oil pressure warning message FIGURE 12-13. The pressure sensor is also commonly called a sending unit since it sends a signal to the light, gauge, or message center in the dash. If the sending unit is designed as part of a warning lamp system, it is made up of a spring-loaded diaphragm and a set of switch contacts and is commonly called a pressure switch. Oil pressure is on the engine side of the diaphragm and a spring is on the other. With the engine off and the ignition switch in the run position, the oil pressure is zero, so the spring holds the diaphragm toward the engine and the switch contacts are closed (i.e., making contact with each other). This causes current to flow from the warning lamp in the dash through the closed switch contacts in the sending unit to ground, which turns on the warning light. When the engine is started, oil pressure increases above spring pressure and the diaphragm is pushed away from the engine, opening the switch contacts and turning off the warning light. In some vehicles, the sending unit sends the electrical signal to the BCM, which is programmed to turn the light on below a certain pressure. This is how the system should work when everything is working normally. If the oil pressure drops below spring pressure while the engine is running, the light will come on, warning the driver of the low oil pressure condition.

If the sending unit is part of an oil pressure gauge system, it usually uses a variable resistor within the sending unit. The variable resistor is moved by the oil pressure moving the diaphragm against the spring pressure. As the pressure increases, the diaphragm is forced against spring pressure and changing the resistance of the variable resistor. This changes the amount of current flowing through the oil pressure gauge and causes it to read higher. If the engine oil pressure drops, then the spring pushes

20
0
162
2.1
mpg
40
0
80
CHECK
ENG OIL
PRESSURE

FIGURE 12-13 If oil pressure falls too low, a pressure sensor in a gallery can **(A)** activate a warning light, **(B)** register on a gauge, or **(C)** turn on a warning message.

the diaphragm toward the engine, again changing the resistance of the variable resistor and the current flowing through the oil pressure gauge, decreasing the pressure reading on the gauge. Some factory-installed oil pressure gauges include a warning light to warn the driver of low oil pressure. In many instances, a driver may not notice that the oil pressure gauge reading has dropped and will keep driving the vehicle, leading to engine damage. But the warning light is designed to catch the driver's attention so that he or she can stop the vehicle and investigate the cause of the low oil pressure.

> **TECHNICIAN TIP**
>
> Some people erroneously refer to the low oil pressure warning system as a low oil level warning system. They think this because, if the oil level gets really low, then the oil pump will draw air into the lubrication system and the oil pressure will fall, turning on the low oil pressure warning light. Unfortunately, if the oil is allowed to get that low, it is doing damage to the engine. A true low oil level warning system is designed to alert the driver when the oil level approaches the "add" mark, which is well before engine damage is being done.

> **TECHNICIAN TIP**
>
> Many vehicle manufacturers have moved to using a switch type sending unit with a gauge. The switch is spring loaded so that it will come on below a pre-determined pressure. But it also allows current to flow through a resistance that is in series with the switch. When the oil pressure is above the spring pressure, the resistor causes the oil pressure gauge to stay mid-scale. When oil pressure falls below this setting, the contacts open and the gauge reads low. This can confuse drivers since the oil pressure remains very steady for many years, and all of a sudden, it drops to zero. As the engine clearances become larger, or if oil becomes thin, oil pressure drops. Once it falls low enough that spring pressure overcomes oil pressure, the gauge will read low or zero.

If the sending unit is part of a driver information system, then the sending unit could be of the switch type or the variable resistance type. It usually also would include a sensor for low oil level monitoring and maybe even an oil temperature monitor. You will need to investigate various manufacturers' driver information systems to familiarize yourself with the different systems and strategies each manufacturer uses.

Oil Analysis

Oil will suspend particles as the engine wears. Analysis of the engine oil is a useful way to see what parts are wearing in the engine. The military as well as many companies use oil analysis to ensure that the engine oil is changed at the appropriate interval. A small tube is slipped down the oil dipstick tube all the way to the oil pan sump. A vacuum device is hooked to this tube to pull a sample of oil from the pan to a collection container. This sample is labeled with the vehicle information and sent to a lab. The lab thoroughly analyzes the oil and reports the findings back to the shop. The report lists physical properties such as viscosity, condensed water, fuel dilution, anti-freeze, acids, metal content, and oil additives. Each of these attributes can be used to determine the condition of the oil as well as the engine. When oil analysis is performed for a particular engine on a regular basis, issues can usually be addressed before they become catastrophic. Oil analysis is typically used in heavy vehicle applications that may use 3 or more gallons (11.4 or more liters) of engine oil. Some race teams will analyze the engine oil to ensure that the engine is not being damaged.

As a technician, a simple test to check for excessive engine wear is to take a white paper towel and wipe the oil from the dipstick on it. Hold the towel to the light and move it back and forth to see if light reflects from metal. If metal is in the oil, there is substantial wear happening inside the engine.

Oil Monitoring Systems

Oil monitoring systems are used to inform the driver when the oil needs to be changed. There are several types of **oil monitoring systems**. Some oil systems are simply timers that keep track of mileage and will activate a warning light to notify the driver when it is time to change the engine oil. Other systems are very sophisticated, analyzing the conductivity of the oil through a sensor in the oil pan and monitoring changes that indicate it is time to change the oil. Depending upon the feedback from the sensor, the monitoring system computer will activate the change oil light or message to warn the driver that it is time to change the oil.

Another monitoring system, called an oil-life monitor, calculates the expected life of the oil and displays it to the driver. The computer receives inputs from several sensors that take into account the number of start-ups, mileage, driving habits/conditions, temperature, length of run time, and other data to calculate the remaining life of the oil, which is displayed as a percentage. When the oil is freshly changed and the oil-life monitor is reset, it will say the oil life is 100%. As the oil life wears out, the monitor will read closer to 0% oil life, informing the driver of the need to change the oil. Since it monitors the conditions the oil is operating under, the life of the oil can change drastically depending on the conditions. For example, if the vehicle were only driven in moderate temperatures for long distances, the oil would be good thousands of miles longer than a vehicle driven in stop-and-go traffic and with long periods of idling. Each vehicle equipped with an oil monitoring system has a specific reset procedure to turn the light or message off after an oil change.

> **TECHNICIAN TIP**
>
> As a technician, you will have to be able to find the procedure to turn the light off and reset the oil monitoring system. Refer to the service manual or owner's manual for resetting procedures. The reset procedures range from something as simple as pushing a button, to having to go through a set of steps, to having to use a dedicated tool.

Types of Lubrication Methods

Pressure System

Modern vehicle engines use a **pressure, or force-feed, lubrication system** where the oil is forced throughout the engine under pressure FIGURE 12-14. In gasoline engines, oil will not flow up into the engine by itself so the oil pump collects it through a pickup tube and strainer and forces it through an oil filter, then into passageways, called galleries, in the engine block. The galleries allow oil to be fed to the crankshaft bearings first, then through holes drilled in the crankshaft to the connecting rods. The oil also moves from the galleries onto the camshaft bearings and the valve mechanism. After circulating through the engine, the oil falls back to the oil sump to cool. This design is called a wet sump lubrication system.

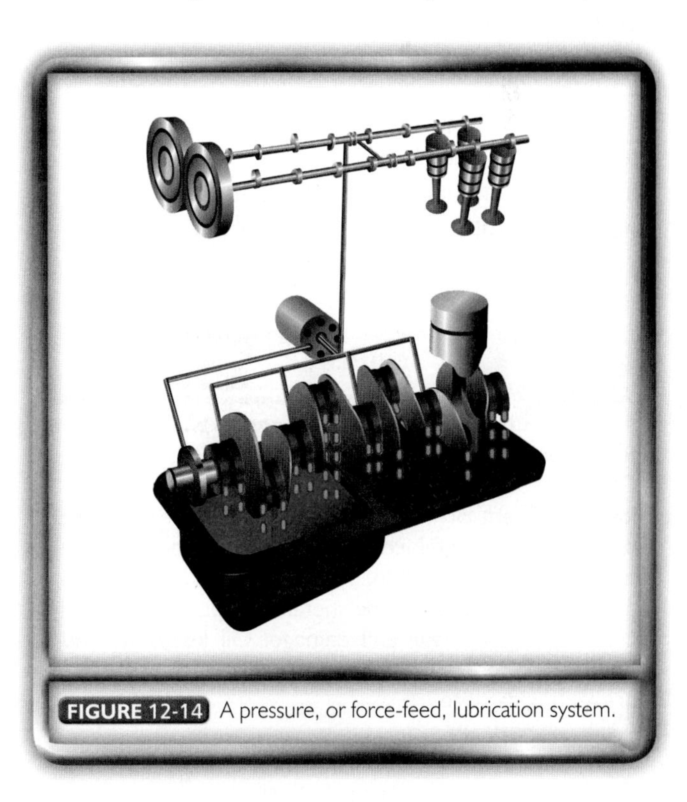

FIGURE 12-14 A pressure, or force-feed, lubrication system.

Some engines use a dry sump lubrication system. It uses all of the parts that make up a wet sump system and it lubricates the engine in the same way. It differs from the wet sump system in the way the oil is collected and stored. In a dry sump system, the oil falls to the bottom of the engine into an oil collection pan. A **scavenge pump** then pumps it to an oil tank where it is stored until the normal oil pump collects it and pumps it through the filter and engine in the normal way. Because there is no oil storage sump under the engine, the engine can be mounted much lower than in a wet sump system, which allows the vehicle to have a much lower center of gravity. The oil tank can be positioned away from the engine where it can get best cooling and the amount of oil in the system can be much greater than in the wet sump system since space is less of an issue.

Diesel engines are lubricated in much the same way as gasoline engines, but there are a few differences. Diesel engines typically operate at the top end of their power range, so their internal operating temperatures are usually higher than those in similar gasoline engines. Thus, the parts in diesel engines are usually more stressed. Since diesel fuel is ignited by the heat of compression, the compression pressures (and compression ratio) are much higher than in gasoline engines. Diesel fuel has more British thermal units (BTUs) of heat energy than gasoline, so it produces more heat when it is ignited, placing more stress on the engine's moving parts. Because of stress from the higher compression and combustion pressures/temperatures, parts have to be much heavier, and with heavier parts, oil must be able to handle higher shear forces. As a result, diesel oils need a different range of properties and are classified differently, usually with a C rating in the API system. It is also common for many diesel engines to use an oil-to-water cooler to cool the oil in the engine. The cooler and oil filter are usually on the same mounting on the cylinder block.

Applied Science

AS-92: Friction: The technician can explain the need for lubrication to minimize friction.

Oil is a good lubricant in an engine because it has a low coefficient of friction. It creates a protective layer between two metal components, which both have a high coefficient of friction. The high coefficient of friction produces heat, causing the metal to expand, potentially creating engine wear and damage. Oil keeps the two metal components from rubbing against each other, thus preventing damage.

Splash Lubrication

Not all lubricated engine components are lubricated by the pressure-fed system. Some are lubricated by the **splash lubrication** method FIGURE 12-15. In this method, the oil is thrown around and gets into spaces that need lubrication. Automotive and diesel engines use splash lubrication for lubricating the cylinder walls, pistons, wrist pin, valve guides, and sometimes the timing chain. The oil that is splashed around usually comes from moving parts that are pressure-fed; as the oil leaks out of those parts as designed, it is thrown around and provides splash lubrication to the needed components.

Most small four-stroke gasoline engines use only splash lubrication to lubricate all of the parts on the engine including the crankshaft bearing, camshaft, and lifters. On horizontal-crankshaft engines, a **dipper** on the bottom of the connecting rod scoops up oil from the crankcase for the bearings. The dipper is also able to splash oil up to the valve mechanism. Alternatively, an **oil slinger** can be driven by the crankshaft or camshaft. A slinger is a device that runs half-submerged in the engine oil. The oil is slung from the slinger upward by centrifugal force to lubricate moving parts. A similar system is used in most small vertical-crankshaft engines. Oil is also splashed up to the valve mechanism from the centrifugal force of the slinger spinning at engine speed.

FIGURE 12-15 A splash lubrication method.

Maintenance and Repair

Tools

The tools for lubrication repair include FIGURE 12-16:

- A variety of oil filter wrenches to remove the oil filter
- A set of wrenches and a socket set to remove the oil drain plug and any engine covers
- A mirror and a quality light for leak testing
- A special socket to remove many of the oil pressure switches or sensors

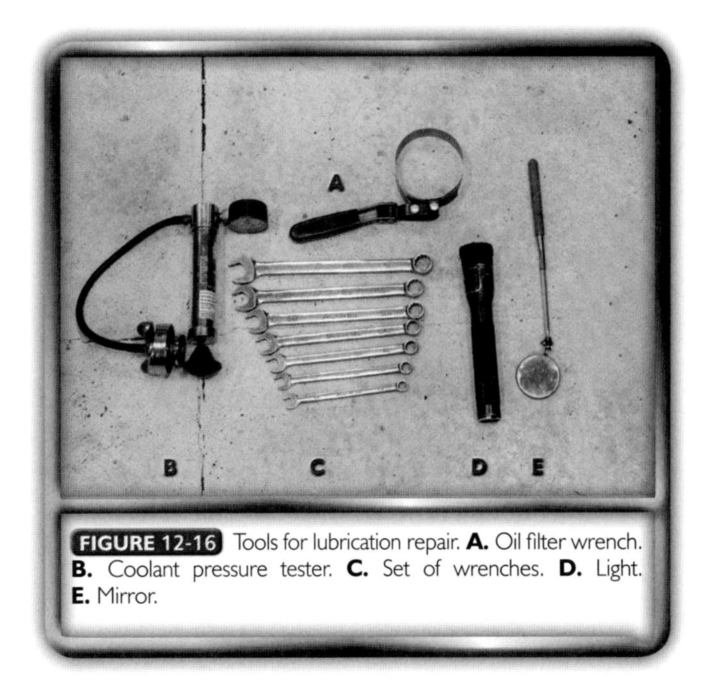
A
B
C
D
E

FIGURE 12-16 Tools for lubrication repair. **A.** Oil filter wrench. **B.** Coolant pressure tester. **C.** Set of wrenches. **D.** Light. **E.** Mirror.

Checking the Engine Oil

Checking the engine oil level regularly is necessary and should be performed during every fuel fill-up or every other fuel fill-up, depending on the age and condition of the vehicle. There is a danger of damaging the engine if the engine oil drops too low in the oil sump. The oil level can be low either because there is an oil leak or because the engine is consuming oil by burning it. Burning engine oil could be due to worn piston rings, worn valve guides, or a malfunction with the positive crankcase ventilation (PCV) system. Checking oil level should also be part of any pretrip check or part of a predelivery inspection on a new car at the dealership. Predelivery inspections are performed on new vehicles before delivering to the purchaser and help to ensure that the vehicle is being delivered in the condition the manufacturer specifies and without any known faults or defects that would reflect negatively on the customer satisfaction index for the manufacturer or dealer.

Always make sure the vehicle is on a level surface and the engine is off before taking a reading. If you do not, you will get inaccurate readings. Also wipe the dipstick off and reinsert it fully before removing it and reading it. When reading it, hold the dipstick horizontal so the oil will not run down the stick. Typically, the amount of oil needed to raise the oil level from the bottom of the "safe" mark on the dipstick to the "full" mark is about a quart. This amount may vary, so always check the service manual to determine the correct quantity. Always install the recommended amount and type of oil given in the service manual. Although fresh oil is translucent and oil that needs to be replaced often looks black and dirty, it is usually difficult to assess the condition of engine oil simply by its color. Oil loses its clean, fresh look very quickly but may still have a lot of life left in it.

The best guide to knowing when to change the oil is the vehicle's oil-life monitor, if equipped. It will tell you the percentage of oil-life remaining before a change is needed. If the vehicle is not equipped with an oil-life monitor, check the oil change sticker on the windshield or ask the owner for oil change records to determine if the oil needs to be changed. This can ensure that the oil is not changed too often, which would be an unnecessary expense for the customer. Our job as technicians is to provide high-quality work only when it is truly needed by the customer. Part of being a professional is letting customers know when they do and when they do *not* need a service performed. Informing the customer of what needs to be done and what does not, along with an explanation, helps to build trust with the customer and often results in the customer returning to your shop for future repairs.

If the oil on the dipstick is not blackish in color but looks milky gray, it is possible that there is water (or coolant) being mixed into the oil. This could indicate a serious problem somewhere inside the engine, such as a leaking head gasket or a cracked head, and you should report this to your supervisor immediately. Engine operating conditions can also influence the oil's condition. For instance, continuously stopping and starting the engine with very short operating cycles can cause condensation to build up inside the engine. An extreme case of this will cause very rapid oil deterioration and will require frequent oil changes. The oil of a vehicle that is running too rich or that has a leaking fuel injector will smell like fuel and will be very thin. These problems can ruin an engine quickly, as oil will not adequately lubricate the moving surfaces in the engine. If you had to add oil to the engine, do not forget to reinstall the filler cap after topping off the oil.

To check the engine oil, follow the steps in SKILL DRILL 12-1.

SKILL DRILL 12-1 Checking the Engine Oil

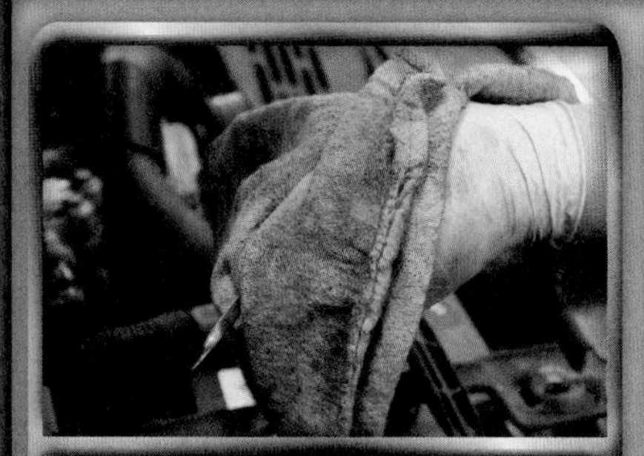

1. Locate the dipstick. With the engine off, remove the dipstick, catching any drops of oil on a rag, and wipe it clean. Observe the markings on the lower end of the stick, which indicate the "full" and "add" marks or specify the "safe" zone.

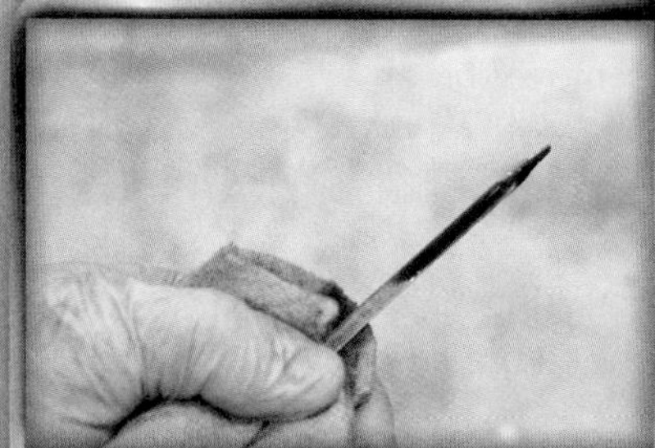

2. Replace the dipstick and push it back down into the sump as far as it will go. Remove it again, and hold it level while checking the level indicated on the bottom of the stick. If the level is near or below the "add" mark, then you will need to determine if the engine just needs topped up to the full level with fresh oil or replaced with new oil and oil filter.

3. Check the oil for any conditions such as unusual color or texture. Report these to your supervisor. Check the oil monitoring system, oil sticker, or service record to determine if the oil needs changed. (Some oil monitoring systems show the percentage of life left in the oil.)

4. If additional oil is needed, estimate the amount by checking the service manual guide to the dipstick markings. Unscrew the filler cap at the top of the engine, and using a funnel to avoid spillage, turn the oil bottle so the spout is on the high side of the bottle and gently pour the oil into the engine. Recheck the oil level.

5. Replace the oil filler cap, and check the dipstick again to make sure the oil level is now correct.

Safety

If the engine has been running, be careful not to burn your hand or arm on the exhaust manifold or any other hot part of the engine when reaching for the dipstick. Remember, the dipstick and the oil on it will also be hot. Dripping oil from the dipstick will smoke or burn if it falls on any hot engine surfaces.

TECHNICIAN TIP

Make sure the hood is secure with a hood prop rod, if necessary. Always make sure you wear the appropriate personal protection equipment before starting the job. It is very easy to think that nothing can happen on a basic job like checking the oil level.

Draining the Engine Oil

Draining the engine oil is a necessary task any time the oil and filter are to be changed or whenever the oil pan needs to be removed for service work. Draining the engine oil for an oil change is necessary after a certain time or mileage interval to remove the dirt and particulates that are suspended in the oil. As the engine wears, the very small pieces of metal will get suspended in the oil. Removing the old contaminated oil helps to make the engine last longer. Always follow the manufacturer's oil change interval, and remember that normal use and severe use have different oil change intervals.

When draining the oil, several precautions are necessary. First, the engine oil is normally changed after the engine is fully warmed up. This helps to stir up any contaminants, making them easier to flush out with the draining of the oil. However, that means that the oil can be 200–300°F (93–149°C), so use disposable gloves and don't burn yourself.

Second, make sure you locate the correct drain plug—or in some cases, the correct *two* drain plugs. Some vehicles have a drain plug on the transmission/transaxle that can be mistaken for the oil drain plug. If in doubt, look it up or ask your supervisor to point it out.

Third, many drain plugs are either angled off of the bottom radius of the oil pan or almost sideways at the bottom side of the pan. This means when the drain plug is removed, hot oil will want to spray sideways. Always make sure you take into consideration what path the oil will take. Oil can shoot out pretty far. The lower the drain pan is compared to the drain plug, the harder it will be to judge the distance the oil will spray.

Fourth, the drain plug gasket can be of the integrated silicone, long-life style that rarely needs to be replaced. The gasket can also be a one-time-use gasket made of plastic, aluminum, or fiber. This type of gasket should be replaced during every oil change since it is crushed to conform to any irregularities of the pan and drain plug. Because it is crushed, it will not conform as easily the next time it is tightened. This means that someone may think it needs to be tightened excessively to prevent seepage. Overtightening can strip the threads on the oil pan, especially if it is made of aluminum, or can strip the threads on the drain plug itself. Replace a non-silicone drain plug gasket every time it is removed.

To drain the engine oil, follow the steps in **SKILL DRILL 12-2**.

> **TECHNICIAN TIP**
>
> When removing the drain plug, be sure to use the proper-sized wrench or socket. Always inspect the drain plug gasket for damage before reusing; some manufacturers require the use of a new drain plug gasket each time the drain plug is removed. Always look up and torque the drain plug to proper specifications, as overtightening could damage the threads of the plug and oil pan, and undertightening could cause an oil leak or the plug to vibrate loose and fall out, resulting in the loss of all the engine oil.

> **TECHNICIAN TIP**
>
> Refer the customer to the owner's manual to determine when the oil should be changed. That could be based on a mileage interval, time interval, or oil-life monitor. You may also need to verify whether the vehicle is operated under normal or severe conditions. Severe conditions may include driving in low temperatures, stop-and-go driving, dusty conditions, short trips, towing, etc. Intervals for severe driving conditions are sooner than normal driving intervals.

Replacing Oil Filters

Oil filters are designed to filter out particles that find their way into the oil. The filter will catch particles that result from carbon from the combustion process that leaks past piston rings or small metal flakes that result from normal engine wear. The engine oil will suspend some of the particles while the heavier particles will fall to the bottom of the oil pan. The oil filter is designed to catch the particles and let the oil flow through. It is critical to change the oil filter at the manufacturer's recommended mileage to help ensure that it does not become clogged.

When changing a spin-on oil filter, be careful of a few things. First, an oil filter wrench is only used to remove an oil filter. It is never used to install an oil filter. Installation must be performed by hand.

Second, the O-ring that seals the spin-on oil filter to the block tends to stick on the engine block when the filter is being removed. This can lead to double-gasketing, which occurs when the new O-ring in the new filter is installed over the old O-ring. Since the groove in the filter is only deep enough to hold the new O-ring, the old one is not held in place. Once the engine is started, the oil pressure pushes it out of place and oil is pumped very quickly out of the engine and onto the floor. This not only makes a huge mess and wastes good oil, but if you don't realize it has happened, the engine could be damaged in

SKILL DRILL 12-2 Draining the Engine Oil

1. Before you begin, clean up any oil spills, obtain the oil drain container (and make sure it has enough room for the oil to be drained), have enough new oil of the correct type to refill the engine, have the correct oil filter, and ensure that the engine oil is up to operating temperature before starting the oil change.

2. Identify the location of the oil drain plug. Some vehicles have two drain plugs, draining separate sump areas. If the drain plug is leaking, damaged, or does not look right, inform your supervisor. Use a box wrench or socket to remove and replace the drain bolt. Be careful that you do not remove the transmission drain plug by mistake.

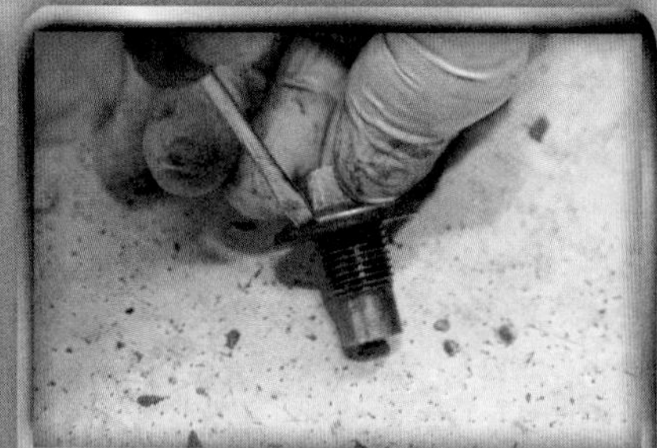

3. Position the drain pan so it will catch the oil. Remove and inspect the drain plug and gasket; replace as necessary.

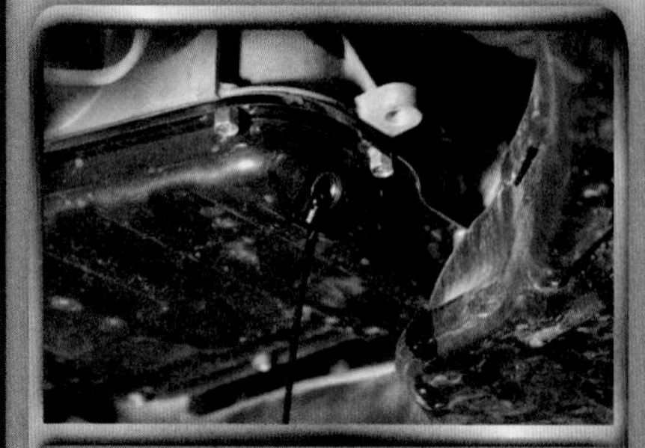

4. Allow the oil to drain while you are dealing with the drain plug, gasket, and oil filter (see Skill Drill 12-3).

5. Screw in the drain plug all the way by hand and then tighten it to the torque specified by the manufacturer. Wipe any drips from the underside of the engine.

6. Safely dispose of the drained oil according to all local regulations.

only a minute or two of running. Always check that the old O-ring was removed with the filter. If it was not, reach up and peel it off of the filter mounting.

Third, when installing the spin-on oil filter, smear a bit of oil on the surface of the O-ring. Doing so lubricates it so that it will spin with the oil filter as it is being tightened. Failure to lube the O-ring can cause it to bind and roll out of the oil filter groove when the filter is being tightened.

Last, when installing the spin-on oil filter, it can be hard to see how it is going on the threaded filter adapter. If you get it cross-threaded, it will leak just like a double-gasketed O-ring. Plus you are likely to damage the threads

TECHNICIAN TIP

To help judge how far to turn the filter to tighten it, mark the outside of the filter with a marker or a dab of oil (but remember to wipe the oil off when you have finished). Do not overtighten the filter. Typically, three-quarters to a full turn is adequate torque for a seal that will not leak, but make sure to follow the tightening instructions for the filter, which are on the filter and/or the box it came in. Be careful not to cross-thread the oil filter on the threaded adapter fitting.

on the adapter, making it harder to install the filter in the future. To prevent this problem, always start the filter by turning it with your fingers. Once you suspect it is started, stop and try to lift the filter off of the adapter. If it comes off, it has not started. Try to start it by finger again; then try to lift it off. If it does not lift off, then it has started onto the threads. Now count the turns that the filter spins on. It should go on at least five full turns before the gasket contacts the filter mounting surface if it is not cross-threaded. You can then tighten it by hand the appropriate amount as specified by the filter manufacturer, typically about three-quarters to one turn.

Manufacturers are returning to using cartridge filters more and more because it is easier to properly dispose of the oil. It also reduces the amount of waste generated from used spin-on filters. When changing a cartridge filter, be aware of the following situations. First, the only parts that get replaced are the paper filter cartridge and the O-rings or seals. All of the other parts are reused, so do not damage them or throw them away during disassembly.

Second, some cartridge filters are near the bottom of the engine, while others are on top. Use the service information to help you locate the filter. If the filter is on the top of the engine, there is a good chance that you will need to prefill the cartridge before installing the filter end cap. Again, check the service information for the vehicle you are working on.

Third, be careful with tightening a cartridge filter, as it is easy to crack or damage the housing—especially if it is plastic. Always follow the manufacturer's torque procedure.

SKILL DRILL 12-3 Replacing a Spin-on Filter
1 Check for new filter availability. Locate the filter being changed. It will usually be located on the side of the engine block or at an angle underneath the engine. Select the proper oil filter wrench.
2 Position a drain pan to catch any oil that will leak from the filter.
3 Remove the filter. Clean the seating area on the engine so that its surface and the surface of the new filter can seal properly. Make sure the O-ring from the removed filter is not still stuck to the filter mounting surface.
4 Confirm you have the correct replacement filter. Smear a little oil on the surface of the new O-ring.
5 Screw in the filter until the filter just starts and ensure that it cannot be pulled off. Then turn the filter by hand until the filter lightly contacts the base. Be careful not to cross-thread the oil filter.

Last, since the filter housing is being reused, it is important that it is clean before being reinstalled. You may need to wash it out in a clean solvent tank. Just be sure that you also remove any solvent residue before reinstalling it.

To replace a spin-on filter, follow the steps in SKILL DRILL 12-3.

To replace a cartridge filter (replaceable element), follow the steps in SKILL DRILL 12-4.

Before removing either type of oil filter, refer to the service information for the vehicle and identify the type of filter required. Make sure a suitable replacement filter is available.

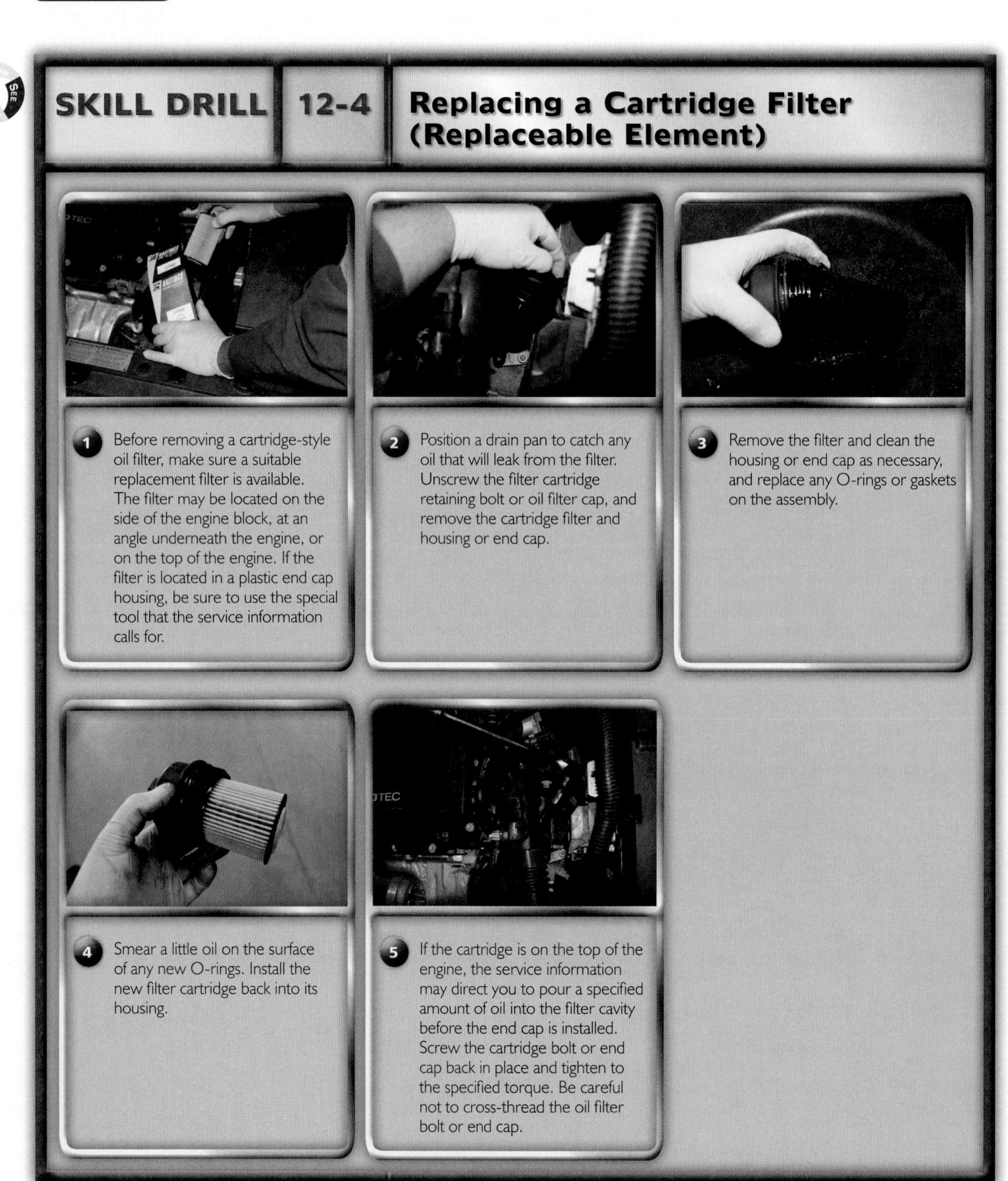

SKILL DRILL 12-4 Replacing a Cartridge Filter (Replaceable Element)

1. Before removing a cartridge-style oil filter, make sure a suitable replacement filter is available. The filter may be located on the side of the engine block, at an angle underneath the engine, or on the top of the engine. If the filter is located in a plastic end cap housing, be sure to use the special tool that the service information calls for.

2. Position a drain pan to catch any oil that will leak from the filter. Unscrew the filter cartridge retaining bolt or oil filter cap, and remove the cartridge filter and housing or end cap.

3. Remove the filter and clean the housing or end cap as necessary, and replace any O-rings or gaskets on the assembly.

4. Smear a little oil on the surface of any new O-rings. Install the new filter cartridge back into its housing.

5. If the cartridge is on the top of the engine, the service information may direct you to pour a specified amount of oil into the filter cavity before the end cap is installed. Screw the cartridge bolt or end cap back in place and tighten to the specified torque. Be careful not to cross-thread the oil filter bolt or end cap.

Refilling Engine Oil

Refilling an engine's oil supply is necessary when performing an oil and filter change. It may also be necessary to refill the engine oil after a lubrication system part has been replaced, if the oil was drained. Always add the recommended amount of oil and grade of oil listed in the service information. After adding the required amount of oil, be sure to start the engine to build oil pressure and fill the oil filter, and then shut the engine off to check for leaks and the level on the dipstick. Fill the oil to the max line and no farther.

To refill the engine oil, follow the steps in SKILL DRILL 12-5.

FULL
OIL LIFE RESET
PRND321

SKILL DRILL 12-5 Refilling the Engine Oil

1. Using the service information, research the correct grade and the quantity of oil you will need to fill the engine. Turn the container of oil so that the spout is on the high side of the bottle. Pour the oil into the funnel carefully so that no oil is spilled onto the outside of the engine, and pour slowly enough to avoid the risk of blowback or overflow. Fill the engine only to the level indicated on the engine dipstick. Replace the filler cap.
2. Start the engine and check the oil pressure indicator on the dash. If the oil pressure is inadequate, stop. Do not continue to run the engine.
3. If the oil pressure is good, turn the engine off and check underneath the vehicle to make sure no oil is leaking from the oil filter or drain plug.
4. With a level vehicle, check the oil level again with the dipstick. It may be necessary to top off the engine by adding a small quantity of oil to compensate for the amount absorbed by the new filter. Do not overfill.
5. Refer to the owner's manual or the service information, and install a static sticker.
6. Reset the maintenance reminder system to remind the owner when the next oil change is due.

Wrap-up

Ready for Review

- Lubrication oil is distilled from crude oil and has additives to prevent acid formation, reduce oxidation, and maintain correct viscosity.
- Functions of oil include reduces friction, cushions, cleans, cools, and seals.
- Viscosity refers to how easily a liquid flows.
- Oil additives include: extreme pressure additives, oxidation inhibitors, corrosion inhibitors, anti-foaming agents, detergents, dispersants, pour point depressants, and viscosity index improvers.
- Engine oil also works to suppress engine noise and protect against corrosion.
- The three types of oils are: conventional, synthetic, and synthetic blend.
- Conventional oil is refined from crude oil and requires additives to function effectively.
- Synthetic oil is developed in a lab, is longer lasting, operates at higher temperatures, protects better against engine wear, and is more costly to manufacture.
- Synthetic blends combine conventional and synthetic oils.
- The American Petroleum Institute classifies oil into groups 1–5.
- Components of a lubrication system include: oil pan, oil sump, pick-up tube, oil pump, oil pressure relief valve, oil filter, spurt holes, and gallery.
- Types of oil pumps are: rotor type, crescent pump, and geared oil pump.
- The two most basic oil filtering systems are full-flow filters (most common) and bypass filters.
- Vehicles are equipped with oil indicators, oil monitoring systems, and some with an oil cooler.
- Types of lubrication systems are: splash and pressure (or force feed).
- Common lubrication system issues are infrequent oil changes, oil leaks, and valve train noise due to low oil pressure.
- Always check a vehicle's service manual when changing engine oil to determine the correct quantity.
- Lubrication repair tools include: oil filter wrench, wrenches and socket set, mirror, good quality light, digital volt ohm meter, and a special socket for removing oil pressure switches or sensors.
- Maintenance and repair procedures include: draining the engine oil; replacing the oil filter; and refilling engine oil.

Key Terms

antifoaming agents Oil additives that keep oil from foaming as it moves through the engine.

bypass filter An oil filter system that only filters some of the oil.

conventional oil Oil that is processed from crude oil; about 20% of oil is additives.

corrosion inhibitors Oil additives that keep acid from forming in the oil.

crescent pump An oil pump that uses a crescent-shaped part to separate the oil pump gears from each other, allowing oil to be moved from one side of the pump to the other.

crude oil Material pulled from the earth, originating from organic compounds broken down over time and formed into petroleum. This material is processed in a refinery to break down into various hydrocarbon substances such as diesel, gasoline, and mineral oil, among others.

detergents Oil additives that help to keep carbon from sticking to engine components.

dipper A type of splash lubricating system used in small engines. It works like a spoon scooping up oil and throwing it upward onto the crankshaft and other wear surfaces.

dispersants Oil additives that keep contaminants held in suspension in the oil, to be removed by the filter or when the oil is changed.

extreme loading Large pressure placed on two bearing surfaces. Extreme loading will try to press oil from between bearing surfaces.

extreme-pressure additive An oil additive that ensures that a protective coating is given to moving engine parts and that keeps oil from being forced out under extreme pressure. Helps oil to cushion components.

full-flow filter An oil filter installed on production cars. This oil filter cleans all oil coming from the oil pump on its way to the lubricated components.

galleries Passageways drilled or cast into the engine block or head(s), which carry pressurized lubricating oil to various moving parts in the engine, such as the camshaft bearings.

geared oil pump An oil pump that has two gears running side by side together to move oil from one side of the pump gears to the other.

gelling A thickening effect of oil in cold weather. This is not a desirable trait for lubricating oil, as it will not flow when it is gelling. Wax content in base stock mineral oil makes gelling worse.

hydro-cracking A process in which group 2 and group 3 oils are refined with hydrogen at much higher temperatures and pressures. This process results in a base mineral oil with many of the higher performance characteristics of synthetic oils.

hydrogenating A process used during refining of crude oil. Hydrogen is added to crude oil to create a chemical reaction to take out impurities such as sulfur.

lubricating oil Processed crude oil with additives to help it perform well in the engine.

lubrication system A system of parts that work together to deliver lubricating oil to the various moving parts of the engine.

mineral oil Base stock processed from crude oil in a refinery, used as the base material of all conventional oil.

oil cooler A device that takes heat away from engine oil by passing it near either engine coolant or outside air. Cooling the engine oil helps to keep it from overheating and breaking down.

oil galleries Oil passages that are drilled into the engine block and cylinder head(s). These passageways carry oil from the oil pump to critical moving parts.

oil monitoring system A system that alerts the driver when it is time to change engine oil. These systems will need to be reset for the customer after an oil change is performed.

oil pan The metal pan that covers the bottom of the engine, contains oil sump where engine oil is held.

oil pressure relief valve A valve usually located in the oil pump that limits the oil pressure. When oil pressure is reached, excessive pressure is bled back to the sump.

oil pump A device that pumps lubricating oil through the engine.

oil pump strainer A screen located on the oil pump pickup that keeps debris from being picked up by the oil pump.

oil slinger A device used on small engines, located on the crankshaft or driven by the camshaft. It works to fling oil up onto moving engine parts.

oil spurt holes Holes drilled into the connecting rod that spray oil up onto the cylinder walls and the piston wrist pins.

oil sump The lower part of the oil pan that holds lubricating oil for the engine. The oil pickup screen sits in this low point.

oxidation inhibitor An oil additive that helps keep hot oil from combining with oxygen to produce sludge or tar.

pickup tube A tube connected to the oil pump that acts like a straw for the oil pump to pull oil from the sump of the oil pan.

polyalphaolefin (PAO) A man-made base stock (synthetic) used in place of mineral oil. Oil molecules are more consistent in size and no impurities are found in this oil since it is made in a lab.

pour point depressants Oil additives that keep wax crystals from forming and causing the oil to gel during cold operation.

pressure, or force-feed, lubrication system A lubrication system that has a pump to pressurize the lubricating oil and push it through the engine to moving parts.

rotor lobes Lobes or rounded edges on rotors that squeeze oil and create pressure.

rotor-type oil pump An oil pump that uses rounded gears to squeeze oil through.

scavenge pump A pump used with a dry sump oiling system to pull oil from the dry sump pan and move it to an oil tank outside the engine.

splash lubrication A lubrication system that relies on oil being splashed onto moving parts by rotating engine parts striking the oil. These systems are typically used in small engines.

synthetic blend A blend of conventional engine oil and pure synthetic oil.

synthetic oil Synthetic oil that, in its pure form, uses man-made base stocks and is not derived from crude oil. This oil lasts longer and performs better than normal oil. The base stock additives are similar to those in conventional oils.

viscosity The ability of a liquid to flow.

viscosity index improver An oil additive that resists a change in viscosity over a range of temperatures.

PROVE
KNOW
SEE
DO

ASE-Type Questions

1. Tech A says that one function of oil is to clean. Tech B says that one function of oil is to cushion. Who is correct?
   a. Tech A
   b. Tech B
   c. Both A and B
   d. Neither A nor B
2. Two techs are discussing 5W20 oil. Tech A says the W stands for "weight". Tech B says the W stands for "Winter." Who is correct?
   a. Tech A
   b. Tech B
   c. Both A and B
   d. Neither A nor B
3. Tech A says that the higher the viscosity number, the thicker the oil. Tech B says that most modern vehicles use single weight oil. Who is correct?
   a. Tech A
   b. Tech B
   c. Both A and B
   d. Neither A nor B
4. Tech A says that spin-on oil filters need RTV gasket sealer to seal the gasket. Tech B says that some oil filters use a replaceable paper filter cartridge. Who is correct?
   a. Tech A
   b. Tech B
   c. Both A and B
   d. Neither A nor B
5. Tech A says that the oil pressure will typically be low if the oil level is at the "add" line on the dipstick. Tech B says that a cracked pickup tube could cause low oil pressure. Who is correct?
   a. Tech A
   b. Tech B
   c. Both A and B
   d. Neither A nor B
6. Tech A says that most oil pumps are of the positive displacement style. Tech B says that oil pumps are designed to deliver more oil than is needed for an engine. Who is correct?
   a. Tech A
   b. Tech B
   c. Both A and B
   d. Neither A nor B
7. Tech A says that it takes about 1 pint of oil to raise the oil level from "add" to "full." Tech B says that it takes about 1 quart to raise it that much. Who is correct?
   a. Tech A
   b. Tech B
   c. Both A and B
   d. Neither A nor B
8. Tech A says that oil pressure is reduced when bearing clearances increase. Tech B says that oil pressure is regulated by the pressure relief valve. Who is correct?
   a. Tech A
   b. Tech B
   c. Both A and B
   d. Neither A nor B
9. Tech A says that a full-flow oil filter filters all of the oil going to the bearings. Tech B says that a bypass filter bypasses the pump, so that any particles in the oil won't damage the pump. Who is correct?
   a. Tech A
   b. Tech B
   c. Both A and B
   d. Neither A nor B
10. Tech A says that it is better to use two O-ring gaskets than just one on an oil filter. Tech B says that it is good practice to replace plastic, fiber, or aluminum drain plug gaskets during every oil change. Who is correct?
    a. Tech A
    b. Tech B
    c. Both A and B
    d. Neither A nor B

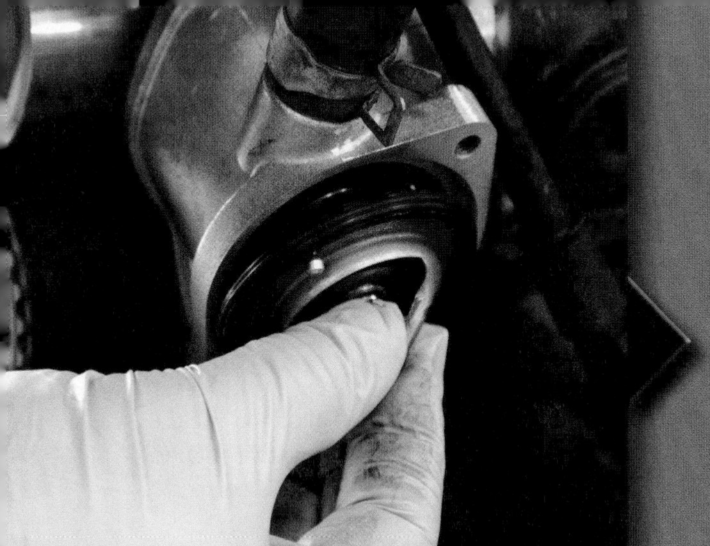

CHAPTER 13

KNOW
SEE
DO
PROVE

NATEF Tasks

Engine Repair Lubrication and Cooling Systems			Page
■ Perform cooling system pressure and dye tests to identify leaks; check coolant condition; inspect and test radiator, pressure cap, coolant recovery tank, and heater core; determine necessary action.	MLR	AST	341–342 See also the HVAC Service chapter.
■ Inspect and test coolant; drain and recover coolant; flush and refill cooling system with recommended coolant; bleed air as required.	MLR	AST	346–349
■ Inspect, replace, and adjust drive belts, tensioners, and pulleys; check pulley and belt alignment.	MLR	AST	349–351
■ Remove, inspect, and replace thermostat and gasket/seal.	MLR	AST	353–354
Heating and Air Conditioning Heating, Ventilation, and Engine Cooling Systems			
■ Inspect engine cooling and heater system hoses; determine necessary action.	MLR	AST	352–353 See also the HVAC Service chapter
Engine Performance General			
■ Verify engine operating temperature; determine necessary action.	MLR	AST	343

Engine Cooling

Know
See
Do

Knowledge Objectives

After reading this chapter, you will be able to:

1. Explain the principles and methods of heat transfer. (pp 320–321)
2. Explain the basic principles of the cooling system. (pp 321–323)
3. Discuss boiling point and pressure, electrolysis, and centrifugal force. (pp 323–325)
4. Describe how the cooling system functions. (pp 325–327)
5. Describe the components of the cooling system. (pp 327–338)

Know
See
Do

Skills Objectives

After reading this chapter, you will be able to:

1. Test the cooling system pressure and verify the engine operating temperature. (pp 341–343)
2. Test the heater control valve. (p 344)
3. Use a hydrometer to test the freeze point of the coolant. (p 345)
4. Use a refractometer to test the freeze point of the coolant. (p 345)
5. Inspect and adjust an engine drive belt. (pp 349–350)
6. Check and replace a coolant hose. (pp 352–353)

Introduction

Cooling systems play a critical role in the life span of the engine. Typically, a great deal of focus is placed on engine lubrication and the maintenance of the engine's lubrication system, but little focus is placed on the engine's cooling system. Yet, because the Department of Transportation has stated that cooling system failure is the leading cause of mechanical breakdowns on the highway, it deserves our attention. The cooling system can have a huge effect on the lubrication system and can also affect engine emissions and fuel economy, thus making its role a significant one.

This chapter will explain the importance of modern cooling system maintenance. We will cover coolant, what it is made of, how it works, and what will happen if the cooling system is not maintained. The chapter will also discuss all the components of the cooling system and how each contributes to the function of the cooling of the engine.

Cooling Fundamentals

Heat is thermal energy. It cannot be destroyed; it can only be transferred. It always moves from areas of higher temperature to areas of lower temperature. This principle is applied to the transfer of heat energy from engine parts to ambient air using the coolant as a medium to carry it. To control this heat transfer, it is necessary to understand how heat behaves. Heat travels in three ways:

1. From one solid to another, by a process called **conduction**.
2. Through liquids and gases by a process called **convection**, whereby heat follows paths called convection currents.
3. Through space, by **radiation** FIGURE 13-1.

Heat Transfer

The internal combustion engine relies on the heat of combustion to produce torque to move the vehicle and

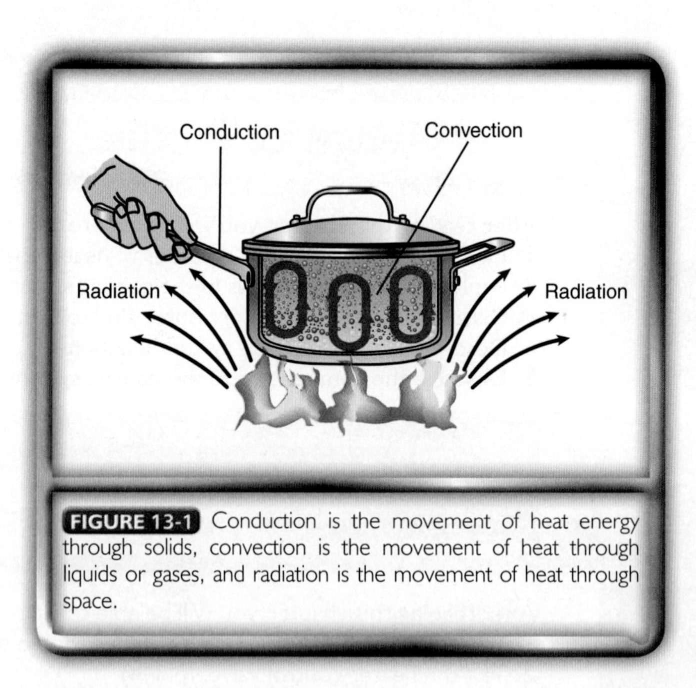
Conduction
Convection
Radiation
Radiation

FIGURE 13-1 Conduction is the movement of heat energy through solids, convection is the movement of heat through liquids or gases, and radiation is the movement of heat through space.

You Are the Automotive Technician

A customer brings his 2009 Honda Accord into your dealership complaining about the coolant boiling over on hot days. The engine gauge gets higher than normal, but never to the red zone, when steam comes out from under the hood. You ask some clarifying questions and he gives these answers; it happens most during stop and go traffic on his way home from work, which is at the hot time of the day. He isn't sure if the electric cooling fan is coming on or not since he is focused on traffic. He says that the quick lube shop takes care of his fluids, so he doesn't know if it is using coolant or not. He agrees to let you diagnose it, so you take it back to the shop and verify that the coolant level is near the full mark. You then take a minute to plan your steps for diagnosis.

1. What are the possible causes for coolant that boils over below the red zone?
2. How can engine operating temperature be verified?
3. What two factors determine the boiling point of coolant?
4. What are some of the most likely causes of coolant that boils over when in the red zone?

Applied Science

AS-27: Heat: The technician can demonstrate an understanding of the effect of heat on automotive systems.

The heat created by burning fuel in the internal combustion engine causes rapid expansions of pressure, which drives the pistons (see the Motive Power Types—Spark-Ignition (SI) Engines chapter). Some of the heat from the combustion process must be dissipated so that it does not overheat or melt engine parts. This is the job of the engine cooling system. The cooling system helps the engine to quickly come up to its specified operating temperature and to maintain that temperature in spite of ambient weather conditions or engine load. If the engine is not allowed to warm up properly, other systems will not operate properly. For example, the engine coolant temperature will greatly affect the engine air–fuel mixture (fuel trim) and thus fuel economy and emissions. Operation of the evaporative emission system and other systems is also affected by engine temperature, so it is important that the cooling system be maintained to operate correctly.

Applied Science

AS-30: Fusion/Vaporization: The technician can demonstrate an understanding of how heat causes a change in the state of matter.

Vaporization and fusion are two ways in which the application of heat can cause matter to change states. Vaporization refers to the transitional phase from liquid to vapor, while fusion refers to the transitional phase from solid to liquid. Both concepts have applications in the shop.

Pressurized cooling systems in motor vehicles are designed to prevent vaporization, in this case from boiling. Water boils at 212°F (100°C) at atmospheric pressure at sea level. When coolant in the cooling system is pressurized, its boiling point is raised, allowing the system to continue to cool the engine at temperatures over 212°F (100°C). Vaporization must be avoided because, unlike liquids, vapors do not effectively remove heat from engine components. Most cooling systems have pressure limits of 14 to 15 pounds per square inch (psi, or 97 to 103 kilopascals [kPa]), effectively raising the boiling point of the coolant by approximately 45°F (25°C).

In contrast, water turns from a liquid to a solid (freezes) at 32°F (0°C). When water freezes, it expands approximately 10%. Pressure from ice is strong enough to break cast iron, which would cause leaks in the cooling system, causing extensive damage to the engine. Antifreeze is used to lower the freezing point of water to prevent freezing of the water and antifreeze mixture, called coolant.

power accessories. Unfortunately, much of the heat produced during combustion is not used productively and must be removed to avoid overheating of the engine. No matter how efficiently fuel burning occurs, and no matter the size of the engine, the heat energy generated never completely transforms into kinetic energy **FIGURE 13-2**. Some heat energy remains unused for powering the vehicle and is typically wasted in three ways: (1) About 33% is wasted by being dumped straight out of the exhaust to the atmosphere (some of this wasted energy can be recovered by a turbocharger); (2) about 33% is wasted by the cooling system, which prevents overheating of the engine components; and (3) about 5% is wasted by internal friction and from radiating off of hot engine components straight to the atmosphere. This leaves only about 25% to 30% of the original energy that is used for powering the vehicle and its accessories. However, turbocharged vehicles recover some of the energy lost from the exhaust, bringing engine efficiency up to near 35%.

Principles of Engine Cooling

From the second law of thermodynamics, we know that heat always moves from hot to cold. These principles are put to use in the automotive cooling system to keep everything working properly. The automotive cooling system provides a means of transferring heat from the hot parts of the engine to ambient air. This can be accomplished through a group of parts working together to circulate coolant throughout a sealed system to carry heat away from those engine parts. Heat can then be released to outside air or to air entering the passenger compartment for comfort purposes.

Manufacturers use various cooling system configurations, but the basic concept is to transfer

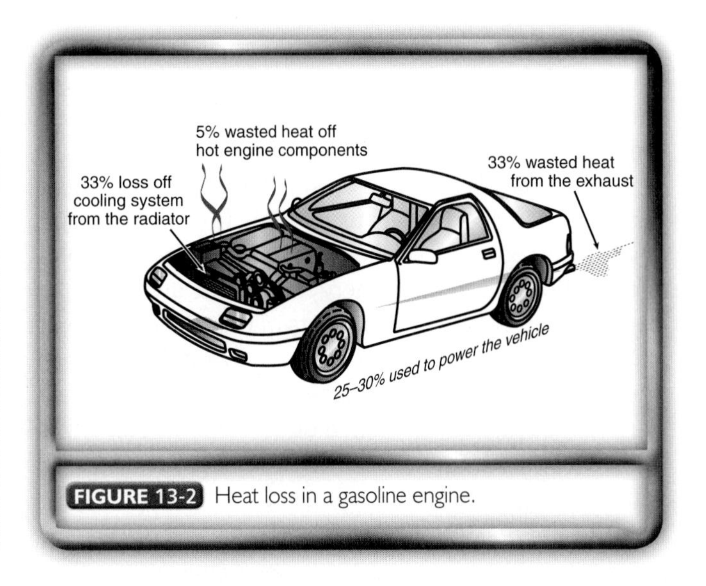
5% wasted heat off
hot engine components
33% wasted heat
from the exhaust
33% loss off
cooling system
from the radiator
25–30% used to power the vehicle

FIGURE 13-2 Heat loss in a gasoline engine.

excessive heat from hotter to cooler environments or materials. Regardless of the parts used by the manufacturer, the job is the same. You might be thinking that if some engine cooling is good, then more must be better. But that is not the case. Engines have an ideal operating temperature somewhere around 200°F (93°C), give or take 20°F (11°C), depending on the vintage of the vehicle. The purpose of the cooling system is to allow the engine to warm up to its optimum temperature as quickly as possible, and then transfer any excess heat energy to the atmosphere, thereby maintaining that ideal temperature.

Most automotive engines are liquid-cooled, although some manufacturers have used air-cooled engines. A liquid-cooled system uses **coolant**, a fluid that contains special anti-freezing and anti-corrosion chemicals mixed with water. In general terms, a water pump causes coolant to flow through passages in the engine, picking up heat along the way, and then through a cooler radiator where it gives up that heat. The radiator accepts hot coolant from the engine and lowers its temperature. As air moves over and through the radiator, the heat energy is transferred from the coolant to the ambient air. The lower-temperature coolant is returned to the engine to absorb more heat energy and continue the cycle.

The circulation of the coolant is controlled by the thermostat. It opens and closes coolant flow from the engine to the radiator. When the engine is cold, coolant circulates through the engine (and heater core) only. Once the engine warms up, the thermostat opens and allows coolant from the engine to flow through the radiator.

Some newer vehicles use a coolant heat storage system (CHSS). This system uses a vacuum-insulated container, similar to a Thermos bottle. The storage container holds an amount of hot coolant and maintains the temperature for up to three days when the engine is shut down. When the vehicle is started the next time, a small electric water pump preheats the engine by circulating this hot coolant through the engine, which greatly reduces hydrocarbon exhaust emissions during start-up and warm-up.

Air cooling is common on smaller internal combustion engines. Most engines use cooling fins. Their design makes the exposed surface area as large as possible, which allows more heat energy to radiate away and be carried off in convection currents in the air. Many small engines also use a fan to direct air through and over the cooling fins, which increases the cooling capacity. Air-cooled engines have fallen out of favor in passenger vehicles because they are harder to maintain at a stable temperature, thereby increasing emissions output of the engine **FIGURE 13-3**.

FIGURE 13-3 A cylinder from an air cooled Volkswagen engine. Note the cooling fins around the cylinder.

Vehicle Coolant

Coolant is a mixture of water and antifreeze, which is used to remove heat from the engine. If an engine did not have the heat removed from it, it would fail very quickly. Coolant absorbs the heat from the engine by convection. Since coolant contacts the hot metal directly, it is a very effective heat sink. The coolant is important for three reasons: (1) It prevents an engine from overheating while in use, (2) it keeps the engine from freezing while not in use in cold climates, and (3) it prevents corrosion of the parts in the cooling system.

Water alone is by far the best coolant there is, since it can absorb a larger amount of heat than most other liquids. But water has some drawbacks. It freezes if its temperature drops below 32°F (0°C) (the temperature at which water becomes a solid). As water freezes, it expands into a solid. If it expands in the coolant passages inside the engine, these passages—typically made of cast aluminum or cast iron—will not flex to allow expansion and will break. This renders the engine inoperative and unrepairable in most cases.

Another thing to realize about using water alone as a coolant is that water is corrosive and causes metal to rust. Think about a piece of unpainted metal that is lying outside in the rain. Rust and corrosion build up quickly on that metal simply because of the reaction (oxidation) of the metal, water, and oxygen. Antifreeze prevents corrosion and rusting through anti-corrosion additives (called corrosion inhibitors) mixed into the solution. Another important note on water is that water contains minerals and will potentially lead to excessive deposits even when added to antifreeze. Because of this, most manufacturers recommend using distilled water for cooling systems.

Antifreeze is mixed with water to lower the freezing point of water and reduce the chances of cracking the engine block, cylinder heads, and other cooling system components. Antifreeze is made from one of two base chemicals—ethylene glycol or propylene glycol—plus a mixture of additives to protect against corrosion and foaming. Ethylene and propylene glycol may achieve a maximum very low freezing point of –70°F (–57°C) when mixed with the appropriate amount of water. **Ethylene glycol** is a chemical that resists freezing but is very toxic to humans and animals. **Propylene glycol** is another chemical that resists freezing but is not toxic and is used in nontoxic antifreezes. Either of these antifreezes will actually freeze around 0°F (–18°C) if not mixed with water, so water is a necessary part of coolant. The freezing point of coolant will vary depending upon how much water is added to the antifreeze FIGURE 13-4. Because antifreeze does not absorb heat as effectively as water, it should not be mixed at a ratio higher than 65% antifreeze and 35% water. Using a higher proportion of antifreeze will actually reduce the cooling quality of the mixture and raise the operating temperature of the engine.

The best coolant is a 50/50 balance of water and antifreeze, making it an ideal coolant for both hot and cold climates and providing adequate corrosion protection. Also, when antifreeze is added at a 50% mixture, the boiling point increases from 212°F (100°C) to around 228°F (109°C). As you can see, this is an extremely beneficial characteristic of antifreeze as manufacturers continue to build engines that are more powerful, create more heat, and operate at higher temperatures.

Antifreeze can be purchased as straight antifreeze (100%) or as a 50/50 premix with water. Straight antifreeze that you buy from the dealer or parts store consists of three parts: glycol (around 96%), corrosion inhibitors and additives (around 2–3%), and water (around 2%).

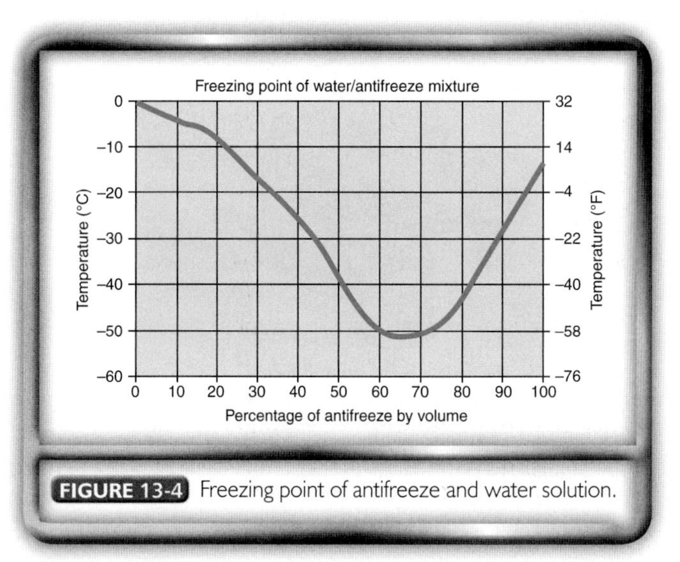
Freezing point of water/antifreeze mixture
Temperature (°C)
0
–10
–20
–30
–40
–50
–60
Temperature (°F)
32
14
–4
–22
–40
–58
–76
0 10 20 30 40 50 60 70 80 90 100
Percentage of antifreeze by volume

FIGURE 13-4 Freezing point of antifreeze and water solution.

Glycol, as discussed previously, keeps the freezing point low and the boiling point high. Corrosion inhibitors and additives prevent corrosion and erosion, resist foaming, ensure coolant is compatible with cooling system component materials and hard water, resist sedimentation, and balance the acid to alkaline content of the antifreeze. Water is added to blend the inhibitors with the glycol.

Antifreeze is an amazing chemical that performs a monumental task in the operation of our vehicles. It works so well that it is often overlooked for maintenance by the customer. However, because the additives wear out and become less effective over time, coolant does need to be changed at recommended intervals. Doing so reduces the possibility of engine damage and failure over time. Likewise, lubrication enhancers, which keep the water pump and seals functioning properly, wear out and need to be replaced.

Boiling Point and Pressure

The **boiling point** of a liquid is the temperature at which it begins to change from a liquid to a gas. Water at sea level atmospheric pressure 14.7 psi (101.4 kPa or 1 atmosphere [atm]) boils at 212°F (100°C). Atmospheric pressure becomes lower as elevation is increased. Because atmospheric pressure is lower at higher elevations (such as in the mountains), the boiling temperature of a liquid in an unsealed system is lower. Think of it as *lower pressure = lower boiling point*. Conversely, raising the pressure has the opposite effect; it raises the boiling point of a liquid. Stated another way, a liquid in a vacuum has a lower boiling point than when that same liquid is at atmospheric pressure. A liquid under pressure higher than atmospheric pressure has a higher boiling point than when that liquid is at atmospheric pressure. Thus, the boiling point of a liquid varies depending upon the surrounding environmental pressure. For a given pressure, different liquids boil at different temperatures.

This principle is used to enable water in the engine's cooling system to remain a liquid at temperatures well above the normal boiling point of 212°F (100°C). The pressurized coolant in the cooling system boils at a

Safety

Because the pressurized coolant in the cooling system boils at a higher temperature than when the radiator pressure cap is removed, you should NEVER remove a radiator pressure cap on a hot engine. If the coolant is above 212°F (100°C), all of the coolant will turn to steam as soon as the pressure is released, pushing superheated steam out the radiator, potentially scalding you.

higher temperature than when the radiator pressure cap is removed (or if the system has a leak).

Over the years, manufacturers intentionally have raised the operating temperature of their engines for more efficient combustion and reduced emissions. A pressurized cooling system can handle the extra heat without boiling over. Pressurizing the cooling system can mean that the cooling system can be downsized (for less weight and space requirement) and still cool the engine effectively. Also, with a higher temperature differential between the cooling system's operating temperature and the outside ambient air, the radiator is more effective at radiating excess heat from the coolant. In today's vehicles, most automotive cooling systems are pressurized at 13–17 psi (89.6–117.2 kPa). However, some factory radiator caps are rated as high as 24 psi (165.5 kPa), and high-performance systems can go as high as 34 psi (234.4 kPa).

TECHNICIAN TIP

The term "psig" is another way of saying the pressure that is read on a normal American pressure gauge. The "g" stands for gauge. So gauge pressure is the amount of pressure measured above 1 atm (atmospheric pressure). A compound pressure gauge typically reads both above and below atmospheric pressure. It measures psig above zero, and inches of vacuum (or mm of mercury) below zero.

In contrast, the term "psia" means *absolute pressure*, which does not include atmospheric pressure. In other words, a psia gauge would read 14.7 psig at sea level. If you want to know the absolute pressure (in psia), just add gauge pressure (psig) to atmospheric pressure (usually considered 14.7 psi at sea level).

Electrolysis

Electrolysis is the process of pulling chemicals (materials) apart by using electricity or by creating electricity through the use of chemicals and dissimilar metals. Electrolysis is used in manufacturing to create some metals, gases, and chemicals. You may have performed electrolysis in a science class by passing electrical current through water to break the hydrogen out of the water. Electrolysis is what takes place in the automotive battery. Two dissimilar metals are submerged in an acid solution, resulting in the reaction that is called electricity. Another common experiment in science class is the potato battery, made from two different types of metal stuck into the potato and used to power a digital clock or a light bulb.

Electrolysis can occur in places where it is not desired and can have undesirable effects. For instance, in automotive cooling systems, electrolysis is possible when the coolant breaks down and becomes more acidic. Many types of metal are used in the engine, such as cast iron, aluminum, copper, and brass. Introducing an acid solution into a mix of metals will produce electricity. When this electricity is produced, the movement of the electrons will begin to erode away the metal in the system. Eventually, pinholes will be created in the thinner, softer cooling system components (typically, the heater core or aluminum cylinder head). To combat electrolysis, the customer needs to have regular scheduled maintenance of the coolant performed, including flushing out of the old coolant and replacing it with new coolant. Electricity can also appear in the cooling system due to faulty grounds on accessories or even the starter motor circuit. Electricity is known to follow the path of least resistance and will be partially carried through the coolant where it can erode metals, if that path is easier than its intended path. We will discuss how to test for electrolysis later in this chapter and will revisit bad grounds at that point.

Centrifugal Force

Centrifugal force is a force pulling outward on a rotating body. For example, if you were to take a tennis ball and tie it to a string and swing it around you, centrifugal force would pull the tennis ball outward making the string taut. Another example of centrifugal force occurs when a vehicle turns a curve. Centrifugal force resists the turning of the vehicle and tries to keep the vehicle moving in a straight line, creating a sliding condition if centrifugal force is great enough. Centrifugal force can be useful in some cases, such as in the water pump. When coolant enters the center of the water pump and the internal rotor spins, centrifugal force moves the liquid outward toward the outlet **FIGURE 13-5**. Centrifugal force

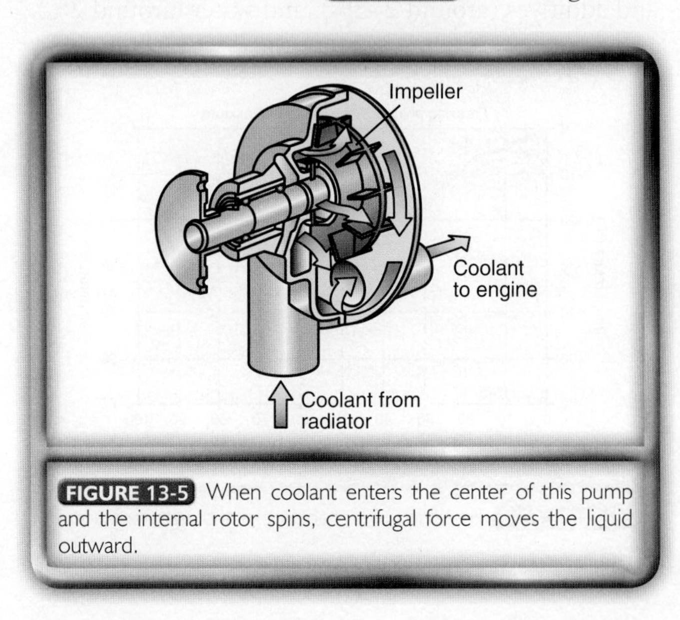
Impeller
Coolant to engine
Coolant from radiator

FIGURE 13-5 When coolant enters the center of this pump and the internal rotor spins, centrifugal force moves the liquid outward.

Applied Science

AS-101: Proportion Mixtures: The technician can correctly mix fluids using proportions.

As discussed earlier, engine coolant is composed of water and antifreeze. The normally recommended mixture of these two liquids is 50/50—50% water and 50% antifreeze—which provides freeze protection to about –34°F (–37°C). Automotive cooling system capacity typically is given in quarts or liters, with smaller vehicles requiring perhaps 5 quarts (or liters) and larger SUVs with air conditioning requiring up to 20 or more quarts (or liters).

If a vehicle's specifications call for a total of 16 quarts of coolant, then a 50/50 mixture would consist of 8 quarts of antifreeze mixed with 8 quarts of distilled water. A 10-quart system would require 5 quarts of each, and so forth. The challenge in ensuring a 50/50 mix is the unknown mixture that remains in the cooling system, since not all of the coolant will drain out. If the system has been flushed with clean water and drained, then to end up with a 50/50 mix, the technician would first add the entire 50% of antifreeze and then top off the rest with clean water, leaving a 50/50 mix. If the coolant was flushed out with a 50/50 mix, then the technician can premix coolant and top the cooling system off with that. After topping off the cooling system, be sure to run the engine to circulate the coolant and then check the mixture's freeze point with a hydrometer or refractometer.

Coolant can now be purchased premixed for convenience, but you will be paying for 50% water, plus the cost of shipping it, so it is less expensive to mix your own coolant.

pushes the coolant into the engine block and head passageways that surround the cylinders. The coolant then travels through the radiator to be cooled.

Cooling Systems

Almost all modern vehicles have engine cooling systems that use a liquid coolant to transfer heat energy from parts of the internal combustion engine to outside air. (Note: Other cooling systems, such as those used for turbocharger intercoolers/aftercoolers or hybrid high-voltage battery packs, may use air-to-air systems to cool the engine's intake air or high-voltage battery). In the engine's liquid-cooled system, coolant is forced to flow around and through parts of the engine to pick up excess heat and carry it through flexible hoses to the radiator. Engine heat is transferred from hotter components to cooler ones. The cooling fan forces air over the fins of the radiator, as necessary, to assist the transfer of heat energy from the coolant to the ambient air **FIGURE 13-6**. The coolant also flows through coolant hoses to the heater core, which is located in the air box in the passenger compartment and provides heat for the passengers when needed. **Cooling hoses** (i.e., radiator hoses and heater hoses) are flexible rubber tubes that connect stationary components of the cooling system, such as the heater core and radiator, to the engine, which is allowed to move on its flexible mounts. Engine movement in its flexible rubber mounts would cause nonflexible coolant hoses to break over time.

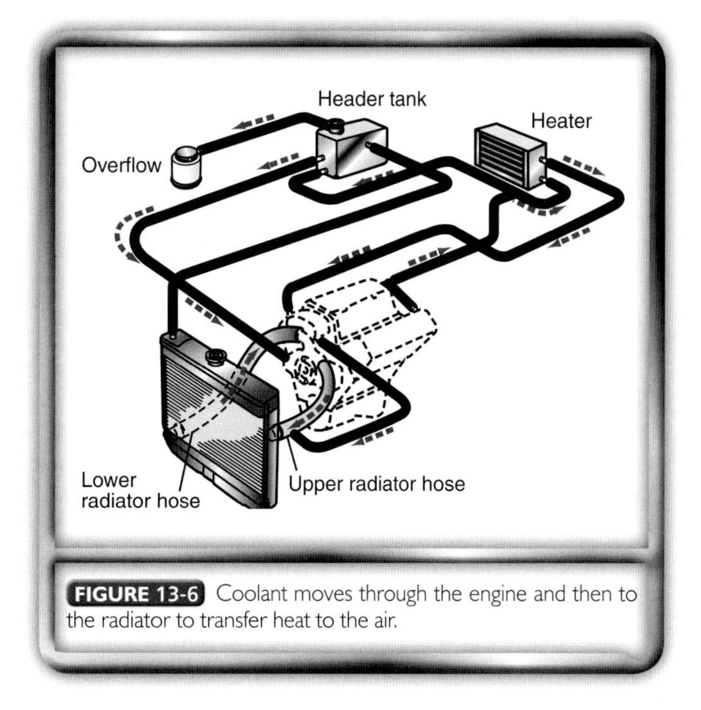
Header tank
Heater
Overflow
Lower radiator hose
Upper radiator hose

FIGURE 13-6 Coolant moves through the engine and then to the radiator to transfer heat to the air.

Air Cooling

Air engine cooling is common on smaller internal combustion engines and was used in the past on some automobiles like the early Volkswagen Beetle and Porsches. Air cooling of an automobile was not ideal from an emissions standpoint; nor did it always provide sufficient cabin heat for the passenger compartment. All automobiles are now water cooled, although small engines can still be found in older automobiles that are air cooled. Air cooling uses heat-dissipating fins on the engine cylinders and heads to allow the movement of air to absorb heat and carry it away from the engine through special ducting. Since the air does the work of keeping the engine cool, an air-cooled system is very simple and light compared to a water-cooled one. This is one of several reasons why most small aircraft engines are air cooled. A major drawback to air cooling is that the engine has to be exposed to the airstream for best cooling. Many motorcycles were air cooled, but as the engines became more powerful, a more effective cooling system became necessary. Most motorcycle engines produced today are water cooled.

Air-cooled engines in automobiles usually are not exposed to the air; rather, the engine is housed in an enclosed engine bay. Still, for a vehicle moving at highway speed, airflow over the engine may be high enough to prevent overheating. At lower speeds or during idling, heat may build up and overheat the engine. One way to remove excess heat from the engine is to use a fan, along with shrouds and ducts, to direct air over or even between the cylinders. An engine that uses these components is called a "forced draft" air-cooled engine. Some air-cooled engines are "open draft" air-cooled, which require the engine to be moving through the air to have sufficient airflow **FIGURE 13-7**.

Liquid Cooling

In modern vehicles, radiators are low and wide to allow the hood to sit lower to the ground for aerodynamics. Because of this design, modern vehicles use a water pump that pulls coolant from the radiator and forces it through passages, called **water jackets**, in the engine block and cylinder head. Coolant absorbs heat by conduction from the engine and becomes hotter. The heated coolant then moves to the radiator for cooling; air flowing over and through the radiator causes heat to be absorbed from the coolant by the air.

All engines operate best when they are at their full operating temperature, commonly referred to as the operating temperature. Most engine wear and high exhaust emissions occur during the warm-up period. Ideally, we want the engine to get to operating temperature as quickly as possible, but not overheat. In order to accomplish this, a thermostat is used to regulate the coolant temperature. The thermostat initially blocks coolant flow to the radiator, keeping coolant circulating in the engine where it heats up quickly and does not pull heat from the warming engine. Once operating temperature is reached, the thermostat starts to open and allows coolant to flow to the radiator to remove excessive heat. The thermostat does not normally open completely, but adjusts between its fully closed or fully open position continually to maintain an optimum engine operating temperature, regardless of engine load.

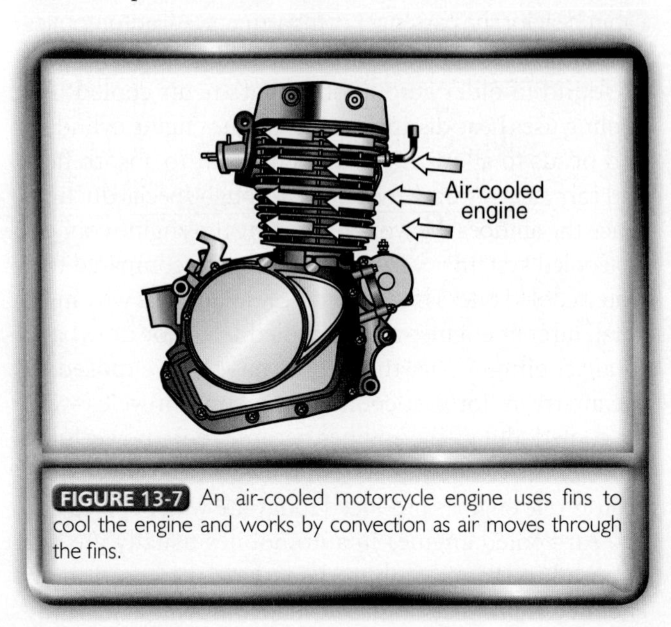
Air-cooled
engine

FIGURE 13-7 An air-cooled motorcycle engine uses fins to cool the engine and works by convection as air moves through the fins.

> **TECHNICIAN TIP**
>
> Preventing overheating is one function of the cooling system. It also helps the engine reach its best operating temperature as soon as possible. Every engine has a temperature at which it operates best. If operated below or above this temperature, ignition and combustion problems may occur. Likewise, the thickness (viscosity) of the lubricating oil in the engine, and in other operating systems, may be affected. An MIL (malfunction indicator lamp) may illuminate if the thermostat has failed and does not allow the engine to reach its normal operating temperature within a specified time. Because of these situations, proper thermostat operation is a very important part of engine maintenance.

Coolant Flow—Normal and Reverse Flow

In a water-cooled cooling system with normal flow, the flow of coolant starts at the water pump. Cold coolant is moved through the engine and starts to warm up as the engine begins to run. The coolant travels up through the engine assisted by the water pump. The pump relies on centrifugal force of the impeller (rotor) to force coolant through the cooling passageways of the engine. The coolant flows around the cylinders where combustion is taking place and picks up excess heat. Heat transfers from around the cylinders to the coolant as it moves past them. It then moves upward through the cylinder head, where it passes over the top of the combustion chamber in the head and flows around the valve guides, all the while picking up more heat as it passes those hotter surfaces.

From the head it will move to the thermostat, which works like a trapdoor: If it is closed, the coolant will continue to circulate within the engine, flowing through a bypass hose or passage to move back down to the water pump, which was the starting point of its journey again. The thermostat is meanwhile sensing the coolant's temperature, and at a specified temperature it begins to open. As the thermostat opens, the coolant begins to flow through the radiator hose and to the radiator. Coolant enters the radiator's inlet tank and then the radiator core, where it flows through small tubes that have heat-dissipating fins on the outside. The tubes act like fins on an air-cooled engine to transfer the coolant's heat to the outside air. As it cools, coolant moves to the cool side of the radiator to begin its journey back to the engine through the other radiator hose. The coolant's return flow to the engine is aided by the suction created by the water pump impeller.

One problem with this normal-flow system was discovered on race cars, which develop more heat than a standard automobile. Because race car engines run hotter, and cylinder heads in general run hotter than engine blocks, the heads would get too hot and fail. The hottest part of any engine is the cylinder head, since this is where the combustion chamber is located. High cylinder head temperatures tend to increase chances of detonation and failure of head gaskets. As a cylinder head heats more than the cylinder block, it will expand further and slide across the head gasket more. When the head does this many times, the gasket is more likely to fail.

In the normal-flow cooling system, coolant goes through the engine block first and then moves to the hottest part—the cylinder head. As a result, the cylinder head operates at a hotter temperature than the cylinder block. Engineers found that if they changed the flow design, they could keep the cylinder head and block closer to the same temperature by pushing coolant through the head first, thus making the head, valves, and head gaskets last longer. Therefore, in some reverse-flow cooling systems, coolant flows to the cylinder heads first and then through the engine block.

In the typical reverse-flow design, coolant starts from the radiator and flows through the radiator outlet hose to the thermostat and then to the water pump. The thermostat is located on the inlet side of the engine to help regulate cold coolant more closely and to help reduce temperature shock to engine components. Coolant moves to the cylinder head first, where it can do the most cooling, then moves through the block and back to the radiator through the other radiator hose. Since the flow through the radiator is the same, it is simply the flow through the engine that has changed. This design differs only in the way coolant flows, head to block; all the components are generally the same. In other reverse-flow designs, coolant may flow from the thermostat in the lower radiator hose to the bottom of the radiator then up to the top of the radiator and back to the cylinder heads, through the block, through the thermostat, and on to the lower radiator.

One problem with the reverse-flow design was easily fixed: As coolant moved through the hottest part of the engine, steam tended to form and get stuck at the head cooling passages, since this is the highest part of the engine. Since the engine will overheat if gas pockets get stuck in the water passageways, the solution was to drill holes in the head for steam to escape and to run a tube from the head back to a **surge tank**, where the steam turns back into coolant and is recycled through the system. The surge tank will be discussed in greater detail later in the chapter.

Cooling System Components

The primary components of a vehicle cooling system are:

- *Radiator*: The radiator is usually made of copper, brass, or aluminum tubes with copper, brass, aluminum, or plastic tanks on the sides or top for coolant to collect in. Air is drawn over the radiator to transfer heat energy to ambient air. The fins on the tubes of the radiator give more surface area for **heat dissipation**—the spreading of heat over a large area to ease heat transfer.
- *Thermostat*: The thermostat regulates coolant flow to the radiator. It opens at a predetermined temperature to allow coolant flow to the radiator for cooling. It also enables the engine to reach operating temperature more quickly for reduced emissions and wear.
- *Recovery system:* The recovery system uses an **overflow tank** to catch any coolant that is released from the radiator cap when the coolant heats up. It works like a catch can.
- *Surge tank*: This pressurized tank is piped into the cooling system. Coolant constantly moves through it. It is used when the radiator is not the highest part of the cooling system. Remember, air collects at the highest point in the cooling system.
- *Water pump*: This pump is used to force coolant throughout the cooling system in order to transfer heat energy. The water pump is typically driven off the engine timing belt or accessory belt. On some engines, it is driven by the camshaft timing chain.
- *Cooling fan*: This fan forces air through the radiator for heat transfer. Cooling fans can be driven by a belt or by an electric motor. The fan can be controlled by viscous fluid or thermostatic sensors, switches, and relays.
- *Radiator hoses*: These hoses are used to connect the radiator to the water pump and engine. They are usually made of formed, nylon-reinforced rubber. Some radiator hoses use coiled wire inside them to prevent hose collapse as the cooling system temperature fluctuates.
- *Heater hoses*: These hoses connect the water pump and engine to the heater core. They carry heated coolant to the heater core to be used to heat the passenger compartment.

- *Drive belts*: These belts provide power to drive the water pump and other accessories on the front of the engine. Three types are used: V-belts, serpentine (also called multi-groove) belts, and toothed belts.
- *Temperature indicators*: Temperature indicators provide information to the operator about engine temperature. The temperature gauge indicates engine temperature continuously. A temperature warning indicator comes on only when the engine is overheating to warn the operator that engine damage will occur if the vehicle is driven much farther.
- *Water jackets*: Water jackets are passages surrounding the cylinders and head on the engine where coolant can flow to pick up excess heat. They are sealed by replaceable core plugs.
- *Heater core*: The heater core is a small radiator used to provide heat to the passenger compartment from the hot coolant passing through it. The amount of heat can be controlled by a heater control valve.
- *Coolant*: Coolant is the liquid used to prevent freezing, overheating, and corrosion of the engine.
- *Auxiliary coolers*: Auxiliary coolers are used to cool automatic transmission fluid, power steering fluid, EGR gasses, and compressed intake air. Each of these coolers transmits heat to either the cooling system or directly to the atmosphere. Because there is such a wide variety of auxiliary coolers, refer to the manufacturer's service information for how to properly inspect the auxiliary cooler for leaks and proper operation.

Radiator

The **radiator** is located in a convenient position under the hood of the vehicle where maximum airflow can pass through it. Its actual location under the hood depends on the engine configuration, the available space, and the shape or line of the hood itself. The radiator consists of top and bottom tanks or side tanks and a core. The radiator core allows the coolant to pass through it in either a vertical or a horizontal cross-flow direction. In addition, the radiator core serves as a good conductor of heat away from the engine.

The materials used in the radiator must be good heat conductors, such as brass, copper, or aluminum. Brass or copper is often used for tanks when combined with a brass or copper core. Modern vehicles often use plastic tanks combined with an aluminum core. This design saves weight and cost while still providing good heat transfer.

The core consists of a number of cooling tubes that carry coolant between the two tanks. The tubes can be in a horizontal (cross-flow) design or a vertical (down-flow) design FIGURE 13-8. In a **down-flow radiator**, the cooling tubes run top to bottom, with the tanks on the top and bottom. In a **cross-flow radiator**, the cooling tubes are arranged horizontally, with one tank on each side. Because of this arrangement, the same amount of cooling area can be achieved without the need for a very tall radiator; instead, it will be wide and short. This design feature allows the hood profile to be lower to allow for better aerodynamics, which improves fuel economy and safety by increasing the driver's vision in front of the vehicle. The function of both types of radiator configurations is the same, which is to cool the coolant before it reenters the engine.

In both the cross-flow and the down-flow design, the core is built of the same components. Although having only cooling tubes exposed to airflow would cool the coolant somewhat, radiators are designed with heat-dissipating fins to allow more surface area to dissipate heat, which is then released to the air. Coolant touches tube walls, and fins touch the tubes, so heat is removed from the coolant by conduction into the cooling fins, then by convection at the surface of the fins. Air rushing by the fins carries the heat away. Liquid coolant emerges cooler at the outlet of the radiator, since the coolant was able to give up much of its heat to the atmosphere.

Radiator Shrouding

In the interest of fuel economy (less drag coefficient), vehicle hood lines have become more streamlined and engine compartments smaller and more crowded. These changes in turn make it more difficult for ram air to flow

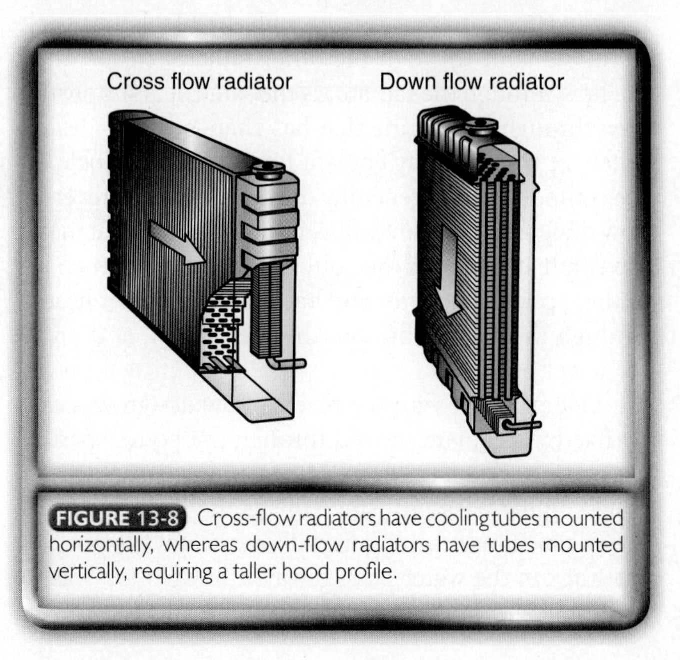
Cross flow radiator
Down flow radiator

FIGURE 13-8 Cross-flow radiators have cooling tubes mounted horizontally, whereas down-flow radiators have tubes mounted vertically, requiring a taller hood profile.

through the radiator and around the engine. Airflow is therefore greatly reliant on shrouding above, behind, and below the radiator to direct ram air to the radiator and from it FIGURE 13-9. Shrouds are also used around the radiator fan to help draw air through the entire radiator core and not just in front of the fan blades. Also, the fan shroud prevents air from simply circulating around the tips of the fan blades, instead of being drawn through the radiator. If the shrouding is removed and not replaced, such as after service has been performed, the engine will not be cooled as efficiently as it should be and will likely overheat, especially on hot days.

Radiator Pressure Cap

If coolant boils, it can be as damaging to an engine as having it freeze. Boiling coolant changes the coolant from a liquid into a gas in the engine water jackets. No liquid is left in contact with the cylinder walls or head, causing heat transfer to stop or slow to the point of overheating. Without cooling, the pistons will seize as temperatures soar with each combustion cycle, and engine meltdown can take place.

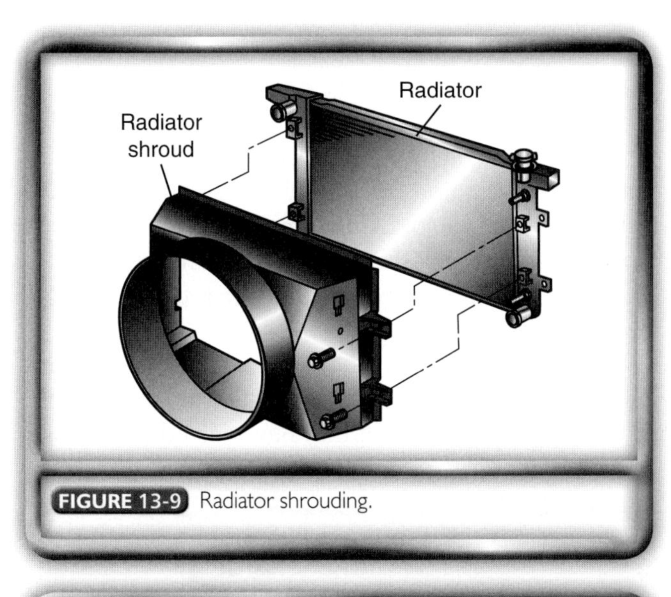
Radiator
Radiator shroud

FIGURE 13-9 Radiator shrouding.

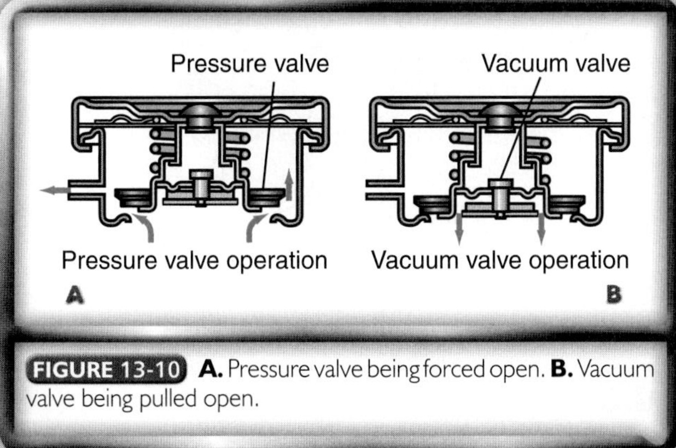
Pressure valve
Vacuum valve
Pressure valve operation
Vacuum valve operation
A
B

FIGURE 13-10 **A.** Pressure valve being forced open. **B.** Vacuum valve being pulled open.

One way to prevent coolant from boiling is to use a radiator pressure cap. As coolant temperature rises, the coolant expands and pressure in the cooling system rises. The increased pressure raises the boiling point of the coolant. Engine temperature keeps rising, and the coolant expands further. Pressure builds against a spring-loaded valve in the radiator cap until, at a preset pressure, the valve opens and releases a small amount of coolant. When this valve opens, the coolant leaves the radiator through the overflow tube to the overflow container FIGURE 13-10. In past designs, the overflow tube would drop the coolant onto the ground, which was an environmental hazard. By releasing coolant into a coolant overflow container, the coolant can be pulled back into the system once it cools.

Coolant loses temperature in the radiator when the engine is off. When coolant cools, it contracts, and with this contraction, it creates a vacuum (low pressure) in the

Applied Science

AS-31: Insulation: The technician can explain the role of insulation in maintaining temperatures.

Certain parts of the vehicle's heating and cooling system, as well as the passenger compartment, must be insulated in order to perform properly. Air-conditioning refrigerant lines, heating ducts, and other areas are insulated to prevent the loss of, or absorption of, heat. Even the hood itself may be insulated, not only to reduce the amount of heat radiated from the engine but also to quiet engine noise from being heard outside the vehicle or inside the passenger compartment.

Applied Science

AS-32: Radiation: The technician can demonstrate an understanding of heat transfer that involves infrared rays.

At one end of the light spectrum, just beyond visibility, lies the infrared portion of light. Infrared is a form of heat energy, and it can be detected by special instruments. Thermography involves the use of heat-sensing instruments to detect heat sources. The amount of radiation emitted by an object increases with temperature; therefore, thermography allows one to see variations in temperature. In the automotive trade, an infrared "temp gun" is pointed at objects to determine their temperature. This method is useful for detecting cylinders that are contributing less power to the engine, finding leaks in air-conditioning systems, and so forth. On the dashboard of many vehicles lies an infrared-sensing "sun-load sensor," which helps automatic HVAC systems to regulate cabin temperature and enables automatic headlight dimming.

radiator. A vacuum valve is located in the radiator cap that will open and allow coolant to be pulled back into the radiator from the overflow container. Because of this design, no coolant is lost as with the older systems that dropped coolant onto the ground. The vacuum valve in the cap also stops low pressure from developing in the radiator and causing collapsed radiator hoses as a result of atmospheric pressure on the outside of the hose crushing the hose against the vacuum in the system.

Surge Tank

Some vehicles are equipped with a surge tank. The surge tank has coolant constantly running through it and is located higher than the top of the radiator. If the radiator sits lower than any other part in the cooling system, then gas will collect in whatever component is highest. On some vehicles this may be the heater core. To solve this problem, engineers have installed a surge tank and placed it so it is the highest component in the system. Thus, any gas in the system will make its way to this tank, ensuring that only liquid coolant circulates through the system. The surge tank has at least one line in and one line out. It is usually made of hardened plastic, which allows for a visual checking of the fluid level through the plastic. This tank is usually where the cooling system is filled or topped off with coolant. In many vehicles with a surge tank, the pressure cap is mounted on the surge tank instead of the radiator FIGURE 13-11.

Recovery System

A coolant recovery system maintains coolant in the system at all times. The recovery system consists of an overflow bottle, a sealed radiator pressure cap, and a small hose connecting the bottle to the radiator neck FIGURE 13-12. As engine temperatures rise, the coolant expands. Pressure builds against a valve in the radiator cap until, at a preset pressure, the valve opens. Hot coolant flows out of the radiator, through the connecting hose, and into an overflow bottle. As the engine cools, coolant contracts and pressure in the cooling system drops below atmospheric pressure. Atmospheric pressure in the overflow bottle opens the vacuum valve in the radiator cap, and overflow coolant flows back into the radiator. Like water, air contains oxygen, which reacts with metals to form corrosion. With use of a recovery system, no coolant is lost and excess air is kept out of the system.

Thermostat and Housing

The **thermostat** is located under the thermostat housing. The thermostat regulates the flow of coolant, allowing coolant to flow from the engine to the radiator when the engine is running at its operating temperature. The thermostat prevents coolant from flowing to the radiator when the engine is cold to allow the engine to warm up more rapidly to reduce engine wear and emissions.

The thermostat is a spring-loaded valve that is controlled by a wax pellet located inside the valve FIGURE 13-13. As the temperature of the coolant rises, the wax pellet will melt and expand, forcing the spring-loaded valve open at a preset temperature. As the valve opens, coolant is allowed to flow through it. The thermostat works like a door to control movement of coolant. When the engine is cold, the door is closed; when hot, the door opens. Some dashboard temperature gauges show a slight swing of engine temperatures as the thermostat cycles slightly toward open or closed.

Some engines are designed such that the coolant bypass passage is directly under the thermostat. In those situations, the thermostat may have a flat disc attached

FIGURE 13-11 A surge tank removes air and gases from the coolant. This is where you normally fill the cooling system.

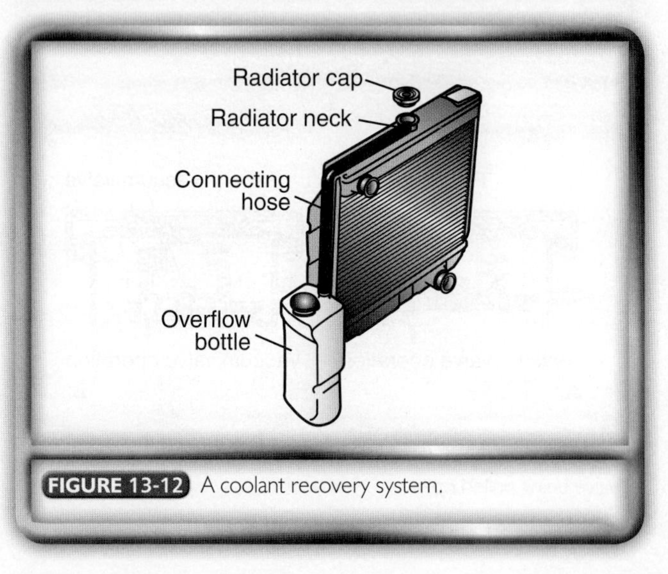
Radiator cap
Radiator neck
Connecting hose
Overflow bottle

FIGURE 13-12 A coolant recovery system.

to the bottom of it, which moves along with the thermostat. When the thermostat fully opens, the flat disc blocks off the bypass passage so that all coolant must flow through the radiator. Yet, when the thermostat partially closes, the bypass passage will be partially open. This helps give more effective cooling when the thermostat is fully open.

Most thermostats have a small hole on one side of the thermostat valve that allows any air in the system to move past the closed thermostat when the valve is closed. This is especially helpful when the cooling system has been drained and is being filled. The hole will usually contain a little pin called a jiggle valve or jiggle pin to help break the surface tension of the coolant and allow any air to flow slowly through the hole. Air trapped in the cooling system is thus able to slowly find its way to the uppermost part of the cooling system where it can be bled. When installing the thermostat, the jiggle valve should be in the uppermost position so that as much air as possible can be bled from the system.

The thermostat and housing are normally located on the outlet side of the coolant flow from the engine. However, on some engines they are located on the inlet side of the engine. The thermostat is identified by being located in the housing connected to the inlet radiator hose. The reason for installing the thermostat on the inlet side is to better control the amount of cold water that rushes into the engine, which can create a temperature shock to the engine.

Some vehicles include a manual bleed valve on the thermostat housing or within a high part of the cooling system. After the vehicle cooling system has been serviced and refilled, the technician should carefully open the bleed valve to vent any trapped air to the atmosphere. It is good practice to bleed the system again once the engine has warmed up.

Water Pump

The water pump is usually belt driven from a pulley on the front of the crankshaft. The engine drives the water pump using an accessory V-belt or the timing belt. Some newer vehicles use an electrically driven water pump. Internally, the water pump has fanlike blades on an impeller or rotor, which is turned by a shaft connected to the pulley. The shaft rides on a heavy-duty double-row ball bearing for long life and to withstand belt tension. The shaft is sealed where it enters the pump chamber. Most water pumps have a small weep hole that sits between the seal and the bearing and vents any coolant that leaks past the seal to be drained to the outside of the engine **FIGURE 13-14**. Checking this hole for signs of coolant leakage is part of the process of inspecting the engine for leaks.

The water pump is usually located at the front of the engine block; a hose typically connects it to the output of the radiator where the relatively cool coolant emerges. Coolant enters the center of the pump. As the impeller rotates, it catches the coolant and flings it outward with centrifugal force. This type of water pump is called a centrifugal pump, meaning that it creates movement of the coolant due to centrifugal force, but does not cause much buildup of pressure. Coolant is driven through the outlet into the water jackets of the engine block and to the cylinder heads. Coolant can be directed to critical hot spots, such as around the exhaust ports in the cylinder head, to stop localized overheating. The cylinder head gasket has holes of various sizes to help determine how

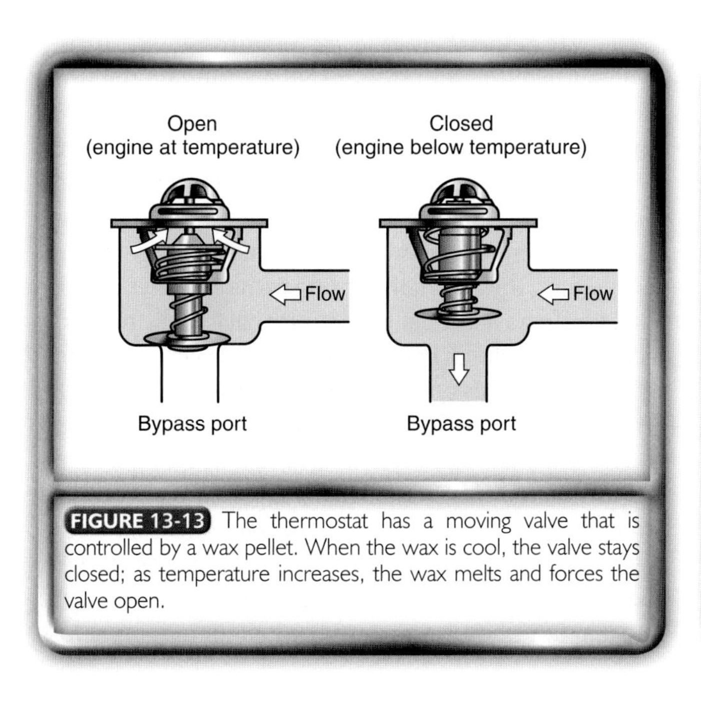
Open
(engine at temperature)
Closed
(engine below temperature)
Flow
Flow
Bypass port
Bypass port

FIGURE 13-13 The thermostat has a moving valve that is controlled by a wax pellet. When the wax is cool, the valve stays closed; as temperature increases, the wax melts and forces the valve open.

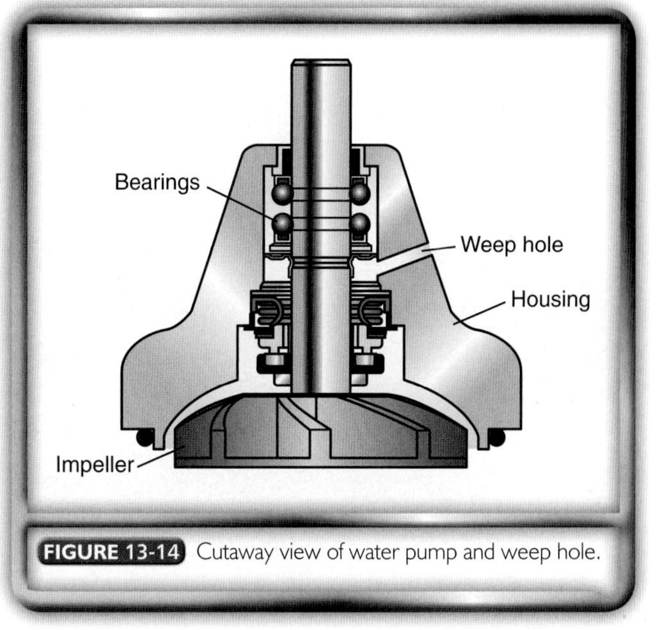
Bearings
Weep hole
Housing
Impeller

FIGURE 13-14 Cutaway view of water pump and weep hole.

much coolant should flow to these and other locations of the head. If the head gasket is not properly installed, cylinder head damage may result from localized overheating.

Replacing a water pump is a fairly common task that used to be performed mostly as a result of noise or leak issues on accessory-belt driven water pumps FIGURE 13-15. But now with many water pumps being driven by timing belts, it is common to replace the water pump along with the timing belt at the belt's recommended replacement schedule FIGURE 13-16. When changing this type of pump, the timing belt will need to be removed, so following the manufacturer's procedure will be necessary to prevent damage to the valves and pistons. Once the drive belt is removed from either style of water pump, the removal of the pump involves the unbolting of the pump, carefully prying it off of the mating surface, cleaning the mounting surface, and re-bolting it back in place with the appropriate gasket or O-ring.

FIGURE 13-15 Replacing a water pump.

FIGURE 13-16 Water pumps are typically driven by timing belts.

Cooling Fan

Cooling fans are used to provide airflow through the radiator core for engine cooling. This is most needed during slow driving or stop-and-go driving. There are two main categories of cooling fans: engine driven and electric. Engine-driven cooling fans may be located on the water pump shaft or in a few cases may be attached directly to the engine crankshaft. Most vehicles today use one or more electrically driven engine cooling fans, which are mounted directly to the radiator. On a fan that is driven by the engine, engine horsepower is directly needed to drive the fan, requiring extra fuel even when the fan is not needed. Such fans are also noisy and dangerous to work around.

It takes a fair amount of energy to turn a fan, which ultimately comes from the crankshaft, consuming energy that could be used to drive the vehicle down the road. Yet, the fan is not needed during cold engine operation. It is also not needed when the vehicle is traveling above about 35 mph (56 kph) and the airflow is strong enough to cool the radiator without using the fan. For years, vehicle manufacturers have sought ways to reduce the energy the fan uses. One type of fan design (called a flex fan) uses flexible steel or plastic blades that straighten out and lessen their **pitch** as engine speed increases. This design increases fuel economy and reduces noise FIGURE 13-17.

Another type of engine-driven fan uses a **viscous coupler** to connect the water pump pulley to the cooling fan FIGURE 13-18. The viscous coupler is called a fan clutch since it can engage and disengage the fan from the pulley. The fan clutch typically uses two discs that have closely fitted interwoven rings and grooves. When viscous silicone oil is allowed to fill the small spaces between the rings and the grooves, it transmits torque from one disc to the other, and is used to transmit torque across the two halves of the hub. A bimetallic spring on the front moves as air temperature from the radiator changes. This spring is attached to a valve that turns and allows more silicone oil to flow into the coupler, thereby transmitting more of the pulley's speed to the fan to move more air. As air temperature decreases from air flowing through the radiator, the bimetallic spring turns the valve and the silicone oil moves out of the coupler back to the reservoir located in the clutch body. This causes the fan to slow and move less air. This type of fan is driven at all times by the accessory belt. The benefit of using a viscous clutch is to increase fuel economy by being able to cycle on and off.

A variation of the clutch fan is the solenoid-controlled fan clutch, which operates in the same manner as the thermostatic fan clutch. The clutch uses oil to control the speed of the fan in relation to engine speed (allows slip to slow fan down) and temperature of the air moving across

FIGURE 13-17 Flex fan.

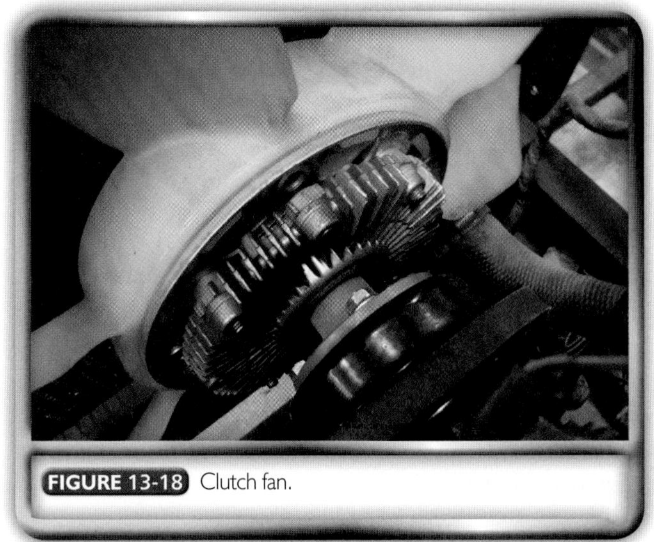
FIGURE 13-18 Clutch fan.

the radiator. The only difference in the operation is that the bimetallic spring is removed and an electric solenoid is installed on the front of the clutch. This solenoid is controlled by the power train control module (PCM), based on engine coolant temperature. As temperature increases, more oil is allowed to flow to the viscous coupler and fan speed increases. As temperature decreases, oil is directed back to the reservoir in the body of the clutch and fan speed decreases. On this type of fan, a feedback sensor provides actual fan speed or rpm information back to the PCM.

As fan designs evolved to increase efficiency, and as more vehicles moved to front-wheel drive, which turns the front of the engine away from the radiator, the electric fan was introduced FIGURE 13-19. Now it is by far the most common and simple type of cooling fan. It can be turned on and off easily whenever it is needed, and it can operate at full speed even though the engine is idling. This versatility makes it very efficient. It only runs when

FIGURE 13-19 Electric fan.

the engine is above the ideal operating temperature. In addition, since it can run at full speed independent of the engine, it can move plenty of air to cool the engine effectively.

Electric fans use an electric motor to turn an attached fan. In most cases, the fan blades are made of plastic, making them safer than metal blades. The blades can be designed to either push or pull air through the radiator, so mounting options are increased. The electric fan is controlled by one of two methods: A control module, such as the PCM, is used to energize a fan relay to turn the fan on and off, or a thermo-control switch is used. The PCM knows the temperature of the engine by means of the coolant temperature sensor. The PCM can then supply either power or ground to the fan relay, energizing the relay and fan.

The **thermo-control switch** is a temperature-sensitive switch that is mounted into the radiator or into a coolant passage on the engine. When engine temperature gets hot enough (say, 215°F [102°C]), the thermo-control switch will close and either send power directly to the fan or cause a relay to be activated, which turns on the fan. Once the engine coolant temperature cools back down, the switch opens and the fan stops.

Thermo-control switches often operate on the bimetallic strip principle. These consist of two different metals or alloys laminated back to back. As different metals and alloys heat and cool, they expand and contract at different rates. That means that if two different metals are joined, and then heated, the greater expansion of one will force the whole strip to flex into a curved shape. As the strip changes shape, it can be designed to complete an electric circuit by closing a switch, which turns the fan on.

With an electric fan, the electricity to run it comes from the alternator, which comes from the engine, which comes from the gasoline fuel. Because an electric fan typically needs to operate only part of the time, fuel is saved whenever it is off. Some manufacturers use multiple fans and control them separately, while others use multispeed fans to provide only enough fan operation to keep the coolant at the proper temperature.

Another type of cooling fan is the hydraulically operated fan. In many cases, it uses power steering fluid from the power steering pump to power the fan **FIGURE 13-20**. Because the power steering pump can create substantial power, hydraulically driven fans can be used to draw a large amount of air through the radiator. They are sometimes used on vehicles with heavy trailer towing capacities, as well as ordinary vehicles. The system consists of the power steering pump, a fluid control device, the hydraulic fan motor, and high-pressure connecting hoses. The fan is typically controlled by a pulse-width–modulated solenoid valve. The solenoid controls how much hydraulic fluid is directed to the fan motor. That way the PCM can vary the signal to the solenoid valve, which controls the amount of hydraulic fluid to the fan motor, which determines how fast it spins. One benefit of the hydraulically controlled fan is that it can be operated at near full speed and force even at idle, similar to an electric fan. Yet it can tap into more engine power than the electric fan, so it can be more heavy duty.

Radiator Hoses

On most vehicles there are two radiator hoses: the upper hose and the lower hose, also called the inlet hose and the outlet hose. **Radiator hoses** are rubber hoses that are subject to high pressure; they are therefore reinforced with a layer of fabric, typically nylon, to give them strength and prevent them from ballooning, and yet still be flexible. They are often molded into a special shape to suit the particular make and model of vehicle. Some radiator hoses, especially lower hoses, have a spiral wire inside to keep the hose from collapsing during heavy acceleration when the water pump is drawing a lot of water from the radiator. The reason radiator hoses need to be flexible is that engines are mounted on flexible engine mounts to reduce noise and vibration. Since the radiator is mounted to the vehicle body, which does not move with the engine, the hoses must be able to move.

The top radiator hose is typically attached to the thermostat housing, which allows the heated coolant to enter the inlet side of the radiator. The bottom or lower radiator hose is connected between the outlet of the radiator and the inlet of the water pump. The radiator hoses are held in position by clamps. These can be spring clamps, wire wound clamps, or worm drive clamps. Radiator hoses deteriorate over time and use. They can also be damaged by oil or fuel leaking on them. Thus, they need to be inspected and changed periodically. Many vehicle manufacturers recommend radiator and heater hose replacement approximately every 4 to 5 years or 48,000 to 60,000 miles (77,000 to 97,000 km). When servicing hoses, be sure to reinstall the clamps correctly or the seal between the hose and the component will leak. Every component has a raised ridge built into it. The hose clamp has to clamp on the inside of this ridge, but not on top of it. If the hose clamp is on top of the ridge, the hose is likely to pop off once the cooling system becomes pressurized **FIGURE 13-21**.

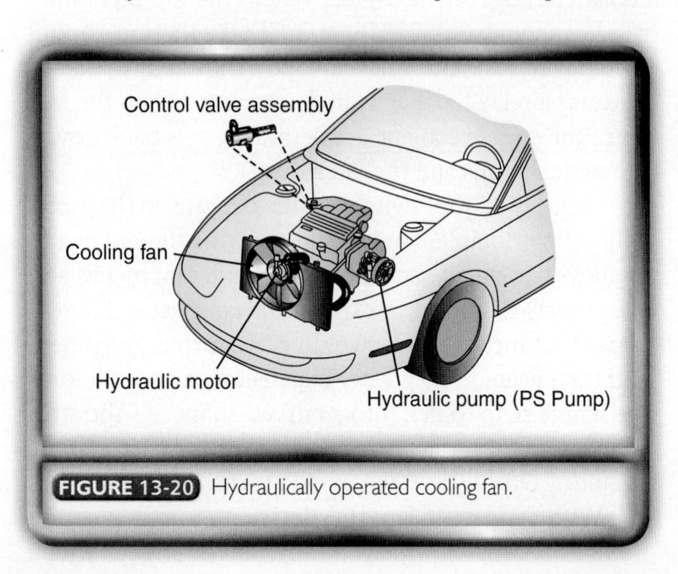
Control valve assembly
Cooling fan
Hydraulic motor
Hydraulic pump (PS Pump)

FIGURE 13-20 Hydraulically operated cooling fan.

Heater Hoses

The heater hoses carry a smaller volume of coolant than do the radiator hoses. Some heater coolant hoses have special shapes and must be ordered specially for the vehicle being serviced. Other heater hoses are straight and can be replaced by heater hose that is supplied on a roll. The construction of the heater hose is the same as the radiator hose, with a reinforcing material embedded into it.

There are two hoses for the heater core: one inlet hose and one outlet hose. The heater hose directs hot coolant to the heater core to provide heat to the inside of the passenger compartment. Some vehicles will use a coolant control valve in line with the heater core hose. The **coolant control valve** controls the flow of hot coolant to the heater core as requested by the driver. The fittings on the valve, like other fittings in the cooling system, usually have a raised ridge to aid in sealing and keeping the hose from blowing off. The heater hoses are sealed and retained by the use of a hose clamp. As with radiator hoses, be sure to install hose clamps correctly. All hoses are subject to hot coolant and

A
B

FIGURE 13-21 **A.** Proper installation of radiator hose clamp. **B.** Improper installation.

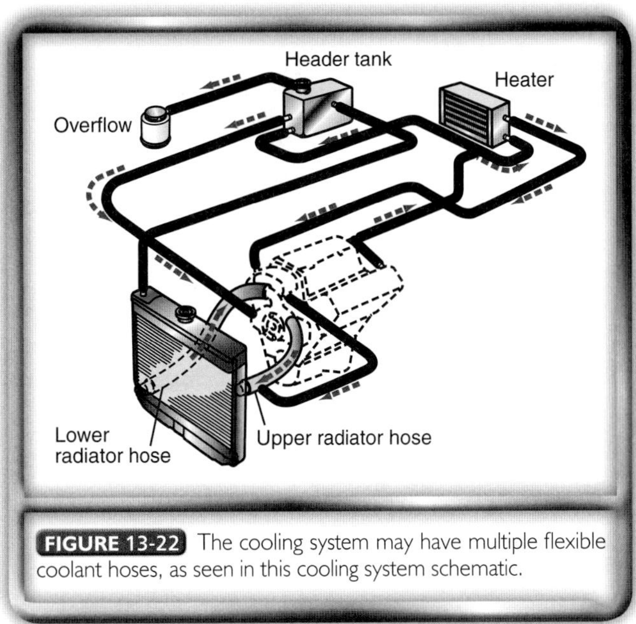
Header tank
Heater
Overflow
Lower radiator hose
Upper radiator hose

FIGURE 13-22 The cooling system may have multiple flexible coolant hoses, as seen in this cooling system schematic.

high underhood temperatures, and they will deteriorate and fail over time. Some coolant hoses are made of silicone, which is designed to withstand heat better and last longer than the standard rubber hose. Be sure to inspect hoses whenever you are servicing the customer's vehicle.

Coolant Hoses

There are additional coolant hoses that carry hot coolant through the cooling system, which are often ignored when checking hoses **FIGURE 13-22**. As part of a maintenance inspection, the technician will inspect the upper and lower radiator hoses along with the heater hoses, but may forget about these other hoses, which can fail if neglected. It is critical that these hoses be checked. Any break in the system will dump the coolant and cause the engine to quickly overheat.

One of the additional hoses is the bypass hose. The bypass hose is typically located on the water pump and connects to the intake manifold on many V-configured engines, such as a V6 or V8. This hose allows the water pump to circulate the water in the engine when the thermostat is closed. This hose is made of the same materials as the radiator hoses and heater hoses. Another coolant hose that may be used is a throttle body coolant line. This hose runs from the intake up to the throttle body to keep the throttle body from freezing during cold outside temperatures when there is high moisture content in the air. The cold wet air being pulled through the throttle plate may create ice, restrict airflow, and cause the throttle to stick. Running coolant through the throttle body eliminates this problem. There are many possible configurations of additional cooling system hoses, such as to remote oil coolers, turbochargers, or even some alternators. In a compressed natural gas vehicle, coolant hoses are routed to the CNG pressure regulator under the vehicle to keep the regulator warm. A similar setup may be used for the engine's idle air control motor and more. The point is to be sure to inspect all of the coolant hoses used on the vehicle.

Drive Belts

Typically, the water pump is turned by a belt that is driven by the crankshaft. This belt may be part of the accessory drive belt system found on the front of the engine. If the belt is located on the front of the engine, it may be tensioned by a separate tensioner or by simply moving a component such as the alternator on slotted bolt holes. Some engines use the camshaft timing belt or chain as the drive for the water pump.

There are four types of drive belts **FIGURE 13-23**:

- *V-type:* A V-type belt has a wedge-shaped interior and sits inside a corresponding groove in the pulley. The sides of the V-belt wedge in the sides of the pulley.

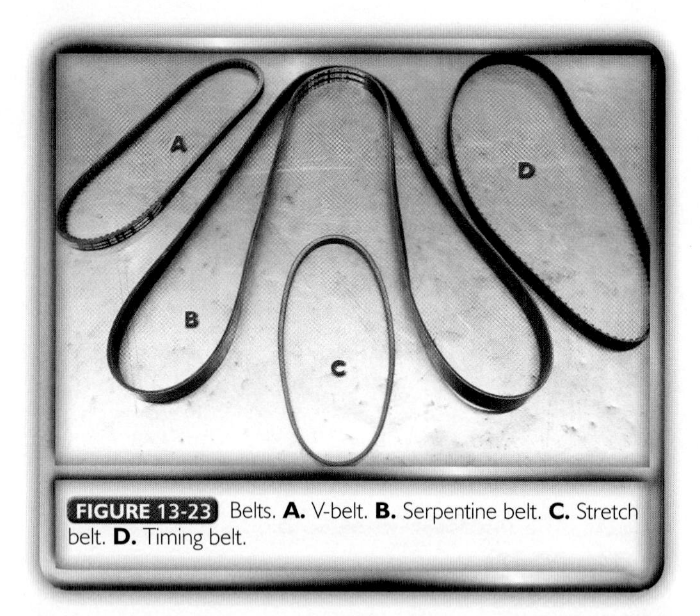
A
B
C
D

FIGURE 13-23 Belts. **A.** V-belt. **B.** Serpentine belt. **C.** Stretch belt. **D.** Timing belt.

- *Serpentine:* A serpentine-type belt, also called a multigroove V-belt, has a flat profile with a number of small V-shaped grooves running lengthwise along the inside of the belt. These grooves are the exact reverse of the grooves in the outer edge of the pulleys; they increase the contact surface area, as well as prevent the belt from slipping off the pulley as it rotates. The serpentine belt is used to drive multiple accessories and to save underhood space forward of the engine. It winds its way around the crankshaft pulley, water pump, alternator, air-conditioning compressor, and tensioner. Most serpentine belts use a spring-loaded tensioner to maintain proper tightness of the belt and prevent it from slipping.
- *Stretch belt:* A stretch belt looks like an ordinary serpentine belt but is found on vehicles without a tensioner. It is made of a special material that allows it to stretch just enough to be installed over the pulleys, but then shrink back to its original size, which is shorter than the distance around the pulleys. This stretchiness keeps the belt properly tensioned. Stretch belts require special tools to install and are usually cut off when being removed.
- *Toothed belt:* The toothed belt has teeth on the inside that are perpendicular to the belt and fit inside the teeth of a gear. Timing belts are always toothed belts to keep the camshaft running exactly half the speed of the crankshaft. To save on labor cost, these belts are generally replaced whenever a water pump replacement is required. And the water pump is generally replaced whenever the timing belt is changed.

The technician must be careful when replacing drive belts to avoid tensioning them too much, or too little. If excessive tension is placed on the belt, the water pump bearing can be overloaded, get hot, and fail due to excessive working load. Follow the manufacturer's service information for correct tensioning.

Tensioners

Tensioners are used to keep the drive belt tight around the pulleys to ensure the least amount of slippage without causing damage to component bearings. Tensioners can be either manual or automatic. Manual tensioners come in a wide variety of configurations. One type uses a pulley that is adjusted by turning a tensioning bolt. When the bolt is tightened, the pulley moves against the belt with increased tension; if the bolt is rotated the other direction, tension decreases. The tensioner is locked in place by tightening the nut on the front of the pulley.

A spring-loaded automatic tensioner is typically used with serpentine accessory belts FIGURE 13-24. This type of tensioner is very simple to operate and adjusts itself, so there is no chance of getting it too tight. However, be sure to note the routing of the serpentine belt when servicing it; there are many pulleys to route around, and it can become confusing if you do not have a routing picture. Automatic tensioners can wear out and cause belt slippage or become noisy. Also, a seized front engine drive component such as a tensioner can cause a no-crank, or slow crank, engine condition that mimics a seized engine. Simply loosening or removing the belt may help to diagnose the problem.

If the water pump is driven by the timing belt, one of two types of tensioners may be used. One type is the spring-loaded tensioner, in which a spring sets the tension and a bolt locks the tensioner into position. The other type is the oil-actuated tensioner. The oil-actuated tensioner uses oil pressure from the engine to provide

FIGURE 13-24 A spring-loaded automatic tensioner is typically used with serpentine accessory belts.

additional tension on the belt. Regardless of the style of tensioner, belt tension can be checked with a belt tension tool and compared to specifications, which are typically published in the service information.

Temperature Indicators

Temperature indicators can come in two forms: a temperature gauge or a temperature light located in the instrument cluster FIGURE 13-25. The two forms are sometimes used in conjunction. Overheating can heavily damage an engine, so a warning indicator is necessary. A temperature warning light is a good indicator of an overheating condition, but it cannot indicate a condition where the engine stays below operating temperature, which causes excess engine wear, increased emission output, and decreased fuel economy. A temperature gauge indicates to the driver whether the temperature is normal, below normal, or above normal. But drivers can forget to monitor it, which means that the engine could overheat without the driver noticing. Thus, a warning light in addition to a temperature gauge gives the best of both worlds.

Temperature gauges and warning lights both operate from a signal sent from a coolant temperature sensor located on the engine in a coolant passage. When engine coolant gets hotter than it should, the sensor causes the warning light or message to turn on to alert the driver that the engine is overheating. The temperature gauge also uses a sensor, which is designed to continuously indicate the temperature of the engine. The sensor for either type of warning device sits in engine coolant so that an accurate reading is always given—that is, as long as there is no air in the cooling system.

There may also be a low coolant indicator that shows when engine coolant level is low. This system works by having a low level sensor in the surge tank or overflow bottle that turns on a warning light in the instrument cluster if the coolant level falls below an acceptable level. If the low coolant indicator illuminates, there is a good chance that the cooling system has a leak that will need to be found.

FIGURE 13-25 **A.** Temperature gauge. **B.** Temperature warning lamp.

Water Jackets

Coolant passages such as water jackets are cast into the block and heads during the manufacturing process. They are designed to allow coolant to circulate around the tops and sides of the cylinders and are critical for the transfer of excess heat energy. It is crucial to the efficiency of heat transfer to keep the coolant passages free of scaling and buildup that can restrict heat transfer and coolant flow by ensuring proper cooling system maintenance. As part of proper maintenance, the technician must drain, flush, and refill the cooling system according to the recommended maintenance intervals. (Also see earlier reference to head gasket design.)

Core Plugs

Core plugs are also known as soft plugs or expansion plugs. These aluminum, brass, or steel plugs are designed to seal the openings left from the casting process where the casting sand was removed FIGURE 13-26. Under some conditions, the core plugs might pop out if the engine coolant is allowed to freeze—that is, if the proper mixture of antifreeze was not used. Because water expands when it freezes, the block or heads can crack internally or externally near the coolant passages. Sometimes the core plug will be pushed out and the coolant will leak out before the block cracks; however, that is not what they are designed for, so do not rely on soft plugs to protect the engine from freezing. Also, core plugs can rust out and start leaking coolant, so do not forget to inspect them when trying to locate a coolant leak.

Heater Core

The heater core is simply a small radiator that is mounted inside the heater box in the passenger compartment.

FIGURE 13-26 Core plugs are designed to seal the openings left from the casting process of the block and heads.

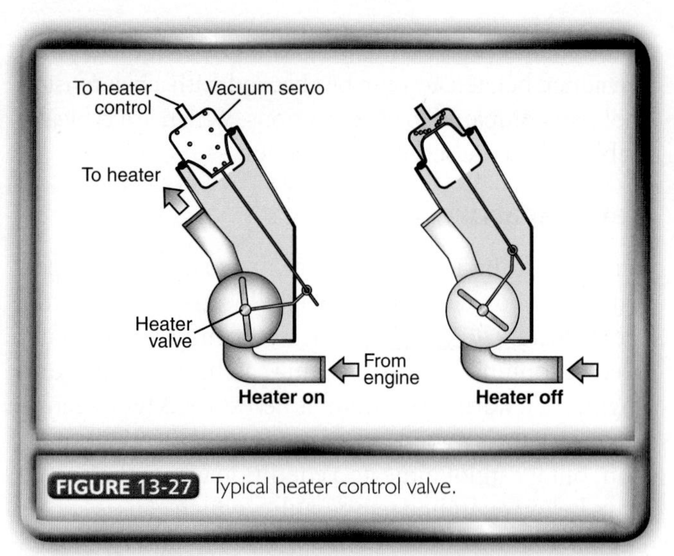
To heater control
Vacuum servo
To heater
Heater valve
From engine
Heater on
Heater off

FIGURE 13-27 Typical heater control valve.

As air is blown past the fins of the core, heat energy is radiated to the air and used to heat the passenger compartment for comfort. The heater core connects to the engine's cooling system and is supplied with hot water by circulation of the water pump. Typically, hot water enters the bottom of the radiator and exits the top; thus, the hot water flows from the bottom to the top of the heater core so more heat can be pulled from the coolant. Heater cores are typically constructed of aluminum, brass, or copper.

Heater Control Valve

If used, the heater control valve is mounted in one of the heater hoses that supply coolant to the heater core. This valve controls the flow of coolant to the heater core to control the temperature of the air desired by the operator. The climate control panel, which is adjusted by the operator, controls this valve FIGURE 13-27.

Air Doors and Actuators

The heater box consists of many air doors, which are plastic or metal flaps that seal off parts of the air box to control airflow FIGURE 13-28. The air doors are moved by one of three methods: cable, vacuum actuator, or electric actuator, called a stepper motor. The **actuator** is a device that is electrically or vacuum controlled and is used to physically move doors within the heater box to control airflow. This system is discussed in detail in the Electronic Climate Control chapter.

The layout and function of the doors depend on the design of the system. Most systems flow air through the evaporator at all times, while air can be diverted around the heater core when heat is not wanted. Also, for best defrost operation, the air is directed first over the evaporator to remove any moisture from the air. Then it is directed over the heater core to warm it up. This process results in dry, warm air to defog or defrost the windshield.

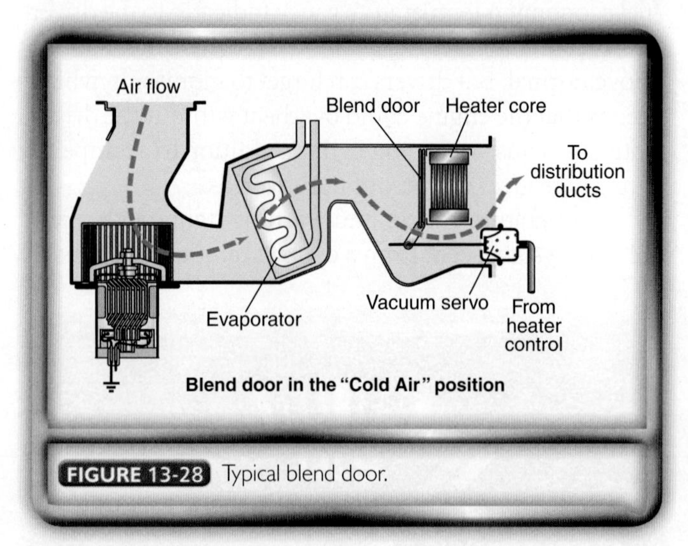
Air flow
Blend door
Heater core
To distribution ducts
Vacuum servo
Evaporator
From heater control
Blend door in the "Cold Air" position

FIGURE 13-28 Typical blend door.

Coolant Types

As mentioned earlier, water-cooled engines must be protected from freezing, boiling, and corrosion. Water absorbs a larger amount of heat than most other liquids. But it freezes at a relatively high temperature, and it is corrosive. Mixing antifreeze with water provides an adequate coolant solution by lowering the freezing point of water, raising the boiling point of water a bit, and providing anti-corrosive properties.

There are several types of coolants available for use in the liquid-cooled automobile engine. The recommended coolant depends on the original equipment manufacturer's (OEM) recommendation. It may be influenced by the metallurgy of the engine parts and the length of time or mileage that the manufacturer has determined between scheduled services.

It is important to note that brands and types of coolant (antifreeze) will differ from one manufacturer to another.

Some believe coolant can be identified according to its color, which may be anything from green or purple to yellow/gold, orange, blue, or pink. OEM cooling system designs and coolant recommendations have changed in recent years, so the color of coolant is no longer a reliable way to identify a particular type of antifreeze. Mixing types of antifreeze can cause a reaction that turns the chemicals in antifreeze to sludge that plugs up the passages in the system, including the radiator and heater core. Always read the container label and follow OEM coolant recommendations.

Most coolant types start with a base of ethylene glycol and add specific corrosion inhibitors, lubricants, and other additives, which all determine the type of coolant it is. Each coolant will have antifoaming and antiscale additives. Maintaining the proper coolant acid/alkaline pH balance is also critical (which will also determine when to perform coolant replacement).

Ethylene glycol is a toxic chemical that works very well as an antifreeze. Ethylene glycol mixes well with water and has a low viscosity, allowing it to circulate easily through the cooling system. Propylene glycol performs essentially the same as ethylene glycol except it is not as toxic. In fact, propylene glycol antifreeze is sold as a nontoxic coolant. The types of ethylene glycol or propylene glycol antifreeze/coolants available, based on the categories of corrosion inhibitors used in them, are as follows:

- Inorganic acid technology (IAT)
- Organic acid technology (OAT)
- Hybrid organic acid technology (HOAT)
- Poly organic acid technology (POAT)

The first category of coolant, IAT, is an early designed chemical formula that became available in the 1930s and was green in color. This coolant is still in use today. It contains phosphate and silicate as corrosion additives. Phosphate protects iron and steel parts, while silicate keeps aluminum from corroding. IAT coolant needs to be changed every 2 years or 24,000 miles (39,000 km), since the additives break down.

The second category, OAT, is a longer-lasting coolant. Called extended-life coolant, it is designed to be changed at 5 years or 150,000 miles (241,000 km), a giant increase in the change interval from IAT coolant. OAT coolant was introduced in North America around 1994 and was intended for certain vehicles of that year and newer. One example of OAT is Dex-Cool, the orange coolant used by GM. The anti-corrosion additives in OAT coolant do not break down as quickly, which explains the longer service time. The primary additives in OAT coolant are organic acids, such as sebacate. These coolants do not use the additives used in IAT coolants.

The third category, HOAT, is a coolant that contains a mixture of inorganic and organic additives. This type of coolant can use silicate and organic acid; it is the best of both worlds of coolants. Some manufacturers found that without silicate, problems arose if the system was not properly serviced, such as oxidation of the coolant, leading to breakdown of the corrosion inhibitors and, ultimately, failure of engine parts and gaskets. Other tests indicate that silicates cause premature water pump failures. Less silicate is present in HOAT coolant than in IAT coolants, so this coolant is still considered extended life and will need to be changed at 5 years or 150,000 miles (241,000 km). An example of this type of coolant is the yellow coolant used by Ford.

The fourth category, POAT, is a relatively new coolant that contains a proprietary blend of corrosion inhibitors. It is a very long-life coolant, providing up to 7 years or 250,000 miles (402,000 km) of protection. It is claimed that it is compatible with most other types of coolant, but check the manufacturer's current service information.

Within the OAT or HOAT classifications, manufacturers may specify different corrosion additives and colored dyes. It is important that you service the vehicle with the coolant that is called for by the manufacturer. In most cases, you should never mix two or more types of coolants and/or refill with a type other than that originally used in a vehicle. Doing so will likely compromise the cooling system's service life and cause premature failure of the system.

Diagnosis

The cooling system is an often overlooked part of the automobile. It does its job very effectively and is rarely thought of, until problems arise. The lack of periodic service of the cooling system according to OEM maintenance schedules is the leading reason that cooling systems fail. Properly performed cooling system maintenance will ensure that the cooling system continues to perform as designed.

Common failures of the cooling system can require repairs ranging from simple to complex. An example of a failure that would require a simple repair is a radiator hose clamp that has not been installed properly and that is creating a leak. The customer notices the leak and brings the vehicle in for service. An example of a more complex repair is a vehicle that needs a new head and block because a severe pH imbalance in the cooling system has heavily corroded the internal metal. Corrosion can build up to the point that normal cooling system operation cannot be restored without replacing multiple parts, including the engine itself, due to corrosion pitting of the engine block or cylinder head, leading to an internal coolant leak. Corrosion can also coat and/or block coolant passages and lead to an engine that runs hotter than normal or overheats.

Another common customer complaint is that the heater does not produce heat when turned on. This issue can result from a group of problems that will have to be diagnosed by the technician, but often the culprit is a stuck-open thermostat that will not let the engine come up to operating temperatures. If the thermostat fails, it can fail in either the open position or the closed position. If it sticks closed, the result will be an overheating condition since coolant cannot get to the radiator to be cooled. If it sticks open, the engine will not warm up fully, leading to excessive engine wear, higher emissions, and reduced fuel economy.

Overheating conditions can have several causes, such as low coolant level due to a leak, a stuck-closed thermostat, a faulty radiator cap, clogged radiator tubes or fins, an inoperative cooling fan, a water pump impeller that is eroded or slipping on the shaft, or a blown head gasket, to name a few. Understanding how the cooling system works, as well as the manufacturer's test procedures, is necessary to successfully diagnose and repair the vehicle.

When diagnosing a cooling system problem, you need to use all of your senses to help determine what is wrong. Your sense of touch can allow you to feel for hot and cold parts in the system. For example, if the engine is overheating, but the upper radiator hose is cold, that could indicate a thermostat that is stuck closed. Your sense of smell could pick up the scent of antifreeze leaking into the passenger compartment from a leaky heater core. Your sense of hearing can tell you that the accessory belt is loose and the water pump is slipping. And your sense of sight could see the telltale stream of coolant leaking out of the water pump weep hole or a rusted-through soft plug. It is advisable not to use your sense of taste when diagnosing cooling system issues.

If the problem cannot be determined by your senses alone, you may have to resort to tools or equipment to help you locate the issue. A cooling system pressure tester will allow you to pressurize the cooling system and radiator cap and check for any visible leaks. Starting the engine and using an exhaust analyzer to sniff the vapors coming out of the neck of the radiator can indicate if there is a small leak from one of the combustion chambers, which is leaking combustion gases into the cooling system. Using a cylinder leakage tester and pressurizing each cylinder can help locate which cylinder has the combustion leak, due to either a blown head gasket or a cracked head. If the leak is a small external leak and the source cannot be located easily, you may need to use a fluorescent dye and black light to help make it stand out better.

An infrared temperature gun is a useful tool that can be used to measure the operating temperature of the engine to verify that the engine really is overheating or not. Or it can be used to check the radiator for cold spots, which would indicate blockage within the core of the radiator. A scan tool can be a quick way to monitor the operating temperature, verify any cooling system diagnostic trouble codes (DTCs), or command the electric fan to come on. As you can see, understanding how cooling systems operate along with observing what is happening, and having a few tools available, can take you a long way toward diagnosing customers' cooling system concerns.

Tools

A properly trained and experienced technician will use special tools for diagnosing and servicing the engine cooling system. These tools include **FIGURE 13-29**:

- *Coolant system pressure tester:* Used to apply pressure to the cooling system to diagnose leakage complaints. Under pressure, coolant may leak internally to the combustion chamber, intake or

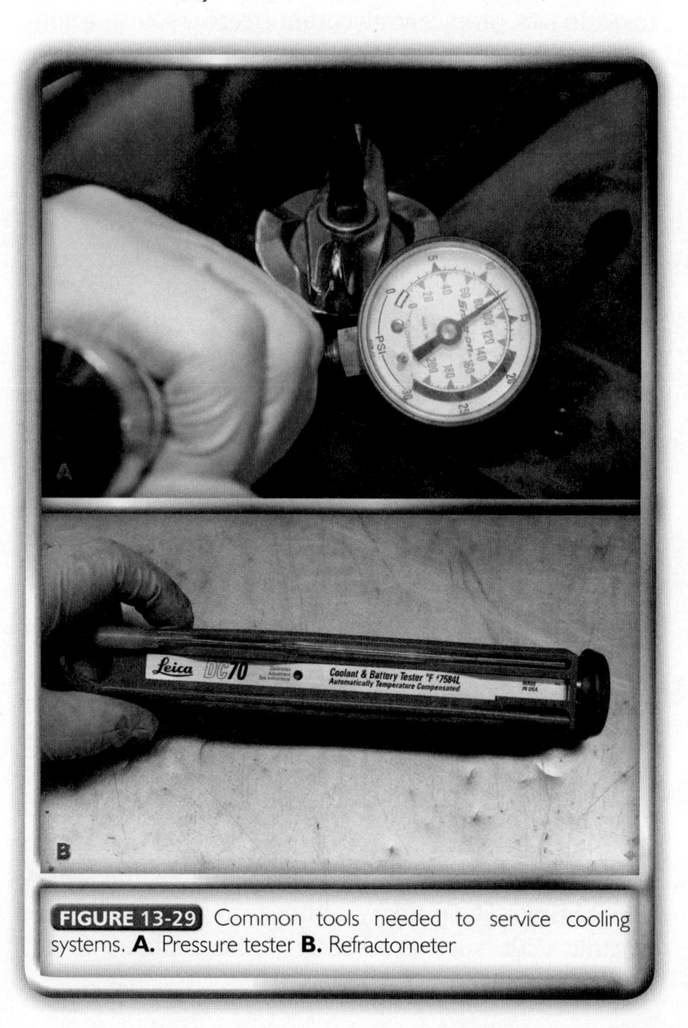
A
PSI
B
Leica DC70
Coolant & Battery Tester °F
Automatically Temperature Compensated

FIGURE 13-29 Common tools needed to service cooling systems. **A.** Pressure tester **B.** Refractometer

exhaust system, or the engine lubrication system. It can also leak externally to the outside of the engine.

- *Hydrometer:* Used to test coolant mixture and freeze protection by testing the specific gravity of the coolant. You must use a hydrometer specifically designed for the antifreeze you are testing.
- *Refractometer:* Used to test coolant mixture and freeze protection by testing the fluid's ability to bend light. This tester can be used with any type of antifreeze.
- *Coolant pH test strips:* Used to test the acid-to-alkalinity balance of the coolant.
- *Coolant dye kit:* Used to aid leak detection by adding dye to coolant and using an ultraviolet light source (black light) to trace to the source of the leak; the dye glows fluorescent when a black light is shined on it.
- *Infrared temperature sensor:* A noncontact thermometer used to check actual temperatures and variations of temperature throughout the cooling system to help pinpoint faulty parts and system blockages.
- *Thermometer:* Used to check the temperature of air exiting the heating ducts.
- *Voltmeter:* Used to check for electrical problems such as cooling fan and temperature gauge issues.
- *Belt tension gauge:* Used to check belt tension.
- *Serpentine belt wear gauge:* Used to check if the serpentine belt grooves are worn past their specifications.
- *Radiator clamp pliers:* Used to safely remove spring-type radiator clamps.
- *Borescope:* Used for examining internal passages for evidence of a coolant leak.
- *Scan tool:* Used to activate the cooling fan through bidirectional controls for testing; to monitor cooling sensor operation and to command air door actuators when testing low heat complaints; and to read DTCs related to cooling system operation.
- *Cooling system flush machine:* Used to flush coolant backward through the system with cleaners that remove corrosion buildup and old coolant. Most of these machines have their own pump so the vehicle does not have to run to perform the flush.
- *Exhaust gas analyzer:* Used to detect exhaust gases that are finding their way into the cooling system due to a leaking head gasket or damaged head or block. Be careful not to allow liquid coolant to be picked up by the analyzer probe.

Visual Inspection

Many times a visual inspection of the cooling system will give you a good indication of any issues. Check the level of the coolant in the overflow bottle and radiator. At the same time, check the condition of the coolant to see if it is cloudy or contaminated. Also check the belt condition and for the proper tension, and check hoses for any leaks or wear. If the sweet aroma of coolant is detected when the engine is first started, check for leaking coolant at the heater box drain, which would indicate a possible cracked or rotted leaking heater core. Check the engine exhaust for white smoke. A head gasket failure or a cracked head or valve seat may cause coolant to leak into the exhaust manifold and be seen as white smoke, especially when combustion pressures are high when accelerating. Also start the engine with the radiator cap off and look for bubbles from combustion in the radiator. Bubbles would indicate a leak in the combustion chamber, likely at the head gasket. Disassembly and inspection would need to occur to verify that it is the head gasket and not a cracked head or block.

Safety

When working around the cooling system, care must be taken particularly if the engine is at operating temperature, as the coolant may be hot enough to scald. Always allow the system to cool before removing the radiator or pressure cap, and use extreme caution when removing the radiator cap. If you must remove the radiator cap from a hot system, wear protective gloves and eyewear and place a cloth fender cover or other large rag on top of the radiator cap before releasing it slowly, to the first (safety) point, to prevent the pressure inside from erupting.

Testing the Cooling System for Leaks

Pressure testing the cooling system for leaks is usually an effective way to locate leaks since it causes coolant to leak out much more quickly, making leaks easier to locate. But before you pressurize the system, make sure it is topped off with coolant or water. Otherwise, the leak could be above the coolant level and only leak air, which is much harder to observe. Topping off leads to quicker pressurization because it removes air, which is compressible. Also, if the system is full of liquid, the pressure reading on the gauge will fall faster if there is a leak.

The pressure tester puts pressure on the cooling system, and with pressure applied, leaks generally show up easily, as identified by coolant coming from the source. The use of a droplight and a mirror may be necessary to see behind the engine or in tight areas. Don't forget to check the heater core in the passenger compartment. If the pressure gauge is losing pressure, ensure that the tester is installed correctly; if it still loses pressure, ensure that the tool is working properly. Once the tool is verified and you cannot find an external leak, you will know that the cooling system may be leaking internally into the engine. Check engine oil for evidence of coolant. It will have a milky appearance on the dipstick. If coolant is not leaking into the oil, it could be leaking into the cylinder. Remove the spark plugs and look for coolant being burned in the cylinders, as evidenced by a color-stained spark plug insulator. A combustion chamber experiencing a coolant leak will appear to be steam cleaned. A borescope can be used to inspect the cylinders through the spark plug holes.

Normally the engine should be off when carrying out any visual inspection of the system or when you connect test equipment such as the pressure tester. However, it is possible that the leak only occurs when the engine is running, such as around the water pump seal, making it necessary to run the engine while testing. If you do have to run the engine after the tester has been installed and pressurized, make sure to watch the pressure gauge and release excess pressure as the engine heats up. When the engine is running, make sure you keep well away from any rotating or hot parts.

Also remember to pressure test the radiator cap, since a leak at the cap will prevent the cooling system from building pressure. Low pressure on the coolant leads to a lower boiling point, which can cause coolant to boil at normal operating temperatures. Many a technician has been fooled into thinking that the vehicle had a serious overheating problem after changing the thermostat, water pump, and so on, when all it needed was a radiator cap.

A pressure tester is normally used to test the cooling system for both internal and external leaks. Most pressure testers are hand operated and come with a number of adapters to fit a variety of cooling systems. Adapters are used to connect the tester to the radiator, surge tank, or radiator cap.

To test the cooling system pressure, follow the steps in SKILL DRILL 13-1.

TECHNICIAN TIP

If you need to replace a pressure cap, use only a cap with the correct recommended pressure. If a cap with a lower pressure rating is installed, it will lower the boiling point of the coolant. Alternatively, a higher rated cap will increase the boiling point and could result in a hose, radiator, or heater core bursting if pressures get too high.

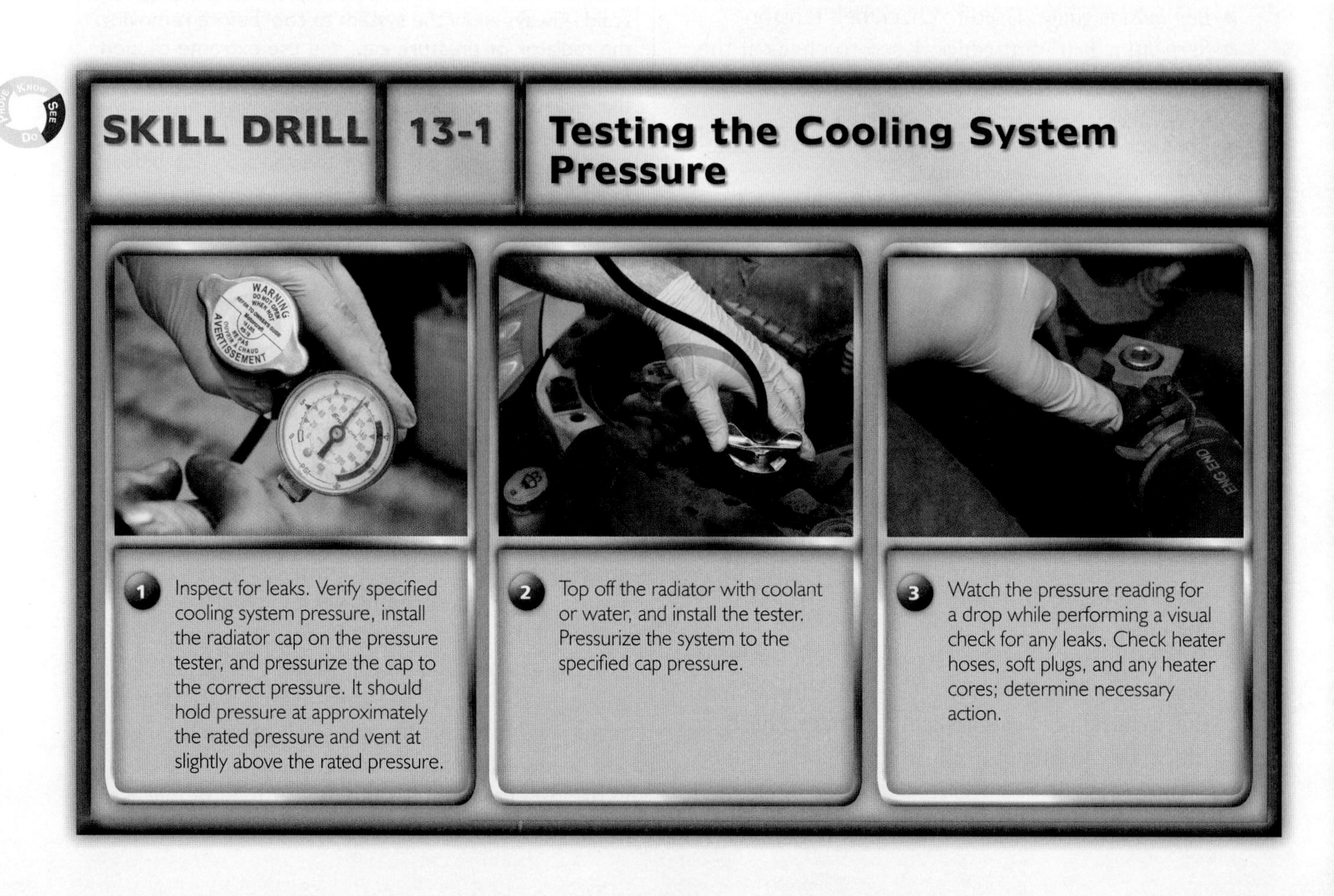
SKILL DRILL 13-1 Testing the Cooling System Pressure
1 Inspect for leaks. Verify specified cooling system pressure, install the radiator cap on the pressure tester, and pressurize the cap to the correct pressure. It should hold pressure at approximately the rated pressure and vent at slightly above the rated pressure.
2 Top off the radiator with coolant or water, and install the tester. Pressurize the system to the specified cap pressure.
3 Watch the pressure reading for a drop while performing a visual check for any leaks. Check heater hoses, soft plugs, and any heater cores; determine necessary action.

Verifying Engine Operating Temperature

Technicians need to verify engine operating temperature whenever the customer complains about an overheating issue, an underheating issue such as inadequate heat from the heater, or poor fuel economy. Verifying the operating temperature involves using an infrared noncontact temperature gun to check whether the on-vehicle temperature indicators, such as the temperature gauge and coolant temperature sensor, are operating accurately. The temperature gun, as described earlier, measures the amount of heat energy (temperature) of an object. Just realize that some objects do not conduct heat as well as others; if you can point the temperature gun at a metal component, it will produce a more accurate reading. If pointed toward the engine's thermostat housing (or next to it), with the engine fully warmed up, a close approximation of the engine's operating temperature can be measured and compared to the specifications. Note that a vehicle with an electric fan will usually have two listed temperatures—one temperature at which the fan should turn on and another temperature at which it should turn off. Anywhere between those temperatures is the operating temperature in this situation. If the operating temperature is correct, verify that the vehicle's temperature gauge is reading accurately. Also, use a scan tool and compare the reading from the coolant temperature sensor to the temperature gun reading to verify that the PCM is receiving the correct temperature signal.

To verify the engine operating temperature, follow the steps in SKILL DRILL 13-2.

Inspecting and Testing Heater Control Valves

Heater control valves control the flow of coolant to the heater core so that the operator can control heater output. If this valve becomes stuck open, the operator will not be able to turn down the heat or the air conditioning will not be as cold as before. If the valve sticks shut, the customer will complain of no heat in the vehicle. The problem can be with the valve or the control system. The valve can get plugged up with contaminants in the coolant, or the lever can slip on the shaft that turns the valve. If it is cable operated, the cable can slip, or even corrode in place. If it is vacuum operated, the diaphragm can get a hole in it, the vacuum hose can leak or fall off, or the vacuum controller

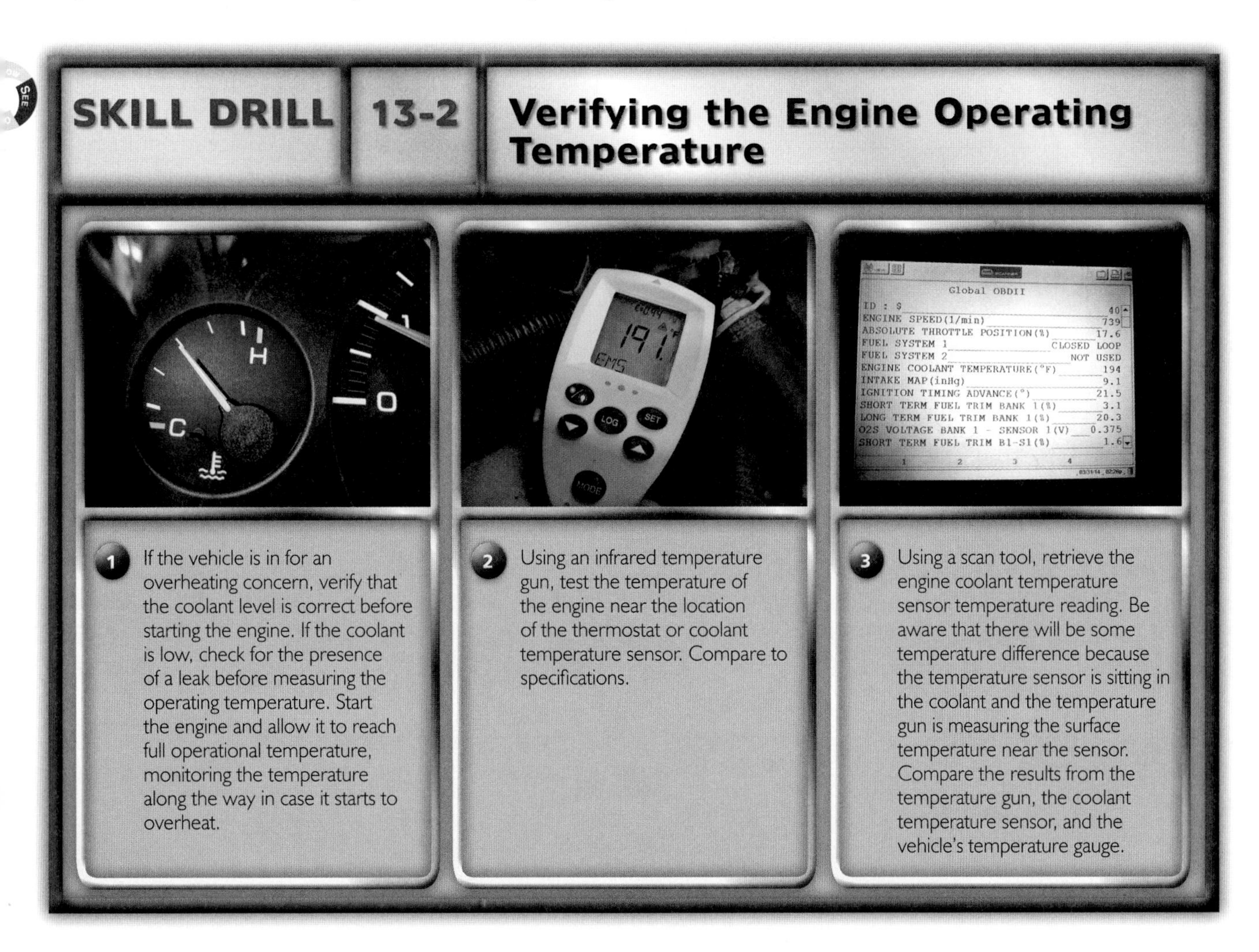
H
C
O
191
EMS
LOG
SET
MODE
Global OBDII
ENGINE SPEED(1/min) 739
ABSOLUTE THROTTLE POSITION(%) 17.6
FUEL SYSTEM 1 CLOSED LOOP
FUEL SYSTEM 2 NOT USED
ENGINE COOLANT TEMPERATURE(°F) 194
INTAKE MAP(inHg) 9.1
IGNITION TIMING ADVANCE(°) 21.5
SHORT TERM FUEL TRIM BANK 1(%) 3.1
LONG TERM FUEL TRIM BANK 1(%) 20.3
O2S VOLTAGE BANK 1 - SENSOR 1(V) 0.375
SHORT TERM FUEL TRIM B1-S1(%) 1.6

SKILL DRILL 13-2 Verifying the Engine Operating Temperature

1. If the vehicle is in for an overheating concern, verify that the coolant level is correct before starting the engine. If the coolant is low, check for the presence of a leak before measuring the operating temperature. Start the engine and allow it to reach full operational temperature, monitoring the temperature along the way in case it starts to overheat.
2. Using an infrared temperature gun, test the temperature of the engine near the location of the thermostat or coolant temperature sensor. Compare to specifications.
3. Using a scan tool, retrieve the engine coolant temperature sensor temperature reading. Be aware that there will be some temperature difference because the temperature sensor is sitting in the coolant and the temperature gun is measuring the surface temperature near the sensor. Compare the results from the temperature gun, the coolant temperature sensor, and the vehicle's temperature gauge.

can quit working. If it is electrically operated, the motor can seize or the circuit can go bad. Heater control valves can also leak coolant, so they need to be inspected for leaks. In fact, one of the first indicators of low coolant in a vehicle is that the heater stops blowing hot air, or blows hot air intermittently. Always verify that the coolant is full before spending too much time tracking down any kind of heater issues.

To test the heater control valve, follow the steps of the SKILL DRILL 13-3.

Maintenance and Repair

Preventive Maintenance Schedules

Preventive maintenance of the cooling system is critical for long life and reliability of the engine. Failure to perform required maintenance will result in cooling system failure, which can lead to breakdowns and major engine damage. Manufacturers publish the required maintenance for the vehicle in the owner's manual and in the service information. The maintenance schedule lists which services are due at a particular mileage or date. With standard IAT coolant, a maintenance schedule will say "every 2 years or 24,000 miles, whichever comes first." Belts and hoses have similar inspection and maintenance requirements. These service intervals are critical to follow, so always check the maintenance schedule for the vehicle you are working on.

EPA Guidelines

As discussed in the coolant section of this chapter, ethylene glycol antifreeze, the most common antifreeze, is highly toxic to humans and animals. Because of this, the Environmental Protection Agency (EPA) has strict regulations for the handling and disposal of vehicle coolant. Coolant should never be dumped into a storm drain or down a shop floor drain. Coolant is a poison and should only be poured into an approved container and either be recycled in house or removed by a licensed recycler.

Care must be taken when a spill occurs when servicing a vehicle; it should be cleaned up promptly according to EPA regulations. Taking a little extra time to place a catch pan under the component being removed can prevent a spill and save time in the long run. Also, coolant should never be mixed with oil or other liquids; separate catch pans should always be used and marked accordingly.

Measuring Freeze Protection

The use of a hydrometer or refractometer is necessary when testing the freeze protection of the coolant in the cooling system. The customer may request this service as part of a winterization package performed by the shop. Any time coolant is replaced in the cooling system, the freeze point should be verified.

The hydrometer is a tool that measures the specific gravity of a liquid. When coolant is drawn into the hydrometer, a float will rise at a certain level depending upon the density of the coolant. Antifreeze has a higher specific gravity than water, so the higher the float rises in the liquid, the greater the percentage of antifreeze in the mix. One drawback to hydrometers is that they are typically antifreeze specific. That means you will need one for ethylene glycol and one for propylene glycol, as

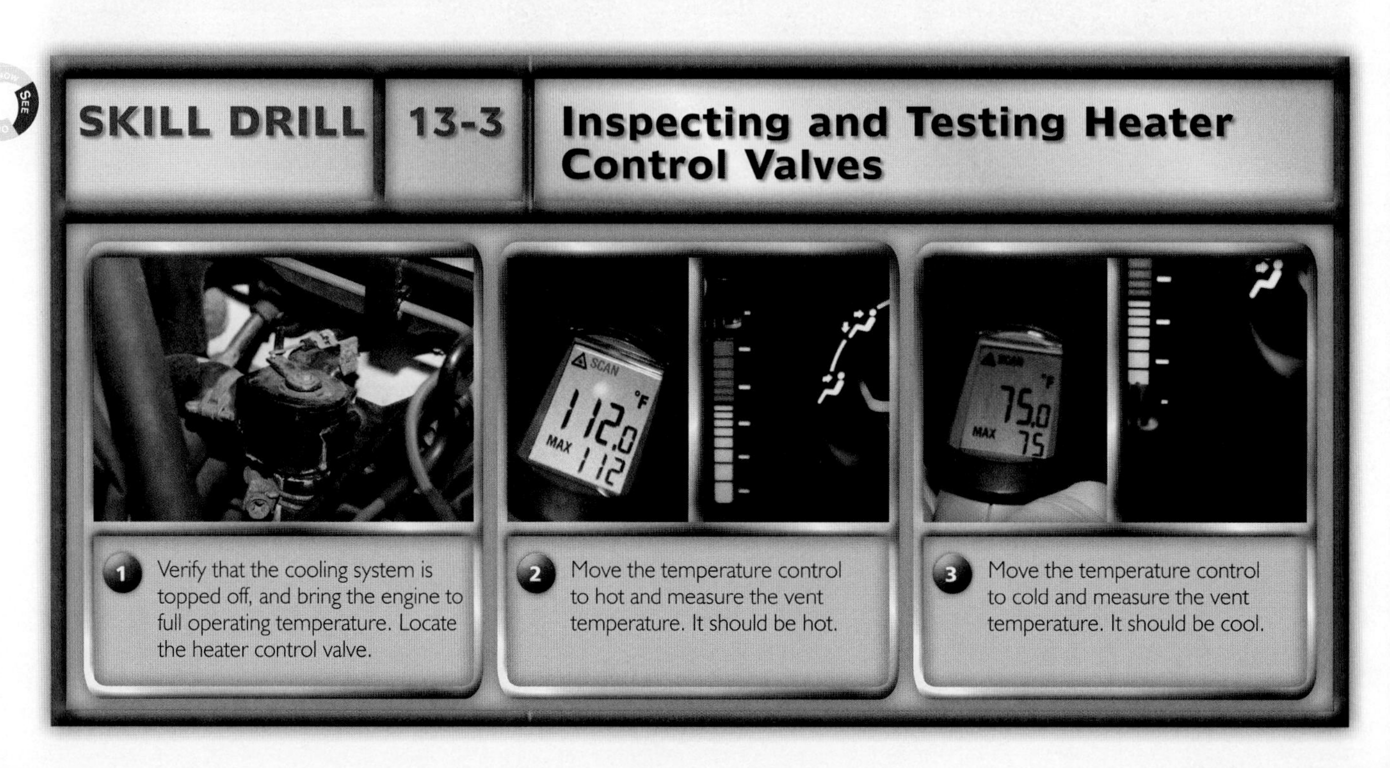
SCAN
112.0
°F
MAX 112
SCAN
75.0
°F
MAX 75

SKILL DRILL 13-3 Inspecting and Testing Heater Control Valves

1. Verify that the cooling system is topped off, and bring the engine to full operating temperature. Locate the heater control valve.
2. Move the temperature control to hot and measure the vent temperature. It should be hot.
3. Move the temperature control to cold and measure the vent temperature. It should be cool.

the specific gravities of the two chemicals are different. Another drawback is that as the temperature of the coolant goes up, the specific gravity goes down. Some hydrometers have a built-in thermometer and a chart, allowing you to compensate for the temperature of the coolant.

A refractometer can also tell the proportions of antifreeze and water in the coolant mix (or the level of freeze protection) by measuring a liquid's specific gravity. It works by allowing light to shine through the fluid. The light bends in accordance with the particular liquid's specific gravity. The bending of the light displays on a scale inside the tool, indicating the specific gravity of the fluid. One nice thing about a refractometer is that it has a scale for both types of antifreeze and reads the freeze point accurately.

To use a hydrometer to test the freeze point of the coolant, follow the steps in SKILL DRILL 13-4.

To use a refractometer to test the freeze point of the coolant, follow the steps in SKILL DRILL 13-5.

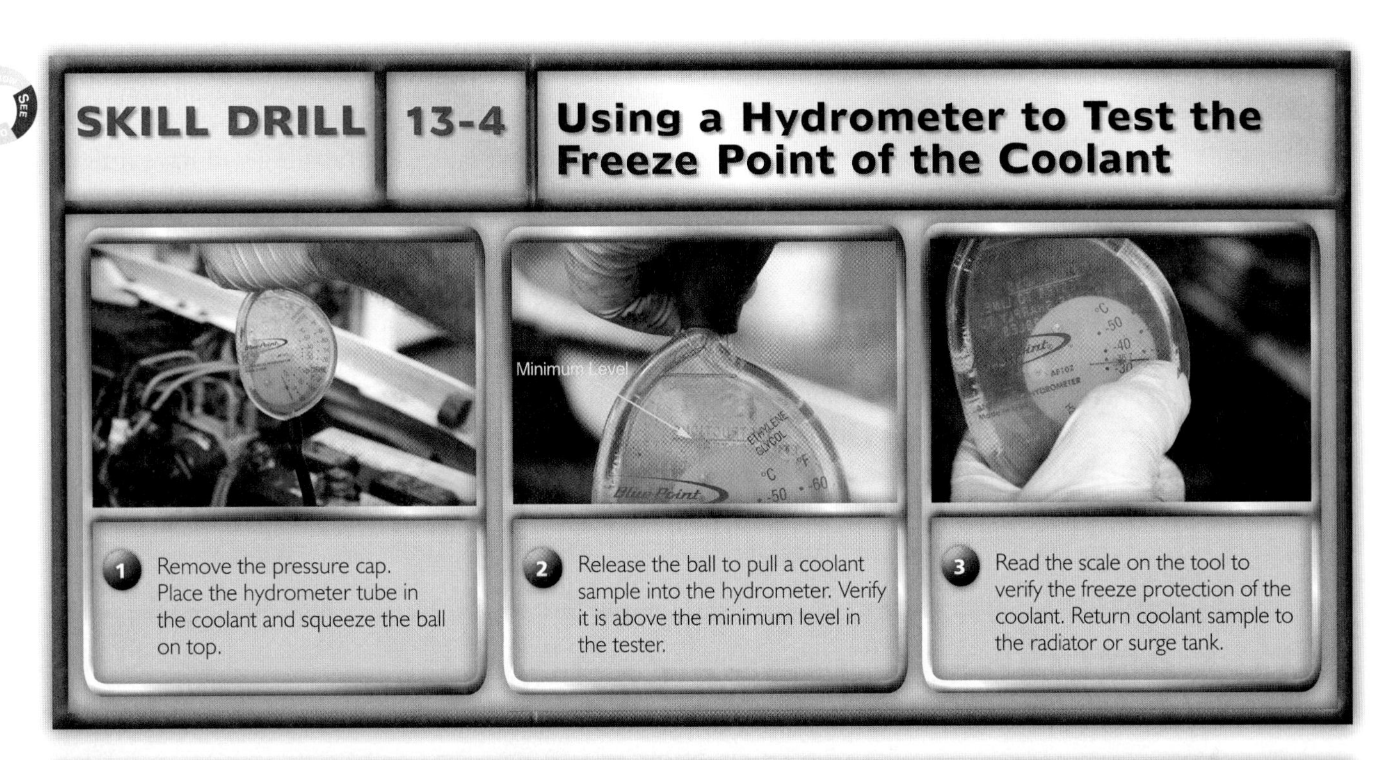
Minimum Level
ETHYLENE GLYCOL
°C
°F
-50
-60
Blue Point

SKILL DRILL 13-4 Using a Hydrometer to Test the Freeze Point of the Coolant

1. Remove the pressure cap. Place the hydrometer tube in the coolant and squeeze the ball on top.
2. Release the ball to pull a coolant sample into the hydrometer. Verify it is above the minimum level in the tester.
3. Read the scale on the tool to verify the freeze protection of the coolant. Return coolant sample to the radiator or surge tank.

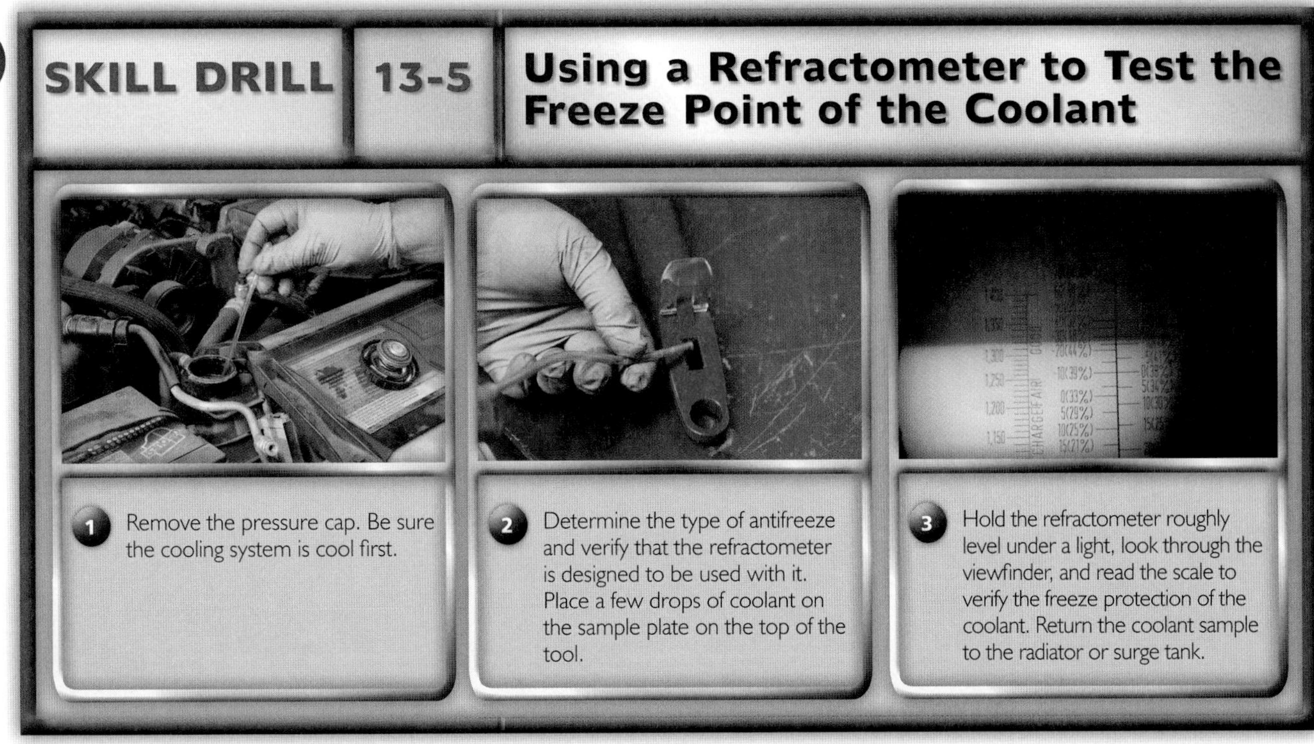

SKILL DRILL 13-5 Using a Refractometer to Test the Freeze Point of the Coolant

1. Remove the pressure cap. Be sure the cooling system is cool first.
2. Determine the type of antifreeze and verify that the refractometer is designed to be used with it. Place a few drops of coolant on the sample plate on the top of the tool.
3. Hold the refractometer roughly level under a light, look through the viewfinder, and read the scale to verify the freeze protection of the coolant. Return the coolant sample to the radiator or surge tank.

Testing the Coolant pH

pH testing is performed whenever cooling system maintenance service is requested, or if there is reason to suspect the coolant has outlived its useful life. It can be done with test strips that turn color based on the level of acidity in the coolant, or with electronic testers that measure the pH of the coolant directly. pH testing of coolant is a great way to determine if the corrosion inhibitors are still working in the antifreeze. As corrosion inhibitors break down over time, the solution of water and antifreeze will become more acidic. As the acid level builds, so will corrosion and electrolysis in the cooling system. If the coolant is left in this acidic condition, it will create permanent erosion to component surfaces that may require replacement of affected components.

To test the coolant pH, follow the steps in SKILL DRILL 13-6.

Testing for Electrolysis

As the search for greater fuel efficiency continues and lighter-weight nonconductive materials are used in our engines and vehicles, problems have arisen that result in the need for new training of technicians. Electrolysis, described earlier in this chapter, is the reaction of different metals to an acid solution to produce electricity. It can result in negative effects on the cooling system. Electrolysis can erode metals from the inside of the cooling system, leading to damage.

Electrolysis can also be due to faulty grounds in the electrical system. If a circuit has a faulty ground, the current will try to find its way back to the battery in whatever way it can. And that can include sending some of the current flow through the coolant. For example, if the engine ground is dirty and has an excessive voltage drop, then when the engine is cranked over, some of the current could flow through the coolant to another ground. Current flowing through the coolant can erode metal surfaces in the cooling system. In this case, the coolant is not at fault, and flushing will have little to no effect on the condition. Repairing the failed ground is the solution in this case. To verify that electricity is finding its way into the cooling system, voltage can be measured when various electrical loads are operated to see if there is any stray voltage in the coolant. If voltages are over 0.3 volts when the load or loads are activated, then you will have to perform electrical diagnosis of the circuit being tested.

To perform electrolysis testing for a suspected coolant problem, follow the steps in SKILL DRILL 13-7.

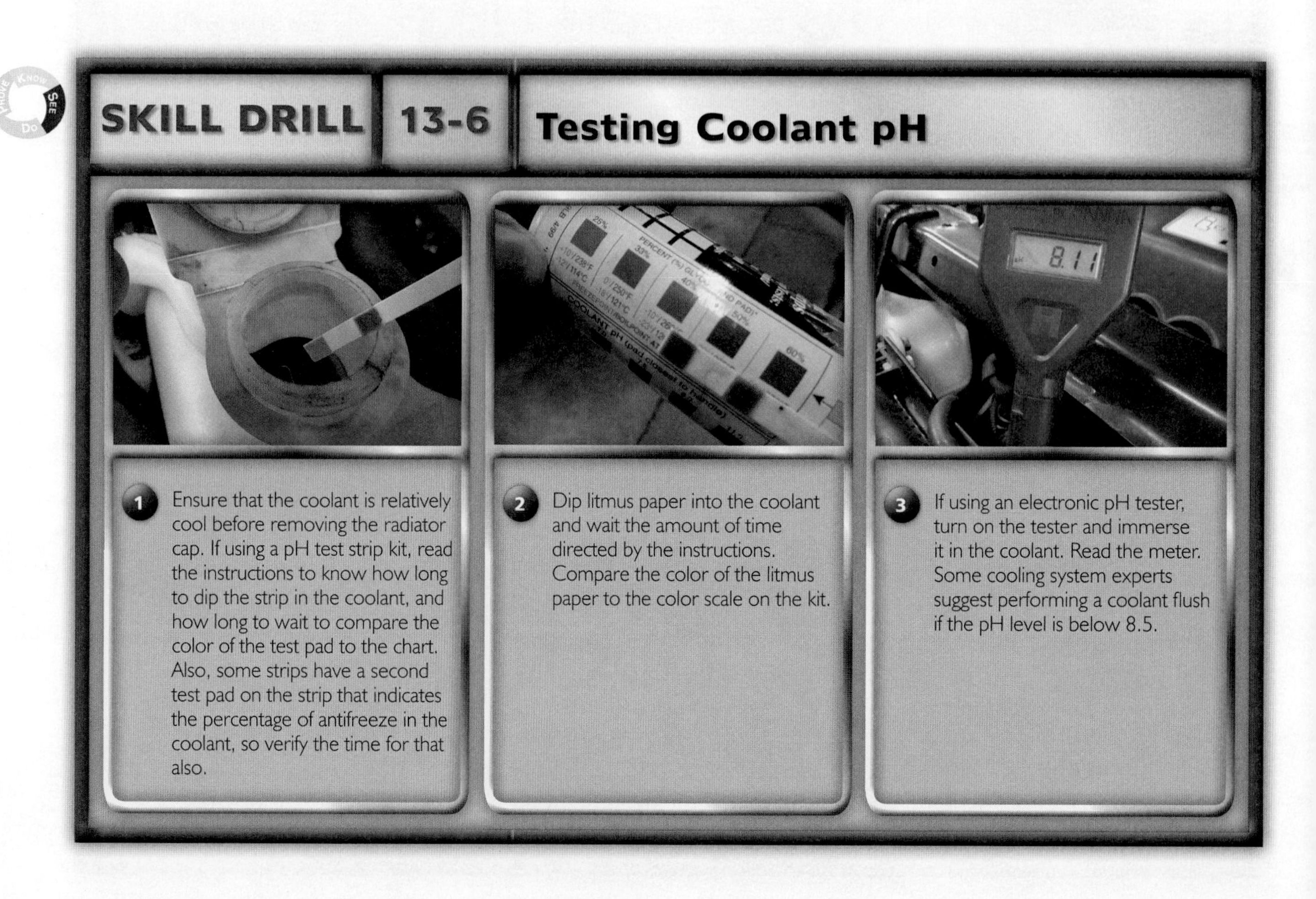
SKILL DRILL 13-6 Testing Coolant pH
8.11
1 Ensure that the coolant is relatively cool before removing the radiator cap. If using a pH test strip kit, read the instructions to know how long to dip the strip in the coolant, and how long to wait to compare the color of the test pad to the chart. Also, some strips have a second test pad on the strip that indicates the percentage of antifreeze in the coolant, so verify the time for that also.
2 Dip litmus paper into the coolant and wait the amount of time directed by the instructions. Compare the color of the litmus paper to the color scale on the kit.
3 If using an electronic pH tester, turn on the tester and immerse it in the coolant. Read the meter. Some cooling system experts suggest performing a coolant flush if the pH level is below 8.5.

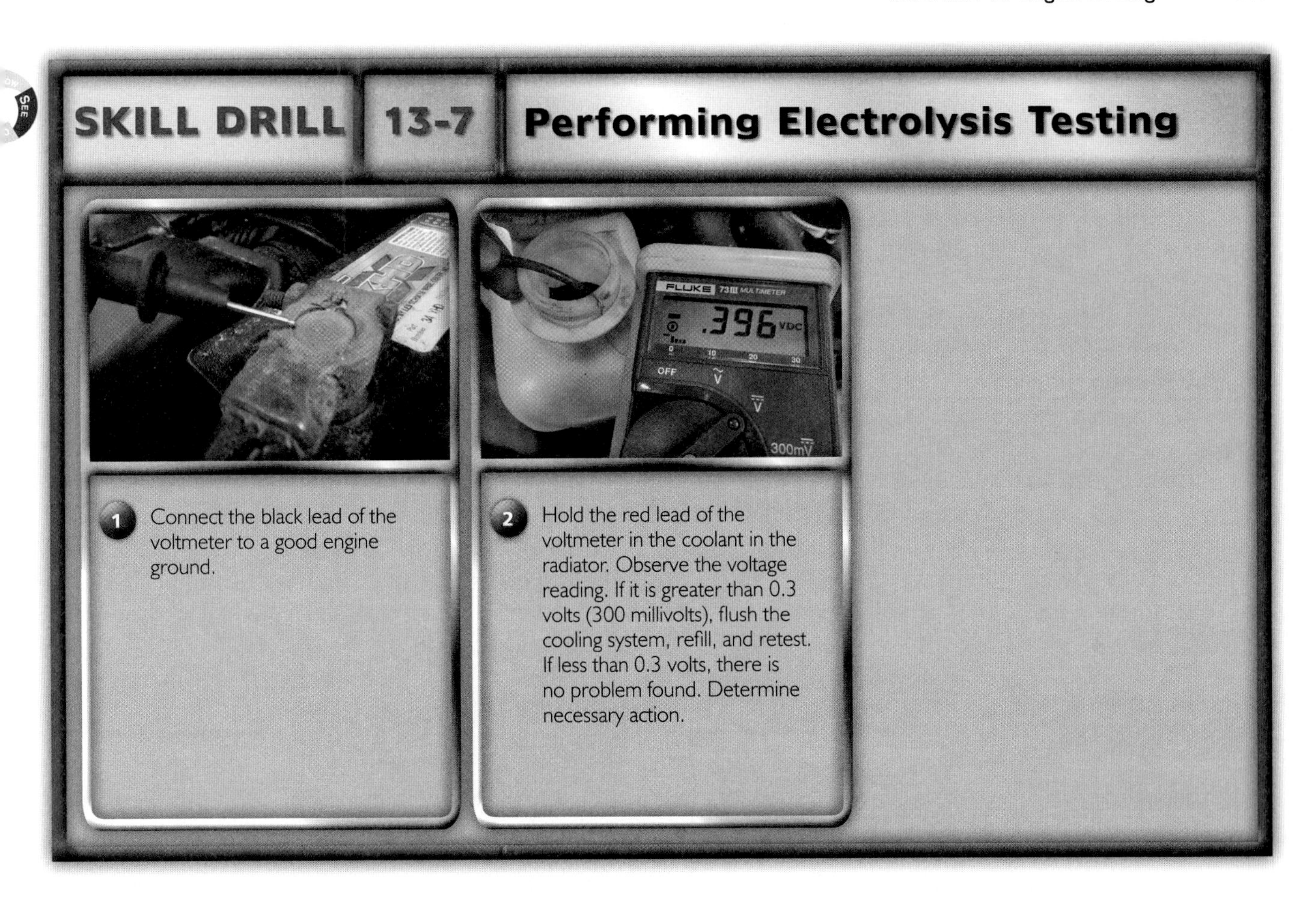
SKILL DRILL 13-7 Performing Electrolysis Testing
FLUKE 73III MULTIMETER
.396 VDC
OFF
300mV
1 Connect the black lead of the voltmeter to a good engine ground.
2 Hold the red lead of the voltmeter in the coolant in the radiator. Observe the voltage reading. If it is greater than 0.3 volts (300 millivolts), flush the cooling system, refill, and retest. If less than 0.3 volts, there is no problem found. Determine necessary action.

Checking and Adjusting Coolant

Checking and adjusting coolant implies two separate tasks. First, is the level at the full mark? Second, is the level of freeze protection appropriate for the climate the vehicle is operated in? Checking coolant level should be part of every oil change so that any leaks can be identified before they become more serious. You may also need to check or adjust coolant level if the customer's low coolant indicator comes on. There are usually two correct level marks on the reservoir because the coolant in the system expands and contracts according to changes in its temperature. The coolant level should not be below the lower mark when the vehicle is cold. It should be near the upper mark when the coolant is hot. If the coolant is indeed low, testing for a coolant leak will be necessary.

Verification of coolant condition can be performed by a checking its pH level with a test strip or electronic tester. Its freeze protection level can be tested with a coolant hydrometer or refractometer. If either of these tests shows that the coolant does not meet specifications, it will need to be flushed and replaced.

To check and adjust coolant, follow the steps in **SKILL DRILL 13-8**:

1. Most modern vehicles have a coolant system that uses a transparent recovery or surge tank as a coolant reservoir. Check the level of coolant in this reservoir; if the engine is hot, the level should be visible near the upper mark. If the engine is cold, it should be at or above the lower mark.
2. Before adding new coolant, check the specific gravity of the coolant in the system with a coolant hydrometer or refractometer. Draw some coolant up into the hydrometer, or place a couple of drops onto the sample plate, and read the freeze protection level on the gauge. These tools will indicate the freezing point of the coolant mixture in the system, so you can tell if it has the right proportions of antifreeze and water.
3. Check the service information for the recommended type and mixture of coolant that will produce an appropriate level of protection for the conditions where the vehicle will be used. Use a funnel to add enough coolant to bring the level up to the appropriate mark. Replace the coolant reservoir cap. If the level was low, find the cause of the loss.

Draining and Refilling Coolant

Draining and refilling coolant will be necessary if the customer requests a preventive maintenance service to flush the cooling system. Another reason you may need to perform this task is if corrosion is discovered in the system or if the coolant was contaminated by an incorrect fluid being added to the radiator, such as mistakenly adding power steering fluid to the coolant reservoir. Any time you have to replace a part of the cooling system, you will have to drain and refill the coolant. The discovery of electrolysis in the radiator will also require flushing the cooling system.

Your shop may have a coolant flushing machine, which will change the steps of the following skill drill. If you are using a flushing machine, follow the directions for the machine you are using.

To drain and refill coolant, follow the steps in SKILL DRILL 13-9.

> **TECHNICIAN TIP**
>
> Air can be trapped in the cooling system, so leave the radiator cap off to allow it to escape, and run the engine until the thermostat opens to allow the coolant to circulate and get rid of trapped air. Fill the radiator, then replace the radiator cap and again bring the engine up to operating temperature.

Flushing the Coolant

Coolant flushing is necessary either as a preventive maintenance service performed by most shops or because the coolant is worn out or contaminated. It will be necessary if the corrosion inhibitors in the coolant are found to be worn out or if some type of contamination is found. Flushing of the coolant is performed in one of two ways: manually or with a flushing machine. Most shops have a coolant flushing machine; if you are using this machine, follow the directions on the machine since they are all different. In this example, we will perform the manual flush.

To flush the coolant, follow the steps in SKILL DRILL 13-10. Be sure you know which direction to turn the drain plug to open. Some drain plugs are quarter-turn valves and are plastic. If turned too far, these drain plugs will break off. These drain plugs cannot always be found as a replacement part, and replacement of the entire radiator may be necessary.

> **TECHNICIAN TIP**
>
> Distilled water is recommended since it has no minerals in it, which would result in deposits in the cooling system. If the vehicle has heavy deposits in the cooling system, the cleaning process may need to be repeated several times to remove all the deposits. If the cooling system has been contaminated with some type of oil, a soapy solution will have to be used to remove the oil residue. This cleaning may need to be repeated until all traces of oil are removed.

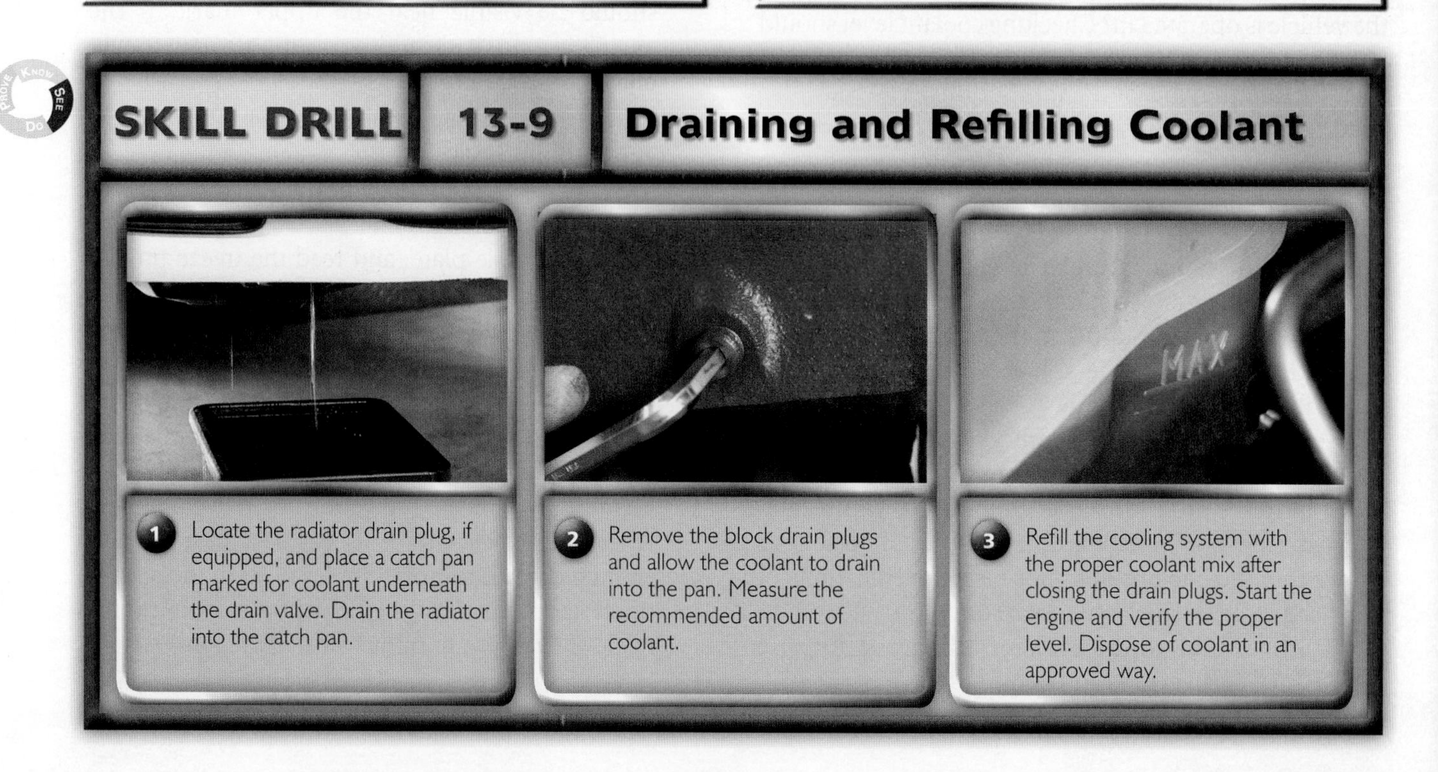
Prove
Know
See
Do
MAX

SKILL DRILL 13-9 Draining and Refilling Coolant

1. Locate the radiator drain plug, if equipped, and place a catch pan marked for coolant underneath the drain valve. Drain the radiator into the catch pan.
2. Remove the block drain plugs and allow the coolant to drain into the pan. Measure the recommended amount of coolant.
3. Refill the cooling system with the proper coolant mix after closing the drain plugs. Start the engine and verify the proper level. Dispose of coolant in an approved way.

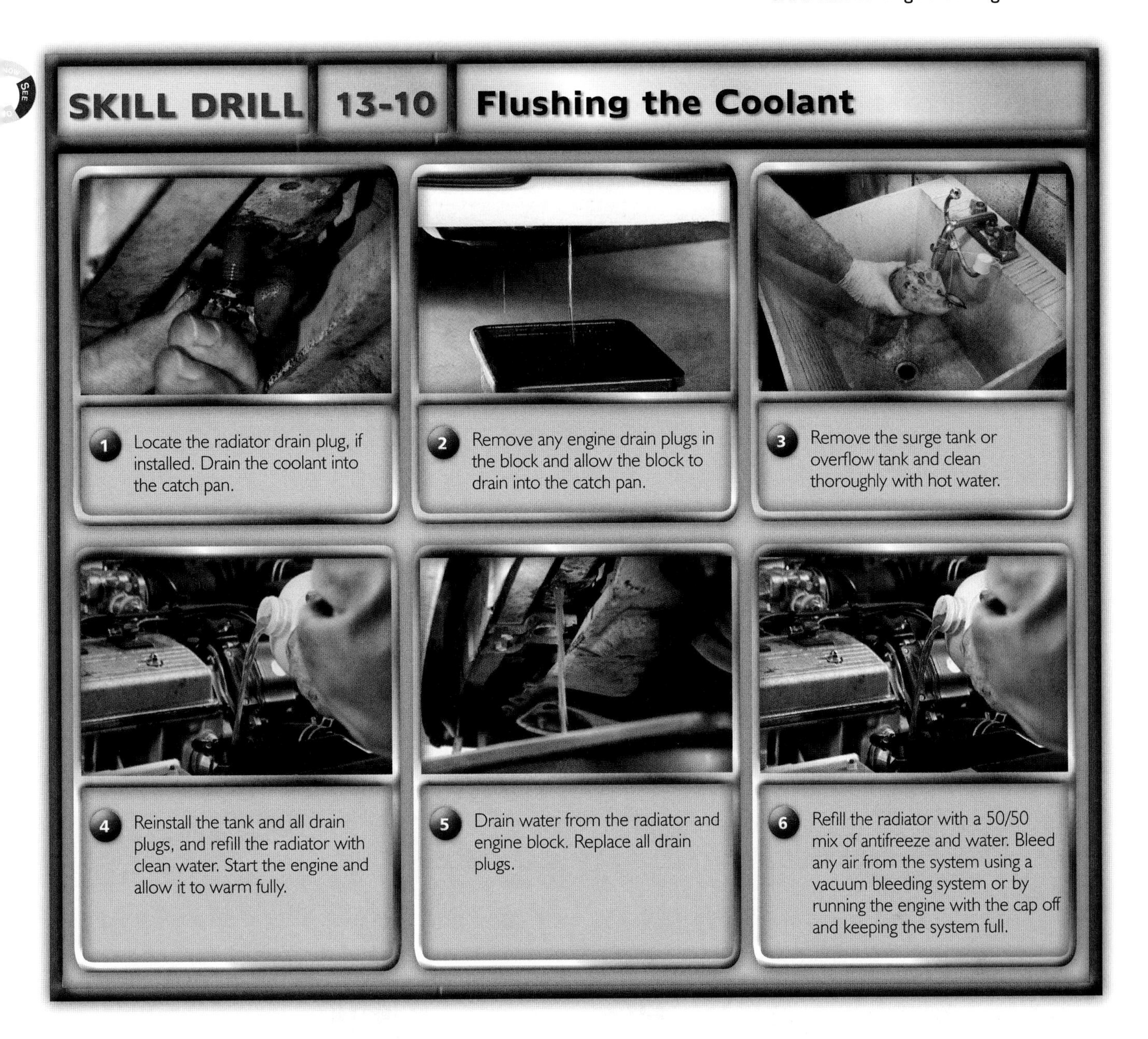
SKILL DRILL 13-10 Flushing the Coolant
1 Locate the radiator drain plug, if installed. Drain the coolant into the catch pan.
2 Remove any engine drain plugs in the block and allow the block to drain into the catch pan.
3 Remove the surge tank or overflow tank and clean thoroughly with hot water.
4 Reinstall the tank and all drain plugs, and refill the radiator with clean water. Start the engine and allow it to warm fully.
5 Drain water from the radiator and engine block. Replace all drain plugs.
6 Refill the radiator with a 50/50 mix of antifreeze and water. Bleed any air from the system using a vacuum bleeding system or by running the engine with the cap off and keeping the system full.

Inspecting and Adjusting an Engine Drive Belt

Inspecting the engine drive belt should be part of any maintenance inspection. Never try to inspect belts with the engine running. Adjusting the drive belt may be necessary if the vehicle is not equipped with an automatic tensioner. Drive belts will stretch over time with use and may require adjustment. When adjusting belts, if they are too loose, they will squeal or chirp and slip. If the belt is too tight, it will put extra force against the bearings on the accessories being turned, which can cause them to wear out prematurely. Conditions to look for on a drive belt include:

- *Cracks:* Cracks in a belt used to indicate that immediate replacement was needed. With today's belts, many manufacturers tolerate a certain number of cracks per inch. Check the manufacturer's specifications before recommending a belt be replaced.
- *Oil contamination:* A belt that has been soaked in oil will not grip properly on the pulleys and will slip. If the oil contamination is severe enough for this to happen, diagnose and repair the cause of the oil contamination and replace the belt.
- *Glazing:* Glazing is shininess on the surface of the belt, which comes in contact with the pulley. If the belt is worn, the glazing could be caused by the belt "bottoming out" in the pulley, and it should be replaced. If it is not old and worn, glazing could simply indicate that the belt is not tight enough.

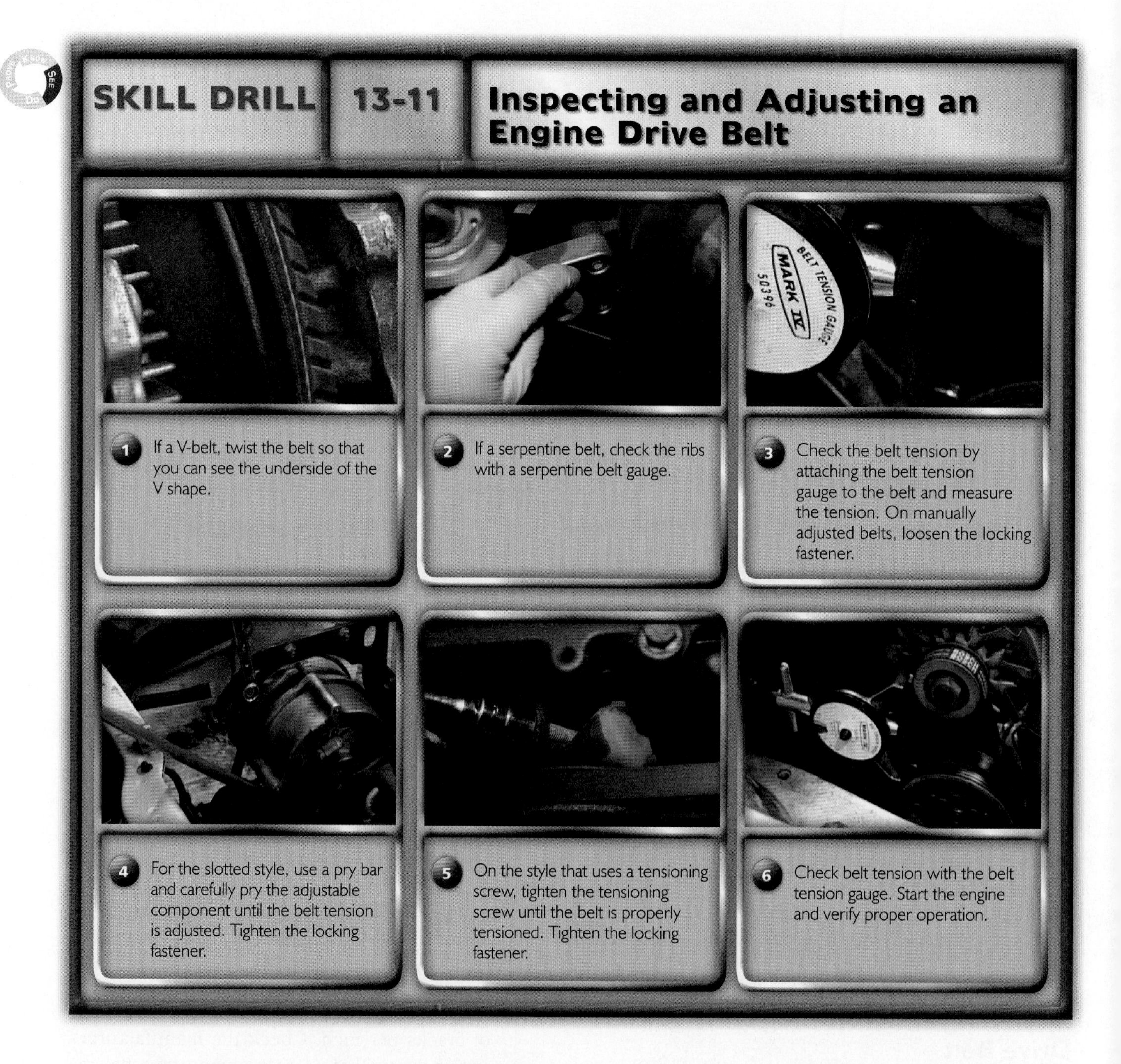
PROVE KNOW SEE DO
BELT TENSION GAUGE
MARK IX
50396

SKILL DRILL 13-11 Inspecting and Adjusting an Engine Drive Belt

1. If a V-belt, twist the belt so that you can see the underside of the V shape.
2. If a serpentine belt, check the ribs with a serpentine belt gauge.
3. Check the belt tension by attaching the belt tension gauge to the belt and measure the tension. On manually adjusted belts, loosen the locking fastener.
4. For the slotted style, use a pry bar and carefully pry the adjustable component until the belt tension is adjusted. Tighten the locking fastener.
5. On the style that uses a tensioning screw, tighten the tensioning screw until the belt is properly tensioned. Tighten the locking fastener.
6. Check belt tension with the belt tension gauge. Start the engine and verify proper operation.

Tightening the belt may be all that is necessary, depending on how bad the glazing is.

- *Tears:* Torn or split belts are unserviceable and should be replaced immediately.
- *Bottoming out:* When V-type or serpentine-type belts become very worn, the bottom of the V-shape may contact the bottom of the groove in the pulley, preventing the sides of the belt from making good contact and wedging with the sides of the pulley groove. This reduced friction causes slippage. A belt worn enough to bottom out should be replaced. V-belts can be inspected for the depth of the belt in the pulley visually. A serpentine belt can be checked with a plastic wear gauge. If the plastic tool is even with the top of the belt ribs, or lower, the belt needs to be replaced.
- *Pulley wear:* Always inspect the pulley when inspecting the belt.

To inspect and adjust an engine drive belt, follow the steps in SKILL DRILL 13-11.

Replacing an Engine Drive Belt

Replacement of an engine drive belt may be necessary when the belt is cracked, glazed, separating, and getting ready to fail. Verifying that the pulley system is not damaged will be the first step if noise is a problem. Perform a pulley alignment check as part of inspecting the drive belt

> **TECHNICIAN TIP**
>
> ***Manual belt tension versus automatic belt tension:*** Many vehicles require the technician to manually adjust the tension on the belt. Other vehicles have an automatic spring tensioning system. There are several different types of tension gauges, so follow the operating instructions for the tool. If you do not have a tension gauge, you can estimate the tension by pushing the belt inward with your thumb. If it is correctly tensioned, you should be able to deflect the belt only about half an inch for each foot of belt span between pulleys.

system if noise is a concern or if belts are being thrown off. Checking pulley alignment is done with a straightedge across the face of the pulleys or with a special laser that fits in the grooves of the pulley. If it is a serpentine belt system, the pulley edges should be within 1/16" (1.6 mm) of alignment with each other.

Another reason to replace belts would be if the customer requests belt replacement as part of the vehicle's preventive maintenance.

To replace a standard engine drive belt, follow the steps in **SKILL DRILL 13-12**.

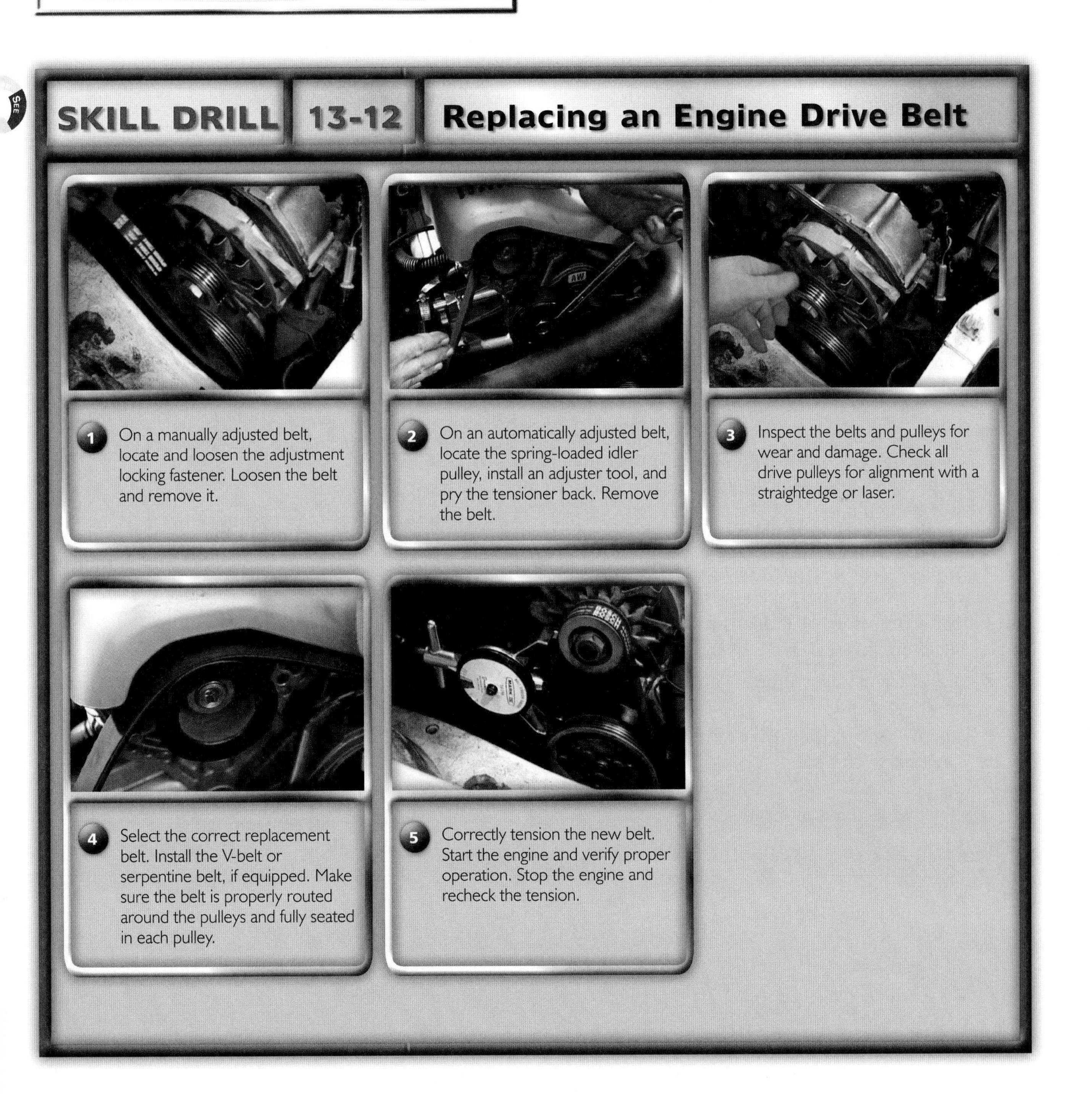

SKILL DRILL 13-12 Replacing an Engine Drive Belt

1. On a manually adjusted belt, locate and loosen the adjustment locking fastener. Loosen the belt and remove it.
2. On an automatically adjusted belt, locate the spring-loaded idler pulley, install an adjuster tool, and pry the tensioner back. Remove the belt.
3. Inspect the belts and pulleys for wear and damage. Check all drive pulleys for alignment with a straightedge or laser.
4. Select the correct replacement belt. Install the V-belt or serpentine belt, if equipped. Make sure the belt is properly routed around the pulleys and fully seated in each pulley.
5. Correctly tension the new belt. Start the engine and verify proper operation. Stop the engine and recheck the tension.

Checking and Replacing a Coolant Hose

Checking and replacing coolant hoses is a very important job of the technician. If the hose is deteriorating, it will eventually burst and coolant will be pumped out of the engine, resulting in overheating. Coolant hoses should be checked anytime the vehicle is in the shop for a maintenance inspection. If you find one defective radiator hose, the chances are that the other hose(s) may be deteriorating in the same way and will soon need to be replaced. For this reason, most technicians will generally replace both radiator hoses at once as a sensible precaution. Do not forget that there may be many hoses in the cooling system and you will need to inspect all of them to ensure proper function of the cooling system. You may need to use a flashlight to inspect the coolant hoses so that you can clearly see if the surface is starting to crack. Radiator hose problems include:

- *Swollen hose:* This hose has lost its elasticity and is swelling under pressure. It may soon rupture; typically you will see a bubble protruding from the side of this hose. Replace this hose immediately.
- *Hardened hose:* This hose has become brittle and will break and leak. Verify hardening by squeezing the hose and comparing it to a known good hose.
- *Cracked hose:* This hose has cracked and will soon start to leak. Verify cracking by a visual inspection.
- *Soft hose:* This hose has become very weak and is in danger of ballooning or bursting. Verify softening by squeezing the hose and comparing it to a known good hose.

Hose clamps come in several forms and will require different tools to properly remove or replace. These clamps secure the hose to the component it is connected to. Be sure to follow proper installation instructions to prevent future leaks from this seal. Types of clamps include:

- *Gear or worm clamp:* Adjust with a screwdriver or nut driver.
- *Banded or screw clamp:* Adjust with a screwdriver.
- *Wire clamp:* This spring clamp is not adjustable. It is fitted and removed with special hose clamp pliers, which have grooved jaws.

TECHNICIAN TIP

"You can't diagnose bad if you don't know good." This saying is very appropriate when checking radiator hoses. It is a good idea to check the feel of radiator and heater hoses on a variety of new vehicles to become familiar with what new hoses feel like. Then it will be easy to identify the bad ones.

Clamps are not expensive, so it is good practice to fit new ones at the same time as new hoses. Even if not corroded, the old clamps may have become distorted when being removed from an unserviceable hose. The time and money associated with replacing clamps are very small when thinking of the results of your customer losing a hose and becoming stranded.

To check and replace a coolant hose, follow the steps in **SKILL DRILL 13-13**. Before you begin, locate both the hoses that carry coolant between the radiator and the engine. One is at the inlet and the other is at the outlet of the radiator. Squeeze each hose. It should feel pliable and springy. If it feels very soft and weak or very hard and brittle, it will need to be replaced. Look for signs of swelling or cracking, particularly near the hose clamps. Check that the clamps are holding the hoses firmly in position and are not damaged or corroded.

Safety

Never try to assess the serviceability of a coolant hose while the engine is hot. Let it cool so that you can handle the hoses comfortably and safely. Always ensure the engine is turned off before attempting to check the coolant hoses, and always wear the appropriate personal protection equipment before starting the job. It is easy to hurt yourself, even when the most exhaustive protection measures are taken.

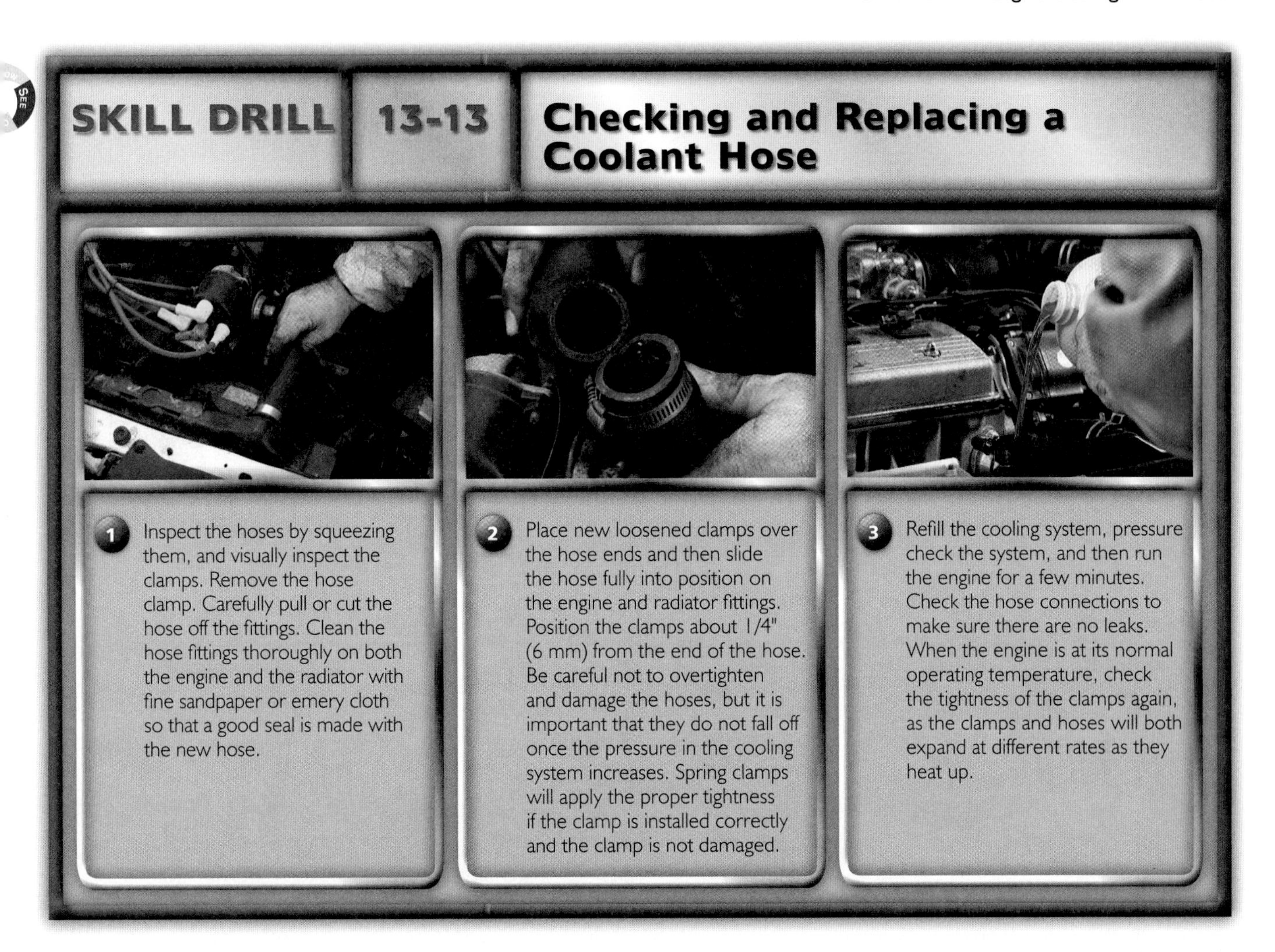
SKILL DRILL 13-13 Checking and Replacing a Coolant Hose

1 Inspect the hoses by squeezing them, and visually inspect the clamps. Remove the hose clamp. Carefully pull or cut the hose off the fittings. Clean the hose fittings thoroughly on both the engine and the radiator with fine sandpaper or emery cloth so that a good seal is made with the new hose.

2 Place new loosened clamps over the hose ends and then slide the hose fully into position on the engine and radiator fittings. Position the clamps about 1/4" (6 mm) from the end of the hose. Be careful not to overtighten and damage the hoses, but it is important that they do not fall off once the pressure in the cooling system increases. Spring clamps will apply the proper tightness if the clamp is installed correctly and the clamp is not damaged.

3 Refill the cooling system, pressure check the system, and then run the engine for a few minutes. Check the hose connections to make sure there are no leaks. When the engine is at its normal operating temperature, check the tightness of the clamps again, as the clamps and hoses will both expand at different rates as they heat up.

Removing and Replacing a Thermostat

It will be necessary to remove and replace a thermostat in the event that the thermostat is found to be faulty, creating either an overheating concern or an underheating concern. You may want to suggest to the customer a thermostat replacement during a cooling system flush or water pump replacement as a precautionary maintenance step. Before starting a repair or service task on the cooling system, allow sufficient time for the system to cool adequately before opening the pressurized system.

Drain at least 50% of the coolant in the system to avoid spills. Once the thermostat has been removed, clean any old gasket material and corrosion that has built up on both sealing surfaces where the thermostat seats. Properly position the thermostat air bleed valve (if equipped). Always install a new gasket and/or O-ring seal when installing the thermostat. Make sure the thermostat is fully seated in the groove and stays there before installing the housing. In most cases, if the thermostat falls out of its recessed groove, one of the thermostat housing ears will break off when the bolts are tightened, and the thermostat itself is likely to be damaged. Tighten the housing bolts to the correct torque. Use the manufacturer's procedure to properly bleed all air from the cooling system.

To remove and replace a thermostat, follow the steps in **SKILL DRILL 13-14**.

Know
See
Do
Prove

SKILL DRILL 13-14 Removing and Replacing a Thermostat

1. Drain the coolant from the cooling system using an approved catch container. Remove the thermostat.

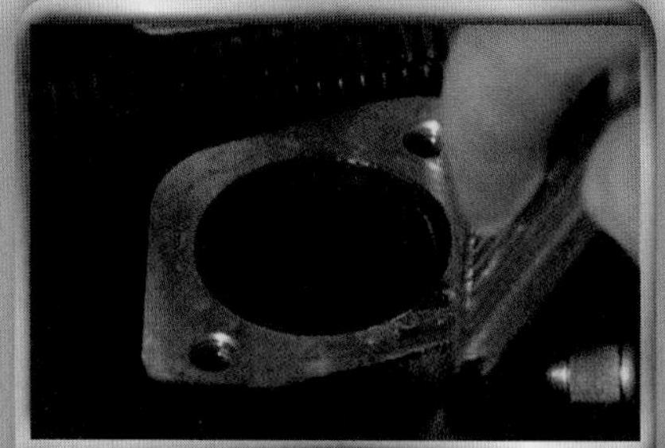

2. Inspect the thermostat housing and clean any gasket material from the mating surfaces. Clean and inspect the thermostat groove.

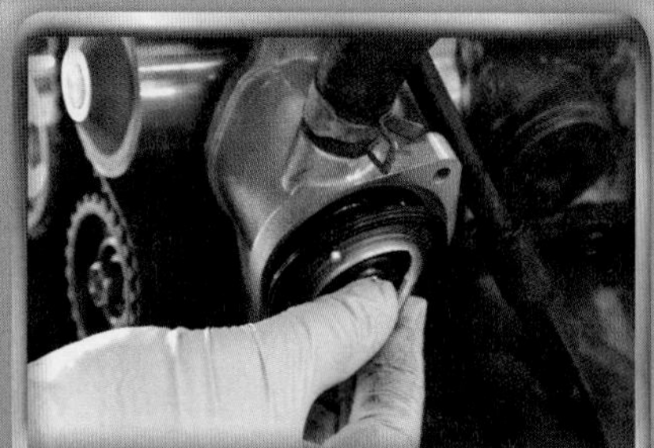

3. Install the new thermostat with the bleed valve in the correct position.

4. Install the gasket or O-ring and thermostat housing.

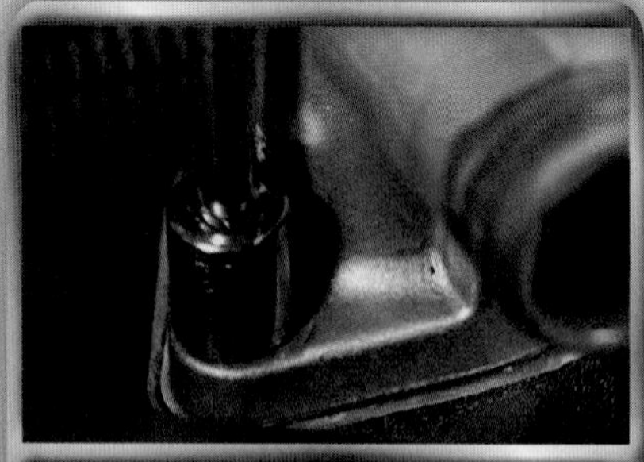

5. Torque to housing specifications.

6. Refill the cooling system to the proper level.

Wrap-up

Ready for Review

- Most cooling systems rely on coolant, a special mix of chemicals (antifreeze) and water.
- Coolant absorbs heat from the engine, is cooled in the radiator, and flows back to the engine to absorb more heat.
- Heat travels in one of three ways: conduction, convection, or radiation.
- Coolant works to keep an engine from overheating and from freezing.
- Coolant must contain antifreeze to prevent the water content from freezing and to reduce corrosion.
- Antifreeze contains either ethylene glycol (toxic) or propylene glycol (nontoxic).
- The combination of water and antifreeze lowers the freezing point and raises the boiling point of both components.
- Manufacturers can create more efficient combustion by raising the engine's operating temperature, creating more pressure, and causing coolant to boil at a higher temperature.
- Radiator caps maintain a specified pressure throughout the cooling system, generally 13–17 psi (89.6–117.2 kPa).
- Changing coolant regularly prevents acid buildup and electrolysis.
- The stationary parts of the cooling system (heater core and radiator) are connected to the engine via radiator and cooling hoses.
- Modern vehicles have replaced the thermo-siphon process for moving coolant through the engine with a water pump that forces coolant through the system.
- An engine thermostat regulates coolant circulation, keeping it in the engine until the engine reaches operating temperature.
- Engineers have developed a reverse-flow cooling system in which coolant is first pushed through the cylinder head, thereby better equalizing temperature between the block and head, which extends the life of the head gasket.
- Engines with the reverse-flow cooling system must have a surge tank to capture steam and reconvert it to coolant.
- The radiator's function is to allow coolant to pass through it and to conduct heat away from the engine.
- Cooling tubes in the radiator core run in a vertical (down-flow) or horizontal (cross-flow) design.
- Radiator pressure caps contain a spring-loaded valve to allow excess coolant to pass into the overflow container, and a vacuum valve to allow coolant to be pulled from the overflow container back into the radiator when it is needed.
- A surge tank is situated as the highest component so that it collects any air present in the system and allows for easy air removal.
- In a recovery system, coolant flows into an overflow container and then back into the radiator so that no coolant is lost.
- The thermostat's valve is controlled by a wax pellet that melts and expands and forces the valve open against spring pressure.
- Thermostats installed on the inlet side of the engine better control the amount of cold water flowing into the engine.
- The water pump uses centrifugal force to drive coolant into the water jackets.
- A fan clutch is driven by an accessory belt and uses a viscous fluid to control speed changes of the fan, determined by air temperature from the radiator.
- A solenoid-controlled fan clutch replaces the bimetallic spring with an electric solenoid controlled by the power train control module.
- Radiator hoses must be correctly clamped to the radiator assembly or a leak will develop.
- Some heater hoses contain a coolant control valve to regulate coolant flow when the air conditioner is turned on.
- The three types of drive belts for the water pump are V-belts, serpentine belts, and toothed belts.
- To ensure minimal slippage, drive belts are tightened around the pulley by tensioners.
- Either a temperature gauge or a temperature light can function as a coolant temperature indicator.
- Coolant passages are critical to the transfer of heat energy so coolant must be serviced regularly to prevent the passages from becoming clogged.
- The heater box contains air doors and actuators that work to control passenger compartment airflow.
- IAT coolant is the standard green coolant used in many vehicles and must be changed every 2 years or 24,000 miles (39,000 km).
- OAT coolant is an extended-life coolant that should be changed every 5 years or 150,000 miles (241,000 km).
- HOAT coolant (yellow) combines inorganic and organic additives and is also an extended-life coolant.
- POAT coolant, the newest type, is a very long-life coolant that should be changed every 7 years or 250,000 miles (402,000 km).

- Cooling systems need regular maintenance to ensure engine longevity.
- Common cooling system diagnostic concerns include coolant leaks, thermostat that is stuck closed or open, faulty water pump, inoperative cooling fan, or failed head gasket.
- Test pH concentration of the coolant to ensure the antifreeze acid inhibitors are working correctly.
- Measure the voltage of the coolant to determine if electrolysis is occurring due to acidic coolant or faulty grounds.
- Always follow EPA regulations for handling and disposing of coolant.
- Coolant condition and level should be checked regularly; coolant should be at the correct level mark (upper or lower) according to engine temperature.
- When removing and replacing a radiator, be sure to properly catch, handle, and dispose of or replace the coolant.
- Do not attempt to remove or replace the thermostat until the engine has cooled for at least 30 minutes.
- Potential engine drive belt problems can be belts that are cracked, oil soaked, glazed, torn, or bottomed out.
- Coolant freeze point can be verified by a hydrometer or refractometer, both of which indicate the specific gravity of the fluid, revealing the ratio of antifreeze to water.

Key Terms

actuator A device that is electrically or vacuum controlled and is used to physically move doors within the heater box to control airflow.

boiling point The temperature at which a substance begins to change from a liquid to a gas.

centrifugal force A force pulling outward on a rotating body.

conduction Movement of heat energy through solids.

convection Movement of heat energy through gases or liquids.

coolant A fluid that contains antifreeze mixed with water.

coolant control valve A valve that blocks off coolant flow to keep hot water from entering the heater core when less heat is requested by the operator.

cooling hoses Flexible hoses that connect the stationary components of the cooling system, such as heater core and radiator, to the engine, which is mounted on flexible mounts.

cross-flow radiator A radiator that uses cooling tubes that run horizontal with tanks on each end. This design allows lower hood profile for better vehicle aerodynamics.

down-flow radiator A radiator that uses cooling tubes that run vertical. This design requires a higher hood profile.

electrolysis The process of pulling metals apart by using electricity or by creating electricity through the use of chemicals and dissimilar metals.

ethylene glycol A chemical used as antifreeze that provides the lower freezing point of coolant and raises the boiling point. It is a toxic antifreeze.

heat dissipation The spreading of heat over a large area to increase heat transfer.

overflow tank A tank used to catch any coolant that is released from the radiator cap (works like a catch can).

pitch The angle of a fan blade. A steeper pitch draws more air, while a shallower pitch draws less air.

propylene-glycol A chemical used as antifreeze. It is labeled as a nontoxic antifreeze.

radiation The movement of energy through space such as the movement of energy from the sun to the earth.

radiator A device that takes hot coolant and cools it by passing heat energy to the surrounding air.

radiator hoses Rubber hoses that connect the radiator to the engine. Because they are subject to pressure, they are reinforced with a layer of fabric, typically nylon.

surge tank A sealed tank that captures coolant coming from the head that has turned to steam and changes the steam back to coolant to be reused by the cooling system.

thermo-control switch A temperature-sensitive switch that is mounted into the radiator or into a coolant passage on the engine to control electric fan operation.

thermostat Located under the thermostat housing, the thermostat regulates the flow of coolant, allowing coolant to flow from the engine to the radiator when the engine is running at its operating temperature.

viscous coupler Called a fan clutch, a hub that connects the water pump drive to the cooling fan using a temperature-sensitive viscous fluid to cause the fan to turn faster as the temperature of the air pulled through the radiator increases.

water jackets The passages in the engine block and cylinder head that surround the cylinders, valves, and ports.

ASE-Type Questions

1. Tech A says that the cooling system is designed to keep the engine as cool as possible. Tech B says that the heater core can remove heat from the cooling system. Who is correct?
   a. Tech A
   b. Tech B
   c. Both A and B
   d. Neither A nor B
2. Tech A says that the thermostat is open until the engine warms up, and then it closes. Tech B says that a faulty radiator cap can be the cause of boiling coolant. Who is correct?
   a. Tech A
   b. Tech B
   c. Both A and B
   d. Neither A nor B
3. Tech A says that when pure antifreeze is used in the cooling system, the protection level is –70°F. Tech B says that pure antifreeze will cool the engine better than water. Who is correct?
   a. Tech A
   b. Tech B
   c. Both A and B
   d. Neither A nor B
4. Tech A says that some drive belts are a stretch fit design. Tech B says that the thermostat may have a bleed valve that should be accurately positioned when the thermostat is replaced. Who is correct?
   a. Tech A
   b. Tech B
   c. Both A and B
   d. Neither A nor B
5. Tech A says that the design of a surge tank system helps to purge air from the cooling system. Tech B says that overflow tanks are pressurized. Who is correct?
   a. Tech A
   b. Tech B
   c. Both A and B
   d. Neither A nor B
6. Tech A says that when you find coolant hoses collapsed, the radiator pressure cap has failed. Tech B says that overflow tanks are reservoirs designed to allow coolant to flow back to the radiator as the engine cools. Who is correct?
   a. Tech A
   b. Tech B
   c. Both A and B
   d. Neither A nor B
7. Tech A says that electric cooling fans operate whenever the engine is running. Tech B says that electric cooling fans are used to cause a large airflow over the radiator at low vehicle speeds. Who is correct?
   a. Tech A
   b. Tech B
   c. Both A and B
   d. Neither A nor B
8. Tech A says that there are a number of coolant types that each has its own life span. Tech B says that mixing of coolants is generally ok, since all coolants use the same chemical base. Who is correct?
   a. Tech A
   b. Tech B
   c. Both A and B
   d. Neither A nor B
9. Tech A says that coolant leaking out of the water pump weep hole is normal. Tech B says that a refractometer measures the specific gravity of a liquid. Who is correct?
   a. Tech A
   b. Tech B
   c. Both A and B
   d. Neither A nor B
10. Tech A says that a cooling system pressure tester can be used to find leaks in the cooling system. Tech B says that the cooling system pressure tester can be used to test the pressure at which the radiator cap vents. Who is correct?
    a. Tech A
    b. Tech B
    c. Both A and B
    d. Neither A nor B

SECTION III

Automatic Transmission

CHAPTER 14

NATEF Tasks

Automatic Transmission and Transaxle

General

		Page
■ Research applicable vehicle and service information, fluid type, vehicle service history, service precautions, and technical service bulletins.	MLR AST	371–372

Knowledge Objectives

After reading this chapter, you will be able to:

1. Describe the principles of operation of the automatic transmission. (pp 362–364)
2. Explain the principles of a torque converter. (pp 364–368)
3. Explain the basic operation of planetary gear sets. (p 370)
4. Identify the different common components of the automatic transmission. (pp 373–375)

Automatic Transmission Fundamentals

KNOW
SEE
DO

Skills Objectives

There are no skills objectives for this chapter.

Introduction

Automatic transmissions were once considered an expensive option on automobiles. Today, the majority of vehicles sold in the United States are equipped with automatic transmissions as standard equipment. Given the number of automatic transmission vehicles being produced, it is necessary for every technician to have a working knowledge of automatic transmission fundamentals even if they may never rebuild a transmission while working in the field. Technicians will come across problems that will mask themselves as transmission problems only to be correctly diagnosed later, after transmission replacement, as a problem relating to an entirely different system, or vice versa. For example, a plugged catalytic converter can make a transmission shift erratically, or a bad vehicle speed sensor can make a transmission not shift at all. In this section, we will cover the types of automatic transmissions, theory of operation, and maintenance procedures of hydraulically and electronically controlled transmissions.

Function of an Automatic Transmission

An automatic transmission has two major functions that separate it from a manual transmission. First, the transmission can select and shift gears without input from the driver. This function is accomplished within the gear train of the transmission along with the aid of the hydraulic system. Second, the transmission can automatically couple and uncouple from the engine when needed, much like a clutch on a manual transmission vehicle but without any work by the driver. This is the function of the torque converter. Without the ability to automatically connect and disconnect the transmission from the engine, a vehicle would stall when it came to a stop, much like a manual transmission vehicle will do if the driver forgets to depress the clutch pedal. These two functions separate automatic transmissions from manual transmissions and will be discussed in depth over the next several chapters.

Types of Automatic Transmissions

There are several types or classifications of automatic transmissions: conventional transmissions, transaxles, dual clutch, continuously variable, a Honda/Saturn type of transmission, and hybrid transmissions. Each of these types of automatic transmissions has elements common to the conventional transmission, but we will explain only the major differences here.

A conventional automatic transmission uses one or more planetary gear sets to create several gear ratios needed to drive the vehicle. Conventional automatic transmissions are typically connected to the engine through a torque converter. The torque converter will be covered in detail later in the chapter. The gears inside a conventional transmission are constantly meshed to each other. Holding devices, such as clutches or bands, will stop the rotation of gears or drive the gears in a planetary gear set in order to create the needed gear ratio.

In the 1970s most manufacturers developed front-wheel drive vehicles for several reasons: improved traction over rear-wheel drive vehicles, less overall

You Are the Automotive Technician

It is your second day as a new technician and you are asked to report to the main office. Your supervisor informs you that your first oil change of the day will include checking and possibly replacing the automatic transmission fluid (ATF). Before you can begin working on the shop floor, your supervisor asks you to review the shop manual for directions on handling and disposing of hazardous fluids. After completing your first oil change, you take a sample of transmission fluid and put it on a piece of white paper towel. Contaminants are left on the towel, indicating that the transmission fluid is dirty. Your recommendation to the customer is to drain and replace the transmission fluid. The customer is adamant about wanting only an oil change at this time.

1. How do you convince the customer that his transmission fluid needs to be replaced?
2. Why is it necessary to check the manufacturer's recommendation and technical service bulletins when replacing any fluid in vehicles?
3. What are some of the additives in automatic transmission fluid and what is their purpose?

weight, and increased passenger compartment space. On front-wheel drive vehicles, a **transaxle** is often used, rather than a typical transmission. A transaxle is a conventional transmission that has a built-in differential and final drive gear FIGURE 14-1. The differential allows for the vehicle to make turns. When a vehicle turns, the wheels on the outside of the turning circle must spin faster than the ones on the inside of the turning circle. Each wheel will follow a circle with a different radius. Without a differential, the wheels would not be able to spin at different speeds, resulting in scuffing of tires, binding in the drive train, and probable broken drive train parts. On most rear-wheel drive vehicles, the differential and final drive gear are located in the rear axle assembly. Some rear-wheel drive vehicles, such as late-model Chevy Corvettes, will also use a transaxle assembly located in the rear of the vehicle while the engine is located in the front of the vehicle. The Corvette uses this transaxle arrangement to better distribute weight between the front and rear wheels to improve handling.

Dual-clutch transmissions are a newer type of automatic transmission that uses two, typically wet, clutches in place of a **standard torque converter** to connect the engine to the transmission FIGURE 14-2. A wet clutch is one that is immersed in hydraulic oil or transmission fluid rather than being dry like a conventional manual transmission clutch. Each clutch is connected to different driving gears. Clutch 1 would be connected to gears 1, 3, and 5, while clutch 2 would power gears 2, 4, and 6. The transmission operates by locking the individual driving gears to the output shaft in order to change the speed of the output shaft. Their operation is similar in some ways to that of a manual transmission, but the changing of gears is controlled by the vehicle computer, not the driver.

Continuously variable transmissions (CVTs) are transmissions that do not use typical gears as in other transmissions. Rather, CVTs commonly use two pulleys that change diameter in response to vehicle load and speed. There is a large, heavy metal belt connecting the two pulleys FIGURE 14-3. When the vehicle is starting from a stop, the input pulley, which is coupled to the engine, has a small

FIGURE 14-1 A typical front-wheel drive vehicle transaxle. Note the differential components inside the case.

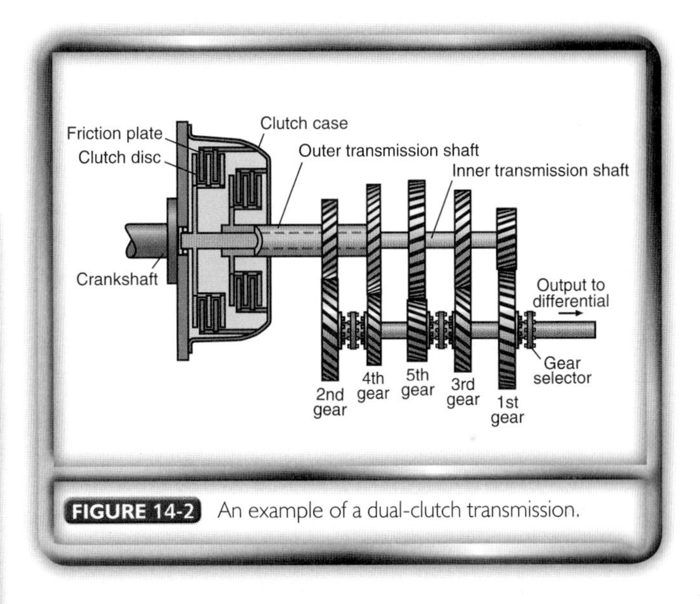
Friction plate
Clutch disc
Clutch case
Outer transmission shaft
Inner transmission shaft
Crankshaft
Output to differential
Gear selector
2nd gear
4th gear
5th gear
3rd gear
1st gear

FIGURE 14-2 An example of a dual-clutch transmission.

FIGURE 14-3 The pulleys and metal belt of a CVT transmission.

diameter while the output pulley, which is coupled to the drive wheels, has a large diameter. This size difference creates a large amount of torque multiplication as the smaller pulley will turn approximately three times for every one turn of the output pulley. When the vehicle reaches cruising speed, the input pulley will have compressed, causing the diameter of the pulley to increase, while the output pulley will reduce in diameter. At this point the output pulley will spin up to three times for every revolution of the input pulley. Using this system, the transmission does not have fixed gear ratios like a conventional transmission; instead it is able to vary the gear ratio infinitely within the changing diameters of the pulleys. This variability allows the engine to operate in its most efficient revolutions per minute (rpm) range to save fuel.

Many Honda and Saturn vehicles use an automatic transmission that more closely resembles a manual transmission, as they do not use planetary gear sets. These transmissions are sometimes called dual-shaft transmissions because they have a main shaft and a countershaft, like in a manual transmission **FIGURE 14-4**. In these transmissions, the synchronizer assemblies that would be in a manual transmission are replaced with multidisc clutch packs to engage the individual gears onto the main shaft.

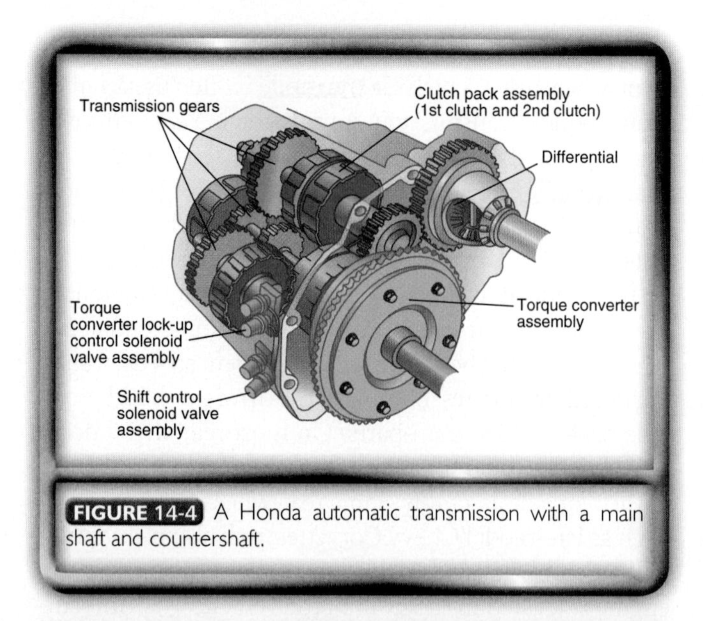
Transmission gears
Clutch pack assembly
(1st clutch and 2nd clutch)
Differential
Torque
converter lock-up
control solenoid
valve assembly
Torque converter
assembly
Shift control
solenoid valve
assembly

FIGURE 14-4 A Honda automatic transmission with a main shaft and countershaft.

Hybrid vehicles use drive trains that can be categorized as series or parallel hybrid drive trains. In a series drive train, the power going into the transmission from the engine is supplemented with power from an electric motor. In a **series hybrid drive train**, the electric motor is not typically able to propel the vehicle on its own. This electric motor is often placed between the engine and the transmission.

A **parallel hybrid drive train** has two or more methods for the power to flow through the transmission. The engine can mechanically send power through the transmission to the wheels, or one or more electric motors can send power through the transmission to the wheels. Either the electric motors or the gasoline engine can propel the vehicle along, individually or in combination.

A **series-parallel hybrid drive train** is designed so that it can function as both a series hybrid and a parallel hybrid. It uses what is called a **power-splitting transmission (PST)** **FIGURE 14-5**. This transmission is sometimes referred to as a type of CVT transmission. It uses a planetary gear set to obtain an infinitely adjustable transmission. It allows power to be applied to the planetary gear set (epicyclic gearing) through three sources: the internal combustion engine (ICE) and two motors/generators. This design is an ingenious application of the planetary gear set, as in its normal use one member is held and another is driven. But in the case of a hybrid vehicle, where you have more than one power source, two components can be driven. Moreover, they can be driven at different speeds, and in the case of the electric motors, they can be driven in reverse. This ability to drive more than one member at various speeds allows the planetary gear to act like a CVT. In this configuration, the planetary gear set acts as a power divider and uses all three power sources or two generators to balance the overall needs of the system, including vehicle speed, traction motor battery charge, and ICE efficiency. This system is operated by sophisticated computer controls. Hybrids and CVT transmissions are covered in greater detail in the chapter on that topic.

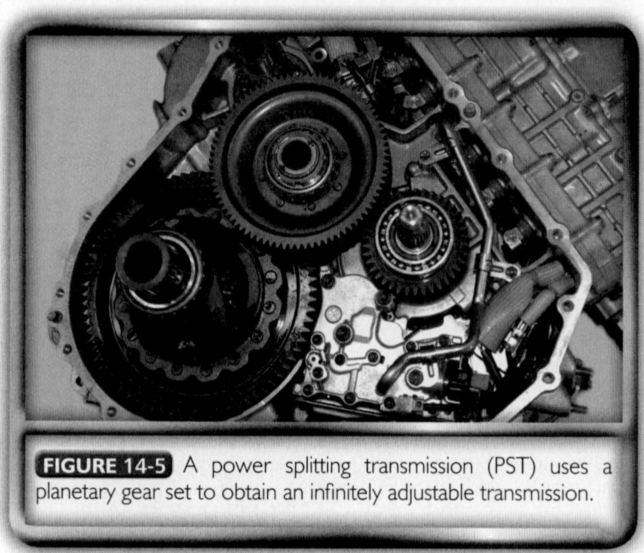

FIGURE 14-5 A power splitting transmission (PST) uses a planetary gear set to obtain an infinitely adjustable transmission.

Torque Converters

Torque Converter Principles

The purpose of a vehicle transmission is to transmit engine torque to the driving wheels. The transmission needs to be able to adapt the engine torque to meet the speed and power demands of the vehicle. In a manual transmission, engine torque is controlled by the driver manually selecting the proper gear. In an automatic transmission, torque is also controlled by selecting the proper gear, but in this case, gear selection is automatic. The transmission also works in concert with the torque converter to modify the engine's torque FIGURE 14-6.

The torque converter is mounted between the engine and the transmission, in the same place as a manual transmission clutch FIGURE 14-7. The torque converter effectively connects the engine flywheel to the input shaft of the transmission. The torque converter does the same job as a manual clutch, transmitting engine torque to the input shaft of the transmission. But it can do one thing a manual transmission clutch cannot do—multiply torque from the engine to the input shaft of the transmission when required by driving conditions. This is one reason that vehicles equipped with automatic transmissions make good tow vehicles. The torque converter can multiply the engine torque when starting from a standstill, which is just what is needed when pulling a boat trailer out of the water on a steep boat ramp. How can it do that, you ask? Well, keep reading and we will explain how each of the torque converter components work together to multiply torque under certain conditions.

FIGURE 14-6 A typical torque converter that has been removed from a vehicle.

Fluid Couplers

Early automatic transmissions used a **fluid coupler** rather than a torque converter. A fluid coupler is basically two fans facing each other FIGURE 14-8. One fan is the driving fan, and it is driven by the engine. The second fan is attached to the input shaft of the transmission. When the fluid is thrown off of the driving fan, it hits the driven fan, causing the second fan to begin to spin. When the second fan spins, the input shaft of the transmission also begins to spin.

The device is called a fluid coupler because none of the converter components are physically connected to the others; rather, the force of the fluid flow causes the transfer of power. This fluid coupler acts as an automatic clutch. At engine idle speeds, it allows the engine to operate while the vehicle is stationary and the transmission is in a drive range, without the driver having to shift the transmission to neutral or step on a clutch pedal.

Modern transmissions no longer use fluid couplers, but the principle of the torque converter operation is still similar to the fluid coupler. In its simplest form, a single-stage torque converter has three elements: the impeller,

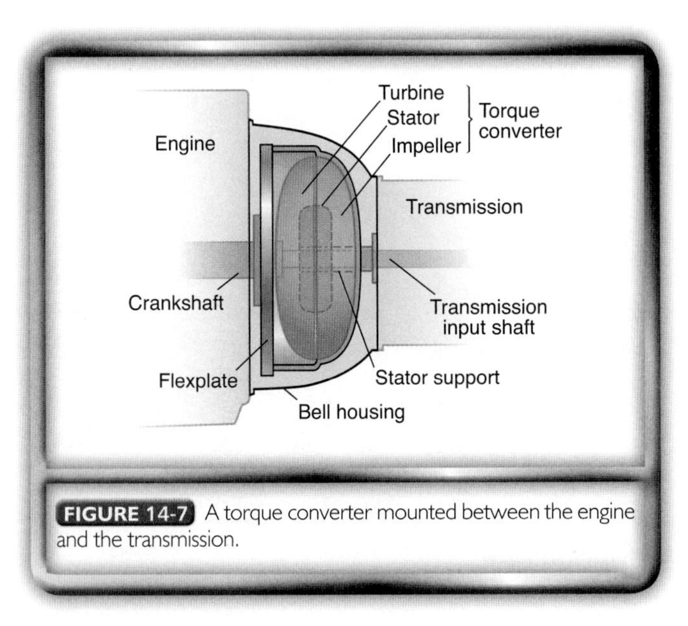
Turbine
Stator
Impeller
Torque converter
Engine
Transmission
Crankshaft
Transmission input shaft
Flexplate
Stator support
Bell housing

FIGURE 14-7 A torque converter mounted between the engine and the transmission.

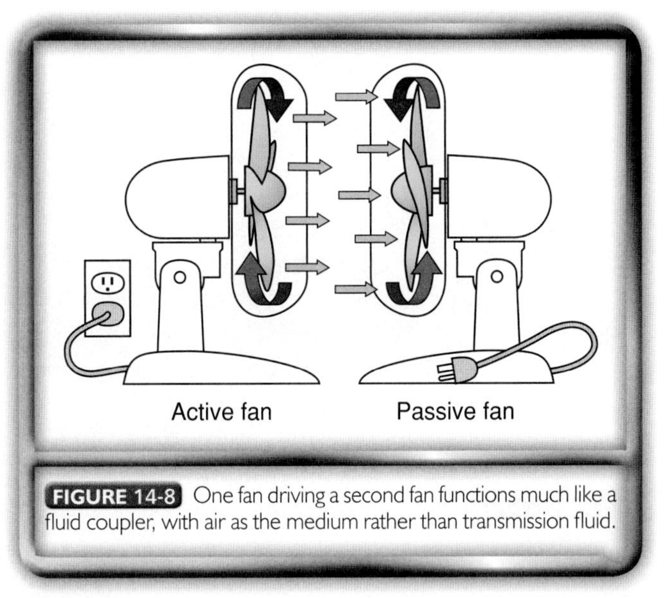
Active fan
Passive fan

FIGURE 14-8 One fan driving a second fan functions much like a fluid coupler, with air as the medium rather than transmission fluid.

the turbine, and the stator FIGURE 14-9. All three have angled or curved vanes and are contained in a single housing. They are separated from each other by thrust bearings, but maintain a close relationship for efficient torque transmission.

The impeller has a large number of vanes attached to the converter housing to form the driving member (like the fan that is plugged in for the fluid coupler) FIGURE 14-10. The vanes rotate with the housing as the engine runs. Each vane has a slight curvature and is set radially in the case.

The turbine is similar in construction to the impeller, but with more vanes and a greater curvature. The direction of curvature of the turbine vanes is opposite to that of the impeller vanes. The turbine is free to rotate in the housing, and the center hub has splines that mate with splines on the input shaft of the transmission FIGURE 14-11. When the fluid coming from the impeller rotates the turbine, the transmission input shaft also rotates.

Both the impeller and the turbine are fitted with a guide ring. This ring helps to secure the vanes in position. It also reduces turbulence as fluid is flowing in a circle from the impeller to the turbine, and back to the impeller again. It also improves torque converter efficiency.

The stator has a small set of curved blades attached to a central hub and is positioned between the impeller and the turbine. The center hub is mounted on a one-way clutch splined to a stator support shaft FIGURE 14-12. The stator support shaft is attached to the transmission case and does not spin. The one-way clutch allows the stator to rotate only in the same direction as the impeller. Trying to rotate the stator in the opposite direction locks the stator on the support shaft and holds it stationary.

FIGURE 14-9 A torque converter that has been cut open to reveal the impeller, turbine, and stator.

FIGURE 14-11 A turbine mounted inside the converter case. Note that the turbine is free to spin inside the housing on bearings.

FIGURE 14-10 An impeller brazed to the housing of the torque converter.

FIGURE 14-12 A stator removed from a torque converter.

Converter Operation

When the engine starts, the transmission pump rapidly fills and pressurizes the converter. The impeller is driven by the engine and turns at crankshaft speed. The turbine is splined to the transmission input shaft. When a gear is selected by the driver, the input shaft becomes locked to the output shaft of the transmission through the various gears, bands, and clutches in the transmission. Centrifugal force throws fluid between the impeller vanes outward, around the back of the guide ring in a forward direction. This is because of the shape of the housing and the curvature of the vanes. With the engine idling, little torque is transferred from the impeller to the turbine, as the fluid flow is too slow. When the engine accelerates, higher impeller speed discharges the fluid across and against the turbine vanes with greater force, causing the turbine to begin to spin and transferring torque to the input shaft of the transmission.

The fluid, still at high velocity, now flows between the turbine vanes. The fluid leaves the turbine in a direction opposite to impeller rotation due to the curvature of the turbine vanes. In a fluid coupler, this fluid flow would then strike the impeller in the opposite direction of impeller rotation, reducing efficiency and torque. In a torque converter, the stator redirects the fluid so that it reenters the impeller in the same direction as impeller rotation **FIGURE 14-13**. The energy that was left in the fluid after turning the turbine is recycled and helps to spin the impeller, which allows the engine to turn faster. This process creates torque multiplication. During torque multiplication, the stator remains stationary while the turbine and impeller spin.

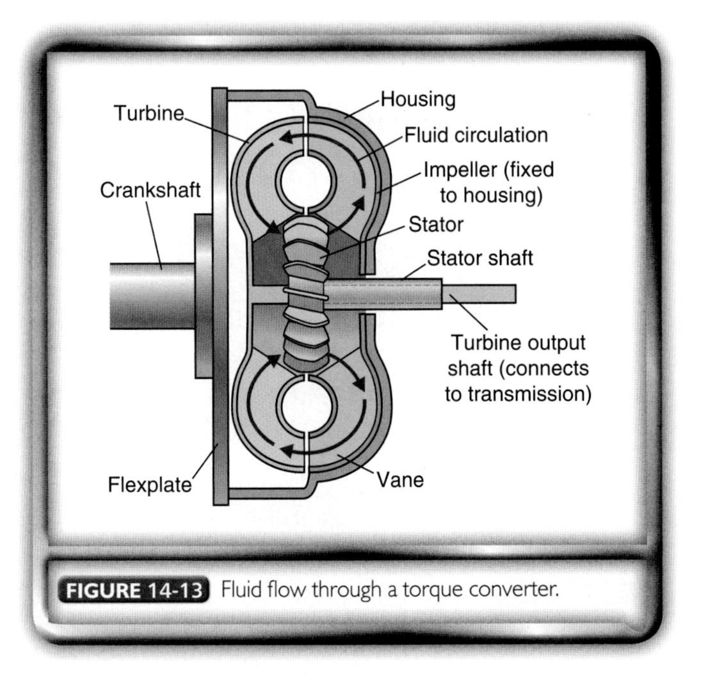
Turbine
Crankshaft
Flexplate
Housing
Fluid circulation
Impeller (fixed to housing)
Stator
Stator shaft
Turbine output shaft (connects to transmission)
Vane

FIGURE 14-13 Fluid flow through a torque converter.

Heat Exchanger

Torque converter slip and loss of power through the transmission produce heat, which must be dissipated. At stall, a lot of engine output is converted into heat, bringing the oil operating temperature closer to its boiling point. Excessive temperature can produce cavitation bubbles in the fluid, which reduce converter efficiency. It can also shorten the life of the transmission fluid greatly. Too hot and it oxidizes; too cold and it does not lubricate as well. Most automatic transmission vehicles use a heat exchanger, sometimes called a transmission cooler, in one tank of the radiator. In this way, the transmission fluid can be cooled, but the engine coolant at the outlet side of the radiator will prevent it from overcooling the transmission fluid.

Fluid flows from the pump to the converter. Since the converter creates a lot of heat, the fluid then flows through the heat exchanger before returning to the transmission where it is used to lubricate the planetary gears and operate the transmission. Heavy-duty vehicles or those with towing packages installed have an extra external transmission cooler installed in front of the radiator to help cool the fluid. When using an external transmission fluid cooler, it is generally agreed that it is best to run the transmission fluid through the external cooler first and then through the cooler in the radiator. Doing so prevents overcooling of the transmission fluid.

TECHNICIAN TIP

If installing an additional transmission cooler onto a vehicle, the lines should be set up so the fluid flows from the converter to the add-on transmission cooler in front of the radiator. From the add-on cooler, it should flow to the factory heat exchanger in the radiator before returning to the transmission. This arrangement allows the fluid to warm up in cold operating conditions to prevent excessive transmission wear and harsh shifting.

Some manufacturers incorporate a transmission fluid warmer that uses engine coolant to warm up the automatic transmission fluid (ATF) quickly and keep it from cooling too much. These warmers are often found on vehicles with CVTs. They help reduce the viscosity of the ATF, which reduces the friction losses of the thicker ATF. At least one manufacturer routes coolant to the warmer assembly, which provides heat to warm up the ATF. The warmer assembly uses a thermostatic valve to direct the flow of ATF through the heated warmer assembly when the ATF is cold, or bypass the heated warmer assembly if the ATF is hot.

Lock-up Converters

Under a drive condition, the impeller and turbine generally never achieve a 1:1 speed ratio. The turbine will almost always spin slightly slower than the impeller. This means that the converter is typically slipping approximately 5% to 10% when comparing engine speed to transmission input speed. During the late 1970s and early 1980s, manufacturers added a lock-up function to the torque converter in their vehicles to deal with this slippage condition.

In a lock-up converter, the impeller and turbine are locked together, when conditions are suitable, to provide a 1:1 drive from the engine to the transmission input shaft. Lock-up normally occurs at higher road speeds and when the vehicle is under light load. Inside the torque converter, there is a large piston that has friction material bonded to its surface near its outside diameter FIGURE 14-14. When the piston is applied with hydraulic fluid from the transmission, the piston and friction material are pressed against the front housing of the torque converter, locking the turbine to the housing. This provides a 1:1 connection from the engine to transmission, with no slippage between components. The lock-up torque converter also helps to reduce transmission fluid temperatures, which in some cases requires an ATF warmer system.

Torsional damper springs are built into the piston assembly. When the clutch is engaged, these springs dampen engine and drive line torsional vibrations. Without these damper springs, every power pulse of the pistons would be felt by the driver as excessive engine vibration.

Gear Train—Principles of Operation

Most automatic transmissions use hydraulic pressure to apply individual clutches and bands in order to hold components of one or more planetary gear sets, called the gear train. A planetary gear set is a device with several gears assembled in a compact design. The planetary gear set has a **sun gear** in the center with smaller **planetary gears** revolving around the sun gear FIGURE 14-15. These planetary gears are held together in a **planet carrier**. The planetary gears revolve inside a larger **ring gear** that wraps around the outside of the whole planetary gear set. When an individual component of a planetary gear set is prevented from turning, one of three gear ratios results: forward torque reduction with a speed increase (overdrive), forward speed reduction with a torque increase, or reverse. Combining two or more planetary gear sets (compound planetary gear sets) creates the needed gear ratios, or speeds, for the modern transmission.

Gear Ratio/Torque Multiplication

Gear ratio refers to the difference in diameter between the driving (input) gear and the driven (output) gear. When you loosen a bolt, what tool do you use? Do you use a socket alone? No, that would not give you much leverage. Instead, you place a long ratchet or breaker bar onto the end of the socket to increase the amount of leverage. This increase in leverage is the same as torque multiplication in a gear ratio.

FIGURE 14-16 shows a gear with 8 teeth driving a gear with 24 teeth. The smaller drive gear will be able to turn three times before the large driven gear turns once. In this scenario, we have created a gear ratio of three to one (3:1). This gear ratio will create three times more torque, but the driven gear will turn at three times less speed and distance, otherwise known as gear reduction. If we were to put 100 foot-pounds (ft-lb; 136 Nm) of torque into this gear system, we would get 300 ft-lb (407 Nm) of torque out, but at one-third the speed and distance.

FIGURE 14-14 A lock-up torque converter piston with friction material bonded to the back of the piston.

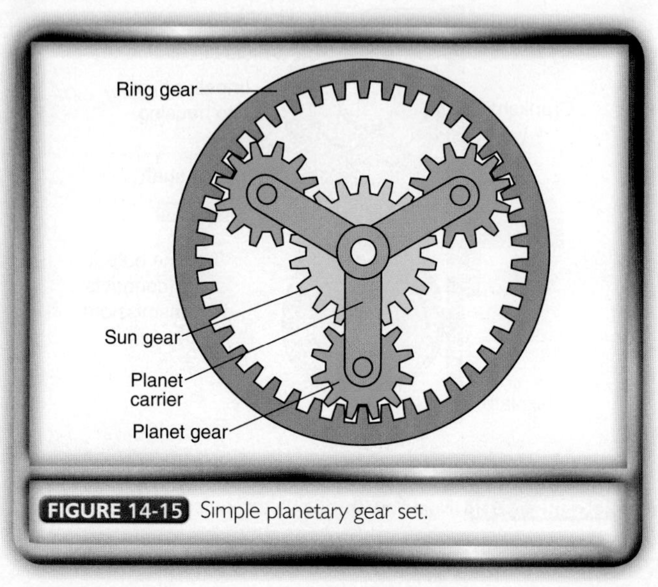
Ring gear
Sun gear
Planet carrier
Planet gear

FIGURE 14-15 Simple planetary gear set.

If we have a gear with 15 teeth driving a gear with only 10 teeth, we will have a gear ratio of 0.67:1. This is an **overdrive** ratio. It will result in less torque being transmitted to the wheels, but will increase wheel speed. Any ratio of less than 1:1 is considered an overdrive ratio. Overdrive ratios are typically used to increase fuel economy while traveling at highway speeds by slowing the engine speed.

A typical automatic transmission will have four or more forward gear ratios and one reverse. Transmission gear ratios vary by transmission and manufacturer but are often approximately 3:1 for first gear, resulting in a large increase in torque, but a major decrease in speed. Second gear is a ratio of approximately 1.75:1, still resulting in a torque increase with a smaller speed decrease. In most transmissions, third gear is a 1:1, or direct, ratio. A direct ratio means that power is sent directly through the transmission with no torque increase or speed increase. Fourth gear is commonly an overdrive ratio of approximately 0.80:1. This ratio means that the engine is turning more slowly than the output shaft of the transmission in order to increase fuel economy. Reverse is often a ratio of approximately 2:1, resulting in a torque increase with a speed reduction.

Early transmissions were simple two-speed automatics with a low gear and a direct gear. As engine size in vehicles decreased, the two gear ratios were no longer adequate to propel the vehicles being produced. Three-speed automatic transmissions became the norm through the early 1980s, when four-speed automatics were installed in vehicles to improve fuel economy. Now with an even greater need to increase fuel economy, manufacturers have turned to adding more gear ratios to their transmissions. Many vehicles are leaving the factory today with five- and six-speed transmissions, with one manufacturer even using an eight-speed automatic. Even with all of these gears, the basic principle of gear reduction and overdrive remains the same.

Gear Set Styles

Individual gears in automatic transmissions are typically one of three types: helical cut, spur (also known as straight-cut gears), or hypoid gears FIGURE 14-17.

Spur gears were used in early transmissions due to ease of manufacturing and lower cost. Spur gears also tend to be much louder and do not offer as much strength as the other types of gears; for this reason, manufacturers usually use helical gears for passenger vehicles.

Helical-cut gears (or simply "helical gears") are cut on a spiral around the axis of the shaft. Helical gears offer the benefit of always having more than one gear tooth in contact with the driving gear, thus increasing the strength. Helical gears are quieter than spur gears but have more thrust motion due to the spiral cut of the gear teeth. Because of this increased thrust, helical gears in an automatic transmission must have a method to control the amount of thrust movement, such as **thrust washers** or **thrust bearings**.

Hypoid gears are often used in the final drive of front-wheel drive transaxles and also in conventional final drives on rear-wheel drive vehicles. Hypoid gears are often used to change the direction of power flow by 90 degrees. They are a type of helical gear in which the axes of the two gears are not aligned FIGURE 14-18. These gears therefore have the thrust action of helical gears along with a scraping action between the teeth. Due to this scraping action and very high pressure on the gear teeth, hypoid gears require a special lubricant to prevent damage.

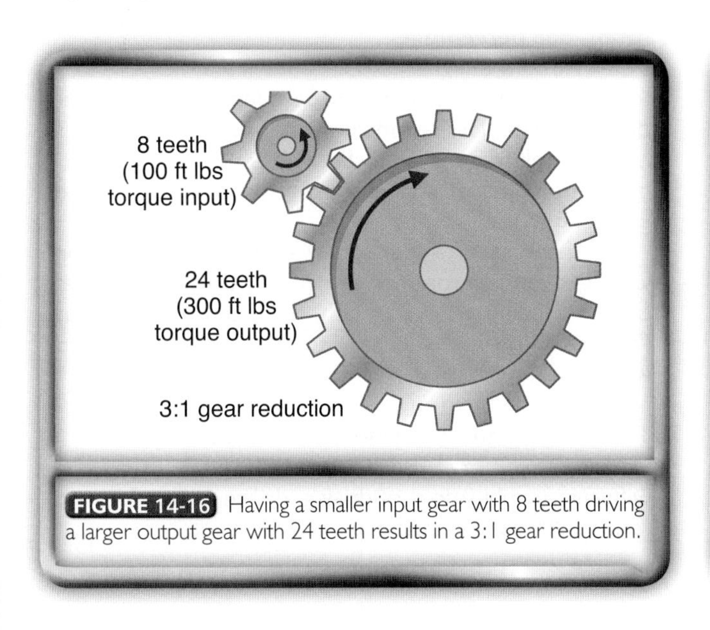
8 teeth
(100 ft lbs
torque input)
24 teeth
(300 ft lbs
torque output)
3:1 gear reduction

FIGURE 14-16 Having a smaller input gear with 8 teeth driving a larger output gear with 24 teeth results in a 3:1 gear reduction.

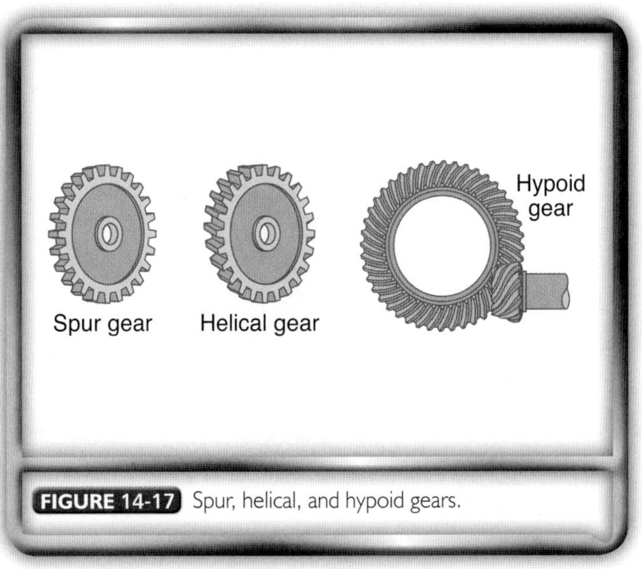
Spur gear
Helical gear
Hypoid
gear

FIGURE 14-17 Spur, helical, and hypoid gears.

Planetary Gear Sets

A simple planetary gear set is the backbone of most modern automatic transmissions. One of their biggest benefits is that they are in constant mesh. And since they involve multiple gears, a variety of speeds can be obtained without having to take them out of mesh or put them back in mesh. As described earlier and shown in FIGURE 14-19, planetary gear sets use either helical gears or straight-cut gears. A simple planetary gear set contains a sun gear in the center with multiple revolving planetary gears around it. The planetary gears are held in place by the planet carrier. On the outside edge of the planetary gears is the ring gear. By holding one of the components (planet carrier, sun, or ring) and driving one of the other components, we can create up to six separate gear ratios—four in the forward direction (two reduction and two overdrive) and two in the reverse direction (one reduction and one overdrive). If any two components are locked together, we end up with another speed—1:1, called direct drive.

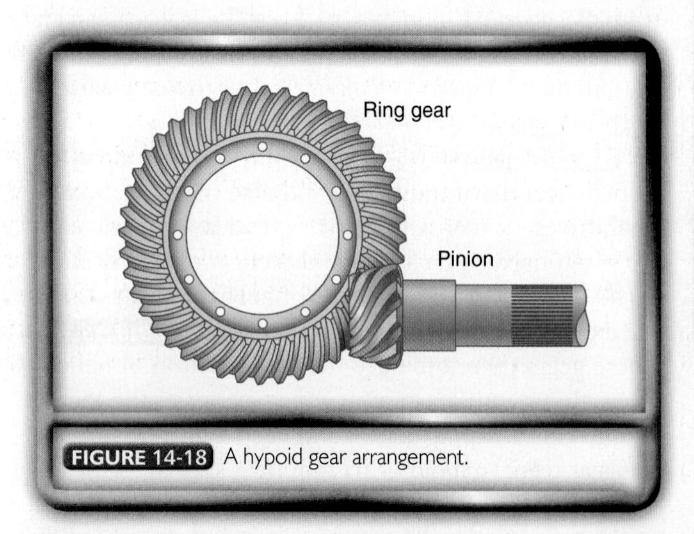
Ring gear
Pinion

FIGURE 14-18 A hypoid gear arrangement.

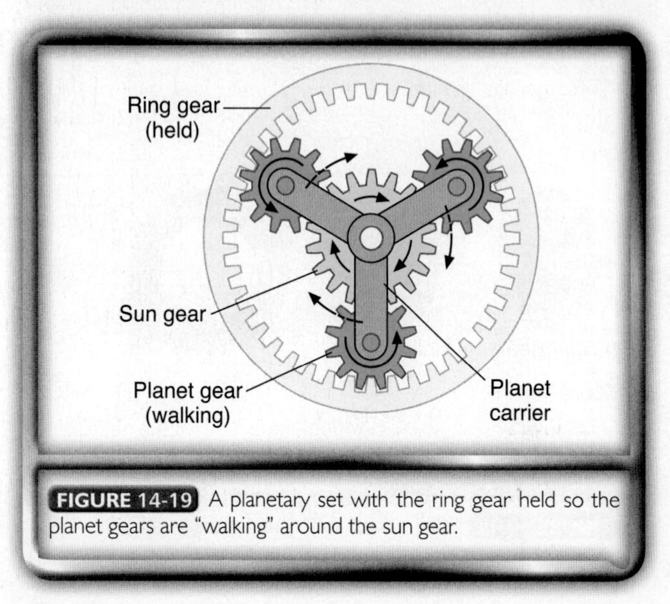
Ring gear (held)
Sun gear
Planet gear (walking)
Planet carrier

FIGURE 14-19 A planetary set with the ring gear held so the planet gears are "walking" around the sun gear.

Just because a planetary gear can obtain four forward gears and two reverse gears does not mean the manufacturer designs the transmission to use each of those ratios. In reality, vehicle manufacturers can obtain only three ratios from any particular planetary gear set due to constraints on transmission design. Manufacturers have to design the planetary gear sets to get the required number of gear ratios as well as gear ratio splits to work with the particular application. The benefit of designing transmissions with planetary gears is that if you need more gear ratios than you have, you can combine multiple planetary gear sets to create the needed ratios FIGURE 14-20.

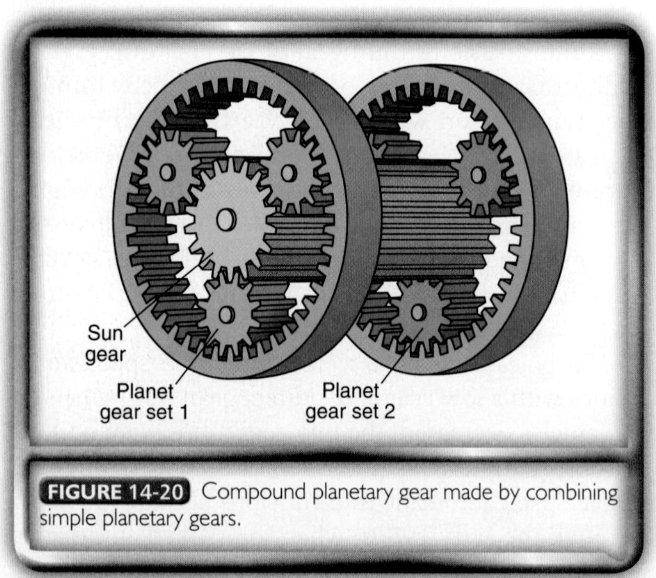
Sun gear
Planet gear set 1
Planet gear set 2

FIGURE 14-20 Compound planetary gear made by combining simple planetary gears.

Applied Math

AM-43: Direct/Inverse Variation: The technician can solve problems requiring the use of fractions, decimals, ratios, and percentages.

When working out gear combinations, it may be necessary to calculate gear ratios based on counting the number of gear teeth. This is simple in the case of differentials and manual transmissions, but the planetary gear sets used in automatic transmissions require more involved calculations.

In the case of a four-speed automatic transmission with an overdrive top gear obtained by driving the planet carrier, the sun gear (30 teeth) held, and the ring gear (72 teeth) driven, the formula to calculate the gear ratio would be:

$$1 / (1 + \text{Sun}/\text{Ring}).$$

The effective ratio is therefore calculated as:

$$1 / (1 + 30/72), \text{ or } 0.71:1.$$

Different combinations of driving, driven, and held gears require different formulae to calculate ratios.

Holding/Driving Gears

As we stated earlier, to create a gear ratio we need to hold one member of a planetary gear set and drive another. There are three basic holding devices used in transmissions today: bands, multidisc clutches, and one-way clutches. These holding devices will either lock two turning members of the transmission together or lock a member to the transmission housing to prevent it from spinning.

The band is a friction-lined steel belt that wraps around the outside of a drum inside the automatic transmission FIGURE 14-21. When a servo applies pressure to one end of the band, it closes the diameter of the band, squeezing the drum and preventing it from turning. The drum is then locked to one member of a planetary gear set.

Multidisc clutches are unique in that they not only can be used to hold a member of the planetary gear set, but they are the only type of component that can be used to drive a member of the planetary gear set. In a multidisc clutch, individual friction discs, often called frictions, are stacked between smooth steel plates, often called steels. Both the frictions and the steels have a hollow center allowing them to wrap around the outside of a hub or drum connected to a member of the planetary gear set FIGURE 14-22. The steels typically have splines, or teeth, on the outside edge to hold them in place inside a drum, while the frictions have splines or teeth on the inside edge to hold them to a member of the planetary gear set. When the steels and frictions are forced together by a hydraulic piston, the separately revolving steels and frictions match speed and lock the drum or hub to the member of the planetary gear set.

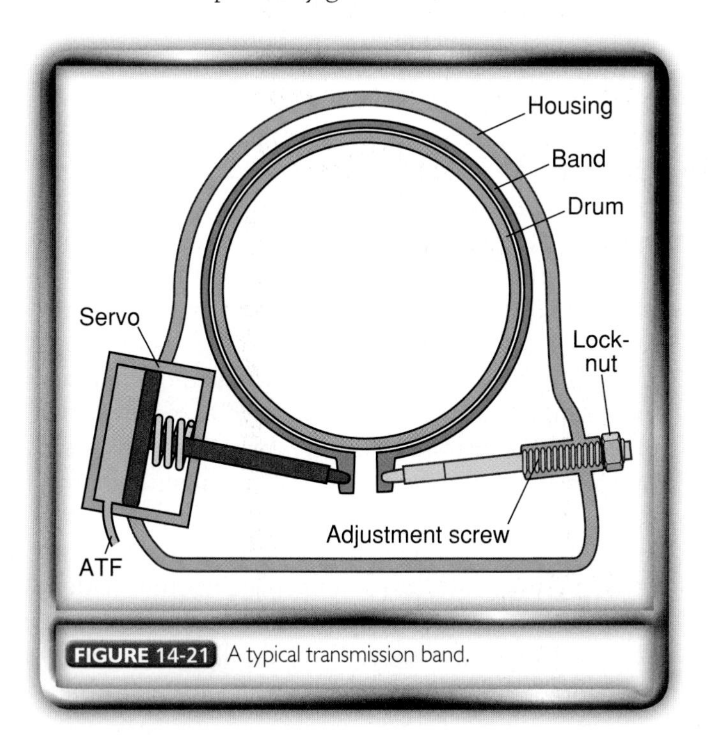
Housing
Band
Drum
Servo
Lock-nut
Adjustment screw
ATF

FIGURE 14-21 A typical transmission band.

FIGURE 14-22 Typical steel and friction discs from a multidisc clutch assembly.

One-way clutches can be either one-way rollers or sprags. Both the one-way roller and the sprag operate on the same principle, but sprags have a greater torque-holding capacity. On both the one-way roller and the sprag, an inside hub is allowed to spin freely in one direction, but spinning the hub in the opposite direction will cause the rollers or sprags to become wedged in place FIGURE 14-23. This wedging action prevents rotation of the hub. In the one-way roller clutch, each roller has a waved compression spring that pushes the roller toward the narrow end of the wedge. Rotating the hub in the opposite direction locks the outer race onto the rollers wedged between the two races. Thus, a one-way clutch allows rotation in one direction but prevents rotation in the opposite direction.

Automatic Transmission Fluids

ATF is a specialized fluid that has been designed for a specific job. The ATF must be able to transfer heat from the internal components of the transmission to the transmission cooler in order to prevent damaging the internal seals of the transmission. The fluid must also lubricate the internal gears, bearings, and bushings of the transmission, yet have a large enough coefficient of friction to allow the clutches to grab and not slip. Coefficient of

TECHNICIAN TIP

When building a performance transmission, it is beneficial on some transmissions to increase the number of individual rollers or sprags to increase holding power. Common performance transmissions have multiple versions of one-way rollers and sprags available.

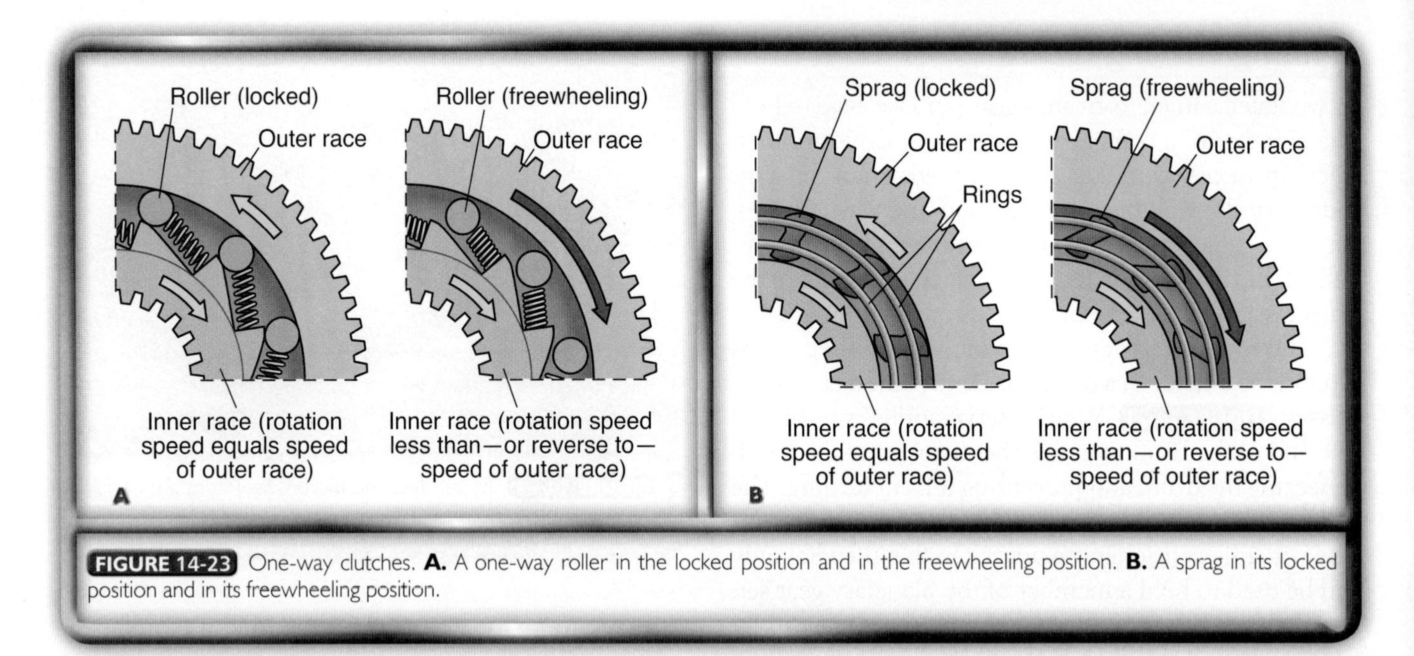
Roller (locked)
Outer race
Inner race (rotation speed equals speed of outer race)
Roller (freewheeling)
Outer race
Inner race (rotation speed less than—or reverse to—speed of outer race)
A
Sprag (locked)
Outer race
Rings
Inner race (rotation speed equals speed of outer race)
Sprag (freewheeling)
Outer race
Inner race (rotation speed less than—or reverse to—speed of outer race)
B

FIGURE 14-23 One-way clutches. **A.** A one-way roller in the locked position and in the freewheeling position. **B.** A sprag in its locked position and in its freewheeling position.

friction is the force required to move two sliding surfaces over each other. ATF fluids are typically dyed red for easy identification and contain many additives such as:

- *Rust and corrosion inhibitors:* These additives prevent the internal parts of the transmission from developing rust and corrosion on metal components. Rust and corrosion can affect the shift quality and longevity of the transmission. As rust particles break off, they become an abrasive in the fluid, causing increased wear.
- *Friction modifiers:* Manufacturers add friction modifiers to the fluid to ensure that the fluid has the proper coefficient of friction in order to produce the desired shift quality. A fluid with a lower coefficient of friction will produce softer, longer shifts, causing an increase in clutch slippage. A fluid with a higher coefficient of friction will cause shorter, harsher shifts, reducing clutch slippage but increasing drive line shock.
- *Seal conditioners:* These additives are designed to help protect the seals inside a transmission and cause the seals to swell slightly to help prevent leaks and clutch slippage.
- *Detergents:* ATF has a large amount of detergent to prevent dirt and other foreign particles from becoming trapped inside the transmission. The detergent causes the dirt and other particles to be attracted to the fluid so they transfer with the fluid. When the fluid passes through the filter, the large particles become trapped in the filter; the small particles are removed during the next transmission fluid change.
- *Antifoam:* These additives help to prevent foaming of the transmission fluid. When moving parts spin through a fluid, they tend to produce air bubbles. These air bubbles can quickly multiply and become foam. Foam is compressible and can cause a transmission to slip because insufficient pressure is applied to the clutches.
- *Viscosity modifiers:* These additives are similar to the engine oil additives that allow us to have multiviscosity engine oils such as 5W-30. These additives allow the fluid to remain thin when the temperature is cold and prevent the fluid from becoming too thin as the transmission fluid warms up.

ATFs can be mineral oil based or a synthetic lubricant. Many late-model vehicles recommend a specific synthetic ATF. Originally, most manufacturers used and recommended General Motors and Ford Motor Company fluids. In the past few decades, most auto manufacturers have developed their own fluids for use in their transmissions. This practice has required repair facilities and quick lube shops to carry many different types of fluids. Some shops carry a few major types of fluids and use those in every vehicle, but that is not recommended as it may cause undesirable transmission operation and may void the transmission warranty. Several vehicle manufacturers have published technical service bulletins (TSBs) related to incorrect fluid use and the negative effects on the transmission. Research all applicable information, including service history and precautions.

ATF needs to be changed periodically to remove dirt and contaminants from the transmission. Technicians used to tell if the transmission fluid needed to be changed by looking at and smelling the fluid. If the fluid was dark or smelled burnt, it needed to be changed. You cannot determine the condition of modern ATF by looks and smell. Some newer synthetic fluids will have a burnt smell when they are brand new and are often darker than mineral-based ATF. To check ATF for contaminants, drop a few drops of transmission fluid onto a white paper towel. The fluid will spread out on the paper towel, but the contaminants will remain where the fluid was dropped.

Flex Plate and Ring Gear

On an automatic transmission there is no flywheel; rather, there is a thin lightweight steel **flex plate**. The flex plate bolts to the rear crankshaft flange in the same manner as a flywheel would. The torque converter is bolted to the flex plate with three or more bolts. Because there is no thrust force of a clutch as in a manual transmission, the flex plate can be significantly lighter than a traditional flywheel FIGURE 14-24. Also, the large mass of the torque converter dampens the engine pulses in a similar manner to a flywheel.

Wrapped around the outside edge of the flex plate is a ring gear that is used when starting the vehicle. The starter pinion gear moves out to contact the ring gear, and the starter motor cranks the engine over when the driver turns the ignition switch to the crank position. This ring gear is not typically a serviceable, separate part of the flex plate. If the ring gear wears out, the entire flex plate will typically need to be replaced. Ring gears on flywheels are often available as separate parts from the flywheel and can be serviced. In some applications, manufacturers weld the ring gear to the torque converter instead of the flex plate.

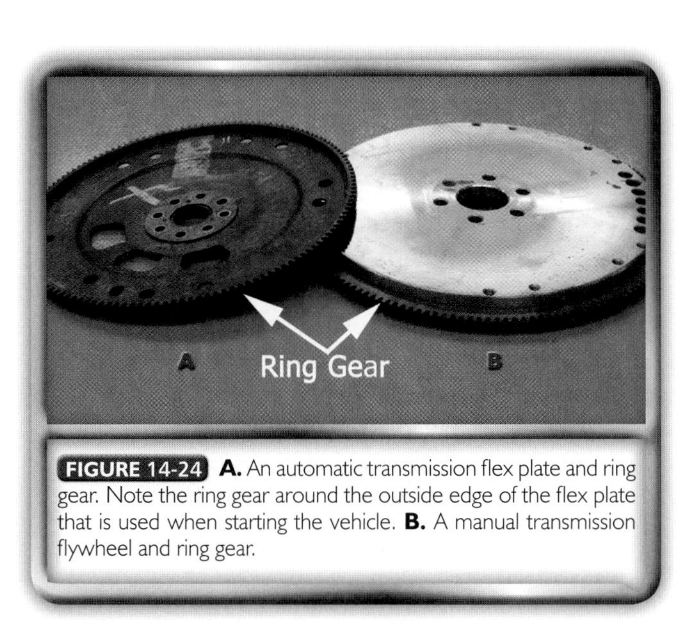
A
Ring Gear
B

FIGURE 14-24 **A.** An automatic transmission flex plate and ring gear. Note the ring gear around the outside edge of the flex plate that is used when starting the vehicle. **B.** A manual transmission flywheel and ring gear.

> **TECHNICIAN TIP**
>
> When a faulty engine or transmission is suspected because of knocking noises, double-check that the flex plate bolts are tight. Loose bolts on the flex plate can sound like a knocking engine. Also, a cracked flex plate can cause a knocking noise that can sound like a defective rod bearing. In some cases, the entire center of the flex plate can break free of the rest of the flex plate, preventing the engine from cranking over when the starter is engaged. It is easy for a technician to think that the engine has a broken crankshaft because the front pulley does not turn when the engine is cranked, when in reality, the outer portion of the flex plate is spinning on the broken center piece.

Case, Extension Housing, and Pan

Modern automatic transmission cases are made of lightweight aluminum and alloys. Early transmission cases were sometimes made of cast iron. When a transmission is new, the manufacturer typically leaves the transmission case uncoated. When the transmission is rebuilt, the rebuilders often paint the transmission a particular color. This serves two purposes: (1) It helps identify a transmission that was previously rebuilt, and (2) it helps seal the transmission after it has been cleaned. Aluminum can become porous after excessive cleaning of the case with detergents and solvents. The paint helps to fill in any case porosity.

On the rear or output side of the transmission, there is an aluminum housing called the **extension housing**. The extension housing is usually bolted to the transmission case with a **gasket** between the housing and the case. The extension housing may contain the vehicle speed sensor drive gear or speedometer drive gear and/or a governor assembly to measure vehicle speed FIGURE 14-25. Inside the end of the extension housing is the extension housing bushing that supports the driveshaft. The extension housing on most four-wheel drive pick-ups and SUVs has a surface that bolts the transmission up to the transfer case.

On the bottom of most transmissions is a sheet metal or aluminum pan. Inside this pan, the transmission filter and possibly the transmission valve body are located. Most front-wheel drive transaxles have a second pan called the side pan, which houses the valve body FIGURE 14-26. The bottom transmission pan is often removed during routine transmission fluid service to change the filter and clean a magnet, if equipped, located inside the pan that catches small particles of steel and iron that are floating in the

Speedometer
cable

FIGURE 14-25 A typical extension housing with the speedometer cable connected.

Side oil pan
Bottom oil pan

FIGURE 14-26 A common front-wheel drive transaxle showing the bottom oil pan and side pan.

fluid. The transmission pan holds about half of the transmission fluid when the vehicle is off. When the vehicle is running, the pump draws fluid from the transmission pan to supply lubrication and pressure to the different parts of the transmission.

Gaskets and Seals

Gaskets are used throughout the automatic transmission. Some gaskets are made from paper, fiber, or cork material that must be replaced every time a component is removed. Other gaskets are a reuseable type with neoprene inserted into a plastic housing. Reuseable gaskets are fairly common for transmission pan gaskets where the part is frequently removed for routine service. Some reusable gaskets have built-in torque limiters. These torque limiters are metal sleeves built in the gasket around the bolt holes to help prevent overtorquing of the gasket.

There are many types of internal seals for an automatic transmission FIGURE 14-27. These internal seals are often the root cause of a transmission slipping and eventually failing. All seals need to be properly lubricated when assembling the transmission to prevent premature failure and to help with installation. Seals are lubricated with ATF, petroleum jelly, or automatic transmission assembly lubricant. Do not use grease to lubricate the seals, as grease can clog up the internal passages of the transmission when the vehicle is put back into service. A description of seals used in a transmission system follows:

- *Square-cut seals:* Square-cut seals can be made from neoprene rubber or Teflon. Teflon seals require special handling and will be discussed separately. Square-cut seals are similar to the seal found inside a brake caliper. They are sometimes located on the piston of a multiple disc clutch.
- *Lip seals:* Lip seals are made from neoprene. Lip seals have a greater sealing ability than a square-cut seal because when pressure is applied to the back of the seal, it forces the seal out against the inside of the clutch drum. These seals are similar to the cup seals located inside a drum brake wheel cylinder. Lip seals can be easily damaged by careless installation and infrequent fluid and filter changes. Lip seals are typically used inside multi-disc clutch assemblies on the piston.
- *Locking seal:* The locking seal is made from cast iron and is similar to a piston compression ring except that the ends overlap and lock together. Locking seals are typically used between the front pump and the rotating clutch drums.
- *O-rings:* O-rings are made from neoprene rubber and are often found sealing external parts of the transmission such as a speedometer cable assembly or governor cover. O-rings can also be used on accumulators and servo covers.
- *Teflon seals:* Teflon seals come in several styles—continuous, butt cut, scarf cut, and step joint. The continuous seal provides the best sealing action and should be used whenever possible, but it does require special tools for proper installation. Teflon seals have replaced the locking seals on most modern transmissions and are found sealing the front pump to input shafts and clutch drums.

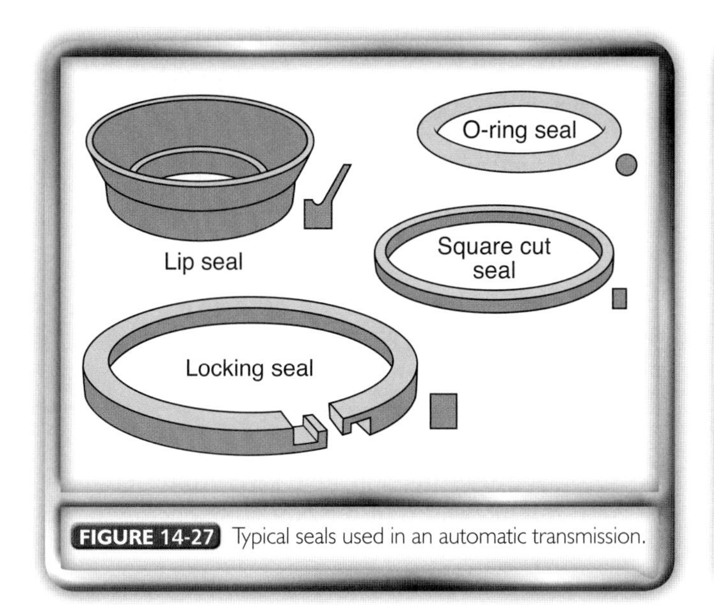
O-ring seal
Lip seal
Square cut seal
Locking seal

FIGURE 14-27 Typical seals used in an automatic transmission.

FIGURE 14-28 A parking pawl assembly on a late-model CVT transmission.

Parking Pawl Assembly

Most automatic transmissions for passenger vehicles include an internal parking mechanism. When the driver shifts the transmission into park, a lever, called a parking pawl, is forced into notches cut into a hardened steel drum on the output shaft of the transmission FIGURE 14-28. This parking pawl prevents rotation of the output shaft when it is engaged. The parking pawl is often operated through a spring in case the driver accidentally places the vehicle into park while it is still moving. In this scenario, the vehicle will make a loud ratcheting noise as the parking pawl bounces against the rotating notches of the output shaft drum. The spring is designed to help minimize damage to the parking pawl and the output shaft. The spring also allows the driver to place the vehicle shift selector into park even when the parking paw does not quite align with the notches in the drum. If this occurs, the gear shift is placed in park but the vehicle may need to roll an inch or two for the parking pawl to engage.

TECHNICIAN TIP

Often, Teflon seals are placed in boiling water prior to assembly to help expand the seal, while the component the seal is being installed on may be placed in the freezer to contract the part.

Wrap-up

Ready for Review

- Automatic transmissions are now standard equipment in vehicles.
- Automatic transmissions contain planetary gear sets.
- Automatic transmissions have four or more forward gear ratios and one reverse ratio.
- Typical forward gear ratios are as follows: first gear, 3:1; second gear, 1.75:1; third gear, 1:1; and fourth gear, 0.80:1.
- Adding more gear ratios to the transmission boosts fuel economy.
- Automatic transmissions select and shift gears without driver input and can couple or uncouple from the engine as necessary.
- Types of automatic transmissions include conventional, transaxle, dual clutch, continuously variable, dual shaft, and hybrid (series or parallel).
- Conventional automatic transmissions have planetary gear sets, connect to the engine via torque converter, and use holding devices to stop one or more parts of the planetary gear.
- Transaxle transmissions add a differential and final drive gear to a standard transmission.
- Dual-clutch transmissions use two wet clutches instead of a standard torque converter.
- Continuously variable transmissions use two moveable pulleys rather than typical gears.
- Honda and Saturn vehicles use dual-shaft transmissions that have a main shaft and a countershaft, as well as multidisc clutch packs.
- Hybrid vehicles often use series transmissions, in which an electric motor supplements power to the transmission.
- A hybrid vehicle may use a parallel hybrid transmission, in which either the engine or an electric motor can power the transmission.
- Automatic transmission gears are typically helical (most commonly used), spur (straight cut), or hypoid.
- Planetary gear sets use either helical- or straight-cut gears and are comprised of three components: planet carrier, sun gear, and ring gear.
- Bands, multidisc clutches, and one-way clutches are the three basic holding devices used in transmissions.
- Automatic transmission fluid (ATF) transfers heat from the internal transmission components to the transmission cooler.
- ATFs are oil-based or synthetic and may contain these additives: rust and corrosion inhibitors, friction modifiers, seal conditioners, detergents, antifoam, and viscosity modifiers.
- Components of an automatic transmission include the flex plate and ring gear; case, extension housing, and pan; gaskets and seals; and parking pawl assembly.
- On automatic transmissions, the flywheel is replaced with a flex plate, with a ring gear wrapped around the outside edge.
- Gaskets may be made of paper, fiber, cork, or neoprene (which may be reusable).
- Types of internal seals include square cut, lip, locking, O-ring, and Teflon.
- A torque convertor works with the transmission to select the proper gear to meet the speed and power demands of the vehicle.
- A single-stage torque converter contains an impeller, a turbine, and a stator.
- A torque converter clutch is used to lock the turbine to the impeller when the vehicle is operating under light loads, to improve fuel economy.

Key Terms

band A metal band with friction material bonded to one side. The band is contracted around a drum to stop the drum from spinning.

coefficient of friction A value assigned to materials to describe the amount of friction when two objects slide against each other.

continuously variable transmission (CVT) A transmission that does not have conventional set gear ratios, but is instead infinitely variable between the transmission's lowest gear ratio and highest gear ratio.

dual-clutch transmission A type of automatically shifting manual transmission in which two separate input shafts are connected to their own clutch. Shifting of the gears alternates between the two input shafts.

extension housing A component of the automatic transmission housing that covers the output shaft of the transmission. The extension housing also supports the end of the driveshaft and may hold components such as the vehicle speed sensor, speedometer drive assembly, and governor assembly.

flex plate Typically a circular steel plate that is bolted to the rear of the crankshaft. The torque converter is bolted to this flex plate. The outside of the flex plate will often have a ring gear that the starter motor engages with to crank the engine over.

fluid coupler A type of hydraulic coupling used on vintage vehicles to connect and transfer power from the engine to the transmission.

gasket A rubber, cork, or paper spacer that goes between two parts to seal the gap between the parts.

gear ratio The ratio of the size or teeth of one gear compared to the size or teeth of a mating gear.

helical-cut gear A type of gear in which the teeth are cut in a spiral down the axis of the gear.

hypoid gear A type of helical gear used to change the direction of motion 90 degrees. The axis of the input gear does not line up on the centerline of the output gear

multidisc clutch A type of holding device used by an automatic transmission to stop the movement of one component of a planetary gear set. It uses several thin friction discs and thin steel plates that are squeezed together when hydraulic pressure is applied to a piston in the clutch.

one-way clutch A type of holding device used by an automatic transmission to stop the movement of one component of a planetary gear set. It allows free spinning in one direction but will lock up when the part attempts to spin in the opposite direction.

overdrive Any gear ratio that results in a torque reduction with a speed increase. Overdrive is used on vehicles to reduce the engine speed when traveling at highway speed in order to save fuel.

parallel hybrid drive train A type of hybrid transmission in which power can flow from either a gasoline engine or an electric motor and any combination of the two.

planet carrier The device that holds the planet gears in place, keeping them equally spaced.

planetary gears The small gears in a planetary gear set that revolve around the sun gear.

power-splitting transmission (PST) A type of hybrid transmission that splits the power flow going to the wheels from one or more electric motors and an internal combustion engine.

ring gear The outer gear of a planetary gear set. The ring gear wraps around the outside of the planetary gears.

series hybrid drive train A type of hybrid transmission in which power flows from the engine through an electric motor. The electric motor supplements the power from the engine to the wheels.

series-parallel hybrid drive train A type of hybrid drive train that can function as both a series hybrid and parallel hybrid. That means the gasoline engine can turn a generator that can be used to power an electric motor. The gasoline engine can also drive the vehicle directly through the transmission. And the electric motor can work in parallel with the gasoline engine to drive the vehicle.

spur gear A type of gear in which the teeth of the gear are cut in a straight line down the axis of the gear.

standard torque converter A hydraulic coupling device consisting of an impeller, turbine, stator, and housing; located between the engine and the transmission.

sun gear The center gear of a planetary gear set around which the other gears rotate.

thrust bearing Also called a Torrington bearing, a small roller bearing assembly with the rollers laid flat axially around the centerline of the bearing. The bearing is used to control forward and backward movement of a part in an automatic transmission.

thrust washer A small steel washer coated with bearing material. The thrust washer is used to control forward and backward movement of a part in an automatic transmission.

transaxle A type of transmission typically used in front-wheel drive vehicles in which the transmission also includes the differential and final drive gear.

ASE-Type Questions

1. Tech A says that the higher the numerical gear ratio (4:1), the more torque that will be applied to the wheels. Tech B says that the lower the numerical gear ratio (2:1), the more torque that will be applied to the wheels. Who is correct?
   a. Tech A
   b. Tech B
   c. Both A and B
   d. Neither A nor B
2. Tech A says that helical-cut gears are stronger than straight cut gears. Technician B says that helical-cut gears are noisier than straight cut gears. Who is correct?
   a. Tech A
   b. Tech B
   c. Both A and B
   d. Neither A nor B
3. Tech A says that a transaxle must have a type of differential assembly to allow the front wheels to turn at different speeds while driving around a curve. Tech B says that a conventional rear wheel drive vehicle will typically use a differential assembly that is located in the rear axle assembly. Who is correct?
   a. Tech A
   b. Tech B
   c. Both A and B
   d. Neither A nor B
4. Tech A says that a parallel hybrid transmission has two or more different devices to propel the vehicle. Tech B says that hybrid power splitting transmissions use 2 adjustable pulleys and a heavy metal belt. Who is correct?
   a. Tech A
   b. Tech B
   c. Both A and B
   d. Neither A nor B
5. Tech A says that planetary gear sets are used in all automatic transmissions. Tech B says that planetary gear sets are often combined together to create the needed gear ratios for a transmission. Who is correct?
   a. Tech A
   b. Tech B
   c. Both A and B
   d. Neither A nor B
6. Tech A says that the impeller is connected directly to the flex plate. Tech B says that the turbine shaft drives the front pump. Who is correct?
   a. Tech A
   b. Tech B
   c. Both A and B
   d. Neither A nor B
7. Tech A says that most automatic transmissions have a ring gear for the starter as part of the flex plate. Tech B says that the ring gear is typically replaceable (interference fit) on a flex plate. Who is correct?
   a. Tech A
   b. Tech B
   c. Both A and B
   d. Neither A nor B
8. Tech A says that a knocking noise in the engine/transmission area is typically a bad front pump in the transmission. Tech B says that a knocking noise in the engine/transmission area is more likely to be loose flex plate bolts. Who is correct?
   a. Tech A
   b. Tech B
   c. Both A and B
   d. Neither A nor B
9. Tech A says that painting a rebuilt transmission helps to identify it as being a rebuilt transmission. Tech B says that painting a rebuilt transmission prevents the housing from leaking due to case porosity. Who is correct?
   a. Tech A
   b. Tech B
   c. Both A and B
   d. Neither A nor B
10. Tech A says that the torque converters multiply the amount of torque transmitted from the engine to the transmission. Tech B says that the torque converter couples and uncouples the engine and transmission as the vehicle stops and starts in traffic. Who is correct?
    a. Tech A
    b. Tech B
    c. Both A and B
    d. Neither A nor B

CHAPTER 15

Know
See
Do
Prove

NATEF Tasks

Automatic Transmission and Transaxle General			Page
■ Check fluid level in a transmission or a transaxle equipped with a dipstick.	MLR	AST	382–383
■ Check fluid level in a transmission or a transaxle not equipped with a dipstick.	MLR	AST	382–383
■ Check transmission fluid condition; check for leaks.	MLR		383–384
■ Diagnose fluid loss and condition concerns; determine necessary action.		AST	383–384
In-Vehicle Transmission and Transaxle			
■ Drain and replace fluid and filters.	MLR	AST	384–385
■ Inspect for leakage; replace external seals, gaskets, and bushings.		AST	384–385
■ Inspect for leakage at external seals, gaskets, and bushings.	MLR		389–390
■ Inspect power train mounts.	MLR	AST	389–392
■ Inspect, adjust, and replace manual valve shift linkage, transmission range sensor/switch, and park/neutral position switch.	MLR	AST	391
Off-Vehicle Transmission and Transaxle			
■ Inspect, leak test, and flush or replace transmission/transaxle oil cooler, lines, and fittings.		AST	393–394

Servicing the Automatic Transmission/ Transaxle

KNOW
SEE
DO
PROVE

Knowledge Objectives

After reading this chapter, you will be able to:

1. Explain the process involved in servicing the automatic transmission, including:
   a. Diagnosing fluid loss and condition concerns. (p 383)
   b. Replacing the fluid and internal filter. (pp 384–386)
   c. Inspecting for leakage and replacing external seals, gaskets, and bushings. (pp 389–390)
   d. Inspecting, replacing, and aligning power train mounts. (pp 389–390)

KNOW
SEE
DO
PROVE

Skills Objectives

After reading this chapter, you will be able to:

1. Diagnose fluid loss and condition concerns, and check fluid level in transmissions with and without a dipstick. (p 383)
2. Replace the fluid and internal filter. (pp 384–385)
3. Inspect for leakage and replace external seals, gaskets, and bushings. (pp 389–390)
4. Inspect, replace, and align power train mounts. (pp 391–392)
5. Inspect, leak test, and flush or replace transmission cooler lines and fittings. (pp 393–394)

Introduction

Most automotive technicians will not perform complete rebuilding of automatic transmissions and transaxles in their shops, but it is very important for technicians to have a good understanding of how the transmission operates and the correct maintenance procedures. A technician who improperly services an automatic transmission can cause it to fail prematurely, leading to internal damage and a large expense for either the customer or shop.

Note, when we say *transmission*, we use the term generically to include transaxles also. When we use transaxle, we generally only mean transaxle. Readers should use their understanding of transmission and transaxle theory to understand the intended meaning. For example, if we are discussing ring and pinion backlash, that can only apply to a transaxle.

General Transmission Maintenance

Most automatic transmissions require some periodic preventive maintenance. This maintenance is designed to reduce transmission failure and save the customer money in the long run. It should include a visual inspection for leaks and a check of the transmission for proper fluid level. Periodic maintenance often also includes transmission fluid and filter replacement, which allows for the inspection of debris or contaminants in the bottom of the transmission pan.

Checking Transmission Fluid

Checking transmission fluid should be done at least at every oil change. Checking the fluid level in an automatic transmission is one of the first steps in diagnosing a transmission problem. Without the proper fluid level, the transmission will not shift properly and may suffer internal damage when the fluid level is too low or too high. If the fluid level is low, it is important to properly identify the source of fluid loss, which we will cover in more depth as we discuss the individual components.

For most, but not all, automatic transmissions, the fluid level is checked with the vehicle idling in park or neutral. Check the service information for the vehicle you are working on. It is important that the vehicle be on level ground to accurately measure the fluid level. When reading a transmission dipstick, it is important to realize that on most transmission dipsticks it only takes a pint of fluid to raise the level from the bottom of the crosshatched area or add mark to the full mark, unlike on the engine oil dipstick, which typically requires 1 quart FIGURE 15-1. In recent years, vehicle manufacturers have been eliminating the transmission dipstick on some of their vehicles. One of the reasons for this is to prevent the vehicle owner from installing the incorrect transmission fluid into a vehicle or overfilling the transmission. Another reason is that by eliminating the transmission dipstick there is one less entry point for dirt and contaminants to enter the transmission.

You Are the Automotive Technician

Today a customer visits your shop with a transmission concern in a 2009 Chevy Impala. He tells you that it takes about 5 seconds for it to go into gear the first thing in the morning, and sometimes the engine revolutions per minute (rpm) flare on an upshift when the engine is cold. You start by checking the fluid level and find it well below the safe mark. It leaves a dark center when placed on a white paper towel. You top it off with about 1.5 quarts of the proper transmission fluid to get it ready for a test-drive. During the test-drive, the customer is thrilled that the flaring on upshifts is gone and the transmission operation feels like normal. You tell the customer that you will still need to perform a visual inspection of the transmission. He authorizes you to perform a full inspection.

1. What might a visual inspection reveal on this vehicle?
2. Why did the transmission flare on upshifts when the engine was cold?
3. Assuming that the visual inspection doesn't find anything indicating that the transmission needs to be rebuilt, what service(s) should be recommended to the customer?

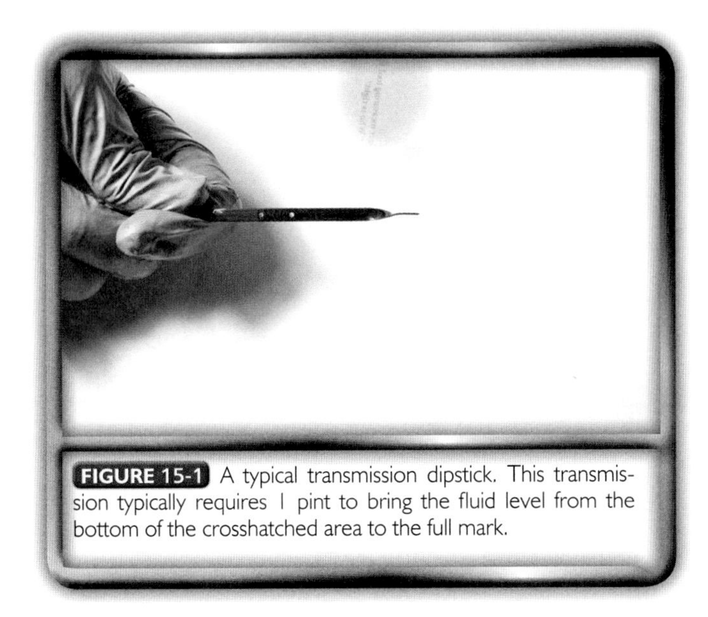

FIGURE 15-1 A typical transmission dipstick. This transmission typically requires 1 pint to bring the fluid level from the bottom of the crosshatched area to the full mark.

On transmissions without a dipstick, it is critical to check the service information for the proper procedure for checking the fluid level. Many late-model Ford and Toyota vehicles have what looks like a drain plug installed in the transmission pan. With the vehicle running, this plug is removed and fluid is forced up into the transmission through this hole. The hole has a tube attached to it inside the transmission. If the fluid level is too high, the fluid will simply drain back out. Allow any excess fluid to drain out of the hole, then reinstall the plug.

General Motors vehicles often have a threaded plug located on the transmission case that you remove while the vehicle is running to check the fluid level. Again, fluid is added until transmission fluid flows out of the hole. Allow the fluid to stop flowing, then reinstall the plug.

Locating Leaks

When fluids leak, they travel downward due to gravity and typically toward the back of the vehicle because of air movement during driving. This fluid travel can make finding a leak more challenging, especially if the vehicle has been leaking for a while. If the transmission has a large amount of oil and dirt on it, locating the leak might require cleaning the transmission case with an engine degreaser or pressure washer. Another option if the leak is hard to locate is to place a leak detection dye in the transmission fluid. After running the transmission for a few minutes, any leaking dye will be visible with a black light.

To diagnose fluid loss and condition concerns and to check fluid level in transmissions with and without a dipstick, follow the steps in SKILL DRILL 15-1. While

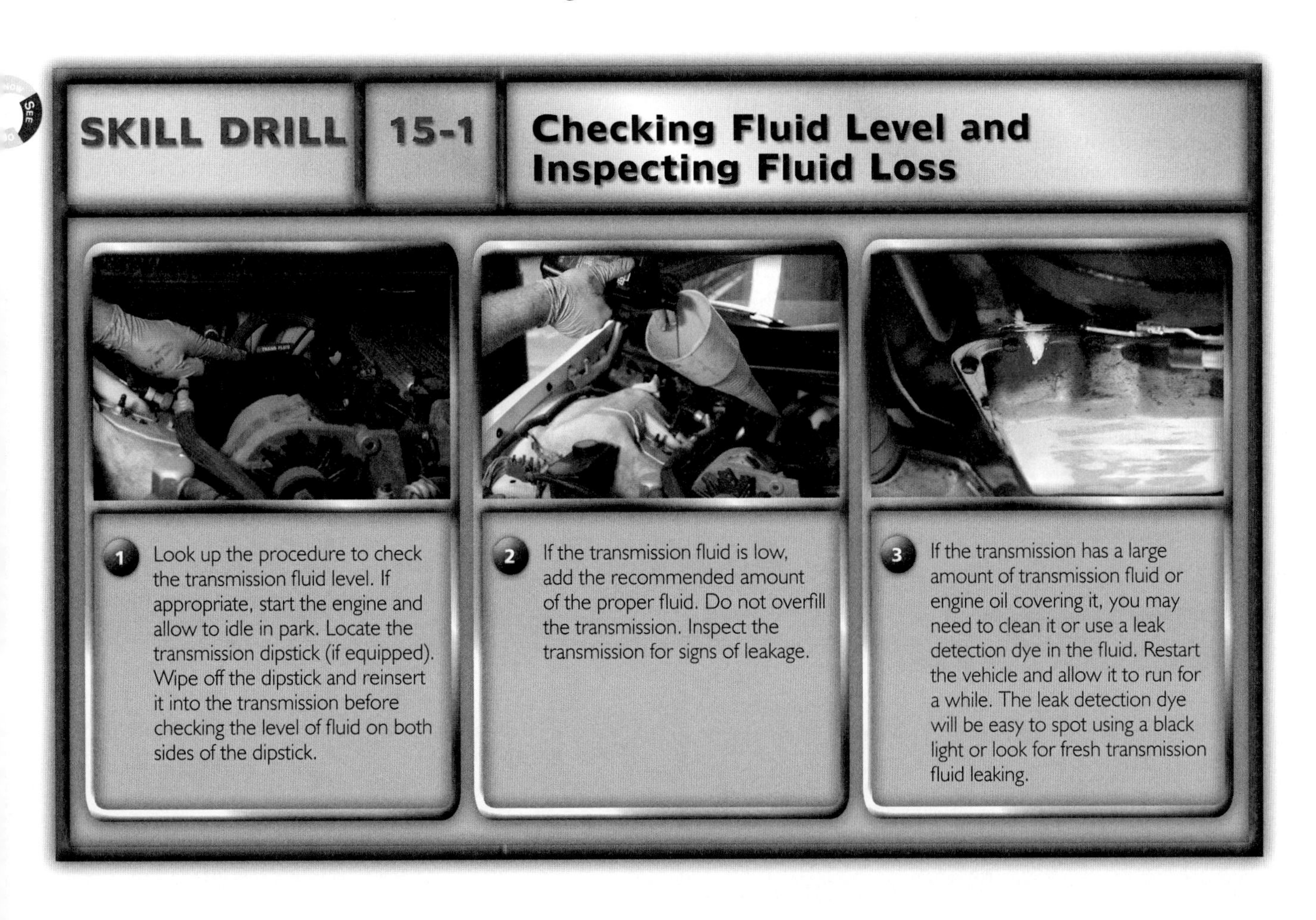

SKILL DRILL 15-1 Checking Fluid Level and Inspecting Fluid Loss

1. Look up the procedure to check the transmission fluid level. If appropriate, start the engine and allow to idle in park. Locate the transmission dipstick (if equipped). Wipe off the dipstick and reinsert it into the transmission before checking the level of fluid on both sides of the dipstick.

2. If the transmission fluid is low, add the recommended amount of the proper fluid. Do not overfill the transmission. Inspect the transmission for signs of leakage.

3. If the transmission has a large amount of transmission fluid or engine oil covering it, you may need to clean it or use a leak detection dye in the fluid. Restart the vehicle and allow it to run for a while. The leak detection dye will be easy to spot using a black light or look for fresh transmission fluid leaking.

inspecting the transmission for leakage, check the transmission pan, area around the entrance of the filler tube to the transmission, extension housing gasket, output shaft seals, selector shaft seal, area around the electrical connectors that go into the transmission case, front pump seals, fluid cooler lines, and fittings. Also, if the vehicle has a vacuum modulator, remove the vacuum hose from the modulator and see if there is any transmission fluid in the hose. If there is, the modulator is bad. Be sure to remove the radiator cap (with vehicle cold) and check for any transmission fluid in the radiator.

Replacing Fluid and Filters

The most common transmission work that the average technician will perform is a visual inspection along with fluid and filter replacement. At the minimum, transmission fluid should be changed according to the manufacturer's maintenance schedule. If the vehicle is used for towing or operates in dusty environments, the fluid should be changed more often. Some manufacturers recommend fluid and filter changes every 25,000 miles (40,000 km), while others advise against changing the fluid for the life of the vehicle because the transmission is sealed—and you will find recommendations everywhere in between.

As discussed in the Automatic Transmission Fundamentals chapter, it used to be possible to check the quality of transmission fluid by looking at its color and smelling it. If the fluid was a darkish red or had a burnt smell to, it was time for fluid replacement. Some modern transmission fluids are a darker red when they are brand new and even have a slightly burnt smell to them. For this reason, it is important to check the fluid in a new way. Take a few drops of transmission fluid and place them on a clean paper towel. The fluid will disperse on the paper towel, but any contaminants will remain where the fluid was placed. If the fluid spot on the paper towel has a darker center, it is a sign that there are contaminants in the transmission fluid and it should be changed FIGURE 15-2.

To replace the fluid and internal filter, follow the steps in SKILL DRILL 15-2.

> **TECHNICIAN TIP**
>
> Some manufacturers install an in-line filter in the cooler line that is replaceable. Be aware of that when you research the replacement procedure for the transmission filter. Also, some transmissions have external filters that look like a typical engine oil filter.

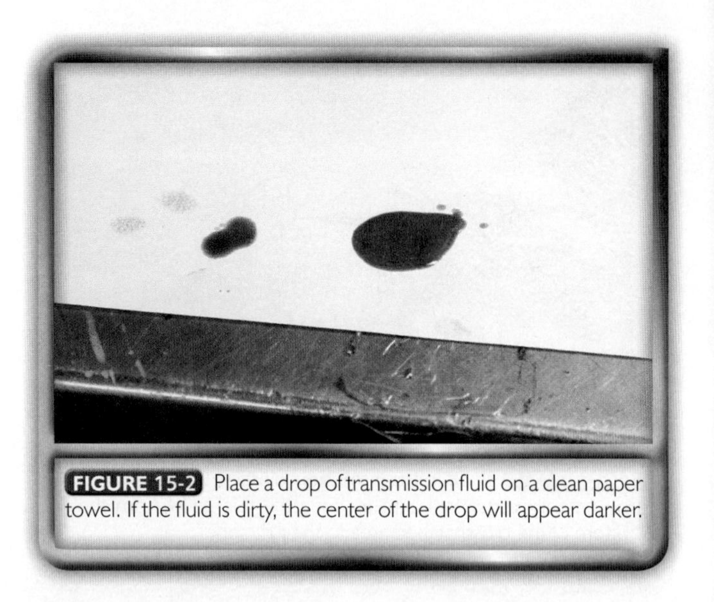

FIGURE 15-2 Place a drop of transmission fluid on a clean paper towel. If the fluid is dirty, the center of the drop will appear darker.

Transmission In-Vehicle Diagnosis

In-vehicle diagnosis enables you to test the transmission in a variety of ways and with a variety of tests that are impossible to reproduce once the transmission is removed from the vehicle. To properly diagnose a transmission (and not simply replace it), you need to do a thorough inspection of the transmission and perform several diagnostic tests. These inspections and tests are done both during a test-drive and in the shop. You will need to use your knowledge of transmissions to determine which tests are necessary based on the customer complaint. Scan tools and pressure gauges are often required to perform those tests. The goal is twofold: (1) diagnose whether the fault is inside or outside of the transmission, and (2) if it is inside of the transmission, then diagnose the faulty components before removing the transmission and tearing it down.

Safety and Precautions

Most of the testing on an automatic transmission requires that the vehicle be running, or even running in a drive gear. Use extreme caution around moving parts of the vehicle to prevent injury. Often, transmissions are located right next to hot exhaust components, such as the catalytic converter and exhaust pipes. Wearing insulated gloves and arm sleeves can help prevent a technician from being severely burned by these components.

Some tests require the vehicle to be "driven" while in the air on a hoist. Vehicle speed should never be allowed to exceed 45 mph (72 kph) on the speedometer, since one wheel's speed may be double that due to the operation of the differential assembly. That means that even though the speedometer reads 45 mph (72 kph), if one drive wheel is stopped, the other wheel is spinning at 90 mph (145 kph). At high speeds, tires can fly apart and send pieces of tire across the shop. Tires that are not in perfect balance can cause the vehicle to shake, which puts it in danger of falling off the hoist.

Often, a road test will need to be completed to properly diagnose the transmission. You may need to use a scan tool to monitor electronic components inside and outside of the transmission during a road test. Distracted driving can lead to an accident; always use the "movie"

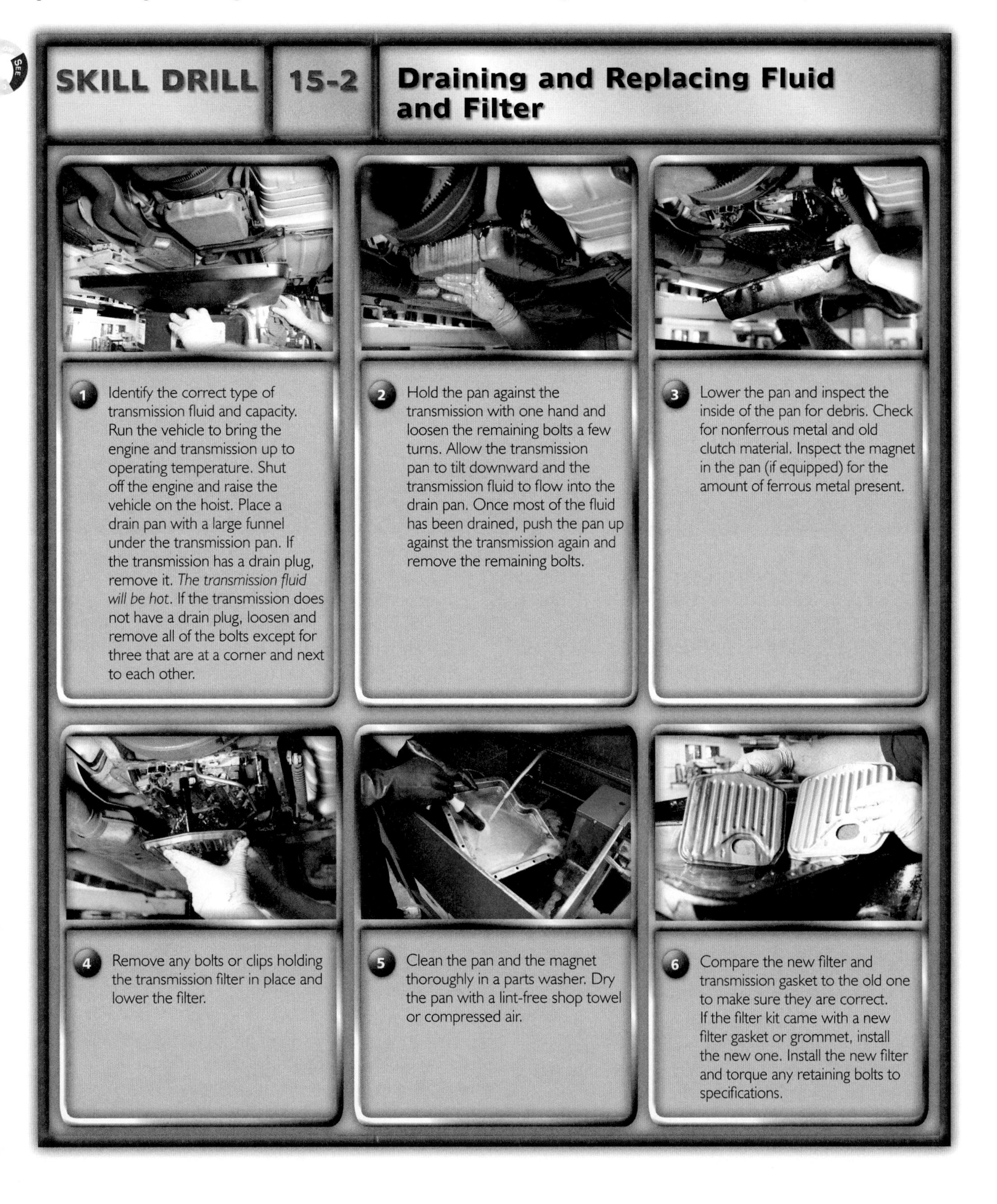

SKILL DRILL 15-2 Draining and Replacing Fluid and Filter

1. Identify the correct type of transmission fluid and capacity. Run the vehicle to bring the engine and transmission up to operating temperature. Shut off the engine and raise the vehicle on the hoist. Place a drain pan with a large funnel under the transmission pan. If the transmission has a drain plug, remove it. *The transmission fluid will be hot*. If the transmission does not have a drain plug, loosen and remove all of the bolts except for three that are at a corner and next to each other.

2. Hold the pan against the transmission with one hand and loosen the remaining bolts a few turns. Allow the transmission pan to tilt downward and the transmission fluid to flow into the drain pan. Once most of the fluid has been drained, push the pan up against the transmission again and remove the remaining bolts.

3. Lower the pan and inspect the inside of the pan for debris. Check for nonferrous metal and old clutch material. Inspect the magnet in the pan (if equipped) for the amount of ferrous metal present.

4. Remove any bolts or clips holding the transmission filter in place and lower the filter.

5. Clean the pan and the magnet thoroughly in a parts washer. Dry the pan with a lint-free shop towel or compressed air.

6. Compare the new filter and transmission gasket to the old one to make sure they are correct. If the filter kit came with a new filter gasket or grommet, install the new one. Install the new filter and torque any retaining bolts to specifications.

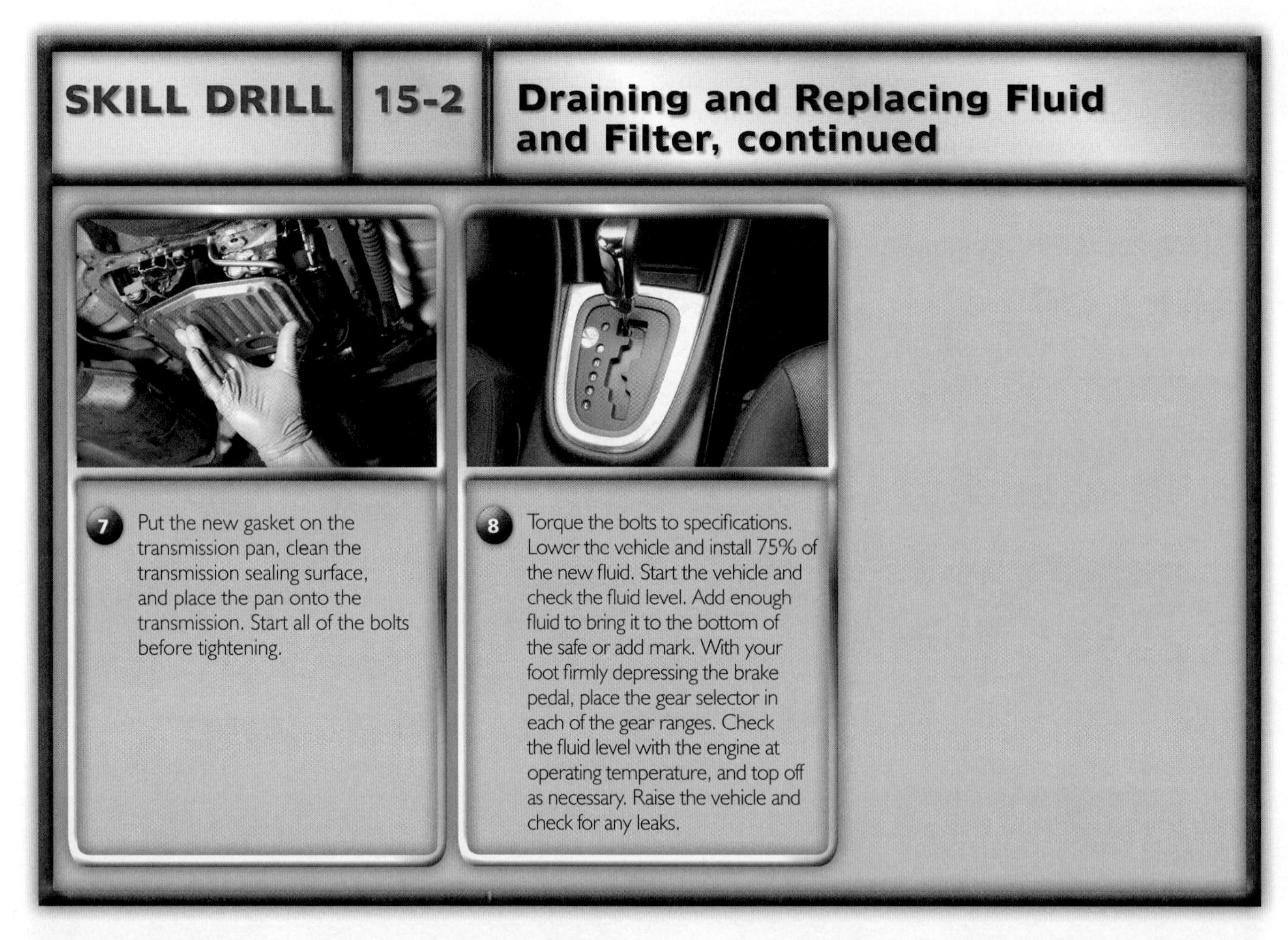
SKILL DRILL 15-2 Draining and Replacing Fluid and Filter, continued
7 Put the new gasket on the transmission pan, clean the transmission sealing surface, and place the pan onto the transmission. Start all of the bolts before tightening.
8 Torque the bolts to specifications. Lower the vehicle and install 75% of the new fluid. Start the vehicle and check the fluid level. Add enough fluid to bring it to the bottom of the safe or add mark. With your foot firmly depressing the brake pedal, place the gear selector in each of the gear ranges. Check the fluid level with the engine at operating temperature, and top off as necessary. Raise the vehicle and check for any leaks.

feature of a scan tool or a data logger to record the information while you test-drive a vehicle, or have another person drive the vehicle while you monitor the scan tool data. Also, you should never drive with a scan tool in front of an airbag in case of an airbag deployment.

Methods of Testing

When diagnosing an automatic transmission, whether it is a hydraulically controlled transmission or an electronically controlled transmission, there are several tests that a technician will perform. Not all of these tests are done on every transmission or for every problem; nor are they always done in the same order. The order and appropriateness of the test depends on the customer complaint, the service procedure listed in the service information, your understanding of how the system operates, and the results of any previous test:

- *Fluid check:* Although we have already discussed how to check transmission fluid, having the proper level of transmission fluid is critical to the proper operation of the transmission and should be double-checked any time there is a possible transmission problem. The fluid in the transmission needs to be at the proper level and in good condition and must be the fluid specified by the manufacturer. It cannot be stressed enough that the wrong fluid or low fluid can cause many issues with an automatic transmission.
- *Road test:* A road test is typically required when the transmission is not so bad that the vehicle cannot easily be driven. In some cases, just driving the vehicle enough to get it in the shop is enough to start the diagnostic process. If the vehicle is brought in on a tow truck, then a test-drive is not an option. If the vehicle can be driven, then a test-drive will give you lots of information and help to verify the customer complaint. What a customer describes as a slipping transmission may not actually be a slipping transmission. The best way to accurately verify the customer complaint is usually by performing a road test.
- *Visual inspection:* A quick check under the hood or under the vehicle often identifies problems that can be causing undesirable transmission operation. For example, on a hydraulically controlled transmission, is the throttle valve cable attached to the throttle body? Did a vacuum hose fall off

that leads to a vacuum modulator? On an electronically controlled transmission, an air intake hose after the mass airflow sensor can cause the transmission to shift erratically. After an oil change, this hose may be left disconnected. Or maybe the customer backed into a curb and kinked the exhaust pipe, causing a restriction that affects the operation of both the engine and the transmission. A quick visual inspection of the entire vehicle can point out issues that relate to the customer concern.

- *Scan of computer for codes (on electronically controlled transmissions):* Scanning the power train control module (PCM) will not necessarily find the exact problem, but it may give the technician a general direction of focus. All codes, not just transmission codes, should be documented and evaluated. Often, a code for the engine may be affecting the transmission operation or vice versa. Once codes are obtained, the diagnostic procedure can be researched in the service information to determine the best way to continue with the diagnosis.
- *Stall test:* A **stall test** checks the torque converter operation and also checks the transmission for slippage by operating the engine at full throttle with the transmission in gear and the brakes applied. It heavily stresses the torque converter and transmission, so any weaknesses that are present will be reflected in the results of the stall test. Because the stall test stresses the drive train so much, many manufacturers do not recommend performing a stall test anymore. It is important to check the service information for the particular vehicle.
- *Hydraulic pressure test:* The **hydraulic pressure test** checks the pump operation, the pressure regulator, and the seals and gaskets inside the transmission. Some transmissions provide a test port for line pressure only, while others provide ports for each individual gear, line pressure, modulator pressure, and so on. The results can be compared against the manufacturer's specifications. Some electronically controlled vehicles have a PID, which can show pressure(s) on a scan tool. Just remember that this information is coming from a pressure sensor and is interpreted by the PCM before being transmitted to the scan tool. Thus, you may have to verify hydraulic pressure manually with a pressure tester.
- *Leak check:* Leak checking the transmission is often done during many other routine services, as mentioned earlier. If a transmission problem is suspected or a low fluid level is found, the transmission should be inspected for leaks. This check can be a visual inspection, or it can be aided by a special fluorescent dye that is added to the transmission fluid.
- *Pan inspection:* **Pan inspection** was discussed as part of the general service of the transmission, under fluid and filter replacement, but removing the transmission pan to check for debris in the pan can be a good indicator of transmission failure and of what part of the components failed. Check the pan for excessive clutch material or metal particles. A small amount of clutch material and metal particles in the pan is due to normal wear and tear over time.
- *Air checking:* **Air checking** or testing uses compressed air to check the different circuits and components in the hydraulic system. Air checking can indicate if a clutch or band is holding pressure and moving. It can also identify a leak in the circuit or unusual application of a band or clutch.
- *Cooler flow test:* A **cooler flow test** uses a flowmeter on the cooler circuit of the hydraulic system of the transmission to help identify poor pump performance, restriction in the cooler, converter clutch problems, and worn spool valves in the valve body.
- *Noise, vibration, and harshness test:* The **noise, vibration, and harshness (NVH) test** describes a process that technicians have always done—listening for noise and feeling for vibrations and harshness. Now there are test tools than can help pinpoint noises in a vehicle while the vehicle is driven, called NVH analyzers.

A technician will use all of the tests just described in conjunction with the service information to make a comprehensive diagnosis of the transmission. By comparing the transmission operation during a test-drive to the correct clutch and band application charts in the service information, the technician can pinpoint the best method for further testing, including applying scan tools, checking on noises heard during the test-drive, pressure testing, air checking, and so on. Another critical step in diagnosis is checking for technical service bulletins (TSBs). In many cases, the manufacturer has identified common problems that occur with a particular vehicle and has provided updated programming, parts, or test procedures to verify the problem. This assistance from the manufacturer can save a technician a lot of time and the customer a lot of money.

If a technician knows how the system works and has access to the right service information, knowledge of the proper tests, and the correct tools, he or she should be able to form a correct diagnosis. Your task as a maintenance and light repair technician is to keep your eyes open looking for any issues that would indicate transmission faults and report them to your supervisor for further diagnosis.

Test-Driving

Test-driving, or performing a road test, is a critical part of the diagnostic procedure. Transmissions operate much differently when they are placed under a load, such as driving up a hill, than they do sitting in a shop on a hoist. A transmission might operate perfectly fine when operated on the hoist, but have a major amount of clutch slippage when taken on a road test. Very few repair shops have access to a chassis dynamometer that would allow them to "test-drive" the vehicle in the shop, so a road test is a great option. Test-driving the vehicle must be done in a safe manner to prevent an accident. If you need to monitor test equipment such as a scan tool or pressure tester, then request the assistance of another technician to operate the vehicle safely.

During the test-drive, it is critical to place the transmission in the same operating conditions as the customer stated the problem occurred in. Did the customer state that the problem occurred during hard acceleration? Or maybe the problem only occurs when the transmission is cold or during shifts.

When test-driving, it is important to test the transmission in many different operating conditions and record the results for further analysis. Test the transmission during light, medium, and hard acceleration. Place the transmission in different gear ranges. For example, does the problem occur only in the overdrive range, or does it still occur in the L2 range? While test-driving, listen for noises that the customer may interpret as a transmission problem but that in fact indicate a problem with another component, such as a U-joint or transmission mount.

Applied Math

AM-53: Word Problem: The technician can evaluate symptoms of problems with a customer or associate technician and identify any relevant missing data required to solve the problem.

Perhaps the most important element of automotive diagnostics is to obtain all of the important information about the problem from the customer. Most customers do not understand the technical operation of their vehicles; they can only describe the symptoms of a problem that they can feel, see, or hear. They may have additional relevant information but not think to include it. It is up to the technician to ask questions that will guide the customer to provide all the information that could help with the diagnosis.

An example might be a complaint of, "The car sometimes seems to rev too hard and then bang into gear." As technicians, we may think this "sounds" like an automatic transmission problem, but to guide our diagnostic process, we need more information from the customer. Clarifying questions in this scenario may include:

- Does the reported problem occur when the vehicle is cold or after driving for a long time?
- Has the transmission been serviced recently?
- How long has the reported problem been occurring?
- Is the vehicle used to carry or tow heavy loads?

Answers to these questions guide us in different directions when looking at a problem and may help us reproduce the required conditions to get a fault to occur during testing. Sometimes it can be useful to take the customer along during a road test to provide further clarification or have him or her reproduce the fault.

Scanning the Transmission Control Module/PCM

A high-quality or factory scan tool can be an invaluable asset while diagnosing an electronically controlled transmission. A code reader can read codes, but a high quality aftermarket scan tool and a factory scan tool can also view live data from sensors and actuators inside the transmission. Further, many high quality scan tools and factory scan tools give the technician **bidirectional control** of the transmission. Bidirectional control means the technician will be able to command different solenoids and actuators "on" and "off" to check their operation. For example, the torque converter clutch (TCC) could be commanded on while the engine is idling in drive with the brakes on. This should kill the engine if the TCC solenoid is operating and the clutch is in good shape. Activating this solenoid and observing the reaction will give you valuable information that helps determine the next steps in the diagnosis process.

Any trouble codes should be researched in the appropriate service information to find the correct diagnostic procedure. Following the diagnostic procedure step by step is critical in a successful repair of the vehicle. The diagnostic procedure will often require the use of a digital volt-ohmmeter (DVOM) to aid in the diagnosis of wiring, switches, solenoids, sensors, and actuators.

To diagnose electronic transmission control systems using appropriate test equipment and service information, follow the steps in SKILL DRILL 15-3.

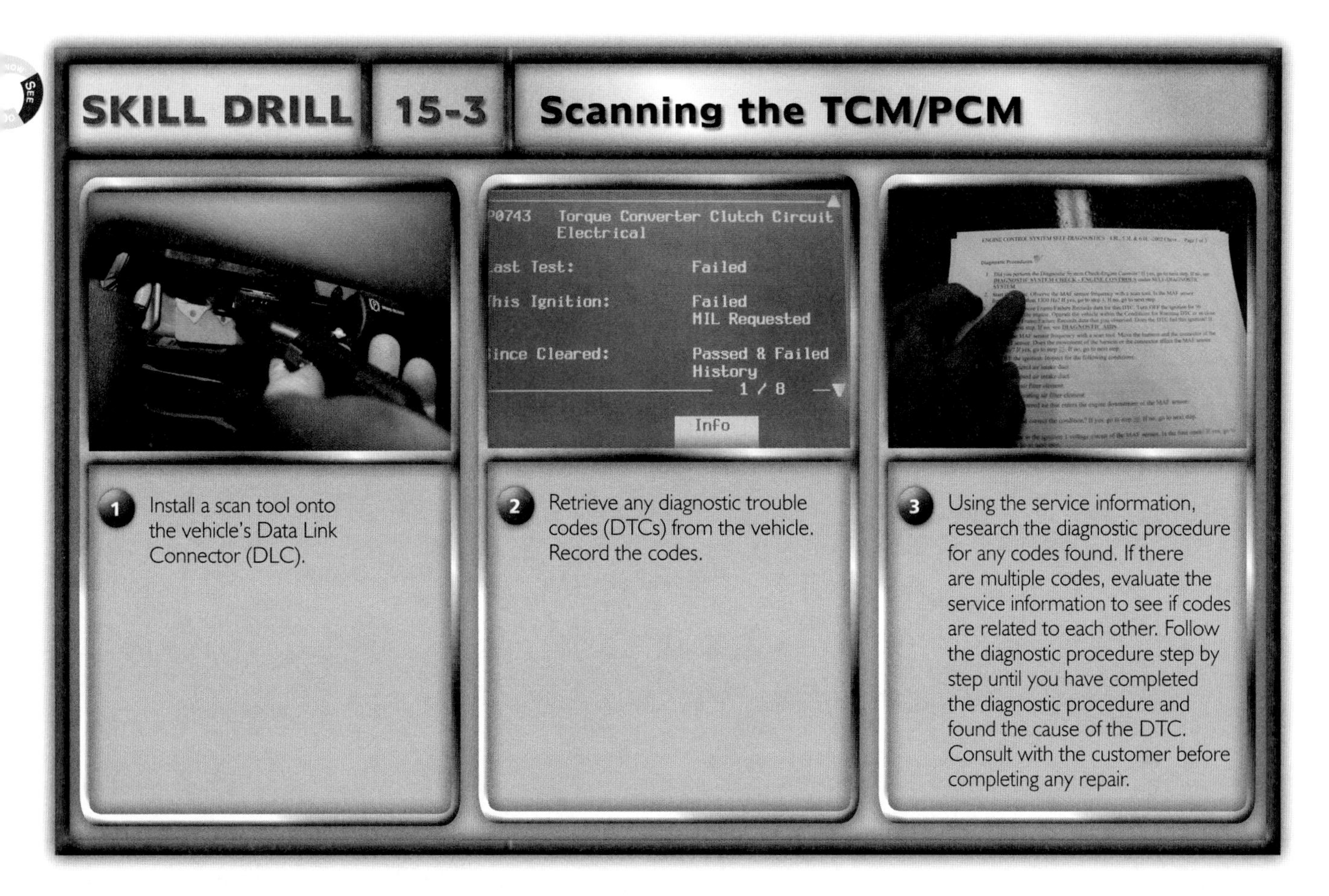
P0743 Torque Converter Clutch Circuit
Electrical
ast Test: Failed
his Ignition: Failed
MIL Requested
ince Cleared: Passed & Failed
History
1 / 8
Info

SKILL DRILL 15-3 Scanning the TCM/PCM

1. Install a scan tool onto the vehicle's Data Link Connector (DLC).
2. Retrieve any diagnostic trouble codes (DTCs) from the vehicle. Record the codes.
3. Using the service information, research the diagnostic procedure for any codes found. If there are multiple codes, evaluate the service information to see if codes are related to each other. Follow the diagnostic procedure step by step until you have completed the diagnostic procedure and found the cause of the DTC. Consult with the customer before completing any repair.

In-Vehicle Transmission Repair

Many automatic transmission repairs can be completed without removing the transmission from the vehicle. Transmission repairs that are completed with the transmission still in the vehicle are often less expensive than pulling the transmission for a complete rebuild because removal and reinstallation of the transmission will take a few hours at a minimum. Examples of typical in-vehicle transmission repairs include replacement of the external gaskets and seals, vehicle speed sensor, shift solenoid, extension housing bushing, and power train mount; repair of the valve body; and adjustment of some servos and bands.

Inspecting and Repairing an External Leak

Transmissions have many external seals and gaskets that can be replaced without removing the transmission from the vehicle. Examples include the extension housing seal, the vehicle speed sensor seal, the pan gasket, and the extension housing gasket. A transmission fluid leak can result in failure of the transmission due to a low fluid level. As a technician, it is important to fix any external leaks on the transmission to prevent this failure.

Some seals, such as the extension housing seal, may require the replacement of the extension housing bushing to properly repair the leak. With a worn bushing, the driveshaft may move up and down excessively, flexing the seal and allowing transmission fluid to flow out of the transmission. Replacement of an extension housing bushing will require the removal of the driveshaft and the extension housing. The bushing can then be driven out using a bushing driver set.

Most seals on the outside of a transmission require specialized tools to be removed and replaced without removing the transmission from the vehicle. Some of these specialty tools are universal types; others are specific for a particular model of transmission.

To inspect for leakage and replace external seals, gaskets, and bushings, follow the steps in SKILL DRILL 15-4.

Inspecting and Repairing Power Train Mounts

The **power train mounts** hold the engine and transmission in the proper position in the vehicle. If the transmission or engine is allowed to move out of position, the shift linkage, or throttle linkage, could become bound or inaccurate, resulting in a safety concern. With the shift linkage bound, the driver might be able to start

SKILL DRILL 15-4 Inspecting for Leakage and Replacing Seals, Gaskets, and Bushings

1. Raise the vehicle on a hoist. Inspect the front pump, output shaft, and selector shaft seals for leakage. Inspect the transmission pan gasket, side pan gasket (if equipped), and extension housing gasket.

2. Inspect the extension housing bushing by moving the driveshaft up and down. If there is excessive movement in the driveshaft, the extension housing bushing must be replaced. Place a drain pan under the extension housing and remove the driveshaft from the vehicle.

3. Remove the extension housing from the transmission. On some older transmissions, the seal and bushing can be replaced with the extension housing still in the vehicle by using a specialty puller.

4. If the bushing requires replacement and is replaceable, use the correct bushing driver and hammer the bushing out of the housing.

5. Use the correct-sized bushing driver to carefully drive the bushing into place. Take note of any lubrication holes that need to be lined up before installation.

6. Use the correct seal installation tool to install the new seal in the housing.

7. Lubricate the edge of the seal with clean transmission fluid and reinstall the extension housing and driveshaft.

TECHNICIAN TIP

A technician was once called by a customer who was on a trip towing his large boat and was experiencing a strange phenomenon. It seemed that the vehicle had developed a mind of its own. As soon as the vehicle would start up a hill, the gas pedal would drop to the floor and the vehicle would go to full throttle. If the driver turned the engine off at the top of the hill and restarted the engine, everything worked fine until the next hill, when the gas pedal would once again drop to the floor. The technician walked the customer through the process of testing the power train mounts, one of which was torn, allowing the engine to move and pulling the throttle linkage open and the pedal to the floor.

a vehicle while it is in gear or have the vehicle in the wrong gear. For example, suppose the driver wants to go in reverse, but as soon as she takes her foot off the brake pedal, the vehicle begins moving forward. Worn power train mounts should always be replaced with the correct part for the vehicle.

Most power train mounts are of the rubber style, which are molded from precisely engineered rubber and with specific shapes and voids. Rubber mounts are subject to cracks and tears that occur over time due to their constant flexing. Their life is also reduced by being saturated with oil, power steering fluid, or gasoline, which can soften the rubber. Power train mounts can also be of the hydraulic style. Hydraulic mounts use silicone hydraulic fluid that is squeezed back and forth between two chambers, similar to the design of a shock absorber. They use a metered orifice between the chambers to control the flow of fluid, which dampens the engine pulsations. Some hydraulic mounts use a computer-controlled electronic control valve that can open an alternate passageway or vary the size of the orifice. This changes the rate of flow between the chambers, thereby allowing the computer to control the amount of dampening that is needed for various operating conditions. Hydraulic mounts should be inspected for leaking and excessive movement. The solenoid valve can also be tested for continuity or commanded to operate with a scan tool. Hydraulic-style power train mounts are typically much more expensive than rubber mounts and may be available only through the manufacturer.

Often, in the event of a broken power train mount, customers complain of a loud thump when they apply the accelerator in drive or reverse and again when they apply the brake pedal. This loud thump may be the engine and/or transmission being pulled up from the broken mount due to the engine's torque, and then being set back down when the brake is applied.

Power train mounts wear out over time, so they need to be inspected periodically. Since leaking fluids can soften the rubber in the mounts over time, it is wise to encourage customers to have leaks repaired before they damage other parts.

To inspect, replace, and align power train mounts, follow the steps in SKILL DRILL 15-5.

Adjusting the Shift Linkage and Transmission Range Sensor

When servicing an automatic transmission, it may be necessary to adjust the shift linkage along with the transmission range sensor. If these are not adjusted properly, the vehicle may not start, or it may start in gear, resulting in a major safety hazard. If the linkage is not adjusted properly, the transmission position indicator (PRNDL indicator) will not be set correctly, the customer will not know which gear the vehicle is in, and the backup or reverse lights may not work.

If the manual valve is not correctly set to the PRNDL indicator, the valve may be placed between two hydraulic passages causing a fluid restriction to the correct hydraulic circuit and possible partial application of the wrong hydraulic circuit. This can cause undesirable transmission operation and damage to the transmission. Or if it is far enough out of adjustment, the valve may supply fluid to the wrong gear, such as neutral when the PRNDL indicator is set to drive.

To inspect, adjust, and replace the manual valve shift linkage, transmission range sensor/switch, and park/neutral position switch, follow the steps in SKILL DRILL 15-6.

1. Look up the proper service procedure in the appropriate service information. Follow the procedure step by step to inspect and adjust the manual valve and transmission range sensor/neutral safety switch.
2. Place the gear selector in the park position.
3. Raise the vehicle on a hoist (if necessary to access the transmission range switch and manual valve linkage).
4. Disconnect the shift linkage from the transmission.
5. Place the manual valve in the park position. The valve should snap into position.
6. The shift linkage should fit right onto the manual valve with no pulling on the linkage or the manual valve.
7. If the linkage does not line up, loosen the adjustment on the shift linkage and adjust the linkage so that it will install properly on the manual valve.
8. Tighten the adjustment on the shift linkage.
9. Double-check that the PRNDL indicator still indicates the vehicle is in park.

Prove
Know
See
Do

SKILL DRILL 15-5 Inspecting, Replacing, and Aligning Power Train Mounts

1. Look up the procedure for checking and replacing power train mounts. Place the vehicle on a hoist to inspect the power train mounts under the vehicle.

2. Use a pry bar to carefully push up on the engine and transmission while watching the power train mounts.

3. Lower the vehicle back down and start the engine. Apply the brake and place the vehicle into gear. Apply the throttle slowly and watch for excessive engine movement on the mounts. Repeat this process of applying the throttle but with the vehicle in reverse to check the opposite mounts.

4. Raise the engine or transmission just far enough that the weight is off of the power train mount. Be *very* careful that you do not cause the vehicle to shift on the hoist!

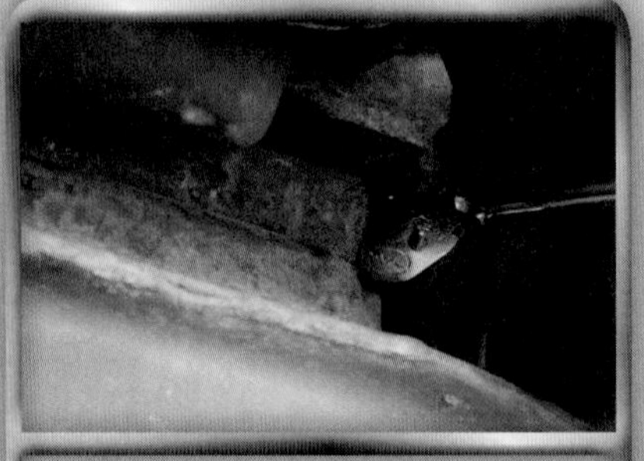

5. Remove the bolts securing the mount to the transmission or engine, and then the bolts securing the mount to the frame of the vehicle.

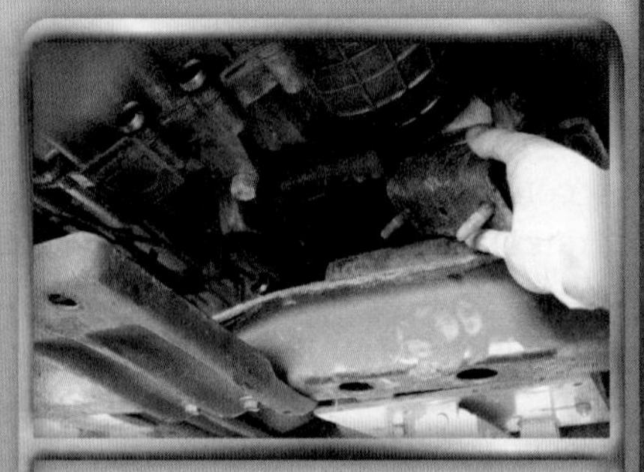

6. Remove the old mount and compare it to the new mount.

7. Place the new mount in the correct position according to the manufacturer's service information, lower the jack slightly, reinstall the bolts, and torque them to specifications.

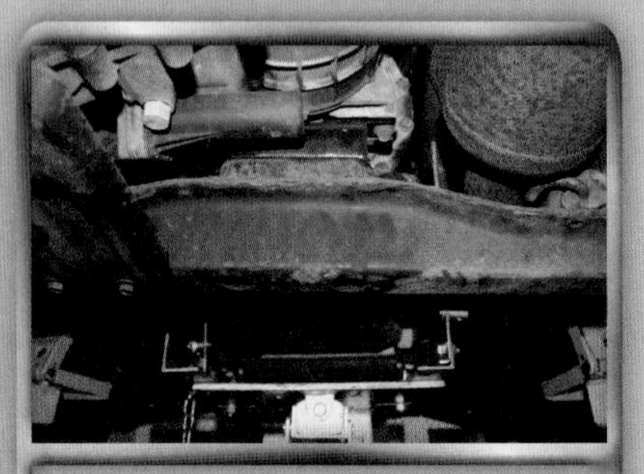

8. Lower the engine or transmission back down. Reinstall any components that were removed to access the power train mount.

10. Use an ohmmeter to check that the neutral safety switch/transmission range switch has continuity on the correct terminals. If not, loosen the switch and adjust its position. If continuity is never obtained, or is obtained in every gear, replace the switch. The vehicle should start only in the park and neutral positions. Make sure the brake pedal is firmly applied, then check that the vehicle starts only in the park and neutral positions.
11. Run the shifter through all of the gear ranges, checking for proper operation.

Inspecting and Cleaning the Transmission Cooler

Before installing a new or rebuilt transmission, it is critical to clean and inspect the transmission fluid cooler and lines. If a transmission suffers catastrophic failure, metal particles and old clutch material can become stuck inside the fluid cooler or lines. Even if this material is not stuck in the cooler, the cooler is still full of old contaminated transmission fluid. This contaminated fluid will contaminate the new transmission as soon as the vehicle is started. Some transmissions have a separate filter located in the cooler lines. These should be replaced, not cleaned. Also be aware that some manufacturers install a check valve assembly in one of the cooler lines to prevent back-drainage of the fluid in the converter when the engine is off. This valve can catch debris, which can cause a restriction or even stick the check valve closed. If this happens, no transmission fluid will get to the planetary gears for lubrication, ruining them pretty quickly. There is debate about whether these check valves can be cleaned adequately since the lines cannot be reverse flushed, so follow the manufacturer's recommendations.

Transmission coolers can be cleaned in one of two ways. The first method is to use a dedicated cleaning system that has a pump that will pulse clean solvent through the transmission cooler and back to the cleaning machine. Dirt and debris will be removed and returned to the cleaning system with the solvent and removed with a filter. The second method of cleaning the transmission cooler involves using an aerosol flushing kit available at many parts stores. The aerosol can is a one-time use system and must be replaced for every transmission. When performing either method, hook up to the transmission cooler so that the solvent will flow backward through the cooler to help dislodge any stuck debris. Cooler lines with check valves cannot be reverse flushed.

A transmission fluid cooler that is leaking could cause the new transmission to fail from low fluid level or could cause anti-freeze to be drawn into the cooler from the radiator, contaminating the fluid. Many times, the transmission fluid will flow into the radiator, causing the anti-freeze to become contaminated with transmission fluid and the transmission to suffer from low fluid level. Transmission lines can also plug up, especially if they have a check valve or filter in them, which would prevent transmission fluid from lubricating the planetary gears, as well as overheat the transmission fluid and transmission.

To inspect, leak test, and flush or replace transmission cooler lines and fittings, follow the steps in **SKILL DRILL 15-7**.

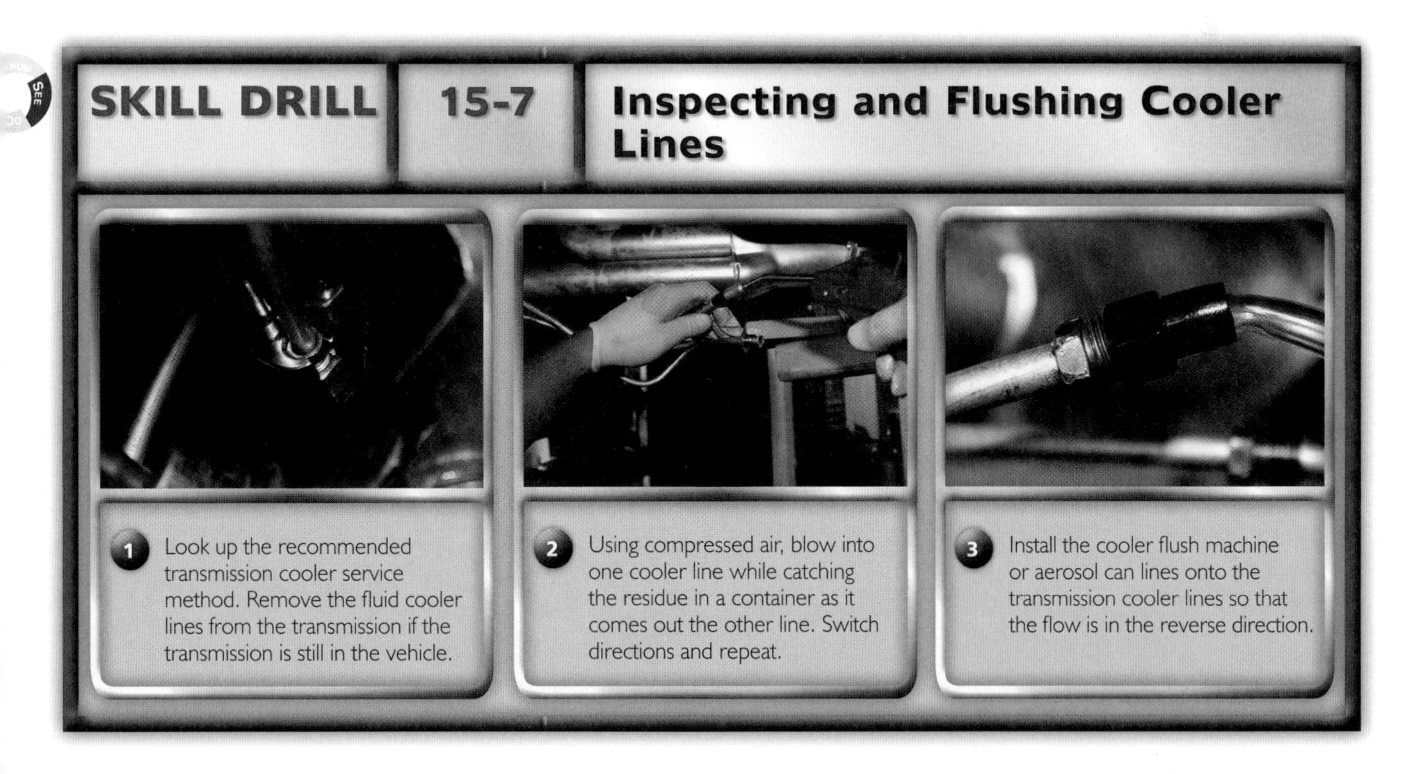
SKILL DRILL 15-7 Inspecting and Flushing Cooler Lines
1 Look up the recommended transmission cooler service method. Remove the fluid cooler lines from the transmission if the transmission is still in the vehicle.
2 Using compressed air, blow into one cooler line while catching the residue in a container as it comes out the other line. Switch directions and repeat.
3 Install the cooler flush machine or aerosol can lines onto the transmission cooler lines so that the flow is in the reverse direction.

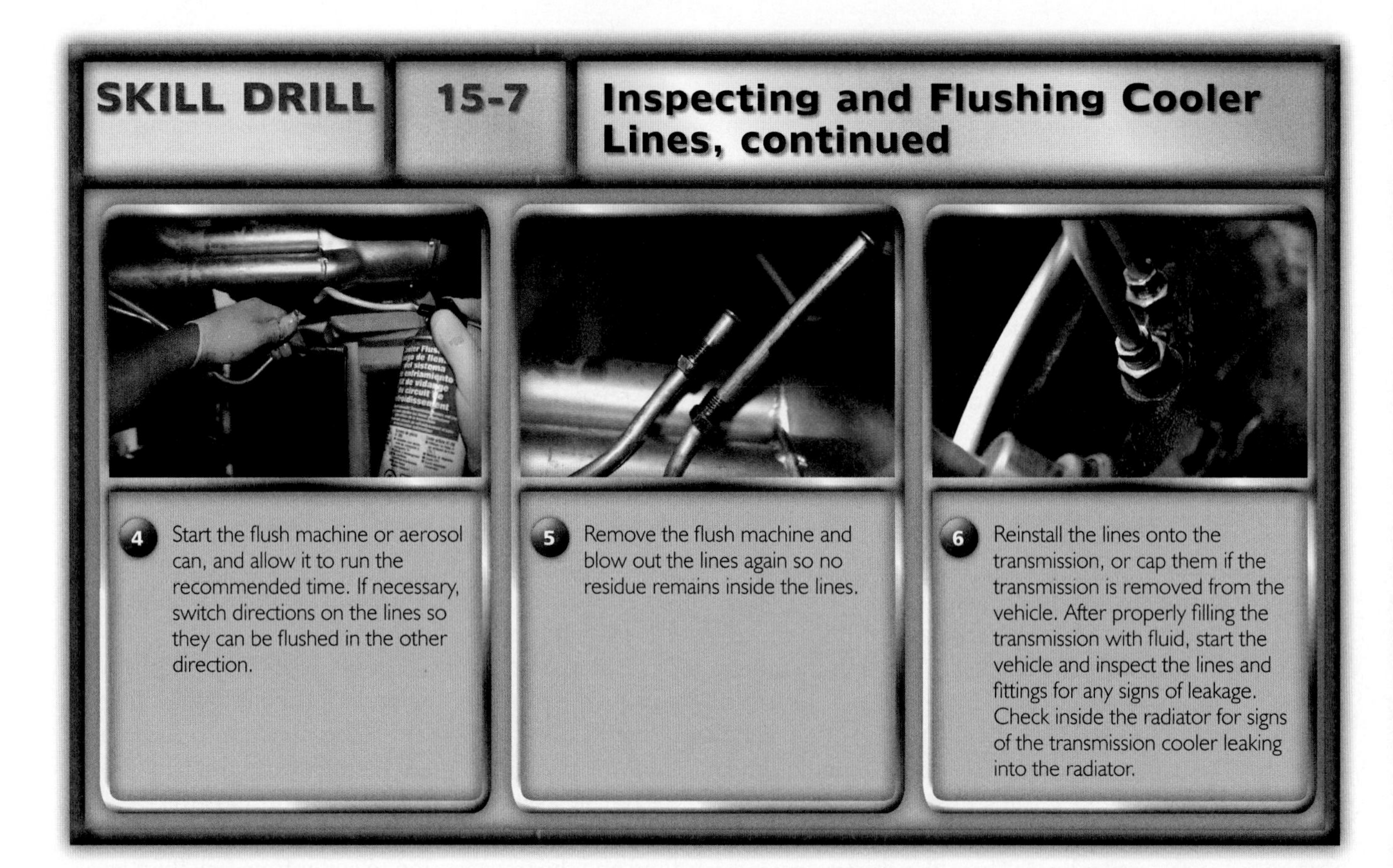

SKILL DRILL 15-7 Inspecting and Flushing Cooler Lines, continued

4. Start the flush machine or aerosol can, and allow it to run the recommended time. If necessary, switch directions on the lines so they can be flushed in the other direction.

5. Remove the flush machine and blow out the lines again so no residue remains inside the lines.

6. Reinstall the lines onto the transmission, or cap them if the transmission is removed from the vehicle. After properly filling the transmission with fluid, start the vehicle and inspect the lines and fittings for any signs of leakage. Check inside the radiator for signs of the transmission cooler leaking into the radiator.

Wrap-up

Ready for Review

- Automatic transmissions require periodic maintenance, which includes checking transmission fluid and replacing fluid and filters.
- If transmission fluid levels are low, identify the source of fluid loss.
- Visually inspect transmission fluid and replace as necessary.
- Diagnosis of transmission problems requires a thorough transmission inspection.
- Use extreme caution and wear proper protective clothing and equipment when diagnosing a transmission in a running vehicle.
- Diagnostic transmission tests include the fluid check, road test, visual inspection, scan of the computer for codes, stall test, hydraulic pressure test, leak check, pan inspection, air check, cooler flow test, and noise, vibration, and harshness test.
- Always perform a diagnostic test-drive under a range of operating conditions.
- Using a factory scan tool allows technicians bidirectional transmission control.
- In-vehicle transmission repairs include replacement of the vehicle speed sensor, extension housing bushing, and power train mount; repair of the valve body and the external gaskets and seals; and adjustments of the servo and bands.
- Leaks from gaskets or seals may require bushing replacement to properly repair the leak.
- Repair of power train mounts is critical for keeping the engine and transmission in proper position.
- Adjust the shift linkage and transmission range sensor as part of automatic transmission servicing.
- Always clean and inspect the transmission oil cooler and lines prior to installing a new or repaired transmission.

Key Terms

air checking The use of compressed air to check clutch and servo operation on transmissions during and after assembly.

bidirectional control The ability to command different solenoids and actuators "on" and "off" to check their operation.

cooler flow test The placement of a specialty measuring device into the transmission cooler line to measure fluid flow to the cooler. Low cooler flow can be a sign of other issues with the pump and lubrication system.

hydraulic pressure test The use of a hydraulic pressure gauge to measure the amount of hydraulic pressure produced in each gear range.

noise, vibration, and harshness (NVH) test A test to measure for any audible noises, vibrations, and harsh operation. It can be completed by the technician with or without the aid of an NVH tester. The tester is used to pinpoint the exact frequencies of the noise and vibrations.

pan inspection The process of removing the transmission pan to check for clutch material, metal, and other debris or contaminants.

power train mount A rubber or metal bracket used to secure the engine and transmission into the vehicle. Some vehicles use hydraulic or electrohydraulic power train mounts.

stall test A test that involves raising the engine rpm to wide-open throttle while the brake is firmly applied and the transmission is in gear. The test is used to check torque convertor and transmission operation on some vehicles.

ASE-Type Questions

1. Tech A says that you should check fluid level in many automatic transmissions with the engine idling and the transmission in park. Tech B says that some transmissions are made without dipsticks. Who is correct?
   a. Tech A
   b. Tech B
   c. Both A and B
   d. Neither A nor B
2. Tech A says that increasing the transmission fluid level from the add mark to the full mark will require a quart of fluid, just like with engine oil. Tech B says that transmission solenoids should be tested electrically and mechanically. Who is correct?
   a. Tech A
   b. Tech B
   c. Both A and B
   d. Neither A nor B
3. Tech A says that transmission pan gaskets are always replaced. Tech B says that some newer transmissions have reusable pan gaskets. Who is correct?
   a. Tech A
   b. Tech B
   c. Both A and B
   d. Neither A nor B
4. Tech A says that the cooler and cooler lines should be flushed as part of a transmission rebuild. Tech B says that when checking the fluid level on the dipstick, always read the highest level on either side. Who is correct?
   a. Tech A
   b. Tech B
   c. Both A and B
   d. Neither A nor B
5. Tech A says that using a scan tool to activate the TCC with the engine idling in drive and the brakes applied is a typical troubleshooting task. Tech B says that diagnosis is a waste of time on a faulty transmission since it will be rebuilt anyway. Who is correct?
   a. Tech A
   b. Tech B
   c. Both A and B
   d. Neither A nor B
6. Tech A says that a stall test checks the torque converter operation and also checks the transmission for slippage. Tech B says the stall test stresses the torque converter and transmission, so any weaknesses will be shown as a result.
   a. Tech A
   b. Tech B
   c. Both A and B
   d. Neither A nor B
7. Tech A says that if the linkage is not adjusted properly, the transmission position indicator (PRNDL indicator) will not be set correctly and the driver may not know which gear the vehicle is in. Tech B says that even if the linkage is not adjusted properly, the backup or reverse lights will still work normally. Who is correct?
   a. Tech A
   b. Tech B
   c. Both A and B
   d. Neither A nor B
8. Tech A says you should check fluid level in all types of automatic transmissions with the engine idling and the transmission in park. Tech B says that a transmission fluid leak can result in failure of the transmission due to a low fluid level. Who is correct?
   a. Tech A
   b. Tech B
   c. Both A and B
   d. Neither A nor B
9. Tech A says that often in the event of a broken power train mount,customers complain of a loud thump when they apply the accelerator in drive or reverse. Tech B says that the loud thump may be the engine and/or transmission being pulled up from the broken mount due to the engine's torque, and then being set back down when the brake is applied. Who is correct?
   a. Tech A
   b. Tech B
   c. Both A and B
   d. Neither A nor B
10. Tech A says that a transmission fluid cooler that is leaking could cause the new transmission to fail from low fluid level. Tech B says that such a leak could cause antifreeze to be drawn into the cooler from the radiator and contaminate the transmission fluid. Who is correct?
    a. Tech A
    b. Tech B
    c. Both A and B
    d. Neither A nor B

CHAPTER 16

KNOW
SEE
DO
PROVE

NATEF Tasks

Automatic Transmission and Transaxle
Off-Vehicle Transmission and Transaxle

Task			Page
■ Describe the operational characteristics of a hybrid vehicle drive train.	MLR	AST	400–402
■ Describe the operational characteristics of a continuously variable transmission (CVT).	MLR	AST	405–406

KNOW
SEE
DO
PROVE

Knowledge Objectives

After reading this chapter, you will be able to:

1. Explain how the hybrid drive system works. (pp 400–402)
2. Discuss and compare hybrid and hybrid electric vehicle models. (pp 402–404)
3. Explain how a continuously variable transmission (CVT) works. (pp 405–406)
4. Explain the operation of electronic continuously variable transmission (ECVT) and variable-diameter pulley CVT. (pp 405–406)

Hybrid and Continuously Variable Transmissions

Skills Objectives

There are no skills objectives for this chapter.

Introduction

With the need for increased fuel economy, lower carbon dioxide emissions, and a smaller global footprint, manufacturers have been working to create more efficient new power train systems. Automobile manufacturers have had hybrid vehicles and vehicles with continuously variable transmissions (CVT) in mass production for more than 20 years. These vehicles are showing up in non-dealer repair facilities in greater numbers every day; therefore, it is important that technicians become familiar with their operation.

Hybrid Drive Systems

A hybrid drive system is defined as a system that uses two or more power sources, such as an internal combustion engine (ICE) and an electric motor, to propel the vehicle. There are many different styles and systems of hybrid vehicles being sold today. We will cover several of the more common hybrid vehicles on the market at the time of this writing—primarily gasoline–electric hybrids—and how they operate. Also expect various other hybrid arrangements, such as diesel–electric hybrids and fuel cell–electric hybrids, in the near future.

Before exploring how a hybrid operates, it is important to first discuss the purpose of a hybrid drive system. Hybrid vehicles have several different functions that separate them from conventional vehicles, such as idle stop and regenerative braking. Not all hybrids have every one of these functions, but often they will have most of them. Hybrids may be considered mild hybrids or full hybrids based on the number of hybrid functions they use. Knowing what functions a hybrid vehicle is equipped with and how the vehicle operates is necessary for two reasons: first, so you will know whether it is operating correctly, and second, so you will know what precautions you need to take in order to work on it safely.

Idle Stop

Idle stop is one of the most common functions of a hybrid vehicle and when used with an integrated starter/generator qualifies the vehicle for mild hybrid status. When the driver stops the vehicle, such as at a stoplight, the power train control module (PCM) shuts off the engine. Shutting off the engine reduces fuel consumption and carbon dioxide emissions. By using high-voltage electric motors, the PCM is able to crank the vehicle over very quickly and smoothly, creating an almost instant start as soon as the driver presses down on the accelerator. This cranking speed can be as high as 1000 revolutions per minute (rpm).

Stopping the engine at stoplights or when idling creates several problems that need to be addressed, such as the operation of the heating and cooling systems when the engine is stopped. In a conventional vehicle, the water pump and air-conditioning compressor are driven by an engine belt. This is not possible on a vehicle with the idle stop function FIGURE 16-1.

Many hybrid vehicles that use idle stop have a small, electric transmission hydraulic pump. This hydraulic

▸ LINK
Refer to the Principles of Heating and Air-Conditioning Systems chapter for more information on the heating and cooling system in hybrid vehicles.

You Are the Automotive Technician

Recently the Express Delivery Company you work for has converted its fleet from diesel to hybrid vehicles. Hybrid vehicles have lower carbon dioxide emissions, increased fuel economy, and a smaller global footprint. These vehicles often use very high-voltage batteries that present a severe shock hazard, which can easily lead to death if handled improperly. Your supervisor has asked you to complete a scheduled maintenance service on one of the hybrid vehicles.

1. Why is it important to fully understand the hybrid system and its operation before attempting any repairs on a hybrid vehicle?
2. What processes do most hybrid vehicles go through as they are braking and coming to a stop?
3. What are the most common types of CVTs being used in vehicles today?

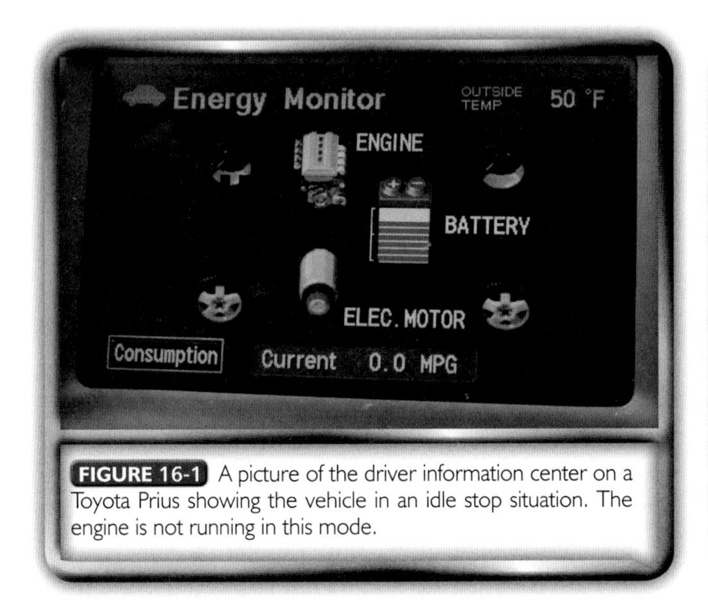
Energy Monitor
OUTSIDE TEMP
50 °F
ENGINE
BATTERY
ELEC. MOTOR
Consumption
Current 0.0 MPG

FIGURE 16-1 A picture of the driver information center on a Toyota Prius showing the vehicle in an idle stop situation. The engine is not running in this mode.

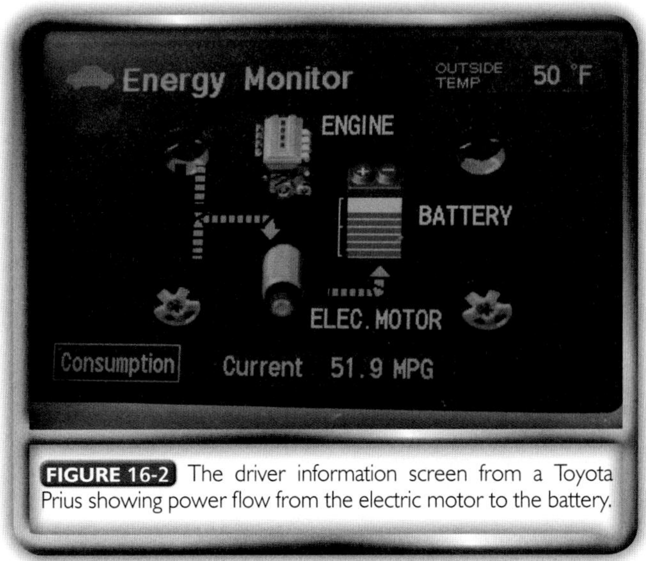
Energy Monitor
OUTSIDE TEMP
50 °F
ENGINE
BATTERY
ELEC. MOTOR
Consumption
Current 51.9 MPG

FIGURE 16-2 The driver information screen from a Toyota Prius showing power flow from the electric motor to the battery.

pump is used to prevent a delay in the engagement of the transmission when the vehicle is restarted.

Torque Smoothing

Torque smoothing refers to the ability of the hybrid vehicle to use an electric motor to help smooth out the power pulses of the ICE and create a flatter torque output curve. This feature is especially helpful on small three- and four-cylinder engines, which tend to produce more engine pulsations at lower engine speeds. When the ICE is on a compression pulse, the electric motor can be used to increase the amount of torque during compression. As the ICE is on a power stroke, the electric motor creates less torque. As the ICE's rpm increases, the torque pulses are needed less and less.

Regenerative Braking

Accelerating a vehicle from a stoplight requires a large amount of energy. When a conventional vehicle is being stopped, most of the kinetic energy of the vehicle's movement is converted into heat by the friction of the brake pads against the brake rotors; therefore, all of this energy is lost on a conventional vehicle. Most hybrid vehicles use **regenerative braking** to ensure that not all of the energy that was used to accelerate the vehicle is lost during braking.

On a hybrid vehicle, when the driver initiates a stop, the electric motor becomes a generator. The kinetic energy of the vehicle's movement is used to turn the generator and create electricity to charge the high-voltage battery. The harder the driver steps on the brake pedal, the more electricity is generated. It is important to remember that the more electricity that a generator is required to produce, the harder it is to turn the generator. This action causes the vehicle to slow down and eventually stop with the help of a conventional braking system FIGURE 16-2.

Regenerative brakes can only develop a certain amount of stopping power. If the driver needs more braking power than the regenerative brakes can supply, mechanical brakes are available as backup. However, they cannot recapture any of the kinetic energy. Judicious use of the brakes on a hybrid vehicle, such that the mechanical brakes are not activated, results in the best fuel economy.

Continuous driving, such as on the interstate, does not offer the regenerative braking system an opportunity to energize the battery. It is during stop-and-go driving that hybrids benefit most from this system, often resulting in a significantly higher gas mileage (MPG) rating during city driving than on the highway. The regenerative braking system also makes hybrids ideal for delivery vehicles and city transit buses that operate in stop-and-go conditions all day long.

Torque Assist

An electric motor is capable of creating its maximum torque as soon as it begins spinning. This torque can be used to help propel the vehicle from a stop, creating **torque assist** for the ICE, which creates its maximum torque much higher in the rpm range. By using an electric motor with an ICE, the overall displacement of the ICE can be reduced. For example, a vehicle that might have needed a 2.0-liter engine to operate might only need a 1.4-liter engine to perform the same way when it is combined with the hybrid electric motor. This reduction in size of the ICE results in a fuel savings, not only during city driving but also on the highway FIGURE 16-3.

Electric-Only Propulsion

On many full hybrids, the vehicle can operate at low speeds using the electric motor only. When a driver presses on the accelerator pedal, the PCM commands the high-voltage battery pack to apply electricity to the

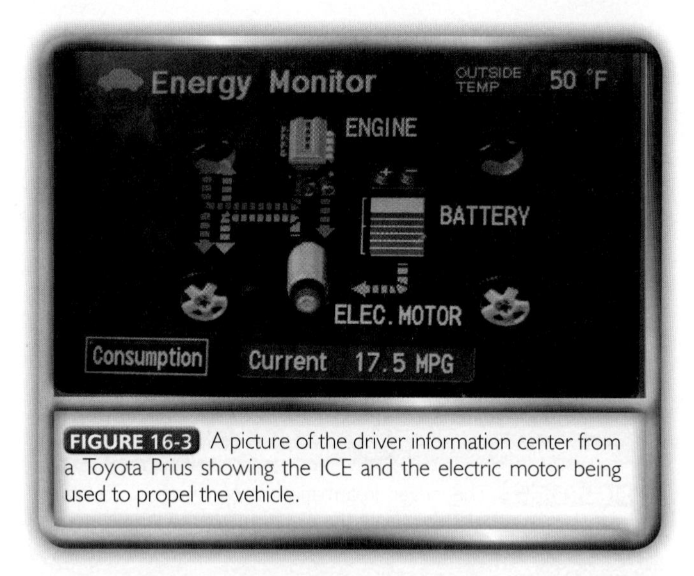

Energy Monitor
OUTSIDE TEMP
50 °F
ENGINE
BATTERY
ELEC. MOTOR
Consumption
Current 17.5 MPG

FIGURE 16-3 A picture of the driver information center from a Toyota Prius showing the ICE and the electric motor being used to propel the vehicle.

electric motor until the vehicle reaches speeds up to approximately 40 miles per hour (64 kilometers per hour) (depending on the model), at which point the PCM starts the ICE to continue accelerating the vehicle **FIGURE 16-4**.

Safety

Extreme caution should be exercised when working around hybrid vehicles. These vehicles often use very high voltages that can cause serious harm or death. Only begin working on a hybrid vehicle after you have had the proper safety training and thoroughly understand the system and its operation, and have the proper safety equipment. Always check with the appropriate service information before attempting any repairs on a hybrid vehicle. In addition to the high voltages, many systems have very strong permanent magnets that will attract any ferrous metal that gets close to them and can pinch your fingers or hand between the part and the magnet. The magnets often cannot be removed without a special tool.

FIGURE 16-4 A driver information center on a Toyota Prius showing the electric motor alone propelling the vehicle.

Hybrid Electric Vehicle Models

Currently, hybrid vehicles are available from almost every vehicle manufacturer, with new models being added every month as the demand for more fuel-efficient vehicles increases. In this section, we will cover some of the more common hybrid vehicle systems used by the different manufacturers.

Belt Alternator Starter

Belt alternator starter (BAS) vehicles have been produced primarily by the General Motors Corporation **FIGURE 16-5**. The BAS unit is a belt-driven alternator and starter motor. Conventional starter motors and alternators operate on nominal 12 volts, while the BAS system uses a 42-volt battery.

When the engine is running, the belt spins the BAS motor, which in turn produces electricity, like a conventional alternator, to charge the high-voltage battery. When the engine is stopped, the BAS motor can crank the vehicle over very quickly through the belt drive. This design allows the vehicle to use the fuel savings of the idle stop function.

As the vehicle is slowing down, the BAS motor is used to produce a large amount of current to charge the battery, while also slowing the vehicle down due to the extra drag of the alternator. This allows the vehicle to capture some of the fuel savings of the regenerative braking.

Honda Integrated Motor Assist

Honda hybrids use a system called the **integrated motor assist (IMA)**. The IMA system uses a thin electric motor in place of a conventional flywheel or flex plate. This electric motor is used to supplement the gasoline engine's

FIGURE 16-5 A BAS system installed on a Chevrolet Malibu.

power when accelerating. The Honda IMA system is classified as a parallel hybrid because the electric motor is operating at the same time as the gasoline engine. The Honda IMA system uses between 144 volts and 158 volts, depending on the year of the vehicle and the specific model of hybrid. Currently, Honda IMA hybrids cannot drive using the electric motor only because the IMA is not able to disconnect from the gasoline engine. Therefore, in order for electricity to be produced, the gasoline engine must be spinning. (It does not have to be using gasoline, though; it can be coasting.)

The electric motor is used to charge the high-voltage battery pack when the vehicle is decelerating, converting some of the kinetic energy of the vehicle motion into electrical energy, rather than wasting some of the energy in heat during braking. The electric motor is also used to rapidly restart the engine after the driver releases the brake pedal.

The Honda IMA system does also use a conventional 12-volt starter to initially start the vehicle when it is cold out or when the high-voltage battery is not charged. The transaxle used in combination with the IMA system can be a conventional automatic transmission, a manual transmission, or, more typically, a CVT. CVTs will be covered later in this chapter. All three types of transmissions have been modified to be smaller so they can fit with the IMA assembly between the engine and the transmission FIGURE 16-6.

Toyota and Lexus Hybrids

Toyota and Lexus hybrids use a power-splitting device that could be considered a type of CVT. These hybrids use voltages from 200 to 650 volts, depending on the application. The Toyota and Lexus hybrids can be classified as a series-parallel hybrid because either the gasoline ICE or the electric motor/generator can propel the vehicle, or both can be used together.

Safety

Because the vehicle can be driven by the electric motor only, and the ICE can be started by the PCM at any time that the key is turned on or the system is powered up by the start button, it is very important that you follow the manufacturer's procedure for testing the vehicle. This imperative could be illustrated by a simple turn signal bulb inspection. You would normally turn the ignition switch to the run position, turn on the turn signal, and then go look at the front and rear turn signal bulbs. Unfortunately, with a hybrid system, the vehicle could start on its own and travel across the shop, putting others and the vehicle in danger. Follow the manufacturer's procedures exactly when working on a hybrid vehicle.

The transaxle contains two electric motor/generators, a final drive gear set, a differential, and a planetary gear set. Each of the electric motor/generators and the ICE are connected to a separate part of the planetary gear set, as shown in FIGURE 16-7.

The ring gear of the planetary gear set is connected to the final drive through a drive chain as in many front-wheel drive (FWD) transaxles. The ring gear is also directly connected to motor/generator 2 (M/G2). The sun gear of the planetary gear set is attached to the motor/generator 1 (M/G1). M/G1 is used as a generator to charge the high-voltage battery pack and to crank the engine over. The planet carrier of the planetary gear set is attached to the ICE.

When starting the gasoline engine, M/G1 spins the planetary carrier, which is attached to the ICE, in order to crank the engine. With the vehicle stopped, M/G2 is basically locked and prevented from turning.

FIGURE 16-6 An electric motor from a Honda IMA system.

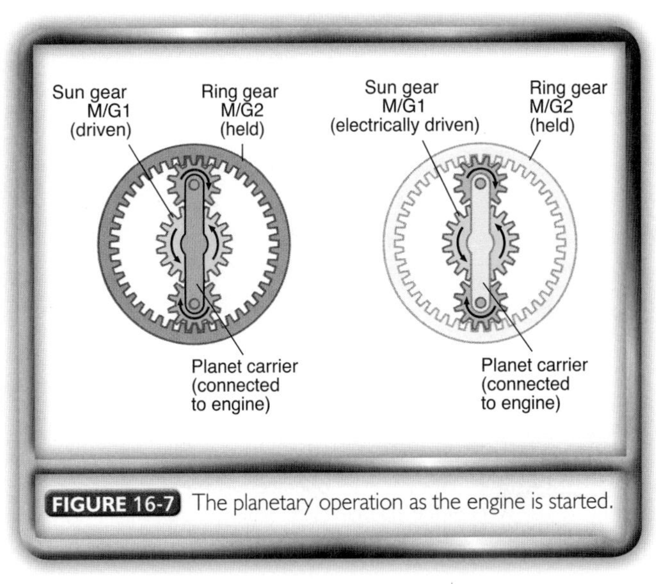
Sun gear
M/G1
(driven)
Ring gear
M/G2
(held)
Sun gear
M/G1
(electrically driven)
Ring gear
M/G2
(held)
Planet carrier
(connected
to engine)
Planet carrier
(connected
to engine)

FIGURE 16-7 The planetary operation as the engine is started.

When the engine starts, M/G1 begins spinning. M/G1 switches to generator mode and begins charging the high-voltage battery pack. M/G2 then begins to spin and the power from the ICE is added to M/G2 to spin the ring gear and propel the vehicle FIGURE 16-8.

Toyota and Lexus hybrids are able to propel the vehicle in electric-only mode at low speeds. During electric-only mode, the ICE is shut down, effectively holding the planet carrier from spinning. High voltage is supplied to M/G2, which spins the ring gear and drives the wheels. M/G1 is allowed to spin freely FIGURE 16-9. In reverse, the current flow to M/G2 is reversed and causes the motor to spin in the opposite direction. In reverse, the ICE is not used to propel the vehicle.

During deceleration at low speeds, the engine is shut off to hold the carrier. M/G1 is allowed to freewheel while M/G2 is driven by the wheels. M/G2 is switched to generator mode and the power generated is used to recharge the high-voltage battery pack FIGURE 16-10.

The vehicle's PCM controls the amount of current produced from M/G2 during deceleration to prevent wheel lock-up and skidding. During electric-only operation, the PCM continuously monitors the battery voltage and restarts the ICE as needed. There is no torque converter or clutch mechanism. There is, however, a damper assembly that is used to cushion the power pulses from the engine and reduce the drive line shock.

Ford Motor Company Hybrids

The Ford Escape and Fusion hybrids (along with the Lincoln and Mercury versions) are very similar in operation to the Toyota system. The Ford transaxle also uses two electric motor/generators that in conjunction with an ICE split power through a planetary gear set. The only major difference between the Ford and the Toyota is that rather than having the two electric motor/generators directly connected to the ring gear and the sun gear, they are attached through a set of transfer gears FIGURE 16-11.

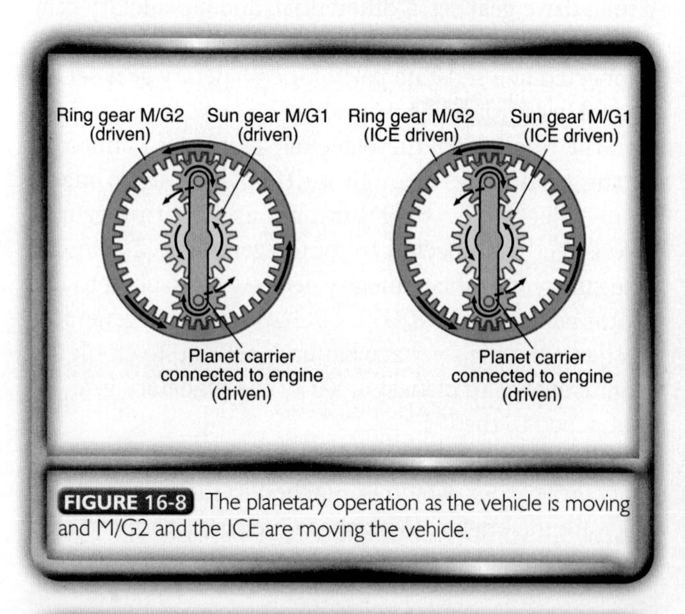
Ring gear M/G2
(driven)
Sun gear M/G1
(driven)
Ring gear M/G2
(ICE driven)
Sun gear M/G1
(ICE driven)
Planet carrier
connected to engine
(driven)
Planet carrier
connected to engine
(driven)

FIGURE 16-8 The planetary operation as the vehicle is moving and M/G2 and the ICE are moving the vehicle.

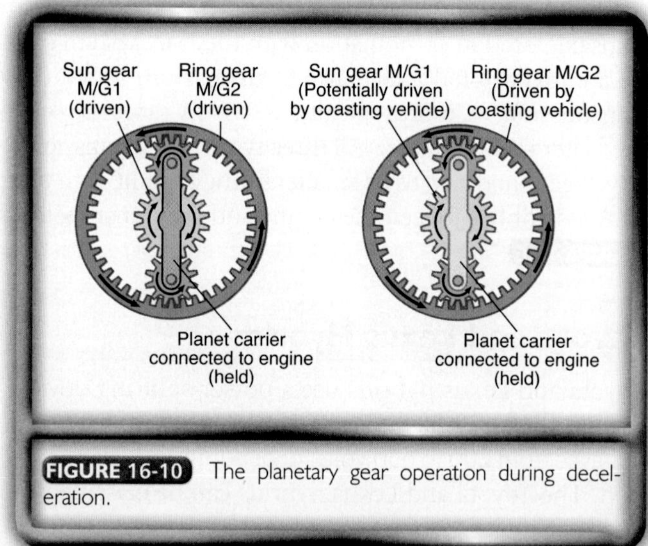
Sun gear
M/G1
(driven)
Ring gear
M/G2
(driven)
Sun gear M/G1
(Potentially driven
by coasting vehicle)
Ring gear M/G2
(Driven by
coasting vehicle)
Planet carrier
connected to engine
(held)
Planet carrier
connected to engine
(held)

FIGURE 16-10 The planetary gear operation during deceleration.

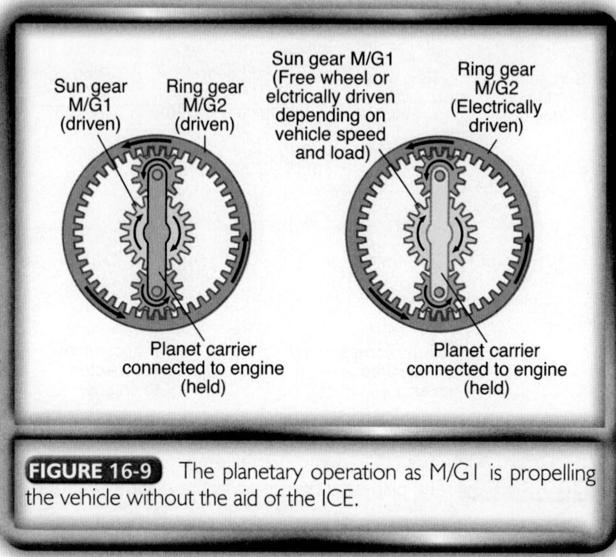
Sun gear
M/G1
(driven)
Ring gear
M/G2
(driven)
Sun gear M/G1
(Free wheel or
elctrically driven
depending on
vehicle speed
and load)
Ring gear
M/G2
(Electrically
driven)
Planet carrier
connected to engine
(held)
Planet carrier
connected to engine
(held)

FIGURE 16-9 The planetary operation as M/G1 is propelling the vehicle without the aid of the ICE.

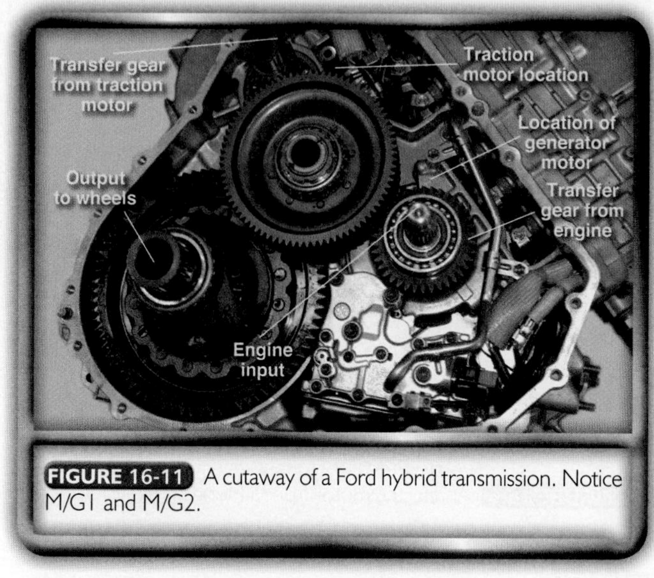
Transfer gear
from traction
motor
Traction
motor location
Location of
generator
motor
Output
to wheels
Transfer
gear from
engine
Engine
input

FIGURE 16-11 A cutaway of a Ford hybrid transmission. Notice M/G1 and M/G2.

Continuously Variable Transmission (CVT)

A CVT has no fixed gear ratios; the transmission can infinitely change the gear ratio within its operational design. Changes to the gear ratio occur in a smooth stepless progression to suit speed and load conditions. This design allows the engine to operate in its most efficient operating rpm range for fuel economy or performance, depending on the driver's demands.

Types of CVTs

There are three basic types of CVTs commonly used in production vehicles. The first type is often referred to as an **electronic continuously variable transmission (ECVT)** and is found in hybrid vehicles. The second type is the most common CVT, called a variable-diameter pulley or Reeves drive CVT. The last type of CVT found in automobiles is a toroidal or roller-based CVT. We will not discuss teroidal type CVT. Feel free to research it on the internet, as it is an interesting CVT.

We have already covered the ECVT because it is the transmission/transaxle found in Toyota and Ford hybrid vehicles. By using the combination of two electric motor/generators and an ICE driven through a specially designed planetary gear set, the manufacturer is able to create an infinite number of gear ratios.

Variable-Diameter Pulley CVT

The **variable-diameter pulley (VDP)** CVT is one of the most common types of CVTs being used in vehicles today. The VDP system operates using two variable diameter pulleys with either a steel or a rubber belt between them. Some of the early CVTs in Europe used a stiff rubber belt, as do many snowmobiles and all-terrain vehicles (ATVs). The rubber belt has a limited service life in an automobile, so most manufacturers use a steel drive belt. Each of the pulleys has two movable drive faces called sheaves. These sheaves can be moved inward or outward, relative to each other, to change the effective diameter of the pulley FIGURE 16-12.

When the vehicle starts from a stop, the input pulley has a small diameter while the output pulley has large diameter. This size difference creates a high torque multiplication (low speed) gear ratio to start the vehicle from a stop. The drive ratio from a stop is approximately 3:1 through the pulleys. As the vehicle gains speed, the input pulley diameter increases, while the output pulley diameter decreases (high speed).

The input pulley diameter is changed by applying hydraulic oil to one of the pulley sheaves to push the two sheaves closer together. The belt is forced to ride higher on the faces of the pulley, changing the effective diameter of the pulley, as shown in FIGURE 16-13. When the two pulleys have the same diameter, the gear ratio of the pulleys is 1:1. As vehicle speed increases, the input pulley continues to increase in diameter, and the output pulley decreases in diameter, to create an overdrive ratio of 1:2, or even greater on some transmissions. Remember that this ratio does not include any final drive gearing, which will reduce the actual gear ratio of the CVT.

Belt tension is maintained by large springs in the output shaft pulley. The springs cause the sheaves of the output pulley to be close together, creating a large-diameter pulley. As the input pulley diameter increases, the springs in the output pulley are compressed, decreasing the diameter of the output pulley. The diameter of the pulleys is controlled to keep the engine operating in its most efficient rpm range.

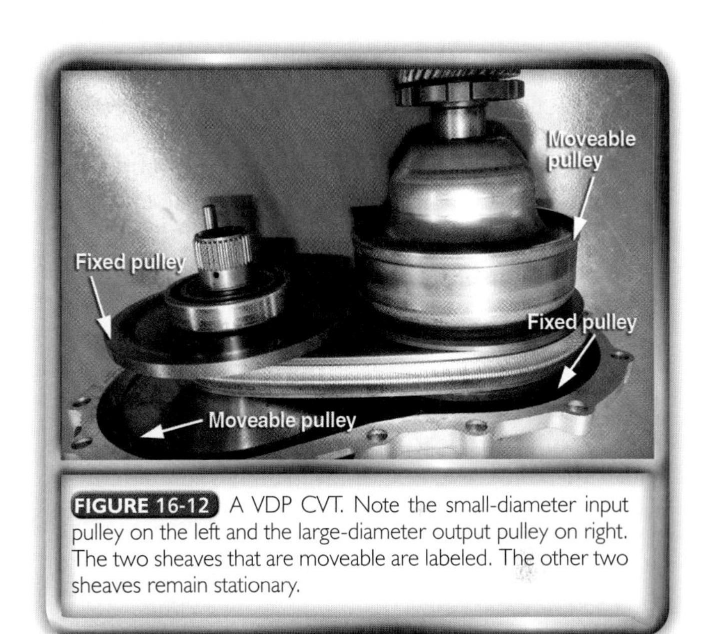
Moveable pulley
Fixed pulley
Fixed pulley
Moveable pulley

FIGURE 16-12 A VDP CVT. Note the small-diameter input pulley on the left and the large-diameter output pulley on right. The two sheaves that are moveable are labeled. The other two sheaves remain stationary.

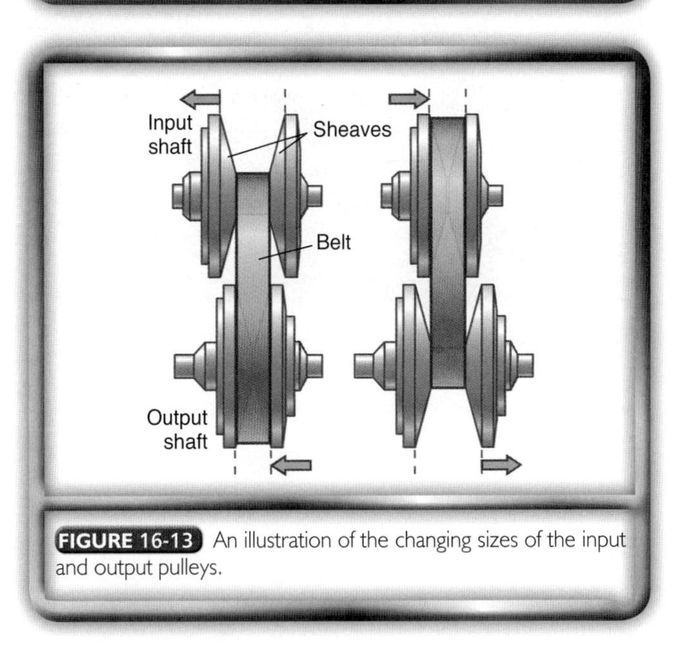
Input shaft
Sheaves
Belt
Output shaft

FIGURE 16-13 An illustration of the changing sizes of the input and output pulleys.

The PCM monitors the speed of the two pulleys to maintain the correct gear ratio. Some CVTs also incorporate a sensor to measure the position of one of the input pulley sheaves. This allows for greater control and monitoring of the CVT.

Some manufacturers have programmed into the PCM regular shift points, at which the pulley sheaves will move to predetermined positions to create the feel of separate conventional shifts. Some manufacturers also allow the driver to manually shift through these predetermined pulley diameters while driving the vehicle.

The steel belt is made up of hundreds of transversely mounted steel plates that are held in place with several steel bands running longitudinally around the edge of the plates. The transverse steel plates grab the sides of the pulley and in turn are pushed by the pulleys. The longitudinal steel bands are used to hold the belt together and keep the steel plates lined up. These bands hold the plates closely together in a very strong and flexible ring. The plates are guided by the bands but not attached to them. Drive is transmitted by compressing the plate elements rather than relying on tension in the band. Each block leaving the primary pulley pushes the blocks ahead of it to the secondary pulley, where the bands keep the blocks in contact with the pulley faces. The blocks are compressed on the drive side and float loosely along the bands on the return side.

The large number of plates that are in contact with the pulleys keeps the surface pressures low on the belt, allowing high torque to be transmitted. The belt is lubricated by transmission fluid sprayed directly onto it at high pressure. A typical steel belt is shown in FIGURE 16-14.

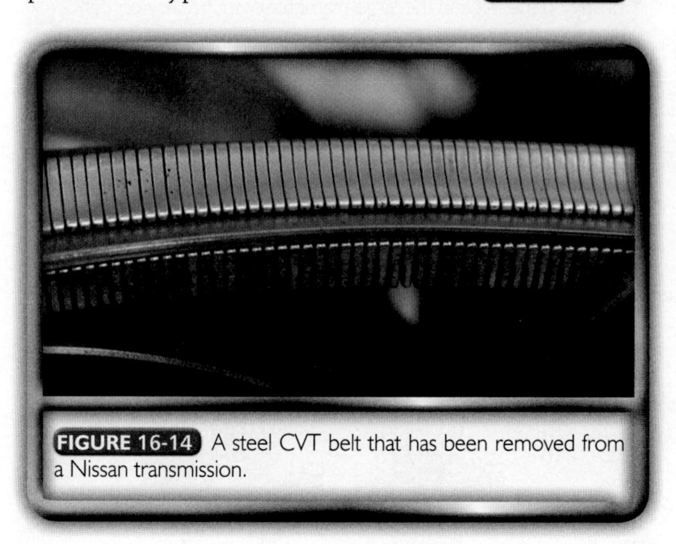

FIGURE 16-14 A steel CVT belt that has been removed from a Nissan transmission.

CVTs require special transmission fluid, and many CVTs have a special transmission oil heater built into them. This heater is used to warm up the transmission oil so the transmission can operate properly during cold weather operation. Filter and fluid change intervals must be adhered to in order to prevent damage to the transmission.

Applied Science

AS-98: Simple Machines: The technician can demonstrate an understanding of how cams, pulleys, and levers are used to multiply forces or change the direction of force in a mechanical system.

Simple machines, such as cams, pulleys, and levers, have become much improved and refined over the years. Looking back into history, we can understand that these three mechanical units have transformed the way that we perform many tasks.

Cams have the ability to change rotary motion to linear motion; for example, a camshaft in an engine. Cams have also been used in printing presses, textile machinery, and machine shop equipment of various types.

Pulleys can be used to change the direction of a force or provide a mechanical advantage with a multiple part line. As an example, raising a flag on a flagpole requires the use of a pulley.

Levers are one of the basic tools that may have been used in prehistoric times. The Greek mathematician, Archimedes, described the use of levers in 260 BC. Examples of levers include pry bars, pliers, claw hammers, and tongs.

As described in our text, the Variable- Diameter Pulley (VDP) continuously variable transmission is one of the most common types of CVT being used in vehicles today. The VDP system operates using two variable diameter pulleys with either a steel or rubber belt between them. The rubber belt has a limited service life in an automobile, so most manufacturers use a steel drive belt. Each of the pulleys has two movable drive faces called sheaves. These sheaves can be moved inward or outward, relative to each other, to change the effective diameter of the pulley.

A CVT is a transmission that can change through an infinite number of gear ratios. This infinite number is limited only between the minimum and maximum capabilities of the particular unit. This contrasts with other mechanical transmissions that offer a fixed number of gear ratios. Fuel economy is enhanced by the engine being allowed to run at its most efficient rpm for a range of vehicle speeds.

Wrap-up

Ready for Review

- Vehicles with continuously variable transmissions (CVTs) are becoming more prevalent.
- A system that uses two or more power sources is a hybrid drive system.
- A hybrid vehicle may have the following functions: idle stop, torque smoothing, regenerative braking, torque assist, and electric-only propulsion.
- Idle stop refers to engine shutoff when the driver stops (but does not turn off) the vehicle.
- A hybrid vehicle that uses an electric motor to smooth out internal combustion engine (ICE) power pulses is using torque smoothing.
- Most hybrid vehicles use braking power to generate electricity to charge the battery (regenerative braking).
- Torque assist refers to using torque to help propel the vehicle when additional torque is needed.
- Common hybrid vehicle systems include belt alternator starter (BAS), Honda integrated motor assist (IMA), Toyota and Lexus hybrids, and Ford hybrids.
- A BAS system uses a 42-volt battery and relies on the belt drive to help quickly crank the vehicle over following an idle stop.
- The IMA system replaces the conventional flywheel with a thin electric motor to supplement the engine's torque during acceleration.
- The Toyota, Lexus, and Ford hybrid systems are series-parallel systems because the ICE and the electric generator can propel the vehicle, either individually or together.
- In Toyota, Lexus, and Ford hybrid systems, the PCM monitors battery voltage; if voltage is low, the ICE is engaged.
- Ford hybrid systems have two electric motors attached through a set of transfer gears.
- A CVT is able to change gear ratios to suit vehicle speed and load conditions for optimum fuel economy and performance.
- Types of CVTs are the electronic continuously variable transmission (ECVT), variable-diameter pulley (VDP) CVT, and toroidal (or roller-based) CVT.
- The most common CVT in vehicles today is the VDP.
- A VDP has two pulleys (input and output) with movable drive faces that can be adjusted to change the pulleys' effective diameter.
- The output pulley of a VDP utilizes large springs to maintain belt tension.
- Manufacturers recommend replacing CVTs as a whole, rather than repairing internal components.
- Change CVT fluid and filters on a regular basis to maintain transmission functionality.
- Toroidal CVTs use curved discs (input and output) with a set of variable-angle rollers instead of pulleys.
- Toroidal CVTs are costly to manufacture, and production is limited.
- In some VDP CVTs, multidisc clutch packs and planetary gear sets are designed to allow transmission operation in reverse and to create a low gear ratio.

Key Terms

belt alternator starter (BAS) A type of hybrid drive system that uses a belt-driven alternator/starter that operates on 42 volts.

continuously variable transmission (CVT) A type of transmission that has no fixed gears, as in a conventional transmission, but rather can adjust gear ratios infinitely within the design of the transmission.

electronic continuously variable transmission (ECVT) A type of hybrid transmission that often uses two electric motors in combination with an ICE. The two electric motors and the ICE transfer power through a planetary gear set, allowing an infinite amount of gear ratios.

hybrid drive system A drive system that uses two or more propulsion systems such as electric motors and an ICE.

integrated motor assist (IMA) A Honda hybrid drive system that uses a moderate-sized electric motor installed between the engine and the transmission.

regenerative braking A type of braking in which the kinetic energy of the vehicle's motion is captured rather than being lost to heat in a conventional braking system.

torque assist Use of an electric motor to supplement the engine's torque whenever additional torque is needed, allowing for a smaller ICE to be used.

torque smoothing A process that uses an electric motor to smooth out engine power pulses when an ICE is operating at low rpm or when the vehicle is using fuel management techniques such as cylinder deactivation.

variable-diameter pulley (VDP) A type of CVT that uses two pulleys with moveable sheaves, allowing the effective diameter of the pulleys to change, resulting in variable gear ratios.

ASE-Type Questions

1. Tech A says that hybrid vehicles have an internal combustion engine and an electric motor. Tech B says that most hybrid vehicles utilize regenerative braking to help improve fuel economy. Who is correct?
   a. Tech A
   b. Tech B
   c. Both A and B
   d. Neither A nor B
2. Tech A says that it is critical to have the proper safety equipment before working on a hybrid. Tech B says that hybrid vehicles can start up or move on their own if not powered down properly. Who is correct?
   a. Tech A
   b. Tech B
   c. Both A and B
   d. Neither A nor B
3. Tech A says that hybrid vehicles will typically use the same transmission as a non-hybrid vehicle. Tech B says that some hybrid transmissions have a small electric fluid pump for when the transmission is in idle/stop mode. Who is correct?
   a. Tech A
   b. Tech B
   c. Both A and B
   d. Neither A nor B
4. Tech A says that BAS vehicles use an alternator to help slow the vehicle and act as a starter. Tech B says that the BAS alternator can be used to propel the vehicle without the ICE. Who is correct?
   a. Tech A
   b. Tech B
   c. Both A and B
   d. Neither A nor B
5. Tech A says that the transmission in a Toyota hybrid has a separate gear to provide reverse. Tech B says that Toyota hybrids use a VDP CVT transmission. Who is correct?
   a. Tech A
   b. Tech B
   c. Both A and B
   d. Neither A nor B
6. Tech A says that some VDP CVTs use a steel belt to transfer power from pulley to pulley. Tech B says that regeneration in a hybrid vehicle is highest during acceleration. Who is correct?
   a. Tech A
   b. Tech B
   c. Both A and B
   d. Neither A nor B
7. Tech A says that some CVTs require a heating system to warm the transmission fluid during cold weather operation. Tech B says that CVTs use conventional automatic transmission fluid. Who is correct?
   a. Tech A
   b. Tech B
   c. Both A and B
   d. Neither A nor B
8. Tech A says that on a VDP CVT, each pulley has a moveable sheave. Tech B says that most CVTs in vehicles use a rubber drive belt between two movable pulleys. Who is correct?
   a. Tech A
   b. Tech B
   c. Both A and B
   d. Neither A nor B
9. Tech A says that regeneration occurs during braking. Tech B says that regeneration charges the main battery pack. Who is correct?
   a. Tech A
   b. Tech B
   c. Both A and B
   d. Neither A nor B
10. Tech A says that the Honda IMA system uses a thin electric motor between the engine and the CVT transmission. Tech B says that the Honda IMA system uses voltages between 144 and 158 volts. Who is correct?
    a. Tech A
    b. Tech B
    c. Both A and B
    d. Neither A nor B

SECTION IV

Manual Transmissions

CHAPTER 17

Prove
Know
See
Do

NATEF Tasks

Manual Transmissions
General

		Page
■ Check fluid condition; check for leaks.	MLR	426–42 430
■ Drain and refill manual transmission/transaxle and final drive unit.	MLR	427–42
■ Check and adjust differential housing fluid level.	MLR	427–42
■ Drain and refill differential housing.	MLR	427

Prove
Know
See
Do

Knowledge Objectives

After reading this chapter, you will be able to:

1. Describe the principle of mechanical advantage. (p 416)
2. Describe the meaning of gear ratio. (pp 416–417)
3. Describe the trade-off between mechanical advantage and the rotational speed of gears. (pp 418–419)
4. Calculate the gear ratio of given sets of gears. (pp 417–418)
5. Describe the principle of power flow. (p 419)
6. Describe the purpose of the drive train, its operation, and components. (pp 419–425)
7. Identify spur and helical gears. (p 421)
8. Describe radial and axial loads. (pp 421–422)
9. Describe the purpose of the clutch. (p 422)
10. Describe the purpose of the transfer case. (pp 424–425)
11. Describe the purpose of the final drive and differential assembly. (pp 424–425)
12. Describe the difference between a live axle and a dead axle. (p 425)
13. Describe preventive maintenance and the importance of lubrication. (pp 425–430)

Manual Transmission/ Transaxle Principles

Know
See
Do

Skills Objectives

After reading this chapter, you will be able to:

1. Check and adjust the gearbox fluid level. (pp 426–427)
2. Check and adjust the differential/transfer case fluid level. (pp 427–428)
3. Change the gearbox fluid. (pp 428–429)
4. Identify the cause of fluid loss in a transmission/transaxle. (pp 428, 430)

Introduction

In this chapter, we will explore the history and principles of the modern manual transmission **drive train** system. Some of those principles involve certain aspects of physics, such as mechanical advantage and gear ratios. Other principles require an understanding of the nomenclature and theory of operation of the major drive train assemblies. Having a good understanding of these principles will give you a framework for performing maintenance and light repair tasks on manual transmission equipped drive trains.

A good starting place is to understand what is meant by "drive train." The drive train consists of the component assemblies that transmit power from the engine all the way to the drive wheels. The manual transmission is at the heart of the drive train and receives power from the engine by way of the clutch assembly. The clutch can be operated by the driver to disconnect and connect the transmission from the engine. The transmission provides the driver with a range of shiftable gears from which to select as he or she is operating the vehicle. In a front-engine, rear-wheel drive vehicle, the transmission sends power to the final drive assembly, which then changes the direction of the twisting force 90 degrees so it can be sent out the axles to the wheels and tires. In a front-engine, front-wheel drive vehicle, the transaxle contains both the transmission and the final drive assembly in a common unit and sends the power out the axles to the front wheels and tires. In four-wheel drive vehicles, the transmission or transaxle sends power to all four wheels and tires.

History of Manual Transmissions

In 1877, a patent for a front-wheel drive carriage with a one-cylinder engine was obtained by George Selden. The "claim to fame" of that vehicle was the transmission FIGURE 17-1. The power from the engine drove a set of bevel gears, which in turn drove a shaft and a pulley. Leather belts were used on a pulley and a geared wheel on the axle to make it move. One small wheel on the engine got the car going by meshing with the ring gear

1877

FIGURE 17-1 The engine and transmission, which were on the front axle, drove this early vehicle.

You Are the Automotive Technician

A customer brings his Buick into the dealership for its 60,000-mile preventive maintenance service appointment. He has faithfully followed the manufacturer's preventive maintenance schedule since he bought the vehicle and would like to have his manual transmission/transaxle and drive train components serviced today. He believes that if you follow the specific manufacturer's schedule, the vehicle will last forever.

1. Why is preventive maintenance so important for the service life of the transmission/transaxle and drive train components?
2. What rationale would you give a customer to have regular maintenance on these parts rather than rebuilding?
3. Why does understanding how the power flows help you to diagnose manual transmission concerns more easily?

on one of the drive wheels. The big wheel on the axle then made the car move along at a staggering, at the time, 20 miles per hour.

This early engine had one belt-driven high gear for speed and one belt-driven low gear for increased torque. If the car needed to climb a hill, the driver had to stop, get out, and change the belt to the lower gear. This setup was similar to a 10-speed bicycle, where the bike has a shifting mechanism to physically move a chain from one gear to another.

In 1894, a couple of Frenchmen, Louis René Panhard and Émile Levassor, designed a front-wheel drive multi-gear manual transmission **FIGURE 17-2**. When they tried to put on a demonstration of their new transmission, the engine in their demo vehicle encountered problems and they were unable to make it move under its own power. One year later, Panhard and Levassor successfully demonstrated their new multi-gear transmission. Their transmission and clutch arrangement is the prototype for most manual transmissions today in that it used a clutch-driven, three-speed, sliding gear transmission. When the driver wanted to shift gears, he or she would push the clutch pedal to disengage the engine. Then the driver would move the shifter lever, which slid the previous gears out of mesh and the newly selected gears into mesh. This process allowed the vehicle to move at higher and lower speeds. This sliding gear arrangement became the basis for nearly all manual transmissions since then, with manufacturers developing enhancements to the design.

Prior to 1898, vehicles were either belt or chain driven. Since the chain or belt was exposed to the elements, this design required frequent maintenance. It could also be dangerous if someone got too close to it.

FIGURE 17-2 Panhard and Levassor's attempt at a front drive axle.

In 1898, Louis Renault connected an engine to a transmission and created a live rear axle by using a metal axle shaft supported by bushings. Renault then adapted a differential-type rear axle that was based on an idea that American C. E. Duryea had back in 1893. The differential assembly had a number of gears set in such a way as to allow each wheel to turn at its own speed when going around a corner. This alleviated the problems of loss of traction and rapid tire wear due to scuffing of tires when making turns with a solid axle.

By 1904, most of the car makers had adopted the sliding gear manual transmission design in one form or another. Many improvements have been made since then, including the invention of the **gear synchronizer** (syncromesh), which applies a friction device between the gear and the shaft to match the gear speed to the shaft speed. As a result, the gear and shaft spin at the same speed, which allows gear selection to be made without "grinding" of the gears. In 1928, Cadillac introduced the first **synchromesh transmission**. Porsche improved the design in 1952 by using moly-coated steel rings, which were more efficient and reliable and were licensed by many of the manufacturers of the time. In the early 1960s, BorgWarner introduced the modern cone-style synchronizer, which is still widely used today.

TECHNICIAN TIP

In the time span between the sliding gear transmission and the synchromesh transmission, there were other attempts to make it easier for the driver to change gears. In 1907, the Ford Model T was equipped with a transmission that used constantly meshed planetary gear sets. These sets consist of a central gear—called a *sun gear*—that is meshed with multiple planetary pinion gears, which are meshed inside of a ring gear. Although this gear arrangement is not common in manual transmissions, it is widely used in automatic transmissions today.

TECHNICIAN TIP

All designs of transmissions since Panhard and Levassor have always had one goal in mind: to make shifting easier for the driver. The easiest transmission to shift is the automatic transmission, which is strictly an American innovation.

Principles of Manual Transmissions

Mechanical Advantage

Mechanical advantage is defined as the amplification of the input force by trading distance moved for greater output force. For example, imagine using a 10' lever to move a large rock. If you place a short section of log (the pivot point) 2' from the end of the lever nearest the rock, you would have a mechanical advantage of 8 to 2 FIGURE 17-3. Ratios are normally expressed as the equivalent of the first number to 1; thus, 8 to 2 would be expressed as 4 to 1, which is written as 4:1. Assuming no frictional loss, a lever with this mechanical advantage would exert four times as much force against the rock as the amount of force being applied by the person to the other end of the lever. So we could say the lever gives a mechanical advantage of 4:1.

Given this 4:1 mechanical advantage, if a person pushes the lever down with a force of 100 pounds (lb), the force the lever generates against the rock is 400 lb. By using a lever, the person achieves more output force than he or she puts in. However, the person also is moving the long side of the lever four times as far as the rock side of the lever. So although the output force is four times greater than the input force, the input distance moved is four times greater than the output distance. Also, the input speed is four times faster than the output speed. Thus, the total amount of work on each end of the lever is the same (work = force × distance); it is simply rearranged to give an increase of the output force. The lesson here is that mechanical advantage can be used to generate a larger output force, but it requires an increase in the input distance and speed.

This concept applies directly to manual transmissions. Each set of gears, called a **gear set**, in the transmission provides a certain amount of mechanical advantage and has a specific speed differential associated with it. For example, in low gear, where the smallest gear in the transmission turns the largest gear in the transmission, one complete turn of the small gear will turn the larger gear only a small portion of a full turn. This provides mechanical advantage and is called gear reduction. At the same time, because the small gear is turning much faster than the output gear, the output speed is slow compared to the input speed. The driver can select the transmission gear set that best matches the operating conditions under which he or she is driving. If driving on rough and hilly off-road terrain, then a lower gear will work well. If driving on a smooth, straight, and level freeway, a higher gear will be best.

Gear Ratios

How do gear sets create mechanical advantage? They do so by having different ratios. Gears with the same number of teeth have a ratio of 1:1, meaning that this set of gears has no mechanical advantage FIGURE 17-4. At the same time, there is no difference of speed between the gears; they each turn at the same speed because they have the same number of teeth. A gear set in which the input gear has half as many teeth as the output gear has a ratio of 2:1. **Gear ratios** can be found by comparing the number of teeth each gear has FIGURE 17-5. If the drive gear (the input gear) has fewer teeth than the driven gear (the output gear), then the gear set will have mechanical advantage because the smaller drive gear has to rotate faster than the larger driven gear, giving an increase in output torque.

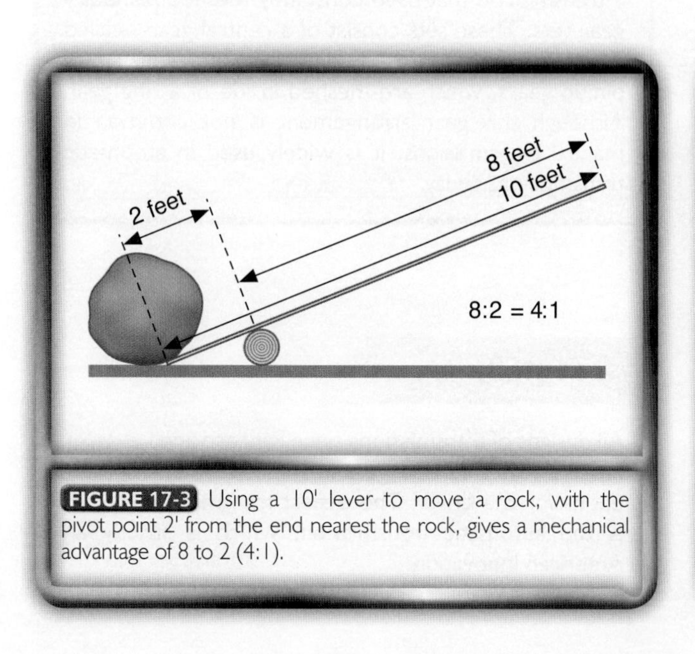
2 feet
8 feet
10 feet
8:2 = 4:1

FIGURE 17-3 Using a 10' lever to move a rock, with the pivot point 2' from the end nearest the rock, gives a mechanical advantage of 8 to 2 (4:1).

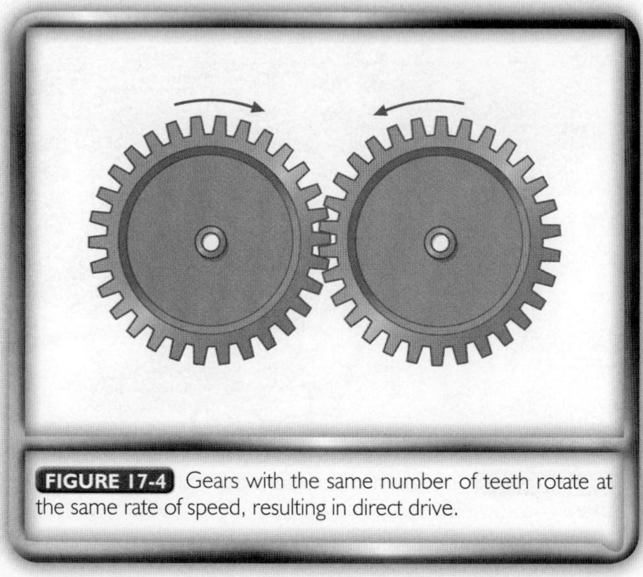

FIGURE 17-4 Gears with the same number of teeth rotate at the same rate of speed, resulting in direct drive.

The terms input gear and drive gear have the same meaning. The same goes for output gear and driven gear. For the sake of simplicity, we will generally refer to the gears as input and output. Note that other textbooks or service information may use the alternate terms.

Calculating the Gear Ratio

Gear ratios of different gear sizes can be calculated by dividing the number of teeth on the driven gear by the number of teeth on the drive gear **FIGURE 17-6**. For example, if the driven gear has 24 teeth and the drive gear has 8 teeth, the gear ratio is 24:8, which reduces to 3:1. In this case, the drive gear has to turn three times to turn the driven gear once. In continuous rotation, the driven gear turns three times slower than the drive gear.

All gear ratios are calculated by the formula:

$$\frac{\text{Driven}}{\text{Drive}}$$

or the number of driven gear teeth divided by the number of drive gear teeth. For example, if the drive gear has 10 teeth and the driven gear has 30 teeth, then the mechanical advantage is 3:1. In this case, the driven gear has three times the output force (torque), but only one-third of the **rotational speed**. In other words, if the drive gear is turning at 100 revolutions per minute (rpm), the driven gear is turning at 33.3 rpm, but with three times the torque. If you were to make the drive gear larger by increasing it to 15 teeth and connect it to a driven gear with 30 teeth, the gear ratio would drop to 2:1, but the speed of the driven gear would increase to one-half as fast as the drive gear. In other words, if the drive gear is turning at 100 rpm, the driven gear is now turning 50 rpm, but with only two times the rational force.

> **Caring for the Customer**
>
> Following manufacturer-recommended shifting speed guidelines will ensure good fuel economy. In fact, many vehicles have an indicator on the dash that signals the driver when an upshift or downshift would provide better fuel economy.

Driving a large gear with a smaller gear results in a **gear reduction**, just as a bicycle with a large gear in the back and a small gear in the front gives you a very low gear ratio. If we think of the radius of each gear as a lever, then a large gear being turned by a small gear results in more leverage (at the large gear) and, therefore, more torque. Also, we turn the input gear quickly but the output gear speed is very low, resulting in gear reduction and higher torque. For example, with a gear ratio of 3:1, if input torque is 100 foot-pounds (ft-lb), then output torque is three times that, or 300 ft-lb. Different gear ratios are used inside the transmission to achieve varied torque to accelerate the vehicle. The increase of torque is referred to as **torque multiplication**.

This is what happens inside of a transmission each time the driver selects a different gear ratio. The output torque and speed can be varied as necessary based on the speed and load of the vehicle. When the vehicle speed is low, the driver selects a lower gear (which has a high gear ratio) so that the engine can be used to accelerate the vehicle. As the engine speed increases, the driver selects the next gear so that the vehicle can be accelerated further. This continues to happen until the vehicle reaches the speed desired by the driver.

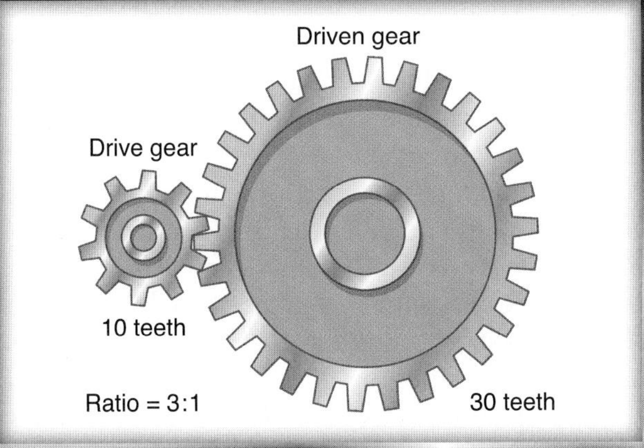

FIGURE 17-5 The mechanical advantage of two gears with a different ratio, which provides torque to get moving.

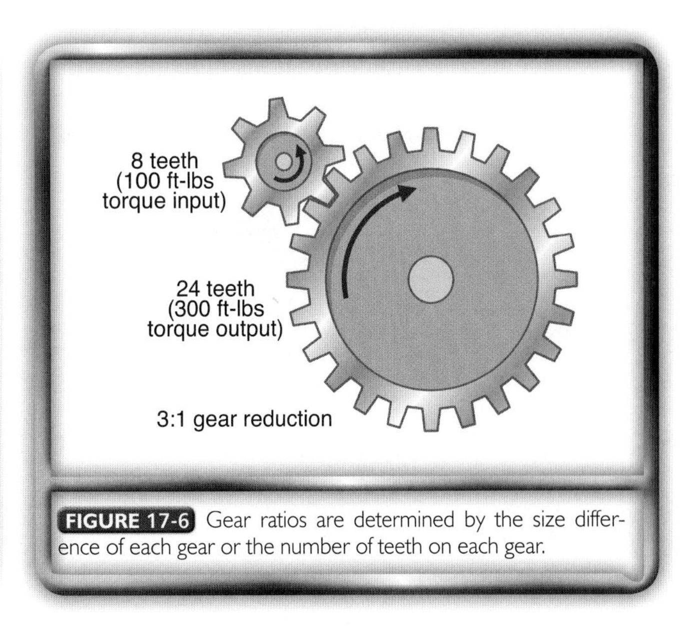
8 teeth
(100 ft-lbs
torque input)
24 teeth
(300 ft-lbs
torque output)
3:1 gear reduction

FIGURE 17-6 Gear ratios are determined by the size difference of each gear or the number of teeth on each gear.

TECHNICIAN TIP

Gear ratio theory will help you to understand how power is distributed and how power and speed vary as the vehicle travels.

Applied Math

AM-35: Standards: The technician can demonstrate conformance to standards defined by the industry and/or manufacturer for the system being analyzed.

A vehicle requires a remanufactured transmission. The owner of the vehicle has indicated to the automotive repair shop service advisor that he would like to inspect the transmission before it is installed. As the owner compares the original five-speed transmission with the remanufactured unit, he has some concerns. The part numbers on the housing are not exactly the same and the customer has some doubts about the remanufactured unit being correct.

Using service information for the customer's vehicle, the technician asks the customer to verify the correct gear ratios for the remanufactured transmission. With the transmission on a work bench, the technician places the shifter into first gear. The service information states that the gear ratio should be 3.5:1 for first gear. This means that the engine would rotate 3.5 times as compared to the output shaft of the transmission rotates 1 time. Using a marker, the technician places reference marks on the input and output shafts of the transmission. The technician rotates the input shaft exactly three and one half turns as the customer observes the output shaft turning exactly one turn. This action demonstrates conformance to the standards of the manufacturer's service information. The same procedure was conducted to indicate a ratio of 2:1 for second gear, 1.4:1 for third gear, 1:1 for fourth gear, and 0.76:1 for fifth gear. After verifying that all gear ratios were correct, the owner was convinced that the remanufactured transmission was correct for his vehicle.

Speed and torque output is the result of which gear ratio is selected and gives the driver a wider range of vehicle speeds to choose from, depending on the road conditions. Controlling an automobile over different terrains and weather conditions is accomplished by using the various gear ratios that are appropriate for those conditions. The ultimate task of the manual transmission is to allow the vehicle to move away from a stop by multiplying the torque through use of low gear, which has a high ratio, and, once moving, to allow the driver to sequentially select higher gears as vehicle speed increases.

In reverse, three gears are in mesh and the input and output gears are meshed with an idler or intermediate gear commonly used in reverse. When two gears are in mesh, the output gear turns in the opposite direction of the input gear. When an idler gear is used between the input and output gears, the output gear turns in the same direction as the input gear. This means the output gear in a three-gear arrangement will rotate in the reverse direction as compared to the output gear on a two-gear arrangement. The **idler gear** simply transfers motion and does not have an effect on the gear ratio of the input to output gears, which is why it is called an idler gear **FIGURE 17-7**.

Output of Different Gear Ratios

As the gear ratio decreases, the output speed increases. This is what happens inside of a transmission each time the driver selects a different gear ratio. The output torque and speed can be varied as necessary based on the speed and load of the vehicle. When the vehicle speed is low, the driver selects a lower gear (which has a high gear ratio) so that the engine can be used to accelerate the vehicle. As the engine speed increases, the driver selects the next gear so that the vehicle can be accelerated further. This continues to happen until the vehicle reaches the speed desired by the driver.

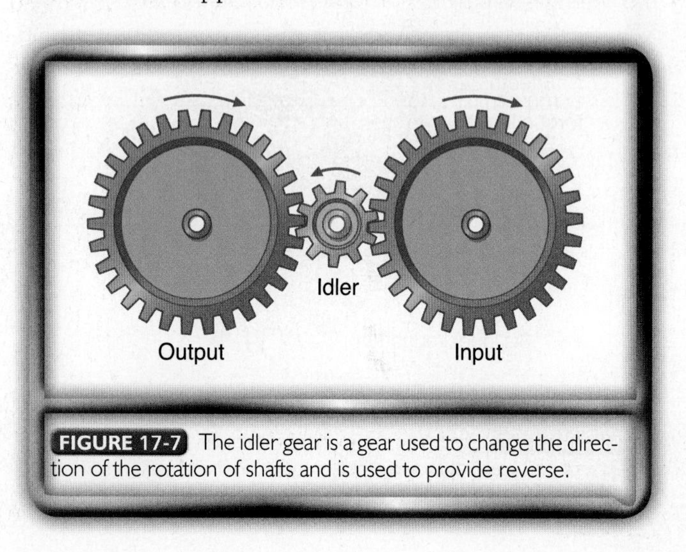
Idler
Output
Input

FIGURE 17-7 The idler gear is a gear used to change the direction of the rotation of shafts and is used to provide reverse.

Speed and torque output is the result of which gear ratio is selected and gives the driver a wider range of vehicle speeds to choose from, depending on the road conditions. Controlling an automobile over different terrains and weather conditions is accomplished by using the various gear ratios that are appropriate for those conditions. The ultimate task of the manual transmission is to allow the vehicle to move away from a stop by multiplying the torque through use of low gear, which has a high ratio, and, once moving, to allow the driver to sequentially select higher gears as vehicle speed increases.

> **TECHNICIAN TIP**
>
> Knowledge of power flow is also an important part of diagnostics. If you understand how the power flows, you will be able to more easily diagnose the manual transmission concern when there is an unusual noise in a particular gear.

Power Flow

Power flow is defined as the path in which power is transmitted through a series of components. There is a power flow for the entire drive train. The engine in the vehicle is the main source of all mechanical power for the vehicle. The power that the engine creates flows from the flywheel, which is bolted to the engine crankshaft, to the clutch assembly, which is bolted to the flywheel. When the clutch is released or the pedal is in the up position, the clutch transmits power from the flywheel to the transmission/transaxle. Power leaves the transmission/transaxle and flows to the final drive assembly, where it changes directions and flows through the axles and out to the wheels. This is a very simple and generic explanation of the path for power to flow from the engine to the tires.

When it comes to the manual transmission, power flows into the transmission through the input shaft, where a gear is used to transfer power to a meshed gear on the countershaft. The countershaft has a number of gears that mesh with gears on the output shaft FIGURE 17-8. The gear the driver selects will determine the power flow from the countershaft to the output shaft. Because of the various gear sets and driver selection, the transmission/transaxle has multiple paths for the power to flow along.

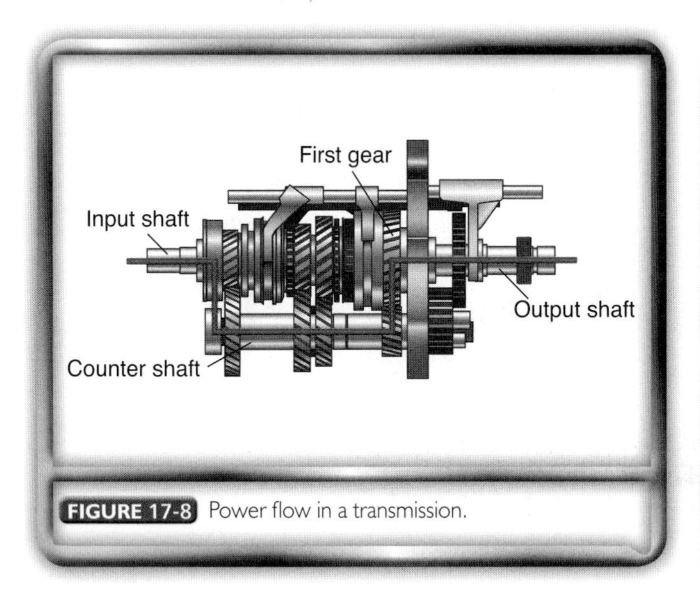
First gear
Input shaft
Output shaft
Counter shaft

FIGURE 17-8 Power flow in a transmission.

Manual Transmission Drive Train Overview

The manual transmission drive train consists of all of the assemblies that transfer power from the engine all the way to the wheels. The **clutch system** is the medium by which the driver can connect and disconnect the engine from the transmission, resulting in the vehicle's forward or rearward movement. On the driver's side, there are usually three pedals on the floor, which, from the driver's right to left, are as follows: the **accelerator pedal**, used for acceleration or deceleration of the engine; the brake pedal, used to stop the vehicle's motion; and the **clutch pedal**, which operates the clutch system. Pushing down on the clutch pedal disconnects the clutch components and allows the selection of the forward or reverse gears within the transmission. Letting the clutch pedal back up reconnects the clutch components and allows the vehicle to move.

The transmission/transaxle is the medium by which the driver selects transitions through the various gear sets to control the speed and power of the vehicle for various types of driving conditions. The term **transmission** relates to layouts where the transmission sends power externally to the final drive assembly and is usually used in rear-wheel drive. The term **transaxle** relates to layouts where the transmission and final drive are integrated into a common assembly and is usually used on front-wheel drive vehicles.

The **final drive assembly** gives the final gear reduction to the drive train and powers the drive wheels through axles FIGURE 17-9. The final drive gear ratio takes the torque from the transmission and increases it further by means of mechanical advantage. This has an effect on the torque applied by the wheels to the ground, the speed of the engine, and the fuel economy. If the final drive has

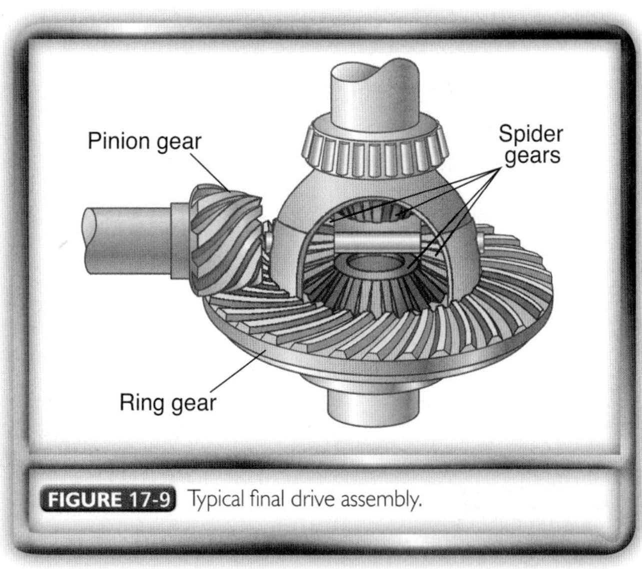
Pinion gear
Spider gears
Ring gear

FIGURE 17-9 Typical final drive assembly.

a high gear ratio (higher numerical number), then the vehicle will have more pulling power but the engine will operate at a higher rpm at any vehicle speed, thereby decreasing the fuel economy. Manufacturers match the final drive gear ratio to the vehicle based on the engine, vehicle weight, and expected use of the vehicle.

When a vehicle travels around a corner, the outside wheel travels a greater distance and thus, turns at a faster rate than the inside wheel. If both wheels were connected to a solid axle, the tires would scuff on the road surface. In modern automobiles, the final drive assembly sits between the ends of two separate axles. The final drive assembly incorporates a set of **differential gears** arranged so that they sit between the two axles. This connects them in such a way that they allow each axle to rotate at its own speed while going around a corner. At the same time, the final drive assembly powers both axles through the differential gear assembly.

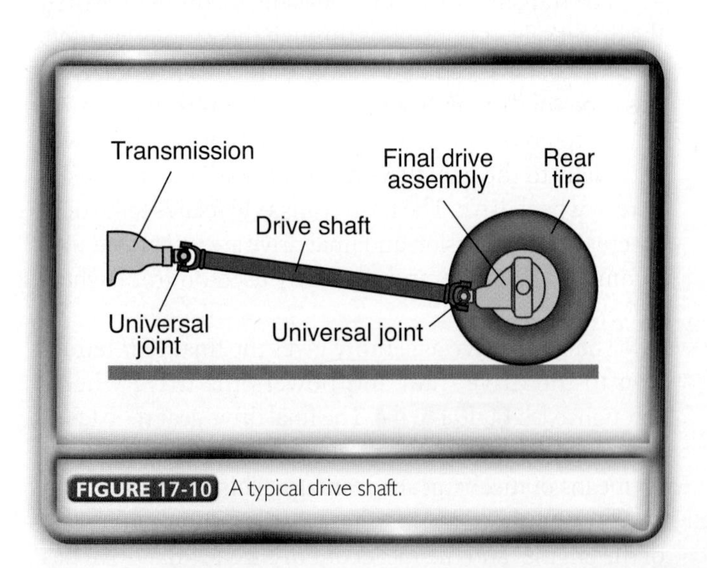
Transmission
Final drive assembly
Rear tire
Drive shaft
Universal joint
Universal joint

FIGURE 17-10 A typical drive shaft.

On rear-wheel drive vehicles, the **drive shaft** transmits power from the transmission to the final drive assembly FIGURE 17-10. The drive shaft uses **universal joints**, which allow the drive shaft to change angles due to the movement of the suspension relative to the body. Since front-wheel drive vehicles incorporate the final drive in the transaxle, no external drive shaft is needed. Both front-wheel drive and rear-wheel drive vehicles use **drive axles** to power the wheels. The axles can be solid, as is the case with many rear-wheel drive vehicles, or flexible **half-shafts**, which use **constant velocity (CV) joints**, as is the case with front-wheel drive vehicles FIGURE 17-11. Front-wheel drive axles must be able to change length as the vehicle goes over bumps and dips and allow for the wheels to be steered. This is provided by different types of CV joints.

Operation

The driver steps on the clutch pedal, which releases the clutch and disconnects the engine from the transmission. Depressing the clutch pedal also closes the contacts of the **clutch safety switch**. The closed clutch safety switch allows the starter motor to crank the engine over when the driver turns the key to the "crank" position. The engine then starts and idles. With the clutch pedal fully depressed, the driver moves the gear shift lever to select first gear or reverse gear. Once in gear, the driver can slowly release the clutch pedal and progressively connect the engine to the transmission.

With the transmission in first gear, the transmission is in the lowest gear; in this gear, the vehicle cannot travel very fast, but it provides the best pulling power. Torque is then sent to the final drive, where its speed undergoes a further gear reduction, which increases the torque again

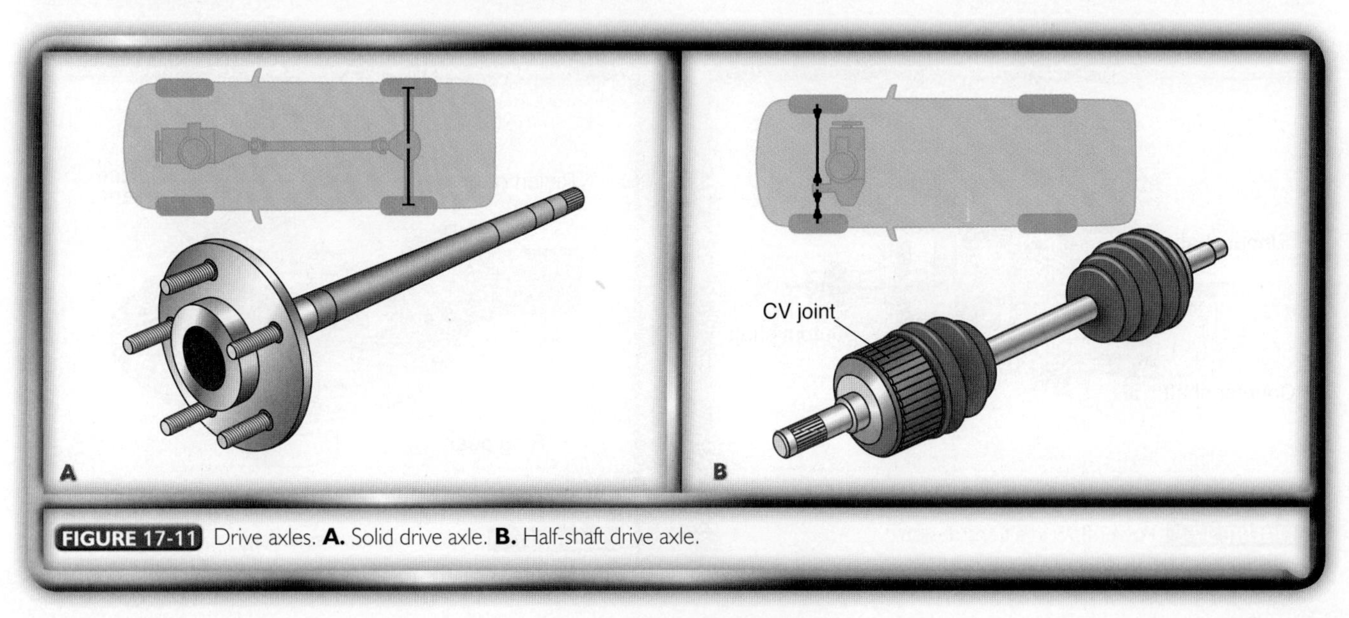
CV joint
A
B

FIGURE 17-11 Drive axles. **A.** Solid drive axle. **B.** Half-shaft drive axle.

before it is sent to the axles. The axles turn the wheels, which are connected to the ground and cause the vehicle to move. When the driver wants to change gears, he or she pushes the clutch pedal and moves the gear shift lever to the next gear position. Once the gear is selected, the driver again slowly releases the clutch pedal to reconnect the engine and transmission and continues driving the vehicle.

Manual Transmission Components

Today's manual transmissions/transaxles are precisely machined, mechanical wonders packed into a relatively small package. Each of the components plays a critical role in allowing the driver to easily operate the transmission. Understanding the main components will give you a good overview of the transmission, which will help you understand how the individual components fit into the overall function of the transmission. Also, understanding the internal workings provides you with a foundation to draw upon when diagnosing transmission problems. We will now cover some of the main components of the manual transmission.

Shafts, Gears, and Bearings

Inside of a manual transmission is a series of shafts, gears, and bearings that make it possible for the driver to select the preferred gear for the road conditions. The availability of several different gear ratios within the transmission allows the vehicle to accelerate from a dead stop almost effortlessly, as well as travel at a variety of speeds without over-revving the engine.

Shafts are used to support gears and are machined precisely to accommodate bearings and individual gears. The surfaces are smooth, allowing the bearings and gears to rotate on a thin film of oil FIGURE 17-12 in order to reduce metal-to-metal friction and prevent catastrophic failure from overheating. Some surfaces on the shaft are **splined** (parallel grooves in a shaft that mate with a component with matching grooves) to allow other parts of the transmission such as synchronizers to be held stationary on the shaft. Other machining may create raised areas on the shafts such as shoulders, which provide a firm support for gears and bearings to butt up against. Alternately, grooves may be cut into the shafts to accommodate **snap rings** and **thrust washers**, which are used for holding the gears in the proper position on the shaft once the gears are installed. The ends of the shafts have machined surfaces to allow for bearings. Bearings are used to center and hold the shafts in alignment so the gears rotate smoothly when in mesh with their mating gears. Friction bearings provide sliding metal-to-metal contact between components and are usually made of brass or bronze. Non-friction bearings provide rolling metal-to-metal contact between components and usually use ball or roller-type bearings.

Gears are round parts with teeth cut on the outside perimeter in order to mate with one or more other gears to achieve a specific gear ratio. The mated gears are called a gear set. Each set is cut on the same angle or pitch to allow for proper contact of the gears with each other. Manual transmission gear teeth are usually of two configurations: spur or helical. **Spur gears** have straight teeth that are parallel to the shaft the gear turns on FIGURE 17-13. They can be noisy during operation. However, they are stronger than helical gears, so they are used in heavy-duty vehicles such as off-road equipment. **Helical gears** have angled teeth that are cut on an angle to the shaft FIGURE 17-14. They operate more quietly and are more commonly used in passenger vehicles.

Bearings are necessary to maintain the position and alignment of the shafts and gears while under two types of loads: radial and axial. **Radial loads** are perpendicular to the shaft and occur because the gears have a tendency to push each other apart as torque is transmitted between

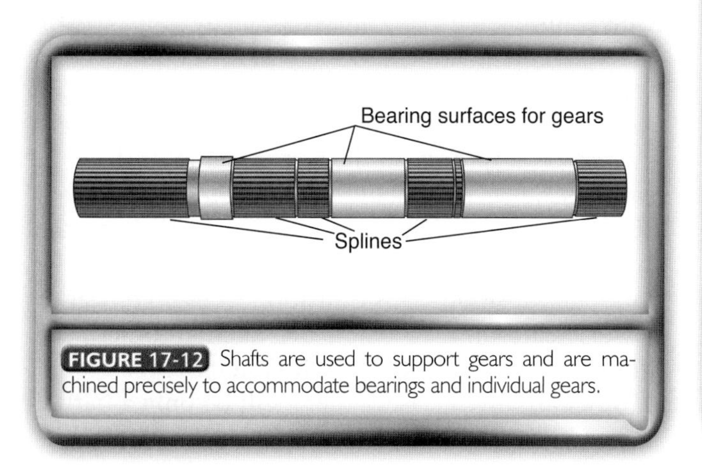
Bearing surfaces for gears
Splines

FIGURE 17-12 Shafts are used to support gears and are machined precisely to accommodate bearings and individual gears.

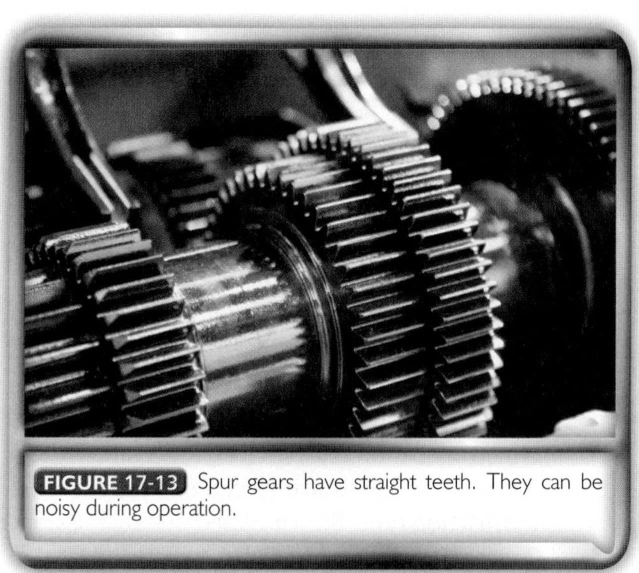

FIGURE 17-13 Spur gears have straight teeth. They can be noisy during operation.

FIGURE 17-14 Helical gears are cut on an angle for better coverage. They operate quietly.

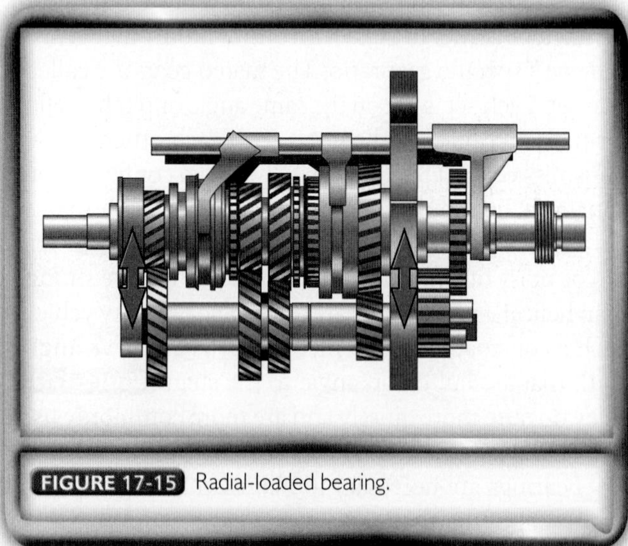

FIGURE 17-15 Radial-loaded bearing.

> **TECHNICIAN TIP**
>
> Manual transmission failures occur, which is why a proper preventive maintenance program is critical to the life of all parts inside the transmission. Proper oil levels, types, and viscosities contribute to longevity of these units.

them while driving FIGURE 17-15. Axial loads are in line with the shaft and occur in transmissions because the cut of the helical gear teeth, which are at an angle to each other, causes a fore and aft load FIGURE 17-16. Bearings also allow shafts and gears to have greater rotational speeds, while at the same time minimizing metal-to-metal friction, which contributes to increased fuel economy and longer transmission life. Bearings can be of the friction type or non-friction type. Both are used in transmissions to resist overheating and keep shafts aligned.

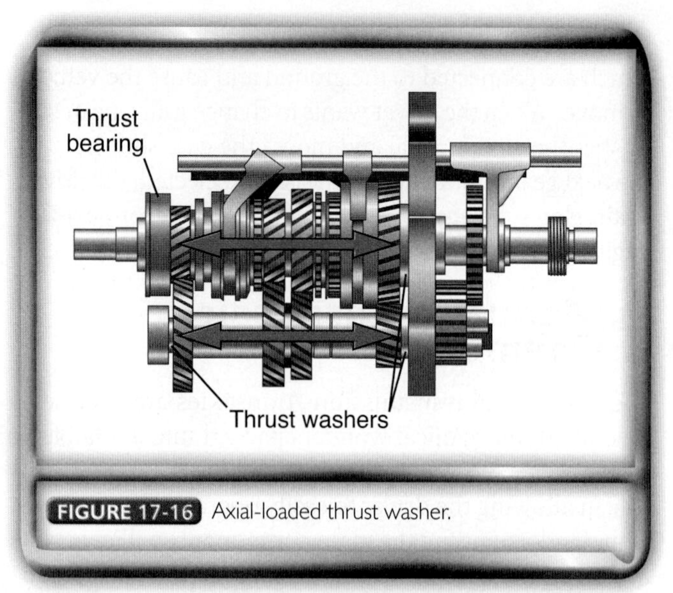
Thrust bearing
Thrust washers

FIGURE 17-16 Axial-loaded thrust washer.

Clutch System

In a manual transmission vehicle, the component that locks the engine and transmission together is the clutch system. The engine is connected to the clutch, and the clutch is connected to the transmission. The clutch is designed so it can connect and disconnect. Imagine a wall-mounted dimmer switch for a ceiling light in a house. When the dimmer switch is in the off position, no electrical power is transmitted to the light, resulting in no illumination of the room. When the clutch pedal is in the depressed or down position, no power is transmitted to the transmission, resulting in no forward movement of the vehicle. When the dimmer switch is in the full on position, electrical power is transmitted to the light bulb, resulting in illumination. Similarly, when the clutch pedal is in the released or up position, power is transmitted to the transmission and forward or rearward movement of the vehicle can be achieved.

Much like the dimmer switch, the clutch pedal requires movement to connect and disconnect power to the transmission many times repeatedly FIGURE 17-17. This movement can cause the clutch components to wear (just as wear can be present in the dimmer switch over time). When the dimmer switch is turned on, there is a drag of amperage on the power source as the light draws power to illuminate a room. This is also what happens when the clutch is released—a drag on the engine is required to get the vehicle to move from the stationary position. This transition from no power to power creates heat, which is detrimental to both the dimmer switch and the clutch system. If the clutch is only partially released, there will be only a partial transmission of the power through the clutch, just like

Caring for the Customer

The clutch system must be inspected and maintained at regular intervals depending on the driver's habits. Customers who tend to slip the clutch, rest their foot on the clutch pedal, or drive aggressively put more wear on the clutch components. It is always a good practice to follow the preventive maintenance schedule to catch a problem before it becomes serious.

power being reduced by the dimmer switch when it is left in a partially on position. The difference is that the dimmer switch is designed to handle the resulting heat, but the clutch is not.

Transmission/Transaxle

Since the invention of the automobile, the need for a device to control engine power and torque for various applications has been satisfied by the transmission. As vehicle design has evolved over the decades, the transaxle was developed **FIGURE 17-18**. The only difference between the transmission and the transaxle is that the transaxle incorporates the final drive assembly in its construction, making the transmission and final drive a single unit. In a vehicle with a transmission, the final drive is a separate unit.

While an automatic transmission shifts by itself, a manual transmission/transaxle requires input from the driver to determine which gear to select. A manual transmission/transaxle uses a series of shafts, gears, and bearings and the driver's input to select the right gear ratio for the situation. Once a gear ratio is selected, the

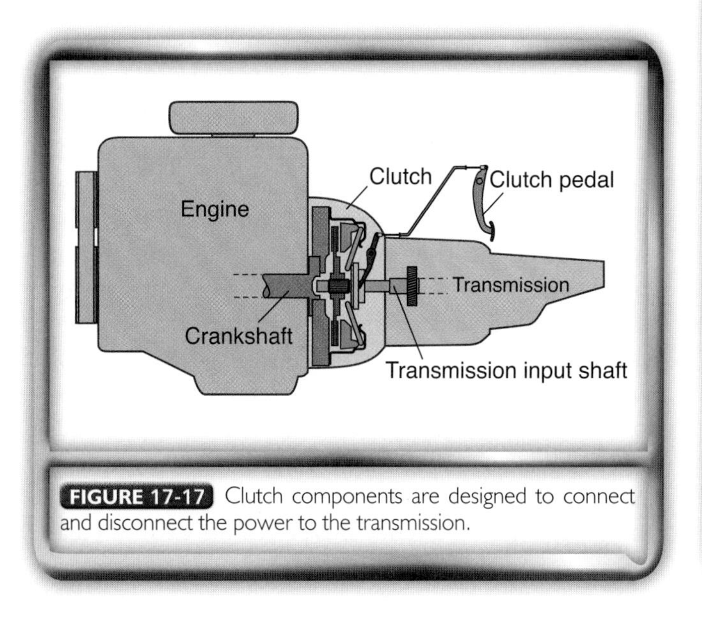
Engine
Clutch
Clutch pedal
Transmission
Crankshaft
Transmission input shaft

FIGURE 17-17 Clutch components are designed to connect and disconnect the power to the transmission.

TECHNICIAN TIP

Most manual transmissions/transaxles are manually shifted, but some are electronically controlled. This type of transmission will be discussed in detail in the Manual Transmissions/Transaxles Basic Diagnosis and Maintenance chapter. In these systems, a computer plays a part in how and when the shift will occur. These new electronic systems require the use of a scan tool to diagnose faults in the transmission as well as to program all parameters for transmission shifting.

TECHNICIAN TIP

The manufacturer determines the gear ratios in the transmission/transaxle based on the power-to-weight ratio, the vehicle size, the application, and the intended use. This concept will be discussed in depth in the Manual Transmissions/Transaxles Basic Diagnosis and Maintenance chapter.

A
B

FIGURE 17-18 Transmissions/transaxles. **A.** Typical rear-wheel drive transmission. **B.** Typical front-wheel drive transaxle.

manual transmission takes the power from the engine and modifies the torque and speed based on the driver-selected gear and sends power to the axles, wheels, and tires. A shifting mechanism is also a part of the transmission/transaxle and is used by the driver to select the appropriate gear for the driving conditions during upshifts and downshifts.

Transmissions/transaxles are rated by the manufacturers for how much twisting force (torque), measured in foot-pounds (ft-lb), they can handle. This rating system ensures that the transmission/transaxle is strong enough for the engine it is used with. Automobile manufacturers design transmissions to be used with their various vehicles—be it a passenger vehicle, pick-up truck, or sport utility vehicle (SUV)—and to meet customer expectations. In some cases, customers have a choice between a five-speed and a six-speed transmission, or between a six-speed and a seven-speed.

Transfer Case

The **transfer case** is typically mounted to the rear of the transmission. Its purpose is to transfer power to both the front and rear axles, providing four-wheel drive so the vehicle can move with more stability in inclement weather and compromised road conditions. Steering ability is also increased, making the vehicle track better in slippery conditions.

The transfer case takes the power from the transmission and directs it to one or both axles, depending on the mode selected FIGURE 17-19. This system requires that the front wheels be powered; thus, a front differential and two front axles were added. A second drive shaft is necessary to provide power to the front axle assembly.

FIGURE 17-19 A typical transfer case used for four-wheel drive.

The transfer case and the manual transmission are similar in operation in that they both have a series of shafts, gears, and bearings and include shift mechanisms. The transfer case can be made of cast iron to provide strength or magnesium or aluminum to lessen the weight. It also is filled with lubricant to reduce friction, increase life span, and maintain quiet operation of the gears by providing a thin film of oil between them.

Transfer cases can be operated manually or electronically. Mechanically shifted transfer cases have a shift lever that is usually next to the transmission gear shift. The transfer case shift lever is also usually shorter, since it is not used as frequently as the transmission gear shift. Electronically shifted transfer cases use either an electronically controlled vacuum actuator or an electric motor to shift the transfer case. Sensors may be used to operate a light that informs the driver which mode is selected.

> **TECHNICIAN TIP**
>
> There are two types of four-wheel drive systems—full-time four-wheel drive and part-time four-wheel drive. These will be explained in greater depth in the Drive Train Components chapter. Most manufacturers of SUVs incorporate some form of four-wheel drive or all-wheel drive as a selling/safety feature to the public. Early four-wheel drive vehicles were not very fuel efficient due to heavy and bulky designs. Over time, manufacturers have made fuel efficiency and safety priorities.

Differential and Final Drive

The term *differential* is used in two different ways. The first is the most technically accurate and refers to the components inside of the differential housing that allow the axles to turn at different speeds when the vehicle is cornering or turning. This is called the differential assembly. Since the outside tire must travel farther when cornering than the inside tire, it must turn at a faster speed. The differential assembly allows this to happen; otherwise, the tires would bind, skip, hop, and slide when going around a corner, which causes them to wear out quickly and could easily cause a loss of vehicle control.

The second way technicians use the term *differential* is as another name for the complete final drive assembly. The final drive assembly provides the final gear reduction necessary for drive train operation. The gear reduction happens because the drive gear (called a pinion gear) is much smaller than the driven gear (called the ring gear). This difference in size results in an increase in mechanical advantage. In addition, the final drive assembly takes the power from the transmission, turns it 90 degrees, and sends it out the axles to the tires. Then the differential assembly allows the tires to travel around corners without binding while the final drive is powering them. Since the differential assembly is housed within the final drive assembly, many technicians simply call the entire final drive assembly the differential. Any time you hear the term *differential*, you need to ask whether the speaker means the final drive assembly or the differential assembly.

There are two types of rear axle assemblies used in modern vehicles: the solid rear axle and the independent rear axle. The **solid rear axle** uses a solid axle housing, which means movement of one wheel affects the other wheel. As the wheel on one side of the vehicle hits a bump, the wheel on the other side pivots, affecting the ride of the vehicle. An **independent rear axle** allows each wheel to move independently of the other wheel, which results in a more comfortable ride and better handling.

Differential assemblies also come in two varieties. First, there is the **open differential assembly**. With the open differential assembly, power is supplied to both wheels equally only when each tire maintains traction, which is not likely on ice and snow. If one wheel is stuck in the snow or ice, the other wheel cannot supply power because of the nature of the open differential assembly. The second type is the **limited slip differential assembly**, which allows both of the rear wheels to supply power to the ground in order to continue forward motion.

> **TECHNICIAN TIP**
>
> If the vehicle is equipped with traction control, the traction control system can help overcome the loss of traction by applying the brakes to the wheel that is slipping. This results in more power being sent to the wheel that is not slipping.

> **TECHNICIAN TIP**
>
> Preventive maintenance is important because the axles are filled with special lubricants and additives that promote long life and maintain quiet operation of the gears. Maintenance schedules help technicians know when each component requires maintenance and when visual and physical inspection are due, thus preventing premature failure.

Drive Axle

The drive axle is the component that supplies the power from the final drive to the wheels. It is part of the **drive axle assembly**. There are two types of axles—live and dead. A **live axle** powers the wheels attached to it. **Dead axles** allow the wheels to freely rotate on the axle assembly and do not drive the wheels.

There are two types of live axles. The first type is the **independent suspension drive axle**. It uses one half-shaft axle for each of the two wheels. These axles must flex to allow suspension movement, so they incorporate what are called constant velocity (CV) joints. CV joints connect the transaxle final drive to the wheels. CV joints are known for their flexibility in allowing greater operating angles; they are used to allow for steering of the front wheels while at the same time supplying them with power. Rubber boots are on each end to contain the lubricant that lubricates each CV joint to maintain its integrity.

The second type of live axle in use today is the **solid axle**. These axles are fitted within a strong housing. The outer ends of the axles have flanges with studs and nuts that are used to secure matching-sized wheels and tires. The other end of the axle has splines that slide into the differential side gears inside the differential housing. This is where the solid axle gets its power from. There are three types of solid live axles used today in rear-wheel drive vehicles: the semi-floating axle, the three-quarter floating axle, and the full floating axle. All three types will be discussed in detail in the Drive Train Components chapter.

Preventive Maintenance

Preventive maintenance is designed to extend the service life of the transmission/transaxle and drive train components. It usually consists of checking and replacing lubricants on a regular basis, lubricating linkage pivot points, performing adjustments such as the clutch adjustment, and inspecting all drive train components for damage or wear. Maintenance also improves the reliability of the vehicle and helps prevent vehicle breakdowns that could leave the occupants stranded. Although most vehicle owners understand this, not all of them choose to have professional preventive maintenance performed on a regular basis. Many owners do not know the extent of the maintenance needed or how it is performed. This is where you come in. By learning how the components operate, what maintenance is needed, and how to perform it, you can help the customer get the maximum reliability and life span out of the vehicle.

Caring for the Customer

Most of the problems that occur in transmissions/transaxles occur because much of the public is unaware that periodic maintenance of the drive train is needed on a regular basis. As a technician, you need to help the customer understand that in almost all cases, maintenance is much less expensive than rebuilding the drive train units.

Lubrication

When it comes to lubrication, every component in the manual transmission requires lubrication according to manufacturer specifications even after the warranty runs out. Clutches, the transmission, the final drive, drive shafts, and drive axles need to be checked or lubricated to maintain their integrity on a regular basis. Proper lubricants will ensure that all manual transmission components last a long time. Manufacturers have used a variety of lubricants for their particular transmissions over the years. The most common lubricant is gear lube. However, some manufacturers have used a specific weight of engine oil. Some manufacturers even specify automatic transmission fluid for their manual transmission. Considering the amount of stress put on the manual transmission, it is important to maintain all lubricants on a regular basis.

The transmission/transaxle and differential lubricant/oil levels keep all rotating parts cool by removing heat and transferring it to the case, which can dissipate the heat to the atmosphere. The lubricant also supplies a thin film of oil between close tolerances of gears, shafts, and bearings to reduce metal-to-metal contact. This oil film prolongs the life of these parts. Improper lubricant/oil levels could cause leaks and unwanted failures to occur.

TECHNICIAN TIP

A good preventive maintenance program will keep on top of all leaks and fluid losses. Always consult manufacturer specifications for correct fluid types.

Components such as CV joints require different types of semisolid lubricants or grease. Considering the amount of torque that CV joints must endure, special lead-based grease is used in most applications. Grease possesses a property called **thixotropy**. This term refers to its ability to be a solid but while under stress to flow or become thin in order to lubricate properly. Many types of semisolid lubricants are in use today. Always remember to consult the manufacturer's service information for correct usage.

Preventive Maintenance

Preventive maintenance is designed to extend the service life of the transmission. It also improves the reliability of the vehicle, and helps to prevent vehicle breakdowns that could leave the driver and passengers stranded. While most vehicle owners understand this, not all of them do. And of those who do, many do not know the extent of the preventive maintenance needed or how it is performed. This is where you come in. By learning what maintenance the manufacturer requires, and how to perform it, you can help the customer get the maximum reliability and life out of the vehicle.

Fluid level and condition should be checked as part of a thorough visual inspection anytime a transmission fault is suspected. Condition and level of the transmission fluid can tell a technician a lot about what is going on inside. For example, if metal is found floating inside the transmission fluid, then the technician knows that the transmission will need to be pulled apart or replaced.

Caring for the Customer

It is always a good idea to keep up with preventive maintenance on a regular basis. Remind the customer that preventive maintenance is the road to long life for the vehicle and can help save thousands of dollars in repairs.

Make it a habit to visually inspect the transmission every time it is in for an oil change or other service so you can catch issues before they become severe.

Checking Gearbox Fluid

As a preventive maintenance task, fluid level of the manual transmission should be checked when other tasks are performed, such as engine oil and filter change or lubrication of steering parts, according to the manufacturer's periodic intervals. In the event of a suspected leak, the transmission fluid level should be checked to prevent catastrophic failure.

To check and adjust the fluid level, follow the steps in SKILL DRILL 17-1.

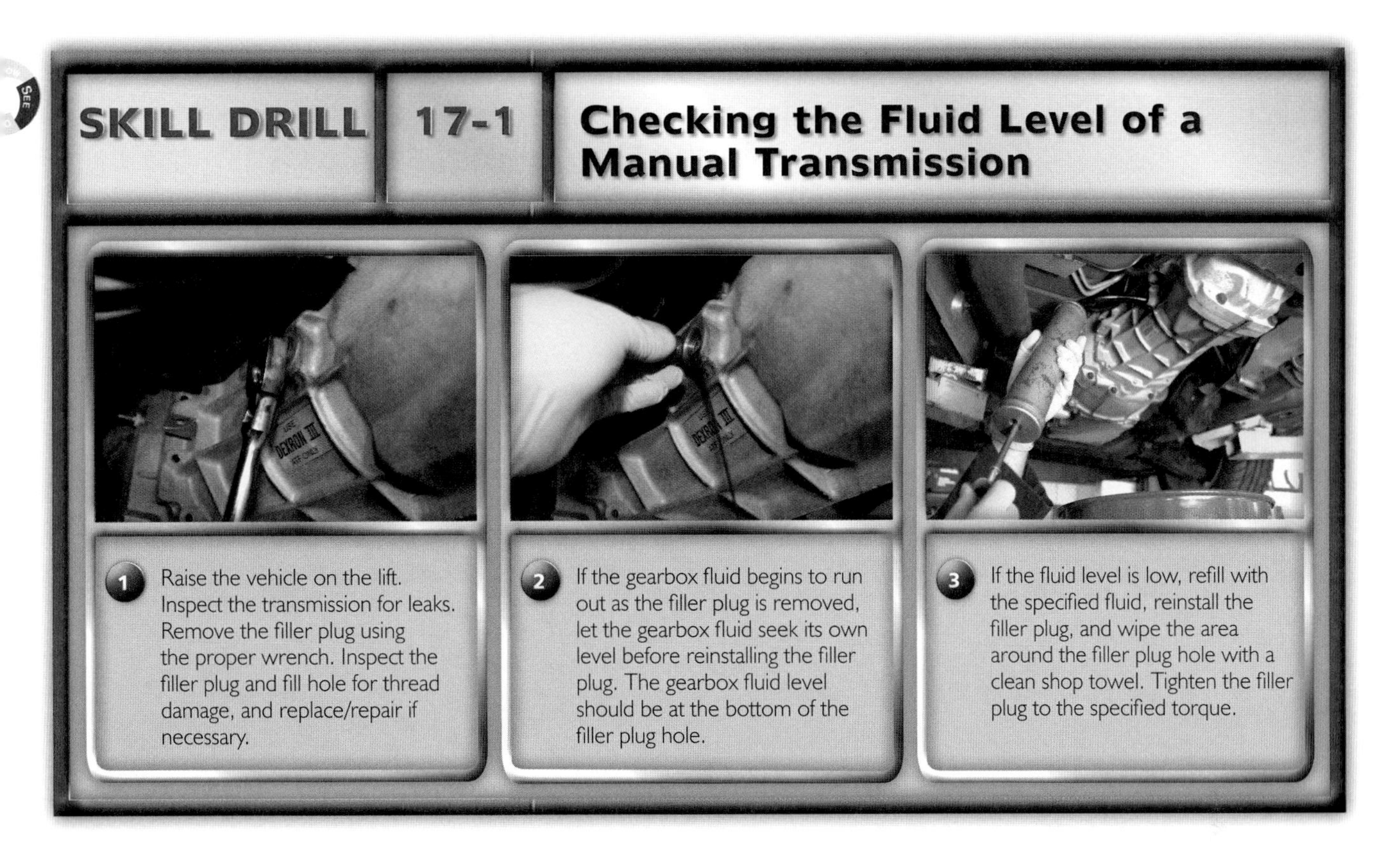
SKILL DRILL 17-1 Checking the Fluid Level of a Manual Transmission
1 Raise the vehicle on the lift. Inspect the transmission for leaks. Remove the filler plug using the proper wrench. Inspect the filler plug and fill hole for thread damage, and replace/repair if necessary.
2 If the gearbox fluid begins to run out as the filler plug is removed, let the gearbox fluid seek its own level before reinstalling the filler plug. The gearbox fluid level should be at the bottom of the filler plug hole.
3 If the fluid level is low, refill with the specified fluid, reinstall the filler plug, and wipe the area around the filler plug hole with a clean shop towel. Tighten the filler plug to the specified torque.

Checking and Adjusting Differential/ Transfer Case Fluid

Checking and adjusting the differential/transfer case fluid level is very similar to the process for checking the transmission fluid level, but there are some differences. First, some differential/final drive assemblies, such as limited-slip and posi-traction assemblies, require specially designed additives or fluid. Transfer cases may also require special lubricants as specified by the manufacturer. Always check the service information for the vehicle you are working on. Differentials and transfer cases generally have fill plugs that can be used when checking the fluid level in the same way a transmission does. However, they often do not have a drain plug. In these cases, either a specific bolt may need to be removed or a cover may need to be unbolted and removed. Follow the service information.

To check and adjust the differential/transfer case fluid level, follow the steps in SKILL DRILL 17-2.

Changing Manual Gearbox and Final Drive Fluid

At the manufacturer's specified intervals, the gearbox fluid must be changed in those vehicles in which manufacturers require it. Gearbox fluid left unchanged will break down from heat and lose its capacity to lubricate all rotating parts, causing premature bearing and gear failure. This potential damage also makes it critical to maintain proper gearbox fluid levels. If the level becomes too low, bearings and gears will starve for lubrication; if levels are too high, aeration of the gearbox fluid will be present and cause premature damage. Regular change intervals help to ensure that none of these conditions occur.

Manual transmissions use fluids specified by the manufacturer. Do not assume that all transmissions use the same fluid. They don't. Some use gear lube of differing viscosities. Some use engine oil of a specified viscosity. And some even specify automatic transmission fluid in the transmission. Therefore, always verify that you are using the specified fluid in a particular vehicle. One other thing to keep in mind, some transaxles use a separate reservoir for the final drive, which is separate from the transaxle reservoir. And in some cases, they use different types of fluid. Always check the manufacturer's specifications before changing out the fluids.

To prepare for a gearbox fluid change, it is a good idea to have the gearbox fluid warm. When it is warm, it will flow better to ensure proper draining. If possible, drive the vehicle until the engine is at operating temperature

SKILL DRILL 17-2 Checking and Adjusting the Differential/Transfer Case Fluid Level

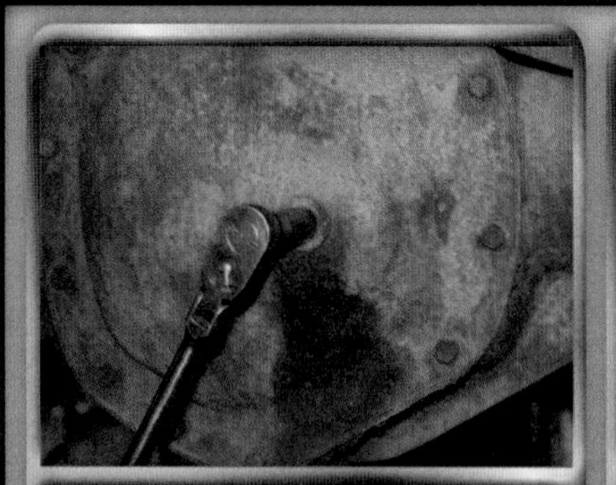

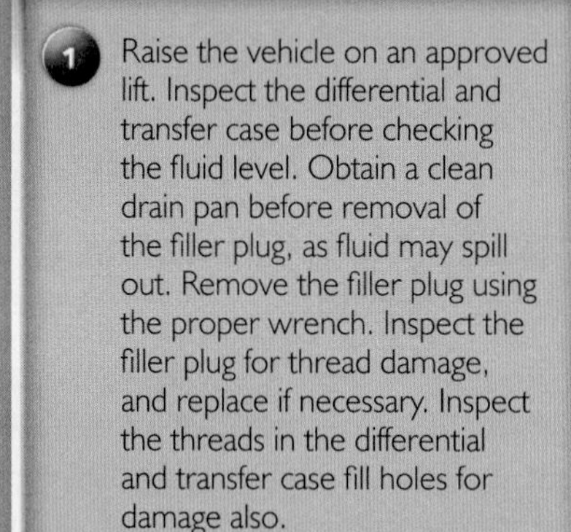

1. Raise the vehicle on an approved lift. Inspect the differential and transfer case before checking the fluid level. Obtain a clean drain pan before removal of the filler plug, as fluid may spill out. Remove the filler plug using the proper wrench. Inspect the filler plug for thread damage, and replace if necessary. Inspect the threads in the differential and transfer case fill holes for damage also.

2. If the fluid begins to run out as the filler plug is removed, let the fluid seek its own level before reinstalling the filler plug. The fluid level should be at the bottom of the filler plug hole.

3. If the fluid level is low, refill with the specified fluid, reinstall the filler plug, and wipe the area around the filler plug hole with a clean shop towel. Tighten the filler plug to the specified torque.

and then change the gearbox fluid. Do not touch the gearbox fluid. It will be hot and could cause burns.

To change the gearbox fluid, follow the steps in SKILL DRILL 17-3.

Identifying the Cause of Fluid Loss

Performing preventive maintenance on a regular basis helps ensure that fluid leaks and concerns are addressed before they can become a major problem. In some cases, repairing fluid leaks and loss requires removal of the transmission. Diagnosing leaks and concerns will require that you put the vehicle on a hoist or jack stands. Noises and shifting concerns can be signs of fluid leaks or problems.

Fluid leaks may be a result of the following conditions:

- Too much fluid in the transmission
- Leaking seals, including:
  - Half-shaft axle seals
  - Input shaft retainer O-rings or lip seals
  - Speed sensor seals or O-ring
  - Backup light switch O-ring
  - Shifting lever shaft seals
  - Transmission rear seal
  - Side covers or access plates
- Improper fluid type
- Transmission case porosity or cracks
- Missing, loose, or stripped case bolts
- Damaged gaskets for case halves
- Loose drain or fill plugs

To identify the cause of fluid loss in a transmission, follow the steps in SKILL DRILL 17-4.

SKILL DRILL 17-3 Changing the Gearbox Fluid

1. Raise the vehicle using an approved lift. Obtain a clean drain pan to put the used fluid in.

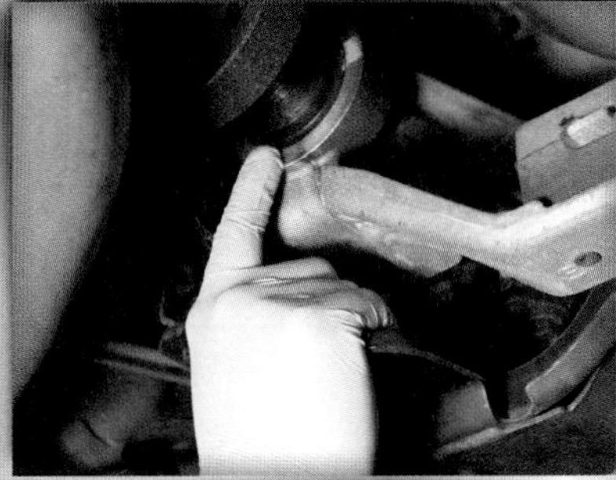

2. Inspect the transmission for leaks.

3. Remove the drain plug from the bottom of the transmission, being careful of the hot gearbox fluid. Let gearbox fluid drain until it has stopped running. If necessary, drain the final drive assembly in the same manner.

4. Replace the drain plug(s) and tighten to specification, and remove the fill plug(s).

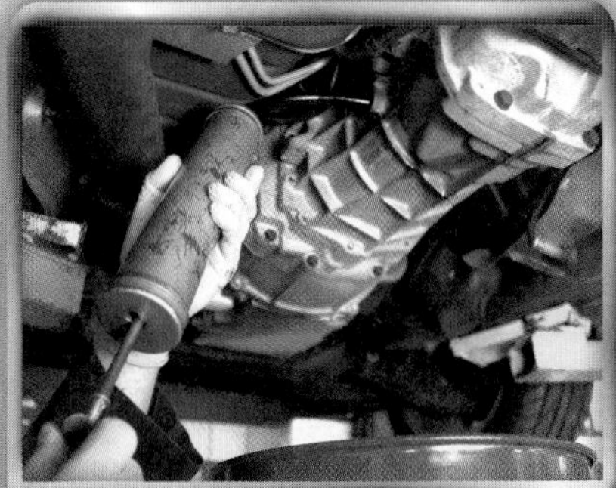

5. Refill the transmission and final drive to the proper level using manufacturer-approved gearbox fluid. Replace the fill plug(s) and tighten. Use a shop towel to wipe away any spillage. Road test the vehicle. If necessary, put the vehicle back on the lift and check for any leaks that may have resulted from the service.

SKILL DRILL 17-4 Identifying the Cause of Fluid Loss in a Transmission

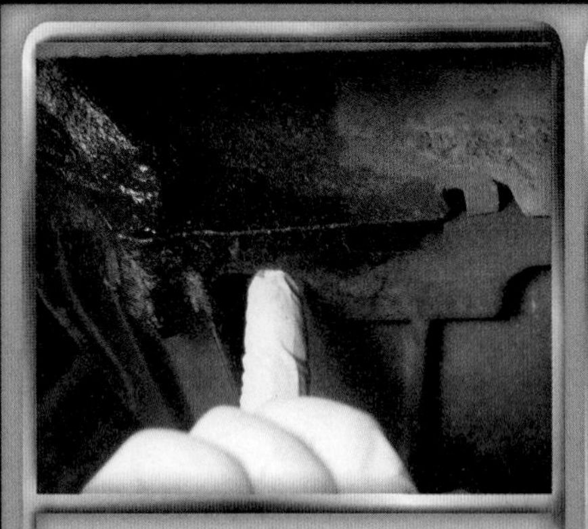

1 Raise the vehicle on a hoist or jack stands. Look for leaks in the transmission bell housing to the engine block (front seal).

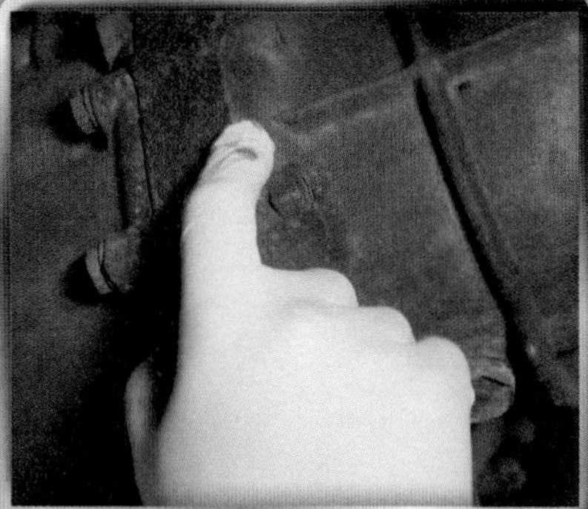

2 Look for leaks in the transmission breather outlet. Look for leaks in all case gasket areas.

3 Look for leaks in the rear tail shaft seal.

4 Inspect for transmission case defects such as cracks and porosity.

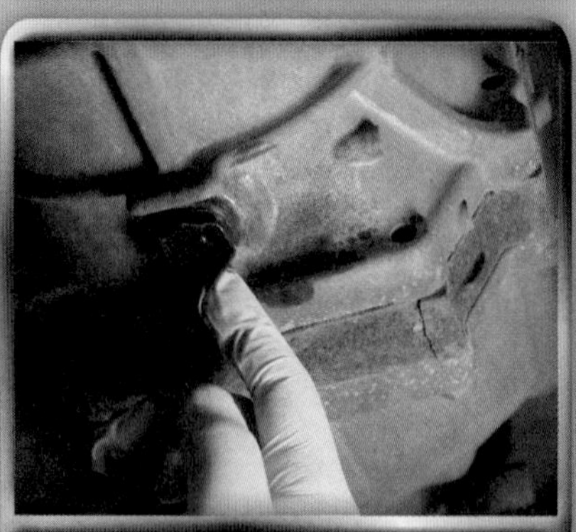

5 Look for leaks at the drain and fill plugs.

6 Check the gear fluid level as you are removing the drain plug, and look for evidence of excess fluid. If found, let the excess fluid drain into a container. If necessary, use your pinky finger to check the level. If the fluid is more than half an inch below the bottom of the threaded hole, add new fluid of the correct viscosity and type.

Wrap-up

Ready for Review

- The drive train comprises component assemblies that transmit power from the engine to the wheels.
- Early engines had belt-driven gears that required drivers to manually change the belt.
- Some form of the multigear transmission, with clutch operation, has been used since its invention in 1894.
- A gear synchronizer matches the gear speed and the shaft speed to allow gear selection without "grinding" the gears.
- Mechanical advantage refers to gaining greater output force by increasing input distance, such that the total work on either end is equal (work = force × distance).
- Each gear set creates mechanical advantage by the ratio of teeth of the input gears to that of the output gears.
- The gear ratio is the number of turns of the input gear, necessary to achieve one turn of the output gear.
- Gear ratios are calculated by the number of driven gear teeth divided by the number of drive gear teeth; as the gear ratio decreases, the output increases.
- Gear ratio theory will help you to understand how power is distributed and how power and speed varies as the vehicle travels.
- Power flow refers to the path by which power is transmitted from one component to another.
- The manual transmission drive train consists of the clutch system, transmission/transaxle, and final drive assembly.
- When depressed, the clutch pedal disconnects the engine from the transmission and allows the driver to change gears.
- Releasing the clutch pedal reconnects the engine to the transmission.
- The main components of a manual transmission are shafts, gears, bearings, and the clutch assembly.
- Shafts support the gears, and bearings maintain the position and alignment of shafts.
- Helical gears have angled teeth; spur gears have straight teeth and are stronger than helical gears.
- Transaxles have final drive assemblies incorporated into their construction.
- Transmissions/transaxles are rated as to how much torque they can handle.
- The transfer case transfers power to both axles to provide four-wheel drive.
- Differential refers to the components that allow the axles to turn at different speeds when a vehicle is cornering.
- The final drive assembly houses the differential and provides the final gear reduction necessary for drive train operation.
- Differentials can be open or limited slip.
- Drive axles supply power from the final drive to the wheels.
- An axle can be live (powers the wheels attached to it) or dead (allows the wheels to rotate freely).
- The two types of live axles are independent suspension and solid (which can be semi-floating, three-quarter floating, or full floating).
- Preventive maintenance extends the service life of the transmission/transaxle and drive train components.
- All components of the manual transmission require lubrication.

Key Terms

accelerator pedal The foot-operated pedal used by the driver to increase and decrease the amount of power the engine develops.

axial load The load applied in line with a shaft. It can be controlled with thrust bearings.

clutch pedal The foot-operated pedal used by the driver to engage and disengage the clutch.

clutch safety switch An electrical switch that is operated by the clutch pedal and keeps the starter motor from cranking the engine over until the clutch is fully depressed.

clutch system A mechanically operated assembly that connects and disconnects the engine from the transmission.

constant velocity (CV) joints Joints commonly used in front-wheel drive vehicles to allow flexibility of the axle while turning.

dead axle An axle that supplies no power to the wheels.

differential gears Gears situated in the final drive assembly that are meshed together and with both axles, allowing the wheels to rotate at different speeds when turning a corner.

drive axle assembly The components that make up the drive axle including the axles, final drive assembly, bearings, and axle housing.

drive axle An axle that provides power to a wheel.

drive shaft The hollow tube with flexible joints on each end that transmits power from the transmission to the final drive unit.

drive train The component assemblies that transmit power from the engine all the way to the drive wheels.

final drive assembly An assembly used to power the drive wheels and allow the wheels to rotate at different speeds as the vehicle turns.

gear A relatively round, rotating part with internal or external teeth that are designed to mesh with another gear for the purpose of transmitting torque.

gear ratio The description of the difference in speed between gears in mesh, determined by comparing the number of teeth on each gear (driven/drive). For example, a gear set that has a drive gear with 5 teeth in mesh with a driven gear of 25 teeth has a gear ratio of 5:1.

gear reduction The use of a small gear to drive a large gear. The result is in an increase in torque but a decrease in speed.

gear set Two or more gears that are in mesh with each other.

gear synchronizer An assembly in the transmission that is used to bring two unequally spinning shafts or gears to the same speed when upshifting or downshifting.

half-shaft An axle that has CV joints on each end and that fits between the transaxle and wheel. Typically, one is used on each side of a vehicle.

helical gears Gears that have teeth set on an angle to the gear face; they operate more quietly than spur gears.

idler gear A gear used in between two gears to change the direction of the rotation of the driveshaft or drive axles in the transmission.

independent rear axle A type of rear suspension system that allows each wheel on the axle to move independently of the other.

independent suspension drive axle A type of suspension that allows each wheel on a drive axle to move independently of the other.

limited slip differential assembly A differential assembly that uses a clutch assembly or gear assembly to allow a limited amount of slip between the two axles. It is used to increase drive wheel traction in slippery conditions.

live axle An axle that provides power to the wheels.

mechanical advantage The process of using a device to get more output force than the amount of input force, with the trade-off being that the input distance is proportionately longer than the output distance.

open differential assembly A differential assembly that allows both axles to turn at their own speed when turning a corner, but is dependent on the traction of the tires to deliver torque to the ground. If one wheel has no traction, all of the engine's torque will be used at that wheel, causing it to simply spin.

power flow The path that power takes from the beginning of an assembly to the end. In a transmission, power flow changes as different gears are selected by the driver.

radial load The load that is perpendicular to a shaft, usually controlled by bearings or bushings.

rotational speed The speed at which an object rotates, measured in revolutions per minute (rpm).

shaft The long, narrow component that carries one or more gears or has gears machined into it.

snap ring The spring-steel C-shaped ring that is fitted in a groove and holds gears, bearings, and shafts in place.

solid rear axle A type of axle that has a one-piece axle housing, so that the action of hitting a bump with one wheel affects the other wheel.

solid axle A type of axle that is not flexible, with splines on one end to fit the final drive unit and a flange on the other end to power the wheel.

splined Typically, a shaft and gear that have parallel grooves machined in them so they mate with each other and lock together rotationally.

spur gears Gears with straight-cut gear teeth.

synchromesh transmission A modern transmission that uses gear synchronizers to match the speeds of gears and shafts during upshifts and downshifts.

thixotropy The ability of a semisolid grease to flow when agitated or stressed.

thrust washers Flat, washer-shaped bearings that provide a wear surface between two rotating components that are loaded axially.

torque multiplication The increase of torque.

transaxle A drive train layout in which the transmission and final drive are integrated into a common assembly; used most often on front-wheel drive vehicles.

transfer case An assembly used in four-wheel drive vehicles to transmit power to either two wheels only or all four wheels.

transmission An assembly that houses a variety of gear sets that allow the vehicle to be driven at a wider range of speeds and terrain conditions than would be possible without a transmission.

universal joint A cross-shaped joint with bearings on each leg where one set of parallel legs is connected to the end of one shaft and the other set of parallel legs is connected to the end of a second shaft. This arrangement allows the shafts to operate at shallow angles to each other.

ASE-Type Questions

1. Tech A says that friction bearings are made up of balls and rollers. Tech B says that non-friction bearings are in sliding contact between moving surfaces. Who is correct?
   a. Tech A
   b. Tech B
   c. Both A and B
   d. Neither A nor B
2. Tech A says that gear ratios are all the same in any five-speed transmission. Tech B says that gear ratios vary from transmission to transmission. Who is correct?
   a. Tech A
   b. Tech B
   c. Both A and B
   d. Neither A nor B
3. Tech A says that a road test is helpful in diagnosing transmission issues. Tech B says that having a thorough understanding of the customer concern is important when diagnosing transmission issues. Who is correct?
   a. Tech A
   b. Tech B
   c. Both A and B
   d. Neither A nor B
4. Tech A says that gear lube can be used in all manual transmissions. Tech B says that some manual transmissions use engine oil as a lubricant. Who is correct?
   a. Tech A
   b. Tech B
   c. Both A and B
   d. Neither A nor B
5. Tech A says that the final drive is used to provide an increase in the rotational speed of the axles. Tech B says that the final drive is used to provide an increase of twisting force to the axles. Who is correct?
   a. Tech A
   b. Tech B
   c. Both A and B
   d. Neither A nor B
6. Tech A says that a gear set that has a drive gear with 9 teeth and a driven gear with 27 teeth has a gear ratio of 3:1. Tech B says that the drive gear is also called the output gear. Who is correct?
   a. Tech A
   b. Tech B
   c. Both A and B
   d. Neither A nor B
7. Tech A says that transmission fluid levels are critical to the life of the transmission. Tech B says that transmission oil should be changed when changing the engine oil. Who is correct?
   a. Tech A
   b. Tech B
   c. Both A and B
   d. Neither A nor B
8. Tech A says that a road test is part of a good process for diagnosing a customer drive train complaint. Tech B says that the ring gear and pinion gear are part of the final drive assembly. Who is correct?
   a. Tech A
   b. Tech B
   c. Both A and B
   d. Neither A nor B
9. Tech A says that the clutch uses a cone-style synchronizer to match the speed of the engine to the manual transmission. Tech B says that the fill plug hole is where to check the fluid level in most manual transmissions. Who is correct?
   a. Tech A
   b. Tech B
   c. Both A and B
   d. Neither A nor B
10. Tech A says that the differential assembly provides a means for the inside and outside wheels to turn at different speeds when going around a corner. Tech B says that the differential assembly provides smooth shifts and reduces gear "grinding" by matching gear speeds. Who is correct?
    a. Tech A
    b. Tech B
    c. Both A and B
    d. Neither A nor B

CHAPTER 18

KNOW
SEE
DO
PROVE

NATEF Tasks

Manual Drive Train and Axles

Clutch

The Clutch System

KNOW
SEE
DO
PROVE

Knowledge Objectives

After reading this chapter, you will be able to:

1. Describe the purpose and operation of the clutch. (p 436)
2. Describe the purpose and operation of each of the major components of the clutch. (pp 437–445)
3. Describe the differences between a standard flywheel and a dual mass flywheel. (pp 438–440)
4. Describe each of the three types of clutch operating systems. (pp 443–445)
5. Describe the maintenance requirements of a clutch system. (pp 445–450)

KNOW
SEE
DO
PROVE

Skills Objectives

After reading this chapter, you will be able to:

1. Check and adjust a mechanical clutch. (pp 445–446)
2. Check and adjust a hydraulic clutch. (pp 446–447)
3. Bleed a hydraulic clutch system using the gravity method. (p 448)
4. Bleed a hydraulic clutch system using the manual method. (pp 448–449)
5. Bleed a hydraulic clutch system using the pressure method. (pp 448, 450)

Introduction

The clutch is a mechanical device located in the bell housing, which sits between the engine and the transmission FIGURE 18-1. The clutch allows the driver to engage and disengage the engine from the transmission while operating the vehicle. The driver controls the operation of the clutch with his or her foot through the clutch pedal. The clutch has a series of components that help to make driving an interactive experience, allowing the driver to control the shifting of gears in the vehicle. An automatic transmission does not use a manual clutch, giving the driver very little control over transmission operation other than to put it in or out of gear.

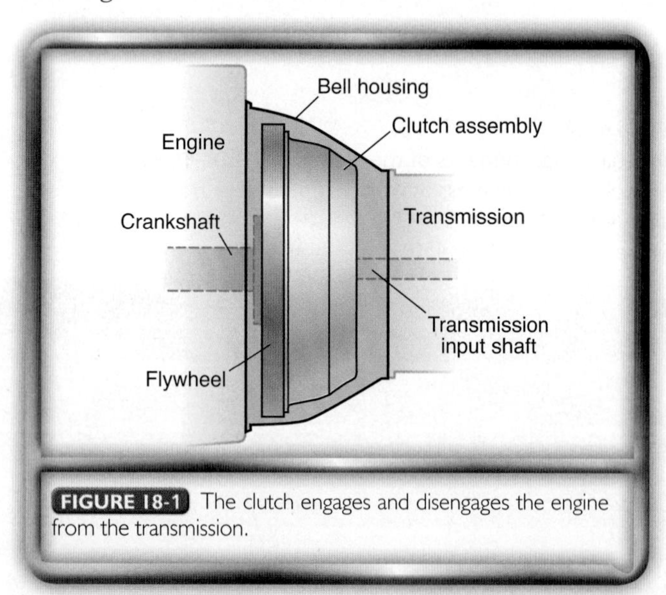
Bell housing
Clutch assembly
Engine
Crankshaft
Transmission
Transmission input shaft
Flywheel

FIGURE 18-1 The clutch engages and disengages the engine from the transmission.

Clutch Principles

The purpose of the clutch is to allow the driver to disconnect and progressively connect the engine to the transmission. It progressively transmits torque from the engine to the transmission. It also allows the driver to disconnect the transmission from the engine for the purpose of shifting between gears while accelerating or decelerating the vehicle.

Automotive manual transmission clutches are dry clutches, as opposed to wet clutches in automatic transmissions, which run in a lubricating fluid. Dry clutches use the friction between the clutch surfaces to transmit torque from the engine to the transmission. The amount of torque a clutch can transmit depends on the amount of friction between the clutch disc and the mating surfaces of the flywheel and pressure plate. This friction is dependent on four variables: the **coefficient of friction** of the clutch disc facings, the diameter of the clutch, the number of clutch discs in the clutch assembly, and the total spring force clamping the parts together.

Increasing the friction of the clutch disc increases the torque-carrying ability, but makes the clutch grab, which makes it more difficult to start from a stop. Increasing the diameter of the clutch gives it more leverage, which increases its torque capacity, but takes up more area. Increasing the number of clutch discs increases torque capacity, but is more complicated due to the extra parts. Increasing the spring force clamping the parts together increases torque capacity, but takes more foot pressure to operate the clutch pedal. Manufacturers balance all of these factors when designing a clutch for a particular application.

You Are the Automotive Technician

A customer brings her 6-year-old Mustang into the shop because the vehicle wants to creep at stop lights as she sits with her foot on the clutch and the transmission in first gear. She says it has been getting worse over the past couple of weeks. The vehicle has about 48,000 miles on it. She just moved into the area a couple of months ago and is looking for a good shop that she can trust. You tell her that her vehicle is equipped with a hydraulic clutch and that she made a good choice to have it looked at since clutch issues that aren't taken care of fairly quickly can shorten the life of the clutch considerably. She agrees to pay the diagnostic fee for determining what is causing the issue. Once the diagnosis is complete, she will decide if she wants the work done or not.

1. What do you suspect is causing the vehicle to creep in this situation?
2. How will you verify your suspicion?
3. What part or parts may need to be replaced to fix this problem?

> **TECHNICIAN TIP**
>
> Two or more clutch plates can be used to form a **multiplate clutch**, increasing the number of facings and the torque capacity. This design is useful where a reduction in clutch diameter is advantageous or where increasing the spring strength is undesirable because it would increase pedal effort and driver discomfort.

Input and Output Shaft Speed

Because vehicles are dependent on shifting between various gears to be able to drive down the road at a variety of speeds, it is important to understand how the transmission input and output shaft speeds play a critical role in shifting. First, you need to understand that output shaft torque and speed can each be increased, but not at the same time. In low gear, the input shaft speed is relatively high, while the output shaft speed is relatively low. This results in an increase of torque from the output shaft. However, the speed of the output shaft (and the speed of the vehicle) is relatively low. This setup makes for good acceleration from a stop or slow speeds. As higher transmission gears are selected, the output shaft speed increases with each higher gear. However, the torque of the output shaft is lessened with each higher gear, allowing the vehicle to travel at higher speeds without over-revving the engine, but with decreased torque.

The second role that the input and output shaft speeds play is during the actual shift. When transitioning from one gear to another, the relative speeds of the shafts must change to allow the gears to shift from one set to another. In order for a gear to be selected, at least one of the shafts must be able to turn freely for this speed change to happen. The input shaft is able to connect to and disconnect from the engine's flywheel through the operation of the clutch, thus allowing the input shaft's speed to change during a shifting of the gears. Since the output shaft is connected directly to the wheels through the drive train components, it cannot be disconnected. This means that any time the vehicle is moving, the output shaft is turning. The faster the vehicle speed, the faster the rotation of the output shaft. This has an impact on shifting because the speeds of both shafts must be such that the individual gears can be selected. The clutch plays the role of engaging and disengaging the input shaft, so the input shaft speed can be changed as needed.

Clutch Components

The main components of a clutch assembly are the **flywheel**, **clutch disc**, **pressure plate**, **throw-out bearing**, **clutch fork**, and **pilot bearing** FIGURE 18-2.

The flywheel bolts onto the rear of the crankshaft, and the pressure plate bolts onto the flywheel. Most light vehicles use a **single-plate clutch** disc with two friction facings attached to a central hub and splined to engage the **transmission input shaft**. The friction facings on the clutch disc are clamped between the flat surfaces of the engine flywheel and the spring-loaded pressure plate. With engine rotation, the flywheel and pressure plate rotate together with the clutch disc. The flywheel and pressure plate are the drive unit, and the clutch disc is the driven unit. Engine torque is transferred from the flywheel and pressure plate through the friction facings of the driven clutch disc to the splines of the input shaft and into the transmission.

Pushing the clutch pedal operates the **release mechanism**, which controls the flow of torque between the engine and the transmission. Depressing the clutch pedal retracts the pressure plate against the force of its springs and frees the friction disc from its clamping action FIGURE 18-3. Releasing the clutch pedal

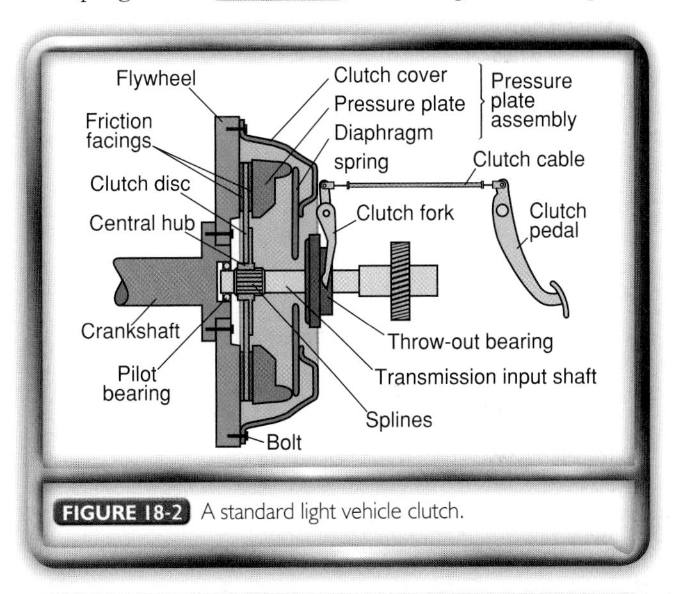
Flywheel
Friction facings
Clutch disc
Central hub
Crankshaft
Pilot bearing
Clutch cover
Pressure plate
Diaphragm spring
Pressure plate assembly
Clutch cable
Clutch fork
Clutch pedal
Throw-out bearing
Transmission input shaft
Splines
Bolt
FIGURE 18-2 A standard light vehicle clutch.

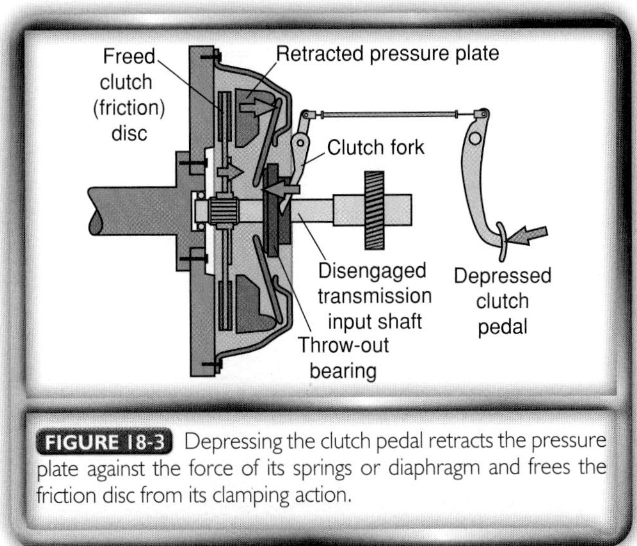
Freed clutch (friction) disc
Retracted pressure plate
Clutch fork
Disengaged transmission input shaft
Throw-out bearing
Depressed clutch pedal
FIGURE 18-3 Depressing the clutch pedal retracts the pressure plate against the force of its springs or diaphragm and frees the friction disc from its clamping action.

reapplies the clamping force and reconnects the engine and transmission by firmly clamping the clutch disc between the pressure plate and the flywheel, allowing them to rotate as a unit FIGURE 18-4.

Flywheel

The main purpose of the flywheel is to smooth out the power pulses from the pistons during the power strokes. It also provides a friction surface for the clutch disc and a mounting surface for the pressure plate FIGURE 18-5. The flywheel is quite heavy. It is usually made of cast iron so that it can store energy from each power pulse from the engine; it uses that energy to keep the crankshaft turning through the intake, compression, and exhaust strokes. However, a heavy flywheel means that it slows the engine's acceleration. A lighter flywheel does not smooth out the power pulses as effectively, but it works well on a drag-racing car, for example, because it allows the engine to accelerate faster.

The flywheel is bolted to the rear of the crankshaft and allows the crankshaft to mate with the transmission via the clutch system. It also incorporates the **flywheel ring gear**, which enables the starter motor drive gear to crank the engine over. In most cases, the ring gear is made of hardened steel and is press-fitted onto the outer edge of the flywheel.

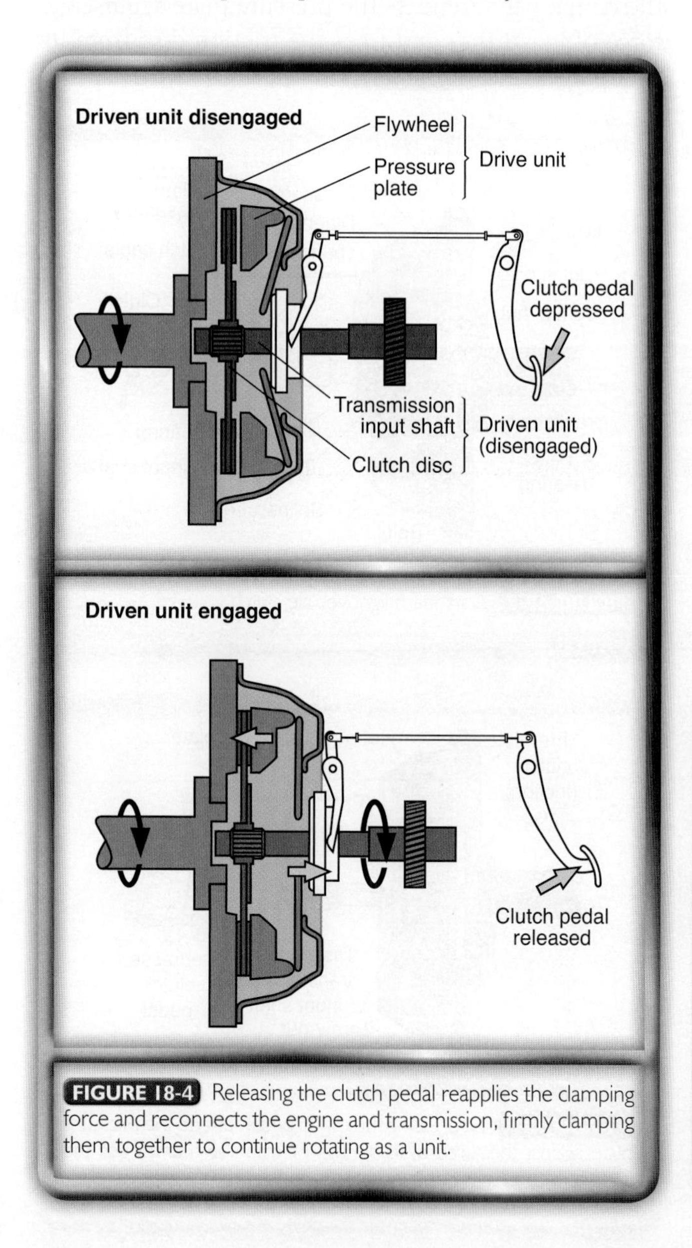
Driven unit disengaged
Flywheel
Pressure plate
Drive unit
Clutch pedal depressed
Transmission input shaft
Clutch disc
Driven unit (disengaged)
Driven unit engaged
Clutch pedal released

FIGURE 18-4 Releasing the clutch pedal reapplies the clamping force and reconnects the engine and transmission, firmly clamping them together to continue rotating as a unit.

Types of Flywheels

There are two main types of flywheels: the single one-piece flywheel and the dual mass flywheel. The single one-piece flywheel is by far the most common on light vehicles and is what most people think of when they think of a flywheel. Its one-piece construction makes it simple, inexpensive, and reliable. It usually has a starter ring gear pressed onto its outer edge and a machined mating surface for the clutch disc. The center of the flywheel has machined holes for bolts to mount it firmly to the flywheel. In some cases, the bolt pattern is equal so it can be mounted in any position. In other cases, where the flywheel is used as the primary method of balancing the engine, it may have offset bolt holes so it can be mounted in only one position on the crankshaft. It is generally designed for a particular application, so do not try to use a flywheel from one type of engine on another type.

Some flywheels are of the stepped style. In this design, the friction surface of the flywheel is recessed, while the outer diameter, against which the pressure plate is bolted, is raised. The depth of the step is critical for proper operation of the clutch assembly. If it is too deep, the clutch will slip or not engage. If it is too shallow, the clutch will be stiff and may not disengage. Both stepped and flat flywheels can be resurfaced if the wear or defects are minor.

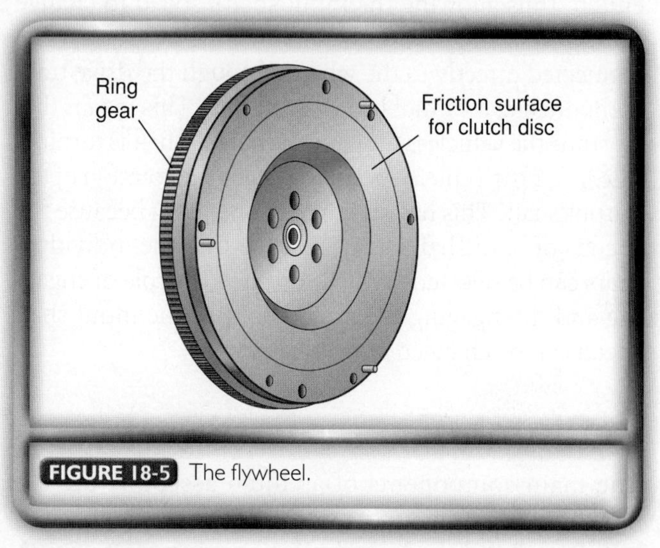
Ring gear
Friction surface for clutch disc

FIGURE 18-5 The flywheel.

> **TECHNICIAN TIP**
>
> Refinishing the flywheel moves the pressure plate toward the engine and away from the throw-out bearing, increasing free-play. If too much material is removed from the flywheel surface, some release mechanisms will not be able to compensate for the loss and the clutch will not fully release. Also, as the flywheel is machined thinner, the clutch center hub may contact the flywheel bolts. So even though most manufacturers do not list a minimum thickness for the flywheel, know that it can cause problems if it becomes too thin.

The dual mass flywheel improves the engine's fuel economy by smoothing out the power pulses and focusing them in the direction of engine rotation. Its inner workings help absorb engine vibrations, thus minimizing gear rattle and putting less strain on the drive train components. This also makes for smoother shifting. There are two basic types of dual mass flywheels. The first is composed of a primary and a secondary flywheel with a series of torsion springs and cushions. The second uses a planetary gear and torsional springs FIGURE 18-6.

In the first type of dual mass flywheel, a friction ring is located between the inner and the outer flywheel that allows the inner and the outer flywheel to slip. This feature is designed to alleviate any damage to the transmission when torque loads exceed the vehicle rating of the transmission. The friction ring is the weak spot in the system and can wear out if excessive engine torque loads are applied. This type of dual mass flywheel also has a center support bearing that carries the load between the inner and the outer flywheel and is fitted with damper springs to absorb shocks.

The second type of dual mass flywheel incorporates planetary gearing along with torsion springs. It is designed for engines with stronger vibrations at lower engine speeds. Some manufacturers use this style for their high-performance vehicles to gain greater driving and shifting comfort. Because of the increased dampening effect at lower engine speeds, the engine can be idled at fewer revolutions per minute (rpm), which reduces fuel consumption slightly.

Dual mass flywheels are most often fitted to light-duty diesel trucks with standard manual transmissions and to higher performance luxury vehicles. However, dual mass flywheels are now being used in economy-type vehicles to dampen vibrations in the drive train. The function of the dual mass flywheel is to absorb torsional crankshaft vibrations, which are twisting forces created in opposite directions. A twisting force happens in one direction when a piston is on the compression stroke and the opposite direction on the power stroke. This vibration is magnified in diesel engines, which have higher compression ratios than gasoline engines. By minimizing the

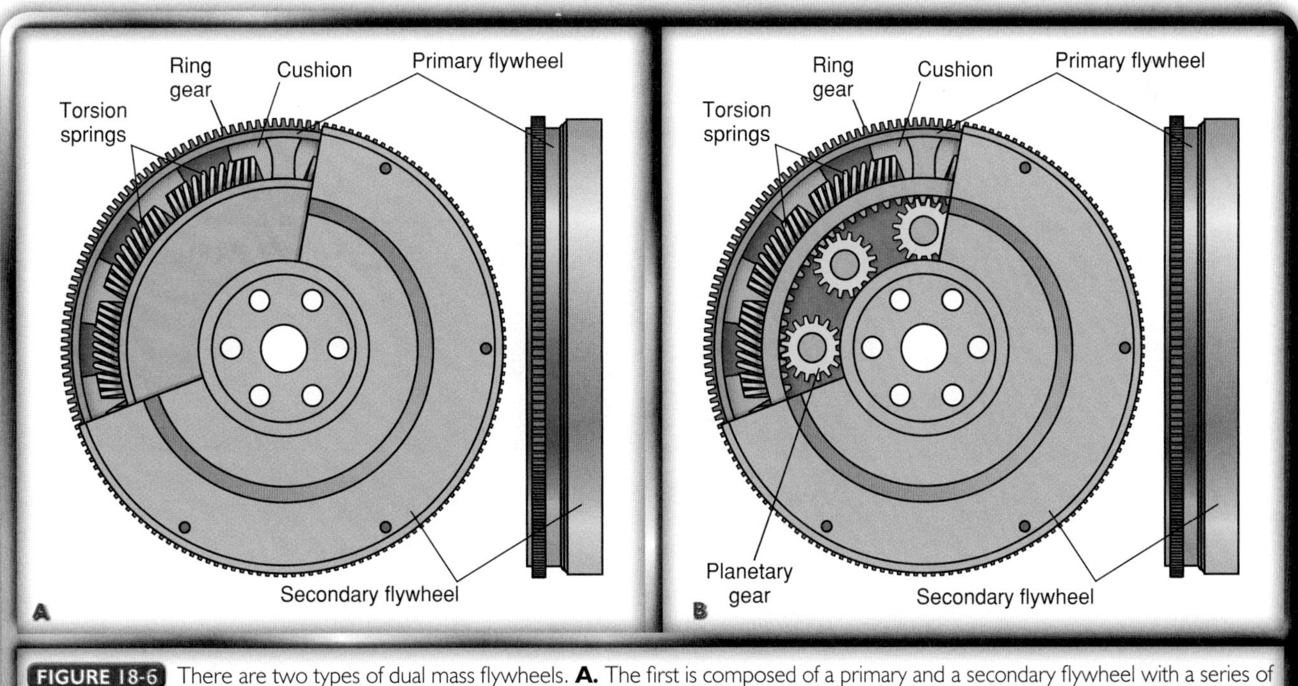
Ring gear
Cushion
Primary flywheel
Torsion springs
Secondary flywheel
A
Ring gear
Cushion
Primary flywheel
Torsion springs
Planetary gear
Secondary flywheel
B

FIGURE 18-6 There are two types of dual mass flywheels. **A.** The first is composed of a primary and a secondary flywheel with a series of torsion springs and cushions. **B.** The second uses a planetary gear and torsional springs.

torsional vibration, the dual mass flywheel eliminates any potential damage to the transmission gear teeth. If the dual mass flywheel were not used, the torsional vibration could cause increased wear or even chipping of the transmission gears.

The dual mass flywheel construction relocates the light-duty torsional damper from the clutch disc in a one-piece flywheel to the engine flywheel on the dual mass flywheel style. This repositioning and heavy-duty torsional damper dampens engine torsional vibrations much more effectively than is possible with standard clutch disc dampening technology.

> **TECHNICIAN TIP**
>
> Dual mass flywheels are designed to provide maximum isolation of the frequency below the engine's operating rpm, usually between 200 and 400 rpm. They are also most effective during engine startup and shutdown.

Pressure Plates

The pressure plate provides the clamping force to clamp the clutch disc between the pressure plate and the flywheel so that torque can be transmitted between those parts. The force is generated by one or more very strong springs. When the driver pushes on the clutch pedal, the spring(s) in the pressure plate are what the driver is pushing against. Pushing the clutch pedal compresses the spring(s) and removes the clamping force from the clutch disc. Releasing the clutch pedal allows the spring(s) to apply their clamping force to the clutch disc again. Most automotive pressure plates are of either the diaphragm spring style or the coil spring style.

Diaphragm Pressure Plate

In light vehicles, the pressure plate is normally a diaphragm type and is serviced as an assembly, which means it is not designed to be disassembled and repaired **FIGURE 18-7**. A **diaphragm pressure plate** consists of a pressed steel cover, a pressure plate with a machined flat surface, a number of spring steel drive straps, and the diaphragm spring. This diaphragm is located inside the clutch cover on two **fulcrum rings**, held in place by a number of rivets passing through the diaphragm. The pressure plate is connected to the cover by the spring steel drive straps, which are riveted to the cover at one end, and two or more projecting lugs on the plate at the other. Retraction clips hold the pressure plate in contact with the outer edge of the diaphragm. During clutch operation, the throw-out bearing pushes on the diaphragm levers. The diaphragm pivots on the fulcrum rings and pulls the outer edge of the diaphragm away from the flywheel. The retraction clips pull the pressure plate away from the clutch disc.

Coil Spring Pressure Plate

The **coil spring pressure plate** uses coil springs to create the clamping pressure and uses release levers to release the clutch disc **FIGURE 18-8**. Typically, three or four release levers are used, depending on if the application is in a car or a truck. The release levers control the movement of the friction portion of the pressure plate. They pivot on the pedestals that are part of the pressure plate housing. When the release bearing pushes

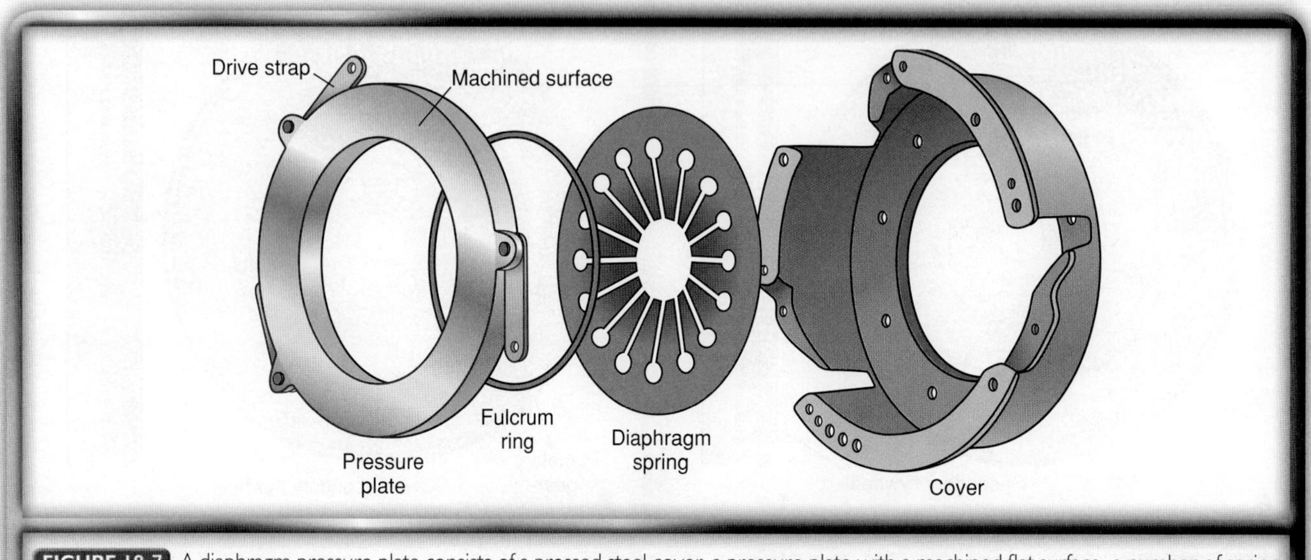
Drive strap
Machined surface
Fulcrum ring
Diaphragm spring
Pressure plate
Cover

FIGURE 18-7 A diaphragm pressure plate consists of a pressed steel cover, a pressure plate with a machined flat surface, a number of spring steel drive straps, and the diaphragm spring.

the levers toward the flywheel, they pivot and pull the friction portion of the pressure plate back toward the driver, which then relinquishes its clamping pressure on the clutch disc. When the clutch pedal is released, the levers return to their rest position, the clamping force is restored to the clutch disc, torque is transmitted, and the vehicle moves forward.

An advantage of the coil spring pressure plate is that the more coil springs there are, the tighter the clamping force and torque capacity. A disadvantage is that if the clutch disc overheats, the springs can become weak and the clamping force is compromised. This slippage causes more heat, which weakens the coil springs even further. Once a clutch starts slipping, it likely will need to be replaced very soon. Additional disadvantages are that the spring pressure is less evenly spaced on many coil spring pressure plates and there are fewer release levers, which can cause uneven wear on the friction surface over time.

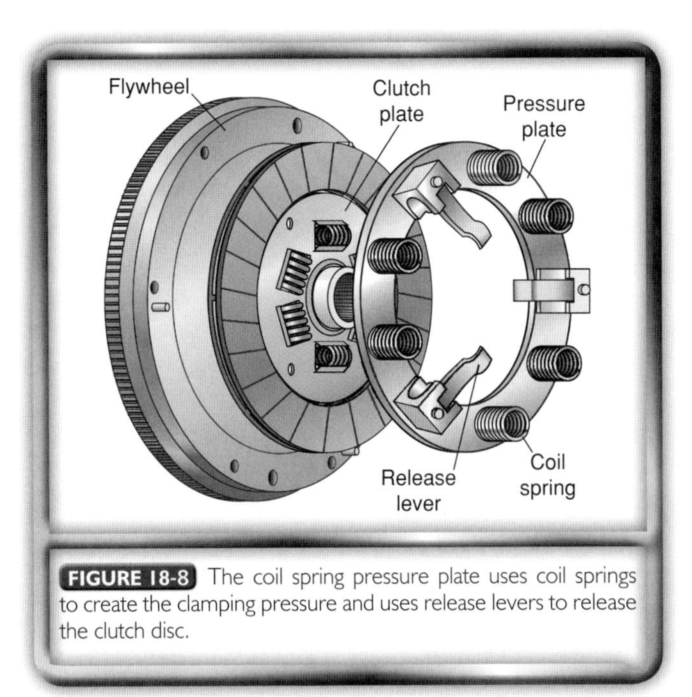
Flywheel
Clutch plate
Pressure plate
Release lever
Coil spring

FIGURE 18-8 The coil spring pressure plate uses coil springs to create the clamping pressure and uses release levers to release the clutch disc.

> **TECHNICIAN TIP**
>
> The coil spring–type pressure plate generally requires more pedal pressure to operate and may be less comfortable to drive. This is why diaphragm pressure plate clutches, which require less pedal effort to operate, are more desirable for light-duty passenger vehicles.

Clutch Disc

The clutch disc is also called a **driven center plate** or a friction disc **FIGURE 18-9**. The clutch disc provides the friction material needed to transmit engine torque from the flywheel and pressure plate to the input shaft of the transmission. On the clutch disc, the friction facings are riveted to waved spring steel segments, which are themselves riveted to a steel disc. The central alloy-steel–splined hub is separate from the steel disc. Drive is transmitted from the steel disc to the hub through heavy torsional coil springs or rubber blocks. This spring hub arrangement dampens torsional vibrations from the engine. It also absorbs shock loads imposed on the drive line by sudden or violent clutch engagement. A molded friction washer between the hub and the spring retaining plate also acts as a damper.

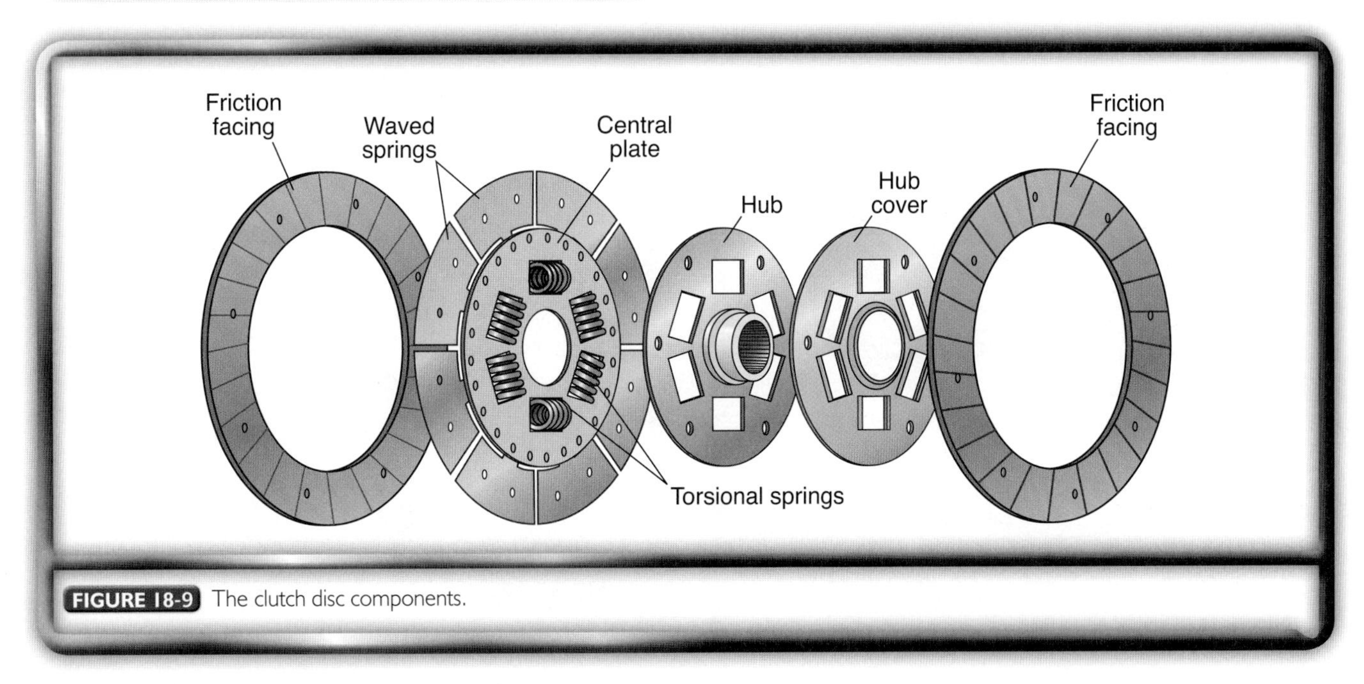
Friction facing
Waved springs
Central plate
Hub
Hub cover
Friction facing
Torsional springs

FIGURE 18-9 The clutch disc components.

> **TECHNICIAN TIP**
>
> The clutch disc friction facings used to be made of a wire-reinforced asbestos composition but now are made of organic resins and copper-reinforced wire. Asbestos is a carcinogen, so using organic materials is safer, which is an advantage for the technician when replacing a clutch assembly.

Waved spring steel segments located between the friction facings cause the facings to spread apart slightly when the clutch is disengaged and to compress as it is engaged FIGURE 18-10. This gives a cushioning effect during clamping of the clutch disc in the pressure plate. These waved springs allow a progressive application of the pressure plate clamping force as the waved springs are being compressed when the pedal is being released. The result is smoother engagement of the clutch when starting from a stop.

Throw-out Bearing and Clutch Fork

The clutch throw-out bearing and clutch fork work together (along with the clutch linkage) to compress the pressure plate springs when the clutch pedal is pressed. Since the pressure plate rotates with the engine flywheel when the engine is running, the throw-out bearing must be able to rotate with the pressure plate while the clutch fork remains stationary. Thus, the throw-out bearing must include a thrust bearing as part of its assembly. Throw-out bearings are usually **thrust-type angular-contact ball bearings** that are pressed onto a **carrier**. The carrier slides on the sleeve of the **front bearing retainer** that extends from the front of the transmission. This is considered a **push-type clutch** design, as the throw-out bearing pushes on the levers of the pressure plate. However, there are pull-type designs used on heavy truck applications. The bearing carrier is located on the clutch release bearing fork FIGURE 18-11.

Moving the clutch release fork (clutch fork) brings the bearing thrust face into contact with the pressure plate levers. This causes the bearing thrust face to rotate against the linear motion of the clutch fork and absorb the rotary motion of the levers. The thrust-type angular contact ball bearing is packed with lubricant during manufacture and requires no periodic maintenance during its service life as long as it is not abused and the clutch free-play is maintained.

The clutch fork is usually made of stamped steel or cast iron. It pivots either in the center or at the end inside the bell housing. The pivot is generally screwed into the bell housing and is usually replaceable. The pivot should be inspected for wear and lubricated whenever the clutch is replaced. The release bearing engages in tabs in the clutch fork and is usually held in place by clips.

Not all release bearings are operated by a clutch fork. Some are operated directly by collar-style slave cylinders. These are sometimes called central or concentric slave cylinders because they are donut shaped and fit around the input shaft. This style uses hydraulic pressure to directly push the release bearing against the pressure plate fingers without the use of a clutch fork.

Pilot Bearing

The pilot bearing is essentially an alignment support bearing for the snout of the input shaft to ride on FIGURE 18-12. It takes two bearings to support a rotating shaft. The pilot bearing is the front bearing, and at the other end of the

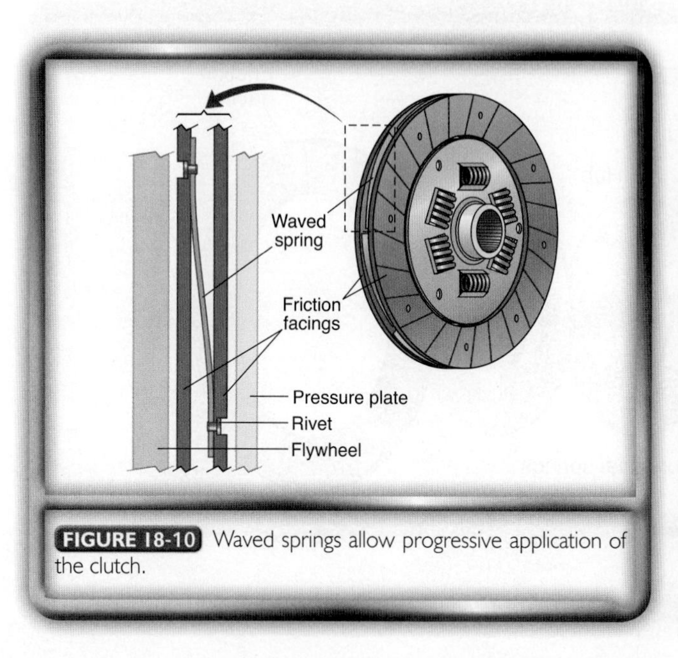
Waved spring
Friction facings
Pressure plate
Rivet
Flywheel

FIGURE 18-10 Waved springs allow progressive application of the clutch.

Clutch release bearing fork
Throw-out bearing

FIGURE 18-11 A clutch release bearing fork.

FIGURE 18-12 Pilot bearing and input shaft.

input shaft is the transmission input bearing. The pilot bearing can be a brass or bronze bushing, a needle-type bearing, or a roller-type bearing FIGURE 18-13. Larger vehicles, such as trucks, may use a ball bearing type. Some of these bearings are installed in the cavity on the end of the crankshaft, or they may be placed or pressed into the center of the flywheel. To access the pilot bearing, should it fail in any way, the transmission and clutch assembly must be removed. Some vehicles do not require a pilot bearing because of the construction of the input shaft. On this type of shaft, the input shaft is long enough (typically front-wheel drive) so it is supported on the front and back of the transaxle case by support bearings.

Clutch Operation

When initially placing the transmission into gear, the transmission input shaft must be disconnected from the engine to prevent gear grinding. In doing so, the transmission input shaft is stopped to allow the shifting of gears on the stopped transmission output shaft. Because both shafts are stopped, the gears can be engaged without grinding. When moving the vehicle from rest, releasing the clutch pedal gradually engages the clutch. As the **friction facings** on the clutch disc initially allow slippage, the torque is applied progressively until the pressure plate and clutch disc are solidly clamped. If the driver releases the clutch pedal properly, the vehicle will move smoothly away from a stop.

While the vehicle is in motion, the transmission of engine torque must be interrupted for shifting of the gears. The input shaft speed must be able to allow the selected gear to match the output shaft speed. Depressing the clutch pedal disconnects the input shaft from the engine so the input shaft speed can allow the desired gear to be engaged. When bringing the vehicle to a stop, the transmission is disengaged by depressing the clutch, which allows the engine to idle while waiting to start moving again.

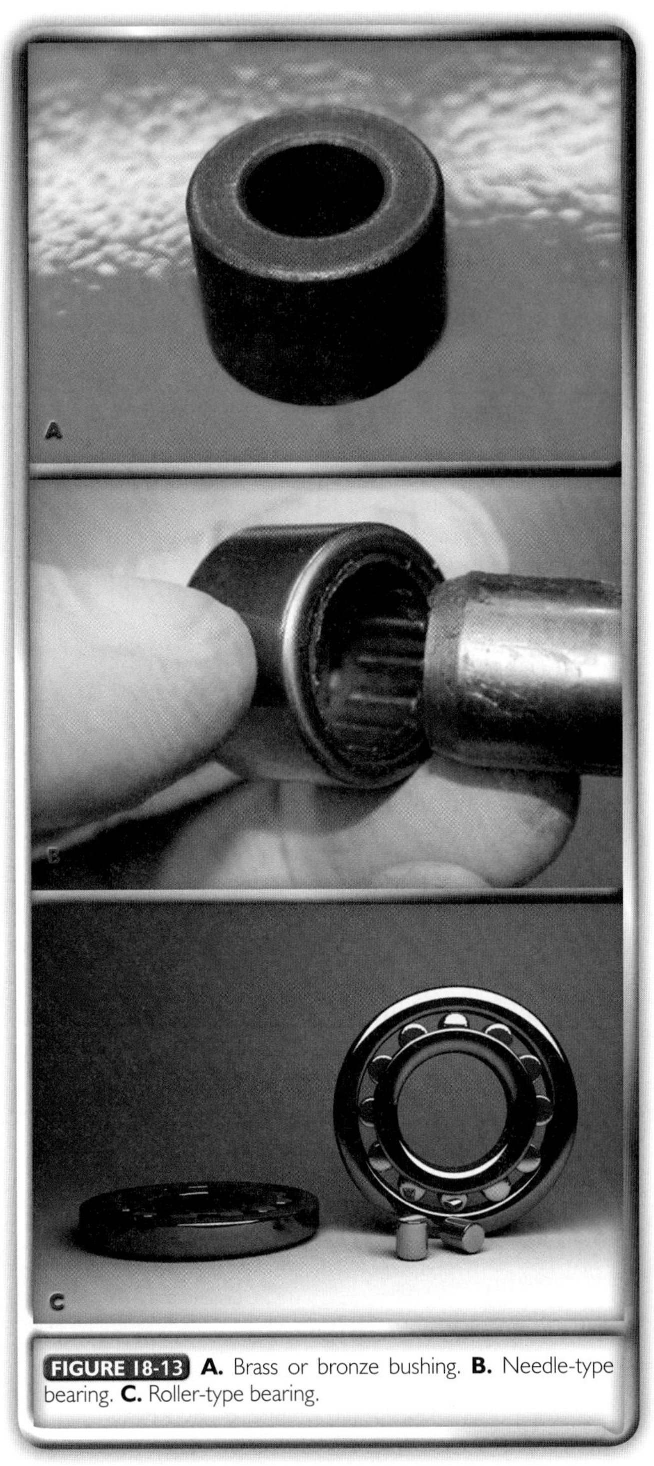
A
C

FIGURE 18-13 **A.** Brass or bronze bushing. **B.** Needle-type bearing. **C.** Roller-type bearing.

Clutch Operating Mechanisms

Movement of the clutch pedal is transferred through an operating mechanism to the clutch assembly on the rear of the flywheel. This mechanism may be one of two types of mechanical systems or a hydraulically operated system. The two types of mechanical systems are the linkage style and the cable style. Linkage-style systems use a system of links, rods, and levers between the clutch pedal and the clutch fork. Cable-operated linkage uses a strong cable in a flexible housing. This style offers more flexibility and is easier to install in the factory. Hydraulic systems use a series of steel, plastic, or reinforced rubber lines along with fluid to accomplish movement for engagement and disengagement of the clutch system.

Caring for the Customer

Regardless of the operating mechanism, it is always a good idea for the driver to make sure when shifting gears to completely remove his or her foot from the clutch pedal to preserve the life of the throw-out bearing and friction facings.

Cable Mechanisms

Cable-operated clutch control systems are easily installed in the vehicle during manufacture and take up less overall engine compartment room. The outer cable housing is fixed to the pedal support inside the vehicle and to the transmission bell housing in the engine compartment. The inner cable connects between the upper end of the clutch pedal and an external lever on the end of the clutch fork FIGURE 18-14. This lever is part of the clutch fork, which operates the throw-out bearing. Depressing the clutch pedal transfers the movement through the cable, and the throw-out bearing thrusts against the levers on the pressure plate, pushing the clutch pressure plate into the released position.

An adjustment on the clutch cable provides for the specified amount of free-play to be maintained between the throw-out bearing and the pressure plate levers when the clutch pedal is in the released position. This free-play prevents constant contact of the bearing with the pressure plate levers and subsequent rotation of the bearing when the engine is running, which would cause it to wear prematurely as well as produce a rotating sound. Some cable-operated clutches are adjusted manually by turning a threaded nut or collar to obtain the proper free-play. Some vehicles use a **quadrant ratchet**, which automatically adjusts the clutch pedal free-play as needed when the pedal is lifted by the driver's toe.

Hydraulic Clutch Mechanisms

In hydraulic clutch release mechanisms, the clutch pedal acts on a master cylinder connected by a hydraulic tube and flexible hose to a slave cylinder mounted on (external type) or in (internal type) the transmission bell housing FIGURE 18-15. The **slave cylinder** operates the clutch fork (external type) or directly on the throw-out bearing (internal type) on some vehicles. With the clutch pedal in the released position, the center valve in the master cylinder is clear of the inlet port and fluid is free to flow to or from the reservoir into the cylinder. This allows for expansion and contraction of the fluid as it heats and cools.

When the clutch pedal is initially depressed, the master cylinder piston moves forward, taking the valve assembly with it. The center valve closes off the inlet port from the reservoir, trapping fluid in the cylinder bore. Further piston movement displaces fluid through the outlet port and into the connecting lines to act on the slave cylinder piston. The movement of the slave cylinder piston is commonly transferred through a pushrod to

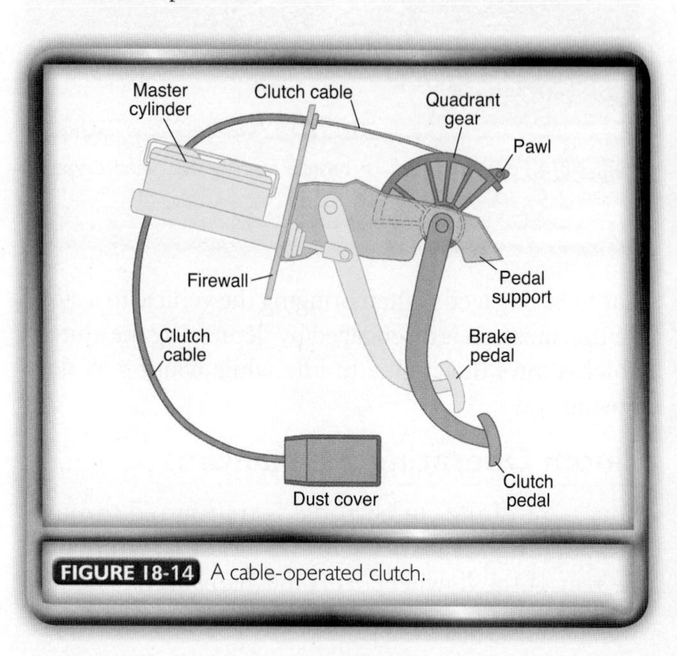
Master cylinder
Clutch cable
Quadrant gear
Pawl
Firewall
Pedal support
Clutch cable
Brake pedal
Dust cover
Clutch pedal

FIGURE 18-14 A cable-operated clutch.

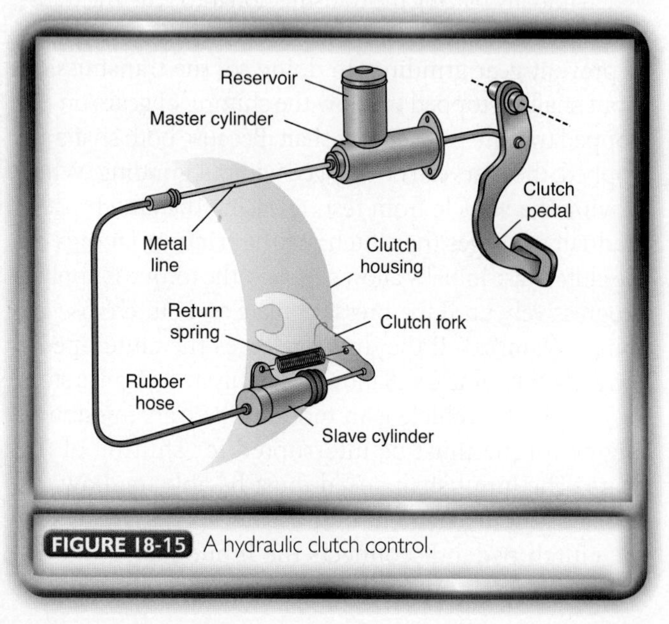
Reservoir
Master cylinder
Clutch pedal
Metal line
Clutch housing
Return spring
Clutch fork
Rubber hose
Slave cylinder

FIGURE 18-15 A hydraulic clutch control.

the clutch release fork to operate the clutch. In other configurations, the slave cylinder is located directly behind the throw-out bearing and pushes directly on it (collar style). When the clutch pedal is released, displaced fluid returns to the master cylinder and the center valve returns to being slightly clear of the inlet port, allowing excess fluid to return to the reservoir. Most hydraulic clutches are self-adjusting since the clutch fork causes the slave cylinder piston to return as far as necessary, venting any excess hydraulic fluid to the master cylinder reservoir. This system automatically compensates for any clutch disc wear and makes it so the clutch, in most cases, does not have to be adjusted.

Lever-Operated Systems

Older technology systems used a series of levers with an equalizing mechanism called a bell crank (equalizer bar) that rotated and was attached to the engine and the vehicle frame **FIGURE 18-16**. The bell crank pivoted in plastic or nylon bushings and wore out over time. Adjustments were made at the end of the lever connected to the clutch fork using a threaded rod and lock nuts. As the clutch plate wore, adjustments were necessary to maintain proper clutch pedal free-play so the clutch would operate correctly.

> **TECHNICIAN TIP**
>
> You might think that because a clutch plate wears over time, the clutch free-play would increase. In fact, it decreases. As the lining wears, the pressure plate levers move backward toward the throw-out bearing, reducing clutch pedal free-play. If the clutch disc wears enough, all of the free-play can be lost, meaning that even with the driver's foot off of the clutch pedal, the linkage is holding some pressure on the lining. This reduces the pressure plate clamping force and, if bad enough, can cause the clutch to slip, leading to a burnt clutch requiring replacement.

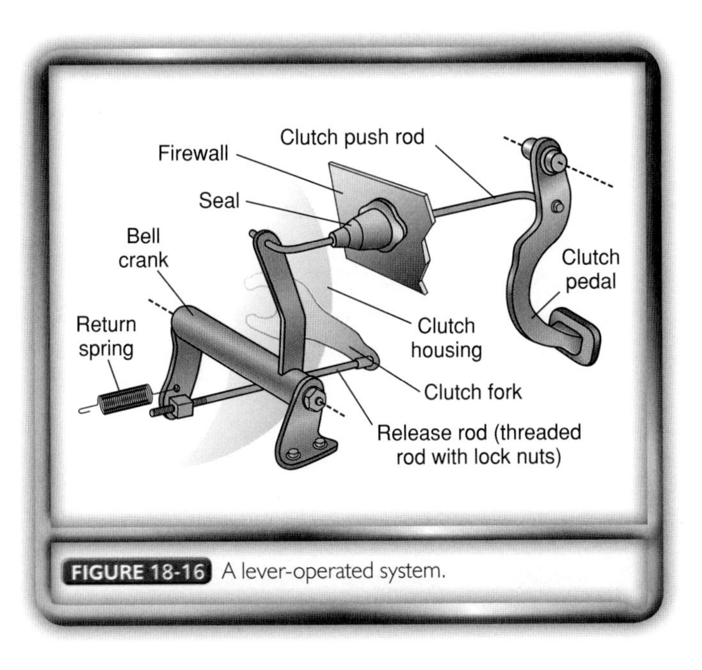
Clutch push rod
Firewall
Seal
Bell crank
Clutch pedal
Return spring
Clutch housing
Clutch fork
Release rod (threaded rod with lock nuts)

FIGURE 18-16 A lever-operated system.

Maintenance and Repair

Preventive Maintenance

Regular preventive maintenance should be performed on the clutch per manufacturer-specified intervals. Clutch pedal free-play should be checked and compared to specifications. Maintaining the specified clutch pedal free-play is critical to maintaining clutch life. This can be accomplished by following the specified adjustment procedures for the clutch system you are maintaining.

The operation of the clutch pedal and return springs should be checked for binding and excessive movement. If a clutch switch is used on the clutch pedal, check that it is functional to prevent cranking the engine while the clutch pedal is released. Mechanical linkage should be inspected for damage and lubricated with specified lubricants at all pivot points.

Hydraulic lines should be checked for leaks at the master cylinder and the slave cylinder. If accessible, pull the boot back on the slave cylinder and inspect it for signs of leakage. Check that all hydraulic lines are not kinked or leaking at their connections. Make sure all hydraulic components are secure in their mountings.

Checking and Adjusting a Mechanical Clutch

As the clutch wears, the friction disc becomes thinner. This results in the pressure plate release levers moving closer to the release bearing and the clutch linkage losing its operational clearance. Some clutches are self-compensating for wear, while others require checking and adjusting. You must refer to the manufacturer's shop information to find out exactly where any adjustment should be made.

It is important to check the clutch linkage mechanism for proper operation and correct the adjustment (free-play) periodically. It is common to do so during every routine maintenance service. If the clutch pedal has too little free-play, the throw-out bearing could remain in contact with the pressure plate levers. As a result, the pressure plate may be unable to apply full pressure, which would result in an incomplete clamping of the disc, leading to premature wear or failure of the clutch assembly and requiring removal and replacement. Also, the pedal will have to be released a long way before the clutch starts to engage. If the adjustment has too much free-play, the clutch pedal may not have enough travel to fully release the pressure plate, causing the gears to clash (grind) when shifting and resulting in heavy synchronizer wear. With this condition, the clutch will start to engage right from the floor when releasing the pedal.

To check and adjust a mechanical clutch, follow the steps in SKILL DRILL 18-1.

Checking and Adjusting a Hydraulic Clutch

It is important to check the clutch hydraulic system and components for proper operation and correct adjustment.

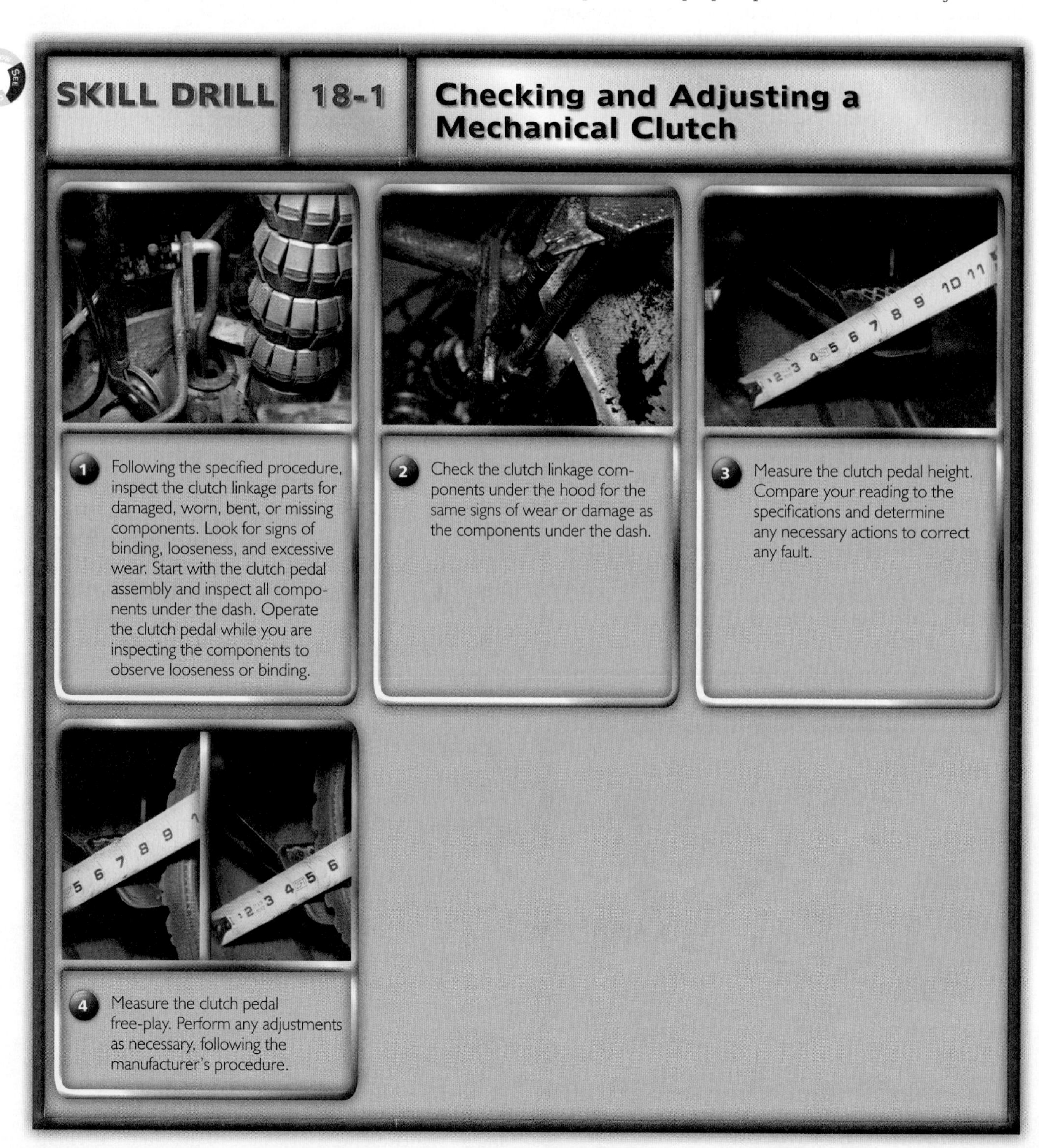
PROVE
KNOW
SEE
DO

SKILL DRILL 18-1 Checking and Adjusting a Mechanical Clutch

1. Following the specified procedure, inspect the clutch linkage parts for damaged, worn, bent, or missing components. Look for signs of binding, looseness, and excessive wear. Start with the clutch pedal assembly and inspect all components under the dash. Operate the clutch pedal while you are inspecting the components to observe looseness or binding.
2. Check the clutch linkage components under the hood for the same signs of wear or damage as the components under the dash.
3. Measure the clutch pedal height. Compare your reading to the specifications and determine any necessary actions to correct any fault.
4. Measure the clutch pedal free-play. Perform any adjustments as necessary, following the manufacturer's procedure.

It is common to do so during periodic routine maintenance service. If the hydraulic clutch system is improperly maintained, clutch operation could be compromised in a similar manner as the operation of a mechanical linkage clutch, resulting in pressure plate, friction disc, and transmission synchronizer failure. Also, improper or old fluid in the hydraulic system can cause master cylinder and slave cylinder damage.

To check and adjust a hydraulic clutch, follow the steps in SKILL DRILL 18-2.

TECHNICIAN TIP

Make sure there are no floor mats or other obstructions that will affect the operation of the clutch pedal.

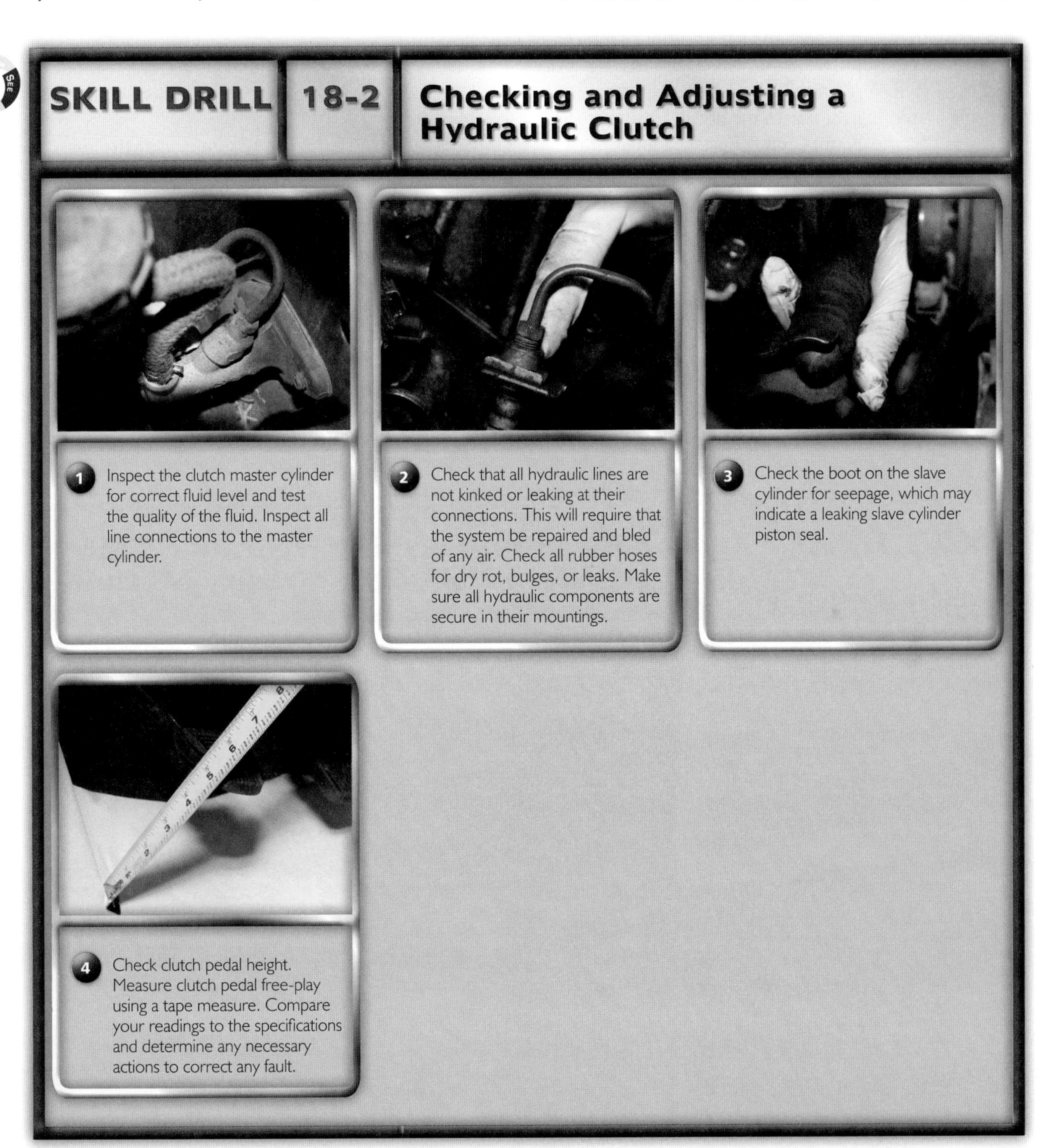

SKILL DRILL 18-2 Checking and Adjusting a Hydraulic Clutch

1. Inspect the clutch master cylinder for correct fluid level and test the quality of the fluid. Inspect all line connections to the master cylinder.
2. Check that all hydraulic lines are not kinked or leaking at their connections. This will require that the system be repaired and bled of any air. Check all rubber hoses for dry rot, bulges, or leaks. Make sure all hydraulic components are secure in their mountings.
3. Check the boot on the slave cylinder for seepage, which may indicate a leaking slave cylinder piston seal.
4. Check clutch pedal height. Measure clutch pedal free-play using a tape measure. Compare your readings to the specifications and determine any necessary actions to correct any fault.

Bleeding a Hydraulic Clutch System

In the case of a hydraulic clutch system failure, it may be necessary to bleed the air from the system. Bleeding is also needed whenever any hydraulic component is replaced or the hydraulic fluid becomes unfit for use due to age or contamination. Not all systems are fitted with a bleeder screw due to how the system is constructed. It may be necessary to bleed the system from the line entering the slave cylinder.

Research the procedure and specifications for bleeding the hydraulic clutch system. There are three types of bleeding: gravity bleeding, manual bleeding, and pressure bleeding. Determine the proper method of bleeding to use by consulting the manufacturer's specifications.

Gravity bleeding uses gravity to push fluid and air from the master cylinder and lines out through the slave cylinder bleeder screw. In most vehicles, the clutch master cylinder is quite a bit higher than the slave cylinder. The weight of the fluid can therefore be used to supply the pressure to push fluid and air out of the system.

To bleed/flush a hydraulic clutch system using the gravity method, follow the steps in SKILL DRILL 18-3.

The manual bleeding method uses the master cylinder to push fluid and air from the system. The procedure usually requires an assistant to hold the clutch pedal down while the other person opens the bleeder valve on the slave cylinder. Pumping of the pedal will result in a single air bubble breaking up into smaller bubbles or foam, which will require more time to bleed the system properly.

To bleed/flush a hydraulic clutch system using the manual method, follow the steps in SKILL DRILL 18-4.

The pressure or vacuum bleeding method uses pressure or vacuum to push or pull fluid and air from the system. This method works well for systems that tend to trap air in the hydraulic system that cannot be bled manually. It does require special bleeding tools or equipment.

To bleed a hydraulic clutch system using the pressure method, follow the steps in SKILL DRILL 18-5.

> **TECHNICIAN TIP**
>
> Be careful of the pressure that comes out of the slave cylinder, as it may splash or spray into your eyes. Also, brake fluid will eat paint, so when handling brake fluid, cover fenders and clean up any spilled fluid with generous amounts of water.

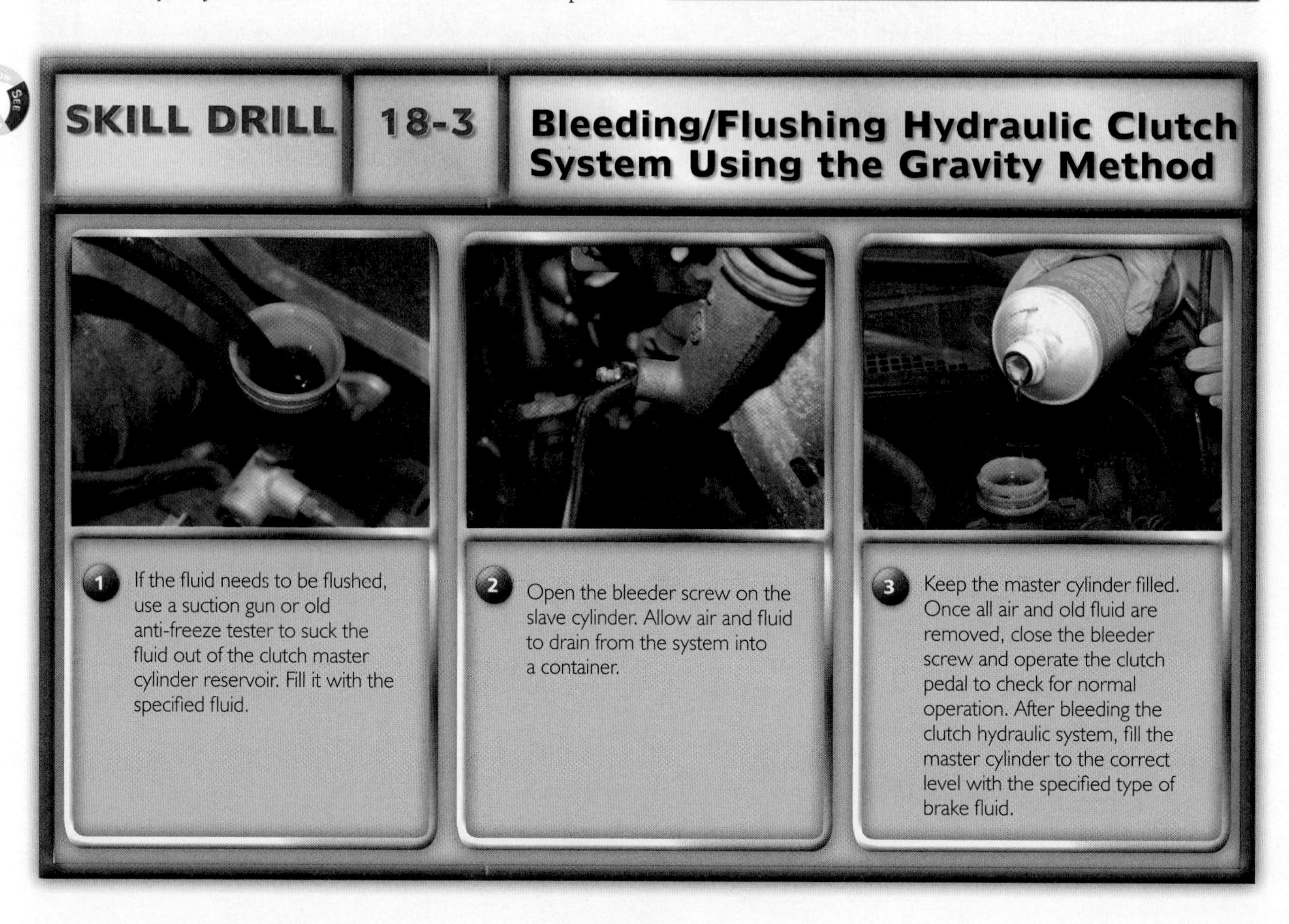
SKILL DRILL
18-3
Bleeding/Flushing Hydraulic Clutch System Using the Gravity Method
1 If the fluid needs to be flushed, use a suction gun or old anti-freeze tester to suck the fluid out of the clutch master cylinder reservoir. Fill it with the specified fluid.
2 Open the bleeder screw on the slave cylinder. Allow air and fluid to drain from the system into a container.
3 Keep the master cylinder filled. Once all air and old fluid are removed, close the bleeder screw and operate the clutch pedal to check for normal operation. After bleeding the clutch hydraulic system, fill the master cylinder to the correct level with the specified type of brake fluid.

SKILL DRILL 18-4 Bleeding/Flushing Hydraulic Clutch System Using the Manual Method

1. Remove all old fluid from the reservoir. Fill it with the specified fluid. Have an assistant depress the clutch pedal slowly.

2. Open the bleeder valve on the slave cylinder and let fluid run out into a container. When all of the fluid stops flowing, close the bleeder valve and slowly release the pedal. Repeat this process until all air and old fluid are removed from the system. After bleeding the clutch hydraulic system, check for correct pedal feel, and fill the master cylinder to the correct level with the specified type of brake fluid.

3. Keep the master cylinder filled. Once all air and old fluid are removed, close the bleeder screw and operate the clutch pedal to check for normal operation. After bleeding the clutch hydraulic system, fill the master cylinder to the correct level with the specified type of brake fluid.

SKILL DRILL 18-5 Bleeding Hydraulic Clutch System Using the Pressure Method

1. Hook up the pressure or vacuum bleeding tool to the vehicle with the correct adapters.

2. Apply pressure or vacuum to the system.

3. Open the bleeder screw and allow the fluid and air to be purged from the system. Repeat this process as necessary. After bleeding, check for correct pedal feel, and fill the clutch master cylinder to the correct level with the specified type of brake fluid.

Wrap-up

Ready for Review

- The clutch is designed to engage and disengage the engine from the vehicle's transmission.
- The driver controls the shifting of gears via the clutch while the vehicle is in operation.
- Dry (automotive) clutches rely on friction to transmit torque from the engine to the transmission.
- There are four variables affecting the clutch torque transmission: amount of friction between the clutch disc and mating surfaces of the flywheel and pressure plate; diameter of the clutch; number of clutch discs in the clutch assembly; and total spring force clamping the parts together.
- Speed and output shaft torque have an inverse relationship: when one is increased, the other is decreased.
- The clutch disengages the input shaft from the engine flywheel in order to switch gears.
- The output shaft cannot be disengaged because it is directly connected to the wheels.
- The clutch assembly is composed of: flywheel, clutch disc, pressure plate, throw-out bearing, clutch fork, and pilot bearing.
- Flywheels are designed to provide a friction surface for the clutch disc and dampen the power pulses from pistons during power strokes.
- Types of flywheels are: single one-piece flywheel (light duty vehicles) and dual mass flywheel (diesel trucks and luxury vehicles).
- A dual mass flywheel can be made of a primary and secondary flywheel with a series of torsion springs and cushions or can use a planetary gear and torsional springs.
- The pressure plate uses springs to clamp the clutch disc between the pressure plate and flywheel, allowing it to transmit torque.
- Pressure plates use diaphragm spring pressure (light-duty vehicles) or coil spring pressure.
- A clutch disc (also known as a driven center plate or friction disc) allows engine torque to transmit from the flywheel and pressure plate to the transmission input shaft by providing necessary friction material.
- The clutch throw-out bearing and clutch fork compress the pressure plate springs.
- Pilot bearings can be brass or bronze bushing, needle type, or roller type and provide alignment support for the input shaft.
- Clutch operating mechanism styles can be linkage, cable, or hydraulic.
- Cable-operated clutch control systems must be adjusted to ensure adequate free-play between the throw-out bearing and pressure plate levers.
- Hydraulic clutch control systems rely on a slave cylinder to operate the clutch fork.
- Perform regular preventive clutch maintenance per the manufacturer's guidelines.
- Check and adjust the clutch linkage mechanism (mechanical or hydraulic) during routine maintenance service.
- Hydraulic clutch systems may need bleeding: if the system fails, when a component is replaced, or if the hydraulic fluid becomes unfit for use.
- Hydraulic clutch systems may be bled via gravity, manually, or via the pressure/vacuum method.

Key Terms

carrier The part of the throw-out bearing assembly that holds the bearing.

clutch disc The center component of the clutch assembly, with friction material riveted on each side. Also called a clutch plate or friction disc.

clutch fork The part of the clutch linkage that operates the throw-out bearing.

coefficient of friction The amount of resistance to movement between any two surfaces that are in contact with each other.

coil spring pressure plate A type of pressure plate that uses coil springs to provide the clamping force.

diaphragm pressure plate A slightly conical, spring steel plate used to provide the clamping force for the clutch assembly.

driven center plate The friction disc that is held firmly against the flywheel by a pressure plate and transfers power from the flywheel to the transmission input shaft.

flywheel A heavy metal disc bolted to the crankshaft that is used to smooth out the engine's power pulses and keep the engine moving through the non-power strokes. Also provides the mating surface for the clutch disc and pressure plate.

flywheel ring gear Large, round, externally toothed gear that is usually press-fitt to the outer diameter of the flywheel and used along with the starter to crank the engine over.

free-play The amount of clearance in the clutch release mechanism as measured at the clutch pedal. The proper amount of free-play is critical to clutch operation and longevity.

friction facing The material riveted to each side of the clutch disc that mates to the flywheel and pressure plate. Used to provide friction and a wear surface for the clutch assembly.

front bearing retainer The housing that bolts the input shaft bearing in place on the front of the transmission.

fulcrum ring A steel ring that is used as a pivot point for the diaphragm spring in the pressure plate.

multiplate clutch A clutch assembly that consists of two or more clutch plates and used to increase the torque-carrying capacity of the clutch.

pilot bearing The bearing or bushing that supports the front of the transmission input shaft.

push-type clutch A typical clutch system used in modern vehicles where the clutch fork pushes the release bearing forward to release the friction facing from the pressure plate.

pressure plate The assembly that applies and removes the clamping force on the clutch disc.

quadrant ratchet The device used in some cable-operated clutches to provide self-adjustment as the clutch disc wears. Some quadrant ratchets adjust if you lift up on the clutch pedal.

release mechanisms Components that operate the clutch. Usually included are the throw-out bearing and the clutch fork. Some manufacturers include the operating system.

single-plate clutch A clutch assembly that uses only one plate to transfer torque from the engine to the transmission. This is the most common type of light vehicle clutch.

slave cylinder The component in a hydraulically operated clutch that converts hydraulic pressure to mechanical movement at the clutch fork.

throw-out bearing The part of the clutch release mechanism that imparts clutch pedal force to the rotating pressure plate levers.

thrust-type angular-contact ball bearing A type of bearing that uses a deep groove in the bearing races where the ball bearings ride; this design is for thrust conditions.

torsional vibrations The speeding up and slowing down of a shaft, which happen at a relatively high frequency. Crankshafts have torsional vibrations due to the power pulses of the pistons.

transmission input shaft The shaft that brings engine torque into the transmission.

ASE-Type Questions

1. Tech A says that the pressure plate friction surface rides on the flywheel friction surface to transmit torque. Tech B says that the flywheel can either be flat or stepped. Who is correct?
   a. Tech A
   b. Tech B
   c. Both A and B
   d. Neither A nor B
2. Tech A says that insufficient clutch pedal clearance (free-play) can cause gear clashing when shifting. Tech B says that when the engine is idling and the clutch pedal is released, the friction disc should stop rotating. Who is correct?
   a. Tech A
   b. Tech B
   c. Both A and B
   d. Neither A nor B
3. Tech A says a dual mass flywheel improves the engine's fuel economy by smoothing out the power pulses and focusing them in the direction of engine rotation.Tech B says there are two types of dual mass flywheel. Who is correct?
   a. Tech A
   b. Tech B
   c. Both A and B
   d. Neither A nor B
4. Tech A says that on larger vehicles, such as trucks, a ball bearing type may used for a pilot bearing. Tech B says that in some applications they may be placed or pressed into the center of the flywheel.. Who is correct?
   a. Tech A
   b. Tech B
   c. Both A and B
   d. Neither A nor B
5. Tech A says that there are three types of mechanical systems used for clutch operation. Tech B says that a hydraulically operated system is also used in some applications. Who is correct?
   a. Tech A
   b. Tech B
   c. Both A and B
   d. Neither A nor B
6. Tech A says that it is important to check the clutch linkage mechanism for proper operation and correct the adjustment (freeplay) periodically. Tech B says that if the clutch pedal has too little free-play, the throw-out bearing could remain in contact with the pressure plate levers. Who is correct?
   a. Tech A
   b. Tech B
   c. Both A and B
   d. Neither A nor B
7. Tech A says that the pilot bearing can be a needle-style bearing. Tech B says that the pilot bearing can be a brass bushing style. Who is correct?
   a. Tech A
   b. Tech B
   c. Both A and B
   d. Neither A nor B
8. Tech A says that when bleeding a clutch hydraulic system, one method uses pressure or vacuum to push or pull fluid and air from the system. Tech B says that this method does not require special bleeding tools or equipment. Who is correct?
   a. Tech A
   b. Tech B
   c. Both A and B
   d. Neither A nor B
9. Tech A says that in a mechanical system if the clutch pedal adjustment has too much free-play, there may not have enough travel to fully release the pressure plate. Tech B says that this condition can cause the gears to clash (grind) when shifting and result in heavy synchronizer wear. Who is correct?
   a. Tech A
   b. Tech B
   c. Both A and B
   d. Neither A nor B
10. Two technicians are discussing pressure plates. Tech A says that diaphragm pressure plates require more pedal effort than coil spring pressure plates. Tech B says that the two types require different free pedal adjustment procedures. Who is correct?
    a. Tech A
    b. Tech B
    c. Both A and B
    d. Neither A nor B

CHAPTER 19

KNOW
SEE
DO
PROVE

NATEF Tasks

Manual Drive Train and Axles Drive Shaft and Half Shaft, Universal and Constant-Velocity (CV) Joint		Page
■ Inspect, service, and replace shafts, yokes, boots, and universal/CV joints.	MLR AST	469
■ Inspect, remove, and replace front-wheel drive (FWD) bearings, hubs, and seals.	MLR AST	472–474
Drive Axle		
■ Inspect and replace drive axle wheel studs.	MLR AST	469–470
Four-Wheel Drive/All-Wheel Drive		
■ Check for leaks at drive assembly seals; check vents; check lube level.	MLR AST	472–473
■ Inspect front wheel bearings and locking hubs; perform necessary actions.	MLR AST	472-473

Basic Drive Layouts

KNOW
SEE
DO

Knowledge Objectives

After reading this chapter you will be able to:

1. Describe rear-wheel drive layout. (pp 456–457)
2. Describe front-wheel drive layout. (p 457)
3. Describe four-wheel drive layout. (pp 457–458)
4. Describe all-wheel drive layout. (p 458)
5. List the three types of shafts that make up the drive line subassemblies. (pp 458–459)
6. Explain the three varieties of drive axles and how each functions. (pp 459–461)
7. Describe universal joints and constant-velocity joints and how they function. (pp 461–463)
8. Explain the terms *final drive* and *differential*. (p 464)
9. Explain the purpose of transfer cases. (p 467)

KNOW
SEE
DO

Skills Objectives

After reading this chapter, you will be able to:

1. Diagnose CV joint issues. (pp 469–470)
2. Measure drive axle flange runout and shaft end play. (pp 469–470)
3. Inspect half-shaft components. (pp 471–472)
4. Inspect fluid leakage. (pp 472–473)
5. Remove and replace a four-wheel drive front wheel bearing. (pp 472–474)

Introduction

In previous chapters we have covered how the engine's torque is modified and delivered through the transmission, whether it is a manual or an automatic type. Now the torque must get delivered to the appropriate wheels. That job is performed by the remainder of the drive train components, such as driveshafts, transfer cases, final drives, differentials, and drive axles. All of these assemblies are made up of subcomponents that allow them to perform their task. Depending on the vehicle, the arrangement of these assemblies can vary. For example, most passenger vehicles are driven by two wheels, while most off-road vehicles are driven by all four wheels. This chapter discusses these various assemblies and components, their layout, how they operate, and ultimately how to maintain them. The drive train operates in harsh conditions. Don't overlook the importance of periodic inspection and maintenance.

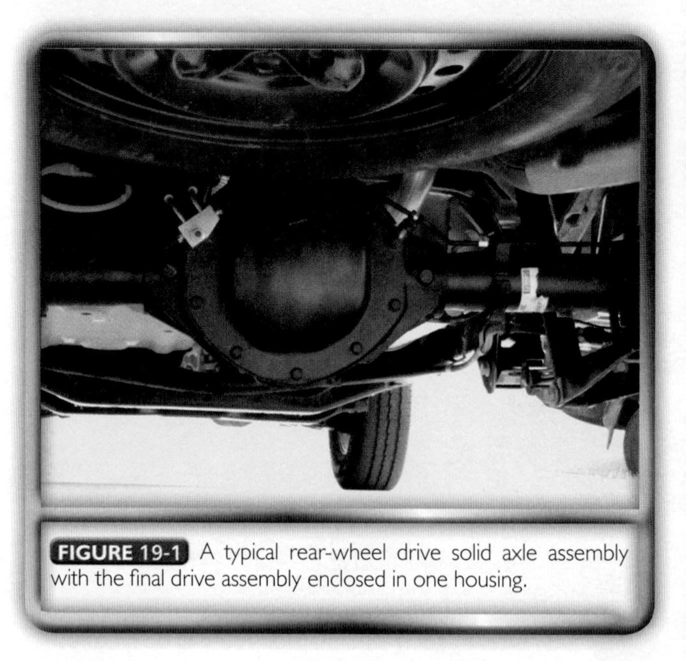

FIGURE 19-1 A typical rear-wheel drive solid axle assembly with the final drive assembly enclosed in one housing.

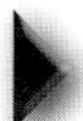

Rear-Wheel Drive Layout

In a conventional rear-wheel drive vehicle, the engine and transmission are mounted longitudinally at the front. Drive from the engine is transmitted to a rear axle assembly by a drive (propeller) shaft. **Beam-type** or solid rear axle assemblies enclose the final drive gears, differential gears, and axle shafts into one housing **FIGURE 19-1**. In vehicles with an independent rear suspension, the final drive unit is mounted on the chassis frame, and drive is transferred to each road wheel through external driveshafts (half-shafts), which have flexible joints on each end. Vehicles with rear- or mid-mounted engines normally use a transaxle in the rear of the vehicle and transfer the drive to the road wheels by external drive half-shafts.

In beam axle or solid rear axle applications, suspension action makes the final drive assembly rise and fall relative to the vehicle frame. This happens as a vehicle goes over bumps and various types of terrain. This movement produces continuous change in the distance from the transmission output shaft to the final drive pinion, and in the angle between the driveshaft and its connections. In addition, the pinion nose is forced up on acceleration by torque and down when the brakes are applied on deceleration.

You Are the Automotive Technician

After a long, icy-cold Michigan winter, Mrs. Simpson visits her local repair shop because she has started to notice an unusual noise that sometimes comes from the front of the vehicle. She drives her vehicle to and from work on Highway 94, which has multiple potholes as a result of the heavy trucking industry and harsh winter weather. You complete an interview with Mrs. Simpson and take her 2006 Toyota Camry for a test-drive, during which you notice that the vehicle makes a popping noise when turning corners. Your preliminary diagnosis is a worn constant-velocity (CV) joint, but you will need to further inspect the vehicle in the service bay. The visual inspection of the underside of the vehicle confirms your preliminary diagnosis: the right front CV joint boot is torn and dripping water. There is also dirt mixed with the little bit of grease still inside the boot.

1. What is likely causing the customer's concern? And what will you recommend to correct it?
2. What are the three different drive axle arrangements used with a rear-wheel drive solid axle? Which drive axle is most commonly used on medium to heavy trucks?
3. What is the difference between a final drive unit and the differential assembly?

Despite these movements, the driveshaft must transfer the drive smoothly. Change in length is accommodated by a sliding coupling built into the driveshaft or through the use of a **slip yoke** on the front of the driveshaft. The slip yoke has splines that mate to the splines on the transmission output shaft. The slip yoke slides in and out on the output shaft, allowing the length changes needed as the suspension moves up and down. If the vehicle uses a **sliding spline driveshaft**, a two-piece driveshaft is joined in the middle with splines. The driveshaft can slide on itself to increase and decrease in length. Universal joints (or simply "U-joints") are fitted at the front and rear ends of the driveshafts to allow for up-and-down suspension movement. The engine crankshaft and driveshaft rotate in line on this arrangement.

As shown in Figure 19-1, the centerline of the rear-wheel drive vehicle is not in line with the axle lines; this means the power needs to be turned 90 degrees to get it to the rear wheels. A ring gear and pinion assembly is commonly used for this purpose. The ring and pinion gear set allows the transfer of power 90 degrees **FIGURE 19-2**. It also reduces the rotational speed of the axles relative to the driveshaft, which increases the torque applied to the wheels.

Front-Wheel Drive Layout

Front-wheel drive vehicle engines may be mounted transversely or longitudinally. **Longitudinally** means the front of the engine is facing the front of the vehicle, while **transverse** mounting means the front of the engine is facing the side of the vehicle; that is, the engine is facing one of the fenders. Most front-engine front-wheel drive vehicles use a transverse-mounted engine coupled to a transaxle. Power is transmitted in a straight line from the engine through the transmission and final drive (differential) gearing and out to the front axles (half-shafts). This design eliminates the need to transfer power 90 degrees as with a rear-wheel drive arrangement.

FIGURE 19-2 The ring and pinion gear set allows power to be transferred ninety degrees from the power source.

Front-wheel drive power reaches the front wheels through the transaxle. In transverse applications, the transaxle is normally mounted at the rear of the engine and a primary shaft engages with the splines of the clutch center plate. When a gear is selected, the drive is transferred to a secondary shaft, and through a secondary shaft pinion, to a helical ring gear attached to the differential case. Drive is then transferred through the differential gears to each driveshaft and into each front wheel.

Four-Wheel Drive Layout

Vehicles with part-time four-wheel drive are designed for optional off-road use. Four-wheel drive can be selected as needed for abnormal surfaces (mud, snow, ice, etc.) and can be disconnected for normal road surfaces. Selection is made by a manual lever or by electronic control via a push button. In such applications, the engine and transmission are normally mounted longitudinally at the front. A transfer case is mounted to the rear of the transmission. The transfer case is a device designed to split the power from the transmission to both the front and the rear drive axles when four-wheel drive is selected. Driveshafts are used to move power from the transfer case to the front and rear drive axles. The transfer case gives the driver control of four possible power transfer options:

1. The selection most often used is two-wheel drive, since most driving is done on clear non-slippery roads. Two-wheel drive sends power to the rear wheels only; the front axle is not being supplied with any power.
2. The next selection is typically neutral, which allows the vehicle to be towed if it is stuck in mud or snow, or towed down the highway with the engine off, such as behind a motor home; no power is being transmitted to either axle in this selection.
3. Another selection is four-wheel drive *high range*, which transmits power to the front and rear drive axles at normal drive speed.
4. The last selection is four-wheel drive *low range*. This position provides a gear reduction inside the transfer case and results in higher torque to the front and rear drive axles. This position causes the vehicle to move slowly while the engine turns at a higher rpm. Thus, to avoid over-revving the engine, the low range should be selected only when driving at slow vehicle speeds.

> **TECHNICIAN TIP**
>
> A neutral position on the transfer case allows an accessory, such as a cable winch or a hydraulically driven dump bed, to be driven from a power take-off (PTO) gear mounted to the side of the transfer case.

The beam-type or solid axle housings enclose the ring gear and pinion and differential gears, and driveshafts supply power from the transfer case. The front drive axle must allow for steering, and to do this, front wheel hubs are mounted to upper and lower ball joints, or pins and bearings. To transfer power to the movable hubs, U-joints must be used in the axle shafts that are splined to the hubs. Newer designs in pick-up trucks and SUVs use **constant-velocity (CV) joint**–type front axles. CV joints allow for smoother transfer of power and allow for the vehicle to turn more tightly without the joint binding. CV joints also allow for differences in working angles, a condition that would have caused vibrations from standard U-joint setups.

All-Wheel Drive Layout

All-wheel drive vehicles are widely used today because they offer both the convenience of not having to select four-wheel drive when needed and the necessary traction when on-road (or occasionally off-road) conditions warrant it. Such vehicles are intended for lighter duty and are sometimes referred to as "boulevard SUVs."

In some all-wheel drive vehicles, only two of the wheels are normally powered, typically the front wheels. In this case, the rear-wheel drive is applied automatically when needed to maintain traction. The driver is not normally aware of when this takes place, but has the peace of mind that it happens when needed. In other all-wheel drive vehicles, all four wheels are powered all of the time, but the torque may be split unevenly when driving under normal conditions.

Drive Line Subassemblies and Components

The drive line subassemblies are made up of driveshafts, axle shafts, and half-shafts. Each shaft transfers torque from one component to the next. Terminology of the components varies depending on the type of drive train. For example, on most rear-wheel drive vehicles, there is one driveshaft from the transmission to the final drive assembly and two axle shafts—one from each side of the final drive to one of the rear wheels. On front-wheel drive vehicles, there are two half-shafts (axles)—one on each side of the transaxle to each of the front wheels. Four-wheel drive and all-wheel drive vehicles use combinations of driveshafts and half-shafts depending on if the axle shafts are independent or non-independent. We will explore each of these types of shafts and the joints that allow them to transfer torque.

Driveshafts—Rear-Wheel Drive

The driveshaft is a device that transfers torque from one component to another, such as from the transmission output shaft to the final drive assembly FIGURE 19-3. The driveshaft is typically made from metal tubing material. The driveshaft can be constructed from steel or aluminum and can come in various sizes and lengths depending upon the application. The driveshaft can be a short one-piece assembly with a U-joint at each end, or in some vehicles with a long wheel base, such as a school bus, the driveshaft can be made up of as many as four separate segments. The driveshaft typically requires the use of joints (described later in this chapter) to allow power to transfer smoothly as the driveshaft follows the movement of the suspension system.

U-joint yokes are typically welded to each end of the tube. The front U-joint connects to the driveshaft's internally splined slip yoke, which engages with splines on the transmission output shaft. The front slip yoke on the driveshaft slides over the output shaft in the transmission and is supported on the outside by a bushing located inside the rear transmission housing. This design enables the slip yoke to move longitudinally and vary the shaft length with suspension movement. The rear U-joint mates with a **companion flange** on the differential pinion shaft. The companion flange is a splined flange that transmits power to the pinion gear as discussed in the differential section.

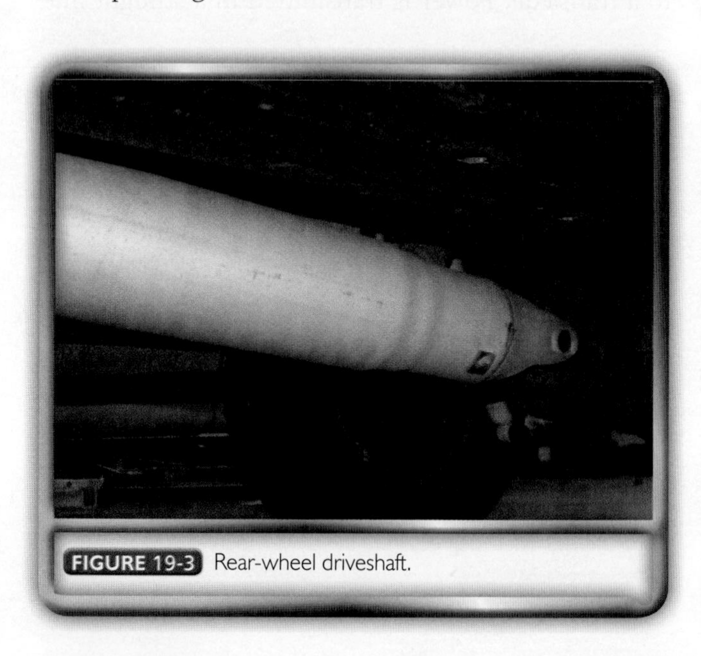

FIGURE 19-3 Rear-wheel driveshaft.

Some applications use a two-piece driveshaft that is able to flex in the middle. The front section of the driveshaft is supported at its rear end by a center bearing, called the carrier bearing. The carrier bearing is bolted to a mounting bracket on the vehicle frame that supports the center of the driveshaft. Since the maximum length of a single section of driveshaft tubing is approximately 72" (183 cm) to prevent twisting of the tube from the torque output, two or more sections may be used. The other reason to use the two-piece driveshaft is because the angle of the U-joint may be too great if the driveshaft were just a single piece. The use of three, or more, U-joints breaks up the excessive angle between the transmission to the rear axle. The U-joint is capable of working at a maximum angle of 3 degrees; beyond this, vibration and additional wear will occur. Be sure to check the drive line angles when diagnosing this concern. Provision is normally made for adjusting the alignment of the two shafts using shims under the carrier bearing.

When working with a two-piece driveshaft or a splined driveshaft, it is critical that the yokes on both halves of the driveshaft be phased correctly, which means the pivot points of the U-joints are lined up in the same exact orientation from one shaft to the other. If the driveshaft halves are not assembled correctly, then vibration will result. With a one-piece driveshaft, the yokes are welded to the tube and cannot be moved. When working on a two-piece driveshaft, be sure to mark the location of each driveshaft half with a marker or white paint mark to ensure the yokes line up FIGURE 19-4.

Driveshafts—Four-Wheel Drive

In four-wheel drive applications, driveshafts transfer the drive from the transfer case (torque splitter) to the final drive units at the front and rear axle assemblies. Each drive shaft has a U-joint at each end to transmit the drive through varying angles, and a sliding joint (slip joint) incorporated into the shaft to accommodate changes in driveshaft length by allowing the driveshaft to slide on the splines of its counterpart.

Axles and Half-Shafts

There are two types of axles used today—the **dead axle** and the **live axle** (**drive axle**). The dead axle does not provide any drive capabilities and is used on the rear of front-wheel drive vehicles, and the front of rear-wheel drive vehicles. It works the same as a trailer axle, allowing the wheels to spin freely and follow the drive axle. The purpose of the drive axle is to transfer the torque that comes from the engine, transmission, driveshaft, and differential to the wheels and tires, propelling the vehicle forward or backward.

Rear-Wheel Drive Solid Axles

Drive axles used with a rear-wheel drive solid axle assembly come in three varieties:

1. **Semi-floating axle**: On the semi-floating axle, the axle shafts are splined to the differential side gears, and the outer bearing is between the outer end of the axle shaft and the inside of the axle housing FIGURE 19-5. Wheel studs are pressed into the axle flange at the end of this type of axle. The axles support the weight of the vehicle and are also subject to bending forces as the vehicle corners. If the vehicle with a semi-floating axle were to hit a curb and break or snap the axle shaft, the wheel would come off of the vehicle.

FIGURE 19-4 The driveshaft yoke alignment is critical for smooth operation.

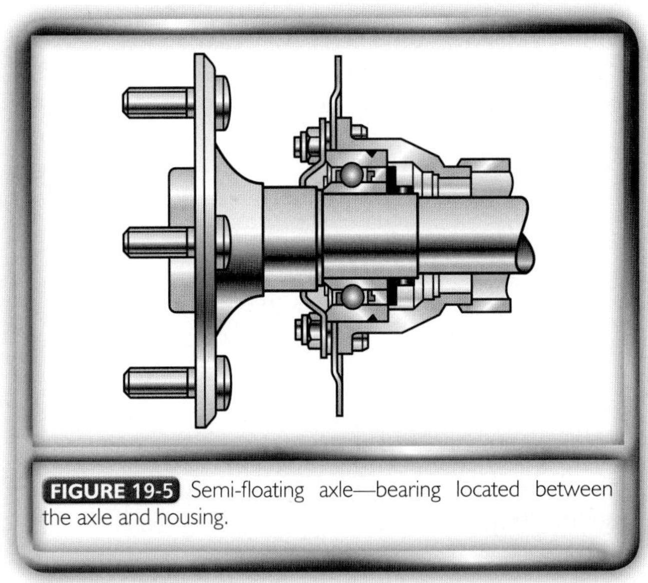

FIGURE 19-5 Semi-floating axle—bearing located between the axle and housing.

2. **Three-quarter floating axle**: On this type of axle, there is a single roller bearing between the hub and the outside of the axle housing FIGURE 19-6. The axle flange is bolted to the housing and stabilizes the wheel vertically, while the vehicle's weight is supported by the hub and the bearing. Three-quarter floating axles were used on older vehicles, such as Chrysler vehicles and pick-up trucks.
3. **Full floating axle**: On the full floating axle, there are two tapered roller bearings between the hub and the outside of the axle housing FIGURE 19-7. This arrangement helps to isolate the weight of the vehicle on the hub and bearings, not on the axle itself. Since full floating axles can carry more weight, they are commonly used on medium- to heavy-duty pick-up trucks. This type of axle floats between the axle side gears and the wheel hub. Torque is delivered to the wheel hub by the flange on the end of the axle that is bolted to the hub. Heavy-duty applications sometimes use conical wedges to keep the full floating axle centered on the hub. The flange requires a gasket or room temperature vulcanizing (RTV) sealer to seal the oil in the axle housing from leaking out while driving down the highway. The inner axle seal is part of the hub and can be serviced only by the removing the wheel and hub assembly.

Whether a vehicle is two-wheel drive, four-wheel drive, or all-wheel drive, axles deliver torque from the differential(s) to the drive wheels. In some four-wheel drive vehicles, the front axle driveshafts are enclosed within an axle housing. They are splined at their inner end to the differential side gears, and to the front wheel hubs at their outer end. A CV joint in each driveshaft allows for greater steering angle movement on turns while continuing to transmit drive to the front wheels.

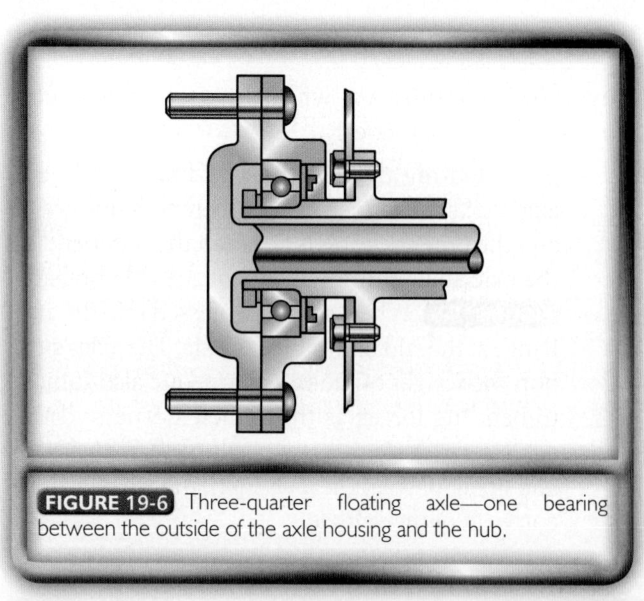

FIGURE 19-6 Three-quarter floating axle—one bearing between the outside of the axle housing and the hub.

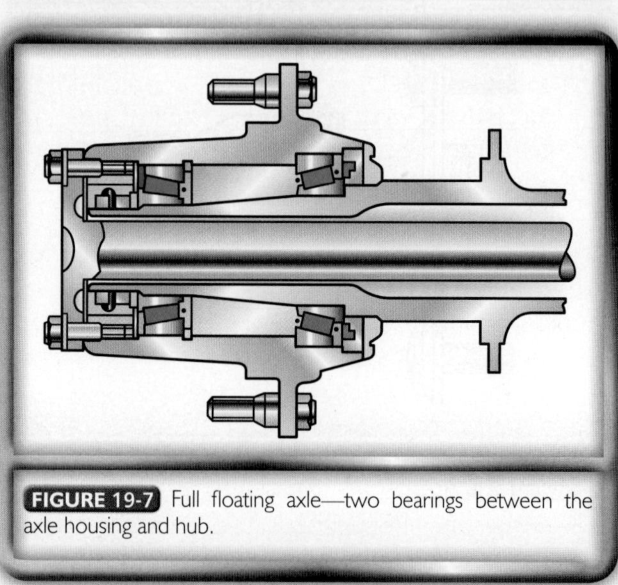

FIGURE 19-7 Full floating axle—two bearings between the axle housing and hub.

> **TECHNICIAN TIP**
>
> Because of their design, full floating axles can be removed without removing the wheels; thus, the vehicle may not even need to be lifted off the ground.

> **TECHNICIAN TIP**
>
> On full floating axles, the two tapered roller wheel bearings that support the hub on the axle housing require adjustment to maintain the proper bearing play as specified by the manufacturer.

Axle Flanges

In most cases, the flange on the end of the axle in either the semi-floating or the full floating axle is a molded part of the axle, whereas the three-quarter floating axle may or may not have a built-in flange as part of it. It is always good practice to check runout on the flange in case of any vibration complaints. If flange damage is diagnosed, replacement of the entire axle shaft will often be required. Also, lug studs are pressed into the axle flange and used to secure the wheel onto the vehicle. It is good practice to inspect the studs for damaged threads, stretching, or even breaking off. Lug studs that are damaged can usually be replaced.

Axle Seals

Axle seals can be of the single-lip or double-lip design depending on the application FIGURE 19-8. The purpose

> **LINK**
> Refer to the Disc Brake Systems chapter for the process of replacing lug studs.

of axle seals is to contain the lubricating fluid in the final drive assembly, to maintain quiet operation, and to seal contaminants out of the sealed cavity. Too much oil inside the axle housing can cause the oil to be forced against the axle seal, which can lead to seepage past the axle seals. Failure of any of the axle shaft bearings or differential bearings can cause leaking of the axle seals as well. Worn bearings allow the axle shafts to move, and the shaft movement will wear the seals quickly and create gaps that the fluid can leak out of.

Sometimes the seal surface on the axle becomes worn or nicked. An aftermarket repair kit called a **speedy sleeve** is available for the seal surface on some axles FIGURE 19-9.

FIGURE 19-8 Single-lip and double-lip seals.

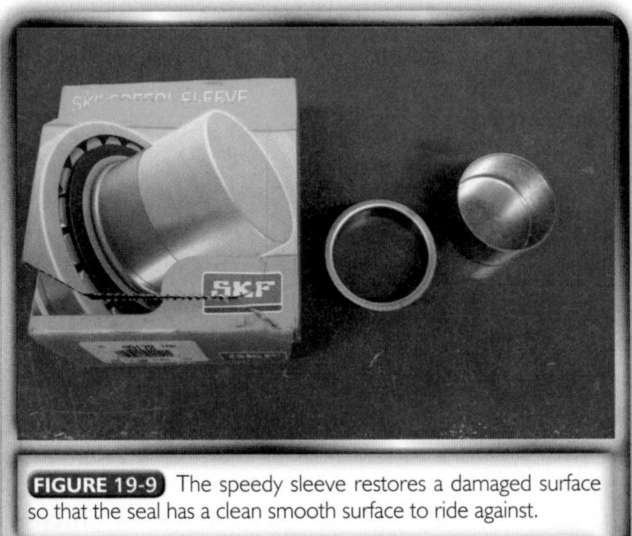
SKF

FIGURE 19-9 The speedy sleeve restores a damaged surface so that the seal has a clean smooth surface to ride against.

> **TECHNICIAN TIP**
> A common issue you might find is the leaking of the axle grease onto the rear drum brakes. Typically, this will be found as part of a state inspection or during a routine brake system inspection. A customer may complain of the rear brakes grabbing. The sticking could be the result of axle gear oil creating a thin, sticky layer on the surface of the brake lining. This in turn makes the brake material grab the drum brake surface and can create a lock-up of the brake, especially at slow speeds.

The speedy sleeve is a thin metal sleeve that fits tightly over the seal surface of the axle, providing a new, undamaged surface for the seal to ride against. The seal is designed slightly oversize to maintain lubrication integrity.

Front-Wheel Drive/All-Wheel Drive Axles/Half-Shafts

In front-wheel drive vehicles and all-wheel drive vehicles, the driveshafts transfer the drive directly from the final drive inside the transaxle to the front wheels. Front-wheel drive vehicles typically use axles called half-shafts, which have an inner and an outer CV joint.

A front-wheel drive transaxle typically does not place the final drive directly in the center of the vehicle; because the final drive is bolted to the end of the transversely mounted engine, it is offset to one side. Thus, the half-shafts are usually different lengths. The use of different-sized axle shafts can cause a problem known as torque steer. **Torque steer** is when the vehicle pulls to one side during hard acceleration. When half-shafts are not equal lengths, more torque is applied to the side with the short half-shaft, creating the pulling condition. In addition to the unequal axle length, the angles at the CV joints are different, which also results in the pulling concern and can create vibration. To combat this condition, many manufacturers use an intermediate shaft FIGURE 19-10. The intermediate shaft is a short section of shaft that typically has a bearing pressed onto it (similar to a carrier bearing). The intermediate shaft makes it so that both half-shafts are the same length from left to right. In some cases the manufacturer uses a longer half-shaft on one side, and a rubber dynamic damper may be fitted to help absorb vibrations, although this does not reduce torque steer issues.

Joints and Couplings

The driveshaft and half-shafts require a flexible joint at either end to allow for angular changes as the suspension travels up and down. There are two common types

FIGURE 19-10 Intermediate shaft.

MADE
IN
USA

FIGURE 19-11 Cross-and-roller U-joint.

of joints used in this way—the U-joint and the CV joint. Both types of joints allow the shaft to transmit torque through a change of drive angle. The U-joint does so with an increase and decrease in velocity as the joint rotates every 90 degrees. A CV joint maintains the same velocity as it goes through its rotation. While both can transfer torque through an angle, the CV joint can do so at a much greater angle than the U-joint, which is why it is used on front half-shafts to accommodate large steering angles. U-joints are typically used on driveshafts because they generally need to accommodate only small angles, although some manufacturers use CV joints to provide a smoother ride, or on off-road vehicles that have been lifted and experience a greater amount of suspension travel. A large amount of torque is transmitted through the driveshaft and half-shafts, so joints can wear over time, making inspection and diagnosis important.

Universal Joints

A **universal joint (U-joint)** is a cross-shaped flexible joint. There are caps that fit over the ends of the cross. Needle bearings fit between the ends of the cross and the caps, allowing the caps to rotate smoothly. The U-joint is considered a non-CV joint. The most common type is a **Hooke's joint** (cross-and-roller joint) FIGURE 19-11. The Hooke's joint consists of a steel cross with four hardened bearing journals, mounted on needle rollers in hardened caps, which locate the cross in the eyes of the yokes. The cross swivels in the yokes as the drive is transferred across the joint. However, the swiveling conflicts with the rotation, and in each revolution the velocity of the yoke changes every 90 degrees due to the angles that the driveshafts are operating on. This change in the angular velocity increases as the angle that the joint operates on increases.

There are two planes of stop/start as the joint flexes due to the cross shape of the joint. As the shaft rotates, it changes the velocity of the shaft up and down and then side to side, creating a speeding up and slowing down of the joint. The sharper the angle of the joint, the more pronounced the velocity change becomes, which may cause a vibration complaint from customers. The effect of the changing velocity can be minimized by having identical non-CV joints at each end of the propeller shaft in phase (in alignment). This is done by having the yokes of the driveshaft in line with each other. An increase in the velocity of the front yoke is canceled out by a similar decrease in the velocity of the rear yoke in each revolution. In some designs, engineers fit a CV joint to the front end of the driveshaft, which allows for an increase of angles of the shafts without creating vibration.

A **double Cardan joint** greatly reduces the change in velocity of a single Cardan joint by using the second joint to cancel out the changes in velocity of the first joint. A double Cardan joint is considered by most technicians to be a CV joint under normal drive line angles. The double Cardan joint uses two Cardan joints housed in a short carrier. Each cross has either a centering ball or a socket that is connected to its back side and joins with its mating component on the other cross. The ball-and-socket assembly keeps each Cardan joint at an equal angle, thereby canceling the change in velocity.

Constant-Velocity Joints

For independent suspension vehicles, the external drive axle shafts (half-shafts) to each road wheel most likely use CV joints at their connecting points. CV joints allow for more torque transfer than U-joints due to their larger bearing surfaces. Also, because of their construction, CV joints can operate at greater angles than U-joints.

Often, a sliding spline or a **plunge-type joint** is used as the inner half-shaft joint to accommodate for changes in shaft length when traveling on different types of terrain. Plunge-type joints allow smooth power flow while allowing the joint to slide in and out, effectively increasing and decreasing the length of the axle shaft during up and down suspension travel. One type of plunge CV joint is the tulip tripod joint. The **tulip/tripod joint** has three equally spaced fingers shaped like a star. On the ends of the star are three round bearing surfaces that sit on needle bearings on each finger. The round bearing surfaces move on the fingers by needle bearings. The outer race has three straight grooves that run from side to side. This configuration allows in-and-out movement of the shaft while allowing flexing FIGURE 19-12.

The **fixed-type joint** does not slide to allow for shaft lengthening or shortening; it simply allows for angle changes as the suspension moves. The fixed joint is typically used on the outboard side of the half-shaft. One type of fixed joint that you will service as a technician is the **Rzeppa joint**. The Rzeppa joint has an inner race, six steel ball bearings, a bearing cage, and an outer race. The ball bearings, retained by a spherical cage, are carried in angular grooves in each race. These balls transfer the drive from one race to the other. The inner race is splined to the axle shaft while the outer race is splined to the wheel hub. The Rzeppa joint has been modified so that it will allow a limited amount of plunge capability.

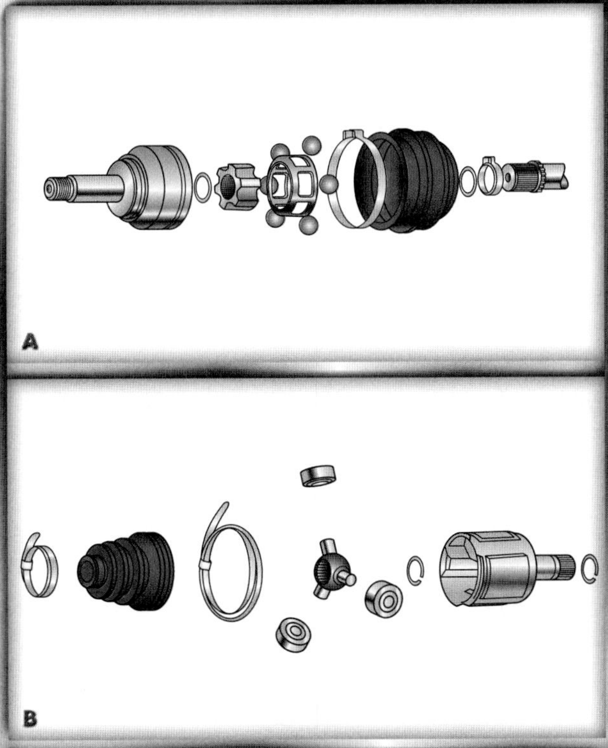

A

B

FIGURE 19-12 The CV joint comes in several forms. The Rzeppa joint **(A)** and the tulip tripod joint **(B)** are two types that are commonly found on half-shafts.

CV Joint Lubrication and Inspection

Each CV joint must be lubricated. Special bearing grease is used to keep the bearing surfaces moving freely. To keep the grease inside the joint, and to keep dirt and debris out, an accordion-type synthetic rubber boot, called a CV boot, is attached to the outside of the joint FIGURE 19-13. The CV boot should be inspected during routine maintenance, such as during an oil change, for cracks or splits. If a boot is leaking, traces of lubricant thrown on nearby components will be noted. In some cases, split-type boots can be used as replacements. Otherwise, the half-shaft will need to be removed to replace the defective boot. If any leakage is noted, the boot should be replaced since dirt and water can enter the joint, causing the joint to ultimately fail.

Although CV joints are larger than U-joints, they are still subject to wear. The indication of excessive wear is typically a clicking or popping noise when the vehicle is driven with the wheels fully turned in one direction or the other. The noise is caused by the drive balls being forced into and out of the wear grooves. Severe cases are indicated by noise at lesser steering angles.

Safety

Some CV joint greases use lead to help cushion the high metal-to-metal contact loads within a CV joint. Always wash your hands thoroughly after working with any CV joint grease.

FIGURE 19-13 CV boot.

Final Drives/Differentials

The terms final drive and differential are confused by technicians. Specifically, the term differential gets used in two different ways. The first is the most technically accurate and refers to the components inside of the differential housing that allow the axles to turn at different speeds when the vehicle is cornering or turning. These components make up what is called the differential assembly. Since the outside tire must travel farther around a corner than the inside tire, it must turn at a faster speed. The differential assembly allows this to happen; otherwise the tires would bind, skip, hop, and slide when going around a corner, which would then cause them to wear out quickly.

The second way technicians use the term "differential" is as another name for the complete final drive assembly. The final drive assembly provides the final gear reduction necessary for drive train operation, and it houses the "differential assembly." The final drive takes the power from the transmission and sends it to the wheels. And the differential assembly within it allows the tires to travel around corners without binding while the final drive is powering them. Since the differential assembly is housed within the final drive assembly, many technicians improperly call the entire final drive assembly the differential. Thus, any time you hear the term "differential," you need to ask whether the person means the final drive assembly or only the differential assembly.

Final drives can be found in axles either at the front or rear of the vehicle or can be found in the transaxle of a front-wheel drive vehicle. The speed reduction gears in the final drive are called the ring and pinion gears. Various "rear axle" ratios are available to suit the demands of the vehicle use. Lower ratios are used to increase low-speed pulling power, while higher ratios are used to improve high-speed fuel economy, such as on the freeway. Some "rear axles" allow for final drive ratios to be quickly changed, such as for racing on different track surfaces (dirt, paved, etc.) or track sizes. If the vehicle uses a front or rear axle, the driveshaft attaches to the final drive. (In the case of a front-wheel drive transaxle, half-shafts attach to the final drive.)

On some of the final drive assemblies manufactured today, the anti-lock brake system (ABS) wheel speed sensor is incorporated in them. Speed sensors read wheel speed and are part of the final drive gear set. If the vehicle is equipped with traction control, the traction control system can overcome the loss of traction by applying more power to the wheel that is not slipping by applying the brake on the wheel that is slipping.

Differential assemblies come in two varieties. First there is the open differential, which means power is supplied to both wheels equally only when each tire maintains traction, which on ice and snow is nearly impossible. If one wheel is stuck in the snow or ice, the other wheel can supply virtually no power due to the nature of the open differential assembly. The second type is the limited slip differential, which allows, under the same conditions, power to be delivered to both of the rear wheels to supply power to the ground to drive the vehicle.

Preventive maintenance of the final drive assembly, regardless of its design, is important, as these axles are filled with special lubricants that promote long life and maintain quiet operation of the gears. Maintenance schedules tell technicians when each component requires maintenance or inspection and thereby help prevent premature failure. More information on final drive assemblies will be provided in subsequent sections in this chapter.

Rear-Wheel Final Drive

In a conventional rear-wheel drive vehicle, such as a pickup truck, a solid axle assembly incorporates and encloses the final drive gears, differential, and axle shafts in one housing. A ring gear and a pinion gear transfer power through 90 degrees and provide a final gear reduction to the driving road wheels. **Hypoid bevel gears** are normally used for this purpose. Hypoid gears are a special design of spiral bevel gears, with the centerline of the pinion below the centerline of the ring gear FIGURE 19-14. This design reduces the height of the driveshaft tunnel, allowing for a flatter vehicle floor pan. The tooth shape also provides a greater area of tooth contact, and therefore greater strength.

In a rear-wheel drive vehicle, the ring gear is bolted to the differential carrier, which is supported in the axle housing or case by tapered roller side bearings, retained by bearing caps and bolts. In some axle designs, threaded adjusting rings engage with threads in the housing and will push against the side bearings of the carrier. These

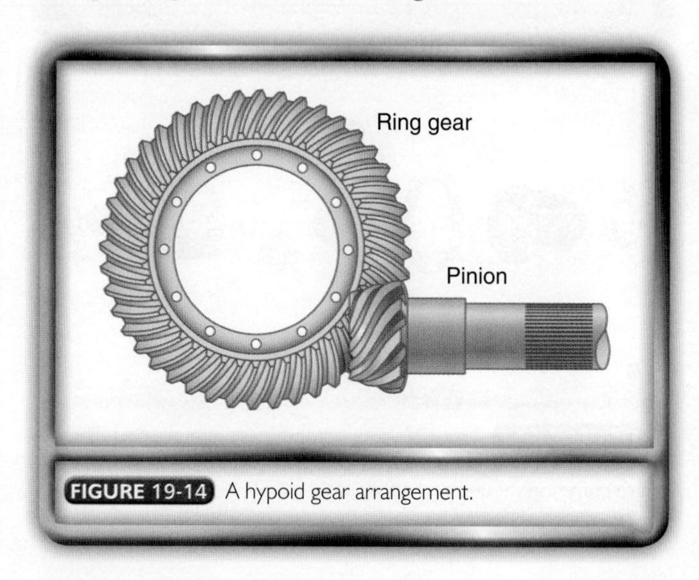
Ring gear
Pinion
FIGURE 19-14 A hypoid gear arrangement.

threaded rings are used to set the carrier bearing preload and a **backlash clearance** between the ring and pinion. Backlash is the amount of movement between the pinion teeth versus the ring teeth. If you hold the ring gear and turn the pinion, you will have a slight clearance back and forth. On other axle designs, shims are used to push against the side bearings to adjust bearing preload and backlash.

The two smaller bevel gears, or pinions, are mounted on a driving pin that passes through the carrier. Two **side gears** mesh with the pinions and are in recesses in the differential carrier. The drive axles are splined to these side gears. With the ring gear bolted to the carrier, the splines on the axle shafts are engaged with the splines in the differential side gears, and drive is transferred through the ring gear to the differential carrier pins, which carry the pinion gears with the carrier. The pinion gears carry the side gears with them, turning the axles and wheels. The pinion and side gears are also called "spider gears."

When the vehicle travels in a straight line, the ring gear rotates the case. The driving pin and pinion gears rotate end over end, carrying the side gears with them. The side gears, which are splined to the axles, then turn the drive axles. There is no relative motion between the pinion gears and the side gears; each side gear turns at the same speed.

As soon as the vehicle turns from a straight-ahead position, the inner wheel slows down and its side gear turns more slowly than the differential case. The turning effort applied to the driving pin allows the pinion gears to rotate slowly on their pin. They walk around the inner side gear while still being turned end over end.

This rotation of the pinion gears makes the outer side gear and its road wheel speed up while the inner side gear and its road wheel slow done in rotation by an equivalent amount. The outer side gear then turns faster than the case. This provides an equal torque to each drive axle while allowing for their rotational speed difference.

Limited Slip Differentials

Limited slip differentials allow normal differential action under normal driving conditions, but when road conditions are not normal, the limited slip differential reduces or prevents differential action so that a wheel cannot spin freely. Drive is maintained to both wheels. There are two main types of limited slip differentials—clutch style and gear style. The clutch-style limited slip differential uses a multiplate clutch pack between each side gear and the differential case. Each clutch pack has two different types of flat steel plates, placed alternately in the pack. One type has internal splines that mate with splines on the side gear pressure ring. The other has driving lugs that locate in slots in the differential carrier.

The outside plate is dished, or cup shaped, to provide initial tension on the clutch pack when the two halves of the carrier are assembled. Four differential pinions are mounted on two driving pins, at right angles to each other, so that they mesh with the side gears. The pinion shafts are relieved, so as not to make contact at their intersection. The ends of the shafts have two flat surfaces forming wedge shapes, which fit into similar wedges in the carrier.

In straight-ahead driving, the driving force through the ring gear to the differential carrier causes the pinion shafts to rotate end over end. This transfers the drive through the pinion gears and the side gears to the axles. There is no relative motion between the gears; however, the resistance at the road wheels forces the pinion shafts up the incline formed by the wedges in the case. As a result, the piston shafts are forced apart and the pinion gears exert a greater force on the side gears and on the clutch packs. The force locks the side gears to the carrier, preventing any sudden spinning of either wheel. Under normal operating conditions, the driving torque is transmitted equally to each axle shaft and wheel, but when patches of loose gravel or mud are encountered, the ratio of torque delivered depends on the traction available at each road wheel.

The greatest amount of torque will be transmitted to the wheel with the most traction. When turning a corner, the limited slip differential gives normal differential action and permits the outer wheel to turn faster than the inner wheel. At the same time, the differential applies the major driving force to the inner wheel, improving stability and cornering.

Torsen Style

Some manufacturers use a gear-style limited slip differential design rather than the usual clutch-type design FIGURE 19-15. This design was used to improve vehicle

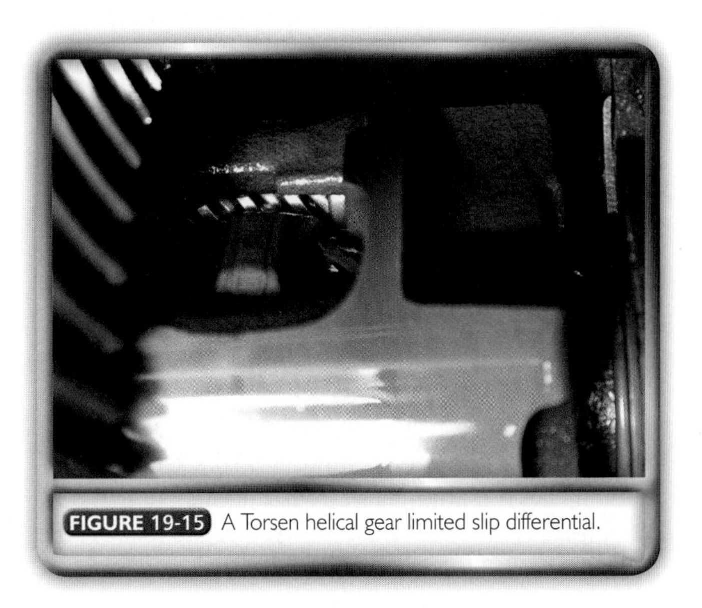

FIGURE 19-15 A Torsen helical gear limited slip differential.

stability and tire traction. Some use gear-based, or torque-biased or torque-sensing (Torsen), units. The heart of these limited slip differentials is the parallel-axis helical gear set. The idea behind the Torsen differential is to multiply the torque available from the wheel that is losing traction and turn it over to the slower turning wheel with better traction. Torque application to the wheel with better traction begins because of the resistance between the sets of gears in mesh.

Helical-geared limited slip differentials respond very quickly to changes in traction. They also do not bind from friction in turns and do not lose their effectiveness since there are no clutches, like a clutch-style unit. The unit described here is the Torsen differential, which is a very popular limited slip differential. Another manufacturer, Eaton, uses a similar design. The side gears of the differential are cut in a worm gear configuration. The pinion gears are also cut with a worm gear cut, and they are splined to each other. When one wheel begins to slip under torque, the worm gears create a locking situation that transfers power to the wheel with greater traction.

> **TECHNICIAN TIP**
>
> Oil changes are required less frequently with gear-style units because there are no clutch discs to wear as the vehicle makes turns, which contaminates the gear oil.

Four-Wheel Drive Differentials

In part-time four-wheel drive vehicles, differentials are fitted to both front and rear axle assemblies. When a two-wheel drive range is selected, the drive is transferred through the rear final drive and the differential gears to the rear axle shafts and road wheels, but not to the front wheels. The differential gears allow the rear wheels to rotate at different speeds when the vehicle is turning, while continuing to transmit an equal turning effort to each wheel. When four-wheel drive is engaged, the drive is transmitted through both front and rear final drive assemblies, and differential action occurs in both.

However, when making a turn, the front wheels travel a greater distance than the rear wheels. This causes a difference in the rotational speeds of the front and rear wheels due to the changing arcs that each wheel is tracing. Since front and rear driveshafts are locked together at the transfer case, the difference in speed cannot be absorbed in the transmission, and the drive lines can be subjected to torsional binding due to the driveshafts being forced to rotate at the same rate of speed. The customer will notice binding of the drive train. If the binding is severe, the tires may chirp, or a popping noise from the drive train may occur.

In off-road conditions, differences in speed between the front and rear driveshafts can be absorbed through slippage of the tires on the ground—be it mud, snow, or ice conditions. On firm road surfaces, only two-wheel drive should be engaged. Using two-wheel drive prevents excessive tire wear and possible damage to the drive lines or other drive train components. It also increases performance and fuel economy.

> **Caring for the Customer**
>
> Differences in wheel speed can also arise from any condition that will cause uneven tire circumferences, such as unmatched tires, unevenly inflated tires, or uneven wear. Whenever excessive binding is experienced in a four-wheel drive vehicle, it is a good idea to check for these issues. Once you have determined that all the tires match and are inflated properly, use a tape measure to measure the circumference of each tire. Manufacturers' recommendations for the maximum difference in tire circumferences typically vary from 0.125″to 0.5″ (3.2 to 12.7 mm). This difference can easily occur when one tire is damaged enough that it has to be replaced, but the other tires are partially worn. Replacing just one tire may not be a viable option, unless the new tire is shaved to match the wear of the other tires.

Four-Wheel Drive Locking Hubs

On part-time four-wheel drives, the front wheels and axle driveshafts are splined together through the differential side gears. When the vehicle is operating in two-wheel drive range, the front axle driveshafts, final drive assembly, and front driveshaft all turn with the road wheels, but do not transmit any drive. The drag from turning all of these components with the wheels while driving down the highway causes reduced fuel economy and vehicle performance. Freewheeling hubs or manually **locking hubs** can be installed on the front hubs to disconnect the hubs from the axle shafts and prevent rotation of the front axle components. This reduces wear and noise and improves performance and fuel economy when driving in a two-wheel drive range.

When "lock" is selected on a manually locking hub, it acts on a sleeve. The sleeve has external splines that engage matching splines on the freewheel hub body, and internal splines to engage splines on the axle shaft. The sleeve slides in and out to lock the two splined components together. In a four-wheel drive range, the drive is transmitted from the axle shaft, through the sleeve, to the hub and road wheel. Unfortunately, in inclement weather conditions, the driver must get out of the vehicle and turn the locking hub knobs located on the front wheels to lock in the front drive axles.

When "free" mode is selected, the compressed spring pushes the sleeve out of engagement, leaving the wheel free to rotate without turning the axle shaft. Most vehicles require slightly reversing the vehicle in order to disengage the sleeve since binding can happen. Reversing the motion of the axle shafts will unbind the sleeve.

Another type of hub is the automatic hub. The automatic hub is factory installed on many newer vehicles. The automatic hub has a spring-loaded sleeve that moves out to engage the hub when power is applied to the front axle. So if four-wheel drive is selected and the vehicle is driven forward, the sleeve will lock the hub to the axle. When four-wheel drive is deactivated, the front axle is not transmitting power, so the spring automatically pushes the sleeve out of engagement and the hub freewheels.

Front-Wheel Drive Differentials

The differential action is the same for front-wheel drive vehicles as it is for rear-wheel and four-wheel drive differentials FIGURE 19-16. The only real difference with a front-wheel drive vehicle is that the differential is located inside the transaxle and is driven by the secondary shaft, which is connected to the pinion drive gear. Some automatic transaxles use a chain to drive the differential assembly.

Transfer Cases

Transfer cases are used in four-wheel drive and all-wheel drive vehicles to split power to the front and rear drive axles. The transfer case, or in some cases a power take-off (PTO), performs this task. A transfer case is used on vehicles that are primarily rear-wheel drive; a PTO (also called a power transfer unit [PTU]) is used on vehicles that are primarily front-wheel drive. The transfer case is typically bolted to the rear of the transmission, while the PTO is bolted to the side of the transaxle. In either situation, transfer cases and PTOs perform the same task, splitting power between the front and rear axles.

Final Drive and Differential Assembly

FIGURE 19-16 A typical front-wheel drive differential.

Four-Wheel Drive Transfer Case

There is a variety of styles of transfer cases used in four-wheel drive vehicles, depending on the manufacturer. If the vehicle uses a front-wheel drive transaxle, then a component similar to a transfer case called the PTO is used. In a typical four-wheel drive vehicle, the transfer case is bolted to the rear of the transmission. The output shaft of the transmission is splined to the input shaft of the transfer case. Power comes into the transfer case through the input shaft and moves to the rear output shaft and, if four-wheel drive is selected, also to the front output shaft. Some transfer cases use a large chain to allow power to move to the front output shaft. The chain rides on bearings on the input shaft and will typically freewheel unless four-wheel drive is selected. When four-wheel drive is selected, the mode fork, which is similar to a shift fork found in a manual transmission, moves a synchronizer sleeve to the input shaft chain sprocket. This locks the chain sprocket to the input shaft and transfers power to the front output shaft. Power then moves out of the transfer case front output shaft to the front driveshaft and to the front axle. In this style of transfer case, the function of four-wheel drive low and neutral is possible through the use of a range fork and a planetary gear set. When the planetary gear carrier is held stationary, a lower gear ratio results than when the sun gear is held.

All-Wheel Drive Transfer Case

Many vehicles today are using transverse front-mounted engines with all-wheel drive. In an all-wheel drive vehicle, both the front drive axle and the rear drive axle propel the vehicle. Depending on the system, the majority of engine drive torque is normally delivered to just one set of wheels, but upon demand, all four wheels receive drive torque and share the load. The transfer case powers both the front and the rear driveshafts, which power both final drive assemblies. Axles may be either solid or half-shafts, depending on whether the vehicle uses an independent suspension.

The all-wheel drive transfer case is bolted to the output of the transaxle FIGURE 19-17. Drive is transferred from the transmission output shaft to an internally splined helical gear on the transfer case input shaft. The internally splined helical gear is constantly meshed with the larger of two idler gear pinions. They are constantly meshed with the high- and low-output pinions on the transfer case output shaft. The low-range output pinion is bolted to a differential case that contains the third set of differential gears. The high range pinion can rotate on needle roller bearings on one side of the differential case.

The idler gear pinions are also separated, with the smaller low-speed gear free to rotate on needle rollers on the idler shaft formed with the high-speed gear. A common selector fork links a splined engagement sleeve on the idler, and a similar sleeve on the output moves the fork to engage the high range and locks the high-output pinion to the differential case.

Drive is transmitted at a one-to-one ratio, through the larger pinion of the idler gear and the locked output pinion, to the differential case. It is then transmitted through the differential gears to the front and rear output shafts, which drive the front and rear driveshafts. Engaging low range moves the selector fork in the opposite direction. This locks the low idler gear pinion to the idler shaft.

From the transmission output, drive is transmitted to the large idler pinion, and through the smaller locked pinion to the low-range output pinion, bolted to the differential case. This double reduction provides a low-output speed ratio of about 2.48 to 1 to both front and rear shafts, which can be used to gain traction in snow and ice or even mud. In addition, in some vehicles, when low range is selected, a geared electric motor automatically operates an engagement sleeve splined to the front output shaft. It engages mating splines on the differential case. This locks out all differential action between the front and rear output shafts; thus, it should only be used in off-road situations so that both the front and rear shafts rotate at the same rate of speed.

In high range, the differential lock is disengaged. Differential action is provided for by the differential gears located in the output case and splined to the output shafts. This design allows for a difference in speed between front and rear wheels when the vehicle is on firm road surfaces.

Transfer Case Differential Action

On all-wheel drive vehicles, when high range is engaged for driving on firm road surfaces, differences in speed between the front and rear wheels while turning and driving into curves must be provided. This can be accomplished by use of a third set of differential gears in the transfer case output assembly. However, the third differential operation means that if a front wheel spins on a slippery surface, virtually no drive is transmitted to the rear wheels.

There are several ways manufacturers have addressed this slipping condition. One of the easiest is to use the traction control system to apply the brake unit at the wheel that is slipping, which increases the amount of torque to the other wheels that have more traction. Other manufacturers use a **viscous coupling** unit between the front and rear driveshafts to act as a limited slip differential and drive both axles if one is slipping FIGURE 19-18. A viscous coupler uses two sets of clutch plates that are alternated front to back. One set of plates is splined to the outer housing (one driveshaft), and the other set of plates is splined to the inner housing (other driveshaft).

FIGURE 19-17 The all-wheel drive transfer case is bolted to the output of the transaxle.

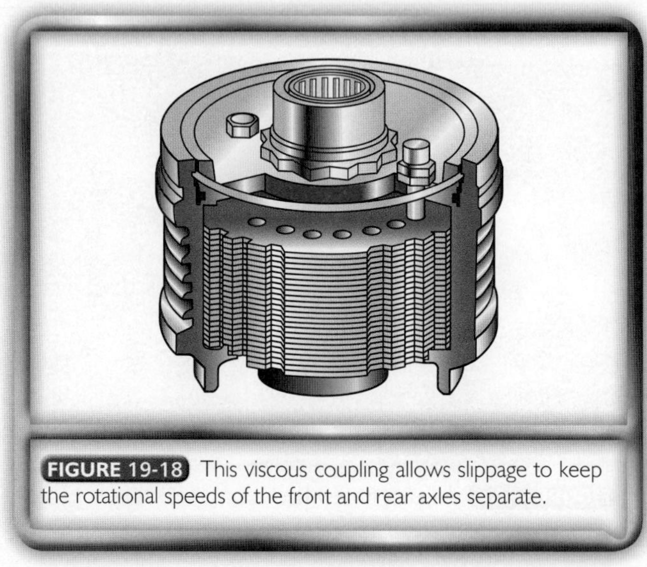

FIGURE 19-18 This viscous coupling allows slippage to keep the rotational speeds of the front and rear axles separate.

In normal driving conditions, the third differential operates to provide the small degree of differential action necessary. In this condition there is only a minor speed difference between the viscous coupling plates, so the viscous coupling allows them to move without much resistance. However, when a wheel spins, there is a higher level of third differential action and a greater speed difference between the front and rear drive shafts. This speed difference also applies to the viscous coupling plates. Fluid in the unit is sheared by the relative motion between them. This shearing action causes the silicone to heat up and become much thicker (higher viscosity), transferring torque to the wheels that are not slipping.

The degree of locking achieved depends on the severity of the wheel slippage occurring. Only under severe conditions is 100% locking achieved. When the plates are fully locked, the fluid starts to cool, and the cycle of shearing and locking starts all over again.

Some manufacturers control the differential action electronically through the use of an electromagnetic clutch to lock the driveshafts together FIGURE 19-19. This device squeezes the clutches together by applying a magnetic force on the clutch discs. In some models, the clutch can be pulse-width modulated, which controls the amount of torque that is being transferred. The use of a control module is necessary to operate this clutch.

Another type of differential used in transfer cases is the Torsen style, which uses gears similar to the version used in final drives. This style is good for splitting torque to each axle as long as the tires maintain traction, but it is not as effective in low-traction conditions.

The last type of coupling device is the mechanical differential lock. This type locks the driveshafts together using a mechanical sleeve that slides over the splines on both shafts. The differential lock is generally activated by a switch on the dash that operates either an electric or a vacuum motor, which engages or disengages the locking sleeve. This type of locking mechanism does not allow for slippage in the transfer case, so it should be used only on slippery surfaces, and disengaged before driving on high-traction surfaces.

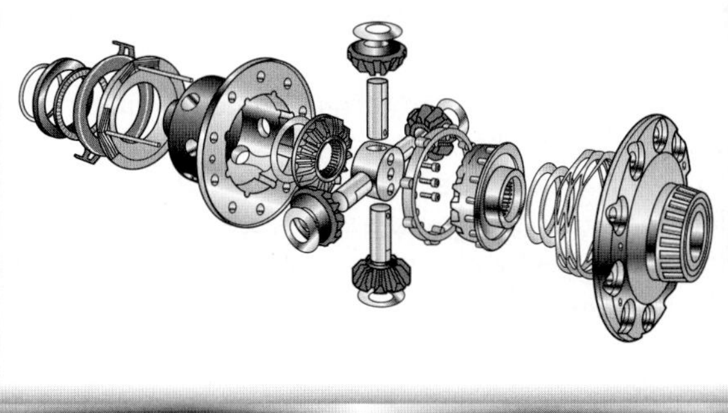

FIGURE 19-19 Some manufacturers control the differential action electronically through the use of an electromagnetic clutch to lock the driveshafts together.

Diagnosis and Maintenance

Diagnosing CV Joint Issues

CV joints have to withstand and transmit tremendous amounts of force when the vehicle is being driven. Grease helps to lubricate and cool the joint, which prevents or reduces wear. CV joints use rubber boots to contain the grease in the joint, while still allowing the joint to pivot. Sometimes the CV joint boots crack or become torn. The grease then runs out and contaminants can get in. This combination of problems causes the joint to overheat and wear out, resulting in a failed CV joint that must be replaced. This is one reason that periodic inspection of the CV boots are important. If caught soon enough, the boot and grease can be replaced before the joint is damaged. One indicator of CV joint wear is clicking or popping noises when cornering. The ball bearings roll into and out of the worn spot in the bearing races, making the popping noise. CV joints that make this noise need to be replaced; they cannot be repaired. A thorough road test along with a visual inspection on a lift may be warranted in order to diagnose CV joint problems.

To diagnose a potential issue with a CV joint, talk to the customer to fully understand his or her concern. Verify the concern with a test-drive or visual inspection, depending on the concern. You should then have enough information to make a diagnosis of the fault.

To diagnose CV joint issues, follow the steps in SKILL DRILL 19-1.

Measuring Drive Axle Flange Runout and Shaft End Play

Once axles have been serviced or replaced, it is a good practice to measure axle flange runout and axle end play. Runout is important to make sure the brake drum or rotor and the tire and wheel assembly will rotate properly and not cause any kind of vibrations. If all repairs have been done properly, runout and end play should be in specifications. Some procedures may differ due to the manufacturer's protocol. Always consult the manufacturer's guidelines and service information to ensure proper procedures for runout and end play.

To measure drive axle flange runout and shaft end play, follow the steps in SKILL DRILL 19-2.

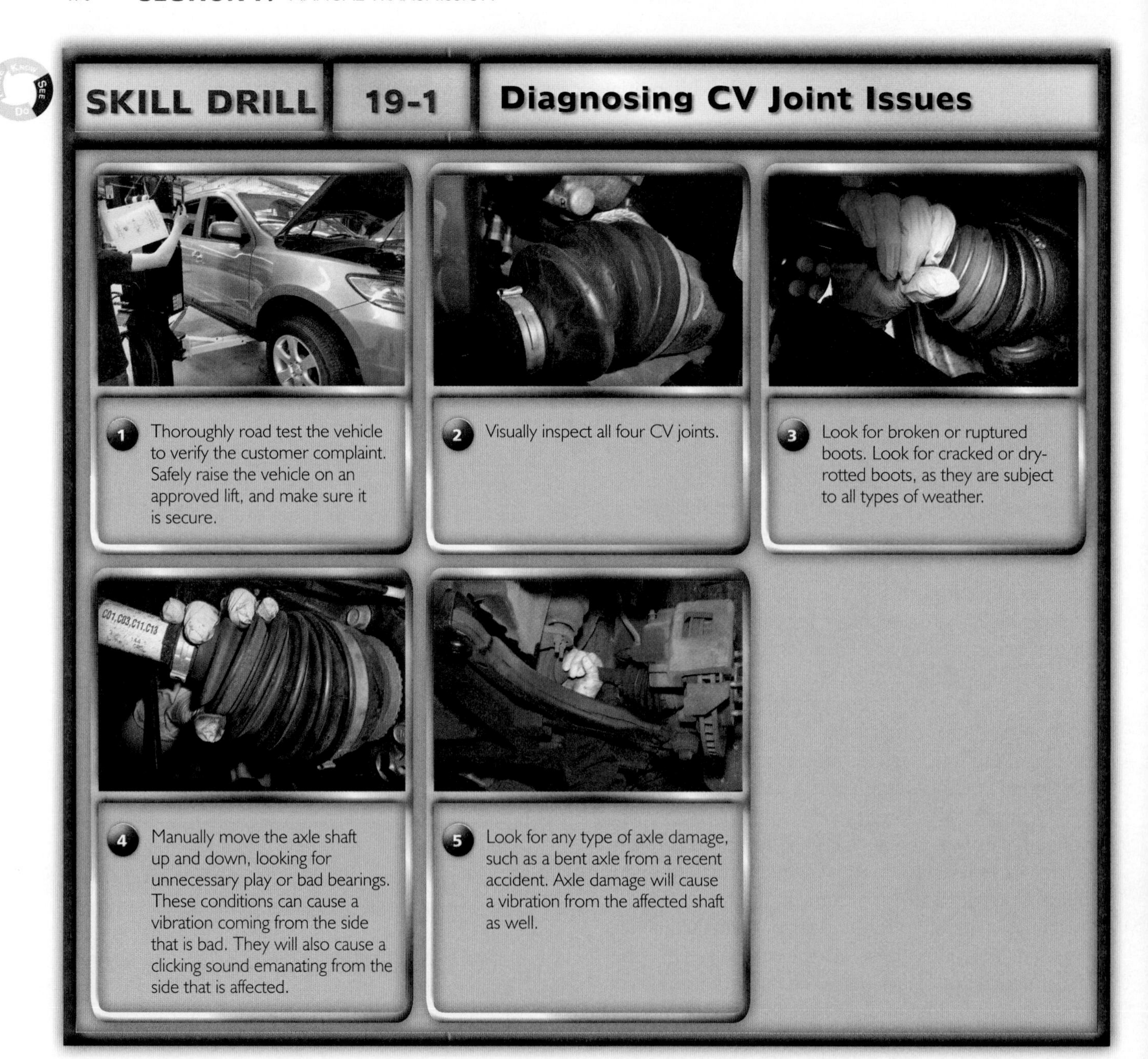
SKILL DRILL
19-1
Diagnosing CV Joint Issues
1 Thoroughly road test the vehicle to verify the customer complaint. Safely raise the vehicle on an approved lift, and make sure it is secure.
2 Visually inspect all four CV joints.
3 Look for broken or ruptured boots. Look for cracked or dry-rotted boots, as they are subject to all types of weather.
4 Manually move the axle shaft up and down, looking for unnecessary play or bad bearings. These conditions can cause a vibration coming from the side that is bad. They will also cause a clicking sound emanating from the side that is affected.
5 Look for any type of axle damage, such as a bent axle from a recent accident. Axle damage will cause a vibration from the affected shaft as well.

Inspecting and Replacing Wheel Studs and Lug Nuts

Lug nuts and studs are what hold the drive wheels in place and have been known to come loose or go bad over time. In some states, the law requires an inspection of the brakes that involves removal of the tires to gain access to the brake system. Lug nuts must be removed to do this. Inspection of the studs should be done in order to look for stretching or thread defects of these studs. If any defects or thread damage is present, the stud should be replaced. Sometimes improper torquing of the lug nuts can cause the studs to fail or lose a wheel when driving. Under- or overtorquing can result in these conditions.

> **TECHNICIAN TIP**
>
> Never use an air gun to torque lug nuts without using a torque stick followed by a torque wrench that is set to the manufacturer's torque specifications; otherwise, lug and stud damage can be present and result in loss of a wheel and tire assembly while driving down the highway.

> **▸ LINK**
>
> Refer to the Disc Brake Systems chapter for the procedure to replace lug studs.

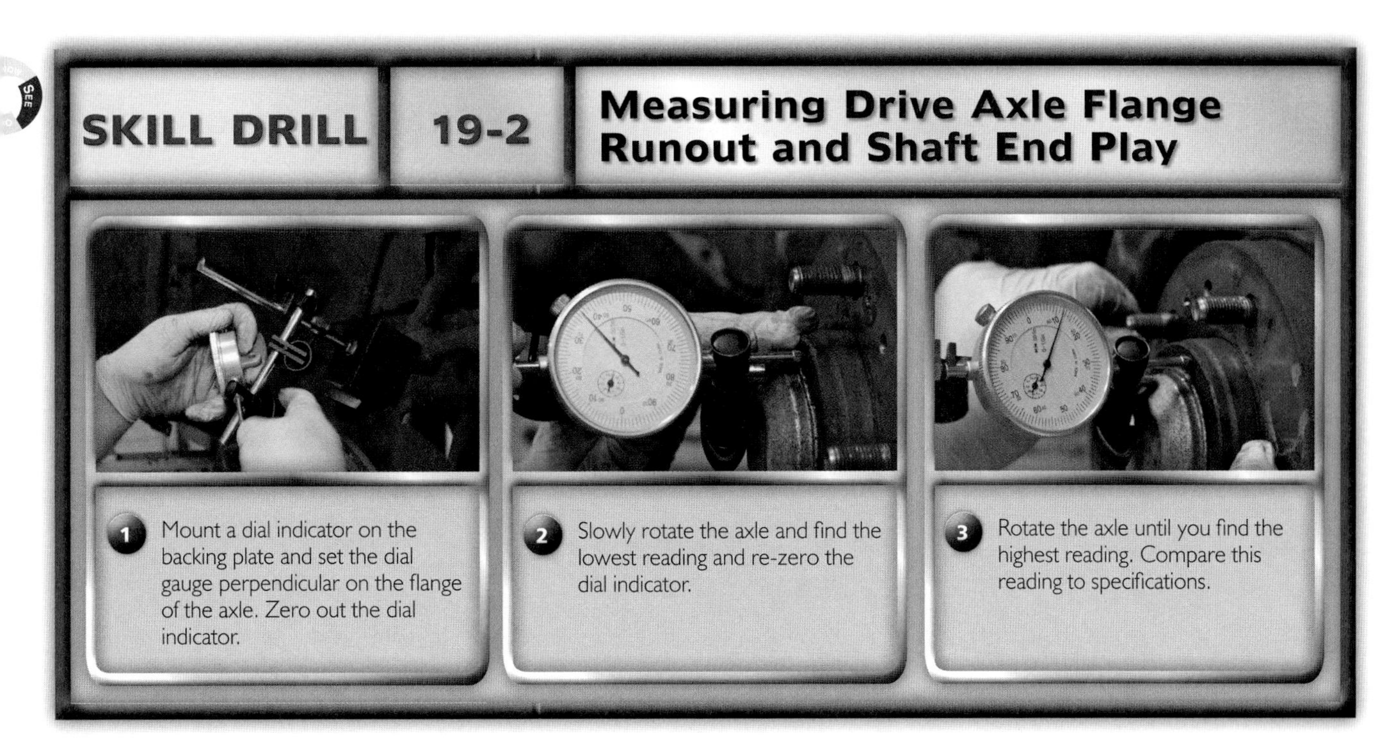
SKILL DRILL 19-2 Measuring Drive Axle Flange Runout and Shaft End Play
1 Mount a dial indicator on the backing plate and set the dial gauge perpendicular on the flange of the axle. Zero out the dial indicator.
2 Slowly rotate the axle and find the lowest reading and re-zero the dial indicator.
3 Rotate the axle until you find the highest reading. Compare this reading to specifications.

Uneven torquing can cause warping, which can cause problems with the brakes.

Inspecting Half-Shaft Components

It is important to make the proper diagnosis before entering into any type of repair. If a repair of the CV joints is necessary, follow all manufacturer guidelines and procedures.

Service of CV joints depends on the type of failure that has occurred. For example, if the axle is clicking when turning sharply, then the joint or the entire half-shaft will need to be replaced. If the CV boot is torn, it can be replaced without replacing the entire joint or shaft. Some can be easy and some can be extremely hard, but a thorough inspection is a good practice to diagnose whether to replace the half-shaft in its entirety or to replace and service one CV joint or boot.

To inspect half-shaft components, follow the steps in SKILL DRILL 19-3.

Inspecting Fluid Leakage

Fluid loss and leaks are a part of the aging process of a vehicle. Fluid leakage concerns are important and should be checked for on a regular basis. Axle seals and pinion seals are usually the likely places to investigate. Seals are subject to expansion and contraction through heat and cold changes that take place on a regular basis. Overfilling of the differential will create a pressure buildup in the differential from foaming of the liquid that the breather cannot handle, so the weakest place to vent pressure will be through the axle seal itself.

A lack of lubrication will cause the axle bearing to heat up and damage the seal. Brake heat that comes from a dragging brake can also cause an axle seal to leak. A bent axle or axle bearing failure will add to the cause of a failure of the seal. Preventive maintenance can identify some of these concerns and should be practiced on a regular basis.

To inspect fluid leakage, follow the steps in SKILL DRILL 19-4.

> **TECHNICIAN TIP**
>
> Some CV joints do not require a retaining ring and just need to be driven off wih a soft metal hammer, preferably a brass one.

Inspecting, Removing, and Replacing Front-Wheel Drive Front Wheel Bearings

Wheel bearings on a front-wheel drive vehicle operate in severe conditions such as puddles, dust and dirt, as well as being subjected to the jarring forces of pot holes. All of that can cause wheel bearings to fail and need replacement. Most manufacturers suggest periodic inspection of the bearings. Because most front-wheel drive wheel bearings are not serviceable, if looseness or roughness is found, then the bearings will need to be replaced. There are two types of non-serviceable wheel bearings; unitized and sealed. See the wheel bearing chapter for more

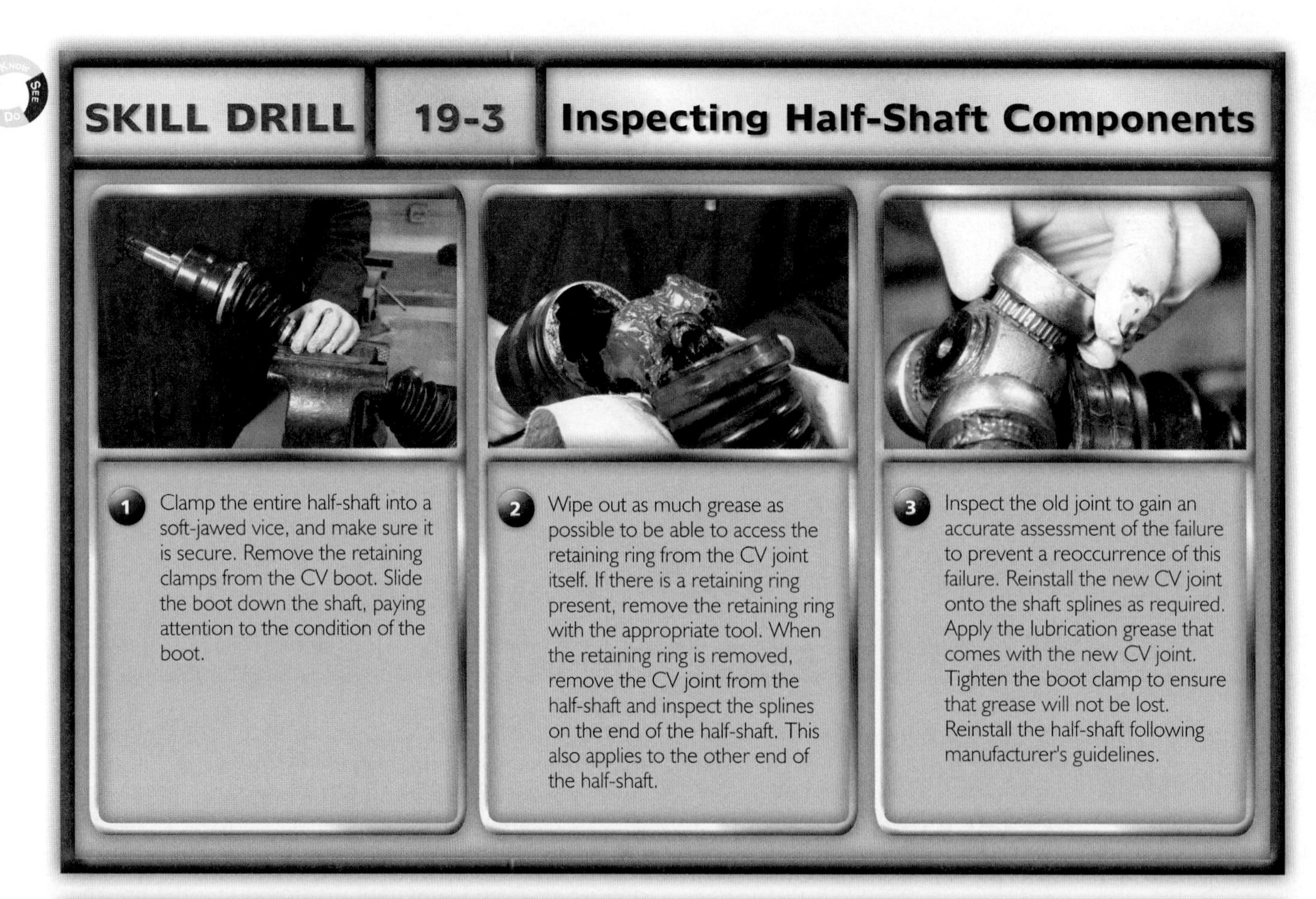
SKILL DRILL 19-3 Inspecting Half-Shaft Components

1 Clamp the entire half-shaft into a soft-jawed vice, and make sure it is secure. Remove the retaining clamps from the CV boot. Slide the boot down the shaft, paying attention to the condition of the boot.

2 Wipe out as much grease as possible to be able to access the retaining ring from the CV joint itself. If there is a retaining ring present, remove the retaining ring with the appropriate tool. When the retaining ring is removed, remove the CV joint from the half-shaft and inspect the splines on the end of the half-shaft. This also applies to the other end of the half-shaft.

3 Inspect the old joint to gain an accurate assessment of the failure to prevent a reoccurrence of this failure. Reinstall the new CV joint onto the shaft splines as required. Apply the lubrication grease that comes with the new CV joint. Tighten the boot clamp to ensure that grease will not be lost. Reinstall the half-shaft following manufacturer's guidelines.

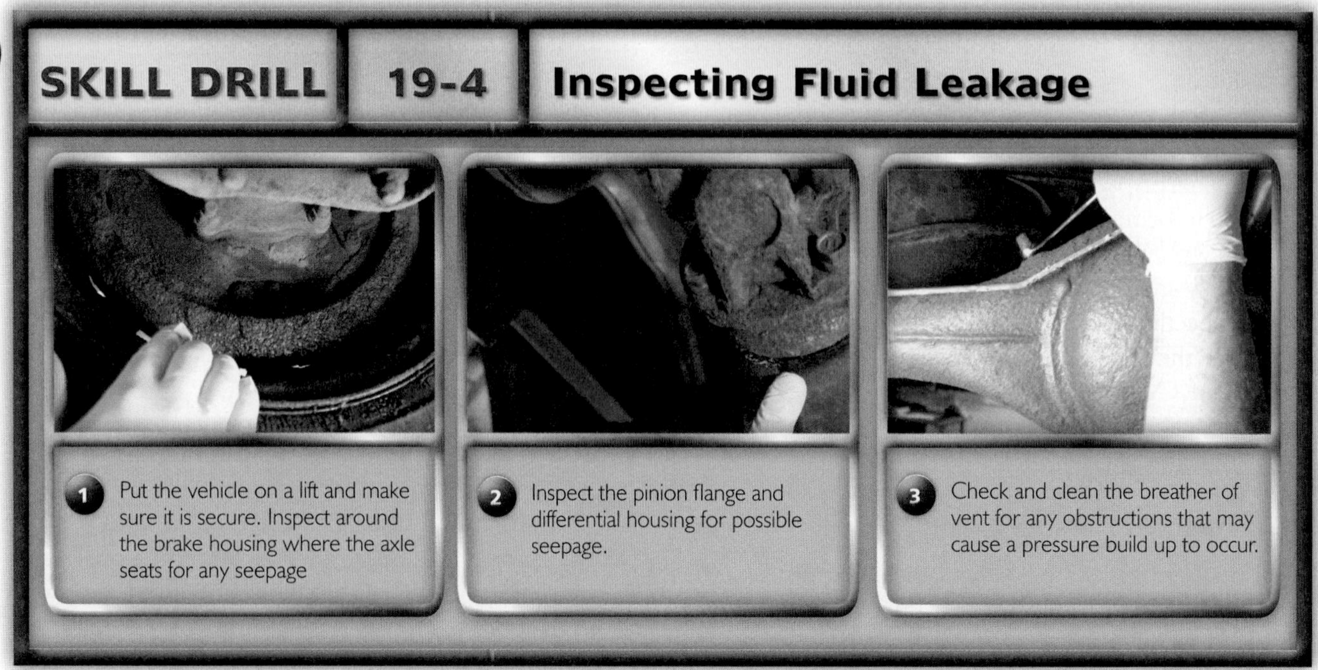
SKILL DRILL 19-4 Inspecting Fluid Leakage

1 Put the vehicle on a lift and make sure it is secure. Inspect around the brake housing where the axle seats for any seepage

2 Inspect the pinion flange and differential housing for possible seepage.

3 Check and clean the breather of vent for any obstructions that may cause a pressure build up to occur.

information on wheel bearing service, along with skill drills showing how to perform that service. When the scheduled maintenance chart or if looseness is present in the bearings, they must be removed and inspected to determine whether they need to be replaced, or just cleaned and repacked with grease. To inspect, remove, and replace front-wheel drive front wheel bearings, follow the steps in SKILL DRILL 19-5.

SKILL DRILL 19-5 Removing and Reinstalling Sealed Wheel Bearings Using the Unitized Wheel Bearing Hub Style

1 Loosen the axle hub nut, if equipped, while the tire is still on the ground. Remove the wheel and brake assembly following the specified procedure. also disconnect the ABS connector and/or sensor if mounted to the hub.

2 If the wheel you are working on is a drive wheel, remove the axle hub nut and tap the drive axle.

3 Unbolt and remove the hub assembly from the steering knuckle. Clean the knuckle assembly and check the hub seat for nicks, burrs, or other damage.

4 Make sure that the replacement hub meets the vehicle specifications by comparing it to the old one.

5 Reassemble the brake assembly and the ABS sensor following the specified procedure.

6 Install the wheel and torque the lug nuts. Install the drive axle nut if equipped. Use a new hub nut if called for by the manufacturer, and torque to specifications.

Inspecting Front Wheel Bearings and Locking Hubs

To connect the front wheels with the front drive axles on a four-wheel drive vehicle, some sort of hub locking mechanism must be used. These vehicles have either automatic locking hubs or manual locking hubs. All of these systems require periodic service and inspection to maintain functionality and prevent early failure of these parts.

To inspect front wheel bearings and locking hubs, follow the steps in SKILL DRILL 19-6.

SKILL DRILL 19-6 Inspecting, Removing, and Replacing Front-Wheel Drive Front Wheel Bearings

1. Raise the front axle off the ground and secure it with jack stands. Loosen the lug nuts, and remove the tire and wheel assembly. Remove the screws from the manual locking hub cap and pull the cap from the axle.

2. Inspect the O-ring on the back side of the cover. Replace it if necessary. Remove the wire ring from the hub, and pull the retaining plate out of the hub. Remove the snap ring from the axle.

3. Remove the locking sleeve from the hub.

4. Remove the bearing retaining nut(s) from the hub assembly to expose the bearings. Then remove the hub and rotor assembly for inspection.

5. Pry out the seal and rear bearing for inspection. Clean and inspect the bearings closely for **brinelling** and bluing due to heat concerns. Replace as necessary.

6. Pack and install new bearings and races using the proper bearing race driver. Install the new seal assembly. Note: When replacing the seal, be sure to put some grease on the spring inside the seal to prevent it from coming off when the seal is driven into the hub.

7. Reinstall the hub and rotor on the axle, and place the outer wheel bearing in the hub. Thread the bearing adjusting nut on by hand. Set the wheel bearing preload following the manufacturer's specifications using the proper tool. Install the locking washer over the adjusting nut.

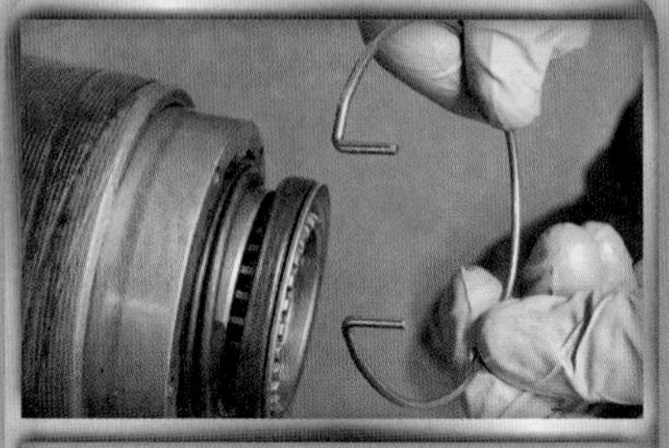

8. Thread the lock nut up against the locking washer and tighten to the specified torque. If necessary, bend the lock tang up against the locking nut. Install the locking sleeve. Install the retaining plate and wire clip.

9. Install a new O-ring on the hub cover, and reinstall the hub cover on the axle. Tighten the hub cover screws to the manufacturer's specifications. Road test the vehicle to ensure that it was repaired properly.

Wrap-up

Ready for Review

- Without a set of gears, flexible joints, and shafts to transfer the power from the engine and transmission, the vehicle would not be able to propel itself up hills, handle turns, or hold itself back as it goes down hills.
- In a conventional rear-wheel drive vehicle, the engine and transmission are mounted longitudinally at the front.
- Vehicles with rear- or mid-mounted engines normally use a transaxle and transfer the drive to the road wheels by independent half-shafts.
- The front-engine front-wheel drive vehicle typically, but not always, uses a crosswise-mounted (transverse) engine coupled to a transaxle.
- CV joints allow for smoother transfer of power and allow for the vehicle to turn more tightly without the joint binding.
- CV joints are most often used on the half-shafts of front-wheel drive vehicles and may be mounted at the end of the drive axles in some rear-wheel drive vehicles.
- The most common type of joint is the universal joint or simply "U-Joint" (the correct term for it is a Hooke's joint).
- The driveshaft itself allows power transfer from one component to another such as from the transmission output shaft to the differential and drive axles.
- The rear-wheel driveshaft transfers the power from the transmission to the final drive at the rear of the vehicle.
- Since the maximum length of a driveshaft is approximately 72" (183 cm), to prevent twisting from the torque output, two or more sections may be used.
- The front section of the two-piece driveshaft is supported at its rear end by a center bearing, called the carrier bearing.
- The U-joint is capable of working at a maximum angle of 3 degrees; beyond this, vibration and damage will result from U-joint binding.
- When working with a two-piece driveshaft or a splined driveshaft, it is critical that the yokes of the driveshaft (the portion of the shaft that has the holes in it for the U-joint end caps to fit into) line up with each other from one end of the driveshaft to the other.
- In front-wheel drive vehicles, the driveshafts transfer the drive directly from the differential inside the transaxle to the front wheels.
- A front-wheel drive transaxle typically does not place the differential directly in the center of the vehicle; instead it is offset to one side since it is bolted to the end of the transversely mounted engine.
- Torque steer is caused by the flexing of the longer half-shaft, resulting in lower torque to one side than the other, creating the pulling condition. To combat this condition, many manufacturers use an intermediate shaft.
- The differential provides the means of transferring power from the driveshaft (propeller) to the drive wheels, while allowing the vehicle to turn smoothly.
- Final drives can be found in axles either at the front or rear of the vehicle or can be found in the transaxle of a front-wheel drive vehicle.
- A ring gear and pinion gear located in the final drive transfer power through 90 degrees and provide a final gear reduction to the driving road wheels.
- The transfer case or power take-off (PTO) allows the transfer of power to the front and rear axles.
- There are different final drive setups. Some are semi-floating and others are full floating axle assemblies. The difference is how they are attached to the final drive.
- The purpose of axle seals is to maintain the required amount of oil in the differential to maintain quiet operation of the differential and related parts and to ensure lubrication for the bearings and gears.

Key Terms

backlash clearance the amount of movement between the pinion teeth versus the ring teeth.

beam-type axle A rear-wheel drive axle assembly that has a solid tube incorporating the differential gears

brinelling Damage done to the surface of a bearing caused by excessive load, which exceeds the limit of the bearing material, typically from shock loads.

companion flange A splined flange that transmits power from the drive shaft to the pinion gear.

constant-velocity (CV) joint A joint used to transmit torque through wider angles and without the change of velocity that occurs in u-joints..

dead axle An axle that does not have the capability to drive the vehicle. It is usually found on the rear of front-wheel drive vehicles.

double Cardan joint A type of joint that uses two Cardan joints housed in a short carrier and that reduces the change in velocity of a single Cardan joint by using the second joint to cancel out the changes in velocity of the first joint.

drive axle See *live axle*.

fixed-type joint A joint that does not slide to allow for shaft lengthening or shortening; it simply allows for angle changes as the suspension moves.

full floating axle An axle that does not support any weight; if removed, the vehicle will still roll on its wheels.

helical-geared limited slip differential A type of differential that responds very quickly to changes in traction and that does not bind from friction in turns or lose its effectiveness since there are no clutches.

Hooke's joint A joint that consists of a steel cross with four hardened bearing journals, mounted on needle rollers in hardened caps, which locate the cross in the eyes of the yokes. The cross swivels in the yokes as the drive is transferred across the joint.

hypoid bevel gear A special design of spiral bevel gear, with the centerline of the pinion below the centerline of the ring gear.

limited slip differential A differential assembly that transmits power to both wheels when one is on a slippery surface, but will still allow slippage on cornering and turns.

live axle An axle that is powered and can move the vehicle. It is usually found on the rear of rear-wheel drive vehicles.

locking hub four-wheel drive front axle hubs that are manually locked or unlocked by turning the knob on the hub.

longitudinal The orientation of the engine in which the front of the engine is facing the front of the vehicle. It is most commonly found in rear-wheel drive vehicles.

plunge-type joint The inner joint on the half shaft that allows for changes in shaft length.

power take-off (PTO) A device attached to the transmission that is gear driven and can be used to run accessories such as winches and towing equipment. It can also refer to the gears that send power to the rear axle in a predominantly front wheel drive vehicle.

Rzeppa joint A type of fixed constant velocity joint that has an inner race, six steel ball bearings, a bearing cage, and an outer race.

semi-floating axle An axle that carries the weight of the vehicle; if removed, there is no way to connect the wheel to the vehicle.

side gear A gear that is splined to the axle shaft and meshes with the spider gears and allows the axles to rotate at their own speeds when cornering and turning.

sliding spline driveshaft A two-piece driveshaft that is joined in the middle with splines. The driveshaft can slide on itself to increase or decrease in length.

slip yoke Part of a two-piece driveshaft that is splined and allows for a change in length of the shaft as the suspension compresses and rebounds.

speedy sleeve An aftermarket repair kit that consists of a think metal sleeve that fits tightly over the seal surface of the axle, providing a new, undamaged surface for the seal to ride against.

three-quarter floating axle An axle on which there is only one wheel bearing which bears the weight of the vehicle, but the axle prevents the wheel from tipping inward or outward.

torque steer A condition in which the vehicle pulls to one side during hard acceleration.

transfer case A component that is bolted to the back of the transmission and connects the front and rear axles via the driveshafts.

transverse The orientation of the engine in which the front of the engine is facing the side of the vehicle.

tulip/tripod joint A constant velocity joint that has three equally spaced fingers shaped like a star. This configuration allows in-and-out movement of the shaft while allowing flexing.

universal joint (U-joint) A cross-shaped flexible joint on which caps fit over the ends of the cross. Needle bearings fit between the ends of the cross and the caps, allowing the caps to rotate smoothly.

viscous coupling An silicone clutch assembly used in all-wheel drive differentials to provide a slight amount of differential action for control of axle rotational speeds.

PROVE
KNOW
SEE
DO

ASE-Type Questions

1. Tech A says that viscous clutch oil should generally be changed at regular intervals. Tech B says that if a viscous clutch fails, it should be replaced. Who is correct?
   a. Tech A
   b. Tech B
   c. Both A and B
   d. Neither A nor B
2. Tech A says that all-wheel drive vehicles have a differential in the middle of the drive train. Tech B says that many all-wheel drive vehicles incorporate a viscous clutch in the center differential. Who is correct?
   a. Tech A
   b. Tech B
   c. Both A and B
   d. Neither A nor B
3. Tech A says that all front wheel hubs lock automatically. Tech B says that all front wheel hubs lock manually. Who is correct?
   a. Tech A
   b. Tech B
   c. Both A and B
   d. Neither A nor B
4. Tech A says that full-floating axles use a single wheel bearing that sits between the axle and axle housing. Tech B says that a differential allows the wheels on a common axle to rotate at different speeds. Who is correct?
   a. Tech A
   b. Tech B
   c. Both A and B
   d. Neither A nor B
5. Tech A says that part-time four-wheel drive does not use a transfer case. Tech B says that a viscous clutch is located in the rear axle. Who is correct?
   a. Tech A
   b. Tech B
   c. Both A and B
   d. Neither A nor B
6. Tech A says that constant-velocity joints are used on some four-wheel drive vehicles. Tech B says that a slip joint is part of a driveshaft. Who is correct?
   a. Tech A
   b. Tech B
   c. Both A and B
   d. Neither A nor B
7. Tech A says that a limited slip differential causes spring loaded clutch plates to provide torque to both wheels. Tech B says that wrong tire sizes can affect the transfer case operation. Who is correct?
   a. Tech A
   b. Tech B
   c. Both A and B
   d. Neither A nor B
8. Tech A says that some transfer cases have a chain inside them to transfer torque to the wheels. Tech B says that a rear-wheel drive axle housing can leak due to being over filled with fluid. Who is correct?
   a. Tech A
   b. Tech B
   c. Both A and B
   d. Neither A nor B
9. Tech A says that CV boots should be patched if they have cracks or splits. Tech B says that CV joints may use a special type of grease, possibly containing lead. Who is correct?
   a. Tech A
   b. Tech B
   c. Both A and B
   d. Neither A nor B
10. Tech A says that u-joints can make a chirping or squeaking nose when they are going bad. Tech B says that u-joints are typically used on front wheel drive axles to provide torque through all angles of steering. Who is correct?
    a. Tech A
    b. Tech B
    c. Both A and B
    d. Neither A nor B

SECTION V

Steering and Suspension

CHAPTER 20

KNOW
SEE
DO
PROVE

NATEF Tasks

Suspension and Steering			Page
■ Inspect tire condition; identify tire wear patterns; check for correct tire size and application (load and speed ratings) and adjust air pressure; determine necessary action.	MLR	AST	502–505
■ Rotate tires according to manufacturer's recommendations.	MLR	AST	505–506
■ Dismount, inspect, and remount tire on wheel; balance wheel and tire assembly (static and dynamic).	MLR	AST	505–513
■ Demonstrate knowledge of steps required to remove and replace sensors in a tire pressure monitoring system.	MLR	AST	513–514, 523–524
■ Dismount, inspect, and remount tire on wheel equipped with tire pressure monitoring system sensor.	MLR	AST	513–514
■ Inspect tire and wheel assembly for air loss; perform necessary action.	MLR	AST	517
■ Repair tire using internal patch.	MLR	AST	518–519
■ Measure wheel, tire, axle flange, and hub runout; determine necessary action.		AST	519–523
■ Identify and test tire pressure monitoring systems (indirect and direct) for operation; verify operation of instrument panel lamps.	MLR	AST	523–524

Servicing Wheels

PROVE
KNOW
SEE
DO

Knowledge Objectives

After reading this chapter, you will be able to:

1. Explain the principles of tire distortion, center of gravity, and wheel offset. (pp 482–484, 486)
2. Describe the components that compose a vehicle's wheel. (pp 484–488)
3. Describe the components of a vehicle's tire. (pp 488–489)
4. Describe the types of tire construction. (pp 489–490)
5. Explain how to decipher the tire markings on the sidewall of each tire. (pp 491–492)
6. Describe the common safety features found on today's tires. (pp 493–496)
7. Describe the components of a standard preventive tire service program. (pp 496–501)
8. Describe the common tire and wheel issues that a driver may experience. (pp 501–502)

PROVE
KNOW
SEE
DO

Skills Objectives

After reading this chapter, you will be able to:

1. Use a tire pressure gauge. (p 503)
2. Adjust the tire pressure. (p 504)
3. Check for tire wear patterns. (pp 504–505)
4. Rotate the tires. (pp 505–506)
5. Dismount a tire. (p 508)
6. Replace a rubber press-fit valve stem. (pp 508–509)
7. Replace a screw-in valve stem. (pp 509–510)
8. Mount a tire. (pp 511–513)
9. Dismount, inspect, and remount a tire and wheel with a tire pressure monitoring system (TPMS). (pp 513–514)
10. Balance a tire. (pp 515–516)
11. Use the spray bottle method to determine the location of air loss. (p 517)
12. Use the dunk method to determine the location of air loss. (p 517)
13. Patch a tire. (pp 518–519)
14. Measure tire runout. (pp 519–521)
15. Measure wheel runout. (pp 521–522)
16. Measure axle flange or hub runout. (pp 522–523)
17. Inspect, diagnose, and calibrate the TPMS. (pp 523–524)

Introduction

The wheel and tire assembly is the only point of contact between the vehicle and the road surface. The entire vehicle literally rests on the wheel and tire assembly. The contact between the tire and the road surface plays a large role in determining how a vehicle handles and rides. Today's newer, lightweight vehicles are more sensitive than ever to minor tire or wheel issues. Poorly maintained wheels and tires will decrease effective handling, fuel economy, and ride quality and increase the potential for accidents or breakdowns.

Paying attention to the wheels and tires can also assist in identifying problems with other vehicle systems, particularly in steering and suspension systems. The wear patterns on a tire correlate with damage to particular vehicle components. Overlooking the wheel and tire assembly may result in missed faults, leading to larger issues and associated costs. It is critical that you be familiar with each part of the wheel and tire assembly and possess the skills necessary to identify and correct problems associated with them.

Principles

Tires and wheels work together to allow the vehicle to roll smoothly down the road. Tires by themselves have very little rigidity; they flex and deform whenever a force is put against them. On the other hand, wheels are very rigid and have no way of absorbing the unevenness of the road surface, so driving would be annoying were they used by themselves. Also, since wheels have a low coefficient of friction, traction would be almost nonexistent. But when you pair a tire with a wheel, you get the rigidity needed to provide directional control (from the wheel), and you get flexibility and traction to grip the road surface while smoothing out the bumps in the surface of the road (from the tire).

Tires on most passenger vehicles are called pneumatic tires because they are filled with pressurized air, which gives them support. Some vehicles, such as forklifts, may use solid rubber tires. These tires are not susceptible to punctures, so they are used where tire hazards are present such as garbage dumps or construction sites. Early pneumatic tires were called tube-type tires because they used an inner tube inside the tire to seal the air in the tire/wheel assembly. Recent vehicles use tubeless tires; these tires are designed to seal tightly to the wheel in such a way that the pressurized air does not leak out.

The air pressure gives the tire its shape when the weight of the vehicle is sitting on it. Air pushes on the entire inside surface of the tire, pushing it outward. Tires on many vehicles are inflated to about 32 pounds per square inch (psi). This means that the air pressure is pushing against every square inch of the inside of the tire. It would not be unreasonable to say there is approximately 1600 square inches of surface area inside a typical passenger car tire. So 32 psi multiplied by 1600 square inches equals 51,200 pounds (lb) of force trying to expand the tire. So why doesn't the tire expand like a balloon? It has lots of strong reinforcing strands molded into it, which gives it strength while still allowing it to be flexible. So the air inside the tire pushes outward on the tire, stretching the strands tightly, which prevents the tire from ballooning. The relatively high pressure in the

You Are the Automotive Technician

A customer brings her 2010 Dodge Caravan to the dealership with the tire pressure light on. The customer tells you that the tires are filled with nitrogen, and on the drive to the dealership, the van pulled to the right. You bring the vehicle into the shop and notice that the right front tire looks low, and the pressure reads 22 psi. You inspect the tire and notice a small screw embedded near the center of the half-worn tread. You mark a big "X" across the tire (centered on the screw) to mark the hole. Air leaks out as you pull the screw out of the tire. You remove the wheel from the vehicle in preparation for repairing the tire.

1. How can you identify if tires have been inflated with nitrogen?
2. What is the proper method of repairing a tire?
3. What are some conditions when a tire should not be repaired?
4. What happens if you repair a high performance speed rated tire?
5. What must be done once the tire is repaired and back on the vehicle?

tire stiffens the tire so that it will support the weight of the vehicle. This design also explains the appearance of a tire that is substantially low on air pressure: The bottom will appear flat, and the sidewall relatively soft. The air pressure is not fully stretching the cords in the tire.

Tire Distortion

During cornering, centrifugal force acts on a vehicle to produce a **side force**. The side force is the pressure on the wheel that pushes it toward the outside or inside of the rim as the vehicle makes a turn. In most instances, the contact of the tire with the surface of the road produces enough friction to prevent this force from actually pushing the wheel and tire sideways across the road surface. However, when the roads are icy, the tire is unable to grip the road surface adequately to generate enough friction to overcome the side force, resulting in the wheels and vehicle skidding sideways during a turn. Without the resistance created by friction, side force will cause the vehicle to continue in a straight line.

The tire provides this opposing force by being able to distort while still gripping the road FIGURE 20-1. Since the tire's construction makes it elastic, it exerts a force, called **cornering force**, that acts between the tread and the road surface. It pulls the distorted rubber back to its normal position. The tire's sideways distortion makes the vehicle follow a path at an angle to the direction the road wheel is pointing. This is called the **slip angle**. As the cornering force increases, so does slip angle.

When a vehicle is being driven into a turn with a decreasing radius, both slip angle and cornering force increase, until a point is reached where the tire slides. At this point, the only resistance comes from sliding kinetic friction across the road surface. The tire grips again only when the vehicle has slowed or the wheels are not turned so sharply—that is, when the side force is reduced to a level the tire can withstand without skidding.

Since both front and rear tires develop a slip angle in a turn, the vehicle's path is determined by the steering of the front tires and the slip angles of both the front and the rear tires. These slip angles depend on the weight distribution within the vehicle, the wheelbase, the tire track, and the overall length of the vehicle. The weight distribution is affected by whether the engine is front, mid, or rear mounted. Another factor is if the vehicle is front- or rear-wheel drive.

During cornering, centrifugal force puts more weight on the outside wheels. Acceleration puts more weight on the rear wheels. Deceleration or braking puts more weight on the front wheels. In a turn, centrifugal force tries to push the vehicle away from the corner. This is resisted by the cornering force of the tires. The tires' slip angles may not be equal, due to the cornering, deceleration, or acceleration forces acting on them. When the front slip angles are larger than the rear slip angles, the vehicle is said to be in an **understeer** condition, which is referred to as the vehicle "pushing" in the corners. Understeer results in the front of the vehicle being pushed toward the outside of the corner. At its worst, it causes the vehicle's front wheels to slide toward the outside of the corner and into the curb or off the track. **Oversteer** is when the rear slip angle is larger than the front slip angle; it is referred to as the vehicle being "loose" in the corners. Oversteer tends to cause the rear of the vehicle to slide toward the outside of the corner. In this situation, the rear wheels lose traction, typically resulting in the vehicle spinning out. When both the front and the rear tires have equal amounts of slip angle, the vehicle is said to have **neutral steer**, in which case the vehicle tends to go in the direction that the front tires are pointing.

Center of Gravity

The center of gravity is the balance point of the entire vehicle. Its actual position depends on location of the engine and transmission FIGURE 20-2. It is always located above

FIGURE 20-1 Tires distort during cornering, providing an opposing force that allows a vehicle to make a turn.

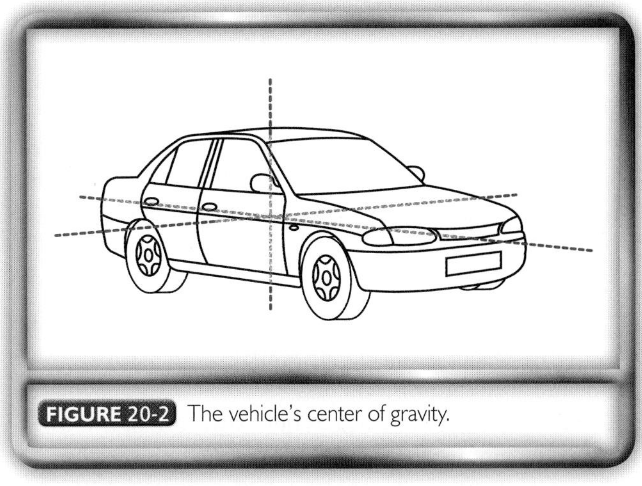

FIGURE 20-2 The vehicle's center of gravity.

the road surface and between the tires. When a vehicle is cornering, this is the point through which all centrifugal force is assumed to act. Its position is determined by the load carried by the front and rear wheels—that is, by how weight is distributed. In a typical rear-wheel drive vehicle, the weight distribution is approximately 60% fore and 40% aft; 60% of the weight is carried on the front wheels, 40% on the rear, and the center of gravity is closer to the rear than the front. On a typical front-wheel drive vehicle, the weight distribution is approximately 75% fore and 25% aft. Lateral, or side-to-side, weight distribution can be expressed in the same way and is affected by things like the location of the fuel tank and battery.

Every vehicle has static weight distribution, whether it is at rest or traveling in a straight line at a steady speed. This distribution is changed laterally by centrifugal force when the vehicle is turning and in a fore-and-aft direction during acceleration or braking.

> **TECHNICIAN TIP**
>
> The height of the center of gravity is determined by the height of the center of the mass above the road surface.

Wheels and Tires

Wheels are usually made from pressed steel or cast aluminium alloy. They are lightweight, yet strong enough to withstand normal operational forces. Alloy wheels are popular because of their appearance and because they are lighter than steel wheels. Aluminium is a better conductor of heat, so alloy wheels can dissipate heat from the brakes and tires more effectively than steel. Alloy wheels are often called mag or magnesium wheels, but wheels made of magnesium are rarely used on vehicles.

The terms wheel and rim are often used synonymously. Technically, the **rim** of a wheel is the outer circular lip of the metal on which the inside edge of the tire is mounted FIGURE 20-3. The purpose of the rim is to hold and seal the tire to the wheel.

FIGURE 20-3 Rim of the wheel.

Rim width is the distance across the **rim flanges** at the **bead seat**. The bead seat is the edge of the rim that creates a seal between the tire bead and the wheel. The rim flange is the exterior lip that holds the tire in place. The rim diameter is the distance across the center of the rim from bead seat to bead seat. The width of the rim and the diameter are traditionally stated in inches, although some are stated in millimeters.

Most passenger vehicle **wheel rims** are of the **drop-center** design. In drop-center rims, the inner section sits lower than the sides FIGURE 20-4. This design allows for tire removal and fitting. The drop-center rim is made in one piece and is permanently fastened to the wheel disc. The drop center is used for mounting and demounting the tire onto the rim. When inflated, the tire is locked to the rim by tapering the bead seat toward the flange, or more commonly by safety ridges or humps, close to the flange.

An important feature in a rim is the location of the drop center in the rim. The drop center can be closer to the front of the wheel or the rear of the wheel, depending on the desired position of the wheel relative to the axle flange. In most stock wheels, the drop center is closer to the front side of the wheel. In **deep dish wheels**, the drop center is closer to the rear of the wheel FIGURE 20-5. Since the drop center is crucial to removing the tire from the wheel, the side of the wheel that is closest to the drop center is the side the tire should be removed from. In fact, it is virtually impossible to remove the tire from the side of the wheel farthest from the drop center.

> **TECHNICIAN TIP**
>
> Rims are stamped with a code. For example, a rim designated 7 JJ by 14 would refer to a rim measuring:
>
> - 7" across the rim flanges
> - 14" in diameter from bead seat to bead seat
> - With the flange profile conforming to a JJ code

> **TECHNICIAN TIP**
>
> Most wheels have ventilation holes in the flange so that air can circulate to the brakes.

FIGURE 20-4 Drop-center rim.

FIGURE 20-5 Deep dish wheel.

With safety in mind, manufacturers and legislators are insisting that passenger cars and light trucks be equipped with safety-type drop-center rims. **Safety-type drop-center rims** have a slight ridge, or hump, at the inside edge of the bead ledges. This ridge helps to hold the tire beads in place when the tire goes flat. In the event of sudden deflation, or blowout, safety ridges prevent the tire from moving down into the well. This helps maintain control of the vehicle while the driver is braking.

Rims can be made from two sections of pressed steel—a flange or disc that is drilled for the wheel fasteners and the rim. The rims for passenger vehicles are usually the **steel-disc type**. The disc may be solid, but the major manufacturers place holes in them to reduce the disc's weight and to provide ventilation for cooling the brakes. The disc is either welded or riveted to the rim and bolted to the axle or axle flange. Additional types of rims can be found in TABLE 20-1.

TECHNICIAN TIP

The tire must be an exact fit on the rim to fulfill a number of functions:

- To ensure that the narrow contact area between the beads of the tire and the rim will seal the air in a tubeless tire.
- To transfer all the forces between the tire and the wheel, without slipping or chafing.
- To ensure that the friction between the tire and the rim prevents the tire from turning on the rim.

TABLE 20-1: Types of Rims

Type	Purpose
Steel rims	Rims that can be painted or chromed. Generally used on bottom-of-the-line vehicles.
One-piece alloy rims	Rims that are constructed in one piece including the well to facilitate the mounting and dismounting of the tire.
One-piece alloy billet rims	Rims that are machined out of a solid piece of alloy.
Two-piece alloy rims	Rims that are constructed as two separate pieces of aluminium, one being the center piece and the other a mounting flange, that are welded together.
Multipiece alloy rims	Rims that are constructed by welding together several separately molded pieces.
Custom rims	Rims that are built to suit the specific, unique needs and requirements of the customer.
Spinning rims (spinners)	Rims that are constructed with a piece that rotates independent from the wheel. High-speed roller bearings placed within the rim create the piece's movement.
Split rims	Rims that are constructed of a single long piece of metal formed into a circle, but the ends are not welded together (a "split" ring). The split allows removal of the outside flange so the tire can be demounted. This type of rim is common on tractor trailers and other big-wheeled trucks.
Semi-drop well rims	Rims constructed of a solid rim to allow removal of the outside flange, as in the split rim.
Drop well rims	Rims constructed with a trough in the center of the rim that is smaller in diameter than the edge by the lip where the bead of the tire seals. The trough allows the tire to be mounted on the rim.
Safety rims	Rims designed to hold the tire bead in place on the rim in the event of inadequate tire pressure.

Safety

The rim width and diameter can also be stated in millimeters. Metric rims are not interchangeable with imperial rims; nor can you fit a metric tire to an imperial rim. Conversely, you cannot fit an imperial tire to a metric rim. Doing so could result in personal injury or a vehicle accident.

Applied Math

AM-27: Distance: The technician can measure distance using a variety of devices to determine conformance to the manufacturer's specifications and tolerances. A technician may be called upon to measure distances with a variety of devices to determine conformance of components to manufacturer's tolerances and specifications. Some examples may include measuring tire tread with a depth gauge, measuring brake pad thickness with a ruler, measuring vehicle ride height with a tape measure, measuring brake disc thickness with a vernier caliper, measuring engine valve clearance with feeler gauges, measuring crankshaft journal thickness with a micrometer, or measuring wheel runout with a dial gauge.

Wheel Offset

The offset of a wheel is the distance from its hub mounting surface to the centerline of the wheel. Offset is important because it is typically used to bring the tire centerline into close alignment with the larger inner wheel bearing, and it reduces load on the stub axle. This requires the inside of the wheel assembly to be shaped so that there is space for the brake assembly, especially disc brakes, which are typically larger in diameter than drum brakes.

The offset can be either zero, positive, or negative:

- **Zero offset**: The plane of the hub mounting surface is even with the centerline of the wheel. Vehicles manufactured in the mid-70s through the 80s were typically built with zero offset wheels.
- **Positive offset**: The plane of the hub mounting surface is shifted from the centerline toward the outside or front side of the wheel. Positive offset wheels are generally found on front-wheel drive vehicles and the newer rear-wheel drive vehicles.
- **Negative offset**: The hub mounting surface is toward the brake side or back of the wheel's centerline. Older model vehicles and specialized high-performance vehicles with deep dish wheels typically have wheels with negative offset.

Wheel Studs and Lug Nuts

Wheels are fastened to the rims by **wheel studs** and **lug nuts**. Wheel studs and lug nuts are highly stressed by loads from the weight of the vehicle and the forces generated by its motion. Wheel studs and nuts are made from heat-treated, high-grade alloy steel. The threads between the studs and the nuts are close fitting and accurately sized. All wheel nuts must be tightened to the correct torque with the proper sequence; otherwise the wheel could break free from the hub.

You must use the correct type of wheel retaining stud or nut—which include **tapered seat**, **flat seat with washer**, or **flat seat without washer** FIGURE 20-6—for the wheel. Tapered seat lug nuts have a tapered end that is placed toward the rim and fit into a matching taper in the rim to help center the wheel on the lug studs. Flat seat studs are flat at the point where it contacts the wheel. Those with washers have a washer affixed to the lug nut enabling it to turn independent from the hex part of the lug nut. When a wheel assembly is changed, it is imperative that the mating surfaces of the wheel inner hub and the axle flange mounting face are clean and free of dirt and mud. After the wheel assembly has been fitted, the **wheel retaining nuts** that hold the wheel onto the vehicle are torqued to the manufacturer's specifications. Many shops request that the customer return and have the lug nut torque rechecked within a few days or about 100 miles. If the nut/stud is overtightened, then there is a good chance that the stud can break due to overstressing, and fatigue fractures can occur.

TECHNICIAN TIP

Don't be like the apprentice technician who was trying to get a vehicle ready for a brake job for the journeyman technician. When the journeyman came into work, the apprentice was just taking off the last wheel and the journeyman could hear the impact wrench hammering away and then the impact wrench zing to full speed. By the time he got to the apprentice, he was on the next to last lug nut. The journeyman stopped him. The apprentice said that all of the lug nuts were rusted on the studs on the right side of the car and every one broke off when he tried to loosen them. The journeyman took the impact wrench, switched directions on it, and proceeded to easily remove the lug nuts. The apprentice was quite embarrassed, especially when the other technicians in the shop started calling him "Lefty."

If a lug nut does not start to loosen quickly when you are trying to remove it, always stop and try to turn it the other direction. It could be a left-hand lug nut, which you will need to turn clockwise to remove. And even if it is a right-hand lug nut, sometimes tightening it just a bit will help break loose any rust so that it will come off easier.

Most lug nuts and studs are right-hand threaded, which means they tighten when turned clockwise. However, some manufacturers use lug nuts and studs with left-hand threads on the right side (passenger side) of the vehicle and right-hand lug nuts and studs on the left side (driver side) of the vehicle. The manufacturers claim that left-hand lug nuts are less likely to back off when used on the right side of the vehicle. This may or may not be true, but properly torqued lug nuts do not generally loosen up, no matter if they are left-hand or right-hand. Left-hand lug nuts can usually be identified by an "L" stamped on the end of the lug stud. When you place the socket or lug wrench over the lug nut, make sure you check for the "L." If there is one, then you will need to turn the lug nut clockwise to loosen it.

The **wheel center** is the part of the wheel containing the holes for the lug studs. It usually has a machined hole in the center, which accurately centers the wheel rim on the axle. In some cases, the fit of the centering hole is snug enough that it can rust in place and stick to the axle. This can require penetrating oil, a hammer, or even heat from a torch to break it loose. Always seek the assistance of your supervisor if you encounter a wheel rusted to the axle flange. The wheel center also provides the required offset from the centerline of the wheel to the face of the mounting flange.

FIGURE 20-6 **A.** Tapered seat lug nut and wheel. **B.** Flat seat with integrated washer and wheel. **C.** Flat seat with separate washer and wheel. **D.** Specialty lugnuts.

Bolt Pattern

The bolt pattern refers to the number and spacing of the lug nuts or wheel studs on the wheel hub on the wheel rim **FIGURE 20-7**. As the studs are most often evenly spaced,

> **TECHNICIAN TIP**
>
> Along with the bolt pattern configuration is **pitch circle diameter (PCD)**. PCD is the diameter of a circle drawn through the center of the wheel's bolt holes. It is a fixed measure set during manufacture that cannot be altered. PCD is measured in both inches and millimeters, and it also indicates the number of studs or bolts the wheel will have. One of the most common configurations has four studs and a PCD of 100 mm, hence the size 4 × 100 designation.

FIGURE 20-7 The bolt pattern refers to the number and spacing of lug nuts or wheel studs on the wheel hub on the wheel rim.

the number of studs determines the pattern. For example, some smaller cars have three studs, some may have four studs, but most passenger cars have five. Pick-up trucks and large SUVs can have as many as 6, 8, or 10 studs. The exact number and pattern of studs vary depending on the vehicle type and manufacturer design.

Tires

Tires are hollow, donut-shaped structures designed to provide traction to the wheel assembly and act as a cushion to absorb shock from road surfaces **FIGURE 20-8**. The air in the tire supports the vehicle's mass, and the tire tread provides frictional contact with the road surface, so the vehicle can maneuver safely. The tire itself is generally composed of the tread, plies or cords, sidewalls, inner liner, and bead. The tread is the exterior rubber portion of the tire that comes in contact with the road. It is configured in a variety of patterns based on the application of the tire, such as for driving in mud and snow. The plies or cords are the reinforcing material that gives the tread and sidewall their ability to hold their shape. The sidewalls are the lightly reinforced sides of the tire that provide lateral strength to the tire and prevent it from ballooning. They do not come into direct contact with the road. The inner liner is a covering of the casing material and seals the air in the tire. Beads are bands of steel wire coated in rubber that give the bead area the stiffness to hold the bead against the bead seat and to seal to the wheel rim. Tires can be inflated through a valve assembly located in the wheel.

Modern tires are made from a range of materials. The rubber used is mostly synthetic, with carbon black added to increase strength and toughness. When used in the tread, this combination gives the tire a long life. Natural rubber is weaker than the synthetic version, so it is used mainly in sidewalls.

Cords of synthetic strands or fabric have high **tensile strength**. Tensile strength is a measure of the innate

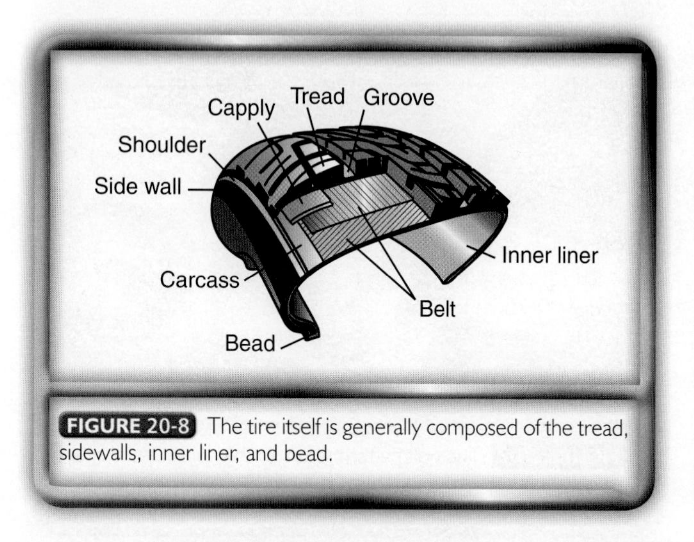
Capply
Tread
Groove
Shoulder
Side wall
Inner liner
Carcass
Belt
Bead

FIGURE 20-8 The tire itself is generally composed of the tread, sidewalls, inner liner, and bead.

Applied Math

AM-28: Distance: The technician can use standard and metric measurement instruments to determine correct sizes and distances.

In practice, both standard and metric measurement instruments must be used to determine correct sizes and distances because specifications may be published in either scale. Some common examples may include, measuring the diameter of wheel rims, which are almost universally measured in inches, and measuring the pitch circle diameter (PCD) of wheel studs, which are usually quoted in millimeters.

strength of a material. Because of their high strength, the cords resist stretching but are flexible under load. The cords are placed in parallel and impregnated with rubber to form sheets called plies or belts. Plies have high strength in one direction and are flexible in other directions. When cotton was used as a cord, the number of plies or layers in a tire was a measure of the tire's strength. Newer cord materials use fewer plies. A modern steel-belted radial tire with a six-**ply rating** may have six plies in the tread but just two plies in its sidewall. Having fewer plies makes the tire more flexible. Higher numbers of plies make a tire's response to bumps harsher, but the tire can withstand punctures much better.

The bead of the tire is made of a cord of high-tensile steel coated with rubber. The end of the plies is wrapped around the bead, which is then wrapped in rubber to stop chafing of the plies and also to seal the bead against the rim. The length of the wire used for the bead determines the rim diameter of the tire. Belts that reinforce the tread area of the tire are typically made of braided, high-tensile steel wire, but they can also be made of rayon or polyester. The inner liner of a tubeless tire is made of soft rubber. The inner liner must be flexible and airtight.

Tire Valve Stems, Cores, and Caps

The **tire valve** is a specially designed opening that allows a tire to be inflated and then automatically closes to prevent air from escaping. It consists of a **valve stem**, into which a **valve core** is threaded, and it is used on virtually all automobile tires. The valve stem is a rubber or steel piece that attaches the valve to the rim of the tire. The valve core is a **Schrader valve** (a spring-loaded, one-way valve) **FIGURE 20-9**. The primary function of the **valve stem cap** is to assist in keeping debris out of the valve stem, which could cause the valve stem core to fail. The valve stem cap is removed to check air pressure and to inflate or deflate the tire. Some valve stem caps come with a built-in tool for tightening or loosening the valve core. In wet climates, the

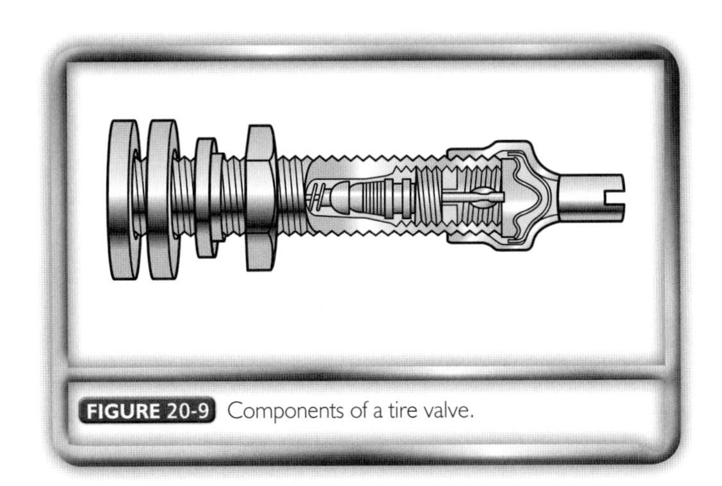

FIGURE 20-9 Components of a tire valve.

valve stem cap keeps mud, water, and ice from entering the valve stem. The valve stem cap can also slow a leak from a valve core, but will not stop a leak completely. In newer vehicles, a green valve stem cap indicates that the tire is filled with nitrogen and, to prevent contamination, should only be topped off with nitrogen.

Types of Tire Construction

Although there are two types of tire construction—**bias-ply** and **radial**—radial tires are by far the most common. In fact, one tire retailer estimates that 98% of the tires sold today for passenger vehicles are radial tires.

Bias-Ply Tires

The bias-ply tire is the older form of tire and is still in use on some trailers and off-road vehicles, primarily because of a slightly lower cost and their more durable construction. Bias tire construction uses body ply cords extended diagonally from bead to bead at 30- to 40-degree angles with successive plies laid at opposing angles, resulting in a crisscross pattern onto which tread is applied. This design provides a strong, stable casing, but with relatively stiff sidewalls. However, during cornering, stiff sidewalls can distort the tread and partially lift it off the road surface, which reduces the friction between the road and the tire.

Radial Tires

Radial tire construction uses the same body ply cords, but they are laid across the tread extending from bead to bead, so the cords end up parallel to each other at approximately 90 degrees to the centerline of the tread. Radial tires are extremely durable and maintain good traction with the road, providing better steering control. Most passenger cars now use radial tires, as do most four-wheel drive vehicles and heavy transport vehicles.

Radial ply tires have much more flexible sidewalls because of their construction FIGURE 20-10. They use two or more layers of **casing plies**, the cords that give the tire shape and strength, with the cord loops, which are loops of high-strength material (typically polyester) inlaid with rubber, running radially from bead to bead. The sidewalls are more flexible because the casing plies do not cross over each other; however, a bracing layer of two or more steel belts running horizontally must be placed under the tread to strengthen and stabilize the tire. The cords of the bracing layers may be of fabric or steel and are placed at 12 to 15 degrees to the circumference line. This design forms triangles where the belt cords cross over the radial cords. The stiff bracing layer links the cord loops together to give stability when accelerating or braking,

> **TECHNICIAN TIP**
>
> The bias-ply tire's stiff sidewalls can make tires run at a higher temperature. This is because, as the tire rotates, the body ply cords in the plies flex over each other, causing friction and heat. A bias-ply tire that overheats can wear prematurely. At the same time, stiffer sidewalls can resist punctures from sharp rocks or other objects better than a radial tire.

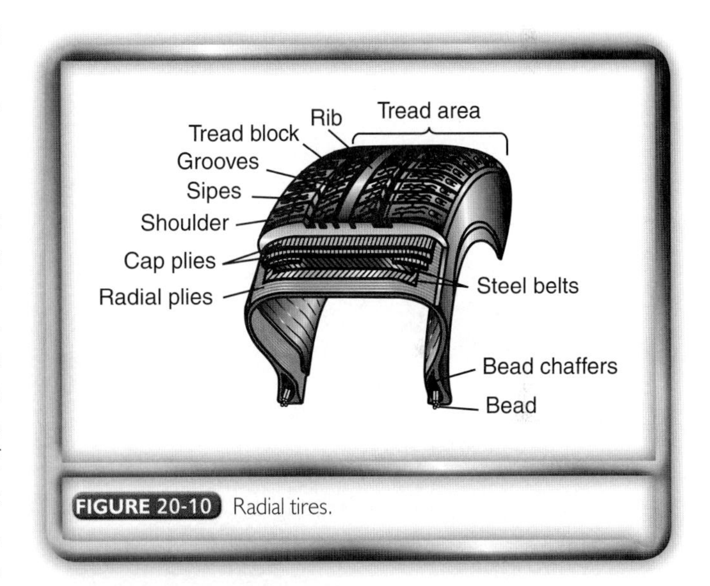
Rib
Tread area
Tread block
Grooves
Sipes
Shoulder
Cap plies
Radial plies
Steel belts
Bead chaffers
Bead

FIGURE 20-10 Radial tires.

> **TECHNICIAN TIP**
>
> The sidewalls of radial tires bulge where the tire meets the road, making it difficult to estimate the inflation pressure visually. Tire pressure needs to be checked with an accurate tire gauge. Using the correct inflation pressures extends the life of the tire and is vital for safety. Sidewalls of an underinflated tire flex too far, which causes the center section of the tread to be pushed up and away from the road surface. This causes wear at the shoulders of the tire. In an overinflated tire, the sidewalls are straightened, which pulls the edges of the tread away from the road and causes wear at the center of the tread.

and it prevents any movement of the cords during cornering. The cord plies flex and deform only in the area above the road contact patch. There are no heavy plies to distort, and flexing of the thin casing generates little heat, which is easily dispersed. A properly inflated radial tire runs cooler than a comparable bias-ply tire, increasing tread life. Also, a radial tire has less rolling resistance as it moves over the road surface, increasing fuel economy.

Tread Designs

Differing tread patterns give manufacturers the ability to design tires for special applications, such as rainy, snowy, muddy, highway, or high-performance driving. Manufacturers spend a lot of money trying to design better tread patterns than their competitors. And when they discover a good design, it can be very profitable. Tire tread patterns can be classified with these general characteristics FIGURE 20-11:

- **Directional tread patterns** are designed to provide a range of attributes during particular driving conditions, such as driving in wet weather where there is a possibility of hydroplaning (sliding across water). The predominate tread pattern is mounted in such a manner as to provide maximum moisture dissipation, thereby creating a drier surface for the tire to adhere to. Specifically,

A
B
C
E

FIGURE 20-11 Tread designs. **A.** Directional tread pattern. **B.** Nondirectional tread pattern. **C.** Symmetric tread pattern. **D.** Asymmetric tread pattern. **E.** Directional and asymmetric tread pattern.

these tread patterns actually pump water out from under the tire, bringing it in direct contact with the surface of the road. This type of tire can only be mounted to the wheel so that it revolves in a particular direction to correspond with the tread pattern. An arrow on the tire sidewall indicates the designed direction of forward travel.

- **Non-directional tread patterns** are designed in such a way that the tire can be mounted on the wheel for any direction of rotation. This allows the tire to be installed on either the left or the right side of the vehicle and to be mounted in multiple directions. These tires are used for general applications when the customer may not be looking for a high-performance tire. They are usually cheaper to manufacture than the specialized tires, and they allow tire stores to stock less tires.
- **Symmetric tread patterns** have the same tread pattern on both sides of the tire and are usually nondirectional tires. As the name indicates, they tend to feature treads that are similar in continuous designs across both sides of the tire tread as well as around the tire. A main feature of most symmetric tires is that they are nondirectional and thus can be fitted in either direction.
- **Asymmetric tread patterns** have a tread pattern that is different from one side of the tire to the other. They are designed to provide good grip when traveling straight and in turns. Asymmetric tires are labeled "outside" on the side of the tire that faces outward from the vehicle.
- **Directional and asymmetric tread patterns** are both directional and asymmetric, which means the tire is designed to rotate in only one direction and has one side that must face outward to ensure that the tire performs as designed under operating conditions.

Tire Markings

Tires come in a variety of sizes and ratings to accommodate the wide range of vehicles and driving situations. To help select the most appropriate tire for a particular application, tires use common sizing and rating systems. All tires meeting legislative codes must have the following information clearly marked on the sidewall:

- Manufacturer or brand name.
- International Organization for Standardization (ISO) tire class:
  - P—passenger
  - LT—light truck
  - C—commercial
  - T—temporary use as a spare wheel
  - No letter designation before the section width—either a European metric tire or an off-road tire
- Section width: Measured in millimeters from sidewall to sidewall.
- Aspect ratio: The height of the sidewall expressed as a percentage of the section width.
- Type of tire construction: R for radial; blank for bias-ply.
- Wheel diameter: Diameter of wheel from bead seat to bead seat, usually measured in inches.
- Speed rating designation: The maximum speed for which a particular tire is rated. Vehicles should not be driven in excess of their speed ratings with the exception of Z-rated tires, which are rated for speeds above 149 miles per hour (mph; 240 kilometers per hour [kph]). Note: Virtually all tires are rated for higher speeds than legal speed limits. Tire speed ratings do NOT give you legal cover for speeding! Speed ratings are as follows:
  - Q—Up to 100 mph (161 kph)
  - R—Up to 106 mph (171 kph)
  - S—Up to 112 mph (180 kph)
  - T—Up to 118 mph (190 kph)
  - U—Up to 124 mph (200 kph)
  - H—Up to 139 mph (224 kph)
  - V—Up to 149 mph (240 kph)
  - W—Up to 168 mph (270 kph)
  - Y—Up to 186 mph (299 kph)
  - Z—149 mph (240 kph) and over
- Maximum air pressure: The maximum pressure that the tire can be inflated to. This does not indicate the vehicle manufacturer's recommended inflation pressure. Always refer to the **tire placard** on the vehicle to determine proper inflation pressures.
- Load index: The maximum amount of weight that a tire can safely carry at the maximum rated tire pressure. When replacing tires, verify that the load index meets the vehicle manufacturer's specifications.
- Uniform Tire Quality Grading (UTQG) system:
  - Tread wear grade: An approximation of how long a tire will last when compared to another tire from the same manufacturer. For example, a tire rated at 450 will last approximately three times as long as one rated 150.
  - Traction grade: A representation of a tire's wet traction characteristics. From highest to lowest: AA, A, B, and C.
  - Temperature grade: A representation of a tire's ability to resist and dissipate heat. From highest to lowest: A, B, and C.

- Department of Transportation compliance symbols and serial numbers, including date of manufacture code:
    - First two letters following the letters "DOT" identify the tire manufacturer and manufacturing plant.
    - The third and fourth letters are codes that indicate the tire's size.
    - The final three or four letters are codes indicating manufacturer-specified characteristics.
    - Week of manufacture: The first pair of digits represent the week of the year in which the tire was manufactured, starting in January.
    - Year of manufacture: The last two digits represent the year of manufacture; for example, a 12 indicates a tire manufactured in 2012.

> **TECHNICIAN TIP**
>
> Radial tires are marked with the section width in millimeters, but with the rim diameter in inches.

A
B

FIGURE 20-12 Tire profile. **A.** Standard-profile tire. **B.** Low-profile tire.

Tire Sizes and Designations

The size of a tire must be appropriate for the vehicle application and intended use. The vehicle manufacturer designates the recommended size and load rating of the tires to be used on each particular vehicle. The bead diameter must match the rim diameter. The section width must be suitable for use on the rim and large enough to have a suitable load-carrying capacity for the vehicle. The overall tire size must allow sufficient clearance between the tire and the chassis and body components.

The section width of the tire is measured in millimeters by the tire manufacturer from sidewall to sidewall when installed on a standard wheel, inflated to its recommended pressure and without any load on it. Section width will vary from manufacturer to manufacturer, so do not assume tires with the same section width are all the same.

The **aspect ratio** of a tire is the ratio of its height to its width. It is usually given as a percentage. Information on tire aspect ratio is now included in the sidewall marking, along with the type of construction and the speed rating. The lower a tire's aspect ratio, the wider the tire is in relation to its height. An aspect ratio of 75 means the height of the sidewall is 75% as much as the section width. Generally, the higher the aspect ratio, the smoother the ride will be, but there will be more flex during corning.

Low-profile tires have very short sidewalls and can be difficult to remove and install **FIGURE 20-12**. They have an aspect ratio as low as 25. The low-profile tire improves corning performance but sacrifices a smooth ride, and there is a greater danger of wheel and suspension damage when hitting potholes. Often, low-profile tires will have a higher speed rating, as there is less centrifugal force trying to throw the tire apart.

Tire Ratings for Tread Wear, Traction, and Temperature

One of the markings on the sidewall of a tire is a **Uniform Tire Quality Grading (UTQG)** rating. As discussed previously, the tire's UTQG rating provides information on three aspects of the tire's durability and operational characteristics: tread wear, traction, and temperature.

The **tread wear grade** comes from testing the tire in controlled conditions. The higher the number, the longer the life expectancy of the tread as compared to another tire from the same manufacturer. Since no one vehicle will be subjected to exactly the same surfaces and at the same speeds as the controlled conditions, the number can only be an indicator of expected tread life in normal conditions. The rating is based on a percentage of the projected wear life. For instance, when looking at two tires from the same manufacturer, one tire rated at 400 has a projected life of four times that of a tire rated at 100.

TECHNICIAN TIP

There are many factors that influence wear, such as vehicle speed, road surface, climate, vehicle wheel alignment, and the driving characteristics of the driver. The rating can only be an indication of the anticipated wear characteristics of the tire in controlled conditions.

A **traction grade** is a letter-based indicator system. The rating is based on the tire's ability to stop a vehicle on wet concrete and asphalt in a straight-line situation. It does not indicate the tire's cornering ability. The tire traction indicators are rated from highest to lowest as AA, A, B, or C. It is important to note that the relevant rating does not indicate hydroplaning resistance, dry or snow traction capacity, or cornering capability in wet, dry, or snow conditions.

The **temperature grade** of a tire is a letter based on a test performed by the tire manufacturer and overseen by the US government. The goal of the test is to determine how well a tire stands up to heat and measures how well the tire dissipates heat. The US government uses the UTQG criteria for tire temperature ratings. The tires are graded from C (least tolerant of heat dissipation) to A (most tolerant of heat dissipation). While a C-graded tire runs hotter, it is not necessarily unsafe.

It is important to remember that these ratings are based on standardized test conditions, and the tests do not reflect tires that are operated in overloaded, under-inflated, and/or misaligned conditions. It should also be noted that one tire might be rated a low A and another a high B, so the actual operating performance differences might be relatively small.

It is not uncommon for there to be differences in UTQG ratings within a given tire design. Sometimes a particular vehicle manufacturer will require certain properties for the tires supplied to their vehicles, which can affect the ratings, both positively and negatively. Sometimes there are differences between small sizes and large sizes of tires in a given design. All of these aspects can affect the actual rating that is put on the sidewall.

Tire Date of Manufacture Coding

The **US Department of Transportation (DOT)** inspects everything and anything pertaining to transportation—including tires. As part of DOT regulations, there must be a tire manufacture date code stamped on the sidewall of every tire. In fact, it is illegal to sell a tire intended for use on a public road within the United States without a DOT stamp. Some manufacturers mold this code on only one sidewall, so you might need to get under the vehicle and look at the inward-facing side of the tire. You will find a three- or four-digit code. This code denotes when the tire was manufactured. For safety concerns and as a rule of thumb, you should never use tires more than 6 years old. The rubber in tires degrades over time, irrespective of whether the tire is being used or not.

Reading the DOT code is relatively simple. A three-digit DOT code was used for tires manufactured before 2000. For example, 176 means that the tire was manufactured in the 17th week of the 6th year of the decade, or 1986.

For tires manufactured in the 1990s, there may be a little triangle after the DOT code. For example, a tire manufactured in the 17th week of 1996 might have the code 176Δ. After 2000, the code was switched to a four-digit code. For example, 30 11 means the tire was manufactured in the 30th week of 2011 **FIGURE 20-13**.

Tire Safety Features

Flat tires are one of the leading causes of vehicle breakdowns. Generally speaking, vehicles cannot be driven with one or more flat tires. Attempting to do so will ruin a potentially reparable tire very quickly. Manufacturers address this situation in various ways. The most common is through the use of tire pressure monitoring systems to monitor the air pressure in each tire and warn the driver

DOT 3011
LMLR5107

FIGURE 20-13 The DOT tire date manufacturing code is a four-digit code.

if one or more tires is low. Another tactic that manufacturers use is run-flat tires. These tires are designed so that they can still be driven for a reasonable amount of time when the tire pressure is low or empty. Similar to the run-flat tires, manufacturers can use self-sealing tires, which resist leaks and help maintain air pressure. The last safety feature involves the use of a spare tire, which is usually of the space-saving type, also called a temporary tire. It is designed to be used for reduced speeds and distances so that a driver can get the vehicle to a service facility. Each of these safety features will be discussed further in the following sections.

> **TECHNICIAN TIP**
>
> In vehicles with a direct TPMS, the dashboard may show:
>
> - The required tire pressure
> - The actual tire pressure
> - The tire pressure status
> - The temperature of the tire
>
> In some vehicles, the driver can use the display control buttons to check the status of each tire.

Tire Pressure Monitoring Systems

Maintaining proper tire pressure is essential for the safety and performance of a vehicle. It also plays a significant role in decreasing fuel consumption, reducing CO_2 emissions, and extending tire life. All tires lose inflation over time and, as many modern vehicles have extended service intervals, tires can become dangerously underinflated without regular checking by the vehicle driver.

In addition to increased fuel consumption and tire wear, long periods of driving with low tire pressures can cause additional stress on the tire sidewalls. This results in increased operating temperatures that can lead to premature tire failure. Tires operating with low pressures can also affect the vehicle's handling and performance. In a worst-case scenario, underinflation can lead to a tire blowout or tread separation. Because of these situations, the Transportation Recall Enhancement, Accountability, and Documentation (or TREAD) Act called for all new passenger vehicles under 10,000 lb (4536 kg) to be equipped with a TPMS by October 1, 2007.

The automated **tire pressure monitoring system (TPMS)** provides a means of reliable and continuous monitoring of the vehicle tire pressure and is designed to increase safety, decrease fuel consumption, and improve vehicle performance. A TPMS monitors the tires for low air pressure and alerts the driver when one or more tires are lower than (or in some cases, higher than) the designated thresholds. This alert can be an illuminated warning lamp or a chime. A TPMS can be fitted to all vehicles using conventional and run-flat tires. With some TPMS systems, drivers can monitor the tire pressures and temperatures from the driver's seat to ensure that their tires are properly inflated under all operating conditions. The TPMS is designed to ignore normal pressure variations caused by changes in ambient temperature.

There are two basic configurations used to monitor the vehicle's tire pressures: direct and indirect. A **direct TPMS** directly measure the tire pressure and sometimes pressure via a sensor that is installed inside each wheel, which helps protect it from damage. There is a sensor with an antenna in each wheel that wirelessly relays the information it senses to receivers located within the vehicle FIGURE 20-14. The receivers send the signal to the control unit. The sensor is able to respond to a drop in pressure of as little as 2 psi (14 kilopascals [kPA]). The control unit sends an appropriate signal to the driver's information circuit or, in some vehicles, the on-board computer, which in turn illuminates a display in the vehicle's multifunction screen to warn the driver of low tire pressure in a certain wheel. An audible and visual warning instantly alerts the driver, allowing time for the vehicle to stop or be driven to a service station.

The sensors are powered by an internal battery that is designed to last between 5 and 10 years. The use of a **centrifugal switch** in the sensor allows the sensor to go to sleep when the vehicle stops, which extends battery life. When the battery goes dead, it will need to be replaced, which usually means that the entire sensor must be replaced because the battery is typically sealed inside the sensor.

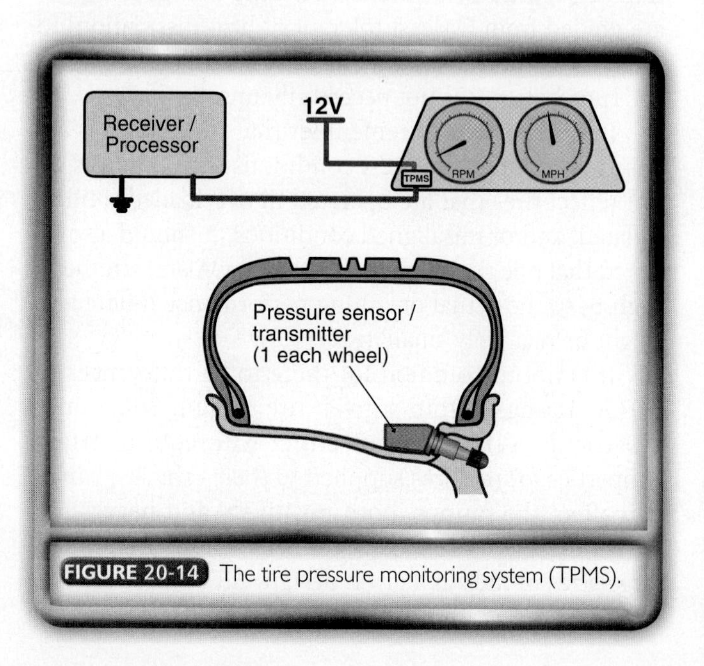
Receiver / Processor
12V
TPMS
RPM
MPH
Pressure sensor / transmitter (1 each wheel)

FIGURE 20-14 The tire pressure monitoring system (TPMS).

A direct TPMS can be of two types: one-way communication or two-way communication. In one-way communication, the TPMS sensor can only transmit to the receiver; it cannot receive any information. In this type of system, the sensors usually use a centrifugal switch to turn them on and off to conserve the battery energy. In a two-way communication TPMS, the sensor can receive signals as well as transmit signals. This allows the control unit to send signals to wake up or cause the sensor to sleep, thus extending the sensor's battery life. The two-way communication system is more complex and expensive than the one-way system.

The wheel sensors are located inside the tire and fastened in some manner to the wheel. Many wheel sensors are integrated into a one-piece design along with the valve stem, while others are a separate unit screwed into the valve stem. The latter style uses a band or strap that fastens around the wheel in the drop center and holds the sensor in place. In a band-style wheel sensor, the sensor is typically located opposite of the valve stem **FIGURE 20-15**. When removing and replacing a tire on a wheel, you must be aware of the sensor's location and take steps to avoid damaging it.

An **indirect TPMS** indirectly monitors tire air pressure. The most prevalent indirect tire pressure monitoring systems in use today utilize the wheel speed anti-lock braking systems (ABS) to measure the difference in the rotational speed of the four wheels. A wheel that is rotating faster than the others indicates that the tire has lower pressure than the other tires. For example, if a tire loses pressure, then its rolling radius is reduced, which increases the speed of rotation. Since it is rolling faster than the other tires, the wheel speed sensor will send a slightly faster wheel speed signal for that wheel to the ABS control unit. The control unit monitors the changes in wheel speed, and when a low tire pressure failure is detected, it sends a signal to the low tire pressure light and/or chime on the dashboard.

> **TECHNICIAN TIP**
>
> Most wheels with TPMS sensors use an aluminium valve stem, which requires a nickel-plated valve core to prevent corrosion. Also, the valve stem acts as the antennae for the TPMS sensor on some applications.

FIGURE 20-15 Band type TPMS sensor.

Run-Flat Tires

The major safety benefit of **run-flat technology** is that it enables a driver to maintain vehicle control if a tire suffers a rapid pressure loss when in motion. In addition, run-flat tires enable the driver to continue the journey within specified speed and distance limits (about 50 mph [80 kph] and at least 50 miles 80 [km]). This alleviates the need to replace the wheel on the side of the road or in an unsafe area. But as with any tire, the run-flat tire cannot continue to be driven if the sidewall has been compromised or blown out. In these instances, the tire needs to be changed. A TPMS is normally mandatory for all run-flat technology applications to monitor the driveability of the vehicle's run-flat tires.

Tire manufacturers also maintain that run-flat technology usually saves weight and space by eliminating the need to carry a spare tire. However, because of their construction, they are generally between two to three times heavier than their conventional counterparts. This adds unsprung weight (weight not held up by the vehicle's springs) to the vehicle, affects the suspension, and can increase fuel consumption.

Because of the extra materials used in the construction of run-flat tires, they are also more expensive to purchase. In addition, run-flat tires are usually harsher riding and noisier in operation, which can be a disadvantage in some applications, such as in luxury cars that are expected to have a quiet, smooth ride. From a manufacturing perspective, the free space created by eliminating a standard spare wheel gives the vehicle manufacturer a range of additional design opportunities, such as providing more storage space in the trunk.

The design features of run-flat technology generally focus on two aspects of operational use: rigidity and heat resistance. The objective is for the tire to support the vehicle's weight when it is rotating with a total air loss. The sidewall is constructed with reinforced rubber and is thicker than in conventional tires, enabling it to carry the vehicle's weight at zero pressure FIGURE 20-16.

The bead shape configuration of the run-flat tire is largely unchanged from conventional tires to enable compatibility with conventional rims. However, the bead wire is normally wider and reinforced to ensure a secure fit on the specialized rim, even at zero pressure. A special bead filler with low heat generation is used as part of the run-flat technology construction to help prevent excess heat buildup that can be generated with zero pressure.

The rim used with some run-flat technology tires is referred to as an **EH2 rim**. EH2 is an abbreviation for double extended hump. These rims have a wider, or more extended, safety hump than a standard safety rim to accommodate the wider and more square-shaped tire bead. The run-flat technology tire bead also has a larger diameter than the standard safety bead of a conventional radial ply tire.

TECHNICIAN TIP

Tire manufacturers will call their run-flat safety tire by various terminologies, but all have the same characteristics. Some run-flat tires are known as:

- Run-Flat Technology (RFT) tires
- Extended Mobility Technology (EMT) tires
- Continuous Mobility Technology (CMT) tires
- Zero-pressure (ZP) tires

EMT tire sidewalls can be six times thicker than the sidewalls of traditional tires. As a result, the manufacturers claim that run-flat tires can be driven at speeds of about 50 mph (80 kph) for at least 50 miles (80 km) in a deflated condition before being damaged. These tires are not indestructible. Major damage that slices the tire casing can still result in complete tire failure.

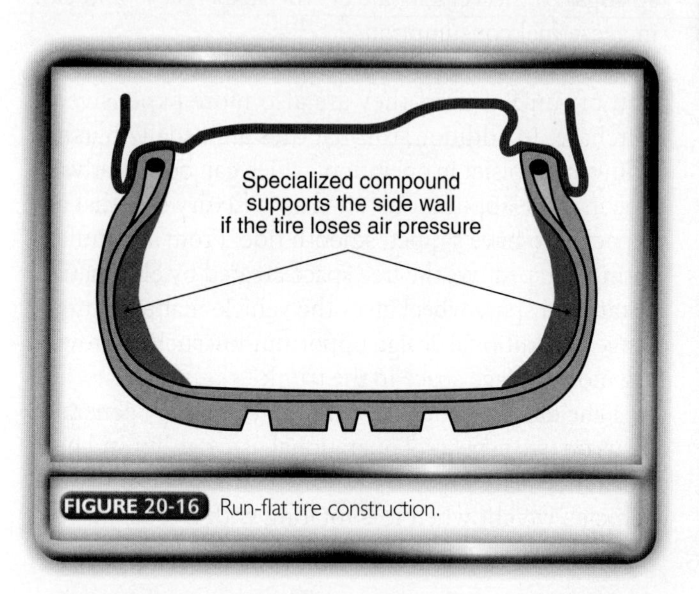
Specialized compound
supports the side wall
if the tire loses air pressure

FIGURE 20-16 Run-flat tire construction.

Self-Sealing Tires

Self-sealing tires were introduced recently to commercial passenger cars. One self-sealing tire manufacturer states that its self-sealing tire is designed to repair most small tread-area punctures instantly and permanently. Self-sealing tires feature standard tire construction with the addition of a flexible and malleable lining inside the tire in the tread area. This lining serves as a puncture sealant that can permanently seal most punctures from nails, bolts, or screws up to 3/16" (or 5 mm) in diameter. Self-sealing tires first provide a seal around the object when the tire is punctured and then fill in the hole in the tread if the object is removed. Most drivers will never even know that they just had a puncture. Because these tires can still leak air from between the bead and the rim or the valve stem and the valve core, they still require a TPMS to detect any low-pressure conditions on 2008 and newer vehicles.

Space-Saver Spare Tires

Space-saver spare tires are designed for emergency use only. They are designed to get the driver to a service center to have the regular tire fixed or purchase a new one. When provided with the vehicle as part of the original manufacturer's equipment, most manufacturers warn not to exceed 50 mph (80 kph) and not to go farther than 50 miles (80 km) on the space-saver spare tire. Some vehicles have miniature or collapsible space-saver spare tires as spares. These normally require a specially charged canister for inflation when being installed. Other vehicles have small, temporary spare tires that have been inflated normally with a compressed air supply but, because of their small size, to a much higher pressure than normal road tires.

Tire Service

A periodic inspection of the tires is necessary to ensure a long life. The tire pressure should be checked and adjusted on vehicles that do not have a TPMS. The tread area is inspected for cuts, flat spotting, or irregular wear patterns. The tread depth is inspected to ensure that it is above the built-in wear indicators, which indicate that the tire is at the end of its legal life and should be replaced. The sidewalls are inspected for cuts or gashes and any signs of damage from impacting solid objects such as curbs. At the same time, vehicle and tire manufacturers recommend that the tires be rotated during each oil change. Tire balance is performed when the tires are new and any time there is a customer concern regarding vibrations that are diagnosed to be caused by tire balance faults, or if tire wear indicates an out-of-balance condition.

Wheel alignment is another service that is performed on occasion. The alignment is normally checked and adjusted in cases such as when there is abnormal tire wear, when steering/suspension parts are replaced, when the vehicle does not handle/drive correctly, and after an accident that could affect the alignment. Most tire stores will try to sell an alignment when new tires are purchased, but if the old tires were wearing normally, then the new tires will wear normally also. Still, some customers like the peace of mind of knowing that the alignment was checked when they get new tires.

▶ **LINK**

Refer to the Servicing Suspension Systems chapter for more detailed information on wheel alignment.

Proper Tire Inflation

Tire inflation pressure is the amount of air pressure in the tire that provides it with load-carrying capacity and affects the overall performance of the vehicle. Vehicle manufacturers determine the tire inflation pressure based on the vehicle's designed load limit, which is the greatest amount of weight a vehicle can safely carry, and the vehicle's tire size. The proper tire pressure for the vehicle is referred to as the recommended cold inflation pressure. It is measured in psi or kPa. You will find this information on the tire placard expressed in psi or kPa **FIGURE 20-17**. The tire placard can be located on the A- or B-pillar door frame, in the glove compartment, or on the fuel filler flap.

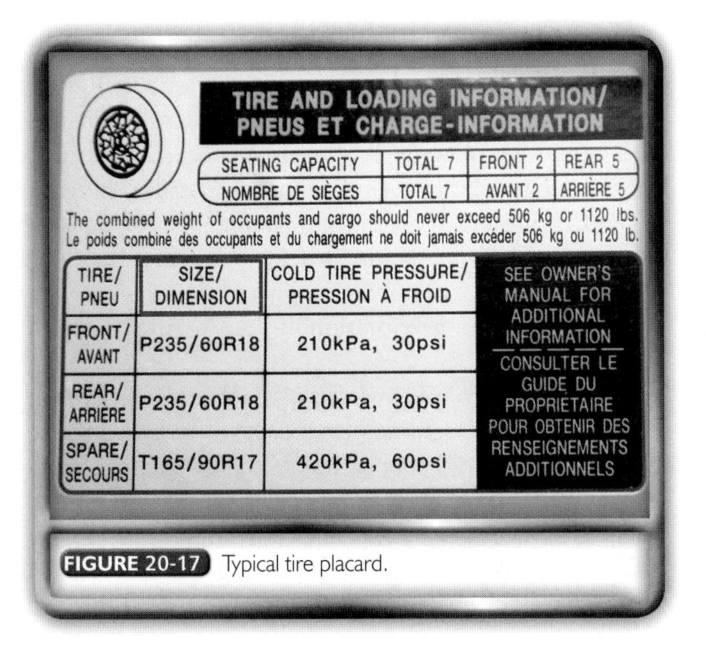
TIRE AND LOADING INFORMATION/
PNEUS ET CHARGE-INFORMATION
SEATING CAPACITY | TOTAL 7 | FRONT 2 | REAR 5
NOMBRE DE SIÈGES | TOTAL 7 | AVANT 2 | ARRIÈRE 5
The combined weight of occupants and cargo should never exceed 506 kg or 1120 lbs.
Le poids combiné des occupants et du chargement ne doit jamais excéder 506 kg ou 1120 lb.
TIRE/ PNEU | SIZE/ DIMENSION | COLD TIRE PRESSURE/ PRESSION À FROID
FRONT/ AVANT | P235/60R18 | 210kPa, 30psi
REAR/ ARRIÈRE | P235/60R18 | 210kPa, 30psi
SPARE/ SECOURS | T165/90R17 | 420kPa, 60psi
SEE OWNER'S MANUAL FOR ADDITIONAL INFORMATION
CONSULTER LE GUIDE DU PROPRIETAIRE POUR OBTENIR DES RENSEIGNEMENTS ADDITIONNELS

FIGURE 20-17 Typical tire placard.

Because tires are designed to be used on more than one type of vehicle, tire manufacturers list the maximum safe inflation pressure on the tire sidewall. This number is the highest amount of air pressure that should ever be put in the tire. The maximum tire pressure should never be exceeded, even when the vehicle's tire placard indicates a higher pressure. As explained earlier, 32 psi of air pressure can generate over 50,000 lb of force on a tire. If the maximum tire pressure is exceeded, the force from the air pressure generates even greater forces and can cause the tire to explode violently. Too many young technicians have lost their life when they overinflated a tire and it blew up in their face. This is one of the more dangerous situations for inexperienced technicians. It is also why it is good to use a tire cage when inflating a tire. If the tire blows up, the explosion will affect your hearing, but the cage is likely to contain most of the tire debris.

To get an accurate pressure reading, the tires must be checked when cold. The term *cold* does not relate to the outside temperature. Rather, a cold tire is one that has not been driven on for at least 3 hours or less than 1 mile (1.6 km). While driving, tires get warmer due to the heat of friction created as the tire materials flex against each other. As tires rotate and the sidewalls flex due to variations in the road surfaces, they generate heat as the layers of plies are forced to accommodate the sidewall flexing. Flexing results in heat. The heated tire materials, in turn, heat the air within the tire. As the air within the tire warms, it expands, causing the air pressure within the tire to increase. To obtain an accurate tire pressure reading, then, you must measure tire pressure when the tires are cold or compensate for the extra pressure in warm tires. Some manufacturers supply this information, while others do not.

TECHNICIAN TIP

According to the US Department of Energy, underinflated tires can lower gas mileage by 0.3% for every 1 psi drop in pressure in all four tires. So running them 10 psi low reduces gas mileage approximately 3%. Underinflation wastes approximately 2 billion gallons of fuel each year in the United States alone.

Nitrogen Fill

Oxygen is harmful to rubber and other tire materials. The oxygen reacts with the rubber through oxidation and causes the rubber to lose its flexibility and sealing ability. This allows oxygen to permeate the rubber and degrade it further over time. Also, as the inner liner oxidizes, more air molecules can pass through it, causing an increased rate of pressure loss. In addition, potential problems can occur from the rust and dust the corrosion of rubber produces, which clog the valve stems, causing them to leak. In recent years, some manufacturers have been filling their tires with pure or nearly pure nitrogen in hopes that the problems associated with oxygen-filled tires can be avoided. Nitrogen is an inert gas that does not react with the rubber compounds in the tire. Nitrogen generators also remove any moisture from the nitrogen gas so corrosion effects are reduced on TPMS sensors and other metal components of the wheels and tires.

Advantages for Nitrogen Fills

While both nitrogen and oxygen can permeate rubber, nitrogen does so at a much slower rate. It might take 6 months to lose 2 psi (14 kPa) with nitrogen, compared to just a month with normal air. In addition, nitrogen is far less reactive. It does not cause rust and corrosion on steel or aluminium, and it does not degrade rubber. Wheel surfaces stay smooth and clean, and rubber remains supple and resilient.

Since tires operate most efficiently when they are at the correct pressure, nitrogen filling can better maintain a tire's performance over time. It will also increase the vehicle's fuel efficiency and tire life by reducing the effects of pressure loss due to permeation. Proper tire inflation also helps prevent accidents by reducing the possibility of blowouts and maintaining maximum tire traction with the road surface.

The air that we breathe and that is typically used to inflate tires chemically consists of 78% nitrogen, 21% oxygen, and 1% other. When using pure nitrogen as an inflation gas, the composition of nitrogen increases from 78% to near 100%. To meet the standards for proper nitrogen fill means that the nitrogen level in the tire must be at 95% or higher. This typically requires two or three inflations and deflations to remove the oxygen. Nitrogen-filled tires can be identified by the green valve stem caps that are placed on the valve stem when the tire is inflated. Although tire manufacturers generally support the use of nitrogen, they do not generally mandate its use based on its ability to better retain a consistent tire pressure over a period of time.

Tire Rotation Pattern

Tire rotation service is the removal and relocation of each tire/wheel assembly on the vehicle. Each tire on the vehicle can wear differently. Regular tire rotation promotes uniform tread wear, extending the life of the set of tires. Uniform tread wear can also boost the vehicle's fuel economy and increase the vehicle's performance. Each manufacturer designates the proper rotation sequence depending on whether the vehicle is front-wheel drive, rear-wheel drive, or all-wheel drive; the type of tires (e.g., directional); and whether a spare tire is involved in the rotation FIGURE 20-18. In general, a four-tire rotation with nondirectional tires can have one of three rotation patterns: forward-cross, rearward-cross, and X pattern. Directional tires require keeping the tires on the same side of the vehicle and generally use a front-to-rear pattern. If the directional tires are differently sized front to rear, then the tires will have to be dismounted and remounted on the wheels from the other side of the vehicle. If the vehicle uses a full-sized spare tire, then the pattern will be one of two five-tire rotations, which are variations of the four-tire forward-cross or rearward-cross pattern. Generally, it is recommended to rotate the tires on vehicles approximately every 5000 miles (8000 km) or with every oil change.

Wheel Balance

Wheels and tires are mass produced so many times that there are small (or sometimes big) imbalances manufactured into them. Also, they are not always perfectly round (concentric), but can still be sold as long as they are within the tolerances specified by the manufacturer. To complicate matters, tolerance stacking can happen. For example, the wheel hub may have an out-of-round tolerance of 0.005" (0.13 mm), the wheel may have a tolerance of 0.005" (0.13 mm), and the tire may have a tolerance of 0.025" (0.64 mm). If all of the tolerances stack up (one on top of another), then the wheel will experience balance and runout issues. Wheels and tires that are not balanced or that are out of balance generally produce an uncomfortable vibration and result in premature wearing of suspension and steering components, as well as uneven tire wear. An out-of-balance tire will cause the vehicle to vibrate at certain speeds, usually between 50 and 70 mph (80 to 113 kph). A tire is out of balance when one section of the tire is heavier or stiffer than the others. One ounce of imbalance on a front tire is enough to cause a noticeable vibration in the steering wheel at highway speeds.

There are two ways wheels can be balanced: off-car and on-car. Although most shops use off-car balancers, if the brake rotor, drum, or hub is out of balance, then a balanced wheel cannot compensate for that, so on-car balancers are used to balance the entire rotating assembly. The only problem with on-car balancing is that the wheel will need to be rebalanced when it is rotated to another

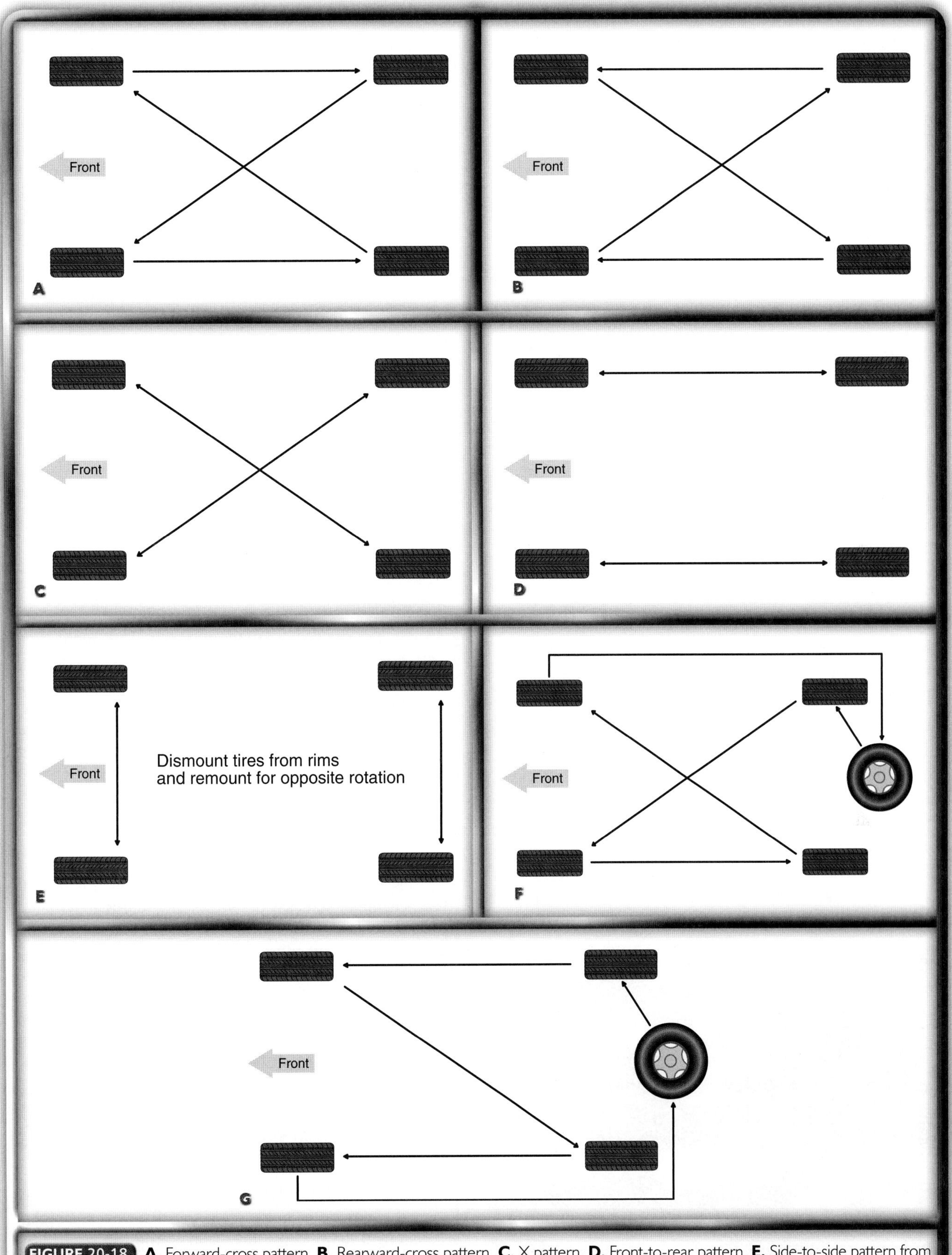
Front
A
Front
B
Front
C
Front
D
Front
Dismount tires from rims
and remount for opposite rotation
E
Front
F
Front
G

FIGURE 20-18 **A.** Forward-cross pattern. **B.** Rearward-cross pattern. **C.** X pattern. **D.** Front-to-rear pattern. **E.** Side-to-side pattern from the other side of the vehicle. **F.** Five-tire forward-cross pattern. **G.** Five-tire rearward-cross pattern.

position on the vehicle. This is one reason that most shops use off-car balancers FIGURE 20-19.

Tires and wheels can be balanced in three ways: static, dynamic, and road force. With static balancing, the tire's imbalance is measured when the tire is stationary. Static balancing does not take into consideration that the tire has width; thus, static balancing can address the imbalance only as it relates to how much weight is needed to counterbalance the imbalance X inches away from the center of the axle. Static balancing assumes the imbalance is centered across the width of the tire. Therefore, it can be effective only when dealing with an imbalance condition that is centered within the width of the tire. **Static imbalance** tends to cause the tire to move purely up and down. Static balancing is no longer an acceptable method of balancing tires on today's vehicles.

Dynamic balancing is performed when the tire is rotating. It takes into consideration that the tire has width; therefore the imbalance is not only a certain weight and distance from the centerline of the axle, but it can also be anywhere within the width of the tire. **Dynamic imbalance** can cause the tire to move side to side as well as up and down. Dynamic balancing is performed by placing specific amounts of weight on each side of the rim to provide the exact counterbalance needed. It can effectively account for an imbalance located anywhere within the volume of the tire/wheel assembly. Dynamic balancing is used in most shops today.

It is possible that the tire and wheel can be perfectly in balance statically and dynamically, yet the vehicle still experiences a shimmy or shake that feels just like an out-of-balance tire. This problem is caused by road force imbalance. Road force imbalance occurs when the wheel or tire is not concentric or when the tire's sidewall has uneven stiffness. As the tire rotates and contacts the surface of the road, any issues with concentricity or sidewall stiffness will push up and down on the vehicle and simulate a tire that is out of balance. Road force balancing a tire gives the best ride quality to owners as it takes into consideration all balance factors related to the wheel and tires.

When dynamically balancing a tire using an off-car balancer, the wheel and tire assembly is mounted on the balancer. It is then spun up to speed so that the precise location and amount of the imbalance can be identified. The balancer then shows the technician where and how much weight to add on each side of the wheel. The wheel is spun up again to ensure that the weights have been affixed in the correct location and there is no more imbalance. If a road force balancer is used, then the tire is run up against a roller and any uneven forces are measured. If an uneven force is encountered, the machine will usually direct you to rotate the tire on the wheel and spin it again to see if there are any concentricity issues with the wheel. It can also tell you where the best location is for the tire on the rim to reduce road force fluctuations. After this process is completed, the wheel is reinstalled on the vehicle and the wheel nuts are torqued to the manufacturer's specification.

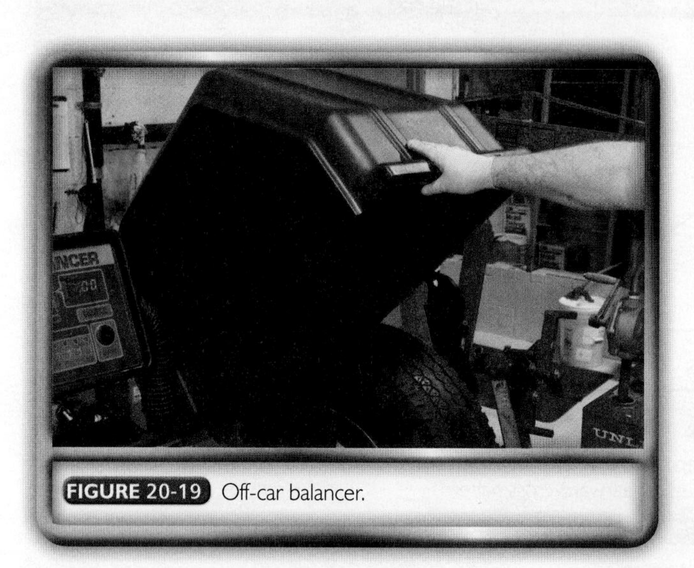

FIGURE 20-19 Off-car balancer.

Applied Science

AS-47: Force, Balance/Unbalanced: The technician can demonstrate an understanding of the role of balanced and unbalanced forces on linear or rotating vehicle assemblies.

When a tire is fitted to a wheel, two imperfectly weighted components are assembled together to form a heavy, large-diameter rotational component. The chances of this assembly having perfect weight distribution are extremely small, hence the importance of adding weight in specific areas to balance the assembly.

A car wheel rotates on a central axis, supported by bearings. When a wheel turning at high speed is out-of-balance, either statically or dynamically, forces are created perpendicular to the rotational axis. These forces are typically experienced as a vibration through the steering wheel if the front wheels are out-of-balance, although in extreme cases a vibration may also be felt through the vehicle's body if the rear wheels are out-of-balance. When a wheel is in perfect balance no forces exist to interrupt the smooth rotation around the central axis.

TECHNICIAN TIP

Not all shimmies and shakes are caused by tire balance issues. Sometimes belts inside the tire carcass break, creating a lump in the tire. Every time the lump hits the road, the tire pushes back. This really is just an extreme case of road force imbalance.

The majority of top-quality tires will hold their balance reasonably well, as long as the vehicle is not driven over potholes. If the driver should notice a vibration that was not there the day before, it is possible that one of the balancing weights fell off. If the driver feels the vibration mostly in the steering wheel, the problem is most likely in a front wheel. If the vibration is mostly in the seat, the problem is probably in one of the rear tires.

Wheel weights come in a variety of styles to fit different rim configurations, so you will need to verify the type of weight needed for a particular wheel. Weights come in 0.25-ounce (7-gram) increments. Although wheel weights have been primarily made of lead for decades, several states have outlawed them because of the potential environmental hazards of lead. In those states, steel weights coated with zinc or another protective layer are being used instead of lead weights. It is good practice to always use new wheel weights when balancing a tire. Do not reuse the old wheel weights, since they are likely to be thrown from the wheel when driven at freeway speeds.

TPMS Service

TPMS sensors need to be treated carefully when tires are being removed and reinstalled. Sometimes normal corrosion can damage the TPMS sensors, but more likely, a careless technician can damage the TPMS sensors by not removing the tire properly. If a sensor is damaged during a tire change, then the entire TPMS sensor unit will generally need to be replaced.

The TPMS sensor unit is a sealed component. Some models are powered by a small sealed disposable battery. These batteries are designed to last for 5 to 10 years without replacement. When the battery does expire, the sensor will need to be removed from the rim and checked. In most instances, the sensor will need to be replaced as a unit. The cost of replacing a battery compared to the sensor may not be economically viable, and new TMPS sensors may need to be installed.

Many TPMS sensors use nickel-plated valve cores in an aluminium valve stem. Never use brass valve cores or unplated brass caps; doing so can cause galvanic corrosion between the two different metals. Many TPMS sensors must be torqued into place. This torque is a very small amount measured in inch-pounds. Be careful as they are easily stripped or broken. Always use new sealing washers with TPMS sensors when removing them from a rim.

Maintenance and Repair

Tires are one of the most maintenance-intensive parts of a vehicle. They require regular visual inspections, pressure inspections, and rotations. Visual inspections of the tires and wheels should be made whenever a vehicle comes into a shop for any work. It is common to check for any unusual wear patterns and for any embedded objects or other signs of damage. If the vehicle is not equipped with a TPMS, then the operator should be encouraged to check the pressure at least monthly. Another task is rotating the tires. Most manufacturers recommend that the tires be rotated at each oil change to even out the wear and extend the life of the tires. Research the vehicle and service information for more information.

Tools

To service tires in an efficient manner, you must have the appropriate tools and equipment. The basic equipment list should consist of:

- Tire pressure gauge: Used to check the air pressure in tires.
- Tread depth gauge: Used to measure the tire's tread depth.
- Valve stem tool: Used to remove and install tubeless valve stems in rims.
- Valve core tool: Used to remove and install valve cores in valve stems.
- Tire-changing machine capable of handling the range of tires that the shop stocks: If the shop handles run-flat tires, then the tire-changing machine must be designed to handle the more robust bead and sidewalls.
- Tire dunk tank: Used to locate leaks in tires and rims.
- Tire spreader: Used to spread the sidewalls of a tire for easier access during tire patching.
- Air tire buffer: Used to lightly buff the inside surface of the tire as preparation for tire patching.
- Patch stitching tool: Used to apply pressure to the patch when positioning it.
- Tire inflation cage: Used to contain the tire and rim during tire inflation in the event of a tire explosion.
- Wheel balancing machine capable of handling the range of tires that the shop stocks.
- Variety of wheel weight styles to cover the various styles of wheels.
- Wheel weight hammer: Used to remove and install wheel weights onto rims.
- TPMS reset tool: Used to reset the TPMS (not required on all TPMS-equipped vehicles).

Common Issues

Common tire and wheel issues include:

- Air loss: The most common issue with tires is air loss. Tires normally lose a small amount of air over time and require periodic refilling. Punctures occur that cause leaks of various sizes. Valve stems and tire beads can also allow air to leak from the tire.

- An out-of-balance tire or wheel: The wheel and tires must be balanced, with the weight equally distributed throughout. When a tire rotates, any points of unequal weight will cause the tire to wobble, placing stress on the shocks, bearings, and wheel assembly. Additionally, the vehicle will vibrate at speeds of about 35 mph (56 kph) and above, it will have a rough ride, and the steering wheel may vibrate. A wheel balancer is used to identify and correct wheel imbalances.
- Excessive loaded radial runout on the tire, wheel, and hub assembly: With radial runout, the tire tread moves up and down. It is caused by incorrect manufacture or by damage to the tire, such as a broken belt. Correction involves replacing the tire.
- Excessive lateral runout on the tire, wheel, and hub assembly: Runout occurs when a part of the wheel assembly becomes bent or was manufactured improperly. The result is a wobble. When lateral runout occurs, the only method for fixing it is to replace the bent or improperly manufactured component.
- Wheel trim imbalance (if fitted): The term "wheel trim" refers to any pieces attached to a wheel that are not necessary for actual wheel function, such as a hubcap or trim ring. Imbalance or wear in trim pieces is corrected by removing or replacing the part.
- Heavy pulling of a vehicle to either the left or the right while the customer is driving is an indication of these possible problems:
    - Mismatched front tire sizes or pressures
    - Tire with broken or misaligned belts
    - Out-of-alignment wheels
    - Worn suspension or steering components
    - A dragging front brake assembly

Using a Tire Pressure Gauge

There are two main types of **tire pressure gauges**: fixed workshop gauges and portable pocket-size gauges FIGURE 20-20. The three most popular types of pocket tire pressure gauges are the pencil type, the dial type, and the digital type. The pencil type looks similar to a pencil and contains a graduated sliding extension that is forced out of the sleeve by air pressure when it is attached to the tire valve. The dial type has a similar chuck to the pencil type but includes a graduated gauge and needle. The digital type can look like any of the others, but it gives a digital reading of the pressure and is generally the most accurate. Some digital pressure gauges can also read the temperature.

MANU
TIRE
BLEED
VALVE
60-200 PSI
LINE PRESSURE
A
B

FIGURE 20-20 Tire pressure gauges. **A.** Fixed workshop gauge. **B.** Portable pocket-size gauge.

TECHNICIAN TIP

A common mistake when inflating tires is to use the pressure listed on the sidewall instead of the tire placard. The pressure listed on the sidewall is the maximum pressure that the tire is designed to withstand and should *never* be exceeded, even when the placard lists a higher pressure! So you should always first check the placard and then verify that it is not higher than the maximum pressure listed on the sidewall. If it is, someone installed underrated tires on the vehicle.

TECHNICIAN TIP

If you check the tire pressures after the vehicle has been driven and the tires are warm or hot, *do not* release this excess pressure. If you bleed the tire pressure down to the manufacturer's recommendation, it will be underinflated when the tire is cold or at normal operating temperature. This could cause premature wear on the tires and handling issues with the vehicle. Most tire manufacturers recommend checking tire pressures before the vehicle has been driven more than 1 mile (1.6 km).

Each tire pressure gauge measures pressures in pounds per square inch (psi), kilopascals (kPa), or **bars**. One bar is equivalent to 14.5 psi or 100 kPa. One psi is equivalent to approximately 7 kPa. Some tire pressure gauges have scales for both units of measurement.

The tire pressure will vary from vehicle to vehicle, its use, and driver preference. Recommended tire pressures are located on the vehicle's tire placard, usually on the driver door pillar. The maximum tire pressure is located on the tire sidewall. Never inflate the tire above the maximum pressure listed on the sidewall. The tire may explode or the wheel rim may give way and cause a blowout, which can easily be fatal.

To use a tire pressure gauge, follow the steps in SKILL DRILL 20-1.

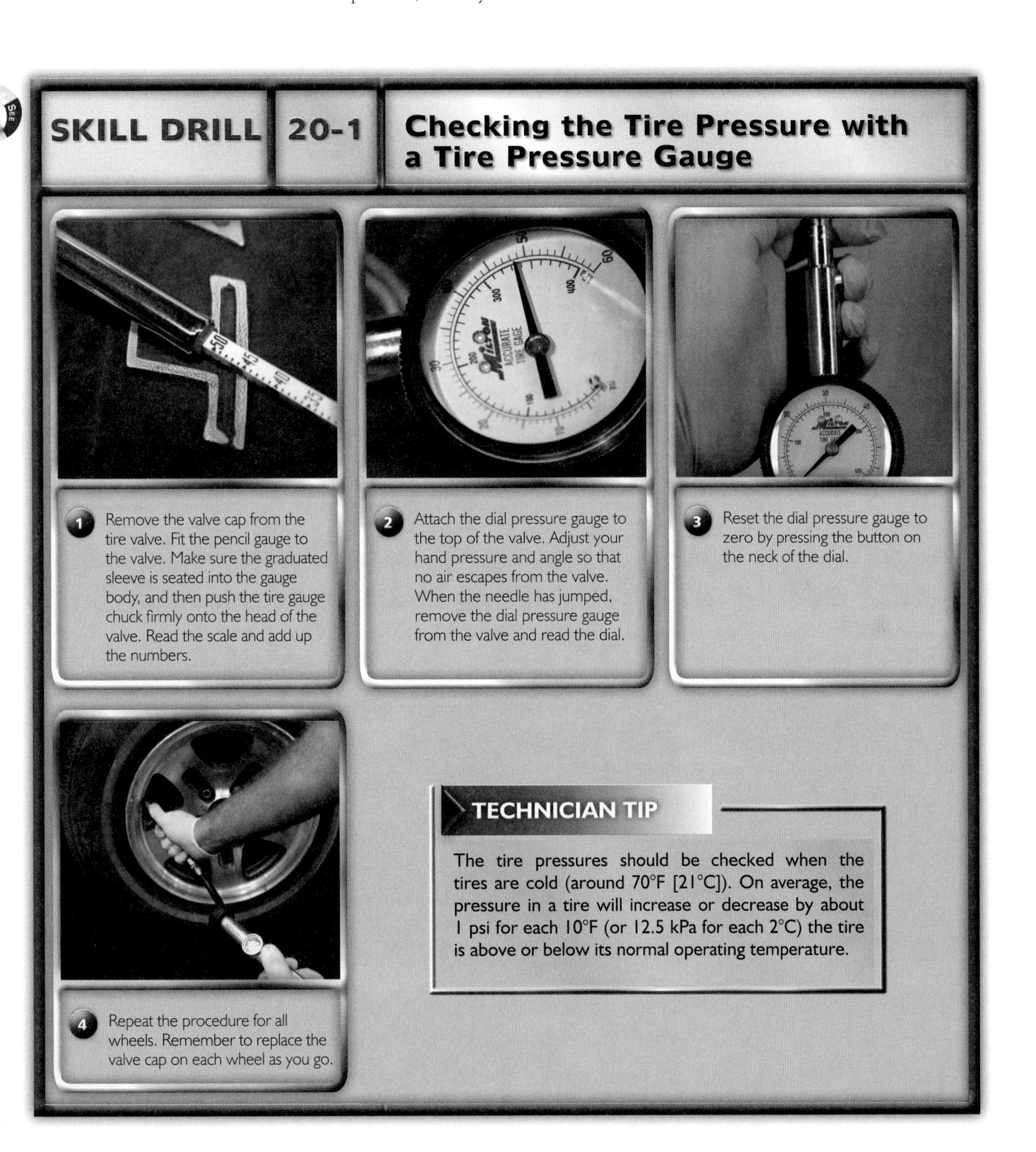
SKILL DRILL 20-1 Checking the Tire Pressure with a Tire Pressure Gauge
1 Remove the valve cap from the tire valve. Fit the pencil gauge to the valve. Make sure the graduated sleeve is seated into the gauge body, and then push the tire gauge chuck firmly onto the head of the valve. Read the scale and add up the numbers.
2 Attach the dial pressure gauge to the top of the valve. Adjust your hand pressure and angle so that no air escapes from the valve. When the needle has jumped, remove the dial pressure gauge from the valve and read the dial.
3 Reset the dial pressure gauge to zero by pressing the button on the neck of the dial.
4 Repeat the procedure for all wheels. Remember to replace the valve cap on each wheel as you go.
TECHNICIAN TIP
The tire pressures should be checked when the tires are cold (around 70°F [21°C]). On average, the pressure in a tire will increase or decrease by about 1 psi for each 10°F (or 12.5 kPa for each 2°C) the tire is above or below its normal operating temperature.

Caring for the Customer

Pocket-type tire pressure gauges are inexpensive and generally more accurate than the gauges provided by service stations. Service station gauges are often damaged by weather, misuse, or being run over. There may also be a significant difference in readings between the tire pressure gauge of one service station and the gauge from another service station. If the same pocket-type tire pressure gauge is always used to check tire pressures, then there will be no variation of readings.

Adjusting Tire Pressure

Even brand new high-quality tires lose air over time, so tire pressure needs to be adjusted periodically. It is good practice to check tire pressure at least monthly to catch a leaking tire. Vehicles that are 2008 model year and newer are required to be equipped with a TPMS, designed to monitor the pressures in each individual tire and alert the driver of a problem if a tire pressure is outside of the specified limits. These vehicles may have a specific tire inflation and TPMS reset procedure required by the manufacturer, so make sure you investigate that before inflating the tire.

Many tires are filled with nitrogen instead of regular air to reduce the amount of air that is lost over time as well as reduce oxidation of the rubber on the inside of the tire. It is best to fill these tires only with nitrogen to avoid introducing oxygen into the tire, but regular compressed air can be used in an emergency. Nitrogen-filled tires can usually be identified by a green cap on the valve stem. Nitrogen-filled tires are best topped off at the manufacturer's dealership or a tire store.

To adjust the tire pressure using a tire pressure gauge, follow the steps in **SKILL DRILL 20-2**.

Checking for Tire Wear Patterns

Tires come in a wide variety of tread patterns. Patterns differ based on the manufacturer and the tire's intended purpose. For example, tires designed to wick water away from the road surface will have deep grooves angled back toward the side of the road. Racing tires will have no grooves, as the smooth tire surface grips dry road surfaces tightly, increasing friction. Regardless of the exact pattern, all four tires should be inspected regularly to ensure they are wearing evenly. Irregular wear patterns are indicative of a problem. Common irregular wear patterns encountered include feathering, one-sided wear, cupping, center wear, and edge wear.

Feathering is observed as a rib with a slightly rounded edge on one side and a sharp edge on the other. This condition can be difficult to identify visually, so the technician should run a hand across the tire in both directions, feeling for the sharp edges. Feathering is most commonly a result of the tires set with excessive toe-in or toe-out.

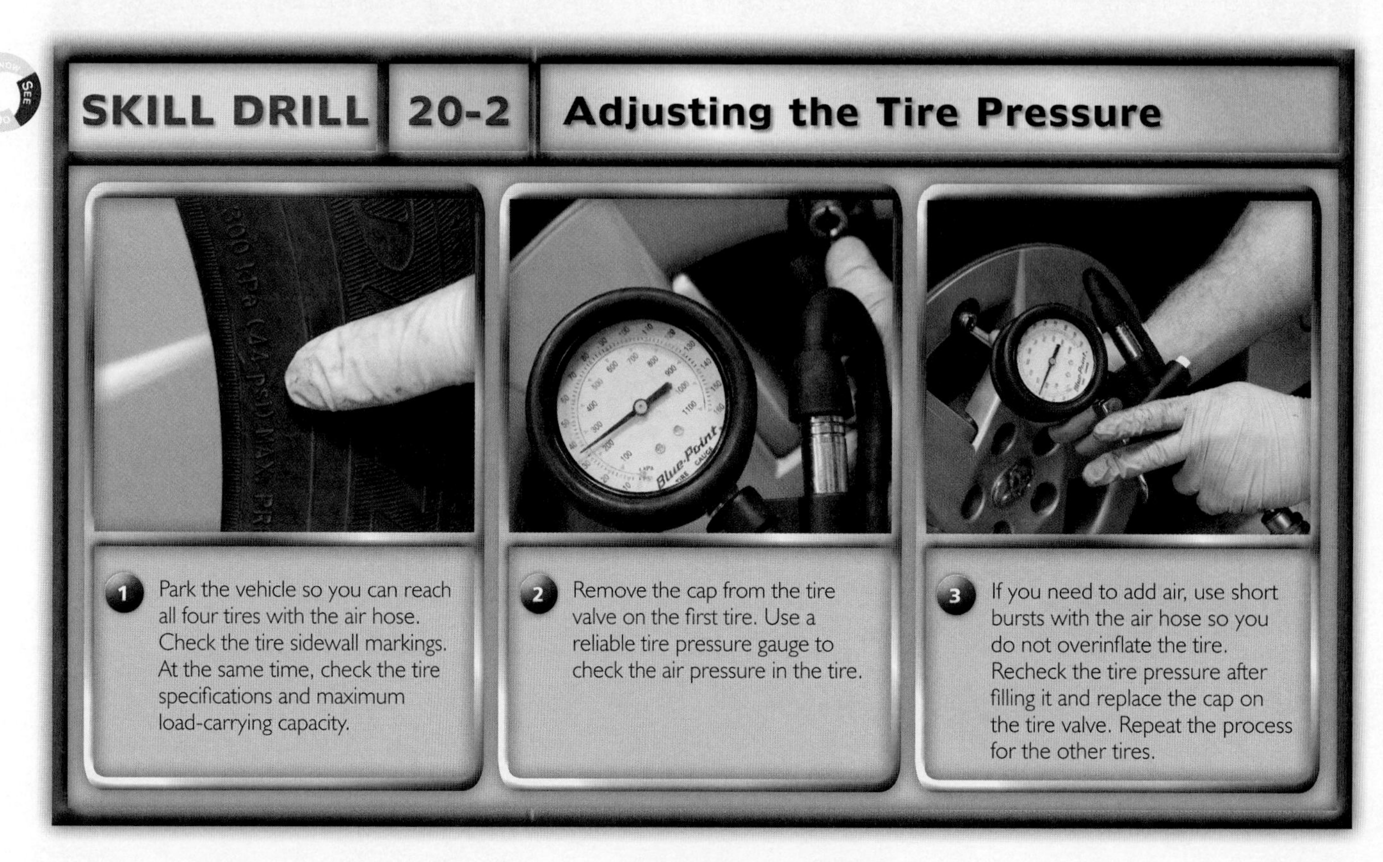

SKILL DRILL 20-2 Adjusting the Tire Pressure

1. Park the vehicle so you can reach all four tires with the air hose. Check the tire sidewall markings. At the same time, check the tire specifications and maximum load-carrying capacity.
2. Remove the cap from the tire valve on the first tire. Use a reliable tire pressure gauge to check the air pressure in the tire.
3. If you need to add air, use short bursts with the air hose so you do not overinflate the tire. Recheck the tire pressure after filling it and replace the cap on the tire valve. Repeat the process for the other tires.

If the tire's sharp edge is toward the outside of the treads, then the tire is toed out. If there are sharp edges toward the inside of the treads, then the tire is toed in. One-sided wear refers to ribs on one side of the tire wearing out faster than those on the other side. This type of wear indicates that the wheels are not properly aligned. Cupping is the appearance of dips around the edge of the tread, usually on just one side of the tire. It occurs when one or more suspension parts are worn or bent. Center wear is when the ribs in the middle of the tire wear faster than those on each side. It results from driving on overinflated tires. Edge wear occurs when the ribs on the outer edges of the tire wear out faster than those in the middle of the tire (the reverse of center wear). It indicates that the vehicle has been driven with the tires consistently underinflated, or the driver regularly corners the vehicle at excessive speeds.

To check for tire wear patterns, follow the steps in SKILL DRILL 20-3.

Rotating the Tires

Rotating the tires to new positions on the vehicle helps to even out the tire wear, which extends their useful life. Manufacturers recommend certain tire rotation patterns for their vehicles, so always research this information for the vehicle you are working on. Many manufacturers recommend tire rotations at every oil change. This means that the tires generally should be rotated at intervals of approximately 5000 to 10,000 miles (8000 to

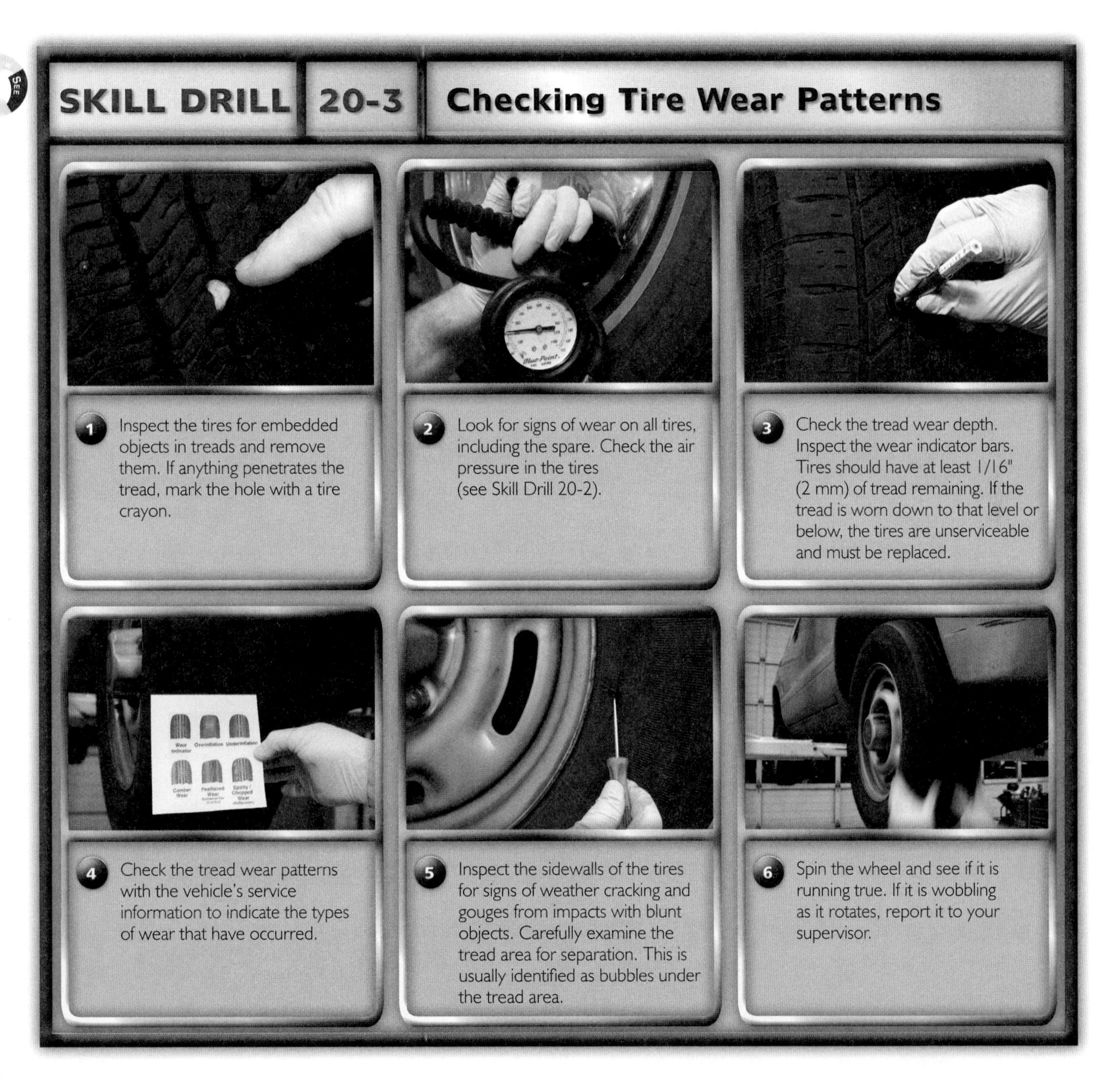
SKILL DRILL 20-3 Checking Tire Wear Patterns
1 Inspect the tires for embedded objects in treads and remove them. If anything penetrates the tread, mark the hole with a tire crayon.
2 Look for signs of wear on all tires, including the spare. Check the air pressure in the tires (see Skill Drill 20-2).
3 Check the tread wear depth. Inspect the wear indicator bars. Tires should have at least 1/16" (2 mm) of tread remaining. If the tread is worn down to that level or below, the tires are unserviceable and must be replaced.
4 Check the tread wear patterns with the vehicle's service information to indicate the types of wear that have occurred.
5 Inspect the sidewalls of the tires for signs of weather cracking and gouges from impacts with blunt objects. Carefully examine the tread area for separation. This is usually identified as bubbles under the tread area.
6 Spin the wheel and see if it is running true. If it is wobbling as it rotates, report it to your supervisor.

16,000 km). When the tires are removed, it is a good time to measure brake lining thickness and look for any leaks or damage to the brake assembly.

To rotate the tires, follow the steps in SKILL DRILL 20-4.

Dismounting a Tire

Tires generally need to be removed from a rim for only a few reasons: replacing old tires with new tires, patching a leaky tire, and possibly switching between snow tires and regular tires. Since the tire is held in place by the air pressure forcing the bead of the tire into the wheel flange, repeatedly removing a tire from its wheels risks damaging the sealing surface of the bead. So it is best to remove the tire only when absolutely necessary.

Dismounting a tire is usually performed on a tire machine, which is very powerful, so use extreme care and closely follow the manufacturer's procedure. Tire machines are strong enough to break the bead loose from the rim as well as hold the rim while the bead is forced over the flange during removal and installation. This means the tire machine has several operations that you must become familiar with. Since different machines

SKILL DRILL 20-4 Rotating the Tires

1. Prepare the vehicle by removing any hubcaps or lug nut covers. If using hand tools, break loose the lug or wheel nuts while some of the weight is still on the ground, then raise the vehicle to a comfortable working position.
2. Remove the lug nuts and place them in a convenient place such as the arm of the hoist.
3. Remove the tire and wheel from the vehicle. Rotate the tires to the new specified position.
4. Reinstall the lug nuts by hand at least two full turns, making sure the correct side of the lug nut is facing the wheel. Do *not* put the nut or stud into the socket of an impact wrench and power them on directly. Tighten the lug nuts to the correct torque in the proper tightening sequence as specified in the service information.

TECHNICIAN TIP

Lug nuts and lug bolts are designed with a specific grade (i.e., strength or amount of holding force) indicating a certain amount of stretch. Why do they stretch? Through proper torque, which stretches the bolt, stretching is what allows the threads of the stud/bolt to tightly mate to prevent them from working loose. Also, the torque listed for lug nuts is a dry torque, meaning that no lubricant should be used. Using a lubricant will cause the lug nuts to be overtorqued, which will likely result in failure.

As with all types of wheels, retorquing lug nuts per the manufacturer's specifications is typically recommended between 25 and 100 miles (40 to 160 km) after the initial tightening. Always refer to the owner's manual for proper factory specifications, which take precedence over any listed recommendations.

have different operating parameters, make sure you understand the manufacturer's specified operating procedure.

The turntable jaws on the tire changer can hold the rim by grasping it from the outside or the inside. When mounting an alloy rim, it is normal that the rim be clamped from the outside, whereas steel rims are clamped from the inside. Always check the instruction manual for the tire changer you are using for the correct method of clamping a rim.

To dismount a tire, follow the steps in **SKILL DRILL 20-5**.

> **TECHNICIAN TIP**
>
> Always remove any balance weights from both sides of the rim before mounting it on the tire changer. If they are not removed, the bead remover could drag the weights around the rim, causing damage to the rim face. This is particularly important with alloy rims. The damage done by the balance weights is not repairable and usually requires the rim to be replaced, costing the shop a lot of money.

SKILL DRILL 20-5 Dismounting a Tire

1. Before removing the tire, check to see if the wheel is equipped with a TPMS sensor. If it is, follow the manufacturer's procedures. Inspect the tread and sidewalls for any sharp cords sticking out that could injure you. If there is any damage, the tire should be discarded.

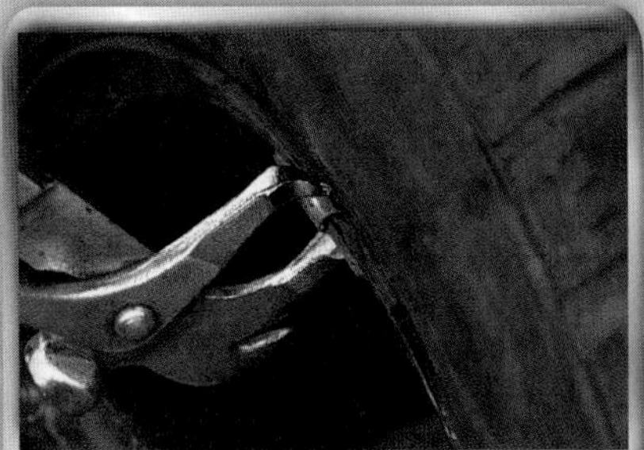

2. Check the wheel for any balance weights, and pry them off with the wheel weight tool.

3. Locate the valve stem, unscrew the dust cap, and store it for later use. Using the valve core tool, unscrew the valve core carefully.

4. Once all the air has been removed from the tire, locate the wheel in the bead breaker with the outside of the rim facing toward the blade. Locate the blade close to the edge of the rim while keeping your hands at a safe distance. Activate the bead breaker, which will force the tire bead away from the edge of the rim and over the safety ridge.

5. Release the blade, turn the wheel one-third to one-half of a turn, reposition the blade, and release this section of the tire as well. Release the blade. Roll the tire away from the machine, and reposition it with the inside of the rim facing toward the blade. Repeat the bead-breaking procedure on all four tires.

6. Set the wheel on the turntable with the shallow dish side of the wheel facing up. Position the wheel and tire assembly on the turntable and activate the jaws so the wheel is centered in the jaws. Activate the turntable to verify that the wheel is centered and securely held.

SKILL DRILL 20-5 Dismounting a Tire, continued

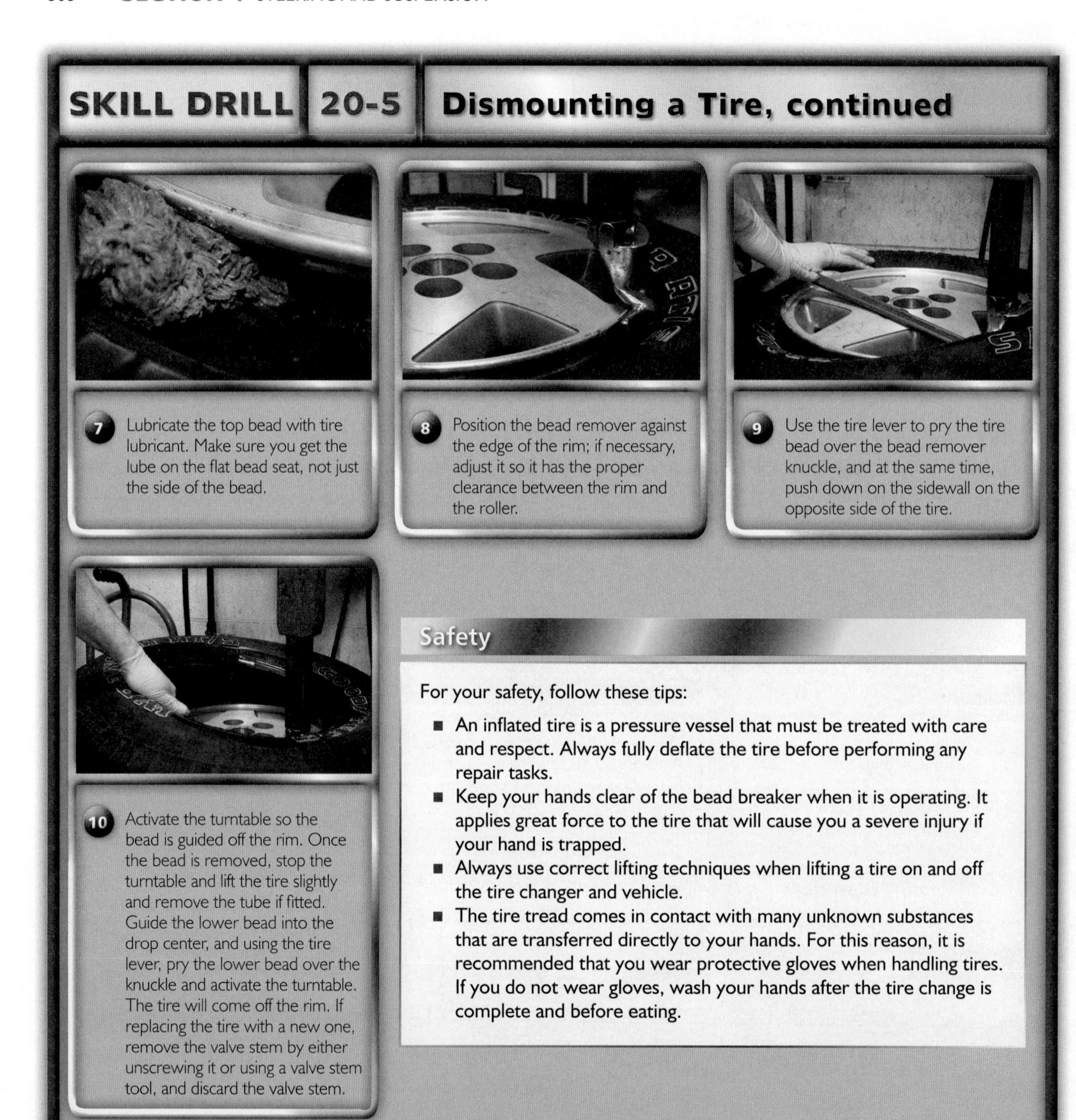

7 Lubricate the top bead with tire lubricant. Make sure you get the lube on the flat bead seat, not just the side of the bead.

8 Position the bead remover against the edge of the rim; if necessary, adjust it so it has the proper clearance between the rim and the roller.

9 Use the tire lever to pry the tire bead over the bead remover knuckle, and at the same time, push down on the sidewall on the opposite side of the tire.

10 Activate the turntable so the bead is guided off the rim. Once the bead is removed, stop the turntable and lift the tire slightly and remove the tube if fitted. Guide the lower bead into the drop center, and using the tire lever, pry the lower bead over the knuckle and activate the turntable. The tire will come off the rim. If replacing the tire with a new one, remove the valve stem by either unscrewing it or using a valve stem tool, and discard the valve stem.

Safety

For your safety, follow these tips:

- An inflated tire is a pressure vessel that must be treated with care and respect. Always fully deflate the tire before performing any repair tasks.
- Keep your hands clear of the bead breaker when it is operating. It applies great force to the tire that will cause you a severe injury if your hand is trapped.
- Always use correct lifting techniques when lifting a tire on and off the tire changer and vehicle.
- The tire tread comes in contact with many unknown substances that are transferred directly to your hands. For this reason, it is recommended that you wear protective gloves when handling tires. If you do not wear gloves, wash your hands after the tire change is complete and before eating.

Replacing a Valve Stem

Valve stems come in a few styles: rubber press-fit valve stems, screw-in valve stems, and TPMS sensor–integrated valve stems. Rubber press-fit stems are normally replaced when new tires are mounted on the rims. Screw-in valve stems normally are not replaced, but may have rubber washers or O-rings that may require replacement when new tires are installed. TPMS-integrated valve stems may be made as part of the valve stem or may screw onto, or snap into, the valve stem, which is replaceable. It is important to know if the TPMS sensor is connected to the valve stem or not so you do not damage it during service and repair. Many TPMS valve stems have valve cores with coated threads and should not be replaced with noncoated threads. They should always be torqued with a valve core torque wrench.

Valve stems can also be damaged by trauma from loose objects on the road, from scraping into curbs or other low structures, or through improper tire changes. Luckily, valve stems are generally inexpensive and relatively easy to replace. To change the valve stem, the wheel must be removed from the vehicle. The tire is then deflated and the top bead broken. On some tires, the sidewall can be pushed down by hand to gain access to the valve stem. In other instances, the tire must be removed from the rim.

After removing the old rubber valve stem, a new one is put into place with some lubricant around the base of the stem. The stem is then pulled into place using the proper installing tool. The tire is reassembled and inflated to the recommended pressure. Spray some soapy water around the valve stem and core to detect air leaks.

For the valve stems that have a threaded shank with a locking nut and sealing washers, the process is similar. The wheel is removed from the vehicle, deflated, and the top bead is broken. The nut on the valve stem is then unscrewed and the stem is removed from the inside of the rim. The old sealing washers can be replaced with new ones. Then the valve stem can be reinstalled in the rim. In some cases only the valve stem core requires replacement. In this case, the old core is screwed out and the new core is installed and the tire pressure re-adjusted to vehicle specifications.

To replace a rubber press-fit valve stem, follow the steps in **SKILL DRILL 20-6**.

To replace a screw-in valve stem, follow the steps in **SKILL DRILL 20-7**.

SKILL DRILL 20-6 Replacing a Rubber Press-Fit Valve Stem

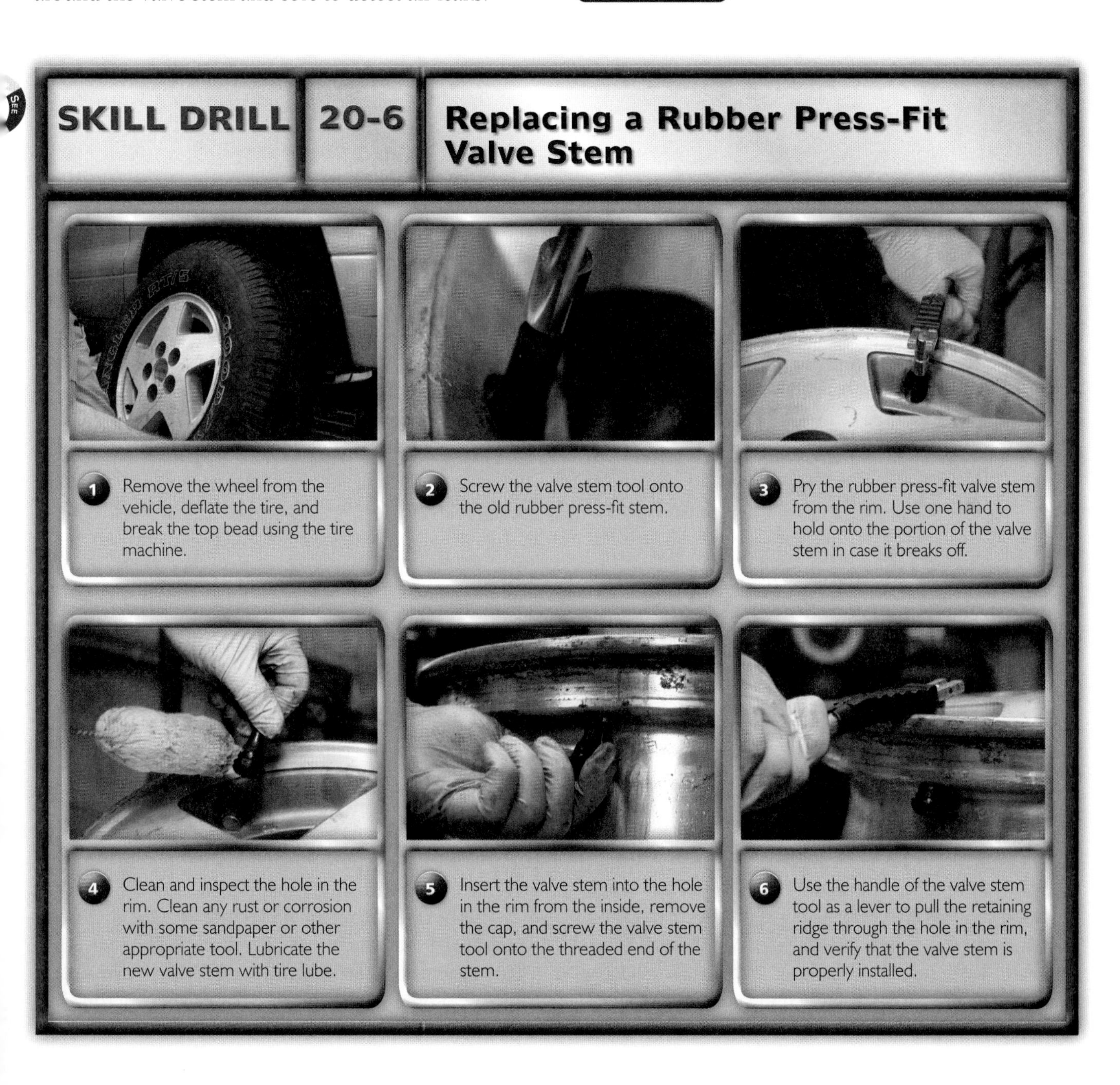

1. Remove the wheel from the vehicle, deflate the tire, and break the top bead using the tire machine.
2. Screw the valve stem tool onto the old rubber press-fit stem.
3. Pry the rubber press-fit valve stem from the rim. Use one hand to hold onto the portion of the valve stem in case it breaks off.
4. Clean and inspect the hole in the rim. Clean any rust or corrosion with some sandpaper or other appropriate tool. Lubricate the new valve stem with tire lube.
5. Insert the valve stem into the hole in the rim from the inside, remove the cap, and screw the valve stem tool onto the threaded end of the stem.
6. Use the handle of the valve stem tool as a lever to pull the retaining ridge through the hole in the rim, and verify that the valve stem is properly installed.

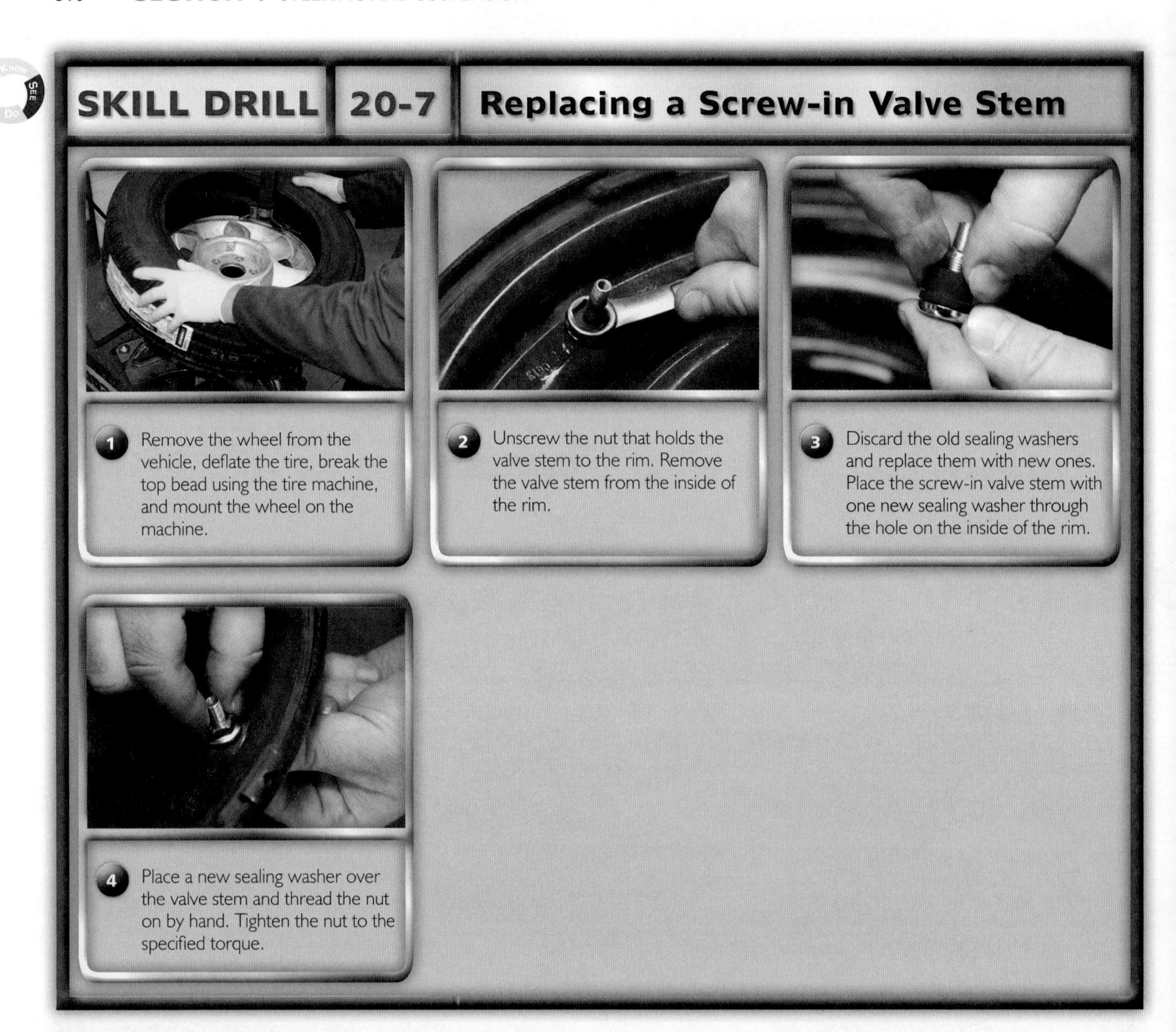
SKILL DRILL 20-7 Replacing a Screw-in Valve Stem
1 Remove the wheel from the vehicle, deflate the tire, break the top bead using the tire machine, and mount the wheel on the machine.
2 Unscrew the nut that holds the valve stem to the rim. Remove the valve stem from the inside of the rim.
3 Discard the old sealing washers and replace them with new ones. Place the screw-in valve stem with one new sealing washer through the hole on the inside of the rim.
4 Place a new sealing washer over the valve stem and thread the nut on by hand. Tighten the nut to the specified torque.

Mounting a Tire

In today's vehicles, mounting a tire means more than just installing a properly sized tire onto the rim. Since tires do not come perfectly round and balanced, most tire manufacturers indicate the tire's highest point with a red dot and the tire's lightest point with a yellow dot. The red dot should be lined up with the rim's lowest point, which is called **match mounting**. The yellow dot should be matched up with the rim's heaviest point, which is called **weight matching**. These points occur innately as part of the manufacturing process because it is impossible to create an absolutely perfect, even, round tire. Slight variations in density and shape of the tire are unavoidable. Matching up the tire and rim using one of these methods will help avoid "tolerance stacking," which is when tolerances in mating parts are aligned in such a way that the tolerances are added together, rather than canceling each other out. In the case of wheels and tires, it would occur when the tire's heavy or high points are aligned with the rim's heavy or high points.

In addition, the type of tread—directional, symmetric, and asymmetric—affects the direction in which tires are mounted on the rims and which side of the vehicle they are installed on. Directional tires are designed to operate better in one direction, requiring that they be mounted accordingly. Symmetric tires can be operated in either direction, so they can be mounted in either direction. Asymmetric tires are generally side specific, but they may also be directional, in which case specific tires must be mounted on certain rims. Do not fit a tire that is too wide or too narrow for the rim. Check the tire manufacturer's recommendation for the correct range of rim sizes for a particular tire.

> **TECHNICIAN TIP**
>
> Most tire changers dismount and mount the tire by turning the turntable clockwise. This is especially helpful to know so you position the tire on the turntable correctly to mount and dismount tires equipped with a TPMS.

The turntable jaws on the tire machine can hold the rim by grasping it from the outside or the inside. When mounting an alloy rim, it is normal that they be clamped from the outside, whereas steel rims are usually clamped from the inside. If the tire is clamped from the outside on the tire machine, it is necessary to release the clamps before fully inflating the tire. Always check the instruction manual for the tire machine you are using for the correct method of clamping a rim.

Inflating a tire for the first time is always dangerous. Some types of tires, such as split rims, must be inflated inside of a tire cage. Doing so contains any pieces if the tire blows up while being inflated. Always follow the manufacturer's guidelines and shop policies when inflating a newly installed tire.

To mount a tire, follow the steps in **SKILL DRILL 20-8**.

SKILL DRILL 20-8 Mounting a Tire

1. Mount the wheel to the tire machine. Examine the wheel and remove any rust or dirt from the rim bead seat.
2. Select the correct type of tubeless valve stem, lube it with tire lube, and insert it through the hole in the rim from the inside. Using the valve stem tool, pull the stem through until its groove locates in the hole. Use the valve core tool to unscrew the valve core from the valve stem.
3. Apply some lubricant to the tire bead and rim ridges.
4. Position the tire on top of the rim so that a portion of the lower bead is positioned in the drop center while keeping the lower bead in the tire machine guide.
5. Activate the turntable and guide the lower tire bead onto the rim.
6. Once the lower bead is fitted, position the upper bead into the guide while holding the other side of the upper bead in the drop center.

SKILL DRILL 20-8 Mounting a Tire, continued

7 Activate the turntable and guide the tire onto the rim. As the turntable rotates, push the sidewall down, keeping your fingers clear of the rim, so that the tire bead is guided below the safety ridge into the drop center.

8 Attach the tire inflator chuck to the valve stem. Stand clear of the tire and inflate it, being careful to not exceed 30 psi (207 kPa) if both beads have not seated against the rim. If they have not seated by 30 psi, deflate the tire and inspect the rim and tire for damage. If they are OK, relube the tire and rim and reattempt to inflate the tire. If it still will not seat the beads by 30 psi, inform your supervisor.

9 Check the location of the bead indicator ridge to make sure the bead is fully seated. If the rim is clamped from the outside, it will be necessary to release the clamps so the tire can inflate fully.

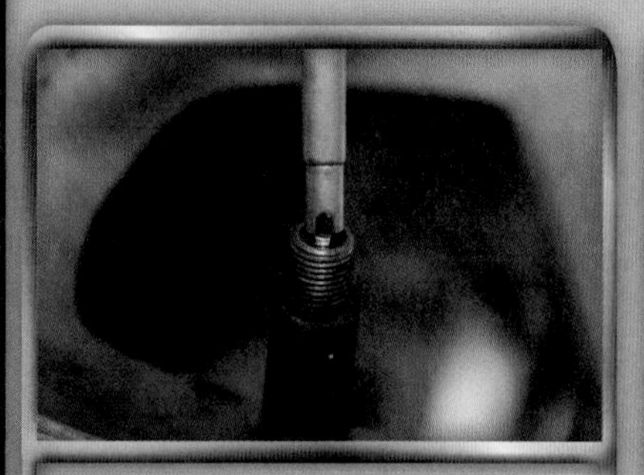

10 When the beads are properly seated, remove the tire inflator chuck, keeping your hands and face clear of the valve stem opening. Once the tire has completely deflated, screw the valve core into the valve stem using the valve core tool.

25
30
35
40
20
45
15
50
10
55
60
psi
bar
80-200 PSI
LINE PRESSURE

11 Reattach the inflator, stand clear, and inflate the tire to the correct pressure as listed on the vehicle's tire placard or in the owner's manual. Be careful to *never* exceed the maximum tire pressure listed on the tire sidewall.

12 Use a soft brush and apply a small amount of soapy water to the bead. If there are any air leaks, they will be indicated by bubbles.

Safety

Overinflated tires can explode. Do not inflate the tire to a pressure greater than what is listed on the sidewall. The possibility of an explosion is why tire inflators have a spring-loaded (dead man's) trigger that does not lock into position. When the tire is being inflated, use a tire cage if required, or an inflator that allows you to stand clear of the tire. Keep hands and body well away from the tire. When a tire explodes, the tire, rim, or components from the tire changer may cause serious injury or death to any person nearby.

Dismounting, Inspecting, and Remounting a Tire on a Wheel Equipped with a TPMS Sensor

Dismounting and mounting tires equipped with a TPMS requires special care to avoid damaging the expensive sensors mounted inside the wheels. There are two general ways that TPMS sensors are mounted in the wheel. The first way involves either attaching it to the valve stem or making it integral to the valve stem, so care must be exercised around the valve stem area. If the TPMS sensor is integrated into the valve stem with a threaded locknut on the valve stem, some manufacturers recommend unscrewing the locknut and pushing the valve stem and TPMS sensor into the tire for safekeeping during disassembly. The second way is by using a band that fits all the way around the drop center of the rim to hold the TPMS sensor to the inside of the wheel. In many cases, the band-style TPMS sensor is positioned 180 degrees away from the valve stem, so care must be exercised on the side opposite of the valve stem. Always check the service information to verify the manufacturer's specified tire dismounting and mounting procedure.

To dismount, inspect, and remount a tire on a wheel equipped with a TPMS sensor, follow the steps in **SKILL DRILL 20-9**.

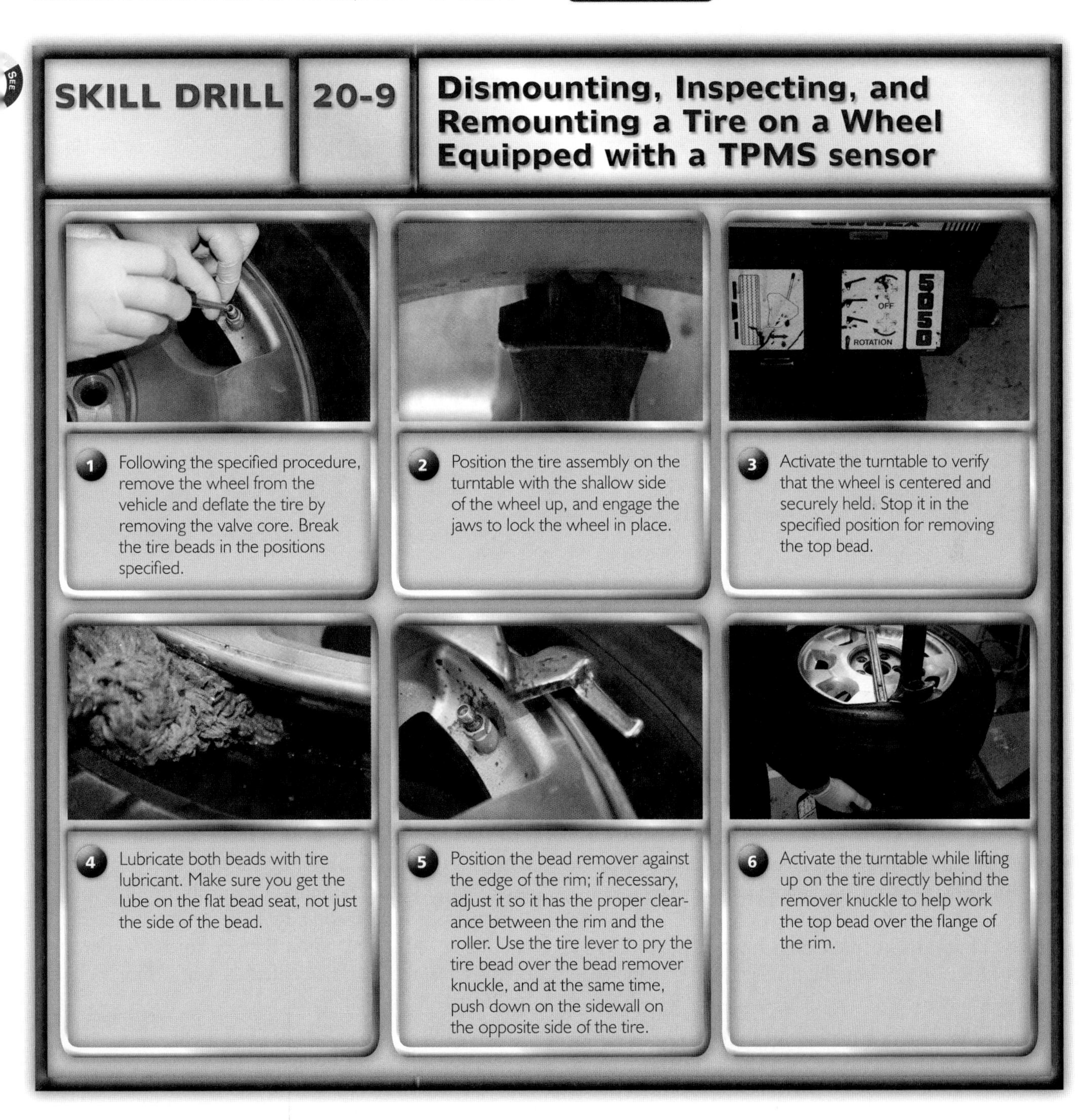
SKILL DRILL 20-9 Dismounting, Inspecting, and Remounting a Tire on a Wheel Equipped with a TPMS sensor
OFF
ROTATION
5050
1 Following the specified procedure, remove the wheel from the vehicle and deflate the tire by removing the valve core. Break the tire beads in the positions specified.
2 Position the tire assembly on the turntable with the shallow side of the wheel up, and engage the jaws to lock the wheel in place.
3 Activate the turntable to verify that the wheel is centered and securely held. Stop it in the specified position for removing the top bead.
4 Lubricate both beads with tire lubricant. Make sure you get the lube on the flat bead seat, not just the side of the bead.
5 Position the bead remover against the edge of the rim; if necessary, adjust it so it has the proper clearance between the rim and the roller. Use the tire lever to pry the tire bead over the bead remover knuckle, and at the same time, push down on the sidewall on the opposite side of the tire.
6 Activate the turntable while lifting up on the tire directly behind the remover knuckle to help work the top bead over the flange of the rim.

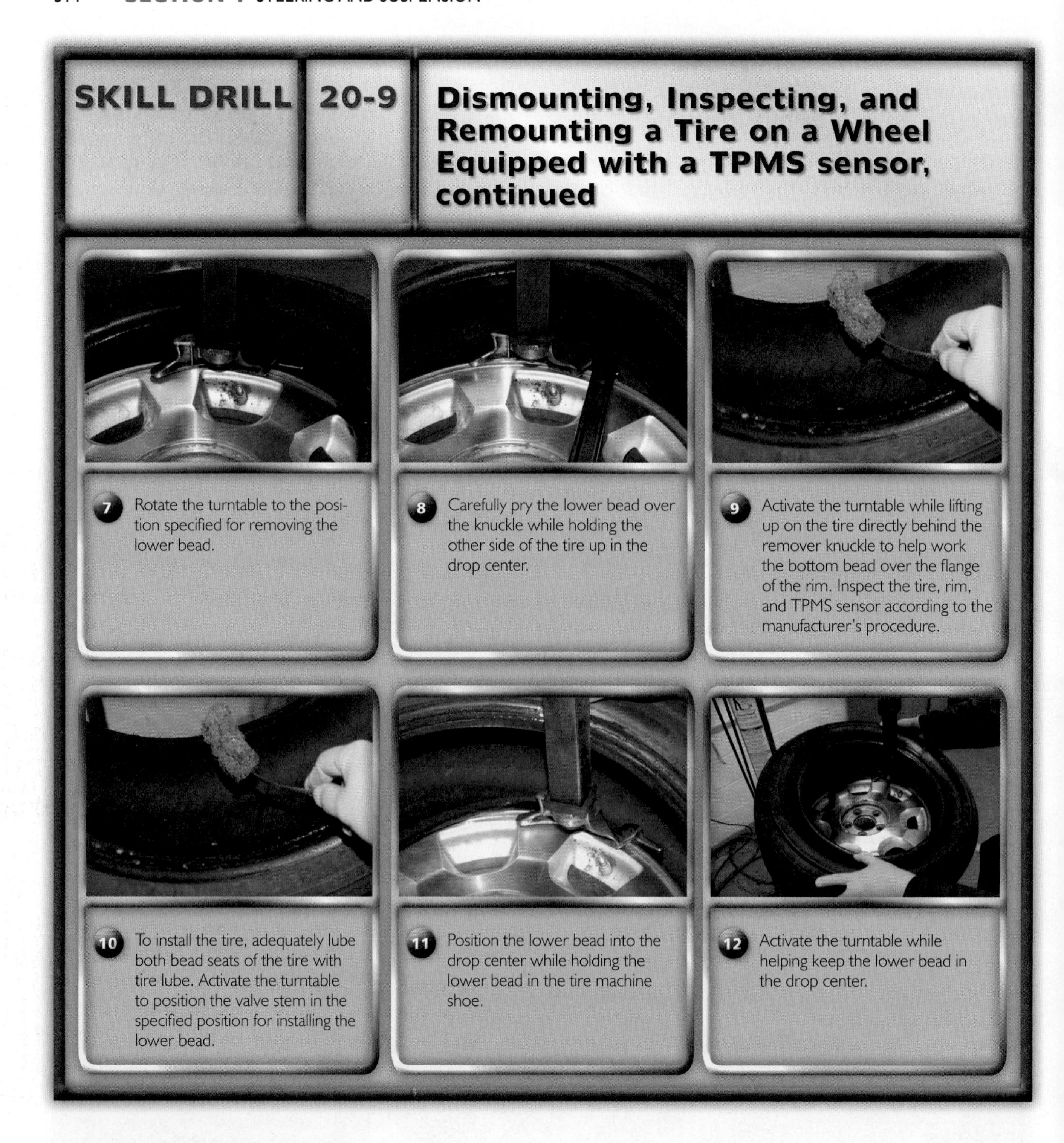
SKILL DRILL 20-9 Dismounting, Inspecting, and Remounting a Tire on a Wheel Equipped with a TPMS sensor, continued
7 Rotate the turntable to the position specified for removing the lower bead.
8 Carefully pry the lower bead over the knuckle while holding the other side of the tire up in the drop center.
9 Activate the turntable while lifting up on the tire directly behind the remover knuckle to help work the bottom bead over the flange of the rim. Inspect the tire, rim, and TPMS sensor according to the manufacturer's procedure.
10 To install the tire, adequately lube both bead seats of the tire with tire lube. Activate the turntable to position the valve stem in the specified position for installing the lower bead.
11 Position the lower bead into the drop center while holding the lower bead in the tire machine shoe.
12 Activate the turntable while helping keep the lower bead in the drop center.

Dynamic Balancing a Tire

A tire that is dynamically in balance is in balance when it is spinning as opposed to when it is stationary. Dynamic imbalance occurs when a spot on either the inside or the outside of the tire's centerline is heavy. This induces a side-to-side imbalance in the tire as it rotates, which can cause a vibration as well as the steering wheel to shimmy. Dynamic imbalance is usually a result of manufacturing variations, but it can be caused by a damaged tire or wheel. Obviously, dynamic imbalance reduces ride quality and tends to increase wear on the tires and on steering and suspension system components. Dynamic balancing of the tires should be performed when new tires are installed on the vehicle as well as any time that tire imbalance is suspected.

Dynamic balancing is performed on a tire balancer that is capable of spinning the tire and then measuring

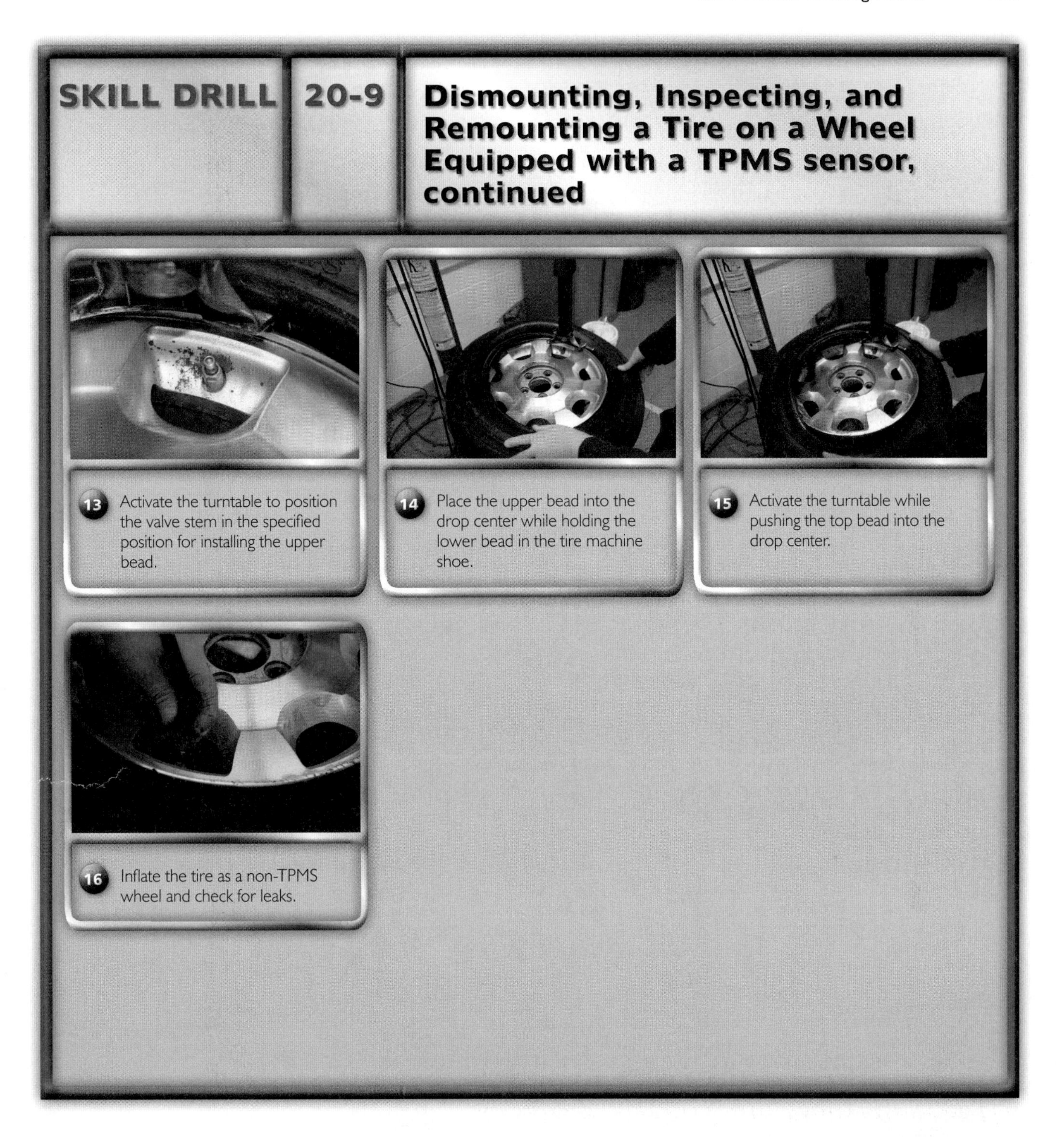

SKILL DRILL 20-9 Dismounting, Inspecting, and Remounting a Tire on a Wheel Equipped with a TPMS sensor, continued

13 Activate the turntable to position the valve stem in the specified position for installing the upper bead.

14 Place the upper bead into the drop center while holding the lower bead in the tire machine shoe.

15 Activate the turntable while pushing the top bead into the drop center.

16 Inflate the tire as a non-TPMS wheel and check for leaks.

the location of any dynamic imbalance. Some balancers are spun at low speed, but others are driven by the balancer at higher speeds. If the tire is spun by the balancer, embedded objects may fly off the tire, so it is important to wear safety glasses. If the wheel balancer is fitted with a safety hood, ensure that it is in place when the wheel is being rotated to further protect against flying objects.

All wheels require one of several specific designs of wheel weights. If the weights fitted to the wheel are not the correct type, they can fly off when the vehicle is driven down the road, causing possible injury or damage. It is good practice to use new wheel weights when balancing a wheel for the same reason. If the vehicle has directional tires, ensure that the wheels are reinstalled in their correct position when balancing is complete.

To balance a tire, follow the steps in SKILL DRILL 20-10.

SKILL DRILL 20-10 Balancing a Tire

TIRE AND LOADING INFORMATION/
PNEUS ET CHARGE-INFORMATION
SEATING CAPACITY | TOTAL 7 | FRONT 2 | REAR 5
NOMBRE DE SIÈGES | TOTAL 7 | AVANT 2 | ARRIÈRE 5
The combined weight of occupants and cargo should never exceed 506 kg or 1120 lbs.
Le poids combiné des occupants et du chargement ne doit jamais excéder 506 kg ou 1120 lb.
TIRE/ PNEU | SIZE/ DIMENSION | COLD TIRE PRESSURE/ PRESSION À FROID
FRONT/ AVANT | P235/60R18 | 210kPa, 30psi
REAR/ ARRIÈRE | P235/60R18 | 210kPa, 30psi
SPARE/ SECOURS | T165/90R17 | 420kPa, 60psi
SEE OWNER'S MANUAL FOR ADDITIONAL INFORMATION
CONSULTER LE GUIDE DU PROPRIETAIRE POUR OBTENIR DES RENSEIGNEMENTS ADDITIONNELS
CM-C08

1. If using hand tools, prepare the vehicle by loosening the lug nuts, and then raise the vehicle into a comfortable working position. Check that the tires fitted to the wheels on the vehicle are the appropriate size and rating for the vehicle.

2. Mark the inside of the wheel or tire in relation to its location on the vehicle and then remove it.

3. Check and adjust the tire pressure before balancing the tire. Mount the wheel and tire on the balancer, putting the inside part of the wheel toward the balancer in most cases. Secure the wheel by screwing the hub nut assembly on the balancer shaft.

4. Calibrate the balancer to the wheel by measuring the width of the rim with a rim caliper, using the gauge on the balancer to determine the offset location of the flange on the wheel, and the diameter of the wheel as listed on the tire. Input these data into the balancer's computer, if fitted. If no computer is fitted, set the balancer adjustments manually according to the instruction manual.

5. If equipped, lower the safety hood over the wheel. Spin the wheel.

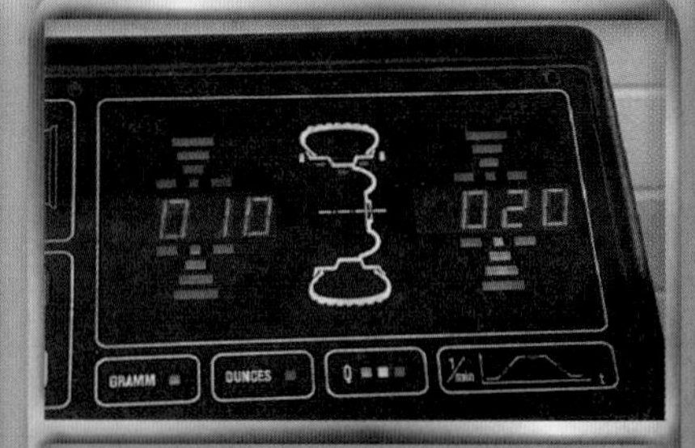
0 10
0 20
GRAMM
OUNCES

6. Read the balancer's analysis. If the wheel is out of balance, you should remove the old weights and recheck the balance of the wheel before adding new weights.

1.25

7. Install new weights as recommended by the machine's display.

ER BALANCER
.00
.00

8. Respin the wheel to check for accuracy of the balancing job and to confirm that balance has been achieved. Repeat the process for the rest of the wheels and tires. Reinstall the wheels and tires to the vehicle.

Inspecting the Wheel Assembly for Air Loss

One of the most frustrating complaints from drivers is that they constantly have to pump their tires up as the result of an air loss somewhere. To efficiently check the suspect tire, it must be removed from the vehicle and aired up to its recommended pressure. A preliminary check can be carried out with a spray bottle of soapy water. You need to spray the soapy water around the valve stem and core. In addition, spray around the bead area. Also spray the entire tread area. If there is any air leakage, soapy air bubbles will indicate where the problem is. Mark the tire where the air bubbles are coming from so that the repairs can be carried out.

Another good method for checking where the air loss is coming from is to immerse the wheel assembly in a container of water. The container must be large enough to immerse the tire either on its side, with the tire completely underwater, or upright, with approximately half the wheel assembly underwater. If there is a leak, it will be obvious by the discharge of air bubbles in the water FIGURE 20-21. Mark the source of the air bubbles. Remove the wheel from the water tank and carry out the appropriate repairs.

To inspect the wheel assembly for air loss using the spray bottle method, perform the steps in SKILL DRILL 20-11.

FIGURE 20-21 A good method for identifying the location of an air leak is to immerse the tire assembly in water and watch for air bubbles.

To inspect the wheel assembly for air loss using the dunk tank method, follow the steps in SKILL DRILL 20-12:

1. Place the tire into the dunk tank and hold it still.
2. Inspect the tire and wheel for any escaping bubbles, including the valve stem and core. If necessary, rotate the wheel assembly so that more of it can be held underwater to inspect for leaks.
3. Mark any leaks in the tire with a tire crayon.

SKILL DRILL 20-11 Inspecting the Wheel Assembly for Air Loss Using the Spray Bottle Method

1. Remove the tire from the vehicle and inflate it to its proper pressure. Using a spray bottle of soapy water, spray the valve stem and core, tire tread, and tire bead area. Inspect the tire, valve stem, and wheel assembly for bubbles.
2. Mark any leaks in the tire with a tire crayon.

Diagnosis

Tire Repair

Driving a short distance on a tire while it is severely underinflated will cause the tire to overheat as well as weaken the sidewall belts, creating a dangerous, nonrepairable condition. The damage is not visible from the outside, so every tire needing repairs must be removed from the wheel for inspection and to assess its repairability. The tire needs to be inspected externally first, then internally for any signs of serious damage, such as chaffing of the sidewalls or cords sticking through the inner liner. If the inspection shows no signs of nonrepairable failure, then the tire can be repaired in accordance with the procedures recommended by the tire associations, including the Rubber Manufacturers Association.

Repairs from any nail or similar object should be limited to the actual tread area. Among the criteria to perform a proper repair are:

- Repairs are limited to the tread area only.
- Puncture injury cannot be greater than 1/4" (6 mm) in diameter.
- Repairs must be performed by removing the tire from the rim/wheel assembly to perform a complete inspection to assess all damage that may be present.

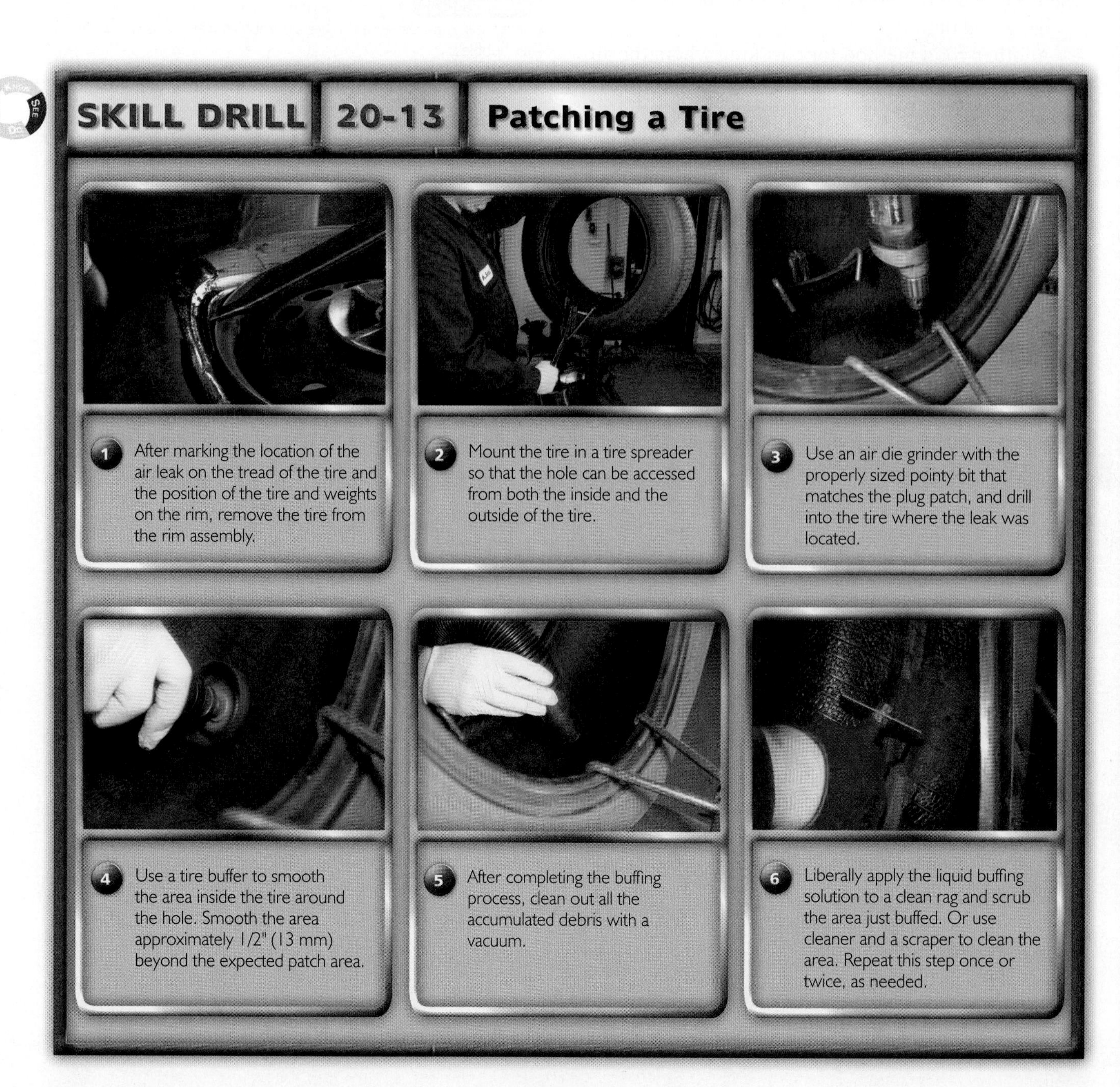

SKILL DRILL 20-13 Patching a Tire

1. After marking the location of the air leak on the tread of the tire and the position of the tire and weights on the rim, remove the tire from the rim assembly.
2. Mount the tire in a tire spreader so that the hole can be accessed from both the inside and the outside of the tire.
3. Use an air die grinder with the properly sized pointy bit that matches the plug patch, and drill into the tire where the leak was located.
4. Use a tire buffer to smooth the area inside the tire around the hole. Smooth the area approximately 1/2" (13 mm) beyond the expected patch area.
5. After completing the buffing process, clean out all the accumulated debris with a vacuum.
6. Liberally apply the liquid buffing solution to a clean rag and scrub the area just buffed. Or use cleaner and a scraper to clean the area. Repeat this step once or twice, as needed.

- Repairs cannot overlap. This means that if there are two or more repairs required to fix the tire, then each repair patch must not overlap.
- A rubber stem, or plug, must be applied to fill the puncture injury, and a patch must be applied to seal the inner liner. A common repair unit is a one-piece unit with a stem and patch portion. A plug by itself is an unacceptable repair.

To patch a tire, you will need a tire machine to remove the tire from the wheel, a buffer to clean the inside of the tire, glue for attaching the patch, and a tire plug patch. The tire plug patch is a superior product to the old-fashioned tire plug, and in many states, it is the only legal way to repair a hole in a tire. It is more expensive but is a much safer alternative for repairing a tire because it patches the inside of the tire in addition to filling the hole in the tire.

To patch a tire, follow the steps in SKILL DRILL 20-13.

Measuring Wheel, Tire, Axle Flange, and Hub Runout

Runout is the side-to-side or up-and-down variation in a part in the wheel assembly. In many cases, runout issues cannot be observed when the vehicle is stationary on the ground. Instead, runout problems can be felt as a vibration while the vehicle is being driven, usually getting more

SKILL DRILL 20-13 Patching a Tire, continued
7 Apply vulcanizing cement evenly to the inner buffed surface of the tire. The cement needs to stand until the cement is relatively dry and is only tacky to touch.
8 After selecting the appropriate tire patch, remove the plastic protective cover that is on the sticky side of the tire patch without getting your fingerprints on the sticky side.
9 Take the pointed part of the patch and push it through the inner side of the tire's hole that was roughed previously, pushing it through to the outside of the tire.
10 Using a pair of pliers, grip the stem of the patch and pull it out so that the disc portion of the patch comes into contact with the cemented area. Pull this pointy part of the patch away from the tire's tread. The sticky side of the patch has now been tightly pressed onto the buffed surface.
11 Use a stitching tool and roll the inner side of the tire patch tight onto the inner surface of the tire. Start at the center of the patch and work outward. Cover the buffed area and newly applied patch with a rubber patch sealant. Trim the plug material even with or just above the tread using a utility knife or other appropriate cutting tool.
12 After the rubber patch sealant has dried, the tire can be reassembled onto the rim in its original position and inflated to the recommended pressure. Check the wheel assembly for balance before it is reinstalled on the vehicle.

noticeable as speed is increased. If the vibration is primarily observed in the steering column or hood, the runout is most likely in one or both of the front wheel assemblies. Vibration felt throughout the entire vehicle suggests that the problem is with one or both of the back wheels.

Runout can be defined as radial or lateral. Radial runout occurs when the component is out of round or off center and is felt more as a vertical vibration. Lateral runout occurs when the component is bent or improperly manufactured and causes the wheels to jiggle side to side, creating a horizontal vibration that feels like a shimmy. Lateral runout is felt in the steering wheel even at slower speeds. Runout of the wheel, tire, axle, and hub are all measured in the same way using a special runout gauge inserted onto the surface of the component being measured.

To measure tire runout, follow the steps in SKILL DRILL 20-14.

SKILL DRILL 20-14 Measuring Tire Runout

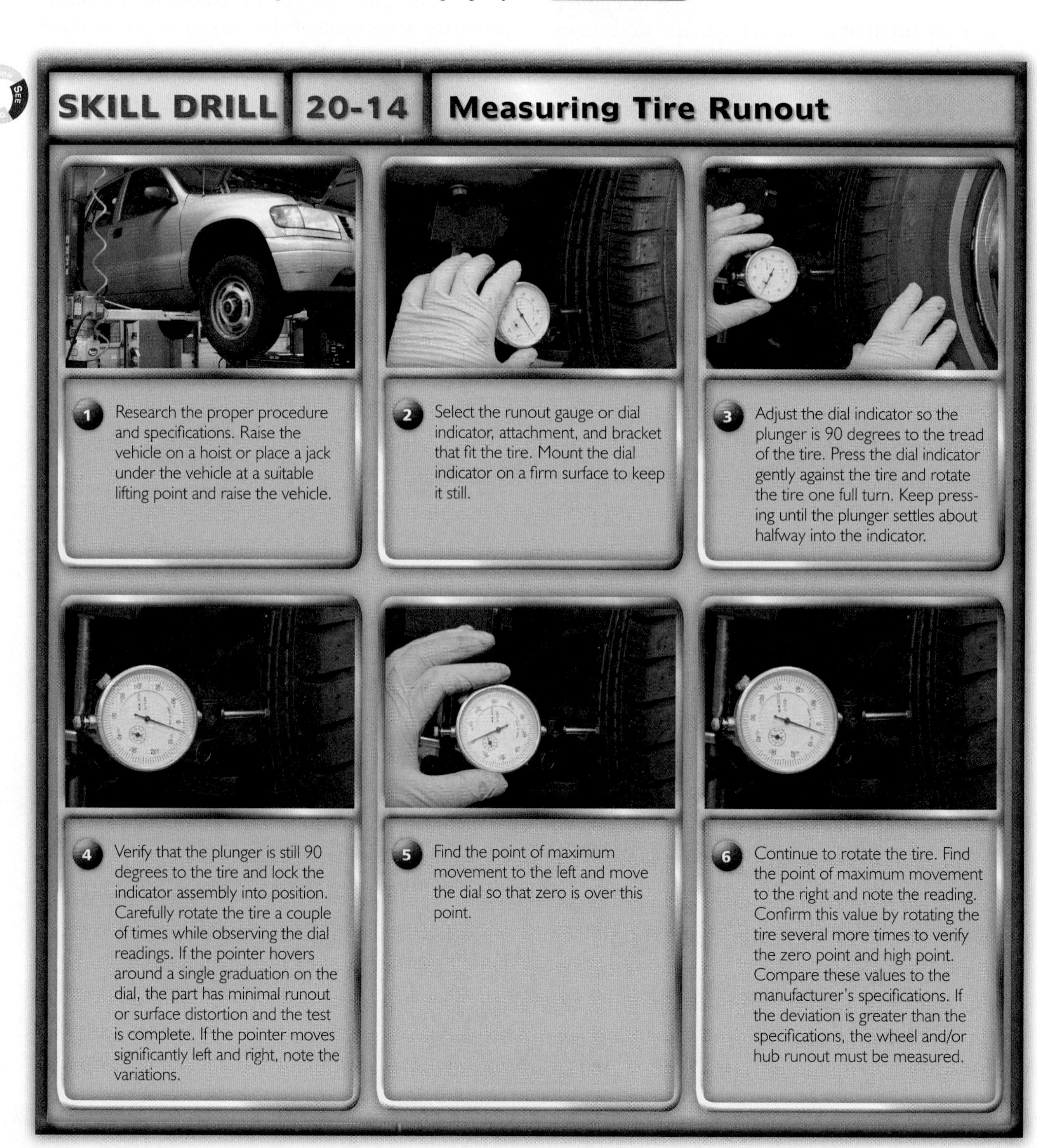

1. Research the proper procedure and specifications. Raise the vehicle on a hoist or place a jack under the vehicle at a suitable lifting point and raise the vehicle.
2. Select the runout gauge or dial indicator, attachment, and bracket that fit the tire. Mount the dial indicator on a firm surface to keep it still.
3. Adjust the dial indicator so the plunger is 90 degrees to the tread of the tire. Press the dial indicator gently against the tire and rotate the tire one full turn. Keep pressing until the plunger settles about halfway into the indicator.
4. Verify that the plunger is still 90 degrees to the tire and lock the indicator assembly into position. Carefully rotate the tire a couple of times while observing the dial readings. If the pointer hovers around a single graduation on the dial, the part has minimal runout or surface distortion and the test is complete. If the pointer moves significantly left and right, note the variations.
5. Find the point of maximum movement to the left and move the dial so that zero is over this point.
6. Continue to rotate the tire. Find the point of maximum movement to the right and note the reading. Confirm this value by rotating the tire several more times to verify the zero point and high point. Compare these values to the manufacturer's specifications. If the deviation is greater than the specifications, the wheel and/or hub runout must be measured.

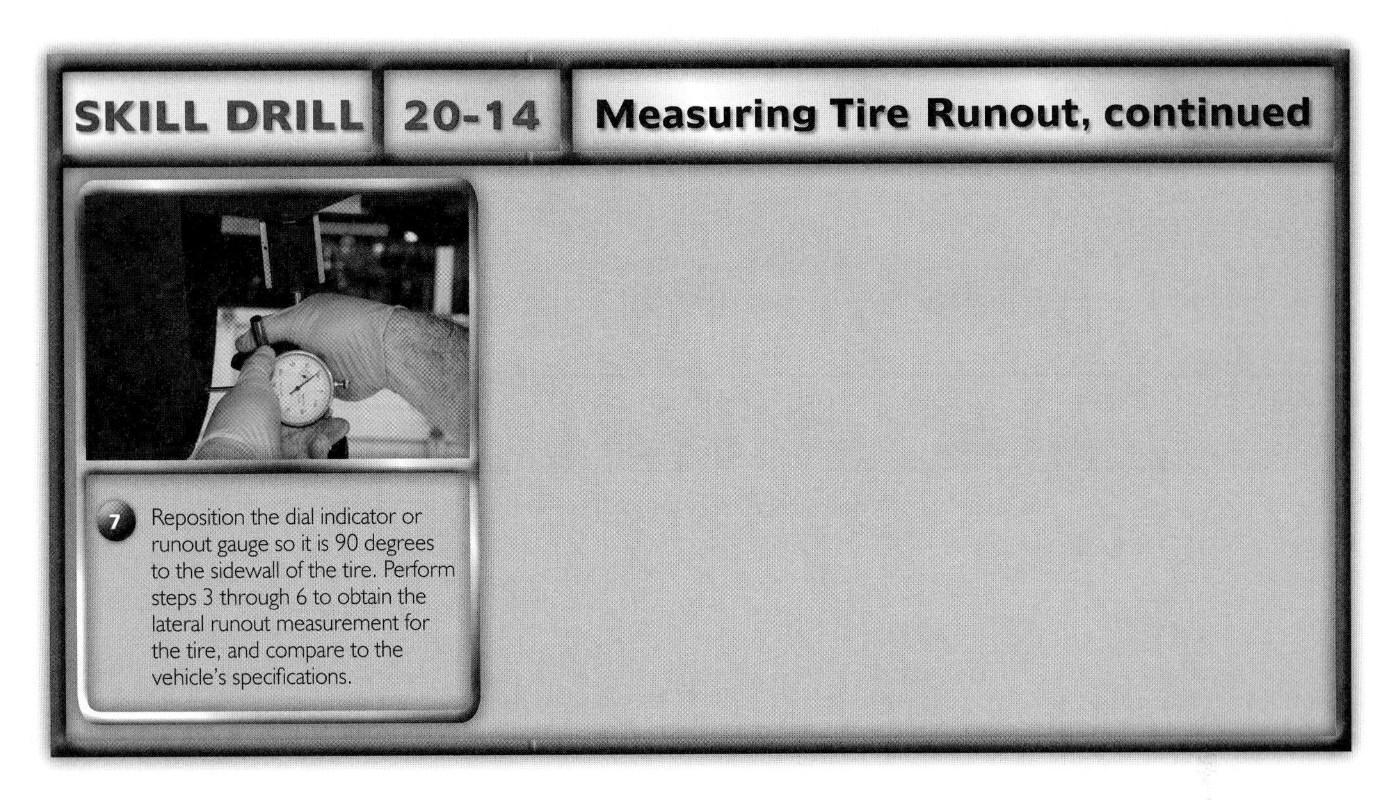

SKILL DRILL 20-14 Measuring Tire Runout, continued

7 Reposition the dial indicator or runout gauge so it is 90 degrees to the sidewall of the tire. Perform steps 3 through 6 to obtain the lateral runout measurement for the tire, and compare to the vehicle's specifications.

To measure wheel runout, follow the steps in SKILL DRILL 20-15.

To measure axle flange or hub runout, follow the steps in SKILL DRILL 20-16.

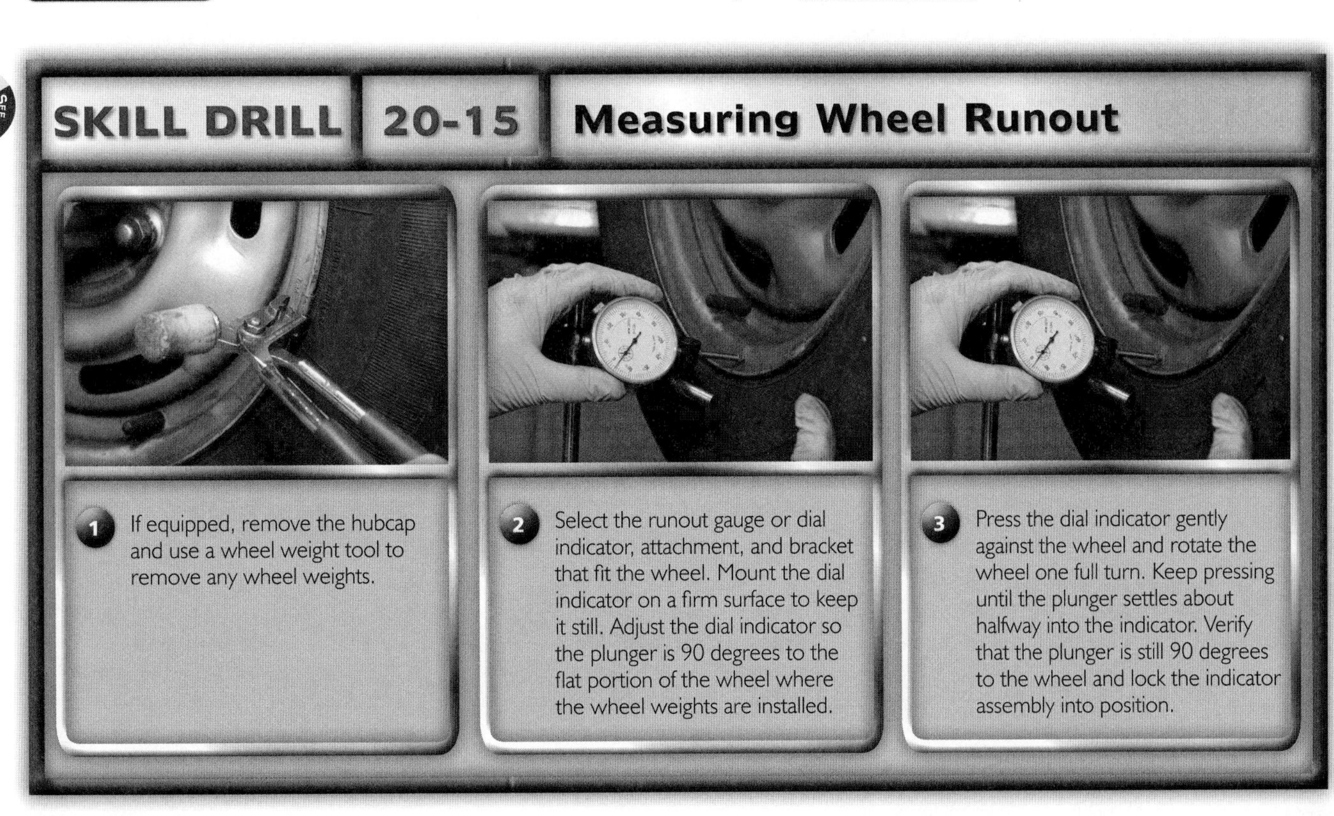

SKILL DRILL 20-15 Measuring Wheel Runout

1 If equipped, remove the hubcap and use a wheel weight tool to remove any wheel weights.

2 Select the runout gauge or dial indicator, attachment, and bracket that fit the wheel. Mount the dial indicator on a firm surface to keep it still. Adjust the dial indicator so the plunger is 90 degrees to the flat portion of the wheel where the wheel weights are installed.

3 Press the dial indicator gently against the wheel and rotate the wheel one full turn. Keep pressing until the plunger settles about halfway into the indicator. Verify that the plunger is still 90 degrees to the wheel and lock the indicator assembly into position.

SKILL DRILL 20-15 Measuring Wheel Runout, continued

4 Rotate the wheel while observing the dial readings. If the pointer hovers around a single graduation on the dial, the wheel has minimal runout or surface distortion and the test is complete. If the pointer moves significantly left and right, note the variations.

5 Find the point of maximum movement to the left and move the dial so that zero is over this point.

6 Continue to rotate the wheel. Find the point of maximum movement to the right and note the reading. Confirm this value by rotating the wheel to verify the zero point and high point. Compare these values to the manufacturer's specifications. If the deviation is greater than the specifications, the axle or hub runout must be measured.

SKILL DRILL 20-16 Measuring Axle Flange or Hub Runout

1 Prepare the vehicle by removing any hubcaps or lug nut covers. With the vehicle on the ground, loosen the lug or wheel nuts. Raise the vehicle and remove the lug nuts and tire.

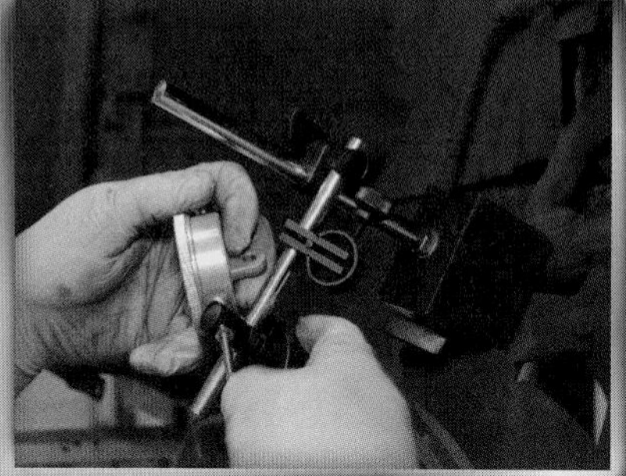

2 Select the runout gauge or dial indicator, attachment, and bracket that fit the axle flange or hub. Mount the dial indicator on a firm surface to keep it still.

3 Adjust the plunger so it is 90 degrees to the axle flange or hub. Press the dial indicator gently against the flat surface of the axle flange or hub and rotate it one full turn. Keep pressing until the plunger settles about halfway into the indicator. Verify that the plunger is still 90 degrees to the tire and lock the indicator assembly into position. Rotate the axle flange or hub while observing the dial readings.

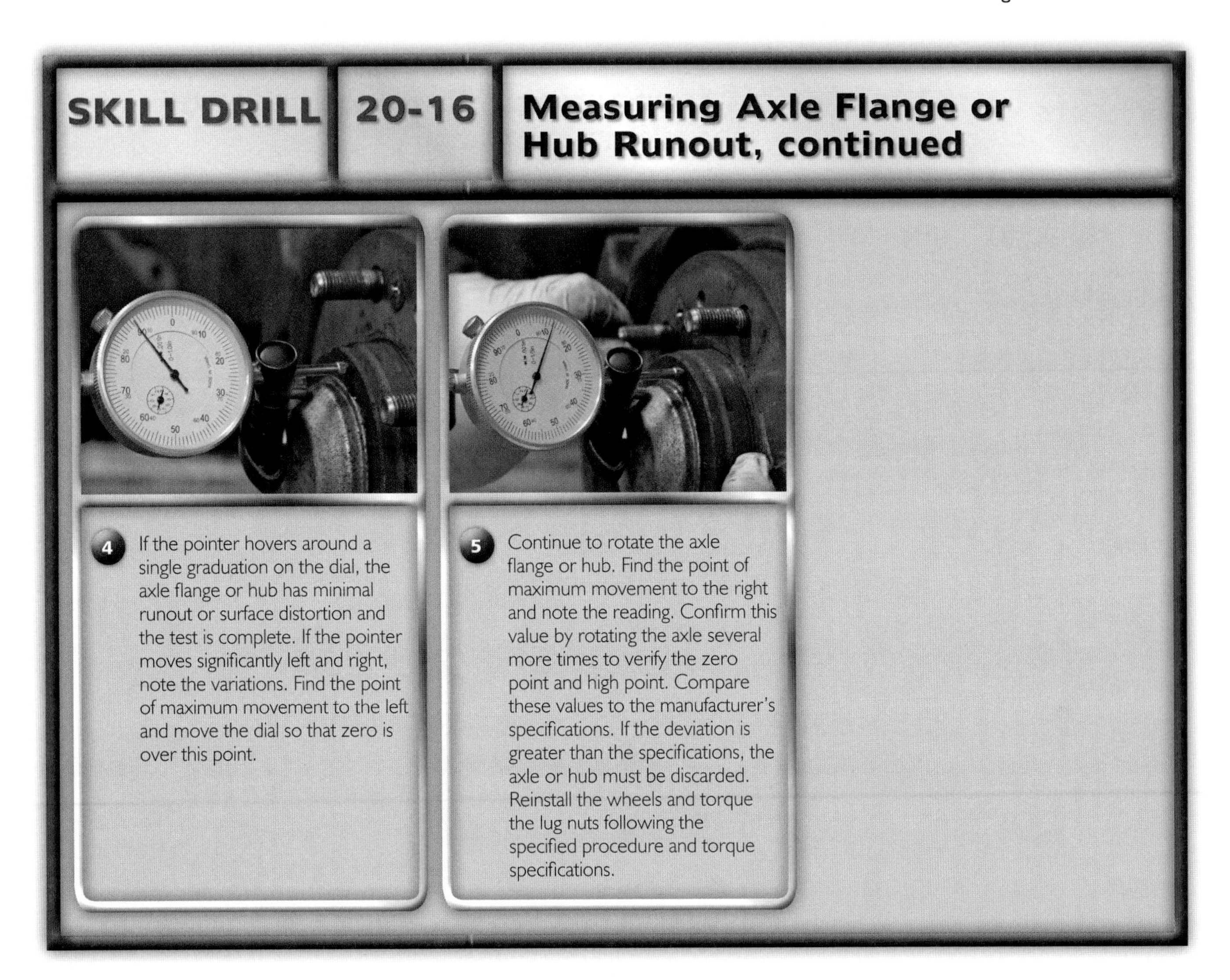
SKILL DRILL 20-16 Measuring Axle Flange or Hub Runout, continued
4 If the pointer hovers around a single graduation on the dial, the axle flange or hub has minimal runout or surface distortion and the test is complete. If the pointer moves significantly left and right, note the variations. Find the point of maximum movement to the left and move the dial so that zero is over this point.
5 Continue to rotate the axle flange or hub. Find the point of maximum movement to the right and note the reading. Confirm this value by rotating the axle several more times to verify the zero point and high point. Compare these values to the manufacturer's specifications. If the deviation is greater than the specifications, the axle or hub must be discarded. Reinstall the wheels and torque the lug nuts following the specified procedure and torque specifications.

Inspecting, Diagnosing, and Calibrating the TPMS

Inspection, diagnosis, and calibration of the TPMS is required in several general situations. Inspection is needed whenever the tires have been dismounted from the wheels. In some cases the TPMS sensor batteries need to be replaced and the sensor mounts need to be inspected. Diagnosis of system faults is required when the system detects a fault and turns on the warning light. This could be caused by one or more tires that are not at the proper pressure, requiring an inspection for leaks or incorrect pressures, or it could be a system fault requiring a scan tool capable of communicating with the TPMS. Calibration of the system is needed on some systems whenever a tire rotation is performed or a sensor is replaced so that the TPMS knows on which wheel each sensor is located.

To inspect, diagnose, and calibrate the TPMS, follow the steps in SKILL DRILL 20-17.

SKILL DRILL 20-17 Inspecting, Diagnosing, and Calibrating the TPMS

1. Turn the ignition key to the run position and observe the TPMS warning light. If the light indicates low tire pressure at any wheel, check the pressure of that wheel with an accurate tire pressure gauge. If incorrect, adjust the pressure using compressed air.

2. If the light indicates a system fault, connect an appropriate scan tool to the system and read any DTCs. Research DTCs in the appropriate service information, and follow the diagnostic steps listed to identify the cause of the fault.

Wrap-up

Ready for Review

- Poorly maintained wheels and tires decrease effective handling and may lead to steering and suspension problems.
- The main principles of understanding service of tires and wheels are: tire distortion, center of gravity, and wheel offset.
- Tire distortion refers to the tire's cornering force countering the side force that occurs when a vehicle corners, to create a slip angle.
- Center of gravity refers to the balance point of the vehicle, which is determined by location of the engine and transmission.
- Wheel offset refers to the distance from the hub mounting surface to the centerline of the wheel.
- Wheel offset can be zero, positive, or negative.
- Tire and wheel assemblies must be balanced to prevent both static and dynamic imbalance.
- Tire and wheel components include the wheel or rim, wheel studs and nuts, wheel center, and tires.
- Rims usually have a deep well—a widened area on one side of the wheel.
- The design of passenger vehicle wheels is generally either well based or drop center.
- Types of rims include: steel, one-piece alloy, two-piece alloy, multipiece alloy, custom, spinning, split, semi-drop well, drop well, and safety.
- Wheel studs and lug nuts fasten the wheels to the rims.
- Wheel retaining studs or nuts can be tapered seat, flat seat with washer, or flat seat without a washer.
- Tires provide the wheel with coverage and protection and absorb shock from road surfaces.
- Tires are composed of treads, sidewalls, inner liners, and beads.
- Synthetic fabric cords are used to create plies, giving the tire strength and flexibility.
- Tires are most commonly either cross-ply or radial (used by most passenger vehicles).

Key Terms

aspect ratio The ratio of sidewall height to section width of a tire.

asymmetric tread pattern A tread pattern that differs on each side and, therefore, is usually directional.

bar A metric unit of measure for pressure.

bead seat The part of the wheel that the tire seals against.

bias-ply A tire constructed in a latticed, crisscrossing structure, with alternate plies crossing over each other and laid with the cord angles in opposite directions.

casing plies A network of cords that give the tire shape and strength; also known as casing cords.

centrifugal switch A switch that is only activated when centrifugal forces are placed on a vehicle.

cornering force The force between the tread and the road surface as a vehicle turns.

deep dish wheel A wheel with negative offset, which gives the outside of the wheel a deep dish appearance. Deep dish refers to the side of the wheel that is farthest from the drop center.

direct TPMS A type of automated tire pressure monitoring system that measures tire pressure and possibly temperature via a sensor installed inside each wheel.

directional and asymmetric tread pattern A tread pattern that is both directional and asymmetric, which means the tire is designed to rotate in only one direction and has one side that must face outward to ensure that the tire performs as designed under operating conditions.

directional tread pattern A tread pattern designed to pump water out from under the tire; each tire must be placed in a particular spot on the vehicle.

drop center A wheel design with part of the center section of the wheel a smaller diameter than the rest. It is used for mounting and demounting the tire.

dynamic imbalance A tire imbalance that causes the wheel assembly to turn inward and outward with each half revolution.

EH2 rim The specialized rim design that is used with some run-flat tires.

Extended Mobility Technology (EMT) Tires with thick sidewalls that allow the tire to be driven on even when it has no air pressure.

flat seat with washer A type of lug nut that is flat where it bolts to the wheel and has a washer affixed that allows it to turn independent of the hex part of the lug nut.

flat seat without washer A type of lug nut that is flat where it bolts to the wheel.

indirect TPMS A type of automated tire pressure monitoring system that uses the anti-lock braking system of a vehicle to measure the difference in the rotational speed of the four wheels to determine tire pressure.

lug nuts Nuts that secure the wheel onto the wheel studs.

match mounting The process of matching up the tire's highest point with the rim's lowest point for the purpose of reducing the tire's radial runout.

negative offset A condition in which the plane of the hub mounting surface is positioned toward the brake side or back of the wheel centerline.

neutral steer A condition in which both the front and the rear tires of a vehicle are experiencing the same slip angle.

nondirectional tread pattern A tread pattern that is nonspecific, allowing the tire to be placed on any wheel of a vehicle.

oversteer A condition in which a vehicle's front slip angles are larger than the rear slip angles. This vehicle is said to be "pushing" in the corners.

pitch circle diameter (PCD) The diameter of the imaginary circle drawn through the center of the wheel bolt holes.

ply rating A rating system that denotes the number of belt layers or plies that make up the tire carcass. In radial tires, ply rating denotes the relative strength of the plies, not the actual number of plies.

positive offset A condition in which the plane of the hub mounting surface is positioned toward the outside or front of the wheel centerline.

radial tire A tire with two or more layers of casing plies and cord loops running radially from bead to bead.

rim the outer circular lip of the metal on which the inside edge of the tire is mounted.

rim flanges The outside edge of the wheel that helps keep the tire from popping off the wheel.

rim width The distance across the rim from one rim flange to the other.

run-flat technology A tire design that allows the vehicle to keep moving under driver control following a puncture or rapid loss of pressure.

safety-type drop-center rim A rim designed with a slight hump at the inside edge of the bead ledges to hold the tire beads in place during a flat tire.

Schrader valve A one-way valve used in a valve stem.

self-sealing tire A tire constructed with a flexible and malleable lining inside the tire around the inner tubeless membrane. The lining can seal small tread-area punctures instantly and permanently.

side force The pressure on the wheel that pushes it toward the outside or inside of the rim as the vehicle makes a turn.

slip angle A tire's sideways distortion that makes the vehicle follow a path at an angle to the direction the road wheel is pointing.

static imbalance A tire imbalance resulting from a heavy spot on a tire; it will vibrate vertically with the heavy area slapping the road surface with each turn of the wheel.

steel-disc–type rim A plain steel wheel that is typically covered by a hubcap.

symmetric tread pattern A tread pattern with the same tread pattern on both sides of the tire; typically nondirectional.

tapered seat A type of lug nut with a tapered end toward the rim that helps center the wheel on the wheel studs.

temperature grade A standardized grading system that indicates the extent to which heat is generated or dissipated by a tire.

tensile strength A measure of how strong a material is as it is being pulled apart.

tire inflation pressure The level of air in the tire that provides it with load-carrying capacity and affects overall vehicle performance.

tire placard A metal, vinyl, or paper tag permanently affixed to a vehicle that indicates the appropriate tire size and inflation pressure for the vehicle.

tire pressure gauge A gauge used to measure the air pressure within a tire.

tire pressure monitoring system (TPMS) An automatic sensor system in most modern vehicles that alerts drivers of tire pressure problems.

tire valve The valve through which air is inserted into a tire to inflate it.

traction grade A standardized grading system that indicates how well a tire will maintain contact with the road surface when wet.

tread wear grade The number imprinted on the sidewall of a tire by the manufacturer as required by the National Highway Traffic Safety Administration (NHTSA) that indicates the tread life of a tire's tread.

understeer A condition in which a vehicle's front wheels turn sharper than the vehicle's direction when the vehicle is steered around a corner. This vehicle is said to be "loose" in the corners.

Uniform Tire Quality Grading (UTQG) A standardized grading system established by the National Highway Traffic Safety Administration (NHTSA) designed to provide tire buyers with a comparative measure of a tire's tread life, traction, and temperature characteristics.

US Department of Transportation (DOT) A federal agency that regulates transportation safety in the United States, including vehicles' wheels and tires. The DOT requires a code—a series of letters and numbers—to be stamped into the sidewall of every tire made for public use in the United States. These codes contain information such as the date of manufacture and the plant where the tire was manufactured.

valve core The one-way spring-loaded valve that screws into the valve stem that allows air to be pumped into a tire and prevents it from flowing out.

valve stem A rubber or steel piece that attaches the tire valve to the rim.

valve stem cap A cap that fits tightly onto the valve stem to prevent debris from clogging it and acts as a secondary seal.

weight matching The process of matching the tire's lightest point with the rim's heaviest point (generally at the valve stem) for the purpose of reducing the tire's radial imbalance.

wheel center The part of the wheel containing the holes for the lug studs.

wheel retaining nuts Lug nuts used to hold the wheel on the hub.

wheel rim The part on which the tire is mounted. Also called a "wheel" or "rim."

wheel studs The threaded fasteners that attach the wheel to the vehicle.

zero offset A condition in which the plane of the hub mounting surface is even with the centerline of the wheel.

ASE-Type Questions

1. Tech A says that when turning a corner, both wheels being steered remain parallel to each other as the wheels are steered. Tech B says that on some vehicles, the rear wheels also can be steered. Who is correct?
   a. Tech A
   b. Tech B
   c. Both A and B
   d. Neither A nor B
2. Tech A says that most wheels have a drop center or deep well that is used in installing a tire on the wheel. Tech B says that the drop center or deep well is used to prevent the tire from coming off the wheel in the case of low tire pressure. Who is correct?
   a. Tech A
   b. Tech B
   c. Both A and B
   d. Neither A nor B
3. Tech A says that all wheels must be torqued to prevent wheels from loosening up and falling off. Tech B says that all wheels must be torqued to prevent overtightening, which can weaken lug studs and warp brake rotors. Who is correct?
   a. Tech A
   b. Tech B
   c. Both A and B
   d. Neither A nor B
4. Tech A says that underinflated tires reduce fuel economy. Tech B says that underinflated tires are unsafe and cause accelerated tire wear. Who is correct?
   a. Tech A
   b. Tech B
   c. Both A and B
   d. Neither A nor B
5. Tech A says that incorrect toe settings will cause feathered wear across the tire tread. Tech B says that underinflated tires have more wear in the center of the tread. Who is correct?
   a. Tech A
   b. Tech B
   c. Both A and B
   d. Neither A nor B
6. Tech A says that tires are marked with a date code indicating the date the tires should be discarded. Tech B says that any tires with a three-digit date code should be discarded. Who is correct?
   a. Tech A
   b. Tech B
   c. Both A and B
   d. Neither A nor B
7. Tech A says that a TPMS system can save fuel over time. Tech B says that a TPMS will help prevent blowouts. Who is correct?
   a. Tech A
   b. Tech B
   c. Both A and B
   d. Neither A nor B
8. Tech A says that the use of nitrogen to fill a tire will prevent the tire from blowing out. Tech B says that when mounting or dismounting a tire on a wheel with a TPMS sensor, you need to position the wheel/tire properly on the tire machine or the TPMS sensor can be easily broken. Who is correct?
   a. Tech A
   b. Tech B
   c. Both A and B
   d. Neither A nor B
9. Tech A says that using a tire plug to repair a hole in a tire is the best and fastest way to fix a tire. Tech B says that using a tire plug patch is the only approved method of repairing a tire in many states. Who is correct?
   a. Tech A
   b. Tech B
   c. Both A and B
   d. Neither A nor B
10. Tech A says that directional tires cannot be rotated. Tech B says that all old wheel weights should be removed before balancing a tire. Who is correct?
    a. Tech A
    b. Tech B
    c. Both A and B
    d. Neither A nor B

CHAPTER 21

Know
See
Do
Prove

NATEF Tasks

Suspension and Steering

Steering Systems

Task			Page
■ Inspect for power steering fluid leakage; determine necessary action.	MLR	AST	552
■ Diagnose power steering gear (non-rack-and-pinion) binding, uneven turning effort, looseness, hard steering, and noise concerns; determine necessary action.		AST	552–553
■ Diagnose power steering gear (rack-and-pinion) binding, uneven turning effort, looseness, hard steering, and noise concerns; determine necessary action.		AST	552–553
■ Determine proper power steering fluid type; inspect fluid level and condition.	MLR	AST	553
■ Replace power steering pump filter(s).	MLR	AST	554
■ Inspect and replace power steering hoses and fittings.	MLR	AST	555–556
■ Inspect rack-and-pinion steering gear; inspect mounting bushings and brackets.		AST	557–558
■ Inspect rack-and-pinion steering gear inner tie-rod ends (sockets) and bellows boots; replace as needed.	MLR	AST	558
■ Inspect pitman arm, relay (center link/intermediate) rod, idler arm and mountings, and steering linkage damper.	MLR	AST	558–559
■ Inspect tie-rod ends (sockets), tie-rod sleeves, and clamps.	MLR	AST	559–560
■ Identify hybrid vehicle power steering system electrical circuits and service and safety precautions.	MLR	AST	561
■ Disable and enable supplemental restraint system (SRS).	MLR	AST	561–562

Servicing the Steering System

NATEF Tasks, continued

Related Suspension and Steering Service

- Inspect electric power assist steering. MLR AST 561

Suspension Systems

- Describe the function of the power steering pressure switch. MLR AST 550

KNOW
SEE
DO
PROVE

Knowledge Objectives

After you have read this chapter, you will be able to:

1. Identify the components of the basic steering system. (pp 532–539)
2. Describe the types of steering boxes, including the rack-and-pinion gearbox and the worm gearbox, and how they function. (pp 539–543)
3. Describe the purpose and types of power steering. (pp 543–550)
4. Explain the various tools and their uses in proper diagnostics of steering systems. (pp 550–553)
5. Describe the maintenance and repair of a steering system. (pp 553–562)

KNOW
SEE
DO
PROVE

Skills Objectives

After reading this chapter, you will be able to:

1. Check and adjust power steering fluid. (p 553)
2. Replace the power steering pump filter(s). (p 554)
3. Inspect power steering hoses and fittings. (pp 555–556)
4. Inspect mounting bushings and brackets. (p 557)
5. Inspect rack-and-pinion steering gear inner tie-rod ends and bellows boots. (p 558)
6. Inspect the idler arm and the pitman arm. (pp 558–559)
7. Inspect the center link (relay rod/intermediate rod). (pp 559–560)
8. Inspect the steering linkage damper. (pp 559–560)
9. Inspect preloaded tie-rod ends. (pp 559–560)
10. Disable and enable the supplemental restraint system (SRS). (pp 561–562)

Introduction

Every driver knows that turning the steering wheel steers the wheels, which steer the vehicle. What is not readily apparent are the many components that are installed between the steering wheel and the wheels that relay the signal and make the wheels steer. This chapter discusses the different steering systems, how they operate, and the purpose and function of each part within them. It also discusses the steps and tools needed to inspect and maintain steering systems. Maintaining a well-functioning steering system is necessary for the safety of the driver, passengers, and others sharing the road.

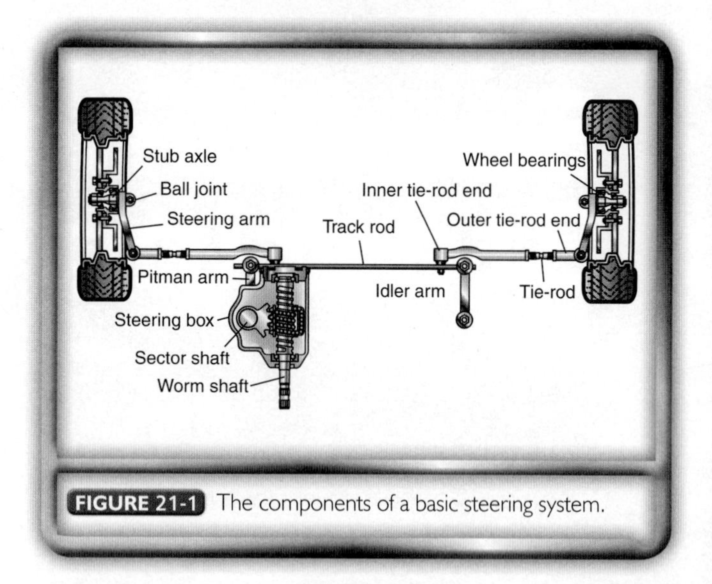
Stub axle
Ball joint
Steering arm
Wheel bearings
Inner tie-rod end
Track rod
Outer tie-rod end
Pitman arm
Idler arm
Tie-rod
Steering box
Sector shaft
Worm shaft

FIGURE 21-1 The components of a basic steering system.

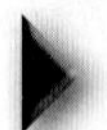

Steering System Overview

The **steering system** provides control over the vehicle's direction of travel, good maneuverability for parking the vehicle, smooth recovery from turns as the driver releases the steering wheel, and minimal transmission of road shocks from the road surface through the steering wheel. As vehicle technology has progressed, steering systems have gone through a number of refinements to enhance vehicle safety, performance, and even fuel economy.

A basic steering system has four main parts: a steering column, a steering box, a steering linkage, and a steering knuckle FIGURE 21-1. Added to the basic steering system is a power assist system that makes it easier for the driver to steer the vehicle. The power steering system can be either a hydraulic type or electric type. In the case of electric power steering, in addition to providing power assist, the system can be integrated with the electronic stability control system, such that the power train control module (PCM) can take command of the steering, if needed, to prevent loss of control of the vehicle. Electric power steering also makes four-wheel steering more of a feasible option.

The **steering column** transmits the driver's steering effort from the steering wheel down to the steering box. The **steering box** converts the rotary motion of the steering wheel to the **linear motion** needed to pivot the wheels. The steering box also uses principles of gear reduction to give the driver mechanical advantage over the wheels, making it easier to steer them. The **steering linkage** transfers the linear steering effort to the wheels by connecting the steering box to the **steering arm** on each

You Are the Automotive Technician

A customer is driving on the highway and notices a burning oil smell and smoke coming from the front of his 6-year-old vehicle with power rack-and-pinion steering. He is able to pull into a visitor's center and check under the vehicle's hood. He identifies a large amount of power steering fluid sprayed all over the engine compartment, and the power steering reservoir is nearly empty. He calls you for advice and wants to know if he can drive it to your shop 35 miles away.

1. What would you advise he do, and why?
2. What are the most likely leak points?
3. While you are working on the vehicle, what other steering-related inspections would you perform?

of the steering knuckles, which pivot on the ball joints, allowing the wheels to steer the vehicle.

There are two main types of steering systems used on vehicles today: rack and pinion and parallelogram. Each one has its strengths and weaknesses, but rack-and-pinion systems are the most commonly used. The rack-and-pinion system gets its name because a rotating pinion gear is used to move a flat, toothed rack FIGURE 21-2. The rack is connected through pivoting socket ends and a **tie-rod** directly to the steering arms. It is a simple, compact system with only a few moving and pivoting parts. It fits well into most engine compartments and takes up less space than other systems, which means it is less likely to get in the way of other components. And because of the fewer parts and the orientation of the pinion gear to the rack, it gives a more precise steering feel, making it more sporty.

The **parallelogram steering system** gets its name because the center link and axle, along with the pitman arm and idler arm, always move parallel to each other FIGURE 21-3. Pivoting tie-rods connect the parallelogram to the steering arms. Parallelogram steering uses a **worm** gearbox, which changes the direction of steering wheel rotation 90 degrees, and a pitman arm and center link to turn the rotary motion into lateral motion. The worm gear design reduces the road shock that is transmitted to the steering wheel, so a parallelogram design provides an advantage especially in off-road four-wheel drive vehicles or non-sporty vehicles.

The **steering knuckles** are stout components that firmly connect the wheels to the suspension and steering systems. They provide a stub axle upon which the wheel bearings ride, or a hub-style wheel bearing assembly that is pressed or bolted onto the steering knuckle. The steering knuckle pivots on one or two ball joints, depending on the type of suspension, which is covered in the Servicing Suspension Systems chapter. The steering arm either is integrated into the casting of the steering knuckle or is bolted on. Either way, it transmits the steering force from the steering linkage to the wheel and tire assembly.

Steering Geometry

The relationships between the steering system, the wheel positions, and the suspension system form what is called the steering geometry. Steering geometry is a geometric arrangement of linkages in the steering of a vehicle designed to solve the problem of keeping the wheels properly oriented through various positions of the steering and suspension systems. As the wheels move up and down relative to the body, the steering linkage swings vertically through an arc. The wheel would thus turn in and out as the vehicle goes over bumps if it were not for steering geometry. In this case, the pivots for the suspension components cause the wheel to go through a similar arc as the steering components, allowing the wheel to track straight ahead, or in a consistent direction if it is in a turn.

Also, when rounding a corner, the inner and outer wheels must trace circles of different radii; otherwise the tires would scrub. This is a challenge because no matter which way the vehicle turns, the inside wheel must always turn more sharply than the outside wheel, which is called toe-out on turns. The Ackermann principle, named after the man who patented it in 1818, provides the needed geometry. The Ackermann principle angles the steering arms toward the center of the vehicle such that imaginary lines drawn from the center of the steering knuckle pivot points, through the center of the outer tie-rod ends,

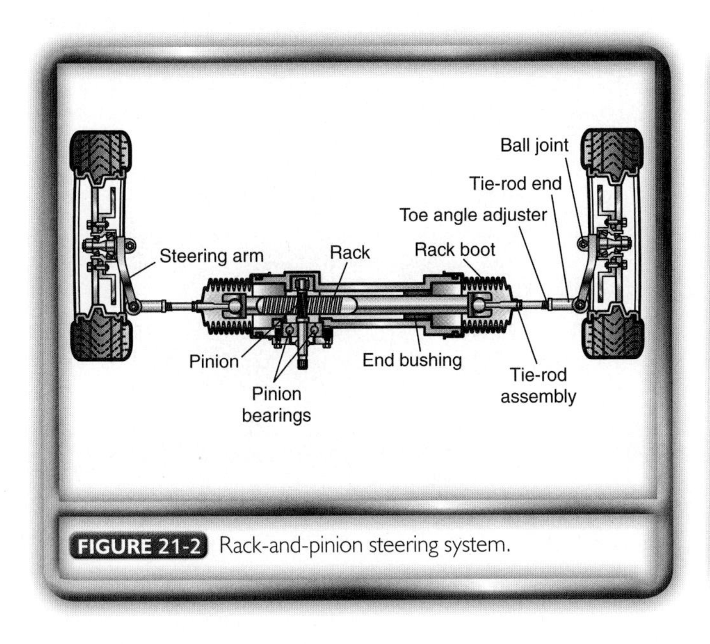
Ball joint
Tie-rod end
Toe angle adjuster
Steering arm
Rack
Rack boot
Pinion
End bushing
Tie-rod assembly
Pinion bearings

FIGURE 21-2 Rack-and-pinion steering system.

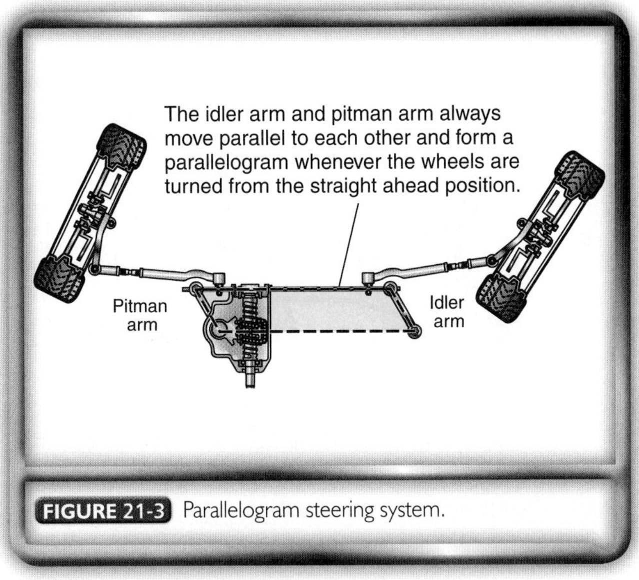
The idler arm and pitman arm always move parallel to each other and form a parallelogram whenever the wheels are turned from the straight ahead position.
Pitman arm
Idler arm

FIGURE 21-3 Parallelogram steering system.

intersect at the center of the rear axle FIGURE 21-4. This angle is what allows the wheels to navigate a corner without scrubbing. Steering geometry and suspension geometry must be within the manufacturer's specifications for the vehicle to operate correctly. If it is not correct, it is usually due to worn or bent components that the technician will have to diagnose and ultimately repair to restore proper operation.

Rack-and-Pinion Steering Gear and Linkage

The **rack-and-pinion steering system** is used on the majority of front-wheel drive vehicles due to the restriction of space under the hood. Rack-and-pinion steering gears are used because their construction makes them compact and lightweight FIGURE 21-5. Their steering response is very sharp because the rack operates directly on the steering knuckle and there is very little sliding and rotational resistance, which gives lighter operation.

The primary components of the rack-and-pinion steering system are:

- **Pinion**: A toothed gear that meshes with the rack. The pinion is connected to the steering column. As the driver turns the steering wheel, the forces are transferred to the pinion, causing the rack to move in either direction. This is achieved by having the pinion in **constant mesh** (constant contact) with the rack.
- **Rack**: A toothed, straight piece of metal that meshes with the pinion in the middle of the rack and has tie-rods on each end that fasten to the knuckle. The rack slides in the housing and is moved by the action of the **meshed pinion** (the pinion it is in contact with). It normally has an **adjustable bushing** positioned opposite the pinion to control the components' meshing, and it has a nylon bushing at the other end. This adjustable bushing allows the technician to adjust play out of the rack and pinion. The function of the rack is to transfer motion to the tie-rod.
- **Inner tie-rod or socket**: The inner tie-rod is attached to the end of the rack and allows for suspension movement and slight changes in steering angles.

FIGURE 21-4 Angling the steering arms inward allows the inner wheel to turn more sharply than the outer wheel.

Pinion
Rack

FIGURE 21-5 The rack-and-pinion steering system. **A.** Pinion and rack. **B.** Inner ball joint or socket. **C.** Tie-rod.

- **Outer tie-rod**: An outer tie-rod end is attached between the tie-rod shaft and the steering arm. It transfers the movement of the rack. The outer tie-rod pivots as the rack is extended or retracted when the vehicle is negotiating turns. Some tie-rods and tie-rod ends are left- or right-hand threaded. This allows toe-in or toe-out to be adjusted to the manufacturer's specifications. Toe-in is a condition where the fronts of the wheels, as seen from above, are closer together than the rears of the wheels. Toe-out is the opposite condition, where the rears of the wheels are closer together than the fronts. A tie-rod end connects the center link to the steering knuckle on vehicles with parallelogram steering systems.
- **Rubber bellows**: The rubber bellows protects the inner joints from dirt and contaminants. In addition, it retains the grease lubricant inside the rack-and-pinion housing. There are two ends of the rack. Each side contains an identical bellows.

Parallelogram Steering Gear and Linkage

The parallelogram steering system is used on larger vehicles where ride comfort is more important than sporty handling. Parallelogram steering linkage is more complicated than the rack-and-pinion linkage, so there are more wear points to know about and inspect. The primary components of the parallelogram steering system, from the gearbox on, are:

- Pitman arm: The pitman arm transfers movement from the steering box to the center link. It is attached to the steering box by a **spline** and nut. Splines are ridges or teeth on a driveshaft that mesh with grooves in a mating piece and transfer torque to it and maintain the angular correspondence between the components. As the driver turns the steering wheel, the steering box mechanism moves the steering linkages via the pitman arm either left or right, depending on the direction in which the steering wheel is turned. The steering box provides the change of angle at 90 degrees to the steering linkage and also provides a steering ratio (the number of turns of the steering wheel compared to the number of turns of the sector shaft) to assist in the ease of turning the steering wheel and linkages.
- Idler arm: The idler arm is attached to the **chassis** (the frame of the vehicle) and is positioned parallel to the pitman arm. The idler arm assembly is the pivoting support for the steering linkage. It consists of a rod that pivots on a bracket bolted to the frame of the vehicle on one end and supports a ball socket on the other end. Generally, an idler arm is attached between the opposite side of the center link from the pitman arm and the vehicle's frame to hold the center link at the proper height so it can accurately relay the pitman arm's movement. Idler arms are generally more vulnerable to wear than pitman arms because of the pivot function built into them.
- Center link: The center link connects the pitman arm to the idler arm. In this way, any movement in the pitman arm is directly applied to the idler arm.
- Tie-rod: The tie-rods connect the center link to the steering arms that are located on the steering knuckles. All movement from the pitman arm is relayed directly to the front wheels, which steer the vehicle.
- Tie-rod end: Tie-rod ends are attached to the tie-rod shaft. They pivot as the rack is extended or retracted when the vehicle is negotiating turns. Tie-rods and tie-rod ends are left- or right-hand threaded. The inner tie-rod ends are attached to either end of the center link and serve as pivot points for the steering gear.
- **Adjustment sleeve**: The adjustment sleeve connects the tie-rod to the tie-rod end. It provides the adjustment point for toe-in or toe-out, depending on the manufacturer's specifications. It is considered a turnbuckle, usually with one end having left-hand threads and the other having right-hand threads. When turning the sleeve, the tie-rods thread apart or together to set the vehicle toe.

TECHNICIAN TIP

Each type of steering system makes provision for adjustment of the linkage to achieve the manufacturer's recommended toe-setting. The toe-setting is the symmetric angle that each wheel makes with the longitudinal axis of the vehicle. The track rods or tie-rod ends are threaded to provide for their lengthening or shortening.

A tie-rod on each side of the vehicle connects each **wheel assembly** to the center link. Each connection point in the linkage system has a pivoting joint, which is a ball-and-socket construction FIGURE 21-6.

Flexible joints on the center link and on the ends of the tie-rods allow for steering and suspension movement. The tie-rods have ball sockets that allow steering movement and movement of the suspension. The tie-rod end

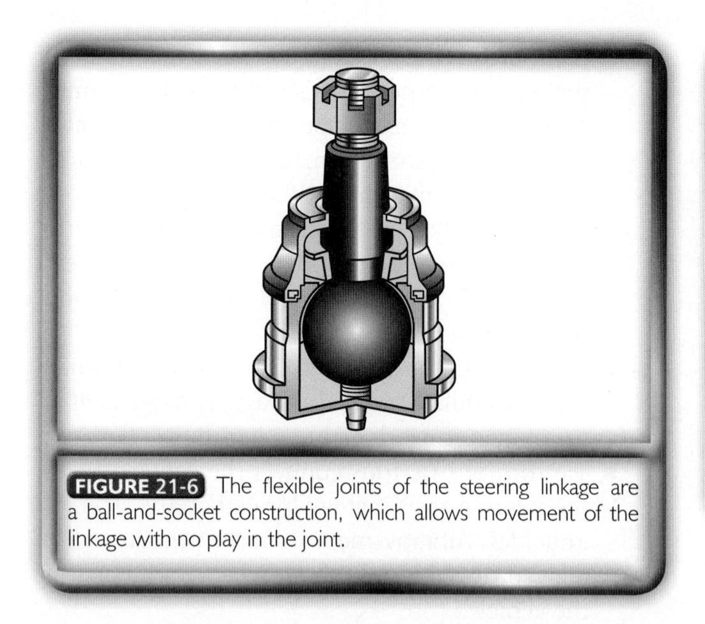

FIGURE 21-6 The flexible joints of the steering linkage are a ball-and-socket construction, which allows movement of the linkage with no play in the joint.

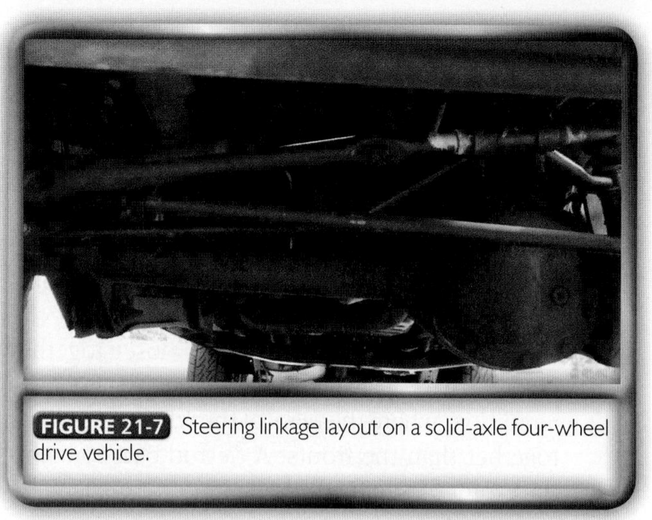

FIGURE 21-7 Steering linkage layout on a solid-axle four-wheel drive vehicle.

swivel joints are at equal heights and pivot so that movement in the suspension does not affect steering operation. Movement of the suspension that does affect steering is called bump steer. **Bump steer** is the undesired condition produced when, upon hitting a bump, the vehicle darts to one side as the steering linkage is pushed or pulled as a result of the travel of the suspension. Typically, bump steer is due to a bent tie-rod end or another bent component that would cause unequal heights of the tie-rod ends. The tie-rod end swivel joints allow the suspension to move up and down without affecting vehicle steering.

In four-wheel drive vehicles with a **beam axle**, a single tie-rod connects the steering arms on each wheel assembly. In this design, the drag link is connected to an arm on the front of the left-hand wheel assembly. Movement of the pitman arm is transferred through the drag link to the left-hand wheel, and through the single tie-rod to the right-hand wheel FIGURE 21-7. The steering box is offset from the steering column, so two universal joints and an intermediate steering shaft are used. Four-wheel drive vehicles of this type often use a **steering damper** on the single tie-rod. It resembles a shock absorber and operates on a similar principle. Specifically, it keeps the steering wheel from shaking when the driver hits a pothole or other road irregularity. The steering damper is mounted between the tie-rod and either the rigid axle or the vehicle frame. When the vehicle is driven over rough terrain, its purpose is to prevent shock forces being transmitted through the steering linkage and back to the steering wheel.

Steering Columns

Effort applied to the steering wheel is transferred down the steering column, or shaft, to a steering box. In early vehicles, the steering column was a straight shaft, running inside a hollow tube. The steering wheel was attached to one end, and the steering box to the other. In many frontal collisions, however, this design caused serious injury to the driver, partly because the steering wheel was forced back toward the driver's head and chest and partly because the sudden stop forced the driver onto the wheel. To reduce this hazard, all steering columns are now fitted with collapsible sections that help protect the driver. During a collision, two forces are applied to the steering column. The first is the force of the steering box being forced toward the steering column and toward the driver. Plastic shear pins allow the lower shaft to move over the upper shaft. The second force is the mass of the driver striking the steering wheel. This force breaks the brackets on the upper part of the column, driving the upper column into the lower column FIGURE 21-8. Most vehicles also integrate a driver's side

FIGURE 21-8 Collapsible steering column.

airbag into the steering wheel for collision protection. This system will be discussed in greater detail in a later section.

The steering column is connected to the input shaft of the steering gear by a flexible joint. This flexible joint allows for smooth turning of the steering wheel since the steering column sits at a different angle than the steering box. It also reduces the transmission of road shocks to the driver. Some steering columns have an **intermediate shaft**, which runs at an angle, from the column to the steering gear. In a collision, the universal joints on the intermediate shaft allow it to fold under, preventing the impact force from being transferred directly to the column FIGURE 21-9.

FIGURE 21-9 Steering column with an intermediate shaft for enhanced protection in an accident.

Some manufacturers fit sensors and an electric motor to the steering column. The sensors in the steering column provide information to a steering control module for electric power steering assist or for the electronic stability control system. The sensors are able to sense rotational direction and speed exerted by the driver and control both the speed and the direction of the electric motor, which is used to provide the electric power steering assist. This system will be discussed further in a later section.

The steering column generally accommodates for an ignition switch and lock assembly, although more new vehicles are coming with a push-button start switch located in the dash. The steering column also incorporates a multifunction switch (or separate switches) that may include switches for lights, turn signal indicators, wipers, and cruise control. The steering wheel itself may have integrated control switches for the entertainment system, a cell phone, and instrument panel display options FIGURE 21-10.

Tilt/Telescoping Mechanism

To compensate for variations in driving positions, many manufacturers have included a steering column tilting and/or telescoping mechanism to their vehicles. These features allow drivers to control the steering wheel position so that it best suits their preferences. The tilting mechanism allows drivers to raise or lower the steering column position, while the telescoping mechanism allows the driver to move the steering wheel closer or farther away. However, the amount of movement in any direction does have its limitations.

The tilt mechanism uses a heavy spring, a pivoting joint, and a ratchet mechanism to operate. These added components make the steering column more complicated to repair. The telescoping mechanism includes a slip joint and locking mechanism. Both of these features can also

A
PUSH
HI
LO
WIPER
OFF
SRC
B

FIGURE 21-10 **A.** Multifunction switch. **B.** Steering wheel entertainment controls.

put the wires in the steering column under additional stress due to more frequent movement, so remember that when diagnosing wiring faults.

Driver's Side Airbag

The driver's side airbag is designed to provide a collapsing cushion that decelerates a driver's head and chest during an accident FIGURE 21-11. One of the leading causes of fatalities in accidents is the rapid deceleration forces that occur within a body during the accident. The body's internal organs cannot handle the force of sudden deceleration, so engineers devise ways to slow the deceleration during an accident. They do this through the use of crumple zones in the vehicle, which fold and crush accordionlike to provide some deceleration. Restraint systems such as tear-away seat belts also are designed to slow the deceleration. Airbags also decelerate the driver and prevent the head from contacting the steering wheel or dash. Side curtain airbags ensure that the driver does not hit the side rail of the roof when involved in a side collision. Next to the seat belt, airbags are the biggest lifesaver in accidents. In most countries, government regulation requires that a vehicle equipped with airbags be capable of having the airbags replaced as part of the repair process of a crashed vehicle. If the airbag has been deployed in an accident, a new airbag and cover must be installed to meet legislative requirements in most states.

When a technician needs to carry out a servicing procedure on the steering column, it is good practice to disarm the triggering system for the driver's side airbag, which is located in the top cover of the steering wheel. If not properly disarmed, the airbag could trigger accidentally, injuring or killing the technician due to the large deployment force created by the ignited propellant, which is rocket fuel. Unintended deployment also creates the need to replace the airbag assembly, which is expensive. Generally, to disarm a driver's side airbag, the correct supplemental restraint system (SRS) fuse must be located and removed, and then verified by turning the ignition switch to run and observing the SRS light, which should remain on. Once the fuse is removed, the negative battery terminal is disconnected and the vehicle is allowed to sit for about 15 minutes to discharge the capacitors. Note that a memory minder SHOULD NOT be used when working on, or around, the SRS system.

Some manufacturers will have you disconnect the airbag connector located under the dash near the steering column. Disconnecting this connector will generally activate a shorting bar in the airbag side of the connector, which will make it much harder for the airbag to accidentally deploy. With the airbag disarmed, you can carry out any needed diagnosis or repair on the steering column. Just remember to rearm the airbag once service is completed. Follow the service information to properly deactivate the airbag prior to steering column diagnosis and repair and to reactivate it when finished.

Because of the critical nature of the airbag, it is imperative that it is always connected electrically to its control module, so it can be deployed when needed. Since the airbag is mounted in the steering wheel, a method of maintaining the electrical connection to the airbag is not as easy. This is overcome by incorporating a clock spring into the steering column. The **clock spring** is a special rotary electrical connector located between the steering wheel and the steering column that maintains a constant electrical connection with the wiring while the vehicle's steering wheel is being turned FIGURE 21-12. The wires from the airbag and its electrical system connect through the clock spring, which coils and uncoils as the wheel is turned, and maintains constant electrical contact. When removing the

35 MPH
032012
VOLVO
FIGURE 21-11 SRS deployed in crash.

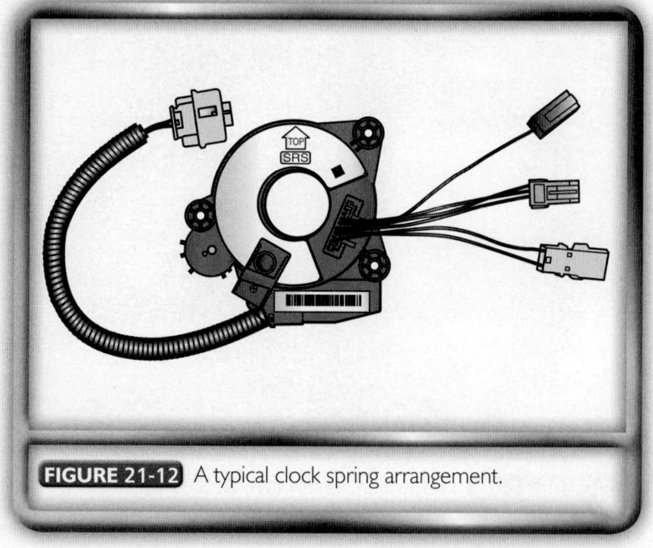
TOP
SRS
FIGURE 21-12 A typical clock spring arrangement.

Safety

Never lean over or in front of an armed airbag when working on the dash, instrument panel, or airbag system. Doing so can cause serious injury or death if it accidentally deploys. Always follow the manufacturer's procedure when disarming and arming the airbag.

airbag assembly from the steering wheel, inspect the wiring and connector of the airbag to clock spring to ensure there is no damage. When the steering wheel is removed and the clock spring is easily visible, inspect it to ensure that it and the clock spring wire is not damaged. Typically, if the electrical wiring inside the clock spring is damaged, an SRS system code will set and the SRS light will be turned on. If it has been damaged in any way, it must be replaced it cannot be repaired.

TECHNICIAN TIP

When removing the rack-and-pinion or steering gear, make sure the wheels are pointing straight ahead before disassembly. Also, either lock the steering column with the ignition key or wrap a seat belt around the steering wheel to prevent the clock spring from being moved off center. Make sure to also reassemble the parts in the straight-ahead position.

Steering Boxes

There are a number of variations for steering boxes. They are either manual steering or power-assisted steering. Manual steering has no power source to help make the wheel easier for the driver of the vehicle to turn, whereas power-assisted steering uses a hydraulic pump or electric motor that aids the driver in turning the wheel. Older vehicles were available with manual steering, and power steering was an expensive option. This is not the case now, as any vehicle purchased will come standard with a form of power steering. The function of all steering boxes is the same, whether manual or power—to transfer the rotary motion of the steering wheel into the side-to-side motion needed to make the wheels pivot left and right.

Steering Box Types

There are two basic types of steering boxes: those with rack-and-pinion gearing FIGURE 21-13 and those with worm gearing and a sector shaft FIGURE 21-14. In both cases, the gearing in the steering box makes it easier for the driver to turn the steering wheel and, hence, the wheels. The variations of steering boxes include:

- The rack-and-pinion gearbox
- The worm gearbox, consisting of:
  - Worm and sector
  - Worm and roller
  - Worm and nut (commonly referred to as the recirculating ball)

Rack-and-Pinion Gearbox

The rack-and-pinion gearbox has a pinion connected to the bottom of the steering column. This pinion runs in mesh with a rack that is connected to the steering tie-rods. This connection gives more direct operation, which enables the driver to feel the road better. Turning the steering wheel rotates the pinion and moves the rack from side to side. On end take-off racks, ball sockets at the end of the rack locate the tie-rods and allow move-

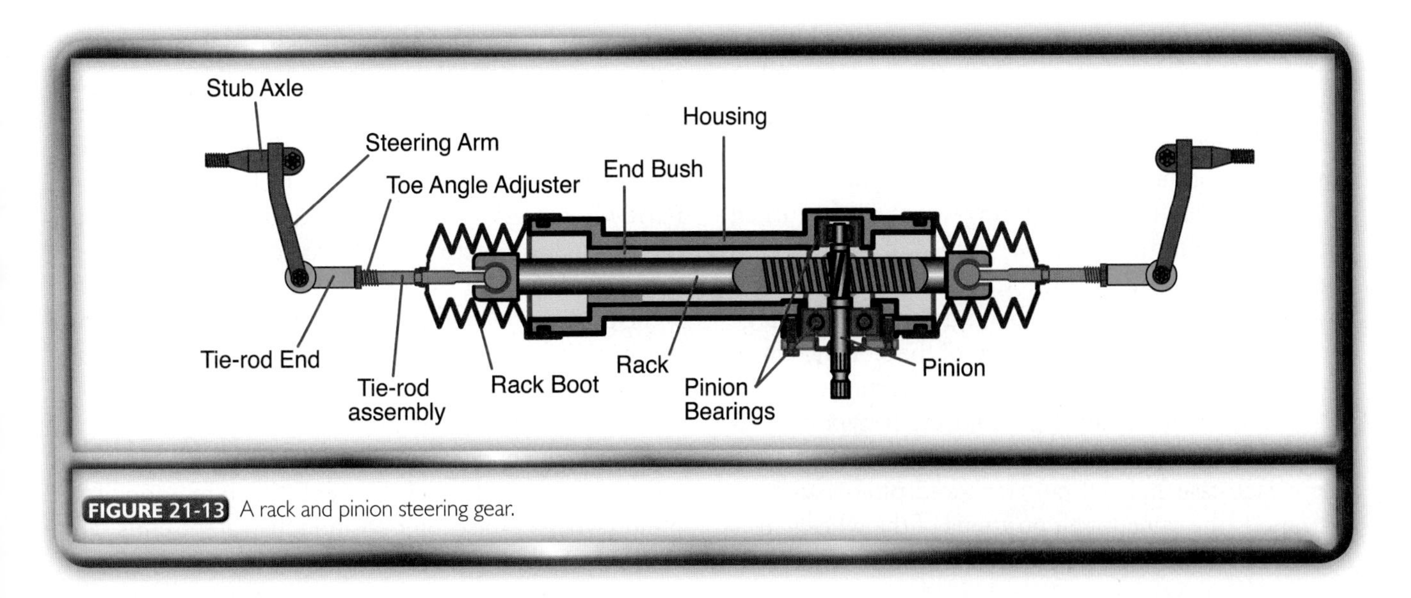
Stub Axle
Housing
Steering Arm
End Bush
Toe Angle Adjuster
Tie-rod End
Tie-rod assembly
Rack Boot
Rack
Pinion Bearings
Pinion

FIGURE 21-13 A rack and pinion steering gear.

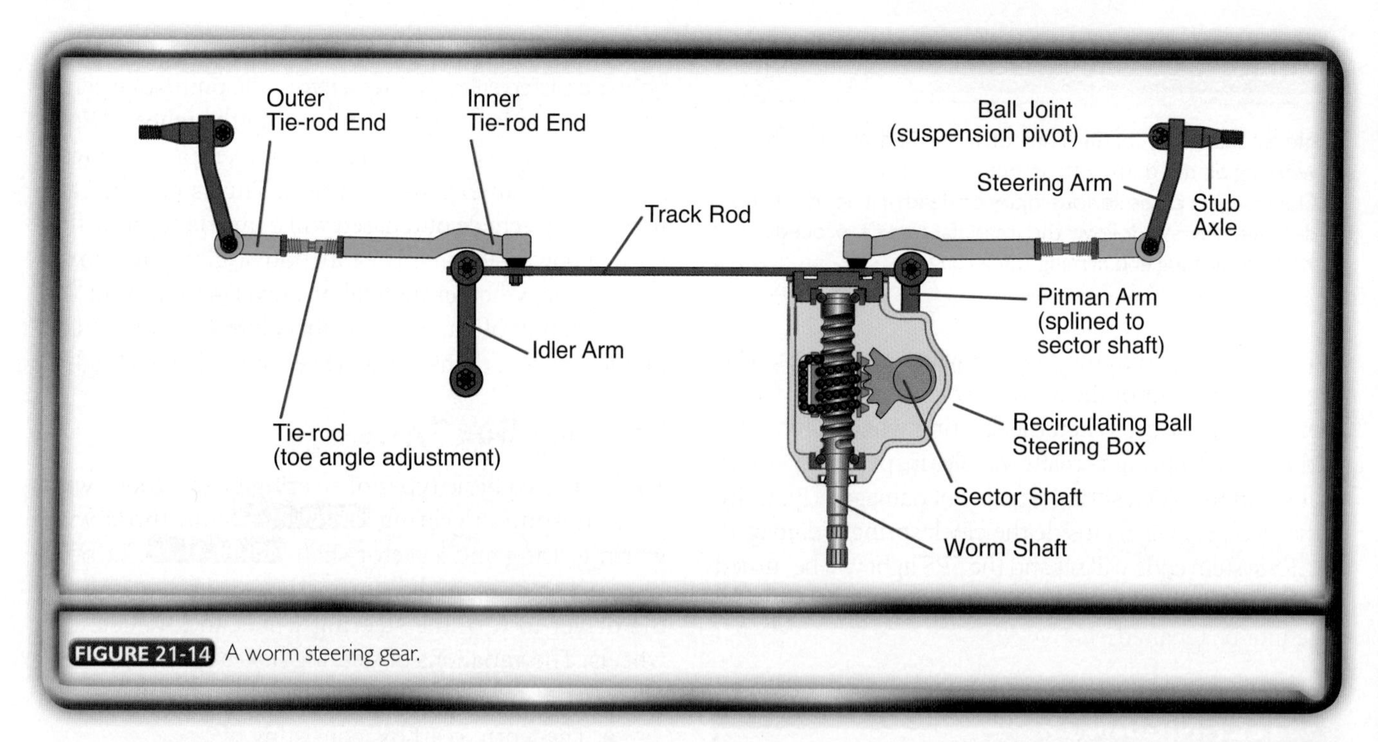
Outer
Tie-rod End
Inner
Tie-rod End
Ball Joint
(suspension pivot)
Steering Arm
Stub
Axle
Track Rod
Pitman Arm
(splined to
sector shaft)
Idler Arm
Recirculating Ball
Steering Box
Tie-rod
(toe angle adjustment)
Sector Shaft
Worm Shaft

FIGURE 21-14 A worm steering gear.

ment in the steering and suspension. On center take-off racks, the tie-rods connect to the center of the rack and pinion. The center of the rack is what moves on this style of rack and pinion.

Both the pinion and the rack teeth are helical gears. If an inclined plane is wrapped around a cylinder, the edge of the plane forms a shape called a **helix**. Rotation of the cylinder causes a point on the helix to move along the surface of the cylinder. The distance the point moves in one revolution of the cylinder is called the **pitch**. The helix shape is commonly used as a thread on nuts and bolts, and also for teeth in steering gears and transmissions. The particular shape and positioning of the teeth in a helical gearing enable smoother and quieter operation for the driver.

Mechanical advantage is gained by the **reduction ratio**, the ratio between the turns of the steering wheel and the angle turned of the wheel (both measured in degrees). The value of this ratio depends on the size of the pinion. A small pinion gives easy steering, but it requires many turns of the steering wheel to travel from lock to lock, which is as far as the steering wheel can be turned from one side to the other. So, instead of a single hard turn of the steering wheel, the driver turns the wheel several times with less force behind each turn. A large pinion means the number of turns of the steering wheel is reduced, but the steering is harder to turn.

Reduction ratios vary depending on the type of vehicle, such as a passenger vehicle versus a tractor trailer. But in each case, in fixed-ratio rack-and-pinion systems, the ratio is the same for all positions of the wheels. It is a fixed ratio, meaning that within a single vehicle, the ratio is the same no matter where the steering wheel is positioned. The rack-and-pinion system produces a ratio between the degrees of steering wheel movement and the degrees of wheel movement. The ratio is called steering ratio and is typically calculated by turning the steering wheel one time and checking the number of degrees that the wheel assembly moves. For example, if one turn of the steering wheel produces 20 degrees of movement at the wheel, then dividing 360 degrees of steering wheel rotation by 20 degrees of wheel movement results in an 18:1 ratio. Steering ratio is not the same on all vehicles and is designed by engineers to provide the best steering response for the vehicle.

In some applications a variable-ratio gear is used, which allows a slow turn rate when the steering wheel is centered and a quicker rate when turned toward the steering lock. This feature provides easier and quicker turning, but keeps the vehicle very stable when traveling straight at high speeds. The variable-ratio rack-and-pinion system uses a specially designed pinion gear tooth, which is more rounded. The rack has teeth that are narrowly spaced in the center and further apart toward the end. Closer teeth provide slower movement of the rack in relation to the turns of the pinion. On other vehicles, it is preferable that the steering be more responsive near the center point, which is ideal for maneuvering at slower speeds. This is accomplished by having widely spaced teeth in the center of the rack and closer spaced teeth near the ends. When designed this way, the steering wheel moves the rack further for each rotation of the pinion when in the center position than at the ends. This also helps prevent stiffer steering toward the full lock positions, since the steering arm leverage is reduced when the wheels are turned sharply.

The rack-and-pinion steering system has the advantages of a large degree of feedback and direct steering feel, meaning the driver can feel the road well. A disadvantage of the rack-and-pinion steering system is that it typically is not manually adjustable. Over time it does wear and develop lash between the pinion teeth and the rack teeth, which is felt as play, or movement, in the steering wheel that does not move the wheels. In many cases, replacement of the rack and pinion is the only cure for excessive lash in the gear teeth.

In the rack-and-pinion steering system, the steering rack is supported at the pinion end by being sandwiched between the pinion and a **spring-loaded rack guide yoke**, sometimes called the rack bearing. Spring-loaded rack guide yokes are made of metal, nylon, or other durable material and have a spring that pushes on the back side of the rack to help reduce the play between the rack and the pinion, while still allowing for relative movement. There may be an adjuster plug that screws into the body of the rack to put pressure on the rack guide yoke. This adjustment produces the correct mesh of the rack teeth to the pinion teeth. It also affects the amount of torque required to turn the pinion. If the setting is incorrect, such as if you are trying to eliminate play in the rack and pinion, turning force of the pinion will become greater and may result in a steering wheel that will not return properly, a condition sometimes referred to as memory steer. Do not adjust the mesh of the rack-and-pinion gears unless directed by service information.

The rack is typically supported at both ends of the **rack housing** or tube by a bushing, a nylon piece that keeps the rack from wearing on the metal housing FIGURE 21-15. Nylon is used because it has a low coefficient of friction and low wear rates. The bushings are an

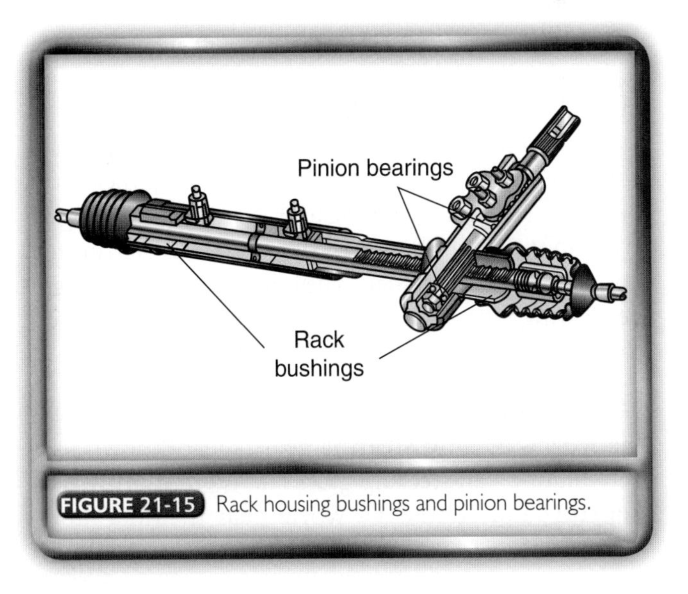
Pinion bearings
Rack
bushings

FIGURE 21-15 Rack housing bushings and pinion bearings.

Applied Math

AM-52: Probability: The technician can relate problem symptoms to the probability of the malfunction of a specific part or system.

A common problem with steering systems, particularly in older vehicles, is excessive free play. Typically, the customer will describe the problem as the steering feeling "loose" or "sloppy." A road test will quickly verify the concern; there will be excessive movement of the steering wheel in the straight-ahead position, before the wheels even begin to turn.

With a pick-up truck that has a basic steering system, the excessive free play could be caused by wear in a number of points within the system. There is a higher probability of the fault being caused within the steering linkage than within the steering gearbox, so components such as tie-rod ends, idler arms and bushings, and pitman arms and bushings should be checked and eliminated first, before inspecting the steering gearbox.

integral part of any steering and suspension system. The bushings enable the flexibility needed to accommodate slight radial or lateral movement to assist in **antibinding**, or release when something gets stuck. However, when the bushings wear beyond the limits, they become a liability because they no longer are effective at eliminating play in the steering rack. Regular maintenance and inspection of the steering system is necessary to ensure the safety of the vehicle and its occupants.

The pinion is supported by two bearings in the rack housing. The bearings must be **preloaded** (already compressed from pressure) to ensure the pinion is in the correct position, relative to the rack, and to eliminate free play.

A rack-and-pinion steering box is normally lubricated by grease. Each end of the rack is protected from dirt and water by a flexible synthetic rubber bellows attached to the rack housing and to the tie-rod. The rubber bellows extends and collapses as the tie-rods move away from and toward the rack housing as the rack moves. On some vehicles, the rubber bellows are interconnected by a tube so that as the steering wheel is moved from side to side, air is transferred from the collapsing bellows side to the expanding bellows side. This process keeps the rubber bellows from collapsing.

With rack-and-pinion steering, the rack is directly connected to the **tie-rod assembly**, which is attached to the steering knuckle. The tie-rod assembly consists of an inner and an outer tie-rod end that are threaded together. The inner tie-rod is threaded onto the rack and has a ball-and-socket swivel joint to allow movement in any direction. The other end of the inner tie-rod is threaded to allow attachment of the outer tie-rod end, which provides the method used to adjust the toe angle.

The steering arm, the **stub axle** knuckle, and the **stub-axle carrier** (the body of the stub axle knuckle) can be forged as one piece, and can be referred to as a steering **knuckle** FIGURE 21-16. They can also be made as separate units and assembled to form one piece.

Worm Gearbox

Worm gear steering boxes made the process of turning the front wheels an easier task for drivers of the early automobile. The worm gearbox uses two gears: a worm and a worm gear (also called a worm wheel). The worm has teeth cut in a helical (spiral) shape and operates the same as a screw. In this case, the helix on the worm moves the worm wheel one tooth for each revolution of the worm. The helix provides smooth and quiet steering operation for the driver. It converts the rotary motion of the steering wheel to the linear motion needed to control the wheels. This system also produces a large **gear reduction**. The **gear ratio** of the gear train within the gearbox is a comparison of the angles of movement between the steering wheel and the wheel assembly and is expressed as a ratio; for example, 18:1. The gear ratio of a worm gearbox increases output torque and reduces the effort the driver has to apply. Within the steering system, gear reduction transforms a large turn of the steering wheel into a smaller turn of the road wheels. Use of gear reduction makes steering easier for the driver. Wheels require a large force to be steered due to the weight of the vehicle pushing the tire into contact with the road. If there were no gear reduction in the steering gear, the driver would not be able to force the tires to pivot on the road's surface.

FIGURE 21-16 Two-piece steering knuckle and steering arm.

Worm gears have another benefit: they do not transmit nearly as much road shock as a rack-and-pinion gear assembly. When the worm is driven (by the steering wheel), the output gear moves easily since each turn of the worm advances the worm wheel one tooth. But if the worm wheel is driven (such as by road shock), the worm wheel teeth butt up against the teeth on the worm, preventing most of the force from being transmitted as rotary motion to the worm. This occurs because most of the force from the output gear is nearly perpendicular to the rotation of the worm gear.

Several forms of the worm gearbox have been used throughout the history of the automobile, although they all use the same component—the worm gear arrangement. Three popular styles have included the worm-and-sector, worm-and-roller, and recirculating ball gearboxes.

Worm-and-Sector Gearbox

The first worm gearbox was of the worm-and-sector style. The worm is meshed with a sector, or portion of a gear, mounted on its own shaft (called a sector shaft), at right angles to the worm. The outer end of the sector shaft has a tapered or straight spline that mates with an internal spline on the pitman arm. As the steering wheel rotates, the worm causes the sector to move through an arc and transfer the motion, through the pitman arm, to the steering linkage. This style of gearbox produced more friction between the gears as the driver turned the steering wheel than later worm gearboxes, which made steering difficult. Variations include the worm-and-roller and the recirculating ball worm gear.

Worm-and-Roller Gearbox

The **worm shaft** in a worm-and-roller steering box has an hourglass shape, and it meshes with a double-track roller, mounted on bearings, on a pin attached to the pitman shaft FIGURE 21-17. This gearbox was an improvement to the worm-and-sector style and reduced the friction due to the roller, which reduced the friction between the two gears. This design makes turning the steering wheel easier. As the driver turns the steering wheel, the worm rotates and the roller rolls against the worm, moving in an arc, following the hourglass shape, and transferring the motion to the pitman shaft. The hourglass shape changes the steering ratio slightly as the steering wheel is turned from the central position toward each lock.

Recirculating Ball Gearbox

The worm-and-nut steering gear is also known as a recirculating ball steering gear. The **recirculating ball steering box** contains a worm gear inside a block

FIGURE 21-17 The worm-and-roller steering gearbox.

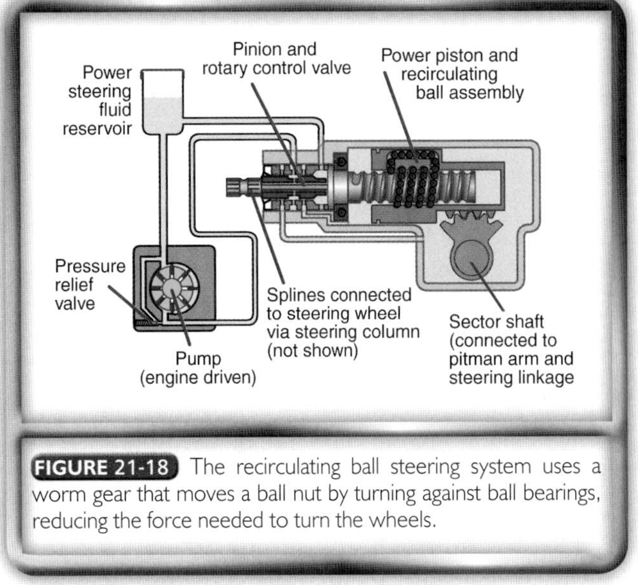
Power steering fluid reservoir
Pinion and rotary control valve
Power piston and recirculating ball assembly
Pressure relief valve
Splines connected to steering wheel via steering column (not shown)
Sector shaft (connected to pitman arm and steering linkage
Pump (engine driven)

FIGURE 21-18 The recirculating ball steering system uses a worm gear that moves a ball nut by turning against ball bearings, reducing the force needed to turn the wheels.

(nut) with a threaded hole in it and gear teeth cut into its outside that engage the sector shaft to move the pitman arm. It was developed in 1940 and is an improved version of the worm-and-sector and worm-and-nut types of worm gear. In the recirculating ball gearbox, both ends of the worm shaft are supported in the housing by angular bearings, which are preloaded to reduce lateral movements known as **end play** and side-thrust movements of the worm gear when it is under load. A ball nut rides on the worm gear, supported on the spiral grooves of the worm and the inside of the nut by many balls FIGURE 21-18. The balls form a low-friction internal thread, which causes the nut to thread up or down on the worm as it rotates. With rotation, the balls are rolled along the grooves, partly in the worm and partly in the nut. When they get to the end of the groove, they circulate by passing through **ball-return guides** to the other end of the nut. Ball-return guides are simply special passages through which the balls move. External teeth on one side of the nut mesh with the teeth of the sector gear formed on the sector shaft, and these transfer the motion through the pitman arm to the steering linkage to produce the left and right motion at the front wheels.

The sector gear and nut teeth are designed so that when the teeth are in the straight-ahead position, they have minimum clearance. This is called the high point. This design reduces free play when the steering wheel is straight. The pitman shaft is supported by two caged needle roller bearings in the steering box housing. The sector teeth are angled, and an adjustment screw on the steering housing cover allows for adjustment of the sector gear height, which provides proper engagement of the sector gear and nut teeth.

TECHNICIAN TIP

On passenger vehicles with independent suspension and a recirculating ball-type steering box, the steering box may be mounted so that the steering linkage is in front of (front steer) or behind (rear steer) the suspension cross member. When the steering linkage is behind the suspension cross member, it is protected by the cross member from possible damage, and the position of the steering box reduces the length of the steering column. This protects the steering box from damage by road debris.

TECHNICIAN TIP

In forward-control vehicles, the steering system is mounted in front of the engine and wheels. The steering box is mounted on the frame, with the pitman arm vertical. A **drag link** is a steel rod that transfers movement of the pitman arm to a **relay lever**. The relay lever is another steel rod that is used to transfer the movement from the drag link to an idler arm. The relay lever has two arms, one connected to the drag link and the other to the idler arm by the track rod. The longitudinal movement of the drag link pivots the relay lever. As a result of these connections, motion is transferred through the track rod to the idler arm and through the tie-rods to the wheels.

Four-Wheel Steering Systems

Some vehicles have **four-wheel steering**, meaning the rear wheels can be steered independently of or in conjunction with the front wheels FIGURE 21-19. The ability to steer the rear wheels improves high-speed handling and increases maneuverability during driving tasks such as U-turns and parallel parking. There are two types of four-wheel steering systems—active and passive. Passive systems use compliant rubber bushings that allow a limited amount of rear-wheel steering, typically toward the inside of the corner, under cornering maneuvers. The passive system operates independently of the steering wheel and driver input, which is why it is called a passive system.

In active four-wheel steering systems, the front wheels are controlled normally, and the rear wheels are typically steered through use of a computer and electric motors. In past designs, rear-wheel steering systems could be controlled mechanically through a direct connection between the front and the rear steering boxes. In modern computer-controlled four-wheel steering, an actuator similar to a front rack-and-pinion assembly attaches to the rear steering knuckles with tie-rod ends. The actuator turns the wheels when commanded by the steering control module. Originally, some actuators were powered hydraulically by the power steering pump and electronic control valves. Most systems still in use today use a rack-and-pinion assembly driven by an electric motor. Some manufacturers have adopted the standard that at low speeds the rear wheels will turn in the opposite direction to the front wheels, providing a substantially reduced turning radius, while at higher speeds the rear wheels will turn in the same direction as the front wheels, producing smaller yaw forces during turning maneuvers. This standard provides better control of a vehicle at high speeds and better handling at low speeds, which is useful for functions like parallel parking. Other manufacturers use systems that disable rear steering at higher speeds and only allow rear steering at slow speeds to allow tighter cornering, such as when backing up a trailer.

Power Steering

As vehicles became heavier in the front end due to the increased use of front-wheel drive and wider low-profile tires, more steering effort became necessary. As a result, **power steering** was introduced. One type has an **engine-driven hydraulic pump** that delivers hydraulic fluid to the power unit at the steering box or rack-and-pinion assembly through connecting hoses and pipes FIGURE 21-20. When the driver moves the wheel, the hydraulic pressure is sent to the rack or steering box. The power steering system is designed so that the vehicle can still be controlled even if the engine or the power steering system were to fail—though greater effort would be required.

There are three types of power steering:

1. Hydraulically assisted power steering
2. Electrically powered hydraulic steering
3. Fully electric power steering

Hydraulically Assisted Power Steering

Hydraulically assisted power steering uses hydraulic fluid under pressure to assist the driver in steering the wheels.

FIGURE 21-19 Four-wheel steering showing the rear wheels being steered in conjunction with the front wheels.

FIGURE 21-20 Power steering fluid being added to a power steering pump reservoir.

This design is especially helpful at slower vehicle speeds when steering wheel turning effort is much higher. An engine-driven hydraulic pump delivers hydraulic fluid to the power unit at the steering gearbox, or rack-and-pinion assembly, through the control valve and connecting hoses and tubes. The fluid reservoir can be mounted on the pump, or it can be remotely mounted. With the engine running, fluid flows continuously from the **power steering pump** to the steering gear control valve and back to the power steering pump. With the steering wheel in the neutral position, minimal pressure is needed to maintain fluid flow, and minimal engine power is needed to operate the system.

Some manufacturers task the power steering system with double duty. The pressure from power steering pumps has been used to power hydraulic brake boosters on hydroboost vehicles. It has also been used to turn the radiator fan on a number of vehicles. Be aware that the power steering system is integrated into those systems on some vehicles.

Power Steering Fluid and Hoses

The hydraulic fluid in a power steering system transmits the pressure from the power steering pump to the working chambers in the power steering gear or rack. The fluid must withstand high temperatures and pressures, and at the same time lubricate the pump and steering gear, while preserving the system seals and pressure hoses. The fluid must also flow freely at very cold temperatures. Many manufacturers have specified certain types of automatic transmission fluid for their power steering systems over the years, while others call for specific formulations of a separate power steering fluid. Since there is typically only a quart or two of power steering fluid in the system, it gets worked pretty hard. The harder it is worked, the hotter it gets. The hotter it gets, the shorter its life. For this reason, some vehicles are equipped with a power steering fluid cooler. This is usually built into the high-pressure line and helps cool the fluid before it gets to the steering gear.

Power steering fluid also gets contaminated with rubber and metallic particles from internal wear in the system. Because of this, some manufacturers install a replaceable filter in the power steering system. While many manufacturers do not specify a power steering fluid change interval, the fluid does degrade over time and becomes contaminated. Many technicians recommend flushing power steering fluid every 50,000 to 100,000 miles, depending on the vehicle and how it is driven.

Power steering hoses are used to carry power steering fluid from the pump to the steering gear. This is the high-pressure hose and is usually made of flexible, high-pressure hose material. The return hose runs from the steering gear back to the pump reservoir and carries fluid under much lower pressure. These hoses must also allow movement between the engine and chassis, so they can't be too stiff. Over time, power steering hoses can become weak or damaged. If they leak, they can quickly cause the system to run dry. And since the pressure is very high, if the high-pressure hose leaks, it can spray hot power steering fluid all over the engine and exhaust. Power steering fluid is flammable, so leaks can cause extreme fire hazards. Because of this, they should be inspected for seepage or wear during each oil change. Also, most power steering hoses use an O-ring to seal the end of each hose to the pump and steering gear. These seals can wear or leak, requiring replacement of the O-ring.

Steering Process

The hydraulic pressure is controlled by a rotary valve located on the input shaft of the steering gear. When the steering wheel is turned, the rotary valve directs fluid to one side or the other of a piston attached to the steering gear. Pressure then increases as required to provide steering assistance.

In a rack-and-pinion steering gear, the piston is formed centrally on the steering rack, and the rack housing provides the working cylinder FIGURE 21-21. Pressure seals at each end of the cylinder isolate the **power section** from the rest of the rack and pinion. Seals in the rotary valve section at the pinion input prevent internal and external fluid leakage.

In a recirculating ball steering box, the power piston and seals slide in a cylinder in the housing FIGURE 21-22. The power piston has an extension formed on one side, with teeth that engage teeth on the sector shaft. Pressure applied to either side of the power piston produces a force, which is transferred through the teeth, to help turn the sector shaft.

Connecting pipes transfer fluid from the rotary valve housing to one side of the piston or the other to provide assistance, which acts directly on the steering gear. The rotary valve is located between the steering gear input shaft and the pinion gear, or worm. It consists of an inner member, which forms part of the input shaft, and a surrounding sleeve member, fixed to the pinion gear or worm. It appears as a shaft within a shaft.

Turning the steering wheel makes both members rotate in the steering gear housing, but it is the slight rotary displacement of the inner member and the sleeve member that controls and directs the power steering fluid flow. This slight rotary displacement is allowed by a **torsion bar**, which is a spring-loaded piece of steel connected to the pinion gear or worm at its bottom end and the input shaft at its top end FIGURE 21-23.

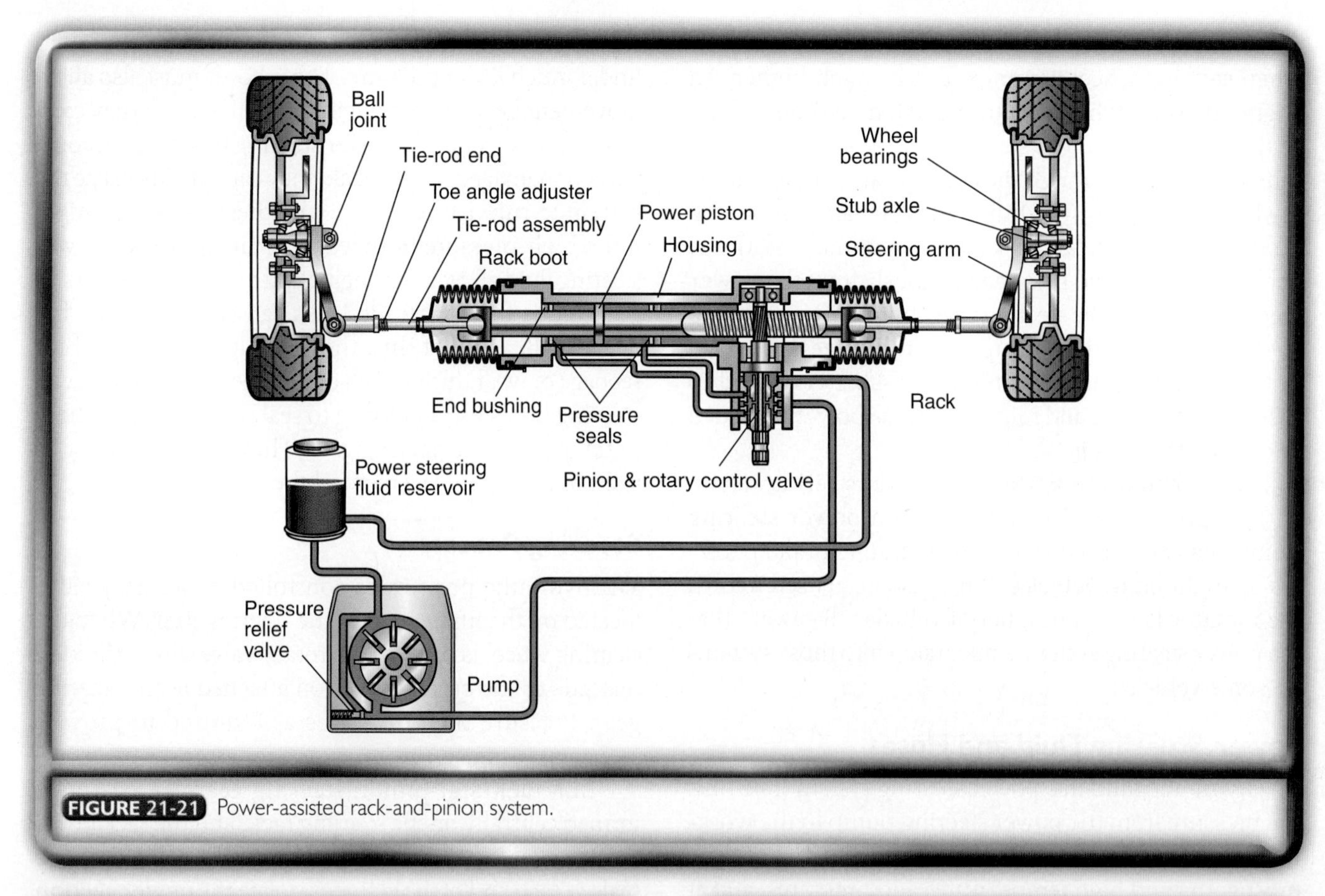
Ball joint
Tie-rod end
Toe angle adjuster
Tie-rod assembly
Rack boot
Power piston
Housing
Wheel bearings
Stub axle
Steering arm
End bushing
Pressure seals
Rack
Power steering fluid reservoir
Pinion & rotary control valve
Pressure relief valve
Pump

FIGURE 21-21 Power-assisted rack-and-pinion system.

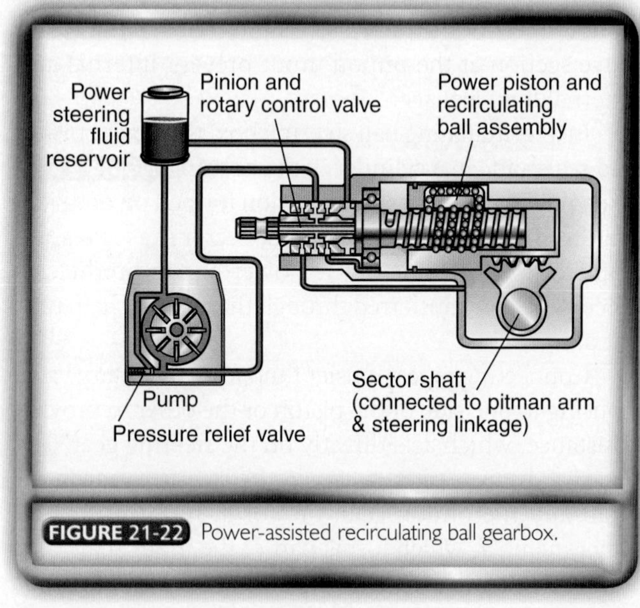
Power steering fluid reservoir
Pinion and rotary control valve
Power piston and recirculating ball assembly
Sector shaft (connected to pitman arm & steering linkage)
Pump
Pressure relief valve

FIGURE 21-22 Power-assisted recirculating ball gearbox.

FIGURE 21-23 Power steering rotary valve and torsion bar.

When the steering wheel is turned, there is resistance from the front wheels at the road surface. This resistance is transmitted through the steering gear so that the input shaft twists slightly on the torsion bar. Since the inner member is also attached to the input shaft, this twisting provides a relative rotary displacement of the inner and outer members. It is this displacement that lets fluid flow through the valve to act on the piston at the steering gear. The input shaft can twist through only a small angle before it contacts a stop on the pinion gear or worm. This is needed as a fail-safe to provide manual steering when power assistance is not available.

With the engine running and the steering in the neutral position, fluid flow is directed into the valve assembly through drilled holes in the outer sleeve FIGURE 21-24. As soon as the steering is turned to the left or right, the

FIGURE 21-24 Drilled passageways through the outer sleeve over the rotary valve.

slight relative movement occurs between the inner and the outer members. In the neutral position, the inner member lets fluid pass equally to both sides of the rack piston and return to the fluid reservoir. Equal, but low, pressure is applied to both sides of the power piston. No power assistance is needed.

When the steering wheel is turned, fluid is restricted from making a free return to the reservoir. It is now directed to the side that matches the turning action. At the same time, fluid on the opposite side is directed to the return circuit, back to the reservoir. Slight rotation of the valve gives a small amount of assistance, which becomes progressively greater as the torsion bar flexes and more assistance is needed. The grooves of the inner member are precisely shaped to meter the flow of fluid between the apply and release passageways.

Flow-Control Valve

All power steering pumps have a **flow-control valve** to vary fluid flow and power steering system pressures. A pressure relief valve prevents excessive pressures from developing when the steering is on full lock (turned all the way to one side) and is held against its stops in that position. The flow-control valve is located at the outlet fitting of the power steering pump and regulates pressures to as high as 1200 to 1500 pounds per square inch (psi), or 8274 to 10,342 kilopascals (kPa). When the flow-control valve is forced open at a steering stop, there is usually an audible whine from this very high pressure.

During slow cornering or when parking, power steering pump speeds are normally low. There is less demand for fluid flow at this time because the engine speed is low, but high pressure is still needed to provide the required assistance. Discharge ports direct fluid to the pressure side outlet and then to the steering gear. The outlet fluid pressure is slightly lower than the internal high pressure coming from the power steering pump. This drop in pressure occurs as the fluid flow passes the needle and orifice in the outlet fitting. This lower pressure is transmitted through a bypass fluid passage to the spring end of the control valve. The pressure difference on the valve causes it to move away from the outlet fitting, but the force of the spring prevents it moving far enough to uncover a return port back to the pump inlet. Movement of the control valve controls the position of the needle valve in the outlet fitting. This controls the fluid flow to the steering gear FIGURE 21-25.

At higher speeds with no steering maneuvers, fluid flow is increased. This reduces pressure at the outlet. The lower pressure is transmitted to the spring end of the

> **Safety**
>
> When replacing or topping off power steering fluid, you must ensure that the correct type and brand of fluid is used. If the wrong type or brand is used, serious damage to the power steering pump and lines can develop, creating a potentially dangerous situation. Different fluids react differently to pressure and temperature changes. Using the incorrect fluid may result in the creation of excessive pressure within the system, bursting the high-pressure lines and potentially spraying fluid at high pressure all over the engine, creating a severe fire hazard. It would also cause a loss of steering assist, which could result in an accident.

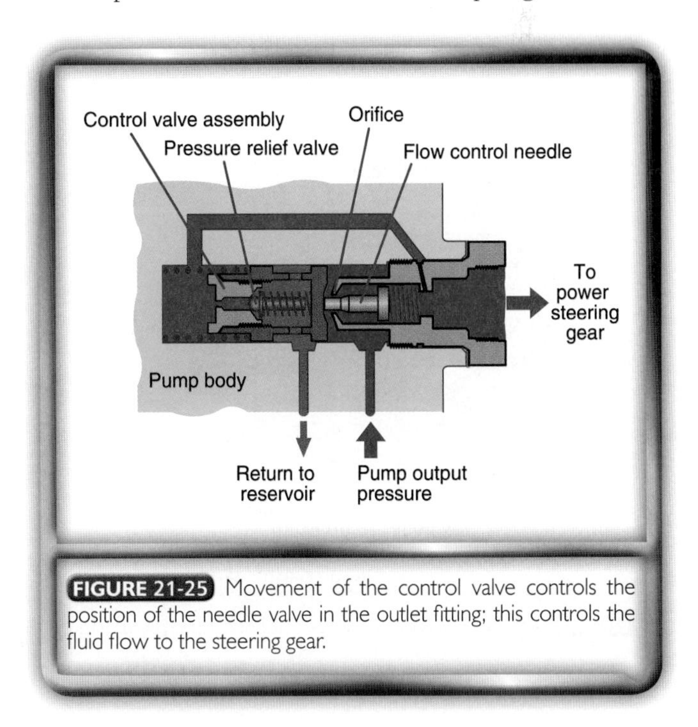
Control valve assembly
Orifice
Pressure relief valve
Flow control needle
To power steering gear
Pump body
Return to reservoir
Pump output pressure
FIGURE 21-25 Movement of the control valve controls the position of the needle valve in the outlet fitting; this controls the fluid flow to the steering gear.

control valve. The valve moves and opens the return port back to the pump inlet. Movement of the control valve also controls the movement of the flow control needle in the outlet fitting. The needle closes in the orifice, and fluid flow to the steering gear reduces.

With the steering wheel held at full lock, the steering rack power piston chamber becomes fully pressurized and fluid flow through the steering gear stops. This high pressure is transmitted back to the spring end of the control valve, opening the pressure relief valve. A small amount of fluid passes through the pressure relief orifice, providing a pressure drop. The valve moves and uncovers the return port to the pump inlet FIGURE 21-26. A predetermined relief pressure is thus maintained.

Idle Speed Strategy

When maneuvering a vehicle at slow speeds, the power steering demand will be high and the engine speed will be low. If the idle speed is not maintained during this condition, the engine could possibly stall. To prevent stalling, engineers program a strategy into the PCM that raises or maintains the idle speed under these conditions. A power steering switch or sensor inputs power steering pressure information to the engine control module, and based on this input and the actual engine idle revolutions per minute (rpm), the PCM is able to determine when additional airflow is needed to raise or maintain the desired engine rpm.

Electric Power Steering

The use of electronics in automotive steering systems enables much more sophisticated control to be achieved. Electric steering is more economical to run and easier to package and install than conventional hydraulic power steering systems and reacts faster to quick steering changes from the driver. Typically, electric and electrohydraulic power steering systems are also lighter and more compact than conventional hydraulic power steering systems. Both the electric power steering system and the electrohydraulic power steering systems are now considered as viable alternatives to conventional hydraulic power steering systems because of their energy efficiency and size.

Electrically powered hydraulic steering (EPHS) replaces the customary drive belts and pulleys that drive a power steering pump in a conventional rack-and-pinion steering system with a brushless motor. This system still uses a pump, but it is driven by an electric motor to reduce power drawn from the engine FIGURE 21-27. Pump speed is regulated by an electronic controller to vary pump pressure and flow. This provides steering efforts tailored for different driving situations. The pump can be run at low speed or shut off to provide energy savings during straight-ahead driving. An EPHS system is said to use only 20% of the engine power used by a standard belt-driven pump and improves fuel mileage by approximately 10%. The engine still contributes power to the steering system through electrical demand on the alternator of the vehicle, but it is greatly reduced from that of hydraulic power steering systems.

Electrically assisted steering (EAS) is a completely electrically powered power-assist system that eliminates all hydraulic components and fluid. An electric motor replaces the hydraulic pump. EAS or direct electric power

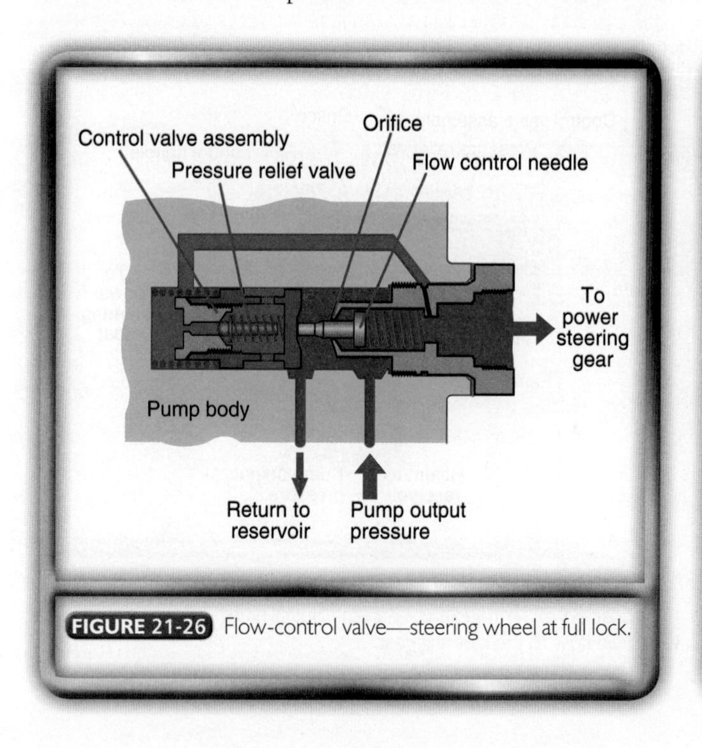
Control valve assembly
Orifice
Pressure relief valve
Flow control needle
To power steering gear
Pump body
Return to reservoir
Pump output pressure

FIGURE 21-26 Flow-control valve—steering wheel at full lock.

FIGURE 21-27 EPHS uses an electric motor to drive the power steering pump.

steering completely eliminates hydraulic fluid and the accompanying hardware from the power steering system, creating a fully **electric power steering (EPS) system**. The reduction of components saves weight and reduces drag on the engine, vastly improving fuel mileage. The EPS system is said to require only 2% of the engine power that a standard belt-driven power steering pump uses. There is still a small amount of power required from the engine, which supplies the electrical demand, but as you can see, it is greatly reduced.

An EPS steering system uses an electric motor attached either to the steering rack or to the steering column via a gear mechanism and torque sensor. A microprocessor or electronic control unit and diagnostic software control the steering dynamics and driver effort. Inputs include vehicle speed, steering wheel torque, angular position, and turning rate.

There are four primary types of electric power assist steering systems:

- Column-assist type: In this system, the **power assist unit**, controller, and **torque sensor** are attached to the steering column. The power assist unit is the electric motor, the controller is the electronic control unit, and the torque sensor measures the load on the steering wheel.
- Pinion-assist type: In this system, the power assist unit is attached to the steering gear pinion shaft. The power assist unit sits outside the vehicle passenger compartment, allowing assist torque to be increased greatly without raising interior compartment noise.
- Rack-assist type: In this system, the power assist unit is attached to the steering gear rack. It is located on the rack to allow for greater flexibility in the layout design FIGURE 21-28.
- Direct-drive type: In this system, the steering gear rack and power assist unit form a single unit. The steering system is compact and fits easily into the engine compartment layout. Direct assistance to the rack enables low friction and **inertia** (resistance to a change in motion), which in turn gives an ideal steering feel.

In these systems, **active control** provides constant feedback from sensors in the vehicle to the **control unit**, which calculates sophisticated computer algorithms. These features allow the steering system to react to the road, the weather, and even the type of driver, and provide assistance to the front or rear road wheels independent of direct driver input. For example, if the electronic stability control system detects the start of an oversteer condition, the control unit can actually steer the wheels in the opposite direction, trying to prevent loss of control of the vehicle. Thus, an EPS system might steer the vehicle opposite of the driver's input, if that input would lessen the control of the vehicle.

FIGURE 21-28 Rack assist steering system.

Basic EPS Operation

A steering sensor is located on the input shaft, where it is bolted to the gearbox housing.

The **steering sensor** performs two functions. First, as a torque sensor, it converts steering torque input and direction into voltage signals for the engine control unit (ECU) to monitor. Second, as a rotation sensor, it converts the rotation speed and direction into voltage signals for the ECU to monitor. An interfaced ECU circuit converts the voltage signals from the torque and rotation sensor into signals that the PCM can process, and ultimately provides the proper output signal to the EPS assembly.

The microprocessor control unit also analyzes inputs from the vehicle's speed and wheel speed sensors. The sensor inputs are then compared to determine how much power assistance is required according to the **forces capability map data** stored in the ECU's memory. These map data are preprogrammed by the manufacturer. The ECU sends the appropriate command to the **power unit**, which supplies the electric motor with the necessary current to operate as commanded. The electric motor then pushes the rack to either the right or the left. The direction of rack movement depends on which way the current flows; reversing the current flow reverses directional rotation of the electric motor. Increasing current to the electric motor increases the amount of power assist.

The EPS system has three operating modes:

- Normal control mode: Provides left or right power assist in response to input from the torque and rotation sensor's inputs
- Return control mode: Assists steering return after completing a turn

- Damper control mode: Adjusts the amount of assist according to the vehicle speed to improve road feel and dampen kickback

If the steering wheel is turned and held in the full-lock position—which is as far as the wheel can turn in one direction—and steering assist reaches maximum, the power unit reduces current to the electric motor to prevent an overload situation that might damage the electric motor. The power unit is also designed to protect the electric motor against voltage surges from a faulty alternator or charging system problem.

The electronic steering control unit is capable of self-diagnosing faults by monitoring the system's inputs and outputs and the driving current of the electric motor. If a problem occurs, the electronic steering control unit turns the system off by **actuating** (turning on) a fail-safe relay in the power unit. This eliminates all power assist, causing the system to revert to manual steering. An in-dash EPS warning light is also illuminated to alert the driver.

Higher Voltage Electrically Assisted Power Steering

Higher voltage electrically assisted power steering systems were developed for modern hybrid vehicles. In hybrid vehicles, the engine is typically off during idling, deceleration, and braking; thus, an EPS system was needed. The higher voltage battery system of the hybrid vehicle provides all the power, with no reliance on engine or hydraulic power. The parts are similar to an electrically assisted power steering system. The electric steering system does not use the full battery voltage from the high-voltage battery pack; instead, it is reduced to a lower voltage through a DC-to-DC converter, which basically just steps the voltage down. Some early hybrids simply used the 12-volt system that was used on gasoline vehicles, but newer models are using voltage as high as 46 volts. One thing to remember is that when voltage goes up, amperage can come down to produce the same wattage. Because of this principle of electricity, smaller gauge wires can be used in the electric steering system.

Diagnosis

Many of the problems associated with steering systems are mechanical, but as more EPS systems are produced, electrical faults are becoming more common. Mechanical joints and bushings, as well as motors, pumps, and switches, wear over time, decreasing in functionality and eventually failing. Sensors also are subject to wear, resulting in inaccurate readings and faulty reactions. The wires are subject to damage and breaks from other mechanical parts, as well as loose connections and wear. When confronted with a steering system problem, it is important to consider both the mechanical and the electrical components before finalizing a diagnosis. Also, since the suspension system is directly related to the steering system and helps to hold the wheels in the proper geometry, you will need to have an understanding of the suspension system. That way you will be able to determine exactly what is causing the customer's concern. Suspension systems are discussed fully in the Servicing Suspension Systems chapter.

Tools and Equipment

Some of the tools used in diagnosing and repairing steering system problems can be broken into two categories: tools for mechanical diagnosis and tools for electrical diagnosis. Tools for electrical diagnosis include the factory scanner and the digital volt-ohmmeter (DVOM). The factory scan tool is recommended by most manufacturers because it can perform tests and identify faults with the electrical portion of steering systems. The scan tool can read almost every system on a vehicle and provides valuable data to assist the technician in identifying problems. It is particularly useful in assessing electronic steering systems for wiring and sensor malfunctions. Typically, electronic steering system faults set a diagnostic trouble code that can be retrieved by the scan tool. Use of the service information to diagnose the fault is necessary as well as a DVOM. The DVOM is used to measure voltage and to check the continuity of the electronic circuit. Breaks in the wiring of an EPS system are not uncommon. When this occurs, the system opens or shorts out. The continuity test can pick up on any opens or shorts and help determine where the problem is located.

Tools and equipment used on the mechanical portion of the steering system include a power steering system pressure tester and various measuring devices, such as dial indicators and belt tension gauges. The mechanical components need to be removed and replaced, requiring tools such as a tie-rod puller, pickle forks, a pitman arm puller, tie-rod sleeve adjusting tools, inner tie-rod socket tools, inch-pound and foot-pound torque wrenches, hammers, air hammers, and pry bars FIGURE 21-29.

The following tools and parts are used in servicing the power steering system:

- Floor jacks and safety stands: Jacks are used to lift a vehicle, and the safety stands provide stability while working on a raised vehicle.
- Pry bar: The pry bar is a lever used to apply pressure for testing purposes or to move various components.

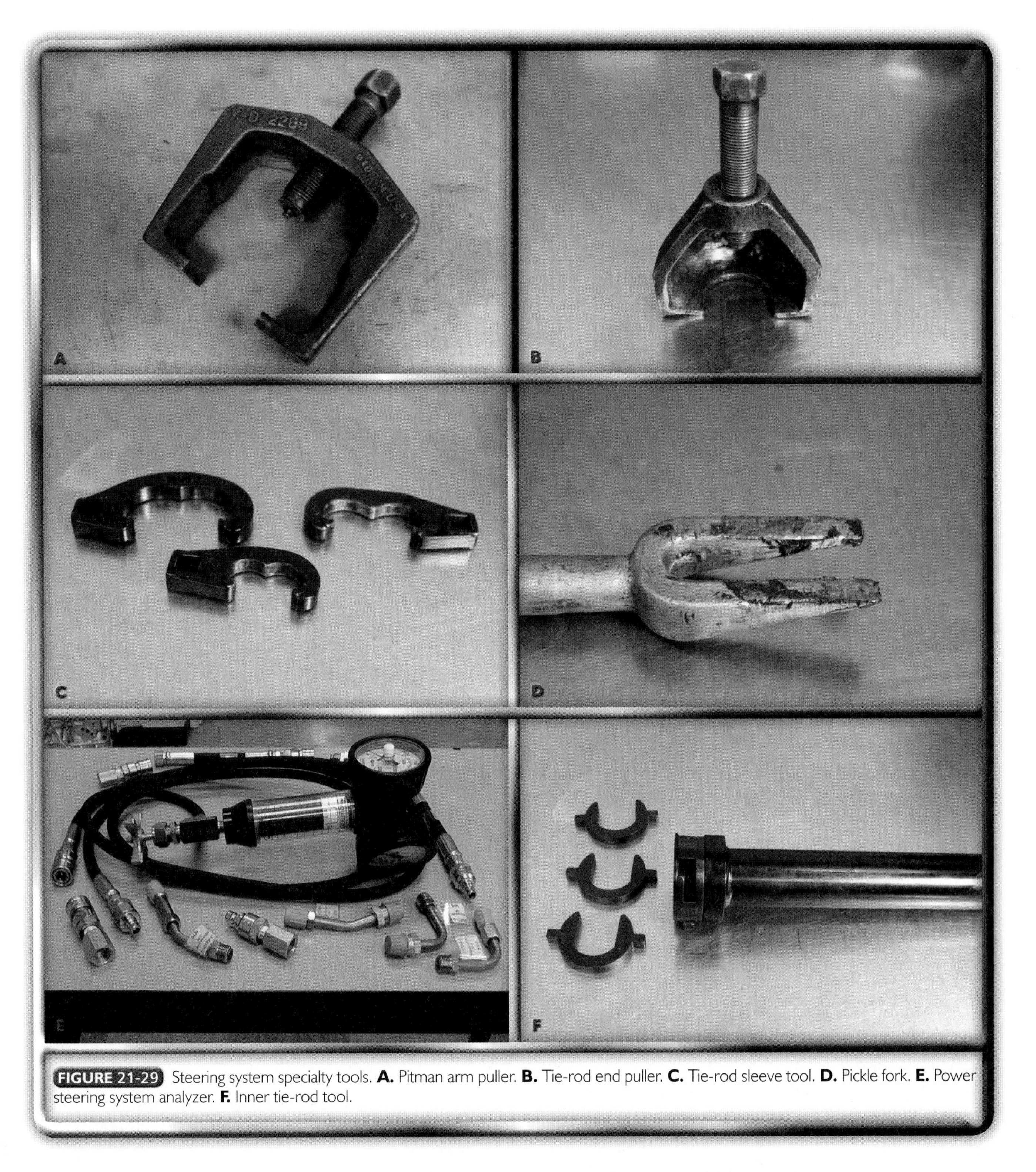
K-D 2289
A
B
C
D
E
F

FIGURE 21-29 Steering system specialty tools. **A.** Pitman arm puller. **B.** Tie-rod end puller. **C.** Tie-rod sleeve tool. **D.** Pickle fork. **E.** Power steering system analyzer. **F.** Inner tie-rod tool.

- Dial indicators: Dial indicators are used to measure the runout or movement on different parts of the steering system, such as play in tie-rod ends.
- Pitman arm puller: This heavy-duty puller is made specially for removing the pressed-on pitman arm from the sector shaft.
- Tie-rod end puller: This tool is used to pull the tapered shaft on a tie-rod end from its mating steering component.
- Tie-rod sleeve adjusting tool: This tool has a tab designed to grab the slot in the sleeve and is used to turn the sleeve when adjusting the toe setting.

- Pickle fork: This U-shaped wedge is used for separating tie-rod ends and is operated by hammer or air hammer. This tool will usually destroy the dust boot during the process, so it is not the best tool to use on tie-rods that will be reused.
- Inner tie-rod end tool: This tool is used to loosen and tighten inner tie-rod ends.
- Manufacturer-specific checking tools: The following tools are made specifically for auto dealerships. There is a wide variety of these tools designed for many different purposes:
  - Power steering system analyzer: This tool includes a pressure and flow gauge set with various fittings to attach in line with the power steering pump. It is used to check volume of fluid flow, maximum pressure, and leaks internal to the steering gear.
  - Scan tool: This tool is used to read codes and data from the vehicle's PCM when diagnosing the vehicle's computer-controlled systems.
  - DVOM: The DVOM, which stands for digital volt-ohmmeter, is used to measure voltage and ohms in a vehicle's electrical systems.
  - Various jumper leads: These are small wires with clips on the ends used to diagnose electrical problems.
  - Circuit tester: This is a test light used to diagnose electrical problems.
  - Belt tension gauge: This tool is designed to measure the amount of flex in a drive belt. Some manufacturers require the use of this tool to adjust proper belt tension.
  - Black light and dye kit: This tool is used to pinpoint fluid leaks. Dye is added to the fluid of the leaking system, and the black light makes the dye glow fluorescent.

Diagnosing Steering Systems

The main problems that arise in the steering system are play and hard steering. The common culprit for these problems is wear or poor lubrication. Play is the wiggling or increased movement of parts that results from wear in the connections between parts. In the steering system, play generally results from worn ball sockets and/or idler arms or too much clearance in the steering gearbox. Hard steering is difficulty in steering the vehicle. There are many faults that can cause hard steering, from low tire pressure to overly tight adjustments in the steering gearbox, to power steering that is not working properly. It is important to thoroughly check the entire steering system to identify all problems when hard steering is the issue. The best way to do this is by physically inspecting each of the components, checking or measuring play, looking for bent or damaged linkage, and testing the operation of the power steering system.

Diagnosing Power Steering Fluid Leakage

Power steering fluid is critical to the proper functioning of the entire steering system. Any power steering fluid leak, no matter how small, is cause for repair. Because a leak can occur anywhere throughout the system, it is necessary to thoroughly inspect it all. One method for checking for leaks is to clean all power steering fluid off the vehicle and then run it for a little while. Turn off the vehicle and reexamine for new leaks. Any drops of fluid are indicative of a leak. Another method uses standard fluorescent dyes. Following the dye manufacturer's instructions, add the appropriate amount of dye to the power steering system. After waiting the recommended amount of time, inspect the vehicle with a black light, which will illuminate the fluorescent dye and make it easy to spot leaks.

Diagnosing Power Steering Gear Issues (Non–Rack and Pinion)

Steering gear issues in a non–rack-and-pinion system can be one of the following: uneven effort needed for turning, looseness of steering, hard steering, unusual noises when steering, or leaks. If the issue is related to the power steering system, such as leaks, noise, or hard steering, you will need to perform a visual inspection of the drive belt and the fluid level and condition, as well as pressure testing of the power steering system if necessary.

If the issue is related to the steering linkage, you will need to perform a visual inspection of the linkage, joints, and steering gear. With the vehicle jacked up and placed on safety stands, have someone turn the steering wheel as you visually inspect the steering linkage. Check for binding, wear or loose connections, and other abnormal conditions. To check for binding issues, it may be necessary to separate the steering linkage to verify that binding is in the steering gearbox, linkage, ball joints, or steering column. For looseness concerns, do not forget to check the universal joint or coupler between the intermediate shaft and the steering gearbox. These components are prone to wear, which creates play. Refer to the manufacturer's service information for diagnostic information and tests for the concern you are working on.

Diagnosing Power Steering Gear Issues (Rack and Pinion)

Diagnosing steering gear issues in a rack-and-pinion system is similar to a non–rack-and-pinion system and includes the same common complaints, such as uneven effort needed for turning, looseness of steering, hard steering, and unusual noises when steering. If the issue is related to the power steering system, perform the inspection and tests associated with the power steering. If the issue is related to the steering linkage, perform a visual and hands-on inspection of the linkage, joints, and steering gear. With the vehicle raised on a hoist or jacked up and placed on safety stands, have someone turn the steering wheel as you visually inspect the steering linkage. Check for binding, wear or loose connections, debris, or any other anomaly.

Maintenance and Repair

The steering system, while being very critical to the safe operation of the vehicle, does not normally require a lot of maintenance. In older vehicles, each of the steering and suspension joints needed to be lubricated with grease during each oil change. Most, but not all, of these joints have been replaced with greased-for-life joints, so most vehicles do not have grease zerks to lubricate the joints. However, always be on the lookout, since many replacement joints use zerk fittings to keep them lubricated. Another area of scheduled maintenance on the steering system is replacement of the power steering belt and also possibly the power steering fluid.

To maintain a safe-operating vehicle, regular inspection of the steering components is essential. This can be performed both by visually inspecting the components and joints for damage, looseness, or leakage and by operating the steering system and looking or feeling for play in the components. Also, listening and feeling the steering components can help identify any needed maintenance or repair. Manufacturers will list the most appropriate method of inspecting and testing their systems. Always refer to the manufacturer's workshop information for these methods and wear specifications.

Checking and Adjusting Power Steering Fluid

The power steering fluid transmits pressure throughout a vehicle's power steering system. It also provides lubrication to the moving parts. It must be able to perform these functions in any weather conditions, maintaining its chemical integrity in the face of subfreezing temperatures or scorching heat. Given its importance, it is critical that the power steering fluid be inspected regularly for both purity (no contamination with debris) and level. The power steering fluid usually has both a hot and a cold indicator on the dipstick to ensure an accurate reading of the fluid level in both conditions. Always refer to the service information for the recommended type of power steering fluid.

To check and adjust power steering fluid, follow the steps in SKILL DRILL 21-1.

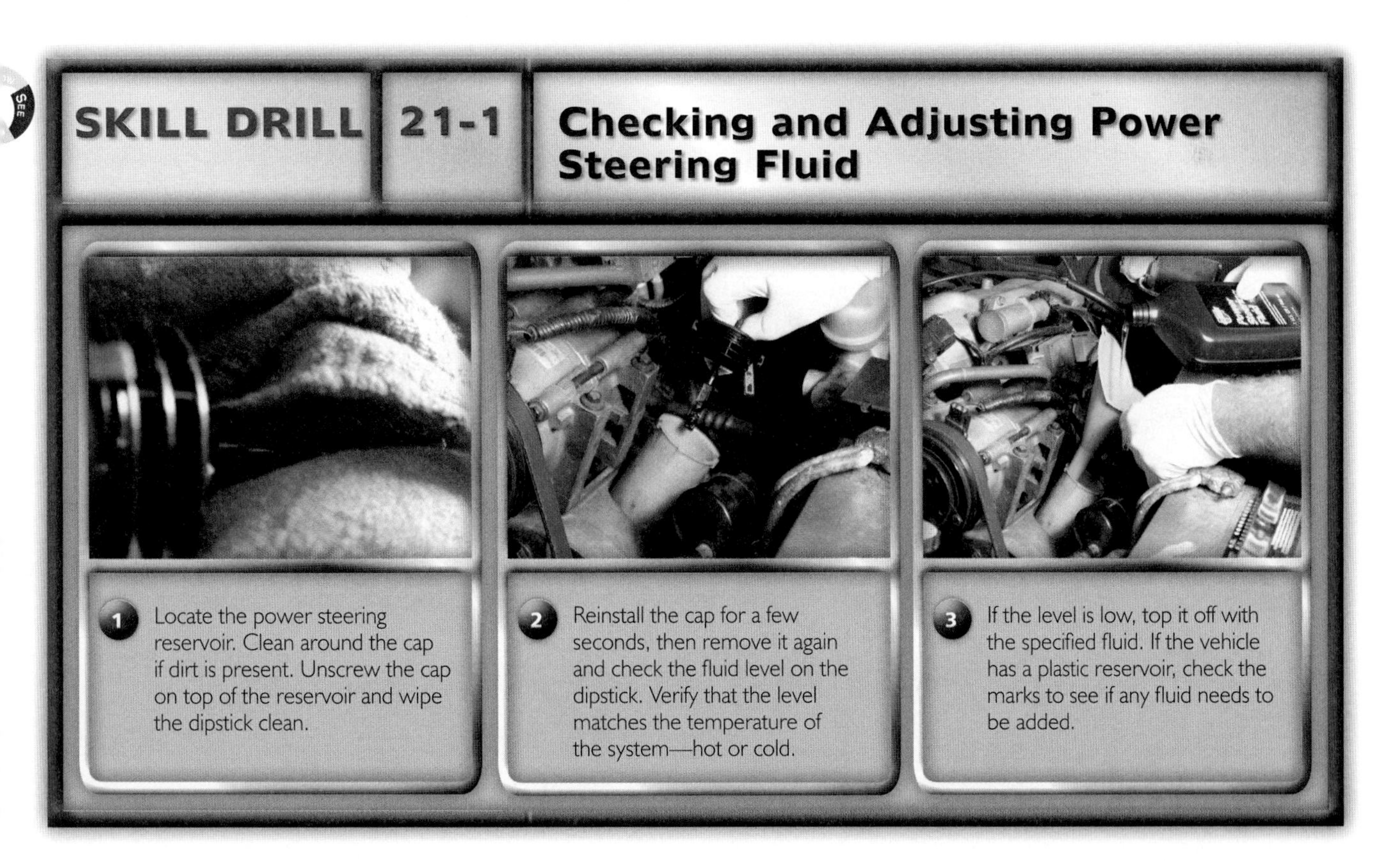
SEE

SKILL DRILL 21-1 Checking and Adjusting Power Steering Fluid

1. Locate the power steering reservoir. Clean around the cap if dirt is present. Unscrew the cap on top of the reservoir and wipe the dipstick clean.
2. Reinstall the cap for a few seconds, then remove it again and check the fluid level on the dipstick. Verify that the level matches the temperature of the system—hot or cold.
3. If the level is low, top it off with the specified fluid. If the vehicle has a plastic reservoir, check the marks to see if any fluid needs to be added.

Replacing Power Steering Pump Filter(s)

Some, but not all, vehicles use a replaceable power steering pump filter. It can be located in the fluid reservoir or in the return line. If it is in the reservoir, it may be a separate filter that sits in the bottom of the reservoir and can be carefully fished out of the reservoir and replaced. Other manufacturers build the filter into the reservoir such that the reservoir and filter are one unit and changed together. If it is an inline filter, it is usually installed in the return line due to the lower pressure. It may be spliced into the hose between the steering gear and the pump, or it could fit inside the return hose where the return hose connects onto the pump. When changing the filter, you may want to consider flushing the power steering system first to remove as much of the old fluid as possible before installing the new filter. Always check the service information to determine the scheduled service interval and the location of the filter.

To replace the power steering pump filter(s), follow the steps in SKILL DRILL 21-2:

1. Research the vehicle you are working on to determine if it has a power steering pump filter, its change interval, and its location.
2. Following the specified procedure, remove the filter.
3. Inspect any hoses or fittings for cracks and damage.
4. Install the new filter, top off the reservoir with the correct fluid, and check for proper operation and leaks.

Flushing a Power Steering System

Flushing the power steering system is the process of removing all the old power steering fluid and replacing it with new. It is performed whenever the manufacturer specifies a fluid change, the fluid appears contaminated or dirty, a major part of the hydraulic steering system is replaced, or there is a serious mechanical problem involving the power steering pump or steering gear that could cause metal shavings to be circulated through the system.

Only use the manufacturer's specified power steering fluid when flushing the system. When the service is complete, inspect for leaks after turning the steering wheel to the full-lock position in both directions and back to the center. Also ensure that none of the power steering hoses makes contact with any of the components. Typically a power steering system flush is performed with a flushing machine that is connected in line with the power steering system pump to remove all old dirty fluid and install new clean fluid without introduction of air. Note that air introduced into the power steering pump can be harmful to the pump since the pump is lubricated by the power steering fluid, and scoring of the pump can result if the pump is run dry. There are several types of flushing machines; if one is not available, flushing will have to be performed as shown in the following skill drill. Be sure to follow the manufacturer's procedure for flushing power steering fluid.

To flush a power steering system, follow the steps in SKILL DRILL 21-3.

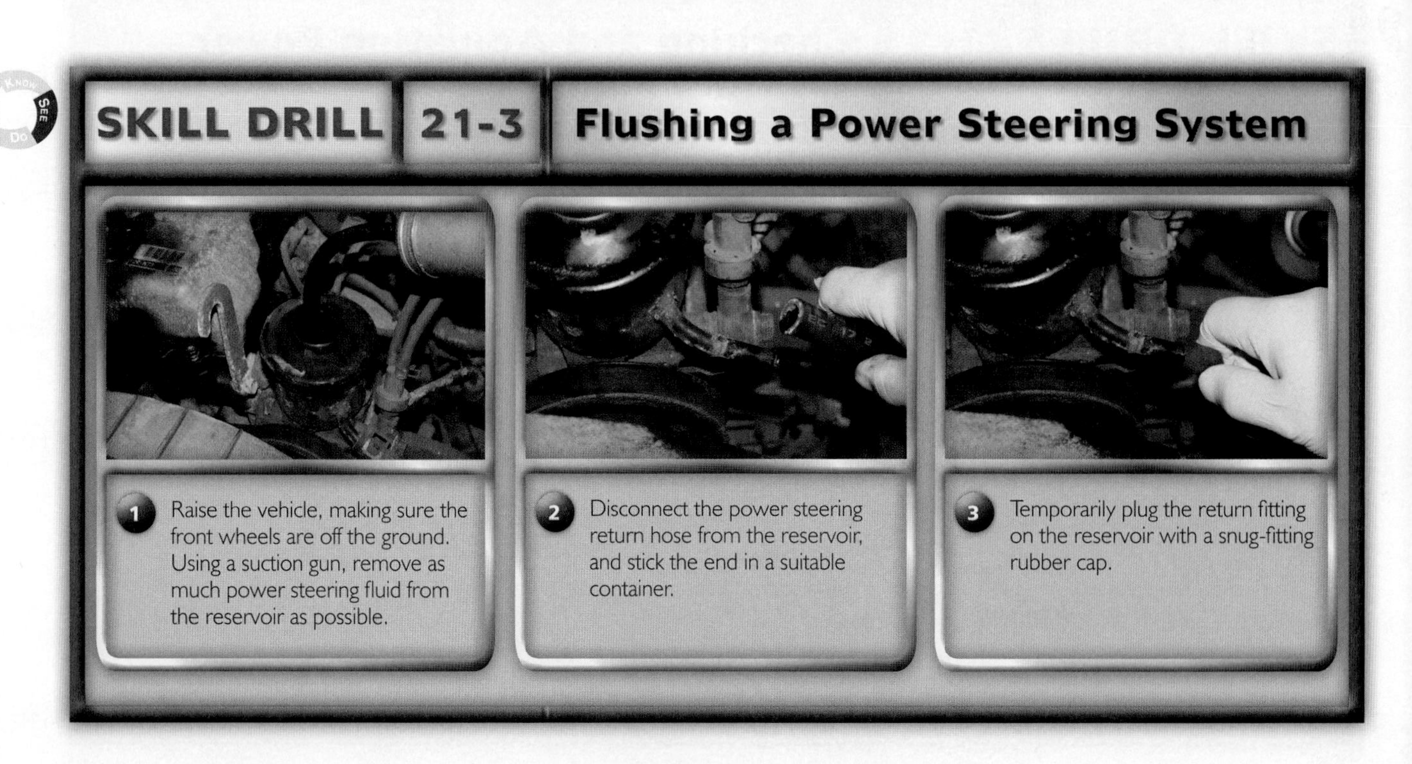
PROVE KNOW SEE DO

SKILL DRILL 21-3 Flushing a Power Steering System

1. Raise the vehicle, making sure the front wheels are off the ground. Using a suction gun, remove as much power steering fluid from the reservoir as possible.
2. Disconnect the power steering return hose from the reservoir, and stick the end in a suitable container.
3. Temporarily plug the return fitting on the reservoir with a snug-fitting rubber cap.

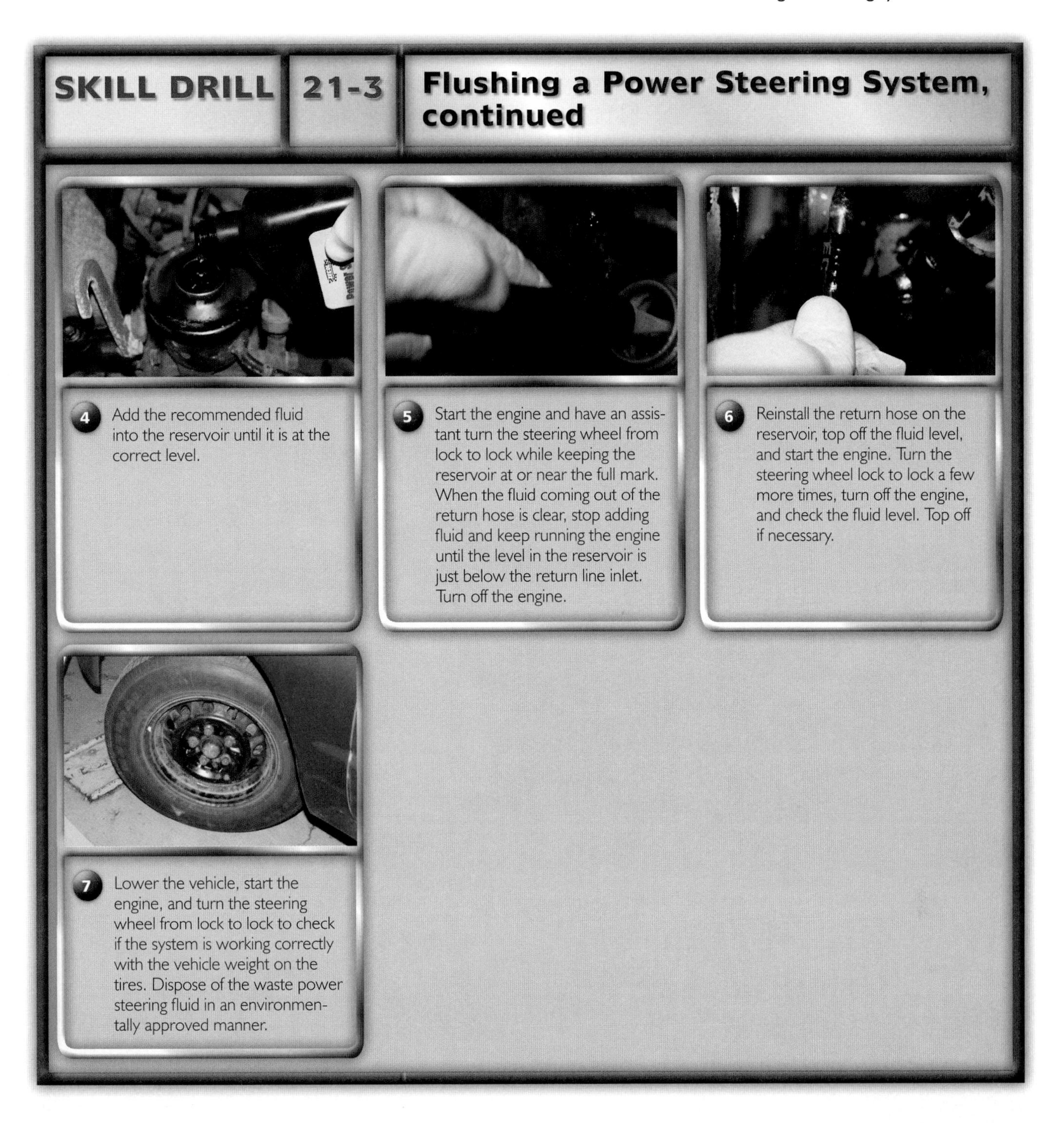
SKILL DRILL 21-3 Flushing a Power Steering System, continued
4 Add the recommended fluid into the reservoir until it is at the correct level.
5 Start the engine and have an assistant turn the steering wheel from lock to lock while keeping the reservoir at or near the full mark. When the fluid coming out of the return hose is clear, stop adding fluid and keep running the engine until the level in the reservoir is just below the return line inlet. Turn off the engine.
6 Reinstall the return hose on the reservoir, top off the fluid level, and start the engine. Turn the steering wheel lock to lock a few more times, turn off the engine, and check the fluid level. Top off if necessary.
7 Lower the vehicle, start the engine, and turn the steering wheel from lock to lock to check if the system is working correctly with the vehicle weight on the tires. Dispose of the waste power steering fluid in an environmentally approved manner.

Inspecting and Replacing Power Steering Hoses and Fittings

Any leakage of power steering fluid out of a power steering pressure hose can be catastrophic. Because it is being actively pumped, the fluid could spray out of the hose at high speed and spray all over the hot engine and exhaust system. The heat of the engine parts will cause the power steering fluid to smoke and billow out from under the hood and even catch on fire. Small leaks or leaks in the return line will result in low fluid level in the power steering reservoir and will leave spots on the floor or parking space. If the fluid level gets low enough, it can cause a buzzing noise when driving. This noise is louder when steering the vehicle. The level of power assist may also fluctuate. If any of these symptoms are present, or to catch issues before they become this severe, it is important that the power steering hoses be inspected regularly and replaced at any sign of wear. Always refer to the manufacturer's workshop information before beginning this operation.

To inspect and replace power steering hoses and fittings, follow the steps in SKILL DRILL 21-4.

SKILL DRILL 21-4 Inspecting and Replacing Power Steering Hoses and Fittings

1 Raise the vehicle on a lift or support it on safety stands. Inspect each of the power steering hoses and fittings for leaks and damage.

2 Place a drain pan under the fitting to be disconnected. Use a flare nut wrench to loosen the fitting while you are holding the nut on the pump or steering gear with a wrench.

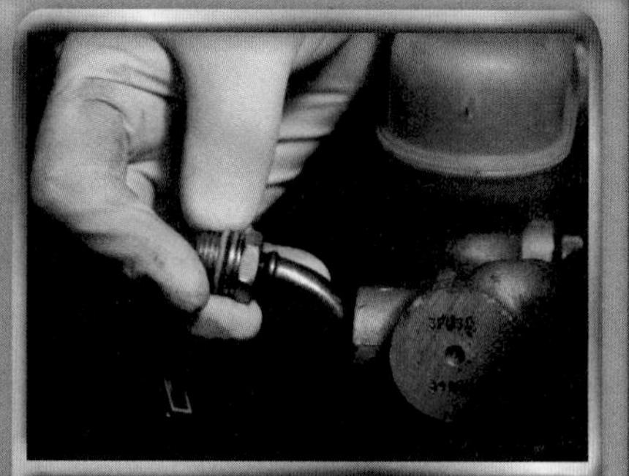

3 If replacing the O-ring, inspect the mating surfaces of the fitting for damage. If no damage is found, replace the O-ring and reinstall the fitting, being careful not to cross-thread or overtighten.

4 If replacing the hose, disconnect the fitting on the other end of the hose. Compare the old and new hoses to verify the correct replacement part.

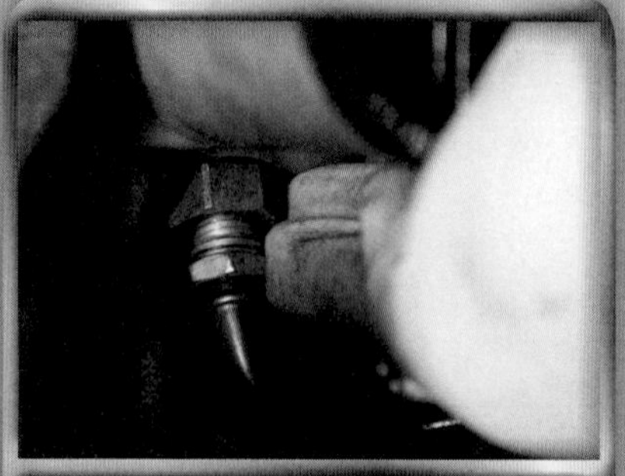

5 Carefully start the fitting on each end of the hose by hand, making sure they are not cross-threaded.

6 Check the routing of the new hoses, ensuring that they do not make contact with any components that could cause a failure to occur; then tighten the fittings to the proper torque.

7 Top off the reservoir with the specified fluid, start the engine, and turn the steering wheel from lock to lock a few times. Check for fluid leaks. Refill the fluid as necessary, and repeat the bleeding process as needed.

Inspecting Mounting Bushings and Brackets

During the normal wear and tear of vehicle use, the rack-and-pinion mounting bushings become compressed, brittle, or torn, and brackets may be damaged or lost. If the vehicle has an oil or power steering fluid leak, the fluid may leak onto the mounting bushings. The oil tends to soften and degrade the bushings. When this happens, the driver typically complains of either loose steering or noises when driving or turning. In either scenario, a quick inspection of these parts is warranted.

To inspect mounting bushings and brackets, follow the steps in SKILL DRILL 21-5.

Inspecting Rack-and-Pinion Steering Gear

Removing and replacing the rack-and-pinion steering gear is not to be undertaken lightly. It should be considered only after carefully examining all parts of the steering system and performing a full diagnosis to ensure the problem is not a result of some other fault. Many symptoms can point to a worn rack-and-pinion assembly, such as tire wear, wandering, and hard or uneven steering. But those symptoms can result from other faults as well. Regardless of the symptoms, all other steering problems should be considered and eliminated before undertaking the removal or replacement of the rack-and-

SKILL DRILL 21-5 Inspecting Mounting Bushings and Brackets
1 Raise the vehicle on a lift, keeping the weight of the vehicle on the wheels, if possible. Inspect the bushings and brackets for any faults.
2 Try moving the rack-and-pinion assembly up and down by hand.
3 Have an assistant rock the steering wheel back and forth while you look for movement in the rack-and-pinion bushings. If the rack moves significantly, place a torque wrench on the mounting bolts and tighten them to specifications. If the rack still moves, then bushing replacement will be necessary.
4 Remove the bracket bolts.
5 Remove the bushings from the rack.
6 Install new bushings in reverse order of removal.

pinion steering gear. Consult the service information for the specific steps to inspect the rack-and-pinion steering gear for the vehicle you are working on.

To inspect a rack-and-pinion steering gear, follow the steps in SKILL DRILL 21-6:

1. Safely raise and secure the vehicle on a hoist.
2. Visually inspect the rack-and-pinion assembly for any damage, worn bushings, fluid leaks, or torn dust boots.
3. Inspect the flexible coupling for wear or damage.

Inspecting Rack-and-Pinion Steering Gear Inner Tie-Rod Ends and Bellows Boots

Over time, the inner tie-rod ends wear and can cause excessive play in the steering linkage. Also, bellows boots may become torn or dislodged from their seat. When bellows boots are torn, dirt or abrasives may enter the unit, accelerating wear of rack-and-pinion seals and bushings. Routine inspection can identify damage early, before additional problems arise. Refer to the appropriate service information when replacing the inner tie-rod ends and bellows boots.

To inspect rack-and-pinion steering gear inner tie-rod ends and bellows boots, follow the steps in SKILL DRILL 21-7.

Inspecting the Pitman Arm, Relay (Center Link/Intermediate) Rod, Idler Arm and Mountings, and Steering Linkage Damper

With any steering complaints, it is necessary to check the components of the steering linkage for wear and damage. Slight problems in any of these components may result in significant steering problems and tire wear. Looseness in the idler arm may cause excessive toe change on rough road surfaces, leading to a wandering condition. Looseness in and of the tie-rod ends may be felt as loose steering and is frequently mistaken as a steering gearbox problem. Because of these issues, each of the steering system joints needs to be inspected for excessive wear or damage. Some vehicles are equipped with a steering damper connecting the frame and center link. This damper minimizes, or dampens, steering-wheel shimmy caused by hitting a bump in the road. Refer to the manufacturer's service information for the procedure and specifications for inspecting these components.

To inspect the idler arm, follow the steps in SKILL DRILL 21-8.

To inspect the pitman arm, follow the steps in SKILL DRILL 21-9.

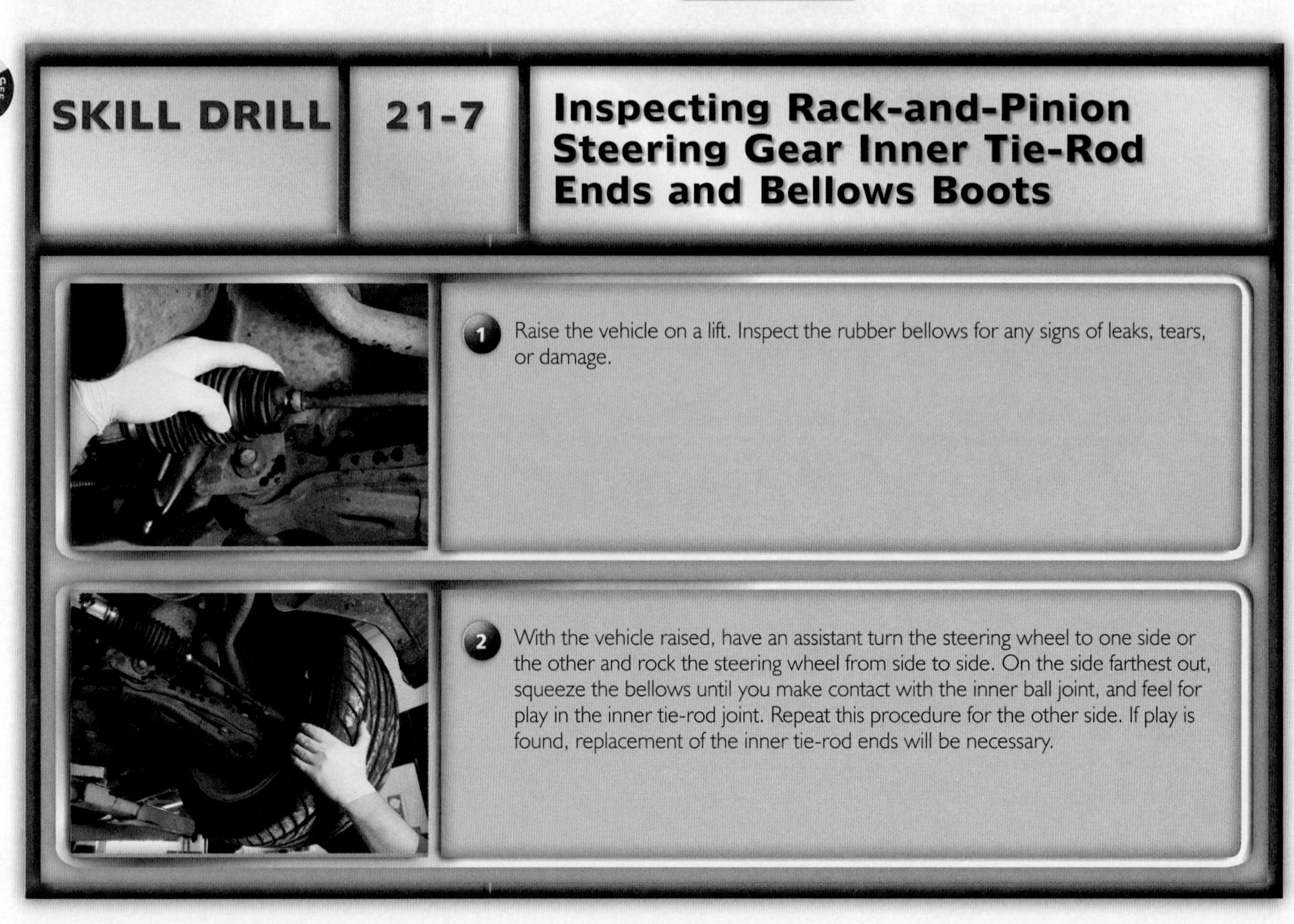
Prove Know See Do

SKILL DRILL 21-7 Inspecting Rack-and-Pinion Steering Gear Inner Tie-Rod Ends and Bellows Boots

1. Raise the vehicle on a lift. Inspect the rubber bellows for any signs of leaks, tears, or damage.
2. With the vehicle raised, have an assistant turn the steering wheel to one side or the other and rock the steering wheel from side to side. On the side farthest out, squeeze the bellows until you make contact with the inner ball joint, and feel for play in the inner tie-rod joint. Repeat this procedure for the other side. If play is found, replacement of the inner tie-rod ends will be necessary.

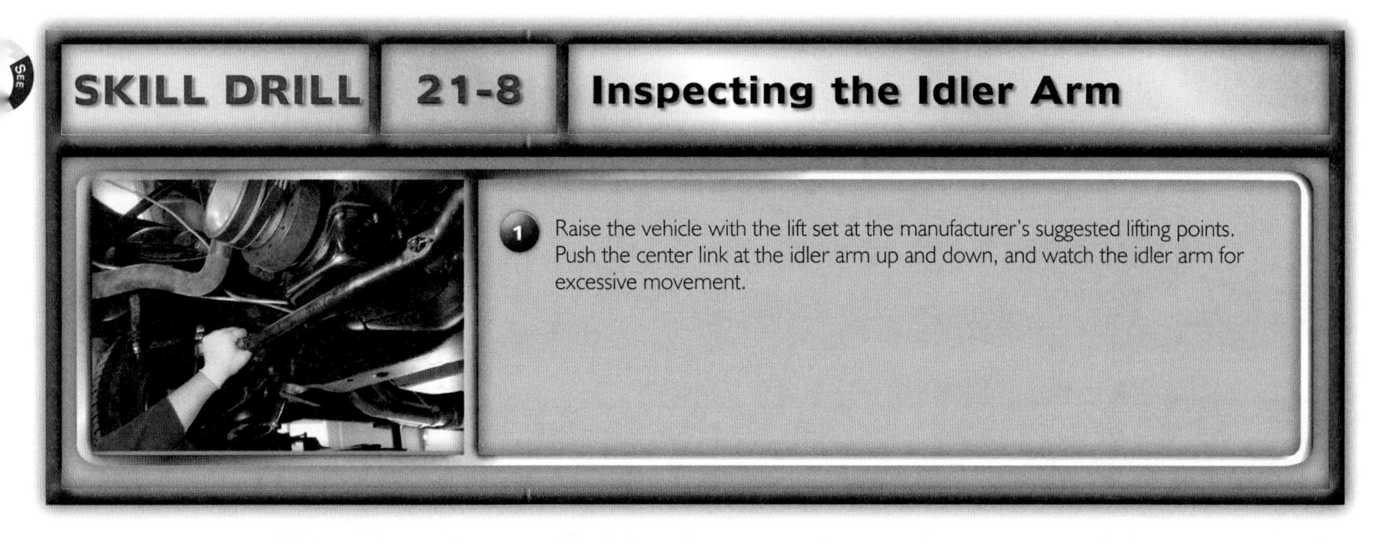

SKILL DRILL 21-8 Inspecting the Idler Arm

1. Raise the vehicle with the lift set at the manufacturer's suggested lifting points. Push the center link at the idler arm up and down, and watch the idler arm for excessive movement.

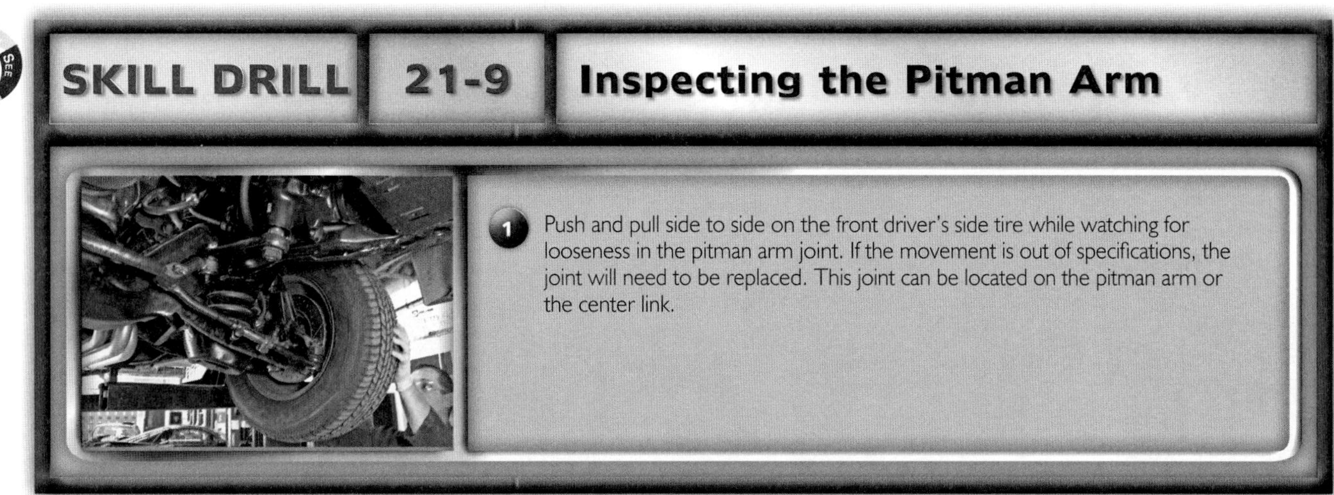

SKILL DRILL 21-9 Inspecting the Pitman Arm

1. Push and pull side to side on the front driver's side tire while watching for looseness in the pitman arm joint. If the movement is out of specifications, the joint will need to be replaced. This joint can be located on the pitman arm or the center link.

To inspect the center link (relay rod/intermediate rod), follow the steps in SKILL DRILL 21-10.

To inspect the steering linkage damper, follow the steps in SKILL DRILL 21-11.

Inspecting Tie-Rod Ends, Tie-Rod Sleeves, and Clamps

Tie-rods make the final connection between the steering linkage and the steering arms. The point of connection with the steering linkage is considered the inner tie-rod end, and the end that connects to the steering arm is considered the outer tie-rod end. Checking tie-rods is important in identifying steering problems because the ends are frequently damaged or worn. There are two basic types of tie-rod ends: spring-loaded and pre-loaded. Each type has its own procedure for inspection and replacement of the ends. Replacement of tie-rod ends requires an alignment to be performed or rapid tire wear will occur. Note: If removing a tie-rod from an aluminum steering knuckle, do not use a pickle fork, as it will damage the soft aluminum. Use the approved tie-rod end puller to separate the end from an aluminum knuckle or steering arm. Be sure to follow the manufacturer's service information for testing and replacement of tie-rod ends.

To inspect preloaded tie-rod ends, follow the steps in SKILL DRILL 21-12.

Safety

On vehicles with high-voltage systems (50 volts or higher), you may be required to wear insulated gloves appropriate for the system voltage you are working on. Always make sure the gloves have been tested for electrical leaks within the required time frame. And always test the gloves before using them by rolling up the sleeve, trapping air inside, and verifying that there are no air leaks. If there are any air leaks, do NOT use them, as electricity could travel through the hole.

SKILL DRILL 21-10 Inspecting the Center Link (Relay Rod/Intermediate Rod)

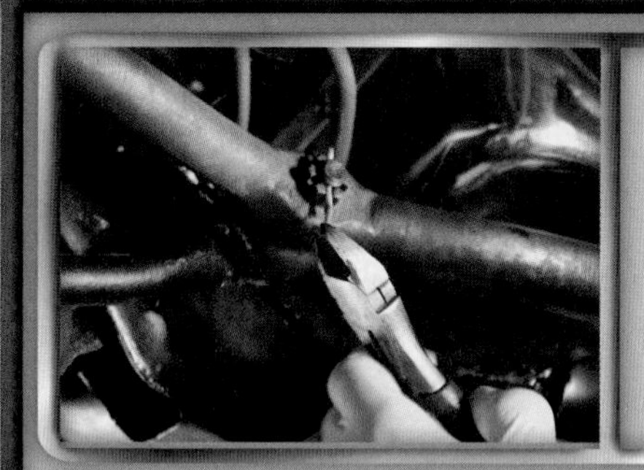

1. Push and pull the tire/wheel assembly from side to side, checking each of the center link joints for excess movement. If the movement is out of specifications, the joint(s) will need to be replaced.

SKILL DRILL 21-11 Inspecting the Steering Linkage Damper

1. Safely raise the vehicle with the lift set at the manufacturer's suggested lifting points. Look for fluid leaking out of the damper or a bent rod in the damper, and check that the bushings are tight in the damper.

2. Grab the wheels and turn them right and left. If the damper is working properly, there should be a fair amount of resistance when trying to turn the wheels quickly. If any of these conditions are found, replacement will be necessary.

3. Grab the damper and wiggle it to check for any looseness. If found, replacement will be necessary.

SKILL DRILL 21-12 Inspecting Tie-Rod Ends

1. With the vehicle's weight on the tires, have an assistant gently rock the steering wheel between the 10 o'clock and the 1 o'clock positions. Note any side-to-side or up-and-down movement in the tie-rod ends. If the ball and socket is worn, replacement will be necessary.

Inspecting Electric Power Assist Steering

On vehicles equipped with EPS, the electric power assist system should be tested any time a driver complains of steering difficulties, either hard or loose. The first step is to verify the concern by starting the vehicle and operating the steering wheel while observing the EPS warning lamp. If the lamp goes out as it should and the power steering feels normal, you may need to perform a test-drive and check the operation of the steering system under driving conditions. The test-drive should confirm the customer's concern and give you valuable information regarding the fault.

If the EPS lamp is off, you will want to perform a visual inspection of the mechanical components such as tire pressure, tires, tie-rod ends, rack bushings, and steering column for excessive play or damage. If the EPS lamp indicates a fault, a scan tool will need to be hooked up to the vehicle's data link connector. The scanner accesses and retrieves data from the vehicle's onboard computer and identifies the diagnostic trouble codes (DTCs). The DTCs are used with the manufacturer's flowchart for that code (found in the service information) to identify the exact problem. Consult the service information for the exact steps for repair or replacement.

Identifying Hybrid Vehicle Power Steering System Electrical Circuits

A technician may be called upon to identify the electrical circuits within the power steering system of a hybrid vehicle, particularly when an electrical problem is suspected. Because the technology in hybrid vehicles varies and is continuously evolving, and because some of these vehicles run on high voltage, the best procedure is to refer to the manufacturer's service information. This information will include a section devoted to diagnosis, along with the wiring diagrams for the various systems. The technician should examine the diagrams and compare them to the systems in the vehicle. Most manufacturers identify their high-voltage wires with specific colors, but there is not a uniform color designation across all manufacturers. Currently, orange, yellow, and blue are used by manufacturers for circuit voltages higher than 12 volts. Always research the color of high-voltage wiring in the service information for any hybrid or electric vehicles prior to working on them.

Disabling and Enabling the SRS

The SRS system must be disabled and enabled while working on or around the steering column, any of the airbags or other pyrotechnic devices, and any of the sensors. Failure to disable the SRS system could cause one or more of the SRS devices to deploy, which can cause serious injury or death, along with an expensive repair. It is important to know that most airbags are inflated by igniting a solid fuel similar to rocket fuel.

Every manufacturer has its own procedures for disabling and enabling the SRS system on its vehicles, and those procedures can be different for each of the vehicle models they sell. Always follow the manufacturer's specified procedure for the model of vehicle you are working on. Also, this is one time that you DO NOT use a memory minder or auxiliary power supply on the vehicle. Doing so could supply power to the SRS system after it has been disabled.

To disable and enable the SRS, follow the steps in SKILL DRILL 21-13.

Safety

Many airbags are now of the two-stage variety so they can deploy with the proper amount of force depending on the severity of the accident, approximate weight of the occupant, etc. This means that even a deployed airbag is still potentially dangerous and needs to be treated with caution during removal. It should be deployed soon after removal, following the manufacturer's specified procedure, which will render it safe for disposal.

Know
See
Do
Prove

SKILL DRILL 21-13 Disabling and Enabling the SRS

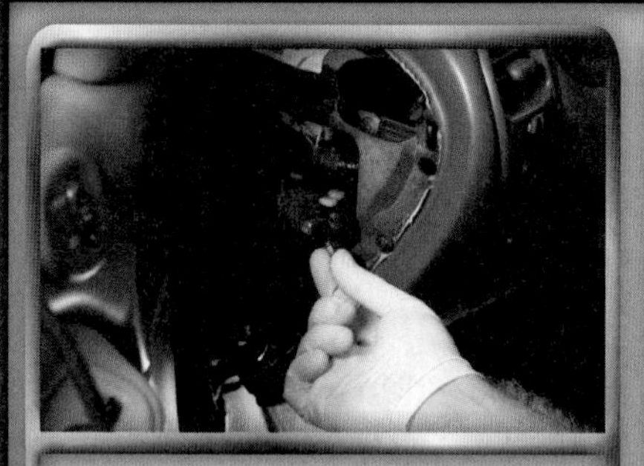

1. Find and remove the SRS fuse. Verify by turning the key on and observing that the SRS light remains lit for at least 30 seconds. If it goes out, you did not remove the correct fuse or all of the required fuses. Make sure the wheels are steered straight ahead. Turn the key off.

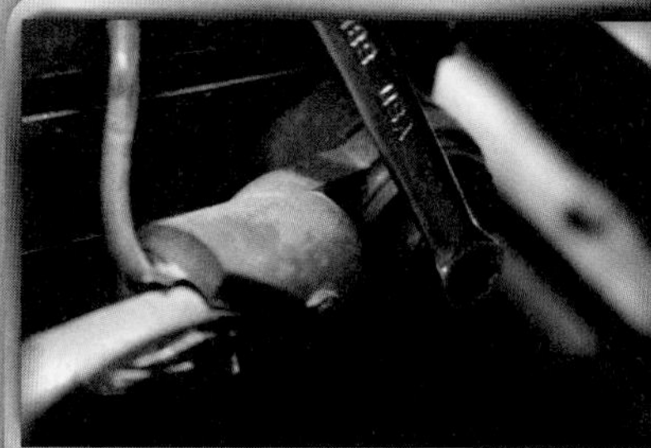

2. Remove the negative battery cable and allow a minimum of 15 minutes to pass to let the SRS system capacitors discharge. Note any radio presets or other memory features of the vehicle that will be erased when the battery is disconnected. *Do not use a memory minder or auxiliary power source!*

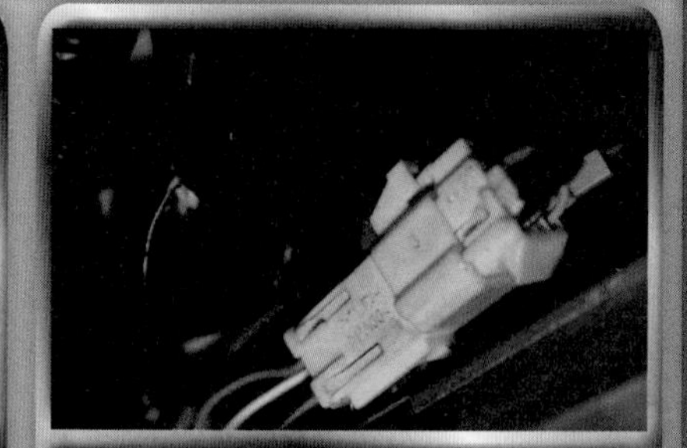

3. To enable the SRS system, verify that all SRS modules, components, and connectors are installed and connected properly.

4. Reinstall the SRS fuse.

LEGEN

5. Reconnect the negative battery terminal and tighten properly.

10
MPH

6. Without being in front of or reaching across the driver's side airbag, turn on the ignition switch and observe the SRS light. It should illuminate briefly and then go out, and stay out. If so, the SRS system should be ready to be placed back into service.

Wrap-up

Ready for Review

- The power steering system can be either a hydraulic or electric type.
- A basic steering system has four main parts: a steering column, a steering box, a steering linkage, and a steering knuckle.
- Steering geometry is a geometric arrangement of linkages in the steering of a vehicle, designed to keep the wheels properly oriented through various positions of the steering and suspension systems.
- The rack-and-pinion steering system is used on the majority of front-wheel drive vehicles because of the space restriction under the hood.
- The parallelogram steering system is used on larger vehicles where ride comfort is more important than sporty handling.
- When servicing the steering column, it is good practice to disarm the triggering system for the drigver's side airbag. If not properly disarmed, it could trigger accidentally.
- Because of the critical nature of the airbag, it is imperative that it is always connected electrically to its control module, so it can be deployed when needed.
- The function of all steering boxes, whether manual or power, is the same: to transfer the rotary motion of the steering wheel into the side-to-side motion needed to make the wheels pivot left and right.
- There are two basic types of steering boxes: those with rack-and-pinion gearing and those with worm gearing and a sector shaft. In both types, the gearing in the steering box makes it easier for the driver to turn the steering wheel and, hence, the wheels.
- Four-wheel steering means the rear wheels can be steered independently of or in conjunction with the front wheels. There are two types: active and passive.
- There are three types of power steering: hydraulically assisted power steering, electrically powered hydraulic steering, and fully electric power steering.
- Electrically powered hydraulic steering replaces the customary drive belts and pulleys that drive a power steering pump in a conventional rack-and-pinion steering system with a brushless motor.
- The steering sensor performs two functions: First, as a torque sensor, it converts steering torque input and direction into voltage signals for the ECU to monitor. Second, as a rotation sensor, it converts the rotation speed and direction into voltage signals for the ECU to monitor.
- Higher voltage electrically assisted power-steering systems were developed for modern hybrid vehicles. The higher voltage battery system of the hybrid vehicle provides all the power, with no reliance on engine or hydraulic power.
- Many of the problems associated with steering system are mechanical, but as more EPS systems are produced, electrical faults are becoming more common. The main problems that arise in the steering system are play and hard steering; common causes are wear and poor lubrication.
- Power steering fluid is critical to the proper functioning of the entire steering system. Any leak, no matter how small, is cause for repair.
- To maintain a safe-operating vehicle, regular inspection of the steering components is essential.
- Removing the rack-and-pinion steering gear should be considered only after examining all parts of the steering system and performing a full diagnosis to ensure the problem is not the result of some other fault.
- Checking tie-rod ends is important in identifying steering problems because the ends are frequently damaged or worn.
- On vehicles equipped with EPS, the electric power assist system should be tested any time the driver complains of steering difficulties, either hard or loose.

Key Terms

active control A system of providing constant feedback from sensors in the vehicle to the control unit.

actuating The act of making something move or work.

adjustable bushing A brace or nylon part that pushes against the rack to adjust the mesh of the rack teeth to the pinion teeth.

adjustment sleeve A component that connects the tie-rods together and to the center link on some applications, providing the adjustment point for toe-in or toe-out, depending on the manufacturer's specifications.

antibinding The release of something when it gets stuck.

ball-return guide A special passage or metal tube through which the balls move in recirculating ball steering boxes.

beam axle A suspension system in which one set of wheels is connected laterally by a single beam or shaft.

bump steer The undesired condition produced when hitting a bump where the vehicle darts to one side as the steering linkage is pushed or pulled as a result of the travel of the suspension.

chassis The frame of a vehicle, to which the suspension pieces attach.

clock spring A special rotary electrical connector located between the steering wheel and the steering column that maintains a constant electrical connection with the wiring system while the vehicle's steering wheel is being turned.

constant mesh A term used to describe two or more parts, such as gears, that are in constant contact with each other.

control unit Any device that controls another object such as a computer.

drag link A steel or iron rod that transfers movement of the pitman arm to a relay lever.

end play Unwanted lateral movements of the worm shaft.

electric power steering system (EPS) A steering system that uses an electric motor and sensors to provide feedback to the vehicle's computer systems to decrease steering effort.

electrically assisted steering (EAS) A power-assist system that uses an electric motor to replace the hydraulic pump to decrease steering effort.

electrically powered hydraulic steering (EPHS) A steering system that uses an electric motor to produce hydraulic assist for steering.

engine-driven hydraulic pump A power steering pump driven by a belt or gear off of the crankshaft.

flow-control valve A valve used in power steering pumps to control the amount of flow out of the power steering pump.

forces capability map data Data preprogrammed into the electronic control unit's memory by the manufacturer and used to determine how much power assistance is needed based on input from the vehicle's speed sensor and steering sensor.

four-wheel steering system A steering system in which the front wheels are controlled normally and the rear wheels use a computer and electric motors to turn the rear linkage.

gear ratio A comparison of the number of turns or speed of the input (first) gear in the train to the number of turns or speed of the output (last) gear in the train.

gear reduction A gear ratio used to make large turns of the steering wheel into smaller turns of the tire to ease steering for the driver.

helix A spiral or coil shape.

inertia The resistance to a change in motion.

inner tie-rod or socket The inner tie-rod is attached to the end of the rack and allows for suspension movement and slight changes in steering angles.

intermediate shaft A steel rod positioned at an angle from the steering column to the steering gear that functions in transferring movement from one to the other.

knuckle The part that contains the wheel hub or spindle and attaches to the suspension components.

linear motion Movement in a straight line.

meshed pinion A pinion when it is mated with the rack.

outer tie-rod The tie-rod attached between the tie-rod and the steering arm. It transfers the movement of the rack, pivoting as the rack is extended or retracted when the vehicle is negotiating turns.

parallelogram steering system A non–rack-and-pinion system that uses a series of parts consisting of the pitman arm, idler arm, center link, and tie-rod assemblies that relays movement from the steering gearbox to the wheel assembly.

pinion A gear located at the end of the steering shaft connected to the rack. It moves the rack from side to side as the pinion rotates, controlling the direction of the wheels.

pitch On a helix, the distance moved in one full revolution of the cylinder.

power assist unit The electric motor in electric power assist steering systems.

power section A chamber in the rack where pressurized fluid acts upon pistons that assist in steering.

power steering An option on a vehicle that allows movement of the steering wheel with decreased driver effort.

power steering pump A small hydraulic pump that provides assistance to the driver when turning the steering wheel.

power unit A belt- or gear-driven pump that produces hydraulic pressure for use in the steering box or rack.

preloaded A part that is already compressed from pressure.

rack A steel rod driven by the pinion with tie-rods on each end or tie-rods connected to the center of the rack.

rack housing The outer shell of the rack-and-pinion steering system that is mounted to the chassis.

rack-and-pinion steering system A steering system composed of a steering wheel, a main shaft, universal joints, and an intermediate shaft. When the steering wheel is turned, movement is transferred by the main shaft and intermediate shaft to the pinion.

recirculating ball steering box A steering box that has worm gear inside a block with a threaded hole in it and gear teeth cut into its outside that engage the sector shaft to move the pitman arm; generally used on trucks and heavy vehicles.

reduction ratio The ratio between the turn of the steering wheel and the turn of the wheel, both measured in degrees.

relay lever A steel rod that transfers movement from the drag link to an idler arm.

rubber bellows Rubber pieces positioned on each end of the rack to protect the inner joints from dirt and contaminants and retain the grease lubricant inside the rack-and-pinion housing.

spline A ridge or tooth on a driveshaft that meshes with grooves in a mating piece and transfers torque to it, maintaining the angular correspondence between them.

spring-loaded rack guide yoke A spring-containing part that pushes on the back side of the rack to help reduce the play between the rack and the pinion while still allowing for relative movement.

steering arm An arm that extends from the steering knuckle. The tie-rods connect to these arms in order to steer the wheels.

steering box A device that converts the rotary motion of the steering wheel to the linear motion needed to steer the vehicle.

steering column A column affixed between the steering wheel and the steering box, usually made to collapse during a crash.

steering damper A device used to prevent shocks from irregular roads from being transmitted through the steering linkage and back to the steering wheel.

steering knuckle The knuckle located between the lower control arm and MacPherson strut or upper control arm, which has a spindle made or bolted onto it to which the wheel hub is attached.

steering linkage Steel rods that connect the steering box to the steering arms on the steering knuckle.

steering sensor A sensor that can read both torque and rotation from the steering wheel.

steering system A term used to describe all of the components and parts involved in steering a vehicle.

stub axle An axle used for one wheel.

stub-axle carrier The body of the stub-axle knuckle.

tie-rod A steering component that transfers linear motion from the steering box to the steering arms at the front wheels.

tie-rod assembly The part that fits between the rack and the steering arms and transfers the movement of the rack.

toe-setting Setting of the toe-in or toe-out of the tires to the centerline of the vehicle.

torque sensor A device used to measure the load on the steering wheel.

torsion bar A spring-loaded piece of steel connected to the pinion gear at its bottom end and the input shaft at its top. Also, a torsion bar is a type of spring that some vehicles use to hold up a corner of the vehicle.

wheel assembly A term used to encompass all components of the wheel and tire.

worm A gear with a helical, threaded shaft that is attached to the steering column and meshes with a worm wheel that transfers motion from the steering wheel to the steering linkage.

worm gear steering A robust steering system frequently used on heavier vehicles that uses a worm to turn a meshed worm wheel to provide gear reduction, making steering easier for the driver.

worm shaft The protrusion of the worm gear that serves as the point of attachment to the steering column.

ASE-Type Questions

1. Tech A says that the steering column uses one or more flexible joints to connect to the steering gearbox. Tech B says that the pitman arm is bolted to the frame and relays the steering linkage movement to the opposite wheel from the steering gearbox. Who is correct?
   a. Tech A
   b. Tech B
   c. Both A and B
   d. Neither A nor B
2. Tech A says that the clock spring assists the turning of the steering wheel on vehicles with EPS. Tech B says that the clock spring is used to transmit an electrical signal to the driver's side airbag. Who is correct?
   a. Tech A
   b. Tech B
   c. Both A and B
   d. Neither A nor B
3. Tech A says that power steering fluid is universal and can be used in virtually any vehicle's power steering system. Tech B says that in a power steering system, the force needed to turn the wheels is created by the hydraulic pump or electric motor. Who is correct?
   a. Tech A
   b. Tech B
   c. Both A and B
   d. Neither A nor B
4. Tech A says that rack-and-pinion steering systems generally do not use power steering due to their lighter duty construction. Tech B says that rack-and-pinion steering systems use a worm gear arrangement to move the rack. Who is correct?
   a. Tech A
   b. Tech B
   c. Both A and B
   d. Neither A nor B
5. Tech A says that to properly check a tie-rod end, the technician should twist the tie-rod end, and any rotational movement means the joint is bad. Tech B says that to properly check tie-rod ends, the vehicle's weight should be on the wheels, and as an assistant wiggles the steering wheel, you can check for movement in the tie-rod ends. Who is correct?
   a. Tech A
   b. Tech B
   c. Both A and B
   d. Neither A nor B
6. Tech A says that worn rack-and-pinion mount bushings can cause excessive play in the steering system. Tech B says that a worn idler arm can cause excessive play in the steering system. Who is correct?
   a. Tech A
   b. Tech B
   c. Both A and B
   d. Neither A nor B
7. Tech A says that when the vehicle is being driven straight ahead, a belt-driven power steering pump will pump fluid continuously, placing a minimal load on the engine. Tech B says that a belt-driven power steering pump is activated by an electromagnetic clutch, so it only pumps fluid when the wheels are being steered. Who is correct?
   a. Tech A
   b. Tech B
   c. Both A and B
   d. Neither A nor B
8. Tech A says that the pressure relief valve maintains a preset minimum pressure in the system. Tech B says that the pressure relief valve prevents excessive pressure. Who is correct?
   a. Tech A
   b. Tech B
   c. Both A and B
   d. Neither A nor B
9. Tech A says that worn tie-rod ends can cause a steering wandering complaint. Tech B says that a hard steering complaint could be caused by a worn power steering pump. Who is correct?
   a. Tech A
   b. Tech B
   c. Both A and B
   d. Neither A nor B
10. Tech A says that a pickle fork is used to hold a tie-rod while it is being tightened. Tech B says that the pitman arm is usually threaded so that the front wheel toe can be adjusted. Who is correct?
    a. Tech A
    b. Tech B
    c. Both A and B
    d. Neither A nor B

CHAPTER 22

KNOW
SEE
DO
PROVE

NATEF Tasks

Suspension and Steering Suspension Systems			Page
■ Inspect, remove, and install front stabilizer bar (sway bar) bushings, brackets, and links.		AST	609–610
■ Inspect shock absorbers; inspect mounts and bushings.	MLR	AST	608–609
■ Inspect front stabilizer bar (sway bar) bushings, brackets, and links.	MLR		609–610
■ Inspect upper and lower control arms, bushings, and shafts.	MLR		612–613
■ Inspect rear suspension system leaf springs, bushings, center pins/bolts, and mounts.	MLR	AST	612–616
Related Suspension and Steering Service			
■ Inspect upper and lower ball joints (with or without wear indicators).	MLR		604–606
■ Inspect suspension system coil springs and spring insulators (silencers).	MLR		611–612
■ Inspect strut cartridge or assembly.	MLR		612–614
■ Inspect front strut bearing and mount.	MLR		612–614
■ Inspect track bar, strut rods/radius arms, and related mounts and bushings.	MLR		613–616
■ Inspect suspension system torsion bars and mounts.	MLR		614–616

Servicing the Suspension System

NATEF Tasks, continued

Suspension and Steering Wheel Alignment		Page
■ Check for front wheel setback; determine necessary action.	AST	599–600
■ Perform pre-alignment inspection and measure vehicle ride height; determine necessary action.	MLR AST	607–608, 616–617
■ Prepare vehicle for wheel alignment on the alignment machine; perform four-wheel alignment by checking and adjusting front and rear wheel caster, camber, and toe as required; center steering wheel.	AST	616–618
■ Check steering axis inclination (SAI) and included angle; determine necessary action.	AST	619–620
■ Check rear wheel thrust angle; determine necessary action.	AST	619–620
■ Check front and/or rear cradle (subframe) alignment; determine necessary action.	AST	619–621

KNOW
SEE
DO

Knowledge Objectives

After reading this chapter, you will be able to:

1. Explain the principles of the suspension system. (pp 571–574)
2. Describe the principle of suspension force and how it affects the suspension system. (pp 572–573)
3. Explain the principles of unsprung weight and dampening. (p 573)
4. Discuss wheel unit location as it relates to the suspension system. (p 573)
5. Describe yaw, pitch, and roll as they relate to the vehicle. (p 574)
6. Describe the purpose and the components of the suspension system. (pp 574–577)
7. Explain the solid axle type of suspension and how it functions. (pp 577–578, 586)
8. Explain the dead axle/live axle types of suspension and how they function. (pp 578, 586)
9. Explain how independent suspension works. (p 587)
10. Explain how rear suspension works. (pp 589–592)
11. Explain the fundamentals and the four basic types of wheel alignment. (pp 594–604)

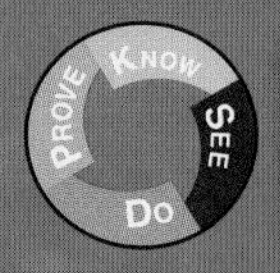
Know
See
Do
Prove

Skills Objectives

After reading this chapter, you will be able to:

1. Inspect upper and lower ball joints. (pp 604–606)
2. Perform ride height diagnosis. (pp 607–608)
3. Check shock absorbers. (p 609)
4. Remove and inspect the stabilizer bar bushings and mount brackets. (pp 609–610)
5. Remove and inspect the sway bar end links. (pp 609–610)
6. Replace a shock absorber. (p 611)
7. Inspect short-/long-arm (SLA) suspension system coil springs and spring insulators. (pp 611–612)
8. Inspect upper and lower control arms and components. (p 612)
9. Lubricate a suspension system and a steering system. (pp 612–613)
10. Inspect the strut assembly, the strut coil spring, and the insulators. (pp 612–614)
11. Inspect a strut coil. (pp 612–614)
12. Inspect leaf springs. (pp 612–615)
13. Inspect strut rods and bushings. (pp 613–615)
14. Inspect the torsion bar. (pp 615–616)
15. Perform a pre-alignment inspection. (pp 616–617)
16. Perform a four-wheel alignment. (pp 616, 618)
17. Check steering axis inclination (SAI). (pp 619–620)
18. Check the rear wheel thrust angle. (pp 619–620)
19. Check cradle alignment. (pp 619, 621)

Introduction

The suspension system of a vehicle is designed to follow the road surface for the purpose of maintaining traction and control of the vehicle, while at the same time providing a smooth ride for the passengers. It is composed of a network of springs, arms, struts, and shocks that work together to achieve these purposes FIGURE 22-1. Wear from extended use is the main cause of suspension problems, though impact from potholes and accidents may cause bent or broken components in the suspension and steering systems. Driver complaints of a bouncy ride, a reduction in steering control, or unusual noises when going over bumps indicate problems in the suspension system. Regular inspection of each component in the suspension system is helpful in identifying wear before it causes severe problems for the owner. Also know that the suspension system interacts very closely with the steering system. Thus, part of the challenge in accurately diagnosing the vehicle is knowing how both systems operate.

Even if all of the suspension and steering system components are in good working condition, they also need to be aligned correctly with each other and with the vehicle's centerline for the vehicle to operate properly and safely. For this reason, the wheels must be in proper alignment from the factory. Technicians need to verify proper alignment typically when the tires are replaced, when parts are replaced, or if a suspension related concern is being diagnosed. This chapter will help you become familiar with the various types of suspension systems, their components, how they operate, and how to inspect and maintain them.

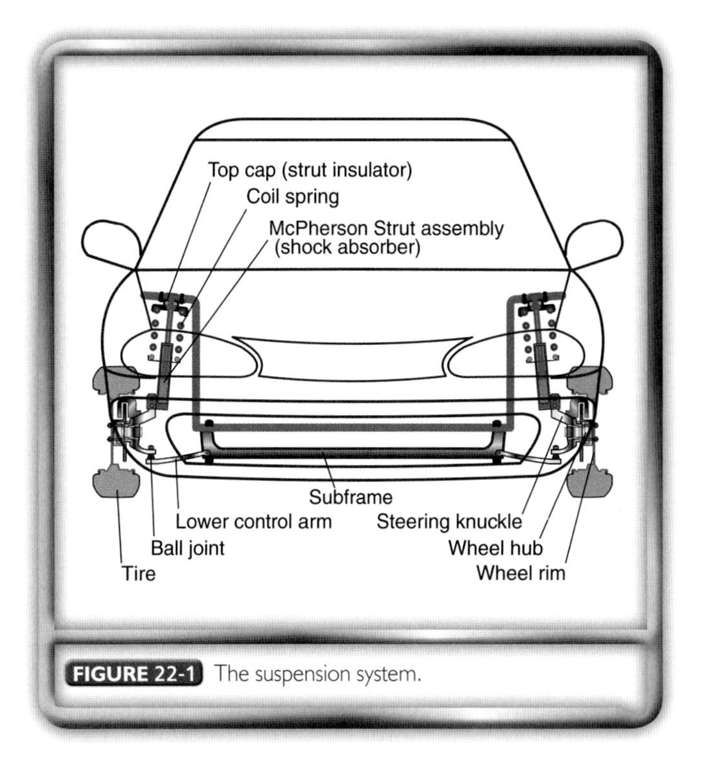
Top cap (strut insulator)
Coil spring
McPherson Strut assembly (shock absorber)
Subframe
Lower control arm
Steering knuckle
Ball joint
Wheel hub
Tire
Wheel rim

FIGURE 22-1 The suspension system.

Suspension System Principles

The **suspension system** isolates the vehicle body from road shocks and vibrations that would otherwise be transferred to the driver and passengers. It also must keep the tires in contact with the road. A suspension system must be strong enough to withstand loads imposed by the vehicle's mass during cornering, accelerating, braking, and uneven road surfaces.

You Are the Automotive Technician

You work for County Fleet Services in the vehicle service department. One of the drivers wrote up a complaint sheet on a relatively new Dodge full-size delivery van with short/long arm suspension on front and leaf-spring suspension on the rear. The truck has a little more than 100,000 miles (160,000 km) on it. The complaint sheet lists several complaints. First, the operator admitted to hitting a curb with the right front wheel. Second, the vehicle pulls hard to the right when driven. Third, it makes an audible clunking noise in the front when going over bumps at around 10 mph (17 kph).

1. What are the potentially damaged components from when the vehicle hit the curb?
2. What will you do to diagnose the pulling condition?
3. What are the possible causes of the clunking noise when hitting a bump?

When a tire hits an obstruction, there is a **reaction force**, meaning the tire will move in response to the force applied by the obstruction. The size of this reaction force depends on the **unsprung mass**, or **unsprung weight**, of each wheel assembly. The sprung mass is that part of the vehicle supported by the springs, such as the body, the frame, the engine, and associated parts. The *unsprung* mass is all the parts of the vehicle that are *not* supported by springs, including the components that follow the road contours, such as wheels, tires, axles, and outboard brake assemblies.

Vehicle ride and handling can be improved by keeping the unsprung mass as low as possible. The heavier the unsprung mass, the harder the vehicle is to control. Think of trying to control a beach ball versus a bowling ball. When large and heavy wheel assemblies encounter a bump or pothole, they experience a larger reaction force, sometimes large enough to make the tire lose contact with the road surface. If the tires are not in contact with the road, they have lost all traction and cannot control the vehicle's direction of travel, a potentially dangerous situation. Some suspension systems are designed to combat that situation, and others are designed to be less costly and complicated.

Suspension Force

Suspension systems must tolerate a huge amount of forces when the vehicle is being driven down the road. Think about all of the weight of the vehicle being supported by the suspension system, and then subjecting the parts in that system to the normal cornering, accelerating, and braking forces, and then adding in the abnormal forces from potholes and speed bumps FIGURE 22-2. Applying a force to an object deforms it. Removing the force allows it to return to its original shape. This characteristic is called **elasticity**. Automotive suspension systems generally use the elastic properties of special metals to provide the springing medium that a suspension system requires.

Springs are located between the frame and the axle assemblies and are shaped to suit specific applications. **Leaf springs** are normally semi-elliptical. They absorb the **applied force** (pressure of the load) by flattening out under load. They are often used at the rear end of a car or truck to help the vehicle carry larger loads. **Coil springs** are formed in a spiral from a single steel rod. They absorb the force of impact by twisting and compressing. They are generally used on smaller vehicles to smooth the ride and improve handling. **Torsion bars** are held rigid at one end and twist around their center as the **control arm** is deflected. Control arms, also known as A-arms or wishbones, attach to the chassis with rubber bushings and allow for the movement of the tire and wheel assembly. Torsion bars all return to their original shape when the **deflecting force** (a force that moves an object in a different direction or into a different shape) is removed. They are typically used in the front of most pick-up trucks because they handle better than leaf springs.

Nonmetallic materials, such as rubber, can provide the main springing action but would not perform as well as a steel spring. Rubber is more commonly used as **stops** to limit extreme suspension movement. Stops, called jounce stops, bump stops, bumper stops, or rebound stops, are rubber parts used to control the movement of suspension components so they do not bang against each other or the frame of the vehicle, damaging the components over time FIGURE 22-3. These stops are typically shaped in a triangle or a cone to provide a collapsible cushion.

FIGURE 22-2 Suspension system subjected to a speed bump.

FIGURE 22-3 Rubber stops.

In light vehicle applications, air is used primarily for ride height control. Rubber bags filled with air are placed at the rear of some vehicles to help support additional weight. This is predominately a function of SUVs for when they are driven off-road, where ground clearance can be a problem.

When a vehicle strikes an uneven surface, the springs are deformed from their original shape. They return to their original position but tend to **overshoot**, or spring back, past their original length following compression, producing oscillations in the spring. **Oscillations** refer to the fluctuating of an object between two states, basically meaning the spring compresses and rebounds over and over again. As a result, the vehicle bounces up and down, making the ride unstable. It can also produce forces that make the tires bounce off the ground and lose their grip on the road.

Unsprung Weight

Most of a vehicle's weight is supported by its suspension system. It suspends the body and associated parts so that they are insulated from road shocks and vibrations that would otherwise be transmitted to the passengers and the vehicle itself. However, other parts of a vehicle are not supported by the suspension system, including the wheels, tires, brakes, axles, and steering and suspension parts not supported by springs FIGURE 22-4. These parts determine a vehicle's unsprung weight. Unsprung weight exerts momentum to the vehicle body whenever the unsprung weight is moved. For example, when a tire hits a speed bump, it moves upward. The heavier it and everything directly connected to it is, the greater the upward force it will generate. In fact, it can have enough force that it keeps on moving upward at the top of the bump. This may cause it to lose traction with the road surface. It also transfers a lot of momentum to the vehicle body, causing it to move upward as it absorbs the energy from the wheel assembly. Conversely, if the wheel and tire are very light, they will not generate as much upward force, so it is easier for the spring to push them back down, maintaining contact with the road. As a general rule, unsprung mass should be kept as low as possible while maintaining enough strength to handle the stresses of the vehicle being driven in rough conditions.

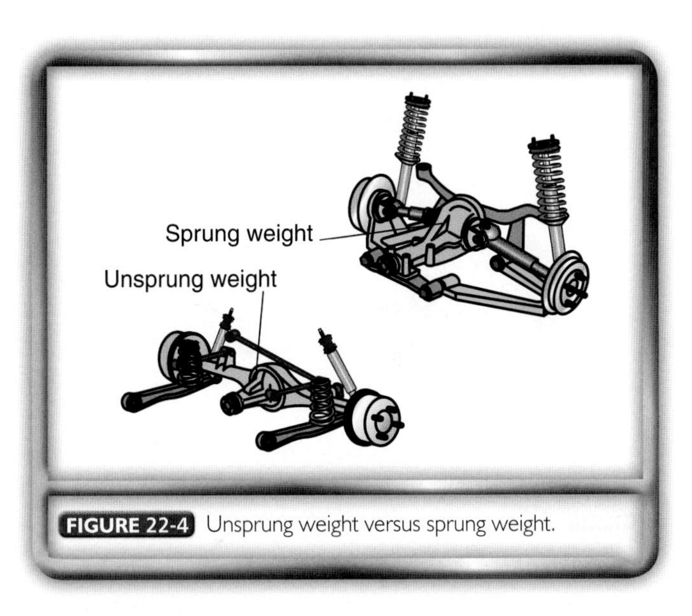
Sprung weight
Unsprung weight

FIGURE 22-4 Unsprung weight versus sprung weight.

Dampening

Different materials have different levels of elasticity. Up to a certain point, they can be deformed and released, and they will try to return to their original condition. Beyond that point, they stay deformed. With some materials, returning to their original state too quickly can produce a bouncing effect (oscillation). Preventing or reducing oscillations is called dampening. It can occur in many different ways. The dampening material absorbs the energy from the oscillation. In a vehicle suspension, a hydraulic shock absorber dampens oscillation in the spring. And rubber bushings dampen road shock. These concepts will be explored in more depth later in this chapter.

Wheel Unit Location

When a vehicle is in motion, certain forces exert pressure against the wheel units: driving thrust, braking torque, and cornering force. **Driving thrust** is the force transferred from the tire contact patch through the axle housing. It places a twisting pressure on the suspension members that push the vehicle along the road. **Braking torque** places a twisting pressure on the axle housing in the opposite direction around its center during braking. **Cornering force** refers to the lateral movement of the axle housing during turning.

These forces are transferred to the frame of the vehicle, but while they act, the wheel units must stay aligned with each other and with the frame. The wheels must be securely located longitudinally, laterally, and vertically while still having the freedom to move vertically to allow for suspension travel and pivot to allow for steering. When a vehicle drives over a bump, the tires are forcibly moved. The suspension system must absorb these forces while maintaining precise control of the wheels. Each of the suspension components contributes to keeping the wheel units in proper alignment.

Yaw, Pitch, and Roll

The terms yaw, pitch, and roll describe the movement of a vehicle around three axes FIGURE 22-5. The x-axis is the imaginary line drawn down the center of the vehicle from front to back. The y-axis is the imaginary line across the vehicle from left to right. The z-axis is the vertical line that runs through the center of the vehicle from top to bottom. **Roll** is vehicular movement along its x-axis. It is the rolling motion you feel when making a sharp corner and is generally what causes rollovers. **Pitch** is movement around the vehicle's y-axis, commonly felt during hard braking or fast acceleration, when the front of the vehicle noses down or rises up slightly. **Yaw** is movement around the z-axis, felt when the vehicle deviates from its straight path, as when the rear wheels slide out during drifting. Movement around each of these axes must be controlled during all of the maneuvers of the vehicle for it to be safe. Many safety systems, such as electronic stability control, are designed to keep vehicles within the safe limits of these axes.

Suspension System Components

A basic suspension system consists of the following parts:

- **Springs**: The spring is the flexible component of the suspension. Basic types are leaf springs, coil springs, and torsion bars. Modern passenger vehicles usually use light coil springs. Light commercial vehicles have heavier springs than passenger vehicles. They can have coil springs at the front and leaf springs at the rear. Heavy commercial vehicles usually use leaf springs, or air suspension.
- **Axles**: Axles are used to drive and/or support the wheels.
- **Shock absorbers**: Shock absorbers dampen spring oscillations by forcing oil through small holes in a piston. The oil heats up as it absorbs the energy of the motion. This heat is then transferred through the body of the shock absorber to the atmosphere.
- **Arms**: Arms are the primary load-bearing elements of a vehicle's suspension system and are commonly known as control arms. They are isolated from the chassis with rubber bushings that allow the up-and-down movement of the tire and wheel assembly.
- **Rods**: Rods are straight pieces of steel used to control motion within the vehicle's suspension system. They typically have pivoting or flexible mounts on each end.
- **Ball joints**: Ball joints are swivel connections mounted in the outer ends of the control arms.

FIGURE 22-6 shows the components of the suspension system.

Springs

Springs suspend the weight of the vehicle on the axles in such a manner that allows the wheels to follow unevenness in the road surface; therefore, springs must be elastic. Most springs are made out of spring steel and sag over time, requiring replacement. Some manufacturers have used composite materials for their leaf springs, which are said to resist sagging better than spring steel, as well as substantially reduce weight. The most common spring configurations are coil springs, leaf springs, and torsion bars.

Yaw
Roll
Pitch

FIGURE 22-5 Yaw, pitch, and roll.

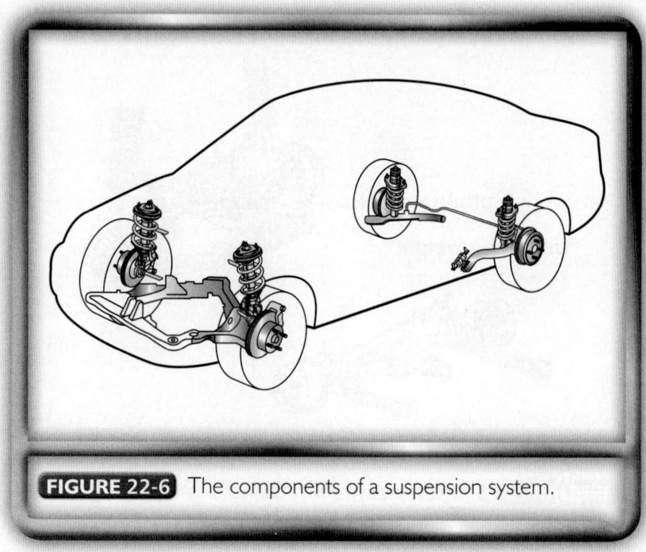

FIGURE 22-6 The components of a suspension system.

Coil Springs

Coil springs, also known as helical springs, are used on the front suspension of most modern light vehicles, and in many cases, they have replaced leaf springs in the rear suspension FIGURE 22-7. A coil spring is made from a single length of special wire, which is heated and wound on a former to produce the required shape. The load-carrying ability of the spring depends on the diameter of the wire, the overall diameter of the spring, its shape, and the spacing of the coils. On a small passenger car, they are lighter and more flexible than springs on a light commercial vehicle, which are more robust and stiff. The stiffer springs are designed to withstand heavier loads, but also make the ride much rougher. Smaller vehicles that do not need to haul heavy loads are built with lighter, flexible springs so they have a smoother ride.

The pitch of a spring is the distance from the center of one coil to the center of the adjacent coil. The coils may be evenly spaced, called **uniform pitch**, or unevenly spaced. The wire can be the same thickness throughout, or it may taper toward the end of the spring. The spring itself may be cylindrical, barrel shaped, or conical. Generally, a cylindrical spring with uniform wire diameter and uniform pitch has a constant rate of deflection, meaning it takes the same amount of force to compress each coil. Its length reduces in direct proportion to the load applied. When the pitch is varied, the deflection rate varies too FIGURE 22-8. The spring is then said to have a **progressive rate of deflection**, meaning it deflects easily under a light load, but its resistance increases as the load increases. This provides a softer ride when the vehicle is lightly loaded than if the vehicle has heavier constant-rate springs. Coil springs can look alike but give very different load ratings, which are often color coded for identification. They also normally use rubber pads at their seats to prevent the transmission of noise and vibration.

As conical and barrel-shaped springs compress, they have the ability to collapse into themselves FIGURE 22-9. This creates a longer suspension travel for a given length of the spring than for a cylindrical spring. The result is a softer ride for light loads and a stiffer ride for heavy loads, which makes them useful in the rear of some pick-up trucks that are also intended as passenger vehicles. As a cylindrical coil compresses, it can become coil-bound, which limits its travel. This can be observed in heavily loaded trucks.

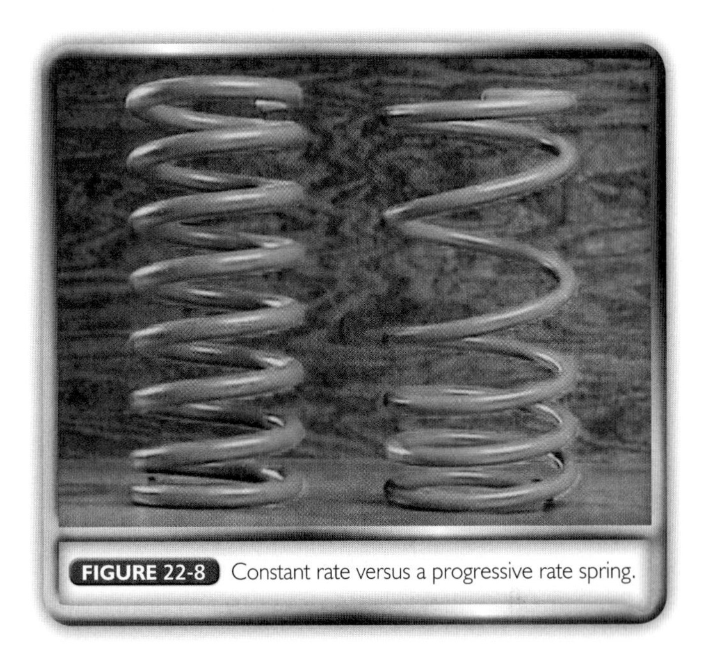

FIGURE 22-8 Constant rate versus a progressive rate spring.

FIGURE 22-7 Coil springs, also known as helical springs, are used on the front suspension of most modern light vehicles.

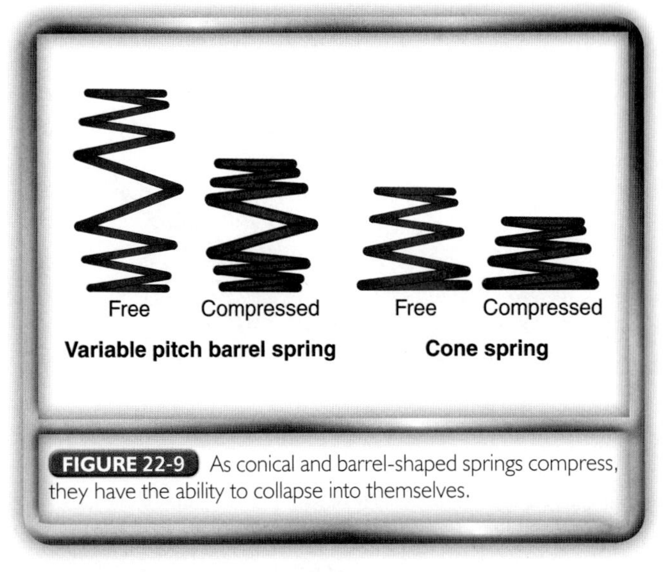

Free
Compressed
Variable pitch barrel spring
Free
Compressed
Cone spring

FIGURE 22-9 As conical and barrel-shaped springs compress, they have the ability to collapse into themselves.

Leaf Springs

The leaf spring is one of the oldest forms of spring. It is usually used on rear-wheel drive vehicles and is mounted longitudinally. Leaf springs consist of one or more flat springs, commonly made of tempered steel FIGURE 22-10. A number of leaves of different length are used to form a multileaf spring. Multileaf springs are used in vehicles that haul heavy loads, such as dump trucks and large pick-up trucks.

The multileaves are held together by a center bolt that passes through a hole in the center of each leaf. The center bolt is also used to locate the spring on the axle. The axle is then clamped to the multileaf spring by U-bolts that wrap around the axle housing and through a spring plate underneath the spring. **Rebound clips** are metal straps wrapped at intervals around the leaf spring to prevent excessive flexing of the main leaf during rebound, and also keep the end of the leaves in alignment.

The longest leaf, called the main leaf, is rolled at both ends to form **spring eyes**. These eyes are used to mount the spring to the frame of the vehicle. Some multileaf springs have the ends of the second leaf rolled around the eyes of the main leaf as reinforcement. This leaf is called the **wrap leaf**.

The front of the multileaf spring is attached to a **rigid spring hanger** on the vehicle frame. This rigid hanger holds the spring and ultimately the axle in position with the frame. The rear of the multileaf is connected to the frame by a **swinging shackle**, which provides a link between the spring eye and a bracket on the frame. This swinging link is needed because the front of the spring is held rigidly to the frame, and as the spring flexes and flattens out under load, the distance between the spring eyes increases. The swinging shackle allows for this lengthening and shortening.

Some multileaf springs have inserts between the leaves of plastic, nylon, or rubber. They act as insulators to reduce noise transfer and friction as the leaves move across each other under load. Some older vehicles completely enclose the leaf springs in grease for this same reason. The spring eyes are fitted with replaceable bushings, usually with a rubber, flexible section, but nylon and urethane bushings are also used, and sometimes bronze for heavy-duty applications. Rubber insulating pads between the spring mounting pad and the spring also act as insulators and, similarly, between the spring plate and the spring. Most springs are arched upward at the ends, but reverse-arch springs are used occasionally, most often when lowering a vehicle. No matter what, leaf springs support the weight of the vehicle while holding the rear axle in line with the frame, as well as the front tires.

Torsion Bars

A torsion bar is a long, alloy-steel bar that is fixed rigidly to the chassis or subframe at one end and to a control arm at the other end FIGURE 22-11. The torsion bar is connected to the control arm in the unloaded condition (no pressure on the bar), and as the suspension control arm is raised, the torsion bar twists around its center, which places it under a **torsional load**. Torsional load is a twisting force that is applied by anchoring one end of an object and then applying a twisting force to the other end.

When the vehicle is placed on the road, with the control arm connected to the suspension assembly, the torsion bar supports the vehicle load and twists around

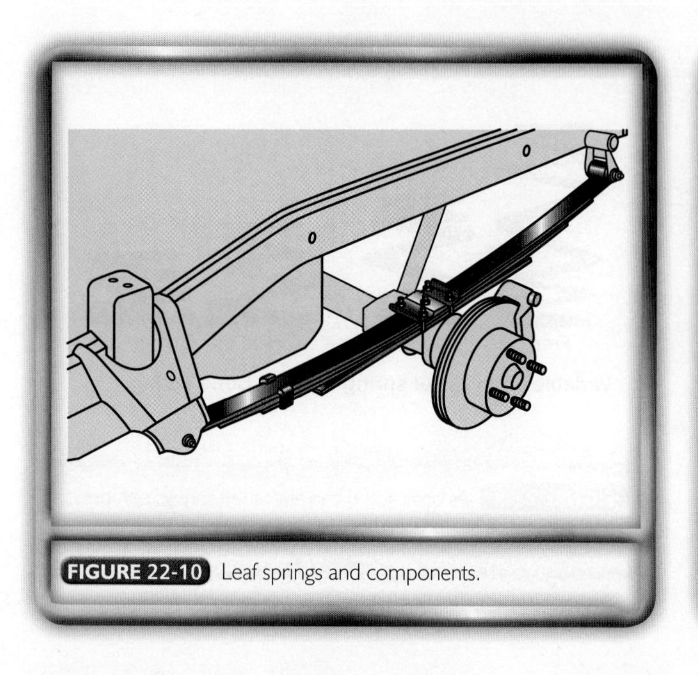
FIGURE 22-10 Leaf springs and components.

FIGURE 22-11 A torsion bar is a long, alloy-steel bar that is attached rigidly to the chassis or subframe at one end and to a control arm at the other.

its center to provide the springing action. Spring rate depends on the length of the torsion bar and its diameter. The shorter and thicker the torsion bar, the stiffer its spring rate. This is useful in heavier vehicles or vehicles that regularly haul loads.

Torsion bars can be used across the chassis frame in a **trailing arm suspension**, or as part of the connecting link between two axle assemblies on a semirigid axle beam. After a lot of use, all springs can sag, including the torsion bar, meaning the ride height on one or both sides of the vehicle will be lower than specified. On many vehicles, it can be adjusted back to the proper ride height by tightening the bolt on the torsion bar adjuster.

Sway Bars

A bar similar to the torsion bar is the **sway bar**, or antiroll bar. The sway bar is used in light vehicles as a stabilizer, or antiroll bar. It is connected to the chassis in the center, and each end is connected to one side of the suspension system FIGURE 22-12. Sway bars are most common on the front suspension since it is most prone to sway, but are also installed on the rear suspension in some vehicles. When the vehicle is turning, centrifugal force acts on the body and tends to make it lean outward (roll). The sway bar uses its connections to each side of the suspension to resist this roll tendency. In this way, the spring on the inside of the corner can assist the spring on the outside of the corner to bear the additional load on the outside wheels. This tends to make the vehicle corner flatter. But because the sway bar can pivot in bushings on the frame, the sway bar just pivots when both wheels go over a speed bump. Also, stiffer roll bars can be installed in a vehicle to enhance its cornering ability.

Rubber Stops

Rubber is used in most suspension systems as stops. If the suspension reaches its limit of travel, stops prevent direct metal-to-metal contact, thereby reducing jarring of the suspension components FIGURE 22-13. The rubber stops protect the suspension parts as when they bottom out. The stops also reduce the shock to the driver as the suspension bottoms out. Stops can be shaped to provide an auxiliary springing function, increasing their resistance progressively with suspension contact. Rubber spring stops can be found on most vehicles. For vehicles with MacPherson **struts**, there is a cone-shaped rubber stop located on the strut below the strut bearing surface. In other applications, these stops are found on the frame of the vehicle where the suspension components will make contact.

> **TECHNICIAN TIP**
>
> Rubber has a number of advantages. It doesn't need to be lubricated, it can be made into any shape, as required, and it is silent during use.

Axles

Axles are shafts to which the wheel assembly is attached. In vehicles, the axle is usually fixed to the wheels, rotating with them. Axles perform many functions. Some are load-bearing elements of the suspension system, helping support the weight of the vehicle. Others are used only to drive the wheels, not support it. They help maintain the position of the wheels relative to each other and the vehicle body.

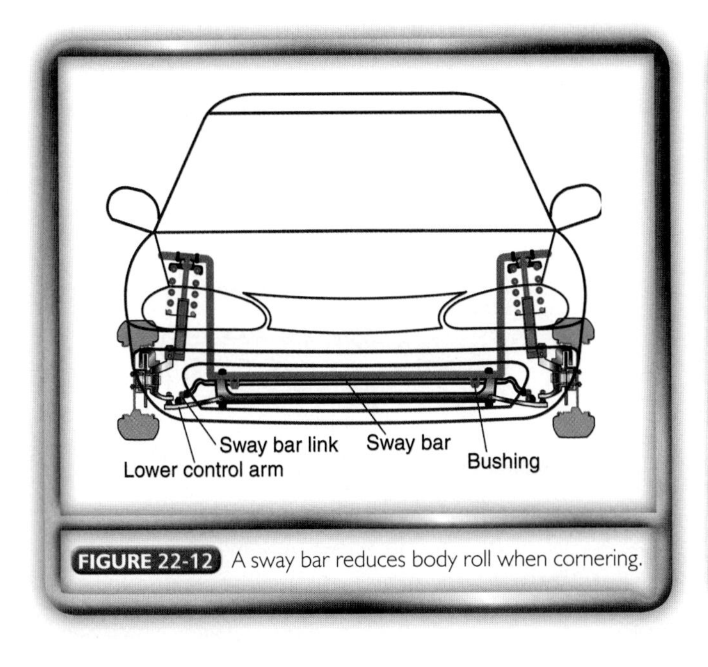
Sway bar link
Sway bar
Lower control arm
Bushing

FIGURE 22-12 A sway bar reduces body roll when cornering.

31061
HELP!
CONTROL ARM BUMPER
TOPE PARA EL BRAZO DE DIRECCIÓN
BUTÉES DU BRAS DE COMMANDE
BAJO EL COCHE • SOUS LA VOITURE
DORMAN

FIGURE 22-13 Variety of rubber stops.

Many different types of axles are available on the market today to suit the needs of vehicle designers. The straight axle or solid axle is a single shaft that connects the front wheels together or the rear wheels together FIGURE 22-14. These axles provide extra support and rigidity to keep the wheels positioned even under heavy loads. Because they are able to withstand extreme stress, straight axles are typically found on many rear-wheel drive vehicles, off-road vehicles, and commercial trucks.

The dead axle is one that does not transmit drive to the wheel, acting only to support it. These axles are used on the rear of some front-wheel drive vehicles and other vehicles that have more than two rear wheel sets to provide added support for carrying heavy loads. Axles use bearings in different arrangements to support the axle or wheel, depending on the type.

In full-floating axles, the axle bearing is placed on the outside of the axle housing. This places all the vehicle weight on the housing and none on the axle itself FIGURE 22-15. The axle in this arrangement functions only in transmitting the rotational torque out to the wheel. In the semi-floating axle, the axle bearing is placed between the axle and the axle housing; therefore, it participates in carrying the load of the vehicle FIGURE 22-16. For more information on wheel bearings and bearing arrangements, see Chapter 27: Wheel Bearings.

FIGURE 22-14 Solid axle.

Shock Absorbers

A shock absorber is a device on a vehicle designed to absorb shock loads caused from driving on irregular surfaces. During compression (jounce), which happens when the tire travels over a bump in the road, the rod and its piston move into the shock absorber. In extension (rebound), which is when the tire travels over a dip in the road, the rod and piston move out of the shock absorber. For dampening to be effective, resistance is needed in both directions, although not in the same proportions. This resistance is provided by the piston forcing oil past disc valves in the piston and the base of the inner tube of the shock absorber FIGURE 22-17. Oil fills the inner tube and surrounds its outer surface to a level that allows a free space or reservoir to exist above it, between the inner and the outer tubes.

A way to think about the basic function of a shock absorber is to think of a rod with a washer fastened to it through the center hole. If a small hole is drilled on the flat of the washer, this will let oil move from one side of the washer to the other. Add some oil to a capped tube and insert the rod and washer into the tube. Add oil to the top, and cap the tube with a sealed cap that will allow the rod to move in and out of the tube but not leak oil. Moving the rod in the oil will produce resistance since oil will be forced through the small hole in the washer. Resistance will be felt in both directions. If the size of the

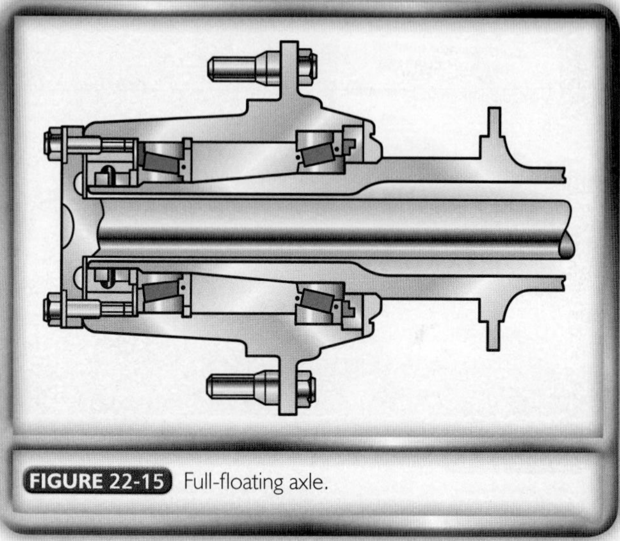
FIGURE 22-15 Full-floating axle.

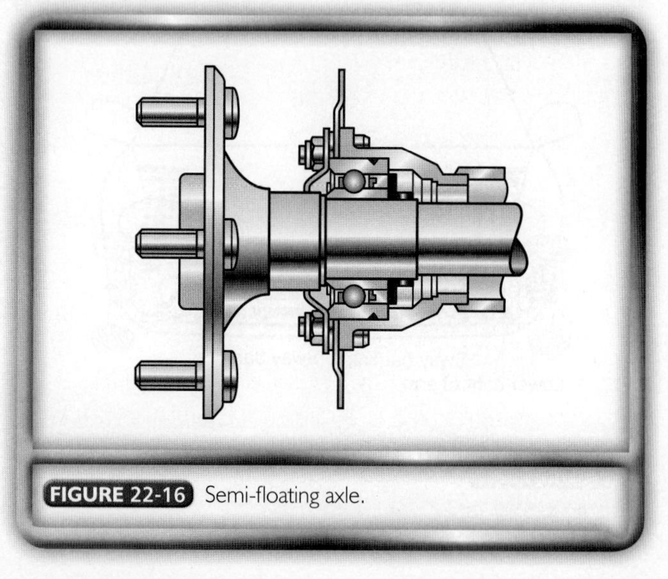
FIGURE 22-16 Semi-floating axle.

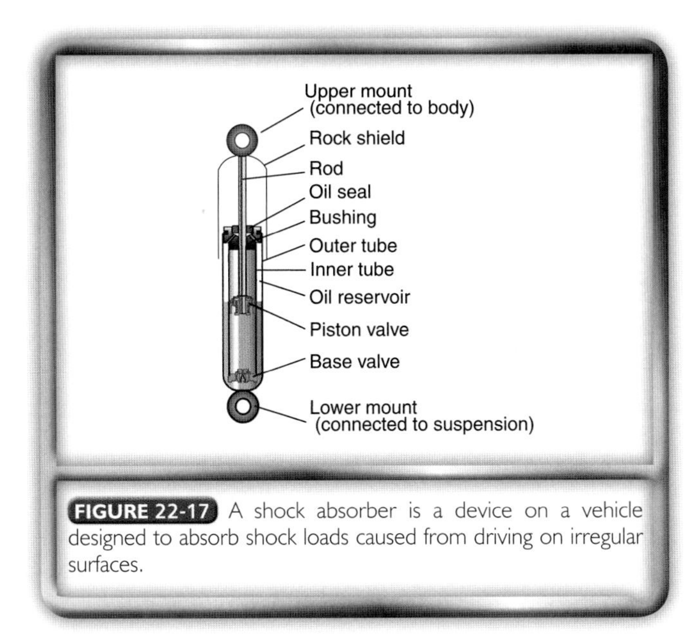
Upper mount
(connected to body)
Rock shield
Rod
Oil seal
Bushing
Outer tube
Inner tube
Oil reservoir
Piston valve
Base valve
Lower mount
(connected to suspension)

FIGURE 22-17 A shock absorber is a device on a vehicle designed to absorb shock loads caused from driving on irregular surfaces.

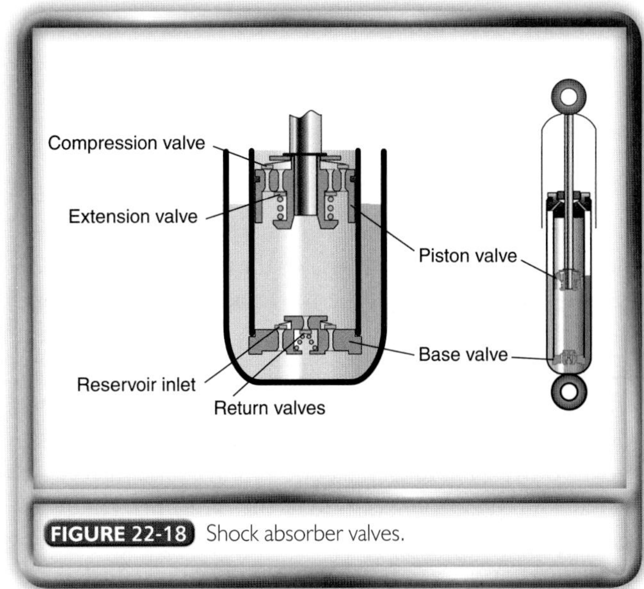
Compression valve
Extension valve
Piston valve
Base valve
Reservoir inlet
Return valves

FIGURE 22-18 Shock absorber valves.

hole in the washer is increased, there will be less resistance. This is the basic operation of the shock absorber, except in a shock absorber, valves can be used to allow different rates of flow on compression and rebound. Thus, the resistance on compression will vary as compared to rebound so that manufacturers can design the desired ride characteristics into the shock absorber.

The valves in the shock absorber provide control over the amount of force required to pass fluid through them at any given piston velocity. They can be made to open in stages, according to fluid pressure FIGURE 22-18. This allows light resistance to motion when the piston moves slowly, and heavy resistance when piston velocity is high.

The rapid movement of the piston, continually forcing the oil backward and forward through the valves, causes the oil to heat up as it absorbs the energy of motion of the springs. The heat is transferred through the outer tube to the outside air. However, the hotter the oil becomes, the greater its tendency to aerate. Aeration occurs because of the high velocity of the oil as it passes through the small passages in the valves. If the velocity is high enough, air dissolved in the oil comes out of the solution as small bubbles and forms foam. As we know from Pascal's law, fluid cannot be compressed, but air can. Air in the shock absorber results in a lack of dampening, which creates a soft, bouncy ride; if the suspension members contact the stops, this creates a harsh ride.

The twin-tube type of shock absorber is the most common. The outer tube is normally attached to the suspension member at its base, and the inner tube provides a working cylinder for a piston that is attached to a piston rod. The piston rod is connected to the vehicle's frame at its outer end, and a bushing in the top of the outer tube keeps the rod in alignment as it moves in and out of the shock absorber, with **suspension action** (or movement of the chassis up and down). A seal above the bushing prevents oil leakage and keeps out dirt and moisture. A **shroud** is a steel, plastic cover, or rubber boot that is typically placed over the shock rod to protect it from damage.

Strut-type Shock Absorbers

The most widely used hydraulic shock absorber is the **direct-acting telescopic type**. It can be fitted to the suspension as a self-contained unit that is designed to control only spin oscillations, or it can be combined with a **suspension strut**, which is used to support the top of the steering knuckle as well as dampen spring oscillations. A suspension strut functions exactly like a shock except it is much stronger since it functions as a structural part of the suspension when it is integrated into MacPherson strut suspensions. On a MacPherson strut suspension system, the top of the hydraulic strut supports the top of the steering knuckle, so it must be much stronger than an ordinary shock absorber. The

> **TECHNICIAN TIP**
>
> Aerated oil has a certain amount of compressibility, so it is unable to provide the dampening force previously achieved in the nonaerated condition, just as a brake pedal will feel spongy when air is present in the brake's hydraulic system. The performance of the shock absorber is thus considerably reduced. This effect is called shock absorber dissolve.

hydraulic shock absorber and the hydraulic strut provide their dampening action by transferring oil under pressure through valves in the piston, which restrict the oil flow.

Gas-Pressurized Shock Absorbers

Fluid fills the chambers above and below the piston of the hydraulic shock absorber. As the piston moves in the cylinder, valves control the movement of oil from one chamber to the other. In a gas shock, pressure on the oil is provided by nitrogen gas at the base of the cylinder, acting on a free-floating separation piston that separates the gas from the oil FIGURE 22-19. On jounce, the piston moves downward, and the penetration of the piston rod displaces a quantity of oil equal to its volume. The separation piston is displaced accordingly, and gas pressure increases. On rebound, the piston and rod move upward, and gas pressure reduces as the separation piston follows the movement. Pressure on the oil is maintained, even when the piston and rod are at the top of their stroke. The pressure applied to the oil keeps air bubbles (or aeration) from forming as easily and thus provides a better job of dampening.

Adjustable Shock Absorbers

In the search for a comfortable ride, while maintaining some level of sporty handling or the ability to handle occasional heavy loads, manufacturers have developed a variety of shock absorbers with enhanced capabilities. As you recall, having a few smaller passageways in a shock absorber causes it to provide a high amount of resistance to jounce and rebound, creating a sporty feel. And larger passageways provide less resistance, creating a smoother ride. Manufacturers have machined more passageways into their shock absorber pistons but then provide either manual, electric, or automatic selection and blockage of certain passageways with valves, depending on the desired ride characteristics. As far as extra loads, some shocks incorporate an expandable air bladder that can be used to support some of the load.

Load-Adjustable Shock Absorbers

When vehicles carry heavy loads, their suspension is compressed, causing the rear of the vehicle to be lower than normal. As a result, steering can become lighter (less responsive), the alignment of the headlights becomes too high, and the compression length of travel of the suspension over bumps is reduced, causing the suspension to bottom out more easily, which is uncomfortable for passengers. To reduce these effects, a **manually adjustable air spring** can be incorporated into each rear shock absorber. This type of shock absorber is commonly referred to as an air shock FIGURE 22-20. The **air spring** consists of a flexible rubber bladder, which seals the outside of the upper and lower halves of the shock absorber. When inflated, the bladder pushes the halves apart.

The shock absorber is a standard hydraulic type, providing normal dampening action, but when a heavy load is placed on the rear of the vehicle, the rubber air bladder can be gas-pressurized to assist the vehicle's springs. By changing the air pressure in the bladder, the ride height can be adjusted, as well as the stiffness of the suspension. Compressed air in the bladder can absorb smaller road shocks and provide better ride characteristics than stiff springs alone.

The rubber air cylinder is connected to a filling valve, similar looking to a tire valve stem, by a flexible plastic hose. Air from a tire pump or air compressor forces more

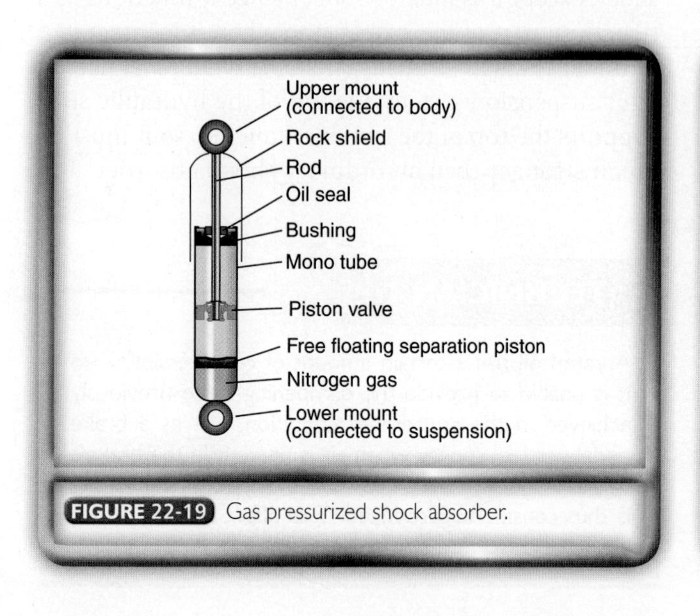
Upper mount
(connected to body)
Rock shield
Rod
Oil seal
Bushing
Mono tube
Piston valve
Free floating separation piston
Nitrogen gas
Lower mount
(connected to suspension)
FIGURE 22-19 Gas pressurized shock absorber.

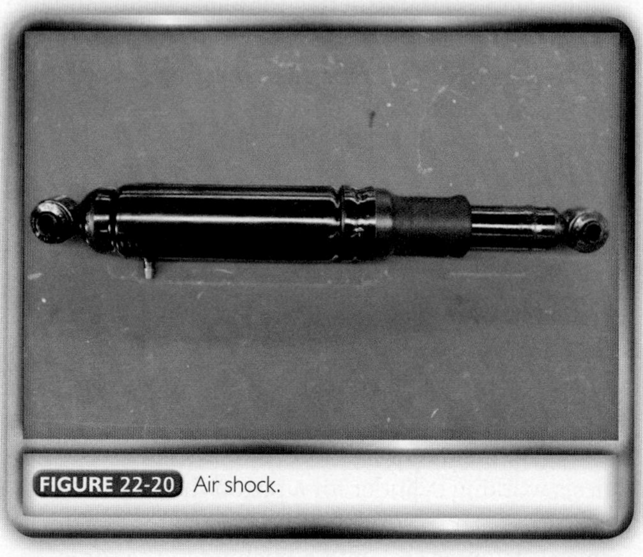
FIGURE 22-20 Air shock.

air into the rubber cylinder, allowing the suspension to support more weight. The maximum air pressure setting must not be exceeded, as excessive air pressure can damage the shock absorber's air spring. When the load is removed, the extra air can be released through the filling valve, which allows the suspension to return to its original settings, just as you would release air from a tire. A minimum air pressure must be maintained in the cylinder to prevent chafing of the rubber as it collapses internally with shock absorber action. Refer to the manufacturer's specifications for the air shock's minimum and maximum air pressure.

Another type of load-adjustable shock absorber uses a coil spring around the outside of the shock. The spring is installed from the factory under tension and connects to both the upper half and the lower half. This tends to push the halves apart, assisting the regular springs in supporting the load.

FIGURE 22-21 Spindle on shock plunger rod.

Manual Adjustable-Rate Shock Absorbers

A **manual adjustable-rate shock absorber** has a manual, external damper rate adjustment. The number of valves and size of the passageways in the piston can then be selected to vary the amount of restriction on the flow of oil through the piston and to vary the force needed to open the valves. Just like in our hole in the washer example from earlier, making the hole larger lets the rod move more freely; whereas, making the hole smaller provides more resistance.

When all of the orifices are open, a small dampening effect is applied to the oil. The spring force applied to the valve can also be reduced to allow the valve to open more easily. This means the oil can flow through the valves more easily, which gives a softer ride, but can also allow more rolling and pitching of the body of the vehicle. Closing some of the orifices, and increasing the spring force applied to the valves, makes it harder for fluid to flow through the piston. This increases the dampening effect of the shock absorber.

The method of changing the position of the valve varies. On some models, it is adjusted by turning a spindle located on the shock plunger rod. Turning the spindle moves the valves and changes the size of the orifices in the valve. On other models, when the shock absorber is extended to its maximum length, a pin is depressed, locking in an adjusting slide on the piston assembly FIGURE 22-21. Twisting the two halves of the shock absorber changes the number of orifices and the spring force on the valves. The first type of adjustable shock absorber can be adjusted with the shock on the vehicle, while the second type must be removed to change the dampening.

Electronic Adjustable-Rate Shock Absorbers

Some vehicles equipped with electronic ride control systems provide driver-selected control of the ride quality. Typically, a switch is located inside the passenger compartment that allows the driver to select sport, touring, or automatic. For example, if the driver selects sport, the ride will become firmer by adjusting the shock dampening. Electronic ride control can also be automatic with no provision for driver control. In automatic ride control, the vehicle's electronic module chooses a softer or firmer ride, sometimes based on the speed of the vehicle or the driving that is being done.

In order to change dampening of the shocks, the shock must be adjustable. Some vehicles use a rotary stepper motor called an actuator to change the dampening. The shock works very similar to the manual adjustment shock that has the spindle that is turned. In the manual adjustable shock, you turn this spindle with an allen wrench or other tool to make dampening changes. In the electronic-controlled shock, the actuator is mounted to the top of the shock and turns the spindle as needed. The actuator changes the number of restrictions or orifices that the oil must pass through. When all orifices are open, oil can flow more easily through the passageways in the piston. Only a small dampening effect is applied to the oil. This provides a dampening force that emphasizes ride comfort when traveling at low speeds. Closing some orifices makes it harder for fluid to flow through the piston. This increases the dampening effect of the shock absorber, providing a firmer ride that is more suitable for higher speeds and faster cornering. The need to increase dampening at high speeds becomes evident when we think about hitting a bump at high speeds, which could cause the wheels to come off the ground, disrupting our ability to steer the vehicle.

Another type of electronic adjustable shock is the solenoid-controlled shock. The solenoid is located in the side of the shock absorber or strut and opens a passageway internal to the shock to allow more fluid to bypass the piston. If the solenoid is commanded closed, the fluid will not be able to bypass, which will result in more dampening. This type of shock is still controlled by the electronic control unit (ECU).

The newest style of electronic adjustable shock uses a special type of fluid called **magneto-rheological fluid**. This fluid has the unique characteristic of changing viscosity when exposed to a magnetic field. General Motors has been using this fluid in vehicles equipped with MagneRide suspension systems. The fluid is mixed with very small ferrous particles that react to magnetic fields. As the fluid is subjected to a magnetic field, the ferrous particles bind together, effectively increasing the viscosity of the fluid. The stronger the magnetic field, the thicker the fluid. The ability to increase and decrease the viscosity of the fluid eliminates the need to change orifice sizes since it is harder to pass a thicker fluid through a hole than a thinner one. Simply varying the magnetic field at the shock absorber causes varied dampening of the suspension FIGURE 22-22. In fact, the viscosity can be changed in a millisecond or less, allowing active dampening of each individual shock absorber as the vehicle is being driven. This means that the power train control module (PCM) can stiffen the appropriate shocks in a continuously active manner as the steering wheel is being turned or the brakes are being applied. On the other hand, a particular shock can be softened as a wheel goes over a bump to prevent the shock from being transmitted as fully to the vehicle. Other manufacturers are beginning to use this technology since it is a faster-acting electronic dampening suspension. This technology is also used in some motor mounts and other applications.

Automatic Load-Adjustable Shock Absorbers

Automatic load-adjustable shock absorbers are also called **self-leveling**, meaning they have a sensor that measures the ride height and uses that information to adjust the load, leveling shocks automatically. An automatic load-adjustable suspension system controls the vehicle ride height automatically, according to the load placed over the rear axle. It consists of air-adjustable shock absorbers fitted to the rear suspension, an electrically driven compressor and air-dryer assembly, a ride height sensor, a control unit, and associated wiring and tubing FIGURE 22-23.

The ride height sensor is mounted to the cross member over the rear axle, and a moveable link connects it to a rear suspension member. As the vehicle is loaded, the normal suspension springs are compressed, which lowers the height of the vehicle. When the ignition is switched on, the control unit senses the lowered ride height and switches on the air compressor. Air is directed to the shock

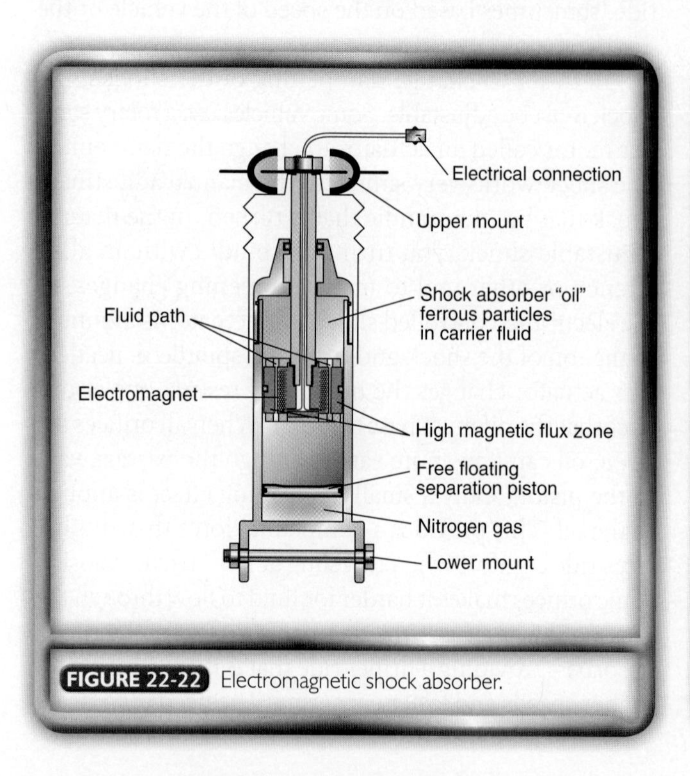
Electrical connection
Upper mount
Shock absorber "oil" ferrous particles in carrier fluid
Fluid path
Electromagnet
High magnetic flux zone
Free floating separation piston
Nitrogen gas
Lower mount

FIGURE 22-22 Electromagnetic shock absorber.

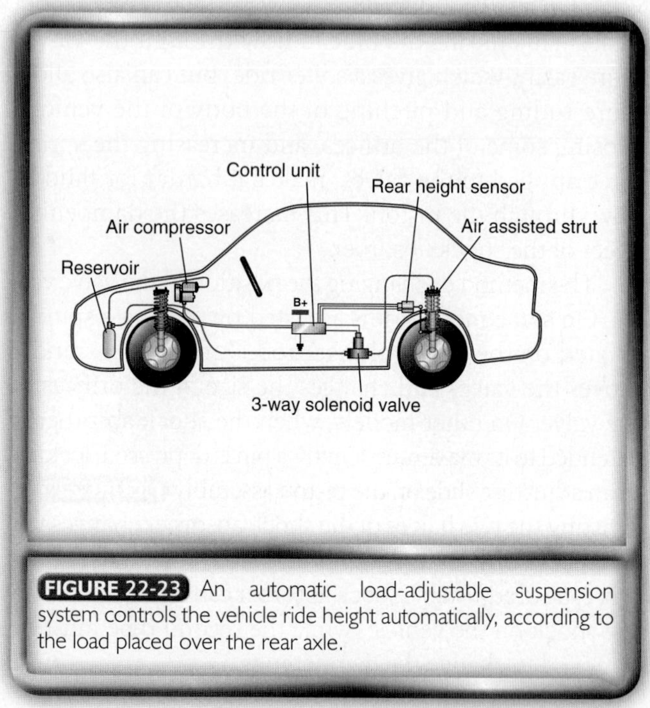
Control unit
Rear height sensor
Air compressor
Air assisted strut
Reservoir
B+
3-way solenoid valve

FIGURE 22-23 An automatic load-adjustable suspension system controls the vehicle ride height automatically, according to the load placed over the rear axle.

absorbers, causing the airbag around them to expand and raise the suspension to the normal **trim height**. If the load is removed, the suspension springs expand, raising the height of the vehicle. The control unit senses the raised ride height, and air is exhausted from the shock absorbers, causing the airbag to deflate and thereby lowering the suspension to the normal ride height.

During normal suspension operation, continual adjustment of vehicle ride height is prevented by a time delay in the control unit. This delay allows the trim height to be adjusted only when the ECU reads an out-of-trim signal for a short period of time—for example, 5 to 15 seconds. Thus, the system does not try to compensate for bumps in the road or weight transfer during braking. The compressor run time or exhaust time is limited to a few minutes. Limiting the operational time prevents it from continuing to operate if the system develops an air leak or if an exhaust vent remains open. If a fault like this develops, most self-leveling systems will set a diagnostic code.

Arms

Arms, commonly known as control arms, are components that serve as a primary load-bearing element of a vehicle's suspension system.

Control arms can be formed in different ways. In the A-arm style, sometimes referred to as a **wishbone control arm**, the arm is a relatively flat triangular part that mounts to the frame or subframe at each leg of the A FIGURE 22-24. These widely spaced mounting points prevent forward or backward movement of the steering knuckle. The mounting points typically use rubber bushings that allow the arm to pivot up and down while dampening or isolating the road shock and vibrations from the rest of the vehicle. The other end of the control arm has a ball joint that connects the control arm to the steering knuckle assembly. This arrangement provides a smooth yet stable ride for the vehicle.

Another type of control arm uses only one contact point at the frame or body FIGURE 22-25. With this style of control arm, another supporting piece called a strut rod or radius rod must be used to keep the control arm from pivoting forward and backward with changes in braking or acceleration. Other types of control arms are made from round tube material and can be used in independent suspensions. These control arms may be called transverse and trailing arms.

Rods

Rods are typically straight pieces of steel used to either transfer motion or prevent motion within a vehicle's suspension system. More specific names are given to rods based on their location or attachments. For example, a suspension system may use tie-rods, lateral rods, tension rods, control rods, panhard rods (track bars), steering track rods, or strut rods. Many of the rods use either a bushing or a joint on one or both ends of the rod. Each of these components is discussed elsewhere in this chapter, but it is important to remember that the exact number and types of rods within a vehicle vary greatly, depending on the make and model of vehicle, as well as its intended use.

Steering Knuckle

The steering knuckle, also known as a stub axle or spindle assembly, can be found in many variations. One type uses a forged piece containing the wheel hub or spindle and attaches to the suspension components. Other knuckles may provide a hole for the axle to pass

FIGURE 22-24 Wishbone control arm.

FIGURE 22-25 Single-point control arm.

through and the wheel hub to mount to FIGURE 22-26. Some knuckles will be cast iron while newer vehicles may have a cast aluminum steering knuckle to reduce unsprung weight as well as total vehicle weight. Typically, the steering knuckle also has a steering arm, which either is cast as part of the knuckle or is a separate piece bolted to the knuckle. The steering arm connects to the steering system and in either form serves to transmit the steering force to the steering knuckle when the driver turns the steering wheel. The steering knuckle pivots on a ball joint on the bottom and either a ball joint or a strut bearing on the top.

Ball Joints

Ball joints are swivel connections mounted in the outer ends of the control arms FIGURE 22-27. Ball joints are typically constructed of a ball and socket. And while ball-and-socket joints are used in most tie-rod ends, the term *ball joints* is typically reserved for the primary joints that the steering knuckle pivots on, and *tie-rod ends* is the term used for the ball-and-socket joints on the steering linkage.

FIGURE 22-26 A type of knuckle that has a hole for the axle to pass through and the wheel hub to mount to.

Suspension ball joints allow the control arms to move up and down with suspension deflection, and also let the wheel and knuckle assembly rotate for steering. The ball joint in most modern vehicles is a sealed, self-contained unit that is replaced as a unit when it is worn out. The ball joint can be fastened to the control arm in several ways. In the past, a ball joint housing was threaded and then screwed into the control arm. This type of ball joint is no longer used and will only be found on classic cars. The ball joint on modern vehicles will either be press-fit into the control arm or held by rivets or bolts. If the ball joint is pressed into the control arm, a special tool called a ball joint press tool will be used to remove and install the joint.

A ball joint is made up of a pressed-steel housing, fitted with **sintered** (bonded using pressure and heat) iron seats and a hardened ball stud. Some ball joints use a Belleville spring to hold tension on the joint, which will need to be compressed when tested. Typically, a taper on the stud locates in a mating taper on the steering knuckle, although some use a straight stud that has a crescent-shaped relief that allows a clamping bolt to orient the stud and clamp it securely. A rubber seal retains grease and keeps out dirt and water. Some ball joints have grease fittings (grease zerks) installed, which allow for periodic lubrication of the moving ball and stationary socket inside the ball joint FIGURE 22-28. Grease fittings can sometimes be found on other suspension components and need to be lubricated as part of a preventive

FIGURE 22-27 Ball joint.

FIGURE 22-28 Some ball joints have grease fittings (grease zerks) installed, which allow for periodic lubrication of the moving ball and stationary socket inside the ball joint.

maintenance program provided by the manufacturer. Most light-duty vehicles manufactured today have maintenance-free suspension components that do not provide access for lubrication. Be sure to check the manufacturer's service information when performing maintenance to see if provisions are provided, or check to see if grease fittings are present on the suspension, steering, and drive line components.

Ball joints can be referred to as loaded or unloaded. A loaded ball joint supports the weight of the vehicle. An unloaded ball joint does not support any weight; it just holds the steering knuckle in position and is referred to as a follower ball joint. For example, in a short/long-arm (SLA) suspension system with an upper and lower control arm, and the coil spring located between the frame and the lower control arm, the lower ball joint is the loaded ball joint **FIGURE 22-29**. This is because the force of the spring is placed against the lower control arm and ball joint. In this situation, the upper ball joint is the follower joint. If the spring is located between the frame and the upper control arm, then the upper ball joint is the loaded joint and the lower ball joint is the follower joint. This distinction becomes important when testing the ball joints for play, as the technician will need to unload the joint to accurately test for play.

Also, the ball joints can be designed to primarily carry either compression loads or tension loads. Compression forces tend to push the ball into the socket, so those types of joints have most of their bearing surface and socket strength near the base of the ball. Tension ball joints are being pulled apart, so they have most their bearing surface and socket strength near the stud end of the ball. Never mix up the positioning of ball joints; doing so will cause them to wear out quickly and fail.

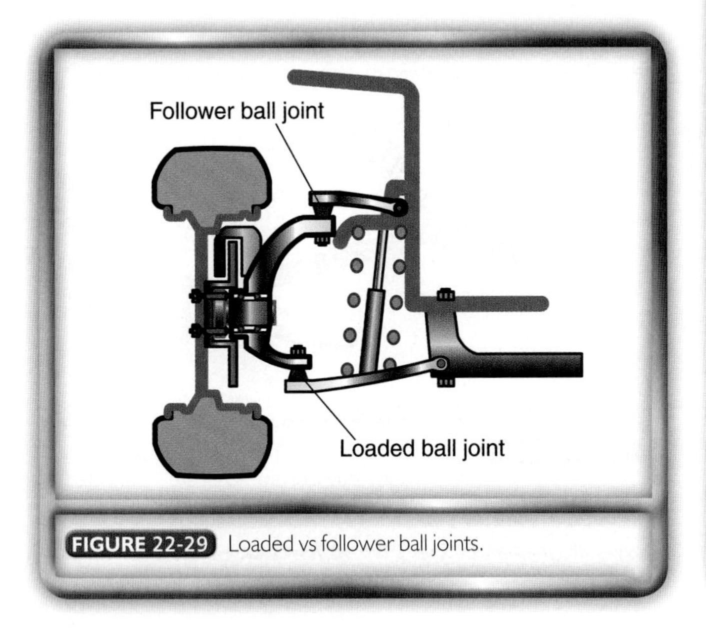
Follower ball joint
Loaded ball joint

FIGURE 22-29 Loaded vs follower ball joints.

Bushings

Bushings act as pivot points and cushions at suspension fulcrum points such as control arm bushings and strut rod bushings, to allow for limited movement of the component, while maintaining its alignment **FIGURE 22-30**. They can be metallic or made of rubber, nylon, or urethane. Many rubber bushings have a metal inner and outer housing to allow for wear surfaces or for being pressed into place. Rubber bushings isolate noise and harshness and dampen unwanted vibrations. The rubber absorbs small impacts from the suspension action, without transmitting them directly to the driver. Rubber requires no lubrication. Rubber bushings can also be used on strut rods. **Rubber-bonded bushings** can be used to mount the steering rack to the vehicle frame.

Spring shackle bushings can be molded to form two halves, to fit into each side of the spring eye on the swinging shackle, which is located on the vehicle frame. With the spring loaded, and the shackle plates tightened, the rubber is compressed in the eye and at the face of the plates. As the spring deflects, the rubber deflects without tearing.

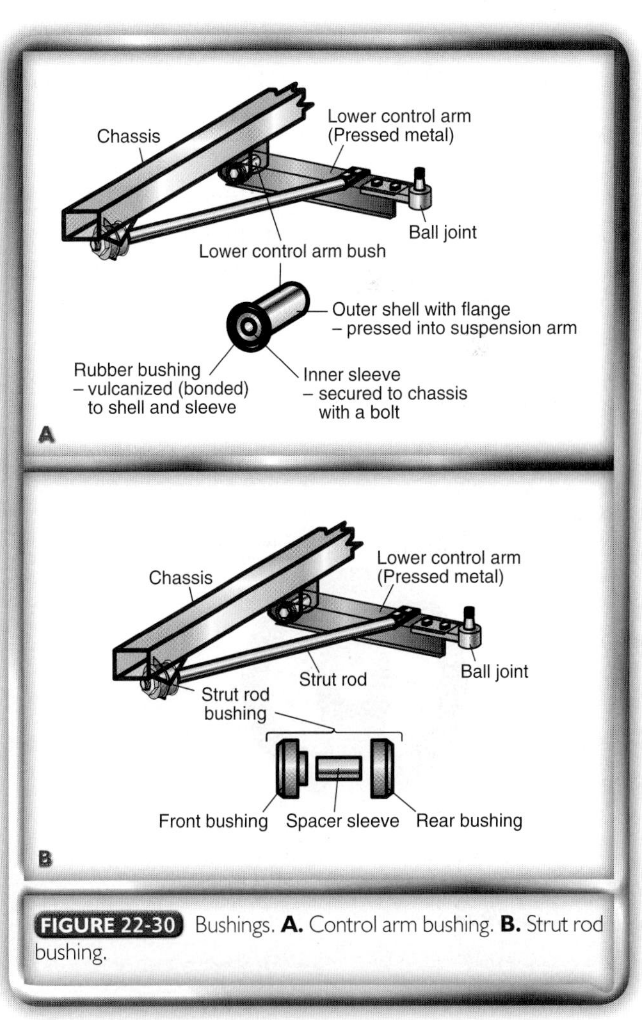
Chassis
Lower control arm
(Pressed metal)
Ball joint
Lower control arm bush
Outer shell with flange
– pressed into suspension arm
Rubber bushing
– vulcanized (bonded)
to shell and sleeve
Inner sleeve
– secured to chassis
with a bolt
A
Chassis
Lower control arm
(Pressed metal)
Strut rod
Ball joint
Strut rod
bushing
Front bushing
Spacer sleeve
Rear bushing
B

FIGURE 22-30 Bushings. **A.** Control arm bushing. **B.** Strut rod bushing.

Rubber-bonded bushings are normally used for the front eye of the spring at the fixed shackle point, and also in control arm applications. The rubber-bonded bushing has a steel outer housing and inner sleeve. The rubber medium is bonded between both to provide flexibility between them. The outer casing is normally pressed into place in the component. Relative movement between the casing and the inner sleeve causes the rubber to flex without tearing.

In control arm applications, particularly at the rear of a vehicle, the rubber bushing may be molded with a voided section FIGURE 22-31. This is known as a **compliance bushing** because it allows the unit or component to comply with a controlled amount of movement in the direction of the void. This movement relative to the vehicle frame may be designed to allow compliance or deflection steer of the road wheels when cornering. Since this influences the steering behavior of the vehicle, it is very important that the voided section is in its correct relative position. It is easy to forget how a bushing was positioned after it is removed. Marking the position with a paint mark is a good way to ensure that the bushing is replaced correctly.

Types of Suspension Systems

Manufacturers use various types of suspension systems, depending on the intended use of the vehicle, cost of manufacturing, and layout of the drive train. One of the simplest designs is the nonindependent, solid axle system, which is fairly inexpensive and not very complicated. Then there are the independent suspension types, such as the MacPherson strut and the SLA suspension systems. Each system comes in various configurations, which we will examine in this chapter. Each design has pros and cons that you need to be aware of when diagnosing and servicing suspension systems. For example, an independent drive axle uses flexible joints in the axle while a solid axle does not; they will create different types of noises when parts are going bad.

Solid Axle

The **solid axle** (beam axle) provides a simple means of mounting the hub and wheel units. Together with leaf springs, it forms an effective, nonindependent suspension system. It is used in the rear suspension of many front-engine, rear-wheel drive vehicles and light commercial vehicles and as the front suspension on many heavy commercial vehicles.

A solid axle is a nonindependent suspension because the wheels on both sides of the axle are connected together. This means when one wheel goes over a bump, the other wheel tilts FIGURE 22-32. This tilting reduces the tire-to-road contact patch, reducing friction. Thus, vehicles with solid axles are said to not handle as well as vehicles with independent suspensions. But they are inexpensive and good for hauling heavy loads.

Dead Axle/Live Axle

The terms **dead axle** and **live axle** refer to whether the axle is a driving axle or not FIGURE 22-33. A dead axle simply holds the wheels in their proper orientation. A good example of a dead axle is a boat trailer. It does not power the wheels at all, just holds them in place. A live axle not only holds the wheels in position, it also drives them. Live axles are connected to the drive train in such a way that power can be transferred through the components in the live axle. Live axles can be part of either a nonindependent or an independent suspension system.

Rubber bushing - vulcanized (bonded) to shell and sleeve
Outer shell - pressed into suspension arm
Cavities - to allow bushing movement
Inner sleeve - secured to chassis with a bolt

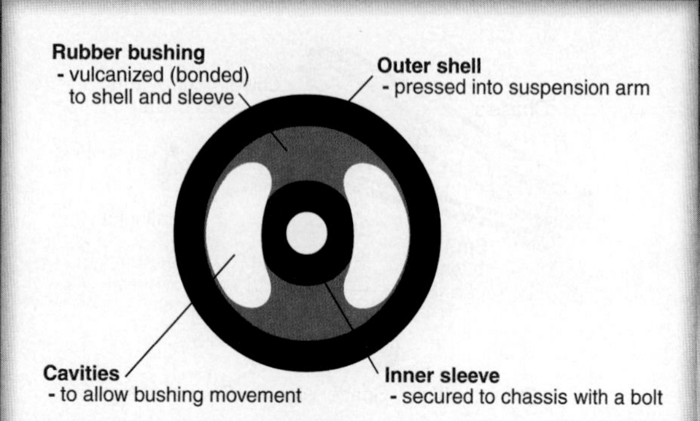

FIGURE 22-31 Compliance bushing.

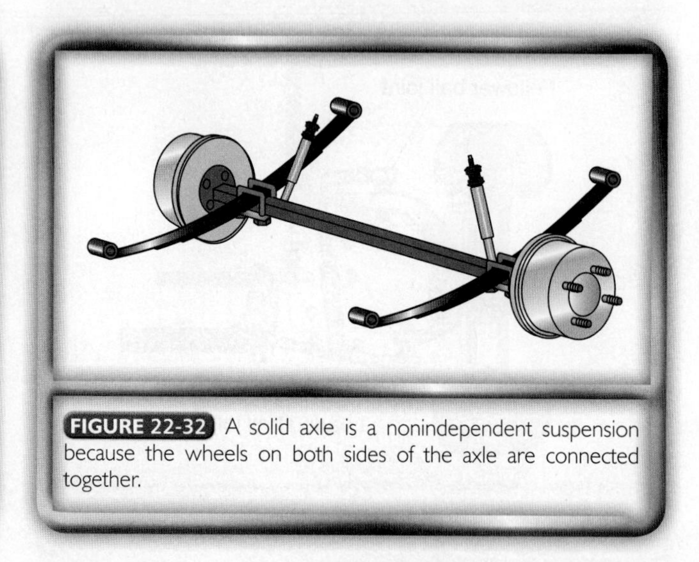

FIGURE 22-32 A solid axle is a nonindependent suspension because the wheels on both sides of the axle are connected together.

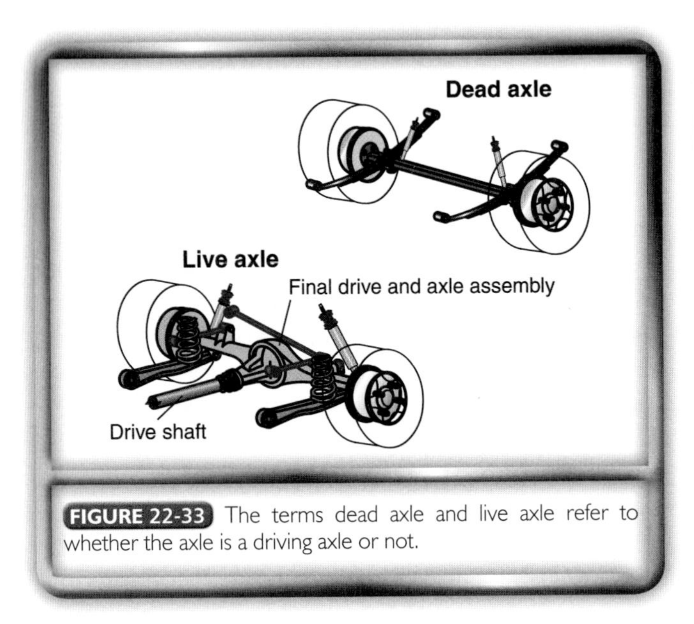
Dead axle
Live axle
Final drive and axle assembly
Drive shaft

FIGURE 22-33 The terms dead axle and live axle refer to whether the axle is a driving axle or not.

On front-wheel drive vehicles, a simple dead axle is used on the rear wheels. On a rear-wheel drive vehicle, the front axle is a dead axle. And on four-wheel drive or all-wheel drive vehicles, both the front and rear axles are live. Again, they can be of the independent or nonindependent styles.

Independent Suspension

An independent suspension allows the wheel on each side of the axle to move up and down independently of each other. In this arrangement, if a wheel on one side hits a road irregularity, it will not upset the wheel on the other side on the same axle. One of the main benefits claimed for **independent suspension** is that unsprung mass can be kept low since a heavy center axle housing is eliminated. One of the simplest, and most common, independent suspension systems is the **MacPherson strut** FIGURE 22-34. It can be used on either the front or the rear of the vehicle. It consists of a spring and heavy-duty shock absorber unit called a strut. The lower end of the strut is connected to the knuckle and located by a ball joint, fitted to the end of the control arm. Its upper end is located in a strut tower formed in the unibody. It sits in a molded rubber mounting. If the strut is on the front, the upper mounting includes a bearing to allow the complete strut assembly to rotate with the steering.

A slightly more complicated, yet common type of independent suspension system is the SLA suspension system FIGURE 22-35. It uses upper and lower control arms to control the movement of the knuckle. It typically uses either a coil spring or torsion bar connected to one of the control arms to support the weight of the vehicle. This system will be discussed further in a following section.

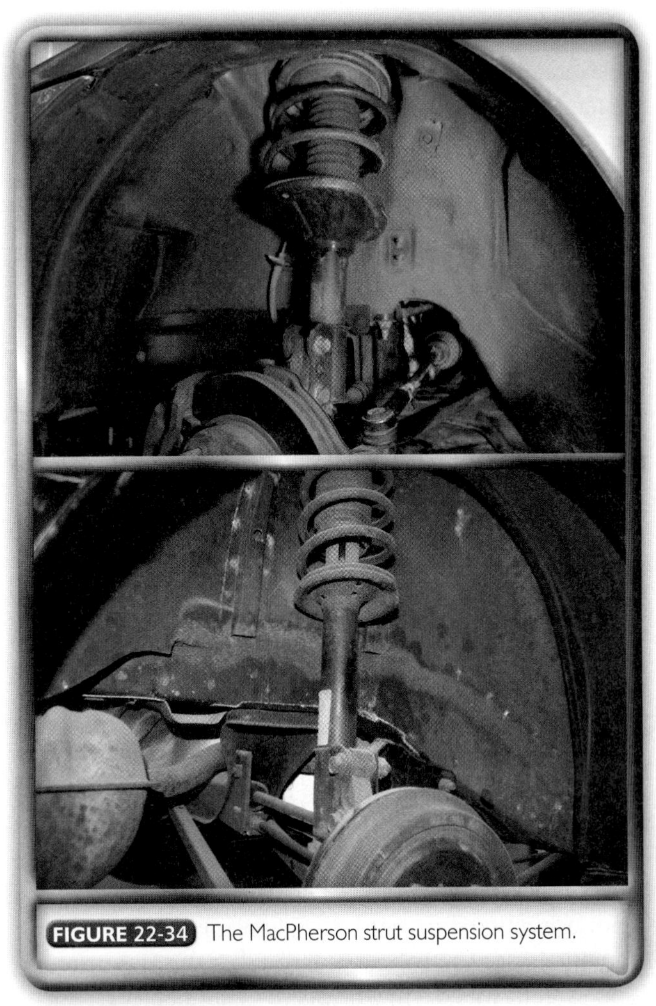

FIGURE 22-34 The MacPherson strut suspension system.

FIGURE 22-35 The SLA suspension system.

Front Suspension

The front wheels of a vehicle can have a different type of suspension system than the rear wheels. The exact type of system used in the front can vary depending on the vehicle type, such as whether it is front-wheel or rear-wheel drive.

The two main types of front suspension systems are the independent and the solid axle systems. In the independent system, the two front wheels can move independently. In the solid axle system, the two wheels are fixed by a rigid axle that binds their movement together. Regardless of design, the primary function of the front suspension system is to keep the tires in constant contact with the road.

Strut Suspension

In strut suspension, the shock absorber is contained inside the strut FIGURE 22-36. It is a direct-acting telescopic-type shock absorber and is a type of hydraulic shock absorber. A coil spring is mounted over the strut, inside the suspension tower of the front wheel housing. The strut has an upper mounting point in the suspension tower.

When used on the front suspension, the strut's upper mounting is bearing-mounted, to allow for the steering movement. The lower control arm is mounted (or held in place) to the frame or subframe by control arm bushings. The outer end of the control arm contains a ball joint and connects the steering knuckle to the control arm. The steering knuckle can then pivot on the ball joint on the bottom of the knuckle and the strut bearing on the top.

SLA Suspension

The **short-/long-arm (SLA) suspension** gets its name from using two different-length control arms, one short and one long. The primary reason that the SLA suspension system was designed was to ensure correct wheel alignment as the vehicle corners. If the arms were the same length, then the wheel would stay perfectly straight as the suspension moved up and down over bumps. This is OK for straight ahead driving, but not OK when cornering. Having arms of the same length would result in incorrect positioning of the tire in relation to the road surface since the body tends to roll. The body roll would tilt the wheel outward (toward positive camber) at the top, reducing the tire-to-road contact patch, which reduces traction. The SLA system, with the short arm on top, tends to pull the tire toward negative camber, keeping the tire-to-road contact patch as large as possible.

The shock absorber is located inside the coil spring and is a direct-acting telescopic-type shock absorber. The coil spring can be mounted either between the frame and the lower control arm (type 1) or between the shock tower and the upper control arm (type 2) FIGURE 22-37. Both control arms pivot on control arm bushings. These bushings twist on the control arm pins, which are bolted to the cross member or subframe of the vehicle. Rubber jounce and rebound stops are used to prevent direct metal-to-metal contact between the control arms and the frame if the suspension should reach its maximum limit of travel.

The steering knuckle is mounted at the ends of the control arms by ball joints and allows both up-and-down and steering movement of the tire. The ball joints can be designed to be mounted so they are under compression or tension forces. Compression forces tend to push the ball into the socket, while on tension pulls the ball away from the socket.

FIGURE 22-36 Strut suspension.

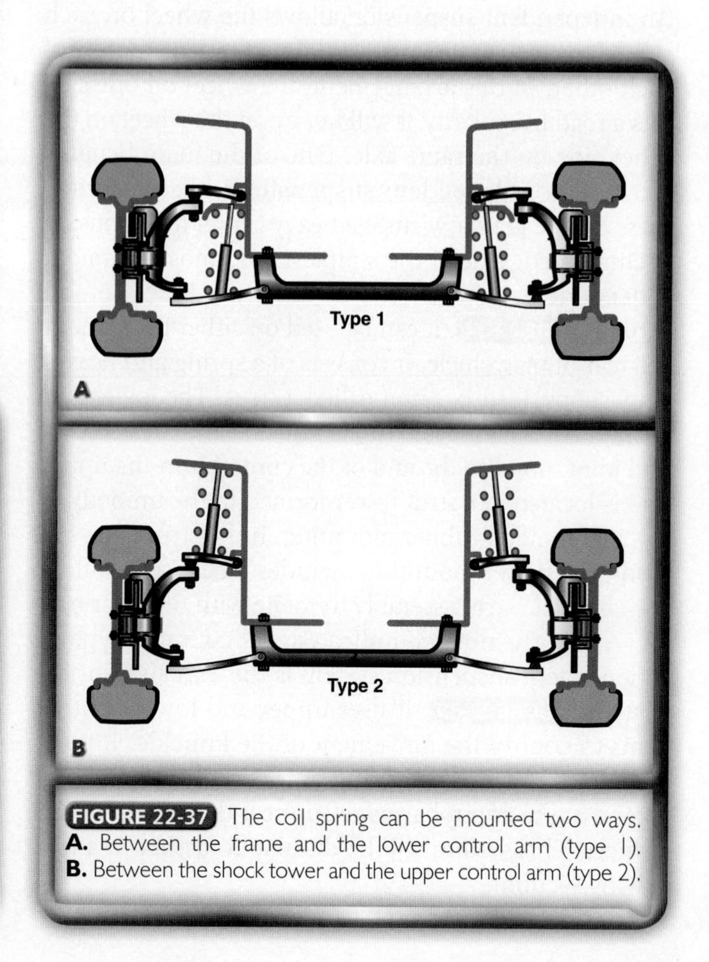
Type 1
A
Type 2
B

FIGURE 22-37 The coil spring can be mounted two ways. **A.** Between the frame and the lower control arm (type 1). **B.** Between the shock tower and the upper control arm (type 2).

There are two arrangements of steering knuckles used on SLA suspensions—short knuckle and long knuckle FIGURE 22-38. The short knuckle design locates the upper ball joint inside of the wheel. The long knuckle design moves the upper ball joint above the tire, meaning the knuckle may even partially wrap around the tire. The long knuckle design affords the manufacturer a more ideal kingpin geometry, as well as better leverage against braking and cornering forces.

Twin I-Beam Suspension

The twin I-beam suspension is a type of independent suspension. It uses separate I-beams for each front wheel that pivot from the opposite side of the vehicle's frame or cross member FIGURE 22-39. This system gives a wide radius that the wheel assembly swings through as the suspension compresses and rebounds. Most twin I-beam systems use a coil spring to support the weight of the vehicle. This means each I-beam must be supported longitudinally, which is accomplished by use of a radius rod. The radius rod connects to the I-beam from the rear and is attached to the vehicle's frame with bushings, which allow the radius rod to pivot slightly as the suspension operates.

Rear Suspension

The main function of the rear suspension system is to keep the rear tires in contact with the road and aligned with the front tires FIGURE 22-40. However, rear-wheel drive or all-wheel drive rear suspension systems are a bit more complicated. In these vehicles, the rear suspension system must not only keep the rear tires in contact with the road and aligned with the front tires, but must also be engineered to transfer engine torque to the rear wheels. And in vehicles with four-wheel steering, the rear suspension must allow the rear wheels to be steered in a similar manner as the front wheels.

FIGURE 22-38 Steering knuckles. **A.** Long knuckle SLA. **B.** Short knuckle SLA.

FIGURE 22-39 Twin I-beam suspension system.

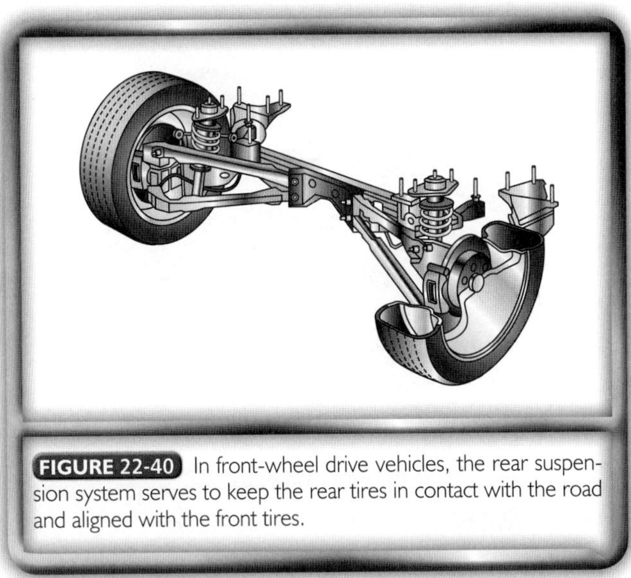

FIGURE 22-40 In front-wheel drive vehicles, the rear suspension system serves to keep the rear tires in contact with the road and aligned with the front tires.

Rear-wheel suspension systems can be of the independent or nonindependent design. It is purely up to the preference of the designer. Many, but not all, rear-wheel drive vehicles use a solid axle, nonindependent suspension system. On front-wheel drive vehicles, the type of rear suspension system leans toward a higher percentage of independent systems, but nonindependent systems are also common.

Rigid-Axle Leaf-Spring Suspension

A rigid-axle leaf-spring suspension can be used in both dead axles and live axles. The front of the leaf spring is attached to the chassis at the rigid spring hanger **FIGURE 22-41**. The spring eyes typically use rubber bushings to connect with the vehicle's frame. The axle housing is rigid between each road wheel. Thus, any deflection to one side is transmitted to the other side. The rear of the leaf spring is attached to the swinging shackle, which allows for suspension movement by allowing the spring to extend or reduce in length, as the vehicle moves over uneven ground.

The top of the direct-acting shock absorber is attached to the chassis and to the spring pad at the bottom. The U-bolts attach the axle housing to the leaf spring. They have a clamping force that helps to keep the leaf spring together. Leaf springs are usually made of tempered steel. They hold the axle in position, both laterally and longitudinally. The leaf spring is usually made up of a number of leaves of different length. The top, or longest leaf, is normally referred to as the main leaf. Most leaf-spring suspensions rely only on the sideways stiffness of the leaf spring to keep the axle in position when turning a corner, while some suspension systems use a rod called a panhard rod to help keep the axle from shifting sideways through turns.

Rigid-Axle Coil-Spring Suspension

In **rigid-axle coil-spring suspensions**, the coil spring is mounted between the axle housing and the vehicle body **FIGURE 22-42**. One drawback of a coil spring is that it cannot provide any side-to-side or front-to-back stability to the axle. All it can do is suspend the body above the axle. Therefore, unlike the with leaf-spring suspension, control rods must be used to control this potential axle movement during braking, acceleration, and cornering. Manufacturers use a variety of configurations to address this concern.

The first style uses lower control arms near each coil spring that are parallel with the **centerline** of the vehicle and connect between the frame and the axle. They maintain the longitudinal position of the axle. The upper control arms are angled toward the center of the vehicle to counteract any lateral forces as well as twisting forces. Another style uses upper and lower control arms that all are parallel with the centerline of the vehicle. They control the twisting force of the axle but cannot control any lateral forces during cornering. One of two methods is used to control the lateral forces—a panhard rod or a Watt's linkage.

A **panhard rod**, also referred to as a track bar, sits parallel with the axle. One end connects to the frame of the vehicle, and the other end connects to the axle **FIGURE 22-43**. The panhard rod uses bushings on each end so the joints can pivot as the suspension compresses and rebounds. The position of the axle is maintained laterally by the rod. A **Watt's linkage** is a bit more complex but functions in a similar way **FIGURE 22-44**. A lever that is able to pivot in the middle is mounted vertically to the rear axle near its center. The top of the lever is connected to a rod that is parallel to the axle and

FIGURE 22-41 A rigid-axle leaf-spring suspension.

FIGURE 22-42 Rigid-axle coil-spring suspension.

mounted high on one side of the frame. The bottom of the lever is connected to a similar rod, which is also parallel to the axle but mounted low on the other side of the frame. These two rods allow up-and-down movement of the axle but prevent lateral movement.

Rigid Nondrive Axle Suspension

A rigid nondrive axle is sometimes referred to as a beam axle. It can come in a variety of configurations. With **rigid nondrive axle suspension**, the longitudinal and lateral position of the axle must be maintained as in all axles, but since it is a dead axle, it typically has to withstand only braking forces. One common rigid nondrive axle suspension uses lower trailing arms connecting the vehicle frame and axle and a strut assembly on top. These trailing arms maintain the longitudinal position of the axle **FIGURE 22-45**, while the springs and strut support the weight of the vehicle and assist in controlling any braking forces. The struts have an upper mounting point in the suspension tower. They are nonsteerable and therefore do not require an upper strut bearing. This type of suspension typically uses a panhard rod to control lateral forces.

Another style of dead axle uses a U-shaped axle beam with a torsion bar mounted inside it. A trailing arm holds the axle longitudinally, a panhard rod holds it laterally, the strut and spring support the weight of the vehicle, and the torsion bar provides a measure of resistance to twisting forces as one wheel goes over a bump.

Other types of dead axles are tube style, using the axle stub shafts as mounting points for the wheel hub. These axles typically use trailing arms with a coil-over-shock arrangement, and a stabilizing bar such as a panhard rod.

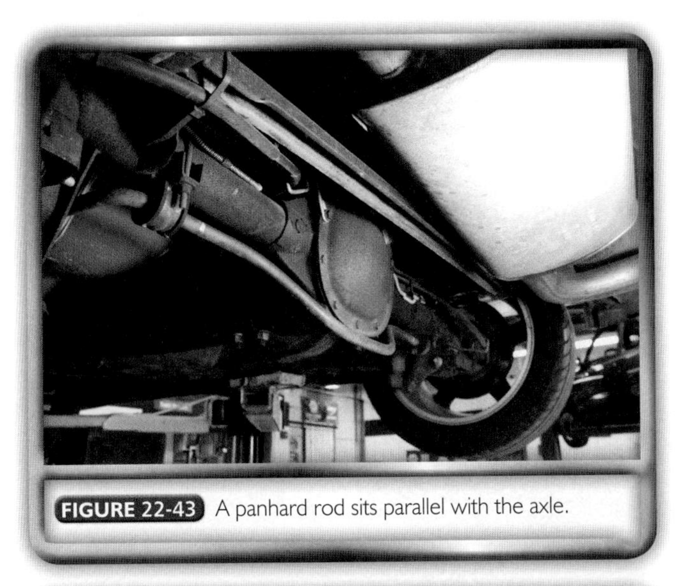

FIGURE 22-43 A panhard rod sits parallel with the axle.

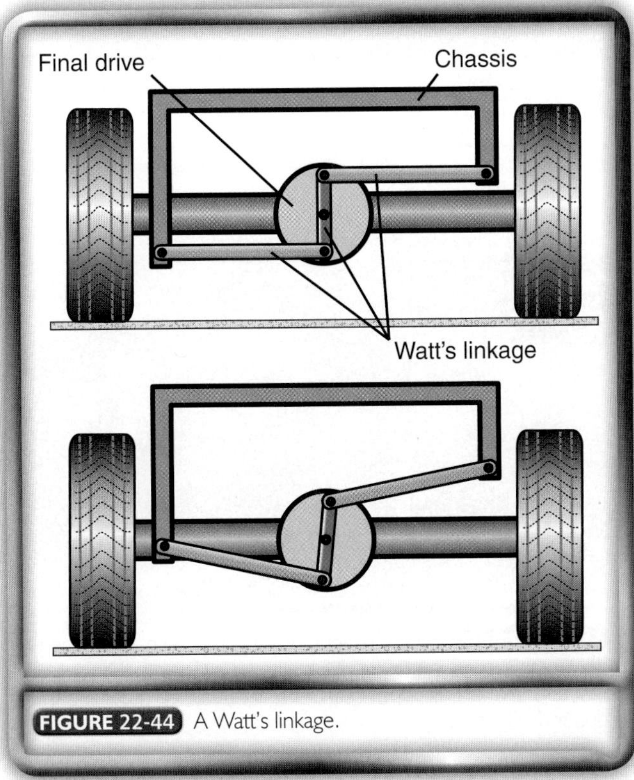
Final drive
Chassis
Watt's linkage

FIGURE 22-44 A Watt's linkage.

Rear Independent Suspension (Nondrive)

The kind of nondrive independent suspension used on the rear of a vehicle can be fairly simple since the wheels typically do not steer or drive the vehicle. In this case, the suspension system only needs to hold the wheels in the proper orientation while the vehicle is being driven. Since it is an independent type of system, each wheel is not connected to the other, so they can move separately. A MacPherson strut system is commonly used at the rear, which can be similar to the front suspension system, using either a wishbone-shaped lower control arm or two control arms, along with a strut assembly. It can also use a trailing arm with a strut assembly and a panhard rod to control all three axes.

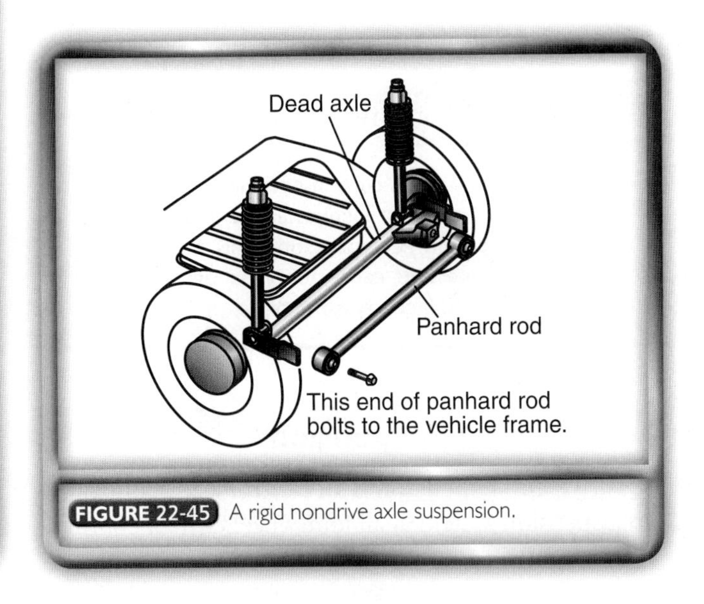
Dead axle
Panhard rod
This end of panhard rod
bolts to the vehicle frame.

FIGURE 22-45 A rigid nondrive axle suspension.

Rear-Wheel Drive Independent Suspension

On rear-wheel drive vehicles with independent rear suspension, the final drive unit is fixed to the vehicle frame FIGURE 22-46. Drive is transmitted to each wheel by **external drive shafts**, shafts that transfer power from the final drive to the live axle. Suspension is normally provided by coil springs, and each wheel unit is located by a combination of lateral and longitudinal control arms, or by trailing arms to the frame. The final drive assembly is normally bolted to the chassis, and since it must absorb the torque reaction, it must be securely fastened. Drive shafts, with either conventional universal joints or constant-velocity joints, rotate and transmit the drive to the wheels. **Universal joints** are placed on the end of a drive shaft to compensate for the up-and-down movement of the rear wheels. When conventional universal joints are used, each drive shaft may have a **splined section**, a special section of the shaft that can move in or out to vary the shaft's length due to changes in the suspension action FIGURE 22-47.

On some vehicles equipped with an independent rear suspension, the drive shafts or half-shafts themselves can be used as the upper link of the suspension, providing the upper pivot point FIGURE 22-48. In this case, the half-shafts are fixed, meaning they do not extend or collapse. This makes the splined section unnecessary, and the shaft can be made as a one-piece unit. The outer wheel bearing hub is held in position laterally and longitudinally at the bottom by a pivot on the end of the lower control arm, and the half-shaft holds the top of the hub in position vertically. Since the hub pivots on both the lower control arm and the half-shaft, the wheel can move up and down. The lower control arm has widely spaced pivots to provide stability. It is longer than the half-shaft, which allows the camber to move slightly positive during cornering, just like an SLA suspension.

FIGURE 22-46 Live independent rear suspension.

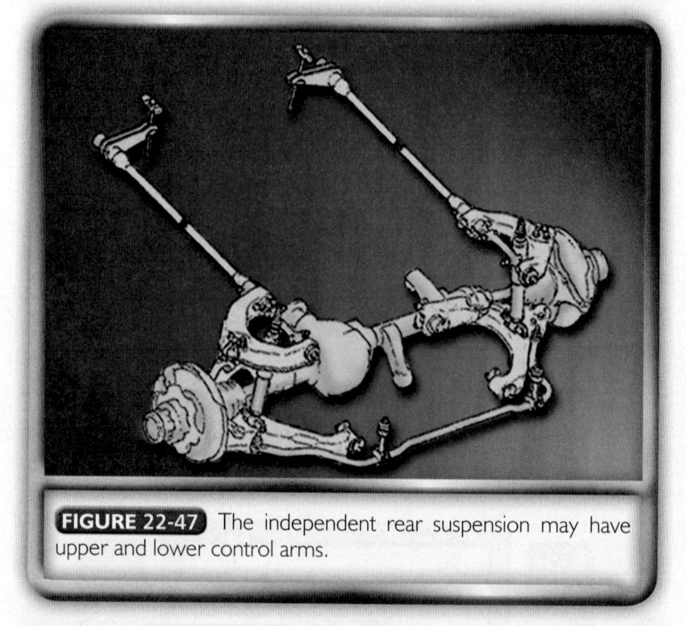

FIGURE 22-47 The independent rear suspension may have upper and lower control arms.

FIGURE 22-48 On some vehicles equipped with an independent rear suspension, the drive shafts or half-shafts themselves can be used as the upper link of the suspension, providing the upper pivot point.

TECHNICIAN TIP

External forces, such as curb impact or a collision, can damage control arms or linkages and move the wheel units from their correct position. This can make a vehicle pull to one side, cause abnormal tire wear, and make the vehicle difficult to control.

Adaptive Air Suspension

Adaptive air suspension is an electronically controlled air suspension system at all four wheels with a continuously adaptive dampening system, meaning it is able to automatically change the dampening power of the shocks when the road conditions change to give the driver a smoother ride. It combines sporty handling with a high level of ride comfort. Additionally, the air suspension allows the speed-dependent lowering of the body; this change in ride height means a low center of gravity, resulting in significantly increased directional stability, as well as increased aerodynamic efficiency. On a bumpy road, it makes the shocks softer so the vehicle rides better. The vehicle's handling characteristics are improved at the same time by the addition or removal of air from the system.

The information obtained from sensors on the axles for ride height, and acceleration sensors on the body for vehicle pitch, is evaluated in the adaptive air suspension's central control unit. This computer can control the adjustment of the individual shock absorbers within milliseconds, depending on driving situations. As long as no higher dampening forces are required—for instance, when driving straight ahead on good roads—the damper settings remain comfortably soft.

Specific adjustments to the dampening force at individual wheels eliminate body movement, which could affect occupant comfort and vehicle control. In some cases, when cornering, braking, or accelerating, adaptive dampening can automatically reduce rolling or pitching movements. Adaptive air suspension also offers the following advantages:

- The vehicle's suspension height remains constant regardless of the load it is carrying.
- Adjustable dampening characteristics and ride height are maintained by a single process, via the manufacturer's "Vehicle Performance" menu, which can be found on the dash or console switch.
- The driver can influence the suspension characteristics, and thus the operating dynamics, as individually preferred. This enables drivers to set the suspension to a sport or performance setting when desired, so that the vehicle will handle better.

Adaptive Air Suspension Operation

On some vehicles, when the ignition is switched on, or when the vehicle's door is opened before ignition, the control system is activated. The height sensor uses the induction principle to constantly monitor the distance between the vehicle's axle and its chassis. If the control system determines that the ride height is too low, it will command that air be added to the appropriate adaptive shock absorbers. When the vehicle is being loaded, unloaded, or lowered due to driver command or vehicle speed, the height sensor monitors the changes and reports them to the control unit. The ECU compares this information to the stored reference values.

The ECU activates either the electric motor of the compressor or the exhaust solenoid valve, which is located on the top of each adaptive shock absorber **FIGURE 22-49**. This also requires the solenoid valve to be actuated or moved to maintain the required level once reached. The adaptive shock absorber solenoid valves are subject to stringent leakage requirements to maintain the vehicle's height even when the system is not being operated.

When the vehicle is being loaded, the compressor delivers air into the four air suspension bellows through fill solenoids or gate solenoids, until the normal level has once again been reached. For additional air delivery or rapid response, the reservoir solenoid valve is opened and air flows directly from the reservoir. When the vehicle is being unloaded, the exhaust solenoid valve is activated. Activation of this valve results in airflow from the air suspension bellows being removed via the air dryer solenoid valve in the compressor, then via the relay valve. The air is then exhausted into the atmosphere through a computer-controlled vent valve. Any dynamic air spring movement while the vehicle is in motion is ignored and does not cause the control system to respond. However, the system can adjust the air pressure based on other parameters such as vehicle speed, driver selection of a different mode, or any automatic adjustments that the control system determines are necessary.

Computer-Controlled Suspension

Just like many other functions on a modern vehicle, the suspension system has been computerized. Computer-

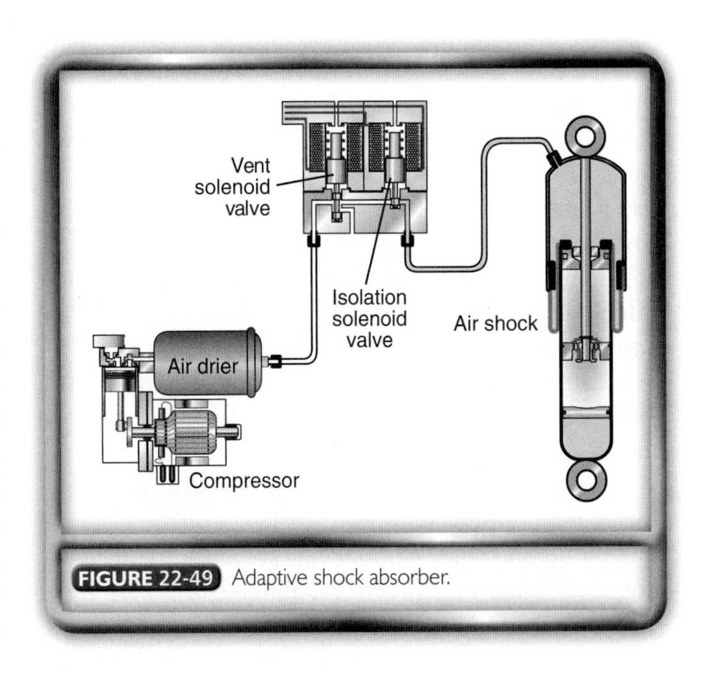
Vent
solenoid
valve
Isolation
solenoid
valve
Air shock
Air drier
Compressor

FIGURE 22-49 Adaptive shock absorber.

controlled suspension systems, often referred to as active or adaptive suspension, use computers to constantly monitor all aspects of the suspension system and ride features to improve vehicle handling and generate a smoother ride. For example, the computer system can set the suspension for sporty handling during situations where precise steering control, fast braking, and high-speed driving are needed. It can then almost instantly shift the suspension system in response to normal driving to provide a smooth ride. Advanced systems are also available that monitor and respond to changes in cargo load and vehicle height. Computer-controlled suspension systems are available on front and rear suspensions. Examples of some computerized suspension systems are:

- Active: Makes adjustments without any driver input
- Hydraulic actuated: Uses fluid to implement changes to the suspension system
- Electromagnetic rheological: Uses an electromagnetic response to make changes to the viscosity of the hydraulic fluid, thereby adjusting the stiffness of the suspension system
- Semi-active: Requires some driver input to change the suspension system
- Solenoid valve actuated: Uses a solenoid valve to change the dampening of the shocks
- Stepper motor actuated: Uses an electric stepper motor to adjust the valving in the shock absorber to change the rate of dampening

Wheel Alignment Fundamentals

All wheels of a vehicle must be correctly positioned in relation to the vehicle and to each other for the vehicle to drive and steer properly. A driver should not need to keep manipulating the steering wheel to maintain the vehicle in a straight-ahead position on straight, level roads. Similarly, little effort should be needed to turn the vehicle into curves or to let it return to the straight-ahead position once the curve has been negotiated. Wheels are positioned on the suspension at certain angles to provide for easy driving of the vehicle. These angles, taken together, determine the vehicle's **wheel alignment**. The alignment is set using the control arms, strut rods, tie-rods, knuckles, and vehicle frame to obtain the proper angles. Alignments should be performed for several reasons, including when handling issues related to alignment angles are found, when tire wear shows any tire wearing angle issue, and when components are replaced that have alignment angle adjustment capabilities. It is also good practice to check vehicles for alignment whenever new tires are being installed. But before you can check alignment, you need to know what the alignment angles are and how they affect driving.

Camber

Camber is the side-to-side vertical tilt of the wheel. It is viewed from the front of the vehicle and is measured in degrees FIGURE 22-50. A wheel that leans away from the center of the vehicle at the top is said to have **positive camber**. A wheel that leans toward the center of the vehicle is said to have **negative camber**. A vehicle with camber pull will pull in the direction of the greatest positive camber. To picture why it pulls in this direction, think of a paper cup lying on its side. When it is rolled, it turns in the direction of the narrower end of the cup. Tires do the same thing in regard to their camber. Camber is affected by ride height and can be seen by looking at the tilt of the wheel in vehicles that are lowered incorrectly. Camber used to be a heavy tire wearing angle when tires were of the bias ply type and had stiff sidewalls. Camber wear is now debatable, given the much more pliable sidewalls in radial tires. It is safe to say that tires can tolerate moderate amounts of improper camber much better than before. There are also studies that say most of what technicians diagnose as camber wear is really toe wear. Pay attention to this debate as it plays out.

> **TECHNICIAN TIP**
>
> Changes in running camber can be caused by driving over road irregularities, load variations, and worn suspension components.

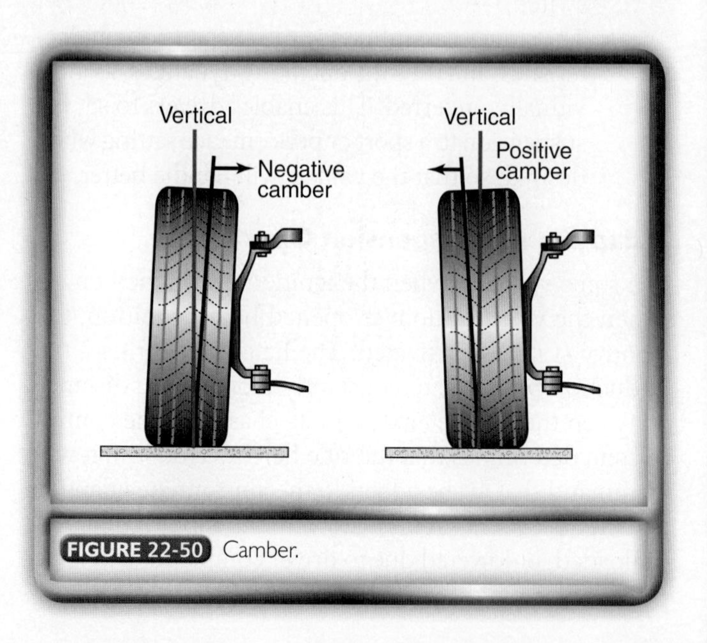
Vertical
Negative camber
Vertical
Positive camber

FIGURE 22-50 Camber.

On earlier vehicles with narrow, large-diameter tires, large camber angles were used to bring the centerline of road contact closer to the steering axis. They also ensured the vehicle weight was carried by the large inner bearing. On modern vehicles, however, tires are much wider and generally smaller in diameter, and large camber angles would cause the tire to ride on the outer edges of the tires. The amount of camber is now reduced so that most vehicles when in forward motion have what is called zero camber, or no tilt, to provide maximum tire patch contact with the road, as well as long tire life.

Caster

Caster is the forward or backward tilt of the steering axis from vertical when viewed from the side of the vehicle FIGURE 22-51. The steering axis is an imaginary line passing through the center of the ball joints on SLA suspensions or passing through the center of the upper strut bearing and lower ball joint on MacPherson strut suspensions. So caster is the tilt of the steering axis from vertical, measured in degrees. Backward tilt from the vertical is positive caster. Forward tilt is negative caster. When a vehicle has positive caster, a line drawn through the steering axis centerline meets the road surface ahead of the vertical centerline of the wheel. The center of the tire contact point is behind the steering axis.

When the wheel is turned to the right, the tire contact point is moved to the left of the direction of travel. Conversely, when the wheel is turned to the left, the contact point is moved to the right of the direction of travel. In forward motion, this generates a self-centering force that helps return the wheels to the neutral position when the steering wheel is released.

Most vehicles have positive caster, because it causes the tires to travel in a straight line with minimal driver action. However, as positive caster increases, more and more effort is needed to turn the steering wheel to overcome the increased self-straightening force. Also, positive caster causes the spindle to tilt as the wheel is steered, and this places more weight on the inside tire because of the body lifting that occurs with the inside tire. This lift can be seen by turning the steering from lock to lock while the vehicle is stationary.

> **TECHNICIAN TIP**
>
> Some vehicles have by design an amount of negative caster, which makes the steering light. Negative caster is created by placing the suspension system pivots so that they are tilted forward from the vertical line. Generally, such vehicles would operate only at low speeds; vehicles with negative caster can become unstable as speed increases. Steering will pull toward the side of the vehicle with the most negative caster. Caster is affected by ride height and on most modern vehicles is a nonadjustable angle without aftermarket components.

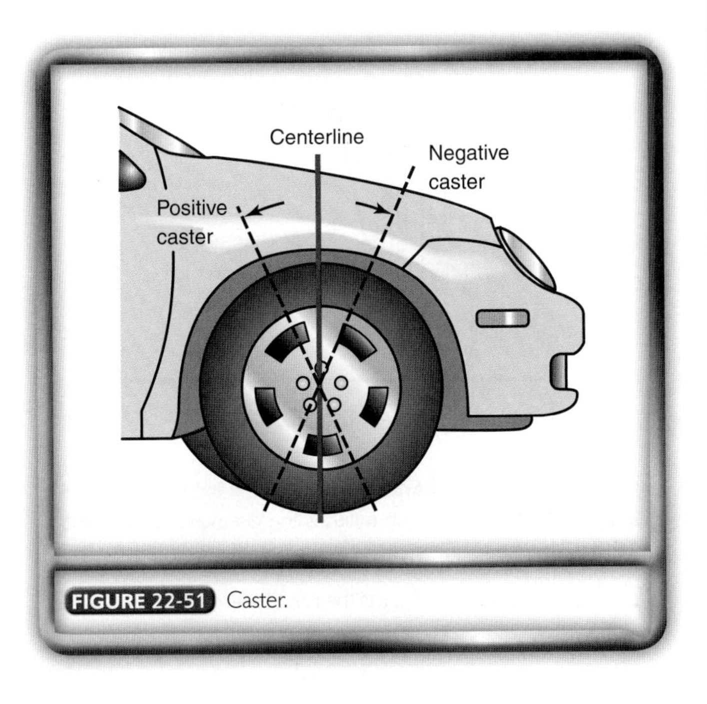
Centerline
Negative caster
Positive caster

FIGURE 22-51 Caster.

> **Applied Math**
>
> ***AM-21: Parallel/Perpendicular: The technician can use measurement devices to determine the parallelism or perpendicularity of chassis, suspension, and other vehicle systems requiring the application of geometric alignment principles.***
>
> A vehicle was purchased at an auction and has been taken to an automotive repair shop for evaluation. When the vehicle was set up on the alignment machine and alignment readings taken, several of the angles were substantially out of specification, including front-wheel setback, rear thrust angle, and SAI. These angles being out of specification indicate the potential of a bent frame or chassis. Upon further examination, the technician observes cracked undercoat and paint on the subframe components, as well as shifting of the engine cradle bolts. This verifies what the alignment angles are telling him; that the chassis is not parallel and perpendicular. The technician knows that the wheels cannot be brought back into proper alignment with the chassis out of alignment.

Steering Axis Inclination

The axis around which the wheel assembly swivels as it turns to the right or left is called the steering axis. It is formed by drawing a line through the center of the upper and lower pivot points of the suspension assembly FIGURE 22-52. Seen from the front of the vehicle, it is tilted inward at the top. The angle formed between this line and the vertical provides the **steering axis inclination (SAI)** angle. Since the SAI is not adjustable, if the camber angle is correct, then the SAI should also be correct; that is, it should match the manufacturer's specifications.

SAI acts with caster to provide a self-centering of the front wheels. When the wheels are in the straight-ahead position, the ends of the stub axles are almost horizontal. When the wheels turn to either side, the effect of SAI is to make the ends of the stub axle tend to move downward, but this tendency is prevented by the wheel and tire on the ground. The stub axle carrier then must move up, which raises the corner of the vehicle. When the steering wheel is released, the weight of the vehicle forces the stub carrier back down, which pushes the wheels back to a central position. When the wheels are turned the other way, the same thing happens. With a perfectly vertical steering axis, no self-centering would occur. The wheel would pivot on a radius, not under the center of the tire patch, but off to the inside of the tire. This would introduce a turning movement on the wheel whenever the tire hit a bump, transmitting road shocks back to the steering wheel, and steering would be difficult to control.

SAI also brings the pivot point close to the center of the tire contact patch at the road surface. For steering purposes, ideally SAI intersects with the camber line (drawn through the center of the tire and the wheel) at the road surface. Any difference in distance between these two lines produces another suspension angle called the scrub radius, which will be discussed further in a later section.

Included Angle

The angle formed between the SAI and the camber line is called the **included angle**, or diagnostic angle. It is found by adding the SAI angle and the camber angle together. If the camber angle is specified as negative, then it is subtracted from the SAI angle. When an angle is referred to as a diagnostic angle, it means the angle cannot be changed but is measured to determine if any parts are bent, such as a spindle, control arm, or steering arm.

Scrub Radius

Scrub radius is also known as steering offset and scrub geometry. It is the distance between two imaginary points on the road surface. One point is the centerline of the tire using the camber line, and the other point is where the SAI centerline contacts the road surface FIGURE 22-53. If these two lines intersect at the center of the tire, at the road surface, then the vehicle is said to have zero offset, or **zero scrub radius**. If the camber line is outside of the SAI line, then it has positive offset or **positive scrub radius**. If the camber line is inside of the SAI line, then

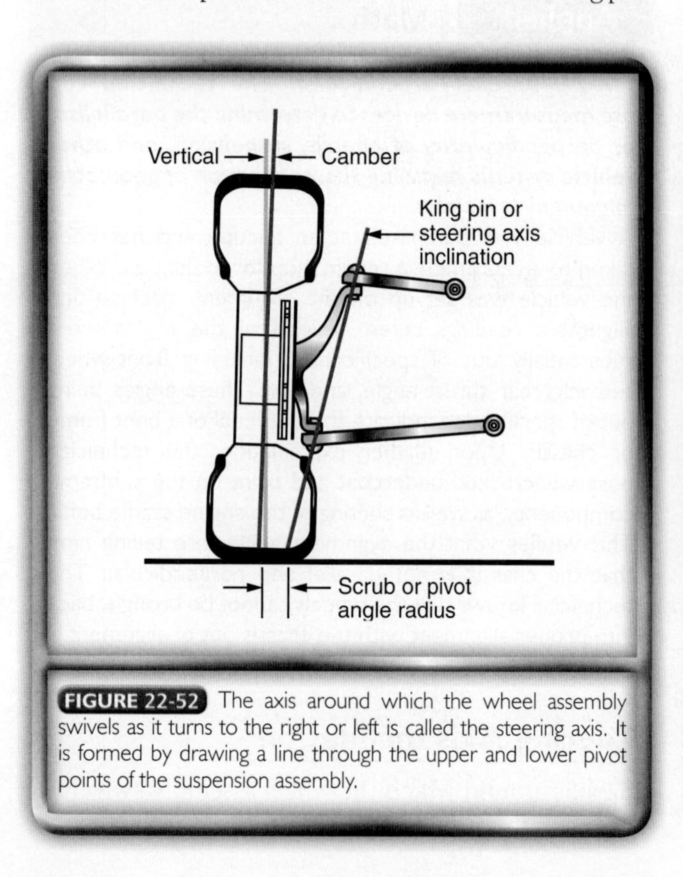
Vertical
Camber
King pin or steering axis inclination
Scrub or pivot angle radius

FIGURE 22-52 The axis around which the wheel assembly swivels as it turns to the right or left is called the steering axis. It is formed by drawing a line through the upper and lower pivot points of the suspension assembly.

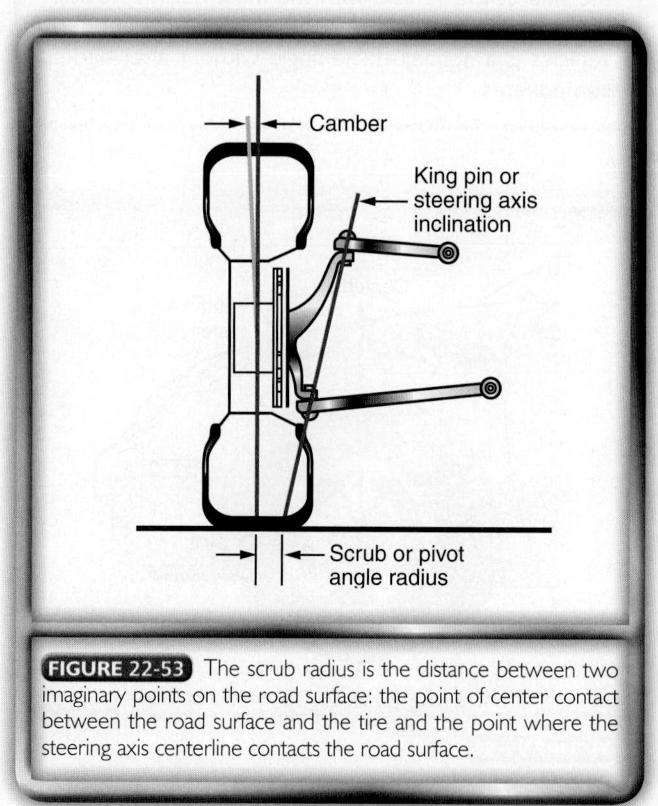
Camber
King pin or steering axis inclination
Scrub or pivot angle radius

FIGURE 22-53 The scrub radius is the distance between two imaginary points on the road surface: the point of center contact between the road surface and the tire and the point where the steering axis centerline contacts the road surface.

it has negative offset or **negative scrub radius**. Scrub radius can be changed accidentally a number of ways. Changing the diameter of wheels and tires affects scrub radius, as does the distance that the center of the wheel and tire sits relative to the vehicle body, which is called wheel offset. SAI and camber also affect scrub radius since we are changing the angles that determine scrub radius.

Incorrect scrub radius can produce undesirable effects. Too much positive scrub radius (the camber line is outside of the SAI line) will cause the vehicle to dart when the brakes are applied. Too much negative scrub radius (the camber line is inside of the SAI line) will cause the vehicle to be unstable while driving (not braking) and will result in less driver feedback. Driver feedback is the feel of the road through the steering wheel. Most front-wheel drive vehicles use a negative scrub radius to provide a measure of safety in the event that one brake circuit fails since they use a diagonal split brake system.

On a rear-wheel drive vehicle with positive scrub radius, the vehicle's forward motion and the friction between the tire and the road cause a force that tends to move the front wheels back. This causes the wheels to toe-out. If it has negative scrub radius, the front wheels again tend to move back and the wheels now toe-in. On front-wheel drive vehicles, the opposite occurs. Positive scrub radius causes toe-in, and negative causes toe-out. During braking, if braking effort is greater on one side of the vehicle than the other, positive scrub radius will cause the vehicle to veer toward the side with the greater braking effort. Negative scrub radius will cause the vehicle to veer away from the side of greatest effort. How much it veers depends on the size of the scrub radius. This is why vehicles with a diagonal-split brake system have negative scrub radius built into the steering geometry. If one half of the brake system fails, then the vehicle will tend to pull up in a straight line.

> **TECHNICIAN TIP**
>
> Since the offset of the wheel rim determines where the centerline of the tire meets the road surface, it is important that the offset is not changed if wheels are being replaced. Changing the rim offset changes the scrub radius and also the predictability of the vehicle handling, especially during brake failure. Also note that if tire size, ride height, or camber adjustment is changed, scrub radius also changes and will affect vehicle handling, potentially creating a safety hazard. Understand that there is a liability risk when modifying the vehicle you are working on.

Toe-in and Toe-out

Toe is the angle of the tires relative to each other when viewed from above. The condition in which the fronts of the wheels are closer together than the rears of the wheels is called **toe-in**. The condition in which the fronts of the wheels are farther apart than the rears is called **toe-out**. Some manufacturers use the terms positive toe for toe-in and *negative toe* for toe-out. Toe can be measure in inches or degrees. The **static toe** setting is designed to compensate for slight wear in steering joints and components, which may cause the wheels to splay outward or inward while the vehicle is being driven. This effect is designed into the vehicle based on several factors, such as front-wheel drive versus rear-wheel drive, front/rear brake system split versus diagonal brake system split, and specific desired handling characteristics. Manufacturers specify the proper static toe for the design of the vehicle such that the wheels will be parallel when the vehicle is in forward motion, which avoids scrubbing of the tires.

Toe-out on Turns

Toe-out on turns is the relative toe setting of the front wheels as the vehicle turns **FIGURE 22-54**. When a vehicle makes a turn, each wheel should rotate with true rolling motion that is free from tire scrub. True rolling motion is obtained only when each wheel is at 90 degrees to a line drawn between the steering axis and the center point of the turn. The steering axis is the point where the tire turns at the knuckle. Because the rear wheels are fixed, the center of the turn will lie somewhere along the centerline of the rear axle, depending on how far

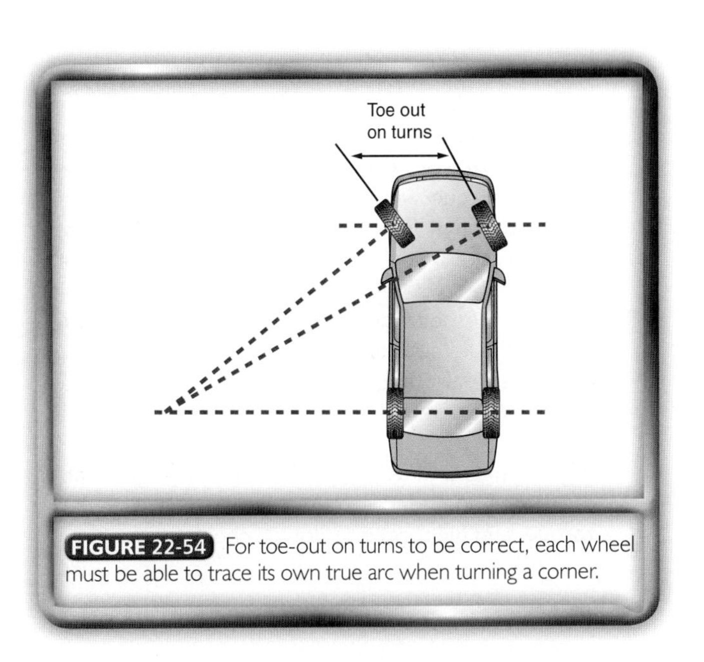
Toe out
on turns

FIGURE 22-54 For toe-out on turns to be correct, each wheel must be able to trace its own true arc when turning a corner.

the steering wheel is turned from the straight-ahead position.

To provide true rolling motion, the inner wheel must be turned through a greater angle than the outer wheel. This allows the inner wheel to turn through a smaller turning radius than the outer wheel. This correct positioning of the wheels when steering around a corner is obtained by use of the **Ackermann principle** and layout. The Ackermann principle is a geometric alignment of linkages in a vehicle's steering such that the wheels on the inside of a turn are able to move in a different circle radius than the wheels on the outside. The inner wheels must move on a circle with a smaller radius, and the outer wheels move on a circle with a larger radius. The **Ackermann angle** is the angle the steering arms make with the steering axis, projected toward the center of the rear axle FIGURE 22-55. The angling of the steering arms forces the inner wheels to turn through a smaller angle when the steering wheel is turned to that side. When the steering wheel is turned the opposite direction, the wheels that were on the outside are now on the inside of the turn and will turn more sharply than the wheels that are now on the outside of the turn. Toe-out on turns is a nonadjustable angle. If it is not correct according to the manufacturer's specifications, then you know that a steering linkage is bent, typically the steering arm. This will also cause the tires to scrub when turning corners.

Applied Science

AS-15: Force: The technician can use a tension gauge such as a torque wrench to measure the force or tension required to tighten connections to manufacturer's specifications.

A good quality torque wrench is one of the technician's most valuable tools. Proper torque applied to fasteners is critical for the repair job to successful. This is true for chassis work as well as for engines.

A torque wrench measures the amount of twisting force or "torque" applied to the fastener. In physics, torque is sometimes called a rotational force. The formula to calculate the torque applied to a bolt is torque = force x distance. In the study of physics, the distance is known as the moment arm. It takes twice the force at half the distance (or moment arm) to equal a certain torque value. It takes half of the force at twice the distance (or moment arm) to equal the same torque value.

When using a torque wrench, the following precautions should be observed:

1. Use manufacturer's service information to obtain the torque specifications.
2. Verify that you have the correct torque wrench for the job that you are doing. The 80/20 rule states that the torque wrench should be used only in the approved range. This would be from 20 to 80 ft.-lb., when using a 0 to 100 ft.-lb. wrench, or 40 to 160 ft.-lb. on a 0 to 200 ft.-lb. wrench.
3. Support the head of the torque wrench with one hand and pull the wrench handle in a steady motion.
4. Use a general crisscross pattern for tightening fasteners unless a manufacturer's torque pattern is available.
5. Tighten nuts and bolts in at least three stages: one-third recommended torque, two-thirds torque, full torque, and full torque to double check, once again.

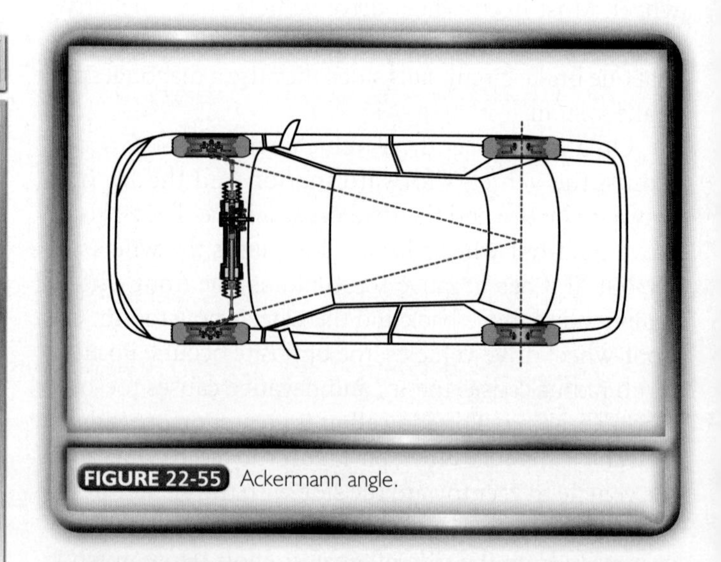

FIGURE 22-55 Ackermann angle.

Applied Science

AS-52: Circular: The technician can demonstrate an understanding of circular motion as it relates to toe and camber on turns.

When you steer a vehicle through a turn, the outside front wheel has to travel a wider arc than the inside wheel; therefore, the inside front wheel must steer at a sharper angle than the outside wheel. To provide true rolling motion, the inner wheel must be turned through a greater angle than the outer wheel. This allows the inner wheel to turn through a smaller turning radius than the outer wheel. With the tires on the turntable, toe-out on turns is measured by the turning angle gauges (turn plates) on the wheel alignment machine. The readings are measured electronically and displayed on the screen. Camber is the vertical angle of the wheels relative to the vehicle. This is best viewed from the front of the car. If the vehicle has negative camber, the tops of the wheels will be closer together than the bottom. During cornering, camber compensates for vehicle weight transfer and body roll.

Turning Radius

Turning radius is a measure of how small a circle the vehicle can turn in when the steering wheel is turned to the limit FIGURE 22-56. All vehicles have stops to limit how far the front wheels can turn. In some designs, these stops can be adjusted as part of a wheel alignment. If the stops are incorrectly adjusted, they could allow too sharp of a turning angle and the steering box could bottom out and be damaged.

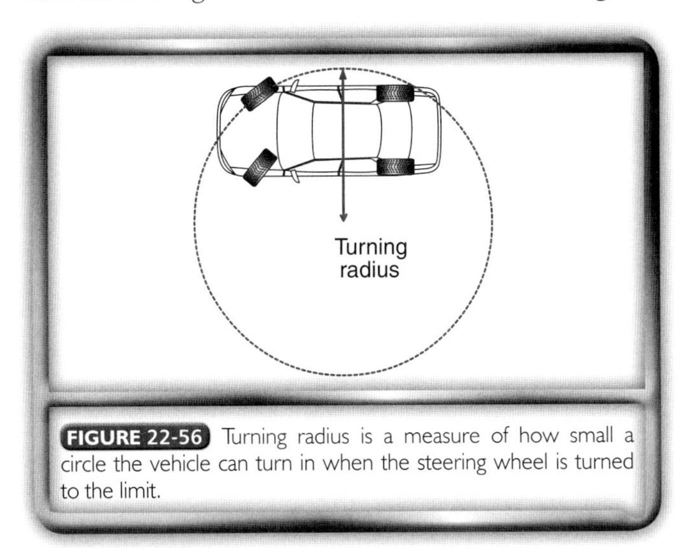
Turning
radius

FIGURE 22-56 Turning radius is a measure of how small a circle the vehicle can turn in when the steering wheel is turned to the limit.

Applied Math

AM-26: Visual Perception: The technician can visually perceive the geometric relationships of systems and subsystems requiring alignment.

Bill is an automotive technician trainee who is working with an experienced technician. Bill is interested in front-end alignment and has performed several alignments with his mentor's assistance. A vehicle has just come into the shop for an alignment, and Bill has been given permission to do this job on his own. The experienced technician will do a final check to ensure everything has been done properly. The shop has the latest type of laser-controlled alignment equipment, so the job will be a lot easier for the technician.

Bill drives the vehicle onto the alignment rack, but before attaching the wheel sensors, he looks the car over. He positions himself at the front of the vehicle, sighting from the front tires toward the rear. Bill wants to see the relationship of the front tires to the rear. He observes that there is a small amount of the rear tread showing on each side and that it appears to be an equal amount of tread on each side. He begins the alignment procedure by attaching the sensors on each wheel. The VIN is scanned into the computerized system, and the alignment system calculates the thrust angle and geometric centerline. The final result is that a slight toe adjustment is needed, but everything else is within specifications. Bill's visual perception of the relationship of the components helped him to predict this reading before the alignment machine verified it.

Applied Math

AM-51: Trial and Error: The technician is able to solve problems by trying a suggested solution and observing the results.

A vehicle with a MacPherson strut design is in the shop for repairs. The technician who is assigned to this project has done similar jobs in the past. The repair order calls for two new front struts plus an alignment. In the past, the technician has done very little regarding marking of the position of the old strut. In this case, the technician is going to try a new method that was suggested by another technician. The new strategy is to employ careful marking of the old start's position. This will include the upper and lower positions of the original strut using a sharp scribe. The technician wants to observe the results of his procedure when the alignment is completed. The strategy is to produce a less involved alignment or perhaps eliminate the need for alignment adjustments to be necessary. The technician understands that this is only a trial and error procedure to be tested and could vary from one type of vehicle to another type. He was pleasantly surprised that the alignment was much closer to the specifications than previous vehicles he hadn't used this process on.

Thrust Angle, Centerlines, and Setback (Tracking)

On a vehicle with independent rear suspension, undertaking a front-wheel-only alignment is considered an inadequate procedure. The rear tires also need to be aligned or they will experience accelerated tire wear and the vehicle will not drive properly. The **thrust angle** refers to the relationship between the centerline of the vehicle and the angle of the rear tires. The term **thrust line** refers to the direction in which the rear wheels are pointing FIGURE 22-57. The thrust angle can be adjusted on vehicles with adjustable rear suspensions. On vehicles that do not have adjustable rear suspensions, a small amount of thrust angle can be compensated for by aligning the front wheels to the rear wheels. Referencing the front steering geometry to the rear is very important.

Ideally, the thrust line and the vehicle's geometric centerline should line up closely. The centerline is drawn through points midway between each pair of wheels; however, the thrust line is not always as straightforward to determine. It is normally perpendicular to the rear axle on solid-axle vehicles. In vehicles with an independent rear suspension, it is derived by splitting the toe angle of each of the rear wheels on the vehicle. For instance, if the right rear wheel is toed-in 6°, and the left rear wheel is at 0°, the thrust line will veer off 3° to the left

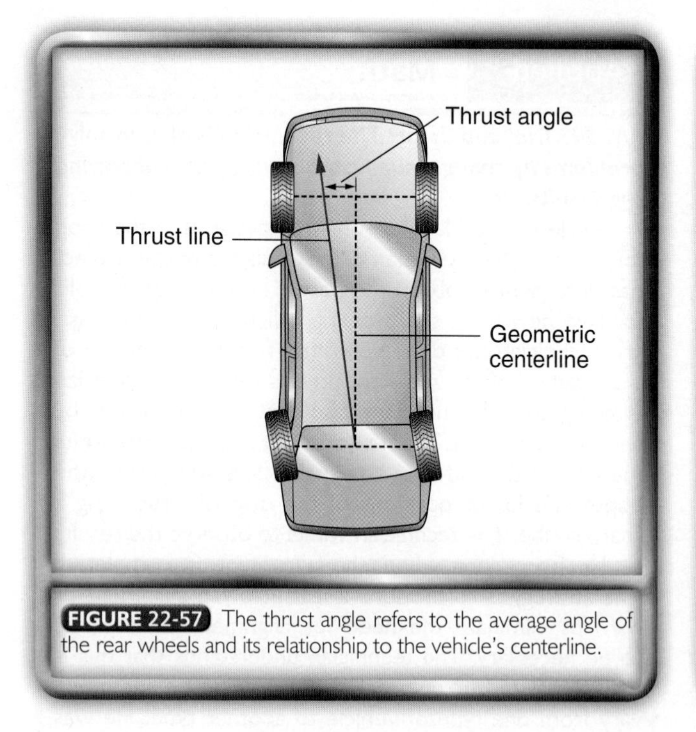
Thrust angle
Thrust line
Geometric centerline

FIGURE 22-57 The thrust angle refers to the average angle of the rear wheels and its relationship to the vehicle's centerline.

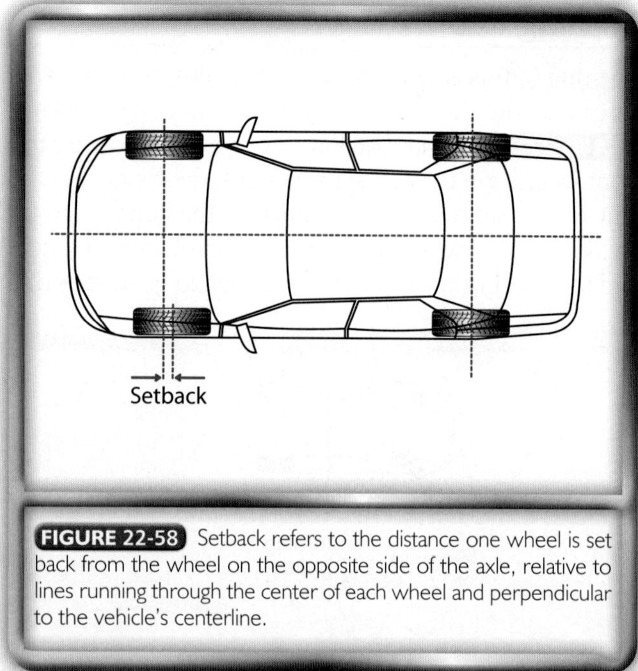
Setback

FIGURE 22-58 Setback refers to the distance one wheel is set back from the wheel on the opposite side of the axle, relative to lines running through the center of each wheel and perpendicular to the vehicle's centerline.

of the vehicle's centerline when the vehicle is moving forward.

Ideally, the thrust and centerlines coincide; however, given the size of a vehicle, the tolerances during manufacture, operational stresses, and component wear, it is rare that they do. If the deviation is very small, then remedial action is normally unnecessary. However, a large deviation can cause considerable concern when the vehicle is being driven, and the cause of this condition needs to be identified and corrected. Under such conditions the rear wheels are steering the vehicle away from its centerline and the driver has to turn the steering wheel to one side to keep the vehicle going in a straight line. Thrust angle issues may be caused by a leaf-spring suspension that has a broken center bolt, a bent axle, a bent frame or unibody, or simply misadjusted rear toe.

Setback is another alignment angle that is not adjustable but that allows the technician to diagnose the vehicle. Setback is the distance one wheel is set back from the wheel on the opposite side of the axle, relative to imaginary lines running through the center of each wheel and perpendicular to the vehicle's centerline **FIGURE 22-58**. Setback is best measured on an alignment machine so it can be measured correctly from the centerline of the vehicle. But an indication of setback can be made by measuring the distance of the wheel base on one side of the vehicle and comparing it to the wheelbase on the other side. If the vehicle has setback, then one wheel base measurement will typically (but not always) be shorter than the other.

Setback can be incorrect due to damage from a collision or due to a cradle that has been installed incorrectly or has shifted. Setback in the front wheels will create a pull condition for the driver to the side with the most setback or the wheel that is farther toward the rear of the car; a setback issue in the rear will pull toward the side with the least setback. Setback due to a cradle shift may also affect the camber from side to side. On a vehicle that has no adjustment for camber, check for a cradle shift by looking for witness marks around the head of the bolt that holds the cradle to the body. If a partial shiny metal ring surrounds the bolt head, then the cradle has shifted. Loosen the cradle bolts and reposition to achieve proper alignment specifications. Usually, setback should be no more than a quarter of an inch from side to side.

TECHNICIAN TIP

In extreme conditions of setback or thrust angle, the tracks the rear tires make are beside those of the front. This condition is known as dog-tracking or crabbing and can cause diagonal tire pattern wear on the rear tires as well as vehicle instability in some driving conditions. A vehicle that is dog-tracking will appear to be driving slightly sideways down the road.

Ride Height

Ride height, sometimes referred to as trim height, is the amount of distance between the ground and a specified part of the vehicle such as the fender well, upper control arm, or rocker panel. Ride height is measured with standard vehicle weight. For cars, it is usually given with no cargo or passengers. Changes in ride height alter the position of the control arms, which can have a detrimental effect on wheel alignment. Ride height that is not within specifications can be caused by improper tires or tire pressure; weak, sagging springs; or bent components such as a control arm or axle, or even a frame or unibody. Ride height should typically not vary by more than half an inch from side to side.

Ground clearance is similar to ride height, but is the distance from the ground to the lowest part of the chassis, typically a cross member, final drive, or oil pan. Ground clearance is especially important for off-road vehicles. Ground clearance can be increased by replacing stock components with aftermarket performance parts, but increasing ground clearance also increases the vehicle's center of gravity, making it more prone to rollover. It also affects scrub radius and potentially other wheel alignment angles. Thus, increasing ground clearance increases the risk of an accident in several ways; consider that carefully before modifying a vehicle in this way.

Applied Science

AS-88: Pneumatics: The technician can demonstrate an understanding of the forces and motions in pneumatic systems.

A vehicle is in the shop due to an inoperative automatic leveling control, which is part of an air suspension system. This vehicle has an (ALC) automatic level system that maintains the correct rear suspension trip height. This height will be maintained even if a heavy weight is placed in the trunk.

Pneumatics is a system operated by compressed air. In the case of the automatic level system, a battery powered air compressor is used to power the system. Nylon air lines connect from the compressor to the rear air shocks to lift the rear of the vehicle to the correct height. The forces involved are linear as the weight of the rear of the vehicle is applied to the air shocks. The vehicle height sensor triggers the air compressor to control the amount of run time needed. When weight is removed from the trunk, the rear of the vehicle will rise. At this point, the vehicle height sensor will give the appropriate signal to the pressure release solenoid valve to release air from the shocks. The body of the vehicle will return to the correct height. This type of system is usually found on luxury vehicles.

The technician inspects the vehicle and discovers a broken airline. After replacing the line, the vehicle is tested by the addition of some heavy items in the trunk. The air compressor starts and the rear of the vehicle rises to the correct trim height. When the weight is removed, the vehicle lowers to the proper height.

Types of Wheel Alignment

Performing a wheel alignment will require the use of an alignment machine. In the past, simpler devices (such as using a measuring tape or a piece of string to set wheel toe) were used to align the vehicle's wheels. Today's vehicles are more sensitive to the position of the wheels, so using a tape measure to set toe is no longer acceptable. The technician will use a computerized alignment machine to ensure all the angles discussed in the previous sections are correct.

The three basic types of wheel alignment are (1) front-end, two-wheel alignment, (2) thrust-angle alignment, and (3) four-wheel alignment. Two-wheel alignment is outdated and almost never performed on modern vehicles, but we will cover it briefly here so you will understand why it would be inappropriate for most vehicles. In front-end, two-wheel alignment, the technician positions the vehicle on the alignment rack and attaches the wheel sensors to the two front wheels. The sensors read the position of both front wheels and provide the measurement to the technician. The two-wheel alignment only compares the front wheel angles to the vehicle's centerline; it does not look at rear wheel position, so it cannot take into account any thrust angle. The technician compares the measurements to the alignment specifications provided by the manufacturer. If they are different, the technician adjusts the angles of the wheels until they match the specifications.

In a thrust-angle alignment, the technician attaches wheel sensors to all four wheels. The front wheels are compared to the angles of the rear wheels and adjusted to them. This technique is typically done on a vehicle with a solid rear axle where no adjustment is possible in the rear. If the thrust is out of specifications, the technician will need to diagnose what is causing the issue, such as a shifted axle or collision damage. If the thrust angle is within specifications, the front wheels are adjusted to compensate for any slight thrust angle of the rear wheels.

In a four-wheel alignment, the technician positions the vehicle on the alignment rack and attaches the wheel sensors to all four wheels. The rear angles are adjusted first so they conform to the vehicle's centerline; then the front wheels are adjusted to conform to the vehicle's centerline and the position of the rear wheels. The four-wheel alignment provides the most accurate alignment of the wheels, if adjustment of the rear suspension is possible.

Remember that anytime a part that has adjustment for alignment angles is removed, an alignment will have to be performed. For example, if the front struts have adjust-

Applied Math

AM-22: Angles: The technician can use angle measurement equipment and techniques to determine any vehicle angle measurement variance from the manufacturer's specifications.

A front-wheel drive vehicle is in the shop for a routine tire rotation. The technician notices that one of the front tires is slightly worn on one side. He reports his findings to the service advisor, who contacts the vehicle owner and obtains authorization for a four-wheel alignment. The technician starts with a pre-alignment inspection including a check for any loose suspension components. No unusual problems are found, and the technician is now ready to use angle measurement equipment and techniques to determine variance from the manufacturer's specifications.

An electronic sensor is attached to each of the four wheels. The technician scans the VIN, and the alignment system automatically goes to the correct specifications for the vehicle. In addition, the video screen of the alignment system gives a step-by-step approach to the procedure. Since there are many different ways to make alignment corrections, the technician is shown the exact procedure for the vehicle being aligned. A color-coded system—red for out of specifications and green for within specifications—is also helpful.

Computer printouts with before and after adjustments will be available to the customer. In this scenario, the alignment equipment indicates that a toe adjustment is needed for the front of the vehicle. As the technician makes the adjustment, the display shows the results on the video screen. When the exact manufacturer's specifications are obtained, the technician locks down the jam nuts to secure the setting.

ment slots and are being replaced, an alignment will need to be performed to ensure the correct wheel alignment angles are restored. If unsure of what parts replacements require an alignment, refer to the manufacturer's service information.

Performing Wheel Alignment

Performing an alignment can be done for maintenance purposes, or it can be done when tires or other steering and suspension components have been replaced. It can also be a helpful diagnostic step when a driver is complaining of uneven tire wear, pulling, hard steering, or wandering conditions. The use of the alignment machine will help you identify problems that might not be identifiable by a visual inspection, such as bent suspension components, worn parts, or improper repairs that have been performed to the steering or suspension system.

While four-wheel alignments are the norm for current vehicles, many technicians jokingly refer to a proper alignment as a five-wheel alignment. This is because the steering wheel also needs to be centered at the completion of a wheel alignment or the customer will be returning for the concern of a crooked steering wheel while driving. Most modern vehicles now use a steering angle sensor that tells the vehicle's stability control module where the steering wheel is pointed. These vehicles may need to have the steering angle sensor recalibrated if changes are made to the alignment or if components are replaced. Typically this process is performed with a scan tool.

To perform the wheel alignment, you will need to first perform a pre-alignment inspection to ensure that the vehicle can be aligned. If any suspension or steering components are found to be loose or damaged, replacement of these components will be necessary before aligning the wheels. The technician will be checking the following primary angles: caster (which is not adjustable on all vehicles and must be checked by turning the wheels of the vehicle in a process called the caster sweep), camber, and toe. The secondary angles that the technician will look at are the SAI, included angle, wheel setback, thrust angle, and toe-out on turns.

The secondary angles are typically not adjustable and, if out of specifications, normally mean that a suspension component or the vehicle frame is bent. When the vehicle has an adjustable rear independent suspension, thrust angle can typically be adjusted by turning tie-rods or turning eccentric bolts to toe the tires in or out to correct the thrust angle. Typically, thrust angle is adjusted as close to the vehicle's centerline as possible.

Adjusting wheel alignment angles must be done in a specific order of caster, camber, and toe. To begin with caster adjustment, locate the method of adjustment for the vehicle you are working on. Most modern alignment machines will include a video to demonstrate how the adjustment process works, but if not, refer to the manufacturer's service information. Not all vehicles have adjustment for caster; if they do not, an aftermarket kit will need to be installed to adjust caster, or the vehicle may need to go to a body shop for frame straightening

For vehicles equipped from the factory with provisions for adjustment, four common types of adjustment systems are used. Shim adjustment for the front wheels was used typically on older rear-wheel drive vehicles and was a bit challenging when adjusting caster **FIGURE 22-59**. In this method, shims are added together or removed from a pack and slipped between the control arm pivot shaft and the vehicle frame at the attachment bolts. This changes the position of the pivot shaft and ultimately the control arm and ball joint, affecting the alignment angles

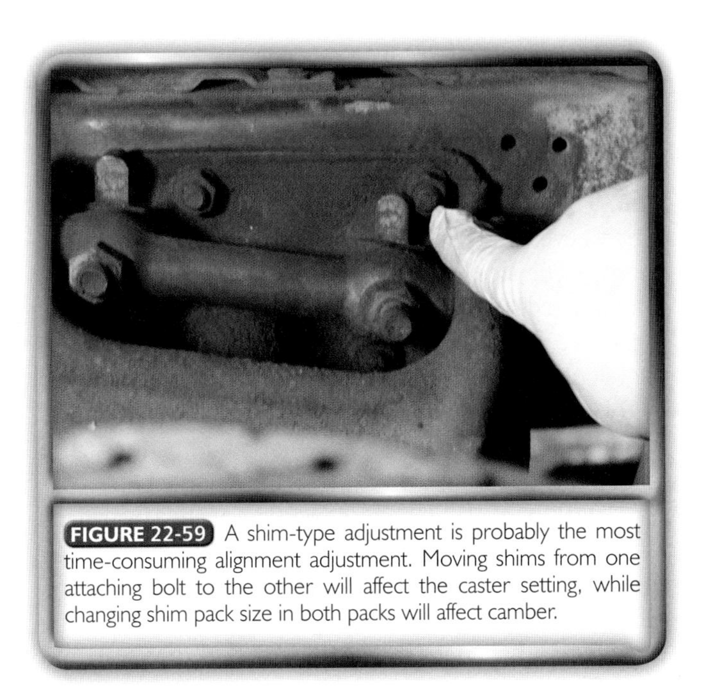

FIGURE 22-59 A shim-type adjustment is probably the most time-consuming alignment adjustment. Moving shims from one attaching bolt to the other will affect the caster setting, while changing shim pack size in both packs will affect camber.

Applied MATH

AM-24: Geometric Figures: The technician can distinguish whether or not the angles between related parts (e.g., suspension components) are within the manufacturer's specifications.

A 3/4 ton pickup truck is in the shop with a driveshaft vibration problem. The owner of the vehicle is requesting an inspection of the rear driveshaft including the measurement of the operating angles.

A driveshaft is a component that connects the transmission (or transfer case) to the axles, transmitting torque from the engine to the driving wheels. This component is also known as a propeller shaft. The cardan style universal joint is sometimes known as the "cross and caps" type. When the driveline has an operating angle of zero, the universal joint is operating under the best possible conditions for long service life. This "perfect" situation is not realistic for a number of reasons. The suspension system will allow the rear axle to move up and down, which will change the operating angle of the driveline. Worn components such as transmission mounts or worn bushings in the spring hangers can change the operating angle.

The technician assigned to the job has a good working knowledge of suspension components and driveline angles. Manufacturer's service information has been accessed and the technician is aware of the 3° maximum operating angle. A special tool called an inclinometer or angle finder will be placed on the driveline to determine the angles at the front and rear of the driveshaft. The operating angles on each end of the driveshaft should be equal to or within 1° of each other. The technician finds that the driveshaft angles are correct, but the rear universal joint is worn, causing the shaft to be out of alignment and balance and creating the vibration. Replacement of the rear universal joint corrects the problem.

Applied MATH

AM-25: Relationships: The technician verifies that the relationship of parallel lines and angles is in conformance with the manufacturer's specifications.

An experienced technician is assigned to assist a technician trainee with an alignment. The shop has recently purchased a state-of-the–art, computerized, laser-operated alignment system. After showing the trainee the basics of a pre-alignment inspection, the vehicle is pulled onto the alignment rack. The technician shows the trainee how to attach a target to each of the four wheels. The target is another name for an electronic device that is attached to each wheel. The VIN number of the vehicle is scanned onto the alignment system. Manufacturer's data will be selected and available for alignment purposes. The experienced technician explained that the alignment system is set up to guide the operator in a step-by-step procedure. On a video screen are instructions that are specific to the exact make and model of the vehicle. There are clear illustrations of all of the adjustments that are needed for each phase of the operation. Concerning the specifications for the vehicle being aligned, caster has a preferred setting of 3.33° with a range of 2.33° to 4.33°. Camber is 0° preferred with a range of -1° to 1°. Toe-in for front is .16" preferred with a range of .11" minimum and .21" maximum. The technician and trainee then compare the alignment readings with the specifications to determine any needed adjustments.

as desired. The attaching bolts fit through the frame of the vehicle and into holes in the cross bar where they are held with nuts. There are two shim packs used—one at the front attaching bolt and one at the rear attaching bolt. Shims are added or removed to shift the ball joint in or out, or back or forward, or a combination of the two. Shim adjustment can affect both caster and camber. If the same amount of shims are taken out of, or added to, each pack, the camber will be changed. If shims are taken from one pack and placed in the other, only the caster will be changed. Shims are available in various thicknesses and typically come in 1/64" (0.015") up to 1/4" (0.250"). Typically, a shim change of 1/32" will move caster by 0.5 degrees, and camber will move around 0.3 degrees with the same shim change.

Shims are still used on some vehicles to adjust rear camber and toe. They are placed behind the backing plate of the brake assembly or behind the hub of the wheel assembly to move the camber or toe to the correct position. These are aftermarket fixes and typically not used from the factory.

Another type of alignment adjustment for caster and camber is the eccentric bolt FIGURE 22-60. The eccentric bolt is slightly egg shaped or has a slightly egg-shaped washer attached to one side of the bolt. This egg shape pushes against ridges in the control arm to change caster and camber. The same strategy applies as with the shim-style adjustment; turning both attaching bolts will move the camber angle. Turning one bolt in one direction and the other bolt in the opposite direction will change caster.

If the vehicle has only one attachment point for the control arm to the body or frame, then it will use a strut rod to support the control arm. Some strut rods have an adjustment nut on the front and the rear of the attachment point to the control arm FIGURE 22-61. If both nuts are moved, then the control arm will be pushed forward or pulled backward, which will affect the caster setting.

FIGURE 22-60 Eccentric bolt adjustment.

The last method of adjusting caster and camber involves the ball joint adjusting sleeve FIGURE 22-62. The adjusting sleeve is used on several four-wheel drive vehicles and mounts into a solid axle or a dual I-beam axle. The ball joint tapered stud fits into the sleeve. This sleeve can be turned to change caster and camber slightly. The sleeve has a slightly offset hole so the ball joint tapered stud can fit into it. When turning the adjusting sleeve, the ball joint stud is pushed either forward or backward, or in or out, changing caster or camber. The factory adjusting sleeve typically only gives a half degree of alignment change, so an aftermarket adjusting sleeve is often installed if more adjustment is needed.

Adjustment of toe is typically accomplished by lengthening or shortening the tie-rod assembly. Lengthening the tie-rod pushes the steering arm and changes the toe setting; shortening moves the steering arm the opposite direction and changes the toe in the other direction. On a vehicle with an adjusting sleeve, the technician must loosen the two clamp bolts that hold the adjusting sleeve tight and turn the sleeve in the proper direction for toe setting FIGURE 22-63. Don't forget to tighten the clamp bolts when the toe is adjusted properly. On a vehicle with a rack-and-pinion steering system, typically the inner tie-rod threads into the outer tie-rod and no adjusting sleeve is used. To lengthen the tie-rod assembly on this vehicle, loosen the lock nut on the outer tie-rod and turn the inner tie-rod in or out to lengthen or shorten the tie-rod assembly. Tighten the lock nut when adjustment is finalized.

Inspecting Upper and Lower Ball Joints

Play in the suspension system can be damaging to other components or can be a major safety hazard on the road. Testing for play requires the proper technique for the

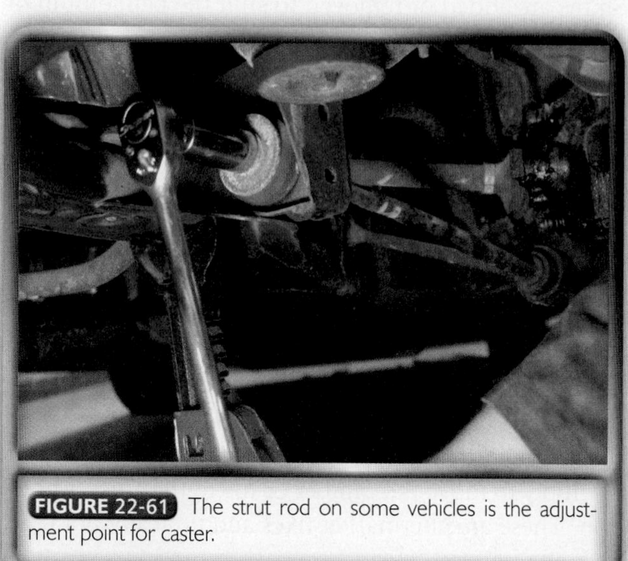

FIGURE 22-61 The strut rod on some vehicles is the adjustment point for caster.

FIGURE 22-62 The adjustable ball joint sleeve gives limited adjustment for caster and camber and is often replaced with an aftermarket part with more adjustment potential.

FIGURE 22-63 The tie-rod assembly comes in two forms and is adjusted by threading the assembly to lengthen or shorten.

results to be accurate. For play to be measured, the joint must be unloaded. This means the joint cannot be under compression or tension forces. In the case of suspension ball joints, the joint cannot be supporting the weight of the vehicle or the force from the vehicle spring when measuring the play.

The method of unloading the ball joints depends on the layout of the suspension. On a type 1 suspension where the coil spring or torsion bar is pushing against the lower control arm, a floor jack must be placed under the lower control arm and the wheel raised off the ground. The weight of the vehicle is thus supported through the spring to the control arm and then the jack, leaving the ball joint only supporting the wheel, tire, spindle, and upper control arm. In this case, a pry bar can then be used to pry the wheel up and down while measuring the ball joint play. The upper ball joint can be tested by pushing in and out on the top of the tire and measuring any play in the joint.

Some manufacturers specify that their type 1 suspensions be tested with the suspension system left hanging. The vehicle would be supported by the frame in this case. Manufacturers may also specify that only hand pressure be applied when checking for play in the joints. Check the service information before testing a particular vehicle.

On a type 2 suspension where the spring is on the top control arm, it is best to fit a wooden block between the upper control arm and the frame, so that the control arm and spring will be held in a position as close to normal ride height as possible. This method allows measurement of the play in the joint where maximum wear occurs. The top of the tire can again be pushed in and out, and measurement of play in the joint can be taken.

In a MacPherson strut suspension with only a lower control arm, testing is performed by raising the vehicle by the frame and allowing the suspension to hang free. This approach tests the point in a position that it does not normally operate in, but if there is play, it will likely still be evident. Since it is a follower joint, most manufacturers say if it has any noticeable play, the joint will need to be replaced.

Be sure to test the ball joint correctly. Refer to the manufacturer's instructions and specifications on how to test these joints, as they are not all tested the same way and may require different tools.

To measure play in the suspension system, follow the steps in SKILL DRILL 22-1.

SKILL DRILL 22-1 Loaded Lower Ball Joint

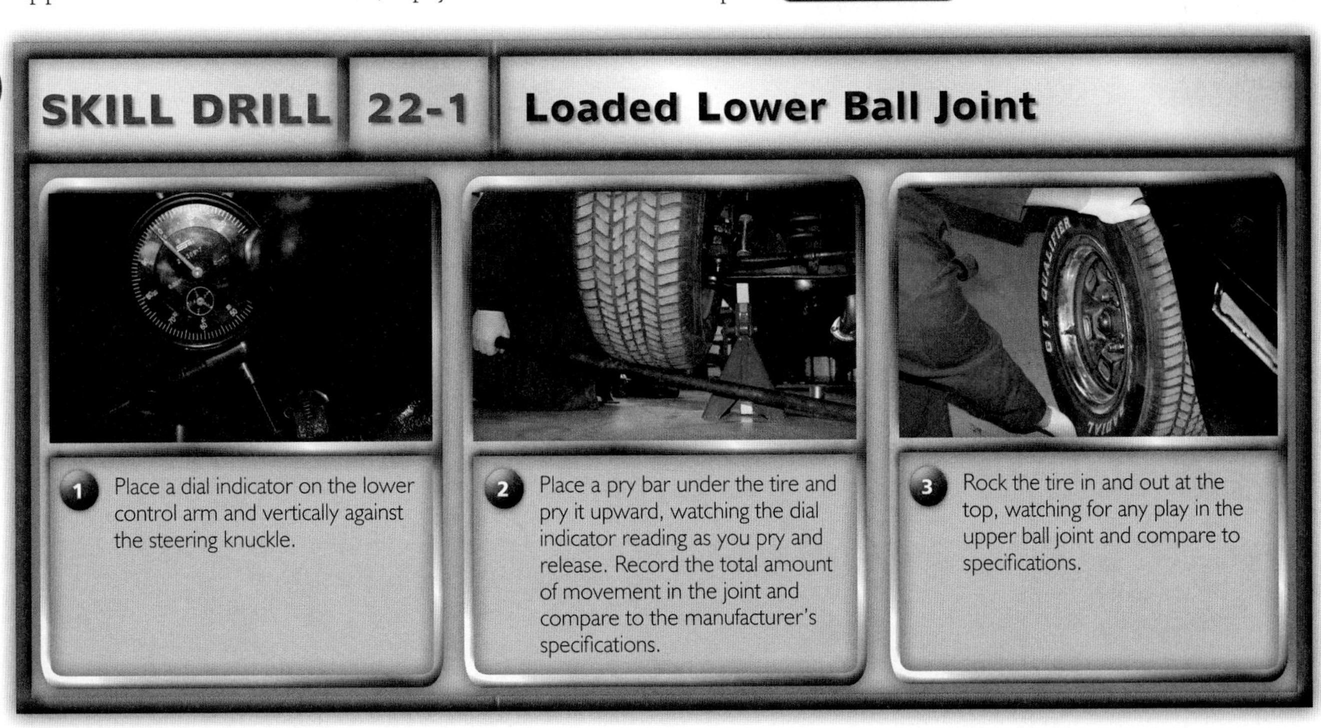

1. Place a dial indicator on the lower control arm and vertically against the steering knuckle.
2. Place a pry bar under the tire and pry it upward, watching the dial indicator reading as you pry and release. Record the total amount of movement in the joint and compare to the manufacturer's specifications.
3. Rock the tire in and out at the top, watching for any play in the upper ball joint and compare to specifications.

To measure play in the suspension system, follow the steps in SKILL DRILL 22-2.

Diagnosing Suspension Noise

A noise that is heard coming from the front end whenever a vehicle hits a bump could indicate a problem with a component of the suspension system. Testing the vehicle while turning and hitting bumps may be necessary to pinpoint the source of the noise. Be sure you have complete information on the customer's concern, such as if the vehicle only makes the noise when cold while going over bumps. In this case, test-driving over bumps while the vehicle is hot will probably not reveal the noise. Suspension system noise can be related to bushings that are worn or broken, ball joints that are worn, spring isolators that have broken or fallen out of place, loose bolts, faulty strut mount or bearing, bushing or joint that has lost its lubrication, or dirt that has gotten into a pivoting point. To diagnose this concern, the use of an assistant to drive the vehicle may be necessary as you listen from different points inside the vehicle to pinpoint if it is a front suspension or rear suspension issue. The use of chassis ears can provide a quick solution to where the noise is originating. Using an assistant allows one person to focus on finding the problem while the other focuses on safe driving.

To diagnose a suspension noise that can be duplicated while not driving, bounce the vehicle up and down while listening for noise. If there are noises, confirm where the noise is coming from. Have an assistant bounce the vehicle while you check for the noise under the vehicle. You can listen by ear or with a stethoscope, or you can feel by hand for vibrations or clunks. Listen around sway bar bushings, control

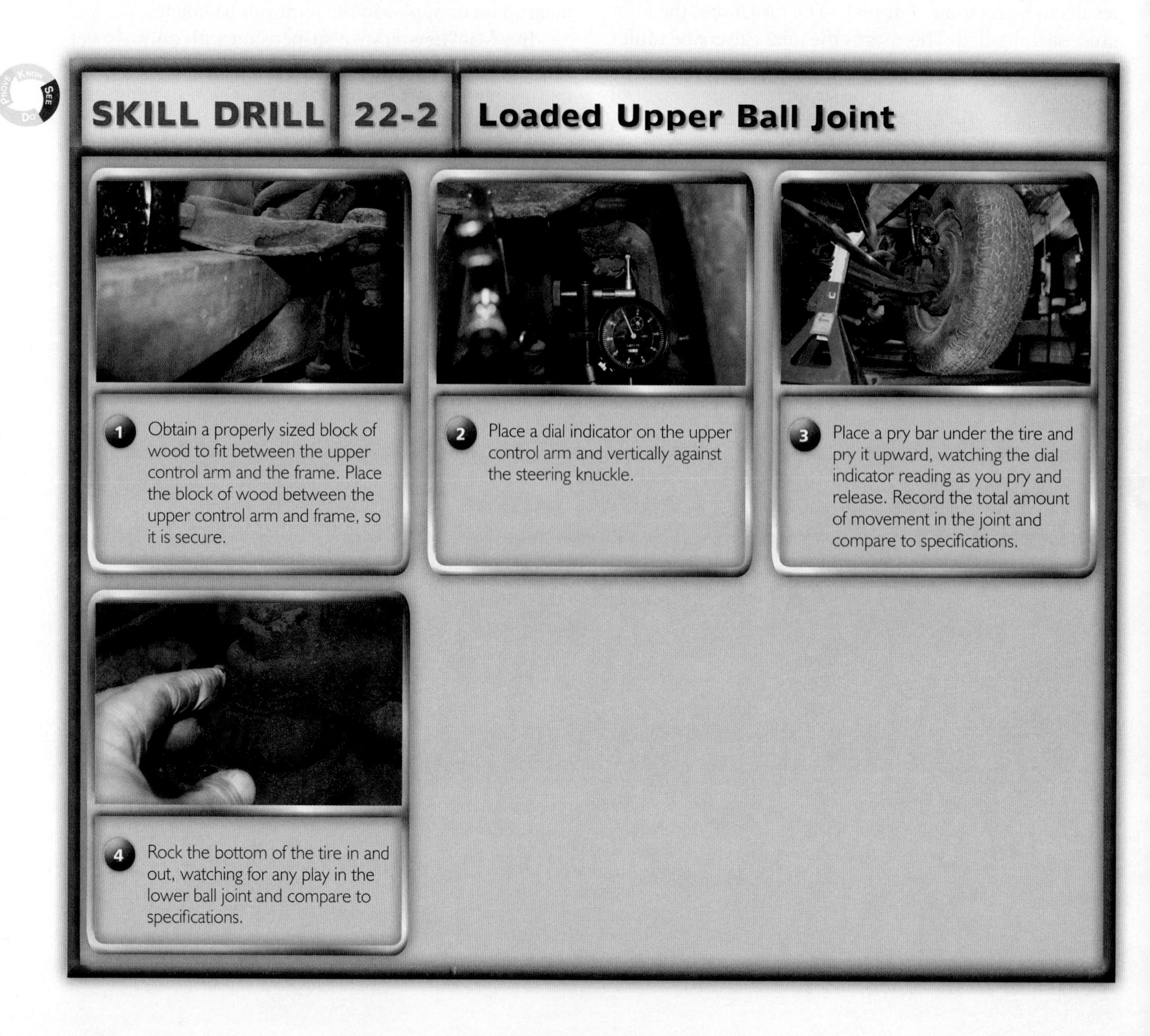

SKILL DRILL 22-2 Loaded Upper Ball Joint

1. Obtain a properly sized block of wood to fit between the upper control arm and the frame. Place the block of wood between the upper control arm and frame, so it is secure.
2. Place a dial indicator on the upper control arm and vertically against the steering knuckle.
3. Place a pry bar under the tire and pry it upward, watching the dial indicator reading as you pry and release. Record the total amount of movement in the joint and compare to specifications.
4. Rock the bottom of the tire in and out, watching for any play in the lower ball joint and compare to specifications.

arm bushings, springs, shock absorbers, component bolts, body panels, steering gear, the MacPherson strut mount, and ball joints. Inspect the component making the noise for damage and replace if necessary. If the noise is found at a component bolt, check the bolt to see if it is loose and retighten to the manufacturer's specifications.

Body Sway

To diagnose body sway, first test-drive the vehicle to verify the customer's concern. Because you will have to swerve from side to side to perform the test, drive the vehicle in a safe area with little to no traffic, such as in a large empty parking lot. While driving the vehicle, move the steering wheel back and forth to make the vehicle swerve slightly, this will shift the vehicle weight from side to side. Observe how much body sway occurs. It may be necessary to compare the sway of the vehicle to a like vehicle to ensure that the condition is not normal. If there is excessive sway, and the suspension is not electronically controlled, then check the vehicle's front and rear (if equipped) sway bar system. Inspect the sway bar bushings, brackets, and link bushings. Bushings should not be cracked and should have little give when pried against. Replacement of faulty components will be necessary.

If the vehicle is equipped with an electronically controlled suspension, it is possible that the system is not providing the active control needed to dampen body sway. In this case, the electronically controlled system will need to be checked for DTCs and diagnosed according to the manufacturer's specified procedure. This can be found in the service information.

Ride Height

The ride height of a vehicle can only be measured if it has matching tires, which are properly inflated, and no additional weight in the vehicle. Once these issues are taken care of, the ride height can be measured as specified by the service information. Most ride height specifications require the measurement to be within half of an inch side to side. If the measured ride height is greater or less than specified, the vehicle is not in correct alignment and may be causing, or contributing to the customer's concern. Check for bent or sagging vehicle springs, bent spring mounting points, a leaking gas pressurized shock absorber, a faulty electronically controlled suspension system, or a bent frame or axle. The use of a measuring tape from a fixed point on the frame or body of the vehicle to the component in question can help determine the cause of improper ride height. If the ride height issue is related to the coil or leaf spring, then replacement of the spring(s) may be necessary. If the ride height issue is on a vehicle equipped with a torsion bar system, then you may be able to adjust the torsion bar so that ride height is returned to specifications.

To perform ride height diagnosis, follow the steps in SKILL DRILL 22-3.

SKILL DRILL 22-3 Ride Height

1. Refer to the manufacturer's service information for correct measurement points and specifications.
2. Check for properly sized, matching, and inflated tires. Correct any issues found.
3. Check the vehicle for any nonstandard loads in the trunk or luggage area. Remove them temporarily while measuring ride height.

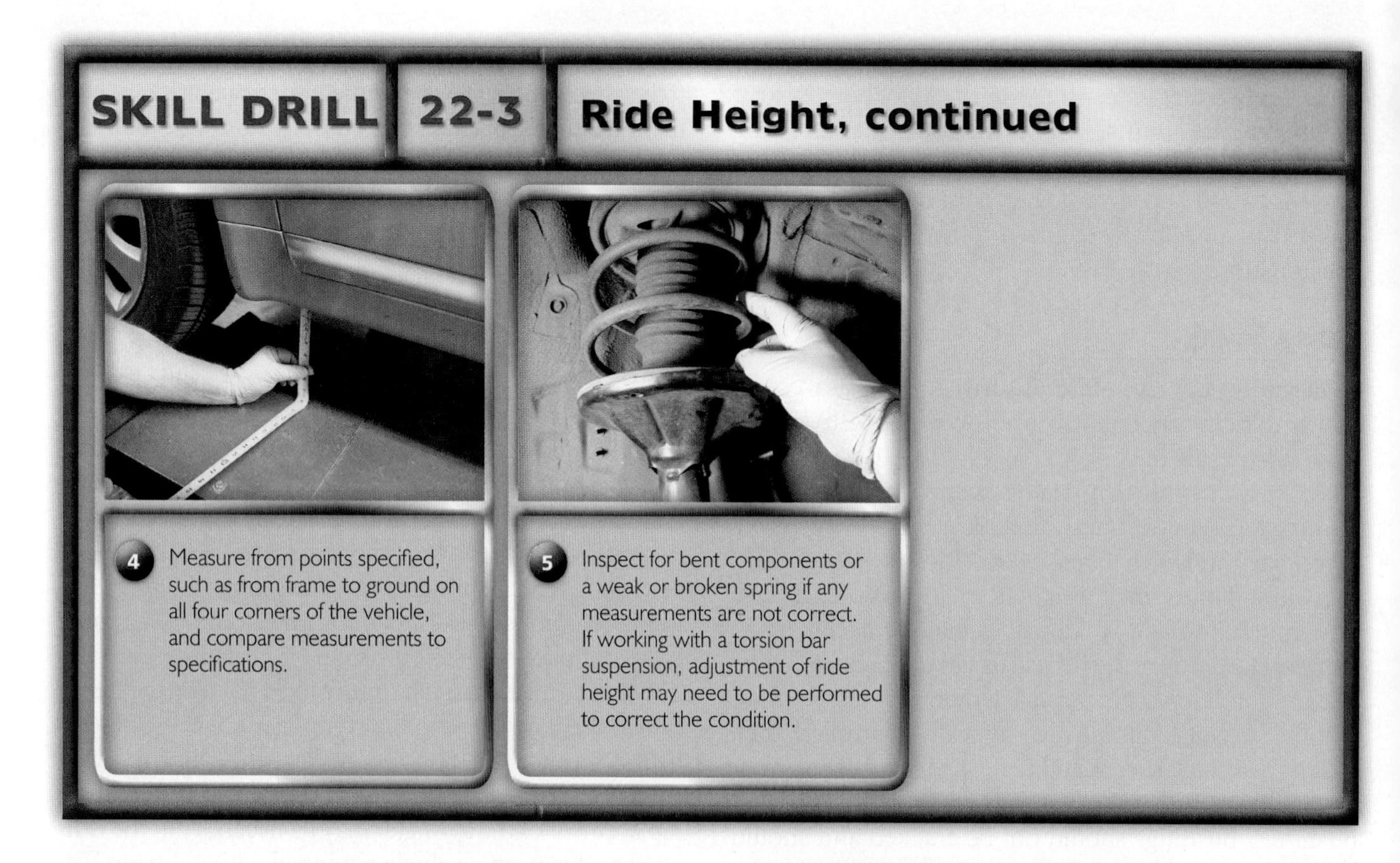
SKILL DRILL 22-3 Ride Height, continued
4 Measure from points specified, such as from frame to ground on all four corners of the vehicle, and compare measurements to specifications.
5 Inspect for bent components or a weak or broken spring if any measurements are not correct. If working with a torsion bar suspension, adjustment of ride height may need to be performed to correct the condition.

Inspecting the Shock Absorbers

Shock absorbers and struts are located near each wheel and dampen body movement from bumps. Common reasons for testing the shock absorbers are unusual tire wear, such as having a cupped appearance. Also, the driver may complain of a soft or bouncy ride. In some cases, a shock absorber can bind up, creating a very stiff ride.

If a vehicle has adjustable shock absorbers, make sure the shock absorber adjustments are the same for the left- and right-hand side. Some shock absorbers contain pressurized gas, which can leak out, causing uneven ride height and shock absorber performance issues. Many of today's vehicles are equipped with a strut-type suspension instead of conventional shock absorbers, but testing either type of system involves the same procedure. Basically, while the vehicle is stationary, push up and down on a strong point at each corner of the vehicle (not the fenders as they can be dented) several times, and watch how the vehicle responds after you release it. Typically, if you let go at the bottom, a good shock will allow the corner of the vehicle to rise and then settle back into position on most vehicles. On some with softer suspensions, it may allow the corner of the vehicle to rise, fall, and rise back into position. Any more oscillations than that indicate worn shock absorbers.

To check shock absorbers, follow the steps in SKILL DRILL 22-4.

Safety

To prevent personal injury, do not puncture or incinerate gas-charged shock absorbers.

Maintenance and Repair

Tools

Many of the tools applied in servicing the suspension system were listed previously with the tools used for diagnosing suspension complaints. In addition, the following tools may be used in maintenance and repair procedures:

- Coil spring compressor: Used to compress coil springs during removal and installation.
- Scan tool: Used to check for codes in the vehicle's computer.
- Spring compressor/tools: Used for changing coil springs.
- Ball joint press tool: Used to remove and replace press-fit ball joints.
- Pickle forks: Used to separate ball joints, but ruins the grease seal.
- Air chisel: Air-operated hammer that can accept a variety of bits including chisels and punches.

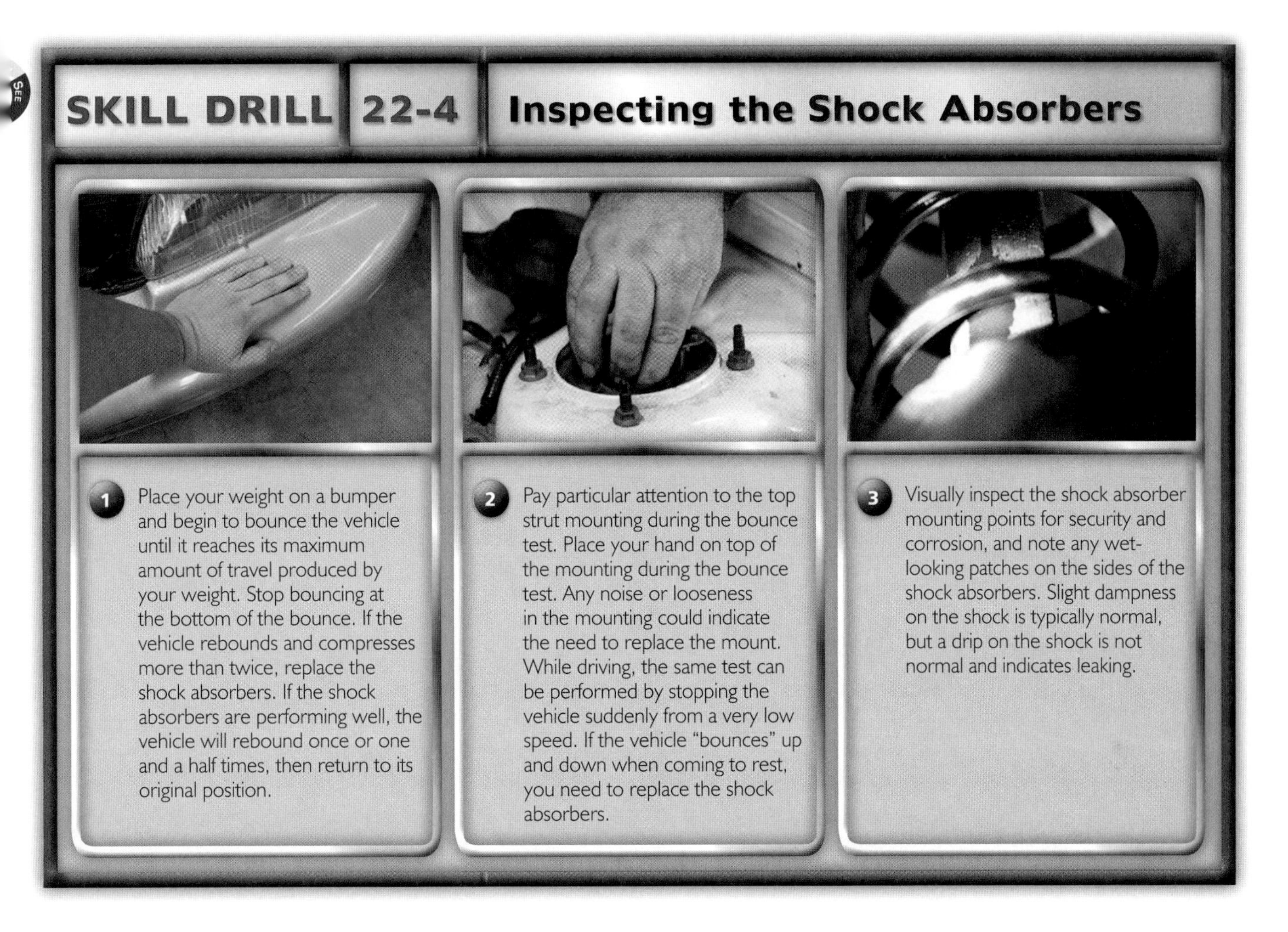
SKILL DRILL 22-4 Inspecting the Shock Absorbers
1 Place your weight on a bumper and begin to bounce the vehicle until it reaches its maximum amount of travel produced by your weight. Stop bouncing at the bottom of the bounce. If the vehicle rebounds and compresses more than twice, replace the shock absorbers. If the shock absorbers are performing well, the vehicle will rebound once or one and a half times, then return to its original position.
2 Pay particular attention to the top strut mounting during the bounce test. Place your hand on top of the mounting during the bounce test. Any noise or looseness in the mounting could indicate the need to replace the mount. While driving, the same test can be performed by stopping the vehicle suddenly from a very low speed. If the vehicle "bounces" up and down when coming to rest, you need to replace the shock absorbers.
3 Visually inspect the shock absorber mounting points for security and corrosion, and note any wet-looking patches on the sides of the shock absorbers. Slight dampness on the shock is typically normal, but a drip on the shock is not normal and indicates leaking.

- Strut compressor: Used to compress MacPherson struts to remove the coil spring.
- Strut servicing kit: Used for changing coil springs on struts.
- Universal strut nut wrench kit: Used to remove a strut.
- 24-mm strut rod socket: Used to remove a strut.

Removing, Inspecting, and Installing Stabilizer Components

The stabilizer components (sway bar) help prevent body roll when cornering. While the stabilizer bar itself rarely gives any trouble, the rubber bushings on the bar and links wear out. This usually results in increased body roll, as well as a clunking noise in the suspension. The stabilizer components should be checked whenever a vehicle is brought into the shop because of handling concerns or suspension-related noises. Before beginning the procedure, research the manufacturer's procedure and specifications for removing and inspecting the stabilizer components.

Note: We will be using the same vehicle to perform most of the SLA-related tasks. Also, we will address each task as a sequence, as if you were doing the entire series of tasks, one after the other. So the disassembly of each component will assume the previously removed components have already been removed. And reassembly will be held off until all of the related tasks are completed.

To remove and inspect the stabilizer bar bushings and mount brackets, follow the steps in SKILL DRILL 22-5.

To remove and inspect the sway bar end links, follow the steps in SKILL DRILL 22-6.

Removing and Replacing Shock Absorbers

Worn shock absorbers will cause the vehicle to ride poorly, especially on rough roads. When the tires encounter a bump in the road, a faulty shock absorber cannot dampen the spring oscillations to promote a smoother ride. The suspension will continue to rebound and bounce. This action is then transferred to the vehicle frame and ultimately to the driver and passengers. Loose or damaged

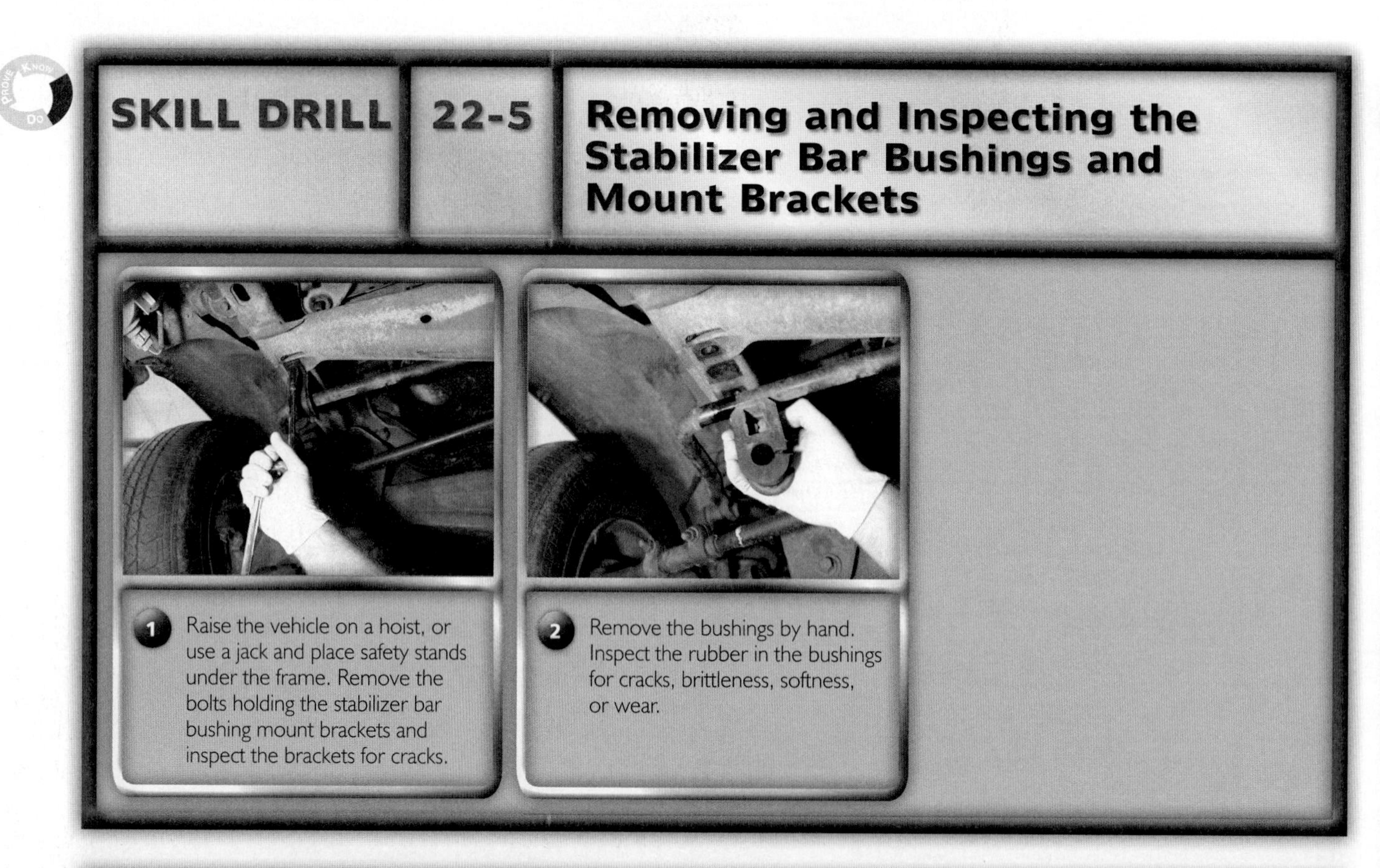

SKILL DRILL 22-5 Removing and Inspecting the Stabilizer Bar Bushings and Mount Brackets
1 Raise the vehicle on a hoist, or use a jack and place safety stands under the frame. Remove the bolts holding the stabilizer bar bushing mount brackets and inspect the brackets for cracks.
2 Remove the bushings by hand. Inspect the rubber in the bushings for cracks, brittleness, softness, or wear.

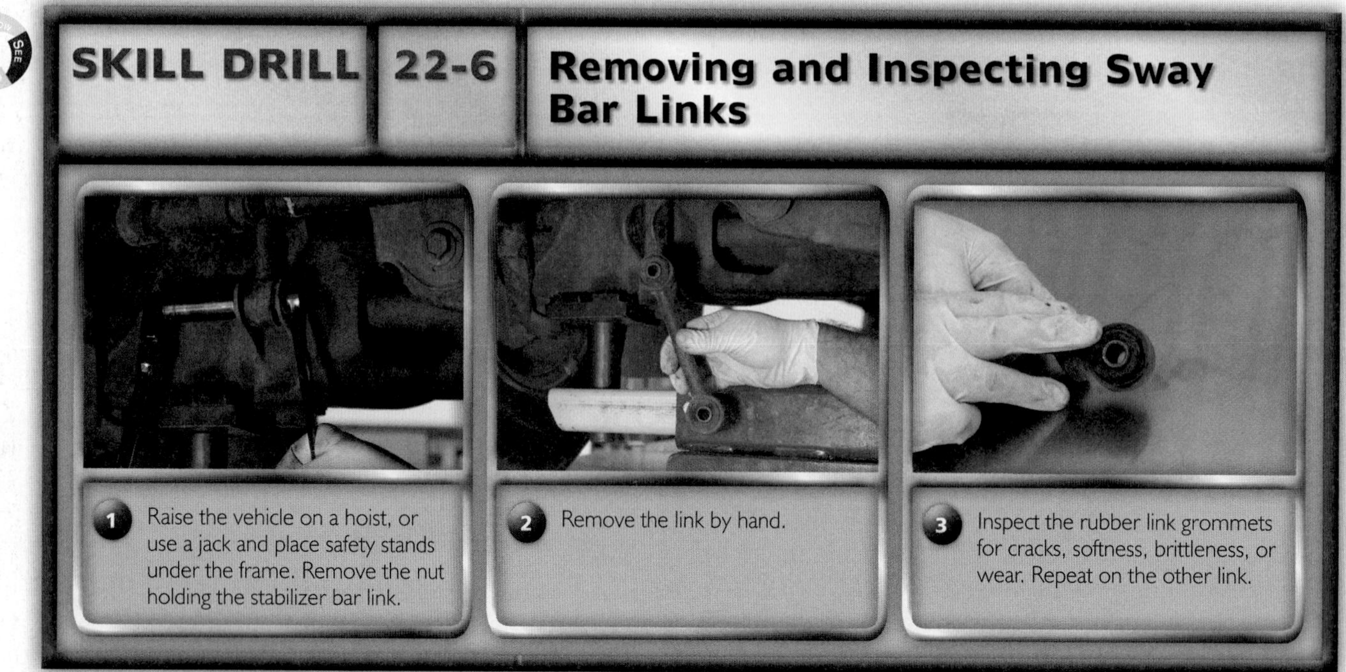

SKILL DRILL 22-6 Removing and Inspecting Sway Bar Links
1 Raise the vehicle on a hoist, or use a jack and place safety stands under the frame. Remove the nut holding the stabilizer bar link.
2 Remove the link by hand.
3 Inspect the rubber link grommets for cracks, softness, brittleness, or wear. Repeat on the other link.

shock absorbers can be distinguished by abnormal, and in some case, loud and unusual noises.

Visually inspect the shock absorbers for any signs of deterioration, such as oil leaking from the shock absorber shaft seal or damaged body. A slight oil film on the shock is considered normal. The mounting bushings must also be carefully inspected for splits and deteriorated or missing rubber mountings. The mounting supports must be checked for good security and tightness.

Many shock absorbers come from the factory pressurized with gas to reduce aeration of the fluid when operating. This pressure tends to expand the shock absorber, making it difficult to install. For this reason, pressurized shocks come compressed with a band holding them

> **TECHNICIAN TIP**
>
> Always replace shock absorbers in pairs so the suspension has the same characteristics for the left and right sides. Shock absorbers are rated for "bump" or "jounce," the rate at which they compress, and "rebound," the rate at which they expand.

> **TECHNICIAN TIP**
>
> Shock absorbers use rubber bushings to isolate them from the vehicle body. Always replace these bushings when replacing the shock absorbers.

together. It is usually easiest to install one end, or in some cases, both ends of the shock before cutting the band.

On some suspension systems (typically nonindependent suspensions), the shocks provide the limit for full extension. This means the shocks may be holding the axle up when the shock is fully extended. In this case, removing the shock could cause the axle to slip, pinching fingers or causing the vehicle to shift on the hoist. It is always good practice to place stands under the axle to support it while the shocks are being removed and installed.

If a shock absorber must be replaced, it is industry practice to replace them as pairs, thus ensuring the ride equilibrium of the vehicle. To replace a shock absorber, follow the steps in SKILL DRILL 22-7.

Inspecting SLA Suspension System Coil Springs and Spring Insulators

Coil springs absorb the road force by twisting, which compresses them. Whenever a driver complains of the way the vehicle sits or an issue related to the ride quality, the coil springs should be inspected for wear and the vehicle's ride height measured.

To inspect SLA suspension system coil springs and spring insulators, follow the steps in SKILL DRILL 22-8.

Inspecting Upper and Lower Control Arms and Components

Control arms themselves do not generally wear out, but the control arm bushings and ball joints do, so you will likely need to remove them to service those components. However, some manufacturers do not sell bushings and ball joints separately, so you may have to purchase the entire control arm and replace it as a unit. Also, control arms can become bent or damaged as the result of a collision or driving through a deep pothole, so control arms do need to be inspected for damage. Lastly, some customers request that the height of their vehicles be lifted or lowered, which can involve modifying suspension components such as springs and control arms with new upgraded ones. Obviously this will change the ride height, alignment, and handling of the vehicle. Only very experienced and highly trained technicians should diagnose and repair these vehicles.

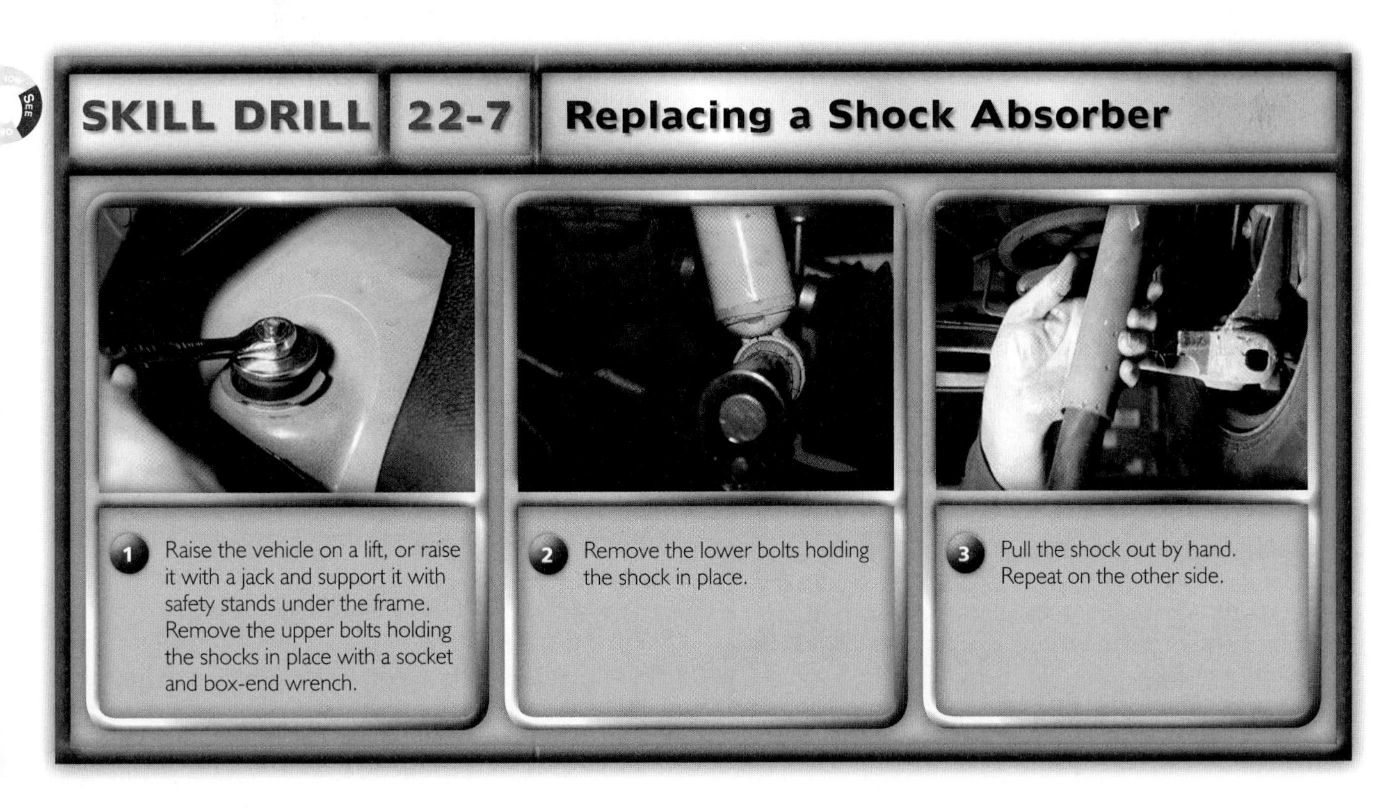
SKILL DRILL 22-7 Replacing a Shock Absorber
1 Raise the vehicle on a lift, or raise it with a jack and support it with safety stands under the frame. Remove the upper bolts holding the shocks in place with a socket and box-end wrench.
2 Remove the lower bolts holding the shock in place.
3 Pull the shock out by hand. Repeat on the other side.

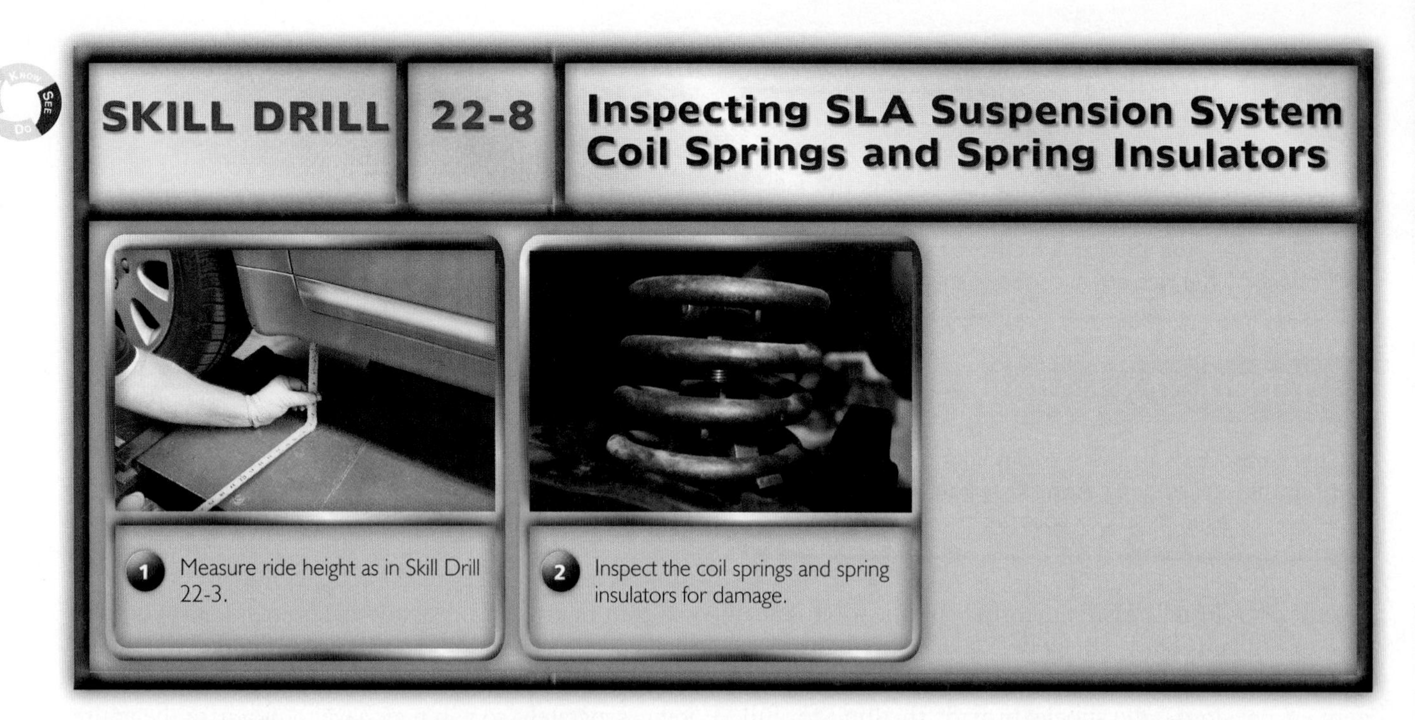
SKILL DRILL 22-8
Inspecting SLA Suspension System Coil Springs and Spring Insulators
1 Measure ride height as in Skill Drill 22-3.
2 Inspect the coil springs and spring insulators for damage.

To inspect upper and lower control arms and components, follow the steps in SKILL DRILL 22-9:

1. Inspect the control arms for any damage, excessive rust, and so on.
2. Inspect the control arm bushings for damage.
3. Using a pry bar, pry against the control arms near the bushings (in several directions) to see if there is excessive movement.

Lubricating Suspension and Steering Systems

To function properly, the suspension and steering system must be lubricated. On most modern vehicles, the joints are sealed and lubricated for life, so there are no grease fittings present. However, some vehicles do have grease fittings installed on them, either from the factory or on aftermarket parts. If grease fittings are present, then lubrication must be performed. Lubrication keeps the parts from rubbing and wearing on each other, which extends their life.

> **TECHNICIAN TIP**
>
> Clean lubricating equipment very carefully. If you don't thoroughly clean the fitting or nozzle before pumping the grease into the fitting, dirt could be forced into the component. Any dirt entering a component will cause premature failure.

To lubricate a suspension system and a steering system, follow the steps in SKILL DRILL 22-10.

Inspecting the Strut Cartridge or Assembly

When a vehicle arrives in the shop with cupped tire wear or if the driver complains of ride comfort problems, the parts of the strut assembly should be checked. Some vehicles have a strut housing that has a replaceable strut insert cartridge, while others are one piece and the entire housing is replaced. In a strut with a strut insert, some manufacturers fill the housing with a lightweight oil to allow heat from dampening to be transferred to the outer housing more efficiently. This oil, along with the fluid inside the strut cartridge, can leak out as well. So be aware of that as you inspect the strut. To inspect the strut cartridge or assembly, follow the steps in SKILL DRILL 22-11.

To inspect the upper strut bearing mount, follow steps in SKILL DRILL 22-12.

Inspecting Leaf Springs

The leaf springs of a vehicle need to be inspected whenever the ride height does not match the manufacturer's specifications. If found to be sagging, bent, or broken, they will need to be replaced. Removal and inspection is also necessary if noise is found to be coming from the leaf spring or bushings in the leaf spring. If new leaf spring bushings will be needed, the use of proper press tools will ensure proper bushing replacement. Remember that when the leaf springs are removed, the axle will not

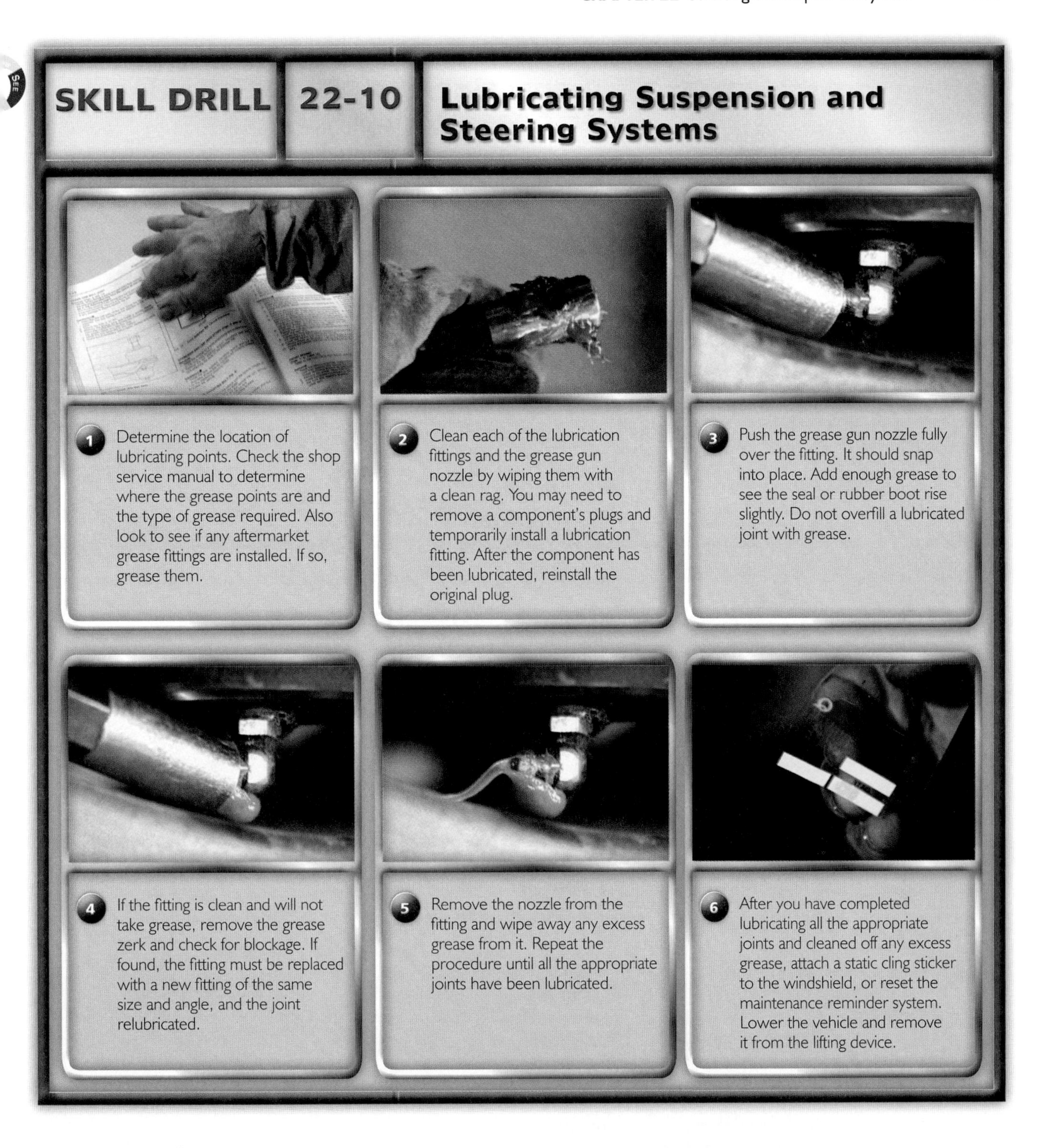
SKILL DRILL 22-10 Lubricating Suspension and Steering Systems
1 Determine the location of lubricating points. Check the shop service manual to determine where the grease points are and the type of grease required. Also look to see if any aftermarket grease fittings are installed. If so, grease them.
2 Clean each of the lubrication fittings and the grease gun nozzle by wiping them with a clean rag. You may need to remove a component's plugs and temporarily install a lubrication fitting. After the component has been lubricated, reinstall the original plug.
3 Push the grease gun nozzle fully over the fitting. It should snap into place. Add enough grease to see the seal or rubber boot rise slightly. Do not overfill a lubricated joint with grease.
4 If the fitting is clean and will not take grease, remove the grease zerk and check for blockage. If found, the fitting must be replaced with a new fitting of the same size and angle, and the joint relubricated.
5 Remove the nozzle from the fitting and wipe away any excess grease from it. Repeat the procedure until all the appropriate joints have been lubricated.
6 After you have completed lubricating all the appropriate joints and cleaned off any excess grease, attach a static cling sticker to the windshield, or reset the maintenance reminder system. Lower the vehicle and remove it from the lifting device.

be supported; the use of screw jacks to support the axle during removal will be necessary.

To inspect leaf springs, follow the steps in **SKILL DRILL 22-13**.

Inspecting Strut Rods and Bushings

The strut rods and bushings hold the control arm and therefore the wheel in position longitudinally. The strut rod bushings wear and degrade over time, requiring replacement whenever they are loose. On some vehicles the strut rod is the adjustment point for caster. An alignment may have to be performed if the bushings get replaced. Refer to the manufacturer's service information to verify if this is needed.

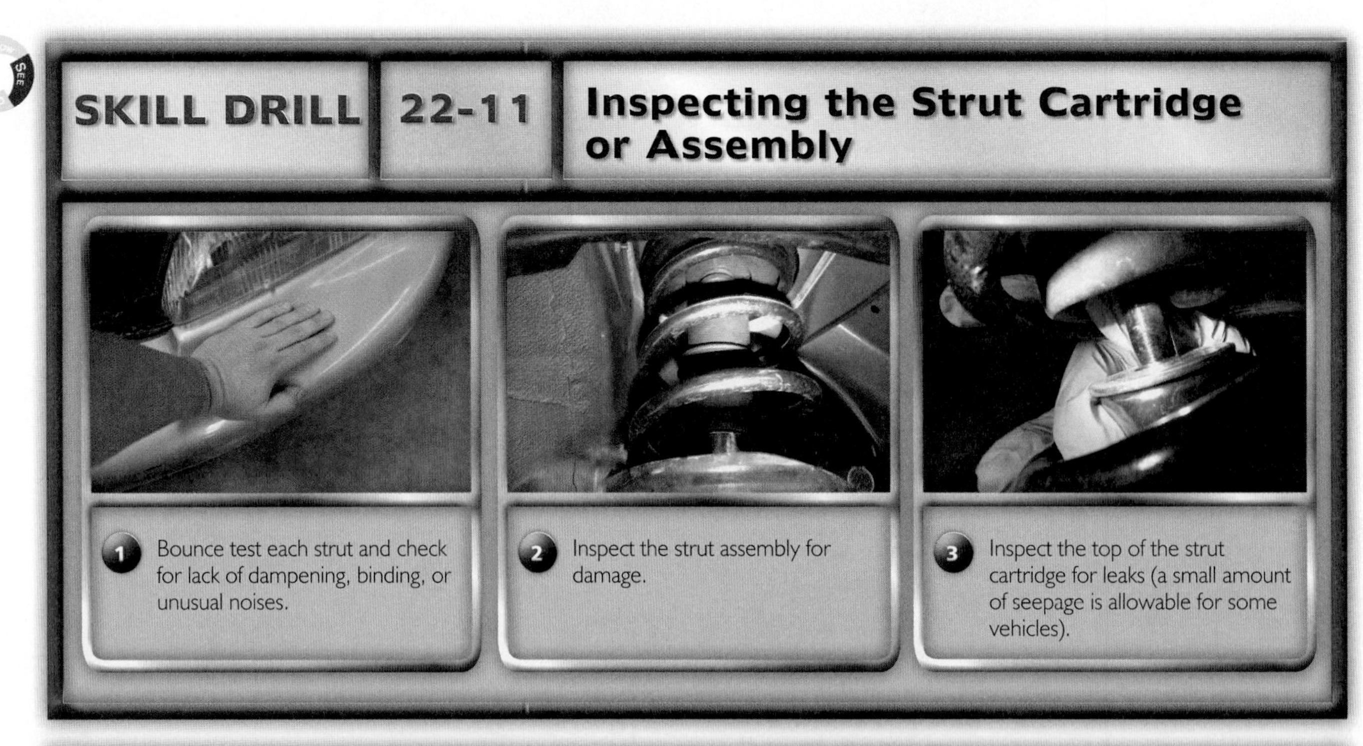
SKILL DRILL 22-11 Inspecting the Strut Cartridge or Assembly
1 Bounce test each strut and check for lack of dampening, binding, or unusual noises.
2 Inspect the strut assembly for damage.
3 Inspect the top of the strut cartridge for leaks (a small amount of seepage is allowable for some vehicles).

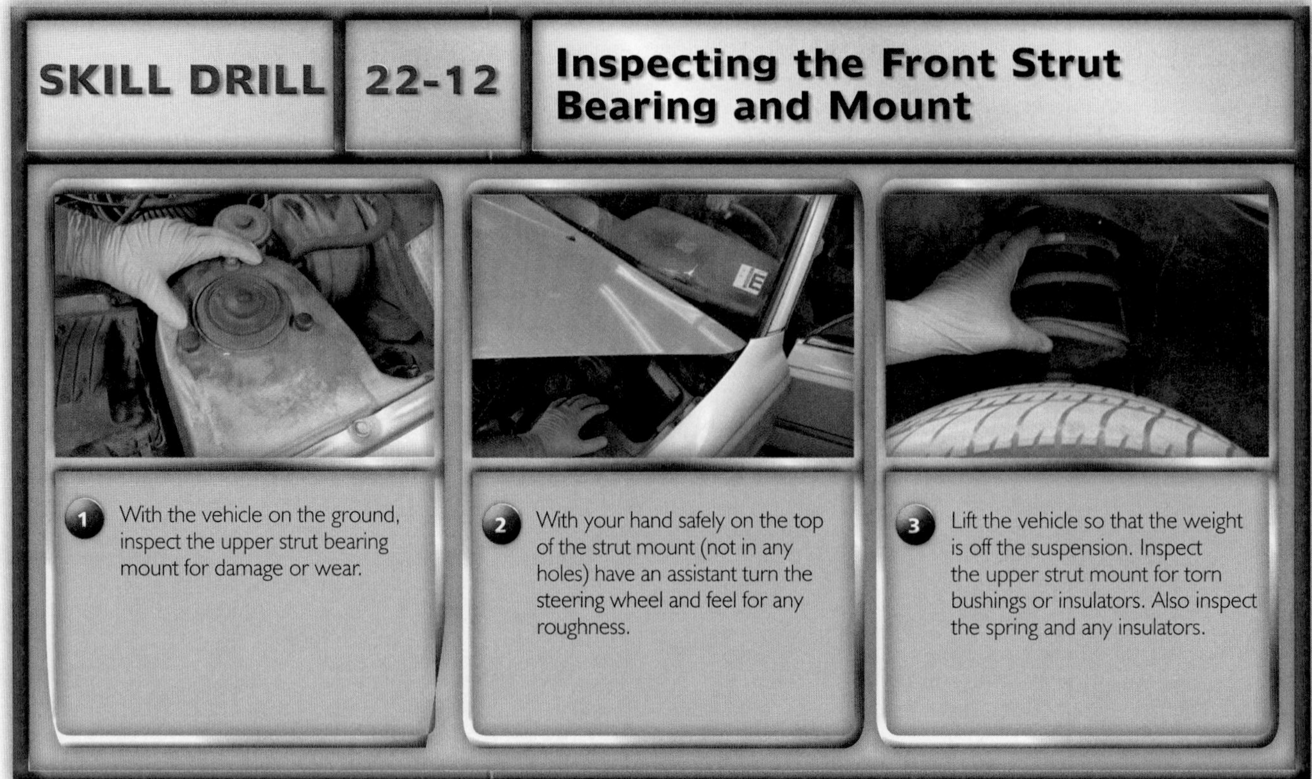
SKILL DRILL 22-12 Inspecting the Front Strut Bearing and Mount
1 With the vehicle on the ground, inspect the upper strut bearing mount for damage or wear.
2 With your hand safely on the top of the strut mount (not in any holes) have an assistant turn the steering wheel and feel for any roughness.
3 Lift the vehicle so that the weight is off the suspension. Inspect the upper strut mount for torn bushings or insulators. Also inspect the spring and any insulators.

To inspect strut rods and bushings, follow the steps in SKILL DRILL 22-14.

Inspecting Torsion Bar Suspension

The torsion bar provides the spring action in a torsion bar front-end suspension system. In many cases, it is adjustable to allow for corrections in ride height. It has a large bolt in the torque arm that, when adjusted, changes the amount of pressure it places on the control arm to raise or lower the suspension. The torsion bar should be checked whenever the driver complains of suspension problems. Torsion bars are typically stamped

SKILL DRILL 22-13 Inspecting Leaf Springs

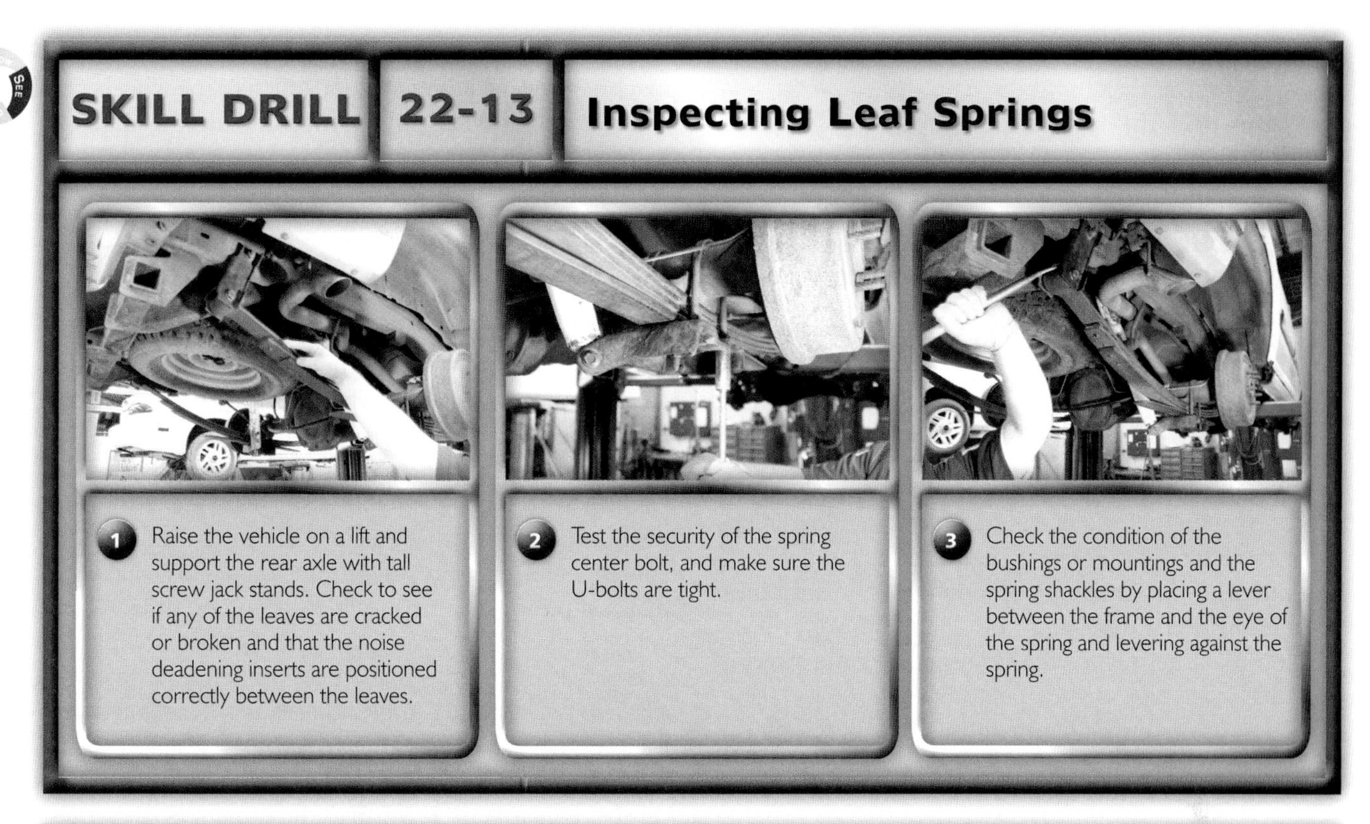

1. Raise the vehicle on a lift and support the rear axle with tall screw jack stands. Check to see if any of the leaves are cracked or broken and that the noise deadening inserts are positioned correctly between the leaves.
2. Test the security of the spring center bolt, and make sure the U-bolts are tight.
3. Check the condition of the bushings or mountings and the spring shackles by placing a lever between the frame and the eye of the spring and levering against the spring.

SKILL DRILL 22-14 Inspecting Strut Rods and Bushings

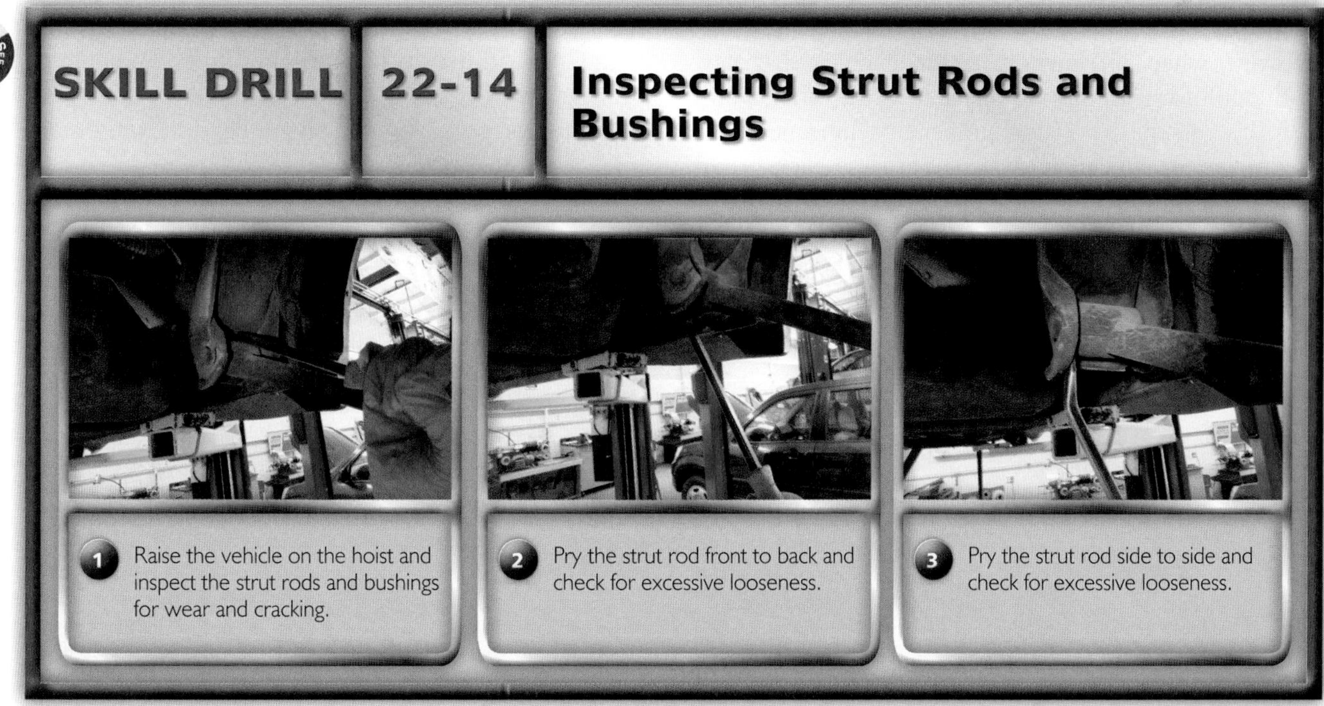

1. Raise the vehicle on the hoist and inspect the strut rods and bushings for wear and cracking.
2. Pry the strut rod front to back and check for excessive looseness.
3. Pry the strut rod side to side and check for excessive looseness.

or marked with a left or right and must be installed in the proper side. If it has marks for left or right, then it is preset for twisting in that specific direction and will not have the same spring force if twisted the opposite way. When replacing torsion bars, if the torsion bars are not marked, then be sure to place a paint mark on them to identify left and right; they have been subjected to torsion in one direction for the life of the vehicle, and installing them backward can result in breakage or incorrect spring rate. The torsion bar may be found on either the lower or upper control arm on certain vehicles. The following skill drill will not be the same for all vehicles. Follow service information for proper operation of this task.

To inspect the torsion bar, follow the steps in SKILL DRILL 22-15.

Performing a Pre-alignment Inspection

Incorrect wheel alignment results in a vehicle that may pull or be hard to steer and causes rapid or improper wearing of the tires. A pre-alignment inspection is performed to ensure that the vehicle is an appropriate candidate for alignment. Worn and loose suspension or steering components, low tire pressure, and heavy objects in the trunk make it impossible to perform an accurate alignment. As with any diagnosis, verifying the customer's concern is the first step. Be sure to test-drive the vehicle prior to the pre-alignment inspection, listening carefully for any unusual noises and noting any improper driving control issues related to the suspension and steering systems.

To perform a pre-alignment inspection, follow the steps in SKILL DRILL 22-16.

Performing Four-Wheel Alignment

Improper wheel alignment results in a vehicle that may be difficult to steer, pulls to one side or the other, wanders, or wears the tires. The alignment machine measures the angles the wheels are at compared to each other and the centerline of the vehicle. Since the alignment machine wheel adapters do not attach to the wheels perfectly straight, the alignment machine has the ability to compensate for any runout in the wheel assemblies so that the alignment machine can ensure it is reading the angle of the wheels accurately, no matter where each tire is positioned.

Alignments always follow a specific order of adjustments. The rear wheels should be adjusted before the front wheels so that the vehicle can be made to track straight down the road. The order is (1) rear caster, (2) camber, and (3) toe; then move to the front to adjust (4) caster, (5) camber, and (6) toe. This sequence is for vehicles with fully adjustable caster, camber, and toe on the front and rear of the vehicle. Performing the alignment adjustment in this way will prevent having to go back and readjust previous settings, which saves you time. Not all vehicles have adjustable caster and camber, so only toe can be set, unless aftermarket components are installed that allow caster and camber adjustment. This skill drill is for a vehicle equipped with two eccentric bolts attaching the lower control arm to the frame, allowing caster and camber adjustment. Perform the alignment as the service information instructs or the alignment machine guides you. This skill drill is not designed to be an accurate example for all vehicles.

To perform a four-wheel alignment, follow the steps in SKILL DRILL 22-17.

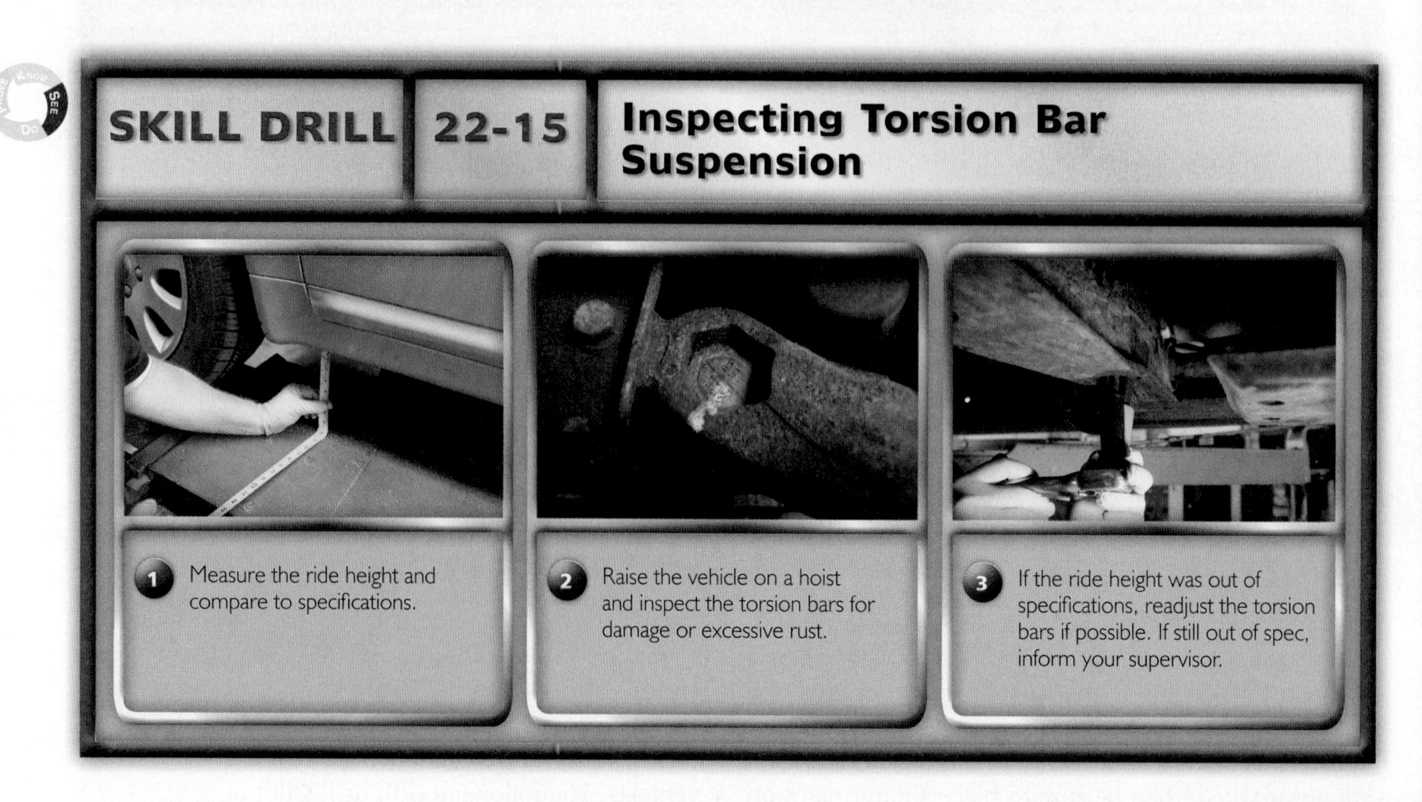
PROVE
KNOW
SEE
DO

SKILL DRILL 22-15 Inspecting Torsion Bar Suspension

1. Measure the ride height and compare to specifications.
2. Raise the vehicle on a hoist and inspect the torsion bars for damage or excessive rust.
3. If the ride height was out of specifications, readjust the torsion bars if possible. If still out of spec, inform your supervisor.

SKILL DRILL 22-16 Preparing a Vehicle for a Wheel Alignment

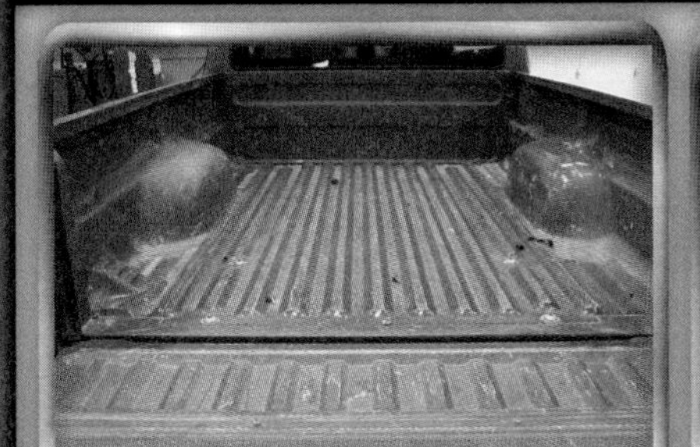

1. Remove any heavy items from the trunk and passenger compartments.

2. Check the size and condition of all four tires. Adjust the air pressure to specifications.

3. Measure the vehicle's ride height.

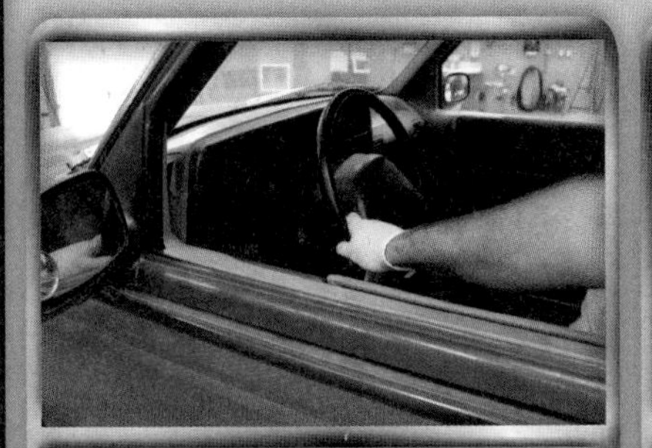

4. Check the play of the steering wheel. Correct any excess play before undertaking the wheel alignment.

5. Bounce each corner of the vehicle to check the correct functioning of the shock absorbers.

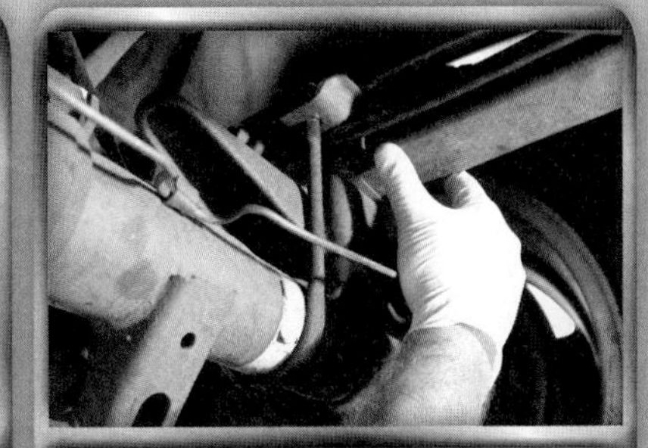

6. With the vehicle raised, inspect all suspension and steering components, including the wheel bearings. Repair or replace all damaged or worn suspension components.

7. Position the vehicle on the wheel alignment ramp, making sure the front tires are positioned correctly on the turntables.

8. Position the rear wheels on the slip plates or rear turntables.

9. Attach the wheel units of the wheel alignment machine.

Prove
Know
See
Do

SKILL DRILL 22-17 Performing Four-Wheel Alignment

1. Position the vehicle on the front-end rack. Raise the vehicle to a comfortable working level, and set the rack on its mechanical locks to provide a level surface.

2. Raise the vehicle with the air jacks on the alignment rack.

3. Attach sensors and compensate each one.

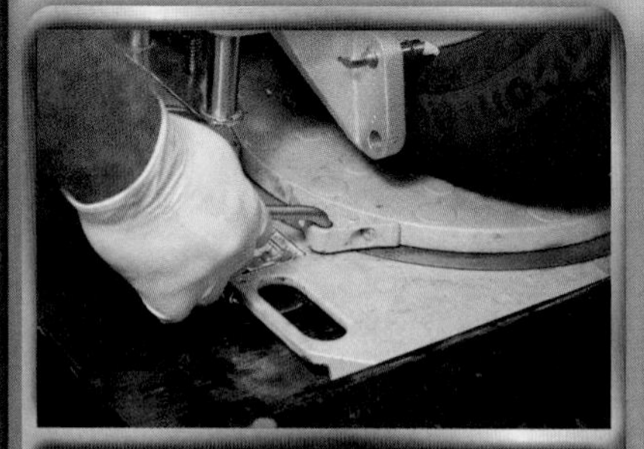

4. Pull the lock pins from the slip plates and turntables.

5. Lower the vehicle as instructed by the machine. Install a brake pedal depressor.

6. Perform a caster sweep by selecting caster sweep on the machine and turning the wheel the number of degrees on the turntables as designnated by the machine.

4.8°
11.4°
-6.6°
-0.7°
1.4°
0.7°
-0.55°
-0.55°
0.00°
OK

7. Take the alignment readings and compare them to the vehicle manufacturer's specifications.

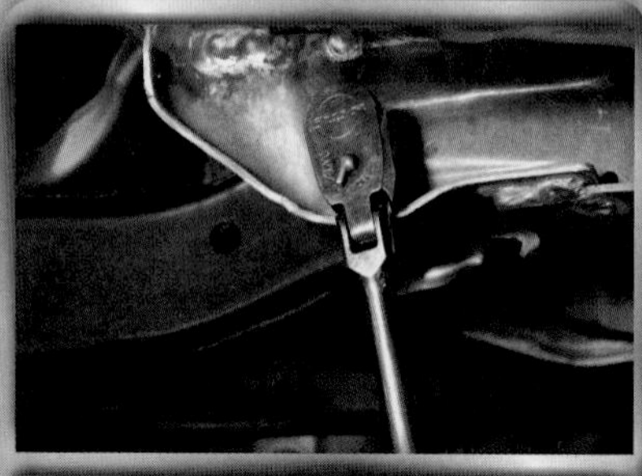

8. Prepare to adjust rear caster, camber, and toe, if possible, by loosening the eccentric bolts.

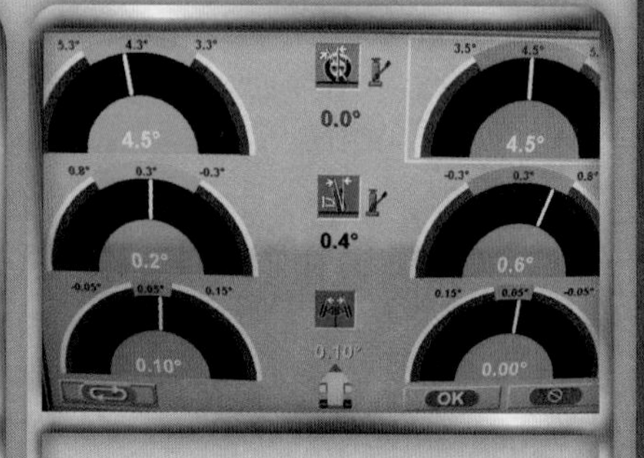
4.5°
0.0°
4.5°
0.2°
0.4°
0.6°
0.10°
0.00°
OK

9. Adjust front caster and camber by turning the eccentric bolts attaching the control arm until alignment is within specifications.

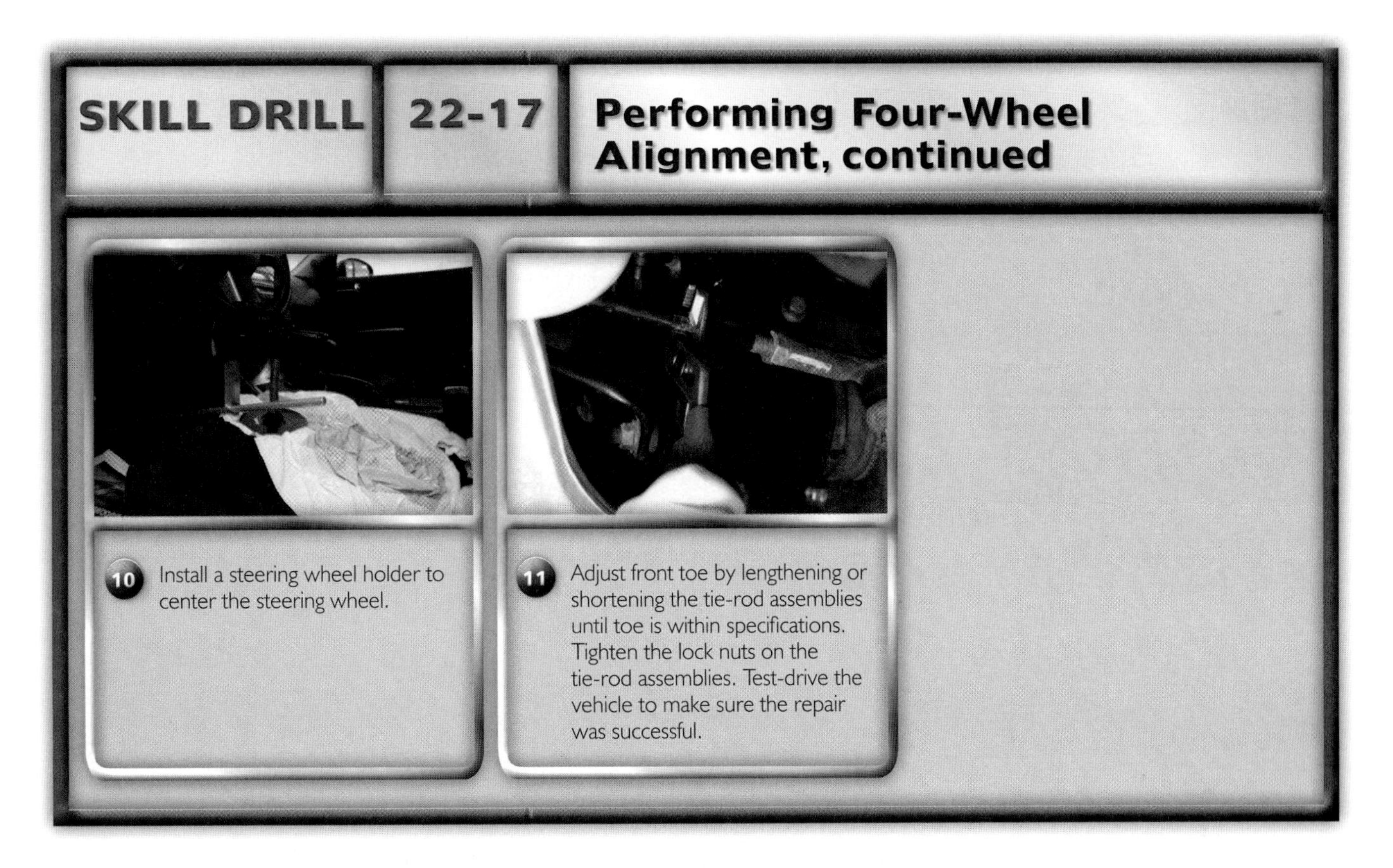
SKILL DRILL 22-17 Performing Four-Wheel Alignment, continued
10 Install a steering wheel holder to center the steering wheel.
11 Adjust front toe by lengthening or shortening the tie-rod assemblies until toe is within specifications. Tighten the lock nuts on the tie-rod assemblies. Test-drive the vehicle to make sure the repair was successful.

Checking SAI and Included Angle

The SAI is the angle formed by an imaginary line running through the upper and lower steering pivots relative to a plumb line—the vertical line created when a weight is hung from a string. It cannot be adjusted, though a technician will on occasion be asked to check the SAI to ensure it is within the manufacturer's specifications after an accident or body repair. Generally, SAI should not vary more than half a degree, plus or minus. If SAI is incorrect, check for a bent strut, bent control arms, or a bent spindle or steering knuckle. If incorrect, SAI will create an issue with the steering wheel not returning to center after cornering.

To check SAI, follow the steps in SKILL DRILL 22-18.

Checking Rear Wheel Thrust Angle

The rear thrust angle refers to the relationship between the rear wheels and an imaginary centerline down the center of the vehicle. Rear thrust angle problems often result from an accident or other impact that bends the rear axle or axle mounting points. Incorrect rear thrust angle can also be caused by wear on independent rear suspension components or incorrectly set rear toe. Incorrect thrust angle will try to steer the vehicle in the direction the wheels are pointing. Think of a monster truck with rear steering that becomes stuck, as you might have seen on TV. The rear of the vehicle will turn in the direction the rear wheels are pointing and the driver will have to turn the front wheels to make the vehicle crab walk in a straight line. As this vehicle moves in a straight line, it will look like the body is sitting sideways. Typically, the steering wheel will be off-center while driving since the driver will have to turn the front wheels to compensate for the rear. The ideal thrust angle will be close to zero, but refer to the manufacturer's specifications for correct thrust angle for the vehicle you are working on.

To check the rear wheel thrust angle, follow the steps in SKILL DRILL 22-19.

Checking Front and/or Rear Cradle Alignment

Damage to the cradle of a vehicle can force the wheels out of alignment, possibly changing caster, camber, and toe and creating pull and tire wear issues. The cradle should always be perpendicular to the centerline of the chassis. It is possible that after an accident the cradle mounting points have moved (bent), and the vehicle will have to be sent to a frame shop to straighten the body before the alignment can be performed.

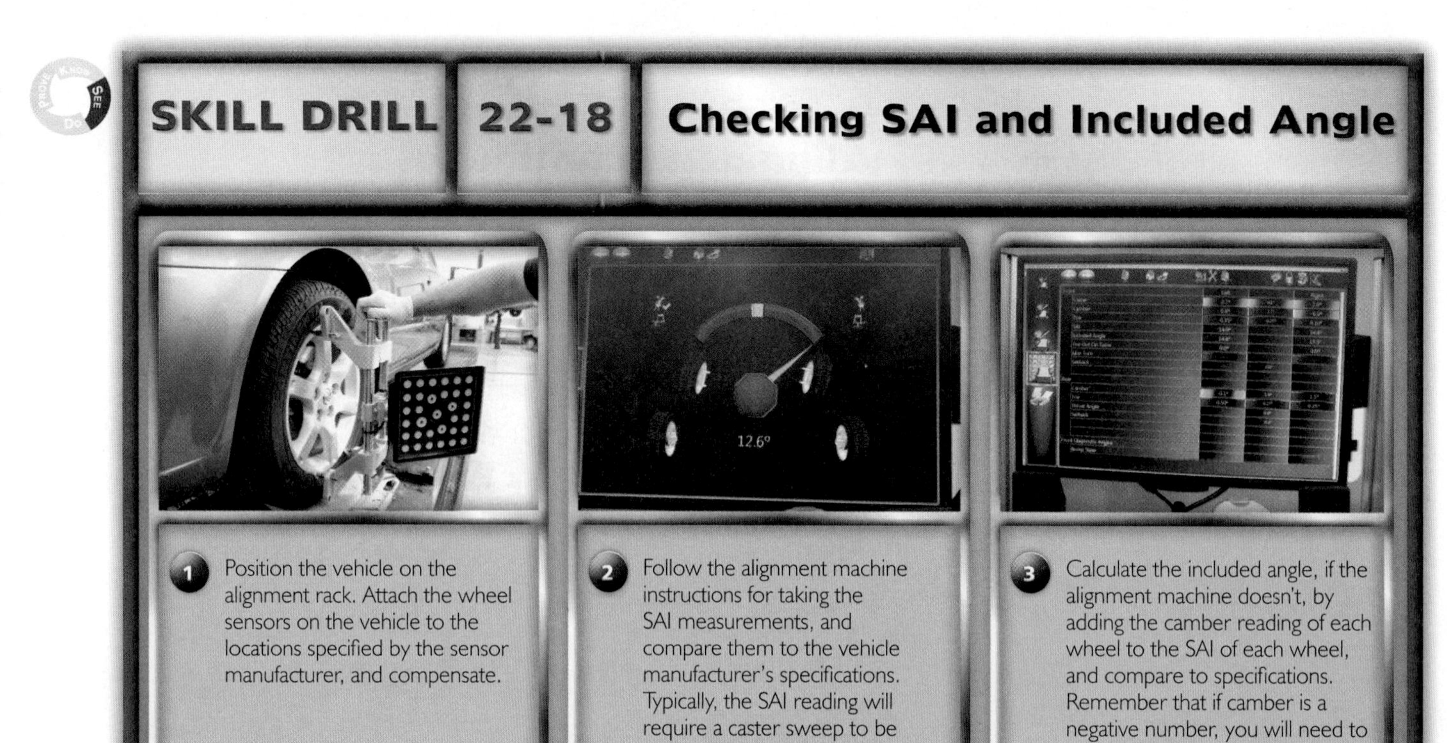
12.6°

SKILL DRILL 22-18 Checking SAI and Included Angle

1. Position the vehicle on the alignment rack. Attach the wheel sensors on the vehicle to the locations specified by the sensor manufacturer, and compensate.
2. Follow the alignment machine instructions for taking the SAI measurements, and compare them to the vehicle manufacturer's specifications. Typically, the SAI reading will require a caster sweep to be performed. SAI is a nonadjustable angle. No changes can be made; the angle will help the technician to verify that suspension components are bent.
3. Calculate the included angle, if the alignment machine doesn't, by adding the camber reading of each wheel to the SAI of each wheel, and compare to specifications. Remember that if camber is a negative number, you will need to subtract the camber from the SAI to get the included angle.

0.45°
-0.5°

SKILL DRILL 22-19 Checking Rear Wheel Thrust Angle

1. Position the vehicle on the alignment rack. Attach the wheel sensors on the vehicle to the locations specified by the sensor manufacturer, and compensate.
2. Thrust angle can be indicated on most alignment machines, although you may have to go to a special screen. Take the thrust angle reading, and compare it to the vehicle manufacturer's specifications.

It is also important to ensure that the cradle is centered when removing and replacing this major component during service, such as when replacing the transmission. It is recommended on some vehicles that an alignment be performed after cradle removal and reinstallation. Refer to the manufacturer's service information on cradle adjustment.

To check cradle alignment, follow the steps in SKILL DRILL 22-20.

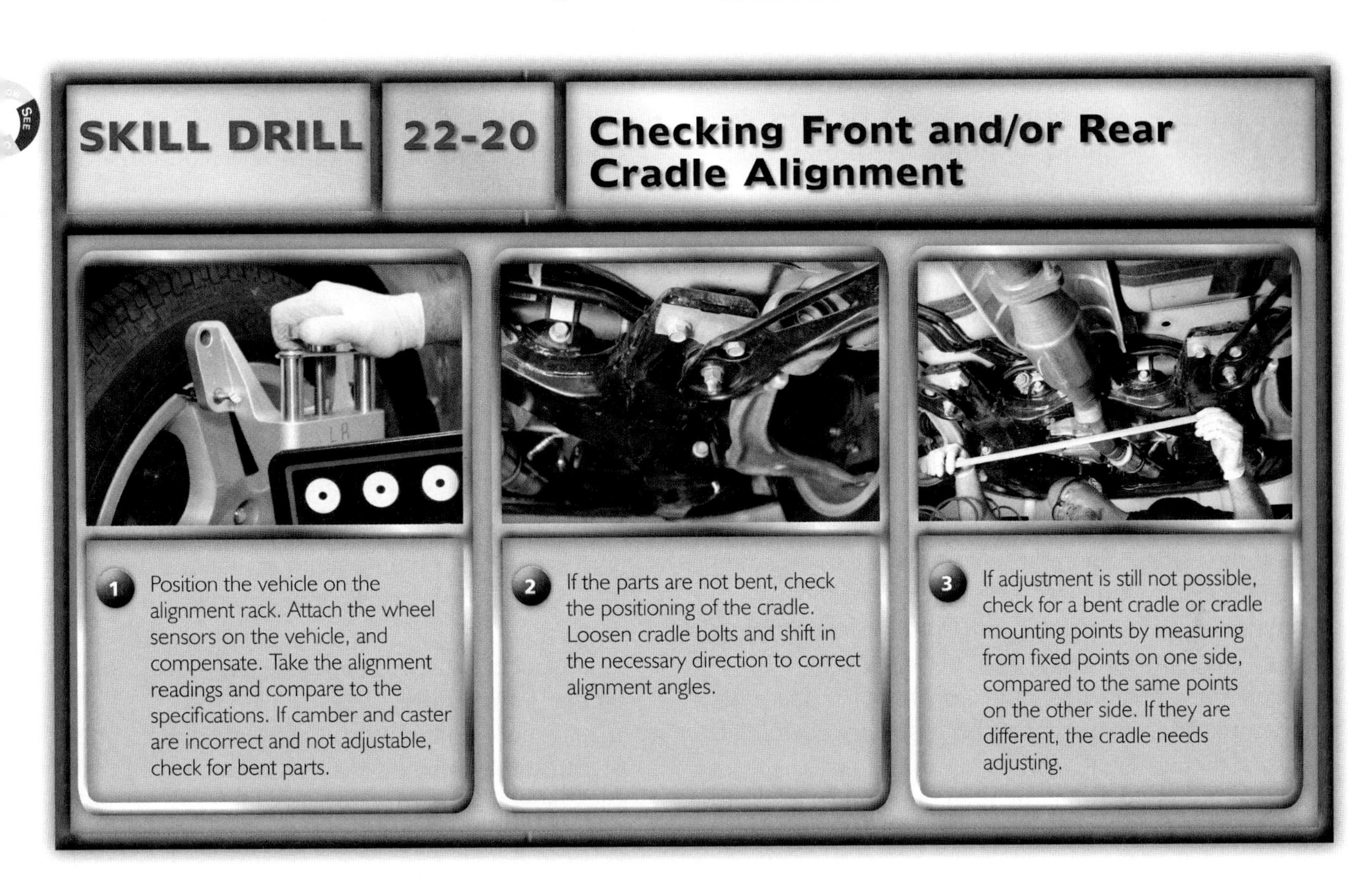
SKILL DRILL 22-20 Checking Front and/or Rear Cradle Alignment
1 Position the vehicle on the alignment rack. Attach the wheel sensors on the vehicle, and compensate. Take the alignment readings and compare to the specifications. If camber and caster are incorrect and not adjustable, check for bent parts.
2 If the parts are not bent, check the positioning of the cradle. Loosen cradle bolts and shift in the necessary direction to correct alignment angles.
3 If adjustment is still not possible, check for a bent cradle or cradle mounting points by measuring from fixed points on one side, compared to the same points on the other side. If they are different, the cradle needs adjusting.

Wrap-up

Ready for Review

- The suspension system is designed to absorb road shock and vibrations.
- Unsprung weight refers to the vehicle parts not supported by springs (wheels, tires, brake and steering assemblies); this weight should be kept as low as possible.
- Metal springs, rubber, and air all work to provide suspension system support by absorbing some amount of force.
- Springs react to road shock by not immediately returning to their original state. They may oscillate—that is, fluctuate in length, until the energy from the road shock is dissipated.
- Vehicle movement may be due to yaw, pitch, or roll.
- Suspension system components include the springs, axles, shock absorbers, arms, rods, sway bars, steering knuckle, bushings, and ball joints.
- Types of springs include coil springs, leaf springs, and torsion bars.
- Coil springs can be cylindrical, barrel shaped, or conical and are used on the front suspension of most modern light vehicles.
- Leaf springs are primarily used on rear-wheel drive vehicles and consist of multiple flat springs made of tempered steel.
- Functions of axles include helping support vehicle weight, maintaining wheel position, providing forward propulsion of the vehicle, and transmitting torque to the wheel.
- Axle types include straight, dead, full-floating, or semi-floating.
- Types of shock absorbers are hydraulic, gas pressurized, and adjustable (which can be load adjustable, annual adjustable rate, electronic adjustable rate, and automatic load adjustable).
- Shock absorbers use the resistance of a rod and piston, and oil and disc valves, to provide a dampening effect on the force created by the bumps and jolts of driving.
- Manually adjustable air springs can be incorporated into rear shock absorbers for vehicles designed to carry heavy loads.
- The dampening rate of electronic adjustable rate shock absorbers can be manually or automatically altered.
- The primary load-bearing elements of a SLA suspension system are known as control arms, which attach to the wheel assembly on one end and the chassis on the other.
- The primary load-bearing elements on a MacPherson strut suspension system is the strut itself.
- Bushings act as bearings at suspension fulcrum points, allowing movement of the component without losing its alignment.
- Types of suspension systems are solid (beam) axles, independent, rear, front, adaptive air, and computer controlled.
- A live axle transfers power from the engine to the wheels; a dead axle does not transmit any drive.
- Independent suspension allows for lower unsprung mass.
- Independent suspension systems adjust wheel camber individually.
- Struts are commonly used in independent suspension systems; the most common type is the MacPherson strut.
- Types of rear suspension systems are rear independent, rear-wheel drive independent, rigid-axle leaf spring, rigid-axle coil spring, and rigid nondrive.
- Rear suspension systems in front-wheel drive vehicles are designed to keep the rear tires in contact with the road, and aligned with front tires.
- The rear suspension system on a rear-wheel drive vehicle must allow for swiveling of the front wheels during steering; on four-wheel steering vehicles, the system must allow for swiveling of rear wheels as well.
- Front suspensions are generally either independent (front wheels move independently) or solid (an axle forces the front wheels to move together).
- Front suspension system types include MacPherson strut, short/long arm (SLA), and torsion bar.
- Adaptive air suspension systems electronically control the height of all four wheels based on vehicle speed and load.

- Types of computer-controlled suspension systems are active, hydraulic actuated, electromagnetic rheological, semi-active, and solenoid/valve actuated.
- Wheel alignment is set using the vehicle's control arms, knuckles, and frame.
- Factors affecting wheel alignment include camber, caster, steering axis inclination, toe-in and toe-out, scrub radius, toe-out on turns, turning radius, thrust angle, and ride height.
- Positive camber refers to the top of tires tilting away from the vehicle; negative camber refers to the top of tires tilting toward the vehicle; zero average camber refers to no tire tilt.
- Caster refers to the angle formed between the centerline of steering axis and true vertical, or the forward/backward tilt of the ball joints.
- Steering axis inclination (SAI) provides the front wheels with a self-centering function; it is formed by drawing a line through the upper and lower pivot points of the suspension assembly.
- Scrub radius (steering offset) is the distance between the center point of the tire contact patch at the road surface and the point of steering axis centerline contact with the road.
- The Ackermann principle ensures that the inner wheels turn at a sharper angle than the outer wheels when turning.
- Thrust angle refers to the relationship of the rear wheels to the vehicle's imaginary centerline.
- When performing a wheel alignment, be sure to check front and rear cradle, thrust angle, wheel setback, wheel camber, caster, toe, SAI, and toe-out on turns.
- There are three basic types of wheel alignment: two-wheel alignment, thrust-angle, and four-wheel alignment.
- A common suspension system problem is excessive play in the parts, usually from wear in the joints and bushings.
- Common tools for maintenance and repair of suspension systems include those used in diagnosis as well as the following: component compression devices, levers, spring compressor tools, a strut-servicing tool kit, a universal strut nut wrench kit, and a 24-mm strut rod socket.
- Wheel alignment servicing equipment is used to measure the steering and suspension alignment angles.

Key Terms

Ackermann angle The angle the steering arms make with the steering axis, projected toward the center of the rear axle.

Ackermann principle The geometric alignment of linkages in a vehicle's steering such that the wheels on the inside of a turn are able to move in a different circle radius than the wheels on the outside.

adaptive air suspension A suspension system that uses rubber bags or bladders filled with air to support the weight of the vehicle.

air spring A part that provides the springing action or auxiliary spring. It is typically used in air suspension systems or heavy truck applications.

applied force Pressure placed on something.

arm The primary load-bearing element of a vehicle's suspension system, commonly known as control arm. Can also mean the steering arm, which applies the driver's turning effort to the steering knuckle.

automatic load-adjustable shock absorber Typically, an air shock absorber used in an automatic load-sensing system that adjusts ride height (ground clearance) automatically such as when additional weight is added to the vehicle.

automatic ride control actuator An electric stepper motor mounted on top of the shock that changes orifice size inside the shock.

axle The shaft of the suspension system to which the tires and wheels are attached; they are used to drive or support the wheels.

ball joint A swivel connection mounted in the outer end of the front control arm. These swivels are typically constructed with a ball and socket to allow pivoting.

braking torque The torque acting to twist the axle housing around its center during braking.

bushing A rubber, nylon, or urethane part that allows for movement while maintaining alignment.

camber The side-to-side vertical tilt of the wheel. It is viewed from the front of the vehicle and measured in degrees. Negative camber is when the top of the tire is closer to the center of the vehicle than the bottom of the tire.

caster The angle formed through the wheel pivot points when viewed from the side in comparison to a vertical line through the wheel.

centerline The imaginary line drawn down the exact center of the vehicle from front to back.

coil spring Spring steel wire that is heated and wound into a coil that is used to support the weight of a vehicle.

compliance bushing A rubber bushing with a voided section molded in it that allows component movement under torque application. It is typically used in control arms on front-wheel drive vehicles to minimize torque steer issues.

control arm The primary load-bearing element of a vehicle's suspension system, commonly referred to as an A-arm or wishbone. These arms may be used as an upper and lower pivot point for the wheel assembly. They attach to the chassis with rubber bushings that allow up-and-down movement of the tire and wheel assembly.

cornering force The force applied to an axle that shifts the axle in relation to the position of the body when turning.

dead axle An axle, used on a rear- or front-wheel drive vehicle that does not drive the vehicle.

deflecting force A force that moves an object in a different direction or into a different shape.

direct-acting telescopic shock absorber A shock absorber designed to reduce spring oscillations.

driving thrust The force transferred from the tire contact patch through the axle housing and front half of the spring to the fixed shackle point that pushes the vehicle along the road.

elasticity The ability to deform and reform into the same shape.

external drive shaft A shaft used to transfer power from the transmission to the live axle.

included angle The angle of camber added or subtracted to the SAI angle. This is the angle of the pivot points in relation to the camber angle of the wheel. Also referred to as the diagnostic angle.

independent suspension A system for allowing the up-and-down movement of one tire without affecting the other tire on that axle.

leaf spring A spring made of one or more flat, tempered steel springs bracketed together that is used in the suspension system to support the weight of the vehicle.

live axle An axle with a final drive unit made into it that transfers the power from the engine to the wheels so the vehicle can move.

MacPherson strut A strut used on an independent suspension where the spring and shock are joined together. Used on most front-wheel drive vehicles.

magneto-rheological fluid A fluid that has the unique characteristic of changing viscosity when exposed to a magnetic field.

manual adjustable-rate shock absorber A shock absorber that allows manual adjustment of the dampening rate.

manually adjustable-air spring A rubber air bag placed inside coil springs to increase the spring's load-carrying ability. It is filled manually through a valve similar to a tire valve stem.

negative camber Tilt of the top of the tire toward the centerline of the vehicle.

negative caster Forward tilt of the wheel pivot points from the vertical line.

oscillation The fluctuation of an object between two states. With regard to suspension springs, it refers to the uncontrolled compression and decompression of the spring following overshoot.

overshoot The amount a spring extends (springs back) past its original length following compression.

panhard rod A metal rod used to hold the dead axle and keep it from moving from side to side through corners. It is mounted on the body or frame of the vehicle and the axle. Also referred to as a track bar.

pitch Movement of a vehicle around its y-axis (the imaginary line across the center of the vehicle from left to right) that causes the vehicle to lower or rise on the front end during quick braking or acceleration.

positive camber Tilt of the top of the tire out from the centerline of the vehicle.

positive caster Backward tilt of the wheel pivot points from the vertical line.

positive scrub radius A condition in which the point of center contact between the road surface and the tire and the point where the steering axis centerline contacts the road surface intersect below the road surface.

progressive rate of deflection The change in deflection rate that occurs as the weight of the vehicle changes. The greater the weight, the lower the rate of deflection due to increased resistance.

reaction force A force that acts in the opposite direction to another force.

rebound clip A metal strap that is warped around the leaf spring to prevent excessive flexing of the main leaf during rebound.

rigid-axle coil-spring suspension A dead axle that uses a coil spring.

rigid nondrive axle suspension A type of dead axle suspension system that is non-independent and uses a beam or solid axle.

rigid spring hanger The rigid part typically welded to the body or frame of the vehicle to which the front of the leaf spring is attached.

rod A straight piece of steel used to transfer motion within the vehicle's suspension system. It typically has treads cut on one or both ends.

roll Movement of a vehicle around its x-axis (the imaginary line down the center of the vehicle from front to back). It is commonly referred to as body roll or lean; when cornering, the body will try to move to the outside of the corner against the suspension.

rubber-bonded bushing A bushing that has a steel outer housing and inner sleeve with rubber inside; also known as a metalastic bushing.

scrub radius The distance between two imaginary points on the road surface—the point of center contact between the road surface and the tire, and the intersecting point where the steering axis centerline and the tire centerline contact the road surface.

self-leveling A vehicle with automatic load-adjustable shock absorbers.

setback The distance one wheel is set back from the wheel on the opposite side of the axle.

shock absorber A device on a vehicle designed to absorb bumps and jolts caused from driving on irregular surfaces and to dampen body movement.

short-/long-arm (SLA) suspension A type of control arm suspension system that uses a short control arm on the top and a long control arm on the bottom. This design ensures correct alignment angles when moving through bumps.

shroud A steel or plastic cover placed over the shock rod.

sintering The process of using pressure and heat to bond metal particles.

solid axle A single piece of steel that provides a simple means of mounting the hub and wheel units. Also called beam axle or straight axle.

splined section A flat key made into a shaft to accommodate changes in shaft length due to movement in wheel camber with suspension action.

spring A resilient steel part that stores energy when compressed and releases energy when released to its original state; available as a leaf spring, coil spring, or torsion bar.

spring eyes Rolled ends of some springs used to mount springs to the chassis.

spring shackle bushing A bushing that is positioned in the shackle that the leaf spring mounts to. Bushings allow the spring shackle to move as the leaf spring dimensions change over bumps.

static toe A setting designed to compensate for slight wear in steering components that may cause the wheels to turn outward or inward while the vehicle is in motion.

steering axis inclination (SAI) The angle formed by an imaginary line running through the upper and lower steering pivots relative to vertical as viewed from the front.

stop A rubber part used to control the movement of control arms (suspension arms).

strut A shock absorber used on a MacPherson strut–type suspension.

suspension action Movement of the chassis up and down.

suspension strut A shock absorber designed to reduce spring oscillations.

suspension system A system within a vehicle designed to isolate the vehicle body from road bumps and vibrations.

sway bar A part used in vehicles as a stabilizer, or antiroll bar. It is connected to the chassis in the center, and each end is connected to one side of the suspension system. It is typically installed on the front, and sometimes the rear suspension.

swinging shackle A shackle connected to the rear of the multileaf spring that allows the leaf spring to move downward when a load is placed on the rear of the vehicle.

thrust angle The angle formed between the centerline of the rear axle in comparison to the centerline of the vehicle.

thrust line The imaginary line drawn through the center of the rear axle.

toe-in When the front of the wheels, as seen from above, are closer together than the rear of the wheels.

toe-out When the rear of the wheels, as seen from above, are closer together than the front of the wheels.

toe-out on turns The difference in turning angle of the inside tire in comparison to the outside tire. This angle difference allows the tires to roll through the corner rather than the inside tire dragging. Also referred to as Ackermann angle.

torsion bar A bar made of a steel alloy that is fixed rigidly to the chassis at one end and the suspension control arm at the other to support the weight of a vehicle.

torsional load A force that is applied by clamping one end of an object to another object that is then twisted.

trailing arm suspension A type of suspension system that uses upper and lower control arms.

trim height The amount of ground clearance a vehicle has, measured from a point on the body or frame depending on the manufacturer. Also known as ride height.

turning radius A measure of how small a circle the vehicle can turn around when the steering wheel is turned to the limit.

uniform pitch A spring whose pitch (the distance from the center of one coil to the center of the adjacent coil) is the same distance throughout.

universal joints Joints placed on each end of a driveshaft that help compensate for movement of the rear end housing up and down.

unsprung mass Any part of the steering and suspension system that is not supported by springs. A large amount of unsprung weight will cause the tire to hop off the ground when hitting bumps, as the weight will overcome dampening of the shock absorbers.

unsprung weight *See* unsprung mass.

Watt's linkage Another name for a rigid-axle coil-spring suspension that uses two bars similar to a panhard rod and a pivot point on the axle to keep the axle from moving in turns.

wheel alignment The practice of aligning the wheels of the vehicle to the centerline of the vehicle and to each other. It ensures that the vehicle will handle correctly and gives best tire wear.

wishbone control arm Another term for an A-arm.

wrap leaf A spring containing spring eyes.

yaw Movement of a vehicle around its z-axis (vertical axis) felt when the vehicle deviates from its straight path, as when skidding sideways and the rear comes around.

zero camber A tire with no tilt or zero camber angle.

zero scrub radius A condition in which the point of center contact between the road surface and the tire and the point where the steering axis centerline contacts the road surface intersect at the road surface.

ASE-Type Questions

1. Tech A says that the wheel and tire are examples of unsprung weight. Tech B says that the exhaust system is an example of sprung weight. Who is correct?
   a. Tech A
   b. Tech B
   c. Both A and B
   d. Neither A nor B
2. Tech A says that thrust angle refers to the direction the front wheels are pointing. Tech B says that scrub radius refers to the vertical centerline of the tire in relation to an imaginary line through the steering knuckle pivots. Who is correct?
   a. Tech A
   b. Tech B
   c. Both A and B
   d. Neither A nor B
3. Tech A says that yaw is when a vehicle deviates from its straight path. Tech B says that roll is felt during hard braking. Who is correct?
   a. Tech A
   b. Tech B
   c. Both A and B
   d. Neither A nor B
4. Tech A says that a vehicle will tend to pull toward the side with the most positive camber. Tech B says that a progressive-rate spring offers a soft ride but can also carry a heavier load. Who is correct?
   a. Tech A
   b. Tech B
   c. Both A and B
   d. Neither A nor B
5. Tech A says that a shock dampens movement of the suspension in both upward and downward movement. Tech B says that a shock only dampens upward movement. Who is correct?
   a. Tech A
   b. Tech B
   c. Both A and B
   d. Neither A nor B
6. Tech A says that ball joints must be unloaded when checking them for wear. Tech B says that ball joints must be loaded when checking them for wear. Who is correct?
   a. Tech A
   b. Tech B
   c. Both A and B
   d. Neither A nor B
7. Tech A says that positive toe is when the front of the tires are farther apart than the rear of the tires. Tech B says that a ball joint in a MacPherson strut suspension is a follower joint (not loaded). Who is correct?
   a. Tech A
   b. Tech B
   c. Both A and B
   d. Neither A nor B
8. Tech A says that a dead axle is designed to carry the weight of the vehicle with no drive capability. Tech B says that checking toe-out on turns is a pre-alignment check. Who is correct?
   a. Tech A
   b. Tech B
   c. Both A and B
   d. Neither A nor B
9. Tech A says that loose ball joints can cause the vehicle to wander. Tech B says that loose control arm bushings can affect alignment angles. Who is correct?
   a. Tech A
   b. Tech B
   c. Both A and B
   d. Neither A nor B
10. Tech A says that the front wheels should be aligned before the rear wheels. Tech B says that front wheel toe should be adjusted after front wheel camber and caster. Who is correct?
    a. Tech A
    b. Tech B
    c. Both A and B
    d. Neither A nor B

SECTION VI

Brakes

CHAPTER 23

KNOW
SEE
DO
PROVE

NATEF Tasks

Brakes General Brake Systems		Page
■ Research applicable vehicle and service information, vehicle service history, service precautions, and technical service bulletins.	MLR AST	642

KNOW
SEE
DO
PROVE

Knowledge Objectives

After reading this chapter, you will be able to:

1. Describe the evolution of braking systems from scrub brakes to brake-by-wire systems. (pp 632–634)
2. List the factors that can influence vehicle braking. (pp 634–635)
3. Identify the two types of brake systems on all vehicles. (pp 635–636)
4. Describe how the principles of kinetic energy, Newton's first law of motion, conservation of energy, and friction apply to the brake system. (pp 636–639)
5. Describe how brake design must account for heat transfer. (p 639)
6. Describe the three causes of brake fade. (pp 639–640)
7. Describe rotational force and weight transfer. (p 640)
8. Describe how the principles of levers and fulcrum apply to the brake system. (pp 640–642)
9. Describe the adjustable brake pedal system. (p 642)
10. Describe the legal standards that apply to brake repair and the range of potential liability of the technician. (p 642)
11. List the types of brake systems and describe how they operate. (pp 642–643)
12. List the types of parking brake systems and describe how they operate. (pp 643-645)

Principles of Braking

Know
See
Do

Skills Objectives

There are no skills objectives for this chapter.

Introduction

The brake system is one of the most critical systems on a vehicle. It allows the driver to slow or stop the vehicle as needed. In ideal situations, the driver will have enough time to anticipate the need to slow down well in advance of an event, allowing the vehicle to slow down gradually. However, many situations require the quick use of a very efficient braking system to avoid an accident. In this chapter, we will explore the history, theory, and operation of modern braking systems.

The History of Brakes

Early automobiles evolved from horse-drawn buggies and used a similar scrub braking system. **Scrub brakes** are a simple mechanical system that uses leverage to force a friction block against one or more wheels. In a buggy, for example, the friction between the two surfaces transformed the energy of the moving buggy into heat energy. As heat was created in the friction materials, the buggy slowed down. The scrub braking system was used for more than 2000 years with virtually no change. It worked reasonably well on dry wheel surfaces made of wood or steel but became quickly outdated once rubber tires were developed around 1900, since the scrubbing action on the softer tires significantly decreased tire life.

Faced with the need to replace the scrub braking system with a system that did not apply friction materials directly to the new rubber tires, designers had to consider other options. One option was the **band brake**. It used a metal band lined with friction material that was operated mechanically to clamp around the outside of a small-diameter wheel or was drum-mounted to the axle or wheel. This system worked well in the forward direction, but the band would try to unwind in the reverse direction; the system was therefore impractical and was abandoned after just a few short years.

The next major development was the **drum brake**, which is similar to the drum brakes that are used today. The drum brake consisted of two brake shoes that would push against the inside of the brake drum. Early drum brake systems were mechanically operated by rods, links, and levers FIGURE 23-1. This worked fine for applying a single brake unit, but as vehicle

FIGURE 23-1 An early drum brake system.

You Are the Automotive Technician

A customer comes into the shop with a brake concern on her 2009 Ford Taurus. She recently drove down a long mountain pass, using her brakes to stay within the speed limit. As she neared the bottom of the pass, the brakes felt like they weren't working, even though the engine was running and she was pushing very hard on the pedal. You recognize the smell of overheated brakes coming from the car. She asks you why her brakes didn't work correctly.

1. How will you explain what happened to the brakes?
2. What would you advise her to do if she is in that situation again?
3. Which type of brakes are more susceptible to this condition?

operating speeds increased, greater braking demands required brake units to be mounted to each wheel. With this mechanically operated system of rods, links, and levers, it was difficult to maintain equal braking forces at each wheel. The old drum braking systems caused the vehicle to veer dangerously to one side when braking. This system also required frequent adjustment of the brakes. Over time, the mechanical drum brake system gave way to the modern hydraulic drum brake system due to its ability to automatically equalize braking forces at each wheel.

Disc brakes were originally developed in the early 1900s but didn't find common use until the 1960s. Because the effectiveness of friction brakes depends on the braking components' ability to dissipate heat quickly into the atmosphere, drum brakes—with their friction materials on the inside—were at a disadvantage. This led to the greater use of **disc brakes** on most vehicles **FIGURE 23-2**. Disc brakes force brake pads against the outside of the brake rotor and create heat where atmospheric air can quickly remove the heat at its source, making them more efficient under prolonged use.

Advanced Brake Systems

Electronic Brake Control

You might think, "If some brake force is good, then more would be better." But this is not the case. Applying too much brake force can cause the tire to lose traction and skid. If this happens, the driver can lose control of the vehicle. This problem led to the design of electronic brake control (EBC) systems. The first versions of EBC systems were the **anti-lock brake systems (ABS)**. ABS systems

FIGURE 23-2 Disc brakes force the brake pads against the outside of the brake rotor.

> **LINK**
> For more information on ABS brake systems, see the chapter Electronic Brake Control.

have helped to reduce the number of vehicle accidents each year. They use a computer to monitor each wheel's speed and either hold, decrease, or apply the hydraulic pressure to each wheel to prevent wheel lock-up and maintain the maximum amount of braking power just short of brake lock-up. Additional safety demands led to the development of traction control systems (TCS) and electronic stability control (ESC). TCS systems help to prevent tires from slipping during acceleration by reducing engine torque and, if necessary, applying brake pressure to the slipping wheels. ESC adds additional functionality to ABS and TCS to help prevent the tires from losing traction when the vehicle is being steered aggressively or evasive maneuvers are being undertaken. In both TCS and ESC, the control unit can independently apply individual brake units even though the driver is not stepping down on the brake pedal.

Brake Assist and Brake-by-Wire Systems

Electronic brake control systems have been further enhanced with additional programmed features such as **brake assist (BA)**. BA gives greater control of the braking system to the computer, which can react more quickly and more deliberately than a driver, especially in a panic situation. An example of BA is the **brake-by-wire system**. A full brake-by-wire system does away with the hydraulic portion of the brake system and replaces it with sensors, wires, an electronic control unit, and electrically actuated motors to apply individual brake units at each wheel. The driver applies foot pressure to a **brake pedal emulator**. This tells the computer how firmly the driver intends to brake. The control unit then sends control signals to the appropriate brake actuators, which generate the commanded clamping force and slow the vehicle. All of this is being monitored by sensors reporting data to the control unit, so the desired braking occurs.

Giving greater control of the braking system to the computer increases driving safety. For example, it takes a certain amount of time and stopping distance for the driver to lift his or her foot from the accelerator pedal, step on the brake pedal, and apply the wheel brake units. In a brake-by-wire system, that time and distance can be reduced. The computer can determine that the driver is quickly releasing the accelerator, which indicates a potential panic stop. As the pedal is being released, the control system immediately applies the brakes lightly,

Caring for the Customer

Many auto insurance companies give their customers a discount when the vehicle is equipped with brake safety features, such as ABS systems, as they help avoid or minimize accidents.

which dries any moisture from the braking surfaces and takes up any clearance in the brake system. This prepares the brakes to be fully applied by the control system if the driver steps on the brake pedal or if the computer detects that a collision is about to happen.

Regenerative Brake Systems

With the pressure to improve fuel economy, some manufacturers have equipped their hybrid vehicles with regenerative braking. Regenerative braking takes brake-by-wire technology to the next level. Instead of applying friction brakes and losing energy as heat, the brake-by-wire system uses the electric motor as a generator, which slows the vehicle by converting the vehicle's kinetic energy into electrical energy FIGURE 23-3. The amount of stopping power is controlled by how much electricity is being generated. The more stopping power needed, the more electrical output is demanded of the generator (up to its maximum rated output) by the control system. The electricity is stored in the vehicle's high-voltage battery and can then be used later by the electric motor to drive the vehicle. This regeneration process makes the vehicle more fuel efficient, especially in stop-and-go traffic. This system still requires traditional friction-based brakes to be used when quick, heavy braking is required. The interaction between the regenerative braking system and the friction braking system must be carefully designed and serviced so that each operates seamlessly with the other.

FIGURE 23-3 A regenerative braking system.

Brake Fundamentals

Several factors can influence vehicle braking. An effective braking system takes all of the following factors into account:

- Road surface: Generally asphalt and concrete road surfaces allow for good braking while gravel surfaces or dirt roads do not.
- Road conditions: Roads that are wet, icy, or covered with loose gravel reduce the tire's traction and result in longer stopping distances. Extremely hot temperatures on asphalt roads can soften the asphalt, making it slippery.
- Weight of the vehicle: Heavier vehicles require more braking force to stop than lighter vehicles and therefore usually have larger wheel brake units. Also, loading down a vehicle increases its stopping distance due to the vehicle's extra mass.
- Load on the wheel during stopping: Heavier loads increase the downward force on the wheels, thereby increasing tire traction FIGURE 23-4.
- Height of the vehicle: Stopping power is exerted at the point where the tire and the road connect. The centerline of the vehicle's weight is above this tire-to-road contact point. The taller the vehicle, the greater the leverage on the contact point. This increases the load on some tires, while decreasing the load on other tires. Thus, controlling the vehicle in a panic situation becomes much more difficult.
- How the vehicle is being driven: Aggressive driving causes the tires to become hot and possibly overheated, thus reducing the tire's ability to obtain maximum traction. Also, increased speed and aggressive handling force the brakes to work under extreme conditions.
- The tires on the vehicle: A tire's composition, tread style, tread condition, and inflation pressure all affect its traction FIGURE 23-5. Manufacturers design tires with different qualities based on vehicle need. Tires are rated for their traction ability. Using the wrong tire will affect the vehicle's stopping power. For example, a tire with tread designed to channel water away from the tire-to-road contact point will have greater traction when the road surface is wet than the tires used on drag race cars, which have a slick tread.

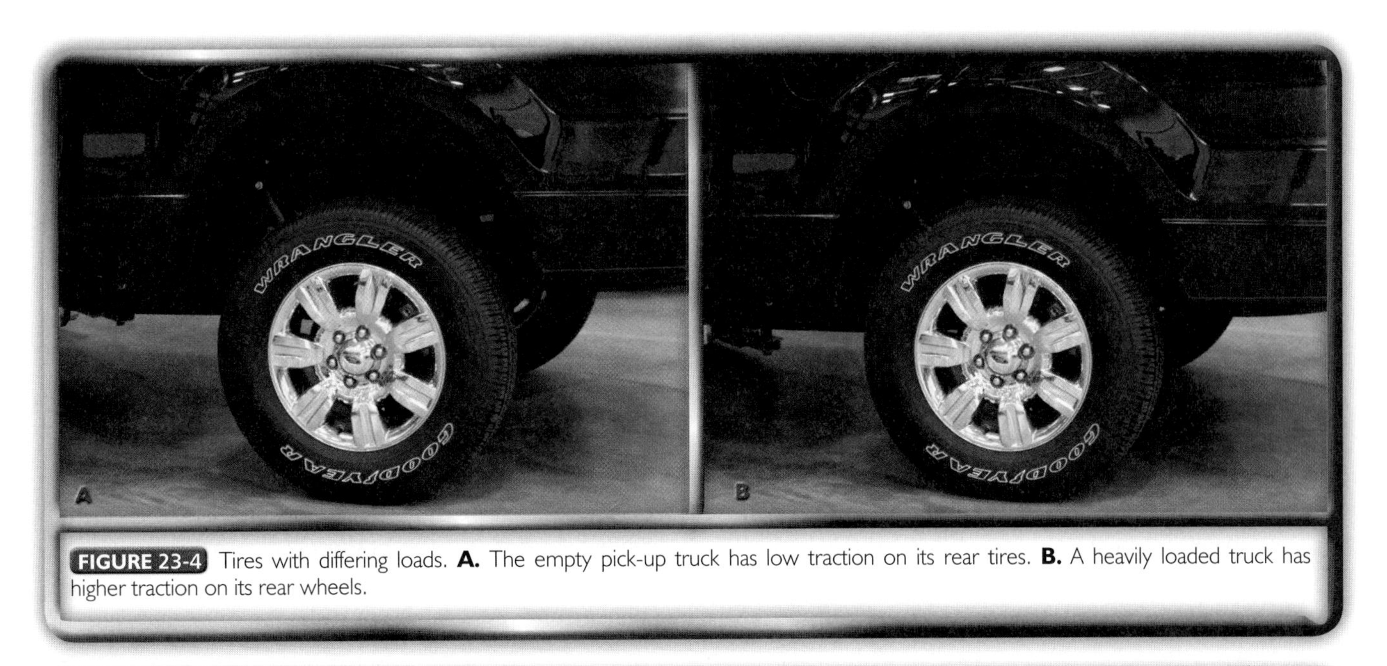
WRANGLER
GOODYEAR
A
WRANGLER
GOODYEAR
B

FIGURE 23-4 Tires with differing loads. **A.** The empty pick-up truck has low traction on its rear tires. **B.** A heavily loaded truck has higher traction on its rear wheels.

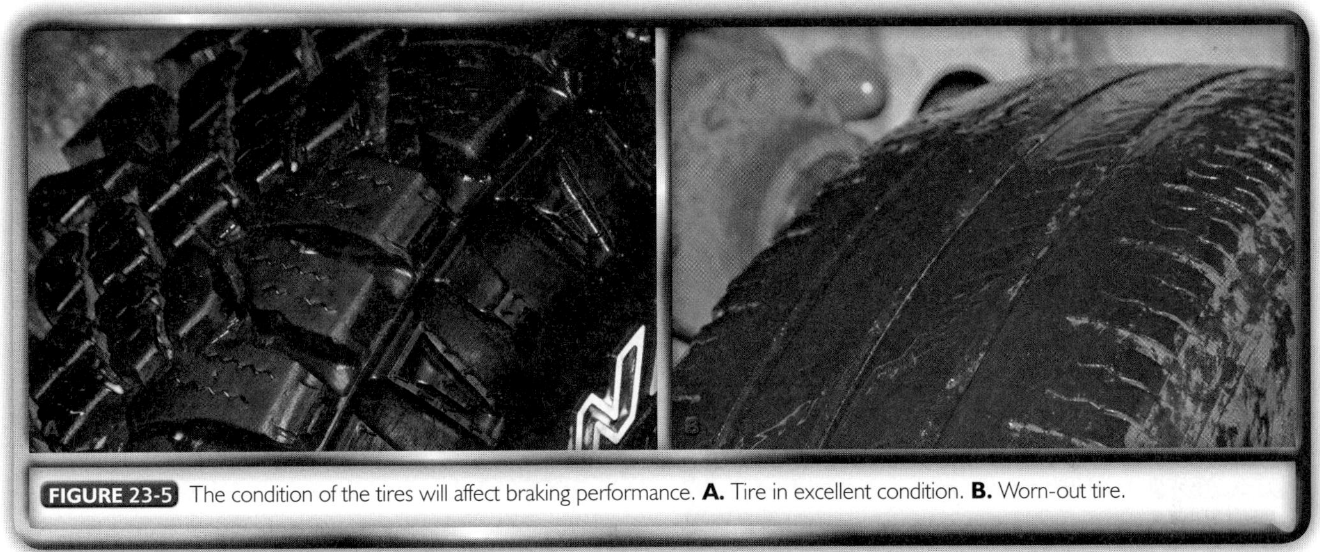

FIGURE 23-5 The condition of the tires will affect braking performance. **A.** Tire in excellent condition. **B.** Worn-out tire.

Brake Systems

There are two brake systems on all vehicles—a service brake and a parking brake. The service brake is used for slowing or stopping the vehicle when it is in motion and is operated by a foot pedal FIGURE 23-6. Service brakes consist of drum and/or disc brakes. Some have disc brakes on the front wheels and drum brakes on the rear wheels, while others have disc brakes on all four wheels. The parking brake is used for holding the vehicle in place when it is stationary. The parking brake is usually operated by hand, but some vehicles use a foot-activated pedal FIGURE 23-7.

Modern braking systems are hydraulically operated and have two main sections: the brake assemblies at the wheels and the hydraulic system that applies them. The driver pushes the brake pedal, which applies mechanical

FIGURE 23-6 A vehicle service brake is used for slowing or stopping a moving vehicle.

force to the pistons in the master cylinder. The pistons apply hydraulic pressure to the fluid in the cylinders. The lines transfer the pressure—which is applied equally in all directions within the confines of the brake lines—to the hydraulic cylinders. The hydraulic cylinders at the wheel assemblies apply the brakes FIGURE 23-8.

Force is transmitted hydraulically through the fluid. For cylinders of the same size, the force transmitted from one is the same value as the force applied to the other. By using cylinders of different sizes, forces can be increased or reduced, allowing designers to obtain the desired braking force for each wheel FIGURE 23-9. The cylinders force friction linings into contact with the braking surfaces. The resulting friction between the surfaces generates heat energy and slows the vehicle.

In drum brakes, the wheel cylinders force brake linings against the inside of the brake drum FIGURE 23-10. In disc brakes, pads are forced against the outside of a brake disc FIGURE 23-11. In both systems, heat spreads into other parts and the atmosphere, so brake linings and drums, pads and discs, and brake fluid must withstand high temperatures and high pressures. On modern vehicles, the basic brake system has some refinements such as a power booster and EBC systems. These help the driver apply the brakes, prevent skidding, and maintain directional control of the vehicle under various driving situations FIGURE 23-12.

Kinetic Energy

Kinetic energy is the energy of an object in motion. All moving objects have kinetic energy. Heavier objects have more kinetic energy than lighter objects moving at the same speed. If the weight doubles, the kinetic

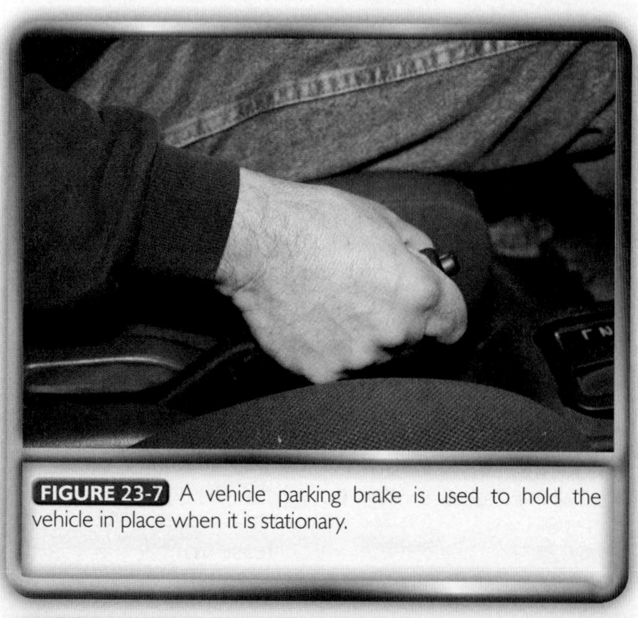

FIGURE 23-7 A vehicle parking brake is used to hold the vehicle in place when it is stationary.

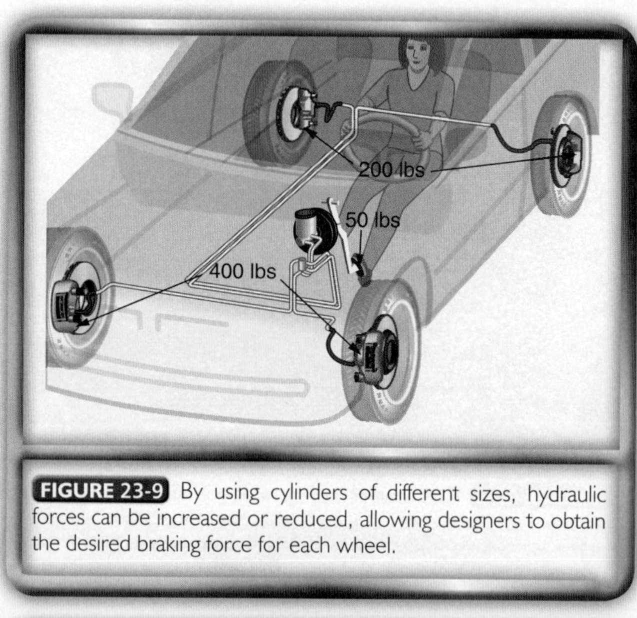
200 lbs
50 lbs
400 lbs

FIGURE 23-9 By using cylinders of different sizes, hydraulic forces can be increased or reduced, allowing designers to obtain the desired braking force for each wheel.

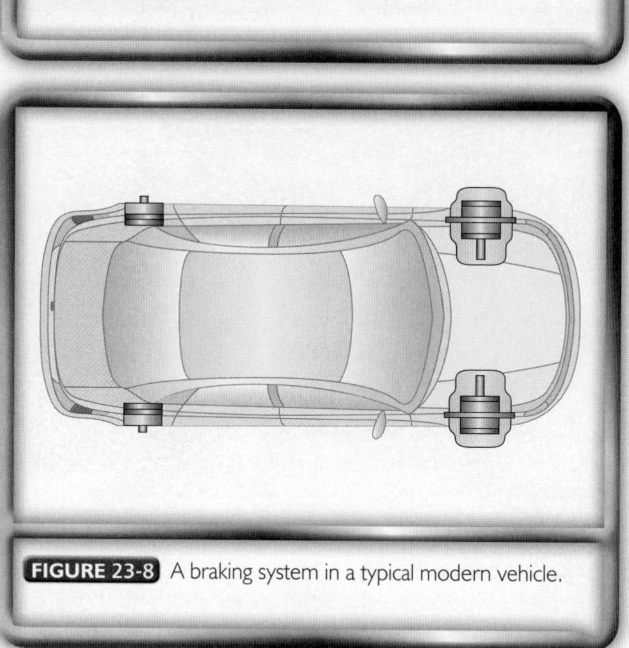

FIGURE 23-8 A braking system in a typical modern vehicle.

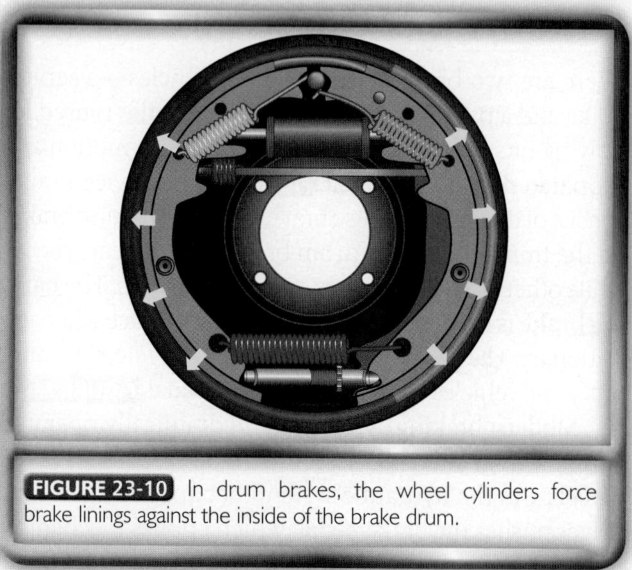

FIGURE 23-10 In drum brakes, the wheel cylinders force brake linings against the inside of the brake drum.

FIGURE 23-11 In disc brakes, pads are forced against the outside of a brake disc.

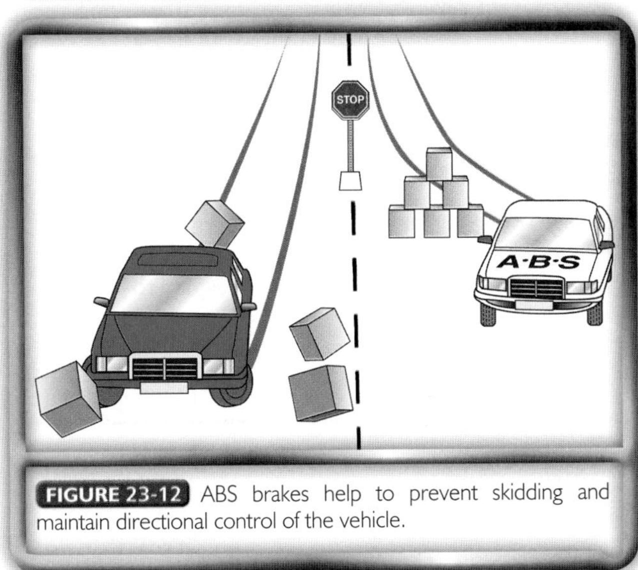
STOP
A·B·S

FIGURE 23-12 ABS brakes help to prevent skidding and maintain directional control of the vehicle.

energy doubles. Faster-moving objects have more kinetic energy than slower-moving objects of the same weight. Kinetic energy increases by the square of the speed. This means that if we double the speed of an object, the kinetic energy will increase by four times. If we triple the speed, the kinetic energy will increase by nine times. Thus, the heavier and faster an object is, the greater its kinetic energy. During braking, all of the kinetic energy in the moving vehicle must be converted to another form of energy (in most cases heat) for the vehicle to stop moving; this is the function of the braking system.

Acceleration and Deceleration

Newton's first law of motion states that "an object will stay at rest or uniform speed unless it is acted upon by an outside force." **Acceleration** refers to an increase in an object's speed. In an automobile, acceleration, or an increase in kinetic energy, is caused by the power from the engine. When the driver steps down on the throttle pedal, the engine's power output is increased and the vehicle accelerates. This acceleration requires a certain amount of energy. The heavier the vehicle, the more energy required to accelerate it to a given speed. A lighter vehicle requires less energy to accelerate; this is why race cars are stripped of all unnecessary weight.

Deceleration refers to a decrease in an object's speed. Remember that an outside force is needed for the speed of an object to change. So we need an outside force to act upon the vehicle to cause it to decelerate. That force comes from the mass of the Earth. If you thought it came from the brakes, you would only be partially correct. Imagine traveling at a high speed in a four-wheel drive vehicle and hitting a bit of a jump. Stepping on the brakes in midair to slow the vehicle wouldn't do you much good, would it? So the brakes only function when they connect the vehicle to the ground or roadway. In fact, that is what they do; they connect the vehicle to the ground through the rolling wheel and tire assembly. In doing so, they apply a varying amount of force from the ground to the vehicle, thereby causing the vehicle to decelerate. The force of the brakes absorbs the kinetic energy of the vehicle. The heavier the vehicle and the faster it is going, the more kinetic energy must be dissipated and the harder the brakes must work.

Applied Science

AS-51: Acceleration/Deceleration: The technician can demonstrate an understanding of a vehicle's acceleration and deceleration as a function of vehicle weight and power.

Kinetic energy is the energy of an object in motion. All moving objects have kinetic energy. Heavier objects have more kinetic energy than lighter objects moving at the same speed. If the weight doubles, the kinetic energy doubles. Energy is needed to start a vehicle. Heat energy is generated in the engine via chemical energy (fuel); it is then converted via mechanical energy to kinetic energy, putting the vehicle in motion. Kinetic energy is converted to heat energy once again through the operation of the brakes. This heat energy is then dissipated in the surrounding air through the brake system, bringing the vehicle to rest.

Newton's first law of motion states that the greater the weight, the more energy is needed to accelerate and maintain speed. For example, it is easier for three people to push a two-door hatchback than an SUV. Also, the more the vehicle weighs, the more energy it takes to decelerate.

Energy Transformation

The law of **conservation of energy** states that energy cannot be created or destroyed. This means that the energy used to cause a vehicle to accelerate and decelerate must be transformed from one form of energy to another. Let's follow the cycle of energy transformation in a typical vehicle.

Gasoline or diesel fuels are potential energy in chemical form. A portion of the fuel's chemical energy is transformed within the engine, first into heat energy and then into mechanical energy. Engines are not very efficient, only transforming about 25% to 35% of the chemical energy into mechanical energy. The rest of the chemical energy is wasted as heat energy, mostly through the exhaust and cooling systems. The mechanical energy is used to accelerate the vehicle, thus converting the mechanical energy to kinetic energy. Once the vehicle is up to speed, the engine only needs to transform enough chemical energy into kinetic energy to overcome wind resistance, climb hills, and power the vehicle's accessories. This is why most vehicles get better fuel economy while operating at steady speeds than in stop-and-go traffic—it takes a lot more energy to accelerate a vehicle than it does to maintain a particular speed.

Does deceleration require an energy transformation? Yes, it does. The kinetic energy has to be removed for the vehicle to decelerate. In other words, the kinetic energy must be transformed into another form of energy for the vehicle to slow down. In a standard vehicle, the braking system transforms the kinetic energy into heat energy **FIGURE 23-13**. In essence, it takes the same amount of energy to slow a vehicle as it does to accelerate it. For safety's sake, we expect a vehicle to stop from a given speed faster than the time it took to accelerate to that speed. For this reason, the braking system can transform energy faster than the engine.

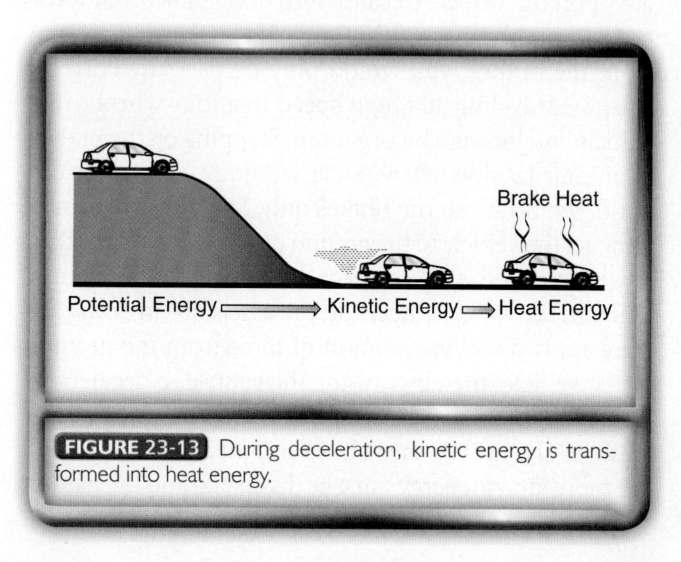
Brake Heat
Potential Energy
Kinetic Energy
Heat Energy

FIGURE 23-13 During deceleration, kinetic energy is transformed into heat energy.

Friction and Friction Brakes

Brakes transform kinetic energy to another form of energy. Standard brakes do this through the principle of friction. **Friction** is the resistance created by surfaces in contact. Static friction is resistance between nonmoving surfaces and is present in parking brakes. Kinetic friction is resistance between moving surfaces and is present in standard brakes. Just as rubbing sandpaper over a block of wood produces heat, operating the brakes causes the moving friction surfaces to come into contact with each other and generate heat. This transformation of energy converts kinetic energy into heat energy and slows the vehicle. If you have seen an old go-kart, you may have noticed the scrub brake. The metal pad scrubbing against the tire causes friction, which slows the go-kart—while also wearing down the tires. As discussed previously, modern vehicles use a more sophisticated braking system with separate braking components that operate more efficiently.

TECHNICIAN TIP

A higher coefficient of friction usually results in a faster wearing of the softer material, such as rubber. This is one reason why the brake lining is designed to be made of softer materials than the drum or rotor, which leads to the wearing out of the brake lining instead of the drum or rotor.

Applied Science

AS-90: Friction: The technician can demonstrate an understanding of friction and its effects on linear and rotational motion.

When adjusting drum brakes, the common method is to adjust the brake and turn the wheel at the same time in order to feel how hard it is to turn the wheel while adjusting the brake. As the brake becomes tighter, the friction between the brake drum and the brake shoe increases; therefore the rotational motion requires more torque or force to produce the same speed of movement.

Linear friction is demonstrated when a heavy object is pulled across a flat surface. The more surface area that is in contact with the object, the harder it is to pull. The larger the surface area that the object is covering, then the greater the force required to move it. For example, try to pull a tool box across a bench. Now lift one end of the toolbox and pull. It is far easier to pull the toolbox with one end lifted because the lifted tool box is in contact with less surface area, reducing the force required to move the box.

Applied Science

AS-91: Friction: The technician can explain the role that friction plays in acceleration and deceleration.
Friction is very important to acceleration and deceleration. A vehicle's tires must be able to keep friction between the tire and the ground in order to propel the car forward. If the tires are not in contact with the road, they will have nothing to push against. No friction is present and the car will not move forward.

Friction is also very important in deceleration, as the tire again has to maintain friction between the road surface and tire. The braking force on the vehicle will also use friction in order to slow or decelerate the vehicle. As the brake pads press against the brake disc, friction is created between the two surfaces. This friction creates heat and slows the vehicle.

The amount of friction between two moving surfaces in contact with each other is expressed as a ratio and is called the **coefficient of friction**. It can be found by comparing the amount of force pushing the two surfaces together to the amount of resistive force generated between the two surfaces sliding against each other. For example, a stationary steel surface pushed against a moving steel surface with 100 lb (45.36 kg) of force might generate 20 lb (9.07 kg) of resistive force. This is expressed as $^{20}/_{100}$ ($^{9.07}/_{45.36}$), which equals a coefficient of friction of 0.20. A stationary block of rubber that is pushed against a moving steel surface with 100 lb of force might generate 125 lb (56.7 kg) of friction. This would be $^{125}/_{100}$ ($^{56.7}/_{45.36}$), which equals a coefficient of friction of 1.25.

Heat Transfer

Heat transfers from a hot area to a cool area. Since there is a lot of kinetic energy converted to heat during the braking process, the brakes must be able to dissipate that heat to the atmosphere effectively. Heat transfer is critical to this process. Heat must continually be transferred away from the friction materials so that the brakes can perform their job of transforming the kinetic energy into heat energy.

Ultimately, most of the heat generated by the braking process radiates into the atmosphere. How it radiates into the atmosphere depends on the type of braking system. In drum brakes, the heat is created inside of the drum and transfers through the drum to the outside surface where it radiates into the atmosphere. In disc brakes, the heat is created on the outer surfaces of the rotors, which are in contact with the atmosphere. Disc brakes also may have internal ventilation to help dissipate the heat transferred from the outer surface even faster.

Brake Fade

In automobiles, **brake fade** is the reduction in stopping power caused by a change in the brake system. Brake fade can be caused by three factors. The first and most common is **heat fade**. Heat fade is caused by the buildup of heat in the braking surfaces, which get so hot they cannot create any additional heat, leading to a loss of friction. Remember, the brakes must transform kinetic energy into heat energy to decelerate the vehicle. If heat energy cannot be generated, then the kinetic energy cannot be reduced and the vehicle will not decelerate. Heat transfer is used to move heat away from the friction surfaces and allow them to continue generating heat. Once the temperature of the friction materials become so hot that they cannot generate any additional heat, the coefficient of friction drops and the brakes cannot generate stopping power until some of the heat dissipates.

A driver will experience heat fade after using the brakes too much, such as during high-performance driving or when going down a long, steep hill, particularly when towing. The brake pedal will be hard, but the braking effect "fades" away and the vehicle's rate of deceleration decreases. This is a dangerous condition and is why many long hills on freeways have truck escape ramps made of sand or some other soft material to slow a vehicle by absorbing the truck's kinetic energy in the soft material.

The second type of brake fade is called **water fade** and is caused by water-soaked brake linings. The water acts like a lubricant and lessens the coefficient of friction between the braking surfaces. This leads to a hard brake pedal but very little braking power. Once the water is removed from the friction surfaces through evaporation, the normal coefficient of friction will be restored.

The third kind of brake fade is called **hydraulic fade** and is caused by the brake fluid becoming so hot

Caring for the Customer

Excessive heat can cause warpage of disc brake rotors and brake drums. Brake fade and rotor warping can be reduced through proper braking technique. When travelling on a long downgrade requiring braking, the driver should simply select a lower transmission gear. Periodic rather than continuous application of the brakes will allow the brakes to cool between applications. Continuous light application of the brakes, sometimes referred to as riding the brakes, can be particularly destructive in both wear and overheating of the brake components.

that it boils. Once it boils, it is no longer only a liquid, converting in part to a vapor, which can be compressed. The brake fluid can no longer transfer force effectively to the wheel brake units and apply them firmly enough to create friction. Since the boiling fluid can be compressed, hydraulic fade can be recognized by the brake pedal becoming soft and having increased pedal travel during heavy brake usage.

Rotational Force

When brakes are operated on a moving vehicle, a **rotational force** is generated. As the wheel rotates, the friction between the brake components tends to twist the brake support in the direction of wheel rotation **FIGURE 23-14**. Since the brake support is ultimately connected to the body of the vehicle, the body too tends to rotate in the same direction. A good example of rotational force is when a motorcycle rider applies the front brake hard enough that the rear wheel is lifted completely off the ground. Rotational forces are usually controlled by the suspension components, but they can become worn and allow movement, which can be felt as a clunk or pop during brake application.

Another result of rotational force is **weight transfer**. The rotational force tends to push the nose of the vehicle down and lift the rear of the vehicle, transferring weight to the front wheels. Rotational force and weight transfer also happen because the centerline of the vehicle is higher than the centerline of the axles; thus, the center of gravity tends to move forward when the brakes are applied firmly **FIGURE 23-15**.

Weight transfer causes the front wheels to have increased traction, allowing them to bear more of the stopping load, and causes the rear wheels to have less traction, reducing the amount of load they can bear. Engineers take this into account when designing the brakes; otherwise the front wheels will not get enough stopping power and the rear will have too much, resulting in rear wheel lock-up and loss of control of the vehicle. Lock-up is avoided by engineering the system with the proper-sized master and wheel cylinders and valving that modifies the hydraulic pressure to the rear wheels under hard braking. This is covered in greater detail in the Hydraulic Components section in the Hydraulics and Power Brakes chapter.

Caring for the Customer

Some owners raise their vehicles for better off-road clearance by installing a lift kit and/or large-diameter tires. Doing so raises the vehicle's center of gravity and increases the amount of weight transfer the vehicle experiences, making it more prone to rear-wheel lock-up and vehicle rollovers. It is important to only use lift kits engineered for the particular vehicle. After installing such a kit, inform the driver of the effect that a higher center of gravity will have on vehicle operation.

Levers and Mechanical Advantage

Brake systems use levers and mechanical advantage to apply service and parking brakes. A simple example of a **lever** is a bar. The point around which a lever rotates and that supports the lever and the load is called the **fulcrum**. A lever allows the user to lift a large load over a small distance at one end by applying a small force over a greater distance from the other end. The effort distance is from

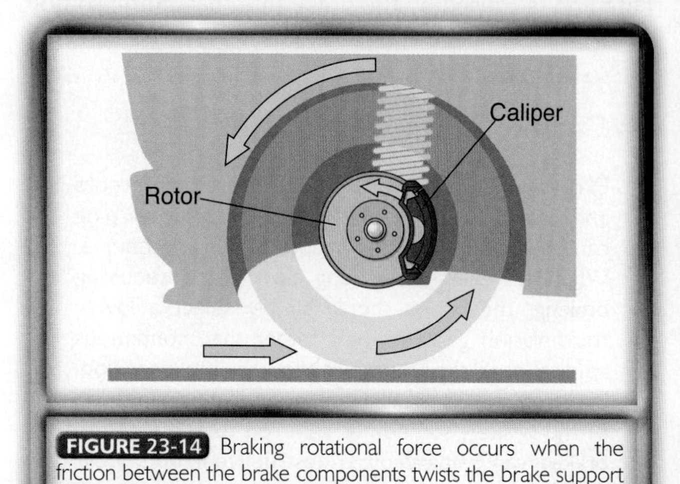
Caliper
Rotor

FIGURE 23-14 Braking rotational force occurs when the friction between the brake components twists the brake support in the direction of the wheel rotation.

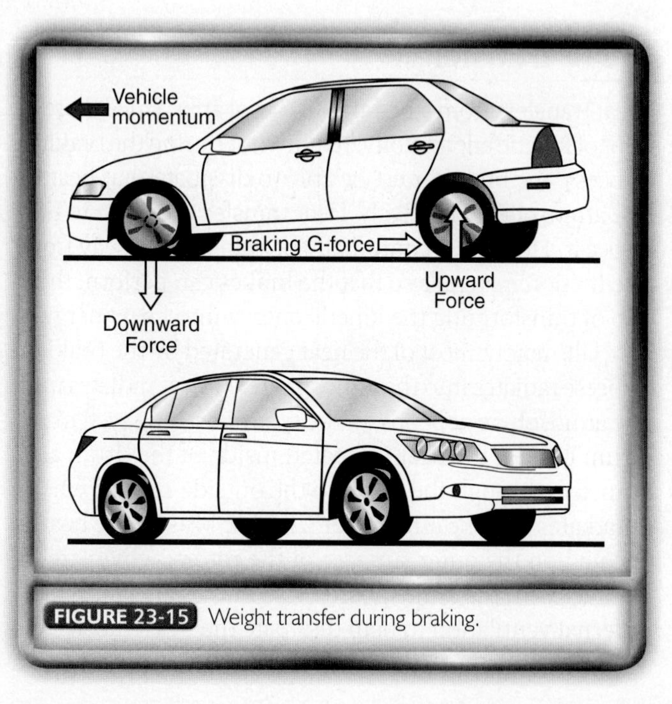
Vehicle momentum
Braking G-force
Upward Force
Downward Force

FIGURE 23-15 Weight transfer during braking.

the fulcrum to the point effort is applied. The load distance is from the fulcrum to the point the load is applied.

The effort required to move a load depends on the relative distance of the load and the effort from the fulcrum. The ratio of load and effort is called **mechanical advantage**. If the effort distance from the fulcrum is greater than the load distance, then the effort required will be less than the load being moved. If the load distance is greater than the effort distance, then the effort required is greater than the load being moved. This is known as a negative mechanical advantage or **mechanical disadvantage**.

Using the right kind of lever in the right way allows a user to move larger loads with less effort. There are three basic types of levers:

1. Lever of the first order: The fulcrum is in the middle, between the load and the effort FIGURE 23-16. Examples are a pry bar or a seesaw. The force applied in this situation is in the opposite direction of the load.
2. Lever of the second order: The load is in the middle, between the effort and the fulcrum FIGURE 23-17. An example is a wheelbarrow. The force applied in this situation is in the direction of the load. Brake pedals are usually of the second order. They pivot at the top end (fulcrum). The foot pressure (effort) is applied to the bottom end. And the master cylinder (load) is applied between the two. Mechanical advantage is engineered into the brake pedal to provide the proper brake pedal application and feel FIGURE 23-18.
3. Lever of the third order: The effort is in the middle, between the load and the fulcrum FIGURE 23-19. An example is an oar when paddling a canoe, where the hand holding the top of the oar is the fulcrum, the other hand holding the middle of the oar is providing the effort, and the water is the load. The force in this situation is in the direction of the load.

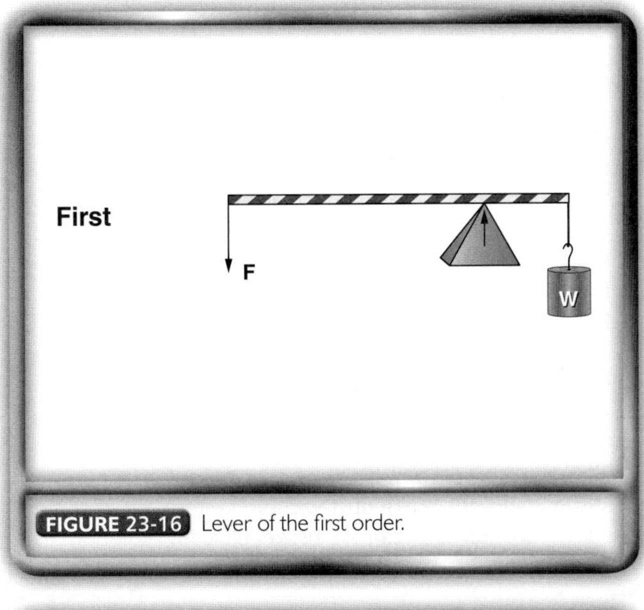
First
F
W

FIGURE 23-16 Lever of the first order.

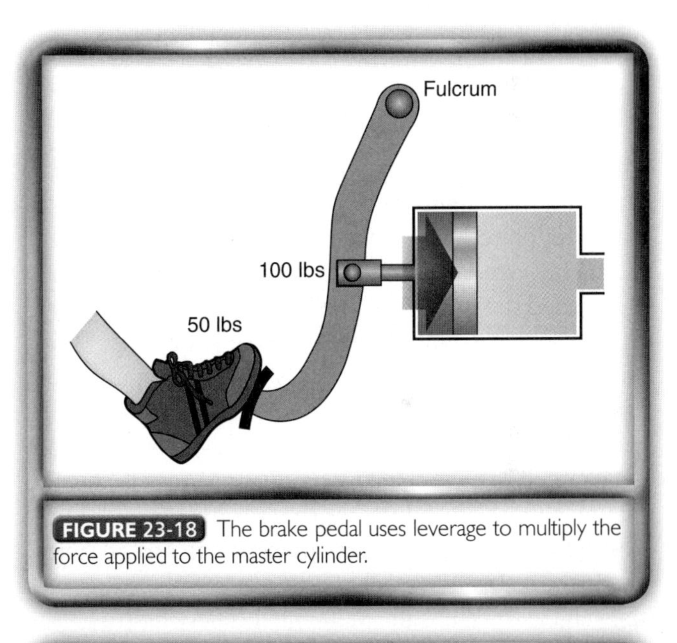
Fulcrum
100 lbs
50 lbs

FIGURE 23-18 The brake pedal uses leverage to multiply the force applied to the master cylinder.

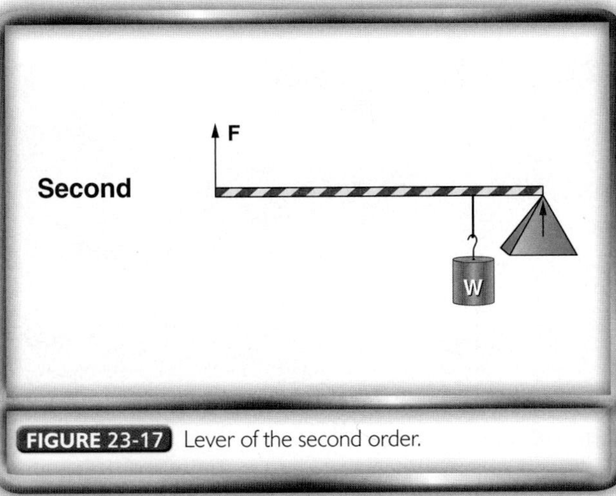
Second
F
W

FIGURE 23-17 Lever of the second order.

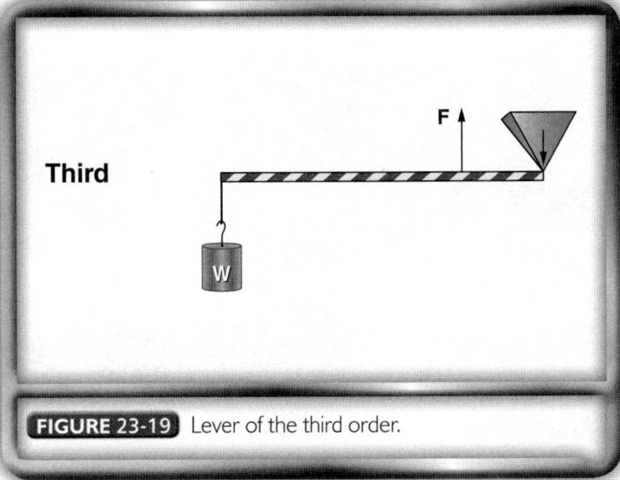
Third
F
W

FIGURE 23-19 Lever of the third order.

Applied Science

AS-12: Levers: The technician can explain how levers can be used to increase an applied force over distance. The lever action is applied many times on a daily basis. The simplest example is the use of a wrench. If a bolt or nut is tight, then instead of using a wrench with a short handle, you can use a wrench with a longer handle. The longer handle improves the lever's mechanical advantage by increasing the ratio of the effort distance to the load distance, thus providing more torque to undo the nut or bolt.

Adjustable Brake Pedal System

Some vehicles come equipped with adjustable pedal assemblies. Such assemblies allow the driver to raise or lower the brake and throttle pedal assembly for personal comfort. These are usually adjusted by electrically driven motors that are operated by a switch on the steering column or dash **FIGURE 23-20**.

Brake Repair Legal Standards and Technician Liability

Brake repair is right up with steering and suspension repair on the liability scale. Improperly repaired brakes can function reasonably well under normal driving situations but can fail during a panic situation when they are needed the most. The likelihood of accidents, injury, or death goes up drastically in those situations. Shops and technicians have been successfully sued for improper brake repairs resulting in large cash settlements. Technicians also risk being found criminally negligent if they are determined to have acted maliciously. Always follow the manufacturer's procedures when servicing brake systems. Research service information, precautions, and technical service bulletins. Never take shortcuts, which could cause the vehicle to be unsafe. Remember, safety first!

Types of Brakes

Now it is time to explore the different types of brakes used on various vehicles. Each vehicle application lends itself to a particular type of brake system. For example, consider trailers. Since they must be able to be hooked up to multiple tow vehicles, connecting a hydraulic brake system becomes difficult due to the leaking of hydraulic fluid as well as air entering the lines. Thus, some heavy trucks use air-operated brakes. That way, when connecting and disconnecting the brake air line, only air will leak, not brake fluid. On passenger-type tow vehicles, electric brakes are often used.

Drum and Disc Brakes

Friction brakes use two kinds of wheel brake units. Drum brakes have a drum attached to the wheel hub and rotate with the tire. Braking occurs by means of stationary brake shoes expanding against the inside of the drum, which creates friction and slows the vehicle. Disc brakes have

Safety

Asbestos is a naturally occurring mineral mined from the earth. Asbestos is a long, very thin fibrous crystal. When asbestos is disturbed, small needle-like fibers can break off and remain airborne, where they are inhaled by people. Since these fibers are so small, they embed themselves deep within lung tissue, causing scarring. Repeated exposure can lead to asbestosis and lung cancer.

While asbestos has been removed from most brake and clutch materials, it is still present in some replacement and old components. Therefore, you must treat all brake and clutch dust as if it contains asbestos. This is accomplished by using an aqueous brake wash station, a HEPA brake dust vacuum system, or, in some states, an aerosol can of brake cleaning solution to carefully wash down the brake components.

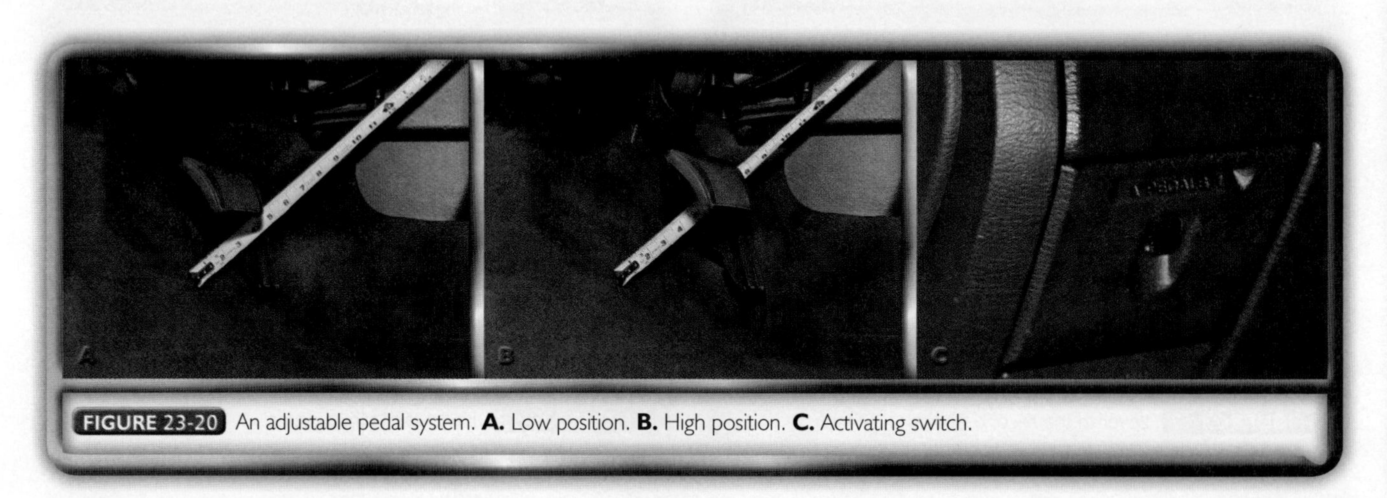

FIGURE 23-20 An adjustable pedal system. **A.** Low position. **B.** High position. **C.** Activating switch.

a disc brake rotor attached to the wheel hub and rotate with the tire. The braking occurs by means of stationary pads clamping against the outside of the rotor, creating friction to slow the vehicle. On light vehicles, both of these systems are hydraulically operated, meaning they use hydraulic fluid to transfer the force from the driver. The brake pedal operates a **master cylinder**. Hydraulic lines and hoses connect the master cylinder to the wheel brake units FIGURE 23-21.

Most modern light vehicles have either disc brakes on the front wheels and drum brakes on the rear or disc brakes on all four wheels. Disc brakes require greater force to operate than drum brakes and usually include a power brake booster to assist the driver by increasing the force applied to the master cylinder when the brake is operated FIGURE 23-22.

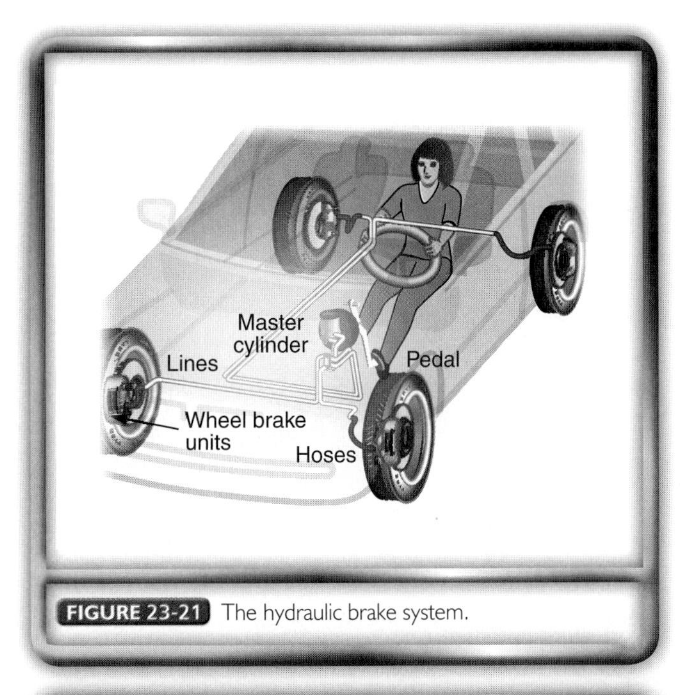
Master cylinder
Lines
Pedal
Wheel brake units
Hoses

FIGURE 23-21 The hydraulic brake system.

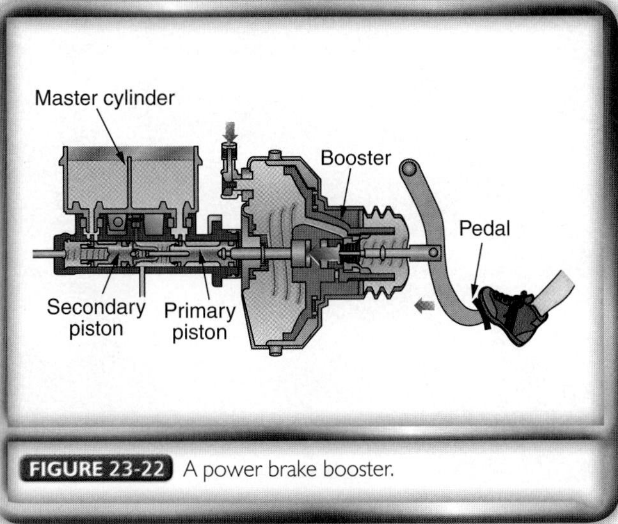
Master cylinder
Booster
Pedal
Secondary piston
Primary piston

FIGURE 23-22 A power brake booster.

Modern drum and disc brake systems are regularly fitted with an ABS that monitors the speed of each wheel and prevents wheel lock-up or skidding, no matter how hard brakes are applied or how slippery the road surface. This allows the driver to better maintain directional control of the vehicle. ABS also generally reduces stopping distances. The system consists of a brake pedal, power booster, master cylinder, wheel speed sensors, the electronic control unit (ECU), and the hydraulic control unit, also called a hydraulic modulator.

> **LINK**
> For more information on air-operated braking systems, see the chapter Hydraulics and Power Brakes.

Parking Brakes

As mentioned previously, all vehicles must be fitted with a service brake and a parking brake. The service brake is usually hydraulically operated and is used while the vehicle is being driven. It applies brake units at all four wheels. The parking brake is mechanically operated to hold the vehicle in place when it is parked. It applies the brake units on two wheels only.

There are several types of parking brakes. Some vehicles equipped with disc brakes incorporate a mechanically operated drum-style parking brake in the center of the rear disc brake rotors, commonly called a **top hat parking brake** design FIGURE 23-23. Other vehicles use a mechanical linkage to directly operate a disc-style service brake FIGURE 23-24.

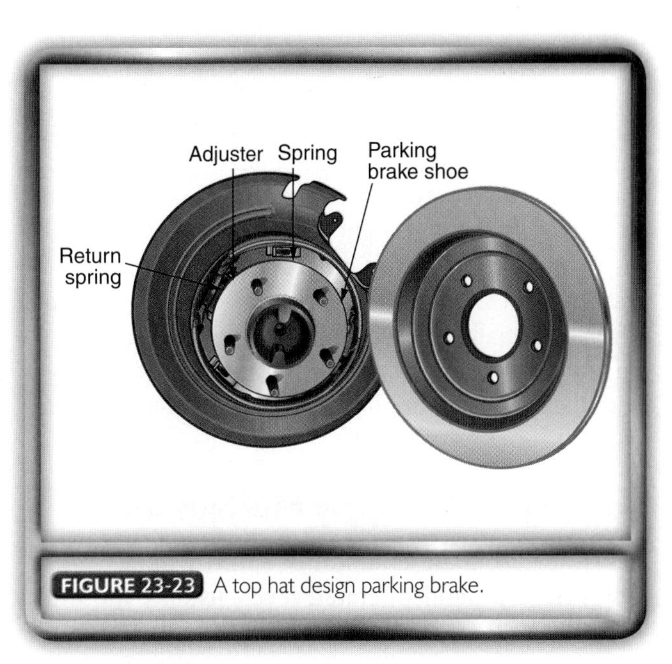
Adjuster
Spring
Parking brake shoe
Return spring

FIGURE 23-23 A top hat design parking brake.

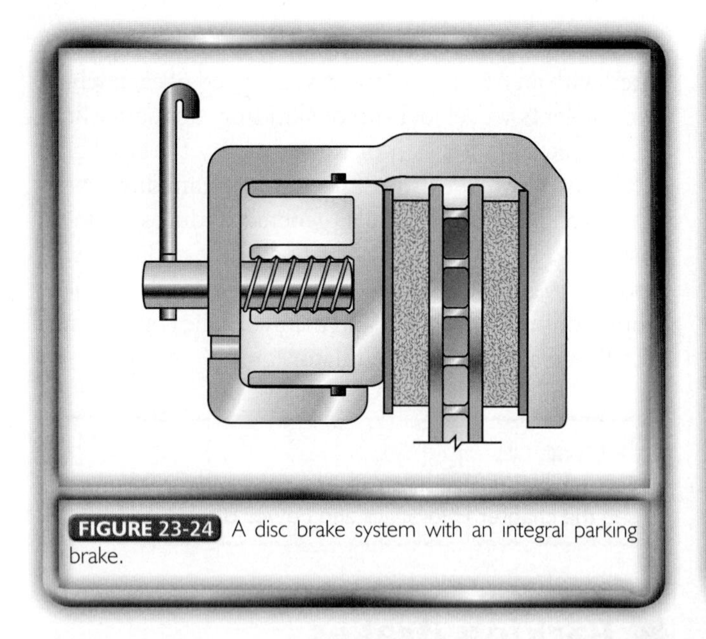
FIGURE 23-24 A disc brake system with an integral parking brake.

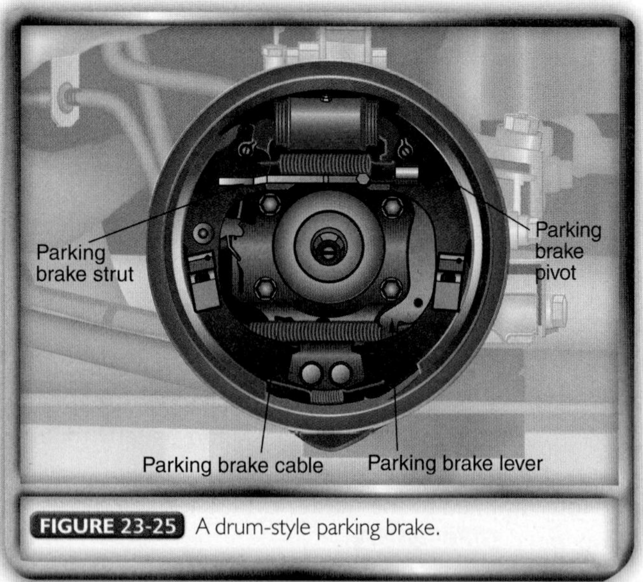
Parking brake strut
Parking brake pivot
Parking brake cable
Parking brake lever
FIGURE 23-25 A drum-style parking brake.

On drum brakes, a **drum-style parking brake** mechanically applies the brake shoes against the drum. The parking brake cable pulls on an actuating lever inside the brake drum assembly FIGURE 23-25. The actuating lever is connected to the secondary brake shoe by a pin or tang and to the primary shoe by a strut. Movement of the lever forces both shoes against the drum.

Less common, older arrangements of parking brakes include a front wheel–mounted parking brake, which activates each front brake caliper, and a **transmission-mounted parking brake**, which uses a small drum brake to prevent the drive shaft from turning FIGURE 23-26. This latter brake is sometimes called a transmission brake.

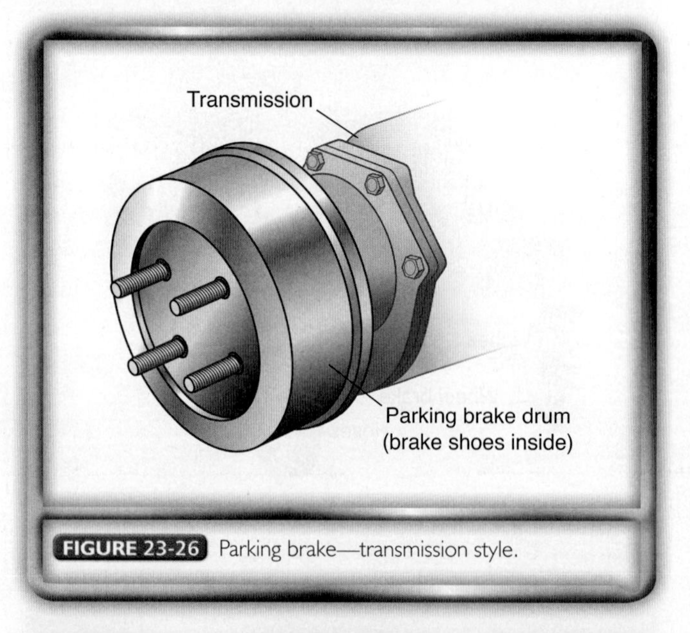
Transmission
Parking brake drum
(brake shoes inside)
FIGURE 23-26 Parking brake—transmission style.

Parking Brake Cables

Parking brake cables transmit force from the parking brake actuating lever to the brake unit. Part of the cable is inside a wound steel housing FIGURE 23-27, which allows it to be somewhat flexible, yet non-compressible to guide the cable and hold everything in place. Other sections of the cable are exposed, which can make them susceptible to damage by being caught on road hazards, especially on off-road vehicles. Also, since the cables are steel, they can rust and stick to the inside of the wound housing. This is especially true where de-icing chemicals are used on roads. Periodic lubrication of the parking brake cables with the lubricant specified by the vehicle manufacturer helps reduce this problem.

FIGURE 23-27 A parking brake cable.

Parking Brake Apply Mechanisms

Parking brakes are commonly applied in two ways. The first is a hand-operated lever, usually mounted between the front seats. The lever has its fulcrum on the bottom end, and the cable is attached a few inches from the fulcrum. The driver grasps the handle on the end opposite of the fulcrum, which gives the driver substantial mechanical advantage and ensures that the parking brake can be firmly applied. The handle contains a ratcheting mechanism that engages automatically when the driver pulls up on the parking brake lever. This mechanism holds the handle in the applied position and maintains tension on the parking brake cables and assembly. The driver can release the mechanism by lifting slightly up on the handle and pushing the release button, which retracts the ratcheting tab and allows the driver to lower the parking brake handle.

The second type of operating mechanism works similarly, but is foot operated. It uses mechanical advantage to firmly apply the parking brake, as well as a ratcheting mechanism to hold it once applied. It is usually mounted under the dash near the kick panel toward the outside of the car. Some foot-mounted parking brake levers can be released by pulling a release handle, which retracts the ratcheting tang and allows the pedal to return to its rest position. Other pedals can be released by simply pushing the pedal a bit farther down, which automatically retracts the ratchet and allows the pedal to return. The last method uses vacuum or electric power to release the parking brake when the gear selector is moved out of the park position.

Parking Brake Adjustment

Parking brake systems incorporate some method of adjustment, although it is not the same for all vehicles. The method of adjustment could be accomplished by an adjustment nut on the cable under the vehicle, an adjustment on the brake lever assembly, or an adjustment at the rear calipers FIGURE 23-28. When adjusting parking brakes, the order of adjustment is as follows: (1) the parking brake cable, which should have slack in it, (2) the service brakes, which are adjusted according to the manufacturer's procedure, and (3) the parking brake. This sequence will ensure that both brake systems are adjusted properly.

A
B
C

FIGURE 23-28 Methods of adjustment. **A.** Parking brake adjustment—under the car. **B.** Parking brake adjustment—brake lever. **C.** Parking brake adjustment—disc brake caliper.

Wrap-up

Ready for Review

- Braking systems evolved from scrub brakes to band brakes to the drum and disc brakes that are used today.
- Electronic brake systems use computer technology to assist with braking by determining speed and needed force to stop.
- The development of electronic brake systems has led to improvements in consumer safety and fuel economy.
- Brake-by-wire systems use computer technology in place of the mechanical or hydraulic connection between the brake pedal and wheel brake units.
- Regenerative brake systems (used in hybrid vehicles) convert a vehicle's energy into electrical energy, which is stored in the battery for later use.
- Factors affecting the effectiveness of braking systems include road surface, road conditions, vehicle weight and height, load on wheels, type of tire, and aggressive vs. defensive driving.
- Every vehicle has two brake systems: service brake (for stopping the vehicle in motion) and parking brake (for holding the vehicle when stationary).
- Hydraulically operated braking systems use a system of cylinders to transfer pressure from the brake pedal to the wheel.
- The braking system converts a vehicle's kinetic energy (the energy of an object in motion) into an alternate form of energy (e.g., heat).
- Acceleration and deceleration determine whether the vehicle's speed is increasing or decreasing. Both require an outside force for action, such as the vehicle's engine (acceleration) or braking system (deceleration).
- The law of conservation of energy requires that energy must be transformed from one form to another; it cannot be created or destroyed.
- Standard brakes use friction to create resistance, thus transforming kinetic energy into heat energy.
- The amount of force pushing two surfaces together compared to the amount of resistive force generated between the two surfaces sliding against each other is called the coefficient of friction.
- Heat energy created by the braking process gets dissipated into the atmosphere.
- Reduction in a vehicle's stopping power (brake fade) can be caused by heat fade, water fade, or hydraulic fade.
- Braking systems create rotational force on the vehicle's suspension, resulting in weight transfer to the front wheels.
- There are three types of levers: lever of the first order (fulcrum in the middle), lever of the second order (load in the middle), and lever of the third order (effort in the middle).
- Technicians can be held liable for improperly repaired brakes.
- Disc brakes and drum brakes are two types of friction brakes that are used on lighter vehicles; both can be equipped with antilock braking systems.
- Parking brake styles include: top hat parking brake, drum-style parking brake, and transmission-mounted parking brake.
- Parking brakes use a ratcheting mechanism to maintain tension on the parking brake cables and assembly when applied.

Key Terms

acceleration An increase in a vehicle's speed.

anti-lock brake system (ABS) A safety measure for the braking system that uses a computer to monitor the speed of each wheel and control the hydraulic pressure to each wheel to prevent wheel lock-up.

asbestos A mineral with needle-like fibers that can become embedded in lung tissue and cause cancer.

band brake A braking system that uses a metal band lined with friction material to clamp around the outside of a wheel or drum.

brake assist (BA) An enhanced safety system built in to some ABS systems that anticipates a panic stop and applies maximum braking force to slow the vehicle as quickly as possible.

brake-by-wire system A braking system that uses no mechanical connection between the brake pedal and each brake unit. The system uses electrically actuated motors to apply brake force.

brake fade The reduction in stopping power caused by a change in the brake system such as overheating, water, or overheated brake fluid.

brake pedal emulator A brake pedal assembly used in electronically controlled braking systems to send the driver's braking intention to the computer; it mimics the feel of a standard brake pedal.

brakes A system made up of hydraulic and mechanical components designed to slow or stop a vehicle.

coefficient of friction The amount of friction between two moving surfaces in contact with each other.

conservation of energy A physical law that states that energy cannot be created or destroyed.

deceleration A decrease in a vehicle's speed.

disc brakes A type of brake system that forces stationary brake pads against the outside of a rotating brake rotor.

drum brakes A type of brake system that forces brake shoes against the inside of a brake drum.

drum-style parking brake A mechanically operated drum brake that can be set while the vehicle is not moving to serve as a parking brake.

friction The resistance created by surfaces in contact. Kinetic friction is resistance to motion when one surface moves over another. Static friction is resistance to motion between two surfaces that are not moving.

fulcrum The point around which a lever rotates and that supports the lever and the load.

heat fade Brake fade caused by the buildup of heat in braking surfaces, which get so hot they cannot create any additional heat, leading to a loss of friction.

hydraulic fade Brake fade caused by boiling brake fluid.

kinetic energy The energy of an object in motion; it increases by the square of the speed.

lever A tool that allows the user to move a large load over a small distance at one end by applying a small force over a greater distance from the other end.

master cylinder Converts the brake pedal force into hydraulic pressure, which is then transmitted via brake lines and hoses to one or more pistons at each wheel brake unit.

mechanical advantage The ratio of load and effort for any simple machine such as a lever.

mechanical disadvantage When the load distance on a lever is greater than the effort distance, which means the effort required to move the load is greater than the load itself.

Newton's first law of motion A physical law that states that "an object will stay at rest or uniform speed unless it is acted upon by an outside force."

parking brake A brake system used for holding the vehicle when it is stationary.

parking brake cable A mechanism used to transmit force from the parking brake actuating lever to the brake unit.

rotational force The force created by the rotating wheel when the brakes are applied; it causes the brake components to twist the brake support and ultimately the vehicle in the direction of wheel rotation.

scrub brakes A brake system that uses leverage to force a friction block against one or more wheels.

service brake A brake system that is operated while the vehicle is moving to slow or stop the vehicle.

top hat parking brake A drum brake that is located inside a disc brake rotor in order to act as a parking brake.

transmission-mounted parking brake A drum brake that is mounted on the drive shaft just after the transmission to serve as a parking brake.

water fade Brake fade caused by water-soaked brake linings.

weight transfer Weight moving from one set of wheels to the other set of wheels during braking, acceleration, or cornering.

ASE-Type Questions

1. Tech A says that regenerative braking converts brake heat into electricity. Tech B says that regenerative braking converts electrical energy into braking energy. Who is correct?
   a. Tech A
   b. Tech B
   c. Both A and B
   d. Neither A nor B
2. Tech A says that an anti-lock brake system (ABS) allows the front wheels to be steered during a panic stop. Tech B says that ABS sensor inputs control wheel speed during brake events. Who is correct?
   a. Tech A
   b. Tech B
   c. Both A and B
   d. Neither A nor B
3. Tech A says that water soaked brake shoes will cause brake fade. Tech B says that disc brakes dissipate heat faster than drum brakes. Who is correct?
   a. Tech A
   b. Tech B
   c. Both A and B
   d. Neither A nor B
4. Tech A says that a brake-by-wire system can start to apply brakes before the driver can step on the brake pedal. Tech B says that brake-by-wire systems use heavy cables to transmit the brake pedal force to the wheel brake units. Who is correct?
   a. Tech A
   b. Tech B
   c. Both A and B
   d. Neither A nor B
5. Tech A says that tire pressure does not affect braking. Tech B says that heavy vehicle loads increase stopping distance. Who is correct?
   a. Tech A
   b. Tech B
   c. Both A and B
   d. Neither A nor B
6. Tech A says that light-duty service brakes are applied hydraulically. Tech B says that light-duty parking brakes are applied hydraulically. Who is correct?
   a. Tech A
   b. Tech B
   c. Both A and B
   d. Neither A nor B
7. Tech A says that the heavier the vehicle, the more stopping power is needed. Tech B says that the faster a vehicle is moving, the more braking power is needed. Who is correct?
   a. Tech A
   b. Tech B
   c. Both A and B
   d. Neither A nor B
8. Tech A says that kinetic energy is created during braking to stop the vehicle. Tech B says that kinetic energy is converted to heat energy during braking. Who is correct?
   a. Tech A
   b. Tech B
   c. Both A and B
   d. Neither A nor B
9. Tech A says that the brake pedal uses leverage to multiply foot pressure. Tech B says that when braking hard while moving forward, the vehicle's weight transfers to the rear wheels, increasing their traction. Who is correct?
   a. Tech A
   b. Tech B
   c. Both A and B
   d. Neither A nor B
10. Tech A says that friction brakes can fade due to overheating of the brake lining. Tech B says that friction brakes can fade due to overheating of the brake fluid. Who is correct?
    a. Tech A
    b. Tech B
    c. Both A and B
    d. Neither A nor B

CHAPTER 24

KNOW
SEE
DO
PROVE

NATEF Tasks

Brakes
Hydraulic System

			Page
■ Select, handle, store, and fill brake fluids to proper level.	MLR	AST	672–674
■ Test brake fluid for contamination.	MLR	AST	672–675
■ Bleed and/or flush brake system.	MLR	AST	675–678
■ Measure brake pedal height, travel, and free play (as applicable); determine necessary action.	MLR	AST	678–679
■ Check master cylinder for internal/external leaks and proper operation; determine necessary action.	MLR	AST	679–680
■ Remove, bench bleed, and reinstall master cylinder.		AST	679–681
■ Diagnose pressure concerns in the brake system using hydraulic principles (Pascal's Law).		AST	680–682
■ Inspect brake lines, flexible hoses, and fittings for leaks, dents, kinks, rust, cracks, bulging, wear, loose fittings and supports; determine necessary action.	MLR	AST	685–686
■ Replace brake lines, hoses, fittings, and supports.		AST	685–686
■ Fabricate brake lines using proper material and flaring procedures (double flare and ISO types).		AST	687
■ Inspect, test, and/or replace components of brake warning light system.		AST	688–690
■ Identify components of brake warning light system.	MLR	AST	688–689

Hydraulics and Power Brakes

NATEF Tasks, continued

Power Assist Units			Page
■ Check brake pedal travel with, and without, engine running to verify proper power booster operation.	MLR	AST	682–683
■ Check vacuum supply (manifold or auxiliary pump) to vacuum-type power booster.	MLR	AST	683–685
■ Inspect vacuum-type power booster unit for leaks; inspect the check-valve for proper operation; determine necessary action.		AST	683–684
Miscellaneous			
■ Check parking brake operation and parking brake indicator light system operation; determine necessary action.	MLR	AST	689–691
■ Check parking brake cables and components for wear, binding, and corrosion; clean, lubricate, adjust or replace as needed.	MLR	AST	691
■ Check operation of brake stop light system.	MLR	AST	691

KNOW
SEE
DO

Knowledge Objectives

After reading this chapter, you will be able to:

1. Describe the principles behind the hydraulic braking system. (pp 653–655)
2. Describe the principles of hydraulic pressure and force, and discuss how the principles apply to the hydraulic braking system. (pp 653–655)
3. Describe the principles of working pressures, input force, and output force, and discuss how the principles apply to the hydraulic braking system. (p 654)
4. Define Pascal's law and discuss how it applies to the hydraulic braking system. (pp 653–655)
5. Describe the role of brake fluid in a hydraulic braking system. (pp 655–656)
6. Describe the purpose of a master cylinder. (pp 656–660)
7. Describe how master cylinders operate within the hydraulic braking system. (pp 656–660)

Knowledge Objectives, continued

8. Describe the purpose of a brake pedal. (pp 660–661)
9. Describe how brake pedals operate within the hydraulic braking system. (p 661)
10. Describe the purpose and standard materials of brake lines. (pp 661–663)
11. Describe how to inspect and replace brake lines and brake hoses. (p 663)
12. List the types of brake line flares. (p 663)
13. Describe the purpose and standard materials of brake hoses. (pp 663–664)
14. List the common issues in brake hoses. (pp 664–665)
15. Describe how a proportioning valve operates. (pp 665–666)
16. Describe the purpose of a metering valve and how it operates. (pp 666–667)
17. Describe the purpose of a pressure differential valve and how it operates. (pp 667–668)
18. Describe how brake warning lights and stop lights operate. (pp 668–669)
19. Discuss how to diagnose common issues with brake warning lights and stop lights. (p 669)
20. Describe the types of power brakes. (pp 669–670)
21. Describe how a vacuum booster operates. (pp 670–671)
22. Discuss how to diagnose common issues with power brake systems. (pp 672–675)
23. Discuss the common questions to ask the customer during diagnosis of a fault in the hydraulic braking system. (pp 680–682)

Know
See
Do
Prove

Skills Objectives

After reading this chapter, you will be able to:

1. Select, handle, store, and fill brake fluid. (pp 672–673)
2. Perform a DVOM–galvanic reaction test. (p 674)
3. Test brake fluid with a brake fluid tester. (p 674)
4. Test brake fluid with brake fluid test strips. (p 665)
5. Perform the manual bleeding method. (pp 675–676)
6. Perform the pressure bleeding method. (pp 675–677)
7. Perform the vacuum bleeding method. (pp 675–677)
8. Measure the brake pedal height. (p 679)
9. Measure the brake pedal free play. (p 679)
10. Measure brake pedal travel. (p 679)
11. Perform a master cylinder inspection. (pp 679–681)
12. Perform master cylinder service and bench bleed. (pp 679–681)
13. Test the brake pedal free travel and check the power assist operation. (pp 682–683)
14. Check the vacuum supply to a vacuum-type power booster. (pp 683–685)
15. Check a vacuum-type power booster unit for leaks and inspect the check valve. (pp 683–685)
16. Inspect the brake lines, brake hoses, and associated hardware. (pp 685–686)
17. Replace the brake lines, hoses, fittings, and supports. (pp 685–686)
18. Perform the ISO flare method on a brake line. (p 687)
19. Perform the double flare method on a brake line. (p 687)
20. Check the brake light warning system. (pp 689–690)
21. Check the parking brake and indicator light system. (p 689)
22. Inspect and maintain parking brakes. (p 691)
23. Check operation of a stop light system. (p 691)

Introduction

In most modern vehicles, the wheel brake units are applied using the principles of hydraulics. This means the brakes are operated by the force transferred by non-compressible brake fluid flowing through the brake lines and hoses. Pressing down on the brake pedal creates pressure in the brake fluid, which transmits that pressure to the brake units, which apply force to the friction materials, which transform the kinetic energy of the moving vehicle into heat energy and cause the vehicle to decelerate.

To make it easier for the driver to apply the brakes, a power booster is fitted to the brake system to increase the driver's brake pedal force to the master cylinder. This power booster can be operated by engine vacuum or through hydraulic pressure, which is usually generated by the power steering pump or an electric-driven pump.

Principles of Hydraulics

Pascal's Law(s)

In the 1600s, Blaise Pascal observed the effects of pressure applied to a fluid in a closed system. **Pascal's law** states that "pressure applied to a fluid in one part of a closed system will be transmitted without loss to all other areas of the system." This law is the principle behind hydraulic brakes. Pressure created in the master cylinder is transmitted through the hydraulic braking system as long as the system remains closed and has no leaks. In a closed system, hydraulic pressure is transmitted equally in all directions throughout the system. What happens to the pressure levels if there is a leak in the system? According to Pascal's law, a substantial leak will prevent the pressure from building up and therefore the pressure within the system will be equally low. This means that the vehicle may lose some or all of its braking ability if a leak develops.

Pascal's law helps in diagnosing problems with the hydraulic braking system. For example, if the brake pedal is squishy (soft or spongy), there is a good chance that the hydraulic braking system has air in it and needs to be bled. If the brake pedal slowly sinks to the floor, there is likely a small leak in the system that needs to be found. If the vehicle pulls to one side, it could be that a brake hose is plugged up and is not transmitting pressure to one of the brake units.

Hydraulic Pressure and Force

Varying amounts of mechanical force can be extracted from a single amount of hydraulic pressure. Since pressure is force per unit area (e.g., 50 pounds per square inch [psi], or 344.7 kPa), the same pressure applied over different-sized surface areas will produce different levels of force FIGURE 24-1. This principle allows engineers to design brakes to have a precise amount of braking force at each wheel. For example, the front wheels

You Are the Automotive Technician

A customer brings his 2007 Chevrolet Tahoe with 96,000 miles to the shop to have a brake concern addressed. The vehicle is regularly driven on the beach and has been pulling to the left, especially after braking. It has gotten worse over the last few weeks. You check the service history and see that the front brake pads were replaced, the rotors refinished, and the brake fluid flushed three years ago at 54,000 miles. Before road testing the vehicle, you ask yourself these questions.

1. What faults in the brakes system could cause the vehicle to pull to the left?
2. How can Pascal's Law be used to help you to diagnose this problem?
3. What are some tests you can perform to help diagnose the fault?

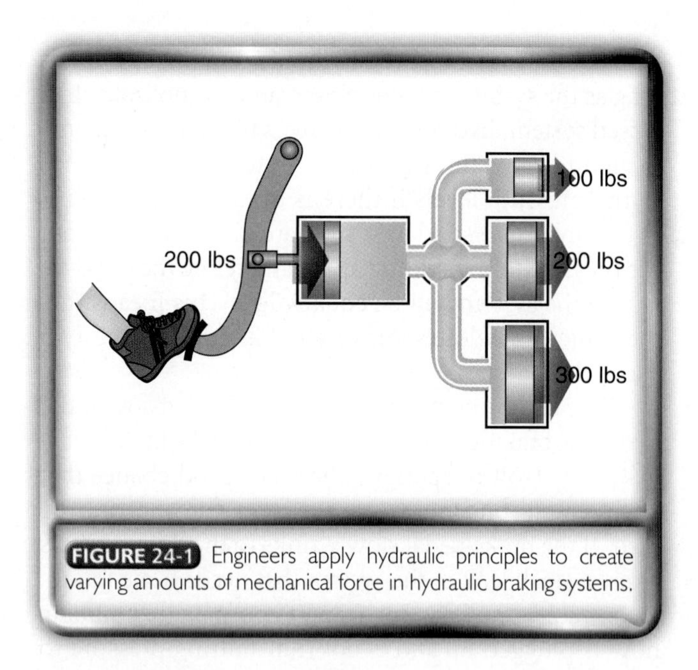
100 lbs
200 lbs
200 lbs
300 lbs

FIGURE 24-1 Engineers apply hydraulic principles to create varying amounts of mechanical force in hydraulic braking systems.

on some front-wheel drive vehicles can produce up to 80% of the vehicle's stopping power due to the weight distribution and weight transfer. For these vehicles to brake smoothly, more pressure must be applied to the front brake units than the rear brake units. This is accomplished through the front and rear brake pistons. The larger brake pistons on the front wheels give greater mechanical force and braking power to the front wheels.

Figure 24-1 illustrates a hydraulic system that has cylinders of different sizes. When the brake pedal is pressed, the force against the piston in the master cylinder applies pressure to the brake fluid. This same pressure is transmitted equally throughout the fluid, but each output piston develops a certain amount of force depending on its diameter (surface area). The top cylinder is smaller than the master cylinder, so the amount of force it exerts will be less than the force applied to the master cylinder. The middle cylinder is the same size as the master cylinder, so the force will be the same. The bottom cylinder is larger than the master cylinder, and so its force will be greater.

There are three variables to consider when talking about pressure and force in hydraulic systems:

- Input force: The force applied to the input piston is measured in pounds (lb), newtons, or kilograms (kg). For example, if 100 lb (45.36 kg) of force were applied to the input piston, this force would be labeled as 100 lb (45.36 kg).
- Working pressure: The working pressure of the hydraulic fluid is expressed as the amount of force per specified area. For example, 100 lb of force per square inch is labeled as 100 psi. It could also be expressed as 689.5 kilopascals (kPa). Note, 1 pascal = 1 newton per square meter, or 1 N/m^2. To find the working pressure, take the input force and divide it by the area of the input piston. The example of 100 lb (45.36 kg) of force applied to a 1-square inch piston creates 100 psi of working pressure. The same 100 lb of force applied to a 0.5-square inch piston creates 200 psi of working pressure (100/0.5 = 200 psi). Conversely, the 100 lb of force applied to a 2-square inch piston creates 50 psi of working pressure.
- Output force: Output force is exerted by the output piston and is expressed as pounds, newtons, or kilograms. Finding this measurement is fairly simple: Take the working pressure and multiply it by the surface area of the output piston. For example, 200 psi of working pressure pushing on a 1-square inch piston exerts 200 lb of force. The same 200 psi of working pressure acting on a 0.5-square inch output piston will create 100 lb of output force. And if 200 psi of working pressure is applied to a 2-square inch output piston, 400 lb of force will be created.

Safety

It is critical that the hydraulic portion of the brake system not have any leaks or weak spots that could fail and cause leaks. Failure of the braking system could occur, putting the driver, passengers, and others in danger. Vehicles operated in corrosive environments, such as in areas where salt and certain de-icers are used, are susceptible to brake line corrosion. Inspect all vehicles carefully for potential brake fluid leaks.

TECHNICIAN TIP

Input force, output force, and working pressure are optimized during the design of the hydraulic system based on a specific vehicle application. This is one reason why it is never acceptable to arbitrarily substitute hydraulic components from another vehicle.

> **TECHNICIAN TIP**

There are very few adjustable components in the hydraulic brake system. One notable exception is the load-sensitive proportioning valve, which is used on some pickup trucks and other load-carrying vehicles. Load-sensing proportioning valves operate so that as load weight increases, more brake pressure is applied to the rear wheels as required.

In the case of a rear-wheel lock-up on one of these vehicles, excessive pressure to the rear brakes may be suspected. To check the operation and adjustment of load-sensing proportioning valves, pressure gauges are fitted in-line to the front and rear brakes. After the hydraulic brake system is opened to install the gauges, air is bled out before accurate readings can be obtained.

The weight on the rear axle must be set according to charts or graphs published by the manufacturer to determine the correct relationship between front and rear pressure at a given load. For example, according to a graph in the service information, if a rear axle is loaded to 1984 lb (900 kg), and front brake pressure is raised to 1138 psi (7846 kPa), then rear brake pressure should fall within the range of 569 to 711 psi (3923 to 4902 kPa). The rear axle is then loaded to 3700 lb (1678 kg). If the rear pressure is outside the specified range, adjustment of the linkage between the proportioning valve and the rear suspension may be required.

Rear Axle Load lb (kg)	Front Brake Pressure psi (kPa)	Rear Brake Pressure psi (kPa)
1984 (900)	1138 (7846)	569–711 (3923–4902)
3699 (1678)	1707 (11769)	1323–1493 (9122–10294)

Hydraulic Components

The hydraulic system is made up of a number of components that work together to transmit the driver's effort to the brake pads or shoes. These components must be able to withstand the force, pressure, and temperatures generated in the hydraulic system. They must also be protected from the elements, as they are generally exposed to weather and road hazards. In this section we will explore each of the basic components of the hydraulic braking system.

Brake Fluid

Types and Characteristics

Brake fluid is hydraulic fluid that has specific properties designed for mobile applications. It is used to transfer force while under pressure through hydraulic lines to the wheel braking units. Braking applications produce heat, so the brake fluid used must have a high boiling point to remain effective under extreme temperatures. If brake fluid boils, it turns from a liquid to a vapor, which is compressible. This will cause a spongy brake pedal and loss of braking ability. Brake fluid must also have a low freezing point so it will not freeze or thicken in cold conditions. If this were to happen, the force from the brake pedal would not be transferred to the wheel brake units.

Standard brake fluid is harmful to painted surfaces because it tends to soften paint; it must therefore be kept off all painted surfaces. Standard brake fluid is also **hygroscopic**, which means it absorbs water. It can absorb water from the atmosphere when it comes into contact with the air in the master cylinder reservoir. Over time, it can even absorb moisture through the flexible brake hoses. Since water boils at a lower temperature than brake fluid, this will gradually reduce the brake fluid's boiling point, making the fluid more likely to boil and cause a hydraulic braking failure. Brake fluid must be flushed periodically to replace old contaminated fluid with new brake fluid to ensure the continued effectiveness of the hydraulic braking system.

> **TECHNICIAN TIP**

Even if they have similar base composition, brake fluids with different Department of Transportation (DOT) ratings should not be mixed.

> **Safety**

Because silicone-based fluid tends to **aerate** (tendency to create air bubbles) when forced at high pressure through small passages, it is *not* to be used in any vehicle equipped with anti-lock brakes (ABS). The control valves in ABS brakes would cause DOT 5 brake fluid to aerate under an active ABS stop. This would lead to a spongy pedal and poor brake application.

> **TECHNICIAN TIP**
>
> If the brake system needs to be bled, then the brake fluid should be tested to see if it needs to be flushed out with and replaced with new brake fluid.

Brake fluids are graded against compliance standards set by the United States Department of Transportation (DOT) TABLE 24-1. Brake fluids that meet these standards qualify for the DOT rating and are considered to be quality brake fluids. Brake fluids are tested to ensure they meet the standards for:

- pH value
- Viscosity
- Resistance to oxidation
- Stability
- Boiling point

Master Cylinder

The master cylinder converts the brake pedal force into hydraulic pressure that is transferred to the wheel brake units. Its mounting ears allow it to be mounted to a power booster or the firewall. The cylinder itself has threaded passageways to which the brake lines firmly connect, and a brake fluid reservoir supplies the brake system with an adequate amount of brake fluid. The master cylinder piston is operated by a pushrod from the power booster or the brake pedal.

While all vehicles manufactured for sale in the United States are required to use tandem master cylinders for safety purposes, we will start our discussion with the less-complicated single-piston master cylinder.

Single-Piston Master Cylinder

Single-piston master cylinders have one piston with two cups: a primary cup and a secondary cup FIGURE 24-2. These cups are also known as seals because they keep the brake fluid from leaking past the piston. When force is

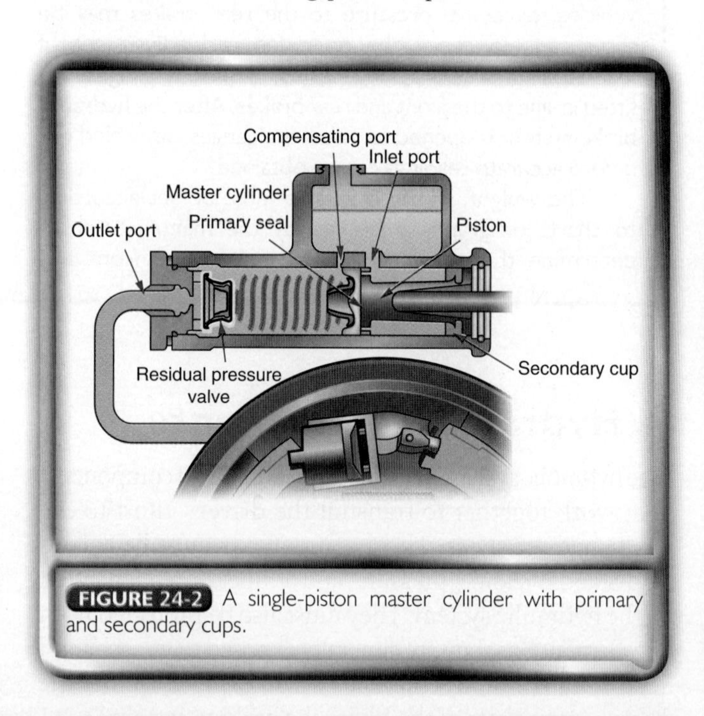
Compensating port
Inlet port
Master cylinder
Primary seal
Outlet port
Piston
Residual pressure valve
Secondary cup

FIGURE 24-2 A single-piston master cylinder with primary and secondary cups.

TABLE 24-1: DOT Ratings for Brake Fluid

Type	Materials	Minimum Dry Boiling Point	Minimum Wet Boiling Point	Additional Specifications
DOT 2	Castor oil-based	Not specified	Not specified	• Outdated type of brake fluid that should not be used in any modern vehicles
DOT 3	Various glycol esters and ethers	401°F (205°C)	284°F (140°C)	
DOT 4	Various glycol esters and ethers	446°F (230°C)	311°F (155°C)	
DOT 5	Silicone-based	500°F (260°C)	356°F (180°C)	• Not hygroscopic, will not absorb water • Less harmful to painted surfaces than glycol-based brake fluids • Provides better protection against corrosion • More suitable for use in wet driving conditions • NOT to be used in any vehicle equipped with anti-lock brakes (ABS)
DOT 5.1	Contains polyalkylene glycol ether	Not specified	375°F (190.6°C)	• Suitable for ABS-equipped vehicles due to high boiling point • More expensive than other brake fluids

Source: United States Department of Transportation, Federal Motor Carrier Safety Administration: S5.1.2 Wet ERBP.

applied to the piston by the pushrod, the **primary cup** seals the pressure in the cylinder, while the **secondary cup** prevents loss of fluid past the rear end of the piston. An **outlet port** links the cylinder to the brake lines. An **inlet port** connects the reservoir with the space around the piston and between the piston cups. A **compensating port** connects the reservoir to the cylinder, just barely ahead of the primary cup.

With the brake pedal in the released position, the compensating port connects the brake system with the reservoir. The compensating port adjusts for changes in the volume of the brake fluid ahead of the piston. This occurs due to the expansion or contraction of the brake fluid as it heats up or cools down. It can also compensate for brake fluid that does not return to the master cylinder due to worn disc brake pads moving the caliper pistons outward, increasing the brake fluid volume in the caliper. In this way, brake fluid can move as needed between the reservoir and the master cylinder bore.

As the pushrod from the brake pedal or power booster moves the piston forward, the compensating port is closed off, trapping brake fluid ahead of the primary cup. Fluid can no longer return to the reservoir. Fluid trapped in the cylinder is then forced from the master cylinder outlet port into the brake lines.

When the brakes are released, the master cylinder piston returns to its original position by action of the spring. When the piston fully returns against its stop, the primary cup uncovers the compensating port. Fluid ahead of the primary cup can now return to the reservoir as needed.

When the brake pedal is released quickly, a spring in the brake pedal pushes the piston back quickly. However, because of the restrictions in the hydraulic system, the brake fluid cannot return as quickly to the cylinder, creating a low-pressure area ahead of the primary cup. As a result, air can be drawn into the system at the wheel cylinders on a drum brake system. To prevent this, small holes are drilled in the piston so that brake fluid from the reservoir can pass through the inlet port and past the edge of the primary cup, thus preventing a vacuum from being created. This is called **recuperation** FIGURE 24-3.

On a drum brake system, when the brake fluid in the lines returns to the master cylinder, brake fluid pressure is held slightly above atmospheric pressure by a valve called the **residual pressure valve**. The residual pressure helps to stop air from entering at the wheel cylinder cups when the brakes are not being applied. The residual pressure valve is located at the outlet end of the master cylinder on single-piston master cylinders, or under the tube seats on tandem master cylinders. Residual pressure valves are not used on disc brake circuits, as the caliper piston seal seals tightly between the piston and bore so air cannot be easily drawn past it into the hydraulic system. Also, the small residual pressure would keep the brake pads slightly applied to the brake rotors causing brake drag, premature wear, and reduced fuel mileage.

Tandem Master Cylinder

With a single-piston master cylinder in the braking system, any fluid leak could mean the whole braking system fails. To reduce this risk, modern vehicles must have at least two separate hydraulic braking systems, hence the development of the tandem master cylinder. If one system fails, the other system can still provide a measure of braking ability, although it will not be as effective. For example, the pressure can be 0 psi (0 kPa) in one circuit and normal in the other circuit. **Tandem master cylinders** combine two master cylinders within a common housing that share a common cylinder bore FIGURE 24-4.

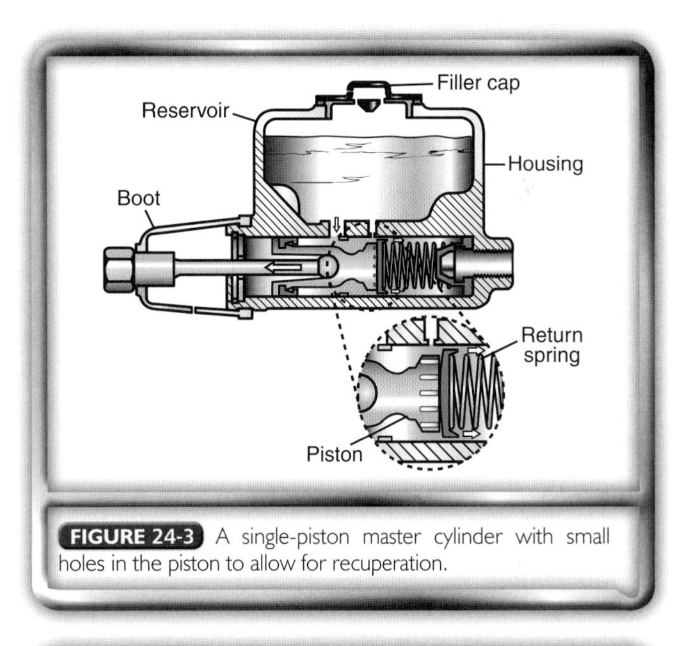
Filler cap
Reservoir
Housing
Boot
Return spring
Piston

FIGURE 24-3 A single-piston master cylinder with small holes in the piston to allow for recuperation.

Secondary piston
Primary piston
Master cylinder

FIGURE 24-4 A tandem master cylinder showing common cylinder.

The two systems can be **split front to rear** so that the front brakes operate from one circuit and the rear brakes from the other. They also can be **split diagonally** so that one front wheel is paired with the rear wheel on the opposite side of the vehicle in one brake circuit, and vice versa in the other circuit.

Like two single-piston cylinders built end to end, a tandem cylinder has a primary piston and a secondary piston. The **primary piston** is in the rear of the cylinder. It is called primary since it is pushed directly by the pushrod. The **secondary piston** is in the front of the cylinder. The secondary piston has a rear-facing seal that seals fluid in the primary chamber and is what ultimately pushes the secondary piston during normal operation. Each half of the cylinder has an inlet port, an outlet port, and a compensating port. There can be two separate reservoirs feeding each half of the cylinder, or just one reservoir divided into separate sections. In the event of a hydraulic leak, a single reservoir with undivided sections would allow brake fluid to become so low in the reservoir that the working side of the system would draw in air and cause the brakes to fail completely.

When the brakes are applied, the primary piston moves forward and closes its compensating port. Continued movement of the piston causes fluid pressure in front of the primary piston to rise, which acts upon the secondary piston, moving it forward and closing its compensating port. Pressure now builds up equally in both circuits of the master cylinder. Both pistons continue moving forward, displace fluid into their separate circuits, and apply the brake units on each wheel.

Just like the single-piston master cylinder, the tandem master cylinder can have problems with a low-pressure area developing when the piston returns quickly but the brake fluid lags. The tandem master cylinder overcomes this by using holes in the piston and grooves in the side of the primary cup. These primary cup grooves allow brake fluid to flow from the inlet port into the low-pressure area, preventing air from entering the system.

If there is a failure in the secondary circuit, the primary system pushes the secondary piston until it contacts the end of the cylinder bore. Once that happens, the primary circuit can start building pressure and operate its brake units. In this situation, it operates but with increased pedal travel. If the primary circuit fails, no pressure is generated to move the secondary piston; thus a rod attached to the front of the primary piston will push the secondary piston directly so that it is still able to generate pressure to operate its brake units. This also results in a lower than normal brake pedal. A differential pressure switch in the master cylinder or hydraulic system can illuminate the brake warning light on the instrument panel, alerting the driver of loss of pressure between the two hydraulic circuits.

Quick Take-up Master Cylinders

Quick take-up master cylinders are used on disc brake systems that are equipped with low-drag brake calipers. These calipers are designed to maintain a larger running clearance between the disc brake pads and rotor. If a standard master cylinder were used, the brake pedal would have to be pushed much farther down before the running clearance would be overcome and the pads would contact the rotor. Hence, a quick take-up master cylinder was designed. It uses a relatively large-diameter piston in the rear of the cylinder to push a large volume of fluid into the hydraulic system at low pressure. This moves the brake pads into contact with the rotor. Once the pressure rises above a predetermined point, a **quick take-up valve** opens and bleeds off any extra pressure created by the large piston **FIGURE 24-5**. At this point a smaller-diameter piston takes over and builds pressure within the hydraulic system to apply the brakes normally.

ABS Master Cylinders

The ABS master cylinder is a tandem master cylinder used in divided systems. It has a primary piston and a secondary piston. It may also incorporate the quick take-up principles of operation. In some applications, the compensating port in the secondary chamber is removed, so there is only an inlet port on the secondary piston. The primary chamber still uses a compensating port and an inlet port. The secondary piston incorporates a center valve that controls the opening and closing of a supply port drilled into the piston. At rest, the supply port is open and connects the reservoir with the front brake circuits. This supply port replaces the compensating port in a normal master cylinder **FIGURE 24-6**. The primary piston still has an inlet port and a compensating port.

When the brake pedal is applied, the primary piston moves and closes its compensating port. Brake fluid pressure in the primary circuit rises and acts with the primary piston spring to move the secondary piston forward, closing the center valve. The pressure builds in the secondary circuit. Pressure keeps building in both circuits and applies force in both circuits. If there is a leak in either circuit, the master cylinder acts like a standard master cylinder and builds pressure in the working circuit.

When the brake pedal is released, the springs in the master cylinder push both pistons back more quickly than the brake fluid can return from the wheel brake units. This creates a low-pressure area in front of each piston and could cause air to be drawn into the system. To prevent this, there are recuperating grooves in the

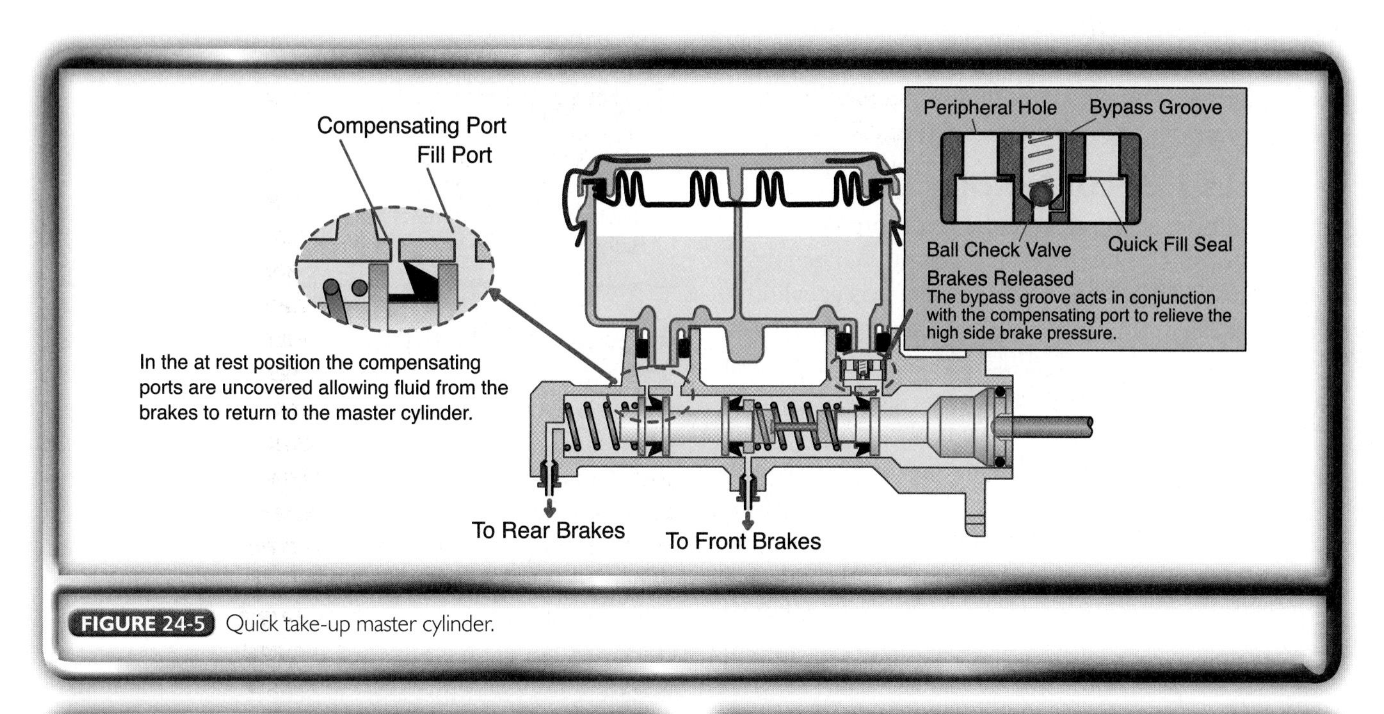
Compensating Port
Fill Port
In the at rest position the compensating ports are uncovered allowing fluid from the brakes to return to the master cylinder.
To Rear Brakes
To Front Brakes
Peripheral Hole
Bypass Groove
Ball Check Valve
Quick Fill Seal
Brakes Released
The bypass groove acts in conjunction with the compensating port to relieve the high side brake pressure.

FIGURE 24-5 Quick take-up master cylinder.

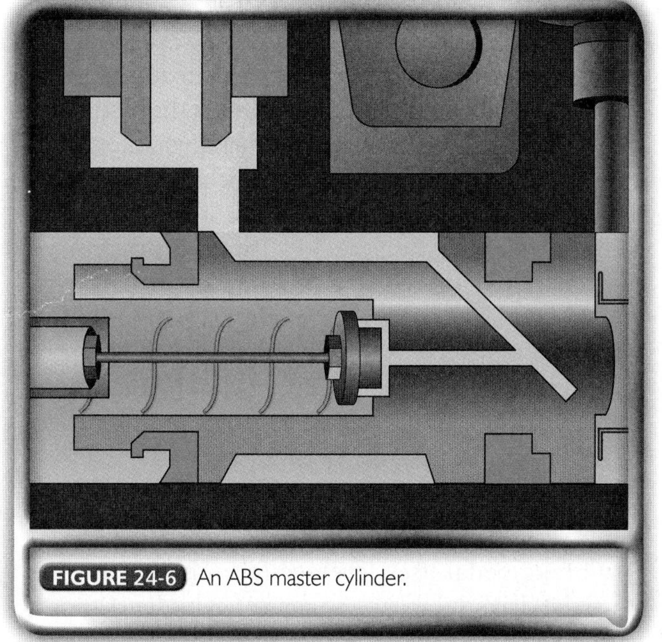

FIGURE 24-6 An ABS master cylinder.

Caring for the Customer

The ABS pedal pulsation has been blamed for actually causing some accidents. Since the ABS system is normally only activated in a panic stop situation, drivers who are unfamiliar with the pedal pulsation have been known to lift their foot off the brake pedal, causing an accident. It is good for drivers to familiarize themselves with the feel of the ABS pedal pulsation by activating the ABS in a safe location, such as an abandoned parking lot. To address this issue, manufacturers have started to move toward electronic braking (brake-by-wire), which prevents hydraulic pulsations from being transmitted to the brake pedal.

primary piston and the seal. Brake fluid at atmospheric pressure flows through the inlet port and past these grooves. When the primary piston is returned fully, any extra brake fluid returning from the wheel brake units displaces brake fluid into the reservoir, through the compensating port. In the secondary circuit, brake fluid at atmospheric pressure is forced back into the inlet port. The inlet port connects with the supply port drilling in the piston. Any difference in pressure lifts the center valve from its seat and lets the brake fluid enter the chamber ahead of the secondary seal, thus preventing low pressures from developing. When the piston has returned to the "rest" position, the seal is pulled off its seat by the action of the link and spring. This lets the brake fluid still returning from the wheel brake units displace the brake fluid back to the reservoir.

If braking conditions are such that the hydraulic modulator must return brake fluid to the master cylinder, then for the front brake circuits, brake fluid is returned to the front section. This forces the secondary piston back against the force of the primary piston spring and the rear brake pressure and pushes both pistons rearward. If enough brake fluid returns, the center valve opens and allows brake fluid to return to the reservoir.

If brake fluid is returned from the rear brake circuit, the secondary and primary pistons tend to be forced apart, causing the primary piston to be driven rearward. If enough brake fluid returns, the compensating port is uncovered and allows brake fluid to return to the reservoir.

The amount of brake fluid that returns to the master cylinder is determined by the degree of ABS control. The driver may be aware of a rising brake pedal during this time.

Reservoirs and Float Switches

Master cylinder reservoirs can be built into the master cylinder housing or can be a separate unit. Built-in reservoirs are made of the same material as the master cylinder, which is usually aluminum or cast iron, and are formed on top of the master cylinder FIGURE 24-7. The reservoir cover on these master cylinders must be removed to inspect the brake fluid level. The cover uses a rubber diaphragm to isolate the brake fluid from the air. These covers are usually held on by bail clips or tabs molded into the cover.

On two-piece master cylinders, the reservoirs are usually made of a see-through plastic material and use grommets or O-rings to seal them to the master cylinder FIGURE 24-8. Because they are see-through, it is usually unnecessary to remove the cover to check the brake fluid level. The covers can be screw-on caps or clip-on covers. The caps usually incorporate a device to minimize contact of the brake fluid with air. Some systems use a disc that floats on the brake fluid to minimize the surface area of the brake fluid in contact with the air.

FIGURE 24-7 Master cylinder with built-in reservoir.

FIGURE 24-8 Two-piece master reservoir.

> **TECHNICIAN TIP**
>
> Master cylinder reservoirs should always have air space at the top of the reservoir to allow for the expansion of brake fluid as it heats up. Never fill master cylinder reservoirs all the way to the top.

To ensure that a leak in one brake circuit will not affect the other circuit, master cylinder reservoirs have two separate chambers. These reservoirs can be two totally separate chambers, or they can use a divider in a common reservoir, which keeps the brake fluid level from falling below a minimum amount.

Most modern master cylinder reservoirs are equipped with a low brake fluid level float switch that turns on the red brake warning light on the instrument panel and/or sets a notification on the driver information system. The warning system can be activated by the float directly or a float with an embedded magnet may activate a switch when the float falls to a certain level. The brake fluid level could be low due to worn brake pad linings or a leak in the system; both situations require further investigation. Adding brake fluid without further investigation into what is causing the low fluid condition could lead to a brake failure, putting the driver and occupants in danger.

Brake Pedals

The brake pedal uses leverage to multiply the effort from the driver's foot to the master cylinder. Different lever designs can be engineered to alter the brake pedal effort required of the driver by using different levels of mechanical advantage. Brake pedals should be mounted securely, free from any excessive sideways movement, and at a height and angle that will allow the driver to quickly move from pressing the accelerator (throttle pedal) to applying the brakes. Brake pedals are covered with a rubber nonslip cover to maintain sure footing. These covers can become worn and lead to slippage, so they need to be inspected periodically.

The brake pedal is usually suspended from a bracket between the dash panel and the firewall FIGURE 24-9. It works as a force-multiplying lever. The pushrod transmits the brake pedal force either directly to the master cylinder or to the power booster. If the power assist

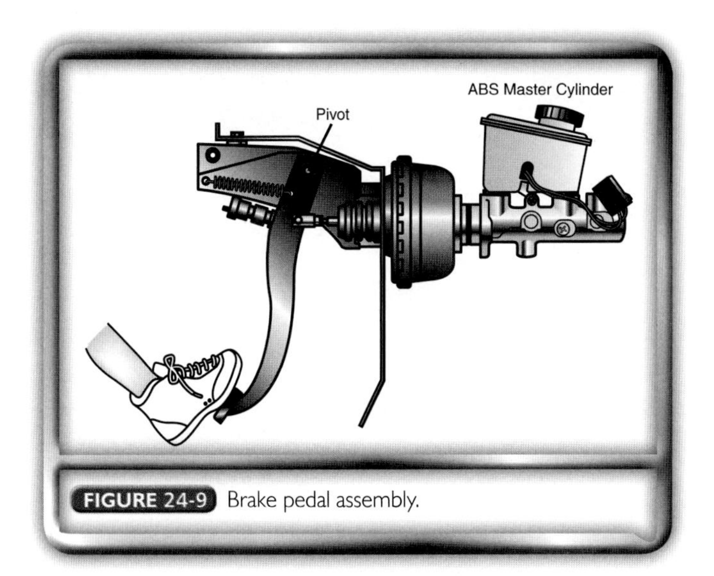
ABS Master Cylinder
Pivot

FIGURE 24-9 Brake pedal assembly.

fails, the brake pedal's leverage is designed to allow the driver to still generate a reasonable braking force at each wheel brake unit but with substantially increased foot pressure.

Brake pedals must be free to return to their starting position when pressure is removed. This allows the master cylinder piston and pushrod to return to their undepressed position. The pedal is enabled to return to its starting position by a return spring. The spring action also causes the brake pedal to push the brake light switch open and stop current flow to the brake lights. When the brake pedal is applied, a lighter spring in the brake light switch causes the brake light switch contacts to close and activate the brake lights. Brake light switches are adjustable on some vehicles. Misadjusted brake light switches can cause the brake lights to stay on when they should be off, or not come on when they are supposed to. Both situations can be corrected by adjusting the switch to the proper position. If the switch is nonadjustable, it will likely need to be replaced if it is not operating correctly.

> **TECHNICIAN TIP**
>
> Changes to how far the pedal travels or to its resistance—if it feels harder or softer than normal—can indicate problems such as a faulty power booster or air in the hydraulic system due to a leak.

> **TECHNICIAN TIP**
>
> When ABS brakes are activated during heavy braking, the pulsations of the system can be felt by the driver through the pedal. This is normal. However, a pulsating pedal during normal or light braking can indicate potential braking system problems, such as a rotor that has thickness variation beyond the manufacturer's specifications or that is possibly warped.

Types of Divided Hydraulic Systems

A wheel's braking ability depends on the load it is carrying; therefore, the type of vehicle is a major factor in determining how its system should be divided. A front-engine rear-wheel drive car has around 40% of its load on its rear wheels and 60% on its front wheels. Its braking system can therefore be divided in a vertical, or front–rear, split. This design puts the front wheels on a different system than the rear wheels. If one half of the system fails—the front or the rear—there is still enough separate braking capability left in the other half to stop the vehicle.

On a front-wheel drive vehicle, a load of about 20% on the rear wheels cannot provide enough braking force to stop the vehicle. Therefore, front-engine, front-wheel drive vehicles use a braking system split in a diagonal, or X, pattern. The left-hand front brake unit is connected to the right-hand rear unit, and the left-hand rear unit is connected to the right-hand front unit. If one system fails, a 50% braking capability is available in the other system.

An alternative arrangement for front-engine, front-wheel drive vehicles is an L split FIGURE 24-10. The front disc brake units have four piston calipers. One inner and one outer piston on each front caliper connect to the right-hand rear brake unit, and the other two pistons of each front caliper connect to the left-hand rear brake unit. As with the diagonal split system, if there is a failure of either half of the system, it still leaves 50% of the braking capability.

> **TECHNICIAN TIP**
>
> When diagnosing and servicing brakes, it is helpful to know how the hydraulic system is divided. If the vehicle is pulling to one side due to a leak in one half of the system, it will generally pull toward the side that is working in the front. Diagnosis and inspection of the other diagonal half will usually lead to the leak. In the same way, if air is trapped in one half of the hydraulic braking system, then bleeding the corresponding diagonal half will make it easier to remove the air.

Brake Lines and Hoses

Brake Lines

Brake lines and hoses carry brake fluid from the master cylinder to the brake units. They are basically the same on all brake systems and passenger vehicles. For most of their length, they are double-walled steel, coated to resist

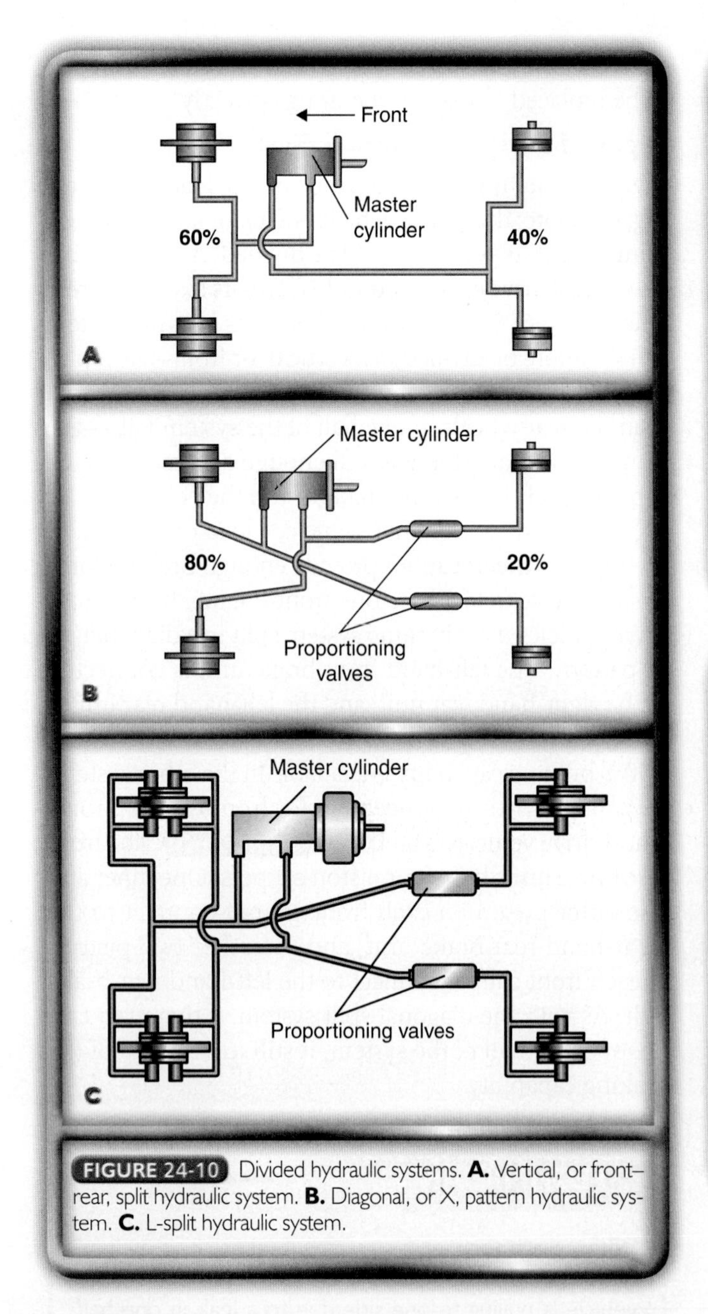
Front
Master cylinder
60%
40%
A
Master cylinder
80%
20%
Proportioning valves
B
Master cylinder
Proportioning valves
C

FIGURE 24-10 Divided hydraulic systems. **A.** Vertical, or front–rear, split hydraulic system. **B.** Diagonal, or X, pattern hydraulic system. **C.** L-split hydraulic system.

FIGURE 24-11 Steel brake line.

FIGURE 24-12 Flexible brake hose.

corrosion, and attached to the body with clips or brackets to minimize damage from vibration FIGURE 24-11. In some vehicles, the brake lines are inside the vehicle to better protect them from corrosion and physical damage. Where the lines must move, flexible brake hoses allow for steering and suspension movement FIGURE 24-12.

Brake Line Materials

The **brake lines** must be able to transmit considerable hydraulic pressure, 1500 psi (10342 kPa) or more during panic stops. They are made of seamless, double-walled steel, rather than a softer but less corrosive, and easier-to-form, material such as copper. They also must conform to applicable standards such as the Society of Automotive Engineers. Only brake lines that meet those standards can be used on vehicles.

If a brake line is damaged, it is common practice to replace the entire brake line with a factory replacement rather than repair it. Also, universal brake lines are available in a variety of lengths that are already factory flared with the correct fitting installed. They just need to be formed with the proper tubing bender to the specified shape following the original brake line routing. Avoid kinks by only using the correct tubing bender. Kinked lines cannot be used or repaired.

Safety

Never substitute a copper, aluminum, or nonapproved line for the original; doing so could lead to a brake failure, which you could be held liable for.

> **TECHNICIAN TIP**
>
> Many brake and fuel lines screw into an adapter. Always use a double wrench method with flare nut wrenches when loosening and tightening brake and fuel lines. This technique will help prevent twisting of the steel lines FIGURE 24-13

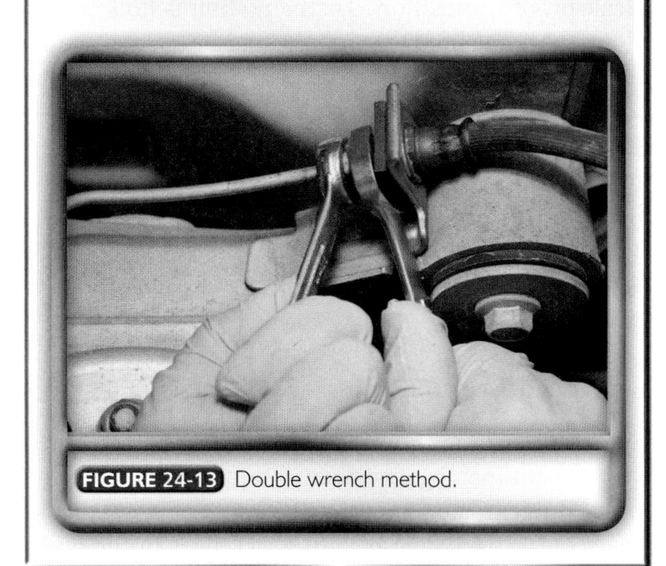

FIGURE 24-13 Double wrench method.

Types of Brake Line Flares

Since brake lines connect all of the various hydraulic braking system components, their ends must make leak-proof connections. This is accomplished by using the following types of flared lines and matching fittings:

- **Inverted double flare**: This type of flare is created by first flaring the end of the tube outward in a Y shape. Then about half of the flared end is folded inside of itself (inverted), leaving a double-thick section of brake line on the flared portion of the Y FIGURE 24-14. The flared portion of the tube is clamped between the mating surfaces of the two fittings to provide a secure, leak-proof connection when performed properly.
- **International Standards Organization (ISO) flare**: This type of flare is sometimes called a "bubble flare." The brake line is flared slightly out and then back in, leaving the brake line "bubbled" near the end FIGURE 24-15. The bubble is then clamped between two matching fittings.

Brake Line Flaring

While it is common practice to replace the entire brake line if it is damaged, sometimes a technician has to fabricate a new one from a section of new universal brake

> **TECHNICIAN TIP**
>
> Flared fittings form a seal by tightly compressing the brake line between the two halves of the fitting. No sealer is needed—nor should it be used—on these types of fittings.

line. Only attempt this when a new factory replacement line is unavailable. Also, ensure that the proper flaring tools are used and the required procedures are followed exactly. Never use compression fittings to splice a section of brake line.

Brake Hoses

A flexible section of the brake lines must be included between the body and suspension to allow for steering and suspension movement. This is accomplished by using flexible hoses made of tough, reinforced tubing. These flexible **brake hoses** transmit the brake system hydraulic

FIGURE 24-14 An inverted double flared line and matching fitting.

FIGURE 24-15 An ISO flared line and matching fitting.

pressures to the wheel units. They also must be tough so as not to be damaged easily by objects thrown by the tires or other hazards. When replacing brake hoses, always make sure they are of the proper length. If they are too short, they can be damaged by being stretched. If they are too long, they can contact moving components such as tires or a suspension member, which could weaken or wear a hole in the hose. This is especially common when a vehicle has a lift kit installed.

Brake Hose Materials

Brake hoses are made of several layers of alternating materials. The inside is a liner that helps seal the brake fluid in and any moisture out. The liner is wrapped with two or more layers of flexible webbing, which are usually embedded in a synthetic rubber material and provide reinforcement for the hose. These layers are covered with a tough flexible outer housing jacket designed to resist abrasion and damage FIGURE 24-16.

While brake hoses are designed to be flexible, they should *never* be pinched, kinked, or bent tighter than a specified radius. Doing so will reduce their life and can cause failure of the brake hose. Some technicians mistakenly use vice grip pliers to crimp a brake hose while disconnected from the caliper or wheel cylinder to prevent brake fluid from leaking out. This practice can damage the brake hose and should be avoided.

> **TECHNICIAN TIP**
>
> *Never* hang a disconnected brake caliper by its flexible brake hose. Doing so can damage the brake hose. Always use a piece of wire or other material (e.g., cable or zip tie) to support the weight of the caliper assembly while hanging on a suspension or other suitable component.

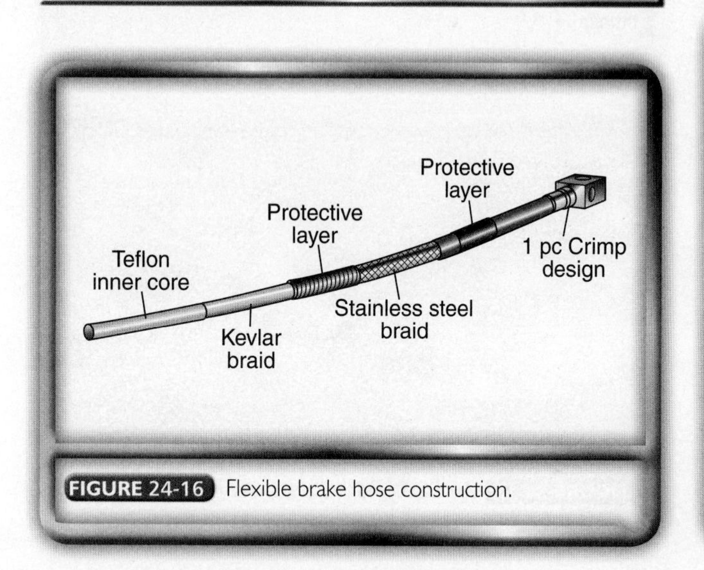
Protective layer
Protective layer
1 pc Crimp design
Teflon inner core
Stainless steel braid
Kevlar braid

FIGURE 24-16 Flexible brake hose construction.

Sealing Washers and Fittings

Many brake hoses use banjo fittings to connect the hose to the wheel unit. These fittings are comprised of the banjo fitting, banjo bolt, and two copper or aluminum sealing washers FIGURE 24-17. The banjo bolt, banjo fitting, and wheel unit usually have sealing ridges machined in them. These ridges dig into the softer sealing washers to ensure a leak-proof connection. The banjo bolt is hollow and allows the brake fluid through the middle to continue on to the wheel unit. It fits in the banjo fitting and clamps it to the wheel unit. The sealing washers fit on both sides of the banjo fitting. One sealing washer is between the head of the banjo bolt and the banjo fitting, while the other sealing washer is between the banjo fitting and the wheel unit. Always use the proper torque when tightening banjo bolts so they are not twisted off or left loose to leak.

Brake hoses need to be inspected periodically for damage or defects. Some possible issues are FIGURE 24-18:

- **Cracks**: The outer layers become brittle and crack over time. Replacement is required.
- **Bulges**: The reinforcing layers become weak and break over time resulting in bulges in the outer cover. Replacement is required.
- **Abrasion or wear**: This usually happens because the brake hose was routed incorrectly or was too

> **TECHNICIAN TIP**
>
> Because the sealing washers are made of soft metal, they become crushed after use. It is good practice to replace them each time the banjo fittings are removed; otherwise leaks could occur.

FIGURE 24-17 Banjo bolt assembly.

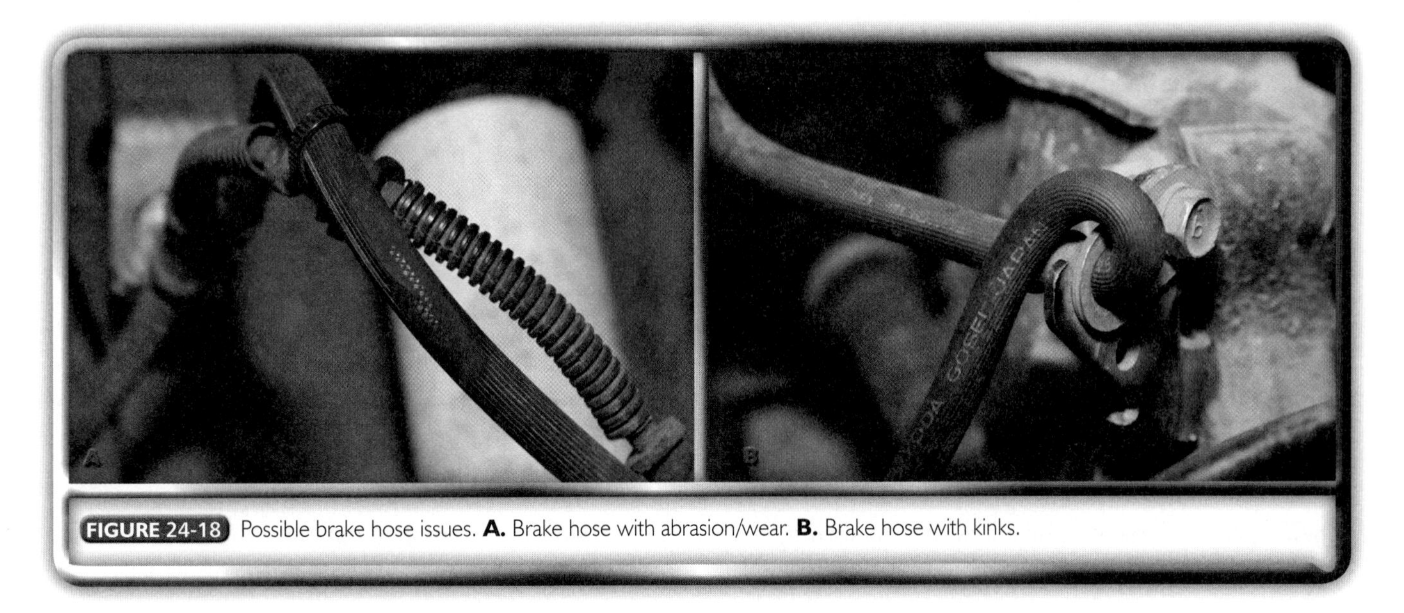
GOSEI JAPAN

FIGURE 24-18 Possible brake hose issues. **A.** Brake hose with abrasion/wear. **B.** Brake hose with kinks.

long or short for the application and the brake hose rubbed on a component, resulting, over time, in the abrasion. Replacement and rerouting are required.

- **Kinks**: Kinking usually happens when the brake hose has been pinched with vice grips or twisted on installation. Replacement is required.
- **Internal deterioration causing blockage of the passageway**: Replacement is required.

Hydraulic Braking System Control

The hydraulic braking system must be controlled accurately to maintain adequate control of the vehicle during braking. As we learned earlier, hydraulic working pressure is equally applied throughout a sealed hydraulic braking system. We also learned that the hydraulic braking system can be designed to optimize the output force at each of the wheel brake units. In a perfect scenario, that would work just fine. But since machines are not perfect, you need to be able to modify the hydraulic pressure to accommodate different scenarios. Components such as proportioning valves, metering valves, pressure differential valves, or anti-lock hydraulic control units are used to modify the pressures within the hydraulic braking system.

Proportioning Valves

Proportioning valves reduce brake pressure to the rear wheels when their load is reduced during moderate to severe braking. Proportioning valves can be pressure-sensitive or load-sensitive. The pressure-sensitive valve is in the master cylinder or in a separate unit in the rear brake circuit, while the load-sensitive type is mounted on the body or on the axle, where it can respond to load changes.

The effectiveness of braking force is determined by tire-to-road friction. The greater the load on the tire, the greater the friction; the greater the friction, the greater the stopping ability. When a vehicle stops abruptly, a portion of the weight on the rear wheels transfers to the front wheels, resulting in greater tire-to-road friction on the front tires and less on the rear. This is called **load transfer**—weight is being transferred from the rear wheels to the front wheels.

If equal braking force is applied to the front and rear wheels during this load transfer condition, the smaller load in the rear can result in the rear wheels locking up. Skidding tires on the surface of the road (kinetic friction) do not have as much friction as rolling tires, and therefore the stopping distance is increased, which can lead to an accident. A pressure-sensitive proportioning valve reduces the pressure applied to the rear brakes under heavy braking to prevent rear wheel lock-up and to help maintain traction.

The load-sensitive proportioning valve reduces rear brake pressure when the vehicle is lightly loaded and allows higher pressure when it is heavily loaded. The load-sensitive proportioning valve is usually located on the chassis and has a lever that is connected to the rear axle. As the vehicle is loaded, the chassis squats on the rear suspension and the lever is moved, applying more force on the load-sensitive proportioning valve. The lever increases or decreases the point at which pressure is limited by the load-sensitive proportioning valve. Heavier loads allow more pressure through the load-sensitive proportioning valve to the rear brakes, and lighter loads restrict pressure through the load-sensitive proportioning valve. A diagonally split system may have two load-sensitive proportioning valves, one for each rear brake unit. Each load-sensitive proportioning valve is mounted on the chassis, around the rear suspension. If the vehicle is equipped with ABS, it may not be equipped with a proportioning valve, as the ABS system can make up for wheel slippage due to the changes in load transfer. This will be covered in detail in the Electronic Brake Control chapter.

Pressure-Sensitive Proportioning Valve Operation

The pressure-sensitive proportioning valve adjusts the braking force to allow for load transfer or variations in loads. During normal braking, the pressure-sensitive proportioning valve's poppet piston is held in a relaxed position by a large pressure spring. The **poppet valve** is held against its retainer by a light return spring, and brake fluid passes freely through the pressure-sensitive proportioning valve to the rear brakes. In this condition, the rear brakes operate normally without any modification to the pressure FIGURE 24-19.

During heavy braking, master cylinder pressure can reach the poppet valve's crack point. The pressure applied to the two different areas of the poppet piston creates unequal forces, which act on the pressure-sensitive proportioning valve. The higher hydraulic pressure moves the poppet piston against the large pressure spring to close the pressure-sensitive proportioning valve. At a specified inlet pressure, the conical section of the pressure-sensitive proportioning valve is held against the seat, which holds the pressure steady to the rear brakes until there is a further change in inlet pressure.

As greater pedal force increases pressure in the master cylinder, brake fluid pressure rises on the smaller end of the poppet piston. This combines with the force of the pressure spring to overcome the lower pressure now on the larger (output) end. As a result, the piston is forced back, opening the poppet valve and allowing pressure to rise to the rear brakes.

The increased pressure now acts on the larger end of the poppet piston and again forces the piston forward to close the poppet valve and hold pressure steady. This repeated action causes a lowering of outlet pressure versus inlet pressure. When the brake pedal is released, the pressure of the rear brake fluid unseats the poppet valve, letting the brake fluid return to the master cylinder. The pressure spring now returns the poppet piston to its relaxed position.

Should the front brake system fail, the warning lamp spool moves forward, taking the poppet valve with it. Pressure in the rear brakes rises and the piston moves forward; however, it cannot close the poppet valve, so full system pressure remains available for the rear brakes in this situation. Should the rear brake system fail, the warning lamp spool will move backward to activate the warning light. The pressure-sensitive proportioning valve cannot operate in this situation.

A diagonally divided system requires one pressure-sensitive proportioning valve for each rear wheel, so they are usually located away from the master cylinder. Each pressure-sensitive proportioning valve operates in a similar way to the pressure-sensitive proportioning valve in the master cylinder, but without the pressure differential warning light circuit.

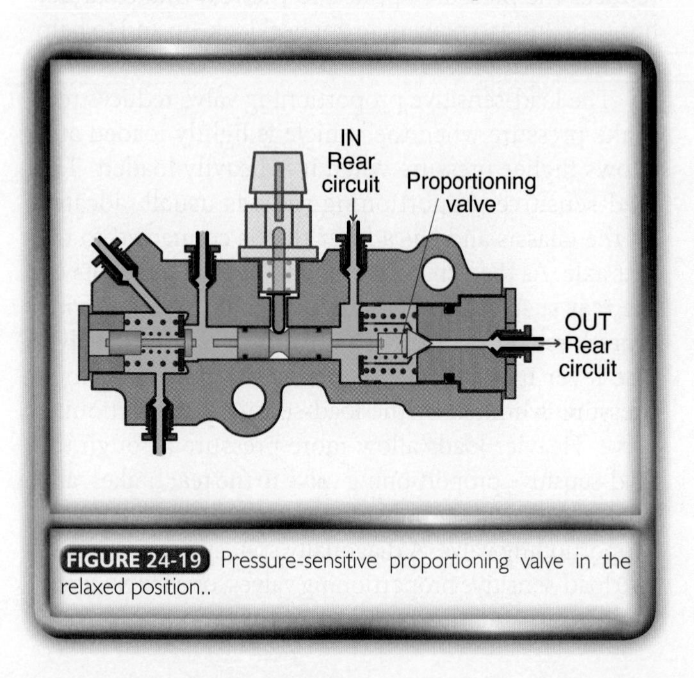
IN
Rear
circuit
Proportioning
valve
OUT
Rear
circuit

FIGURE 24-19 Pressure-sensitive proportioning valve in the relaxed position..

Adjustable Proportioning Valves

After-market adjustable proportioning valves are available for performance applications. They have a method of adjusting the proportioning valve's crack point and can be customized to the specific vehicle. Adjustable proportioning valves are popular with kit car builders who use components from a variety of vehicles that were not originally designed to work together. Adjustable proportioning valves are not recommended for most applications due to the amount of trial and error necessary to set them properly.

Metering Valves

Metering valves are used to hold off the application of the front brakes on vehicles with disc brakes on the front wheels and drum brakes on the rear wheels FIGURE 24-20. Drum brakes use springs to return the brake shoes to their rest position. This means that it takes a certain amount of hydraulic pressure to overcome the tension of the return springs and move the shoes to contact the drums. Disc brakes use the much smaller force of the square-cut O-ring to return the caliper piston to its rest position. Thus, very little hydraulic pressure is needed to move the brake pads into contact with the rotor.

FIGURE 24-20 A metering valve.

Vehicles handle better when the rear brakes engage before the front brakes. This helps keep the vehicle tracking straight while the brakes are initially applied. The metering valve keeps the front disc brakes from being applied until the rear drum brakes have had a chance to overcome the tension of the return springs.

Metering Valve Operation

The metering valve operates like a radiator cap. It has a relatively heavy spring that holds the metering valve closed until a specified pressure is reached FIGURE 24-21. Pressure rises in the hydraulic braking system, overcomes the rear brake return spring tension, and starts to apply the rear brakes. As pressure continues to rise above the metering valve's crack point, brake fluid flows to the front disc brake calipers and starts to apply the front brakes. Since the metering valve only has hydraulic pressure on the inlet side, any pressure above its crack point will hold it open.

When the brake pedal is released, the metering valve is pushed closed by the spring and a fluid return valve opens up, allowing brake fluid to flow freely back to the master cylinder. During bleeding, if there is air in the lines, it may be difficult to raise the brake fluid pressure enough to open the metering valve. This makes it almost impossible to bleed any air out of the front part of the hydraulic braking system. Most metering valves are designed so that they can be manually held in the open position to allow bleeding to take place. Also, many pressure bleeders operate at an insufficient pressure to open the metering valve, and the valve will have to be held open manually.

Vehicles equipped with a diagonally split system are generally front-wheel drive. They usually do not use metering valves for two reasons. First, the torque of the spinning engine during braking compensates for the earlier application of the front brake pads and offsets not having a metering valve. Second, since up to 80% of the braking occurs at the front wheels, they need to be applied as quickly as possible to start braking the vehicle effectively.

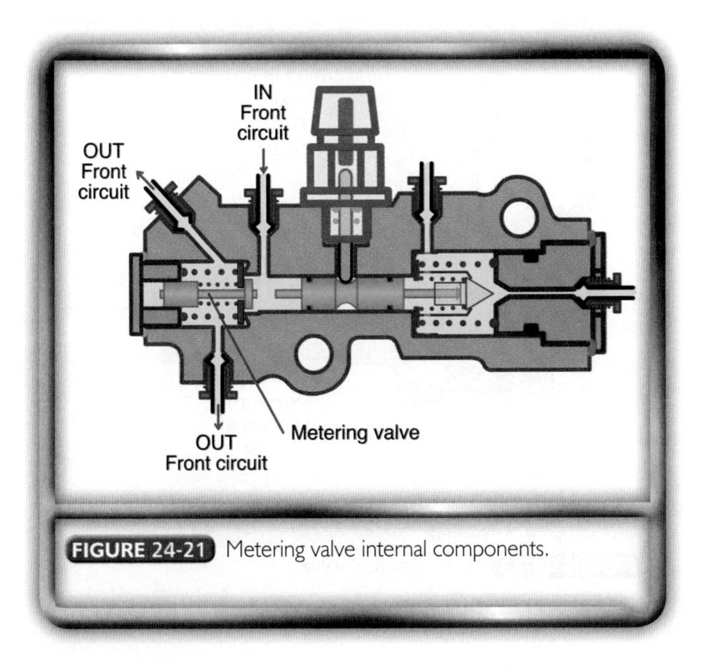
IN
Front
circuit
OUT
Front
circuit
OUT
Front circuit
Metering valve
FIGURE 24-21 Metering valve internal components.

Pressure Differential Valve

A pressure differential valve monitors any pressure difference between the two separate hydraulic brake circuits. If there is a moderate leak anywhere in the system, it will illuminate the brake warning light on the instrument panel. Sometimes the light will only flicker, or come on

Safety

After bleeding the hydraulic braking system, always remember to remove the tool that is holding open the metering valve. Failure to do so could cause the vehicle to brake improperly.

TECHNICIAN TIP

On a front–rear split system, there can also be a pressure difference if the rear drum brake shoes are grossly underadjusted. When the brake pedal is pushed, the shoes do not make contact. The primary piston moves so far that it contacts the secondary piston, which starts to apply the front brakes. This raises the pressure in the secondary circuit higher than in the primary circuit, moving the pressure differential valve toward the primary circuit and thus illuminating the brake warning light.

when the brake pedal is pushed, indicating a small leak. The valve can be located in the master cylinder or in the combination valve.

Pressure Differential Valve Operation

The pressure differential valve is connected between the two halves of the hydraulic braking system so pressure is applied to each end of the pressure differential valve. As long as the pressure stays the same in both circuits, the pressure differential valve remains in the same position and the light stays off. A moderate leak in the hydraulic brake system will lower the pressure on that side of the circuit. This system will allow the higher pressure in the nonleaking side to push the pressure differential valve off-center toward the side with the leak. The pressure differential switch will then close and illuminate the brake warning light on the instrument panel, telling the driver that there is a serious leak in the hydraulic brake system that needs to be diagnosed FIGURE 24-22.

During hydraulic braking system bleeding, the pressure differential valve may need to be centered. Most pressure differential valves have springs that help center them. Applying the brakes firmly will cause the pressure to equalize, and the spring returns the pressure differential valve to center. On vehicles without this feature, once the hydraulic braking system has been bled, you must bleed a small amount of brake fluid out of the opposite hydraulic circuit to allow the pressure differential valve to move back to center. Follow the manufacturer's procedure.

Combination Valve

The combination valve can combine the pressure differential valve, metering valve, and proportioning valve(s) in one unit FIGURE 24-23. Some combination valves combine just the pressure differential valve and proportioning valve(s). On others, just the pressure differential valve and metering valve are combined. Each valve operates individually as it was designed and is collected in one unit. Combination valves are not serviceable. If they become faulty, they must be replaced.

Electronic Brake Proportioning

Many ABS-equipped vehicles integrate an electronic brake proportioning function within the hydraulic control unit on vehicles that require it. This function reduces hydraulic pressure to the rear wheels under heavy braking, similar to the proportioning valve. However, in these vehicles the pressure reduction is handled electronically and can compensate for differences in traction by monitoring wheel slip.

Brake Warning Light and Stop Lights

Red lights are used on vehicles as warning devices to warn drivers and others of specific conditions. When a red light

FIGURE 24-22 A pressure differential valve with a leak in the hydraulic braking system.

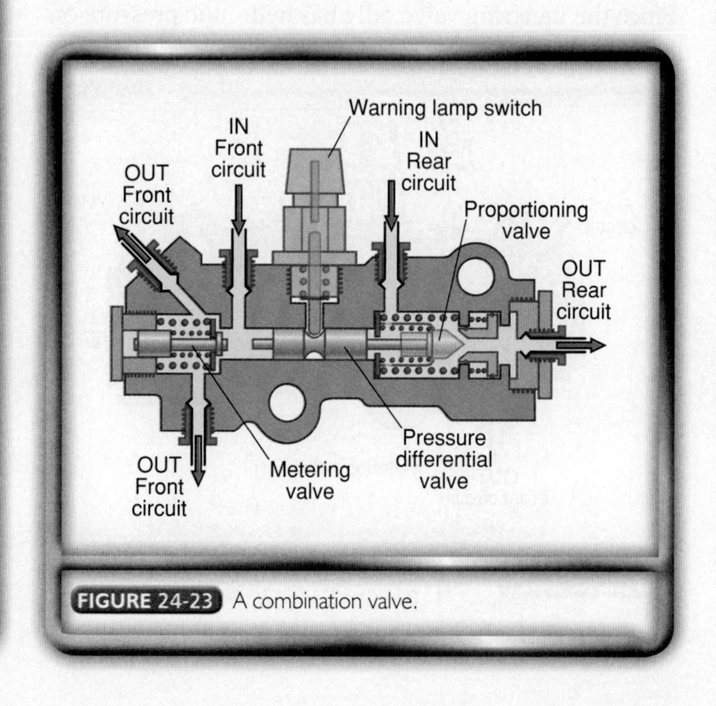
Warning lamp switch
IN
Front
circuit
IN
Rear
circuit
OUT
Front
circuit
Proportioning
valve
OUT
Rear
circuit
OUT
Front
circuit
Metering
valve
Pressure
differential
valve

FIGURE 24-23 A combination valve.

comes on, the driver should take notice and respond appropriately. There are two general categories—the brake warning light and stop lights. The brake warning light is a single light located in the instrument panel, while the stop lights are made up of at least three lights at the rear of the vehicle.

Brake Warning Light

The brake warning light is designed to warn the driver of a condition in the braking system that needs attention. Usually the light can be illuminated by four causes FIGURE 24-24. The first is if the parking brake is engaged. The light is turned on by the parking brake lever or pedal when the parking brake is applied. This is to alert the driver that it is on so the driver will release it before driving. The second reason the brake warning light comes on is because the brake fluid level is too low in the master cylinder reservoir. This could be caused by a leak in the hydraulic braking system or worn brake pads on the disc brakes. On vehicles without ABS, the third cause of the brake warning light coming on is unequal pressure in the hydraulic brake system, which causes the pressure differential valve to activate the brake warning light switch. The fourth cause of the brake warning light illuminating is called a "prove out" or "proffing" circuit. On most vehicles designed without controller area network bus (CAN-bus), turning the ignition switch to the "crank" position causes the warning light to illuminate so the driver knows the bulb is good.

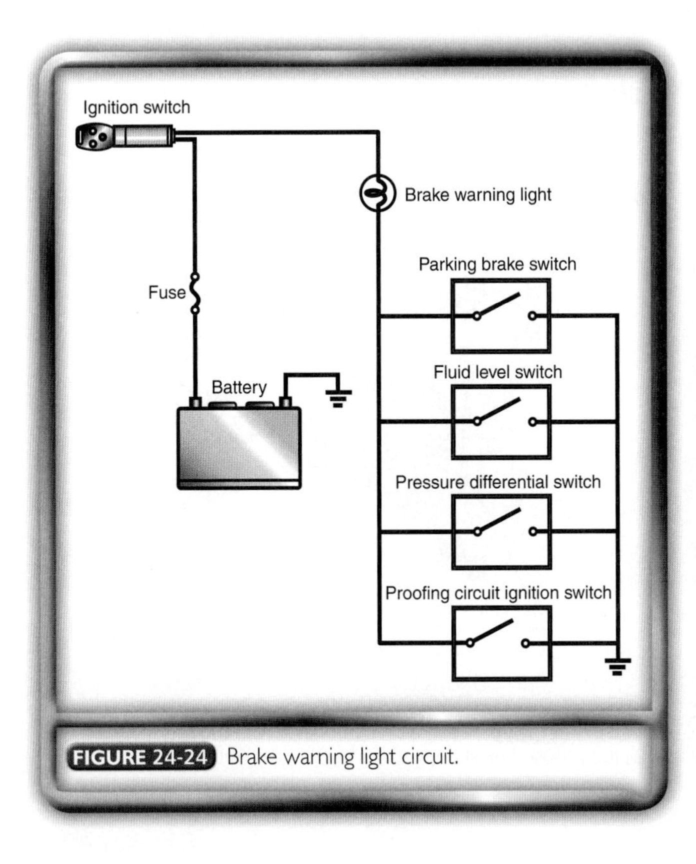
Ignition switch
Brake warning light
Parking brake switch
Fuse
Fluid level switch
Battery
Pressure differential switch
Proofing circuit ignition switch

FIGURE 24-24 Brake warning light circuit.

Stop Lights

Stop lights are designed to warn others that the vehicle is braking. This information is critical to help avoid accidents. The regular stop lights are mounted on the rear of the vehicle and must conform to federal laws for brightness and location. They are activated by a normally closed stop light switch located on the brake pedal assembly. When the driver applies the brake, the brake pedal moves away from the stop light switch. A spring in the switch closes the contacts, allowing current to flow and illuminate the stop lights. Releasing the brakes causes the brake pedal to force the stop light switch open, turning the stop lights off.

In 1986, North America mandated that all new passenger vehicles be equipped with a center high mount stop lamp (CHMSL). Light trucks and vans were added in 1994. This lamp is located higher than the regular brake lights, near the centerline of the vehicle FIGURE 24-25. It is designed to be more in the driver's line of sight while he or she is looking down the road to anticipate traffic hazards. This higher-mounted lamp helps reduce rear-end collisions by being more visible to drivers, giving them more warning time for stopping.

Power Brakes

Types and Purpose

A power booster or power brake unit uses an external source of force to multiply the driver's pedal effort and apply that to the master cylinder pistons, thus increasing the hydraulic pressure available from the master cylinder. There are two main types of power brake units: vacuum-

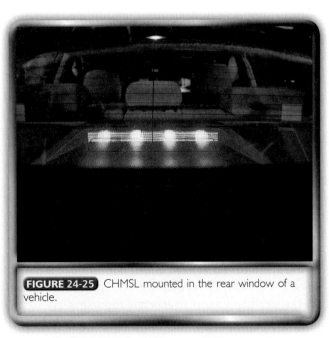

FIGURE 24-25 CHMSL mounted in the rear window of a vehicle.

assist and hydraulic-assist. The vacuum-assist power booster is the most common.

Units on gasoline engines use the vacuum produced in the intake manifold to power the brake booster. This supplies approximately 20″ of vacuum to the booster. Vehicles with diesel engines do not have manifold vacuum, so they are fitted with an engine-driven vacuum pump.

The vacuum-assisted power booster operates between the brake pedal and the master cylinder. It uses the difference between engine vacuum and atmospheric pressure to increase the force that acts on the master cylinder pistons. The level of assistance this power booster gives depends on the pressure applied to the brake pedal and the pressure difference between the vacuum side of the booster and the atmospheric pressure side.

The hydraulic-assisted power booster operates between the brake pedal and the master cylinder. It usually uses hydraulic pressure from the power steering pump to increase the force that acts on the master cylinder. The level of assistance this power booster gives depends on the pressure applied to the brake pedal and the hydraulic pressure in the system.

Vacuum Booster

The most common types of vacuum boosters are the single diaphragm and the dual diaphragm. Just as the names imply, they have either one or two diaphragms that are used to extract power from atmospheric pressure. Using two diaphragms allows the diameter of the booster to be smaller, although it is a bit longer than a single-diaphragm unit.

Vacuum boosters consist of the following:

- A housing, which encases all of the other parts
- One or two sealed diaphragms, which transmit the force to the master cylinder
- A diaphragm return spring, which pushes the diaphragm back when the brake pedal is released
- A control valve, which controls vacuum and atmospheric pressure to each chamber
- A one-way check valve, which holds vacuum in the booster when it is higher than intake manifold vacuum
- Seals, which prevent air leaks

How much force can a vacuum booster create? Let's do the math using a panic stop situation. The booster receives approximately 20" (51 cm) of vacuum from the intake manifold. That is equal to about 10 psi (69 kPa) of pressure since 2" (5.1 cm) of vacuum equals 1 psi (6.9 kPa). So the booster diaphragm can generate approximately 10 psi (69 kPa). If the diaphragm has a circumference of 12" (31 cm), then it has an area of approximately 113 square inches (729 cm^2). Therefore, 10 psi (69 kPa) × 113 square inches (729 cm^2) = 1130 lb (513 kg). That means that a 12" (24-cm) booster can add 1130 lb (513 kg) of force to whatever the driver's foot effort is after being multiplied through the leverage of the brake pedal. That force is magnified further by the hydraulic system. This is why a vehicle weighing thousands of pounds can be stopped with minimal foot pressure.

Vacuum Booster Operation

When the driver steps on the brake pedal, it moves the brake pedal pushrod forward, which transmits movement through the power unit to the master cylinder piston to apply the brakes. It also operates a control valve that controls the flow of vacuum and atmospheric pressure to each side of the diaphragm. How it works depends on the position of the control valve.

A hose connects the intake manifold to a vacuum check valve on the power brake unit. With the engine running, the check valve allows air to be evacuated from the booster, but not to return. Vacuum in the intake manifold is used to evacuate the power unit. The valve stays open until vacuum in the unit is as high as or higher than manifold vacuum. It then seals the booster off from the intake system. It also holds vacuum in the booster in the case of an engine failure where it will allow at least one full boosted brake application.

The booster chambers are separated by a flexible rubber diaphragm attached to the diaphragm plate. It is held in the off position by a large-diaphragm return spring FIGURE 24-26. The master cylinder pushrod and the control

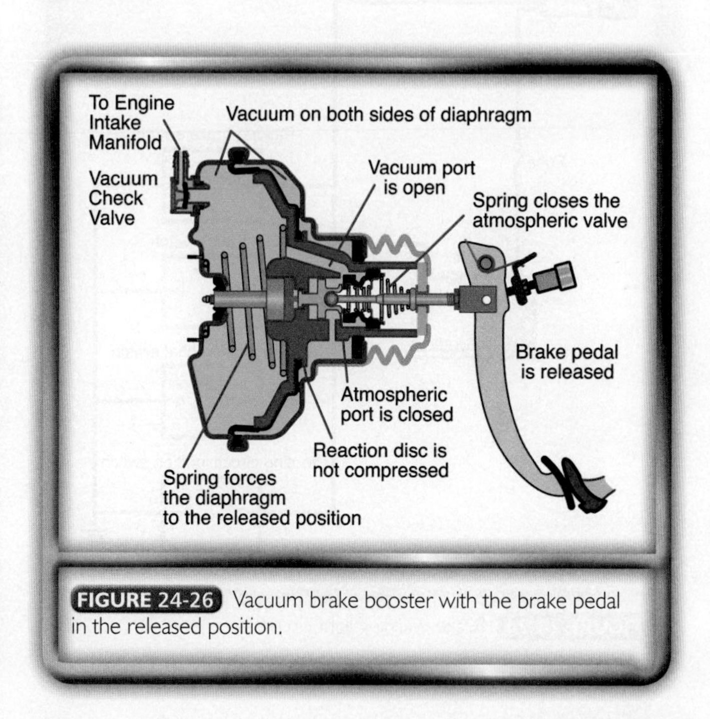
To Engine Intake Manifold
Vacuum on both sides of diaphragm
Vacuum Check Valve
Vacuum port is open
Spring closes the atmospheric valve
Brake pedal is released
Atmospheric port is closed
Reaction disc is not compressed
Spring forces the diaphragm to the released position

FIGURE 24-26 Vacuum brake booster with the brake pedal in the released position.

valve assembly are centrally located on each side of the plate. The master cylinder pushrod normally incorporates a system to provide an adjustment for pushrod length. The adjustable length provides the proper clearance between the master cylinder pushrod and the master cylinder piston. The length normally does not need to be adjusted, but if adjustment is required, use the proper tools and follow the service information completely.

As the brakes are applied, the pedal pushrod and plunger move forward in the diaphragm plate, which brings the vacuum valve into contact with the vacuum port seat. This closes the vacuum port, sealing off the passage connecting the two chambers and holding the pressure and vacuum steady in each chamber. This is called the hold position.

Further movement of the pushrod and plunger moves the atmospheric valve away from the atmospheric port seat FIGURE 24-27. Air at atmospheric pressure comes in through the air filter in the rear of the unit and enters the chamber behind the diaphragm. The difference in pressure now on both sides of the diaphragm moves the diaphragm plate forward, and it takes the master cylinder pushrod with it, applying greater force to the master cylinder. In this position, called the apply position, the vacuum valve is closed and the atmospheric valve is open.

Once the brake pedal stops moving, the atmospheric pressure continues to build up in the rear chamber. As hydraulic pressure rises, a counterforce acts through the master cylinder pushrod and the reaction disc. This counterforce allows the diaphragm plate and control valve to continue moving forward a little bit until the movement causes the atmospheric valve to close off the atmospheric port. Closing off the atmospheric port stops the atmospheric pressure from entering the booster, which causes it to hold in that position, ready for increased or decreased pedal pressure from the driver.

During application, the reaction force against the valve plunger works against the driver to close the atmospheric port. With both the atmospheric and the vacuum ports closed, the power unit is in a hold position. It stays this way until increased pedal force reopens the atmospheric port, causing more boost; or a drop in pedal force reopens the vacuum port, reducing boost. When the force on the pedal is held constant, and both the vacuum valve and the atmospheric valve are closed, the valve always returns to the hold position.

When the brake pedal is released, the atmospheric valve is closed and the vacuum valve opens. As a result, any atmospheric pressure is evacuated from the rear chamber, through the front chamber, out the booster, through the check valve, and into the intake manifold. This reduces the atmospheric pressure pushing on the diaphragm plate. The return spring then pushes the diaphragm plate back to its off position. With the driver's foot off of the brake pedal, the vacuum valve remains open, ensuring that there is equal vacuum on both sides of the diaphragm plate ready for the next application.

When the engine is switched off or stops for any reason, no manifold vacuum is available to supply the booster. The vacuum remaining in the booster, held by the one-way check valve, will provide for at least one power-boosted brake application. After this, the brakes will still operate, but without power assistance, they require more brake pedal effort from the driver.

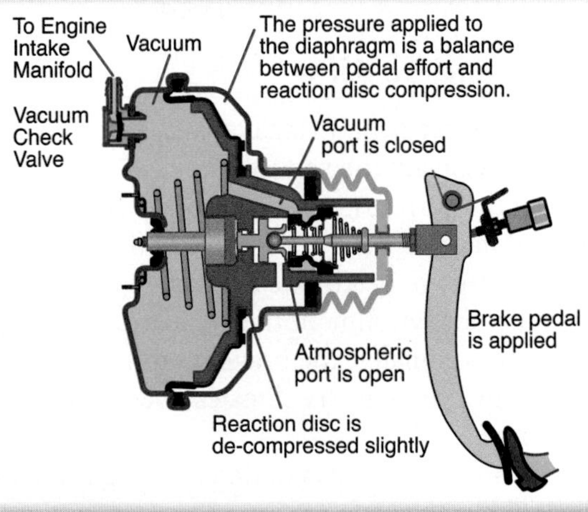

FIGURE 24-27 Vacuum brake booster with the brake pedal in the applied position.

Hydraulic Brake Booster

Purpose and Operation

Although not as common as a conventional brake system fitted with a vacuum booster, many vehicles are now equipped with hydraulically assisted brake boosters. The hydraulic booster system uses hydraulic pressure generated by the power steering pump rather than engine vacuum to provide the required power FIGURE 24-28. This application is particularly suitable to vehicles with diesel engines, as a separate vacuum source does not have to be provided for the system to operate. While hydraulic brake boosters use power steering fluid to operate the booster, the master cylinder portion of the system still uses brake fluid. Do not make a mistake and put power steering fluid in the master cylinder reservoir or brake fluid in the power steering pump reservoir.

Because the hydraulic booster system uses fluid pressure from the existing power steering pump, the

Accumulator
Hydraulic booster
FIGURE 24-28 Hydraulic power brake booster.

booster uses the pressure from the power steering fluid that is always circulating through it as the source of pressure applied against the master cylinder actuating piston. The hydraulic pressure generated by the power steering pump is stored in an accumulator, routed to the hydraulic booster unit, and applied as mechanical force to the master cylinder when the brake pedal is applied.

The booster can generate pressures of 1200 to 2000 psi (8274 to 13790 kPa) to activate the master cylinder. Hydraulic boosters can be completely separate components from the master cylinder, or integrated components with the master cylinder. As a safety measure, part of the hydraulic booster system includes an accumulator, which assists in maintaining a reserve of system pressure. Some are nitrogen pressurized while others are spring loaded, depending on the application. Should pressure in the hydraulic system be lost, such as when the engine stalls or the power steering pump drive belt breaks, the hydraulic booster system's accumulator is designed to store sufficient pressure to provide for a few full-power applications. Once this accumulated pressure is used up, the hydraulic booster system resorts to manual brake function, requiring much higher pedal pressure.

Diagnosis

Tools

Brake bleeder wrenches are used to open and close bleeder screws. They come in a variety of configurations and are designed to fit into the tight space where the bleeder screw is located. They are also usually designed with six sides to decrease the likelihood of rounding off the bleeder screw hex head.

Vacuum brake bleeders can be operated by hand, by air, or by electricity. The hose from the vacuum bleeder is placed onto the end of the bleeder screw and the bleeder screw is opened. The vacuum is applied and pulls brake fluid from the hydraulic braking system through the bleeder screw; this fluid is captured in a container for later disposal.

Pressure brake bleeders provide a reservoir of brake fluid under pressure. The pressure bleeder usually mounts to the master cylinder reservoir and supplies a steady stream of clean brake fluid for bleeding or flushing. With the master cylinder pressurized, the bleeder screws on the wheel brake units can be opened one at a time and bled or flushed of old brake fluid and air.

Proportioning valve/metering valve gauge sets are used to test the operation of the proportioning valve and metering valve. The gauge set is connected to the output line of the appropriate valve and the brake pedal is activated. The pressures are monitored and compared to specifications FIGURE 24-29.

Brake Fluid Handling

You need to understand how to select and handle brake fluid as it is the life-blood of the hydraulic braking system. Failure to do so could cause damage to the hydraulic braking system and an unsafe situation for the driver and passengers. Brake fluid levels should be inspected during every oil change. But since brake fluid is considered to be a non-top off fluid, if it is below the minimum level in the reservoir, the cause of the low brake fluid level needs to be identified and corrected. Normally, topping off the brake fluid should only be performed when the brakes are being repaired or serviced.

To select, handle, store, and fill brake fluids to proper level, follow the steps in SKILL DRILL 24-1.

Brake Fluid Testing

Brake fluid replacement is a maintenance item for virtually all vehicles. Consult the vehicle's service information to determine the correct intervals for brake fluid flushing. Some manufacturers neglect to specify this time frame, so you will need to determine the proper interval based on the type of environment the vehicle is driven in. In humid or wet climates, the brake fluid may need to be flushed every 2 years. In dry climates, every 4 years might be appropriate.

There are several ways of determining if the brake fluid should be flushed:

- Time/mileage: The manufacturer may specify a time/mileage interval for flushing the brake fluid.

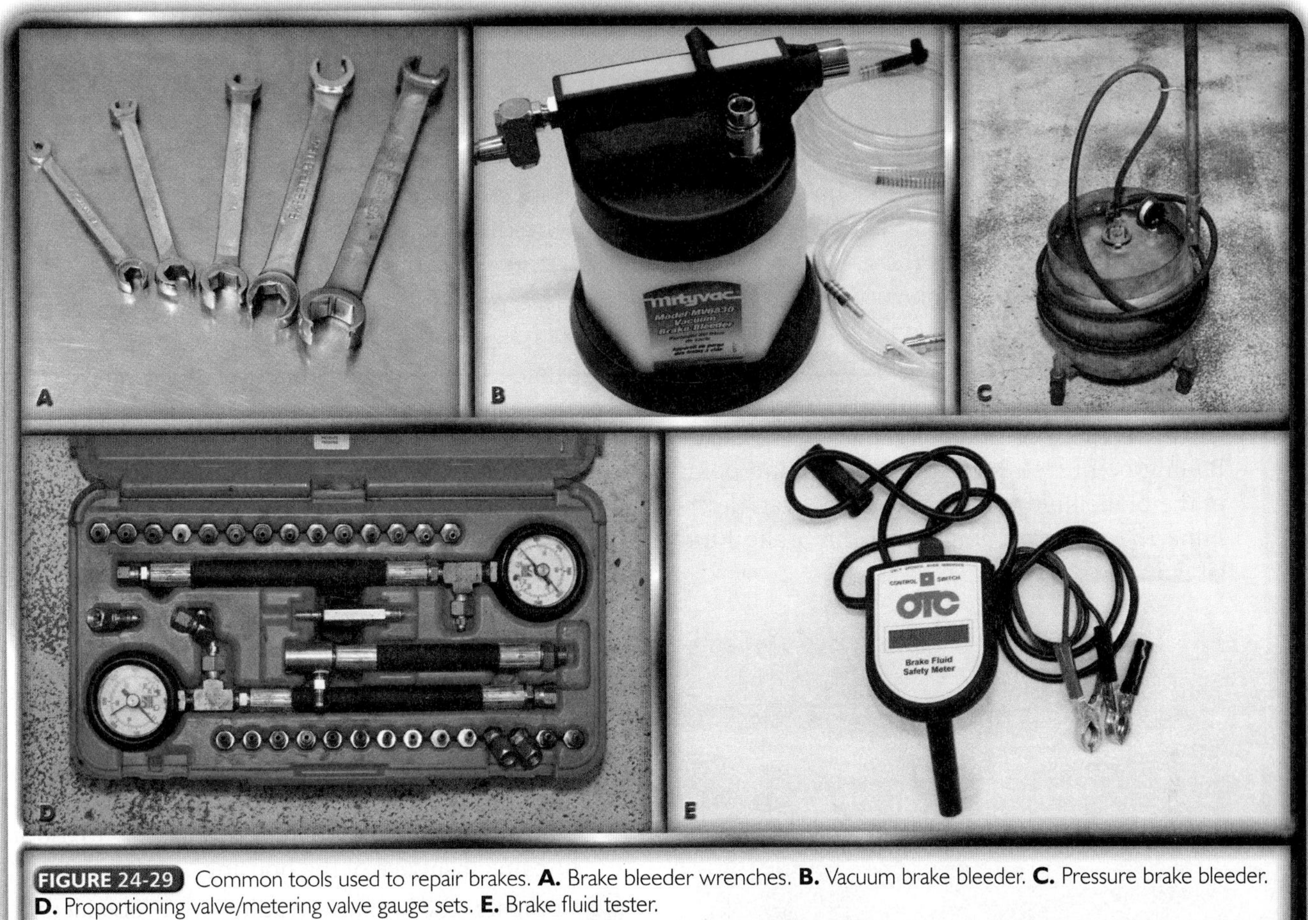
A
B
C
D
E
OTC
Brake Fluid Safety Meter

FIGURE 24-29 Common tools used to repair brakes. **A.** Brake bleeder wrenches. **B.** Vacuum brake bleeder. **C.** Pressure brake bleeder. **D.** Proportioning valve/metering valve gauge sets. **E.** Brake fluid tester.

SKILL DRILL 24-1 Selecting, Handling, Storing, and Filling Brake Fluid

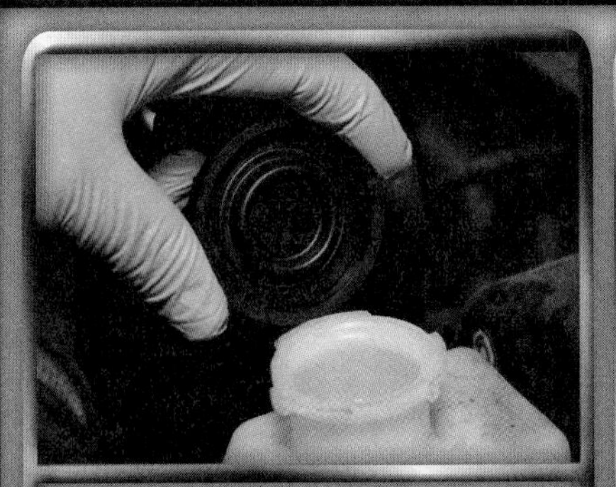

1. Research the specified type of brake fluid in the appropriate service information. Wipe around the master cylinder reservoir cover to prevent any dirt from entering the system. Remove the reservoir cover.

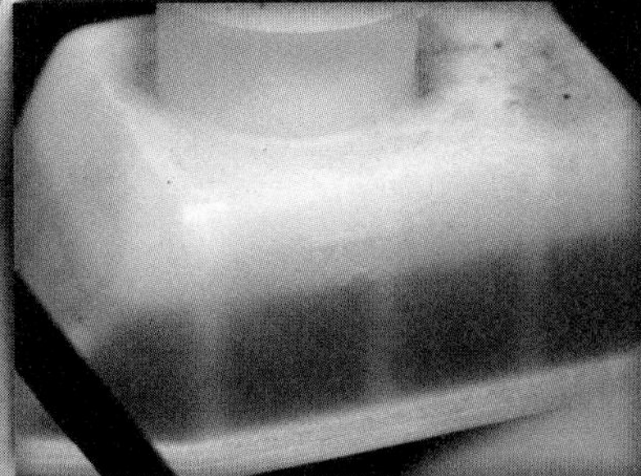

2. Check the fluid level in the reservoir. The fluid should be near the full mark on the side of the cylinder or within half an inch of the top of each chamber if there are no marks. A low level could be caused by worn brake linings/pads or a slow leak in the hydraulic braking system. Investigate these possibilities fully and inform your supervisor of your findings.

3. Once you are sure there are no unresolved issues, add the manufacturer's recommended brake fluid to bring the level to the full mark. Replace the cover and check that it is properly seated. Check for any leaks around the master cylinder. Dilute any brake fluid that may have been spilled with fresh clean water.

- DVOM–galvanic reaction test: The majority of today's braking systems use a combination of dissimilar metals. Manufacturers use aluminum in pistons and housings, and steel in brake lines and some wheel cylinders. When moisture mixes with brake fluid, a galvanic reaction (corrosion) can occur. The higher the moisture content in brake fluid, the higher the galvanic reaction and the greater the erosion/corrosion it causes. The DVOM–galvanic reaction test uses a DVOM to measure the voltage created by the galvanic reaction due to the level of moisture in the fluid **FIGURE 24-30**.
- Boiling point test: Measuring the boiling point of the brake fluid using a special tool can determine the moisture content of the brake fluid **FIGURE 24-31**.
- Test strip: Measuring specific chemicals/metals in the brake fluid can indicate whether there is a chemical breakdown of the brake fluid. Brake fluid test strips contain special color-changing pads that react in the presence of moisture or specific chemicals that have built up in the fluid and that indicate the need for flushing the brake fluid **FIGURE 24-32**.

To test the brake fluid for contamination, you can use the DVOM–galvanic reaction test, the brake fluid tester, or brake fluid test strips. For all three tests, follow these steps first: Brake fluid condition and level should be inspected at every oil change and the fluid replaced according to the manufacturer's recommended service schedule, or when it fails the following tests. Clean around the master cylinder cap to prevent contaminants from entering the reservoir. Remove the master cylinder reservoir cap.

To perform a DVOM–galvanic reaction test, follow the steps in **SKILL DRILL 24-2**:

1. Set the DVOM to DC volts. Insert the red lead in the "v/Ω" slot and the black lead in the "common" slot.
2. Place the red voltmeter probe in the reservoir brake fluid, and place the black lead on the metal housing of the master cylinder. Make sure to use an unpainted surface of the housing.
3. Compare the voltage reading you obtained to specifications. Less than 0.3V is OK. More than 0.3V means the fluid needs to be flushed.

To test brake fluid with a brake fluid tester, follow the steps in **SKILL DRILL 24-3**:

1. Follow the directions for the tester you are using.
2. Test the brake fluid. This is usually accomplished by placing an amount of brake fluid from the

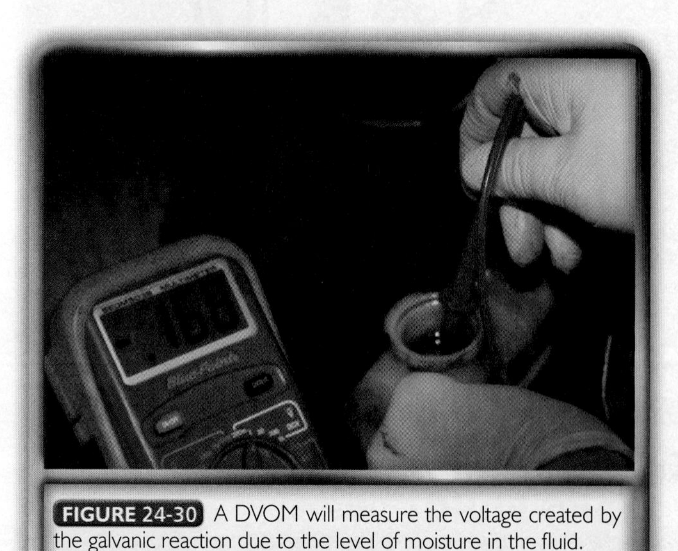

FIGURE 24-30 A DVOM will measure the voltage created by the galvanic reaction due to the level of moisture in the fluid.

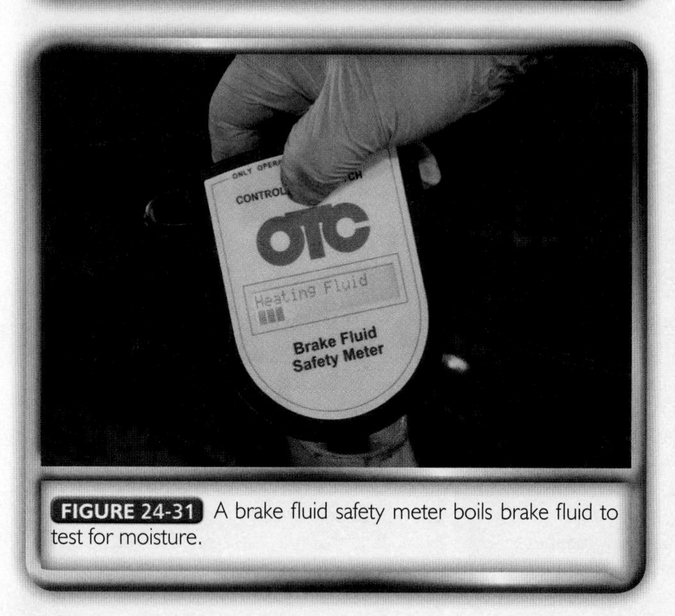
OTC
Heating Fluid
Brake Fluid
Safety Meter

FIGURE 24-31 A brake fluid safety meter boils brake fluid to test for moisture.

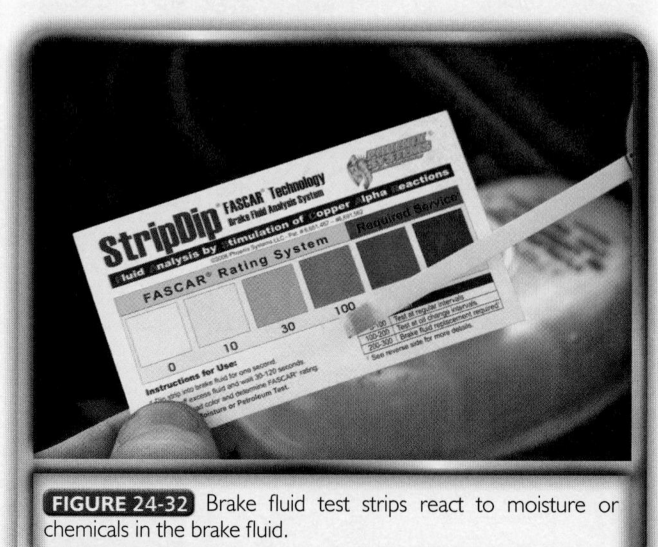
StripDip
FASCAR Technology
Brake Fluid Analysis System
FASCAR® Rating System
Required Service
0
10
30
100

FIGURE 24-32 Brake fluid test strips react to moisture or chemicals in the brake fluid.

master cylinder into the tester. Some testers are designed to be placed directly into the brake fluid.

3 Compare the results you obtained to specifications. Most testers will tell you the boiling point of the fluid or the percent of moisture in the fluid.

To test brake fluid with a brake fluid test strip, follow the steps in SKILL DRILL 24-4:

1 Follow the directions for the brake fluid test strips you are using.

2 Test the brake fluid. Most test strips need to be dipped into the brake fluid for a specified amount of time (usually about 1 or 2 seconds).

3 Shake off excess fluid. An additional amount of specified time is allowed to pass before comparing the colored pad with the color chart to determine the level of contaminates or pH level.

4 Compare the results you obtained to specifications.

Maintenance and Repair

Bleeding

When pressure is applied to brake fluid in a hydraulic braking system, the brake fluid can not be compressed into a smaller volume, and therefore the pressure rises within the hydraulic braking system. Pressure is transmitted throughout the hydraulic braking system without loss. If air enters the hydraulic braking system, it can be dangerous. Unlike fluids, gases are compressible; when pressure is applied to air (a gas), the air decreases its volume and the pressure does not build up as quickly throughout the hydraulic braking system. The brakes will feel spongy and will not be fully functional. **Bleeding** the brakes means removing air from the hydraulic braking system so that only the brake fluid is left in the system.

There are a number of different brake bleeding methods. The three most common are:

- **Manual bleeding**: Using a helper to manually operate the brake pedal while you open and close the bleeder screws on the wheel units to allow the air and old brake fluid to be pushed out of the hydraulic braking system.
- **Pressure bleeding**: Using clean brake fluid under pressure from an auxiliary tool or piece of equipment to force the air and old brake fluid from the hydraulic braking system.
- **Vacuum bleeding**: Using a vacuum bleeder to pull the air and old brake fluid from the hydraulic braking system.

For all three methods, follow these general steps first: Remove as much of the old brake fluid from the reservoir as possible using a suction gun, old antifreeze tester, or turkey baster. Refill the master cylinder reservoir using the specified fluid type. Then determine which method of bleeding you will use. Also research the service information to obtain the bleeding sequence for the vehicle.

The manual bleeding method requires the least amount of equipment and tools. It requires more time if a large percentage of the brake fluid needs changed. It also is less effective at removing trapped air in systems that have high spots in the brake lines or in vehicles that have a large vertical drop between the master cylinder and the wheel brake units, such as a truck that has been lifted. This method is best when only a small amount of brake fluid needs to be bled, such as after replacing front brake calipers, or when more expensive equipment is not available.

To perform the manual bleeding method, follow the steps in SKILL DRILL 24-5. Be sure that you DO NOT bleed the system so much that the reservoir runs dry and admits air into the hydraulic braking system. If this happens, it will be much harder to bleed the hydraulic braking system since air is compressible, making it harder to build pressure within the hydraulic braking system.

The pressure bleeding method uses equipment that can provide a continuous supply of brake fluid under pressure to the master cylinder reservoir. It may also include small-diameter hoses that attach to the bleeder screws and recover all of the old brake fluid. Since this method takes a bit of work to connect the equipment to the vehicle, it is best used when the hydraulic system needs a full flush or on systems that have a tendency to trap air, making manual bleeding much more difficult. To perform the pressure bleeding method, follow the steps in SKILL DRILL 24-6.

To perform the vacuum bleeding method, follow the steps in SKILL DRILL 24-7.

After performing one of these three methods, follow these steps:

1. Double-check that all bleeder screws are properly tightened.
2. Replace all bleeder screw dust caps when finished.
3. Refill the master cylinder to the proper level and reinstall the master cylinder reservoir cap.
4. Start the vehicle and check for proper brake pedal feel (it should be firm and high).
5. Verify that there are no leaks at each bleeder screw.
6. Dispose of any old brake fluid in an environmentally approved method.

SKILL DRILL 24-5 Performing Manual Bleeding

1. Ask an assistant to slowly push the brake pedal down, keeping his or her left foot underneath the pedal to limit full pedal travel.

2. Install a clear hose on the farthest bleeder screw. Open the bleeder screw one-quarter to one-half turn. Observe any old brake fluid and air bubbles coming out. When the brake fluid stops, close the bleeder screw lightly, and then have the assistant slowly release the brake pedal. Repeat these steps until there are no more air bubbles or old fluid coming out of the hose. Close off the bleeder screw and tighten it to the manufacturer's specifications. Check the level in the master cylinder reservoir, top it off, and reinstall the reservoir cap. Repeat this bleeding procedure for each of the brake units, moving closer to the master cylinder, one wheel at a time.

3. Close off the bleeder screw and tighten it to the manufacturer's specifications. Check the level in the master cylinder reservoir, top it off, and reinstall the reservoir cap. Repeat this bleeding procedure for each of the brake units, moving closer to the master cylinder, one wheel at a time.

TECHNICIAN TIP

One other method that you need to know about is gravity bleeding. This method relies on the master cylinder being mounted higher than the wheel brake units. Because gravity tries to pull the brake fluid down, gravity bleeding can occur just by opening one or more bleeder screws. If the height difference is great enough, the brake fluid will slowly drain out of the system. A technician can use this method to start the bleeding process while working on other wheel brake units. However, gravity bleeding can be a disadvantage. If a technician inadvertently leaves a hose disconnected or a bleeder screw open, *all* of the brake fluid can drain out of the system, leaving it full of air and harder to bleed. Be very careful and do not leave the hydraulic braking system open for too long.

TECHNICIAN TIP

Never run the master cylinder dry during bleeding; doing so will make it much more difficult to bleed!

TECHNICIAN TIP

Many manufacturers recommend that brake fluid be changed every 2 to 4 years. Consult the vehicle's owner manual for the specified intervals for the model you are working on and the type of replacement brake fluid recommended.

SKILL DRILL 24-6 Performing Pressure Bleeding

1 Prepare the pressure bleeder and install it on the vehicle.

2 Install a clear hose on the farthest bleeder screw, and open it one-quarter to one-half turn. Observe any old brake fluid and air bubbles coming out.

3 Close off the bleeder screw when the brake fluid is clear and has no bubbles. Tighten it to the manufacturer's specifications. Repeat this procedure for each of the wheel brake units, moving closer to the master cylinder, one wheel at a time.

SKILL DRILL 24-7 Performing Vacuum Bleeding

1 Prepare the vacuum bleeder for use. Install the vacuum bleeder on the farthest bleeder screw, and open it one-quarter to one-half turn.

2 Operate the vacuum bleeder to pull brake fluid from the bleeder screw. Observe any old brake fluid and air bubbles coming out. Close off the bleeder screw and tighten it to the manufacturer's specifications. Check the level in the master cylinder reservoir and top it off. Repeat this procedure for each of the brake units, moving closer to the master cylinder, one wheel at a time.

TECHNICIAN TIP

Note that air can be drawn around the threads of the bleeder screw, so those can fool you into thinking there is still air in the system.

> **TECHNICIAN TIP**
>
> When bleeding the brakes, top off the brake fluid after bleeding each wheel brake unit.

Flushing Process

Flushing brake fluid is similar to brake bleeding except that it is designed to not only remove any trapped air, but to also replace all of the old brake fluid with new brake fluid. A flush using clean brake fluid can be performed to remove any remaining residue and all air. Usually clean brake fluid of the proper type for the vehicle is used for flushing a hydraulic braking system. However, if the hydraulic braking system has been contaminated with petroleum products or other improper fluids, some manufacturers specify flushing it with clean alcohol. The alcohol will help dissolve any oil in addition to flushing the system. Once the alcohol flush is complete, dry compressed air can be used to blow out the majority of the alcohol.

Inspecting Brake Pedal

Brake pedal height, free play, and travel are critical for proper brake operation. Having the proper brake pedal height helps to ensure that the brake pedal has enough starting height to fully apply force to the brakes even if one half of the hydraulic system is rendered useless by a leak. In other words, there needs to be a specified distance the brake pedal can travel before it contacts the floor or anything else. **Free play** is the amount of clearance between the brake pedal linkage and the master cylinder piston. To measure it, you can apply very light hand pressure to the brake pedal, measuring how far the pedal travels before you start to feel resistance **FIGURE 24-33**.

Brake pedal travel is sometimes called reserve pedal. Travel is the distance the brake pedal travels, from its rest position to its applied height. Travel is measured by reading brake pedal height and subtracting the height from the floor **FIGURE 24-34**. For example, if the brake pedal height is 8″ (203.2 mm) and the travel takes it down to 5″ (127 mm) off the floor, then the travel is 3″ (76.2 mm). Reserve pedal is the measurement from the floor to the applied brake pedal and represents how much reserve is left for the brake pedal to travel if needed **FIGURE 24-35**.

FIGURE 24-33 To measure free play, apply light hand pressure to the brake pedal and measure how far the pedal travels before you feel resistance.

FIGURE 24-34 Travel is measured by reading brake petal height and subtracting the height from the floor.

FIGURE 24-35 Reserve pedal is the measurement from the floor to the applied brake pedal.

To measure brake pedal height, follow the steps in SKILL DRILL 24-8:

1. Research the procedure and specifications for measuring brake pedal height, travel, and free play for the vehicle you are working on. Some manufacturers specify how much travel the brake pedal should have while others specify how much reserve pedal should remain when the brake pedal is fully applied. Know which process applies to the vehicle you are working on.
2. Remove any removable floor mats or anything lying on the floor near the brake pedal.
3. With the engine off, measure the brake pedal height between the two specified points using a measuring stick.
4. Compare this reading to the specifications and determine any necessary actions.

TECHNICIAN TIP

Make sure you understand and observe all legislative and personal safety procedures when carrying out tasks. If you are unsure of what these procedures are, ask your supervisor.

Applied Science

AS-96: Contamination: The technician can demonstrate an understanding of how a contaminated liquid can cause a chemical reaction that results in the deterioration of performance.

As moisture levels increase in brake fluid, the boiling point of the brake fluid decreases. This chemical reaction results in the deterioration of the brake fluid's performance. In any liquid, when boiling occurs, the liquid turns to vapor. Brakes work on the principle of liquid being incompressible; however, vapor is compressible. The result of brake fluid boiling in brake systems is a spongy pedal and a loss of braking effort at the wheels, including potential for complete brake failure. SAE field tests have documented that the average 1-year-old car has approximately 2% moisture in the brake fluid, making regular brake fluid changes necessary to ensure safety.

Safety

Never use any petroleum- or mineral-based products, such as gasoline or kerosene, to clean a hydraulic braking system or its components. They are not compatible with the seals used in the braking system and will result in a failure of the hydraulic braking system and its components. This failure may result in injury to the passengers or damage to the vehicle.

To measure brake pedal free play, follow the steps in SKILL DRILL 24-9:

1. Research the specified procedure to measure the pedal free play.
2. Use light hand pressure to apply the brake pedal until all clearances are taken up, while measuring the distance the brake pedal moved.
3. Compare this reading to the specifications and determine any necessary actions.

To measure brake pedal travel, follow the steps in SKILL DRILL 24-10:

1. Research the specified procedure to measure the brake pedal travel or reserve pedal height.
2. Start the engine. This will allow the booster to operate normally.
3. Apply the brake pedal with the specified force.
4. Measure the brake pedal travel or reserve height.
5. Compare this reading to the specifications and determine any necessary actions.

Inspecting Master Cylinder

Inspecting the master cylinder for internal and external leaks is usually performed under the following conditions: the brake pedal sinks when the brakes are applied, the brake fluid is low in the reservoir, the brake warning light is on, or the brake pedal reserve height is too low. To check the master cylinder for internal or external leaks and proper operation, follow the steps in SKILL DRILL 24-11.

Master Cylinder Service and Bench Bleeding

Removing and bench bleeding the master cylinder are usually only performed when the master cylinder is being replaced. Bench bleeding makes bleeding the hydraulic system much easier by removing all of the air from the master cylinder. Failure to bench bleed the master cylinder prior to installing it into the hydraulic brake system will prevent the master cylinder from building much brake fluid pressure. As a result, very little brake fluid will be bled out of each wheel cylinder or caliper, increasing the time it takes to bleed the hydraulic brake system.

To remove, bench bleed, and reinstall the master cylinder, follow the steps in SKILL DRILL 24-12.

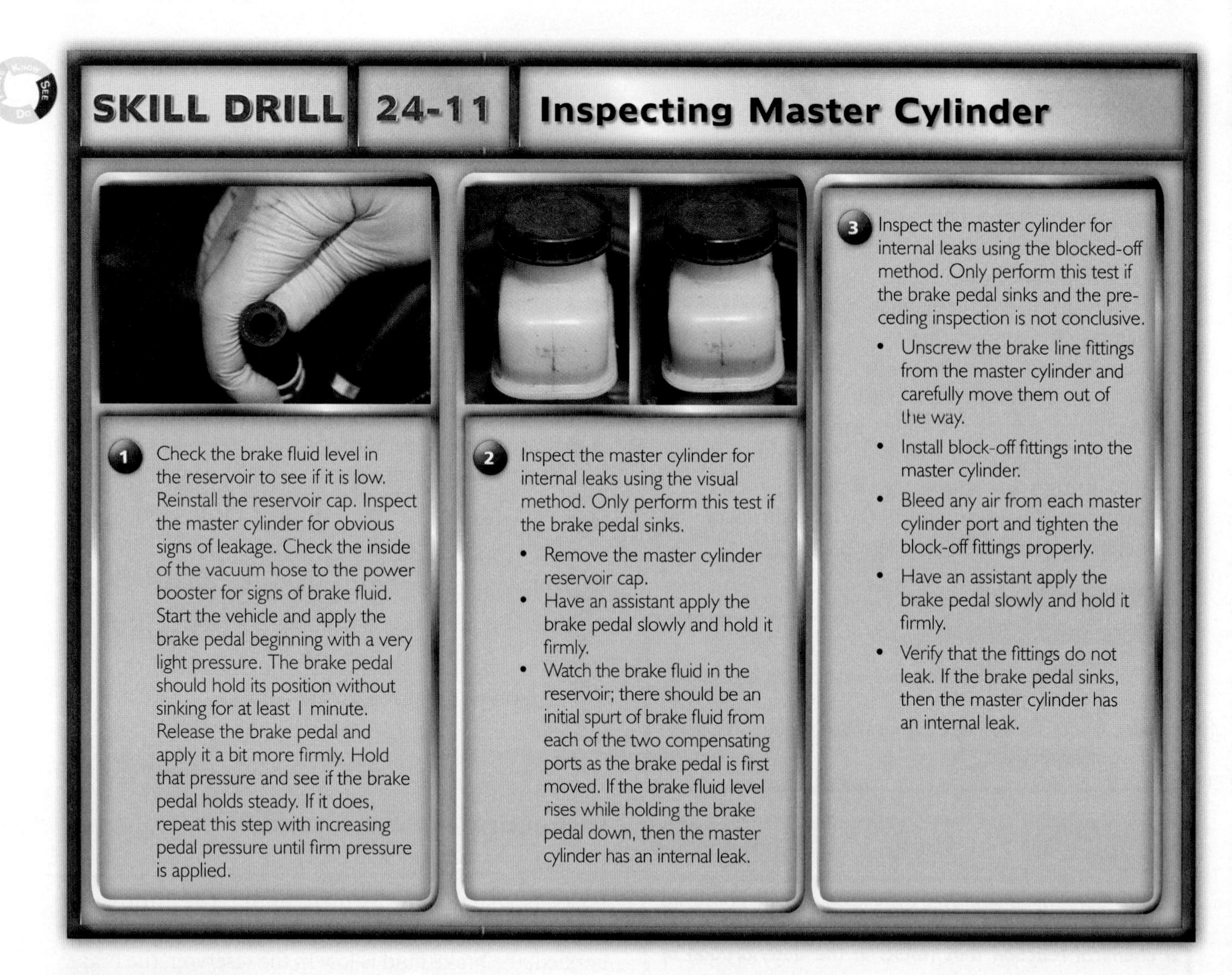
SKILL DRILL 24-11 Inspecting Master Cylinder

1 Check the brake fluid level in the reservoir to see if it is low. Reinstall the reservoir cap. Inspect the master cylinder for obvious signs of leakage. Check the inside of the vacuum hose to the power booster for signs of brake fluid. Start the vehicle and apply the brake pedal beginning with a very light pressure. The brake pedal should hold its position without sinking for at least 1 minute. Release the brake pedal and apply it a bit more firmly. Hold that pressure and see if the brake pedal holds steady. If it does, repeat this step with increasing pedal pressure until firm pressure is applied.

2 Inspect the master cylinder for internal leaks using the visual method. Only perform this test if the brake pedal sinks.
• Remove the master cylinder reservoir cap.
• Have an assistant apply the brake pedal slowly and hold it firmly.
• Watch the brake fluid in the reservoir; there should be an initial spurt of brake fluid from each of the two compensating ports as the brake pedal is first moved. If the brake fluid level rises while holding the brake pedal down, then the master cylinder has an internal leak.

3 Inspect the master cylinder for internal leaks using the blocked-off method. Only perform this test if the brake pedal sinks and the preceding inspection is not conclusive.
• Unscrew the brake line fittings from the master cylinder and carefully move them out of the way.
• Install block-off fittings into the master cylinder.
• Bleed any air from each master cylinder port and tighten the block-off fittings properly.
• Have an assistant apply the brake pedal slowly and hold it firmly.
• Verify that the fittings do not leak. If the brake pedal sinks, then the master cylinder has an internal leak.

Diagnosis

Overview

Diagnosis of hydraulic braking system faults begins with an understanding of the system being worked on and familiarity with Pascal's law. Add to that the customer's description of the concern and you will have enough to start investigating the cause of the customer concern. It is good practice to gather as much related information as possible about the concern from the customer. The more information you obtain, the better chance you will have in diagnosing the issue. Ask the customer questions such as:

- Does the brake pedal sink under hard pressure? Or light pressure?
- Does the vehicle pull to the left when braking? Or the right?
- Does the wheel lock up under hard brake pressure? Or light pressure?

Once you have an understanding of how the vehicle is acting, try to determine what conditions are present with the concern by asking questions such as:

- Does it happen when it is wet? Dry? Or always?
- Does it happen when it is hot? Cold? Or always?
- Does it happen when you are driving at highway speeds? At stop-and-go speeds? Or always?
- Does it happen when you are carrying a heavy load? Light load? Or always?

If the vehicle is safe to drive, it is common practice to test-drive the vehicle to verify the customer concern. If it is an intermittent problem or if it is hard to reproduce, you may need to take the customer along on the test-drive to point out what she or he is experiencing. While on the test-drive, reproduce the conditions that the customer identified and observe the concern. Do your best to determine where the fault is located by safely operating the vehicle in a variety of manners.

SKILL DRILL 24-12 Performing Master Cylinder Service and Bench Bleeding

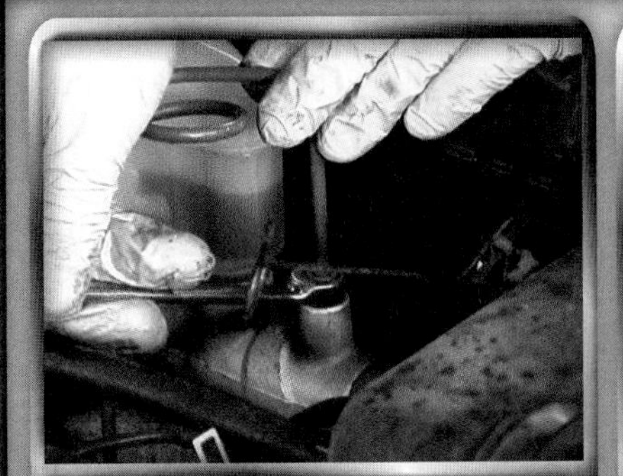

1. Compare the new unit to the old one to verify that it is the correct replacement. If it is not, inform your supervisor/instructor. Remove all of the old brake fluid from the master cylinder reservoir. Remove the master cylinder brake lines using a flare wrench and, if necessary, the double wrench method.

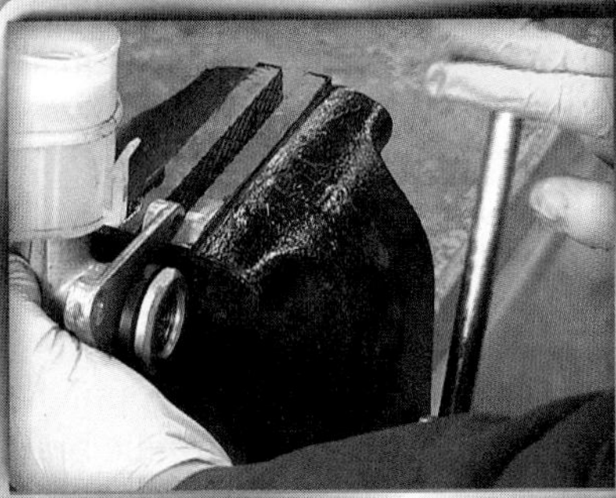

2. Remove the nuts holding the master cylinder to the power brake booster. Remove the master cylinder. Mount the master cylinder in a vise with the reservoir facing up.

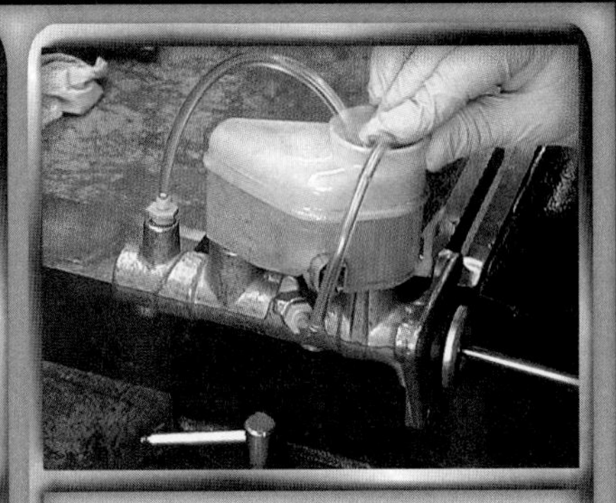

3. Install the bleeder lines into the master cylinder outlet ports with the ends of the lines deep within the master cylinder reservoir below the normal fluid level. Fill the reservoir about half full with clean brake fluid. With an appropriate tool, slowly push the master cylinder piston into the bore. Allow the piston to return to its rest position. Repeat the last two steps until all air bubbles and old fluid have been removed from the master cylinder.

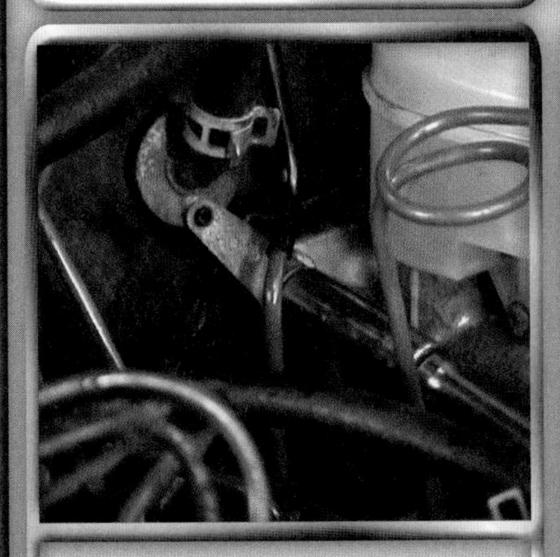

4. Place the master cylinder on the power booster and install the nuts just far enough to hold it from falling off.

5. Carefully line up the brake lines and start them by using your fingers to thread them into the master cylinder outlet ports at least four or five threads from when they first catch. To prevent cross threading, do not use a wrench to start the threads.

6. Tighten the bolts connecting the master cylinder to the power booster to their proper torque. Tighten the brake line fittings using a flare nut or line wrench. Use the double wrench method if the master cylinder is fitted with an adapter. Top off the master cylinder and bleed all wheel brake units to remove any remaining air. Start the engine and check brake pedal feel to verify proper height and firmness and that there is no sinking condition. Visually inspect all fittings and bleeder screws to make sure they are not leaking.

As you are gathering information, compare what is happening in the vehicle with your knowledge of the hydraulic braking system and Pascal's law to identify possible causes of the fault. If the fault is fairly substantial, the cause may be easy to identify. If this situation is not easily identified, then determine whether further test-driving will be useful.

Once the test-drive has accomplished as much as possible, it is time to identify the cause of the concern. Doing so may involve further testing in the shop or it could require disassembly and inspection of the suspected component or system. If you have been thorough in your diagnostic process, this should lead you to the cause of the fault. If not, take what you learned on the further diagnosis and/or inspection, determine what the next best step is, and perform it. Continue this process until you have identified the cause of the fault.

Once the cause of fault is identified, consider if it is the root cause. For example, if the customer concern is that the brake pedal is spongy, you cannot stop your diagnosis when you find low brake fluid level in the master cylinder reservoir. Adding brake fluid and bleeding the brakes might restore proper function to the brake pedal, but you have to ask, "Why was the brake fluid low?" It is likely that there is a leak in the hydraulic braking system that will cause the customer concern to return. In this case, the root cause might be a leaky wheel cylinder. Because the brake fluid was low, you should perform a visual inspection of the hydraulic braking system to verify there are no leaks.

Diagnosing Power Brake Systems

All power brake systems should be inspected and tested whenever the customer complains that the brakes are dragging, the brake pedal is harder to push than normal, the pedal height has changed, or if the engine operation changes more than a minimal amount when the brake pedal is applied. Vacuum boosters should also be tested if you determine that the vehicle has an unlocated vacuum leak. Single-diaphragm and dual-diaphragm vacuum brake boosters are diagnosed in the same manner. The following tests can be performed on single-diaphragm and dual-diaphragm boosters:

- Brake pedal free travel: Tests to see if there is the proper brake pedal linkage clearance
- Performance/operation test: Tests to see if the booster is operational
- External leak test: Tests for leaks to the atmosphere
- Internal leak test: Tests for leaks between the booster chambers

Testing Power Booster

Power booster testing starts with a brake pedal free travel test and then follows up with a performance test to see if the booster is operating properly. The brake pedal free travel is critical for proper brake operation. The proper amount of free travel ensures that the brake pedal linkage allows the master cylinder piston to return to its proper rest position and uncover the compensating ports. Insufficient free travel can cause the brakes to drag due to trapped fluid pressure in front of the piston not being able to return to the reservoir through the blocked compensating ports. Excessive free travel is not good either, as it reduces the amount of reserve pedal for braking in the event of a hydraulic brake system leak.

As important as brake pedal free travel is, it normally does not need to be adjusted since the components are locked in place. The situations that would call for adjusting it include the following: someone has changed the adjustment setting, the brake pedal linkage has been repaired or adjusted, the linkage has worn over time leading to increased free travel, or the power booster is being replaced. Just changing the master cylinder does not normally require brake pedal free travel adjustment; however, it is good practice to verify that it is within specifications. If adjustment is needed, the manufacturer usually incorporates a locking adjustment rod between the power booster and the brake pedal.

After verifying that the free travel is correct, it is time to performance test the power booster. To do so, operate the booster to test its ability to provide boost to the master cylinder. To test pedal free travel and check power assist operation, follow the steps in **SKILL DRILL 24-13**. Because the brake pedal responds differently on vacuum-assisted, hydraulic-assisted, and other vehicles, consult the service information to verify the specific testing procedure and results for the vehicle you are working on.

> **TECHNICIAN TIP**
>
> Holding the brake pedal in a steady manner should not affect the operation of the engine. If the engine runs rough when the brake pedal is held down or changes substantially when the brake pedal is released, it could indicate a vacuum leak in the booster. Perform the external and internal leak tests to identify any faults.

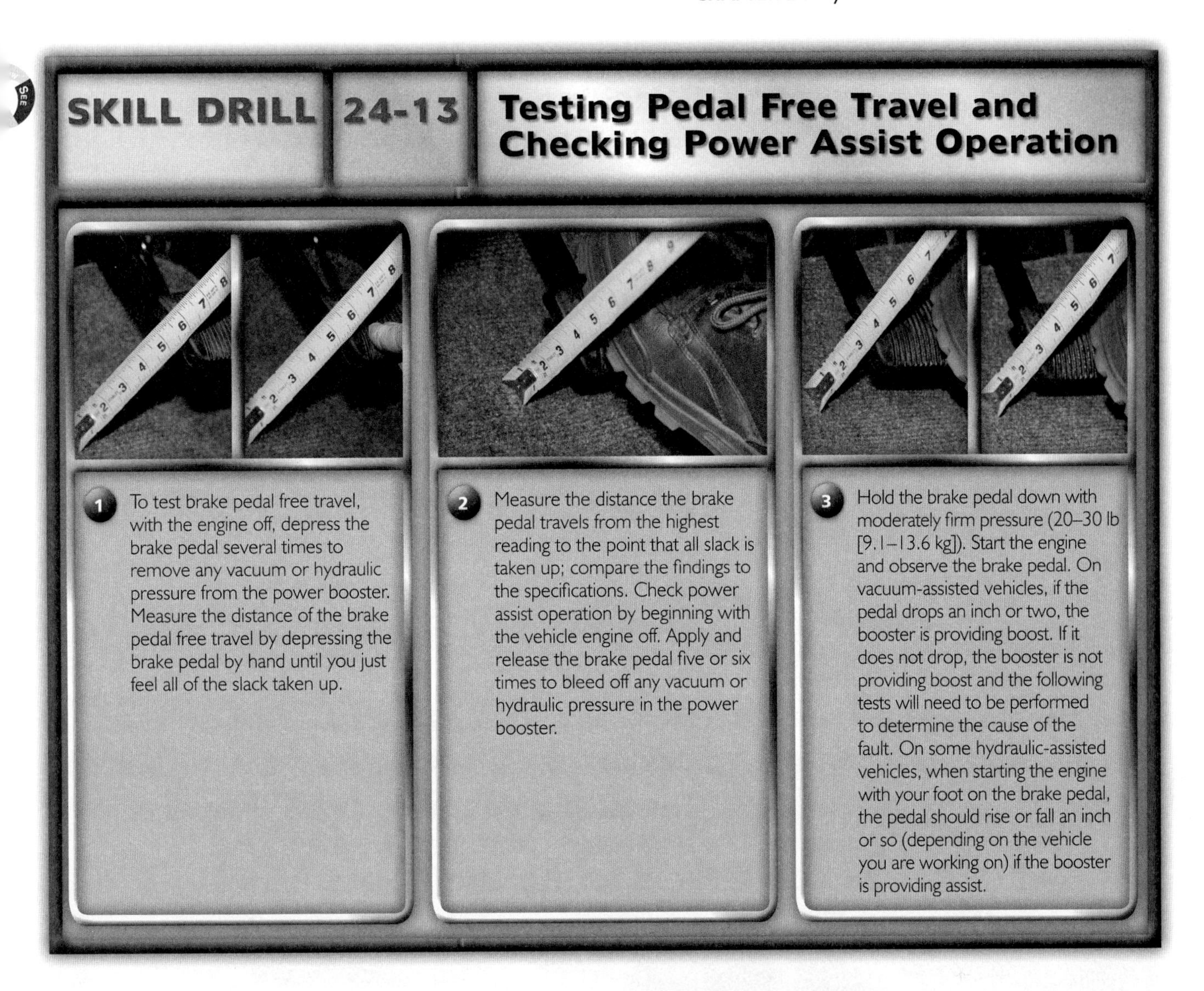
SKILL DRILL 24-13 Testing Pedal Free Travel and Checking Power Assist Operation
1 To test brake pedal free travel, with the engine off, depress the brake pedal several times to remove any vacuum or hydraulic pressure from the power booster. Measure the distance of the brake pedal free travel by depressing the brake pedal by hand until you just feel all of the slack taken up.
2 Measure the distance the brake pedal travels from the highest reading to the point that all slack is taken up; compare the findings to the specifications. Check power assist operation by beginning with the vehicle engine off. Apply and release the brake pedal five or six times to bleed off any vacuum or hydraulic pressure in the power booster.
3 Hold the brake pedal down with moderately firm pressure (20–30 lb [9.1–13.6 kg]). Start the engine and observe the brake pedal. On vacuum-assisted vehicles, if the pedal drops an inch or two, the booster is providing boost. If it does not drop, the booster is not providing boost and the following tests will need to be performed to determine the cause of the fault. On some hydraulic-assisted vehicles, when starting the engine with your foot on the brake pedal, the pedal should rise or fall an inch or so (depending on the vehicle you are working on) if the booster is providing assist.

Checking Vacuum Supply to Vacuum-Type Power Booster

The brake booster must have an adequate amount of vacuum to operate correctly. Insufficient vacuum will require the driver to increase foot pressure to activate the brakes. Excessive vacuum is not usually a problem because the booster is designed to work using maximum engine vacuum. Many manufacturers specify a minimum of 16 inches of mercury (in. Hg; 406 mm Hg) of intake manifold vacuum. To check vacuum supply to a vacuum-type power booster, follow the steps in SKILL DRILL 24-14.

Checking Vacuum-Type Power Booster Unit for Leaks and Inspecting the Check Valve

Vacuum leaks in the power booster require increased driver foot pressure to activate the brakes. Since the vacuum normally comes from the intake manifold, a leaky power booster can affect the operation of the engine by changing the air/fuel mixture. Power boosters can leak internally or externally. Perform the external leak test before the internal leak test to avoid confusion in identifying the cause of the leak. To inspect the vacuum-type power booster unit for leaks and inspect the check valve for proper operation, follow the steps in SKILL DRILL 24-15.

TECHNICIAN TIP

Engines with modified camshafts regularly have decreased amounts of manifold vacuum due to the high-duration camshaft. This lowered vacuum results in higher foot pressure required to stop the vehicle. An auxiliary vacuum pump may be needed to provide adequate braking. Also, vehicles operated at high altitude will always have less vacuum. The general rule of thumb is that you will lose 1 in. Hg (25 mm Hg) for every 1000″ (305 m) of altitude gained.

SKILL DRILL 24-14 Checking Vacuum Supply to Vacuum-type Power Booster

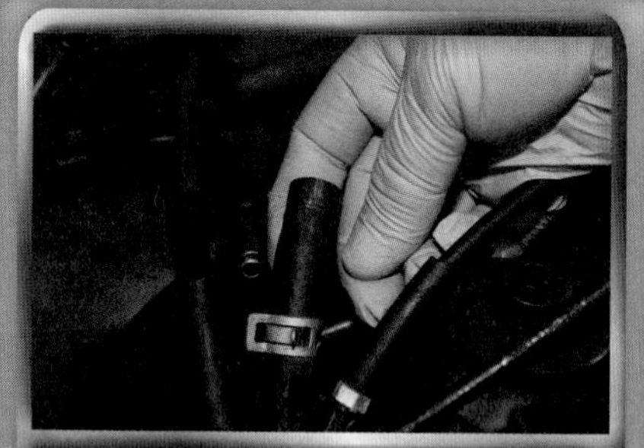

1. With the engine off, remove the inlet hose from the vacuum-type booster.

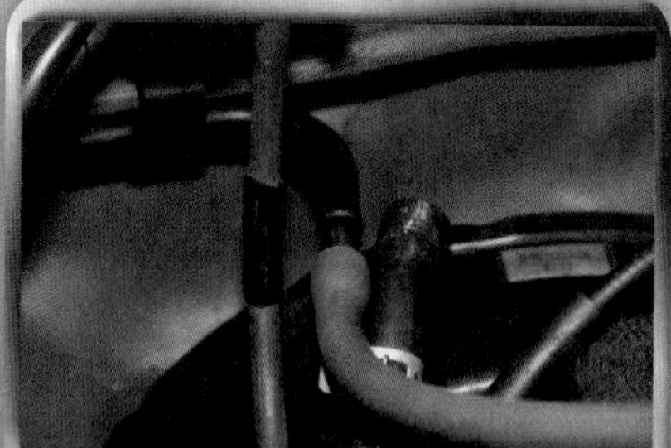

2. Connect a vacuum gauge to the vacuum supply end of the hose.

3. Start the engine and read the vacuum supply available to the vacuum-type booster. Vacuum should be greater than 16 in. Hg (406 mm Hg) on most vehicles. If the reading is insufficient, check for vacuum leaks or restrictions in the supply hose or for an improperly tuned engine.

SKILL DRILL 24-15 Checking Vacuum-Type Power Booster Unit for Leaks and Inspecting the Check Valve

1. The first step is to perform an external leak test. Start the engine and allow it to run for at least 10 seconds. With your foot *off* of the brake pedal, turn the engine off. Wait at least 10 minutes, then apply the brake pedal with moderately firm pressure (20–30 lb [9.1–13.6 kg]). Note the feel and pedal reserve height. Apply the brake pedal a couple more times with the same moderately firm pressure. Each application should result in a higher brake pedal as the vacuum is released from the booster.

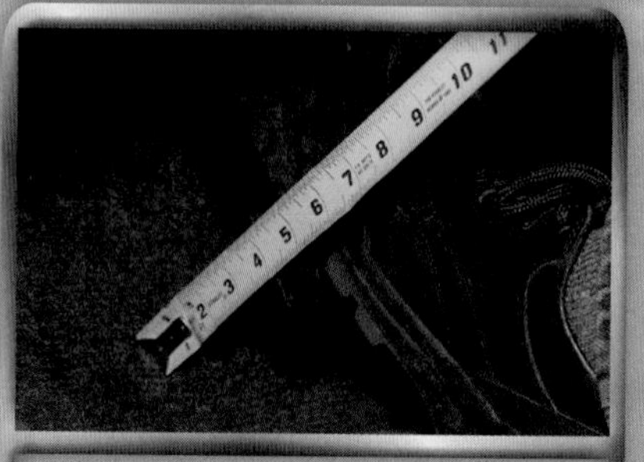

2. The second step is to perform an internal leak test. Begin by starting the engine and letting it idle. Apply the brake pedal with firm pressure (30–50 lb [13.6–22.7 kg]). Without moving your foot, shut off the engine and observe the brake pedal for approximately 1 minute. If it stays steady, there are no internal leaks. If the brake pedal rises, there is an internal leak.

00:30

3. The third step is to perform a check valve operation test. Start the engine and allow it to run for 30 seconds to evacuate the booster.

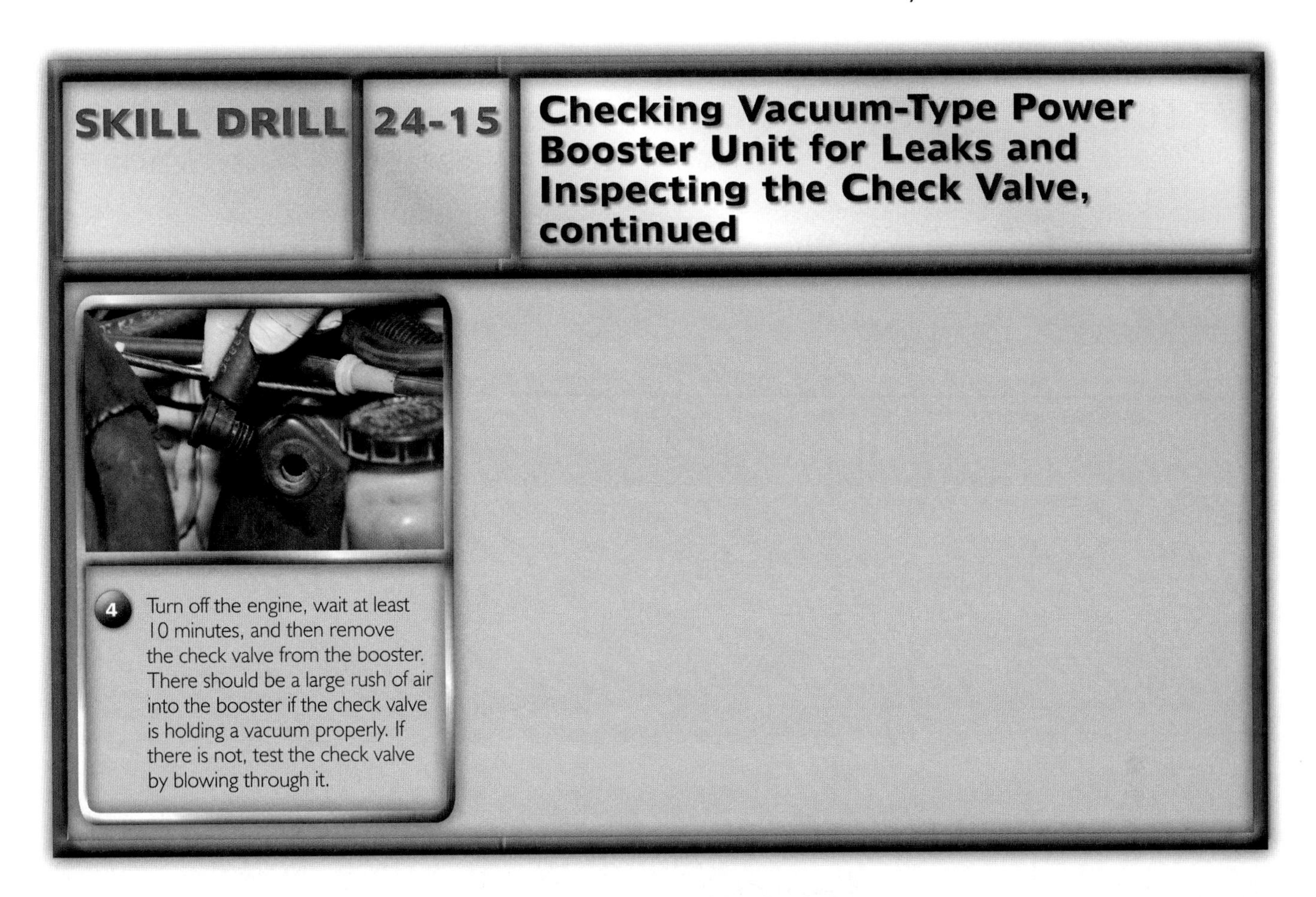
SKILL DRILL 24-15
Checking Vacuum-Type Power Booster Unit for Leaks and Inspecting the Check Valve, continued
4 Turn off the engine, wait at least 10 minutes, and then remove the check valve from the booster. There should be a large rush of air into the booster if the check valve is holding a vacuum properly. If there is not, test the check valve by blowing through it.

Inspecting Brake Lines and Hoses

Inspecting brake lines and brake hoses can show where maintenance is needed to prevent vehicle breakdowns and unsafe vehicle operation. Regular inspection of these components is recommended by all manufacturers. Be sure to take into account regional differences, such as regions that are highly susceptible to corrosion from de-icing chemicals or high humidity. Also, off-road vehicles may be more prone to dents, kinks, and cuts. Inspect all vehicles carefully.

To inspect brake lines, brake hoses, and associated hardware, follow the steps in SKILL DRILL 24-16. In step one, pay special attention to any low spots in steel lines, as they can collect water inside them and rust from the inside out.

Replacing Brake Lines, Brake Hoses, Fittings, and Supports

To replace brake lines, brake hoses, fittings, and supports, follow the steps in SKILL DRILL 24-17.

Applied Science

AS-87: Hydraulics: The technician can explain how fluid pressure transmits force from one location to another.

Pascal's law states that incompressible liquids transmit pressure in all directions. This is the basic principle underpinning the operation of hydraulic braking systems on motor vehicles. When braking, brake pedal pressure is applied, via the master cylinder, to the brake fluid. The hydraulic fluid under pressure pushes against the caliper or wheel cylinder pistons, forcing friction material against the brake discs or drums to stop the movement of the vehicle.

For the sake of simplicity, let's think of a hydraulic brake system like a tube of toothpaste. Start with a full tube (no air). If you punch a hole in the tube and squeeze, toothpaste (a thick liquid) will be displaced from the hole. If you punch three holes through various parts of the tube and squeeze in only one place, toothpaste will be displaced from all three holes. This illustrates that force applied to a liquid in one area is transferred to all areas within a container.

Prove
Know
See
Do

SKILL DRILL 24-16 Inspecting Brake Lines, Brake Hoses, and Associated Hardware

1. Safely raise the vehicle on a hoist. Trace all brake lines from the master cylinder to each wheel's brake assembly. Inspect the steel brake lines for leaks, dents, kinks, rust and cracks.

2. Inspect all flexible brake hoses for cracks, bulging, and wear.

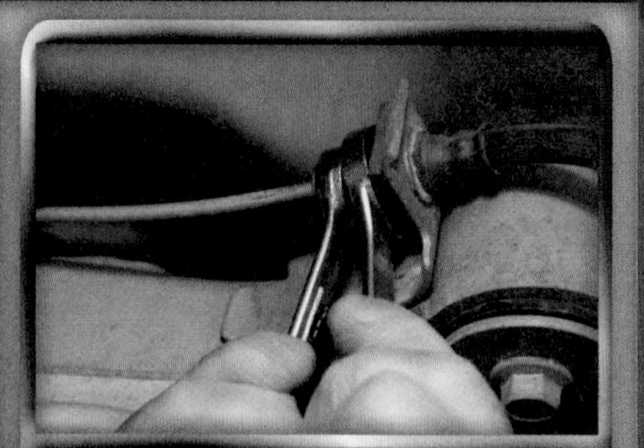

3. Tighten any loose fittings and supports.

Prove
Know
See
Do

SKILL DRILL 24-17 Replacing Brake Lines, Hoses, Fittings, and Supports

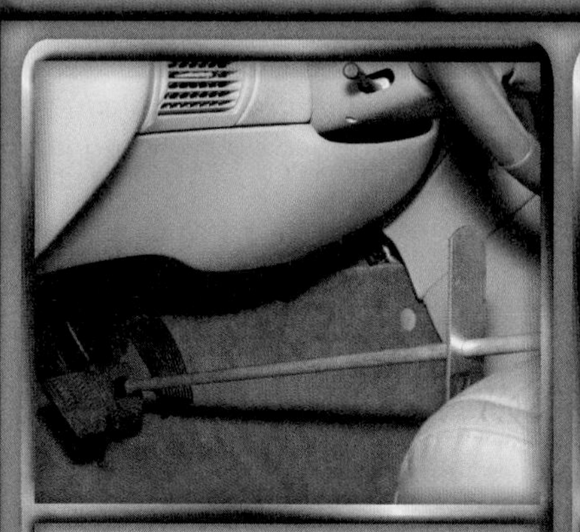

1. To prevent an excessive amount of brake fluid from leaking out of the hydraulic brake system while the brake line or brake hose is removed from the vehicle, depress the brake pedal with a brake pedal depressor. This will push the master cylinder piston past the compensating ports and prevent brake fluid from leaving the reservoir.

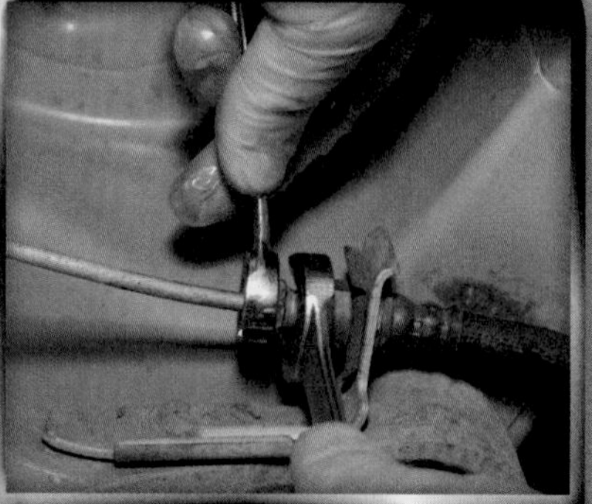

2. Remove the stop light fuse to avoid draining the battery. Safely raise the vehicle on a hoist. Using flare nut wrenches and the double wrench method, carefully remove any brake lines, hoses, fittings, and supports that are to be replaced. Inspect all components for damage and wear.

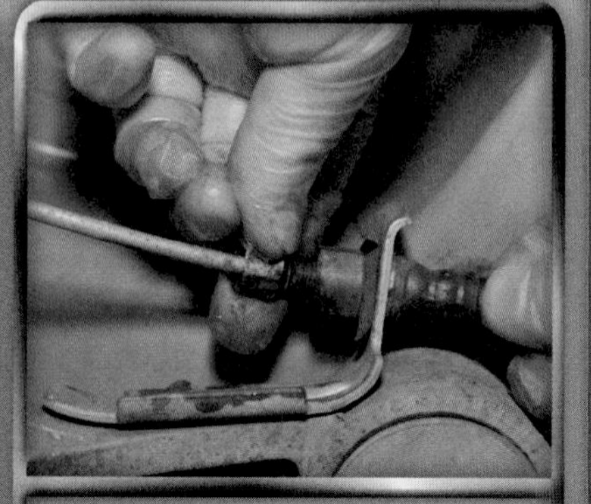

3. Carefully reassemble the removed components, but until everything is assembled, tighten any fittings or supports by using your fingers only. Once everything is assembled, tighten each fitting and support using flare nut wrenches and the double wrench method wherever two fittings connect. Bleed the hydraulic braking system to remove any trapped air. Start the vehicle to verify proper brake pedal height, firmness, and feel. Reinstall the brake light fuse if removed.

Brake Line Flaring

To fabricate brake lines, decide whether you will be using the double flare or ISO method. First select new, double-walled brake line of the specified diameter. Make sure the end you are flaring is cut smooth and square, without dings or gouges. Clean up with a file or recut the end with a tubing cutter. Obtain the flaring tool for the type of flare you are fabricating: double flare or ISO.

To perform the double flare method, follow the steps in SKILL DRILL 24-18.

To perform the ISO flare method, follow the steps in SKILL DRILL 24-19:

1. Install the proper fitting onto the brake line. You may want to tape it out of the way temporarily.
2. Use a bench vise to hold the brake line clamping tool.
3. Select the proper adapter to match the tubing size. Use it to set the height of the tube in the clamp. Tighten down the clamp securely.
4. Insert the adapter into the tubing, and install the flaring tool onto the clamp and over the adapter.
5. Tighten down the flaring tool until the adapter touches the clamp.
6. Remove the flared line from the clamp and inspect it.

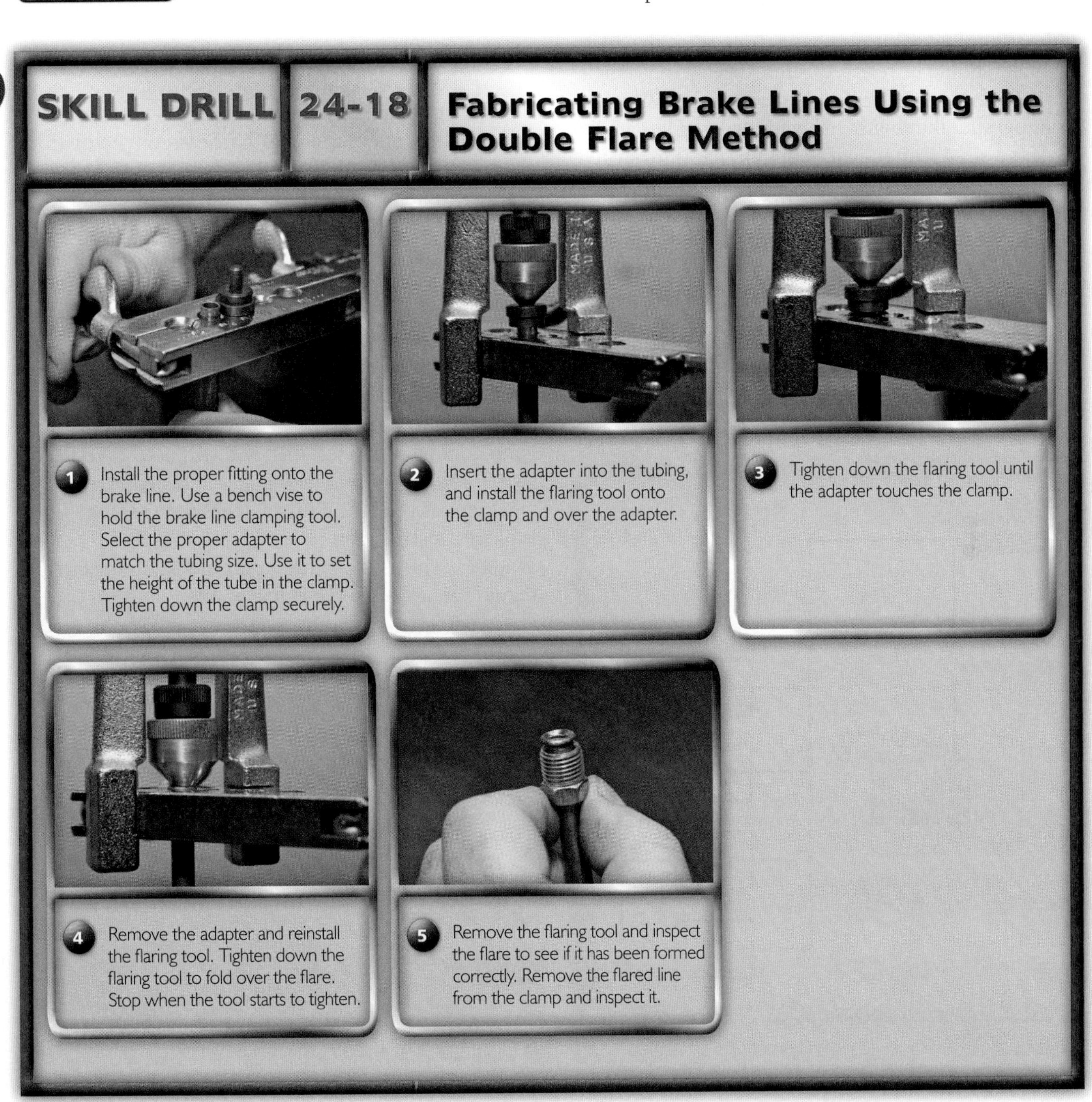
SKILL DRILL 24-18 Fabricating Brake Lines Using the Double Flare Method
1 Install the proper fitting onto the brake line. Use a bench vise to hold the brake line clamping tool. Select the proper adapter to match the tubing size. Use it to set the height of the tube in the clamp. Tighten down the clamp securely.
2 Insert the adapter into the tubing, and install the flaring tool onto the clamp and over the adapter.
3 Tighten down the flaring tool until the adapter touches the clamp.
4 Remove the adapter and reinstall the flaring tool. Tighten down the flaring tool to fold over the flare. Stop when the tool starts to tighten.
5 Remove the flaring tool and inspect the flare to see if it has been formed correctly. Remove the flared line from the clamp and inspect it.

Diagnosing Brake Warning Lamp

A mechanical brake warning lamp system (non-CAN-bus) circuit is a simple light bulb in series with as many as four switches that are connected in parallel with each other FIGURE 24-36. Each switch can illuminate the warning lamp under the right conditions. The warning lamp should be off when the ignition key is in the "run" position if the parking brake is released and there are no faults in the hydraulic system. When the ignition is turned to the "crank" position, the warning lamp should illuminate. In the "run" position, the warning lamp can be illuminated only when one of the switches is closed. One switch is on the parking brake assembly and illuminates the warning lamp when the parking brake is applied. This alerts the driver that the parking brake should be released before driving the vehicle. The second switch is located on the pressure differential assembly and illuminates the warning lamp if there is a moderate-sized hydraulic system leak. The third switch, if equipped, is located on the master cylinder reservoir and illuminates the warning lamp if the fluid level falls below a certain point. The last switch, if equipped, is located on the ignition switch and acts as a bulb check feature, which illuminates the warning lamp when the ignition switch is in the "crank" position.

When diagnosing the brake warning lamp, it is good to start by verifying that the bulb is operational using the circuit's bulb check feature if equipped. To do so, turn the ignition key to the "crank" position. The brake warning lamp on the dash should illuminate on most vehicles. If the bulb illuminates, then you know the bulb is good, it has power, and the ground circuit through the ignition switch is operating as it should. If it does not illuminate, first check the fuse with a test light FIGURE 24-37. If the fuse is OK, remove the bulb and verify that it is not burned out by measuring its resistance with an ohmmeter and comparing it to specifications or the resistance of a known good bulb.

If the brake warning lamp illuminated in the "crank" position, turn the ignition key to the "run" position. The brake warning lamp should be off. If it is, apply the parking brake. The warning lamp should illuminate. If it does not illuminate, you will need to refer to the vehicle's wiring diagram to determine the best strategy to diagnose the system. If it is similar to the one in Figure 24-25, then locate the parking brake switch, disconnect the wire harness connector from the switch, and jump it to ground with a jumper wire. With the ignition switch on, the brake warning light should now be illuminated. If it is, then the switch either needs adjustment or replacement. If it is not, then there is a problem between the switch and the bulb. Use the same process for the low brake fluid switch, the pressure differential switch, and the ignition switch.

If the brake warning lamp always stays on in the "run" position, you will need to disconnect each of the four switches one at a time, checking to see if the warning lamp goes off. If it does, then you will need to test each switch and determine whether it is adjusted properly, or whether it is shorted. If the switches test OK, then there is likely a short circuit in one of the wires leading to the switches. This is the hardest part of testing the circuit; thankfully, it doesn't happen very often.

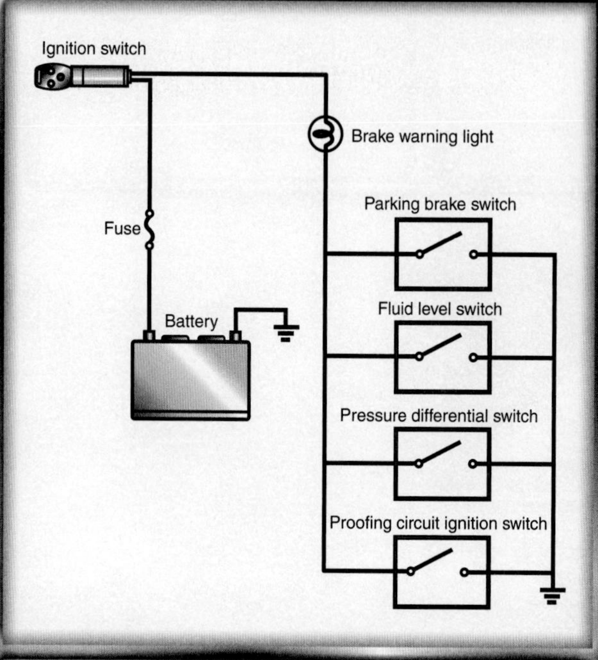

Ignition switch
Brake warning light
Parking brake switch
Fuse
Fluid level switch
Battery
Pressure differential switch
Proofing circuit ignition switch

FIGURE 24-36 Brake warning light circuit.

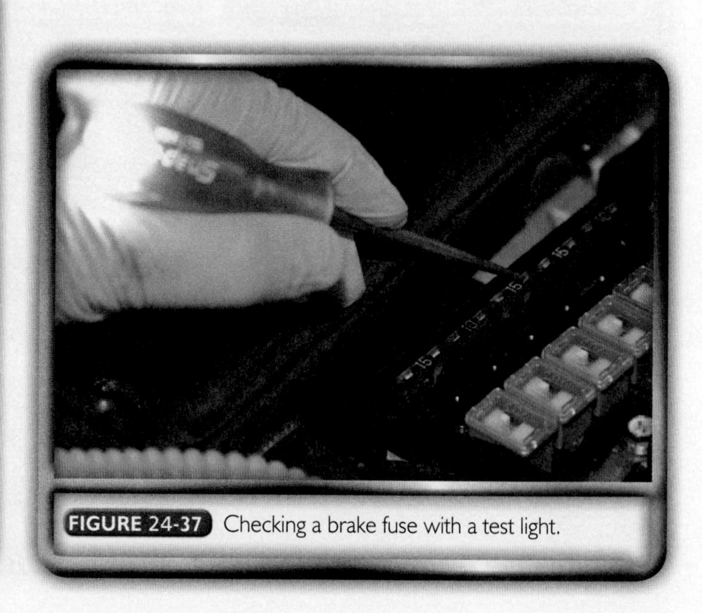

FIGURE 24-37 Checking a brake fuse with a test light.

In a CAN-bus circuit, the parking brake sensor and the low brake fluid sensors send signals over the CAN-bus network regarding their status **FIGURE 24-38**. The appropriate module will then signal the instrument panel module to illuminate the brake warning light. Diagnosis involves using a scan tool capable of interrogating the system, a wiring diagram, and a digital volt-ohmmeter (DVOM) to perform specific tests.

> **LINK**
> Refer to the Disc Brake System chapter for more information on parking brakes.

Checking the Brake Warning Light System

To check a brake warning light system on a non-CAN-bus system, follow the steps in **SKILL DRILL 24-20**.

Checking the Parking Brake and Indicator Light System

To check the parking brake and indicator light system operation, follow the steps in **SKILL DRILL 24-21**.

1. Count the number of clicks it takes to apply the parking brake and compare that to the manufacturer's specifications. If incorrect, follow the specified procedure to adjust it.
2. With the parking brake applied, turn the ignition switch to the "run" position. The red brake warning lamp should be illuminated.
3. Release the parking brake. The warning lamp should turn off. If it does, the parking brake warning light system is operating properly.
4. If the lamp does not turn off, disconnect the wire to the parking brake switch. If the light turns off, test the parking brake switch.
5. If it does not turn off, check the operation of the other warning lamp switches and circuit.

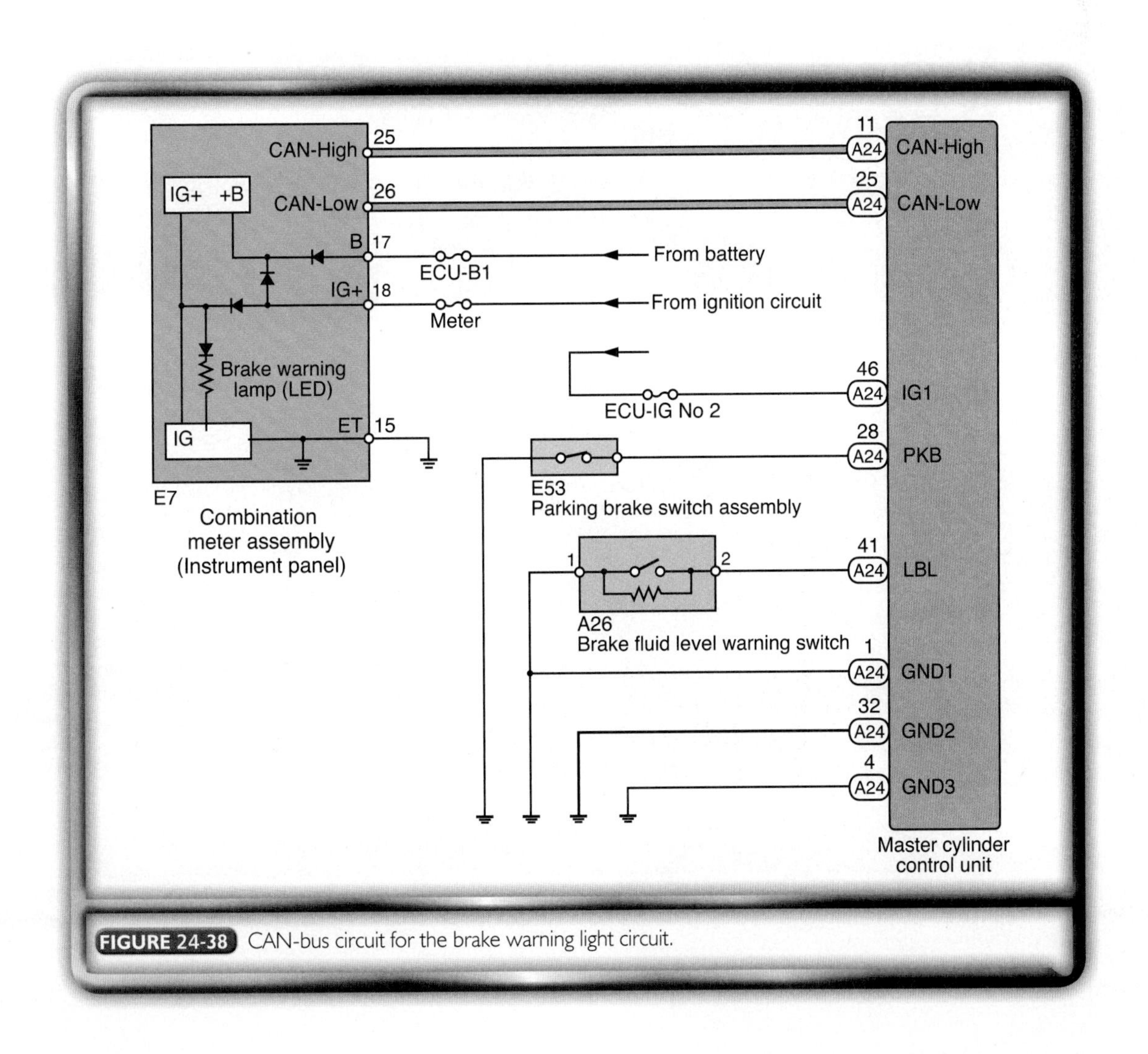

CAN-High
25
IG+ +B
CAN-Low
26
B
17
ECU-B1
From battery
IG+
18
Meter
From ignition circuit
Brake warning
lamp (LED)
ECU-IG No 2
ET
15
IG
E7
Combination
meter assembly
(Instrument panel)
E53
Parking brake switch assembly
1
2
A26
Brake fluid level warning switch
11
A24
CAN-High
25
A24
CAN-Low
46
A24
IG1
28
A24
PKB
41
A24
LBL
1
A24
GND1
32
A24
GND2
4
A24
GND3
Master cylinder
control unit

FIGURE 24-38 CAN-bus circuit for the brake warning light circuit.

Prove
Know
See
Do

SKILL DRILL 24-20 Checking the Brake Warning Light System in a Non-CAN-bus System

1. Perform a bulb check and observe the brake warning light. If it is on, go to step 2. If it is off, check the fuse with a test light. If it is OK, check the warning lamp bulb with an ohmmeter.

2. Make sure the parking brake is released and turn the ignition key to the "run" position. The brake warning lamp should be off. If not, go to step 6.

BRAKE

3. If the warning lamp is off, apply the parking brake. The lamp should illuminate. If it does, check the operation of the other switches. If they work fine, there are no faults present in the system.

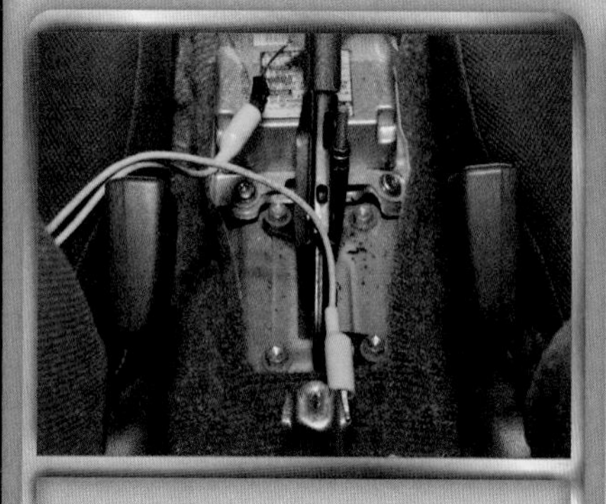

4. If the brake warning light is off when the parking brake is on, disconnect the wire from the parking brake switch and ground the wire. The brake warning light should illuminate. If it does, test the parking brake switch with a DVOM.

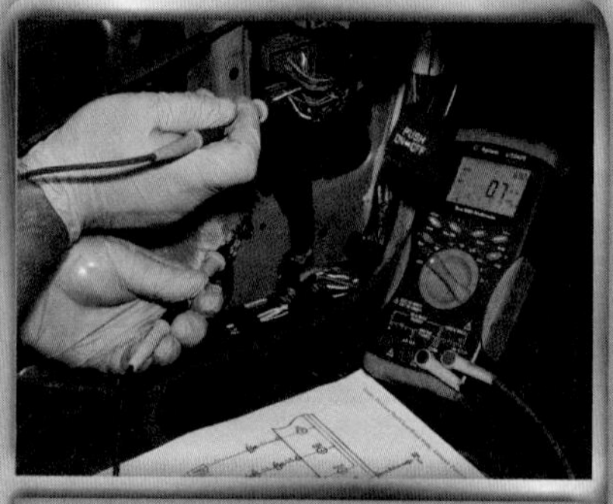

5. If the warning lamp does not illuminate with the parking brake wire grounded, suspect an open circuit between the parking brake wire and the warning lamp. Use a DVOM and wiring diagram to diagnose the fault.

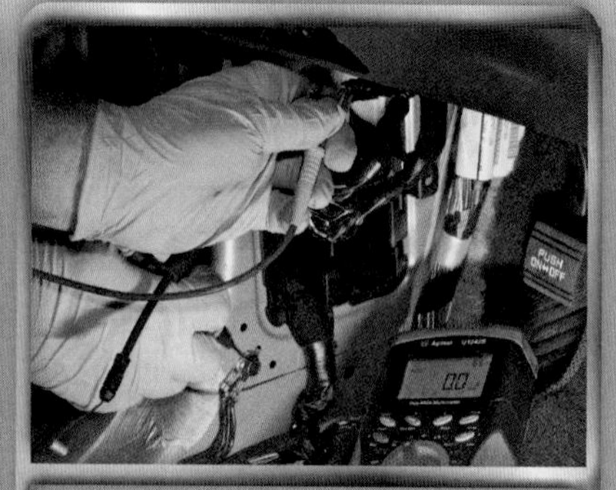

6. If the light stayed on in step 2, apply and release the parking brake several times. If this turns it off, clean or adjust the parking brake mechanism or switch. If it is still on, then, one at a time, disconnect each of the switches that activate it: parking brake, low fluid level, pressure differential, and ignition. If disconnecting one of the switches turns the light off, then test that switch for misadjustment or a shorted condition. If the warning lamp is still on, suspect a short to ground in the wiring harness between the switches and the warning lamp bulb. Use a wiring diagram and DVOM to identify the location of the fault.

Inspecting and Maintaining Parking Brakes

To inspect and maintain parking brakes, follow the steps in SKILL DRILL 24-22.

Diagnosing Stop Light

The mechanical system (non-CAN-bus) circuit is simply a normally closed switch in series with two to six brake light bulbs connected in parallel with each other. This circuit is also protected by a fuse. Some vehicles use separate fuses for the center high mount stop lamp (CHMSL) and the side stop lights. The switch is turned on and off by the movement of the brake pedal. Diagnosis starts with operating the stop lights and observing their reaction, and comparing that to a wiring diagram to see how the manufacturer has wired the circuit. If they do not illuminate at all, check components common to all of the stop lights such as the fuse, stop light switch, and stop light ground circuit. If individual lights do not illuminate, check those bulbs to see if they are burned out, or if they have bad connections, terminals, or wires.

Checking Operation of a Stop Light System

The stop lights are capable of operating at all times on most vehicles. This means the stop lights should come on whenever the brake pedal is pressed, regardless of whether the key is on or off. Checking the operation of the stop lights involves a visual inspection of each bulb. If the bulbs are on even when the brake pedal is released, suspect a misadjusted brake pedal, a defective brake switch, or a short to power in the circuit. If none of the bulbs light up when the brake pedal is depressed, suspect a fault that is common to all of the bulbs such as the fuse, brake switch, feed wire, or ground wire. If there is a problem with only some of the bulbs, suspect a fault that is common to only the bulbs that do not operate, such as the bulbs or the individual wires. In any case, you will need to use the DVOM to locate the open circuit, high resistance, or short circuit.

To check the operation of the brake stop light system and determine any necessary action, follow the steps in SKILL DRILL 24-23:

1. Verify that the stop lights are off when the brakes are released. If the lights are on, test the operation of the brake pedal and brake switch.
2. Observe the stop lights when the brake pedal is applied. All lights including the CHMSL should be illuminated.
3. If some or all of the stop lamps do not illuminate, test them with a DVOM.
4. If the bulbs are OK, consult the wiring diagram to determine potential causes of the fault in the circuit.
5. Use the wiring diagram and a DVOM to identify the cause of the fault.

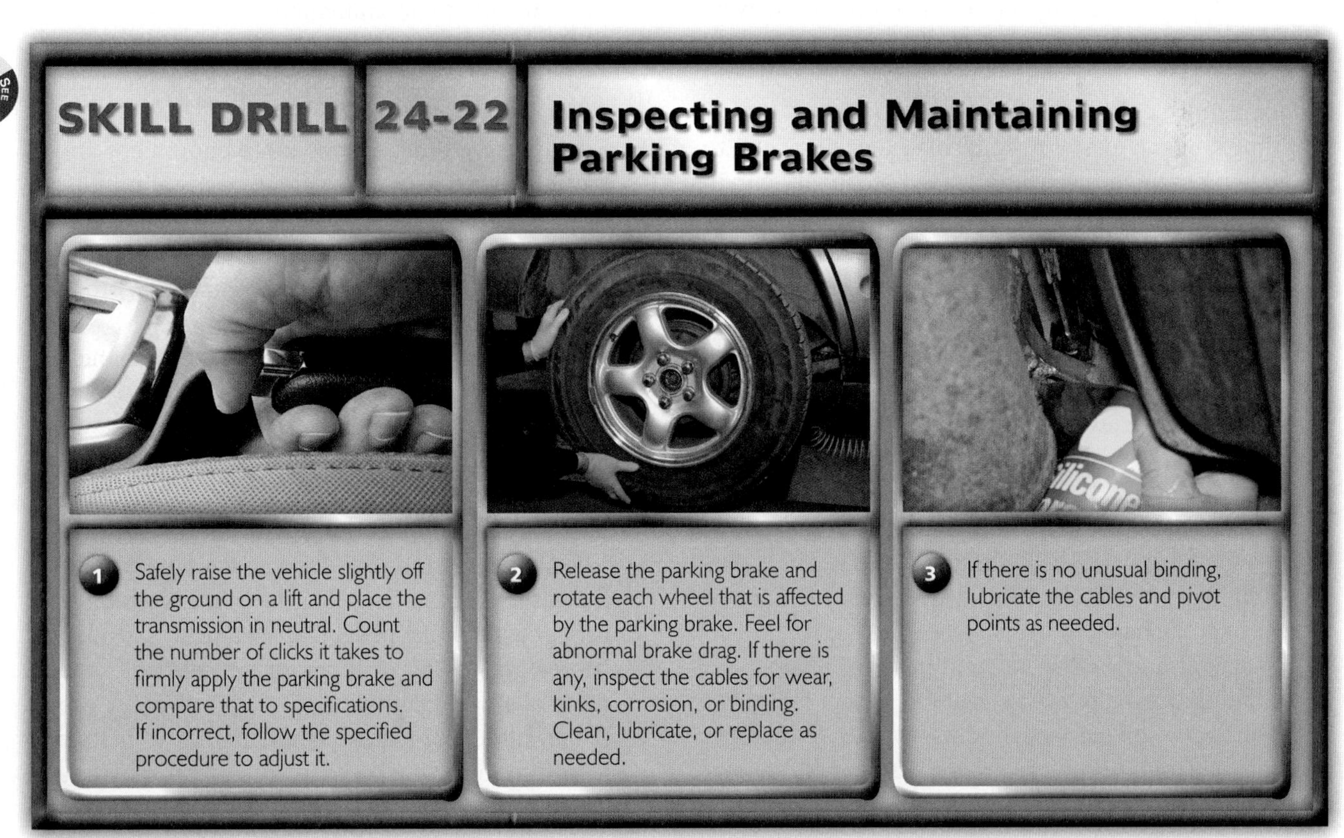
SKILL DRILL 24-22 Inspecting and Maintaining Parking Brakes
1 Safely raise the vehicle slightly off the ground on a lift and place the transmission in neutral. Count the number of clicks it takes to firmly apply the parking brake and compare that to specifications. If incorrect, follow the specified procedure to adjust it.
2 Release the parking brake and rotate each wheel that is affected by the parking brake. Feel for abnormal brake drag. If there is any, inspect the cables for wear, kinks, corrosion, or binding. Clean, lubricate, or replace as needed.
3 If there is no unusual binding, lubricate the cables and pivot points as needed.

Wrap-up

Ready for Review

- The principle behind hydraulic brakes is Pascal's Law, which states that pressure applied to a fluid in one part of a closed system will be transmitted without loss to all other areas of the system.
- A substantial leak in the hydraulic braking system will prevent enough pressure from building to exert the necessary braking force.
- Engineers design brakes that have precise (but unequal from front to back) amounts of braking force at each wheel.
- The three variables related to pressure and force in hydraulic systems are: input force, working pressure, and output force.
- Main components of the hydraulic braking system are: brake pedal, brake fluid, and master cylinder.
- The brake pedal multiplies force from the driver's foot to the master cylinder.
- Brake fluid has a high boiling point, a low freezing point, and is hygroscopic (absorbs water).
- Brake fluids are graded by the Department of Transportation on: pH value, viscosity, resistance to oxidation, stability, and boiling point.
- Master cylinders convert force exerted from the brake pedal into hydraulic pressure to activate wheel brake units.
- Types of master cylinders are: single piston and tandem (required on modern cars).
- Single piston master cylinders use a primary cup to seal pressure in the cylinder and a secondary cup to prevent fluid loss.
- A single piston master cylinder traps brake fluid and forces it into the brake lines.
- Residual pressure valves are used on drum brake systems to maintain brake fluid pressure and prevent air entry when the brakes are off.
- Modern vehicles have tandem master cylinders to ensure braking ability in at least one circuit despite a leak.
- Differential pressure switches monitor loss of pressure between the hydraulic circuits.
- Braking units can be split front-to-rear, diagonally, or in an L shape.
- Diagonal and L-shaped braking splits retain 50% braking capability even if half the system fails.
- Quick take-up master cylinders work to compensate for the large running clearance maintained by low-drag brake calipers.
- It can be dangerous to add brake fluid without diagnosing the reason for a low fluid level.
- Always ask customers questions to gather diagnostic information; try a test drive to understand what the customer is experiencing.
- Always try to discern the root cause of a vehicular problem.
- Common tools that are used to repair hydraulic brake systems are: brake bleeder wrenches, vacuum brake bleeders, pressure brake bleeders, and valve gauge sets.
- Bleeding the brakes removes air form the hydraulic braking system.
- The three most common brake bleeding methods are: manual, pressure, and vacuum (gravity is also used).
- Flushing the brake fluid involves bleeding out the air and replacing the old brake fluid with new.
- Always select the proper grade of brake fluid for the vehicle you are working on.
- Determining if brake fluid should be flushed can be done by: time/mileage, DVOM-galvanic reaction test, boiling point test, or test strip.
- DVOM-galvanic reaction test, brake fluid testers, and brake fluid test strips can all be used to check for brake fluid contamination.
- Manual bleeding requires the least amount of tools and is best when a small amount of bleeding is needed.
- Pressure bleeding requires more equipment and is best when the hydraulic system needs a full flush.
- After bleeding, always check that bleeder screws are properly tightened with no leaks, refill master cylinder and reinstall reservoir cup, and properly dispose of brake fluid.
- Brake pedal inspection includes brake pedal height, free play, and travel.
- Free play is the clearance between the brake pedal linkage and master cylinder piston.
- Brake pedal travel is the distance from its rest position to its applied height.
- Check the master cylinder for leaks if: the brake fluid is low in the reservoir, the brake warning light is on, or the brake pedal reserve height is too low.
- Inspect the master cylinder for internal leaks only if the brake pedal sinks.
- Bench bleed the master cylinder prior to installing it to minimize time needed to bleed the hydraulic brake system.

- Brake lines are made of double-walled steel and coated to help resist corrosion.
- Damaged brake lines should be replaced not repaired; always use the correct tubing bender to avoid kinks.
- The two types of brake line flares are inverted double and ISO.
- Brake hoses transmit the brake system hydraulic pressures to the wheel units and must be of the proper length to be effective.
- Pinching or kinking a brake hose can cause it to fail.
- Inspect brake hoses for: cracks, bulges, abrasion or wear, kinks, and internal breakdown.
- Hydraulic braking systems use proportioning valves, metering valves, pressure differential valves, or anti-lock hydraulic control units to modify hydraulic pressure.
- Proportioning valves reduce brake pressure to the rear wheels and are pressure-sensitive or load-sensitive.
- Load-sensitive proportioning valves adjust rear brake pressure according to the weight of the vehicle's load.
- Pressure-sensitive proportioning valves use a poppet piston to limit the rate of braking pressure increase to the rear brakes.
- Metering valves work to ensure rear brake pressure is applied before front brake pressure.
- The combination valve combines individually operating proportioning valves, metering valve and pressure differential valve in one unit and cannot be repaired.
- Brake warning lights alert drivers to: engagement of the parking brake, low brake fluid intake, and unequal pressure in the hydraulic brake system.
- Stop lights are mounted on the rear of a vehicle and alert other drivers that the vehicle is being braked.
- As of 1986, all vehicles must have a center high-mount stop lamp (CHMSL) to reduce incidence of rear-end collisions.
- Power brake units are either vacuum assist (most common) or hydraulic assist.
- Vacuum boosters have single or dual diaphragms to extract power from atmospheric pressure and transmit force to the master cylinder.
- A 12-inch vacuum booster is capable of generating enough psi to stop a vehicle weighing thousands of pounds.
- A vacuum booster works off of the difference between manifold vacuum and atmospheric pressure; a difference in these pressures creates more force on the master cylinder pistons.
- Inspect and test power brake systems whenever the customer complains that the brakes are dragging, the brake pedal is harder to push than normal, the pedal height has changed, or the engine operation changes more than a minimal amount when the brake pedal is applied.

Key Terms

aerate The tendency to create air bubbles in a fluid.

bleeding The process of removing air from a hydraulic braking system.

brake fluid Hydraulic fluid that transfers forces under pressure through the hydraulic lines to the wheel braking units.

brake hose A flexible section of the brake lines between the body and suspension to allow for steering and suspension movement.

brake lines Made of seamless, double-walled steel, and able to transmit over 1000 psi (6895 kPa) of hydraulic pressure through the hydraulic brake system.

CAN-bus circuit A two-wire communication network that transmits status and command signals between control modules in a vehicle.

compensating port Connects the brake fluid reservoir to the master cylinder bore when the piston is fully retracted, allowing for expansion and contraction of the brake fluid.

free play The amount of clearance between the brake pedal linkage and the master cylinder piston.

hygroscopic A substance that attracts and absorbs water (e.g., brake fluid).

inlet port Connects the reservoir with the space around the piston and between the piston cups in a brake master cylinder.

input force The force applied to the input piston, measured in either pounds or kilograms.

International Standards Organization (ISO) flare A method for joining brake lines, also called a bubble flare. Created by flaring the line slightly out and then back in, leaving the line bubbled near the end.

inverted double flare A method for joining brake lines that forms a secure, leak-proof connection.

load transfer Weight transfer from one set of wheels to the other set of wheels during braking, acceleration, or cornering.

manual bleeding A bleeding method where one person manually operates the brake pedal while the other person opens and closes the bleeder screws on the wheel brake units to allow the air and old brake fluid to be pushed out.

metering valve A valve used on vehicles equipped with older rear drum/front disc brakes to delay application of the front disc brakes until the rear drum brakes are applied. Located in line with the front disc brakes.

output force Force that equals the working pressure multiplied by the surface area of the output piston, expressed as pounds, newtons, or kilograms.

outlet port Links the cylinder to the brake lines.

Pascal's law The law of physics that states that pressure applied to a fluid in one part of a closed system will be transmitted equally to all other areas of the system.

poppet valve A valve that controls the flow of brake fluid at usually preset pressures.

pressure bleeding A bleeding method that uses clean brake fluid under pressure from an auxiliary tool or piece of equipment to force the air and old brake fluid from the hydraulic braking system.

pressure differential valve A valve that monitors any pressure difference between the two separate hydraulic brake circuits; it usually contains a switch to turn on the brake warning light when there is a pressure difference.

primary cup A seal that holds pressure in the master cylinder when force is applied to the piston.

primary piston A brake piston in the master cylinder moved directly by the pushrod or the power-booster; it generates hydraulic pressure to move the secondary piston.

proportioning valves Valves used mostly on older vehicles equipped with rear drum brakes to reduce rear wheel hydraulic brake pressure under hard braking or light loads. Located in line with the rear brakes.

quick take-up master cylinders Cylinders used on disc brake systems that are equipped with low-drag brake calipers to quickly move the brake pads into contact with the brake rotors.

quick take-up valve A valve used to release excess pressure from the larger piston in a quick take-up master cylinder once the brake pads have contacted the brake rotors.

recuperation Process by which brake fluid moves from the reservoir past the edges of the seal into the chamber in front of the piston. This prevents air from being drawn into the hydraulic system caused by low pressure when the brake pedal is released quickly.

residual pressure valve (residual check valve) In drum brake systems, a valve that maintains pressure in the wheel cylinders slightly above atmospheric pressure so that air does not enter the system through the seals in the wheel cylinders.

secondary cup A seal that prevents loss of fluid from the rear of each piston in the master cylinder.

secondary piston A piston that is moved by hydraulic pressure generated by the primary piston in the master cylinder.

single-piston master cylinder A master cylinder with a single piston that creates hydraulic pressure for all wheel units. If there is a leak in the system, there is a loss of pressure for all wheel units.

split diagonally A brake system in which the left front wheel is hydraulically paired with the right rear wheel and the right front wheel is paired with the left rear. This preserves 50% of the braking capability if one of the brake circuits begins to leak.

split front to rear A brake system in which the front brakes operate on one hydraulic circuit and the rear brakes from the other.

tandem master cylinder A master cylinder that has two pistons that operate separate braking circuits so that if a leak develops in one circuit, the other circuit can still operate.

vacuum bleeding Bleeding process that uses a vacuum bleeder to pull the air and old brake fluid from the system.

working pressure The pressure within a hydraulic system while the system is being operated.

ASE-Type Questions

1. Tech A says that hydraulic pressure is applied equally in all directions throughout a closed system. Tech B says that air in the hydraulic system will cause the brake pedal to be spongy. Who is correct?
   a. Tech A
   b. Tech B
   c. Both A and B
   d. Neither A nor B
2. Tech A says that a brake pedal that does not return all the way will cause the brake warning light on the instrument panel to stay on. Tech B says that when bleeding brakes, you should normally start at the wheel that is closest to the master cylinder. Who is correct?
   a. Tech A
   b. Tech B
   c. Both A and B
   d. Neither A nor B
3. Tech A says that brake fluid should periodically be checked for excessive moisture content. Tech B says that brake fluid should be replaced every 12,000 miles. Who is correct?
   a. Tech A
   b. Tech B
   c. Both A and B
   d. Neither A nor B
4. Tech A says that DOT 5 brake fluid should be used in all vehicles today because it is silicone based and will not absorb water. Tech B says that mixing DOT 4 and DOT 3 is not recommended because of different boiling points, but both are hydroscopic. Who is correct?
   a. Tech A
   b. Tech B
   c. Both A and B
   d. Neither A nor B
5. Tech A says that the secondary piston in a master cylinder is operated by hydraulic force. Tech B says that the brake pedal return spring returns the master cylinder pistons to their original position. Who is correct?
   a. Tech A
   b. Tech B
   c. Both A and B
   d. Neither A nor B
6. Tech A says that the low level brake fluid switch on a master cylinder will turn on the brake warning light when the system is low on fluid. Tech B says that the low level switch also monitors the condition of the fluid and will activate the warning light when the brake fluid needs to be replaced. Who is correct?
   a. Tech A
   b. Tech B
   c. Both A and B
   d. Neither A nor B
7. Tech A says that the metering valve controls pressure to the rear brakes. Tech B says that the proportioning valve controls pressure to the front brakes. Who is correct?
   a. Tech A
   b. Tech B
   c. Both A and B
   d. Neither A nor B
8. Tech A says that the vacuum booster uses vacuum and atmospheric pressure to multiply the driver's foot pressure applied to the master cylinder push rod. Tech B says that the vacuum booster increases the vacuum in the brake system. Who is correct?
   a. Tech A
   b. Tech B
   c. Both A and B
   d. Neither A nor B
9. Tech A says that bench bleeding a master cylinder will prevent having to bleed air from the brake lines during replacement. Tech B says that bench bleeding the master cylinder makes bleeding the brakes on the vehicle easier. Who is correct?
   a. Tech A
   b. Tech B
   c. Both A and B
   d. Neither A nor B
10. Tech A says that a faulty vacuum booster can affect engine operation. Tech B says that steel brake line can be replaced with a copper line, since it is easier to bend into shape. Who is correct?
    a. Tech A
    b. Tech B
    c. Both A and B
    d. Neither A nor B

CHAPTER 25

NATEF Tasks

Brakes General Brake Systems			Page
■ Describe procedure for performing road test to check brake system operation, including an anti-lock brake system (ABS).	MLR	AST	713
■ Identify and interpret brake system concern; determine necessary action.		AST	713–714
Hydraulic System			
■ Diagnose poor stopping, pulling or dragging concerns caused by malfunctions in the hydraulic system; determine necessary action.		AST	714
Disc Brakes			
■ Diagnose poor stopping, noise, vibration, pulling, grabbing, dragging or pulsation concerns; determine necessary action.		AST	714
■ Remove and clean caliper assembly; inspect for leaks and damage/wear to caliper housing; determine necessary action.	MLR	AST	716–717
■ Clean and inspect caliper mounting and slides/pins for proper operation, wear, and damage; determine necessary action.	MLR	AST	717
■ Check brake pad wear indicator; determine necessary action.	MLR	AST	718
■ Remove, inspect and replace pads and retaining hardware; determine necessary action.	MLR	AST	718–719
■ Lubricate and reinstall caliper, pads, and related hardware; seat pads and inspect for leaks.	MLR	AST	719–722
■ Retract and readjust caliper piston on an integrated parking brake system.	MLR	AST	721–723
■ Clean and inspect rotor, measure rotor thickness, thickness variation, and lateral runout; determine necessary action.	MLR	AST	723–725
■ Remove and reinstall rotor.	MLR	AST	723–727

Disc Brake System

NATEF Tasks, continued

Task	Level	Pages
■ Refinish rotor on vehicle; measure final rotor thickness and compare with specifications.	MLR AST	724–729
■ Refinish rotor off vehicle; measure final rotor thickness and compare with specifications.	MLR AST	727–731
■ Inspect and replace drive axle wheel studs. (NATEF, Drive Axles)	MLR AST	727–733
■ Install wheel and torque lug nuts. (NATEF, Drum Brakes)	MLR AST	734–735
■ Describe importance of operating vehicle to burnish/break-in replacement brake pads according to manufacturer's recommendations.	MLR AST	734–735

Know
See
Do

Knowledge Objectives

After reading this chapter, you will be able to:

1. Describe the components of the disc brake system. (pp 699–700)
2. Describe how the components of the disc brake system work together during braking operations. (pp 700–701)
3. Describe the advantages and disadvantages of the disc brake system. (pp 701–702)
4. Describe the purpose of disc brake calipers. (pp 702–703)
5. Describe the components of disc brake calipers. (pp 703–705)
6. Describe the purpose of disc brake pads. (pp 705–706)
7. Describe the principle of the coefficient of friction and how it affects brake lining materials. (pp 706–708)
8. Describe the components that are employed to prevent noise in disc brakes. (pp 708–709)
9. Describe the types of wear indicators for disc brakes. (pp 709–710)
10. Describe the purpose of disc brake rotors. (p 710)
11. Describe the types of disc brake rotors. (pp 711–712)
12. Describe how the parking brake system operates in a disc brake system. (pp 712–713)
13. Describe the types of parking brakes in a disc brake system. (pp 712–713)
14. Describe the process of diagnosing issues with a disc brake system. (pp 713–715)

Know
See
Do
Prove

Skills Objectives

After reading this chapter, you will be able to:

1. Remove and inspect the caliper. (pp 716–717)
2. Inspect caliper mountings, slides, and pins. (p 717)
3. Inspect brake pads and wear indicators. (p 718)
4. Check the brake pads. (pp 718–719)
5. Disassemble the caliper. (pp 719–720)
6. Reassemble the caliper. (pp 720–722)
7. Retract and readjust the piston on an integrated parking brake. (pp 721–723)
8. Inspect and measure the disc brake rotor. (pp 723–725)
9. Remove and reinstall the disc brake rotor. (pp 723–727)
10. Refinish the disc brake rotor while it is on the vehicle. (pp 724–729)
11. Refinish the disc brake rotor while it is off the vehicle. (pp 727–731)
12. Inspect and replace wheel studs. (pp 727, 731–733)
13. Install a wheel, torque lug nuts, and make final checks and adjustments. (pp 731, 734–735)

Introduction

Disc (also spelled disk) brakes are so named because they create braking power by forcing flat friction pads against the sides of a rotating disc. This disc is also called a disc brake rotor, or rotor. The vehicle wheels are bolted to the disc FIGURE 25-1. The applied force is created in the caliper, which straddles the pads and rotor. Higher applied forces can be used in disc brakes than in drum brakes, because the design of the rotor is stronger than the design of the drum FIGURE 25-2. Since heat is generated on the outside surfaces of the rotor, it can be easily transferred to the atmosphere. Disc brakes are effective at creating substantial braking power using a fairly simple design that is relatively easy for technicians to service and repair.

TECHNICIAN TIP

The purpose of the disc brake system is to provide an effective means to slow the vehicle under a variety of conditions in an acceptable distance and manner. The better a braking system can do this, the more likely the vehicle will avoid an accident.

FIGURE 25-1 Disc brake operation.

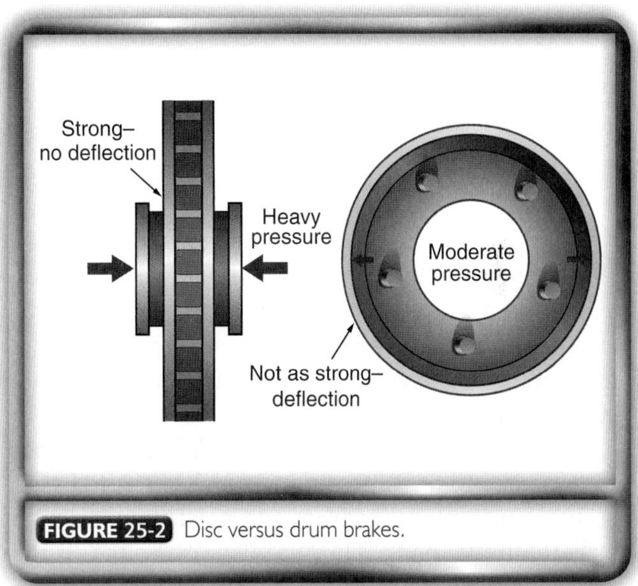
Strong–
no deflection
Heavy
pressure
Moderate
pressure
Not as strong–
deflection

FIGURE 25-2 Disc versus drum brakes.

You Are the Automotive Technician

A customer comes into the service department. She has been experiencing a pulsating brake pedal and high pitched sqealing during braking on her 2009 Town and Country minivan, which has 41,000 miles on the odometer. After reviewing the vehicle's service history on your computer, you notice the vehicle has never had any brake service. You advise the customer that you will need to complete a more thorough inspection to determine what is causing the issues. After completing a visual inspection of the brakes, and measurement of the rotor's thickness and parallelism, you see that the front brake linings have worn down to the wear indicators and the rotors are warped beyond specifications. You inform the customer of your findings and recommend that the vehicle needs new front brake pads installed, and the rotors refinished. You also recommend that the brake fluid be flushed, since the fluid is beyond the end of its two-year life.

1. What conditions can cause a rotor to become warped?
2. What conditions would require replacement of the rotors rather than just refinishing them?
3. What are the relatively common maximum specifications for rotor runout and thickness variation?

Purpose and Overview

Disc brakes operate on the same principle as all friction brakes. They generate stopping power by applying friction materials to moving surfaces, thus transforming the vehicle's kinetic energy into heat energy. This is accomplished by disc brake calipers using hydraulic pressure from the master cylinder to create a mechanical clamping action, forcing the brake pads onto the surface of the rotor, creating friction. As the vehicle's kinetic energy is transformed into heat energy, the vehicle's speed decreases.

Disc Brake System

Modern passenger vehicles are almost always equipped with disc brakes on at least the front two wheels, and many manufacturers are using them on all four wheels. The primary components of the disc brakes are:

- Rotor
- Caliper
- Brake pads FIGURE 25-3

The **rotors** are the main rotating part of this brake system. They are durable and resist being damaged by the high temperatures that occur during braking. In high-performance vehicles, the rotors are made from composite materials, ceramics, or carbon fiber; otherwise, they are usually made of cast iron.

The **caliper** straddles the rotor and houses the disc brake pads and an activating piston(s). The calipers use hydraulic pressure from the master cylinder to apply the brake pads. They are usually bolted to the steering knuckle or, in the case of a nonsteering axle, to a suspension component. Calipers need to be inspected at the same time as the brake pads.

The **disc brake pads** are located inside the caliper or caliper mounting bracket. The pads clamp onto the rotor to slow or stop the vehicle. The disc brake pad consists of a friction material bonded or riveted to a steel backing plate. With this design, the pads will wear out over time and need to be replaced periodically.

Disc Brake Operation

Disc brakes can be used on all four wheels of a vehicle, or a combination of brake types can be used, with disc brakes on the front wheels and drum brakes on the rear. When the brake pedal is depressed, a **pushrod** transfers the force through a **brake booster** to a hydraulic master cylinder. The master cylinder converts the pedal force into hydraulic pressure, which is then transmitted via brake lines and hoses to one or more pistons at each brake caliper FIGURE 25-4. The pistons operate on friction pads to provide a clamping force on a rotor that is attached to the wheel hub. This clamping action is designed to stop the rotation of the rotor and the wheel.

The rotors are free to rotate with the wheels due to wheel bearings and the hubs that contain them. The hub can be part of the brake rotor or a separate assembly that the rotor slips over and is bolted to by the lug nuts

FIGURE 25-3 The disc brake system.

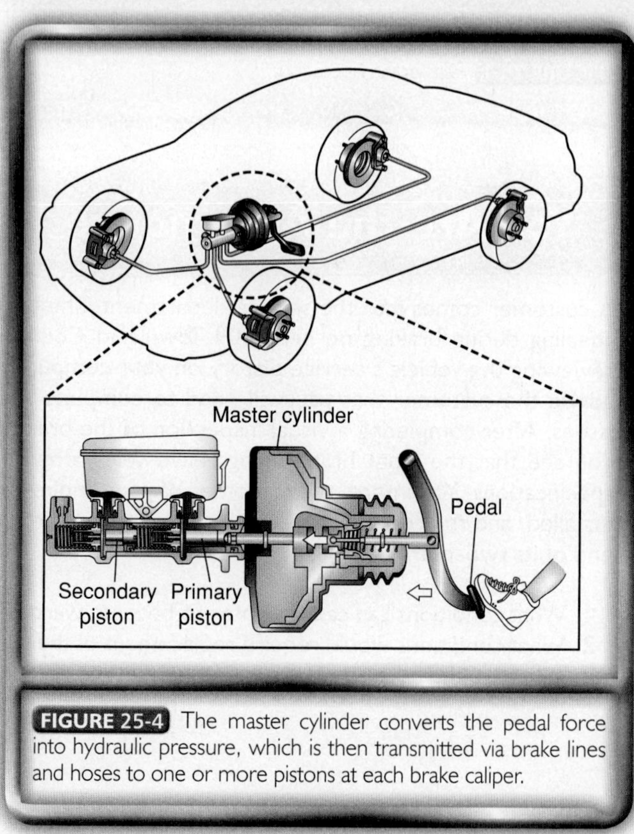
Master cylinder
Pedal
Secondary piston
Primary piston

FIGURE 25-4 The master cylinder converts the pedal force into hydraulic pressure, which is then transmitted via brake lines and hoses to one or more pistons at each brake caliper.

FIGURE 25-5. On rear-wheel drive vehicles, the rotor is mounted onto the driving axle or hub and may be held in place by the wheel. On front-wheel drive vehicles, it can be mounted on the front hub and wheel bearing assembly.

The brake caliper assembly is normally bolted to the vehicle axle housing or suspension FIGURE 25-6. In most cases, the brake is positioned as close as possible to the wheel, but there are exceptions. Some high-performance cars with **independent rear suspension (IRS)** use inboard disc brakes on the rear wheels. The calipers are mounted on or next to the differential, which is directly mounted to the vehicle body. Manufacturers claim improved vehicle handling for this design because it reduces the vehicle's unsprung weight by taking the differential assembly and brakes from the suspension and mounting them to the body. Because the wheels and axles are now lighter, the vehicle's springs can do a better job of keeping the wheels on the ground, especially on uneven road surfaces.

FIGURE 25-5 The hub and hubless rotors.

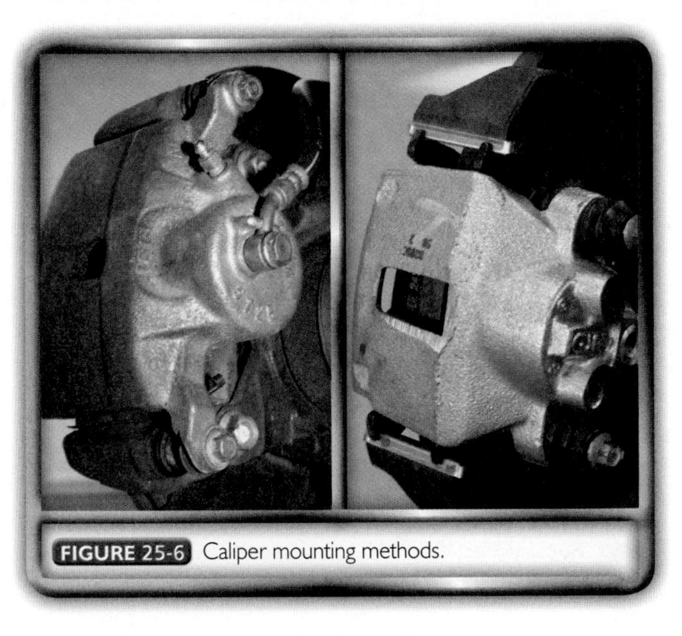

FIGURE 25-6 Caliper mounting methods.

Disc brake pads require much higher application pressures to operate than drum brake shoes because they are not self-energizing. This additional clamping pressure is created by increasing the diameter of the caliper pistons. Unfortunately, this means the brake pedal travel is lengthened to move the additional fluid being displaced by the larger caliper pistons. Building in more pushrod travel would require more room under the dash. Manufacturers have overcome this problem by equipping most disc brake systems with a power booster. Because of the high forces needed to apply a disc brake, using it as a parking brake is more challenging. Some manufacturers have chosen to design more complicated calipers, while others have built an auxiliary drum brake assembly into the center of the rear disc brake rotors to provide for parking brake operation. This is referred to as a top hat design.

Advantages and Disadvantages

Disc brakes have a number of advantages over drum brakes. They also have some disadvantages. In most cases, the advantages outweigh the disadvantages. One of the biggest advantages is that disc brakes can generate and transfer greater amounts of heat to the atmosphere; because most of the friction area of a rotor is exposed to air, cooling is far more rapid than for a drum brake. This faster cooling makes them better suited for high-performance driving or heavy-duty vehicles and reduces the likelihood of brake fade.

Also, because of their shape, rotors tend to scrape off water more effectively. After being driven through water, disc brakes operate at peak performance almost immediately. Further, due to their design, disc brakes are self-adjusting and do not need periodic maintenance or rely on a self-adjusting mechanism that is prone to sticking (see the Disc Brake Calipers section). Lastly, in most cases, disc brakes are also easier to service than drum brakes.

While disc brakes have a number of benefits over drum brakes, there are some disadvantages. Probably the most apparent disadvantage is that disc brakes are much more prone to noise. Their design tends to create squeals and squeaks, which can be very annoying. Many a technician has spent time servicing perfectly functional disc brakes due to excessive noise complaints. Another issue is that the rotors warp easier than in drum brake systems. Since the brake pads are pressing on each side of the rotor, thickness variations of as small as 0.0003" (0.0076 mm) can cause brake pedal pulsations, requiring resurfacing or replacement. The last disadvantage is that since disc brakes are not self-energizing, they need higher clamping forces, which requires a power booster. This also makes it harder to use them as effective parking brakes.

> **TECHNICIAN TIP**
>
> While there may appear to be more disadvantages to disc brakes versus drum brakes, the advantages are generally considered much more critical than the disadvantages. Thus, disc brakes are preferred over drum brakes in most applications.

Disc Brake Calipers

In most applications, the disc brake caliper assembly is bolted to the vehicle axle housing, or **steering knuckle**, and clamps the brake pads onto the rotors to slow the vehicle. There are two main types of calipers: **fixed calipers** and **sliding or floating calipers** FIGURE 25-7. Sliding or floating calipers are the most common type used in passenger vehicles because they are easier to build and are more compact. All calipers are fitted with a **bleeder screw** on the top of the piston bore to allow for the removal of air within the disc brake system as well as to help in performing routine brake fluid changes.

Fixed calipers are rigidly bolted in place and cannot move or slide. This makes their application of braking forces more precise than floating calipers. They commonly have one to four pistons on each side of the rotor FIGURE 25-8. When the brakes are applied, hydraulic pressure forces the pistons on both sides of the caliper inward, causing the brake pads to come in contact with the rotor FIGURE 25-9. Once the pad-to-rotor clearance is taken up, the hydraulic pressure rises equally on each side of the caliper, applying both brake pads equally.

The sliding or floating caliper has brake pads located on each side of the rotor, but all of the pistons are only on one side, usually the inside of the rotor. Thus, the hydraulic force is generated on one side of the rotor, but the unique design applies equal braking force to both sides of the rotor. This distribution of force is possible because the caliper is mounted on pins, or slides, that allow it to move (float or slide) from side to side as necessary. This movement allows pistons on one side of the rotor to generate force on both sides of the rotor at the same time.

FIGURE 25-8 Fixed calipers with multiple pistons.

FIGURE 25-7 Fixed and sliding/floating calipers.

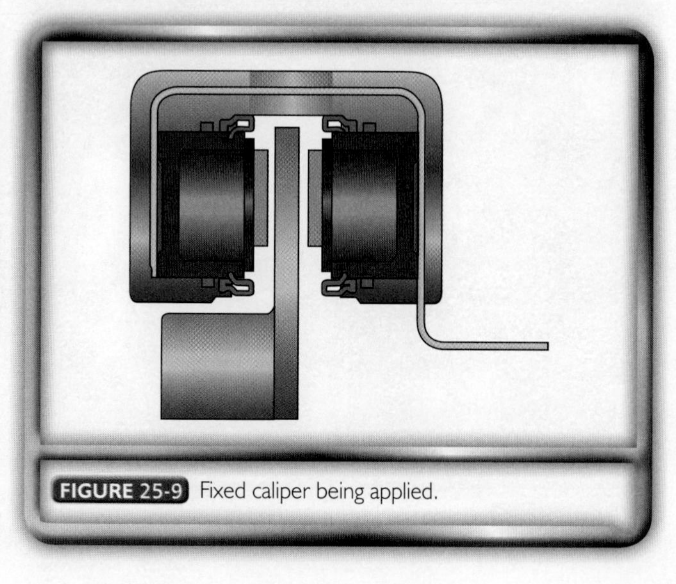

FIGURE 25-9 Fixed caliper being applied.

When the brakes are applied, hydraulic pressure forces the piston toward the rotor. This takes up any clearance between the brake pad and rotor and starts to push the pad into the rotor. Since the caliper is free to move on the pins or slides, it gets pushed away from the rotor, pulling the outer brake pad into contact with the outside of the rotor. Once all clearance is taken up on the outer brake pad, the clamping force will increase equally on both brake pads, applying the brakes FIGURE 25-10.

O-Rings

In disc brake calipers, the piston is sealed by a stationary square section sealing ring, also called a square cut O-ring FIGURE 25-11. This O-ring has a square cross-section and is fitted in a machined groove in the caliper. The O-ring is compressed between the piston and caliper housing, creating a positive seal to keep the high-pressure brake fluid from leaking out. It also prevents air from being drawn into the system when a low-pressure situation is created in the hydraulic system when the brake pedal is released quickly.

When the brakes are applied, the piston moves outward, slightly deforming the O-ring seal FIGURE 25-12. When the brakes are released, the elasticity or flexibility of the seal causes it to return to its original shape. This action of the sealing ring retracts the piston to provide a small running clearance between the rotor and pads. As the brake pads wear, the piston needs to move outward a bit farther than the sealing ring can stretch or flex. The sealing ring is designed to allow the piston to slide through it in this situation, taking up the extra clearance and making the disc brakes self-adjusting.

FIGURE 25-10 Sliding/floating caliper application.

TECHNICIAN TIP

Since the force generated by the O-ring to retract the piston is fairly small, any corrosion or buildup on the piston or bore will cause the piston to stick and not retract. This holds the brakes in the applied position, causing brake drag, overheated brakes, and poor fuel economy. Technicians can identify this situation by using an infrared temperature gun to measure the temperature of each brake rotor after test-driving the vehicle. The temperatures should be approximately the same on each side. If they are not, suspect a stuck or binding caliper.

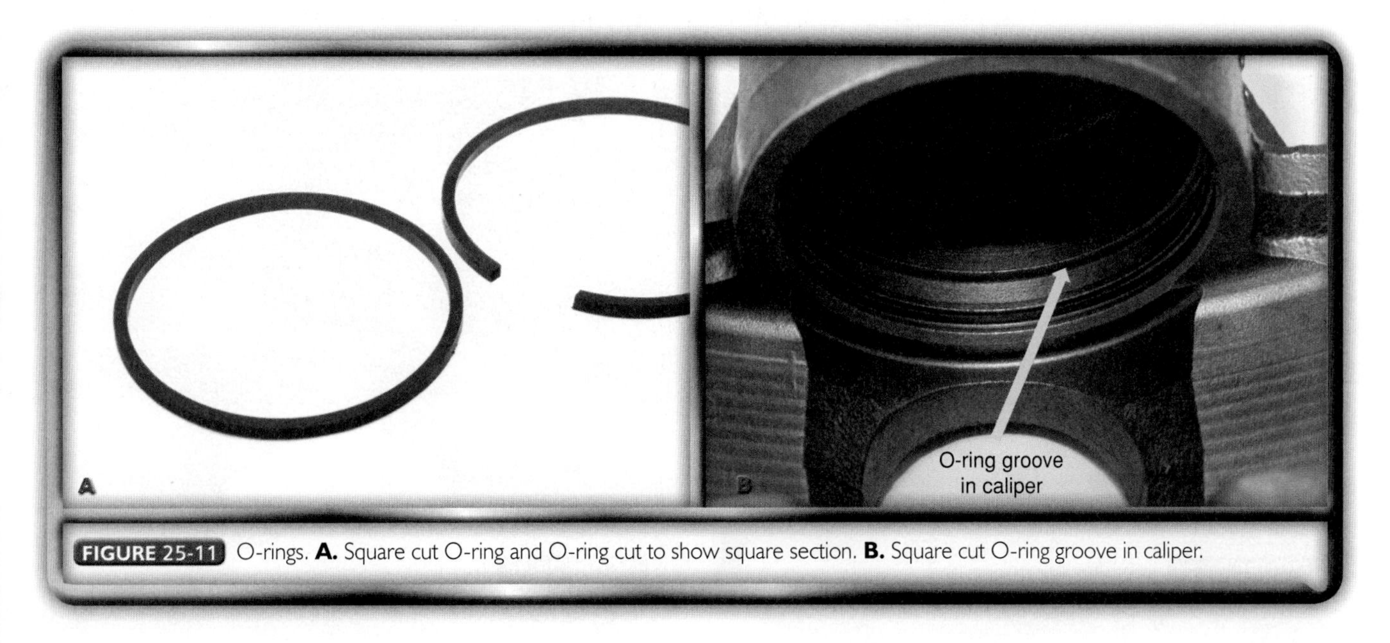
A
B
O-ring groove
in caliper

FIGURE 25-11 O-rings. **A.** Square cut O-ring and O-ring cut to show square section. **B.** Square cut O-ring groove in caliper.

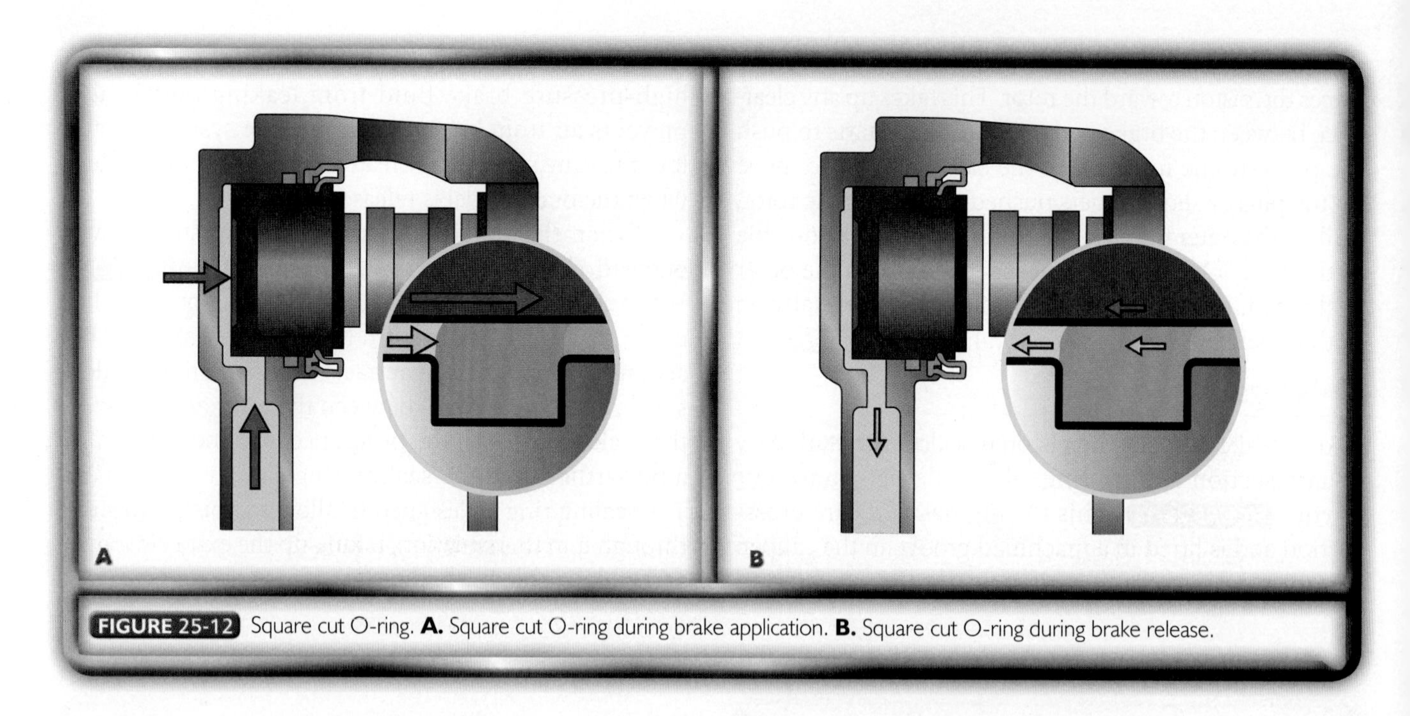
A
B

FIGURE 25-12 Square cut O-ring. **A.** Square cut O-ring during brake application. **B.** Square cut O-ring during brake release.

Some calipers, sometimes called **low-drag calipers**, are designed to maintain a larger brake pad-to-rotor clearance by retracting the pistons a little bit farther. This is accomplished by modifying the sealing groove in the caliper so the outside of the groove is slightly angled toward the rotor **FIGURE 25-13**. This position allows the seal to flex a bit farther upon brake application and then retract the piston a greater distance. These systems use a "quick take-up" or "fast fill" master cylinder to maintain adequate brake pedal reserve height.

The primary sealing surface is the outside diameter of the piston. It is critical that this surface be smooth and free of pitting or rust; therefore, steel pistons are chrome plated. This gives the surface a hard, wear-resistant, and corrosion-resistant finish. Chrome can still rust, but it is much more corrosion resistant than steel. Another way manufacturers have dealt with the corrosion issue is by making pistons out of a **phenolic resin**. Pool balls also are made from phenolic resin, which is very dense when it hardens and does not corrode or rust, making for a good sealing surface in brake systems. Although the phenolic pistons themselves do not corrode, the cast iron bore of the caliper does corrode and rust and can therefore cause a phenolic piston to seize in the bore **FIGURE 25-14**.

Phenolic pistons transfer heat slower than steel pistons **FIGURE 25-15**, which is a good thing because they transfer less heat from the brake pad to the brake fluid.

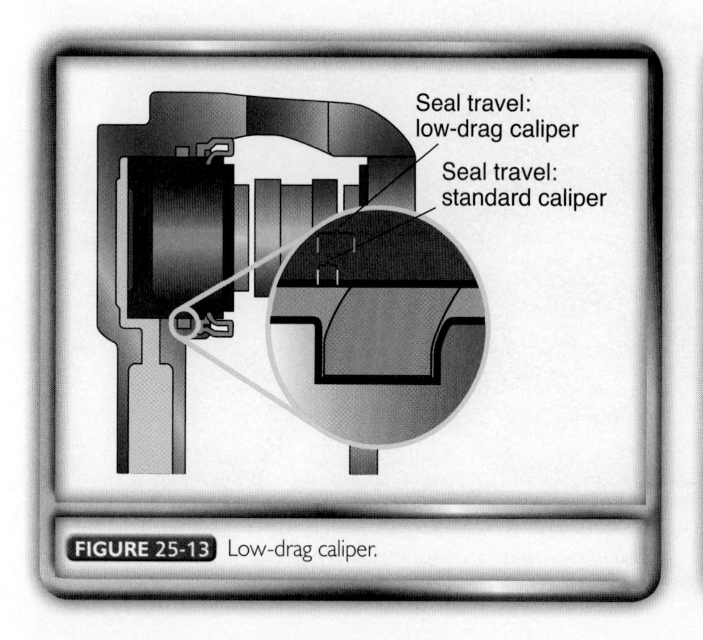
Seal travel:
low-drag caliper
Seal travel:
standard caliper

FIGURE 25-13 Low-drag caliper.

FIGURE 25-14 Corroded caliper piston bore.

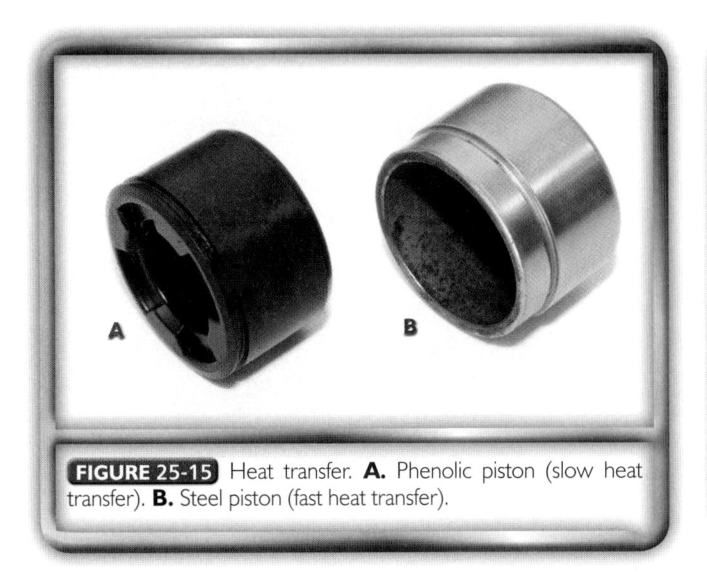
A
B

FIGURE 25-15 Heat transfer. **A.** Phenolic piston (slow heat transfer). **B.** Steel piston (fast heat transfer).

FIGURE 25-16 Floating caliper guide pins.

FIGURE 25-17 Sliding caliper.

This helps prevent boiling of the brake fluid in the caliper under heavy brake usage. Calipers with phenolic pistons are therefore less susceptible to brake failure from boiling brake fluid.

There is also a dust boot that seals the surfaces of the piston and caliper bore from outside dirt and moisture. This seal connects to both the piston and the caliper and must be expandable to allow the piston to move outward as the brake pads wear. It also must be free from cuts and holes; otherwise the piston and bore could corrode and cause the piston to bind in the bore, causing brake drag.

Caliper Lubrication

Floating calipers are mounted in place by **guide pins** and **bushings** FIGURE 25-16. The pins allow the caliper to move in and out as the brakes are operated and as the brake pads wear. Since the calipers move on the pins, the bushings must be lubricated with high-temperature, waterproof disc brake caliper grease when they are serviced. This will help prevent them from binding or sticking. Inspecting, cleaning, and lubricating the pins and pin bores, including any bushings and dust boots, are important steps in disc brake repair.

Sliding calipers have matching machined surfaces on the caliper and caliper mount that allow the caliper to slide in the mount FIGURE 25-17. The sliding mount holds the caliper in position and prevents it from rotating when the brakes are applied. The machined mounts allow the caliper to move side to side as necessary to operate the brakes or adjust for brake pad wear. The surfaces must be cleaned and lubricated with the same high-temperature, waterproof grease as the floating calipers when the calipers are serviced. Sliding calipers are held in place by a spring steel clip or shim that is bolted to the caliper mount.

Disc Brake Pads and Friction Materials

Disc brake pads consist of friction material bonded or riveted onto a steel **backing plate** FIGURE 25-18. **Bonded linings** are more common on light-duty vehicles since they are less expensive to build and the bonding agent can fail under the very high temperatures of heavy-duty use. **Riveted linings** are used on heavier-duty or high-performance vehicles. Metal rivets provide a mechanical connection to hold the lining to the backing plate that is less susceptible to failure under high temperatures. Since the rivets actually pinch some of the lining between the rivet head and the backing plate, the linings must be changed sooner than bonded linings. Otherwise, the rivet heads would contact the rotor and wear a groove in the face of the rotor. The backing plate has **lugs** that correctly position the pad in the caliper assembly and help the backing plate maintain the proper position to the

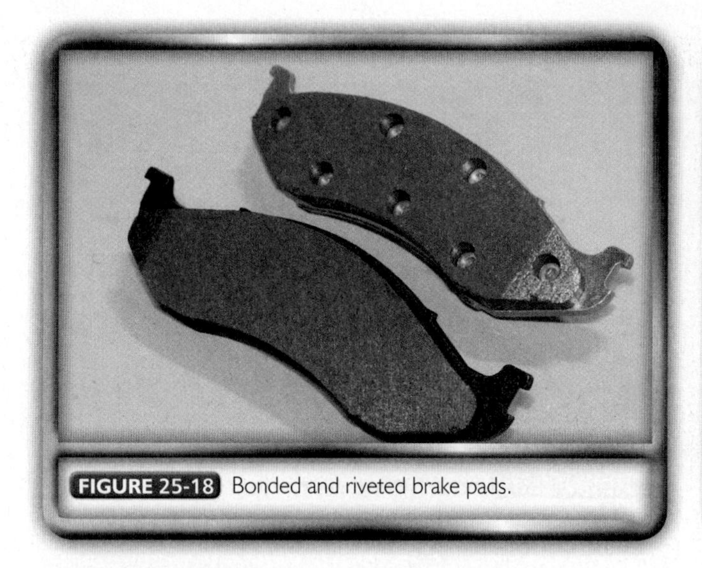
FIGURE 25-18 Bonded and riveted brake pads.

FIGURE 25-19 Brake pad locating lugs.

rotor FIGURE 25-19. Disc brakes are usually designed so that the thickness of the pads can be checked easily once the wheel has been removed. Most disc brakes also are designed to allow the pads to be replaced with a minimum of disassembly.

Some pads have a groove cut into the friction surface. This groove helps ventilate gases that build up at the surface of the friction material under heavy brake application. It also can help modify the harmonic vibration quality of the friction material to reduce brake squeal. On some pads, the depth of this groove is set so that as the pad wears thinner, the remaining groove gets smaller; when it can no longer be seen, the pad should be replaced.

The composition of the friction material affects brake operation. Materials that provide good braking with low pedal pressures tend to lose efficiency when they get hot, thus increasing the stopping distance. They also tend to wear out quicker. Materials that maintain a stable friction coefficient over a wide temperature range generally require higher pedal pressures to provide efficient braking. They also tend to put added wear on the disc brake rotor, reducing its useful life FIGURE 25-20.

FIGURE 25-20 Brake rotor wear.

Brake Friction Materials

Friction is the force that acts to prevent two surfaces in contact from sliding against each other. The amount of friction between two surfaces is expressed as a ratio and is called the coefficient of friction. When friction occurs, the kinetic energy (motion) of the sliding surfaces is converted into thermal energy (heat). Some combinations of materials, such as a hockey puck on ice, have a very low coefficient of friction. There is very little friction between them and therefore almost no sliding resistance. Rubber tires against a dry hard road surface have a high coefficient of friction, which means they tend to grip and resist sliding against each other.

Disc brake pads and drum brake linings are made from materials that have a moderate coefficient of friction TABLE 25-1. They also must be able to absorb and disperse large amounts of heat without their braking performance being adversely affected. As the heat in brake pads and linings builds up, the coefficient of friction capability of the material—and consequently its

TABLE 25-1: Brake Lining Coefficient of Friction (Sliding)

Materials Involved	Coefficient of Friction—Dry Sliding
Rubber and concrete	.6–.85
Steel and cast iron	.23
Copper and cast iron	.29
Brass and cast iron	.3
Leather and oak	.52
Brake lining (FF rating)	.35–.45

Applied Math

AM-17: Charts/Tables/Graphs: The technician can interpret charts, tables, and graphs to determine the manufacturer's specifications for a given system.

Algebra (9–12)

C3: Draw reasonable conclusions about a situation being modeled.

Representation

A2: Select, apply, and translate among mathematical representations to solve problems.

Technicians regularly apply math concepts to disc brake diagnosis and repair. For example, a technician will measure the amount of rotor thickness variation and runout if there is a brake pedal pulsation problem. Let's say the technician performed these measurements and came up with a thickness variation of 0.0025" (0.064 mm) and a runout of 0.0015" (0.038 mm) on the left front rotor. Next the technician looks up the manufacturer's specification chart and found that the maximum allowable thickness variation is 0.0005" (0.013 mm) and the maximum allowable runout is 0.003" (0.076 mm) for the vehicle being worked on. Using the information from the chart, the technician determines that the thickness variation is excessive by 0.002" (0.051 mm) (0.0025" [0.064 mm] – 0.0005" [0.013 mm] = 0.002" [0.051 mm]) and the runout is OK since it is under the maximum allowable specification. But even so, since the thickness variation is out of specifications, the rotor will need to be refinished or replaced to bring it back within specification.

stopping power—is reduced. This is called brake fade. Minimizing or overcoming fade is a major factor in the design of brakes and the development of brake friction materials.

Brake friction materials were historically made from asbestos compounds because of the excellent heat resistance of that material. Now that asbestos has been proven to be toxic, it is generally banned and is not normally used. Today, brakes are manufactured from a variety of different materials, including:

- Non-asbestos organic (NAO) materials—Organic materials such as Kevlar and carbon
- Low-metallic NAO materials—Small amounts of copper or steel and NOA materials
- Semimetallic materials—A higher quantity of steel, copper, and/or brass
- Ceramic materials—Ceramic fiber materials and possibly a small amount of copper

The choice of brake lining compound depends on the application. Lighter passenger vehicles generate less heat in the brakes than heavy or high-performance vehicles.

Safety

Don't assume that a brake pad doesn't contain asbestos; it is still found in some applications.

Living in a very hilly region of the country, or where there is a lot of stop-and-go traffic, will put added demands on the brake pads. The optimum brake composition for any given vehicle or use is a combination of weighted qualities, including:

- Stopping power
- Heat absorption and dispersion
- Resistance to fade
- Recovery speed from fade
- Wear rate
- Performance when wet
- Operating noise
- Price

For instance, owners of small economy vehicles tend to value a longer pad life and minimal operating noise rather than resistance to fade in extreme conditions. Owners of high-performance cars, however, may consider fade resistance and stopping power at high speeds more important than noise levels or wear rate.

The Society of Automotive Engineers (SAE) has adopted letter codes to rate brake lining materials' coefficient of friction. The rating is written on the edge of the friction linings and is called the **edge code** FIGURE 25-21. The lower the letter, the less friction the material has, and the harder the brake pedal must be applied to achieve a given amount of stopping power.

BK NS265H(FF)
4Y15FC

FIGURE 25-21 Brake lining edge code.

These code letters represent the following coefficients of friction:

- C: ≤ 0.15
- D: 0.15–0.25
- E: 0.25–0.35
- F: 0.35–0.45
- G: 0.045–0.55
- H: > 0.55
- Z: Unclassified

The lining is tested both cool and hot. The rating is a two letter designation such as "FF." The first letter is for the cool performance and the second letter is for the hot performance. For example, FF has a cool coefficient of friction of 0.35–0.45 and the same coefficient of friction at the hot temperature. It also is very possible that the hot and cold ratings differ from each other. For example, if the rating is FE, the coefficient of friction reduces as the temperature of the lining heats up. Notice that the coefficient of friction range is quite wide for each letter designation. Linings with the same letter ratings may not have the same braking performance as each other. This means that an EE-rated lining from one manufacturer is likely to have different braking characteristics than an EE-rated lining from another manufacturer. Always use high-quality brake lining from reliable companies to help avoid brake issues.

FIGURE 25-22 Brake pad shims and guides.

FIGURE 25-23 Example of brake pad retainers.

FIGURE 25-24 Brake lining grooves and contouring.

Anti-Noise Measures

Disc brakes are more prone to annoying brake squealing than are drum brakes. Brake squealing is caused by vibrations set up between the brake pad and rotor. Manufacturers have addressed this problem in a number of ways:

1. Using softer linings with a higher coefficient of friction, which are less prone to noise than harder linings with a lower coefficient of friction
2. Adding **brake pad shims and guides** to the brake pads, which help cushion the brake pad and absorb some of the vibration FIGURE 25-22
3. Using springs to tightly hold the pads in place to minimize vibration FIGURE 25-23
4. Contouring and grooving the lining material in a way that minimizes vibration FIGURE 25-24
5. Incorporating **bendable tangs** on the brake pad backing plate that allow technicians to crimp the tangs so they are more firmly mounted in the caliper FIGURE 25-25

Technicians also can apply noise-reducing compounds to the brake pads. One is a type of high-temperature liquid rubber compound that is applied to

DELCO
MORAINE

FIGURE 25-25 Brake pad bendable tangs.

the back of the brake pad. When it cures, it stays flexible and absorbs brake pad vibrations and helps reduce brake noise. Another compound is a specially designed liquid that is applied directly to the face of the lining material. This compound helps to modify the lining's coefficient of friction slightly, making it less likely that the lining will squeal. Make sure you apply the correct compound to the correct side of the brake pad.

Applied Science

AS-36: Sound: The technician can demonstrate an understanding of the role sound plays in identifying various problems in the vehicle.

Sound is a series of waves that travel through a gas, liquid, or solid and can often be heard by the human ear. Sound waves are created by vibrating objects, such as a guitar string. Moving objects that are in sliding contact with each other are highly likely to create sound. One example of this is fingernails dragging on a chalkboard. The fingernails vibrate on the surface of the chalkboard and create sound waves that are then heard by the ear.

Technicians commonly use differences in sound to assist in diagnosing disc brake problems. For example, brake pads that are worn down to the metal backing plate make a deep grinding noise when the brakes are applied. Listening to hear which wheel or wheels the noise is coming from helps identify the source of the problem. In the same way, if the disc brakes are equipped with a scratcher style of brake warning system, the brakes will make a high-pitched screeching noise. Many times this noise will happen when the vehicle is being driven when the brakes are not applied. One way to help determine which side the noise is coming from is by driving the vehicle next to a concrete traffic wall or building. If the noise is on that side, it will get much louder than when not near the wall.

TECHNICIAN TIP

Some manufacturers claim that refinishing their rotors removes enough material from the rotor that it can cause the brakes to squeal due to less mass, which changes the harmonic vibration qualities of the rotor. They recommend replacing the rotors any time the rotors are worn enough to need resurfacing.

Wear Indicators

Some manufacturers provide a means of notifying the driver that the brake pad linings are worn to their minimum limit. This helps ensure that the brake linings do not wear down to the point that they cannot properly perform their job anymore. Excessively thin brake linings tend to heat up quicker than thicker linings, which can lead to premature brake fade. Not all manufacturers use a brake lining wear indicator. In those cases, it is especially important to inspect the brakes at regular intervals, usually during tire rotations or oil changes.

Types

Some manufacturers use a mechanically operated wear indicator to notify the driver that the brake pads are worn to their minimum limit. This is achieved by a spring steel **scratcher** mounted to the brake pad FIGURE 25-26. Part of the scratcher extends below the brake pad backing plate at the lining's minimum wear thickness.

FIGURE 25-26 The scratcher brake wear indicator.

> **TECHNICIAN TIP**
>
> In many cases, the scratchers will start to make noise when the brakes are not applied and stop making noise when the brakes are applied, as applying the brakes tends to dampen the vibrations.

When the friction material wears down far enough, the scratcher contacts the surface of the rotor and makes a squealing noise similar to fingernails on a chalkboard. This distinctive noise means the brakes need service right away. When you replace the brake pads, make sure they come equipped with new scratchers set to the correct depth so they can function the next time the pads wear down.

Some manufacturers use a warning lamp or warning message on the dash to alert the driver that the lining is worn to its minimum thickness. These systems have an electrical contact installed on the brake pad at the point of the lining's minimum wear thickness. When the pad wears to this minimum thickness, the contact touches the rotor as the brakes are applied, prompting a warning light or warning message that tells the driver the disc brake pads are due for replacement. These contacts can be manufactured into the pad or they can be clipped onto the pad. The contacts are normally replaced when the pads are replaced. Make sure that either the contacts come with the new pads or order them along with the pads.

Disc Brake Rotors

The brake disc or rotor is the main rotating component of the disc brake unit. The wheel is bolted to the rotor and they rotate together, leading some manufacturers to integrate the anti-lock brake system (ABS) tone wheel into the rotor. Since friction between the rotor and brake pads generates great amounts of heat, rotors must be able to withstand high temperatures. The pads are also forced onto the surface of the rotor with potentially thousands of pounds of force, so the rotor must be strong and have a durable surface. The rotors are usually made of cast iron. To reduce weight, some manufacturers use a two-part rotor with a cast iron disc and a stamped steel center hat. This style of rotor is called a composite rotor. Some heavy-duty and/or high-performance vehicles have rotors made of reinforced carbon, carbon ceramic, or composite ceramic substances to reduce weight and withstand much higher temperatures.

Since the rotor surfaces are squeezed between two brake pads, any unevenness of the rotor surfaces will cause pulsation of the brakes as the thicker and thinner portions pass between the brake pads. The rotor surfaces must be parallel to each other to avoid this situation. Rotors can fail in two ways: parallelism, which is also called thickness variation, and lateral runout. **Parallelism** is the most critical condition. If the rotor's thickness varies by as little as 0.0003" (0.0076 mm), the rotor will tend to push the brake pads outward at any high spots. This tends to create more pressure on the brake pads and slows the vehicle down faster at that point. It also pushes up on the brake pedal as fluid is being forced back to the master cylinder. The result is a pulsation of the brake pedal and a surging of the vehicle while braking, which is usually more noticeable at lower braking speeds.

Lateral runout, also called warpage, is the side-to-side movement of the rotor surfaces as the rotor turns. A warped rotor can be within specifications for parallelism but out of specification for lateral runout. Lateral runout tends to move the caliper pistons in the same direction as each other, so brake fluid is not pushed back to the master cylinder. However, the caliper tends to be moved side to side. This movement can cause the steering wheel to shimmy as the warped rotor follows the brake pads, if the lateral runout is greater than about 0.003" (0.076 mm).

Also, runout causes the pads to rub on high spots of the rotor when the brakes are not being applied, causing uneven wear and/or the depositing of pad material on the rotor, which leads to thickness variation concerns.

For proper operation, rotors must maintain their shape and resist warpage under high heat and pressure conditions. Because of these requirements, they are usually made of cast iron. On motorcycles, rotors are often made of stainless steel for cosmetic reasons. Disc brakes also are equipped with a dust shield to help protect the rotor. Dust shields help keep dust, water, and other road debris away from the inside surface of the rotor. They also can help direct air flow to the rotor to assist with heat transfer to the atmosphere. Dust shields are commonly made of stamped sheet metal, but they also can be made of plastic. Dust shields can become damaged during brake repair so always inspect them for proper clearance before installing the wheel assembly.

> **TECHNICIAN TIP**
>
> Rotors can be warped by improperly torquing the lug nuts. Always use a properly calibrated torque wrench (or the proper torque stick if the shop policy allows) to torque the lug nuts to the manufacturer's specified torque.

Types of Rotors

Rotors can be solid or ventilated FIGURE 25-27. Solid rotors are less expensive and usually found on smaller vehicles. Ventilated rotors are used to improve heat transfer to the atmosphere. These passageways are designed to use centrifugal force to cause air to flow through the center of the rotor when it is rotating. Ventilated rotors are used on heavier vehicles or high-performance vehicles. Some ventilated rotors are directional, meaning they are designed to force air through the rotor in one direction only FIGURE 25-28. If the rotor is rotated in the wrong direction, it will not pump air properly and will overheat easier.

Disc brake rotors with holes or slots machined into their surface dissipate heat quicker FIGURE 25-29. They also help to remove water quickly from the surface of the pad in wet driving conditions. Since the pads wipe across the holes or slots, the surface of the pad is prevented from becoming hard and glassy smooth from the friction and heat of use. However, this scraping action reduces the overall life of the brake pad, so these types of rotors are generally only used in high-performance or race vehicles.

Most disc brake rotors are stamped with the manufacturer's minimum thickness specification FIGURE 25-30. This minimum thickness ensures an adequate amount of

> **TECHNICIAN TIP**
>
> If you hear a loud scraping or grinding noise when you test-drive a vehicle after servicing the brakes, check to see if the dust shield is contacting one of the rotors. If so, it can make a lot of loud grinding noises. Since it is thin sheet metal, chances are good that it is bent. It can usually be bent back into shape easily.

A
B

FIGURE 25-27 Rotors. **A.** Standard solid rotors. **B.** Ventilated rotors.

Direction of rotation

FIGURE 25-28 Directional ventilated rotor.

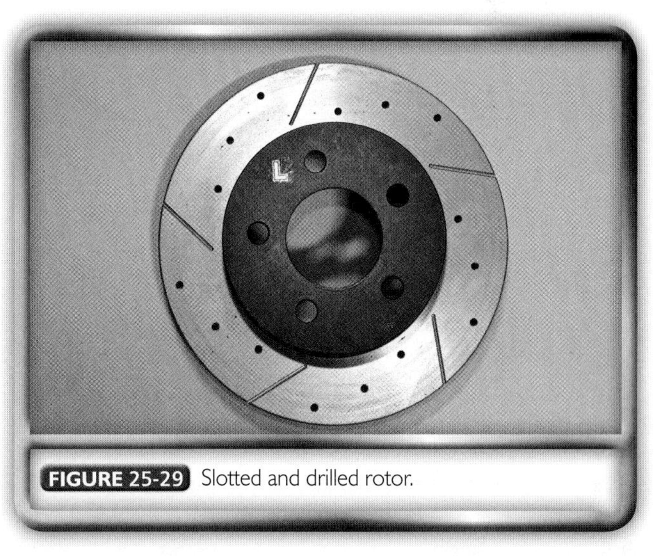

FIGURE 25-29 Slotted and drilled rotor.

5599 MIN THK 9.5 MM R5

FIGURE 25-30 Rotor with minimum thickness stamped on it.

thermal mass for stopping power FIGURE 25-31. When material is removed, there is not as much material to absorb heat and the rotor heats up faster. The excess heat can lead to brake fade sooner. Also, when the brake pads wear, if the thickness of the rotor were below this minimum, the piston could be pushed out beyond the edge of the sealing ring, which would cause the brakes to lose hydraulic pressure and fail. Make sure the rotors are always above the manufacturer's minimum thickness before putting them back in service.

Parking Brakes

Parking brakes are designed to hold the vehicle stationary when parked. Manufacturers are required to design the vehicle so the parking brake will hold the vehicle for a given amount of time on a specified grade in both directions. The parking brake must be separately activated from the service brakes, and the driver must be able to latch it into the applied position. Parking brakes can be foot operated or hand operated. Since disc brakes require higher applied forces to operate, they are a bit more difficult to use as parking brakes. However, manufacturers have overcome this challenge in a couple of ways.

Types of Parking Brakes

Currently most parking brakes are mechanically applied by use of a cable and ratcheting lever assembly. Parking brakes on disc brake units are primarily of two types: an integrated parking brake caliper and the top hat drum style. Alternatively, electric parking brakes are being used on some vehicles. The electric motor can pull on a conventional parking brake cable, or the electric motor can be mounted on the caliper and directly drive the caliper piston to apply force to the brake pads.

Integrated Mechanical Parking Brake Calipers

The integrated parking brake mechanically forces the disc brake piston outward, forcing the brake pads to clamp the rotor when the parking brake is applied FIGURE 25-32. A lever on the back side of the caliper is pulled by the parking brake cable. The lever converts that motion to rotary motion on a shaft that enters the rear of the caliper cylinder. The shaft uses a seal to prevent fluid leakage from the bore. The shaft has a coarse thread machined into it, which threads into a nut assembly inside the caliper piston. As the shaft is turned by the parking brake lever, the nut causes the piston to be forced outward, applying the brakes. Releasing the parking brake cable allows a spring to unwind the shaft and release the pressure on the brake pads.

Top Hat Design Parking Brake

The top hat design gets it name from the shape of the rotor. The rotor has a deeper offset than normal, giving the appearance of a top hat. The offset portion allows room for a drum surface within the center of the rotor. Drum brake shoes are mechanically forced outward into contact with the inside of the brake drum, which locks the wheel. Releasing the parking brake allows the springs to retract the brake shoes from contact with the drums.

Electric Parking Brake

The electric parking brake uses an electric motor to apply the disc brake assemblies. The cable style uses an electric motor to pull standard parking brake cables, which apply standard integrated mechanical parking brake calipers. The electrically integrated caliper style uses an electric motor mounted on the caliper to directly apply the brakes. Pushing a parking brake button on

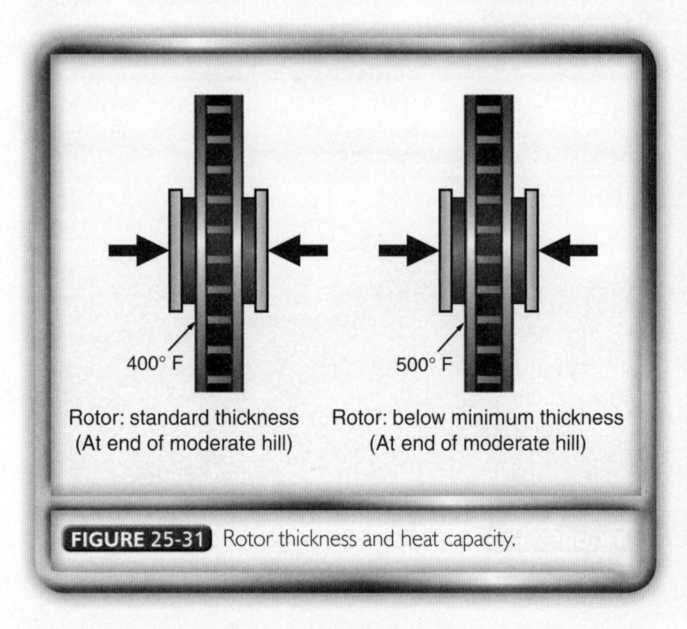
400° F
500° F
Rotor: standard thickness
(At end of moderate hill)
Rotor: below minimum thickness
(At end of moderate hill)

FIGURE 25-31 Rotor thickness and heat capacity.

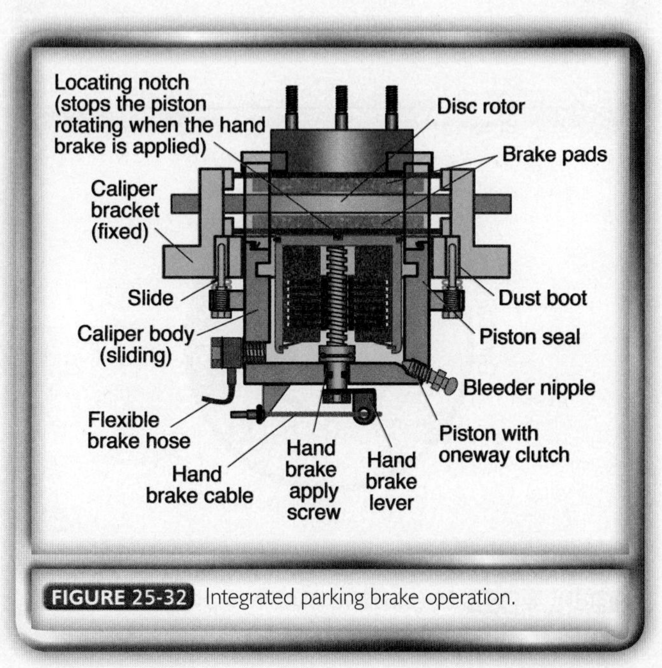
Locating notch
(stops the piston
rotating when the hand
brake is applied)
Disc rotor
Brake pads
Caliper
bracket
(fixed)
Slide
Dust boot
Caliper body
(sliding)
Piston seal
Bleeder nipple
Flexible
brake hose
Piston with
oneway clutch
Hand
brake cable
Hand
brake
apply
screw
Hand
brake
lever

FIGURE 25-32 Integrated parking brake operation.

the dash causes the motor to either tension the cable or directly apply the parking brake. Electric parking brakes also can be integrated with the controller area network bus (CAN-bus) system to provide additional features beyond just holding the vehicle when it is parked. It can be used to automatically hold the vehicle while it is stopped on a hill to prevent it from rolling backward or forward. It also can be automatically released by the vehicle's **electronic control module (ECM)** when the throttle is applied for starting to move away from the stop. It also may work with the vehicle's proximity detector when backing up. If the system detects the vehicle getting too close to an object, the ECM can apply the electric parking brake to stop the vehicle and prevent it from striking the object.

Diagnosis

Disc brake diagnosis usually starts with understanding the customer's concern. Communicating directly with the customer is the best way to do that, but the customer is not always available. An experienced service advisor will gather the required information, so you should read the service advisor's notes on the repair order carefully or speak with him or her directly. Once you understand the customer's concern, a test-drive is usually needed to verify the accuracy of the concern. This is a good opportunity to test the brakes under a variety of conditions. Replicating the customer concern is important in order to address the situation that the customer is experiencing.

During the test-drive, find a safe place to operate the brakes at a variety of speeds with a variety of brake pedal pressures, especially trying to mimic the conditions the customer described. It is may be necessary to go on a test drive with the customer driving, allowing him or her to operate the vehicle in the way that makes the problem evident and point out the particular situation he or she is experiencing. Also, it is good to have the customer along in case the problem does not occur, in which case he or she won't think you don't believe them or are ignoring the issue.

If there is a concern related to the anti-lock brake system (ABS) that requires a test drive, extreme caution is required so that an accident doesn't happen. Since ABS operates only during extreme braking or poor traction conditions, you run the risk of being rear-ended by a vehicle behind you or losing control of the vehicle if you apply the brakes hard enough to activate the ABS. So make sure the vehicle is being tested away from all other traffic. Remember that if the yellow ABS warning lamp is illuminated, the ABS system is deactivated, and you should not try to activate ABS on a test drive. If the yellow ABS lamp is off, the ABS system should be active and ready to activate. It is helpful when testing ABS to do so on a surface with limited traction, such as wet pavement or a dirt road. When you do apply the brakes firmly, ABS activation can typically be felt as pulsations in the brake pedal and possibly the steering wheel. The vehicle should brake quickly while maintaining steering control. In some cases, a "poor traction" lamp may illuminate, telling you that the ABS system had to activate. This warning lamp will usually turn off after several seconds. If the yellow ABS warning lamp illumines, it typically means that the vehicle's ECM has observed a fault in the ABS system and will need to be checked for DTCs.

Once the customer concern has been verified, you will hopefully have enough information to know how best to proceed. This could be as simple as performing a visual inspection of the brake fluid level and condition, removing the wheels to disassemble and inspect the brake units, looking up technical service bulletins, or reviewing the diagnostic troubleshooting chart for the particular symptom in the service information to determine the next step.

Suspension and steering system faults can appear to be brake system faults. An example of this is a pulling condition while braking. If the strut rod bushings on the suspension are worn, then braking the vehicle will cause the wheel to move rearward; at the same time, that will cause the steering angle to change, causing the wheel to point in a direction other than straight down the road, imitating a brake pull.

The braking system on a vehicle must be restored to its proper operation. Diagnosis of any problem must identify all issues that would prevent the brakes from operating normally. Lawyers and technicians have been known to say, "He who touched the brake system last, owns it!" What this means is that if there is a problem in the brake system and you inspected it or worked on it, you are very likely liable for anything that went wrong with it. Brake system failures are more likely to lead to vehicle accidents than failures of most systems. Any diagnosis and subsequent repairs need to be thorough and complete.

> **TECHNICIAN TIP**
>
> One way to help identify if a problem is coming from the front or rear brakes is to test-drive the vehicle in a safe place at a relatively low speed and lightly apply the parking brake. If the condition is still present, the problem is with the rear brakes, since the parking brakes are usually on the rear wheels. If the condition is not present, the problem is likely with the front brakes.

Tools

The tools that are used to diagnose and repair brake systems include:

- Brake lining thickness gauges—Used to measure the thickness of the brake lining
- Brake wash station—Used to clean drum and disc brake dust
- Caliper piston pliers—Used to grip caliper pistons when removing them
- Disc brake rotor micrometer—Used to measure the thickness and parallelism of a rotor
- Dial indicator—Used to measure the lateral runout (side to side) of the rotor
- Parking brake cable pliers—Used to install parking brake cables
- Caliper piston retracting tool—Used to retract caliper pistons with integrated parking brakes
- C-clamp—Used to push pistons back into the caliper bore on non-integrated parking brakes
- Off-car brake lathe—Used to machine drums and rotors that are off the vehicle
- On-car brake lathe—Used to machine rotors that are on the vehicle
- Caliper dust boot seal driver set—Consists of a driver and a variety of adapters used to install various sizes of dust boot seals FIGURE 25-33

Diagnosing Disc Brakes

To diagnose poor stopping, noise, vibration, pulling, grabbing, dragging, or pulsation concerns and determine any necessary actions, follow the steps outlined in the remainder of this chapter. While braking concerns are generally easier to diagnose than most of the other systems on the vehicle, the large variety of conditions listed makes it imperative that you have a good understanding of disc brake and hydraulic theory. It also helps to use all of your senses to assist you in identifying the location of the fault. As a reminder, TABLE 25-2 lists some of the common faults to consider for each concern.

Verify the customer concern by operating the vehicle if safe to do so. Depending on the concern, it may be as simple as stepping on the brake pedal without moving the vehicle and feeling the pedal sink to the floor, or it could require a more detailed test-drive to observe the fault the customer is describing. Regardless of the condition, it is almost always good practice to research any technical service bulletins (TSBs) for the particular situation. If no related TSBs are found, research the service information to familiarize yourself with the system and the manufacturer's diagnostic procedure for the condition. Perform any diagnostic tests to identify the cause of the condition. This could be a visual inspection or any other prescribed test, such as a power booster test. It could also involve a detailed testing sequence, such as testing the proportioning and metering valves. Once you have identified the cause of the fault, determine the action that will rectify the fault.

TABLE 25-2: Common Brake Issues

Concern	Fault
Poor stopping	• Power booster not operating properly • Internal master cylinder leak; air in the hydraulic system • Metering valve or proportioning valve blocking fluid flow • Improperly adjusted drum brakes • Improper friction lining material • Contaminated linings
Noise	• Friction lining material too hard • Lining worn down to metal • Worn caliper slides/guide pins • Component-specific noises
Vibration	• Improper friction lining material • Rotor surface finish not correct • Foreign object (mud, rocks, etc.) in rotor • Warped rotor • ABS operating
Pulling	• Plugged or restricted brake hose • Stuck caliper piston • Seized caliper guide pins • Contaminated lining • Lining worn down to metal • Air in the hydraulic system
Grabbing	• Contaminated lining • Stuck caliper piston • Internal master cylinder leak • Misadjusted drum brakes
Dragging	• Stuck caliper piston • Seized caliper guide pins • Misadjusted master cylinder pushrod length • Binding brake pedal • Plugged restricted brake line or hose
Pulsation	• Warped rotors • Rotor parallelism • ABS operation

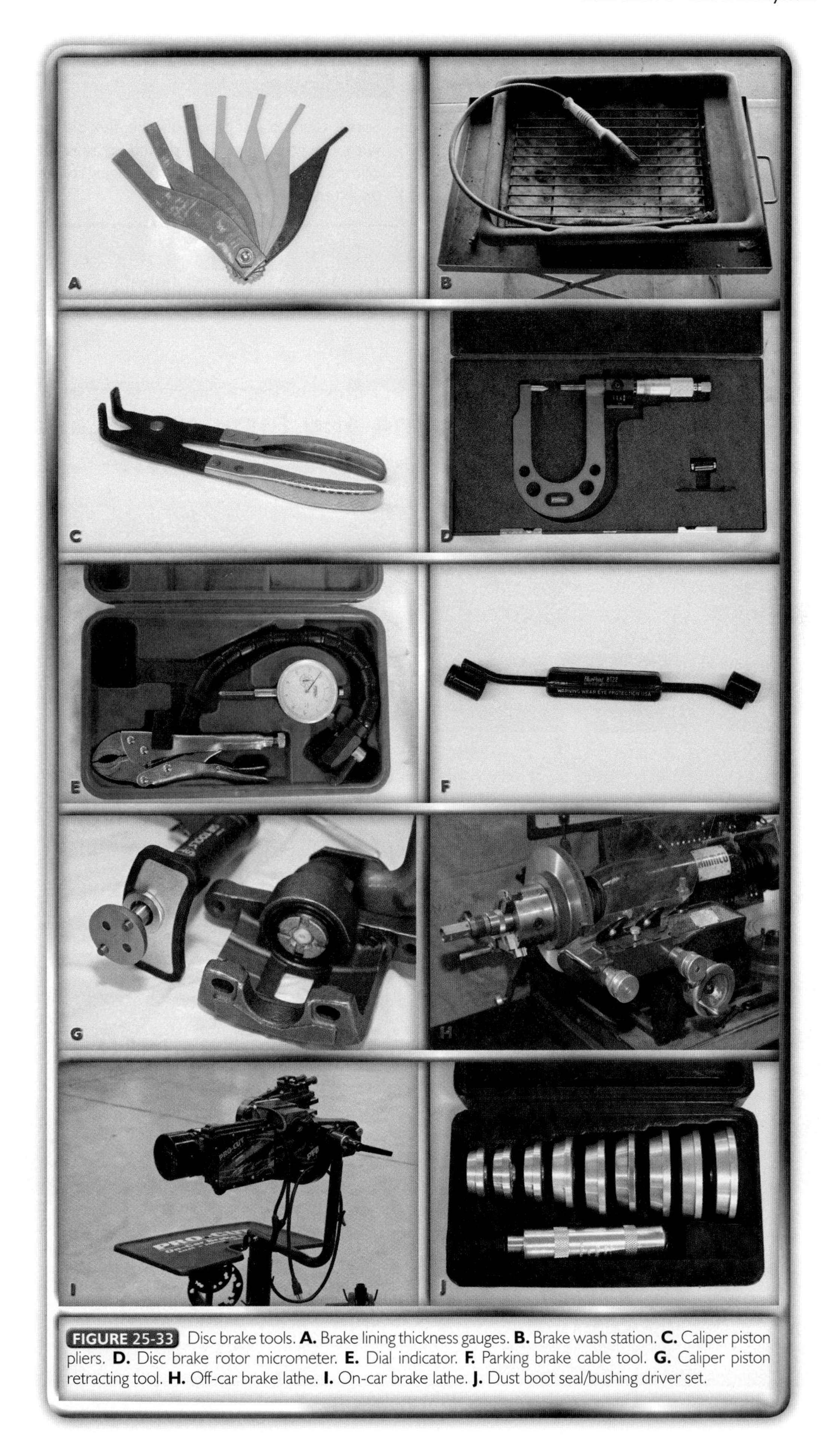
A
B
C
D
E
F
G
H
I
J

FIGURE 25-33 Disc brake tools. **A.** Brake lining thickness gauges. **B.** Brake wash station. **C.** Caliper piston pliers. **D.** Disc brake rotor micrometer. **E.** Dial indicator. **F.** Parking brake cable tool. **G.** Caliper piston retracting tool. **H.** Off-car brake lathe. **I.** On-car brake lathe. **J.** Dust boot seal/bushing driver set.

Maintenance and Repair

Removing and Inspecting Calipers

Removing the caliper is necessary for replacing the brake pads on most vehicles. It also allows access for machining of the rotors on the vehicle, removal of the rotors for replacement, or machining of the rotors off the vehicle. Further, it allows for a thorough inspection of the caliper, pads, and rotor to determine the cause of a brake concern. To remove the caliper assembly, inspect for leaks and damage to the caliper housing, and determine any necessary actions, follow the steps in **SKILL DRILL 25-1**.

> **TECHNICIAN TIP**
>
> Some technicians pinch off the flexible brake hoses with vice grip pliers. This should be avoided because it crimps the hose, potentially damaging it internally and/or externally.

SKILL DRILL 25-1 Removing and Inspecting Calipers

1. Research the procedure for removing the caliper in the appropriate service information. Loosen the bleeder screws slightly and then retighten them.

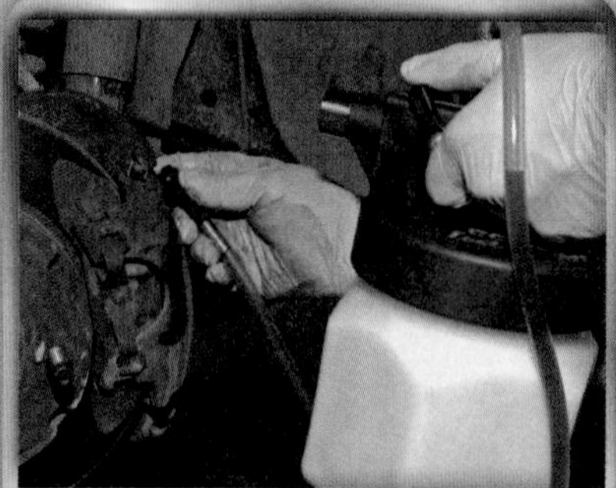

2. If the caliper is being rebuilt or a new caliper will be installed, it is good practice to flush the old brake fluid from the system at this time. Leave the master cylinder reservoir level low to prevent overflowing.

3. Use a brake pedal holding tool to slightly apply the brakes and block off the compensating ports in the master cylinder to avoid excess fluid leakage.

4. Remove the brake line or hose from the caliper. Be careful not to lose the sealing rings.

5. Push the caliper pistons back into their bores slightly. While many use a screwdriver as shown, a pry bar is a safer choice.

6. Remove the caliper assembly from its mountings.

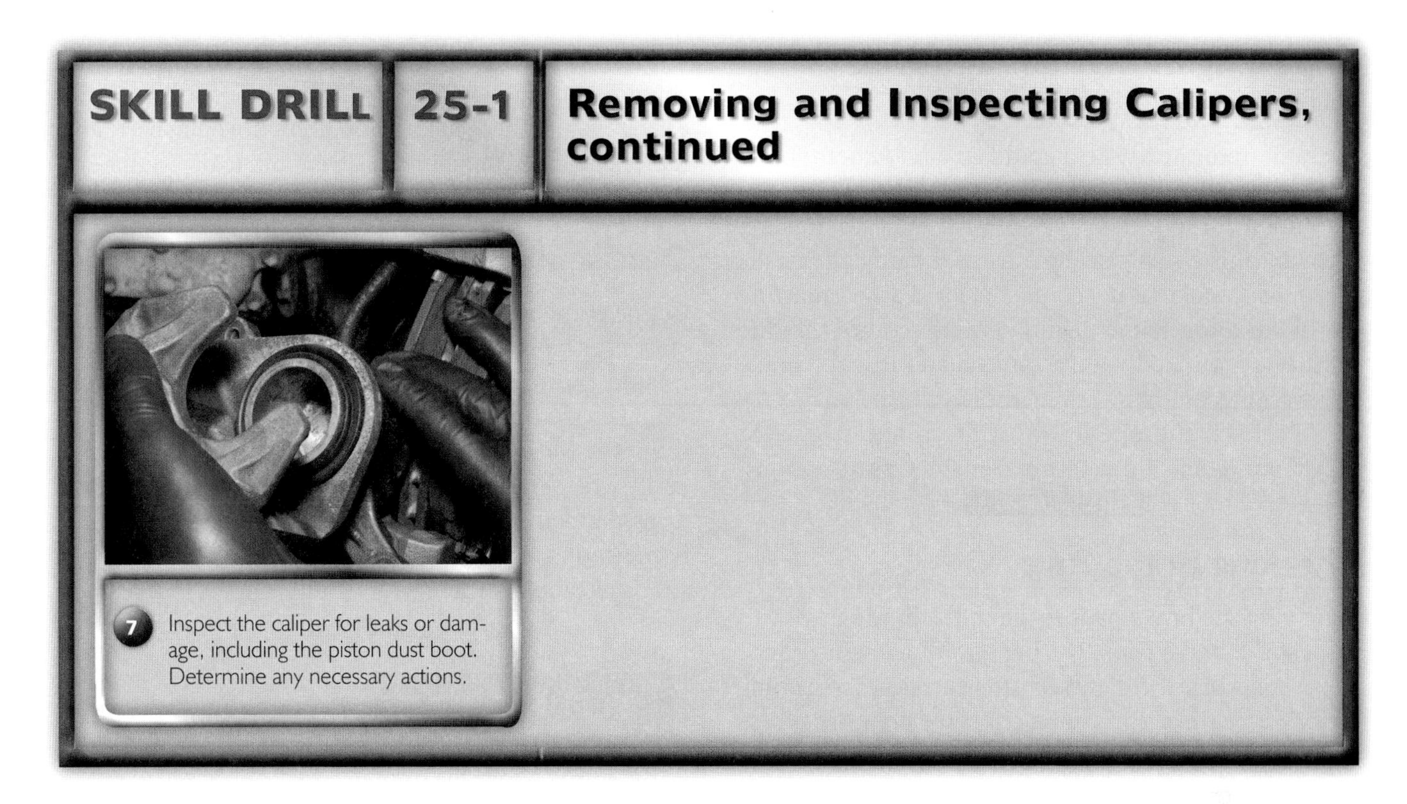
SKILL DRILL 25-1 Removing and Inspecting Calipers, continued

7 Inspect the caliper for leaks or damage, including the piston dust boot. Determine any necessary actions.

Inspecting Caliper Mountings, Slides, and Pins

The caliper mountings and slides/pins are placed under heavy loads and forces. They also operate in harsh environments. It is common that they experience wear over time. They can also corrode and bind up. Clean caliper mountings and slides/pins thoroughly, and inspect them closely.

To clean and inspect caliper mountings and slides/pins for operation, wear, and damage and to determine any necessary actions, follow the steps in SKILL DRILL 25-2.

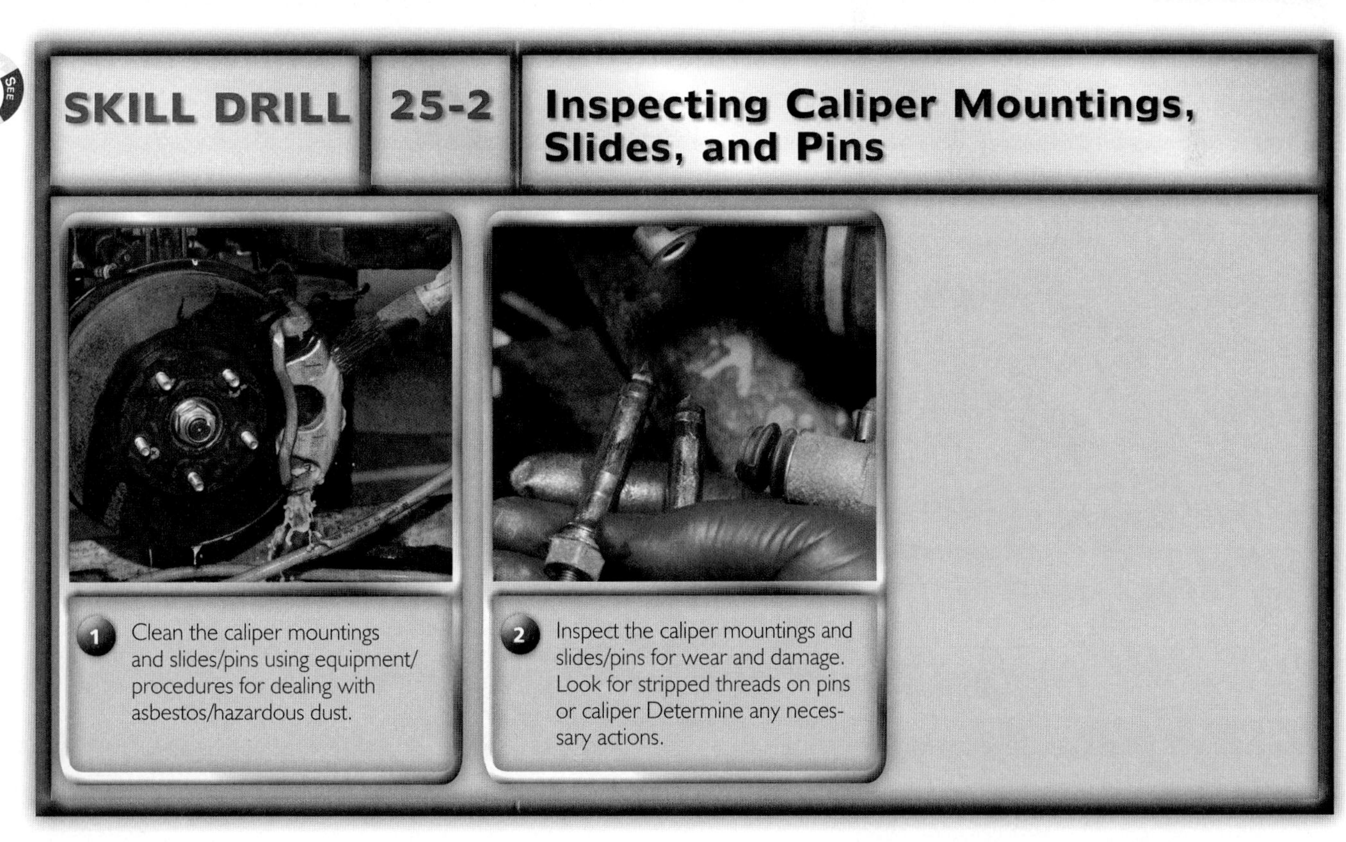
SKILL DRILL 25-2 Inspecting Caliper Mountings, Slides, and Pins

1 Clean the caliper mountings and slides/pins using equipment/procedures for dealing with asbestos/hazardous dust.

2 Inspect the caliper mountings and slides/pins for wear and damage. Look for stripped threads on pins or caliper Determine any necessary actions.

Inspecting Brake Pads and Wear Indicators

The wear indicator system could be a scratcher type or a sensor type. It is also very possible that the vehicle does not incorporate any type of wear indicator system. Checking this system usually consists of verifying that the sensor or scratcher is not contacting or nearly contacting the brake rotor. Some manufacturers require that the sensor be grounded with a test lead and that the brake pad warning lamp or warning message come on.

To check the operation of the brake pad wear indicator system and determine any necessary actions, follow the steps in **SKILL DRILL 25-3**.

Checking Brake Pads

Removing the brake pads is the most thorough way to inspect the brake pads. During a routine maintenance inspection where there are no customer concerns regarding the brakes, a simple measurement of the lining thickness is usually adequate. But if there are customer concerns with the brakes, it may be necessary to remove the pads for a more detailed inspection. This could show cracks in the lining or other defects that wouldn't be otherwise seen from the outside. It also allows for a more thorough inspection of the retaining hardware. Also pay attention to the way the brake pads come off, as some pads have slight differences (such as locating nipples) that make it easy to install them incorrectly. To remove, inspect, and replace pads and retaining hardware and to determine any necessary actions, follow the steps in **SKILL DRILL 25-4**.

Disassembling Calipers

Calipers are disassembled and cleaned for a couple of reasons. The first is to diagnose a brake system concern related to one or more calipers. For example, if the vehicle has a brake pull, it could be caused by a sticking caliper piston. Disassembling the caliper will allow you to verify whether that is the case or not. They also need to be disassembled and cleaned if they are going to be rebuilt. Some shops rebuild the calipers themselves, but most shops just replace them with rebuilt calipers if necessary.

> **TECHNICIAN TIP**
>
> Because you have the rotor exposed, skip ahead to the sections on inspecting and servicing rotors, and complete the tasks listed there. This will save you time and effort. Pick up here once you are done with the rotor.

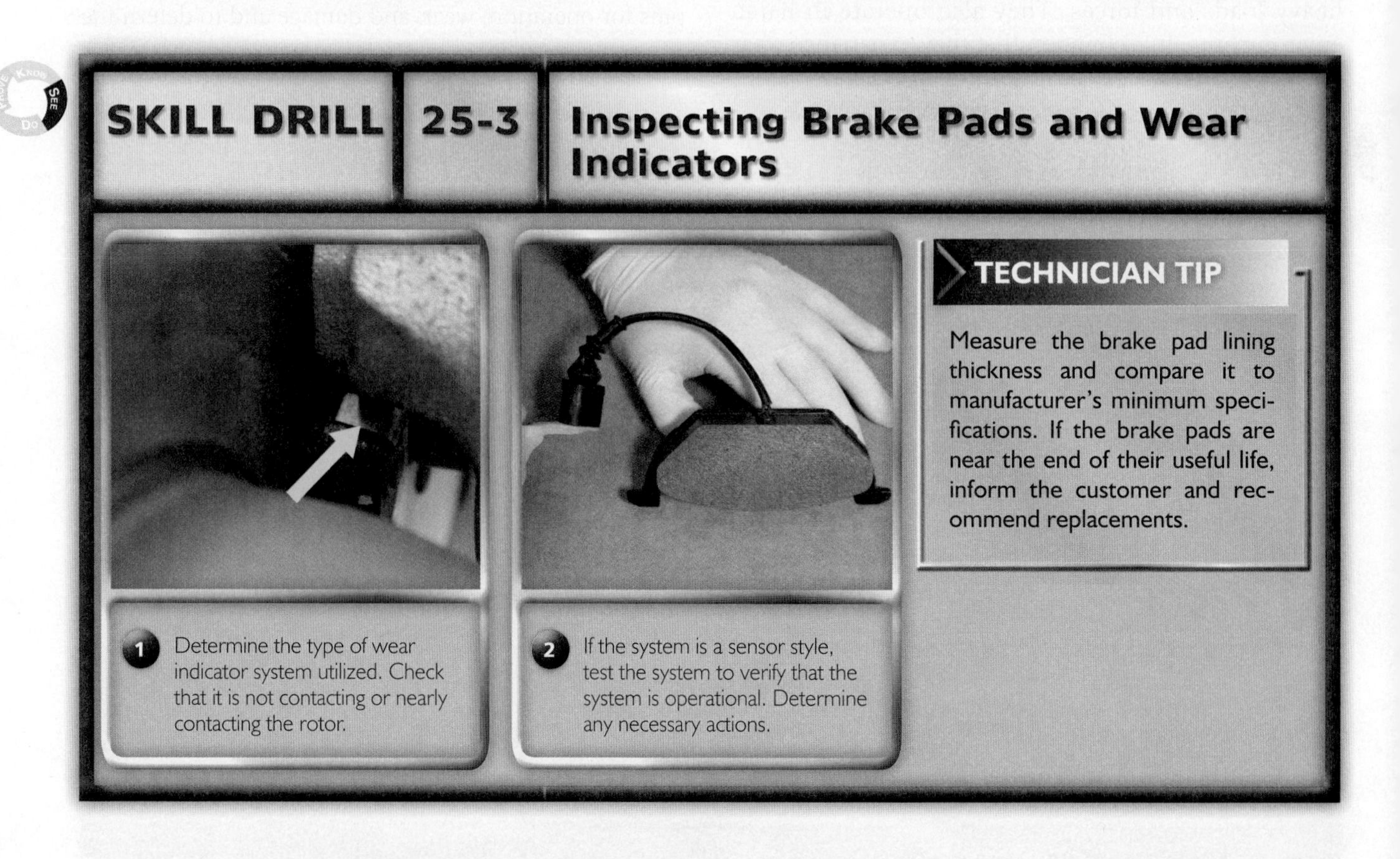
SKILL DRILL 25-3 Inspecting Brake Pads and Wear Indicators
TECHNICIAN TIP
Measure the brake pad lining thickness and compare it to manufacturer's minimum specifications. If the brake pads are near the end of their useful life, inform the customer and recommend replacements.
1 Determine the type of wear indicator system utilized. Check that it is not contacting or nearly contacting the rotor.
2 If the system is a sensor style, test the system to verify that the system is operational. Determine any necessary actions.

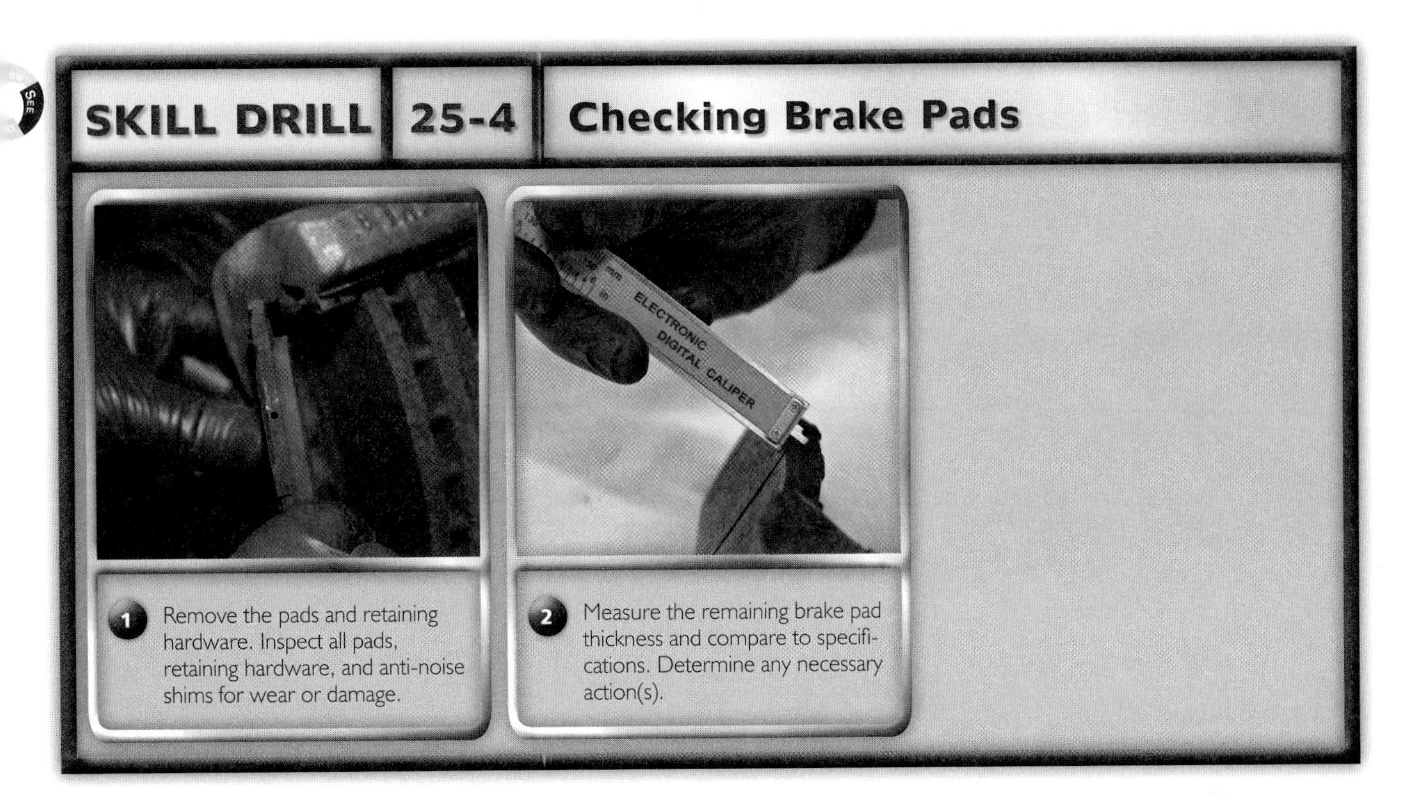
ELECTRONIC DIGITAL CALIPER

SKILL DRILL 25-4 Checking Brake Pads

1. Remove the pads and retaining hardware. Inspect all pads, retaining hardware, and anti-noise shims for wear or damage.
2. Measure the remaining brake pad thickness and compare to specifications. Determine any necessary action(s).

Disc brake calipers are usually side specific, meaning they are designed to be installed on a particular side of the vehicle. Failure to install them on the correct side usually results in the bleeder screws being on the bottom of the caliper cylinder. This will prevent air from being bled from the caliper and result in a very spongy brake pedal.

To disassemble and clean the caliper assembly; inspect parts for wear, rust, scoring, and damage; and replace the seal, boot, and damaged or worn parts, follow the steps in **SKILL DRILL 25-5**.

SKILL DRILL 25-5 Disassembling Calipers

1. Disassemble the caliper, following the service manual procedure.
2. Clean all of the caliper parts following the service manual procedure.
3. Inspect each of the parts for damage, rust, and wear. Check the caliper pin bores or bushings for wear or damage.

SKILL DRILL 25-5 Disassembling Calipers, continued

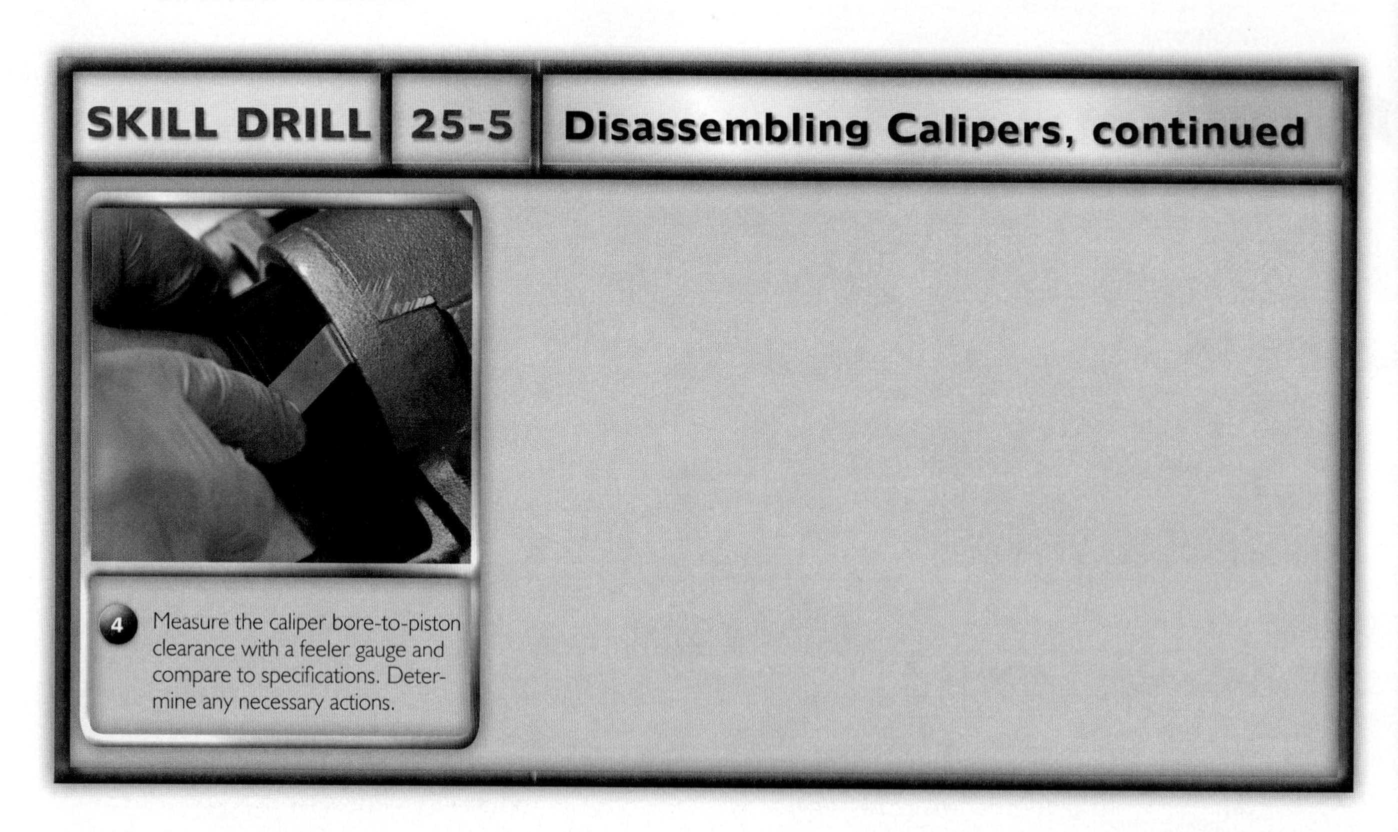

4 Measure the caliper bore-to-piston clearance with a feeler gauge and compare to specifications. Determine any necessary actions.

Reassembling Calipers

Reassembling the caliper requires patience and attention to detail. Ensure that the sealing ring groove is spotless and that the O-ring gets seated fully in the groove. Use clean brake fluid or approved caliper piston assembly lube on the piston and sealing ring prior to installing it. Also check the service manual to see when the piston dust boot needs to be installed. Some calipers require the dust boot to be installed in the caliper before installing the piston. In this case, a special technique using air pressure to "balloon" the dust boot is required so the piston can slip inside it. Ask your supervisor to demonstrate this technique.

To reassemble, lubricate, and reinstall the caliper, pads, and related hardware; seat pads; and inspect for leaks, follow the steps in SKILL DRILL 25-6. When seating the pads (step 6), place your left foot under the brake pedal so that when applying the pedal with your right foot, the pedal does not push the master cylinder pistons farther into the master cylinder bore, which could dislodge sludge or cut the lips of the master cylinder primary seals. Applying the brake will force the brake caliper pistons to adjust to the proper clearance for proper brake application. You may need to start the vehicle to enable the power booster to help you fully apply the brakes, especially if the vehicle is equipped with integrated parking brake calipers.

TECHNICIAN TIP

In some cases, the piston cannot be removed with compressed air due to the piston being seized in the bore. If this happens, reinstall the calipers on the vehicle without the pads, bleed the brakes, and use the brake pedal to force the stuck piston out of the caliper. You may have to block any nonseized pistons so they don't pop out; that way, just the seized piston gets pushed out.

Safety

If using compressed air to remove the piston, be very careful, as the piston can pop out with great force, enough to break finger bones or pinch fingers off. Always use an approved cushion between the caliper piston and caliper housing. Keep your fingers away from the area.

SKILL DRILL 25-6 Reassembling Calipers
1 Make sure the rotor has been properly installed on the hub/spindle and the hub surface is free of rust or dirt.
2 Reassemble the caliper assembly, following the manufacturer's procedure. Lubricate the sealing ring, piston, and other moving parts. Be careful to not pinch, twist, or cut the sealing ring and dust boot.
3 Assemble the pads, hardware, and caliper on the caliper mountings using the specified lubricant. Lubricate all moving parts.
4 Reinstall the brake line fittings using two new copper washers (if equipped). Place one between the brake line fitting and the head of the banjo bolt and the other between the brake line fitting and the caliper.
5 Tighten the brake line fitting and caliper bolts to the proper torque. Bleed the brakes following the manufacturer's procedure.
6 Seat the pads by applying the brake pedal several times, not allowing the pedal to go all the way to the floor.

Retracting and Readjusting Pistons on an Integrated Parking Brake

Retracting the caliper piston on an integrated parking brake system is different than on a standard caliper. Since the integrated parking brake system uses a threaded shaft to force the piston outward from the caliper bore, it cannot just be retracted with a C-clamp. The piston will need to be screwed back in on the threaded shaft to retract it into the bore. This is accomplished by using a tool that mates to slots, grooves, or holes in the outer face of the piston. The tool is then turned by hand or wrench to screw the piston back into the bore. Be careful to not tear the piston dust boot during this operation.

To retract the caliper piston on an integrated parking brake system, follow the steps in SKILL DRILL 25-7.

SKILL DRILL 25-6 Reassembling Calipers, continued

7 If the brake pedal is spongy, you will need to bleed the brakes of any remaining trapped air in the system.

8 Inspect the system for any brake fluid leaks, no matter how small.

SKILL DRILL 25-7 Retracting and Readjusting Pistons on an Integrated Parking Brake

1 Research the procedure for retracting the caliper piston. Select the proper adapter or tool to match the caliper piston.

2 Install the tool and turn it in the direction that causes the piston to retract.

3 Continue turning until the piston is lightly seated at the bottom of its bore.

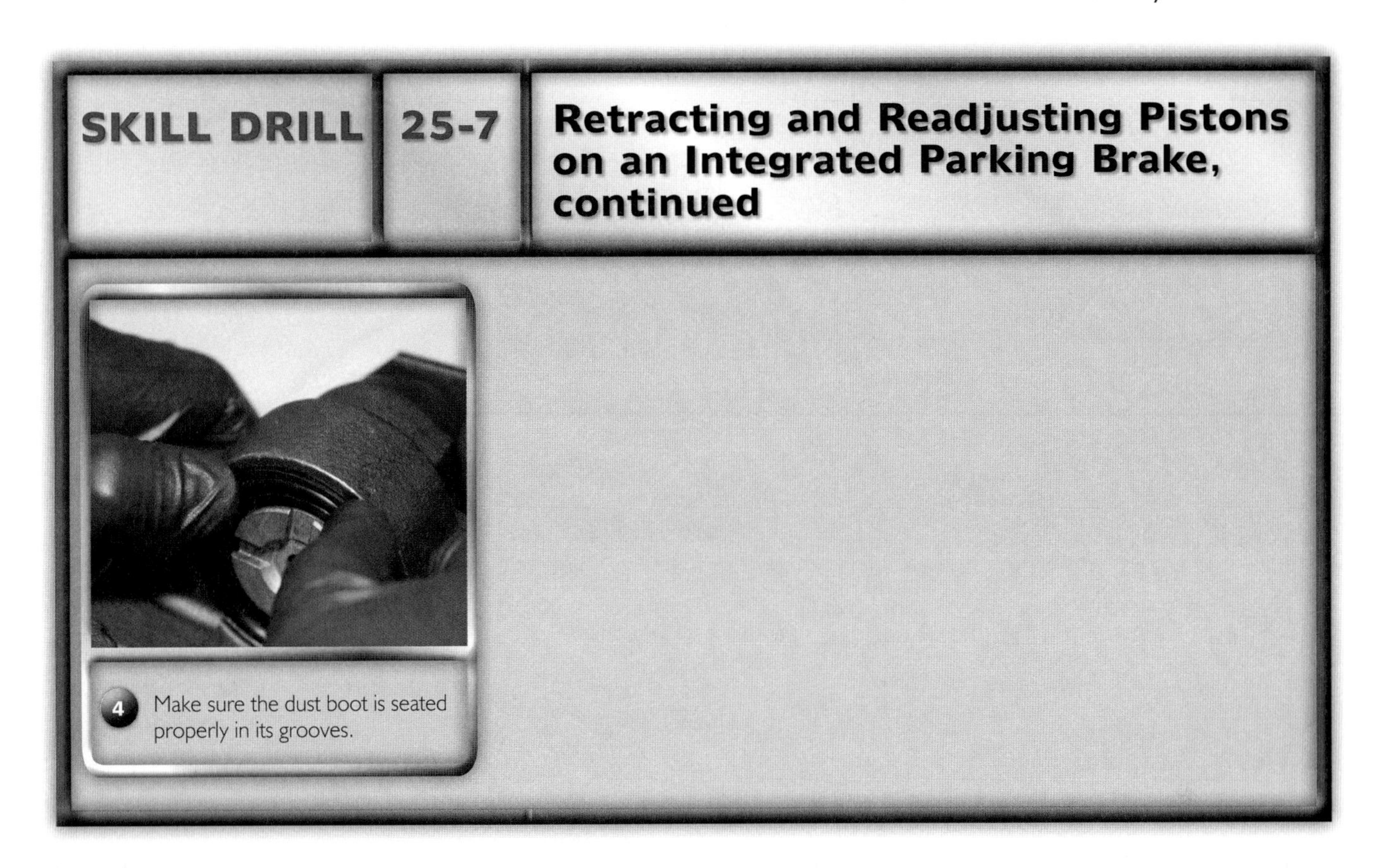
SKILL DRILL 25-7 Retracting and Readjusting Pistons on an Integrated Parking Brake, continued

4 Make sure the dust boot is seated properly in its grooves.

Before starting, research the procedure for retracting the caliper piston on an integrated parking brake system in the appropriate service information, paying close attention to which direction the piston needs to be turned. Select the proper adapter or tool to match the caliper piston. There are several types of tools that work. One is a multisided cube with a variety of projections of varying configurations on each side. This cube fits on the end of a ratchet. The ratchet and tool need to be held tightly against the piston so it does not slip. There are other more application-specific tools that use the caliper housing to keep the tool from slipping out of the holes in the piston. This style works the best if you have access to one.

Inspecting and Measuring Disc Brake Rotors

The rotor thickness, lateral runout, and thickness variation must be within specifications for the rotor to function properly. Rotors that are too thin cannot handle as much heat and will experience brake fade sooner than thicker rotors will. They also may cause the piston to be pushed out of the caliper bore far enough that the sealing ring no longer seals the piston. This would lead to a lack of braking action on at least half of the system.

Excessive thickness variation will cause brake pedal pulsation and the vehicle to have a surging feeling while coming to a stop. Excessive lateral runout tends to cause the steering wheel to shimmy. It also can cause an excessive thickness variation problem due to the high spot of the rotor continuously hitting the brake pad while driving down the road. This constant rubbing on the high spot of the rotor will wear it slightly, leading to excessive thickness variation across the face of the rotor.

To clean, inspect, and measure rotor thickness, lateral runout, and thickness variation and to determine any necessary action(s), follow the steps in SKILL DRILL 25-8.

> **TECHNICIAN TIP**
>
> Before machining the rotor, check to see how badly it is scored. Remember that removing 0.015" (0.38 mm) on each side of the rotor results in the thickness being reduced by 0.030" (0.76 mm). Many rotors only start with 0.060" (1.52 mm) of machinable material when they are new.

SKILL DRILL 25-8 Inspecting and Measuring Disc Brake Rotors

1. Research the procedure and specifications for inspecting the rotor. If you have not already done so, remove the caliper assembly, brake pads, and any hardware. Clean the rotor with approved asbestos removal equipment.

2. Inspect the rotor for hard spots or hot spots, scoring, cracks, and damage.

3. Measure the rotor thickness at the deepest groove or thinnest part of the rotor and compare to specifications. If undersize, replace it; if it is too thick, machine it to specfications.

4. Set up a dial indicator to measure lateral runout. Rotate the rotor and find the lowest spot on the rotor, then zero the dial indicator.

5. Slowly rotate the rotor to find the highest spot on the rotor. Read the dial indicator showing maximum runout.

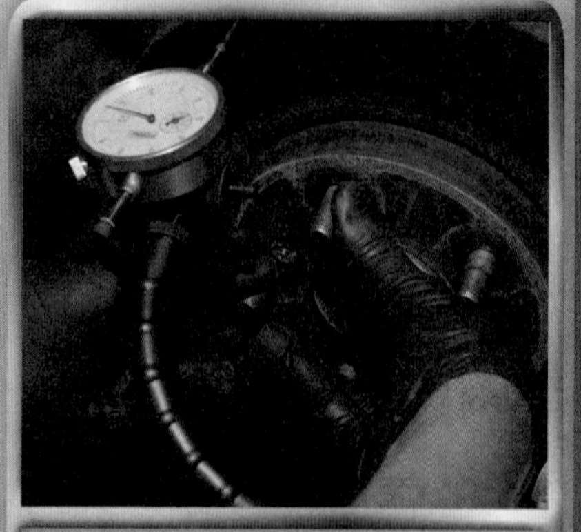

6. Keep turning the rotor to make sure the dial indicator does not read below zero. If it does, rezero the dial caliper on the lowest spot. Keep turning the rotor to find the highest spot and reread the dial indicator. Compare all of your readings to the specifications and determine if the rotor is fit for service, is machinable, or needs to be replaced.

Removing and Reinstalling Rotors

Removing the rotor is usually required when the rotor needs to be replaced because it is under the specified minimum thickness or would be after machining. It also would need to be removed to be refinished on an off-car brake lathe or to service the wheel bearings or axle shaft. Also, hubless rotors that are being machined with an on-car brake lathe need to be removed to clean off the rust and dirt accumulated between the rotor and the hub.

Rotors are designed to be mounted in one of two ways: hub style or hubless style. The hub style has the wheel bearing hub cast into the rotor. This style generally requires disassembly of the wheel bearing hub to remove the rotor from the vehicle. The hubless style uses a wheel bearing hub separate from the rotor, with the rotor held onto the hub by the wheel studs and lug nuts. Some hubs also use small screws to hold the rotor on the hub whenever the wheel is removed from the vehicle. Removing hubless rotors is generally easier than removing hub-style rotors, although some manufacturers design their rotors to unbolt from the rear side of the bearing hub. In these applications, the wheel bearing hub must be removed before the rotor can be removed from the hub.

To remove and reinstall the rotor, follow the steps in SKILL DRILL 25-9. As always, begin by researching the procedure for removing and reinstalling the brake rotor in the appropriate service information.

SKILL DRILL 25-9 Removing and Reinstalling Rotors

1. Research the procedure for removing and reinstalling the brake rotor. If you have not already done so, remove the caliper assembly, brake pads, and any hardware. If the caliper mount straddles the rotor, remove it.
2. To remove the hubless-style rotor, mark the rotor for proper reinstallation.
3. If there are screws or speed nuts holding the rotor to the hub, remove them.
4. Remove the rotor from the hub.
5. To remove the hub-style rotor, remove the wheel bearing locking mechanism.
6. Remove the wheel bearing adjusting nut, thrust washer, and outer bearing.

SKILL DRILL 25-9 Removing and Reinstalling Rotors, continued

7 Follow the steps of the inner bearing and grease seal removal procedure (detailed in the Wheel Bearings chapter) if the rear bearing must be removed.

8 To reinstall a hubless-style rotor, clean all mounting surfaces on the hub and rotor and remove any burrs.

9 Slip the rotor over the wheel studs.

10 If the rotor uses small screws to hold the rotor to the hub, reinstall those and tighten to the proper torque.

11 Spin the rotor to ensure it spins true and does not contact any other components such as the dust shield.

12 To reinstall a hub-style rotor, see the wheel bearing service skill drills in the Wheel Bearing chapter. Be sure to properly lock the adjustment nut in place once adjustment is completed.

13 Spin the rotor to ensure it spins true and does not contact any other components such as the dust shield.

Refinishing Rotors on Vehicle

Rotors need to be refinished when they have excessive runout, thickness variation, or grooving. A brake lathe refinishes the rotor surfaces by removing metal and truing the surfaces. If the grooving or surface defects are too great, the rotor may require the removal of too much metal to satisfactorily refinish the surfaces. The rotor thickness should always be remeasured once the refinishing is complete to ensure it is above the manufacturer's minimum thickness.

Rotors can be refinished while on the vehicle or off the vehicle. On-vehicle refinishing is preferred by most manufacturers (those who allow refinishing of their rotors) because it minimizes runout issues between the hub and rotor. Since the rotor is being machined as it is mounted on the vehicle, it is being refinished true to the hub and other brake components. This minimizes any lateral runout issues. To refinish a rotor while it is on the vehicle and to measure final rotor thickness, follow the steps on **SKILL DRILL 25-10**. Before starting, research the brake lathe manufacturer's procedure for properly refinishing the rotor. Follow those guidelines completely.

Refinishing Rotors off Vehicle

Refinishing a rotor while it is off the vehicle is a bit different than on-vehicle refinishing. The major difference is in the setup. Hub-style and hubless-style rotors each

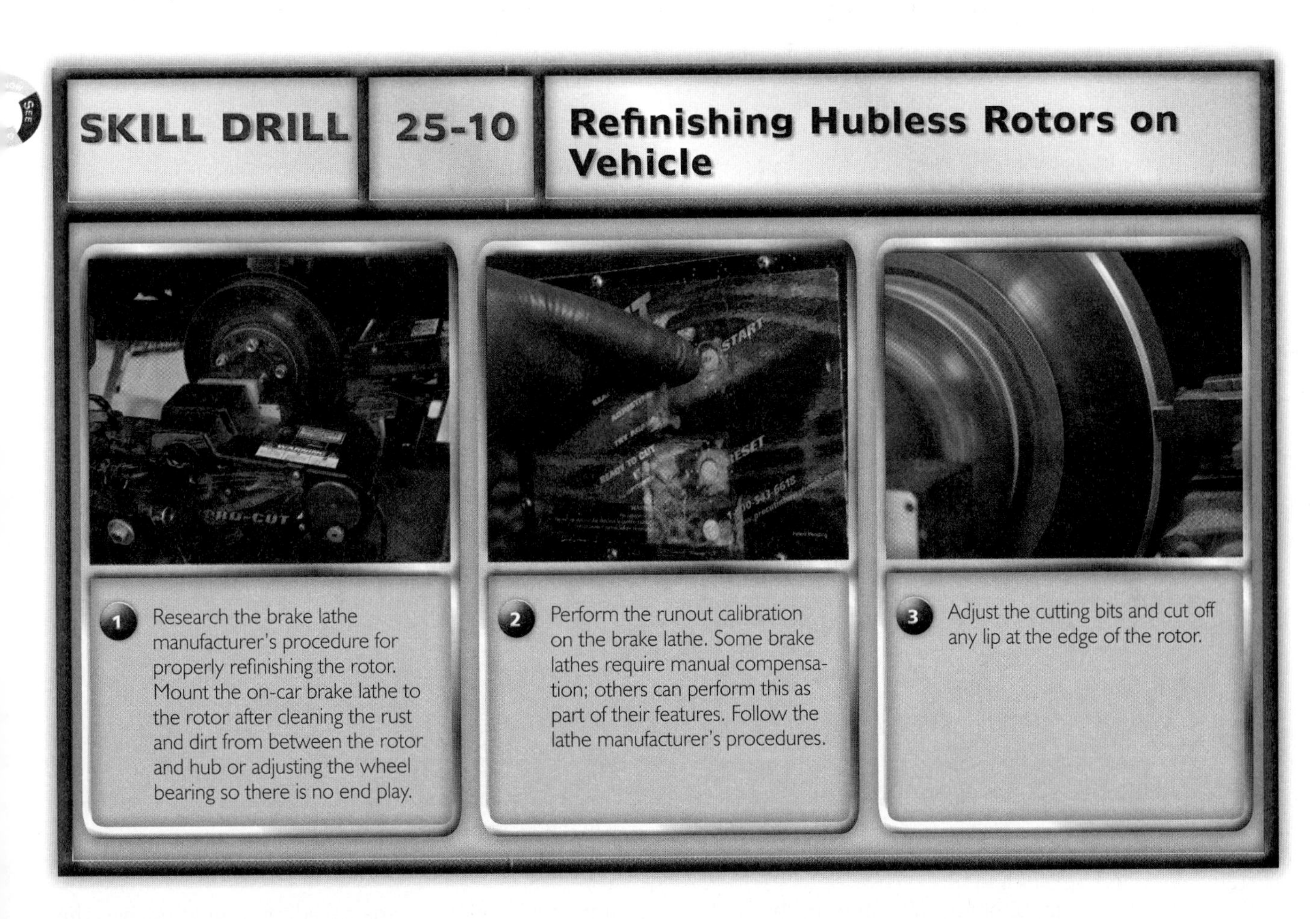
START
RESET
PRO-CUT

SKILL DRILL 25-10 Refinishing Hubless Rotors on Vehicle

1. Research the brake lathe manufacturer's procedure for properly refinishing the rotor. Mount the on-car brake lathe to the rotor after cleaning the rust and dirt from between the rotor and hub or adjusting the wheel bearing so there is no end play.
2. Perform the runout calibration on the brake lathe. Some brake lathes require manual compensation; others can perform this as part of their features. Follow the lathe manufacturer's procedures.
3. Adjust the cutting bits and cut off any lip at the edge of the rotor.

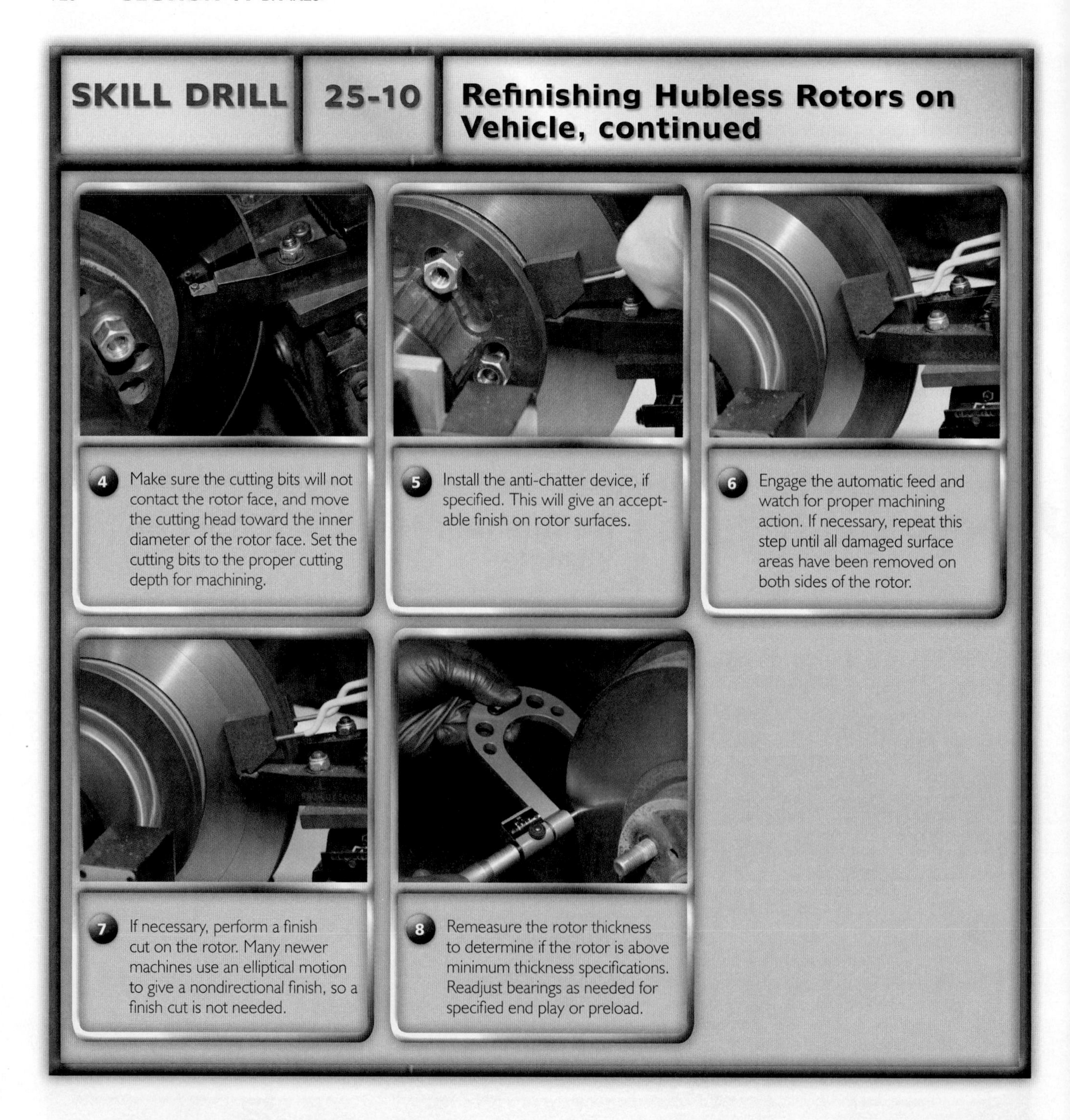
SKILL DRILL
25-10
Refinishing Hubless Rotors on Vehicle, continued
4 Make sure the cutting bits will not contact the rotor face, and move the cutting head toward the inner diameter of the rotor face. Set the cutting bits to the proper cutting depth for machining.
5 Install the anti-chatter device, if specified. This will give an acceptable finish on rotor surfaces.
6 Engage the automatic feed and watch for proper machining action. If necessary, repeat this step until all damaged surface areas have been removed on both sides of the rotor.
7 If necessary, perform a finish cut on the rotor. Many newer machines use an elliptical motion to give a nondirectional finish, so a finish cut is not needed.
8 Remeasure the rotor thickness to determine if the rotor is above minimum thickness specifications. Readjust bearings as needed for specified end play or preload.

require their own way of being mounted on the brake lathe. Most hub-style rotors use the **bearing races** to drive and center the rotor on the lathe spindle. Thus, bearing adapters of the proper size need to be selected and used (see the Wheel Bearings chapter). The spindle nut then clamps the rotor onto the spindle through these bearing adapters and races. Hubless rotors are centered using a spring-loaded centering cone to align the rotor's centering hole with the spindle. Clam shell clamps are then used on each side of the rotor to clamp it to the lathe spindle. Composite rotors use a special adapter which drives the rotor from the center hole and, at the same time, clamps it firmly between solid plates.

To refinish a rotor while it is off the vehicle and measure final rotor thickness, follow the steps in **SKILL DRILL 25-11**. Before starting, research the brake lathe manufacturer's procedure for properly refinishing the rotor. Follow those guidelines completely. After refinishing the rotor, wash it in hot soapy water solution or parts-washing cabinet to remove any metal particles and dry thoroughly.

SKILL DRILL 25-11 Refinishing Rotors off Vehicle

1. Research the brake lathe manufacturer's procedure for properly refinishing the rotor. Clean nicks, burrs, or debris from the mounting surfaces of the rotor including the centering hole.
2. Mount the rotor. Check that the rotor is running true on the lathe.
3. Install the anti-chatter band or anti-chatter pucks on the rotor.
4. Position the cutting head about one-quarter the way in from the outer diameter of the rotor. Turn on the lathe.
5. Set the cutting bits to the proper cutting depth for machining the ridge.
6. By hand, move the cutting head outward toward the ridge. Slowly remove the ridge.

Inspecting and Replacing Wheel Studs

Wheel studs need to be replaced when they have been damaged or broken off due to improper installation or normal wear and tear. Wheel studs can be damaged by being overtightened and stretched. Look for a necked-down or thinned-out section of the stud, which is most likely to happen within the threaded area of the stud. Stretched studs need to be replaced. Studs can also have their threads damaged by cross-threading or seizing of the lug nut on the stud. It is best to replace the stud and nut if this occurs. Lastly, wheel studs may even break off if they are overtightened beyond their stretch point. It is always a good idea to consider replacing all of the studs on a wheel (and maybe the ones on the other wheels also) if one stud is broken off, as it is likely that all of the others have been weakened.

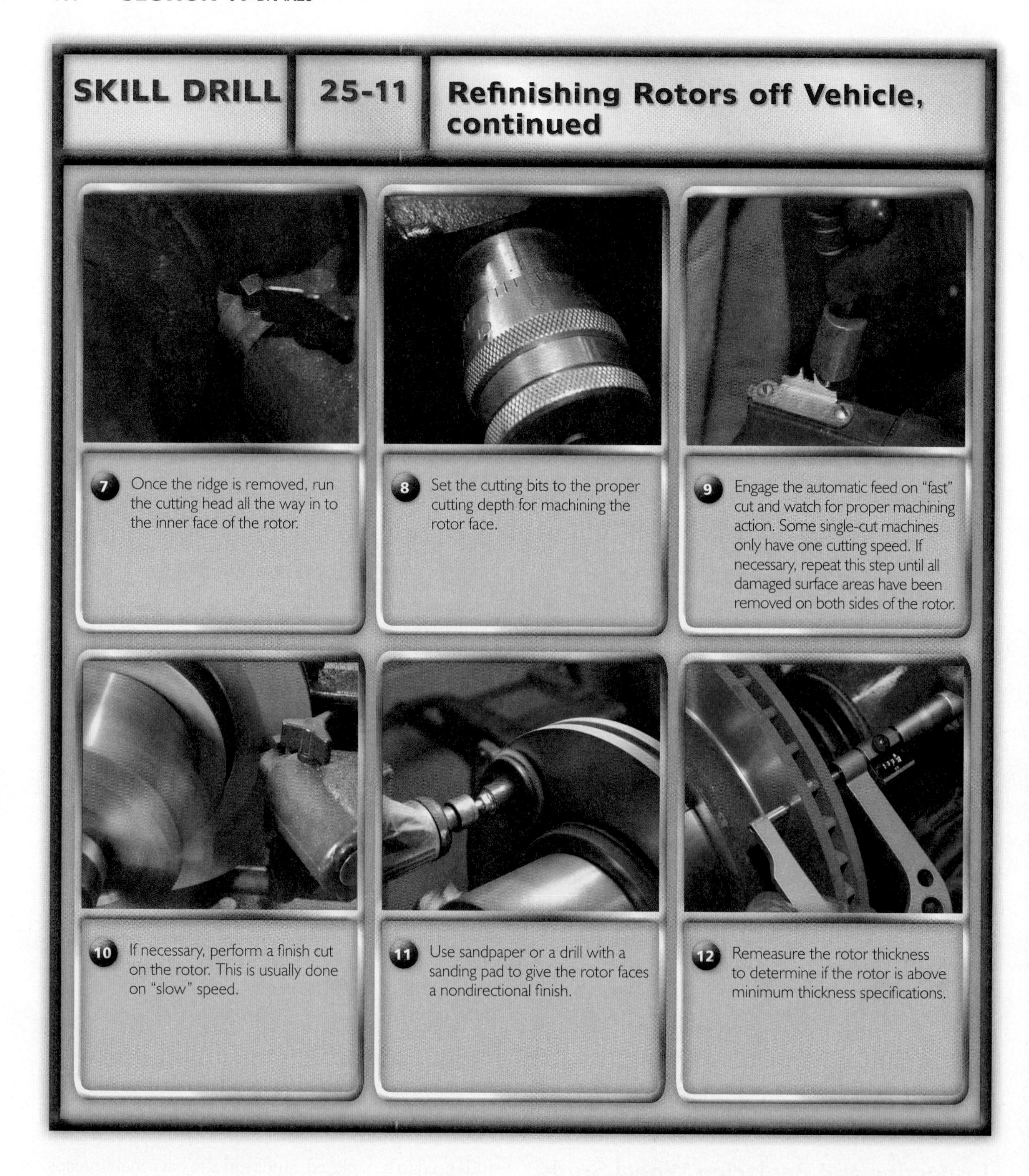
SKILL DRILL
25-11
Refinishing Rotors off Vehicle, continued
7 Once the ridge is removed, run the cutting head all the way in to the inner face of the rotor.
8 Set the cutting bits to the proper cutting depth for machining the rotor face.
9 Engage the automatic feed on "fast" cut and watch for proper machining action. Some single-cut machines only have one cutting speed. If necessary, repeat this step until all damaged surface areas have been removed on both sides of the rotor.
10 If necessary, perform a finish cut on the rotor. This is usually done on "slow" speed.
11 Use sandpaper or a drill with a sanding pad to give the rotor faces a nondirectional finish.
12 Remeasure the rotor thickness to determine if the rotor is above minimum thickness specifications.

Some vehicles are designed to allow for the removal and replacement of the wheel studs while the hub and wheel flange are still installed on the vehicle. The manufacturer may have provided a recessed spot in the steering knuckle where the studs have enough clearance to be removed; thus, the flange needs to be positioned in that particular position. Other vehicles do not have enough clearance on the back side for the stud to be removed; thus, the hub and flange must be removed from the vehicle.

There are two primary methods of replacing lug studs: the **drawing-in method** and the **hydraulic press method**. The drawing-in method uses the lug nut to draw in the wheel stud. It is accomplished by inserting the new stud into the wheel stud hole in the flange, installing enough heavy-duty washers over the stud to allow the lug nut to draw the wheel stud into the flange when tightened. The lug nut is placed flat side in, on the stud, and tightened. Make sure that as the stud is pulled in the lug nut does not run out of threads on the stud. If it does, remove the nut and add washers. Keep tightening the lug nut until the wheel stud bottoms out in the flange. Verify that the head of the stud is fully seated in the flange.

The hydraulic press method uses a press to force the wheel stud into the flange until it bottoms out. This method requires the hub and flange to be removed from the vehicle. Make sure the flange is positioned and supported properly on the press table. Sometimes it is best to use a short piece of pipe (a bit longer than the wheel stud) to support the flange while the stud is being pressed in. Once the stud is installed, verify that it is fully seated in the flange.

To inspect and replace wheel studs, follow the steps in SKILL DRILL 25-12.

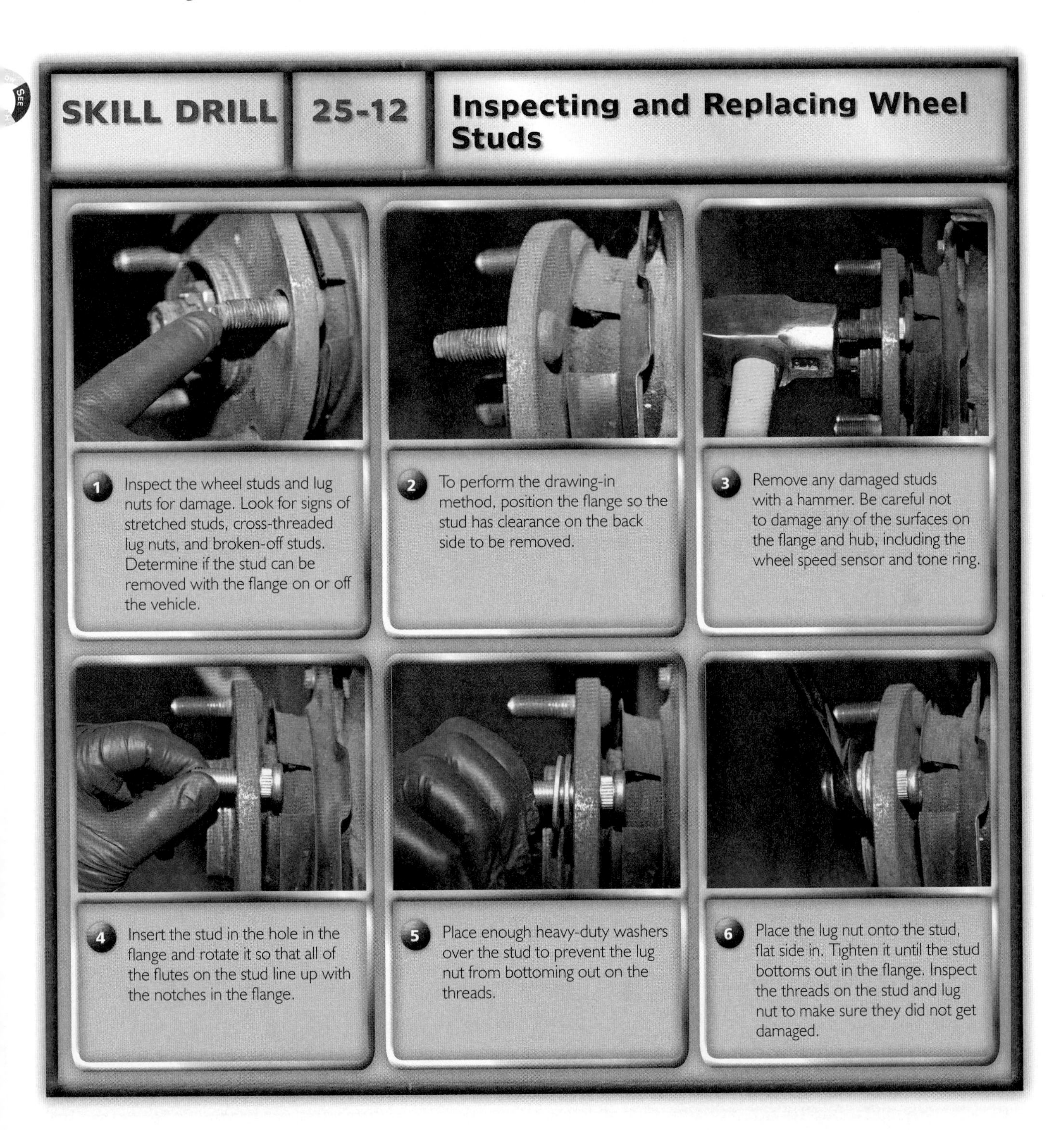
SKILL DRILL
25-12
Inspecting and Replacing Wheel Studs
1 Inspect the wheel studs and lug nuts for damage. Look for signs of stretched studs, cross-threaded lug nuts, and broken-off studs. Determine if the stud can be removed with the flange on or off the vehicle.
2 To perform the drawing-in method, position the flange so the stud has clearance on the back side to be removed.
3 Remove any damaged studs with a hammer. Be careful not to damage any of the surfaces on the flange and hub, including the wheel speed sensor and tone ring.
4 Insert the stud in the hole in the flange and rotate it so that all of the flutes on the stud line up with the notches in the flange.
5 Place enough heavy-duty washers over the stud to prevent the lug nut from bottoming out on the threads.
6 Place the lug nut onto the stud, flat side in. Tighten it until the stud bottoms out in the flange. Inspect the threads on the stud and lug nut to make sure they did not get damaged.

SKILL DRILL 25-12 Inspecting and Replacing Wheel Studs, continued

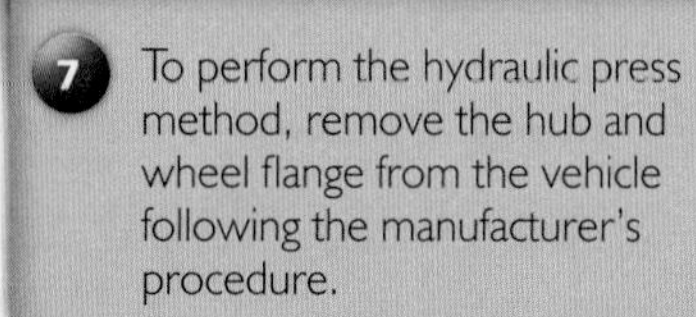

7 To perform the hydraulic press method, remove the hub and wheel flange from the vehicle following the manufacturer's procedure.

8 Use the press to push out any damaged lug studs.

9 Insert the new lug stud into the wheel flange hole. Line up the flutes on the stud with the notches in the flange.

10 Support the hub and flange so the press is pushing the stud straight into the flange.

11 Push the stud in until it bottoms out in the flange.

12 To complete the drawing-in method and the hydraulic press method, verify that each stud is fully seated in the flange.

13 Reinstall the hub and flange on the vehicle if it was removed.

Installing Wheels, Torquing Lug Nuts, and Making Final Checks

This step, while fairly simple, can result in problems if it is not done properly. Overtightening the lug nuts can cause the wheel studs to break either immediately, or worse, after the vehicle has been driven for a period of time. Overtightening also can cause warpage of the rotors, which results in the need to refinish or replace them. Undertightening can lead to loosening of the lug nuts and result in the wheel working its way off the vehicle. This can cause the driver to lose control of the vehicle and potentially result in an accident. Lug nuts should be tightened to the proper torque, in the specified sequence. All manufacturers specify the sequences for each of their vehicles. The torque pattern is usually in some form of a star or cross.

Be careful which way you install the lug nuts. Many wheels use a tapered hole that matches the tapered end of the lug nut and centers the wheel on the wheel flange. Other wheels use a flat surface that matches flat surfaces on the lug nuts. But no matter what, the lug nut surface *must* match the mating surface of the wheel. Always check that these surfaces match.

When installing lug nuts, the weight should be off the vehicle so that the wheel is off the ground or is barely touching the ground. The lug nuts should easily center the wheel on the hub. This is especially important on aluminum wheels that use a flat lug nut seating surface. The lug nuts can dig into the sides of the lug nut holes and cause the wheel to not center properly. Once the lug nuts are against the wheel, work the wheel onto the lug nut shafts. Then you can torque them down properly. Once the lug nuts are torqued properly and the brake system checked, it is time for a test drive to verify proper brake operation, and to burnish the new brake pads and rotor surfaces. Burnishing, also called bedding in, is the process of transferring pad material onto the rotor evenly, as well as cooking off the resins that are used to bind the friction material together in the pad. Burnishing results in long, quiet brake life, which results in satisfied customers.

For burnishing to happen properly, the rotor and pad material need to be heated slowly and evenly. This is done by making a specified number of stops from a specified speed, with the appropriate wait times between stops. In some cases, brake lining manufacturers want you to perform a series of stops at light to moderate brake application. Other manufacturers specify a series of moderate to heavy stops. Always check the manufacturer's procedure to burnish the brakes once the brake job is complete. This process will help avoid the dreaded disc brake squeal.

To install the wheel, torque lug nuts, and make final checks and adjustments, follow the steps in **SKILL DRILL 25-13**.

> **TECHNICIAN TIP**
>
> There is some controversy regarding the use of a lubricant or antiseize on wheel studs and lug nuts. Since the purpose of a lubricant or antiseize is to prevent the components from sticking, CDX errs on the side of not using those products, for fear of the lug nuts coming loose. Also, the torque given for the lug nuts is dry (no lubricant) so torquing them to specifications would lead to overtorquing. At the same time, in areas of the country prone to rust, it is understandable why some want to put a very light amount of antiseize only on the threads of the wheel stud, being careful not to get any on the contact seat of the wheel and lug nut. Doing so would prevent rust from building up on the threads. However, the lug nut torque would need to be reduced due to the lubricant. CDX prefers to install lug nuts dry and avoid this issue altogether. Many shops have their customers sign on the repair order that they will return and the wheel torque will be rechecked after 50 to 500 miles of driving to make sure the wheels have not loosened.

SKILL DRILL 25-13 Installing Wheels, Torquing Lug Nuts, and Making Final Checks

1 Start the lug nuts on the wheel studs, being careful to match up the surfaces. The lug nuts should be able to be turned by finger.

2 Carefully run all of the lug nuts down so they are seated in the wheel. The wheel should be centered on the hub.

3 Lower the vehicle so the tires are partially on the ground to keep them from turning while tightening the lug nuts.

4 Use a torque wrench to tighten each lug nut to the proper torque in the proper sequence.

5 Once all of the lug nuts have been torqued, go around them again, this time in a circular pattern to ensure that you did not miss any in the previous pattern.

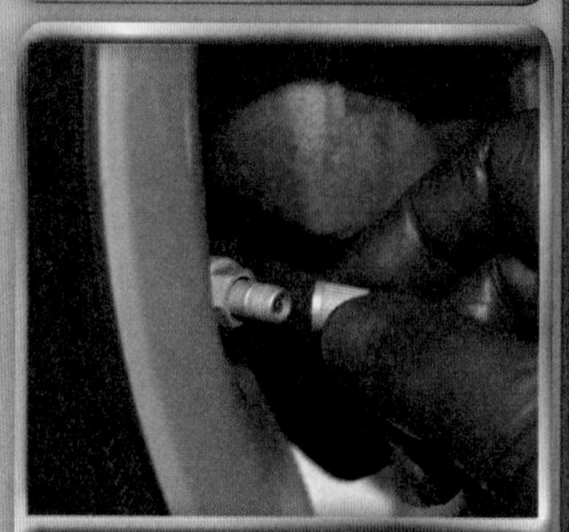

6 If the vehicle was equipped with hubcaps and valve stem caps, reinstall them.

SKILL DRILL 25-13 Installing Wheels, Torquing Lug Nuts, and Making Final Checks, continued

7. Check the brake fluid level in the master cylinder reservoir. Start the vehicle and check the brake pedal for proper feel and height. Check the parking brake for proper operation. Also inspect the system for any brake fluid leaks and loose or missing fasteners.

Wrap-up

Ready for Review

- Disc brakes create braking power by forcing flat friction pads against the outer faces of a rotor.
- The vehicle's kinetic energy is transformed into heat energy by the disc brake components, which slow the vehicle when applied.
- Disc brake assemblies consist of a caliper, brake pads, and a rotor.
- Caliper pistons use hydraulic pressure to create a clamping force of the brake pads to the faces of the rotor.
- Disc brake pads require much higher application pressures to operate than drum brake shoes, because they are not self-energizing.
- Advantages of disc brakes over drum brakes: more effective at transferring heat to the atmosphere, self-adjusting, resistant to water fade, and easier to service.
- Disadvantages of disc brakes compared to drum brakes: more prone to noise, more prone to pedal pulsations due to warpage, and more difficult to use as an emergency brake.
- Disc brake calipers come in two main styles: fixed and floating/sliding.
- In disc brake calipers, the piston is sealed by a square cut O-ring.
- Floating/sliding calipers require clean and lubricated pins, bushings, or guides for proper operation.
- Brake pad lining is either riveted or bonded to the pad backing plate.
- Brake pad lining is available in a variety of materials with varying amounts of coefficient of friction.
- Brake pads may use shims, spacers, guides, and bendable tangs to help minimize squealing.
- Brake pad wear indicators, if used, can be of the mechanical or electronic type.
- Rotors rotate with the wheels and are usually made of durable cast iron with friction surfaces that run true and parallel.
- Brake rotors can be solid or ventilated.
- Disc brake parking brakes can be of the integrated caliper style, top hat drum style, electric pull-cable style, and the integrated electric motor caliper style.
- Diagnosing brake faults requires good information from the customer, an adequate test-drive when possible, and a good understanding of brake theory.

Key Terms

backing plate A metal plate to which the brake lining is fixed.

bendable tangs Small tabs on the brake pad backing plate that are crimped on to the caliper, creating a secure fit and reducing noise.

bearing races Hardened metal surfaces that roller or ball bearings fit into when a bearing is properly assembled.

bleeder screw A screw that allows air and brake fluid to be bled out of a hydraulic brake system when it is loosened and seals the brake fluid in when it is tightened.

bonded linings Brake linings that are essentially glued to the brake pad backing plate; more common on light-duty vehicles.

brake booster A vacuum or hydraulically operated device that increases the driver's braking effort.

brake lining thickness gauge A tool used to measure the thickness of the brake lining.

brake pad shims and guides Small pieces of metal that cushion the brake pad and absorb some of the vibration, helping to cut down on unwanted noise.

brake wash station A piece of equipment designed to safely clean brake dust from drum and disc brake components.

bushing An insert with an inner bearing surface that is fitted into a hole in an object, allowing the object to rotate or slide on a pin or shaft.

caliper A hydraulic device that uses pressure from the master cylinder to apply the brake pads against the rotor.

caliper dust boot seal driver set A set of drivers used to install metal-backed caliper dust boot seals.

caliper piston pliers A tool used to grip caliper pistons while removing them.

caliper piston retracting tool A tool used to retract caliper pistons on integrated parking brake systems.

C-clamp A tool used to push pistons back into the caliper bore on non-integrated parking brakes.

dial indicator Tool used to measure the lateral runout of the rotor.

disc brake pads Brake pads that consist of a friction material bonded or riveted to a steel backing plate; designed to wear out over time.

disc brake rotor micrometer A specially designed micrometer used to measure the thickness of a rotor.

drawing-in method A method for replacing wheel studs that uses the lug nut to draw the wheel stud into the hub or flange.

edge code A code printed on the edge of a friction lining that describes its coefficient of friction.

electronic control module (ECM) A computer that receives signals from input sensors, compares that information with preloaded software, and sends an appropriate command signal to output devices; used to manage the anti-lock brake system (ABS).

fixed caliper A type of brake caliper bolted firmly to the steering knuckle or axle housing, having at least one piston on both sides of the rotor.

guide pins Pins that allow the caliper to move in and out as the brakes operate and as the brake pads wear.

hydraulic press method A method for replacing wheel studs that uses a press to force the wheel stud into the flange until it bottoms out.

independent rear suspension (IRS) A type of suspension system where each rear wheel is capable of moving independently of the other.

lateral runout Also called warpage, the side-to-side movement of the rotor surfaces as the rotor turns.

low-drag caliper A caliper designed to maintain a larger brake pad-to-rotor clearance by retracting the pistons farther than normal.

lug A flange that is shaped to assist with aligning objects on other objects.

off-car brake lathe A tool used to machine (refinish) drums and rotors after they have been removed from the vehicle.

on-car brake lathe A tool used to machine (refinish) rotors while they are still attached to the vehicle.

parallelism Also called thickness variation; both surfaces of the rotor should be perfectly parallel to each other so that brake pulsations do not occur.

parking brake cable pliers A tool used to install parking brake cables.

phenolic resin A material used to create some brake pistons that is very resistant to corrosion and heat transfer.

pushrod (braking system) A mechanism used to transmit force from the brake pedal to the master cylinder.

riveted linings Brake linings riveted to the brake pad backing plate with metal rivets and used on heavier-duty or high-performance vehicles.

rotor The main rotating part of a disc brake system.

scratcher A thin, spring steel wear indicator that is fixed to the backing plate of the brake pad; it emits a high-pitched squeal when the brakes are applied if the brake pads have become too thin.

sliding or floating caliper A type of brake caliper that only has piston(s) on the inboard side of the rotor. The caliper is free to slide or float, thus pulling the outboard brake pad into the rotor when braking force is applied.

solid rotor A type of brake rotor made of solid metal.

square cut O-ring An O-ring with a square cross-section that is used to seal the pistons in disc brake calipers.

steering knuckle A device that connects the front wheel to the suspension; pivots on the top and bottom, thus allowing the front wheels to turn.

ventilated rotor A type of brake rotor with passages between the rotor surfaces that are used to improve heat transfer to the atmosphere.

wheel studs Threaded fasteners that are pressed into the wheel hub flange and used to bolt the wheel onto the vehicle.

ASE-Type Questions

1. Tech A says that disc brakes operate on the principle of friction. Tech B says that disc brakes operate on the principle of regeneration. Who is correct?
   a. Tech A
   b. Tech B
   c. Both A and B
   d. Neither A nor B
2. Tech A says that some vehicles use fixed calipers. Tech B says that some vehicles use sliding/floating calipers. Who is correct?
   a. Tech A
   b. Tech B
   c. Both A and B
   d. Neither A nor B
3. Tech A says that disc brakes require higher application pressures than drum brakes. Tech B says that disc brakes are self-energizing. Who is correct?
   a. Tech A
   b. Tech B
   c. Both A and B
   d. Neither A nor B
4. Tech A says that fixed calipers use one or more pistons only on one side of the rotor. Tech B says that sliding/fixed calipers use one or more pistons on both sides of the rotor. Who is correct?
   a. Tech A
   b. Tech B
   c. Both A and B
   d. Neither A nor B
5. Tech A says that calipers use a round section O-ring to seal each piston. Tech B says that calipers use a square section O-ring to seal each piston. Who is correct?
   a. Tech A
   b. Tech B
   c. Both A and B
   d. Neither A nor B
6. Tech A says that pistons plated with chrome resist rust. Tech B says that pistons made of phenolic resin do not corrode and rust. Who is correct?
   a. Tech A
   b. Tech B
   c. Both A and B
   d. Neither A nor B
7. Tech A says that some vehicles are equipped with a spring-steel brake pad wear indicator that drags on the rotor when the lining thickness is low. Tech B says that some vehicles are equipped with an electric brake pad wear sensor that activates a warning on the dash. Who is correct?
   a. Tech A
   b. Tech B
   c. Both A and B
   d. Neither A nor B
8. Tech A says that rotors should be measured for thickness variation (parallelism). Tech B says that rotors should be measured for lateral runout. Who is correct?
   a. Tech A
   b. Tech B
   c. Both A and B
   d. Neither A nor B
9. Tech A says that rotors that are too thin cannot handle as much heat and will experience brake fade sooner. Tech B says that brake pedal pulsation is the result of air in the hydraulic system. Who is correct?
   a. Tech A
   b. Tech B
   c. Both A and B
   d. Neither A nor B
10. Tech A says that a micrometer is used to measure rotor thickness variation. Tech B says that a micrometer is used to measure rotor lateral runout. Who is correct?
    a. Tech A
    b. Tech B
    c. Both A and B
    d. Neither A nor B

CHAPTER 26

Know
See
Do
Prove

NATEF Tasks

Brakes Drum Brakes			Page
■ Diagnose poor stopping, noise, vibration, pulling, grabbing, dragging or pedal pulsation concerns; determine necessary action.		AST	754
■ Remove, clean, inspect, and measure brake drum diameter; determine necessary action.	MLR	AST	756–757
■ Refinish brake drum and measure final drum diameter; compare with specifications.	MLR	AST	758
■ Remove, clean, and inspect brake shoes, springs, pins, clips, levers, adjusters/self-adjusters, other related brake hardware, and backing support plates; lubricate and reassemble.	MLR	AST	759–761
■ Inspect wheel cylinders for leaks and proper operation; remove and replace as needed.	MLR	AST	762
■ Pre-adjust brake shoes and parking brake; install brake drums or drum/hub assemblies and wheel bearings; make final checks and adjustments.	MLR	AST	763
■ Install wheel and torque lug nuts.	MLR	AST	764

Drum Brake Systems

Know
See
Do

Knowledge Objectives

After reading this chapter, you will be able to:

1. List the components of the drum brake system. (pp 742–743)
2. Describe how the components of the drum brake system work together during the braking process. (pp 743–744)
3. Describe the principle of self-energization. (pp 743–744)
4. Define and describe servo action. (p 744)
5. Describe the types of drum brake systems. (pp 744–745)
6. Describe the types of brake drums. (pp 745–746)
7. Describe the purpose of the backing plate and its components. (pp 746–747)
8. Describe the purpose of the wheel cylinder and its components. (pp 747–748)
9. Describe the types of wheel cylinders. (p 748)
10. Describe the purpose of brake shoes and linings. (p 749)
11. Describe the two processes of attaching lining to brake shoes. (pp 750–751)
12. Describe the common brake noises that indicate an issue with the drum brakes. (p 751)
13. Describe the purpose of springs and hardware in the drum brake system. (pp 751–752)
14. Describe the types of springs used in drum brake systems. (pp 751–752)
15. Describe the types of self-adjusters used in drum brake systems. (pp 752–754)
16. Describe how the parking brake system operates in a drum brake system. (p 754)
17. Describe the process of diagnosing issues with drum brakes. (p 754)

Know
See
Do

Skills Objectives

After reading this chapter, you will be able to:

1. Remove, clean, inspect, and measure the brake drums. (pp 756–757)
2. Refinish a brake drum. (p 758)
3. Disassemble and reassemble duo-servo brakes. (pp 759–760)
4. Disassemble and reassemble non-servo brakes. (pp 759–761)
5. Remove, inspect, and install wheel cylinders. (p 762)
6. Pre-adjust brakes and install brake drums and wheel bearings. (p 763)
7. Install wheel, torque lug nuts, and make final checks. (p 764)

Introduction

Drum brakes get their name from the rotating drum-shaped component called a brake drum (or simply drum). The drums are bolted to the vehicle's axle hubs by the lug nuts. This means the wheels and drums rotate together. Friction lining on brake shoes is forced against the inside of the drums by hydraulic wheel cylinders, causing friction and absorbing the vehicle's kinetic energy. Since heat is created inside of the drums, the heat has to transfer through the drum material before it can be transferred to the atmosphere. Situations such as heavy loads or long downhill grades where the brakes are used heavily can lead to overheating of the lining, drums, or brake fluid, resulting in a loss of braking, called brake fade.

Most drum brakes require the removal of the drum to inspect the condition of the brake lining and inside drum surface. Drum brake design requires more parts and components, so service and repair can be a bit more complicated than for disc brakes. However, drum brakes are generally less expensive to manufacture and easier to adapt a parking brake to.

Drum Brake Systems

While many vehicles use disc brakes on all four wheels, drum brakes can be found on the rear wheels of vehicles with a combination of disc and drum brakes, and on all four wheels of older vehicles. Drum brakes can be designed to match the braking requirements of various vehicles. Heavier duty vehicles like pick-up trucks use larger diameter brake drums and shoes, as well as wider brake shoes and drum surfaces. These factors allow the drum brakes to create, absorb, and transfer a greater amount of heat energy. The main components of the drum brake system are **FIGURE 26-1**:

- **Brake drum**: The brake drum fits over the brake linings and forms the braking surface for the brake linings. It is usually made from cast iron and machined so the inside surface rotates true.
- **Backing plate**: The backing plate is made from stamped steel and is bolted to the steering or suspension components. It supports the wheel cylinder(s), brake shoes, and hardware.
- **Wheel cylinder**: The wheel cylinder is attached to the backing plate. The wheel cylinder pistons

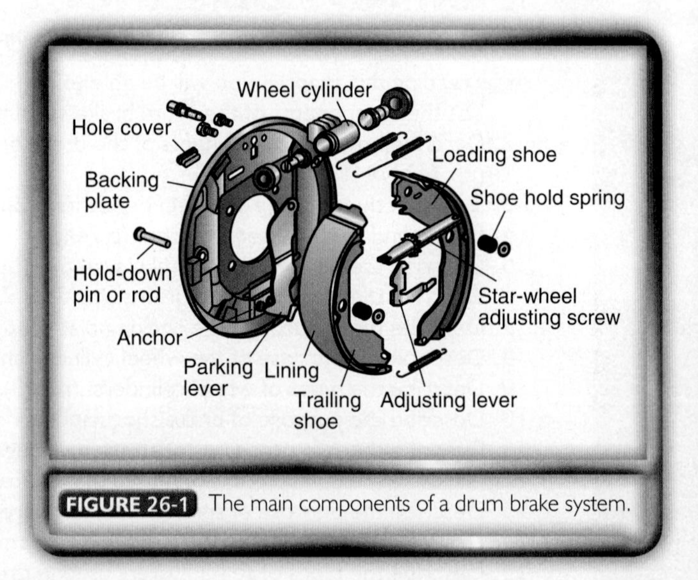
Wheel cylinder
Hole cover
Loading shoe
Backing plate
Shoe hold spring
Hold-down pin or rod
Star-wheel adjusting screw
Anchor
Parking lever
Lining
Trailing shoe
Adjusting lever

FIGURE 26-1 The main components of a drum brake system.

You Are the Automotive Technician

You are working in San Francisco, CA, on your company's fleet vehicles, which are about 6 years old. Today you are performing a rear brake inspection on a light duty truck. The driver has indicated that the parking brake isn't able to completely hold the vehicle on some of the steepest hills he has to park on. You operate the parking brake and notice that it can be pushed all the way to the floor before it is completely tight. This means you will have to visually inspect the rear brake assemblies.

1. How is the parking brake similar to and different from the rear drum brakes?
2. What are the possible faults in the service brakes (drum brake style) that could cause the parking brake to be out of adjustment?
3. In what order should the drum brakes and parking brakes be adjusted?

push the brake shoes into contact with the brake drum to slow or stop the vehicle.

- Brake shoes: The brake shoe consists of the steel shoe and the brake lining friction material. The brake shoes are held against the backing plate by hold-down springs and clips.
- Springs and clips: Return springs retract the brake shoes when the brakes are released. Other springs work with the self-adjuster and with parking brake linkage operation.
- Automatic brake self-adjuster: The automatic self-adjuster automatically adjusts the brakes to maintain a specified amount of running clearance between the shoes and drum. It operates in one of two ways—either when using the brakes while backing up or as part of applying the parking brake. It also makes periodic brake adjustment unnecessary.
- Parking brake mechanism: The parking brake linkage mechanically operates the brake shoes (service brakes) to hold the vehicle stationary when the driver applies the parking brake.

Drum Brake Operation

Drum brakes were once common on all four wheels of a vehicle, but now they are usually found only on the rear wheels in disc–drum applications. In drum brake systems, when the brake pedal is depressed, a pushrod transfers the force to a hydraulic master cylinder. The master cylinder converts the brake pedal force into hydraulic pressure, which is then transmitted without loss via the brake lines and hoses to one or two wheel cylinders at each drum brake assembly. The pistons within each wheel cylinder are forced outward by the hydraulic pressure and apply force to the brake shoes, forcing them into each rotating drum FIGURE 26-2. Since the brake shoes are anchored to the backing plate, preventing them from rotating freely with the drum, the friction generated between the moving surfaces slows down the rotation of the drum and the wheel.

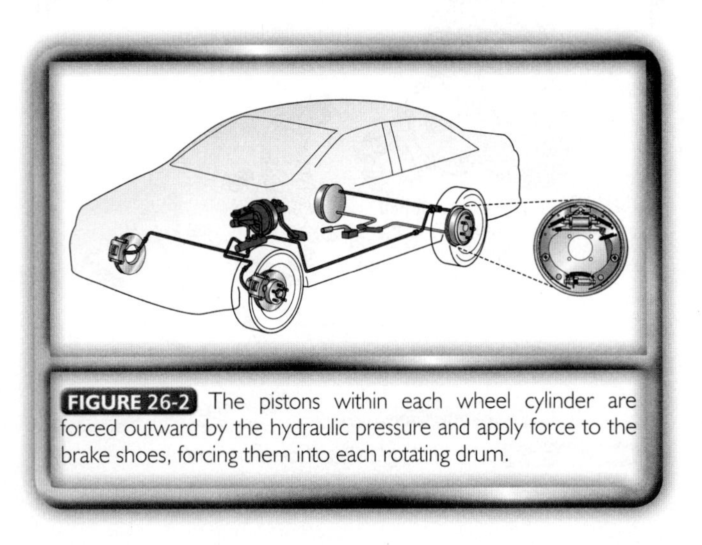

FIGURE 26-2 The pistons within each wheel cylinder are forced outward by the hydraulic pressure and apply force to the brake shoes, forcing them into each rotating drum.

The drums are free to rotate with the wheels due to wheel bearings in the hub or on the axle. The hub can be part of the drum or a separate assembly that the drum slips over and is bolted to by the wheel and lug nuts. On most rear driving wheels, the drum slips over the axle flange and is held on by the wheel and lug nuts.

Each drum brake has two brake shoes with a friction material called a lining attached. These shoes expand against the inside surface of a brake drum and slow the wheel. The harder the linings are forced against the brake drum, the greater the braking force applied. They can be expanded mechanically or hydraulically. Drum brake systems need to be adjusted to allow for wear of the lining. As the lining wears, the brake shoes must be pushed farther outward to contact the drum. This wearing causes only the top portion of the linings to contact the drum, reducing the surface area of the lining that can dissipate the created heat. Also, if they are not adjusted, the brake pedal reserve height will be too low to be safe.

TECHNICIAN TIP

Servicing the wheel bearings is a common part of a brake job if the vehicle has serviceable wheel bearings. If the vehicle uses non-serviceable bearings, the bearings should be checked during a brake job and replaced if they are worn out. See the Wheel Bearings chapter for more information on wheel bearings and service.

Self-Energizing and Servo Action

Drum brakes are self-energizing. This means they can increase the force with which they are applied. When brake shoes come into contact with the moving drum, the friction tends to carry them in the direction the drum is rotating. Because the brake shoes are inside the drum and anchored at one end, this has a wedging effect on the brake shoe. This wedging effect assists the driver in applying the brakes, making it so the driver does not have to push so hard on the brake pedal FIGURE 26-3. Brake shoes are designed in a leading or trailing manner. Leading shoes are installed so the direction they are applied is the same as the forward rotation of the drum. Leading shoes are self-energizing. Trailing shoes are installed so the direction they are applied is opposite of the forward rotation of the drum. Trailing shoes are not self-energizing. In fact, they tend to have reduced

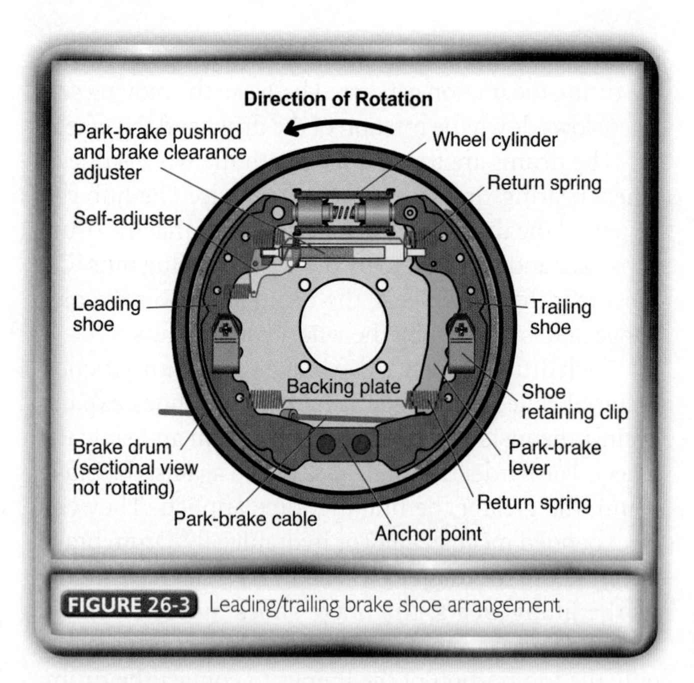
Direction of Rotation
Park-brake pushrod and brake clearance adjuster
Wheel cylinder
Return spring
Self-adjuster
Leading shoe
Trailing shoe
Backing plate
Shoe retaining clip
Brake drum (sectional view not rotating)
Park-brake lever
Return spring
Park-brake cable
Anchor point

FIGURE 26-3 Leading/trailing brake shoe arrangement.

energization, meaning they are not nearly as efficient at developing braking force as leading shoes are.

Servo action as related to brakes means that one brake shoe, when activated, applies an increased activating force to the other brake shoe, in proportion to the initial activating force. This further enhances the self-energizing feature of some drum brakes. We will cover this topic in greater depth later in this chapter.

Types of Drum Brake Systems

There are three types of drum brake systems: twin leading shoe, leading/trailing shoe (also called single leading shoe), and duo-servo. Each type uses similar drum brake components but functions a bit differently. All three types are self-energizing in at least one direction. The first two types are non-servo brakes. The duo-servo drum brake system uses servo action in both directions. Each of the three types have pros and cons and designers use the type that best fits the vehicle application.

Twin Leading Shoe Drum Brake Systems

The twin leading shoe drum brake system is the least common type in modern automotive use. This system was once popular on front wheels because it is very efficient at braking in the forward direction. Since the vehicle travels much faster forward than it does in reverse, this matched the braking needs well. The large forward stopping power the twin leading shoe drum brake system generated also allowed the system to operate without a power brake booster.

Twin leading shoe drum brake systems use two single-piston wheel cylinders (also called single-acting wheel cylinders)—one near the top of the backing plate and one near the bottom. Each wheel cylinder activates one of the brake shoes. The brake shoes are anchored at the closed end of the opposite wheel cylinder. It is called a twin leading shoe drum brake system because both shoes are arranged in a leading shoe (self-energizing) configuration in the forward direction. This arrangement gives very good stopping power in the forward direction. When applied in the reverse direction, the braking force is much less, only about 30% as efficient. This type of drum brake system was usually accompanied by one of the other types of brakes on the rear wheels to be used as a parking brake. The twin leading shoe drum brake system is very well suited for motorcycles since they are driven mostly in the forward direction and rarely reverse.

Leading/Trailing Shoe Drum Brake Systems

The leading/trailing shoe drum brake system is very common on the rear wheels of front-wheel drive vehicles due to their equal braking forces in both the forward and reverse direction. This system uses a single wheel cylinder with two pistons (also called a double-acting wheel cylinder), usually mounted near the top of the backing plate FIGURE 26-4. Each piston operates one of the brake shoes. Each shoe is anchored at the bottom of the backing plate. This arrangement makes one shoe a leading shoe and the other a trailing shoe. In the forward direction, the front piston forces the front brake shoe into the drum, and it acts like a leading shoe. The rear piston pushes the rear brake shoe into contact with the drum, but it acts as a trailing shoe, so it does not create as much braking power.

When the brakes are applied when the car is reversing or facing uphill, the rear shoe becomes a leading shoe and the front shoe becomes a trailing shoe. The leading/

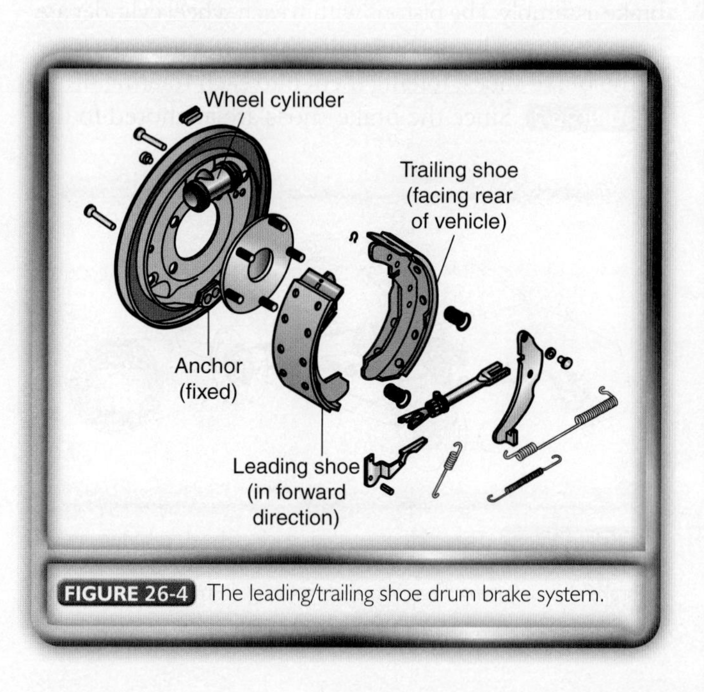
Wheel cylinder
Trailing shoe (facing rear of vehicle)
Anchor (fixed)
Leading shoe (in forward direction)

FIGURE 26-4 The leading/trailing shoe drum brake system.

trailing shoe drum brake system works equally well in both directions. It is also important to note that it does not provide maximum braking in either direction; it tends to produce a lesser but equal amount of force in both directions. This makes it ideal for the rear wheels of front-wheel drive vehicles since approximately 70–80% of the braking power needed under heavy braking occurs at the front wheels and only 20–30% at the rear wheels.

Duo-Servo Drum Brake Systems

Duo-servo drum brake systems get their name from using the servo action in both the forward and reverse direction. Like the leading/trailing system, the system uses a single wheel cylinder with two pistons (also called a double-acting wheel cylinder), usually mounted near the top of the backing plate FIGURE 26-5. The bottom of each brake shoe is not anchored to the backing plate but is connected by an adjustable, floating link. This configuration allows the bottom of the brake shoes to move in the direction of the drum. What keeps the shoes from just spinning around with the drum? There is an anchor pin at the top of the backing plate above the wheel cylinder that prevents each shoe from rotating past that point. The shoes can move away from the anchor pin, but they are stopped by it when they rotate toward it.

When the brakes are applied, the front piston overcomes the weaker front return spring tension to move the forward shoe into contact with the drum. When the shoe contacts the drum, the friction causes it to start to rotate with the drum. This puts a small force through the bottom connecting link and applies (servo action) the bottom of the rear shoe, pushing it into contact with the rotating drum. The top of that shoe is thus carried into the anchor pin at the top of the backing plate, causing both shoes to stop rotating. The brakes generate a small amount of force at this point.

As the driver applies more force to the brake pedal, the forward piston in the wheel cylinder pushes the front shoe harder into the rotating drum, which causes the front shoe to apply more force to the rear shoe. This forces the rear shoe harder into the drum as the anchor pin prevents it from rotating. Since hydraulic pressure is the same on both pistons in the wheel cylinder, the rear piston also tends to push the rear shoe outward into the drum, which helps apply it, although not in a completely complimentary direction.

Since the front shoe multiplies the force applying the rear shoe, the rear shoe does more of the braking work. If the linings were the same length front to rear, then the rear one would wear out much faster. This is why manufacturers put more lining on the rear shoe than on the front shoe. They might also use linings with different coefficients of friction for each of the shoes to get the desired braking load between the two shoes. It is important, therefore, to install the correct shoe in the correct position. Failure to do so will cause the brake linings to wear unevenly, as well as work improperly.

Brake Drums

Brake drums provide the rotating friction surface that the brake lining contacts. They are usually made from cast iron due to its ability to withstand high temperatures, absorb a lot of heat, and maintain its shape. To enhance the cooling of the brake drum, some manufacturers add cooling fins to the outside of the brake drum, while others make the brake drum out of aluminum FIGURE 26-6.

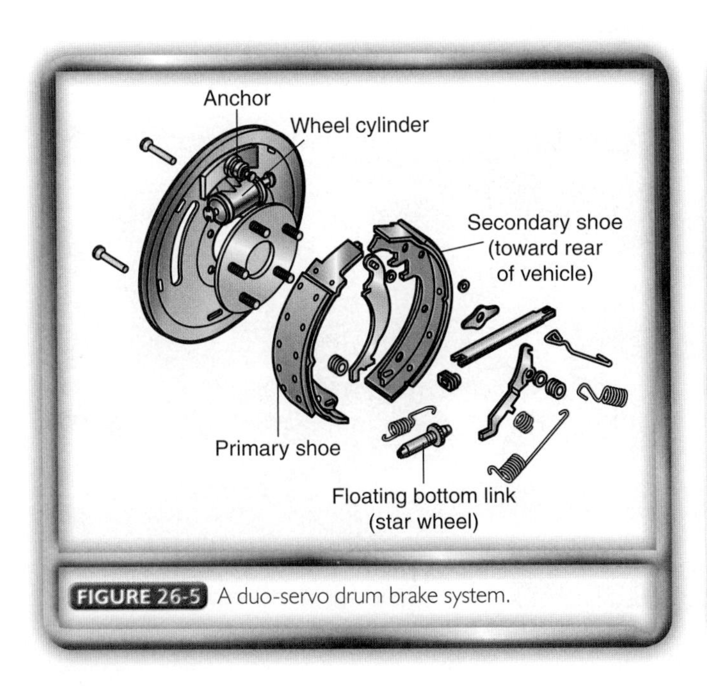
Anchor
Wheel cylinder
Secondary shoe
(toward rear
of vehicle)
Primary shoe
Floating bottom link
(star wheel)

FIGURE 26-5 A duo-servo drum brake system.

A
B

FIGURE 26-6 Brake drums. **A.** Without cooling fins. **B.** With cooling fins.

Brake drums are machined to a specific diameter from the manufacturer, which is called its standard diameter. Manufacturers specify the maximum allowable inside diameter a brake drum can be worn or machined to and usually stamp or cast that specification on the outside of the brake drum. This specification is commonly 0.060" (1.524 mm) over the standard diameter on many brake drums, but it can be as low as 0.030" (0.762 mm) over standard, or as high as 0.090" (2.286 mm) over standard on some passenger vehicles. Always check the manufacturer's specifications. Remember that taking 0.015" (0.381 mm) off of one side of the brake drum surface also removes 0.015" (0.381 mm) from the other side for a total of 0.030" (0.762 mm).

Brake drums that are heavily grooved or warped will likely need to be replaced. Even if they are not grooved, they need to be measured since they may have been refinished one or more times before, making them oversized. Never put an oversized brake drum back in service, because it does not have as much mass to absorb brake heat, and it also is not as strong as a drum that is within specifications.

Types of Brake Drums

Like rotors, brake drums can have an integrated hub called a hub-style drum or a separate hub called a hubless-style drum. Hubless drums are the most common in passenger vehicles because of the high percentage of sealed wheel bearings being used. Since the wheel bearings in this case do not need to be packed with grease periodically, they do not need to be removed unless they wear out. Manufacturers design the brake drum to slip over the lug studs on the wheel flange and to be held on by the wheel and lug nuts. Hubless drums are less expensive to replace when they no longer meet the manufacturer's specifications.

Hub-style drums have a one-piece integrated hub/drum assembly. The wheel bearings are housed in the hub and are usually serviceable. If they are serviceable, then it is standard procedure to pack the wheel bearings with the specified grease and replace the grease seals during a brake job. More steps are required to remove hub-style drums from the vehicle than hubless drums, and they are more expensive to replace.

Backing Plate

All of the brake unit components, except the brake drum, are mounted on a backing plate bolted to the vehicle axle housing or suspension. The backing plate is usually pressed into a very specific configuration from heavy-gauge steel FIGURE 26-7. It has a raised edge on its outer surface that fits into a groove or recess in the brake drum and helps keep out dust, dirt, and water spray. It also has holes stamped in it for the wheel cylinder, hold-down pins and the parking brake cable to pass through. Some vehicles have one or two openings in the backing plate to allow for manual adjustment of the brake shoes. These holes are plugged with rubber grommets that need to be reinstalled after adjusting the brakes.

Anchor Pins and Pad Surfaces for Shoes

One of the most important components of the backing plate is the **anchor pin** (or anchor block). The anchor pin must be able to take all of the braking force when the brakes are applied, so it must be strong and firmly attached to the backing plate FIGURE 26-8. The anchor pin may also hold the shoe guide, return springs, and self-adjuster cable on duo-servo–style brakes.

The inside surface of the backing plate has flat or raised brake shoe contact pads stamped into it. The brake shoes

FIGURE 26-7 The backing plate.

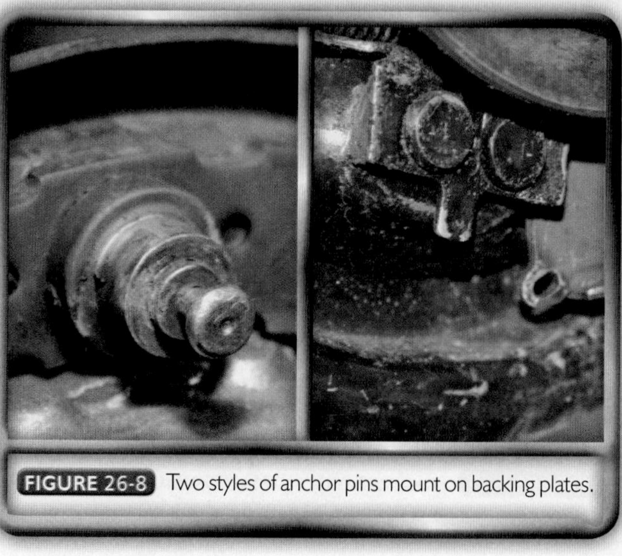

FIGURE 26-8 Two styles of anchor pins mount on backing plates.

are held against the brake shoe contact pads by spring pressure and are free to move side to side. Over time, the brake shoes can wear a groove in the surface of the contact pad. During brake shoe replacement, these contact pads need to be cleaned and inspected. If there is no wear, then a very light coat of white lithium grease can be applied to the contact pads to lessen any wear during the life of the new brake shoes. If there is light wear, this can be cleaned up with a file or small handheld grinder. If the grooves are too deep, the backing plate will need to be replaced.

Wheel Cylinders

The wheel cylinder is located inside the brake drum and is either bolted or firmly clipped to the backing plate FIGURE 26-9. It converts hydraulic pressure from the master cylinder into mechanical force that pushes the brake linings against the inside of the brake drum.

Wheel cylinders usually contain one cylinder housing, one or two pistons, a lip seal for each piston, a spring and expander set, a dust boot for each open end of the cylinder, a pushrod for each piston, and a bleeder screw FIGURE 26-10. Wheel cylinder housings are usually made of cast iron or aluminum alloy, and they operate under extreme pressures and temperatures.

The **cylinder bore**, or inside diameter of the cylinder, is created by drawing a properly sized ball bearing through the bore FIGURE 26-11. This technique gives the surface a hard, smooth finish. It is also why most manufacturers recommend replacing, rather than honing, the wheel cylinder if it has pits or corrosion. Cylinder bores on aluminum wheel cylinders are usually anodized to help resist corrosion. They also should not be honed, as this would remove the protective finish. Some cylinder bores are sleeved with stainless steel to be longer wearing and more resistant to corrosion.

FIGURE 26-9 The wheel cylinder mounted on the backing plate.

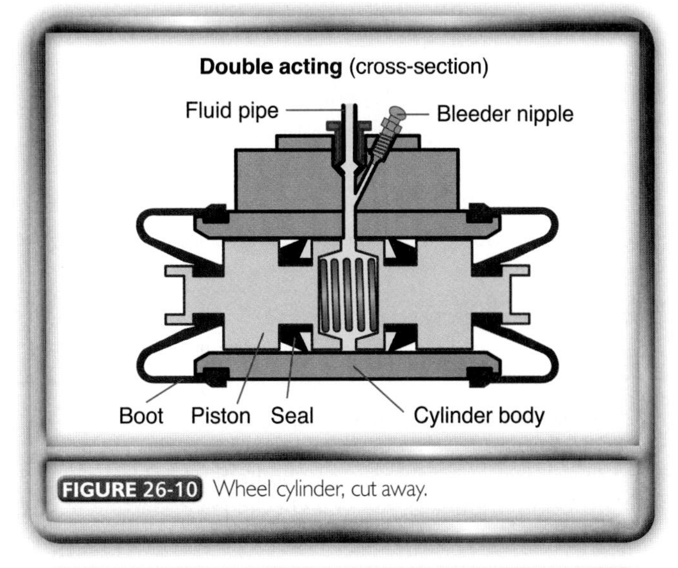
Double acting (cross-section)
Fluid pipe
Bleeder nipple
Boot
Piston
Seal
Cylinder body

FIGURE 26-10 Wheel cylinder, cut away.

FIGURE 26-11 Wheel cylinder components.

No matter the type of material used, the cylinder and pistons are manufactured to a precise diameter. This provides the proper amount of clearance between them. It also maintains the proper tension of the piston seal to the cylinder bore, which helps hold pressure in and the air out. These are other reasons why honing the cylinder bore is frowned upon.

Contamination, particularly from water, lowers the boiling point of the brake fluid (which is hygroscopic) and may cause pitting and rusting of the inner surface of the wheel cylinder. Such damage can result in leakage of brake fluid from the cylinder or stuck pistons. The sealing surface in a wheel cylinder is the inside surface of the cylinder bore. This surface must be clean, smooth, and free of pitting. The wheel cylinder cups the seal against the surface of the cylinder bore and prevents the brake fluid from leaking out of the cylinder. Hydraulic pressure forces the lip of the seal into the surface of the cylinder bore even harder when the brakes are applied. The sealing cups are made of materials that are compatible with the type of brake fluid specified for the particular vehicle. Using the wrong seal compound in a brake system or mixing the wrong brake fluid in the brake system can cause seal damage and brake failure. Always verify that the brake fluid and components are compatible with each other.

> **TECHNICIAN TIP**
>
> During a brake inspection, it is good practice to carefully peel back the dust boot from the wheel cylinder and see if there is any brake fluid behind the dust boot. If there is, the wheel cylinder is starting to leak and should be replaced.

Wheel cylinder pistons are usually made of anodized aluminum. They have a built-in mating surface for the pushrods to engage. Most pistons use a flat surface that supports the piston seal, but some pistons use a seal that fits within a machined groove at its inner end. Piston-to-cylinder clearance is critical for proper operation, so verify that the cylinder and piston are not worn beyond the specified clearance.

Wheel cylinders may be fitted with a spreader and a light expansion spring to keep the lips of the seal in contact with the cylinder bore during times of low pressure, such as during retraction and while at rest. This helps keep air from being drawn into the cylinder. A flexible dust boot fits over the open ends of the cylinder and allows for piston movement. At the same time, it helps keep brake dust and moisture away from the inside of the cylinder and piston.

Wheel cylinders are fitted with a bleeder screw to allow for bleeding of air and old brake fluid from the hydraulic brake system. The bleeder screw is a hollow screw. It has a taper on the end that mates with a matching tapered seat in the wheel cylinder. These tapered seats seal when the bleeder screw is closed. The bleeder screw has been cross-drilled into the center hole just above the taper. This way, when the bleeder screw is loosened slightly, the tapered seat opens and brake fluid enters the cross-drilled passage into the center hole and flows out the end of the bleeder screw. Tightening the bleeder screw closes off the tapered seat and holds pressure in the wheel cylinder. Bleeder screws have a small rubber dust cap that fits over the exposed end of the screw to keep water, dirt, and debris from entering the center hole and plugging it up or rusting it in place. Always remember to replace these caps when you finish bleeding the drum brakes.

Types of Wheel Cylinders

Wheel cylinders come in different configurations. They are either single acting or dual acting **FIGURE 26-12**. Single-acting cylinders use a single piston, meaning that the force is generated in one direction only. Dual-acting cylinders use two pistons opposite of each other, meaning that the force acts in two different directions. Most modern vehicles use double-acting wheel cylinders because they are simpler to design, install, and bleed. Dual-acting wheel cylinders use a common cylinder with a piston and lip seal in each end. There is usually a coil spring with expanders on each end, positioned between the lip seals. The expander helps to hold the seal lips against the cylinder bore when there is little or no hydraulic pressure.

Single-acting wheel cylinders are used on some non-servo drum brakes. Each wheel cylinder only has one piston, so the cylinder bore is closed off at the opposite end. There are two of these cylinders on each wheel assembly, one for each brake shoe. The wheel cylinder is very similar to the double-acting cylinder in that it is made of the same materials and has an aluminum piston, a lip seal, a spring and expander, a dust boot, a pushrod, and a bleeder screw.

> **TECHNICIAN TIP**
>
> One way to help identify if a problem is coming from the front or rear brakes is to test-drive the vehicle in a safe place at a relatively low speed and lightly apply the parking brake. If the condition is still present, the problem is with the rear brakes, since the parking brakes are usually on the rear wheels. If the condition is not present, the problem is likely with the front brakes.

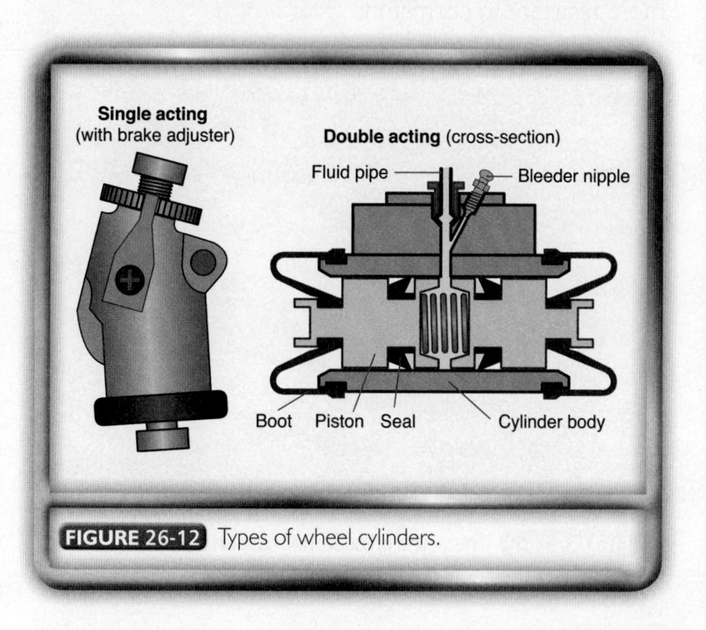
Single acting
(with brake adjuster)
Double acting (cross-section)
Fluid pipe
Bleeder nipple
Boot
Piston
Seal
Cylinder body

FIGURE 26-12 Types of wheel cylinders.

Brake Shoes and Linings

The drum brake system uses metal brake shoes that have holes, slots, and tabs for springs and hardware to attach to. The brake shoes also have friction material called linings attached to them. Linings can be riveted but are more often bonded to the brake shoes.

Brake Lining Materials

The composition of the lining material affects brake operation. Materials that provide good braking with low pedal pressures tend to lose efficiency when they get hot FIGURE 26-13. This means the stopping distance will be increased. They also tend to wear out more quickly. Materials that maintain a stable friction coefficient over a wide temperature range generally require higher pedal pressures to provide efficient braking. They also tend to put added wear on the brake drum friction surface, reducing its useful life. Drum brakes are usually designed so that the condition of the lining can only be checked once the drum has been removed.

Brake lining selection requires knowledge of the customer expectations and driving habits. For example, you will need to choose a different lining material for a vehicle that regularly carries heavy loads versus one that is road raced on a track on the weekends. Selecting lining that does not match the driver's needs will result in a lack of customer satisfaction and vehicle repair returns.

Primary and Secondary Brake Shoes

The terms primary and secondary refer to the brake shoes in a duo-servo brake system. The primary shoe goes toward the front of the vehicle, and the secondary shoe goes toward the rear of the vehicle FIGURE 26-14. In most cases, the primary and secondary metal shoes are the same, but the linings installed on the brake shoes are of different length. Since the primary shoe applies the secondary shoe, the secondary shoe is responsible for doing most of the braking work. Therefore, the primary shoe lining is shorter in length, and the secondary shoe lining is longer. The primary lining may also have a different coefficient of friction than the secondary lining. New shoes are normally labeled with "pri" (for primary) or "sec" (for secondary) on the edge of the lining. Verify that you are installing the lining in the proper position.

Safety

Brake friction materials were historically made from asbestos compounds because of the excellent heat resistance of that material. Asbestos compounds are now known to be toxic and are generally banned. Do not assume that a brake shoe does not contain asbestos, as it is still found in some applications. Brakes are now manufactured from a variety of different materials that may be non-asbestos organic (NAO), low-metallic NAO, semimetallic, and ceramic.

TECHNICIAN TIP

As the heat in brake pads and linings builds up, the coefficient of friction capability of the material—and consequently its stopping power—is reduced. This reduction is called brake fade. Minimizing or overcoming brake fade is a major factor in the design of brakes and the development of brake friction materials.

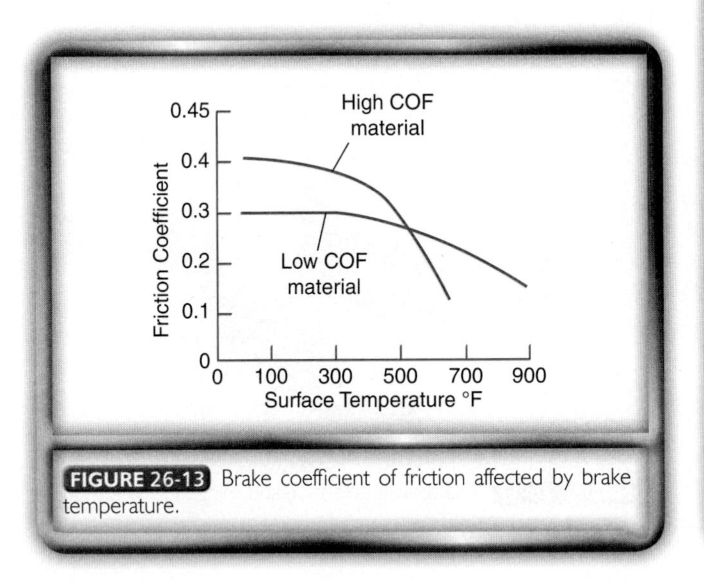
High COF material
Low COF material
Friction Coefficient
0.45
0.4
0.3
0.2
0.1
0
0
100
300
500
700
900
Surface Temperature °F

FIGURE 26-13 Brake coefficient of friction affected by brake temperature.

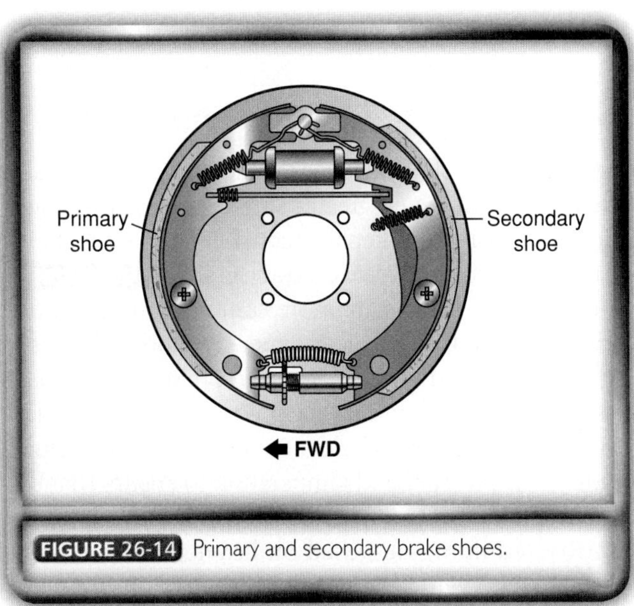
Primary shoe
Secondary shoe
FWD

FIGURE 26-14 Primary and secondary brake shoes.

TECHNICIAN TIP

New technicians tend to make a couple of rookie mistakes when it comes to duo-servo brake installation. The first relates to the way the new brake shoes are packaged in their box. The manufacturer generally puts the brake shoes in the box in like pairs. What this means is that both primary shoes are in the bottom of the box and both secondary shoes are in the top of the box (or vise versa). When students remove the top two shoes to install them, and compare them to each other, they find that the shoes match (they shouldn't if they are for a duo-servo system). The students assume the matching shoes belong on the same side of the vehicle and install them accordingly **FIGURE 26-15**. They then do the same with the other two brake shoes (which also match each other) on the other side of the vehicle. So both primary shoes are now installed on one side of the vehicle, and both secondary shoes are installed on the other side.

The second mistake involves installing the shoes in the wrong position on the backing plate. When students install the brake shoes on the first assembly, they may look carefully at the assembly and determine (correctly) that the primary shoe goes on the forward side of the backing plate, which for the driver's side is the left side of the backing plate. They then determine that the secondary shoe goes on the right side of the backing plate. When they move to the passenger side of the vehicle, they believe they have already determined that the primary shoe goes on the left side of the backing plate just like the other side. Unfortunately, that is the *rear* side of the backing plate and the secondary shoe should be installed in that position. So, the vehicle has the brake shoes installed correctly on one side but incorrectly on the other side **FIGURE 26-16**. Watch for these mistakes as you perform brake inspections and service.

FIGURE 26-15 A common installation error: The primary shoes are on one side of the vehicle, and the secondary shoes are on the other.

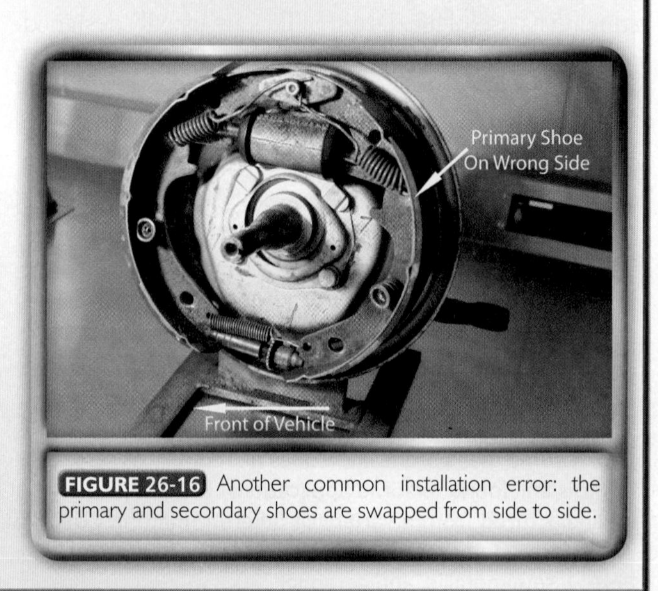
Primary Shoe
On Wrong Side
Front of Vehicle

FIGURE 26-16 Another common installation error: the primary and secondary shoes are swapped from side to side.

Riveted and Bonded Friction Materials

Lining on brake shoes is much thinner than on disc brake pads due to the much greater surface area of the brake shoe lining. Drum brake shoes consist of friction material or lining bonded or riveted onto a steel shoe **FIGURE 26-17**. Bonded brake linings are more common on light-duty vehicles since they are less expensive to build. Also, lighter vehicles do not subject the brake linings to as much heat, so the bonding agent is not as likely to fail as it would on heavier vehicles. Bonded linings are glued under high pressure and temperature to ensure that the bonding is as strong as possible.

Riveted linings are used on heavier duty or high-performance vehicles. Metal rivets, usually made of

FIGURE 26-17 The drum brake shoe and lining.

copper or aluminum, provide a mechanical connection to hold the brake lining to the shoe. This means rivets are less susceptible to failure under high temperatures. However, since the rivets actually pinch some of the brake lining between the rivet head and the metal shoe, the brake linings cannot wear down as much before the rivets contact the drum. Riveted linings must be changed sooner than bonded linings to prevent the rivet heads from contacting the drum and wearing a groove in the friction surface.

Coefficient of Friction Edge Coding

The Society of Automotive Engineers has adopted codes to rate brake lining materials' coefficient of friction. The rating is written on the edge of the friction linings and is called the edge code. The Disc Brake System chapter discusses these ratings in detail.

Drum Brake Noises

Drum brakes are not prone to squealing like disc brakes are, but that does not mean they never make noise. One of the most common sounds that drum brakes make is a groaning noise. It can be caused by excessive brake dust in the drum that causes the brakes shoes to skip and catch, which sounds like a groan. Removing the drum and cleaning the excess brake dust or replacing the brake shoes due to wear usually resolves this issue FIGURE 26-18.

Another noise that drum brakes can make is a grinding noise. If the friction lining wears all the way down to the metal shoe, the shoe and drum can make a metal-on-metal grinding noise. This noise can only be resolved by replacing the brake shoes and refinishing or replacing the drum. Keeping drum brakes from making unwanted noises is pretty simple—keep them clean and inspect the brake lining thickness periodically, replacing it when it gets to the specified minimum thickness.

The last common noise that drum brakes can make is a clicking noise. This can be caused by two situations. First, it could be that the brake shoes have worn grooves in the contact pads on the backing plate and are causing the clicking noise when the shoe moves into and out of the groove. Second, it could be that the brake drum's surface finish cut is too rough and acts like the threads on a screw. When the lining contacts the surface of the drum, the lining follows the threaded finish of the drum and the linings thread themselves away from the backing plate. When the brakes are released, the hold-down springs snap the brake shoes back against the backing plate.

Springs and Hardware

Drum brakes use a variety of springs and hardware to control the action of the brake shoes FIGURE 26-19. Each type of brake uses its own arrangement of these components. Pay close attention to how they are installed before removing them. It is good practice to only disassemble and reassemble the brake components on one side of the vehicle at a time. That way you can refer to the other side if you forget how something came apart. Generally speaking, there are several categories of springs used in drum brakes: return, hold-down, and specialty.

Return Springs

Return springs retract the brake shoes when the driver releases the brake pedal FIGURE 26-20. Each return spring either connects to one brake shoe and the backing plate anchor pin or directly to the other brake shoe. In both cases, they pull the brake shoes back into their rest

FIGURE 26-18 Brake dust.

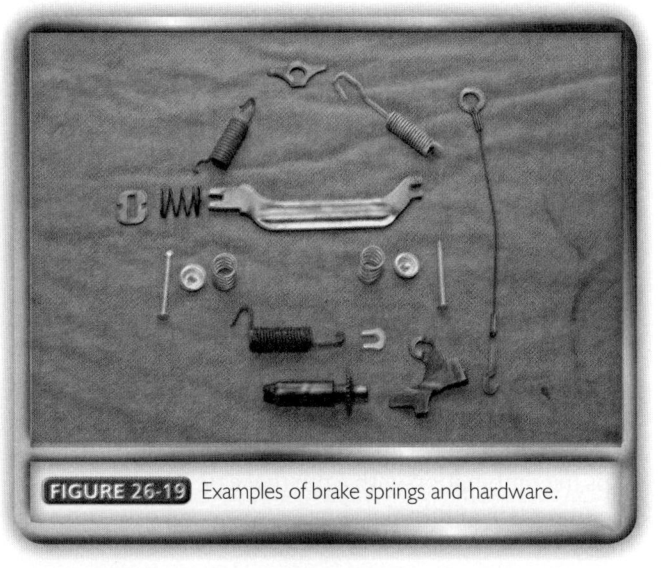

FIGURE 26-19 Examples of brake springs and hardware.

Brake shoe return springs

FIGURE 26-20 Common drum brake return springs.

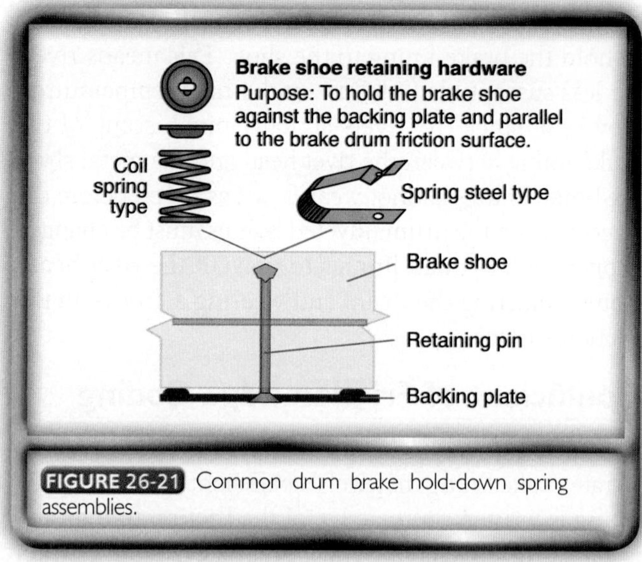
Brake shoe retaining hardware
Purpose: To hold the brake shoe against the backing plate and parallel to the brake drum friction surface.
Coil spring type
Spring steel type
Brake shoe
Retaining pin
Backing plate

FIGURE 26-21 Common drum brake hold-down spring assemblies.

position. Return springs can integrate one or more coil springs in the length of the spring or it can be a large U-shaped spring. Return springs are generally quite stiff, making them a challenge to install. Brake pliers can make installation easier. Even though return springs may look the same front to rear within a particular brake assembly, be aware that they can have different amounts of strength. On duo-servo brakes, the primary return spring is weaker than the secondary return spring, so the primary shoe can be applied before the secondary shoe.

The coils on return springs should be tightly wound together, meaning that the coils should be touching each other, with no space between them. Any space indicates that the return spring has been stretched and needs to be replaced. Return springs are normally replaced in sets. If one spring needs to be replaced, they all should be replaced to avoid mismatched components. Also, due to the high temperatures and the large number of apply and return cycles that drum brake springs must endure, some manufacturers and shops recommend replacing the return springs and hardware during every brake job.

Hold-Down Springs

Hold-down springs do just what their name suggests—they hold the brake shoes against the backing plate FIGURE 26-21. They can be coil springs in combination with a spring retainer and a pin, sometimes referred to as a brake nail, that extends through the backing plate, brake shoe, and center of the spring; or they can be coil springs lying on their side and connected to the pin beside them. They can also use U-shaped spring steel clips in combination with a pin that extends through the backing plate and brake shoe.

Specialty Springs

Specialty springs are used to return links and levers on the parking brake system or the self-adjuster mechanism. Specialty springs can be of all different shapes and sizes and can be used to push or pull components into proper position. Be sure to install each specialty spring in the correct position so that each of the brake systems works as intended. If in doubt, check the other wheel brake unit or the service information to see how it is assembled.

Self-Adjusters

Brake shoe lining wears over time and increases the clearance between the brake lining and drum. This increased clearance causes the wheel cylinder pistons to travel farther to move the brake shoes out to contact the surface of the drums. It also causes the brake pedal to travel farther before activating the brakes, reducing the reserve pedal height, which leaves the driver vulnerable if a hydraulic failure occurs. To safeguard against these dangers, all manufacturers have been required since 1968 to incorporate a self-adjusting mechanism into their drum brake systems that is capable of maintaining proper shoe-to-drum clearance.

Types of Self-Adjusters

The first type of self-adjuster is used on most duo-servo brakes. It has an adjustable threaded star wheel assembly holding the bottoms of the brake shoes apart. The link has three main parts: the threaded barrel, the nonthreaded barrel (and possible thrust washer), and the star wheel, which is threaded on one end and smooth on the other FIGURE 26-22. Both barrels have slots that fit to tabs on

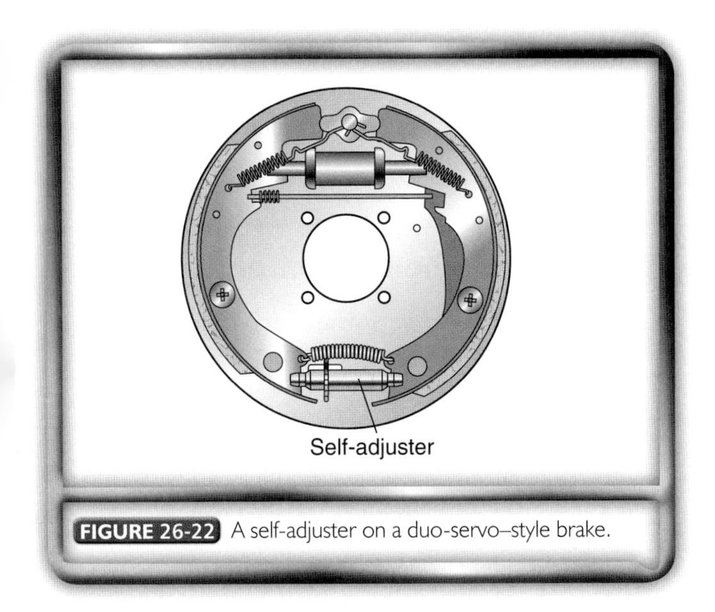
Self-adjuster

FIGURE 26-22 A self-adjuster on a duo-servo–style brake.

the brake shoes, preventing them from turning. The star wheel's threaded end screws into the threaded barrel. The smooth end of the star wheel fits into the nonthreaded barrel FIGURE 26-23. As the star wheel is turned, the thread causes the self-adjuster to lengthen. This takes up excess brake shoe clearance, as needed. The question is what turns the star wheel?

A movable self-adjuster link is held against the star wheel. The link is moved up and down by the action of applying the brakes while the vehicle is backing up. If the link moves far enough, it will catch another tooth of the star wheel and the spring action will turn the star wheel one tooth, adjusting the brakes shoes outward just a bit. This process continues until the brake shoe clearance is taken up enough so that the self-adjuster link cannot move far enough to catch another tooth on the star wheel. As the brake linings wear, the clearance increases and the movement of the link increases to the point that it catches another tooth. This continues for the life of the brake lining.

The self-adjuster link is moved by a cable or rod, which is connected to the anchor pin at the top of the backing plate. The movement of the secondary brake shoe, when the brakes are applied while backing up, causes the self-adjuster link to be pulled by the cable or rod. The position of the link and cable or rod is critical to the operation of the self-adjuster assembly. The link should be level with the star wheel and close to its centerline. Also, the star wheel assembly is side specific, meaning that the threads on each star wheel are opposite of each other, so they turn in opposite directions.

A similar style of self-adjuster works off of the parking brake assembly. It is usually used on non-servo brakes. The star wheel linkage is threaded and is usually mounted between the brake shoes just below the wheel cylinder. There is a pivoting self-adjuster link attached to one brake shoe, and a spring pulls the lever down. As the parking brake is applied, the parking brake lever pushes the star wheel linkage toward the other shoe. The end of the linkage pivots the self-adjuster link upward against spring pressure. If it travels far enough, it will catch the next tooth. As the parking brake is released, the spring pulls the self-adjuster link down and rotates the star wheel one tooth. This expands the star wheel linkage and reduces the brake shoe clearance slightly. This process continues until the excess clearance of the brake shoe to the drum is taken up. The self-adjuster link will then be unable to catch another tooth until the clearance opens a bit more as the brake linings continue to wear.

TECHNICIAN TIP

Be careful to not switch the self-adjusters from one side of the vehicle to the other. If this happens, the self-adjuster will retract the adjustment, causing the brake shoe clearance to increase as the brakes adjust. The customer will report that the brake pedal keeps getting lower and lower but was fine when they picked up the vehicle.

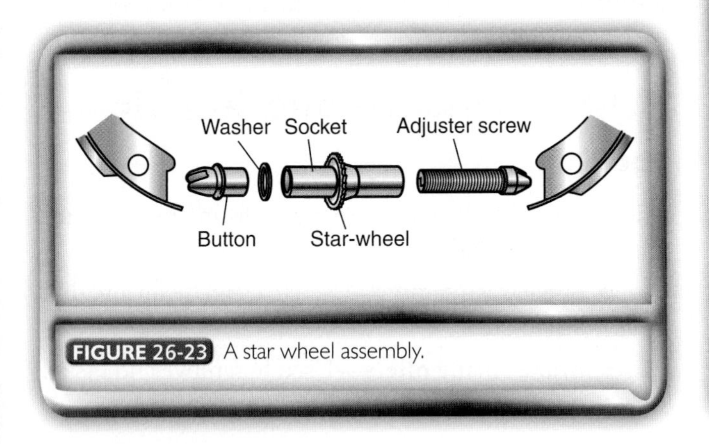
Washer
Socket
Adjuster screw
Button
Star-wheel

FIGURE 26-23 A star wheel assembly.

Caring for the Customer

Some drivers never use their brakes when backing up. Instead, they back up slowly, put the transmission in first gear, and use their clutch or automatic transmission to stop the vehicle and start going forward at the same time. Backing without braking prevents the self-adjusters from adjusting the drum brakes on vehicles equipped with this style of self-adjuster. Educating customers on how the self-adjuster works will help them keep their brakes adjusted, as well as get longer life out of the linings.

Some manufacturers use a ratcheting-style self-adjuster. This type uses two toothed pieces held in contact with each other by spring pressure. They can slide over each other in one direction, but hold in the other direction. The two pieces allow excessive shoe-to-drum clearance to be taken up when the brake pedal is applied and then prevent the shoes from fully returning to their rest position when the brakes are released. As the service brakes are applied, the shoes move apart. If they travel far enough, the toothed pieces slide over each other until the shoes contact the drum. When the brakes are released, the components allow a small amount of inward brake shoe movement to occur, which creates the proper shoe-to-drum clearance. This style of self-adjuster generally can be adjusted in one brake pedal application, reducing the amount of time spent pre-adjusting the brake shoes when they are being replaced.

Parking Brake Systems

Drum parking brake systems mechanically apply the regular service brake shoes. Since drum brakes are self-energizing, it is easier to generate the force needed to apply them mechanically than it is to apply disc brakes. The parking brake cable attaches to the bottom of the parking brake actuating lever in the drum brake assembly. The other end of the lever is attached to the top end of one of the brake shoes with a pin or tang. A strut rod runs from near the top of the actuating lever to the other brake shoe **FIGURE 26-24**. When the cable is pulled, the lever pivots on the strut rod, pushing the top of the brake shoe rearward and the strut rod forward. Since the strut rod is connected to the other shoe, pulling the lever forces the brake shoes apart and into firm contact with the drum, holding the vehicle stationary. Releasing the cable allows the brake retracting springs to pull the brake shoes away from the drums.

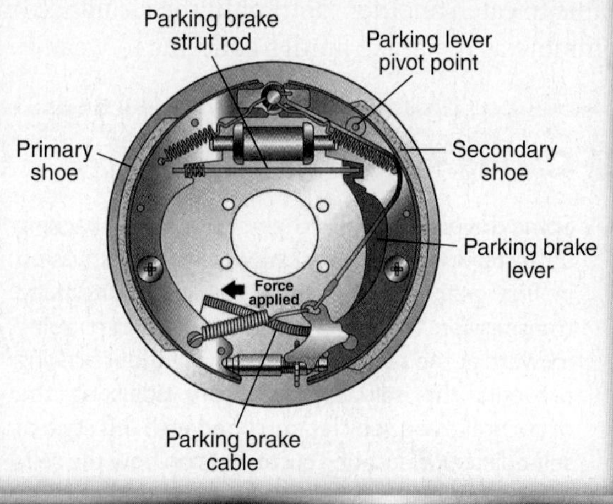

FIGURE 26-24 A parking brake assembly for a drum brake.

Caring for the Customer

It is common to have more than one condition present in a brake system when you diagnose it, such as worn brake shoes, a leaky wheel cylinder, and a leaky seal in the master cylinder. It is good practice to perform a thorough inspection of the brake system whenever one condition is present to determine if any others are present at the same time. This prevents you from having to go back to the customer to get permission to perform the additional work after he or she has agreed to the initial repair, giving the customer cause to doubt your competence or integrity.

Diagnosis

Diagnosing Drum Brakes

To diagnose issues with the drum brakes, verify the customer concern by operating the vehicle if it is safe to do so. Depending on the concern, it may be as simple as stepping on the brake pedal without moving the vehicle and feeling the brake pedal sink to the floor, or it could require a more detailed test-drive to observe the fault the customer is describing. Never test-drive the vehicle if the brake pedal goes to the floor. Depending on the condition, it is good practice to research any technical service bulletins (TSBs) for the particular situation. If no related TSBs are found, research the service information to familiarize yourself with the drum brake system and the manufacturer's diagnostic procedure for the condition. Perform any diagnostic tests to identify the cause of the condition. Diagnosis could involve a visual inspection or any other prescribed tests. It could also involve a detailed testing sequence. Once you have identified the root cause of the fault, determine the action that will rectify the fault.

Maintenance and Repair

Tools

The tools used to diagnose and repair drum brake systems include **FIGURE 26-25**:

- Brake wash station—Used to clean drum and disc brake dust.
- **Brake spring pliers**—Used to remove and install return springs.

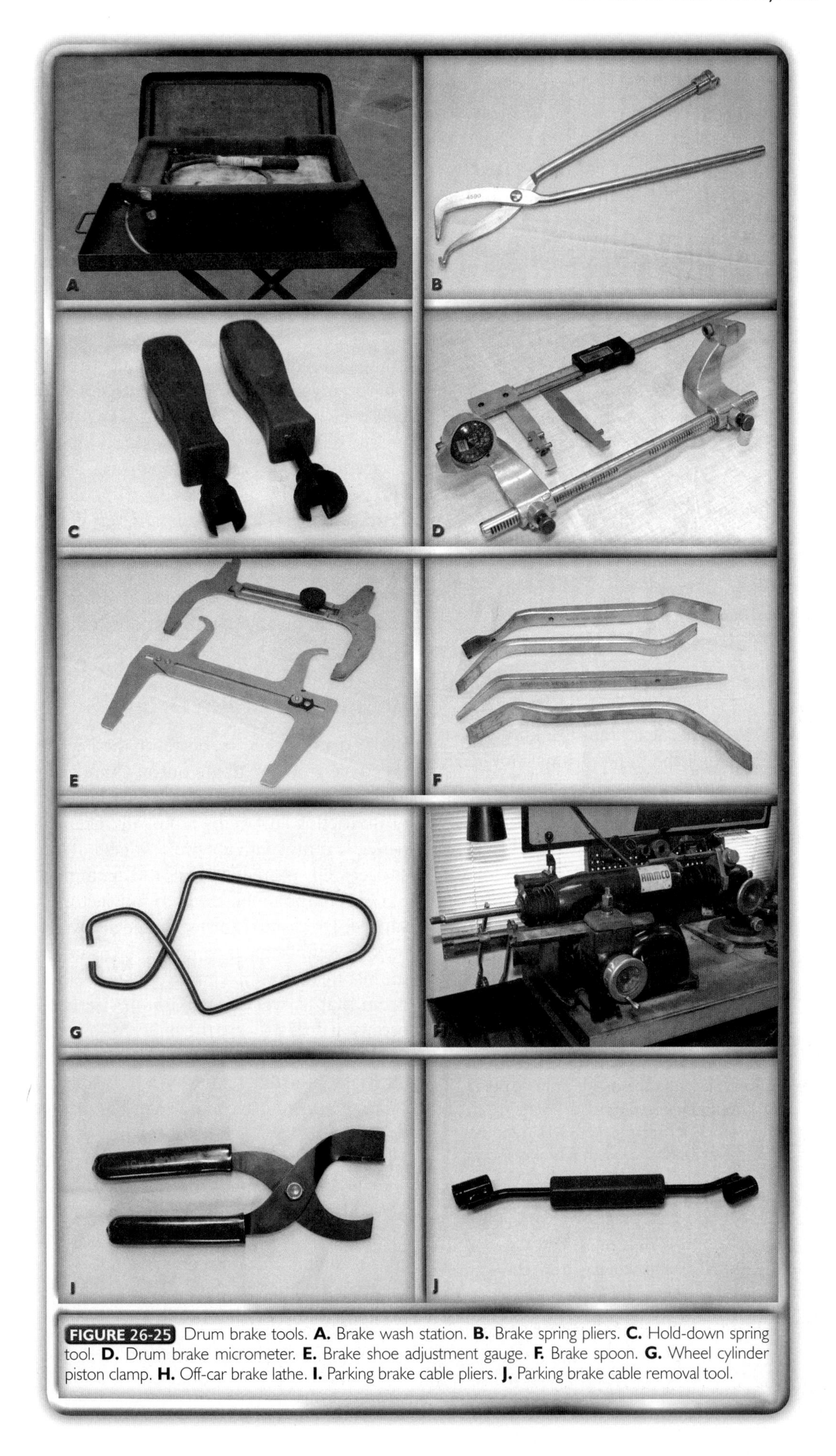
A
B
C
D
E
F
G
H
I
J

FIGURE 26-25 Drum brake tools. **A.** Brake wash station. **B.** Brake spring pliers. **C.** Hold-down spring tool. **D.** Drum brake micrometer. **E.** Brake shoe adjustment gauge. **F.** Brake spoon. **G.** Wheel cylinder piston clamp. **H.** Off-car brake lathe. **I.** Parking brake cable pliers. **J.** Parking brake cable removal tool.

- **Hold-down spring tool**—Used to remove and install hold-down springs.
- **Drum brake micrometer**—Used to measure inside brake drum diameter.
- **Brake shoe adjustment gauge**—Used to pre-adjust brake shoes before installing the drum.
- **Brake spoon**—Used to adjust brake shoes when the drum is installed.
- **Wheel cylinder piston clamp**—Used to hold the pistons in the wheel cylinder while the brake shoes are removed.
- **Off-car brake lathe**—Used to machine drums and rotors that are off the vehicle.
- **Parking brake cable pliers**—Used to install parking brake cables on the parking brake lever.
- **Parking brake cable removal tool**—Used to remove the parking brake cable from the backing plate.

Removing, Cleaning, Inspecting, and Measuring Brake Drums

Brake drums need to be removed for a variety of reasons, such as inspecting the thickness of the brake linings, checking for wheel cylinder leaks, and packing wheel bearings. While removed, the brake drums should be inspected visually for any damage. They should also be measured with a drum micrometer to verify that they are smaller than the specified maximum diameter. If not, they need to be replaced.

> **TECHNICIAN TIP**
>
> Once the brake drum is loose from the hub, it can sometimes be difficult to remove it from over the shoes due to wear on the drum friction surface. The wear leaves a lip on the outer edge of the brake drum that the brake shoes hit when the brake drum is being pulled off. This condition prevents the brake drum from being removed. If it occurs, you will need to manually back off the self-adjuster with a brake spoon so that the brake shoes are not expanded as far. Once the star wheel is backed off, the lip of the brake drum should slide over the brake shoes and you can clean, inspect, and measure it. Just remember that you will have to hold the self-adjuster link away from the star wheel so that the star wheel can be backed off.

Before removing the brake drum, you need to determine if it is a hub style, or hubless (slip-off) style. Most light-duty vehicles now use hubless drums. You can usually tell which style of brake drum you are working on by looking at the holes for the lug studs. If there is clearance between the stud and drum, it is likely a hubless brake drum. You can also look at the clearance between the center hole of the brake drum and the hub. A hubless brake drum will have a parting line at the centering hole. A hub-style brake drum will appear to be one solid piece.

Because of the tight clearances between the hub and brake drum on a slip-off style brake drum, the surfaces can rust together. You may have to use a medium or large ball-peen hammer to hammer on the drum between the lug studs. Make sure you do not hit the lug studs because you will damage them. Some drums can be rusted on very solidly. If you are having difficulty breaking the drum loose, seek the assistance of your supervisor. A torch may be needed to heat up the drum to break the rust bond.

To remove, clean, inspect, and measure brake drums and determine any further actions, follow the steps in SKILL DRILL 26-1.

Refinishing Brake Drums

Brake drums need to be refinished when they have excessive grooving or are out-of-round. They are refinished using a brake lathe. A **brake lathe** refinishes the drum friction surface by removing metal and making it perfectly round with the proper finish. If the grooving or surface defects are too great, the drum may require the removal of too much metal to satisfactorily refinish the surface. The drum diameter should always be remeasured once the refinishing is complete to ensure that it is under the manufacturer's maximum diameter. Never put a brake drum that is over the maximum size back in service, because it does not have the ability to absorb as much heat.

Hub-style and hubless-style drums are mounted on the brake lathe differently. Most hub-style drums use the bearing races to drive and center the drum on the lathe spindle. Bearing adapters of the proper size need to be selected and used. The spindle nut then clamps the drum onto the spindle through these bearing adapters and races.

Hubless drums can be mounted on the composite rotor adapter or centered using a spring-loaded centering cone to align the drum's centering hole with the spindle. Clam shell clamps are then used on each side of the drum to clamp it to the lathe spindle.

SKILL DRILL 26-1 Removing, Cleaning, Inspecting, and Measuring Brake Drums

1. To remove a hubless-style drum, first make matching marks on the drum and hub for reinstallation in the correct position.
   - If there are screws or speed nuts holding the drum to the hub, remove them following the specified procedure. The speed nuts can be discarded and are not needed upon reassembly. The screws will be reused.
   - Remove the drum from the hub.

2. To remove a hub-style drum, first remove the wheel bearing locking mechanism (cotter pin, lock nut, or peened washer).
   - Remove the wheel bearing adjusting nut, thrust washer, and outer bearing.
   - If the rear bearing needs to be removed for service, or replacement of the drum, remove the inner bearing and grease seal.

3. Reinstall the adjusting nut onto the spindle about five turns. Grasp the drum/hub assembly on the top and bottom and push it toward the center of the vehicle. Hold slight downward pressure as you firmly pull the drum/hub assembly toward yourself. This should cause the adjusting nut to catch the wheel bearing and pull it and the seal out of the rear of the hub. The grease seal will need to be replaced with a new one. Once the drum is removed, clean, inspect, and measure it. Clean the drum with approved asbestos removal equipment. Inspect the drum for hard spots/hot spots, scoring, cracks, and damage.

4. Measure the drum diameter at the deepest groove or most worn part of the drum and compare to specifications. If it is over the size limit, it will need to be replaced. If it needs to be machined and is below the maximum diameter, check to see how badly it is scored.

8500

5. Find the smallest diameter of the drum and write down the reading.

8500

6. Find the largest diameter of the drum and write down that reading. Calculate the difference between the two readings, which is the out-of-round measurement and compare it to specifications. Determine any necessary action.

To refinish a brake drum and measure final drum diameter, follow **SKILL DRILL 26-2**. Before starting, research the brake lathe manufacturer's procedurefor properly refinishing the drum. Follow those guidelines.

SKILL DRILL 26-2 Refinishing Brake Drums

1. Research the brake lathe manufacturer's procedure for properly refinishing the drum. Clean any nicks, burrs, or debris from the mounting surfaces of the drum. Mount the drum on the brake lathe. Check to see that the drum is running true on the lathe. If it wobbles, turn off the lathe, dismount the drum, and recheck for burrs, debris, or any other condition that causes it to wobble.

2. Install the anti-chatter band on the drum to prevent vibration during machining.

3. Set the position of the cutting tool so that the brake drum is close to the brake lathe when the cutting bit is in the far corner of the drum. Make sure the cutting bits will not contact the face of the drum, and move the cutting head about 0.5" (12.7 mm) in from the outside of the drum. Turn on the brake lathe and set the depth of the cutting tool so it just touches the surface of the drum. Slowly remove the ridge.

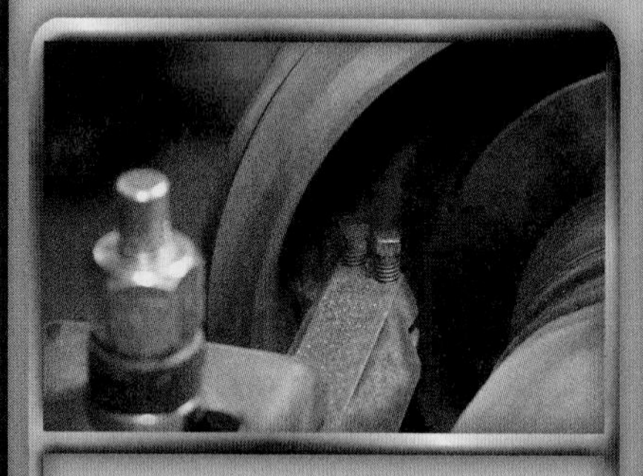

4. Run the drum all the way in so the cutting bit is in the inner corner of the drum.

5. Set the cutting bit to the proper depth and lock it in place. Engage the automatic spindle feed and set it to the proper speed (if equipped), lock it in place, and watch for proper machining action. Repeat this step until the worn surface areas have been removed all the way around the surface of the drum. If the brake lathe is not a single-cut machine, perform a finish cut on the drum.

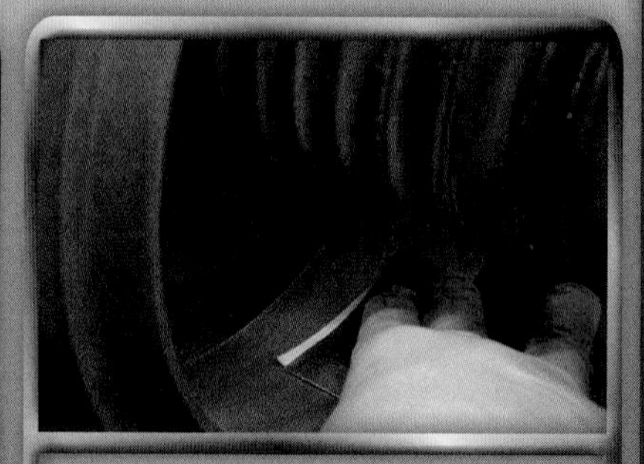

6. Move the drum well away from the cutting bit and use sandpaper to give the drum surface a non-directional finish. Remeasure the drum diameter and discard if above specifications.

Applied Science

AS-37: Vibrations/Waves: The technician can demonstrate an understanding of the types and causes of vibrations caused by out-of-balance or excessively worn systems.

Sound is very important in diagnosing problems in a motor vehicle. Sound is a series of waves that travel through a gas, liquid, or solid, many of which can be heard by the human ear. For example, the solid rumble strips on the sides of the highway make a continuous noise or vibration when driven over by a motor vehicle.

Sound can help you to diagnose a worn wheel bearing that needs replacing. As a wheel bearing becomes worn, the case hardening on the bearing race begins to wear away due to constant friction between the bearing race and the bearing rollers. As the case hardening starts to wear, the bearing race develops low spots in the race. As the flat bearing rollers start to roll over the high and low spots in the bearing race, a noise will occur.

To diagnose the noise of a worn bearing in a motor vehicle, you can hoist the vehicle, spin the wheel, and listen for a noise. Or you can test-drive the vehicle and gently turn the steering wheel from side to side. As the vehicle moves from side to side, more weight is placed on each side of the bearing due to centrifugal force. You will hear a louder noise as you turn away from the side with the faulty bearing.

TECHNICIAN TIP

Since it can be hard to remember where all of the parts fit inside of a drum brake assembly, it is good practice to disassemble only one side at a time, leaving the other side as a reference for when you reassemble the first side. Or, use a digital camera to take a couple of reference pictures before disassembly.

Caring for the Customer

If one wheel cylinder is leaking, how long until the other wheel cylinder starts leaking? And if it does leak, will it contaminate the new brake lining? Take into consideration the age and condition of the components when you inspect the system and give the customer your recommendation.

Removing, Cleaning, and Inspecting Brake Shoes and Hardware

Drum brakes need to be disassembled for a variety of reasons such as when the brake lining has worn beyond specifications, the wheel cylinders are faulty, the self-adjuster is stuck or damaged, or the axle seal has failed and leaked gear oil or wheel bearing grease onto the brake lining. Drum brakes are generally more complicated to change than disc brake pads, so care needs to be taken when working on them. There is usually a combination of springs, links, levers, guides, and retainers. It is easy to install these items incorrectly. It is good practice to carefully examine each brake assembly before disassembling to verify that it was assembled correctly previously.

Brake shoes and springs are always replaced in axle sets. If one rear brake assembly has linings contaminated with grease from a failed axle seal, the lining on both wheel brake units will need to be replaced. The same goes with springs. The other parts are left to the discretion of the technician and any shop policies.

Regarding star wheel assemblies, there is some controversy as to whether the threads should be lubricated. The argument on one side is that if you do not lubricate the threads, then they will be likely to rust and freeze up. The other side argues that any lubricant on the threads will attract brake dust and gum up the threads. There is some truth to both arguments. CDX would suggest using a light coating of lubricant on the threads in areas where the star wheel is likely to come in contact with salt, mud, or water because rust and corrosion are a greater hazard than dust gumming up the threads. In areas where the assembly is unlikely to come in contact with those conditions, use no lubricant on the threads. But always follow the manufacturer's recommended procedure, if specified.

To remove, clean, inspect, and reassemble a duo-servo brake, follow the steps in **SKILL DRILL 26-3**. In the appropriate service information, research and follow the procedure for disassembling the brake assembly. Manufacturers use many drum brake configurations, so the following steps are general in nature and should not be substituted for the manufacturer's procedure.

To disassemble, clean, inspect, and reassemble a non-servo brake, follow the steps in **SKILL DRILL 26-4**.

SKILL DRILL 26-3 Removing, Cleaning, Inspecting, and Reassembling a Duo-Servo Brake

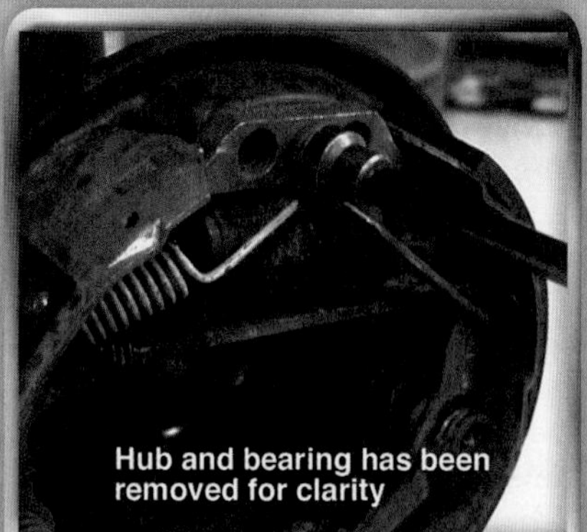
Hub and bearing has been
removed for clarity

1. Research the procedure for disassembling the brake assembly. Clean brake shoes, hardware, and backing plates using equipment and procedures for dealing with asbestos/dust.

2. To disassemble a duo-servo brake, first remove the return springs, cable guide (if installed), and shoe guide. Remove the parking brake strut and spring. Remove the primary shoe hold-down spring, retainer, and pin. Remove the self-adjuster spring and star wheel assembly and primary shoe.

3. Remove the secondary hold-down spring, retainer, pin, and secondary shoe. Disassemble the parking brake lever from the brake shoe and hardware from the backing plate. Finally, clean and inspect all parts according to the manufacturer's procedure.

4. To reassemble a duo-servo brake, first reassemble the parking brake lever on the brake shoe and parking brake cable. Reassemble the star wheel assembly, lubricate the floating end, and set aside. Also lubricate the pads on the backing plate. Install both shoes to the backing plate with the hold-down spring assemblies. Install the shoe guide and self-adjuster cable over the anchor pin.

5. Install the cable guide and return spring in the secondary shoe. Also align the wheel cylinder pushrod in the shoe. Position the secondary shoe in place and use brake spring pliers to install the return spring over the anchor pin. Install the parking brake strut rod onto the secondary shoe, and pull the primary shoe engaged with the parking brake strut rod. Install the return spring in the primary shoe and use brake spring pliers to stretch the return spring over the anchor pin. Install the self-adjuster link, cable, and spring into position. Install the star wheel between the bottoms of the two shoes. Finally, check the fit of all springs, clips, and levers.

SKILL DRILL 26-4 Disassembling, Cleaning, Inspecting, and Reassembling a Non-Servo Brake

1. Research the procedure for disassembling the brake assembly. Clean brake shoes, hardware, and backing plates using equipment and procedures for dealing with asbestos/dust. To disassemble a non-servo brake disassembly, first remove the hold-down springs, retainers, and pins. Spread the shoes apart and remove the parking brake strut and self-adjuster components.

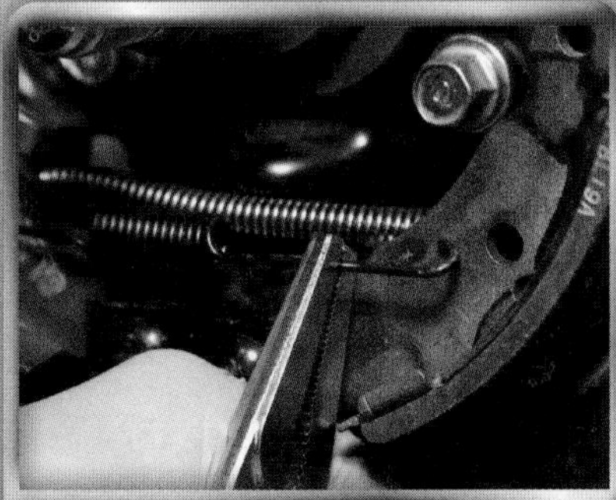

2. Remove the return springs. Disassemble the parking brake lever from the brake shoe and hardware from the backing plate. Finally, clean and inspect all parts.

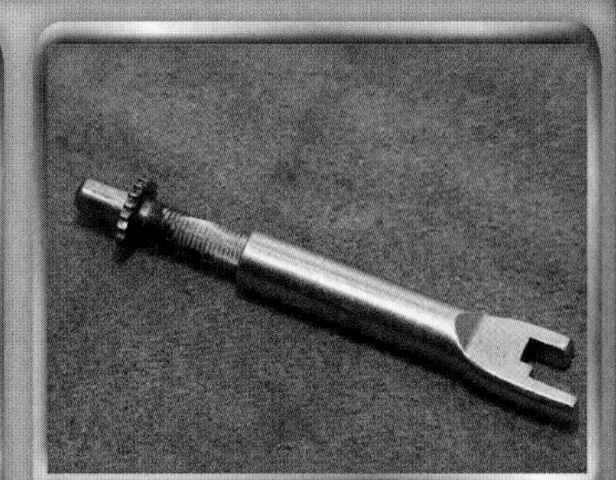

3. To reassemble a non-servo assembly, first assemble and lube the self-adjuster/parking brake strut assembly. Lube the backing plate pads. Place one shoe on the backing plate and install the hold-down spring and pin. Place the self-adjuster/parking brake strut on the installed brake shoe.

4. Place the retracting springs on both shoes, and fit the loose shoe to the backing plate, being sure to line up the wheel cylinder pushrods, the self-adjuster, and the parking brake mechanism. Install the hold-down spring and pin. Check the fit of all springs, clips, and levers.

Removing, Inspecting, and Installing, Wheel Cylinders

If a wheel cylinder is leaking or binding, there is a good chance that the cylinder bore is corroded and pitted, requiring removal and replacement of the wheel cylinder. Wheel cylinders also need to be removed if the backing plate is being replaced. Very few shops rebuild wheel cylinders anymore. If you are reusing the wheel cylinder, make sure the bleeder screw can be opened. Because they are hollow, they break off easily, making bleeding virtually impossible.

To remove, inspect, and install wheel cylinders, follow the steps in SKILL DRILL 26-5.

Pre-Adjusting Brakes and Installing Drums and Wheel Bearings

Pre-adjusting the brake shoes and parking brake is a routine step in a drum brake job. It saves time because it is faster to adjust the brakes with the drum off than it is when the drum is installed. The pre-adjustment sequence is important. Start by making sure the parking brake is fully released. Then look at the shoes to make sure the parking brake adjustment is not holding the brake shoes in the applied position. You can see this by verifying that the brake shoes are up against their stops on the top and bottom of each shoe. If they are not firmly against them, loosen the parking brake adjustment. Then adjust the service brakes. Once they are adjusted, adjust the parking brake.

Prove
Know
See
Do

SKILL DRILL 26-5 Removing, Inspecting, and Installing Wheel Cylinders

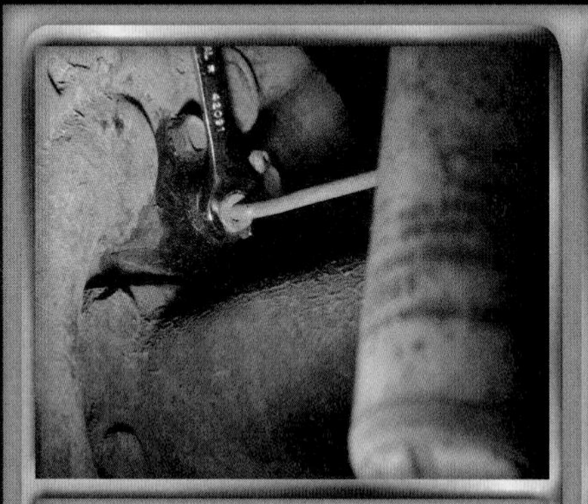

1. Use a flare nut or line wrench to unscrew the brake line from the wheel cylinder. Remove the wheel cylinder from the backing plate.

2. Peel back the dust boots and check for brake fluid behind them. If any is found, the piston seal is leaking and the wheel cylinder should be replaced.

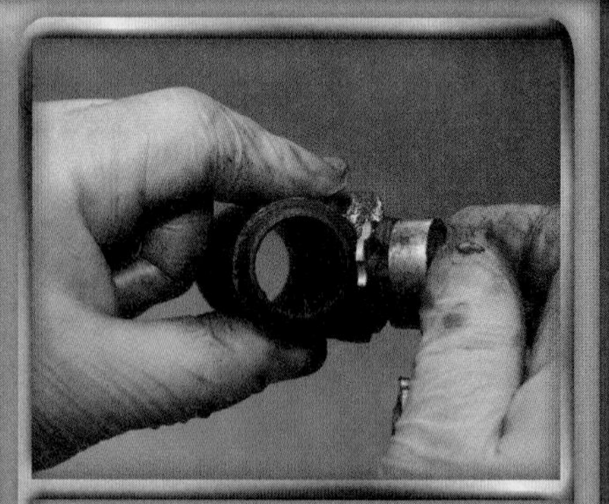

3. Disassemble the wheel cylinder and inspect each part. Determine any necessary actions.

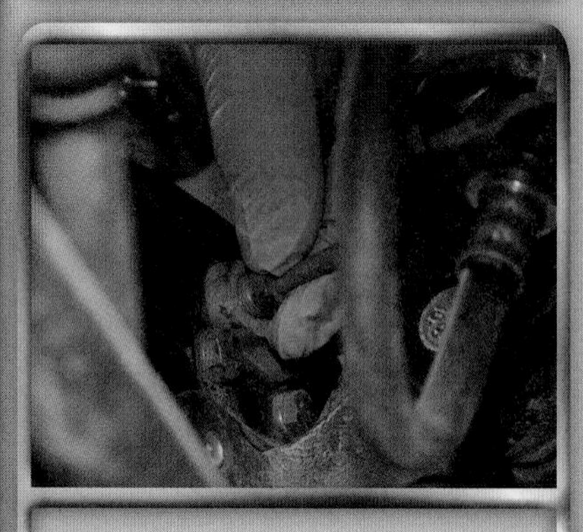

4. If the cylinder can be reused, rebuild it, preferably with new seals and dust boots. If not, replace it with a new wheel cylinder. Reinstall the brake line by hand. Install and tighten any mounting screws. After that, tighten the brake line with a flare nut or line wrench.

> **TECHNICIAN TIP**
>
> When reinstalling the wheel cylinder on the backing plate, it is best to first start the brake line three or four full turns using just your fingers. This will help prevent cross-threading the wheel cylinder and make it much easier to start the brake line. Otherwise, you risk ruining the wheel cylinder and brake line fitting.

To pre-adjust brake shoes and the parking brake and to install brake drums or drum/hub assemblies and wheel bearings, follow the steps in SKILL DRILL 26-6.

Installing Wheels, Torquing Lug Nuts, and Making Final Checks

This procedure, while fairly simple, can result in problems if it is not performed properly. Overtightening the lug nuts can cause the wheel studs to break either immediately or, worse, after the vehicle has been driven for a period of time. Undertightening can lead to loosening of the lug nuts and result in the wheel working its way off the vehicle. This can cause the driver to lose control of the vehicle and potentially result in an accident.

Lug nuts should be tightened to the proper torque, in the specified sequence. All manufacturers specify these details for each of their vehicles. The torque pattern is usually either in some form of a star or cross. Be careful which way you install the lug nuts. Many wheels use a tapered hole that matches the tapered end of the lug nut and centers the wheel on the wheel flange. Other wheels use a flat surface that matches flat surfaces on the lug nuts. No matter

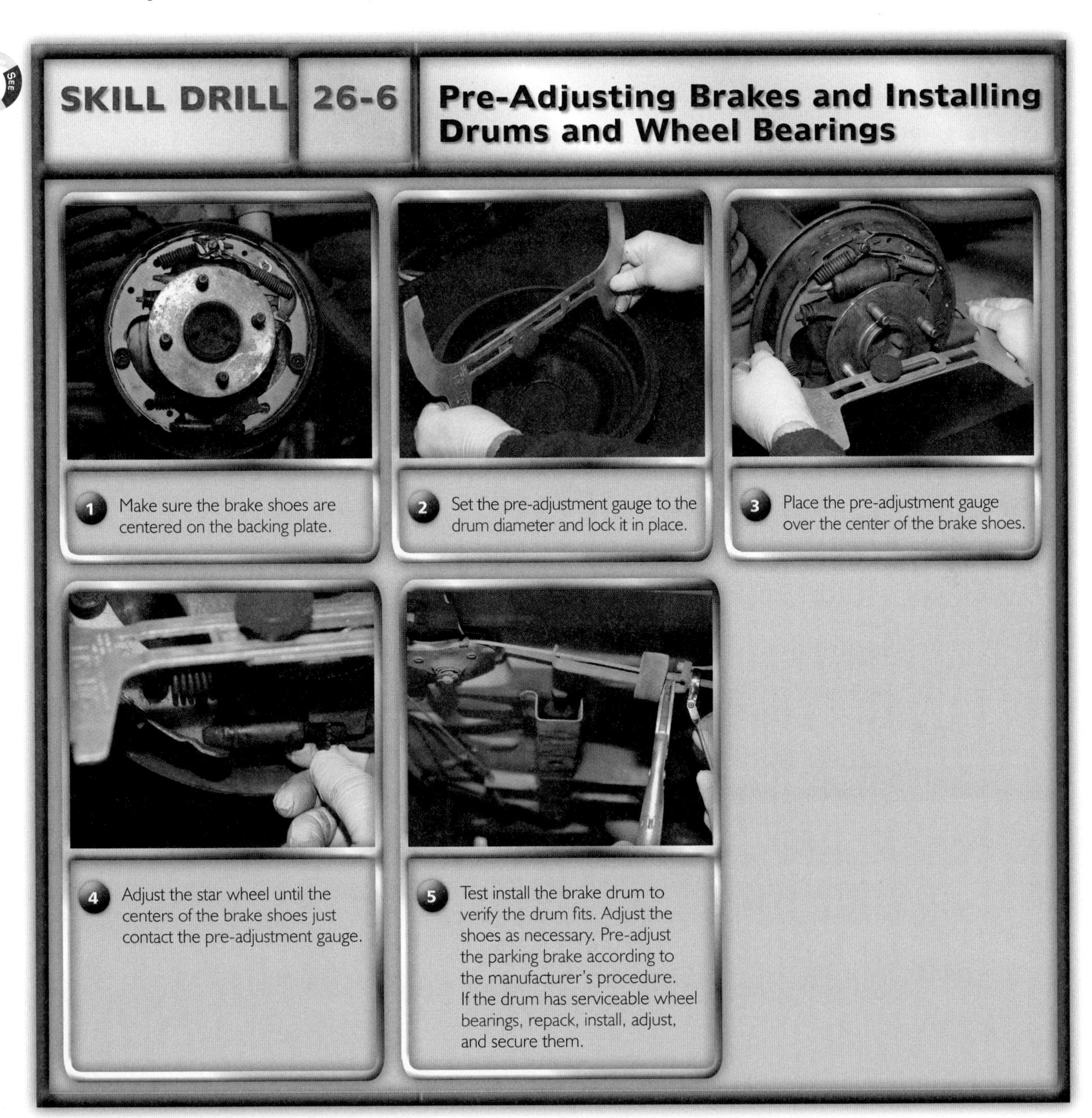

SKILL DRILL 26-6 Pre-Adjusting Brakes and Installing Drums and Wheel Bearings

1. Make sure the brake shoes are centered on the backing plate.
2. Set the pre-adjustment gauge to the drum diameter and lock it in place.
3. Place the pre-adjustment gauge over the center of the brake shoes.
4. Adjust the star wheel until the centers of the brake shoes just contact the pre-adjustment gauge.
5. Test install the brake drum to verify the drum fits. Adjust the shoes as necessary. Pre-adjust the parking brake according to the manufacturer's procedure. If the drum has serviceable wheel bearings, repack, install, adjust, and secure them.

what, the lug nut surface **must** match the mating surface of the wheel. Always check that these surfaces match.

When installing lug nuts, the weight should be off the vehicle. The lug nuts should easily center the wheel on the hub. Proper centering is especially important on aluminum wheels that use a flat lug nut sealing surface. The lug nuts can dig into the sides of the lug nut holes and cause the wheel to not center correctly. Once the lug nuts are up against the wheel, work the wheel up onto the lug nut shafts. Then you can torque them down properly.

There is some controversy regarding the use of a lubricant or antiseize on wheel studs and lug nuts. Since the purpose of a lubricant or antiseize is to prevent the components from sticking, the lug nuts may loosen up. The torque given for the lug nuts assumes that the lug stud is dry (no lubricant), so torquing them to specifications would lead to overtorquing. In areas of the country that are prone to rust, it is understandable why some want to put a very light amount of antiseize only on the threads of the wheel stud, being careful not to get any on the contact seat of the wheel and lug nut; doing so would prevent rust from building up on the threads. However, the lug nut torque would need to be reduced due to the lubricant. To avoid this issue, install the lug nuts dry.

To install the wheel, torque lug nuts, and make final checks and adjustments, follow the steps in **SKILL DRILL 26-7**.

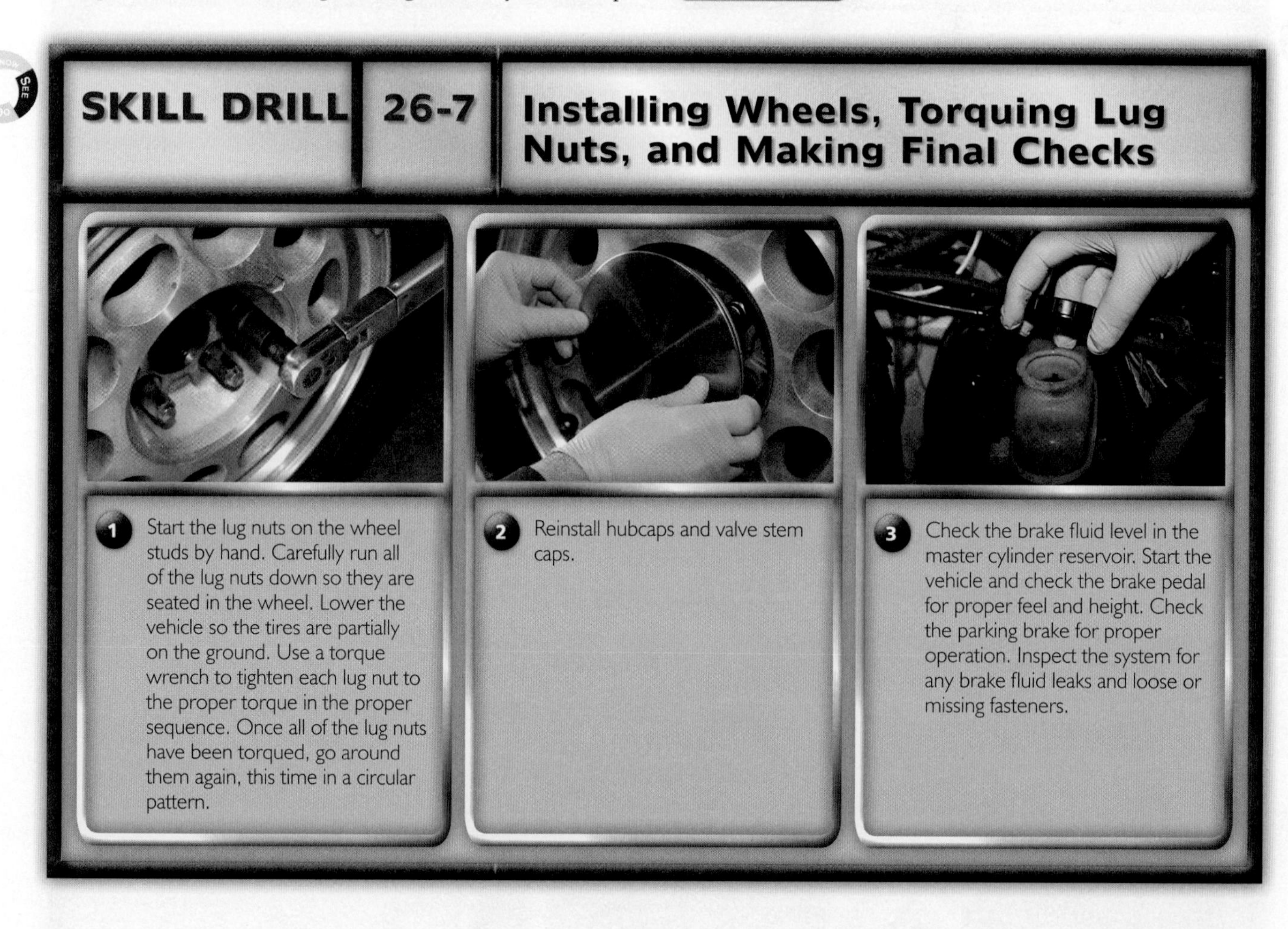
Prove Know See Do

SKILL DRILL 26-7 Installing Wheels, Torquing Lug Nuts, and Making Final Checks

1. Start the lug nuts on the wheel studs by hand. Carefully run all of the lug nuts down so they are seated in the wheel. Lower the vehicle so the tires are partially on the ground. Use a torque wrench to tighten each lug nut to the proper torque in the proper sequence. Once all of the lug nuts have been torqued, go around them again, this time in a circular pattern.
2. Reinstall hubcaps and valve stem caps.
3. Check the brake fluid level in the master cylinder reservoir. Start the vehicle and check the brake pedal for proper feel and height. Check the parking brake for proper operation. Inspect the system for any brake fluid leaks and loose or missing fasteners.

Wrap-up

Ready for Review

- The main components of the drum brake system are: brake drum, backing plate, wheel cylinder, brake shoes, springs and clips, automatic brake self-adjuster, and parking brake mechanism.
- Drum brakes are usually located on the rear wheels of disc-drum applications.
- Hydraulic pressure forces pistons to move the brake shoes into contact with the brake drums.
- Leading brake shoes are applied in the same direction as the brake drum's forward rotation and are self-energizing; trailing brake shoes are applied in the opposite direction of the brake drum's forward rotation and are not self-energizing.
- Drum brake systems can be: twin leading shoe (least common), leading/trailing shoe, and duo servo.
- Twin leading shoe brake systems are more efficient in forward braking than reverse braking.
- Leading/trailing shoe brake systems provide equal, but not maximum, braking in both directions.
- Duo-servo drum brake systems use servo action for the front brake shoes to multiply the force to the rear shoes, causing rear brake shoes to do more braking work.
- Brake drums are machined to the manufacturer's specified standard diameter and should be replaced once refinished beyond specifications.
- Brake drums styles are hub or hubless (most common in passenger vehicles).
- All brake unit components (except brake drum) are mounted to the backing plate.
- Brake shoe contact pads provide a smooth surface for the brake shoes to ride on.
- Wheel cylinders contain a housing, pistons, piston lip seals, spring and expander set, dust boots, push rods, and a bleeder screw.
- Wheel cylinders should be replaced rather than honed if corrosion or pitting occurs.
- Wheel cylinders are single acting (one piston, force generated in one direction) or dual acting (two pistons, force generated in two directions).
- Steel brake shoes have lining material bonded (or riveted) to them to create friction for braking.
- Duo-servo brake systems have primary brake shoes (front of vehicle, shorter shoe lining) and secondary brake shoes (rear of vehicle, longer shoe lining).
- Drum brakes may make the following noises: groaning (excess brake dust in the drum), grinding (worn friction lining), or clicking (grooves worn into backing plate contact pads or rough finish cut on the drum).
- Drum brakes use return, hold-down, and specialty springs.
- Drum brakes must have self-adjusters to maintain proper shoe-to-drum clearance.

Key Terms

anchor pin A component of the backing plate that takes all of the braking force from the brake shoes.

automatic brake self-adjuster A system on drum brakes that automatically adjusts the brakes to maintain a specified amount of running clearance between the shoes and drum.

backing plate A stamped steel plate, bolted to the steering or suspension, which supports the wheel cylinder, brake shoes, and other hardware.

brake drum A short, wide, hollow cylinder that is capped on one end and bolted to a vehicle's wheel; it has an inner friction surface that the brake shoe is forced against.

brake lathe A tool used to refinish the drum surface by removing a small amount of metal and returning it to a concentric, non-directional finish.

brake shoe A steel shoe and brake lining friction material that apply force to the brake drum during braking.

brake shoe adjustment gauge An adjustable tool used to pre-adjust the brake shoes to the diameter of the brake drum.

brake spoon A tool used to adjust the brake lining-to-drum clearance when the drum is installed on the vehicle.

brake spring pliers A tool used for removing and installing brake return springs.

cylinder bore The inside diameter of a cylinder.

drum brake micrometer A tool used for measuring the inside diameter of the brake drum.

duo-servo drum brake system A system that uses servo action in both the forward and reverse direction.

hold-down springs Springs that hold the brake shoes against the backing plate.

hold-down spring tool A tool used for removing and installing hold-down springs.

leading shoes Brake shoes that are installed so that they are applied in the same direction as the forward rotation of the drum and thus are self-energizing.

leading/trailing shoe drum brake system Type of brake shoe arrangement where one shoe is positioned in a leading manner and the other shoe in a trailing manner.

off-car brake lathe A tool used to machine (refinish) drums and rotors after they have been removed from the vehicle.

parking brake cable pliers A tool used to install parking brake cables.

parking brake cable removal tool A tool used to compress the spring steel fingers of the parking brake cable so that the cable can be removed from the backing plate.

parking brake mechanism A mechanism that operates the brake shoes or pads to hold the vehicle stationary when the parking brake is applied.

return springs Springs that retract the brake shoes to their released position.

self-energizing The property of drum brakes that assists the driver in applying the brakes; when brake shoes come into contact with the moving drum, the friction tends to wedge the shoes against the drum, thus increasing the braking force.

servo action A drum brake design where one brake shoe, when activated, applies an increased activating force to the other brake shoe, in proportion to the initial activating force; further enhances the self-energizing feature of some drum brakes.

specialty springs Springs used to return links and levers on the parking brake system or the self-adjuster mechanism.

springs and clips Various devices that hold the brake shoes in place or return them to their proper place.

trailing shoes Brake shoes installed so that they are applied in the opposite direction to the forward rotation of the brake drum; not self-energizing and less efficient at developing braking force.

twin leading shoe drum brake system Brake shoe arrangement in which both brake shoes are self-energizing in the forward direction.

wheel cylinder A hydraulic cylinder with one or two pistons, seals, dust boots, and a bleeder screw that pushes the brake shoes into contact with the brake drum to slow or stop the vehicle.

wheel cylinder piston clamp A tool that prevents the pistons from being pushed out of the wheel cylinders while the brake shoes are being replaced.

ASE-Type Questions

1. Tech A says that parking brakes on drum brake vehicles use separate brake shoes for back up in an emergency. Tech B says that parking brakes on drum brake vehicles mechanically operate the standard drum brake shoes. Who is correct?
   a. Tech A
   b. Tech B
   c. Both A and B
   d. Neither A nor B
2. Tech A says that most brake drums are designed to be machined if minor surface issues are present. Tech B says that brake drums can be reused if they are machined over specifications, as long as the surface is smooth. Who is correct?
   a. Tech A
   b. Tech B
   c. Both A and B
   d. Neither A nor B
3. Tech A says that duo-servo brake shoes are only anchored on the top. Tech B says that typically duo-servo brake shoes adjust automatically during normal brake applications in a forward direction. Who is correct?
   a. Tech A
   b. Tech B
   c. Both A and B
   d. Neither A nor B
4. Tech A says that when inspecting brake shoes, if the shoes are unequally worn, this could be caused by a stuck wheel cylinder piston. Tech B says that the lining on the primary shoe is typically shorter in length and is installed toward the front of the vehicle. Who is correct?
   a. Tech A
   b. Tech B
   c. Both A and B
   d. Neither A nor B
5. Tech A says that it is almost impossible to install self-adjusters on the wrong side of the vehicle. Tech B says that grease seals can be reused. Who is correct?
   a. Tech A
   b. Tech B
   c. Both A and B
   d. Neither A nor B
6. Tech A says to use an air hose to clean the backing plate of dust and contamination. Tech B says to use a brake cleaning solution to clean the backing plate of dust and contamination. Who is correct?
   a. Tech A
   b. Tech B
   c. Both A and B
   d. Neither A nor B
7. Tech A says that riveted lining is usually for heavy duty or high performance vehicles. Tech B says that you need to identify each shoe individually to help ensure proper installation. Who is correct?
   a. Tech A
   b. Tech B
   c. Both A and B
   d. Neither A nor B
8. Tech A says that a grinding noise in drum brakes generally requires replacing the brake shoes and resurfacing or replacing the drums. Tech B says that a click noise in drum brakes requires replacing the brake shoes and resurfacing or replacing the drums. Who is correct?
   a. Tech A
   b. Tech B
   c. Both A and B
   d. Neither A nor B
9. Tech A says that brake shoe linings saturated with brake fluid from a leaky wheel cylinder can be cleaned with brake cleaner and reused as long as they aren't worn out. Tech B says that brake shoes should be replaced in axle sets. Who is correct?
   a. Tech A
   b. Tech B
   c. Both A and B
   d. Neither A nor B
10. Tech A says that when performing a brake job on the rear axle of an older vehicle, inspection finds brake fluid under the dust boot; this suggests wheel cylinder replacement on both rear wheels. Tech B says that when a drum brake return spring has failed, springs on both rear wheels need to be replaced. Who is correct?
    a. Tech A
    b. Tech B
    c. Both A and B
    d. Neither A nor B

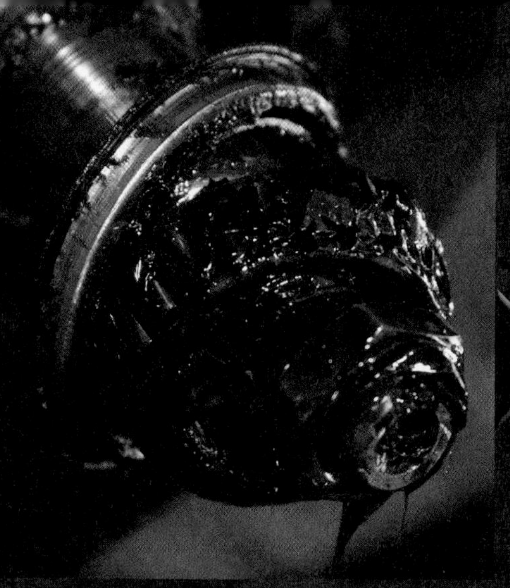

CHAPTER 27

KNOW
SEE
DO
PROVE

NATEF Tasks

Brakes Miscellaneous		Page
■ Diagnose wheel bearing noises, wheel shimmy, and vibration concerns; determine necessary action.	AST	778–779
■ Remove, clean, inspect, repack, and install wheel bearings; replace seals; install hub and adjust bearings.	MLR AST	779–783
■ Replace wheel bearing and race.	MLR AST	782–783
■ Remove and reinstall sealed wheel bearing assembly.	AST	783–785
Suspension and Steering Related Suspension and Steering Service		
■ Remove, inspect, and service or replace front and rear wheel bearings.	AST	779–785

KNOW
SEE
DO
PROVE

Knowledge Objectives

After reading this chapter, you will be able to:

1. Describe the components of a wheel bearing. (pp 770–771)
2. Describe the advantages and disadvantages of serviceable and sealed wheel bearings. (p 771)
3. Describe the difference between friction and anti-friction bearings. (p 771)
4. Describe advantages and disadvantages of ball and roller types of wheel bearings. (pp 771–775)
5. Describe how side load (thrust) impacts bearing selection. (pp 771–772)
6. Describe the purpose of double-row wheel bearings. (p 773)
7. Describe a unitized wheel bearing hub. (p 773)
8. Describe the purpose of grease seals. (pp 776–777)
9. Describe the different wheel bearing lubricant designations. (pp 776–777)
10. Describe wheel bearing end play and preload. (p 777)
11. Describe the process of diagnosing wheel bearing concerns. (pp 778–779)

Wheel Bearings

Know
See
Do

Skills Objectives

After reading this chapter, you will be able to:

1. Remove, clean and inspect wheel bearings. (pp 779–780)
2. Pack wheel bearings by hand. (pp 779–781)
3. Pack wheel bearings using a bearing packer. (p 779)
4. Install wheel bearings. (pp 779–782)
5. Install the locking mechanism on a wheel bearing. (pp 781–783)
6. Replace a wheel bearing and race. (pp 782–783)
7. Remove and reinstall a sealed wheel bearing using the unitized wheel bearing hub style. (pp 783–785)

Introduction

Wheel bearings are a commonly overlooked component. All wheel bearings used to be the serviceable type, requiring periodic maintenance every 24,000–30,000 miles (38,624–48,280 km), consisting of disassembly, cleaning, inspecting, reassembly, and adjusting. With the introduction of sealed wheel bearings that do not need periodic service, many manufacturers switched to using them on most of their lighter duty vehicles. As a result, many technicians do not give the wheel bearings as much consideration as they once did. However, both types of wheel bearings can fail, and vehicles with serviceable wheel bearings still need maintenance, so it is important that you become familiar with wheel bearings.

In this chapter, you will learn about each wheel bearing component and the role wheel bearings play in helping to keep the vehicle safe. Because wheel bearings can require maintenance, you will learn how to accurately diagnose common issues and recommend the proper service or repair to the customer. You will also learn how to properly maintain and, if necessary, replace today's wheel bearings.

Wheel Bearings Overview

Wheel bearings play a critical role in the vehicle by allowing the wheels to roll with a minimum of friction while still maintaining accurate wheel positioning under all driving conditions. Most wheel bearing assemblies include the following components: an **outer race**, an **inner race**, **roller bearings** or **ball bearings**, and a **bearing cage** to hold the rollers or balls in place FIGURE 27-1. The rollers or balls are made of hardened metal and roll between the two races. The races are also made of hardened metal and are carefully formed to match the contour of the rollers or balls, so all of the components roll easily against each other.

Each race either fits firmly within a housing or fits firmly on a shaft. In many situations, the races are an **interference fit** with the housing or shaft, which means they must be pressed into place with a high amount of force. In other words, the races are designed so that when they are installed, they should not rotate in or on their respective components. The rollers or balls are specifically designed to provide the rolling function. Because the races, rollers,

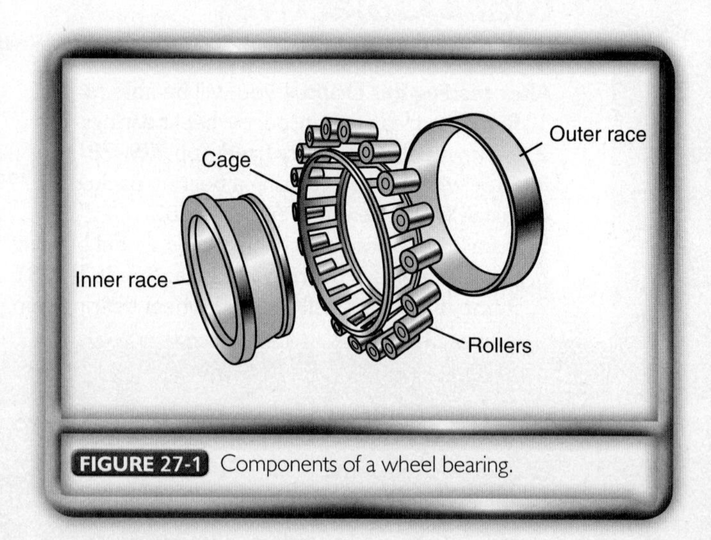
Outer race
Cage
Inner race
Rollers

FIGURE 27-1 Components of a wheel bearing.

You Are the Automotive Technician

A customer pulls her 2003 Ford F250 pick-up truck into your shop complaining that the vehicle is making a howling sound when driving more than 20 mph. The noise seems to gradually increase as the speed of the vehicle increases. She is concerned that the vehicle might break down and leave her stranded. You ask her where the noise is coming from and she explains it is coming from the center or rear of the vehicle. You notice that the truck is equipped with a solid live rear axle, and the tires are in good shape, with a fairly smooth highway tread on them.

1. On a test drive, how can you determine whether the noise is coming from a wheel bearing or a transmission bearing?
2. What bearing arrangements can be used on a solid live rear axle?
3. How are rear wheel bearings lubricated on a solid live rear axle?

and balls are made of hardened metals, they are designed to resist wear and damage. However, overloading the vehicle can put the wheel bearings under a greater load than they are rated for, which can cause them to fail. In the same way, using improper or insufficient lubricant can cause them to fail. Wheel bearing failure is discussed in detail later in this chapter.

There are two categories of wheel bearings: **serviceable bearings** and **sealed bearings**. Serviceable bearings are designed so they can be disassembled and serviced, while sealed bearings are not. Serviceable bearings must be serviced periodically by disassembling, cleaning, inspecting, repacking them with the specified lubricant, reinstalling, and adjusting them. Sealed bearings are designed so they cannot be disassembled or adjusted. Sealed bearings are manufactured with the proper clearance and filled with the specified lubricant from the factory FIGURE 27-2. They are designed to last the life of the vehicle, but bearings do wear out or fail occasionally and need to be replaced. We will discuss sealed bearing failure and replacement in detail later in the chapter.

> **TECHNICIAN TIP**
>
> Roller and ball bearing assemblies are called **anti-friction bearings** because the components are in rolling contact with one another and therefore have minimal friction. A sleeve-type bearing, or **bushing**, such as a clutch pilot bushing, is called a **friction bearing**, as the components are in sliding contact with one another. Anti-friction bearings run much more freely than friction bearings.

Wheel Bearing Types

Wheel bearings commonly are of the following types: cylindrical roller bearing, tapered roller bearing, ball bearing, double-row ball bearings, and double-row tapered roller bearings. Each one is designed for a particular application. For example, roller bearings support the load over a larger surface area so they can carry heavier loads than ball bearings. Manufacturers determine the type of wheel bearing they will use, based on the particular application and its requirements. You will need to be familiar with each type of wheel bearing to successfully service a variety of vehicles.

Cylindrical Roller Bearings

Cylindrical roller bearing assemblies use rollers that are cylindrical in shape, so that the races are parallel to each other with the rollers between them FIGURE 27-3. This type of wheel bearing assembly is used in situations where the wheel bearing is not subject to side loads. It is common in rear axles of rear-wheel drive vehicles, where the rear axles are held from moving side to side by means other than the wheel bearings, such as a differential assembly that uses thrust bearings to prevent the axle from moving side to side. Since all side-to-side movement is controlled within the differential assembly, the cylindrical roller bearing assemblies solely support the vehicle's weight.

In many instances, cylindrical roller bearing assemblies use the surface of the axle as the inner bearing race. The cylindrical roller bearings ride directly on the axle shaft. In this situation, if the cylindrical roller bearing assembly fails, the axle shaft most likely will need to be replaced along with the bearing assembly. Some bearing

FIGURE 27-2 Sealed bearing.

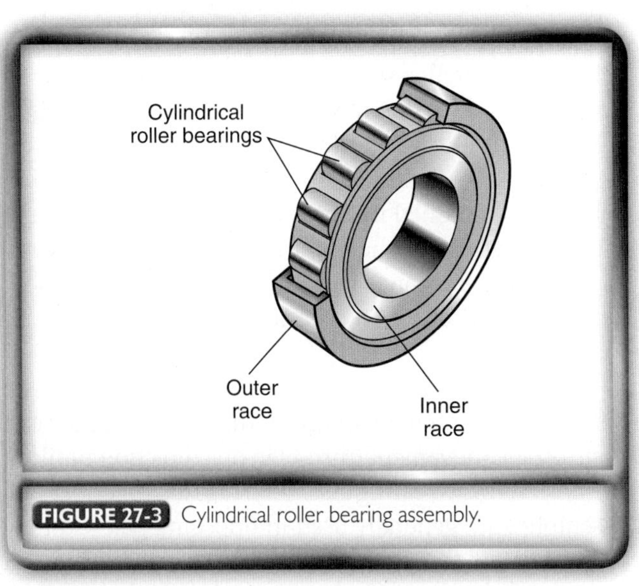
Cylindrical roller bearings
Outer race
Inner race

FIGURE 27-3 Cylindrical roller bearing assembly.

manufacturers have designed replacement cylindrical roller bearing assemblies that ride farther out on the axle shaft than the original bearing, so the axle may not need to be replaced in this situation.

Cylindrical roller bearing assemblies are manufactured to have the proper running clearance between the rollers and races, so no adjustment of this type of wheel bearing is needed. However, they do require lubrication to cushion the rollers and races while operating. Lubrication also removes the heat generated between the rolling surfaces and transmits it to the housing and ultimately the atmosphere. This transfer of heat is usually accomplished by the **gear lube**, which is filled high enough in the differential housing to flow outward to the cylindrical roller bearings. The gear lube is retained in the housing by a **grease seal**, which is located in the outer end of the axle housing outside of the cylindrical roller bearing assembly. This arrangement allows the cylindrical roller bearing assembly to be lubricated while still retaining the gear lube in the housing. At the same time, any dirt and contaminants are sealed out of the housing.

Tapered Roller Bearings

Tapered roller bearing assemblies are commonly used where heavier loads need to be supported and the wheel bearings are put under a side load (thrust) condition. Wheel bearing side load conditions occur when the vehicle is cornering. When the wheel is being turned, the vehicle wants to keep going straight. This causes the bottom of the outside wheel to be pushed inward and the bottom of the inside wheel outward, which puts them both under a side load condition. In this situation, cylindrical roller bearing assemblies would just allow the wheel to slide sideways on the axle, which means they cannot control the side load (thrust) condition. However, tapered roller bearing assemblies can.

With tapered roller bearing assemblies, the races and rollers are tapered in such a manner that all of the tapered angles meet together at a common point **FIGURE 27-4**. This design allows the tapered rollers to freely roll between the angled inner and outer races. The tapered rollers are contained in a bearing cage, which holds the tapered bearings to the inner race as a unit. The inner race is called the cone. The outer race is called the cup. The cone and cup make up a tapered roller bearing assembly.

Because the components are on an angle to the centerline of (and not parallel to) the axle shaft, they can control side movement (thrust) in one direction unlike a cylindrical roller bearing assembly. Tapered roller bearing assemblies are generally used in opposing pairs so they can control side movement (thrust) in both an inward and outward direction. When used in pairs, the individual tapered roller bearing assemblies are generally referred to as inner (or inboard) and outer (or outboard) bearings. The inner bearing assembly is closer to the centerline of the wheel so it supports most of the vehicle weight. Because of this, the inner bearing assembly is typically larger than the outer bearing assembly.

Some manufacturers have designed double-row tapered roller bearing assemblies, which combine two opposing tapered roller bearing assemblies into one unit. This design provides excellent side thrust–carrying capacity and at the same time excellent load-carrying capacity. For more information, see the section Sealed Wheel Bearings.

Because tapered roller bearing assemblies use tapered components, the wheel bearing assembly must be adjusted to have the proper **running clearance** between the tapered rollers and races when the bearing assemblies are installed. The running clearance is the amount of space between components during operation. If the tapered roller bearing clearance is too tight, the components will bind and overheat due to increased pressure and because the rollers squeeze out too much grease, making the lubricating film too thin. If the tapered roller bearing is adjusted with too much clearance, excessive side-to-side and up-and-down movement will occur, which can cause the components to hammer against each other, damaging the surfaces of the tapered roller bearings and races.

Lubrication of serviceable tapered wheel bearing assemblies is usually accomplished in one of two ways—wheel bearing grease or gear lube. If wheel bearing grease is specified, the tapered wheel bearing will need to be packed with new grease before installing it, since the grease is very thick and does not flow unless it is heated

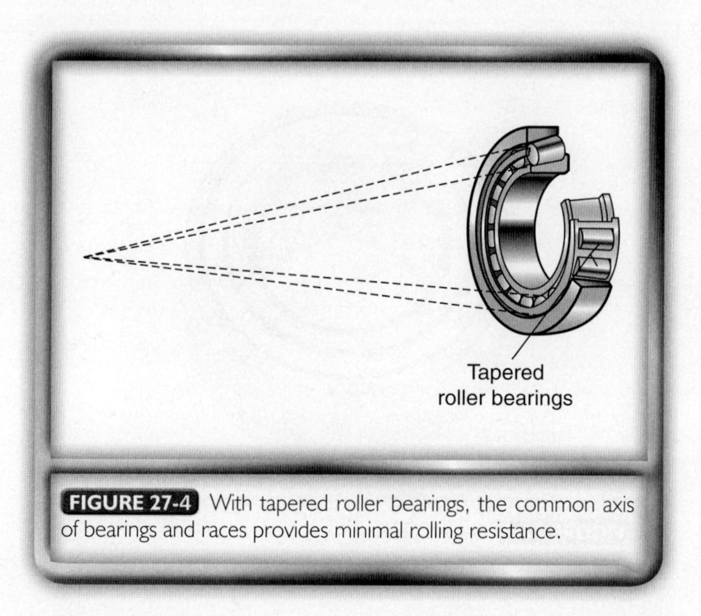
Tapered
roller bearings

FIGURE 27-4 With tapered roller bearings, the common axis of bearings and races provides minimal rolling resistance.

up. Packing a bearing means that the spaces between the rollers and races are completely filled with grease. Packing is best performed with a bearing packing tool, but it can be successfully performed by hand; it just takes a bit longer. This grease, plus a small reserve amount, will provide lubrication for the tapered wheel bearing assembly as it is in service. For detailed information on this procedure, see the Wheel Bearing Maintenance section.

Some tapered wheel bearing assemblies are lubricated with gear lube from the axle housing just like the cylindrical bearing assemblies. They do not need to be packed since gear lube flows relatively easily and fills the spaces once the proper amount of gear lube is added to the axle housing. Keeping the gear lube at the proper level is critical for long life of a tapered wheel bearing assembly. If the gear lube gets too low, the tapered wheel bearing assemblies will be starved for lubrication, overheat, and become damaged. Some front axle housings on four-wheel drive vehicles use separate, sealed bearing chambers to hold a quantity of gear lube. In either type of system, grease seals help retain the gear lube in the system as well as seal out contaminants.

Ball Bearings

Deeply grooved ball bearing assemblies are used as wheel bearings on a lot of light-duty vehicles because they have a lower rolling resistance. The much smaller contact area between the balls and races prevents a ball bearing assembly from being used on larger vehicles, which experience higher loads. Ball bearing assemblies consist of an inner race, an outer race, ball bearings, and a ball bearing cage. The balls roll in deep channels in the races. Side loads are controlled by the balls rolling against the sides of the channels. Since there is much less surface area between the balls and the sides of the channels compared to the tapered roller bearing, ball bearing assemblies are limited in how much side load they can handle. At the same time, the small surface area allows them to roll freer than roller bearings, and they therefore help manufacturers decrease drag on a vehicle, which increases fuel efficiency. Ball bearing assemblies depend on lubricants similar to roller bearings; but in most cases, they are usually designed as a sealed bearing assembly. This means that the proper type and amount of lubrication is sealed inside the ball bearing assembly by the manufacturer and never needs routine maintenance or packing. But if ball bearings become worn or faulty, they must be replaced. This will be discussed further in Skill Drill 27-7: Removing and Reinstalling Sealed Wheel Bearings Using the Unitized Wheel Bearing Hub Style.

> **TECHNICIAN TIP**
>
> Ball bearings roll easier than roller bearings since they have a smaller contact area; thus, they provide a small increase in vehicle efficiency.

Ball bearing assemblies also come in a **double-row ball bearing assembly** configuration FIGURE 27-5. The double-row configuration gives the ball bearing assembly twice the surface contact area so it can control greater amounts of loads and side loads than a single-row bearing assembly. Virtually all wheel bearings using a ball bearing assembly are of the double-row ball bearing variety, and they are commonly used in automotive light vehicle applications.

The outer race is usually a one-piece unit, while the inner race is usually two separate pieces. The inner races are manufactured to create the correct running clearance when the double-row ball bearing assembly is torqued in place. In automotive wheel bearing applications, the double-row ball bearing assembly may come as a **unitized wheel bearing hub** with the bearing assembly installed in the hub and the wheel flange installed in the center of the bearing assembly FIGURE 27-6. In this way, the old ball bearing assembly can be unbolted, and a new one bolted in its place with minimal labor and no adjustments needed. This is virtually a zero maintenance system until it wears out, and then it is usually replaced as a unit.

Seals and Axle Seals

All wheel bearings rely on some sort of seal to keep the lubricant in and contaminants out. Some wheel bearings have the seal built right into the bearing assembly, such as the sealed bearings that will be covered in detail in the

FIGURE 27-5 A double-row ball bearing assembly.

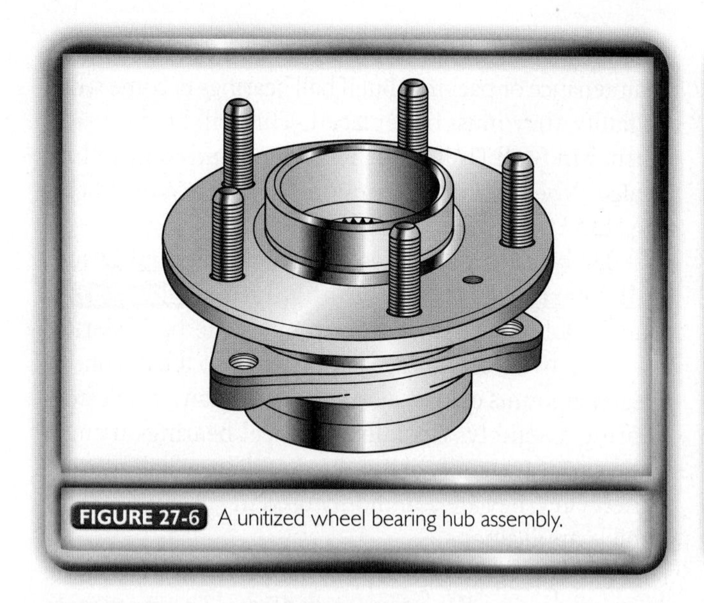

FIGURE 27-6 A unitized wheel bearing hub assembly.

FIGURE 27-7 Components of a typical seal.

next section. Other wheel bearings rely on a completely separate grease seal. Wheel bearing grease seals seal against a rotating surface so that lubricants cannot leak from the bearing side of the seal past the shaft to the other side of the seal. They also prevent any dirt and contaminants from getting past the seal into the bearing. In some applications, the grease seal is a press-fit into the axle housing, which is stationary, and seals against the axle shaft, which is rotating. In other applications, the grease seal is press-fit into the wheel hub, which rotates, and seals against the spindle, which does not rotate.

Most axle seals consist of a stamped sheet metal case and flexible sealing lip with an internal **garter spring** **FIGURE 27-7**. The metal seal case is constructed to be a press-fit when installed in the housing. The outside surface of the metal case usually comes precoated with a thin layer of sealer compound to seal minor surface imperfections between the seal case and the housing. The sealing lip is carefully designed and precisely manufactured so that it will seal the specified lubricant. Many seals use a garter spring to help hold the lips of the seal in contact with the shaft it is sealing. The garter spring helps maintain an adequate seal if the parts are slightly out of alignment or if there is a small amount of runout or clearance between the seal and shaft.

> **TECHNICIAN TIP**
>
> Grease seals are designed to be used only one time. If you have to remove a seal for any reason, replace it with a new one. Failure to do so will likely result in a leaky seal. Also, if you damage a seal during installation, you should replace it with a new one. Always use care when installing seals, and use the correct installation tool.

Seals come in a variety of configurations, so it is critical to use the specified seal for the application you are servicing. The sealing lip can also be made from a variety of materials. Always purchase seals from a reputable manufacturer so you can be confident it will do its job and last a long time. When you install a seal, always remember to pre-lube the sealing lip with a small amount of oil or grease. This will prevent it from overheating during the initial use resulting in premature failure of the seal.

Sealed Wheel Bearings

Some vehicles use sealed wheel bearings. These bearing assemblies are designed and manufactured as completely sealed units. They can be single row or double row, depending on the vehicle application, and can be made up of ball, cylindrical roller, or tapered roller types of bearings. The bearing assemblies are prefilled with lubricant and have integrated grease seals built into them to contain the lubricant. They also are manufactured with the proper running clearance, so they do not need to be adjusted. This saves the vehicle manufacturer money by decreasing the time it takes to install them during vehicle assembly. It also makes for a more reliable and consistent installation process since every unit comes preset at the proper clearance. This style of wheel bearing assembly is also beneficial to vehicle owners since it is designed to last the life of the vehicle during normal use and does not need periodic maintenance, which saves owners money.

Another application for sealed wheel bearings is unitized wheel bearing hubs. These usually include either a double-row ball bearing assembly or a double-row tapered roller bearing assembly installed in a housing that is bolted onto the knuckle or axle housing. In many cases, it also has the wheel flange pressed into the inner race of the wheel bearing. This unit can easily be unbolted from the suspension and replaced as a unit—bearing, hub, and flange. Unitized wheel bearing hubs also provide the benefits offered by the sealed wheel bearing, so manufacturers have embraced them for many of their vehicles. On some vehicles equipped with ABS brakes, the ABS sensor is integrated into the unitized wheel bearing assembly.

Wheel Bearing Arrangements for Rear Drive Axles

Rear drive axles come in three different designations: full floating, semi-floating, and ¾ floating. Each designation refers to how the axle and wheel are supported by the wheel bearings. It is also important for you to understand the differences so that you will be able to service each style properly. In a full floating axle arrangement, the axle only carries a twisting force. The weight of the vehicle is fully carried by a pair of tapered roller bearing assemblies, which ride between the hub and axle tube FIGURE 27-8. The axle does not carry any of the vehicle load since the wheel is bolted directly to the bearing hub. The hub also controls side thrust. Full floating axles handle heavy loads better than the other styles, so they are used in heavy-duty applications such as one-ton pickups, trucks, and vans.

In a semi-floating axle, the wheel flange is part of the axle, which is supported by a single bearing assembly (usually a ball or cylindrical roller bearing style) near the flange end of the axle FIGURE 27-9. The bearing assembly rides between the axle and the axle tube, so all of the weight is put on the axle flange, which transfers the weight to the wheel bearing assembly. In this case, the axle and bearing assembly each carry the full weight of the vehicle. The axle also provides the twisting force for the wheel. This arrangement is generally considered the lightest duty of the three types of axle designations.

In a ¾-floating axle design, there is a single bearing assembly (usually a ball or cylindrical roller bearing style) between the outside of the axle tube and the hub FIGURE 27-10. The axle has a wheel flange that bolts to the hub and provides lateral support for the hub and wheel, while the bearing assembly supports the weight of the vehicle. The axle also provides the twisting force for the wheel. This arrangement is generally considered heavier duty than the semi-floating axle, but lighter duty than the full floating axle.

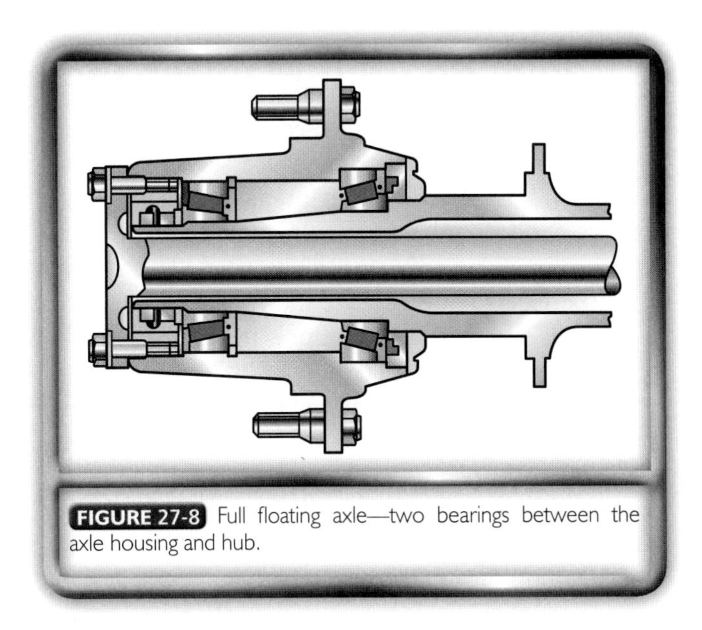

FIGURE 27-8 Full floating axle—two bearings between the axle housing and hub.

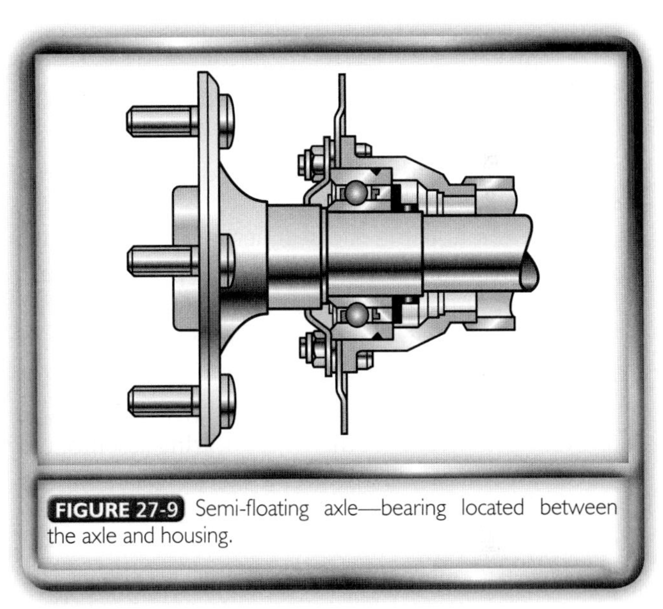

FIGURE 27-9 Semi-floating axle—bearing located between the axle and housing.

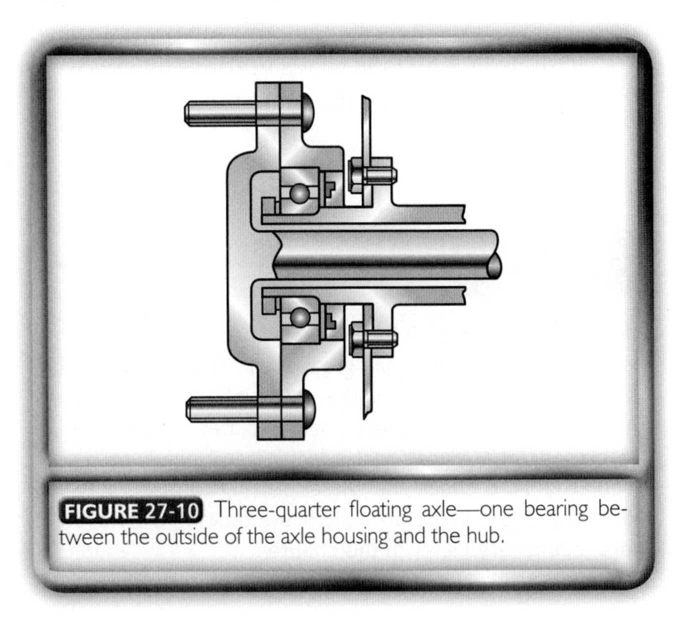

FIGURE 27-10 Three-quarter floating axle—one bearing between the outside of the axle housing and the hub.

Wheel Bearing Maintenance

While sealed wheel bearings are used on a higher percentage of vehicles and require no maintenance, serviceable wheel bearings do need periodic maintenance. Maintenance consists of disassembling, cleaning, inspecting, repacking, installing, and adjusting the bearings. This is commonly performed during brake shoe/pad replacement or at intervals specified by the vehicle manufacturer, usually around 24,000–30,000 miles (38,624–48,280 km). A normal part of servicing wheel bearings includes the replacement of the old grease seals with new ones along with the **cotter pin** (if used), which retains the wheel bearing adjusting nut. A cotter pin is a soft metal pin that can be bent into shape and is used to retain the bearing adjusting nut. Ensure that the correct replacement parts and grease are available before starting the job.

Lubrication

All wheel bearings require lubrication to extend their useful life. There are two common types of lubricants used—gear lube and bearing grease. Each application specifies one or the other. They cannot be substituted, due to the different housing and seal designs each lubricant demands. Gear lube is somewhat thicker than engine oil. Since gear lube flows much easier than grease, the bearing assembly runs in a housing partially filled with gear lube. The gear lube is thin enough to flow around and between the rollers, lubricating them and helping to prevent overheating of the wheel bearing assemblies.

In many rear-wheel drive vehicles, the wheel bearing assemblies are open to the axle housing, which is partially filled with gear lube that also lubricates the differential assembly. Maintenance of this system involves draining the old gear lube and refilling the system with the specified new gear lube. In most cases, this can be performed without disassembling the wheel bearings by removing a drain plug or bolt and filling the system through the **fill plug** FIGURE 27-11. A fill plug is usually threaded and can be removed to allow the level of a fluid to be checked and filled. Some manufacturers have chosen to use a rubber fill plug that snaps into the fill hole. The level of gear lube should normally be within 0.25" (6.35 mm) of the bottom of the fill plug hole.

In order to properly perform maintenance on wheel bearings, you will need to understand the different characteristics of gear lube and bearing grease. This will help ensure that you select the proper lubricant for the task you are performing. Gear lube is classified by the Society of Automotive Engineers (SAE) according to its viscosity and by the American Petroleum Institute (API) according to its service grade. **Viscosity** refers the thickness of the gear lube; the higher the number, the thicker the gear lube. Vehicle manufacturers specify a certain viscosity of gear lube based on the climate the vehicle is operated in or the load it is carrying, so understanding viscosity is very important when servicing vehicles.

Standard viscosities for gear lube are 70W, 75W, 80W, 85W, 90, and 140. The W stands for "winter" or the gear lube's cold temperature viscosity. The non-W ratings are the viscosity of the gear lube at a predetermined hot temperature. Similar to engine oil, gear lube is available in multiviscosity configurations such as 75W–90, 80W–90, or 85–140. Unlike engine oil, the temperature for the W rating varies according to the standard being met. For example, 70W has a maximum allowable temperature for its viscosity of −67°F (−55°C), while 85W is −10°F (−23°C). The manufacturers have gone to great lengths to specify the proper gear lube for their vehicles. Make sure you follow their recommendations when choosing the gear lube for a particular vehicle.

> **TECHNICIAN TIP**
>
> If the level of gear lube is lower than it should be, suspect a leaking axle shaft grease seal. This can usually be verified by looking at the inside of each tire and the back side of the brake backing plate. If gear lube is present, the grease seal is leaking and needs to be replaced. Also check the wheel bearing to make sure it is not faulty; to do so, follow the bearing diagnosis procedure listed later in this chapter.

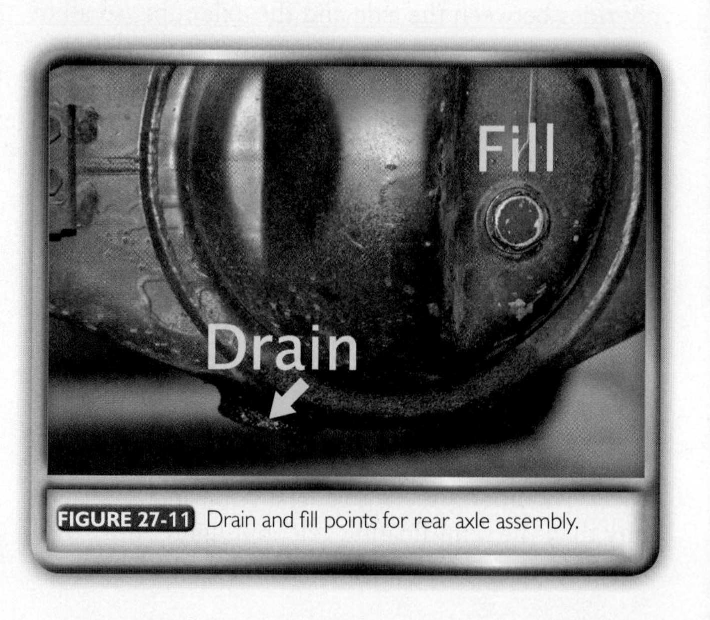
Fill
Drain

FIGURE 27-11 Drain and fill points for rear axle assembly.

Current ratings of the API service grade are GL-1, GL-4, and GL-5. Generally, the higher the number, the better the lubricant. GL-1 has minimal additives, which makes it unsuitable for modern applications, although it is still used in some heavy truck manual transmissions. GL-4 is intended for use with bevel-type gears operating under moderate speeds and loads, such as in many manual transmissions. GL-5 has about twice as much extreme pressure additive as GL-4, so it is intended for most differentials that use hypoid-type gears operating under high-speed/low-speed, high-torque, and shock-load conditions. It can also be used in some manual transmissions. Always check the manufacturer's specifications to determine the proper gear lube for the application you are working on.

Most serviceable wheel bearings require **grease** as their lubricant. Grease is made of a base oil, plus a thickening agent, and specific additives to meet the requirements of the application. **Lithium soap** is a common thickening agent in automotive grease. Other greases use calcium or **molybdenum thickening agents**. Some add small amounts of copper and/or lead to enhance the grease's ability to withstand extreme pressures.

Automotive wheel bearing grease is a thickened lubricant, designated as a plastic solid. This means that while it is thick enough at room temperature to maintain its shape if left undisturbed, it is thin enough to be squeezed into and out of small spaces. Its consistency is similar to a glob of gel toothpaste.

The thickness of grease is graded by the **National Lubricating Grease Institute (NLGI)** TABLE 27-1.

Since it does not flow at room temperature, the grease needs to be packed into the spaces around the rollers when the wheel bearing assemblies are installed. This also needs to be done when the grease wears out and must be replaced. Packing a wheel bearing assembly can be done by hand or with a **bearing packer**, which is a tool that forces grease into the spaces between the bearing rollers. Packing a bearing assembly should be done only after thoroughly cleaning and inspecting the rollers and races for wear, damage, or corrosion. If any of these are present, the bearing assembly should be replaced.

TABLE 27-1: NLGI Rating System

NLGI Number	Consistency
00	Semifluid
0	Very soft
1	Semisoft
2	Soft—Common wheel bearing grease
3	Semifirm
4	Firm
5	Very firm

Courtesy of the National Lubricating Grease Institute

Adjustment

All wheel bearings need the proper **end play** or **preload** to operate correctly. End play, in the context of wheel bearings, refers to the amount of inward and outward movement of the hub due to the clearance within the bearing assembly. Preload refers to the absence of clearance in the bearing and the specified amount of pressure forcing the bearing components together. Sealed bearings and double-row bearing assemblies come from the manufacturer with the proper clearance machined into them. These wheel bearings are designed so that when the components are tightened together, the races butt up against each other in such a way that the proper clearance is maintained. For these wheel bearings, it is only critical that the retaining bolt or bolts are torqued to the proper specification. This is usually quite high and can typically exceed 200 foot pounds (ft-lb; 271.1 newton meters [Nm]). Be sure to check the manufacturer's torque specifications for the application you are working on.

On adjustable wheel bearings, the proper clearance must be set using the **adjusting nut**. In this case, the adjusting nut is only tightened lightly so that a small amount of clearance or preload is maintained between the rollers and races, depending on the manufacturer's specifications. The adjusting nut is then locked in place by a locking mechanism so that it cannot loosen. This is critical to prevent the wheel from falling off and causing injury. The most common locking mechanism uses a **keyed washer** (hardened), adjusting nut, **lock cage**, and cotter pin FIGURE 27-12. On

FIGURE 27-12 Typical cotter pin-style wheel bearing locking mechanism.

four-wheel drive vehicles, the locking mechanism commonly includes a keyed washer (hardened), adjusting nut, **keyed lock washer** (or tang washer), and **lock nut** FIGURE 27-13. To learn more about the procedure for adjusting wheel bearings, see Skill Drill 27-1.

Diagnosis

Wheel bearings can be damaged from excessive loads such as overloading the vehicle, shock loads such as hitting a large pot hole, improper adjustment, or just plain wear over time. The wheel bearings must hold up under difficult circumstances, so suspect faulty bearings whenever an unusual rumbling, whirring, howling, or rough sound comes from the wheel areas when the vehicle is being driven. The noise usually can be heard once the vehicle gets up to 15–20 mph (24.1–32.2 kph) and gets louder as the vehicle speeds up.

Loose or worn wheel bearings can also cause the vehicle to wander, shimmy, or vibrate. For these concerns, it is best to lift the wheels off the ground and check the wheel bearings for looseness by grabbing the tire at the 6 o'clock and 12 o'clock positions and lightly wiggling it back and forth. Watch the inside of the wheel to see if the play is coming from the wheel bearings and not the ball joints. Then grab the wheel at the 3 o'clock and 9 o'clock positions and again lightly wiggle the wheel back and forth. Watch to see if the play is coming from the wheel bearings and not the tie rod ends. If there is play in the wheel bearings and the vehicle uses sealed bearings, they will need to be replaced. If the vehicle uses serviceable bearings, the maximum allowable play is approximately 0.010" (0.254 mm). If greater than that, they will need to be disassembled, cleaned, inspected, repacked, reinstalled, and readjusted if they are still in good condition.

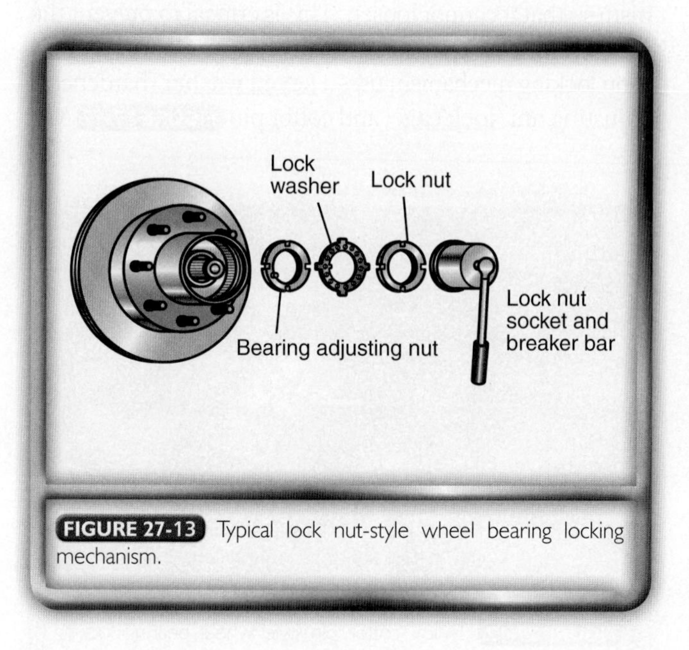
Lock washer
Lock nut
Lock nut socket and breaker bar
Bearing adjusting nut

FIGURE 27-13 Typical lock nut-style wheel bearing locking mechanism.

One way to isolate a wheel bearing noise from a transmission noise is to drive the vehicle at the speed at which it is making the noise and then shift into a higher or lower transmission gear while maintaining the same speed. If the noise speeds up or slows down, then it is a transmission-related issue. If it stays relatively the same, accelerate, coast, and decelerate the vehicle. If the noise changes, suspect the differential or universal joints. If the noise stays relatively steady, it is most likely related to the wheel bearings.

To determine which side the bearing noise is coming from, you can sometimes drive the vehicle at the speed at which it is making the noise and then lightly rock the car side to side using the steering wheel. If the noise gets louder when the car is steered right, then it is usually the left side with the bad bearing, and vise versa. Only perform this test in a safe place such as an abandoned parking lot. Another challenge is distinguishing a wheel bearing noise or a tire noise. The best approach to this problem is to drive over different road surfaces such as asphalt and concrete. If the noise changes, it is likely a tire problem. If the noise does not change, it is likely to be a faulty wheel bearing.

If you cannot determine the source of the noise on a test-drive, you might be able to determine the source of the noise by placing the vehicle on a hoist and rotating the wheels. If the vehicle has a MacPherson strut suspension, raise and support the vehicle and spin the wheel by hand while holding on to the coil spring with the other hand, feeling for a vibration or roughness. The spring tends to magnify the wheel bearing roughness, which can be felt with some practice. If the suspect wheel is a drive wheel, have an assistant drive the vehicle in gear while on the hoist, and listen to the wheel bearings with a stethoscope. Since the vehicle is running on the hoist, this can be a hazardous situation and must only be performed under the close guidance of your supervisor.

Failure Analysis

Wheel bearings can be inspected and determinations made about why the wheel bearing failed. Getting to the source of the problem is important to ensure that the same thing does not happen to the new wheel bearings. Failure analysis starts with removing the faulty wheel bearing and cleaning it and the races thoroughly. Once they are clean, visually inspect the wheel bearing components and compare your findings to the wheel bearing manufacturer's failure analysis chart. This information should lead you to what caused the wheel bearing failure.

Once the cause of the wheel bearing failure has been determined, measures will need to be taken to ensure that the failure does not repeat itself. For example, if the bearing and race surfaces show signs of rust or corrosion, you will want to inspect and replace the grease seals along with replacing the wheel bearing assembly. Also, if the wheel bearing is so worn that there are metal shavings in the wheel hub and grease, a thorough cleaning of the wheel hub will be required so that all of the metal shavings are removed and will not ruin the new bearing assembly.

Some wheel bearing failures involve the races spinning in either the machined bore of the wheel hub or on the surface of the spindle/axle. This can lead to wear of the wheel hub or spindle/axle, which requires replacement of these components. Be sure to inspect the wheel hub and spindle/axle closely for any damage every time the wheel bearings are removed and serviced.

Maintenance and Repair

Tools

Here is a list of common tools used to maintain and repair wheel bearings:

- Bearing packer
- Seal puller
- Wheel bearing race installer/seal installer set
- Wheel bearing lock nut sockets
- Cotter pin removal tool
- Dust cap pliers

Repacking and Adjusting Wheel Bearings

Serviceable wheel bearings should be serviced periodically according to the manufacturer's scheduled maintenance chart, whenever brake work is being performed, or if a faulty wheel bearing is suspected. When servicing wheel bearings, it is critical that the proper grease is used. Also avoid mixing different types of grease by thoroughly cleaning all old grease from the wheel bearings. Another option is to use a bearing packer, with the same kind of grease, to force the old grease out of the wheel bearings FIGURE 27-14. Make sure the grease in the bearing packer is not contaminated with dirt or debris and is correct for the vehicle being serviced.

When reinstalling wheel bearings, it is critical to follow the manufacturer's adjustment procedure. Always use new grease seals and cotter pins (if used). Doing so will prevent grease leaks and ensure that the adjusting nut does not back off, causing an unsafe driving situation.

To remove, clean, inspect, repack, and install wheel bearings, and to install the locking mechanism, follow the steps in Skill Drills 1–7. To remove, clean, and inspect the wheel bearings, follow the steps in SKILL DRILL 27-1.

To pack grease by hand, follow the steps in SKILL DRILL 27-2. Some technicians use a bearing packer as shown in Figure 27-14. It is important to ensure:

- That the bearing packer has the proper grease and that it is uncontaminated.
- That the wheel bearing is placed on the packer with the narrow side down.
- That the packer cone is placed on the top of the wheel bearing.
- That the packer's instructions are followed to pack the bearing. After packing, place the bearing in a clean location to prevent contamination.

FIGURE 27-14 A bearing packer.

Prove
Know
See
Do

SKILL DRILL 27-1 Removing, Cleaning, and Inspecting Wheel Bearings

1. Remove the wheel bearing dust cap with dust cap pliers or a narrow cold chisel and hammer.

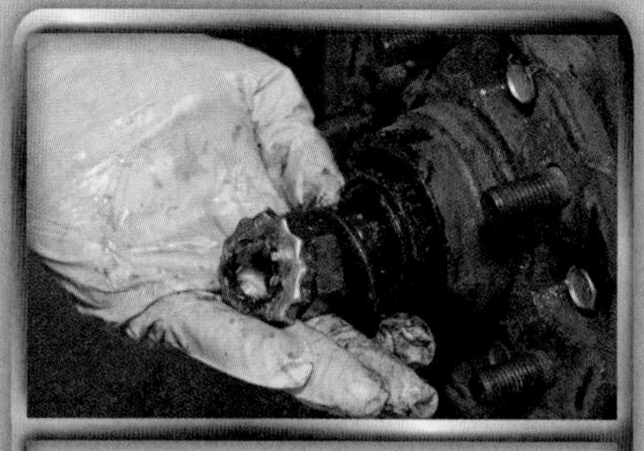

2. Remove the locking mechanism. Remove the adjusting nut, keyed washer, and outer bearing. Reinstall the adjusting nut approximately five turns back onto the spindle.

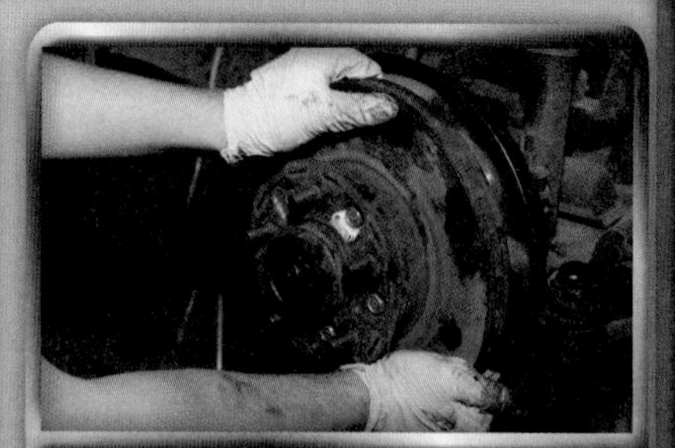

3. Grasp the drum/rotor at the 1 o'clock and 7 o'clock positions or 11 o'clock and 5 o'clock positions. While holding downward pressure, quickly pull the drum/rotor toward you. The adjusting nut should catch the inner bearing race and pop the grease seal and bearing out of the hub, leaving them sitting on the spindle.

4. Wipe any old grease off of the wheel bearings, races, and spindle with a rag and give them a quick visual inspection. Consult the bearing diagnosis chart to identify any faults.

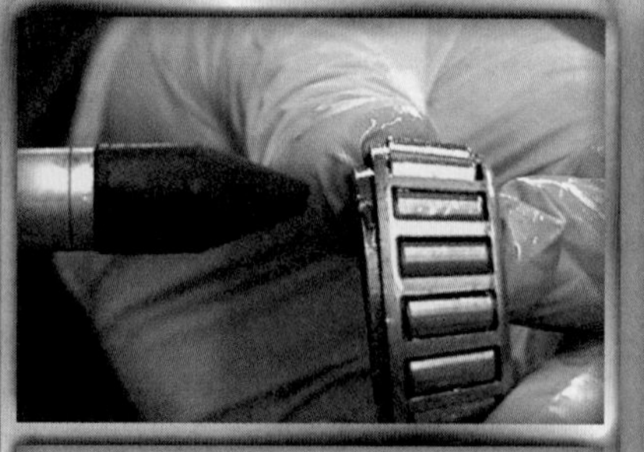

5. If the wheel bearings are in serviceable condition, completely clean the wheel bearings, races, and hub. If using solvent to clean any of the components, make sure there is no solvent-contaminated grease left on the parts.

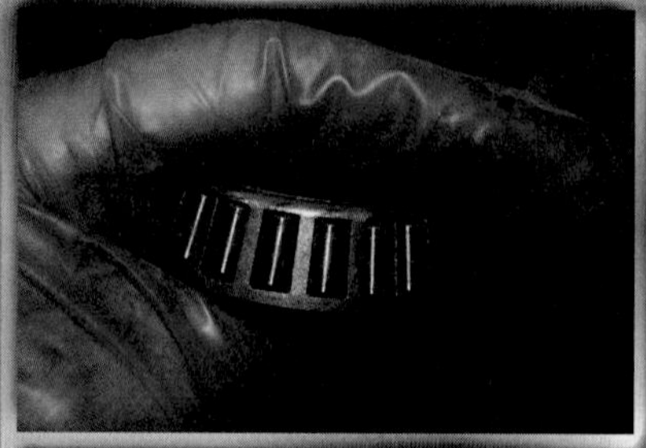

6. Give the parts a final inspection, and consult the bearing diagnosis chart if there are any signs of damage. Using the specified grease, pack both wheel bearings, being careful to keep dirt and debris out of the grease (see Skill Drills 27-2 and 27-3).

SKILL DRILL 27-2 Packing Grease by Hand

1 Using a pair of latex or nitrile (nitro) gloves, place a small glob of grease in the palm of your nondominant hand. Place the index finger of your other hand through the bearing center hole with the larger diameter facing down.

2 Push the large diameter of the bearing down the edge of the grease into your palm. This should force grease into the space between the bearings and races. Continue this process until grease comes out of the top of the bearing.

3 Carefully turn the bearing as a unit to a new space, and keep forcing grease between the bearings. Do this until all of the spaces are full.

4 Smear some grease around the outside of the bearing. Repeat this process on the other bearing.

To install wheel bearings, follow the steps in SKILL DRILL 27-3.

To install the locking mechanism, follow the steps in SKILL DRILL 27-4.

TECHNICIAN TIP

Some technicians simulate the preload torque by placing a 12" crescent wrench on the nut and using the hanging weight of the crescent wrench when it is parallel to the ground. Do not let it drop into position; just lower the handle to where it stops turning the nut. This should be when the handle is approximately level. If not, reposition the crescent wrench on the nut and allow it to lower until it stops parallel.

SKILL DRILL 27-3 Installing Wheel Bearings

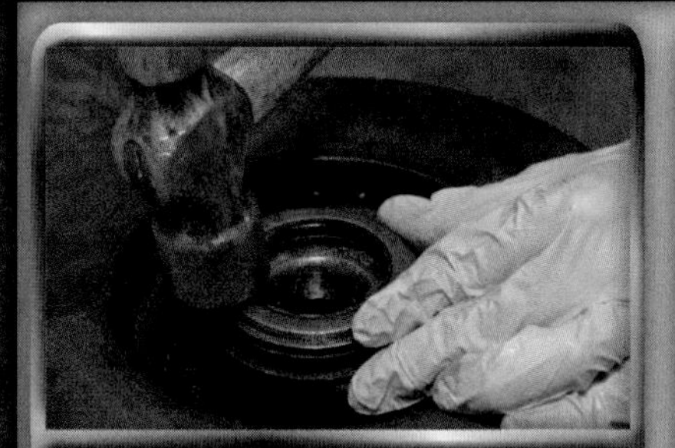

1. Place a small amount of extra grease in the center of the hub. Do not fill it completely (Not very much grease is needed to keep the bearings lubricated, so go easy on the amount of grease you put in teh hub). Place the inner wheel bearing in its race, narrow side toward the race. Install the new grease seal, being careful not to damage it. Place a small amount of grease on the lip of the seal to provide it with initial lubrication.

2. Without getting grease on the drum/rotor, carefully install it on the spindle, making sure the inner bearing fully seats against the spindle flange. Install the outer bearing on the spindle and into the race.

3. Install the keyed washer and adjusting nut on the spindle and tighten until finger tight. Tighten the adjusting nut to the specified seating torque (usually about 20 ft-lb [27.1 Nm]) while turning the drum/rotor. This squeezes the excess grease out from between the wheel bearings and races while seating the bearings. Loosen the adjusting nut approximately one-sixth to one-quarter turn without turning the drum/rotor, and then tighten the adjusting nut to the specified preload torque. This is usually about 15–25 in.-lb (1.69–2.82 Nm).

SKILL DRILL 27-4 Installing the Locking Mechanism

1. Install the locking mechanism. If it is a *cotter pin*, insert the new cotter pin through the **castellated nut** or locking cage and spindle. The short leg of the cotter pin should be against the castellated nut and the long leg should be toward you. With the cotter pin fully engaged in the notch, bend the outer leg toward you and up over the end of the spindle. Cut it off just short of the spindle. Also cut the short leg off so it does not extend beyond the nut or cage. Make sure the cotter pin will not hit the inside of the dust cap.

2. If it is a *bendable tang locking style*, then place the tang washer against the adjusting nut and thread the locking nut up against it. Torque the locking nut to the specified torque, and bend the appropriate tang out toward you against the flat side of the locking nut with a small pry bar to lock the adjustment in place.

3. If it is a *locking nut style*, then tighten the lock nut to the specified torque. This is usually a substantial torque of 50 ft-lb (67.79 Nm) or more.

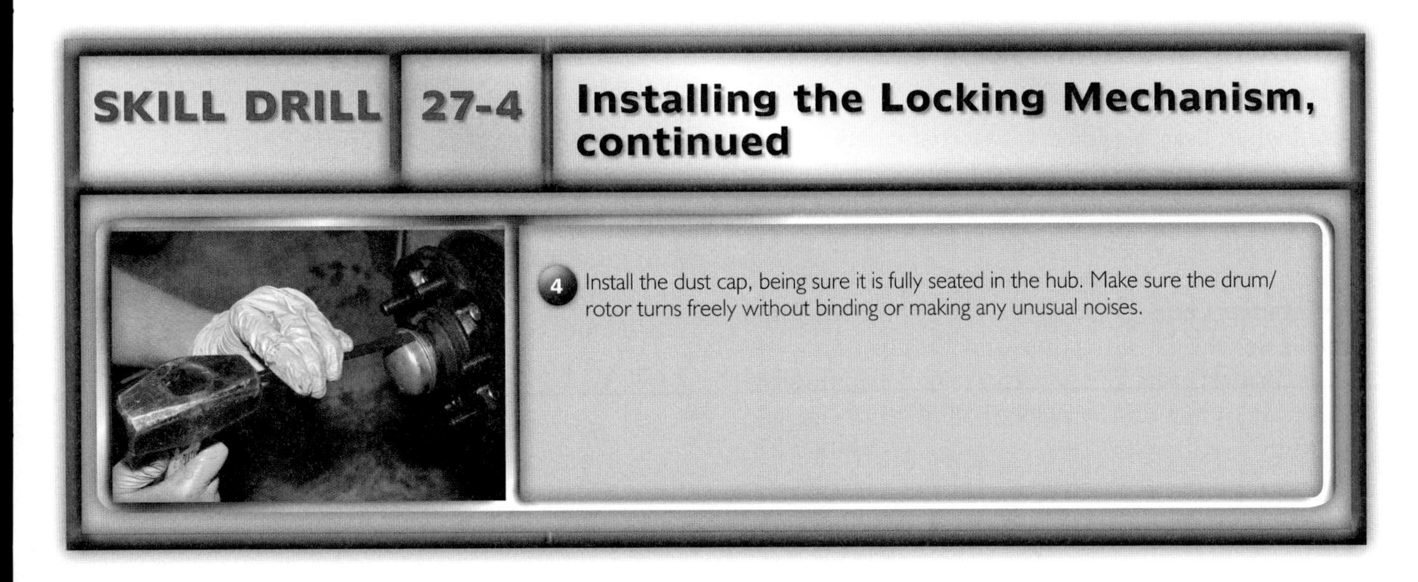
SKILL DRILL 27-4 Installing the Locking Mechanism, continued

4 Install the dust cap, being sure it is fully seated in the hub. Make sure the drum/rotor turns freely without binding or making any unusual noises.

Replacing Wheel Bearings and Races

Wheel bearings and races need to be replaced only when they are damaged. If one part of the wheel bearing is damaged, all parts must be replaced. So if the tapered roller bearings are damaged, both the bearing and the race of that bearing need to be replaced at the same time. On serviceable bearings, the inner race, roller bearings, and bearing cage are one unit, which generally slips off of the spindle. The outer race is usually press-fit into the hub and will need to be driven or pressed out and a new one press-fit back in. It is critical that the seat in the hub be spotlessly clean with no burrs or the bearing race will not seat properly and the bearing will fail prematurely.

To replace a wheel bearing and race, follow the steps in SKILL DRILL 27-5.

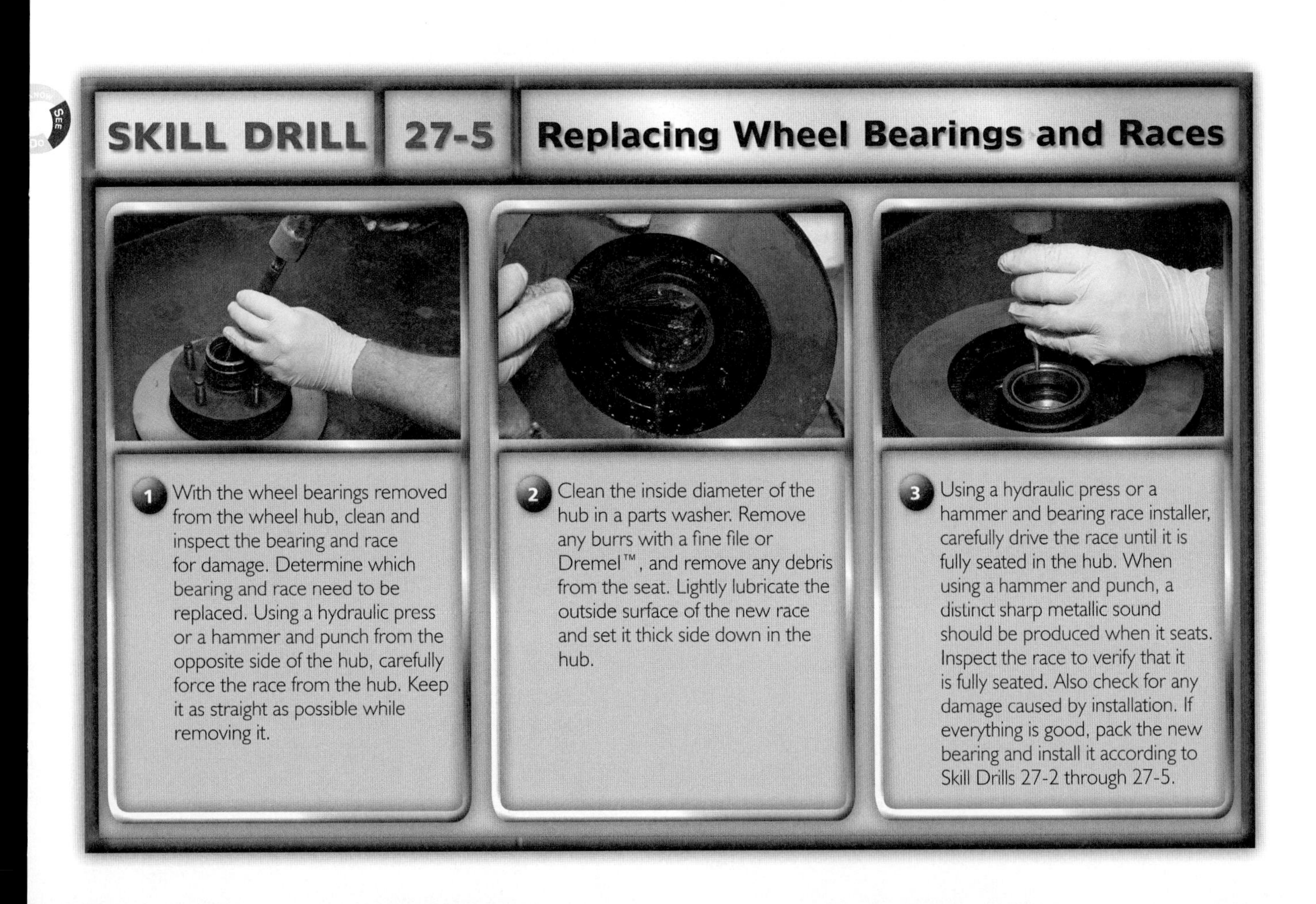
SKILL DRILL 27-5 Replacing Wheel Bearings and Races

1 With the wheel bearings removed from the wheel hub, clean and inspect the bearing and race for damage. Determine which bearing and race need to be replaced. Using a hydraulic press or a hammer and punch from the opposite side of the hub, carefully force the race from the hub. Keep it as straight as possible while removing it.

2 Clean the inside diameter of the hub in a parts washer. Remove any burrs with a fine file or Dremel™, and remove any debris from the seat. Lightly lubricate the outside surface of the new race and set it thick side down in the hub.

3 Using a hydraulic press or a hammer and bearing race installer, carefully drive the race until it is fully seated in the hub. When using a hammer and punch, a distinct sharp metallic sound should be produced when it seats. Inspect the race to verify that it is fully seated. Also check for any damage caused by installation. If everything is good, pack the new bearing and install it according to Skill Drills 27-2 through 27-5.

Removing and Reinstalling Sealed Wheel Bearings

Sealed wheel bearings come in two configurations. The first is a replaceable sealed bearing only. On most front wheels, this wheel bearing is pressed between the hub and wheel flange and is the more difficult of the two to replace. The second configuration consists of a unitized wheel bearing hub including a sealed wheel bearing, a removable wheel bearing hub, and possibly the wheel flange. In most cases, this type can be unbolted from the suspension system and a new one bolted in its place, and it is ready to go.

The replaceable bearing style needs to be pressed apart with a hydraulic press or a special sealed bearing removal/installing tool. If using the hydraulic press method, the steering knuckle will need to be removed from the vehicle so it can be placed on the hydraulic press. If the special sealed bearing tool is used, most bearings can be removed while the steering knuckle is still installed on the vehicle, which can save the technician a fair amount of time. To remove and reinstall a sealed wheel bearing assembly using the unitized wheel bearing hub style, follow the steps in SKILL DRILL 27-6.

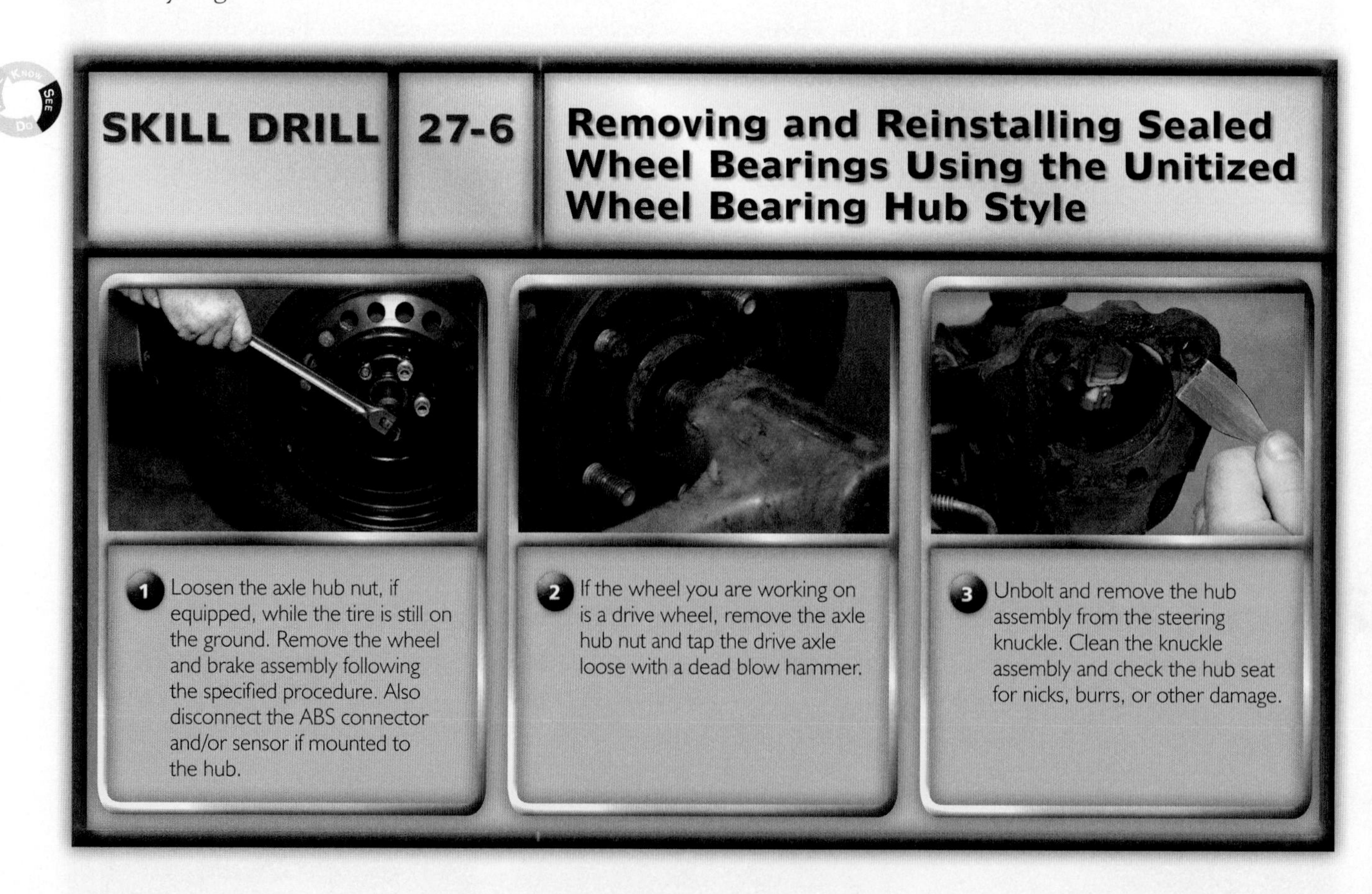
PROVE KNOW SEE DO
SKILL DRILL 27-6 Removing and Reinstalling Sealed Wheel Bearings Using the Unitized Wheel Bearing Hub Style
1 Loosen the axle hub nut, if equipped, while the tire is still on the ground. Remove the wheel and brake assembly following the specified procedure. Also disconnect the ABS connector and/or sensor if mounted to the hub.
2 If the wheel you are working on is a drive wheel, remove the axle hub nut and tap the drive axle loose with a dead blow hammer.
3 Unbolt and remove the hub assembly from the steering knuckle. Clean the knuckle assembly and check the hub seat for nicks, burrs, or other damage.

SKILL DRILL 27-6 Removing and Reinstalling Sealed Wheel Bearings Using the Unitized Wheel Bearing Hub Style, continued

4 Carefully compare the new hub to the old one, then fit the new hub assembly (over the axle shaft, if equipped) to the knuckle, making sure it is fully seated in place, and torque the mounting bolts to the specified torque. Reassemble the brake assembly and ABS sensor following the specified procedure, install the wheel, and torque the lug nuts. Install the drive axle nut, if equipped. Use a new hub nut if called for by the manufacturer, and torque to specifications.

5 Reassemble the brake assembly and ABS sensor, if removed, following the specified procedure, install the wheel, and torque the lug nuts. Be sure the correct ends of the lug nuts are facing the wheel.

6 Install the drive axle nut, if equipped. Use a new hub nut if called for by the manufacturer, and torque to specifications.

Wrap-up

Ready for Review

- Wheel bearings allow wheels to roll with minimum friction.
- Wheel bearing assemblies include: outer race, inner race, roller or ball bearings, and a bearing cage.
- Categories of wheel bearings are serviceable or sealed.
- Types of wheel bearings are: cylindrical roller bearing, tapered roller bearing, ball bearing, double-row ball bearing, and double-row tapered roller bearings.
- Cylindrical roller bearing assemblies have parallel races flanking the rollers and are most commonly used in rear axles of rear-wheel drive vehicles.
- Cylindrical roller bearing assemblies rely on lubrication to cushion the rollers and transfer heat to the atmosphere.
- Tapered roller-bearing assemblies have tapered rollers housed in a bearing cage, are used for heavier loads, are used in pairs, and control side movement.
- Tapered roller bearing assemblies must be adjusted for proper running clearance.
- Ball bearings are used in light-duty vehicles, are designed as a manufacturer-sealed bearing assembly, and should be replaced as a unit.
- Wheel bearings are sealed to keep out contaminants and contain the lubricant.
- Serviceable wheel bearings need periodic maintenance, including replacing old grease seals and the cotter pin.
- Wheel bearings are lubricated by gear lube or bearing grease.
- Gear lube is classified by viscosity (thickness) and service grade.
- Bearing grease is graded by thickness; it holds its shape at room temperature.
- For correct operation, wheel bearings must be adjusted for proper end play preload.
- Wheel bearing locking mechanisms include a keyed washer, adjusting nut, lock cage, and cotter pin.
- Damage to wheel bearings may be from: vehicle overload, shock loads, improper adjustment, or wear over time.
- Wheel bearing assembly diagnosis may include wiggling the tire (with vehicle lifted) by hand, by test-driving, or placing on a hoist and rotating the wheels.
- Determine the cause of wheel bearing failure so that the new bearings are not damaged for the same reason.

Key Terms

adjusting nut The nut used to adjust the end play or preload of a wheel bearing.

anti-friction bearing Wheel bearing assemblies that use surfaces that are in rolling contact with each other to greatly reduce friction compared to surfaces in sliding contact.

ball bearings The rolling components of a wheel bearing consisting of hardened balls that roll in matching grooves in the inner and outer races.

bearing cage The component in a wheel bearing that maintains the proper spacing between the roller bearings or ball bearings.

bearing packer A tool that forces grease into the spaces between the bearing rollers.

bushing A sleeve type bearing made of metal or plastic bearing material used to support a rotating shaft.

castellated nut An adjusting nut with slots cut into the top such that it resembles a castle; used with a cotter pin to prevent the nut from turning.

cotter pin A one-use soft metal pin that can be bent into shape and is used to retain bearing adjusting nuts.

cylindrical roller bearing assembly A type of wheel bearing with races and rollers that are cylindrical in shape and roll between inner and outer races, which are parallel to each other.

double-row ball bearing assembly A single ball bearing assembly using two rows of ball bearings riding in two channels in the races.

end play The in-and-out movement of the hub caused by clearance within the wheel bearing assembly.

fill plug Usually a threaded plug that can be removed to allow the level of a fluid to be checked and filled. This could also be a rubber snap fit plug.

friction bearing A bearing that uses sliding motion between components, such as a clutch pilot bearing.

garter spring A coiled spring that is fitted to the inside of the sealing lip of many seals, used to hold the lip in contact with the shaft.

gear lube A type of lubricant primarily used to lubricate transmission and differential gears but also used to lubricate some wheel bearings.

grease A lubricating liquid thickened to make it suitable for use with many wheel bearings.

grease seal A component that is designed to keep grease from leaking out and contaminants from leaking in.

inner race The inside component of a wheel bearing that has a smooth, hardened surface for rollers or balls to ride on.

interference fit A condition when two parts are held together by friction because the outside diameter of the inner component is slightly larger than the inside diameter of the outer component.

keyed lock washer The washer that fits between the adjusting nut and the lock nut; the face of the washer is drilled with a series of holes that mate to a short pin from the adjusting nut, locking it to the spindle. Also referred to as a tang washer.

keyed washer The washer that fits between the adjusting nut and the wheel bearing and that has the center hole keyed to fit a slot on the spindle or axle tube.

lithium soap A thickening agent for grease to give it the proper consistency.

lock cage The stamped sheet metal cap that fits over the bearing adjustment nut and is secured by a cotter pin going through it and the spindle/axle.

lock nut The nut that holds the adjusting nut from turning; usually tightened much tighter than the adjusting nut.

molybdenum thickening agent A compound used in some greases to give it the needed consistency.

National Lubricating Grease Institute (NLGI) An organization that grades the thickness of automotive and industrial grease.

outer race The outside component of a wheel bearing that has a smooth, hardened surface for rollers or balls to ride on.

preload A condition where the wheel bearing components are forced together under pressure and therefore have no end play.

roller bearings The rolling components of a wheel bearing consisting of hardened cylindrical or tapered rollers.

running clearance The amount of space between wheel bearing components while in operation.

sealed bearings Wheel bearings that are assembled by the manufacturer with the proper lubrication and sealed for life; cannot normally be disassembled.

serviceable bearings Wheel bearings that can be disassembled, cleaned, inspected, packed, reinstalled, and adjusted.

tapered roller bearing assembly A type of wheel bearing with races and rollers that are tapered in such a manner that all of the tapered angles meet at a common point, which allows them to roll freely and yet control thrust.

unitized wheel bearing hub An assembly consisting of the hub, wheel bearing(s), and possibly the wheel flange, which is preassembled and ready to be installed on a vehicle.

viscosity The measurement of the thickness of a liquid.

wheel bearing A component that allows the wheels to rotate freely while supporting the weight of the vehicle, made up of an inner race, outer race, rollers or balls, and a cage.

ASE-Type Questions

1. Tech A says that cylindrical roller bearings can carry more weight than similarly sized ball bearings. Tech B says that tapered roller bearings used in opposing pairs, control side thrust. Who is correct?
   a. Tech A
   b. Tech B
   c. Both A and B
   d. Neither A nor B
2. Tech A says that a tapered roller bearing assembly has less rolling resistance than a similarly sized ball bearing assembly. Tech B says that the bearing assembly in a unitized wheel bearing assembly can normally be disassembled, cleaned, and repacked. Who is correct?
   a. Tech A
   b. Tech B
   c. Both A and B
   d. Neither A nor B
3. Tech A says that over time a grease seal can wear a groove in the sealing surface of the axle or shaft. Tech B says that grease seals need to be replaced every time the bearing is removed. Who is correct?
   a. Tech A
   b. Tech B
   c. Both A and B
   d. Neither A nor B
4. Tech A says that in a full floating axle, the axle does not support the weight of the vehicle. Tech B says that when installing tapered wheel bearings, the final torque should be about 20 ft/lbs. Who is correct?
   a. Tech A
   b. Tech B
   c. Both A and B
   d. Neither A nor B
5. Tech A says that serviceable wheel bearings can be repacked by removing the dust cap, filling it with grease, and reinstalling it. Tech B says that the cotter pin must be replaced with a new one every time it is removed. Who is correct?
   a. Tech A
   b. Tech B
   c. Both A and B
   d. Neither A nor B
6. Tech A says that the grease level in the final drive is okay as long as you can touch the level with your finger. Tech B says that the grease level should normally be no more than ¼" below the threads on the fill plug hole. Who is correct?
   a. Tech A
   b. Tech B
   c. Both A and B
   d. Neither A nor B
7. Tech A says that wheel bearings need to be replaced as a set, bearing and race. Tech B says that the wheel bearings and races on both sides of the vehicle must be replaced if one side fails. Who is correct?
   a. Tech A
   b. Tech B
   c. Both A and B
   d. Neither A nor B
8. Tech A says that unitized hubs have a wheel nut with a higher installation torque than serviceable wheel bearings. Tech B says that unitized hubs have the proper bearing end play designed into the assembly once they are torqued properly. Who is correct?
   a. Tech A
   b. Tech B
   c. Both A and B
   d. Neither A nor B
9. Tech A says when installing a bearing race you should use a 3-lb hammer and a brass drift. Tech B says that when installing a bearing race you should use a 3-lb hammer and a ⅜" drive extension. Who is correct?
   a. Tech A
   b. Tech B
   c. Both A and B
   d. Neither A nor B
10. Tech A says that when a race is fully seated, a sharp metallic sound will be produced when installation is complete. Tech B says that to be sure a race is fully seated, the wheel bearing adjusting nut should be tightened to at least 100 ft-lbs of torque, which will finish seating it. Who is correct?
    a. Tech A
    b. Tech B
    c. Both A and B
    d. Neither A nor B

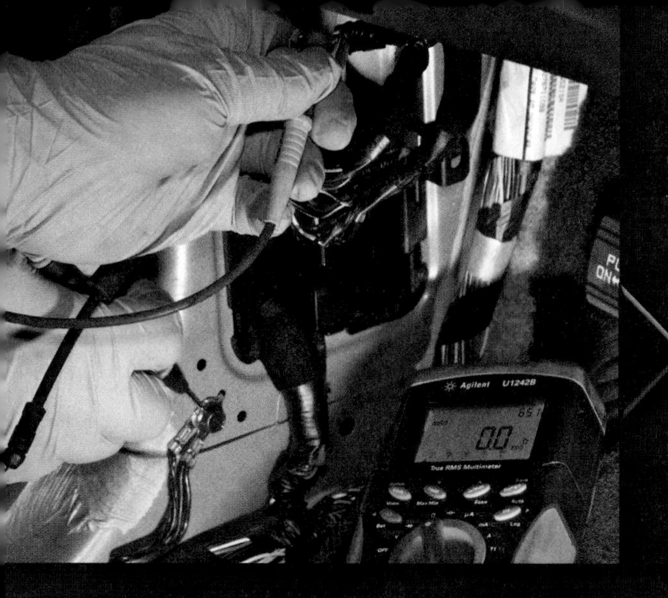

CHAPTER 28

NATEF Tasks

Brakes
Electronic Brakes, Traction and Stability Control Systems

Task		Page
■ Identify traction control/vehicle stability control system components.	MLR AST	802–805

Knowledge Objectives

After reading this chapter, you will be able to:

1. Describe the safety advantages of EBC systems. (p 792)
2. Describe the three most common EBC systems. (pp 792–793)
3. Describe additional functions that can be built into basic EBC systems. (pp 792–793)
4. Describe the purpose and function of the steering wheel position sensor. (p 793)
5. Describe understeer and oversteer conditions. (p 793)
6. Describe the basic principles of operation of anti-lock brake systems. (pp 793–794)
7. Describe the purpose, function, and types of ABS master cylinders. (pp 794–797)
8. Describe the purpose, function, and types of hydraulic control units. (pp 797–799)
9. Describe the difference between hydraulic control units with different numbers of channels. (pp 798–799)
10. Describe the purpose, function, and types of accumulators. (p 790)
11. Describe the purpose, function, and types of wheel speed sensors. (pp 799–801)
12. Describe the purpose and function of the brake switch. (p 801)
13. Describe the basic principles of operation of traction control. (pp 802–803)
14. Describe the methods used by the traction control system to reduce engine torque. (p 803)
15. Describe the purpose and function of the yaw sensor. (pp 793, 804)
16. Describe the basic principles of operation of electronic stability control. (pp 803–805)

Electronic Brake Control

Know
See
Do

Skills Objectives

There are no skills objectives for this chapter.

Introduction

Electronic brake control (EBC) systems have greatly increased the safety of vehicles over the years by integrating computer controls into the braking system. Standard hydraulic brake systems have limitations on how effectively they can stop a vehicle. The driver can only input braking force to the system through the brake pedal, which applies hydraulic pressure at predetermined ratios to the front and rear brakes. In a panic situation, the driver is unable to apply the exact amount of force to maintain the maximum amount of braking. Too little force and the vehicle does not stop as quickly. Too much force and the tires skid, making the vehicle's stopping distance longer. At the same time, if the front wheels skid, the driver will lose the ability to steer the vehicle. If the rear wheels skid, the car could spin out and possibly roll over.

Even if the driver could apply the perfect amount of braking force, there is no way to accommodate different amounts of traction at each wheel, such as when one or two wheels are on pavement and the other tires are on loose gravel. This situation can also lead to a loss of control of the vehicle.

In the quest for increased safety, manufacturers developed a series of EBC systems. The first-generation EBC system was the anti-lock brake system (ABS). The ABS system was designed to prevent wheels from locking up under braking conditions and shorten most panic stop distances. ABS systems also helped the driver maintain steering control of the vehicle. The Principles of Braking chapter covers this topic in detail.

Basic Operation of Electronic Brake Control Systems

ABS systems use a computer that monitors the speed of each wheel as the brakes are applied. If one or more wheels begin to lock up, the computer sends electrical signals to **solenoid valves** that momentarily hold or release hydraulic pressure to that wheel until it speeds up and starts rolling again. Once that happens, the computer allows hydraulic pressure to be applied to that wheel again, slowing it down. This process is repeated very rapidly as the vehicle is brought to a stop. Because the tires remain in rolling contact with the road surface, the vehicle can be steered, allowing the driver to maintain directional control (steerability) of the vehicle and thereby decreasing the chances of a collision. These actions are completely dependent on the driver applying pressure to the brake pedal.

While the basic ABS system does a good job of managing the braking effort of the driver in a panic stop situation, it is limited to using the hydraulic pressure the driver exerts on the system. This means that the standard ABS system by itself cannot increase the hydraulic pressure in the ABS system; nor can it apply hydraulic pressure separate from the driver. As long as the driver is exerting firm pressure on the brake pedal, ABS can work to minimize the stopping distance and steerability of the vehicle.

The second enhancement to the EBC system was the **traction control system (TCS)**. With the addition of a high-pressure pump and a few **isolation valves** to

You Are the Automotive Technician

A long-time customer brings his 2007 Ford Explorer into the shop to get his brakes inspected. He claims that the brake pedal pulsates when he applies the brakes. You ask him if he has had any recent work done on the vehicle. He explains that he recently had new tires put on. He also explains that while leaving the parking lot, a car pulled out in front of him and he had to lock up the brakes to avoid hitting him. He was startled by heavy brake pulsations, which have gotten worse each time he uses the brakes. He is wondering if there is a problem with the anti-lock brakes.

1. Is there a problem with the ABS system? What will you say to the customer?
2. What do you suspect is causing the pedal pulsations, and how did it occur?
3. What could cause the ABS warning lamp to be illuminated?

the basic ABS system, manufacturers found that they could assist the driver in minimizing wheel slip while the vehicle is being accelerated. This is especially effective on slippery road surfaces such as gravel, snow, and ice. In most vehicles, the vehicle's traction is only as good as the traction on the tire with the least traction. So if one tire is on a patch of ice, the vehicle may not have enough traction to move, and will ultimately become stuck. The TCS system applies brake pressure to the slipping tire, which causes more of the engine's torque to be transmitted to the wheel or wheels with the most traction. If necessary, the TCS system can also request that the engine's power train control module reduce the power output of the engine to further enhance traction. These actions are automatic and do not require any input from the driver.

The next enhancement to the EBC system was the **electronic stability control (ESC) system**. ESC takes the ABS and TCS systems to the next level. By adding sensor information regarding the driver's directional intent (from the **steering wheel position sensor**) and sensor information regarding the vehicle's actual direction (from the **yaw sensor**), the EBC module (EBCM) can detect the start of an **understeer**, **oversteer**, or potential rollover condition. Understeer and oversteer are conditions that happen when a vehicle is traveling too fast for a particular corner. During understeer, the vehicle's front wheels are turned more sharply than the vehicle's path FIGURE 28-1. The front tires are actually sliding somewhat sideways toward the outside of the corner. The greater the understeer, the more the tires slide. Understeer is also referred to as "push," as in "the vehicle is pushing in the corners."

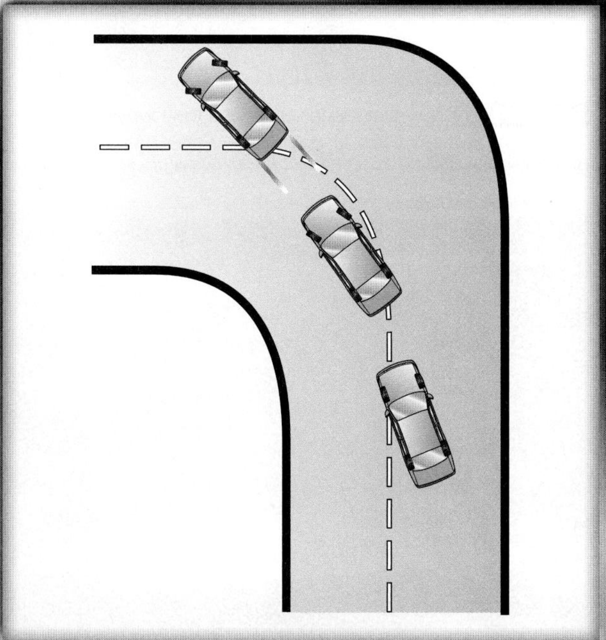

Oversteer is just the opposite. It occurs when the vehicle is turning more sharply than the front wheels are being steered. This happens when the rear tires are sliding sideways toward the outside of the corner. Oversteer is also referred to as "loose," as in "the vehicle is getting loose in the corners." Most passenger vehicles are designed to have a bit of understeer because this condition is easier for a driver to recover from than an oversteer.

Using information provided by the sensors of the ESC system, plus the wheel speed sensors, the EBCM monitors the stability of the vehicle and can command individual brakes to be applied and request decreased engine torque as necessary. For example, if a vehicle is traveling too fast around a right-hand corner and the front wheels are starting to lose traction (understeer), the control system can apply the right rear brake to help pivot the vehicle around the right rear tire, assisting it to turn and at the same time slowing the vehicle slightly. If additional measures are needed, additional brakes can be applied and the engine torque reduced. The control system performs these functions automatically without any driver input other than steering the vehicle in the direction intended.

FIGURE 28-1 During understeer, the vehicle's front wheels are turned more sharply than the vehicle's path.

Caring for the Customer

It is important for customers to know that ABS, TCS, and ESC are not guarantees of avoiding an accident. These systems are designed to help drivers who are driving in a responsible manner to avoid an accident. Drivers can easily exceed the ability of these systems.

Anti-Lock Braking System Overview

The ABS system is designed to prevent wheels locking or skidding, no matter how hard the brakes are applied or how slippery the road surface, and to maintain steering control of the vehicle. The primary components of the ABS braking system are:

- ABS master cylinder: Creates hydraulic pressure for each of the two hydraulic brake circuits.
- EBCM or electronic control unit (ECU): An onboard computer that is programmed to monitor sensor data and send output control signals to

electronic solenoid valves, which modify brake pressure to individual wheel brake units.

- **Hydraulic control unit (HCU)** or modulator: Contains electric solenoid valves controlled by the EBCM to modify hydraulic pressure in each hydraulic circuit **FIGURE 28-2**. Most systems also contain an **accumulator** to store brake fluid under pressure.
- Power booster: Boosts driver brake pedal force on the master cylinder.
- **Wheel speed sensor**: A device that monitors wheel speed and sends that signal to the EBCM.
- **Brake switch**: An on/off switch that informs the EBCM of whether or not the driver is applying the brakes.

The EBCM may be located inside the vehicle, mounted near the HCU, or it could be integrated into the HCU. In many cases, it is a separate module from the power train control module and may be part of the vehicle's **body control module (BCM)**. The body control module is the computer that controls the electrical system in the body of the vehicle. The EBCM receives input signals from the ABS sensors, compares that data to information stored in its memory, decides what actions are necessary, and sends output commands to the HCU.

The HCU or modulator is connected in-line with the brake lines between the master cylinder and the wheel brake units. It houses electric solenoid valves that control the flow of brake fluid to each wheel. The HCU receives operating signals from the EBCM to control the brakes under ABS conditions.

The power booster and master cylinder assembly is mounted on the firewall. In most current applications, these components operate similarly to non-ABS power boosters and tandem master cylinders. Some manufacturers use a portless master cylinder to allow brake fluid to return to the master cylinder reservoir more easily than a master cylinder fitted with a compensating port. When the brakes are operating without ABS action, the brake pressure is controlled by the driver's foot pressure, which is assisted by the power booster. In other words, the ABS system only affects brake pressure when one or more wheels are starting to skid.

The wheel speed sensor consists of a toothed tone wheel (or tone ring) that rotates with the road wheels and a pick-up assembly that generates a speed signal. The wheel speed sensor is located near the wheel hub in many applications **FIGURE 28-3**. The wheel speed sensor sends an electrical signal that varies with the speed of the wheel to the EBCM. Wheel speed sensors can be **variable reluctance sensors** (magnetic induction), generating an analog AC sine wave signal **FIGURE 28-4**. Wheel speed sensors can also be of the magneto-resistive or

FIGURE 28-3 A wheel speed sensor and tone wheel.

FIGURE 28-2 A hydraulic control unit (HCU).

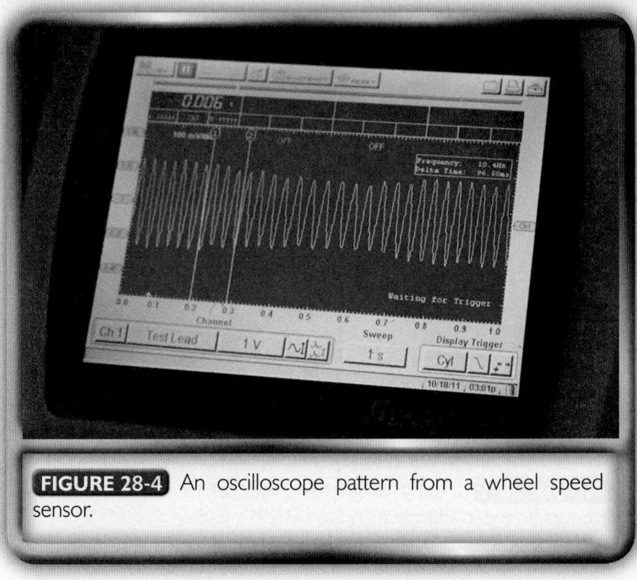
Waiting for Trigger
Ch 1
Test Lead
1 V
Channel
Sweep
Display Trigger
Cyl

FIGURE 28-4 An oscilloscope pattern from a wheel speed sensor.

Hall effect type, generating a digital square wave signal. These signals can be used by the EBCM to determine the speed of each wheel. We will cover the operation of these sensors in much greater depth in the ABS Components section.

Anti-Lock Braking System Operation

Applying brakes too hard or on a slippery surface can cause the wheels to lock. When the wheels lock, steering control is lost and, in most cases, longer stopping distances result due to the reduced friction of the sliding tire. The ABS system prevents the wheels from locking or skidding, no matter how hard the brakes are applied or how slippery the road surface. Steering stays under control and the stopping distances are generally reduced.

When the ignition switch is turned on, the ABS controller illuminates the yellow ABS warning lamp and performs an automatic self-check of the system. If the system check passes, the controller will extinguish the warning lamp indicating to the driver that the ABS system is functional. Some ABS systems will perform an additional self-check once the vehicle is traveling greater than approximately 3–5 mph (4.8–8 kph). Failures in the ABS system will cause the controller to illuminate the ABS warning light in the instrument panel.

As the wheels start to turn, the wheel speed sensors generate small electrical signals and send them to the EBCM. When the brakes are applied, the wheels' rotational speed is reduced. As the speed changes, the signal sent to the EBCM changes in like manner. If the control unit detects that a wheel might be slowing too quickly and starting to lock, it sends an output signal to the appropriate solenoid valve in the HCU to modify the hydraulic pressure to the affected wheel brake unit.

Principles of ABS Braking

Braking force and the tendency of the wheels to lock up are affected by a combination of factors such as the friction of the road surface; the type, condition, and loading of each tire; and the difference between the vehicle speed and the speed of the wheels. It should be noted that maximum traction happens with approximately 10–20% tire slip. Thus, maximum braking traction occurs when the wheels are rotating 10–20% slower than the vehicle speed. In the same way, maximum traction during acceleration occurs when the wheels are rotating 10–20% faster than the vehicle speed. At the same time, traction falls off quickly above 20% wheel slip, which is why ABS is so effective. It allows just enough slip to keep the tires at close to their maximum traction. It does so by rapidly modulating the hydraulic pressure in the vehicle's brake system.

During normal braking, as the rotational speed of each wheel falls equally, no ABS intervention is needed. In this condition, the EBCM does not energize the solenoid valves in the hydraulic unit. The master cylinder hydraulic pressure is applied to the wheel brake units, and the ABS is not involved. However, even though the ABS is passive during normal braking, the EBCM is constantly monitoring the speed of each wheel, looking for any wheel that begins to decelerate more rapidly than any of the other wheels.

If one wheel speed sensor signals more severe wheel deceleration—which means the wheel is beginning to slip—the EBCM sends current to the appropriate solenoid valve FIGURE 28-5. The first level of valve action isolates that brake circuit from the master cylinder. This stops the braking pressure at that wheel from rising and keeps it constant. If the wheel speed sensors indicate that the wheel is still decelerating too rapidly, the EBCM commands the appropriate solenoid valve to release braking pressure. The solenoid valve opens a passage from the brake circuit, releasing the hydraulic pressure to that brake unit. Brake fluid is released from the specific brake circuit back to the master cylinder. Pressure in the brake circuit is reduced so that the wheel is not being braked.

If the wheel speed sensors indicate that reducing the brake pressure is allowing the wheel to roll again, the EBCM stops sending current to the hydraulic unit and de-energizes the solenoid valves. This lets the hydraulic pressure increase so that the brake is again applied by the master cylinder pressure. This cycle repeats itself at up to 16 times per second. It is normal in an ABS system for

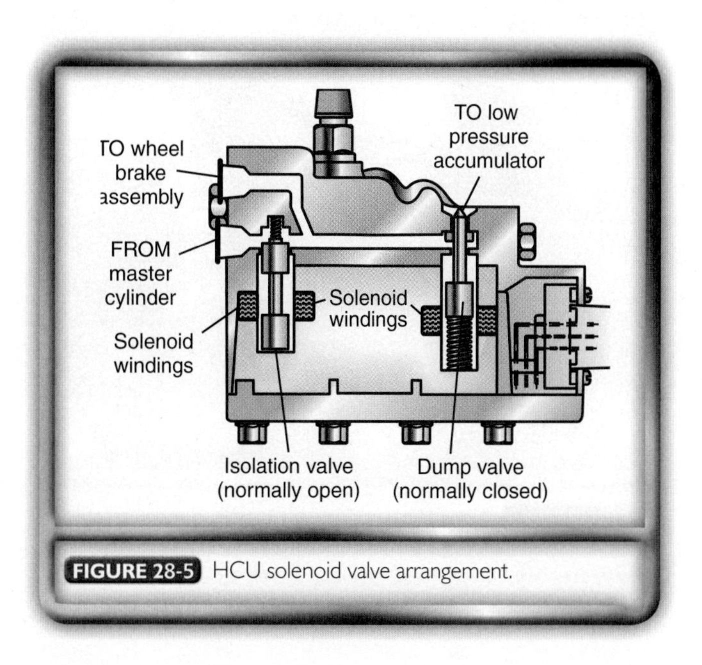
TO low pressure accumulator
TO wheel brake assembly
FROM master cylinder
Solenoid windings
Solenoid windings
Isolation valve (normally open)
Dump valve (normally closed)

FIGURE 28-5 HCU solenoid valve arrangement.

Caring for the Customer

Drivers need to be taught to expect ABS brake pedal pulsation when in a panic stop. Some drivers who have never experienced this actually let up on the brake pedal because of the rapid pulsations and accompanying noise. When in a panic stop, drivers should push hard on the brake pedal and not let up until the vehicle is stopped or the vehicle is out of danger.

the valves in the HCU to keep changing position as they modulate the brake pressure that is being applied. These changes in valve position normally cause rapid hydraulic pulsations, which can be felt by the driver through the brake pedal. The solenoid valves also make a fairly loud clicking noise as they cycle on and off.

ABS Components

ABS Master Cylinder

ABS master cylinders come in two major configurations: integral and nonintegral FIGURE 28-6. **Integral ABS systems** are mostly found on older vehicles. They combine the tandem master cylinder, HCU, and power booster in one unit. The power booster consists of a high-pressure electric pump and accumulator that operates the integrated master cylinder. Brake fluid passes from the master cylinder portion of the assembly to the HCU portion where pressures are modified by the computer-controlled solenoid valves.

Nonintegral ABS systems use a fairly standard tandem master cylinder and a typical vacuum or hydraulic power booster. The booster assists the driver in applying force to the master cylinder. The master cylinder sends fluid under pressure to the HCU, which is a separate assembly that is installed in-line with the brake lines between the master cylinder and the wheel brake units. If the pressure needs are modified, the computer-controlled solenoid valves in the HCU will carry out the commands.

Purpose and Operation of the ABS Master Cylinder

Nonintegral ABS master cylinders are usually identical to non-ABS master cylinders. They both use primary and secondary pistons in a common housing with a **common bore**. Some of these master cylinders utilize a portless ABS master cylinder design, which does not use a compensating port on the secondary circuit. Instead, the secondary piston incorporates a center valve FIGURE 28-7 that controls the opening and closing of a supply port in the piston. At rest, the supply port is open and connects the reservoir with the front brake circuit. The primary piston still uses an inlet port and a compensating port; therefore, the portless design is only used on the secondary circuit.

When the brake is applied, the primary piston moves and closes its compensating port. Fluid pressure in the primary circuit rises. It acts with the primary piston spring to move the secondary piston forward, closing the center valve. Pressure builds in the secondary circuit. Pressure keeps building in both circuits and applies the brakes in both circuits.

FIGURE 28-6 Nonintegral and integral master cylinder assemblies.

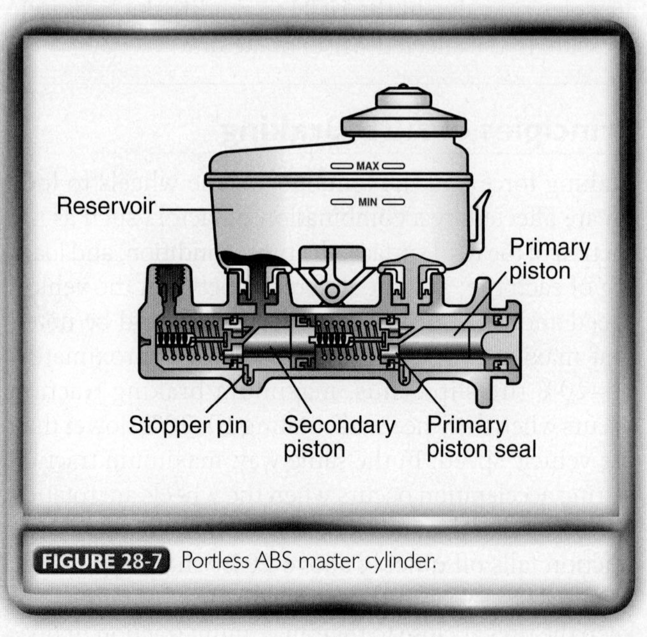
MAX
MIN
Reservoir
Primary piston
Stopper pin
Secondary piston
Primary piston seal

FIGURE 28-7 Portless ABS master cylinder.

If braking conditions are such that the hydraulic modulator must return brake fluid to the master cylinder, then, for the front brake circuits, brake fluid is returned to the front section. This forces the secondary piston back against the force of the primary piston spring and the rear brake pressure. If enough brake fluid returns, the center valve opens and allows the brake fluid to return to the master cylinder reservoir. If brake fluid is returned from the rear brake circuit, the secondary and primary pistons tend to be forced apart, which generally moves the primary piston rearward. If it travels far enough, brake fluid will return to the reservoir through the compensating port.

The amount of brake fluid that returns to the master cylinder is determined by the degree of anti-lock braking control. With as many as 16 ABS control cycles per second, the rapid changes in hydraulic pressure cause brake fluid pulsations to be sent back to the master cylinder; these pulsations can be felt by the driver at the brake pedal.

Hydraulic Control Unit (HCU)

In a standard ABS system, the HCU houses electrically operated hydraulic control valves (solenoid valves) that control brake pressure to specific wheel brake circuits. Each separate hydraulic circuit within the HCU has one or two solenoid valves that provide three operating conditions: apply, hold, and release. During the apply mode, the solenoid valves allow brake fluid to freely flow through the HCU hydraulic control circuit to the specific brake circuit. In this case, the driver is in full control of the brakes through the master cylinder.

In the hold mode, a solenoid valve "isolates" the master cylinder from the brake circuit. This prevents brake pressure from building any further. The brake pressure to the wheel is held at that level until the solenoid valve is commanded to change its position. In the release mode, a solenoid valve "dumps" the brake circuit pressure to the wheel, allowing it to start rolling again. The solenoid valve opens a passage back to the accumulator where brake fluid is stored until it can be returned by an electric pump to the master cylinder reservoir.

The isolation valve and dump valve can be separate valves or they can be combined into a common assembly.

> **TECHNICIAN TIP**
>
> Many, but not all, HCUs are sealed units and cannot be serviced. If you are working on a vehicle with a sealed HCU and it is faulty, it will have to be replaced. This can be quite costly.

Either way, they open and close passageways. However, if they are separate valves, they use a separate **electric solenoid** to operate each valve. If the valve and electric solenoid are combined in a common assembly, then they have one electric solenoid that operates the valve in three positions—one position for apply, one for hold, and one for release.

Purpose and Operation of the HCU

The ABS control module (or EBCM) sends commands in the form of electrical signals to the HCU. The HCU executes the commands, using one or two solenoid valves for each hydraulic circuit, depending on the type of HCU. Since the control valves are situated between the master cylinder and the wheel brake units, they can allow, block, or release hydraulic pressure going to the brake units.

In a normal non-ABS braking scenario, brake pedal force is transmitted to the master cylinder, then through the non-energized open isolation valve to the brake unit at the wheel. When the signals from the wheel speed sensors show no tendency for the wheels to lock up, the EBCM does not send any control current to the solenoid valves. The solenoid valves are not energized and the hydraulic pressure from the master cylinder flows freely through the HCU to the brake units at each wheel.

When the control unit detects any lock-up tendency, it sends a command current to the isolation solenoid valve. This current causes the solenoid valve to close, isolating the brake circuit from the master cylinder. That holds the hydraulic pressure between the solenoid valve and the brake circuit constant—regardless of whether the master cylinder hydraulic pressure rises or falls.

If the wheel speed sensors signal that excessive wheel deceleration is continuing, the control module commands the dump valve to open. This reduces the braking pressure by opening a passage from the brake circuit to the accumulator. A pump in the HCU sends brake fluid back to the master cylinder, pushing one or both pistons rearward in the bore.

If the sensors indicate that the lower pressure has allowed the wheel to speed up, the EBCM de-energizes the solenoid valve(s), closing the dump valve and opening the isolation valve. The hydraulic pressure from the master cylinder is again allowed to apply the brakes, and the wheel is again slowed. This process continues until the vehicle comes to a stop or the driver lifts his or her foot from the brake pedal. In most standard ABS systems, the hydraulic pressure in the brake circuits can never rise above the master cylinder pressure.

Types of HCUs

There are a number of HCUs that vehicle manufacturers use, and they generally fall into a few categories. The first category relates to how many channels the system has. A **channel** generally means the number of electrical wheel sensor circuits and hydraulic circuits a system has FIGURE 28-8. A single-channel system uses one sensor circuit with the speed sensor typically located in the differential and one hydraulic control circuit to control both rear wheels.

A two-channel system is similar but uses two separate speed sensors and hydraulic control circuits, one for each rear wheel. The two hydraulic control circuits apply brake pressure separately to the rear wheels. A three-channel system is configured so that each front wheel has its own speed sensor and hydraulic control circuit, while the rear brakes use a single speed sensor with a single hydraulic control circuit. A four-channel system uses separate speed sensors and hydraulic control circuits for each of the four wheels.

Another difference among types of HCUs is the number of solenoid valves per hydraulic control circuit. Some HCU units use a single, three-position solenoid valve per circuit, while others use dual, two-position valves per hydraulic circuit. The first position of the single, three-position valve allows brake fluid to flow through the apply port, while blocking the release port. The second position blocks the apply port and the release port. The third position blocks the apply port and opens the release port. Thus, the single, three-position valve has all three conditions—apply, hold, and release.

The dual, two-position valve style of HCU uses one solenoid valve to open and close the apply port. This is commonly called the isolation valve. When this valve is not energized, the apply port is open. The second solenoid valve opens and closes the release port. When this valve is not energized, the release port is blocked. The EBCM operates each of these valves independently to

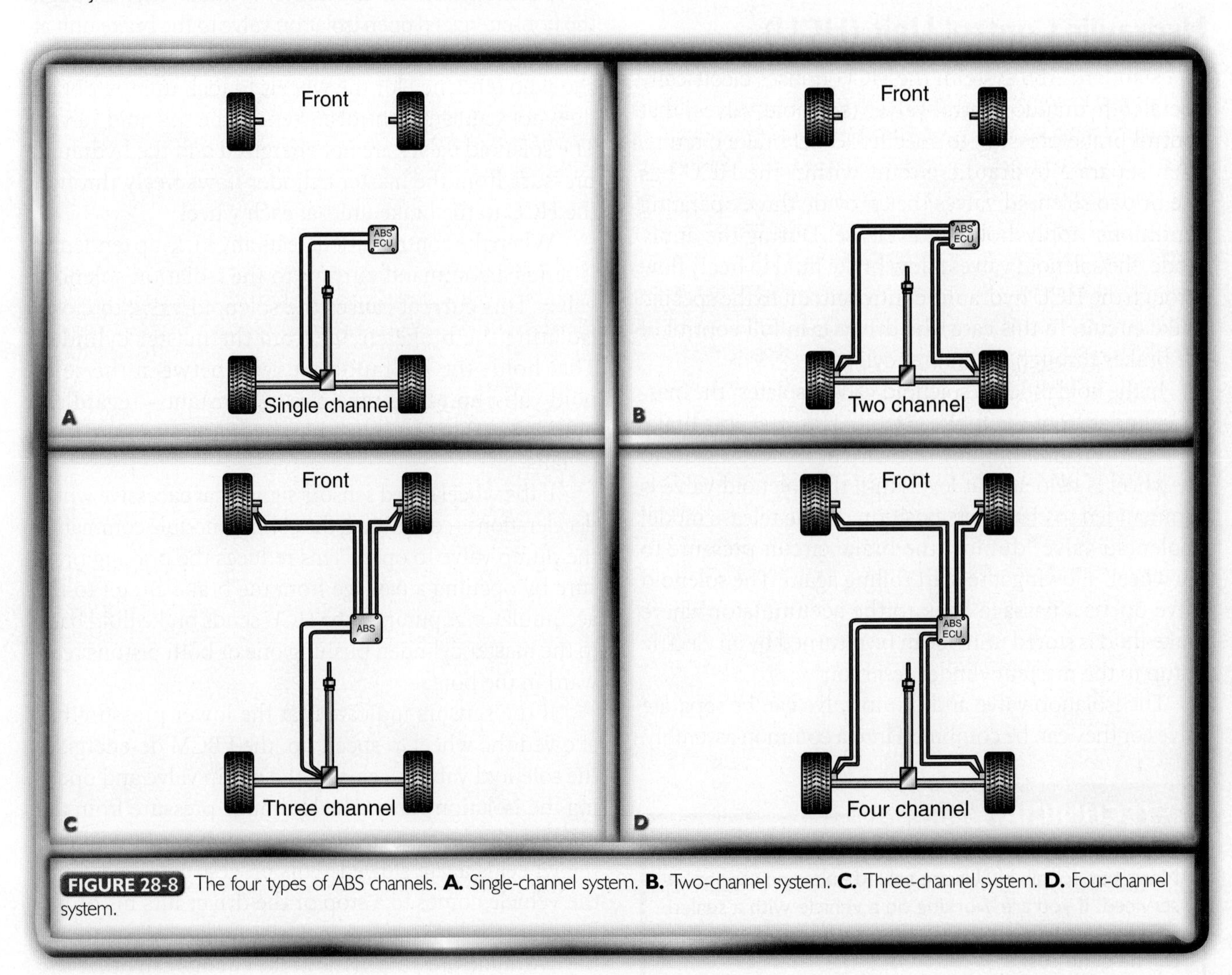
Front
ABS ECU
Single channel
A
Front
ABS ECU
Two channel
B
Front
ABS
Three channel
C
Front
ABS ECU
Four channel
D

FIGURE 28-8 The four types of ABS channels. **A.** Single-channel system. **B.** Two-channel system. **C.** Three-channel system. **D.** Four-channel system.

obtain apply, hold, and release functions. Because there are twice as many solenoid valves and each valve needs its own electrical control circuit, the EBCM is more complicated and costly to build. Therefore, EBCMs are specifically designed to work with only the specified type of HCU, and EBCMs and HCUs cannot be randomly interchanged.

Another difference between HCUs is the type of accumulator used, low pressure or high pressure. **Low-pressure accumulators** hold brake fluid in a spring-loaded chamber when it is released by the dump valves during an EBC event. The hydraulic pressure remains fairly low since an electric pump returns the released brake fluid to the master cylinder when brake fluid in the accumulator reaches a certain point. When the electric pump turns on, the fluid returning to the master cylinder pushes the brake pedal toward the driver's foot, causing the brake pedal to rise. This can be confusing to drivers because it feels like someone is under the dash pushing the brake pedal back toward them.

High-pressure accumulators are used to store brake fluid under high pressure for one of two purposes: to be used as a power booster for applying the integrated master cylinder or to be used to independently apply the wheel brake units when the EBCM commands it. When used as a power booster, pressure in the accumulator is maintained by a high-pressure electric pump. The pump is activated by a pressure switch and relay when the hydraulic pressure falls below a certain point. When the pressure reaches the specified upper pressure limit, the pressure switch opens and deactivates the electric pump. The hydraulic pressure is then used to boost the driver's foot pressure on the master cylinder when the driver depresses the brake pedal. If the high-pressure pump fails for any reason, the accumulator holds enough brake fluid at high pressure to apply the brakes 10 to 20 times before the boost is used up. If that occurs, the brakes will still operate but will require much higher foot pressure.

The accumulator used to supply brake pressure to the HCU also uses a high-pressure pump, pressure switch, and relay to maintain an operating pressure of approximately 1200–2700 psi (8274–18,616 kPa), depending on the system FIGURE 28-9. The high-pressure pump pushes the brake fluid against a high-pressure nitrogen chamber, which holds pressure on the brake fluid. The hydraulic pressure is used to independently apply the brakes during a TCS or ESC event. If the high-pressure pump fails while driving and the hydraulic pressure falls below the pump's specified "on" pressure, the EBCM will disable the ABS system and illuminate the yellow warning lamp alerting the driver to an ABS system fault.

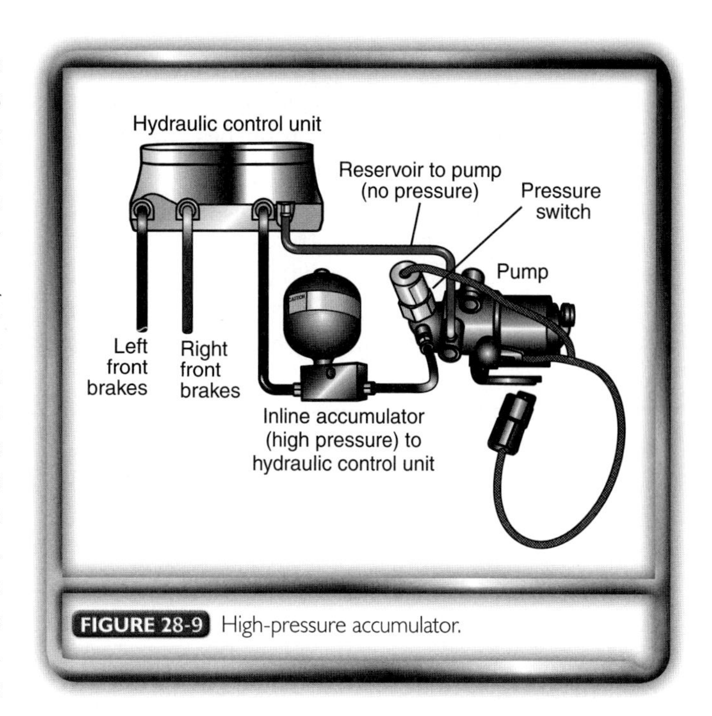
Hydraulic control unit
Reservoir to pump (no pressure)
Pressure switch
Pump
Left front brakes
Right front brakes
Inline accumulator (high pressure) to hydraulic control unit

FIGURE 28-9 High-pressure accumulator.

Safety

Be careful to follow the manufacturer's procedures when working on EBC systems. High-pressure brake fluid stored in the accumulator is dangerous.

Wheel Speed Sensors

Wheel speed sensors create electrical signals based on the rotational speed of each wheel they monitor. Wheel speed sensors do so by using principles of electromagnetism to generate an analog or digital electrical signal. This signal is read by the EBCM to determine the speed of each wheel, as well as the rate of deceleration of each wheel. This information is used to determine if a wheel is starting to lock up and skid.

A wheel sensor assembly consists of a toothed tone wheel (or tone ring) that rotates with the wheels and a stationary pick-up assembly attached to the hub or axle housing. The **pick-up assembly** and **tone wheel** do not touch each other; a small gap, called an **air gap**, must be maintained at the specified clearance. Since there is no mechanical connection, there is virtually no wear unless a foreign object gets between them. As each tooth of the tone wheel approaches the pick-up, a small voltage is created that pushes current flow in one direction inside the pick-up assembly. As each tooth leaves the pick-up assembly, voltage is generated that pushes current flow in the opposite direction. This process creates a full-cycle sine wave for each tooth on the tone wheel FIGURE 28-10. The faster the wheel is turned, the faster the sine wave rises and falls. The speed at which the sine wave rises and falls is referred to as frequency. Frequency is measured in hertz, where one hertz equals one full-cycle sine wave per second.

The height of the sine wave, called its amplitude, also tends to change with speed. At very slow vehicle speeds, when the vehicle is just creeping along, the amplitude of the sine wave is very low. As the speed increases, so does the amplitude, along with the frequency. This alternating current sine wave signal is sent to the ECU, which evaluates and compares it to other speed sensor signals to determine if a wheel is about to lock up.

Types of Wheel Speed Sensors

The three most common types of wheel speed sensors are the variable reluctance (magnetic induction style), **magneto-resistive**, and **Hall effect** styles. The variable reluctance type is simpler and usually less expensive for manufacturers to use. This style is sometimes called a passive system since it is self-contained and needs no outside power to function. Magnetic induction occurs when the teeth on the tone wheel pass the sensor, creating an analog AC voltage signal. The faster the tone wheel rotates, the faster the AC signal frequency. This AC signal is sent to the ECU where it is processed and then compared to the AC signals from the other wheels.

Low speed (A)
Moderate speed (B)
High speed (C)

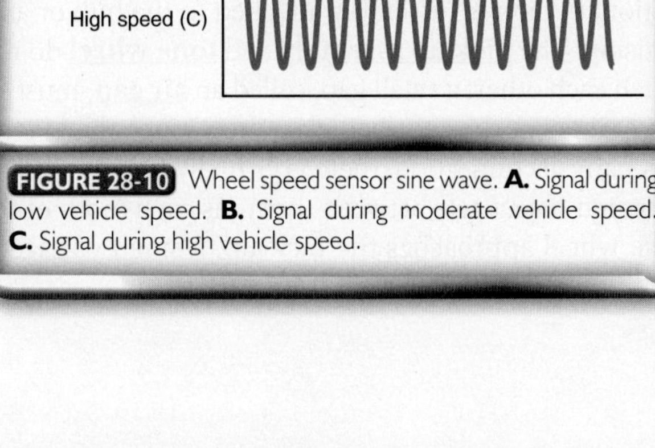

FIGURE 28-10 Wheel speed sensor sine wave. **A.** Signal during low vehicle speed. **B.** Signal during moderate vehicle speed. **C.** Signal during high vehicle speed.

Most variable reluctance wheel speed sensors are two-wire sensors, which complete the circuit back to the ECU. The variable reluctance sensor assembly consists of a coil of wire around a permanent magnet, with each end of the coil connected to one of the wheel speed sensor terminals, which connect directly into the EBCM. Since this type of sensor operates on principles of magnetism, the air gap between the toothed tone wheel and sensor is critical. If the air gap is too small, the parts could contact each other, damaging them. If the air gap is too large, the sensor output signal to the ECU could be too weak and trigger a code or cause the sensor to work intermittently.

One drawback to the variable reluctance sensor is that since it depends on the speed of movement of the tone wheel to create a signal, it does not function effectively below vehicle speeds of around 5 mph (8 kph). In other words, the amplitude of the sine wave it creates at slow speeds is not high enough for the EBCM to read it. This can prevent the ABS from functioning during the last part of a braking event. On a very slippery road surface such as ice, the lack of ABS functionality at that speed could lengthen the stopping distance significantly.

The magneto-resistive and Hall effect sensor systems are called active systems because they require an outside power source to operate. If the sensor loses power or ground, it cannot generate an output signal. The power wire originates from the EBCM and normally supplies the magneto-resistive or Hall effect sensor systems with a reference voltage of between 5 and 12 volts, depending on the manufacturer. This helps ensure that the sensor is not affected by changes in the vehicle's electrical system voltage. A signal wire transmits the output signal from the sensor to the EBCM. The magneto-resistive and Hall effect sensors can be a three-wire arrangement, with the third wire being a dedicated ground, or a two-wire arrangement with ground being provided by the chassis.

The magneto-resistive speed sensor and Hall effect wheel speed sensor types operate similar to all Hall effect sensors. A reference voltage and ground are supplied to the sensor assembly, where internal circuitry causes a small current to flow across the semiconductor bridge/Hall material. If the bridge/Hall material is exposed to a magnetic force, the magnetism forces the current to flow to one side of the bridge/Hall material. This produces a small difference in voltage across the sides of the bridge/Hall material FIGURE 28-11. This voltage is then amplified and processed into a digital "on" signal (circuit is pulled to ground) and sent to the EBCM. As the magnetic field is removed, the small signal voltage across the bridge/Hall material falls to 0V. The signal sent to the EBCM will be a digital "off" signal (reference voltage). As the magnetic field is alternately applied and removed, the sensor will send a digital square wave on/off signal corresponding to the changes in the magnetic field. Because the magnetic field does not have to be moving for the bridge/Hall effect voltage to be created, the sensor works all the way down to 0 mph (0 kph). This allows the ABS to continue functioning until virtually reaching a full stop.

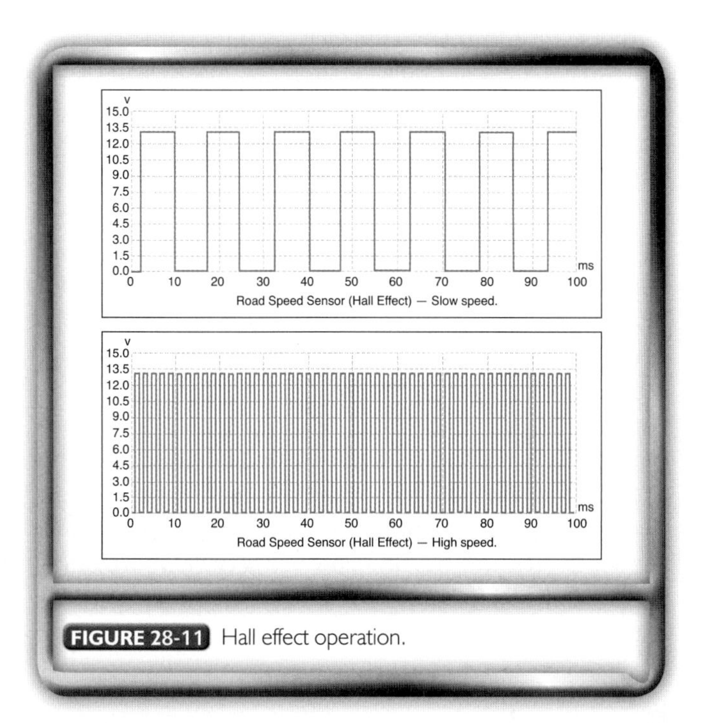
V
15.0
13.5
12.0
10.5
9.0
7.5
6.0
4.5
3.0
1.5
0.0
ms
0 10 20 30 40 50 60 70 80 90 100
Road Speed Sensor (Hall Effect) — Slow speed.
V
15.0
13.5
12.0
10.5
9.0
7.5
6.0
4.5
3.0
1.5
0.0
ms
0 10 20 30 40 50 60 70 80 90 100
Road Speed Sensor (Hall Effect) — High speed.

FIGURE 28-11 Hall effect operation.

> **TECHNICIAN TIP**
>
> Testing wheel speed sensors is dependant on knowing which kind of sensor the vehicle uses. Do not assume all two-wire sensors are of the variable reluctance style. With the ignition switch set to the "run" position and the wheels stationary, use your digital volt-ohmmeter (DVOM) to properly back-probe both sensor wires for voltage. If neither wire has voltage, suspect a variable reluctance sensor. If one of the two wires has a reference voltage, you are likely dealing with a magneto-resistive or Hall effect sensor.

Brake Switch

In addition to activating the rear brake lights, the brake switch sends an electrical input signal to the EBCM telling it if the driver is applying the brakes or not. If the brakes are being applied, the EBCM will activate the appropriate solenoid valves if the wheel speed sensors signal that the wheels are starting to lock up. If the brake switch indicates that the brakes are not being applied and the wheel speed sensors are showing unequal speeds indicating a slippery road surface, the EBCM on some vehicles will illuminate a low traction warning lamp alerting the driver to the low traction condition.

The brake switch is a normally closed switch, meaning that if the switch is not affected by any outside force, electrical current will flow through it. The brake pedal pushes the brake switch open when the brakes are released. As soon as the driver steps on the brake pedal, the spring in the brake switch closes the contacts and sends electrical current (signal) to activate the brake lights. This electrical signal is also sent to the EBCM, signaling it that the driver is applying the brakes. In some systems, the brake switch is only used to signal the body control module, which then sends current to illuminate the brake lights.

More advanced EBC systems may use a brake pedal position sensor, which indicates how far and fast the brake pedal is being pushed. It sends a variable signal based on the application of the brakes, which the EBCM uses to determine brake pedal travel and speed. This gives the EBCM additional information about the type of braking that is being performed, which can be used to modify the ABS intervention.

ABS Electronic Brake Control Module (EBCM)

The EBCM is made up of electronic circuitry to process input signals, an electronic data processor, computer memory, and output drivers to control the output devices such as the electric solenoid valves. The EBCM is programmed from the manufacturer to make brake control decisions and send output commands to the controlled devices based on sensor input data, which are compared to the data maps in its memory. These maps are designed to account for all of the reasonable braking conditions that the vehicle could experience. The EBCM continuously monitors the sensor data for any indication that one or more wheels are about to lock up.

The EBCM receives signals from several sources **FIGURE 28-12**. A switch at the brake pedal provides a brake on/off condition or, on some vehicles, a brake pedal position signal. An input from the ignition switch signals that the driver has turned the ignition on. Some control units monitor the battery voltage and use the rise in charging system voltage to indicate that the engine is actually running. The **vehicle speed sensor** reports the speed of the vehicle. Each of these input signals is used by the EBCM to know if a wheel starts to lock while the driver is applying the brakes and which ABS actions are necessary to prevent a full skid condition.

Some ABS control modules have additional functionality designed into them. One example is electronic brake proportioning. This feature does away with the mechanical proportioning valve and duplicates that action electronically by using the ABS valves to reduce rear brake hydraulic pressure under moderate brake pedal application. The EBCM restricts pressure to the rear wheels based on how hard the brake pedal is being applied. In this case, the EBCM does not wait until a wheel sensor reports that one or both rear wheels are locking up; instead, it reduces rear brake pressure slightly before lock-up occurs. It does this during moderate and heavy braking because of weight being transferred from the rear wheels to the front wheels, reducing the traction at the rear wheels.

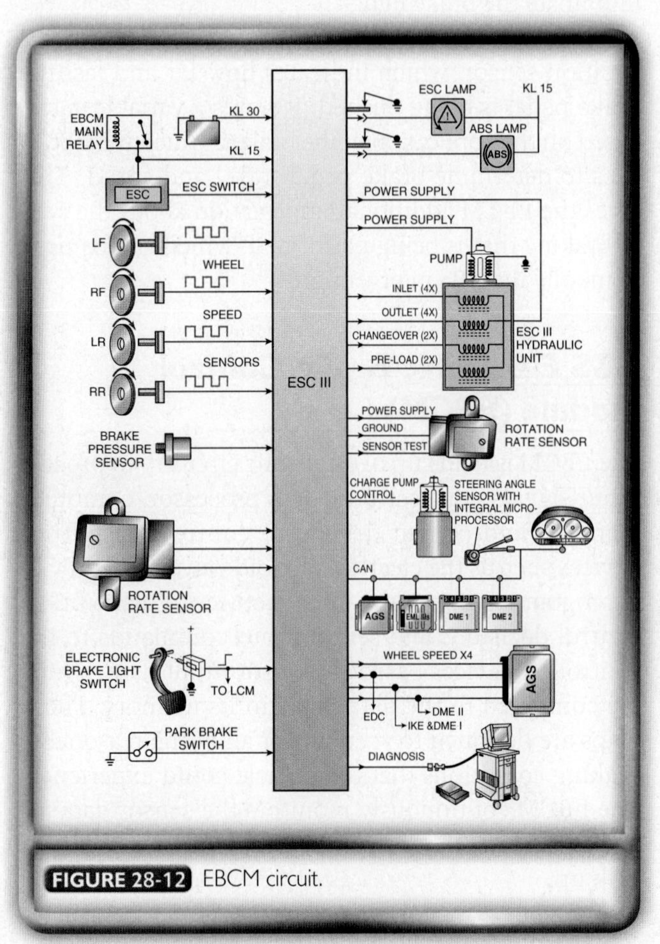
EBCM MAIN RELAY
KL 30
KL 15
ESC LAMP
KL 15
ABS LAMP
ESC
ESC SWITCH
POWER SUPPLY
POWER SUPPLY
LF
RF
LR
RR
WHEEL
SPEED
SENSORS
PUMP
INLET (4X)
OUTLET (4X)
CHANGEOVER (2X)
PRE-LOAD (2X)
ESC III HYDRAULIC UNIT
ESC III
BRAKE PRESSURE SENSOR
POWER SUPPLY
GROUND
SENSOR TEST
ROTATION RATE SENSOR
CHARGE PUMP CONTROL
STEERING ANGLE SENSOR WITH INTEGRAL MICRO-PROCESSOR
CAN
ROTATION RATE SENSOR
AGS
DME 1
DME 2
WHEEL SPEED X4
AGS
ELECTRONIC BRAKE LIGHT SWITCH
TO LCM
EDC
DME II
IKE &DME I
PARK BRAKE SWITCH
DIAGNOSIS

FIGURE 28-12 EBCM circuit.

The EBCM performs an automatic system self-check and warning lamp bulb check on the ABS system every time the key is turned to the "run" position. If the EBCM detects a fault, the ABS warning lamp will remain on and most, but not all, systems store the fault in the EBCM memory. The faults are stored as diagnostic trouble codes (DTCs) for retrieval by technicians when diagnosing ABS system faults.

Some ABS systems provide **blink codes**, also known as flash codes, through the ABS warning lamp when a specific terminal is grounded or two specific terminals are shorted together. If a code is stored in the EBCM memory, the EBCM will blink the ABS warning lamp in a manner that indicates a particular trouble code. For example, a code 12 would be one blink followed by a short pause, then two rapid blinks followed by a long pause. Each code is usually displayed three times before the next code is displayed. Once all codes have been displayed, the codes will start at the beginning again.

Other ABS systems require a scan tool that connects to the EBCM or power train control module data link connector to read the **fault codes**. Fault codes indicate which circuit is experiencing a fault, such as an open left front wheel speed sensor circuit. The fault codes also can indicate if there is a condition the EBCM determines is out of acceptable tolerances, such as wheel speeds that do not match within the specified tolerance. The cause could be as simple as having a tire of the wrong size installed on the vehicle or having properly sized tires not inflated to the same pressure. Technicians use service information to determine how to diagnose the problem and locate the cause of the fault.

Caring for the Customer

It is important for the customer to know that the ABS system is disabled when the ABS yellow warning lamp is on. The brakes will work normally, but without ABS function.

Traction Control System (TCS) Overview

While a basic ABS system can prevent skidding by holding or releasing individual brake circuit pressure, it has no ability to apply the brakes apart from the driver-created hydraulic pressure. This system works fine as long as the tire slippage is a result of the driver applying the brakes. However, tires also slip because the engine torque accelerating them exceeds their traction with the road surface; in this scenario, they can slip, spin, or break loose, causing a loss of control of the vehicle. The TCS system was developed to prevent the drive wheels from slipping while the vehicle is being accelerated. It is active up to a manufacturer-specified speed. Above that speed, traction control is deactivated by the EBCM because further acceleration is unlikely to cause the wheels to lose traction.

To obtain traction control capabilities, manufacturers have added a few design features to the basic ABS system, one of which is a high-pressure electric pump that maintains high-pressure brake fluid in an accumulator. This pressure is used to activate brake units on the drive wheels independently of the driver. The sensors are the same as in the ABS system, but the ability to apply the individual drive wheel brakes is needed; thus, two to four extra solenoid valves, called **boost valves**, are added to the HCU **FIGURE 28-13**. These boost valves direct hydraulic pressure from the accumulator to the ABS solenoid valves so that individual wheel brake units can be applied independently. Additional programming is added to the EBCM to control the high-pressure pump and extra HCU valves and to decide when each of them needs to be activated.

Operation of the TCS

When the TCS is active, the EBCM monitors the speed of the individual drive and nondrive wheels along with the vehicle speed from the vehicle speed sensor. If the driven wheels are accelerating at different speeds from each other or the nondriven wheels, the EBCM can identify which wheel or wheels are slipping. It will then take action to reduce the torque to the appropriate wheels by first applying the brake to any wheels that are slipping. It does this by activating the isolation valve to close off the supply port from the master cylinder. It then activates the boost valve to pressurize the brake circuit on the spinning wheel to slow it down. If that is not enough to prevent the slippage, the EBCM will request reduced power from the engine. This can be accomplished by reducing the throttle plate opening, by shutting down one or more fuel injectors, by reducing the engine timing, or by selecting a higher gear in the transmission. Once the wheel speeds return to proper parameters, the EBCM will return the TCS system to normal and continue to monitor the wheels for slippage.

Some TCS systems can be temporarily deactivated by a TCS function switch located on the dash or center console. If the driver deactivates TCS, the system will not intervene during wheel slip. Drivers will disable the TCS for a variety of reasons. They might be climbing a long hill on a rough gravel road, which would continuously activate traction control, overheating the brakes. Or they might want to show off by "roasting" the tires or experience driving without traction control such as on a racetrack. The TCS will automatically default back to "on" during the next ignition switch cycle. In most cases, if the TCS is deactivated, the ABS system will still be active.

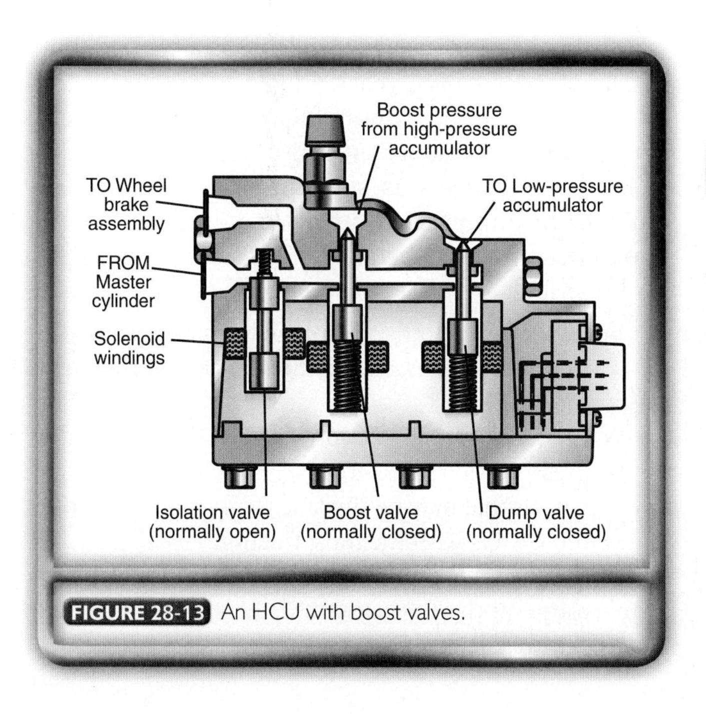

Boost pressure from high-pressure accumulator
TO Wheel brake assembly
TO Low-pressure accumulator
FROM Master cylinder
Solenoid windings
Isolation valve (normally open)
Boost valve (normally closed)
Dump valve (normally closed)

FIGURE 28-13 An HCU with boost valves.

> **TECHNICIAN TIP**
>
> Manufacturers use various strategies in their TCS systems, and not all of them apply the brakes as a first step. Some of them reduce engine power first. Even so, EBCMs today operate very fast, so there may only be a few milliseconds between each action.

Electronic Stability Control (ESC) Overview

ABS does a good job of preventing wheels from locking up under hard braking or poor traction conditions and allows the driver to maintain directional control of the vehicle. TCS also does a good job of maintaining traction when the vehicle is driven in a relatively straight line. However, drivers can lose directional control of the vehicle while driving aggressively, taking emergency steering actions, or if there are sudden changes in the traction of the road surface while in a turn. These situations can cause the vehicle to understeer (push) or oversteer (fishtail). It can also cause vehicles with a high center of gravity, such as an SUV, to roll over. All of these situations can lead to serious accidents.

If any of these situations are imminent, the ESC system can independently activate individual wheel brake units as necessary to help keep the driver from losing control of the vehicle. ESC utilizes the ABS and TCS systems, but with a few enhancements to more actively interface with the vehicle's operation in maintaining directional stability while the vehicle is being steered. A US Insurance Institute for Highway Safety 2006 study estimated that if all vehicles were equipped with ESC, approximately 10,000 fatal accidents in the United States could be avoided each year. This finding led the Department of Transportation to require that all vehicles of less than 10,000 lb (4536 kg) gross vehicle weight, and manufactured after September 1, 2011, be equipped with an ESC system that meets their minimum specifications.

The ESC system integrates a yaw sensor, **steering angle sensor**, and sometimes a **roll-rate sensor** into the basic ABS and TCS systems. It also adds new programming parameters into the EBCM to monitor the vehicle's stability, as well as added output command capabilities to apply individual drive wheel and nondrive wheel brake units independent of the driver. The yaw sensor measures the amount of directional rotation of the vehicle on its vertical axis. In other words, it tells the EBCM the rate at which the vehicle is turning. The steering angle sensor tells the computer what the driver's directional intent is. If equipped, the roll-rate sensor tells the computer the rate of roll and the amount of roll that the vehicle is experiencing. The EBCM continuously monitors these signals and compares them to preprogrammed scenarios and decides which, if any, brake units need to be applied, and if engine torque needs to be reduced to keep the vehicle stable.

Safety

Most standard passenger vehicles are designed with a bias toward understeer. It is generally agreed that understeer is easier for the average driver to recover from. However, many performance vehicles are designed with a slight bias toward oversteer, which can be managed by an experienced driver while driving aggressively.

TECHNICIAN TIP

The yaw sensor operates similarly to a Wii or other video game controllers. Its internal circuitry senses movement and sends an output signal directly related to the movement it senses.

Operation of ESC

If the ESC system is activated, the ECBM monitors the yaw sensor signal, the steering angle sensor signal, and the roll-rate sensor signal, as well as the wheel speed sensor signals. If the vehicle is beginning to understeer, oversteer, or roll, the EBCM will detect it in the signal values. It will then apply up to three wheel brake units to help bring the vehicle back within proper stability parameters. If that does not stop the stability issue, the EBCM will request a reduction in engine power through the power train control module to help slow the vehicle further. On most vehicles, the EBCM will illuminate a warning lamp on the dash or sound a beeper signifying when the ESC system has detected the start of a skid and reacted to it. This way the driver will be informed that he or she is on the verge of losing control of the vehicle.

On most vehicles, the ESC system defaults to "on" so it is always active. Some vehicles have a switch on the dash or center console to temporarily deactivate the system. This can be useful when driving in mud or sand when traction is virtually nonexistent and the ESC system cannot function effectively. Even though some ESC systems can be turned off, they may still monitor the operation of the vehicle and reactivate the ESC system under certain situations, such as driving above a specified speed or if a spin is detected while the brakes are being applied.

Some ESC systems incorporate a switch that allows the driver to select one or more varying levels of assist from the ESC, such as "touring," "track," or "sport." This option allows the driver to experience differing levels of wheel slip by being able to push the vehicle closer to the edge of control than when ESC is fully activated, while still having the ESC system available as a backup, but with limited assistance. When driving on a racetrack, for example, the driver may want full control of the vehicle instead of being limited by the ESC system.

In the continuous search for new bells and whistles to impress customers and enhance safety, manufacturers have designed other features into ESC systems, such as:

- Hill assist: Holds the brake pressure until the throttle is depressed and the vehicle starts to move forward.
- All-wheel drive traction control: Applies brake pressure as needed to any of the four individual wheels that may be slipping to maintain power to the wheels with the most traction.
- Engine braking control: Increases the engine torque if the ESC system detects wheel slippage during deceleration.

> TECHNICIAN TIP

Many ESC-equipped vehicles monitor signals from other sensors as well to help prevent a loss of control of the vehicle; these sensors include the throttle position sensor, vehicle speed sensor, and brake pedal position sensor. When diagnosing an ESC system fault, research the sensors monitored by the EBCM.

- Panic stop assist: Detects a driver's rapid throttle release and lightly applies the brakes to dry the rotors and prepare the brakes for a panic stop.
- Accident avoidance: Works in conjunction with adaptive cruise control to monitor objects in front of the vehicle. If the ESC system detects an imminent collision, it can apply the brakes or boost the brake pressure over driver pressure.
- Hill descent control: Works in conjunction with the ESC system to control the speed of the vehicle when going down loose, rough, or slippery slopes.
- Trailer sway control: Detects trailer sway and uses the ESC system to keep it under control.
- Optimized hydraulic braking: Monitors brake pressure in each brake circuit and increases it above boosted pressure if deemed necessary.

Wrap-up

Ready for Review

- Electronic brake control systems integrate computer controls to prevent wheel lock-up, shorten panic stop distances, help drivers maintain steering control, and improve vehicle stability.
- Basic anti-lock brake systems control hydraulic pressure hold and release via solenoid valves, but cannot function independently of the driver's applied brake pressure.
- Traction control systems minimize wheel slip by automatically applying brake pressure to a slipping wheel's brake unit and reducing engine output.
- Electronic stability control systems use steering wheel position sensors, yaw sensors, and wheel speed sensors to independently monitor vehicle stability and apply brakes as necessary.
- Primary components of an anti-lock braking system are: ABS master cylinder, electronic brake control module/electronic control unit, hydraulic control unit/modulator, power booster, wheel speed sensor, and brake switch.
- Braking force and wheel lock-up are affected by friction of road surface and type, condition, and loading of each tire.
- Maximum traction occurs with 10–20% tire slip.
- Wheel speed sensors signal the EBCM, which sends current to the solenoid valve, which then holds or releases hydraulic braking pressure.
- ABS master cylinders are integral (mainly in older vehicles) or nonintegral with the HCU.
- Solenoid valves provide three operating conditions: apply, hold, and release.
- The hydraulic control unit executes the commands of the ABS control module.
- Hydraulic control units differ by number of channels (one, two, three, or four), number of solenoid valves (single or dual), and type of accumulator (low or high pressure).
- Wheel speed sensors send electric signals to the EBCM to determine speed and rate of deceleration for each wheel.
- Wheel sensor assemblies consist of a toothed tone wheel and a pickup assembly, separated by an air gap.
- Types of wheel speed sensors are: variable reluctance, magneto-resistive, and Hall effect.
- The EBCM consists of electronic circuitry, electronic data processor, computer memory, and output drivers.
- The EBCM receives input signals from: the brake switch, ignition switch, vehicle speed sensor, wheel speed sensors, and sometimes the battery.
- The ESC system includes a yaw sensor (directional rotation), steering angle sensor (driver's directional intent), and roll-rate sensor (rate and amount of vehicle roll).
- Some TCS and ESC systems can be manually deactivated by the driver.

Key Terms

accumulator A storage container that holds pressurized brake fluid.

air gap The space or clearance between two components, such as the space between the tone wheel and the pick-up coil in a wheel speed sensor.

blink codes Codes used to communicate DTCs; they are given by the EBCM as a series of blinks illuminated by the ABS warning lamp.

body control module (BCM) The computer that controls the electrical system in the body of a vehicle, including power windows, door locks, heating and A/C systems, and in some cases the EBC system.

boost valve A valve located in the HCU that is controlled by the EBCM; it allows brake fluid under high pressure to flow into the HCU hydraulic circuits to apply the brakes when commanded.

brake switch The electrical switch that is activated by the brake pedal; it turns on the brake lights and signals the EBCM that the brakes are being applied.

channel The number of wheel speed sensor circuits and hydraulic circuits the EBCM monitors and controls.

common bore When a single cylinder is used for two pistons. A tandem master cylinder would be an example of two pistons in one bore.

electric solenoids An electrically operated valve, which in brake systems is used to control the flow of brake fluid in the hydraulic system.

electronic brake control (EBC) system A hydraulic brake system that has integrated electronic components for the purpose of closely controlling hydraulic pressure in the brake system.

electronic stability control (ESC) system A computer-controlled system added to ABS and TCS to assist the driver in maintaining vehicle stability while steering.

fault codes An alphanumeric code system used to identify potential problems in a vehicle system.

Hall effect An electrical effect where electrons tend to flow on one side of a special material when exposed to a magnetic field, causing a difference in voltage across the special material. When the magnetic fields is removed, the electrons flow normally and there is no difference of voltage across the special material. This effect can be used to determine the position or speed of an object.

high-pressure accumulator A storage container designed to contain high-pressure liquids such as brake fluid.

hydraulic control unit (HCU) An assembly that houses electrically operated solenoid valves used in electronic braking systems; also called a modulator.

integral ABS system A brake system in which the master cylinder, power booster, and HCU are all combined in a common unit.

isolation valve The valve in the HCU that either allows or blocks brake fluid that comes from the master cylinder from entering the HCU hydraulic circuit.

low-pressure accumulator A storage container for brake fluid coming from the release valves, which is under relatively low pressure.

magneto-resistive sensor A type of wheel speed sensor that uses an effect similar to a Hall effect sensor to create its signal.

nonintegral ABS systems A brake system in which the master cylinder, power booster, and HCU are all separate units.

oversteer A condition in which the rear wheels are slipping sideways toward the outside of the turn.

pick-up assembly A component with a wire coil wrapped around a ferrous metal core; it is used to generate an electrical signal when a magnetic field passes through it.

roll-rate sensor A sensor that measures the amount of roll around the vehicle's horizontal axis that a vehicle is experiencing.

solenoid valve An electrically operated valve that when used in brake systems is designed to control the flow of brake fluid in the hydraulic system.

steering angle sensor A sensor that measures the amount of turning a driver desires. This information is used by the ESC system to know the driver's directional intent.

steering wheel position sensor A sensor that signals to the EBCM both the position and speed of the steering wheel.

tone wheel The part of the wheel speed sensor that has ribs and valleys used to create an electrical signal inside of the pick-up assembly.

traction control system (TCS) A computer-controlled system added to ABS to help prevent loss of traction while the vehicle is accelerating.

understeer A condition in which the front wheels are turned further than the direction the vehicle is moving and the front tires are slipping sideways toward the outside of the turn.

variable reluctance sensor A type of wheel speed sensor that uses the principle of magnetic induction to create its signal.

vehicle speed sensor The component that creates an electrical signal based on the speed of the vehicle, which is sent to the EBCM.

wheel speed sensor A device that creates an analog or digital signal according to the speed of the wheel.

yaw sensor A sensor that measures the amount a vehicle is turning around its vertical axis. This information is used by the ESC system to know how much a vehicle is turning.

ASE-Type Questions

1. Tech A says that an anti-lock brake system (ABS) helps shorten the stopping distance during a panic stop. Tech B says that antilock brake systems work by increasing the hydraulic pressure in the brake system so the brakes can be applied harder. Who is correct?
   a. Tech A
   b. Tech B
   c. Both A and B
   d. Neither A nor B
2. Tech A says that traction control can reduce the power output of the engine to increase traction. Tech B says that electronic stability control increases the risk of rollover. Who is correct?
   a. Tech A
   b. Tech B
   c. Both A and B
   d. Neither A nor B
3. Tech A says that an electronic braking system has sensors that monitor wheel speed. Tech B says that under steer is generally easier to recover from than over steer. Who is correct?
   a. Tech A
   b. Tech B
   c. Both A and B
   d. Neither A nor B
4. Tech A says that ABS controls braking every time the brakes are used. Tech B says that during an ABS event, it is normal for the brake pedal to pulsate. Who is correct?
   a. Tech A
   b. Tech B
   c. Both A and B
   d. Neither A nor B
5. Tech A says that during anti-lock braking, brake fluid may be returned to the master cylinder. Tech B says that solenoid valves in the hydraulic control unit will isolate the master cylinder from the brake circuit when it is in the "hold" mode. Who is correct?
   a. Tech A
   b. Tech B
   c. Both A and B
   d. Neither A nor B
6. Tech A says that mismatched tires may cause the ABS system to register a fault code. Tech B says that a traction control system may automatically apply brake pressure to a wheel brake unit even if the vehicle is not being braked. Who is correct?
   a. Tech A
   b. Tech B
   c. Both A and B
   d. Neither A nor B
7. Tech A says that an ABS key-on system test checks for faults in the vehicle's base brake system. Tech B says that on most vehicles ABS DTCs are stored in memory for later retrieval. Who is correct?
   a. Tech A
   b. Tech B
   c. Both A and B
   d. Neither A nor B
8. Tech A says that a yaw sensor tells the computer the vehicle's actual direction. Tech B says that raising a vehicle's curb height has no effect on the electronic stability control system. Who is correct?
   a. Tech A
   b. Tech B
   c. Both A and B
   d. Neither A nor B
9. Tech A says that some hydraulic control units can boost the brake pressure higher than the pressure created by the driver. Tech B says that the dump valve can release pressure in the brake system when ABS is applied during a panic stop. Who is correct?
   a. Tech A
   b. Tech B
   c. Both A and B
   d. Neither A nor B
10. Tech A says that some ABS wheel speed sensors create a square wave digital pattern. Tech B says that some wheel speed sensors create an AC sine wave pattern. Who is correct?
    a. Tech A
    b. Tech B
    c. Both A and B
    d. Neither A nor B

40

SECTION VII

Electrical

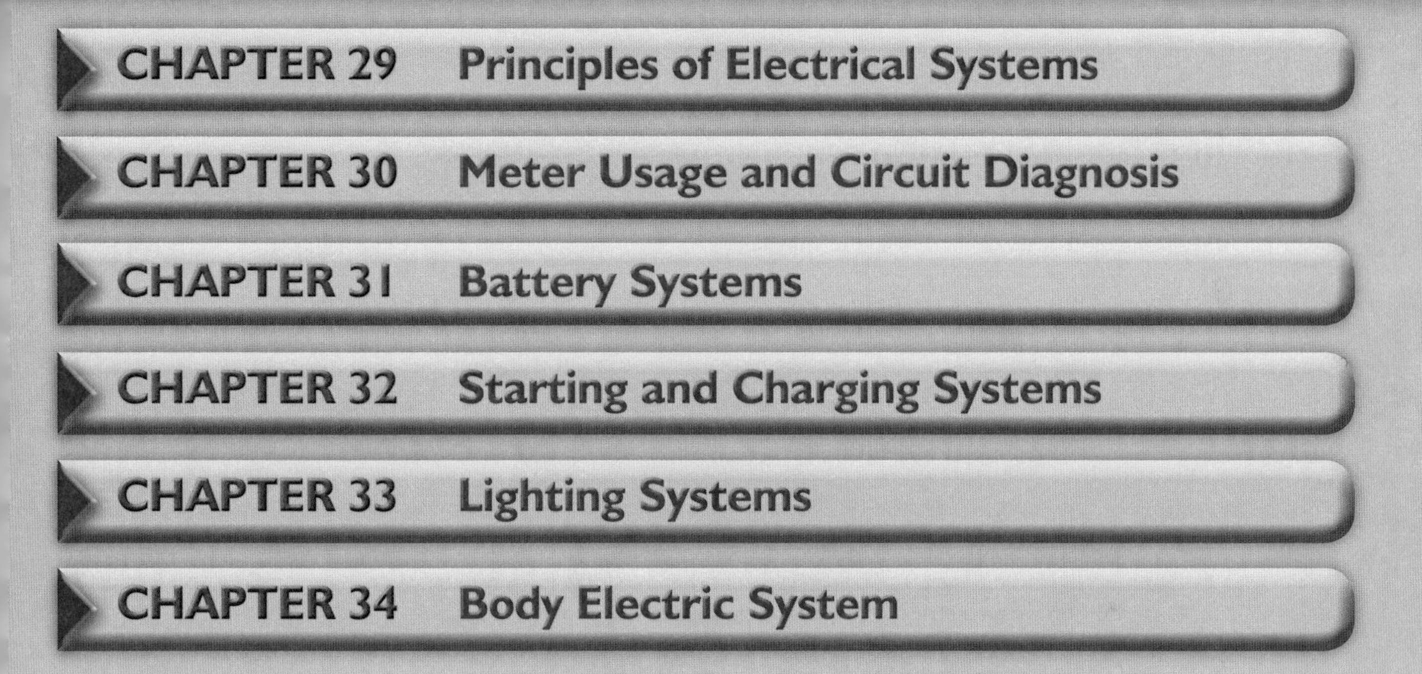

CHAPTER 29 Principles of Electrical Systems
CHAPTER 30 Meter Usage and Circuit Diagnosis
CHAPTER 31 Battery Systems
CHAPTER 32 Starting and Charging Systems
CHAPTER 33 Lighting Systems
CHAPTER 34 Body Electric System

CHAPTER 29

KNOW
SEE
DO
PROVE

NATEF Tasks

Electrical/Electronic Systems
General Electrical System

Task			Page
■ Replace electrical connectors and terminal ends.	MLR	AST	841–842
■ Perform solder repair of electrical wiring.	MLR	AST	842–843

KNOW
SEE
DO
PROVE

Knowledge Objectives

After reading this chapter, you will be able to:

1. Describe the basic principles of electricity and the units of voltage resistance and current flow. (pp 814–817)
2. Describe common electrical terms and their application. (pp 814–824)
3. Describe common semiconductors, how they work, and their use. (pp 817–818)
4. Identify the difference between AC and DC. (pp 819–820)
5. Undertake basic Ohm's law calculations. (pp 824–826)
6. Describe series and parallel circuits. (pp 828–830)
7. Describe electrical and electronic components and their application. (pp 830–836)
8. Describe the characteristics of wires, cables, harnesses, and shielding, and explain their correct application. (pp 837–839)

Principles of Electrical Systems

Know
See
Do

Skills Objectives

After reading this chapter, you will be able to:

1. Strip wire insulation. (p 841)
2. Install a solderless terminal. (pp 841–842)
3. Solder wires and connectors. (pp 842–843)

Introduction

The application of electrical principles in the repair of modern vehicles has become increasingly important for vehicle technicians as the electrical and electronic complexity of vehicles has increased. As hydrocarbons become scarcer and more expensive, the increased use of sophisticated electrical and electronic systems in vehicles to improve efficiency and economy will continue into the future. This trend is supported by the increasing popularity of hybrid vehicles and the investment by manufacturers in future technology, such as electric vehicles and fuel cell technology. To work on the current and future vehicles, it is increasingly important for the technician to have a sound understanding of electrical terminology, the behavior of electricity, and electrical component and circuit theory. The technician also needs to be able to read wiring diagrams, measure electrical quantities in the shop, calculate electrical values, and understand the quantities used. Your success as a technician will depend on your ability to apply these electrical principles and understand how they relate to the operation of virtually every vehicle system.

Electrical Fundamentals

Understanding the behavior of electricity can be more difficult than understanding other concepts such as four-stroke engine theory or the operation of disc brakes. For all intents and purposes, electricity cannot be seen, so you will have to use your imagination and visualize what it is doing. At the same time, electricity is governed by the laws of physics, so learning how electricity behaves can be approached in a logical manner, as with any other science. By applying yourself, over time it will make more and more sense.

In this chapter, we will explore the various types of circuits and how electricity behaves within each type. We will also explore electrical components and see how they either use electricity to perform various types of work or control electricity so that it can be applied to various devices in an appropriate manner.

To get started, it is helpful to know that electricity is made up of tangible objects. Even if we cannot normally see these objects with our eyes, we can imagine them in our minds. In fact, it may be helpful to think of electricity as nothing more than the movement of specific particles from one point to another. Imagine a line of marbles rolling through a tube or drops of water through a pipe. The moving marbles or drops of water can perform work if they are directed against another object with force. In the same way, electricity can perform work if it is directed at objects that can extract energy from the moving particles, such as lights and electric motors. That is where some of electricity's magic comes in. The moving electrical particles carry a negative charge and are attracted to a positive charge or are repelled by a negative charge. These attractive and repelling forces are what cause the particles to move and perform work. As we continue, just remember that electricity is the movement of particles from one place to another. The fascinating way it does this will be explained next.

You Are the Automotive Technician

The customer has complained that the fog lights no longer illuminate when turned on. Checking for a blown fuse is one of the first steps in diagnosing an electrical problem on any system in a car. The fuse box on the vehicle you are working on today is located on the passenger's side cabin. The inside cover of the fuse box identifies the location of the fog light fuse. You test it with a DVOM and find battery power on only one side of the fuse, which indicates that it is blown. You then disconnect the wiring harness connectors from both fog lights and measure the resistance at the harness connector, between the input wire and the frame of the vehicle. The ohmmeter reads 0.2 ohms indicating a short circuit to ground. You see that the vehicle has had a winch installed recently. As you visually inspect the area, you see a bundle of wires pinched between the winch bracket and the vehicle's frame. Loosening the winch bracket and removing the wires causes the ohmmeter to read an expected OL. To permanently solve the problem you will need to perform wire repairs on each of the damaged wires.

1. What caused the fuse to blow?
2. What other types of circuit protection devices do manufacturers use?
3. What is the process for repairing wires in a harness?

Basic Electricity

All questions about the nature of electricity lead to the composition of matter. All matter is made up of atoms FIGURE 29-1. Every atom has a nucleus, with at least one positively charged proton and, in most atoms, at least one neutron that has no charge. Moving around the nucleus are one or more negatively charged electrons. Electrons travel in different rings or shells around the nucleus. Each ring or shell can contain a specific maximum number of electrons. Any additional electrons must fit into the next higher ring or shell. With equal numbers of protons and electrons, the charges within an atom cancel each other out, leaving the atom with no overall charge. In this state, the electrons and protons are content to stay in the atom as they are.

An atom with more electrons than protons has an overall negative charge and is called a negative ion FIGURE 29-2. Ion simply means the atom has an imbalance of electrical charges due to the gain or loss of electrons. This negative ion is not balanced, so it is looking for a change. Since the electrons have the same negative charge, they repel one another, and the repelling force wants to push one of the electrons away from the atom.

A deficiency of electrons gives the atom an overall positive charge. This atom is called a positive ion. It is also not balanced and is looking for a change. In this case, it is exerting an attracting force on electrons to try to pull one into its atom from another atom. If a negative ion and positive ion are close enough, the negative charge of the negative ion exerts a repelling force on the extra electron, causing it to be pushed away from its atom; at the same time, the positive ion exerts an attracting force on the extra electron. These repelling and attracting forces cause the electron to be pushed and pulled from the negative atom to the positive atom, balancing both atoms out. The flow of electrons from atom to atom is called current flow and is the basic concept of electricity.

Not all atoms can give up or accept electrons easily. Materials that can do so easily are called conductors, while those that cannot do so easily are called insulators FIGURE 29-3A. The explanation of what makes a good conductor or a good insulator is quite complex and is found in the theories of quantum mechanics, which address the arrangement and behavior of electrons around the nuclei of atoms. To simplify matters, it is safe to say that in some materials there are electrons, called **free electrons**, located on the outer ring, called the valence ring. These electrons are only loosely held by the nucleus and are free to move from one atom to another when an electrical potential (pressure) is applied. In fact, atoms with fewer electrons in the valence ring are the best **conductors**, one electron being the best conductive material. This is because the single electron by itself in the valence ring is held the most loosely by the nucleus. Materials made up of atoms with one to three valance ring electrons are considered conductors. The more atoms that have free electrons a particular

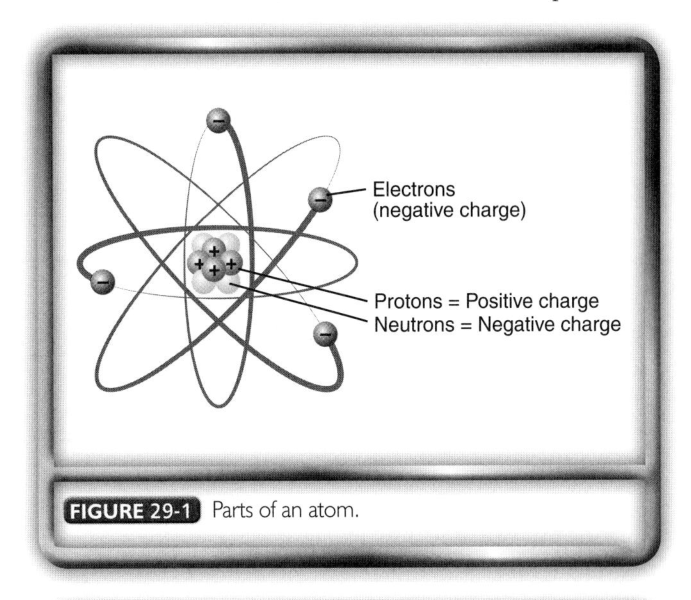
Electrons
(negative charge)
Protons = Positive charge
Neutrons = Negative charge

FIGURE 29-1 Parts of an atom.

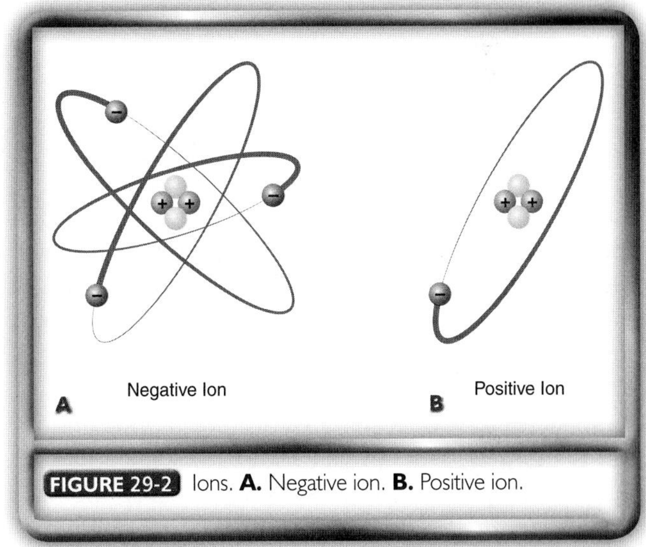
A
Negative Ion
B
Positive Ion

FIGURE 29-2 Ions. **A.** Negative ion. **B.** Positive ion.

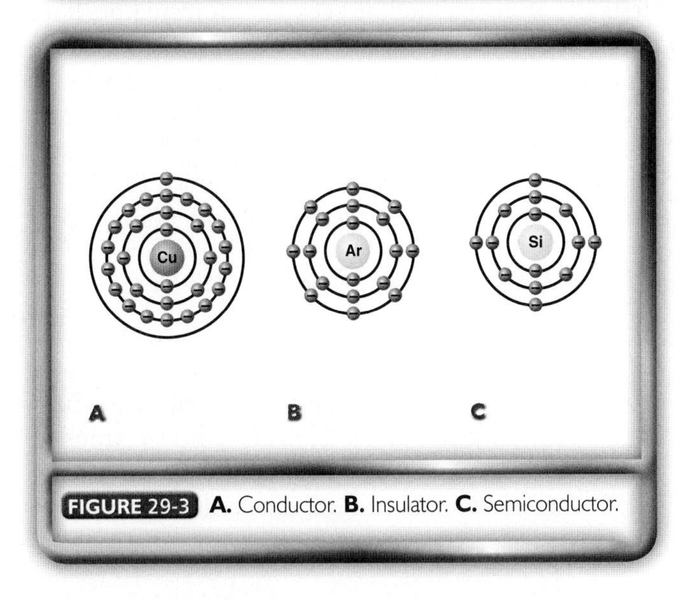
Cu
Ar
Si
A
B
C

FIGURE 29-3 **A.** Conductor. **B.** Insulator. **C.** Semiconductor.

material has, the better it can conduct electrons. Metals typically have lots of free electrons because of the atoms' structure and are therefore good conductors.

Every substance, even air, will conduct an electrical current if enough electrical pressure (voltage) is applied to it, but the word *conductor* normally is used for materials that allow current flow with little resistance. Most metals are good conductors. The most common conductor used in automobiles is copper. It is used in virtually all of the wiring that connects automotive components together. The more electrons a conductor must carry, the heavier the gauge or thickness the wire needs to be.

Materials that do not conduct electrons easily are called **insulators**. Most plastics are good insulators. The plastic covering on a wire is an example of this. The ceramic portion of a spark plug is also a good insulator. In insulators, electrons in the valence ring are bound much more tightly to the nucleus. A good insulator does not support current flow because it has no or very few free electrons, and the electrons it does have cannot move freely; therefore, an insulator prevents the movement of electrons when an electrical potential is applied. Insulators are made up of atoms that have five to eight valence ring electrons. The greater the number of valence ring electrons, the better the insulator FIGURE 29-3B.

Semiconductors are materials that conduct electricity more easily than insulators but not as well as conductors. Semiconductors such as silicon are crucial in electronics. They are used to make electronic components, such as transistors and microchips, that can switch the material from a conductor to an insulator and back again very quickly and without mechanical means. Atoms that have four valance ring electrons are considered semiconductors FIGURE 29-3C. Note that because the semiconductor material has precisely four electrons, it is only one electron away from becoming an insulator or a conductor. If an electron is added, it becomes an insulator; if an electron is removed, it becomes a conductor. Thus, the semiconductor material can be used as a switch to control whether electrons flow though the semiconductor material or are stopped by it. All we have to do is add or subtract electrons from the semiconductor material, which we will explore further in a later section.

Movement of Free Electrons

Free electrons are necessary for electrical current, but for the free electrons to move easily, they need two things—a complete pathway, or circuit, and a force that makes them move. The force from a battery can cause electrons to move. Like charges repel, so the negative electrons repel each other and are forced from the negative terminal of the battery. Unlike charges attract, so the electrons are attracted toward the positive protons in the positive side of the battery. In this case, free electrons flow in one direction only. This is called direct current. Most, but not all, circuits in passenger vehicles operate on direct current. The larger the charge between the negative and the positive terminal, the more strongly the positive terminal attracts and the negative terminal repels the free electrons. This attraction/repelling acts as a force driving the electrons along. The greater the force, the stronger the electrical current. The force is called **electromotive force**, and it is also referred to as voltage. So you could say that voltage is the force that motivates electrons to move and is measured in volts.

> **TECHNICIAN TIP**
>
> Since electrical current is the flow of electrons, it is natural to say that the direction of current is the direction in which the free electrons move—from negative to positive—which is called the **electron theory**. However, before the discovery that they are negatively charged, it was thought the natural way for electrons to flow was from positive to negative, which is called the **conventional theory**. Most wiring diagrams are written from the conventional theory perspective, while electronic circuits are typically designed and operate on the electron theory perspective. Thus, both concepts are still in use. In fact, a third theory exists that closely mirrors the conventional theory, called the **hole theory**. It states that while negative electrons do move from negative to positive, holes move from positive to negative as electrons move from atom to atom; in this case, holes (current) flow from positive to negative, and are sometimes called "positive holes." What's most important to remember is that voltage causes current to flow through conductive paths (resistance). We will be using the conventional and hole theories when explaining the electrical concepts throughout this text unless otherwise noted.

Electrical Resistance

Also affecting the current flow in a circuit is **electrical resistance**, measured in **ohms**. All materials have resistance—even good conductors. There are four factors that determine the level of electrical resistance:

1. Type of material: This refers to how many free electrons a material has.
2. Length of the conductor: As length increases, so does resistance.

3. Diameter of the conductor: The larger the conductor, the greater the amount of current it can carry.
4. Temperature of the conductor: The higher the temperature, the harder it is for free electrons to pass through and the higher the electrical resistance.

While all materials have some resistance to current flow based on the number of free electrons the material has, a **resistor** is a component designed to extract energy from the current flow by forcing it through a restriction in the circuit. A typical resistor has a set resistance, usually marked or coded on its surface. Electrical resistance is somewhat like the electrical equivalent of friction in the mechanical world: It is the degree to which a material opposes, or resists, the passage of an electrical current. Good conductors have low resistance, while insulators have high resistance. Electrical energy lost through resistance is converted into heat.

Resistance is measured in ohms. Under most conditions, except temperature change, the resistance of an object is a constant and does not depend on the amount of the voltage or the amount of current passing through it. At the same time, **Ohm's law** tells us that if we increase current flow through a resistance, the voltage used by that resistance will increase. So in that sense, the resistance did not change, but the voltage drop did FIGURE 29-4. When diagnosing circuits, we usually use a voltmeter to look for excessive voltage drops that reduce the available voltage at the load. An ohmmeter would not normally work in this case, since it generally cannot read less than 0.1 ohms. This amount of resistance in a 10-amp circuit would cause a 1.0-volt drop, which is way beyond the allowable maximum voltage drop for a wire, which will be discussed further in the Meter Usage and Circuit Diagnosis chapter. The relationships between current, voltage, and resistance are calculated using Ohm's law. This concept will be discussed in detail later in this chapter.

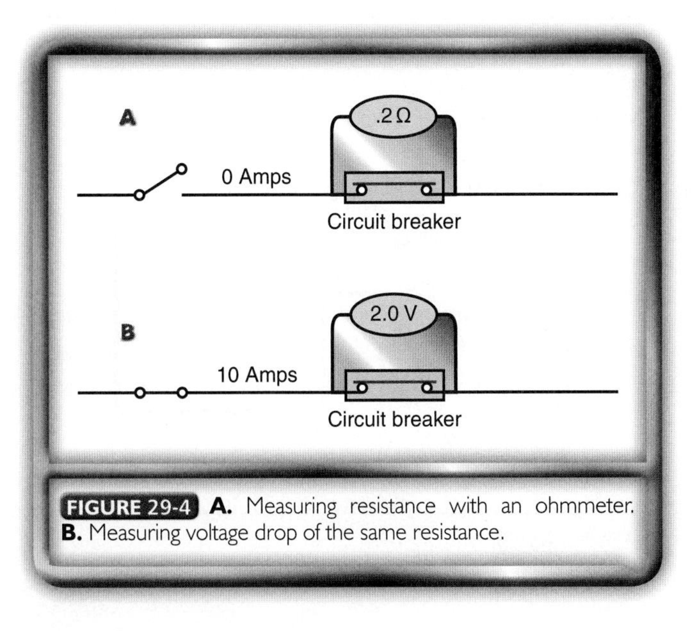
A
.2Ω
0 Amps
Circuit breaker
B
2.0 V
10 Amps
Circuit breaker

FIGURE 29-4 **A.** Measuring resistance with an ohmmeter. **B.** Measuring voltage drop of the same resistance.

Semiconductors

The term electronics usually refers to devices in which *electrons* are conducted through a vacuum, gas, or **semiconductor**. Automotive applications such as electronic control units mostly use semiconductors such as diodes, transistors, and power transistors. A semiconductor's electrical resistance is higher than that of most conductors, but lower than that of most insulators. A semiconductor's conducting ability depends on two kinds of **charge carriers**:

- The first type of charge carrier is the negative electron. This kind of semiconductor contains an excess of free electrons. They can be made to flow and carry charge.
- The second type of charge carrier is the hole. Holes occur when an electron moves from its existing place to a new place, leaving a void where it was. Because the holes are positive, a voltage can make them move toward the negative pole. When connected in a circuit, both the electrons and the holes move, but in opposite directions.

The number of charge carriers, either an excess of electrons or deficiency of electrons (causing holes in a material), can be altered by **doping**, or adding very small quantities of impurities to a semiconductor material. A doped semiconductor always has an excess of one type of charge carrier. For example, electrons in excess make it an **N-type** semiconductor. N stands for negative. Holes in excess make it a **P-type** semiconductor. P stands for positive. Each of these materials responds to positive or negative current flow oppositely.

Semiconductor Operation

Most electronic components combine P-type and N-type semiconductors. The point where they join is called the **PN junction**. In this area, the **depletion layer** occurs, and some electrons and holes cancel each other out and few charge carriers are present. The depletion layer is very thin and acts like an insulator.

A **diode** is one P-type semiconductor material joined to one N-type semiconductor material with a single PN junction. If it is connected to a voltage source so that the P region is connected to a negative pole and the N region to a positive pole, then the negative pole attracts the holes, and the positive pole attracts the electrons. This enlarges the depletion layer and the insulated space. As a result, current cannot flow across the junction.

Semiconductors are very versatile substances and are widely used to make various electronic components. Their conductivity can be manipulated and precisely controlled by doping with impurities to make transistors. They can also be designed to vary their conductance in magnetic fields to make Hall-effect devices and to vary their light to make photoelectric diodes and transistors. Semiconductor devices are replacing many other kinds of switching devices such as mechanical switches and relays. They are small, light, and use low operating voltages. They are reliable, require no maintenance, and are relatively easy to manufacture, but they are sensitive to heat and voltage spikes.

Electrical Circuits

Electrical circuits are designed to perform electrical work in a controlled manner. They can be compared to a small city; the roads are like wires, the stoplights are like switches, and businesses are like electrical devices where work happens. And cars are like electrons that deliver the workers to the workplace. Electrical circuits can be very basic, consisting of a power supply, a fuse, a switch, a component that performs work, and wires connecting them all together FIGURE 29-5. The power source—for example, the battery—creates a potential difference across its terminals measured in volts. It pushes a flow of electrons (current flow), measured in amps, when the switch is in the closed position completing the path. The current flows through the fuse into the circuit wires to the lamp where the resistance of the lamp filament causes it to glow, producing light. The current continues to flow through the lamp filament and the return pathway through the wires back to the battery to complete the circuit. When the switch is moved to the open position, the current path is broken and current flow stops, turning the lamp filament off.

A circuit can be much more complex than the one just described. But even then, most circuits contain a power source, circuit protection device, control mechanism, load, and connecting wires. As you understand the principles of electricity and how it behaves, you will be able to understand more complicated circuits.

Applied Science

AS-57: Conductors: The technician can explain the difference between an electrical conductor and an insulator.

The electrical conductivity of a material refers to the freedom of the electrons within the atoms of the material to move around. Materials with high electron mobility are known as conductors, while materials with low electron mobility are called insulators. High electron mobility allows electrons to freely flow when a voltage is applied across two points of the material.

Most familiar conductors are metallic, although there are nonmetallic conductors such as graphite and salt solutions. Silver is the best conductor, but copper is most commonly used for electrical wiring due to many desirable properties including high tensile strength and ductility.

An insulator is a material that resists the flow of an electrical charge. Glass and paper are both very good insulators, but polymers and plastics are more commonly used to insulate wiring. The purpose of an insulator in electrical applications is to support or separate conductors without allowing current flow through themselves.

TECHNICIAN TIP

One thing to know about current flow in a circuit: It doesn't flow like dominoes, with a little bit of delay between each domino. Current flow is more like ball bearings lined up touching each other inside a closely fitting pipe. As you push on a ball bearing at one end, the ball bearing at the other end falls out. Current flow works the same way, except the effect of current flow travels at the speed of light. Thus, if you add an electron at one end of a wire that is 186,000 miles (300,000 km) long, an electron at the other end of that wire will be pushed out 1 second later. That is why we say that current flow stays the same throughout a series circuit. As one electron is moved, all of the others move with it.

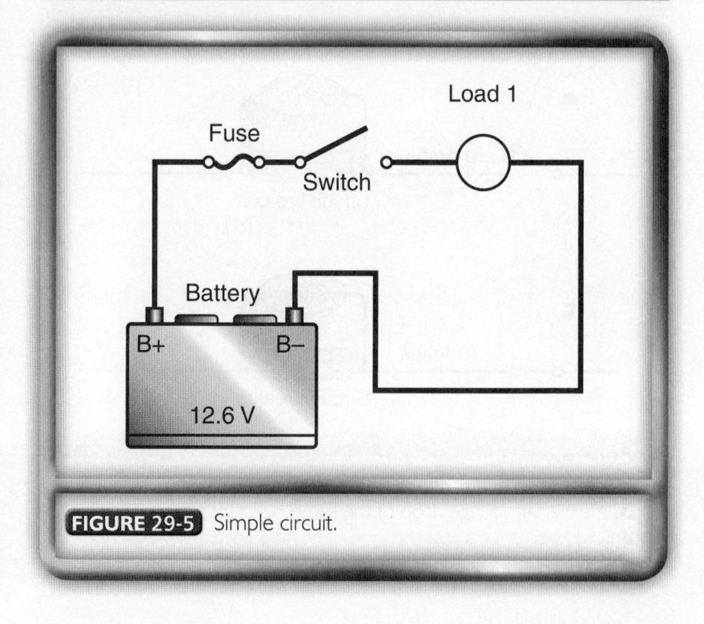
Load 1
Fuse
Switch
Battery
B+
B–
12.6 V

FIGURE 29-5 Simple circuit.

Volts, Amps, and Ohms

Volts, amps, and ohms are three basic units of electrical measurement. Voltage is the potential or electrical pressure difference between two points in an electrical circuit and is measured in **volts**. For example, the voltage of a typical car battery is 12 volts. This is the potential difference or electrical pressure between the positive and the negative battery terminal. It can be measured with a voltmeter or **multimeter** set to read voltage. Voltage can be measured by hooking a voltmeter across two parts of a circuit where you want to measure the difference in volts. It might be easier to understand if you think of voltage as the electrical force or pressure in a circuit or battery, just like the water pressure that exists in the bottom of a full tank of water or a home plumbing service.

The ampere, or **amp**, is the unit used to describe how much current or how many electrons are flowing at a given point in a given amount of time when work is being performed—for example, when a lamp is operating. An amp is a measure of the number of electrons flowing past a given point in 1 second. An amp is equal to 6.28 billion billion electrons past a given point in 1 second. Yes, billion billion is correct. To say it another way, think of a pile of 1 billion electrons. One amp would equal the number of elections in 6.28 billion of those piles travelling past a given point in a circuit in 1 second. That is impressive! No wonder we can't see them! And just to get you thinking, a starter motor may draw about 200 amps. Amperage, or current flow, can be thought of as a faucet being turned on and water flowing. Each drop of water is like an electron. Current flow is measured in amps by placing an **ammeter** into the circuit so that the current flows through the meter.

The ohm is the unit used to describe the amount of electrical resistance in a circuit or component. The higher the resistance, the less current (amps) that will flow in the circuit for any particular voltage. The lower the resistance, the higher the current that will flow in the circuit. Using the water analogy, if you kink a hose with the water running, less water will come out of the hose for a given pressure. If you kink the hose more, more resistance will be added and even less water will flow through the hose. Lessening the kink will lower the resistance and allow more water to flow. Resistance in a simple electrical circuit works the same way.

An ohmmeter is used to measure the amount of resistance in a component or circuit. The ohmmeter pushes a small amount of current through the part being tested, so an ohmmeter is usually used on a component or wire that has been disconnected from the rest of the circuit. The amount of resistance in the component changes the amount of current that the ohmmeter can push through the component. The more current that the ohmmeter can push through the component, the lower the resistance will read on the ohmmeter.

Direct Current and Alternating Current

Electrons need to flow in a circuit for work or action to be undertaken. For example, the action of a lamp glowing brightly is caused by the flow of electrons through the filament, heating it up and causing it to glow. There are two fundamental types of **current flow**: **direct current (DC)** and **alternating current (AC)** FIGURE 29-6. DC is produced by a battery. The battery maintains the same positive and negative **polarity**; therefore, the current flows in one direction only. The characteristics of DC are the fixed polarity of the applied voltage and the flow of charges in only one direction. It is possible to have varying DC; however, the charges always flow in the one direction and the applied voltage polarity remains the same.

AC is the type of current in your home electricity supply. It continuously changes its direction of current flow, and the alternating voltage repeatedly reverses or alternates its polarity. Thus, the current flow moves back and forth within a circuit. AC is produced in what is called a **sine wave**. It operates on a cycle, gradually building to a maximum current flow in one direction (positive value), then gradually reducing to zero, then gradually building to a maximum current flow in the other direction (negative value), and finally gradually reducing back to zero current. In most cases, this cycle can occur many times a second. For example, the AC flow in the house supply changes direction 60 times per second. **Hertz** is the measurement of frequency and indicates the number

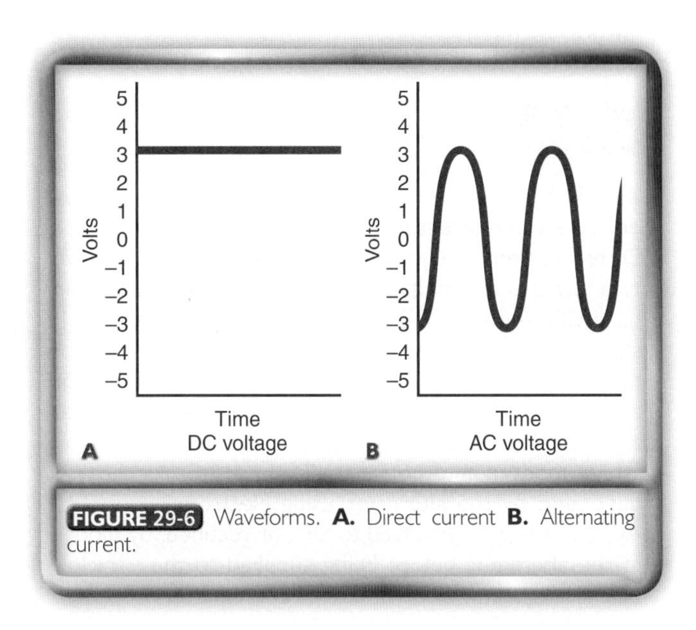
5
4
3
2
1
0
–1
–2
–3
–4
–5
Volts
Time
DC voltage
A
Volts
Time
AC voltage
B

FIGURE 29-6 Waveforms. **A.** Direct current **B.** Alternating current.

of cycles per second. So, since the AC supply in the home typically changes polarity 60 times a second, its frequency is 60 hertz, or 60 Hz. Hertz simply means "cycles per second."

AC is used in vehicles to a lesser extent than DC. Alternators use it to create current flow to charge the battery and run the electrical accessories. The AC is first transformed to DC before it leaves the alternator so it can be effectively put to use in the DC electrical system.

AC is used in the electric motors on most hybrid vehicles. Since those motors generally require high amounts of electrical power, and because AC is more efficient than DC, AC is more advantageous for that application. The AC is created by a sophisticated electronic inverter.

Some manufacturers use sensors that create an AC signal that varies in frequency. This varying signal is sent to the vehicle's computer as an indication of changes within the system being monitored. The computer can use that signal to make adjustments based on its programmed software.

In general, electrical components are designed to work on either AC or DC, but not both. For example, a DC motor will not work on AC, and vice versa. Devices can be made to convert or change AC to DC and DC to AC. For example, a battery charger that has an input AC of 110 volts at 60 Hz power can change this to 14 volts DC through a transformer and rectifier to charge a battery.

TECHNICIAN TIP

While the United States has chosen 60 Hz for the electrical grid, many other countries use 220 volts at 50 Hz and have different-shaped plugs. If you travel to these countries, make sure to purchase the proper converter or transformer so your electrical devices will work and not be damaged.

Applied Science

AS-58: AC/DC: The technician can explain the difference between direct and alternating current.

Direct current (DC) and alternating current (AC) are two forms of electricity that are produced differently and have different uses. DC electricity is the simpler form. It starts in one place and then flows in the same direction to its destination. AC electricity flows in one direction for a period of time, then changes direction over and over again continuously.

In modern automotive applications, AC electricity is generated by the alternator using electromagnets. The AC electricity is converted to DC, or rectified, by diodes in the alternator before being supplied to the vehicle's electrical systems or being stored in the battery.

Applied Science

AS-53: Electricity: The technician can demonstrate an understanding of and explain the properties of electricity as they relate to lighting, engine management, and other electrical systems in the vehicle.

Most automotive electrical systems use 12-volt DC electricity supplied from the vehicle's battery to power items such as light bulbs, electric motors, and heater elements. Some circuits may use switching with varying degrees of resistance to control the output from the circuit's load; examples may include interior blower fan motors that run at varying speeds and the vehicle's fuel gauge, which uses a variable resistor to determine the position of the gauge.

Engine and power train management systems are also powered from the vehicle's 12-volt battery but use various other voltages to monitor operating parameters via sensors. Some sensors operate using a reference voltage, generally 5 volts, which is modified to determine operating parameters. Examples could be a digital crankshaft position/speed sensor or a digital mass airflow meter. The reference voltage is effectively switched "on" or "off" by the digital sensor, producing a square-wave output with a frequency that changes according to the engine speed or airflow rate.

Some sensors generate their own voltage; examples include zirconia oxygen sensors, analog crankshaft or camshaft position sensors, which generate AC voltage, and piezoelectric knock sensors. Voltages generated from these sensors are monitored by the electronic control unit (ECU) to determine engine operating parameters.

Some computer-controlled devices can simply be turned on and off. A cooling fan may be turned on when the coolant reaches a temperature of 219°F (104°C) for example and turned back off when the coolant temperature falls below 201°F (94°C) for example. Pulse-width modulation provides a means for a computer to control a device with variable operating parameters. Fuel injectors, for example, need to be open for differing amounts of time depending on the fueling requirements of the engine. An ECU can control injector opening time by sending a pulsed signal with shorter or longer duration.

Applied Math

AM-14: Mentally: The technician can determine the proper mathematical operation (addition, subtraction, multiplication, or division) and mentally arrive at the solution.

Determining the operating parameters of electrical circuits can require a selection of different mathematical operations. Some examples may include adding the resistance of individual components in a series circuit to determine the total resistance of the circuit, dividing the voltage by the resistance to determine the current flow in a parallel circuit, or multiplying the amperage of a circuit by its resistance to determine the voltage a device is using.

Applied Math

AM-44: Formulas: Using formulas, the technician can predict the outcome(s) under different variations.

Ohm's law, a mathematical formula, can be applied to predict the outcome of changes made to electrical systems. Say we have a 12-volt automotive electrical circuit to drive a bulb in an interior light. A customer has complained that the interior light in his car is not bright enough and has requested that a higher wattage bulb be fitted. (Caution: We are only using this as an example. Additional wattage creates additional heat, which can cause the fuse to blow, or in an extreme case, a fire. It is recommended that you never modify a vehicle from the manufacturer's original condition.) The resistance of bulbs varies according to their wattage. Generally, the higher the wattage, the lower the resistance.

The original 5-watt bulb fitted to the vehicle had a resistance of 30 ohms. Through Ohm's law, we know that current flow equals voltage divided by resistance, or in this case 0.4 amps. The new 10-watt bulb to be fitted has half the resistance, 15 ohms. Current flow in the circuit is now calculated as 12 volts divided by 15 ohms, which is 0.8 amps, which provides twice the wattage.

Applied Math

AM-46: Equivalent Form: The technician can write or rewrite an algebraic equation to solve for any unknown variables.

Ohm's law is commonly used to calculate the value of an unknown variable from known values in electrical circuits. The equation is commonly stated as voltage (V) equals current flow (A) multiplied by resistance (R), or $V = AR$. To calculate current flow or resistance, instead of voltage, the equation must be rewritten. To apply the rules of basic algebra, anything we do to one side of the equation we must also do to the other. To calculate current flow, we need the A by itself on one side of the equation, so we divide both sides by R to arrive at $A = V/R$. To calculate resistance, the R must stand alone, so we divide both sides of the equation by A to arrive at $R = V/A$. Ohm's law is commonly represented in a triangle or circle format, making the correct algebraic equation very simple to find.

Devices are also available to change DC into AC, and are called **inverters**. For example, an inverter could have an input of 12 volts DC and convert that to 110 volts AC at 60 Hz. AC and DC power sources can be of any voltage and are not limited to the relatively low 12 volts DC found in the batteries on vehicles or the 110 volts AC found in the home power supply. For example, some hybrid vehicles use high-voltage DC invertors drawing 200 to 300 volts DC to power the 500-volt three-**phase** AC to power the main electric traction motors or accessory motors. Phase refers to the number of separate staggered **power windings** in the motor or alternator. Generally, three-phase motors or alternators produce more output than single-phase motors or alternators because they can maintain a much more even voltage compared to single-phase AC.

Power (Source or Feed) and Ground

Power and ground are terms to describe the beginning and end of a circuit. Power, source, and feed signify the supply side (beginning) of the circuit, where the electricity originates. Ground signifies the return side of the circuit **FIGURE 29-7**. In conventional theory, the supply side is the positive side of the circuit, and the return side is the negative side of the circuit, which we will be using throughout this text. In a vehicle, the positive battery post is considered the source. The power or feed side of a circuit refers to the wires and components that originate at the positive post of the battery and end at either a switch or a load, whichever occurs first.

Ground is a term used by technicians to indicate the portion of the circuit that returns current flow to the negative side of the battery. The ground side of the circuit starts at the negative post of the battery and ends at either a load or a switch, whichever occurs first. The term ground is also used to mean a direct connection with the negative side of the circuit, as in "the switch is grounded." Also, if you are told to ground something, that means it needs to be connected to the negative side of the circuit. Many vehicles connect the chassis and body to the negative battery terminal, which means most of the metal components on the vehicle are grounded. As a result, many manufacturers use the chassis as the return path to the negative battery terminal, as this cuts down on the amount of wire needed in the vehicle. At the same time, many

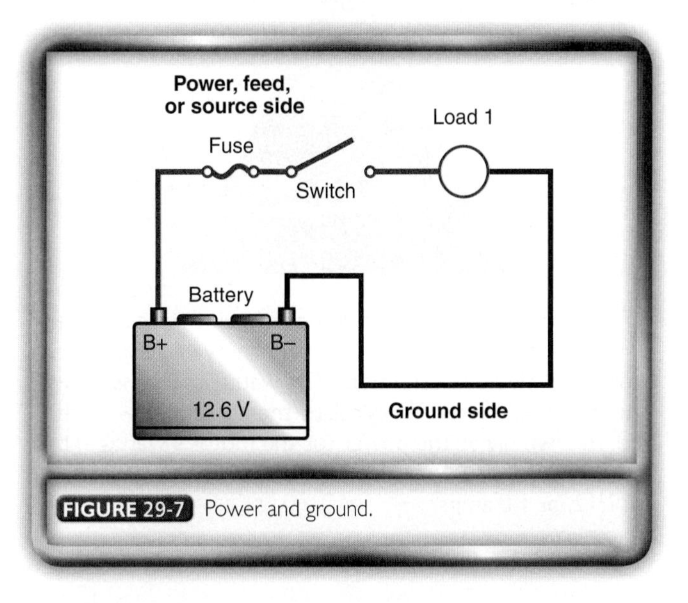
Power, feed, or source side
Load 1
Fuse
Switch
Battery
B+
B–
12.6 V
Ground side

FIGURE 29-7 Power and ground.

computer circuits use dedicated ground wires from their sensors back to the computer so that the electrical signal is accurate and not affected by any stray electrical signals on the ground circuit.

Continuity, Open, Short, and High Resistance (Voltage Drop)

The terms *continuity*, *open*, *short*, and *high resistance* are often used to describe a circuit's or component's condition. For example, the wiring harness could be described as having a short or the connector as having an open circuit. **Continuity** is achieved when an electrical circuit has a continuous and uninterrupted electrical connection and is thereby capable of conducting current and working as designed. No continuity means there is a break in the circuit and current cannot flow past the break. It can be measured with a digital volt-ohmmeter (DVOM) in ohms between two points in a circuit. For example, if a technician suspects that a circuit has a break or bad connections in the wiring, the continuity could be measured between two points. A faulty circuit has high resistance or no continuity. A circuit with continuity has very low resistance. But be careful, checking the circuit for continuity cannot determine all electrical faults. If the continuity test determines that there is a break in the circuit, you can bank on that and track it down to determine the fault. However, if the continuity test determines that there is continuity, you still don't know for sure that the circuit is good. It is possible that while the circuit has continuity, it has excessive resistance that could affect the operation of the electrical device under normal current flow. Thus, continuity testing is limited in what it can indicate. It is a great test for determining whether a wire or component is open or whether two circuits are shorted together.

The term **open** describes a low-voltage circuit that does not have a complete circuit and therefore cannot conduct current. In other words, the circuit does not have continuity. For example, when a switch is turned off, the circuit is open and no current can flow. Open can also be used to describe a fault in a circuit. For example, if the fuse is open-circuited, which describes a blown fuse, no

Applied Math

AM-48: Algebraic Expressions: The technician can use Ohm's law and the power law to determine circuit parameters that are out of tolerance.

The power law, or Watt's law, is a mathematical equation describing the relationship of voltage, current, and power in electrical circuits. Power may be defined as the amount of work done in a given period of time. Understanding this equation is useful in calculating characteristics within circuits. The power law is written as

Power (watts) = Voltage (volts) × Current (amps).

An unknown parameter can be calculated from any two known parameters. Like Ohm's law, the power law is commonly represented in a triangle diagram, as shown here:

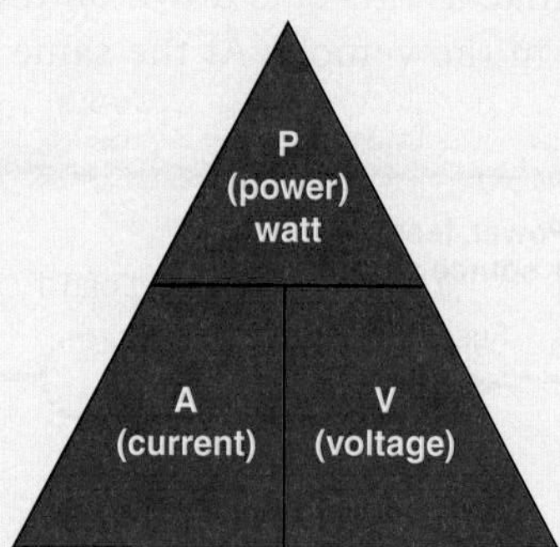
P
(power)
watt
A
(current)
V
(voltage)

For example, we have an electrical circuit driving a power window motor in a passenger car. The vehicle operates on a 12-volt electrical system. The wattage of the window motor is 22 watts. To calculate the current flow in the circuit, we divide the power (or the motor's wattage) by the voltage, or P/V. In this case the amperage would be 22/12, or 1.8 amps.

Applied Science

AS-60: Ground: The technician can demonstrate an understanding of the problems associated with having an electrical circuit inadequately grounded.

Ground problems can present some of the most challenging issues encountered in automotive diagnostics. Let's illustrate why ground points are so important on motor vehicles. In a simple circuit, we might have a battery, a fuse, and a load, all connected by wire. In automotive applications, manufacturers take advantage of the conductivity of metal car and truck bodies by connecting the ground side of electrical components to the vehicle's body or chassis. The negative side of the battery is also connected to the body, so instead of electrical current returning to ground via wiring, it is conducted through the body.

If we have a component with no ground connection, we have an open circuit and no current flow. Loose or dirty ground connections create a point of high resistance in the circuit, resulting in lower current flow and excessive voltage drop. This results in lamps illuminating dimly, electric motors not working or not working at full speed, and running problems in computer-controlled systems. In some circuits, issues may be encountered with electricity finding alternative paths to ground. You may sometimes see vehicles with brake lights flashing along with, or opposite to, turn signal lights. This is commonly caused by a poor ground in the taillight circuit.

current will be able to flow. A multimeter or test lamp can be used to test for an open circuit. An open circuit has infinite resistance—so much resistance that it is not measurable.

The term **short**, in its purest definition, describes a circuit fault in which current takes a shorter path, resistance-wise, through an accidental or unintended route. The low-resistance fault causes abnormally high current flow in the circuit and may cause the circuit protection devices, such as fuses or circuit breakers, to open the circuit. An example of a pure short would be insulation on the windings within a relay coil that has worn through and is allowing current to bypass many of the windings FIGURE 29-8. In this case, resistance decreases, amperage increases, and the magnetic field created by the winding becomes weaker, potentially causing the relay to not operate.

A pure short circuit is not the only type of short circuit. There are three additional types of short circuits that you need to understand. The first is a short to ground. In this case, the circuit has an unintended path directly to ground. For example, if the wire from the brake switch to the brake lights rubs through the wire insulation on a sharp edge of a body panel, the bare wire may make contact with the metal panel and cause a short to ground when the brake pedal is pressed FIGURE 29-9. A short to ground causes increased current flow and will typically blow the circuit fuse.

Another type of short is a short to power. In this case, the circuit has an unintended path directly to a power source. An example would be two wires in a harness that have melted together, one that supplies power to the blower motor and one that feeds power from the brake light switch to the brake lights FIGURE 29-10. In this example, turning on the ignition switch would cause the brake lights to come on because power would be sent to the blower fuse and then, due to the short in the wiring, to the brake lights.

Unintended **high resistance** in a circuit causes a reduction in current flow in the circuit as well as a drop in voltage at the resistance. Both of these cause the intended circuit device to not operate effectively or at all. Unintended high resistance can also cause an overheating condition at the area of resistance, which can melt wire insulation or plastic **connectors**. This condition can be caused by a number of faults, including corroded or loose harness connectors, wire that is too thin for the circuit current flow, incorrectly connected terminals, and poorly soldered joints FIGURE 29-11.

Voltage drop is another name for high resistance, and voltage drop testing is the best way of finding high resistance in the feed side or ground side of the circuit. For a voltage drop to occur, two conditions must present: resistance and current flow. Thus, a voltage drop in

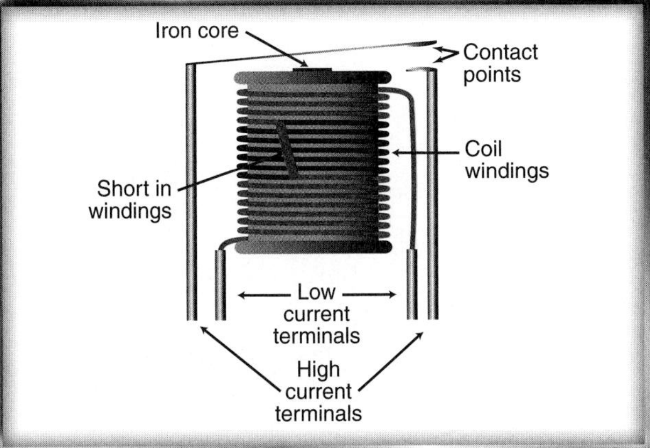

FIGURE 29-8 Short circuit.

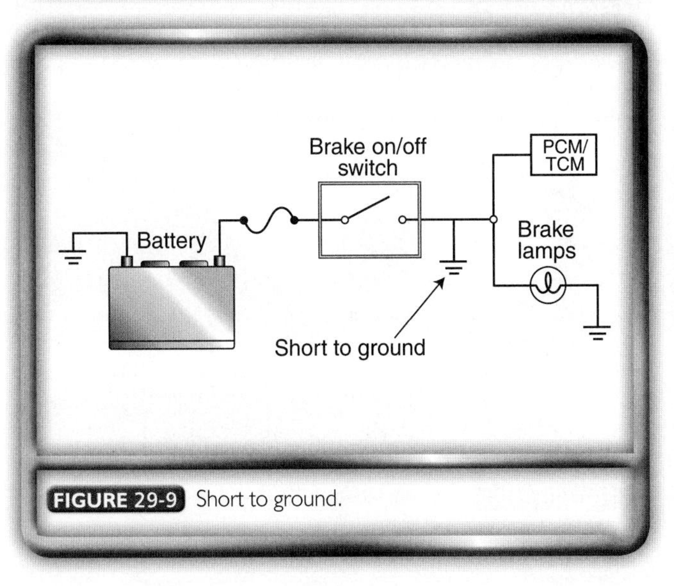
Brake on/off switch
PCM/ TCM
Battery
Brake lamps
Short to ground
FIGURE 29-9 Short to ground.

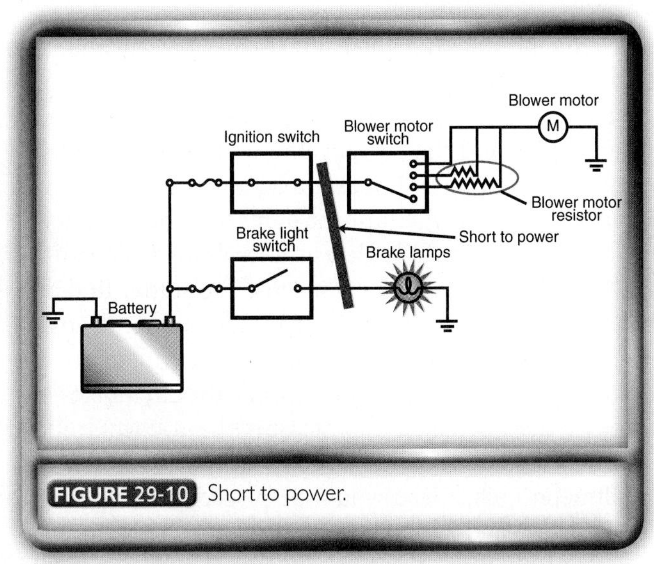
Blower motor
M
Ignition switch
Blower motor switch
Blower motor resistor
Brake light switch
Short to power
Brake lamps
Battery
FIGURE 29-10 Short to power.

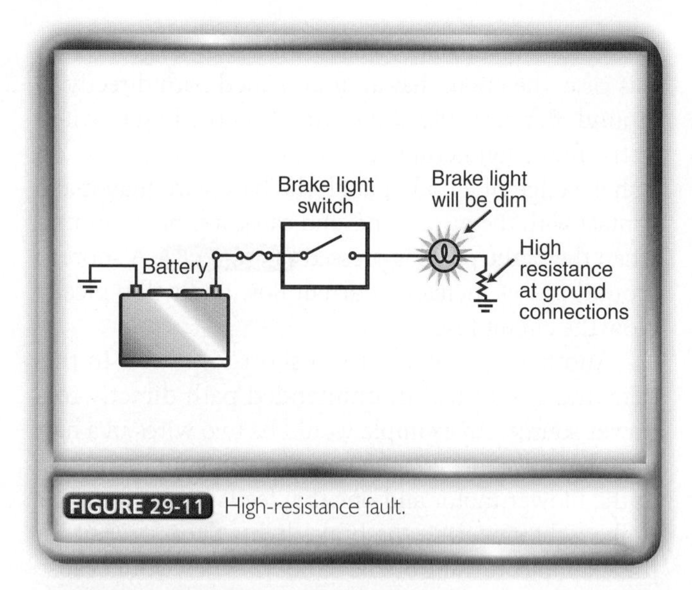
Brake light switch
Brake light will be dim
Battery
High resistance at ground connections

FIGURE 29-11 High-resistance fault.

> **TECHNICIAN TIP**
>
> Since current flowing through a resistance causes heat, you can sometimes locate the high resistance in the circuit just by feeling the wires and connections. Using the very simple theory that resistance causes heat and therefore heat causes even more resistance then changes in current (amps) in a circuit will change as the circuit gets hotter. So, when working on circuits for a long period of time, expect the amperage readings on a DVOM to change because of the heat generated in the circuit. Remember: if resistance goes up, current flow will go down; and if resistance goes down, current flow will go up.
>
> For example, if one of the battery posts is corroded between the post and the battery cable and if you operate the starter for several seconds and then feel each battery terminal, the one with excessive resistance will be warmer than the other.

a circuit indicates that there is resistance present and current is flowing, or trying to flow, through the resistance. If the high-resistance fault is excessive, it will reduce both the voltage and the current flow in the circuit, affecting its performance. For example, a voltage drop in the headlight circuit will cause the lights to be dim, reducing their performance. A high resistance in the main battery lead to the starter motor will cause the starter to crank the engine over slowly or not at all. The voltage drop can be measured in a circuit by placing a voltmeter across two different points in a circuit while the circuit is being operated. For example, to measure the voltage drop in the main positive battery lead to the starter motor, the voltmeter's black lead would be placed on the positive battery lead and the red lead would be placed on the main battery lead of the starter motor, and the voltage would then be read on the meter while the engine is cranked FIGURE 29-12.

Ohm's Law and Circuits

Ohm's law helps us to understand the relationship between volts, amps, and ohms. They always have to balance out. If they do not, you made a mistake. Ohm's law tells us that it takes 1 volt to push 1 amp through 1 ohm of resistance. That gives us the relationship among the three units. Volts and resistance are physical things. Volts are the surplus of electrons creating electrical pressure. Resistance is the physical restriction of the conductor. Amps are the amount of electrons moved. That means that amps are the result of both the volts and resistance. For example, if resistance doubles and voltage stays the same, current flow must be cut in half. To illustrate this relationship, consider the following: If you steadily push (voltage) a loaded wheelbarrow twice as far up a hill (ohms), you will only move half the amount of dirt in a given amount of time FIGURE 29-13. It is the same with the electrical circuit: If the pressure (volts) stays the same but the restriction

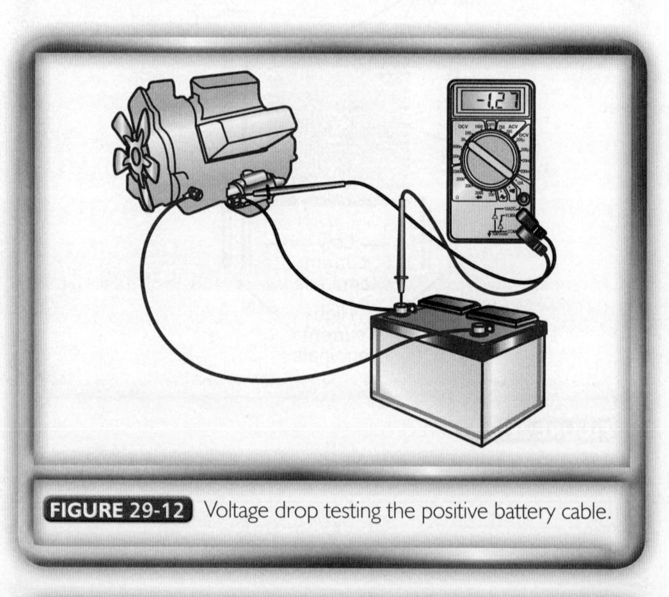
-1.27

FIGURE 29-12 Voltage drop testing the positive battery cable.

FIGURE 29-13 Current flow is the result of voltage and resistance.

(ohms) doubles, then the electrons (amps) will be reduced by half. Conversely, if the voltage is doubled and the resistance stays the same, then amperage will double.

If you understand the preceding, then you are well on your way to diagnosing electrical problems. Here is a question. If the amps in a circuit are lower than they should be, what are the two possible causes? First, the source voltage could be low. In that case, you would use a voltmeter to measure the source voltage at the battery. The second possibility is that the resistance in the circuit is too high. In that case, you would use a voltmeter to see if there is an excessive voltage drop on both sides of the circuit that would be caused by high resistance. If the voltage drop is within specifications, you would use an ohmmeter to measure the resistance of the load.

Most of the time when circuits fail it is because the current flow is too low or nonexistent. Yes, it is possible that the battery is dead or discharged, but more likely there is high resistance as a voltage drop either in the feed side or the ground side of the circuit. Or the electrical device has too much resistance or is open. Performing a voltage drop test on both sides of the circuit will quickly identify if there is an excessive voltage drop present. And a resistance check of the electrical device will indicate a high resistance or open condition in the component. Knowing the specifications that go along with these steps will enable you to repair more than half of the electrical problems on a vehicle.

Circuits are made up of components and interconnecting conductors, such as wires, arranged to manage and control the flow of electrons to perform specific electrical tasks. Understanding circuits and how to take electrical measurements is essential to perform electrical repair activities. Circuits come in two basic configurations: series circuits and parallel circuits. The two types can also be combined into what is called a series-parallel circuit. Understanding how electricity behaves within each of these circuits will help you know how the circuit operates and how to approach diagnosis. It will also allow you to apply Ohm's law correctly to each type of circuit. We will look at the types of circuits further after finishing our discussion of Ohm's law.

Ohm's Law and Ohm's Law Calculations

Because Ohm's law is a relationship between volts, amps, and ohms, and because they must always balance out, if we know any two of the values, then we can calculate the third. If resistance stays the same but voltage rises, then the greater force pushes more current through the circuit. If resistance stays the same but voltage decreases, then less current will flow through the circuit. That means that the total current flow of a circuit in amps always equals the voltage divided by the resistance.

In calculating Ohm's law, R stands for resistance, V for voltage, and A for current (A is for amps).* Depending on which value you wish to solve for, you will apply one of the following three formulas:

- $A = V/R$
- $V = A \times R$
- $R = V \div A$

Voltage can vary across different points in a circuit, but determining the current at any point can be found without an ammeter by using Ohm's law.

Using the Ohm's law circle will help you remember which math operation to use FIGURE 29-14. All you have to do is place your finger over the value you are looking for. If you place your finger on the top value (volts), then you would multiply amps by resistance. If you place your finger on one of the side values, then you would divide volts by the other value. This means two things. First, the values always have to balance. And second, as long as you know any two values, the third can be calculated. This is especially helpful when determining current flow, because instead of breaking

Applied Science

AS-70: Ohm's Law: The technician can demonstrate an understanding of and explain the use of Ohm's law in verifying circuit parameters (resistance, voltage, amperage).

Ohm's law quantifies the relationship between amperage, voltage, and resistance in any given circuit. It provides a means to calculate any one of these parameters from the values of the other two. Ohm's law is easiest applied through the use of a circle diagram like the one shown here:

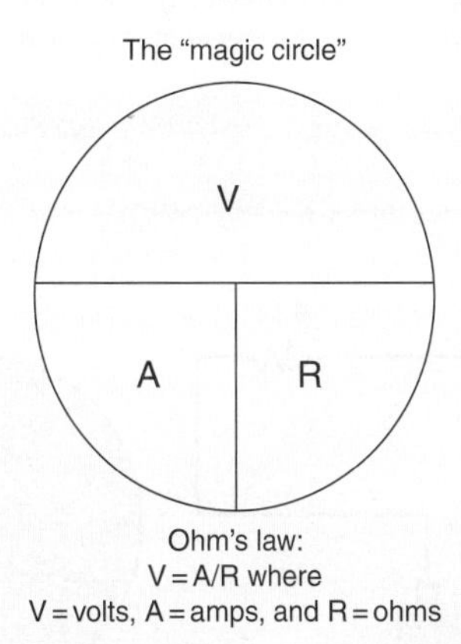
The "magic circle"
V
A
R
Ohm's law:
V = A/R where
V = volts, A = amps, and R = ohms

These diagrams are used by placing your finger over the parameter you are trying to calculate, then reading the remainder of the diagram to identify the calculation you need to perform. For example, if you need to work out the amperage flowing in the circuit, block off the A, and your calculation is V ÷ R, or voltage divided by resistance. For a 12-volt automotive circuit with 20 ohms of resistance, your calculation is 12 ÷ 20, to arrive at 0.6 amps.

into a circuit to measure current with a meter, if the voltage and resistance are known, Ohm's law may be used to calculate amps.

For example, battery voltage can be measured. Let's use 12 volts. The value of the resistor, 4 ohms, is on its casing. Current then equals voltage (12 volts) divided by resistance (4 ohms). We can quickly calculate that there are 3 amps of current flowing through every point in the circuit FIGURE 29-15.

Solving Ohm's Law

Using the rules of Ohm's law gives an accurate method of determining values in an electrical circuit. To assist with these problems, use the Ohm's law circle FIGURE 29-16. If the value of V and R are known, then to find A, V is divided by R. Place your thumb over A and the circle tells you this formula. Similarly, if V and A are known, then R can be found by dividing V by A. If A and R, are known, then V is found by multiplying A by R.

In the circuit diagram in FIGURE 29-17, the value of the amperage is not known. The applied voltage is 12 volts (V) and the resistance is 4 ohms (Ω). To find the value of A, simply divide V by R, or 12 by 4. The value of A is 3 amps (A).

In the circuit diagram in FIGURE 26-16, the value of the applied voltage is not known but the amperage and resistance are. To find the value of V, multiply A by R, or 6 amps by 4 ohms. The answer is 24 volts.

In the circuit diagram in FIGURE 26-17, the value of the current flow is unknown. To find the value of A, divide V by R, or in this case, 12 volts divided by 3 ohms. The value of A is 4 amps.

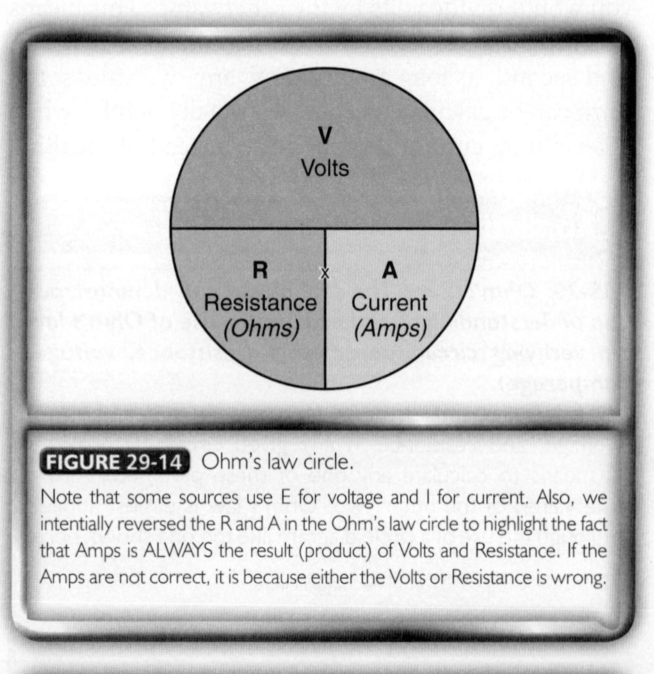
V
Volts
R
Resistance
(Ohms)
A
Current
(Amps)

FIGURE 29-14 Ohm's law circle.

Note that some sources use E for voltage and I for current. Also, we intentially reversed the R and A in the Ohm's law circle to highlight the fact that Amps is ALWAYS the result (product) of Volts and Resistance. If the Amps are not correct, it is because either the Volts or Resistance is wrong.

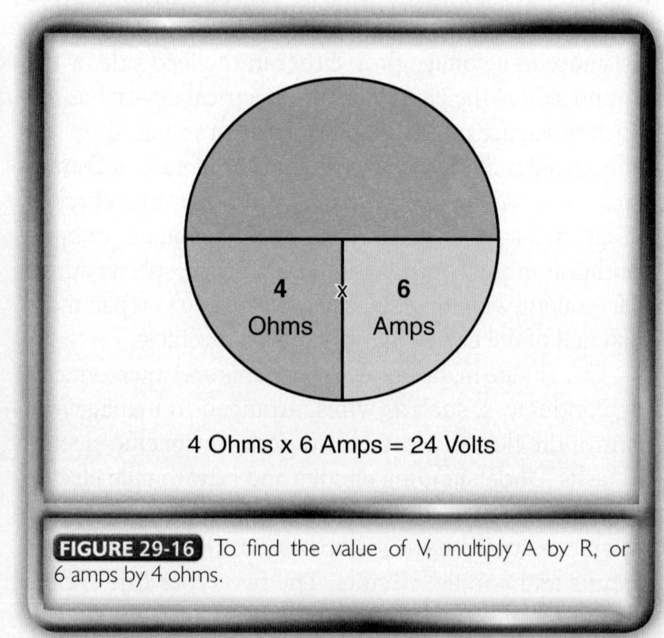
4
Ohms
6
Amps
4 Ohms x 6 Amps = 24 Volts

FIGURE 29-16 To find the value of V, multiply A by R, or 6 amps by 4 ohms.

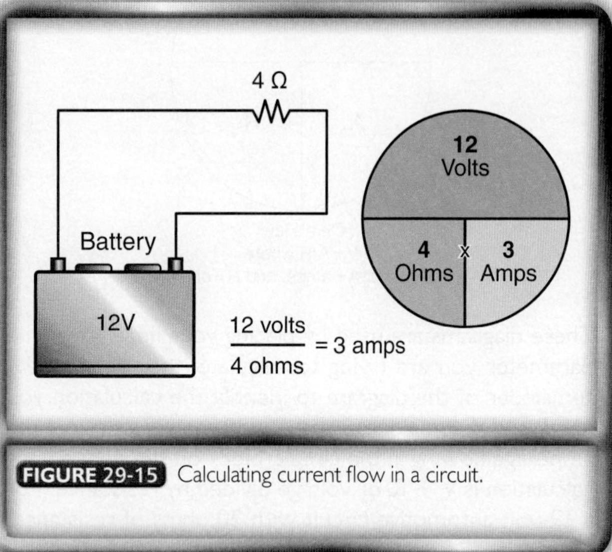
4 Ω
Battery
12V
12 volts / 4 ohms = 3 amps
12
Volts
4
Ohms
3
Amps

FIGURE 29-15 Calculating current flow in a circuit.

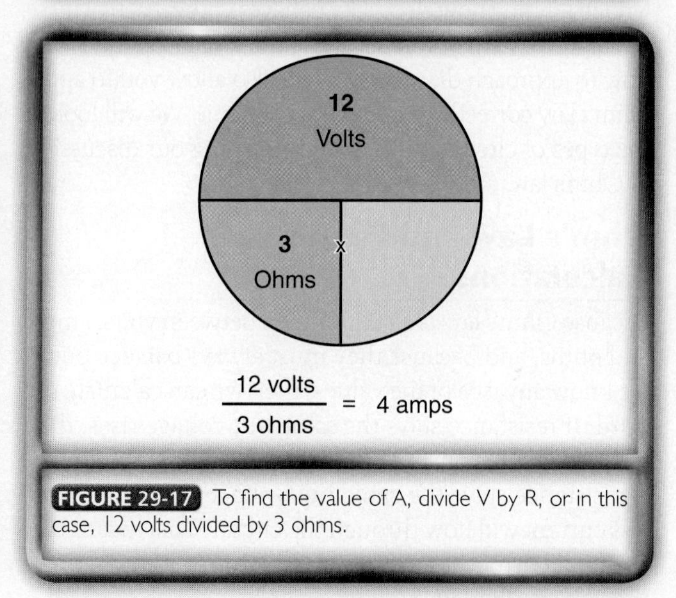
12
Volts
3
Ohms
12 volts / 3 ohms = 4 amps

FIGURE 29-17 To find the value of A, divide V by R, or in this case, 12 volts divided by 3 ohms.

Electrical Power and the Power Equation

Energy is the potential to do work. However, work is done only when the energy is released. A disconnected battery is not doing work, but it has the potential to do work and is therefore a source of energy. The difference in electron supply at the battery terminals creates electrical force and is sometimes called the potential difference. In the case of a standard charged automotive battery, it has a potential of approximately 12 volts. Tapping this potential means turning one form of energy, the battery's chemical energy, into another form of energy, electrical energy.

Turning one form of energy into another is called energy transformation. The amount of energy transformed is the amount of work done. When a person's legs turn the pedals of a bicycle, chemical energy (from oxygen and food) is being turned into mechanical energy. A motorcycle engine turns chemical energy into thermal energy, and then into mechanical energy. In each case, work is being done, but there is a difference with the motorcycle—it does the work more quickly, delivering more mechanical energy faster. That difference is called power. Power is the rate at which work is performed. It is also known as the rate of transforming energy. In an electrical circuit, power refers to the rate at which electrical energy is transformed into another kind of energy.

The unit of electrical power is the watt. One watt is produced when 1 volt causes 1 amp of current to flow. From this comes the power equation: P, the power in watts, equals V, the voltage in volts, multiplied by A, the current in amps. This calculation is applied similarly to Ohm's law and is typically represented as a triangle FIGURE 29-18.

When current flows in a circuit with a resistor in it, the resistor becomes hotter as it converts electrical energy into heat energy. If this circuit is powered by a 12-volt battery with a current of 2 amps, using the power equation ($P = V \times A$) we can determine that the resistor is using 24 watts of power.

It is also possible to simplify and transpose the power equation. If power equals voltage times current, then:

- Voltage equals power divided by current: $V = P \div A$
- Current equals power divided by voltage: $A = P \div V$

Solving Power Equations

Electrical power is a measurement of the rate at which electricity is consumed or created. When used in relation to loads, it is a measure of electricity consumed. A light bulb uses a certain amount of electrical power, but the power used is not an indication of brightness; it is a measure of power consumption. When used in relation to

Applied Science

AS-71: Resistance: The technician can demonstrate an understanding of the relationship of resistance to heat, voltage drop, and circuit parameters.

The electrical resistance of a component is the component's opposition to the flow of electrical current. Any resistance in a circuit creates a voltage drop across the resistive component, be it a resistor, a bulb, an electric motor, or merely a wire. The amount of voltage drop is proportional to the amount of resistance. Resistors work by dissipating energy in the form of heat; therefore, for a given amount of current flowing in a circuit, the higher the resistance of a component, the more heat it will produce.

Let's look at an example using a rear window defogger. The defogger elements form a resistor in the circuit. In this case, heat is produced by the resistor grid to defog the window. The resistance of each grid line creates a steady voltage drop across the length of the grid line. Current flowing through the grid line then creates heat. Broken grid lines cannot conduct current flow, so there is no voltage drop, nor heat generated in that grid line. Battery voltage (12 volts) is applied across the element when you switch on the defogger. If you were to measure the voltage at the center of one of the grid lines in the element, you should expect to see a voltage of approximately 6 volts. If the grid is burned open on the ground side, then the voltage would read about 12 volts, since there cannot be a voltage drop if there is no current flow. If the grid was burned open on the power side, the voltage would near 0 volts because the current flow cannot get past the open circuit to the middle of the grid line. Moving the voltmeter toward the side with the break can pinpoint the exact location of the broken grid line so that repairs can be made.

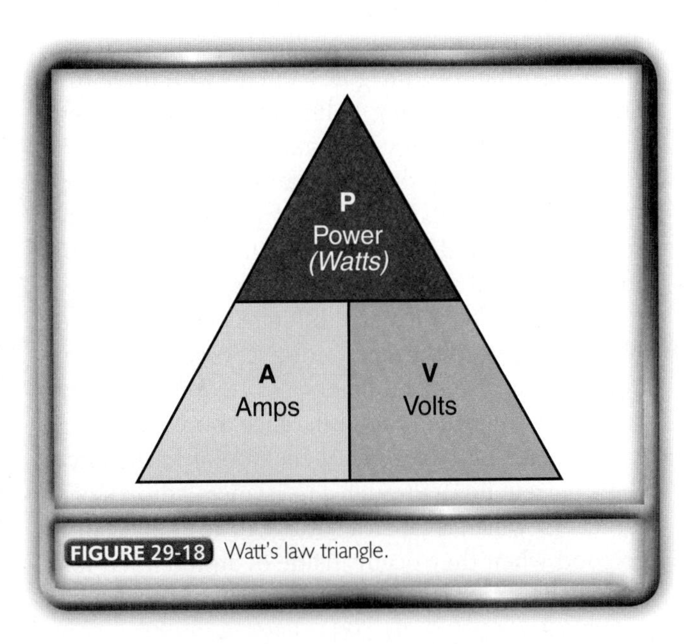
P
Power
(Watts)
A
Amps
V
Volts

FIGURE 29-18 Watt's law triangle.

generators, it is a measure of electrical power produced. One volt pushing 1 amp equals 1 watt of electrical power. To calculate power, the current flow in the circuit is multiplied by the voltage used. So,

$$P = A \times V, \text{ or Watts} = \text{Amps} \times \text{Volts}$$

This is demonstrated by the diagram in FIGURE 29-20. For reference purposes, 746 watts equal 1 horsepower.

If a 12-volt circuit with a single light has a current flow of 5 amps, then applying the formula will yield:

- $P = A \times V$
- $P = 5\ A \times 12\ V$
- $P = 60\ W$

The power consumed by the circuit is 60 watts, and the bulb will carry a rating of 60 watts. This rule can be applied to any circuit where the voltage and current flow are known. However, if the values of voltage or current flow are not known, then Ohm's law can be used to determine the missing value. As an example: $V = A \times R$. By expanding $P = A \times V$, it can be said that

$$P = A \times (A \times R), \text{ or } P = A^2 \times R.$$

Similarly, by applying $A = V \div R$, we have

$$P = (V \div R) \times V, \text{ or } P = V^2 \div R.$$

Series Circuits

A series circuit is the simplest type of electrical circuit. In a series circuit, there is only one path for current to flow. All of the current flows to each component in turn. It also means that all the electrons flow at the same rate throughout all parts of the circuit. Current is equal everywhere within a series circuit.

In a series circuit, if there is more than one resistance in the circuit, those resistances are connected one after the other; thus the resistances add up. The total resistance in a series circuit is the sum of all of the individual resistances. For example, imagine a circuit with three resistors in series, each having 4 ohms of resistance, powered by a 12-volt battery. Total resistance of the three 4-ohm resistors is 12 ohms, since resistance adds up in a series circuit. According to Ohm's law, if 12 volts is applied to a circuit that has 12 ohms of resistance, the resulting current flow will be 1 amp.

However, the voltage at different points within the circuit changes, as the electromotive force, or pressure, drops from a potential difference of 12 volts as it leaves the battery to virtually no difference, no voltage at all, as it returns to the battery. At each point in the circuit where current flows through a resistance, a drop in voltage occurs, which is called a **voltage drop**. Voltage drops are good when they occur inside of an intended load. They are bad when they occur where they are not wanted.

In FIGURE 29-19, after the first resistor, voltage has dropped from 12 to 8 volts. After the second, it is down to 4 volts. After the third, it is 0 volts. The voltage drop across each resistor can be found by subtracting the voltage after a resistor from the voltage before it, or the difference can be measured. The voltmeter will read 4 volts in each case because that is the difference between the two points, the potential difference, or voltage.

Ohm's law can be used in series circuits to calculate voltage, resistance, and current. Any one of these can be calculated as long as the values of the other two are known.

The series circuit laws listed here provide a summary of how electricity behaves in a series circuit, which is defined as a circuit with multiple loads but only one path for current to flow:

- Current flow stays the same in a series circuit. Current flow is the same in all parts of the circuit.
- Voltage drops as current goes through resistance(s) in series. The applied voltage is equal to the sum of the individual voltage drops (Kirchhoff's voltage law).
- Resistance adds up in series. Total circuit resistance is equal to the sum of the individual resistances; for example, $R_T = R_1 + R_2 + R_3$, and so on.

Parallel Circuits

In a series circuit, components are connected like links in a chain. If any link opens, current to all of the components is cut off. In a parallel circuit, all components are connected directly to the voltage supply FIGURE 29-20. If any connection or component fails in a parallel circuit, current continues to flow normally through the remaining circuits. This is one reason why parallel circuits are used

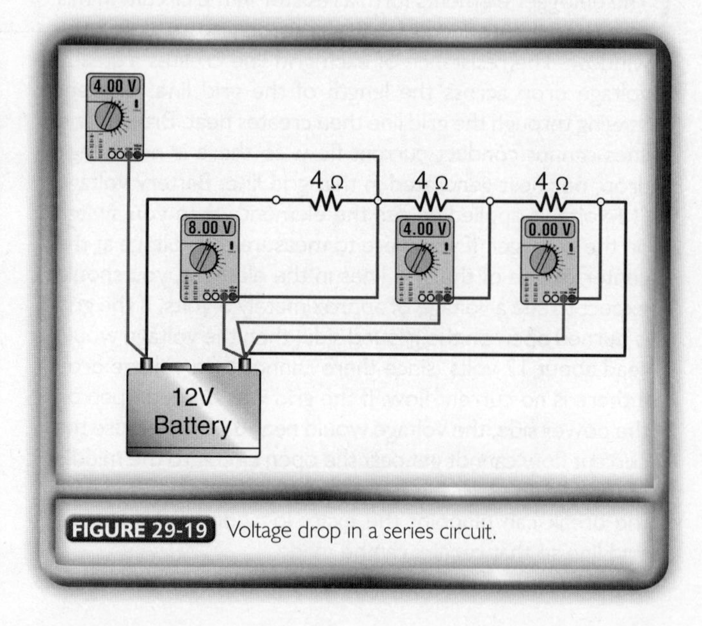
4.00 V
4 Ω
4 Ω
4 Ω
8.00 V
4.00 V
0.00 V
12V
Battery

FIGURE 29-19 Voltage drop in a series circuit.

in automotive applications, such as headlight and taillight systems. If one lamp fails, current continues to flow through the other lamps in parallel. In a series circuit, all would go out, which could be disastrous.

Also, since all components connect directly to the battery terminals, the metal of the vehicle's chassis can become one of the conductors. One terminal of the battery and one terminal of each component can be connected anywhere on the body or chassis to complete the circuit. This is called a common, or ground, connection. It saves a lot of connecting wire.

While electricity always behaves according to the laws of physics, when it operates in a parallel circuit, there are some additional laws you need to know. The parallel circuit laws listed here should be applied when working with parallel circuits:

- The voltage across all branches of a parallel circuit are equal.
- The total current in a parallel circuit equals the sum of the current flowing in each branch of the circuit.
- The total resistance of a parallel circuit decreases as more branches are added. Total parallel circuit resistance will always be less than the lowest branch resistance.

Let's look at those laws a bit more closely. A feature of a properly working parallel circuit is that the voltage across each branch is the same as the other branches. No matter how many branches are added, or removed, as long as they are in parallel, the voltage across them will be the same as across each of the other branches, including the battery. Another feature of a parallel circuit is that the current flowing in each branch is determined by the resistance of that branch along with the voltage used by that branch.

In a parallel circuit where the resistors in each branch are the same, the current flowing in each branch is also the same. The sum of their individual currents is equal to the total current flowing in the entire parallel circuit. When the resistances are not equal, the current divides in accordance with the resistance of each branch, but the total current flow is still the sum of the currents flowing in each branch FIGURE 29-21.

Parallel Circuit Resistance

Resistance in a parallel circuit is not as easily calculated as it is in a series circuit, because as branches are added, another path for current to flow to ground is added. Adding extra paths reduces the circuit's total resistance to current flow. For example, if you have a 12-volt parallel circuit with three branches, each branch having a 12-ohm resistor that allows 1 amp of current flow, and you then add another parallel branch with a 12-ohm resistor to the circuit, the result will be the opposite of what might be expected. Current increases from 3 amps to 4 amps. This is because in a parallel circuit adding more branches provides more pathways, but decreases the overall circuit resistance; thus, current flow increases. This is like having a freeway with three lanes and bumper-to-bumper traffic. If you add a fourth lane, the resistance to flow decreases and cars can move more easily. Another visual example would be if you had a bucket full of water and the bucket had three holes in the bottom. If another hole were added, the total flow out of the bucket would speed up, which means the resistance to flow decreases. To calculate resistance, use the formula in FIGURE 29-22 and substitute the value of each resistor in the place of R_1, R_2, etc.

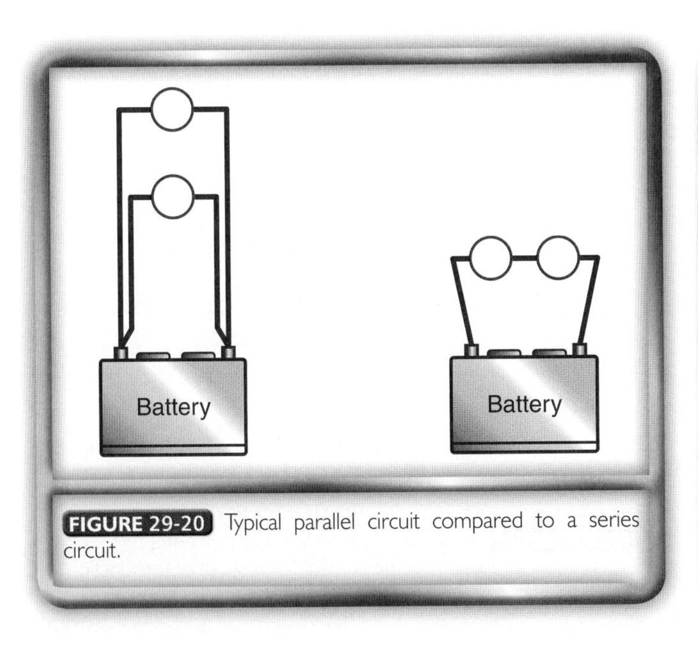
Battery
Battery

FIGURE 29-20 Typical parallel circuit compared to a series circuit.

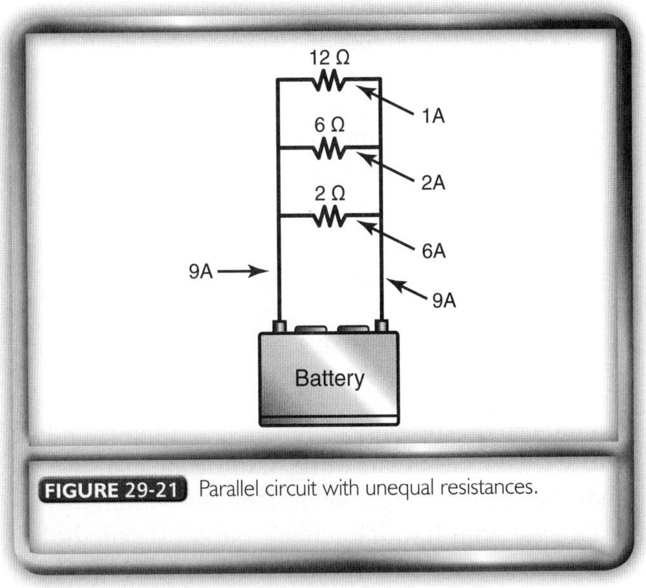
12 Ω
6 Ω
2 Ω
1A
2A
6A
9A
9A
Battery

FIGURE 29-21 Parallel circuit with unequal resistances.

$$R_T = \frac{1}{\frac{1}{R1} + \frac{1}{R1} + \frac{1}{R1}}$$

2 resistors in parallel

$$R_T = \frac{R1 \times R2}{R1 + R2}$$

FIGURE 29-22 Calculating parallel resistance with uneven resistances.

Series-Parallel Circuits

When electrical components are wired together one after another so that there is only one path for current flow, they are said to be wired "in series." When they are wired together side by side, so there is more than one path for current to flow, they are said to be wired "in parallel." A **series-parallel circuit** is made of both a series circuit and a parallel circuit. The series circuit can be before or after the parallel portion of the circuit. Series-parallel circuits can be analyzed using the same electrical laws that apply to separate series or parallel circuits; you just have to apply the series laws to the series portion and the parallel laws to the parallel portion.

A circuit for dash lights is an example of a series-parallel circuit in an automotive application. In this situation, a variable resistor is connected in series with a number of dash lights, which are connected in parallel to each other. When the variable resistor is turned, the resistance changes. As the resistance increases, the voltage drop across the potentiometer increases and the current flow decreases. This lowers the voltage and current flow to the dash lights, making the dash lights dimmer. When the variable resistor is turned such that its resistance is lowered, the voltage drop across it is reduced and the current flow in the circuit increases, making the dash lights brighter. Since the dash lights are in parallel, they each receive the same amount of voltage, and the total circuit current flow is divided equally between them, making them equally bright as one another.

Kirchhoff's Current Law

Kirchhoff's current law describes a fundamental electrical principle and is used by technicians in understanding how all electrical circuits work. Many technicians would understand the principle behind the law without necessarily associating it with Kirchhoff. Simply stated, the law is that current entering any junction is equal to the sum of the current flowing out of the junction. For example, in a junction of three conductors, current is flowing in at 10 amps from conductor A and out by the other two conductors, B and C **FIGURE 29-23**. According to Kirchhoff's current law, the sum of the current in conductors B and C will equal the current flowing into the junction at conductor A, or 10 amps.

Electrical Components

Electrical components such as switches, fuses, circuit breakers, resistors, capacitors, and relays are all used in a circuit to modify or manage the flow of current. Each component performs a specific task within the circuit and will be connected into its particular circuit. To ensure the components' correct operation, they will often have terminals numbered or marked with the connections and be referenced in wiring diagrams or schematics.

Some components are **polarity sensitive**. This means they must be connected into the circuit with the correct polarity to each lead. For example, some capacitors, and most semiconductor components, are polarity sensitive. Polarity-sensitive components have the polarity marked on at least one connection to ensure that the user connects them into the circuit correctly.

Switches

A **switch** is an electrical device used to turn the current on and off in a circuit. When turned off, switches open the circuit, stopping current flow; when turned on, they close the circuit, allowing current to flow. For example, switch off—light goes out; switch on—light comes on. There are many different types and configurations of switches, including toggle switches, push-button switches, and specialty switches for turn signal indicators and windshield

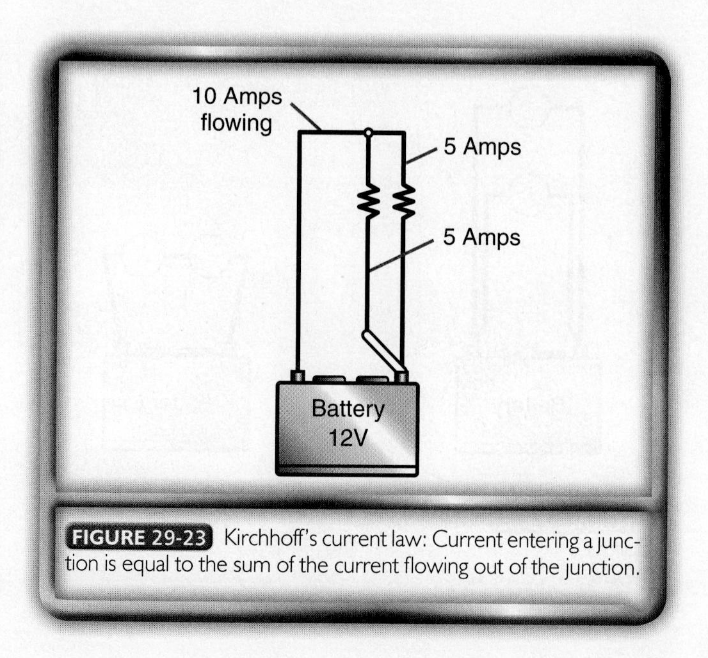
10 Amps flowing
5 Amps
5 Amps
Battery
12V

FIGURE 29-23 Kirchhoff's current law: Current entering a junction is equal to the sum of the current flowing out of the junction.

wipers FIGURE 29-24. The most basic switches have only two terminals and are simply on or off.

More complex switches have many terminals and contacts inside them to switch a number of circuits at the same time. The **turn signal switch** is an example of a more complex switch. It has three positions: center for off, pushed in one direction for the left turn signals, pushed in the other direction for the right turn signals. **Circuit or schematic diagrams** show switches, their contacts, and the surrounding circuits so that the technician can identify how they operate in a circuit. The terminals on the switch are often numbered or lettered to indicate the correct way of connecting them into their circuits and to show the mating connectors in the wiring diagrams.

Fuses, Fusible Links, and Circuit Breakers

Fuses and **circuit breakers** are designed to protect electrical circuits by opening the circuit if the current flow is excessive. The most common kinds of circuit protection devices are fuses, fusible links, circuit breakers, and positive temperature coefficient (PTC) thermistor protection devices. Fuses and circuit breakers are rated in amps, and their ratings are usually marked on them. Fusible links are typically rated by their wire size.

Fuses are typically used in lighting and accessory circuits where current flow is usually moderate. Usually, a fuse contains a metal strip that is designed to overheat and melt when subjected to a specified excessive level of current flow, breaking the circuit and stopping the excessive current flow from potentially damaging the wiring harness and more valuable components. Fuses come in a variety of configurations, from cylindrical glass cartridge fuses to plastic blade fuses FIGURE 29-25. They also come in a variety of sizes and amp ratings. Fuses are typically housed in fuse boxes located around the vehicle, typically under the hood and/or dash.

A fusible link is made of a short length (usually 6" [15 cm] or less) of smaller diameter wire that has a lower melting point than standard wire and insulation that is fire resistant. Fusible links are typically placed near the battery to protect the wiring harness between the battery and any fuse boxes. In most cases, they are used to carry higher current flows than fuses, and typically feed power to one or more circuits FIGURE 29-26. Fusible links are fairly durable, and do not fail very often, unless there is a substantial short circuit in the system or the fusible link wire is abused by excessive flexing or pulling on it. Some newer vehicles use maxi-fuses, which are large blade-type fuses, instead of fusible links.

Circuit breakers are different from fuses and fusible links in two ways. First, they are not destroyed by excess current. And secondly, they can be reset, either automatically or manually. In a circuit breaker, a bimetallic strip heats up and bends, opening a set of contacts and breaking the circuit when current flow becomes excessive. In most types, as the strip cools, it resumes its original shape. The contacts then close, completing the circuit once more. These are called self-resetting circuit breakers. Manual breakers must be reset by hand, which could involve flipping a lever or inserting a small rod to reset the bimetal spring once it cools down.

PTC thermistors are also used as circuit protection devices. They have very low resistance at room temperature, but increase in resistance as the temperature increases. If too much current starts to flow through a PTC, the small voltage drop creates heat in the PTC.

FIGURE 29-24 Typical automotive switches.

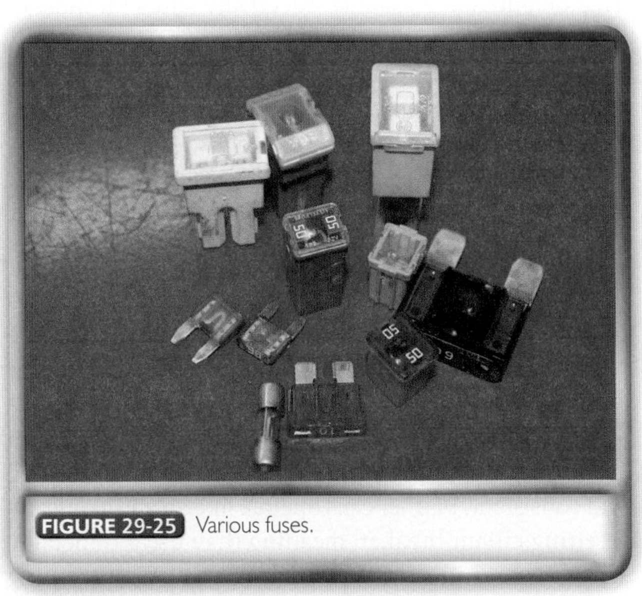

FIGURE 29-25 Various fuses.

FIGURE 29-26 A fusible link is typically placed near the battery and carries the current needed to power an individual circuit or a range of circuits.

The increased heat produces increased resistance, which further increases the voltage drop. This cycle continues quickly until the PTC reaches its maximum resistance. This heightened resistance effectively shuts off most of the current flow to the protected device. PTCs generally reset once power is removed and they are allowed to cool. They are typically integrated into components such as power window motors and door locks.

Flasher Can/Control

The **flasher can** is the control mechanism for the turn signal lights on the vehicle. As the name suggests, it flashes or turns the turn signal lights on and off at a regular rate to indicate a change in the vehicle's direction. Flasher cans are mechanical devices, while flasher controls are generally electronic devices FIGURE 29-27. Both types perform the same job, but the electronic version is more reliable and consistent. Flasher cans operate like an automatically resetting circuit breaker, meaning they use a bimetallic strip to open and close the switch contacts. This opening and closing gives them a distinctive clicking sound that, along with the turn signal indicator lights on the dash, tells the driver when the turn signals are on so that they remember turn them off when needed. Electronic flasher controls control the on/off function electronically, which means they can be designed to operate over a wider range of current flow, which makes them ideal for trailer towing. In many cases, the hazard lamps are also operated by a flasher can or flasher control.

DOT APPROVED
2x27W+5W
4x27W
MAX 6 LAMPS
SAE J945, J590
FMVSS 108

FIGURE 29-27 Flasher control and flasher can.

Relays

Relays are switches that are turned on and off by a small electrical current. They are ideal for using a small current to control a larger current. An example would be the horn circuit. A small current can be turned on and off by the horn switch in the steering wheel, using a light-duty switch and wires. The small current is then used to activate the relay, which sends the larger current to the horn. Thus, larger wires are needed only up front where they can be shorter, and smaller wires can be used to run up the steering column. Most electrical components found in a motor vehicle are controlled by relays. ECUs use relays to control components such as fuel pumps, headlights, and the cooling fan. All of these circuits carry large electrical loads.

The relay is made up of an electromagnet, a set of switch contacts, terminals, and the case. The electromagnet is a winding of fine metal-insulated wire wrapped around an iron core. Each end of the winding is connected to one of the terminals. The contacts usually consist of three contacts—two fixed and one movable. The movable contact is fixed to a spring-loaded armature blade and is held against one of the fixed contacts, which is called the **normally closed (NC)** contact. When the relay coil is activated, the electromagnet pulls the movable armature blade contact away from the NC contact and against the normally open (NO) contact, sending power out to the controlled device. It also opens the NC contact points on that type of relay.

When the contact points are closed, current flows across the contact points and out to the electrical device to the rest of the circuit. As long as the small control current flows through the relay windings, the much larger current for the load will flow through the relay's contact points. A **solid-state relay** acts like a mechanical relay but does not have any moving parts. This means that electronic relays do not use mechanical switches, but instead use transistorized circuitry to turn the circuit on and off. They also do not make any sound, unless they were specifically designed with components to do that.

Automotive relay terminals use one of two standard labeling systems: 85, 86, 30, 87a, and 87 or 1, 2, 3, 4, 5 FIGURE 29-28.

- 85 or 1 = One end of the relay winding
- 86 or 2 = The other end of the relay winding
- 30 or 3 = Common—movable switch contact
- 87a or 4 = NC fixed contact to the common
- 87 or 5 = NO fixed contact to the common

When electromagnetic relays are de-energized, the collapse of the magnetic field induces a large voltage spike in the relay coil windings. If unchecked, this voltage can be transmitted back into the circuit where it can damage electronic components. Some relays deal with this danger by placing either a suppression diode or a resistor in parallel with the winding FIGURE 29-29. Doing so reduces the voltage spike by shunting the voltage spike from the output side of the coil back to the input side of the coil. This design prevents the voltage from spiking so high when the relay is de-energized. When replacing a relay that has spike protection, make sure to use a new relay that is specified for the application.

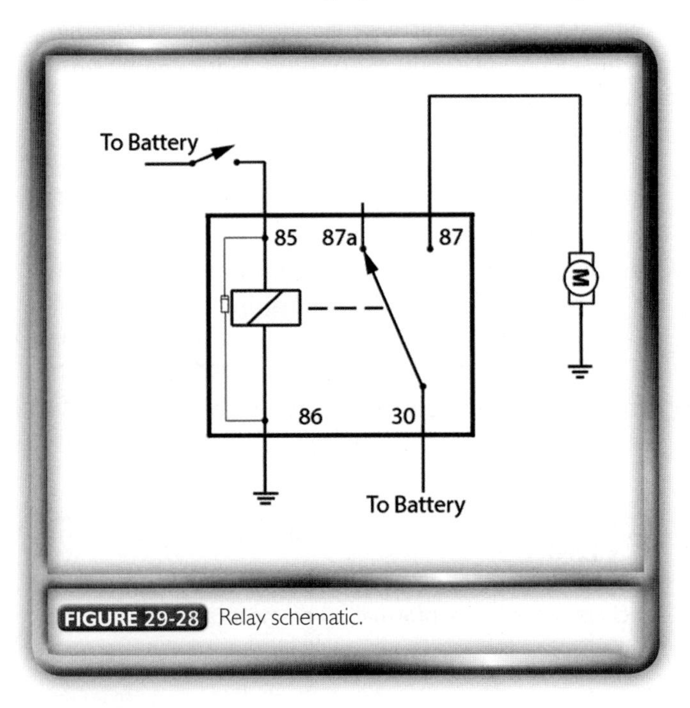
To Battery
85
87a
87
86
30
To Battery
M

FIGURE 29-28 Relay schematic.

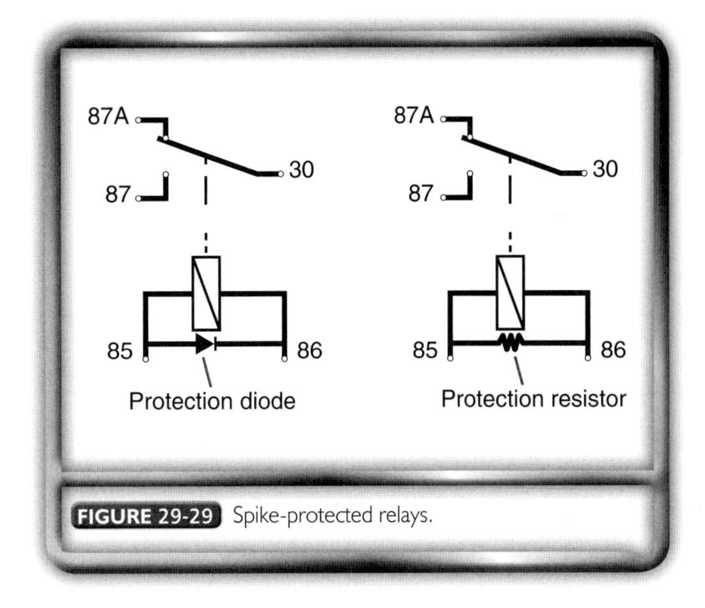
87A
30
87
85
86
Protection diode
87A
30
87
85
86
Protection resistor

FIGURE 29-29 Spike-protected relays.

Solenoids

A **solenoid** is an electromechanical device that coverts electrical energy into mechanical linear (back-and-forth) movement. Solenoids can be used to pull or push. In a simple solenoid, insulated wire is wound many times around a hollow cylindrical form. A sliding mild steel core is made to fit inside the hollow form. When the winding is energized, the resulting magnetic field attracts the mild steel, drawing it into the form and producing linear motion. Solenoids can be very strong and produce a lot of mechanical energy. Solenoid design may incorporate

Applied Science

AS-61: Parallel/Series Circuits: The technician can explain current flow and voltage in series and parallel circuits.

The terms "series" and "parallel" describe different ways in which components in a circuit can be connected. In a series circuit, all components are connected along a single path. Electricity can flow only one way, so the flow of electrons, or the current flow, within the circuit is the same at all points. The voltage in the system will change at different points due to voltage drops at various resistors. In a parallel circuit, components are connected so that the circuit divides into two or more paths before recombining. All components are connected to the same voltage supply, so the same voltage is applied to all components. Current flow in different branches of a parallel circuit changes depending on the resistance in each branch; therefore, different branches of the circuit may experience differing amperage if their resistance values are different.

return springs, multiple windings, electrical contacts, and mechanical connections.

Fuel injectors and starter motor solenoids are two of the many solenoid-type components used in a motor vehicle. The operation of a solenoid is similar to a relay, but where a relay uses a magnetic field to close an electrical circuit, a solenoid uses a magnetic field to create lateral movement and, in the case of a starter solenoid, to also close heavy electrical contacts. The metal core, used by the electromagnet to strengthen the magnetic field, is referred to as an **armature**. It is spring loaded so that it is positioned partially outside the electromagnetic coil and is free to move in and out. When the coil is energized, the magnetic field draws the armature into the center of the coil. If the armature is attached to a lever or plunger, it will be forced to move as well. Stopping current flow causes the electromagnet to de-energize and the spring pushes the armature out again.

Another device that uses a solenoid is a vehicle horn. When the armature is drawn in by the electromagnetic coil, it opens a set of electrical contacts so that current flow through the coil is stopped. This stoppage causes the armature to move out again, closing the contacts, drawing the armature back in. This process occurs at very high speeds. The vibration caused by the rapid movement is transferred to a diaphragm, and the familiar horn sound is produced.

Applied Science

AS-62: Short Circuit: The technician can demonstrate an understanding of the processes used to locate a short circuit in an electrical/electronic system.

Two types of short circuit can occur in electrical systems. In a short to ground, electrical current finds its way to ground before it was intended, usually due to compromised wiring insulation that allows wiring to touch the metal vehicle body. In a short to power, a circuit is exposed to voltage flowing in another circuit, generally also due to broken wiring insulation. The effect of either type of short will depend on the layout of the circuit and where the short occurs in relation to the load.

The most common indicator of a short circuit is a fuse blowing due to excessive current flow. Traditionally, diagnosing the location of the short has required being able to segment the circuit by disconnecting fuses, components, switches, or harness plugs and checking individual sections of the circuit for integrity. Electronic short-circuit finders are now available that send an electrical signal along the circuit. A receiver is run along the circuit until it stops receiving a signal, at which point the location of the short has been found.

Applied Science

AS-69: Fuse: The technician can explain the role of a fuse or fusible link as a protective device in an electrical or electronic circuit.

A fuse, or fusible link, is a form of overcurrent protection device. It consists of a conductive metal strip that melts when subjected to more than a specified level of current. When the fuse "blows," the circuit is broken and no current flows in the remainder of the circuit. Fuses are installed for two reasons: They can prevent excessive current flow from damaging more expensive components elsewhere in the circuit, and they can prevent overheating within wiring and components, which could potentially cause a fire.

▸ LINK

Refer to the Batteries, Starting, and Charging Systems chapter for a detailed description of the starter solenoid operation.

Motors

While solenoids use magnetic fields to create lateral movement, electric motors use magnetic fields to create rotary movement. Motors consist of two main components: the armature and the field. The armature contains electromagnetic coils. The field contains either electromagnets or permanent magnets. The interaction between the magnetic fields of the stationary field coils and the magnetic fields of the moveable armature coils causes the armature to rotate. Since the armature coils can be energized and create electromagnetic fields, those fields can be turned on and off so that they attract and repel the fields of the stationary magnetic fields. The design and orientation of the electromagnetic coils ensure that the armature continues to turn as it rotates through various positions. The armature is connected to the electrical supply by a set of carbon brushes that contact a **commutator**, which is a segmented component of the armature. The commutator and brushes act as switches to control the current flow through the windings of the armature FIGURE 29-30. The brushes allow the electrical connection to occur even when the armature is spinning.

▸ LINK

Refer to the Batteries, Starting, and Charging Systems chapter for more information on motors.

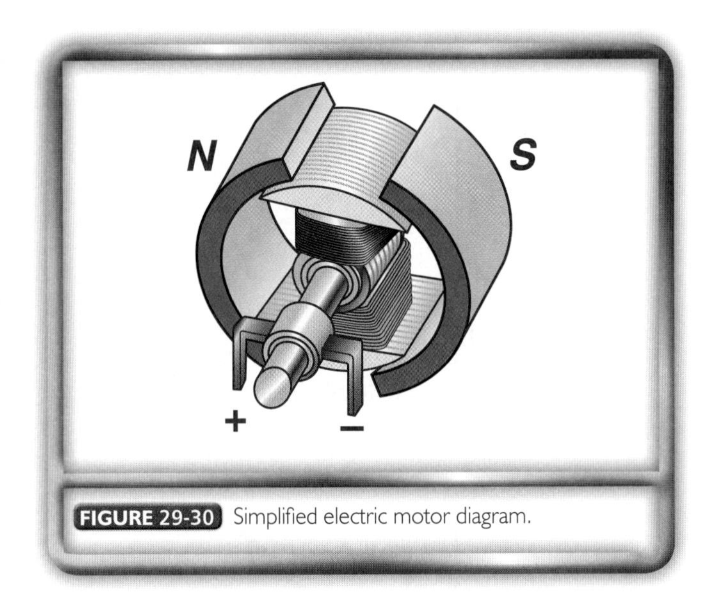
N
S
+
–
FIGURE 29-30 Simplified electric motor diagram.

Ignition Coils and Transformers

Ignition coils and transformers both operate under the principles of electromagnetic induction. They use electromagnetism to produce electricity, rather than mechanical movement. An ignition coil can be described as a **step-up transformer**. This is because the output can be 60 kilovolts (or more), which is higher than the input, nominally 12 volts.

Two sets of coil windings are used. One coil, referred to as a **primary winding**, is wound around a second, the **secondary winding**. The primary coil typically has 200 to 300 turns of light-gauge wire while the secondary has approximately 30,000 to 60,000 turns of very fine wire. When current is passed through the primary winding, the magnetic field builds surrounding both the windings. When the current is turned off, the magnetic field collapses with enough speed to induce high voltage in the primary winding (self induction) and very high voltage in the secondary winding (mutual induction) by the rapidly moving (collapsing) magnetic field. Voltage is induced into each of the thousands of windings of the secondary coil. This voltage is strong enough to overcome the infinite resistance of the spark plug gap and push current across the gap, causing a spark with enough heat to ignite the airfuel mixture in the cylinder.

> **TECHNICIAN TIP**
>
> You might expect a transformer to be a great way to boost the amount of electrical power that is transmitted, but it isn't. The amount of power after the transformation is relatively the same as before the transformation. For example, if we raise the voltage from 12 volts to 120 volts, the amperage will decrease from, say, 10 amps to 1 amp. Thus, the wattage stays the same:
>
> 12 volts × 10 amps = 120 watts
> 120 volts × 1 amp = 120 watts
>
> Also, remember that transformers are not 100% efficient, so some of the power is lost as heat.

The **transformer action** causes heat to be produced. In the past, the internal coils were immersed in cooling oil, allowing the heat to be conducted to the case. Modern ignition coils do not use oil. They are usually constructed using a heat-conducting hard resin and are cooled by their location on a heat sink or in a stream of air. The advent of computer controls has allowed the time that current flows through the primary windings to be minimized to reduce heat and electrical loads, while still providing enough spark to ignite the airfuel mixture

Step-down transformers operate under the same operating principles. The only difference is that the secondary coil has fewer turns than the primary, providing a lower induced output. These transformers are used on power poles to lower the voltage to your house or school and on low-voltage devices in your home that are plugged into your 110-volt outlets, such as cell phone chargers.

Resistors

Resistors are electrical components that resist a current running through them. Putting a resistor in a circuit causes a drop in voltage across the resistor. It also reduces the amperage in the circuit. Resistors are commonly used to control the voltage and amperage that reaches various components. It is important to remember that each electrical component has its own resistance. Most high-wattage resistors that can carry large amperage contain a coil of high-resistance wire wound around a ceramic form to dissipate heat.

Fixed Resistors

Fixed resistors are generally cylinders with connecting metal leads projecting along the axis of the cylinder at each end. Most axial resistors are marked with a series of colored stripes to indicate their resistance and tolerance levels. Fixed resistors can be manufactured as very tiny devices without leads and can be built into integrated circuits with many other miniaturized components.

Variable Resistors

Resistors found on circuit boards are normally fixed in value. Some resistors found in the motor vehicle are variable. **Variable resistors** can have their value altered by movement of a slide or by temperature change. The three types of variable resistors are rheostats, potentiometers, and thermistors. Variable resistors can be linear, meaning their resistance value varies proportionally with movement or temperature change, or nonlinear, meaning the resistance change is not proportional with movement.

Rheostats

A **rheostat** is a mechanical variable resistor with two connections. It consists of a resistance wire wrapped in a loose coil connected to the supply at one end only. A moveable wiper is connected to the other circuit connection and is made to move over the wire manually FIGURE 29-31. When the wiper is close to the beginning of the coil, the total resistance value is very small. As the wiper is positioned closer to the end of the coil, the resistance value increases. Rheostats are commonly used in dash light dimmer circuits and some fuel gauge sender units. They alter the current flow and voltage in a circuit.

Potentiometers

Potentiometers are mechanical variable resistors with three connections, two fixed and one moveable. They act as voltage dividers and as such alter the voltage in a circuit. A resistance wire is wrapped between two fixed connections. One fixed connection is attached to the electrical supply, the other to a ground. The third moveable connection is moved across the coil by a wiper in a similar fashion to a rheostat. The variable voltage output is taken from this point. Throttle position sensors are potentiometers.

Thermistors

As mentioned earlier, thermistors are conductors in which resistance value is affected by temperature. There are two types: **negative temperature coefficient (NTC)** and **positive temperature coefficient (PTC)** FIGURE 29-32. NTC thermistors alter their resistance value inversely to temperature. As the temperature increases, resistance value decreases. PTC thermistors alter their resistance value proportionally to temperature. As temperature rises, so does the resistance value. NTC thermistors are the most common and are used in circuits for ECU inputs. They are the sensing elements of devices such as coolant and air temperature sensors.

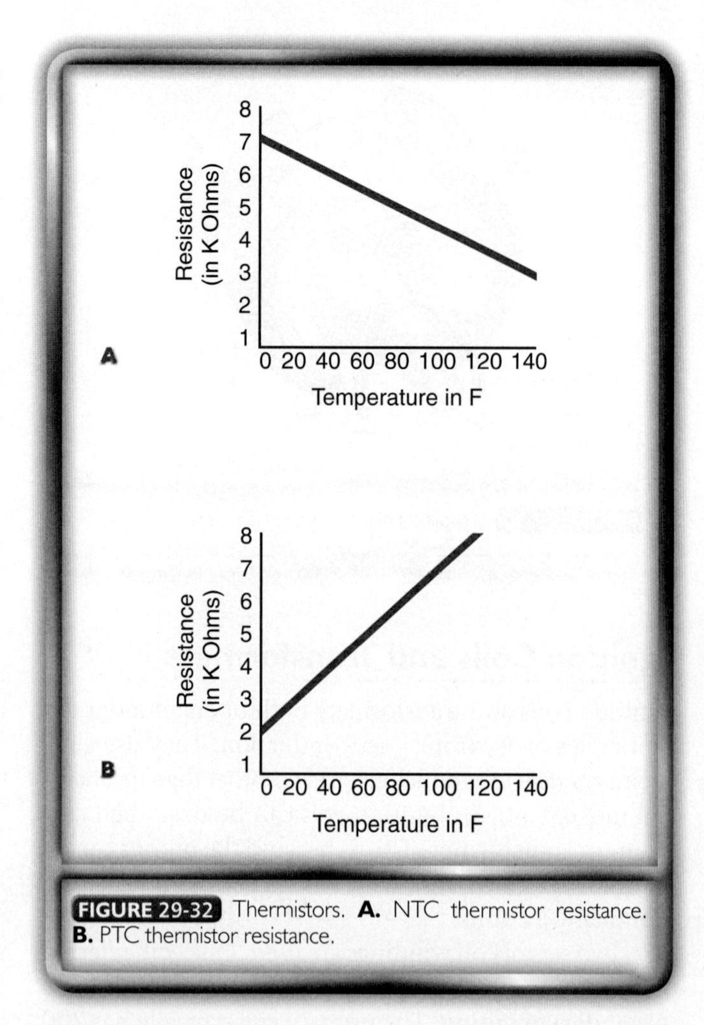
A
Resistance (in K Ohms)
1 2 3 4 5 6 7 8
0 20 40 60 80 100 120 140
Temperature in F
B
Resistance (in K Ohms)
1 2 3 4 5 6 7 8
0 20 40 60 80 100 120 140
Temperature in F

FIGURE 29-32 Thermistors. **A.** NTC thermistor resistance. **B.** PTC thermistor resistance.

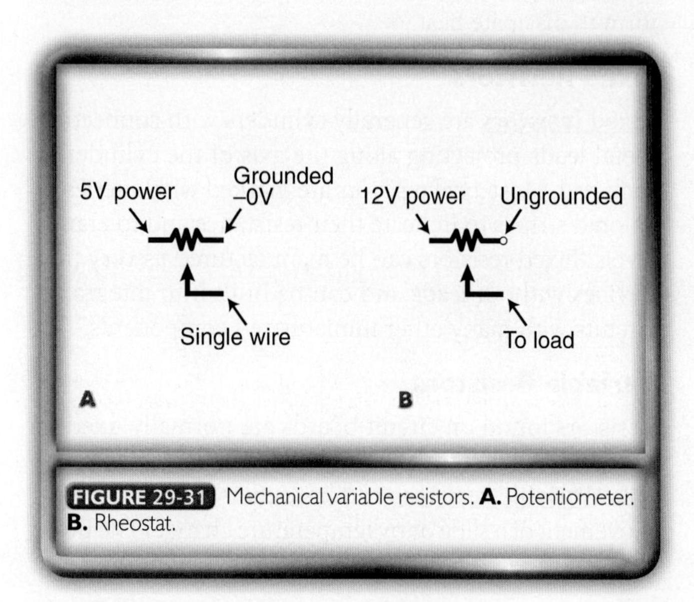
5V power
Grounded –0V
12V power
Ungrounded
Single wire
To load
A
B

FIGURE 29-31 Mechanical variable resistors. **A.** Potentiometer. **B.** Rheostat.

Resistor Ratings

Resistance is measured in ohms, represented by the Greek letter omega (Ω). Resistors are rated in ohms as well, to indicate how strongly they will oppose any current flowing through them. Because resistors work by converting some of the electrical energy passing through them into heat, they also have a power rating. Only the resistance value is marked. The resistor's power rating is determined by its size.

Regardless of their power rating, resistors are small, so identification by numbers is impractical. To identify their value, many resistors are marked with four or five colored bands. Each color represents a numeric resistance value. The color bands are set close to each other and read from left to right. The last band, or tolerance band, is spaced farther apart. FIGURE 29-33 shows the resistor colors.

Wires and Wiring Harnesses

Wires and wiring harnesses are the arteries of the vehicle's electrical system, and as such they need to be kept in good condition, free of any damage or corrosion. They carry the electrical power and signals through the vehicle to control virtually all of the systems on a vehicle. As technology in vehicles has increased, so, too, has the number of wires and cables installed on these vehicles. Although wireless communication is being used in some vehicle security, entertainment, and tire pressure monitoring systems, wires are still the dominant signal carriers in a vehicle. To help protect wires and keep them organized, they are bundled together in a wiring harness. A number of wiring harnesses are located throughout the vehicle.

Wires

Electrical wires are used to conduct current around the vehicle. Wire can also be referred to as cable, although cable typically refers to large-diameter wire. Automotive **wire** is commonly a multistranded copper core wrapped with seamless plastic insulation. Copper is typically used as it offers low electrical resistance and remains flexible even after years of use. The insulation is designed to protect the wire and prevent leakage of the current flow so that it can get to its intended destination. **Ribbon cable** is a series of wires that are formed side by side and joined along the wire insulation; they are flat like a ribbon **FIGURE 29-34**. Ribbon cable works well when several wires run from one component to another. The ribbon design groups them so they can be routed neatly and easily. Ribbon cable is often found inside computers and other electronic components. It is used for connecting between **printed circuits** or between printed circuits and other components. Some wires, especially signal wires and communication wires, are shielded, which helps to prevent electromagnetic interference, also referred to as "noise."

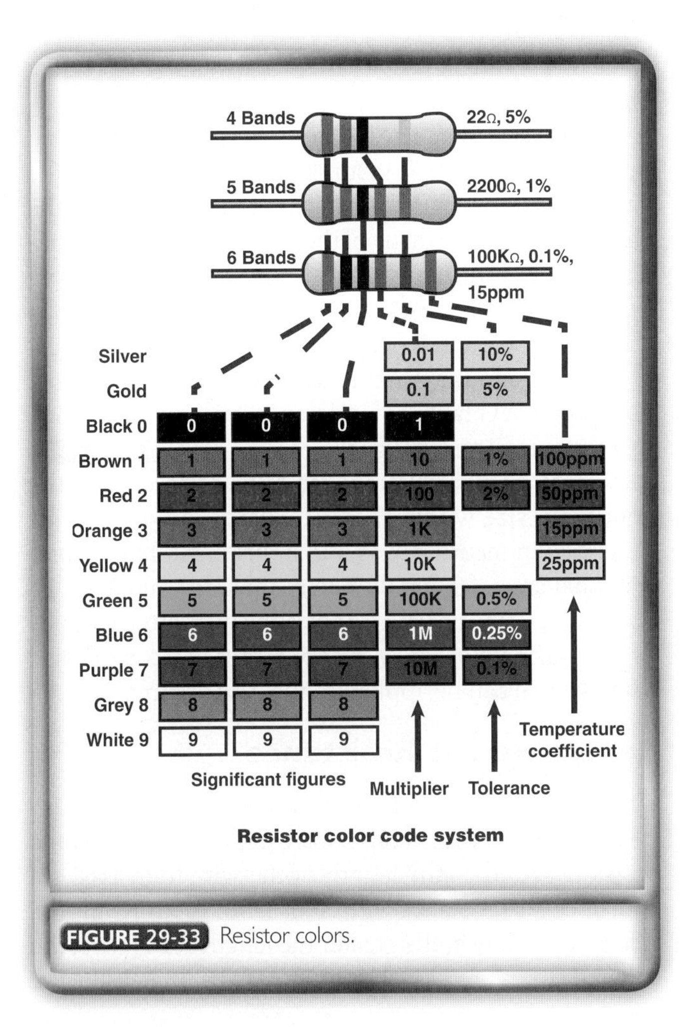
4 Bands
22Ω, 5%
5 Bands
2200Ω, 1%
6 Bands
100KΩ, 0.1%, 15ppm
Silver
Gold
Black 0
Brown 1
Red 2
Orange 3
Yellow 4
Green 5
Blue 6
Purple 7
Grey 8
White 9
0.01
0.1
1
10
100
1K
10K
100K
1M
10M
10%
5%
1%
2%
0.5%
0.25%
0.1%
100ppm
50ppm
15ppm
25ppm
Significant figures
Multiplier
Tolerance
Temperature coefficient
Resistor color code system

FIGURE 29-33 Resistor colors.

Shielding

In certain locations within a vehicle and in environments where strong electromagnetic interference (EMI) is present, wiring harnesses are subject to a situation where unwanted electromagnetic induction occurs. This interference is referred to as electrical noise or EMI noise. To prevent noise, some vehicles use **shielded wiring harnesses**. The type of shielding used can be one of three forms: twisted pair, Mylar tape, and drain lines.

Twisted Pair

Twisted pair uses two wires delivering signals to a common component. The wires are uniformly twisted through the entire length of the harness and end at a terminating

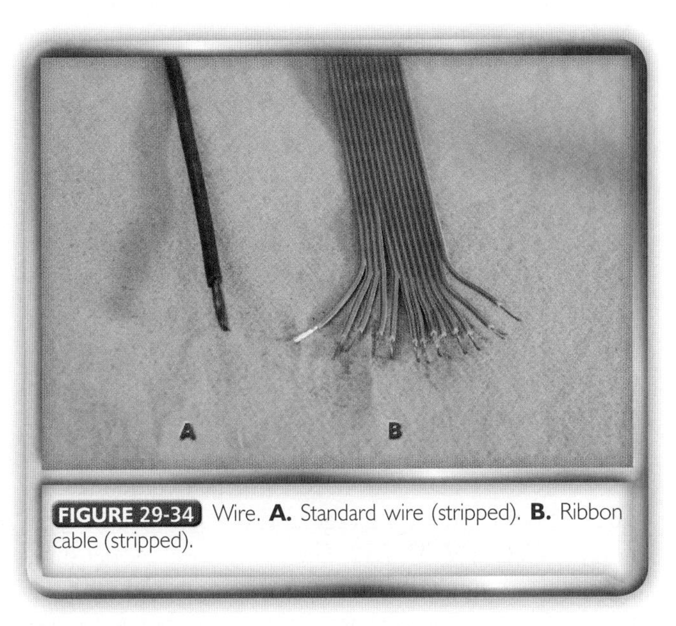
A
B

FIGURE 29-34 Wire. **A.** Standard wire (stripped). **B.** Ribbon cable (stripped).

> **LINK**
> Refer to the On-Board Diagnostics chapter for more information on control with the CAN-bus.

resistor. The twisted wires along with the terminating resistor have the effect of canceling any noise that occurs in the wires, reducing the loss of data in the transmitted signals. The controlled area network, or CAN, bus in a modern vehicle may use one or more twisted pairs to connect all the vehicle control units with common data line(s) to share information.

Mylar Tape

Mylar tape is an electrically conductive material that is wrapped around a wiring harness inside the outer harness layer. Any noise that attempts to reach the wires inside the shield are absorbed by the Mylar, where it will be conducted to ground via a ground connection. The shielding is important to prevent electrical noise penetrating into the electrical wiring. If the harness is exposed, the Mylar will have to be rewrapped so that noise cannot penetrate into the harness.

Drain Lines

A **drain line** is a noninsulated wire that is wrapped within a wiring harness. The drain wire is connected to ground at the harness source end and conducts any noise to ground, negating the noise effect. If the drain wire is cut, it will be inoperative, so it is important that the wire not be cut or left disconnected.

Wire Sizes

Wire size is very important for the correct operation of electrical circuits. Selecting a wire gauge that is too small for an application will have an adverse effect on the operation of the circuit. This will cause voltage drop and poor performance, or, in extreme cases, the wire will get hot enough to melt the insulation. Selecting a wire gauge that is too large increases costs and weight and the size of wiring harnesses.

The resistance of a wire affects how much current it can carry. Even good conductors have a slight amount of resistance. The resistance of a wire is determined by its length, diameter, construction material, and temperature. The longer the wire and the smaller the diameter, the higher the resistance. The shorter the wire and the larger the diameter, the lower the resistance.

There are two scales used to measure the sizes of wires: the metric wire gauge and the **American wire gauge (AWG)** TABLE 29-1. The metric system measures the cross-sectional area of the conductor in square millimeters. The AWG system uses a rating number; the larger the rating number, the smaller the wire and the lower its current-carrying capability. Most countries use the metric scale. American manufacturers are split, with some using AWG and others using the metric scale.

TABLE 29-1: Metric Wire Size Comparison and American Wire Gauge (AWG)

Metric Wire Sizes	AWG Wire Sizes
0.22	24
0.35	22
0.5	20
0.8	18
1.0	16
2.0	14
3.0	12
5.0	10
8.0	8
13.0	6
19.0	4
32.0	2

To select the correct wire gauge for any given application, it is best to refer to a wire chart. Manufacturers and standards bodies use wire gauge charts to define how much current each wire gauge can carry safely and efficiently. A vehicle uses a variety of wire sizes depending on the requirements of each particular circuit.

The correct wire size for an application can be looked up on a wire size chart if you know the amperage of the circuit and the length of the wire. But be careful of the chart you use, since many of them allow up to a 10% voltage drop over the length of the wire, which is way more than is allowed in most automotive circuits. For example, if a 12-volt circuit is designed for a maximum current flow of 10 amps and is approximately 20" (6.1 meters) long, using the AWG table as a reference, you can determine that the correct wire gauge to use is 12 AWG TABLE 29-2.

There are two different methods of describing the conductor size within these standards. A wire may be described in metric size as 5.0, indicating it has a cross-sectional area of 5.0 millimeters squared (mm^2). It can also be expressed as 10/0.5, indicating there are 10 strands of wire, each with a cross-sectional area of 0.5 mm^2. The same system can be applied to the AWG rating.

Length Versus Resistance

Copper is used to conduct electrical current because of its low resistance value. However, it does offer some resistance, and as the length of the wire increases, so, too, does the resistance within the wire. To overcome the effect of resistance, the greater the length of the wire, the larger the cross-sectional area needs to be. Increasing the

TABLE 29-2: AWG Wire Sizes Based on Amperage and Wire Length*

Circuit Amps	Wire Length from Battery to Load						
	2 Feet	5 Feet	7.5 Feet	10 Feet	15 Feet	20 Feet	25 Feet
2	20	20	20	18	18	18	16
5	18	18	18	18	16	14	14
8	18	16	16	14	14	12	12
10	16	16	16	14	12	12	10
12	16	16	14	14	12	12	10
15	16	16	14	12	10	10	8
18	16	14	12	12	10	8	8
20	14	14	12	10	10	8	8
25	14	12	12	10	8	8	6
30	12	12	10	10	8	6	6

*Chart is based on a maximum 0.4-volt drop per wire size; shorter distances are less than a 0.4-volt drop.

cross-sectional area overcomes the resistance and maintains the current-carrying capacity of the circuit. Refer to TABLE 29-2 for information on wire size and current-carrying capacity.

Terminals and Connectors

Terminals are installed to the ends of wires to provide low-resistance termination to wires. They allow electricity to be conducted from the end of one wire to the end of another wire. In many cases, they allow the wires to be disconnected and reconnected. They come in many different types and sizes to suit various wire sizes and termination requirements FIGURE 29-35. For example, there are **push-on spade terminals**, **eye ring terminals** to accommodate screws, **butt connectors**, and **male and female terminals** that are designed to be separated and reconnected. Most terminals are the crimp type, which require the use of special tools to crimp the terminal to the end of the wire. They can be insulated or noninsulated. Some **solder-type terminals**, which require the use of a soldering iron and solder, are still in use and require the use of electric or gas soldering irons, flux, and solder to make the connection. When soldering wiring, always use a rosin or rosin-core solder; never use an acid-core solder, since acid can cause corrosion and high resistance over time.

Terminals can be installed as a single terminal on a wire or grouped together in a wiring harness with a connector housing, also called **wiring harness connectors**. Connector housings have male and female sides and are usually shaped so that they can be connected in only one way. They will often incorporate a locking mechanism so the plug cannot accidentally work loose. Many of these connectors are weatherproofed to keep moisture out. Special tools are usually needed to insert and remove the terminals from the connector housing.

Wiring Harnesses

Wiring harnesses, also known as wiring looms or cable harnesses, are used throughout the vehicle to group two or more wires together within a sheath of either insulating tape or tubing FIGURE 29-36. Often, harnesses on modern vehicles contain many wires, each terminating at crimped terminals inserted into connector or harness plugs. There are usually a number of harnesses within the vehicle interconnecting with various connector plugs, as

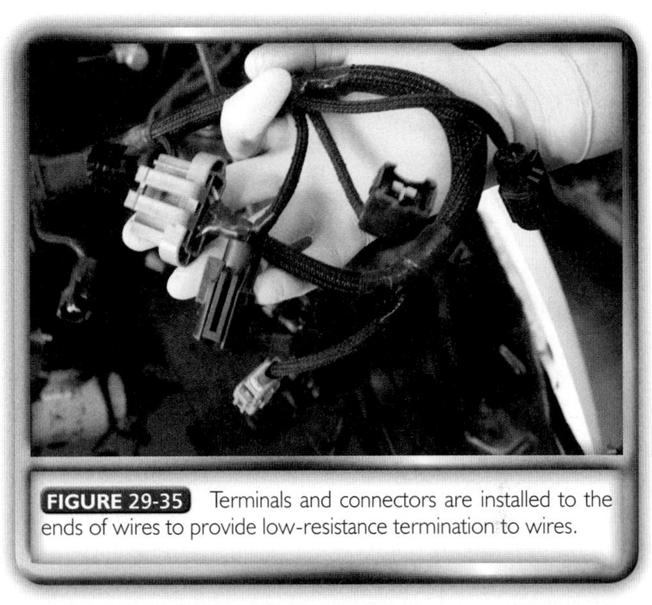

FIGURE 29-35 Terminals and connectors are installed to the ends of wires to provide low-resistance termination to wires.

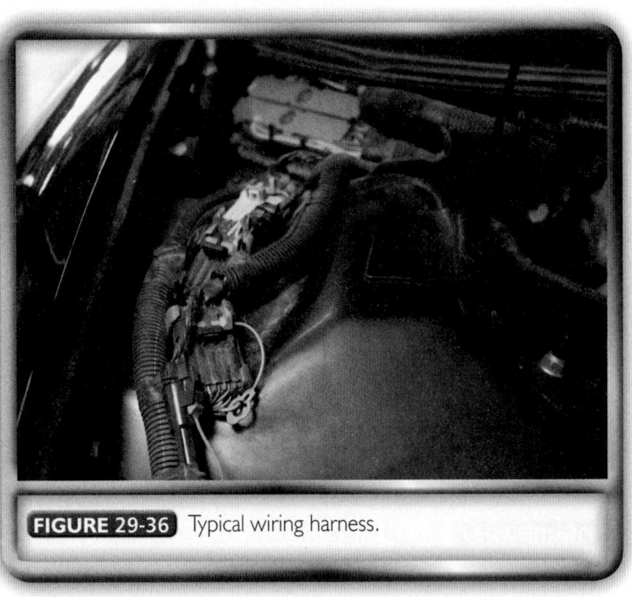

FIGURE 29-36 Typical wiring harness.

required to form the wiring system of the vehicle. Wiring harnesses run around the engine bay, through the dash and interior cabin, and to the rear of the vehicle. They are attached to the vehicle with harness fasteners such as body clips or wire ties, and rubber sealing grommets are used when the harness passes through the metal bodywork.

Wiring Diagram Fundamentals

Wiring diagrams, also known as electrical schematics or electrical diagrams, use abstract graphical symbols to represent electrical circuits and their connection or relationship to other components in the system. They are essentially a map of all of the electrical components and their connections FIGURE 29-37. The wiring on modern vehicles is very complex, with many wires and components interconnected. A single wiring diagram of the whole vehicle would be very difficult to read. To make it easier, the wiring diagrams are split up into systems and subsystems to reduce the complexity on each page. For example, there is a wiring diagram for the starter system, a separate one for the charging system, and others for the engine, transmission, anti-lock brakes, headlights, taillights, and so on.

Wiring diagrams contain large amounts of information in the form of lines and symbols. The technician will need to decode this information by interpreting the symbols and connections and relating them to the actual components on the vehicle. To assist in understanding the wiring diagrams, manufacturers supply keys on the diagrams, which are lists of the component symbols and their names, wiring color codes, harness connectors, and pin numbers. Armed with all of this information, the

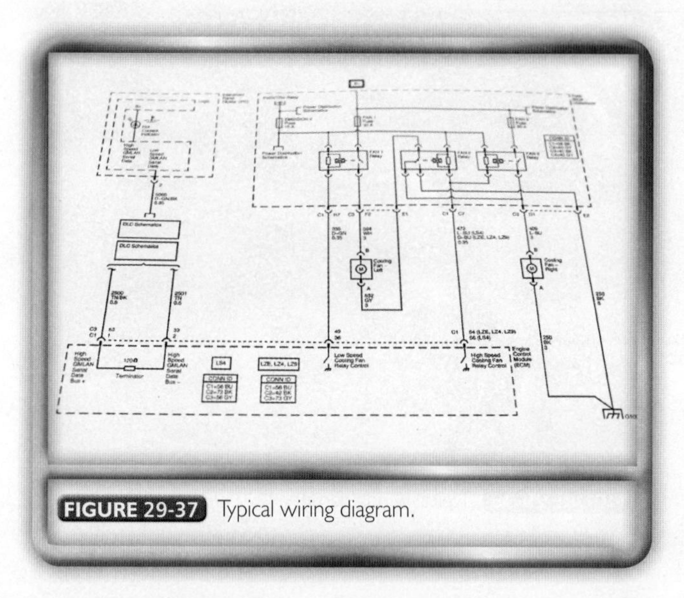

FIGURE 29-37 Typical wiring diagram.

TECHNICIAN TIP

Modern vehicles have many electrical components, wiring connectors, and wires. To work on vehicles, you need an understanding of how all the components are assembled together and arranged in circuits. Electrical symbols and circuit diagrams are a way to provide this information in a logical way that represents the physical wiring harness and components attached to vehicles FIGURE 29-38. Every electrical device and component has a corresponding electrical symbol. Many of the symbols are standardized and used universally by manufacturers, although in some cases, variations may exist. Manufacturers' diagrams and manuals contain keys to identifying the various symbols used and their meaning.

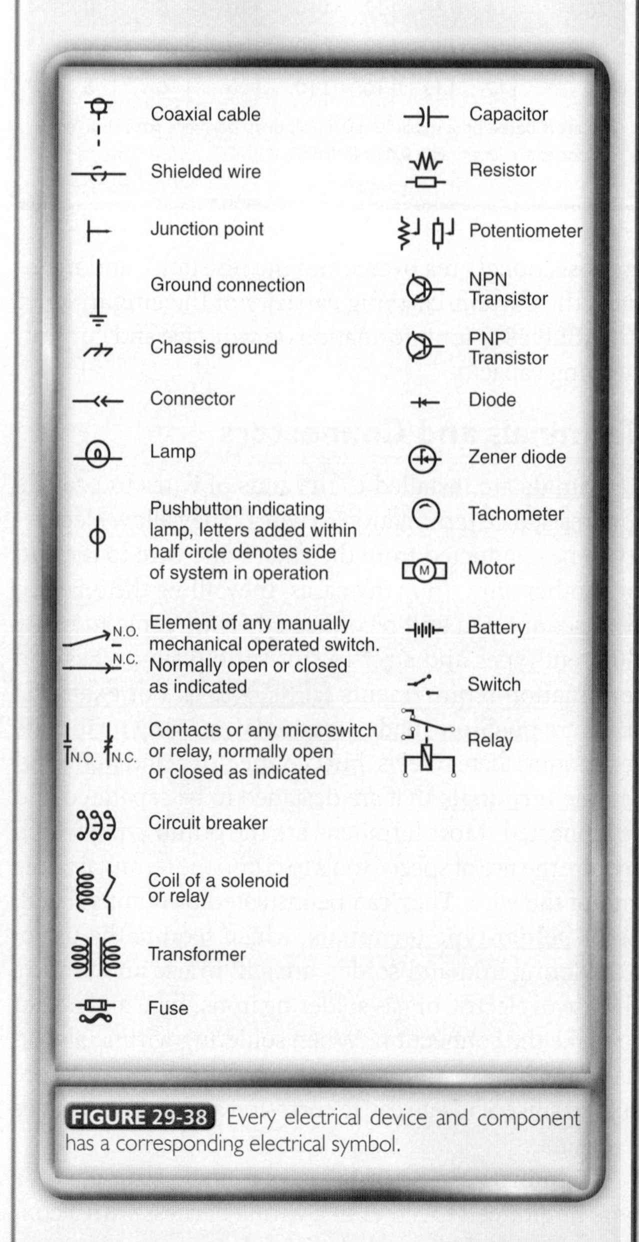
Coaxial cable
Capacitor
Shielded wire
Resistor
Junction point
Potentiometer
Ground connection
NPN Transistor
Chassis ground
PNP Transistor
Connector
Diode
Lamp
Zener diode
Pushbutton indicating lamp, letters added within half circle denotes side of system in operation
Tachometer
M
Motor
N.O.
N.C.
Element of any manually mechanical operated switch. Normally open or closed as indicated
Battery
Switch
N.O.
N.C.
Contacts or any microswitch or relay, normally open or closed as indicated
Relay
Circuit breaker
Coil of a solenoid or relay
Transformer
Fuse

FIGURE 29-38 Every electrical device and component has a corresponding electrical symbol.

technician can read the wiring diagram and identify circuits as they relate to the actual components and circuits on the vehicle.

Wire Maintenance and Repair

Wires are generally trouble free and long lasting. But they can be damaged. Generally speaking, any issues with wiring are more likely to be with the terminals than with the wires themselves. Terminals can corrode, lose their tension, or push back up inside the connector, leading to poor connections and voltage drops. If you suspect a problem with a wire, first inspect the ends. If no problems are found, look for mechanical damage to the wire or wiring harness itself. When a wire is damaged, it is usually due to one of several conditions. One possibility is that the wire has been physically broken, such as a wire that was not disconnected when removing a major component such as the engine or transmission. Another issue is when a wire gets pinched between components such as between the engine and the transaxle when replacing a clutch. The pinched wire can cause either a short circuit or an open circuit. Wires can also be misrouted so that they lay on a hot surface such as the exhaust manifold, which melts the insulation and causes the wires to short. In all of these cases, the problem can typically be spotted visually. One problem that may be harder to spot is if a circuit shorts out and melts one or more wires together within a harness. In this case, you may have to open up the wiring harness and inspect the wires. Next, we will cover how to repair wires, terminals, and connectors.

Stripping Wire Insulation

An insulating layer of plastic covers electrical wire used in automotive wiring harnesses. When electrical wire is joined to other wires or connected to a terminal, the insulation needs to be removed. Wire stripping tools come in various configurations, but they all perform the same task. The type of tool you use or purchase will depend on personal preference and the amount of electrical wire repairs you perform. A good pair of wire strippers removes the insulation without damaging the wire strands. Never use a knife or other type of sharp tool to cut away the insulation, as it often cuts away some of the strands of wire as well. This is known as ringing the wire, which effectively reduces the current-carrying capacity of the wire

To strip wire insulation, follow the steps in SKILL DRILL 29-1.

Installing a Solderless Terminal

Solderless terminals are used by the factory throughout the vehicle, primarily at connectors. If a wire itself needs to be repaired, it should be soldered back together instead of using solderless terminals to reconnect the wires. Solderless terminals are quick to install and effective at conducting electricity across joints that are designed to be disconnected. Solderless terminals require a clean, tight connection. It is important to make sure the wire and the connection are clean before attaching any terminals. You should use connections that match the size of the wire. Many solderless connectors are color coded for the size of wire they are designed to work with, such

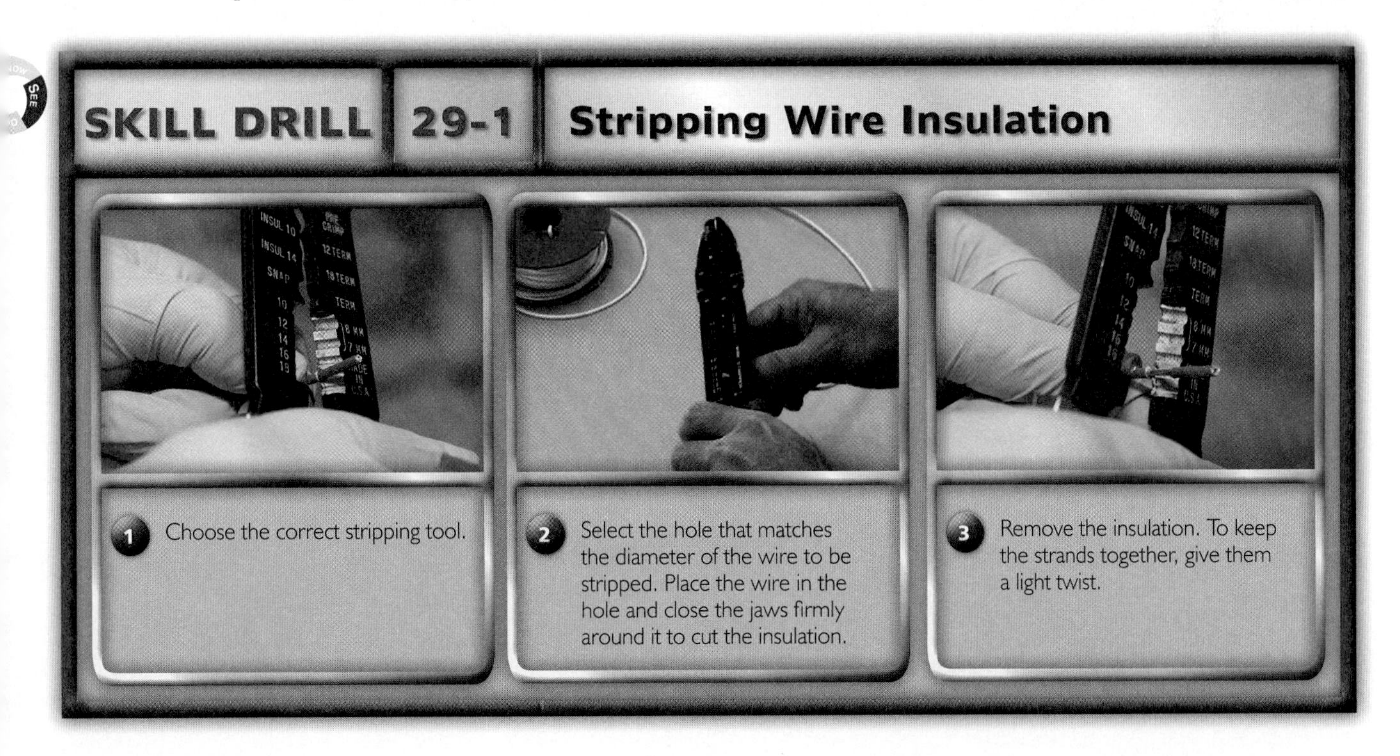
SEE

SKILL DRILL 29-1 Stripping Wire Insulation

1. Choose the correct stripping tool.
2. Select the hole that matches the diameter of the wire to be stripped. Place the wire in the hole and close the jaws firmly around it to cut the insulation.
3. Remove the insulation. To keep the strands together, give them a light twist.

as yellow 12-10 AWG, blue 16-14 AWG, and red 22-18 AWG. Use the correct wire stripper to strip only as much insulation off as needed to allow the wire to fully engage the terminal. To keep the wires together after stripping them, give them a slight twist. Do not twist the wire too much; otherwise you risk a poor wire-to-terminal connection. Use the correct crimping tool for the connection. Using the wrong type of tool will cause the connection to have a poor grip on the wire.

To install a solderless terminal, follow the steps in SKILL DRILL 29-2.

Soldering Wires and Connectors

Solder used in automotive electrical applications is an alloy typically made up of 60% tin and 40% lead. Solder needs to change from a solid state into liquid easily and return to its solid state quickly. Solder is available as solid or flux cored. Solid solder requires an external flux to be applied in the soldering process. Flux is needed to prevent the metals from being joined due to oxidization

Safety

While soldering is generally thought of as a simple process, it can be very dangerous. The solder, soldering iron, and wires are very hot and can cause severe burns. Be careful what you grab or where you set hot items. Molten solder can be flicked by a springy wire up into your eyes, so always wear safety glasses or goggles.

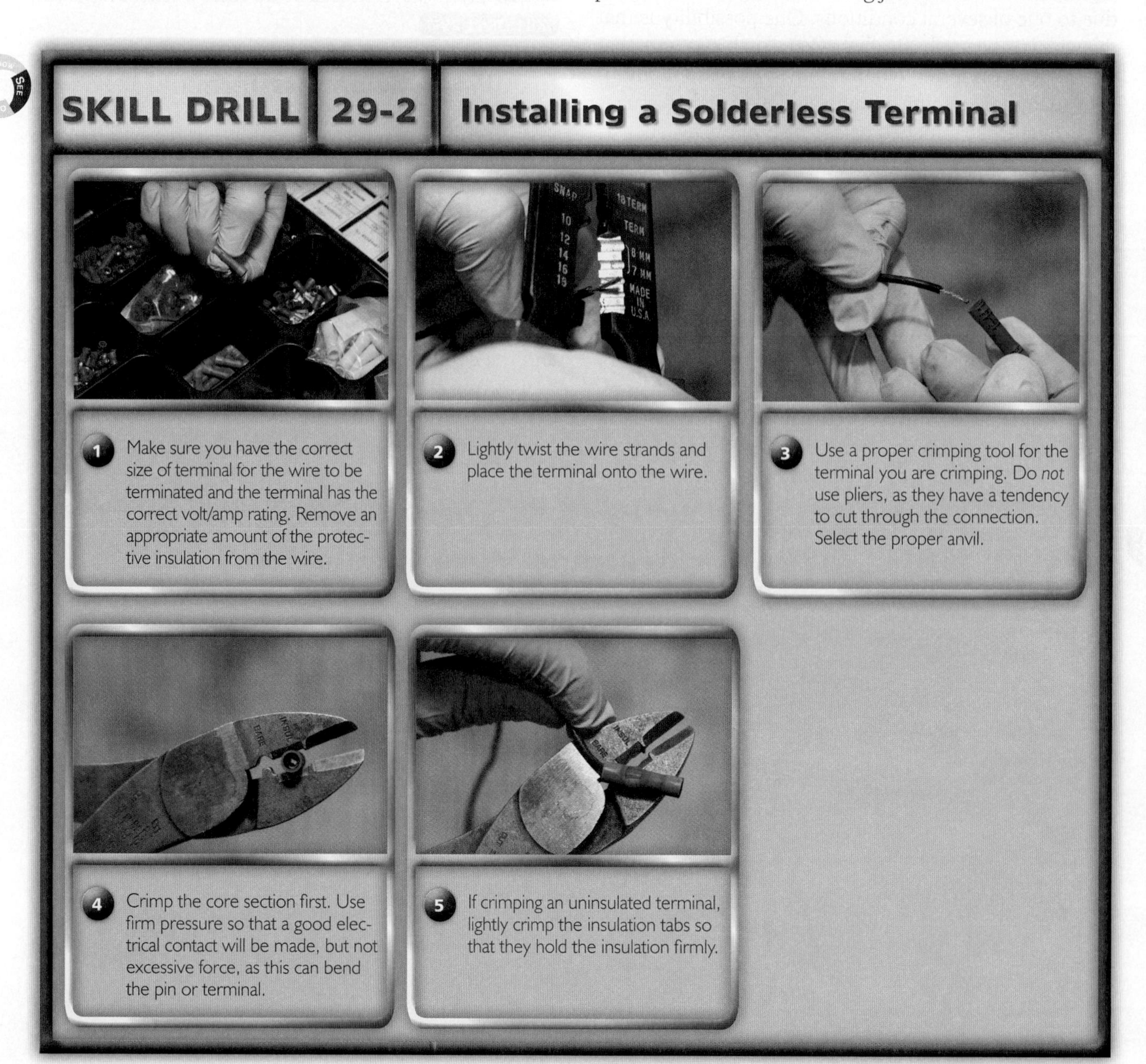

SKILL DRILL 29-2 Installing a Solderless Terminal

1. Make sure you have the correct size of terminal for the wire to be terminated and the terminal has the correct volt/amp rating. Remove an appropriate amount of the protective insulation from the wire.
2. Lightly twist the wire strands and place the terminal onto the wire.
3. Use a proper crimping tool for the terminal you are crimping. Do *not* use pliers, as they have a tendency to cut through the connection. Select the proper anvil.
4. Crimp the core section first. Use firm pressure so that a good electrical contact will be made, but not excessive force, as this can bend the pin or terminal.
5. If crimping an uninsulated terminal, lightly crimp the insulation tabs so that they hold the insulation firmly.

> **TECHNICIAN TIP**
>
> One mistake students make is trying to apply the solder directly to the tip of the soldering iron while the iron is heating up the wires. This does melt the solder, but it is likely that the wire is not hot enough for the solder to stick to it; instead the solder just globs on top of the wires, leading to what is called a cold joint. A cold joint has high resistance and the wires are likely to break loose from the solder. One sign that the solder joint is good is that you can clearly see the outline of the wires on the surface of the solder, all the way around the joint.

when they are heated. Flux-cored solder has a bead of flux within the center of the solder. Flux in flux-cored solder can have either an acid base or a rosin base. Acid flux is designed to be used on nonelectrical metal joints such as radiators and must be removed after the soldering process so that the joint does not corrode. Rosin flux solder is used on electrical connections because it is much less likely to corrode the metals than acid flux. Acid flux and rosin flux also come in paste form that can be brushed onto the joint if using solid-core solder.

Solder is applied with a hot soldering iron. The soldering iron is heated electrically or by an external source such as a butane or oxyacetylene torch. The soldering iron tip absorbs heat that is then applied to the materials to be joined. Once they are hot enough, solder can be melted between the components. It solidifies as it cools, "gluing" the metal pieces together.

For a connection to be successful, the soldering iron needs to be clean and "tinned." Cleaning may be as simple as heating the tip and wiping it on a damp cloth. Or, with the soldering iron cold, you may need to use a file to remove oxidized metal and reshape it so it can effectively transfer heat to the wires. The tinning process assists in transferring heat to the wire, by leaving a small amount of liquid solder on the tip which increases the surface area where the tip contacts the wires. To tin the soldering iron, the tip is heated and a small amount of solder is applied to the tip. Excess solder is removed with a cloth rag. The soldering iron tip is heated and then applied to the wire so heat is transferred to the wire. The solder is then applied to the wire opposite the soldering iron. Once the wire is up to soldering temperature, it will melt the solder and pull the solder into the strands of wire producing a strong, effective joint. Do not apply too much heat to the wire or two things will happen. First, the solder will be drawn too far up the strands of wire making a very long, nonflexible joint that is subject to breaking. The second problem is that the insulation may overheat and melt.

To solder wires and connectors, follow the steps in SKILL DRILL 29-3.

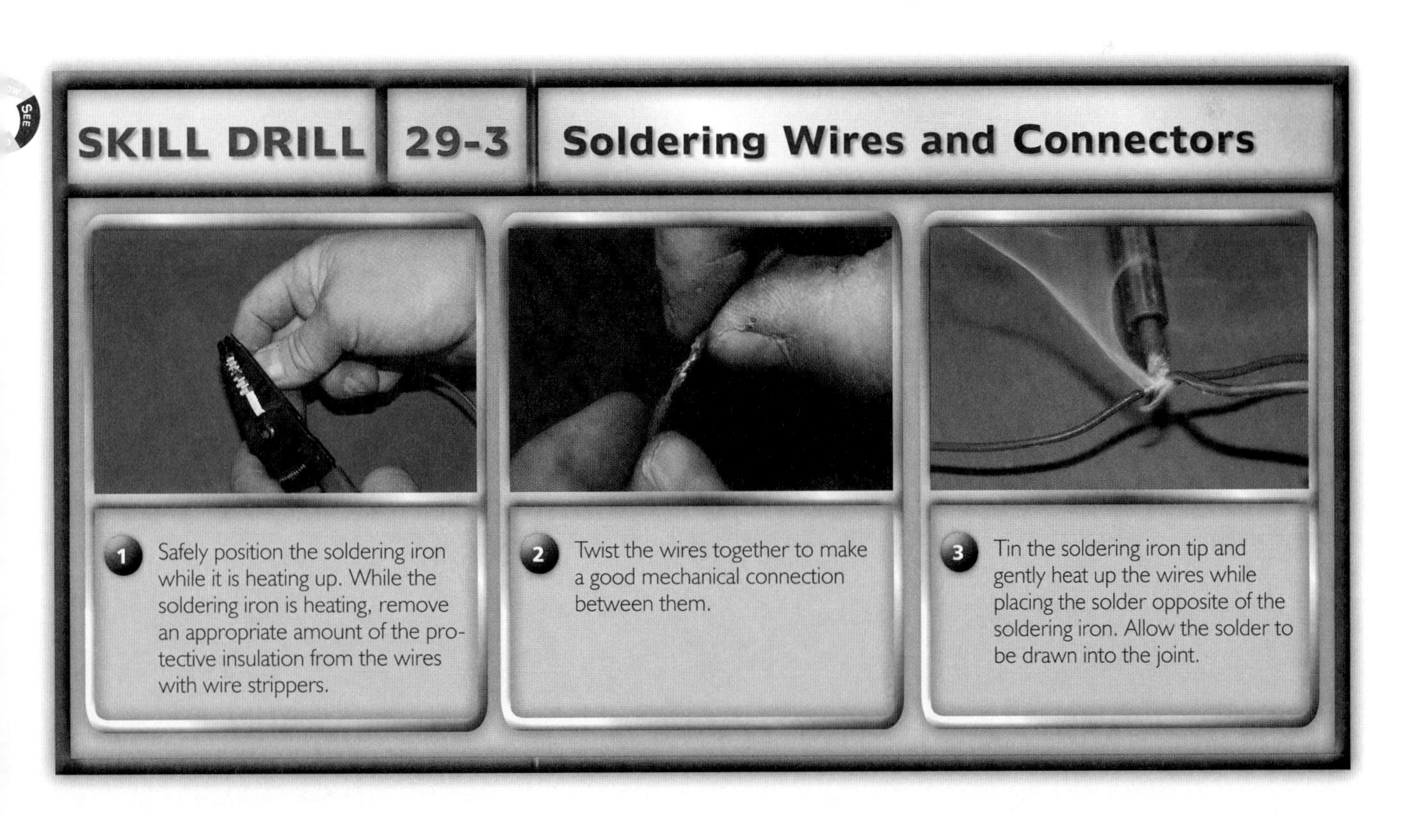
SEE
SKILL DRILL 29-3 Soldering Wires and Connectors

1. Safely position the soldering iron while it is heating up. While the soldering iron is heating, remove an appropriate amount of the protective insulation from the wires with wire strippers.
2. Twist the wires together to make a good mechanical connection between them.
3. Tin the soldering iron tip and gently heat up the wires while placing the solder opposite of the soldering iron. Allow the solder to be drawn into the joint.

SKILL DRILL 29-3 Soldering Wires and Connectors, continued

4. A good solder joint where the solder has been drawn in.

5. Once the electrical connection has been made and it has cooled enough for you to handle it, slide the insulator sleeve cover over the joint and use a heat gun to shrink the tubing around the joint.

6. To solder a wire to a terminal connector, it is best to crimp it in place as before and use the solder to "glue" the joint together. Place the heated iron onto the terminal to get it hot enough to melt the solder applied to the end of the crimped wire tabs. Some solder will be pulled between the terminal and the wire. Cover the terminal with heat-shrink tubing.

Wrap-up

Ready for Review

- Increasingly, vehicle technicians must have an understanding of the electrical principles involved in vehicle system operation.
- Atoms contain negatively charged electrons moving around a nucleus, in which there are positively charged protons and neutrons with no charge.
- Atoms with excess electrons have a negative charge and create a negative ion; those deficient in electrons have a positive charge and create a positive ion.
- Free electrons can move from one atom to another if an electrical potential is applied.
- Materials with many free electrons are good electrical conductors.
- Copper is the most common conductor.
- Insulators are materials that do not conduct current easily; an example is plastic.
- Semiconductor refers to a material that conducts electricity more easily than an insulator, but not as well as a conductor.
- Free electrons require a pathway or circuit, and a force to act upon them, such as a battery.
- Like charges repel, and unlike charges attract.
- The attraction of free electrons that creates a force is called voltage.
- The four factors that determine electrical resistance level are the type of material and the length, size, and temperature of the conductor.
- Electrical resistance refers to the degree to which a material opposes the passage of an electrical current.
- Resistance is measured in ohms and is constant in an object unless the temperature changes.
- A semiconductor's ability to conduct electricity depends on negative electrons and holes.
- The number of charge carriers in a semiconductor can be changed by adding small quantities of impurities (doping).
- The PN junction of a semiconductor is located at the depletion layer.
- Semiconductors can prevent or allow current flow, depending on connection to a current source.
- Semiconductor materials include silicon, germanium, gallium-arsenide, and silicon carbide.
- Electrical circuits contain a power supply, a current flow on/off switch, a functional component, a conductive pathway, and a protection device (e.g., a fuse).
- Voltage is the electrical pressure difference between two points in an electrical circuit.
- The ampere (amp) is the unit used to describe how much current is flowing at a given point within a circuit when the functional component is operational.
- The ohm is the unit used to describe electrical resistance in a circuit or component.
- Direct current (DC) flows in one direction only; alternating current (AC) continuously changes its direction of flow.
- Electrical components can work only on AC or DC, but not both.
- Circuits may be described in terms of continuity, open, short, and high resistance.
- Relays are used to control circuits that carry high current flow; they can be normally open (NO) or normally closed (NC).
- Solenoids operate similarly to a relay, but create lateral movement rather than closing a circuit.
- Electric motors rely on magnetic fields to create rotary movement.
- Ohm's law states that the total resistance of a circuit always equals the voltage divided by the amperage.
- The term "work" refers to transforming one form of energy into another.
- Power refers to the rate at which work is done, or the rate of transforming energy.
- The watt is the unit of power.
- Kirchhoff's current law states that electrical current entering any junction is equal to the sum of the current flowing out of the junction.
- In a series circuit, current can flow in only one path and all electrons flow at the same rate.
- Voltage drop refers to the pressure lost by driving the current through a resistor.
- The electrical properties of a series circuit are as follows: current flow is the same in all parts of the circuit; the applied voltage is equal to the sum of the individual voltage drops; and total circuit resistance is equal to the sum of the individual resistances.

- All components in a parallel circuit are directly connected to the voltage supply; hence the voltage across each component is equal to battery voltage.
- Parallel circuit laws are as follows: the voltage across all branches of a parallel circuit are the same; the total current equals the sum of the current flowing in each branch; the amount of current in each branch is inversely proportional to the resistance of the branch; and the total resistance of a parallel circuit can be calculated as $R_T = (R_1 \times R_2)$ divided by $(R_1 + R_2)$.Or $R_T = 1/\ 1/R_1 + 1/R_2 + 1/R_3$.
- Series-parallel circuits contain both a series circuit and a parallel circuit.
- Electrical components must be correctly connected onto circuits and may have numbered or marked terminals to ensure proper connection.
- Circuit protection devices, which break the circuit during excessive current flow, are fuses, fusible links, and circuit breakers.
- Most vehicle wires are braided copper with plastic insulation, but other types are shielded wires and ribbon.
- Wire shielding to prevent noise (unwanted electromagnetic induction) can be twisted pair, Mylar tape, or drain lines.
- Proper operation of electrical circuits requires correct wire size.
- Length and diameter of a cable determine its resistance.
- Copper has low resistance value, although as the wire length increases, so does resistance within the wire; therefore, the cross-sectional area needs to increase to overcome resistance.
- Terminals and connectors are fitted to the ends of cables to provide low-resistance cable termination.
- Terminals can be push-on spade terminals, eye ring terminals, and solder-type terminals.
- Connectors can be permanent cable joiners, wiring harness connectors, or male or female connectors.
- Wiring harnesses are used to bind wires together within a sheath of insulating tape or tubing.
- Wiring diagrams are generally split up into systems and subsystems.
- Electrical measurement tools include the ammeter, voltmeter, ohmmeter, and digital multimeter.

Key Terms

alternating current (AC) A type of current flow that flows back and forth.

American wire gauge (AWG) A standard used to identify different wire sizes.

ammeter A device used to measure current flow.

amp An abbreviation for amperes, the unit for current measurement.

armature The rotating wire coils in motors and generators. It is also the moving part of a solenoid or relay, and the pole piece in a permanent magnet generator.

butt connector A crimp or solder joint that creates a permanent connection.

charge carrier A mobile particle that has a positive or negative electrical charge.

circuit or schematic diagram A pictorial representation or road map of the wiring and electrical components.

circuit breaker A device that trips and opens a circuit, preventing excessive current flow in a circuit. It is resettable to allow for reuse.

commutator A device made on armatures of electric generators and motors to control the direction of current flow in the armature windings.

conductor A material that allows electricity to flow through it easily. It is made up of atoms with one to three valance ring electrons.

connector The plastic housing on the end of a wiring harness that holds the wire terminals in place. It can also refer to a type of wire terminal that connects wires together or to a common point such as a bolt.

continuity A conductive path between two points.

conventional theory The theory that electrons flow from positive to negative.

current flow The flow of electrons, typically within a circuit or component.

depletion layer An area of neutral charge in semiconductors.

diode A two-lead electronic component that allows current flow in one direction only.

direct current (DC) Movement of current that flows in one direction only.

doping The introduction of impurities to pure semiconductor materials to provide N- and P-type semiconductors.

drain line A wire included in a harness with one end grounded to reduce interference or noise being induced into the harness.

electrical power A measurement of the rate at which electricity is consumed or created.

electrical resistance A material's property that slows down the flow of electrical current.

electromotive force An electrical pressure or voltage.

electron theory The theory that electrons, being negatively charged, repel other electrons and are attracted to positively charged objects; thus electrons flow from negative to positive.

energy The ability to do work.

eye ring terminal A type of crimp or solder terminal that has an enclosed eyelet to connect the terminal with a bolt or screw.

fixed resistor A resistor that has a fixed value.

flasher can A mechanism that turns the vehicle's turn signal and hazard flasher bulbs on and off.

free electron An electron located on the outer ring, called the valence ring, that is only loosely held by the nucleus and that is free to move from one atom to another when an electrical potential (pressure) is applied.

fuse A safety device that self-destructs to prevent excessive current flowing in a circuit in the event of a fault.

ground The return path for electrical current in a vehicle chassis, other metal of the vehicle, or dedicated wire.

hertz The unit for electrical frequency measurement.

high resistance The resistance of a component or circuit relative to a low resistance. It can also refer to a faulty circuit where a section or component has excess unwanted resistance.

hole theory The theory that as electrons flow from negative to positive, holes flow from positive to negative.

insulator A material that has properties that prevent the easy flow of electricity. These materials are made up of atoms with five to eight electrons in the valance ring.

invertor A device that changes direct current into alternating current.

Kirchhoff's current law An electrical law stating that the sum of the current flowing into a junction is the same as the current flowing out of the junction.

male and female terminal A crimp or solder terminal on which the male and female ends join to create a removable low-resistance connection.

multimeter A test instrument used to measure volts, ohms, and amps. A digital multimeter may also be called a digital volt-ohmmeter (DVOM).

mylar tape Polyester film that may be metalized and incorporated into a wiring harness to provide electrical shielding.

negative temperature coefficient (NTC) A characteristic of materials whereby resistance decreases as temperature increases.

normally closed (NC) An electrical contact that is closed in the at-rest position.

normally open (NO) An electrical contact that is open in the at-rest position.

N-type Semiconductor material with a small amount of extra electrons.

ohm The unit for measuring electrical resistance.

Ohm's law A law that defines the relationship between current, resistance, and voltage.

open A term used to describe a circuit that does not have a complete path for current to flow.

phase A term used to describe one set of windings from an alternator or alternating current electric motor.

PN junction The junction between N- and P-type semiconductor materials.

polarity The state of charge, positive or negative.

polarity sensitive A term used to describe a component that must be connected into a circuit with the correct polarity to its terminals.

positive temperature coefficient (PTC) A characteristic of materials whereby resistance increases as temperature increases.

potentiometer Also called a pot, a three-terminal resistive device with one terminal connected to the input of the resistor, one terminal connected to the output of the resistor, and the third terminal connected to a movable wiper arm that moves up and down the resistor.

power The rate at which work is done; electrical power is measured in watts.

power winding The current-carrying winding in an alternator or motor.

primary winding The coil of wire in the low voltage circuit that creates the magnetic field in a step-up transformer.

printed circuit The fine copper strip or track attached to an insulated board for mounting and connecting electronic components.

P-type Semiconductor material with holes where electrons are missing.

push-on spade terminal A disconnectable type of crimp or solder terminal used to terminate electrical wires.

resistor A component designed to have a fixed resistance.

rheostat An adjustable resistor that varies current flow through a circuit.

ribbon cable A type of flat harness in which cables are insulated from each other but joined together side by side.

secondary winding The coil of wire in which high voltage is induced in a step-up transformer.

semiconductor A material used to make microchips, transistors, and diodes.

series-parallel circuit A circuit that has both a series and a parallel circuit combined into one circuit.

shielded wiring harness A wiring harness that has shielding built into it to protect it from induced electrical interference.

short Also called a short circuit, the flow of current along an unintended route.

sine wave A mathematical function that describes a repetitive waveform such as an alternating current signal.

solder-type terminal A terminal that requires soldering to fasten the terminal to the cable or wire.

solenoid An electromagnet with a moving iron core that is used to cause mechanical motion.

solid-state relay A relay that performs the function of a mechanical relay but using only electronic components.

step-down transformer A transformer used to reduce the voltage, such as to allow a battery charger operated on 120 volts to charge a 12-volt battery.

step-up transformer A transformer used to increase the voltage from a lower input voltage to a higher output, such as an ignition coil.

switch An electrical device with contacts that turns current flow on and off.

terminal A means of providing a low-resistance connection/termination at the end of a wire.

thermistor A temperature-sensitive resistor. Its resistance varies substantially with temperature change.

transformer action The transfer of electrical energy from one coil to another through induction in a transformer.

turn signal switch A switch that turns the left and right turn signal lights on and off.

twisted pair Two conductors that are twisted together to reduce electrical interference.

variable resistor A component that has a mechanism for varying resistance.

volt The unit used to measure potential difference or electrical pressure.

voltage drop The amount of potential difference between two points in a circuit.

watt The unit for measuring electrical power.

wire A conductor usually made of multistranded copper with an external insulated coating.

wiring diagram A schematic drawing and symbol representation of the wiring and components; also called electrical schematic.

wiring harness A collection of wires or cables insulated from each other but bound together.

wiring harness connector A plug that contains multiple terminals with male and female ends.

work The process by which one type of energy is transformed into another type of energy.

ASE-Type Questions

1. Tech A says that if the specified fuse keeps blowing, it is generally OK to replace it with a larger fuse. Tech B says that a fusible link is one type of circuit protection device. Who is correct?
   a. Tech A
   b. Tech B
   c. Both A and B
   d. Neither A nor B
2. Tech A says that the movement of electrons in a circuit is called current flow. Tech B says that the movement of electrons in a circuit is measured in amps. Who is correct?
   a. Tech A
   b. Tech B
   c. Both A and B
   d. Neither A nor B
3. Tech A says that electromotive force is also known as voltage. Tech B says that when electrons flow in one direction only, this is DC. Who is correct?
   a. Tech A
   b. Tech B
   c. Both A and B
   d. Neither A nor B
4. Tech A says that 18 AWG wire is larger than 12 AWG wire. Tech B says that the larger the diameter of the conductor, the more electrical resistance it has. Who is correct?
   a. Tech A
   b. Tech B
   c. Both A and B
   d. Neither A nor B
5. Two technicians are discussing electron flow. Tech A says that in "conventional theory" current is believed to flow from positive to negative. Tech B says that in "electron theory" current is believed to flow from negative to positive. Who is correct?
   a. Tech A
   b. Tech B
   c. Both A and B
   d. Neither A nor B
6. Tech A says that hertz is the number of cycles per second. Tech B says that hertz is the amount of current flow produced by an alternator. Who is correct?
   a. Tech A
   b. Tech B
   c. Both A and B
   d. Neither A nor B
7. Two technicians are discussing a series circuit with four resistors of various resistances. Tech A says that current flow will be different in each resistor. Tech B says that current flow will be the same in each resistor. Who is correct?
   a. Tech A
   b. Tech B
   c. Both A and B
   d. Neither A nor B
8. Tech A says that a voltage drop is typically used to find excessive resistance in a circuit. Tech B says that high resistance creates heat at the point of resistance in the circuit. Who is correct?
   a. Tech A
   b. Tech B
   c. Both A and B
   d. Neither A nor B
9. Tech A says that in a series circuit with two resistors of 120 ohms each, the total circuit resistance is 240 ohms. Tech B says that in a parallel circuit with two resistors of 120 ohms each, the total circuit resistance is 240 ohms. Who is correct?
   a. Tech A
   b. Tech B
   c. Both A and B
   d. Neither A nor B
10. Tech A says that a relay is a one-way electrical check valve used in alternators to change AC into DC. Tech B says that a relay uses electromagnetism to open or close a switch. Who is correct?
    a. Tech A
    b. Tech B
    c. Both A and B
    d. Neither A nor B

FLUKE 73III MULTIMETER
.000
VDC
OFF
300mV
10A
300 mA
COM

CHAPTER 30

KNOW
SEE
DO
PROVE

NATEF Tasks

Electrical/Electronic Systems General Electrical System			Page
■ Demonstrate the proper use of a digital multimeter (DMM) when measuring source voltage, voltage drop (including grounds), current flow, and resistance.	MLR	AST	852–869, 877–879
■ Demonstrate knowledge of electrical/electronic, parallel, and series-parallel circuits using principles of electricity (Ohm's Law).	MLR	AST	869–873
■ Use wiring diagrams to trace electrical/electronic circuits.	MLR		878–879
■ Use wiring diagrams during diagnosis (troubleshooting) of electrical circuit problems.		AST	878–879
■ Check operation of electrical circuits with a test light.	MLR	AST	881–882
■ Check operation of electrical circuits with fused jumper wires.	MLR	AST	882
■ Demonstrate knowledge of the causes and effects from shorts, grounds, opens, and resistance problems in electrical/electronic circuits.	MLR	AST	883–884
■ Inspect and test fusible links, circuit breakers, and fuses; determine necessary action.	MLR	AST	884
■ Inspect and test switches, connectors, relays, solenoid solid-state devices, and wires of electrical/electronic circuits; determine necessary action.		AST	884

Meter Usage and Circuit Diagnosis

Knowledge Objectives

After reading this chapter, you will be able to:

1. Explain how to set up a digital volt-ohmmeter (DVOM). (p 852)
2. Describe how to measure volts, ohms, and amps. (pp 856–857)
3. Understand the use of the DVOM in taking voltage measurements. (pp 858–863)
4. Understand the use of the DVOM in taking current measurements. (pp 863–867)
5. Understand the use of the DVOM in measuring volts, ohms, and amps in a parallel circuit. (pp 869–872)
6. Understand the use of the DVOM in measuring current and voltage in a series-parallel circuit. (pp 872–873)
7. Understand the use of the DVOM in measuring voltage and amperage in a circuit with a variable resistor. (pp 873–875)

Skills Objectives

After reading this chapter, you will be able to:

1. Use Ohm's law to diagnose circuits. (pp 877–879)
2. Use wiring diagrams to diagnose electrical circuits. (pp 878–879)
3. Use a DVOM to measure voltage. (p 881)
4. Check circuits with a test light. (pp 881–882)
5. Check circuits with fused jumper leads. (p 882)
6. Locate opens, shorts, grounds, and high-resistance faults. (pp 883–884)
7. Inspect and test circuit protection devices. (p 884)
8. Inspect and test switches, connectors, relays, solenoid solid-state devices, and wires. (p 884)

Introduction

Digital volt-ohmmeters (DVOMs) and oscilloscopes are electrical measuring tools frequently used to diagnose and repair electrical faults. Like many diagnostic tools, practice is required to understand how the DVOM and oscilloscope are used to take electrical measurements and connect them into electrical circuits to ensure correct readings are obtained. Once a reading is obtained, it needs to be interpreted and applied, in conjunction with knowledge of electrical theory, to diagnose the circuit being tested. This chapter provides an explanation of how to use and set up a DVOM for measuring voltage, amperage, and resistance.

This chapter also has a number of exercises that will expand your knowledge on using a DVOM, allowing you to practice taking readings and apply the results. It also relates the practical circuit examples and DVOM readings to Ohm's law calculations. Basic oscilloscope use and typical waveforms are also covered. Knowing how to properly use DVOMs and oscilloscopes along with interpreting and applying their readings will allow you to diagnose electrical faults, making you very valuable to your employer.

Digital Volt-Ohmmeter

A **digital volt-ohmmeter (DVOM)** or digital multimeter (DMM) is a versatile and useful piece of test equipment **FIGURE 30-1**. It is called a digital meter because the meter gives a numerical reading on a digital display. An analog meter, by comparison, uses a needle that hovers over a series of scales, requiring the technician to determine the numerical value of the reading. Digital meters are easier to read, which means that a technician is less likely to get the wrong reading. The DVOM tends to be the first test tool selected for electrical diagnosis and repairs. Basic DVOMs can measure alternating current (AC) and direct current (DC) voltage, AC and DC amperage, and resistance. Most modern DVOMs can also measure frequency and temperature and have a dedicated diode test capability.

DVOMs come in a variety of layouts and quality. You will want to get used to the meters in your shop so you will know their capabilities and how to use them. Most

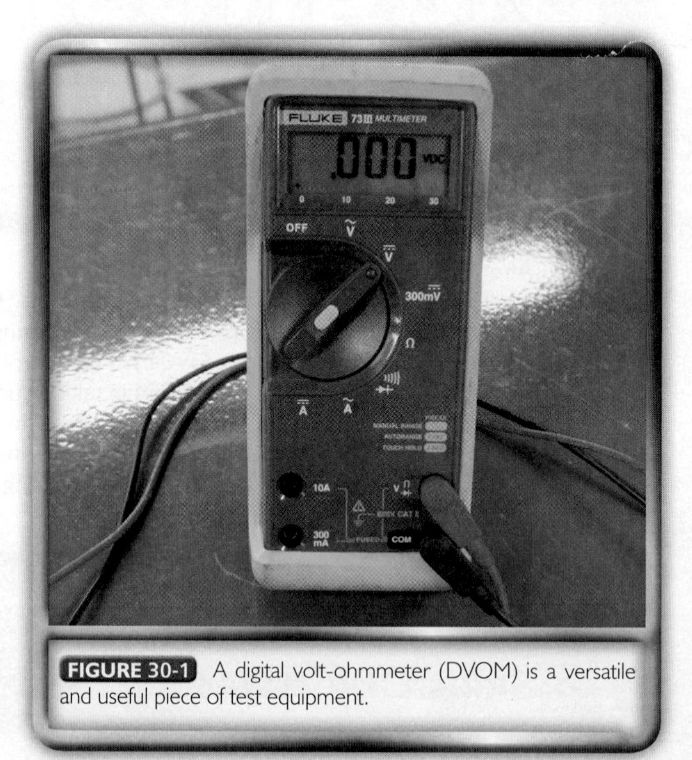
FLUKE 73III MULTIMETER
.000
VDC
OFF
300mV
10A
300 mA
COM

FIGURE 30-1 A digital volt-ohmmeter (DVOM) is a versatile and useful piece of test equipment.

You Are the Automotive Technician

Your supervisor requested that you train the shop apprentice on how to use a DVOM. You will be using the DVOM to teach the apprentice how to take simple measurements that will come in handy when doing vehicle inspections such as measuring battery and charging system voltage; testing a fuse to see if it is blown; and how to perform a voltage drop on a simple circuit. The apprentice explains what volts, ohms, and amps are, so you show him how to set up the meter for each of these tests. Once he is competent in setting up the meter, you show him how to take each type of reading. The following is the list of questions your supervisor has asked you to review with the new employee after the hands-on training:

1. What are the most common measurements taken by a DVOM, and how is the meter hooked up in the circuit for each one?
2. Describe the different ways that a voltage drop can be measured.
3. What two things are needed to have a voltage drop?

DVOMs of average quality are "fused," meaning that one or more "fast-blow" fuses are included inside the DVOM. If the amperage is too high, the fuse will blow, protecting the meter. If the meter is unfused, it will not be protected and could be damaged if used incorrectly when measuring amperage.

DVOMs and test leads also should have a CAT rating listed on the front. CAT is short for "category." Each level, or CAT, is designed to work safely on higher-powered electrical systems TABLE 30-1. CAT ratings were not designed initially for automotive meters since most vehicles use low voltage, but with more and more hybrid and electric vehicles on the road, which operate on very high voltages, CAT ratings are becoming important for automotive technicians. Hybrid vehicles typically require meters and test leads rated as CAT III or CAT IV. Another thing to keep in mind if you are working on high-voltage systems is that you need to wear a pair of certified and tested rubber-insulated gloves, most likely with leather protectors over top. Always use the proper CAT-rated meter and leads along with the proper personal protective equipment when working on high-voltage systems.

DVOM Use

DVOMs are used to take many different electrical measurements on electrical circuits and are one of the first tools used when conducting electrical repair or diagnosis work. As a voltmeter, the DVOM can measure electrical voltage within circuits; for example, the available voltage at a fuse, switch, or lamp. The DVOM can also measure resistance of a component, connector, or cable, such as the resistance of an ignition coil to check against specifications. DVOMs can also measure current flow in circuits, such as when the amount of current flow through a fuse needs to be checked against specifications. Clearly, a DVOM is a very versatile tool, explaining why it is the most commonly used electrical diagnosis tool. In the next several sections we will further explore DVOMs and how to use them.

TABLE 30-1: Meter CAT Ratings

Overvoltage Category	Short Description	Examples
CAT I	Electronics	Low-power electronic equipment such as copiers, etc.
CAT II	Single-phase plug-in tools and equipment	Portable tools, appliances, etc.
CAT III	Three-phase fixed equipment and single-phase commercial lighting	Equipment in fixed installations (this is the minimum rating required for hybrid vehicles)
CAT IV	Three-phase utility connection, any outdoor wires	Main power wires from the utility company; outside wire for lighting (this rating is for heavier-duty meters and leads for hybrid vehicles)

DVOM Components

There are two main components of a DVOM, the main instrument body and the test leads that connect the DVOM to the circuit being tested. The DVOM main instrument body has a function switch to choose the type of electrical measurement to be taken, digital display to report the readings, and sockets to connect test leads. Test leads are used to connect the DVOM to or into the circuit being tested and come in pairs: one red, the other black. Basic leads have a probe on one end for making the connection with the electrical circuit being tested and a connector on the other end for plugging into the sockets of the DVOM. A wide variety of test leads and adapters are available to make it easier to use the DVOM; for example, alligator clips enable hands-free connection of the leads. Adapters such as temperature probes and inductive current clamps connect to the input sockets of the DVOM and convert temperature or current flow into a voltage that can be measured by the DVOM.

Ranges and Scales

DVOMs read very small quantities in the one-ten thousandths of a unit range up to very large quantities in the range of millions of units in the case of resistance measurements. It is not possible for DVOMs to effectively and accurately measure such ranges with only a single range or scale; they must have multiple ranges or scales. But before we can talk about those ranges, we need to understand that the DVOM screen can only display four or five digits. This means that symbols must be used to substitute for some of the digits. TABLE 30-2 shows the common symbols, their prefix, and the factor they represent. You will

TABLE 30-2: DVOM Values

Factor	Prefix	Symbol
1,000,000	mega	M
1,000	kilo	k
1	No prefix	
0.001	milli	m
0.000001	micro	μ

have to place the appropriate electrical symbol, V, A, or Ω, behind the factor symbol based on what you are measuring. For example, 2168 mV would be the same as 2168 millivolts. It could also be called 2.168 volts, since there are 1000 millivolts in 1 volt. Either designation is correct. The challenge is taking the meter reading and making sense of it, which takes practice.

Once you understand the symbols and what value they represent, you are ready to decide which range to set the meter to. TABLE 30-3 lists a typical set of DVOM ranges; however, there is no single range or scale value used by DVOM manufacturers. The resolution indicates the accuracy of the count within any given range and is different for each range. To achieve the most accurate reading, always select the lowest range possible for the value being measured. For example, if you are measuring 12 volts, you should select the 60-V range, because 6 volts would be too low and 600 volts would be less accurate.

Most modern DVOMs have an automatic ranging capability while maintaining the ability to be used in a manually selected range, which means the user can determine the range. When used in the auto range, the DVOM selects the best range for the value being measured so that the technician does not have to be concerned with manually setting the range FIGURE 30-2. But be careful! The meter does not give you flashing light warnings that it has changed ranges, so it is extremely easy to miss that. Many a technician has been led down the wrong diagnostic path by thinking the 12.6 on the meter was volts when in fact the meter had auto-ranged to millivolts; so instead of having full power, the battery being tested had almost *no* power. To prevent this mistake, many instructors require their students to use only manual ranging when using their meter.

TABLE 30-3: DVOM Ranges

Function	Range	Resolution
mV DC	0–600.0 mV	0.1 mV
V DC	0–6.000 V	0.001 V
	0–60.00 V	0.01 V
	0–600.0 V	0.1 V
	0–1000 V	1 V
Ohms	0–600.0 Ω	0.1 Ω
	0–6.000 kΩ	0.0001 kΩ
	0–60.00 kΩ	0.01 kΩ
	0–600.0 kΩ	0.0001 MΩ
	0–40.00 MΩ	0.01 MΩ

Min/Max and Hold Setting

Many DVOMs have special settings incorporated into their design to assist you in taking measurements of rapidly changing values or to freeze the display so that an individual reading is not lost. In the **min/max setting**, the DVOM will record in memory the maximum and minimum reading obtained during the time the DVOM is connected to a source to take a reading. The min/max setting is often used to measure vehicle battery voltage while the engine is cranking or the battery is charging. During cranking of the starter motor, current is at its highest, but for only a fraction of a second when the engine initially starts to crank. Cranking is also when the battery voltage is at its lowest. In min/max mode, a DVOM will capture the minimum and maximum battery voltage FIGURE 30-3. A limitation in the use of the DVOM

Agilent U1242B
AUTO
68.3
0.0
m V
True RMS Multimeter
Setup
Shift
Hold
Range
Save
View
Max Min
Scan
Auto
Bat
mA
Log
OFF

FIGURE 30-2 Meter set to auto range and reading mV.

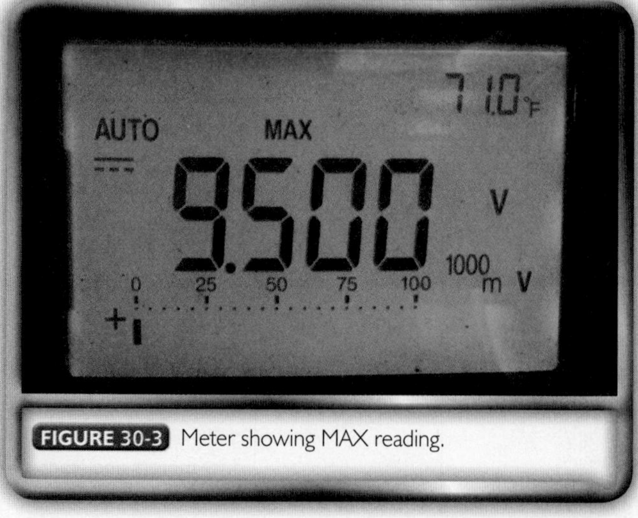
AUTO
MAX
9.500
V
71.0
1000
m V

FIGURE 30-3 Meter showing MAX reading.

is the sample rate. The sample rate is the speed at which the DVOM can sample the voltage. The DVOM does not continuously sample the voltage; rather, it checks the voltage at regular intervals or at a sample rate. While this occurs quickly—for example, every 100 milliseconds—it does mean that if a transient voltage occurs between samples, it will not be recorded by the DVOM. Where quicker sample rates are required, other tools such as oscilloscopes can be used.

The **hold function** allows the display to be frozen. When the hold function is activated, the display will hold the value on the display until the function or DVOM is turned off FIGURE 30-4. A variation of the hold function is the "auto hold" function found on some DVOMs. When activated, the auto hold function takes a measurement and freezes or holds the display until the function or DVOM is turned off. This function can be useful when taking measurements in difficult locations, such as underneath a dash where you may not be able to watch the meter display while making the meter connections.

Setting Up a DVOM

To set up a DVOM to take accurate measurements, you need to know if you will be measuring resistance, voltage, or current. You should also know the reading that you are expecting so you can be sure to set up the meter appropriately. If very high voltages are to be measured, it is important to make sure the DVOM and leads match the appropriate CAT rating for use at the voltages you will be testing. All of this information will determine the way in which you set up the DVOM, including the connections you need to make on the DVOM and the range you select. Resistance measurements should be undertaken with the circuit disconnected. If measuring the resistance of components, they should be removed from the circuit. The following steps describe how to set up a DVOM:

1. Know what you are testing—volts, amps, or ohms.
2. Know the value you expect to be reading (specification).
3. Select leads and probes to suit the measuring task.
4. Connect the leads to the DVOM.
5. Use the function switch to select the type of measurement to be undertaken (e.g., resistance, volts, or amps; DC or AC).
6. Select the correct meter range if you are using a manual range meter.
7. Connect the leads to the circuit being tested.
8. Read the meter display.

Test Leads: Common and Probing

Many people incorrectly label the red lead as positive and the black lead as negative. However, if you look at your meter near the test lead terminals, you will not see a "+" or a "–" anywhere. What you will see is "A" (typically 10 A), "mA," "common," and "V/Ω" FIGURE 30-5. Common just means that the terminal is "common" to all of the functions of the meter. In other words, this lead does not need to be moved when different functions of the meter are typically accessed. On the other hand, the red lead does have to move, depending on what function of the meter is being used. That is why it is labeled with the V/Ω symbol, and not "+." If you find this distinction questionable, consider the following: When we measure various electrical signals at the same time on an oscilloscope, we need more than just the red lead. In fact, we typically use a yellow, a blue, and a green test lead. In all of these situations, the test lead (no matter the color) acts as a probe into the circuit. So rather than referring

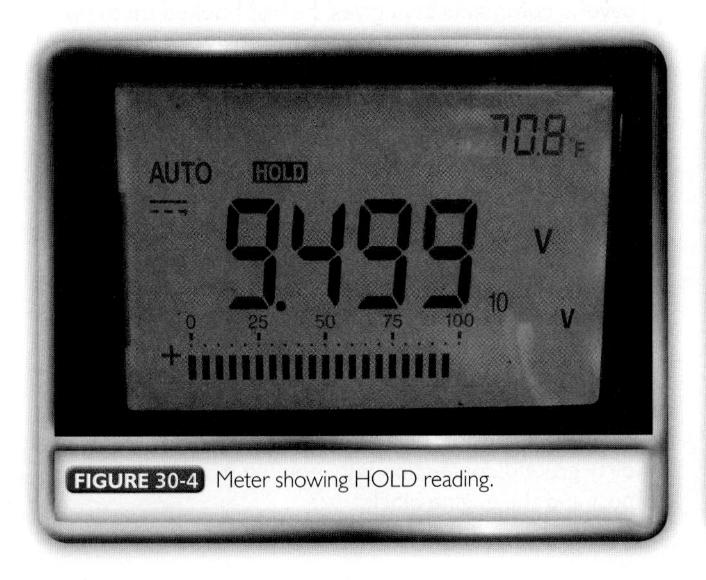
70.8 °F
AUTO
HOLD
9.499
V
0 25 50 75 100
10
V

FIGURE 30-4 Meter showing HOLD reading.

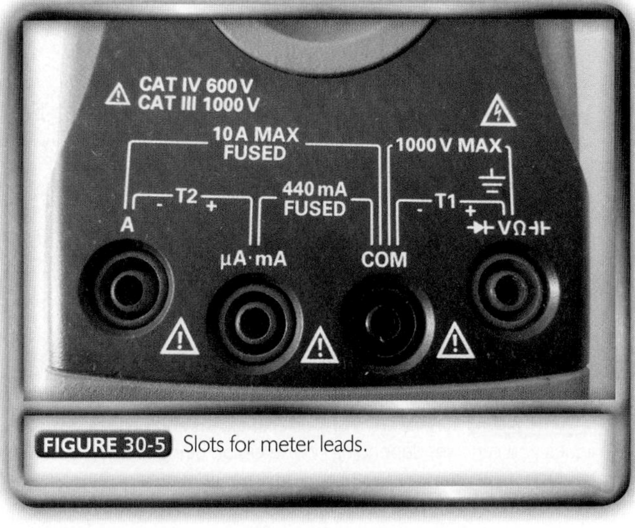
CAT IV 600 V
CAT III 1000 V
10 A MAX
FUSED
1000 V MAX
T2
440 mA
FUSED
T1
A
µA·mA
COM
VΩ

FIGURE 30-5 Slots for meter leads.

to the red lead as the positive lead, it is more accurate to refer to it as the probing lead for the DVOM. Then we can introduce probing leads of other colors when we use an oscilloscope.

The other important note is that the meter screen will always read what the probing lead is touching. For example, if the common lead is touching the battery's negative post and the probing lead is touching the positive post, the meter screen will display a "+" before the reading. That means that the probing lead is touching something more positive than the common lead. If we reverse the leads, the meter screen will display a "–" before the number, meaning that the probing lead is touching something more negative than the common lead. When you understand this concept, rather than jumping to the conclusion that "the meter leads are hooked up backward," you will be ready to start diagnosing all kinds of strange electrical problems, especially with ground issues and charging system issues.

Probing Techniques

A **probing technique** is the way in which the DVOM probes are connected into circuits. There are many different types of probes and probing techniques you can use, depending on the circuit being tested. Some examples are alligator clips, fine-pin probes, and insulation piercing clips **FIGURE 30-6**. Make sure you know the voltage limits of the probes you use, since high-voltage measurements require special probes that are designed for that purpose.

Never use excessive force when probing; doing so may bend or damage connectors and terminals. The standard probe leads that are supplied with a DVOM are basic straight metal probes useful for making quick measurements in circuits, but they do require the use of both hands to hold them in place. Leads with alligator clips, which come in various sizes, allow the DVOM leads to be clipped onto the circuit and held in place, freeing up your hands for other tasks. These clips are particularly useful for connecting to larger terminals, such as battery terminals.

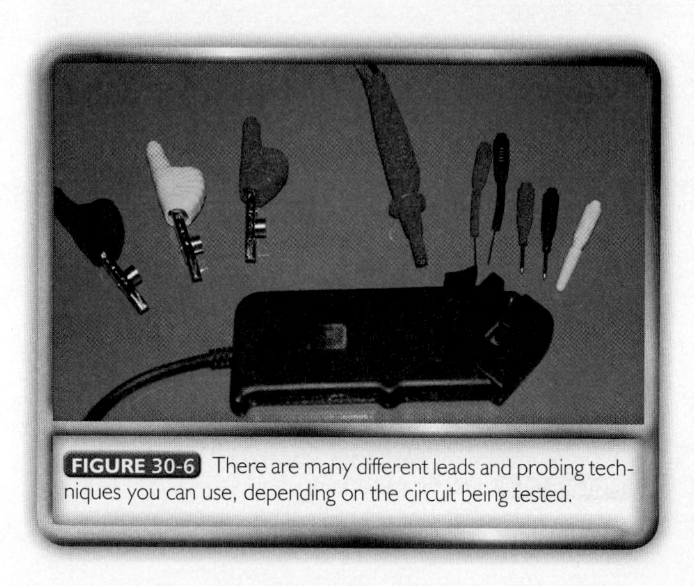

FIGURE 30-6 There are many different leads and probing techniques you can use, depending on the circuit being tested.

Back-probing occurs when the probe is pushed in from the back of a connector to make a connection. To perform this task, very fine pins are used to reduce the possibility of damage. The pins are designed to slip into the back of connectors and provide contact without causing damage. Insulation piercing probes are also available but should be used with caution. They have sharp fine pins that pierce the insulation on conductors to create a connection. Remember to always reinsulate the hole that the probe makes to prevent any corrosion. Use liquid insulation or a similar product to reinsulate; do not use room temperature vulcanizing (RTV) silicone, which attracts moisture as it cures, potentially causing corrosion. Since it may result in damage to the insulation or conductor, this type of probe should be used only as a last resort.

Measuring Volts, Ohms, and Amps

The most common measurements taken with DVOMs are voltage, resistance, and current. To take voltage measurements, the probing lead (red) is connected to the volts/

> **TECHNICIAN TIP**
>
> A technician recently posted an electrical problem on a technical forum. He said that he had hooked up a voltmeter with the black (common) lead on the negative battery terminal and the red (probing) lead on the vehicle engine ground with the engine running. The meter read a negative number. He asked the forum if he had the meter leads hooked up backward. He received several comments saying yes, he had hooked them up backward. However, those technicians were not correct. His probing lead was registering a reading that was more negative than the common lead. But what could be more negative than the negative post of the battery? When the engine is running, the alternator can be more negative than the negative battery post. So what his DVOM was trying to tell him was that there was a voltage drop between the negative battery post and the alternator frame. If he would have understood that the probing lead was not lying to him, that it was reporting exactly what it was touching compared to what the common lead was touching, then he could have started down the path to diagnosing what it indicated. In this case, he should have been looking for a dirty ground connection between the negative battery post and the engine block.

ohms, or V/Ω, terminal, and the common lead (black) is connected to the common, or COM, terminal of the DVOM. An appropriate range or auto range is selected on either AC or DC voltage, depending on the voltage to be measured. The probing lead is typically connected to the positive side of the circuit being tested, and the common lead to the negative side. Watch your screen. If the "+" or "–" is not what you were expecting, check the leads to verify they are connected the way you intended. If you still get an unexpected reading, stop and analyze the situation. Ask yourself, what could cause the meter to read that way? Then brainstorm the options.

Most DVOMs can measure milliamps or 10 to 20 amps directly through the meter. The correct range needs to be selected, along with AC or DC. The red probe is connected to the A terminal, and the black lead is connected to the COM terminals. On some DVOMs, there may be a separate mA terminal that the red probe plugs into to measure milliamps. To measure current, the DVOM is connected in series with the circuit, with the probing lead closest to the positive terminal of the power supply or battery. Quality DVOMs typically have an internal fuse that will blow if excessive current flows through it. This fuse is designed to help prevent damage to the meter.

If larger amperage needs to be measured, then current clamps can be connected to the DVOM, and, depending on their range, they can measure high currents, such as starter motor current draw of 400 amps or more. Current clamps are available in a variety of current-measuring ranges. The current clamp fastens around the conductor and measures the strength of the magnetic field produced from current flowing through the conductor and outputs a voltage that the DVOM reads as voltage, which is directly related to the amount of current flowing in amps. When using current clamps, the DVOM is set to read volts. Current clamps also have the advantage that they clamp around the conductor, so the circuit does not need to be broken into to insert the DVOM in series as you would with standard probes on an ammeter.

To accurately measure the resistance of a component, you should remove or isolate the component from the circuit. Doing so removes the possibility of any parallel circuit resistance affecting the resistance measurement. If you need to measure resistance in a circuit, always make sure the power is disconnected. In order to read resistance, batteries inside the DVOM supply the circuit with power to take the measurement. If power is not removed from the circuit being tested, it disrupts the measurement and can provide a false reading or potentially damage the DVOM. To take resistance measurements, the red (probing) lead is connected to the V/Ω terminal, and the black (common) lead is connected to the COM terminal of the DVOM. You will need to select an appropriate range or auto range to measure resistance. The red probing lead is connected to one side of the component being tested, and the black common lead is connected to the other side.

Applied Math

AM-1: Whole Numbers: The technician can add whole numbers to determine measurement conformance with the manufacturer's specifications.

An alternator is being tested to determine if it meets manufacturer's specifications. If an alternator is damaged due to a blown diode or similar problem, it is usually out of specifications by a wide margin. For this type of alternator the output specification is 95 amperes. The technician tests the alternator that puts out 65 amps. The service material states a good alternator will provide an output that is within 15 amps of its rated value. The technician adds 15 amps to the original 65 amps which is a total of 80 amps. This is below the specifications of 95 amps for this type of alternator.

In this example, we are working with whole numbers. If a number has a negative sign, a decimal point, or a part that's a fraction, it is not considered a whole number.

Applied Math

AM-2: Decimals: The technician can add decimal numbers to determine conformance with the manufacturer's specifications.

A starter has been rebuilt and the technician wants to check the pinion clearance. A feeler gauge will be used to determine this clearance. Manufacturer's specifications for this clearance are from 0.010″ to 0.140″, with 0.070″ considered the midpoint. The technician's feeler gauge set only goes to 0.045″, which fits too loosely in the gap. He places a 0.025″ blade next to the 0.045″ blade, which together, fits in the gap with just the right tension. The selected gauges are 0.025″ plus 0.045″ to equal a total of 0.070″.

In this example, we are working with decimal numbers. Decimals are numbers that are expressed using a decimal point.

TECHNICIAN TIP

DVOMs come in many forms. Always follow the specific manufacturer's instructions in the use of the DVOM or serious damage either to the DVOM and/or to the electrical circuit could result.

Voltage Exercises

The following voltage exercises are designed to explain the use of the DVOM in taking DC voltage measurements. Examples are given to show the use of different ranges on the meter display and voltage drops in the series circuits across equal and unequal loads. It is important to understand that the sum of the series voltage drops equals the supply voltage as explained in Kirchhoff's voltage law.

Voltage Ranges

Typically, a DVOM has both an auto range and a manual range capability. The way in which you select auto range and manual range will vary depending on the DVOM. Different DVOMs have different range settings. For example, one DVOM's setting could be 6 V, 60 V, and 600 V, and another's 4 V, 40 V, and 400 V. FIGURE 30-7 shows a circuit with two resistors in a series with a 12-volt DC supply. Various DVOM ranges can be compared by measuring the voltage drops across each of the resistors. The DVOM has the following ranges: 600.0 mV, 6.000 V, 60.00 V, 600.0 V, and 1000 V. TABLE 30-4 provides results of voltmeter readings and a DVOM's display to show how different ranges affect the way in which the DVOM readings are displayed.

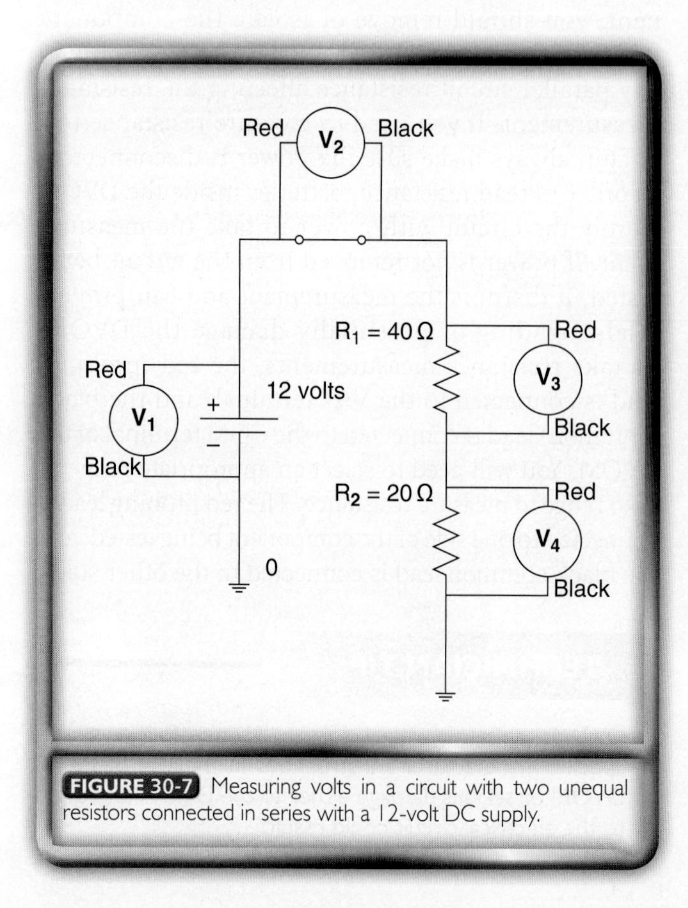
Red
V_2
Black
$R_1 = 40\,\Omega$
Red
V_3
Black
Red
12 volts
+
−
V_1
Black
$R_2 = 20\,\Omega$
Red
V_4
Black
0

FIGURE 30-7 Measuring volts in a circuit with two unequal resistors connected in series with a 12-volt DC supply.

Voltage Drop

Voltage drop is measured with a voltmeter and is the potential difference between two points in a circuit. The sum of all the voltage drops in a series circuit equals the supply voltage, while the voltage drop across all parallel circuit branches is the same. Voltage drop does occur in all parts of the circuit, but in a correctly working vehicle circuit, the vast majority of voltage drop is across

TABLE 30-4: Example of the Effect of Different Ranges on DVOM Readings

Voltmeter	Range	Meter Display	Explanation
V_3 V_4	Auto range Auto range	8.00 4.000	Auto ranging selects the correct range for the voltage being read.
V_3	6 V	OL	OL means overload and indicates the voltage being read is higher than the maximum allowed for the range.
V_4	6 V	4.000	The 6-V range is the best range to most accurately measure 4 V. Note how it has three digits after the decimal point.
V_3	60 V	8.00	The 60-V range is the best range to most accurately measure 8 V.
V_4	60 V	4.00	Four volts can also be read on the 60-V range; however, when compared to the 6-V range, there are two digits rather than three after the decimal point. This reading will not be as accurate on this range.
V_3 V_4 V_3 V_4	600 V 600 V 1000 V 1000 V	8.0 4.0 8 4	On these ranges, the DVOM still reads but the measurements are not as accurate. To get the most accurate reading, a DVOM range should be selected that is slightly higher than the reading expected.

the component or load we want to do work, such as the headlight bulb.

Unwanted voltage drop becomes a problem if it becomes excessive and occurs in parts of the circuit other than the load. For example, ideally the only resistance in the circuit would be the headlight bulb. If this were the case, then all of the battery voltage would be dropped (used up) across the headlight bulb. In practice, however, resistance exists in the cables and connectors within the circuit. In a good circuit, the resistance of the cables, terminals or connectors, and switches is very low, causing small and insignificant amounts of voltage drop. A problem arises when excessive voltage drop occurs in the circuit cables, connectors, and switches, which reduces the efficiency of the circuit. Excessive voltage drop is a fault in the circuit and can cause problems; for example, it will result in yellow or dim headlights. To test for unwanted voltage drop of the conductors, switches, and connectors, measure the voltage across each of these parts of the circuit and add the voltage drops together. In a 12-volt system, the total unwanted voltage drop across each side of the whole circuit should not exceed 0.5 volts or 1.0 volt for a 24-volt circuit. And individual voltage drops across an individual wire, connection, or common switch should be less than 0.2 volts.

To measure voltage drop, the DVOM needs to be used on the voltage range. To perform this measurement process, you will need to set the function switch to "auto range volts DC" on the DVOM (some technicians prefer to use manual range, so they will not be fooled by auto range), and connect the black lead to COM and the red

Applied Math

AM-5: Decimals: The technician can subtract decimal numbers to determine conformance with the manufacturer's specifications.

A technician is performing a battery state of charge test using a hydrometer. This procedure can be used on automotive batteries that have removable individual filler caps. The tube of the hydrometer is inserted into one of the battery cells. The technician will gently draw electrolyte into the hydrometer. The float indicator will rise and float freely. The specific gravity can be obtained by reading the indicator at eye level. When doing this procedure, it is important to consider the hazards of battery electrolyte, which contains sulfuric acid. Eye protection and rubber gloves are needed for personal protection. After reading the hydrometer, the electrolyte is returned to the cell from which it was withdrawn. The same procedure will be repeated for the other five cells.

Manufacturer's specifications state that a fully charged battery should show a specific gravity of approximately 1.260 with electrolyte temperature at 80° Fahrenheit. The results of the readings of each cell will be compared to a chart that shows specific gravity as compared to state of charge. If the electrolyte temperature is above or below 80° Fahrenheit, corrections must be made by one of several methods. In this case, the technician consulted a temperature correction chart.

The technician observed that at 40° F, the correction factor would be to subtract 0.016 points. The reading for cell one was 1.240. To compensate for the huge temperature difference between 80° and 40° Fahrenheit, corrections are needed. In this example, we have 1.240 minus (-) 0.016 = 1.224 for the adjusted specific gravity of one of the battery cells. The next step would be to look at the readings for the other five cells of the battery.

Applied Math

AM-3: Mentally: The technician can mentally add two or more numbers to determine conformance with the manufacturer's specifications.

AM-6: Mentally: The technician can mentally subtract decimal and whole numbers to arrive at a difference for comparison with the manufacturer's specifications.

In this scenario, a technician is using a DVOM to test the resistance of a coil pack for a V-6 engine. The ignition coil pack is suspected to be faulty due to a failed power balance test in which the cylinder was not properly contributing to the performance of the engine. Since coil designs are different, manufacturers' testing procedures vary. With the key off and the battery lead to the coil disconnected, the ohmmeter function of the DVOM will be used to check resistance. The technician will measure the resistance of the primary and secondary windings. In this case, the specifications for the primary windings are 0.3–1.0 ohms. Before taking this reading, the technician checks the resistance in the leads of his DVOM. This was determined to be 0.2 ohms of resistance and will be subtracted (mentally) from the primary resistance reading. Using service information, the technician places the leads of the DVOM in proper slots of the component and obtains a reading of 0.8 ohms. He mentally subtracts 0.2 ohms for the resistance in the meter leads for a corrected reading of 0.6 ohms. This is within specifications for the primary windings.

The next step is the readings for the secondary windings of the coil pack. The manufacturer's specifications are 8000 ohms–9000 ohms. The technician places the meter leads as shown in the service information and obtains a reading of 6,200 ohms. Mentally, the technician subtracts this and records the information on the repair order. The coil pack is 1,800 ohms below minimum specifications. The technician will install a known good component (coil pack) for a test to see how the engine performs.

(probing) lead to V/Ω. Voltage drop can be measured across components, connectors, or cables. The probing lead of the DVOM is normally connected to the point in the circuit where you want to know the voltage. For example, if you want to know what the voltage is at the positive post of the battery, then you would connect the red lead to the positive post of the battery and the black lead to the negative post of the battery. The voltmeter would then read the amount of voltage greater than is at the negative terminal.

If you are performing a voltage drop test, for example, on the feed side of the horn circuit, you could connect the black lead to the positive terminal of the battery and the red lead to the input wire of the horn (the wire connected to the horn). When you activate the horn, the voltmeter will read the amount of voltage drop in the feed side of the circuit. For example, it might be –4.2 volts. This means that the voltage is 4.2 volts less at the input of the horn (red lead) than it is at the positive battery post (black lead). In this case, the "–" means less than. So there are 4.2 volts less at the horn than at the positive battery post. Since the voltage drop is more than 0.5 volts, this is an excessive voltage drop in that portion of the circuit, and the voltmeter leads will need to be moved wire by wire closer together until the point of the voltage drop is located.

You could make the same measurement with the DVOM leads reversed. If you place the red lead on the positive battery post and the black lead on the input of the horn, the meter would then read 4.2 volts. In this case it shows positive. This is because the red lead is on the positive post of the battery, which is 4.2 volts higher than the horn input where the black lead is connected. As you can see, voltmeter leads can be hooked up in a couple of ways. Just remember that the meter always reads what the red lead is touching.

FIGURE 30-8 shows a series circuit of two resistors with a 12-volt battery and switch. In this example of how to measure voltage drop, the voltage in various parts of the circuit will be measured with the switch in the open position. **TABLE 30-5** gives an explanation of the voltage measurements and validates the measurements with Ohm's law calculations with the switch in the open position.

FIGURE 30-9 shows a series circuit of two resistors with a 12-volt battery and switch. In this example of how to measure voltage drop, the voltage in various parts of the circuit will be measured with the switch in the closed position. **TABLE 30-6** gives an explanation of the voltage measurements and validates the measurements with Ohm's law calculations with the switch in the closed position.

Unwanted voltage drops in vehicle circuits can cause real problems and faults. For example, a corroded or bad chassis ground can cause a voltage drop that reduces the

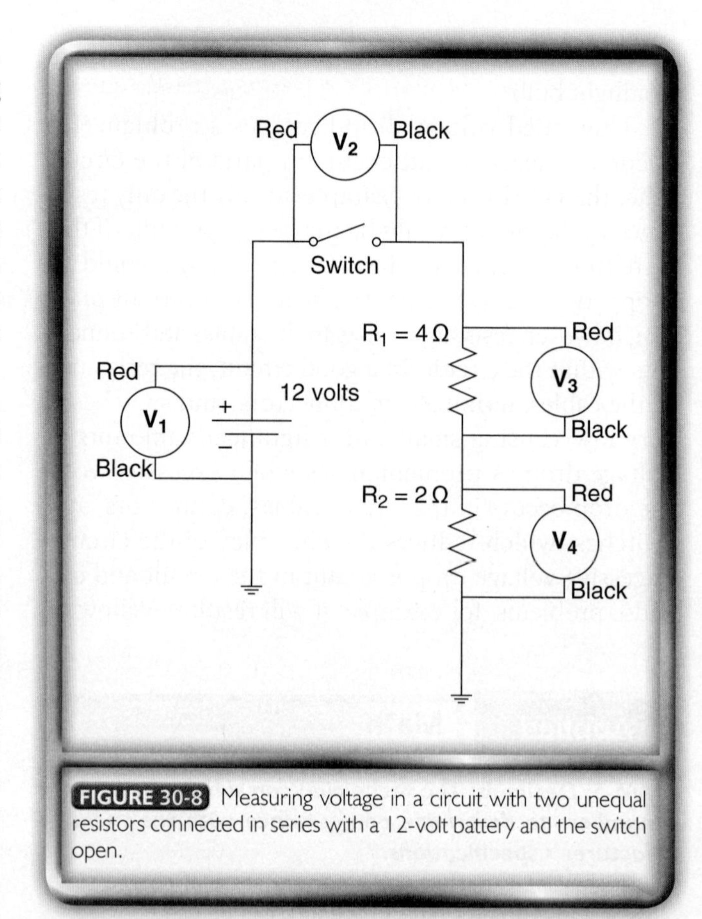
Red
V2
Black
Switch
R1 = 4 Ω
Red
V3
Black
Red
V1
Black
12 volts
+
–
R2 = 2 Ω
Red
V4
Black

FIGURE 30-8 Measuring voltage in a circuit with two unequal resistors connected in series with a 12-volt battery and the switch open.

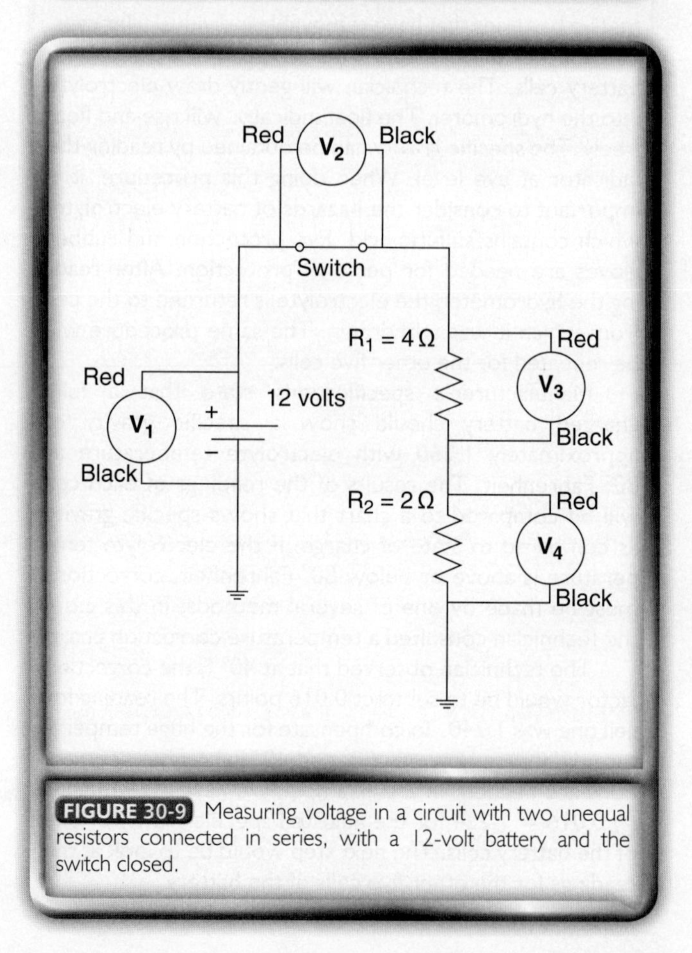
Red
V2
Black
Switch
R1 = 4 Ω
Red
V3
Black
Red
V1
Black
12 volts
+
–
R2 = 2 Ω
Red
V4
Black

FIGURE 30-9 Measuring voltage in a circuit with two unequal resistors connected in series, with a 12-volt battery and the switch closed.

TABLE 30-5: Explanation of Voltage Measurements in Figure 30-8

Measured Voltage	Explanation
V_1 = 12 V	V_1 is measuring the voltage directly across the supply battery, so the voltage reading will be the battery voltage.
V_2 = 12 V	With the switch in the open position, no current flows in the circuit. The probing lead is connected directly to the battery via the cable, while the black lead is connected to the negative battery terminal via the two series resistors. Because no current flows in the circuit, there is no voltage drop across the two resistors; therefore, the entire battery voltage drop is across the open circuit switch.
V_3 = 0 V	No current is flowing in the circuit; therefore, resistor R_1 has no voltage drop across it. This can be calculated using Ohm's law: Voltage Drop = Resistance × Current = 4 Ω × 0 A = 0 V drop This would be the same as having a garden hose with a kink in it but with the water shut off at the house. The pressure would be the same on both sides of the kink in the hose, since there is no flow.
V_4 = 0 V	No current is flowing in the circuit; therefore, resistor R_2 has no voltage drop across it. This can be calculated using Ohm's law: Voltage Drop = Resistance × Current = 2 Ω × 0 A = 0 V drop

TABLE 30-6: Explanation of Voltage Measurements in Figure 30-9

Measured Voltage	Explanation
V_1 = 12 V	V_1 is measuring the voltage directly across the supply battery, so the voltage reading will be the battery voltage.
V_2 = 0 V	With the switch in the closed position, current flows in the circuit. The switch contacts ideally will have no resistance when closed, so the voltage drop across the contacts will be 0 V. In actual circuit operation, there will always be a slight amount of resistance that will drop a slight amount of voltage in a good switch, but for our examples in this chapter, we will assume there is none.
V_3 = 8 V	With the switch closed, current can flow in the circuit. The amount of voltage drop across R_1 will be 8 V. This can be calculated using Ohm's law: Voltage Drop = Resistance × Current = 4 Ω × 2 A (see note below) = 8 V drop Note: To calculate total circuit current, use this formula: $I_T = V_T \div R_T$ = 12 ÷ 6 Ω = 2 A
V_4 = 4 V	With the switch closed, current can flow in the circuit. The amount of voltage drop across R_2 will be 4 V. This can be calculated using Ohm's law: Voltage Drop = Resistance × Current = 2 Ω × 2 A = 4 V drop

voltage and current available to components. **FIGURE 30-10** shows a simple circuit with a bulb connected via a switch across a 12-volt circuit. In this circuit, a corroded ground connection has caused a resistance that is dropping 2 volts across it. **TABLE 30-7** analyzes the voltage drops across the corroded ground connection and explains how it reduces the voltage across the bulb, which in turn will cause poor illumination.

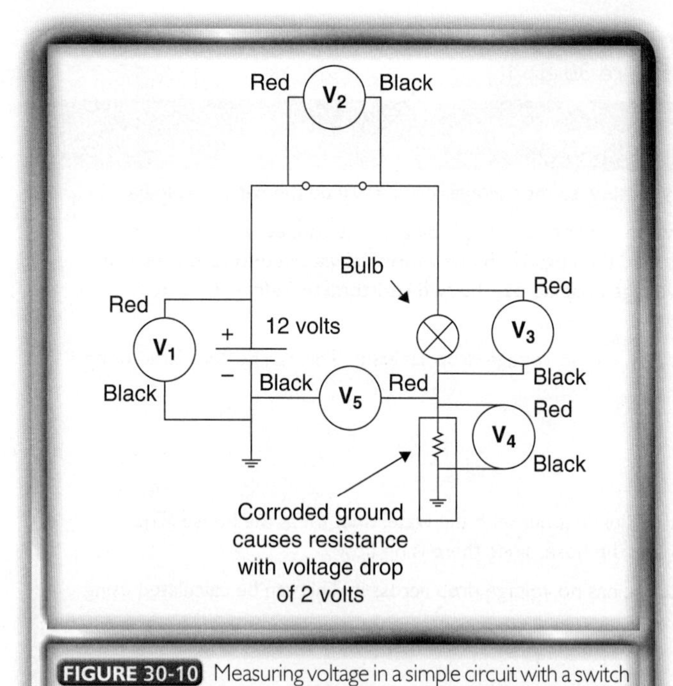
Red
V2
Black
Bulb
Red
Red
12 volts
+
V1
V3
−
Black
Black
V5
Red
Black
Red
V4
Black
Corroded ground causes resistance with voltage drop of 2 volts

FIGURE 30-10 Measuring voltage in a simple circuit with a switch and one bulb, but with high resistance due to a corroded ground.

TABLE 30-7: Analysis of Voltage Drops in Figure 30-10

Measured Voltage	Explanation
V_1 = 12 V	V_1 is measuring the voltage directly across the supply battery, so the voltage reading will be the battery voltage.
V_2 = 0 V	With the switch in the closed position, current flows in the circuit. The switch contacts ideally will have no resistance when closed, so the voltage drop across the contact will be 0 V.
V_3 = 10 V	With the switch closed, current can flow in the circuit. The amount of voltage drop across the bulb is 10 V, because 2 V is being dropped across the corroded ground connection.
V_4 = 2 V	With the switch closed, current can flow in the circuit. The amount of voltage drop across the corroded ground connection is 2 V. This amount of voltage drop robs the bulb of part of the source voltage and would cause the bulb to be very yellow and dim. The box around the resistor and ground indicates the resistance is within the ground connection. High resistance always robs voltage from the designed loads in the circuit and reduces amperage in the circuit.
V_5 = 2 V	V_5 is measuring the same voltage as V_4; the red and black leads of both DVOMs are connected to points with the same potential.

Applied Math

AM-4: Whole Numbers: The technician can divide whole numbers to determine differences for comparison with the manufacturer's specifications.
AM-7: Whole Numbers: The technician can divide whole numbers to determine differences for comparison with the manufacturer's specifications.
Battery load testing is a procedure that uses a simulated starter current draw on a battery. The results of this test can be compared to manufacturer's specifications for the condition of the battery. There are a number of steps to complete regarding a battery load test using a carbon pile unit. One of the steps is to use one-half CCA rating to determine the load to be applied to the battery. CCA stands for cold cranking amps, which is one of the battery's primary ratings. In this example, we have a 770 CCA battery and the load to be applied will be one-half of that amount. To determine this, we can divide by two to give us the 385 CCA load to apply. Another way to describe this would be: 770 CCA/2 = 385 CCA (test load).

In this example, we are dividing whole numbers. Division is the opposite of multiplication.

Note that an incandescent bulb filament is a heating element and its resistance varies greatly as the current going through it varies.

Voltage Drop Across Multiple Loads

To measure voltage drop, the DVOM is used on the voltage range. Select "auto range volts DC" on the DVOM, and connect the black lead to COM and the red lead to V/Ω. Voltage drop can be measured across components, connectors, or cables, but current has to be flowing to get an accurate measurement. Remember, the leads when checking voltage can be placed in either direction. Just remember which way you placed them so you understand what the reading means. We will show the red lead on the most positive side for purposes of the following diagrams.

In **FIGURE 30-11**, the resistors in the series circuit each have the same value—3 ohms. **TABLE 30-8** lists the circuit voltages and provides an explanation for each.

Voltage Drop Across Unequal Loads

To measure voltage drop, the DVOM must be set on the voltage range. Select "auto range volts DC" on the DVOM, and connect the black lead to COM and the red lead to V/Ω. Voltage drop can be measured across components, connectors, or cables accurately *only* when current is flowing. Remember, the leads when

Applied Math

AM-8: Decimals: The technician can divide decimal numbers to determine measurement conformance with the manufacturer's specifications.

In this scenario, a technician is installing a new starter on a Chevrolet automobile. This type of starter requires a shim or series of shims between the starter mounting flange and the engine block.

The manufacturer's specifications for this operation are 0.020 inch to 0.060 inch clearance between the pinion gear and flywheel. There is also a note of caution in the manufacturer's service information. The note of caution states: Failure to correct a clearance problem can lead to broken flywheel teeth or starter motor housings.

The technician measured the clearance and found it to be 0.010 inch. He needs to install the starter with the proper number of shims to equal the mid-point of the specifications. This would equal 0.040 inch clearance, so he needs to increase the clearance by 0.030 inch to reach his goal. The service information states that each shim will increase the clearance approximately 0.005 inch.

The technician is aware that he needs to divide 0.030 inch by 0.005 inch to determine the number of shims required to meet the mid-point of the specifications. We have 0.030 inch divided by 0.005, which equals six shims required. The technician installs six shims and measures the clearance at approximately 0.040, which is well within the specified range.

checking voltage can be placed in either direction. Just remember which way you placed them so you understand what the reading means. We will show the red lead on the most positive side for purposes of the following diagrams.

FIGURE 30-12 shows that the resistors in the series circuit have different values; R_1 is 4 ohms and R_2 is 2 ohms. **TABLE 30-9** lists the circuit voltages and provides an explanation for each.

Current Exercises

In this section, the exercises are designed to explain the use of the DVOM when taking DC current measurements. Undertaking the exercises will improve your understanding of Ohm's law and current measurements. Examples are given to demonstrate measuring current and to show the magnetic fields produced around a conductor when current flows. It is important to understand that current is the same in all parts of a properly working series circuit. Always remember that an ammeter must be connected in series within the circuit. That means that the circuit must be broken in two and each end of the ammeter connected to one of the two broken ends. This method will ensure that all of the current flowing through the circuit flows through the ammeter.

In this exercise, voltage and current measurements will be taken. For voltage measurements, select "auto range volts DC" on the DVOM, and connect the red lead to V/Ω and the black lead to COM. For current measurements, select "auto range amps DC" on the DVOM.

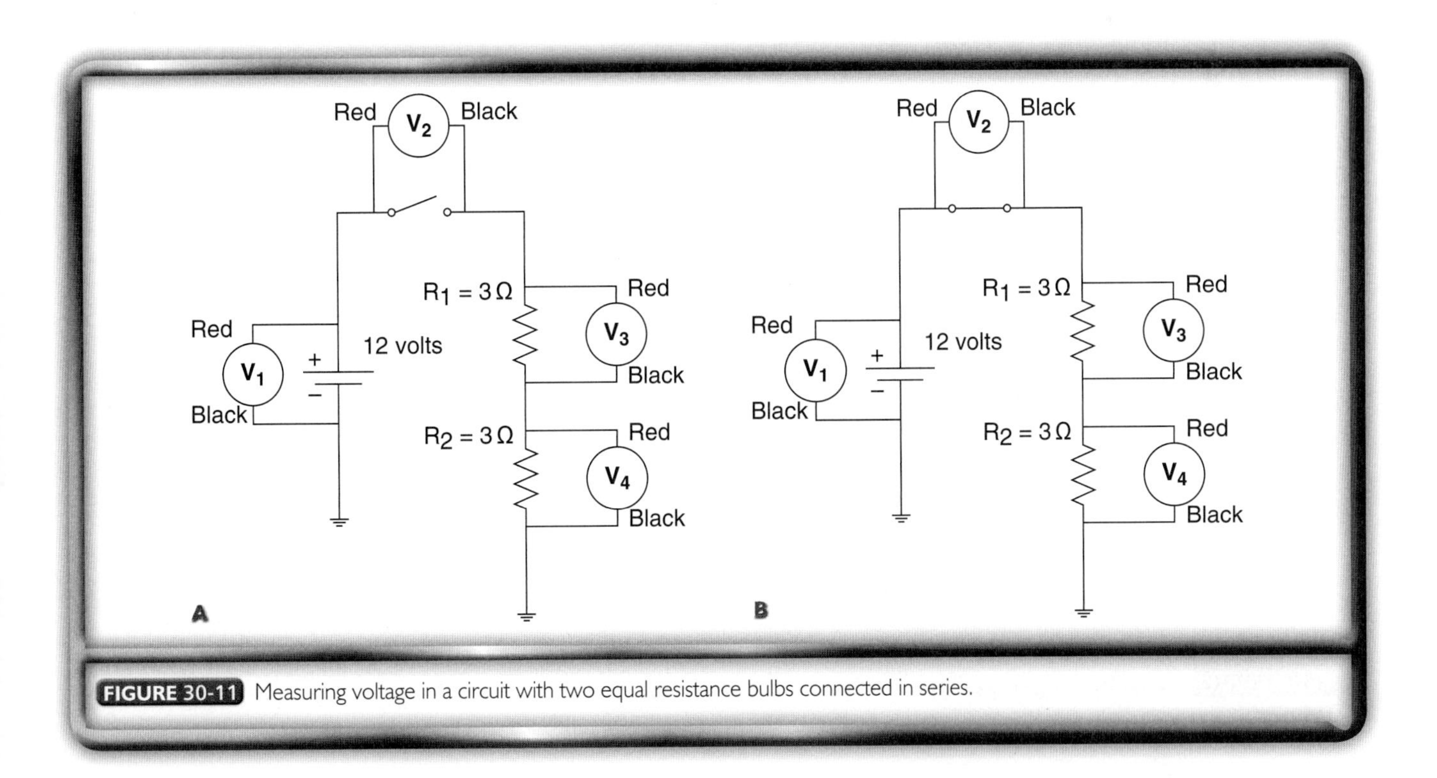
Red
V2
Black
R1 = 3 Ω
Red
V3
Black
Red
V1
Black
12 volts
R2 = 3 Ω
Red
V4
Black
A
B

FIGURE 30-11 Measuring voltage in a circuit with two equal resistance bulbs connected in series.

TABLE 30-8: Explanation of Circuit Voltages in Figure 30-11

Figure	Measured Voltage	Explanation
A B	$V_1 = 12$ V $V_1 = 12$ V	V_1 is measuring the voltage directly across the supply battery, so the voltage reading will be the battery voltage regardless of the position of the switch.
A	$V_2 = 12$ V	With the switch in the open position, no current flows in the circuit. The red DVOM lead is connected directly to the battery via the cable, while the black lead is connected to the negative battery terminal through the two series resistors. Because no current flows in the circuit, there is no voltage drop across the two resistors; therefore, the entire battery voltage drop is across the open circuit switch.
B	$V_2 = 0$ V	The switch contacts ideally will have no resistance when closed, so the voltage drop across the contacts will be 0 V.
B	$V_3 = 6$ V	With the switch closed, the amount of voltage drop across R_1 will be 6 V. This can be calculated using Ohm's law: Voltage Drop = Resistance × Current = 3 Ω × 2 A (see note below) = 6 V drop Note: To calculate total circuit current, use this formula: $I_T = V_T \div R_T$
B	$V_4 = 6$ V	With the switch closed, the amount of voltage drop across R_2 will be 6 V. This can be calculated using Ohm's law: Voltage Drop = Resistance × Current = 3 Ω × 2 A = 6 V drop R_1 and R_2 are of the same resistance, so they will have the same voltage drop. Summing the voltage drops of R_1 and R_2 will equal the supply voltage: V_T = The sum of the voltage drops in a series circuit = VD R_1 + VD R_2 = 6 V + 6 V = 12 V

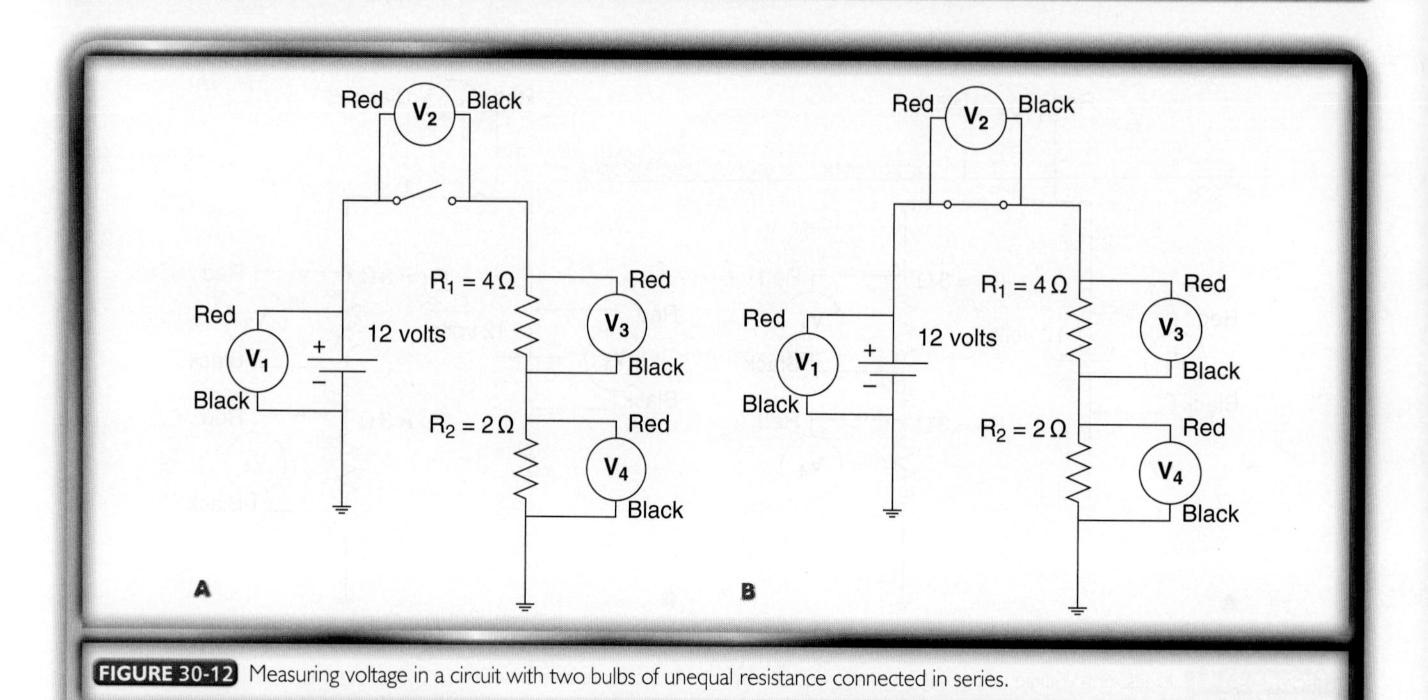
Red
V_2
Black
$R_1 = 4\,\Omega$
Red
V_3
Black
Red
V_1
Black
12 volts
+
−
$R_2 = 2\,\Omega$
Red
V_4
Black
A
Red
V_2
Black
$R_1 = 4\,\Omega$
Red
V_3
Black
Red
V_1
Black
12 volts
+
−
$R_2 = 2\,\Omega$
Red
V_4
Black
B

FIGURE 30-12 Measuring voltage in a circuit with two bulbs of unequal resistance connected in series.

TABLE 30-9: Explanation of Circuit Voltages in Figure 30-12

Figure	Measured Voltage	Explanation
A B	$V_1 = 12$ V $V_1 = 12$ V	V_1 is measuring the voltage directly across the supply battery, so the voltage reading will be the battery voltage regardless of the position of the switch.
A	$V_2 = 12$ V	With the switch in the open position, no current flows in the circuit. The red DVOM lead is connected directly to the battery via the cable, while the black lead is connected to the negative battery terminal via the two series resistors. Because no current flows in the circuit, there is no voltage drop across the two resistors; therefore, the entire battery voltage drop is across the open circuit switch.
B	$V_2 = 0$ V	With the switch in the closed position, current flows in the circuit. The switch contacts ideally will have no resistance when closed, so the voltage drop across the contacts will be 0 V.
B	$V_3 = 8$ V	With the switch closed, current can flow in the circuit. The amount of voltage drop across R_1 will be 8 V. This can be calculated using Ohm's law: Voltage Drop = Resistance × Current = 4 Ω × 2 A (see note below) = 8 V drop Note: To calculate total circuit current, use this formula: $I_T = V_T \div R_T$
B	$V_4 = 4$ V	With the switch closed, current can flow in the circuit. The amount of voltage drop across R_2 will be 4 V. This can be calculated using Ohm's law: Voltage Drop = Resistance × Current = 2 Ω × 2 A = 4 V drop R_1 and R_2 are of different resistances, so each will have a voltage drop proportional to its resistance. In a series circuit, the higher resistance will have a greater proportion of the voltage drop. You will notice that R_1 has twice the amount of resistance that R_2 has; thus it takes twice the amount of voltage to push current through R_1 as it does through R_2. Summing the voltage drops of R_1 and R_2 will equal the supply voltage: V_T = The sum of the voltage drops in a series circuit = VD R_1 + VD R_2 = 8 V + 4 V = 12 V

Connect the red lead to the A socket and the black lead to the COM socket. If using a manual-range DVOM, you will need to select an appropriate range.

FIGURE 30-13 shows a circuit with a single resistor with a 12-volt DC supply. The DVOM will be used to measure both voltage and current. **TABLE 30-10** provides an explanation of the DVOM readings and shows how they relate to Ohm's law.

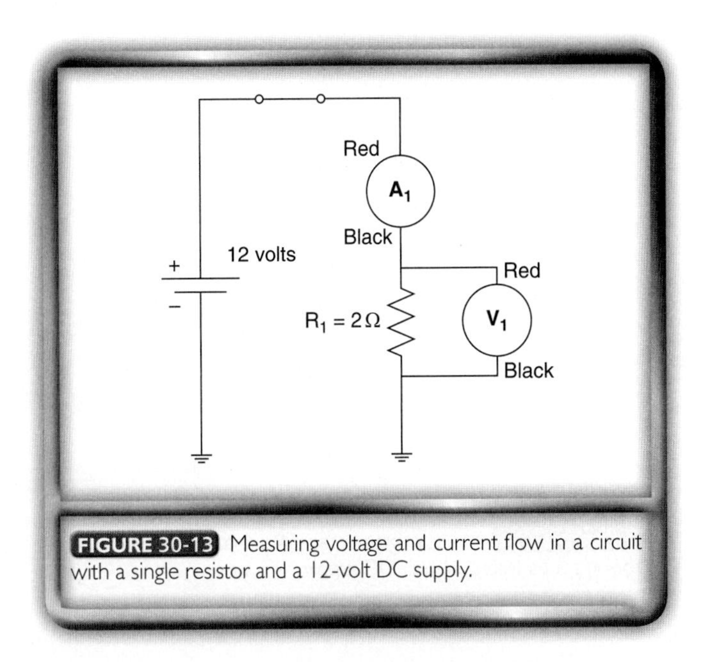

Red
A_1
Black
12 volts
+
−
Red
$R_1 = 2\Omega$
V_1
Black

FIGURE 30-13 Measuring voltage and current flow in a circuit with a single resistor and a 12-volt DC supply.

Measuring Current

To conduct this exercise, the DVOM must be set to read "DC amps." The red lead will be connected to the A socket and the black lead connected to the COM socket. If using a manual-range DVOM, select an appropriate range. If unsure which range is appropriate, start with the largest range and work down.

TABLE 30-10: Explanation of DVOM Readings in Figure 30-13

Measurements	Explanation
$V_1 = 12$ V	With the switch closed, current will flow through the resistor. The amount of voltage drop across R_1 will be 12 V—the full battery voltage. This can be calculated using Ohm's law: Voltage Drop = Resistance × Current = 2 Ω × 6 A (see note below) = 12 V drop. Note: To calculate total circuit current, use this formula: $I_T = V_T \div R_T$ $= 12 \div 2\ \Omega$ $= 6$ A
$A_1 = 6$ A	With the switch closed, the current flow through the resistor will be 6 amps. Since there is only one resistor in the circuit, its current flow will be the same as total current flow for the circuit.

FIGURE 30-14 shows a circuit with two resistors in series with a 12-volt DC supply. The DVOM can be connected in various parts of the circuit to measure the current flow. **TABLE 30-11** shows the results and an explanation of the ammeter readings in a series circuit.

Current and Magnetic Fields

In this example, a relay controlled by a switch will be used to switch the current through a resistor. The compass is used to demonstrate that a magnetic field is produced

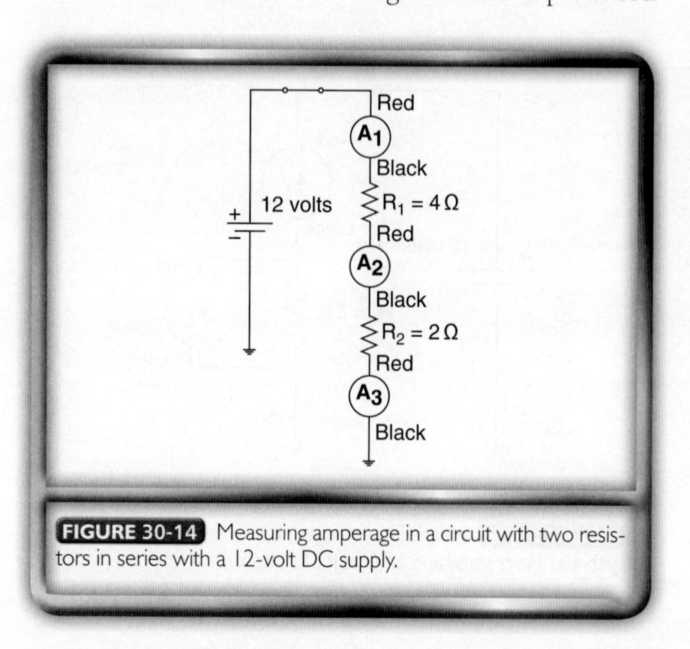
Red
A1
Black
12 volts
R1 = 4 Ω
Red
A2
Black
R2 = 2 Ω
Red
A3
Black

FIGURE 30-14 Measuring amperage in a circuit with two resistors in series with a 12-volt DC supply.

Applied Math

AM-10: Whole Numbers: The technician can multiply whole numbers to determine differences for comparison with the manufacturer's specifications.

An automotive battery is composed of six individual cell compartments within a case. The individual cells are joined by cell connectors in series with one another. Each cell has an open circuit voltage of approximately 2.1 volts at 80° Fahrenheit. When fully charged, a 12-volt automotive battery has an actual open circuit voltage of 12.6 volts at 80°. For easy calculations with whole numbers, we have 2 volts × 6 = 12 volts, which is why we refer to it as a 12-volt battery.

A technician was in the process of checking valve springs for proper tension during the overhaul of a V-8 engine. The valve springs did not meet manufacturer's specifications and all new valve springs are needed. There are four valve springs per cylinder × eight cylinders. We have whole numbers to multiply, which can be written as 4 × 8=32. A quantity of 32 new valve springs is needed to complete the cylinder head work.

Applied Math

AM-9: Mentally: The technician can mentally divide decimal and whole numbers to determine conformance with the manufacturer's specifications.

In this scenario, the technician is using a DVOM to measure cooling fan current flow in amps, and will determine circuit resistance in ohms using Ohm's law.

The first step is to locate proper service information for the vehicle that would cover the following items: fuse block diagram, cooling fan circuit diagram, and specifications or current flow for cooling fan motor. The cooling fan relay will then be removed. The DVOM will be set up to measure current by placing the red lead to the 10A connection on the meter. The black lead will be placed in the COM connection. In this testing procedure, the DVOM is connected in series with the red lead in socket 30 and the black lead in socket 87. With the cooling fan motor in operation, the technician observes a reading of 3 amps. The specifications for this vehicle call for a range of 2.3–4.6 amps to operate the cooling fan motor.

To determine the resistance of this circuit, we will use the formula, R = V/A. This is a form of Ohm's law (Voltage = Amps × Resistance); R = 12 volts/3 amps = 4 ohms of resistance. The technician was able to calculate this mentally using Ohm's law. In this example, whole numbers were used but a similar procedure would be used with decimals. For example, if the resistance was 3.5 volts, our formula would be R = 12 volts/3.5 amps = 3.42 ohms. For the decimal portion of this example, the technician may need a calculator, but mentally, the formula would be used.

TABLE 30-11: Explanation of DVOM Readings in Figure 30-14

Measured Current	Explanation
A_1 = 2 A	With the switch closed, the current will flow through the series circuit. The amount of current flow through R_1 will be 2 A, or 2000 milliamps (mA). This can be calculated using Ohm's law. As this is a series circuit, the current flow in the circuit will be the same in all parts of the circuit. To calculate the current flow in the series circuit: Current = Voltage ÷ Resistance = 12 V ÷ 6 Ω (see note below) = 2 A Note: To calculate the total circuit current, use this formula: $I_T = V_T \div R_T$
A_2 = 2 A	With the switch closed, the current flow will be the same in all parts of the series circuit; therefore, current flow on the ammeter will always be the same regardless of its position in the circuit. The same current flow will be read on A_1, A_2, and A_3.

around the relay winding when the current flows through it. To conduct this experiment, set the DVOM to measure "DC amps." Connect the red lead to the A socket and the black lead to the COM socket. If using a manual-range DVOM, select an appropriate range.

FIGURE 30-15 shows a circuit with a relay controlled by a switch and a single resistor with a 12-volt DC supply.

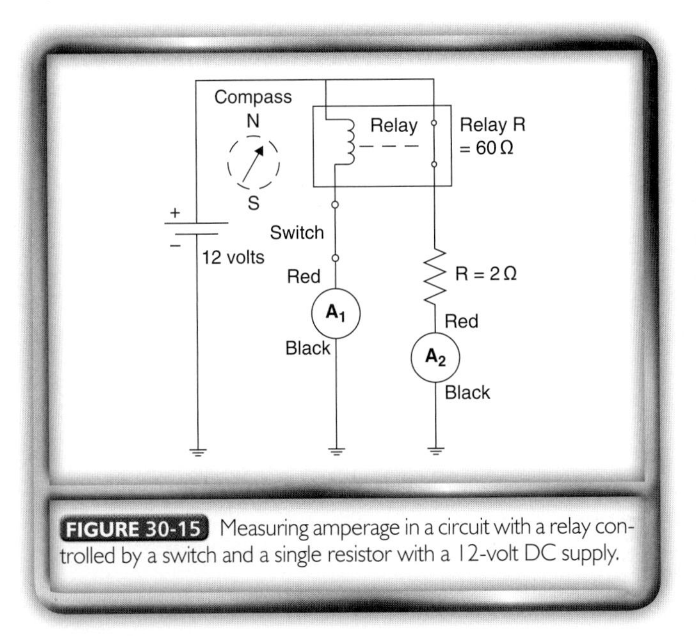
Compass
N
S
Relay
Relay R
= 60 Ω
+
−
12 volts
Switch
Red
A_1
Black
R = 2 Ω
Red
A_2
Black

FIGURE 30-15 Measuring amperage in a circuit with a relay controlled by a switch and a single resistor with a 12-volt DC supply.

The compass is used to show that when energized the relay winding produces a magnetic field. The DVOM will be used to measure current. TABLE 30-12 shows the current flow through the circuit and provides an explanation of the circuit, current flow, and how Ohm's law calculations can be used.

Resistance Exercises

In this section, the exercises are designed to explain the use of the DVOM in measuring resistance. Resistance measurements are used to check components or circuits against the manufacturer's specifications; for example, the resistance of sensors. Examples are given to demonstrate measuring resistance and to describe how the resistance affects current flow. It is important to understand that current flow is inversely proportional to resistance. The higher the resistance, the less current that will flow. The reverse is also true: The lower the resistance, the higher the current flow.

TABLE 30-12: Explanation of DVOM Readings in Figure 30-15

Measured Current	Explanation
A_1 = 200 mA	When the switch is closed, the current will flow through the relay winding. The magnetic field generated by current flowing through the winding will cause the main relay contacts to close, which in turn will supply current to the resistor. The compass positioned near the winding will change its heading indicating the presence of a magnetic field from the winding. The amount of current through the relay winding is 200 mA. The resistance of the winding can also be calculated using Ohm's law if the current flow through the winding resistance is known: R = V ÷ I = 12 ÷ 0.2 A = 60 Ω
A_2 = 6 A	With the switch closed, the relay contact will close and the current flow through the resistor will be 6 A. As there is only one resistor in the circuit, its current flow will be the same as total current flow for the circuit. To calculate the current flow in the resistor circuit, use this formula: Current = Voltage ÷ Resistance = 12 volts ÷ 2 Ω = 6 A

Measuring Resistance

In this exercise, a resistance measurement will be taken. For resistance measurements, you need to select "auto range Ω" on the DVOM, and connect the red lead to V/Ω and the black lead to COM. If using a manual-range DVOM, select an appropriate range by starting at the highest range and working your way down. Resistance measurements should only be taken with power disconnected, and ideally, with the component disconnected from the circuit.

FIGURE 30-16 shows a circuit with a lamp in series with a resistor and a 12-volt DC supply. The DVOM will be used to measure resistance. TABLE 30-13 shows the measurement that can be expected from the circuit.

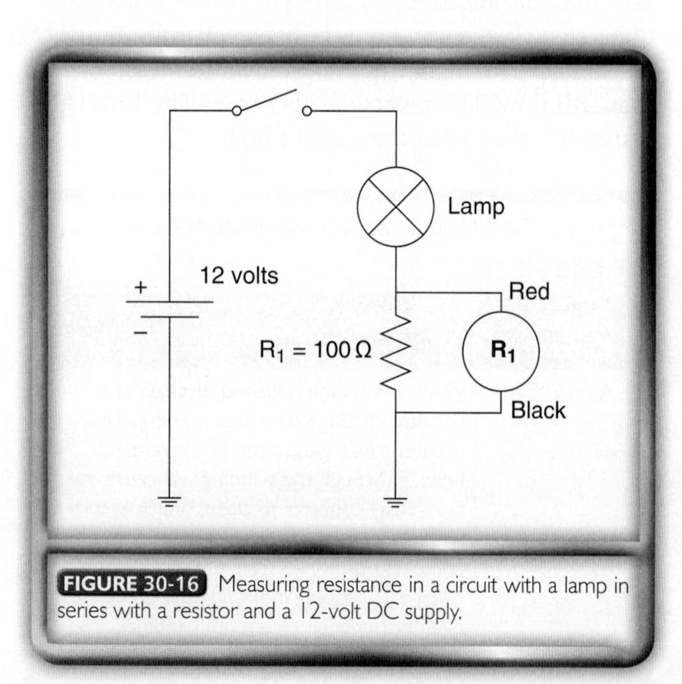
Lamp
12 volts
+
–
Red
R_1 = 100 Ω
R_1
Black

FIGURE 30-16 Measuring resistance in a circuit with a lamp in series with a resistor and a 12-volt DC supply.

TABLE 30-13: Explanation of DVOM Readings in Figure 30-16

Measurement	Explanation
R_1 = 100 Ω	The switch should be open to measure resistance. If possible, one lead of the resistor should be disconnected from the circuit. The DVOM leads should be connected to the V/Ω and COM sockets. The DVOM switch should be placed in the Ω or resistance position. Reversing the DVOM connections will have no effect on the DVOM reading.

Resistance Effects on Current—Exercise 1

In this exercise, resistance, voltage, and current measurements will be taken. For resistance and voltage measurements, select "auto range volts DC" on the DVOM, and connect the red lead to the V/Ω and the black lead to COM. Always make resistance measurements with the component disconnected from the circuit. For current measurements, select "auto range amps DC" on the DVOM. The red lead will be connected to the A socket and the black lead connected to the COM socket. If using a manual-range DVOM, select an appropriate range.

FIGURE 30-17 shows a circuit with a resistor and a 12-volt DC supply. The DVOM will be used to measure resistance, voltage, and current. TABLE 30-14 shows the measurements that a DVOM would read in the circuit, explains the readings, and describes how Ohm's law is applied.

Resistance Effects on Current—Exercise 2

In this exercise, resistance, voltage, and current measurements will be taken. For resistance and voltage measurements, you will need to select "auto range volts DC" on the DVOM, and connect the red lead to V/Ω and the black lead to COM. Always make resistance measurements with the component disconnected from the circuit. For current measurements, select "auto range amps DC" on the DVOM. The red lead will be con-

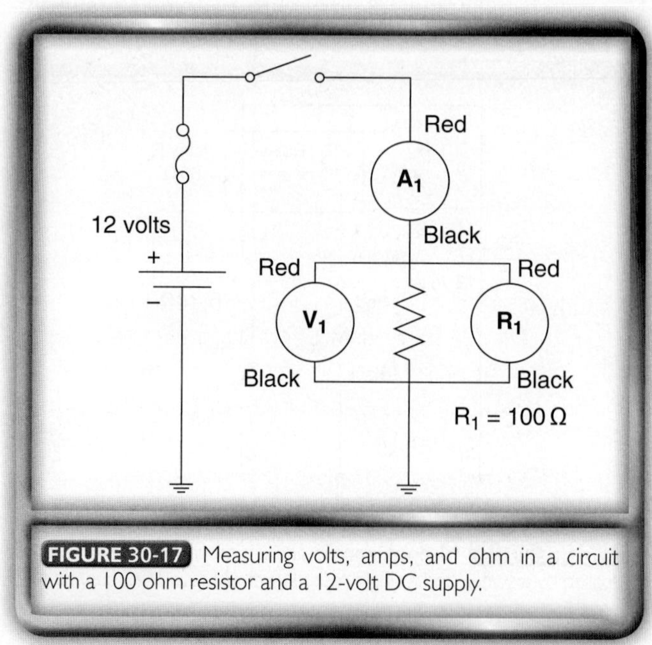
Red
A_1
12 volts
Black
+
–
Red
Red
V_1
R_1
Black
Black
R_1 = 100 Ω

FIGURE 30-17 Measuring volts, amps, and ohm in a circuit with a 100 ohm resistor and a 12-volt DC supply.

TABLE 30-14: Explanation of DVOM Readings in Figure 30-17

Measurements	Explanation
R_1 = 100 Ω	The switch should be open to measure resistance. If possible, one lead of the resistor should be disconnected from the circuit. Reversing the DVOM connections will have no effect on the DVOM reading. Resistance can be calculated if the voltage and current are known: Resistance = Voltage ÷ Current = 12 V ÷ 0.12 A = 100 Ω
V_1 = 12 V	With the switch closed, V_1 = 12 V. This can also be calculated if the current flow and resistance are known: Voltage Drop = Resistance × Current = 100 Ω × 0.12 A = 12 V drop Note: In practice, fuses have a very low resistance and, therefore, will have a very small voltage drop.
A_1 = 0.12 A	With the switch closed, A_1 = 0.12 A. To calculate the current flow: Current = Voltage ÷ Resistance = 12 V ÷ 100 Ω = 0.12 A

nected to the A socket and the black lead connected to the COM socket. If using a manual-range DVOM, select an appropriate range.

FIGURE 30-18 shows a circuit with a resistor and a 12-volt DC supply. The DVOM will be used to measure resistance, voltage, and current. TABLE 30-15 shows the measurements of the circuit by a DVOM, explains the measurement, and describes how Ohm's law is applied.

Parallel Circuit Exercises

In this section, the exercises are designed to explain the use of the DVOM in measuring volts, amps, and ohms in a parallel circuit. Parallel circuits are commonly used in the vehicle's electrical system, especially for lights. Understanding how they work and the relationship between voltage, amperage, and resistance in parallel circuits will help you to diagnose electrical faults. Examples are given to demonstrate how to measure volts, amps, and ohms and to show how current flows and voltage drops in a parallel circuit. It is important to remember the laws for a parallel circuit: resistance goes down when more parallel paths are added, current flow from individual legs add up in parallel, and voltage stays the same at all common parallel circuit inputs. The following exercises help to reinforce the understanding of these laws.

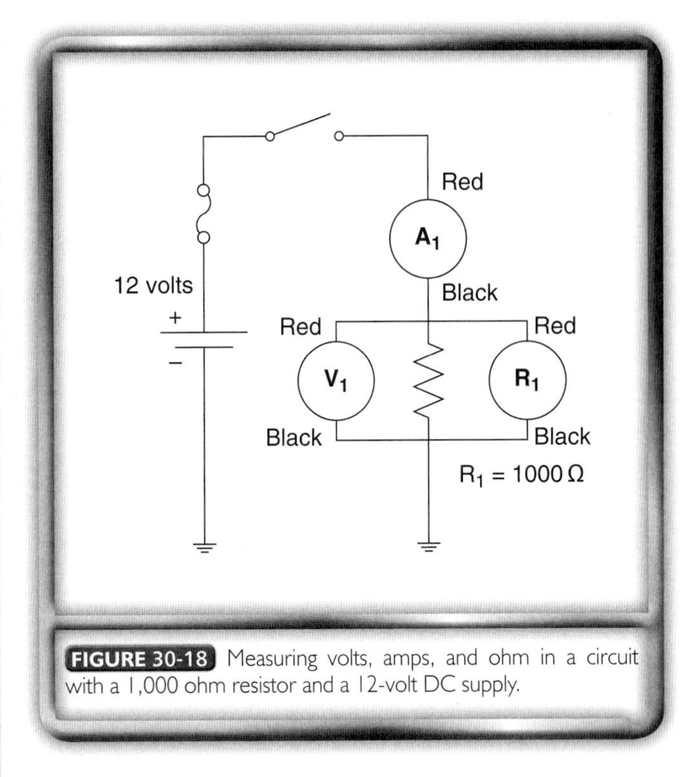
Red
A1
12 volts
+
−
Black
Red
Red
V1
R1
Black
Black
R1 = 1000 Ω

FIGURE 30-18 Measuring volts, amps, and ohm in a circuit with a 1,000 ohm resistor and a 12-volt DC supply.

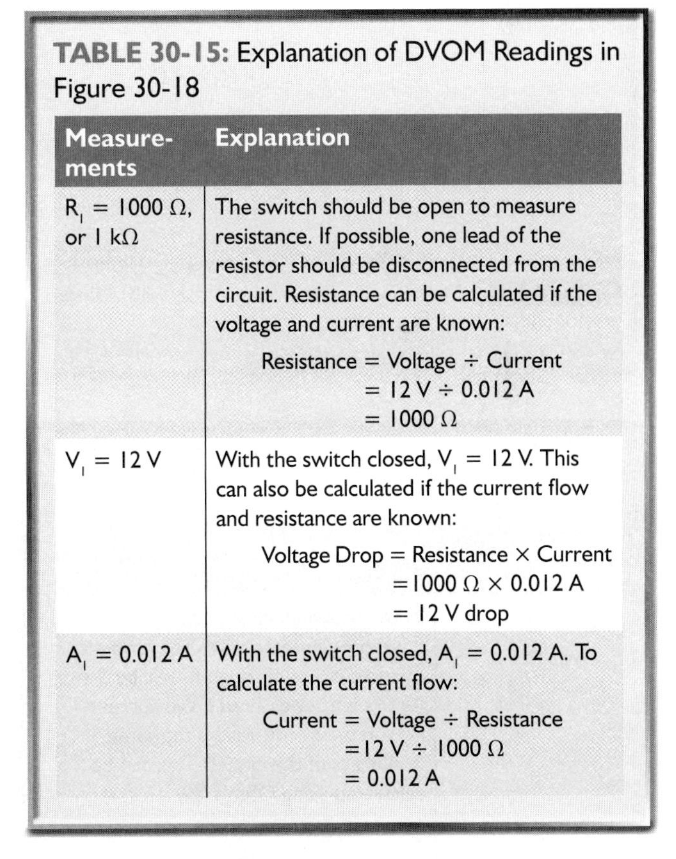

TABLE 30-15: Explanation of DVOM Readings in Figure 30-18

Measurements	Explanation
R_1 = 1000 Ω, or 1 kΩ	The switch should be open to measure resistance. If possible, one lead of the resistor should be disconnected from the circuit. Resistance can be calculated if the voltage and current are known: Resistance = Voltage ÷ Current = 12 V ÷ 0.012 A = 1000 Ω
V_1 = 12 V	With the switch closed, V_1 = 12 V. This can also be calculated if the current flow and resistance are known: Voltage Drop = Resistance × Current = 1000 Ω × 0.012 A = 12 V drop
A_1 = 0.012 A	With the switch closed, A_1 = 0.012 A. To calculate the current flow: Current = Voltage ÷ Resistance = 12 V ÷ 1000 Ω = 0.012 A

Parallel Circuits—Exercise 1

To conduct this exercise, the DVOM must be set to read "DC amps." Connect the red lead to the A socket and the black lead to the COM socket. If using a manual-range DVOM, select an appropriate range.

FIGURE 30-19 shows a circuit with a single resistor and a 12-volt DC supply. The DVOM can be connected in various parts of the circuit to measure the current flow. TABLE 30-16 provides the measurements taken of the circuit by a DVOM, explains the circuit and the measurements, and describes how Ohm's law is applied.

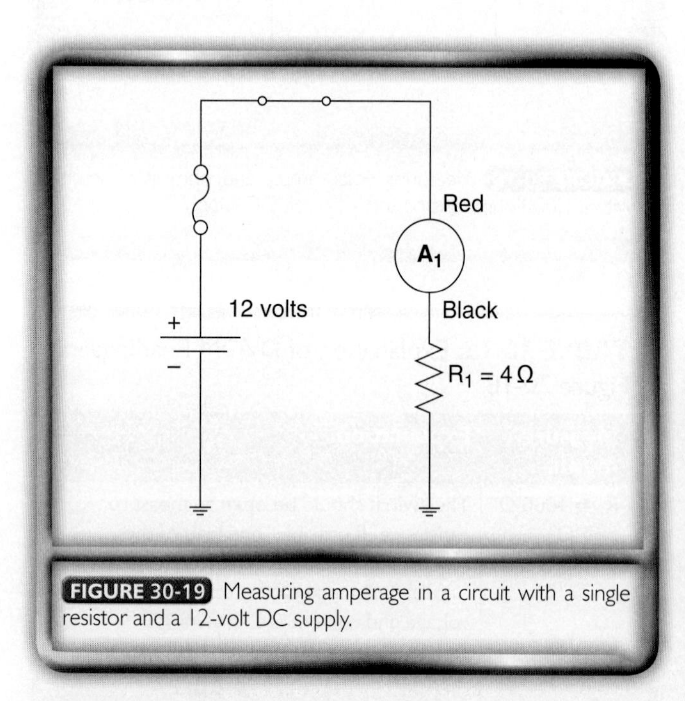
Red
A_1
12 volts
Black
+
−
$R_1 = 4\,\Omega$

FIGURE 30-19 Measuring amperage in a circuit with a single resistor and a 12-volt DC supply.

TABLE 30-16: Explanation of DVOM Readings in Figure 30-19

Measured Current	Explanation
$A_1 = 3$ A	With the switch closed, current will flow through the circuit. The amount of current flow through R_1 will be 3 A. As this is a series circuit, the current flow in the circuit will be the same in all parts of the circuit. This can be calculated using Ohm's law: Current = Voltage ÷ Resistance = 12 V ÷ 4 Ω = 3 A

Parallel Circuits—Exercise 2

To conduct this exercise, the DVOM must be set to read DC amps. Connect the red lead to the A socket and the black lead to the COM socket. If using a manual-range DVOM, select an appropriate range.

FIGURE 30-20 has two resistors in parallel. The additional resistor in parallel will cause an increase in circuit current flow and a decrease in total circuit resistance. TABLE 30-17 provides the measurements taken of the circuit by a DVOM, explains the circuit and the measurements, and describes how Ohm's law is applied.

Parallel Circuits—Exercise 3

To conduct this exercise, the DVOM must be set to read DC amps. Connect the red lead to the A socket and the black lead to the COM socket. If using a manual-range DVOM, select an appropriate range.

FIGURE 30-21 has three resistors in parallel. With the additional resistors, the total circuit current will

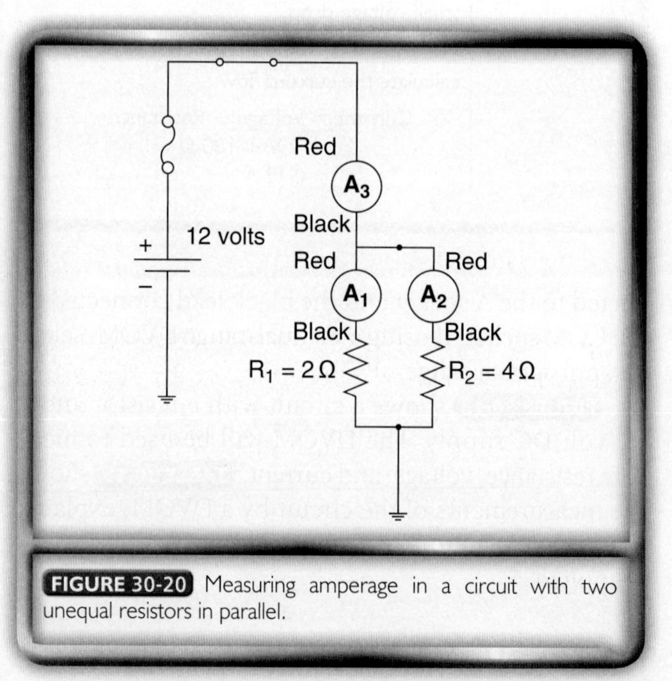
Red
A_3
Black
12 volts
+
−
Red
Red
A_1
A_2
Black
Black
$R_1 = 2\,\Omega$
$R_2 = 4\,\Omega$

FIGURE 30-20 Measuring amperage in a circuit with two unequal resistors in parallel.

Safety

Notice how the current in the circuit increases with each additional load. This is also what happens with a power strip; each time an additional item is plugged in, the current increases. Overloading the circuit may cause the protection device to trip or in extreme cases could cause a fire. Never overload an electrical circuit, whether on a vehicle or in the shop.

TABLE 30-17: Explanation of DVOM Readings in Figure 30-20

Measured Current	Explanation
$A_3 = 9$ A	With the switch closed, the current will flow through the circuit. Due to its position in the circuit, A_3 will measure total current flow or I_T and will be 9 A.
$A_1 = 6$ A	A_1 is positioned so that it only measures the current flow through R_1, and its current flow will be 6 A.
$A_2 = 3$ A	A_2 is positioned so that it only measures the current flow through R_2, and its current flow will be 3 A.
The current flows can be calculated using Ohm's law in two ways:	
Calculate current flow through each resistor and add them together: $IR_1 = VR_1 \div R_1$ $= 12\text{ V} \div 2\ \Omega$ $= 6\text{ A}$ $IR_2 = VR_2 \div R_2$ $= 12\text{ V} \div 4\ \Omega$ $= 3\text{ A}$ $I_T = IR_1 + IR_2$ $= 6 + 3$ $= 9\text{ A}$	Calculate total resistance R_T and use it to then calculate I_T total current: $R_T = \frac{1}{\frac{1}{R_1} + \frac{1}{R_2}}$ $R_T = \frac{1}{\frac{1}{2} + \frac{1}{4}}$ $R_T = 1.3333\ \Omega$ $I_T = V_T \div R_T$ $= 12\text{ V} \div 1.3333\ \Omega$ $= 9.0002\text{ A}$ Note: R_T is 1.3 recurring. It has been rounded to four decimal places; this gives the variance of 0.0002 in the I_T calculation. In practice, this small variation can be ignored.

Applied Math

AM-47: Specified Symbols: The technician can use conventional symbols (E for voltage, etc.) to solve problems using formulas such as Ohm's law, E=IR.

Voltage, current, and resistance have a specific relationship to each other. This concept forms the basis for electrical diagnosis.

George Ohm discovered that it takes one volt to push one amp through one ohm of resistance. Ohm's law is E = I × R or Voltage = Amps × Resistance. If you know two of the three values for an electrical circuit, you can find the missing one. To find resistance, the formula is volts divided by amps. To find voltage, the formula is amp multiplied by resistance. To find current, or amps, the formula is volts divided by resistance.

In this example, we have an electrical circuit that has a current flow of 2 amps being pushed by 12 volts. We want to find the resistance. Our formula will be R=V/A:

R = V/A

R= 12 volts/2 amps

R= 6 ohms, which is our circuit resistance.

Applied Math

AM-45: <, >, =, e.g.: The technician can interpret symbols to determine conformance with the manufacturer's specifications.

In this scenario, we will look at three of the most common symbols used in technical manuals.

<, > These symbols are lesser than: <, and greater than: >. An example of this would be describing the specification for the maximum limit for an A.C. voltage from an alternator (< .5 volts A.C).

= This symbol is a mathematical symbol used to indicate equality. An example would be the formula for Ohm's law which is E = I X R

"e.g." means "for example." It comes from the Latin expression, *exempli gratia*, for the sake of an example. An example of this would be: The technician will use a precision measuring instrument (e.g., micrometer) to measure the part.

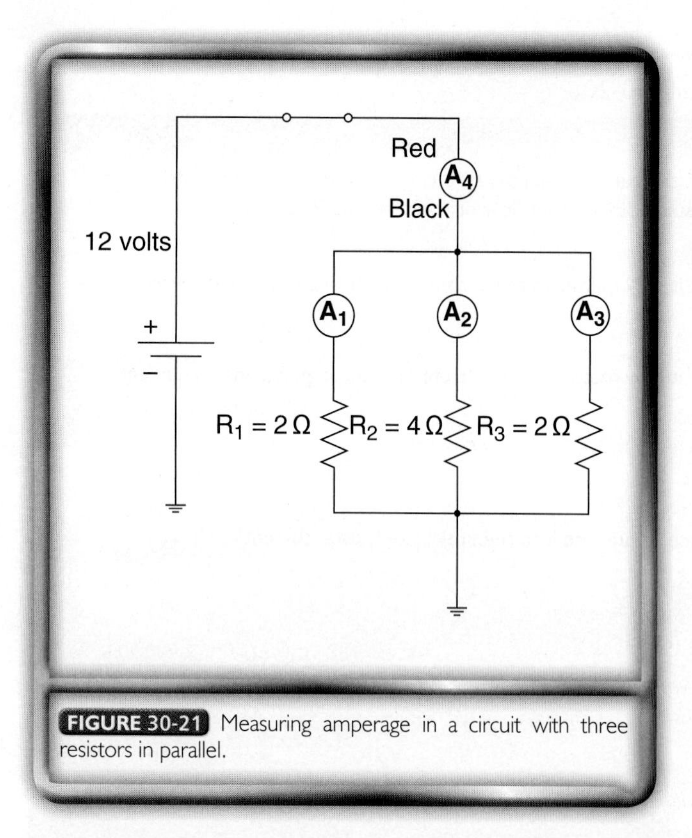

Red
A4
Black
12 volts
+
–
A1
A2
A3
R1 = 2 Ω
R2 = 4 Ω
R3 = 2 Ω

FIGURE 30-21 Measuring amperage in a circuit with three resistors in parallel.

increase while the total circuit resistance will decrease. **TABLE 30-18** provides the measurements taken of the circuit by a DVOM, explains the circuit and the measurements, and describes how Ohm's law is applied.

Series-Parallel Circuit Exercise

In this section, the exercise is designed to explain the use of the DVOM in measuring current and voltage in a series-parallel circuit. Series-parallel circuits are found in vehicles, such as in dash light dimmer circuits, although they are not as common as parallel circuits. Typically, a series-parallel circuit occurs when unwanted resistance shows up in series with a parallel circuit. For example, if the brake light switch contacts become worn out, they can create a voltage drop in series with the brake lights, causing them all to be dimmer than they should be. Understanding how series-parallel circuits work and the relationships between current flow, voltage drops, and resistance will help you diagnose these types of electrical faults. Examples are given to demonstrate measuring

TABLE 30-18: Explanation of DVOM Readings in Figure 30-21

Measured Current	Explanation
$A_4 = 15$ A	With the switch closed, the current will flow through the circuit. Due to its position in the circuit, A_3 will measure total current flow or I_T and will be 15 A. The total current in the circuit increases as additional load or resistances are added in parallel.
$A_1 = 6$ A	A_1 is positioned so that it only measures the current flow through R_1, and its current flow will be 6 A.
$A_2 = 3$ A	A_2 is positioned so that it only measures the current flow through R_2, and its current flow will be 3 A.
$A_3 = 6$ A	A_3 is positioned so that it only measures the current flow through R_3, and its current flow will be 6 A.
The current flows can be calculated using Ohm's law in two ways:	
Calculate current flow though each resistor and add them together: $IR_1 = VR_1 \div R_1$ $= 12\text{ V} \div 2\ \Omega$ $= 6\text{ A}$ $IR_2 = VR_2 \div R_2$ $= 12\text{ V} \div 4\ \Omega$ $= 3\text{ A}$ $IR_3 = VR_3 \div R_3$ $= 12\text{ V} \div 2\ \Omega$ $= 6\text{ A}$ $I_T = IR_1 + IR_2 + IR_3$ $= 6 + 3 + 6$ $= 15\text{ A}$	Calculate total resistance R_T and use it to then calculate I_T total current: $R_T = \frac{1}{\frac{1}{R_1}+\frac{1}{R_2}+\frac{1}{R_3}}$ $R_T = \frac{1}{\frac{1}{2}+\frac{1}{4}+\frac{1}{2}}$ $R_T = 0.8\ \Omega$ $I_T = V_T \div R_T$ $= 12\text{ V} \div 0.8\ \Omega$ $= 15\text{ A}$

voltage and current and to show how current flow and voltage drop are affected by resistance in a series-parallel circuit. It is important to understand that to analyze and calculate current flow and voltage drop, the total resistance of the circuit needs to be considered. The voltage drop across the parallel branch will be the same for all resistances in the parallel branch, and the sum of the current flow in each branch is equal to the total parallel circuit current flow. These exercises also examine how the addition of resistors in series to a parallel circuit affects the circuit current flow and circuit resistance.

In this exercise, voltage and current measurements will be taken from the series-parallel circuit formed by resistors R_1, R_2, R_3, and R_4. See **FIGURE 30-22**. To measure voltage drop, the DVOM must be set on the voltage range. Select "auto range volts DC" on the DVOM, and connect the black lead to COM and the red lead to V/Ω. Voltage drop can be measured across components, connectors, or cables as long as current is flowing in the circuit. The red lead of the DVOM is normally connected to the positive side of the component. To measure current, the DVOM must be set to read DC amps. Connect the red lead to the A socket and the black lead to the COM socket. If using a manual-range DVOM, select an appropriate range. **TABLE 30-19** provides the measurements taken of the circuit by a DVOM, explains the circuit and the measurements, and describes how Ohm's law is applied. Please note that calculations have been rounded to four decimal places.

Variable Resistors

In this section, the exercises are designed to explain the use of the DVOM in measuring voltage and amperage in a circuit with a variable resistor, as well as a potentiometer. Understanding the relationships between voltage, resistance, and current as the variable resistor is adjusted will help you diagnose electrical faults. Examples are given to demonstrate measuring voltage and current and to show how current flows and how voltage drop and current are affected by the position of the wiper of the potentiometer. It is important to understand that as the position of the wiper of the potentiometer is changed, so too is the voltage and current flow to a load connected to the potentiometer.

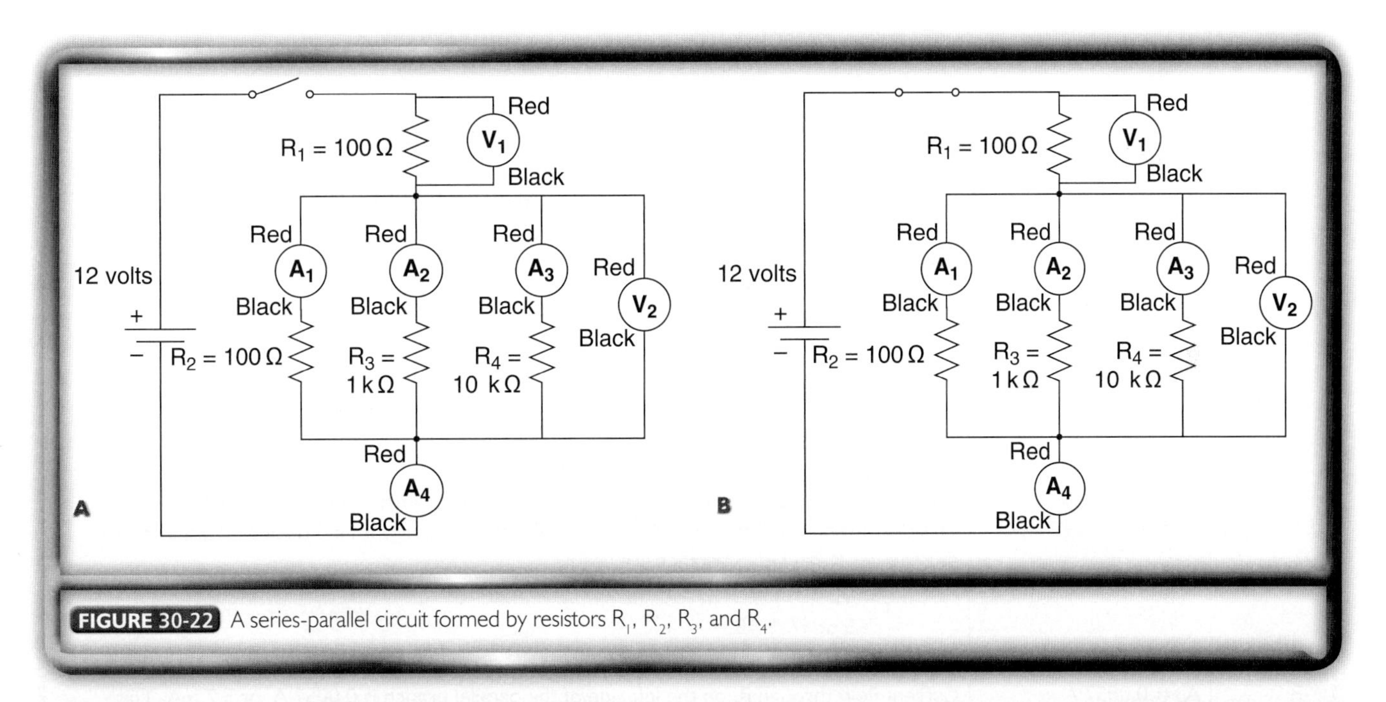
A
12 volts
+
-
R1 = 100 Ω
R2 = 100 Ω
R3 = 1 kΩ
R4 = 10 kΩ
V1
V2
A1
A2
A3
A4
Red
Black
B

FIGURE 30-22 A series-parallel circuit formed by resistors R_1, R_2, R_3, and R_4.

TABLE 30-19: Explanation of DVOM Readings in Figure 30-22

Figure	Measurement	Explanation
A	$V_1 = 0$ V	With the switch off, there will be no current flow in the circuit, and as V_1 is positioned after the switch, the voltmeter red lead has no circuit to the positive battery terminal.
B	$V_1 = 6.31$ V	With the switch closed, the current can flow in the circuit. The amount of voltage drop across R_1 will be 6.31 V. This can be calculated with Ohm's law, which will require a number of steps:

(continues)

TABLE 30-19: Explanation of DVOM Readings in Figure 30-22 *(continued)*

Figure	Measurement	Explanation
		1. Calculate total resistance R_T. To do so, first calculate the resistance of the parallel branch: $R_{PB} = \frac{1}{\frac{1}{R_1}+\frac{1}{R_2}+\frac{1}{R_3}}$ $R_{PB} = 1\frac{1}{100}+\frac{1}{1000}+\frac{1}{10000}$ $R_{PB} = 90.0901\ \Omega$ Next, sum the series resistor R_1 and the total resistance of the parallel branch R_{PB}: $R_T = R_1 + R_{PB}$ $= 100 + 90.0901$ $= 190.0901\ \Omega$ 2. Now that resistance total is known, the total circuit current can be calculated I_T: $I_T = V_T \div R_T$ $= 12\text{ V} \div 190.0901$ $= 0.0631\text{ A, or } 63.1\text{ mA}$ 3. Voltage drop across R_1 can now be calculated using the total current flow I_T and the resistance of R_1 (see note). $\text{VD } R_1 = I_T \times R_1$ $= 0.0631 \times 100$ $= 6.31\text{ V}$ Note: I_T is used because R_1 is in series with the parallel branches; therefore, current flow through R_1 will be the same as I_T.
A	$V_2 = 0\text{ V}$	With the switch off, there will be no current flow in the circuit, and as V_2 is positioned after the switch, the voltmeter red lead has no circuit to the positive battery terminal.
B	$V_2 = 5.6847\text{ V}$	The amount of voltage drop across the parallel branches will be 5.6847 V. This can also be calculated with Ohm's law by using the figures calculated earlier in the experiment. Resistance of the parallel branches and I_T: $R_{PB} = 90.0901\ \Omega$ $I_T = 0.0631\text{ A, or } 63.1\text{ mA}$ $\text{VD Parallel Branch} = I_T \times \text{Resistance } R_{PB}$ $= 0.0631\text{ A} \times 90.0901\ \Omega$ $= 5.6847\text{ V}$
B	$A_1 = 0.0568\text{ A}$	Current flow through R_2 on the left side of the parallel branches is 0.0568 A, or 56.8 mA. This can also be calculated with Ohm's law. To calculate current flow through R_2, the voltage drop across R_2 and its resistance are used: $IR_2 = VDR_2 \div R_2$ $= 5.6847 \div 100$ $= 0.0568\text{ A, or } 56.8\text{ mA}$
B	$A_2 = 0.0057\text{ A}$	Current flow through R_3 on the left side of the parallel branch is 0.0057 A, or 5.7 mA. This can also be calculated with Ohm's law. To calculate current flow through R_2, the voltage drop across R_2 and its resistance are used: $IR_2 = VDR_2 \div R_2$ $= 5.6847 \div 1000$ $= 0.0057\text{ A, or } 5.7\text{ mA}$

(continues)

TABLE 30-19: Explanation of DVOM Readings in Figure 30-22 *(continued)*

Figure	Measurement	Explanation
B	$A_3 = 0.0006$ A	Current flow through R_3 on the left side of the parallel branches is 0.0006 A, or 0.6 mA. This can also be calculated with Ohm's law. To calculate current flow through R_2, the voltage drop across R_2 and its resistance are used: $IR_2 = VDR_2 \div R_2 = 5.6847 \div 10{,}000 = 0.0006$ A, or 0.6 mA
B		The series current in the circuit splits across the parallel branches of resistance. The amount of current through each part of the parallel branch is dependent on the resistance of each branch. The higher the resistance of the branch, the less current that flows through it. Adding the parallel branches' current equals the total current I_T: $I_T = IR_2 + IR_3 + IR_4 = 0.0568 + 0.0057 + 0.0006 = 0.0631$ A, or 63.1 mA

Applied Math

AM-12: Mentally: The technician can mentally multiply numbers that include decimal numbers to determine conformance with the manufacturer's specifications.

In this scenario, a technician is conducting a voltage drop test on the positive side of the starter circuit. As described in the text, a voltage drop occurs when current flows through a resistance. The higher the resistance, the higher the voltage drops. So we could say that a voltage drop test checks for excessive resistance in a circuit. When testing for a voltage drop, always have the circuit operating. That way, the circuit will have current flowing so any voltage drops will be evident.

The technician begins by placing the DVOM selector on the 20V DC scale. He starts testing at the battery and checks step by step all the way to the starter motor using the direct method of voltage drop testing. The technician uses both test leads on the same side of the circuit. The tests include battery post to cable clamp, cable clamp to the end of the cable at the solenoid, and from the solenoid to the starter motor terminal. At each of the test points, an assistant cranked the engine over to load the circuit. Each of the three connection points had a reading of 0.30 volt. The technician mentally multiplied those decimal numbers to obtain a total of 0.90 volt (3×0.30 volt $= 0.90$ volt). This reading is in excess of the manufacturer's specifications of 0.5 volt. The technician will now clean each of the connection points and retest.

Variable Resistors Exercise

In this exercise, a variable resistor is used as a potentiometer, or voltage divider. For voltage measurements, you will need to select "auto range volts DC" on the DVOM and connect the red lead to V/Ω and the black lead to COM. For current measurements, select "auto range milliamps DC" on the DVOM. Connect the red lead to the A socket and the black lead to the COM socket. If using a manual-range DVOM, you will need to select an appropriate range.

FIGURE 30-23 shows circuits with a 250-Ω variable resistor in the circuit as a voltage divider with a 12-volt DC supply. In Figure 30-29A, the wiper of the variable resistor is set so that minimum voltage will occur at V_1. In Figure 30-29B, the variable resistor is set so that maximum voltage can occur at V_1. Only two states for the variable resistor are analyzed in this section, although the variable resistor is continuously variable and the voltage at V_1 will vary depending on the position of the wiper. The DVOM will be used to measure voltage V_1, a voltage divider output from the variable resistor VR_1. TABLE 30-20 provides the measurements taken of the circuit by a DVOM and explains the circuit and the measurements. When the wiper in Figure 30-29 is at the upper or lower limits, in practice there may be a small amount of the variable resistor left on the outer edges.

Electrical Circuit Testing

Electrical circuit testing begins with understanding circuit types and how electricity behaves within them. Add to that the ability to use meters and oscilloscopes to measure the values of voltage, amperage, and resistance, along with understanding how to read wiring diagrams so you will know how the circuits are constructed, and you will be well on your way to diagnosing electrical faults successfully. Those are the concepts we will be exploring in this section. Feel free to refer back to the previous circuits to help you remember how electricity behaves, as well as how meters are hooked up for specific measurements.

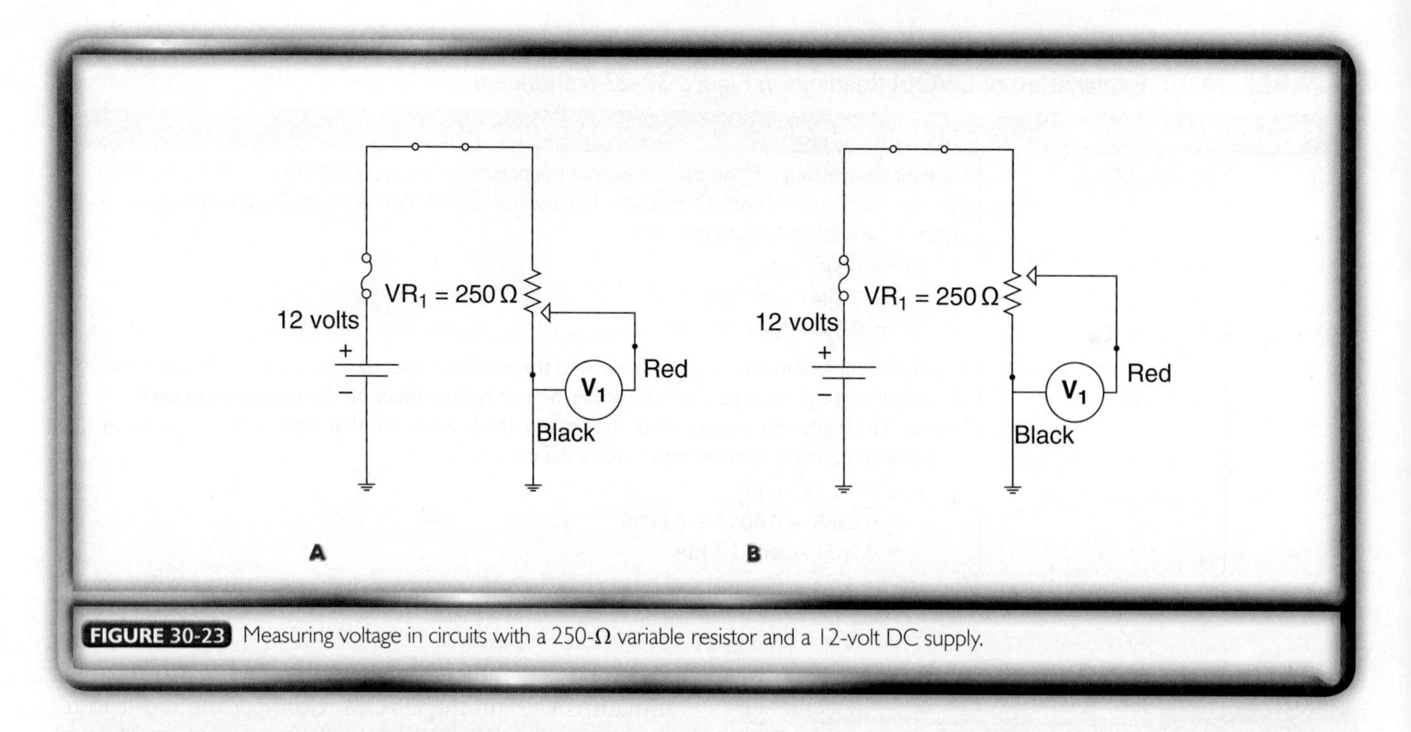
12 volts
VR$_1$ = 250 Ω
+
−
Red
V$_1$
Black
A
12 volts
VR$_1$ = 250 Ω
+
−
Red
V$_1$
Black
B

FIGURE 30-23 Measuring voltage in circuits with a 250-Ω variable resistor and a 12-volt DC supply.

TABLE 30-20: Explanation of DVOM Readings in Figure 30-23

Figure	Voltage Measurements	Explanation
A	$V_1 = 0.005$ V	With the switch in the closed position, current can flow in the circuit. The fixed resistor (250 Ω) between the two outer legs of the variable resistor will have a consistent current flow and voltage drop of 12 V. The variable wiper provides a varying voltage output depending on the wiper's position, which can be read on V_1. With the wiper in the position shown in Figure 30-29A, V_1 will read very close to ground potential because almost all of the voltage was dropped through the fixed resistor; hence, the reading of 0.005 V.
B	$V_1 = 12$ V	With the wiper in the position shown in Figure 30-29B, V_1 will read very close to supply potential; hence, the reading of 12 V.

Let's kick this off by seeing how Ohm's law can help us predict the behavior of electricity.

Using Ohm's Law to Diagnose Circuits

Ohm's law can be used in two ways to help in diagnosing electrical circuit faults. The first is by using it to perform the math to predict and verify measurements. The second way is by using the relationships it demonstrates to guide you through the diagnosis process.

When using Ohm's law in the first way, it is used to calculate electrical quantities in a circuit and is valuable in cross-checking actual measured results within the circuit. For example, if the resistance and voltage of a circuit are known, then the theoretical current can be calculated using Ohm's law. The calculated result can then be compared to the measured results from an ammeter to determine if the circuit is functioning correctly. Technicians will often do a quick calculation, sometimes just in their head, to obtain an approximate value of an electrical quantity before they take actual measurements. Doing so allows them to anticipate what they will be measuring and to set the measuring tool to the correct range. Always remember that a calculation may only yield an approximate value; in actual circuits, variations or tolerances exist in components, causing differences between calculated values and actual measurements.

Using Ohm's law the second way helps you to understand the relationship between volts, amps, and ohms. For example, if voltage stays the same but resistance decreases, amperage must increase. In the case of a short circuit, the resistance decreases and the amperage increases, potentially blowing the fuse. In the opposite scenario, where resistance increases, current flow decreases FIGURE 30-24. This is the case when a corroded or loose connection introduces excessive resistance to the circuit. It also results in less electrical power (volts and amps) to operate the intended load.

What does Ohm's law tell us to expect when the voltage changes? If voltage decreases and the resistance stays the same, then amperage will decrease FIGURE 30-25. This results in less power being able to operate the load. If the voltage increases and the resistance stays the same, then amperage will increase. If amperage and voltage both increase, then the electrical power operating the load will also increase. This condition can shorten the life of, or even burn out, the load.

So, how do amperage changes affect volts and amps? That is a good question. But if you think about it, amperage is a result of, or product of, the voltage and resistance. Amperage cannot exist without both voltage and resistance—a means of pushing the amperage (voltage) and a path for the amperage to flow (resistance). If you ask yourself, what is the amperage doing in a circuit? the answer will always be, it is doing whatever the voltage and resistance allow it to do. If the amperage is low, then you know that one of two conditions is present—either the voltage is low or the resistance is high. If the amperage is high, then either the voltage is high or the resistance is low. Understanding this relationship between volts, amps, and ohms will help you know what test you need to perform next during diagnosis.

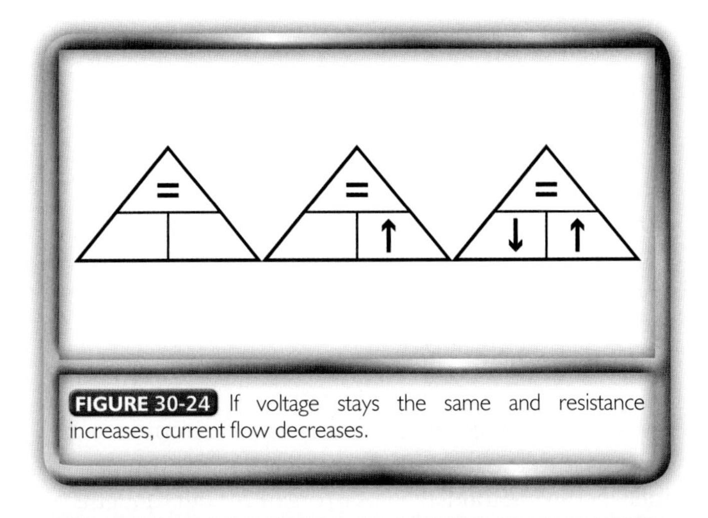
=
=
↑
=
↓
↑

FIGURE 30-24 If voltage stays the same and resistance increases, current flow decreases.

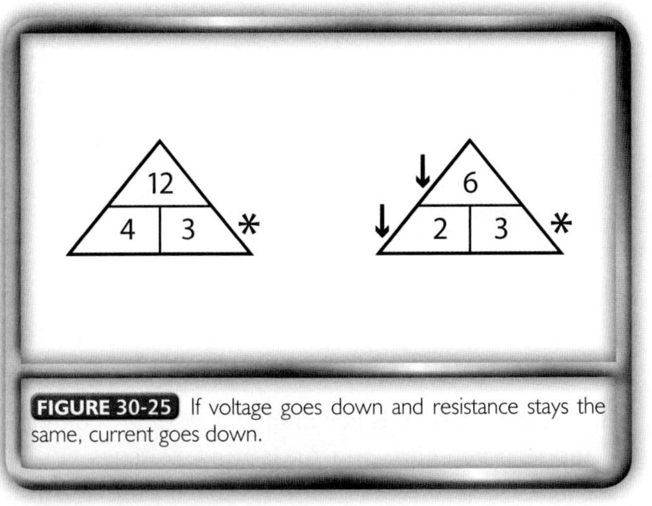
12
4
3
*
↓
6
↓
2
3
*

FIGURE 30-25 If voltage goes down and resistance stays the same, current goes down.

Since amperage is a product of voltage and resistance, it is a good idea to keep your eye on the amperage. What this means is that if you have a circuit fault, you can generally see what the amperage is doing; it is either high or low. If you truly cannot see what the current is doing, like in a solenoid, you will have to measure it. But in most cases, you can see it; the fuse blew because the current was too high, the lights are dim because the current is too low, etc. If current is low (most common scenario), then Ohm's law tells you that it is because either the voltage is low or the resistance is high. On the flip side, if your eye determines that the current is high, then either the voltage is high or the resistance is low.

For example, let's say that the left front headlight is dim. Your eye determines that the current in that circuit is low. Thus, either the voltage is low or the resistance is high. Now you just have to test for those two things. Use a voltmeter to measure the voltage at the battery. If low, determine why the battery voltage is low. If good, check the voltage across both sides of the headlight with the circuit on. It should be within 1.0 volt of the battery voltage. If not, then switch to looking for the high resistance. This is accomplished by first measuring the voltage drop on each side of the headlight. If there is an excessive voltage drop on one side, follow the circuit back toward the battery to identify the cause. If the voltages on both sides of the headlight are within specifications, the problem is most likely the headlight itself. You may be able to check the resistance of the headlight itself and compare it to a known good bulb. Or you may have to measure the current flow through the bulb and compare that to specifications, since its resistance increases greatly due to heat when it is illuminated.

If the current flow appears too high, then the circuit may have too much voltage or too little resistance. Measuring the battery voltage is an easy way to check for too much voltage. Using an ohmmeter to check the resistance of the load and comparing that to specifications will tell you if it is shorted. If it is not, then use the ohmmeter to check the wire harness for any short circuit conditions.

To use Ohm's law to diagnose circuits, follow the steps in SKILL DRILL 30-1:

1. Identify the circuit to be tested and determine the expected voltage, current, and resistance of the component or circuit. Using Ohm's law, calculate the expected voltage, current flow, or resistance of the circuit.

2 Set up the DVOM for a continuity or resistance check. Make sure there is no power connected to any circuit that you test for continuity. Next prepare the DVOM for testing just like you did for voltage by inserting the black probe into the COM terminal and the red probe into the V/Ω terminal.

3 Turn the rotary dial of the DVOM to the mode for measuring ohms, which also measures continuity. The digital display should now give you an "Out of Limits" reading indicating that there is not a continuous circuit connection between the two probes (some meters show "OL," and others place "1" on the left of the display). Touch the probe ends together. The display should now give a zero reading, or very close to zero, which indicates no resistance. This means there is a continuous circuit through the probes. Some DVOMs also indicate continuity with an audible tone.

4 Check a fuse. One typical use of the test is to determine whether a fuse needs to be replaced. If the fuse has been overloaded and "blown," then it will no longer complete a circuit when a DVOM is used to test it. To check this, place the black probe on one end of the fuse and the red probe on the other. If the fuse is functioning correctly, then the reading will be zero, indicating a complete, or closed, circuit. If the fuse is open, then there will be no reading and no tone, indicating an incomplete, or open, circuit.

5 A continuity or resistance test is used to check for a broken circuit caused by a break in a cable or lead or caused by a component becoming disconnected. The same test can also confirm whether there is continuity between components that are not supposed to be connected, a condition known as a short circuit. This test can also be used to check circuits that are suspected to have a high resistance.

6 Compare the test results with the calculated results from step 1. Key things to note are any variations between the calculated and measured results. Determine whether the variations can be accounted for within the tolerances of the components or whether a fault exists.

TECHNICIAN TIP

When using an ohmmeter to measure resistance or to check continuity with a DVOM, the circuit must be powered down to avoid a wrong reading. The best way to ensure this is by disconnecting the component from the circuit.

Using Wiring Diagrams to Diagnose Electrical Circuits

Vehicle wiring diagrams or schematics may be available as paper-based manuals, computer programs, or online resources. They are produced by manufacturers and some aftermarket publishing companies. Increasingly, repair information is accessed via the Internet using subscription services that are regularly updated. To use wiring diagrams, an understanding of the symbols, abbreviations, and connector coding used in the diagrams is required. These are usually found on the diagram or in information pages. See the chapter Lighting Systems for examples of some of the common symbols used.

Reading a wiring diagram is like reading a road map. There are a lot of interconnected circuits, wires, and components to decipher. Learning to read wiring diagrams takes a bit of time and experience, but knowing that circuits usually consist of a power source, a switch, a load, and a ground is a good start. Jorge Menchu of AESWave has been promoting a novel approach of using color crayons to help understand how a particular circuit in a wiring diagram operates. The following is a paraphrased version of that process.

Begin by printing out a copy of the wiring diagram for the circuit being diagnosed. Color all of the wires green that are directly connected to "ground". Color all of the wires red that are "hot" at all times. Color all of the wires orange that are "switched to power." Color all of the wires yellow that are "switched to ground." If there are any wires that reverse polarity, such as power window motor wires, mark those with side-by-side orange and yellow lines. Finally, color any variable wires, such as signal wires, blue.

Coloring the wires on the wiring diagram in this way does several things. First, it forces you to determine what each wire in the diagram does, which helps you get the total picture. Second, it helps to organize your thoughts so that you can understand how electricity flows through the circuit. Third, it helps to keep you from losing your place or forgetting what a particular wire does. And fourth, it can give you confidence that you have properly diagnosed the problem when you know why the circuit is not working properly and exactly where the problem is located **FIGURE 30-26**.

To use wiring diagrams to diagnose electrical circuits, follow the steps in **SKILL DRILL 30-2**.

Using a DVOM to Measure Voltage

The electrical system is becoming increasingly complex on modern vehicles, and measuring voltages with a DVOM is a very common task when diagnosing electrical

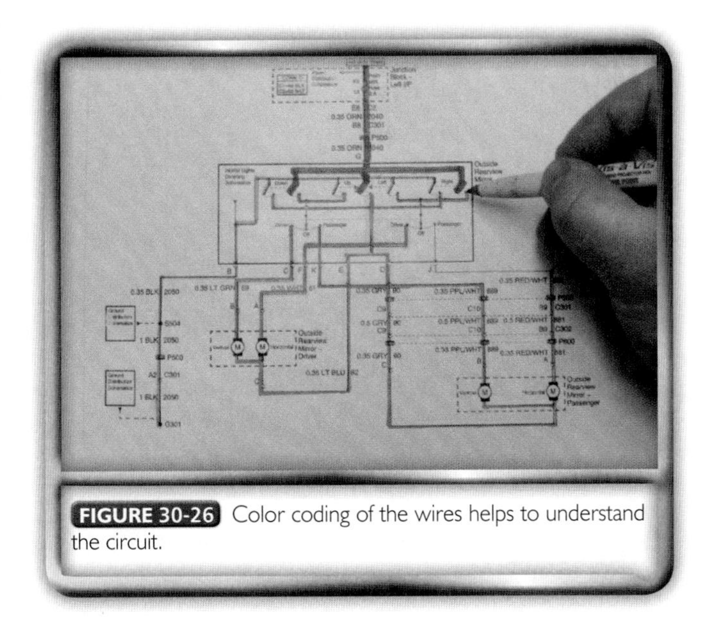

FIGURE 30-26 Color coding of the wires helps to understand the circuit.

faults. For most measurements, set the DVOM to auto range for ease of use. Select DVOM leads and probe ends to match the task at hand; for example, if you need to take a measurement but require both hands to be free, use probe ends with alligator clips. Ensure that you do not exceed the maximum allowable voltage or current for the DVOM. If you are measuring high voltages, wear appropriate personal protective equipment, such as high-voltage safety gloves, long-sleeved shirts and pants, and protective eyewear, and remove any personal jewelry or items that may cause an accidental short circuit.

When using a voltmeter for measuring voltage, you have a couple of options. One is just a simple voltage test. This typically involves placing the common lead on a good ground and the red probing lead on the input side of an electrical component. Doing so will give you a reading of how much more voltage is at the probing lead than is at the common lead. But that only gives us an indication of voltage. It does not tell us how much voltage we started with or how much voltage did not make it through the circuit. Therefore, be careful when using this test to determine if the voltage is good.

A better test is a voltage drop test. A voltage drop occurs when current flows through a resistance. The higher the resistance, the higher the voltage drop. We could say that a voltage drop test measures for excessive resistance in a circuit. When testing for a voltage drop, always have the circuit turned on. That way, the circuit will have current flowing, thereby making voltage drops evident. Just to be clear, in a real circuit, no current flow means no voltage drop.

There are two ways to do a voltage drop test: the direct method and the indirect method **FIGURE 30-27**. The direct method uses both test leads on the same side of the circuit. It will directly read how much voltage is lost between those two points. The indirect method leaves the black lead on the negative battery terminal (or other good ground) all the time. The probing lead is moved from one point (generally the positive battery terminal) to another point (generally the input of the load). The

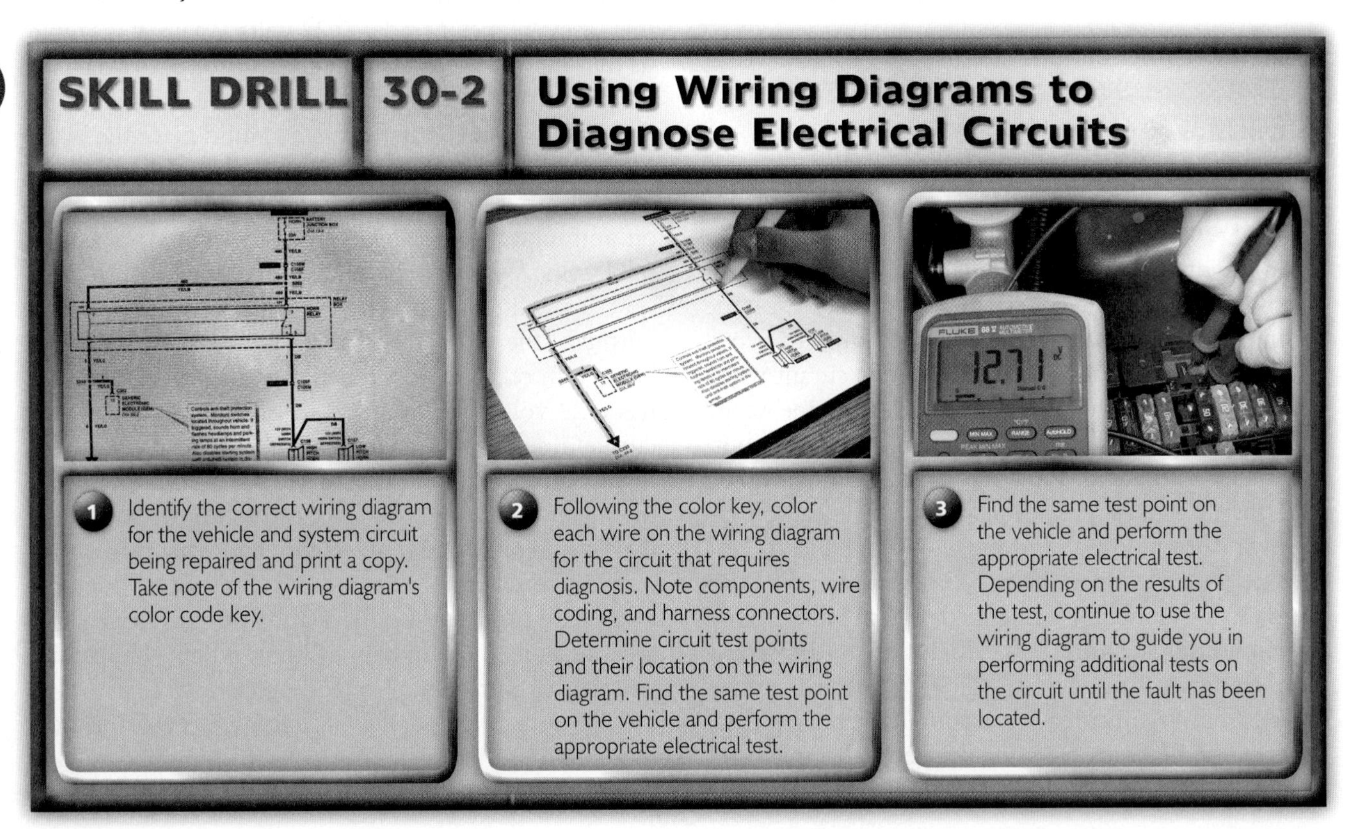

SKILL DRILL 30-2 Using Wiring Diagrams to Diagnose Electrical Circuits

1. Identify the correct wiring diagram for the vehicle and system circuit being repaired and print a copy. Take note of the wiring diagram's color code key.
2. Following the color key, color each wire on the wiring diagram for the circuit that requires diagnosis. Note components, wire coding, and harness connectors. Determine circuit test points and their location on the wiring diagram. Find the same test point on the vehicle and perform the appropriate electrical test.
3. Find the same test point on the vehicle and perform the appropriate electrical test. Depending on the results of the test, continue to use the wiring diagram to guide you in performing additional tests on the circuit until the fault has been located.

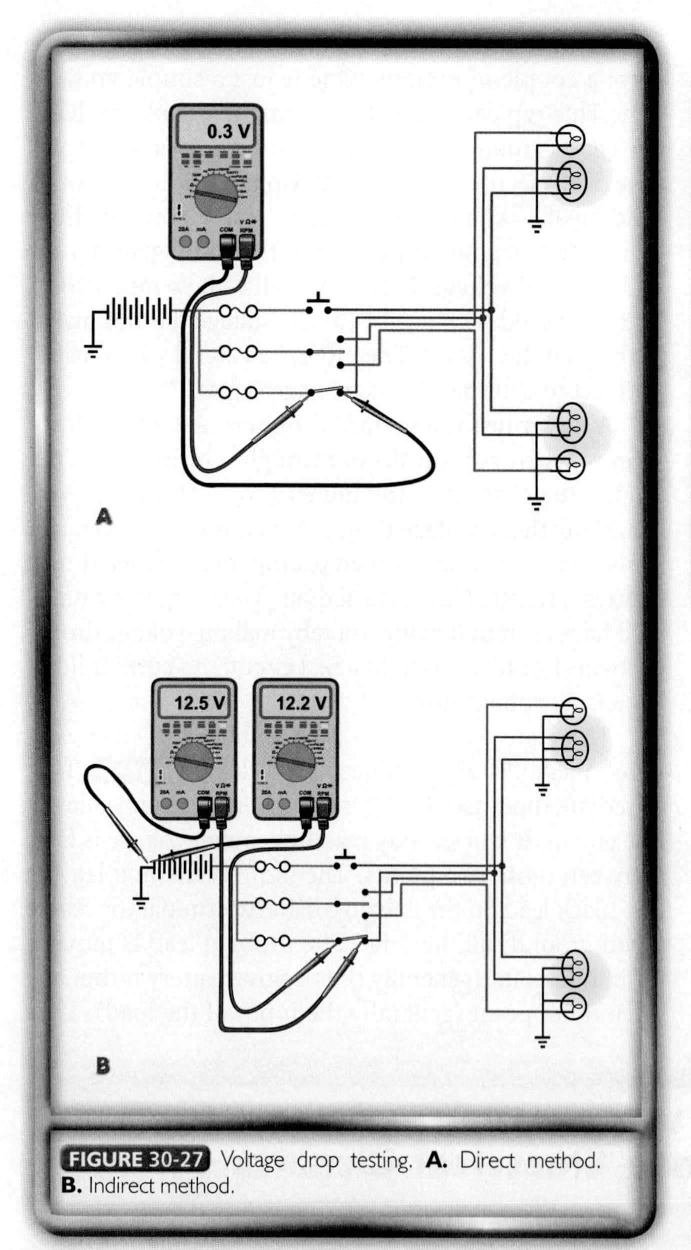
0.3 V
A
12.5 V
12.2 V
B

FIGURE 30-27 Voltage drop testing. **A.** Direct method. **B.** Indirect method.

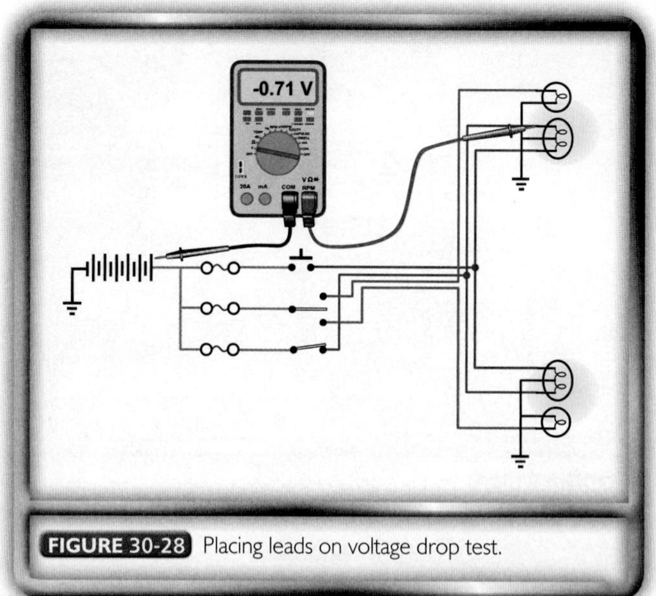
-0.71 V

FIGURE 30-28 Placing leads on voltage drop test.

second reading is then subtracted from the first reading to give the amount of the voltage drop. As you can see, the first method requires no math, so it is less prone to errors.

So how do you place the leads in the circuit when performing a direct voltage drop test? Let's assume we are checking the positive side of the circuit for voltage drops. If we stick with the idea that the red lead is the probing lead, then it makes sense to place the black lead on the positive battery post and probe with the red lead. Let's pretend we are measuring the voltage drop on the positive side of the circuit feeding the low beam filament on the left headlight. With the headlights on low beam, the voltmeter reads –0.71 volts FIGURE 30-28. Wait a minute, there is that negative reading again. Remember, we are measuring voltage drop, so it makes sense that the meter would read that the voltage is 0.71 volts *less than* (–) the voltage at the black lead. By the way, a 0.71-volt drop is beyond the 0.5-volt drop maximum allowed on one side of a circuit; thus, each part of the feed side of the circuit needs to be voltage drop tested to find the excessive voltage drop.

And how should the leads be placed when checking voltage drop on the ground side of the circuit? If we are looking to measure voltage drop, then we need to place the black lead on the output terminal of the headlight and the red lead on the negative battery terminal. Turn on the low beam headlights and measure the voltage drop. In this case, the meter reads –0.24 volts. Again, it is telling us that the voltage is dropping, this time 0.24 volts, on the return trip to the negative battery terminal.

To look at it another way, you could place the black lead on the negative battery terminal and the red lead on the output side of the headlight. Turn the headlight on and take the reading again. This time it measures 0.24 volts. Why isn't it negative this time? Good question. It is telling us that there are 0.24 volts more at the output of the headlight than at the negative post of the battery. In other words, the negative side of the circuit has 0.24 volts more at the start of the return path for current flow than it does at the end of the path, which is the negative battery terminal. Thus, we could hook up the meter either way; we just need to know which way we have it connected in the circuit and what reading we expect, whether it is negative or positive. Just don't get in the habit of ignoring the + and – signs. These signs are indicators that can help us know what is happening within a given circuit.

The other method of voltage drop testing is the indirect method. This method involves taking two voltage readings and subtracting them from each other to determine the voltage drop. This method is useful when working far away from the battery, where connecting one of the voltmeter leads to the battery is not possible, such as when checking lights at the rear of a vehicle. The indirect method involves first measuring the voltage at the battery with the electrical device turned on. This is the base reading. The second measurement is taken at the load that is being tested while the circuit is on. The leads are placed on the input to the load and the ground near the load. This will give the voltage that is available to the load. The last thing to do is subtract the voltage at the load from the battery voltage; any difference is the voltage drop in the system. Note, however, that the drop could be on the power side or the ground side of the circuit, so further testing must be performed if the voltage drop is excessive.

To use a DVOM to measure voltage, follow the steps in **SKILL DRILL 30-3**.

Checking Circuits with a Test Light

Nonpowered test lamps are useful in determining if electrical power is present in a part of a circuit. But you should always first test the test light on a known good power and ground before using it to test a circuit. It is possible that the bulb in the test light is burned out. You want to know that before performing any tests. If the test light illuminates, the two ends of the test light are touching both a power and a ground. If the light does not illuminate, the circuit is missing one or both of those elements or the test light is faulty. Test lights are great to grab to perform simple tests such as testing fuses. The test light lead can be quickly grounded and the probe end touched to each end of the suspect fuse. If both ends light, the fuse itself is good (but the fuse box terminal could be loose). If only one side of the fuse lights the test lamp, then the fuse is blown.

To avoid damaging the test light, make sure the circuit voltage you are testing does not exceed the test light's rating. Most test lights are rated for 6- or 12-volt systems, and using the light in a 24-volt system will usually blow the bulb. You should *not* use a test light to test SRS (supplemental restraint systems), as unintended deployment of the airbags could result, a very dangerous and costly mistake. Also, using a test light on a computer circuit designed for very small amounts of current flow can damage the circuit.

To check circuits with a test light, follow the steps in **SKILL DRILL 30-4**.

Checking Circuits with Fused Jumper Leads

Jumper leads can be used in a number of ways to assist in checking circuits. They can be created by the technician or purchased in a range of sizes, lengths, and fittings, or connectors. They are used to extend connections to allow circuit readings or tests to be undertaken with a DVOM, an oscilloscope, current clamps on fuses, relays, and connector plugs on components. In some circumstances, jumper leads may provide an alternate current or ground source for components being tested. Regardless of their application, it is important that the circuit remain

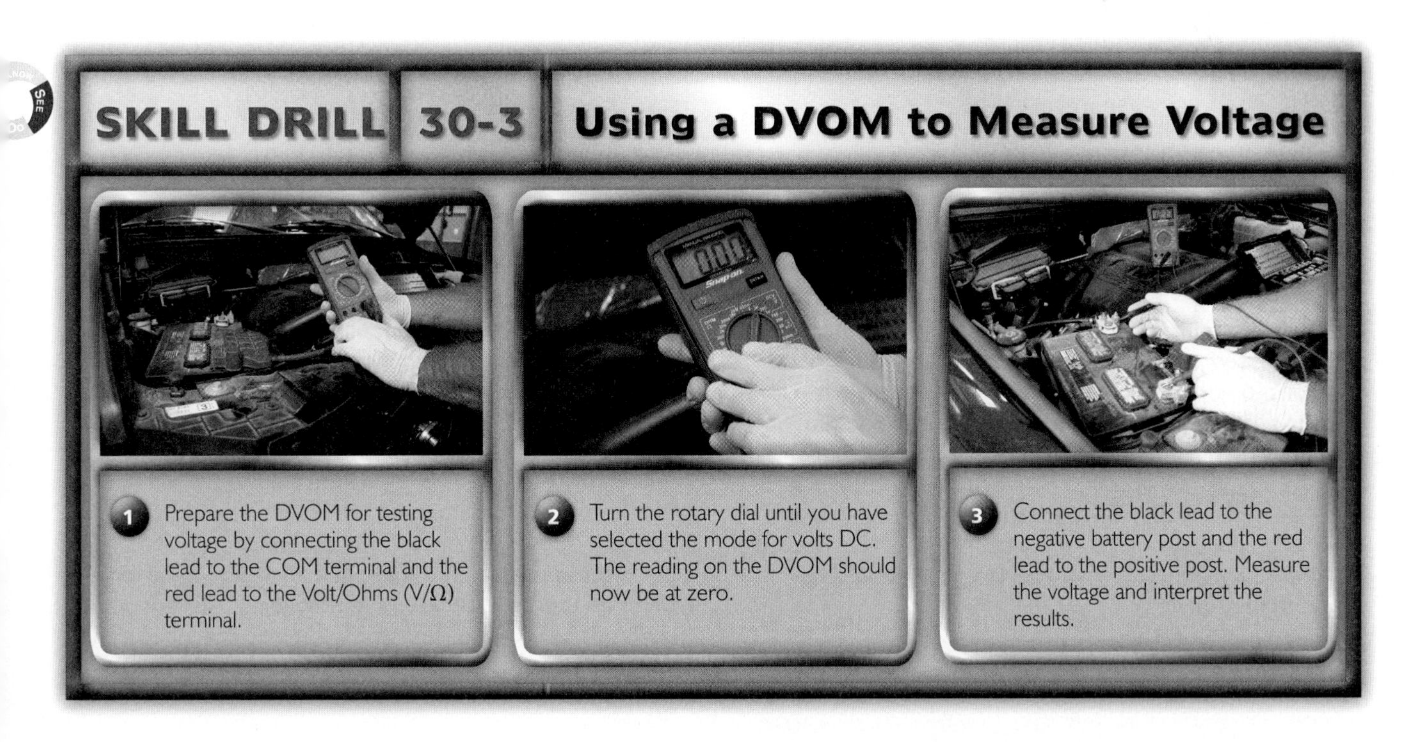

SKILL DRILL 30-3 Using a DVOM to Measure Voltage

1. Prepare the DVOM for testing voltage by connecting the black lead to the COM terminal and the red lead to the Volt/Ohms (V/Ω) terminal.
2. Turn the rotary dial until you have selected the mode for volts DC. The reading on the DVOM should now be at zero.
3. Connect the black lead to the negative battery post and the red lead to the positive post. Measure the voltage and interpret the results.

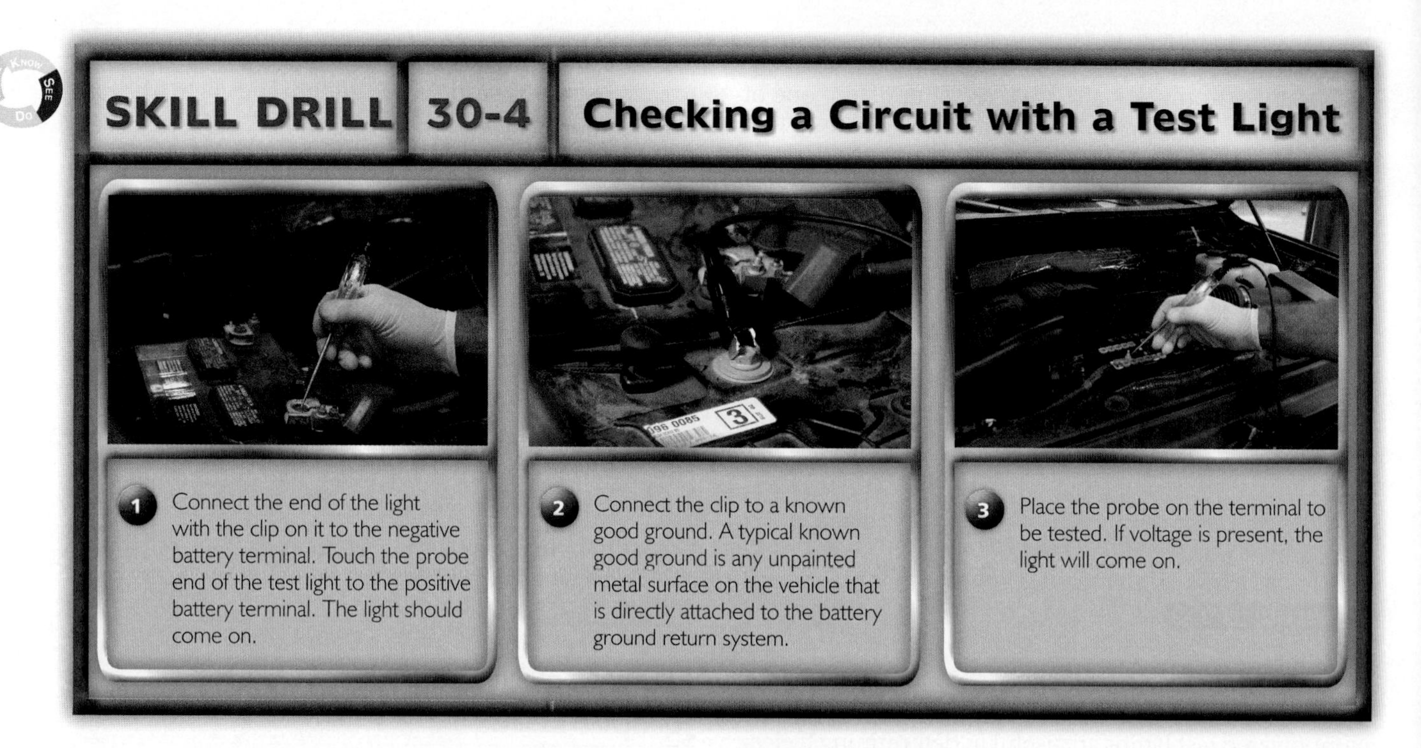
SKILL DRILL 30-4 Checking a Circuit with a Test Light

1. Connect the end of the light with the clip on it to the negative battery terminal. Touch the probe end of the test light to the positive battery terminal. The light should come on.
2. Connect the clip to a known good ground. A typical known good ground is any unpainted metal surface on the vehicle that is directly attached to the battery ground return system.
3. Place the probe on the terminal to be tested. If voltage is present, the light will come on.

protected by a fuse of the correct size. To determine the correct size of fuse for any particular application, refer to the manufacturer's information.

To check circuits with fused jumper leads, follow the steps in SKILL DRILL 30-5:

1. Identify the circuit to be checked and determine the fuse rating for the circuit.
2. Select appropriate jumper leads with the correct fuse rating.
3. Install the jumper lead into the circuit. Perform any required circuit checks. Never use a jumper lead to jump across a load; doing so bypasses circuit resistance and will likely cause excessive current to flow in the circuit.

Safety

Be very careful how you hook up any type of jumper leads, fused or unfused. If you hook them up to the wrong branch of a circuit, especially electronic circuitry, damage can be extensive. There is the old "magic smoke" saying: "Electrical and electronic components work off of the principle of magic smoke. Once the magic smoke is allowed to escape from the component, the component will never function again." Don't use jumper leads in a way that would let the "magic smoke" out of the circuit.

Applied Science

AS-77: Capacitance: The technician can demonstrate an understanding of the role of capacitance in timer circuits such as RC timers or a MAP sensor.

Sensors are the components of the system providing input to the computer making it possible for it to carry out its operations.

The MAP sensor, or manifold absolute pressure sensor, plays a big role in proper engine performance. There are several different types of MAP sensors. Some of the popular styles are the variable voltage MAP sensor, the variable-inductance MAP sensor, and the variable-capacitance MAP sensor. Here, we will focus on the variable-capacitance MAP sensor.

The variable-capacitance MAP sensor consists of two aluminum oxide plates in a chamber that is connected by tubing to the engine's intake manifold. This sensor is capable of generating an output signal in hertz proportional to the change in manifold pressure. This is the key point that the technician should understand. The electrical output signal to the computer is directly proportional to engine load as the manifold pressure changes. At engine idle, the vacuum is at approximately 17–21 in. Hg. at sea level. Under this condition, the MAP sensor hertz will be approximately 95. When the engine is at wide open throttle, the vacuum is almost zero inches of mercury, which is converted to a hertz reading of approximately 160. The MAP sensor sends the proportional signal to the computer as a result in changes in engine load. The computer responds by providing more or less fuel to the injectors as well as performing a number of other vital tasks.

Locating Opens, Shorts, Grounds, and High Resistance

DVOMs, test lamps, and simulated loads tend to be the tools used most often for locating opens, shorts, grounds, and high-resistance faults. Refer to the chapter Principles of Electrical Systems for more information on opens, shorts, grounds, and high resistance faults. An **open circuit** is a break in the electrical circuit where either the power supply or ground circuit has been interrupted. Most open circuits can be located by probing along the circuit at various points testing for power and by checking for an effective ground at the ground point. A systematic check of the circuit is required by first performing a voltage drop check on each side of the affected circuit. An open circuit will cause a voltage drop equal to the source voltage. Once the voltage drop is isolated to one side of the circuit, voltage drop testing can continue on that side, working the leads closer together in steps. Also, use your understanding of electrical systems to consider the most likely places for the open circuit, such as a blown fuse or a faulty switch. And don't forget that the load could also be open. If the voltage drop test on each side of the circuit is within specifications, use an ohmmeter to check whether the load is open, if possible. Some loads such as diodes cannot be tested with a standard ohmmeter. In this case, follow the manufacturer's diagnostic procedure.

Shorts, or **short circuits**, can occur anywhere in the circuit and can be difficult to locate, especially if it is intermittent. A short is a circuit fault in which current travels along an accidental or unintended route and can be thought of as a shorter path for current to flow. The short may occur within the load, such as shorted relay windings, or it can be in the wiring, where a wire is shorted to ground or to supply voltage. A short will typically cause lower than normal circuit resistance. The low-resistance fault would cause an abnormally high current flow in the circuit and may cause the circuit protection devices, such as fuses or circuit breakers, to open the circuit. A short to supply voltage may cause the circuit to remain live even after the switch is turned off. For example, a short between a wire with power on all the time and a wire switched by the ignition switch would cause the circuit controlled by the ignition switch to remain on even after the switch is turned off. Just remember that shorts can be caused by faulty components or damaged wiring.

Shorts that happen within components, such as a relay coil, can usually best be tested by comparing the reading of an ohmmeter to specifications. Shorts that occur in wire harnesses are usually best tested by disconnecting each end of the affected harness and using an ohmmeter to test for unwanted continuity between various wires. A reading on the ohmmeter when connected to two separate wires indicates a short circuit between them. A true short between wires would be indicated by a very low ohm reading, typically around 1 ohm or less.

Grounds is a term often used in conjunction with shorts and is usually a reference to a short to ground. An initial test can be conducted by carrying out resistance checks or disconnecting the load. For example, if testing the blower motor, first disconnect the blower motor. If the short is still in place, then the wiring between the fuse or circuit breaker and the load must be at fault. To further narrow down the site of the short to ground, inspect the wiring harness, looking for obvious signs of damage. Another test can be conducted by connecting a test lamp or buzzer in place of a fuse. Current will flow through the test lamp or buzzer and find a ground through the short. Parts of the circuit can then be disconnected along the wiring harness to narrow down the location of the short. Specialized short circuit detection tools are also available. They work by sending a signal through the wiring harness where a short is suspected. A receiving device is then moved along the wire loom and will indicate when a short is located. This type of device can be very useful in situations where it is difficult to access the wiring, such as within large wire looms or under vehicle trim.

Short to power refers to a condition where power from one circuit leaks into another circuit. A short to power situation usually causes strange electrical issues. In some cases, one or more circuits will operate when they should not. Or in the case of sensor wires, the incorrect signals caused by the short to power can cause the computer to make very wrong decisions based on the faulty data. In this case, the engine, transmission, or other computer-controlled component can react strangely. Shorts to power are diagnosed first with a voltmeter to check for the unwanted voltage. Next, an ohmmeter is used to isolate the problem in the wire harness.

High resistance refers to a circuit where there is unintended resistance, which then causes the circuit to not perform properly. It can be caused by a number of faults, including corroded or loose harness connectors, incorrectly sized cable for the circuit current flow, incorrectly fitted terminals, and poorly soldered joints. The high resistance causes an unintended voltage drop in a circuit when the current flows. This drop reduces the amount of voltage that can be used by the load. The high-resistance fault will also reduce the current flow in the circuit. The reduction in voltage and current to the load reduces the amount of electrical power to load (Power =

Voltage × Current), affecting its performance. Unwanted high resistance can best be located by conducting a voltage drop test in the power and ground circuits.

If the high resistance is within the load, such as a relay coil, then the resistance can be checked with an ohmmeter and compared to specifications. Some devices, such as a fuel injector or ignition coil, may need further testing using an oscilloscope. In this way, the waveform can be evaluated, which can indicate issues that an ohmmeter cannot identify as easily.

Inspecting and Testing Circuit Protection Devices

Protection devices are designed to prevent excessive current from flowing in the circuit. Protection devices like fuses and fusible links are sacrificial, meaning that if excessive current flows, they will blow or trip and have to be replaced. Circuit breakers can be reset. Once they trip, they either reset automatically or require a manual reset by pushing a button or moving a lever. Fuses, fusible links, and circuit breakers are available in various ratings, types, and sizes, and must always be replaced with the same rating and type.

> **TECHNICIAN TIP**
>
> It is fine to condemn fuses if they are obviously blown, but if they appear intact, do not rely on your eyes. Over time, fuses heat slightly and cool. This heating and cooling process can cause the fuse to become brittle and crack. The crack can be very fine, almost invisible, yet not conduct electricity, leading your diagnosis astray.

In most vehicles, protection devices are situated in the power or feed side of the circuit. A blown or faulty fuse can be tested using a DVOM or test lamp. A good fuse will have virtually the same voltage on both sides. A blown fuse will typically have battery voltage on one side of the fuse and 0 volts on the other side. They can also sometimes be visually inspected. This may require the removal of the fuse from the fuse holder. The fusible element should be intact and, if measured by an ohmmeter, should have a very low resistance. The contacts on both the fuse and the fuse holder should be clean and free of corrosion and should fit snugly together.

To inspect and test circuit protection devices, follow the steps in **SKILL DRILL 30-6**:

1. Identify the protection device to be inspected and tested.
2. Conduct a visual inspection.
3. Set up a DVOM to read volts or use a test lamp.
4. Energize the affected circuit, if necessary.
5. Test for voltage on both sides of the circuit protection device. Determine and perform any necessary actions.

Inspecting and Testing Switches, Connectors, Relays, Solenoid Solid-State Devices, and Wires

Inspection of electrical devices and wires usually starts with a visual inspection of the electrical circuit and is followed up with electrical testing. The visual inspection looks for breakage, corrosion, or deformity and includes examination of the insulation for any worn or melted spots. In the case of switches, solenoid contacts, and relay contacts, an electrical inspection is necessary. For example, all switches would require voltage drop testing to see if they operate properly without excessive resistance. Additionally, solenoid and relay contacts can wear out and produce excessive resistance, so performing a voltage drop test on them is a valid testing procedure. Some solenoids can be disassembled and visually inspected. In this case, the solenoid cap may be removed and the contacts visually inspected. Typically, if there is an excessive voltage drop across the contacts, the contacts will be pitted and burned. Measuring resistance also comes into play when a shorted relay or solenoid winding is suspected.

DVOMs and test lamps are used for most basic testing, with more specialized test equipment, such as oscilloscopes, being used if necessary. It is important to note that test lamps should not be used on electronic circuits due to their higher current draw, which could overpower the electronic components. Some tests, such as resistance tests, can be conducted on components in or out of the circuit. In-circuit tests are often preferred, as they usually provide the opportunity to test the component under load or during operational conditions. After in-circuit testing, components can be removed for individual testing, if required.

Manufacturers produce diagnostic flowcharts that guide the technician through a diagnostic sequence based on test results. In complex circuits, it is good practice to gather as much information as possible about the operation of the circuit and the customer concern. With that information, and the diagnostic flowchart, formulate a testing sequence for diagnosing the fault. Going through this process will help you to understand the problem and to identify possible causes, and a potential sequence of testing.

Wrap-up

Ready for Review

- The digital volt-ohmmeter (DVOM) or digital multimeter (DMM) is electrical measurement tool used to diagnose and repair electrical faults.
- To properly use a DVOM requires time and effort to learn the parts and how it works.
- The DVOM can measure volts, ohms, and amps in a circuit.
- An advanced DVOM can measure frequency, temperature, and has a dedicated diode test capability.
- A DVOM is the first tool used to take electrical measurements.
- The DVOM allows the technician to see the movement of electrical impulses that cannot be seen without some type of electrical test equipment.
- The DVOM can measure electrical volts within circuits.
- The DVOM can measure ohms, which is the resistance of a circuit.
- The DVOM can measure amps, which is the current flow of a circuit.
- The main parts of the DVOM is the main body and the two current leads.
- The main body has a function switch, a connection point for the leads, and a digital display to show values.
- The leads are black for negative and red for positive connections.
- There is a wide selection of leads for the DVOM to enhance the testing capabilities.
- Before you can use a DVOM, the technician needs to know the quantity of the measurement (volt, ohm, or amp).
- The DVOM can read a wide range of scales depending what position is selected.
- The DVOM can read from low to high values.
- The DVOM in auto range will select the best value for the range being measured.
- The min/max setting gives the technician the ability to measure circuits that are only on momentarily.
- The hold function freezes the value measured.
- There are many different ways to probe a circuit depending on the circuit being tested.
- The probes should never be forced as this could damage the circuit being tested and the probes being used.
- If the technician uses the back probe method, the holes probed need to be resealed to keep moisture out.
- The most common measurements taken with the DVOM are voltage, current, and resistance.
- Depending on measurements taken, the leads need to be in the correct location on the body of the DVOM.
- If the leads are connected in the wrong place on the DVOM, it could cause a fuse to blow.
- When voltage is measured, the leads are placed parallel to the circuit being measured.
- When current is measured, the leads are placed in series with the circuit being measured.
- When resistance is measured, the component should be isolated from the circuit so no power is present.
- The meter is very useful in finding opens, shorts, grounds, and high resistance.

Key Terms

digital volt-ohmmeter (DVOM) A test instrument with a digital display for measuring voltage, resistance, and current. Also called a digital multimeter (DMM).

grounds Fault conditions in a circuit where the circuit is unintentionally contacting a grounded component or wire. This may result in a short, in the case of a power wire, or it could cause a circuit to stay live in the case of a switched ground circuit.

high resistance A term that describes a circuit or components with more resistance than designed.

hold function A setting on a DVOM to store the present reading.

min/max setting A setting on a DVOM to display the maximum and minimum readings.

open circuit A circuit that has a break that prevents current from flowing.

probing technique The way in which test probes are connected to a circuit.

short circuit A condition in which the current flows along an unintended route.

short to power A condition in which current flows from one circuit into another.

ASE-Type Questions

1. Tech A says that total resistance goes up as more parallel paths are added. Tech B says that total amperage goes up as more parallel paths are added. Who is correct?
   a. Tech A
   b. Tech B
   c. Both A and B
   d. Neither A nor B
2. Tech A says that when reading DC voltage on a meter, a "+" before the number means that there is a higher voltage at the red lead than the black lead. Tech B says that a "–" before the number means that there is a lower voltage at the red lead than the black lead. Who is correct?
   a. Tech A
   b. Tech B
   c. Both A and B
   d. Neither A nor B
3. Tech A says that to read amperage the meter needs to be hooked up in series in a circuit. Tech B says that to read amperage at a load, place one lead of the ammeter on the input side of the load and the other lead on the output. Who is correct?
   a. Tech A
   b. Tech B
   c. Both A and B
   d. Neither A nor B
4. Tech A says that when checking amperage on a battery, hook the red lead to positive and the black lead to ground. Tech B says that a resistance reading on a light bulb requires the DVOM to be hooked to each side of the bulb and the switch turned on. Who is correct?
   a. Tech A
   b. Tech B
   c. Both A and B
   d. Neither A nor B
5. Tech A says that when checking a voltage drop across an open switch, a measurement of 12 volts means the circuit is open. Tech B says that when checking voltage drop across an open switch, a measurement of 12 volts means the switch contacts are closed. Who is correct?
   a. Tech A
   b. Tech B
   c. Both A and B
   d. Neither A nor B
6. A customer complains of slow engine cranking. Tech A says that the starter is faulty and should be replaced. Tech B says that performing a voltage drop test on the high current side of the starter circuit is a valid test in this situation. Who is correct?
   a. Tech A
   b. Tech B
   c. Both A and B
   d. Neither A nor B
7. Tech A says that when resistance increases, current flow decreases. Tech B says that when voltage decreases, current increases. Who is correct?
   a. Tech A
   b. Tech B
   c. Both A and B
   d. Neither A nor B
8. Tech A says that an open circuit will typically cause higher current flow, which will blow the fuse. Tech B says that a short to ground can typically be found by checking voltage at different points in the circuit. Who is correct?
   a. Tech A
   b. Tech B
   c. Both A and B
   d. Neither A nor B
9. Tech A says that when a fuse has popped, it just needs to be replaced, since it performed its job. Tech B says that when a fuse has blown, the circuit needs to be diagnosed because the fuse was probably not the problem. Who is correct?
   a. Tech A
   b. Tech B
   c. Both A and B
   d. Neither A nor B
10. Technician A says that the black voltmeter lead stays on the negative battery terminal whenever you perform a "direct voltage drop test." Technician B says that an "indirect voltage drop test" is used to accurately measure current flow in a circuit. Who is correct?
    a. Tech A
    b. Tech B
    c. Both A and B
    d. Neither A nor B

CHAPTER 31

KNOW
SEE
DO
PROVE

NATEF Tasks

Electrical/Electronic Systems

General Electrical Systems Diagnosis

Task	MLR	AST	Page
■ Measure key-off battery drain (parasitic draw).	MLR		908–909
■ Diagnose the cause(s) of excessive key-off battery drain parasitic draw, determine necessary action.		AST	908–909

Battery

Task	MLR	AST	Page
■ Perform battery state-of-charge test; determine necessary action.	MLR	AST	900–901
■ Confirm proper battery capacity for vehicle application; perform battery capacity test; determine necessary action.	MLR	AST	901–902
■ Identify electronic modules, security systems, radios, and other accessories that require reinitialization or code entry after reconnecting vehicle battery.	MLR	AST	902–903
■ Maintain or restore electronic memory functions.	MLR	AST	902–903
■ Inspect and clean battery; fill battery cells; check battery cables, connectors, clamps, and hold-downs.	MLR	AST	904–905
■ Perform slow/fast battery charge according to manufacturer's recommendations.	MLR	AST	905
■ Jump-start a vehicle using jumper cables and a booster battery or an auxiliary power supply.	MLR	AST	905–907

Battery Systems

KNOW
SEE
DO

Knowledge Objectives

After reading this chapter, you will be able to:
1. Describe battery types, ratings and sizes, and construction. (pp 890–892)
2. Explain the operation of lead-acid batteries. (p 893)

KNOW
SEE
DO

Skills Objectives

After reading this chapter, you will be able to:
1. Perform a battery state-of-charge test using a hydrometer, refractometer, or DVOM. (p 901)
2. Test battery capacity. (p 902)
3. Identify electronic modules, security systems, radios, and other accessories that require reinitialization or code entry following battery disconnect. (pp 902–903)
4. Maintain or restore electronic memory functions. (pp 902–903)
5. Inspect, clean, fill, or replace the battery, battery cables, clamps, connectors, and hold-downs. (pp 904–905)
6. Charge a battery. (pp 904–906)
7. Jump-start a vehicle. (p 907)
8. Measure parasitic draw with a standard parasitic load test and a Chesney parasitic load test. (p 909)

Introduction

The electrical system on modern vehicles is becoming increasingly complex with an increasing reliance on electrical power to assist in the management and control of not only the engine and emissions system, but also almost all aspects of the vehicle, including brakes and suspension, navigation, entertainment, information retrieval, and much more. Almost every system on modern vehicles relies on electrical and electronic components and theory, electronic control modules, and networking systems to connect everything together.

Fundamental to the automobile is the 12-volt storage battery, the engine starting system, and the electrical charging system. Once the engine is started, all of the vehicle's electrical systems rely on the charging system to provide sufficient power output and precise voltage control for the vehicle's on-board electrical and electronic circuits. Let's start with the battery, which provides the necessary standby (and reserve) power to get things started.

The Battery

As you learned in the Principles of Electrical Systems chapter, electricity is a very flexible and useful energy that can be used easily in a variety of ways. But one drawback to electricity is that it cannot be stored easily in its electrical form for later use. This means that electricity must be stored in another form of energy and reconverted to electricity when needed. This is where batteries enter the discussion.

Batteries were developed in the early 1800s, and since that time many varieties and designs have been developed. The battery is part of everyday life and is widely used in modern electrical and electronic devices. Batteries store electricity in chemical form, which is possible because electricity causes a chemical reaction within the battery. In other words, the electrical energy is transformed into chemical energy. The chemical reactions change the composition of the chemicals, which then are stored until the electrical energy is needed. When electricity is needed, the chemicals react with each other, transforming the chemical energy back into electrical energy.

A battery consists of two dissimilar metals, an insulator material separating the metals, and an **electrolyte**, which is an electrically conductive solution **FIGURE 31-1**. The strength of the battery depends on the materials used.

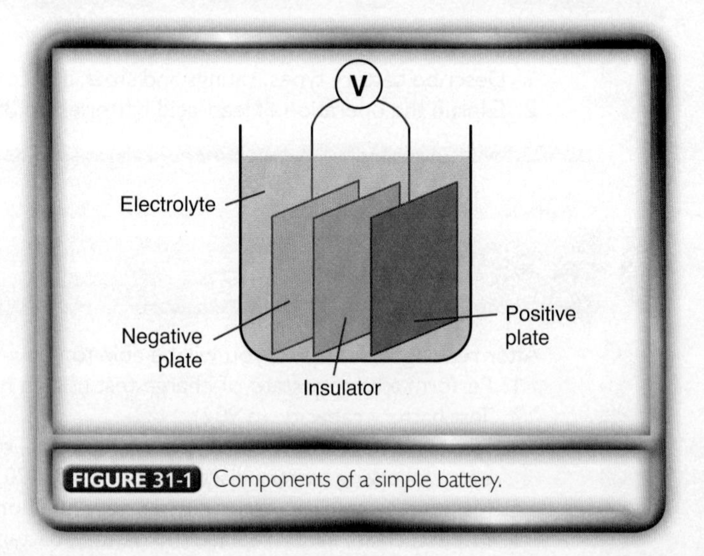
V
Electrolyte
Negative plate
Insulator
Positive plate

FIGURE 31-1 Components of a simple battery.

You Are the Automotive Technician

A seven year old vehicle has just been towed into the shop with a no-crank condition. The driver of the vehicle informs you that it was acting strange; the wipers were running slow, the headlights were dim, and the battery light was on. He pulled off the highway and a few minutes later the engine died and wouldn't start. He thinks that the vehicle needs a new battery, but agrees to let you diagnose the problem. After writing up the repair order and looking up the service history, you inspect the vehicle visually. The shop apprentice has already partially charged the battery. You notice that the battery is the original one and the terminals are quite dirty. After using a battery terminal tool to clean the battery terminals, you test the battery with a conductance tester and find it has degraded from its original 650 CCAs to 185 CCAs. With a booster battery connected, the vehicle starts and runs normally. You test the alternator output and find its maximum output is about 15 amps, and the alternator ripple indicates faulty diodes or stator assembly. The last test you perform is a starter draw test. The specifications are 150–190 amps and it measures 165 amps.

1. Why did the vehicle act strange and die?
2. Which parts need to be replaced and why?
3. If the starter still wouldn't crank, nor make any noise, after the battery was replaced and the terminals cleaned, what would you test and why?

The traditional automotive battery type is the lead-acid battery. It is available in many different shapes, sizes, and designs to meet the requirements for various applications. For example, the battery used for starting a vehicle's engine is different from the marine deep cycle battery. Each requires different design characteristics for obviously different applications. Vehicle batteries are designed to provide high current draws for short periods of time, while deep cycle batteries supply smaller, continuous loads over longer periods of time. Although the size, case configuration, and design may change, the fundamental components and their operation remain the same.

Lead-Acid Flooded Cell and Gel Cell Batteries

The wet cell lead-acid battery is the main storage device in automotive use. It is called a flooded cell battery because the lead plates are immersed in a water–acid electrolyte solution. An automotive battery can supply very high discharge currents while maintaining a high voltage, which is useful when cold starting. It gives a high power output for its compact size, and it is rechargeable.

The standard 12-volt car battery consists of six cells connected in series. Each cell has a nominal 2.1 volts, for a total of 12.6 volts for a fully charged "12-volt" battery. Each cell contains two sets of electrodes (called plates), one set of lead (Pb) and the other set of lead dioxide (PbO_2), in an electrolyte solution of diluted sulfuric acid (H_2SO_4). As the battery discharges, the sulfuric acid is absorbed into the lead plates and both of the plates slowly turn into lead sulfate. At the same time, the strength of the electrolyte becomes less acidic as the acid is absorbed into the plates. Recharging the battery reverses this process.

In a conventional open wet cell battery, charging generates hydrogen and oxygen gas by separating them from the water in the electrolyte, creating a highly explosive mix. Overcharging or rapid charging causes some gas to escape from the battery; this is called **gassing**. The sulfuric acid contained in batteries is highly corrosive and can also be very harmful to metal, painted surfaces, and skin. Always wear protective clothing and use extra care when handling batteries.

In automotive storage batteries, the main storage device is the wet cell. The nominal 2.1 volts of each cell does not depend on the size of the cell; however, its current capacity does. The surface area of the plates in a cell determines the cell's current capacity. In a lead-acid battery, positively and negatively charged plates are assembled so that they are alternated. All of the positive plates are connected to each other in parallel, and all of the negative plates are connected to each other in parallel **FIGURE 31-2**. The more plates, the greater the current capacity of the cell. Since the plates are arranged alternately, they need to be close to each other but not touching. If they touch, an internal short circuit in the cell will occur, which is typically what has happened in a battery with a "dead" cell. The positive and negative plates have shorted together and therefore discharge that cell completely. Normally, the plates are kept from touching each other by separators, usually made of plastic.

The battery's six 2.1-volt cells are connected in series to form the battery, which gives the battery a nominal voltage of 12.6 volts. The cells are sealed from each other and filled with dilute sulfuric acid. The battery case is usually made of plastic or hard rubber. With the cells in series, one end of the battery is connected to the negative post and the other end is connected to the positive post **FIGURE 31-3**.

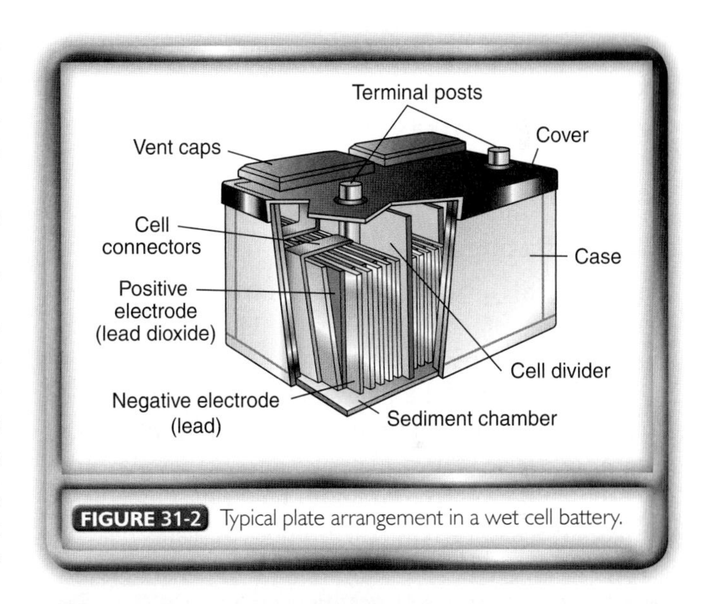
Terminal posts
Vent caps
Cover
Cell connectors
Case
Positive electrode (lead dioxide)
Cell divider
Negative electrode (lead)
Sediment chamber

FIGURE 31-2 Typical plate arrangement in a wet cell battery.

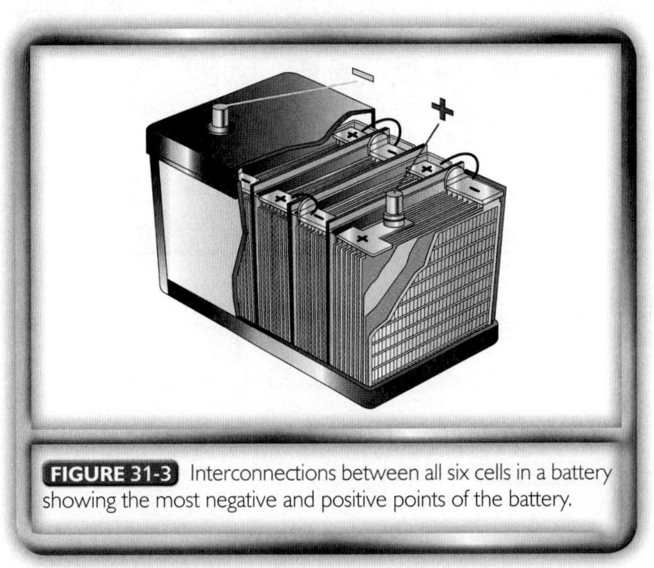
+

FIGURE 31-3 Interconnections between all six cells in a battery showing the most negative and positive points of the battery.

Ratings and Sizing

Batteries have different ratings and sizing to fit the needs of a variety of vehicles. Ratings have to do with the electrical specifications of a battery, while sizing has to do with the physical attributes of the battery. Both are important when selecting or replacing a battery. Physical attributes of the automotive battery include the size of the battery case, the arrangement of the battery terminals (top or side mounted), and the size or type of battery terminal post (round-tapered posts or screw-on terminals).

Batteries sizes are designated by the Battery Council International (BCI) and given a group number. Individual groups are specified by dimension in length, width, and height. Note that a physically larger battery does not necessarily mean a higher electrical capacity, so always check the ratings in addition to the BCI group size. Other designations relate to the **battery terminal configuration**, which refers to the placing of the positive and negative terminals on the battery FIGURE 31-4. The position of the battery posts varies with each layout. Battery catalogs will specify the correct battery for each vehicle and terminal layouts. Different types of battery posts are also available for batteries, including lug terminals, side terminals, and standard posts FIGURE 31-5.

Battery Ratings

The **electrical capacity**, or the amount of charge a typical lead-acid battery can store, is determined primarily by the total surface area of the plates, but also to some extent by the thickness of the plates. The more plate surface area there is, the higher the electrical capacity of the battery. Automotive battery plates tend to be manufactured in a standard size, so a common method of increasing surface area is to increase the number of plates per cell. For example, a 12-volt 11-plate cell will have a higher capacity than a 12-volt 9-plate cell.

There are several methods used to rate automotive battery capacity. The three most common are **cold cranking amps (CCA)**, **cranking amps (CA)**, and **reserve capacity**. CCA measures the load in amps that a battery can deliver for 30 seconds while maintaining a voltage of 1.2 volts per cell (7.2 volts for a 12-volt battery) or higher at 0°F (–18°C). CA measures the same thing, but at a higher temperature—32°F (0°C). This can cause confusion since a 500-CCA battery has about 20% more capacity than a 500-CA battery, so it is important to keep the ratings straight. Reserve capacity is the time in minutes that a new fully charged battery at 80°F (27°C) will supply a constant load of 25 amps without its voltage dropping below 10.5 volts for a 12-volt battery. This rating approximates the amount of time that a vehicle can be driven before the battery dies, if the charging system fails completely. The CCA, CA, and reserve capacity are typically marked on automotive batteries, and technicians use these ratings when testing battery performance and when selecting batteries for particular vehicle applications.

Low-Maintenance and Maintenance-Free Batteries and Cells

There are many types of batteries, with variations of cell design available for vehicles. Some batteries are specifically designed for starting, some for extended-load marine usage, some for low-maintenance or maintenance-free applications. Low-maintenance batteries require little, if any, topping off of the water in the electrolyte. The plates and venting system are designed so that they do not normally gas and release water vapor to the atmosphere. Low-maintenance batteries still have

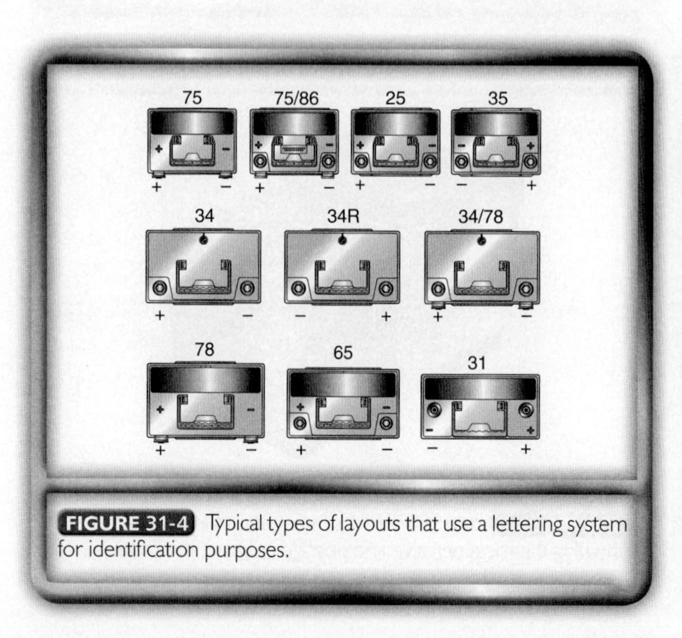
75
75/86
25
35
34
34R
34/78
78
65
31

FIGURE 31-4 Typical types of layouts that use a lettering system for identification purposes.

6024

FIGURE 31-5 Battery posts. **A.** Side terminal. **B.** Standard post.

removable caps so that electrolyte can be checked and topped off if necessary.

> **TECHNICIAN TIP**
>
> Since lead is relatively soft, when it is used in the lead plates of a battery it is prone to bending and stretching. Many years ago, antimony was added to the plates to strengthen them, but this caused the cells to gas off water, which caused the electrolyte level to fall over time, requiring periodic topping off. Calcium was added to one or both plates to reduce water usage.

Maintenance-free batteries are fully sealed and do not require the electrolyte to be topped off. In some cases they use a gel-type electrolyte instead of a liquid. **Absorbed glass mat** batteries have the electrolyte absorbed within a mat of fine glass fibers **FIGURE 31-6**. The plates in this type of fully sealed battery can be made flat or wound in a cylindrical cell. Because the electrolyte in absorbed glass mat batteries is a gel, which does not spill, this type of battery is especially handy for rough handling or tipping. In fact, this type of battery can even be mounted on its side and still perform well. Thus the absorbed glass mat battery is especially suited for off-road and racing vehicles.

A sealed or low-maintenance battery typically has no removable cell covers, so you cannot adjust or test the fluid levels inside. However, some of these batteries do have a visual indicator (a single-cell hydrometer float) that provides information on the status of the charge and condition of one of the battery cells. Each manufacturer provides details of these visual indicators; refer to these when performing an inspection.

OPTIMA

FIGURE 31-6 AGM battery.

Battery Charging and Discharging Cycle

In a discharged lead-acid cell, the active material of both plates becomes lead sulfate, and the electrolyte becomes mostly water as the acid is absorbed into the plates. The result is a very weak sulfuric acid solution in the electrolyte. When being charged, the battery is connected to a direct current (DC) electrical supply with electrical pressure (voltage) higher than that of the battery's total cell voltage. The charging device acts like an electron pump, forcing electrons to move from the positive plates to the negative plates in the battery.

At the negative plates, sulfate is discharged, which changes the chemical composition of the plates back into sponge lead and also creates a stronger solution of sulfuric acid in the electrolyte. At the same time, lead peroxide is formed at the positive plates, which helps to restore the cell's electrical potential or voltage.

The charging process increases the amount of acid in the electrolyte, making the electrolyte stronger. When further charging no longer makes the electrolyte stronger, charging is complete. Connecting a lead-acid battery to a load causes chemical changes as the battery discharges. At the positive plate, sulfate from the sulfuric acid in the electrolyte joins with lead to form lead sulfate, and oxygen from the plate joins the hydrogen from the electrolyte to form water. Lead sulfate also forms at the negative plate, as sponge lead forms with sulfate from the electrolyte **FIGURE 31-7**.

Overall, the percentage of acid in the electrolyte falls, and the percentage of water rises, reducing the strength of the electrolyte. As the cell discharges, the plates develop the same composition, which reduces the potential of the cell. Recharging the battery restores the difference between its sets of plates.

Battery Temperature Monitoring

Battery temperature plays an important role in the performance of a battery, and every battery has an ideal operating temperature range. In cold weather, battery performance drops dramatically due to a slowing of the chemical reaction process. At hotter temperatures, battery performance increases, but if the temperature increases too high, battery life may be compromised. Some vehicles monitor the battery temperature by placing a temperature probe in contact with the battery case **FIGURE 31-8**. The power train control module (PCM) then controls the levels of current flow and voltage at which the battery is charged. Generally speaking, the colder the battery temperature, the higher the rate of charging; and the hotter the battery temperature, the slower the rate of charging.

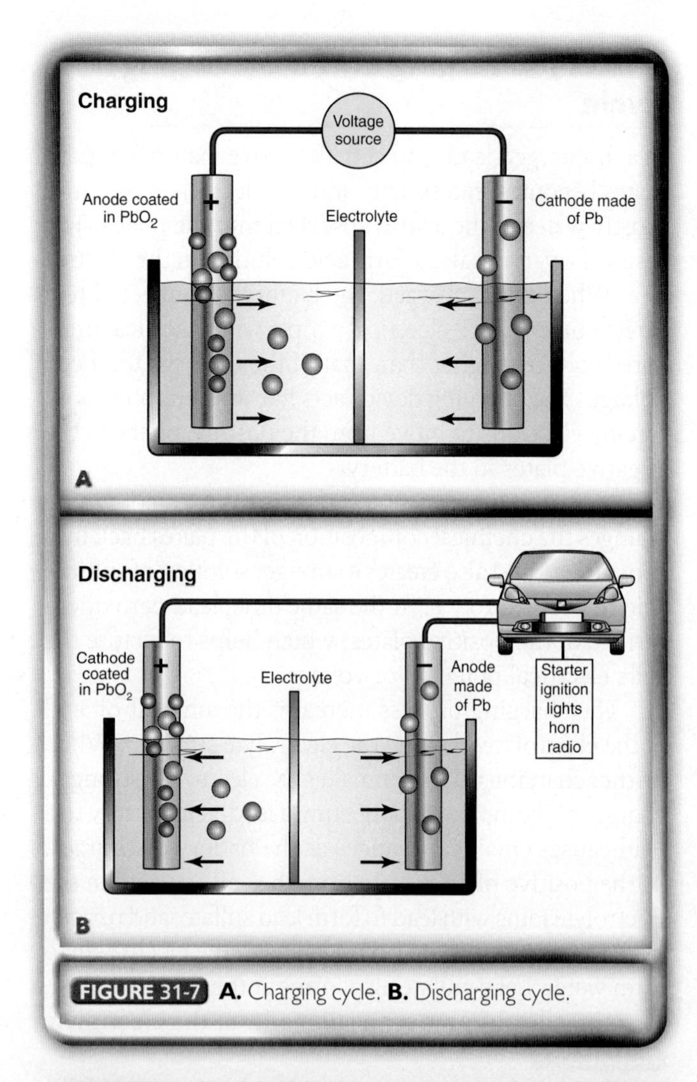
Charging
Voltage source
Anode coated in PbO_2
Electrolyte
Cathode made of Pb
A
Discharging
Cathode coated in PbO_2
Electrolyte
Anode made of Pb
Starter ignition lights horn radio
B

FIGURE 31-7 **A.** Charging cycle. **B.** Discharging cycle.

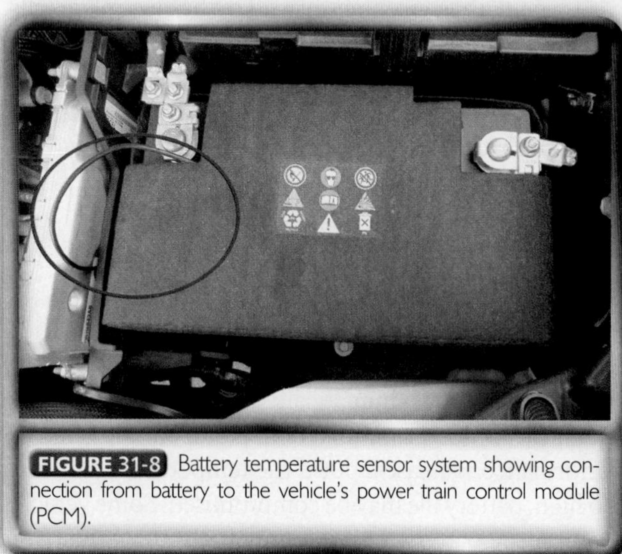

FIGURE 31-8 Battery temperature sensor system showing connection from battery to the vehicle's power train control module (PCM).

Smart chargers and battery management systems use the feedback from the temperature probe to manage the charge rate of a battery, ensuring the battery is at capacity and the temperature is within the optimal range, thereby promoting longer battery life.

Battery Operating Conditions

Batteries have a range of operating conditions under which the best possible performance and lifetime can be achieved. They should be kept clean, dry, and fully charged; have minimal vibration and the correct level of electrolyte; be kept at a moderate temperature (e.g., 77°F [25°C]); and be well secured. A battery's lifetime is shortened by the following conditions:

- Being fully discharged or having deep discharge cycles
- Remaining over- or undercharged
- Experiencing high discharge rates for extended periods
- Experiencing excessive vibration
- Being exposed to extremes of temperature
- Having dirt or moisture around the case
- Developing corrosion

Poor maintenance and operating conditions reduce the battery's operating life.

> **TECHNICIAN TIP**
>
> Back in the day when many people worked on their own cars, a very handy do-it-yourselfer bought a top-shelf battery for his vehicle from the local parts store. After a couple of weeks, the customer brought the battery back saying it had a dead cell. The store employee checked it out and sure enough, it had a dead cell, so they gave him a new battery. A few weeks later, the customer returned with the same problem. The store employee apologized profusely and gave him another battery. Sure enough, the customer was back within the month with another bad battery. By this time, the owner figured something had to be going on, so he went to the customer's home to check it out. When he got there, he saw a beautiful 57 Chevy with a tilt front end. One quick look told him everything he needed to know. When the tilt front end was installed, the battery tray had to be removed. The customer found a nice new spot to mount the battery tray, bolting it right on the top of the upper control arm for the suspension. So every bump in the road bounced the battery and literally shook it to death. Needless to say, the customer ended up paying for a few ruined batteries.

Rechargeable Cell Batteries

Batteries and cells continue to be developed to create more efficient, higher density batteries. Consumer electronic devices such as mobile phones and laptop computers have been driving the development of new battery technologies such as nickel-cadmium (Ni-Cd), nickel-metal hydride (Ni-MH), and lithium ion (Li-ion). All of these are types of rechargeable cell batteries, as are lead-acid batteries. Nickel-cadmium batteries contain older technology and have been replaced by nickel-metal hydride batteries; as both have a nominal cell voltage of 1.2 volts. The nickel-metal hydride battery can have two to three times the energy density of a nickel-cadmium battery, which means that for the same size case, they can store two to three times the energy. This makes nickel-metal hydride batteries especially useful for drive motor applications such as in hybrid electric, plug-in hybrid, and battery electric vehicles. They also tend not to have the memory effect that plagued the nickel-cadmium batteries of the past. The memory effect required nickel-cadmium batteries to be fully discharged between charge cycles to ensure maximum performance of the battery was maintained.

The lithium ion is a newer type of rechargeable cell and is now used in many consumer electronic devices, such as cell phones and laptop computers. Such applications paved the way for further breakthroughs in the use of lithium-ion batteries in hybrid-electric or battery-electric vehicles; these vehicles use what is known as the rechargeable energy storage system (RESS). A lithium-ion battery has one of the highest energy density ratios of common batteries in production today. This high energy density means the battery can store more energy than comparable batteries of other types. This is a real advantage for vehicle applications. They also have a low self-discharge rate, which means they can sit on the shelf for long periods without discharging. They do have a shelf-life even if they are not used. For example, they typically last for up to 5 years from the date of manufacture, whether they are used or not.

The actual cell voltage depends on the final materials used to make the cell. The typical cell voltage for a lithium-ion battery is 3.6 volts. In contrast, cell voltage of a nickel-cadmium or nickel-metal hydride battery is 1.2 volts, and a typical lead-acid battery is 2.1 volts. Like all batteries, the lithium-ion cell has an anode, a cathode, and an electrolyte. When discharging, the lithium ions are removed from the anode and added into the cathode. When the cell is charging, the reverse occurs.

Lithium-ion batteries may suffer from **thermal runaway** and cell rupture if overheated or overcharged. In extreme cases, thermal runaway may result in an explosion. Extreme care should be taken when handling or charging lithium-ion batteries; always follow the manufacturer's recommendations. In hybrid or electric vehicle applications, many small dry cell battery-sized cells are connected in series and in parallel arrangements to form a battery pack that delivers the power requirements of the vehicle. Following safety precautions is extremely important because RESS battery packs develop voltages in excess of 200 volts.

Advantages of lithium-ion batteries include:

- High energy density: There is more power per pound.
- Low self-discharge: Self-discharge is typically less than half of that of nickel-cadmium.
- Low maintenance: No periodic discharge required.
- No memory
- Low internal resistance: They are good for high current requirements.

Applied Science

AS-54: Batteries: The technician can demonstrate an understanding of the electrochemical reactions that occur in wet cell and dry cell batteries.

A vehicle that has a no crank condition is towed into a dealership. The technician assigned to the job has completed his diagnosis of the problem and determined that the vehicle has a faulty battery. An apprentice technician working under his supervision also discovered that the hold down clamp on the battery was missing.

At break time, the apprentice asked the technician why he thought that the battery failed. The technician explained his thoughts by going back to the basics of battery construction and the electrochemical reactions that occur during various events. The battery case can be thought of as a container. Inside this container are six separate compartments or cells, which are the energy producing units. Each cell has a number of plates soaked in an electrolyte solution of about 64% water and 36% sulfuric acid. The plates are separated into the anode or negative side and the cathode or positive side.

As stated in our text, connecting a lead acid battery to a load causes chemical changes as the battery discharges. At the positive plate, sulfate from the electrolyte joins with lead to form lead sulfate, and oxygen from the plate joins the hydrogen from the electrolyte to form water. Lead sulfate also forms at the negative plate, as sponge lead forms with sulfate from the electrolyte. Overall, the percentage of acid in the electrolyte falls, and the percentage of water rises, which reduces the strength of the electrolyte. As the cell discharges, the plates develop the same composition, which reduces the potential of the cell. Recharging the battery again restores the difference between its sets of plates.

The technician explained his theory of the failure of the battery to the missing hold down clamp. With the battery not being securely fastened, plate material breaks off and drops down into the bottom of the battery case. This will eventually cause the plates to short out. He went on to explain that all batteries will eventually wear out but the excessive vibration shortened the life of the battery.

Disadvantages of lithium-ion batteries include:

- Need for circuit protection to ensure current and voltage are within safe limits
- Limited shelf-life, even if not used
- Sensitivity to high temperatures
- Increased cost of manufacturing (however, these costs are being reduced as research improves the technology)
- Potential for damage if completely discharged

It should be noted that battery research is extremely intensive, driven by the search for evermore energy-dense renewable energy storage systems. As new developments find their way to market, expect to see even more variations of lithium-type batteries being used in hybrid electric and battery electric vehicles.

Battery Cables and Terminals

Battery cables and terminals are designed to carry high discharge currents that are required during cranking of the automotive engine. Battery cable terminals are usually made of lead or zinc-plated brass. There are a number of designs, the most common being a cone design that provides a large surface contact area with the ability to tighten the terminal onto the battery post using a nut and bolt. The tapered cone allows easy removal of the clamp when the bolt is loosened. The larger positive and smaller negative terminals are slightly different in size to ensure correct connection of the cables when installing or servicing the battery FIGURE 31-9.

Another type of battery terminal is the side terminal. It gets its name because the battery connection is on the side of the battery. The terminal is a flat circle with a center bolt that bolts the terminal tightly to the battery connection. Side terminal batteries seem to avoid some, but not all, of the oxidation issues of a top-post battery. One shortcoming of a side terminal battery is that it is harder to get a good connection when using jumper cables or a jumper box to jump-start the vehicle. One less common battery terminal is a flat terminal with a hole through the center. The post on the battery sticks up vertically with at least one side flat and a matching hole through the post. The battery terminal butts up against the flat post, and a bolt inserted through the battery post and terminal holds them firmly together.

FIGURE 31-9 Battery terminals.

TECHNICIAN TIP

Installing a battery into a vehicle backwards instantly destroys expensive on-board electronics, as some technicians and do-it-yourself vehicle owners have unfortunately discovered.

Applied Science

AS-55: Acids/Bases: The technician can identify the effects of the pH of a solution on various systems.

A technician has replaced a heater core in a vehicle, a task that required many hours of labor due to its location. The technician filled the cooling system with the type of antifreeze recommended by the manufacturer with a 50/50 mix of distilled water. After running the engine to check for leaks, the technician used a coolant test strip to verify the proper pH level of the coolant. The test strip indicated a pH level of 10, which is in the correct range of 9.8 to 10.2 pH. Any reading below 9.0 indicates that the coolant may cause damage to the water pump, radiator, heater core, or other components. This condition is known as electrolysis.

An acid is a substance that produces hydrogen ions. A base is a substance that produces hydroxide ions. The pH scale is used to tell how acidic or base a substance is. A hand-held refractometer is a precision optical device used to measure the concentration or mix ratio of liquids. This instrument is more accurate than test strips for pH testing.

In addition to pH testing of the cooling system, brake fluid can be also checked with test strips or a refractometer. The safe range for brake fluid ranges from 7.0 to 11.5 on the pH scale. Battery electrolyte can be tested with a hydrometer or a refractometer. When a battery is discharging, the specific gravity of the electrolyte is dropping. When a battery is being charged, the situation is reversed. Electric current is forced into the battery by the vehicle's alternator or a battery charger. The specific gravity of the battery goes up as a result.

> **TECHNICIAN TIP**
>
> Corrosion from the battery can creep into and destroy a battery cable beneath the insulation and may not be visible. An engine cranking voltage drop test is the most reliable way to detect such high resistance caused by corrosion.

Battery cables are usually made of many fine strands of copper wire bound tightly together and insulated to make a cable with high current capacity. There are a number of cable sizes available to handle various current capacities. For example, a small-displacement spark-ignition engine requires far less current to crank than, for example, a high-compression diesel (compression-ignition) engine of the same displacement. Battery terminals are usually crimped or soldered onto the battery cables to ensure strong, low-resistance connections. Often, heat-shrink tubing with sealing adhesive is used over the joint to ensure it is kept clean and protected from corrosion. Battery cables should be protected from chafing or damage, and terminals should be kept clean and free of corrosion.

> **TECHNICIAN TIP**
>
> When buying battery cables or jumper cables, be careful to verify the wire size. Some wire manufacturers place very thick insulation over a small wire size, making the cable look bigger than it is. Remember, it is the size of the wire that determines current flow, not the size of the insulation.

Battery Condition

Batteries do not last forever. Over time and use, the plates start to lose effectiveness as lead paste falls off the plates and collects in the bottom of the battery case. This type of damage is especially likely to develop in a battery subjected to high vibration and shock, as when subjected to off-road travel. As plate material becomes deposited in the bottom of the battery case, it eventually shorts out the plates and renders that cell useless, which causes the battery to fail under load.

A battery may also become sulfated, meaning the surfaces of the plates harden, making it more difficult for the acid to be absorbed into the plate. As a result, the battery can no longer readily accept a charge or cannot adequately discharge under load. Leaving a battery on a slow charger overnight and then finding that it fails a load test in the morning is an indication of a sulfated battery. Sulfated batteries cannot create the necessary current flow and should be replaced and recycled.

Parasitic Draw

Parasitic draw refers to the current draw that occurs once the vehicle has been turned off and the systems have shut down. All modern vehicles have a certain minimum amount of parasitic current draw that is used by the vehicle's **keep alive memory (KAM)** circuits. KAM systems maintain memory functions and monitor systems. For example, the vehicle's theft-deterrent system is part of this parasitic current draw. Excessive parasitic draw will discharge the battery prematurely. Typically, when the ignition is switched off, the vehicle's engine stops and the vehicle systems begin to shut down, which is called "going to sleep" or "entering sleep mode." Vehicle systems will turn off at different rates and do not necessarily immediately turn off as soon as the ignition is off. For example, some vehicles may take up to a couple of hours before the last system goes to sleep and the parasitic draw reaches its minimum value. A low-amp clamp capable of measuring milliamps or an ammeter is the tool commonly used to measure parasitic draw from the battery. We will explore another option when we get to the parasitic draw skill drill SKILL DRILL 31-9. Manufacturers will specify how much parasitic draw is acceptable and the waiting period required after the ignition is switched off before the measurement can be accurately taken.

Jump Starting

Jump starting of a vehicle requires the use of a slave battery along with high-current–capacity leads made with clamps on each end that can connect over the battery terminals. The slave battery is connected in parallel from the slave (charged) battery to the host (discharged) battery to provide additional capacity to crank and start the vehicle. Jump starting should be performed with caution, as incorrect polarity or voltage spikes can cause damage to the sensitive electronic components installed on either of the vehicles. The safest way to deal with a discharged battery is to remove and charge it or replace it. If jump starting must be undertaken, make sure the slave battery is fully charged. Use jumper leads equipped with electrical spike protection. Spike-protected leads have a built-in device to prevent damaging electrical spikes from reaching electronic equipment. It is important to ensure that the leads are connected with the correct polarity to prevent damage to electronic components and to connect and disconnect leads in the correct sequence as explained in the skill drill on jump-starting a vehicle SKILL DRILL 31-7.

Safety

Never allow a spark or flame around a battery, and never try to jump-start a frozen, faulty, or open-circuit battery; doing so could cause the battery to explode, causing injury.

Battery Service Precautions

When servicing batteries, always ensure that you have the right personal protective equipment (e.g., safety eyewear, gloves, and shop clothing). Never wear any conductive jewelry, such as neck chains, watches, or rings, when working on or near batteries as they may provide an accidental short-circuit path for high currents. If the battery is being, or has been recently, charged, ensure that the space around the battery is well ventilated. Avoid making any sparks, which may ignite the gassing hydrogen–air mixture. Never create a low-resistance connection or short across the battery terminals. Always remove the negative or ground terminal first when disconnecting battery cables, as doing so reduces the possibility of a wrench creating an accidental short to ground from the positive terminal to any grounded metal surface, which would cause a very large spark.

Safety

The editor has been in the vicinity of two batteries when they blew up. One was from across the shop and sounded like a bomb going off. A student had been welding a van door when a spark from the welding ignited the hydrogen gases. Fortunately, the battery was on the opposite side of the door from where the student was working. The battery case was blown apart and acid was thrown 5 to 10 feet in all directions. Fortunately, no students were within that range. Always keep sparks away from batteries.

Battery Recycling

Batteries contain many environmentally damaging chemicals and metals. If they find their way into a landfill, the acid and metals can contaminate the soil and waterways. Correct disposal of batteries by recycling them is good for the environment, and the precious metals can be reclaimed for reuse. Many municipalities require battery recycling and levy a "core charge" on every new automotive battery sold. The core charge is refunded if an old battery is brought in and exchanged for the new one. This process helps prevent batteries from being discarded in the trash or left lying around. Check local laws and regulations to ensure that batteries are disposed of correctly.

Battery Maintenance

Batteries require regular maintenance consisting of inspection, cleaning, testing, and charging when discharged. Good times to check batteries are during oil changes and in the fall, prior to cold weather setting in, which makes the battery work harder.

Ensure the battery electrolyte level is correct by checking the markings on the case or by looking in each cell to ensure the plates are well covered **FIGURE 31-10**. Make sure the exterior case is dry and free of dirt. Dirt on top of the battery can actually cause premature self-discharge of the battery as current "leaks" across the path of dirt or grime. This mixture can become conductive and drain the battery over time. To tell if the surface of the battery needs to be cleaned, use a digital volt-ohmmeter (DVOM) set to volts to measure the voltage on the surface of the top of the battery. You can do this by placing the black lead on the negative battery post and rubbing the red lead around the top of the battery, measuring the voltage present there. Any voltage over about 0.2 volts means the battery should be cleaned with a mixture of baking soda and water, but make sure not to get any of that mixture down inside of the battery, as it will tend to neutralize the electrolyte, ruining the battery.

Keeping the battery and terminals clean is one of the best maintenance tasks for the money. The lead in the battery posts and terminals oxidizes over time. Unfortunately, lead oxide is an insulator. Therefore, if the lead surfaces of the post and terminal oxidize, the insulator effect can cause the vehicle to not crank over, stranding the driver. Lead oxide can be identified by its dark gray or black color. The only effective way of removing it is with

FIGURE 31-10 Checking battery electrolyte levels and state of charge using a hydrometer.

Applied Science

AS-56: Density/Specific Gravity: The technician can explain the role of specific gravity in determining the condition of the system.

A technician is assigned to perform a battery state-of-charge (SOC) test on an automotive battery with removable filler caps. This procedure is a specific gravity test using a battery hydrometer.

The technician would normally use an electronic battery tester for a capacitance test, but due to technical difficulties, it has to be repaired. This type of test is used often on today's vehicles but sometimes other methods are used, such as the battery hydrometer.

When working with battery electrolyte, there are important safety precautions to take. Eye protection is a must and suitable gloves should be worn while working with batteries. Clothing can be damaged as well as the vehicle's paint by battery electrolyte, which is about 36% sulfuric acid.

Observing the safety precautions, the technician uses a hydrometer to draw some electrolyte from each cell and record the information on a sheet of paper. As stated in our text, a very low overall reading of 1.150 or below indicates a low state of charge. A high overall reading of about 1.280 indicates a high state of charge. The reading from each cell should be the same. If one or two cells are .050 different from the rest, it indicates there is something wrong with the battery. See temperature corrections chart to adjust for temperature variations that are above or below 70°F (21 degrees C) for the battery electrolyte temperature.

Safety

To ensure safety when working on batteries, take the following precautions:

- Make sure the hood is secured with a hood stay rod.
- Don the appropriate personal protection equipment before starting the job. Remember that batteries contain acid; if this acid is splashed in your eyes, it can blind you or seriously damage your eyes.
- Follow the manufacturer's personal safety instructions to prevent personal injury or damage to the vehicle you are working on.

a special battery terminal scraper or wire brush, which will restore the lead to its shiny silver color **FIGURE 31-11**. Once the battery terminal is reinstalled and tightened, the terminals should be coated with a battery oxidation inhibitor spray to help slow down the oxidation process.

Batteries sometimes need to be recharged when lights are left on (a parasitic drain) or when the vehicle has not been driven for several weeks or months. Knowing how to properly diagnose and recharge a battery is an important task that you will need to become proficient with. Performing a battery state-of-charge test with a hydrometer or refractometer is a good indicator of whether the battery needs to be charged or not. Another maintenance check of the battery is the conductance test, which indicates the capacity of the battery and how much life is left in the battery.

A
B
FIGURE 31-11 **A.** Heavily oxidized battery post. **B.** Clean battery post.

Testing Battery State of Charge and Specific Gravity

While the capacitance test is the preferred test of battery condition, other tests may still be used. One of those tests is the state-of-charge test. State-of-charge testing tells us how charged or discharged a battery is, not how much capacity it has. The degree of the battery's charge is handy to know when testing starting and charging system issues, as well as just about any other electrical issue. Unfortunately, most batteries are of the low-maintenance or no-maintenance type and may not provide access to the

> **TECHNICIAN TIP**
>
> When performing a state-of-charge test, keep these tips in mind:
>
> - When filling a battery that is not fully charged, never fill it to the top of the full line, as charging the battery will raise the electrolyte level.
> - Small amounts of electrolyte in the hydrometer may leak out and damage the vehicle's paint or your clothing.
> - Do not inadvertently remove electrolyte from one cell or add it to another cell when testing; doing so will cause incorrect readings.

electrolyte in the cells for state-of-charge testing. Older batteries with removable caps may be tested for sufficient state of charge by testing the electrolyte for acid content.

Recall that the acid level drops as the battery becomes discharged. One of the most accurate ways of testing the state of charge is to use a hydrometer or refractometer to measure the specific gravity of the electrolyte in each of the battery's cells. The higher the specific gravity, the higher the percentage of acid in the electrolyte, which corresponds to a high battery state of charge.

The hydrometer's reading, unlike that of the refractometer, must be corrected for electrolyte temperature. Since the hydrometer draws electrolyte into it to raise a float, the electrolyte level must be at least slightly above the top of the plates. If it is not, then distilled water will need to be added and the battery fully charged.

A very quick indicator of battery state of charge is the open circuit voltage test. This test uses a DVOM to accurately measure the voltage of a battery that has been sitting with no charge for at least 10 minutes. The voltage reading can roughly indicate the battery state of charge. For example, 12.6 volts or above indicates a fully charged battery, 12.4 volts indicates a charge of approximately 75%, and 12.0 indicates a battery with almost no charge TABLE 31-1.

TABLE 31-1: State of Charge as Indicated by Voltage Reading

Voltage	Percentage of Charge
12.6 or greater	100
12.4–12.6	75–100
12.2–12.4	50–75
12.0–12.2	25–50
11.7–12.0	> 0–25
0.0–11.7	0 (no charge)

To perform a battery state-of-charge test, follow the steps in SKILL DRILL 31-1.

Testing Battery Conductance

When in doubt of how well a battery can meet demands placed upon it, it should be tested. The use of electronic battery testers has by and large replaced the need for hydrometer and other invasive types of battery testing. In fact, many manufacturers are now requiring the use of a conductance test instead of a high-amperage load test in order for warranty coverage to be considered FIGURE 31-12. Many of the testers have integrated printers, and for the battery to be warranted, a printout of the test result has to accompany the replaced battery.

The conductance tester sends low-frequency signals into the cells to determine the battery's ability to conduct current. The greater the ability to conduct current, the higher the CCA capacity of the battery. Since batteries deteriorate over time, their CCA capacity also deteriorates. The conductance tester is able to predict a battery's CCA capacity by measuring its conductance, which provides a near linear comparison between the two. Since conductance testing takes only a minute or two to complete, it is a good way to show customers the status of their battery and how that condition changes over time. If the conductance test shows that the battery no longer meets specifications, then customers will know that the battery is at the end of its useful life and must be replaced to avoid it failing and leaving them stranded.

Testing Battery Capacity

The load test has been used for years to test a battery's capacity and internal condition, but some manufacturers have been saying that their batteries should *not* be load tested, and instead should be conductance tested. They

GOOD, RECHARGE
MIDTRONICS
MDX-600
BI-MA

FIGURE 31-12 Conductance tester being used.

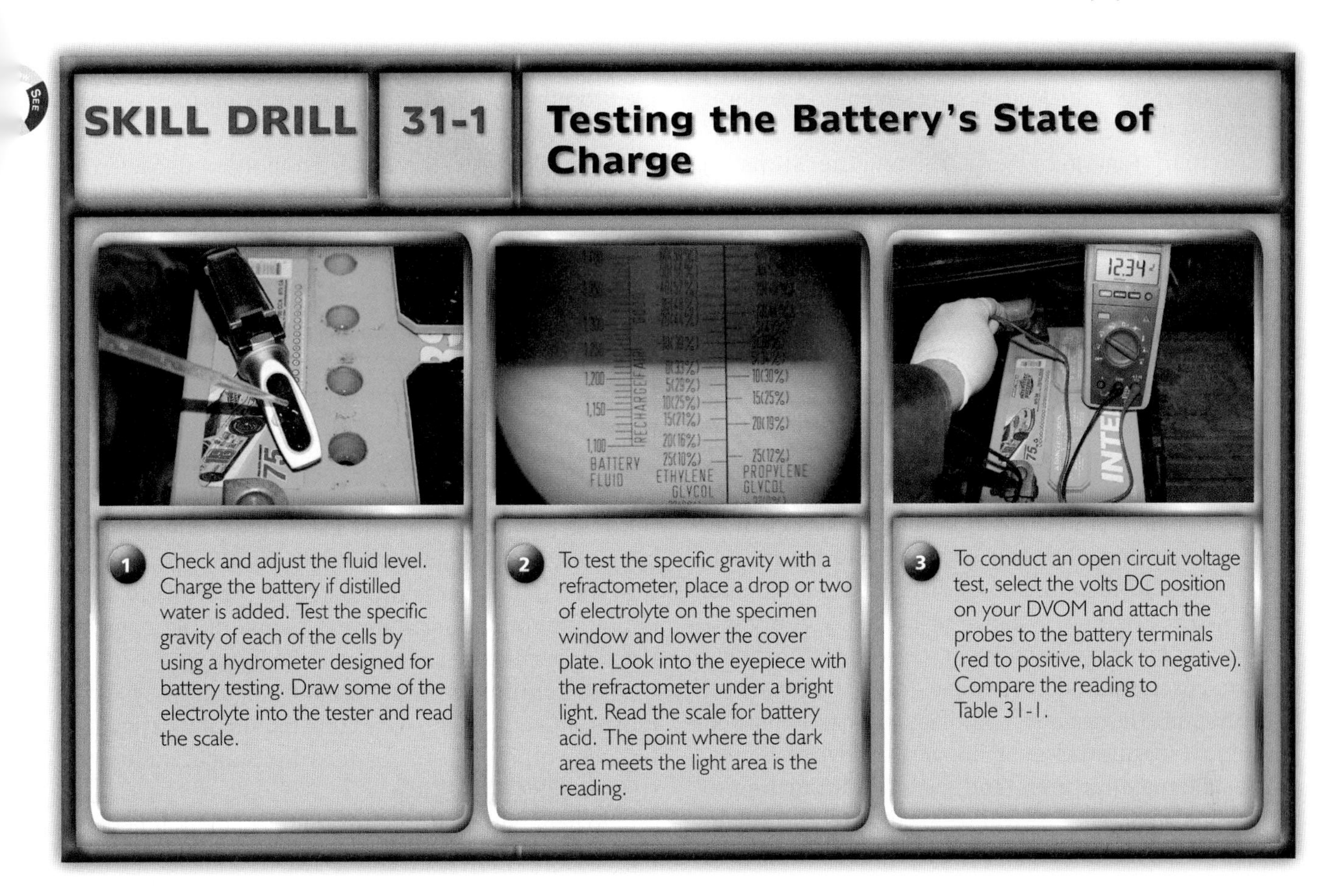

SKILL DRILL 31-1 Testing the Battery's State of Charge

1. Check and adjust the fluid level. Charge the battery if distilled water is added. Test the specific gravity of each of the cells by using a hydrometer designed for battery testing. Draw some of the electrolyte into the tester and read the scale.

2. To test the specific gravity with a refractometer, place a drop or two of electrolyte on the specimen window and lower the cover plate. Look into the eyepiece with the refractometer under a bright light. Read the scale for battery acid. The point where the dark area meets the light area is the reading.

3. To conduct an open circuit voltage test, select the volts DC position on your DVOM and attach the probes to the battery terminals (red to positive, black to negative). Compare the reading to Table 31-1.

claim that load testing can damage the battery. Therefore, always check the service information before performing a load test.

As the name suggests, the load test subjects the battery to a high rate of discharge, and the voltage is then measured after a set time to see how well the battery creates that current flow. In other words, if the battery can maintain a high rate of discharge for a specified time and the voltage is still relatively high, then you know the battery is in good shape. Conversely, if the voltage falls off fairly quickly, the battery is not in very good condition. It is kind of like two people running a mile sprint. The one who does it in 5 minutes is likely in pretty good shape. The one who takes 20 minutes is likely in poor shape. It is similar with batteries. The faster the rate at which a battery can create current flow, the higher its voltage, indicating a higher capacity. Another way to think of a load test is that we are testing the battery's ability to produce the high starting current, while maintaining enough voltage to operate the ignition and electronic control systems.

You will remember that CCAs reflect the load in amps that a battery can deliver for 30 seconds while maintaining a voltage of 7.2 volts or higher at 0°F (−18°C). Since vehicle and battery manufacturers specify the CCA rating for every vehicle and battery, that rating is used to calculate the load placed on the battery when load testing. The battery can be either in or out of the vehicle but must be at, or near, a full state of charge for the test to be accurate. The electrolyte temperature should be approximately 70°F (21°C) for the most accurate results, because a cold battery cannot produce current flow as efficiently and will show a false fail result. When load testing a battery, use the following testing parameters:

Test load = half the CCA of the battery you are testing (verify it is sized correctly for the vehicle)

Load test time = 15 seconds

Results: Pass = 9.6 volts or higher; Fail = less than 9.6 volts

If the battery fails the load test, one further test is required before condemning the battery. The battery needs to be slow charged until it is fully charged (can take up to 20 hours), then repeat the load test. If it still

TECHNICIAN TIP

Technicians used to perform a 3-minute charge test on batteries if they failed the load test. But this test is being discouraged by battery and vehicle manufacturers due to its potential of damaging the battery or vehicle. Thus, we will not discuss this test method further.

fails, the battery is sulfated and needs to be replaced. If it passes, test the vehicle's charging system to see if it is charging the battery properly.

To load test a battery, follow the steps in SKILL DRILL 31-2.

Identifying Modules that Lose Their Initialization During Battery Removal

Many electronic modules in vehicles, such as radio and driver-specific presets, require a small amount of power to maintain their KAM (memory). When the battery is disconnected from the vehicle, the memory of specific electronic systems is usually lost. For some systems this can be annoying. The PCM may lose its adaptive learning data, which means the vehicle will have to relearn this information during a period of driving that could take several days. For other systems, such as the security system, loss of memory may prevent the vehicle from being restarted or the radio from being used. At the very least, it may require the dealer or manufacturer to be contacted for vehicle-specific codes to reinitiate the vehicle systems. Check the manufacturers' and owners' information to determine what systems will be affected by the power loss. You will need to identify any system that will require security or initialization codes to be reentered, and ensure the procedure and equipment are available to reinitialize systems or modules.

In some cases, it may be possible to use a 9-volt memory minder or memory saver to maintain the vehicle's memory while the vehicle battery is disconnected. This should supply enough power to maintain the memory for small jobs such as changing the battery—provided the vehicle doors or trunk are not opened, causing the interior lights to illuminate and essentially drain the 9-volt battery. Many technicians advocate using an external 12-volt DC power supply connected to the data link control with a suitable cable. If the cigarette lighter socket is always powered on, this too can be used for supplying power to the vehicle while the battery cables and connectors are being serviced. Just remember that providing power back into the circuit makes the system susceptible to short circuits by providing a ground to any of the powered wires or terminals.

To identify electronic modules, security systems, radios, and other accessories that require reinitialization or code entry following battery disconnect, follow the steps in SKILL DRILL 31-3.

To maintain or restore electronic memory functions, follow the steps in SKILL DRILL 31-4.

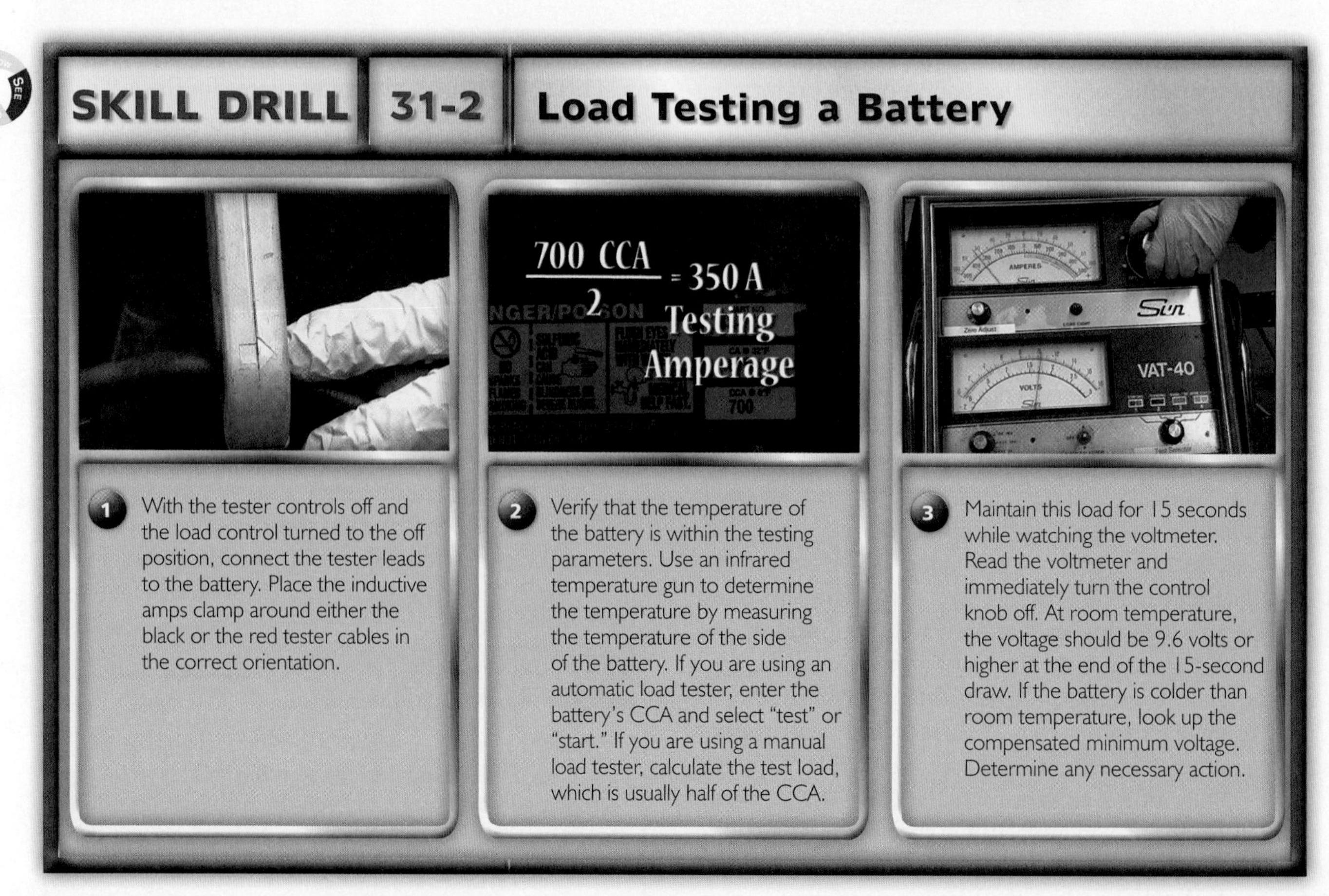
SKILL DRILL 31-2 Load Testing a Battery
700 CCA / 2 = 350 A
Testing Amperage
VAT-40
1 With the tester controls off and the load control turned to the off position, connect the tester leads to the battery. Place the inductive amps clamp around either the black or the red tester cables in the correct orientation.
2 Verify that the temperature of the battery is within the testing parameters. Use an infrared temperature gun to determine the temperature by measuring the temperature of the side of the battery. If you are using an automatic load tester, enter the battery's CCA and select "test" or "start." If you are using a manual load tester, calculate the test load, which is usually half of the CCA.
3 Maintain this load for 15 seconds while watching the voltmeter. Read the voltmeter and immediately turn the control knob off. At room temperature, the voltage should be 9.6 volts or higher at the end of the 15-second draw. If the battery is colder than room temperature, look up the compensated minimum voltage. Determine any necessary action.

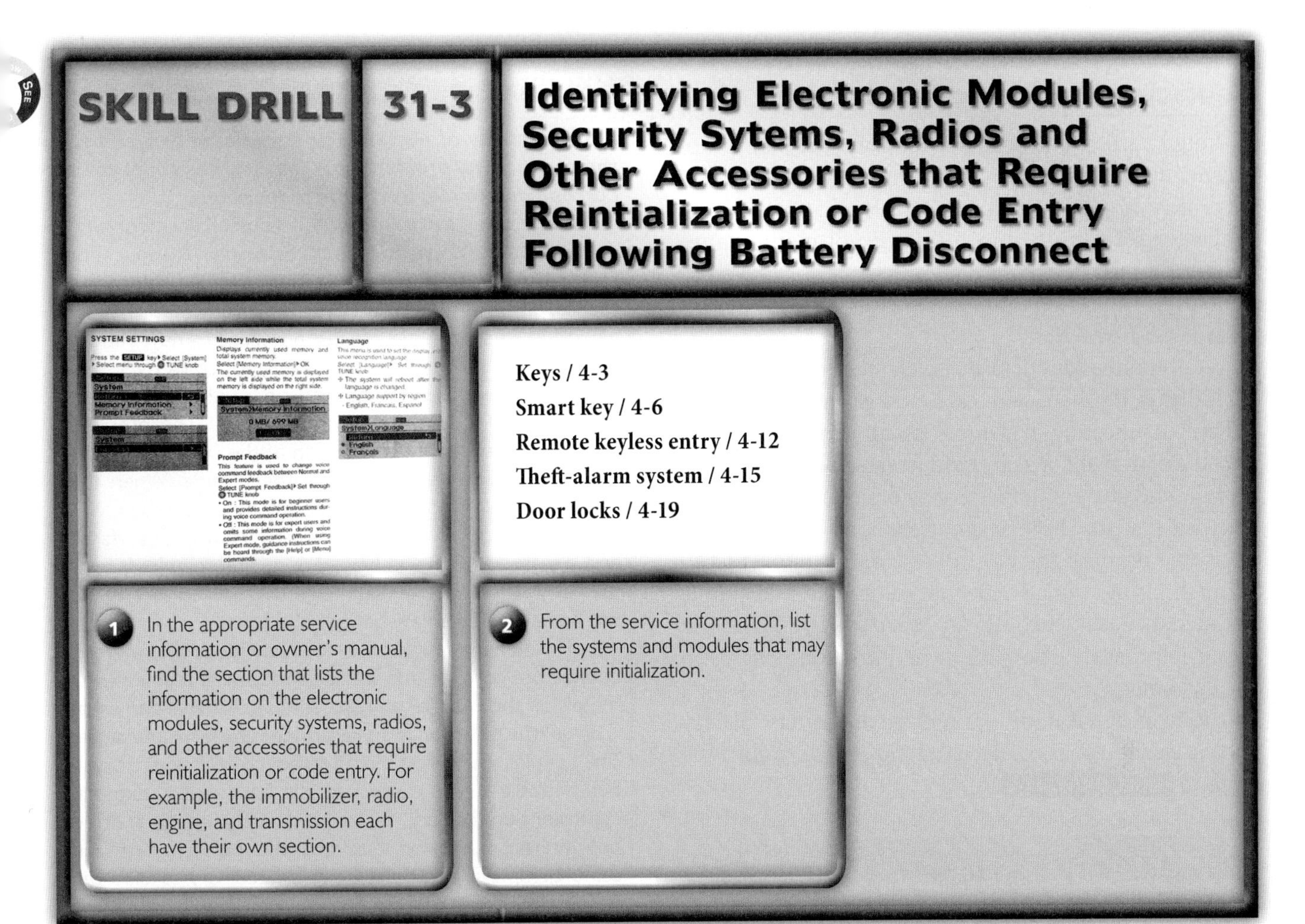
SKILL DRILL 31-3
Identifying Electronic Modules, Security Sytems, Radios and Other Accessories that Require Reintialization or Code Entry Following Battery Disconnect
Keys / 4-3
Smart key / 4-6
Remote keyless entry / 4-12
Theft-alarm system / 4-15
Door locks / 4-19
1 In the appropriate service information or owner's manual, find the section that lists the information on the electronic modules, security systems, radios, and other accessories that require reinitialization or code entry. For example, the immobilizer, radio, engine, and transmission each have their own section.
2 From the service information, list the systems and modules that may require initialization.

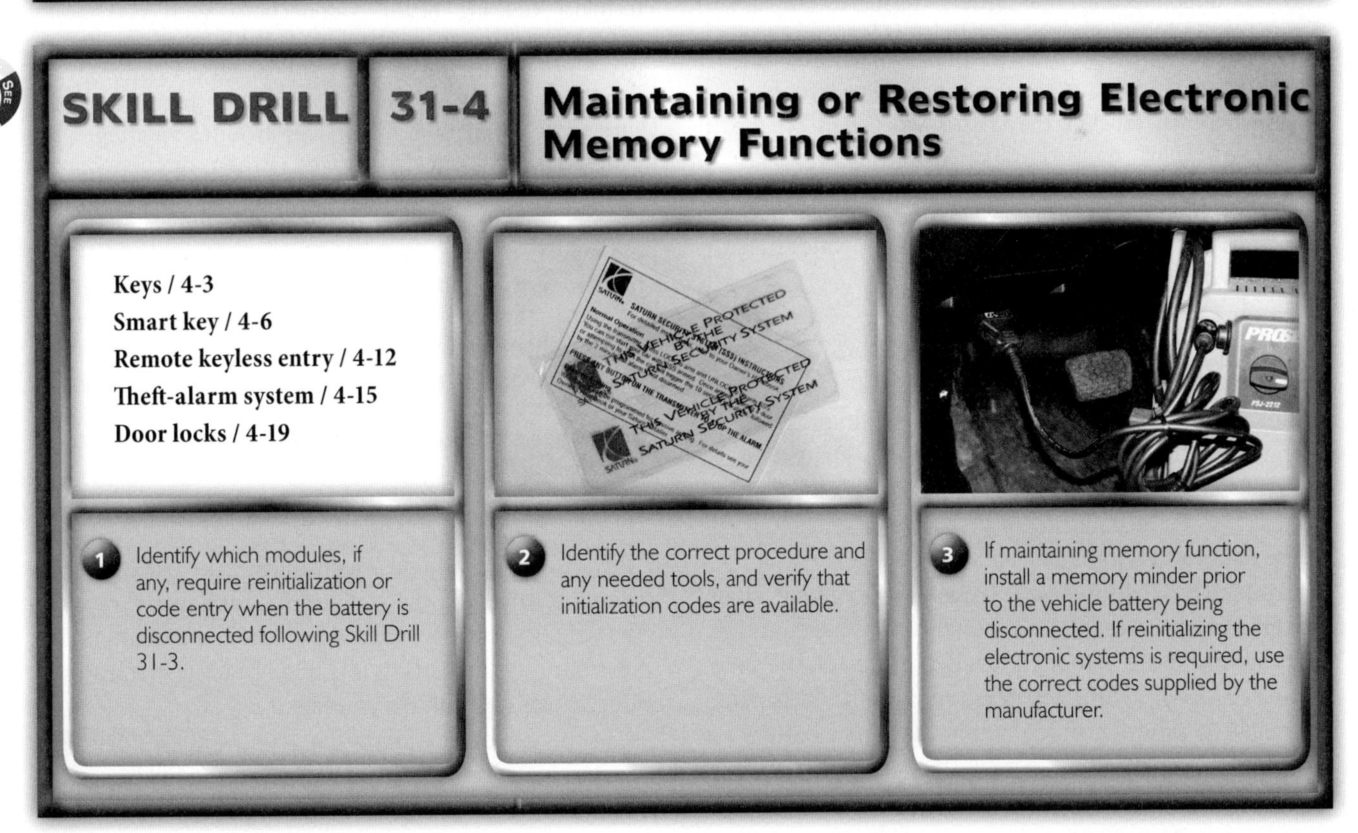
SKILL DRILL 31-4
Maintaining or Restoring Electronic Memory Functions
Keys / 4-3
Smart key / 4-6
Remote keyless entry / 4-12
Theft-alarm system / 4-15
Door locks / 4-19
1 Identify which modules, if any, require reinitialization or code entry when the battery is disconnected following Skill Drill 31-3.
2 Identify the correct procedure and any needed tools, and verify that initialization codes are available.
3 If maintaining memory function, install a memory minder prior to the vehicle battery being disconnected. If reinitializing the electronic systems is required, use the correct codes supplied by the manufacturer.

Inspecting, Cleaning, Filling, and Replacing the Battery and Cables

As noted earlier, batteries last longer if they are properly maintained. In fact, one of the most common causes of vehicle no-starts is dirty/corroded battery cables. Inspecting, cleaning, and filling (if not maintenance free) are common tasks that should be performed every 6 months to 1 year on top-post batteries, and 1 to 2 years on side-post batteries.

Automotive batteries can look lighter than they really are. Always lift them with care, and get help if needed. When reconnecting the battery, be sure you do not connect the battery incorrectly (with reverse polarity); doing so will send current in the reverse direction through the electrical system. The reverse current flow will likely damage some or all of the electronic control units (ECUs) throughout the vehicle. So what started out as a simple maintenance task becomes an expensive diagnosis and repair job that the shop has to perform at no charge to the customer.

To inspect, clean, fill, or replace the battery, battery cables, clamps, connectors, and hold-downs, follow the steps in SKILL DRILL 31-5.

Safety

When disconnecting the battery terminals, always remove the negative terminal completely first and install the negative terminal only after the positive terminal is fully tightened. Once the negative terminal is removed, if the wrench touches the chassis when it is on the positive terminal, no spark will be created because there is no path back to the negative terminal. You still need to be careful that the wrench does not bridge straight from the positive battery terminal to the negative battery terminal, as that would cause a huge spark.

Charging the Battery

Vehicle batteries may become discharged and require charging particularly if the vehicle has been sitting idle without starting for more than a couple of weeks or if the charging system is faulty. Ideally a battery is fully charged before being tested for faults. Battery state of charge can be determined by a battery tester. If charging is needed, slow charging is less stressful on a battery than fast charging is. It can take more than 20 hours depending on the state of charge. Some manufacturers recommend removing the negative battery terminal while charging a battery to reduce risk to the vehicle's electronics. If the battery needs to be disconnected during charging, remember to verify if the vehicle's adaptive memory needs to be maintained. After charging the battery, it is good practice to clean the battery posts and cable terminals.

To charge a battery, follow the steps in SKILL DRILL 31-6.

Applied Science

AS-74: Activity of Metals: The technician can explain the conductivity problems in a circuit when connectors corrode due to electrochemical reactions.

A dealership technician has a do-it-yourself neighbor who enjoys working on vehicles in his driveway. The neighbor has questions from time to time for the professional technician. The do-it-yourselfer is restoring a fairly old vehicle in his spare time. He just purchased a new battery and a new starter, but the engine will not crank over. The technician demonstrated how to do a voltage drop test using a DVOM (digital volt-ohm meter). The problem was in a battery cable connection at the starter solenoid mounted on the fender well of the vehicle. When the cable end was removed from the solenoid, corrosion was found. After removing the corrosion from both surfaces and reattaching the cable, the engine cranked over properly. The do-it-yourself neighbor realized that he did not actually need a new battery and starter.

This is an example of a conductivity problem when connectors corrode due to electrochemical reactions. All metals on the vehicle can rust. Battery terminal corrosion is one of the main concerns regarding vehicle maintenance. The terminal corrosion can be removed with a wire brush but periodic maintenance will still be needed. External corrosion on battery terminals is very easily spotted but internal corrosion between the battery post and cable clamp will not be seen. It is necessary to take the connection apart and clean each surface with a battery terminal cleaning brush. Connections with corrosion problems will increase resistance at the battery terminals, which will reduce the voltage to the electrical system.

When working with automotive batteries, be sure to keep safety in mind. This includes wearing eye protection and suitable gloves. When disconnecting battery cables, there is a definite order to follow. As stated in our text, always remove the cable clamp from the negative terminal first. The negative terminal is marked with a minus sign. Then remove the positive terminal, the one with the plus sign. You will later replace them in reverse order, positive cable first, and then the negative cable. While they are disconnected, bend the cables back, or if necessary, tie them out of the way, so that they cannot fall back and touch the terminals accidentally.

SKILL DRILL 31-5 Inspecting, Cleaning, Filling, and Replacing the Battery and Cables

1. Remove the cable clamp from the negative terminal first. Then remove the positive terminal. Bend the cables back out of the way so that they cannot fall back and touch the battery terminals accidentally.

2. Remove the battery hold-downs or other hardware securing the battery.

3. Keeping it upright, remove the battery from its tray and place it on a clean work surface. Inspect the battery for damage.

NAPA POWER

4. Measure the voltage on the top of the battery with a DVOM. Place the black lead on the negative post and move the red lead across the top of the battery until you find the highest reading.

POWER

5. Carefully clean the battery case and the battery tray.

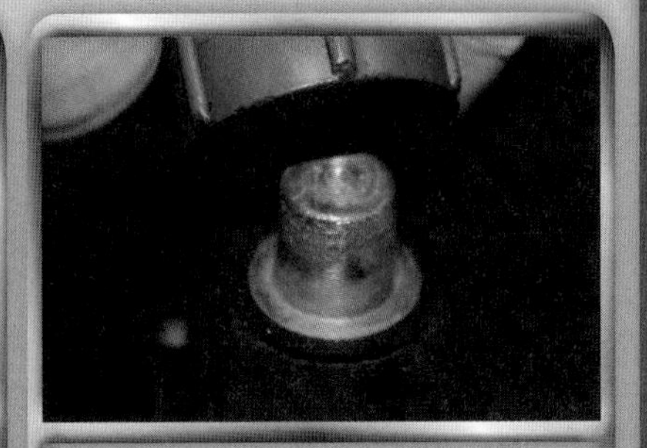

6. Clean the battery posts with a battery terminal tool. Clean the cable terminals with the same battery terminal tool. Examine the battery cables for fraying or corrosion.

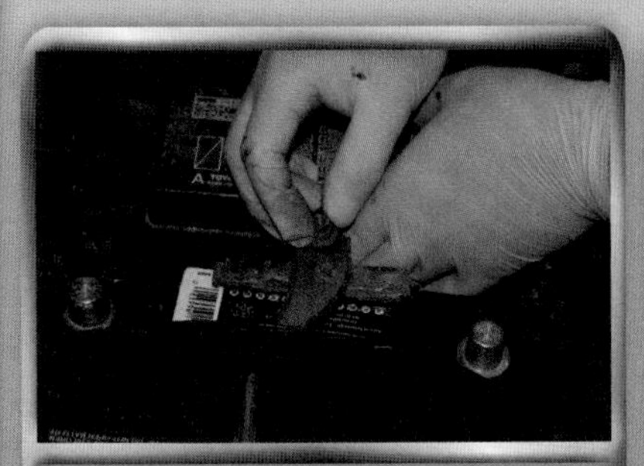

7. Reinstall the cleaned and serviced battery. Replace the hold-downs and make sure the battery is securely held in positions. If installing a new battery, ensure that it meets the original manufacturer's specifications.

8. Reconnect the positive battery terminal and tighten it in place. Once the positive terminal is finished, reconnect the negative terminal and tighten it.

9. Coat the terminal connections with anti-corrosive paste or spray to keep oxygen from the terminal connections. Test that you have a good electrical connection by starting the vehicle.

SKILL DRILL 31-6 Charging a Battery

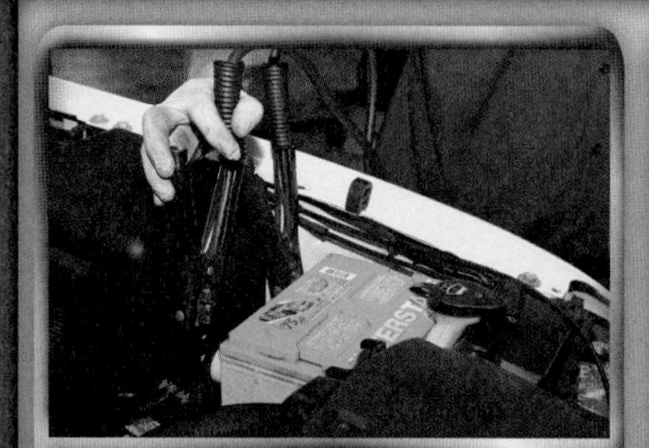

1. Verify whether the battery needs to be disconnected during charging and, if so, whether the adaptive memory needs to be maintained. Inspect the battery casing and ensure that the battery has not been frozen. Verify that the charger is unplugged and off. Connect the red lead to the positive terminal and the black lead to the negative terminal.

6 VOLT
12 VOLT
OFF
DC AMPERES

2. Turn the charger on to a slow, automatic charge.

STATE OF HEALTH

3. Once the battery is charged, turn the charger off. Allow the battery to stand for at least 5 minutes before testing the battery. Using a capacitance tester, load tester, refractometer, or hydrometer, test the charged state of the battery.

Applied Science

AS-72: Voltage: The technician can demonstrate an understanding of and explain system voltage generation, uses, and characteristics.

Voltage generation in the majority of modern automotive applications relies on an engine-driven alternator. Using the principle of electromagnetic induction, alternators generate alternating current (AC) electricity through the use of a moving magnet within a coil of wire. AC electricity needs to be converted to direct current (DC) before being used in automotive systems or stored in a battery. The AC electricity is "rectified," or converted to DC, by being passed through a bridge of diodes mounted in the alternator. Diodes are small solid-state devices that allow current flow in only one direction. The resulting DC electricity can be used to power various vehicle systems, including processing modules, electric motors, and lights, and can also be used to charge the vehicle's battery.

Generators, which produce DC electricity, were once commonly used in automotive applications but were replaced by alternators when small, inexpensive diodes became available. Alternators are more practical, simpler to produce, and less maintenance-intensive.

Applied Science

AS-64: Motors: The technician can demonstrate an understanding of the role of the generator/alternator in maintaining battery and system voltage.

A vehicle is in the shop for an illuminated battery light on the instrument panel. The repair order states that the customer had to jump-start the vehicle in order to drive it to the shop. An apprentice technician has been given the job of diagnosing this vehicle with the help of an experienced technician, if required. The apprentice starts by verifying the customer's concerns and finds the vehicle once again requires a jump start. When the engine starts, the battery light on the dash remains on. Checking under the hood, the apprentice finds what appears to be a new battery. Reading further on the repair order, the customer states that he replaced the battery two days ago. The apprentice connects his DVOM (digital volt-ohm meter) and obtains a reading of 10.2 volts. It is obvious to the apprentice that the alternator is not charging at all. The experienced technician performs a voltage drop test and agrees that a new or remanufactured alternator should be installed.

As stated in our text, the alternator converts mechanical energy into electrical energy by electro-magnetic induction. In a simple version, a bar magnet rotates in an iron yoke, which concentrates the magnetic field. A coil of wire is wound around the stem of the yoke. As the magnet turns, voltage is induced in the coil, producing a current flow. A typical charging voltage will be from 13.8 to 14.2 volts DC, which will keep the battery fully charged at 12.6 volts at 70°F (21degrees C).

Jump-Starting the Vehicle

Before attempting to jump-start a vehicle, you need to make sure the battery is not frozen. You cannot jump-start a frozen battery. Before you disconnect the service battery from the discharged battery, it is good practice to place a load across the discharged battery, such as turning on the headlamps, to absorb any sudden rise in voltage that may occur as the alternator suddenly increases its output. There are many sensitive electronic devices in most modern vehicles that are very susceptible to voltage surges. One method of reducing the risk of damage to such devices is using jumper leads that have a built-in surge protector. Separate surge protector devices can also be used to reduce the possibility of such surges and voltage spikes.

An option that is less risky when jump-starting a vehicle is the use of a jump box. A jump box does not involve a charging system, which lessens the risk of voltage spikes. This device contains a relatively large battery and has short cables and spring-loaded clamps attached to it that can be connected directly to the dead battery. It may produce enough electrical energy to start the vehicle.

Another risk is overheating and damaging the vehicle's alternator. With all of the electrical draws on the vehicle, today's alternators work harder than ever. Adding the job of fully recharging the battery on top of the regular electrical loads can push an alternator into the danger zone. Because of the risk of damaging the electronics and alternator, many manufacturers (and tow companies) are now refusing to jump-start newer vehicles or authorize that practice. They now recommend either externally charging the battery or replacing the battery with a charged battery.

To jump-start a vehicle, follow the steps in SKILL DRILL 31-7.

SKILL DRILL 31-7 Jump-Starting a Vehicle
1 Position the vehicle with the charged battery close to the vehicle with the discharged battery, but not touching. Connect the red or orange lead to the positive terminal of the discharged battery.
2 Connect the other end of this red or orange lead to the positive terminal of the charged battery.
3 Connect the black lead to the negative terminal of the charged battery.

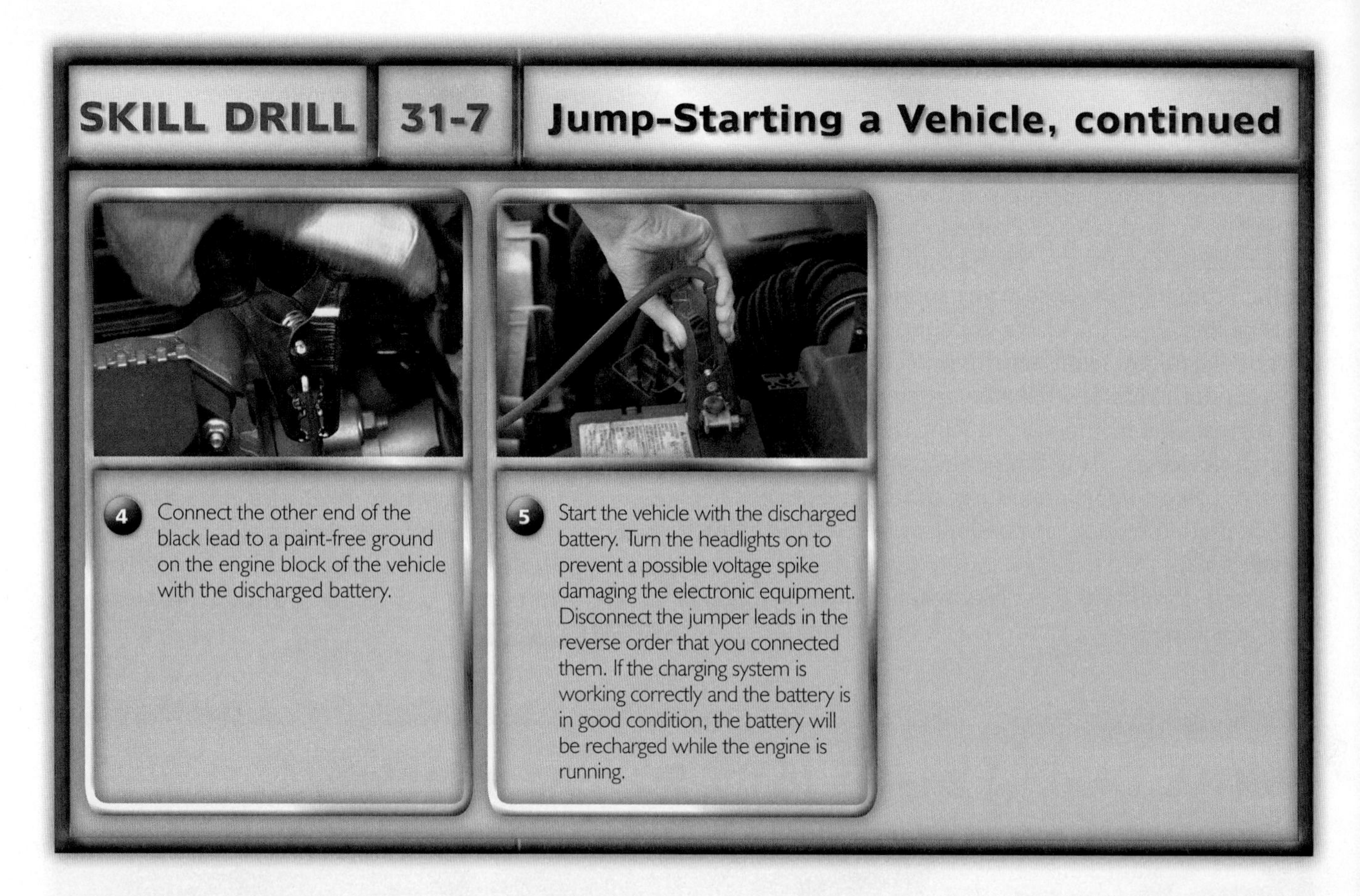
SKILL DRILL 31-7 Jump-Starting a Vehicle, continued
4 Connect the other end of the black lead to a paint-free ground on the engine block of the vehicle with the discharged battery.
5 Start the vehicle with the discharged battery. Turn the headlights on to prevent a possible voltage spike damaging the electronic equipment. Disconnect the jumper leads in the reverse order that you connected them. If the charging system is working correctly and the battery is in good condition, the battery will be recharged while the engine is running.

Measuring Parasitic Draw

All modern vehicles have a small amount of current draw when the ignition is turned off. This charge is used to run some of the vehicle systems, such as the security system and radio memory. The vehicle computer systems also require a small amount of power to maintain the computer memory while the vehicle is off. The parasitic current draw should be a relatively small amount of current, since excessive draw will discharge the battery over a short amount of time.

Parasitic current draw does not necessarily immediately drop to its lowest level the instant the ignition is turned off. This usually occurs over a period of time as various systems go into hibernation or sleep mode, which can take up to a few hours. Consult the manufacturer's service information to determine the maximum allowable parasitic current draw and the time period, after the ignition is turned off, and the time it takes the modules to go to sleep.

Parasitic current draw can be measured in several ways, the most common being the process of using an ammeter capable of measuring milliamps and inserting it in series between the battery post and the battery terminal. The ammeter is usually put in series with the negative battery lead. If the vehicle is equipped with systems or modules that will require electronic memory to be maintained, follow the procedure for identifying modules that lose their initialization during battery removal and maintain or restore electronic memory functions. Note that the timers may reset during the process of disconnecting the battery terminal and connecting the ammeter in series, so you may have to wait for the timers to go back to sleep. If excessive parasitic draw is measured, disconnect fuses or systems one at a time while monitoring parasitic current draw to determine the systems causing excessive draw.

Disconnecting the battery can be avoided if a sensitive low-current (i.e., milliamps) clamp is available. The low-amp **current clamp** measures the magnetic field generated by a very small current flow through a wire or cable. Placing the low-amp current clamp around the negative battery cable will allow you to measure the parasitic draw. If excessive parasitic draw is measured, disconnect fuses or systems one at a time while monitoring parasitic current draw to determine the systems causing the excessive draw.

The last way to measure a parasitic draw is a bit controversial, but it is well worth trying out since it can save a lot of time and requires no special tools other than a DVOM. It is named the Chesney parasitic load test after its creator, Sean Chesney. Instead of using an ammeter to measure the draw, an ohmmeter is used. Before doing anything, set the ohmmeter to ohms (the lowest scale), touch the meter leads together, and read the screen. The reading is the resistance of the meter leads and is called the "delta" value, which is the meter's true zero when used with those leads. Typically an ohmmeter will read about 0.1 ohms when the leads are touched together. Remember this number for later. Some meters have a delta feature that recalibrates the ohmmeter to zero when the leads are placed together and the delta button is pushed. If your meter has this delta feature, you can use it so that you will not have to remember the delta reading.

Next, with the battery terminals still connected to the battery, place the black lead on the negative post of the battery and the red lead on an unpainted surface of the alternator housing. Read the ohmmeter and subtract the delta value from the reading. This reading corresponds to the relative parasitic draw on the system.

Through testing, Chesney found that a draw of about 35 milliamps equaled an ohm reading of about 0.3 ohms delta (above the delta value) on a DVOM with 10 megohms of impedance, and about 0.6 ohms delta on a DVOM with 20 megohms of impedance FIGURE 31-13. Anything above those readings indicates an excessive parasitic draw. You may be skeptical of this method, so go out and try it on any vehicle. Simulate a parasitic draw by opening the driver's door, which illuminates the dome light, and watch the ohmmeter. It went up, right? Close the door. As soon as the light went off, the ohmmeter reading went back down, right? If you use this test and find an excessive draw, you can pull fuses one at a time, watching for the ohmmeter reading to decrease. If it does not decrease after removing all of the fuses, suspect an unfused circuit such as the alternator diodes or the ignition circuit on some vehicles.

To measure parasitic draw with a standard parasitic load test, follow the steps in SKILL DRILL 31-8.

To measure parasitic draw with a Chesney parasitic load test, follow the steps in SKILL DRILL 31-9.

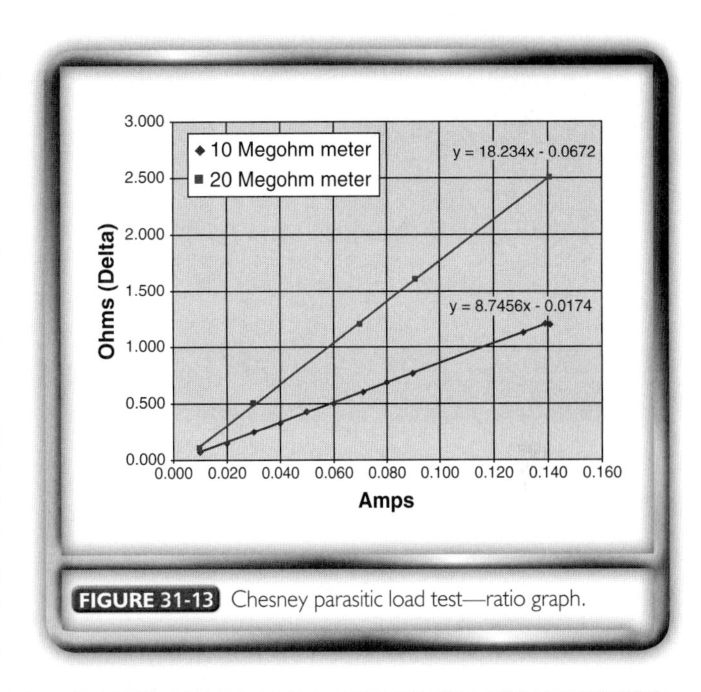
3.000
2.500
2.000
1.500
1.000
0.500
0.000
Ohms (Delta)
◆ 10 Megohm meter
■ 20 Megohm meter
y = 18.234x - 0.0672
y = 8.7456x - 0.0174
0.000 0.020 0.040 0.060 0.080 0.100 0.120 0.140 0.160
Amps

FIGURE 31-13 Chesney parasitic load test—ratio graph.

SKILL DRILL 31-8 Measuring Parasitic Draw—Standard Test

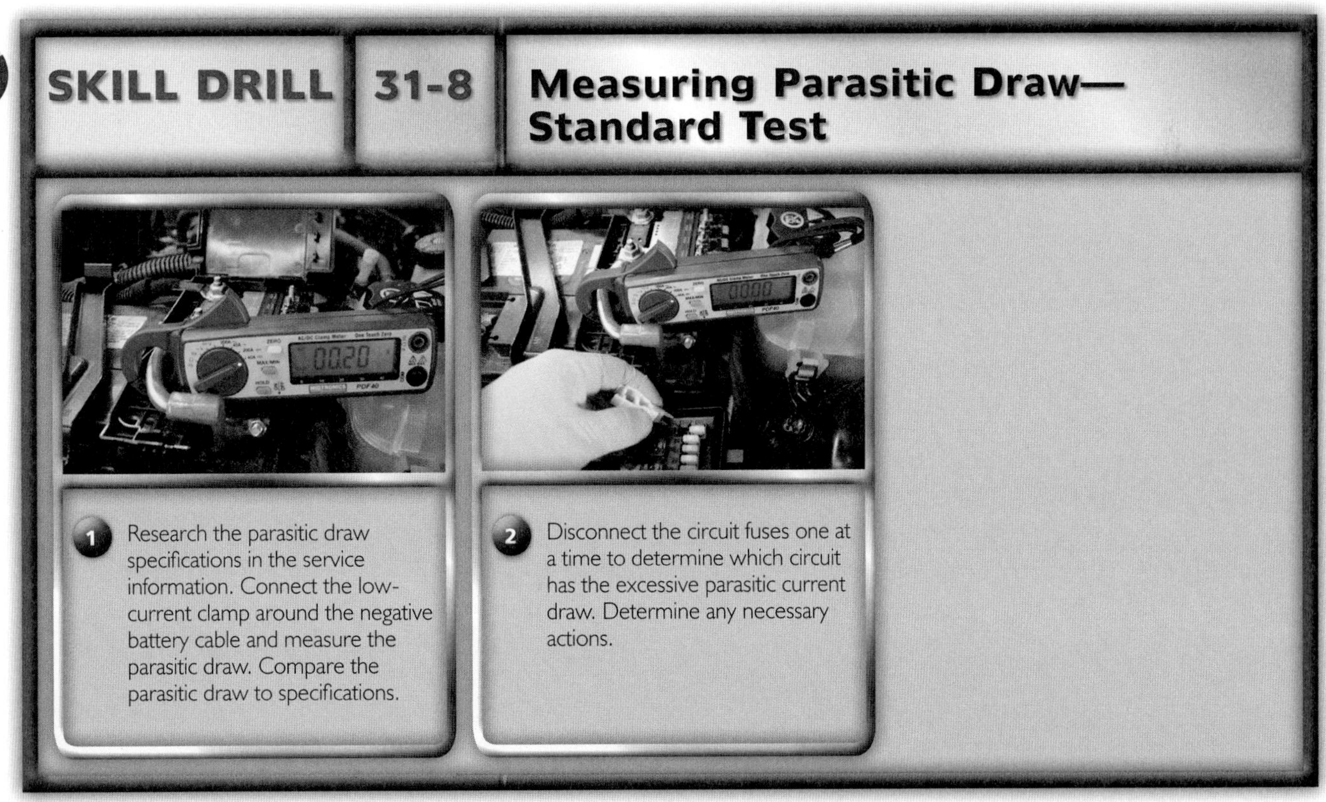

1. Research the parasitic draw specifications in the service information. Connect the low-current clamp around the negative battery cable and measure the parasitic draw. Compare the parasitic draw to specifications.

2. Disconnect the circuit fuses one at a time to determine which circuit has the excessive parasitic current draw. Determine any necessary actions.

Prove
Know
See
Do

SKILL DRILL 31-9 Measuring Parasitic Draw—Chesney Parasitic Load Test

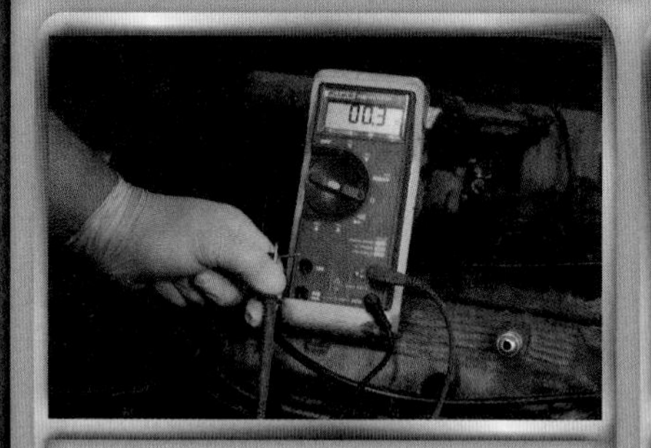

1. Set the DVOM to read ohms (lowest scale if available). Connect the leads together and read the meter screen. This is the meter's delta reading.

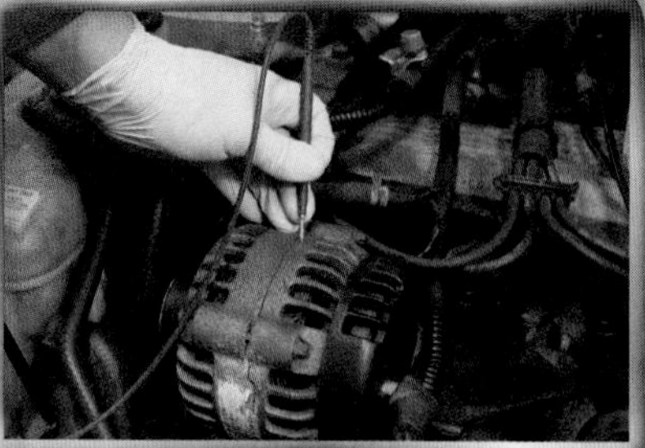

2. Place the black meter lead on the negative battery post and the red lead on the alternator case.

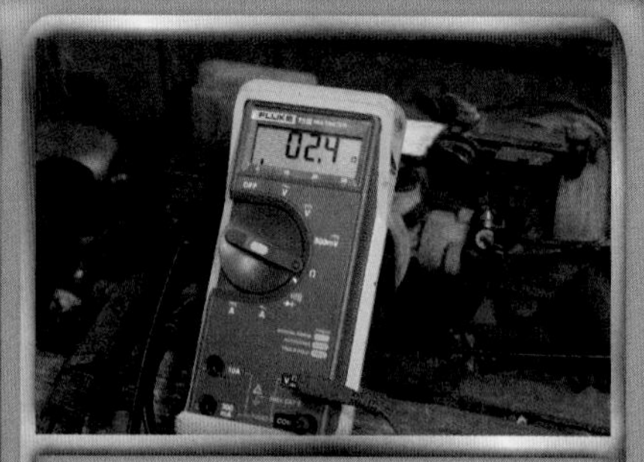

3. Read the meter and compare the reading to the Chesney parasitic load ratio graph. If there is excessive parasitic load, pull fuses one at a time to identify the faulty circuit.

Wrap-up

Ready for Review

- The primary components of the battery are the case, cover, vent caps, plates, separators, electrolyte, and terminals.
- Batteries operate by storing electrical energy in chemical form.
- The discharge of electrolytes produces battery current.
- The standard automotive battery has 2.1 volts per cell, with six cells holding 12.6 volts on a fully charged battery.
- Batteries are classified into groups, and only certain groups and layouts will fit certain vehicle applications.
- Batteries are rated by electrical capacity, cold cranking amps, and amp hour ratings.
- There are two chemicals that make the battery a safety hazard: hydrogen gas and sulfuric acid.
- The absorbed-glass mat battery is good for rough handling and can be mounted on its side compared to the electrolyte battery.
- Battery temperature plays a critical part in battery life. When a battery is cold, it takes more power to start the vehicle; when a battery is to hot, its life is diminished significantly.
- Lithium-ion batteries are the future and are especially being used in hybrids. However, they have not replaced the conventional battery in most applications.
- There are two ways to connect the battery to the vehicle: the top-post design and the side-post design.
- Batteries must be kept free of corrosion, as corrosion is the fastest way to destroy a battery and cable.
- If a vehicle seems to have a dead battery after sitting, the battery needs to be checked for parasitic draw.
- Jump-starting a vehicle is one of the simplest automotive tasks to perform, but done incorrectly, it can cause battery and possible vehicle damage. Always ensure the proper polarity when connecting the dead and good batteries together.
- When servicing a battery, always wear the proper personal protective equipment.
- Battery maintenance requires inspecting, cleaning, testing, and charging. Always follow all applicable technical data when performing battery maintenance.
- Batteries need to be recycled once their life cycle is used up. They contain hazardous materials that cannot be put in a landfill.
- The best way to test a battery's capacity and internal condition is through a battery load test.

Key Terms

absorbed glass mat A type of lead-acid battery.

battery terminal configuration The placement of positive and negative battery terminals.

cold cranking amps (CCA) A standard for rating the ability of a vehicle battery to supply high current under cold operating conditions.

cranking amps (CA) A standard similar to CCA, but that measures the battery's function at a higher temperature—32°F (0°C)

current clamp A device that clamps araound a conductor to measure current flow. It is often used in conjunction with a DVOM.

electrical capacity The ability of a circuit or component to carry electrical loads.

electrolyte The liquid in lead-acid battery cells. It is a mixture of about 67% water and 33% sulfuric acid.

gassing The escape of gas from the battery.

keep alive memory (KAM) A certain minimum amount of parasitic current draw that is used by the vehicle's circuits to maintain memory functions and monitor systems.

parasitic draw Unwanted drain on the vehicle battery when the vehicle is off.

reserve capacity A standard used to specify the time in minutes that a battery will supply a load of 25 amps at 80°F (27°C) without its voltage dropping below 10.5 volts.

thermal runaway A cycle during battery charging in which heating lowers resistance, which in turn increases current flow, which in turn further increases heat created. During this cycle, dangerous gases may build up, creating the potential for an explosion or damage through excessive current flow.

ASE-Type Questions

1. Tech A says that a battery stores electrical energy in chemical form. Tech B says that a battery creates direct current. Who is correct?
   a. Tech A
   b. Tech B
   c. Both A and B
   d. Neither A nor B
2. Tech A says that a 12-volt battery has six cells. Tech B says that the more plates a cell in a battery has, the more voltage it creates. Who is correct?
   a. Tech A
   b. Tech B
   c. Both A and B
   d. Neither A nor B
3. Tech A says that a parasitic draw is measured in volts. Tech B says that pulling fuses one at a time can help locate a parasitic draw. Who is correct?
   a. Tech A
   b. Tech B
   c. Both A and B
   d. Neither A nor B
4. Tech A says that when disconnecting the battery, the negative terminal should be disconnected first. Tech B says that baking soda and water will remove oxidation from battery terminals. Who is correct?
   a. Tech A
   b. Tech B
   c. Both A and B
   d. Neither A nor B
5. Tech A says that checking the specific gravity will indicate the battery's cold cranking amps. Tech B says that a battery load test should be performed when the battery is heavily discharged. Who is correct?
   a. Tech A
   b. Tech B
   c. Both A and B
   d. Neither A nor B
6. Tech A says that before attempting to jump-start a vehicle, you need to make sure the battery is not frozen. Tech B says that it is good practice to place a load across the discharged battery, such as turning on the headlamps, to absorb any sudden rise in voltag.e Who is correct?
   a. Tech A
   b. Tech B
   c. Both A and B
   d. Neither A nor B
7. Tech A says that there is an additional method to measure a parasitic draw using a DVOM. Tech B says that the method is known as the Chesney parasitic load test after its creator, Sean Chesney. Who is correct?
   a. Tech A
   b. Tech B
   c. Both A and B
   d. Neither A nor B
8. Tech A says that a thermal runaway can occur during battery charging in which heating increases resistance and decreases the potential for an explosion or damage through excessive current flow. Tech B says that a thermal runaway can occur during battery charging in which heating lowers resistance and increases the potential for an explosion or damage through excessive current. Who is correct?
   a. Tech A
   b. Tech B
   c. Both A and B
   d. Neither A nor B
9. Tech A says that some manufacturers recommend removing the negative battery terminal while charging a battery to reduce risk to the vehicle's electronics. Tech B says that this is not necessary since all the electronics are protected. Who is correct?
   a. Tech A
   b. Tech B
   c. Both A and B
   d. Neither A nor B
10. Tech A says that a cold cranking amps (CCA) ratings are a standard for determining the ability of a vehicle battery to supply high current under cold operating conditions. Tech B says that cranking amps (CA) is similar to CCA, but measures the battery's function at a higher temperature—32°F (0°C). Who is correct?
    a. Tech A
    b. Tech B
    c. Both A and B
    d. Neither A nor B

CHAPTER 32

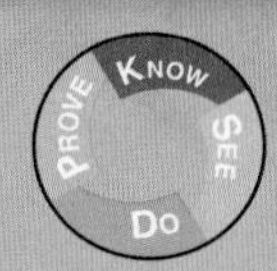
Know
See
Do
Prove

NATEF Tasks

Electrical/Electronic Systems

Starting Systems			Page
■ Perform starter current draw test; determine necessary action.	MLR	AST	925–926
■ Perform starter circuit voltage drop tests; determine necessary action.	MLR	AST	925–926
■ Inspect and test switches, connectors, and wires of starter control circuits; determine necessary action.	MLR	AST	927
■ Inspect and test starter relays and solenoids; determine necessary action.	MLR	AST	927–930
■ Remove and install starter in a vehicle.	MLR	AST	930
■ Differentiate between electrical and engine mechanical problems that cause a slow-crank or no-crank condition.	MLR	AST	930–931
Charging System			
■ Perform charging system output test; determine necessary action.	MLR	AST	937–938
■ Perform charging circuit voltage drop tests; determine necessary action.	MLR	AST	937–938
■ Inspect, adjust, or replace generator (alternator) drive belts, check pulleys, and tensioners for wear; check pulley and belt alignment.	MLR	AST	939–940
■ Remove, inspect, and reinstall generator (alternator).	MLR	AST	939–940
■ Diagnose (troubleshoot) charging system for cause of undercharge, no-charge, or overcharge conditions.		AST	939–940

Starting and Charging Systems

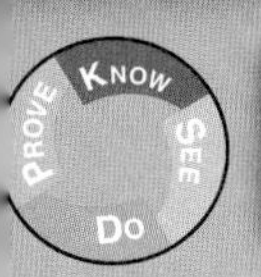
KNOW
SEE
DO
PROVE

Knowledge Objectives

After reading this chapter, you will be able to:
1. Explain the operation of the starting system and its components. (pp 916–925)
2. Explain the operation of the charging system and its components. (pp 932–937)

KNOW
SEE
DO
PROVE

Skills Objectives

After reading this chapter, you will be able to:
1. Test the starter draw and the starter circuit voltage drop. (pp 925–926)
2. Inspect and test the starter control circuit, relays, and solenoids. (pp 927–930)
3. Remove and install a starter in a vehicle. (pp 930–931)
4. Perform a charging system output test and a charging circuit voltage drop test. (pp 937–938)
5. Replace an alternator. (pp 939–940)

Introduction

The starting system provides a method of rotating (cranking) the vehicle's internal combustion engine (ICE) to begin the combustion cycle. In early vehicles, this was done by the use of a hand-crank handle. Modern vehicles use an electric starter motor that draws its electrical power from the vehicle's battery. The starter is designed to work for short periods of time and must crank the engine at sufficient speed in order for it to start. Modern starting systems are very effective provided that they, and the battery, are well maintained.

Engine Starting (Cranking) Systems

The starting/cranking system consists of the battery, high- and low-amperage wires, a solenoid, a starter motor assembly ring gear, and the ignition switch. On PCM-activated starting systems, there is also the PCM, a relay, and all of the related sensors that feed information to the PCM. A control circuit determines when and if the cranking circuit will function.

The control circuit starts sometimes with a fuse, the ignition switch (or PCM circuitry), the starter relay, a safety switch, and/or a combination relay/starter solenoid. All vehicles equipped with an automatic transmission use a neutral safety switch or a similar device, and many vehicles equipped with a manual transmission have a clutch safety switch.

An on-board computer (PCM) and a security system may also determine if and when the starting system will function.

During the cranking process, two actions occur. The pinion of the starter motor engages with the flywheel ring gear, and the starter motor then rotates to turn over, or crank, the engine. The starter motor is an electric motor mounted on the engine block or transmission. It is typically powered by the 12-volt storage battery, although some hybrid vehicles use the high-voltage battery to operate the starter motor. It is designed to have high turning effort (torque) at low speeds. The starter cables are the heaviest in the vehicle since they carry the high current needed by the starter motor. The starter motor causes the engine flywheel and crankshaft to rotate from a resting position and keeps them turning until the engine fires and runs on its own.

Starter Motor Principles

The starter motor converts electrical energy to mechanical energy for the purpose of cranking the engine over. There are three sections to the typical starter—the electric motor, the drive mechanism, and the solenoid. The starter motor is mounted on the transmission or cylinder block in a position to engage a ring gear around the outside edge of the engine flywheel, flex plate, or torque converter. Starting is usually accomplished by the operator activating a starter switch built into the ignition lock assembly, or a start button. A relatively small current flows through a neutral safety switch or clutch switch to a starter relay that controls a larger current to operate the starter solenoid, which

You Are the Automotive Technician

The owner of an 8 year old Ford F-150 4X4 has her vehicle towed to your shop because it wouldn't start. She tells you that her son was out four-wheeling and got stuck in a large mud hole. The engine died and wouldn't restart. Now the lights dim considerably each time she tries to start the engine. She agrees to let you diagnose the problem while she waits in the customer lounge. You verify the problem by trying to crank the engine over. The starter motor clicks once, and the head lights dim considerably.

1. What are the most likely faults that would cause an engine to not crank over?
2. What starting system components are likely NOT causing this problem?
3. If the problem is not an electrical fault, what could be causing the concern?
4. What tests will you perform to diagnose the problem, and what results will you be expecting?

is typically mounted atop the starter motor. The solenoid plunger moves the drive pinion gear into engagement with the ring gear and also closes a set of heavy-duty contacts. This allows a very large current to flow from the battery to the starter motor, rotating the armature and drive pinion gear, causing the crankshaft to rotate. When the engine starts and is able to run on its own, the operator usually releases the key and the solenoid spring withdraws the pinion gear from the ring gear and brings the armature to a halt. On many modern vehicles, the PCM signals the relay to continue the cranking process once a crank signal is received from the operator until the vehicle starts or the starting operation times out.

Direct-Drive/Gear Reduction Styles

Starter motors can be designed to drive the ring gear in one of two ways: either direct-drive or gear reduction. In the direct-drive system, the starter drive is mounted directly on one end of the armature shaft. The starter drive transfers the rotating force of the armature directly to the engine flywheel FIGURE 32-1. In this arrangement, the only gear reduction is the reduction between the pinion gear and the ring gear.

Gear reduction starters use an extra gear between the armature and the starter drive mechanism. They have a reduction of about 4:1. The gear reduction allows the starter to spin at a higher speed with lower current FIGURE 32-2. It also enables the starter to be downsized yet create a higher torque output. Two types of gearing systems are normally used: spur gears or planetary gears. Spur gears require the armature to be offset via a gear housing that holds the starter drive. A gear reduction system using planetary gears does not require an offset housing; the planetary gears are housed in the drive-end housing in line with the starter drive.

FIGURE 32-1 Armature and starter drive from a direct-drive starter.

Starter Motor Construction, Including the Brake Washer

A starter motor normally consists of the following components: field coils or large permanent magnets, an armature, a commutator, brushes, a drive pinion with an overrunning clutch, and a drive pinion engagement solenoid and shift fork FIGURE 32-3. The armature is the revolving component of the DC motor. The armature shaft is supported at each end by bushings or bearings pressed into end frames, which locate the armature centrally in the outer casing (i.e., the "barrel") of the motor and between the field coils or permanent magnets.

The commutator end frame carries copper-impregnated carbon brushes, which conduct current through the armature when it is being rotated in operation. The brushes are mounted in brush holders and are kept in contact with the commutator by tensioned spiral springs.

FIGURE 32-2 Gear reduction starter.

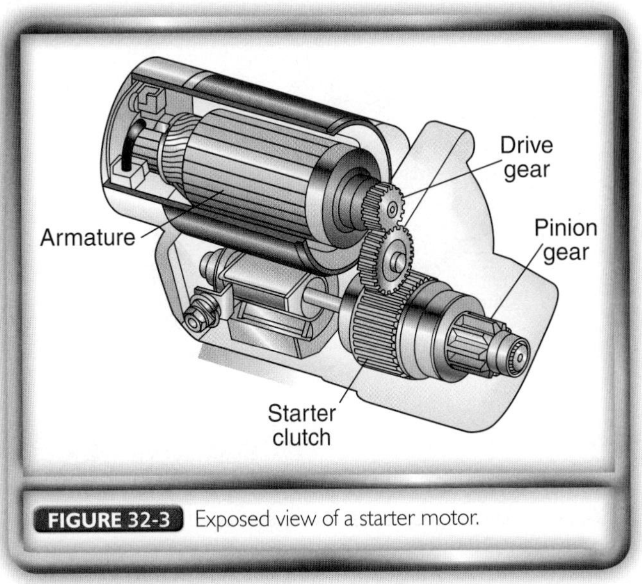
Drive gear
Pinion gear
Armature
Starter clutch

FIGURE 32-3 Exposed view of a starter motor.

Half of the brushes are connected directly to the end frame and ground the armature windings via the engine block to the negative battery terminal. The other brushes are insulated from the end frame and connect to the positive battery terminal via the main starter solenoid input terminal. This connection is direct from the solenoid in the case of a permanent magnet starter, and is indirect via the electromagnetic field poles in a series-wound motor FIGURE 32-4. A brake washer, typically made of leather or fiber, is placed around the armature shaft between the commutator and end housing. This acts as a friction brake to help slow the starter motor when the starter is disengaged. It also acts as an insulator for the commutator.

Starter Magnet Types

Starter motors use two magnet types: electromagnetic and permanent magnet FIGURE 32-5. Electromagnetic fields are formed by current flow through heavy strip copper windings, wound around iron pole shoes, which are then fastened to the starter case/barrel. Permanent magnets are located similarly but do not need electricity and therefore occupy less space. The case is made of iron and serves to concentrate the magnetic field produced by the field magnets.

Starter motors with electromagnetic field windings for light vehicle applications are typically series-wound motors. Because the resistance of the field and armature windings is low, the current flow is high when the motor starts under load, and this generates a strong magnetic field that will produce high torque at low speeds. This high initial torque drops sharply as the motor speed increases because of the **counter-electromotive force (CEMF)** or voltage generated in the armature windings as the motor armature spins in the magnetic field. The CEMF increases with armature speed and opposes current flow. It reduces both current flow and torque output. The faster the motor turns, the less current it draws and the less torque it develops. For example, on a typical V6 engine with standard

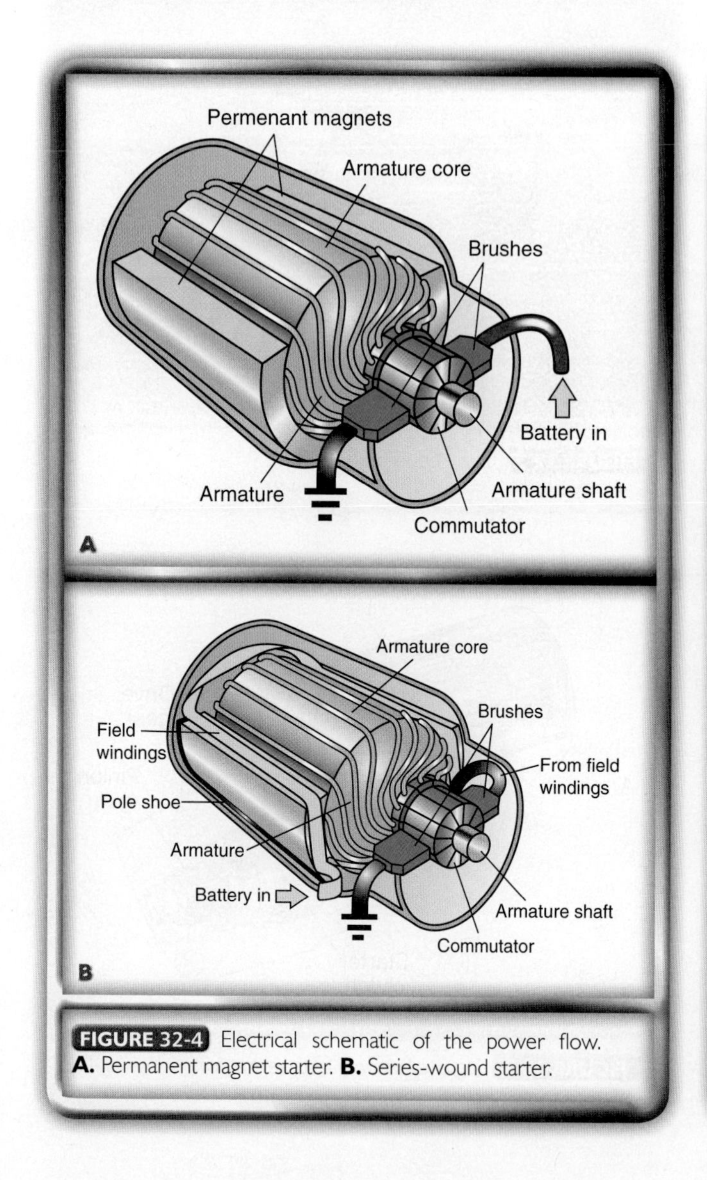
Permenant magnets
Armature core
Brushes
Battery in
Armature
Armature shaft
Commutator
A
Armature core
Brushes
Field windings
From field windings
Pole shoe
Armature
Battery in
Armature shaft
Commutator
B

FIGURE 32-4 Electrical schematic of the power flow. **A.** Permanent magnet starter. **B.** Series-wound starter.

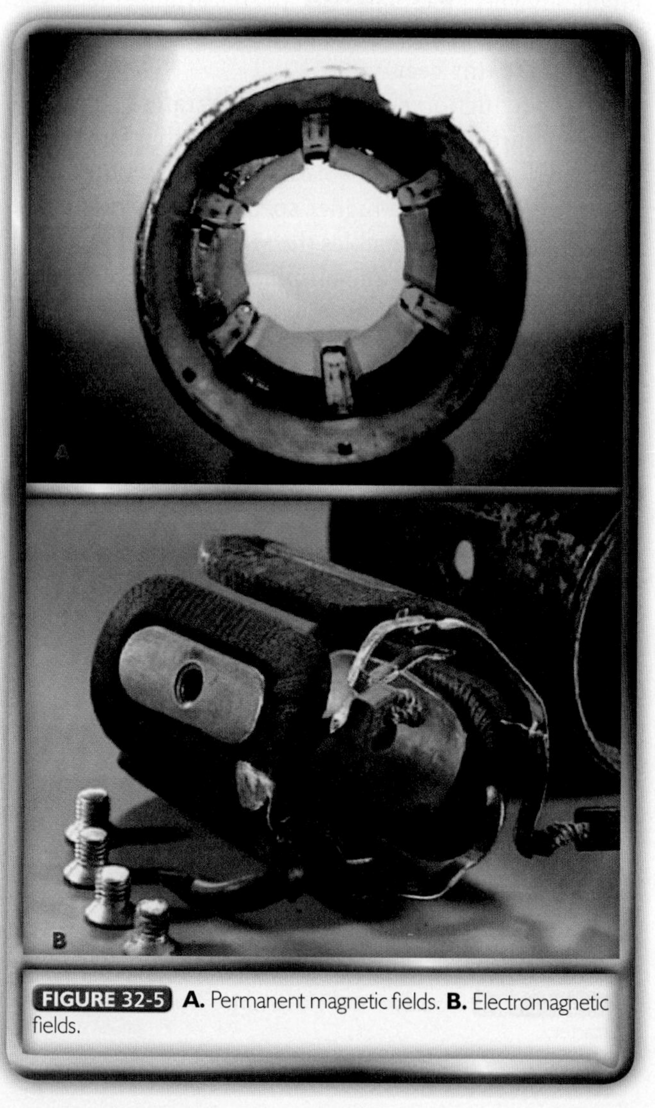
A
B

FIGURE 32-5 **A.** Permanent magnetic fields. **B.** Electromagnetic fields.

compression, the initial surge through the starter is usually over 500 amps, but as the armature starts to spin, the CEMF opposes the current flow, reducing it to around 120 amps (average) within about a second. This initial surge and subsequent drop of amperage can be observed on an oscilloscope when testing the starter motor.

Some series-wound motors have parallel-wired field windings, but they are still wired in series with the armature. These starters are referred to as series-parallel–wound starter motors. By connecting the field windings in this way, more current can flow in the circuit, and an overall increase in torque is obtained.

Starter Motor Engagement

Engagement is provided by operation of the ignition switch in the start position or when commanded by the PCM, which activates a starter-mounted solenoid whose plunger is engaged with the end of a pinion shift lever and operating fork. Solenoid operation moves the operating fork, causing the pinion to engage with the ring gear and also causing the plunger contacts to bridge with the main starter terminals FIGURE 32-6. The fork is located in a guide ring on the pinion drive, which is coupled to the pinion gear via a roller-type overrunning clutch. It is designed to transmit drive in one direction only and freewheel in the opposite direction.

The pinion drive is mounted on a slight helix that is machined onto the armature shaft to form a very coarse thread. This arrangement allows the pinion drive to rotate slightly when it is moved toward the ring gear. This feature, together with a chamfer on the leading edge of the ring gear and pinion gear teeth, is designed to assist the teeth in meshing. However, if the pinion gear teeth butt against the ring gear teeth and engagement is prevented, the guide ring continues its axial movement by sliding over the sleeve of the drive and compressing a meshing spring until the solenoid plunger contacts bridge the main terminals and the armature begins to turn.

Slight armature rotation and the force from the meshing spring push the pinion teeth into mesh with the ring gear. The meshing spring forces the pinion farther into the ring gear until the pinion contacts a stop ring on the armature shaft. This prevents further axial movement. The starter drive is locked to the shaft via the helix. The one-way clutch drives the pinion gear and transfers the armature rotation to the ring gear.

The pinion has only a small number of teeth compared to the ring gear, usually around 17:1, meaning the armature will rotate 17 times for each revolution of the flywheel. The gear reduction with this ratio also multiplies the torque from the starter motor 17 times, allowing a relatively small electric motor to turn the much larger ICE. If a gear reduction starter is used, then the torque is multiplied further, giving more cranking power from the same size starter motor.

As soon as the engine starts, it may easily run at 1000 revolutions per minute (rpm) or more. If still engaged, the engine would then turn the starter pinion gear about 17 times faster, or 17,000 rpm. Turning that fast would destroy the armature. At this instant, the freewheeling of the overrunning clutch prevents the armature from turning too fast should the driver not release the ignition key from the start position.

The pinion remains meshed as long as the engaging lever is held in the engaged position. Releasing the starter switch (or the PCM terminating the crank signal) allows the solenoid plunger return spring to disengage the pinion gear from the ring gear by returning the engaging lever, starter drive, and pinion gear to their original position FIGURE 32-7.

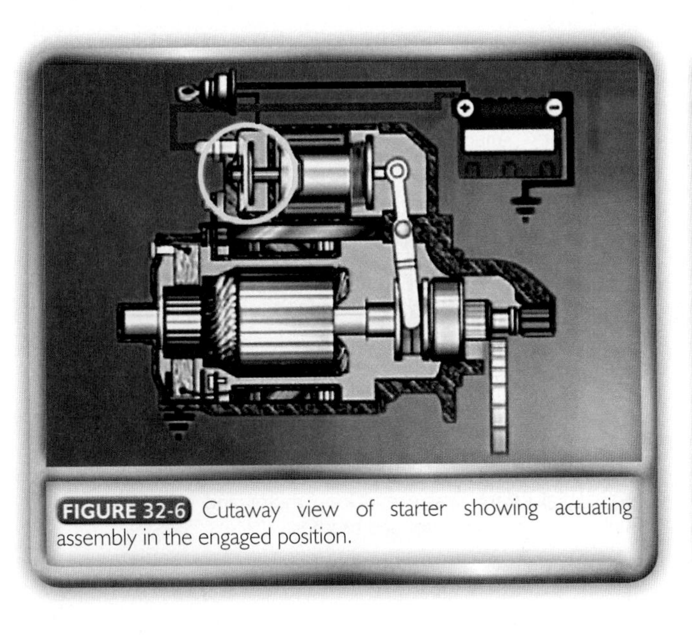

FIGURE 32-6 Cutaway view of starter showing actuating assembly in the engaged position.

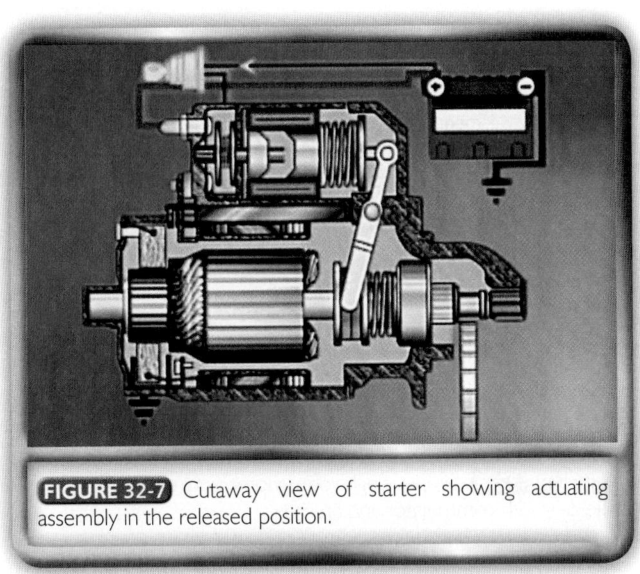

FIGURE 32-7 Cutaway view of starter showing actuating assembly in the released position.

Commutation and Brushes

When current flows in a conductor, an electromagnetic field is generated around it. If the conductor is placed so that it cuts across a stationary magnetic field, the conductor will be forced out of the stationary field. This occurs when the lines of force of the stationary field are distorted by the electromagnetic field around the conductor and try to return to a straight-line condition. Reversing the direction of current flow in the conductor will cause the conductor to move in the opposite direction. This is known as the motor effect and is greatest when the current-carrying conductor and the stationary magnetic field are at right angles to each other.

A conductor loop that can freely rotate within the magnetic field is the most efficient motor design. In this position, when current flows through the loop, the stationary magnetic field is distorted and the lines of force try to straighten. This forces one side of the loop up and the other side of the loop down, thus turning the loop **FIGURE 32-8**. The turning motion is called the motor effect and causes the loop to rotate until it is at 90 degrees to the magnetic field. To continue rotation, the direction of current flow in the conductor must be reversed at this static neutral point. A commutator is used to continually reverse the current flow to maintain rotation of the loop **FIGURE 32-9**. For example, a commutator consists of two semicircular segments that are connected to the two ends of the loop and are insulated from each other. Carbon-impregnated brushes provide a sliding connection to the commutator to complete the circuit and allow current to flow through the loop.

Rotation begins with both sides of the conductor loop cutting the stationary field. When the loop passes the point where the field is no longer being cut, the momentum of rotation carries the loop and the commutator segments over so that the brushes maintain current flow in the same direction in each side of the loop relative to the stationary field.

This process will maintain a consistent direction of rotation of the loop. In order to achieve a uniform motion and torque output, the number of loops must be increased. The additional loops smooth out the rotational forces. A starter motor armature has a large number of conductor loops and therefore has many segments on the commutator **FIGURE 32-10**.

Solenoid Operation

The solenoid on the starter motor performs two main functions: It switches the high current flow required by the starter motor on and off, and it engages the starter drive with the ring gear. The solenoid is typically a cylindrical

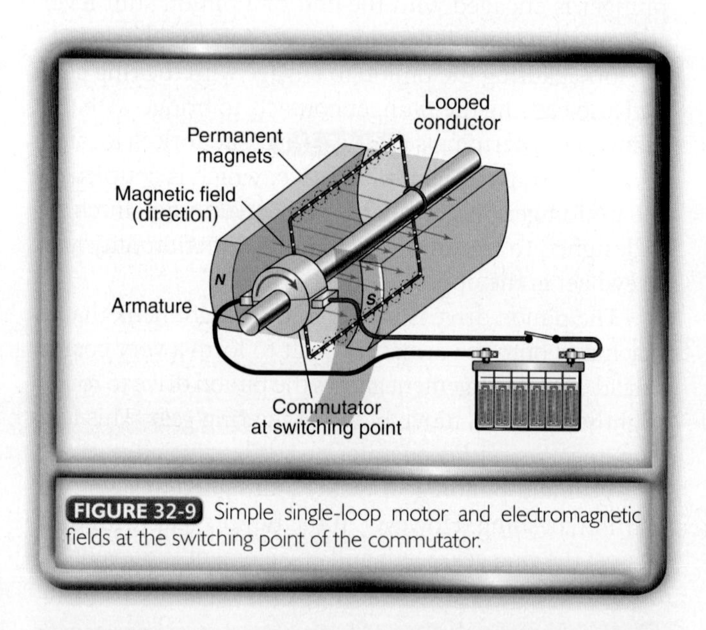
Looped conductor
Permanent magnets
Magnetic field (direction)
N
S
Armature
Commutator at switching point

FIGURE 32-9 Simple single-loop motor and electromagnetic fields at the switching point of the commutator.

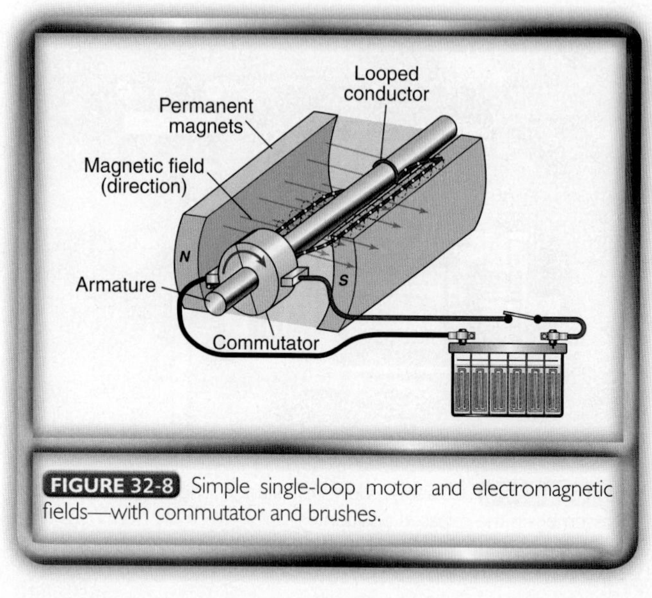
Looped conductor
Permanent magnets
Magnetic field (direction)
N
S
Armature
Commutator

FIGURE 32-8 Simple single-loop motor and electromagnetic fields—with commutator and brushes.

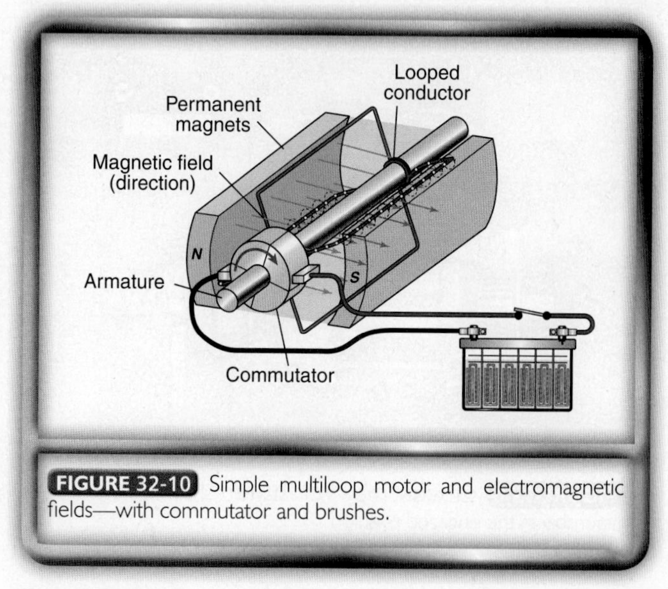
Looped conductor
Permanent magnets
Magnetic field (direction)
N
S
Armature
Commutator

FIGURE 32-10 Simple multiloop motor and electromagnetic fields—with commutator and brushes.

Applied Science

AS-75: Electromagnetism: The technician can explain the relationship between current in a conductor and strength of the magnetic field.

Electromagnetism can be defined as the physical relationship between a magnet and electricity. Michael Faraday is best known for his discoveries of electromagnetism back in 1831. His biggest breakthrough was his invention of the electric motor.

Today's automotive electrical systems use a variety of electromagnetic devices to accomplish a wide range of tasks. We have both AC and DC electric motors/generators when you consider hybrid vehicles. Automotive starters and generators (alternators) operate on the electromagnetic principle. Electric fuel pumps, cooling fan motors, and windshield wiper motors all produce a turning force based on the principles of magnetic fields.

The basic concept of the electromagnetic principle is to place a rotating armature inside of field windings. The field windings are stationary insulated electrical wires formed into a circular pattern. A magnetic field is created when current flows through the field winding. The armature spins as a result of the magnetic field. An example of this would be a starter motor.

In the case of a charging system, we can see the relationship of the output of the generator (alternator) voltage by increasing the number of turns, or windings, in the stator. We could also increase the output voltage by the rotor's magnetic field being increased.

device mounted on the starter motor FIGURE 32-11. It is constructed with two electrical windings, a pull-in winding and a hold-in winding, which will be explained in a moment. One end of the solenoid has a moving soft iron plunger, which is connected to a lever that moves the starter drive. The other end has an insulated cap with electrical connections to the solenoid windings along with a set of high-current contacts and a movable copper disc that completes the cranking circuit when the solenoid plunger is drawn forward FIGURE 32-12. Once the cranking circuit is completed, current flows from the battery to the starter fields and armature.

The starter control circuit activates the solenoid winding to draw the plunger forward. The control circuit can be activated directly by the ignition switch on some vehicles or by the PCM on other vehicles. When the control circuit is activated, it supplies battery power to the two windings in the starter solenoid. One of these is a pull-in winding, which draws a higher current and creates a stronger magnetic field than the other winding—the hold-in winding. The inputs of both windings are connected to the S-terminal (control circuit) on the solenoid. Both windings are wound in the same direction

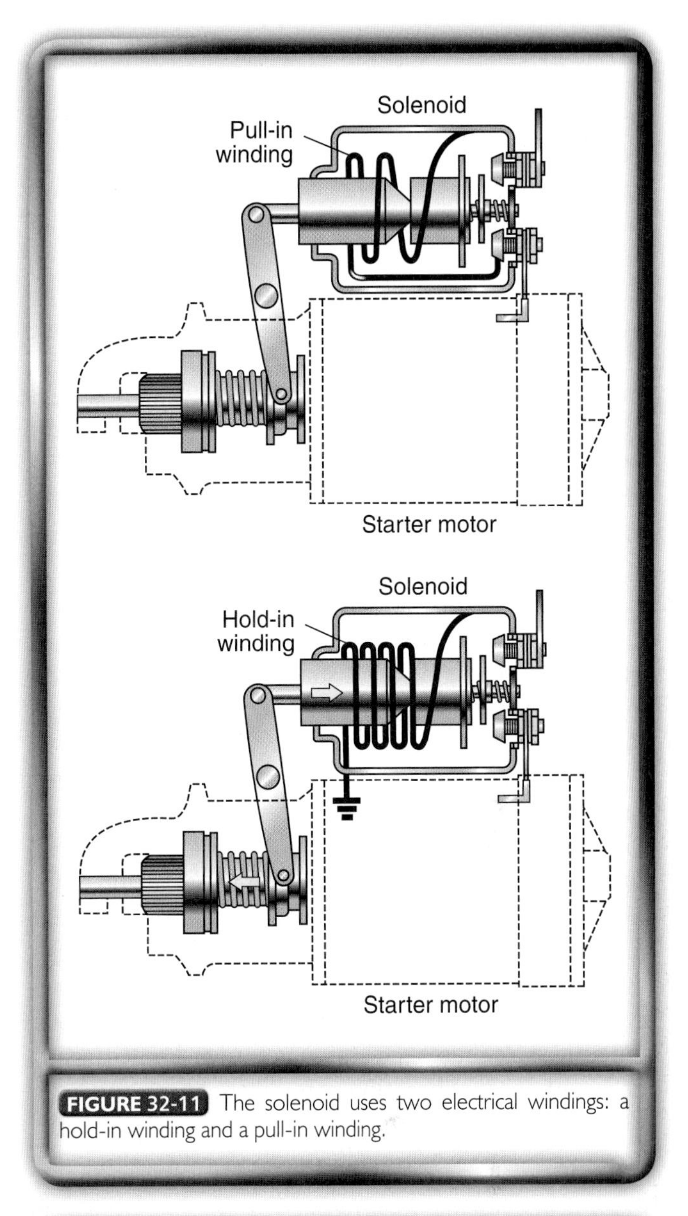
Solenoid
Pull-in
winding
Starter motor
Solenoid
Hold-in
winding
Starter motor

FIGURE 32-11 The solenoid uses two electrical windings: a hold-in winding and a pull-in winding.

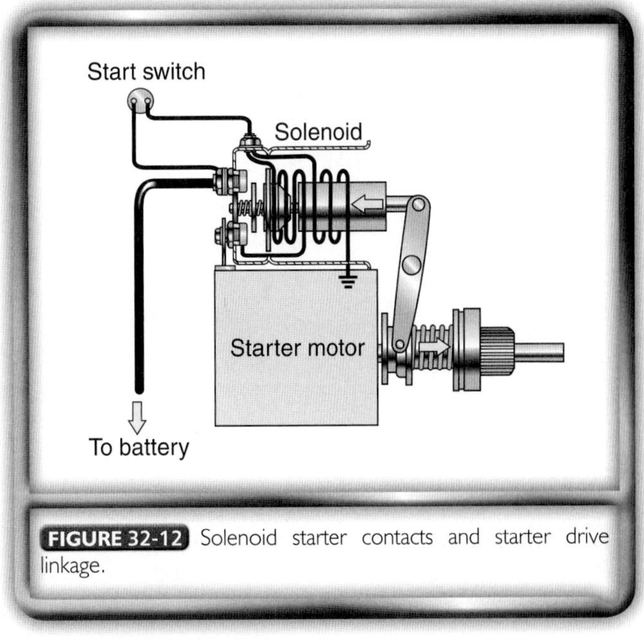
Start switch
Solenoid
Starter motor
To battery

FIGURE 32-12 Solenoid starter contacts and starter drive linkage.

in the solenoid housing. The output of the pull-in winding is connected to the main starter terminal leading to the field and armature windings, which provides ground to the pull-in winding until the solenoid contacts close. The output of the hold-in winding is connected to ground on the starter casing, which provides ground to the hold-in winding at all times.

When the starter is activated, current passes through both starter windings. The magnetic fields from both windings work together to attract the solenoid plunger toward the main starter terminals in the solenoid cap FIGURE 32-13. Plunger movement also operates the shift fork lever, thus engaging the drive pinion with the flywheel ring gear. The plunger contacts a switching pin, which transfers the motion through a contact spring, closing the main solenoid terminals. This allows a large current to flow from the battery through the starter motor windings, causing armature and pinion rotation, and rotation of the engine crankshaft. However, closing the contacts does another very important task; it shorts-to-power the output wire of the pull-in winding, resulting in two sequential actions. First, the short-to-power means that the pull-in winding has battery voltage applied to both the input and the output of the winding, stopping the current flow through the pull-in winding and stopping that magnetic field. But the hold-in winding still has power from the control circuit, so it continues to hold the plunger in place while the starter cranks. In fact, during engine cranking, the action of the helix on the rotating armature shaft causes the pinion gear to be held firmly in mesh with the flywheel ring gear. The hold-in winding is used only to ensure that the moving contact continues to bridge the main starter terminals FIGURE 32-14.

Once the engine starts, the control circuit is deactivated, and now is when the second action comes into play. The current stops flowing through the control circuit to supply the input of the hold-in and pull-in windings, but the output of the pull-in winding is still activated through the bridged solenoid contacts, so current flows backwards through the pull-in winding and then forward through the hold-in winding FIGURE 32-15. Since

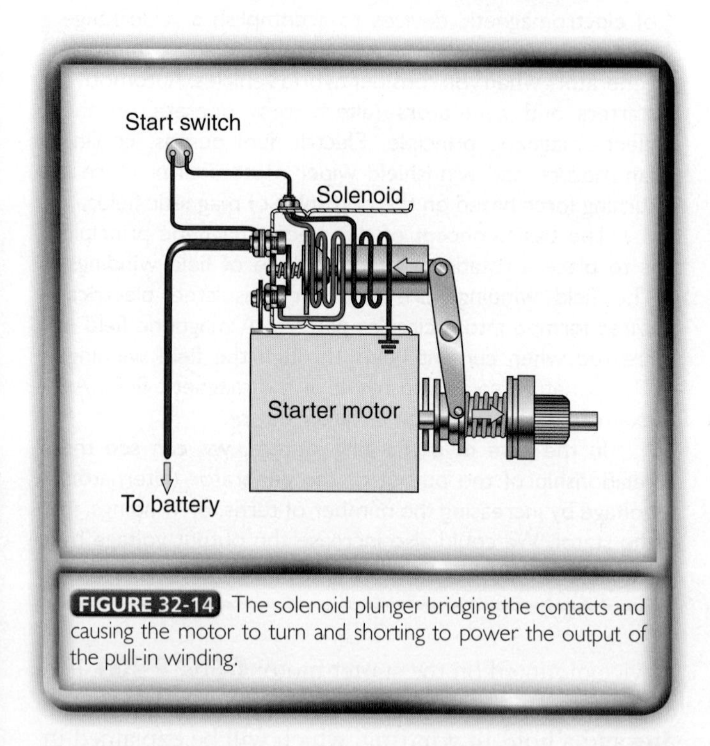
Start switch
Solenoid
Starter motor
To battery

FIGURE 32-14 The solenoid plunger bridging the contacts and causing the motor to turn and shorting to power the output of the pull-in winding.

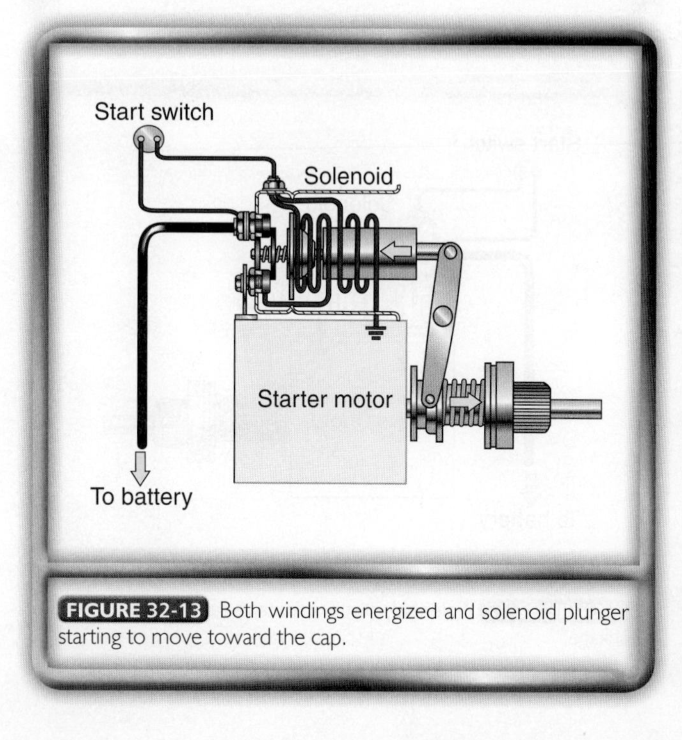
Start switch
Solenoid
Starter motor
To battery

FIGURE 32-13 Both windings energized and solenoid plunger starting to move toward the cap.

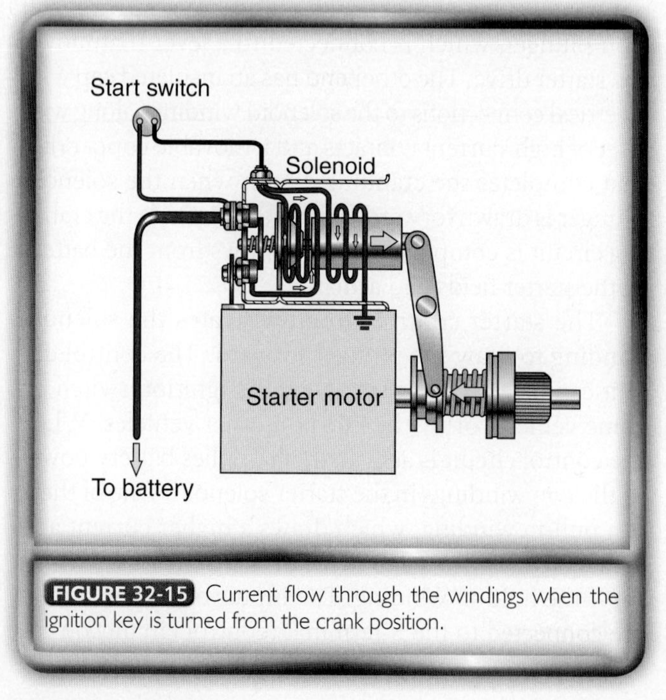
Start switch
Solenoid
Starter motor
To battery

FIGURE 32-15 Current flow through the windings when the ignition key is turned from the crank position.

the current flows in the two windings are opposite to each other, the two magnetic fields oppose each other and tend to cancel each other out, thereby allowing the plunger return spring to retract the plunger. This disconnects the power from the pull-in and hold-in windings as well as the starter motor, causing it to stop cranking the engine. As the return spring in the solenoid returns the plunger, it also retracts the pinion gear to its rest position.

Ford Starter with Moveable Pole Shoe

Some Ford vehicles use a separate starter relay in the engine compartment, instead of a solenoid, to control the high current for the starter motor. A spring-loaded pole shoe on the starter itself is magnetically pulled into position when current is supplied to the starter **FIGURE 32-16**. As the pole shoe moves into position, a shift fork attached to it engages the starter drive with the flywheel ring gear, thereby negating the need for a separate starter solenoid. Other functions of this type of starter are similar to those described previously.

Starter Control Circuit

The starter control circuit provides a means of operating the starter motor only within certain parameters, such as when the transmission is in park, the clutch is depressed, the brake pedal is applied, or the proper ignition switch is being used. These requirements help prevent accidentally starting the vehicle in gear **FIGURE 32-17**, which could cause an accident or injury, and also help prevent the vehicle from being stolen. For many years, manufacturers have placed switches in series with the starter solenoid windings, which prevents the starter from being activated unless each of the switches is closed. If the vehicle was equipped with an automatic transmission, then a neutral safety switch was incorporated into the shifter linkage so that the switch was only closed when the transmission was in park or neutral. If the vehicle was equipped with a standard transmission, then a clutch switch was installed such that it was closed by pressing the clutch pedal to the floor. Newer vehicles with their computer controls can monitor that information, and more, so that the starter will not activate until all of the required parameters are met. Once they are met, the PCM either activates a starter relay, which activates the starter solenoid, or the PCM activates the solenoid directly. With PCM-controlled starters, the starter control circuit becomes part of the vehicle theft-deterrent system, since the starter action can be disabled to prevent the vehicle from being started and stolen, as you will see in the next section.

FIGURE 32-16 Ford moveable pole shoe starter.

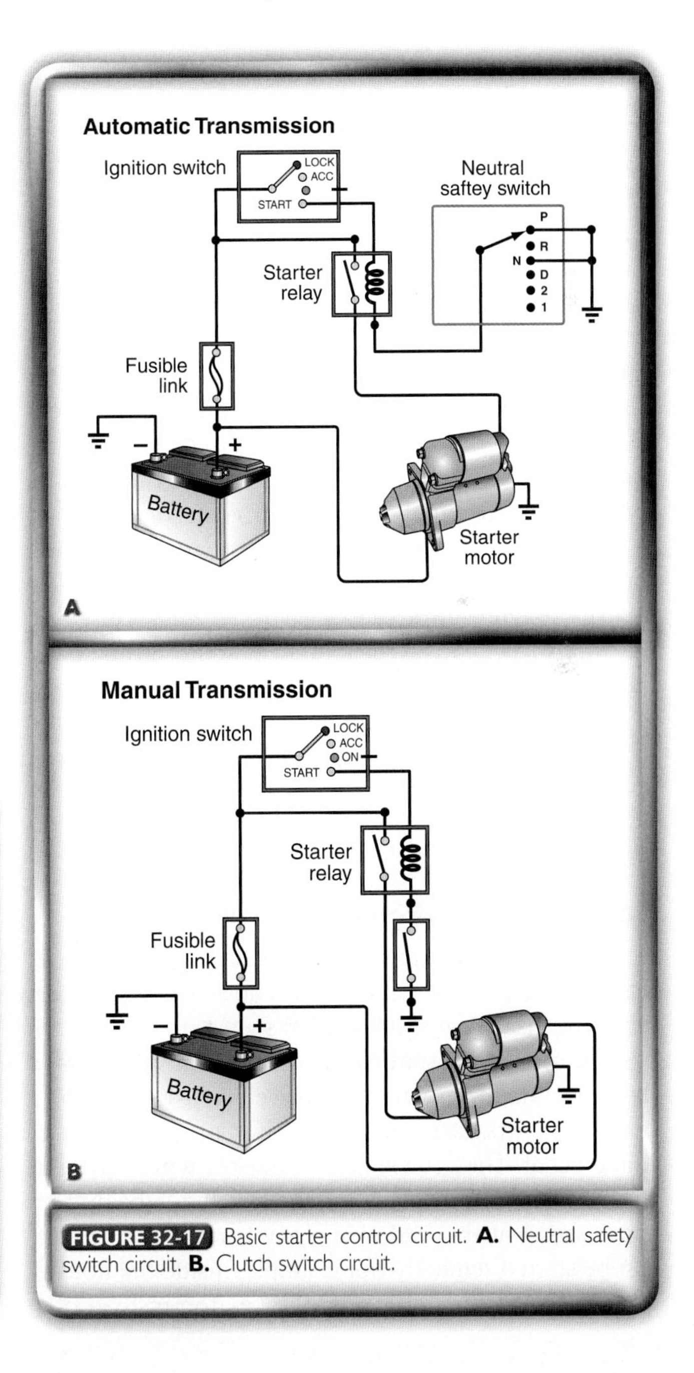
Automatic Transmission
Ignition switch
LOCK
ACC
START
Neutral
saftey switch
P
R
N
D
2
1
Starter
relay
Fusible
link
Battery
Starter
motor
A
Manual Transmission
Ignition switch
LOCK
ACC
ON
START
Starter
relay
Fusible
link
Battery
Starter
motor
B

FIGURE 32-17 Basic starter control circuit. **A.** Neutral safety switch circuit. **B.** Clutch switch circuit.

Vehicle Immobilization Systems

There are many different names given to vehicle immobilization systems. Each manufacturer produces its own version, each with subtle differences. Vehicle immobilizers generally comprise a computer-managed security system that disables the vehicle starter and engine systems by using an electronic system to uniquely identify each vehicle key by a security code system. Some keys have a built-in electronic circuit board used to store the code. This system makes it very difficult to start the vehicle with anything other than a correctly coded vehicle key. It also means that the key not only needs to be cut to fit the lock, but it must also be coded electronically to match the vehicle. Key coding is usually done with a scan tool with the correct software and a pass-through device that enables the body control module (BCM) to be programmed from the Internet.

The key identification system has two states of operation: mobilized and immobilized (or secure). When mobilized, the vehicle and engine components are allowed to operate normally. While in the immobilized or secure state, the key identification system is activated to protect the vehicle and prevent the engine from starting and/or cranking. The system is set to immobilize when the engine is switched off and the key removed. Usually the system will incorporate a flashing warning lamp on the dash to identify that it is immobilized. To mobilize the system, the key needs to be inserted into the ignition switch and turned to the on position, or the operator has to be in possession of the electronic smart key, step on the brake pedal, and push the start button. The vehicle's security system will check to see if the key that is inserted has the correct code to enable the system. If the codes are recognized, the system will allow the engine to start.

Some General Motors vehicles have used a key with a built-in resistor. Only when the key with the correct value of resistance is inserted into the ignition switch will the immobilizer module enable the starter control circuit to operate.

Keyless Starting/Remote Starting

Immobilizer systems now use keyless starting. The vehicle has a start button on the dash and does not require the key to be inserted into an ignition switch. In this type of wireless system, the start button will start the vehicle only if the key is in the proximity of the vehicle—for example, in the driver's pocket—and if the driver is stepping on the brake pedal. The vehicle detects the key wirelessly and mobilizes the system so the engine can start if the button is pressed. A further variation of this is where the vehicle can be started remotely (for example, inside the house) by pressing a start button on the key fob instead of a button on the dash. This is handy in hot or cold climates when warming or cooling the vehicle is desired prior to entering the vehicle.

Starter Drives and the Ring Gear

The starter drive transmits the rotational drive from the starter armature to the engine via the ring gear that is mounted on the engine flywheel, flex plate, or torque converter. The starter drive is composed of a pinion gear, an internal spline that mates with the slightly curved external spline on the armature shaft, an overrunning clutch, and a return spring. The pinion gear is small in comparison to the ring gear, which means the starter turns many times faster than the engine ring gear FIGURE 32-18. This also gives a large amount of mechanical advantage to the starter motor, allowing it to crank over the much larger ICE.

The overrunning clutch drives the pinion gear in one direction, while allowing it to freewheel in the opposite direction. The overrunning clutch uses roller bearings housed between an inner and an outer shell. The outer shell has tapered ramps built into it in which the roller bearings ride FIGURE 32-19. Springs push the rollers toward the tapered ends of the ramps. In the forward direction, the rollers roll slightly between the tapered ramps and are pinched between the inner and outer shells, thereby locking the assembly and driving the pinion gear. In the opposite direction (once the engine starts), the rollers roll up the inclined ramps against spring pressure, unlocking the rollers and allowing the pinion gear to freewheel. The overrunning clutch prevents the starter motor from being driven by the engine once the engine starts, which would spin the armature faster than it

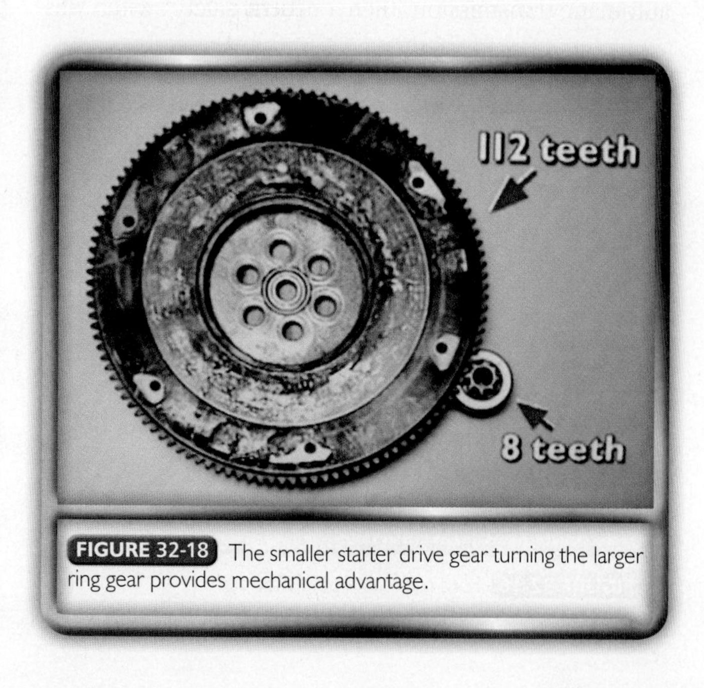
112 teeth
8 teeth
FIGURE 32-18 The smaller starter drive gear turning the larger ring gear provides mechanical advantage.

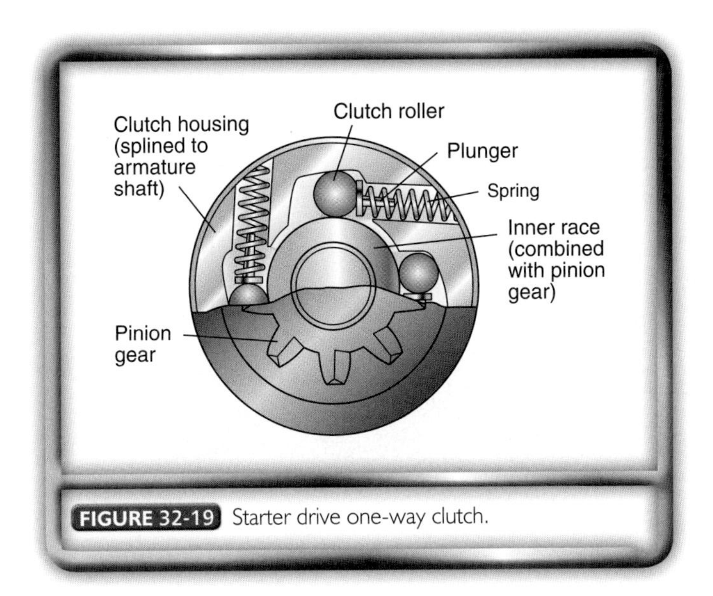
Clutch housing (splined to armature shaft)
Clutch roller
Plunger
Spring
Inner race (combined with pinion gear)
Pinion gear

FIGURE 32-19 Starter drive one-way clutch.

could handle. Without the overrunning clutch, the vehicle engine would overspeed the starter motor, causing significant damage.

When the starter solenoid is activated, the starter drive teeth engage the ring gear. The solenoid plunger is connected to the starter drive by a lever and pushes the starter drive into mesh with the ring gear. It also retracts the starter drive once the solenoid has been deactivated.

Starter Location Variation

Engine design usually dictates the location of the vehicle starter motor. Traditionally, most starter motors are mounted on one side of the engine so they can mesh with the ring gear. Starter motors can be difficult to see by just looking into the engine bay; they are often tucked up under exhaust manifolds or engine covers. On transverse engines, they are often mounted on the side closest to the firewall, which can make them difficult to locate. Starter motors are sometimes more easily accessed from underneath the vehicle. Often engine covers and components will need to be removed to gain access to difficult starter motor locations. On some engines, such as the General Motors Northstar engine, the starter motor is mounted at the top of the engine under the intake manifold. You may have to check the service information to locate the starter motor on some vehicles.

Hybrid Vehicle Starters

Hybrid vehicles use both an ICE and electric motors to power the vehicle's drive train, although some manufacturers have released (so-called) hybrid vehicles that are driven entirely by an ICE and use only an idle-stop feature. Most hybrid vehicles use a high-voltage electric motor for engine start-up, auxiliary power, and regenerative braking functions. Regardless of the hybrid configuration, the ICE still requires a method to crank it over. On most hybrid vehicles, this task is undertaken by the hybrid's main electric drive motor, which can spin the ICE at a much faster and smoother rate, causing it to start almost instantly. On some hybrids, a more conventional ICE starter is also provided to start the engine if the main high-voltage battery bank is discharged.

Starter Draw Testing

Testing starter motor current draw is a good indicator of overall starter motor performance. Manufacturers will specify the current draw for starter motors, and any tests must be performed with a fully charged and correct capacity battery for the vehicle. Starter motors can be tested in two ways: on vehicle or off vehicle. The on-vehicle test is usually called a starter draw test, while the off-vehicle test is called a no-load test. Manufacturers will provide specifications for one or both of the tests.

Ideally, the starter motor current draw should be tested under load, which is often easier to accomplish while the starter motor is mounted in the vehicle. Starter current draw is at its highest when the starter pinion gear first engages with the engine flywheel. As the starter motor and engine cranking speed increase, the current draw decreases and quickly stabilizes once the engine reaches full cranking speed. There is a variety of starter test equipment used to test starter draw. Each device will operate slightly differently, but all should have an inductive high-current ammeter to measure the cranking current flow and a voltmeter to measure the cranking voltage. The inductive ammeter is better to use than a standard ammeter because it does not require any battery cables to be removed; it is quickly clamped around the main starter cable. When conducting the test, the engine must be disabled so it will crank but not start. The current flow and voltage will be measured during cranking and compared to specifications.

To test the starter draw, follow the steps in **SKILL DRILL 32-1**.

Testing Starter Circuit Voltage Drop

The electrical circuit of the starter motor consists of a high-current circuit and a control circuit. The high-current circuit consists of the battery, main battery cables to the starter motor solenoid, solenoid contacts, and heavy ground cables back to the battery from the engine and chassis. The control circuit activates the solenoid and can either be PCM controlled or non-PCM controlled.

> **▸ LINK**
> Refer to the Meter Usage and Circuit Diagnosis chapter for more information on DVOMs.

SKILL DRILL 32-1 Testing the Starter Draw

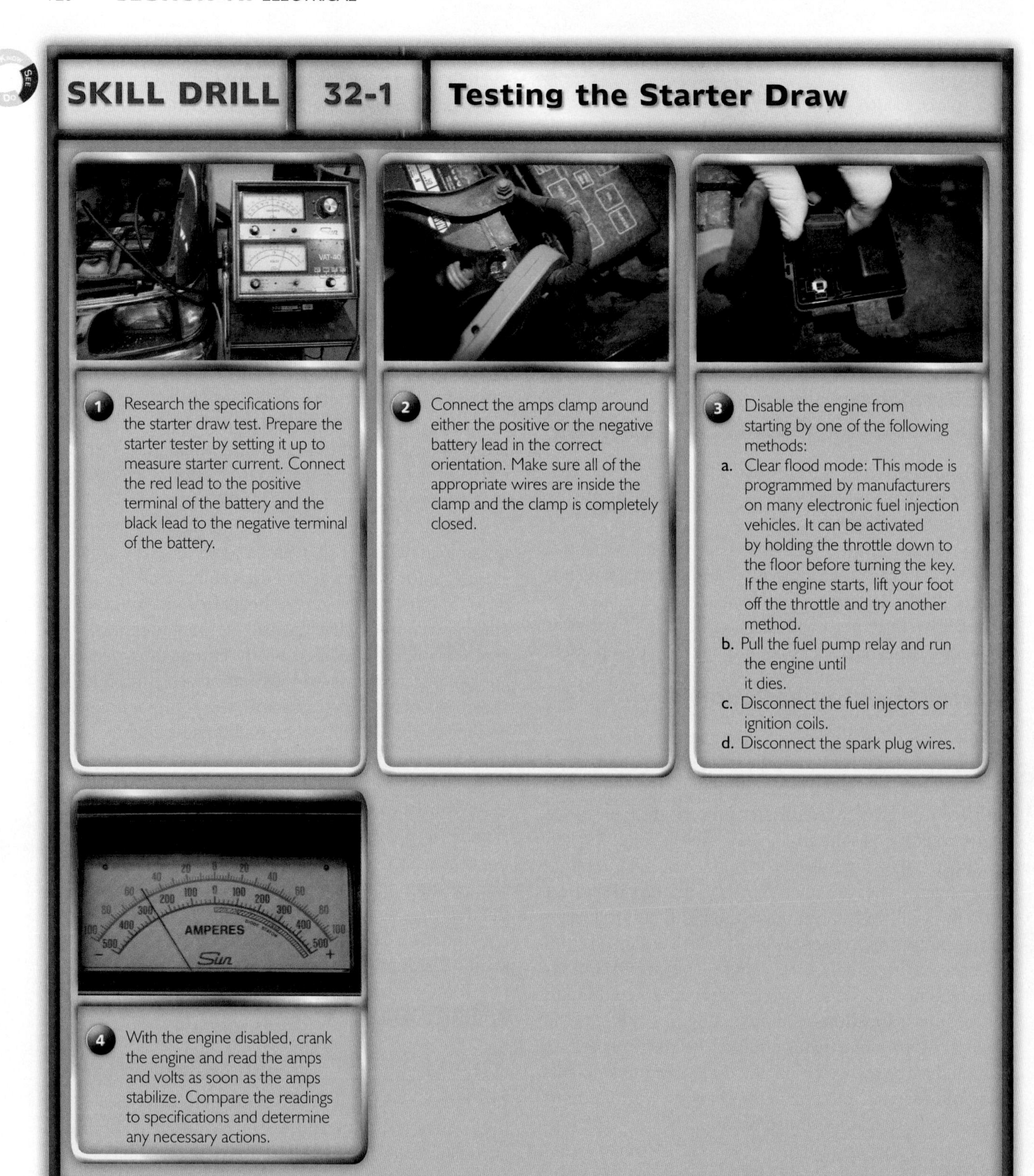
VAT-40
AMPERES
Sun

1. Research the specifications for the starter draw test. Prepare the starter tester by setting it up to measure starter current. Connect the red lead to the positive terminal of the battery and the black lead to the negative terminal of the battery.

2. Connect the amps clamp around either the positive or the negative battery lead in the correct orientation. Make sure all of the appropriate wires are inside the clamp and the clamp is completely closed.

3. Disable the engine from starting by one of the following methods:
   a. Clear flood mode: This mode is programmed by manufacturers on many electronic fuel injection vehicles. It can be activated by holding the throttle down to the floor before turning the key. If the engine starts, lift your foot off the throttle and try another method.
   b. Pull the fuel pump relay and run the engine until it dies.
   c. Disconnect the fuel injectors or ignition coils.
   d. Disconnect the spark plug wires.

4. With the engine disabled, crank the engine and read the amps and volts as soon as the amps stabilize. Compare the readings to specifications and determine any necessary actions.

We will look at testing the control circuit voltage drop in the next section. Voltage drop can occur across both the high-current and control circuits; however, the high-current circuit is more susceptible to voltage drop due to the much larger amount of current flowing in the circuit. One thing to remember is that when testing the voltage drop on the high-current side, for the measurement to be meaningful, the starter must be activated by the solenoid. The starter does not necessarily have to turn, but the solenoid must at least click when the ignition switch is engaged. If the solenoid does not click, then you will need to test the control side of the starter circuit.

A voltmeter or DVOM is used to measure voltage drop across all parts of the circuit. A voltmeter with a minimum/maximum range setting is very useful when measuring voltage drop because it will record and hold the maximum voltage drop that occurs for a particular operation cycle.

Voltage drop is tested while the circuit is under load. The DVOM is connected in parallel across the component or part of the circuit that is to be tested for voltage drop. Usually the most efficient method is to test large sections of the circuit first and, if required, narrow down the test to individual components to identify precisely where excessive voltage drop is located. For example, you can connect the black probe to the ground side of the starter motor and the red probe to the negative battery terminal, operate the starter with the engine disabled, and record the voltage drop across the ground circuit while the starter motor is cranked. Manufacturers will specify the maximum allowable voltage drop, but a rule of thumb is no more than 0.5 volts (500 millivolts) for a 12-volt circuit.

The same test should also be performed on the positive side of the circuit. On most vehicles, the starter cable is connected to the input of the solenoid, while the output of the solenoid is connected to the input of the starter motor. Since the heavy contacts are located between the input and the output terminals of the solenoid, where possible, it is best to measure the voltage drop from the positive battery post to the starter motor input (not the solenoid input). That way you are measuring any voltage drop across the solenoid contacts, which are a high-probability failure point. Check the service information for safe methods of disabling the engine so it will not start.

To test starter circuit voltage drop, follow the steps in **SKILL DRILL 32-2**.

> **TECHNICIAN TIP**
>
> A faulty battery will affect voltage drop tests, so always ensure that the battery is fully charged and in good condition before performing tests.

Inspecting and Testing the Starter Control Circuit

The starter control circuit activates the starter solenoid, which activates the starter motor. If there is a problem in the starter control circuit, the vehicle will likely not crank over at all, or maybe intermittently. The control circuit is made up of the battery, fusible link, ignition switch,

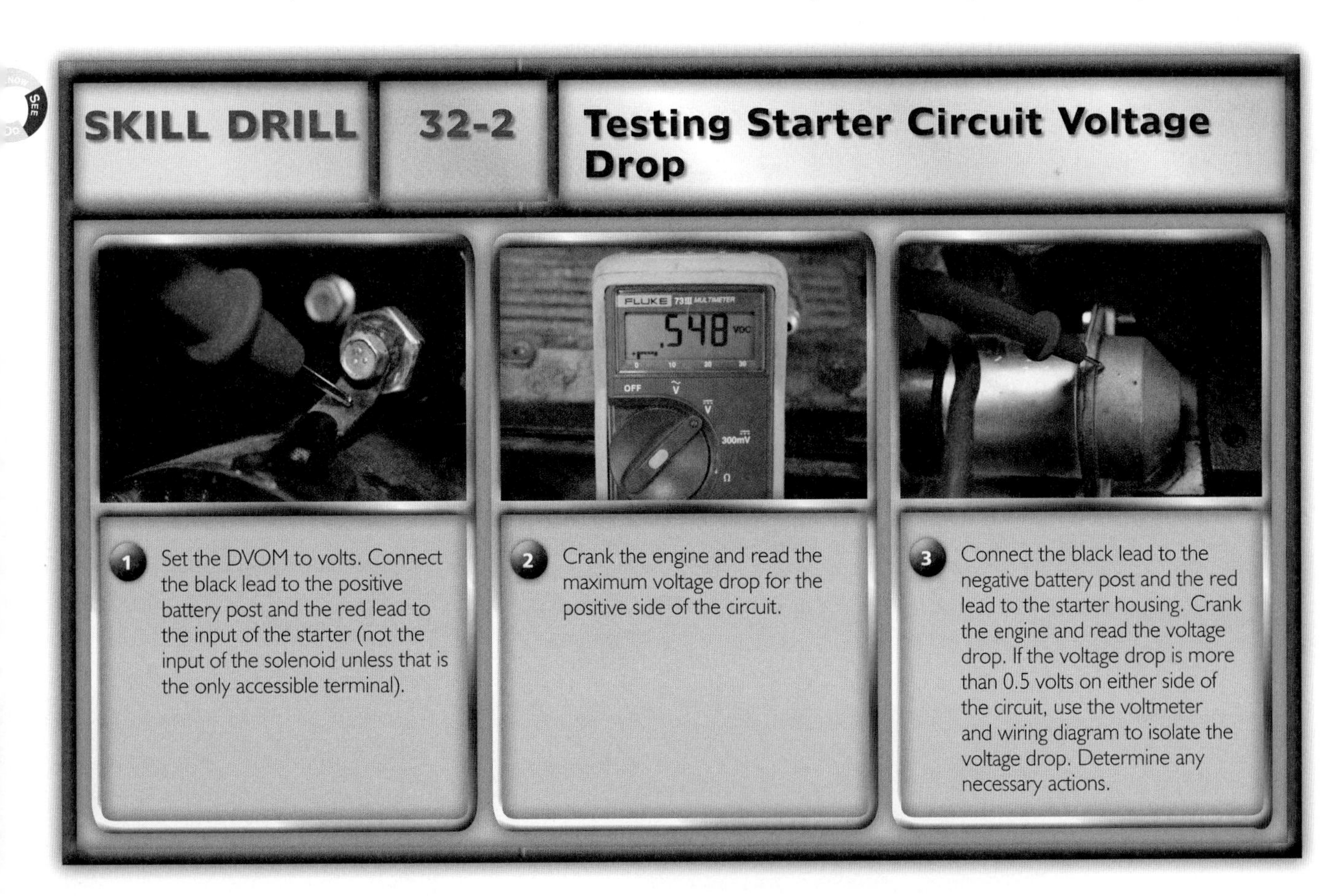
SKILL DRILL 32-2 Testing Starter Circuit Voltage Drop
FLUKE
548
1 Set the DVOM to volts. Connect the black lead to the positive battery post and the red lead to the input of the starter (not the input of the solenoid unless that is the only accessible terminal).
2 Crank the engine and read the maximum voltage drop for the positive side of the circuit.
3 Connect the black lead to the negative battery post and the red lead to the starter housing. Crank the engine and read the voltage drop. If the voltage drop is more than 0.5 volts on either side of the circuit, use the voltmeter and wiring diagram to isolate the voltage drop. Determine any necessary actions.

neutral safety switch (automatic vehicles), clutch switch (manual vehicles) starter relay, and solenoid windings. If the starter is controlled by the PCM, then you must be aware of all of the circuits, such as the immobilizer circuit and the PCM itself.

Before performing any tests, you should know and confirm the customer's concern. The manufacturer's wiring diagrams should be consulted to determine the circuit operation and to identify all components in the starter control circuit.

Once an understanding of the customer concern and circuit operation is obtained, it is time to test. Start by placing the DVOM's red lead on the starter input terminal and the black lead on the starter housing. Measure the voltage with the key in the crank position. At that point, assuming a fault in the control circuit is present, the voltage at the control circuit will be less than about 10.5 volts. If it is, you will need to perform voltage drop tests on the power side of the control circuit to determine which side(s) of the circuit the voltage drop is located on. If the voltage drop is less than 0.5 volts, then the voltage drop on the starter ground circuit should be measured with the voltmeter. If the voltage drop is excessive, perform individual voltage drops on the ground leg. If both the control circuit power and the ground circuit voltage are within specifications, the resistance of the solenoid pull-in and hold-in windings will need to be measured. If out of specifications, the solenoid or starter motor and solenoid will need to be replaced.

To inspect and test the starter control circuit, follow the steps in **SKILL DRILL 32-3**.

Inspecting and Testing Relays and Solenoids

The starting system typically contains solenoids and relays that activate the control circuit. The solenoid is mounted on the starter motor, while the starter circuit relay is usually in or near the main fuse box with other similar devices.

Before performing any tests, ensure that the vehicle battery is charged and in good condition. The manufacturer's wiring diagrams should be checked to determine the circuit operation, identification, and location of all components in the starter circuit.

Relays must be tested in two or three ways depending on the relay. The simplest test is to measure the resistance of the relay winding. If it is out of specifications, the relay will need to be replaced. If it is OK, the contacts will need to be tested for an excessive voltage drop. The best way to do this is by using an adapter that fits between the relay and the relay socket. This will allow the normal circuit current flow to flow through the contacts so that a voltage drop measurement can be taken. Any excessive voltage drop across the relay contacts will require

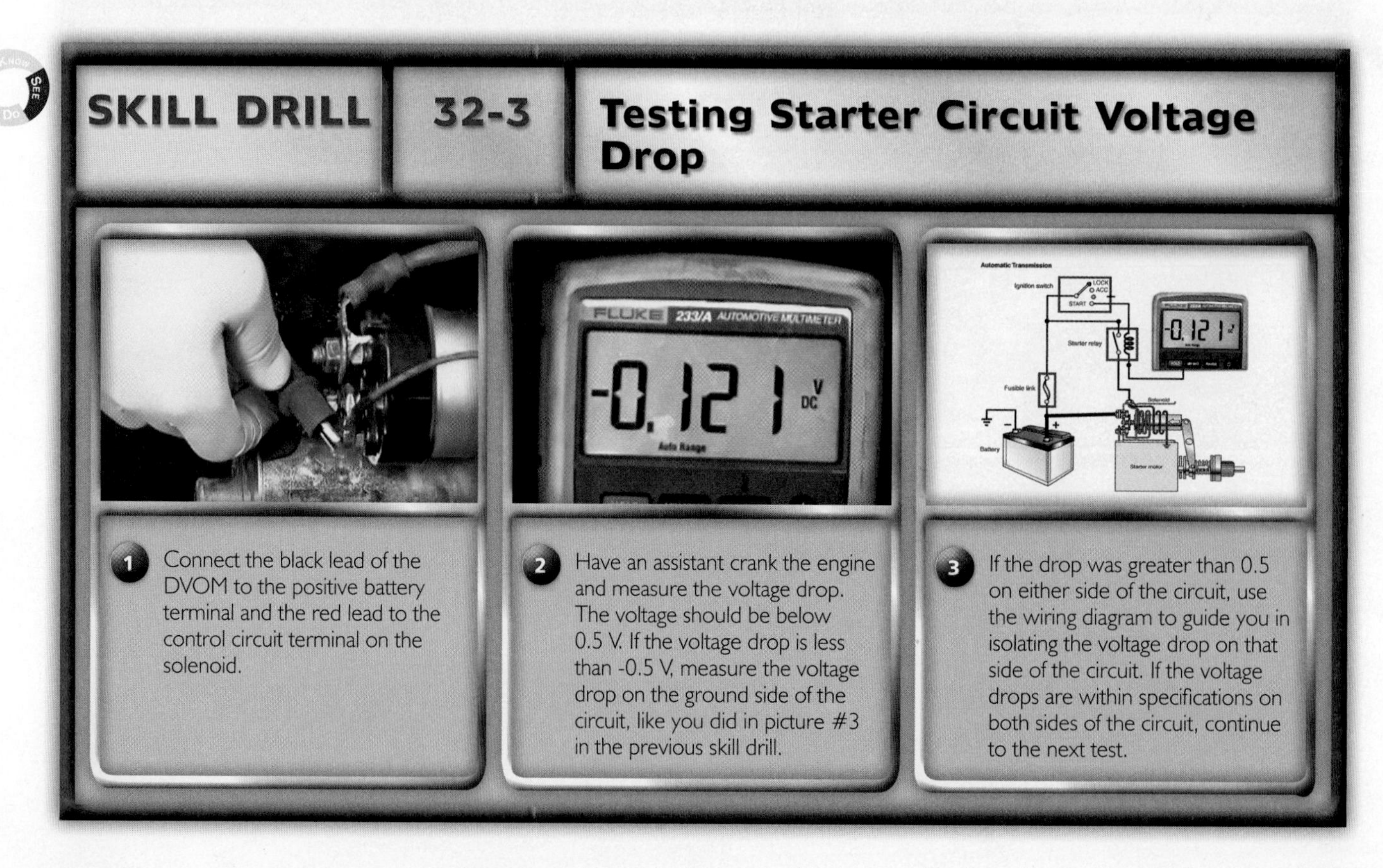

KNOW
SEE
DO
PROVE
FLUKE 233/A AUTOMOTIVE MULTIMETER
-0.121 V DC
Auto Range
Automatic Transmission
Ignition switch
LOCK
ACC
START
Starter relay
Fusible link
Battery
Solenoid
Starter motor
-0.121

SKILL DRILL 32-3 Testing Starter Circuit Voltage Drop

1. Connect the black lead of the DVOM to the positive battery terminal and the red lead to the control circuit terminal on the solenoid.
2. Have an assistant crank the engine and measure the voltage drop. The voltage should be below 0.5 V. If the voltage drop is less than -0.5 V, measure the voltage drop on the ground side of the circuit, like you did in picture #3 in the previous skill drill.
3. If the drop was greater than 0.5 on either side of the circuit, use the wiring diagram to guide you in isolating the voltage drop on that side of the circuit. If the voltage drops are within specifications on both sides of the circuit, continue to the next test.

the replacement of the relay. The last test is used only on relays with a suppression diode in parallel with the relay winding. Connect a reasonably fresh 9-volt battery across the relay winding terminals in one direction, and then switch polarity by turning the battery around. If the diode is good, the relay should click in one direction and not in the other FIGURE 32-20. If it clicks in both directions, the diode is open. If it does not click in either direction, the relay winding is open or the diode is shorted.

9V
Energizer
03-2016
ALKALINE BATTERY

FIGURE 32-20 Testing a relay with a 9v battery.

Solenoids can be difficult to test on the vehicle due to poor access, and tests will usually be limited to voltage and voltage drop tests on the main contacts. For other tests, such as pull-in and hold-in winding tests, the starter motor will usually need to be removed. Care should be taken when testing relays and solenoids to ensure that cables are not shorted to ground and the engine is not accidentally cranked over.

The first test to perform is a voltage drop test across the solenoid contacts. Place the red lead on the solenoid B-positive input and the black lead on the solenoid B-positive output. The voltage drop should be less than 0.5 volts. If not, replace the starter assembly. Testing of the solenoid winding requires partial disassembly of the solenoid. Therefore, it is usually best to disconnect the control circuit connector from the solenoid and use a jumper wire to activate the solenoid. If the solenoid and starter operate, there is probably a fault in the vehicle's control circuit that needs further testing. If the solenoid or starter does not work (and the ground circuit is good), then the starter is likely faulty and will need to be replaced.

To inspect and test relays and solenoids, follow the steps in SKILL DRILL 32-4.

SKILL DRILL 32-4 Inspecting and Testing Relays and Solenoids

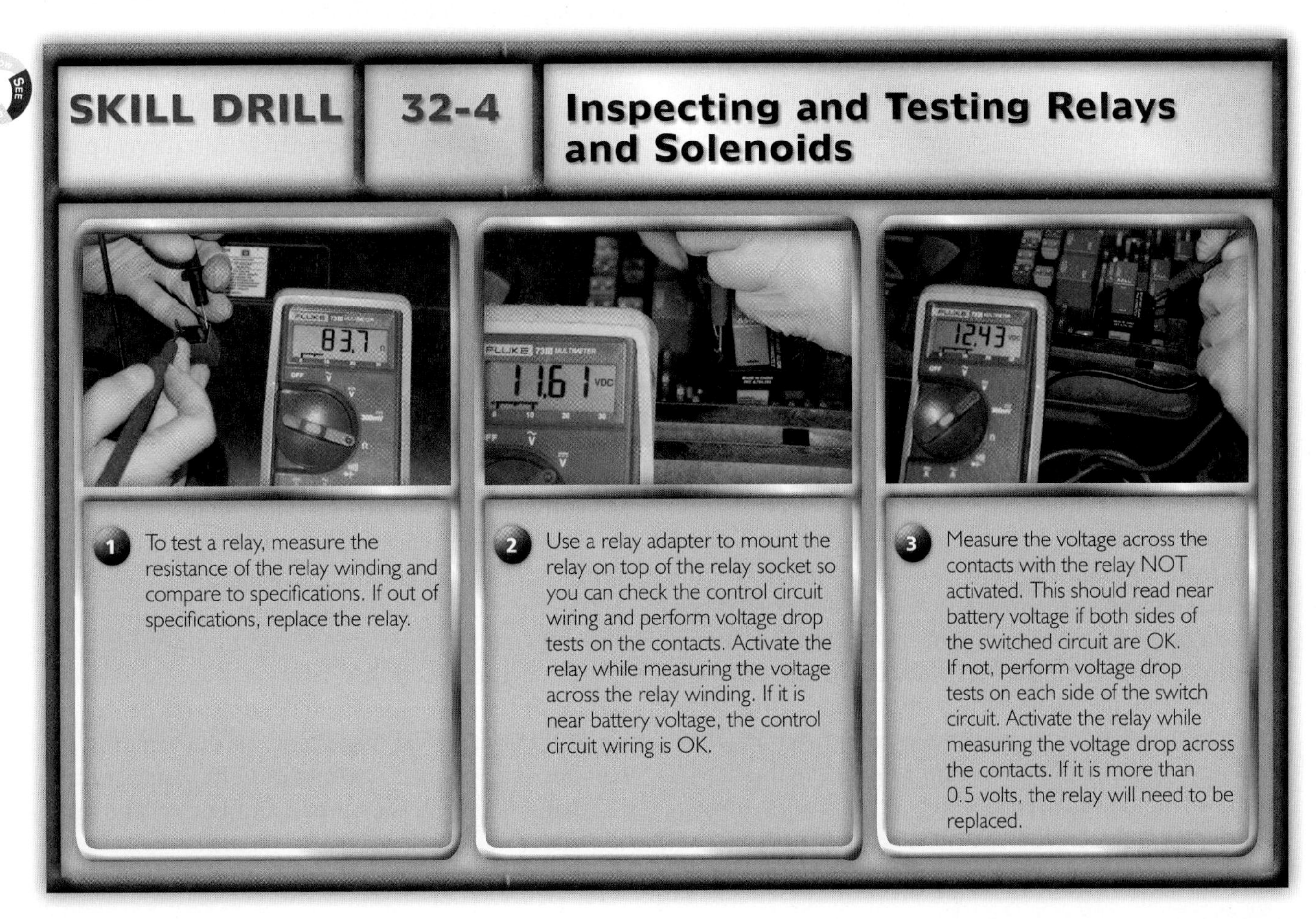
83.7
FLUKE
11.61 VDC
12.43

1. To test a relay, measure the resistance of the relay winding and compare to specifications. If out of specifications, replace the relay.

2. Use a relay adapter to mount the relay on top of the relay socket so you can check the control circuit wiring and perform voltage drop tests on the contacts. Activate the relay while measuring the voltage across the relay winding. If it is near battery voltage, the control circuit wiring is OK.

3. Measure the voltage across the contacts with the relay NOT activated. This should read near battery voltage if both sides of the switched circuit are OK. If not, perform voltage drop tests on each side of the switch circuit. Activate the relay while measuring the voltage drop across the contacts. If it is more than 0.5 volts, the relay will need to be replaced.

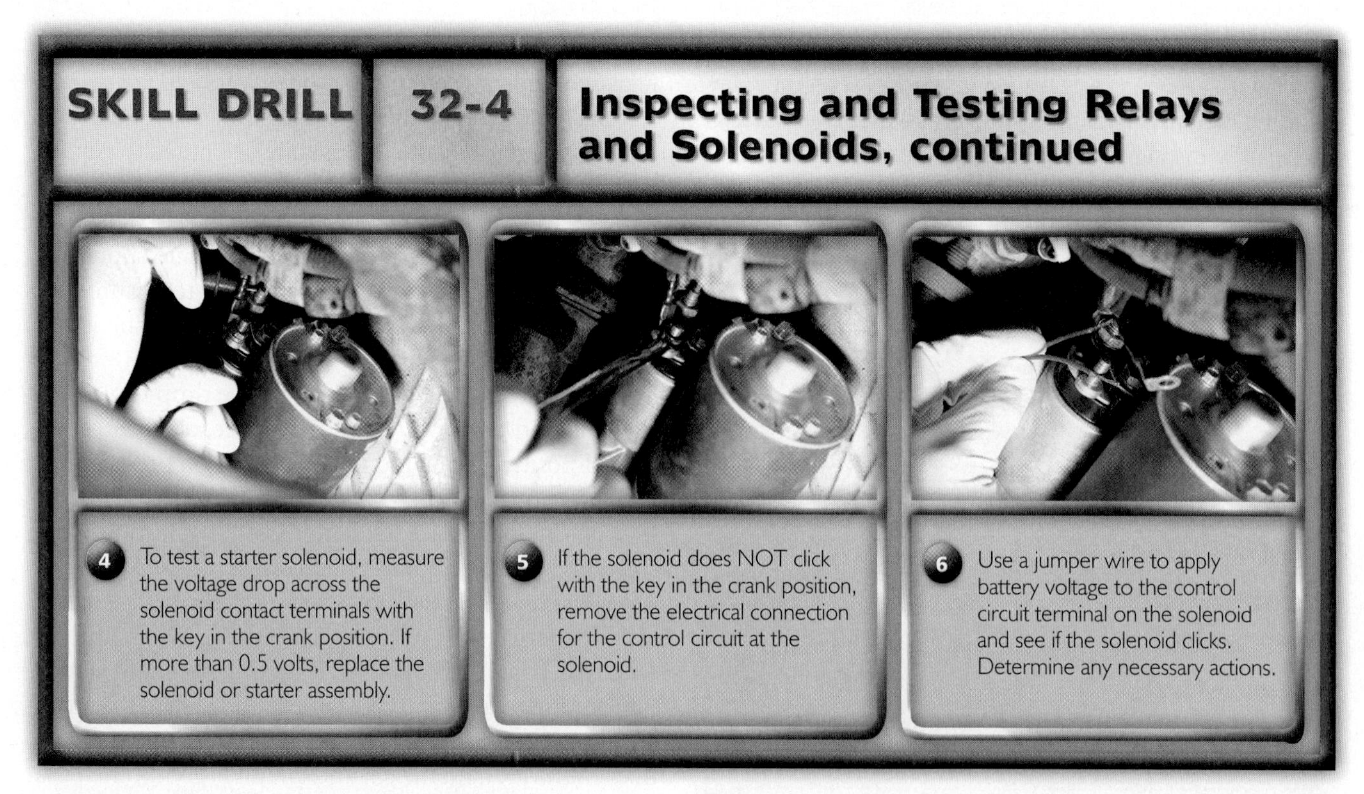
SKILL DRILL
32-4
Inspecting and Testing Relays and Solenoids, continued
4 To test a starter solenoid, measure the voltage drop across the solenoid contact terminals with the key in the crank position. If more than 0.5 volts, replace the solenoid or starter assembly.
5 If the solenoid does NOT click with the key in the crank position, remove the electrical connection for the control circuit at the solenoid.
6 Use a jumper wire to apply battery voltage to the control circuit terminal on the solenoid and see if the solenoid clicks. Determine any necessary actions.

Removing and Installing a Starter

Starter motors are usually located close to the flywheel end of the engine. They can be in difficult-to-reach locations, and some engine components or covers may need to be removed to gain access. In most cases, the starter can be accessed more easily from underneath the vehicle. Always disconnect the negative battery lead before attempting to remove or install a starter motor, and be sure to use a memory minder if specified by the manufacturer.

To remove and install a starter in a vehicle, follow the steps in SKILL DRILL 32-5.

Differentiating Between Electrical and Mechanical Problems

Failure to crank over properly, whether a slow-crank or a no-crank condition, can be caused by electrical or mechanical problems. For example, slow cranking could result from an electrical fault such as high resistance in the solenoid contacts. This problem could be resolved by replacing the starter with a new or remanufactured unit. But the slow-crank condition could also be caused by a mechanical engine fault such as a spun main bearing that is causing a lot of drag on the crankshaft, preventing the starter from cranking it over at normal speed. In this case, the entire engine will need to be rebuilt. As you can imagine, telling customers that they need a new starter motor when in fact they need a new engine (costing 10–20 times as much money) will not make them very happy with you. It is important to be able to differentiate between the two types of faults so that a wrong diagnosis can be avoided and the problem fixed appropriately the first time.

Typical electrical problems that can cause starting system problems include loose, dirty, or corroded terminals and connectors, a discharged or faulty battery, a faulty starter motor, or a faulty control circuit. Mechanical problems that may cause starting system problems include seized pistons or bearings, hydrostatic lock from liquid in the cylinder(s) (e.g., a leaky fuel pressure regulator or water ingestion during off-road operation), incorrect ignition or valve timing, a seized alternator or other belt-driven device, and so on. Gathering as much customer and vehicle information as possible will assist in narrowing down the options of what is causing the fault.

The order in which various tests are undertaken is determined by the likelihood of a particular fault occurring given the facts you gather. For example, if the vehicle is in a parking lot, there is a better chance that the fault is an electrical fault in the starting system than if the vehicle is out in the woods, in the middle of a huge puddle of mud and water, which would tend to move the odds toward a hydrolocked or seized engine. You will also need to consider the ease of conducting a particular test or performing a visual inspection for determining the fault. For example, it is easier to perform a starter draw test than it is to pull the oil pan and inspect the main bearings. Always check for the most common and easiest faults first.

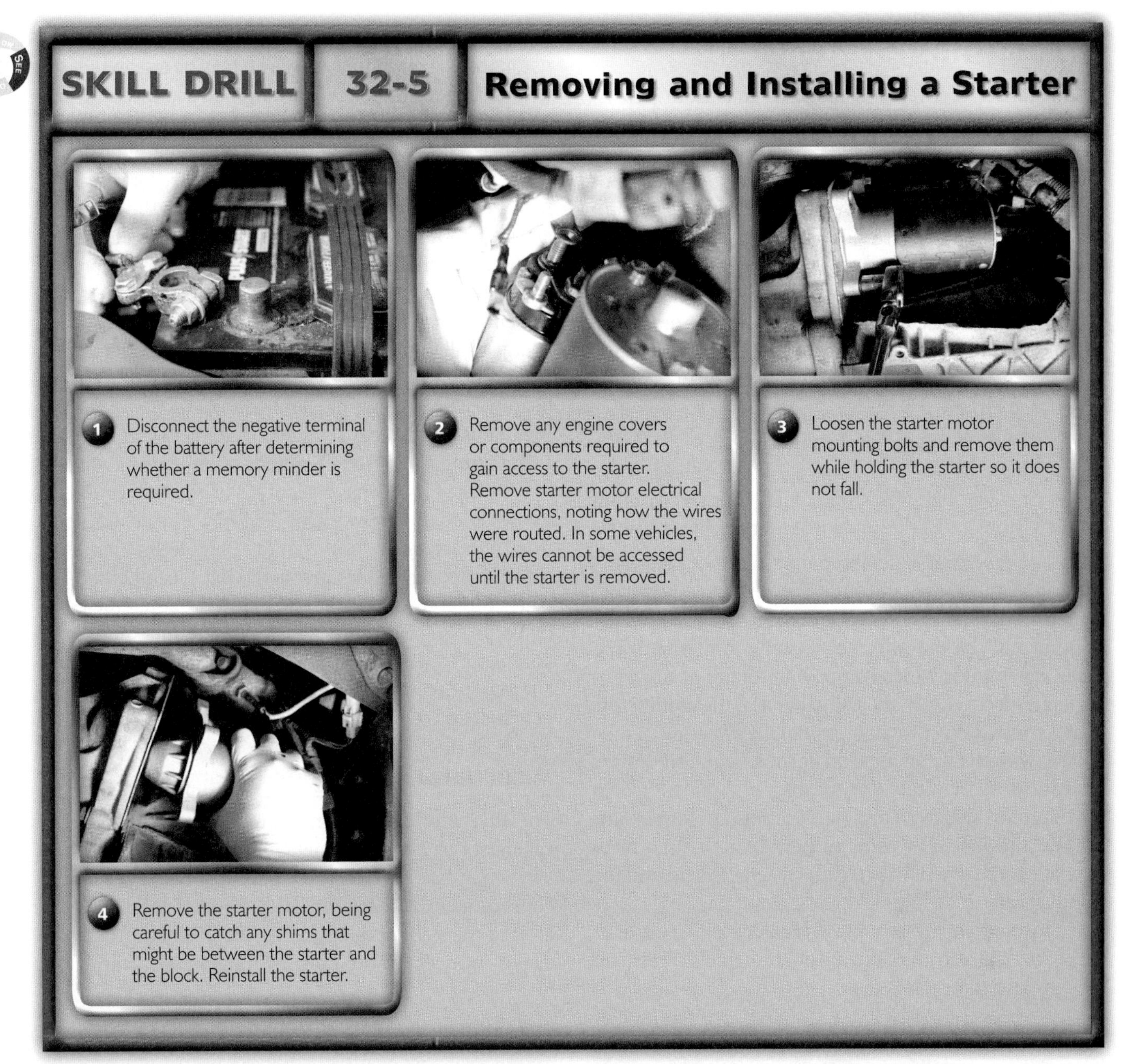
SKILL DRILL 32-5 Removing and Installing a Starter
1 Disconnect the negative terminal of the battery after determining whether a memory minder is required.
2 Remove any engine covers or components required to gain access to the starter. Remove starter motor electrical connections, noting how the wires were routed. In some vehicles, the wires cannot be accessed until the starter is removed.
3 Loosen the starter motor mounting bolts and remove them while holding the starter so it does not fall.
4 Remove the starter motor, being careful to catch any shims that might be between the starter and the block. Reinstall the starter.

If possible, measure starter motor current draw; excessive draw may indicate a starter motor electrical fault or a mechanical engine fault. A slow crank accompanied with low draw typically points to high resistance in the main starter circuit or the starter itself. A slow crank accompanied by a high draw could be due to a fault in the starter or to engine mechanical fault. If a mechanical fault is suspected, check the oil and coolant for signs of contamination. If the coolant and oil are mixing, suspect a head gasket or cracked head/block issue. If the oil and coolant are not contaminated, turn the engine over by hand to see if it is tight compared to a similar known good engine. If it is harder to turn than it should be, remove the accessory drive belt, spin each of the accessories, and try to turn the engine over again. If still hard to turn over, you will have to go deeper in your visual inspection and start disassembling components based on the information you have gathered along the way. For example, if the crankshaft cannot be turned a complete revolution, remove the spark plugs and see if liquid is ejected out of one or more spark plug holes. If so, the engine was hydrolocked and you will need to determine the cause. If no liquids are ejected, then you will need to disassemble the engine further until you determine the cause of the mechanical resistance.

The important thing to remember is that slow-crank and no-crank conditions can be caused by both electrical and mechanical faults, so don't jump to conclusions. You need to identify the root cause of the fault so you can advise the customer on what is needed to repair the vehicle.

Charging Systems

Compared to older vehicles, modern vehicles are increasingly dependent on electronic and electrical systems that require a constant and reliable supply of electrical power. Alternators (sometimes called AC generators, or just generators) supply the electrical energy required for modern vehicles FIGURE 32-21. The terms generator and alternator are often used interchangeably to describe the electrical generating component. Strictly speaking, the DC generator has not been used on most vehicles since the 1960s. Thanks to solid state electronics and circuitry, alternators have taken over due to their superior operating characteristics, including:

- Greater wattage output at lower rpm
- Higher rpm
- Smaller physical size and weight for a given output
- Greater reliability and longer service life (brushes)

Both DC generators and alternators produce electricity by relative movement of conductors in a magnetic field, which induces an electrical potential or voltage within the conductors. The key difference between an alternator and a DC generator is which component rotates or moves to generate electricity. In the DC generator, the conductors that generate power rotate as part of the armature, which rotates within a magnetic field created by the stationary pole shoes. In the alternator, the magnetic field is created by the rotor, which rotates within the stationary stator windings to generate electricity there. In both cases, there is relative movement between the magnetic field and the conductors.

The charging system provides electrical energy for all of the electrical components on the vehicle. The main parts of the charging system include the battery, the alternator, the voltage regulator (which may be integrated into the alternator), a charge warning light, and wiring that completes the circuits.

The battery stores an electrical charge in chemical form, acts as an electrical dampening device for variations in voltage or voltage spikes, and provides the electrical energy for cranking the engine. Once the engine is running, the alternator—which is connected to the engine and driven by a drive belt—converts some of the mechanical energy of the engine into electrical energy to supply energy to all the electrical components of the vehicle. The alternator also charges the battery to replace the energy used to start the engine. The voltage regulator circuit maintains optimal battery state of charge by sensing and maintaining a required charging system output voltage.

Older vehicles have separate (discrete) regulators mounted on the firewall FIGURE 32-22. The next generation of charging systems included regulators that were incorporated inside the alternator. More recently, the PCM is used to control the charging system more efficiently by controlling alternator output based on a number of parameters such as electrical load, engine load and rpm, alternator capability, battery temperature, fuel economy benefits, and more.

Alternator Principles

The alternator converts mechanical energy into electrical energy by electromagnetic induction. In a simplified version, a bar magnet rotates in an iron yoke, which concentrates the magnetic field. A coil of wire is wound around the stem of the yoke. As the magnet turns, voltage is induced in the coil, producing a current flow

FIGURE 32-21 Alternator.

AMERICAN BOSCH
RAB 128 5
ALTERNATOR
REGULATOR
MADE IN U.S.A

FIGURE 32-22 External voltage regulator.

FIGURE 32-23. When the north pole is up and south is down, voltage is induced in the coil, producing current flow in one direction. As the magnet rotates, and the positions of the poles reverse, the polarity of the voltage reverses as well and, as a result, so does the direction of current flow. Current that changes direction in this way is called alternating current, or AC. In this example, the change in direction occurs once for every complete revolution of the magnet.

Alternating Current

The value of the electromotive force (EMF) or voltage potential induced by an AC generator depends on four factors. The first is the strength of the magnetic field. Increasing the strength of the magnetic field increases the value (voltage output) of the induced EMF. The second factor is the speed at which the magnet rotates. The third factor is the relative distance between the magnet and conductors, and the last factor is the number of turns of wire on the stationary coil.

A single-phase AC generator has only one stationary coil, which creates a single sine wave. In a typical automobile alternator, three or possibly four separate coils of wire, or phase windings, are common. The windings are arranged so that when the magnet is rotated, it generates a three-phase (or four-phase) output. The phases are equally spaced in time, and this results in a phase shift of, in the case of a three-phase AC generator, one phase every 120 degrees FIGURE 32-24.

Alternator Components

The alternator consists of a stationary winding assembly called the stator, a rotating electromagnet called the rotor with a slip ring, a brush assembly, a rectifier assembly, two end frames, and a cooling fan and drive pulley FIGURE 32-25. A voltage regulator monitors battery voltage and varies current flow through the rotor field circuit, thus controlling the strength of the magnetic field

FIGURE 32-23 Electromagnetic induction.

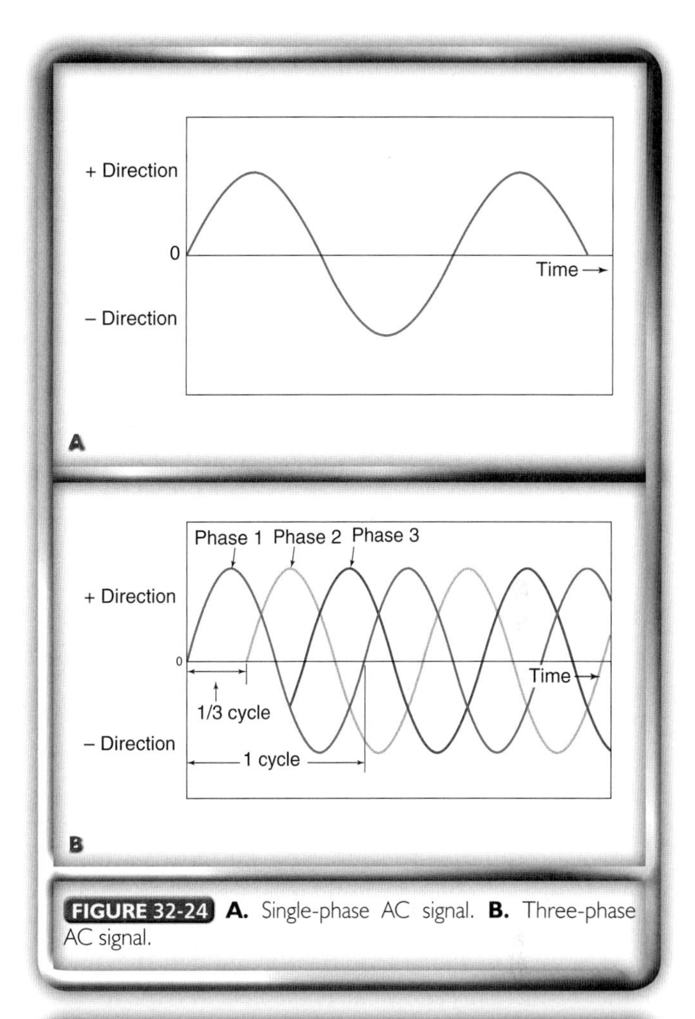
+ Direction
0
Time
– Direction
A
Phase 1
Phase 2
Phase 3
+ Direction
0
Time
1/3 cycle
– Direction
1 cycle
B

FIGURE 32-24 **A.** Single-phase AC signal. **B.** Three-phase AC signal.

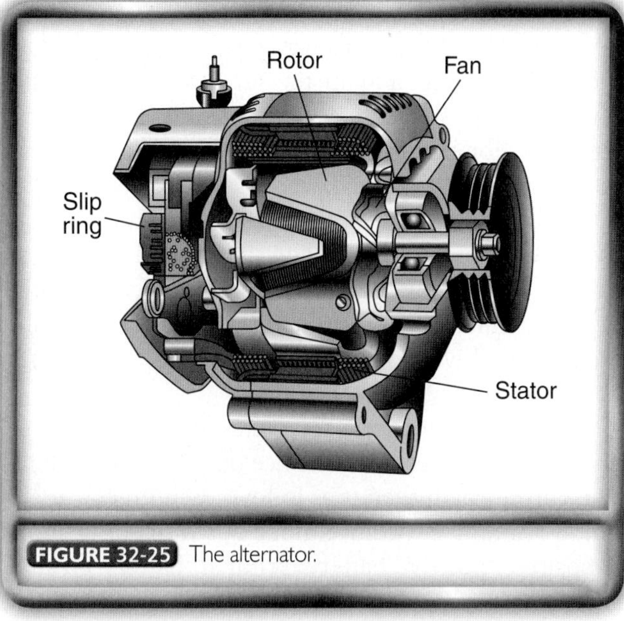
Rotor
Fan
Slip ring
Stator

FIGURE 32-25 The alternator.

of the rotating magnet. Field current varies as required to perhaps 5 or more amps to keep up with the output demand of the electrical system of perhaps 120 or more amps for a typical automobile. The voltage regulator's job then is to control the output of the alternator so that the system voltage is maintained within specified limits.

Rectification

Rectification is a process of converting AC into the DC that is required by the battery and nearly all of the automobile systems. To change AC to DC, automotive alternators use a rectifier assembly consisting of diodes in a specific configuration. Remember that a diode allows current to flow in one direction but blocks the flow of current in the other direction. A so-called three-phase "bridge" rectifier has a minimum of six diodes (three positive and three negative) to rectify the AC output of the stator windings to DC output from the rectifier. A diode bridge gets its name from two diodes in series bridged with a wire. If one end of a stator winding is connected between the diodes on the bridge, then the current flows through the ground diode into the winding and out of the winding and through the positive diode. In a three-phase alternator, one side of each winding is connected to one of the bridges. Since the other end of each winding is connected to at least one other winding, a complete path from the negative diode through a stator winding(s) and the positive diode can be completed as needed.

As the rotor rotates, each time the magnetic field changes from north to south and south to north, the polarity of each phase winding reverses and, as a result, the current changes direction. No matter what direction the current is flowing in the stator windings, the diodes in the rectifier only allow current to flow into the rectifier and out of the rectifier in one direction (DC). So the diodes take the current flowing no matter what direction through the stator windings and use the current flow (even if it is reversed) to push electrons out of the rectifier's positive terminal. For example, as the rotor turns, it induces a voltage in a stator winding, which generates current flow in one direction. In this position, and with this polarity, the current path is as follows: output of winding A, positive diode A, alternator terminal B-positive, positive battery terminal, battery ground (B-negative), alternator ground, negative diode B, output of winding B, neutral or star point FIGURE 32-26.

When the rotor's magnet rotates further, windings B and C come under the influence of the magnetic field. The current path then is as follows: winding C, at star point, winding B, positive diode B, alternator terminal B-positive, positive battery terminal, battery ground, alternator ground, negative diode C, output of winding C FIGURE 32-27. As the rotor moves through its various positions, individual phase currents change in magnitude and polarity, but the output current to the battery and the electrical circuits remains in one direction only. This is because the individual phase windings are set 120 degrees apart (three-phase system).

Thus, two things are happening. First, the three phases are split so that as the voltage in one phase is falling, the voltage in the next phase is still rising. As the second phase is falling, the third phase is rising. And as the third phase is falling, the first phase is rising again FIGURE 32-28.

Second, by redirecting the current so that it is flowing in the positive direction, the diodes effectively flip all of the current flow activity, from below the neutral point of

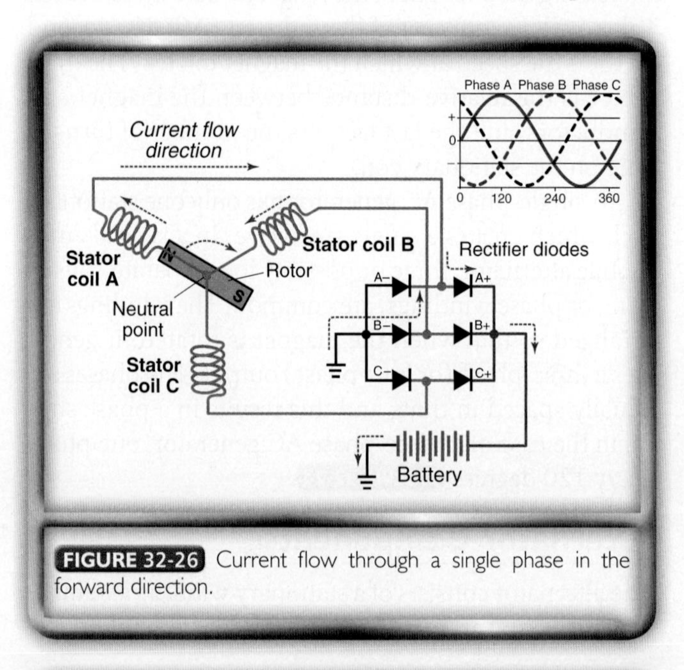
Phase A Phase B Phase C
+
0
–
0 120 240 360
Current flow direction
Stator coil B
Rotor
Stator coil A
Neutral point
Stator coil C
Rectifier diodes
A–
A+
B–
B+
C–
C+
Battery

FIGURE 32-26 Current flow through a single phase in the forward direction.

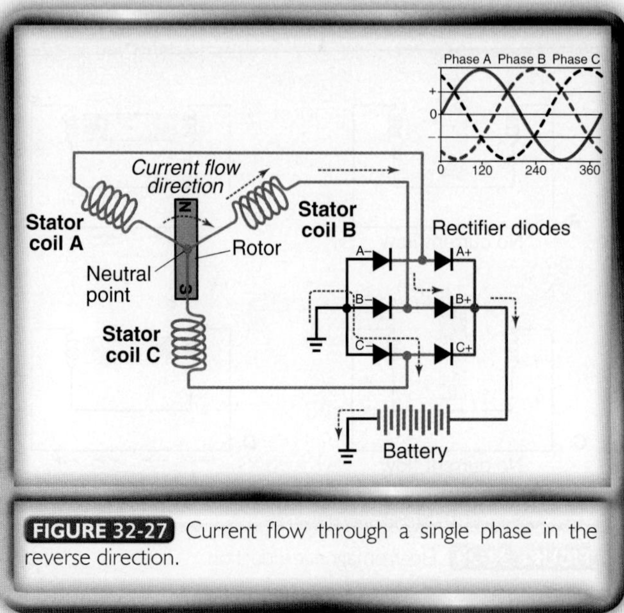
Phase A Phase B Phase C
+
0
–
0 120 240 360
Current flow direction
Stator coil A
Stator coil B
Rotor
Neutral point
Stator coil C
Rectifier diodes
A–
A+
B–
B+
C–
C+
Battery

FIGURE 32-27 Current flow through a single phase in the reverse direction.

the graph to the positive side, which smoothes out the power flow even further FIGURE 32-29.

The top of the waveform is called the alternator ripple. A ripple that is consistent across each winding indicates that the stator windings and diodes are each creating current flow and voltage consistently. Inconsistent ripple indicates a fault in either the diodes or the stator windings.

Study the illustrations carefully so that you understand the role the diode bridge plays in providing the relatively smooth DC output required by the automobile's systems.

Rotor Circuit

Current is provided to the rotor by means of the copper slip rings on the rotor and brushes. The rotor can be supplied with power in a variety of ways. On older vehicles, rotors on many vehicles were supplied power by means of three extra diodes, called a diode trio, and connected to the bridge rectifier circuit FIGURE 32-30. These extra diodes are known as field diodes or exciter diodes, and the alternator is said to be self-exciting. However, this self-excitation can only occur when the alternator is producing an output.

When the ignition is on, current flows from the positive battery terminal through the ignition switch and charge indicator lamp to the L terminal of the alternator FIGURE 32-31. The circuit is completed through the slip rings and rotor field winding, and through the voltage regulator, to ground on the vehicle frame.

The small amount of current flowing in the circuit illuminates the indicator lamp and provides the initial excitation of the field winding. This slightly magnetizes the rotor iron claw pole shoes and produces a weak magnetic field to get the generation process started.

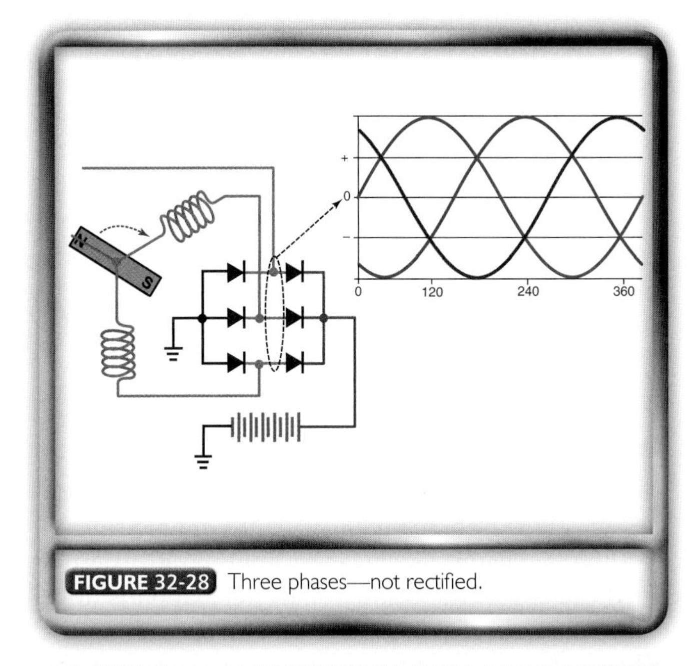
+
0
−
0
120
240
360
N
S

FIGURE 32-28 Three phases—not rectified.

RENARD
5205
USA0860

FIGURE 32-30 Diode trio supplies power to the rotor in some alternators.

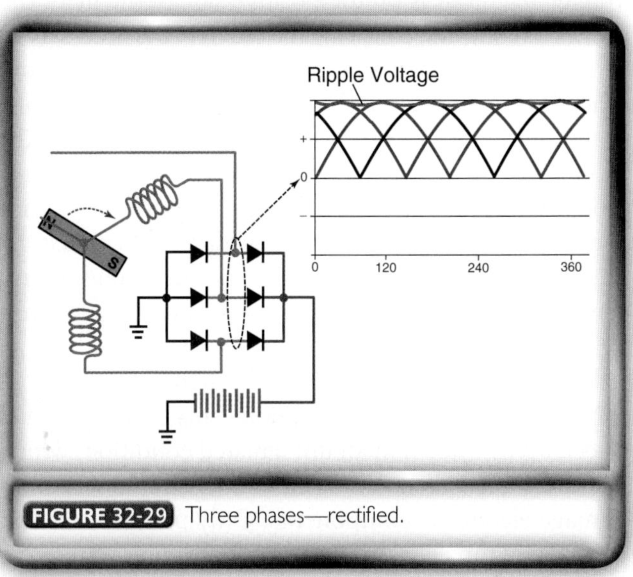
Ripple Voltage
+
0
−
0
120
240
360
N
S

FIGURE 32-29 Three phases—rectified.

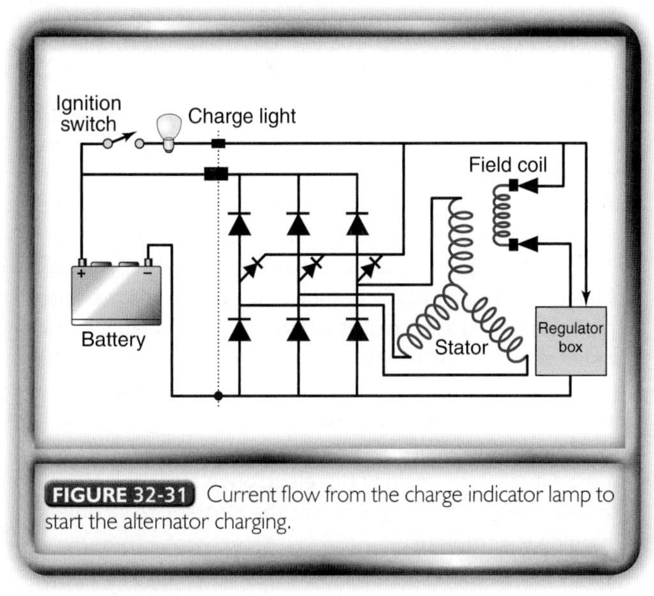
Ignition switch
Charge light
Field coil
Battery
Stator
Regulator box

FIGURE 32-31 Current flow from the charge indicator lamp to start the alternator charging.

When the rotor is driven (turned by the pulley) from the engine crankshaft, the rotating magnetic field induces a voltage in the stator phase windings, which is then fed to the bridge rectifier to create DC. From there, DC goes to the B-positive alternator output terminal. Stator output is also fed to the exciter diodes so that DC current can flow to the field circuit, restricted only by the resistance of the field winding (and the regulator circuit). This strengthens the magnetic field, and the output voltage rises quickly.

The voltage regulator takes control of the field circuit to limit field current to maintain a preset regulated output voltage at the B-positive terminal voltage of approximately 14 volts. As the voltage on each side of the charge indicator lamp is now equal (between the lamp and the diode trio), there is no current flow through the lamp, and the lamp is turned off.

Applied Science

AS-73: Electrochemical Reactions: The technician can demonstrate an understanding of the ion transfer process that occurs in an automotive battery.

A vehicle is in the shop for routine maintenance and a general inspection is being performed. The technician observes that the battery appears to be old and finds a code on the battery indicating it was manufactured six years ago.

At lunch time, the technician discusses the topic of batteries with another technician. He has the opinion that an automotive battery should be replaced every five years to prevent possible starting problems. Jim does not agree as he believes there are too many variables to make this determination. This leads to a discussion of how a lead acid battery works.

As stated in our text, in a discharged lead-acid cell, the active material of both plates becomes lead sulfate, and the electrolyte becomes mostly water as the acid is absorbed into the plates. The result is a very weak sulfuric acid solution in the electrolyte. When being charged, the battery is connected to a DC electrical supply with electrical pressure (voltage) higher than that of the battery's total cell voltage. The charging device acts like an electron pump, forcing electrons to move from the positive plates to the negative plates in the battery.

At the negative plates, sulfate is discharged, which changes the chemical composition of the plates into sponge lead and also creates a stronger solution of sulfuric acid in the electrolyte. At the same time, lead peroxide is formed at the positive plates, which helps to restore the cell's electrical potential or voltage.

The charging process increases the amount of acid in the electrolyte, making the electrolyte stronger. When further charging no longer makes the electrolyte stronger, charging is complete.

The alternator is now charging and since the output voltage at the B-positive alternator terminal is greater than that of the battery, current flows to the battery to begin the recharging process.

Voltage Regulation

The alternator's output is determined by the amount of current flowing through the rotor. The greater the current flow through the rotor, the stronger the magnetic field generated. The stronger the magnetic field, the stronger the alternator output. The voltage regulator monitors battery voltage and adjusts the current flow through the rotor appropriately.

When the engine is running and voltage output is low, the regulator allows more current to flow through the rotor field winding. This increased current flow strengthens the magnetic field, which raises the induced voltage in the stator windings, and alternator output then increases. As the output voltage increases to the maximum regulated voltage, the voltage regulator reduces the current flow through the rotor, reducing alternator output. Regulator switching takes place in milliseconds, so the voltage to the battery is fairly constant. This process occurs quickly enough to maintain consistent system voltage even as loads are switched on or off. Today's field circuits are electronically controlled by a pulse-width–modulated signal, for even smoother regulation and quicker control.

An A- or B-Type Regulating Circuit?

Switching of the field current may be done on the positive side of the rotor windings or on the ground side. In an A-type regulating circuit, alternator B-positive output is fed directly to the rotor; voltage regulation is done on the ground side of the field. In a B-type circuit, the voltage regulator is on the positive side of the field; the ground is constant. Knowing the difference is necessary in order to properly bypass a voltage regulator (full-fielding) when diagnosing some charging systems. For example, many alternators are designed with A-type circuits and a grounding tab on the regulator. The grounding tab provides a method of full-fielding the charging system with the engine running. The tab is grounded by placing a small metal rod or screw driver on the metal tab and then shorting it out by moving the side of the metal rod against the alternator frame. This grounds the A-type field causing full current to flow through the rotor, causing full alternator output. Caution: This procedure puts the charging system in an unregulated condition, which can cause the system voltage to increase high enough to damage electronic components. Only perform this test at idle, and for a few seconds. If the charging system is a

B type, then battery power needs to be fed to the field. This is usually accomplished by using a test lead or jumper lead to supply power to the correct terminal. Make sure you do not mix up the types of charging systems or supply power or ground to the wrong place, as you can damage the electronic components.

Charging System Output Test

Vehicle charging systems are voltage regulated, which means that the alternator will try to maintain a set voltage across the electrical systems. As electrical load current increases in the vehicle systems, voltage starts to drop. The voltage regulator senses this voltage drop and increases the current output of the alternator, which in turn increases system voltage to try to maintain the correct voltage in the system. The testing of an alternator output initially involves the testing of the system's regulated voltage using a voltmeter. Regulated voltage is the voltage at which the regulator is allowing the alternator to create only a small charge due to the battery being relatively charged, as evidenced by the greatly reduced current output. Regulated voltage should be between the manufacturer's specified minimum and maximum regulated voltage. If it is incorrect, verify that there are no voltage drops on the alternator and regulator. If no voltage drops are found, the regulator is likely faulty and will need to be replaced.

Once the regulated voltage is confirmed, it is time to check the charging system output. This is done by using an external electrical load such as a carbon pile to reduce the battery voltage, thereby tricking the regulator into full-fielding the alternator, making it produce maximum amperage output. This output is read using an inductive ammeter and should then be compared to the manufacturer's rated output specifications. An alternator that puts out within 10% of its rated output is OK. Less than that indicates a faulty regulator, faulty alternator, or excessive voltage drop(s) on the alternator output or ground circuits.

> **TECHNICIAN TIP**
>
> Back in the day of DC generators, it was acceptable to test the charging system by removing one of the battery terminals from the battery post. If the engine kept running, the charging system was working. If the engine died, the charging system was not working. On alternator-equipped vehicles, doing this test is very risky, since any voltage spike caused from disconnecting the battery terminal can destroy any of the electronics in the vehicle. Thus, this test is no longer valid on virtually all vehicles on the road today.

To perform a charging system output test, follow the steps in **SKILL DRILL 32-6**:

1. Connect a charging system tester to the battery with the red lead to the positive post, the black lead to the negative post, and the amps clamp around the alternator output wire.
2. Start the engine, turn off all accessories, and measure the regulated voltage at around 1500 rpm. The regulated voltage is the highest voltage the system achieves once the battery is relatively charged, as evidenced by the ammeter reading less than about 15–20 amps when the amps clamp is around the alternator output cable. Typical regulated voltage specifications are wider than they used to be due to the ability of the PCM to adjust the output voltage for a wide range of conditions. Thus, typical readings could be about 13.2–15.5 volts on newer vehicles and 13.5–14.5 volts on older vehicles. Always check the specifications.
3. Operate the engine at about 1500 rpm and either manually or automatically load down the battery just enough to obtain the maximum amperage output without pulling battery voltage below 12.0 volts. This reading should be compared against the alternator's rated output. Normally, readings more than 10% out of specifications indicate a problem.

Testing Charging System Circuit Voltage Drop

An excessive voltage drop in the charging system output and ground circuit tends to cause one of two problems: (1) The battery is not be fully charged because although the alternator is creating the specified voltage, the voltage drop is reducing the amount of voltage to the battery, or (2) the battery is fully charged, but the alternator is working at a higher voltage to do so, potentially overheating it. Which of the two issues is occurring depends on where the voltage is sensed. If it is sensed at the alternator, then the battery will generally be undercharged. If the voltage is sensed at the battery, then the alternator will work at the higher voltage. Knowing the system will help you diagnose voltage drop issues in the output and ground circuits of the charging system.

The external alternator output circuit components consist of the wires and fuse or fusible link between the positive battery post and the alternator output terminal, and the ground wire back to the battery from the engine and chassis. Voltage drop may occur anywhere in the output current circuit and ground circuit but is especially common at the terminals and connectors due to the high charging system current flowing through them. Even a small amount of resistance can cause significant voltage drop when conducting these higher levels of current flow.

As with testing for voltage drop at the starter circuit, a voltmeter or DVOM is used to measure voltage drop across all parts of the circuit. A voltmeter with a minimum/maximum range setting is very useful when measuring voltage drop, as it will record and hold the maximum voltage drop that occurs for a particular operation cycle. Voltage drop tests are only valid when the circuit is under load, because voltage drops can only occur when current is flowing. The greater the flow, the greater the voltage drop, if resistance is present. Therefore, when testing for voltage drop, always perform the test when the circuit is being operated.

To measure for voltage drop, the DVOM is connected in parallel across the component, cable, or connection that is to be tested. Usually it is most efficient to first measure the voltage drop on both the entire positive side and the entire negative side of the circuit, and if required, narrow down the test to individual components to identify precisely where excessive voltage drop is located (individual voltage drops in a simple circuit add up). For example, you can connect the black probe to the output side of the alternator and the red probe to the positive post of the battery. Then, operate the charging system under a heavy load by turning on as many electrical items as possible or by using a load tester to load down the battery. Record the voltage drop across the output side of the circuit while the alternator is fully charging. Then perform the same test on the ground side of the circuit from the negative battery terminal to the frame of the alternator. Manufacturers will typically specify the maximum allowable voltage drop, but a rule of thumb is no more than 0.5 volts (500 millivolts) for each side of a 12-volt circuit.

To perform a charging circuit voltage drop test, follow the steps in SKILL DRILL 32-7.

Replacing an Alternator

Alternators need to be replaced whenever they are electrically or mechanically faulty. Electrical faults include no-charge, undercharge, or overcharge conditions. Mechanical faults include worn and noisy bearings, or other internal or external mechanical damage. When replacing an alternator, there are some precautions, the

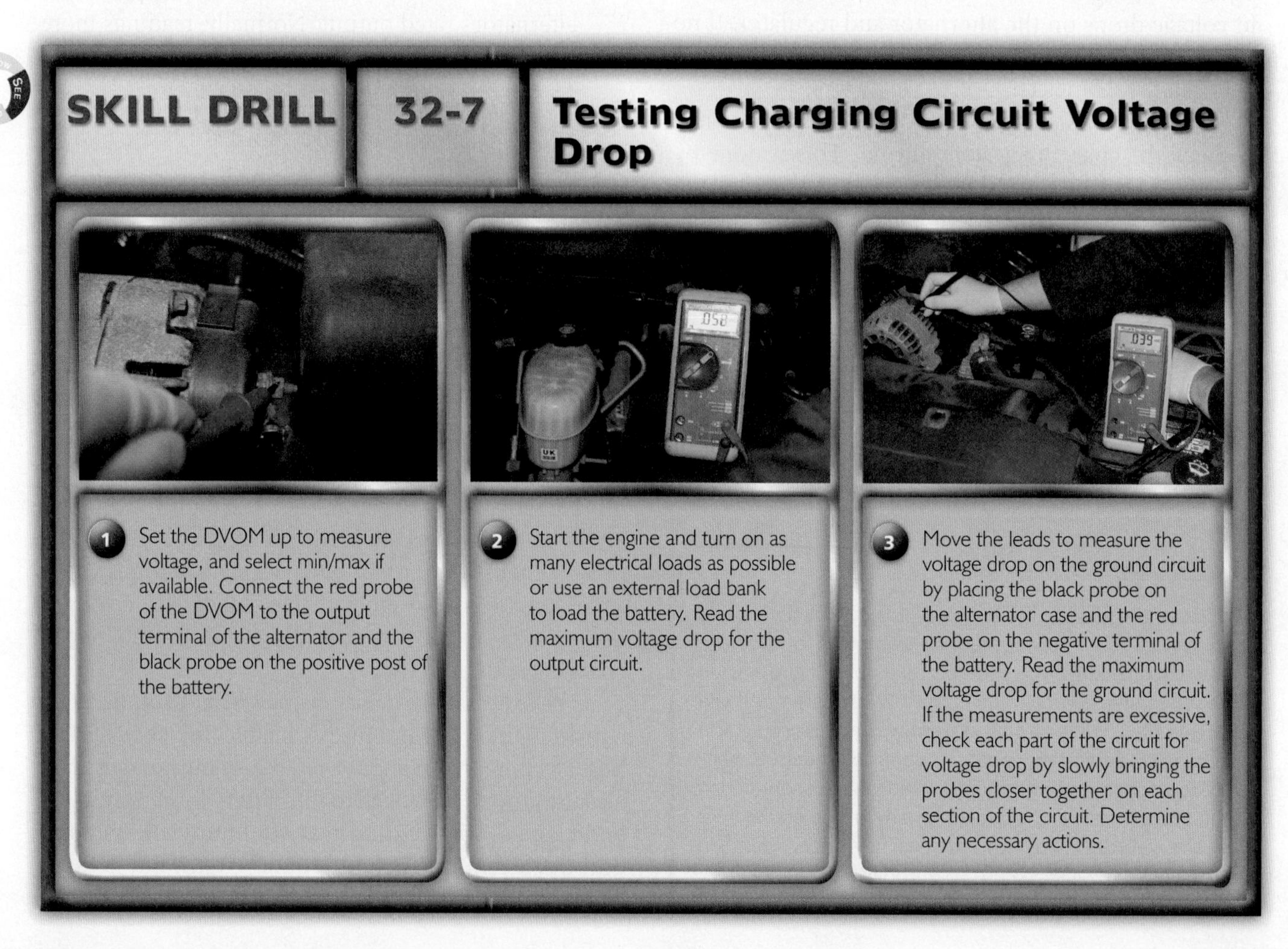

SKILL DRILL 32-7 Testing Charging Circuit Voltage Drop

1. Set the DVOM up to measure voltage, and select min/max if available. Connect the red probe of the DVOM to the output terminal of the alternator and the black probe on the positive post of the battery.

2. Start the engine and turn on as many electrical loads as possible or use an external load bank to load the battery. Read the maximum voltage drop for the output circuit.

3. Move the leads to measure the voltage drop on the ground circuit by placing the black probe on the alternator case and the red probe on the negative terminal of the battery. Read the maximum voltage drop for the ground circuit. If the measurements are excessive, check each part of the circuit for voltage drop by slowly bringing the probes closer together on each section of the circuit. Determine any necessary actions.

first being that battery voltage is always present at the output terminal of the alternator. This means that if the battery terminal is not removed from the battery and a wrench is placed on the output terminal of the alternator, a very large spark could occur if the wrench touches something metal. So always disconnect at least one battery terminal prior to removing the alternator. Also, check the manufacturer's information regarding maintaining the adaptive memory, if necessary.

The alternator must not be operated with the battery disconnected or with the terminals at the back of the alternator disconnected. Even though most vehicle electrical systems are described as being 12 volt, they typically operate at between 13.8 to 14.5 volts. If the system is not operating in this range, the drive belt may have become loose, or excessive voltage drops in the charging or voltage-sensing circuit may be the cause. If all of these components check out, the alternator, external voltage regulator, internal regulator, or even the built-in voltage-regulating circuit in the ECM/BCM may be faulty. Make sure you have identified the cause of the fault before removing the alternator.

To replace an alternator, follow the steps in SKILL DRILL 32-8.

Diagnosing Undercharge and Overcharge

Undercharging and overcharging are both bad for a vehicle. Undercharging leads to electrical systems that do not function fully, and the battery may not fully charge, leading to an early death due to sulfation. Overcharging can lead to short life of bulbs and other electrical devices, while at the same time overcharging the battery, which can increase gassing and loss of water from the electrolyte. Maintaining a proper charge is critical to long life and proper operation of the electrical system.

The voltage regulator maintains a constant voltage output from the alternator up to the maximum output current. Always check the manufacturer's specifications for alternator regulated voltages; more and more manufacturers are using PCM-controlled charging systems, which means the voltages can have a wider range than non-PCM-controlled systems.

As a rule of thumb, for a typical non-PCM-controlled 12-volt charging system, the regulated alternator output voltage should be between 13.8 and 14.5 volts. If the voltage measured is outside of the manufacturer's specifications, further testing will need to be performed to determine the cause.

For this task, we will assume that the charging system is charging (not a no-charge condition) and that it is either not charging fully or is overcharging. If the system is overcharging, it can almost always be tracked to either a faulty voltage regulator or a faulty regulator ground, both of which can cause the alternator to overcharge.

An undercharge condition has many more potential causes, such as a loose drive belt, voltage drop in the charging system wiring, faulty regulator, worn brushes in the alternator, high resistance in the rotor, open or shorted diodes, open or shorted stator windings, or even a shorted cell on a battery. Always check for the easiest

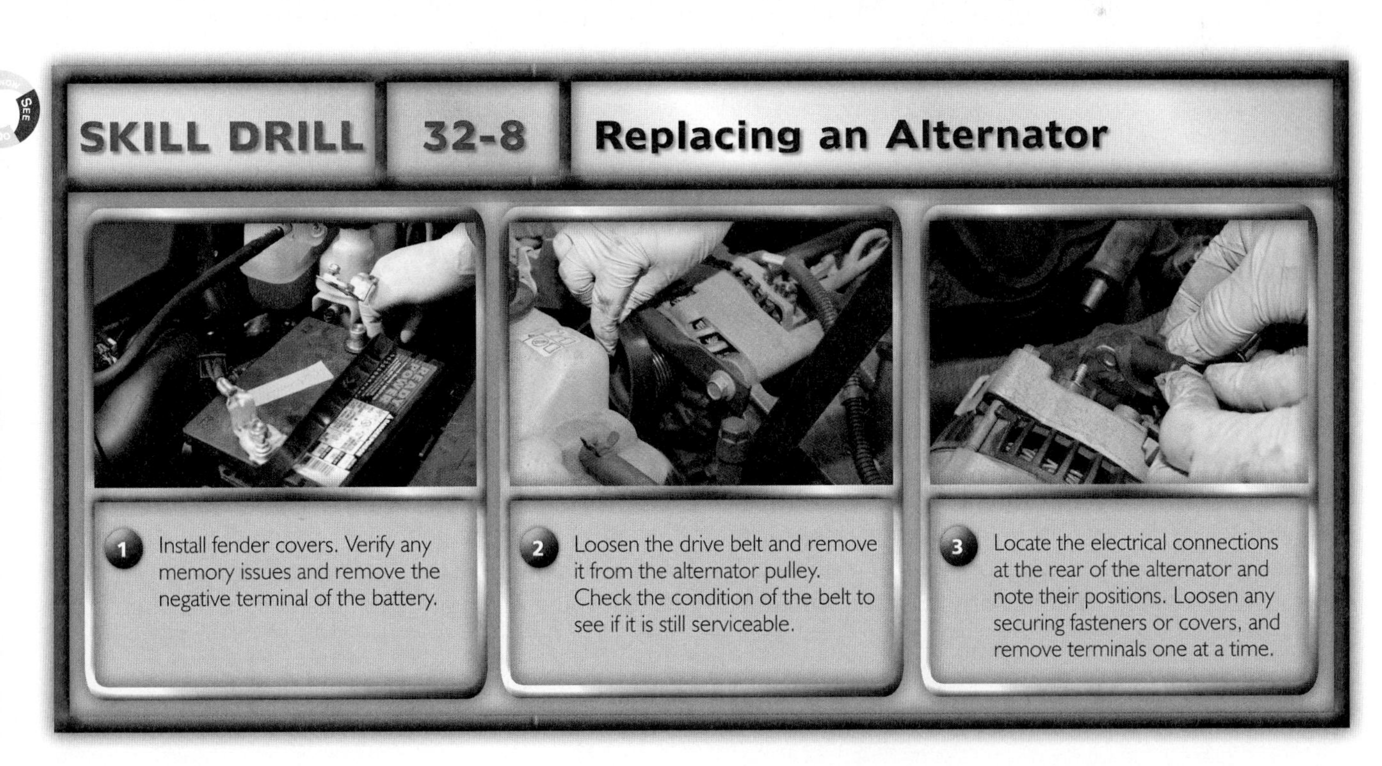
SKILL DRILL 32-8 Replacing an Alternator
1 Install fender covers. Verify any memory issues and remove the negative terminal of the battery.
2 Loosen the drive belt and remove it from the alternator pulley. Check the condition of the belt to see if it is still serviceable.
3 Locate the electrical connections at the rear of the alternator and note their positions. Loosen any securing fasteners or covers, and remove terminals one at a time.

SKILL DRILL 32-8 Replacing an Alternator, continued
4 Loosen the securing fasteners that hold the alternator to its mounting bracket(s), making sure the alternator is supported. Remove the alternator.
5 Reinstall the alternator. Situate the alternator in the mounting bracket(s) and, while still supporting the alternator, loosely start the securing fasteners that hold the alternator to its mounting bracket(s).
6 Reinstall the electrical wires to their correct terminals, referring to the manufacturer's information. Check the security of any fastening devices.
7 Install the drive belt over the alternator drive pulley and, using the correct tools, adjust the belt to the correct tension.
8 Reattach to the negative post of the battery. Make sure the fastener is tight and replace any battery terminal covers.
9 Turn the ignition to the on position and make sure the charge light on the instrument panel illuminates. Start the engine see if the charge light goes off. Measure the regulated voltage and maximum alternator amperage output. Remove the fender covers and return any tools used to their correct place.

and most common faults first. For example, check that the drive belts are not slipping, particularly under load. Also verify that the battery does not have a shorted cell and that its capacity is adequate.

If nothing obvious can be found wrong, then you will need to dig deeper. One way to do this is to use an oscilloscope to check the alternator ripple. The ripple will indicate faulty stator windings or diodes, meaning the alternator needs to be replaced. If the ripple is OK and the voltage output is low, then testing for voltage drops on the output and ground circuit is a good step. If voltage drops are found, then they will need to be repaired and the system retested. If there are no voltage drops, then the fault is likely to be located inside of the alternator, such as a faulty regulator, worn brushes, or a faulty rotor, which would also require replacement of the alternator.

Wrap-up

Ready for Review

- The starting system provides a method of rotating (cranking) the vehicle's internal combustion engine (ICE) to begin the combustion cycle.
- The starting system consists of a battery, cables, a solenoid, a starter motor, a ring gear, and an ignition switch.
- The starter motor converts electrical energy to mechanical energy.
- Some starters operate through gear reduction, giving the same amount of torque at less size and weight.
- A starter motor is basically an electromagnet.
- The starter motor pinion must mesh with the engine ring gear to turn the engine over and allow the vehicle to start.
- Once the engine starts running on its own, the starter must disengage from the ring rear to avoid damaging the starter or the ring gear.
- The solenoid on the starter motor performs two main functions: It switches the high current flow required by the starter motor, and it engages the starter drive with the ring gear.
- Vehicle immobilizers generally comprise a computer-managed security system that disables the start and engine systems by using an electronic system to uniquely identify each vehicle key by a security code system.
- Hybrid vehicles use both an ICE and electric motors to power the vehicle's drive train.
- Testing starter motor current draw is a good indicator of overall starter motor performance.
- Compared to older vehicles, newer vehicles put a higher demand on the charging system, as many systems are required not only to operate the vehicle but also to operate an array of entertainment systems.
- The DC generator has not been used on vehicles since the 1960s.
- The AC generator, or alternator, is used on today's vehicles both to recharge the vehicle battery and to run numerous other electrical accessories on the vehicle.
- The alternator converts mechanical energy into electrical energy.
- The alternator changes AC to DC by using a rectifier with diodes to allow electrical current to flow in one direction only.
- The alternator has a regulator, either built in or external, to keep the alternator from overcharging the battery.
- The more amps the alternator can produce, the more accessories the vehicle electrical system can handle.
- The first item that should be checked if an alternator is not charging according to the manufacturer's specifications is the belt tension and condition.

Key Terms

counter-electromotive force (CEMF) Voltage created in the field windings as the motor rotates, which opposes battery voltage and limits motor speed.

current clamp A device that clamps around a conductor to measure current flow. It is often used in conjunction with a DVOM.

hold-in winding A low-current winding found in starter solenoids that holds the plunger in the activated position.

pull-in winding A high-current winding found in starter solenoids that pulls the solenoid plunger into the activated position.

rectification A process of converting AC into DC required by the battery and nearly all of the automobile systems.

ASE-Type Questions

1. Tech A says that some starters use gear reduction to improve efficiency. Tech B says that a starter converts electrical energy to mechanical energy. Who is correct?
   a. Tech A
   b. Tech B
   c. Both A and B
   d. Neither A nor B
2. Tech A says that the pull-in winding is short-circuited when the solenoid is fully engaged. Tech B says that the starter drive has a built-in one-way clutch. Who is correct?
   a. Tech A
   b. Tech B
   c. Both A and B
   d. Neither A nor B
3. Tech A says that a voltage drop of 0.8 volts on the starter ground circuit is within specifications. Tech B says that high starter draw current could be caused by a spun main bearing in the engine. Who is correct?
   a. Tech A
   b. Tech B
   c. Both A and B
   d. Neither A nor B
4. Tech A says that the first item to check if an engine does not crank is the voltage to the S-terminal on the starter. Tech B says that the first item to check if an engine does not crank is battery voltage. Who is correct?
   a. Tech A
   b. Tech B
   c. Both A and B
   d. Neither A nor B
5. Tech A says that the voltage regulator controls the strength of the rotor's magnetic field. Tech B says that the voltage regulator is installed between the output terminal of the alternator and the positive terminal of the battery. Who is correct?
   a. Tech A
   b. Tech B
   c. Both A and B
   d. Neither A nor B
6. Tech A says that overcharging can lead to short life of bulbs and other electrical devices. Tech B says that maintaining a proper charge is critical to long life and proper operation of the electrical system. Who is correct?
   a. Tech A
   b. Tech B
   c. Both A and B are correct
   d. Neither A nor B
7. Tech A says that an excessive voltage drop in the alternator output circuit will likely cause a high charging system voltage. Tech B says that the alternator output circuit voltage drop must be checked with the charging system under a heavy load. Who is correct?
   a. Tech A
   b. Tech B
   c. Both A and B are correct
   d. Neither A nor B
8. Tech A says that most hybrid vehicles use the high voltage electric motor to start the engine. Tech B says that most hybrid engines need to crank over more slowly than regular engines. Who is correct?
   a. Tech A
   b. Tech B
   c. Both A and B are correct
   d. Neither A nor B
9. Failure to crank over properly, whether a slow-crank or a no-crank condition can be caused by electrical or mechanical problems. Tech A says that failure to crank over properly is always caused by mechanical problems. Tech B says that failure to crank over properly is always caused by electrical problems.
   a. Tech A
   b. Tech B
   c. Both A and B are correct
   d. Neither A nor B
10. Tech A says that the starter drive uses a pinion gear on an internal spline that mates with a slightly curved external spline on the armature shaft with an overrunning clutch, and a return spring. Tech B says that on some engines the starter motor is mounted at the top of the engine under the intake manifold. Who is correct?
    a. Tech A
    b. Tech B
    c. Both A and B are correct
    d. Neither A nor B

CHAPTER 33

Know
See
Do
Prove

NATEF Tasks

Electrical/Electronic Systems Lighting Systems			Page
■ Identify system voltage and safety precautions associated with high-intensity discharge headlights.	MLR	AST	958–960
■ Inspect interior and exterior lamps and sockets including headlights and auxiliary lights (fog lights/driving lights); replace as needed.	MLR	AST	960–961
■ Aim headlights.	MLR	AST	962–963
Required Supplemental Tasks Shop And Personal Safety			
■ Demonstrate awareness of the safety aspects of high voltage circuits (such as high intensity discharge (HID) lamps, ignition systems, injection systems, etc.).	MLR	AST	958–960

Lighting Systems

Know
See
Do

Knowledge Objectives

After reading this chapter, you will be able to:

1. Describe different types of lighting found on a vehicle and the function of each type. (pp 946–958)
2. Explain the operation and benefits of various lighting systems. (pp 950–958)

Know
See
Do

Skills Objectives

After reading this chapter, you will be able to:

1. Check lighting and peripheral systems. (p 960)
2. Check and change an exterior light bulb. (p 961)
3. Check and change a headlight bulb. (pp 961–962)
4. Aim headlights. (pp 962–963)

Introduction

Well-designed vehicle lighting systems enhance vehicle safety by increasing the driver's visibility while operating the vehicle and by clearly signaling the driver's intent to those around the vehicle. Lighting systems are also used inside the vehicle to indicate messages to the driver and provide convenience to any occupants. Manufacturers continue to improve and develop their lighting systems as new technology becomes available. Modern lighting system features include the increased use of light-emitting diode (LED) and xenon lighting, electronic body control units to manage lighting, and high-intensity discharge (HID) lamps, which are much brighter than the traditional sealed-beam or halogen units. Many vehicles also have systems that warn you if lamps are not working properly.

Lighting Systems

Lighting systems improve visibility at night and make a vehicle visible to other road users. A lighting switch activates taillights, park lights, and headlights to allow the driver to see ahead and be seen from the side and rear. A beam selector switch allows the driver to change the beams from high to low, or vice versa, as required. Brake lights operate when the brake pedal is depressed or when a vehicle control module is automatically applying the brakes. Red or amber turn signals alert other drivers of a change in direction and are mounted so they can be seen from the front, the rear, and sometimes the sides of the automobile. The emergency flasher system operates both front and rear turn signals at the same time as a warning to others. Other circuits operate courtesy, or convenience, lights, back-up (reverse) lights, fog lights, and fault indicators.

Types of Lamps

Modern vehicles use many different kinds and sizes of lamps, also known in some places as light bulbs or light globes. There are several lamp types available, including standard incandescent lamps, halogen lamps, vacuum tube fluorescent (VTF) lighting, HID xenon gas systems, LEDs, and more. Conventional incandescent lamps are being replaced in many applications by these other more efficient types of lights.

Incandescent and Halogen

Incandescent lamps consist of one or more filaments that heat up to approximately 5000°F (2760°C) and glow white hot FIGURE 33-1. The filament material does not burn because most of the oxygen in the bulb has been replaced by inert gases that stop combustion from occurring. The power in watts consumed is often marked on the lamp; wattage (work performed) is found by multiplying the voltage used by the lamp by the current flowing through it. The higher the wattage, the more light that can be created when compared to a similar type of bulb. Incandescent bulbs are inefficient, converting only about 10% of the electricity to visible light.

Halogen lamps are another type of incandescent lamp, but they are filled with a halogen gas such as

You Are the Automotive Technician

A customer brings his 2010 Dodge Avenger into the auto dealership for a 60,000 mile service checkup. You take the vehicle back to the service bay. Part of the 60,000 mile service is to check the lighting and peripheral systems. Your coworker operates each of the lights while you check the front lights and then the rear lights. You notice that the center high mount stop light (CHMSL) on the trunk lid is not functioning, but the brake lights are working normally. The customer agrees to allow you to diagnose it. After referring to the manufacturer's information and wiring diagrams, you see that the CHMSL is on the same fuse as the brake lights, so that does not need to be investigated further. You see also that the brake switch feeds both the CHMSL and brake lights, so that does not need to be investigated further. Based on your reading of the wiring diagram, you determine that the problem is between the brake switch and CHMSL, between the CHMSL and the ground, or the CHMSL bulbs or unit are faulty. You test the power and ground at the CHMSL terminals with the brake pedal applied. You find 12.2 volts available. Since the CHMSL is a sealed LED-style assembly, you know it will need to be replaced. The customer approves the repair, and you install the new CHMSL and test the vehicle again. Your coworker verifies that the light is working properly. You review the work and invoice with the customer, thank him for his business, and set him up in the automated email system to send a reminder to schedule his next maintenance visit.

1. Why didn't you have to check the fuse or brake switch?
2. What did the 12.2 volt reading at the CHMSL terminals tell you?
3. How do wiring diagrams save time?

FIGURE 33-1 Incandescent bulb with single filament.

FIGURE 33-2 Halogen bulb.

bromine or iodine FIGURE 33-2. These lamps have a much longer life and are generally brighter and produce more light per unit of power consumed. However, they become very hot in use. They are manufactured from highly heat-resistant materials, and the bulbs must be handled carefully because they are sensitive and can be damaged even by finger oil residue left by fingerprints.

Vacuum Tube Fluorescent

Vacuum tube fluorescent (VTF), also called vacuum fluorescent display (VFD), is used for instrumentation displays on vehicle instrument panel clusters. This type of lighting emits a very bright light with high contrast and can display in various colors. Usually VTF displays are of bar graphs, seven-segment numerals, multisegment alphanumeric characters, or a dot-matrix pattern. VTF displays include different kinds of alphanumeric characters and symbols to alert drivers of various conditions.

High-Intensity Discharge

High-intensity discharge (HID) headlamps produce light with an electric arc rather than a glowing filament FIGURE 33-3. The high intensity of the arc comes from metallic salts that are vaporized within an arc chamber. HIDs produce more light for a given level of power consumption than ordinary tungsten or halogen bulbs. Automotive HID lamps are commonly called "xenon headlamps," though they are actually metal halide lamps that contain xenon gas. The light from HID headlamps exhibits a distinct bluish tint as compared with the yellow-white color of tungsten-filament headlamps.

HID headlamp bulbs do not run on low-voltage direct current; they require a **ballast** with an internal or an external igniter that is either integrated into the bulb or included as a separate unit or part of the ballast. The ballast increases the voltage substantially and controls the current to the bulb.

FIGURE 33-3 HID headlamp assembly.

HID headlamps produce between 2800 and 3500 lumens from between 35 and 38 watts, while halogen filament headlamp bulbs produce between 700 and 2100 lumens from between 40 and 72 watts at 12.8 volts. The advantage of using HID headlight systems is that they offer substantially greater luminance than halogen bulbs (about 3000 lumens versus 1400 lumens for comparable halogen bulbs). If the higher-output HID light source is used in a well-engineered headlamp optic, the driver gets more usable light. Studies indicate that drivers react faster and more accurately to roadway obstacles when using good HID headlamps than when using halogen headlamps; therefore, good HID headlamps contribute to driving safety.

The contrary argument is that HID headlamps can impact negatively the vision of oncoming traffic due to their high intensity and the "flashing" effect caused by the rapid transition between low and high illumination in the field of illumination. This potential distraction increases the risk of a head-on collision between a vehicle using HID headlamps and a blinded oncoming driver. Scientific studies of headlamp glare from HID systems has shown that for any given intensity level, the light from HID headlamps is 40% more glaring than the light from tungsten-halogen headlamps.

Some countries mandate that HID headlamps may only be installed on vehicles (except motorcycles) with lens-cleaning systems (to reduce glare) and automatic self-leveling systems (which prevent dazzling oncoming traffic). These systems are usually absent on vehicles not originally equipped with HID lamps, so if a halogen headlamp is retrofitted with an HID bulb, light distribution with illegal levels of glare will be produced.

Another disadvantage of HID headlamps is that they are significantly more costly to produce, install, purchase, and repair. However, some of this cost is offset by the longer lifespan of the HID burner relative to halogen bulbs.

Light-Emitting Diode

Light-emitting diodes (LEDs) have been used for some time in various automotive applications, such as warning indicators and alphanumeric displays. More recent developments in LED technology have seen the production of a wider range of colors and LEDs that are brighter than previous types. It is now possible to get LEDs that emit bright red, green, blue, yellow, and clear or white light. This has made it possible to use LEDs for many new applications, such as more general lighting applications. For example, LEDs are now often used for stop lights, turn signals, and interior lighting on vehicles FIGURE 33-4.

One of the advantages of LEDs is that they turn on instantly. This is particularly useful in brake lights, as they can reduce the braking light response time by two-tenths of a second. This translates to an extra 16' (4.9 meters) of stopping distance for vehicles traveling at highway speeds. LEDs also have better visibility in inclement weather, operate at cooler temperatures, consume less energy, are much smaller, and can last up to 100 times longer, reducing the cost of servicing. LEDs can be specifically designed for LED lighting and also as LED replacement bulbs for more traditional bulb holders.

For automotive applications, a number of LEDs are grouped together to provide the amount of light required for the application. Additionally, LED light lenses are specifically designed with light-focusing prisms and lenses to focus the light generated by the LEDs. A typical LED has a voltage drop of 1.2 to 3.5 volts across it, depending upon the color, when it is forward biased and emitting light.

FIGURE 33-4 LED lights.

When used in automotive lighting, many LEDs are required to give off a specified amount of light. To do so they are usually connected in groups called series strings. A number of series strings are then connected in parallel until enough LEDs are connected to give off the required amount of light.

LEDs work best when the voltage to them and the current flow through them remains constant at a preset level. There are two main ways to achieve this; the first is via a resistor. The second and more preferred way is through the use of a voltage regulation circuit.

Some LED lights are multivoltage, which means they can work on both 12- and 24-volt systems. These lights are normally used in aftermarket products, which can be installed in a wide range of vehicles.

Lamp/Light Bulb Information

All lamps or light bulbs have letters and numbers stamped on them that typically indicate their part number and often the operating voltage and power consumed. For instance, in a bulb marked 12V/21W, the filament will consume 21 watts of power when 12 volts is applied across the filament. While the wattage is not necessarily an indication of light output, it can be generally assumed that the higher the wattage, the greater the light output.

Lamps and light bulbs come in a variety of configurations to fit the various applications within a vehicle. One designation is how many filaments the bulb has FIGURE 33-5. Single-filament bulbs are common for use as courtesy lights, dash lights, and warning lights. Dual-filament bulbs have two filaments of different wattage; one filament emits a small amount of light, and the

FIGURE 33-5 Dual-filament bulb.

FIGURE 33-6 Bayonet-style bulbs.

second filament emits more light. These bulbs work well as a combination taillight and brake light. Headlights can also be dual-filament bulbs. In some cases, the low beam filament is lower wattage than the high beam filament, but not always. In a headlight, the filaments are positioned to give a different profile of light. Low beams emit light closer to the vehicle and angled slightly toward the side of the road, while high beams tend to focus farther down the road and straight ahead.

Another feature that differs among lights is the type of base on the lamp—in other words, what type of socket it is retained in. Bayonet-style bulbs have been around for a long time. They get their name from the two retaining pins on the side of the base FIGURE 33-6. The pins follow slots in the side socket and at the bottom, and the slots turn sideways into a small pocket. The pins are retained in the pocket by the spring-loaded base in the bottom of the socket, which pushes the bulb upward. This design resists vibration very well. Removal of the bulb requires carefully pushing in on the bulb and rotating the bulb slightly counterclockwise and pulling it out. One or two electrical contacts are built into the bottom of the bulb's base. If the bulb is a dual-filament bulb with two contacts on the base, then the pins will be unequal height so that the contacts will be registered properly with the contacts in the socket.

Many newer bulbs use a wedge base either made from the glass bulb itself or with a built-in plastic base FIGURE 33-7. The bulbs are pushed straight into the socket, and tension from the socket retains the bulb. The electrical contact on the glass-based bulbs is made by wires extending from the base of the bulb and bent over opposite sides of the wedge.

Dome lights use festoon lights, which have a base on each end of a cylindrical light bulb FIGURE 33-8. Each end

FIGURE 33-7 Wedge-style bulbs.

FIGURE 33-8 Festoon-style bulbs.

of the filament is connected to one of the bases. Generally, the bases fit in spring steel contacts, which hold the light bulb securely in place.

Types and Styles of Lighting Systems

There are many different styles and types of lights. Each style and type is designed to perform specific roles. For example, warning lamps, turn indicators, stop lights, taillights, courtesy lamps, and headlamps all perform different roles. Lamp locations, color, and brightness are governed by regulations to ensure consistency and safety in the application of lighting on vehicles. Lighting regulations should always be consulted before modifying or adding to any of the vehicle lighting systems. Well-maintained lighting systems improve road safety for all drivers.

Courtesy Lights

Courtesy lights or lamps are used to provide ambient lighting in the cabin. They are usually low-intensity or low-wattage bulbs and can be overhead, in the doors, glove compartment, and the trunk. Door and latch switches control the various lamps for the trunk and glove compartment. Courtesy lights are usually controlled by the vehicle body computer with inputs from the ignition and door switches either in the handle, latch, or door pillar. Courtesy lights may be designed with timing circuits that allow for the cabin lamps to stay on for a short period after all the doors are shut or the vehicle is locked.

Warning Lights

Warning lamps are usually part of the instrument cluster and are controlled by electronic control units in the vehicle on a modern vehicle. Warning lamps provide the vehicle operator with information regarding the operation of the main vehicle systems, such as the vehicle battery charge level, oil pressure level, and airbag system status FIGURE 33-9. When the ignition initially comes on, the warning lamps usually light up as part of a self-test to show that they are in working order. Once the engine starts, the warning lamps should extinguish and not come on again while the engine is running, unless there is a system fault. Some vehicles have warning lights that self-test while the vehicle is being cranked. This function is performed by the "proofing circuit" in the ignition switch, which grounds certain warning lights when turned to the "crank" position.

40
80
BRAKE
ABS
210
100
260

FIGURE 33-9 Warning lamp.

Park/Tail/Marker/License Lights

Park, tail, and marker lights are all low-intensity or low-wattage bulbs used to mark the outline or width of the vehicle. Park and tail lamps tend to be installed close to the corners of the vehicle. Park lamps are placed to the front of the vehicle, or in some cases they are incorporated in the headlight assembly and are white or yellow in color. Tail lamps are red and usually installed in a cluster assembly with the stops lamps at the rear of the vehicle.

License plate lamps produce a white light and are designed to illuminate the lettering on the license plate at night without the white light itself being seen from the rear. The bulbs are connected in parallel to each other so that the failure of one filament will not cause a total circuit failure. A license plate illumination lamp or lamps are usually connected in parallel to the taillights and operate whenever the taillights are on.

Taillights are usually incorporated in a cluster assembly at the rear of the vehicle. Government regulations control the height of the lamps and their brightness.

Park lights are located at the front of the vehicle and are used at night when the vehicle is parked on the side of the road and are also on anytime the headlights are on. They use low-wattage bulbs and may have a lens or diffuser that makes the emitted light widespread. In some cases, park lights are incorporated in the headlight assembly. Park lights operate when the light switch is moved to the park light position. For safety reasons, park lights and taillights continue to operate when the light switch is moved to the headlight position. The bulbs are connected in parallel with each other.

> **TECHNICIAN TIP**
>
> In many vehicles produced before the mid-1960s, front park lights turn off when the headlights are on. The thinking was that if the headlights are on, then the park lights were unnecessary. The problem arose when a headlight failed and only one light illuminated on the front of the vehicle, mimicking a motorcycle, which gave the impression of the vehicle being narrower than it is. Designing the park lights to stay on with the headlights helped to prevent this unsafe situation.

On computer-controlled lighting systems, the park lights and taillights are BCM controlled. The lights are supplied with power and ground through a networked light controller. The controller is connected to a network/bus system by the twisted pair of communication wires. The park light switch is hardwired to a module. When the park light switch is activated, the module sends a park light request out on the network where the appropriate controllers pick up the message and supply power or ground to the appropriate light bulb filaments to illuminate the park lights.

Marker lights are used to mark the sides of some vehicles are often located down the sides of the vehicle or trailer. They can be located on the front and rear fenders. On newer vehicles, they are sometimes placed on side-view mirrors, or between the front and the rear doors on large SUVs or pick-ups FIGURE 33-10. Red marker lamps face toward the rear, and yellow lamps face toward the front of the vehicle. These lights are designed to work when the park lights or headlights are selected and sometimes operate as turn signals so a driver can warn others of his or her intent to switch lanes or turn a corner.

FIGURE 33-10 Marker lights on an SUV.

Government regulations control the positioning of lights, including the height of the lamps' beam and their brightness. The park, tail, marker, and license plate lamps operate when the headlight switch is in both the park and the headlight-on positions. The bulbs are connected in parallel to each other so that the failure of one filament will not cause a total circuit failure. Tail and park lamps may use separate fuses, so if one circuit fails the other will continue to operate.

Brake Lights and CHMSL

Brake lights, which may also be called stop lights, are red lights mounted to the rear of the vehicle. They are usually incorporated in the taillight cluster. Many vehicles by law now have a higher additional third brake light mounted on top of the trunk lid or on the rear window. This light is called a center high mount stop light (CHMSL), or "chimsul" FIGURE 33-11. The brake lights are activated whenever the driver operates the foot brake to slow or to stop the vehicle or when a control module automatically applies the brakes. The lighting circuit consists of the battery, fusible links and fuses, a brake light switch, brake light bulbs, wiring to connect the components, and the ground circuit to return current from the light to the battery. It may also include a BCM to command the lights on when the proper inputs are present.

On older vehicle models, when the operator of the vehicle depresses the brake pedal, a switch mounted on the pedal support closes. This allows the electrical current to flow from the battery through the fuse, through the switch, to the brake lamp and to return to the battery by the ground circuit. When the driver releases the pedal, it returns to the rest position and opens the brake switch. The flow of electrical current stops and the brake lamps

FIGURE 33-11 Center high mount stop light.

are extinguished. Today, computer-controlled brake lights are activated by the body control module (BCM) when the computer sees an input from the brake pedal switch.

Applied Science

AS-33: Refraction: The technician can demonstrate an understanding of refraction as it occurs in systems that employ fiber optics.

A vehicle is in the shop for repairs to the lighting system. The repair order cites as the customer concern that the illumination for the console-mounted shifter indicator is not working. The driver is unable to determine which gear is selected for the automatic transmission at night.

Ethan is the apprentice technician at the dealership who was given the assignment of solving this concern. The first step is to verify the customer concern by covering the windows of the vehicle to simulate night conditions. Ethan looks up the manufacturer's information on a shop computer. Expecting to find an illustration showing the location of a bulb for illumination, he finds the procedure for removal of the illumination control. He then begins the disassembly procedure to get to the components involved. Rather than a conventional light socket and bulb, Ethan finds a fiber-optic lighting assembly that provides illumination for the shifter indicator.

Fiber optics components have been used by Mercedes-Benz, BMW, Daimler, Audi, Porsche, Volvo, and Cadillac. Some of the applications include dashboard lights, interior lights, taillights, and entertainment and information systems.

Refraction is defined as the change in direction of light due to a change in speed as it passes from one medium to another. A reference for the path of light is described in respect to the normal path of light. If light enters a new medium and is slowed down, it bends to the normal path. If it speeds up, it bends away from the normal path.

Aftermarket lighting accessories that are available today include fiber-optic taillights with reverse lights for certain vehicles. These lights are advertised to be considerably brighter than stock units and to light up faster and run cooler. Due to the use of fiber rather than light bulbs, fiber-optic lights are said to be vibration-proof.

Back-up Lights

The back-up lights, also called reverse lights, are white lights mounted at the rear of a vehicle. They provide the driver with vision behind the vehicle at night and also alert other drivers to the fact that the vehicle is in reverse. The lighting circuit consists of the battery, fuses and fusible links, the ignition switch, the back-up light (reverse) switch or a combined transmission back-up light/neutral safety switch on the transmission, back-up lamps, wiring to connect the components, and the ground circuit to allow current to return to the battery through the vehicle chassis.

When the ignition is on, and the vehicle is placed in reverse gear, the current flows from the battery, through the ignition switch, and through the closed reverse lamp or transmission position switch on the transmission. Electrical current then flows out of the closed switch to the back-up lamps and returns to the battery by the vehicle chassis ground circuit. Modern vehicles use network/bus systems and the BCM to command the back-up lights to come on.

Back-up lights are the only white lights on the rear of the vehicle. Since they operate only in reverse, other drivers can tell that the driver is backing up. This is why it is illegal to have broken tail/brake/turn signal lenses in the rear of the vehicle since white light would be visible, confusing other drivers.

Turn Signal Lights

Turn signal indicators are located on the extreme corners of the vehicle. They are usually amber in the front and can be either red or amber in the rear. A column-mounted switch, operated by the driver, commands a pulsing current to the indicator lights on one side of the vehicle or the other. These pulsing lights warn other road users of the driver's intended change of direction.

Once activated, they continue until the switch is cancelled either by the operator or by a cancelling mechanism in the switch. The cancelling mechanism operates to return the switch to its central or "off" position after a turn has been completed and the steering wheel is returned to the straight-ahead position. The circuit consists of the battery, fusible links and fuses, the ignition switch, the flasher unit, a three-position switch used as the direction indicator switch, the lights at the front and rear of the vehicle, indicator lights mounted in the instrument cluster to indicate to the driver which way the switch has been operated, wiring to connect all of the components, and the ground circuit to return the electrical current to the battery.

If the indicator switch is turned to indicate a right-hand turn, current from the battery typically flows through the fusible link to the ignition switch, where it is directed through a fuse to the flasher unit. The flasher unit uses a timing circuit to pulse the current flowing out of the flasher unit 60 to 120 times per minute. This pulsing current is directed through the indicator switch to the right-hand indicator lights at the front and rear of the vehicle, causing the lamps to flash on and off. An indicator light on the instrument cluster also blinks in sync with the turn signals. The operation of the flasher unit also produces a clicking sound to audibly inform the driver that the indicators are in operation.

When the turn signal switch is returned to the off position, no current flows through the flasher unit, so the timer circuit is switched off. When the turn signal switch is turned in the opposite direction, it directs the pulsing current to the left-hand lights at the front and rear of the vehicle as well as the left-hand indicator light on the instrument cluster. Older vehicles used a thermo-mechanical flasher unit that relied on heat from the current flow to cause the flasher unit to work. It is very important to use bulbs of the proper wattage on all types of flasher units, as the speed of the flash may be incorrect if incorrect bulbs are used.

These indicators can also be computer controlled. The BCM commands the appropriate turn indicators to come on as it sees an input from the turn signal switch, and flashes it at the proper rate. The computer turns off the turn signals when a steering angle sensor signals the steering wheel is being centered. It can also cancel the turn indicators if the vehicle is driven for a programmed amount of time or distance without the steering wheel being turned. Often a chime will alert the driver if the turn indicator has been left on for too long. On many computer-controlled turn signals, the turn signals will not work at all when the computer senses the wrong amperage flow.

Turn Signal Lights—Domestic and Import Systems

All turn signal lamps flash, but there are variations in layout and design. This is most noticeable when comparing some domestic and imported vehicles. Imported vehicles tend to have separate amber-colored turn signal lamps on both the front and the rear of the vehicle. Some domestic vehicles use the rear brake lamps as turn signals by flashing the brake lamp on one side to indicate the turn. Wiring schematics should always be checked because the dual function of the brake lamps means the wiring for brake lamps on vehicles with this feature is different than those where the brake lamps perform only during braking **FIGURE 33-12**. In such cases, current for the brake lights must flow first from the brake switch and then through the turn signal switch, and on to the individual brake lights. This design tends to make the study of the current path more complicated, since there are two inputs—one for the turn signals and one for the brake lights. So the turn signal switch is much more complicated on a domestic-style turn signal switch than an import-style switch.

Hazard Warning Lights

All modern vehicles are equipped with hazard warning lights. This circuit is similar to the turn indicator lights except that it simultaneously causes a pulsing in all exterior indicator lights and both indicator lights on the instrument panel. Hazard lights can warn other road users that a hazardous condition exists or that the vehicle is standing or parked in a dangerous position on the side of the road. The hazards also use a flasher unit that can be a separate unit or the same as that used for the turn signals. The BCM may control the hazard lights when it sees an input from the hazard switch or an input from the restraints control module indicating a vehicle crash.

Daytime Running Lights

Daytime running lights (DRLs) are an additional safety feature designed on vehicles to improve the vehicle's visibility to other drivers in all weather conditions. They are existing lights that turn on when the vehicle is running and turn off when the engine stops. The lamps on the front are the headlights, which are typically operated at about a 60% power level, providing light without excessively decreasing bulb life or using full electrical power. The lamps used on the rear in DLR systems are the taillights.

DLRs are mandatory on modern vehicles licensed in Canada and some other countries. In the United States, DRLs are permitted but not required. Their use is somewhat controversial. First, if they are too bright, they can cause daytime glare. Second, they tend to mask the visibility of turn signals, making it harder for other drivers to determine a vehicle's intent. Overall, they have not been proved to reduce accidents or increase safety. They also require energy to operate, which reduces fuel economy and increases carbon dioxide emissions.

Headlights

Headlights are built into the front of a vehicle to illuminate the road ahead of the vehicle when driving at night or in other conditions of reduced visibility. In headlights, most vehicles require two beams to provide for a high beam and low beam operation. The beams are created by separate filaments, included either in one light bulb or in separate bulbs. These filaments must be positioned correctly in relation to the highly polished reflector. This is called focusing and is carried out when designing the light assembly and lens for the vehicle. The high beam filament is positioned at the focal point of the reflector to project the maximum amount of light forward and parallel to the reflector axis **FIGURE 33-13**. This light is then shaped by the lens, which is made up of many small glass or plastic prisms fused together. These prisms bend the light horizontally and vertically to achieve the desired light pattern for road illumination.

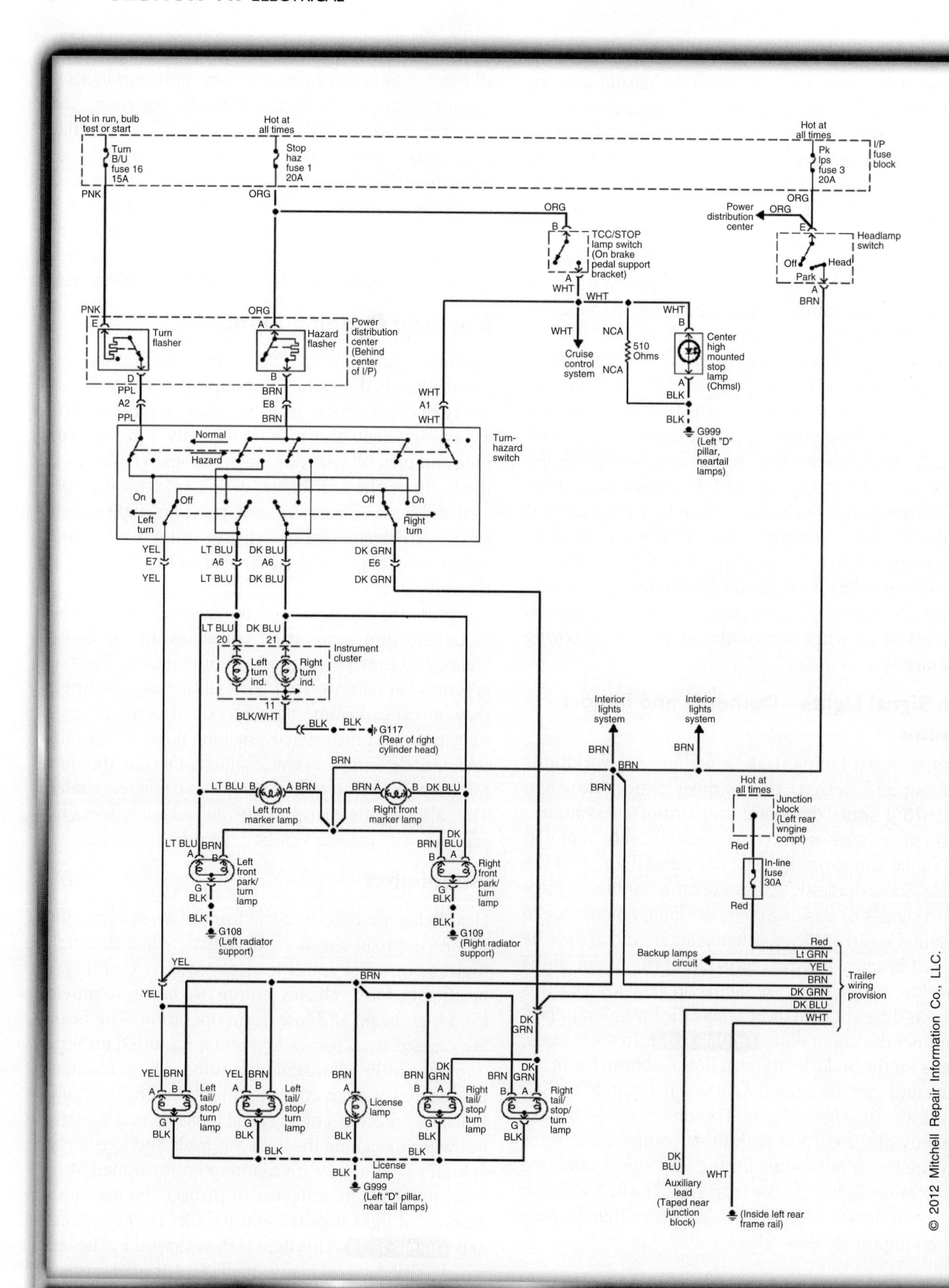
Hot in run, bulb test or start
Hot at all times
Hot at all times
Turn B/U fuse 16 15A
Stop haz fuse 1 20A
Pk lps fuse 3 20A
I/P fuse block
Power distribution center
TCC/STOP lamp switch (On brake pedal support bracket)
Headlamp switch
Turn flasher
Hazard flasher
Power distribution center (Behind center of I/P)
Cruise control system
510 Ohms
Center high mounted stop lamp (Chmsl)
G999 (Left "D" pillar, neartail lamps)
Turn-hazard switch
Normal
Hazard
Left turn
Right turn
Instrument cluster
Left turn ind.
Right turn ind.
G117 (Rear of right cylinder head)
Interior lights system
Left front marker lamp
Right front marker lamp
Junction block (Left rear wngine compt)
Left front park/ turn lamp
Right front park/ turn lamp
In-line fuse 30A
G108 (Left radiator support)
G109 (Right radiator support)
Backup lamps circuit
Trailer wiring provision
Left tail/ stop/ turn lamp
License lamp
Right tail/ stop/ turn lamp
G999 (Left "D" pillar, near tail lamps)
Auxiliary lead (Taped near junction block)
(Inside left rear frame rail)
© 2012 Mitchell Repair Information Co., LLC.

FIGURE 33-12 Typical wiring diagram showing domestic-type turn signals.

FIGURE 33-13 High and low beam filament position in relation to the reflector.

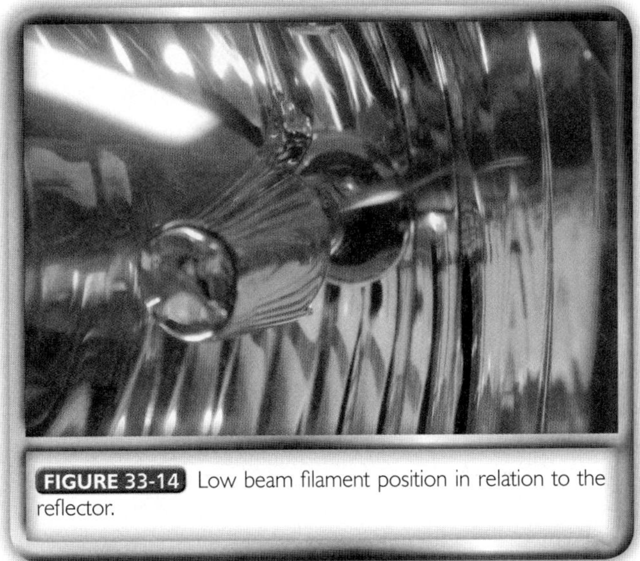

FIGURE 33-14 Low beam filament position in relation to the reflector.

The low beam filament is often placed above and slightly to one side of the high beam filament. Mounting the low beam filament in this position produces a beam of light that is projected downward and toward the curb side FIGURE 33-14. With this arrangement, the high beam filament produces the most concentrated light output, while the low beam filament gives a downward and dispersed beam that is less likely to blind oncoming drivers.

Headlight Design

Generally speaking, the headlight circuit consists of the battery, the fusible link or maxi-fuse, headlight fuses, the headlight switch, the headlight relay(s), the beam selector switch, headlights, the high beam indicator light, wiring of a suitable size to carry the electrical current through the circuit, and the ground circuit. Modern vehicles use the BCM to manage headlight functions.

On older, noncomputer-controlled systems, when the headlights are switched on, current is supplied from the battery and proceeds through the fusible link or maxi-fuse, headlight fuse(s), headlight switch, and dimmer switch, reaching either the low or the high beams. In more recent, noncomputer-controlled systems, some vehicles use relays to control the current through the low or high beam circuits. In this configuration, the beam selector switch either powers or grounds the relay windings in each of the relays, depending on the position of the beam selector switch. Activating the beam selector switch in the low beam position creates a magnetic field inside the low beam relay that closes the relay contacts, which allows electrical current to flow to the low beams. Activating the beam selector switch in the high beam position creates a magnetic field inside the high beam relay that closes the relay contacts, turning on the high beams.

The beam selector switch is a single-pole, double-throw switch, meaning it has one movable pole but makes contact in two positions. In the high beam position, the current is switched to the high beam circuit. In the low beam position, the current is switched to the low beam circuit. The beam selector switch can be set to switch a common power input to two outputs, or it can switch a common ground input to two outputs.

As with other advanced-technology on-board systems, modern vehicles use a network/bus system to manage these and other headlight and dimmer functions. On many vehicles, the headlight switch and dimmer switch are just inputs to a control module that sends a headlight "on" or "off" request over the network. The appropriate light controller processes the request and actually commands the lights on or off, sometimes with the help of relays—especially for high beams.

A sealed-beam headlight has a highly polished aluminized glass reflector that is fused to the optically designed lens. It is a completely sealed unit that has the filaments accurately positioned in relation to the reflector. Most older vehicles used two dual-filament 7" (178-mm) round lamps; for a time, four single-filament 5.25" (133-mm) round lamps were used. Other older vehicles used two large dual-filament 7.875" (200-mm) rectangular lamps, or four smaller rectangular single-filament lamps. Regardless of size, when a filament fails in a sealed-beam light, the whole sealed unit must be replaced.

A semi-sealed beam headlight uses a replaceable bulb with a prefocus collar. The collar locates the bulb in the headlight and also controls the correct positioning of the filaments to the reflector and lens FIGURE 33-15. Some replaceable headlight bulbs have a partial shield below the low beam filament. This shield prevents light from the filament from striking the lower

FIGURE 33-15 Replaceable halogen bulb.

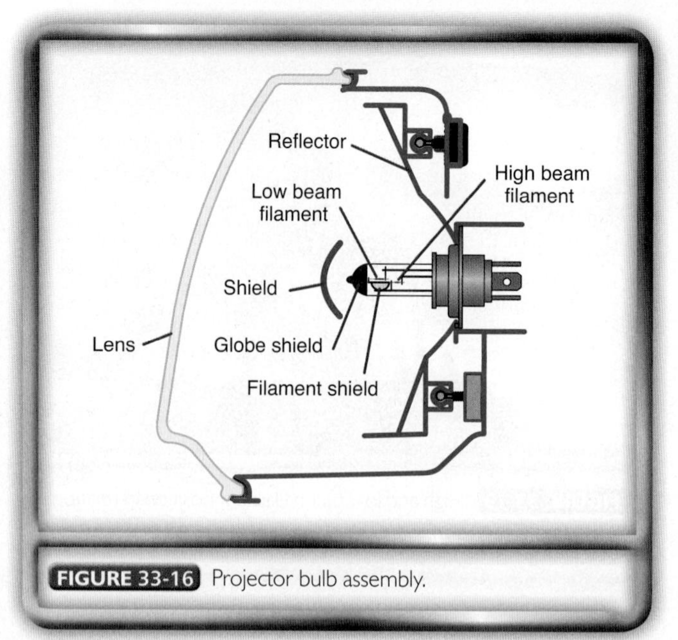
Reflector
Low beam filament
High beam filament
Shield
Lens
Globe shield
Filament shield

FIGURE 33-16 Projector bulb assembly.

part of the reflector, which would be reflected higher than the midpoint of the lamp. The shield provides the primary shape of the low beam. The final shaping of the beam is carried out by small cylindrical prisms in the headlight lens. This provides a low beam that is asymmetrical. The asymmetrical lens pattern causes light to be thrown upward at a 15-degree angle on the curb side to better illuminate objects, persons, or animals close to the road.

Types of Headlights

Headlight systems have traditionally used reflector-type lighting systems. In a reflector headlight, the light from the bulb is reflected forward by a specially shaped reflector. An alternative is a projection-type headlight system. This type of headlight often has a smaller front lens; however, it produces a high-intensity forward beam. It uses a lens system to project the light forward, rather than the traditional reflector system FIGURE 33-16. A projector-style light can use a standard incandescent bulb, or more commonly, an HID light.

HID lights use light from an electric arc rather than heating up a filament until it glows FIGURE 33-17. High voltage is applied to tungsten electrodes. Xenon gas inside the bulb is then ionized and creates an electrical path between the electrodes, which lowers the resistance of the gap. As the temperature rises, metallic salts are vaporized and provide a stable arc, emitting much light. To initially jump the gap, a ballast and igniter raise the vehicle's low-voltage direct current (DC) to as much as 25,000 volts alternating current (AC). Once the light

FIGURE 33-17 HID headlight assembly.

reaches full operation, voltage is maintained between approximately 40 and 85 volts AC, depending on the system. HID lights give off a brighter and bluer light than halogen bulbs with less electrical energy, so they help fuel efficiency slightly. They last two to four times as long as a halogen bulb but are quite a bit more expensive. Also, they take up more room in the engine compartment.

Some vehicles use LED lights as headlights. They are not currently as bright as HID lights but are at least as bright as halogen lights. LED lights are known for low power consumption, but for LEDs to create enough light to function as headlights, they must consume almost as much energy as HID lights. Still, LED technology continues to improve. One drawback of current LED headlights is that high temperatures degrade or damage them. Thus, heat sinks and cooling measures are needed, which add complexity, cost, and space.

Night vision is another relatively new technology that enhances a driver's visual perception in dark or poor weather conditions. There are two types of night vision systems: active and passive. Active systems use an infrared light generator that projects infrared light in front of and to the side of the roadway ahead. A special camera picks up the reflected infrared radiation. The image is then displayed either on the windshield using a heads-up display or on an LCD screen on the dash or navigation system.

Passive night vision systems use a heat-sensing camera (thermal imaging) to pick up thermal radiation emitted by objects. This system does not have an infrared light source on the vehicle. The captured thermal image is then displayed either on a heads-up display or on an LCD screen. One benefit of the thermal system is that it can be programmed to recognize pedestrians and animals and can then either place an outline around them on the display or flash a warning symbol.

Driving Lights

Driving lights are used to supplement vehicle headlight systems. The driving lights are installed on the front of the vehicle and provide higher intensity illumination over longer distances than standard headlight systems **FIGURE 33-18**. Vehicle design rules and regulations specify the limitations in relation to the positioning and lens configuration of driving lights. It is essential that the local regulations are adhered to when mounting or adjusting driving lights.

There are many types of driving lights available. They come in different sizes, shapes, lens pattern, and bulb wattage. In some instances, a single driving light can be installed to suit particular applications, but lights are normally installed in pairs.

Most driving lights use quartz halogen bulbs in the 55- to 120-watt range. The quality of the reflector is extremely important in driving lights to get optimum performance. Driving lights are wired so that they operate only when the high beam is operating. This safety feature ensures that driving lights turn off when the headlights are switched from high to low beam, thus ensuring that oncoming traffic is not blinded by excessive light. While many performance vehicles come equipped with driving lights, they can be added to almost any vehicle. If they are, a relay and circuit breaker should always be used for circuit protection reasons.

Fog Lights

Fog lights are used with other vehicle lighting in poor weather such as thick fog, driving rain, or blowing snow. Because fog is made up of water droplets suspended in the air, it can reflect headlights back into the driver's eyes at night. In such conditions, fog lights can help drivers see farther ahead and illuminate the road's edges at reasonable speeds. They are used with park lights and low beam headlights but not with high beams.

Most older fog lights have yellow-colored reflectors, although more recently, white fog lights have become more widely used because yellow lenses reduce fog light brilliance by about 30%. Fog lights typically use quartz halogen bulbs and are available in different shapes and sizes. Fog lights are usually mounted lower than headlights and tend to be aimed straight forward and low **FIGURE 33-19**. Fog light lenses have a sharp cutoff pattern

FIGURE 33-18 Vehicle with factory driving lights.

FIGURE 33-19 Vehicle with factory fog lights.

so that most of the light projected remains below the driver's eye level.

Fog lights are typically wired with a relay and circuit breaker. The method of connection of fog lights will depend on local regulations. They may be wired to work only with park lights and to turn off when headlights are used or to work when high beams are used. The BCM normally controls the function of the fog lights if they are installed as original equipment.

Cornering Lights

To improve visibility during night driving, some vehicle manufacturers provide cornering lights FIGURE 33-20. Cornering lights are white lights usually installed into the bumper or fender and are designed to provide side lighting when the vehicle is turning corners. The additional lighting provided by cornering lights helps the driver to see the curb and any obstacles that may not be illuminated by the headlights. Cornering lights turn on only when the headlights and turn signal switches are on, and turn off automatically when the turn signal cancels. Even though they come on with the turn signals, their light is steady; that is, they don't blink.

Lighting Circuits

Each lighting circuit has particular operating characteristics based on its purpose and the system design. Knowing how a circuit is designed to operate and how it interacts with other related circuits will help you to better know how to go about diagnosing the system. A typical lighting circuit may be made up of the battery, fuses or circuit breakers, switches, relays, lamps, and wiring to connect the components. Manufacturers design the circuits to operate in specific ways and then create schematics or wiring diagrams, which are a diagrammatic layout of the entire circuit to assist in the repair and maintenance of lighting circuits. Learning how to read wiring diagrams takes time and practice. Understanding circuit design, operation, and wiring diagram information can then be used to diagnose circuit faults.

FIGURE 33-20 Cornering lights.

Lighting System Wiring Diagrams

The layouts of electrical circuits and their components are shown as diagrams made up of symbols and connecting lines. Being able to read a wiring diagram is probably the most important skill when trying to trace and correct a fault in an electrical system.

Not all wiring diagrams use the same symbols or the same numbering system. It is helpful to refer to the manufacturer's service information for specific details on how to read a particular wiring diagram.

The illustrations below show some of the common symbols and what they represent.

1. FIGURE 33-21 shows the battery and fuse symbols.
2. FIGURE 33-22 shows the ground and connector symbols.
3. FIGURE 33-23 shows the switch symbols.
4. FIGURE 33-24 shows the resistors, coils and relay symbols.
5. FIGURE 33-25 shows the semiconductor symbols.
6. FIGURE 33-26 shows the capacitor and device symbols.
7. FIGURE 33-27 shows the motors, generators, and solenoid symbols.
8. FIGURE 33-28 shows the gauges and warning device symbols.

HID Safety Precautions

HID lamps produce a very bright white light. Manufacturers use various designs of HID lamps. Regardless of the design, they generally require a high-voltage spark of up to 25,000 volts to start and a high operating voltage (e.g., 40–85 volts AC) to maintain light. To generate the voltages required to operate, a transformer and electronic circuitry called a ballast are used to supply electrical components.

Several safety precautions should be taken when working on HID systems. There is a risk of electrocution, burns, or shock from the high voltages generated by the HID system. If diagnosing the HID system, be very careful when working on the system when it is live. You should wear safety glasses, high-voltage safety gloves, and safety boots, and you should ensure that

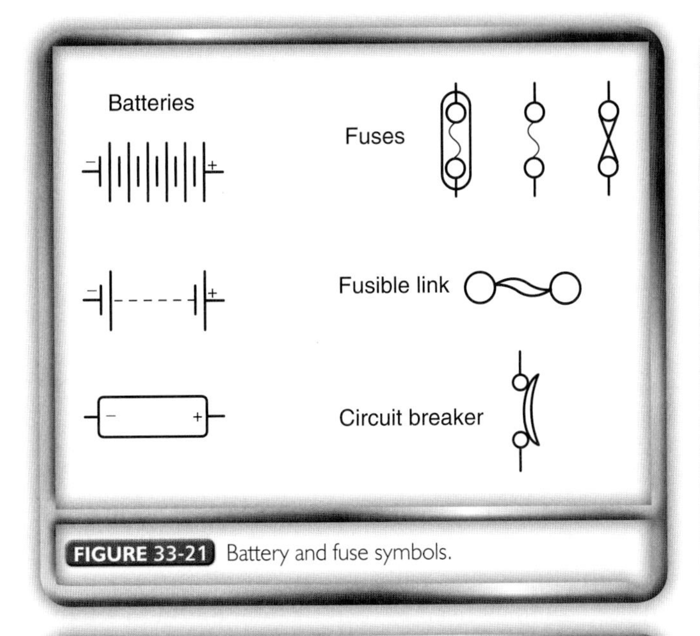
Batteries
Fuses
Fusible link
Circuit breaker

FIGURE 33-21 Battery and fuse symbols.

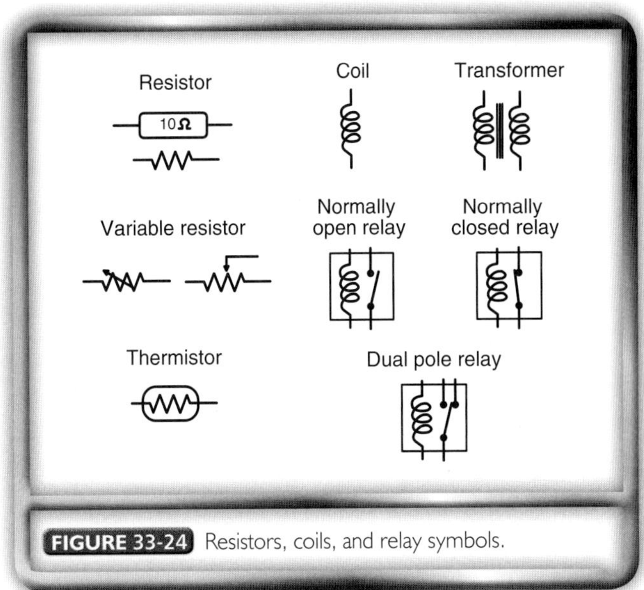
Resistor
10Ω
Coil
Transformer
Variable resistor
Normally open relay
Normally closed relay
Thermistor
Dual pole relay

FIGURE 33-24 Resistors, coils, and relay symbols.

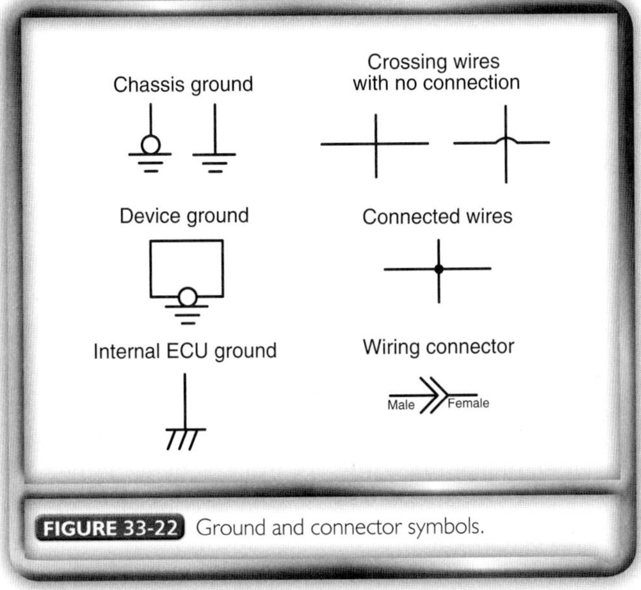
Chassis ground
Crossing wires with no connection
Device ground
Connected wires
Internal ECU ground
Wiring connector
Male
Female

FIGURE 33-22 Ground and connector symbols.

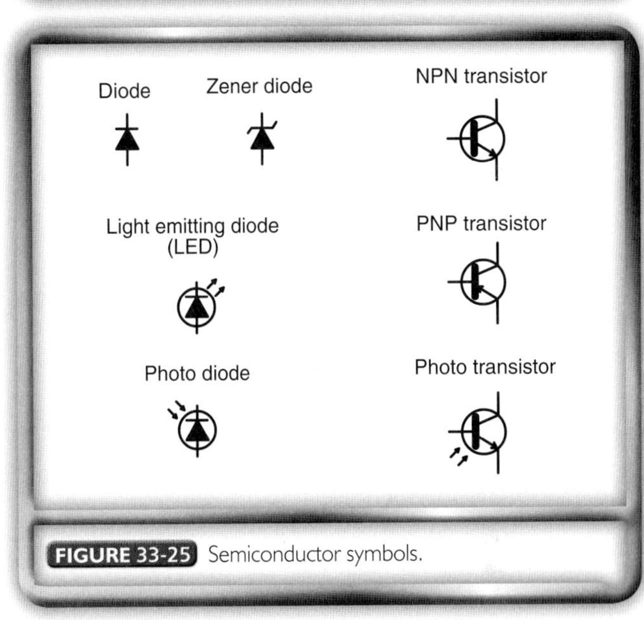
Diode
Zener diode
NPN transistor
Light emitting diode (LED)
PNP transistor
Photo diode
Photo transistor

FIGURE 33-25 Semiconductor symbols.

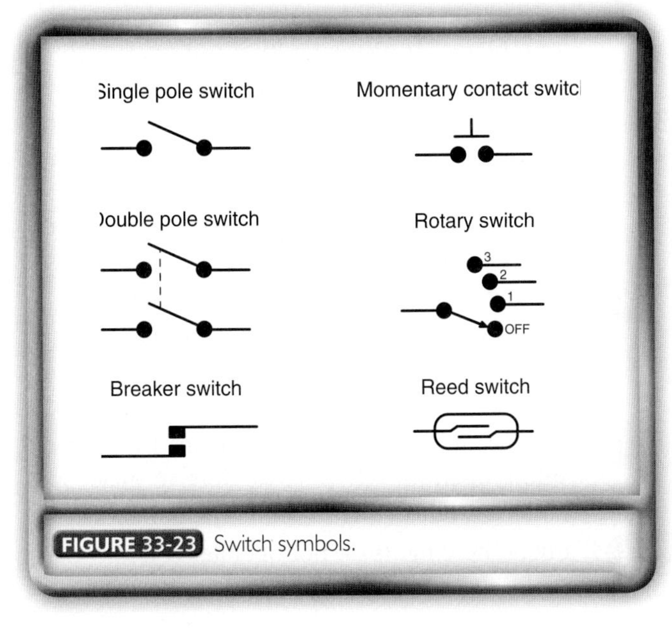
Single pole switch
Momentary contact switc
Double pole switch
Rotary switch
3
2
1
OFF
Breaker switch
Reed switch

FIGURE 33-23 Switch symbols.

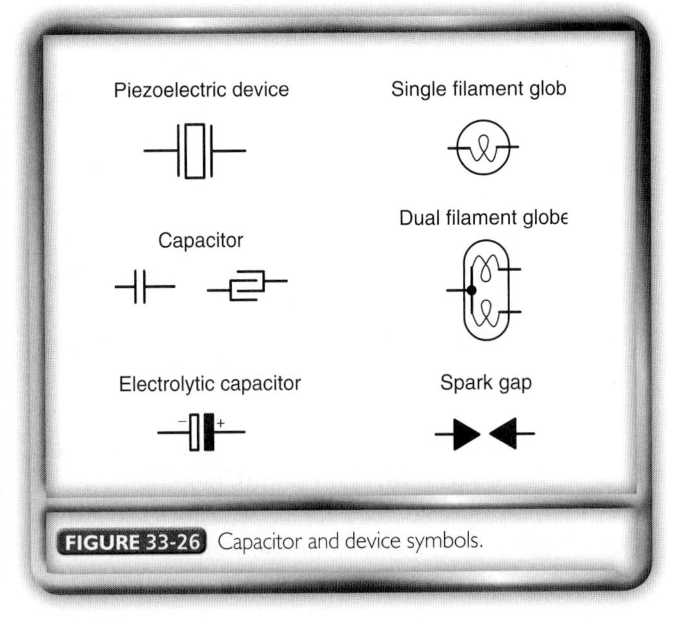
Piezoelectric device
Single filament glob
Capacitor
Dual filament globe
Electrolytic capacitor
Spark gap

FIGURE 33-26 Capacitor and device symbols.

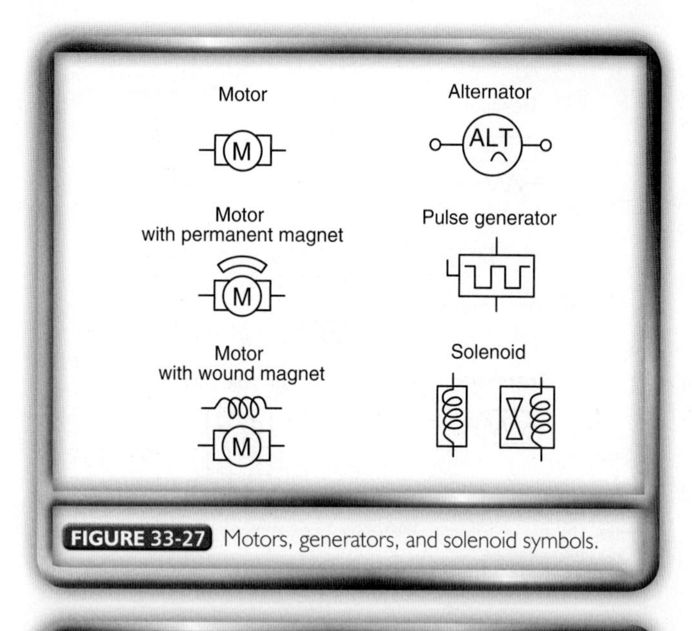
Motor
Alternator
M
ALT
Motor
with permanent magnet
Pulse generator
M
Motor
with wound magnet
Solenoid
M

FIGURE 33-27 Motors, generators, and solenoid symbols.

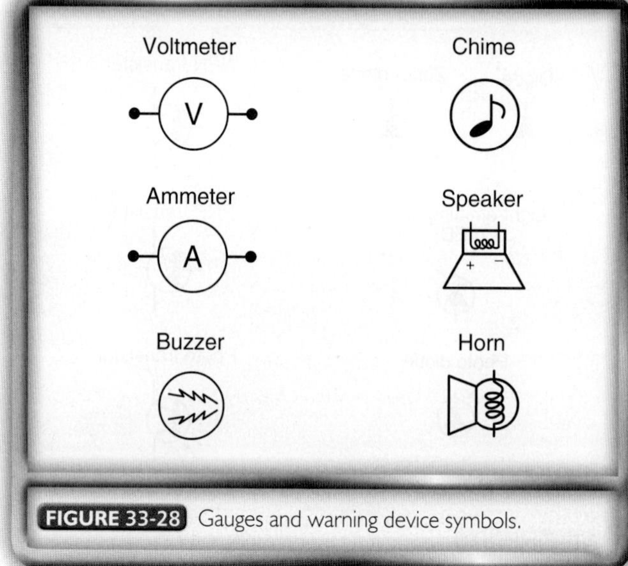
Voltmeter
Chime
V
Ammeter
Speaker
A
Buzzer
Horn

FIGURE 33-28 Gauges and warning device symbols.

the vehicle, engine compartment, and ground under the vehicle are dry. Do not touch the ballast while it is operating; it will often be generating a lot of heat. Persons with active electronic implants, such as heart pacemakers, should not work on HID headlamps. If changing out the bulb, make sure the headlights are turned off. The manufacturer may specify that the battery be disconnected when replacing the bulb. If so, follow the manufacturer's instructions.

There is also a risk of injury caused by exposure to ultraviolet light produced by the HID lamp if the lamp is operated outside of its housing. Once ignited, the pressure inside an HID bulb can build up to a very high pressure (around 220 pounds per square inch, 1517 kilopascals) due to the high operating temperature (about 1500°F [816°C]). This pressure creates a potential explosion hazard, so do not attempt to power an HID bulb outside of the headlamp assembly to test it or operate it near flammable gases or liquids. Also, the bulb must be maintained in a horizontal position when it is on; otherwise it may overheat and fail. HID headlamps use various heavy metals in their construction; therefore, it is important to always dispose of the bulbs in an environmentally friendly way. Avoid breaking bulbs, as there is also a risk of poisoning caused by inhalation or skin contact of heavy metal vapors and toxic salts.

Checking Lighting and Peripheral Systems

When checking lighting and peripheral systems, be sure to work in a systematic manner to avoid missing a faulty bulb or other component. A vehicle may have warning lights that will activate only if that circuit is in use. You may need to turn that circuit on to see the warning light. If you are unsure of where these are, ask your supervisor.

To check lighting and peripheral systems, follow the steps in SKILL DRILL 33-1.

1. In a darkened area, turn on or activate the ignition. The dash warning lights should be displayed. Start the engine. If any warning light stays on after the engine is started, it could indicate a problem in one of the vehicle's safety or mechanical systems. If you are unsure about what any of the warning lights mean, consult the owner's manual.
2. Make sure the vehicle's horn is working. If the horn is not working, locate it under the hood with the help of manufacturer's information. Check the wiring to make sure there is a good contact. If necessary, use a wiring diagram and DVOM to isolate the fault.
3. Have someone stand behind the vehicle to report any problems. Turn the ignition to run. Switch on the park lights, taillights, marker lights, and license plate lights. Do the same for left and right turn indicator lights. Depress the brake pedal to make sure the brake lights work and have the proper intensity. Also, place the transmission in reverse and check the back-up lights.
4. With someone in front of the vehicle, make sure the high and low headlight beams, park lights, turn signals, driving lights, fog lights, and cornering lights are all working properly.
5. With the interior light switch in the correct position, open the driver's side door to make sure the interior lights work.
6. If any of these lights do not operate, you may need to replace a bulb, or diagnose the fault.

Safety

The glass in a light bulb is thin, and if it breaks, it is extremely sharp. Since bayonet-style lights need to be pushed in to be released, and they can become corroded in place, and it may take a lot of force to push them in. Placed under such high pressure, the glass can break and severely cut the skin and even the tendons in fingers. If a bulb does not come out easily, stop, use a folded rag, and try to remove it again. If it shatters, the rag will help to protect your fingers.

Checking and Changing an Exterior Light Bulb

Light bulbs have a limited life span and burn out occasionally. Inspecting the lighting system's operation periodically, such as during oil changes, will help identify any light bulb issues. If none of the bulbs in a particular circuit is working, there may be a bigger electrical problem to resolve, requiring diagnosis. Many tail, brake, and signal light bulbs have more than one filament inside them. These bulbs normally have offset pins to ensure proper orientation of the electrical contacts in the socket.

Be sure to look carefully at the bulb you are replacing to make sure you do not try to force the bulb in the wrong way. Also, make sure you don't replace a dual-filament bulb with a single-filament bulb since that can short both lighting circuits together, causing the lights to work very strangely. Some bulbs have a colored glass envelope that enables them to be used with a clear lens. If you replace a bulb of this type, make sure you replace it with one of the same color.

To check and change an exterior light bulb, follow the steps in SKILL DRILL 33-2.

TECHNICIAN TIP

A customer with sealed-beam headlights once complained of poor headlight performance. When the technician turned on the lights, they both worked but didn't seem to create much light. As the technician opened the hood to investigate further, he noticed something strange. The headlights were shining light out the back of the lights, illuminating the engine compartment. He inspected the lights and found that the metallic reflector in the sealed beams had pretty much all flaked away, allowing most of the light to exit the rear of the bulb, instead of being reflected forward. Replacing the sealed-beam headlights with new ones fixed the customer's concern.

Checking and Changing a Headlight Bulb

There are many types of headlight bulbs available. Always make sure you replace a bulb with one of exactly the

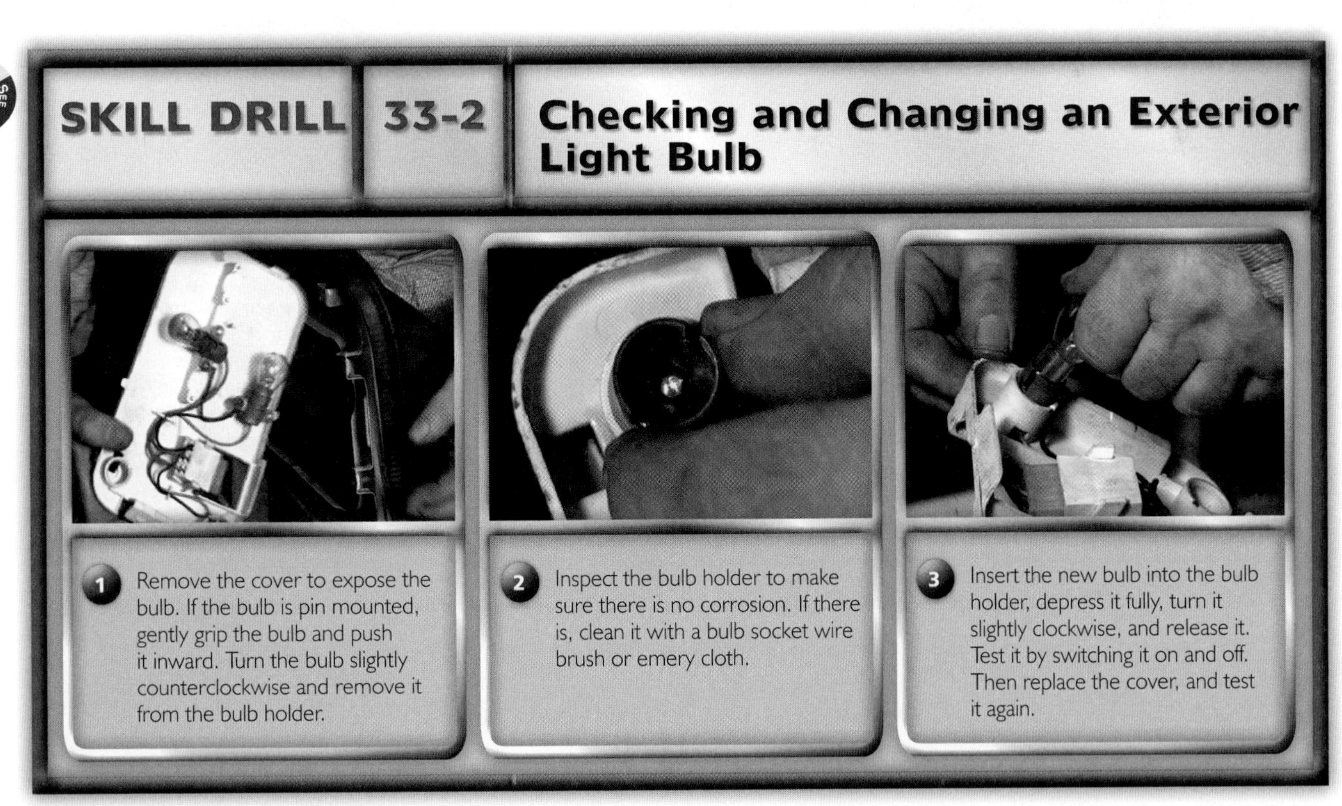

SKILL DRILL 33-2 Checking and Changing an Exterior Light Bulb

1. Remove the cover to expose the bulb. If the bulb is pin mounted, gently grip the bulb and push it inward. Turn the bulb slightly counterclockwise and remove it from the bulb holder.
2. Inspect the bulb holder to make sure there is no corrosion. If there is, clean it with a bulb socket wire brush or emery cloth.
3. Insert the new bulb into the bulb holder, depress it fully, turn it slightly clockwise, and release it. Test it by switching it on and off. Then replace the cover, and test it again.

same type. Sealed-beam units require that the whole light be replaced when one filament has failed. If the reflector in the sealed-beam light shows signs of degradation, it also indicates that you must change the unit. If both lights operate but are not bright when switched on, start the engine to see if this solves the problem; the battery may be in a poor state of charge. When replacing a halogen bulb, avoid touching it with your fingers, which can leave a residue from your fingers on the outer surface. This residue can cause the bulb to crack or shatter and burn out after a short time of operation. If you inadvertently touch the bulb, clean it with alcohol and a lint-free cloth. Do not use gasoline or paraffin to clean the bulb.

To check and change a headlight bulb, follow the steps in SKILL DRILL 33-3.

Aiming Headlights

Although the principle of aiming headlights is the same in the majority of cases, the legal rules can differ from region to region. Be sure to check the requirements for your location. If you are unsure of what these are, ask your supervisor. Some manufacturers may suggest that the headlights be aimed on high beam, others on low beam, and in cases of separate high and low beams, both beams may need to be aimed independently. The manufacturer may also suggest that a load be placed in the vehicle, to simulate the ride height of the vehicle when it is travelling down the road. Headlights are typically aligned both vertically and horizontally so that as much of the road is illuminated as possible, without blinding oncoming traffic. Some vehicles have headlights that adjust automatically; do not try to adjust those unless you are diagnosing a fault in the system.

When aiming or aligning headlights, there are a couple of possible methods to utilize. The first, while no longer commonly used, involves an on-vehicle headlight aligner. This method was used extensively on sealed-beam headlights. The aligners are calibrated to the floor at the point where the front and rear wheels contact the concrete. Then the aligners are installed on the headlights with a built-in suction cup, which holds them in place. The aligners use a set of mirrors that can be calibrated

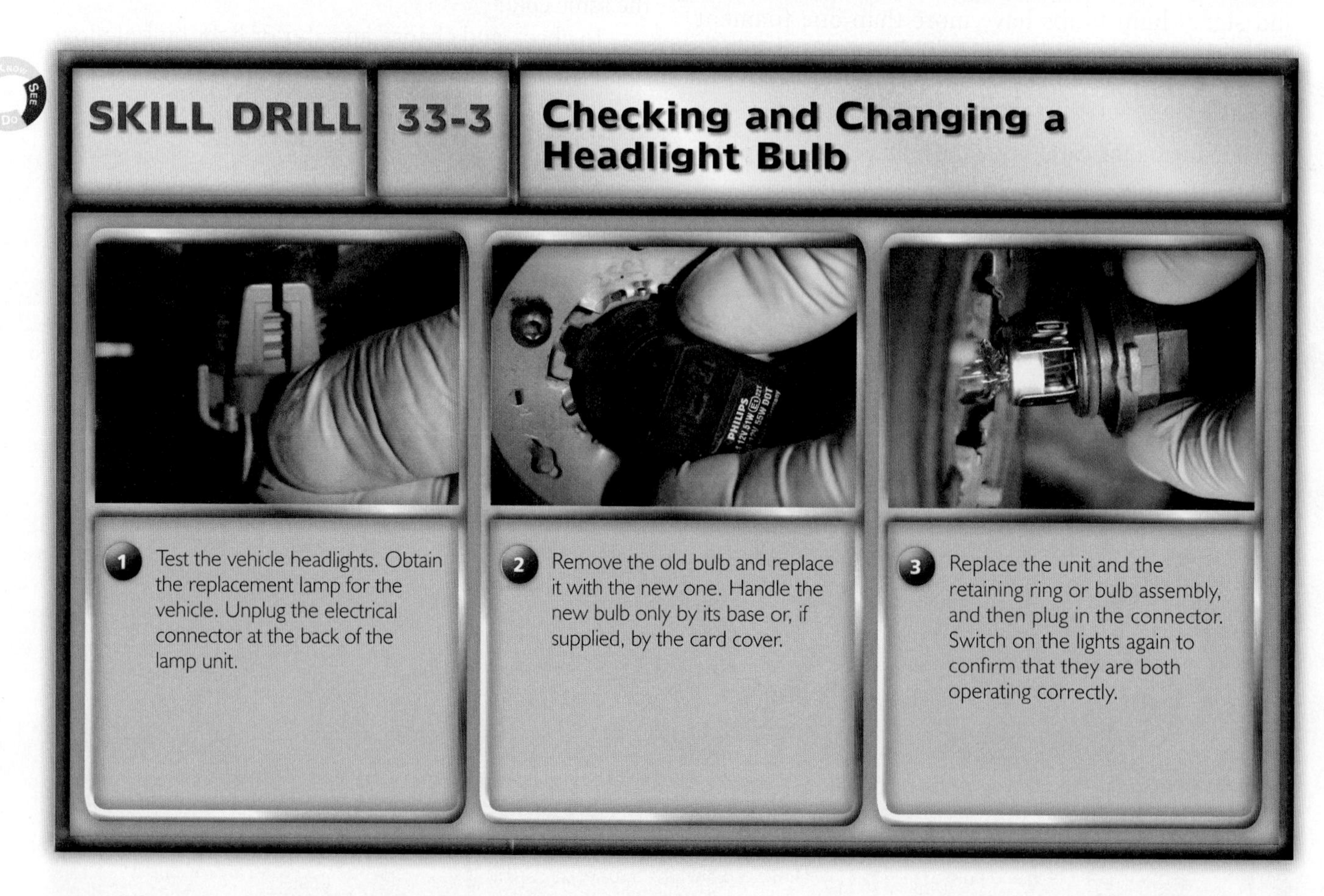

SKILL DRILL 33-3 Checking and Changing a Headlight Bulb

1. Test the vehicle headlights. Obtain the replacement lamp for the vehicle. Unplug the electrical connector at the back of the lamp unit.
2. Remove the old bulb and replace it with the new one. Handle the new bulb only by its base or, if supplied, by the card cover.
3. Replace the unit and the retaining ring or bulb assembly, and then plug in the connector. Switch on the lights again to confirm that they are both operating correctly.

to local regulations so that the headlights can be aligned properly.

With the introduction of aerodynamic headlights using removable halogen bulbs, off-vehicle headlight aligners became more popular. These aligners sit in front of the vehicle after being calibrated for the floor slope and orientation with the vehicle. With the headlights on, adjustments can be made by following the instructions on the aligner. Refer to the manufacturer's information for specific information regarding headlight aiming.

To aim headlights, follow the steps in SKILL DRILL 33-4.

Headlight Brightness

Headlight brightness is critical to safe driving. Too dim, and the road ahead will not be adequately illuminated. Too bright, and the life of the headlight will be shortened, making it prone to early burnout. In most cases, the headlights are more likely to be too dim than too bright. Bulbs that are too bright indicate that either the charging system voltage is too high and needs to be measured with a DVOM or someone may have replaced the headlights with an aftermarket set, which may be illegal. Checking bulb numbers will verify this condition.

If the headlights are too dim, there can be several causes. The most common one is high resistance in the light circuit. This can be checked by measuring the voltage drop on both the power side of the bulb and the ground side. The voltage drop should be less than 0.5 volts on each side. If an excessive voltage drop is indicated, use a wiring diagram to research the circuit. Once you know how it is wired, use the DVOM to isolate the voltage drop by using the meter to measure each segment of the circuit. When the high resistance is located, perform the needed repair, whether that is a wire repair or a connector, switch, or relay replacement. If the voltage drop is less than 0.5 volts on each side, suspect the light bulb is wearing out. One way to verify this is with a light intensity meter. This meter can measure the amount of light energy the lamp is producing, so you can compare that to specifications. If the light is being supplied with the specified voltage, but it is not creating enough light, the bulb will need to be replaced.

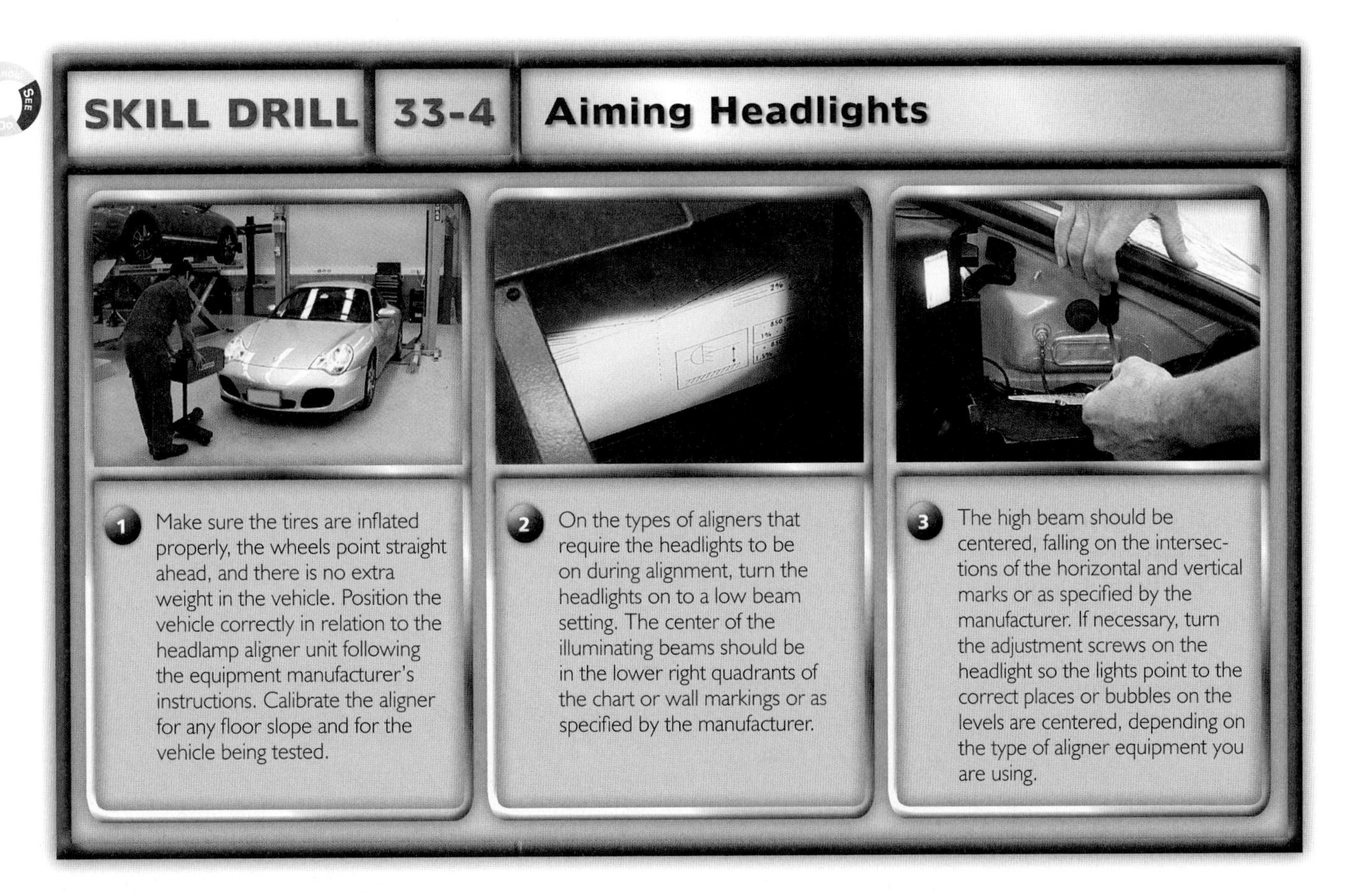
SKILL DRILL 33-4 Aiming Headlights
1 Make sure the tires are inflated properly, the wheels point straight ahead, and there is no extra weight in the vehicle. Position the vehicle correctly in relation to the headlamp aligner unit following the equipment manufacturer's instructions. Calibrate the aligner for any floor slope and for the vehicle being tested.
2 On the types of aligners that require the headlights to be on during alignment, turn the headlights on to a low beam setting. The center of the illuminating beams should be in the lower right quadrants of the chart or wall markings or as specified by the manufacturer.
3 The high beam should be centered, falling on the intersections of the horizontal and vertical marks or as specified by the manufacturer. If necessary, turn the adjustment screws on the headlight so the lights point to the correct places or bubbles on the levels are centered, depending on the type of aligner equipment you are using.

Wrap-up

Ready for Review

- Incandescent lamps consist of one or more filaments, which heat up until they glow.
- Halogen lamps have a much longer life and are generally brighter and produce more light per unit of power consumed, but they become very hot during use.
- High-intensity discharge (HID) headlamps produce light with an electric arc rather than a glowing filament.
- Light-emitting diodes (LEDs) have been used for some time in various automotive applications, such as warning indicators and alphanumeric displays.
- One of the advantages of LEDs is that they turn on instantly.
- All lamps or light bulbs have letters and numbers stamped on them that indicate the power consumed by bulb operation at the nominal operating voltage.
- Lighting regulations should always be consulted before modifying or adding to any of the vehicle lighting systems.
- Park, tail, and marker lamps are all low-intensity or low-wattage lamps used to mark the outline or width of the vehicle.
- Brake lights, which may also be called stop lights, are red lights mounted to the rear of the vehicle.
- Reverse lights, also called back-up lights, are the bright white lights on the back of the vehicle that allow the operator to see behind the vehicle when backing up.
- Hazard lights can warn other road users that a hazardous condition exists or that the vehicle is standing or parked in a dangerous position on the side of the road; they normally use the same bulbs as the turn signal indicators.
- The low beam is usually set to the outside of the front, and the high beams are closer to the front center of the vehicle.
- The driving lights are installed on the front of the vehicle and provide higher intensity illumination over longer distances than standard headlight systems.
- Warning lamps provide the vehicle operator with information regarding the operation of the main vehicle systems, such as the vehicle battery charge, oil pressure level, and airbag system status.
- A typical lighting circuit is made up of the battery, fuses or circuit breakers, switches, lamps, and wiring to connect the electrical circuit.
- For motor vehicles and trailers, two red tail lamps operate when the headlight switch is in the park position and the headlight position.
- Daytime running lights (DRLs) automatically operate when the vehicle is running and turn off when the engine stops.
- The layouts of electrical circuits and their components are shown as diagrams made up of symbols and connecting lines.
- Being able to read and interpret electrical circuit layouts can cut a technician's troubleshooting time in half; this is a skill all technicians need to learn.
- When checking lighting and peripheral systems, be sure to work in a systematic manner or you could miss a faulty bulb or other component.
- If all of the bulbs on one fuse do not work, check the fuse.
- When replacing a bulb, always ensure there is no corrosion in the bulb socket, as this will shorten the life of the new bulb and add resistance in the circuit.
- Always make sure you replace a bulb with one of exactly the same type.
- It is critical that headlights be aimed correctly so as not to impair an oncoming vehicle and to allow correct visibility for the driver.

Key Terms

ballast A device that increases lighting voltage substantially and controls the current to the bulb.

halogen lamp A type of bulb that produces a bright white light.

high-intensity discharge (HID) A type of lighting that produces light with an electric arc rather than a glowing filament.

incandescent lamp The traditional bulb that uses a heated filament to produce light.

light-emitting diode (LED) A type of lighting various automotive applications, such as warning indicators and alphanumeric displays.

vacuum tube fluorescent (VTF) A type of lighting used for instrumentation displays on vehicle instrument panel clusters. This type of lighting emits a very bright light with high contrast and can display in various colors. Also called vacuum fluorescent display (VFD).

ASE-Type Questions

1. Tech A says that a voltage drop on the ground side of a bulb won't affect its brightness because the electricity has already been used up. Tech B says that a voltage drop is one way to determine if there is unwanted resistance in a circuit. Who is correct?
   a. Tech A
   b. Tech B
   c. Both A and B
   d. Neither A nor B
2. Tech A says that incandescent bulbs resist vibration well. Tech B says that HID headlamps require up to approximately 25,000 volts to start. Who is correct?
   a. Tech A
   b. Tech B
   c. Both A and B
   d. Neither A nor B
3. Tech A says that many automotive light bulbs have more than one filament inside. Tech B says that some lights use a filament made of quartz. Who is correct?
   a. Tech A
   b. Tech B
   c. Both A and B
   d. Neither A nor B
4. Tech A says that LED brake lights illuminate faster than incandescent bulbs. Tech B says that LED brake lights have more visibility and last longer. Who is correct?
   a. Tech A
   b. Tech B
   c. Both A and B
   d. Neither A nor B
5. Tech A says that if the brake light switch is open, neither brake light will illuminate. Tech B says that the back-up lights are connected in parallel with the tail lights. Who is correct?
   a. Tech A
   b. Tech B
   c. Both A and B
   d. Neither A nor B
6. Tech A says that some brake lights get power from the brake switch through the turn signal switch. Tech B says many turn signals use amber lights. Who is correct?
   a. Tech A
   b. Tech B
   c. Both A and B
   d. Neither A nor B
7. Tech A says that daytime running light systems illuminate the tail lights to enhance visibility. Tech B says that the CHMSL is illuminated when the tail lights are activated. Who is correct?
   a. Tech A
   b. Tech B
   c. Both A and B
   d. Neither A nor B
8. Tech A says that some turn signals are flashed by a flasher can. Tech B says that some turn signals are flashed by the BCM. Who is correct?
   a. Tech A
   b. Tech B
   c. Both A and B
   d. Neither A nor B
9. Tech A says that setting the tire pressure is part of a headlight adjustment. Tech B says that some headlight aligners require the headlights to be on during the alignment process. Who is correct?
   a. Tech A
   b. Tech B
   c. Both A and B
   d. Neither A nor B
10. Tech A says that if a bulb is dim when operated, the circuit likely has a short to ground. Tech B says that if a bulb is dim, you should perform a voltage drop test on the power and ground side of the bulb. Who is correct?
    a. Tech A
    b. Tech B
    c. Both A and B
    d. Neither A nor B

LOCK
BACK ONLY
HEAT OFF

CHAPTER 34

KNOW
SEE
DO
PROVE

NATEF Tasks

Electrical/Electronic Systems Horn and Wiper/Washer			Page
■ Diagnose (troubleshoot) causes of incorrect horn operation; determine necessary action.		AST	973–975
■ Diagnose (troubleshoot) windshield washer problems; determine necessary action.		AST	978–979
Accessories			
■ Describe the operation of keyless entry and remote start systems.	MLR	AST	975, 983–985
■ Remove and reinstall door panel.	MLR	AST	976
■ Verify windshield wiper and washer operation; replace wiper blades.	MLR	AST	978–979
■ Disable and enable airbag system for vehicle service; verify indicator lamp operation.	MLR	AST	983–984

Body Electrical System

Knowledge Objectives

After reading this chapter, you will be able to:

1. Explain the principles of operation of the CAN-bus system. (pp 968–969)
2. Describe the different network configurations of the CAN-bus system. (pp 968–969)
3. Explain the purpose of the different electric motor types—brush, brushless, permanent magnet, and stepper. (pp 970–971)
4. Describe the operation of the horn system. (pp 972–973)
5. Describe the operation of the wiper system. (pp 976–977)
6. Describe the purpose and operation of the supplemental restraint system (SRS). (pp 979–980)

Skills Objectives

After reading this chapter, you will be able to:

1. Diagnose the horn system. (pp 974–975)
2. Remove the door panel. (p 976)
3. Test the washer system. (pp 978–979)
4. Disable and enable the supplemental restraint system (SRS). (pp 983–984)

Introduction

Electrical systems on modern vehicles are becoming increasingly complex with the addition of a range of electronic and accessory systems, such as global positioning systems, entertainment systems, security systems, electric seats, and heated glass. Many of these systems are controlled by body computer systems. Increasingly, the electrical and electronic assemblies are interconnected through vehicle data networks that require sophisticated diagnostic techniques. The shop technician requires an in-depth knowledge of these systems, including how they work and interconnect through the vehicle network. We will start with some of the basic principles so that you will have a knowledge base upon which you can build your further studies.

CAN-bus System

The terms **controller area network (CAN)** and **bus** are used together (often as "CAN-bus") to describe the data-sharing network in vehicles. The many sensors and electronic control modules can share information across a common network using the CAN-bus protocol to communicate efficiently and effectively. CAN-bus is a broad protocol developed by Bosch to share data and information across a network. In electrical and electronic systems, a bus is a means of connecting many electrical or electronic components for either data or power sharing. There are several signal protocols that have been developed for use with second-generation on-board diagnostics (OBDII), including SAE J1850 PWM, SAE J1850 VPM, ISO 9141-2, ISO 14230 KW, and ISO 15765 CAN-bus (C&B).

Within the CAN-bus system design, there are several different network layouts or designs, and there may be a gateway or hub controller, but no single dominant electronic control module; each receives the same data and simply chooses the data it needs to work effectively. It is a robust system, and many modules can send and receive data without corruption or interference. The CAN-bus system continues to develop and, although standards are in place, manufacturers may use different terminology to describe their particular systems. As CAN-bus has developed, so too have the network speeds. CAN-bus A is a low-speed network, CAN-bus B is a medium-speed network, and CAN-bus C is a high-speed network. Higher-speed networks are used for critical data such as supplemental restraint systems, anti-lock brake systems, and engine controls. Lower-speed networks are used for lesser priority data such as data related to entertainment systems. CAN-bus systems will continue to evolve and new standards will be developed; however, the fundamental operating principles are likely to remain the same. And since CAN-bus-compliant diagnostic systems have been required on all vehicles sold in the United States since 2008, it is even more important that you be familiar with them.

Principles of Operation

The CAN-bus system uses digital data, called binary data, which have only two states: 0 or 1. All the data can be coded in binary form using a series of 0s and 1s. Each 0 or 1 is called a bit of information, and a group of eight bits is called a byte. The 0s and 1s are represented on the data bus as low and high voltages FIGURE 34-1. Each module on the data bus sees all data, so along with the

You Are the Automotive Technician

A 2010 minivan comes into the dealership due to the power window not working properly. The customer informs you that the "one-touch" function works sometimes and not others. After performing a VIN check for service history, you look up technical service bulletins (TSBs) and notice one related to the "one-touch" feature on this vehicle. The issue may be related to a binding window track, plus there is a software update to help address the issue down the road.

The first step is to verify if there is an overcurrent condition on the window motor. You connect the scan tool and see a code indicating an overcurrent shutdown on the driver's window. Next, you clean out the exposed window track with a clean shop rag. You then spray silicone lubricant into the window track and operate the window several times. Because the window is moving smoothly, the software can be updated. You follow the flash reprogramming steps detailed in the manufacturer's guide, which allows a slightly higher current flow in the circuit, which will prevent the computer from disabling the feature. Once the update is complete, you verify that the "one-touch" feature is functioning properly.

1. What is a CAN-bus system?
2. What was causing the high current condition?
3. Why is it important to look for TSBs before diagnosing a problem?

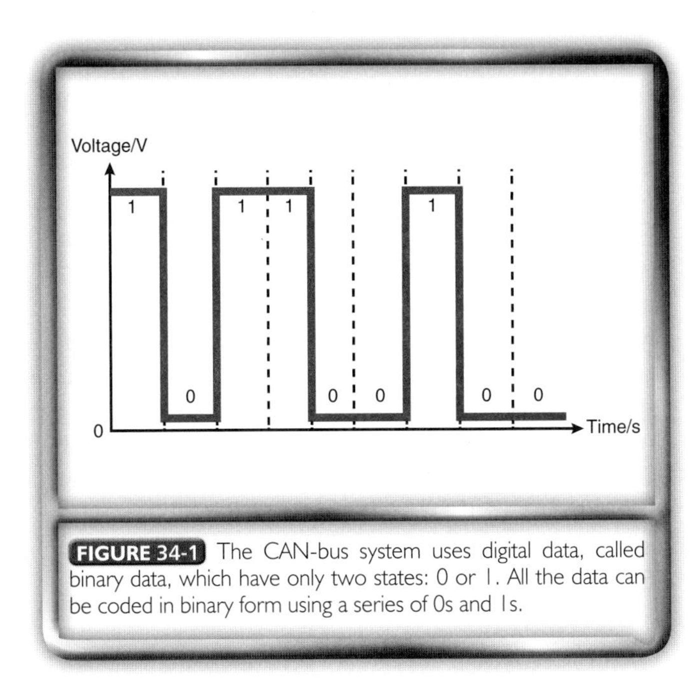
Voltage/V
1
1
1
1
0
0
0
0
0
0
Time/s

FIGURE 34-1 The CAN-bus system uses digital data, called binary data, which have only two states: 0 or 1. All the data can be coded in binary form using a series of 0s and 1s.

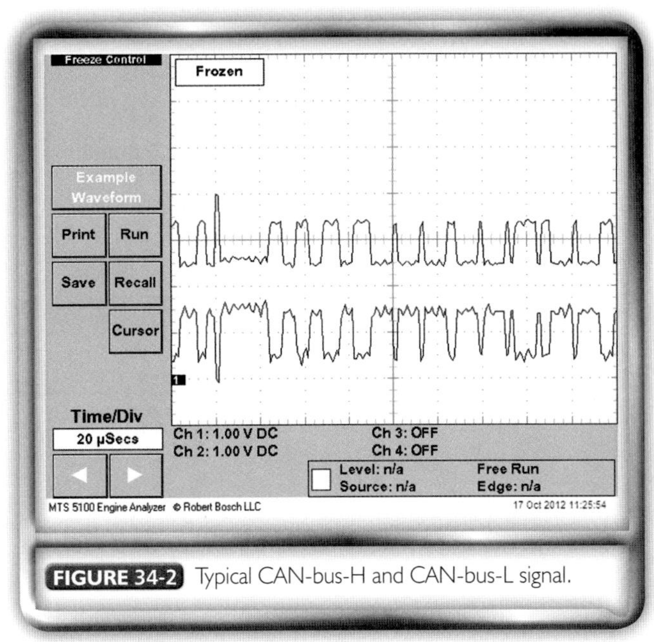
Freeze Control
Frozen
Example Waveform
Print
Run
Save
Recall
Cursor
Time/Div
20 μSecs
Ch 1: 1.00 V DC
Ch 2: 1.00 V DC
Ch 3: OFF
Ch 4: OFF
Level: n/a
Source: n/a
Free Run
Edge: n/a
MTS 5100 Engine Analyzer © Robert Bosch LLC
17 Oct 2012 11:25:54

FIGURE 34-2 Typical CAN-bus-H and CAN-bus-L signal.

actual data, other information like message headers is required to identify sender and recipient modules along with message priority, wake-up commands, and state of health messages. These details are all coded in binary form and sent along the data bus. The data are grouped into blocks of data, each with a beginning and an end, and each module is capable of reading the binary data, interpreting the required data, and sending its own messages along the data bus.

Some networks transmit and receive signals over a single wire, but most have dual wires and are commonly called "CAN-bus high (H)" and "CAN-bus low (L)," with the same message sent on both lines FIGURE 34-2. This system provides redundancy in the case of a fault or interference on a single line. The signal on each CAN-bus line is a differential signal, meaning they are a mirror image, or opposite polarity, of each other. The actual voltages used on the data lines to represent a 0 or 1 will vary with each manufacturer.

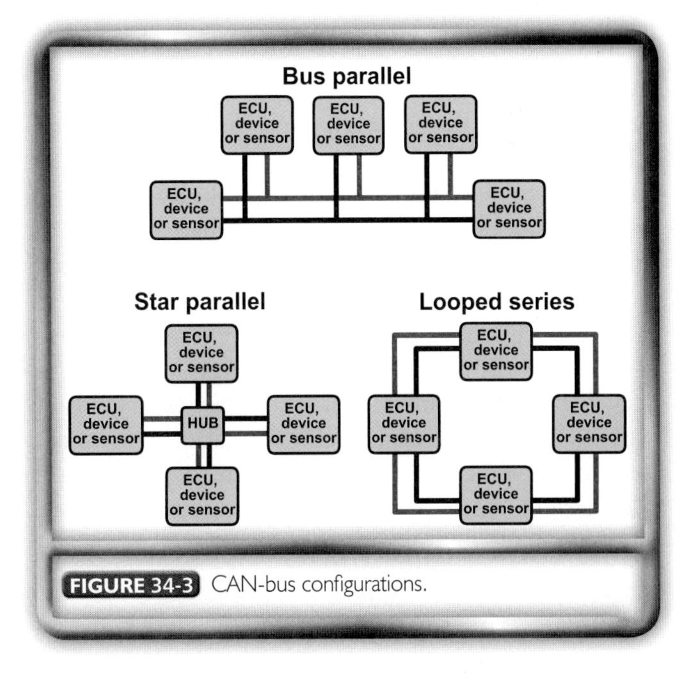
Bus parallel
ECU, device or sensor
Star parallel
HUB
Looped series

FIGURE 34-3 CAN-bus configurations.

Configurations and Terminal Resistors

The network configurations, or how the network connects to each module, will vary with each manufacturer. Some use a simple series configuration; others use variations of series networks and parallel network connections with descriptive names, such as looped series, star parallel, or bussed parallel FIGURE 34-3. Regardless of how the network is physically connected, the CAN-bus-H and CAN-bus-L system will have terminating resistors connected to the data lines to form a loop through the resistors. The value of resistors can vary by manufacturer, but high-speed CAN-bus systems tend to use dual 120-ohm resistors, giving a total of 60 ohms per pair since they are connected in parallel, but typically at opposite ends of the bus FIGURE 34-4.

The resistors can be connected externally in the wiring harness or connectors but are usually integrated internally into modules. The data lines are also twisted together with a specific twist rotation per length. This twisting, in combination with the terminating resistors, reduces the amount of interference on the data lines. The CAN-bus system has a **data link connector (DLC)** that provides a connection into the data network. The DLC is also used to connect scan tools into the network. It can also be used to conduct voltage and waveform tests on the CAN-bus.

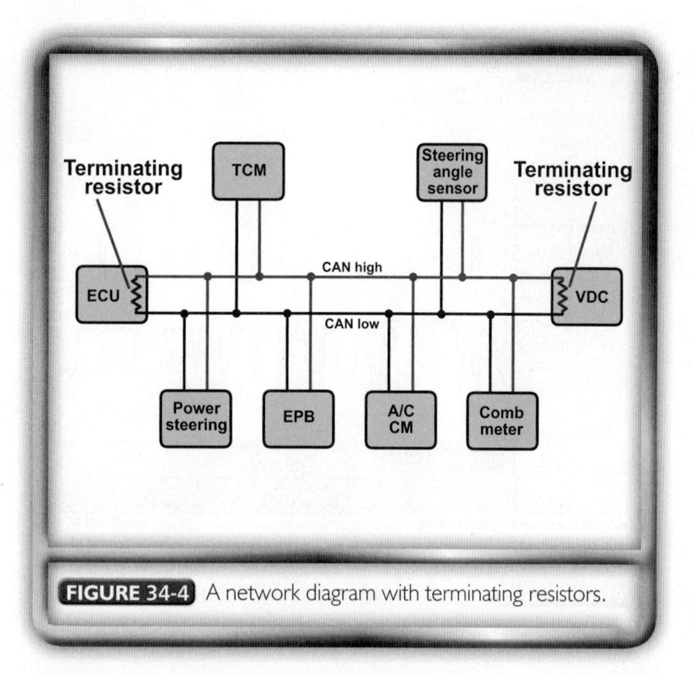
Terminating resistor
TCM
Steering angle sensor
Terminating resistor
CAN high
ECU
VDC
CAN low
Power steering
EPB
A/C CM
Comb meter

FIGURE 34-4 A network diagram with terminating resistors.

Electric Accessory Motors

Electric motors rotate as a result of the interaction of magnetic fields; that is, magnetic poles repel each other, and opposite poles attract. Two magnetic fields are required for motor action: one in the casing and the other in the rotating armature. The magnetic field in the casing can be generated by permanent magnets or many windings of fine copper wire wound in loops called field coils. The armature's magnetic field is generated in loops of wire that form the armature windings. Motor action occurs through the interaction of the magnetic fields of the field coils and the armature, which causes a rotational force to act on the armature, creating the turning motion **FIGURE 34-5**. From there, the rotary motion can be used to drive a variety of devices. Many times, the speed of the motor must be geared down so that more torque can be obtained, such as with windshield wipers and many actuators. Most of the time, the gears are located inside the motor housing, so if one or more gears go bad (e.g., stripped teeth), then the motor may still spin but the output gear or lever will not move as designed. Thus, listening for motor rotation can help you diagnose the problem. For example, if the windshield wipers do not move when activated, yet you can hear the motor running, you know that the electrical circuitry is working but the movement isn't getting from the motor to the wipers. This example could be an internal gear problem in the motor, or it could be a problem with the wiper linkage. But at least you will have a good head start on diagnosing the fault.

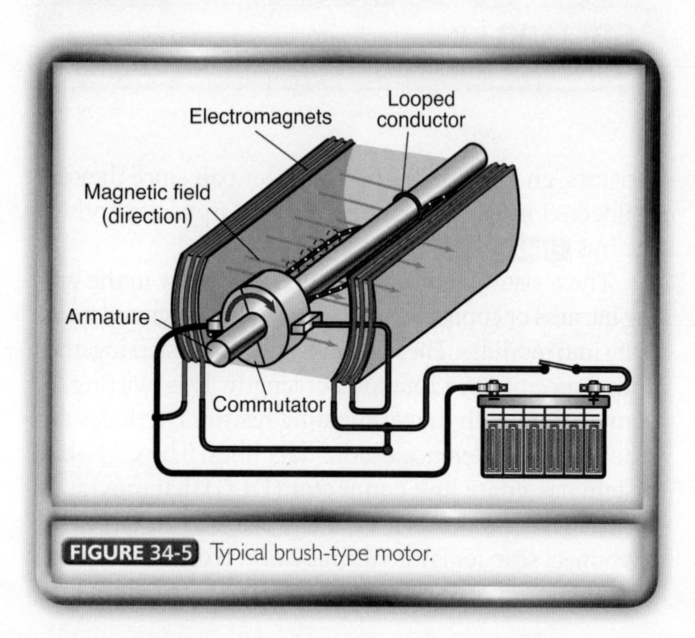
Electromagnets
Looped conductor
Magnetic field (direction)
Armature
Commutator

FIGURE 34-5 Typical brush-type motor.

Motor Types—Brush, Brushless, Permanent Magnet, and Stepper Type

Electric motors are designed to perform specific functions. They all work on the same fundamental principle of the interaction of magnetic fields; however, their construction varies. One of the most common types of DC electric motors is the **permanent magnet type**. In this type of motor, the magnetic field in the casing is produced by permanent magnets, while the armature has an electromagnetic field generated by passing electrical current through loops or windings to produce the motor action. Power is supplied to the armature loops by brushes riding on the commutator, which continually changes the current flow in the armature loops as it rotates. This changes the polarity of the magnetic field in the armature, producing the motor action effect as the armature magnetic field interacts with the permanent magnets in the casing.

A **brushless DC motor**, as the name suggests, does not have any brushes and is sometimes called an "electronically commutated motor." In this type of motor, an electronic control module replaces the brushes and commutator. A brushless motor has permanent magnets rotating around a fixed armature or stator. Having a fixed stator eliminates the need to have brushes. The current flow still needs to be continually alternated in the stationary stator to produce motor action, and this is achieved by an electronic control module. A brushless DC motor has several advantages over brush motors, including improved efficiency and reliability. In addition, brushless motors create less electrical interference because there are no sparks created by brushes making and breaking contact on the commutator.

A **stepper motor** is a type of brushless motor with a key difference: It is designed to rotate in fixed steps

Applied Science

AS-66: Electricity/Measurement: The technician can demonstrate an understanding of the correct procedure to measure the electrical parameters of voltage, current, and resistance.

A vehicle is in the shop for multiple interior electrical problems. The systems affected are the power seats, power windows, power door locks, and interior lighting. This problem was initially intermittent, but at this point the affected systems are not functioning.

The technician assigned to this repair has a good knowledge of troubleshooting automotive electrical circuits with a DVOM. He often helps other technicians who are in need of assistance on electrical concerns. In order to explain voltage, current, and resistance, the technician likes to use an analogy of a water hose. The water pressure available signifies voltage, the flow of water through the hose is the current measured in amps, and a kink or crimp in the hose is like the resistance in the electrical circuit. Resistance in a water hose application can be wanted or unwanted according to the purpose. When watering small plants, we want more resistance in the hose to reduce the amount of water flow. In the electrical system, there are times when we want increased resistance to reduce voltage, such as for low-speed windshield wiper operation.

In repairing the vehicle, the technician will do a voltage drop test to determine if there is a bad ground causing the multiple circuit problems. He is using a long jumper wire along with his DVOM to accomplish the test. The technician attaches a long jumper lead to the negative battery post, which connects to the COM or black test lead of the DVOM. The DVOM is set to read DC volts, and the red lead is used to check the ground side of the components in question. This test will be performed with each separate component under load, such as when attempting to operate a window. A good ground should have a reading of 0.10 volt or less. The technician finds a very high reading for each of the affected circuits and determines that the problem is in a corroded multiple ground connection point. Using the manufacturer's service information, the technician finds the four ground connections secured by a single bolt behind the driver's side kick panel. Each ground connector is cleaned on both sides with emery cloth. The frame location is cleaned also and the bolt securely tightened. The DVOM reading is now 0.07 volt, and all circuits are working properly.

AS-67: Ammeter/Voltmeter: The technician can demonstrate an understanding of how to correctly measure electrical current and voltage in a circuit.

The digital volt-ohmmeter (DVOM) is the testing and measuring device used by most technicians working on today's vehicles. While separate ammeters are available for measuring current in amperes, and separate voltmeters are available for measuring voltage in a circuit, for the purposes of this article, we will consider the DVOM as being the meter of choice.

To measure electrical current with the DVOM, it is helpful to know that current is the volume of electrons flowing in a circuit. Amps and milliamps are a measure of the volume of electrons. To measure current below 10 amps, place the meter in series with the load. If the current is expected to be above 10 amps, an inductive pickup must be used. Turn off the power to the circuit and determine where the test leads should be attached. Put the black test lead into the COM input jack. Plug the red test lead into the 10 amps or 300 milliamps position and select DC amps. Connect the test probe's tips to the circuit across the break so current will flow through the meter in series. Turn on the circuit and view the reading on the meter.

To measure voltage with a DVOM, it is helpful to know that voltage is the electrical pressure that causes electricity to flow. Voltage is the difference in electrical potential between the "hot" side of the battery and the "ground" side. To make a voltage measurement, the meter leads must be connected across the load or component being measured. When testing an automotive battery, you must wear safety glasses. Place the red lead on the positive post of the battery. Place the black lead on the negative post of the battery. A fully charged automotive battery should be approximately 12.66 volts at 70°F (21°C).

through a set number of degrees. The stepper motor is controlled by an electronic microcontroller and has a number of wound coils, each controlled independently by the controller. Each time the controller energizes a coil for a short period of time, the motor armature turns a set number of degrees and stops FIGURE 34-6. For example, if a motor were to turn 20 degrees for each step, it would require a minimum of 18 pairs of coils—one coil for each 20 degrees of rotation (totaling 360 degrees). Energizing each coil in rapid succession creates rotational movement. Stepper motors can also be used to rotate a short distance and then stop or go in the reverse direction for a set number of degrees by controlling each coil individually through the microcontroller. Stepper motors are increasingly used in vehicles; for example, the electronic throttle body uses a stepper motor to open and close the throttle plate one step at a time, as directed by the power train control module (PCM).

Blower Motor and Circuits

The **blower motor** in a vehicle is usually the permanent magnet type and moves air over the air-conditioning evaporator and heater core. The blower motor circuit incorporates a speed control for the motor. Speed can be

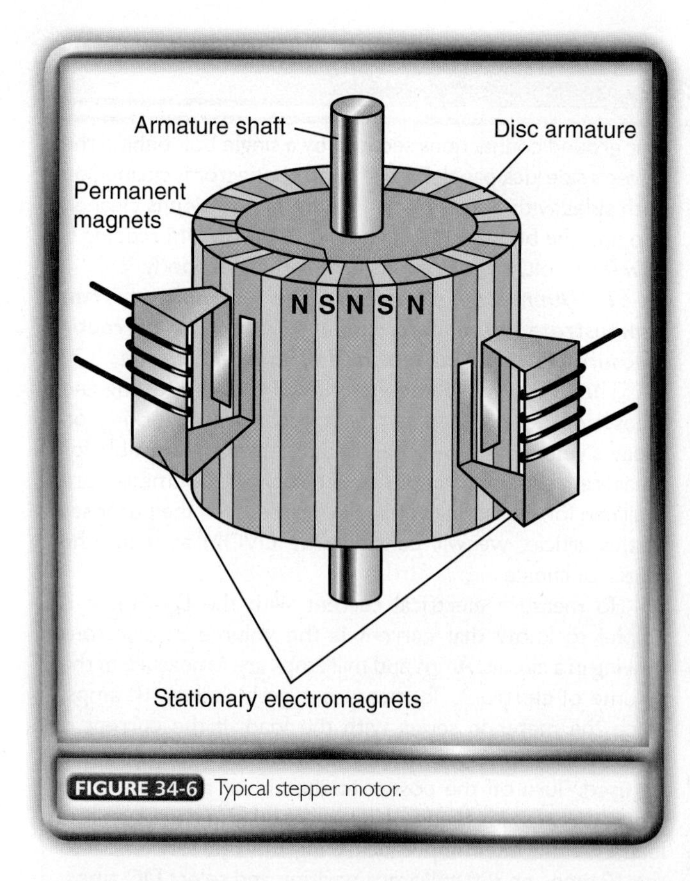

Armature shaft
Disc armature
Permanent magnets
N S N S N
Stationary electromagnets

FIGURE 34-6 Typical stepper motor.

controlled by using a number of resistors connected in series and a switch to select between combinations of resistors or a more complex electronic speed control module. The blower motor circuit consists of the power supply, fuse, on/off switch, speed control, relay, and the motor itself FIGURE 34-7. In vehicles equipped with air conditioning, the blower motor control circuit is incorporated into the control circuits for the air-conditioning system.

Cooling Fans and Circuits

Electric cooling fans for the radiator are increasingly common, particularly for transversely mounted engines and as supplementary cooling fans for vehicles equipped with air conditioning. Cooling fans in modern vehicles are usually switched by relays, which are controlled by an electronic control unit based on information from the coolant temperature sensor. Control units can be quite complex and can incorporate variable speed and on/off control. The control circuits are designed to ensure that the operating temperature of the engine is kept as close as possible to the temperature at which the engine operates most efficiently.

The basic electric cooling fan circuit contains the battery or power supply, fuse, relay, fan control circuits, and fans FIGURE 34-8. The actual circuit and its complexity will vary by manufacturer and vehicle model. The circuit diagram or schematic for the fan system should be examined before attempting any diagnosis.

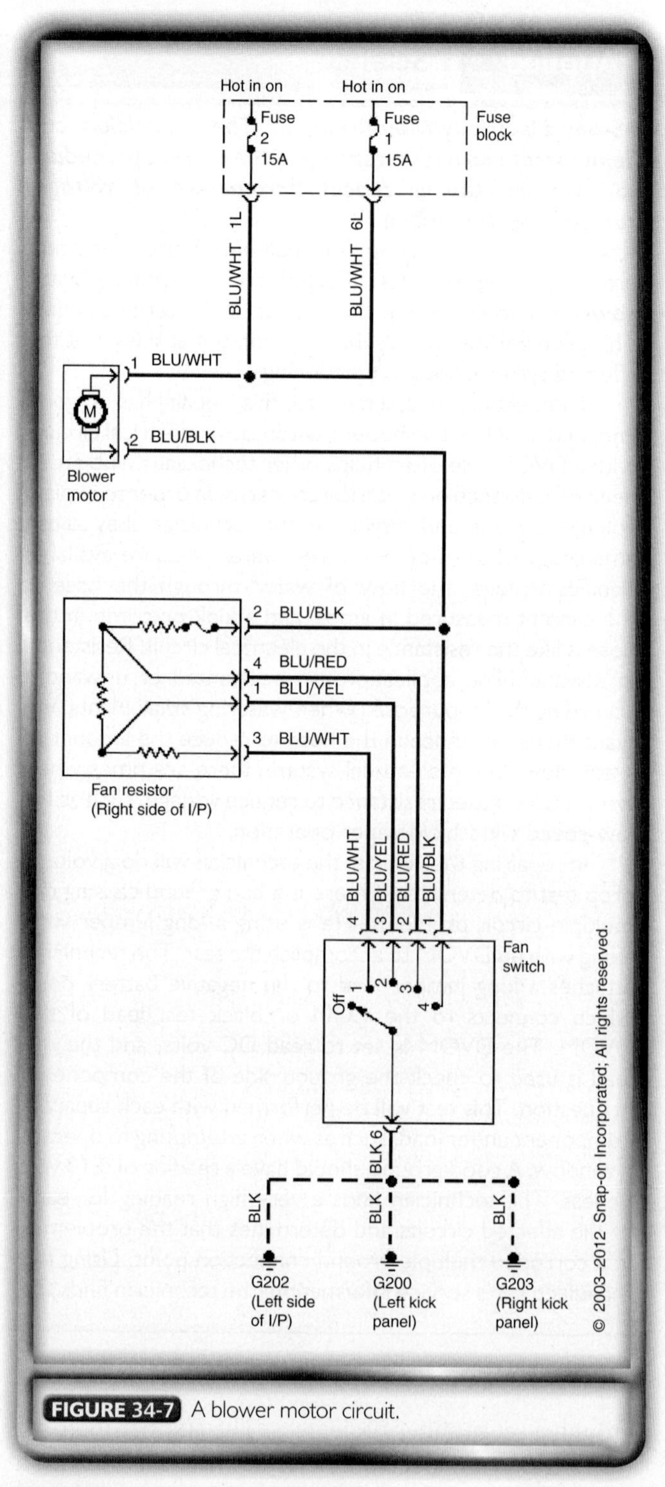

Hot in on
Hot in on
Fuse 2 15A
Fuse 1 15A
Fuse block
BLU/WHT 1L
BLU/WHT 6L
1 BLU/WHT
2 BLU/BLK
Blower motor
2 BLU/BLK
4 BLU/RED
1 BLU/YEL
3 BLU/WHT
Fan resistor (Right side of I/P)
4 BLU/WHT
3 BLU/YEL
2 BLU/RED
1 BLU/BLK
Fan switch
Off
BLK 6
BLK
BLK
BLK
G202 (Left side of I/P)
G200 (Left kick panel)
G203 (Right kick panel)
© 2003–2012 Snap-on Incorporated; All rights reserved.

FIGURE 34-7 A blower motor circuit.

Horn Systems

The vehicle horn is a sound making safety device to warn others of a vehicle's presence. Legislation requires vehicles to have a working horn and in most cases also prescribes the sound level required to be made by the horn. Single horns may be installed but often they will be installed in pairs, one each of a high and low note to produce a harmonious sound and to give redundancy if one horn fails.

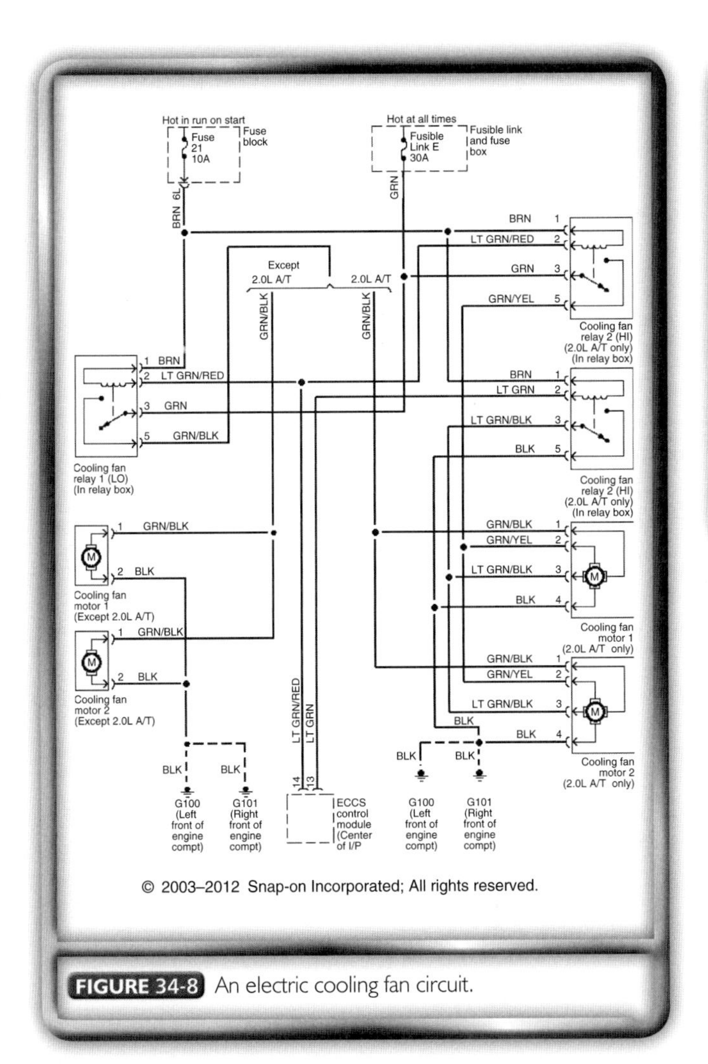
Hot in run on start
Fuse 21 10A
Fuse block
Hot at all times
Fusible Link E 30A
Fusible link and fuse box
BRN 6L
GRN
BRN
LT GRN/RED
GRN
GRN/YEL
Except 2.0L A/T
2.0L A/T
GRN/BLK
Cooling fan relay 2 (HI) (2.0L A/T only) (In relay box)
BRN
LT GRN/RED
GRN
GRN/BLK
BRN
LT GRN
LT GRN/BLK
BLK
Cooling fan relay 1 (LO) (In relay box)
Cooling fan relay 2 (HI) (2.0L A/T only) (In relay box)
GRN/BLK
BLK
Cooling fan motor 1 (Except 2.0L A/T)
GRN/BLK
GRN/YEL
LT GRN/BLK
BLK
Cooling fan motor 1 (2.0L A/T only)
GRN/BLK
BLK
Cooling fan motor 2 (Except 2.0L A/T)
GRN/BLK
GRN/YEL
LT GRN/BLK
BLK
LT GRN/RED
LT GRN
Cooling fan motor 2 (2.0L A/T only)
BLK
BLK
G100 (Left front of engine compt)
G101 (Right front of engine compt)
ECCS control module (Center of I/P)
G100 (Left front of engine compt)
G101 (Right front of engine compt)
© 2003–2012 Snap-on Incorporated; All rights reserved.

FIGURE 34-8 An electric cooling fan circuit.

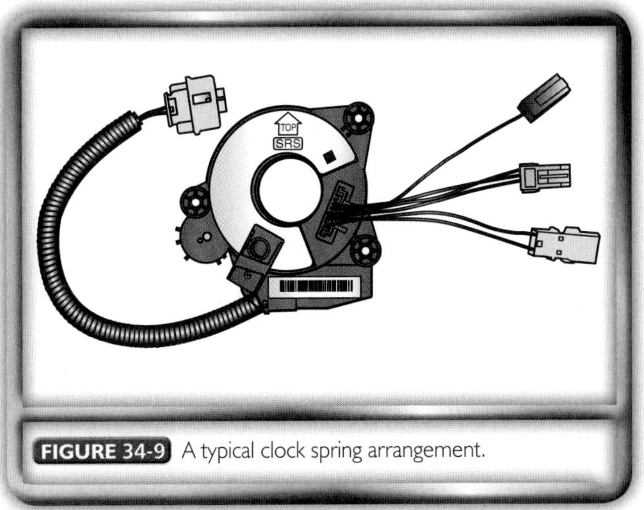
TOP
SRS

FIGURE 34-9 A typical clock spring arrangement.

> **TECHNICIAN TIP**
>
> Vehicles without a driver's side airbag usually use a slip ring and brush assembly in place of a clock spring to transmit the electricity across the rotating steering wheel connection.

Horn, Relay, Switch, and Clock Spring

The sound of a horn is produced by the vibration of a metal diaphragm, which is operated by an electromagnet switched by a set of contacts. The diaphragm is connected to an armature that moves inside an electromagnet. When the electromagnet is on, the diaphragm is pulled by the armature toward the electromagnet; as this occurs, a trip ring opens the contacts, allowing the diaphragm to spring back to its original position. This cycle happens many times a second, producing sound through the rapid vibration of the diaphragm.

The horn switch is usually mounted in the steering wheel and requires a method to maintain an electrical connection to the circuit as the steering wheel rotates. On vehicles with a driver's side airbag, the clock spring performs this function. The clock spring is also used to carry the electrical signals for the driver airbag circuit and may be used for sound system or cruise control circuits if they are built into the steering wheel. The clock spring is a rotating device with flexible ribbon cable and rotates as the steering wheel rotates FIGURE 34-9. It is designed to turn two or three times in each direction from the center point and cannot rotate endlessly in a single direction. It must be adjusted when it is installed to match the position of the steering wheel to avoid it reaching the end of its travel in any single direction.

The horn circuit is made up of the battery power supply, a fuse or circuit breaker, a relay, the horn switch, and the clock spring. The horn switch is usually a grounding circuit. The switch grounds the relay winding, which in turn supplies power through the relay contacts to operate the horn FIGURE 34-10. The horns on many newer vehicles can be operated by pressing the panic button on a fob. They may chirp when locking or unlocking and honk when a breach of security has happened. In most cases, these horns are operated by a body computer when the correct inputs arrive.

Testing the Horn System

The horn circuit can fail in many ways. Any of the components in the circuit can go bad, as can the wiring. Using a DVOM to measure voltages and test voltage drops on fuses, relays, switches, and power and ground connection will tell you how to proceed when testing the circuit. The horn switch is usually mounted within the steering wheel and is usually connected through the steering column by a clock spring. The clock spring must be correctly centered when it is installed to ensure it has enough travel in each direction. The horn switch usually grounds the horn relay winding, which in turn sends power to the horn.

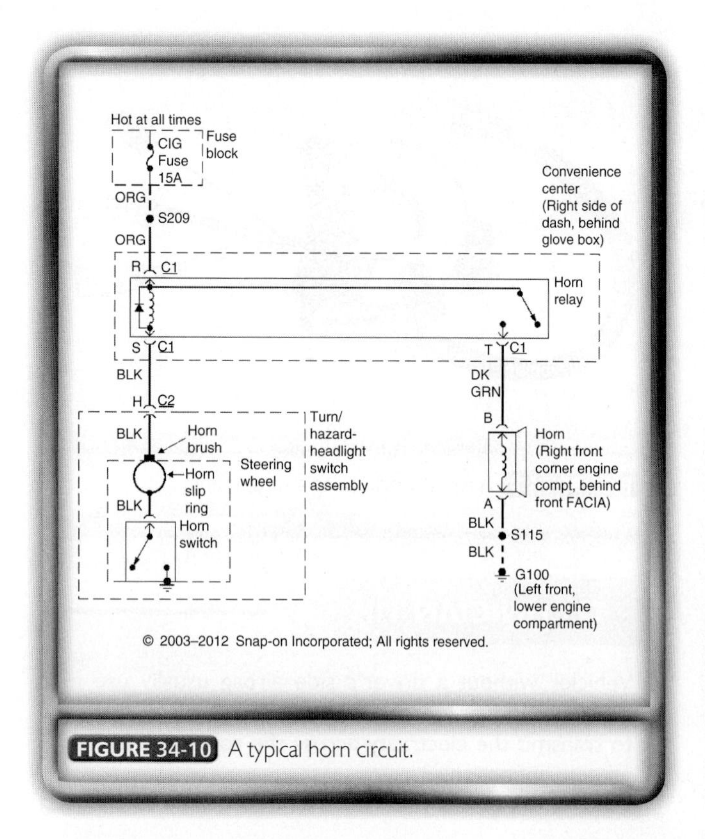
Hot at all times
CIG Fuse 15A
Fuse block
ORG
S209
ORG
Convenience center (Right side of dash, behind glove box)
R C1
Horn relay
S C1
T C1
BLK
DK GRN
H C2
BLK
Horn brush
Turn/ hazard- headlight switch assembly
Steering wheel
Horn slip ring
BLK
Horn switch
B
Horn (Right front corner engine compt, behind front FACIA)
A
BLK
S115
BLK
G100 (Left front, lower engine compartment)
© 2003–2012 Snap-on Incorporated; All rights reserved.

FIGURE 34-10 A typical horn circuit.

When testing the horn, it may be easiest to first test to see if power is getting to the horn when the horn is activated since it is not uncommon for horns to go bad, especially if they are rarely used or are overused. If power is getting to the horn, check the voltage drop on the ground side. If the voltage drop is fine, the horn is bad. In this case, tap the horn while it is energized. It is possible the contacts inside the horn are dirty or rusty, and tapping on the horn may free them up. If so, you will know that the rest of the circuit is operational. You will probably want to replace the horn since it is likely to go bad again soon.

If the horn does not have power when activated, it is good to go to the horn relay to perform the next tests. At the relay, you have access to each of the legs in the circuit—power from the horn fuse, the output terminal to the horn, power from the fuse feeding the winding, and the horn switch terminal. Using the DVOM and a jumper lead, you can check each of these legs. Remove the relay and using the DVOM, check for power from each fuse. If present, use the jumper lead from the horn fuse input to the horn output (at the relay connector) and see if the horn honks. If it does not honk, check the wiring between the relay and the horn. If it does honk, use a DVOM to check the continuity of the horn switch leg with the horn switch depressed. There should be continuity between the horn switch terminal on the relay and ground. If there is, then the relay is faulty.

To diagnose the horn system, follow the steps in **SKILL DRILL 34-1**.

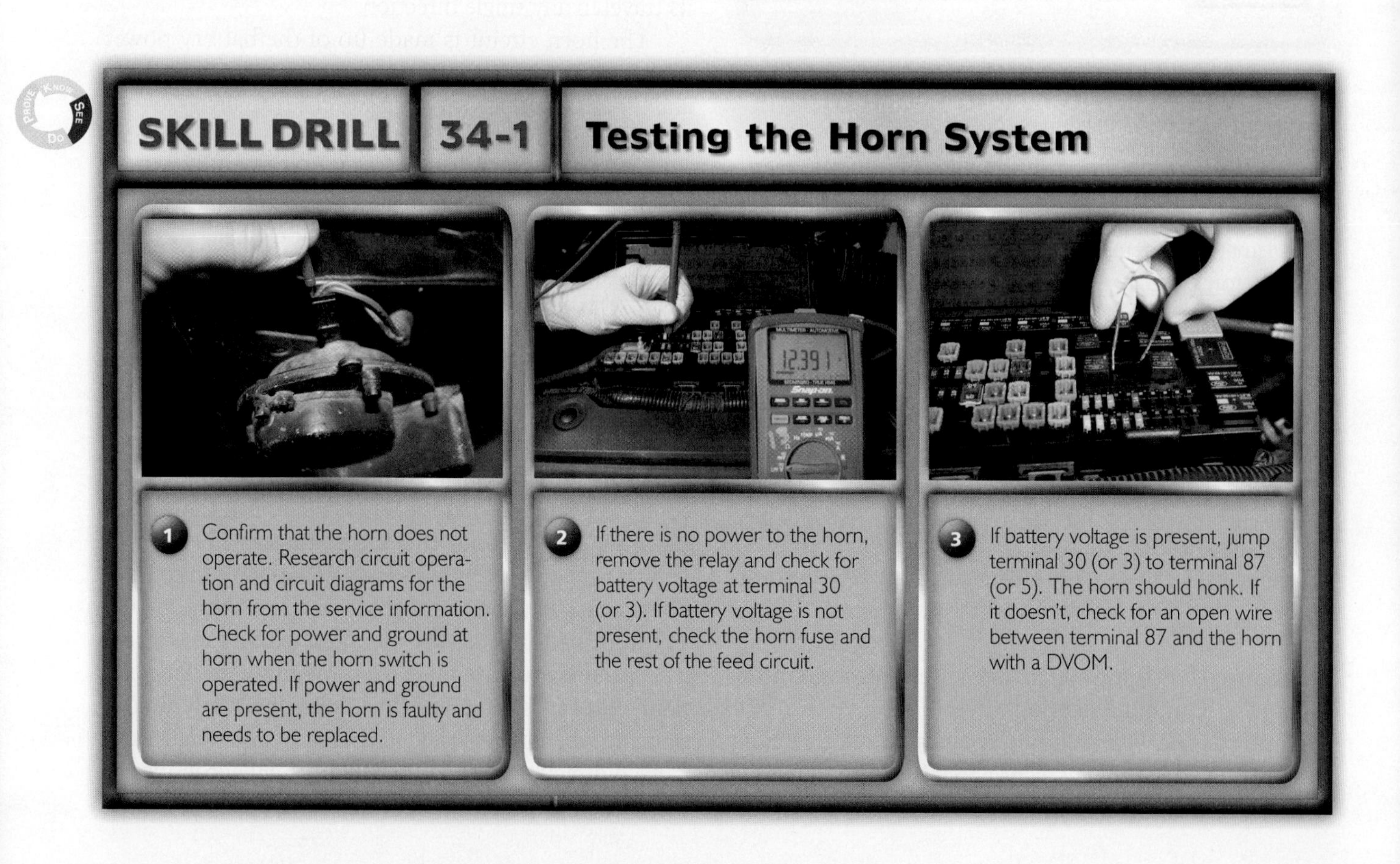

SKILL DRILL 34-1 Testing the Horn System

1. Confirm that the horn does not operate. Research circuit operation and circuit diagrams for the horn from the service information. Check for power and ground at horn when the horn switch is operated. If power and ground are present, the horn is faulty and needs to be replaced.

2. If there is no power to the horn, remove the relay and check for battery voltage at terminal 30 (or 3). If battery voltage is not present, check the horn fuse and the rest of the feed circuit.

3. If battery voltage is present, jump terminal 30 (or 3) to terminal 87 (or 5). The horn should honk. If it doesn't, check for an open wire between terminal 87 and the horn with a DVOM.

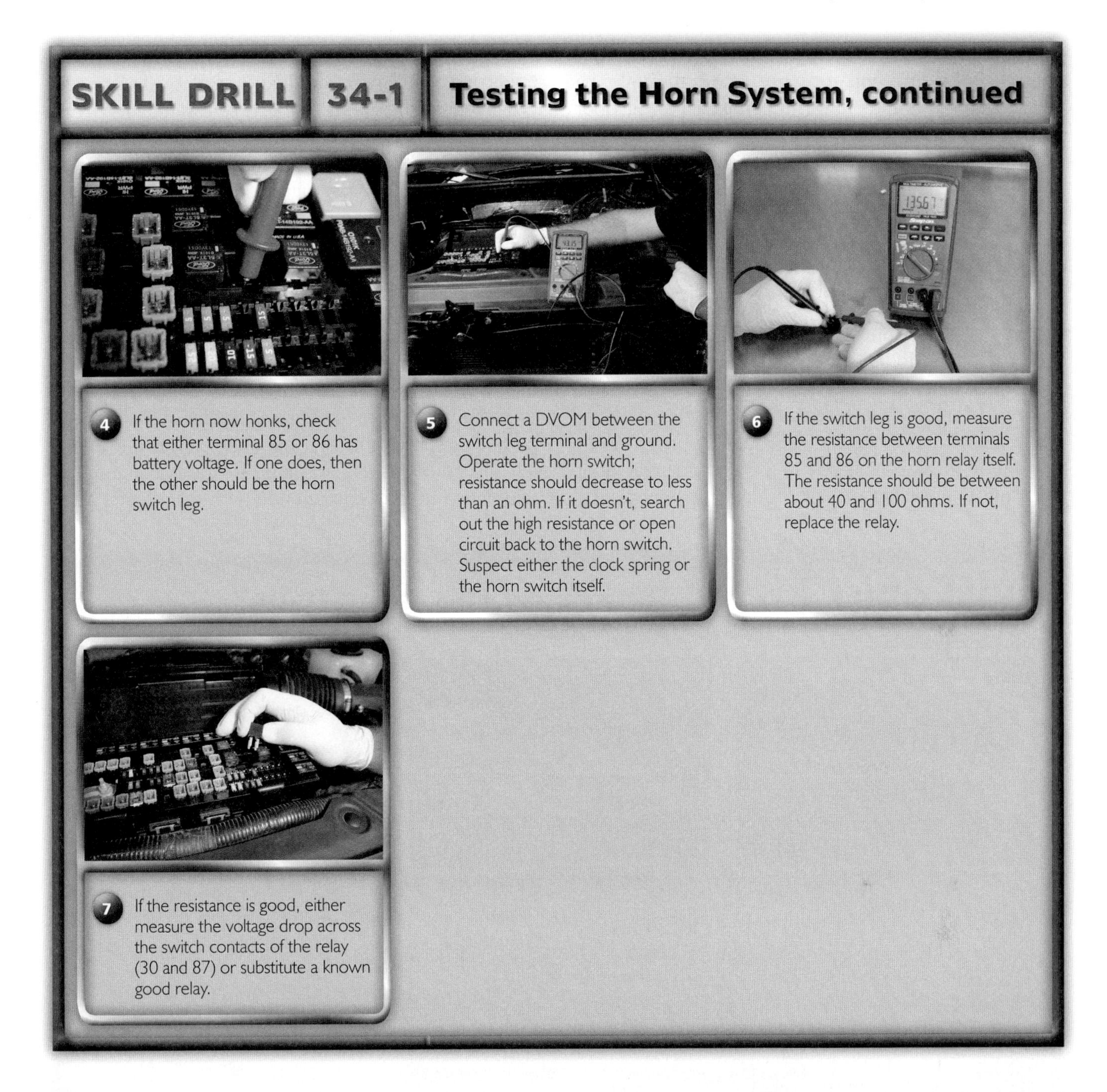
SKILL DRILL 34-1 Testing the Horn System, continued
4 If the horn now honks, check that either terminal 85 or 86 has battery voltage. If one does, then the other should be the horn switch leg.
5 Connect a DVOM between the switch leg terminal and ground. Operate the horn switch; resistance should decrease to less than an ohm. If it doesn't, search out the high resistance or open circuit back to the horn switch. Suspect either the clock spring or the horn switch itself.
6 If the switch leg is good, measure the resistance between terminals 85 and 86 on the horn relay itself. The resistance should be between about 40 and 100 ohms. If not, replace the relay.
7 If the resistance is good, either measure the voltage drop across the switch contacts of the relay (30 and 87) or substitute a known good relay.

Power Door Locks

Power or electric door locks are a common option in modern vehicles and are installed in each door. They are often integrated with the vehicle's security system and remote locking systems and are called central locking systems. Many vehicles also have trunk locks incorporated into the vehicle's electric locking system. The driver's side door is usually a master door lock, which means that when it is locked or unlocked with the key (or the remote fob) the other locks follow suit.

Power door locks use an electrical actuator to move the mechanical door lock mechanism. There are two main types of actuators: a DC motor actuator and a solenoid type. The DC reversible permanent magnet motor type is enclosed in a single casing with a number of gears for speed reduction that connect to a rack-and-pinion gear set for conversion of the rotational motion into linear motion to operate the lock. A centrifugal clutch built into the motor main gear allows the door locks to be operated manually.

The solenoid-type actuator has a permanent magnet with a north and south pole mounted on a moving plunger and a stationary coil wound around the outside. It can move in both directions. The magnetic fields of the permanent magnet on the plunger react with the magnetic fields of the coils producing linear movement of the plunger.

The plunger's direction of movement can be reversed by controlling the direction of current flow in the coil. The connecting rod of the plunger is connected to the door locking mechanism. The electric door lock circuit consists of the power supply, fuses or circuit breakers, the actuator (motor or solenoid), relays, switches, and cabling. Relays are typically used to switch the motors or solenoids.

Removing the Door Panel

Removing door panels requires the removal of the arm rest, door lever, window crank, and any switch panels mounted on the door. In most cases, the door panel itself will be attached to the door using clips, so they will have to be pried out of their holes. Some manufacturers use a few screws to provide extra security. To pry the door panel from the door, it is best to use a nonmetallic door panel tool to prevent damage to the door or paint finishes. Special tools may be required to release the clip that holds the manual window handles in place, if equipped. Preserve the inner lining for reuse by carefully removing it from the door frame. Carefully examine the door lining for screws and fastenings that may need to be removed before attempting to pry off the door panel.

To remove the door panel, follow the steps in SKILL DRILL 34-2.

Wiper/Washer System

The wiper and washer system is an important vehicle safety system. The wipers ensure that the driver has a clear line of sight through the windshield by removing any excess moisture from the glass. The wipers usually have a number of speeds and intermittent operation for varying rainfall conditions. The washers provide a cleaning spray that, when used in conjunction with the wipers, helps

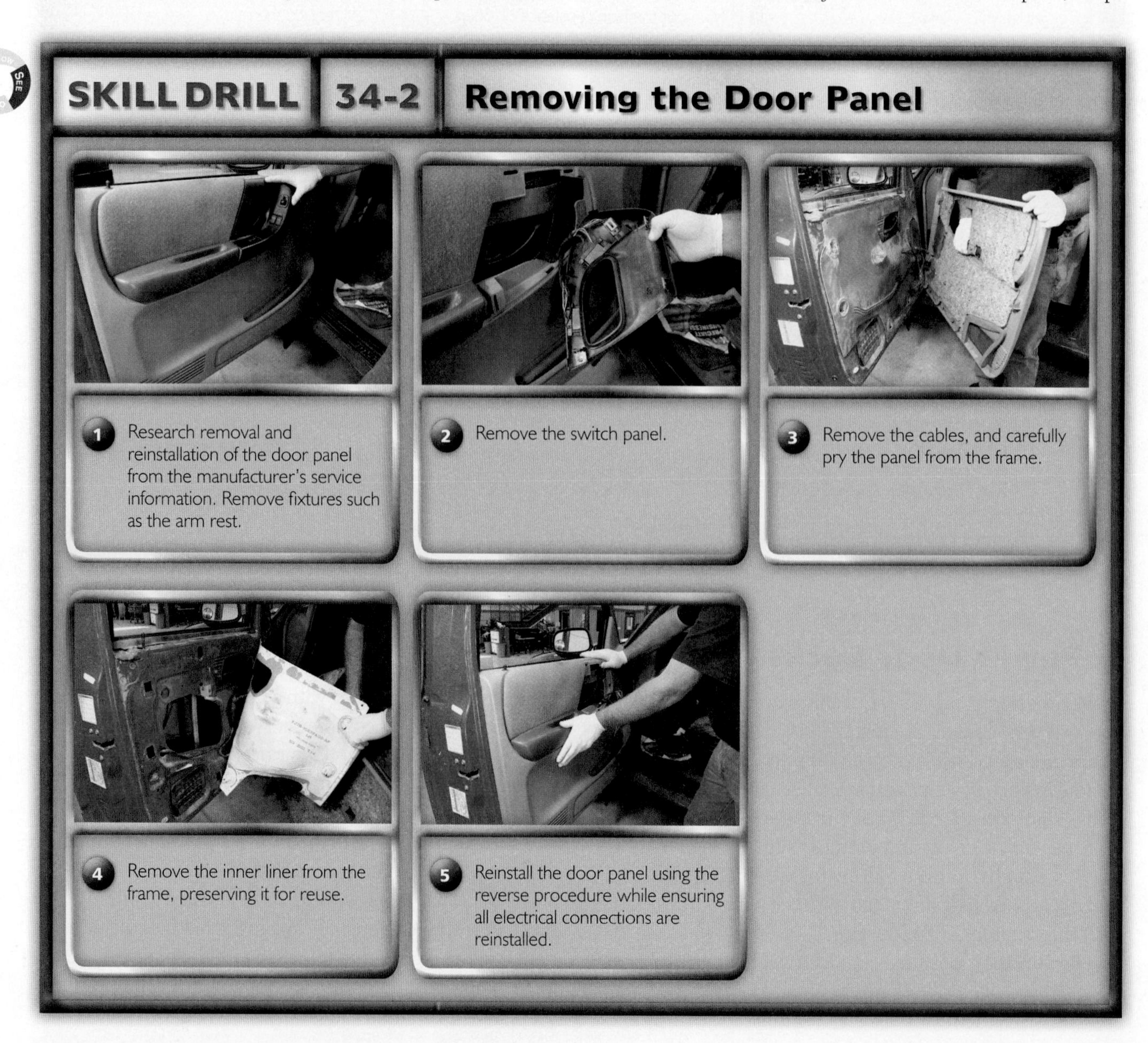
PROVE KNOW SEE DO

SKILL DRILL 34-2 Removing the Door Panel

1. Research removal and reinstallation of the door panel from the manufacturer's service information. Remove fixtures such as the arm rest.
2. Remove the switch panel.
3. Remove the cables, and carefully pry the panel from the frame.
4. Remove the inner liner from the frame, preserving it for reuse.
5. Reinstall the door panel using the reverse procedure while ensuring all electrical connections are reinstalled.

to clean road grime from the windshield. Some vehicles use a wiper and washer for the rear glass, and even some headlights as well.

Wiper and Delay Circuits

The wiper motor will usually have a high and low speed and a time delay or intermittent operation. Intermittent operation will be controlled by a timer circuit, which may be a discrete electronic timer or controlled by the vehicle body computer. Incorporated into the circuit and activated by the motor gear is a parking switch to ensure that the motor stops when the wiper blades are in the park position. The DC motor is dynamically braked to make sure the motor stops instantly without overrun in the park position. To provide high and low speed, the wiper motor is equipped with three brushes. Two brushes are placed 180 degrees apart, as they are in a standard motor, while the additional or third brush is located off-center. When current is switched from the low-speed brush to the high-speed brush, it provides higher rotational speed of the armature due to the different interaction of the magnetic fields.

The wiper circuit consists of the battery, a fuse or circuit breaker, the ignition switch, the wiper switch, an intermittent timer and/or body computer, and the motor assembly with park switch FIGURE 34-11. The park switch

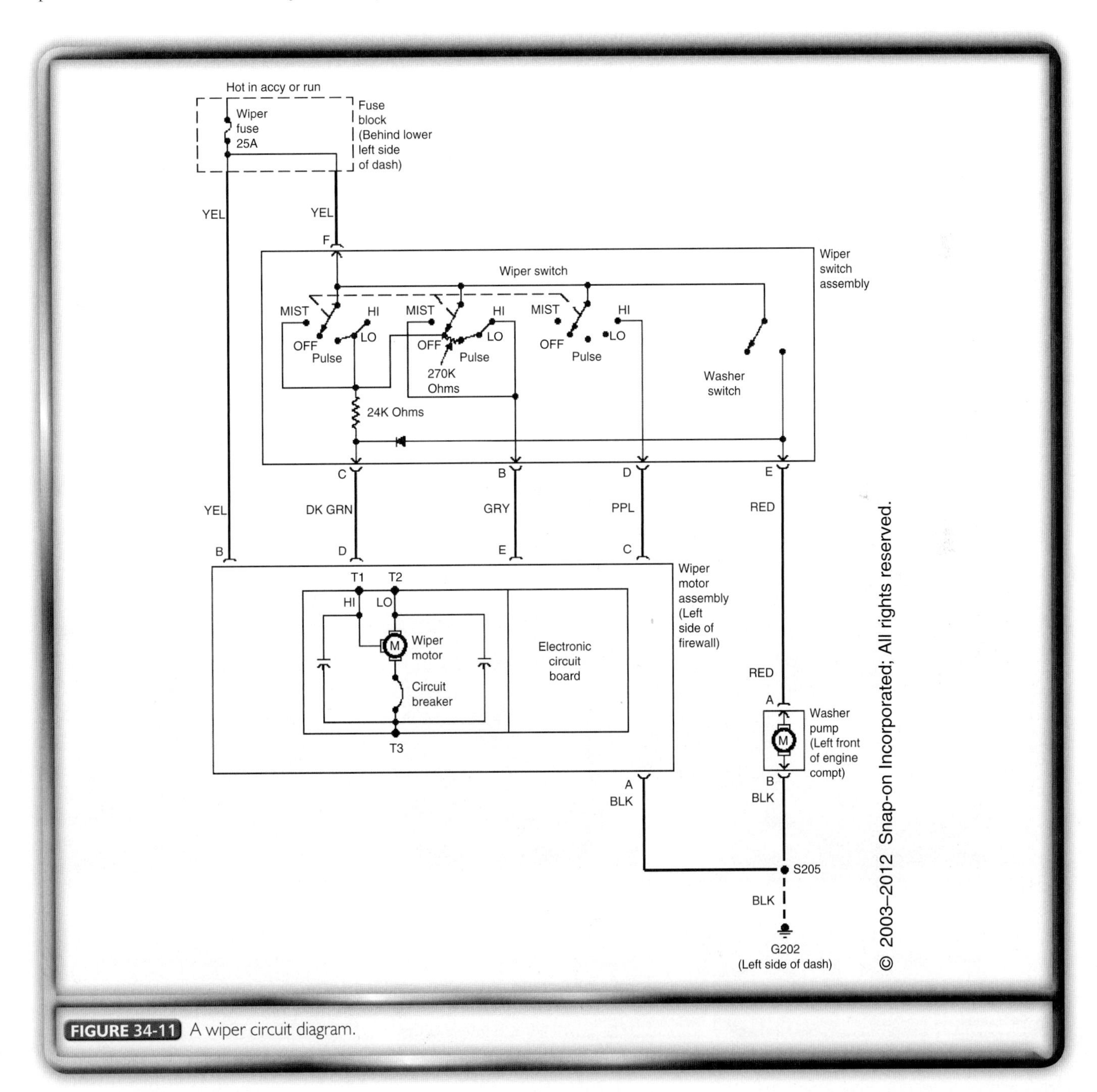
Hot in accy or run
Wiper fuse 25A
Fuse block (Behind lower left side of dash)
YEL
YEL
F
Wiper switch
Wiper switch assembly
MIST
HI
LO
OFF
Pulse
MIST
HI
LO
OFF
Pulse
270K Ohms
MIST
HI
LO
OFF
Pulse
Washer switch
24K Ohms
C
B
D
E
YEL
DK GRN
GRY
PPL
RED
B
D
E
C
T1
T2
HI
LO
Wiper motor
Circuit breaker
Electronic circuit board
T3
Wiper motor assembly (Left side of firewall)
RED
A
Washer pump (Left front of engine compt)
B
BLK
A
BLK
S205
BLK
G202 (Left side of dash)
© 2003–2012 Snap-on Incorporated; All rights reserved.

FIGURE 34-11 A wiper circuit diagram.

is built inside the motor and gearbox housing and switches a power feed to the low-speed brush when the wiper switch is in the off position and the wiper blades are in the park position. This dynamically brakes the motor because power is now applied across both brushes in the motor, bringing the motor to a quick stop. Intermittent operation is achieved by pulsing the low-speed circuit with a temporary power, causing the motor to move off the park position. With the power pulse removed, the motor continues on a single wipe of the windshield through the park switch until it again reaches the park position.

Wiper circuits can also be ground-switched circuits. For example, the ignition switch provides a power feed to the motor through a fuse or circuit breaker, and the wiper switch, depending on the switch position, switches the high- or low-speed brush to ground. Some vehicles use a rain sensor mounted in or near the windshield, which will signal the body computer to operate the wipers accordingly.

Testing the Washer System

The windshield and back window washer systems are made up of the washer bottle to hold the washer fluid, a DC electric pump, nozzles to spray the glass, and tubing to carry the washer fluid from the pump to the nozzles. The DC motor on the pump is a permanent magnet motor and has power supplied to one brush from the ignition circuit and the other brush grounded by the switch. The switch for the washer is usually located on the same switch assembly as the wipers. Operating the washer switch will usually also operate the wipers for at least one cycle; however, some systems allow for multiple wipe cycles before parking the wiper blades.

Both the electrical circuit and the pump discharge circuit will need to be tested for correct operation. The electrical circuit consists of the power supply, fuse, switch, and DC pump motor and can be tested with a test lamp or DVOM. The pump or washer fluid discharge circuit is made up of the pump, the washer fluid supply or tank, the tubes that carry the washer fluid to the washer nozzles, and the nozzles. You may find that blowing air through the discharge circuit and nozzles cleans out any debris that may be plugging the pump. Just be careful that you don't overpressurize the system and cause an inaccessible hose to be blown off of a fitting. Also, ensure adequate washer fluid in the tank before conducting any tests.

To test the washer system, follow the steps in SKILL DRILL 34-3.

Testing the Wiper System

The windshield wipers can fail in a number of ways. First, they may completely not work, such as when a fuse or motor is bad. Second, they may work on only some speeds, such as when the switch or one of the brushes in the motor is faulty. Third, they may not work on the intermittent speed, such as when the delay module is faulty. Fourth, they may not park, as when the park contacts in the motor are faulty or the wiper switch is bad. Each of these faults can be diagnosed by using a DVOM and referring to the wiring diagram to locate the fault. Another fault with wiper systems is that the linkage wears out, which can prevent one or both of the wiper arms from

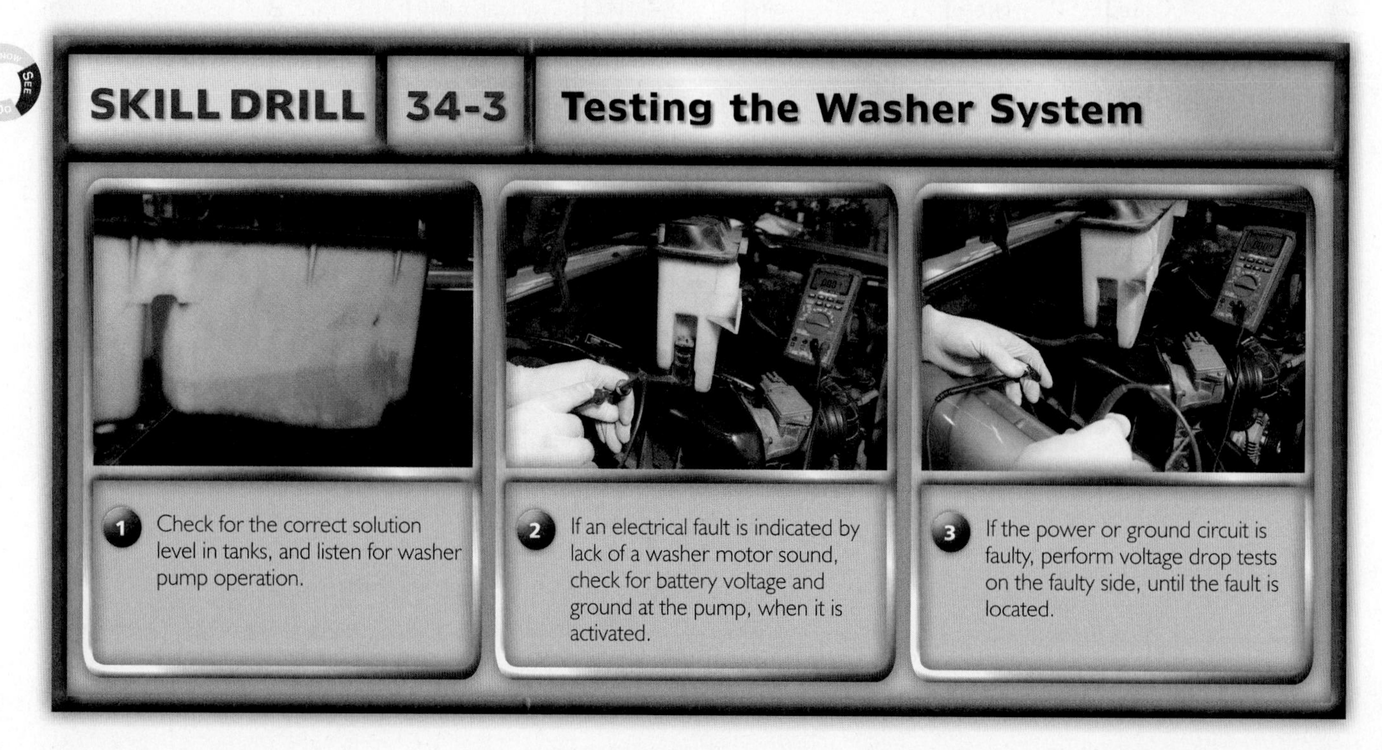
PROVE KNOW SEE DO
SKILL DRILL 34-3 Testing the Washer System
1 Check for the correct solution level in tanks, and listen for washer pump operation.
2 If an electrical fault is indicated by lack of a washer motor sound, check for battery voltage and ground at the pump, when it is activated.
3 If the power or ground circuit is faulty, perform voltage drop tests on the faulty side, until the fault is located.

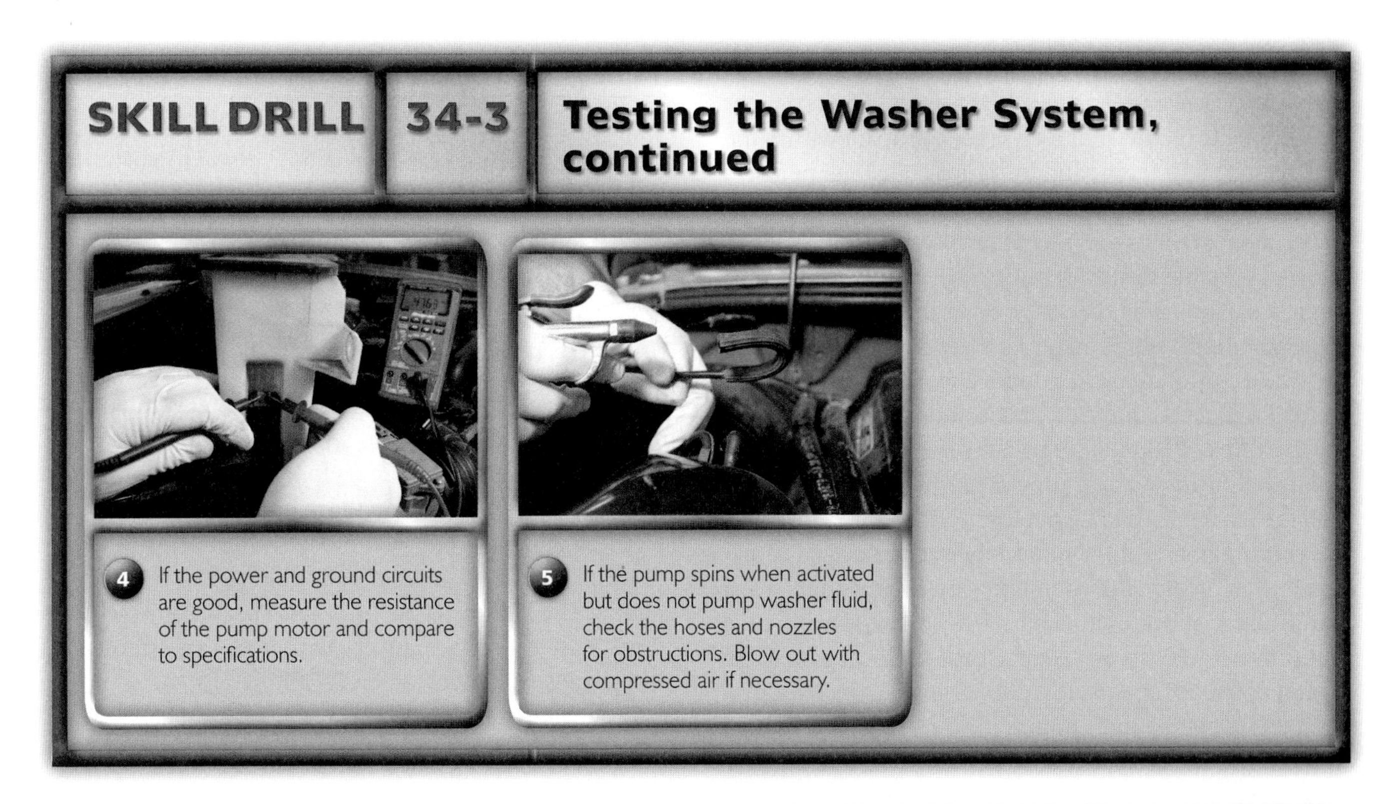

SKILL DRILL 34-3 Testing the Washer System, continued

4. If the power and ground circuits are good, measure the resistance of the pump motor and compare to specifications.

5. If the pump spins when activated but does not pump washer fluid, check the hoses and nozzles for obstructions. Blow out with compressed air if necessary.

operating. To diagnose this, you will want to inspect the linkage for loose or disconnected joints.

This activity will require you to work with motors, gears, and mechanical levers, which may create a crush injury hazard; keep fingers away from mechanisms. Always wear the correct protective eyewear and clothing, use the appropriate safety equipment, and apply fender covers, seat protectors, and floor mat protectors.

Supplemental Restraint Systems

The supplemental restraint system (SRS) is used to describe passenger safety devices installed on vehicles such as airbags and seat belt pre-tensioners FIGURE 34-12. Manufacturers continue to develop and improve airbag technology to make vehicles safer. When first introduced, a single airbag was usually installed on the driver's side. Now, it is not unusual for modern vehicles to have six airbags, along with side-impact protection known as side curtains.

Purpose and Operation of the SRS

Vehicle safety systems are designed to protect occupants during accidents and can be classified as primary (passive) systems and secondary (active) systems. Primary systems are ready to operate in any accident. They include bumper bars, body panels, seat belts, crumple zones, and collapsible steering columns. A secondary system has to be activated to work and is only necessary in severe

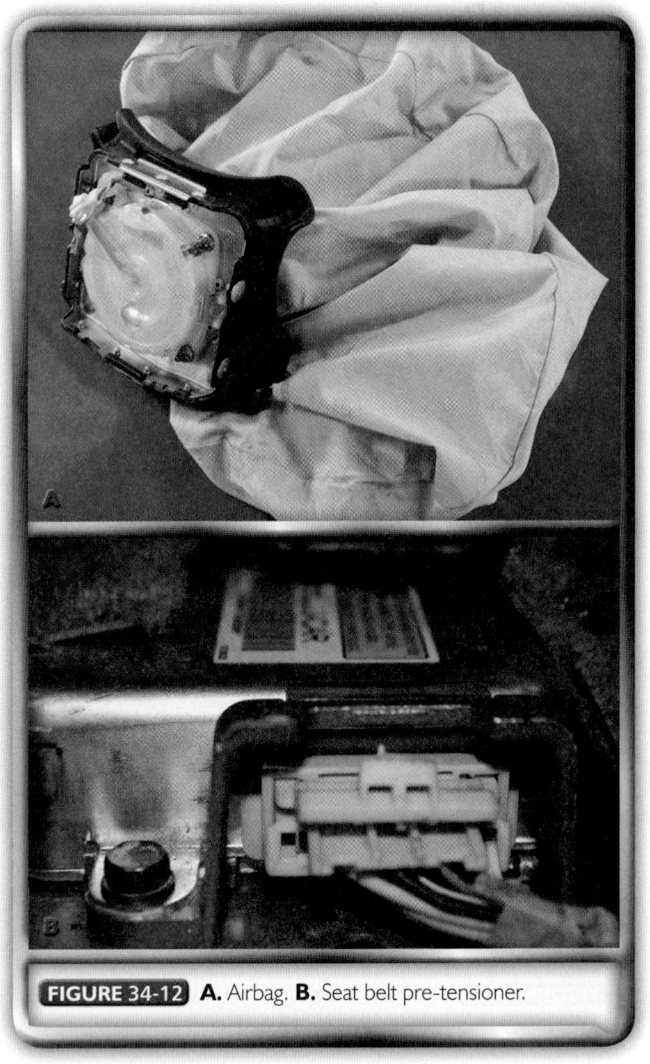
A
B

FIGURE 34-12 **A.** Airbag. **B.** Seat belt pre-tensioner.

accidents. The two most popular types of secondary systems are SRS airbags and seat belt pre-tensioners.

Seat belts secure and restrain the occupant within the seat and vehicle cabin, and in minor collisions perform their task well. In a more severe impact, inertia causes the occupant to move further and with greater force. This increases the possibility of injury caused by the restraining force exerted by the seat belt or from the occupant striking interior equipment. In these situations, airbags provide additional protection for the occupants.

If a vehicle is equipped with an airbag, it deploys during a severe collision, offering a greater degree of protection from injury. Airbags provide cushioning against the effects of inertia. The bag deploys toward the occupant's approaching body, inflated rapidly by pressurized nitrogen gas. Typically, inflation takes no longer than three hundredths (0.03) of a second. The airbag is not a nice soft pillow, but a strong counterforce to react against the inertia of the occupants. It is not designed to be comfortable; it is designed to minimize injury. Immediately after absorbing the momentum, the airbag deflates, having done its job.

Airbags and Pre-tensioners

Airbags are usually described as the SRS, but in some countries, wearing seat belts is not mandatory. In this case, airbags become the primary restraint mechanism, and they need to trigger at lower speeds and be larger in volume. There are a number of different types of airbags. Their size and location is determined by the type of protection they offer FIGURE 34-13.

The most common location for an airbag is in the center of the steering wheel. Here, it protects the driver from frontal impacts. Airbags are also commonly installed on the passenger side of dashes for the same reason. Side-impact airbags are located in the sides of front seats to protect the occupants from side impacts. Curtain side airbags are located in the side edge of roof linings to protect the occupant's head from side impacts. The airbag assembly consists of a nylon bag, **squib**, igniter, gas generator, and airbag triggering mechanism FIGURE 34-14.

There are two types of airbag triggering mechanisms: electrical and mechanical. Most airbags are triggered electrically, with a small electrical current delivered from a

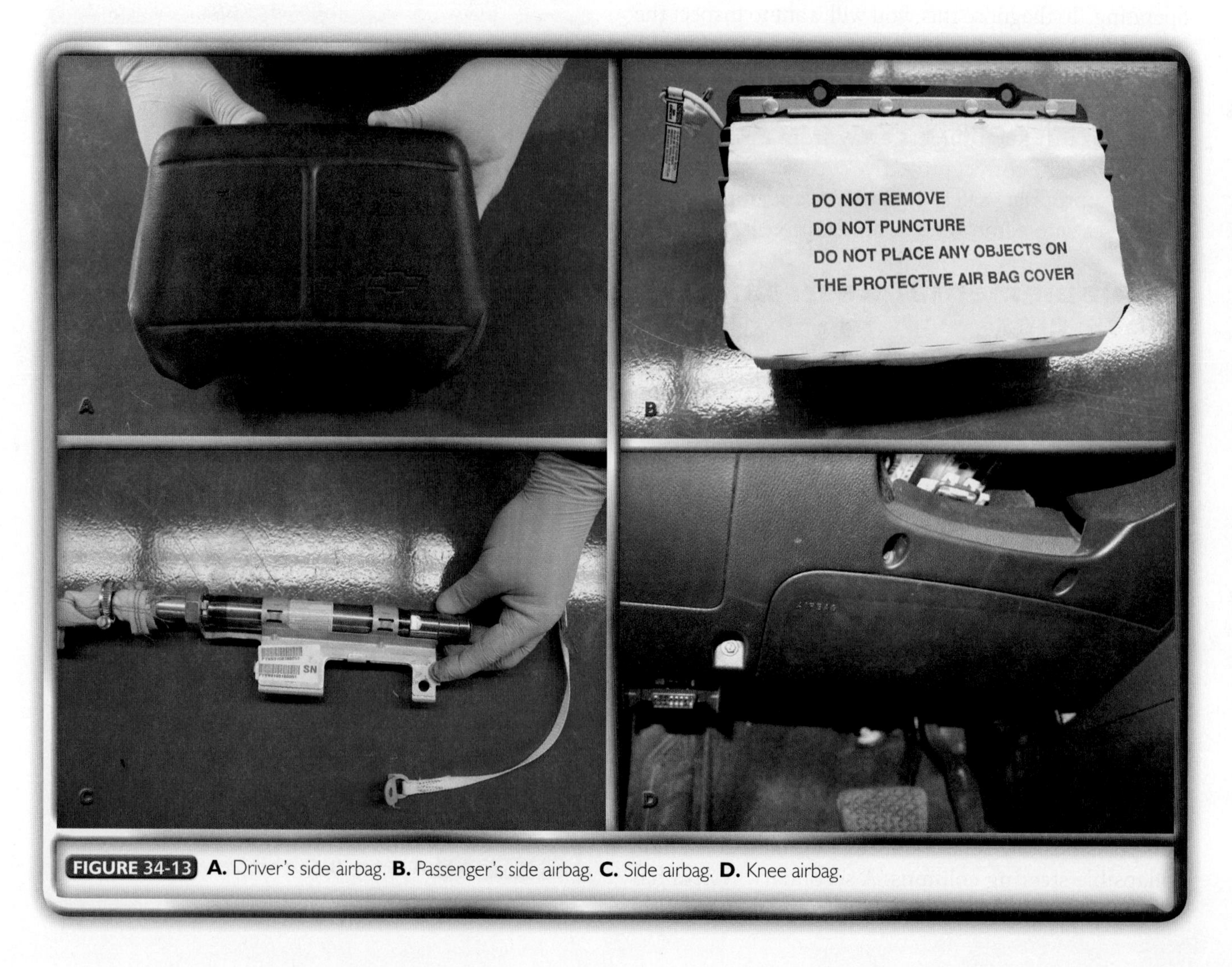
A
B
DO NOT REMOVE
DO NOT PUNCTURE
DO NOT PLACE ANY OBJECTS ON
THE PROTECTIVE AIR BAG COVER
C
SN
D

FIGURE 34-13 **A.** Driver's side airbag. **B.** Passenger's side airbag. **C.** Side airbag. **D.** Knee airbag.

Safety

Airbags, when they deploy, inflate toward the occupant at more than 100 mph (160 kph). Because of this force and speed, they have been known to break wrists and even cause death when not used properly. Always keep the seat positioned so you are at approximately arm's length from the steering wheel; that is, the steering wheel should be at least 10" to 12" (25 to 50 cm) from your chest. Also make sure your hands are in the 9 o'clock and 3 o'clock positions. The old 10 and 2 position can lead to your hands being thrown back toward you or outward (remember that 100+ mph), both of which can injure you.

remote SRS control unit. Mechanically activated systems use inertia to move a triggering pin. Regardless of the type of triggering mechanism, the airbag deploys due to simultaneous explosions occurring within the squib, the igniter, and the gas generator. These three parts are located in a metal housing attached to the back of the airbag assembly.

When the control unit determines that the airbag should be deployed, the electrical current triggers the squib. The heat generated causes the igniter to burn, which in turn explodes the gas generator. The high-pressure nitrogen gas is produced and the airbag rapidly inflates. When the airbag assembly is mounted, it sits behind a pad, which may have a fracture line cast into the inner face. When the airbag deploys, the force of the generated gas causes the cover pad to rupture, allowing the bag to fully inflate.

Mechanically deployed airbags do not have any electrical circuitry. The squib is ignited with a firing pin. Under severe deceleration, inertia causes a steel ball to release a firing pin into the squib. Once the squib has been triggered, the deployment process is identical to electrically triggered airbags. The airbag is fully inflated within three hundredths (0.03) of a second, cushioning the head and upper chest of the occupant as it moves forward.

The airbag is made from nylon and is folded into the front face of the assembly. Older airbags were coated in cornflower, which acts as a lubricant for the fabric during deployment. Newer ones use either more slippery fabric or silicone to allow the airbag to inflate without binding. Relatively large holes are usually located in the rear face of the airbag to allow the nitrogen gas to escape. This deflates the airbag and provides a slightly cushioned surface, rather than a hard one, to help protect the occupant.

A new type of airbag was recently released called a pedestrian airbag. It is located under the rear edge of the hood. When a collision with a pedestrian is imminent, the hood retracts slightly and the airbag inflates to cover a portion of the windshield FIGURE 34-15. This system can protect pedestrians from direct impact with the windshield.

Seat Belt Pre-tensioners

Seat belt pre-tensioners are used to tighten the seat belt in a severe frontal accident. Both mechanical and electronic control systems are available. The most common type relies on an explosive charge that is detonated electronically by a sensor within the seat belt tensioning mechanism FIGURE 34-16. This explosion moves a piston that pulls on a steel cable causing the belt to tighten by approximately 4" (100 mm). The design allows for the belt to tension before the occupant has moved forward in the seat.

Mechanical systems rely on inertia to move a sensing mass. This releases a spring to pull on a cable, thus tightening the belt. Once the pre-tensioner has triggered,

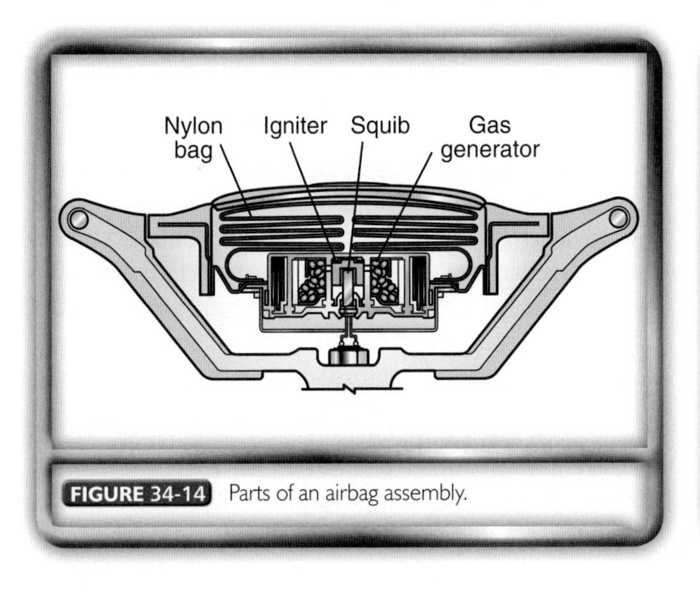
Nylon bag
Igniter
Squib
Gas generator

FIGURE 34-14 Parts of an airbag assembly.

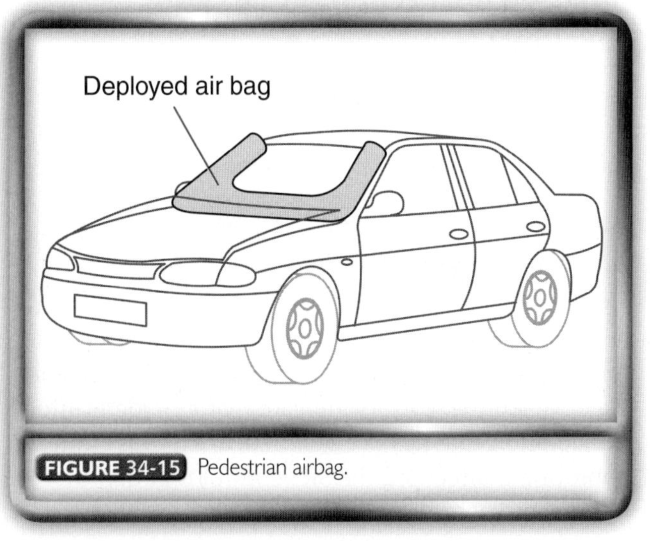
Deployed air bag

FIGURE 34-15 Pedestrian airbag.

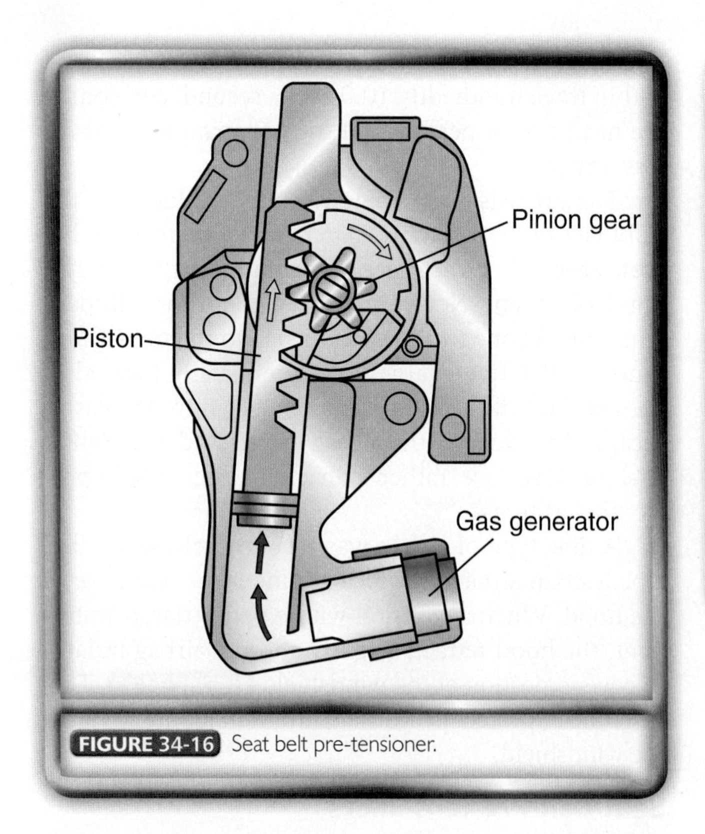
Pinion gear
Piston
Gas generator

FIGURE 34-16 Seat belt pre-tensioner.

MADE IN CANADA
A9982NXP17A
4L14-14B006-AA

FIGURE 34-17 Typical crash sensors.

a ratchet prevents the seat belt from loosening. When the seat belt is removed from the buckle, it cannot be reinserted, and the assembly will need to be replaced.

Rip stitching is used on seat belts in conjunction with an airbag and seat belt pre-tensioners. During a collision, the pre-tensioners initially pull the seat belt tight; however, the stitching gradually tears, allowing the occupant to move forward into the airbag at a controlled rate.

For safety reasons, these belts must be replaced once they have had their stitching ripped. Manufacturers generally fit warning labels within the fold to indicate the belt is to be replaced when the label is revealed. Ripping the stitching exposes the warning label.

Sensors, Control Module, and Circuitry

Crash sensors can be installed in various positions throughout the vehicle. Their location depends upon the direction of deceleration they are designed to detect. Some manufacturers place the sensors within the PCM. Others are located behind the front bumper, headlights, and dash FIGURE 34-17.

Side-impact sensors are located in the doorsills or B-pillar. They inform the SRS control unit of a side impact and whether to deploy the left or right side airbags. When the sensors indicate that a predetermined deceleration rate has been exceeded and it is from the appropriate direction, the SRS control unit deploys the relevant airbags.

If the collision is from the front, the driver and passenger airbags will deploy. If the collision is from the side, the sensor determines whether the seat-mounted airbag or the curtain airbags for one side of the vehicle will deploy. With more refined designs, the passenger airbag deploys only if there is an occupant in the seat. Deployment can also depend on the weight of the occupant and whether the passenger airbag switch, if equipped, is turned on.

To prevent incorrect and unnecessary deployment, systems include a safing sensor mounted within the SRS control unit FIGURE 34-18. The SRS control unit will only pass current through the squib if both the safing sensor and a crash sensor indicate simultaneously that a predetermined deceleration rate has been exceeded.

Capacitors within the SRS control unit are used to store electricity and act as a backup power supply if the vehicle has its battery destroyed or disconnected in an accident. The capacitors supply the electricity required to keep the SRS system operational for a short time. If a fault is detected in the system, the SRS warning light is illuminated and stays on.

Some seat-mounted side-impact airbags also operate without electricity. When the side of a vehicle is crushed inward, a detonator mounted on the lower outside edge of the seat is activated. Pyrotechnic tubes connect the detonator to the airbags, which in turn ignite the squib. Many vehicles use two-stage side-impact bags. This design provides protection to an occupant's upper torso over a more extended time.

Smart Airbag Technology

Manufacturers continue to improve the safety devices installed on vehicles, including airbags. Smart airbag

FIGURE 34-18 Safing sensor is typically located in the SRS control unit.

Safety

While an airbag is powerful enough to counteract the weight of a moving body during an accident, it doesn't take much electricity to ignite one. In fact, a fresh 9-volt battery will provide more than enough electrical energy to set it off. In the same way, an ordinary test lamp connected to 12 volts can ignite the airbag if the wrong wire is probed. Always be careful when working around SRS systems.

Safety

Just because an airbag has been deployed doesn't mean it is safe. Dual-stage airbags may be designed with two ballistic charges, and only one of them may have been deployed. Airbags must have all charges deployed before disposal. But only do so according to the manufacturer's service information.

technology is the use of intelligence in the control of airbag deployment in the event of an accident rather than deployment with maximum force. The improvements include the use of information regarding the severity of the accident, seat position, and weight of the occupant as inputs for controlling airbag deployment. Airbags in systems with smart technology are capable of varying the size and force of the airbag as needed. These adjustments can be performed in one of several ways: diverting some of the gas from the airbag inflation system into the dash, using a dual-chamber airbag, or using a dual-stage airbag that has two charges that can be used individually or together. It is now possible for the control systems to deploy the airbags with a more appropriate amount of force, customizing the protection to the occupant.

Disabling and Enabling the SRS

The SRS system must be disabled and enabled while working on or around the steering column, any of the airbags or other pyrotechnic devices, and any of the sensors. Failure to disable the SRS system could cause one or more of the SRS devices to deploy, which can cause serious injury or death, along with an expensive repair. It is important to know that most airbags are inflated by igniting a solid fuel similar to rocket fuel.

Every manufacturer has its own procedures for disabling and enabling the SRS system on its vehicles, and those procedures can be different for each of the vehicle models they sell. Always follow the manufacturer's specified procedure for the model of vehicle you are working on. Also, this is one time that you DO NOT use a memory minder or auxiliary power supply on the vehicle. Doing so could supply power to the SRS system after it has been disabled.

To disable and enable the SRS, follow the steps in SKILL DRILL 34-4.

Safety

Many airbags are now of the two-stage variety so they can deploy with the proper amount of force depending on the severity of the accident, approximate weight of the occupant, etc. This means that even a deployed airbag is still potentially dangerous and needs to be treated with caution during removal. It should be deployed soon after removal, following the manufacturer's specified procedure, which will render it safe for disposal.

Keyless Entry and Remote Start

In the quest to make vehicle operation more convenient for drivers and passengers, manufacturers have added a number of features to attract customers to their brand of vehicle. Two such features are keyless entry and remote starting capability. Keyless entry allows the vehicle's doors to be locked and unlocked with the push of a button. Remote start allows the driver to start the vehicle's engine remotely. This is very handy in extremely cold or hot climates, as the vehicle's interior can be warmed or cooled as needed prior to the occupants entering the vehicle. Let's take a brief look at these two systems.

Vehicle Locking and Keyless Entry

Door lock systems have come a long way. Initially, all locks were operated manually. A key was inserted in the

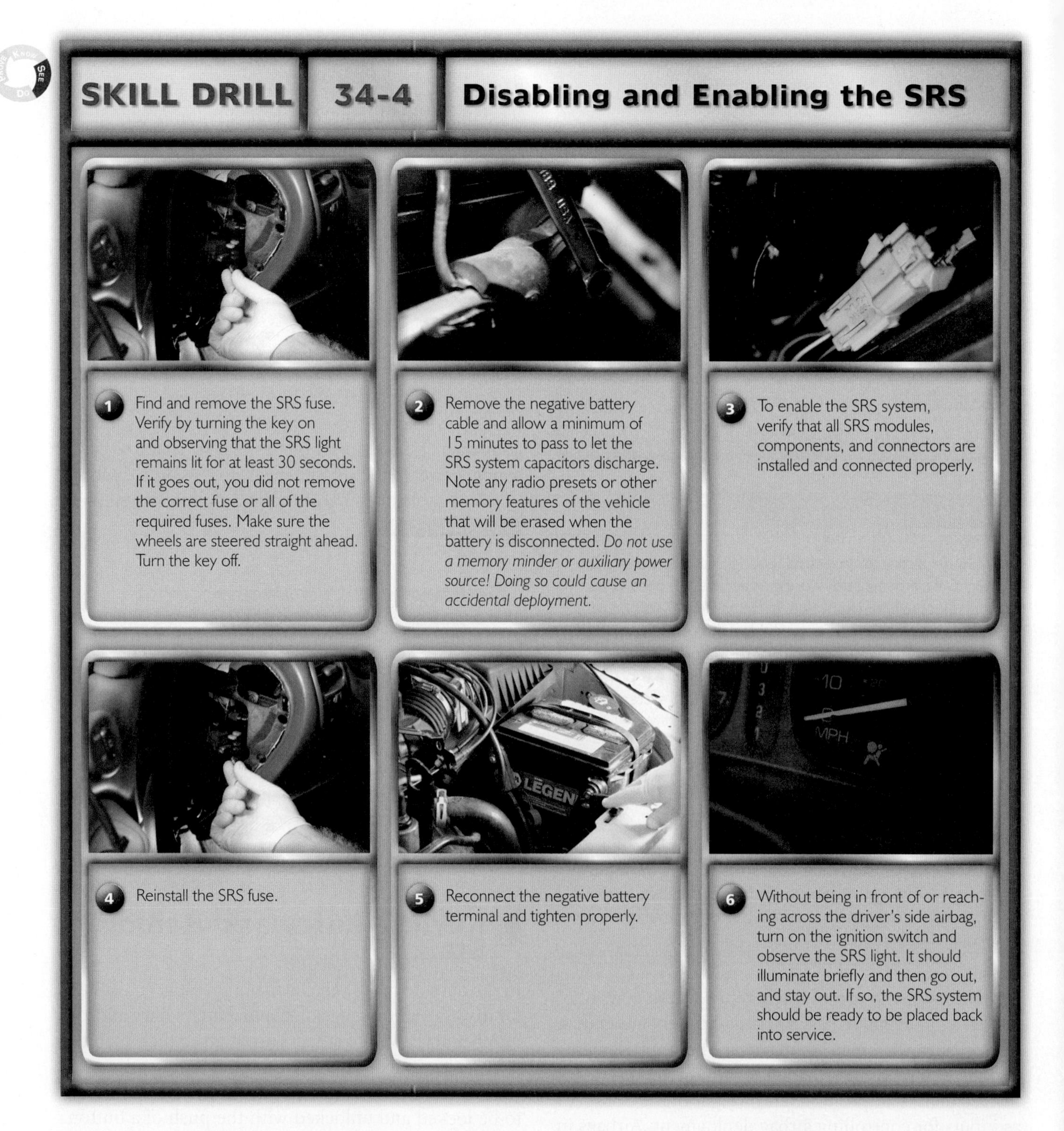

SKILL DRILL
34-4
Disabling and Enabling the SRS
1 Find and remove the SRS fuse. Verify by turning the key on and observing that the SRS light remains lit for at least 30 seconds. If it goes out, you did not remove the correct fuse or all of the required fuses. Make sure the wheels are steered straight ahead. Turn the key off.
2 Remove the negative battery cable and allow a minimum of 15 minutes to pass to let the SRS system capacitors discharge. Note any radio presets or other memory features of the vehicle that will be erased when the battery is disconnected. Do not use a memory minder or auxiliary power source! Doing so could cause an accidental deployment.
3 To enable the SRS system, verify that all SRS modules, components, and connectors are installed and connected properly.
4 Reinstall the SRS fuse.
5 Reconnect the negative battery terminal and tighten properly.
6 Without being in front of or reaching across the driver's side airbag, turn on the ignition switch and observe the SRS light. It should illuminate briefly and then go out, and stay out. If so, the SRS system should be ready to be placed back into service.

door lock, and when turned, it would unlock only that door. The remaining doors needed to be unlocked manually, via the lock knob or lever. Releasing the key would return it to the same position it was in when inserted so it could be removed. When central locking was introduced, the lock mechanism on the driver's door had a microswitch that, when turned, activated electric solenoids on the remaining doors and trunk and unlocked or locked them. Further enhancement allowed manufacturers to introduce a security system that automatically locked the doors once the vehicle had reached a preset speed. This feature is mandatory in some countries.

Dead locking adds a further level of security. If the key is turned a quarter turn and removed, a second microswitch activates small electric motors in each door lock mechanism, mechanically locking them.

In keyless systems, remote control keys and key fobs transmit a coded signal that is received by the vehicle's theft-deterrent module. If the code meets preset criteria, the module closes a switch that enables either the driver's door or all doors to be locked and unlocked as required. Pressing the button a second time when locking some vehicles activates the dead lock actuators and deadlocks the vehicle.

For the remote key and computer to exchange information, wireless communication is needed. High-frequency electromagnetic fields (i.e., RF signals) are used. This system relies on the same basic technology as cell phones, TV, and radio, but at much lower power.

The remote fob can have one button for locking and unlocking; two buttons, where one locks and the other unlocks; three buttons, where the third button activates the trunk or tailgate; four buttons, where the fourth activates a panic alarm; or five buttons, where the fifth remotely starts the vehicle. Some vehicles actively transmit a radio code looking for a specific key. As the driver approaches the vehicle, the vehicle locates the key and the theft-deterrent module prepares to unlock the vehicle. On some vehicles, when the driver leaves the vehicle and the key is out of range, the theft-deterrent module locks the vehicle.

When keyless entry is used, personalization of systems is possible. They can be programmed to recognize different keys, with each driver having his or her own specific key. This allows for different settings to be made that are unique to each driver. When a specific key is identified, the theft-deterrent module communicates with the body control unit. Specific settings are remembered from that key, so the seat, steering wheel, and mirror position automatically adjust to the driver as well as climate control settings for cabin temperature and system modes. Entertainment system settings such as radio station presets, volume and audio settings, and transmission shift point preferences can all change to the driver's individual preferences. This system also allows for a valet key, or even a "teen driver" key to be used, limiting engine power, vehicle speed, and maximum radio volume, as well as preventing other vehicle settings from being changed.

Engine and Transmission Immobilization and Remote Start

Immobilization occurs when the theft-deterrent system prevents the vehicle's engine from starting or the transmission from operating without the properly authorized key. Audible and visible alarms may be activated when the locking or immobilization systems are tampered with. The immobilization system is enabled when the lock button is pressed on the remote key, when the doors are locked manually with the door key, or when a period of time has elapsed, typically 15 seconds, after the engine has stopped. The immobilization system is disabled by pressing the unlock button on the remote fob.

The key fob and theft-deterrent computers have to be capable of transmitting and receiving coded information. Operational characteristics vary greatly among manufacturers, and because it is a theft-deterrent system, details are a closely kept secret.

Some vehicles are equipped with a remote start function. This allows the engine to be started remotely by use of the key fob or, in some cases, a smart phone. Some remote start systems have bi-directional communication. That is, the fob or smart phone will show that the engine did or did not start and what the inside vehicle temperature is in real time. This allows the operator to know when the vehicle is ready to be driven. The remote start system ties into the vehicle's PCM and BCM. If the BCM determines that the vehicle meets all of the criteria to be started, it communicates with the PCM to crank over and start the engine. Remote start systems can also control the vehicle's heating and air conditioning systems to warm or cool the vehicle, as well as operate the window defrost systems. In extremely cold or hot temperatures, this functionality can even be life saving.

Wrap-up

Ready for Review

- Electrical systems on modern vehicles are becoming increasingly complex with the addition of a range of electronic and accessory systems, such as global positioning systems, entertainment systems, security systems, electric seats, and heated glass. Many of these systems are controlled by body computer systems.
- The controller area network (CAN-bus) and the bus system are used together in vehicle terminology (often called "CAN-bus") to describe the data-sharing network in vehicles. The many sensors and engine control units or modules can share information across a common network using the CAN-bus protocol to communicate efficiently and effectively with low data loss.
- Electric cooling fans for the radiator are increasingly common, particularly for transversely mounted engines and as supplementary cooling fans for vehicles equipped with air conditioning.
- The sound of a horn is produced by the vibration of a metal diaphragm, which is operated by an electromagnet switched by a set of contacts.
- Technicians today need to know how to service all the accessories behind the door panels. This is a critical skill that must be mastered without damaging the accessory, wiring, or door panel.
- The wiper and washer system is an important vehicle safety system. The wipers ensure that the driver has a clear line of sight through the windshield by removing any excess moisture from the glass.
- Vehicle safety systems are designed to protect occupants during accidents; they can be classified as primary, or passive, systems and secondary, or active, systems.
- Seat belt pre-tensioners are used to tighten the seat belt in a severe frontal accident; both mechanical and electronic control systems are available.
- Crash sensors can be installed in various positions throughout the vehicle. Their location depends upon the direction of deceleration they are designed to detect.
- Keyless entry allows the vehicle's doors to be locked and unlocked with the push of a button, or even just by walking up to the vehicle with the key fob in a pocket.
- Remote start allows the driver to start the vehicle's engine remotely. This is very handy in extremely cold or hot climates.

Key Terms

blower motor An electric motor, usually the permanent magnet type, that moves air over the air-conditioning evaporator and heater core.

brushless DC motor An electric motor that does not have any brushes and is sometimes called an "electronically commutated motor." In this type of motor, an electronic control module replaces the brushes and commutator.

bus The data transport system for electronic control modules.

controller area network (CAN) The network that connects the vehicle's electronic control modules.

data link connector (DLC) The port to which a scan tool can be connected.

permanent magnet electric motor An electric motor in which the magnetic field in the casing is produced by permanent magnets, while the armature has an electromagnetic field generated by passing electrical current through loops or windings, thereby producing the motor action.

squib The component inside the airbag inflator that triggers the airbag deployment.

stepper motor A type of brushless motor with a key difference: It is designed to rotate in fixed steps through a set number of degrees.

supplemental restraint system (SRS) A passenger safety system, such as airbags and seat belt pre-tensioners.

ASE-Type Questions

1. Tech A says that CAN A is a low-speed data network. Tech B says that CAN C is a high-speed network. Who is correct?
   a. Tech A
   b. Tech B
   c. Both A and B
   d. Neither A nor B
2. Tech A says that CAN C uses two 120-ohm resistors with a total circuit resistance of 60 ohms. Tech B says that CAN C uses two 120-ohm resistors with a total circuit resistance of 240 ohms. Who is correct?
   a. Tech A
   b. Tech B
   c. Both A and B
   d. Neither A nor B
3. Tech A says that a twisted pair of wires in a wire loom makes it easier to route wires to their destination. Tech B says that the twisted pair of wires transmit signals of opposite polarity on the two lines. Who is correct?
   a. Tech A
   b. Tech B
   c. Both A and B
   d. Neither A nor B
4. Two technicians are discussing windshield washers that aren't working. Tech A says that the windshield washer motor could be faulty. Tech B says that the washer nozzles could be plugged up. Who is correct?
   a. Tech A
   b. Tech B
   c. Both A and B
   d. Neither A nor B
5. Tech A says that stepper motors are used as blower motors to achieve various speeds controlled by the driver. Tech B says that stepper motors are used where precise movement must occur, such as in electronic throttle controls. Who is correct?
   a. Tech A
   b. Tech B
   c. Both A and B
   d. Neither A nor B
6. Tech A says that some airbags are dual stage and can have two charges in them. Tech B says that airbags must be manually deflated after being deployed. Who is correct?
   a. Tech A
   b. Tech B
   c. Both A and B
   d. Neither A nor B
7. Tech A says that the clock spring is a device used in the steering wheel to transmit signals across the rotating electrical connection. Tech B says that the clock spring must be wound correctly during installation, as it only allows turning both ways a certain number of rotations. Who is correct?
   a. Tech A
   b. Tech B
   c. Both A and B
   d. Neither A nor B
8. Tech A says that most SRS systems use a safing sensor to reduce the possibility of accidental deployment of the airbags. Tech B says that airbags are designed to act like a nice soft pillow in an accident. Who is correct?
   a. Tech A
   b. Tech B
   c. Both A and B
   d. Neither A nor B
9. Tech A says that if airbags have been deployed, the affected seat belts and pre-tensioners need replaced. Tech B says that there are relatively large holes in the rear of an airbag that allow it to quickly deflate after deployment. Who is correct?
   a. Tech A
   b. Tech B
   c. Both A and B
   d. Neither A nor B
10. Tech A says that in some vehicles, airbag deployment can be based on the speed of the impact and the weight of the driver. Tech B says that the SRS seat belt pre-tensioners tighten the seat belt when you connect the seat belt. Who is correct?
    a. Tech A
    b. Tech B
    c. Both A and B
    d. Neither A nor B

150
10
5
50

SECTION VIII

Heating and Air Conditioning

CHAPTER 35

Know
See
Do
Prove

NATEF Tasks

Heating and Air Conditioning General A/C System			Page
■ Performance test A/C system; identify problems.		AST	1007–1008
Refrigeration System Component			
■ Inspect A/C condenser for airflow restrictions; perform necessary action.	MLR	AST	1008
■ Inspect and replace A/C compressor drive belts, pulleys, and tensioners; determine necessary action.	MLR	AST	1009–1010
Operating Systems and Related Controls			
■ Identify the source of A/C system odors.	MLR	AST	1006

Principles of Heating and Air-Conditioning Systems

KNOW
SEE
DO
PROVE

Knowledge Objectives

After reading this chapter, you will be able to:

1. Explain the licensure requirements for working on an air-conditioning system. (p 993)
2. Explain the principles of the heating, ventilation, and air-conditioning (HVAC) system. (pp 994–998)
3. Explain the three methods of heat transfer. (pp 995–996)
4. Describe heat energy and how it is measured. (p 996)
5. Explain how a fixed orifice tube air-conditioning system operates. (p 1001)
6. Explain the difference between an accumulator and a receiver/filter/drier. (pp 1001–1002)
7. Explain how a thermal expansion valve air-conditioning system operates. (pp 1001–1002)
8. Describe heating system components and operation. (pp 1002–1003)
9. Describe the principles of air-conditioning service process. (pp 1006–1007)
10. Explain the process of performance testing the air-conditioning system. (pp 1007–1008)

KNOW
SEE
DO
PROVE

Skills Objectives

After reading this chapter, you will be able to:

1. Performance-test the air-conditioning system. (pp 1007–1008)
2. Inspect the evaporator housing water drain. (p 1009)
3. Inspect and test the HVAC control cables. (pp 1009–1010)
4. Inspect the air-conditioning system heater ducts, doors, and cabin filters. (pp 1010-1011)

Introduction

This chapter will explain the processes involved in regulating the temperature inside the passenger compartment of a vehicle. The quality and temperature of the surrounding air strongly influence a driver's performance and concentration. Within a passenger vehicle, the heating, ventilation, and air-conditioning (HVAC) system is designed to maintain a comfortable temperature in the vehicle cabin and also provide fresh, filtered, quality air on a constant basis. Depending on the outside temperature and the desired cabin temperature, the supplied air is either heated, cooled, or both.

The HVAC system of most passenger vehicles uses the heat created by normal engine operation to raise the temperature in the passenger compartment. Refrigerant is used to cool the air in the passenger compartment. To ensure that the air brought into the vehicle is free from dust and debris, many vehicles pass the air through a cabin air filter that removes foreign particles. Without proper maintenance, the HVAC system can break down, resulting in an unpleasant ride for the passengers, particularly during the summer and winter months. Accordingly, it is critical that the automotive technician be familiar with the components of the HVAC system and understand how each component works so that the system can be maintained and serviced when necessary.

History of Automotive Heating and Cooling

There is some debate about the origins of systems for heating the passenger compartment of vehicles. What has been confirmed is the use of gas lamps in the early 1900s for heat. Passengers would bring a small gas lamp into the compartment for heat, but it was not connected to the vehicle in any way. Around 1917–1920, some vehicles transferred exhaust gas through pipes into the compartment to provide heat. The first use of air heated from normal engine operation to warm the passenger compartment dates from the late 1920s. These vehicles had rudimentary blowers that simply funneled air from around the engine into the cabin. By the 1930s, the first true heating systems using engine coolant, similar to what is still used today, were developed.

Automotive air conditioning has a long history, beginning with a discovery by Michael Faraday. In 1820, Faraday discovered how to create cool air by passing air over an evaporating coil of compressed ammonia. Although this was a great advance in comfort, ammonia is a caustic agent and hazardous to humans, causing skin burns, lung damage, and possibly asphyxiation. In 1902, Willis Carrier invented and patented the first electric air conditioner. A great advance was made in 1928 when a research division of General Motors produced **chlorofluorocarbons (CFCs)**, a chemical compound containing chlorine, fluorine, and carbon. CFCs made it possible for

You Are the Automotive Technician

A customer brings his vehicle to the auto shop for a routine maintenance check. He will be driving his vehicle from New York to Florida this fall and won't be returning until the following spring. He is worried how his vehicle's HVAC system will perform during his long trip and during his stay in Florida. He isn't familiar with auto shops in Florida, so he wants you to inspect the system and suggest any repairs it may need.

1. What are the two types of automotive air-conditioning systems?
2. Refrigerants are another important part of the HVAC system. Why is identifying refrigerants becoming an important part of repairing air-conditioning systems?
3. What license is required for technicians to work with refrigerants?

air-conditioning systems to be used by consumers with no apparent harm, unlike the ammonia systems.

In 1939, Packard introduced the first automotive air-conditioning system as an add-on luxury unit FIGURE 35-1. The add-on was offered for $274, which in today's money would be more than $4000. Automotive air conditioning is now standard on most production vehicles because of customer demand as well as the increased fuel economy that comes from increased aerodynamic efficiency. Having the windows rolled up while driving at moderate and high speeds reduces wind drag and increases aerodynamic efficiency in most vehicles.

HVAC Legislation

Automotive air conditioning is federally regulated by the Environmental Protection Agency (EPA). Section 609 of the Clean Air Act (CAA)—the federal law that regulates air emissions from stationary and mobile sources—contains all of the motor vehicle air-conditioning (MVAC) requirements and laws. Among other things, this law authorizes the EPA to establish National Ambient Air Quality Standards (NAAQS) to protect public health and public welfare and to regulate emissions of hazardous air pollutants.

This act sets the standards for shops that do air-conditioning work. It mandates that each shop maintain a current government-issued license and stipulates what certifications are required for technicians doing MVAC procedures. It also outlines the specific refrigerants that can be safely used for each application and how refrigerants must be stored and reclaimed, even citing the specific approved equipment technicians may use.

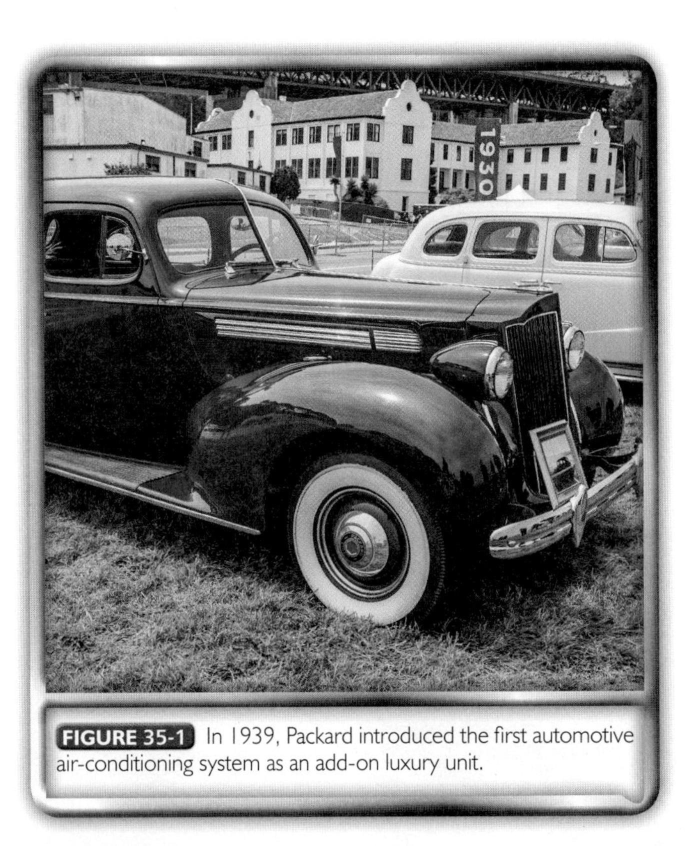
1930

FIGURE 35-1 In 1939, Packard introduced the first automotive air-conditioning system as an add-on luxury unit.

> **TECHNICIAN TIP**
>
> Almost all manufacturers rely on the air conditioner's ability to remove moisture from the air to meet the defrost time standard set by the U.S. Department of Transportation.

Licensure

Automotive air-conditioning service and repair technicians need to have a special license FIGURE 35-2. The license is granted after passing the 609 test, which is a self-study course that can be found online through companies such as Automotive Service Excellence (ASE), Mobile Air Conditioning Society (MACS), and Mainstream Engineering. Passing the test results in a lifelong license. Since the license never expires, the technician is responsible for keeping up to date with all new regulations and technology. The 609 license also allows the technician to purchase a few select refrigerants, such as R-12 and R-134a (refrigerants are identified with a letter R, followed by a series of numbers that indicate their chemical composition). The 609 license does not mean that the technician knows how to repair the automotive air-conditioning systems, but that the technician knows the laws and will comply with all regulations.

THIS CERTIFICATE HEREBY CONFIRMS

Henry Ford

has successfully completed
the ASE Refrigerant Recovery & Recycling
Review and Certification Program
This day of April 10, 1998

111-11-1111 MVAC
Certification Number

Ronald H. Weiner
President, ASE

FIGURE 35-2 EPA 609 license.

Applied Science

AS-29: Expansion/Contraction: The technician is able to demonstrate an understanding of the expansion and contraction of system parts as a result of heat generated during the use of the system.

When matter is heated, it expands, or becomes larger in size. Conversely, when cooled, it contracts, or becomes smaller (assuming the change in temperature does not cause the matter to change state). Thermal expansion (or TX) valves, found in many air-conditioning systems, operate via these principles. The function of a TX valve is to regulate to flow of liquid refrigerant from the evaporator back to the compressor, thereby also regulating the temperature of refrigerant.

The valve is actuated against spring pressure by a temperature-sensing bulb, filled with a similar gas to the refrigerant used in the air-conditioning system. As the refrigerant temperature at the evaporator outlet increases, the pressure in the bulb increases due to expansion of the gas and causes the TX valve to open. When the evaporator outlet temperature drops, the pressure in the bulb decreases as the gas contracts and allows spring pressure to close the valve.

Applied Science

AS-84: Relative Humidity: The technician can demonstrate an understanding of and discuss relative humidity in terms of its effect on automotive heating and air-conditioning systems.

Relative humidity is essentially a measure of how moist the air is, or in more detail, the amount of water vapor in the air expressed as a percentage of the amount that the air can "hold" at a given temperature. The warmer air is, the more moisture it is able to hold.

In a car air-conditioning system, warm air is forced through a cold (below dew point) evaporator core. This condenses the water vapor in the air into its liquid form and drains it away, much like the way water condenses on the outside of a cold soda can. Thus, water vapor in the incoming air is removed and the relative humidity in the vehicle's cabin is lowered. On humid days, the system removes more water vapor from the air, and you may notice larger than usual amounts of water draining from the evaporator onto the ground underneath the vehicle.

While you may expect heating the incoming air to have the opposite effect, in reality this is not the case. Cool air is passed through a hot heater core (generally heated by coolant from the engine's cooling system), which also has a drying effect, lowering the relative humidity in the cabin.

TECHNICIAN TIP

The equipment used to recover refrigerants from MVAC systems is also covered in the 609 MVAC laws. The technician is responsible for using properly certified equipment when servicing MVAC systems. The current fine for not complying with the 609 laws is $37,500 per day per incident. This fine is applicable to the person or entity not in compliance with the 609 regulations.

HVAC Principles

The function of air conditioning in the HVAC system is to reduce the temperature and humidity inside the passenger compartment to a level that ensures passenger comfort **FIGURE 35-3**. The HVAC system achieves this by removing excess heat from the passenger compartment through a series of thermal and chemical transformations. In other words, heat is removed from the passenger compartment and transferred by the air-conditioning system to the outside air.

The HVAC system is governed by the principles of physics just like all of the other systems on a vehicle. Understanding the physics will help you to know when a system is operating properly and when it needs to be serviced. One of the simplest concepts concerns heat transfer: Heat always transfers from hot objects to cold objects. Another concept concerns density: Liquids are denser than gases. Thus liquids tend to be pulled to the bottom by gravity, and gases tend to float to the top.

Heat
Air
Heat
Air
Heat
Air

FIGURE 35-3 The HVAC system reduces the temperature inside the passenger compartment by removing excess heat through a series of thermal and chemical transformations.

Another simple concept is the relationship between temperature and pressure: When pressure is raised on a gas, its temperature also rises; when pressure is lowered, so does its temperature. These and other principles will be explored in greater depth in the following sections.

Cold and Hot

The conditions "cold" and "hot" are more of a feeling than a science. Cold is simply a relative term for the absence of heat, or it can be regarded as a condition that exists after heat has been removed. Heat energy is in all matter, from gases (oxygen), to liquids (water), to solids (metal). One might think that 32°F (0°C) is cold, but more heat energy is present than at –19°F (–28°C). Heat energy cannot be created or destroyed; it can only be transferred from one object to another. Heat always travels from a warmer object to a cooler object.

Consider this age-old question: Does ice cause your hand to be cold, or does your hand warm up the ice? The answer is that your hand is warming up the ice and the extreme transfer of heat energy makes your hand feel cold. The warming of the ice is known as **heat transfer**. Heat transfer can take place by one of three methods: conduction, convection, or radiation. The HVAC system relies on all three types of heat transfer. **Conduction** is the process of transferring heat through matter by the movement of heat energy through solids from one particle to another. For example, if you hold a lighter up to a steel pipe, the heat from the flame will travel through the steel, eventually heating the entire pipe.

Heat transfer by **convection** is the circulatory movement that occurs in a gas or fluid with areas of differing temperatures due to the variation of the density and the action of gravity. Consider a container of water being heated on a stove. If you put a drop of food coloring in one part of the water and start to heat the water, you can readily see the circulation of the water within the container. As the water heats up, it expands and becomes lighter than the surrounding water. This causes a column of water to rise to the top; the cooler water then falls to the bottom. Thus, a cycle occurs of warmer water rising to the top, pushing cooler water to the bottom. The convection currents have the same effect of a small pump pushing the water around in a set pathway.

Radiation is the transfer of heat through the emission of energy in the form of invisible waves FIGURE 35-4. The sun radiates energy to the earth over the vast miles of outer space; the electromagnetic radiation readily travels through the vacuum of space. When this energy is absorbed, it becomes converted to heat—that is, the heat you feel as the sun touches your body on a warm day. Of course, the direction in which the radiation travels can be changed or redirected, as when a sheet of shiny aluminum foil reflects the sun's rays and bounces the energy in another direction.

The cooling cycle begins in the passenger compartment with the radiation of heat from the rays of the sun

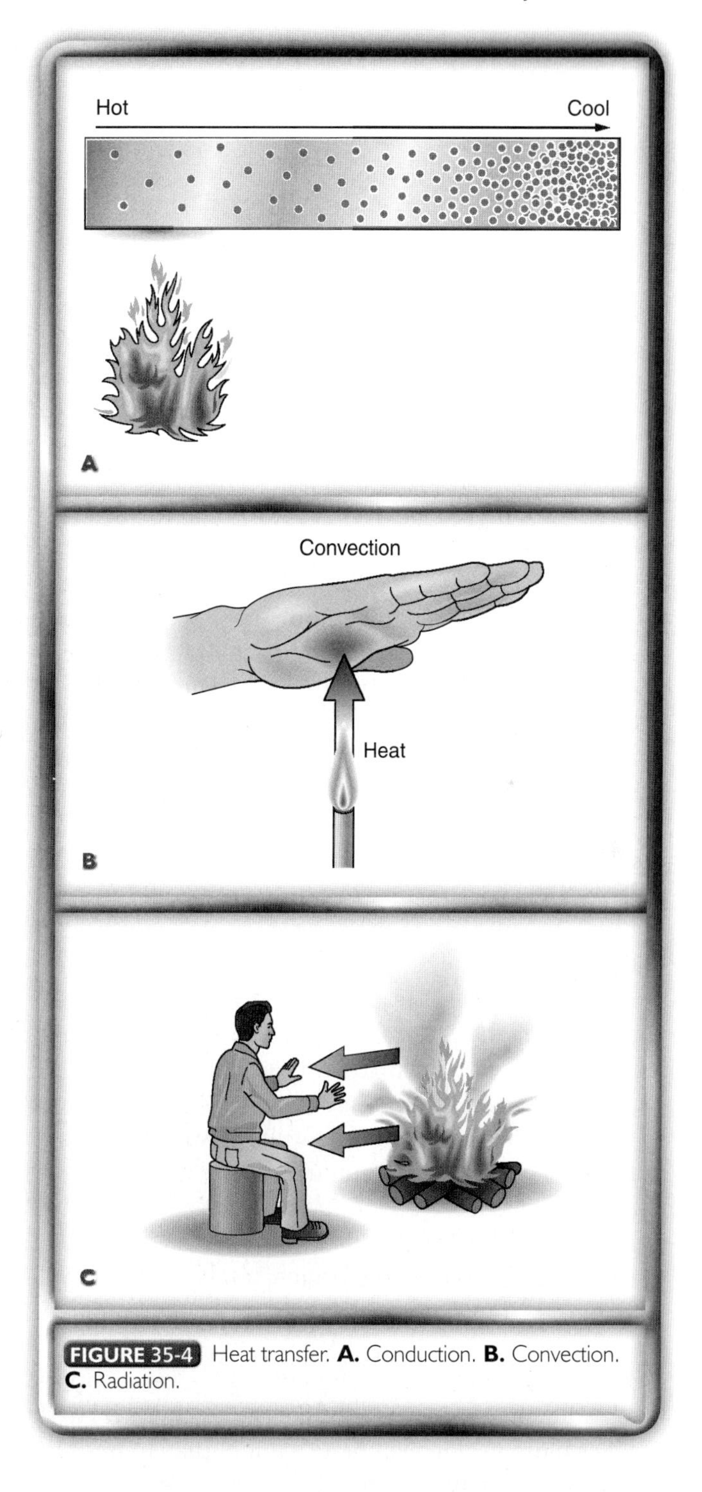
Hot
Cool
A
Convection
Heat
B
C

FIGURE 35-4 Heat transfer. **A.** Conduction. **B.** Convection. **C.** Radiation.

penetrating through the windows. The interior air heats up and the driver turns on the air-conditioning function of the HVAC system. Convection currents from the heated air in the passenger compartment flow over an evaporator core of refrigerant, causing a conduction of heat through the metal coils of the evaporator. The metal coils of the evaporator then transfer the heat by conduction to the refrigerant, causing convection currents to transfer heat through the refrigerant. The refrigerant is then circulated by the compressor and carried to the condenser where conduction and convection dissipate the heat to the surrounding air and ultimately to the atmosphere.

Heat Energy

Heat energy is measured in **British thermal units (Btu)**. The Btu is a measurement of heat quantity and is a standard unit of measurement of heat energy. It describes the amount of heat it takes to move temperature up or down in degrees. One pound of water at **atmospheric pressure** and at a temperature of 32°F (0°C) would require 1 Btu of energy added to increase the temperature 1 degree Fahrenheit. A change in the temperature of 1 pound of water from 32°F (the freezing point of water) to 212°F (100°C) (the boiling point of water) would require 180 Btu of heat energy.

Water cannot get any hotter than 212°F at atmospheric pressure. The temperature will not rise because the molecules have reached their maximum speed of movement at atmospheric pressure. Temperature is increased only by moving the molecules faster. If the water is exposed to any more energy, it will start to change its state of matter from a liquid to a gas: steam. Turning a pound of water at 212°F at atmospheric pressure into steam requires 970 Btu. The heat required to change the water at its maximum temperature from a liquid to a gas is called **latent heat of evaporation**. This latent heat is called "hidden heat" because it cannot be felt or measured with a thermometer. Heat that can be felt and measured with a thermometer is called sensible heat. The amount of heat given up by steam to turn back into a liquid is the same 970 Btu and is called **latent heat of condensation**.

Taking the same pound of water from a liquid to a solid is called freezing. You must remove heat from the liquid to make ice. At 32°F, the molecules in the water cannot move any slower without changing state. At 32°F, the **latent heat of freezing** begins. It takes the removal of 140 Btu from 1 pound of 32°F water to change its state into ice.

The changing of state in liquids, referred to as vaporizing and condensing, is the basis of air conditioning. It takes more heat to evaporate a liquid than to freeze a liquid. This is why air conditioning uses the process of evaporating a liquid to absorb a large amount of heat energy. By evaporating liquids, the air conditioner can remove the heat from the cabin air, which contains the heat to cause the vaporization, thereby making the occupant feel cool. It is the same principle by which sweat cools human beings. Heat is absorbed by the evaporating sweat droplets on the skin, thereby removing heat from the body and cooling it. Similarly, by evaporating liquids, the air conditioner can remove large amounts of heat from the air and make the occupant feel cooler.

Refrigerant Principles

Manipulating nature's law of **vaporization** and **condensation** of liquids and gases is how the air conditioner forces ambient passenger compartment air to become cool and less humid for the driver and passengers of the vehicle. For the cycle of vaporization and condensation to occur, the air conditioner needs a fluid that vaporizes and condenses at the correct temperature and pressure. It also must be able to change its state in the continuous cycle of vaporization and condensation without breaking down. The fluid used for these purposes is **refrigerant**. The refrigerant in the air-conditioning system must have a boiling point well below freezing to manipulate its boiling and condensing points by changing pressure **FIGURE 35-5**. The super low boiling point of most

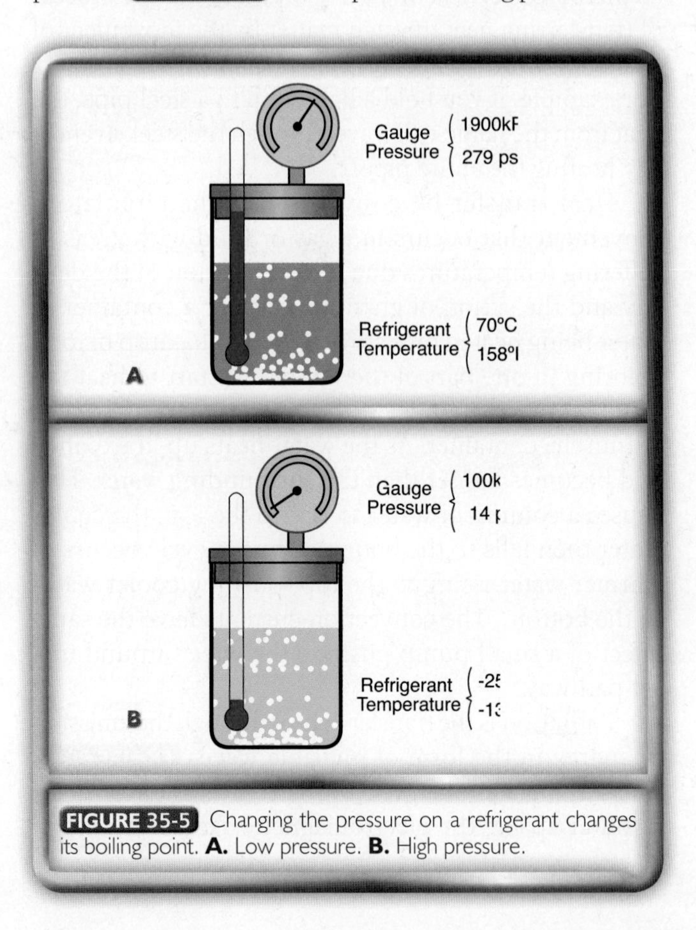
Gauge Pressure
Refrigerant Temperature
70°C
A
Gauge Pressure
Refrigerant Temperature
B

FIGURE 35-5 Changing the pressure on a refrigerant changes its boiling point. **A.** Low pressure. **B.** High pressure.

refrigerants allows the system to control the vaporization and condensation point of the refrigerant at normal ambient temperatures. A commonly used refrigerant is R-134a, a hydrofluorocarbon that contains none of the ozone-depleting chlorine found in old refrigerants.

With the use of refrigerants, maintaining vaporization and condensing points at normal ambient temperatures is simply done by raising or reducing the pressure of the refrigerant. At atmospheric pressure, R-134a boils at about –15°F (–26°C), so in most normal conditions it is in its gaseous state. By adding a small amount of pressure to the refrigerant, the boiling point of the refrigerant will rise. Indeed, a low pressure (approximately 15 pounds per square inch [psi], or 103 kilopascals [kPa]) in a refrigerant can force the boiling point of the refrigerant to be just above freezing (32°F [0°C]). Likewise, to allow the R-134a to condense back into a liquid, its boiling point can be increased well above the ambient temperature by further increasing its pressure. Forcing the refrigerant's boiling point so that it is well above ambient temperatures allows it to be cooled by ambient air so that it will condense back into a liquid within the condenser and stay a liquid all the way to the restriction.

With the refrigerant boiling below the temperature of the air in the passenger compartment, the air conditioner will forcefully remove the heat from the passenger compartment's air by using the heat from the air in the passenger compartment to boil the refrigerant. R-134a under low pressure (15–25 psi [103–172 kPa]) boils at about 32°F (0°C). Warm air from the passenger compartment is circulated from the passenger cabin across the evaporator containing R-134a, causing it to boil. As R-134a boils, it absorbs that heat and pulls it along with the moving R-134a away from the evaporator. The process continually repeats as the fan circulates the air, and the operating air-conditioning system continually circulates refrigerant, resulting in a continual supply of cool air to the cabin. The air returning to the passenger compartment will feel cool to the driver and passengers because the heat was removed from the air when the heat was used to boil the refrigerant. The heat from the air is absorbed by the refrigerant, changing the state of the refrigerant from liquid to gas, while at the same time cooling the air.

If the temperature of the refrigerant falls below the freezing point of water during this process, the air conditioner must shut off. The air passing over the evaporating refrigerant is full of moisture, so the extreme heat removal will cause any moisture in the air to condense on the cold surface of the evaporator. The water vapor in the air could freeze on the outside of the evaporator and block the airflow that is needed to cause the refrigerant to vaporize. The air must keep flowing over the evaporator, renewing the heat source to keep the refrigerant evaporating (boiling) efficiently without freezing.

Applied Science

AS-23: Phases/States: The technician can explain in detail the three states of matter.

Solids, liquids, and gases are the three most common states of matter on earth. The distinction between them is based on characteristics relating to the shape and volume of the piece of matter in question.

Solid matter retains a fixed volume and shape. There are many examples of solid matter used in motor vehicles, from the cast iron, steel, and aluminum used to build engines, to the fabric and plastic materials used in interiors. Liquid matter retains a fixed volume but the shape adapts to the shape of the container they are held within. Again, there are many liquids used in motor vehicles. In the case of gases, the matter does not retain a fixed volume, but expands to fill whatever volume is available. Air-conditioning refrigerant is an interesting example of a compound that takes the form of both a liquid and a gas in different sections of the air-conditioning system.

Applied Science

AS-28: Conduction/Convection: The technician is able to explain the concept of heat transfer in terms of conduction, radiation, and convection in automotive systems.

Heat can be transferred via three methods; conduction, convection, and radiation. Put simply, conduction is the transfer of heat through solid matter, convection is the transfer of heat through liquid or gas relying on the movement of currents, and radiation is the transfer of heat energy through space by means of electromagnetic waves.

All three of these methods of transfer come into play when trying to keep the inside of your car cool. The heat you feel in the cabin originates from the sun. The sun's heat travels by radiation, and you feel it coming through the glass windows into the vehicle cabin. Heat is transferred through the cabin via convection, with the hot glass panels heating the air inside and causing it to move in currents. When turned on, the air-conditioning system moves the hot air through the cold evaporator core. The heat is moved to the evaporator core via convection and dissipated through the metal evaporator core by conduction.

Differential Gas Pressure

Every vehicle's air conditioner has a low side (approximately 20–40 psi [138–276 kPa] depending on outside temperature) and a high side (approximately 170–230 psi

[1172–1586 kPa]) FIGURE 35-6. The low side is designed to allow easy transformation of the refrigerant from a liquid to a gas. The high side enables the transfer of heat out of the refrigerant to the atmosphere so it changes back from a gas to liquid.

Starting at the compressor, a low-pressure gas is compressed into a high-pressure gas and is pumped into the condenser located in the front of the vehicle radiator. The gaseous refrigerant is cooled by the air passing through the condenser and leaves the condenser as a high-pressure liquid. The high pressure is required to enable the change from gas to liquid. From there, the liquid travels through a small orifice (restriction) that reduces the pressure (a fixed orifice tube or thermal expansion valve). After the restriction, the low side of the system begins. The low-pressure liquid leaves the metering device and travels to the evaporator, which is usually located under the dash. As the low-pressure liquid travels through the evaporator, a fan blows the warm to hot cabin air across the fins, adding heat to the refrigerant until it boils. As it boils, it absorbs heat from the air and the refrigerant is transformed back into a gas. The gaseous refrigerant then travels back to the compressor to start the cycle over.

Air-Conditioning Components and Operation

Each HVAC system uses refrigerant and four major components. Each component has a specific job and purpose. The components are the compressor, condenser, restriction, and evaporator FIGURE 35-7. The air-conditioning cycle starts with the **compressor**. The compressor changes a low-pressure refrigerant gas to a high-pressure gas. The compressor also provides the needed refrigerant movement in the system. Without the movement of refrigerant, the system could not exchange the heat from the condenser and the evaporator. Moving refrigerant also allows for the pressure drop to occur in the restriction. Without movement, the restriction could not drop the pressure. Refrigerant enters the compressor as a low-pressure gas from the evaporator. The compressor's function is to increase the pressure of the gaseous refrigerant and then push it into the condenser.

Forcing a gas to become a liquid is achieved through condensing. So the next component after the compressor in the air-conditioning system is the **condenser**. Hot high-pressure gas enters the condenser from the compressor. The gas flows through a series of coils in the condenser and ambient air passes over the outside of the finned coils. The engine's radiator fan and/or dedicated condenser fans move ambient air across the condenser coils and fins. The cooler outside air removes the heat from the hot high-pressure gas and the gas begins to condense into a liquid. Emerging from the outlet of the condenser is a relatively hot, high-pressure liquid. The condenser transforms gas to liquid on the high side of the system.

The air conditioner is a **closed loop system**, meaning that nothing else enters or exits the system; the refrigerant just continues to cycle through the system, changing

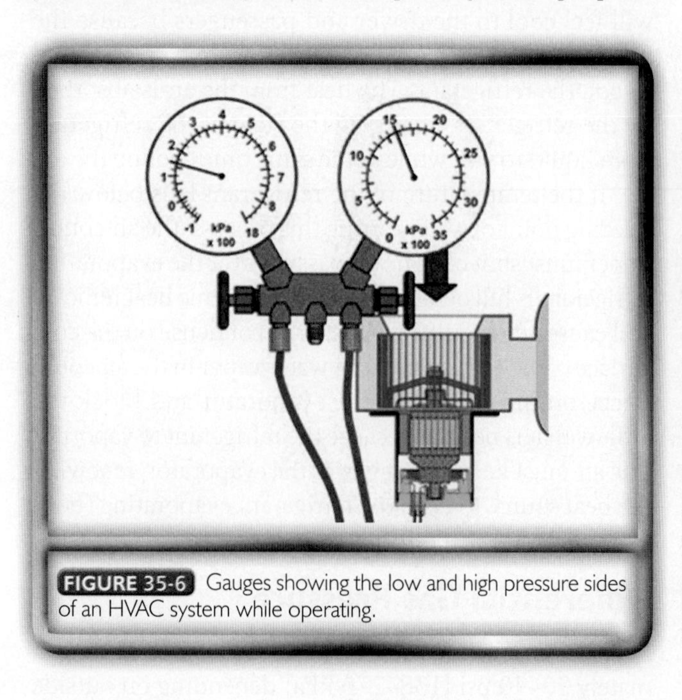
kPa
x 100
kPa
x 100

FIGURE 35-6 Gauges showing the low and high pressure sides of an HVAC system while operating.

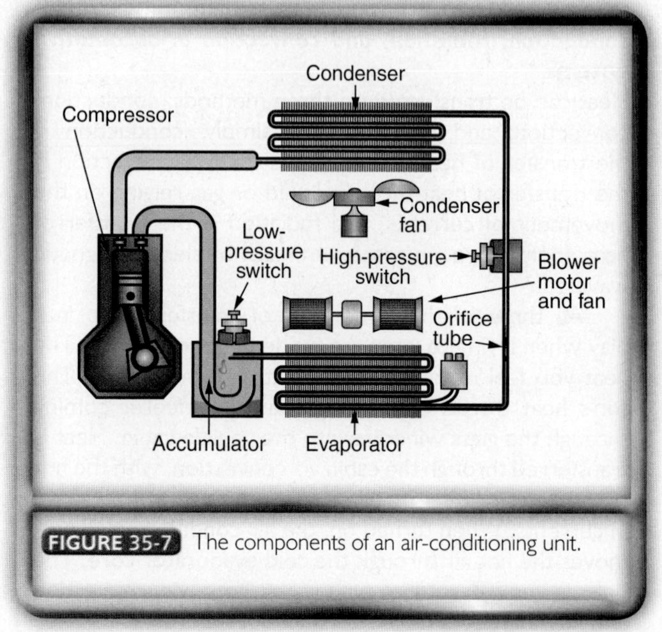
Condenser
Compressor
Condenser fan
Low-pressure switch
High-pressure switch
Blower motor and fan
Orifice tube
Accumulator
Evaporator

FIGURE 35-7 The components of an air-conditioning unit.

pressure and state to complete the task of cooling the cabin. Before the liquid can be evaporated back into a gas for the compressor, the pressure needs to be dropped so the boiling point can be lowered below the passenger compartment air temperature, thus allowing vaporization to remove the heat from the passenger compartment air. Dropping pressure occurs by flowing a liquid through a **restriction**.

The restriction lowers the pressure using the Bernoulli principle. Daniel Bernoulli stated that if the flow of a fluid remains constant, the energies of the fluid remain constant; changing one of the two energies (up or down) affects the other energy oppositely. The two energies in fluid are velocity and pressure. These energies react opposite to each other. When velocity increases, the pressure must drop if the flow remains constant. The restriction causes a significant increase in refrigerant velocity because the compressor is constantly moving fluid in the closed loop system.

The fluid flowing through the restriction is a liquid. Liquids are considered incompressible (Pascal's law). Forcing a noncompressible fluid through a small orifice causes the velocity in the restriction to rise. If the velocity of the liquid rises, the pressure of the liquid must drop according to the Bernoulli principle. Raising the velocity and dropping the pressure is how the restriction transforms the high-pressure liquid refrigerant to a low-pressure liquid refrigerant. The reduced pressure reduces the boiling point of the refrigerant and turns the refrigerant into a low-pressure liquid ready for the evaporator to vaporize the liquid into a gas.

The next component in the air-conditioning system is the **evaporator**. The evaporator transforms low-pressure liquid to a low-pressure gas. The transformation from liquid to gas begins when the air from the passenger compartment passes over the evaporator coils and fins. The pressure on the refrigerant is held between 20 and 40 psi (138 and 276 kPa); the pressure on the low side of the system reduces the refrigerant's boiling point to a bit over 33°F (1°C). The liquid refrigerant absorbs heat from any source available as it boils. This heat comes from the air flowing through the evaporator core.

The vaporization of the refrigerant is forced to happen just above the freezing point of water so that the evaporator core will not freeze. Any heat source will amplify the boiling process. By moving air across the evaporator coils, the convection currents pass over the evaporator coils, causing conduction of heat to the refrigerant through the tubes of the evaporator. The conduction of heat through the coils then provides the needed energy to boil (evaporate) the liquid refrigerant to a gas. It also strips the air of much of its heat energy and moisture, making the air flowing from the duct cool and crisp.

Refrigerant

Proper air-conditioning operation requires that all of the components, including the refrigerant, work efficiently. Without proper refrigerant levels, or if any one component is not functioning properly, the air conditioner will not cool the passenger compartment effectively. Each component requires that the refrigerant level be correct and that the previous component deliver the refrigerant to it in the correct state. The evaporator requires a low-pressure liquid; the compressor requires a low-pressure gas; the condenser requires a high-pressure gas; and the restriction requires a high-pressure liquid.

Types of Refrigerant

Dichlorodifluoromethane (R-12), a member of the CFC family of gases, was the first common refrigerant to be used in an automotive air conditioner. The first part of the word refers to chlorine, a primary component of CFCs that is banned by the U.S. government in refrigerants because of its detrimental effects on the atmosphere. It is nonflammable, nontoxic, and stable at all temperatures; does not react with aluminum, steel, or copper; and is soluble in mineral oils. It has a boiling point of –21.8°F (–29.9°C). In the early 1990s, R-12 was found to be one of the leading causes of the depletion of the ozone layer and was outlawed for new vehicle installation. Although you will not find R-12 in today's production vehicles, you may still have customers with older cars using R-12.

Tetrafluoroethane (R-134a) was the replacement for R-12. It is a hydrofluorocarbon, or HFC. Although R-134a has a boiling point of –15.3°F (–26.3°C), which is nearly the same as R-12's boiling point, R-134a can only be substituted for R-12 (retrofitted) by following a specific procedure. The common refrigerant R-134a uses a polyalkalene glycol (PAG) oil to lubricate the air-conditioning components, and R-12, the less common refrigerant, uses mineral oil. One reason it is so important to always use the correct refrigerant is that PAG oil mixed with mineral oil creates a hazardous gas that can corrode the air-conditioning system. The mixture is also considered a contaminant and must be handled as hazardous waste. To help prevent the wrong lubricant or refrigerant being installed during servicing, the service ports on air-conditioning systems have been changed so that the service equipment for an R-12 system cannot be connected to an R-134a system. Common PAG oils are PAG 46, PAG 100, PAG 133, and PAG 150.

> **TECHNICIAN TIP**
>
> Identifying refrigerants has become an important part of repairing air-conditioning systems. The accidental mixing of refrigerants or the mixing of different types of refrigerant oil could cause damage to the system and the machines that service air conditioners. Before reclaiming a system, you need to identify the type of refrigerant in the vehicle to prevent the accidental contamination of the refrigerant in your recovering machine.

R-134a is nonflammable and is accepted by the automotive world to be safe for automotive air conditioners. R-134a, which is a liquid, boils well below normal room temperatures and, in vaporizing, will absorb tremendous amounts of heat without increasing its own temperature. Unfortunately, recent discoveries show that R-134a is a major contributor to greenhouse gases, so it is being phased out. Tetrafluoropropene (HFO-1234yf) is the preferred replacement.

HFO-1234yf is the latest refrigerant for mobile air-conditioning systems. It has a greatly reduced global warming potential (GWP) of 4, compared to a GWP of 1430 for R-134a refrigerant. Its atmospheric lifetime is only 11 days, compared to 13 years for R-134a. It is slightly flammable, but the safety risk has been determined to be significantly less than the risk associated with gasoline. Also, HFO-1234yf is more costly to produce than R-134a, so that will impact customers as their systems need servicing. HFO-1234yf uses a PAG-type oil with different additives on belt-driven compressors and polyolester (POE) oil for electrically driven compressors. HFO-1234yf uses service ports that are different than those used with R-12 or R-134a, so contamination issues can be avoided FIGURE 35-8.

A
B
FIGURE 35-8 Service ports. **A.** R-12. **B.** R-134a.

Refrigerant Oils

The oil used in refrigeration systems must be compatible with the refrigerant used. The old refrigerant R-12 used mineral oil. R-134a uses a PAG oil and POE oil is recommended for use with HFO-1234yf FIGURE 35-9. The oil is necessary to keep moving parts in the compressor lubricated and is used on the gaskets and seals to protect and help seal. It must be able to move throughout the system without foaming and be compatible with the refrigerant and the pressure changes taking place. The oil is picked up and carried throughout the system in the refrigerant, so some oil will be found in all the major air-conditioning system components (compressor, evaporator, receiver dryer or accumulator, and condenser). The oil in the compressor is just as important as oil in an engine. Without it, the compressor will overheat and destroy itself.

Mineral oil is clear to light yellow, and PAG oil is usually a light blue color. As the oil picks up dirt or becomes contaminated, it will turn brown or black, depending on the level of contamination.

POE oil can sometimes be used with R-134a. It can also be recommended when retrofitting R-134a in R-12 systems since POE oils are not as reactive to small traces of mineral oil residue. Both POE and PAG oils absorb moisture, so be sure to cap the oil bottle whenever you are not pouring it.

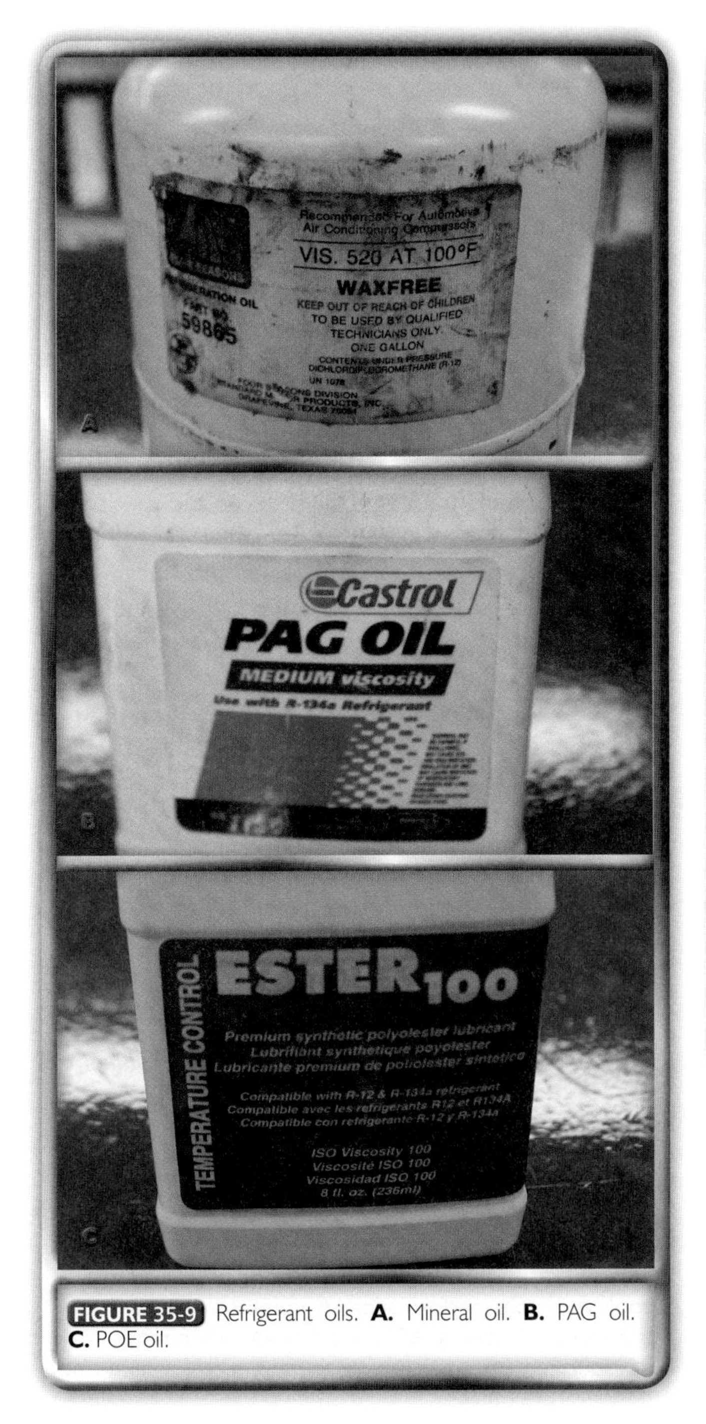
VIS. 520 AT 100°F
WAXFREE
Castrol
PAG OIL
MEDIUM viscosity
ESTER100
TEMPERATURE CONTROL
A
B
C

FIGURE 35-9 Refrigerant oils. **A.** Mineral oil. **B.** PAG oil. **C.** POE oil.

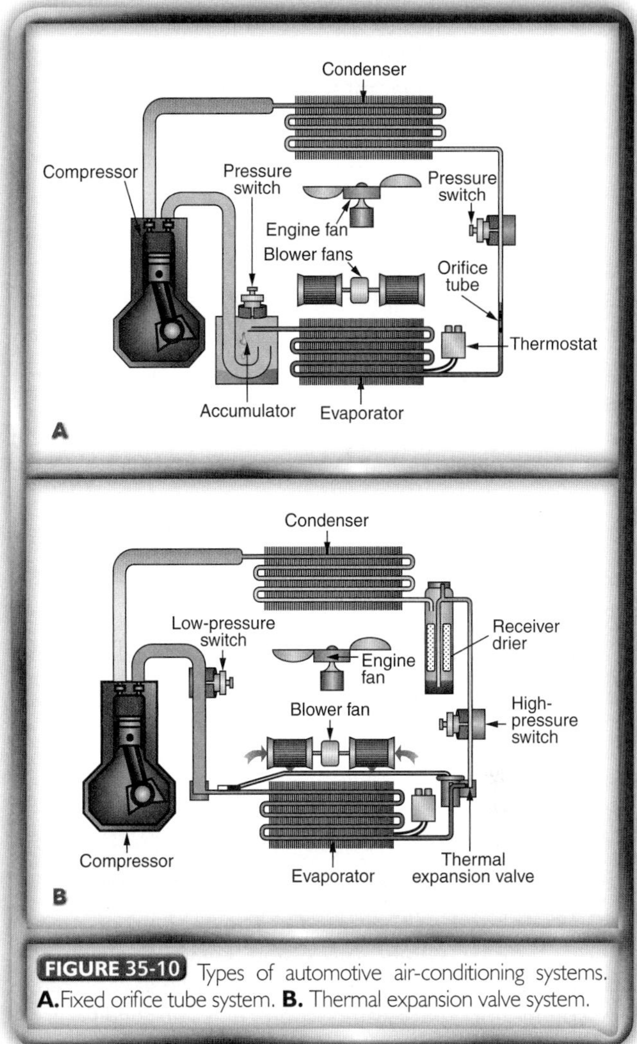
Condenser
Compressor
Pressure switch
Pressure switch
Engine fan
Blower fans
Orifice tube
Thermostat
Accumulator
Evaporator
A
Condenser
Low-pressure switch
Engine fan
Receiver drier
Blower fan
High-pressure switch
Compressor
Evaporator
Thermal expansion valve
B

FIGURE 35-10 Types of automotive air-conditioning systems. **A.** Fixed orifice tube system. **B.** Thermal expansion valve system.

Types of Automotive Air-Conditioning Systems

There are two definitive system types: **fixed orifice tube system** and **thermal expansion valve (TXV) system** FIGURE 35-10. The difference is that the TXV is adjustable based on the temperature of the outlet pipe from the evaporator, whereas the fixed orifice tube provides a nonadjustable passage for the refrigerant to pass through. Each type of air-conditioning system contains one subcomponent that is vital to the operation and efficiency of the air-conditioning unit. The type of restriction being used will determine which subcomponent is required. Fixed orifice tube systems use an **accumulator** to ensure that a pure gas is delivered to the compressor, and TXV systems use a receiver filter drier to ensure that a pure liquid is delivered to the restriction.

The fixed orifice tube system has the accumulator on the low side line between the evaporator and the compressor. Since this system cannot adapt to temperature changes in the cabin, it is likely that during cooler weather or as the cabin temperature decreases the refrigerant in the evaporator will not fully boil. This means that some liquid refrigerant will still be present as it heads for the compressor. Since liquid cannot be compressed, its presence in the compressor may cause damage from trying to compress a noncompressible substance. The accumulator's job is to prevent liquid from getting into the compressor and causing damage. Liquid and gaseous refrigerant are both able to enter the accumulator. In the accumulator, the liquid falls to the bottom because it is heavier, and the gas rises to the top. The outlet of the accumulator only draws from the top; therefore, it only allows gaseous refrigerant to reach the compressor. The liquid in the bottom is heated by the gas passing through it and heat from the engine compartment, and it boils and rises to be used as a gas.

The TXV system has a receiver dryer in the high side line between the condenser and the TXV. This system can adapt to the temperature changes in the evaporator, so unlike the fixed orifice system, it does not need the safety device for the compressor. The receiver dryer also lets in liquid and gaseous refrigerant, but it actually draws the liquid from the bottom on the outlet side. The receiver stores the accumulated liquid refrigerant in case of a sudden change of temperature in the cabin. If the cabin is cool because the air conditioning has been on for a while and the customer opens a window or door, hot air rushes in, raising the outlet temperature of the evaporator and causing the TXV to rapidly open. This rapid opening stimulates a rush of the extra liquid refrigerant from the receiver to the evaporator to keep it from drawing a vacuum and becoming inefficient.

Applied Science

AS-19: Fahrenheit/Centigrade: The technician measures system temperatures and converts them to degrees Fahrenheit or degrees Centigrade as required.
A common HVAC-related concern is air-conditioning systems failing to cool effectively. Prior to carrying out any diagnosis, technicians must determine whether or not the system is operating properly. This is determined by measuring the output temperature at the center vents in the vehicle's dash.

Once the vent temperature has been measured, it should be compared to manufacturer's specifications to determine if the system is operating effectively. Measuring instruments are available reading in either degrees Centigrade or degrees Fahrenheit. The unit of measurement in which specifications are published may vary according to the manufacturer. It may be necessary to convert the measured temperatures from degrees Centigrade to degrees Fahrenheit, or vice-versa, to determine if the reading meets specifications.

Heating System Components and Operation

Many of the components used to warm the passenger cabin of a vehicle also function in removing heat from the engine. The key shared components are the radiator, thermostat, water pump, and upper and lower radiator hoses. As the engine heats up from the process of burning fuel to create power, the coolant in the engine is also heated, reaching temperatures of 180–205°F (82–96°C) under normal conditions and 235°F (113°C) or more in hot climates or under heavy vehicle loads. The heat from the hot coolant opens the thermostat and the water pump pushes the coolant into the radiator, which is located in front of the engine. Airflow from the vehicle moving and/or the cooling fans passes over the radiator and the heat is transferred to the air, warming the air and reducing the temperature of the coolant. The coolant is then cycled back through the engine to restart the process. Heated coolant is also pumped to a heater core where the blower causes air to flow through the heater core and is warmed. The heated air is directed into the passenger compartment.

Just as the pressure inside of the air-conditioning system is manipulated to control the boiling point of the refrigerant, the cooling system is kept under pressure to prevent the coolant from boiling at the normal boiling point of water, which is 212°F (100°C). The cap holds the pressure at approximately 8–20 psi (55–138 kPa) depending on what the manufacturer designed the system to be safely pressurized to. Raising the pressure 1 psi (7 kPa) raises the boiling point of water approximately 3°F, so water in a cooling system with a

Applied Math

AM-40: Proportion: The technician can solve problems that determine the proportion of variables of a solution and determine if that proportion is within the manufacturer's specifications.
Engine coolant is composed of a mixture of antifreeze, commonly ethylene glycol or propylene glycol, and water. Different operating temperature ranges may require different ratios of antifreeze to water to ensure adequate cooling system performance. A common mixture ratio is 50% antifreeze to 50% water, but other ratios may be specified by antifreeze manufacturers for extreme temperature ranges.

Coolant concentration can be checked with an antifreeze hydrometer, which indicates the proportion of antifreeze in the system. Coolant concentration should be checked during vehicle servicing. Topping up cooling systems with water is a common practice, but the proportion of antifreeze in the system is reduced. If measurement indicates that the proportion of antifreeze in the system is low, some coolant must be drained from the system, which can then be refilled with antifreeze to the correct proportion. Too much antifreeze in the system can cause poor cooling, if this occurs some coolant must be drained from the system and the system refilled with water to the correct proportion.

Safety

In the same way that liquid refrigerant boils when its pressure is lowered, so too does coolant. If an engine is overheating, never remove the radiator pressure cap. If you do, and the coolant is above 212°F (100°C), then the coolant will instantly turn into steam and shoot out of the radiator like a geyser, potentially burning you badly. Let all engines cool before opening the radiator pressure cap.

15-psi (103-kPa) radiator cap will not boil until 45°F above 212°F, or 257°F (125°C). And if the water is mixed with anti-freeze, the boiling point will be even higher.

Heater Core

In the heating system, two hoses run from the engine to a **heater core** (small radiator). The heater core is located inside the cabin in the plastic box with the air-conditioning evaporator. As air is moved through the fins of the heater core, hot air is removed and sent out of the vents to heat the passenger cabin. The heater core is made from tubes that have thin metal fins connected to them, which increase the surface area tremendously. Since the tubes are also made of relatively thin metal, they can corrode from the inside and develop pinhole leaks from old acidic anti-freeze. Changing a heater core can be a time-consuming and costly job in many of today's vehicles, so regular cooling system maintenance can pay off for a customer.

Heater Control Valve and/or Blend Door

To adjust the amount of heat delivered to the cabin, some heating systems use a control valve on the inlet of the heater core to control the flow of hot coolant through the heater core. The valve can be mechanically operated by a cable, vacuum operated by a vacuum diaphragm, or electrically operated by an electric motor. Other vehicles use a blend door to control how much airflow goes through the heater core based on the driver's request using the temperature settings on the dash. Blend doors can be operated mechanically, by vacuum, or by electric motors. Most vehicles either use a heater control valve or a blend door to control the amount of heat delivered to the passenger compartment FIGURE 35-11.

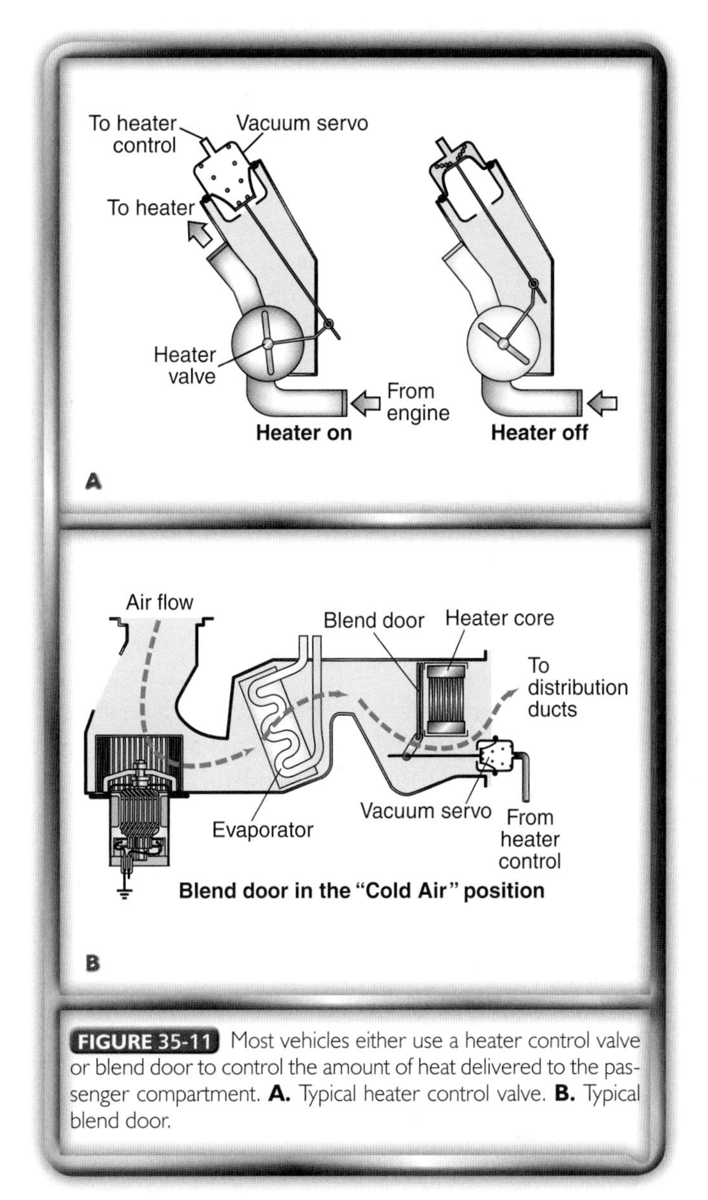

To heater control
Vacuum servo
To heater
Heater valve
From engine
Heater on
Heater off
A
Air flow
Blend door
Heater core
To distribution ducts
Vacuum servo
Evaporator
From heater control
Blend door in the "Cold Air" position
B

FIGURE 35-11 Most vehicles either use a heater control valve or blend door to control the amount of heat delivered to the passenger compartment. **A.** Typical heater control valve. **B.** Typical blend door.

Heating and Ventilation

To improve driver and passenger safety, a supply of fresh air is necessary to maintain comfort and reduce fatigue. Fresh air is drawn from outside usually through air ducts at the base of the windshield and directed to the passenger compartment. The air is then delivered through a system of ducts and air doors, which are positioned to direct air to particular points inside the passenger compartment.

Vehicle Heating and Ventilation Components

Some of the heat generated by the burning fuel in the engine is removed by the cooling system. The hot coolant is pumped through a heater core usually located in the vehicle cabin. As cool air blows across the heater core, the air is heated by the warm coolant. The coolant is then pumped back through the engine to pick up heat from the engine and the cycle continues. In the dash is a control system for the blower fan speed. The blower fan blows the warm or cool air out of the ducts. The control system also has a temperature control that either opens a blend door that determines how much air blows across the heater core or around it, or controls a heater control valve that varies the amount of hot water being pumped through the heater core. In most vehicles, all air flows through the evaporator on its way to the heater core.

If cold air is desired, then the air-conditioning system is activated to cool the evaporator. If the cool or cold setting is selected, then either the blend door will divert the air around the heater core or the heater control valve will prevent coolant from flowing through it. If warm or hot air is desired, then the air conditioner will be off and either the blend door will divert the air through the heater core or the heater control valve will allow hot coolant to flow through the heater core. If defrost is desired, then both the air conditioner and the heater will operate. The air first goes through the evaporator, and most of the moisture is pulled from the air. Then the air is directed through the heater core where it is heated. This causes hot, dry air to be blown onto the windshield, which defrosts it quickly.

Another control regulates location of airflow. There are several doors designed to direct the air to the feet (floor ducts), head (vent ducts), windshield (defrosting ducts), or a combination of locations, such as the feet and windshield. This control also has a vent setting that allows fresh air in, then directs it to the vents. Vehicles with air conditioning can have a recirculation switch or lever, or they can have a "max" or "maximum" setting. This setting closes the door to the outside air to allow the air-conditioning system to work with only the air already present in the cabin. Using only the air within the cabin produces better cooling because the air-conditioning system will be cooling air that has already been through the air-conditioning system rather than hot, muggy air from outside the vehicle. Recirculation can also be used on some vehicles to help keep the moisture out when using the defroster.

Applied Science

AS-9: Scientific Methods: The technician develops a theory relative to the cause of the problem based on the information provided, then tests the hypothesis to determine the solution.

A vehicle is presented to the workshop with an air conditioning problem. The customer is concerned that all air from the ventilation system is being directed to the windshield and that turning the direction control to either the face or feet positions has no effect.

The vehicle in question uses a vacuum-operated system to control blend-door positions in the HVAC system. The technician forms a theory that the system may have a vacuum leak, based on the fact that, in the event of no vacuum, the system defaults to defroster operation to ensure the driver retains visibility and is able to safely operate the vehicle.

The technician first confirms that the HVAC vacuum line is connected to the engine's intake manifold then forms a hypothesis that the vacuum leak is occurring within the HVAC system located inside the vehicle's cabin. He is able to confirm this hypothesis by connecting a vacuum pump to the HVAC line in the engine bay and confirming that the system does not hold vacuum. Individual components and sections of vacuum line in the cabin are then individually tested to ensure they hold vacuum. A common failure in this scenario is an internal vacuum leak in the direction control assembly.

Vehicle Heating and Ventilation Operation

Air doors can be controlled by cables, **vacuum servos**, or **electric servos**. Servos are devices designed to do work. They are hooked to the ventilation doors and open and close them according to the request from the control assembly. Vacuum servos use a vacuum control at the control head. Vacuum is supplied by the engine and run into the control head with a small hose called a vacuum hose (it is normally black). The control head can route this vacuum to the correct servo by turning the dial on the control head. Each setting has a different-colored hose coming out and going to a separate servo or, in some cases, to a dual servo that can move in two directions. Traditionally, these systems have doors that can be only opened or closed, because they either have vacuum pulling on a diaphragm or they do not. Newer vehicles have electric servos. They are the same as the old, mechanical servos except instead of vacuum, they use electric motors to open and close the doors. These can be adapted to only partially open a door. Most of these systems are computer controlled so the system knows when a door opens and when it does not and can set trouble codes if a door malfunctions. In this way, the servos can direct air to the vent ducts, floor ducts, windshield ducts, and rear passenger compartment ducts.

A fan, usually driven by an electric motor, is used to assist the air to flow through the radiator and condenser when demands are high or when vehicle speeds are low. When vehicle speeds are low, there may not be enough airflow to cool the coolant and the refrigerant. In these conditions, the fan comes on to pull the air through the radiator and the condenser to keep the vehicle from overheating and also to allow the refrigerant to condense. Some vehicles have two or more fans, typically one for the radiator and one or more for the condenser. They frequently are positioned side by side and attached to the radiator, just as in applications with one fan. Each fan has different controls regulating when they come on or turn off. Most vehicles with electric fans will turn on at least one fan when the air conditioning is on to aid in the cooling of the refrigerant.

The heating system of most passenger vehicles uses hot engine coolant flowing through a **heater core**, which is usually mounted under the dash **FIGURE 35-12**. The heater core is connected to the engine's cooling system by flexible rubber hoses, which allow for movement and a reduction in the level of engine noise and vibration transmitted into the passenger compartment. The heater core is a small radiator consisting of **tubes**, **fins**, and **tanks**. The tubes are the metal pipes running side to side or up and down that the coolant travels through. Fins are small, flat metal pieces placed between the tubes to help transfer heat from the coolant to the air. The fins are in direct contact with the hot pipes and absorb the heat. The heat is then absorbed by the air flowing through the fins, warming the air, which is then blown back into the passenger cabin. Metal or plastic tanks line the sides of the tubes, connecting them together and assisting with coolant flow. The coolant flow is created by the engine water pump directing the coolant through the heater core and then back to the engine. In some applications, a heater control valve is located in one of the heater coolant hoses to adjust the quantity of coolant flowing through the heater core.

The coolant enters the heater core from the warm engine, and the air that is passed over the heater core from the passenger compartment cools the coolant in the heater core. The transfer of heat from the hot coolant to the air passing over the heater core is what causes the temperature to rise in the air duct. The air that has been heated by the heater core is warm but still moist because the heat from the heater core cannot condense the moisture out of the air. This condition of warm moist air does not have an adverse effect on the passengers in most cases.

Defroster

When the air conditioner is allowed to operate during the defrost cycle, the air is dried from the moisture removal occurring as air passes over the evaporator before passing over the heater core. The result of air passing over both cores is dry and heated air. The dry hot air from the defrost duct hits the windshield, and the moisture from the glass is quickly drawn into the air. The defrost time of passenger vehicles has decreased considerably because of the air conditioner being switched on during the defrost cycle.

Blower Motors

Blower motors are electric motors that determine the rate of air flow out of the vents. Attached to the spinning shaft of the motor is what is called the "squirrel cage," a plastic cage with fins to pull or push air **FIGURE 35-13**. The speed is controlled by the driver (except in electronically controlled systems) through the fan switch and a series of resistors to limit the fan speed. Blower motors can be positioned either before the evaporator and heater core or after in the HVAC system. When placed after, they pull the air through the evaporator and heater core in the box. Placing the blower before pushes air through the evaporator and heater core in the box.

Blower Motor Resistor Packs/Speed Controls

The resistor pack or resistor block is the most common blower motor control. It uses resistors in series to regulate the speed of the fan **FIGURE 35-14**. The more resistance there is in the circuit, the less current available to spin the fan. The lowest speed (speed 1) passes the current through

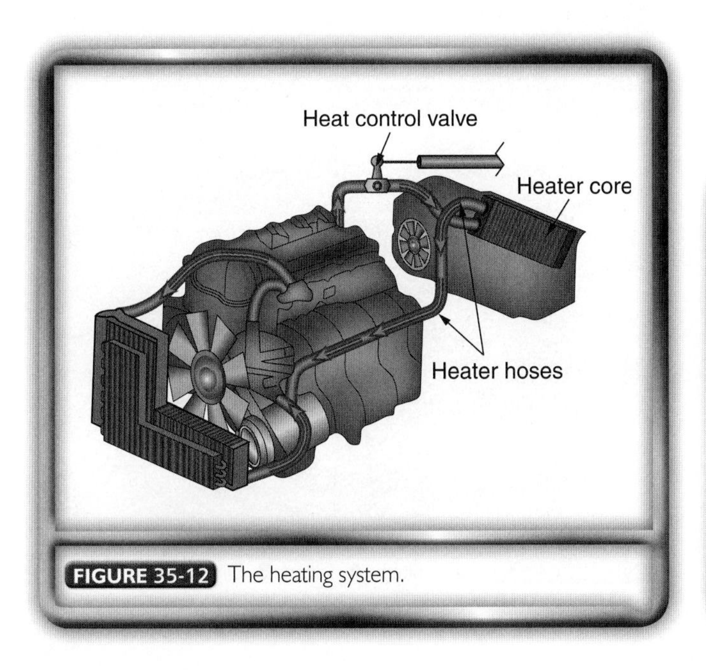
Heat control valve
Heater core
Heater hoses

FIGURE 35-12 The heating system.

FIGURE 35-13 Blower motor and squirrel cage fan.

several resistors. The highest speed uses no resistors so the motor has full current flow. The amount of resistors in a pack depends on the number of different speed settings.

On vehicles with electronic air-conditioning systems or automatic systems where the customer just sets a desired temperature, the fan is controlled by a variable resistor called a rheostat that allows the computer to change fan speed infinitely by varying resistance such as a light dimmer in a house. Other systems use **pulse width modulation** to control fan speed. Normally this is done by controlling "on" time compared to "off" time on the ground side of the circuit. The longer the on time, the faster the fan will spin.

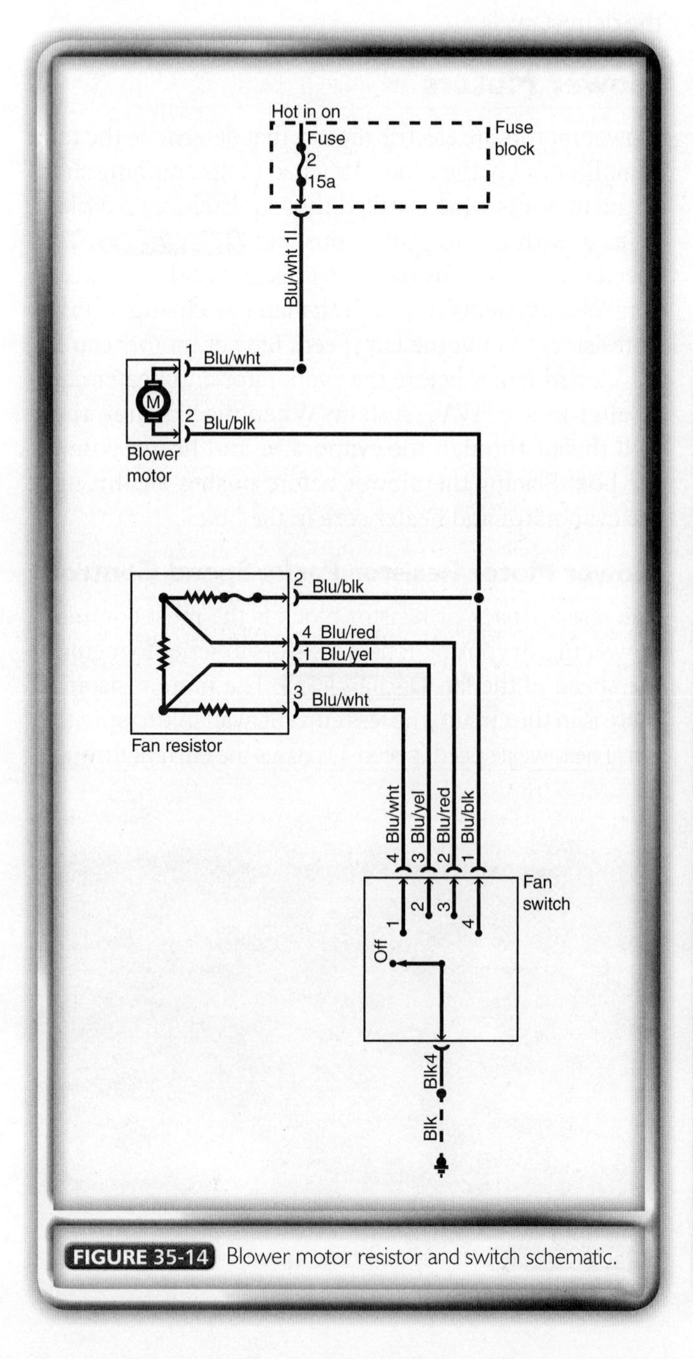
Hot in on
Fuse
2
15a
Fuse
block
Blu/wht 11
1 Blu/wht
M
2 Blu/blk
Blower
motor
2 Blu/blk
4 Blu/red
1 Blu/yel
3 Blu/wht
Fan resistor
4 Blu/wht
3 Blu/yel
2 Blu/red
1 Blu/blk
Fan
switch
1
2
3
4
Off
Blk4
Blk

FIGURE 35-14 Blower motor resistor and switch schematic.

Cabin Air Filters

Many manufacturers have added cabin air filters to the inlet side of the heating/air-conditioning box where fresh air enters the cabin. This filter is designed to catch dust and outside contaminates so they do not get blown into the cabin. Many are paper just like the air filter for the engine and as such should be checked regularly and replaced when they begin to clog or they will cause the system to be inefficient due to poor airflow FIGURE 35-15. Some manufacturers are using activated charcoal cabin filters, which help trap odors and airborne pollutants such as carbon monoxide and oxides of nitrogen. Cabin air filters usually should be replaced once a year or between 12,000 and 15,000 miles.

HVAC Developments

With the advent of electric and hybrid passenger cars, the HVAC system continues to evolve. The heater core in your car may soon be a thing of the past; reversing the refrigerant flow through the air-conditioning system would turn your evaporator core into a condenser and

FIGURE 35-15 Cabin filters. **A.** Clean. **B.** Dirty.

provide ample heat for the passenger compartment. This is the same principle that heat pumps operate on. They can reverse the flow of refrigerant, which turns them from a heater to an air conditioner.

Another development is electric compressors, which are already taking the place of less-efficient belt-driven compressors. The amount of energy loss from the drive belt and electric clutch is too high for hybrid and electric vehicles that need to conserve all the power possible. As passenger cars evolve, so must the air-conditioning system; greater efficiency and less power consumption will be the drivers of new air-conditioning systems FIGURE 35-16.

Performance Testing

The pretest and inspection of the air-conditioning system are the first step in the diagnostic process. **Performance testing** is the term used to describe the standard air-conditioning testing process. You need to look at all of the components and compare how the air-conditioning unit is functioning versus how it is designed to function. When testing the air-conditioning system, make sure to have all of the controls at the maximum settings. The heater fan needs to be on the highest speed. The heater control knob should be on the coldest setting. The airflow should be set to the dash vents. An external fan needs to be supplying air to the condenser to simulate driving conditions.

The engine's rpm should be at 1200, which is the ideal and average rpm for the majority of air-conditioning systems on vehicles. Before testing the air-conditioning system, let the system stabilize for a few minutes to allow the refrigerant to equalize and the temperatures to reach the proper level.

To performance test an air-conditioning system, follow the steps in SKILL DRILL 35-1.

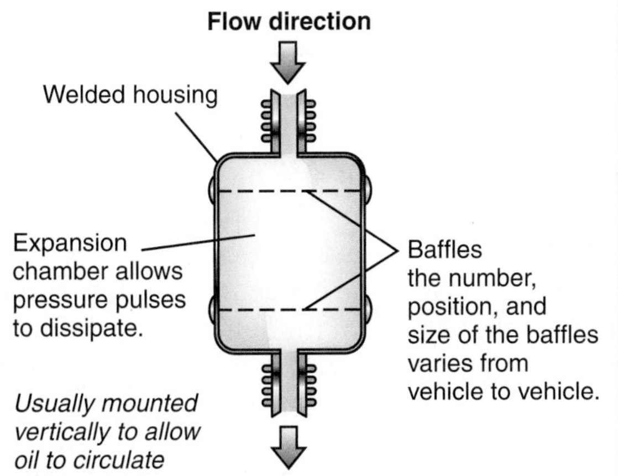

Flow direction
Welded housing
Expansion chamber allows pressure pulses to dissipate.
Baffles the number, position, and size of the baffles varies from vehicle to vehicle.
Usually mounted vertically to allow oil to circulate

FIGURE 35-16 The muffler is constructed of a hollow cylinder with baffling.

> **TECHNICIAN TIP**
>
> Performance testing of the air-conditioning system must be done before and after the repair. Doing so will help ensure that you identify any faults before starting the repairs, as well as verify that the faults are completely repaired.

Abnormal Noises

The compressor is the most common source of abnormal noises arising from the air conditioner. If the compressor fails internally, it may make a knocking noise. Restrictions are another cause of odd noises. Restrictions rattle the air-conditioning pipes, especially if the restriction comes and goes. While performance testing the system, abnormal noises can occur while the air-conditioning system is operating. Listen for noises that may occur when the compressor clutch is engaged. If the noise disappears when the compressor clutch

> **Applied Math**
>
> ***AM-33: Temperature: The technician can use standard and metric temperature measurement instruments to measure system temperature and determine conformance to metric specifications.***
>
> The most common air conditioning concern encountered in the workshop environment is the air-conditioning system failing to effectively cool the cabin of the vehicle. Technicians need to determine whether the system is operating effectively before proceeding with diagnosis. This is determined by measuring the vent temperature as the air enters the vehicle cabin.
>
> This test involves a thermometer being inserted into the air vents and the temperature being measured with the air-conditioning controls being set to cold and the fan set to its highest speed (the remainder of this test procedure is outlined in the Performance Testing section of the text).
>
> Once the vent temperature is measured, it must be compared to the manufacturer's specifications to determine if the system is operating effectively. If specifications are published in metric units, either a metric thermometer should be used or readings must be converted from Fahrenheit to Centigrade to determine if the measured temperature conforms to specifications.

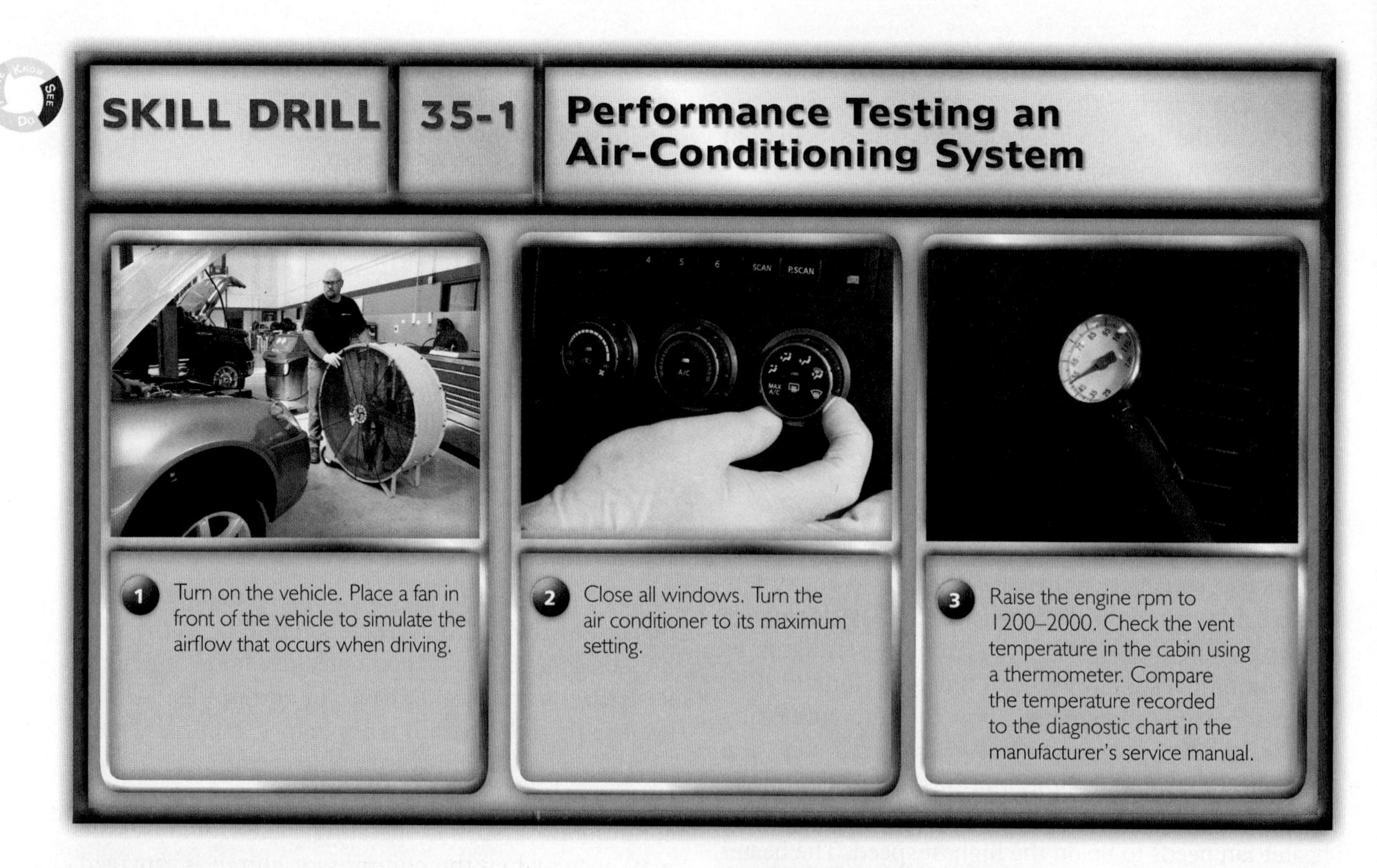
SKILL DRILL 35-1 Performance Testing an Air-Conditioning System
1 Turn on the vehicle. Place a fan in front of the vehicle to simulate the airflow that occurs when driving.
2 Close all windows. Turn the air conditioner to its maximum setting.
3 Raise the engine rpm to 1200–2000. Check the vent temperature in the cabin using a thermometer. Compare the temperature recorded to the diagnostic chart in the manufacturer's service manual.

TECHNICIAN TIP

As a general rule, the duct temperature should be no greater than 17°F above the evaporator temperature. The optimum vent temperature is from 38°F to 48°F. The air-conditioning clutch cycle should not allow the duct temperature to have greater than a 5° swing from high to low while staying within the range of 38°F to 48°F. If the swing is out of the 5° range, the thermal switch or the pressure cycle switch may need to be replaced, if equipped.

TECHNICIAN TIP

There are factory adjustments on both the thermal cycle switch and the pressure cycle switch. The adjustments are for achieving optimum performance at the factory. Trying to adjust either of the switches because of an incorrect temperature swing may mask the faulty switch for a short time. If these switches are incorrectly functioning, replacement is the proper and recommended procedure for the repair.

disengages, then the noise is from the air-conditioning system. Be sure to listen for noises under the hood as well as in the vehicle's passenger compartment. Turn off and on the compressor clutch and move the controls on the dash, listening to determine whether the noises appear and disappear.

Inspecting the Condenser for Airflow Restrictions

The condenser is normally inspected when high-side pressures are too high and the system is not cooling well. Road debris, leaves, and animal fur and feathers are common culprits, but anything that sits in front of the condenser can cause this issue. This inspection should also be performed with any air-conditioning tune-up or inspection, such as those offered by many shops before summer. Use a flashlight on the back of the condenser. Look in from the outside of the vehicle for the light coming through the condenser. Move the light across the entire condenser. If the light is not showing, the condenser needs to be cleaned.

When cleaning the condenser for debris, shop air or a water hose may be used to remove the debris, but be careful to not fold over the fins. If the shop air and a water hose do not remove the restriction, the condenser must be removed and professionally cleaned.

Inspecting the Evaporator Housing Water Drain

As the air-conditioning system is running, the evaporator will sweat water throughout the day. The water collected needs to be drained from the evaporator housing. A drain hose is connected to the evaporator housing and exits through the vehicle's firewall. Checking that the drain is not plugged is a common diagnostic procedure.

To inspect the evaporator housing water drain, follow the steps in SKILL DRILL 35-2:

1. Determine that the drain tube is clogged by allowing the air-conditioning system to run while observing the drain tube for water drops. In the case of a plugged drain, no water or very few drops are found.
2. Carefully use low-pressure shop air and an air nozzle to blow air into the drain tube. Note that water will come out of the drain tube when the clog is removed and will result in a large discharge of malodorous water; stand back.
3. When the water has completely drained, the task has been performed. Advise the customer to periodically check for a water puddle under the vehicle; if one is not present, the clog may have reoccurred, and removal of the air box may be necessary to open the air box and clean out any remaining debris.

Cabin Air Filter

Many vehicles now include a cabin air filter in the HVAC system to filter the air before it enters the system. The filter is housed in the air box and can be accessed from one of a variety of positions, depending on the vehicle. The access may be from under the hood near the firewall, under the windshield, or behind the glove box. It is usually fairly easy to remove and replace once you find the access cover. This filter should be inspected during every service and replaced according to the manufacturer's specified interval, typically once a year or every 12,000 to 15,000 miles (19,000 to 24,000 kilometers [km]). When inspecting the cabin air filter, use the same guidelines as for an engine air filter. Hold it up to a light and look at it to see if the light shines through or if it is blocked from being dirty. Also check it for any cracks, tears, or deformities that would cause it to be ineffective.

Inspecting and Replacing a Drive Belt

Inspecting the drive belt of the compressor is an important part of air-conditioning maintenance and repair. If the belt is worn, the engine cannot drive the compressor properly. On hot days, the refrigerant pressures are high and the compressor needs an effective drive belt to prevent slipping and causing excessive heat buildup around the clutch. The air-conditioning system requires that the compressor move the refrigerant at the correct velocity for the cooling of the passenger compartment to be at its peak efficiency. The drive belt is the first link in the system and needs to be in good condition and proper tension to ensure efficient air conditioning.

Inspecting and Testing the Heater Control Valves

The heater control valves should be tested if the customer complains of no heat or poor air conditioning. The heater control valve, if equipped, regulates coolant flow to the heater core for heat and limits flow for air conditioning. Some are vacuum controlled and some are cable controlled. Cable-controlled models must be checked to ensure that the cable is free and working. Vacuum-controlled models should be checked to ensure that the vacuum is supplied to the valve at the right time and that the valve will hold vacuum. If there is a problem with cable or vacuum operation, then the control head in the dash will probably have to be removed, inspected, and repaired. If the cable or vacuum is working, then the operation of the valve should be checked. Have someone move the temperature lever from hot to cold while watching the valve. If the cable or vacuum servo is moving the control arm on the valve, then the valve is probably okay and the problem is elsewhere in the system, although the valve could be plugged or slipping on the shaft. Therefore, you may have to remove it from the heater hose and visually inspect that the valve opens and closes.

Inspecting and Testing HVAC Control Cables

Inspecting and testing system control cables and linkages usually will be needed only when the air conditioner or heater is not delivering the proper temperature of air or is delivering airflow to a different mode than selected. This will happen when a cable is binding, is broken, or has popped off its linkage at the door or control head. The HVAC control panel will need to be visually inspected and tested, requiring you to gain access to the cables and linkages. Access is different for each vehicle, so research the procedure in the appropriate service information.

To inspect and test the HVAC control cables, follow the steps in SKILL DRILL 35-3.

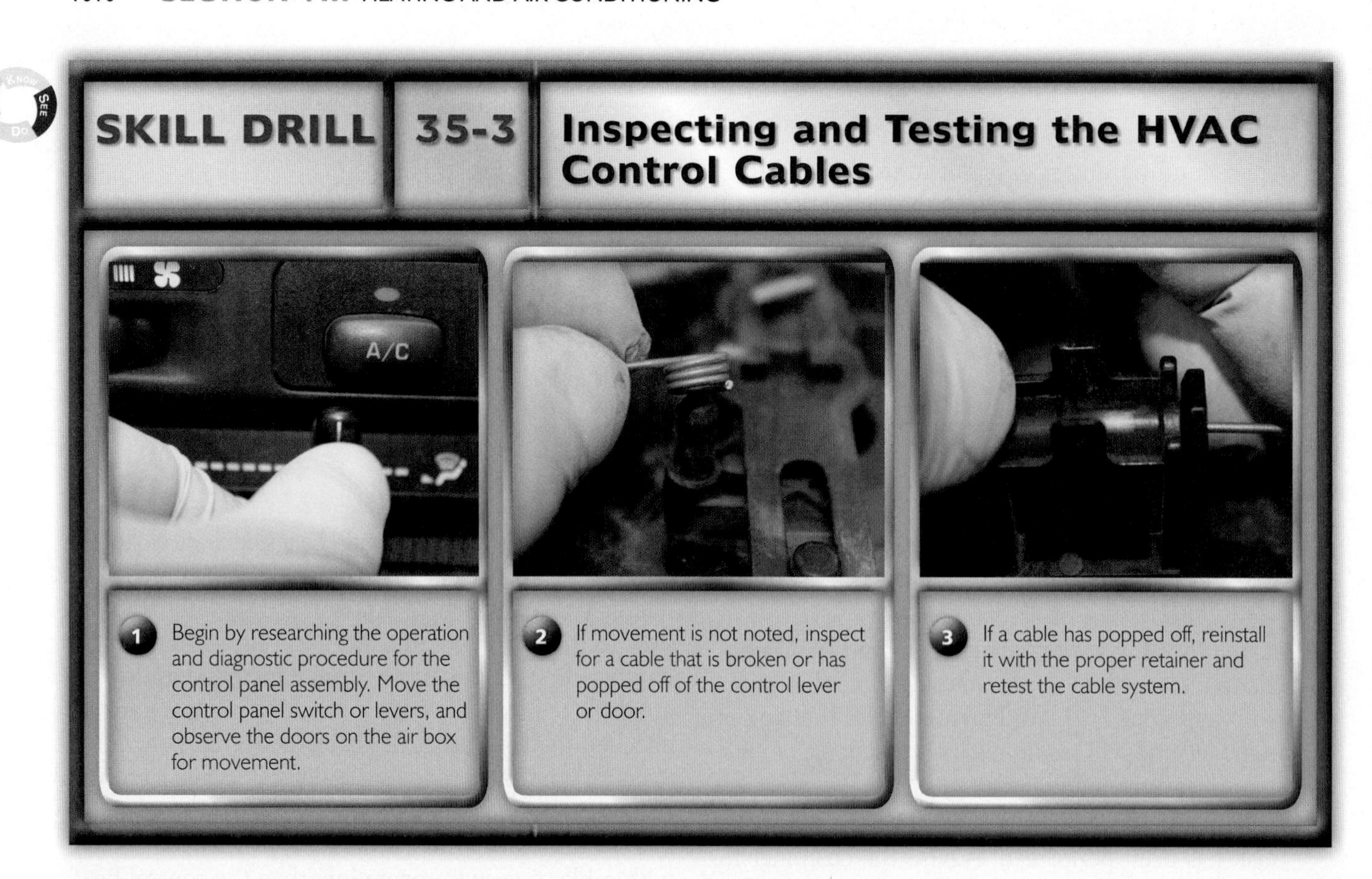
SKILL DRILL 35-3 Inspecting and Testing the HVAC Control Cables
A/C
1 Begin by researching the operation and diagnostic procedure for the control panel assembly. Move the control panel switch or levers, and observe the doors on the air box for movement.
2 If movement is not noted, inspect for a cable that is broken or has popped off of the control lever or door.
3 If a cable has popped off, reinstall it with the proper retainer and retest the cable system.

Inspecting the HVAC System: Heater Ducts, Doors, and Cabin Filters

Because the HVAC system ducts and doors direct airflow to specific areas within the passenger cabin, it is important that they function as shown on the control panel; for instance, if you select floor mode, air should come out at the floor. Inspecting the HVAC system ducts is accomplished by operating the system in all positions and verifying that it is being controlled appropriately. If not, each position on the HVAC control panel will indicate the air door or duct that is affected.

This inspection of the ducts and doors offers a good opportunity to inspect any cabin filters to see if they need to be replaced. In systems where the cabin air filter is in the fresh air intake, you can use an anemometer to check the difference in the speed of the vent airflow with the system in recirculation mode compared to fresh air mode. Any difference indicates a filter restriction. In systems where the cabin air filter filters recirculated air as well, you will need to remove the cabin air filter and hold it up to a light to determine if it needs to be replaced.

To inspect the heater ducts, doors, and cabin filters, follow the steps in SKILL DRILL 35-4.

SKILL DRILL 35-4 Inspecting the Heater Ducts, Doors, and Cabin Filters

1. Start the vehicle and turn the fan switch to the maximum setting.

2. Turn the mode selector through all the positions and make sure the air is distributed through the appropriate vents. Turn the mode selector to dash vents and recirculate.

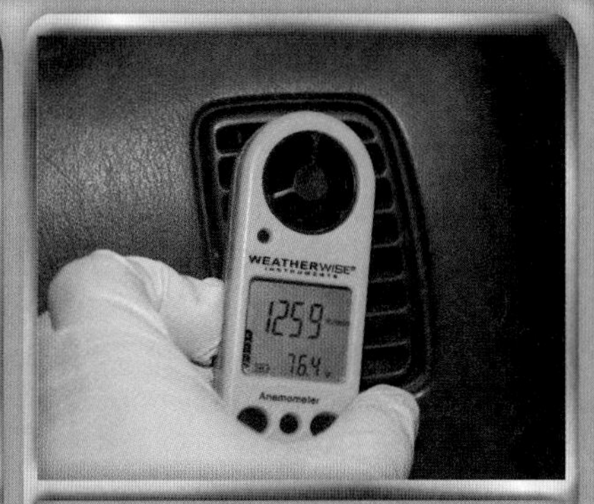
WEATHERWISE
1259
76.4
Anemometer

3. Take an average airflow measurement from all vents (800 fpm minimum average). If no flowmeter is available, test the amount of airflow with your hand or a piece of paper and compare to a similar vehicle.

4. Move the fresh air/recirculate control to the fresh air position and retest the airflow to see if the cabin filter is plugged. Make sure at least one window or door is open to avoid restricting airflow. The airflow should not drop.

5. If the cabin air filter filters all air in the system, remove the cabin air filter and hold it up to a light to see if it is plugged. Replace it if it is restricted or damaged.

Wrap-up

Ready for Review

- The heating, ventilation, and air conditioning (HVAC) system maintains a comfortable temperature inside a vehicle and uses an air filter to provide fresh, filtered air.
- The vehicle heating system and automotive air conditioning system were developed in the 1930s.
- The Environmental Protection Agency regulates automotive air conditioning via Section 609 of the Clean Air Act.
- Automotive HVAC technicians must obtain a license to verify that they are familiar with federal rules and regulations.
- HVAC systems use heat transfer to ensure temperature comfort inside a vehicle.
- Heat transfer can take place via conduction, convection, or radiation.
- A vehicle's air conditioner transforms the refrigerant from a liquid to a gas and back to liquid.
- Heat energy (the amount of heat needed to move a temperature up or down by degrees) is measured in British thermal units (BTUs).
- The temperature at which a liquid changes to gas is called latent heat of evaporation; likewise, the temperature at which a liquid forms a solid (ice) is called latent heat of freezing.
- Vehicle air conditioners use a refrigerant for the vaporization and condensation process.
- HVAC systems have four major components: evaporator, compressor, condenser, and the restriction.
- The compressor is designed to increase the pressure of the refrigerant (in gas form) and push it into the condenser.
- A vehicle's air conditioner is a closed loop system.
- The condenser is designed to move gas through a series of coils and cool it into a liquid.
- The restriction works to transform high pressure liquids into low pressure liquids.
- The evaporator vaporizes liquid into gas as it removes heat energy from the passenger compartment.
- Each HVAC system component requires the refrigerant to be delivered in the proper state and at the correct level.
- Refrigerant moves through the air conditioning system because of the high pressure and volume of gas leaving the compressor.
- The velocity and pressure of the refrigerant changes when it moves through the restriction.
- Bernoulli's principle states that the speed/flow of a liquid changes in opposition to the liquid's pressure (when one increases, the other decreases).
- Pascal's law states that liquid cannot be compressed.
- Automotive air conditioners can be fixed orifice tube systems or thermal expansion valve (TXV) systems.
- Fixed orifice tube systems use an accumulator to prevent liquid from entering the compressor.
- TXV systems use a receiver filter dryer to draw in and store liquid refrigerant.
- Air doors are controlled by cables, vacuum servos, or electric servos.
- Vehicle heating systems rely on a hot engine coolant flowing through a heater core—a small radiator consisting of tubes, fins, and tanks.
- Performance testing of the air-conditioning system is one of the first steps to diagnosis.
- A performance test involves external cooling for the condenser, running the engine between 1200–2000 RPMs, placing the air-conditioning on max cold, placing the fan on high, measuring the duct temperature, and then comparing the duct temperature to a system performance chart from the manufacturer.
- Air-conditioning system inspection should include possible condenser airflow restrictions, evaporator housing water drain, air filter, hoses and belts, coolant pressure, radiator cap vacuum and pressure, cooling fan, fan clutch, fan shroud, air dams, and heater control valves.

Key Terms

accumulator The air-conditioning component used on fixed orifice systems to protect the compressor by storing liquid refrigerant so it does not reach the compressor.

air-conditioning compressor clutch The device which connects and disconnects the drive pulley to the compressor shaft and operated by electro-magnetism.

atmospheric pressure The pressure of the air surrounding everything caused by gravity and the weight of air. The higher from sea level, the lower the atmospheric pressure.

British thermal unit (Btu) A measure of heat energy. It takes 1 Btu to raise the temperature of 1 pound of water 1°F.

chlorofluorocarbon (CFC) A manufactured compound designed to be used as a refrigerant. It is now illegal due to the high chlorine content.

Clean Air Act (CAA) A policy signed into law in 1990 that sets standards for air pollution to eliminate ozone-depleting elements.

closed loop system A totally self-contained system with no materials entering or exiting.

compressor A belt- or electrically driven device designed to increase refrigerant pressure and cause refrigerant to travel through the air-conditioning system.

condensation The changing of a gas into a liquid through cooling.

condenser The air-conditioning component located in the front of the vehicle designed to allow high-pressure refrigerant to change states from gas to liquid.

conduction The process of transferring heat through matter by the movement of heat energy through solids from one particle to another.

convection The process of transferring heat by the circulatory movement that occurs in a gas or fluid as areas of differing temperatures exchange places due to variations in density and the action of gravity.

desiccant A drying agent used in air-conditioning systems to absorb moisture.

dichlorodifluoromethane (R-12) An inert, colorless gas that can be used as a refrigerant. It is stored in white containers.

electric servo An air-conditioning door actuator controlled by electricity.

Environmental Protection Agency (EPA) A government agency concerned with air quality and pollution issues related to the environment.

evaporator The air-conditioning component normally located in the passenger compartment designed to allow low-pressure refrigerant liquid to change states to a gas.

fin A small, flat piece of metal placed between the tubes to help with the transfer of heat from the coolant to the air, refrigerant to air, or air to refrigerant. The metal heats up due to contact with the hot pipes in the case of a radiator or heater core and from hot air in the case of an evaporator.

fixed orifice tube system A system with a fixed orifice tube that uses an accumulator between the evaporator and the compressor.

heat transfer The flow of heat from a hotter part to a cooler part; it can occur in solids, liquids, or gases.

heater core A heat-exchanging device that transfers heat converted by the fuel burning in the engine to the passenger compartment.

latent heat of condensation The amount of heat removal necessary to change the state from a gas to a liquid without changing the actual gauge temperature.

latent heat of evaporation The amount of heat required to change the state from a liquid to a gas without raising the actual gauge temperature.

latent heat of freezing The amount of heat removal required to change the state from a liquid to a solid without changing the actual gauge temperature.

low-pressure cycling switch A device installed on the low-pressure line or the accumulator to turn the air-conditioning clutch on and off at specified pressures.

performance testing The process of recreating a driving situation to check air-conditioning performance and vent temperature.

pulse width modulation A digital on/off electrical signal used as a variable control for devices such as solenoids.

radiation The transfer of heat through the emission of energy in the form of invisible waves.

receiver filter drier (RFD) The air-conditioning component used on TXV systems to filter and store liquid refrigerant to supply liquid refrigerant to the TXV. It is located between the condenser and the TXV.

refrigerant The name given to a chemical compound designed to meet the needs of the refrigeration system.

restriction A blockage that partially stops or slows the flow of a material such as refrigerant.

tanks Metal or plastic pieces that line the pipes used to connect the tubes together to allow the coolant to continue to flow.

tetrafluoroethane (R-134a) An inert colorless gas that can be used as a refrigerant. It is stored in light blue containers.

thermal expansion valve (TXV) system A system with a valve designed to sense evaporator outlet temperature and vary the inlet orifice size accordingly.

tubes Metal pipes running side to side or up and down that the coolant or refrigerant travels through.

vacuum servo An air-conditioning door actuator controlled by a vacuum.

vaporization The changing of a liquid to a gas through boiling.

XH-7 A form of desiccant used with pure R-134a.

XH-9 A form of desiccant used when the refrigerant may not be pure, such as with some imports.

ASE-Type Questions

1. Tech A says that one advantage of an air conditioner is that the system removes water from the air. Tech B says that air conditioners are needed to remove moisture from the inside of the windshield to meet the mandated defrost time. Who is correct?
   a. Tech A
   b. Tech B
   c. Both A and B
   d. Neither A nor B
2. Tech A says that the EPA regulates automotive air-conditioning systems. Tech B says that EPA tests air-conditioning systems every 5 years. Who is correct?
   a. Tech A
   b. Tech B
   c. Both A and B
   d. Neither A nor B
3. Tech A says that an accumulator creates the pressure needed for the air-conditioning system to operate. Tech B says that the high side refers to refrigerant entering the compressor. Who is correct?
   a. Tech A
   b. Tech B
   c. Both A and B
   d. Neither A nor B
4. Tech A says that heat is removed from the passenger compartment by the heater core. Tech B says that heat in the cab is removed through by the refrigerant and is released to the outside air at the condenser. Who is correct?
   a. Tech A
   b. Tech B
   c. Both A and B
   d. Neither A nor B
5. Tech A says that conduction is when heat transfers through solids. Tech B says that radiation is when heat travels through space. Who is correct?
   a. Tech A
   b. Tech B
   c. Both A and B
   d. Neither A nor B
6. Tech A says that the air-conditioning compressor creates high-pressure liquid. Tech B says that the metering device creates a physical change in refrigerant from a liquid to a gas. Who is correct?
   a. Tech A
   b. Tech B
   c. Both A and B
   d. Neither A nor B
7. Tech A says that when an air-conditioning system freezes up, the refrigerant freezes and stops the cooling process. Tech B says that when an air-conditioning unit freezes up, the evaporator coils are covered with frozen water molecules that stop airflow across the coils, thus preventing cooling. Who is correct?
   a. Tech A
   b. Tech B
   c. Both A and B
   d. Neither A nor B
8. Tech A says that the evaporator is on the high side of the system. Tech B says that the condenser transfers heat to the atmosphere. Who is correct?
   a. Tech A
   b. Tech B
   c. Both A and B
   d. Neither A nor B
9. Tech A says that R-134a replaced R-12 as an approved refrigerant. Tech B says that HFO-1234yf refrigerant is flammable. Who is correct?
   a. Tech A
   b. Tech B
   c. Both A and B
   d. Neither A nor B
10. Tech A says that the engine thermostat controls the available coolant temperature for the heater system. Tech B says that the heater core can have engine coolant or refrigerant flowing through it depending on whether heat or cool is commanded. Who is correct?
    a. Tech A
    b. Tech B
    c. Both A and B
    d. Neither A nor B
11. Tech A states that an air-conditioning performance test usually requires that an auxiliary condenser fan be used during the test. Tech B states that a performance test will show if the air-conditioning system is contaminated with sealer. Who is correct?
    a. Tech A
    b. Tech B
    c. Both A and B
    d. Neither A nor B

SECTION IX

Engine Performance

CHAPTER 36

NATEF Tasks

Engine Performance Ignition System			Page
■ Remove and replace spark plugs; inspect secondary ignition components for wear and damage.	 MLR	 AST	1040–1043

Knowledge Objectives

After reading this chapter, you will be able to:

1. Explain the basic principles of a modern ignition system. (pp 1020–1025)
2. Describe the functions of the major components in an ignition system. (pp 1025–1030)
3. Describe the various types of ignition systems. (pp 1030–1037)
4. Explain the process involved in diagnosing ignition system issues. (p 1037)
5. Safely perform the NATEF tasks related to ignition systems. (pp 1037–1043)
6. List the steps involved in maintaining and repairing ignition system components. (pp 1040–1043)

Ignition Systems Overview

Know
See
Do
Prove

Skills Objectives

After reading this chapter, you will be able to:

1. Perform a spark test. (pp 1037–1038)
2. Inspect secondary circuits. (pp 1038–1039)
3. Test the ignition coil. (pp 1038–1040)
4. Test a spark plug wire. (pp 1039–1041)
5. Inspect a distributor cap and rotor. (pp 1039–1041)
6. Replace the spark plugs and spark plug wires. (pp 1042–1043)

Introduction

The air–fuel mixture inside each cylinder must be ignited for it to release its energy and create pressure to force the piston down the cylinder on the power stroke. Gasoline engines use the heat of a **high-voltage spark** to ignite the mixture. The purpose of the ignition system is to create the high-voltage spark and deliver it at the right time to each cylinder.

The ignition system consists of a primary (low-voltage) circuit and a secondary (high-voltage) circuit. The primary circuit connects and disconnects the ignition coil, which changes the low voltage of the vehicle battery into the high voltage needed to create the spark that is sent across the spark plug electrodes. The secondary circuit distributes the high voltage from the coil, or coils, to the spark plug at each cylinder. Although there are several types of ignition systems, the common components include the spark plugs, the ignition coil, and a device for triggering the ignition coil.

For an engine to run smoothly and efficiently, the high-voltage spark must jump across the spark plug electrode as the piston approaches top dead center of the **compression stroke**. The ignition system must also be able to advance or retard the timing of the spark, based on engine conditions such as load, speed, and driver input. This chapter explains the principles and operation of modern ignition systems and covers basic diagnosis, maintenance, and repair.

Ignition Principles

When the driver turns the key to the start position (or presses the electronic start button), an electrical connection is made between the vehicle battery and the primary winding of the ignition coil. As the engine is cranked, a switching circuit turns the primary ignition coil circuit on and off. The coil's function is to amplify the battery's low voltage and high current into very high voltage and low current. This high voltage is delivered from the ignition coil to each cylinder, where the spark plugs are installed **FIGURE 36-1**. As the high

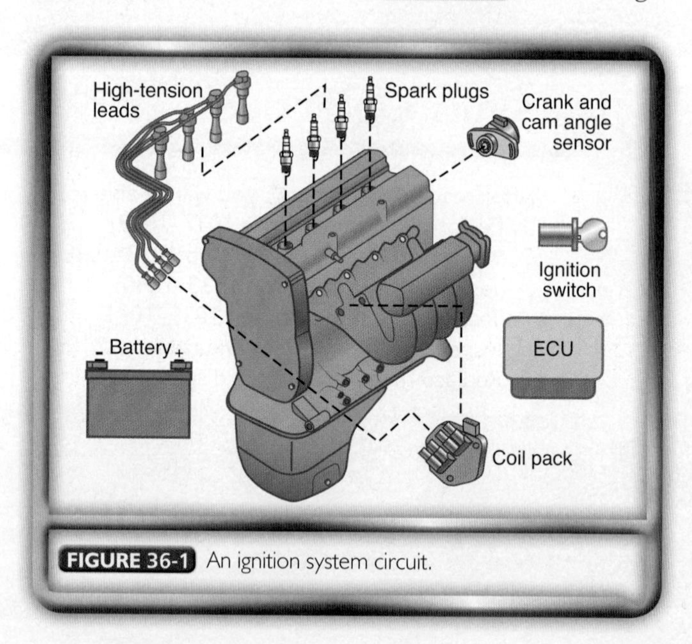
High-tension leads
Spark plugs
Crank and cam angle sensor
Ignition switch
Battery
ECU
Coil pack

FIGURE 36-1 An ignition system circuit.

You Are the Automotive Technician

Today a customer visits your shop for a scheduled 60,000 mile service on her 2009 vehicle. The service information says to replace the spark plugs and inspect the secondary ignition system, consisting of the ignition coils and spark plug boots. When you twist the spark plug boots to pull them off of the plugs, several of the boots tear, requiring replacement. After the boots are off, you use compressed air (while wearing safety glasses) to blow out any debris from around the spark plugs. You remove the plugs one at a time and inspect them. The deposits are light and show that they are burning correctly—not too hot nor too cold. The gaps are worn as expected. You inspect the ignition coils. The terminals and insulation look good, and you will be replacing all of the boots.

1. How would you prevent the boots from sticking to the spark plugs the next time?
2. How would you test to see if the ignition system was working on a vehicle that cranked but didn't start?
3. If this customer drove only short trips of a mile or two, would you recommend a spark plug with a hotter heat range or colder heat range? If so, why?

Applied Science

AS-76: Coil: The technician can explain how a coil can increase the battery voltage needed to fire a spark plug.

An ignition coil is a step-up transformer, increasing the vehicle's battery voltage to a high voltage necessary to fire the spark plugs and ignite the air–fuel mixture in the cylinders. Coils operate via the concept of electromagnetic induction, which dictates that a moving magnetic field (or a change in a stationery magnetic field in the case of an ignition coil) can induce a current in a wire exposed to the field.

The internal makeup of a coil is basically an iron core with two windings of wire, both wound around the core. The secondary winding is wound with considerably more turns than the primary, typically at a ratio of about 100:1.

In operation, battery voltage is applied to the primary winding, creating a magnetic field. This process is called saturation. The secondary winding is exposed to this field. To create a spark, the primary circuit is interrupted, or turned off, by a power train control module, ignition module, or breaker points. This interruption causes the magnetic field to collapse and a high voltage to be induced into the secondary winding. The increase in voltage is provided by the difference in the number of turns between the windings. Current in the secondary winding is directed to the spark plugs.

voltage pushes current across the spark plug electrodes, the air–fuel mixture is ignited, causing very high pressure, which in turn pushes the piston down on the power stroke.

The ignition system has undergone changes in technology over the decades to meet requirements for dependability, reduced maintenance expectations, and increasingly strict emission standards. The original system was the **contact breaker point ignition system**—a mechanical system with a switch, called **contact breaker points**, that was opened and closed as the engine was running FIGURE 36-2. The points turned the primary ignition circuit on and off, which created a spark that was distributed to each spark plug in the firing order.

The first advancement was the replacement of the mechanical switch with an electronic switching device FIGURE 36-3. This device lacked moving components, meaning minimal wear on the switching device and very little, if any, maintenance. The device was called an **electronic ignition system—distributor type**, since it still used a distributor to dispense the spark to the various cylinders.

The next advancement was eliminating the distributor by using dedicated ignition coils—one coil for each pair of cylinders. This was called a **waste spark ignition system** FIGURE 36-4. A four-cylinder engine would have two ignition coils, a six-cylinder engine would have three coils, and so on. Eliminating the distributor meant doing away with the last mechanical component of the ignition system, which again resulted in increased reliability and reduced maintenance issues.

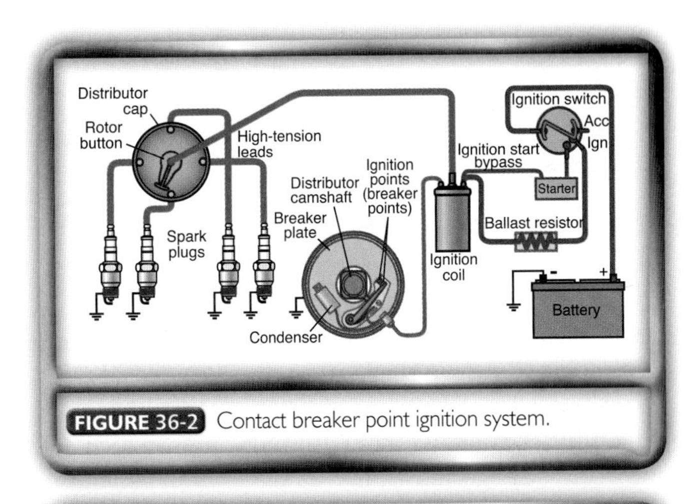
Distributor cap
Rotor button
High-tension leads
Ignition points (breaker points)
Distributor camshaft
Breaker plate
Spark plugs
Condenser
Ignition switch
Acc
Ign
Ignition start bypass
Starter
Ballast resistor
Ignition coil
Battery

FIGURE 36-2 Contact breaker point ignition system.

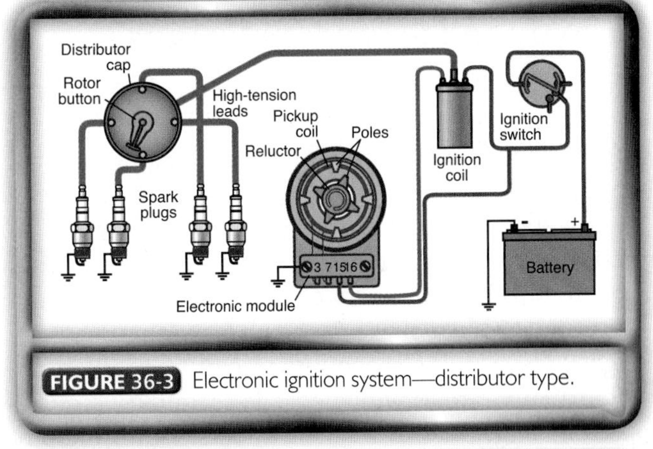
Distributor cap
Rotor button
High-tension leads
Pickup coil
Poles
Reluctor
Spark plugs
Electronic module
Ignition coil
Ignition switch
Battery

FIGURE 36-3 Electronic ignition system—distributor type.

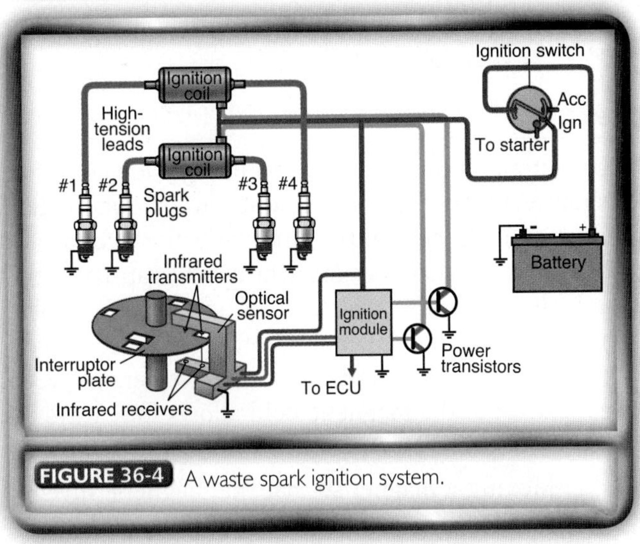
Ignition coil
High-tension leads
Ignition coil
#1
#2
Spark plugs
#3
#4
Infrared transmitters
Optical sensor
Interruptor plate
Infrared receivers
Ignition module
To ECU
Power transistors
Ignition switch
Acc
Ign
To starter
Battery

FIGURE 36-4 A waste spark ignition system.

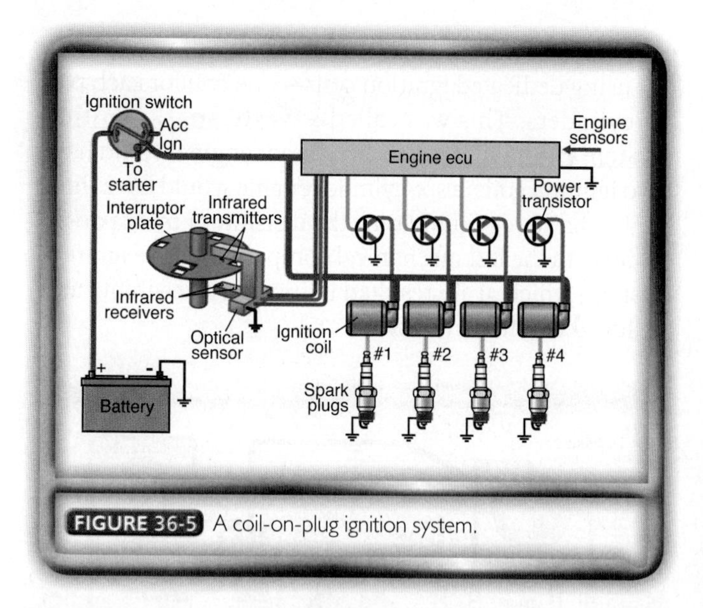

Ignition switch
Acc
Ign
To starter
Engine sensors
Engine ecu
Power transistor
Interruptor plate
Infrared transmitters
Infrared receivers
Optical sensor
Ignition coil
#1
#2
#3
#4
Spark plugs
Battery

FIGURE 36-5 A coil-on-plug ignition system.

The latest development has been to give each cylinder its own ignition coil. This is called a **direct ignition system** or **coil-on-plug** ignition system FIGURE 36-5. This system puts the ignition coil directly on top of the spark plug, thus eliminating the spark plug wires, which are subject to damage and wear.

Primary and Secondary Circuits

The ignition system uses an **induction coil** to convert relatively low-voltage and high-current flow into very high-voltage and very low-current flow. The low-voltage side is called the **primary circuit**, and the high-voltage side is called the **secondary circuit**. The battery supplies the low-voltage and high-current flow to power the primary circuit. The induction coil steps up the low voltage in the primary circuit to the high voltage in the secondary circuit. A problem in the primary circuit will affect the secondary circuit, so technicians need a complete understanding of both circuits when diagnosing faults relating to the ignition system TABLE 36-1.

TABLE 36-1: Primary and Secondary Circuit Components

Contact Breaker System	
Primary Circuit Components	**Secondary Circuit Components**
Battery	Ignition coil—secondary winding
Ignition switch	Coil wire
Ballast resistor	Distributor cap
Ignition coil—primary winding	Rotor
Capacitor	Spark plug wires
Contact breaker points	Spark plugs
Electronic Ignition—Distributor-Style System	
Primary Circuit Components	**Secondary Circuit Components**
Battery	Ignition coil—secondary winding
Ignition switch	Coil wire
Ignition coil—primary winding	Distributor cap
Ignition module	Rotor
Triggering device	Spark plug wires
	Spark plugs
Electronic Ignition—Distributorless-Style System	
Primary Circuit Components	**Secondary Circuit Components**
Battery	Ignition coils—secondary windings
Ignition switch	Spark plug wires
Ignition coils—primary windings	Spark plugs
Ignition module	
Triggering device	
Direct Ignition System	
Primary Circuit Components	**Secondary Circuit Components**
Battery	Ignition coils—secondary windings
Ignition switch	Spark plugs
Ignition coils—primary windings	
Ignition module	
Triggering device	

Faraday's Law

Most automotive ignition systems use ignition coils that operate on the principles of an induction coil. Automotive induction coils step up the nominal battery voltage of 12 volts to the voltage needed to bridge the gap across the spark plug electrodes, which can be up to 100,000 volts. These induction coils operate according to Faraday's law.

Faraday's law states that relative movement between a conductor and a magnetic field allows four ways by which voltage can be induced in a conductor:

1. Moving a magnet so that the magnetic lines of force cut across a conductor, as in an alternator.
2. Moving a conductor so that it cuts across the stationary magnetic field, as in a generator.
3. Starting, stopping, or changing the rate of current flow in a conductor. This causes the conductor

to induce an electromagnetic field into itself and occurs in the primary windings of an ignition coil. This process is called self-induction.

4. Starting, stopping, or changing the rate of current flow in a conductor that is positioned close to a second conductor. This is called mutual induction. It is used to induce high voltage in the secondary winding of the ignition coil.

When any of these methods are used to induce voltage in a conductor, the value of that voltage depends on the density, or strength, of the magnetic field. The stronger the field, the greater the **induced voltage**. It is also influenced by the number of turns of the coil. The more turns, the greater the induced voltage. The speed at which the lines of force are cut also affects the voltage induced. The greater the speed, the greater the induced voltage. In the induction coil, the secondary winding has many thousands of turns of fine enameled copper wire. The primary winding, with a few hundred turns of relatively heavy wire, is positioned close to the secondary winding. A soft iron core is positioned centrally to concentrate the magnetic field. Current flow through the primary winding establishes a magnetic field around the windings. The higher the current flow, the stronger the field.

Sudden interruption of the primary current effectively disconnects the battery from the coil and current flow ceases. As a result, there is no externally applied voltage source to dictate the voltage value across the ends of the primary winding. The magnetic field collapses into the iron core, returning its stored energy to the coil by cutting across the coil's primary and secondary windings. This produces a self-induced voltage in the primary winding and a mutually induced voltage in the secondary winding.

The maximum value of the secondary voltage is partly determined by the ratio of the number of turns in the secondary winding to the number of turns in the primary winding (in this case, approximately 100 to 1) and by the value of the self-induced voltage in the primary winding (in this case, 300 volts). If this coil is 100% efficient, the maximum voltage available from the secondary winding would be 300 volts multiplied by 100, or 30,000 volts.

Since the value of the self-induced voltage in the primary winding is also influenced by the rate of collapse of the magnetic field, which is determined by the rate of change of the current flow through the coil, it is essential that the primary current be switched off as quickly as possible. All ignition systems make provisions to ensure that this occurs. This subject will be covered in greater detail later in this chapter.

Required Voltage Versus Available Voltage

Understanding the terms "required voltage" and "available voltage" will help you diagnose ignition systems. **Required voltage** is the amount of voltage required to initially get current to jump the spark plug gap. When the voltage reaches the point where current is flowing in the secondary circuit, the required voltage drops to a much lower level, just sufficient enough to sustain current flow and the spark. This gives the air–fuel mixture the opportunity to ignite during the duration of the spark.

The other factor is available voltage. **Available voltage** is the maximum amount of voltage available to try to push current to jump the spark plug gap if the gap were infinite. In other words, available voltage is the maximum amount of voltage that the ignition coil can put out. It is very important that the available voltage is always higher than the required voltage FIGURE 36-6. If the available voltage falls below required voltage, or if required voltage is ever higher than the available voltage, there will not be enough voltage to push current across the gap and create a spark. Since the spark between the spark plug electrodes is required to ignite the air–fuel mixture, higher required voltage or lower available voltage will prevent the spark from occurring, which causes the cylinder to not fire, which is called a misfire.

As a vehicle is driven over time, generally the required voltage will increase while the available voltage decreases. The required voltage usually increases primarily because

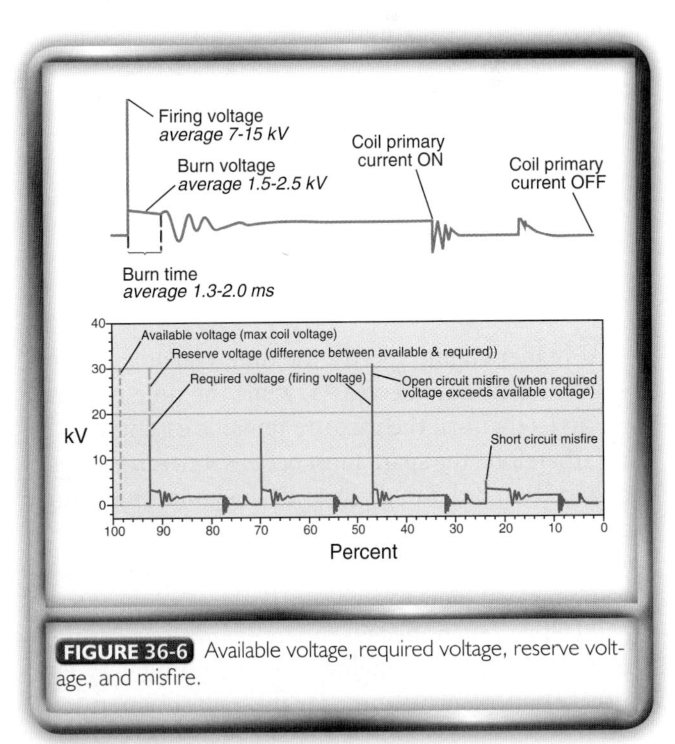

Firing voltage
average 7-15 kV
Burn voltage
average 1.5-2.5 kV
Coil primary
current ON
Coil primary
current OFF
Burn time
average 1.3-2.0 ms
Available voltage (max coil voltage)
Reserve voltage (difference between available & required))
Required voltage (firing voltage)
Open circuit misfire (when required
voltage exceeds available voltage)
Short circuit misfire
kV
40
30
20
10
0
100
90
80
70
60
50
40
30
20
10
0
Percent

FIGURE 36-6 Available voltage, required voltage, reserve voltage, and misfire.

of the growing gap of the spark plug as it wears over time. However, it can also increase due to any open circuits in the secondary side of the circuit, such as a broken rotor tip or an open spark plug wire. Manufacturers design their ignition systems to have an amount of reserve voltage above the required voltage so that misfire is prevented. But if the vehicle's ignition system is not maintained, this reserve voltage is reduced and the engine is prone to misfire, especially when accelerating or climbing a hill. Inspecting all of the components and replacing any that are worn will restore the available voltage to what it should be and reduce the required voltage to within specifications. This will restore the ignition system to its proper operation.

> **TECHNICIAN TIP**
>
> Required voltage is increased by spark plug gaps that are too wide or worn, compression pressures that are higher than normal, or lean mixtures. Available voltage is affected by faults in the primary or secondary circuits such as shorted coil windings or high resistance in the primary circuit.

Spark Timing

The timing of the spark is critical to the smooth and efficient operation of the engine. For any given engine speed and load, the correct **spark timing** varies according to a number of factors, including:

- Air–fuel ratio
- Detected knock
- Engine speed
- Engine load
- Engine temperature
- Air temperature
- Transmission gear selected
- Throttle position

At higher engine speeds, the time available to burn the air–fuel mixture decreases, while the time required to completely burn the mixture remains essentially the same; therefore, the spark must occur sooner in the cycle (advanced) in order to give the air–fuel mixture enough time to burn and create maximum cylinder pressure soon after top dead center. As the throttle is opened and the engine load increases, the spark does not need to be advanced as much, because there is more pressure in the cylinders and the engine is not spinning very fast; thus, there is plenty of time for the air–fuel mixture to burn. However, as the engine's revolutions per minute (rpm) continue to increase, especially under a light load, the timing must be advanced significantly. If the timing is advanced too far, then the engine begins to knock. If it is equipped with a knock sensor located on the engine block, the sensor sends a signal to the **power train control module (PCM)**. The PCM may also be called an **engine control module (ECM)** or an **electronic control unit (ECU)**. The PCM then retards the timing to decrease or eliminate the knock. At lower engine temperatures, the fuel does not atomize as quickly and requires the spark to be advanced.

In early vehicles that use a distributor, base spark timing is set at idle speeds by positioning the distributor body in relation to its rotating cam. The timing is almost always indexed to the **number one cylinder**, and the contact breaker points are operated in turn by each cam lobe to provide the same timing point for succeeding cylinders in the firing order. This initial setting, which in most, but not all, cases occurs before top dead center, allows time for maximum pressure in the cylinder to develop, just as the piston is descending on the power stroke.

Today's vehicles use electronically triggered ignition systems. The timing is engineered into the design of the engine and is not adjustable. The timing components are fixed in position within the distributor (if used) or on the engine block and crankshaft or flywheel **FIGURE 36-7**. The initial timing specification is programmed into the PCM software.

As engine speed increases, there is increasingly less time for the air–fuel mixture to be ignited and for this maximum pressure to develop; therefore, the ignition point must be advanced. That is, it must start earlier in

FIGURE 36-7 A crankshaft position sensor.

relation to the piston's position during the compression stroke. This adjustment must occur automatically in relation to engine speed and engine load.

Older vehicles with nonelectronically controlled spark timing and early electronic ignition systems use mechanical means to adjust spark timing according to engine rpm and load. To advance the timing in response to rpm, a centrifugal type of **advance mechanism** is used, called a mechanical advance. This device is located either above or below the distributor base plate and rotates with the distributor shaft. As engine speed rises, the flyweights on the advance mechanism are thrown outward by centrifugal force. Since the distributor cam is able to pivot on the distributor shaft a limited number of degrees, the weights act against their springs and move the distributor cam forward, advancing the timing.

The load-sensitive advance mechanism, called the **vacuum advance unit**, is operated by **intake manifold vacuum** via a port on the **throttle body** FIGURE 36-8. It acts to adjust the timing based on engine vacuum, which changes as engine load changes. The port is connected by a vacuum line to a sealed chamber on one side of a spring-loaded diaphragm. A mechanical link on the other side connects the diaphragm to the **distributor base plate**, also called the **breaker plate**. The distributor base plate is a moveable metal plate located in the distributor, beneath the distributor cap on which the contact breaker points are mounted. As vacuum is applied, the diaphragm moves against the spring to rotate the base plate, and since the base plate carries the contact breaker points, the contacts meet the distributor cam earlier in rotation, advancing the spark.

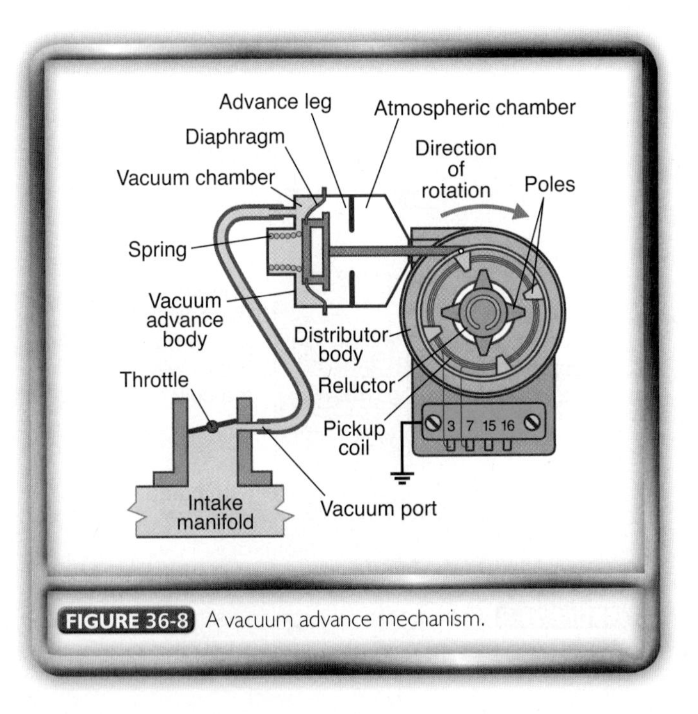
Advance leg
Atmospheric chamber
Diaphragm
Direction of rotation
Vacuum chamber
Poles
Spring
Vacuum advance body
Distributor body
Throttle
Reluctor
Pickup coil
3 7 15 16
Intake manifold
Vacuum port

FIGURE 36-8 A vacuum advance mechanism.

Today's vehicles all use the PCM to control spark timing. Various sensors, such as the throttle position sensor, mass airflow sensor, rpm signal, and many other engine sensors, send input to the PCM. The ideal spark timing for all engine conditions is programmed into the PCM using software. The PCM then calculates the timing and controls the ignition coils either directly or through a driver located on the coil.

Standard Components of an Ignition System

Most ignition systems include a battery, ignition switch, ignition coil(s), high-tension leads (also called spark plug wires), and spark plugs. The battery is the same one used to start the vehicle and provide electrical power to all electrical loads when the engine is not running. The ignition switch is used to connect the ignition system to the battery during operation and disconnect it from the battery to turn the engine off. The ignition coil is needed to amplify the battery voltage into very high voltage.

The high-tension leads connect the coil to the distributor cap center terminal and the distributor cap side terminals to the terminals on the top of the spark plugs. On distributorless and coil-on-plug systems, the high-tension lead connects directly from the coil to the spark plug. Coil-on-plug systems have no high-tension leads at all. The spark plugs are threaded into the top of each cylinder and provide a place for the spark to jump within the combustion chamber.

Battery

An automotive battery is a chemical-electrical device that provides voltage to all electrical loads while the engine is not running, and when the loads exceed the output of the alternator. The **battery** supplies the electrical energy to the ignition circuit during start-up. Most modern vehicles use a 12-volt lead acid rechargeable battery located in the engine compartment, in the trunk, or under the rear seats. Once the engine is started, the alternator provides power for all electrical loads by charging the battery.

Ignition Switch

The **ignition switch** has more functions than simply starting and stopping the engine. It provides a way to disconnect most electrical accessories from the battery with an ignition key. The common position of an ignition switch include:

- Lock and off: The key can only be removed from the lock position. When this occurs, all nonessential electrical circuits are disabled and the steering column lock is enabled. If equipped, the engine immobilizer and theft-deterrent system are normally activated at this time. Many modern vehicles also include an off ignition point. Turning the key from the lock to the off position unlocks the steering column, but it does not enable any electrical systems or disable the engine immobilizer or theft-deterrent system.

- Accessory: This position allows power to be supplied to the vehicle entertainment system, the blower fan, and in some vehicles the wipers, electric windows, and sunroof. The features enabled by the accessory position are mainly for passenger convenience. Prolonged use of any of them without the engine running will drain the battery.
- On/run: When the switch is turned to the on position, most warning lamps on the instrument panel should illuminate. This is to test the operation of the lamps. On vehicles that are not equipped with engine immobilizers, this position also activates the accessories and ignition system. Vehicles that are equipped with engine immobilizers do not normally activate these systems until the key is turned to the start position.
- Start/crank: The start position activates the starter motor relay and/or solenoid, which enables the engine to crank and start the engine. Vehicles without engine immobilizers can start immediately, as the required electrical systems will have already been activated when the key was turned to the on position. In vehicles equipped with engine immobilizers, a number of the essential electrical systems are not normally enabled until the key is turned to the start position. When this occurs, communication between various control units determines whether to allow the engine to start or not. Starting is achieved by deactivating the immobilizer and activating the ignition, fuel, and charging systems. There may be a slight delay while this communication is occurring.

The key itself can consist of two parts. The first is a mechanical type that works in the key barrel and turns to unlock the steering column and switch through the various stages of off, accessories, on, and start. Many modern vehicles now come equipped with an immobilizer system that disables the ignition, fuel, and starter systems unless a transponder device with the correct code is within close range of a receiver in the vehicle. The immobilizer system uses a randomly selected **rolling code**—a constantly changing, numeric code that is communicated with the engine immobilizer and security system by a radio frequency signal. The frequency transmitter is usually located in the key assembly itself and is usually powered by magnetic induction through a winding around the key barrel. The receiver is often also found in the steering column, near the key barrel. If the correct code is not recognized, or if someone attempts to start the vehicle by some other means, the system will remain armed and prevent the vehicle from starting. In some vehicles, the starting system may be disabled in place of, or in addition to, the fuel and ignition systems.

In many automatic transmission vehicles, the ignition switch also has a transmission shift interlock device connected to it. In these vehicles, the gear selector must be moved into the park position before the key can be removed from the lock position. In the same way, the transmission shift lever cannot be moved out of park until the key has been turned to the on/run position and the brake pedal has been depressed.

Ignition Coil

Ignition coils are basically **step-up transformers**. Ignition coils are electrical devices that amplify the low voltage available from the vehicle's battery to the very high voltage needed for the current to jump the electrodes of the spark plugs, thereby causing spark FIGURE 36-9. There are two sets of windings in an ignition coil: the **primary winding** and the **secondary winding**.

When battery voltage pushes current through the primary windings of an ignition coil, a magnetic field is created. When the primary circuit is opened, the collapsing magnetic field induces a voltage of more than 20,000 volts in the secondary winding. This voltage pushes current through the secondary circuit to the electrodes of the spark plugs, creating the needed spark for the power strokes.

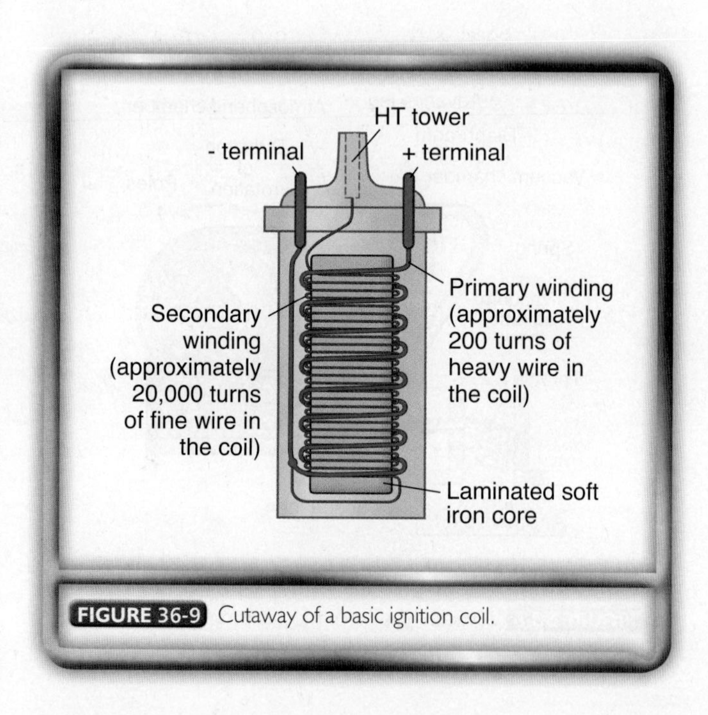
HT tower
- terminal
+ terminal
Primary winding (approximately 200 turns of heavy wire in the coil)
Secondary winding (approximately 20,000 turns of fine wire in the coil)
Laminated soft iron core

FIGURE 36-9 Cutaway of a basic ignition coil.

Applied Science

AS-65: Transformers: The technician can explain the ignition coil transformer's role in generating the high voltage required to fire a spark plug.

The 12-volt battery voltage used in light vehicles is insufficient to jump spark plug gaps. Much higher voltage is needed to fire the plugs and initiate combustion, especially considering the high pressures and turbulent conditions inside the cylinders. Automotive ignition systems are designed to allow a modest battery voltage to generate the very high voltages required to fire the spark plugs.

The ignition coil is a step-up transformer. The function of a transformer is to transfer voltage from one circuit to another, either as a higher voltage (as in this case) or as a lower voltage (referred to as a step-down transformer).

Depending on the ignition system, the 12 volts applied to the coil may be amplified to between 10,000 and 60,000 volts via a process called electromagnetic induction.

A standard ignition coil has a rod-shaped laminated iron core, which is located centrally by an insulator at its base. The secondary winding, with 15,000 to 30,000 turns of very thin **enameled copper wire**, is wound around the core and is insulated from the core by layers of treated insulated paper. The primary winding, with a few hundred turns of much heavier copper wire, is wound on the outside of the secondary. A shield of soft iron surrounds the outer windings, and the complete assembly is inserted into a one-piece steel or aluminum container or encased in an epoxy housing. On older coils, the container is then filled with special oil, which provides good electrical insulation and permits rapid heat dissipation. Epoxy-encased coils are cooled by the surrounding air.

The coil has two terminals, positive and negative, for external connection to the primary circuit. The ends of the primary winding are connected internally to each of these terminals. Provisions are also made externally for a heavy insulated center terminal to connect the high-tension coil leads.

One end of the secondary winding is connected to this center terminal, and the other end is connected either to one end of the primary winding or in some applications to a separate ground. On waste spark systems, each end of the secondary winding is attached to a spark plug with a spark plug wire (two plugs per coil). Coil-on-plug and coil-near-plug systems usually have one end of the secondary winding grounded and the other end connected to the high-tension terminal of the spark plug.

High-Tension Leads

High-tension leads, also known as HT leads or spark plug wires, connect the secondary ignition components together, such as the coil to the distributor cap and the distributor cap to the spark plugs. High voltage from the ignition coil pushes current to the distributor cap and on to the spark plugs along these leads and jumps across the spark plug gap, creating the hot spark needed for combustion. The high-tension leads conduct the high output voltage generated in the secondary ignition circuit when each ignition pulse occurs. They link the **high-tension terminal(s)** of the ignition coil, the distributor cap, and spark plugs.

With the higher voltages that today's electronic ignition systems have to endure because of the increased spark plug gaps and leaner air–fuel mixtures, the insulation material on the high-tension leads is now much thicker than in earlier models. The core of the high-tension lead is typically made of carbon-impregnated linen or fiberglass FIGURE 36-10. It has a specific resistance, or opposition, to current flow that helps reduce the radio frequency interference emitted from the high-tension leads. A crimped terminal at each end provides for connection of the components.

Coil Wire

If a distributor is used, typically a coil wire is used to transmit the high voltage from the ignition coil to the center terminal of the distributor cap. On systems where the coil is mounted inside the distributor, there is no coil wire. The high voltage is transmitted through a terminal in the distributor cap. On systems that do not use a distributor, there is no coil wire. Instead, the high-tension leads connect the terminals of coil packs directly to the terminals of the spark plugs.

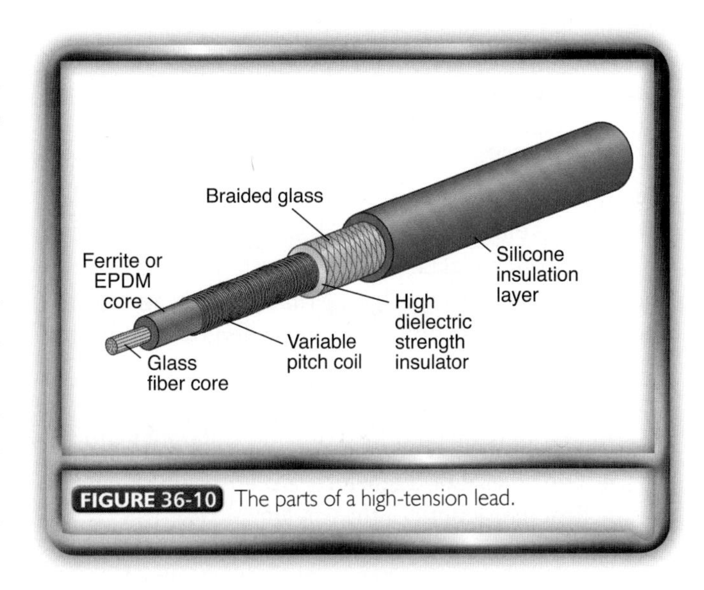
Braided glass
Ferrite or EPDM core
Silicone insulation layer
High dielectric strength insulator
Variable pitch coil
Glass fiber core

FIGURE 36-10 The parts of a high-tension lead.

> **TECHNICIAN TIP**
>
> With the high voltage capacity of today's ignition systems, the quality of the spark plug wires, in particular the insulation, is of utmost importance. As the current is conducted down the leads, a magnetic field around the lead is induced. If the insulation around the cable is insufficient and the leads are not spaced far enough apart and run parallel to each other, then an **induced voltage** can be generated in the other wires. In some instances this could lead to premature firing of the adjacent spark plug when it is not in sequence. Remember that compression pressures increase required voltage, so the cylinder with lower cylinder pressure (the one not near top dead center) is easier to fire than the one that is near top dead center. Severe engine damage can result when the firing order of the engine has two side-by-side cylinders fire one after the other, causing ignition in the following cylinder well before it is up on the compression stroke. Make sure the plug wires are routed and secured according to the manufacturer's specifications.

Spark Plug

The **spark plug** consists of a plated metal shell with a ceramic insulator and an electrode extending through the center of the insulator. Threads on the metal shell allow it to be screwed into the cylinder head. A short side electrode is attached to one side and bent toward the center electrode. The electrodes are made from a special alloy wire with a manufacturer-recommended gap between them. The spark bridges this gap to ignite the air–fuel mixture in the combustion chamber. When the spark jumps from one electrode to the other (usually from the center electrode to the side electrode), it ignites the air–fuel mixture inside the cylinders.

Most modern spark plugs are made of a ceramic heat insulator, partially covered by a steel shell that threads into the cylinder head at the top of the combustion chamber FIGURE 36-11. All spark plugs include at least one side electrode and may have as many as four side electrodes. Spark plugs either use a taper design or a washer type of gasket to form a seal between the spark plug and the cylinder head. Modern spark plugs also include an internal resistor to suppress voltage spikes when the spark plug is energized. The reduced voltage spikes prevent radio frequency interference.

Spark plugs are identified by three different features:

- Thread size or diameter
- Reach or length of the thread
- Heat range or operating temperature

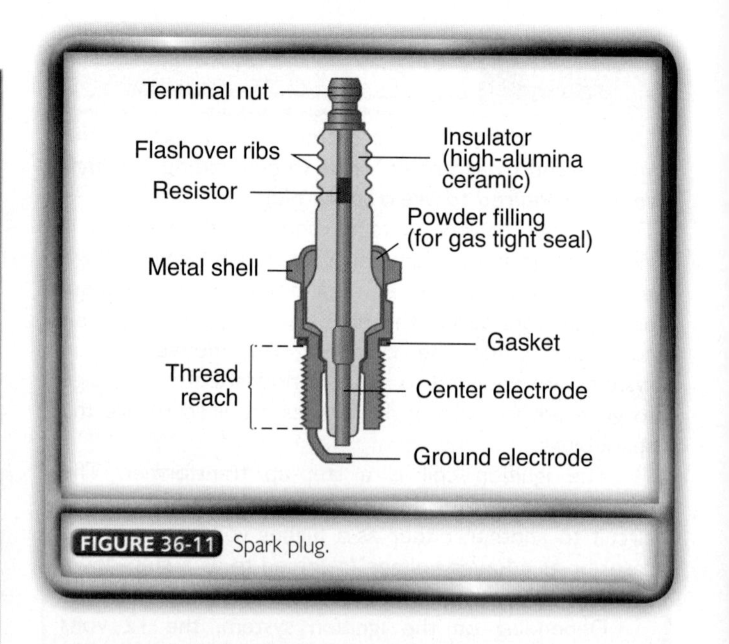
Terminal nut
Flashover ribs
Resistor
Metal shell
Thread reach
Insulator (high-alumina ceramic)
Powder filling (for gas tight seal)
Gasket
Center electrode
Ground electrode

FIGURE 36-11 Spark plug.

Spark Plug Components

The metal case of a spark plug removes heat from the insulator and passes it on to the cylinder head. It also provides structural strength to cope with the torque force applied when tightening the plug into place. The case also acts as the ground for the current passing through the electrodes.

The insulator covering the center electrode is usually made from an aluminum oxide ceramic with a high tolerance to heat and electrical voltage. The ribbing design, the exact composition of the insulator material, and the length of the insulator can all partly determine the heat range of the plug. For example, a spark plug with a shorter path for heat to flow from the center of the spark plug to the coolant flowing through the cylinder head has a cooler heat range. A spark plug with a longer path for heat to flow has a hotter heat range.

The spark plug seals the combustion chamber when installed, and the seals make sure it is kept airtight. The seal can be a hollow metal washer, which at the correct torque setting is partially crushed between the flat surface of the head and the plug just above the threads. Or the seal can be provided by a carefully machined taper on the spark plug body that mates with a matching machined taper in the spark plug hole in the cylinder head.

A terminal at the outer end of the spark plug connects it electrically to the ignition system. Most ignition leads clip on the spark plug. In a few applications, they may be held in place by a threaded nut. The side electrode runs very hot and is usually made of nickel steel or another high-temperature metal and welded to the side of the metal spark plug case. Some spark plug designs have multiple side electrodes that create the gap between the side of the center electrode and the side electrode.

The **center electrode** is the hottest part of the spark plug. Generally it takes less voltage for a spark to jump from a hot surface to a cooler surface, so many older ignition systems were designed to jump from the center electrode to the side electrode. However, with today's high-energy ignition systems, this is no longer a factor. The electrons stream from the sharp edges of the electrodes, and as these edges erode and become less sharp, it becomes more difficult for the electrons to jump the air gap, causing an increase in the required voltage. It used to be necessary to maintain spark plugs by sandblasting built-up deposits from the internal surfaces and filing the electrodes sharp again, but as low-erosion materials such as platinum and iridium have become available, this is not necessary. Spark plugs now usually last a lot longer (up to 100,000 miles [160,000 km]) and are replaced rather than refurbished. Be careful when installing plugs on some waste spark systems, which use polarity sensitive spark plugs that have platinum only on one electrode and therefore need to be installed in the correct spark plug hole. Manufacturer's service information will provide this information.

> **TECHNICIAN TIP**
>
> The same spark plug can sometimes be used in different engines with different gap settings; therefore, the gap should be checked with an accurate spark plug gauge and, if necessary, adjusted according to the specifications in the service information when the spark plug is first installed. The gap is critical to engine performance. A narrow gap may give a spark too weak to ignite the air–fuel mixture effectively. A gap too wide may fail to produce any spark at all. Either way, the wrong gap will reduce engine power and fuel efficiency and will increase emissions. One exception to the gapping rule is iridium spark plugs. The gap should not be adjusted, as the iridium is brittle and can snap off. Verify that their gap meets specifications. If the gap is wrong, they will have to be replaced.

Spark Plug Size

Spark plug size refers to the diameter of the threads of the spark plug. Nearly all of today's light-duty vehicles use either a 14-millimeter (mm) or an 18-mm spark plug, although some manufacturers use 16-mm "high-thread" spark plugs or even 12-mm long-reach spark plugs **FIGURE 36-12**. Most manufacturers have been switching toward smaller plugs to allow for larger or more valves in the cylinder head. Both the Society of Automotive Engineers (SAE) and the International Organization for Standardization (ISO) have a set of standards that cover length, hex size, thread diameter, and thread pitch.

Spark Plug Reach

Spark plug reach is the distance from the seat of the spark plug to the end of the spark plug threads. The purpose of spark plug reach is to ensure that the spark plug electrodes are in the most efficient position for combustion within the cylinder. If the reach is too long, the piston may strike the spark plug while moving up. If the reach is too short, the spark may occur inside of the threaded spark plug hole, resulting in a misfire. Some spark plugs are only threaded on the bottom half or in the case of "high thread" plugs, the top half of their reach. Always install the specified spark plug for the engine you are working on **FIGURE 36-13**.

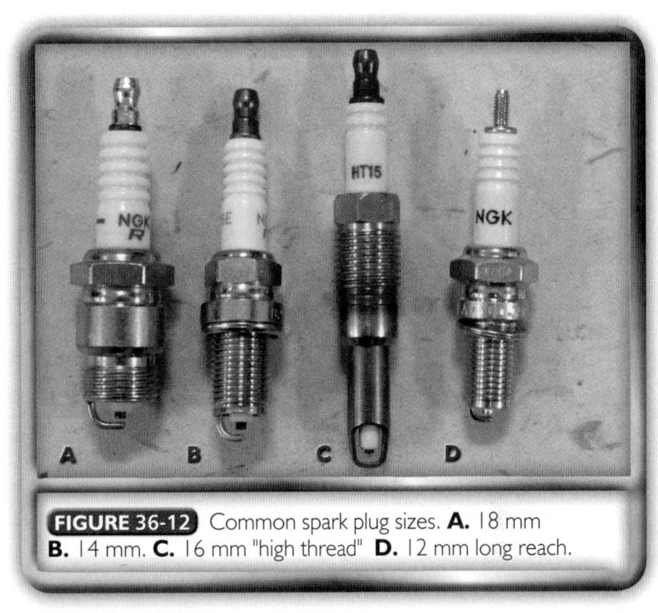
HT15
NGK
A
B
C
D

FIGURE 36-12 Common spark plug sizes. **A.** 18 mm **B.** 14 mm. **C.** 16 mm "high thread" **D.** 12 mm long reach.

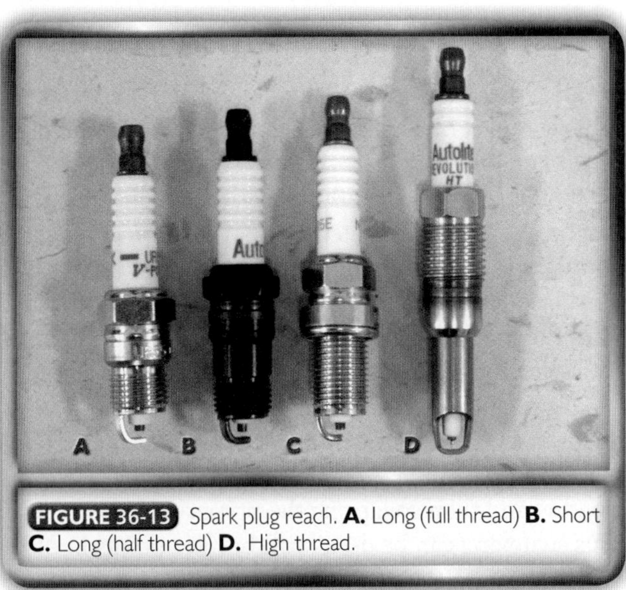
A
B
C
D

FIGURE 36-13 Spark plug reach. **A.** Long (full thread) **B.** Short **C.** Long (half thread) **D.** High thread.

Heat Range

Spark plugs should operate between average temperatures of 746°F and 1460°F, or 400°C and 800°C. This is referred to as the **heat range**. The operating temperature of a spark plug refers to the temperature at the sparking tip of the spark plug inside a running engine. The temperature that a spark plug will reach depends on the distance the heat must travel from the insulator on the firing end to reach the outer shell of the plug and enter the cylinder head and the water jacket. If the heat path is long, the spark plug will retain more heat and therefore will run at a higher temperature than one with a short heat path. If the tip is too hot, pre-ignition can occur.

If it is too cold, deposits may form on the insulator, causing spark energy loss. Hot-rated spark plugs are better insulators, keeping more of the engine heat in the tip of the spark plug. A cold-rated plug conducts more of the heat out of the spark plug tip. The heat range of a spark plug is affected by a wide range of characteristics, including its design profile and the types of material used in its manufacture, as well as the operating conditions of the engine.

TECHNICIAN TIP

Spark plug cooling is affected by spark plug torque. Since almost all of the heat from the spark plug must be transferred through the threads of the spark plug to the cylinder head, properly torquing the spark plugs will keep the threads in contact with the head, allowing heat to transfer more quickly. This allows the plug to operate at its designed temperature, instead of overheating and causing pre-ignition.

Types of Ignition Systems

Several types of ignition systems have been used over the years. Contact breaker point ignition systems were used on earlier vehicles and relied on mechanical devices to create the spark. On later vehicles, the mechanical contact breaker was eliminated, and an electronic means of connecting and disconnecting the primary circuit was used. Modern vehicles no longer use a distributor and send the high voltage from the coil packs or individual coils directly to the spark plugs.

The main difference among these systems is in the way the primary circuits are controlled to produce the secondary spark. The primary circuit is switched on and off, thus creating and then collapsing the primary magnetic field. This switching can be done with breaker points in older vehicles or by electronic switches in modern vehicles.

Contact Breaker Point Ignition Systems

Contact breaker point ignition systems were used on early-model vehicles, providing a mechanical means of quickly connecting and disconnecting the primary side of the ignition coil to ground. The contact breaker is a mechanically operated electrical switch that is fixed to the distributor base plate and opened and closed by the distributor cam with the rotation of the engine. This process builds up and collapses the magnetic field in the ignition coil in order to create a high-voltage output of the ignition coil.

Located in the distributor, the contact points are opened by **cam lobes**, or protrusions on the otherwise round distributor shaft, and closed by a spring. The number of lobes is equal to the number of cylinders, so that the contact breaker points open the circuit and activate the ignition coil at the end of each compression stroke for each cylinder. In order for the spark plugs to fire at the correct moment, the distributor must be installed in the right position. Most manufacturers specify that the ignition **rotor** be located under the distributor cap terminal of the number one cylinder with the piston of the number one cylinder at top dead center of the compression stroke.

Contact breaker point ignition systems provide a simple means of establishing and interrupting the current flowing in the primary ignition circuit. A basic system consists of:

- The battery: Provides a source of energy.
- The ignition switch: Provides the driver control over system operation.
- An ignition coil: Provides step-up transformer action.
- Contact breaker points: Opened and closed by lobes on the distributor cam as the engine rotates to make and break the primary circuit at the correct time in the ignition cycle **FIGURE 36-14**.
- A **capacitor**: Assists in the rapid collapse of the ignition coil's magnetic field. Any voltage surge across the contacts will charge the capacitor, rather than cause damaging arcing. The condenser is typically mounted on the breaker plate or on the side of the distributor.
- A distributor: Rotates at half the speed of the crankshaft to house the contact breaker points and distribute the high voltage from the ignition coil and spark plugs, thus igniting the air–fuel mixture in each cylinder in the correct firing order.
- Connecting wires and leads suitable for conducting the current flowing in the ignition system, at the appropriate voltage level.

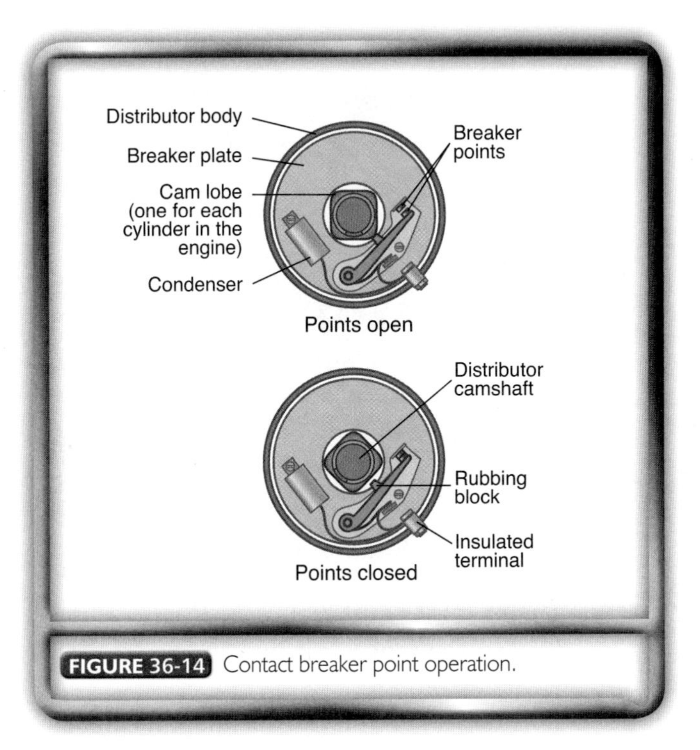

Distributor body
Breaker plate
Cam lobe (one for each cylinder in the engine)
Condenser
Breaker points
Points open
Distributor camshaft
Rubbing block
Insulated terminal
Points closed

FIGURE 36-14 Contact breaker point operation.

Opening and closing the contact breaker switches the primary current off and on. When the contacts begin to separate, the primary current tends to flow on, producing an arc across the contacts. The capacitor absorbs this surge of **inductive current** by providing a very short-term, alternative path, in parallel with the opening contacts. The capacitor charges to the peak value of the primary winding voltage. By the time this has occurred, the gap between the contacts is too wide for a spark to discharge between them. This abrupt interruption of the primary circuit assists in the rapid collapse of the magnetic field and, hence, an increase in the value of the voltage induced in the primary and secondary windings. The high voltage induced in the secondary winding rises to a value great enough to bridge the gap across the spark plug. The process then repeats itself many times per second.

TECHNICIAN TIP

The secondary spark occurs when the points open, not when they close. It is the rapid collapse of the magnetic field that induces the high voltage in the secondary windings. Knowing that the spark occurs just as the points open helps a technician static-time an engine after an engine rebuild or when the distributor has been removed.

Distributors

The **distributor's** main function is to distribute the spark to the spark plugs in the correct sequence and at the correct time in the engine cycle FIGURE 36-15. It includes a distributor cap, rotor, switching device, and a shaft with cam lobes for operating the switching device. The switching device is used to connect and disconnect the primary circuit. The distributor also houses the vacuum and mechanical (centrifugal) timing advance mechanisms on older engines. These are used to advance the timing of the spark under certain driving conditions.

The **distributor cap** covers the end of the distributor to protect the components inside. It also provides a connection point between the rotor and the spark plug leads. The rotor is a high-voltage rotating switch that transfers

TECHNICIAN TIP

The condenser is a critical component of the primary circuit in point-type ignition systems. Without it, the points arc as they are opened. This arcing causes a slow stopping of the primary current flow, which causes a slow collapsing of the magnetic field in the ignition coil, which in turn causes low voltage output of the secondary windings. If you have weak spark output on a point-type ignition system, do not be like a former student and overlook the very simple and inexpensive condenser. This student ended up replacing the spark plugs, spark plug wires, cap, rotor, points, ignition coil, and carburetor before he asked for help. The wise old technician, after listening to his story, pulled out a used condenser and connected it to the negative side of the coil and ground with a couple of test leads and asked the student to try starting the engine. The student was amazed when it started right up and ran like new.

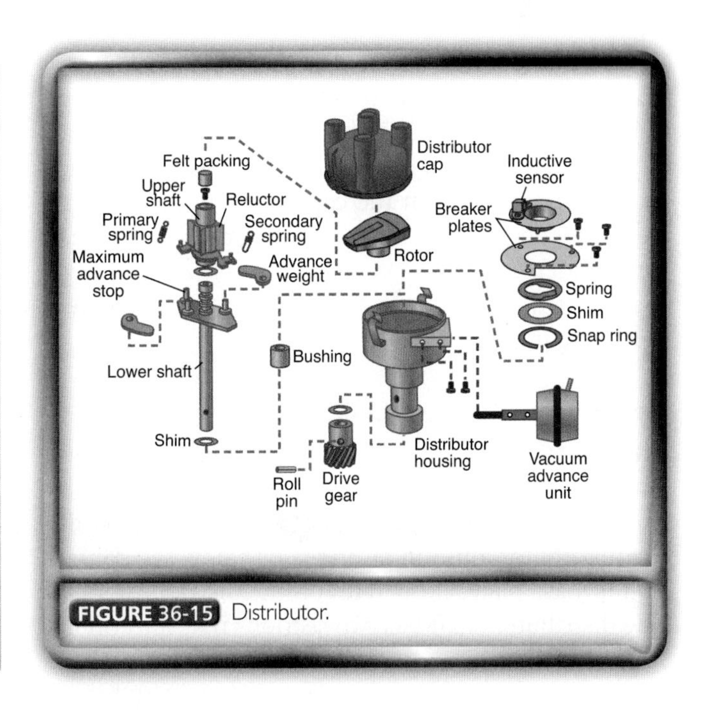

Felt packing
Upper shaft
Reluctor
Primary spring
Secondary spring
Maximum advance stop
Advance weight
Distributor cap
Inductive sensor
Breaker plates
Rotor
Spring
Shim
Snap ring
Bushing
Lower shaft
Shim
Roll pin
Drive gear
Distributor housing
Vacuum advance unit

FIGURE 36-15 Distributor.

the secondary voltage from the center terminal of the distributor to the side terminals. The distributor distributes the high-voltage pulses to the individual spark plug wires in the correct sequence and at the correct instant in the engine cycle. In some applications, the ignition coil is mounted inside of the distributor; the cap covers the coil and provides an electrical path from the coil's output terminal to the center of the rotor. In other applications, the ignition coil is bolted to the top of the distributor cap on the outside and covered with a plastic shield. In this instance, the center of the coil sits right above the rotor, and a hole drilled in the cap allows a spring-loaded button to transfer the current pushed by the high voltage directly to the center of the rotor.

An insulated **rotor arm** with a brass or steel electrode is keyed to the shaft directly above the cam and rotates within a molded insulated distributor cap held by clips or screws on the distributor housing. The distributor cap has the same number of connecting terminals for the spark plug wires as there are spark plugs, and a central terminal is connected to the high-tension lead from the ignition coil. An internal spring-loaded carbon brush conducts each high-voltage pulse from the central terminal to the center of the rotor electrode as it turns.

The high-voltage spark is timed to occur when the rotor electrode is aligned with a fixed electrode inside the distributor cap. The high voltage bridges the small gap between the electrodes, driving current through the ignition terminal for that cylinder and bridging the gap at the spark plug.

As the rotor turns inside the distributor cap, the high-voltage electrical surges take place successively for each cylinder according to the firing order. This is accomplished by arranging the high-tension leads, according to their place in the firing order, on the distributor cap. For example, an in-line four-cylinder engine typically has a firing order of 1-3-4-2. If the distributor shaft were designed to spin clockwise, the high-tension leads would be arranged on the cap with cylinder 3 positioned 90 degrees clockwise from cylinder 1. The lead for cylinder 4 would be 90 degrees clockwise from cylinder 3, and the lead for cylinder 2 would be 90 degrees clockwise from cylinder 4.

Centrifugal Advance Units

The **centrifugal advance mechanism** (also called mechanical advance) controls ignition timing in relation to engine speed **FIGURE 36-16**. It is located within the distributor and can be above or below the contact points' base plate. It operates on the distributor shaft. The distributor shaft has two sections that turn on the same axis. The lower shaft is driven by the camshaft, and the upper shaft controls the opening time of contact points. Both shafts are joined by the centrifugal advance mechanism. Its function is to turn the upper shaft forward within limits in relation to the lower shaft, proportional to engine speed.

FIGURE 36-16 Centrifugal advance mechanism.

Vacuum Advance Units

The vacuum advance mechanism controls **ignition advance** in relation to engine load. At light load, an engine is more efficient when the timing is advanced slightly. Under heavy load, the timing must be retarded slightly to avoid "pinging" or spark knock. Its function is to improve fuel economy and, in doing so, reduce exhaust emissions. Vacuum is routed from the carburetor to a spring-loaded diaphragm housing attached to the distributor. The diaphragm is attached to a pull rod that, when operating, acts on the distributor base plate, turning it opposite to the direction of distributor shaft rotation **FIGURE 36-17**. The movement results in the contact points' opening time being advanced during light engine loads and retarded during heavy engine loads.

Manufacturers designed their vacuum advance to operate on one of three types of vacuum: ported, manifold, or venturi **FIGURE 36-18**. It is obtained through a small slit in the throttle bore located just above the throttle plate. This slot has no vacuum at idle, creating no vacuum advance at idle. As the throttle is opened, the vacuum to the slit increases, causing some vacuum advance, which tapers off at wide-open throttle. Manifold vacuum is obtained through a small hole in the throttle bore just below the throttle plate. It provides strong vacuum at idle and less vacuum as the throttle is opened. Venturi vacuum is obtained from a port that is connected to the smallest

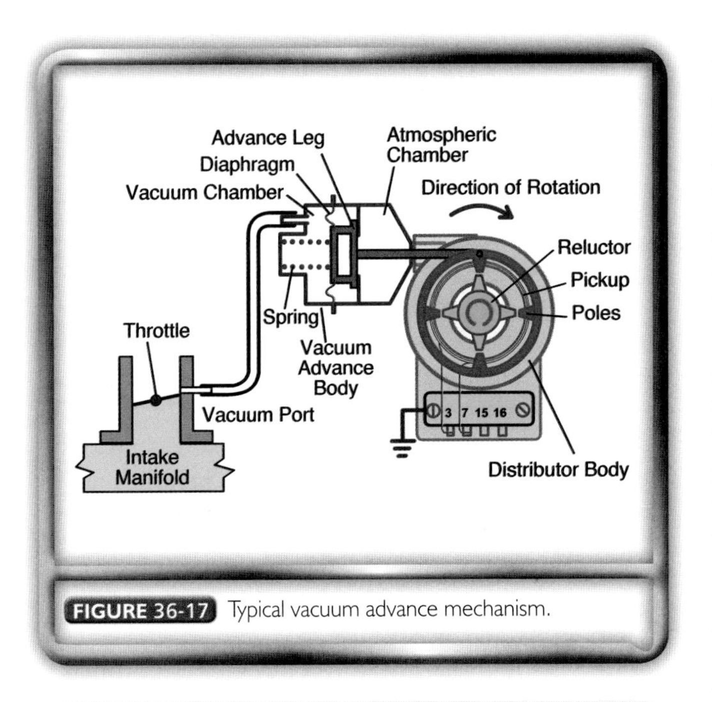
Advance Leg
Diaphragm
Vacuum Chamber
Atmospheric Chamber
Direction of Rotation
Reluctor
Pickup
Poles
Throttle
Spring
Vacuum Advance Body
Vacuum Port
Intake Manifold
Distributor Body

FIGURE 36-17 Typical vacuum advance mechanism.

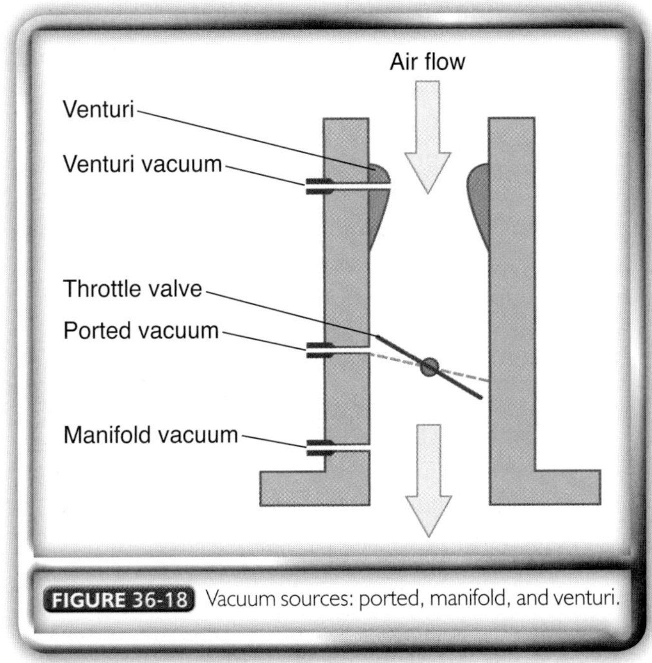
Air flow
Venturi
Venturi vacuum
Throttle valve
Ported vacuum
Manifold vacuum

FIGURE 36-18 Vacuum sources: ported, manifold, and venturi.

diameter of the venturi. This system has no vacuum at idle, but as airflow increases through the venturi, the vacuum increases. The vacuum in each of these systems acts on the vacuum diaphragm causing the timing to advance as vacuum increases, or retard as vacuum decreases. Since the vacuum responds differently in each type of vacuum, the manufacturer would specify the base timing and the advance curve profile for the engine.

Engine Spark Timing

Engine manufacturers include timing marks on their engines so that the technician can check and adjust the engine timing if some conditions have changed. There are two types of timing on gasoline engines: valve timing and ignition timing. Valve timing refers to the position of the valves in relation to the piston stroke. During the four-stroke cycle, the valves must open and close at the proper times. Engine manufacturers place marks on the gears, sprockets, or pulleys and the corresponding surfaces of the block and head to allow the valve timing to be properly set whenever the valve timing components are being replaced.

The ignition timing refers to the point at which the spark plug "fires" near the end of the compression stroke. On older vehicles with distributors, the base timing can be adjusted by rotating the position of the distributor housing in relation to the engine. On newer engines, the timing is not adjustable since the computer controls it based on all of the sensor information.

Electronic Ignition Systems

In **electronic ignition systems**, the contact breaker points are eliminated and the primary circuit is switched or triggered electronically with a power transistor located in the ignition module. In general, an electronic ignition system will have a stationary component and a component that spins with the distributor shaft, which is driven by the camshaft. When the spinning component and the stationary component interact as designed, a signal is sent to the ignition module where the transistor switches the primary circuit on and off, creating and collapsing the magnetic field in the coil primary winding. This is typically accomplished through the use of an inductive pickup, a **Hall-effect switch**, or an **optical sensor**. Many of the components, such as the battery, ignition switch, spark plugs, and wiring, in an electronic ignition system are essentially the same as those in a contact breaker point ignition system. The following sections describe only those components of an electronic ignition system that are not part of a contact breaker point ignition system.

> **TECHNICIAN TIP**
>
> Some newer engines still use a distributor for distributing the high-voltage spark, but they use a crankshaft position sensor to control the timing of the spark. Turning the distributor on this application interferes with the rotor to cap alignment. It does not actually change the timing. So just because it has a distributor does not mean that adjusting it will change the spark timing.

Components of Distributor-Type Systems

Early electronic ignition systems included an ignition module and a triggering device coupled with a standard distributor. The triggering device can be a magnetic pulse generator, also known as a pickup coil, a Hall-effect switch, or an optical sensor. The triggering device sends signals to the ignition module to open and close the primary circuit. This causes a magnetic field to build up and collapse in the primary winding in the same way that the point ignition system does. The collapsing magnetic field in the primary circuit induces a voltage into the secondary windings of the ignition coil, producing the high voltage needed for sparking. This high voltage pushes current to the spark plugs, where the current jumps across the spark plug electrodes, creating the heat to ignite the air–fuel mixture.

Ignition Modules

Ignition modules are used in virtually every type of ignition system except the contact breaker point system. In its simplest form, it uses the information from the triggering device to turn the primary circuit on and off. As technology progressed, processing power was added to the module so that the dwell time could be modified. Thus, the dwell time could be shortened during low engine rpm and lengthened as rpm increased. This flexibility helps to prevent overheating of the ignition coil and transistor during low speed while still maintaining adequate time for coil saturation during all engine speeds. Further refinement saw current-limiting circuitry added to the ignition module, which allowed for the use of low-impedance ignition coils. After that, manufacturers started to use their PCMs to work along with the ignition module. The module typically provided for base timing while the engine was being started and then switched over and allowed the PCM to control ignition timing through the ignition module once the engine was running. In early electronic-ignition vehicles, the ignition module was typically located in one of three places: in the distributor, on the distributor, or away from the distributor on the firewall, inner fender, or air cleaner housing. On many waste spark systems, the ignition module is located either under the ignition coils or within the coil assemblies. On newer vehicles, the ignition module functions are completely controlled by the PCM, in many cases eliminating the need for an external ignition module.

Induction-Type Systems

Induction-type systems are electronic systems that use a magnetic pulse generator, also called a variable reluctor sensor (VR sensor), to generate an AC signal. They come in a variety of configurations, but all of them have a **stator** (also called a pickup coil) mounted on the distributor body and a rotor unit (also called a **reluctor** or trigger wheel) attached to the distributor shaft FIGURE 36-19. The reluctor has one tooth for each cylinder. As it spins, the teeth interact with the stator to trigger the ignition module. The stator may have only one projection with a stationary coil of fine enameled wire wound around it, or it may have a circular permanent magnet with a number of projections or teeth corresponding to the number of engine cylinders, and a stationary coil of fine enameled copper wire wound on a plastic reel and positioned inside or around the magnet. As the reluctor rotates, the teeth on the reluctor approach and leave the stator teeth, changing the air gap between them. As this occurs, the strength of the magnetic field changes, increasing as the teeth approach, reaching a maximum when they are in alignment and decreasing as they move away.

Hall-Effect Sensors and Operation

Another type of electronic ignition system is the Hall-effect type. In Hall-effect systems, a Hall-effect generator, also called a Hall-effect sensor or switch, can be located inside the distributor to signal an ECU to turn the primary circuit on and off. Hall-effect generators operate by using a potential difference, or voltage, created when a current-carrying conductor is exposed to a magnetic field. If a magnetic field is applied at right angles to the direction of current flow in a conductor, the lines of magnetic force permeate the conductor and the electrons flowing in the conductor are deflected to one side of the conductor. This deflection creates a potential difference or voltage across the conductor. The stronger the magnetic field, the higher the voltage. This dynamic is called the Hall-effect voltage, and if the magnetic field is alternately shielded and exposed, it can be used to trigger a switching device. Hall devices are made of semiconductor material, which can quickly respond when shielded from or exposed to a magnetic field.

FIGURE 36-19 Types of inductive ignition pickup coils.

In a distributor, the Hall-effect generator and its **integrated circuit** are located on one leg of a U-shaped assembly, mounted on the distributor base plate FIGURE 36-20. An integrated circuit is a semiconductor chip that contains miniature versions of various electrical components within one housing. A permanent magnet is located on the other leg, and an air gap is formed between them. An **interrupter ring**, which has the same number of blades and windows as engine cylinders, is rotated by the distributor shaft, moving the blades through the air gap. The purpose of an interrupter ring is to systematically block and expose the magnetic field. The ring is shaped like a very shallow cup with slits, or windows, cut into it at evenly spaced intervals. It is made of a ferrous metal.

When a window is aligned with the assembly, the magnetic field is at its strongest, and its lines of magnetic force permeate the Hall generator material. The Hall generator material creates a voltage that is used to switch the primary circuit to ground. When the interrupter ring rotates so that the blade aligns with the assembly, the magnetic field is shielded from the generator, and the Hall material does not create a signal voltage; thus, the primary circuit is not switched to ground. With continuous rotation, the blades repeatedly move in and out of the air gap, and the signal voltage turns on and off repeatedly. This can be used to control the operation of the ignition coil primary circuit.

Optical-Type Sensors

Another type of electronic ignition system uses a light-emitting diode (LED) and a phototransistor to create an optical sensor FIGURE 36-21. The optical sensors located inside the distributor can be used to sense the position of the crankshaft and send an appropriate voltage signal to the ignition module or PCM. A signal rotor plate is attached to the distributor shaft. Although various designs are used, a typical rotor plate has 360 slits at 1-degree intervals on its outer edge. Inboard of these slits are four slits on a four-cylinder engine, six slits on a six-cylinder engine, and so on. One slit is larger than the others to identify the position of the number one cylinder to the PCM.

As the rotor plate turns, it passes between an LED above the rotor plate and a phototransistor below the plate. When provided with a suitable voltage, LEDs transmit a fine beam of light. Phototransistors receive this light and use it to make a voltage output signal. When a slit is in alignment, the light beam passes through it and a signal is transmitted to the control unit. When the slit is out of alignment, the light beam is interrupted and the signal falls to zero.

The control unit uses the signals it receives at every 1 degree to gauge engine rpm and **crank angle position** in 1-degree increments. It uses the signals from the inner slits to gauge the piston position, with the signature slit identifying the number one piston. The signals from both sets of diodes are converted to on/off pulses in the sensor's

> **TECHNICIAN TIP**
>
> The optical sensor is very precise due to the small slits that the light passes through. However, because they are so small, they can easily become blocked by dirt, debris, or even oil. Make sure the slits in the rotor plate stay clean when working around it.

FIGURE 36-20 Hall-effect setup in a distributor.

FIGURE 36-21 Optical sensor ignition system.

internal circuitry. This on/off pulse is then used by the ignition module and/or PCM to know when the spark needs to occur in each cylinder.

Components of Distributorless-Type Systems

In **distributorless ignition systems**, also known as electronic ignition systems, the distributor is eliminated and replaced by multiple ignition coils. In waste spark systems, there is one ignition coil for each pair of companion cylinders. For direct ignition systems, there is one ignition coil for each cylinder. Signals from a **crankshaft position sensor** FIGURE 36-22 and, if equipped, a **camshaft position sensor** are used by the PCM to control the on/off signal to the primary windings of the coils. Both of these sensors are either Hall-effect or induction-type sensors to let the PCM know the positions of the crankshaft and the camshaft. Not all manufacturers use a camshaft position sensor, as the PCM only needs to know when the number one cylinder is at top dead center to give the proper spark timing on waste spark systems.

With waste spark systems, each spark plug is fired by a high-voltage impulse from an ignition coil shared with a companion cylinder. The distributorless systems that have a dedicated coil for each spark plug are referred to as coil-on-plug or coil-over-plug systems. The main advantage of the distributorless ignition system is the elimination of all the mechanical parts included in a distributor assembly such as bushings, bearings, the breaker plate assembly, and advance mechanisms. Also, the distributorless ignition system has eliminated maintenance items such as a distributor cap, rotor, contact points, and condenser.

Waste Spark Ignition System

In a waste spark system for a six-cylinder engine, three ignition coils, each with their own primary and secondary windings, can be combined to form one coil pack or can be three separate coils. Each ignition coil serves two cylinders, with each end of the secondary winding attached by a high-tension lead to a spark plug. These two plugs are on companion cylinders—that is, cylinders where the pistons reach top dead center at the same time. The cylinder on the compression stroke is said to be the **event cylinder**, because it is the one getting ready to produce power, and the cylinder on the exhaust stroke is the **waste cylinder**, since the spark has no effect on engine operation FIGURE 36-23.

When the high voltage is induced in the secondary winding, the secondary circuit is completed by current flowing through the high-tension lead to the center electrode on one spark plug, bridging the gap and creating a spark in that cylinder, traveling through the cylinder head, bridging the spark plug gap in the companion cylinder, and flowing back through that high-tension lead to its starting point at the ignition coil. The cylinder on the compression stroke with its charge of fuel and air is "fired" by its spark, driving the piston down on the power stroke, while the spark at the plug of the cylinder on exhaust simply serves to complete the circuit, and is "wasted."

When the crankshaft rotates through one revolution, the roles are reversed, and the waste cylinder becomes the event cylinder. Firing of both spark plugs again takes place, and this cylinder now drives its piston down on the power stroke. This same process occurs on each pair of companion cylinders as they approach the top dead center position. The primary circuit in each coil must

FIGURE 36-22 The interrupter rings on a six-cylinder engine's crankshaft pulley.

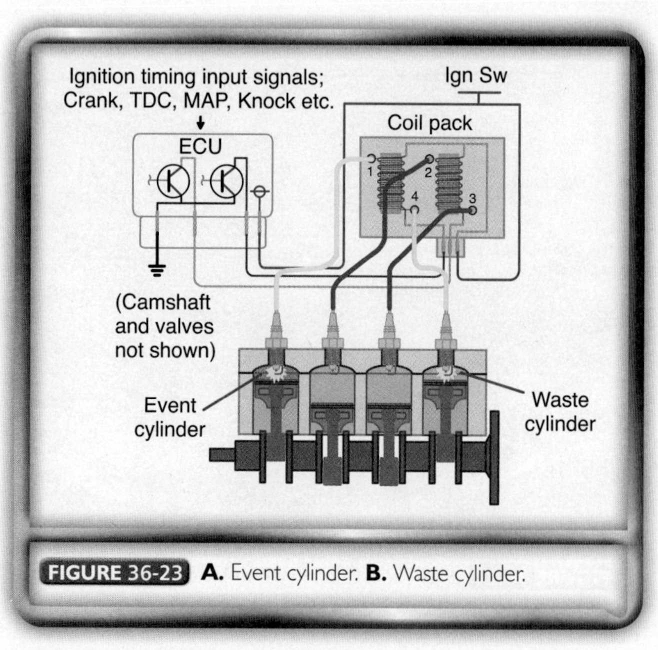
Ignition timing input signals;
Crank, TDC, MAP, Knock etc.
Ign Sw
Coil pack
ECU
1
2
3
4
(Camshaft
and valves
not shown)
Event
cylinder
Waste
cylinder

FIGURE 36-23 **A.** Event cylinder. **B.** Waste cylinder.

therefore trigger at the correct time in each crankshaft revolution. Timing is controlled by the PCM based on all of the engine sensor input.

Direct Ignition System

Most current production gasoline engines use a single ignition coil for each cylinder. These ignition systems are similar to waste spark ignition systems but use one ignition coil for each cylinder rather than shared coils or a coil pack. In these systems, the coils can be all separate coils with spark plug boots or can be placed in an insulated cassette with each coil attached to a spark plug boot and connected directly to its spark plug FIGURE 36-24. This design eliminates the necessity for high-tension leads and reduces the possibility of current not making it to the spark plug.

The same sensor inputs previously discussed allow the PCM to determine ignition firing order and to set ignition timing according to operating conditions. Some manufacturers use the term direct ignition to identify their waste spark systems. Other manufacturers refer to their coil-on-plug ignition systems as direct ignition systems.

Diagnosing Ignition System Issues

Concerns relating to the ignition system typically involve drivability. They may be nonstarting, hard starting, lack of power, misfiring, or any concern related to how smooth or responsive an engine is. After verifying the concern and any related concerns, perform a visual inspection with the engine off and again with the engine running. Look for loose connections, broken or corroded terminals, and maintenance items that appear to need replacement. Also, check for the high-tension leads to see if they are resting on hot engine parts or arcing. If an engine is running rough or lacks power, use a scan tool to check for misfire data or any DTCs. If it is not an OBDII vehicle, remove and inspect the spark plugs.

FIGURE 36-24 A direct ignition coil and boot.

> **Safety**
>
> While the secondary voltage is very high (up to 100,000V), the current flow is very low. Because the current flow is so low, an ignition system shock is unlikely to kill you directly (unless you have a pacemaker), but it could hurt you. If you get shocked by the high voltage, it will hurt, and you will likely jerk away from it. This can cause you to get tangled up in the fan belts, or ram your head into the hood safety latch, which could seriously injure you. Always respect secondary ignition systems and work around them carefully.

The condition of the spark plugs, when viewed on the electrodes side, can give a good indication of major engine problems. For example, if the electrodes are covered in oil, there may be worn valve seals or oil-control piston rings. If the electrodes are covered with black carbon, the engine may be running rich. Inspect the rotor and the inside of the distributor cap for cracks and carbon tracks. Replace any parts that are worn, cracked, or broken. A spark test should be performed to see if there is an adequate spark at the spark plug while the engine is being cranked, and always refer to the manufacturer's recommended procedure once you have completed a visual inspection and performed a spark test. Test-drive the vehicle once the repair is completed.

Spark Testing

A spark test should be performed when an engine will not start, has one or more cylinders misfiring, or has other drivability problems, such as a lack of power, or stalling. A spark tester can look like a regular spark plug, but it has a large alligator clip attached to its side, or it can be an adjustable tester that allows you to adjust the gap. If the spark jumps across the specified gap of the spark tester, then the spark is high enough to jump across the spark plug gap in the combustion chamber.

To perform a spark test, follow the steps in SKILL DRILL 36-1.

Inspecting the Ignition Primary and Secondary Circuits

The primary and secondary wiring should be checked for cuts, abrasions, and signs of arcing. The

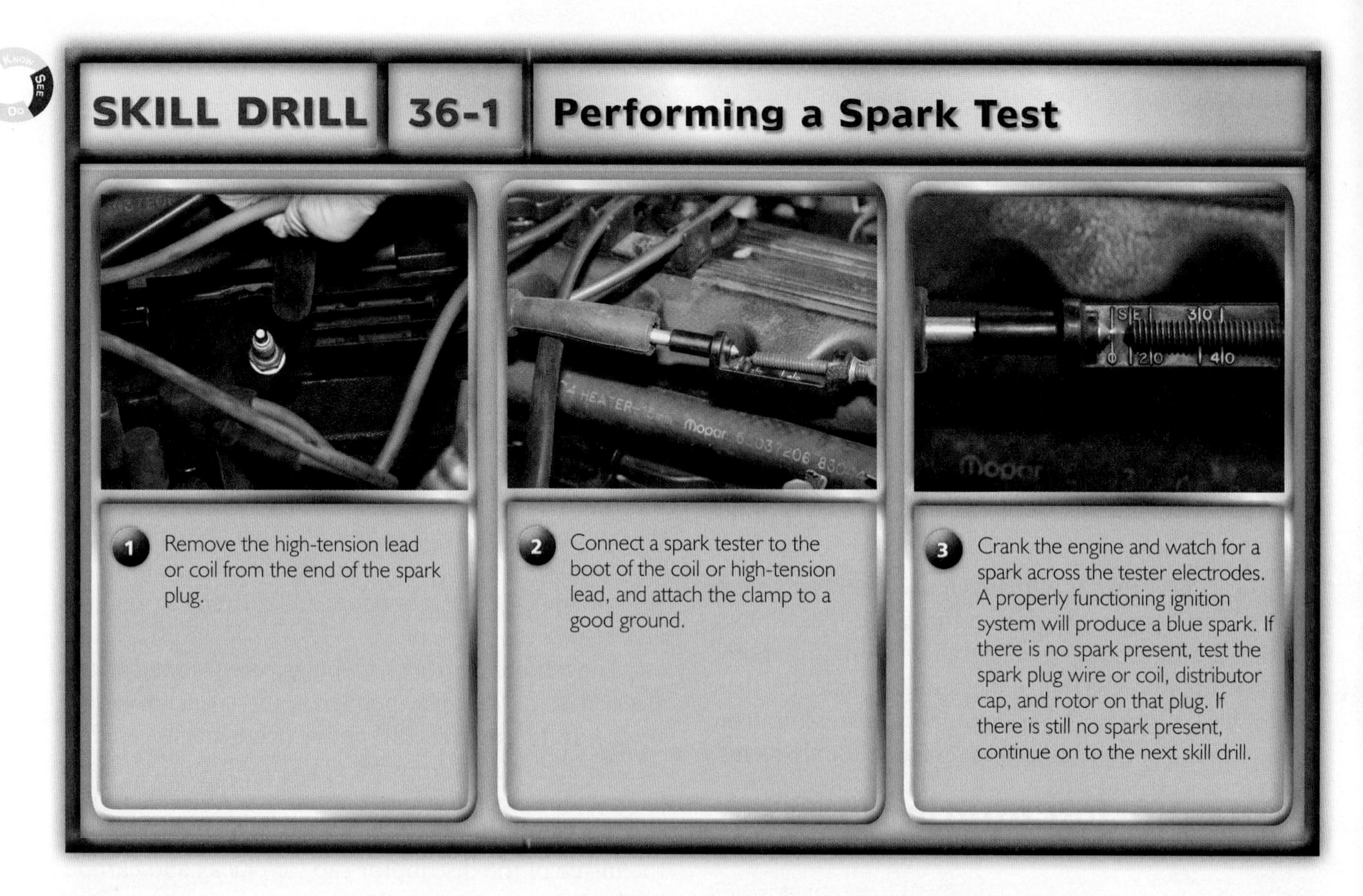
SKILL DRILL 36-1 Performing a Spark Test
1 Remove the high-tension lead or coil from the end of the spark plug.
2 Connect a spark tester to the boot of the coil or high-tension lead, and attach the clamp to a good ground.
3 Crank the engine and watch for a spark across the tester electrodes. A properly functioning ignition system will produce a blue spark. If there is no spark present, test the spark plug wire or coil, distributor cap, and rotor on that plug. If there is still no spark present, continue on to the next skill drill.

primary wires are the two to four smaller wires attached to the ignition coil(s), and the secondary wires are the larger wires leading from the coil pack to the spark plugs or from the distributor cap to the spark plugs, depending on the type of ignition system. Loose or corroded wires can also cause an ignition system to perform poorly.

To inspect the primary and secondary circuits, follow the steps in SKILL DRILL 36-2.

> **TECHNICIAN TIP**
>
> Many technicians have been fooled by using one of the engine's spark plugs as a spark tester. They plug an old spark plug in a spark plug boot, lay it on a good engine ground, and crank the engine. They observe a spark jumping across the standard spark plug gap and assume that the spark is fine. But it takes a LOT more voltage to jump a standard spark plug gap inside the cylinder under compression pressures, than outside of the cylinder at atmospheric pressure. So while the spark may jump the standard spark plug gap outside the engine, it may be too low to jump it inside the engine, fooling you into thinking the spark is fine and sending you on a wild goose chase. This is why spark testers use a much larger gap.

Testing the Ignition Coil

Whether an engine uses a single ignition coil, an **ignition coil pack**, or one coil for each cylinder, it is critical that the ignition coil or ignition coils are operating properly. A faulty ignition coil may cause hesitation under acceleration or may prevent an engine from starting. Ignition coils can fail in a few ways. The primary and secondary windings may be open or shorted. A DVOM is used to measure the resistance of the primary and secondary windings and compared to factory specifications. Another way ignition coils can fail is breakdown of the insulating material. This can happen if the secondary terminal of the coil becomes carbon tracked and allows voltage to push current to ground; or if there is an internal breakdown of the insulation, the voltage can push current to the primary circuit or ground. Finding breakdowns in coil insulation requires the coil to be activated and the available voltage to be measured on an oscilloscope and compared to specifications. If there is a weak spark or no spark during the spark test and the spark plug wires and primary circuit have been tested and are found to be satisfactory, the ignition coil may be faulty.

To test the ignition coil, follow the steps in SKILL DRILL 36-3.

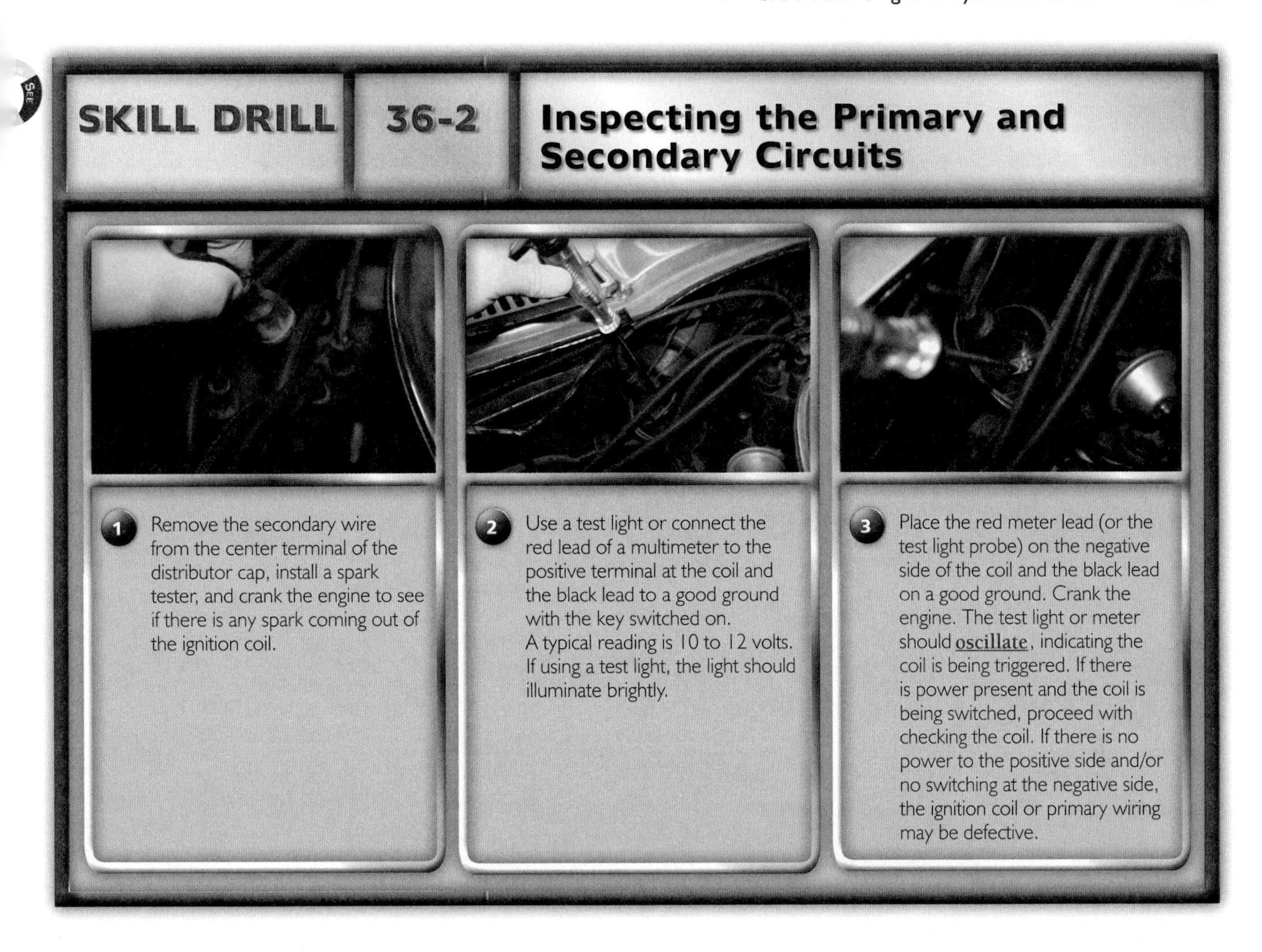
SKILL DRILL 36-2 Inspecting the Primary and Secondary Circuits
1 Remove the secondary wire from the center terminal of the distributor cap, install a spark tester, and crank the engine to see if there is any spark coming out of the ignition coil.
2 Use a test light or connect the red lead of a multimeter to the positive terminal at the coil and the black lead to a good ground with the key switched on. A typical reading is 10 to 12 volts. If using a test light, the light should illuminate brightly.
3 Place the red meter lead (or the test light probe) on the negative side of the coil and the black lead on a good ground. Crank the engine. The test light or meter should oscillate, indicating the coil is being triggered. If there is power present and the coil is being switched, proceed with checking the coil. If there is no power to the positive side and/or no switching at the negative side, the ignition coil or primary wiring may be defective.

Testing the Spark Plug Wire

A faulty spark plug wire may cause a misfire, high exhaust emissions, poor fuel economy, and/or a lack of power. Over time, spark plug wires become brittle and frayed and tend to have higher resistance; they can internally burn in two, causing an open. An open spark plug wire can cause the engine to run poorly or may cause the cylinders with the faulty wires to misfire. Misfires can cause catastrophic damage to the catalytic converters on the vehicle, so misfires are serious issues if left undiagnosed and not repaired.

If the vehicle has an intermittent misfire and is equipped with spark plug wires, you can use a spray bottle with plain water to mist the wires while the engine is running. Or you can use a grounded test lead and run it along the wires with the engine running. If the spark plug wires have a weak spot in the insulation, you should be able to see and hear the spark jumping to another wire, the test lead, or conductive engine part. If the vehicle is equipped with a coil-on-plug system, or if the spark plug wires fit down inside of a recessed well, then you can use insulated pliers to carefully lift the coil or plug wire boot off the spark plug while the engine is running and see if the spark is jumping through a hole or crack in the boot to the side of the spark plug well or the grounded test lead.

To test a spark plug wire, follow the steps in SKILL DRILL 36-4.

Inspecting the Distributor Cap and Rotor

A defective distributor cap or rotor can also prevent a spark plug from firing or cause a weak spark. If an engine has a misfire or exhibits a lack of power, poor fuel economy, or high emissions, the distributor cap and rotor should be inspected. Distributor caps and rotors become carbon tracked over time. This means that the high voltage ionizes the surface of the plastic parts and eventually can create a path to ground or to another spark plug terminal. This carbon track will allow electricity to flow along that path instead of firing the proper spark plug. Carbon tracks look like small hairline cracks but can become much more noticeable over time. A faulty distributor cap or rotor may also cause an engine to run rough, backfire, or not start at all.

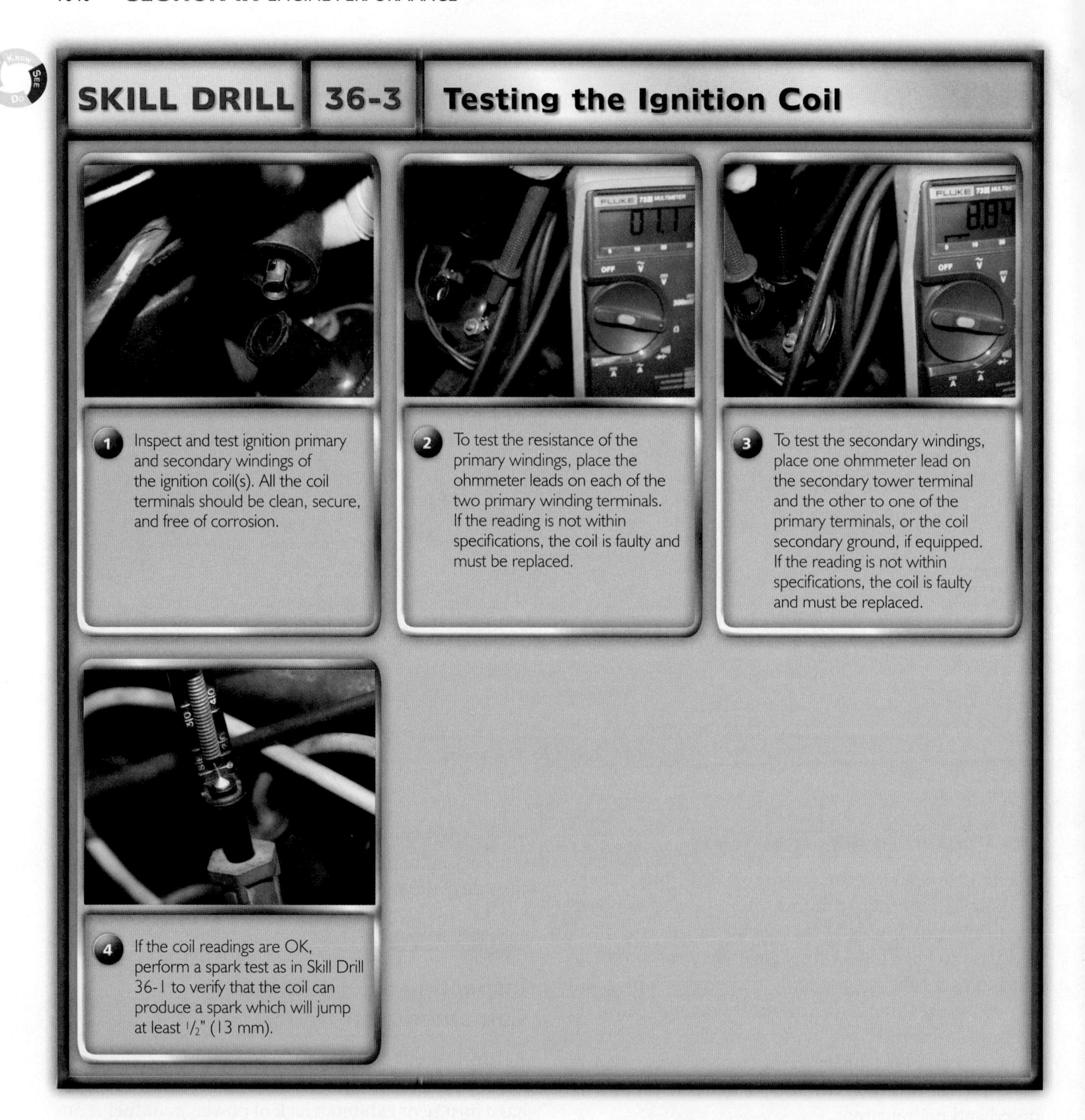
SKILL DRILL
36-3
Testing the Ignition Coil
1 Inspect and test ignition primary and secondary windings of the ignition coil(s). All the coil terminals should be clean, secure, and free of corrosion.
2 To test the resistance of the primary windings, place the ohmmeter leads on each of the two primary winding terminals. If the reading is not within specifications, the coil is faulty and must be replaced.
3 To test the secondary windings, place one ohmmeter lead on the secondary tower terminal and the other to one of the primary terminals, or the coil secondary ground, if equipped. If the reading is not within specifications, the coil is faulty and must be replaced.
4 If the coil readings are OK, perform a spark test as in Skill Drill 36-1 to verify that the coil can produce a spark which will jump at least 1/2" (13 mm).

To inspect a distributor cap and rotor, follow the steps in SKILL DRILL 36-5.

Removing and Replacing Secondary Ignition Components

As the vehicle ages, the components of the secondary ignition system will wear. Periodic replacement of the spark plugs and high-tension leads (spark plug wires) or coil boots is required to maintain vehicle performance and to meet emission standards. The main components to be replaced on today's vehicles are the spark plugs and the high-tension leads (if equipped) and coil-on-plug coil boots on some applications. High tailpipe emissions, hard starting, or misfiring under load may indicate a need for service of these ignition components.

Servicing the Spark Plug

According to most maintenance schedules, the spark plugs should be replaced every 30,000 to 50,000 miles

SKILL DRILL 36-4 Testing a Spark Plug Wire

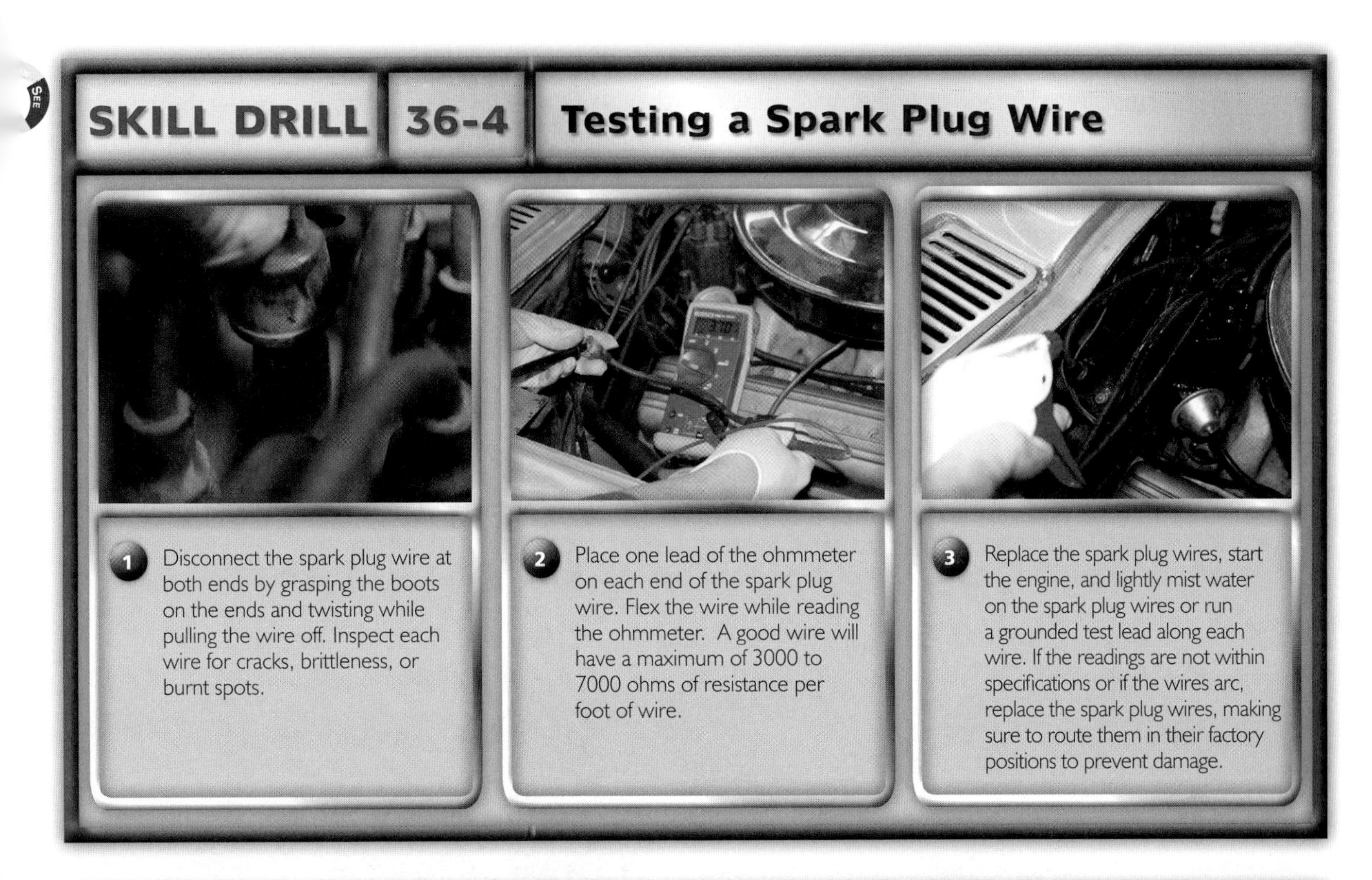

1. Disconnect the spark plug wire at both ends by grasping the boots on the ends and twisting while pulling the wire off. Inspect each wire for cracks, brittleness, or burnt spots.
2. Place one lead of the ohmmeter on each end of the spark plug wire. Flex the wire while reading the ohmmeter. A good wire will have a maximum of 3000 to 7000 ohms of resistance per foot of wire.
3. Replace the spark plug wires, start the engine, and lightly mist water on the spark plug wires or run a grounded test lead along each wire. If the readings are not within specifications or if the wires arc, replace the spark plug wires, making sure to route them in their factory positions to prevent damage.

SKILL DRILL 36-5 Inspecting a Distributor Cap and Rotor

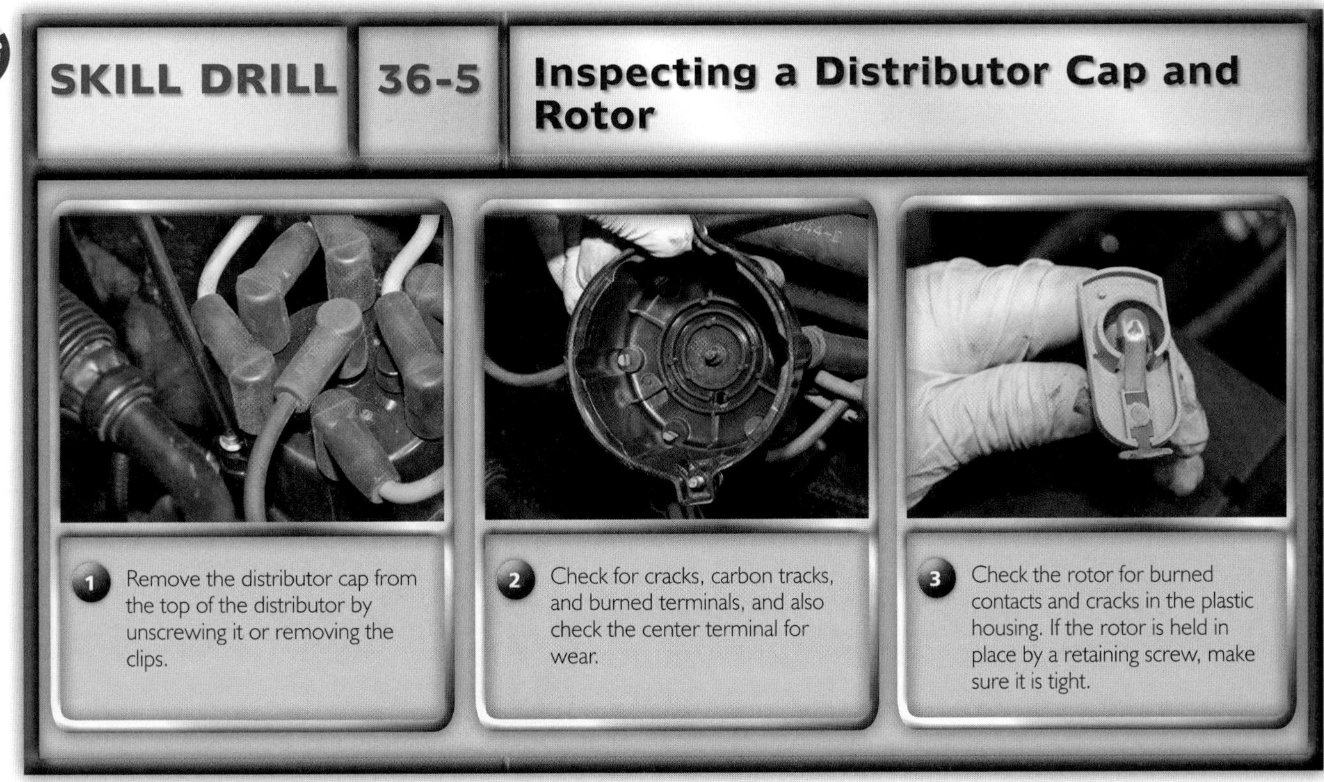

1. Remove the distributor cap from the top of the distributor by unscrewing it or removing the clips.
2. Check for cracks, carbon tracks, and burned terminals, and also check the center terminal for wear.
3. Check the rotor for burned contacts and cracks in the plastic housing. If the rotor is held in place by a retaining screw, make sure it is tight.

(50,000 to 80,000 km). Some newer vehicles use high-performance spark plugs that are made with platinum, iridium, or gold palladium and do not require replacement until the engine reaches 100,000 miles (160,000 km). When service is needed, avoid attaching the spark plug wires to the wrong cylinder by replacing the spark plugs one at a time. Note that some manufacturers recommend that the spark plugs only be replaced on a cold engine to avoid damaging the threads in the cylinder head. Check the service procedure before attempting to replace the spark plugs on a hot engine. Some manufacturers have very specific procedures for removing their spark plugs, and the procedure should be followed exactly or broken-off plugs can occur. Even when following exact procedures, some applications still result in broken-off spark plugs, and the proper tools and procedures will need to be followed for replacement.

It is quicker to set the spark plug gap on all of the new spark plugs at one time. Although most spark plugs come pre-gapped, they should be checked to make sure they were not damaged during shipping. Some spark plugs, such as those made with iridium, are not to be adjusted; if the gap is off, they are to be replaced, as they break very easily.

To replace the spark plugs, follow the steps in **SKILL DRILL 36-6**. If the gap of the spark plug is correct, there will be a slight drag between the gapping tool gauge and the spark plug electrodes as the gauge is installed and removed. If the gap is too big, the outer electrode should be bent down slightly until it is correct. If the gap is set too small, bend the outer electrode away from the center electrode until the gapping tool fits snugly between the two electrodes.

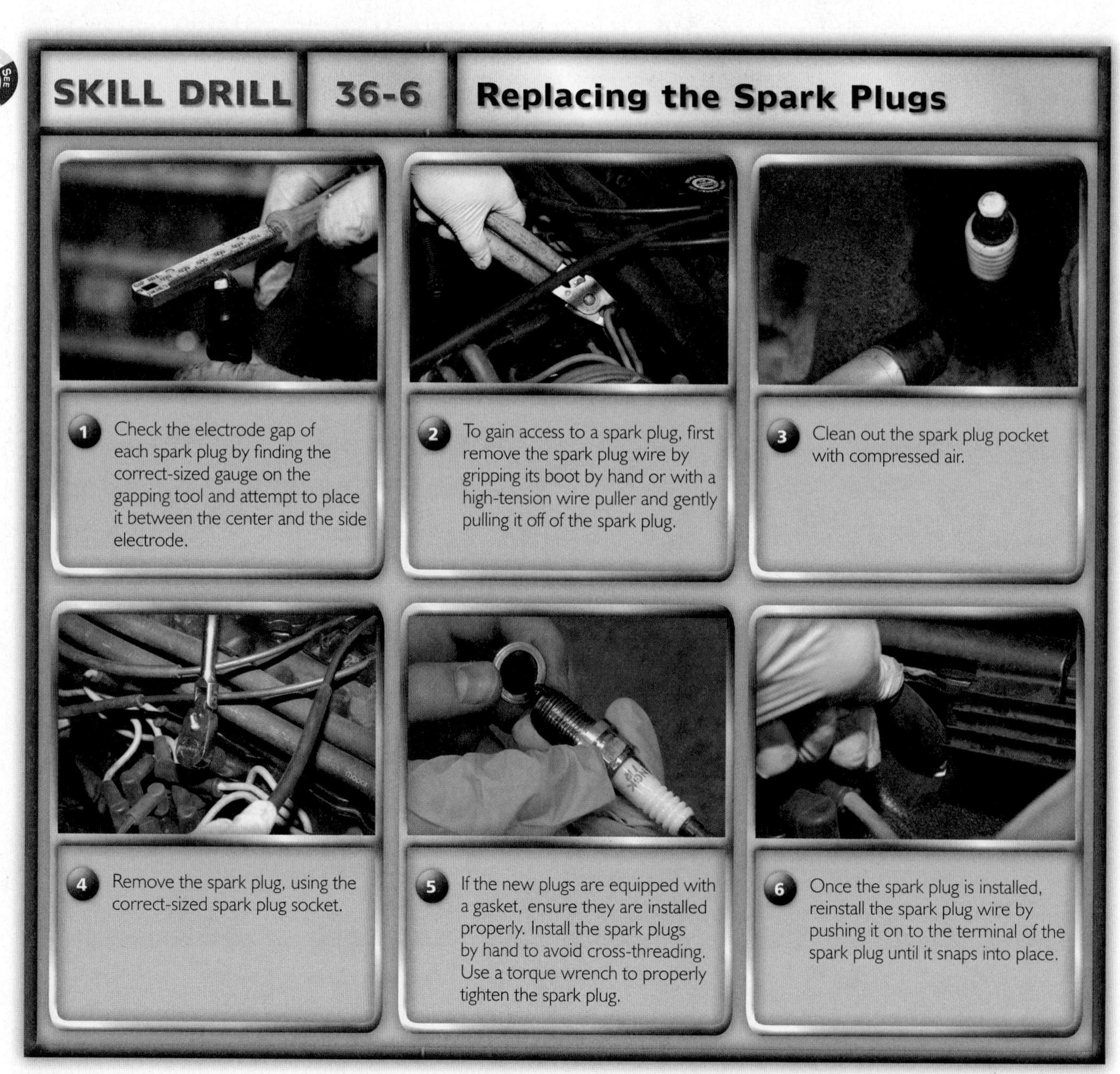

SKILL DRILL 36-6 Replacing the Spark Plugs

1. Check the electrode gap of each spark plug by finding the correct-sized gauge on the gapping tool and attempt to place it between the center and the side electrode.
2. To gain access to a spark plug, first remove the spark plug wire by gripping its boot by hand or with a high-tension wire puller and gently pulling it off of the spark plug.
3. Clean out the spark plug pocket with compressed air.
4. Remove the spark plug, using the correct-sized spark plug socket.
5. If the new plugs are equipped with a gasket, ensure they are installed properly. Install the spark plugs by hand to avoid cross-threading. Use a torque wrench to properly tighten the spark plug.
6. Once the spark plug is installed, reinstall the spark plug wire by pushing it on to the terminal of the spark plug until it snaps into place.

Replacing the Spark Plug Wires

The spark plug wires, high-tension leads, or COP boots should be replaced periodically. There is not usually a recommended replacement interval stated in the owner's maintenance schedules for spark plug wires. Many shops recommend replacement at about the 100,000-mile (160,000-km) range. When replacing a set of plug wires, replacing one spark plug wire at a time will help prevent you from getting the wires and cylinders mixed up. It is also good to lay out the wires shortest to longest so that you can match up the wires if they are not numbered. Some spark plug boots are designed to use a high-temperature dielectric grease to prevent the boots from sticking to the spark plug porcelain. In some cases, you will need to burp any trapped air from the spark plug wire boots with a small dull screwdriver so that the air does not push the boots back off.

To replace the spark plug wires, follow the steps in SKILL DRILL 36-7.

SKILL DRILL
36-7
Replacing the Spark Plug Wires
1 Remove one end of the wire (or boot) from the distributor cap, coil pack, or COP coil. Remove the other end from the spark plug with a high-tension wire puller by twisting the boot on the spark plug while gently pulling it off.
2 If dielectric grease is specified for the spark plug boots, use a cotton swab to spread a small amount around the inside of the boot.
3 Install the new spark plug wire by pushing one end onto the spark plug and the other onto the distributor cap, coil pack, or COP coil. The spark plug wires should be routed in their factory positions to prevent damage.

Wrap-up

Ready for Review

- Ignition systems have a primary (low-voltage) circuit to connect and disconnect the ignition coil and a secondary (high-voltage) circuit to send voltage from the battery to the spark plug.
- Common components of an ignition system are the spark plugs, high tension leads ignition coil, and ignition-coil triggering device.
- Principles of an ignition system involve a circuit activating the ignition coil, which converts the battery's low voltage to high voltage. The voltage then travels to the spark plug in each cylinder, igniting the air–fuel mixture and creating enough pressure to push down the pistons.
- The original contact breaker ignition system was replaced with an electronic ignition system of the distributor type.
- Modern systems are direct ignition systems (or coil-on-plug), which have a dedicated coil for each cylinder.
- The amount of available voltage should always be higher than the amount of required voltage.
- As ignition components age and become worn, required voltage increases and available voltage decreases.
- Spark timing is affected by any of these factors: air–fuel ratio, detected knock, engine speed, engine load, engine temperature, and throttle position.
- Spark timing must be correct in order to give the air–fuel mixture enough time to burn.
- Modern vehicles have electronically programmed spark timing via the PCM; older vehicles mechanically advance or retard the spark timing.
- Common points on an ignition switch are the lock and off functions and the accessory, on/run, and start/crank positions.
- Automatic transmission vehicles may employ a transmission shift interlock device to ensure that the gear selector is in park before key removal can occur.
- Standard ignition coils contain primary and secondary windings around a rod-shaped laminated iron core.
- The main difference among types of ignition systems is the method used to control the primary circuit to produce the secondary spark.
- In the primary circuit, a magnetic field develops that is interrupted by the ignition triggering device, thus collapsing the field and returning stored energy to ignition coil terminals.
- Because the secondary winding has approximately 100 times as many turns as the primary winding, it can produce 100 times greater voltage.
- Basic contact breaker point ignition systems consist of the battery, ignition switch, ignition coil, contact breaker points, capacitor, distributor, and appropriate voltage-connecting wires and leads.
- The purpose of the distributor is to transfer the spark to the spark plugs with the correct sequence and timing.
- The distributor cap provides rotor and spark plug lead connection.
- The distributor controls ignition timing in relation to speed via a centrifugal advance mechanism and ignition timing in relation to vehicle load via a vacuum advance mechanism.
- Vehicles regulate voltage to the ignition system via a ballast resistor, which is inserted in the primary circuit and lowers the voltage.
- Spark plugs all have at least one, and up to four, side electrodes, as well as an internal resistor to suppress voltage spikes and prevent radio frequency interference.
- Spark plugs are identified by thread size or diameter, reach or length of thread, and heat range or operating temperature.
- Spark plug components include the metal case, insulator, terminal, side electrode, and center electrode.
- To work effectively, spark plugs must have proper reach (distance from sealing area to end of spark plug threads) and proper heat range (operating temperature, generally 746°F to 1,460°F [400°C to 800°C]).
- High-tension leads carry a high-voltage spark from the ignition coil to the distributor cap and on to the spark plugs.
- Engine timing can refer to valve timing or ignition timing.
- Electronic ignition systems electronically trigger the primary circuit (rather than using a contact breaker).
- The triggering device of an electronic ignition system can be a magnetic pulse generator (pickup coil) or a Hall-effect switch or an optical sensor.
- Ignition modules process information from various sensors and then interrupt the signal to the primary winding of the ignition coil.

- Induction-type systems use a magnetic pulse generator with a stator and a reluctor attached to the distributor body and shaft, respectively.
- Induction-type systems produce an alternating current voltage.
- Hall-effect systems use a potential difference, or voltage, which is used as a switch device.
- In a Hall-effect system, the magnetic field is alternately blocked and exposed by an interrupter ring.
- Some ignition systems use a phototransistor to receive light from an LED and transform it into a voltage output signal.
- In distributorless ignition systems, the distributor is eliminated so crankshaft and camshaft position sensors help determine when to send a signal to the coil's primary windings by monitoring which cylinder is approaching its power stroke.
- In a six-cylinder, waste spark engine, each set of two cylinders is paired with an ignition coil. The cylinders alternate between an event cylinder and a waste cylinder.
- The first step in diagnosing ignition system issues is to conduct a visual inspection to look for loose connections, broken or corroded terminals, or any components that need replacing.
- Inspect the primary and secondary circuit wiring for cuts, abrasions, and signs of arcing.
- Test the ignition coil for primary and secondary winding resistance.
- If the vehicle will not start, performing a spark test is a good step.
- Test to ensure that the spark plug wire, distributor cap and rotor, crankshaft and camshaft position sensors, and ignition modules are in proper working order.
- Always follow manufacturer-recommended procedure for diagnosing each ignition system component.
- Spark plugs and spark plug wires will wear over time and require replacement; check the manufacturer's recommendations for replacement schedules.

Key Terms

advance mechanism A device used to trigger an earlier spark based on engine conditions.

available voltage The maximum amount of voltage that the induction coil secondary is capable of putting out.

battery An electrochemical device used to supply voltage to a vehicle's electrical systems.

breaker plate The movable plate which the breaker points are mounted on and which pivots as the vacuum advance pulls on it.

cam lobes Raised areas or protrusions on an otherwise round shaft.

camshaft position sensor A sensor mounted near the camshaft and used to send camshaft and valve position information to the PCM.

capacitor (condenser) A self-contained unit that is connected electrically in parallel with the contact breaker points and used to assist the rapid collapse of the magnetic field in the coil by preventing the contact breaker points from arcing. Also used on some coils to reduce radio frequency interference.

center electrode The electrode located in the center of a spark plug. It is the hottest part of the spark plug.

centrifugal advance mechanism An ignition timing device, located above or beneath the distributor base plate, that rotates with the distributor cam and is used to advance the spark. As engine speed rises, the flyweights on the advance mechanism are thrown outward by centrifugal force. Since the distributor cam is able to pivot on the distributor shaft, the weights act against their springs and move the distributor cam forward.

coil-on-plug A type of ignition system used on late-model vehicles that uses one coil placed above each spark plug.

compression stroke The stroke in the four-stroke cycle in which the air–fuel mixture is compressed.

contact breaker point ignition system A type of ignition system that uses a mechanical means of turning the primary circuit on and off.

contact breaker points A mechanically operated electrical switch that is fixed to the distributor base plate and opened and closed by the distributor cam with the rotation of the engine. The contacts normally form a self-contained unit, fixed to the base plate by a retaining screw engaged in a slot in the fixed contact.

crank angle position The position of the crankshaft, measured in degrees.

cranking Rotating the engine by turning the ignition key to the start position.

crankshaft position sensor A sensor mounted near the crankshaft and used to send engine speed and position signals to the PCM.

direct ignition system May refer to a waste spark ignition or a coil-on-plug ignition system, in which the coils are directly attached to the spark plugs.

distributor The part of an ignition system that distributes the spark to the spark plugs in the correct sequence and at the correct time. It includes a distributor cap, rotor, shaft, and usually a switching device.

distributor base plate A round metal plate near the top of the distributor that is attached to a distributor housing; also called a breaker plate.

distributor cap The top portion of a distributor, used to make a connection between the spinning rotor and the high-tension leads.

distributorless ignition system An ignition system that does not include a distributor. It uses signals from the crankshaft position sensor and the camshaft position sensor sent to the PCM to determine when to send a signal to the ignition module.

electronic control unit (ECU) A computer that controls the ignition and fuel control and emissions control systems on an engine; also called the engine control module (ECM) or power train control module (PCM).

electronic ignition system—distributor type An ignition system that uses a distributor but replaces the contact points with an electronic triggering device.

electronic ignition system An ignition system that uses a nonmechanical (electronic) method of triggering the ignition coil's primary circuit.

enameled copper wire Wire that uses a thin layer of enamel as insulating material. The thinness of the insulation allows the wire to be closely wound in a coil, creating a dense magnetic field when current flows through it.

engine control module (ECM) A computer that controls the ignition and fuel control and emissions control systems on an engine; also the electronic control unit (ECU) or power train control module (PCM).

event cylinder The cylinder that uses the spark to ignite the air–fuel mixture on a waste spark ignition system.

Hall-effect switch The portion of an electronic ignition system used to trigger the ignition system. Hall-effect switches operate by using a potential difference, or voltage, created when a current-carrying conductor is exposed to a magnetic field. If a magnetic field is applied at right angles to the direction of current flow in a conductor, the lines of magnetic force permeate the conductor, and the electrons flowing in the conductor are deflected to one side. This deflection creates a potential difference across the conductor. The stronger the magnetic field, the higher the voltage.

heat range The rating of a spark plug's operating temperature.

high-tension leads The heavy insulated wires used to connect the distributor cap terminals to the spark plugs, and the ignition coil to the distributor cap, or on waste spark systems, the coils to the spark plugs.

high-tension terminals The terminals on the coils and distributor cap that the high-tension leads are connected to.

high-voltage spark The electrical arc that takes place between the center and the side electrode of a spark plug.

ignition advance The means of causing the spark to occur earlier within the compression stroke for better performance and fuel economy during changing engine conditions.

ignition coil A device used to amplify an input voltage into the much higher voltage needed to jump the electrodes of a spark plug.

ignition coil pack A group of two or more ignition coils housed in one assembly.

ignition module An electronic component that electronically controls the ignition coil or coils.

ignition switch A switch operated by a key or start/stop button and used to turn on or off a vehicle's electrical and ignition system.

induced voltage The creation of voltage in a conductor by movement of a magnetic field that is near that conductor.

induction coil An electrical transformer that uses magnetic fields to produce high-voltage pulses from low-voltage direct current.

induction-type system A type of ignition system that uses a magnetic pulse generator to trigger the spark.

inductive current The current that has been created across a conductor by moving it through a magnetic field.

intake manifold vacuum Pressure that is less than atmospheric pressure that develops in the intake manifold of a running engine equipped with a throttle plate. It is a measure of the vacuum in the intake manifold.

integrated circuit A semiconductor chip that contains miniature versions of various electrical components within one housing.

interrupter ring A ferrous metal ring, shaped like a very shallow cup with slits or windows cut into it at evenly spaced intervals. The ring has the same number of blades and windows as engine cylinders and is rotated by the engine moving the blades through an air gap. The purpose of an interrupter ring is to systematically block, and expose, the magnetic field in a Hall-effect sensor in order to turn the primary ignition circuit on and off.

number one cylinder Typically the cylinder located farthest forward on the engine. It is the first cylinder in the firing order.

optical sensor A sensor that generates a voltage when excited by a beam of light.

oscillate To cycle above and below a given value.

power train control module (PCM) A computer that controls the ignition and fuel control and emissions control systems on an engine; also called the electronic control unit (ECU) or engine control module (ECM).

primary circuit The low-voltage circuit that turns the coil on and off.

primary winding The low-voltage coiled copper wiring found in an ignition coil.

raster The scope pattern where all of the ignition firing sequences are stacked vertically on top of each other.

reluctor A rotating, toothed wheel that changes the reluctance of a material to conduct magnetic lines of force.

required voltage The amount of voltage needed to push current across the electrodes of a spark plug located in the combustion chamber.

rolling code A constantly changing, randomly selected numeric code that is communicated with the engine immobilizer and security system.

rotor A high-voltage rotating switch that transfers voltage from the distributor cap's center terminal to the outer terminals.

rotor arm The portion of the rotor that extends toward, but not touching, the outer distributor cap terminals.

secondary circuit The part of an ignition system that operates on higher voltage and delivers the necessary high voltage to the spark plugs.

spark plug A device that provides a gap for the high-voltage spark to occur in each cylinder.

spark plug reach The length of the spark plug from the seat to the end of the threads.

spark timing The point at which a spark occurs at the spark plug relative to the position of the piston.

stator Portion of an electronic ignition system that is mounted to the base of the distributor. It has a circular permanent magnet with a number of projections or teeth corresponding to the number of engine cylinders, and a stationary coil of fine enameled copper wire wound on a plastic reel and positioned inside the magnet.

step-up transformer An electrical device containing many turns of wire, used to amplify low voltage into high voltage.

throttle body The housing on an intake manifold that is used to control the amount of filtered air that enters the cylinders.

vacuum advance unit A mechanism that controls ignition timing advance in relation to engine load and causes the spark at the spark plug to occur sooner based on engine conditions. Its function is to improve fuel economy and, in doing so, reduce exhaust emissions.

waste cylinder The cylinder in a waste spark ignition system that receives a spark near the top of its exhaust stroke.

waste spark ignition system An ignition system in which each ignition coil serves two cylinders, with each end of the secondary winding attached by a high-tension lead to a spark plug. The spark is used to ignite the air–fuel mixture in one cylinder and has no effect on the other cylinder.

ASE-Type Questions

1. Tech A says that contact breaker points are a mechanical switch that opens and closes once for every ignition spark that is created. Tech B says that contact breaker points send high voltage directly from the points to the spark plugs. Who is correct?
   a. Tech A
   b. Tech B
   c. Both A and B
   d. Neither A nor B
2. Tech A says that as engines gain miles, the spark plug gap increases, which raises the ignition system's available voltage. Tech B says that misfire occurs when required voltage is higher than available voltage. Who is correct?
   a. Tech A
   b. Tech B
   c. Both A and B
   d. Neither A nor B
3. Tech A says that as engine RPM increases, spark timing generally increases. Tech B says that as engine load increases, spark timing generally decreases. Who is correct?
   a. Tech A
   b. Tech B
   c. Both A and B
   d. Neither A nor B
4. Tech A says that a Hall-Effect switch uses light to turn a circuit on and off. Tech B says that waste spark systems don't need distributors. Who is correct?
   a. Tech A
   b. Tech B
   c. Both A and B
   d. Neither A nor B
5. Tech A says that coil-on-plug ignition systems use one coil to fire two cylinders. Tech B says that you should twist spark plug boots before removing them. Who is correct?
   a. Tech A
   b. Tech B
   c. Both A and B
   d. Neither A nor B
6. Tech A says that the ignition system will maintain spark at the spark plug for approximately 23 degrees of crankshaft rotation. Tech B says that the duration of spark in the spark plug only lasts 2 to 3 degrees of crankshaft rotation. Who is correct?
   a. Tech A
   b. Tech B
   c. Both A and B
   d. Neither A nor B
7. Tech A says that the positive side of the coil primary circuit is switched. Tech B says that the negative side of the coil primary circuit is switched. Who is correct?
   a. Tech A
   b. Tech B
   c. Both A and B
   d. Neither A nor B
8. Tech A says that one main advantage of distributorless ignition systems is no moving parts to maintain. Tech B says that the coil-on-plug ignition system uses a rotor to distribute the spark to each cylinder. Who is correct?
   a. Tech A
   b. Tech B
   c. Both A and B
   d. Neither A nor B
9. When removing spark plugs, Tech A says that you should blow around each spark plug to remove any debris that could fall into the cylinder. Tech B says that on engines that have more than about 100,000 miles, you should adjust the spark plug gap to about half the specified gap. Who is correct?
   a. Tech A
   b. Tech B
   c. Both A and B
   d. Neither A nor B
10. Tech A says that dielectric grease applied to the inside of the spark plug boot is used to keep the boot from sticking to the spark plug porcelain. Tech B says that spark plug boots may need to be "burped" so that the air doesn't push the boot off the spark plug. Who is correct?
    a. Tech A
    b. Tech B
    c. Both A and B
    d. Neither A nor B

CHAPTER 37

NATEF Tasks

Engine Performance Fuel, Air Induction, and Exhaust Systems			Page
■ Replace fuel filter(s).	MLR	AST	1067–1068
■ Inspect and test fuel pumps and pump control systems for pressure, regulation, and volume; determine necessary action.		AST	1067–1070
■ Check fuel for contaminants; determine necessary action.		AST	1070–1072
■ Inspect and test fuel injectors.		AST	1071–1073

Knowledge Objectives

After reading this chapter, you will be able to:

1. Explain the principles of the gasoline fuel system. (pp 1053–1054)
2. Describe the characteristics of gasoline fuel. (pp 1054–1055)
3. Explain stoichiometric ratio and how it applies to engine fuel. (p 1056)
4. Discuss the components of the fuel supply system. (pp 1058–1063)
5. Describe the differences between single-point and multipoint injection systems. (pp 1064–1065)
6. Explain the principles and components of the EFI fuel supply system. (pp 1064–1066)

Gasoline Fuel Systems

Skills Objectives

After reading this chapter, you will be able to:

1. Replace fuel filters. (pp 1067–1068)
2. Inspect and test fuel pumps and pump control systems for pressure, regulation, and volume. (pp 1068–1071)
3. Check fuel for contaminants and quality. (pp 1071–1072)
4. Inspect and test fuel injectors. (pp 1071–1073)

Introduction

Today's gasoline **fuel systems** must meter a precise amount of fuel into the engine under a wide range of operating conditions. The most important job of the fuel system is optimizing engine performance while keeping fuel consumption and emissions to a minimum. Although carburetors were commonly used on vehicles up until about 30 years ago, they didn't perform these jobs adequately FIGURE 37-1. Their limitations prompted the development of fuel injection, starting with mechanically operated systems that typically sprayed a continuous flow of fuel through fuel injectors at each individual intake port in the intake manifold. These systems were sometimes referred to as "bug sprayers" since they put out a continuous fine mist. The amount of fuel sprayed was controlled mechanically by an airflow-operated fuel distributor. The more air that entered the engine, the more fuel that was sprayed.

Mechanical fuel injection still could not meet the increasingly stringent emissions standards, so electronic fuel injection (EFI) was introduced. In this way, fuel delivery could be controlled electronically, allowing continuous adjustments to the air–fuel ratio. Most early EFI systems used throttle body injection (TBI), wherein one or two injectors were mounted in a throttle body. These systems looked like a simplified carburetor. As technology progressed, multipoint fuel injection (MPFI or just PFI) became more prevalent, involving one injector installed in the intake manifold near the intake port of each cylinder. This design allowed more equal distribution of fuel among the cylinders, which improved fuel economy and reduced emissions further. But even that wasn't the end of the line for new innovations. Gasoline direct injection (GDI) places the fuel injectors in the cylinder head where they can spray fuel directly into the combustion chamber. This technology allows manufacturers to operate the engine on much leaner mixtures than has otherwise been possible during certain engine operating conditions.

To make EFI of any type function correctly, an electronic control unit (ECU), also called a power train control module (PCM), is needed to determine the proper quantity of fuel to be delivered. For the PCM to make the proper determination, information from a variety of electronic sensors is needed. It is the wide variety of information that allows the fuel injection system to operate so precisely and efficiently. As a maintenance and light repair technician, it is critical that you have a basic understanding of how these systems and components operate so that you will be able to properly inspect and maintain them for your customers. This understanding will also prepare you for further training on the deeper theory and diagnosis of the fuel system.

You Are the Automotive Technician

A new customer brings her late model vehicle into your shop complaining that it hasn't been "running right" for the last few weeks. She took it to another shop where the technician said it needed a tune-up and changed the spark plugs, oxygen sensors, fuel filter, and air filter. It improved, but then started getting worse. At first the MIL came on intermittently, but now is on most of the time. The vehicle seems to be low on power, as well, and yesterday, it didn't start. When it started today, she thought she should bring it in. You explain that you will need to diagnose the problem. She authorizes the diagnostic charge. You scan the PCM and find a P0171 (system too lean bank 1), and a P0174 (system too lean bank 2). Since the oxygen sensors are new and look like they are OEM replacements, you decide to perform a fuel pump pressure and volume test. You will also perform an alcohol content test on a small sample of the fuel after the volume test.

1. Why do you suspect a fuel pump problem in this situation?
2. If the fuel pump passes the pressure test, should you perform the volume test? Why or why not?
3. How could too much alcohol in the gasoline cause the engine to run too lean?

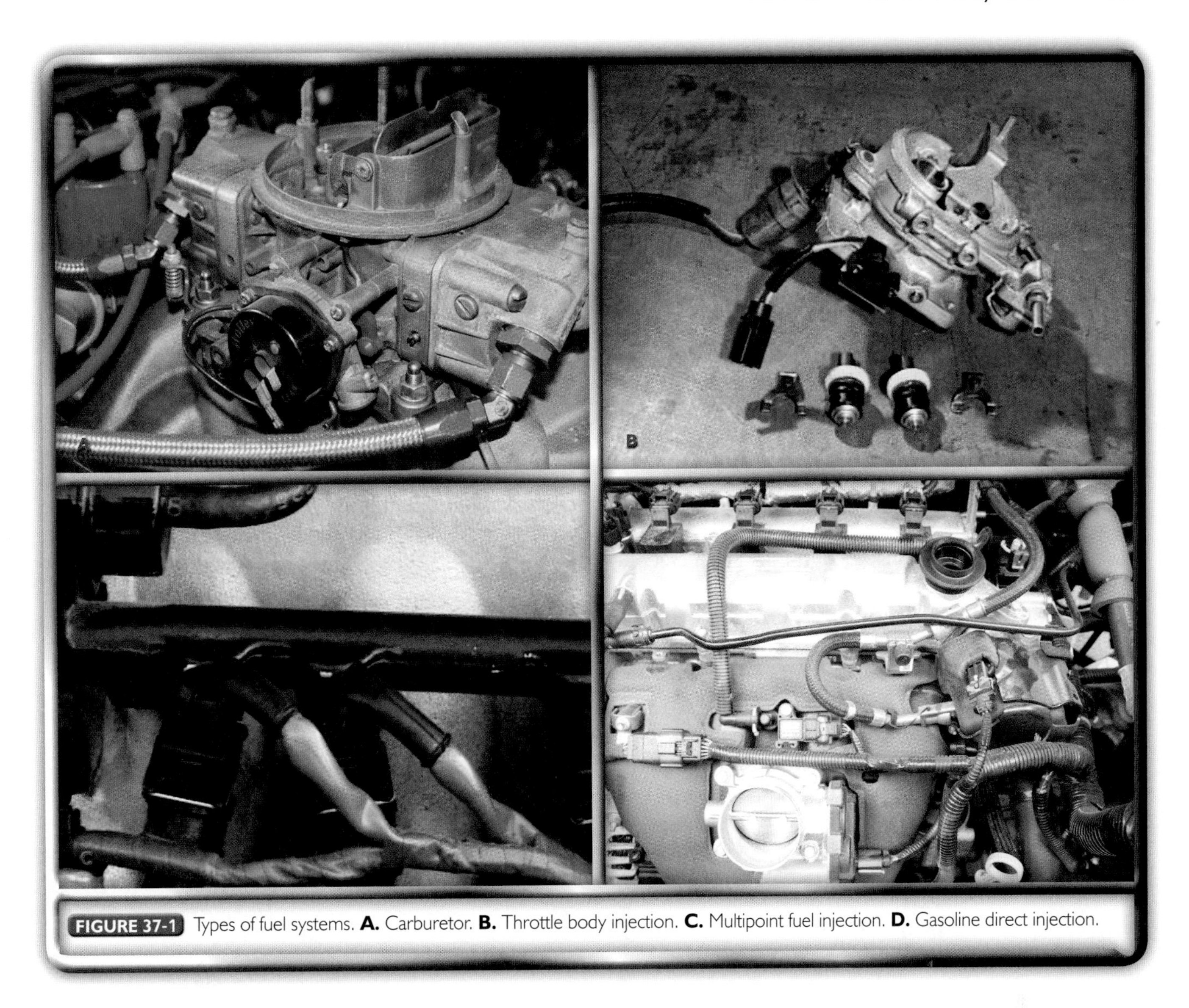
B

FIGURE 37-1 Types of fuel systems. **A.** Carburetor. **B.** Throttle body injection. **C.** Multipoint fuel injection. **D.** Gasoline direct injection.

Gasoline Fuel System Principles

The purpose of a fuel system is to provide the ideal air–fuel mixture for the operating conditions of the internal combustion engine. Liquid fuel will not burn. Fuel needs to be vaporized, turning from a liquid to a gas. It then needs to be mixed with the proper amount of air. It takes time and temperature for fuel to vaporize fully. The smaller the liquid droplets, the faster they can be vaporized. The process of making the droplets small is called atomization. A fuel system needs to atomize the fuel as small as possible so that it can be vaporized before it is ignited.

As explained in the introduction, older cars and trucks used a carburetor to atomize the fuel and mix it with air. Modern gasoline-powered vehicles use EFI systems, which atomize the fuel into much smaller particles, giving superior efficiency and performance over carburetors.

One of the reasons that carburetors cannot atomize fuel as efficiently as fuel injection systems is because the principles of operation are different. Pressure differential is central to all fuel systems. The greater the differential, the easier it is to atomize the fuel. A carburetor works off of pressures below atmospheric pressure (vacuum), which involves a relatively low pressure differential. Fuel injection, in contrast, works off of pressures above atmospheric pressure, which generally involves a much higher pressure differential FIGURE 37-2. With a very small pressure difference, as in a carburetor, fuel passages must be much larger. This means the fuel entering the airstream in a carburetor is in much larger droplets than fuel that is sprayed out of a very small hole at high pressure in a fuel injection system.

Modern fuel injection systems have three subsystems:

- **Fuel supply system**: This system provides pressurized, filtered gasoline to the fuel injectors or carburetor (in older vehicles). The fuel supply system draws in gasoline from the gas tank (fuel cell) and delivers it under pressure to a fuel metering device. Today's vehicles typically use an in-tank electric fuel pump. Older vehicles used a mechanical fuel pump that was typically mounted on the engine and driven by the camshaft.

- **Air supply system**: The air supply system, also called the induction system, provides clean filtered air for combustion in the engine. An air filter is a paper filter or **element** that filters the incoming dirty/dusty air. The element is usually housed in a plastic or metal air cleaner housing located in the engine compartment. Engineers have made numerous configurations to prevent water and dirt intrusion. In addition, air intake sounds have been carefully analyzed, and intake systems have been engineered to give the optimum vehicle performance while providing smooth and quiet operation.
- **Fuel metering system**: This system constantly meters and adjusts the amount of fuel that the engine is burning. The most common type of EFI fuel metering is multipoint fuel injection. Although specific systems vary, many of the systems have similar parts. For example, most vehicles with multipoint fuel injection systems have sensors, fuel injectors, and a PCM.

FIGURE 37-2 The main difference between carburetion and fuel injection is that carburetion works off of pressures below atmospheric pressure fuel is pulled out of the carburetor by vacuum, but fuel is sprayed under pressure out of the fuel injector.

Gasoline Fuel

Gasoline fuel is derived from crude oil. Crude oil is taken out of the ground as a liquid mixture of highly flammable compounds of hydrogen and carbon, called hydrocarbons, together with impurities. It is then processed into many fuel and lubricant products at an oil refinery through the fractional distillation process in which the crude oil is heated in the base of a tower and allowed to condense at different temperatures (levels) of the tower. More volatile compounds rise to the top of the tower, while less volatile compounds stay low in the tower FIGURE 37-3.

Gasoline is very volatile, mixing easily with air to form gas or vapor. The more effectively liquid gasoline is changed into vapor, the more efficiently it burns in the engine. Thus, high volatility is desirable. However, gasoline vapor allowed to mix with air in the open is highly explosive; therefore, it can be very dangerous, and gasoline must be handled with care. High volatility also can create excessive hydrocarbon emissions, which, if vented to the atmosphere, contribute to air pollution and smog. If liquid gasoline is heated, it is even more volatile. If it vaporizes in the fuel pump, bubbles of vapor can block the flow of fuel and stop the engine. This situation is called **vapor lock**.

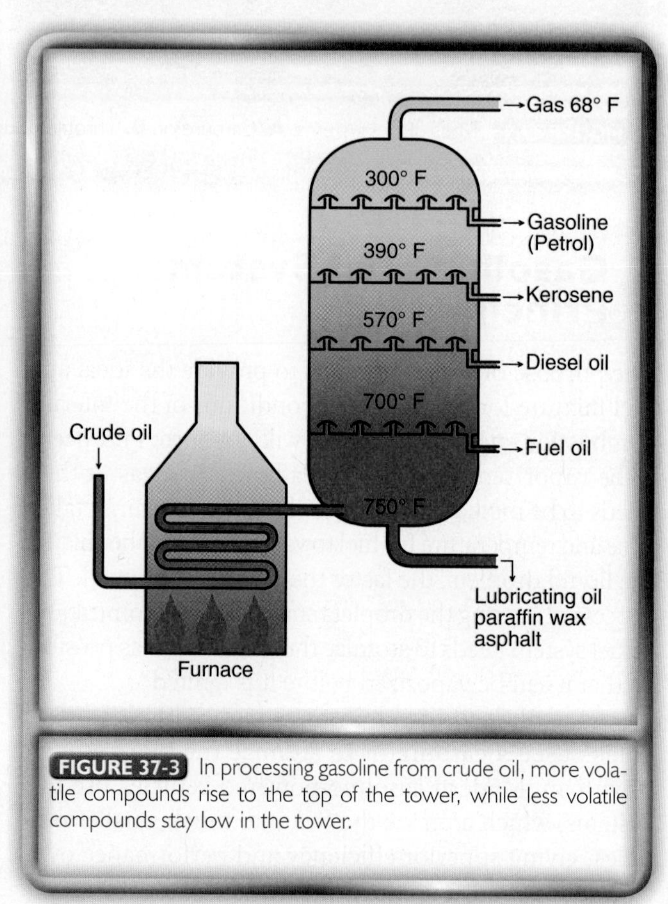
Gas 68° F
300° F
Gasoline (Petrol)
390° F
Kerosene
570° F
Diesel oil
700° F
Fuel oil
750° F
Crude oil
Lubricating oil
paraffin wax
asphalt
Furnace

FIGURE 37-3 In processing gasoline from crude oil, more volatile compounds rise to the top of the tower, while less volatile compounds stay low in the tower.

A typical gasoline is mainly a mixture of paraffins, naphthenes, aromatics, and olefins, together with some other organic compounds and contaminants such as sulfur. Some of these contaminants can cause corrosion, so they must be removed. Tight regulations in some countries limit the allowed proportion of aromatics, olefins, and sulfur in gasoline. Gasoline in its raw processed form is not suitable for use in vehicle engines; it must be enhanced with different additives such as detergents, octane boosters, and oxygenates such as ethanol. Detergents help to keep the fuel system clean, especially the fuel injector nozzles and intake valves. Octane boosters make it harder to ignite the gasoline, and oxygenates add oxygen to the fuel, which helps reduce carbon monoxide pollutants by slightly leaning out the air–fuel mixture.

When a mixture of gasoline (petrol) and air is compressed inside an engine cylinder, it heats up. If the compression of the engine is high enough, and if the fuel is able to ignite easily enough, the air–fuel mixture may spontaneously ignite before the spark plug is fired at the optimum ignition moment. This is called pre-ignition, better known as **knocking**.

Gasoline fuel can be modified during processing by including additives so that it is less prone to spontaneously ignite. This ignition characteristic is known as its **octane rating**. The less easily the fuel ignites, the higher the octane rating. Higher compression engines are more susceptible to engine knock, so they require fuels with a higher octane rating—that is, fuels that ignite less readily.

A gasoline's octane rating is measured by the producer. There are two different methods used to measure the octane rating of a fuel—the Research Octane Number (RON) and the Motor Octane Number (MON). Depending on the composition of the fuel, the MON of a modern gasoline will be about 8 to 10 points lower than the RON; however, there is no direct link between RON and MON. Both are measurements of a fuel's resistance to knock, but the MON is a better measure of how the fuel behaves when under load.

In most countries, including the whole of Europe and much of the rest of the world, the RON rating is the one that is usually displayed on the pump at filling stations. In the United States and Canada, and some other countries, the displayed fuel rating is an average of the RON and the MON rating: (RON + MON)/2. Consequently, whatever the rating may be called at the pump, the rating number for identical fuels will on average be about 4 to 5 points higher in Europe than they will appear to be in the United States.

There is a popular belief that fuels with higher octane ratings will improve performance in vehicles that are designed to run on fuels with lower octane ratings. This is largely a myth, although some premium fuels do have higher energy ratings. Higher-powered engines usually have a higher compression ratio, so they generally require more expensive higher-octane fuels to prevent pre-ignition and detonation. Higher octane does not in itself mean higher energy output, so a fuel designed for a high-compression engine will not necessarily deliver any more power in a lower compression engine. Engines perform best when used with the fuel that has the engine manufacturer's recommended octane rating.

Octane can be boosted with additives. Prior to the introduction of catalytic converters, tetraethyl lead was added to boost octane. Lead was also used to lubricate valve faces and seats, which slowed down wear. But lead also would coat the catalytic converter and oxygen sensor, rendering them inoperable. So leaded fuel was phased out for general vehicle use, and unleaded fuel took its place. So-called "unleaded gasoline" may contain small amounts of lead, but maximum levels are tightly controlled. Octane is now boosted with additives of ethanol, aromatic hydrocarbons, and ethers.

Controlling Fuel Burn

For gasoline to burn properly, it must be mixed with the right amount of air. For a gasoline engine, the air–fuel ratio by mass is about 14.7 to 1. By volume, it is about 11,000 to 1—not much gasoline, but lots of air. A lean air–fuel mixture has more air in proportion to the amount of fuel. A slightly lean mixture gives good fuel economy and low exhaust emissions—suitable for cruising conditions. A mixture that is too lean can make an engine run rough and overheat. A rich air–fuel mixture has less air in proportion to the amount of fuel. A slightly rich mixture can produce more power at lower temperatures, but the extra fuel it uses steps up fuel consumption and greatly increases emissions. A mixture that is too rich fouls spark plugs and causes incomplete burning, and that reduces power.

Combustion

In normal combustion, the spark plug ignites the mixture, and a small ball of flame forms around the tip of the plug FIGURE 37-4. The piston finishes compressing the mixture. The flame spreads faster and moves evenly to halfway through the mixture, and the piston reaches top dead center. The flame picks up more speed, then shoots out to consume the rest of the mixture. Combustion ends with the piston a short way down the cylinder. Ideally, this would completely burn all of the fuel that entered the cylinder, extracting the maximum thermal energy from the gasoline.

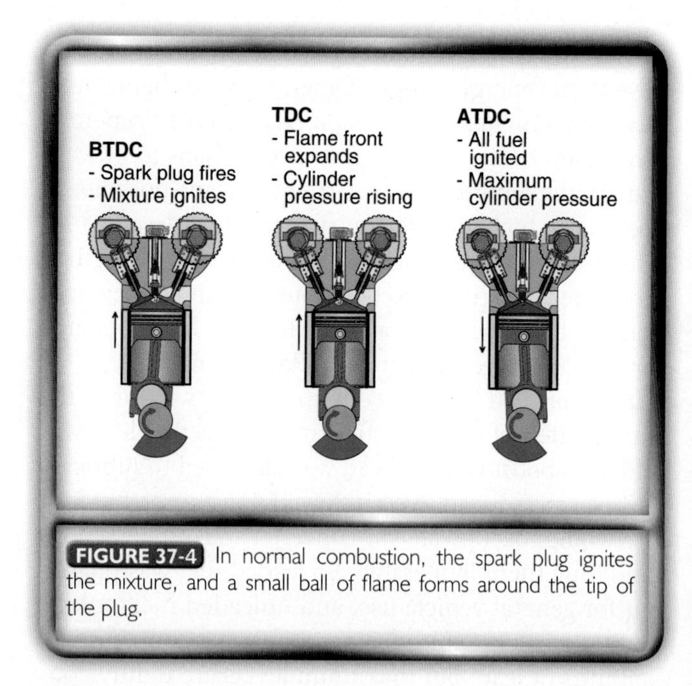
BTDC
- Spark plug fires
- Mixture ignites
TDC
- Flame front expands
- Cylinder pressure rising
ATDC
- All fuel ignited
- Maximum cylinder pressure

FIGURE 37-4 In normal combustion, the spark plug ignites the mixture, and a small ball of flame forms around the tip of the plug.

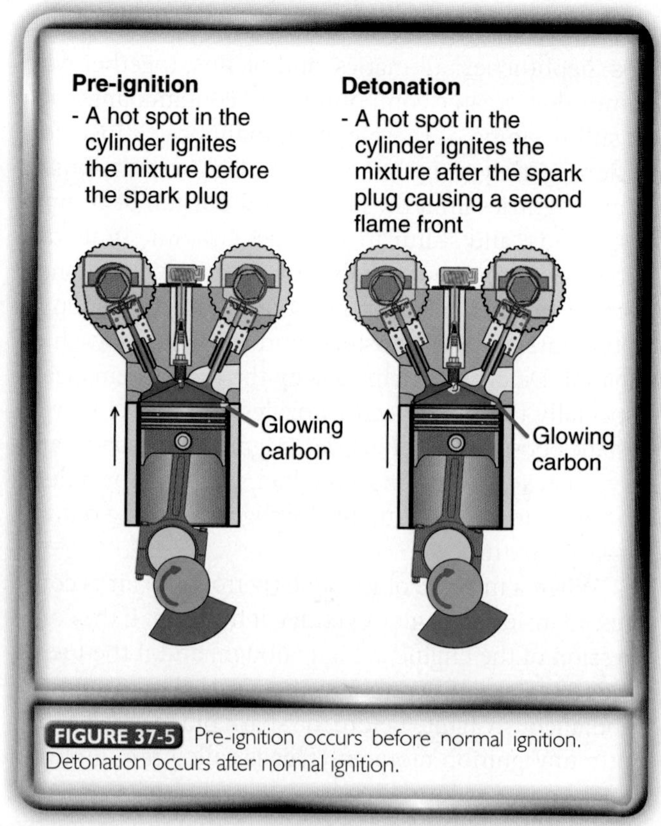
Pre-ignition
- A hot spot in the cylinder ignites the mixture before the spark plug
Detonation
- A hot spot in the cylinder ignites the mixture after the spark plug causing a second flame front
Glowing carbon
Glowing carbon

FIGURE 37-5 Pre-ignition occurs before normal ignition. Detonation occurs after normal ignition.

Detonation/Pre-ignition

Detonation is a violent collision of flame fronts in the cylinder, caused by uncontrolled combustion. It occurs after the spark plug has fired. The sudden rise in pressure can cause the remainder of the mixture to ignite spontaneously creating a second flame front that collides with the first front, making a knocking sound FIGURE 37-5. Sustained detonations can raise temperatures enough to cause pre-ignition, also called auto-ignition. Pre-ignition occurs before normal combustion, when something in the combustion chamber heats up enough to ignite the mixture before the spark plug fires. A mixture may also ignite simply because it is unstable under the higher heat and pressure. Detonation and pre-ignition can cause severe damage and must be avoided. Many engine management systems use knock sensors to detect detonation, and the PCM retards ignition timing to certain limits to try to stop it.

An engine that keeps running after it is switched off is said to be running-on or **dieseling**. That's because, as in a diesel engine, the fuel is igniting just from heat with no spark from the plug. This situation may even cause an engine to run backwards for a brief time when it comes to a stop. Dieseling can be caused by a high idling speed, an overheated engine, too many carbon deposits in the chamber, or use of a gasoline with an octane rating that is too low. On carburetors, it can be prevented by a special valve in the carburetor idle circuit that cuts off fuel when the ignition is turned off, or a solenoid can be used to return the **throttle** to a below-idle position. Fuel-injected vehicles do not experience dieseling unless there is a leaking injector when the ignition is turned off and the PCM shuts off the injector(s).

Stoichiometric Ratio

The term **stoichiometric ratio** describes the chemically correct air–fuel ratio necessary to achieve complete combustion of the fuel and air. In other words, it is when all of the oxygen completely combines with the fuel, leaving no molecules of either remaining. All of the oxygen and fuel have been chemically combined through complete combustion. It is represented by the Greek letter lambda (λ). For gasoline fuel, the stoichiometric air–fuel ratio is 14.7 parts air to 1 part fuel by mass, not volume. By volume, that equals 11,000 gallons or liters of air to every 1 gallon or liter of fuel—a ratio of 11,000:1. So if the air–fuel mixture is at the stoichiometric air–fuel ratio of 14.7 to 1, then the lambda value is 1 ($\lambda = 1$).

If an air–fuel mixture has a higher figure, say a lambda value of 1.05, there is more air in proportion to the fuel than 14.7 to 1; in fact, it is about 15.5:1, and the mixture is slightly lean. A mixture with a lower lambda value, say 0.95, has proportionately less air than fuel, approximately 14.0:1, and the mixture is slightly rich.

The exhaust gas oxygen sensor (often written as "O_2" sensor) is also called the lambda sensor, since it can be used to indicate the amount of oxygen in the exhaust so that the PCM can maintain a lambda that oscillates just above and below 1. The upstream oxygen sensor is usually installed in the exhaust manifold, where it measures the percentage of oxygen in the exhaust gases. A high percentage of oxygen may mean too little fuel is entering the engine, the mixture is too lean, and lambda is greater than 1. The sensor delivers this information to the PCM, which adjusts the mixture accordingly. Similarly, a low percentage of oxygen may indicate too much fuel is entering the engine, the mixture is too rich, and lambda is less than 1. Different fuels have a different stoichiometric ratio. For instance, methanol's air–fuel ratio is 6.4:1, and ethanol's is 9:1, again measured by mass not volume.

Internal Combustion Requirements

There are three key components of internal combustion:

1. Air: Air is an oxygen-rich combustible gas.
2. Fuel: In this chapter, the fuel referred to is gasoline.
3. Pressure/vacuum differential: Pressure or vacuum is used to force the first two components into the combustion chamber, where they are compressed and ignited.

Air

Air is one of the essential components of the internal combustion engine. The components of air are a mixture of gases and small particles, which vary in composition. There are four primary components of the earth's atmosphere: nitrogen, oxygen, argon, and carbon dioxide FIGURE 37-6.

The density of air is its mass per unit volume. Thus, a volume of air at high density has a higher mass than the same volume at low density. And if there is a larger mass of air, it will contain proportionally more oxygen. The density of air in the atmosphere changes at different temperatures and altitudes. That means the air that enters an engine at different locations could have very different amounts of oxygen. The amount of oxygen in air directly affects how well it supports combustion, so it can be important in determining an air–fuel ratio for an engine.

Fuel

As described throughout this chapter, gasoline is the fuel for the process of internal combustion. Derived from crude oil (petroleum), gasoline can be a powerful form of energy when mixed with air and pressurized.

Pressure

Pressure and negative pressure, or **vacuum**, are terms used daily in the automotive industry. Manufacturers recommend a pressure to which tires need to be inflated. And manifold vacuum is used to operate a power brake booster. Gases exert pressure on all bodies they make contact with. This applies also to the air in the earth's atmosphere. Air has mass, and as a result it exerts pressure, called atmospheric pressure, not only on the earth's surface, but also on all objects on the earth's surface.

Atmospheric pressure varies with altitude. At sea level, it is calculated as 14.7 pounds per square inch (psi), or 101 kilopascals (kPa). But if this is so, why does a pressure gauge read zero when it is not in use? This is because the gauge indicates only pressure above atmospheric pressure. This reading is called gauge pressure FIGURE 37-7. If you needed to know absolute pressure, an absolute pressure gauge would be required, and it would read 14.7 psi at sea level. Absolute pressure equals gauge pressure plus atmospheric pressure. Readings on

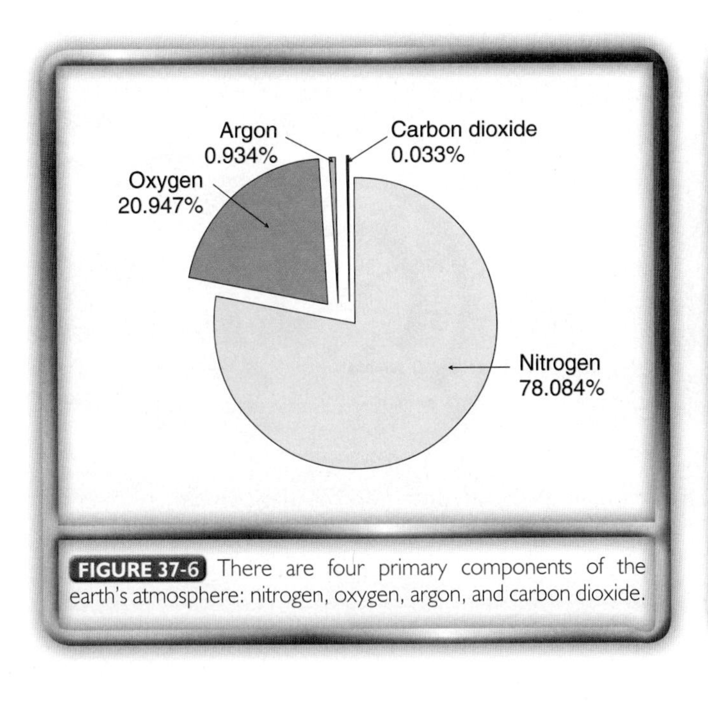
Argon
0.934%
Carbon dioxide
0.033%
Oxygen
20.947%
Nitrogen
78.084%

FIGURE 37-6 There are four primary components of the earth's atmosphere: nitrogen, oxygen, argon, and carbon dioxide.

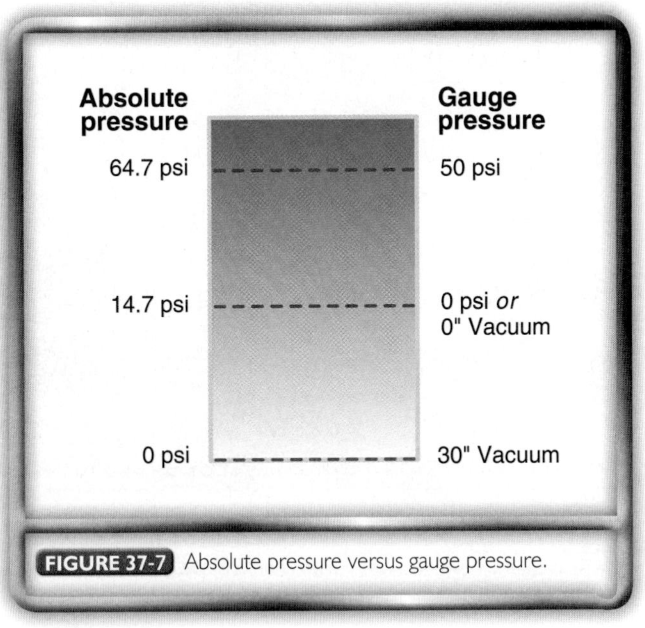
Absolute pressure
Gauge pressure
64.7 psi
50 psi
14.7 psi
0 psi or
0" Vacuum
0 psi
30" Vacuum

FIGURE 37-7 Absolute pressure versus gauge pressure.

an oil pressure gauge, or a tire gauge, should really have 14.7 psi added to them (at seal level) for true pressure. It is normal practice, however, for the gauge reading alone to be taken as the accepted value since atmospheric pressure is present at sea level.

If pressure being measured is below atmospheric pressure, a pressure gauge with its zero reading is of no value. Therefore, for pressures below atmospheric pressure, as in manifold vacuum, a vacuum gauge is normally used.

In a gasoline engine, the position of the throttle plate controls the volume of air, or air–fuel mixture, entering the manifold. At **idle** speed, the pistons draw air away from the manifold at a faster rate than it can pass the throttle plate into the manifold, creating a high vacuum, or low pressure. At wide-open throttle, depending on load, the vacuum is much less, and pressure in the manifold rises closer to atmospheric pressure FIGURE 37-8.

A vacuum gauge can be calibrated in inches of mercury in a scale reading from 0" to 30", or if using millimeters of mercury, the scale reads from 0 to 760 mm. The scale is derived from the fact that atmospheric pressure at sea level supports a column of mercury 30" (760 mm) high. This glass tube, closed at one end, is filled with mercury, then inverted in a bowl of mercury. The space above the mercury is a vacuum, and atmospheric pressure on the exposed surface of the mercury supports the column. As noted, atmospheric pressure supports a 30" (760-mm) column of mercury at sea level, but at higher altitude, its height falls, which indicates that atmospheric pressure at that altitude is less. Thus, this scale can be used to indicate the degree of vacuum, or depression, that exists below atmospheric pressure. At idle speeds, a vacuum gauge connected to the intake manifold will indicate a reading of approximately 15" to 21" (308 to 530 mm) of mercury, depending on altitude.

Some engine management systems signal changes in atmospheric pressure by using a barometric pressure sensor in the PCM. This is because, above sea level, air pressure is reduced; to maintain the correct air–fuel ratio, a vehicle must reduce the amount of fuel delivered to the engine.

Electronic Fuel Injection Fuel Supply Components

The fuel supply system consists of several components that all play integral roles in delivering gasoline to the fuel injection system, including the following:

- Fuel tank
- Fuel filler neck
- Gas cap
- Evaporative emission control system (EVAP)
- Fuel pump relay
- Fuel pump
- Fuel tank sending unit
- Fuel filter
- Fuel lines
- Fuel rail
- Fuel pressure regulator
- Fuel injector(s)

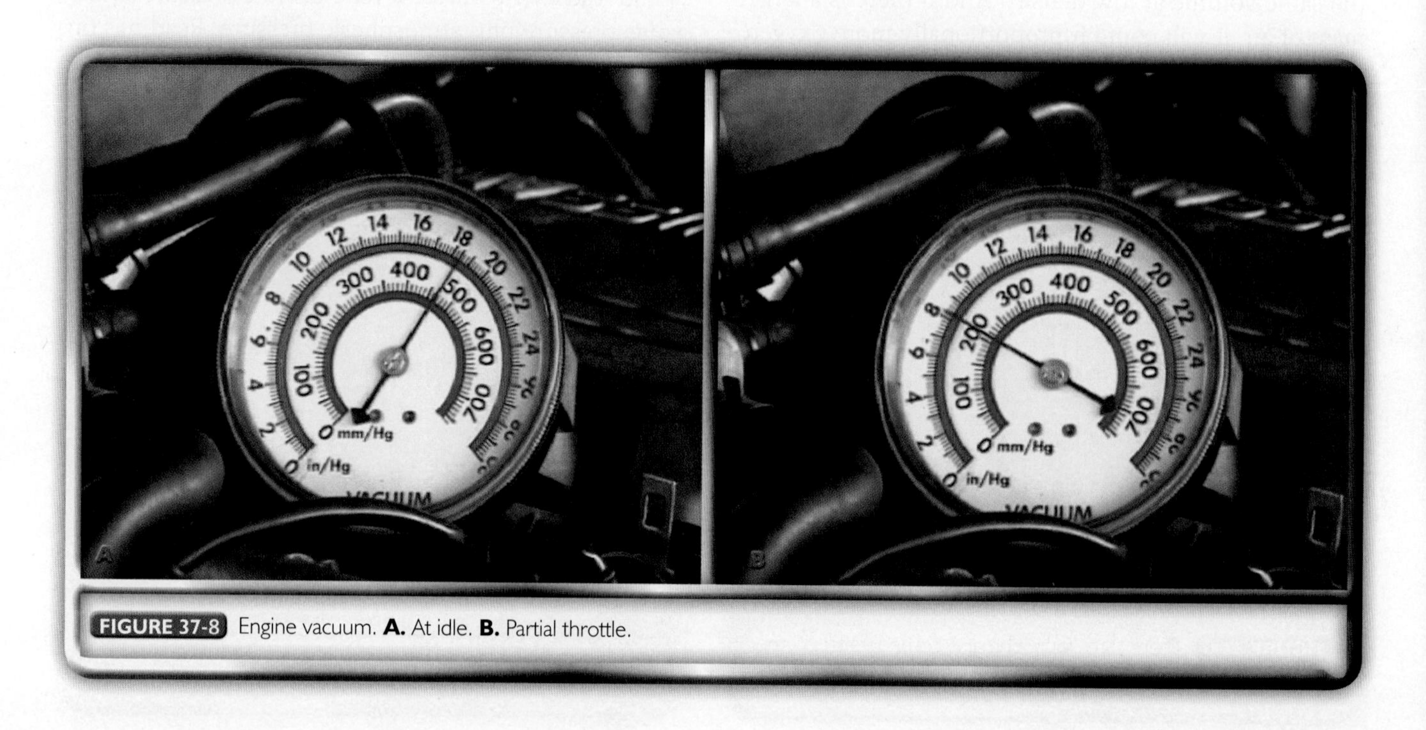
A
B
mm/Hg
in/Hg
VACUUM

FIGURE 37-8 Engine vacuum. **A.** At idle. **B.** Partial throttle.

Fuel Tank

The fuel tank (or gas tank, as it is sometimes called) is the primary reservoir of the on-board fuel supply. The typical fuel tank of modern vehicles consists of a gas cap, filler neck, fuel, fuel pump, and gauge sending unit FIGURE 37-9. Its primary function is to safely hold an adequate supply of gasoline for prolonged engine operation.

Where the tank is mounted depends on where the engine is and on space and styling. Safety demands that it be positioned well away from heated components and outside the passenger compartment. Tanks are made either of tinned sheet steel that has been pressed into shape or of nonmetallic materials. Aluminum or steel is used on commercial vehicles. The metal tank is usually in two parts, joined by a continuous weld around the flanges where the parts fit together. Baffles make the tanks more rigid. They also prevent the surging and sloshing of fuel and ensure that fuel is available at the pickup tube.

Because fuel expands and contracts as temperature rises and falls, fuel tanks are vented to let them breathe. Modern emission controls prevent tanks from being vented directly to the atmosphere. They must use evaporative control systems. Vapor from the fuel tank is vented through a charcoal canister where fuel vapors are stored until they are burned in the engine. A vapor or vent line with a check valve connects the space above the liquid fuel with the canister. This valve opens above a specified pressure and lets through vapor but not liquid.

Liquid fuel closes the check valve and blocks the line, which stops it from reaching the charcoal. Some systems have a small container, called a liquid–vapor separator, above the fuel tank. It also prevents liquid fuel from reaching the charcoal.

Fuel Filler Neck

The fuel filler is where fuel enters the tank. The fuel filler neck is a pipe that extends above the fuel tank FIGURE 37-10. On older unleaded gasoline vehicles with catalytic converters, the filler neck was designed to prevent leaded fuel being added. Its diameter is smaller than those on leaded vehicles, and a trapdoor inside the filler can be opened only by the nozzle of the unleaded gasoline spout. The location of the filler neck depends on the design of the vehicle and location of the tank. The filler neck can incorporate the use of a blowback ball valve to prevent fuel from leaking from the vehicle during fill-ups and to deter gas theft.

Safety

Never use a hose and your mouth to siphon gasoline from a vehicle. It is easy to swallow or inhale the gasoline, which is poisonous. If gas needs to be removed from a vehicle, always use a gas caddy with a suction pump.

Gas Cap

Modern vehicles are required by the Environmental Protection Agency (EPA) to have a nonvented gas cap. This nonvented cap prevents fuel vapors from being

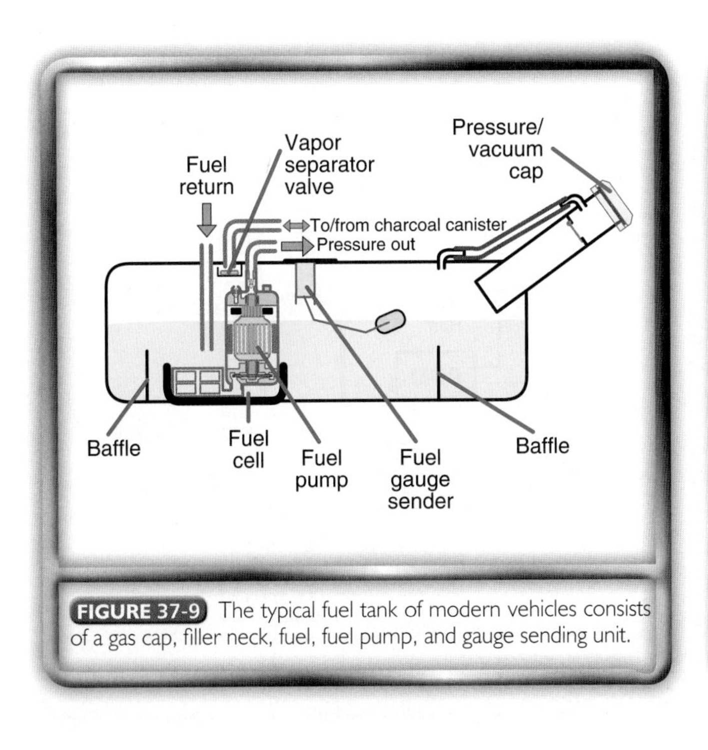
Vapor separator valve
Pressure/ vacuum cap
Fuel return
To/from charcoal canister
Pressure out
Baffle
Fuel cell
Fuel pump
Fuel gauge sender
Baffle

FIGURE 37-9 The typical fuel tank of modern vehicles consists of a gas cap, filler neck, fuel, fuel pump, and gauge sending unit.

FIGURE 37-10 The fuel filler neck.

directly vented to the atmosphere, which wastes gasoline and contributes to air pollution. To help ensure that the cap is tightened properly, many of these caps use a ratchet system. Drivers tighten the cap until it ratchets. Newer Ford vehicles are using an Easy Fuel capless system FIGURE 37-11. There is no gas cap to remove when refueling the vehicle. When the properly sized nozzle is placed on the top of the cap, latches release that open the valve and allow the nozzle to be fully inserted. This cap also reduces the amount of gasoline vapors that escape to the atmosphere when compared to a standard cap.

> **TECHNICIAN TIP**
>
> A loose or leaky gas cap can cause the malfunction indicator lamp (MIL) to illuminate on the dash when the evaporative emission system monitor runs and the leak is detected. Always check the tightness of the cap if an evaporative emission system leak code is present. If the cap is tight, you may want to test the cap for leaks on a cap tester before digging into the evaporative emission system to locate the leak.

TIGHTEN TO CLICK
REMOVE SLOWLY
Easy Fuel
B

FIGURE 37-11 Gas caps. **A.** Standard gas cap. **B.** New capless system.

Fuel Pump Relay

Fuel pumps can draw a considerable amount of current while they run. To carry that high current load, modern vehicles use a **fuel pump relay**. The relay is an electromagnetically operated switch that basically activates the fuel pump when the ignition is turned on for priming the fuel system, when the engine is cranked, and when the engine is running. As low-amperage current is passed through the winding in the relay, a magnetic field is created that pulls the contacts together, controlling the larger current flow going to the fuel pump FIGURE 37-12. The current operating the fuel pump relay winding is typically controlled by the PCM. In most cases, the PCM grounds the winding when it wants the fuel pump to operate.

Fuel Pump

Most fuel-injected vehicles use one or two electrical **fuel pumps** to supply the fuel system with pressurized fuel. The pump either is mounted on the frame or, more likely, is located inside the fuel tank. If located in the tank, the pump is of the submersible type. Electric fuel pumps can be of the low-pressure type or the high-pressure type, depending on the fuel system used on the vehicle.

The fuel pump is electrically operated and electronically controlled. It is driven by a permanent-magnet electric motor, a sealed unit integral with the pump FIGURE 37-13. Fuel flows through the pump and around

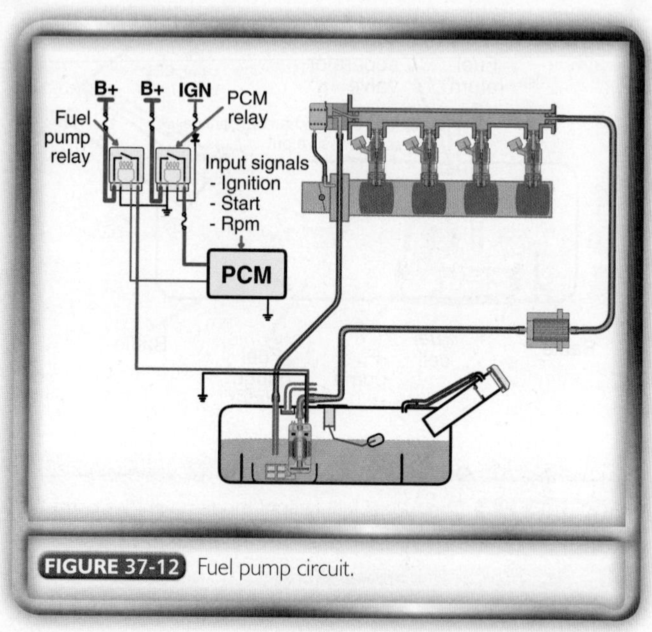
B+
B+
IGN
PCM relay
Fuel pump relay
Input signals
- Ignition
- Start
- Rpm
PCM

FIGURE 37-12 Fuel pump circuit.

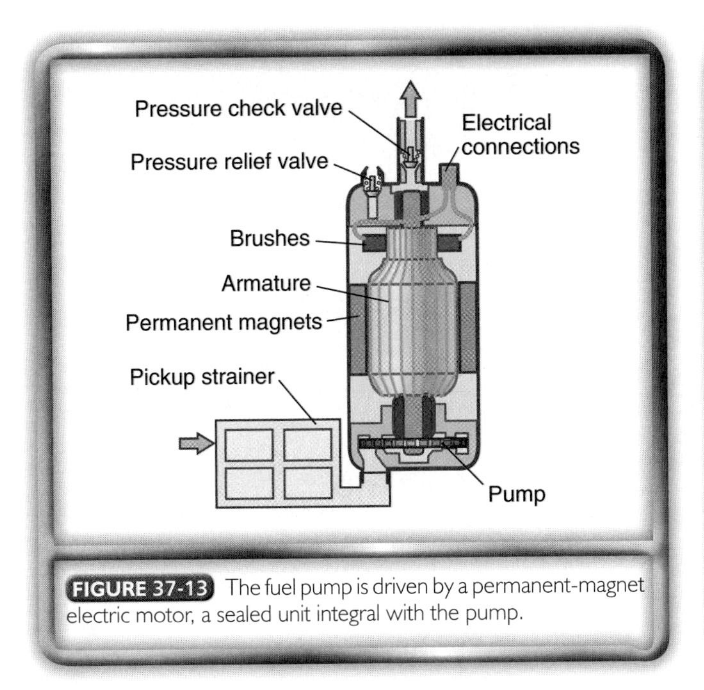
Pressure check valve
Pressure relief valve
Electrical connections
Brushes
Armature
Permanent magnets
Pickup strainer
Pump

FIGURE 37-13 The fuel pump is driven by a permanent-magnet electric motor, a sealed unit integral with the pump.

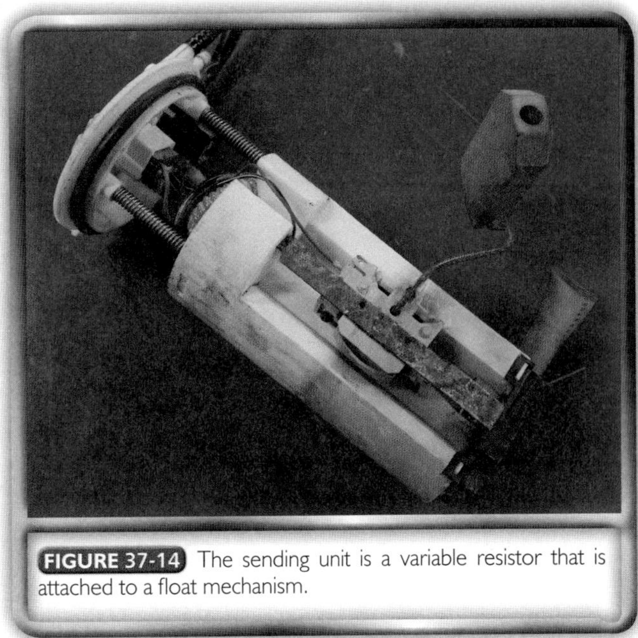

FIGURE 37-14 The sending unit is a variable resistor that is attached to a float mechanism.

the electric motor when it is running. There is never an ignitable mixture (of air and fuel); only fuel is inside the pump housing, so there is virtually no danger of explosion. The pump is designed to deliver more fuel than the maximum requirement of the engine, so pressure in the fuel system is maintained at all times. Either a fuel pressure regulator maintains fuel pressure between the pump and the injectors or the speed of the pump is varied to maintain the correct pressure. Electric fuel pumps use various types of pump chambers, one of which is the roller cell. In this style, rollers float in channels in an offset rotor. As the rotor turns, the rollers are thrown outward, drawing fuel in as the space between the rollers expands, and forcing fuel out as the space decreases. Other types are the peripheral type and the side channel pump.

Fuel Tank Sending Unit

For obvious reasons, it is important for the driver to know how much fuel the vehicle has in the tank. The primary job of the **sending unit** is to send constant electrical signals to the gas gauge located in the driver information center or to the BCM, which then controls the gas gauge. The sending unit is a variable resistor that is attached to a float mechanism FIGURE 37-14. As the fuel level changes, so does the resistance and in turn the amount of current sent to the fuel gauge. This current directly indicates an accurate amount of fuel in the tank. On today's EFI vehicles, the sending unit is incorporated with the fuel pump and, in some cases, a replaceable or nonreplaceable fuel filter. The entire assembly has three jobs: pick up fuel from the bottom of the tank by way of the fuel pump, strain (filter/clean) the fuel and pressurize it, and, of course, report the level of fuel in the tank at the driver information center. These systems are meant to last at least the life of the warranty.

Filter Sock

Fuel contamination can be extremely detrimental to the fuel supply system as well as the engine itself. To this end, a **filter sock** is the first line of defense and is incorporated into the end of the fuel pickup tube. The sock typically consists of a fine mesh, which prevents most small particles from being drawn into the fuel pump and sent through the rest of the fuel system.

Fuel Lines

Fuel lines are usually made of metal tubing or synthetic materials. A fuel supply line carries fuel from the tank to the engine. A return line may also be provided to allow excess fuel to return to the tank. Returning the excess fuel helps prevent the formation of vapor that can occur in the fuel supply during hot conditions. Other lines that run along with the fuel lines include evaporative emission system lines, which connect between the fuel tank, charcoal canister, and intake manifold FIGURE 37-15. These lines can be damaged by rust or foreign objects or even by lifting a vehicle improperly with a jack or hoist.

Fuel Filter

The **fuel filter** typically consists of a pleated paper filter housed in a sealed container. Its primary function is to prevent contaminants from reaching the injectors. The paper filter can also prevent small amounts of water from get-

FIGURE 37-15 Fuel and evaporative emission lines.

ting past it since the paper absorbs the water, causing the fibers in the filter to swell and preventing any liquid from getting past it. Most fuel filters are directional, meaning they must be installed in the proper direction. Usually an arrow on the filter indicates the direction of flow.

Fuel Rail

A **fuel rail** is a special manifold designed to provide a reservoir of pressurized fuel for the fuel injectors. The gasoline is fed from the fuel tank by way of the fuel lines. The fuel, under pressure of course, is supplied by the fuel pump. The fuel rail can also serve as a mounting place for the fuel pressure regulator. The couplings where the fuel lines meet the fuel rail are usually sealed by flared ends, quick-connect high-pressure O-rings, or banjo fittings FIGURE 37-16. These methods ensure a sealed, leak-proof joint between the parts. Many, but not all, fuel rails provide a means for connecting a fuel pressure tester to the rail. This design, called a Schrader valve, uses a one-way valve to hold pressure in the system while the pressure tester is connected and disconnected to the fuel rail. Schrader valves usually are covered by a screw-on cap with a seal inside to prevent leaks in the event the Schrader valve goes bad.

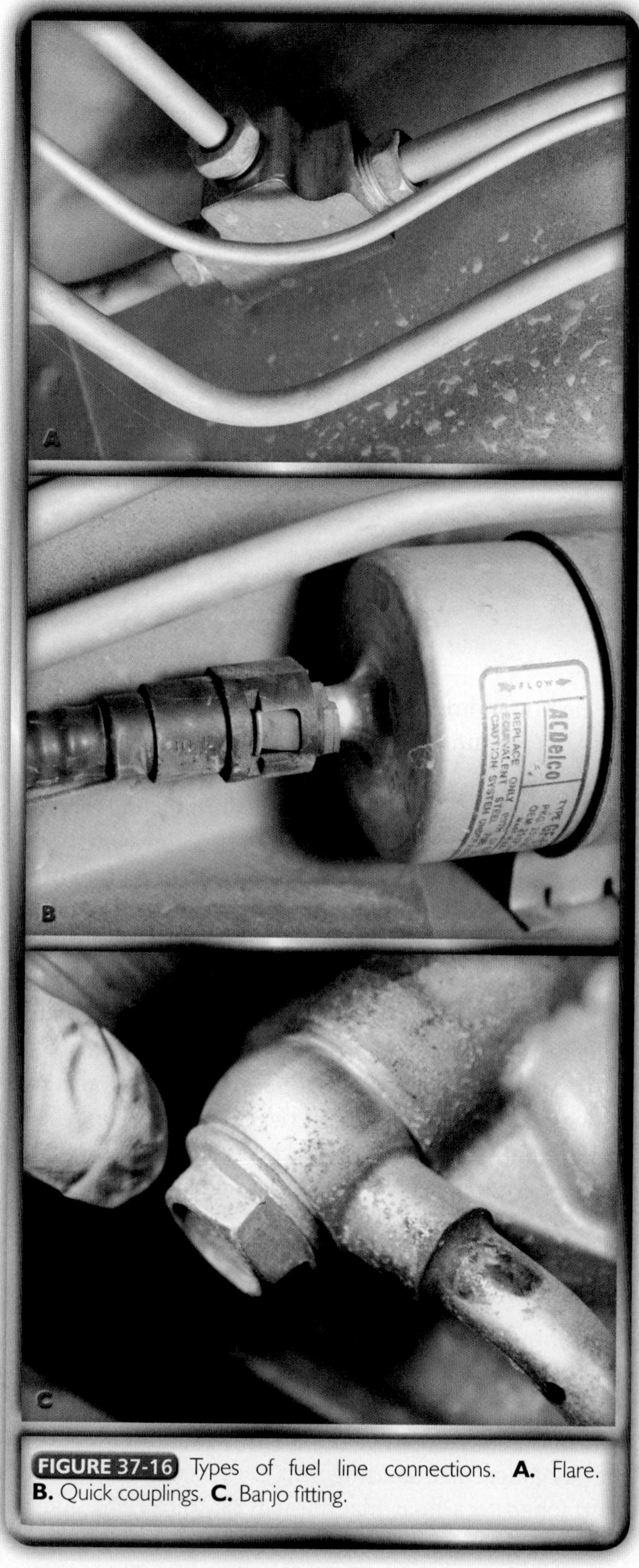
A
ACDelco
B
C

FIGURE 37-16 Types of fuel line connections. **A.** Flare. **B.** Quick couplings. **C.** Banjo fitting.

Fuel Pressure Regulator

Fuel pressure must be regulated in some manner. On port fuel-injected engines, the fuel pressure needs to be maintained above manifold pressure. Since manifold pressure changes with engine load, fuel pressure also needs to change with it. Some vehicles use a pressure regulator on the fuel rail, some are in the fuel tank, and others control fuel pressure by controlling the speed of the fuel pump.

A **fuel pressure regulator** mounted on the fuel rail incorporates a diaphragm-operated valve FIGURE 37-17. On one side of the valve is a pressure spring and engine vacuum. On the other side of the diaphragm is fuel pressure from the fuel pump. Movement of the diaphragm opens and closes the valve, which vents pressure back to the fuel tank through a return line. Fuel pressure builds against the diaphragm, and once it hits the preset pressure, the valve will open slightly and bleed off pressure. This action reduces the pressure on the diaphragm closing the valve. With the valve closed, the pressure rises again, until the valve once again opens.

This process is repeated over and over to maintain the pressure in a fuel system. However, this system does not adjust the pressure when the engine load is increased. The spring-loaded vacuum chamber is connected by a manifold vacuum line to the intake manifold. The vacuum pulls against spring pressure to modify the pressure at which the valve opens to allow fuel to return to the fuel tank. As the driver accelerates, the manifold vacuum diminishes. That, in turn, allows more spring pressure to push on the diaphragm, which then requires more fuel pressure to open the valve, providing higher fuel pressure in the fuel rail to maintain a consistent pressure drop across the injectors.

A
B
FIGURE 37-17 A fuel pressure regulator mounted on the fuel rail incorporates a diaphragm-operated valve.

Fuel Injector

The modern fuel injector is simply a spring-loaded, electric-solenoid spray nozzle FIGURE 37-18. It incorporates a filter screen in the inlet and is usually sealed with O-rings to the fuel rail and intake manifold. The nozzle can be of several types, such as rotating disc style, pintle style, and ball-valve style. Each type has its own pros and cons. Its job is to spray the proper amount of gasoline in the proper pattern either into the intake ports, directly into the combustion chamber, or into a prechamber in response to signals from the PCM. It is positioned between the fuel rail and the intake manifold, or in the case of a GDI fuel system, between the fuel rail and the combustion chamber.

As you know, fuel is pressurized and waiting in the fuel rail. When the PCM sends an electric signal to the fuel injector, the injector opens for a specified time and then the current is stopped and an internal spring returns the injector to the closed position, where it waits for the next "on" command. This happens repeatedly hundreds of times per minute at each fuel injector. The fuel injectors are designed and built to very exacting tolerances, giving them a high degree of fuel delivery precision and a long service life.

The response time to lift the injector needle to the fully open position is about 1 millisecond. If battery voltage is low, this response time takes longer and the engine receives less fuel. The PCM can compensate for this delay in opening time by extending the pulse width of the injector(s).

FIGURE 37-18 The modern fuel injector is a spring-loaded, electric-solenoid spray nozzle.

Electronic Fuel Injection Principles

EFI systems employ electronically controlled injectors to spray the fuel into either the intake system or the cylinder directly. The following discussion covers the basic EFI systems you will encounter as an automotive technician and then describes specifically how these systems operate.

Types of EFI Systems

There are three basic EFI systems: throttle body injection, also called single-point injection; multipoint fuel injection; and gasoline direct injection, or simply direct injection FIGURE 37-19. The specific characteristics of each of these designs will be explained further, but they all operate on similar principles: Fuel is supplied to the injectors at the specified pressure, the PCM sends an electric signal to each injector to cause it to open for a certain amount of time (pulse width), and fuel is injected into the intake manifold or combustion chamber.

Throttle Body Injection Systems

Throttle body injection (TBI), also known as single-point injection or central-point injection, is a system with one or two fuel injectors located centrally on the intake manifold, right above the throttle plates. Fuel is sprayed into the top center of the throttle body and then atomized with the incoming filtered air. This air–fuel mixture is then delivered to each of the engine's cylinders evenly. TBI is a simpler system, requiring only one or two injectors, meaning the PCM can be of a simpler, less powerful design. And since the fuel is sprayed above the throttle plates, it is at atmospheric pressure, so the pressure drop across the injector is always the same. Thus, fuel pressure does not need to change with throttle opening or engine load.

In TBI systems, the central injector is normally triggered on every ignition pulse. However, if there are two injectors, alternate triggering may be used. At idling speeds, the frequency may be less to provide finer control. TBI is the predecessor to modern-day multipoint (or multiport) fuel injection.

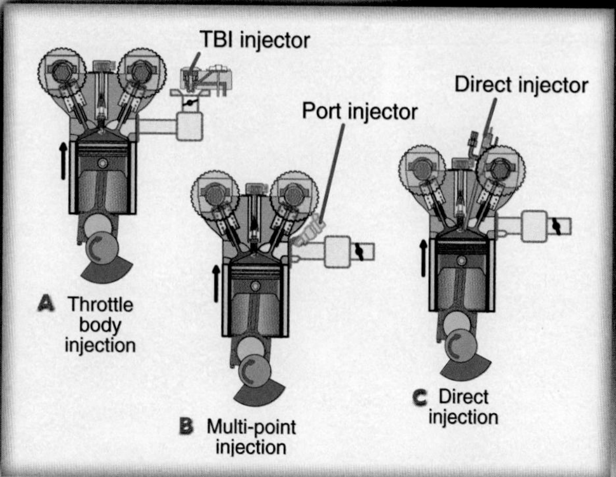

TBI injector
Direct injector
Port injector
A Throttle body injection
B Multi-point injection
C Direct injection

FIGURE 37-19 The three basic systems. **A.** Throttle body injection. **B.** Multipoint fuel injection. **C.** Direct injection.

Multipoint Fuel Injection Systems

In **multipoint fuel injection (MPFI)** systems, a fuel injector is used for each cylinder. The injector is located in the intake manifold near each intake valve and sprays fuel toward the valve. Each injector is connected to the fuel rail, which supplies the injector with fuel under pressure. Each injector also has an electrical connector that provides it with power and ground. Most electronic fuel injectors are supplied with constant battery voltage when the ignition key is in the run or crank position. The PCM then switches the negative side of the injector circuit to ground to turn it on. When the PCM switches the negative side of the circuit off, the spring in the injector closes the injector, and fuel stops spraying.

On return-style MPFI systems, a fuel pressure regulator inlet is connected to the fuel rail, and an outlet lets fuel return to the tank. A control diaphragm and pressure spring determine the exposed opening of the outlet and the amount of fuel that can return. Thus, the strength of the pressure spring determines fuel pressure in the fuel rail and keeps it at a fixed value. However, the pressure in the intake manifold varies considerably with changes in engine speed and with load, so the pressure drop across the injector must also be taken into account.

For any injection duration, if fuel is held at constant pressure, then as manifold pressure varies, so does the amount of fuel delivered. That means fuel pressure must be held constant above manifold pressure. This pressure is held by sealing the spring housing of the pressure regulator and letting it sense manifold pressure via a connecting hose. Then, when manifold pressure changes, so does the fuel pressure.

When manifold pressure is low (high vacuum), as it is at idling, fuel pressure is low. As manifold pressure rises (low vacuum), toward open throttle, fuel pressure rises. Since the injectors are all subjected to the same pressure, they all inject an equal amount of fuel. The quantity of fuel delivered is thus controlled accurately by the pulse width of the injector.

Note that manifold pressure sensing is not required in TBI systems, as the injection occurs above the throttle plate, at atmospheric pressure; thus fuel pressure is determined by the force of the regulator spring acting on the diaphragm. The injectors are sealed into the manifold by O-rings that prevent air entering at that point. The O-rings, together with plastic caps on the injector nozzles, also act as a barrier to heat being transferred to the injector body.

For a short time after an engine is switched off, the engine temperature keeps rising, which can produce vapor in the fuel lines. A check valve in the pump maintains the fuel pressure in the system after engine shut down, preventing the fuel from boiling (vaporizing) as it absorbs heat from the engine (heat soak) **FIGURE 37-20**. This pressure will diminish in about 20 to 30 minutes, but it ensures effective hot-starting capability of the engine.

When the engine is running, the circulation of fuel ensures that cool fuel is delivered at all times and that vapor formation in the lines is prevented. The pump control circuit normally allows the pump to operate for only a few seconds when the ignition is switched on; this is for priming the system. The pump control circuit allows the pump to operate during cranking and when the engine is running above a specified minimum revolutions per minute (rpm).

Gasoline Direct Injection Systems

With the pressures to reduce emissions and increase fuel economy, as well as gain an advantage over the competition and offset the escalating price of crude oil, manufacturers have looked to new technologies in fuel injection. Just as TBI replaced carburetion, gasoline direct injection (GDI) is the natural successor to indirect fuel injection. While indirect fuel injection atomizes fuel at or near the intake valve, GDI systems take their design cues from diesel technology by spraying the fuel directly into the cylinder **FIGURE 37-21**. Because of this direct injection, engines can run on extremely lean fuel mixtures—much leaner than stoichiometric (14.7 parts fuel to 1 part air). Their fuel mixtures can be as lean as 65 to 1!

The fuel injector of each cylinder is located in the cylinder head. Fuel is directly sprayed into the combustion chamber as an atomized mist at the precise time it is needed, depending on the operating conditions of the engine. The reason this type of engine can run so lean is because the injector can place the fuel in a localized spot surrounding the spark plug. This is called a stratified charge because the fuel is mixed with air in just a small area, not thoroughly dispersed among the entire amount of air in the combustion chamber.

So far GDI engines still use spark plugs. Use of spark plugs provides the computer with more choices as to when the fuel gets injected. For example, during heavy load conditions, a slightly rich mixture is injected during the intake stroke. This gives more time for the larger amount of fuel to mix more fully with the air, creating maximum power and reduced spark knock. During moderate engine loads, just enough fuel is injected during the intake stroke to create a stoichiometric air–fuel ratio, to again fully mix with the air. This results in good power and a very clean burn. Under light load or cruise conditions, if the fuel pump is designed to deliver the high pressures needed to overcome the compression pressures, the fuel is injected as described earlier, during the latter stages of the compression stroke, and is placed near the spark plug. This small amount of air and fuel is surrounded by a larger amount of air, which helps insulate the cylinder walls from the heat of combustion. This design reduces

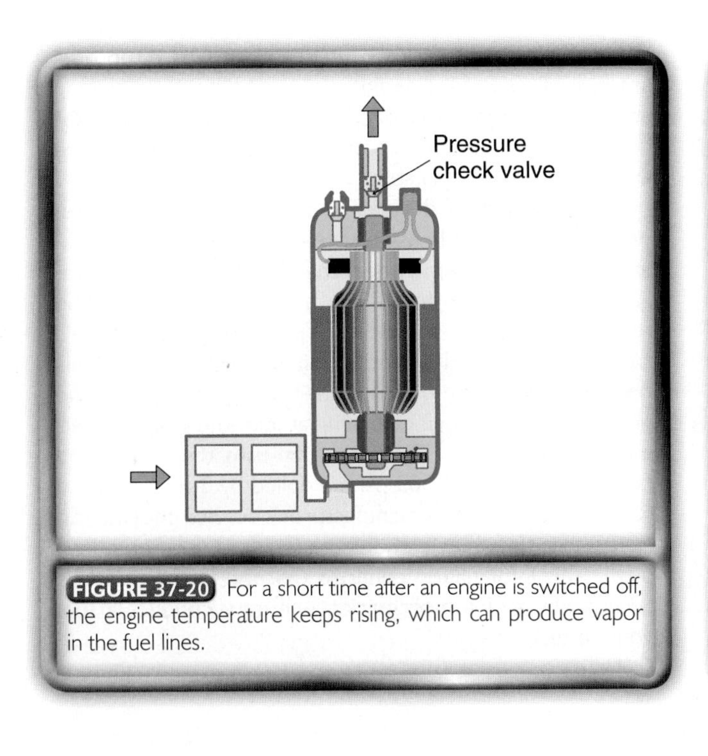
Pressure
check valve

FIGURE 37-20 For a short time after an engine is switched off, the engine temperature keeps rising, which can produce vapor in the fuel lines.

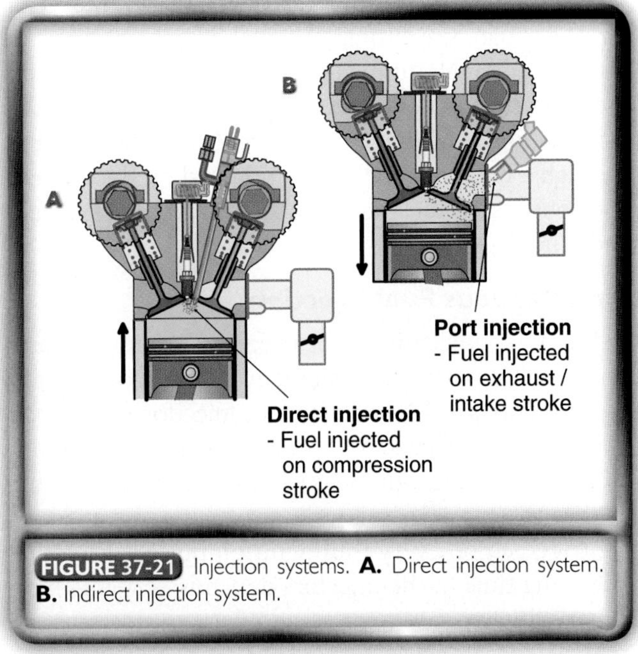
A
B
Port injection
- Fuel injected
on exhaust /
intake stroke
Direct injection
- Fuel injected
on compression
stroke

FIGURE 37-21 Injection systems. **A.** Direct injection system. **B.** Indirect injection system.

heat loss in the combustion chamber and increases fuel economy.

GDI fuel systems can be of either a low-pressure variety (only inject during the intake stroke or early in the compression stroke) or a high-pressure variety (can inject during the intake stroke, the compression stroke, and potentially the power stroke).

Operation of EFI Systems

As mentioned previously, the three EFI systems—TBI, MPFI, and GDI—all share certain operative principles. To properly diagnose and service these systems, the technician must understand such processes as the injection of fuel, delivery of air, and management of combustion.

Returnless Fuel Injection Systems

New vehicles have been using **returnless fuel injection systems** for the past 10 years or so. Manufacturers turned to using returnless fuel systems to reduce evaporative emissions. On a return-type system, the fuel returning to the tank is hot from engine heat. Hot fuel will readily vaporize and make the evaporative system work harder, requiring additional fuel vapor storage capacity. Since no hot fuel is returned to the tank in a returnless system, the fuel in the tank stays relatively cool, thus minimizing vaporization.

There are two types of returnless systems. One uses a pressure regulator in the fuel tank (mechanical), and the other controls the speed of the fuel pump to modify pressure (electronic). The in-tank regulator uses a spring-loaded pressure regulator similar to the type mounted to the fuel rail, except it does not change with manifold pressure and therefore does not use a vacuum hose. Excess fuel pressure is simply vented into the tank.

On the electronically controlled system, the PCM sends a square wave (digital) signal, which controls the speed of the fuel pump. The faster it turns, the higher the pressure and flow. The lower it turns, the lower the pressure and flow. The PCM monitors the fuel pressure through a fuel pressure sensor mounted on the fuel rail and controls the fuel pump based on engine speed, load, and other factors.

Simultaneous Fuel Injection

In MPFI, the injectors can be triggered in various ways. The simplest way is to trigger them at the same time or in groups. This is called simultaneous injection or grouped injection, and the injectors operate twice per cycle—once each crankshaft revolution, each time delivering half the fuel for the cycle. In a six-cylinder engine, the injectors are triggered on every third ignition pulse. The actual operating time of the injectors depends very much on battery voltage.

Sequential Fuel Injection

Sequential injection means injection occurs in the sequence of the firing order. The injectors follow the firing order of the engine. Each injector opens only once in each cycle, to deliver the fuel needed. Because each injector is controlled separately, the PCM needs to have individual drivers to turn each injector on and off. This system requires more computing power to manage each injector circuit. It also requires more wires back to the PCM, since each injector requires its own circuit. Since each injector fires only once per cycle, the timing of the injection pulse is important, and, therefore, the position of the number 1 cylinder and the camshaft must be known. This also adds to the complexity of the system over a TBI or simultaneous-injection system. Added load placed on the engine during idle can be compensated for by increasing the passageway of an idle speed control device or by opening the throttle plate slightly on drive-by-wire systems. Doing so lets more air bypass the throttle plate. This air has been measured by the airflow meter, so extra fuel is metered to maintain the same air–fuel ratio. The extra mixture thus delivered increases engine torque and maintains idle speed.

Applied Math

AM-18: Standard/Metric: The technician can measure/test with tools designed for standard or metric measurements, and then convert the measurement to the system used by the manufacturer for specifications and tolerances.

A vehicle is in the shop for engine performance concerns. The vehicle has been running badly for about 2 weeks according to the repair order information. The symptoms are lack of power and engine stalling at times. Performing an underhood visual inspection, the technician does not find anything unusual. A scan tool check indicates there are trouble codes available.

The technician decides to check the fuel pressure, which is a quick and easy test. As he looks in his toolbox for the gauge, he remembers that he loaned his pressure gauge to someone and it has not been returned. The technician has one other fuel pressure gauge that is calibrated only in the metric unit bar. He connects this pressure gauge to the Schrader valve and starts the engine. With the engine running at idle, the gauge shows a reading of 3 bars. The technician uses the conversion factor of 1 bar = 14.503 psi multiplied by 3 to obtain the result of 43.5 psi. The manufacturer's service information states that the vehicle should have 44 psi plus or minus 3 psi. This information confirms that the fuel pressure is acceptable, and the technician will now conduct a fuel volume test.

Maintenance and Repair

Replacing a Fuel Filter

Fuel filters are a maintenance item and need to be replaced according to the manufacturer's specified replacement schedule, or anytime restricted flow is encountered. Fuel filters can be located in a variety of places depending on the vehicle. Common locations are under the vehicle in the fuel line, under the hood in the engine compartment, and inside the fuel tank as part of the fuel pump assembly. Since fuel pressure is maintained in all electric fuel pump systems, even when the engine is not running, it is important to bleed the pressure off before opening the system so that fuel does not spray everywhere. There are several ways to relieve the static pressure in the fuel system before removing the fuel lines. One way is to remove the fuel pump relay or the fuel pump fuse and run the engine until it dies. Another method is to connect a fuel pump gauge that has a bleed valve to the fuel rail test point, and bleed the excess pressure from the system into a gas can. No matter how you bleed the static pressure in the fuel system, vent the pressure in the gas tank by removing the gas cap. Doing so will reduce the amount of gas that dribbles out of the lines when removing the filter. Always refer to the service information for the specific procedure for removing and replacing the fuel filter for the vehicle you are working on.

Some vehicles use metal or plastic lines that bolt onto the filter, using either a flared fitting or a banjo bolt. For either type, you will need to use the double wrench method to unbolt the line; otherwise you may twist or kink the metal or plastic line. The double wrench method uses two wrenches, one on the filter nut and the other on the flare nut or banjo bolt. Use the wrench on the filter nut to prevent the filter from twisting while applying force to the other wrench. Often you can place the wrench handles so they are at a slight angle to each other and squeeze them together to break the fittings loose.

Safety

Gasoline fuel vapor is explosive and highly flammable. Be careful not to spill any fuel onto a hot engine component where it could evaporate, ignite, and start a fire. Also take care not to cause any sparks while you are changing a fuel filter. Collect the gasoline waste in a metal container and dispose of it in an environmentally prescribed way. Always wear the appropriate personal protection equipment before starting the job.

Many newer vehicles use quick couplers to retain the fuel lines on the fuel filter. These couplers make it very quick and easy for the factory to install the filter since the fuel filter lines only have to be pushed into or onto the filter inlet and outlet. The quick coupler may use a plastic clip or a coiled spring to retain the line on the filter. Only use the proper release tool when removing the line; otherwise you can damage the fitting or line. Also, most quick coupler systems use O-rings to seal the fuel line to the filter. Make sure the O-rings are in good shape or replace them with new ones.

If the fuel lines connecting the fuel tank to the filter are flexible hoses rather than metal lines, check their condition to determine whether it is necessary to replace the hoses and clamps when you replace the filter. Some replacement filters come with these items; when they are supplied, you should always use them. If they are not supplied, but you need to replace them anyway, obtain a sufficient length of the proper type of new fuel line and suitable clamps. There are different types of clamps for flexible fuel lines, including spring type, worm type, or rolled edge. You will need to use the appropriate tool when installing new clamps on the hoses.

Some manufacturers have been installing the fuel filter in the fuel tank along with the fuel pump assembly. The only way to get to the pump and filter is through the top of the fuel tank. Sometimes manufacturers provide a removable access cover under the backseat that will allow you to get to the top of the tank. Other times the tank will need to be removed to gain access. Once the covers are removed, the fuel pump assembly can be carefully removed and the filter replaced.

To replace a fuel filter, follow the steps in **SKILL DRILL 37-1**.

Inspecting and Testing Fuel Pumps

Fuel pumps need to be tested if a vehicle experiences low engine power or if the vehicle will not start due to a fuel-related issue. Some shops will test a fuel pump's performance, looking to see if it is nearing a failure. There are several ways to test a fuel pump: pressure/volume test, lab scope inductive current flow test, and scan tool data stream test. Each will be described in this section.

The pressure/volume test measures the fuel pressure being delivered to the fuel rail along with the volume of the fuel pump. Many, but not all, fuel-injected engines provide a test port that a fuel pressure tester can connect to. Once connected, the pressure can be measured with either just the key on or with the engine running. Manufacturers will give pressure specifications to compare the pressure readings with. If the pressure is low, and the system uses a return line from the pressure regulator on the fuel rail, you may need to pinch off the return line to see if the pressure goes up due to a faulty pressure regulator. If the pressure is within specifications, turn the engine off, but watch the pressure gauge. It should stay steady. If it drops, there is a leak in the system, either at the pressure regulator or at the check valve in the fuel pump.

The pressure may be within specifications and hold pressure when the engine is off, but the fuel pump volume may be low. Specifications are given in volume per amount of time, such as 1 pint in 30 seconds or 28 lb per hour, which will usually need to be converted to volume per amount of time. The volume is measured with the engine idling. Most EFI fuel pressure gauges have a valve that will allow fuel to be taken from the rail without killing the engine and then caught in a calibrated container. If the fuel flow is low, check to see if the fuel filter is plugged and restricting the flow. If the filter is OK, you may need to remove the fuel pump from the fuel tank and inspect the fuel sock at the bottom of the fuel pump to see if it is plugged. If all of the filters are

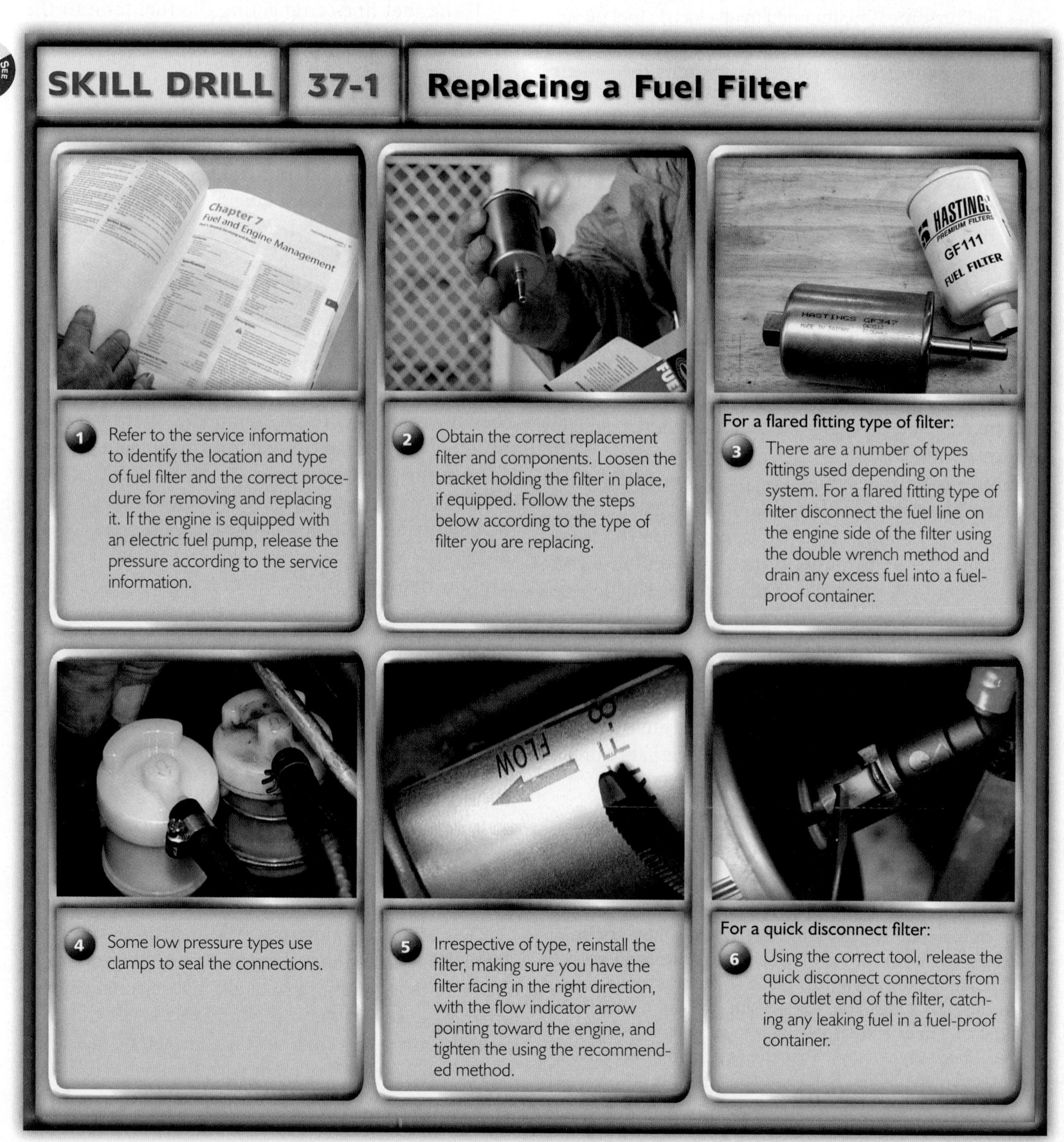

SKILL DRILL 37-1 Replacing a Fuel Filter

1. Refer to the service information to identify the location and type of fuel filter and the correct procedure for removing and replacing it. If the engine is equipped with an electric fuel pump, release the pressure according to the service information.

2. Obtain the correct replacement filter and components. Loosen the bracket holding the filter in place, if equipped. Follow the steps below according to the type of filter you are replacing.

For a flared fitting type of filter:

3. There are a number of types fittings used depending on the system. For a flared fitting type of filter disconnect the fuel line on the engine side of the filter using the double wrench method and drain any excess fuel into a fuel-proof container.

4. Some low pressure types use clamps to seal the connections.

5. Irrespective of type, reinstall the filter, making sure you have the filter facing in the right direction, with the flow indicator arrow pointing toward the engine, and tighten the using the recommended method.

For a quick disconnect filter:

6. Using the correct tool, release the quick disconnect connectors from the outlet end of the filter, catching any leaking fuel in a fuel-proof container.

SKILL DRILL 37-1 Replacing a Fuel Filter, continued
7 Release the quick disconnect connectors from the inlet end of the filter, and remove the filter from the lines.
8 Reinstall the filter, with the flow indicator arrow pointing toward the engine, and fully engage the lines, making sure they are secure.
9 Wipe any residual fuel off with a clean shop rag, and write the date and mileage on the filter with permanent marker. Remember to replace the fuel pump fuse, if removed.
10 Turn the key to the on position for 5 seconds, but do not start the engine, and then turn it back to off. Repeat the process two more times, checking the filter connections for leaks. If no leaks are found, start the vehicle, letting it run for 2 to 3 minutes before shutting it off. Recheck the filter connections for leaks.

not restricted but the pump volume is low, the pump will need to be replaced.

Some technicians like to use their lab scope to display the trace for the fuel pump's current flow. As each pair of segments of the fuel pump's commutator aligns with the brushes, current flows through the connected windings in the armature. If there is high resistance or a bad connection in one of the commutator segments or armature windings, the current flow will decrease. Since each pair of segments is connected to a different set of windings, the current flow can change for each set, if the resistance is different from each other. This will be evident on the lab scope by current pulses of different height in a repeating pattern.

Another technique to identify a fuel delivery fault is to use a scan tool and a test-drive. If possible, set the scan tool to record rpm, VSS, front oxygen sensors, short-term fuel trim, and long-term fuel trim, and then go on a test-drive. In a safe place and manner, briefly drive the vehicle under heavy load and at higher rpm. After returning to the shop, look at the recording; if you see a lean oxygen signal with a large increase in fuel trim, a fuel delivery problem is indicated. This problem could be as simple as a restricted fuel filter or something more severe such as a faulty pump or plugged fuel injectors.

To inspect and test fuel pumps, follow the steps in **SKILL DRILL 37-2**. Note in Step 3 if the fuel pressure is low, you may want to momentarily pinch off the return line, if equipped, which deadheads the pump. If the pressure was low before pinching off the return line and rises after pinching it off, the pressure regulator is faulty. If the pressure does not rise, either the fuel filter is restricted or the pump is likely to be faulty.

Checking Fuel for Contaminants and Quality

It is easy to forget that fuel by itself can cause drivability issues if it becomes contaminated or old, or even if it is

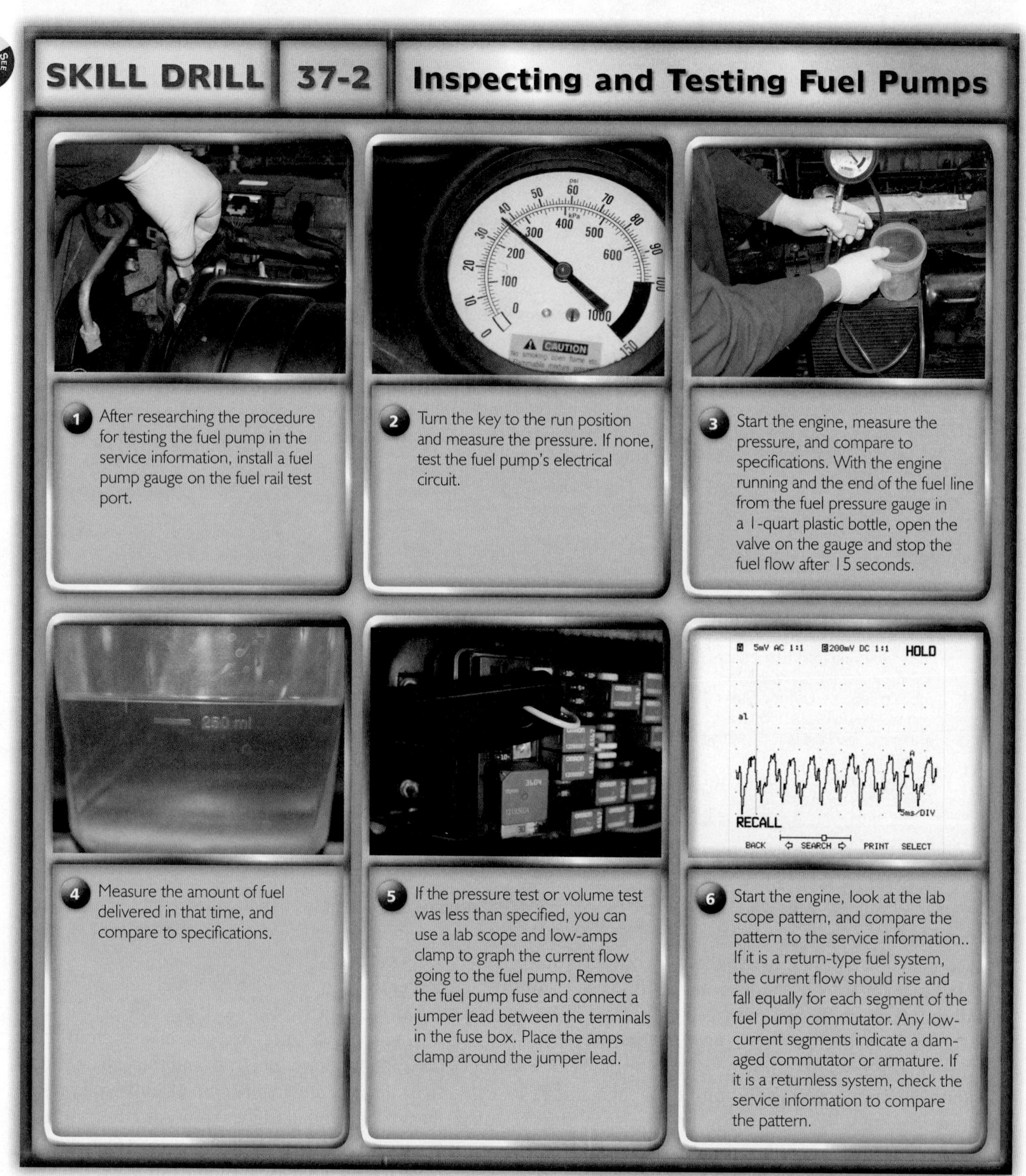
PROVE
KNOW
SEE
DO
psi
kPa
CAUTION
RECALL
HOLD
5ms/DIV
BACK
SEARCH
PRINT
SELECT

SKILL DRILL 37-2 Inspecting and Testing Fuel Pumps

1. After researching the procedure for testing the fuel pump in the service information, install a fuel pump gauge on the fuel rail test port.
2. Turn the key to the run position and measure the pressure. If none, test the fuel pump's electrical circuit.
3. Start the engine, measure the pressure, and compare to specifications. With the engine running and the end of the fuel line from the fuel pressure gauge in a 1-quart plastic bottle, open the valve on the gauge and stop the fuel flow after 15 seconds.
4. Measure the amount of fuel delivered in that time, and compare to specifications.
5. If the pressure test or volume test was less than specified, you can use a lab scope and low-amps clamp to graph the current flow going to the fuel pump. Remove the fuel pump fuse and connect a jumper lead between the terminals in the fuse box. Place the amps clamp around the jumper lead.
6. Start the engine, look at the lab scope pattern, and compare the pattern to the service information.. If it is a return-type fuel system, the current flow should rise and fall equally for each segment of the fuel pump commutator. Any low-current segments indicate a damaged commutator or armature. If it is a returnless system, check the service information to compare the pattern.

SKILL DRILL 37-2 Inspecting and Testing Fuel Pumps, continued

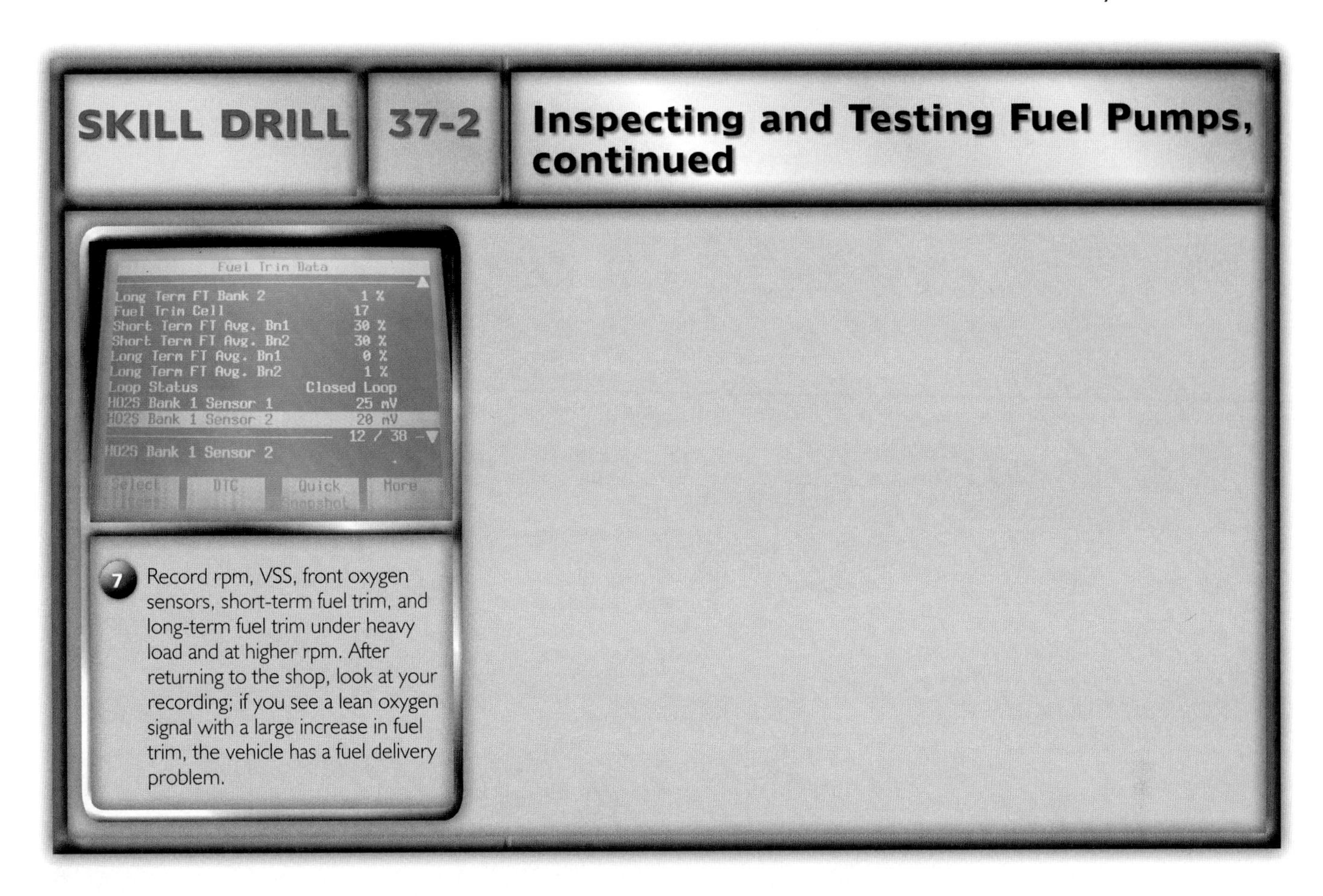
Fuel Trim Data
Long Term FT Bank 2 1 %
Fuel Trim Cell 17
Short Term FT Avg. Bn1 30 %
Short Term FT Avg. Bn2 30 %
Long Term FT Avg. Bn1 0 %
Long Term FT Avg. Bn2 1 %
Loop Status Closed Loop
HO2S Bank 1 Sensor 1 25 mV
HO2S Bank 1 Sensor 2 20 mV
12 / 38
HO2S Bank 1 Sensor 2
DTC
Quick Snapshot
More

7. Record rpm, VSS, front oxygen sensors, short-term fuel trim, and long-term fuel trim under heavy load and at higher rpm. After returning to the shop, look at your recording; if you see a lean oxygen signal with a large increase in fuel trim, the vehicle has a fuel delivery problem.

the wrong fuel for the vehicle. In fact, with more people owning diesel passenger vehicles and light trucks, you may encounter vehicles filled with the wrong fuel, such as a diesel car filled with gasoline, or vice versa. Also, higher blends of gasoline and alcohol make it easy to fill up a standard gasoline vehicle with E-85, which is 85% alcohol and 15% gasoline. A flex fuel vehicle will operate correctly on that blend, but a non–flex fuel vehicle will not. Anytime a vehicle is not running properly and other common causes have not identified the issue, you will want to check the fuel for contaminants and quality.

Short of sending fuel out to be tested by a lab, there are some simpler tests that can be done. All require getting a sample from the fuel supply, which is best taken from the fuel rail or where the gas enters the carburetor. That way you will be testing the fuel that the engine is running on. You will want to collect a cup or two of fuel in a clear container, preferably not glass, which can break easily. Allow the fuel to settle and look at it. Is it the right color? Is it cloudy? Does it have a separation line due to being contaminated with water? Does it smell right? If any of those conditions are not correct, you will need to drain the fuel system, flush it out, and replace the fuel filters. If the fuel passes the visual inspection, it is time to perform an alcohol content test. For this test, you will use a tall 100-mL graduated cylinder. A mixture of 10 mL of clean water and 90 mL of gasoline are carefully agitated for 30 seconds. The mixture is allowed to settle for a minute or two. Any alcohol in the fuel will absorb the water, raising the level above the original 10 mL. Each mL above 10 equals the percentage of alcohol in the gasoline. Most vehicles can tolerate 10% alcohol without causing any drivability issues. And flex fuel vehicles can typically operate on 85% alcohol.

To check fuel for contaminants and quality, follow the steps in SKILL DRILL 37-3.

Inspecting and Testing Fuel Injectors

Fuel injectors can fail electrically or mechanically. They can also become plugged or deposits can build up on the nozzle, affecting the spray pattern of the injector. If the injector fails completely, it will cause the cylinder to misfire. If the injectors have a poor spray pattern due to deposits, the engine may experience general roughness or random misfires that are not isolated to one or two cylinders. Before specifically testing an injector, it should be identified as causing a drivability issue. In other words, the ignition system, compression, vacuum leaks, and other engine mechanical faults can cause

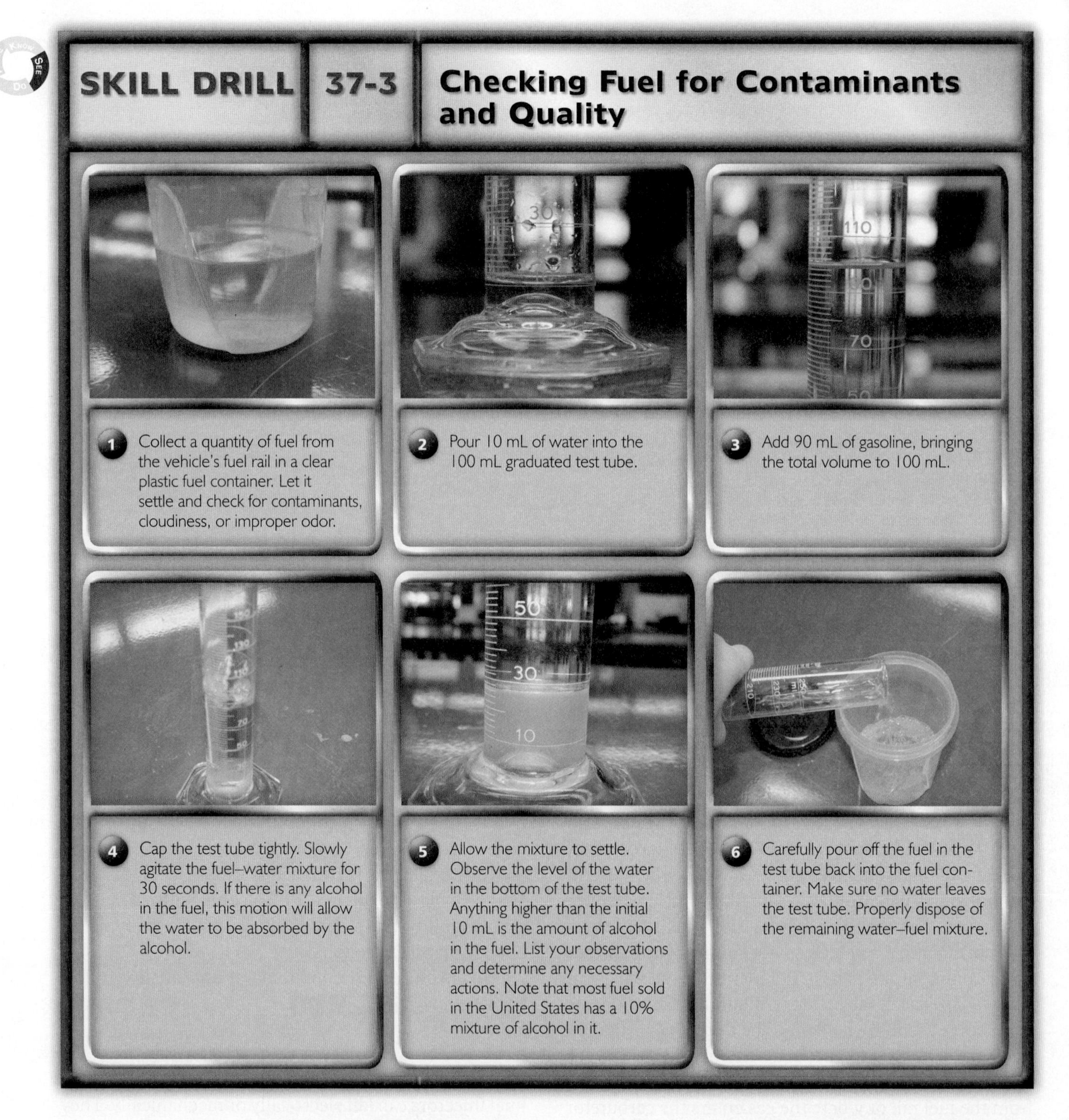
SKILL DRILL 37-3 Checking Fuel for Contaminants and Quality
1 Collect a quantity of fuel from the vehicle's fuel rail in a clear plastic fuel container. Let it settle and check for contaminants, cloudiness, or improper odor.
2 Pour 10 mL of water into the 100 mL graduated test tube.
3 Add 90 mL of gasoline, bringing the total volume to 100 mL.
4 Cap the test tube tightly. Slowly agitate the fuel–water mixture for 30 seconds. If there is any alcohol in the fuel, this motion will allow the water to be absorbed by the alcohol.
5 Allow the mixture to settle. Observe the level of the water in the bottom of the test tube. Anything higher than the initial 10 mL is the amount of alcohol in the fuel. List your observations and determine any necessary actions. Note that most fuel sold in the United States has a 10% mixture of alcohol in it.
6 Carefully pour off the fuel in the test tube back into the fuel container. Make sure no water leaves the test tube. Properly dispose of the remaining water–fuel mixture.

one or more cylinders to not work correctly, just like a fuel injector problem. Use all of your diagnostic skills and tools to narrow the fault down to the injectors. For example, you may need to retrieve the codes, read the data stream, or access mode 6 data to help you narrow down the area of the fault. If you suspect a fuel injector is causing the fault, you can quickly measure the resistance of the injector winding and compare it to specifications. Any improper resistance will require replacement of the injector.

If the injector resistance and on/off signal are good, you can perform an injector pressure drop test to see if the injector is restricted with deposits. This test uses a fuel pressure gauge and injector pulsing tool. The fuel pressure gauge is connected to the test port in the fuel rail, and the pulsing tool is connected to the battery and the suspect injector. The pulse tool pulses the injector a certain number of times, for a certain amount of time. The idea is that you will pressurize the fuel rail by turning the key to the on position and charging the fuel rail.

Then start the pulse tool, which will pulse the injector the set amount of times. Read the pressure on the fuel pressure gauge, and compare this reading to the pressure reading after doing the same test on another injector. If the flow is the same between the two injectors, the pressure at the end of each test should be within a few psi of each other. If not, the one with the higher pressure at the end of the test is not allowing as much fuel to flow as the other, which could indicate deposit buildup on the nozzle or a restricted filter screen on the injector.

To inspect and test fuel injectors, first research the fuel injector testing procedure and specifications for the vehicle in the appropriate service information. Inspect the fuel injectors for leaks and damage, then follow the service information to test the fuel injectors. If the information does not provide a method for testing the injectors, follow the steps in SKILL DRILL 37-4.

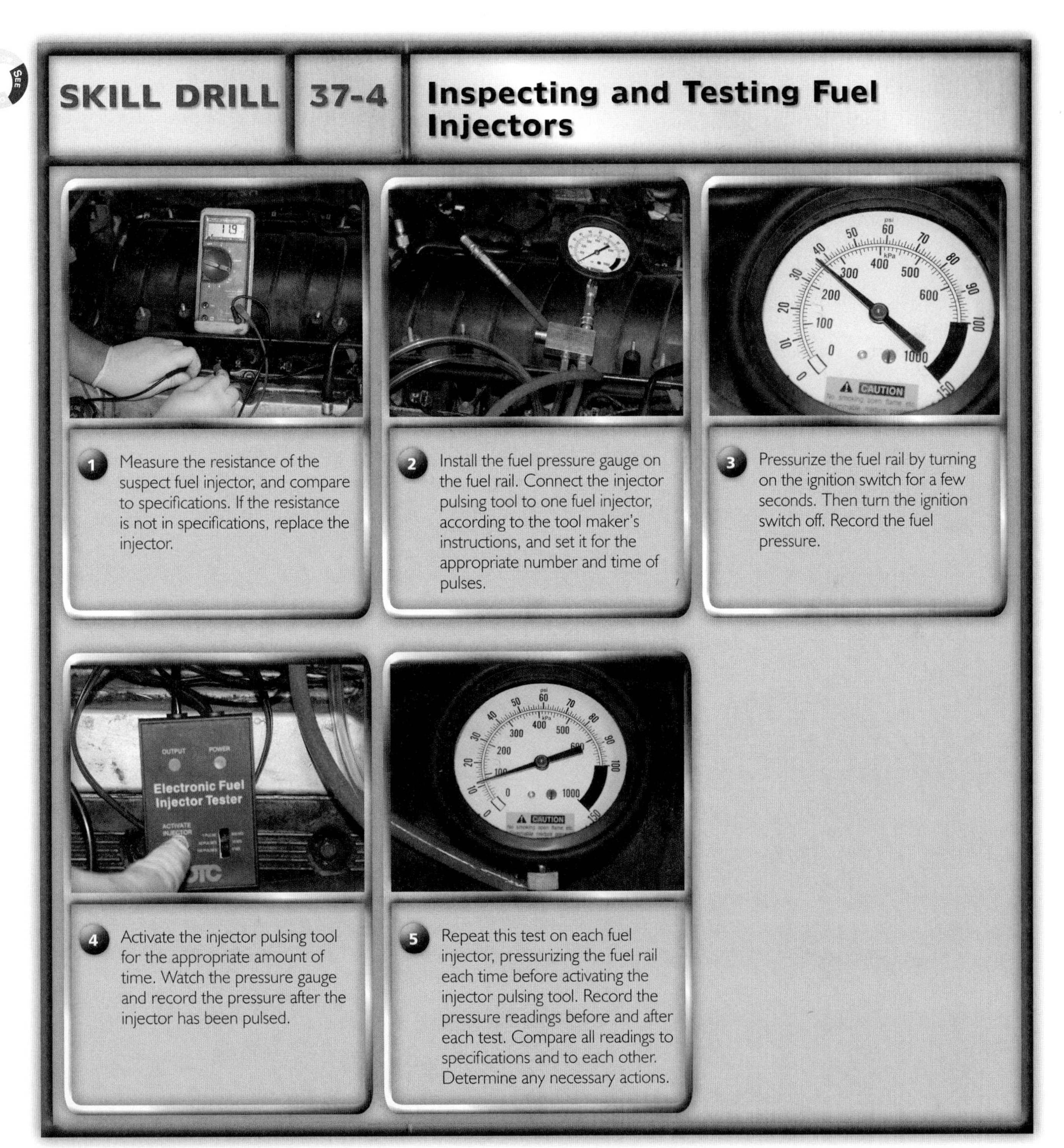
Electronic Fuel Injector Tester
CAUTION

SKILL DRILL 37-4 Inspecting and Testing Fuel Injectors

1. Measure the resistance of the suspect fuel injector, and compare to specifications. If the resistance is not in specifications, replace the injector.

2. Install the fuel pressure gauge on the fuel rail. Connect the injector pulsing tool to one fuel injector, according to the tool maker's instructions, and set it for the appropriate number and time of pulses.

3. Pressurize the fuel rail by turning on the ignition switch for a few seconds. Then turn the ignition switch off. Record the fuel pressure.

4. Activate the injector pulsing tool for the appropriate amount of time. Watch the pressure gauge and record the pressure after the injector has been pulsed.

5. Repeat this test on each fuel injector, pressurizing the fuel rail each time before activating the injector pulsing tool. Record the pressure readings before and after each test. Compare all readings to specifications and to each other. Determine any necessary actions.

Wrap-up

Ready for Review

- The most important job of the fuel system is optimizing engine performance while keeping fuel consumption and emissions to a minimum.
- As a technician you must be able to properly inspect, diagnose, and repair fuel system components for your customers, thus keeping their vehicles running at optimum efficiency and performance.
- Modern fuel injection has three subsystems: fuel supply, air supply, and fuel metering.
- Vapor lock occurs when vapor forms in the fuel line; the bubbles of vapor block the flow of fuel at the pump and stop the engine.
- Engines perform best when used with the fuel that has the engine manufacturer's recommended octane rating.
- Combustion is the burning of the air–fuel mixture.
- Detonation is when the entire mixture explodes instead of burning smoothly across the combustion chamber.
- Gasoline must be burnt in a controlled manner or it will burn either too fast or too slow.
- The term stoichiometric ratio describes the chemically correct air–fuel ratio necessary to achieve complete combustion of the fuel and oxygen in the air.
- Air is one of the essential components of the internal combustion engine.
- Fuel pumps can be electrical or mechanical. The most common today are electrical and are installed in the fuel tanks.
- Most of today's vehicles use electronic fuel injection (EFI), which is better for fuel economy and emission controls.
- The typical fuel tank (or gas tank, as it is sometimes called) of modern vehicles consists of a gas cap, filler neck, fuel, fuel pump, and gauge sending unit. The tank's primary function is to hold an adequate supply of fuel.
- Modern vehicles are required by the Environmental Protection Agency (EPA) to have a nonvented gas cap. This nonvented cap prevents the dangerous fuel vapors from being directly vented to the atmosphere.
- There are three types of electronic fuel injection—throttle body injection (TBI), port fuel injection (PFI), and gas direct injection (GDI).
- If the fuel system is maintained, it will give many years of dependable service to the vehicle's owner.
- Always refer to the manufacturer's technical data for the latest service information on the specific vehicle that is being serviced or repaired.

Key Terms

air supply system Equipment in a motor vehicle that delivers air to the engine.

detonation The condition in which the remaining fuel charge fires or burns too rapidly after the initial combustion of the air–fuel mixture. It is audible through the combustion chamber walls as a knocking noise.

dieseling A condition in which the engine continues to run after the ignition key is turned off. Also referred to as run-on.

element The replaceable portion of a filter, such as an air filter element or oil filter element.

filter sock The first line of defense in the fuel supply system. The sock typically consists of a fine mesh, which prevents most small particles from being drawn into the fuel pump and sent through the rest of the fuel system.

fuel filler neck The upper end of the fuel filler tube leading down to the fuel tank, which accepts the fuel hose nozzle at the gas station pump.

fuel filter A device that removes impurities (dirt and water) from the fuel before they reach the carburetor or injection system. Filters may be made of metal or plastic screen, paper, or gauze.

fuel metering system Equipment in a motor vehicle that delivers the proper amount of fuel to each cylinder.

fuel pressure regulator A system that controls the pressure of fuel entering the injectors.

fuel pump A mechanically or electrically driven vacuum device used to draw fuel from the tank and force it into the fuel system.

fuel pump relay A relay to turn on or off the high-amperage circuit of the fuel pump.

fuel rail Tubing that connects several injectors to the main fuel line.

fuel supply system Equipment in a motor vehicle that delivers fuel to the engine.

fuel system Equipment in a motor vehicle that delivers fuel to the engine.

gasoline A volatile, flammable liquid mixture of hydrocarbons, obtained from crude oil and used as fuel for internal combustion engines.

gasoline direct injection (GDI) A fuel injection system in which fuel is sprayed directly into the combustion chamber.

gauge sending unit A device used for transmitting a signal to control a fuel gauge.

idle The speed at which an engine runs without any throttle applied.

indirect fuel injection Any fuel injection that is not sprayed directly into the combustion chamber.

knocking A noise heard when the air–fuel mixture spontaneously ignites before the spark plug is fired at the optimum ignition moment.

multipoint fuel injection (MPFI) An injection system in which fuel is injected into the intake ports just upstream of each cylinder's intake valve, rather than at a central point within an intake manifold. Also called multiport injection.

octane rating A standard measure of the performance of a motor or aviation fuel. The higher the octane number, the more heat the fuel can withstand before self-igniting.

pressure The force per unit area applied to the surface of an object.

returnless fuel injection system A type of injection system in which no hot fuel is returned to the tank, thus keeping the fuel in the tank relatively cool and minimizing vaporization.

sending unit The component in the fuel supply system responsible for sending constant electrical signals to the gas gauge located in the driver information center.

stoichiometric ratio The optimum ratio of air to fuel for combustion—14.7 parts air to 1 part fuel by weight.

throttle A device used to produce acceleration by controlling the air–fuel mixture.

throttle body injection (TBI) A fuel injection system that uses one or more fuel injectors mounted above or in the throttle body itself. Also called single-point injection.

vacuum A pressure in an enclosed area that is lower than atmospheric pressure.

vapor lock A situation in which vapor forms in the fuel line, and the bubbles of vapor block the flow of fuel and stop the engine.

ASE-Type Questions

1. Tech A says that most electric fuel pumps are now mounted inside of the fuel tank. Tech B says that fuel flows through the center of the electric pump and is used to cool the pump. Who is correct?
   a. Tech A
   b. Tech B
   c. Both A and B
   d. Neither A nor B
2. Tech A says that the stoichiometric ratio is 14.7 gallons of air to 1 gallon of fuel. Tech B says it is 14.7 lbs of air to 1 lb of fuel. Who is correct?
   a. Tech A
   b. Tech B
   c. Both A and B
   d. Neither A nor B
3. Tech A says that some throttle plates are not mechanically connected to the gas pedal, but are operated by an electric motor. Tech B says that too much alcohol in gasoline can cause the engine to not run properly. Who is correct?
   a. Tech A
   b. Tech B
   c. Both A and B
   d. Neither A nor B
4. Tech A says that high octane fuel is harder to ignite than lower octane. Tech B says that using high octane fuel in an engine designed for lower octane will produce better fuel economy and power. Who is correct?
   a. Tech A
   b. Tech B
   c. Both A and B
   d. Neither A nor B
5. Tech A says that dieseling in a car today indicates a possible leaking injector. Tech B says that a tripped inertia switch means that there is a possible short in the fuel pump circuit. Who is correct?
   a. Tech A
   b. Tech B
   c. Both A and B
   d. Neither A nor B
6. Tech A says that a lambda greater than 1 means the engine is running rich. Tech B says that the amount of oxygen in the exhaust indicates how rich or lean the mixture is. Who is correct?
   a. Tech A
   b. Tech B
   c. Both A and B
   d. Neither A nor B
7. Tech A says that gauge pressure indicates pressure above atmospheric pressure. Tech B says that atmospheric pressure increases as elevation increases. Who is correct?
   a. Tech A
   b. Tech B
   c. Both A and B
   d. Neither A nor B
8. Tech A says that fuel pressure is regulated by a fuel pressure regulator on some vehicles. Tech B says that fuel pressure is regulated by controlling the speed of the fuel pump on some vehicles. Who is correct?
   a. Tech A
   b. Tech B
   c. Both A and B
   d. Neither A nor B
9. Tech A says that measuring the alcohol content in gasoline involves using water. Tech B says that as long as the fuel pressure is correct, you don't have to worry about fuel pump volume. Who is correct?
   a. Tech A
   b. Tech B
   c. Both A and B
   d. Neither A nor B
10. When testing fuel injectors, Tech A says that the resistance can be tested and compared to specifications. Tech B says that resistance can be tested by measuring the fuel pressure drop when activating them with an injector pulse tool. Who is correct?
    a. Tech A
    b. Tech B
    c. Both A and B
    d. Neither A nor B

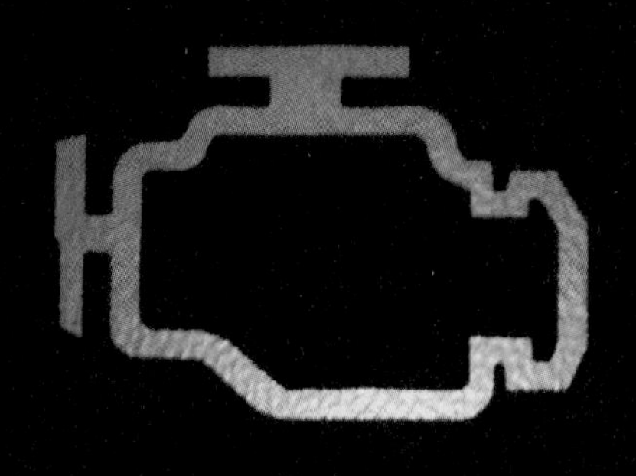

CHAPTER 38

KNOW
SEE
DO
PROVE

NATEF Tasks

Engine Performance
General Engine Diagnosis

Task			Page
■ Diagnose engine mechanical, electrical, electronic, fuel, and ignition concerns; determine necessary action.		AST	1091
Computerized Engine Controls			
■ Describe the importance of running all OBDII monitors for repair verification.	MLR	AST	1087–1090
■ Retrieve and record diagnostic trouble codes, OBD monitor status, and freeze-frame data; clear codes when applicable.	MLR	AST	1092–1093

On-Board Diagnostics

KNOW
SEE
DO
PROVE

Knowledge Objectives

After reading this chapter, you will be able to:

1. Explain what volatile organic compounds (VOCs) are and how they relate to vehicle emissions. (p 1080)
2. List some of the pollutants emitted by vehicles. (p 1080)
3. List the various sensors of the EFI system. (pp 1082–1087)
4. Explain the causes of engine knock. (p 1086)
5. Explain the origins and purpose of OBDI and OBDII systems; explain the importance of monitoring on-board systems and reporting vehicle emission–related faults. (p 1087)
6. Describe the role of controller area networks (CANs). (p 1088)
7. Explain the purpose and function of DTCs. (pp 1088–1089)
8. Describe how scan tools work and what is involved in using them. (pp 1090–1091)
9. Explain the purpose and function of control modules such as the power train control module (PCM), the body control module (BCM), and the transmission control module (TCM). (p 1089)

KNOW
SEE
DO
PROVE

Skills Objectives

After reading this chapter, you will be able to:

1. Retrieve and record DTCs, OBD monitor status, and freeze-frame data; clear codes when applicable. (pp 1092–1093)

Introduction

The automobile we drive today has certainly evolved significantly—even over the last few years. Yet despite all the innovations, **emissions** from automobiles can still harm the environment, as well as our health, and therefore need to be monitored and kept in check.

In the United States, Congress has passed federal emission regulations, starting with the **Clean Air Act** in 1963. This basic research program was expanded in 1967 to help curb emissions from automobiles. Major amendments to the law, requiring regulatory controls for air pollution, were enacted in 1970, 1977, and 1990.

In some parts of the country (usually urban areas) where noncompliance with clean air laws exists, auto technicians know that vehicle emission testing and repair remedies are a big part of day-to-day business. Today, when a vehicle's **malfunction indicator lamp (MIL)**—formerly called a "check engine light"—is illuminated it means the vehicle is not complying with clean air regulations; in the interest of public health, keeping cars running clean is a mandate. Low tailpipe emissions also mean a vehicle is running efficiently, which helps to conserve energy.

Pollutants

Vehicles emit evaporative emissions, known as **volatile organic compounds (VOCs)**, to the atmosphere. VOCs may be fuel or oil vapors emitted from the fuel tank, fuel lines, engine crankcase, or elsewhere. In earlier vehicles, engine draft tubes spewed VOCs from the crankcase onto the road, as evidenced by dark center-of-lane deposits on uphill stretches of our highways. Likewise, hot summer days once meant the smell of gasoline fumes around filling stations and parked cars—but not today!

Vehicles can also emit harmful emissions from the tailpipe. These pollutants include:

- **Carbon monoxide (CO)**
- **Hydrocarbons (HCs)**, or VOCs
- **Particulate matter (PM)**
- **Carbon dioxide (CO_2)**
- **Sulfur dioxide (SO_2)**
- **Oxides of nitrogen**—nitric oxide (NO) and nitrogen dioxide (NO_2)

Oxides of nitrogen and hydrocarbons react together to create ground-level ozone, which is considered a health hazard. Ground-level ozone especially affects children, the elderly, and those with respiratory problems. On "ozone alert days," such people are advised to stay indoors, and the operation of VOC-spewing lawn and garden equipment is discouraged. Some of the preceding gases also contribute to the greenhouse effect.

All of these pollutants to one degree or another are monitored and controlled by efficient on-board systems using state-of-the-art electronics. Computers run vehicle systems through self-tests at engine start-up and continue to do so once underway. If anything is out of the ordinary, the driver is alerted, a snapshot of operating conditions is saved for technicians to examine later, and, if needed, alternate operating strategies are initiated to protect the vehicle and the environment.

There have been many strategies implemented to clean up vehicle emissions, and in more recent years, closed-loop electronic systems have assumed the major responsibility. The following is an abbreviated timeline

You are the Automotive Technician

Jim, a new customer, brings his vehicle into your shop for an illuminated malfunction indicator lamp (MIL). He says it has been on for about a week and wants to know if you have one of "those computers" that will tell you what is wrong with his vehicle. You tell him, as you chuckle, that you wish there was a tool you could buy that would do that, but you do have several scan tools and the training to know how to use them. With that and some good technical service information, you can diagnose what is causing the MIL to be on, so it can be fixed right the first time. Jim says that makes sense, as one of his co-workers had a similar problem and the shop he went to told him that the vehicle needed a particular part, but that part didn't fix the problem. The co-worker ended up buying several parts over a couple of visits and the MIL always came back on. Jim agrees to let you diagnose the problem.

1. What does the MIL being illuminated indicate?
2. What is "freeze frame" data? And how can it help you diagnose the problem?
3. What do monitors that report "passed" and "failed" indicate?

of the many strategies devised for curtailing light-duty vehicle emissions in the United States since the 1960s:

1961—First positive crankcase ventilation (PCV) systems required in California
1964—Sealed crankcase systems replace crankcase "draft tubes"
1968—Controls for crankcase VOCs, tailpipe CO, and hydrocarbons (PCV, AIR, etc.)
1969—Commencement of limiting oxides of nitrogen emissions by retarding ignition and valve timing
1971—Introduction of evaporative emission (EVAP) control systems (charcoal canisters)
1973—Exhaust gas recirculation (EGR) systems used to control oxides of nitrogen
1975—Unleaded gasoline phase in
1975—Oxidizing catalytic converters introduced
1981—Closed-loop systems and three-way catalysts introduced; first-generation on-board diagnostics (OBDI) enacted nationwide (OBDI started with California vehicles)
1996—Second-generation on-board diagnostics (OBDII) enacted nationwide
1998—Commencement of vehicle refueling emission controls
2003—Widespread adoption of controller area network (CAN) communication systems (originated in 1998 with Robert Bosch–equipped vehicles like Volkswagens)

Before we look at the on-board-diagnostics (OBD) system theory, let's look at some of the sensors that are used by OBD systems to monitor the operation and efficiency of the powertrain. A basic understanding of these sensors will help you understand how the OBD system operates. It will also make it easier to see how the OBD system can identify **faults** in the powertrain.

Electronic Fuel Injection Sensors

Early fuel injection systems were mechanically timed. Although considered advanced technology for the era, those systems were soon phased out by modern-day EFI. The current EFI systems are constantly adjusting for various conditions and requirements to produce high levels of power at an acceptable and efficient rate. Many sensors are required to properly make the necessary adjustments for today's fuel emission requirements. But before we discuss each sensor, we need to explore the various types of electrical signals.

Digital Versus Analog Signals

Analog produces a signal that is smooth and gradually changing in strength, whereas a digital signal is a direct on/off with no in-between transition. Although a reliable system, analog signals lack the true reaction timing of the new age of digital signals. The advent of digital technology has given rise to higher powered processors that allow better control and monitoring of the systems on the vehicle, including the fuel injection system FIGURE 38-1.

Frequency

Sound travels through the air by producing pressure waves—areas of high pressure and areas of low pressure. The rate at which these waves reach our ears is called **frequency**. It is measured in cycles per second, where a cycle is the distance between waves, or wavelength. The higher the frequency, the higher the pitch of the sound FIGURE 38-2.

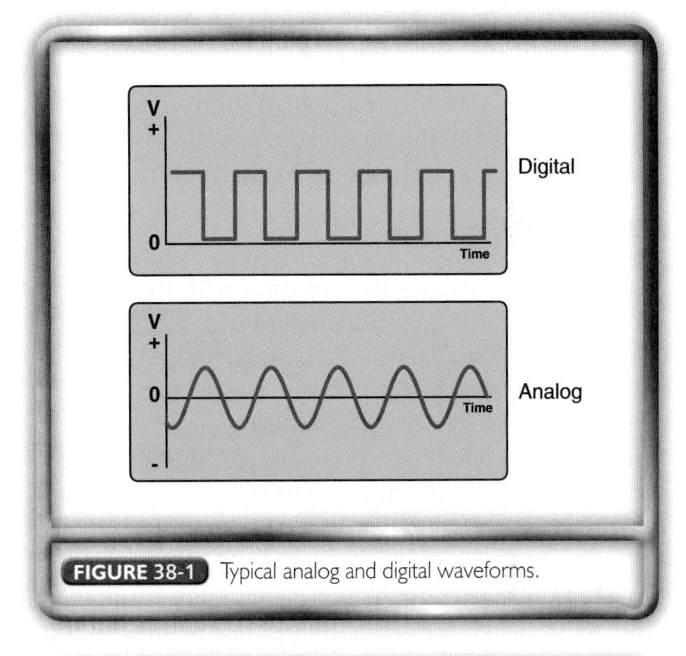
V
+
0
Time
Digital
V
+
0
-
Time
Analog

FIGURE 38-1 Typical analog and digital waveforms.

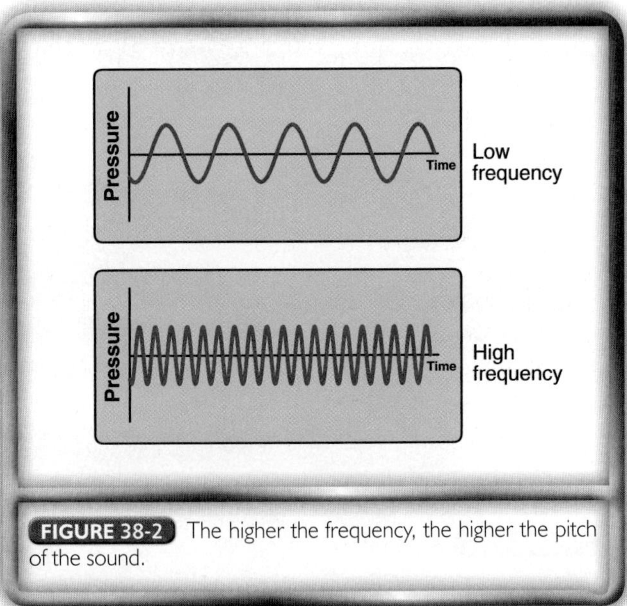
Pressure
Time
Low frequency
Pressure
Time
High frequency

FIGURE 38-2 The higher the frequency, the higher the pitch of the sound.

The range of human hearing is approximately 20 cycles per second to 20,000 cycles per second. An engine produces sounds across a wide range of frequencies. The mufflers and resonators in the engine exhaust system reduce these sounds to an acceptable level.

Potentiometer

A **potentiometer** is a mechanically variable resistor that, in EFI applications, is normally a film type. It can be linear or circular in construction and has three electrical connecting points. Two are at the ends of the resistor, and a third is attached to a center sliding contact, arranged to move across the resistor. A reference voltage is applied to the resistor so that a steady current flows through it. As the center sliding contact moves across the resistor, it measures the voltage at the point it is in contact with and provides a reference voltage for that position.

In automotive applications, the circular form is commonly used as a throttle position sensor, with the center contact attached to the throttle plate. The throttle plate position can then be monitored by the control unit.

Thermistors

A resistor that changes its resistance with the changes in temperature is called a **thermistor** FIGURE 38-3. Thermistors are used in various temperature-related controls on modern vehicles. Coolant temperature sensors, fuel temperature sensors, and ambient temperature sensors are just a few types. For example, the cabin temperature sensor's internal resistance may decrease when the cabin temperature increases. This resistance change causes a change in a voltage signal that could be used by the HVAC system to increase the air-conditioning airflow or to lower the vent temperature by moving the blend door. As a result, the system can maintain a driver-selected temperature.

EFI Sensors

The sensors used in an EFI system include:

- Crankshaft position sensor (CKP sensor)
- Ignition pickup
- Camshaft position sensor (CMP sensor)
- Throttle position sensor (TPS)
- Engine coolant temperature sensor (ECT sensor or CTS) and intake air temperature sensor (IAT sensor)
- Oxygen sensor (before and after catalytic converts) (O_2 sensor or HO_2S)
- Manifold absolute pressure sensor (MAP sensor)
- Barometric pressure sensor (BARO sensor)
- Air-conditioning compressor clutch signal
- Knock sensor
- Vehicle speed sensor (VSS)
- Inertia sensors
- Fuel pressure sensors

Crankshaft Position Sensor

Crank angle sensing sends information on the speed and position of the crankshaft to the **power train control module (PCM)** for the control of ignition timing and injection sequencing. The control unit can then trigger the ignition and injection to suit virtually all operating conditions. The **crankshaft position (CKP) sensor** may be mounted externally on the crankcase housing or it may be inside the housing of the ignition distributor. There are different kinds of CKP sensors.

Inductive-type sensors sense the movement of the ring gear teeth on the flywheel, or a toothed disc on the crank pulley FIGURE 38-4. These sensors do not make

FIGURE 38-3 A thermistor.

FIGURE 38-4 An inductive-type sensor and toothed wheel.

physical contact. The sensor is mounted on the crankcase housing. It consists of a stator, with a central permanent magnet, and a soft iron core surrounded by an induction winding. The housing around all of these components is insulated from them.

The stator is positioned so that it has a very small clearance, or air gap, between the end of the soft iron core and the flywheel teeth. As the flywheel rotates, the teeth approach and leave the stator, and the air gap changes. As this occurs, the strength of the magnetic field changes. The winding is part of a complete circuit, so changing the magnetic field produces an alternating voltage and current.

A Hall-effect CKP sensor measures engine speed, represented in rpm of the crankshaft. The sensor is in very close proximity to a metal disc that is typically attached to the crankshaft or camshaft. Around the circumference of the disc there are evenly spaced teeth or cogs (square, even serrations) FIGURE 38-5. The sensor is stationary and usually located in the engine block, with an O-ring to seal in engine oil. It contains a magnetic coil, which reacts with the magnetic field as each cog passes by the tip of the sensor. When the crankshaft spins, induction current is set up around the magnetic coil. The cog edge of the crankshaft obstructs the sensor's magnetic field, creating a signal. This is what gives the PCM a measurement of the engine rpm.

Camshaft Position Sensor

The camshaft position (CMP) sensor (or cam sensor) sends constant data to the computer to let it know which cylinder is on its power stroke as well as the position of the camshaft and valve. It does this by constantly reading a magnetic point on the camshaft or on the distributor housing FIGURE 38-6. The CMP sensor works in conjunction with a knock sensor and the computer to keep the ignition timing adjusted for all load conditions, thus reducing pinging and knocking.

Throttle Position Sensor

The throttle position sensor (TPS) gathers information on throttle position to allow the control unit to make adjustments according to operating conditions. It is located on the throttle body and operated by rotation of the throttle shaft. A potentiometer-type sensor monitors throttle position over its full range. One end has a 5-volt reference voltage from the control unit FIGURE 38-7. The other is connected to the control unit ground. A third wire runs from a sliding contact in the TPS sensor to the input circuits of the control unit. The sensor works like a variable resistor. As the angle of the throttle valve changes, so does the voltage signal along the third wire.

FIGURE 38-6 The camshaft position (CMP) sensor sends data to the computer to let it know which cylinder is on its power stroke as well as the position of the camshaft and valve.

FIGURE 38-5 A Hall-effect CKP sensor measures engine speed, represented in rpm of the crankshaft.

FIGURE 38-7 A potentiometer-type sensor monitors throttle position over its full range. One end has a 5-volt reference voltage from the control unit.

At closed throttle, the reading is usually below 1 volt. As the throttle valve opens, the voltage signal rises. At wide-open throttle, it is about 4.5 volts. This ongoing monitoring of throttle position provides accurate data for the control unit, allowing control over a wider range of operating conditions.

Engine Temperature Sensors

To maintain the air–fuel ratio within an optimum range, the control unit must take account of coolant temperature and air temperature. Extra fuel is needed when the engine is cold, and when the air is colder, and therefore denser.

The **coolant temperature sensor (CTS)** is immersed in coolant in the cylinder head, block, or intake manifold. It consists of a hollow threaded pin that has a resistor sealed inside it **FIGURE 38-8**. This resistor is made of a thermistor semiconductor material whose electrical resistance falls as temperature rises. The signal from the CTS is used by the PCM to control the mixture of the engine throughout its operating temperature.

Air temperature is one factor that changes the density of air, so air temperature needs to be monitored by the PCM to better judge how much fuel needs to be injected. An air temperature sensor does just that. If the air temperature sensor is installed in the airflow sensor, it is positioned in the airstream and is called an **intake air temperature (IAT) sensor** **FIGURE 38-9**. When it is installed in the intake manifold, it is located in one of the intake runners and is called a manifold air temperature (MAT) sensor. In both cases, it relays information on air temperature and, therefore, the density of the air. The control unit can then vary the injector pulse width accordingly.

Oxygen Sensor

An **oxygen sensor (before and after catalytic converter)** is positioned in the exhaust pipe and provides the engine management PCM with an electrical signal that relates to the amount of oxygen in the exhaust gas. The PCM uses this and other information to determine the correct amount of fuel to be injected into the engine.

Originally, automotive oxygen sensors were stoichiometric sensors. Although still in use today, they indicate only if the air–fuel ratio is rich (deficient oxygen) or lean (excess oxygen). They do not indicate how rich or how lean. Their output signal changes almost vertically on either side of an air–fuel ratio of stoichiometric, 14.7:1. It is the "Nernst cell" inside the sensor that produces this signal voltage. The Nernst cell operates by comparing the amount of oxygen in the exhaust gas to oxygen levels in the outside air **FIGURE 38-10**. To operate, this cell needs to be hot, approximately 600°F (315°C) or more. Exhaust gas can heat the sensor; however, when an internal heater is added, the sensor becomes operational more quickly and is called a heated oxygen sensor (HO_2S). This is most relevant when the sensor is positioned in cooler parts of the exhaust system away from the exhaust manifold.

As emission standards become tighter for both gasoline and diesel engines, a more precise signal is required. In these systems, the broad-band oxygen sensor (or wide-band oxygen sensor) informs the PCM of a range of air–fuel ratios from 9:1 to atmospheric air. These systems are ideal for optimum emissions for vehicle gasoline or diesel engines, particularly where the incoming air is unthrottled and not restricted by a throttle butterfly lean-running GDI engine.

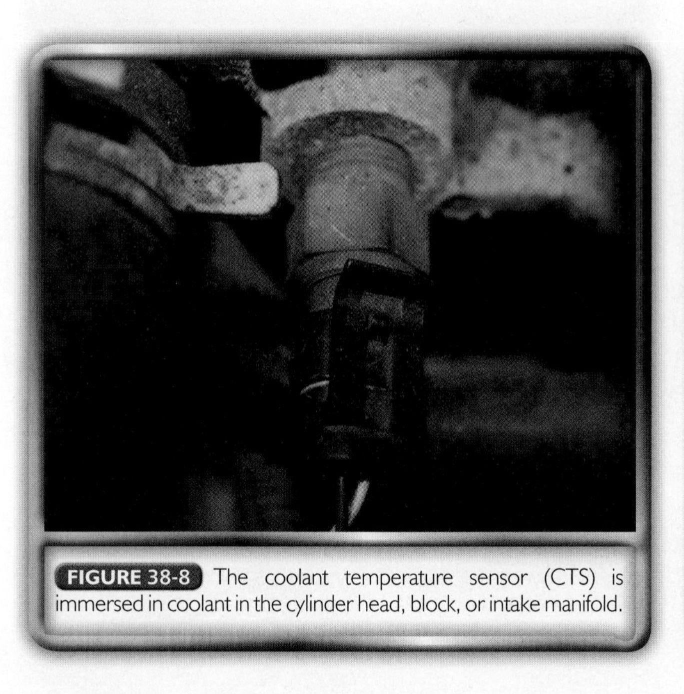

FIGURE 38-8 The coolant temperature sensor (CTS) is immersed in coolant in the cylinder head, block, or intake manifold.

FIGURE 38-9 Intake air temperature (IAT) sensor.

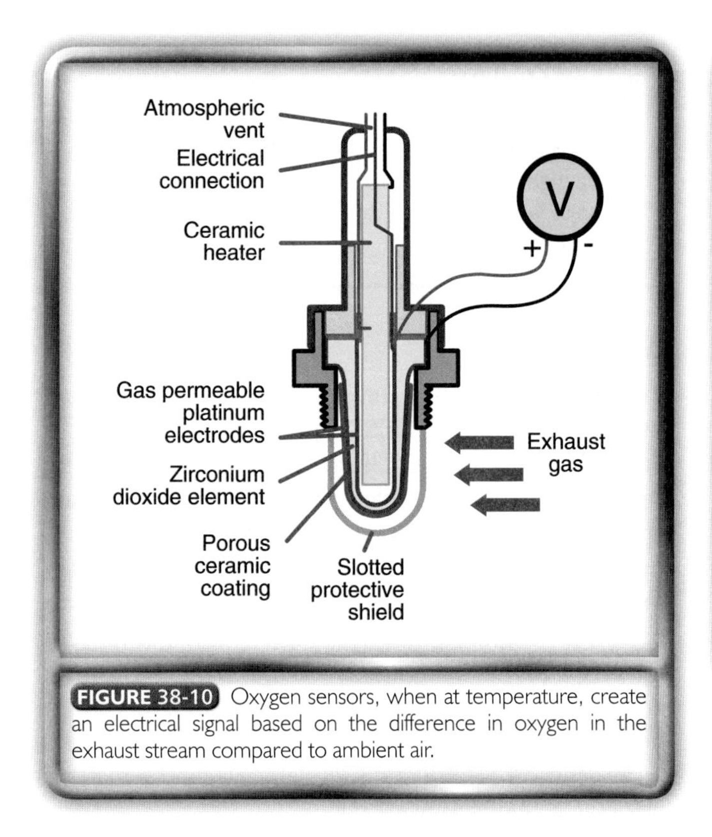
Atmospheric vent
Electrical connection
Ceramic heater
V
+
-
Gas permeable platinum electrodes
Exhaust gas
Zirconium dioxide element
Porous ceramic coating
Slotted protective shield

FIGURE 38-10 Oxygen sensors, when at temperature, create an electrical signal based on the difference in oxygen in the exhaust stream compared to ambient air.

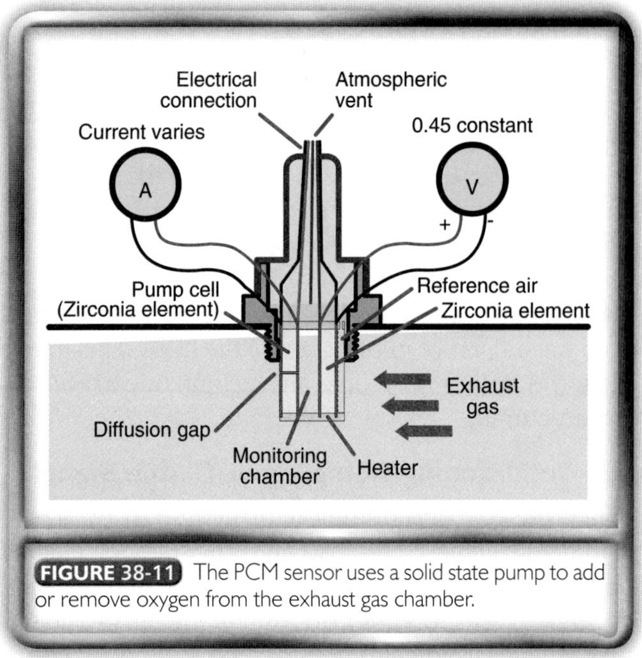
Electrical connection
Atmospheric vent
Current varies
0.45 constant
A
V
+
-
Pump cell (Zirconia element)
Reference air
Zirconia element
Exhaust gas
Diffusion gap
Monitoring chamber
Heater

FIGURE 38-11 The PCM sensor uses a solid state pump to add or remove oxygen from the exhaust gas chamber.

The wide-band oxygen sensor is far more sophisticated in operation than the earlier sensors, but it does include some similar parts. The Nernst cell is still used; however, the exhaust gas oxygen levels are referenced to a sealed chamber of air within the sensor and not outside air. These sensors have an electrical heating element that heats the sensor quickly from a cold start, typically in less than 10 seconds. This is a shorter time than that taken by the older sensors. This faster heating is achieved because the sensors have far less material within the sensing element.

Current through the heater is controlled by the PCM, allowing the correct operating temperature to be continuously maintained. A minute chamber within the sensor has access to the exhaust gas. It is this chamber that the Nernst cell samples exhaust gas from. This sensor uses a solid state pump to add or remove oxygen from the exhaust gas chamber FIGURE 38-11.

The computer controls the current flowing through the pump so that the Nernst cell output is at stoichiometric. Current flowing in one direction through the pump adds oxygen, while current in the opposite direction removes oxygen. The value and direction of current required to do this represents the level of oxygen in the exhaust gas. Reading this current allows the PCM to control the amount of fuel delivered and maintain correct emission levels.

Since 1996, nearly all manufacturers install an oxygen sensor before and after the catalytic converter to test for correct operation. For a catalytic converter to change exhaust gases correctly, it needs to be capable of storing and releasing oxygen from the catalyst. When this happens, the amount of oxygen entering the converter will differ from that leaving. The PCM uses these two signals along with response time to determine if the catalytic converter is functioning. If a malfunction is detected for a predetermined period, the MIL will be illuminated. Many manufacturers also use the rear oxygen sensor to fine-tune the fuel trim.

Manifold Absolute Pressure Sensor

Changes in engine speed and load cause changes in intake manifold pressure. A **manifold absolute pressure (MAP) sensor** measures these pressure changes and converts them into an electrical signal. The signal may be an output voltage or a frequency. By monitoring output signals, the PCM senses manifold pressure and uses this information to calculate the basic fuel requirement. The MAP sensor can use a piezoelectric crystal. If there is a change in the pressure exerted on this crystal, the resistance changes. This alters its output signal.

During idling, manifold pressure is low (high vacuum), which produces a comparatively low MAP output. With wide-open throttle, manifold pressure is higher, closer to atmospheric pressure (low vacuum), and voltage output is higher. Another type of MAP sensor that has been used by some manufacturers is one that sends a varying frequency to the PCM. As the sensor measures low manifold pressure, it sends a frequency signal. Frequency can be read on a digital volt-ohmmeter that has a frequency function.

Barometric Pressure Sensor

A barometric pressure (BARO) sensor measures barometric pressure, which helps to calibrate the fuel injection system. The barometric pressures at sea level and in Denver, Colorado, which is called the mile-high city because of its high altitude, are extremely different. The vehicle must function properly at both locations or anywhere in between. The BARO sensor works in conjunction with the MAP sensor to provide constant pressure difference information to the PCM. This information is critical for proper air–fuel mixture as well as ignition timing.

Air-Conditioning Compressor Clutch Signal

When the air conditioning is turned on, it creates a load on the engine. This load, in turn, drags the engine down, especially during engine idle conditions on smaller engines. In vehicles equipped with the circuitry to do so, the clutch electrical circuit signals the PCM that the air conditioning has been turned on and that there will therefore be greater load on the engine. To counteract this load, the PCM sends a command to the engine idle speed controller to open slightly to maintain an acceptable engine rpm. This ultimately gives the driver smooth and quiet engine operation during idle with the air conditioning on.

Applied Science

AS-83: Barometric Pressure: The technician can demonstrate an understanding of the relationship of barometric pressure to engine performance.

Atmospheric pressure is a measure of the pressure exerted by the weight of the atmosphere. This is also called barometric pressure because barometers are used to measure it. The term barometer comes from the Greek words for weight and measure. A mercury barometer compares atmospheric pressure to a column of mercury and measures the results in inches or millimeters of mercury.

A barometric pressure (BARO) sensor measures barometric pressure and is crucial to most fuel injections systems. The barometric pressure varies by geographic elevation. The vehicle must function flawlessly in any given location. Accurate pressure readings are critical for proper air–fuel mixture as well as ignition timing.

The principle of the operation of barometric sensors is based upon the flexing of a silicon chip. The output voltage signal varies based upon the amount that the chip flexes due to barometric pressure. The PCM uses this information along with other data to determine the proper adjustments that should be made to the fuel system as well as other systems.

TECHNICIAN TIP

Another way of preventing engine knock is to use fuel with a higher octane rating. This makes the fuel harder to ignite and slower to burn, both of which reduce engine knock.

Knock Sensor

Engine knock occurs in the combustion chamber when there is an unwanted spike in pressure caused by pre-ignition or detonation. This unwanted and damaging event can be caused in different ways. Some vehicles are equipped with a knock sensor, the function of which is to monitor the noise that is created by the pressure spike. This noise, or "knock," can be created by an excessive load on the engine, ignition timing that is too advanced, or overheating of the engine. The PCM can adjust the ignition timing to help reduce the knocking, except in the case of engine overheating. In addition, adjustments to the ignition timing and fuel delivery can be made if the vehicle begins to overheat.

The sensor is screwed into the engine block, where it is influenced by all engine vibrations FIGURE 38-12. Using a piezoelectric crystal, the sensor produces a signal voltage proportional to the vibrations applied to it. The PCM interprets the strength, frequency, and timing of the signal to determine if knock has occurred. While knock sensor technology has improved, it cannot always know the difference between engine knock and a loose air-conditioning compressor bracket that rattles when it is on. In this situation, the rattling air-conditioning compressor bracket causes a noise that the knock sensor

FIGURE 38-12 The sensor is screwed into the engine block, where it is influenced by all engine vibrations.

picks up as engine knock. But since the "knock" in this case does not go away as the timing is retarded, the PCM gradually reduces ignition advance until it reaches its limits, causing low power, poor fuel economy, and possible engine overheating. Monitoring the knock sensor signal and amount of timing retard on a scan tool will help you identify this issue.

Vehicle Speed Sensor

The vehicle speed sensor (VSS) is a detection device that sends the vehicle speed information (i.e., how fast the vehicle is traveling) to the ECM. The VSS is sometimes located in the instrument cluster; however, most manufacturers mount these sensors on the transmission or transfer case.

Fuel Pressure Sensor

Most vehicles now use a fuel pressure sensor mounted on the fuel rail FIGURE 38-13. This sensor allows the PCM to monitor the fuel pressure in the fuel rail so that it can control the speed of the fuel pump to maintain the correct pressure in the system.

Switches

While at idle, engine speed can be adversely affected by fairly minor changes in load. Loads from transmissions, power steering pumps, and air-conditioning compressors are examples. For optimum engine control, it is necessary for the PCM to be informed of these loads before the engine speed drops. Switches are used to inform the PCM when the power steering pump pressure is high, automatic transmission drive gear is selected, and the air-conditioning compressor is engaged. The result is excellent PCM control of idle speed as loads vary on the engine.

FIGURE 38-13 Fuel pressure sensor mounted on the fuel rail.

On-Board Diagnostic Systems

OBD systems are a great resource to help the technician work more efficiently and remove some of the guesswork involved in diagnosing problems in today's sophisticated vehicles. These systems use powerful on-board computers in harmony with sophisticated diagnostic equipment to pinpoint problems in vehicle systems and components. Various on-board computers (sometimes referred to as **modules**) inform the vehicle operator when a fault occurs and assist technicians in identifying and repairing malfunctioning circuits or components.

In the United States, two different types of OBD systems have been used. The first generation of on-board diagnostic (**OBDI**) systems operated under manufacturer standards, starting with California vehicles and becoming nationwide in 1981. The second generation of on-board diagnostic (**OBDII**) systems operate under standards set by the Society of Automotive Engineers (SAE) to conform with US Environmental Protection Agency (EPA) regulations. Some manufacturers started using OBDII with a few of their models in 1994 and 1995 to become familiar with the systems, but for the 1996 model year, OBDII was standardized and initiated nationwide.

Where OBDI monitored mainly for parts and wiring malfunctions, OBDII is an enhanced diagnostic system that identifies faults in anything that may affect the vehicle's emission system. OBDII tests vehicle operating systems for faults affecting vehicle drivability and those that may affect vehicle safety and emission efficiency. OBDII constantly monitors and manages some of the electronics that control the vehicle's emission systems, which in turn enables much tighter standards to be enforced, with cutoff points far lower than those previously possible.

Both OBDI and OBDII systems provide a certain degree of commonality in that all vehicle manufacturers must adhere to certain standards regarding nomenclature (names of parts) and fault description codes. This means that any so-called "generic" OBDII faults and background data can be accessed and read by **aftermarket** as well as original equipment manufacturer (OEM) test equipment.

Both OEM and aftermarket OBDII scan tools serve to access OBD information via the **data link connector (DLC)**. The DLC enables the scanner to access data stored in the vehicle's various computers FIGURE 38-14. The DLC itself is a 16-pin connector with a common (SAE J1962) size and shape. Regardless of vehicle make and model, its location is now fairly standardized as being within 2' of the steering wheel below the driver's side instrument panel.

FIGURE 38-14 The data link connector (DLC) enables the scanner to access data stored in the vehicle's various computers.

OBD Terminology

The automotive technician needs to know and understand the "lingo" used in the diagnosis and repair of automobiles in the service bay. Before the SAE published the appropriate "recommended practices," OEMs used nonstandardized nomenclature. The SAE has helped to standardize automotive terms used by engineers and technicians alike. A complete listing of OBDI and OBDII terms is available from the SAE (SAE J1930).

CAN-Bus

Standard copper wiring bundles on vehicles have become a major weight and cost issue due to the increased interconnectivity required between on-board computers and components. To simplify wiring, controller area networks (CANs) have become commonplace in today's vehicles. A CAN is a localized (on-board) vehicle network that enables computers and components to send and receive signals across a shielded twisted pair of wires. The wires are shielded by being twisted around one another and carrying balanced (+ and –) signals to reduce the likelihood of radio frequency interference into the network. The shielded pair of wires forms a common loop around the vehicle to connect components and handle encoded messages between components. Thus, the various computers/modules can network, or "talk," to one another. For example, a throttle position sensor or coolant temperature sensor may provide valued information to a number of other on-board modules to serve their respective needs.

The CAN-bus is constantly monitored by the OBDII system. Additionally, for diagnostic purposes, data can be accessed by the technician using the appropriate scan tool to either read data or command certain actuator functions to operate and be tested **FIGURE 38-15**.

Diagnostic Trouble Codes

Diagnostic trouble codes (DTCs) indicate the component or circuit in which a fault has been detected. Codes are "set" (stored) in one or more of the vehicle's on-board computers once a fault is detected. A fault is generated when values being monitored determine the emissions would be 1.5 times the EPA Federal Test Procedure (FTP). For example, a short or open in the engine's coolant temperature circuit will cause the fuel system to run rich, increasing the emissions so a DTC will be set. Also, if two sensors send conflicting data, a fault is recorded and the MIL is illuminated. Some DTCs set due to implausibility and conditions that are out of parameters, but it is not always a case of a failed component or wiring. Understanding how the affected system operates is very important when troubleshooting the OBDII system. If you don't know how it works, how can you fix it? Locating, reading, and understanding the strategy used by the manufacturer to generate the DTC is of utmost importance.

Emission-related DTCs are the same (generic) across all vehicle makes and models, as are the SAE-recommended names used to describe components and systems. Any number of on-board computer modules

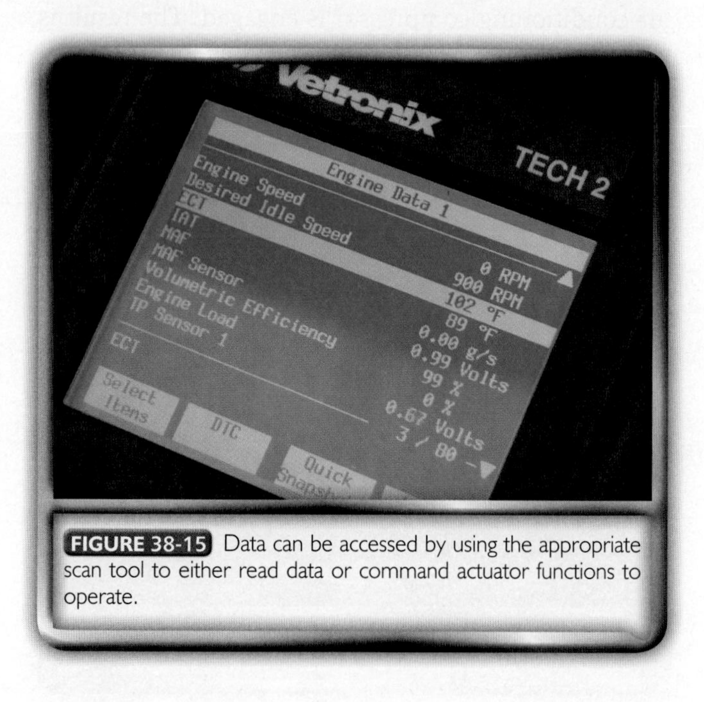
Vetronix
TECH 2
Engine Data 1
Engine Speed
Desired Idle Speed
ECT
IAT
MAF
MAF Sensor
Volumetric Efficiency
Engine Load
TP Sensor 1
ECT
0 RPM
900 RPM
102 °F
89 °F
0.00 g/s
0.99 Volts
99 %
0 %
0.67 Volts
3 / 80
Select Items
DTC
Quick

FIGURE 38-15 Data can be accessed by using the appropriate scan tool to either read data or command actuator functions to operate.

may communicate with one another using standardized digital "languages." Nonmanufacturer-specific codes—those that are in any way emission related—are now the same from one vehicle to the next. Refer to SAE J2012 for more information on interpreting generic DTCs. Refer to OEM service manuals for interpreting OEM-specific (nongeneric) system codes.

If a vehicle system reports that a fault exists, the MIL located in the instrument cluster will likely illuminate FIGURE 38-16. Sometimes it takes two consecutive drive cycles, or "trips," to illuminate the MIL. The MIL alerts the driver that there is a problem. Even a loose gas cap will trigger a DTC and illuminate the MIL under certain conditions. Catalytic converter input and output are monitored and compared. If the converter's efficiency is out of range, the MIL will illuminate and a DTC will set.

If the catalytic converter is at risk, such as from overfueling or a continuous misfire, the MIL will flash, thus telling the driver to stop the vehicle immediately to avoid serious damage to the converter. Once a malfunction occurs, the MIL will remain on until the system returns to normal or the fault is seen as repaired; alternately, the code may be cleared from memory by the technician using a scan tool. OBD systems store DTCs in the computer's so-called keep alive memory (KAM). The codes remain in memory until power is disconnected for older vehicles; for newer vehicles, DTCs are saved even if the vehicle's battery is disconnected. DTC information remains stored in the respective control module's long-term memory regardless of whether a "hard" (continuous) or an intermittent fault has set the code.

FIGURE 38-16 The malfunction indicator lamp (MIL).

A DTC may be generated by any of the numerous computer modules on board. It serves not only to inform the driver of a fault, but also to enable the automotive technician to determine where the fault has occurred. DTCs are used in conjunction with diagnostic flowcharts found in the manufacturer's service information to assist technicians in determining the likely cause of a failure.

Both OBDI and OBDII systems monitor engine sensors, fuel delivery components, and emission control devices that, if faulty, will cause problems. Simpler OBDI systems are normally limited to the detection of an open or short in a sensor or wiring. But OBDII systems monitor all emission-related components and circuits for opens, shorts, abnormal operation, and more.

OBDII codes use a series of letters and numbers grouped together to identify which system, component, or circuit is at fault. The first character of the code is a letter that identifies whether the fault is located within the power train (P), body (B), chassis controller (C), or communication system (U). The next four characters are numbers, starting with 0 or 1. A 0 indicates a generic OBDII code; a 1 indicates an OEM code. The next three numbers identify the system and component related to the fault. Refer to DTC charts (on the Internet or in service literature) for a complete listing of the hundreds of possible codes. The list grows constantly as on-board systems become even more sophisticated and unique, as with hybrid-electric vehicles.

Freeze-Frame Data

Since OBDII came about in 1996, technicians have had the ability to access freeze-frame snapshots that are automatically recorded in the vehicle's power train control module (PCM) when a vehicle fault occurs. If a more serious fault supersedes another previously less-serious recorded fault, freeze-frame data are updated. Difficult-to-find intermittent faults can thus be diagnosed by carefully reviewing data stored just before, during, and after the fault occurred. During a test-drive, such recorded data give the technician a valuable "instant replay" of what happened and when. For example, if the vehicle experienced a misfire while crossing a rough set of railroad tracks but at no other time. Modern scan tools can retrieve freeze-frame data and display them (via a graphing scan tool) for analysis after the fact FIGURE 38-17.

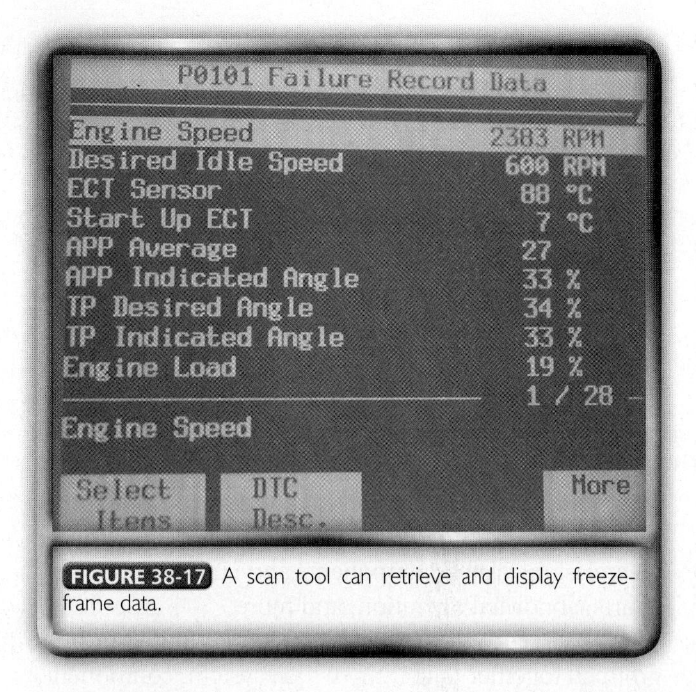
P0101 Failure Record Data
Engine Speed 2383 RPM
Desired Idle Speed 600 RPM
ECT Sensor 88 °C
Start Up ECT 7 °C
APP Average 27
APP Indicated Angle 33 %
TP Desired Angle 34 %
TP Indicated Angle 33 %
Engine Load 19 %
1 / 28
Engine Speed
Select Items
DTC Desc.
More

FIGURE 38-17 A scan tool can retrieve and display freeze-frame data.

System Monitors

OBDII standards dictate that a vehicle's computer (PCM) must monitor emission systems with two priorities in mind. The first is the **continuous monitoring** of systems and components that could contribute to major emission failures. Possible faults include engine misfiring and an incorrect air/fuel mixture, which are monitored on a continuous basis by the PCM. Lower-priority faults are monitored on a **noncontinuous** basis. In such cases, systems are checked only once during each engine **warm-up cycle**, or even less often, depending on certain circumstances such as ambient temperatures or fuel level.

Each time the engine is started, the PCM checks that components such as the oxygen sensor, catalytic converter, and other engine systems are functioning correctly. If a fault is detected, the MIL is illuminated, indicating that the vehicle needs attention.

If the condition is intermittent and the faulty system once again operates normally, the MIL will turn off after the vehicle has operated through three warm-up cycles, but the DTC will remain logged in the PCM's memory as a **history code** for a set period. If the fault does not reoccur within 40 drive cycles, the code will automatically be erased.

Drive Cycles

A **drive cycle** is essentially considered to include the following events: A vehicle starts, warms up, is accelerated, cruises, slows down, accelerates once more, decelerates, stops, and cools down. The EPA has established "drive cycles" for emission testing of various kinds of vehicles, and the light-duty vehicle (240-second) drive cycle is the basis for how OBDII **monitors** (tests) are run. A complete driving cycle should include diagnostics on all systems and be completed in under 15 minutes; however, sometimes certain monitors cannot be run during a drive cycle if qualifying conditions for running that particular monitor are not met. For example, an evaporative emission (EVAP) monitor will not run if the fuel tank is nearly full or nearly empty. In some cases, particular monitors cannot run until after others have been run and passed. EVAP monitoring will also not run if the engine coolant temperature monitor has not passed. State-run emission inspection stations in the Unites States will sometimes allow a vehicle to pass an emission inspection, even if one or two monitors have not run and passed.

Scan Tools

Essentially, a **scan tool** ("scanner") is a device able to electronically communicate with and extract data from the vehicle's one or more on-board computers. On-board computer modules include the PCM, **electronic brake control module (EBCM)**, **body control module (BCM)**, **transmission control module (TCM)**, and perhaps numerous others. Simple scan tools from the 80s could read and erase fault codes and little more. But as on-board systems became more complex, so too did professional-grade scan tools used in the service bay. Today, these scanners are sold to consumers.

Cost and complexity increase commensurate with the bells and whistles desired in a scanner. Automotive technicians today are finding that they must use faster and more accurate diagnostic instruments, such as graphing scan tools, to see hidden faults in component or system waveforms. Scanners are now used to monitor engine compression, vacuum, internal engine anomalies, and so forth. Called **bidirectional scanners**, they are used to cause various components and systems to operate for test purposes. Scanners are used along with digital storage oscilloscopes, portable five-gas **emission analyzers**, and other diagnostic equipment for much more effective time-saving diagnostic routines.

The scan tool is not a "magic bullet," however. A fault code found does not necessarily point directly to the problem. For example, a *P0171 Fuel System Too Lean* code could be caused by a defective oxygen sensor, but it

Applied Science

AS-18: Time: The technician uses direct and indirect methods to measure time and compare the results to the manufacturer's specifications.

A technician is troubleshooting a vehicle that has an intermittent problem with hesitation on acceleration. The technician has started his evaluation by conducting a visual inspection. After this, he uses a scan tool to check for codes but does not find any. He checks fuel pressure and volume, and both are within the manufacturer's specifications. The technician checks for service bulletins for this symptom but has not found any leads in this area.

Another technician suggests confirming that the injector pulse width meets the manufacturer's specifications, since he has a similar vehicle that had problems in this area. The technician checks the service manual and finds that the injector pulse width should be 2.5 to 2.7 milliseconds at engine idle. The manual also gives other pulse-width specifications for other engine speeds. Using a scan tool, the technician is able to verify that the pulse width is within the manufacturer's specifications at all published engine speeds. The scan tool data is on a direct-time basis as real-time engine data is being used.

Pulse width is the amount of time measured in milliseconds that a fuel injector delivers fuel to the cylinder. The injector pulse width depends on the input signals supplied to the PCM from its various engine sensors. The pulse width expands on acceleration and contracts under lighter loads.

could also be caused by an underreporting mass airflow sensor, a vacuum leak, use of the wrong fuel, and so on., so further testing is often required.

Training and experience play a major role in effectively using these modern information-gathering tools. Understanding the principles of combustion theory, internal combustion engine operation, and emissions are essential ingredients for success. Something that is often forgotten in this electronic age is that engines, transmissions, and braking systems are still, by nature, mechanical devices. Electronics can control and monitor them, but they cannot overcome large physical defects. For instance, low compression due to a burned valve may go undiagnosed if a code is not set. After the scanner is used to read any codes, but before any electronic troubleshooting begins, a thorough visual examination of the mechanical parts of the system involved should be performed. Simple faults like a cracked or loose vacuum hose, or even a loose gas cap, may easily be found and corrected—whether a code is set or not.

Indeed, the field is demanding. It requires extensive training and also a sizeable investment. Opportunities abound for the technician who understands the theory and masters the use of the scanner to quickly and efficiently analyze, diagnose, and solve problems on today's advanced vehicle engine systems.

Diagnosis and Testing

Diagnosing Engine Concerns

Modern vehicle engine systems are complex systems that have developed to provide performance and efficient use of fuel while ensuring that exhaust emissions meet strict environmental regulations. To achieve these demands, engineers have improved the performance of mechanical components and used computer control of the electrical, ignition, and fuel systems to ensure the highest possible efficiency while reducing exhaust emissions. Each of these systems must be working together, each interacting with the other correctly to ensure optimal engine operation. A fault in one system will affect the performance of other systems. For example, a plugged injector may cause a cylinder misfire, reducing engine power and also affecting the secondary ignition voltages. Diagnosis of the engine requires that you understand each of these systems, how they operate, and how their performance affects other systems and components.

To diagnose correctly, test for the cause of the customer's concern to verify the fault. Determine what faults may cause the symptoms and conduct mechanical, electrical, ignition, and fuel system checks to correctly identify the location and types of faults. It is also possible that a vehicle may have multiple faults; for example, a plugged injector may have been caused by poor-quality fuel.

Test equipment will need to be used to diagnose engine faults. This equipment may include OBD scanners, digital storage oscilloscopes, compression gauges, digital volt-ohmmeters (DVOMs), fuel system pressure gauges, and flowmeters. You will need to interpret the test results, compare the results to the manufacturer's specifications, and then apply the test results in a diagnostic pathway.

Retrieving and Recording DTCs, OBD Monitor Status, and Freeze-Frame Data

Modern vehicles are required to meet strict environmental emission regulations over the life of their operation. In order to meet these standards, vehicles are equipped with sophisticated electronic control units and sensors to monitor and adjust the engine fuel and the ignition and emission systems and to provide diagnostic capability to meet the required standards. Retrieving and recording DTCs, monitor status, and freeze-frame data are integral steps in diagnosing faults within vehicle systems. The technician must be able to do so anytime a vehicle sets a DTC or fails emission monitors.

Every vehicle sold is required to meet a drive cycle, which is designed to simulate actual driving conditions. The OBDII system constantly tests and analyzes each system's performance over the drive cycle. This is achieved through a set of PCM programs called monitors, which test each system's operation. The monitor will set a pass or fail based on each system test. The electronic systems will also record and store data for diagnostic purposes. The PCM will set and store DTCs if a fault is detected. Freeze-frame data are also stored, which provide a snapshot of particular PIDs before, during, and after the time of the fault being detected. Never delete or reset the diagnostic data until all testing has been completed. Ensure that any codes or data are recorded and safely stored.

To retrieve and record DTCs, OBD monitor status, and freeze-frame data, follow the steps in SKILL DRILL 38-1.

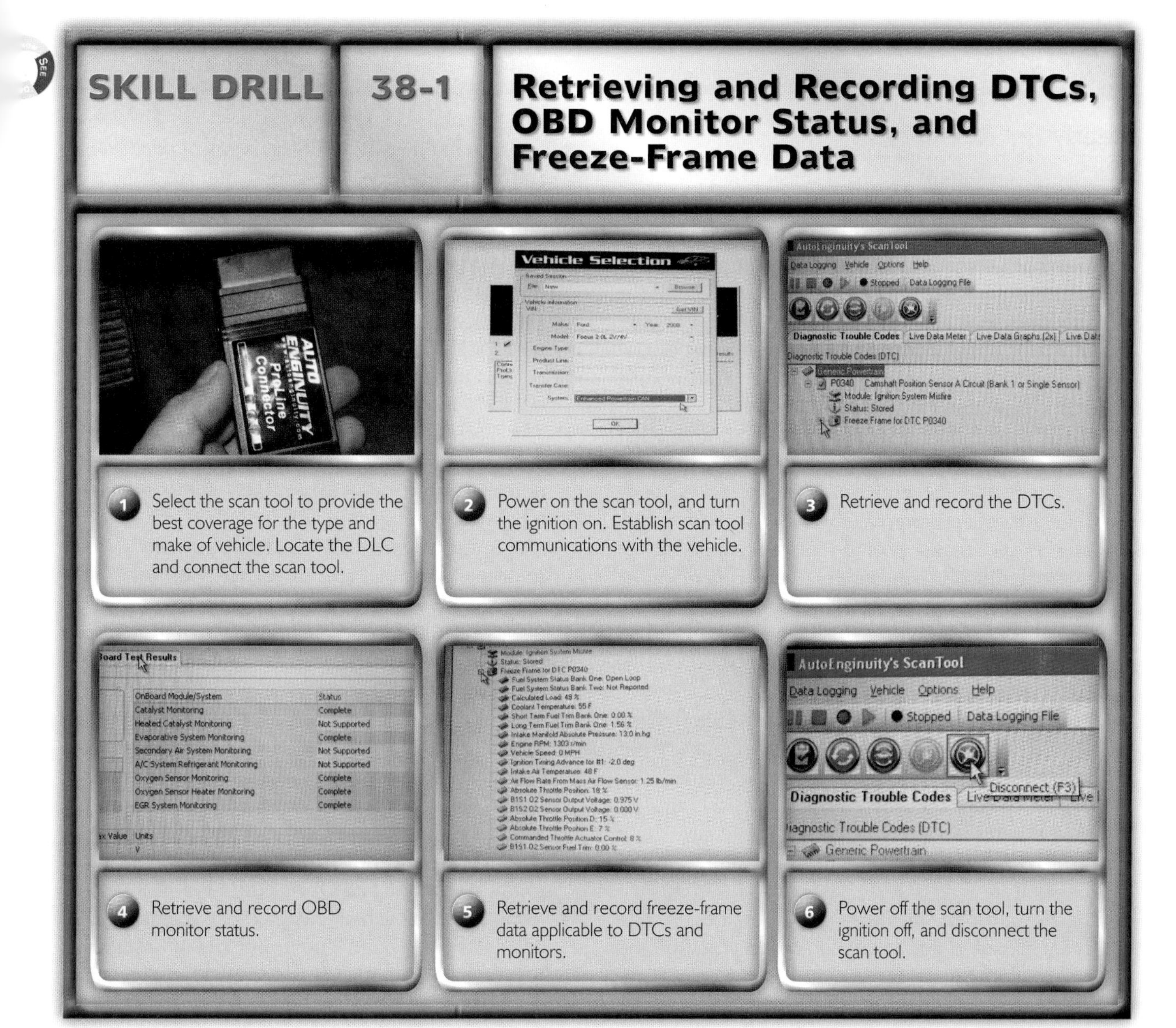

SKILL DRILL 38-1 Retrieving and Recording DTCs, OBD Monitor Status, and Freeze-Frame Data

1. Select the scan tool to provide the best coverage for the type and make of vehicle. Locate the DLC and connect the scan tool.
2. Power on the scan tool, and turn the ignition on. Establish scan tool communications with the vehicle.
3. Retrieve and record the DTCs.
4. Retrieve and record OBD monitor status.
5. Retrieve and record freeze-frame data applicable to DTCs and monitors.
6. Power off the scan tool, turn the ignition off, and disconnect the scan tool.

Wrap-up

Ready for Review

- Second-generation on-board diagnostics (OBDII) started in late 1995 and became standard in 1996. All vehicles use the same generic adapter for a generic scan tool to connect to the vehicles computer.
- Since California's emission laws of the 1960s, the standards for emissions have gotten more stringent, requiring many changes to subsequent vehicles.
- Airflow and volume are critical in ensuring the engine has the correct ratio of air to fuel.
- All electronic fuel systems use sensors and other devices to tell the PCM how much fuel is needed for a given engine operating condition.
- The crankshaft position (CKP) sensor uses information on the speed and position of the crankshaft to control ignition timing and injection sequencing.
- The camshaft position (CMP) sensor sends constant data to the computer to let it know which cylinder is on its power stroke as well as the position of the camshaft and valve.
- The throttle position sensor (TPS) gathers information on throttle positions to allow the control unit to make adjustments according to operating conditions.
- Engine coolant temperature maintains the air–fuel ratio within an optimum range. The control unit must take account of coolant temperature and air temperature.
- Manifold absolute pressure (MAP) measures changes in engine speed and load and converts the findings into an electrical signal to control engine operations.
- The vehicle speed sensor (VSS) is a detection device that sends the vehicle speed information (i.e., how fast the vehicle is traveling) to the electronic control module.
- OBD systems help the technician work more efficiently and help take the guesswork out of diagnosing problems on today's sophisticated vehicles.
- OBD systems are a great resource, using powerful on-board computers in harmony with sophisticated diagnostic equipment to pinpoint problems in vehicle systems and components.
- Both OEM and aftermarket OBDII scan tools serve to access OBD information via the data link connector (DLC).
- The Society of Automotive Engineers (SAE) has standardized the terminology of parts and systems nomenclature (J1930) and across-the-board identification of generic DTCs (J2012).
- Diagnostic trouble codes (DTCs) are usually set after the vehicle has had two drive cycles with the same malfunction.
- Codes on OBD systems are categorized as power train (P), body (B), chassis controller (C), and communications system (U).
- Freeze-frame data are the best way for a technician to determine the conditions under which a concern happens which then helps determine the cause of the DTC.
- Scan tools, a lab scope, and a digital volt-ohmmeter (DVOM) are a technician's best tools when it comes to troubleshooting an OBD code.
- Always refer to the manufacturer's service information and follow the diagnostic flowcharts to ensure that the vehicle malfunction is identified and repaired correctly.
- Always use wiring diagrams when diagnosing any electric/electronic circuits in the OBD system, and do not forget about the grounds.

Key Terms

aftermarket That segment of the trade that supplies parts, services, and repair for vehicles outside of the original equipment manufacturer (OEM) or the dealer network.

barometric pressure (BARO) sensor A sensor that measures atmospheric pressure.

bidirectional scanners Scanners used to monitor engine compression, vacuum, internal engine anomalies, and so forth by causing various components and systems to operate for test purposes.

body control module (BCM) An electronic unit that monitors and regulates electronic devices in the vehicle.

camshaft position (CMP) sensor A detection device that signals to the PCM the rotational position of the camshaft.

carbon dioxide (CO_2) A vehicle emission that is considered a primary greenhouse gas, though not toxic and not yet regulated.

carbon monoxide (CO) A vehicle emission produced by partially burned fuel that is colorless, odorless, and highly toxic and that causes asphyxiation when inhaled.

Clean Air Act Federal legislation enacted in the United States to reduce pollution, in part from automobiles.

code Another name for a fault code; *see* DTC.

continuous monitoring A term that describes OBDII monitors that run continuously throughout the drive cycle.

controller area network (CAN) A localized (on-board) vehicle network that enables computers and components to send and receive signals across a shielded twisted pair of wires.

coolant temperature sensor (CTS) A thermistor usually screwed into a cylinder head water jacket. Usually the CTS is a negative temperature coefficient thermistor, or a resistor whose resistance varies, with temperature varying a voltage signal to the PCM.

crankshaft position (CKP) sensor A sensor similar to a Hall-effect switch that is used to monitor crankshaft position and speed.

data link connector (DLC) A device that enables a scan tool to access data stored in the vehicle's various computers.

diagnostic trouble code (DTC) A computer-driven on-board report regarding component or system faults following the running of monitors.

drive cycle A series of prescribed automobile operating conditions during which emissions testing is performed.

electronic brake control module (EBCM) The module that controls and monitors the anti-lock braking system.

emissions Tailpipe and volatile organic compound pollutants emitted by the automobile.

emission analyzer A service bay or lab device used for detecting/measuring vehicle emissions.

fault *See* diagnostic trouble code (DTC).

freeze-frame A feature of OBDII that records events before, during, and after a fault occurs.

frequency The rate of change in direction, oscillation, or cycles in a given time.

history code A fault code that has occurred but is not current and is saved in the PCM's memory for 40 drive cycles.

hydrocarbon (HC) A microscopic unburned fuel particle that contributes to photochemical smog and helps form ground-level ozone.

inductive-type sensor A sensor mounted on the crankcase housing that is used to sense the movement of the ring gear teeth on the flywheel, or a toothed disc on the crank pulley.

intake air temperature (IAT) sensor A sensor that measures the temperature of the incoming air through the air filtration system.

knock sensor An engine sensor that detects preignition, detonation, and knocking.

malfunction indicator lamp (MIL) An indicator located in the instrument cluster that illuminates when the power train control module (PCM) detects a fault in one of the vehicle systems. Formerly called a check engine or service engine soon light.

manifold absolute pressure (MAP) sensor A detection device that measures absolute air pressure in the intake manifold.

module An electronic computer or circuit board that controls specific functions.

monitor An OBDII test run to ensure that a specific component or system is working properly.

noncontinuous monitor A monitor that runs only once per drive cycle.

OBDI The first generation of on-board diagnostic systems that originated for California vehicles.

OBDII The second generation of on-board diagnostic systems, which have been in effect for all US vehicles since 1996.

oxides of nitrogen A vehicle emission that contributes to ground-level ozone. Oxides of nitrogen are produced when nitrogen and oxygen react during combustion, given sufficient temperatures and pressures. Forms include nitrogen oxide and nitrogen dioxide.

oxygen sensor (before and after catalytic convertor) An exhaust sensor used to measure the amount of oxygen in the exhaust gases produced by the engine PCM, used to determine fuel mixture and spark timing.

particulate matter (PM) Unseen microscopic particles of carbon consisting of soot (especially prominent with diesel exhaust). PM clogs the lungs and is carcinogenic.

potentiometer A variable resistor that can be used to adjust voltage in a circuit.

power train control module (PCM) The module that controls and monitors the engine ignition, fuel, and emission system functions.

SAE J1930 An SAE standard for across-the-board standardization of parts and systems nomenclature.

SAE J2012 An SAE standard for across-the-board identification of generic DTCs.

scan tool A plug-in electronic device for extracting and interpreting fault codes (DTCs) in the automobile, plus much more.

sulfur dioxide (SO_2) A pollutant resulting from sulfur in motor fuel and contributing to acid rain.

thermistor A device that changes its resistance in relation to heat.

throttle position sensor (TPS) A potentiometer that sends an analog signal to the electronic control unit that corresponds to the position of the throttle valve.

transmission control module (TCM) An electronic computer that controls transmission function; it may include adaptive learning capabilities for driver preferences.

volatile organic compound (VOC) The hydrocarbons in petroleum products that contribute to combustion.

warm-up cycle One drive cycle, during which the vehicle starts out cold, warms up, and then cools down after the driving cycle.

ASE-Type Questions

1. Tech A says that on OBDII vehicles, it is a good idea to clear the codes before diagnosis, and see if they reset. Tech B says that the DTC will tell you what part needs to be changed. Who is correct?
   a. Tech A
   b. Tech B
   c. Both A and B
   d. Neither A nor B
2. Tech A says that OBDI and OBDII use different DLC connectors. Tech B says that OBDII standardizes the designations for diagnostic trouble codes (DTCs). Who is correct?
   a. Tech A
   b. Tech B
   c. Both A and B
   d. Neither A nor B
3. Tech A says that monitors are designed to test if emission systems are working properly. Tech B says that monitors are designed to store sensor data about a fault if a DTC is set. Who is correct?
   a. Tech A
   b. Tech B
   c. Both A and B
   d. Neither A nor B
4. Tech A says that control modules communicate back and forth today using a CAN, which is a bundle of many individual wires, specially designed for fast communication speed. Tech B says that OBDII mandates that a DTC must be set if the emissions are more than 1.5 times the EPA FTP. Who is correct?
   a. Tech A
   b. Tech B
   c. Both A and B
   d. Neither A nor B
5. Tech A says that OBDII will allow a technician to hook up a generic scan tool to read DTCs and clear DTCs. Tech B says that when the MIL is on, the vehicle should not be driven. Who is correct?
   a. Tech A
   b. Tech B
   c. Both A and B
   d. Neither A nor B
6. Tech A says that something as simple as a loose gas tank fill cap will turn on the MIL. Tech B says that every digit of a DTC has identifying characteristics. Who is correct?
   a. Tech A
   b. Tech B
   c. Both A and B
   d. Neither A nor B
7. Tech A says that a "P" in the DTC stands for a powertrain code. Tech B says a "U" stands for an undetermined code. Who is correct?
   a. Tech A
   b. Tech B
   c. Both A and B
   d. Neither A nor B
8. Tech A says that on OBDII systems, the KAM stores DTCs forever. Tech B says that on OBDII systems, the KAM is erased when the battery is disconnected. Who is correct?
   a. Tech A
   b. Tech B
   c. Both A and B
   d. Neither A nor B
9. Tech A says that the MIL can turn off if the fault doesn't reappear in a certain number of tests. Tech B says that when an MIL is activated, the PCM stores the DTC until a predetermined number of drive cycles have been performed or cleared by a scan tool. Who is correct?
   a. Tech A
   b. Tech B
   c. Both A and B
   d. Neither A nor B
10. Tech A says some mechanical engine problems can cause OBDII DTCs to be set. Tech B says that OBDII codes only monitor the emission control system components. Who is correct?
    a. Tech A
    b. Tech B
    c. Both A and B
    d. Neither A nor B

CHAPTER 39

KNOW
SEE
DO
PROVE

NATEF Tasks

Engine Performance Fuel, Air Induction, and Exhaust Systems			Page
■ Inspect integrity of the exhaust manifold, exhaust pipes, muffler(s), catalytic converter(s), resonator(s), tailpipe(s), and heat shield(s); determine necessary action.	MLR	AST	1117–1119

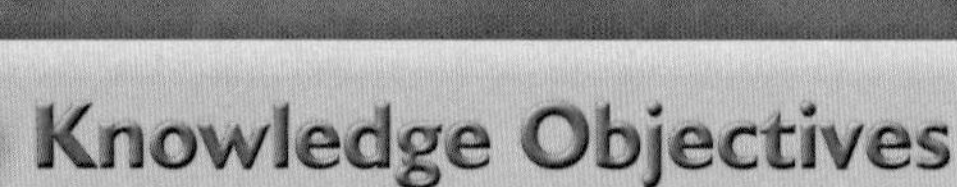

Knowledge Objectives

After reading this chapter, you will be able to:

1. Explain the basic principles of the intake system and its components. (pp 1100–1104)
2. Describe the functions of the exhaust system and its components. (pp 1111–1116)
3. Safely perform the NATEF tasks related to air induction and exhaust systems. (pp 1116–1117)

Induction and Exhaust

Know
See
Do
Prove

Skills Objectives

After reading this chapter, you will be able to:

1. Inspect the integrity of the exhaust manifold, exhaust pipes, muffler(s), catalytic converter(s), resonator(s), tailpipe(s), and heat shield(s). (pp 1117–1119)

Introduction

The intake and exhaust systems are critical parts of the internal combustion engine. The intake system ensures that clean, dry air is supplied to the engine, which is then mixed with fuel and burned in the combustion chamber, creating the thermal expansion that pushes the pistons down the cylinder. Clean, dry air is essential for proper combustion and a long-lasting engine, since dirt would get between the close-moving parts and cause premature wear of the engine. In fact, it takes only a tablespoon or two of dirt entering the engine through the intake system to ruin an engine. The intake system must provide a sealed passageway to the combustion chambers to ensure that no contaminants leak into the system and that no air is allowed to bypass the airflow sensor, which could create a drivability problem. The intake system also controls the amount of air entering the engine, by use of a throttle plate, which is how engine revolutions per minute (rpm) and power are controlled.

The exhaust system provides a path for the burned exhaust gases to safely exit the engine and travel out the rear of the vehicle. It also provides a method of reducing the noise from the power pulses and includes components that help reduce the harmful emissions in the exhaust stream. Getting rid of exhaust gases is just as important as getting air into the engine. If exhaust gases cannot leave the engine easily, then air will not be able to enter the engine easily. An efficient, free-flowing exhaust system will assist the engine in creating maximum power with minimal emissions. In this chapter, we will explore the operation and maintenance of both the intake and the exhaust systems.

The Intake System

The intake system is primarily designed to control the flow of air delivered to the combustion chamber. In most fuel-injected and carbureted engines, fuel is mixed in the intake system so air and fuel are being delivered together. In diesel and gasoline direct-injection engines, fuel is injected directly into the combustion chamber where it is mixed with air; thus, only air (plus any positive crankcase ventilation and evaporative emissions) flows through the intake system. For any fuel to burn efficiently, no matter where it is injected, it must be vaporized and fully mixed with the proper amount of air. Vaporization starts when the fuel system atomizes the fuel by breaking it up into very small particles by spraying it into the charge of air. These small particles make it much easier to vaporize the fuel. Heat and low pressure also may be used to vaporize the atomized fuel.

Intake System Components

The primary components of the automotive intake system are the intake manifold, the throttle body, and the air induction system. The intake manifold is bolted to the cylinder head. Its construction and design depend on the engine for which it is created. The intake manifold directs airflow into each cylinder FIGURE 39-1, and when restricted by the throttle plate, it provides a source of vacuum for systems such as the power brake system.

The intake manifold creates a mounting place for a throttle body assembly. In throttle body injection, one or two fuel injectors, which are mounted in the top of the throttle body, spray fuel down into the intake manifold.

You Are the Automotive Technician

A customer comes into the dealership complaining that her 12-year-old Ford Mustang doesn't idle as well as it should and the malfunction indicator lamp (MIL) is illuminated. You scan it for codes and notice that it has a P0131 (Circuit Low Voltage B1S1), a P0171 (Fuel Trim Lean B1), and a P0300 (Engine Misfire) detected. As an apprentice technician, you refer to the Ford Motor Company's service information to look up the process for diagnosing the codes. You notice that there could be several things that cause those codes, including a vacuum leak, weak oxygen sensor, and dirty fuel injectors. You decide to start by looking for a vacuum leak because you hear what sounds like a leak when the vehicle is running.

1. What are the different ways of locating a vacuum leak?
2. What are the possible places that a vacuum leak can occur?
3. How does a vacuum leak affect a vehicle equipped with a mass airflow sensor?

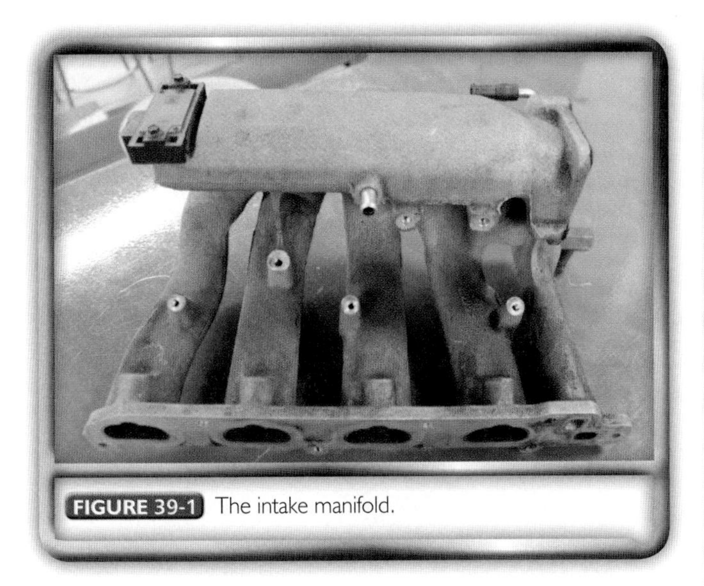

FIGURE 39-1 The intake manifold.

In a port fuel-injected engine, a throttle body is bolted to the opening of the intake manifold and the injectors are mounted in the intake manifold near the intake valves FIGURE 39-2. The throttle body controls airflow with a butterfly valve or valves, also called throttle valves. The throttle valves are opened and closed either by a throttle cable or, if the engine uses an electronic throttle control, by an electric motor that opens and closes the throttle plates. Attached to the throttle body is a throttle position sensor, which provides throttle position information to the engine computer. The throttle body also includes vacuum ports for the operation of vacuum-controlled devices such as evaporative emission systems and the power brake booster.

The air induction system consists of the following components: an air cleaner and housing, solid and flexible-duct tubing, connectors, and sometimes a mass airflow sensor. The air induction system draws in ambient air through a filter from the environment, or a turbocharger or supercharger can push air through the induction system FIGURE 39-3. The inlet opening of the induction system may be located in various positions under the hood depending on the available space for the automotive engineer to work with.

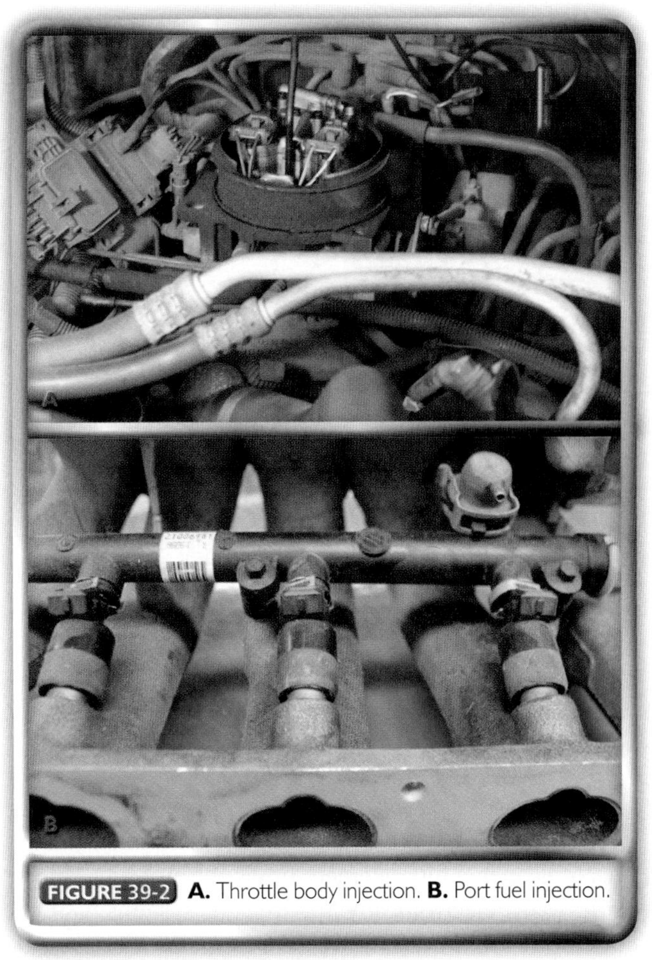
A
B

FIGURE 39-2 **A.** Throttle body injection. **B.** Port fuel injection.

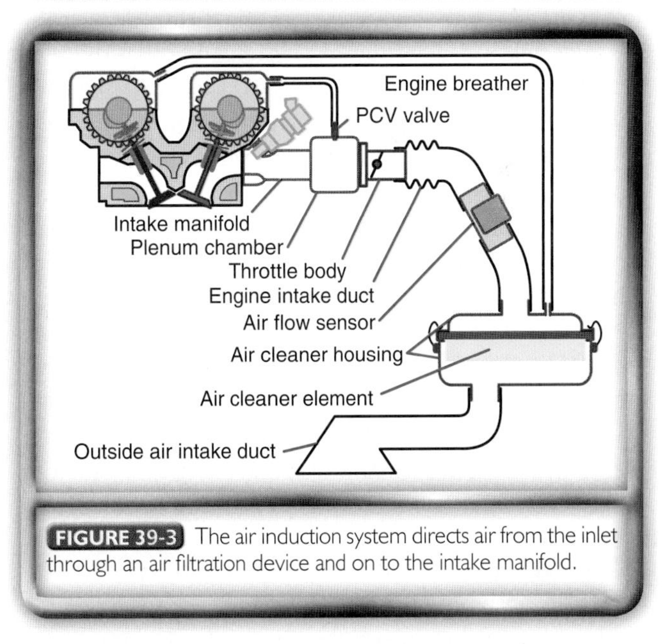
Engine breather
PCV valve
Intake manifold
Plenum chamber
Throttle body
Engine intake duct
Air flow sensor
Air cleaner housing
Air cleaner element
Outside air intake duct

FIGURE 39-3 The air induction system directs air from the inlet through an air filtration device and on to the intake manifold.

Air Cleaner

The air cleaner filters the incoming air. In past designs, the air cleaner housing was made of stamped metal and housed a round air filter. Most air cleaners are now made of plastic and can vary in shape from square to round. The air cleaner element or filter may be manufactured from pleated paper or from oil-impregnated cloth or felt; in much older vehicles, it was manufactured in an oil bath configuration. Another function of the air cleaner is to muffle the noise of the intake pulses and the incoming air, which travels at high speeds. The air cleaner can also act as a flame arrester. If a gasoline engine backfires, the air cleaner can contain the flame within the intake manifold or carburetor. The location of the air cleaner depends on the available space and the hood design.

A lot of air passes through the intake system into the engine. In a gasoline engine, the air–fuel mixture, by weight, is about 15 parts air to 1 part fuel. By volume, that's 10,000 times more air than fuel. When an engine consumes 10 gallons of gas, the air filter will have filtered 100,000 gallons of air. The air–fuel mixture enters the engine, so the air needs to be clean. Any abrasives that enter the engine can quickly cause wear and damage.

> **TECHNICIAN TIP**
>
> One way to tell if a pleated paper air filter needs to be changed is by holding it up to a light and seeing how much light passes through it. Just because it is a bit dirty on the outside doesn't mean it needs to be replaced. In fact, a lightly plugged filter prevents particles from going through the filter better than a brand new filter. But if it is too plugged, it will restrict airflow to the engine. If you can see a lot of light through it, it is reusable. If it restricts the light very much, it should be replaced.

An air cleaner on a multipoint electronic fuel-injected engine usually has a different shape from that on a carbureted engine, but it serves the same purpose. In many vehicles, the air cleaner is mounted where it can obtain cool, clean air. The air from the air cleaner is then carried to the throttle body by a long, flexible duct. Inside the air cleaner, a filter element filters the air and reduces noise. Many electronically fuel-injected systems have an airflow sensor after the air cleaner element, which accurately measures all air entering the engine and adjusts the air–fuel mixture accordingly; it is essential that there be no air leaks after the airflow sensor, as leaks will upset the air–fuel mixture. It is interesting to note that a **mass airflow (MAF) sensor** can measure air entering the engine down to tenths of a gram per second.

One type of air cleaner system is the long-life filtration system that is currently used on the Ford Focus. This air cleaner assembly is a nonserviceable unit that is designed to last 150,000 miles (240,000 km) or more. It is made to also capture any hydrocarbons being released from the throttle body and then allow them to be pulled back into the engine as air flows across the filter. The filter element is made of specially designed foam. This filter can be serviced only by replacement of the entire assembly.

Ducting

Ducting can be made of hardened plastic with flexible rubber couplings to absorb engine movement. It may have a MAF sensor in line and be retained with worm-style clamps to seal the duct to the sensor. The ducting is what connects the ridged air cleaner to the throttle body of the intake manifold. Some ducting also includes air dampening, sometimes referred to as a Helmholtz resonator. A **Helmholtz resonator** is a container that is sealed and specially shaped to cancel noise created by pressure waves. The pressure wave bounces off the walls of the resonator and collides with the incoming waves, canceling the noise. On the vehicle, the resonator is a tube that is connected to the air ducting and is simply a sealed chamber that is open where it is connected to the air duct **FIGURE 39-4**.

FIGURE 39-4 The air duct on some vehicles contains a resonator to cancel air noise as air flows through the intake.

> **Applied Science**
>
> ***AS-38: Amplification: The technician can explain to a customer how sound can be amplified in a vehicle due to resonant cavities and other physical characteristics of the vehicle.***
>
> The noise level of a vehicle plays an important role in the overall satisfaction rating by the owner. A quiet vehicle is expected by the majority of vehicle owners. Some vehicle owners prefer the sound of a high-performance vehicle, and the noise level is not as much of a concern. Air intake and exhaust systems can be manufactured and modified for a variety of different sounds.
>
> Back in 1863, physicist Herman Von Helmholtz did many studies regarding air-dampening devices. He discovered a resonator that uses the principle of sound waves colliding, resulting in the concept of canceling noise. The resonator can be used in the exhaust system to assist the muffler in further reducing noise. The resonator can also be used in the induction system. The benefit is the ability to muffle airflow noise. The Helmholtz resonator is basically a simple device consisting of a cavity with one or more short narrow tubes. For each application, the device must be precisely tuned. Concerning the air induction system, the resonator is installed between the air filter and the engine inlet. The design of the Helmholtz resonator creates a sound frequency that cancels out some of the engine noise. On some vehicles, there is a vacuum-activated valve that disables the effects of the resonator at certain rpm.

Applied Science

AS-39: Carriers/Insulators: The technician can demonstrate an understanding of how sound generated in one place can be carried to other parts of the body or engine through metal and materials.

Sound travels through steel approximately 17 times faster than through the air. This is because the molecules in steel are closer together. Sound is produced when an object vibrates. Vibrations can pass from molecule to molecule quickly in materials such as steel.

When a vehicle has a bad wheel bearing that is producing a rumbling sound, it is often difficult to tell which of the four wheels the noise is coming from. In this case, you might try driving the vehicle alongside a building or a concrete block wall. Sound waves travel in all directions from their source. Some of them will strike the wall, and the noise will be reflected back toward the vehicle. A greater proportion of the sound waves will strike the wall when it is near the side of the vehicle with the faulty wheel bearing, meaning more sound waves will be reflected toward the vehicle. Thus, if the noise is louder when the passenger side is near the wall, the technician will know the faulty bearing is on the passenger side.

A mechanic's stethoscope can also be used to locate sounds on vehicles. The tip of the metal probe can be used to trace the sound to the source of the problem. There are now electronic devices that can be used to locate sounds on vehicles.

The pressure waves created when the engine pulls air into the air duct produce a loud suction sound that can be unpleasant to the owner. Use of the resonator minimizes the noise produced in the air intake system.

Intake Manifolds

The intake manifold is usually a cast-iron, aluminum, or plastic part with several tubular branches. In a carbureted engine, the intake manifold directs the air–fuel mixture into the engine. The cross-sectional area of each tube needs to be kept small to maintain the high air speeds that improve vaporization. At the same time, intake manifold tube size should not be too small, since that restricts the airflow to the engine at higher speeds.

Intake Materials

Intake manifolds were originally made from cast iron, and later from light alloy metal castings. In modern vehicles, the intake manifold is made from special heat-resistant polymers and plastics FIGURE 39-5. Manifolds using this type of construction lighten manifold weight by up to 50% and contribute to higher fuel efficiency. These intake manifolds are normally molded from a glass fiber–reinforced grade of crystalline polymer that consists of a blend of syndiotactic polystyrene and polyamide. The polyamide nylon–based materials provide a good solution for these components because of their mechanical properties and their ease of processing during their manufacture. This type of material is ideally suited for replacing metal in under-the-hood applications because of its strength, stiffness, and chemical resistance under high-temperature operating conditions. In addition, intake manifolds made from polyamide nylon have improved the environmental performance of vehicles because of their light weight, which translates to improved fuel economy. The plastic can also be recycled, similar to cast iron and aluminum. The use of plastic has enabled more efficient airflow into the engine due to smoother surfaces of the manifold and has allowed for easier shaping of the manifold, creating better airflow characteristics.

FIGURE 39-5 Plastic intake manifold.

Application of Intake Manifolds

The intake manifold has several tubular branches and carries air and/or air–fuel mixture from the air cleaner to the cylinder head. In carbureted engines and in throttle body injection systems, the intake manifold directs the air–fuel mixture into the engine. On many engines, the intake manifold has a mounting for the throttle body and a flange that bolts it onto the cylinder head. The cross-sectional area of each tube needs to be kept small to maintain the high air speeds that improve speed and turbulence. Yet, it cannot be too small, since that would restrict the airflow to the engine at higher engine speeds.

Cylinder heads that have intake and exhaust manifolds on opposite sides of the engine are known as cross-flow heads. That means the intake manifold is on one side and the exhaust manifold is on the other FIGURE 39-6. This design tends to produce more power because the flow of air moves more easily across the

FIGURE 39-6 Cross-flow head.

head rather than coming in and then turning back out the same side. Most modern engines are set up with a cross-flow cylinder head. The cross-flow head contains individual branches or ports to carry air and fuel into the combustion chamber. In past designs, two cylinders could share an intake port, but this design did not allow for free flow and was replaced with individual ports to allow for more power.

Variable Intake Systems

The air intake manifold for an electronic fuel injection multipoint engine normally has long branches of equal length. The long branches increase the pulsing effect of the airflow at lower engine rpm and help charge the cylinders. The more air drawn into the cylinder, the denser the air/fuel mixture is when the intake valve closes. The increased density of the air/fuel mixture determines how much pressure develops in the cylinder during combustion and the amount of force on the piston to turn the crankshaft.

The characteristic torque curve of a naturally aspirated engine depends mainly on how the engine's mean pressure changes across the rpm operating range. The design of the intake system largely determines the mass of air that can be drawn into a cylinder at a given engine speed; thus, the intake system largely determines the engine's torque curve. In general, a long intake manifold produces high torque at lower engine rpm because of the increased amount of time between the air pulses due to the inertia of the long column of air. The increased time between the pulses matches the longer time between lower rpm. Higher torque is obtained at higher engine rpm with a shorter intake manifold because of the shorter amount of time between the pulses due to the inertia of a shorter column of air. This ram air effect allows for more total airflow at and near the tuned rpm.

Manifolds that respond to changes in engine load and speed by changing their effective length in two or three stages are called variable inertia, or intake charging systems FIGURE 39-7. The primary section is long and narrow for the low range of rpm. The secondary section is shorter and wider for the high range of rpm. This combination maintains a high-speed airflow in the system. The three-stage manifold extends the torque curve even more, so that the torque curves overlap each other as advantageously as possible.

The different manifold stages are controlled by valves that are computer controlled by the engine management system to open at a specified engine speed and extend the torque output. The system is called intake manifold runner control (IMRC). Specific intake runner stages can be opened or closed off so that air is forced to run through the other set of runners. The runners are closed off by a butterfly-type valve that is moved by a stepper motor or vacuum actuator. The stepper motor or supply of vacuum is controlled by the engine control module.

Intake Air Heating

Heating of the intake manifold is required in a carbureted or throttle body–injected engine to provide greater vaporization of the fuel and to ensure that fuel does not collect on the cold walls, creating a lean mixture. Port fuel-injected or gasoline direct-injected intake manifolds do not normally need to be heated, since the manifold does not carry fuel. Also, the MAF sensor and intake air temperature sensor monitor the mass and temperature of the air entering the engine and send signals to the PCM

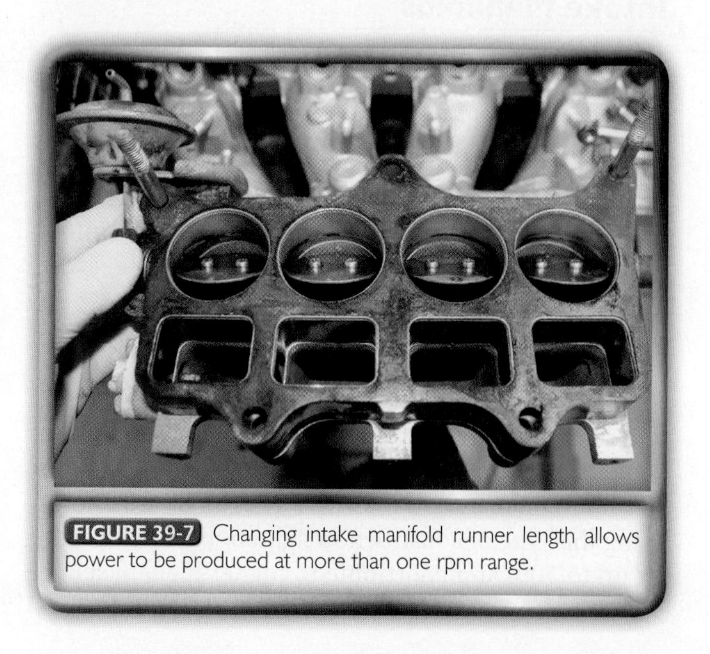
FIGURE 39-7 Changing intake manifold runner length allows power to be produced at more than one rpm range.

so it can trigger the injectors to spray the proper amount of fuel to mix with the air.

There are several methods that manufacturers have used to heat intake manifolds, including hot engine coolant, hot exhaust gases, and electric heaters. Flowing hot engine coolant from the cooling system through passageways in the intake manifold heats the manifold FIGURE 39-8. However, it takes a while for the coolant to become hot, so this is not the fastest way to heat the intake manifold. Coolant continuously circulates through the manifold, even when the engine is fully warmed up.

Exhaust gases can also be directed through passageways in the intake manifold on V-type engines during engine warm-up. The hot exhaust gases are hot immediately and therefore heat the manifold up more quickly than coolant does. A heat riser valve at the end of the exhaust manifold blocks most of the exhaust gases from exiting through the exhaust pipe. A passageway in the cylinder head directs the exhaust gases through a passageway in the cylinder head, through a chamber in the bottom of the intake manifold, out the passageway in the other cylinder head, and to the exhaust pipe on the other side of the engine. Once the engine is warm, the heat riser opens the valve in the exhaust, and exhaust gases can flow normally out of the exhaust pipe. If the heat riser valve sticks closed, the engine will run hotter than normal and will likely be low on power.

Electric heaters have also been used to preheat the air. A preheat grid is typically placed between the intake manifold and the throttle body FIGURE 39-9. During cold engine operation, current flows through the heating grid, warming the air passing through it. Once the engine reaches a certain temperature, the current flow to the grid is turned off and the engine operates normally. If the heater stays on too long, the heater grid can melt down, dropping particles down the intake manifold, which can damage the engine.

Another method of helping the fuel to vaporize in the intake manifold on carbureted and throttle body–injected engines is to warm the incoming air by passing it through a shroud around the exhaust manifold. This method was called an early fuel evaporation (EFE) system FIGURE 39-10. An enormous amount of heat passes

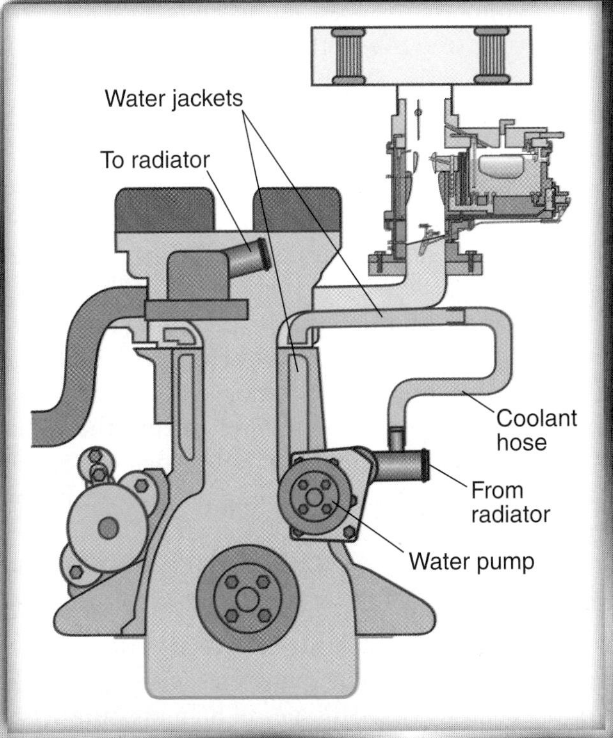

FIGURE 39-8 Using hot engine coolant to heat the manifold.

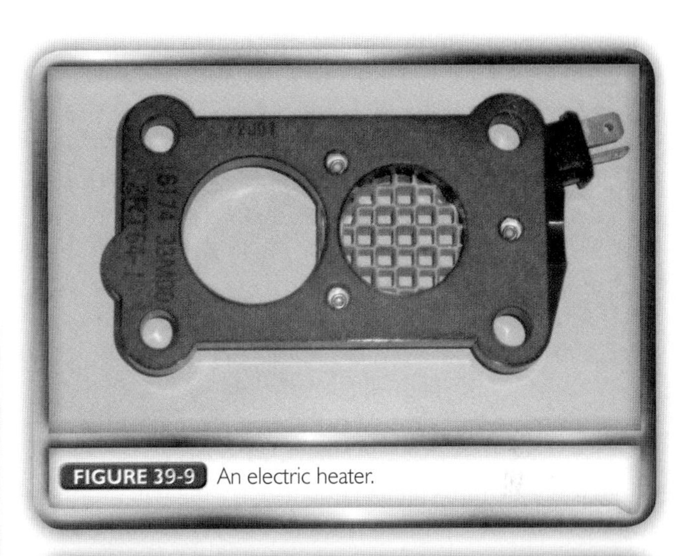

FIGURE 39-9 An electric heater.

FIGURE 39-10 The heated air intake system, found on carbureted and throttle body injection systems, is used to ensure that fuel does not collect on the cold intake manifold.

through the exhaust manifold and is used to heat the incoming air. The heated air then enters the air cleaner and proceeds through the throttle body and intake manifold while it mixes with the fuel.

Once an engine is hot, the incoming air can become too hot, so the amount of hot air entering the engine needs to be controlled. On vehicles with emission controls, air cleaners use a thermostatic valve to control how much hot air enters the air cleaner. These systems are called heated air cleaners (HAC) and heated air systems (HAS). When the engine is started, only heated air is used. As engine temperature rises, the valve opens and blends cold ambient air with the hot air. This ensures that the temperature of the air supplied to the engine stays fairly constant. This valve can be a simple thermostatic (mechanical) type. Another way to control the amount of hot air is to use a vacuum control unit and a control valve mounted inside the air cleaner unit. The vacuum control unit has a diaphragm attached to the control valve. When a cold engine starts, vacuum from the intake manifold moves the diaphragm. It opens the valve and hot air flows into the air cleaner while closing the ambient air intake. A heat-sensitive valve in the air cleaner responds to changes in air temperature. Below a certain level, it opens, letting hot air flow into the air cleaner. As the temperature rises, it slowly closes, reducing the flow of hot air and blending in cooler air. When carburetors and the throttle body injection units were no longer installed in vehicles, heated intake air was no longer needed.

With a multipoint injection setup, the intake manifolds carry air only, so heating of the intake manifold is not needed. Also, the cross-sectional area of the tubes can be larger. Because more air can flow, the engine will produce more power. Fuel is injected directly into the intake ports of the cylinder head. The other possible fuel delivery method is the gasoline direct-injection system, which directs fuel straight into the combustion chamber. This system uses an intake similar to the multipoint injection setup, flowing air only through the intake. The fuel-injected engine manifold has a **plenum chamber** that provides a reservoir of air and helps prevent interference with the flow of air between individual branches. The plenum chamber is a large portion of the intake manifold after the throttle plate and before the intake runner tubes FIGURE 39-11.

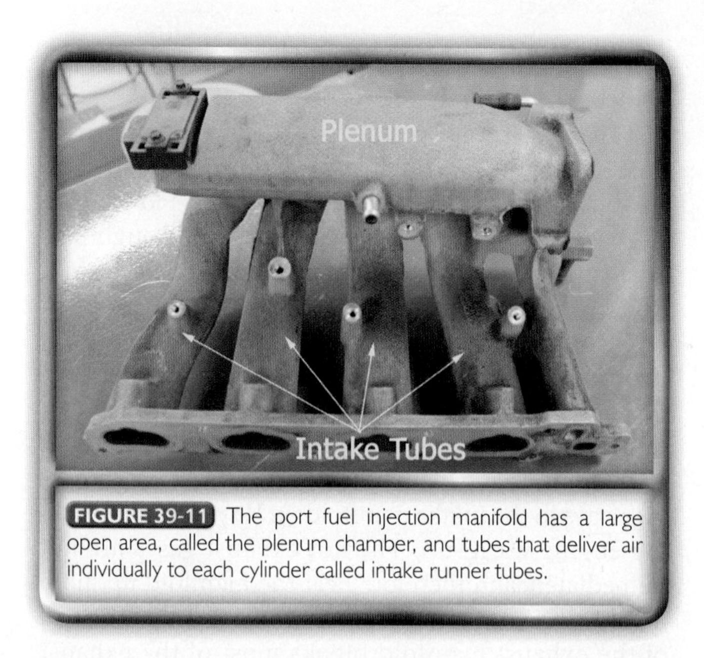
Plenum
Intake Tubes

FIGURE 39-11 The port fuel injection manifold has a large open area, called the plenum chamber, and tubes that deliver air individually to each cylinder called intake runner tubes.

Volumetric Efficiency

Volumetric efficiency compares the volume of air entering a cylinder during intake to the internal volume of the cylinder when the piston is at bottom dead center. It is usually expressed as a percentage. In a stock naturally aspirated engine, one without forced induction, volumetric efficiency can almost never be 100%. This is because of the resistance to the airflow that occurs at the throttle body, manifold, and intake valve FIGURE 39-12. However, some highly modified engines can exceed 100% due to the valve overlap being matched to the intake and exhaust manifold sizes and lengths, which maximize the ram air effect at the tuned rpm.

To understand volumetric efficiency, you must have a good understanding of the physics of airflow. Air likes to move in a straight manner and is affected by bends in the tubing that is used in the intake. Sharp bends force the air to move to the opposite side of the tube and force the air to pile up, slowing the airflow. Air also works like a bearing surface: Air near the surface of the manifold slows as friction of the tube wall resists its motion, while air in the center of the airstream tends to speed up as it moves over top of the slower air. All of these factors slow the airflow and reduce volumetric efficiency.

With forced induction, the incoming air is compressed by some sort of pump or compressor. Because of this greater pressure, a greater volume and mass of air is forced into the cylinder during the intake stroke, which takes the volumetric efficiency to well above 100%, increasing the engine's power output proportionately.

Back-Pressure

Back-pressure in an exhaust system refers to a buildup of pressure in the system that interferes with the outward flow of exhaust gases. This area of high pressure acts as a kind of wall to stop gas flow. It can be caused by a blockage in a muffler or a similar restriction. One common cause of excessive back-pressure is a catalytic converter

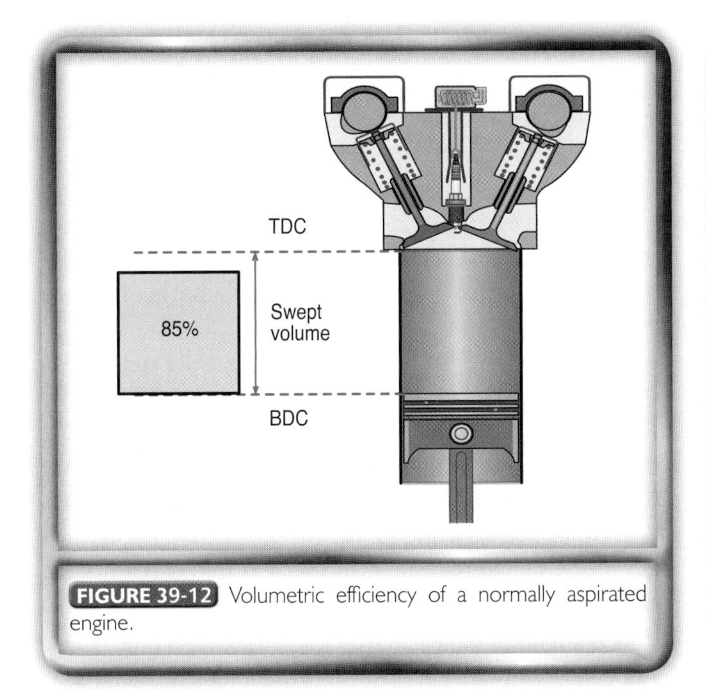
TDC
85%
Swept volume
BDC

FIGURE 39-12 Volumetric efficiency of a normally aspirated engine.

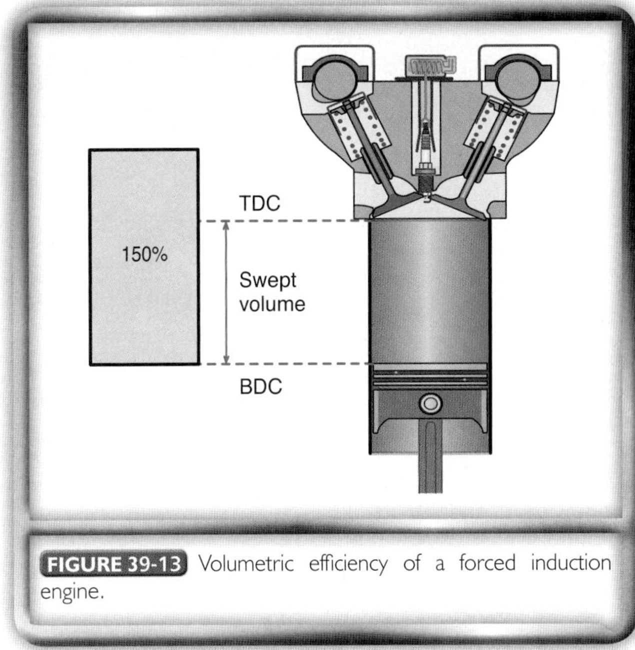
150%
TDC
Swept volume
BDC

FIGURE 39-13 Volumetric efficiency of a forced induction engine.

that has melted down and created a restriction in the exhaust stream. Catalytic converters become hotter as the combustible mixture is increased, such as from a misfire. The catalyst in the converter will melt if it gets hot enough and essentially block off the entrance to the small passageways. Back-pressure typically should be no more than 2.5 pounds per square inch (psi), or 17.2 kilopascals (kPa). If it is greater, it can create performance issues, as it will cause exhaust to back up into the combustion chamber, minimizing the amount of fresh air (combustible mixture) flowing into the engine. This reduces volumetric efficiency and engine power output.

Forced Induction

One way to improve engine output is to increase the amount of the air–fuel mixture that is burned in the cylinder (increasing volumetric efficiency). Volumetric efficiency can be boosted the most by what is called **forced induction**. Forced induction increases air pressure in the intake manifold above atmospheric pressure. Thus, an engine using forced induction can have a volumetric efficiency well above 100% FIGURE 39-13.

One way to achieve forced induction is by using a turbocharger. A turbocharger uses energy that is normally wasted through the exhaust. Exhaust gases enter a turbine and make it spin. The turbine is connected to one end of a shaft, and a compressor is connected to the other. The more exhaust gases the engine produces, the faster the turbocharger spins and the more air is compressed and forced into the engine. Another way to achieve forced induction is to use a supercharger. A supercharger is turned by the crankshaft, compresses the air, and forces it into the engine. The faster the engine turns, the more air is moved by the supercharger.

Supercharger Systems

Power is produced when a mixture of air and fuel is burned inside an engine cylinder. If more air is forced into the cylinder, then more fuel can be burned and more power produced with each power stroke. A **supercharger** compresses the air in the intake system to above atmospheric pressure, which increases the density of the air entering the engine. Naturally aspirated engines operate with uncompressed air at atmospheric pressure, 14.7 psi (101 kPa). But a supercharger boosts that pressure another 6 psi (41.4 kPa) or higher.

In a supercharged system, there is a greater air mass flow rate—that is, a higher density and speed of airflow. Air pressure is increased by the compressor on the way into the engine and more fuel is added, which creates more pressure and power. The increased pressure causes the exhaust gases to exit much more rapidly, making the timing and exhaust sizing less important. Also, any residual gases will have less of an effect on the airflow entering the combustion chamber, since the supercharger boosts the manifold pressure substantially.

Although some of the extra power produced must be used to drive the supercharger, the net result is more total power from the crankshaft. The supercharger may include a **bypass valve** system that allows the supercharger to "idle" when "high power" is not required, releasing the pressure back to the supercharger inlet and allowing the engine to run without boost. The bypass valve can be mounted remotely or directly onto the intake port FIGURE 39-14.

FIGURE 39-14 The supercharger compresses air to feed to the intake and is run by the engine crankshaft.

It allows air to move back past the compressor portion of the supercharger, keeping boost pressure low.

Several types of superchargers are manufactured for use on vehicles. The oldest version is the roots-style supercharger, which uses lobes to move air. This type of the supercharger does not compress air at the lobes, but rather pushes air around the sides of the housing and into the intake. It uses the stacking of the air against the intake valves to build boost pressure as the lobes come together and prevent air from leaking back between them. Another version of the supercharger is the twin screw type. The twin screw supercharger compresses air between the screws and forces it into the intake. This compressor design is very efficient but very expensive. Many aftermarket high-performance superchargers are centrifugal. This supercharger shaft is turned by a drive belt from the crankshaft and spins a compressor wheel, similar to what is used in the turbocharger. The supercharger shaft is connected by a set of gears to create a higher speed of the compressor. Since compressing air heats the air up, a heat exchanger can be located between it and the intake manifold. The heat exchanger is like a radiator that the air flows through to cool it before entering the engine.

Turbocharger Systems

A **turbocharger** is a forced induction system that uses wasted kinetic energy from the exhaust gases to increase the intake pressure. Like superchargers, turbochargers increase the amount of air that flows into the engine, but they have a negative effect on the flow of air out of the engine. This means that for maximum power output, valves, cam timing, and exhaust system design are more important in turbocharged systems than in supercharged systems.

The turbocharger uses exhaust gases to turn a turbine fan. A shaft connects the turbine to a centrifugal compressor FIGURE 39-15. The compressor compresses the air and forces it under pressure into the intake manifold. Since the turbine is turned by exhaust gases, it runs at very high temperatures. It, along with the compressor, can rotate at well over 100,000 rpm. The turbocharger needs a good supply of clean oil to lubricate the bearings and carry excess heat away from the turbocharger. Some engines also supply coolant to the turbocharger body to improve cooling.

Higher engine speeds mean increased exhaust gas volume, and that makes the turbocharger spin faster and force more air into the cylinders, which can damage the engine if allowed to get too high. When pressure increases in an engine, so does cylinder temperature. As the temperature increases, the possibility of detonation also increases, since the gasoline will ignite before the piston reaches the proper position in the cylinder. To control this risk of detonation, a device called a **wastegate** is installed on the exhaust inlet of the turbocharger. When air pressure in the intake manifold reaches a preset level, the wastegate automatically directs the exhaust gases so they bypass the turbine FIGURE 39-16. The wastegate can also be computer controlled to reduce intake air pressure in the case of detonation or knocking.

On a mechanically operated wastegate, the spring pressure in the diaphragm controls the pressure at which the wastegate valve opens. The wastegate actuator is a spring-loaded pressure diaphragm that moves when air pushes against it. The air moves into the chamber of the wastegate actuator and presses on the diaphragm, overcoming the spring force. This causes the control linkage to push the wastegate open, allowing exhaust gases to bypass the turbine wheel, which reduces the boost pressure. This process happens over again, and as pressure

FIGURE 39-15 The turbocharger compresses air to feed to the intake and is run by exhaust gases.

FIGURE 39-16 The turbocharger wastegate actuator controls the amount of boost pressure going to the intake manifold.

FIGURE 39-17 The blow-off valve is a spring-loaded valve that releases excessive pressure in the air intake tube going to the intake manifold.

drops, the wastegate closes and allows exhaust to flow to the turbine wheel again. The wastegate actuator gets pressure from a line connected to the intake manifold. The wastegate can be computer controlled by a boost solenoid that delays the intake pressure from reaching the wastegate actuator. The computer receives information from the manifold absolute pressure sensor, which tells how much pressure is in the intake manifold.

A pressure relief valve may also be installed so that if the wastegate should fail, it can prevent an abnormal rise in manifold pressure. This relief valve is also known as a **blow-off valve**. A blow-off valve works against spring pressure, and as boost pressure rises above a predetermined amount, the pressure will push the valve against the spring pressure and open it, allowing excess pressure to "blow off" into the atmosphere.

The blow-off valve may also vent the pressure to the air cleaner box to reduce the turbocharger pressure release noise. The blow-off valve is located in the air intake tubing connected to the intake manifold. It is also used to ensure that when the throttle is abruptly shut, pressure does not rise excessively between the throttle body and the turbocharger compressor wheel FIGURE 39-17. If pressure rises excessively, **compressor surge** will occur. Compressor surge is when manifold pressure rises above normal and works against the spinning exhaust turbine wheel, slowing it considerably. The pressure wave can then flow backward out of the compressor, creating a fluttering noise and continued pressure waves. Compressor surge, which is recognizable by a rapid fluttering sound, can be damaging to the compressor wheel, since the backing up pressure wave forces the wheel to slow.

Since the turbocharger uses the energy of the exhaust gases, there is a short delay between when a driver opens the throttle and when maximum power is available. This delay is called turbo lag, and on larger engines, it can be quite noticeable if the turbocharger is not sized correctly. Because a turbocharger recycles heat energy that would otherwise be lost, a turbocharged engine can increase an engine's efficiency and fuel economy—as long as the vehicle is being driven conservatively. However, even though a turbocharger may seem to be offering additional energy for nothing, it can introduce problems of its own. The extra heat and power it generates can put an extra

Applied Science

AS-40: Decibels/Intensity: The technician can demonstrate an understanding of how sound intensity can be measured.

The degree of loudness is measured in units called decibels (dB). The average human can hear sounds between 0 and 120 dB. One-time exposure to noises above 120 dB, or sustained exposure above 85 dB, can damage the ears. Decibels can be measured with a sound pressure level meter. These meters are available in analog and digital styles.

As a baseline, the decibel level of some common sounds are as follows:

- Conversational speech at a distance of 3 feet: 60 dB
- A diesel truck engine at a distance of 30 feet: 90 dB
- A chain saw at a distance of 3 feet: 110 dB
- A jet aircraft at takeoff at a distance of 150 feet: 150 dB

Technicians should be concerned about the decibel rating of sounds in the workplace as well as the exposure time. The length of time that a person is exposed to the sound is a very important factor. For example, the CDC recommends that a person should be exposed to a sound pressure level of 100 dB for no more than 15 minutes. Ear protection should be worn to protect your hearing based on the decibel rating and exposure time.

load on the engine's cooling and lubrication systems. This is why most turbocharged vehicles have shorter service intervals for oil changes than nonturbocharged vehicles.

As the air passes through the turbocharger, it heats up. Hot air is less dense than cool air, so it tries to expand again, and some of the benefits of compressing it are lost. To stop this expansion and improve efficiency, some engines use an intercooler to cool the compressed air. It fits between the turbocharger and the engine. It typically uses outside air to cool the compressed air, but on some applications, it may use the engine's cooling system to cool the compressed air.

When the turbocharger housing is large, boost pressure is higher at high speed, but lag is worse for a given exhaust flow. When the housing is small, boost pressure is high at lower speeds, but a restriction occurs in the exhaust system at high rpm. To combat turbo lag and avoid creating a restriction, several designs have been made. The first is the twin scroll turbocharger, which uses two passageways into the turbine housing from the exhaust manifold. The one passageway is controlled by a flap that can be closed to accelerate the exhaust flow, making the turbocharger operate at a higher boost at low engine speeds.

Another way to improve the turbo lag issue is to use twin turbochargers. Many manufacturers use two small turbochargers (one on each bank of the engine) that can spin up more quickly, thereby creating boost sooner. The turbo lag is decreased as boost is created at a lower engine speed, and yet additional boost is created at a higher speed since there are two turbochargers to deal with the total exhaust flow.

The final way to create boost pressure without lag is to use a variable-geometry turbocharger. The variable-geometry turbocharger uses a set of movable vanes or fingers that change the flow of exhaust gases through the turbine housing. Under low exhaust speed, the fingers are positioned so that the exhaust gases spin the turbine faster, creating boost. Under high rpm, the speed of the exhaust gases is very high; therefore, the fingers are moved so they do not overspeed the turbine while also not restricting the exhaust flow and creating backup of exhaust, which would lower power. This type of turbocharger offers the best of both worlds. Currently it is used on Ford's Powerstroke series of diesels.

Another new development in turbocharger technology is used on the BMW engine. The engine design uses reverse flow cylinder heads. The center of the V-type engine, which normally was for intake, is now for the exhaust passages. Exhaust leaves the head and moves into the twin turbochargers, one per engine bank. The intake manifold is now on the outside of the head. The different positioning of the turbochargers keeps exhaust temperatures high and produces more turbine speed, which increases the efficiency of the turbocharger. The catalytic converter also gets up to temperature faster, reducing emissions.

Applied Science

AS-41: Frequency/Hertz: The technician can explain how frequency of a sound can be used to identify normal and abnormal operating systems.

A vehicle is making a high-pitched whining sound upon acceleration. The sound seemed very abnormal to the owner of the vehicle, and it is now in the shop for diagnosis and repair. The technician test-drives the vehicle to verify the concern.

In a short distance, the technician verifies the high-pitched whining sound. The technician uses a mechanic's stethoscope to discover that the abnormal sound is coming from the alternator. Further diagnostic testing reveals that the alternator has a bad diode that is causing the whining sound. The recommendation to the customer is to replace the alternator.

Concerning the properties of sound, frequency is the number of waves produced in a given time. The frequency of sound waves determines the audible pitch, either high or low. Hertz is the unit used to measure the frequency of sound waves or pitch.

AS-42: Hearing: The technician can demonstrate an understanding of the role of listening for unusual sounds as part of a troubleshooting process.

A vehicle has been towed to a dealership with a no-start condition. A technician has been assigned to determine the cause of the problem. To assure that the cranking voltage will be sufficient, the technician connects a booster pack to the battery. While an assistant attempts to start the vehicle, the technician listens to the cranking rhythm of the engine. The engine has a very uneven cranking rhythm, which indicates uneven compression between cylinders. Using diagnostic equipment, the technician verifies that the engine has very low compression on several cylinders and has a broken timing belt. When the timing belt broke, many of the engine's valves were bent, resulting in the low compression.

Listening for unusual sounds can be an essential part of a troubleshooting process. It is helpful to use other methods as well to verify the diagnosis.

Intercoolers

A turbocharger or supercharger is used to increase the volume of air in the engine cylinder by compressing the air above atmospheric pressure. However, when air is compressed, it heats up, which causes the volume of the gas to increase, which lowers the air density. Hot air under pressure in a cylinder contains fewer oxygen molecules than cooler air at the same pressure in the same volume.

The purpose of an intercooler is to reduce the intake air temperature up to a few hundred degrees Fahrenheit before it enters the intake manifold. Decreasing air temperature increases the density of the pressurized air and improves engine efficiency. The intercooler is most efficient when the turbocharger's boost pressure is near its maximum, typically above 15 psi, or 100 kPa. Most intercoolers operate on an air-to-air principle, by feeding compressed air from the turbocharger through the intercooler and then into the intake manifold. The intercooler works like a radiator. Inside it, the air passes through small tubes with thin fins attached. The heated compressed air flowing through the intercooler heats up the fins and the tubes, and as the vehicle moves forward, the cool outside air flowing across the fins pulls heat away from the tubes and fins. This heat transfer occurs constantly during engine operation. Some larger engine applications have a liquid-operated intercooler FIGURE 39-18. In this system, the air is fed through small tubes in a heat exchanger, and the vehicle coolant absorbs the heat and transfers it to the engine cooling system.

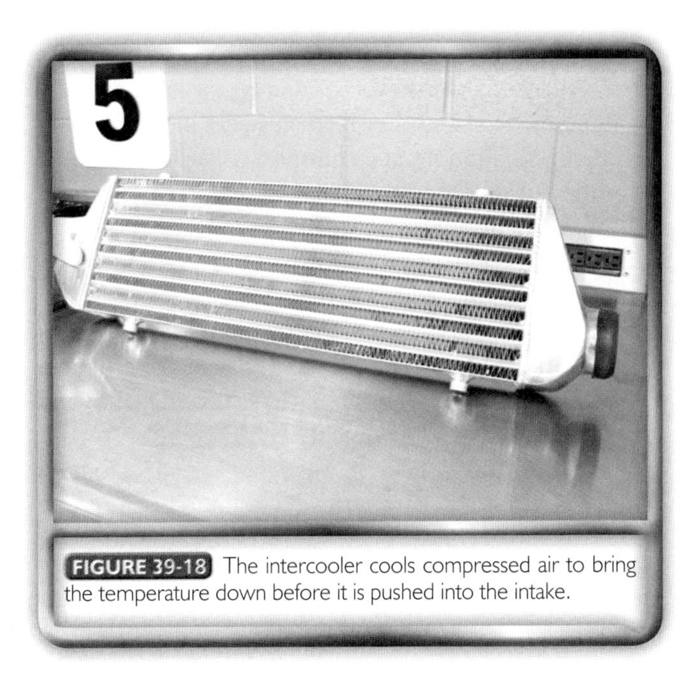
5

FIGURE 39-18 The intercooler cools compressed air to bring the temperature down before it is pushed into the intake.

The Exhaust System

The exhaust system is made up of several components that work together to perform four main functions: remove exhaust gases from the engine, quiet the exhaust noise, ensure that poisonous exhaust gases do not enter the passenger compartment, and reduce harmful emissions in the exhaust stream FIGURE 39-19. Exhaust flow is described as follows: Burned gases exit the cylinder through the exhaust port and pass into the exhaust manifold. The first pipe is usually called the engine pipe or down pipe. The down pipe is connected to the outlet of the manifold, which carries the exhaust gases to the catalytic converter. Catalytic converters were introduced in vehicles in the mid-1970s and were designed to reduce exhaust emissions. The exhaust exits the converter and continues on through an intermediate pipe to the muffler, which reduces exhaust noise. Exhaust gases are then either passed through a resonator or simply discharged to the atmosphere through a tailpipe, usually at the rear, to the side or above the vehicle.

During engine operation, each time an exhaust valve opens, a pulse of hot exhaust gases is forced into the exhaust manifold. These hot gases produce a lot of noise, some of it at very high frequency. Even while quieting the exhaust noise, the exhaust system can be designed to enhance engine operation and efficiency. In fact, a well-designed system can improve drivability and performance.

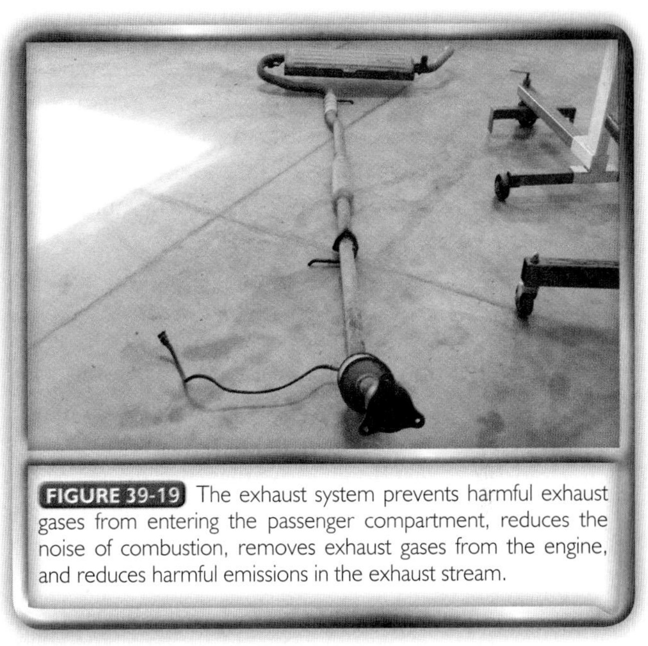

FIGURE 39-19 The exhaust system prevents harmful exhaust gases from entering the passenger compartment, reduces the noise of combustion, removes exhaust gases from the engine, and reduces harmful emissions in the exhaust stream.

Exhaust System Components

Exhaust Manifold

The exhaust manifold is bolted to the engine's cylinder head. It also usually provides a mounting place near its outlet for the oxygen sensor, since it is advantageous to position the sensor as close to the cylinders as possible. This position will help it warm up faster during a cold start. The exhaust manifold can be of a one-piece or a two-piece construction. It is usually made from either cast iron or stainless steel. Due to the extreme temperatures generated at the exhaust manifold, heat shields can be installed to protect other vehicle components from heat damage.

On many current vehicles, the exhaust manifold is often replaced with a header. The **header** is an exhaust manifold made of mandrel-formed steel tubes that are of equal lengths and join at a common collector. **Mandrel forming** is the use of a special pipe-bending tool to ensure that piping bends in a smooth arc and will not collapse, which would create a partial restriction. The equal length of the pipes ensures that the exhaust pulses create a more equal airflow out of each cylinder. Exhaust manifolds can be restricting, forcing the pistons to work harder to push the exhaust gases out. A header is freer flowing, allowing gases to leave the engine quickly FIGURE 39-20.

The headers also provide a **scavenging** effect to help remove exhaust gases from the cylinders. The outgoing pulse from one cylinder is timed to arrive at the junction at exactly the right time to help draw out the pulse from another cylinder. This setup is called tuned exhaust, and the lengths of the header tubes determine the rpm range they are tuned to. Tuned exhaust is widely used on high-performance vehicles and race cars. Performance gains can be realized by ensuring that exhaust gases flow freely, so that the engine can pull air in and push exhaust out efficiently. When a Formula One car is produced, extreme attention is given to exhaust tuning to ensure that the exhaust will flow correctly, resulting in the maximum power for the engine.

Engine Pipe

The engine pipe, or down pipe, is attached to the exhaust manifold and connects to the catalytic converter. The engine pipe is usually made of a nickel chromium material, which resists rust and corrosion to ensure it is long lasting. Some exhaust down pipes may also use stainless steel to ensure long life. The engine pipe may be attached to the exhaust manifold by spring-loaded bolts that allow the exhaust to move slightly as the engine moves in its mounts. Some engine pipes also have flexible connectors that allow flexing of the engine pipe as the engine moves in its mounts FIGURE 39-21.

Flexible Connections

There may be a flexible connection between the engine pipe and an intermediate pipe. The flexible connector is used close to the gap. Its main functions are to allow engine movement and to reduce vibration without passing it along the exhaust—especially in front-wheel drive vehicles FIGURE 39-22. The flexible connector also helps with the alignment of the pipes as the engine moves under load.

Catalytic Converter

A catalytic converter is used to convert unacceptable exhaust pollutants, such as carbon monoxide,

FIGURE 39-21 The engine pipe connects the exhaust manifold to the catalytic converter and may contain a flexible connector.

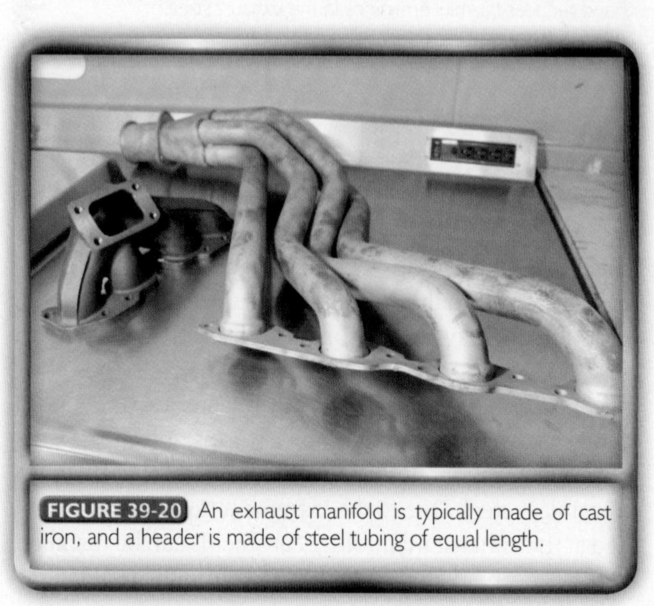

FIGURE 39-20 An exhaust manifold is typically made of cast iron, and a header is made of steel tubing of equal length.

FIGURE 39-22 The flexible connector is used to allow the pipe to flex as the engine moves.

hydrocarbons, and oxides of nitrogen into less dangerous substances. Three-way converters convert oxides of nitrogen back into nitrogen and oxygen, and the hydrocarbons and carbon monoxide to water and carbon dioxide. Older two-way catalytic converters converted hydrocarbons and carbon monoxide to water and carbon dioxide, but were not able to convert the oxides of nitrogen. A catalytic converter fits in line with the exhaust system. It is located close to the exhaust manifold so that it can reach its operating temperature as soon as possible FIGURE 39-23. Some manufacturers install a catalytic converter in the base of the exhaust manifold and another one downstream before the muffler.

Catalytic converters can become contaminated by lead and silicone. Leaded fuel must not be used in an engine with a catalytic converter, because lead will coat the catalyst and prevent it from doing its job. Some types of silicone sealer will also coat the catalyst. Once coated, the converter will most likely need to be replaced.

The catalytic converter operates by beginning and then maintaining a chemical reaction in the exhaust gases. It usually creates heat as it is converting the harmful gases to less harmful ones, so it can get extremely hot. Because of this, it has a heat shield to prevent heat from radiating to bodywork and other parts. The catalytic converter is covered in greater detail in the Emission Control chapter.

Exhaust Brackets

The exhaust components are supported along the length of the vehicle by brackets suspended from the underbody. The supports are usually rubber mounted and help isolate the vibrations of the exhaust from the main body of the vehicle. Rubber is preferred because of its natural dampening effect FIGURE 39-24.

FIGURE 39-23 The catalytic converter is located after the engine pipe and before the muffler. It changes harmful gases into nonharmful gases to be released to the atmosphere.

FIGURE 39-24 The exhaust is supported by rubber mounts that ensure that vibration is not felt by the driver.

Intermediate Pipe

The intermediate pipe connects the catalytic converter to the muffler. This pipe can be made to fit inside of the pipe of the catalytic converter and may be sealed with an exhaust clamp. The pipe may also have flanges on the ends that bolt to a flange on the catalytic converter and will have a gasket between the bolted flanges to seal the exhaust in.

The Muffler System

The function of a vehicle's muffler is to minimize the sounds coming from the exhaust system. These sounds originate from the combustion process within the engine. Exhaust noise becomes an issue as vehicle systems become generally quieter and as the number of vehicles on our roads increases.

To understand the operation of modern exhaust noise reduction systems, it is helpful to understand what sound is. We sense sound with our eardrum, located within the ear. The eardrum is made to move by variations in air pressure. Variations in air pressure can be created when a force is placed upon an object. An example is clapping your hands. As the two hands collide, they push the air surrounding them away. The moving air creates a wave of air pressure, or a sound wave. This sound wave moves your eardrum, which is interpreted as sound by your brain.

The engine produces noise, since each combustion process is a rapid burning of air and fuel—a controlled explosion. These explosions create a great deal of noise if they are not absorbed or canceled. *Noise absorption* refers to putting a sound material around a perforated pipe that the exhaust gases flow through. This is similar to placing noise-absorbing materials inside the walls of a house to make the rooms quieter. *Noise cancellation* is a system that prevents the sound waves from leaving the exhaust

Applied Science

AS-43: Noise/Acoustics: The technician can demonstrate an understanding of why the acoustics of the vehicle affect specific noises.

The acoustics of a vehicle is related to the behavior of sound waves in an enclosed space. Noise can enter the passenger compartment from a number of sources. The road noise when driving is one source of noise. Engine noise, tire noise, wind noise, and the noise of other vehicles are other sources. Dampening material around the vehicle cabin is a very good method of noise reduction.

Current automotive technology includes improvements in acoustic materials around the passenger compartment. Insulation is placed in trunk panels, rear wheel wells, doors, and the roof, as well as under the carpet. All of this insulation reduces unwanted environmental noise.

Today's vehicles differ widely in the way they are manufactured as related to noise and acoustic factors. On some vehicles, to reduce weight and be more price competitive, insulation and dampening materials have been reduced. In comparison, luxury vehicles may have more than 100 pounds of sound-deadening material placed carefully in the most needed areas to ensure a quiet environment.

Technicians should understand that noises may not be the same in all vehicles due to variations in manufacturing. The acoustics of a particular vehicle may differ widely as compared to another. On one type of vehicle, it may be typical for the driver to report a squealing sound from under the hood before a water pump failed. On another, the engine covers and multiple layers of dampening material between the engine and the passenger compartment may have a different effect on the driver hearing abnormal engine sounds.

AS-44: Overtones/Harmonics: The technician can explain that the presence of overtones may indicate changes in vibration in systems.

A technician in a luxury car dealership has replaced a number of water pumps on a certain model of a popular vehicle. The published labor rate for this water pump replacement is 11.2 hours. This greatly exceeds the average water pump replacement labor rate by three or four times.

The technician has observed that the water pump on this particular vehicle tends to have a slightly noisy bearing before it fails. As a preventive measure, the technician uses a stethoscope to listen to the sound of the water pump bearing when vehicles of this model are in for basic service. The pump sounds are checked with the stethoscope at idle, at 1000 rpm, and again at 1500 rpm. Over the years, the technician has developed the listening skills with his stethoscope to evaluate the condition of the water pump bearing on this particular vehicle model. When an abnormal condition exists during the stethoscope evaluation, the technician is aware of the situation and can detect the presence of an overtone, which is a higher tone above the average tone. This condition may indicate the first sign of a bearing with excessive vibration. The technician will make a record of his findings on the repair order to alert the owner of this concern. It would be better for the owner to schedule this service rather than having a water pump failure on a long trip.

system by canceling them out inside the muffler. These systems create gas pressures that are equal in force but opposite in direction to the noise source. These generated pressures are known as anti-noise. Any remaining sound is referred to as residual noise.

The muffler is designed to quiet the noises of combustion without restricting exhaust flow to the point of adversely affecting performance. The goal is to produce a vehicle that is smooth and quiet as well as powerful. A muffler may use a dissipative technique, which is sound absorption, or a noise-canceling technique, or both. Exhaust noise can be reduced by various means, including baffles and chambers, variable-flow exhaust, and electronic mufflers.

TECHNICIAN TIP

Pedestrians are faced with the opposite problem when dealing with hybrid and electric vehicles—the vehicles are too quiet. It is easy for pedestrians who are visually or hearing impaired, or who just aren't paying close attention, to walk out in front of one of these vehicles while it is operating on electric power. Federal guidelines are being written to address this issue.

Baffles and Chambers

The dissipative type muffler uses a perforated tube or baffle that is wrapped in fiberglass material, and this will absorb the noise of combustion as gases flow past. The baffle then gets welded or bolted into the exhaust pipe. Typically, aftermarket motorcycle mufflers have removable baffles to allow the owner to rewrap the fiberglass insulation or to remove it if a louder exhaust note is wanted.

The noise-canceling technique uses a large chamber that the exhaust pipe enters. The exhaust flows into the large chamber, and the exhaust gases bounce off of the chamber's wall. The exhaust gases bounce back toward the incoming gases, and the pressure waves collide, canceling the noise. The exhaust gases then flow out the opposite pipe to the tailpipe. There are several variations to the design of the noise-canceling muffler, which are intended to produce less back-pressure FIGURE 39-25.

FIGURE 39-25 The muffler is one of two types of designs, either the dissipative type or the noise-canceling type.

Variable-Flow Exhaust

A moveable valve built within the exhaust system is used to change the path for exhaust to flow as well as the amount of exhaust back-pressure. This system is used on many high-end performance vehicles to ensure they meet noise restrictions. The system operates in two stages. In the first stage, when the engine rpm and throttle position are low, the exhaust takes a longer route through two or more mufflers/resonators. This design provides a longer path through silencers before the exhaust is expelled. It also provides a small amount of back-pressure, which further lowers the exhaust noise as well as the hydrocarbon emissions during valve overlap at low rpm. When the throttle is opened and engine speed increases, the second stage is activated. A valve opens and allows the exhaust to bypass some of the silencers in the system, making the exhaust path more free-flowing. The valve can be operated by:

- Exhaust gas pressure
- Vacuum diaphragm
- Electronic actuator

Adding a variable-flow exhaust to the baffle or chamber system reduces emission noise. This is because the system can partially respond to changes in engine speed and load. A version of this system is typically found on high-end exotics such as Ferrari, Aston Martin, or Lamborghini.

Electronic Mufflers

Any restriction to exhaust flow in the exhaust system creates back-pressure. Although some back-pressure can be beneficial, excessive back-pressure reduces volumetric efficiency. This in turn reduces engine efficiency. Electronic mufflers are designed to produce anti-noise without restricting exhaust flow. This computer-controlled system uses a microphone to detect the sound waves produced within the exhaust system. A computer-driven loudspeaker is operated to generate equal but opposite sound waves to cancel the exhaust noises. This use of opposing sound waves is sometimes called anti-noise. The anti-noise is applied to the exhaust stream in an electronic muffler. The result is a virtually silent exhaust without generating additional and unwanted back-pressure across all engine operating conditions. This system increases fuel economy and reduces exhaust emissions. The electronic muffler is a research part at the moment and has never been released on a production vehicle.

TECHNICIAN TIP

Some vehicles use the audio system to cancel noise inside the passenger compartment in order to combat engine noise. This is done in two ways. The first is to use the entertainment system to actively cancel engine and road noise. The second way is to use a speed-sensitive entertainment system that adjusts the volume of the entertainment system according to vehicle speed: low volume at low speed and higher volume at higher speed. This helps overcome objectionable noise.

Resonator

Some manufacturers use a resonator in the exhaust system. It is located between the muffler and the exhaust outlet. Its function is to reduce any resonance levels that the muffler could not adequately suppress FIGURE 39-26. Some manufacturers may use more than one resonator to quiet the combustion noises even further. Some

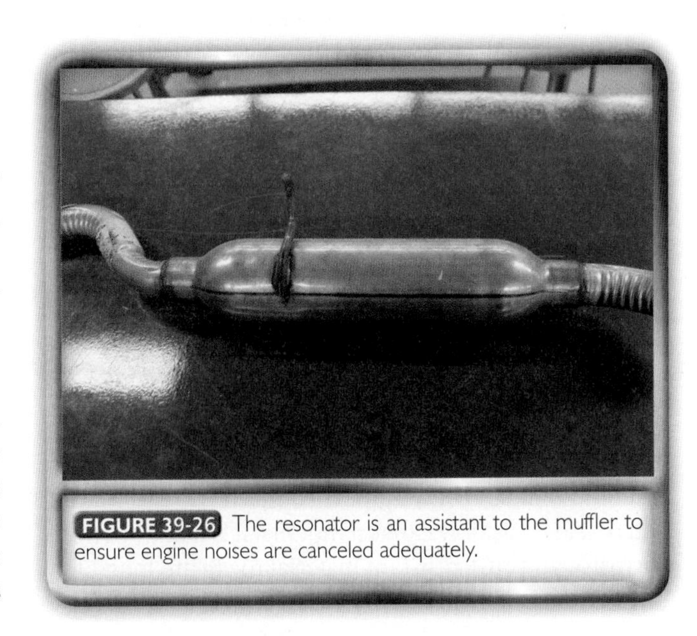

FIGURE 39-26 The resonator is an assistant to the muffler to ensure engine noises are canceled adequately.

resonators work on the Helmholtz principle—namely that air blown across a tube connected to a rounded container will create a vibration, and noise is produced, similar to air blown across a bottle. This principle is then used to cancel noise by bouncing waves off of each other, reducing their intensity, which lowers the exhaust noise.

Applied Science

AS-45: Pitch/Frequency: The technician can explain the relationship of pitch to frequency.

Heinrich Hertz, a German physicist, was the first to prove the existence of electromagnetic waves. He did so by engineering a radio wave transmitter. In honor of his work, the unit for measuring frequency, hertz, is named after him. Because it is named after a person, its abbreviation (Hz) begins with a capital letter.

Frequency is the number of sound waves produced in a given time. The frequency of a sound wave determines its pitch, described in terms of how "high" or "low" the sound is. Humans can perceive sound waves ranging from 20 Hz (lowest pitch) to 20,000 Hz (highest pitch).

The concept of sound is based on the principle that a sound wave begins with a vibrating object. The frequency of a sound wave, or Hz, can be expressed as 1 Hz = 1 vibration/second. A diesel-powered generator used for backup electrical purposes is a 60-Hz unit, which is standard for the industry.

AS-46: Resonance: The technician can demonstrate an understanding of what happens when an object resonates.

In physics, resonance refers to the amplitude at which an object vibrates at a given frequency. There are a number of different types of resonance, including mechanical resonance. When a large group of soldiers are marching across a bridge, they are told to break step in order to avoid damaging the bridge's structure. If the soldiers' footsteps were to fall simultaneously, extreme vibrations could result, which the bridge might not be able to withstand.

In automotive applications, a vehicle with a tire that is out of balance vibrates when traveling at a certain speed. Resonance issues are often experienced in exhaust systems that have been modified and can produce a droning noise from vibration. Vehicle manufacturers in some cases have found it necessary to add mass (weight) to the various exhaust components to change the resonance frequency.

Tailpipe

The tailpipe takes the exhaust gases away from the vehicle. Its exit point must not allow any of the exhaust gases to enter the vehicle. The tailpipe is connected to the muffler and is held by flexible exhaust mounts. It is made of a non-corrosive and rust-resistant material to ensure long life.

Exhaust Gaskets

Exhaust components are sometimes bolted together. If they are, they may need to have a gasket to seal them. Exhaust gaskets can be found between the engine cylinder head and the exhaust manifold, the engine pipe and the catalytic converter, and possibly the catalytic converter and the muffler. The exhaust is extremely hot, so the gaskets must withstand the temperatures without burning **FIGURE 39-27**. Exhaust gaskets can be multilayered high-temperature alloys that are formed with graphite or mica to provide a good seal as exhaust components move with expansion and contraction. Donut gaskets are another type of exhaust gasket. They use spiral wound steel and filler material, which is shaped into a round design, that, when installed in ball-shaped pipe, provides seal while allowing the pipes to be joined even if they are slightly out of line. Some of these gaskets also allow for slight movement of the engine.

Diagnosis and Testing

Inspecting the Throttle Body and the Induction System

The throttle body and the induction system ensure that the engine gets airflow into the cylinders. The throttle body allows control of engine rpm. If the induction system gaskets leak, engine performance problems will result. Some vehicles use a MAF sensor to send airflow information to the PCM. The PCM uses this information to accurately deliver fuel. If air leaks are present in the induction system downstream of the MAF sensor, then the sensor will not be able to measure the air coming into the engine.

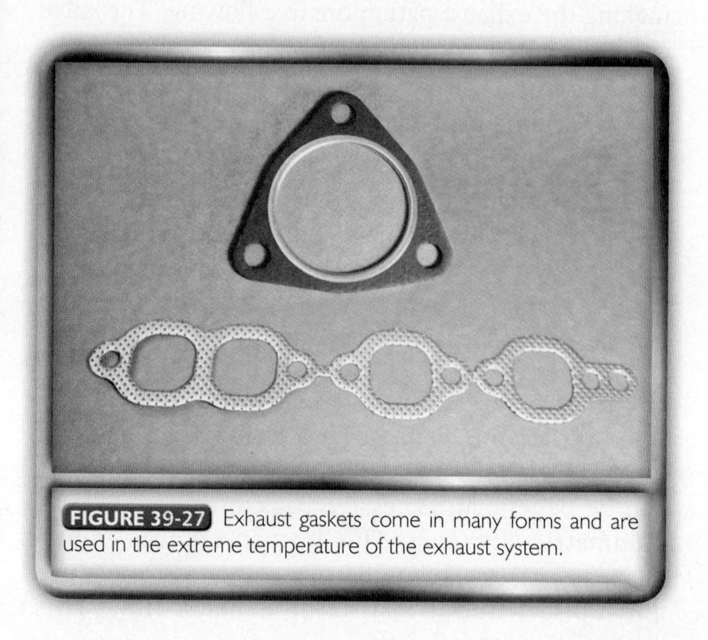

FIGURE 39-27 Exhaust gaskets come in many forms and are used in the extreme temperature of the exhaust system.

This additional air is sometimes referred to as "false air." As a result, the PCM will not deliver enough fuel based on the MAF signal and the engine will tend to run lean.

There are several ways to test for air leaks, including using a substitute fuel to artificially enrich the mixture at the point of the leak, using a smoke machine to fill the intake system and show any external leaks, and using an electronic stethoscope (or piece of heater hose) to listen for and pinpoint the leak. The use of a substitute fuel such as acetylene, propane, or carburetor cleaner is a quick and accurate method, but you risk catching the engine on fire. The technician carefully directs a small amount of fuel toward any suspected leaking components FIGURE 39-28. If an intake gasket is leaking, the vacuum will pull the gas into the intake manifold and the engine rpm will increase, or smooth out. If the engine has an idle control system, the rpm may not change much, except slightly when you uncover the leak and when you pull the fuel away. You may need to disable the system, or hold the throttle open just enough that the control system is not controlling the idle. You may also be able to use a scan tool to watch oxygen, short-term fuel trim, and injector pulse-width readings while applying and removing the acetylene or propane.

Leaks can also happen in the duct work, hoses, and diaphragms that are connected to the intake manifold, creating a false air condition. While the acetylene and propane may still find the leak, a smoke machine is invaluable. The smoke machine pushes smoke at low pressure out of the hose and into the intake manifold. The smoke machine can then be used to fill the entire intake system with smoke. If there are any leaks, the smoke will leak from inside the system to the outside. So anywhere the smoke is leaking from is an air leak. A high-intensity light can be used to make the smoke more visible.

To inspect the throttle body, air induction system, and intake manifold for leaks, follow the steps in SKILL DRILL 39-1.

Safety

Be careful using carburetor cleaner, or any flammable liquid, on a hot engine. Carburetor cleaner is a flammable material.

FIGURE 39-28 To find a leaking intake manifold gasket, a technician can use acetylene, propane, or carburetor cleaner to enrich the mixture.

Inspecting the Exhaust System

Inspection of the exhaust system is a necessary task as an automotive technician. Exhaust inspection is part of any mandatory state inspection process, since a leak will result in possible injury or death to the passengers due to carbon monoxide poisoning. Also, most municipalities have noise ordinances limiting the amount of noise an exhaust can emit. Special care should be taken to ensure that the exhaust system is not leaking. Exhaust leaks will create a black carbon marking.

A quick test for exhaust leaks is to use a rag to block off the exhaust flow from the tailpipe; if the exhaust system is not leaking, pressure will build and force the rag out of the pipe. If there are leaks in the exhaust, then hissing will be heard from the exhaust system through the leaks. It may be necessary to have an assistant perform this test (block off the tailpipe with a rag) while the technician listens for exhaust leaks. A mechanic's stethoscope can help pinpoint small leaks while this test is being performed. Another testing option is to use a smoke machine with an exhaust pipe adapter to fill the exhaust system with smoke. With the engine off, any signs of smoke will pinpoint leaks in the exhaust system. Remember that smoke will fill the cylinder of the engine on the cylinder that has an exhaust valve open. If both intake and exhaust valves are open due to overlap, then you may see smoke coming from the air cleaner assembly. This is considered normal and should not be confused as a leak from the exhaust.

The exhaust pipes can rust out over time. The water and corrosive chemicals in the exhaust stream corrode the pipe. A good way to test the integrity of the pipe is to use a large pair of adjustable pliers to squeeze the pipe. If it is springy or crushes easily, the pipe needs to be replaced. Make sure you check any low spots in the system along with bends in the pipe, as these are weak spots.

To inspect the exhaust system for leaks, follow the steps in SKILL DRILL 39-2.

Prove
Know
See
Do

SKILL DRILL 39-1 Inspecting the Throttle Body, Air Induction System, and Intake Manifold

1. Start the engine and let the idle stabilize. Using an acetylene or propane testing tool, place the hose near the suspected leak area.

2. Open the fuel valve to slowly release the acetylene or propane.

x1000r/min

3. On vehicles without an idle control system, observe the rpm and smoothness of the engine. If the engine speed increases or smoothes out, then a vacuum leak is present. Determine any necessary repairs. On vehicles with an idle control system, connect a scan tool and select data stream. Observe the oxygen, short-term fuel trims, and injector pulse width as you are moving the acetylene or propane around.

4. Shut off the engine and connect a smoke machine to the intake manifold. Start the smoke machine and inject smoke into the intake manifold.

5. Using a bright light, look around the engine compartment for traces of smoke. Any smoke coming from the air cleaner inlet is normal. Determine any necessary action(s).

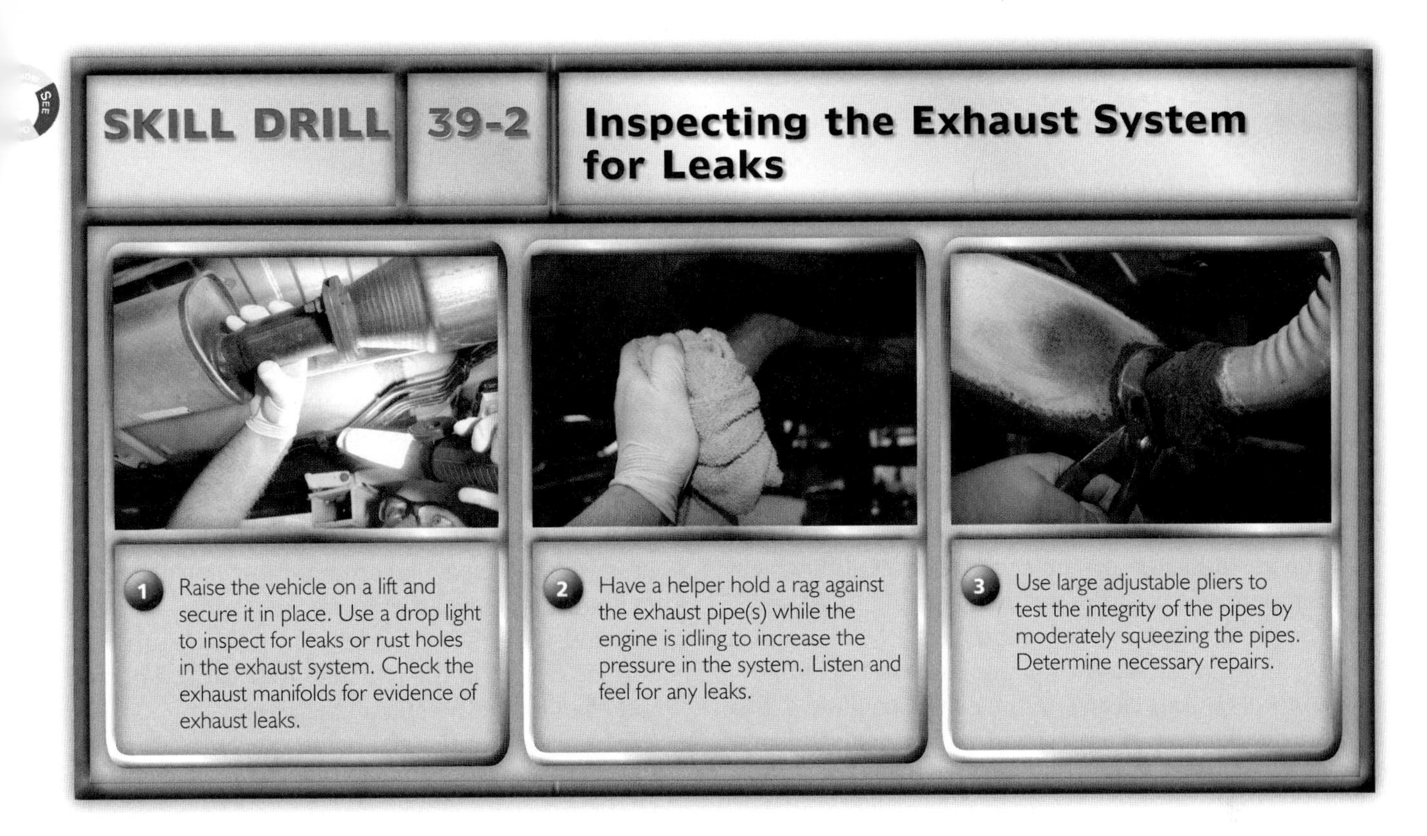

SKILL DRILL 39-2 Inspecting the Exhaust System for Leaks

1. Raise the vehicle on a lift and secure it in place. Use a drop light to inspect for leaks or rust holes in the exhaust system. Check the exhaust manifolds for evidence of exhaust leaks.
2. Have a helper hold a rag against the exhaust pipe(s) while the engine is idling to increase the pressure in the system. Listen and feel for any leaks.
3. Use large adjustable pliers to test the integrity of the pipes by moderately squeezing the pipes. Determine necessary repairs.

Wrap-up

Ready for Review

- The intake system ensures that clean, dry air is delivered to the engine to be mixed with fuel.
- Clean air is essential to a long-lasting engine.
- The intake system ensures that air and fuel are delivered to the engine efficiently.
- The primary components of the intake system are the intake manifold, the throttle body, and the air induction system.
- There are two types of intake manifolds: wet and dry.
- The air induction system consists of the following components: an air cleaner and housing, solid and flexible-duct tubing, and connectors.
- Ducting can be made of plastic for movement and connects the air cleaner to the intake manifold.
- The intake manifold provides a path for fuel and air to travel to the engine combustion chambers.
- Volumetric efficiency compares the volume of air entering a cylinder during intake to the internal swept volume of the cylinder when the piston is at bottom dead center.
- Back-pressure typically should never get higher than 3 psi (20.7 kPa). If it is greater, it can create poor performance issues, as it will cause exhaust to back up into the combustion chamber, minimizing the fresh airflow into the engine.
- Forced induction increases air pressure in the intake manifold above atmospheric pressure.
- A supercharger compresses the air intake to above atmospheric pressure, which increases the intake air density to the engine.
- A turbocharger is a forced induction system that uses wasted kinetic energy from the exhaust gases to increase the intake pressure.
- When using a turbocharger, exhaust gases turn the turbine, which in turn pulls in fresh air at a higher rate than normally aspirated engines.
- When air is compressed, it heats up; to keep the heating process to a minimum, an intercooler is used to cool the air prior to being injected into the engine.
- The exhaust system involves many components that work together to remove the by-products of combustion from the engine.

- The primary components of the exhaust system are the exhaust manifold, engine pipe (sometimes called the down pipe), catalytic converter, intermediate pipe, muffler, tailpipe, and exhaust brackets.
- The exhaust manifold provides a path for exhaust gases to escape the engine. In a high-performance engine, headers are tuned for better engine breathing.
- The flexible connector allows movement between the engine and the rest of the exhaust system and keeps the pipes aligned under a load.
- A catalytic converter is used to convert unacceptable exhaust pollutants, such as carbon monoxide, certain hydrocarbons, and oxides of nitrogen, into less dangerous substances.
- There may be one or two heated oxygen sensors after the catalytic converter.
- The rubber exhaust brackets support the system and allow movement and dampening action in the exhaust system.
- The function of a vehicle's muffler is to minimize the sounds coming from the exhaust system.
- The baffles in the exhaust system help to muffle the noises that the engine makes during normal operation.
- The tailpipe prevents the harmful exhaust fumes from entering the passenger compartment.
- Gaskets are used throughout the exhaust system to make a tight, leak-free system.
- The throttle body and the induction system ensure that the engine gets airflow into the cylinders and must be inspected for proper operation.
- Refer to applicable manufacturer's information when inspecting the induction system or the exhaust system.

Key Terms

blow-off valve A valve that allows the release of excessive boost pressure from the turbocharger when the throttle plate is quickly closed.

bypass valve The pressure control valve of the supercharger. When the bypass valve opens, it lets air move around the supercharger compressor section, reducing the boost pressure.

compressor surge The backup of air against the throttle plate as it is closed. The turbocharger is still spinning, pressurizing air, when the throttle plate is closed. Air will stack up, creating a rapid slowing of the turbocharger compressor wheel. This can damage the compressor wheel.

forced induction The pressurization of airflow going into the cylinder through the use of a turbocharger or supercharger.

header A specially tuned exhaust manifold typically made of exhaust pipes. These pipes are usually made equal length to ensure equal flow between cylinders.

Helmholtz resonator A device that uses the principle of noise cancellation through the collision of sound waves. When necessary, the resonator is used in addition to the muffler to cancel additional sounds. This resonator may also be used on the induction system to muffle noise of airflow through the induction system. It is named after physicist Hermann Von Helmholtz.

mandrel forming The special bending of pipe to ensure the pipe does not collapse. The use of a pipe bender with mandrels allows for very tight bends without creating kinks or reducing the size of the pipe.

mass airflow (MAF) sensor The PCM input sensor that tells the computer the amount of air coming into the engine. The MAF sensor allows the correct calculated amount of fuel delivery to the engine. It is usually located in the ducting of the air cleaner system.

plenum chamber A large portion of the intake manifold after the throttle plate and before the intake runner tubes. The plenum provides a reservoir of air and helps prevent interference with the flow of air between individual branches.

scavenging The process of exhaust flow pulling fresh air into the cylinder as it creates a low-pressure area in the cylinder as it moves out of the cylinder.

supercharger A device that pressurizes airflow into the engine, working similar to a turbocharger. The supercharger is driven by the crankshaft through a belt or gears and does require power from the engine.

turbocharger A device that pressurizes airflow into the engine. The turbocharger works similar to a supercharger, but is driven by the exhaust gases.

wastegate A pressure regulator device that allows control of the pressure produced by the turbocharger. The wastegate moves to allow exhaust gases to bypass the turbine wheel of the turbocharger and flow down the exhaust pipe.

ASE-Type Questions

1. Tech A says that coolant circulates through some intake manifolds to help warm them up. Tech B says that some intake manifolds use an electric heater grid to warm up the intake air. Who is correct?
   a. Tech A
   b. Tech B
   c. Both A and B
   d. Neither A nor B
2. Tech A says that in some gas engines, the intake manifold runner length can be changed. Tech B says that some intake systems use resonators to quiet intake noise. Who is correct?
   a. Tech A
   b. Tech B
   c. Both A and B
   d. Neither A nor B
3. Tech A says that a good way to check the integrity of exhaust pipes is to tap on them with the handle of a screw driver. Tech B says that small exhaust leaks can be found with a smoke machine. Who is correct?
   a. Tech A
   b. Tech B
   c. Both A and B
   d. Neither A nor B
4. Tech A says that scavenging creates a low pressure in the cylinder by means of the exhaust gases flowing through the exhaust pipe. Tech B says that back pressure in the exhaust system increases the scavenging effect. Who is correct?
   a. Tech A
   b. Tech B
   c. Both A and B
   d. Neither A nor B
5. Tech A says that shorter intake manifolds produce higher torque at lower rpm. Tech B says that longer intake manifolds produce higher torque at high engine speeds. Who is correct?
   a. Tech A
   b. Tech B
   c. Both A and B
   d. Neither A nor B
6. Tech A says that air becomes heated as a supercharger compresses it. Tech B says that a turbocharger pulls the exhaust gases out of the engine, thereby increasing the scavenging effect. Who is correct?
   a. Tech A
   b. Tech B
   c. Both A and B
   d. Neither A nor B
7. Tech A says that a wastegate designed to direct waste gases to the intake manifold. Tech B says that a blow-off valve vents excess boost pressure from the turbocharger when the throttle is closed quickly. Who is correct?
   a. Tech A
   b. Tech B
   c. Both A and B
   d. Neither A nor B
8. Tech A says that the exhaust system is usually suspended from the underbody by rubber mounts. Tech B says that some engines use a flexible pipe between the engine pipe and intermediate pipe. Who is correct?
   a. Tech A
   b. Tech B
   c. Both A and B
   d. Neither A nor B
9. Tech A says that a catalytic converter operates best at cold temperatures. Tech B says that the catalytic converter is typically located after the muffler. Who is correct?
   a. Tech A
   b. Tech B
   c. Both A and B
   d. Neither A nor B
10. Tech A says that small vacuum leaks can be found with a vacuum gauge. Tech B says that the catalytic converter can be ruined if it becomes contaminated with lead or silicone. Who is correct?
    a. Tech A
    b. Tech B
    c. Both A and B
    d. Neither A nor B

CHAPTER 40

Know
See
Do
Prove

NATEF Tasks

Engine Performance

Emission Control Systems

		Page
Inspect, test, and service positive crankcase ventilation (PCV) filter/breather cap, valve, tubes, orifices, and hoses; determine necessary action.	MLR AST	1144–1145

Know
See
Do
Prove

Knowledge Objectives

After reading this chapter, you will be able to:

1. Explain the composition of air in the atmosphere. (pp 1126–1127)
2. Describe the types of exhaust emissions released from the internal combustion engine. (pp 1128–1132)
3. Discuss how emissions can be reduced. (pp 1132–1135)
4. Define the term stoichiometric ratio. (p 1134)
5. List the types of emission control devices used. (pp 1135–1139)

Emission Control

Skills Objectives

After reading this chapter, you will be able to:

1. Inspect and service the PCV system. (p 1145)

Introduction

Emissions are the release of substances into the atmosphere. They can occur naturally, from forest fires, volcanoes, and the decomposition of natural materials. Emissions can also be man-made, such as from vehicles and industrial sites. In automotive applications, most **emissions** are the by-product of combustion and are emitted from the exhaust system. Not all emissions from combustion are considered hazardous. Those emissions from the automobile that are hazardous can be managed by carefully designing the engine, accurately controlling the air to fuel ratio, or converting them to nonharmful or less harmful gases through the use of add-on emission control devices. Today's vehicle technology has reduced the harmful emissions a vehicle produces to almost zero. This chapter will detail the methods and control devices designed to either reduce those harmful emission gases or convert them into less harmful or nonharmful elements.

Composition of Air

The air we breathe is composed mainly of two gases: nitrogen and oxygen. Nitrogen by far makes up the largest percentage of air (78%). It is an inert gas, which means it does not react easily with other compounds. Oxygen (21%) is the second most abundant element in air. It is a highly reactive gas, which means it combines readily with almost all other elements. In many cases, oxygen reacts through the process of combustion, which is also called oxidation. These two gases account for approximately 99% of the content of air. That leaves 1% for all of the other elements found in air, including carbon dioxide and argon.

The level of oxygen in the atmosphere is critical to humans. The gases in our atmosphere provide a balanced environment for plant, animal, and human life. Humans breathe in oxygen and exhale carbon dioxide; trees and plants take in carbon dioxide and give back oxygen. This process is part of the oxygen cycle **FIGURE 40-1**. There is also a nitrogen cycle, in which nitrogen from our atmosphere is converted to usable food for plants by bacteria in the ground. There is also a carbon cycle. Carbon fuels are burned and produce carbon dioxide in

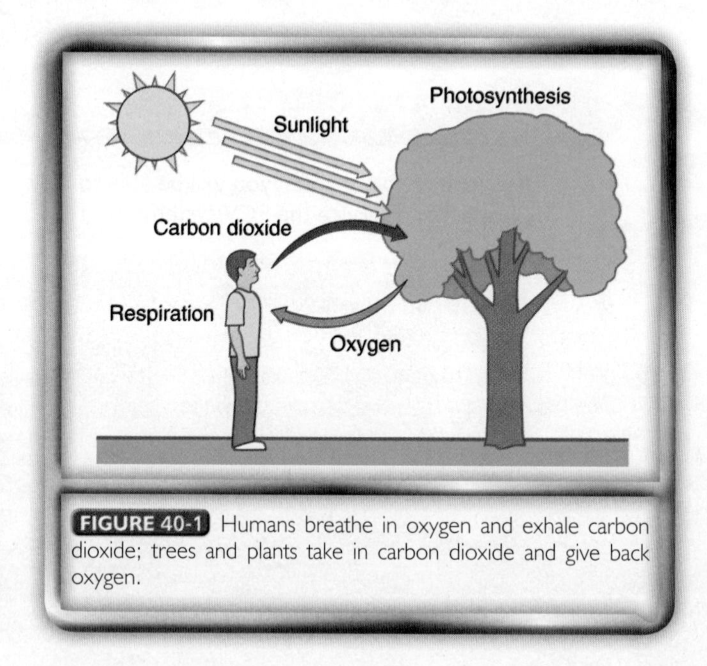
Photosynthesis
Sunlight
Carbon dioxide
Respiration
Oxygen

FIGURE 40-1 Humans breathe in oxygen and exhale carbon dioxide; trees and plants take in carbon dioxide and give back oxygen.

You Are the Automotive Technician

A customer brings her 8-year-old car into your shop for an oil change. She is concerned because her oil life monitor indicates the oil needs changed at a much lower mileage this time compared to past years. She is worried that her vehicle is worn out. You assure her that she did the right thing to bring it in and have it diagnosed, and you compliment her on paying attention to the changes in her vehicle's operation. In the shop, you start your inspection by pulling the dipstick and looking at the oil. It is black, but it also looks just a little milky. You inspect the air filter and see that there is a bit of oil spray and a small amount of oil in the bottom of the air cleaner housing. Suspecting a fault in the Positive Crankcase Ventilation system, you inspect the PCV valve and vacuum hose. The valve doesn't rattle when you shake it. And the hose is quite a bit softer than it should be.

1. What made you suspect that the PCV system was faulty?
2. Why did the oil life monitor indicate a shorter oil life?
3. How did oil get into the air cleaner?
4. What work will you recommend for this customer?

the air, which is then converted to carbon and oxygen by plants. The carbon is used to grow the plant while oxygen is given back to the air.

While nitrogen and oxygen make up 99% of the air, the other 1% contains a variety of gases TABLE 40-1. Some of these gases can be useful in different ways. As a technician, while welding, you may have to use carbon dioxide, argon, or helium to keep oxygen away from the weld. These gases are used because if oxygen is allowed to come in contact with the molten metal of the weld, oxidation will occur and the weld will be weak and could fail. Neon is a gas, drawn from the atmosphere, that produces light when exposed to electricity and is used as an accent light in some show cars.

Sources of Emissions

The term *emission*, when used in automotive circles, normally refers to the pollution produced by a light vehicle during operation or while sitting stationary. All fuels, with the exception of pure hydrogen, produce pollution. **Emission control systems** are designed to limit the pollution caused by the storing and burning of various fuels. Emissions from current gasoline-fueled motor vehicles usually come from three sources: the fuel system, the crankcase, and the tailpipe.

The fuel tank allows liquid fuel to evaporate into a gas. If not controlled, those vapors can escape into the atmosphere and are called evaporative emissions. When gasoline or other hydrocarbon fuel is burned in the combustion chamber along with the oxygen and nitrogen from the air, emissions are created. Some of the emissions are pollutants and are released from the exhaust system in the form of gases. These emissions are called tailpipe emissions. Some of the combustion gases leak past the compression rings and cylinder walls and find their way into the crankcase. These blow-by gases create pressure in the crankcase and if not controlled are vented into the atmosphere and are called crankcase emissions.

In a **compression-ignition engine** (diesel engine), emissions are created in the combustion chamber the same way as they are in spark-ignition engines and escape to the atmosphere through the exhaust and the crankcase breather. Diesel fuel does not evaporate as easily as gasoline, so evaporative emissions are not a major concern on vehicles powered by diesel fuel.

TABLE 40-1: Percentages of Gases Contained in the Atmosphere

Gas	Percentage
Nitrogen (N_2)	78.08
Oxygen (O_2)	20.95
Water (H_2O)	0 to 4, variable
Argon (Ar)	.93
Carbon dioxide (CO_2)	.0360, variable
Neon (Ne)	.0018
Helium (He)	.0005
Methane (CH_4)	.00017, variable
Hydrogen (H_2)	.00005
Oxides of nitrogen (NO_X)	.00003, variable
Ozone (O_3)	.000004

Regulated Emissions

Manufacturers are required by law and the Environmental Protection Agency (EPA) to control the emissions produced by their vehicles. The EPA requires every manufactured power train to pass a federal emission test before it can be sold in the United States. This test is called the Federal Test Procedure (FTP) and is designed to determine the emission output of that particular vehicle as classified by year, make, model, and drive train. The test uses a dynamometer that will duplicate the normal driving pattern of the typical commuter, known as the FTP drive cycle. As the vehicle is operated according to the FTP drive cycle, the emission output is monitored in grams per mile (g/mi). For the vehicle to pass, the emissions must stay under the limits for that type of vehicle. Other countries have other agencies that regulate emissions, but any vehicle entering the United States must pass the US FTP test.

Not only must the vehicles pass the test before they can be sold, they must be capable of detecting an emission failure over their life, as they are being operated. As of 1996, all vehicles must meet the **on-board diagnostics II (OBDII)** standard. OBDII is an automotive self-diagnostic system mandated by the EPA that requires a warning light to alert the driver of an emission system fault. The EPA requires that when a vehicle's emissions deviate from the FTP limit by 1.5 times, the warning light (malfunction indicator lamp [MIL]) must turn on and one or more specific diagnostic trouble codes (DTCs) be set in memory.

If the vehicle begins to run rich—for example, due to a leaking fuel injector—and the emission output exceeds 1.5 times the FTP limit, the engine management system must be able to detect the rich condition. The engine control module (ECM) will then turn the MIL on to warn the driver that the vehicle has a fault and requires service. The OBDII system was developed purely with the intent of keeping vehicles emission-compliant and warning drivers if they are not.

Regulated air pollutants can be divided into two groups: gases and particulates. The primary pollutant gases from vehicles include hydrocarbons, carbon monoxide, oxides of nitrogen, and sulfur dioxide. These pollutants can have a damaging effect on people, the atmosphere, and the natural environment. Particulates, often referred to as **particulate matter**, are tiny particles of solid or liquid suspended in the air. Particulate matter is graded in a size range from 10 nanometers to 100 micrometers in diameter. Particulates of less than 10 micrometers are dangerous to humans because they can easily become airborne and reach the lungs. Smaller particles also tend to stay airborne longer than larger particles, which settle more quickly.

Many countries have recognized the global effects that the continual release of pollutants into the earth's atmosphere can have. These countries have developed emissions laws or follow an international protocol on emission control standards. Vehicle manufacturers are required to comply with these laws to ensure that the emissions from the vehicles they produce meet the emission control standards.

Manufacturers design emission control systems for their vehicles, which monitor and control emissions so that they do not exceed the emission control limits. A **limit value** is the maximum amount of emissions that a vehicle is permitted to emit. Limit values are assigned to different classifications of vehicles. Passenger and light vehicle limit values are normally given in grams per mile in the United States and grams per kilometer in Europe. These regulations have become progressively more stringent as government regulations become tougher in an effort to further reduce vehicle emissions.

In the quest to meet the tougher emission control standards, many manufacturers are turning to hybrid technologies, which couple two power sources together (electric and gas). Hybrid vehicles have reduced emission output and meet tougher fuel economy standards. Alternative fuels, such as compressed natural gas (CNG) and propane, are also being used more frequently in the attempt to further reduce pollutions. Ever-stricter emission control is at the forefront of vehicle design and construction.

> **TECHNICIAN TIP**
>
> Historically, the regulated emissions have been hydrocarbons, carbon monoxide, oxides of nitrogen, and particulate matter. In recent years, carbon dioxide has been added to the list of emissions that are being regulated. Not all scientists agree with this regulation since carbon dioxide is necessary for plant life and is given off in human respiration.

Types of Emissions

Internal combustion engines produce several emission gases as part of the conversion process of turning fuel (chemical energy) into mechanical energy. There are three categories of emission gases: nonharmful, harmful, and debatable. The nonharmful gases are water (H_2O), nitrogen (N_2), and oxygen (O_2). The harmful gases are carbon monoxide (CO), oxides of nitrogen (NO_X), and sulfur dioxide (SO_2). The debatable gas is carbon dioxide (CO_2). Each of these gases will be explained in the following sections.

Water

Water is a natural by-product of complete combustion and is not harmful to the environment or our air quality. Water is formed by the engine when two hydrogen molecules from the fuel are drawn into the combustion chamber and are combined with one oxygen molecule FIGURE 40-2. Water is emitted as a result of complete combustion of hydrogen and oxygen. We could say that water is a by-product of completely burned hydrogen fuel. In fact, burning 1 gallon of gasoline in an engine creates about 1 gallon of water. Thus, water is formed in all internal combustion engines and is discharged along with all normal combustion gases through the exhaust system.

> **TECHNICIAN TIP**
>
> In a gasoline engine, about 1 gallon of water is created for every 1 gallon of gasoline burned. This water usually leaves the exhaust system as superheated steam since it is produced under very high combustion temperatures. If the exhaust pipe is cool because the engine was not running very long, the steam can condense into water and drip out of the tailpipe. Water also mixes with any sulfur dioxide in the exhaust and creates sulfuric acid. This water and sulfuric acid can sit in low spots in the exhaust system and rust or corrode any steel and iron components. Many manufacturers use exhaust system pipes and mufflers made of stainless steel, which resists rust and corrosion.

Carbon Dioxide

Carbon dioxide is a by-product of complete combustion, along with water. When complete combustion of air and fuel occurs, one carbon molecule combines with two

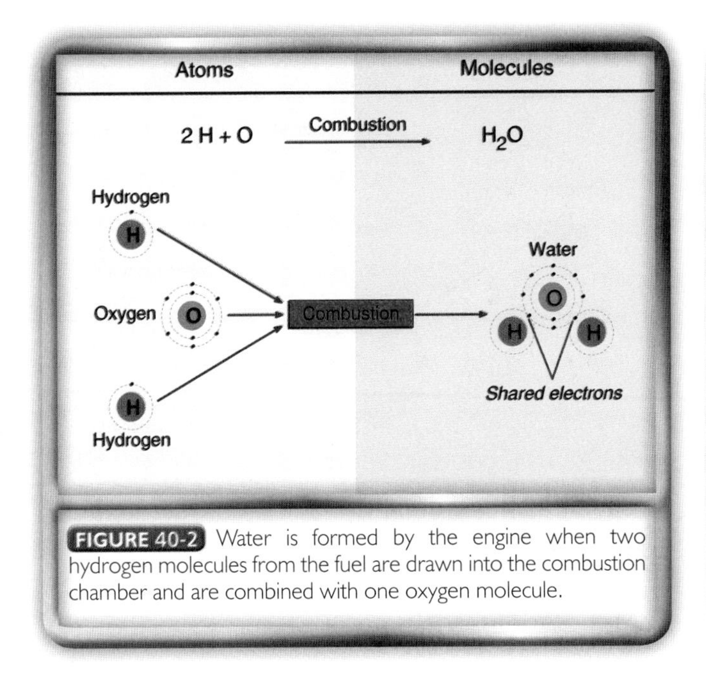
Atoms
Molecules
2 H + O
Combustion
H2O
Hydrogen
H
Oxygen
O
Combustion
Water
O
H
H
Shared electrons
H
Hydrogen

FIGURE 40-2 Water is formed by the engine when two hydrogen molecules from the fuel are drawn into the combustion chamber and are combined with one oxygen molecule.

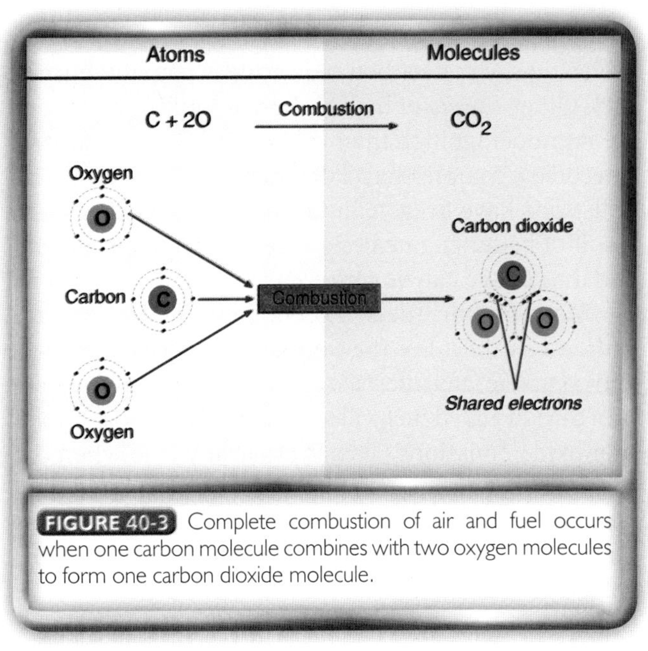
Atoms
Molecules
C + 2O
Combustion
CO2
Oxygen
O
Carbon dioxide
C
Carbon
C
Combustion
O
O
O
Shared electrons
Oxygen

FIGURE 40-3 Complete combustion of air and fuel occurs when one carbon molecule combines with two oxygen molecules to form one carbon dioxide molecule.

oxygen molecules to form one carbon dioxide molecule FIGURE 40-3. So we could say that carbon dioxide is completely burned carbon fuel. Carbon dioxide is not normally considered a poisonous gas; in fact, humans exhale it as our bodies use the oxygen we breathe in, and plants use the carbon from carbon dioxide for growth while releasing the oxygen back into the atmosphere. However, some scientists consider carbon dioxide a serious contributor to global warming, and the EPA has labeled it as a pollutant. Thus, manufacturers are now finding ways to reduce it. Carbon dioxide is believed to act as a blanket, trapping heat and thereby raising the temperature of the earth's atmosphere. Since motor vehicles are a major source of carbon dioxide, governments are seeking ways to regulate them with the goal of reducing the total amount of carbon dioxide released into the atmosphere.

Carbon dioxide is also formed inside of catalytic converters. The catalytic converter completes the combustion process by adding another oxygen molecule to the carbon monoxide (CO) to convert it to carbon dioxide (CO_2). In addition, carbon dioxide is produced by diesel, liquid petroleum gas (LPG), propane, CNG, or any other carbon-based fuel used in a vehicle with an internal combustion engine.

Hydrocarbons

Gasoline, diesel, LPG, and natural gas are all hydrocarbon compounds. **Hydrocarbons** are created when raw fuel evaporates into the atmosphere or when it does not burn at all in the combustion chamber and is exhausted out the tailpipe. In other words, hydrocarbon emissions are unburned fuel that escapes to the atmosphere.

Gasoline needs to evaporate easily so that it can mix with air to burn properly in an internal combustion engine. But this property also means it evaporates easily into the atmosphere at ordinary temperatures and pressures. For example, when a vehicle is being refueled, hydrocarbon vapors can escape from the filler neck into the atmosphere. When the vehicle is left in the sun, the temperature of the fuel increases, and fuel can evaporate from the tank.

TECHNICIAN TIP

Hydrocarbon emissions react with oxides of nitrogen (NO_x) in the presence of sunlight to produce **photochemical smog**, a brown haze that hangs in the sky, typically seen over large cities. Smog is a major health issue to humans because it affects lung tissue. Hydrocarbons are a major component of photochemical smog.

Carbon Monoxide

Carbon monoxide is a colorless, odorless, tasteless, flammable, and highly toxic gas. It is a product of the incomplete combustion of carbon and oxygen. The incomplete combustion can result from either too much fuel (carbon) or not enough air (oxygen). In these conditions, the carbon can only attach itself to one oxygen molecule, creating carbon monoxide FIGURE 40-4. We could say that carbon monoxide is partially burned fuel. Other causes of high carbon monoxide emissions are improper ignition timing, low combustion temperature, or low compression of the engine. Carbon monoxide emissions have been reduced in modern vehicles as a result of better engine design, better fuel management, and the use of catalytic converters in the exhaust system.

Most engine fuels, except pure hydrogen, are carbon-based. Unless the combustion process is perfect and complete, any internal combustion engine operating on a carbon-based fuel will tend to produce some carbon monoxide emissions. This is especially true when the combustion temperature is low, such as during a cold start, when there is not enough oxygen present to completely burn the fuel, or when there is insufficient time in the combustion chamber for complete combustion.

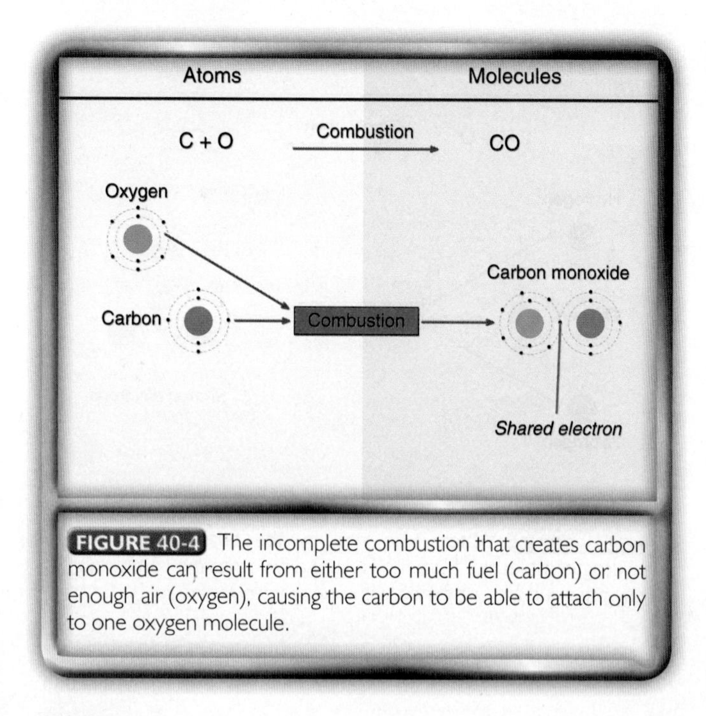
Atoms
Molecules
C + O
Combustion
CO
Oxygen
Carbon
Combustion
Carbon monoxide
Shared electron

FIGURE 40-4 The incomplete combustion that creates carbon monoxide can result from either too much fuel (carbon) or not enough air (oxygen), causing the carbon to be able to attach only to one oxygen molecule.

Applied Science

AS-24: Chemical Reactions: The technician can demonstrate an understanding of the chemical reactions that occur in the automotive engine that are related to the combustion of fuels and the operation of the catalytic converter.

An automotive teacher asks a student to use a hacksaw to cut apart a failed catalytic converter for evaluation purposes. When the converter is cut into two pieces, it is evident that the converter had melted down. The students find six large pieces of material that resemble rocks. The ceramic catalyst was damaged because of a super-heated condition that resulted from unburned fuel entering the converter. This teaching aid provides an introduction to the catalytic converter and how it works and relates to the combustion of fuels in an automotive engine.

The stoichiometric ratio is the ratio of air to fuel at which all of the oxygen in the air and all of the fuel are completely burned. This is the ratio of 14.7 parts of air to 1 part of fuel. Maintaining close control of the air–fuel ratio allows an engine to run cleaner than ever. In many cases, precise control of the air–fuel ratio has made the job of hydrocarbon (HC) and carbon monoxide (CO) related emission control devices much easier, since they are dealing with much smaller volumes of the pollutants. Catalytic converters use a base structure of ceramic material coated with precious metals to react with and break up or combine gases in the exhaust system. The catalytic converter cleans up the pollutants left over from combustion, and tailpipe emissions are reduced.

In the case of the failed converter that was cut apart for evaluation, the engine had a misfiring cylinder as a result of a faulty spark plug. The check engine light that was illuminated on the dash was ignored by the vehicle owner for about one month, resulting in the failure of the converter. The unburned fuel from the misfiring cylinder was ignited in the converter, causing overheating of the ceramic monolith.

Toxicity

Carbon monoxide is an extremely poisonous gas. Since you cannot see it or smell it, it is very dangerous. Inhaling carbon monoxide in a confined space can be lethal. Because it is known to come from the exhaust system, it is important not to allow any engine to run inside a workshop without venting the exhaust gases directly to the open air outside.

Victims of **carbon monoxide poisoning** can sometimes look healthy and pink-cheeked. This is because concentrations of carbon monoxide in the bloodstream give the blood a brighter red color than normal. Carbon monoxide binds much more easily than oxygen with hemoglobin, which is the blood component that carries life-giving oxygen around the body. As the hemoglobin becomes saturated with carbon monoxide, it becomes unable to carry oxygen. When the brain is starved of oxygen, the victim becomes unconscious, resulting in brain damage or death. Early signs of carbon monoxide poisoning include headaches, nausea, weakness, and irritability.

Since carbon monoxide is absorbed so easily by red blood cells, the following agencies set limits for the permissible exposure limit (PEL) for the workplace:

- OSHA PEL is 50 parts per million (ppm) for an 8-hour shift.
- The National Institute for Occupational Safety and Health (NIOSH) PEL is 35 ppm for an 8-hour shift with a ceiling of 200 ppm for any length of time.
- The American Conference of Governmental Industrial Hygienists (ACGIH) PEL is 25 ppm for an 8-hour shift and a 40-hour workweek.

Exposure levels of 400 ppm may be fatal in as little as 3 hours, and 6400 ppm may be fatal in as little as

30 minutes. As you can see, it doesn't take much carbon monoxide in the air to be hazardous. To further help you understand the smallness of the PELs, consider that 1% carbon monoxide equals 10,000 ppm of carbon monoxide. Vehicles with an emission-related problem can run perfectly well and still easily have carbon monoxide tailpipe readings between 3% and 5%, which equates to 30,000–50,000 ppm—more than 1000 times the allowable PELs given in the preceding list.

Safety

Be sure when working in a shop environment with a vehicle running that you provide adequate ventilation by using an exhaust extraction device (fan system and exhaust hoses designed to draw exhaust gases from the vehicle's exhaust pipe and push them outside of the shop). Small amounts of carbon monoxide can kill if proper ventilation is not provided.

Oxides of Nitrogen

Air that is drawn from the atmosphere into an engine contains almost 80% nitrogen, which is normally considered to be an inert gas. Under the high temperature and pressure of combustion, nitrogen may combine with oxygen to produce **oxides of nitrogen** FIGURE 40-5. Since nitrogen is inert, it is typically produced in large amounts only when combustion temperatures of around 2500°F (1400°C) and above occur. A lean mixture will result in higher oxides of nitrogen because lean mixtures burn faster than rich mixtures, resulting in an excessive combustion temperature. The increase of available oxygen can oxidize the nitrogen at those high temperatures.

Oxides of nitrogen are claimed to be major contributors to photochemical smog, along with hydrocarbons and sunlight. For example, the brown-looking cloud that often hangs over large cities is photochemical smog. Oxides of nitrogen irritate the eyes, nose, and throat. In extreme cases, such as regular exposure to high concentrations, coughing and lung damage can occur.

Sulfur Dioxide

Gasoline and diesel fuels contain sulfur as part of their chemical makeup. When sulfur burns in the combustion chamber, one sulfur molecule combines with two oxygen molecules, creating sulfur dioxide. Sulfur dioxide mixes with water vapor formed during the combustion process and produces sulfuric acid FIGURE 40-6. This corrosive compound is emitted into the atmosphere through the exhaust. Sulfuric acid is a major environmental pollutant, coming back to earth in contaminated rainwater, called acid rain. This acid rain has been responsible for degrading vast areas of arable land. As a result, the reduction or removal of sulfur from motor fuels has become a major part of most countries' vehicle emission control programs.

High sulfur levels in fuel, when combined with water vapor, can also cause corrosive wear on valve guides and cylinder liners, which can lead to premature engine failure. Using proper lubricants and draining oil at the correct intervals help combat this effect and reduce the degree of corrosive damage. Many manufacturers have been using stainless steel in their exhaust pipes and mufflers to help resist corrosion caused by sulfur in these components.

Sulfur reduces catalyst efficiency in modern vehicles, and vehicles operating with higher sulfur gasoline have higher emissions than vehicles operating on lower sulfur

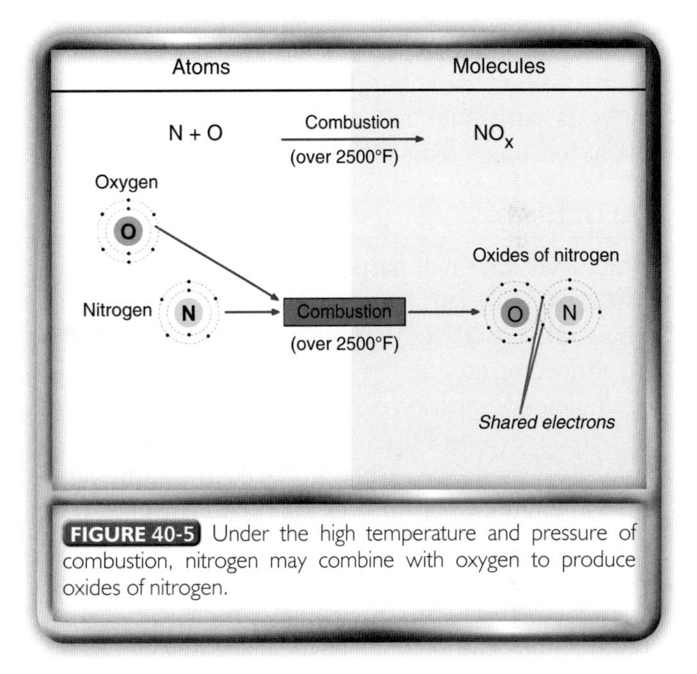
Atoms
Molecules
N + O
Combustion
(over 2500°F)
NOx
Oxygen
O
Oxides of nitrogen
Nitrogen
N
Combustion
(over 2500°F)
O
N
Shared electrons

FIGURE 40-5 Under the high temperature and pressure of combustion, nitrogen may combine with oxygen to produce oxides of nitrogen.

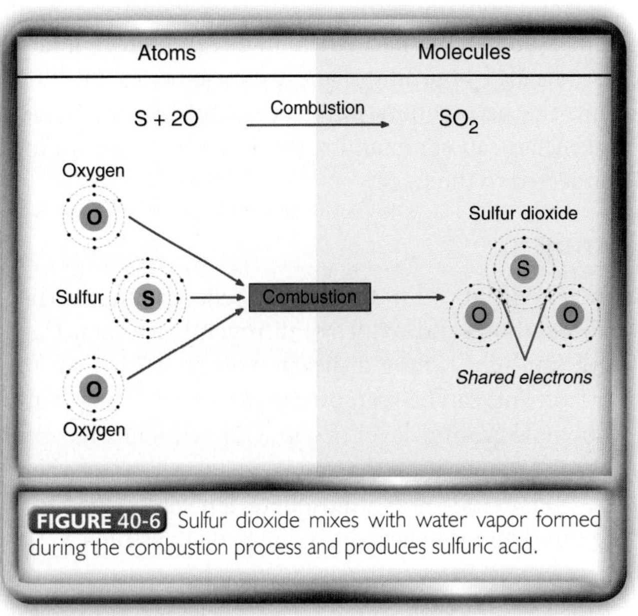
Atoms
Molecules
S + 2O
Combustion
SO2
Oxygen
O
Sulfur dioxide
S
Sulfur
S
Combustion
O
O
Shared electrons
O
Oxygen

FIGURE 40-6 Sulfur dioxide mixes with water vapor formed during the combustion process and produces sulfuric acid.

gasoline. There is evidence that in some instances, sulfur in gasoline may also degrade the performance of oxygen sensors, which may contribute to higher tailpipe emissions.

Although regulations have reduced the permissible levels of sulfur in fuel, there are some side effects from using low-sulfur diesel fuel. The refining process used to reduce the sulfur level can reduce the natural lubricating properties of the diesel fuel, which is essential for the lubrication and operation of fuel system components such as fuel pumps and injectors. These components either need to be manufactured with higher quality materials or special lubricants need to be used to provide the required level of protection.

To reduce the sulfur content, oil companies change the overall chemical composition of the fuel, which can affect fuel pump seals, engine seals, and O-rings, some of which react to changes in fuel composition by swelling or shrinking. This problem can be fixed by performing regular maintenance of the fuel system and by replacing the seals with ones made of materials that are less susceptible to swelling or shrinking.

Particulates

Particulates are small particles of solid matter that are suspended in the air. Particulates from modern engines are usually small particles of carbon **FIGURE 40-7**. In spark-ignition engines, particulates are caused by incomplete combustion of rich air–fuel mixtures. In this case, the hydrogen burns away from the hydrocarbon molecule, leaving the carbon by itself. In compression-ignition engines, particulates are caused by either too rich of a mixture or a poorly mixed air–fuel mixture. This produces very rich areas in the combustion chamber, even though the overall mixture could be very lean. Newer compression-ignition engines use a particulate filter to catch and hold the particulates in the exhaust stream. In some systems, the particulate filter can be regenerated periodically by burning off the carbon particles. The ECM controls the regeneration process automatically, or a technician can command regeneration with a scan tool connected to the ECM.

Smog

Smog is produced in the atmosphere when unburned hydrocarbons and oxides of nitrogen react chemically with sunlight. Smog appears reddish brown on the horizon and can be seen over major cities. Smog is also known as ground-level ozone. Ozone blocks harmful ultraviolet light from the sun in the upper atmosphere; however, in the lower atmosphere, it creates irritation of the lungs and is believed to contribute to asthma.

FIGURE 40-7 Particulates from modern engines are usually small particles of carbon.

Controlling Emissions

Manufacturers are relatively free to determine how they will meet the standards, as long as they do meet the standards. They design systems and processes that will effectively and cost efficiently meet the standards. There are a couple of strategies that manufacturers use. The first is to design the engine in such a way as to reduce emissions as much as possible, such as building turbulence-enhancing strategies and precisely controlling valve and spark timing. The second strategy is to closely control the air–fuel mixture under all driving conditions, thereby minimizing emission output. The third strategy is to warm up the engine as quickly as possible, as well as operate it at higher temperatures than older engines. The final strategy is to integrate precombustion and post-combustion add-on devices that are designed to further reduce emission output.

> **TECHNICIAN TIP**
>
> Manufacturers continue to produce cleaner and more efficient vehicles. Most vehicles will use similar emission controls; however, you should always refer to the service information for a description and operation of the emission system before attempting to diagnose or repair it.

Combustion

Since most emissions are by-products of combustion, accurately controlling combustion within the cylinders can minimize emission output. For fuel to burn efficiently, it needs to be fully evaporated and completely mixed with the right proportion of air. This is pretty easy to do in the controlled environment of a laboratory, but doing so repeatedly at a high rate of speed in very short periods of time under a huge variety of conditions is much more difficult. These are the conditions we are dealing with inside automotive combustion chambers. Thus, maintaining low emission output is a challenge and requires all of the engine's systems and components to be working properly for combustion to occur efficiently. In fact, a good general test that will tell you the overall condition of the engine and its control systems is an emission test. If the vehicle passes the emission test with clean results, that is a good indication that all of the engine systems and the engine itself are operating well.

Combustion Chamber Design

Combustion chamber design can affect the combustion process, which also affects the level of emissions. In the combustion chamber where surface temperatures are low, the combustion flame can be **quenched** FIGURE 40-8. The flame temperature drops so low in these areas that the flame goes out, or is quenched. Fuel left unburned in these zones is then exhausted as hydrocarbon and carbon monoxide emissions.

If the spark plug is positioned near the center of the combustion chamber so that the **flame front** travels evenly through the combustion chamber, combustion is more complete. The flame front is the rapid burning of the air–fuel mixture that moves outward from the spark plug across the cylinder. The flame front can be extinguished in cold areas of the cylinder, such as near the corner of the head and cylinder wall. Proper placement of the spark plug can help to minimize this effect.

The designs of intake ports and cylinder heads can aid in swirling mixtures as they travel to the combustion chamber. Swirling of the air and fuel helps to create a proper mixture of air and fuel vapors. If fuel does not stay in the air when being drawn into the combustion chamber, the mixture can fluctuate excessively and create drivability problems and excessive emissions, showing us how important proper movement of air is in the engine.

Gas flow rate affects the ability of air to hold fuel. Fast-moving air tends to hold fuel better than slow-moving air, which allows fuel to fall out of the airstream FIGURE 40-9. Fast-moving air more easily causes swirling of the air and fuel. Gas flow rate can be increased by the use of smaller intake ports. This design works well at keeping good airflow at low engine revolutions per minute (rpm). But at high rpm, it can restrict the airflow too much and reduce engine power. Some manufacturers overcome this problem by using two or more intake valves in each cylinder. With both valves open at high rpm, the overall size of the intake port opening is then increased and the gas flow rate increases. The more air that can flow into an engine, the more efficient that engine, and with better efficiency comes less emissions.

Changing valve timing also alters the combustion process. Reducing the valve overlap reduces the **scavenging effect**, which is when the exhaust gases moving out of the combustion chamber create a low-pressure area in the exhaust manifold, helping to pull air and fuel into the cylinder. If the valve overlap is excessive, unburned air and fuel can be pulled out of the exhaust valve, which will increase hydrocarbon emissions.

FIGURE 40-8 Quench areas in a combustion chamber.

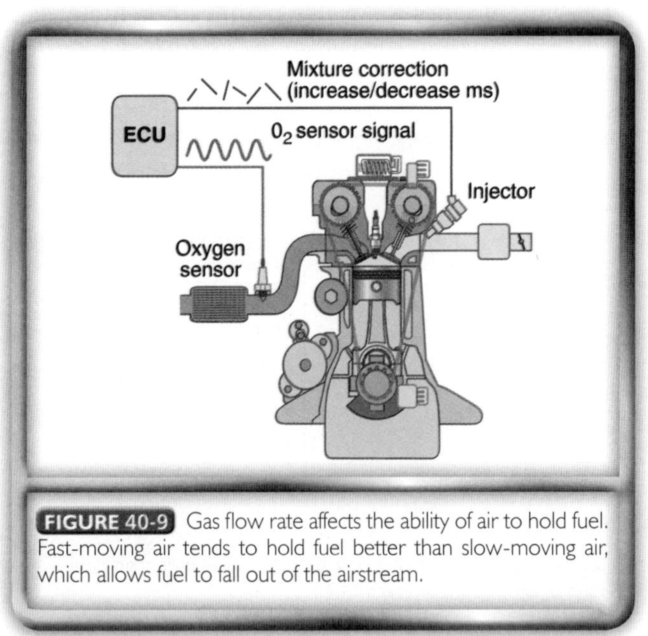
Mixture correction
(increase/decrease ms)
ECU
0_2 sensor signal
Injector
Oxygen
sensor

FIGURE 40-9 Gas flow rate affects the ability of air to hold fuel. Fast-moving air tends to hold fuel better than slow-moving air, which allows fuel to fall out of the airstream.

Stoichiometric Ratio

The stoichiometric ratio, also referred to as lambda, is the ratio of air to fuel at which all of the oxygen in the air and all of the fuel are completely burned. As you can imagine, complete combustion reduces hydrocarbons and carbon monoxide. The typical stoichiometric ratio for gasoline is 14.7:1 (14.7 parts air to 1 part gasoline by weight or mass). This ratio equates to a lambda reading of 1.0. Each fuel has its own stoichiometric ratio TABLE 40-2. As the air–fuel ratio moves away from the stoichiometric point, the hydrocarbons and carbon monoxide emissions increase. Maintaining close control of the air–fuel ratio allows an engine to run cleaner than ever. In many cases, precise control of the air–fuel ratio has made the job of hydrocarbon and carbon monoxide emission control devices much easier since they are dealing with much smaller volumes of the pollutants.

A rich condition means more fuel is introduced than the engine can completely burn. This is anything lower (richer) than 14.7:1 or less than 1.0 lambda. When this condition occurs, hydrocarbons can only partially burn because of the lack of oxygen. This rich condition creates large amounts of carbon monoxide. If excessively rich, some of the hydrocarbons will not burn at all, leaving hydrocarbons to pass through the engine unburned. Elevated amounts of carbon monoxide in the exhaust are a good indicator that the engine is running rich.

A lean condition means more air is introduced than the engine can completely burn. This is anything above (leaner than) 14.7:1 or greater than 1.0 lambda. When this condition occurs, not all of the hydrocarbons burn because the flame cannot reach some of the hydrocarbon molecules due to the excessive amount of oxygen and nitrogen molecules. Thus, the hydrocarbon molecules are pushed out of the exhaust pipe unburned. Elevated hydrocarbon readings (with low carbon monoxide readings) are a good indicator of a lean condition.

Carbon dioxide is a good indicator of whether the fuel is burning completely. For example, high readings of 12% to 15% of carbon dioxide in the exhaust indicate proper combustion efficiency. A smaller percentage of carbon dioxide in the exhaust indicates that combustion is not complete, indicating a rich or lean mixture, ignition problems, lowered compression, or exhaust system leak.

TABLE 40-2: Stoichiometric Ratios for Various Fuel Types

Fuel Types	Stoichiometric Ratio
Gasoline	14.7
No. 2 Diesel	14.7
Methanol	6.45
Ethanol	9.00
Propane	15.7
Compressed Natural Gas	17.2
Hydrogen	34.3

Source: Department of Energy website. Stoichiometric ratio is the ratio of air to fuel, expressed 14.7:1.

> **TECHNICIAN TIP**
>
> Carbon dioxide is a gas that manufacturers are trying to reduce. It is believed to contribute to global warming, and laws are underway that will require manufacturers to reduce its creation. Some of the ways that carbon dioxide can be reduced is by making vehicles smaller, lighter, and more aerodynamic; using smaller, more fuel-efficient engines; and using technology to shut down the engine when the vehicle is decelerating or stopped at a stop light.

Controlling Air–Fuel Ratios

Precise control of the air–fuel ratio is one of the main strategies for minimizing a vehicle's emission output. Keeping the air–fuel ratio close to the stoichiometric point produces minimal hydrocarbon and carbon monoxide emissions. Electronic fuel injection and engine management systems can adjust the air–fuel mixture within certain limits as parts wear and thereby maintain proper control of the air–fuel ratio over a broad range of conditions. These systems closely control the air–fuel ratio entering each cylinder and ensure the ignition timing matches operating conditions. Sensors around the engine send information about airflow, coolant temperature, throttle position, engine speed, and other inputs to the ECM. The ECM uses this information to set fuel and ignition settings, which change as sensor data change. The ECM has a programmed memory that works like a reference chart. The manufacturer's engineers program the ECM to constantly adjust the fuel and spark depending on the values received from the sensors. For example, as airflow rises, the fuel increases proportionately.

Fuel delivery is controlled by the fuel injector. The typical fuel injector is simply an electric solenoid. When electrical current flows in the fuel injector winding, a magnetic field is produced (electromagnet), causing the fuel injector to open and allow fuel to flow through it into the intake manifold. The ECM (or power train control module [PCM]) opens the fuel injector for a longer or shorter period of time, creating more or less fuel delivery. The longer the fuel is delivered, the richer the mixture, and vice versa.

Changes in operating conditions can change mixture conditions. For instance, if an engine is being driven at moderate speed and the throttle is suddenly closed, any fuel condensed on the intake manifold walls or intake port of the cylinder head will be drawn into the cylinders. A smaller amount of air moves into the combustion chamber with the throttle plates closed, so turbulence tends to be poor, which can lead to incomplete combustion and the release of unburned gases into the exhaust.

TECHNICIAN TIP

The pulse width of the fuel injector is a piece of data that can be read on a scan tool or lab scope to assist the technician in testing fuel delivery. The pulse width is the amount of time the fuel injector is turned on and fuel is sprayed into the intake manifold. It is measured in milliseconds. The longer the pulse width, the more fuel is delivered to the engine.

To reduce this effect, the ECM detects that the throttle is being closed through the use of the throttle position sensor (TPS) and will reduce the fuel spray by reducing the on time of the injectors. If the engine is being used to slow the vehicle, the injectors can be completely shut off to save fuel and reduce pollution. This is called fuel cutoff mode. Newer engines with electronic throttle control can move the throttle plate independent of driver input. This feature allows the computer to control the throttle opening as well as the fuel injection pulse width to create a proper mixture during all driving conditions.

Precombustion/Postcombustion Treatment

The pollution emitted from the internal combustion engine can be reduced by taking actions both prior to combustion and after combustion. Precombustion treatment focuses on assuring that combustion happens in a controlled and complete manner that minimizes postcombustion pollutant gases. There are two primary precombustion emission control systems: the heated air intake system and the exhaust gas recirculation system. The heated air intake system was used on throttle body–injected (and carbureted) engines. It was designed to keep the air entering the engine at a constant temperature of approximately 100–110°F (38–43°C) to help vaporize the fuel in the intake manifold. The better vaporized the fuel, the more likely it could be distributed evenly within the air, and the cleaner the combustion gases. This system will be discussed further in the Emission Control Systems section.

Most port fuel injection systems do not need a heated air intake system because the fuel is sprayed into the intake manifold right next to the intake valve. The injector sprays a fine mist of fuel, which is easier to vaporize. Plus it does not have to sit or travel along a cold intake manifold where it can condense out of the air. Most new vehicles monitor the intake air temperature and use that to determine the mass of the air entering the engine and therefore know exactly how much fuel to inject.

The second precombustion emission control system is the exhaust gas recirculation system. This system recirculates some of the inert exhaust gases back into the intake manifold when combustion temperatures are high enough to create oxides of nitrogen. The inert gases help lower peak combustion temperatures below the threshold at which oxides of nitrogen are created. Exhaust gas recirculation systems will be covered in greater depth in the following Emission Control Systems section.

Postcombustion emission control systems deal with the remaining pollutants that are left over from the combustion process. There are two primary postcombustion systems: the secondary air injection system and the catalyst system. The secondary air injection system helps to complete the burning of hot hydrocarbons and carbon monoxide in the exhaust system by adding oxygen to the exhaust stream. The oxygen in the air reacts with the hydrocarbons and carbon monoxide and converts them to carbon dioxide and water.

The catalyst system reduces oxides of nitrogen back into nitrogen and oxygen and oxidizes hydrocarbons and carbon monoxide. Both of these systems help reduce tailpipe emissions to near zero if the engine and all of the systems are operating as designed. Both of these systems are covered in greater depth in the following section.

Emission Control Systems

Emission control systems have been created by manufacturers to minimize the amount of pollution released into the atmosphere from a vehicle and its internal combustion engine. Before the days of emission control systems, vehicles and engines produced very large amounts of pollutants, as evidenced by the number of smog days in many big cities. Even though there are now many more vehicles and many more miles driven, the number of pollution days in a year has been reduced substantially and continues to decline in most areas.

One of the earliest control devices was the positive crankcase ventilation (PCV) system. The system was first used around 1961 and later became a mandatory emissions device. PCV systems stop the release of hydrocarbons from the crankcase of the engine to the atmosphere. Another control device is the evaporative control system, known as the EVAP system. This system was used beginning around 1972 and later became a mandatory emission system. It is used to stop the release of hydrocarbons from the fuel tank to the atmosphere.

Exhaust gas recirculation (EGR) systems began to appear on the automobile around 1972 and became a mandatory part of emission controls. These systems control the release of oxides of nitrogen to the atmosphere by controlling the temperature of the combustion process. The use of a system called secondary air injection began in the late 1960s to limit hydrocarbon release from the engine during cold engine operation. The system injects air into the exhaust stream to mix with the hydrocarbons and aid in the conversion process as the exhaust exits the combustion chambers. Catalytic converters found their way onto the automobile around 1973. Catalytic convertors are used to reduce remaining pollutants in the exhaust stream before they leave the tailpipe. As catalytic converters were introduced, leaded gas was phased out. Lead in the gas would contaminate (coat) the catalyst in the convertor and render it inoperative.

Catalytic Converters

Catalytic converters are a primary emission control device. They perform a final cleanup of the tailpipe emissions on a properly running engine equipped with functioning emission control systems. Catalytic converters are not designed to handle the emission output of a poorly running engine or one with faulty emission control systems. Catalytic converters create heat as they convert harmful gases into less harmful gases. Forcing converters to deal with more gases than they are designed to handle can cause them to overheat. In some cases, they may even melt down internally, which ruins them.

Catalytic converters use a base structure of ceramic material coated with precious metals to react with and break up or combine gases in the exhaust system FIGURE 40-10. The term catalyst refers to a material that causes a chemical reaction without itself being consumed or changed in the reaction. Specific precious metals have the ability to act as a catalyst that can convert harmful exhaust gases to nonharmful or less harmful gases. Catalytic converters come in two types: oxidizing and reduction. Each type is used to react with particular gases.

The reduction catalyst contains a platinum and rhodium coating, which helps to reduce the oxides of nitrogen molecules into their base compounds. When a nitric oxide or nitrogen dioxide molecule comes into contact with the catalyst coating, the coating strips the nitrogen atom out of the molecule and retains it. This frees up the one or two oxygen atoms in the molecule, which combine in pairs to form molecules of oxygen. The nitrogen atoms bond with other nitrogen atoms that are retained in the catalyst and form molecules of nitrogen; thus, two molecules of nitric oxide become one molecule of nitrogen and one molecule of oxygen, or two molecules of nitrogen dioxide become one molecule of nitrogen and two molecules of oxygen FIGURE 40-11.

The second type of catalyst is the oxidizing catalyst. It oxidizes any unburned hydrocarbons and carbon monoxide as they travel over the platinum and palladium coating. This aids the reaction of the carbon monoxide and hydrocarbons with any remaining oxygen in the

FIGURE 40-10 Catalytic converters use a base structure of ceramic material coated with precious metals to react with and break up or combine gases in the exhaust system.

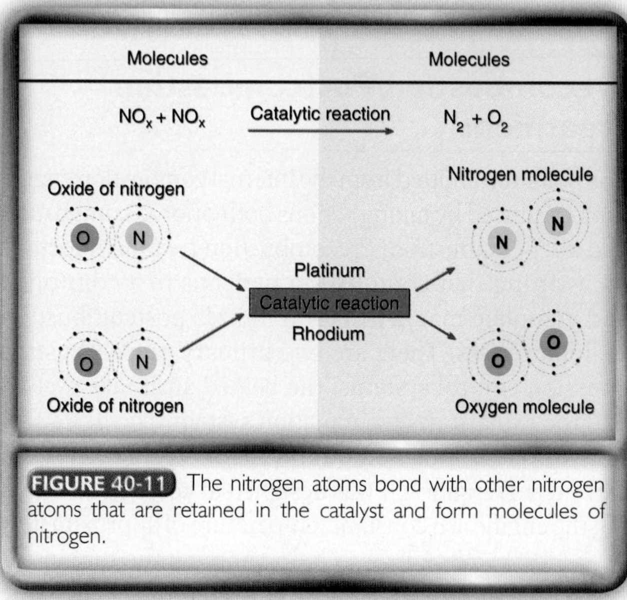
Molecules
Molecules
$NO_x + NO_x$
Catalytic reaction
$N_2 + O_2$
Oxide of nitrogen
Nitrogen molecule
O
N
N
N
Platinum
Catalytic reaction
Rhodium
O
N
O
O
Oxide of nitrogen
Oxygen molecule

FIGURE 40-11 The nitrogen atoms bond with other nitrogen atoms that are retained in the catalyst and form molecules of nitrogen.

exhaust gas FIGURE 40-12. Each carbon monoxide (CO) molecule combines with an oxygen (O) molecule to make one less-harmful carbon dioxide (CO_2) molecule. And two hydrogen (H) atoms combine with one oxygen (O) molecule to form one nonharmful water (H_2O) molecule.

Catalytic converters are referred to as either two-way or three-way catalytic converters. The **two-way catalytic converter** was the first type of catalytic converter designed. The two-way catalytic converter is an oxidizing catalyst and is named because it converts two gases, hydrocarbons and carbon monoxide, to carbon dioxide and water. The early two-way catalytic converters used a bed of catalytic pellets (pellet-style converter) that the exhaust passed through. More recent versions of the two-way (and three-way) catalytic converters are designed with a honeycomb catalytic element. The honeycomb structure provides long narrow passageways for the exhaust gases to flow through, which ultimately helps the gases to come in contact with the catalyst materials on the sides of the honeycomb walls. This contact between the gases and the catalyst promote oxidation of the hydrocarbons and carbon monoxide once the catalyst reaches its operating temperature.

Safety

Catalytic converters must be above approximately 500°F (260°C) to begin conversion. Typically, they operate at 900–1600°F (482–871°C). Catalytic converters can cause serious burns, so use gloves and heat protection sleeves when working around a hot catalytic converter.

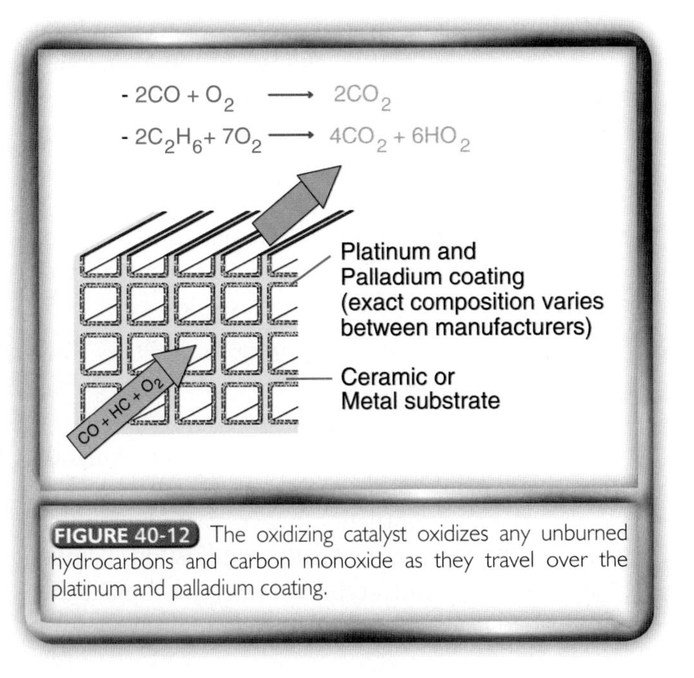

- 2CO + O2 → 2CO2
- 2C2H6+ 7O2 → 4CO2 + 6HO2
Platinum and Palladium coating (exact composition varies between manufacturers)
Ceramic or Metal substrate
CO + HC + O2

FIGURE 40-12 The oxidizing catalyst oxidizes any unburned hydrocarbons and carbon monoxide as they travel over the platinum and palladium coating.

TECHNICIAN TIP

Catalytic converters may contain rhodium, palladium, platinum, or cerium. These materials are more valuable than gold and should be recycled. Catalytic converters have become a target for thieves, who cut them out of the exhaust system while a vehicle is in a parking lot or driveway.

Modern vehicles operating on petroleum-based fuels are fitted with three-way catalytic converters. **Three-way catalytic converters** contain both a reduction catalyst and an oxidizing catalyst. The term three-way is in relation to the three regulated emissions the three-way catalytic converter is designed to convert: carbon monoxide, hydrocarbons, and oxides of nitrogen. The reduction catalyst is in front and converts the oxides of nitrogen, nitric oxide, and nitrogen dioxide back into harmless nitrogen and oxygen molecules. The oxidizing catalyst then uses the oxygen from the reduction catalyst to oxidize the hydrocarbons and carbon monoxide into water and carbon dioxide.

Because of strict emission requirements, vehicles with three-way catalytic converters require a feedback system on the fuel system. The ECM monitors the oxygen content in the exhaust stream by using an exhaust gas oxygen (EGO) sensor, also known as a lambda sensor, mounted in the exhaust manifold. This sensor tells the engine computer how much oxygen is in the exhaust. The computer uses this information to control the pulse width of the fuel injectors.

The ECU can increase or decrease the amount of oxygen in the exhaust by adjusting the air–fuel ratio. The ECU ensures that the air–fuel ratio cycles at close to the stoichiometric point in normal driving conditions. This ensures that there is always sufficient oxygen in the exhaust system to allow the oxidization catalyst to deal with unburned hydrocarbons and carbon monoxide.

TECHNICIAN TIP

Each style of catalytic converter is designed for a specific vehicle; one size does not fit all. A converter intended for the treatment of a four-cylinder engine will not be efficient on an eight-cylinder engine. Be sure to install the correct catalytic converter in the correct vehicle. Always check the manufacturer's specifications before making a repair. Be careful with aftermarket catalytic converters, which may not use as much catalyst agent (precious metals) as the emission system requires.

Applied Science

AS-89: Catalytic Converter: The technician can explain the principles by which a catalytic converter modifies emission gases at the atomic level to provide a lower level of HC, CO, and NO_x in the final exhaust. One of the greatest emission devices to be installed on vehicles is the catalytic converter. This component will last for the life of the vehicle if given proper care. Proper care for the converter would include maintaining the engine according to the manufacturer's service information. If the engine is operating normally, the converter won't have to work hard to accomplish its task. Catalytic converters are designed to provide control of hydrocarbons (HC), carbon monoxide (CO), and oxides of nitrogen (NO_x). Emissions are passed through the converters catalytic inlaid materials. Catalytic converter's may contain materials such as rhodium, palladium, platinum, or cerium. All of these special materials are considered to be precious metals. The reduction catalyst is in front and converts the oxides of nitrogen, nitric oxide, and nitrogen dioxide back into harmless nitrogen and oxygen molecules. The oxidizing catalyst then uses the oxygen from the reduction catalyst to oxidize the hydrocarbons and carbon monoxide into water and carbon dioxide.

A catalytic converter can be checked with an infrared noncontact thermometer. The outlet temperature should be 30 to 100 degrees higher than the inlet temperature at 2,500 rpm. There are several other tests that can be performed to verify that the catalytic converter is working properly. The manufacturer's service information should be consulted for more details.

Catalyst Monitoring

Any vehicle produced after 1996 monitors catalyst efficiency by using two oxygen sensors **FIGURE 40-13**. One oxygen sensor is in front of the catalytic converter, as in the past, and indicates the amount of oxygen in the exhaust stream as it leaves the cylinders. The reading from this sensor normally toggles rich and lean as the ECM is controlling the air–fuel ratio. The second oxygen sensor is located after the catalytic converter and measures the oxygen in the exhaust stream after it leaves the catalytic converter. Since the converter uses oxygen to oxidize the hydrocarbons and carbon monoxide, the oxygen content is normally lower after the converter and results in a higher and steadier oxygen sensor voltage. The catalyst monitor tracks both oxygen sensor readings to ensure that the gases are being effectively converted by the catalytic converter. As the catalytic converter fails, the rear sensor tends to track the oscillations of the front oxygen sensor. The ECM monitors these two oxygen sensor signals and will turn on the MIL and set a DTC once the catalyst efficiency degrades to a predetermined point.

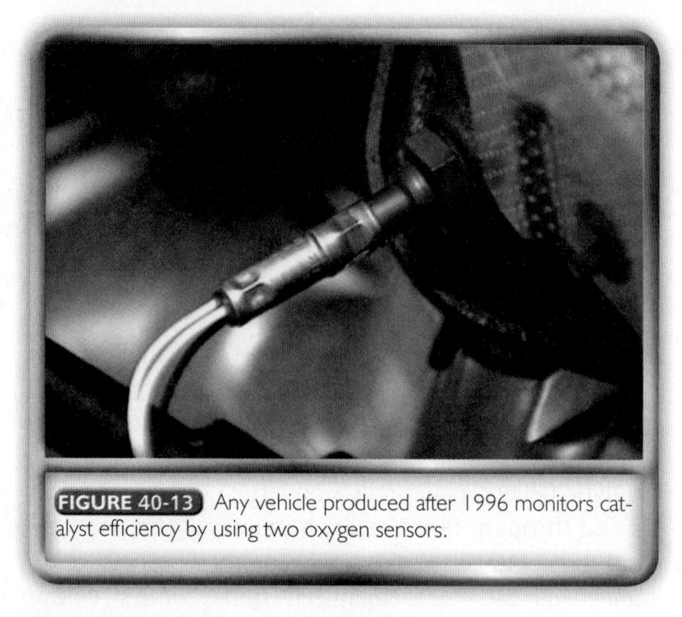

FIGURE 40-13 Any vehicle produced after 1996 monitors catalyst efficiency by using two oxygen sensors.

Crankcase Emission Control

While the engine is running, some gases from the combustion chamber leak past the piston rings and the cylinder walls, down into the crankcase. This leakage is called **blow-by**. To prevent pressure buildup during operation, the crankcase must be ventilated. Unburned fuel (hydrocarbons) and water from condensation also find their way into the crankcase and sump. When the engine reaches its full operating temperature, the water and fuel in the crankcase evaporate. In older vehicles, crankcase vapors were vented directly to the atmosphere through a **breather tube** or road-draft tube. It was shaped so that air flowing past it while the vehicle was being driven helped draw the vapors from the crankcase. This resulted in blow-by gases being vented directly to the atmosphere.

Modern vehicles are required to direct crankcase blow-by gases and vapors back into the intake manifold where they can be returned to the combustion chamber to be burned. A common method of directing gases and vapors back to the intake is through the emission control system called the **positive crankcase ventilation (PCV)** system **FIGURE 40-14**. The PCV system regulates the flow of blow-by gases between the crankcase and the intake manifold.

Types of PCV Systems

There are three main types of PCV systems: **variable orifice**, **fixed orifice**, and **separator** type. All three types do the same job—ventilate blow-by gases back to the intake manifold to be burned in the combustion chamber.

In a variable-orifice type of system, a replaceable, spring-loaded **PCV valve** regulates gas flow. The position

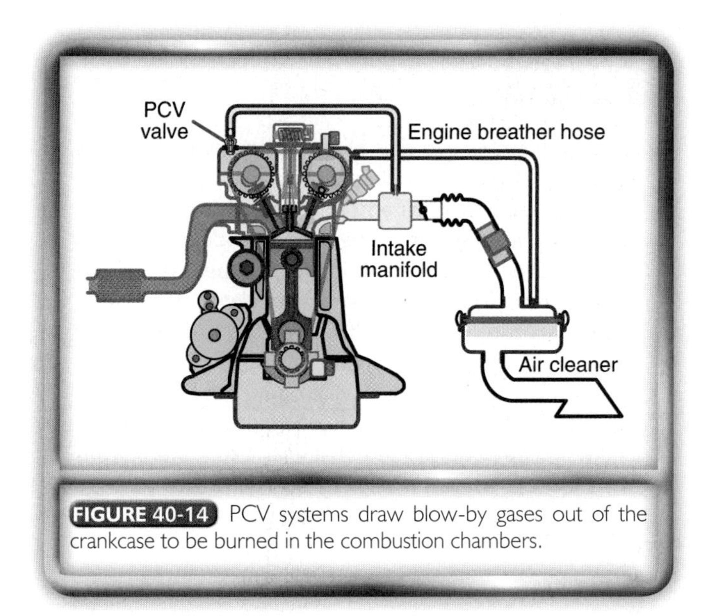
PCV valve
Engine breather hose
Intake manifold
Air cleaner

FIGURE 40-14 PCV systems draw blow-by gases out of the crankcase to be burned in the combustion chambers.

of the PCV valve is controlled by the pressure in the manifold. With the engine off, the spring holds the PCV valve in the closed position, and air cannot enter the inlet manifold. This allows the engine to start. At idle, intake manifold pressure draws the PCV valve to the other end of the PCV valve's housing, where it allows only a small, measured amount of gases and air past the PCV valve. At wider throttle openings, the PCV valve plunger position allows maximum flow through the PCV valve's housing, which gives maximum crankcase ventilation and tends to match the higher amount of blow-by gases under that condition.

The PCV system is designed to remove more air than just blow-by gases, so there should almost always be more ventilation capacity than the amount of blow-by. The additional air that the system removes comes from a fresh air intake hose or tube, usually attached to the air cleaner assembly. The fresh air intake hose directs filtered air to one side or end of the crankcase. This intake point is usually as far as possible from the PCV valve to ensure that as much of the blow-by gases are pulled from the crankcase as possible, giving good ventilation.

The PCV system has two main purposes, to remove blow-by gases from the crankcase in a manner that is not harmful to the environment and to prevent a buildup of pressure in the crankcase. Modern PCV systems are of the closed (sealed) type. This means both ends of the PCV system are connected to the intake system. The PCV valve is connected directly to the intake manifold below the throttle plate, while the fresh air hose is connected to the air intake above the throttle plate. Having a closed system means any gases that cannot be handled through the vacuum side of the system are directed back through the fresh air connection to the air cleaner assembly, where they are drawn into the intake airstream, and burned in the combustion chamber.

The fixed-orifice type of PCV system usually involves a screw-in fitting with a small hole drilled in it. The hole creates a predetermined vacuum leak that draws a predetermined amount of crankcase vapors from the crankcase. Engineers have factored the vacuum leak into the engine management system to ensure the correct air–fuel mixture. The fixed orifice is typically mounted on or in the intake manifold.

The separator type of PCV system involves a valve that is hooked to the pressure side of the crankcase, an oil return line at the bottom of the valve, and a suction line on the other side. Oil that is mixed with blow-by gases enters the separator, and the heavy oil tends to fall out of the mixture to the bottom of the valve and return to the crankcase. The separator type is used on turbocharged applications since turbocharged systems pressurize the intake system and would close off a standard PCV valve.

Common PCV Failures

PCV failures can occur and potentially create drivability problems for the customer. The most common problem is when the PCV system has a vacuum leak. The hose connecting the PCV valve to the intake manifold can crack and create a vacuum leak. Vacuum leaks tend to cause a lean air–fuel mixture and create a rough idle, which is most noticeable while the vehicle is stopped at a stop light.

PCV systems can also become clogged. Over time, especially if the vehicle's oil changes are neglected, the PCV valve or hose can plug up with sludge. If this happens, the PCV system cannot ventilate the crankcase and blow-by gases will contaminate the oil further, which creates more sludge throughout the engine. Another common failure from a clogged PCV valve or hose is oil being pushed up into the housing. If oil is found in the air filter housing, the PCV system is either being overwhelmed by the blow-by gases (the piston rings are worn out), or the suction side of the PCV system is clogged/restricted. This causes the pressure to build up in the crankcase, which then forces oil mist up the fresh air hose to the air cleaner housing. In this case, check that there is strong vacuum present at the PCV valve when the engine is idling and that the valve is not restricted. Also test the crankcase pressure using a blow-by gauge.

Repeat engine oil leaks may be the result of excessive pressure in the crankcase. If this pressure cannot be removed, it will continue to build and eventually either push oil past the seals or in some cases even push oil seals and gaskets out of position, causing an oil leak. In the event of multiple gasket or seal failures or repeat failures, be sure to check that the PCV system is operating correctly by testing for the proper PCV system flow.

Exhaust Gas Recirculation System

The **exhaust gas recirculation (EGR) system** was designed by automotive engineers in the 1970s to control the emission of oxides of nitrogen. Nitrogen is oxidized in large amounts once combustion temperatures reach approximately 2500°F (1371°C) FIGURE 40-15. This temperature is reached when the vehicle is under moderate to heavy loads and the air–fuel ratio is at stoichiometric or leaner. EGR systems were designed to operate during those times. As with all vehicle technology, EGR systems have evolved over time, and some newer engines use variable valve timing to draw some exhaust gases back into the cylinder through the exhaust valve, which is held open a little longer than typical.

> **TECHNICIAN TIP**
>
> Many people believe that all emission control devices kill engine power and use extra gasoline. While there may have been a small amount of truth to that when some of the systems were first introduced, that is almost never the case any longer. In the case of the EGR system, exhaust gases are recirculated only during partial throttle operation. If any power is lost at that time, the throttle can be opened slightly to make up for it. And when the throttle is wide open, the EGR system does not operate, so there is no impact at that time. Lastly, it could be argued that the extra inert gases from the EGR system help maintain a higher average cylinder pressure, which makes up for less air–fuel entering the cylinder.

Purpose and Operation

An **EGR valve** connects the exhaust port, or manifold, and the intake manifold FIGURE 40-16. If engine operating conditions are likely to produce oxides of nitrogen, the EGR valve opens, letting some burned exhaust gases pass from the exhaust into the intake system. During combustion, an amount of fresh air–fuel mixture is displaced by inert exhaust gases that do three things. First, they make it so there is not quite as much burnable mixture, which helps keep the temperature from rising as high as it otherwise would. Second, since they are inert and mix thoroughly with the rest of the air–fuel mixture, they cause the mixture to burn a bit slower, and therefore cooler, as the flame front must travel farther to burn around the inert molecules. Third, the inert gases absorb some of the heat of the burning gases. These three situations lower the peak combustion temperature, thus reducing the formation of the oxides of nitrogen.

The EGR valve can open only under the conditions that create oxides of nitrogen. Since oxides of nitrogen are not created in a cold engine, the EGR valve is unable to open until after the engine achieves its normal operating temperature. Another situation where the combustion temperatures are low is when the vehicle is at or near idle. The EGR valve does not operate at idle because there is only a small amount of air–fuel mixture being burned, so the combustion temperature is well below 2500°F (1371°C). There is one condition when oxides of nitrogen are being created in large amounts and the EGR valve does not operate: when the vehicle is operated at WOT.

FIGURE 40-15 The exhaust gas recirculation (EGR) system was designed by automotive engineers in the 1970s to control the emission of oxides of nitrogen. Nitrogen is oxidized in large amounts once combustion temperatures reach approximately 2500°F (1371°C).

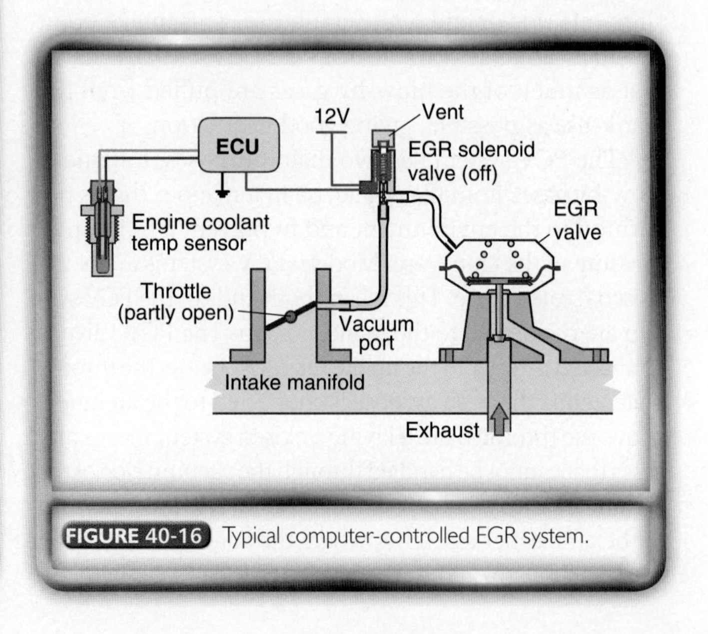
12V
Vent
ECU
EGR solenoid valve (off)
EGR valve
Engine coolant temp sensor
Throttle (partly open)
Vacuum port
Intake manifold
Exhaust

FIGURE 40-16 Typical computer-controlled EGR system.

> **TECHNICIAN TIP**
>
> In the combustion chamber, higher combustion temperatures tend to create more power. But high temperatures also create very high amounts of oxides of nitrogen. One way to overcome this is by understanding the difference between high peak-combustion temperature and high average-combustion temperature. High peak temperatures last for a very small time. While they produce a sharp spike in pressure, it does not last long and tends to give a hammer blow to the piston, which is not very effective in pushing it down the cylinder. The high average-combustion temperature maintains high average pressure, which is good for a longer, smoother push of the piston. It produces good power while minimizing the creation of oxides of nitrogen.

In this condition, the EGR system is shut off so that full engine power is available for emergency needs such as avoiding an accident. But most passenger vehicles do not operate very often or for very long at WOT, so the overall amount of oxides of nitrogen created is not substantial.

Some manufacturers have been able to accomplish the same reduction in oxides of nitrogen by using variable valve timing on their engines instead of the traditional EGR system. In situations where oxides of nitrogen can be created, the ECM retards the exhaust camshaft so that the exhaust valves are held open during the first part of the intake **stroke**. As the piston moves down slightly, the lower cylinder pressure pulls some of the exhaust gases back into the combustion chamber. These exhaust gases are used to dilute the air–fuel mixture with inert gases just like an external EGR system does. In this case, the ECM controls how long the exhaust valve remains open, which then affects the amount of exhaust gases that are retained in the cylinder. This is sometimes referred to as an internal EGR system, and the beauty is that it uses only the variable valve timing components, which are used for other fuel economy and drivability reasons. So there are fewer components to install and go bad.

Computer Monitoring Strategies

With the introduction of OBDII, monitoring of the EGR system was made mandatory by the EPA, and each manufacturer became responsible for ensuring its system runs a self-test to verify it is operating correctly. The test is called an **EGR system monitor**. The ECM will run a test of the system to ensure that it is working properly. Preprogrammed conditions must be met prior to the monitor running; for example, the engine temperature, throttle position, and vehicle speed all must be within certain parameters. Also, other system monitor tests, such as the catalyst efficiency monitor or oxygen sensor monitor, may need to have passed prior to the running of the EGR system monitor test.

Manufacturers have slightly different monitoring strategies for the EGR system. But once the parameters for running the monitor are met, all of the manufacturers have the ECM command the EGR valve to open and then watch for a sensor to report an expected change. This expected change could be an increased temperature of the EGR flow while the EGR valve is open as measured by a temperature sensor in the EGR passageway **FIGURE 40-17**. Or, it could be a certain amount of pressure drop in the intake manifold as measured by the MAP sensor when the EGR valve opens. Or, it could be the reduction in exhaust oxygen as measured by the oxygen sensor while the EGR valve is open. Another system uses a differential pressure sensor to measure the pressure drop of exhaust gases flowing through a restriction in the EGR passageway. Regardless of the type of monitoring, if the ECM sees a result that is outside of its expected readings, it will illuminate the MIL, set a DTC, and store freeze-frame data in the ECM memory.

> **TECHNICIAN TIP**
>
> It is important to know that the results of monitor tests are erased when DTCs are cleared. Since it can take days, weeks, or in some cases months for the monitors to run, it may be prudent to leave any DTCs in memory and let the ECM turn off the MIL once you have completed the repairs on the vehicle.

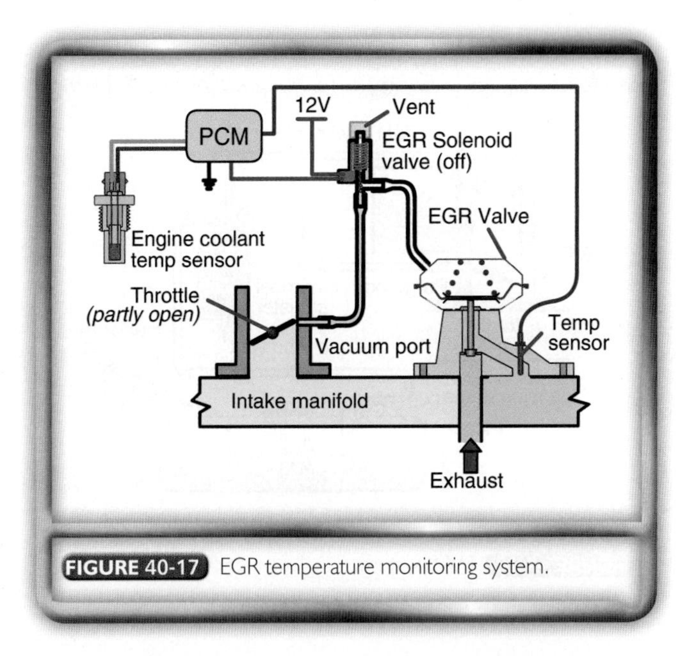
12V
Vent
PCM
EGR Solenoid valve (off)
EGR Valve
Engine coolant temp sensor
Throttle (partly open)
Vacuum port
Temp sensor
Intake manifold
Exhaust

FIGURE 40-17 EGR temperature monitoring system.

Evaporative Emission Control

The **evaporative emission (EVAP) system** is designed to ensure that hydrocarbons are not released into the atmosphere when fuel in the fuel tank begins to vaporize and build pressure. The EVAP system uses a charcoal canister and a series of hoses and valves to capture the hydrocarbon vapors that would normally be lost from the fuel tank and then deliver them to the intake manifold to be burned in the engine's combustion chambers FIGURE 40-18. The EVAP system stores the fuel vapors in the charcoal canister until the ECM determines they can be burned in the engine without affecting the drivability of the vehicle. Once the ECM determines that the conditions are right for burning off of the vapors, it will control the amount of vapors being released to the engine. The EVAP system also incorporates a monitoring system to ensure that there are no leaks in the fuel storage system, as well as verify that the vapors are being delivered, as designed, to be burned.

Computer Monitoring Strategies in the EVAP System

The EVAP system monitoring is a bit different from the other emission control monitors. EVAP monitoring is required not only to detect faults that prevent proper purging of the canister but also to detect any leaks greater than 0.020" (0.51 mm) in the system. Manufacturers are free to design their own monitoring systems as long as the system can accurately detect the minimum specified fault. Because manufacturers have the ability to design their own systems, there is a wide variety of strategies and components used by the manufacturers. We will explore some of the more common strategies in this section.

In some cases, manufacturers use dedicated sensors such as a **purge switch**, which is located in the purge line and senses the flow of gases or the pressure drop caused by the flow of gases that are being purged FIGURE 40-19. The purge switch then signals the ECM that purge is actually happening. Other EVAP monitoring strategies use the oxygen sensors to measure the decrease in exhaust oxygen content when the EVAP system is being purged. Another method is to accurately calculate the amount of fuel vapor in the purged gases by using the fuel trim correction data during purge.

Newer EVAP systems monitor purge operation by reading a **fuel tank pressure sensor**. The ECM system closes the **vent solenoid**, which seals off the EVAP system from outside air. The purge valve is opened to allow manifold vacuum to pull a vacuum on the system. If the purge system is operating correctly, the fuel tank pressure sensor will report an increase in vacuum that is within the specified pressure and time factors for the conditions currently present in that vehicle FIGURE 40-20. If the system passes the purge test, the ECM commands the purge valve to close, thus sealing off the EVAP system from manifold vacuum. Since the vent solenoid is still closed, the EVAP system is completely sealed. The ECM monitors the fuel tank pressure sensor for a set time and looks for any loss of vacuum. If noted, the ECM will set a DTC based on the calculated size of the leak. The ECM is required to detect leaks as small as 0.020" (0.51 mm) (small leak). Larger leaks will set a separate DTC.

Secondary Air Injection

Secondary air injection is less common now than it was in previous years. There are several reasons for this. The first reason is improved engine design, which causes the

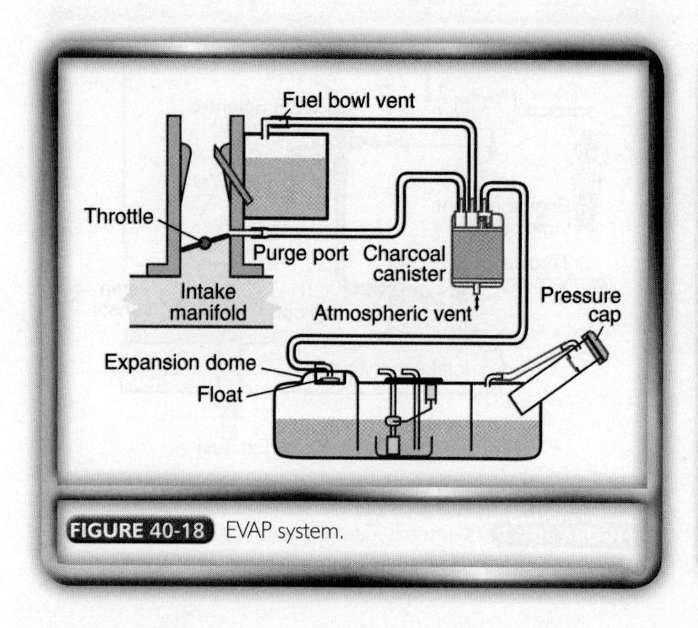
Fuel bowl vent
Throttle
Purge port
Charcoal canister
Intake manifold
Atmospheric vent
Pressure cap
Expansion dome
Float

FIGURE 40-18 EVAP system.

FUEL
FLAMMABLE
CAUTION

FIGURE 40-19 Purge switch.

engine to warm up much quicker and therefore emit fewer emissions. Improved engine design also enhances turbulence and mixing of the air and fuel, which has the effect of reducing the emissions. The second reason that engines run much cleaner is due to the much more accurate fuel delivery to the combustion chamber. And the last reason is due to the use of highly efficient three-way catalytic converters. In fact, many new vehicles are able to meet the tightened emission regulations even without the secondary air injection system. Of those vehicles that are equipped with a secondary air injection system, many only operate during engine warm-up to burn off the increased hydrocarbons and carbon monoxide as well as help heat up the catalytic converter quicker.

When older carbureted and throttle body–injected engines were started up cold, they needed a richer mixture to operate due to the cold intake manifold surfaces, which condensed fuel out of the air and created a lean condition. This rich mixture resulted in the excessive release of hydrocarbons and carbon monoxide from the tailpipe until the engine warmed up. To reduce hydrocarbons and carbon monoxide, the secondary air injection system was added. It injected air (oxygen) into the hot exhaust gases as they left the combustion chamber. The extra oxygen caused the hot hydrocarbons and carbon monoxide to burn, converting them into water and carbon dioxide. The burning of the hydrocarbons and carbon monoxide also added extra heat to the exhaust stream, which helped warm up the catalytic converter more quickly, making it operational sooner. Once the catalytic converter heated up, the air (oxygen) was switched from upstream (near the exhaust valves) to downstream, where it entered the oxidizing catalyst in the converter. The extra oxygen was used to help oxidize any remaining hydrocarbons and carbon monoxide in the converter.

Secondary air injection systems use three valves to control airflow in the system. The **air switching valve** is used to switch air from upstream to downstream once the engine reaches the specified temperature. The **air diverter valve** diverts the injection air from the exhaust stream to the air cleaner assembly whenever additional air in the exhaust stream could cause backfiring in the exhaust, such as during deceleration or WOT. The last type of valve used in the system is a check valve **FIGURE 40-21**. It prevents hot exhaust gases from traveling backward through the hoses and valves to the air pump, which would overheat and ruin the hoses, valves, and pump in short order.

Early secondary air injection systems used a thermal vacuum switch in the vacuum line to control the switching valve. When the engine was cold, the thermal vacuum switch allowed vacuum to the switching valve, which moved the switching valve to the upstream position. Once the specified engine temperature was reached, the thermal vacuum switch would block the vacuum from reaching the switching valve and a spring moved the switching valve to the downstream position. In later designs, the air switching valve and diverter valve were operated by an electrical actuator controlled by the ECM for more precise control of the air injection system.

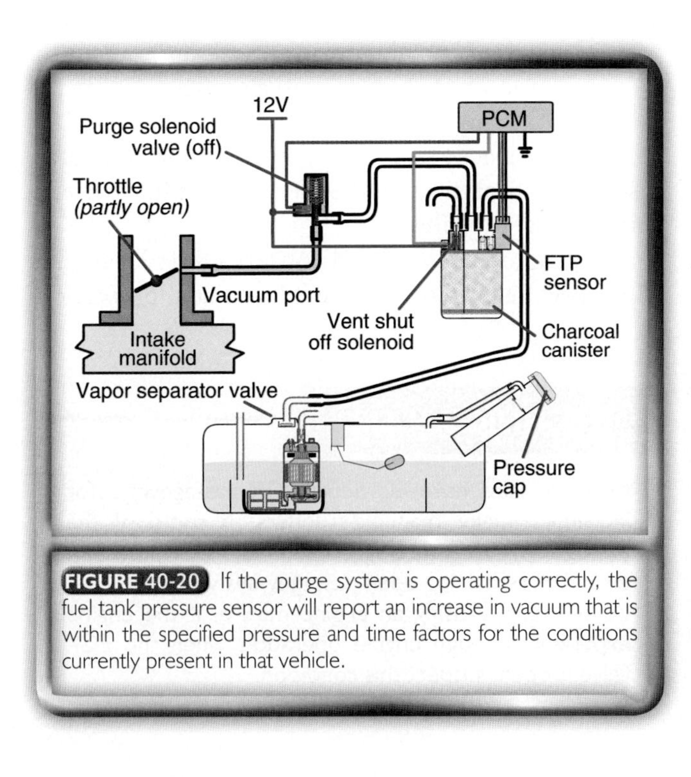
12V
PCM
Purge solenoid valve (off)
Throttle (partly open)
Vacuum port
Intake manifold
Vent shut off solenoid
FTP sensor
Charcoal canister
Vapor separator valve
Pressure cap

FIGURE 40-20 If the purge system is operating correctly, the fuel tank pressure sensor will report an increase in vacuum that is within the specified pressure and time factors for the conditions currently present in that vehicle.

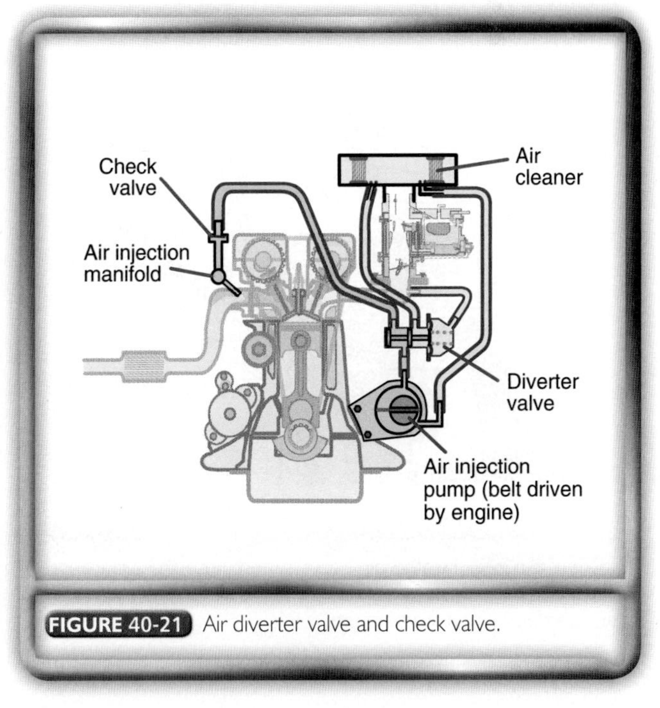
Check valve
Air cleaner
Air injection manifold
Diverter valve
Air injection pump (belt driven by engine)

FIGURE 40-21 Air diverter valve and check valve.

Heated Air Intake Systems

Fuel must be in a vapor form for it to burn. Liquid fuel will not burn. So the challenge is to get liquid fuel to fully vaporize by the time it needs to be ignited, not much sooner and not later. Intake manifolds carry the fuel. Fuel tends to condense on the inside surface of the cold manifold. One method of minimizing this problem is use of a **heated air intake system**. This system collects hot air from around the exhaust manifold and mixes it with outside air entering the air cleaner assembly **FIGURE 40-22**. The system maintains a specified air temperature of air entering the engine. This simple system uses a temperature-sensitive valve inside the air cleaner. It operates a flap that blends the hot air with cool air, so that the intake manifold receives air at about 100–110°F (38–43°C), regardless of the outside air temperature. Maintenance of this consistent temperature assists in the proper **vaporization** of the fuel, particularly when the engine is cold.

Vaporization is also assisted in some engines, such as in the Toyota Prius, by circulating stored hot liquid coolant through passages in the intake manifold and cylinder head, thereby preheating them right before the engine is started. Another past method of preheating fuel and air mixtures before entering the combustion chamber was to use a hot wire mesh under the throttle body to assist in heating air to promote the vaporization of the fuel. Fuel will not mix easily in cold air temperatures, so the use of a heating grid assures a more combustible fuel mixture.

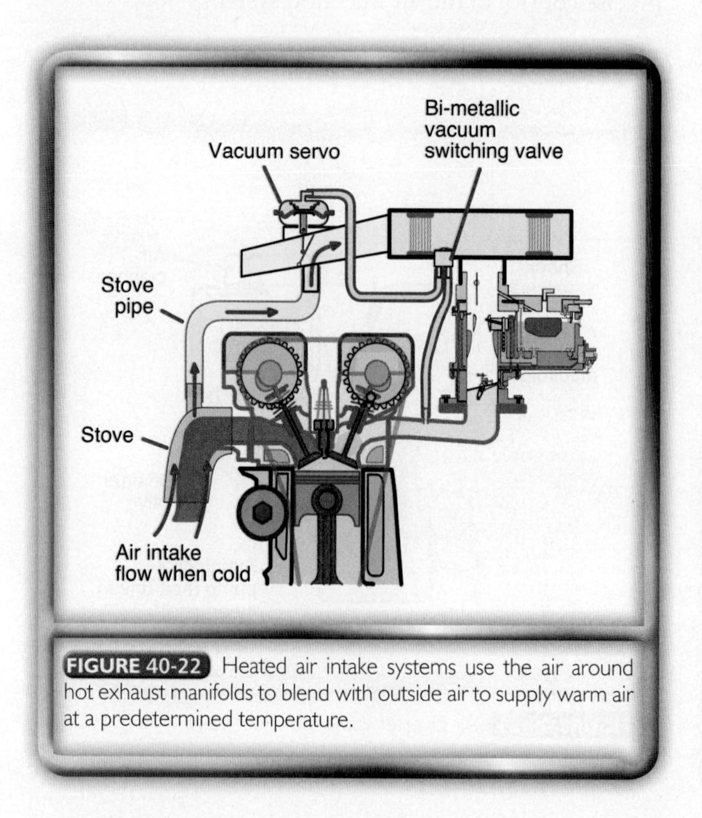
Bi-metallic
vacuum
switching valve
Vacuum servo
Stove
pipe
Stove
Air intake
flow when cold

FIGURE 40-22 Heated air intake systems use the air around hot exhaust manifolds to blend with outside air to supply warm air at a predetermined temperature.

Diagnosis

With emission control systems, often the first indication of any trouble is an illuminated MIL on the dash. In many cases, the vehicle may not exhibit any drivability issues. If the vehicle is equipped with an OBDII system, then using any stored DTCs will help isolate the fault. Diagnosis of emission control systems often starts with a good scan tool to access any DTCs. Once you have a DTC, service information, and any related technical service bulletins, you will have the information to determine the steps to locate the cause of the fault. If the vehicle's ECM has bidirectional capability, it may be helpful to operate suspect components and observe the results. For example, if there is a DTC regarding the canister vent solenoid, you might want to command it to close and then check to see if it indeed did close, both electrically and mechanically.

If there are no DTCs present, then having a good understanding of the types of emission control systems the vehicle is equipped with is a good place to start. This can best be found by researching the "description and operation" of the systems in the service information. Use that information plus any "symptom diagnosis" procedures to start diagnosing the system. Also, understanding the following information will help you track down the cause of the fault.

Diagnosing PCV-related Concerns

A PCV system is used to remove blow-by gases from the crankcase in an environmentally friendly manner. If blow-by gases are not removed from the crankcase, pressure can build up and cause oil seals and gaskets to leak oil. Replacement of seals or gaskets might temporarily fix the problem until excessive pressure pushes the seal or gasket out of place again. Proper testing of the PCV valve system is critical to get to the root cause of the concern and avoid repeat failures.

To diagnose PCV-related concerns, first locate the PCV valve. Refer to the service information for location

TECHNICIAN TIP

Many vehicles have individual EGR passageways for individual intake manifold runners. If some of the passageways become clogged, too much EGR gases will go to the remaining open passageways when the EGR valve opens, causing an engine misfire. If the engine experiences rough engine operation when the EGR valve is open, suspect this condition.

of the PCV valve and hoses. If the PCV valve is located in the valve cover, remove the PCV valve from the cover and ensure that a strong vacuum is coming through the valve with the engine running. This ensures the PCV valve and hose are clear. Reinstall the PCV valve into the valve cover and remove the breather tube from the air cleaner assembly. With the engine still running, check that vacuum builds up in the breather tube (and crankcase), indicating that the breather tube is clear and there is not excessive blow-by gases. Inspect all hoses for softening, brittleness, cracks, kinks, and holes. Cracks in hoses can result in vacuum leaks, which can create a poor idle situation. Inspect the PCV valve and ensure it has the correct part number for the vehicle. If the incorrect part is found, or the valve is sludged up or sticky, replace it with a new PCV valve.

Inspecting and Servicing the PCV System

The PCV system draws crankcase gases out of the crankcase and burns them in the engine to reduce crankcase emissions. It is an important system that needs to be serviced on a regular maintenance interval determined by the manufacturer and published in its service information. A PCV valve test should be performed as part of a thorough tune-up service. Failure of the PCV system can result in drivability issues or repeat oil seal failures, creating oil leaks on the engine. Repeat oil seal or gasket failures are noted by checking vehicle service history and noting multiple replacements of a specific seal or gasket.

To test the PCV system, follow the steps in SKILL DRILL 40-1.

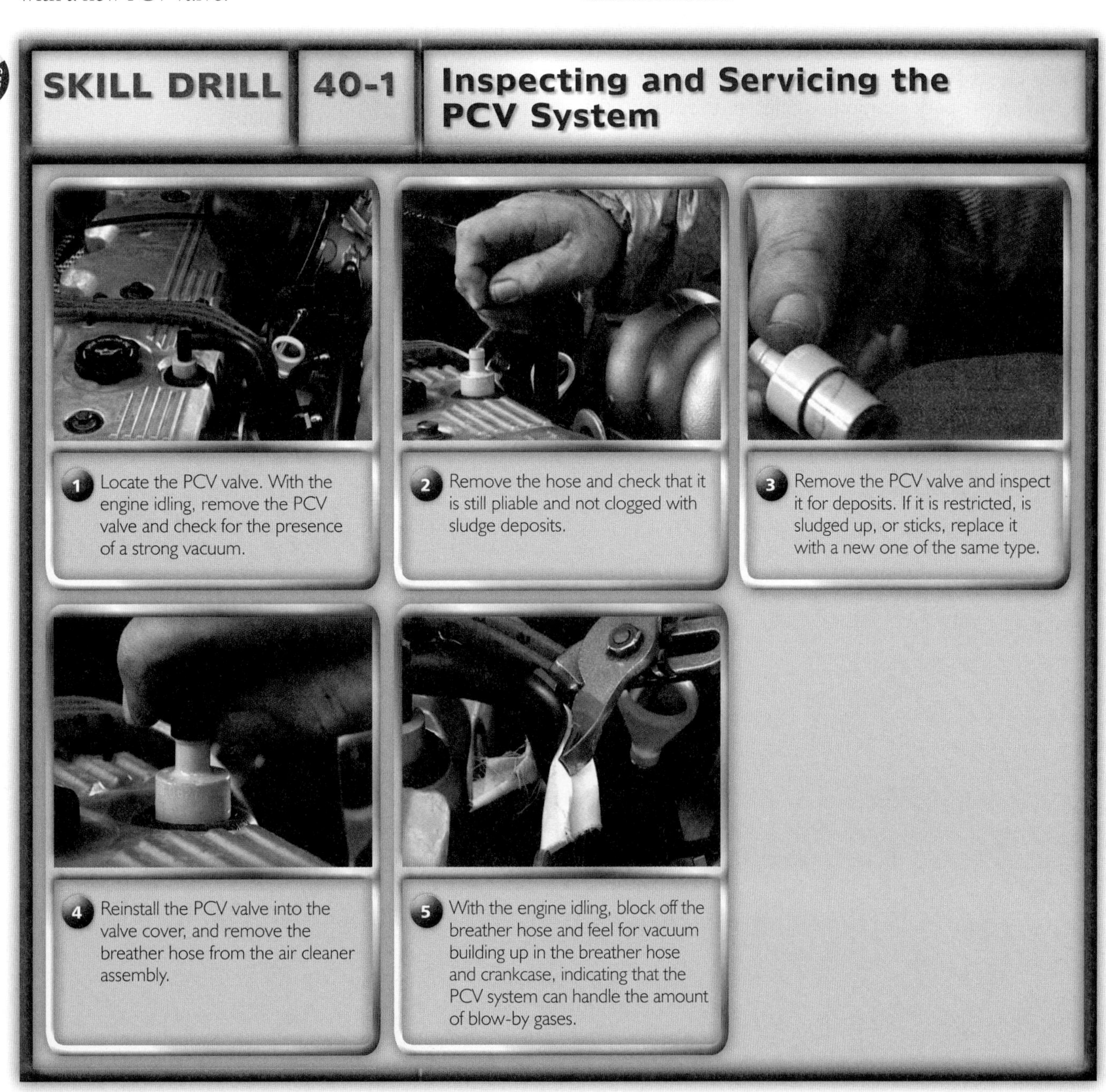
SKILL DRILL 40-1 Inspecting and Servicing the PCV System
1 Locate the PCV valve. With the engine idling, remove the PCV valve and check for the presence of a strong vacuum.
2 Remove the hose and check that it is still pliable and not clogged with sludge deposits.
3 Remove the PCV valve and inspect it for deposits. If it is restricted, is sludged up, or sticks, replace it with a new one of the same type.
4 Reinstall the PCV valve into the valve cover, and remove the breather hose from the air cleaner assembly.
5 With the engine idling, block off the breather hose and feel for vacuum building up in the breather hose and crankcase, indicating that the PCV system can handle the amount of blow-by gases.

Wrap-up

Ready for Review

- In automotive applications, most emissions are the by-product of combustion and are emitted from the exhaust system.
- Not all emissions from combustion are considered hazardous.
- The term "emission", when used in automotive circles, normally refers to the pollution produced by a light vehicle during operation or while sitting stationary.
- The fuel tank allows liquid fuel to evaporate into a gas; if not controlled, those vapors can escape into the atmosphere and are called evaporative emissions.
- In a compression-ignition diesel engine, emissions are created in the combustion chamber the same way as in spark ignition engines and escape to the atmosphere through the exhaust and the crankcase breather.
- Manufacturers are required by law and the Environmental Protection Agency (EPA) to control the emissions produced by their vehicles.
- The federal test procedure (FTP) requires all manufacturers to pass a federal emission test before vehicles can be sold in the United States.
- Not only must the vehicles pass the test before they can be sold, but also they must be capable of detecting an emission failure over the life of the vehicle, as they are being operated.
- As of 1996, all new vehicles most meet the OBDII standard, meaning all vehicles must have the same self diagnostic connectors.
- The EPA requires that when a vehicle's emissions deviate from the FTP limit by 1.5 times, the warning light (malfunction indicator lamp) must turn on and one or more specific diagnostic trouble codes (DTC) set in memory.
- The OBDII system was developed purely with the intent of keeping vehicles emission compliant and warning drivers if they aren't.
- Regulated air pollutants can be divided into two groups: gases and particulates.
- Many countries follow an international protocol on emissions requiring vehicle manufacturers to comply with these laws.
- Historically, the regulated emissions have been hydrocarbons, carbon monoxide, oxides of nitrogen, and particulate matter. In recent years, carbon dioxide has been added to the list of emissions that are being regulated.
- There are three categories of emission gasses: non-harmful, harmful, and debatable.

Key Terms

air diverter valve A valve that changes secondary airflow from the exhaust stream to the air cleaner or vice versa.

air switching valve The valve used to switch secondary air from near the exhaust valve (upstream) to the catalytic converter (downstream) for the purpose of oxidizing hydrocarbons and carbon monoxide.

blow-by Pressure that leaks past the compression rings during compression and combustion.

breather tube A tube used in the PCV system to allow fresh air into the engine crankcase.

carbon dioxide A by-product of complete combustion, carbon dioxide is a chemical compound made up of two oxygen molecules bonded to a single carbon molecule.

carbon monoxide A poisonous gas released during combustion of rich air–fuel mixtures.

carbon monoxide poisoning Exposure to higher than tolerable levels of carbon monoxide, resulting in headaches, fatigue, or loss of consciousness, eventually resulting in death.

compression-ignition engine An engine that uses the heat of compression to ignite the air–fuel mixture; also known as a diesel engine.

EGR system monitor A control module diagnostic test that is run to ensure that the EGR valve and passageways are operating properly.

EGR valve A valve that connects the exhaust port, or manifold, and the intake manifold. If engine operating conditions are likely to produce oxides of nitrogen, the EGR valve opens, letting some burned exhaust gases pass from the exhaust into the intake system.

emission A gas that is released to the atmosphere; usually refers to a harmful gas.

emission control system A system of devices that are designed to control or reduce harmful gases released to the atmosphere.

evaporative emission (EVAP) system A system used to capture vapors or gases from an evaporating liquid.

exhaust gas recirculation (EGR) system A system that recirculates a portion of burned gases back into the combustion chamber to displace air and fuel and cool combustion temperatures.

fixed-orifice PCV system A system in which a hole of a predetermined size is used as a means of pulling crankcase vapors into the intake manifold to be burned.

flame front The rapid burning of the air–fuel mixture that moves outward from the spark plug across the cylinder.

fuel tank pressure sensor A sensitive pressure sensor mounted in the fuel tank or EVAP system used to monitor the system for leaks.

heated air intake system A system that uses hot air from around the exhaust manifold to warm the air going into the intake manifold.

hydrocarbon A molecule made up of hydrogen and carbon. It is considered a harmful vehicle emission.

lambda The ratio of air to fuel at which all of the oxygen in the air and all of the fuel are completely burned; See also *stoichiometric ratio*.

limit value The maximum amount of emissions that a vehicle is permitted to emit. Values are assigned to different classifications of vehicles.

on-board diagnostic II (OBDII) This generation of self-diagnostic systems mandated standardized diagnostic trouble codes and a data link connector. It also mandated monitoring of certain emission systems, such as the catalytic converter, oxygen sensor, EGR, and evaporative emissions.

oxides of nitrogen Gas created when nitrogen is combined with oxygen under the high temperature and pressure of combustion.

particulate matter Particles that are heavier than air that are released during combustion. It is the black smoke that is commonly emitted from a diesel engine.

PCV valve A valve that controls the amount of crankcase ventilation flow that is allowed and varies with changes in manifold pressure.

photochemical smog A brown haze that hangs in the sky, typically seen over large cities. Smog is a major health issue to humans because it affects lung tissue.

positive crankcase ventilation (PCV) system A system that draws blow-by gases from the crankcase into the intake to be burned.

purge switch A device used to show the computer when purge is occurring. It is used as a feedback device to allow the computer to determine whether flow is happening.

quenched The state in a combustion chamber in which the flame cannot burn due to cold surfaces or poor distribution of the fuel mixture.

scavenging effect A condition caused by moving columns of air, which create a low-pressure area behind them, resulting in a pulling force that is used to pull the remaining burned gases from the combustion chamber. Valve timing affects the amount of scavenging effect an engine has.

separator PCV system A PCV system that uses a device that uses gravity to allow oil to fall to the bottom of the valve and be returned to the crankcase; the valve prevents liquid from traveling to the intake manifold.

stoichiometric ratio The exact ratio between air and fuel, at which both are burned completely. See also *lambda*.

stroke The movement of the piston in the engine from top dead center to bottom dead center, or vice versa. There are four strokes: intake, compression, power, and exhaust.

three-way catalytic converter A converter that changes hydrocarbons, carbon monoxide, and oxides of nitrogen into harmless elements.

two-way catalytic converter A converter that changes only hydrocarbons and carbon monoxide into harmless elements.

vaporization The ability of a liquid to evaporate.

variable-orifice PVC system A system in which a replaceable, spring-loaded PCV valve regulates gas flow. The position of the PCV valve is controlled by the pressure in the manifold.

vent solenoid A solenoid that allows fresh air to enter the evaporative system during a purge event. Also used for an evaporative system monitoring test.

ASE-Type Questions

1. Tech A says that the purge valve is part of the evaporative emission system. Tech B says that OBDII systems must illuminate the MIL when the emissions exceed 1.5 times the FTP. Who is correct?
   a. Tech A
   b. Tech B
   c. Both A and B
   d. Neither A nor B
2. Tech A says that carbon monoxide is partially burned fuel. Tech B says that oxides of nitrogen are unburned fuel. Who is correct?
   a. Tech A
   b. Tech B
   c. Both A and B
   d. Neither A nor B
3. Tech A says that hydrocarbons are a result of complete combustion. Tech B says that a catalytic converter creates a chemical reaction, changing carbon monoxide and hydrocarbons to water and carbon dioxide. Who is correct?
   a. Tech A
   b. Tech B
   c. Both A and B
   d. Neither A nor B
4. Tech A says that allowing hot exhaust gases into the engine through the EGR valve helps to warm up the engine during warm-up. Tech B says that rich fuel mixtures will create low amounts of carbon monoxide. Who is correct?
   a. Tech A
   b. Tech B
   c. Both A and B
   d. Neither A nor B
5. Tech A says that burning gasoline in an engine creates water as a by-product of combustion. Tech B says that variable valve timing can be used to reduce oxides of nitrogen, eliminating the need for an EGR valve on some engines. Who is correct?
   a. Tech A
   b. Tech B
   c. Both A and B
   d. Neither A nor B
6. Tech A says that the PCV system recirculates exhaust gases into the intake manifold. Tech B says that the PCV system recirculates blow-by gases into the intake manifold. Who is correct?
   a. Tech A
   b. Tech B
   c. Both A and B
   d. Neither A nor B
7. Tech A says that variable orifice PCV valves allow maximum PCV flow at idle. Tech B says that lean means there is not enough air in the air–fuel mixture. Who is correct?
   a. Tech A
   b. Tech B
   c. Both A and B
   d. Neither A nor B
8. Tech A says that the EVAP system stores escaping hydrocarbons until the engine can burn them. Tech B says that catalytic converters were designed for regular leaded gas. Who is correct?
   a. Tech A
   b. Tech B
   c. Both A and B
   d. Neither A nor B
9. Tech A says that the EGR valve is open fully at idle so that the engine will not die. Tech B says that oxides of nitrogen are created in large amounts when the combustion temperature is above 2500°F (1400°C). Who is correct?
   a. Tech A
   b. Tech B
   c. Both A and B
   d. Neither A nor B
10. Two technicians are discussing PCV system failures. Tech A says that the hose to the PCV valve can crack and cause a large vacuum leak. Tech B says that the hose to the PCV valve can become plugged with sludge restricting PCV flow. Who is correct?
    a. Tech A
    b. Tech B
    c. Both A and B
    d. Neither A nor B

FLEX
FUEL

CHAPTER 41

KNOW
SEE
DO
PROVE

NATEF Tasks

Engine Repair General			Page
■ Identify hybrid vehicle internal combustion engine service precautions.	MLR	AST	1158–1160
Electrical/Electronic Systems Battery			
■ Identify high-voltage circuits of electric or hybrid electric vehicles and related safety precautions.	MLR	AST	1159–1160
■ Identify hybrid vehicle auxiliary (12v) battery service, repair, and test procedures.	MLR	AST	1161

KNOW
SEE
DO
PROVE

Knowledge Objectives

After reading this chapter, you will be able to:

1. Define what is meant by "alternative fuel." (p 1152)
2. Describe the three basic hybrid drive configurations. (p 1155)

Electric and Hybrid Electric Vehicles

Skills Objectives

There are no skills objectives in this chapter.

Introduction

The use of alternative fuels in the internal combustion engine is nothing new. Back between 1890 and 1896, Henry Ford designed one of his first vehicles—the Quadricycle—to run on ethanol derived from local farm crop waste (Ford's Model T also ran on ethanol). Most of the earliest automobiles and trucks operated either on electricity or by using external combustion steam engines fueled with paraffin or internal combustion engines running on "town gas" produced from coal. But for a number of reasons (both political and practical), once discovered, petroleum replaced almost all other options for motor fuel used in light-duty road vehicles. Petroleum-based fuels have dominated the transportation sector for the last century. Presented with a long-standing record of gasoline use, some people question the logic of switching back to alternative fuels for powering our road vehicles.

Alternative Fuels

What are "alternative fuels," alternative fuel vehicles (AFVs), and alternative energy sources? An **alternative fuel** is essentially anything other than a petroleum-based motor fuel (gasoline or diesel fuel) that is used to propel a motorized vehicle. Alternative fuels may be liquid or gas (or electric) and contain a variety of latent heat energy for use in the internal combustion engine. An alternative fuel vehicle, then, is a vehicle powered by something other than petroleum. One example is an electric vehicle, which is fueled by electricity generated in a variety of ways (more on this later). Here is a list of some of the recognized alternative fuel vehicles currently produced:

- Flexible-fuel vehicles (FFVs)
- Dedicated and bi-fuel compressed natural gas vehicles (CNGVs)
- Liquefied natural gas vehicles
- Liquid petroleum gas (LPG, also called propane) vehicles
- Hydrogen-powered internal combustion engine (ICE) vehicles
- Battery electric vehicles (BEVs)
- Hybrid electric vehicles (HEVs)
- Hydrogen fuel cell (electric) vehicles (FCVs)

Some of the alternative fuels include:

- Ethanol (alcohol)
- Methanol (alcohol)
- Biodiesel
- Methane: compressed natural gas (CNG) and liquefied natural gas (LNG)
- Liquefied petroleum gas (LPG, also called propane) from methane
- Synthetic fuels
- Electricity (not a fuel, per se, but an energy source)

While the topic of alternative fuels is an entire subject itself, we will focus in this chapter primarily on the fundamentals of electric and hybrid electric vehicles. Both technologies are seeing continued growth in terms of number of vehicles produced. You will likely come in contact with these types of vehicles in regular shops, so you should know the basic fundamentals of their operation as well as safe work practices. When working with

You Are the Automotive Technician

A Toyota Prius hybrid, which is a high-voltage vehicle, is brought into the shop for a regular 120,000-mile service, requiring replacement of the spark plugs and other maintenance items. You know that you need to follow the latest safety precautions when servicing a high-voltage vehicle. First, you do some research on the Toyota website and locate the service information for this make and model. Next, you create a service plan to prepare the workspace for safety and determine which tools are needed and which technicians are trained to perform the work.

1. Why is it important to read the Toyota service information for the hybrid vehicle prior to servicing?
2. Why is it necessary to inform or work with someone else while you are servicing a high-voltage vehicle?
3. What is the standard equipment needed to work on high-voltage vehicles?
4. Why must the main high-voltage battery pack be disconnected before servicing a high-voltage vehicle?

electric and hybrid electric vehicles, be sure to follow ALL of the manufacturers, safety procedures and precautions.

Battery Electric Vehicle Technology

Battery electric vehicle (BEV) principles were used more than a century ago, before the advent of gasoline-powered internal combustion vehicles. With modern-day improvements in vehicle systems and battery technology, electric vehicles are returning to the marketplace. Because more than 75% of daily commuters drive no more than 40 miles (about 65 km) a day, electric vehicles are becoming viable, as they can now deliver that range without needing to consume any gasoline or diesel fuel at all, and therefore, produce no emissions.

BEVs first enjoyed a brief resurgence during the late 1990s in the United States with a number of OEMs offering them for lease. These included GM's EV!, Toyota's RAV4 EV, Ford's Electric Ranger pick-up, and Nissan's Altra station wagon/crossover vehicle, to name a few. These vehicles were preproduction or limited production test vehicles mainly for California commuters, police or postal fleets, and other limited-range applications. The limitations included the lack of a recharging infrastructure and lack of a single charge port configuration; various conductive hookups were used along with the innovative inductive "paddle." The vehicles also suffered from disappointing range issues. Where lead-acid batteries offered a limited range-to-weight ratio, the nickel metal hydride batteries proved expensive and at the time somewhat unreliable. Thus, most BEVs of that period were recalled by the OEMs and crushed. But, the knowledge and technology gains from those electric vehicles propelled a new generation of HEVs and BEVs forward to the marketplace. As a result of improved development in battery technology and propulsion system management algorithms, many manufacturers are now entering the BEV market.

Electric Motors

Vehicles that include electric drive motors have many advantages over traditional vehicles. Lower noise and gas emissions are among the major benefits. Other benefits include fewer moving parts, fewer maintenance requirements, good low-speed torque output, and increased reliability.

Many applications of the alternating current (AC) and direct current (DC) electric motor are in use today. Different vehicle manufacturers apply these varying operating systems to fill chassis demands.

In vehicles designed for highway use, drive motor systems are computer controlled. The computer controls the direction, frequency, order, and amplitude of current flowing through the motor(s). The magnetic field produced by this current reacts with permanent magnets in the motor, causing the motor's rotor to rotate. Smaller non-road (golf cart style) or low-speed neighborhood electric road vehicles (NEVs) may use DC motors and relays to control the drive system. However, it is important to note that the AC systems used in on-road vehicles operate on dangerously high voltages, some as high as 500 to 650 volts.

The electric motor is connected to road wheels typically via planetary gears. A few vehicles use so-called wheel motors, which are built into the wheel hub to save valuable cargo-carrying space normally displaced by the drive system.

During deceleration or vehicle braking, the electric motor connected to the drive line serves as a generator to create energy normally lost as heat from friction created by braking. This energy, captured as high current during regenerative braking, is routed back into the battery for storage. The electric motor in some power trains is also used as a generator to provide partial recharging of batteries when the vehicle is coasting. This energy must be strictly controlled by the battery pack controller or serious damage to the battery system will result.

The most popular types of electric motors used are brushless, multiphase, synchronous, and permanent magnet motors.

- Brushless: Brushes and commutators are not used.
- Multiphase: The stator contains more than one winding, usually three.
- Synchronous: The speed of the rotor is synchronized to the frequency of current flowing through the **stator windings**. This design maintains excellent power and efficiency characteristics even at low speeds.
- Permanent magnet: The rotor is made from very powerful rare earth permanent magnet alloys—typically, neodymium-iron-boron or samarium-cobalt.

BEVs and Sustainable Energy Sources

When coupled with sustainable or renewable energy sources, the BEV can truly serve as an emissions-free vehicle. Sustainable energy may be provided by unlimited sources of supply. These sources include:

- Solar panels and reflectors (to drive steam turbines)
- Wind generators
- Tidal and wave-power generators
- Geothermal sources

These sources and others offer limitless energy sustainability, without the use of fossil fuels like petroleum or coal. The BEV itself normally uses only one power source—the battery. The battery powers traction motors to propel the vehicle. The vehicle is returned to a charging station to maintain the energy FIGURE 41-1. Alternatively, the batteries may be quickly swapped at a "refueling" station. With a BEV, the average distance is limited to the storage capacity of the battery and the efficiency of its motor. Most BEVs can travel about 80 to 100 miles (129 to 161 km) on a single charge, with some exceptions. Coda Automotive reportedly uses a lithium-iron phosphate battery pack and AC electric motor with 134 horsepower in their BEV. This plug-in electric sedan will travel 90 to 125 miles (145 to 201 km) on less than $4 of electricity. The Tesla Roadster is reportedly the first production automobile to use lithium-ion battery cells and the first production BEV (all-electric) to travel more than 200 miles (322 km) per charge. With such promising battery and vehicle technology, BEV range will likely extend to more than 300 miles (483 km) in the not-too-distant future.

The Chevy Volt is known as an extended-range electric vehicle. It uses a lithium-ion battery that can be recharged from a domestic electrical power outlet (110 or 220 volts AC). This vehicle, however, is not a pure electric vehicle but a form of hybrid vehicle, as it also has a small gasoline/petrol-powered engine that drives a generator to provide electric power, should the vehicle travel beyond its battery-only range.

Electric vehicles for road use today use AC motors. The DC motors used in electric concept cars were originally carryovers from the electric forklift industry. DC installations tend to be simpler and less expensive than an AC system. AC installations allow the use of a three-phase AC motor. A typical automotive AC drive motor would run at 240 volts with a 300-volt battery pack. AC motors and controllers often incorporate a "regen" feature like that used with many commercial hybrid vehicle applications. This means that during braking, the motor functions as a generator to deliver otherwise lost kinetic energy into power to recharge the batteries.

Hybrid Electric Vehicles

If you consider diesel-electric submarines or diesel-electric locomotives, you will realize that the hybrid drive concept is anything but new FIGURE 41-2. Light- and

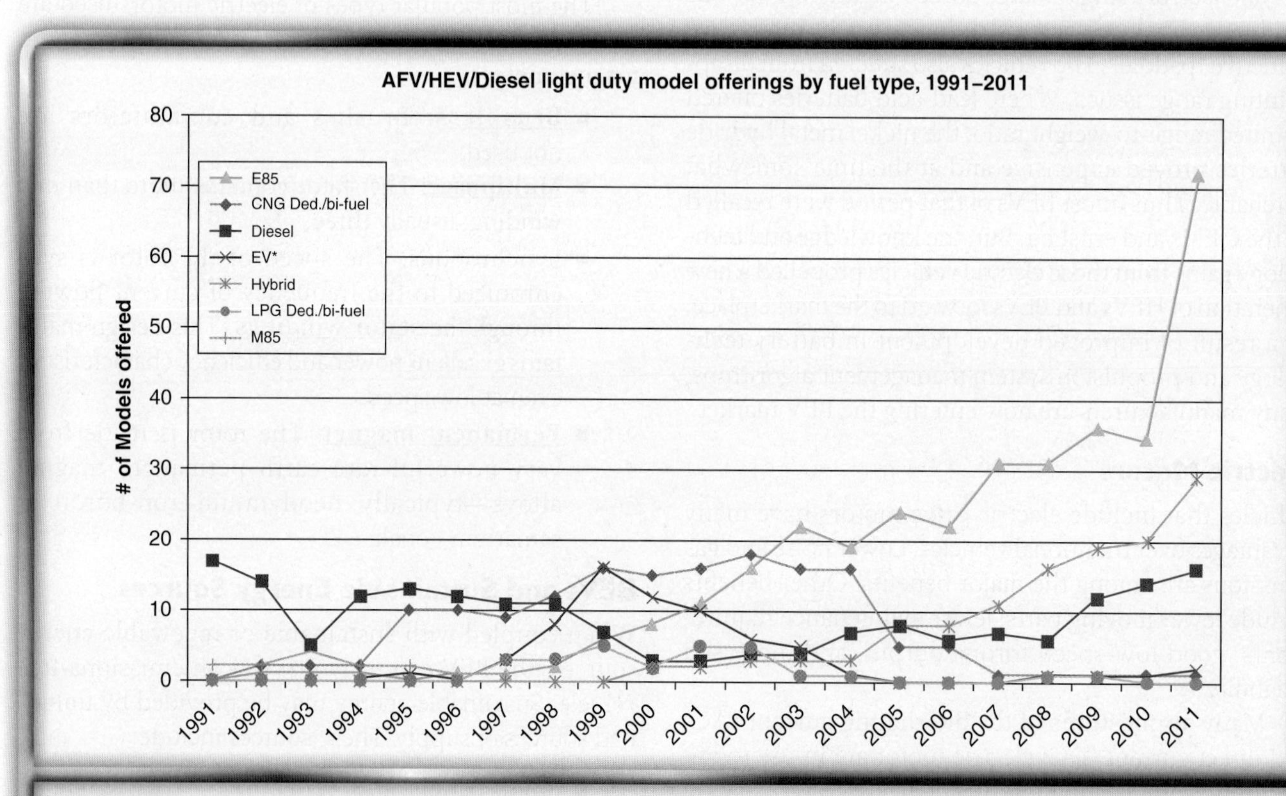
AFV/HEV/Diesel light duty model offerings by fuel type, 1991–2011
# of Models offered
E85
CNG Ded./bi-fuel
Diesel
EV*
Hybrid
LPG Ded./bi-fuel
M85
0
10
20
30
40
50
60
70
80
1991
1992
1993
1994
1995
1996
1997
1998
1999
2000
2001
2002
2003
2004
2005
2006
2007
2008
2009
2010
2011

FIGURE 41-1 Notice that starting from 1999, close to 3 million hybrids rank second highest among AFVs in the United States. These numbers will continue to climb in the coming years. Note also that as of 2011 there are more than 7 million E85 (85% ethanol) FFVs on US roads. Most owners of these FFVs are unaware that they can handle alcohol fuel.

ELECTRIC

FIGURE 41-2 Ford Focus–Electric being charged.

medium-duty hybrids now come in a variety of configurations. Power from the ICE (running on natural gas, diesel, propane, or gasoline) combines with auxiliary backup or primary power from electric batteries, ultra- or supercapacitors, hydraulic-pneumatic accumulators, or even flywheels operating at super-high revolutions per minute (rpm). Other power options, such as microturbines, are used in nonroad special-purpose hybrids. US light-duty hybrids are almost exclusively gasoline-electric.

Hybrid electric vehicles (HEVs) use a combination of electric power and an ICE. They combine the different advantages of ICEs and electric motors to provide a vehicle that operates more efficiently. Usually, the engine drives a generator to provide the electricity, which is stored in batteries that then drive an electric motor. The engine may also drive the wheels directly. Hybrid vehicles are designed to drive like conventionally powered vehicles, while producing significantly lower emissions and increased fuel economy.

In conventional vehicles that have only an ICE, the engine must be large enough and powerful enough to produce momentary torque sufficient for rapid acceleration at low speeds or from a stationary position. Such an engine is larger than necessary for highway cruising, which requires far less power. The parasitic losses of the larger engine take their toll on fuel economy. A vehicle that has only an electric motor has its own complications. It must carry a large volume of heavy batteries to give it sufficient range to be useful, and these must be recharged or replaced when discharged.

While electric motors produce their maximum torque at stall speed, a gasoline engine is more efficient at higher rpm. Combining a small but efficient gasoline engine that is designed to operate at its optimum peak torque rpm with an electric motor that can double as a generator to recapture braking energy is both effective and efficient.

Hybrid Drive Configurations

There are three basic kinds of hybrid drive configurations:

- Series hybrid: The gasoline engine is used only to drive a generator and charge a battery, which produces power to drive an electric motor. The electric motor then drives the wheels of the vehicle. The gasoline engine is really only a battery charger inside an electric vehicle.
- Parallel hybrid: The engine always drives the wheels and keeps the batteries charged. The electric motor acts like a large starter motor, helping the engine to crank over when more power is needed, particularly when starting from rest or when accelerating rapidly. This allows the engine to be smaller and lighter and more fuel efficient than if it were the sole source of power in the vehicle.
- Series-parallel hybrid: This design allows both the engine and the motor to drive the vehicle, or either one by itself, under the control of an on-board computer that determines the optimum combination of power delivered to the wheels at any time. The engine can shut down completely when the batteries are charged. When needed, the gasoline engine fires up again to assist in driving the wheels or to recharge the battery. The engine can be optimized for efficiency within a narrow rpm range, and the overall combination of both power sources takes up little more room than a conventional all-purpose gasoline engine, and yet can deliver lower emissions and much greater fuel economy. This design is used by the Toyota Prius and Ford Escape.

Almost all hybrids (except the Chevy Volt) transfer motive power to the wheels in either the parallel or the series-parallel drive configuration.

A variety of transmissions, clutches, and other features are used depending on the desired amount of performance (or alternatively, fuel economy) and the selling price. Some hybrids come with manual or automatic (up to eight speeds) planetary gear set transmissions; others come with continuously variable transmissions (some with sporty "paddle" type shifters). High-voltage controls vary also, along with the types of batteries and capacities, type of battery cooling, and so on. There may be one, two, or more high-voltage **electric machines** (drive motors/generators) used. These may be three-phase AC permanent magnet or inductive motors. Usually, the ICE provides power when the vehicle is traveling at higher speeds, and the electric motor is used when slowing to a halt and at lower speeds. The parallel hybrid arrangement is best suited to vehicles that travel greater distances between stops, such as more traditional passenger vehicles and delivery trucks.

Hybrid Vehicle Efficiency

HEVs are able to offset ICE efficiency by using smaller volumetric engine size and by running the ICE at the optimal torque and speed. Efficiency is also achieved through regenerative braking and by using displacement-on-demand cylinder deactivation, power-on-demand, and idle stop. **Regenerative braking** occurs when the drive motor(s) act as generators to recharge the traction batteries during deceleration or when braking. This feature reportedly saves around 10–15% on fuel consumption. **Displacement-on-demand** deactivates cylinders when operating under cruise or coasting conditions to save fuel. The **power-on-demand** feature temporarily shuts off the ICE when it is not needed, such as when idling or coasting. Drive may also be provided instead only by the electric motor, without burning fuel, thus saving energy and reducing emissions. **Idle stop** turns off the ICE when the vehicle is at a standstill. Expect all of these features to be more widely used as newer vehicles hit the market. Other fuel-saving features include variable valve timing, Atkinson cycle (five-cycle) or Miller cycle (five-cycle with low rpm boost) engines, and similarly interesting innovations.

Hybrid vehicle types are classified by body style and by the degree of performance and luxury they offer. But technically speaking, they are also classified by how far they can be driven on batteries alone. For example, a "full hybrid" can cruise a limited distance without the engine running. A "partial hybrid" runs on ICE power at all times except when stopped. The vast majority, perhaps 90% of US registered HEVs, are full hybrids using drive systems with one or more planetary gear sets licensed from, or similar to, Toyota's Hybrid Synergy Drive design. A number of other OEMs are using the GM-originated Two-Mode hybrid drive system.

> **▸ LINK**
> Refer to the Motive Power Types chapter for more on these engines.

Hybrid System Components

The ICE in a hybrid vehicle is designed to operate only within its most efficient operating range, typically somewhere between 2000 and 4500 rpm, where engine peak **volumetric efficiency** and peak torque are developed. Its construction has lighter internal components than would otherwise be required, resulting in an efficient engine with low frictional qualities. It may also incorporate other fuel-efficient technologies such as engine cylinders that can be selectively shut down, multi-runner intake manifolds, and throttleless intake manifolds.

A powerful permanent magnet brushless motor/generator is mounted adjacent to the engine FIGURE 41-3. It draws power from the battery to drive the vehicle in situations involving low load and speed, and it assists the engine to provide more power during acceleration. During deceleration and braking, it functions as a generator, reclaiming kinetic energy by converting it to electrical energy and storing it in the battery.

Often, a power splitting assembly is mounted between the ICE (engine) and the electric motor FIGURE 41-4. This device functions as a **continuously variable transmission (CVT)** and transaxle assembly. The CVT does not "shift" from one gear to another in the usual sense; rather, it continuously varies the amounts of speed and torque from the engine and the motor to the wheels, selecting the best (most efficient) engine and motor rpm balance for any given driving condition.

Batteries have transitioned from lead-acid in early electric vehicles to sealed nickel–metal hydride 200- to 300-volt battery packs to sealed lithium-ion battery packs, which provide higher power output and are lighter than other battery types FIGURE 41-5. Their output may be inverted and raised to 650 volts by the power inverter to power the electric drive motors (also called electric machines, because they also generate electricity during overrun situations, such as when coasting). Hybrid battery packs are generally made up of a lot of small individual battery cells that are connected in series. They are

FIGURE 41-3 Main traction motor.

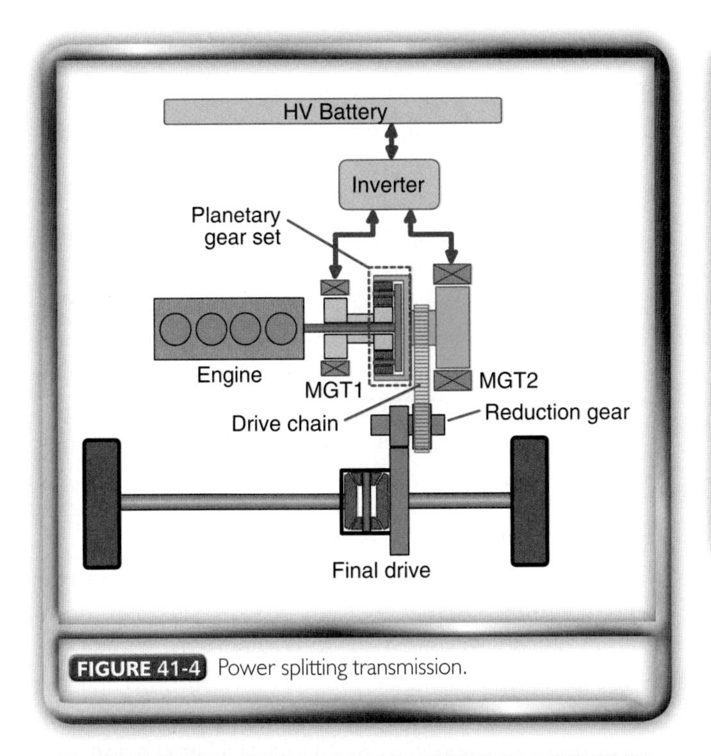
HV Battery
Inverter
Planetary gear set
Engine
MGT1
MGT2
Drive chain
Reduction gear
Final drive

FIGURE 41-4 Power splitting transmission.

FIGURE 41-5 A battery pack installed in a Toyota Prius.

monitored and managed by a control unit that controls the rate of charge and monitors their temperature.

A small permanent magnet brushless motor/generator replaces the engine flywheel **FIGURE 41-6**. It functions as the engine's starter motor and battery charger. It also provides additional power for the larger main motor/generator. A motor control unit controls the delivery of electrical current to and from the battery and the electric motors. It has its own cooling system to control its operating temperature. It also contains an AC to DC

FIGURE 41-6 Flywheel-mounted motor/generator.

converter used to charge the battery, and a DC to AC power **inverter** to change direct current from the battery into alternating current to power the electric motors.

Hybrid Vehicle Operation

When the vehicle is moving from a stationary position, and when traveling at low to moderate speeds, the main electric motor/generator drives the vehicle. At these speeds, the ICE is less efficient and is normally used only to charge the battery.

During normal driving, the ICE starts and drives the generator and the power splitter/divider. Power from the generator is used to drive the electric motor. The motor control unit controls the **power divider/splitter** so that the drive remains at its most efficient. When accelerating and when using power from the ICE, the control unit draws power from the battery and directs it to the electric motor/generator, providing more power to the wheels than the ICE could supply on its own.

During deceleration and braking, the ICE is turned off. Inertia from the wheels drives the electric motor/generator, using the current produced to charge the battery. Normally this energy would be wasted as heat, but in the hybrid, it is recovered and reused. The **retarding effect** (vehicle slowing) caused by this system provides the same deceleration as normal engine braking would. Gentle application of the brake pedal does not apply the brakes. The braking effect is achieved by using the electric motor/generator, which converts the vehicle's inertial momentum into electrical energy to charge the battery.

When the vehicle is stationary and the brakes are applied, the ICE is stopped and power is not applied to the electric motor/generator. No fuel is burned and no emissions are produced. Releasing the brakes applies power to the electric motor. Moving the accelerator pedal activates the electric motor and, if required, the ICE to drive the vehicle.

Types of Hybrids and Electric Vehicles

There are various kinds of electric and hybrid vehicles on the market today. They may be classified by body style, but how is the *degree* of hybridization described? There seems to be some confusion. HEVs may be classified by the type of drive configuration used—such as planetary gear sets, multiple electric machines, and continuously variable transmissions. Other descriptions are thrown around with abandon. The following are some widely used descriptions you should be familiar with, but don't be surprised if other designations (often created for marketing appeal) are used for these hybrid vehicles.

Battery Electric Vehicles

BEVs need recharging when batteries are low. In the past, lead-acid or nickel-metal hydride batteries were typically used. Now lithium-ion and other types of batteries are used for greater range. Early BEVs include GM's EV-1, Ford's EV Ranger, Toyota's RAV-4 EV, and Nissan's Altra. Most of these early electric vehicles have been reclaimed and scrapped by the OEMs. Now, a whole new generation of electric vehicles is becoming available, such as the Nissan Leaf FIGURE 41-7. Watch for more BEVs to be released soon.

Hybrid Electric Vehicles

HEVs have two power sources, typically a gasoline ICE and high-voltage batteries working in both series and parallel. HEVs are not typically electric grid rechargeable, although some have been converted to plug-in HEVs (see the next section) for more than 100 mpg (43 km/L). HEV types include micro, partial, and full hybrid vehicles.

- Micro-hybrids include GM's Silverado and Sierra with start/stop features.
- Partial hybrids include Honda's Civic and Insight, in which the engine (ICE) does not shut off while the vehicle is underway.
- Full hybrids include the Toyota Prius models, the Ford Escape hybrid, and the Mercury Mariner hybrid. These and many others (perhaps 90%) of the market are considered full hybrids, as they can be driven short distances and at low speeds using only the (high-voltage) batteries.

FIGURE 41-7 Nissan Leaf.

Plug-in Hybrid Electric Vehicles

Many manufacturers are entering the **plug-in hybrid electric vehicle (PHEV)** market. A PHEV is different in that only one power source, the battery, is used to propel the vehicle for a certain distance, limited by the storage capacity of the battery and the efficiency of the motor. A PHEV-20, for example, is designed to go 20 miles (32 km) before the batteries need charging and the ICE is needed; a PHEV-40 can go 40 miles (64 km), etc. The ICE may also start up for added power before the batteries need a recharge. Ford, Toyota, and other light duty vehicle OEMs have PHEVs on test. PHEV automobiles achieve great fuel economy with some getting more than 100 mpg (43 km/L). Medium-duty vehicles from Mercedes-Benz and others offer PHEVs for commercial use. International Truck and Engine sells a PHEV school bus. Combined with FFV capability, PHEVs offer a good gasoline per gallon equivalent.

Extended-Range Electric Vehicles

Extended-range electric vehicles (EREVs) are plug-ins that have a relatively small auxiliary ICE to drive a generator for charging the batteries. The Chevy Volt is a series EREV.

Fuel Cell (Electric) Vehicles

FCVs are considered hybrid vehicles because they have two power sources. The sources typically are a hydrogen fuel cell "stack" and a storage device from which electric power is drawn. Regenerative braking electrical energy may be stored in the vehicle's high-voltage battery pack, or as with Honda's early FCX and others, in ultra- or supercapacitors, which can more quickly be charged or provide acceleration power as needed.

Hybrid Vehicle Service

Before attempting to perform service operations on any hybrid vehicle, read the manufacturer's service information for the vehicle you are about to service. The service manual will instruct you in how to properly follow all safety procedures. The most important rule to remember is, never work on a high-voltage vehicle without first notifying someone who is trained in dealing with high-voltage electrocution. You need a responsible person in your work environment to check on you as you work around high voltage.

The matter of servicing hybrids safely is to be taken seriously. Always follow the manufacturer's safety and service procedures to keep out of trouble. There are many safety features built into hybrid vehicles to prevent accidental shock, but once you decide to venture into high-voltage areas, be prepared to spend some money on safety equipment. This is no time to pinch pennies! Some of the standard equipment for servicing HEV systems includes:

- OEM or equivalent scan tools
- A high-quality (three-phase CAT III or CAT IV) digital volt-ohmmeter (DVOM) with appropriate high-voltage leads FIGURE 41-8
- Insulated gloves rated for 5000 volts and certified to 1000 volts (Class 0) FIGURE 41-9
- Safety cones and safety tape (to mark off service areas) and other such items
- A retrieval hook in case someone becomes disabled from electrical shock

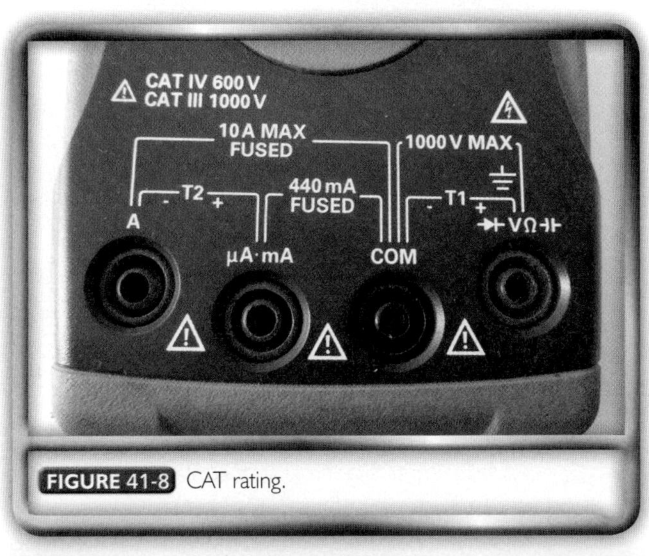
CAT IV 600 V
CAT III 1000 V
10 A MAX
FUSED
1000 V MAX
T2
440 mA
FUSED
T1
A
VΩ
µA·mA
COM
FIGURE 41-8 CAT rating.

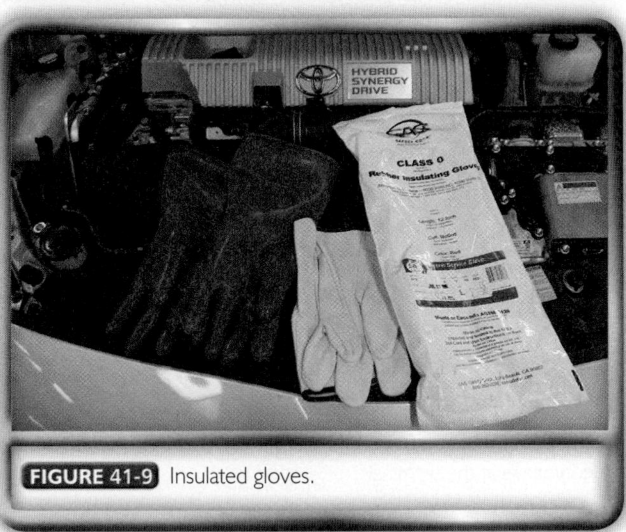
HYBRID
SYNERGY
DRIVE
CLASS 0
FIGURE 41-9 Insulated gloves.

If you decide to service electric and hybrid vehicles, get the proper training on the high-voltage areas as well as a full understanding of how they operate. Stay alert and continually practice situational awareness.

Besides the high voltage dangers of a hybrid or electric vehicle, there are other precautions you need to be aware of. One of the first is that the vehicle should be completely powered down before working on it, since the ICE can start at any time it deems necessary. The vehicle should be in park, with the parking brake applied, and the power button powered down. The keyless fob, if equipped, should be more than 15' (4.6 m) from the vehicle.

Safety

Always make sure there is someone in your work environment who is trained in the safety procedures regarding high-voltage electrocution to check on you whenever you work around high-voltage systems.

Identifying and Disabling the High-Voltage System

There are plenty of opportunities to service HEVs without venturing into the high-voltage areas of the vehicle, such as changing oil. Just because you are not working on the main traction motor doesn't mean that you won't come into contact with other high voltage circuits. In many hybrid and electric vehicles, high voltage is used to operate a variety of accessories, such as power steering and air-conditioning, so you need to be aware that high voltage wires can be located nearly anywhere in the vehicle. These high voltage wires are recognized by orange (usually) convolute or wiring FIGURE 41-10. Some vehicles have used other colors, such as blue, to designate high-voltage wiring. Avoid working on these high-voltage areas of a hybrid vehicle without first having the proper training, service information, and experienced help on hand. The main high-voltage battery pack must be disconnected before service is performed on or around the high-voltage components. Every manufacturer has a different way of disconnecting high-voltage batteries from the main electrical system, but it usually involves a service plug that is removed from near the battery or a battery module switch that is turned to the off position, both of which will disconnect the battery from the high voltage system.

FIGURE 41-10 High-voltage wiring.

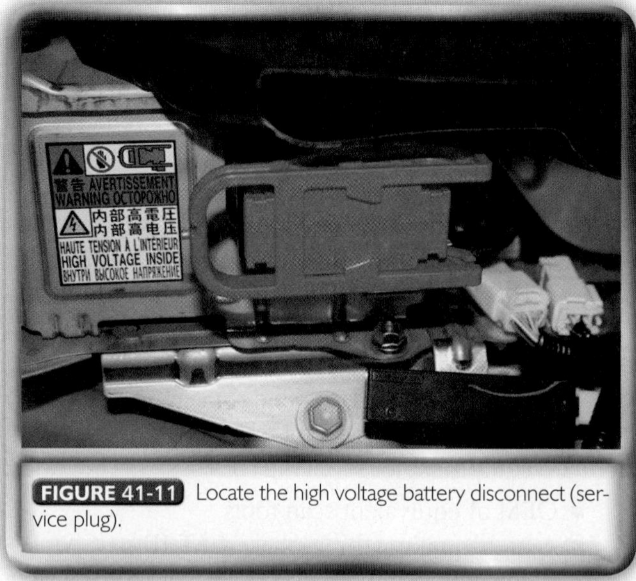

警告 AVERTISSEMENT
WARNING ОСТОРОЖНО
内部高電圧
内部高电压
HAUTE TENSION À L'INTERIEUR
HIGH VOLTAGE INSIDE
ВНУТРИ ВЫСОКОЕ НАПРЯЖЕНИЕ

FIGURE 41-11 Locate the high voltage battery disconnect (service plug).

Before you disable the high voltage system, make sure you are wearing the appropriate PPE. Locate the high voltage battery disconnect (service plug) **FIGURE 41-11**. Release the lock, release the lever, and remove the service plug. Store it in a safe place where it cannot be reinserted accidentally. Wait for the specified time for the residual electricity to bleed off. Locate the high voltage access panel. Remove the bolts that secure the cover **FIGURE 41-12**. Then remove the cover, and, using the correctly rated meter, measure that there is no voltage at the specified terminals **FIGURE 41-13**.

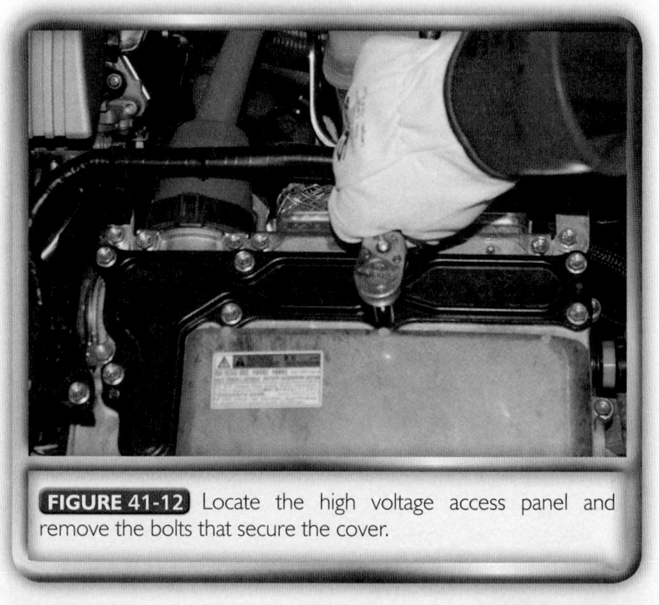

FIGURE 41-12 Locate the high voltage access panel and remove the bolts that secure the cover.

Hybrid ICE Service Precautions

Hybrid vehicle ICEs require maintenance and service like other ICEs, such as changing the oil and filter and replacing belts (on those equipped with accessory drive belts). The last thing you want is to be electrocuted or have the engine start up while you are working on it. All hybrids are designed to operate uniquely; therefore, there are precautions specific to each vehicle model. Don't assume that the safety precautions for an older model are the same for a newer model, and vice versa. The first precaution is to make sure you have been trained to work on the particular hybrid or electric vehicle. If you are not properly trained to work on that particular hybrid vehicle, you should not work on it. Before starting any diagnostic, maintenance, or repair work, always check the service information for the specific safety or procedural requirements that the manufacturer has specified. Also, know how to power down the high-voltage system, and remember that it takes 5 to 15 minutes for the electrical charge to bleed off.

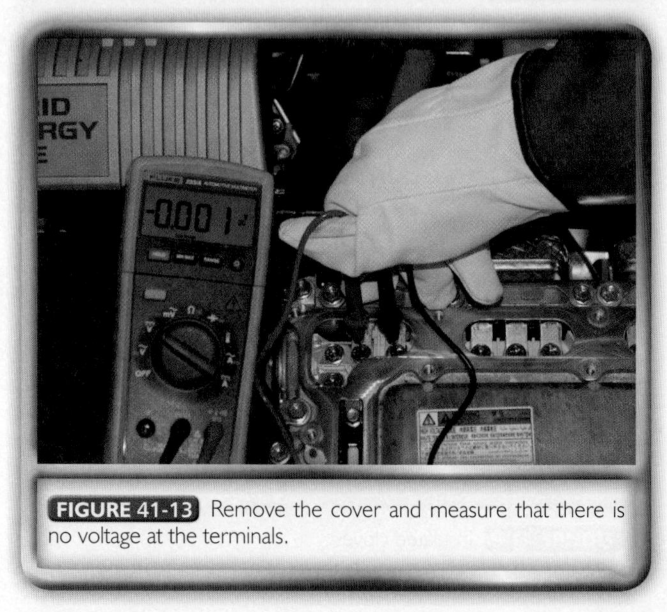

FIGURE 41-13 Remove the cover and measure that there is no voltage at the terminals.

Hybrid Auxiliary (12v) Battery Service

On most hybrid vehicles, the 12-volt auxiliary battery is used to power up the vehicles computers and run virtually all of the accessories. Because it powers up the computers it is critical to starting the vehicle, even though it is generally not used to crank the engine over; that is typically done by one of the traction motors and high voltage battery. This means that the 12v battery in a hybrid vehicle is generally smaller than in a standard vehicle, making the battery is more susceptible to parasitic current draws, since they don't have as much current capacity. It is also located separately from the traction batteries; typically either under the hood, or in the trunk. In most cases, the 12v battery is charged from an inverter built into the hybrid electronic controller, instead of a separate alternator **FIGURE 41-14**.

In most hybrids, the 12v battery is of the absorbed glass mat (AGM) construction. This battery is sensitive to overcharging, which can damage it, so a special battery charger is required whenever charging is needed. Some manufacturers recommend removing the 12v battery from the vehicle while it is charging to prevent any damage to the vehicle's electrical system. But this can erase the computer and entertainment memories, as well as activate the anti-theft system, so always follow the manufacturer's procedure when disconnecting a battery. Also, most manufacturers prohibit hybrid vehicles from being used to jump start another vehicle, due to the reduced size of the auxiliary battery, and the potential damage to the hybrid electrical system. The 12v battery can be tested in a similar manner to a lead-acid flooded cell battery, with either a load tester or a conductance tester, as described in the Battery Systems chapter and the Starting and Charging Systems chapter. Again, it is preferable to remove the battery from the vehicle during testing.

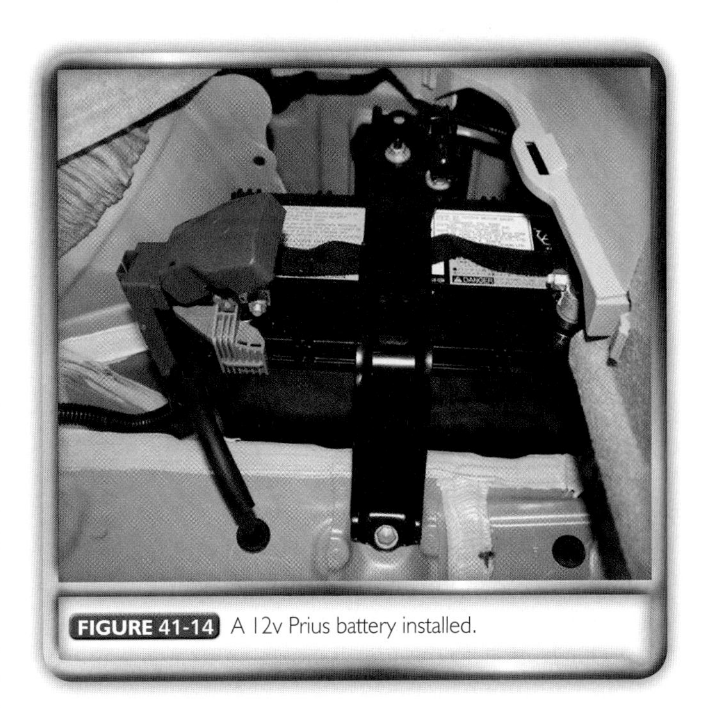
FIGURE 41-14 A 12v Prius battery installed.

Wrap-up

Ready for Review

- An alternative fuel is any fuel that powers a vehicle that is not petroleum-based motor oil.
- Alternative fuels are not new; they have been around since the 1890s.
- The electric motor shows great promise because it has fewer moving parts, less maintenance requirements, good low-speed torque output, and increased reliability.
- The computer gives the electric motor new life and has some advantages; the biggest disadvantage is the electric motor must have a battery to run it.
- Battery electric vehicles (BEVs) are making a comeback with the addition of computer technology and lithium batteries.
- The Chevy Volt was supposed to be the first BEV, but it is really a hybrid, since it has a gasoline engine to recharge the battery.
- Hybrids have been used since World War II.
- The locomotives on the railroad tracks today are diesel electric; the engine charges the batteries and the locomotive runs on the batteries.
- Many city buses are diesel electric, which demonstrates that hybrid technology is not new; it is being redefined, with the new vehicles using computers to control operations.
- The engine in hybrids can be much smaller, as its main purpose is to recharge the hybrid's battery. The hybrid gets most of its power from the battery running the electrical drives.
- When you think of hybrids, think of electrical circuitry. There are series, parallel, and series parallel designs.
- On series hybrids, the engine runs only to supply the electric motor or charge the batteries.
- On parallel hybrids, the engine runs to charge the battery and directly assist propelling the vehicle.

- On series-parallel hybrids, the engine runs to charge the battery, operate the electric motor, and assist with propelling the vehicle all at the same time.
- Hybrids offset the power lost by internal combustion engines (ICEs) in several ways. One of the most efficient is the regenerative braking system.
- There are numerous hybrids, from plug-in to extended-range. They all work basically the same way: They allow the vehicle to be propelled by the electrical power. Thus, they are more fuel efficient.
- The hybrid normally starts out on electrical power, and as the need changes, the engine will come on to assist or recharge the batteries, depending on the design.
- The ICE is turned off during deceleration and braking.
- The ICE needs to start and run at higher rpm for peak efficiency.
- Hybrids can be dangerous. Always refer to the appropriate repair information.
- In hybrids, it is usually the orange wires that indicate high voltage. Other colors may be used, so check the manufacturer's information. Always wear special gloves to remove the access plugs to disable hybrids.
- Anytime service is performed, the technician needs to ensure that the hybrid is not in the ready mode and that everything is off.

Key Terms

alternative fuel A nonpetroleum-based motor fuel.

battery electric vehicle (BEV) A vehicle powered by battery only.

brushless An electric motor without brushes.

continuously variable transmission (CT) A transmission without individual gears or gear ratios.

displacement-on-demand A feature that allows cylinders to be taken off-line when not needed, such as at vehicle cruise.

electric machine Another name for a traction motor with regenerative capability.

hybrid electric vehicle (HEV) A vehicle that uses two power sources for propulsion, one of which is electricity.

idle stop A feature that turns off the internal combustion engine when the vehicle is at a standstill.

inverter A device that converts direct current to alternating current.

multiphase An electric motor that operates through more than one phase.

parallel hybrid A hybrid vehicle driven simultaneously by an internal combustion engine and an electric machine.

permanent magnet A material with natural or man-made constant magnetic properties.

plug-in hybrid electric vehicle (PHEV) A hybrid electric vehicle in which only one power source, the battery, is used to propel the vehicle for a certain distance, limited by the storage capacity of the battery and the efficiency of the motor.

power divider/splitter A device that receives power from an internal combustion engine and electric machine to power a hybrid electric vehicle.

power-on-demand A feature that shuts down the engine when not needed to save fuel.

regenerative braking A feature that allows drive motors to act as generators to recharge the traction batteries during deceleration or when braking.

retarding effect The result of retarding (slowing) the vehicle.

series hybrid A hybrid electric vehicle powered by an internal combustion engine, but driven by battery.

series-parallel hybrid A hybrid electric vehicle that uses the internal combustion engine and/or the battery pack for propulsion.

stator winding A winding in an alternator that creates the current output, or a winding in a motor that creates the needed magnetism for the motor to rotate.

volumetric efficiency A measure of how well an internal combustion engine can breathe at a given rpm at wide-open throttle.

PROVE
KNOW
SEE
DO

ASE-Type Questions

1. Tech A says that alternative fuels may be liquid or gas (or electric) and contain a variety of latent heat energy for use in the internal combustion engine. Tech B says that an alternative fuel vehicle is a vehicle powered by something other than petroleum. Who is correct?
   a. Tech A
   b. Tech B
   c. Both A and B
   d. Neither A nor B
2. Tech A says that battery electric vehicle's (BEV's) were introduced more than a century ago. Tech B says that BEV's have only been around for approximately the past 10 years. Who is correct?
   a. Tech A
   b. Tech B
   c. Both A and B
   d. Neither A nor B
3. Tech A says that high voltage wires in hybrid and electric vehicles are usually a special color. Tech B says that special high voltage shoes should be worn when working on high voltage vehicles. Who is correct?
   a. Tech A
   b. Tech B
   c. Both A and B
   d. Neither A nor B
4. Tech A says that the electric motors used in all automotive applications are direct current, or DC, motors. Tech B says that the electric motors used in all automotive applications are alternating current, or AC motors. Who is correct?
   a. Tech A
   b. Tech B
   c. Both A and B
   d. Neither A nor B
5. Tech A says that in a hybrid vehicle the engine usually drives a generator to provide the electricity, which is stored in batteries that then drive an electric motor. Tech B says that the engine may also drive the wheels directly as well. Who is correct?
   a. Tech A
   b. Tech B
   c. Both A and B
   d. Neither A nor B
6. Tech A says that in hybrid vehicles the main high-voltage battery pack must be disconnected before service is performed on or around the high-voltage components. Tech B says that this is not necessary because the system has built in protection devices. Who is correct?
   a. Tech A
   b. Tech B
   c. Both A and B
   d. Neither A nor B
7. Tech A says that on most hybrid vehicles, a 12-volt auxiliary battery is used to power up the vehicles computers and run most of the accessories. Tech B says that the 12-volt auxiliary battery is typically used to crank the ICE power unit when starting. Who is correct?
   a. Tech A
   b. Tech B
   c. Both A and B
   d. Neither A nor B
8. Tech A says that the 12v battery in a hybrid vehicle is generally smaller than in a standard vehicle. Tech B says that the battery is more susceptible to parasitic current draw, as they do not have as much current capacity. Who is correct?
   a. Tech A
   b. Tech B
   c. Both A and B
   d. Neither A nor B
9. Tech A says that that hybrids have a feature that allows the traction motor's batteries to be charged when the vehicle is braking. Tech B says this is known as regenerative braking. Who is correct?
   a. Tech A
   b. Tech B
   c. Both A and B
   d. Neither A nor B
10. Tech A says that when servicing a hybrid electric vehicle, it is OK to leave the power switch on as long as the ICE and electric motor are not operating. Tech B says when performing service on a hybrid electric vehicle, the key fob should be more than 15 feet away from the vehicle. Who is correct?
    a. Tech A
    b. Tech B
    c. Both A and B
    d. Neither A nor B

APPENDIX A

2013 NATEF Automobile Accreditation Task List Correlation Guide

NATEF 2013 Tasksheet Title	MLR NATEF Reference number; Priority Level	AST NATEF Reference number; Priority Level	Chapter Number
Safety and Foundation			
A. General Safety			
Identify general shop safety rules and procedures.	0A1; P-1	0A1; P-1	3
Identify marked safety areas.	0A6; P-1	0A6; P-1	3
Identify the location and the types of fire extinguishers and other fire safety equipment; demonstrate knowledge of the procedures for using fire extinguishers and other fire safety equipment.	0A7; P-1	0A7; P-1	3
Identify the location and use of eye wash stations.	0A8; P-1	0A8; P-1	3
Identify the location of posted evacuation routes.	0A9; P-1	0A9; P-1	3
Locate and demonstrate knowledge of material safety data sheets (MSDS).	0A15; P-1	0A15; P-1	3
B. Personal Safety			
Comply with the required safe use of safety glasses, ear protection, gloves, and shoes, during lab/shop activities.	0A10; P-1	0A10; P-1	4
Identify and wear appropriate clothing for lab/shop activities.	0A11; P-1	0A11; P-1	4
Secure hair and jewelry for lab/shop activities.	0A12; P-1	0A12; P-1	4
C. Tool Safety			
Identify tools and their usage in automotive applications.	0B1; P-1	0B1; P-1	6
Identify standard and metric designation.	0B2; P-1	0B2; P-1	6
Utilize safe procedures for handling of tools and equipment.	0A2; P-1	0A2; P-1	6
Demonstrate safe handling and use of appropriate tools.	0B3; P-1	0B3; P-1	6
Demonstrate proper cleaning, storage, and maintenance of tools and equipment.	0B4; P-1	0B4; P-1	6
Demonstrate proper use of precision measuring tools (i.e. micrometer, dial-indicator, dial-caliper).	0B5; P-1	0B5; P-1	6
D. Vehicle Protection and Jack and Lift Safety			
Identify purpose and demonstrate proper use of fender covers, mats.	0C2; P-1	0C2; P-1	7
Utilize proper ventilation procedures for working within the lab/shop area.	0A5; P-1	0A5; P-1	4
Identify and use proper placement of floor jacks and jack stands.	0A3; P-1	0A3; P-1	7
Identify and use proper procedures for safe lift operation.	0A4; P-1	0A4; P-1	7
Engine Repair			
A. Vehicle, Customer, and Service Infromation			
Complete work order to include customer information, vehicle identifying information, customer concern, related service history, cause, and correction.		1A1; P-1	11

NATEF 2013 Tasksheet Title	MLR NATEF Reference number; Priority Level	AST NATEF Reference number; Priority Level	Chapter Number
Research applicable vehicle and service information, such as internal engine operation, vehicle service history, service precautions, and technical service bulletins.	1A1; P-1	1A2; P-1	11
Identify hybrid vehicle internal combustion engine service precautions.	1A7; P-3	1A9; P-3	41
B. Fastener Repair			
Perform common fastener and thread repair, to include: remove broken bolt, restore internal and external threads, and repair internal threads with thread insert.	1A6; P-1	1A7; P-1	6
C. Engine Mechanical Testing			
Inspect engine assembly for fuel, oil, coolant, and other leaks; determine necessary action.	1A3; P-1	1A4; P-1	11
Verify operation of the instrument panel engine warning indicators.	1A2; P-1	1A3; P-1	8
E. Cylinder Head Removal, Inspection, and Installation			
Remove and replace timing belt; verify correct camshaft timing.	1A5; P-1	1A6; P-1	11
F. Cylinder Head Dissasembly, Inspection, and Repair			
Adjust valves (mechanical or hydraulic lifters).	1B1; P-1	1B4; P-1	11
J. Miscellaneous In-Vehicle Engine Tasks			
Install engine covers using gaskets, seals, and sealers as required.	1A4; P-1	1A5; P-1	11
K. Lubrication System Service			
Perform engine oil and filter change.	1C5; P-1	1D10; P-1	12
L. Cooling System Service			
Perform cooling system pressure and dye tests to identify leaks; check coolant condition and level; inspect and test radiator, pressure cap, coolant recovery tank, and heater core and galley plugs; determine necessary action.	1C1; P-1	1D1; P-1	13
Inspect, replace, and adjust drive belts, tensioners, and pulleys; check pulley and belt alignment.	1C2; P-1	1D3; P-1	13
Remove, inspect, and replace thermostat and gasket/seal.	1C3; P-1	1D7; P-1	13
Inspect and test coolant; drain and recover coolant; flush and refill cooling system with recommended coolant; bleed air as required.	1C4; P-1	1D4; P-1	13
Automatic Transmission and Transaxle			
A. Vehicle, Customer, and Service information			
Check fluid level in a transmission or a transaxle equipped with a dip-stick.	2A2; P-1	2A4; P-1	15
Check fluid level in a transmission or a transaxle not equipped with a dip-stick.	2A3; P-1	2A5; P-1	15
Check transmission fluid condition; check for leaks.	2A4; P-2		15
Diagnose fluid loss and condition concerns; determine necessary action.		2A3; P-1	15
Drain and replace fluid and filter(s).	2B4; P-1	2B4; P-1	15
Describe the operational characteristics of a continuously variable transmission (CVT)	2C1; P-3	2C4; P-3	16
Describe the operational characteristics of a hybrid vehicle drive train.	2C2; P-3	2C5; P-3	16
D. Maintenance and Repair			
Inspect, adjust, and replace external manual valve shift linkage, transmission range sensor/switch, and park/neutral position switch.	2B1; P-2	2B1; P-2	15
Inspect for leakage at external seals, gaskets, and bushings	2B2; P-2		15
Inspect for leakage; replace external seals, gaskets, and bushings.		2B2; P-2	15
Inspect, replace and align powertrain mounts.	2B3; P-2	2B5; P-2	15

(continued)

NATEF 2013 Tasksheet Title	MLR NATEF Reference number; Priority Level	AST NATEF Reference number; Priority Level	Chapter Number
Inspect, leak test, and flush or replace transmission/transaxle oil cooler, lines and fittings		2C2; P-1	15
Manual Drive Train and Axles			
A. Vehicle, Customer, and Service Information			
Research applicable vehicle and service information, fluid type, vehicle service history, service precautions, and technical service bulletins.	3A1; P-1	3A2; P-1	14
Describe the operational characteristics of an electronically controlled manual transmission/transaxle.	3C1; P-3	3C2; P-3	16
B. Transmission/Transaxle Maintenance			
Check fluid condition; check for leaks.	3A3; P-1		17
Check fluid condition; check for leaks; determine necessary action		3A3; P-1	17
Drain and refill manual transmission/transaxle and final drive unit.	3A2; P-1	3A4; P-1	17
C. Clutch Maintenance			
Check and adjust clutch master cylinder fluid level.	3B1; P-1	3B5	18
Check for system leaks.	3B2; P-1		18
Bleed clutch hydraulic system.		3B4; P-1	18
G. Drive Shaft, Half Shaft, Universal, and Constant-Velocity Joint Diagnosis and Repair			
Inspect, service, and replace shafts, yokes, boots, and universal/CV joints.	3D2; P-2	3D4; P-1	19
Inspect, remove and replace front wheel drive (FWD) bearings, hubs, and seals.	3D1; P-2	3D3; P-1	19
H. Drive Axle Diagnosis and Repair			
Check and adjust differential housing fluid level.	3E2; P-1	3E1: 2; P-1	17 19
Drain and refill differential housing.	3E3; P-1	3E1: 3; P-1	17 19
Clean and inspect differential housing; check for leaks; inspect housing vent.	3E1; P-2	3E1: 1; P-2	19
J. Drive Axle Shaft			
Inspect and replace drive axle wheel studs.	3E1:1; P-2	3E2:1; P-1	19
K. Four-Wheel Drive/ All-Wheel Drive Component Diagnosis and Repair			
Inspect front-wheel bearings and locking hubs	3F1: P-3		19
Inspect front-wheel bearings and locking hubs; perform necessary action(s).		3F2; P-3	19
Check for leaks at drive assembly seals; check vents; check lube level.	3F2; P-3	3F3; P-3	19
Identify concerns related to variations in tire circumference and/or final drive ratios.		3F4; P-3	19
Suspension and Steering Systems			
A. Vehicle, Customer, and Service information			
Research applicable vehicle and service information, such as suspension and steering system operation, vehicle service history, service precautions, and technical service bulletins.	4A1; P-1	4A1; P-1	Chapter Number
B. Wheel and Tire Maintenance			
Inspect tire condition; identify tire wear patterns; check for correct tire size and application (load and speed ratings) and adjust air pressure; determine necessary action.	4D1; P-1	4F1; P-1	20
Rotate tires according to manufacturer's recommendations.	4D2; P-1	4F3; P-1	20
Dismount, inspect, and remount tire on wheel; Balance wheel and tire assembly (static and dynamic).	4D3; P-1	4F6; P-1	20
Demonstrate knowledge of steps required to remove and replace sensors in a tire pressure monitoring system.	4D8; P-2	4F11: P-1	20

NATEF 2013 Tasksheet Title	MLR NATEF Reference number; Priority Level	AST NATEF Reference number; Priority Level	Chapter Number
Dismount, inspect, and remount tire on wheel equipped with tire pressure monitoring system sensor.	4D4; P-2	4F7; P-2	20
C. Wheel and Tire Diagnosis			
Inspect tire and wheel assembly for air loss; perform necessary action.	4D5; P-1	4F8; P-1	20
Repair tire using internal patch.	4D6; P-1	4F9; P-1	20
Measure wheel, tire, axle flange, and hub runout; determine necessary action.		4F4; P-2	20
Identify and test tire pressure monitoring systems (indirect and direct) for operation; verify operation of instrument panel lamps.	4D7; P-2	4F10; P-2	20
D. Power Steering Pump Maintenance and Service			
Determine proper power steering fluid type; inspect fluid level and condition.	4B2; P-1	4B9; P-1	21
Replace power steering pump filter(s).	N/A	N/A	21
Flush, fill, and bleed power steering system.	4B3; P-2	4B10; P-2	21
Remove, inspect, replace, and adjust power steering pump belt.	4B5; P-1	4B12; P-1	13
Inspect for power steering fluid leakage; determine necessary action.	4B4; P-1	4B11; P-1	21
Inspect and replace power steering hoses and fittings.	4B6; P-2	4B15; P-2	21
E. Steering Gear Service			
Inspect rack and pinion steering gear inner tie rod ends (sockets) and bellows boots.	4B1; P-1		21
F. Steering Linkage Service			
Inspect pitman arm, relay (centerlink/intermediate) rod, idler arm and mountings, and steering linkage damper.	4B7; P-1		21
Inspect tie rod ends (sockets), tie rod sleeves, and clamps	4B8; P-1		21
H. Steering Column Service			
Disable and enable supplemental restraint system (SRS).	4A2; P-1	4B1; P-1	21
I. Front Suspension Service-Long and Short Arm			
Inspect and replace front stabilizer bar (sway bar) bushings, brackets, and links.	4B15; P-1		22
Inspect suspension system coil springs and spring insulators (silencers).	4B13; P-1		22
Inspect upper and lower control arms, bushings, and shafts.	4B9; P-1		22
Inspect and replace rebound and jounce bumpers.	4B10; P-1		
Inspect upper and lower ball joints (with or without wear indicators).	4B12; P-1		22
J. Font Suspension Service-Strut and Torsion Bar			
Inspect strut cartridge or assembly.	4B16; P-1		22
Inspect front strut bearing and mount.	4B17; P-1		22
Inspect track bar, strut rods/radius arms, and related mounts and bushings.	4B11; P-1		22
Inspect suspension system torsion bars and mounts.	4B14; P-1		22
L. Rear Suspension Service			
Inspect, remove, and replace shock absorbers; inspect mounts and bushings.	4B20; P-1	4D1; P-1	22?
Inspect rear suspension system lateral links/arms (track bars), control (trailing) arms.	4B18; P-1		22
Inspect rear suspension system leaf spring(s), spring insulators (silencers), shackles, brakets, bushings, ccenter pinks/bolts, and mounts.	4B19; P-1		22
M. Electronically Controlled Steering and Suspension Service			
Inspect electric power assist steering.	4B21; P-3	4C19; P-3	21

(continued)

NATEF 2013 Tasksheet Title	MLR NATEF Reference number; Priority Level	AST NATEF Reference number; Priority Level	Chapter Number
Describe the function of the power steering pressure switch.	4B23; P-3	4D3; P-3	21
Identify hybrid vehicle power steering system electrical circuits and safety precautions.	4B22; P-2	4B18; P-2	21
N. Wheel Alignment Diagnosis, Adjustment, and Repair			
Perform prealignment inspection and measure vehicle ride height; determine necessary action.	4C1; P-1		
Perform prealignment inspection and measure vehicle ride height; perform necessary action.		4E2; P-1	22
Prepare vehicle for wheel alignment on the alignment machine; perform four wheel alignment by checking and adjusting front and rear wheel caster, camber; and toe as required; center steering wheel.		4E3; P-1	22
Check toe-out-on-turns (turning radius); determine necessary action.		4E4; P-2	22
Check SAI (steering axis inclination) and included angle; determine necessary action.		4E5; P-2	22
Check rear wheel thrust angle; determine necessary action.		4E6; P-1	22
Check for front wheel setback; determine necessary action.		4E7; P-2	22
Check front and/or rear cradle (subframe) alignment; determine necessary action.		4E8; P-3	22
Reset steering angle sensor		4E9; P-2	22
Brakes			
A. Vehicle, Customer, and Service Information			
Research applicable vehicle and service information, such as brake system operation, vehicle service history, service precautions, and technical service bulletins.	5A1; P-1	5A2; P-1	23
Identify and interpret brake system concerns; determine necessary action.		5A1; P-1	25
Describe procedure for performing a road test to check brake system operation, including an anti-lock brake system (ABS).	5A2; P-1	5A3; P-1	25
B. Fluid Testing and Maintenance			
Select, handle, store, and fill brake fluids to proper level.	5B4; P-1	5B9; P-1	24
Test brake fluid for contamination.	5B7; P-1	5B13; P-1	24
Bleed and/or flush brake system.	5B6; P-1	5B12; P-1	24
C. Master Cylinder Testing and Service			
Measure brake pedal height, travel, and free play (as applicable); determine necessary action.	5B1; P-1	5B2; P-1	24
Check master cylinder for external leaks and proper operation.	5B2; P-1		24
Remove, bench bleed, and reinstall master cylinder.		5B4; P-1	24
D. Brake Lines and Hoses Inspection and Repair			
Inspect brake lines, flexible hoses, and fittings for leaks, dents, kinks, rust, cracks, bulging, wear; tighten loose fittings and supports; determine necessary action.	5B3; P-1	5B6; P-1	24
Replace brake lines, hoses, fittings, and supports.		5B7; P-2	24
Fabricate brake lines using proper material and flaring procedures (double flare and ISO types).		5B8; P-2	24
E. Disc Brake Inspection, Maintenance, and Service			
Diagnose poor stopping, noise, vibration, pulling, grabbing, dragging or pulsation concerns; determine necessary action.		5D1	25
Remove and clean caliper assembly; inspect for leaks and damage/wear to caliper housing; determine necessary action.	5D1	5D2	25

NATEF 2013 Tasksheet Title	MLR NATEF Reference number; Priority Level	AST NATEF Reference number; Priority Level	Chapter Number
Clean and inspect caliper mounting and slides/pins for proper operation, wear, and damage; determine necessary action.	5D2	5D3	25
Check brake pad wear indicator; determine necessary action.	5D10	5D11	25
Remove, inspect and replace pads and retaining hardware; determine necessary action.	5D3	5D4	25
Reasasemble, lubricate, and reinstall seat pads and caliper, pads, and related hardware; inspect for leaks.	5D4	5D5	25
Retract and re-adjust caliper piston on an integral parking brake system.	5D9	5D10	25
Describe importance of operating vehicle to burnish/break-in replacement brake pads according to manufacturer's recommendations.	5D11	5D12	25
F. Rotor Inspection and Service			
Clean and inspect rotor; measure rotor thickness, thickness variation, and lateral runout; determine necessary action	5D5; P-1	5D6; P-1	25
Remove and reinstall rotor.	5D6; P-1	5D7; P-1	25
Refinish rotor off vehicle; measure final rotor thickness and compare with specifications.	5D8; P-1	5D9; P-1	25
Refinish rotor on vehicle; measure final rotor thickness and compare with specifications.	5D7; P-1	5D8; P-1	25
Inspect and replace wheel studs.	5F6; P-1	5F7; P-1	25
G. Drum Brake Inspection, Maintenance, and Service			
Diagnose poor stopping, noise, vibration, pulling, grabbing, dragging or pedal pulsation concerns; determine necessary action.		5C1; P-1	26
Remove, clean, inspect, and measure brake drum diameter; determine necessary action.	5C1; P-1	5C2; P-1	26
Refinish brake drum and measure final drum diameter; compare with specifications.	5C2; P-1	5C3; P-1	26
Remove, clean, and inspect brake shoes, springs, pins, clips, levers, adjusters/self-adjusters, other related brake hardware, and backing support plates; lubricate and reassemble.	5C3; P-1	5C4; P-1	26
Inspect wheel cylinders for leaks and proper operation; remove and replace as needed.	5C4; P-2	5C5; P-2	26
Pre-adjust brake shoes and parking brake; install brake drums or drum/hub assemblies and wheel bearings; make final checks and adjustments.	5C5; P-2	5C6; P-2	26
Install wheel and torque lug nuts.	5A3; P-1	5A4; P-1	26
H. Parking Brake Inspection and Service			
Check parking brake cables and components for wear, binding, and corrosion; clean, lubricate, adjust or replace as needed.	5F2; P-2	5F3; P-2	24
Check parking brake operation and parking brake indicator light system operation; determine necessary action.	5F3; P-1	5F4; P-1	24
I. Power Booster Inspection			
Check brake pedal travel with, and without, engine running to verify proper power booster operation.	5E1; P-2	5E1; P-2	24
Check vacuum supply(manifold or auxiliary pump) to vacuum-type power booster.	5E2; P-1	5E2; P-1	24
Inspect the vacuum-type power booster unit for leaks; inspect the check valve for proper operation; determine necessary action.		5E3; P-1	24

(continued)

NATEF 2013 Tasksheet Title	MLR NATEF Reference number; Priority Level	AST NATEF Reference number; Priority Level	Chapter Number
J. Hydraulic System Diagnosis and Service			
Diagnose pressure concerns in the brake system using hydraulic principles (Pascal's Law).		5B1; P-1	24
Diagnose poor stopping, pulling or dragging concerns caused by malfunctions in the hydraulic system; determine necessary action.		5B5; P-1	25
K. Wheel Bearing Inspection, Maintenance, and Service			
Remove, clean, inspect, repack, and install wheel bearings; replace seals; install hub and adjust bearings.	5F1; P-1	5F2; P-1	27
Replace wheel bearing and race.	5F5; P-2	5F6; P-2	27
Remove and reinstall sealed wheel bearing assembly.		5F8; P-2	27
Diagnose wheel bearing noises, wheel shimmy, and vibration concerns; determine necessary action.		5F1; P-3	27
L. Brake Warning Light and Stop Light inspection and Service			
Check operation of brake stop light system; determine necessary action	5F4; P-1	5F5; P-1	24
Identify components of the brake warning light system	5B5; P-3	5B11; P-2	24
Inspect, test, and/or replace components of brake warning light system.		5B10; P-3	24
M. Electronic Brake Control Maintenance and Service			
Identify traction control/vehicle stability control system components.	5G1; P-3	5G2; P-3	28
Describe the operation of a regenerative braking system.	5G2; P-3	5G3; P-3	16
Electrical			
A. Vehicle, Customer, and Service Information			
Demonstrate knowledge of electrical/electronic series, parallel, and series-parallel circuits using principles of electricity (Ohm's Law).	6A2; P-1	6A2; P-1	30
B. Battery Diagnosis and Service			
Perform battery state-of-charge test; determine necessary action.	6B1; P-1	6B1; P-1	31
Confirm proper battery capacity for vehicle application; perform battery capacity test; determine necessary action.	6B2; P-1	6B2; P-1	31
Identify electronic modules, security systems, radios, and other accessories that require reinitialization or code entry after reconnecting vehicle battery.	6B8; P-1	6B8; P-1	31
Maintain or restore electronic memory functions	6B3; P-1	6B3; P-1	31
Inspect and clean battery; fill battery cells; check battery cables, connectors, clamps, and hold-downs.	6B4; P-1	6B4; P-1	31
Perform slow/fast battery charge according to manufacturer's instructions.	6B5; P-1	6B5; P-1	31
Jump-start vehicle using jumper cables and a booster battery or an auxiliary power supply.	6B6; P-1	6B6; P-1	31
Measure key-off battery drain (parasitic draw)	6A8; P-1		31
Identify hybrid vehicle auxiliary (12v) battery service, repair,	6B9	6B9; P-3	41
C. Starting System Diagnosis and Repair			
Perform starter current draw tests; determine necessary action.	6C1; P-1	6C1; P-1	32
Perform starter circuit voltage drop tests; determine necessary action.	6C2; P-1	6C2; P-1	32
Inspect and test switches, connectors, and wires of starter control circuits; determine necessary action.	6C5; P-2	6C5; P-2	32
Inspect and test starter relays and solenoids; determine necessary action.	6C3; P-2	6C3; P-2	32
Remove and install starter in a vehicle.	6C4; P-1	6C4; P-1	32

NATEF 2013 Tasksheet Title	MLR NATEF Reference number; Priority Level	AST NATEF Reference number; Priority Level	Chapter Number
Differentiate between electrical and engine mechanical problems that cause a slow-crank or no-crank condition.		6C6; P-2	32
D. Charging System Diagnosis and Repair			
Inspect, adjust, or replace generator (alternator) drive belts; check pulleys, and tensioners for wear; check pulley and belt alignment.	6D2; P-1	6D3; P-1	23
Perform charging system output test; determine necessary action.	6D1; P-1	6D1; P-1	32
Perform charging circuit voltage drop tests; determine necessary action.	6D4; P-1	6D5; P-1	32
Remove, inspect, and re-install generator (alternator).	6D3; P-1	6D4; P-1	32
Diagnose (troubleshoot) charging system for the cause of under-charge, no-charge, or overcharge conditions.		6D2; P-1	32
E. Lighting System Diagnosis and Repair			
Identify system voltage and safety precautions associated with high intensity discharge headlights.	6E3; P-2	6E4; P-2	33
Inspect interior and exterior lamps and sockets including headlights and auxiliary lights (fog lights/driving lights); replace as needed.	6E1; P-1	6E2; P-1	33
Aim headlights.	6E2; P-2	6E3; P-2	33
F. Fundamentals			
Use wiring diagrams to trace electrical/electronic circuits .	6A3; P-1	6A7; P-1	30
Use wiring diagrams during the diagnosis (troubleshooting) of electrical/electronic circuit problems.	N/A	N/A	30
Demonstrate the proper use of a digital multimeter (DMM) when measuring source voltage, voltage drop, (including grounds), current flow and resistance.	6A4; P-17	6A3; P-1	30
Check operation of electrical circuits with a test light.	6A6; P-2	6A5; P-2	30
Check operation of electrical circuits with fused jumper wires.	6A7; P-2	6A6; P-2	30
Inspect and test fusible links, circuit breakers, and fuses; determine necessary action.	6A9; P-1	6A9; P-1	30
Demonstrate knowledge of the causes and effects from shorts, grounds, opens, and resistance problems in electrical/electronic circuits.	6A5; P-1	6A4; P-1	30
Inspect and test switches, connectors, relays, solenoid solid state devices, and wires of electrical/electronic circuits; determine necessary action.		6A10; P-1	30
G. Wire Repair			
Replace electrical connectors and terminal ends.	6A11; P-1	6A11; P-1	29
Perform solder repair of electrical wiring.	6A10; P-1	6A13; P-1	29
H. Horn and Wiper/Washer diagnosis and Repair			
Diagnose (troubleshoot) causes of incorrect horn operation; perform necessary action.		6G1; P-1	34
Verify windshield wiper and washer operation; replace wiper blades	6F5; P-1	6H10; P-1	34
Diagnose (troubleshoot) windshield washer problems; perform necessary action.		6G3; P-1	34
J. Accessories Diagnosis and Repair			
Describe the operation of keyless entry/remote-start systems.	6F3; P-3	6H8; P-3	34
K. Accessories Diagnosis and Repair (SRS, etc)			
Disable and enable an airbag system for vehicle service; verify indicator lamp operation.	6F1; P-1	6H5; P-1	34
Remove and reinstall the door panel.	6F2; P-1	6H6; P-1	34

(continued)

NATEF 2013 Tasksheet Title	MLR NATEF Reference number; Priority Level	AST NATEF Reference number; Priority Level	Chapter Number
HVAC			
A. Vehicle, Customer, and Service Information			
Identify hybrid vehicle A/C system electrical circuits and the service/safety precautions.	7B2; P-2	7B4; P-2	41
B. Preliminary Testing			
Performance test A/C system; identify problems.		7A3; P-1	35
Inspect A/C condenser for airflow restrictions; determine necessary action.	7B3; P-1		35
Inspect A/C condenser for airflow restrictions; perform necessary action.		7B7; P-1	35
Inspect evaporator housing water drain; perform necessary action.		7B10; P-1	35
Identify the source of A/C system odors.	7D2; P-2	7D7; P-2	35
D. Refrigeration System Component Diagnosis and Repair			
Inspect and replace A/C compressor drive belts, pulleys, and tensioners; determine necessary action.	7B1; P-1	7B1; P-1	35
E. Heating, Ventilation, and Engine Cooling Systems Daignosis and Repair			
Inspect engine cooling and heater system hoses; perform necessary action.	7C1; P-1	7C1; P-1	13
Inspect and test heater control valve(s); perform necessary action.		7C2; P-2	35
F. Operating Systems and Related Controls Diagnosis and Repair			
Inspect A/C-heater ducts, doors, hoses, cabin filters and outlets; perform necessary action.	7D1; P-1	7D6; P-3	35
Engine Performance			
B. Mechanical Engine Testing			
Perform engine absolute (vacuum/boost) manifold pressure tests; determine necessary action.	8A2; P-1	8A5; P-1	11
Perform cylinder power balance test; determine necessary action.	8A3; P-1	8A6; P-2	11
Perform cylinder cranking and running compression tests; determine necessary action.	8A4; P-1	8A7; P-1	11
Perform cylinder leakage test; determine necessary action.	8A5; P-1	8A8; P-1	11
Diagnose abnormal engine noises or vibration concerns; determine necessary action.		8A3; P-3	11
C. Camshaft Timing			
Verify correct camshaft timing.		8A11; P-1	11
D. Engine Operating Temperature			
Verify engine operating temperature; determine necessary action.	8A6; P-1	8A10; P-1	13
E. Ignition System			
Remove and replace spark plugs; inspect secondary ignition components for wear and damage.	8A7; P-1	8C4; P-1	36
F. Fuel and Induction System Testing			
Inspect and test fuel pumps and pump control systems for pressure, regulation, and volume; perform necessary action.		8D2; P-1	37
Check fuel for contaminants; determine necessary action.		8D1; P-2	37
Inspect and test fuel injectors.		8D6; P-2	37
Replace fuel filter(s).	8C1; P-1	8D3; P-1	37
Inspect, service, or replace air filters, filter housings, and intake duct work.	8C2; P-1	8D4; P-1	8

NATEF 2013 Tasksheet Title	MLR NATEF Reference number; Priority Level	AST NATEF Reference number; Priority Level	Chapter Number
H. Exhaust System Testing			
Inspect condition of exhaust system hangers, brackets, clamps, and heat shields; repair or replace as needed.	8C4; P-1	8D9; P-1	8
Inspect integrity of the exhaust manifold, exhaust pipes, muffler(s), catalytic converter(s), resonator(s), tail pipe(s), and heat shields; perform necessary action.	8C3; P-1	8D8; P-1	39
Check and refill diesel exhaust fluid (DEF).	8C5; P-3	8D11; P-3	8
Perform exhaust system back-pressure test; determine necessary action.		8D10; P-2	39
I. Powertrain Control System Testing			
Describe the importance of running all OBDII monitors for repair verification.	8B2; P-1	8B4; P-1	38
Retrieve and record diagnostic trouble codes, OBD monitor status, and freeze frame data; clear codes when applicable.	8B1; P-1	8B1; P-1	38
J. PCV System Testing			
Inspect, test, and service positive crankcase ventilation (PCV) filter/breather cap, valve, tubes, orifices, and hoses; perform necessary action.	8D1; P-2	8E2; P-2	40
N. General Driveability and Emission Diagnosis			
Diagnose engine mechanical, electrical, electronic, fuel, and ignition concerns; determine necessary action.		8A9; P-2	38

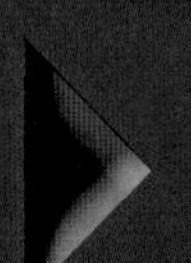

APPENDIX B
NATEF Integrated Applied Academic Skills Correlation Guide

Applied Math	Chapter	Applied Science	Chapter	Applied Communication	Chapter
AM-1	30			AC-1	9
AM-2	30	AS-2	3	AC-2	9
AM-3	30	AS-3	3	AC-3	9
AM-4	30	AS-4	3	AC-4	9
AM-5	30	AS-5	3	AC-5	9
AM-6	30	AS-6	11	AC-6	9
AM-7	30	AS-7	5	AC-7	9
AM-8	30	AS-8	5	AC-8	9
AM-9	30	AS-9	25	AC-9	9
AM-10	30	AS-11	5	AC-10	9
AM-12	30	AS-12	23	AC-11	9
AM-14	39	AS-15	22	AC-12	9
AM-16	11	AS-18	38	AC-13	9
AM-17	25	AS-19	35	AC-14	9
AM-18	37	AS-23	35	AC-15	9
AM-21	22	AS-24	40	AC-16	9
AM-23	25	AS-25	12	AC-17	9
AM-24	22	AS-27	13	AC-18	9
AM-25	22	AS-28	35	AC-19	9
AM-26	22	AS-29	35	AC-20	9
AM-27	20	AS-30	13	AC-21	9
AM-28	20	AS-31	13	AC-22	9
AM-29	12	AS-32	13	AC-23	5
AM-30	12	AS-33	33	AC-24	9
AM-33	35	AS-34	11	AC-25	9
AM-35	17	AS-35	11	AC-26	9
AM-36	8	AS-36	25	AC-27	9
AM-40	35	AS-37	26	AC-28	9
AM-44	29	AS-38	39	AC-29	9
AM-45	30	AS-39	39	AC-30	9
AM-46	29	AS-40	39	AC-31	9
AM-47	30	AS-41	30	AC-32	9
AM-48	29	AS-43	14, 39	AC-33	9
AM-50	8	AS-44	39	AC-34	9

Applied Math	Chapter	Applied Science	Chapter	Applied Communication	Chapter
AM-51	22	AS-45	39	AC-35	9
AM-52	21	AS-47	20	AC-36	9
AM-53	15	AS-39	10		
		AS-51	23		
		AS-52	22		
		AS-53	29		
		AS-54	31		
		AS-55	31		
		AS-56	31		
		AS-57	29		
		AS-58	29		
		AS-60	29		
		AS-61	29		
		AS-62	29		
		AS-64	31		
		AS-65	36		
		AS-66	34		
		AS-69	29		
		AS-70	29		
		AS-71	29		
		AS-72	31		
		AS-73	32		
		AS-74	31		
		AS-75	32		
		AS-76	36		
		AS-77	30		
		AS-83	38		
		AS-84	35		
		AS-87	24		
		AS-88	22		
		AS-89	40		
		AS-90	23		
		AS-91	23		
		AS-92	12		
		AS-96	24		
		AS-97	10		
		AS-98	16		
		AS-99	10		
		AS-101	11		
		AS-103	12		

GLOSSARY

abrasive discs (cutting wheels) Abrasive wheels or flat discs fitted to bench, pedestal, and portable grinders.

acceleration An increase in a vehicle's speed.

accelerator pedal The foot-operated pedal used by the driver to increase and decrease the amount of power the engine develops.

accessory drive pulley A round circular metal disc attached to the front of the engine crankshaft with a rubber/fiber belt that helps operate automotive accessories.

accumulator (heating and cooling system) A device placed between the evaporator and the compressor to collect liquid refrigerant and prevent it from entering the compressor.

accumulator (manual transmission) A device used to reduce the speed of clutch or band application to help prevent harsh shifting.

accumulator (brakes) A storage container that holds pressurized brake fluid.

Ackermann angle The angle the steering arms make with the steering axis, projected toward the center of the rear axle.

Ackermann principle The geometric alignment of linkages in a vehicle's steering such that the wheels on the inside of a turn are able to move in a different circle radius than the wheels on the outside.

active control A system of providing constant feedback from sensors in the vehicle to the control unit.

actuating The act of making something move or work.

actuator (heating and cooling system) A device that is electrically or vacuum controlled and is used to physically move doors within the heater box to control airflow.

adaptive air suspension A suspension system that uses rubber bags or bladders filled with air to support the weight of the vehicle.

adjustable bushing A brace or nylon part that pushes against the rack to adjust the mesh of the rack teeth to the pinion teeth.

adjusting nut The nut used to adjust the end play or preload of a wheel bearing.

adjustment sleeve A component that connects the tie-rods together and to the center link on some applications, providing the adjustment point for toe-in or toe-out, depending on the manufacturer's specifications.

advance mechanism A device used to trigger an earlier spark based on engine conditions.

aerate The tendency to create air bubbles in a fluid.

after top dead center (ATDC) The position of the piston once it has moved beyond top dead center.

aftermarket That segment of the trade that supplies parts, services, and repair for vehicles outside of the original equipment manufacturer (OEM) or the dealer network.

air checking The use of compressed air to check clutch and servo operation on transmissions during and after assembly.

air diverter valve A valve that changes secondary airflow from the exhaust stream to the air cleaner or vice versa.

air drier A device fitted to compressed air lines to remove moisture.

air drill A compressed air–powered drill.

air gap The space or clearance between two components, such as the space between the tone wheel and the pick-up coil in a wheel speed sensor.

air hammer A tool powered by compressed air with various hammer, cutting, punching, or chisel attachments. Also called an air chisel.

air impact wrench An impact tool powered by compressed air designed to undo tight fasteners.

air nozzle A compressed air device that emits a fine stream of compressed air for drying or cleaning parts.

air ratchet A ratchet tool for use with sockets powered by compressed air.

air spring A part that provides the springing action or auxiliary spring. It is typically used in air suspension systems or heavy truck applications.

air supply system Equipment in a motor vehicle that delivers air to the engine.

air switching valve The valve used to switch secondary air from near the exhaust valve (upstream) to the catalytic converter (downstream) for the purpose of oxidizing hydrocarbons and carbon monoxide.

air-conditioning compressor clutch The mechanical coupler that is electromagnetically engaged and provides a way of uncoupling the compressor from the accessory drive belt.

air-conditioning machine A machine designed to recover, recycle, evacuate, leak test, and recharge (R/R/R) the air-conditioning system.

air-conditioning pressure sensor A sensor that gives an input signal of refrigerant pressure in the air—conditioning system to the ECU.

air-conditioning system pressure The refrigerant pressure contained within the air-conditioning system.

Allen wrench A type of hexagonal drive mechanism for fasteners.

alloy The mixture of materials to make a substance that has properties different from the original materials. Aluminum alloy has silica added to make it perform better than pure aluminum.

all-wheel drive (AWD) A drive train arrangement in which all of the wheels drive the vehicle.

alternating current (AC) A type of current flow that flows back and forth.

alternative fuel A nonpetroleum-based motor fuel.

aluminum rod A lightweight, strong, either cast or forged metal shaft that connects the piston assembly to the crankshaft assembly.

ambient air temperature sensor A thermistor that is used to measure the air temperature outside the vehicle.

American Petroleum Institute (API) The organization responsible for setting the standards for all American petroleum products including natural gas and biodiesel fuels.

American wire gauge (AWG) A standard used to identify different wire sizes.

ammeter A device used to measure current flow.

amp An abbreviation for amperes, the unit for current measurement.

anchor pin A component of the backing plate that takes all of the braking force from the brake shoes.

anemometer A device that measures airflow in feet per minute (fpm).

angle grinder A portable grinder for grinding or cutting metal.

anisotropic An object that has unequal physical properties, along its various axes. Used in head gaskets to pull heat laterally from the edge surrounding the combustion chamber to the water jacket.

antibinding The release of something when it gets stuck.

antifoaming agents Oil additives that keep oil from foaming as it moves through the engine.

anti-friction bearing Wheel bearing assemblies that use surfaces that are in rolling contact with each other to greatly reduce friction compared to surfaces in sliding contact.

anti-lock brake system (ABS) A safety measure for the braking system that uses a computer to monitor the speed of each wheel and control the hydraulic pressure to each wheel to prevent wheel lock-up.

applied force Pressure placed on something.

arc joint pliers Pliers with parallel slip jaws that can increase in size. Also called Channellocks.

arm The primary load-bearing element of a vehicle's suspension system, commonly known as control arm. Can also mean the steering arm, which applies the driver's turning effort to the steering knuckle.

armature The rotating wire coils in motors and generators. It is also the moving part of a solenoid or relay, and the pole piece in a permanent magnet generator.

asbestos A mineral with needle-like fibers that can become embedded in lung tissue and cause cancer.

aspect ratio The ratio of sidewall height to section width of a tire.

aspirator A tube that is used to direct airflow across the cabin air temperature sensor.

asymmetric tread pattern A tread pattern that differs on each side and, therefore, is usually directional.

Atkinson cycle An engine cycle that uses a longer effective exhaust stroke than intake stroke to reduce exhaust emissions. This type of engine is widely used in hybrid-electric vehicles.

atmospheric pressure The pressure of the air surrounding everything caused by gravity and the weight of air. The higher from sea level, the lower the atmospheric pressure.

automatic brake self-adjuster A system on drum brakes that automatically adjusts the brakes to maintain a specified amount of running clearance between the shoes and drum.

automatic climate control system A system that automatically adjusts the heating or cooling to meet a specified temperature demanded by the passengers.

automatic load-adjustable shock absorber Typically, an air shock absorber used in an automatic load-sensing system that adjusts ride height (ground clearance) automatically such as when additional weight is added to the vehicle.

automatic oiler A device fitted to compressed air systems to oil air tools.

Automotive Service Excellence (ASE) An independent, nonprofit organization dedicated to the improvement of vehicle repair through the testing and certification of automotive professionals.

Automotive Youth Educational Systems (AYES) An independent, nonprofit organization that is a partnership between automotive manufacturers, their dealerships, and affiliated secondary automotive programs.

available voltage The maximum amount of voltage that the induction coil secondary is capable of putting out.

aviation snips A scissor-like tool for cutting sheet metal.

axial load The load applied in line with a shaft. It can be controlled with thrust bearings.

axle The shaft of the suspension system to which the tires and wheels are attached; used to transmit driving torque to the wheels.

back clearance The area or space behind the piston rings when the rings are in the piston ring grooves.

backing plate (disc brakes) A metal plate to which the brake lining is fixed.

backing plate A stamped steel plate, bolted to the steering or suspension, which supports the wheel cylinder, brake shoes, and other hardware.

backlash clearance The amount of movement between the pinion teeth versus the ring teeth.

baffle A plate installed vertically in the fuel tank to control sloshing of the fuel.

balance shaft A metal shaft attached and located inside the engine cylinder block assembly to counteract crankshaft vibrations.

ball bearings The rolling components of a wheel bearing consisting of hardened balls that roll in matching grooves in the inner and outer races.

ball hone An assembly of metal rods, with abrasive stones attached, that is inserted into the cylinder and spun to break the glazing off the cylinder walls and make a new crosshatched pattern.

ball joint A swivel connection mounted in the outer end of the front control arm. These swivels are typically constructed with a ball and socket to allow pivoting.

ball-peen (engineer's) hammer A hammer that has a head that is rounded on one end and flat on the other; designed to work with metal items.

ball-return guide A special passage or metal tube through which the balls move in recirculating ball steering boxes.

ballast A device that increases lighting voltage substantially and controls the current to the bulb.

band brake A braking system that uses a metal band lined with friction material to clamp around the outside of a wheel or drum.

band A metal band with friction material bonded to one side. The band is contracted around a drum to stop the drum from spinning.

bar A metric unit of measure for pressure.

barometric pressure (BARO) sensor A sensor that measures atmospheric pressure.

barrier cream A cream that looks and feels like a moisturizing cream but has a specific formula to provide extra protection from chemicals and oils.

base circle The rounded bottom part of the camshaft (off the lobe) where the valves remain closed or at rest.

battery charger A device that charges a battery, reversing the discharge process.

battery electric vehicle (BEV) A vehicle powered by battery only.

battery An electrochemical device used to supply voltage to a vehicle's electrical systems.

baulk-ring synchromesh unit A synchronizer used in all current transmissions. It uses a blocking ring. Also called a blocker ring synchromesh unit.

bead seat The part of the wheel that the tire seals against.

beam axle A suspension system in which one set of wheels is connected laterally by a single beam or shaft.

beam-type axle A rear-wheel drive axle assembly that has a solid tube incorporating the differential gears.

bearing cage The component in a wheel bearing that maintains the proper spacing between the roller bearings or ball bearings.

bearing crush The force created to seat the bearing by the extra bearing material when the ends of the bearing inserts touch each other and are forced against each other.

bearing inserts Components made out of soft metal materials that are replaceable and come in pairs; also called half-shell bearings.

bearing packer A tool that forces grease into the spaces between the bearing rollers.

bearing races Hardened metal surfaces that roller or ball bearings fit into when a bearing is properly assembled.

bedding-in The process of a valve wearing into the valve seat and creating a positive seal around the whole diameter.

before top dead center (BTDC) The position of the piston when it has not yet reached top dead center.

belt alternator starter (BAS) A type of hybrid drive system that uses a belt-driven alternator/starter that operates on 42 volts.

belt routing label A label that lists a diagram of the serpentine belt routing for the engine accessories.

bench grinder (pedestal grinder) A grinder that is fixed to a bench or pedestal.

bench vice A device that securely holds material in jaws while it is being worked on.

bendable tangs Small tabs on the brake pad backing plate that are crimped on to the caliper, creating a secure fit and reducing noise.

bias-ply A tire constructed in a latticed, crisscrossing structure, with alternate plies crossing over each other and laid with the cord angles in opposite directions.

bidirectional control The ability to command different solenoids and actuators "on" and "off" to check their operation.

bidirectional scanners Scanners used to monitor engine compression, vacuum, internal engine anomalies, and so forth by causing various components and systems to operate for test purposes.

billet The roughly shaped steel piece that has been cast or forged but has not undergone its final machining.

bimetal Aluminum, tin, and silicon alloy metals placed together with steel to form one piece of material and used for bearing materials.

bleeder screw A screw that allows air and brake fluid to be bled out of a hydraulic brake system when it is loosened and seals the brake fluid in when it is tightened.

bleeding The process of removing air from a hydraulic braking system.

blind rivet A rivet that can be installed from its insertion side.

blink codes Codes used to communicate DTCs; they are given by the EBCM as a series of blinks illuminated by the ABS warning lamp.

block deck The "top" of the engine block and cylinder bore where the cylinder head is bolted on.

blocking ring A synchronizer part that increases or decreases a gear's speed to match shaft speed so that the synchronizer sleeve can lock the gear to the shaft. Also called baulk ring.

blow-by Pressure that leaks past the compression rings during compression and combustion.

blow-off valve A valve that allows the release of excessive boost pressure from the turbocharger when the throttle plate is quickly closed.

blowby gas The result of combustion gases leaking past the compression rings and getting into the crankcase.

blower motor An electric motor, usually the permanent magnet type, that moves air over the air-conditioning evaporator and heater core.

bob weights Weights used during the balancing process that are used to mimic the exact weight of the piston and connecting rod weights for that particular rod bearing journal.

body control module (BCM) The computer that controls the electrical system in the body of a vehicle, including power windows, door locks, heating and A/C systems, and in some cases the EBC system.

boiling point The temperature at which a substance begins to change from a liquid to a gas.

bolt A type of threaded fastener with a thread on one end and a hexagonal head on the other.

bolt cutters Strong cutters available in different sizes, designed to cut through non-hardened bolts and other small-stock material.

bonded linings Brake linings that are essentially glued to the brake pad backing plate; more common on light-duty vehicles.

boost valve A valve located in the HCU that is controlled by the EBCM; it allows brake fluid under high pressure to flow into the HCU hydraulic circuits to apply the brakes when commanded.

bore A tool used to make a hole in or through an object.

bored out An object that has been bored.

boring bar A long bar used to position and align a single-point tool, such as an engine cylinder block boring machine, for boring operations.

bottom dead center (BDC) The position of the piston at the end of its stroke when it is closest to the crankshaft.

bottoming tap A thread-cutting tap designed to cut threads to the bottom of a blind hole.

box-end wrench A wrench or spanner with a closed or ring end to grip bolts and nuts.

brake assist (BA) An enhanced safety system built in to some ABS systems that anticipates a panic stop and applies maximum braking force to slow the vehicle as quickly as possible.

brake booster A vacuum or hydraulically operated device that increases the driver's braking effort.

brake drum A short, wide, hollow cylinder that is capped on one end and bolted to a vehicle's wheel; it has an inner friction surface that the brake shoe is forced against.

brake fade The reduction in stopping power caused by a change in the brake system such as overheating, water, or overheated brake fluid.

brake fluid Hydraulic fluid that transfers forces under pressure through the hydraulic lines to the wheel braking units.

brake hose A flexible section of the brake lines between the body and suspension to allow for steering and suspension movement.

brake lathe A tool used to refinish the drum surface by removing a small amount of metal and returning it to a concentric, non-directional finish.

brake lines Made of seamless, double-walled steel, and able to transmit over 1000 psi (6895 kPa) of hydraulic pressure through the hydraulic brake system.

brake lining thickness gauge A tool used to measure the thickness of the brake lining.

brake pad shims and guides Small pieces of metal that cushion the brake pad and absorb some of the vibration, helping to cut down on unwanted noise.

brake pedal emulator A brake pedal assembly used in electronically controlled braking systems to send the driver's braking intention to the computer; it mimics the feel of a standard brake pedal.

brake shoe A steel shoe and brake lining friction material that apply force to the brake drum during braking.

brake shoe adjustment gauge An adjustable tool used to pre-adjust the brake shoes to the diameter of the brake drum.

brake spoon A tool used to adjust the brake lining-to-drum clearance when the drum is installed on the vehicle.

brake spring pliers A tool used for removing and installing brake return springs.

brake switch The electrical switch that is activated by the brake pedal; it turns on the brake lights and signals the EBCM that the brakes are being applied.

brake technician A technician who specializes in working on vehicle brake systems.

brake wash station A piece of equipment designed to safely clean brake dust from drum and disc brake components.

brake-by-wire system A braking system that uses no mechanical connection between the brake pedal and each brake unit. The system uses electrically actuated motors to apply brake force.

brakes A system made up of hydraulic and mechanical components designed to slow or stop a vehicle.

braking torque The torque acting to twist the axle housing around its center during braking.

breaker plate The movable plate which the breaker points are mounted on and which pivots as the vacuum advance pulls on it.

breather tube A tube used in the PCV system to allow fresh air into the engine crankcase.

brinelling Damage done to the surface of a bearing caused by excessive load, which exceeds the limit of the bearing material, typically from shock loads.

British thermal unit (Btu) A measure of heat energy. It takes 1 Btu to raise the temperature of 1 pound of water 1°F.

broach-style surfacer A tool used in resurfacing the engine block.

brushless An electric motor without brushes.

brushless DC motor An electric motor that does not have any brushes and is sometimes called an "electronically commutated motor." In this type of motor, an electronic control module replaces the brushes and commutator.

bucket-style lifter A bucket-shaped lifter assembly that sits on top of the valves and is operated directly by the camshaft. It can be hydraulic or mechanical.

bump steer The undesired condition produced when hitting a bump where the vehicle darts to one side as the steering linkage is pushed or pulled as a result of the travel of the suspension.

bushing An insert with an inner bearing surface that is fitted into a hole in an object, allowing the object to rotate or slide on a pin or shaft.

butt connector A crimp or solder joint that creates a permanent connection.

bypass filter An oil filter system that only filters some of the oil.

bypass valve The pressure control valve of the supercharger. When the bypass valve opens, it lets air move around the supercharger compressor section, reducing the boost pressure.

C-clamp A clamp shaped like the letter C; it comes in various sizes and can clamp various items.

cabin air temperature sensor A thermistor that measures air temperature inside the vehicle.

caliper A hydraulic device that uses pressure from the master cylinder to apply the brake pads against the rotor.

caliper dust boot seal driver set A set of drivers used to install metal-backed caliper dust boot seals.

caliper piston pliers A tool used to grip caliper pistons while removing them.

caliper piston retracting tool A tool used to retract caliper pistons on integrated parking brake systems.

cam The egg-shaped lobe machined to a shaft used to cause opening and closing of the valves of a four-stroke cycle engine.

cam lobe centerline The location of the cam lobe in relation to top dead center of the engine in degrees.

cam lobe ramp The rise of the lobe from the base circle to the top of the lobe, which is where the valve starts to lift, on the side opposite of where it starts to close.

cam lobe separation The number of degrees between the centerline of the intake lobe and the centerline of the exhaust lobe; this with cam duration determines the amount of valve overlap.

cam lobes Raised areas or protrusions on an otherwise round shaft.

camber The side-to-side vertical tilt of the wheel. It is viewed from the front of the vehicle and measured in degrees. Negative camber is when the top of the tire is closer to the center of the vehicle than the bottom of the tire.

cam-in-block engine An engine in which the camshaft is located in the engine block rather than on the cylinder head.

camshaft A shaft with lobes that operates the valve mechanisms controlling valve opening time and duration. Also, it can be used to drive fuel injection pumps and mechanical fuel pumps.

camshaft follower A slider or roller placed in direct contact with the lobes of the OHC camshaft that pushes on the tip of the valve to open it.

camshaft lobe The eccentric "egg-shaped" portion of the camshaft that pushes on the valve lifter or camshaft follower.

camshaft position (CMP) sensor A sensor mounted near the camshaft and used to send camshaft and valve position information to the PCM.

CAN-bus circuit A two-wire communication network that transmits status and command signals between control modules in a vehicle.

canted valves A valve arrangement in the cylinder head where the valves are at an angle to the cylinder bore. Canting the valves can make for a straighter path for air to flow into and out of the intake and exhaust ports.

capacitor (condenser) A self-contained unit that is connected electrically in parallel with the contact breaker points and used to assist the rapid collapse of the magnetic field in the coil by preventing the contact breaker points from arcing. Also used on some coils to reduce radio frequency interference.

carbon monoxide poisoning Exposure to higher than tolerable levels of carbon monoxide, resulting in headaches, fatigue, or loss of consciousness, eventually resulting in death.

carrier The part of the throw-out bearing assembly that holds the bearing.

casing plies A network of cords that give the tire shape and strength; also known as casing cords.

cast rod A connecting rod that is created by the metal casting process.

castellated nut An adjusting nut with slots cut into the top such that it resembles a castle; used with a cotter pin to prevent the nut from turning.

caster The angle formed through the wheel pivot points when viewed from the side in comparison to a vertical line through the wheel.

casting line A by-product of the metal casting process that forms a line found on parts that are cast in metal.

center bolt A fastener or bolt found in the middle of the harmonic balancer or cam sprocket that attaches it to the crankshaft or the camshaft.

center electrode The electrode located in the center of a spark plug. It is the hottest part of the spark plug.

center punch Less sharp than a prick punch, the center punch makes a bigger indentation that centers a drill bit at the point where a hole is required to be drilled.

centerline The imaginary line drawn down the exact center of the vehicle from front to back.

centrifugal advance mechanism An ignition timing device, located above or beneath the distributor base plate, that rotates with the distributor cam and is used to advance the spark. As engine speed rises, the flyweights on the advance mechanism are thrown outward by centrifugal force. Since the distributor cam is able to pivot on the distributor shaft, the weights act against their springs and move the distributor cam forward.

centrifugal force A force pulling outward on a rotating body.

centrifugal switch A switch that is only activated when centrifugal forces are placed on a vehicle.

cetane number A rating of the ignition quality of diesel fuel.

chamfer A rounded or angled edge located on the blocking ring, with ridges machined into it to help grab the cone surface of the gear.

chamfering The process of cutting into the top of the oil passage hole with a specialized chamfering tool or regular drill bit to make the top of the oil hole more like a 45-degree angle, to keep the edge from digging into the bearing the way a 90-degree edge would.

channel The number of wheel speed sensor circuits and hydraulic circuits the EBCM monitors and controls.

charge (heating and cooling system) The amount of refrigerant present in the system or the process of installing refrigerant in the system.

charge carrier A mobile particle that has a positive or negative electrical charge.

chassis technician A technician who specializes in working on vehicle suspension and steering systems.

chassis The main support frame in a vehicle. It includes the running gear, such as suspension, the engine, and the drive train.

check valve Also known as a shuttle valve, a valve that allows the flow of hydraulic oil in one direction only. It is typically used to allow oil to escape quickly from an application device when shifting gears.

chlorofluorocarbon (CFC) A manufactured compound designed to be used as a refrigerant. It is now illegal due to the high chlorine content.

circuit breaker A device that trips and opens a circuit, preventing excessive current flow in a circuit. It is resettable to allow for reuse.

circuit or schematic diagram A pictorial representation or road map of the wiring and electrical components.

Clean Air Act (CAA) A policy signed into law in 1990 that sets standards for air pollution to eliminate ozone-depleting elements.

cleaning gun A device with a nozzle controlled by a trigger fitted to the outlet of pressure cleaners.

climate control system A system that provides the heating and cooling of air inside the passenger compartment for passenger comfort.

clock spring A special rotary electrical connector located between the steering wheel and the steering column that maintains a constant electrical connection with the wiring system while the vehicle's steering wheel is being turned.

closed loop system A totally self-contained system with no materials entering or exiting.

clutch disc The center component of the clutch assembly, with friction material riveted on each side. Also called a clutch plate or friction disc.

clutch fork The part of the clutch linkage that operates the throw-out bearing.

clutch pedal The foot-operated pedal used by the driver to engage and disengage the clutch.

clutch safety switch An electrical switch that is operated by the clutch pedal and keeps the starter motor from cranking the engine over until the clutch is fully depressed.

clutch system A mechanically operated assembly that connects and disconnects the engine from the transmission.

coarse (UNC) Used to describe thread pitch; stands for Unified National Coarse.

code Another name for a fault code; ***see*** DTC.

coefficient of friction A value assigned to materials to describe the amount of friction when two objects slide against each other.

coil bind A result of excessive valve lift. When the coils of the spring touch each other, the spring breaks, flattening the cam lobe and bending the pushrod.

coil spring pressure plate A type of pressure plate that uses coil springs to provide the clamping force.

coil spring Spring steel wire that is heated and wound into a coil that is used to support the weight of a vehicle.

coil-on-plug A type of ignition system used on late-model vehicles that uses one coil placed above each spark plug.

cold chisel The most common type of chisel, used to cut cold metals. The cutting end is tempered and hardened so that it is harder than the metals that need to be cut.

collet A cone-shaped tool that encloses and grips a rod or shaft when inserted into the sleeve of a lathe or other machine.

column inertia The principle that as a column of air flows, it creates inertia, which keeps air flowing until its inertia energy is spent; sometimes referred to as a "ram effect" when using tuned intake or exhaust systems.

combination pliers A type of pliers for cutting, gripping, and bending.

combination wrench A type of wrench that has an open end on one end and a box-end wrench on the other.

combustion chamber The area of an engine in which the air/fuel mixture is burnt. It consists of the bottom of the cylinder head and the top of the piston.

combustion pressure The force exerted by the expanding gases during the burning process. It is what causes the internal combustion engine to operate.

common bore When a single cylinder is used for two pistons. A tandem master cylinder would be an example of two pistons in one bore.

common rail system (CRS) A diesel fuel injection system that uses a pump to develop high-pressure fuel directed to an accumulator or rail.

common rail A type of injection system using a common fuel manifold from which individual injectors are fed high-pressure fuel.

commutator A device made on armatures of electric generators and motors to control the direction of current flow in the armature windings.

companion flange A splined flange that transmits power from the drive shaft to the pinion gear.

compensating port Connects the brake fluid reservoir to the master cylinder bore when the piston is fully retracted, allowing for expansion and contraction of the brake fluid.

compliance bushing A rubber bushing with a voided section molded in it that allows component movement under torque application. It is typically used in control arms on front-wheel drive vehicles to minimize torque steer issues.

compressed air equipment Tool or machinery that operates on compressed air.

compression ratio (CR) The volume of the cylinder with the piston at bottom dead center as compared to the volume of the cylinder at top dead center, given in a ratio such as 9:1 CR.

compression ring A metal ring found inside the grooves on the side of the engine piston.

compression ring groove A square groove found on the outside of the piston skirt in which the piston ring fits.

compression stroke The stroke of the piston during which air and fuel is being compressed into a small area prior to ignition.

compression tester A device used to measure the amount of compression pressure a cylinder can generate.

compressor A belt or electrically driven device designed to increase refrigerant pressure and cause refrigerant to travel through the air-conditioning system.

compressor surge The backup of air against the throttle plate as it is closed. The turbocharger is still spinning, pressurizing air, when the throttle plate is closed. Air will stack up, creating a rapid slowing of the turbocharger compressor wheel. This can damage the compressor wheel.

concentricity (valve) A term used to describe a valve seat where the valve seat and valve stem share a common center. In this design, the valve can seal against the seat no matter how it is rotated.

concentricity (hole) The roundness of a hole. If the hole is not round it can also be referred to as out of round.

condensation The changing of a gas into a liquid through cooling.

condenser The air-conditioning component located in the front of the vehicle designed to allow high-pressure refrigerant to change states from gas to liquid.

conduction The process of transferring heat through matter by the movement of heat energy through solids from one particle to another.

conductor A material that allows electricity to flow through it easily. It is made up of atoms with one to three valance ring electrons.

connecting rod A cast or forged metal rod that connects the engine pistons to the engine crankshaft.

connector The plastic housing on the end of a wiring harness that holds the wire terminals in place. It can also refer to a type of wire terminal that connects wires together or to a common point such as a bolt.

conservation of energy A physical law that states that energy cannot be created or destroyed.

constant mesh A term used to describe two or more parts, such as gears, that are in constant contact with each other.

constant velocity (CV) joints Joints commonly used in front-wheel drive vehicles to allow flexibility of the axle while turning.

contact breaker point ignition system A type of ignition system that uses a mechanical means of turning the primary circuit on and off.

contact breaker points A mechanically operated electrical switch that is fixed to the distributor base plate and opened and closed by the distributor cam with the rotation of the engine. The contacts normally form a self-contained unit, fixed to the base plate by a retaining screw engaged in a slot in the fixed contact.

continuity A conductive path between two points.

continuous monitoring A term that describes OBDII monitors that run continuously throughout the drive cycle.

continuously variable transmission (CT) A transmission without individual gears or gear ratios.

continuously variable transmission (CVT) A type of transmission that has no fixed gears, as in a conventional transmission, but rather can adjust gear ratios infinitely within the design of the transmission.

control arm The primary load-bearing element of a vehicle's suspension system, commonly referred to as an A-arm or wishbone. These arms may be used as an upper and lower pivot point for the wheel assembly. They attach to the chassis with rubber bushings that allow up-and-down movement of the tire and wheel assembly.

control unit Any device that controls another object such as a computer.

controller area network (CAN) A localized (onboard) vehicle network that enables computers and components to send and receive signals across a shielded twisted pair of wires.

convection The process of transferring heat by the circulatory movement that occurs in a gas or fluid as areas of differing temperatures exchange places due to variations in density and the action of gravity.

conventional oil Oil that is processed from crude oil; about 20% of oil is additives.

conventional theory The theory that electrons flow from positive to negative.

convertible A vehicle that converts from having an enclosed top to having an open top by a roof that can be removed, retracted, or folded away.

coolant When anti-freeze concentrate is mixed with water, the resulting mixture is called engine coolant. Most manufacturers recommend a 50/50 mixture.

coolant control valve A valve that blocks off coolant flow to keep hot water from entering the heater core when less heat is requested by the operator.

coolant label A label that lists the type of coolant installed in the cooling system.

coolant temperature sensor (CTS) A thermistor usually screwed into a cylinder head water jacket. Usually the CTS is a negative temperature coefficient thermistor, or a resistor whose resistance varies, with temperature varying a voltage signal to the PCM.

cooler flow test The placement of a specialty measuring device into the transmission cooler line to measure fluid flow to the cooler. Low cooler flow can be a sign of other issues with the pump and lubrication system.

cooling hoses Flexible hoses that connect the stationary components of the cooling system, such as heater core and radiator, to the engine, which is mounted on flexible mounts.

core plug A metal cap for the holes that are used to remove core sand used during the casting process.

cored solder Solder that is in the form of a hollow wire. The center is filled with flux, which is used as a cleaning agent while the solder is being applied to the metal surfaces.

cornering force (suspension system) The force applied to an axle that shifts the axle in relation to the position of the body when turning.

cornering force (wheels) The force between the tread and the road surface as a vehicle turns.

corona-suppression An electronic sniffer used for detecting refrigerant leaks.

corrosion inhibitors Oil additives that keep acid from forming in the oil.

cotter pin A one-use soft metal pin that can be bent into shape and is used to retain bearing adjusting nuts.

coupe A two-door vehicle that has seating for two people and may have a small rear seat.

crank angle position The position of the crankshaft, measured in degrees.

crank core The rough, unfinished crankshaft assembly that has just left the foundry or forging area.

crankcase The bottom area of the engine cylinder block where the crankshaft is located.

cranking Rotating the engine by turning the ignition key to the start position.

crankshaft A part mounted in the lower side of the engine block that has offset journals that rotate to change the up-and-down motion of the pistons into rotary motion at the crankshaft.

crankshaft journals Smooth, curved, machined areas where other parts fit to the crankshaft.

crankshaft position (CKP) sensor A sensor used by the PCM to monitor engine speed. It can be one of three types of sensors—Hall effect, magnetic pickup, or optical.

crescent pump An oil pump that uses a crescent-shaped part to separate the oil pump gears from each other, allowing oil to be moved from one side of the pump to the other.

crimp The bent shape of the oil ring expander that allows it to provide outward force on the oil rings.

cross-arm A description for an arm that is set at right angles or 90 degrees to another component.

cross-cut chisel A type of chisel for metal work that cleans out or cuts key ways.

cross-flow radiator A radiator that uses cooling tubes that run horizontal with tanks on each end. This design allows lower hood profile for better vehicle aerodynamics.

crosshatch A pattern of lines placed at angles to each other, appearing as a series of Xs across a surface.

crossover utility vehicle (CUV) A vehicle that is a cross between an SUV and a passenger vehicle.

crude oil Material pulled from the earth, originating from organic compounds broken down over time and formed into petroleum. This material is processed in a refinery to break down into various hydrocarbon substances such as diesel, gasoline, and mineral oil, among others.

cubic boron nitride (CBN) cutter An engine block resurfacing tool used on cast iron parts.

current clamp A device that clamps around a conductor to measure current flow. It is often used in conjunction with a DVOM.

current flow The flow of electrons, typically within a circuit or component.

curved file A type of file that has a curved surface for filing holes.

CV joint CV is an abbreviation for constant velocity, a type of universal joint used on the drive axles or half-shafts of a vehicle. Usually refers to front-wheel drive vehicles.

cylinder bore The hole in the engine block that the piston fits into.

cylinder head The part of the engine that is bolted to the engine block and caps off the top of the combustion chamber.

cylinder leakage tester A device that pumps air into the cylinder and measures the percentage of air that is leaking out of the cylinder.

cylindrical roller bearing assembly A type of wheel bearing with races and rollers that are cylindrical in shape and roll between inner and outer races, which are parallel to each other.

data link connector (DLC) The connector through which the scan tool communicates to the vehicle's computers; it will display the readings from the various sensors and can retrieve trouble codes, freeze-frame data, and system monitor data.

dead axle An axle that does not have the capability to drive the vehicle. It is usually found on the rear of front-wheel drive vehicles.

dead blow hammer A type of hammer that has a cushioned head to reduce the amount of head bounce.

deceleration A decrease in a vehicle's speed.

deck The surface area at the top of the engine block against which the cylinder head seals.

deep dish wheel A wheel with negative offset, which gives the outside of the wheel a deep dish appearance. Deep dish refers to the side of the wheel that is farthest from the drop center.

deflecting force A force that moves an object in a different direction or into a different shape.

degree wheel A disc with 360 one-degree markings near its outer edge; it bolts to the front of the crankshaft and is used to check valve and cam timing.

depletion layer An area of neutral charge in semiconductors.

depth filter A hydraulic filter that has thick filter media to trap dirt and other particles of various sizes as they pass through the filter.

depth micrometer A measuring device that accurately measures the depth of a hole.

detent mechanism The mechanism that holds or helps hold the shift rail into position to ensure that the gear does not pop out when selected and to let the driver feel when a shift is completed.

detent valve See ***kickdown valve***.

detergents Oil additives that help to keep carbon from sticking to engine components.

detonation The condition in which the remaining fuel charge fires or burns too rapidly after the initial combustion of the air–fuel mixture. It is audible through the combustion chamber walls as a knocking noise.

diagnostic trouble code (DTC) A code set by the computer indicating system or component malfunction.

diagonal cutting pliers Cutting pliers for small wire or cable.

dial indicator An accurate measuring device where measurements are read from a dial and needle.

diaphragm pressure plate A slightly conical, spring steel plate used to provide the clamping force for the clutch assembly.

dichlorodifluoromethane (R-12) An inert, colorless gas that can be used as a refrigerant. It is stored in white containers.

die stock A handle for securely holding dies to cut threads.

diesel exhaust fluid (DEF) A mixture of urea and water that is injected into the exhaust system of a late-model diesel-powered vehicle to reduce exhaust nitrogen oxide emissions.

diesel exhaust fluid (DEF) A urea chemical reactant specifically designed for use in selective catalytic reduction systems to reduce nitrogen oxides.

diesel particulate filter (DPF) A filter that converts particulate matter, or soot, into ash.

dieseling A condition in which the engine continues to run after the ignition key is turned off. Also referred to as run-on.

differential gear set The arrangement of gears between two axles that allows each axle to spin at its own speed when the vehicle is going around a corner.

differential gears Gears situated in the final drive assembly that are meshed together and with both axles, allowing the wheels to rotate at different speeds when turning a corner.

digital volt-ohmmeter (DVOM) A test instrument with a digital display for measuring voltage, resistance, and current. Also called a digital multimeter (DMM).

diode A two-lead electronic component that allows current flow in one direction only.

dipper A type of splash lubricating system used in small engines. It works like a spoon scooping up oil and throwing it upward onto the crankshaft and other wear surfaces.

direct burning The phase of combustion after ignition when the rest of the fuel is injected into the combustion chamber and there is a more gradual pressure change in the cylinder.

direct current (DC) Movement of current that flows in one direction only.

direct drive A condition in which the engine and transmission output are turning at the same rate of speed.

direct fuel injection A fuel injection system in which the fuel is injected directly into the combustion chamber.

direct ignition system May refer to a waste spark ignition or a coil-on-plug ignition system, in which the coils are directly attached to the spark plugs.

direct TPMS A type of automated tire pressure monitoring system that measures tire pressure and possibly temperature via a sensor installed inside each wheel.

direct-acting telescopic shock absorber A shock absorber designed to reduce spring oscillations.

directional and asymmetric tread pattern A tread pattern that is both directional and asymmetric, which means the tire is designed to rotate in only one direction and has one side that must face outward to ensure that the tire performs as designed under operating conditions.

directional tread pattern A tread pattern designed to pump water out from under the tire; each tire must be placed in a particular spot on the vehicle.

disc brakes A type of brake system that forces stationary brake pads against the outside of a rotating brake rotor.

disc brake pads Brake pads that consist of a friction material bonded or riveted to a steel backing plate; designed to wear out over time.

disc brake rotor micrometer A specially designed micrometer used to measure the thickness of a rotor.

dispersants Oil additives that keep contaminants held in suspension in the oil, to be removed by the filter or when the oil is changed.

displacement-on-demand A feature that allows cylinders to be taken off-line when not needed, such as at vehicle cruise.

distributor base plate A round metal plate near the top of the distributor that is attached to a distributor housing; also called a breaker plate.

distributor cap The top portion of a distributor, used to make a connection between the spinning rotor and the high-tension leads.

distributor The part of an ignition system that distributes the spark to the spark plugs in the correct sequence and at the correct time. It includes a distributor cap, rotor, shaft, and usually a switching device.

distributorless ignition system An ignition system that does not include a distributor. It uses signals from the crankshaft position sensor and the camshaft position sensor sent to the PCM to determine when to send a signal to the ignition module.

doping The introduction of impurities to pure semiconductor materials to provide N- and P-type semiconductors.

double Cardan joint A type of joint that uses two Cardan joints housed in a short carrier and that reduces the change in velocity of a single Cardan joint by using the second joint to cancel out the changes in velocity of the first joint.

double flare A seal that is made at the end of metal tubing or pipe.

double-clutching A technique used to shift gears when a nonsynchronized transmission is used. The driver must push the clutch in multiple times to change gears.

double-insulated Tools or appliances that are designed in such a way that no single failure can result in a dangerous voltage coming into contact with the outer casing of the device.

double-row ball bearing assembly A single ball bearing assembly using two rows of ball bearings riding in two channels in the races.

down-flow radiator A radiator that uses cooling tubes that run vertical. This design requires a higher hood profile.

drag link A steel or iron rod that transfers movement of the pitman arm to a relay lever.

drain line A wire included in a harness with one end grounded to reduce interference or noise being induced into the harness.

drawing-in method A method for replacing wheel studs that uses the lug nut to draw the wheel stud into the hub or flange.

drift punch A type of punch used to start pushing roll pins to prevent them from spreading.

drill chuck A device for securely gripping drill bits in a drill.

drill press A device that incorporates a fixed drill with multiple speeds and an adjustable worktable. It can be free-standing or fixed to a bench.

drill vice A tool with jaws that can be attached to a drill press table for holding material that is to be drilled.

drivability technician A technician who diagnoses and identifies mechanical and electrical faults that affect vehicle performance and emissions.

drive axle assembly The components that make up the drive axle including the axles, final drive assembly, bearings, and axle housing.

drive axle An axle that provides power to a wheel.

drive shaft The hollow tube with flexible joints on each end that transmits power from the transmission to the final drive unit.

drive train A term used to identify the engine, transmission/transaxle, differential, axles, and wheels.

driven center plate The friction disc that is held firmly against the flywheel by a pressure plate and transfers power from the flywheel to the transmission input shaft.

driving thrust The force transferred from the tire contact patch through the axle housing and front half of the spring to the fixed shackle point that pushes the vehicle along the road.

drop center A wheel design with part of the center section of the wheel a smaller diameter than the rest. It is used for mounting and demounting the tire.

drum brake micrometer A tool used for measuring the inside diameter of the brake drum.

drum brakes A type of brake system that forces brake shoes against the inside of a brake drum.

drum-style parking brake A mechanically operated drum brake that can be set while the vehicle is not moving to serve as a parking brake.

dry flanged sleeve A metal cylinder with a flange embedded into the block pressed into an engine cylinder to give it a new wear surface. The flanged sleeve is held in by the cylinder head.

dry sleeve A metal cylinder that is pressed into an engine cylinder block that does not come in direct contact with coolant. It is held in place with an interference fit.

dual overhead cam (DOHC) engine An engine design that is like the overhead cam engine but with two camshafts used per cylinder head; one operates the intake valves and the other operates the exhaust valves.

dual-clutch transmission A type of automatically shifting manual transmission in which two separate input shafts are connected to their own clutch. Shifting of the gears alternates between the two input shafts.

dual-drive air-conditioning compressor An air compressor drive used on some hybrid vehicles. The compressor can be driven by the accessory belt or by an electric motor.

dual-mass flywheel (DMF) A type of flywheel that eliminates excessive transmission gear rattle, reduces gear change/shift effort, and increases fuel economy.

duo-servo drum brake system A system that uses servo action in both the forward and reverse direction.

duration The amount of time the valve stays open, given in degrees of rotation of the crankshaft.

duty cycle Another term for pulse-width modulation.

dynamic imbalance A tire imbalance that causes the wheel assembly to turn inward and outward with each half revolution.

ear protection Protective gear worn when the sound levels exceed 85 decibels, when working around operating machinery for any period of time, or when the equipment you are using produces loud noise.

edge code A code printed on the edge of a friction lining that describes its coefficient of friction.

effective stroke The duration of plunger stroke with the spill port covered, which determines the amount of fuel injected.

EGR system monitor A control module diagnostic test that is run to ensure that the EGR valve and passageways are operating properly.

EGR valve A valve that connects the exhaust port, or manifold, and the intake manifold. If engine operating conditions are likely to produce oxides of nitrogen, the EGR valve opens, letting some burned exhaust gases pass from the exhaust into the intake system.

EH2 rim The specialized rim design that is used with some run-flat tires.

elasticity The amount of stretch or give a material has.

electric machine Another name for a traction motor with regenerative capability.

electric power steering system (EPS) A steering system that uses an electric motor and sensors to provide feedback to the vehicle's computer systems to decrease steering effort.

electric servo An air-conditioning door actuator controlled by electricity.

electric servo motor Also referred to as an electric actuator, a motor that provides movement to operate the air doors in an air box to control air temperature and air movement.

electric solenoids An electrically operated valve, which in brake systems is used to control the flow of brake fluid in the hydraulic system.

electrical power A measurement of the rate at which electricity is consumed or created.

electrical resistance A material's property that slows down the flow of electrical current.

electrical technician A technician who diagnoses, replaces, maintains, identifies fault with, and repairs electrical wiring and computer-based equipment in vehicles.

electrically assisted steering (EAS) A power-assist system that uses an electric motor to replace the hydraulic pump to decrease steering effort.

electrically powered hydraulic steering (EPHS) A steering system that uses an electric motor to produce hydraulic assist for steering.

electrolyte (batteries) The liquid in lead-acid battery cells. It is a mixture of about 67% water and 33% sulfuric acid.

electromagnetic clutch arrangement An arrangement used in hybrid air-conditioning systems to drive the compressor. The air-conditioning clutch is an electromagnetic clutch that works by creating a strong magnetic field that pulls the clutch into mesh with the pulley on the air compressor.

electromotive force An electrical pressure or voltage.

electron theory The theory that electrons, being negatively charged, repel other electrons and are attracted to positively charged objects; thus electrons flow from negative to positive.

electronic brake control (EBC) system A hydraulic brake system that has integrated electronic components for the purpose of closely controlling hydraulic pressure in the brake system.

electronic brake control module (EBCM) The module that controls and monitors the anti-lock braking system.

electronic continuously variable transmission (ECVT) A type of hybrid transmission that often uses two electric motors in combination with an ICE. The two electric motors and the ICE transfer power through a planetary gear set, allowing an infinite amount of gear ratios.

electronic control module (ECM) A computer that receives signals from input sensors, compares that information with preloaded software, and sends an appropriate command signal to output devices; used to manage the anti-lock brake system (ABS).

electronic control unit (ECU) A computer that controls the ignition and fuel control and emissions control systems on an engine; also called the engine control module (ECM) or power train control module (PCM).

electronic control unit (ECU) (heating and cooling system) When referring to the HVAC system, the electronic module that makes the "decisions" of the climate control system settings based on input sensors and the module programming.

electronic diesel control (EDC) A computer or electronic control unit that controls diesel fuel injection systems.

electronic ignition system An ignition system that uses a nonmechanical (electronic) method of triggering the ignition coil's primary circuit.

electronic ignition system—distributor type An ignition system that uses a distributor but replaces the contact points with an electronic triggering device.

electronic pressure control (EPC) solenoid A pulse width–modulated solenoid used to control transmission line pressure in an automatic transmission.

electronic reverse lockout An electronic solenoid used to prevent accidental engagement into reverse gear while the vehicle is moving forward.

electronic stability control (ESC) system A computer-controlled system added to ABS and TCS to assist the driver in maintaining vehicle stability while steering.

element The replaceable portion of a filter, such as an air filter element or oil filter element.

emission analyzer A service bay or lab device used for detecting/measuring vehicle emissions.

emission control system A system of devices that are designed to control or reduce harmful gases released to the atmosphere.

emission A gas that is released to the atmosphere; usually refers to a harmful gas.

enameled copper wire Wire that uses a thin layer of enamel as insulating material. The thinness of the insulation allows the wire to be closely wound in a coil, creating a dense magnetic field when current flows through it.

end play (transmission) Referring to the input or output shaft, fore-and-aft movement in the transmission.

end play (wheels) The in-and-out movement of the hub caused by clearance within the wheel bearing assembly.

end play (manual transmission) Unwanted lateral movements of the worm shaft.

energy The ability to do work.

engine balancer An expansive bench unit complete with computer controls, a lathe and drill press for machining metal for the balancing procedure, and all necessary adapters for most applications of crankshaft assemblies.

engine bearing A specially designed metal piece that supports circular moving parts.

engine block deck The portion of the engine cylinder block on which the head gasket lies on and to which the cylinder head is bolted.

engine block dowel pinhole The hole where the engine cylinder block dowel pins are fixed.

engine configuration The way engine cylinders are arranged—for example, V, flat, or in-line.

engine control module (ECM) A computer that controls the ignition and fuel control and emissions control systems on an engine; also the electronic control unit (ECU) or power train control module (PCM).

engine coolant temperature (ECT) sensor A sensor that changes resistance based upon coolant temperature; also known as a thermistor.

engine coolant temperature sensor A thermistor that measures the temperature of the engine coolant.

engine displacement The size of the engine given in cubic inches, cubic centimeters, and liters. It is found by multiplying the piston displacement by the number of cylinders the engine has. Sometimes called "swept volume."

engine-driven hydraulic pump A power steering pump driven by a belt or gear off of the crankshaft.

epitrochoid curve The circular movement around the perimeter of another circle. This is the movement that the rotary engine uses to ensure that the rotor stays in contact with the housing.

ethylene glycol A chemical used as anti-freeze that provides the lower freezing point of coolant and raises the boiling point. It is a toxic anti-freeze.

evaporative emission (EVAP) system A system used to capture vapors or gases from an evaporating liquid.

evaporator temperature sensor A thermistor that reads the temperature of the evaporator, used to ensure that the evaporator does not freeze.

evaporator The air-conditioning component normally located in the passenger compartment designed to allow low-pressure refrigerant liquid to change states to a gas.

event cylinder The cylinder that uses the spark to ignite the air–fuel mixture on a waste spark ignition system.

exhaust gas recirculation (EGR) valve A valve that allows a controlled amount of exhaust gas into the intake manifold during a certain period of engine operation. Used to lower nitrogen oxide exhaust emissions.

exhaust stroke The stroke in an engine cycle when the piston moves up, with the exhaust valve(s) open, exhausting the burned exhaust gases out through the exhaust system.

exhaust valve The valve through which exhaust gases are forced out of the combustion chamber.

expander The part of an oil control ring that holds the ring against the cylinder wall.

Extended Mobility Technology (EMT) Tires with thick sidewalls that allow the tire to be driven on even when it has no air pressure.

extension housing A component of the automatic transmission housing that covers the output shaft of the transmission. The extension housing also supports the end of the driveshaft and may hold components such as the vehicle speed sensor, speedometer drive assembly, and governor assembly.

external combustion engine An engine that runs on heat applied externally to the cylinder. For example: the steam engine.

external drive shaft A shaft used to transfer power from the transmission to the live axle.

extreme loading Large pressure placed on two bearing surfaces. Extreme loading will try to press oil from between bearing surfaces.

extreme-pressure additive An oil additive that ensures that a protective coating is given to moving engine parts and that keeps oil from being forced out under extreme pressure. Helps oil to cushion components.

eye ring terminal A type of crimp or solder terminal that has an enclosed eyelet to connect the terminal with a bolt or screw.

fast chargers A type of battery charger that charges batteries quickly.

fasteners Devices that securely hold items together, such as screws, cotter pins, rivets, and bolts.

fault codes An alphanumeric code system used to identify potential problems in a vehicle system.

fault *See* diagnostic trouble code (DTC).

feedback signal A voltage signal sent back to an electronic control unit. The feedback signal is how the control module is able to interpret temperature or other information from its sensors.

feeler gauge A thin blade device for measuring space between two objects.

ferrous metals Metals that have an iron compound in their makeup or that are magnetic.

fill plug Usually a threaded plug that can be removed to allow the level of a fluid to be checked and filled. This could also be a rubber snap fit plug.

fillet area The area of the crankshaft that meets up with the rod bearing journal or main bearing journal.

fillet The radius portion of an inside corner that reduces stress at the corner.

filter sock The first line of defense in the fuel supply system. The sock typically consists of a fine mesh, which prevents most small particles from being drawn into the fuel pump and sent through the rest of the fuel system.

fin A small, flat piece of metal placed between the tubes to help with the transfer of heat from the coolant to the air, refrigerant to air, or air to refrigerant. The metal heats up due to contact with the hot pipes in the case of a radiator or heater core and from hot air in the case of an evaporator.

final drive assembly An assembly used to power the drive wheels and allow the wheels to rotate at different speeds as the vehicle turns.

final drive A component that provides a final gear reduction and allows for the difference in speed of each wheel when cornering.

fine (UNF) Used to describe thread pitch; it stands for Unified National Fine.

finished rivet A rivet after the completion of the riveting process.

fire rings Steel rings integrated into the cylinder head gasket nearest the combustion chambers that provide extra sealing to seal in the high combustion pressures.

fixed caliper A type of brake caliper bolted firmly to the steering knuckle or axle housing, having at least one piston on both sides of the rotor.

fixed orifice tube system A system with a fixed orifice tube that uses an accumulator between the evaporator and the compressor.

fixed resistor A resistor that has a fixed value.

fixed-orifice PCV system A system in which a hole of a predetermined size is used as a means of pulling crankcase vapors into the intake manifold to be burned.

fixed-type joint A joint that does not slide to allow for shaft lengthening or shortening; it simply allows for angle changes as the suspension moves.

flame front The front edge of the burning air/fuel mixture in the combustion chamber.

flame front The rapid burning of the air–fuel mixture that moves outward from the spark plug across the cylinder.

flame propagation The movement of the flame through the combustion chamber during the combustion process.

flame spread The phase of combustion in which there is a sharp pressure rise in the combustion chamber because of the sudden combustion of the fuel.

flare nut wrench A type of box-end wrench that has a slot in the box section to allow the wrench to slip through a tube or pipe. Also called a flare tubing wrench.

flashback arrestor A spring-loaded valve installed on oxyacetylene torches as a safety device to prevent flame from entering the torch hoses.

flasher can A mechanism that turns the vehicle's turn signal and hazard flasher bulbs on and off.

flat blade screwdriver A type of screwdriver that fits a straight slot in screws.

flat seat with washer A type of lug nut that is flat where it bolts to the wheel and has a washer affixed that allows it to turn independent of the hex part of the lug nut.

flat seat without washer A type of lug nut that is flat where it bolts to the wheel.

flat tappet A camshaft specifically designed to push on flat bottom lifters (nonroller types). It typically has a higher rolling resistance than the roller-style camshafts.

flathead engine An L-head engine with valves in the block.

flat-nosed pliers Pliers that are flat and square at the end of the nose.

flex hone A machine tool with abrasive stones that is used to refinish the inside of the cylinder walls.

flex plate A metal part attached to the rear of the crankshaft that connects to the torque converter in a vehicle with an automatic transmission.

floating pin A round metal pin that has a very small clearance but is free to float in the piston and connecting rod.

flow-control valve A valve used in power steering pumps to control the amount of flow out of the power steering pump.

fluid coupler A type of hydraulic coupling used on vintage vehicles to connect and transfer power from the engine to the transmission.

fluid dissipater A silicone fluid component that allows the mass of a fluid type harmonic balancer to rotate at a more constant speed than the crankshaft to help even out the torsional vibrations of the crankshaft.

flux A liquid or paste that protects a soldering or welding joint from oxidization.

flywheel ring gear Large, round, externally toothed gear that is usually press-fitt to the outer diameter of the flywheel and used along with the starter to crank the engine over.

flywheel The heavy, circular flat plate that keeps the engine rotating when power is not produced, such as on the exhaust, intake, and compression strokes.

force The effort to produce a push or pull action.

forced induction The pressurization of airflow going into the cylinder through the use of a turbocharger or supercharger.

forces capability map data Data preprogrammed into the electronic control unit's memory by the manufacturer and used to determine how much power assistance is needed based on input from the vehicle's speed sensor and steering sensor.

forcing screw The center screw on a gear, bearing, or pulley puller. Also called a jacking screw.

forged connecting rod A strong metal connecting rod hammered into shape by large presses used to connect the piston to the crankshaft.

four-post hoist A type of hoist that the vehicle is driven onto that uses two long, narrow platforms to lift the vehicle.

four-stroke engine An engine that uses four strokes—intake, compression, power, and exhaust—to complete its cycle.

four-wheel drive (4WD) A drive train layout in which the engine drive has either two wheels or four wheels depending on which mode is selected by the driver.

four-wheel steering system A steering system in which the front wheels are controlled normally and the rear wheels use a computer and electric motors to turn the rear linkage.

fracture split A method used on powdered metal connecting rods where the big end of the connecting rod is broken in half and can be identified by a ragged finish of the big end's parting surfaces.

free electron An electron located on the outer ring, called the valence ring, that is only loosely held by the nucleus and that is free to move from one atom to another when an electrical potential (pressure) is applied.

freewheeling engine An engine that has enough clearance between the piston and the valves so that in the event the timing belt or chain breaks, the valves that are hanging all the way open will not contact the piston, thus preventing engine damage.

freeze-frame A feature of OBDII that records events before, during, and after a fault occurs.

frequency The rate of change in direction, oscillation, or cycles in a given time.

friction The resistance created by surfaces in contact. Kinetic friction is resistance to motion when one surface moves over another. Static friction is resistance to motion between two surfaces that are not moving.

friction bearing A bearing that uses sliding motion between components, such as a clutch pilot bearing.

friction facing The material riveted to each side of the clutch disc that mates to the flywheel and pressure plate. Used to provide friction and a wear surface for the clutch assembly.

front bearing retainer The housing that bolts the input shaft bearing in place on the front of the transmission.

front-wheel drive (FWD) A drive train layout in which the engine drives the front wheels.

fuel cell An electro-chemical device that uses hydrogen and oxygen to create electricity.

fuel cell (electric) vehicle (FCV) A vehicle that converts fuel to electricity in a direct electrochemical process, with more energy extracted from the fuel source than in traditional internal combustion engines.

fuel filler neck The upper end of the fuel filler tube leading down to the fuel tank, which accepts the fuel hose nozzle at the gas station pump.

fuel filter A device that removes impurities (dirt and water) from the fuel before they reach the carburetor or injection system. Filters may be made of metal or plastic screen, paper, or gauze.

fuel metering system Equipment in a motor vehicle that delivers the proper amount of fuel to each cylinder.

fuel pressure regulator A system that controls the pressure of fuel entering the injectors.

fuel pump A mechanically or electrically driven vacuum device used to draw fuel from the tank and force it into the fuel system.

fuel pump relay A relay to turn on or off the high-amperage circuit of the fuel pump.

fuel rail Tubing that connects several injectors to the main fuel line.

fuel shutoff mode A safety precaution by which fuel is shut off when certain conditions are met during a vehicle crash.

fuel supply system Equipment in a motor vehicle that delivers fuel to the engine.

fuel system Equipment in a motor vehicle that delivers fuel to the engine.

fuel tank pressure sensor A sensitive pressure sensor mounted in the fuel tank or EVAP system used to monitor the system for leaks.

fulcrum ring A steel ring that is used as a pivot point for the diaphragm spring in the pressure plate.

full floating axle An axle that does not support any weight; if removed, the vehicle will still roll on its wheels.

full-flow filter An oil filter installed on production cars. This oil filter cleans all oil coming from the oil pump on its way to the lubricated components.

fuse A safety device that self-destructs to prevent excessive current flowing in a circuit in the event of a fault.

galleries Passageways drilled or cast into the engine block or head(s), which carry pressurized lubricating oil to various moving parts in the engine, such as the camshaft bearings.

garter spring A coiled spring that is fitted to the inside of the sealing lip of many seals, used to hold the lip in contact with the shaft.

garter spring lip seal A seal that has a spring to maintain pressure on the seal's surface to prevent leakage.

gas direct injection (GDI) cylinder head A cylinder head designed to accept a gasoline injector directly in the combustion chamber instead of in the intake manifold.

gas welding goggles Protective gear designed for gas welding; they provide protection against foreign particles entering the eye and are tinted to reduce the glare of the welding flame.

gasket A rubber, cork, or paper spacer that goes between two parts to seal the gap between the parts.

gasket scraper A broad sharp flat blade to assist in removing gaskets and glue.

gasoline A volatile, flammable liquid mixture of hydrocarbons, obtained from crude oil and used as fuel for internal combustion engines.

gasoline direct injection (GDI) A fuel injection system in which fuel is sprayed directly into the combustion chamber.

gauge sending unit A device used for transmitting a signal to control a fuel gauge.

gear A relatively round, rotating part with internal or external teeth that are designed to mesh with another gear for the purpose of transmitting torque.

gear lube A type of lubricant primarily used to lubricate transmission and differential gears but also used to lubricate some wheel bearings.

gear pullers A tool with two or more legs and a cross bar with a center forcing screw to remove gears.

gear ratio The ratio of the number of turns that a drive gear must complete to turn the driven gear one turn. Typically this is a calculation of the driven gear to the drive gear. Ratios are listed, for example, as 2:1 or 4.3:1.

gear reduction The use of a small gear to drive a large gear. The result is in an increase in torque but a decrease in speed.

gear set Two or more gears that are in mesh with each other.

gear shift lever The lever that the driver uses to shift the transmission.

gear synchronizer An assembly in the transmission that is used to bring two unequally spinning shafts or gears to the same speed when upshifting or downshifting.

geared oil pump An oil pump that has two gears running side by side together to move oil from one side of the pump gears to the other.

gelling A thickening effect of oil in cold weather. This is not a desirable trait for lubricating oil, as it will not flow when it is gelling. Wax content in base stock mineral oil makes gelling worse.

girdle A metal device connected to the bottom of the engine cylinder block to create strength for the main bearing caps.

governor pressure The pressure created by the governor, which is used to make the shift valves upshift and is proportional to vehicle speed.

governor A device that controls how much fuel is delivered to the injector.

gradient resistance Resistance encountered when a vehicle travels up a hill, requiring torque to be applied to overcome it.

gravity pouring The casting process used for creating metal parts.

grease A lubricating liquid thickened to make it suitable for use with many wheel bearings.

grease seal A component that is designed to keep grease from leaking out and contaminants from leaking in.

grinding wheels and discs Abrasive wheels or flat discs fitted to bench, pedestal, and portable grinders.

ground The return path for electrical current in a vehicle chassis, other metal of the vehicle, or dedicated wire.

grounds Fault conditions in a circuit where the circuit is unintentionally contacting a grounded component or wire. This may result in a short, in the case of a power wire, or it could cause a circuit to stay live in the case of a switched ground circuit.

guide pins Pins that allow the caliper to move in and out as the brakes operate and as the brake pads wear.

half-shaft An axle that has CV joints on each end and that fits between the transaxle and wheel. Typically, one is used on each side of a vehicle.

Hall-effect An electrical effect where electrons tend to flow on one side of a special material when exposed to a magnetic field, causing a difference in voltage across the special material. When the magnetic field is removed, the electrons flow normally and there is no difference of voltage across the special material. This effect can be used to determine the position or speed of an object.

Hall-effect switch The portion of an electronic ignition system used to trigger the ignition system. Hall-effect switches operate by using a potential difference, or voltage, created when a current-carrying conductor is exposed to a magnetic field. If a magnetic field is applied at right angles to the direction of current flow in a conductor, the lines of magnetic force permeate the conductor, and the electrons flowing in the conductor are deflected to one side. This deflection creates a potential difference across the conductor. The stronger the magnetic field, the higher the voltage.

halogen lamp A type of bulb that produces a bright white light.

hard rubber mallet A special-purpose tool with a head made of hard rubber; often used for moving things into place where it is important not to damage the item being moved.

hard shifting A shifting problem in which the shifter will not move smoothly into the desired gear, requiring excessive force by the driver to set it into gear.

hardened seat A valve seat that has undergone a heat-treating process to become more robust and capable of withstanding the severe demands of today's vehicles and drivers.

harmonic balancer A round metal disc connected to the front of the crankshaft that smoothes out torsional vibrations created by the crankshaft.

hatchback A vehicle that has a shared passenger and cargo area; it typically is available in three- and five-door arrangements.

hazard Anything that could hurt you or someone else.

hazardous environment A place where hazards exist.

hazardous material Any material that poses an unreasonable risk of damage or injury to persons, property, or the environment if it is not properly controlled during handling, storage, manufacture, processing, packaging, use and disposal, or transportation.

head gasket A thin piece of material, often a multilayered, bimetallic sheet used to seal the cylinder head assembly to the engine block.

header A specially tuned exhaust manifold typically made of exhaust pipes. These pipes are usually made equal length to ensure equal flow between cylinders.

headgear Protective gear that includes items like hairnets, caps, or hard hats.

heat buildup A dangerous condition that occurs when the glove can no longer absorb or reflect heat and heat is transferred to the inside of the glove.

heat dissipation The spreading of heat over a large area to increase heat transfer.

heat fade Brake fade caused by the buildup of heat in braking surfaces, which get so hot they cannot create any additional heat, leading to a loss of friction.

heat range The rating of a spark plug's operating temperature.

heat transfer The flow of heat from a hotter part to a cooler part; it can occur in solids, liquids, or gases.

heated intake system A system that uses hot air from around the exhaust manifold to warm the air going into the intake manifold.

heated diode A sniffer that uses electricity to determine if there is a refrigerant leak; considered the best sniffer for R-134a.

heater control cables Cables that control the air doors in an air box as part of the air distribution system.

heater core A heat-exchanging device that transfers heat converted by the fuel burning in the engine to the passenger compartment.

heavy line technician A technician who undertakes major engine, transmission, and differential overhaul and repair.

helical gears Gears that have teeth set on an angle to the gear face; they operate more quietly than spur gears.

helical-cut gear A type of gear in which the teeth are cut in a spiral down the axis of the gear.

helical-geared limited slip differential A type of differential that responds very quickly to changes in traction and that does not bind from friction in turns or lose its effectiveness since there are no clutches.

helix The curve created by a smooth spiral and used in the angle of gear teeth and coil springs.

Helmholtz resonator A device that uses the principle of noise cancellation through the collision of sound waves. When necessary, the resonator is used in addition to the muffler to cancel additional sounds. This resonator may also be used on the induction system to muffle noise of airflow through the induction system. It is named after physicist Hermann Von Helmholtz.

hemispherical cylinder head A combustion chamber that is hemispherical in shape with the valves in a crossflow arrangement and the spark plug near the center of the cylinder head directly over the top of the piston.

hertz The unit for electrical frequency measurement.

high resistance A term that describes a circuit or components with more resistance than designed.

high resistance The resistance of a component or circuit relative to a low resistance. It can also refer to a faulty circuit where a section or component has excess unwanted resistance.

high-intensity discharge (HID) A type of lighting that produces light with an electric arc rather than a glowing filament.

high-pressure accumulator A storage container designed to contain high-pressure liquids such as brake fluid.

high-tension leads The heavy insulated wires used to connect the distributor cap terminals to the spark plugs, and the ignition coil to the distributor cap, or on waste spark systems, the coils to the spark plugs.

high-tension terminals The terminals on the coils and distributor cap that the high-tension leads are connected to.

high-voltage spark The electrical arc that takes place between the center and the side electrode of a spark plug.

history code A fault code that has occurred but is not current and is saved in the PCM's memory for 40 drive cycles.

hold function A setting on a DVOM to store the present reading.

hold-down spring tool A tool used for removing and installing hold-down springs.

hold-down springs Springs that hold the brake shoes against the backing plate.

hole theory The theory that as electrons flow from negative to positive, holes flow from positive to negative.

hollow punch A punch with a center hollow for cutting circles in thin materials such as gaskets.

honing The smoothing-out process of the cylinder walls performed after the boring process. This is the final step in refinishing the cylinder; it creates the proper crosshatched pattern necessary for the piston rings to seal and seat into to give the combustion chamber the proper seal.

Hooke's joint A joint that consists of a steel cross with four hardened bearing journals, mounted on needle rollers in hardened caps, which locate the cross in the eyes of the yokes. The cross swivels in the yokes as the drive is transferred across the joint.

horizontally opposed engine An engine with two banks of cylinders, 180 degrees apart, on opposite sides of the crankshaft. It is also called a flat engine or a boxer engine.

horsepower An amount of work performed in a given time.

hoses Flexible lines used to direct liquids or gases.

hybrid drive system A drive system that uses two or more propulsion systems such as electric motors and an ICE.

hybrid electric vehicle (HEV) A vehicle that uses two power sources for propulsion, one of which is electricity.

hydraulic actuator A hydraulically controlled cylinder that engages or disengages the clutch pedal.

hydraulic control unit (HCU) An assembly that houses electrically operated solenoid valves used in electronic braking systems; also called a modulator.

hydraulic fade Brake fade caused by boiling brake fluid.

hydraulic jack A type of vehicle jack that uses oil under pressure to lift vehicles.

hydraulic press method A method for replacing wheel studs that uses a press to force the wheel stud into the flange until it bottoms out.

hydraulic pressure test The use of a hydraulic pressure gauge to measure the amount of hydraulic pressure produced in each gear range.

hydraulic valve lifter A small mechanical cylinder with a hydraulically operated internal piston used to automatically take up the slack (valve clearance) in the valve train.

hydraulically actuated electronically controlled unit injector (HEUI) A diesel fuel injection system that operates by drawing fuel from the tank using a tandem high- and low-pressure fuel pump.

hydro-cracking A process in which group 2 and group 3 oils are refined with hydrogen at much higher temperatures and pressures. This process results in a base mineral oil with many of the higher performance characteristics of synthetic oils.

hydrodynamic seal Oil seal flutes or swirls that are part of the oil seal and that create a pumping action to return oil to the transmission as the shaft rotates, enabling lubrication.

hydrogenating A process used during refining of crude oil. Hydrogen is added to crude oil to create a chemical reaction to take out impurities such as sulfur.

hydrometer A tool that measures the specific gravity of a liquid.

hypereutectic piston An aluminum piston that is cast with a 16% to 19% silicon content and that has minimal expansion rates.

hypoid bevel gear A special design of spiral bevel gear, with the centerline of the pinion below the centerline of the ring gear.

hypoid gear A type of helical gear used to change the direction of motion 90 degrees. The axis of the input gear does not line up on the centerline of the output gear

idle The speed at which an engine runs without any throttle applied.

idle stop A feature that turns off the internal combustion engine when the vehicle is at a standstill.

idler gear A gear used in between two gears to change the direction of the rotation of the driveshaft or drive axles in the transmission.

ignition The lighting of the fuel and air mixture in the combustion chamber.

ignition advance The means of causing the spark to occur earlier within the compression stroke for better performance and fuel economy during changing engine conditions.

ignition coil A device used to amplify an input voltage into the much higher voltage needed to jump the electrodes of a spark plug.

ignition coil pack A group of two or more ignition coils housed in one assembly.

ignition delay/lag period The time it takes for the fuel to ignite after the fuel is injected into the engine.

ignition module An electronic component that electronically controls the ignition coil or coils.

ignition switch A switch operated by a key or start/stop button and used to turn on or off a vehicle's electrical and ignition system.

impact driver A tool that is struck with a hammer to provide an impact turning force to remove tight fasteners.

incandescent lamp The traditional bulb that uses a heated filament to produce light.

included angle The angle of camber added or subtracted to the SAI angle. This is the angle of the pivot points in relation to the camber angle of the wheel. Also referred to as the diagnostic angle.

independent rear axle A type of rear suspension system that allows each wheel on the axle to move independently of the other.

independent rear suspension (IRS) A type of suspension system where each rear wheel is capable of moving independently of the other.

independent suspension A system for allowing the up-and-down movement of one tire without affecting the other tire on that axle.

independent suspension drive axle A type of suspension that allows each wheel on a drive axle to move independently of the other.

indirect fuel injection A fuel injection system in which the fuel is injected into a separate chamber in the cylinder head, often called a prechamber.

indirect TPMS A type of automated tire pressure monitoring system that uses the anti-lock braking system of a vehicle to measure the difference in the rotational speed of the four wheels to determine tire pressure.

induced voltage The creation of voltage in a conductor by movement of a magnetic field that is near that conductor.

induction coil An electrical transformer that uses magnetic fields to produce high-voltage pulses from low-voltage direct current.

induction hardening A process for hardening metal by touching it to a device that raises the temperature of the part with heat or magnets and then suddenly cooling it in water, oil, or another chemical.

induction-type system A type of ignition system that uses a magnetic pulse generator to trigger the spark.

inductive current The current that has been created across a conductor by moving it through a magnetic field.

inductive-type sensor A sensor mounted on the crankcase housing that is used to sense the movement of the ring gear teeth on the flywheel, or a toothed disc on the crank pulley.

inertia The resistance to a change in motion.

injector A valve that is controlled by a solenoid or spring pressure to inject fuel into the engine.

inlet port Connects the reservoir with the space around the piston and between the piston cups in a brake master cylinder.

in-line engine An engine in which the cylinders are arranged side by side in a single row.

inner race The inside component of a wheel bearing that has a smooth, hardened surface for rollers or balls to ride on.

inner tie-rod or socket The inner tie-rod is attached to the end of the rack and allows for suspension movement and slight changes in steering angles.

input force The force applied to the input piston, measured in either pounds or kilograms.

input shaft speed sensor A sensor inside the transmission that measures the rpm of the input shaft. Also called a turbine shaft sensor.

inside micrometer A micrometer designed to measure internal diameters.

insulator A material that has properties that prevent the easy flow of electricity. These materials are made up of atoms with five to eight electrons in the valance ring.

intake air temperature (IAT) sensor A sensor that measures the temperature of the incoming air through the air filtration system.

intake manifold vacuum The measure of the pressure that is less than atmospheric pressure that develops in the intake manifold of a running engine equipped with a throttle plate.

intake port The port through which the air or air/fuel mixture travels from the throttle body area to the combustion chamber.

intake stroke The stroke in an engine cycle when the piston moves from top dead center (TDC) to bottom dead center (BDC).

intake valve The valve through which air and fuel enter the combustion chamber.

integral ABS system A brake system in which the master cylinder, power booster, and HCU are all combined in a common unit.

integral valve guide A valve guide machined into the cylinder head during cylinder head construction.

integrated circuit A semiconductor chip that contains miniature versions of various electrical components within one housing.

integrated motor assist (IMA) A Honda hybrid drive system that uses a moderate-sized electric motor installed between the engine and the transmission.

interference angle The built-in differences in the angles between the valve seat and the valve face for the purpose of providing quick wearing-in of the surfaces; there usually must be between ½ and 1 degree of difference.

interference engine An engine that has minimum clearance between the valves and the pistons during normal operation; in the event that the timing belt or chain breaks, the open valves will be contacted by the piston and bend the valves, possibly breaking the piston.

interference fit A condition when two parts are held together by friction because the outside diameter of the inner component is slightly larger than the inside diameter of the outer component.

interlock mechanism A mechanical device that prevents engagement of two different gears at the same time.

intermediate shaft A steel rod positioned at an angle from the steering column to the steering gear that functions in transferring movement from one to the other.

intermediate tap One of a series of taps designed to cut an internal thread. Also called a plug tap.

internal combustion engine An engine that burns a fuel internally and creates movement due to thermal expansion of gases.

International Standards Organization (ISO) flare A method for joining brake lines, also called a bubble flare. Created by flaring the line slightly out and then back in, leaving the line bubbled near the end.

interrupter ring A ferrous metal ring, shaped like a very shallow cup with slits or windows cut into it at evenly spaced intervals. The ring has the same number of blades and windows as engine cylinders and is rotated by the engine moving the blades through an air gap. The purpose of an interrupter ring is to systematically block, and expose, the magnetic field in a Hall-effect sensor in order to turn the primary ignition circuit on and off.

inverted double flare A method for joining brake lines that forms a secure, leak-proof connection.

inverter A device that converts direct current to alternating current.

invertor A device that changes direct current into alternating current.

isolation valve The valve in the HCU that either allows or blocks brake fluid that comes from the master cylinder from entering the HCU hydraulic circuit.

jack stands Metal stands with adjustable height to hold a vehicle once it has been jacked up.

journal saddle A semicircular cut located at the bottom of the engine block that is used to support the engine crankshaft.

keeper groove A groove machined into the top of the valve stem near the tip of the valve that is used to "lock in" the valve keepers to help retain the valve spring onto the valve assembly.

keepers Locking devices that keep the valve retained by the valve spring seat.

keyed lock washer The washer that fits between the adjusting nut and the lock nut; the face of the washer is drilled with a series of holes that mate to a short pin from the adjusting nut, locking it to the spindle. Also referred to as a tang washer.

keyed washer The washer that fits between the adjusting nut and the wheel bearing and that has the center hole keyed to fit a slot on the spindle or axle tube.

kickdown valve A type of spool valve that is connected to the throttle on the vehicle. The valve is used to force a downshift when the throttle is opened all the way, assuming the governor pressure is below a specified point. Kickdown valves are also called detent valves.

kinetic energy The energy of an object in motion; it increases by the square of the speed.

Kirchhoff's current law An electrical law stating that the sum of the current flowing into a junction is the same as the current flowing out of the junction.

knock sensor An engine sensor that detects pre-ignition, detonation, and knocking.

knocking A noise heard when the air–fuel mixture spontaneously ignites before the spark plug is fired at the optimum ignition moment.

knuckle The part that contains the wheel hub or spindle and attaches to the suspension components.

knurled A process in which a drill bit with a spiral groove is threaded through or run through the valve guide to create raised ridges on either side of the groove, effectively shrinking the size of the valve guide.

labor guide A guide that provides information to make estimates for repairs.

lambda The ratio of air to fuel at which all of the oxygen in the air and all of the fuel are completely burned; See also ***stoichiometric ratio***.

latent heat of condensation The amount of heat removal necessary to change the state from a gas to a liquid without changing the actual gauge temperature.

latent heat of evaporation The amount of heat required to change the state from a liquid to a gas without changing the actual gauge temperature.

latent heat of freezing The amount of heat removal required to change the state from a liquid to a solid without changing the actual gauge temperature.

lateral runout Also called warpage, the side-to-side movement of the rotor surfaces as the rotor turns.

leading shoes Brake shoes that are installed so that they are applied in the same direction as the forward rotation of the drum and thus are self-energizing.

leading/trailing shoe drum brake system Type of brake shoe arrangement where one shoe is positioned in a leading manner and the other shoe in a trailing manner.

leaf spring A spring made of one or more flat, tempered steel springs bracketed together that is used in the suspension system to support the weight of the vehicle.

lemon law buyback A consumer protection law used in some states to identify a new vehicle that has undergone several unsuccessful attempts to repair the same fault.

lever A tool that allows the user to move a large load over a small distance at one end by applying a small force over a greater distance from the other end.

L-head A type of four-stroke internal combustion engine having both intake and exhaust valves located in one side of the engine block, which are operated by lifters actuated by a single camshaft. It is sometimes called a flat head because there are no valves in the head.

lift The amount the valve will open. The more the valve lifts off its seat, the more air can get into and out of the engine.

lift pump A pump that transfers fuel from the fuel tank to the fuel injection system; also called a transfer pump or supply pump.

lifter A cylindrical component that rides on the camshaft lobe to transmit lobe movement to the valves through a linkage system.

light line technician A technician who diagnoses and replaces the mechanical and electrical components of motor vehicles.

limit switches Switches that turn off power flow to an electric motor when a particular limit is reached.

limit value The maximum amount of emissions that a vehicle is permitted to emit. Values are assigned to different classifications of vehicles.

limited slip differential assembly A differential assembly that uses a clutch assembly or gear assembly to allow a limited amount of slip between the two axles. It is used to increase drive wheel traction in slippery conditions.

limp-in mode A transmission operating mode in which limited computer controls are needed to operate for the purpose of getting the vehicle to a shop.

line bored/line honed A process for correcting a mainline that is out of line.

line pressure A hydraulic pressure that is used to apply bands and clutches, and is regulated by the pressure regulator valve.

line pressure sensor A variable resistor sensor used to monitor line pressure. It sends a signal back to the PCM where it can be translated into a psi reading.

linear motion Movement in a straight line.

lines Term used interchangeably with pipes or tubes.

lip-type dynamic oil seal A seal with a precisely shaped dynamic rubber lip that is held in contact with a moving shaft by a garter spring. An example would be a valve seal or camshaft seal.

lithium soap A thickening agent for grease to give it the proper consistency.

live axle An axle that is powered and can move the vehicle. It is usually found on the rear of rear-wheel drive vehicles.

load transfer Weight transfer from one set of wheels to the other set of wheels during braking, acceleration, or cornering.

lobe The raised portion on a camshaft; used to lift the lifter and open the valve.

lock cage The stamped sheet metal cap that fits over the bearing adjustment nut and is secured by a cotter pin going through it and the spindle/axle.

lock nut The nut that holds the adjusting nut from turning; usually tightened much tighter than the adjusting nut.

locking hub four-wheel drive front axle hubs that are manually locked or unlocked by turning the knob on the hub.

locking pliers A type of plier where the jaws can be set and locked into position.

lockout solenoid The cam and lock pin operated by an electronic solenoid that keeps the reverse gear in lockout until it is selected.

lockout/tagout A safety tag system to ensure that faulty equipment or equipment in the middle of repair is not used.

long block An engine assembly that includes the short block and adds the valve train cylinder heads, timing cover, oil pan, and, in some cases, manifolds.

longitudinal The orientation of the engine in which the front of the engine is facing the front of the vehicle. It is most commonly found in rear-wheel drive vehicles.

lost foam A metal casting process that uses a foaming process to create the pattern of the part being cast in metal.

low-drag caliper A caliper designed to maintain a larger brake pad-to-rotor clearance by retracting the pistons farther than normal.

low-pressure accumulator A storage container for brake fluid coming from the release valves, which is under relatively low pressure.

low-pressure cycling switch A device installed on the low-pressure line or the accumulator to turn the air-conditioning clutch on and off at specified pressures.

lube technician A technician who carries out scheduled maintenance activities on a range of mechanical and related vehicle components.

lubricating oil Processed crude oil with additives to help it perform well in the engine.

lubrication system A system of parts that work together to deliver lubricating oil to the various moving parts of the engine.

lug A flange that is shaped to assist with aligning objects on other objects.

lug nuts Nuts that secure the wheel onto the wheel studs.

lug wrench A tool designed to remove wheel lugs nuts that is commonly shaped like a cross.

MacPherson strut A strut used on an independent suspension where the spring and shock are joined together. Used on most front-wheel drive vehicles.

magnafluxing An electromagnetic process used to locate cracks in ferrous engine blocks and cylinder heads and other ferrous metal parts.

magnetic pickup tools An extending shaft, often flexible, with a magnet fitted to the end for picking up metal objects.

magneto-resistive sensor A type of wheel speed sensor that uses an effect similar to a Hall effect sensor to create its signal.

magneto-rheological fluid A fluid that has the unique characteristic of changing viscosity when exposed to a magnetic field.

main bearing A bearing that supports the crankshaft in the block and provides a lubrication surface for the main journals.

main bearing caps Sturdy caps placed over the main journals of the crankshaft assembly and fastened with either two or four bolts.

main bearing journal A bearing surface that supports the crankshaft in the engine block.

main cap girdle A metal attachment that strengthens and connects all the main bearing caps together. It can be integral from the main bearing caps, or separate.

main journal The smooth machined area of the crankshaft assembly that allows the crankshaft to rotate within the main bearings.

mainline The imaginary centerline down the engine cylinder block.

mains The specific round smooth journals of the crankshaft that rotate in main bearings.

male and female terminal A crimp or solder terminal on which the male and female ends join to create a removable low-resistance connection.

malfunction indicator lamp (MIL) An indicator located in the instrument cluster that illuminates when the power train control module (PCM) detects a fault in one of the vehicle systems. Formerly called a check engine or service engine soon light.

Mallory metal A tungsten alloy of copper and nickel that is used as a metal substitute added to the crankshaft counterweight for balancing purposes.

mandrel The shaft of a pop rivet.

mandrel forming The special bending of pipe to ensure the pipe does not collapse. The use of a pipe bender with mandrels allows for very tight bends without creating kinks or reducing the size of the pipe.

mandrel head The head of the pop rivet that connects to the shaft and causes the rivet body to flare.

manifold absolute pressure (MAP) sensor A vacuum sensor that is attached to the intake manifold by a passageway or vacuum hose. The sensor measures engine intake manifold pressure to determine engine load and sends a corresponding signal to the PCM.

manual adjustable-rate shock absorber A shock absorber that allows manual adjustment of the dampening rate.

manual bleeding A bleeding method where one person manually operates the brake pedal while the other person opens and closes the bleeder screws on the wheel brake units to allow the air and old brake fluid to be pushed out.

manual climate control system A climate control system fully controlled by the operator.

manual lever position (MLP) switch A switch that is used by the PCM to tell which gear range the driver has selected with the shift lever.

manually adjustable-air spring A rubber air bag placed inside coil springs to increase the spring's load-carrying ability. It is filled manually through a valve similar to a tire valve stem.

master cylinder Converts the brake pedal force into hydraulic pressure, which is then transmitted via brake lines and hoses to one or more pistons at each wheel brake unit.

match mounting The process of matching up the tire's highest point with the rim's lowest point for the purpose of reducing the tire's radial runout.

measuring tape A thin measuring blade that rolls up and is contained in a spring-loaded dispenser.

mechanical advantage The process of using a device to get more output force than the amount of input force, with the trade-off being that the input distance is proportionately longer than the output distance; the ratio of load and effort for any simple machine such as a lever.

mechanical disadvantage When the load distance on a lever is greater than the effort distance, which means the effort required to move the load is greater than the load itself.

mechanical fingers Spring-loaded fingers at the end of a flexible shaft that pick up items in tight spaces.

mechanical jack A type of vehicle jack that uses mechanical leverage to lift a vehicle.

mechanical pressure control regulator valve A spool valve and spring assembly that are used to control the amount of line pressure in a transmission.

memory saver (memory minder) Battery backup device for vehicle computer systems.

meshed pinion A pinion when it is mated with the rack.

metallurgical bonding A process of sintering metals until they are fused together as one metal.

metering valve A valve used on vehicles equipped with older rear drum/front disc brakes to delay application of the front disc brakes until the rear drum brakes are applied. Located in line with the front disc brakes.

microleak detector A solution used to detect refrigeration leaks.

micrometer An accurate measuring device for internal and external dimensions. Commonly abbreviated mic.

micron A unit of measurement equal to 0.000039" (0.001 mm).

micron gauge A device designed to measure vacuum very precisely.

Miller cycle An engine cycle that uses a longer exhaust stroke than intake stroke through delayed closing of the intake valve. This engine uses a supercharger to pressurize air into the cylinder when needed.

min/max setting A setting on a DVOM to display the maximum and minimum readings.

mineral oil Base stock processed from crude oil in a refinery, used as the base material of all conventional oil.

minivan A lighter-duty van used for carrying six to eight occupants or light cargo.

modulator pressure A pressure created by the vacuum modulator that is proportional to engine load. Modulator pressure is used to delay transmission upshifting based upon engine load. It may also be used to raise line pressure to more firmly apply bands and clutches under higher engine loads.

module An electronic computer or circuit board that controls specific functions.

moly The abbreviation for the lubricant called molybdenum disulfide.

molybdenum thickening agent A compound used in some greases to give it the needed consistency.

monitor An OBDII test run to ensure that a specific component or system is working properly.

Morse taper A tapered mounting shaft for drill bits and chucks in larger drills and lathes.

muffler A device to quiet the pipes of the air-conditioning system with baffles placed inside to deaden the sound of refrigerant moving.

multidisc clutch A type of holding device used by an automatic transmission to stop the movement of one component of a planetary gear set. It uses several thin friction discs and thin steel plates that are squeezed together when hydraulic pressure is applied to a piston in the clutch.

multilayer steel (MLS) head gasket A gasket composed of multiple layers of steel and coated with a rubberlike substance that adheres to metal surfaces. They are typically used between the cylinder head and the cylinder block.

multimeter A test instrument used to measure volts, ohms, and amps. A digital multimeter may also be called a digital volt-ohmmeter (DVOM).

multiphase An electric motor that operates through more than one phase.

multiplate clutch A clutch assembly that consists of two or more clutch plates and used to increase the torque-carrying capacity of the clutch.

multipoint fuel injection (MPFI) An injection system in which fuel is injected into the intake ports just upstream of each cylinder's intake valve, rather than at a central point within an intake manifold. Also called multiport injection.

mylar tape Polyester film that may be metalized and incorporated into a wiring harness to provide electrical shielding.

National Automotive Technicians Education Foundation (NATEF) An accrediting body for secondary and post-secondary automotive training programs; an independent, nonprofit organization under the umbrella of the ASE.

National Lubricating Grease Institute (NLGI) An organization that grades the thickness of automotive and industrial grease.

needle roller bearing Typically a small-diameter pin rolling bearing that can be held in a cage or placed into the inside diameter of a hole.

needle-nosed pliers Pliers with long tapered jaws for gripping small items and getting into tight spaces.

negative camber Tilt of the top of the tire toward the centerline of the vehicle.

negative caster Forward tilt of the wheel pivot points from the vertical line.

negative offset A condition in which the plane of the hub mounting surface is positioned toward the brake side or back of the wheel centerline.

negative scrub radius A condition in which the point of center contact between the road surface and the tire and the point where the steering axis centerline contacts the road surface intersect above the road surface.

negative temperature coefficient (NTC) A characteristic of materials whereby resistance decreases as temperature increases.

negative temperature coefficient (NTC) thermistor A thermistor that gains resistance as temperature goes down and loses resistance as temperature goes up.

neutral steer A condition in which both the front and the rear tires of a vehicle are experiencing the same slip angle.

Newton's first law of motion A physical law that states that "an object will stay at rest or uniform speed unless it is acted upon by an outside force."

nippers (pincer pliers) Pliers designed to cut protruding items level with the surface.

nitriding A metal surfacing process that uses nitrogen ammonia gas to create a very thin, highly hardened surface.

nitridization process The nitriding metal surfacing process in which nitrogen ammonia gas is used inside a furnace and heated up and then cooled.

noise, vibration, and harshness (NVH) test A test to measure for any audible noises, vibrations, and harsh operation. It can be completed by the technician with or without the aid of an NVH tester. The tester is used to pinpoint the exact frequencies of the noise and vibrations.

noncontinuous monitor A monitor that runs only once per drive cycle.

nondirectional tread pattern A tread pattern that is nonspecific, allowing the tire to be placed on any wheel of a vehicle.

nonintegral ABS systems A brake system in which the master cylinder, power booster, and HCU are all separate units.

non-integral valve guide Also called a replaceable valve guide, a valve guide that is pressed into the cylinder head after the head has been constructed. These guides can be removed and replaced.

normally closed (NC) An electrical contact that is closed in the at-rest position.

normally open (NO) An electrical contact that is open in the at-rest position.

N-type Semiconductor material with a small amount of extra electrons.

number one cylinder Typically the cylinder located farthest forward on the engine. It is the first cylinder in the firing order.

nut A fastener with a hexagonal head and internal threads for screwing on bolts.

Occupational Safety and Health Administration (OSHA) Government agency created to provide national leadership in occupational safety and health.

octane rating A standard measure of the performance of a motor or aviation fuel. The higher the octane number, the more heat the fuel can withstand before self-igniting.

off-car brake lathe A tool used to machine (refinish) drums and rotors after they have been removed from the vehicle.

offset area An area on the crankshaft that is offset from the crankshaft centerline and that becomes a counterweight.

offset screwdriver A screwdriver with a 90-degree bend in the shaft for working in tight spaces.

offset vice A vice that allows long objects to be gripped vertically.

ohm The unit for measuring electrical resistance.

Ohm's law A law that defines the relationship between current, resistance, and voltage.

oil control ring The widest of the metal rings on the piston head assembly that controls oil flow to and from the cylinder walls.

oil cooler A device that takes heat away from engine oil by passing it near either engine coolant or outside air. Cooling the engine oil helps to keep it from overheating and breaking down.

oil filter wrench A specialized wrench that allows extra leverage to remove an oil filter when it is tight.

oil monitoring system A system that alerts the driver when it is time to change engine oil. These systems will need to be reset for the customer after an oil change is performed.

oil pan The metal pan that covers the bottom of the engine, contains oil sump where engine oil is held.

oil pressure relief valve A valve usually located in the oil pump that limits the oil pressure. When oil pressure is reached, excessive pressure is bled back to the sump.

oil pump A device that pumps lubricating oil through the engine.

oil pump strainer A screen located on the oil pump pickup that keeps debris from being picked up by the oil pump.

oil ring groove A metal groove cut into the piston head assembly designed to hold the oil control ring, which lubricates the cylinder wall and pistons.

oil seal Any seal used to seal oil in and dirt, moisture, and debris out.

oil slinger A device that rides partially in the transmission fluid; as it spins, it flings oil to lubricate the internal workings of the transmission.

oil spurt holes Holes drilled into the connecting rod that spray oil up onto the cylinder walls and the piston wrist pins.

oil sump The lower part of the oil pan that holds lubricating oil for the engine. The oil pickup screen sits in this low point.

oiler A device used to add oil to the air-conditioning system.

oil galleries Oil passages that are drilled into the engine block and cylinder head(s). These passageways carry oil from the oil pump to critical moving parts.

on/off–type signal A signal that is either a 12-volt signal or zero volts. Typically, switches provide on/off signals. Some systems use a 5-volt reference signal instead of a 12-volt signal.

on-board diagnostic II (OBDII) This generation of self-diagnostic systems mandated standardized diagnostic trouble codes and a data link connector. It also mandated monitoring of certain emission systems, such as the catalytic converter, oxygen sensor, EGR, and evaporative emissions.

on-car brake lathe A tool used to machine (refinish) rotors while they are still attached to the vehicle.

one-way clutch A type of holding device used by an automatic transmission to stop the movement of one component of a planetary gear set. It allows free spinning in one direction but will lock up when the part attempts to spin in the opposite direction.

open circuit A circuit that has a break that prevents current from flowing.

open differential assembly A differential assembly that allows both axles to turn at their own speed when turning a corner, but is dependent on the traction of the tires to deliver torque to the ground. If one wheel has no traction, all of the engine's torque will be used at that wheel, causing it to simply spin.

open A term used to describe a circuit that does not have a complete path for current to flow.

open-end wrench A wrench with open jaws to allow side entry to a nut or bolt.

optical sensor A sensor that generates a voltage when excited by a beam of light.

orifice A precisely sized hole used to reduce the speed and pressure of hydraulic oil flowing to a clutch or band.

O-ring seal A seal that is a complete circle. If a cutaway is done, it will also be a complete circle. These seals are usually set into a groove that is machined into the housing or part that does not move and is intended to be sealed.

O-ring valve stem seal A seal used where the valve spring retainer attaches to the valve stem to seal the juncture and prevent excessive oil from leaking into the valve stem.

oscillate To cycle above and below a given value.

oscillation The fluctuation of an object between two states. With regard to suspension springs, it refers to the uncontrolled compression and decompression of the spring following overshoot.

outer race The outside component of a wheel bearing that has a smooth, hardened surface for rollers or balls to ride on.

outer tie-rod The tie-rod attached between the tie-rod and the steering arm. It transfers the movement of the rack, pivoting as the rack is extended or retracted when the vehicle is negotiating turns.

outlet port Links the cylinder to the brake lines.

output force Force that equals the working pressure multiplied by the surface area of the output piston, expressed as pounds, newtons, or kilograms.

outside micrometer A precision measuring instrument meant to measure the outside of components. It is usually accurate to 0.0001" (0.0025 mm).

overcharging Overfilling of the air-conditioning system; may result in poor cooling or mechanical failure of the system.

overdrive Any gear ratio that results in a torque reduction with a speed increase. Overdrive is used on vehicles to reduce the engine speed when traveling at highway speed in order to save fuel.

overflow tank A tank used to catch any coolant that is released from the radiator cap (works like a catch can).

overhauling The process of refurbishing the transmission to like-new condition.

overhead cam (OHC) engine An I-head engine with the camshaft located on top of the cylinder head rather than in the block.

overhead valve (OHV) engine An engine in which the valves are positioned in the cylinder head assembly, directly over the top of the piston.

overshoot The amount a spring extends (springs back) past its original length following compression.

oversteer A condition in which a vehicle's front slip angles are larger than the rear slip angles. This vehicle is said to be "pushing" in the corners.

owner's manual An informational guide supplied by the manufacturer; it contains basic vehicle operating information.

oxidation inhibitor An oil additive that helps keep hot oil from combining with oxygen to produce sludge or tar.

oxides of nitrogen A vehicle emission that contributes to ground-level ozone. Oxides of nitrogen are produced when nitrogen and oxygen react during combustion, given sufficient temperatures and pressures. Forms include nitrogen oxide and nitrogen dioxide.

oxyacetylene torch A gas welding system that combines oxygen and acetylene.

oxygen sensor (before and after catalytic convertor) An exhaust sensor used to measure the amount of oxygen in the exhaust gases produced by the engine PCM, used to determine fuel mixture and spark timing.

P-type Semiconductor material with holes where electrons are missing.

paddle A shifting mechanism or electronic control usually attached to the steering wheel.

pan inspection The process of removing the transmission pan to check for clutch material, metal, and other debris or contaminants.

panhard rod A metal rod used to hold the dead axle and keep it from moving from side to side through corners. It is mounted on the body or frame of the vehicle and the axle. Also referred to as a track bar.

parallax error A visual error caused by viewing measurement markers at an incorrect angle.

parallel hybrid A hybrid vehicle driven simultaneously by an internal combustion engine and an electric machine.

parallel hybrid drive train A type of hybrid transmission in which power can flow from either a gasoline engine or an electric motor and any combination of the two.

parallelism Also called thickness variation; both surfaces of the rotor should be perfectly parallel to each other so that brake pulsations do not occur.

parallelogram steering system A non–rack-and-pinion system that uses a series of parts consisting of the pitman arm, idler arm, center link, and tie-rod assemblies that relays movement from the steering gearbox to the wheel assembly.

parasitic loss A loss of engine efficiency caused by internal friction, inefficient breathing, etc.

parking brake A brake system used for holding the vehicle when it is stationary.

parking brake cable A mechanism used to transmit force from the parking brake actuating lever to the brake unit.

parking brake cable pliers A tool used to install parking brake cables.

parking brake cable removal tool A tool used to compress the spring steel fingers of the parking brake cable so that the cable can be removed from the backing plate.

parking brake mechanism A mechanism that operates the brake shoes or pads to hold the vehicle stationary when the parking brake is applied.

parts program A computer software program for identifying and ordering replacement vehicle parts.

parts specialist The person who serves customers at the parts counters.

Pascal's law The law of physics that states that pressure applied to a fluid in one part of a closed system will be transmitted equally to all other areas of the system.

PCV valve A valve that controls the amount of crankcase ventilation flow that is allowed and varies with changes in manifold pressure.

peening A term used to describe the action of flattening a rivet through a hammering action.

performance testing The process of recreating a driving situation to check air-conditioning performance and vent temperature.

permanent magnet A material with natural or man-made constant magnetic properties.

permanent magnet electric motor An electric motor in which the magnetic field in the casing is produced by permanent magnets, while the armature has an electromagnetic field generated by passing electrical current through loops or windings, thereby producing the motor action.

personal protective equipment (PPE) Safety equipment designed to protect the technician, such as safety boots, gloves, clothing, protective eyewear, and hearing protection.

phase A term used to describe one set of windings from an alternator or alternating current electric motor.

phenolic resin A material used to create some brake pistons that is very resistant to corrosion and heat transfer.

Phillips head screwdriver A type of screwdriver that fits a head shaped like a cross in screws.

photochemical smog A brown haze that hangs in the sky, typically seen over large cities. Smog is a major health issue to humans because it affects lung tissue.

photodiode An electronic component that creates a varying voltage or current output based on the amount of light striking it.

pick-up A vehicle that carries cargo; it has stronger chassis components and suspension than a sedan.

pick-up assembly A component with a wire coil wrapped around a ferrous metal core; it is used to generate an electrical signal when a magnetic field passes through it.

pickup tube A tube connected to the oil pump that acts like a straw for the oil pump to pull oil from the sump of the oil pan.

pilot bearing The bearing or bushing that supports the front of the transmission input shaft.

pin punch A type of punch in various sizes with a straight or parallel shaft.

pinion shaft On a drive axle using a ring-and pinion gear assembly, the input component that drives the ring gear.

pip mark A small indent or dimple on the piston ring that indicates which side of the ring is installed upward. It is also used on some timing sprockets.

pipe wrench A wrench that grips pipes and can exert a lot of force to turn them. Because the handle pivots slightly, the more pressure put on the handle to turn the wrench, the more the grip tightens.

piston The round metal plug found inside the engine cylinder that moves up and down inside the cylinder.

piston assembly All of the parts of the piston including the piston, piston rings, and piston pin.

piston clearance The clearance between the piston and the cylinder wall that allows for lubricating oil to reduce friction.

piston displacement The volume of air that is moved by the piston from bottom dead center to top dead center.

piston engine An internal combustion engine that uses cylindrical pistons moving back and forth in a cylinder to extract mechanical energy from chemical energy.

piston pin (wrist pin) A round circular metal manufactured part that attaches the piston assembly to the connecting rod assembly.

piston pin boss The reinforced area of the piston where the piston wrist pin attaches the piston to the connecting rod.

piston ring A metal ring that is placed in a square groove around a piston for sealing purposes.

piston ring groove A square-cut groove located on the piston designed to hold a metal piston ring.

piston skirt The area below the ring groove area of the piston that prevents the piston from cocking and becoming jammed in the cylinder bore.

piston slap An engine noise caused by excessive clear-ance between the piston skirt area and the cylinder wall.

piston stroke The distance the piston travels through the engine cylinder from top dead center to bottom dead center.

pitch circle diameter (PCD) The diameter of the imaginary circle drawn through the center of the wheel bolt holes.

pitch (brakes) Movement of a vehicle around its y-axis (the imaginary line across the center of the vehicle from left to right) that causes the vehicle to lower or rise on the front end during quick braking or acceleration.

pitch (bolts) On a helix, the distance moved in one full revolution of the cylinder.

pitch The angle of a fan blade. A steeper pitch draws more air, while a shallower pitch draws less air.

planet carrier The device that holds the planet gears in place, keeping them equally spaced.

planetary gears The small gears in a planetary gear set that revolve around the sun gear.

plasma cutter A tool that uses electricity and compressed gas to produce a stream of high-temperature gas to cut metal.

Plastigauge® The trademarked name for a plastic gauging material used to check the clearances between two surfaces.

plenum chamber A large portion of the intake manifold after the throttle plate and before the intake runner tubes. The plenum provides a reservoir of air and helps prevent interference with the flow of air between individual branches.

pliers A hand tool with gripping jaws.

plug-in hybrid electric vehicle (PHEV) A hybrid electric vehicle in which only one power source, the battery, is used to propel the vehicle for a certain distance, limited by the storage capacity of the battery and the efficiency of the motor.

plunge-type joint The inner joint on the half shaft that allows for changes in shaft length.

ply rating A rating system that denotes the number of belt layers or plies that make up the tire carcass. In radial tires, ply rating denotes the relative strength of the plies, not the actual number of plies.

PN junction The junction between N- and P-type semiconductor materials.

pneumatic jack A type of vehicle jack that uses compressed gas or air to lift a vehicle.

pocket bearing A roller in the rear of the input shaft that supports the front of the main shaft.

polarity The state of charge, positive or negative.

polarity sensitive A term used to describe a component that must be connected into a circuit with the correct polarity to its terminals.

policy A guiding principle that sets the shop direction.

pollutant A potential threat to human health or the environment resulting from excessive amounts of chemicals and waste.

polyalphaolefin (PAO) A man-made base stock (synthetic) used in place of mineral oil. Oil molecules are more consistent in size and no impurities are found in this oil since it is made in a lab.

polycrystalline diamond (PCD) cutter An engine block resurfacing tool used on aluminum parts.

pop rivet gun A hand tool for installing pop rivets.

poppet (mushroom) valve A cam-operated, spring-loaded mushroom-type valve used to control intake into, and exhaust out of, the combustion chamber.

poppet valve A valve that controls the flow of brake fluid at usually preset pressures.

positive camber Tilt of the top of the tire out from the centerline of the vehicle.

positive caster Backward tilt of the wheel pivot points from the vertical line.

positive crankcase ventilation (PCV) system A system that draws blow-by gases from the crankcase into the intake to be burned.

positive offset A condition in which the plane of the hub mounting surface is positioned toward the outside or front of the wheel centerline.

positive scrub radius A condition in which the point of center contact between the road surface and the tire and the point where the steering axis centerline contacts the road surface intersect below the road surface.

positive temperature coefficient (PTC) A characteristic of materials whereby resistance increases as temperature increases.

positive valve stem seal A valve seal located at the top of the valve guide that is a more positive seal than an umbrella or O-ring seal.

potentiometer A variable resistor that can be used to adjust voltage in a circuit.

pour point depressants Oil additives that keep wax crystals from forming and causing the oil to gel during cold operation.

powdered metal rod A connecting rod manufactured through the process of heat, compression, and forging of powdered metals into a connecting rod.

power The rate at which work is done; electrical power is measured in watts.

power assist unit The electric motor in electric power assist steering systems.

power chip An aftermarket performance programmable chip marketed to increase horsepower and mileage of electronically controlled diesel engines.

power divider/splitter A device that receives power from an internal combustion engine and electric machine to power a hybrid electric vehicle.

power flow The path that power takes from the beginning of an assembly to the end. In a transmission, power flow changes as different gears are selected by the driver.

power section A chamber in the rack where pressurized fluid acts upon pistons that assist in steering.

power steering An option on a vehicle that allows movement of the steering wheel with decreased driver effort.

power steering pump A small hydraulic pump that provides assistance to the driver when turning the steering wheel.

power stroke The stroke during which combustion is pushing the piston from top dead center to bottom dead center in the cylinder. This stroke is where power is produced.

power take-off (PTO) A device attached to the transmission that is gear driven and can be used to run accessories such as winches and towing equipment. It can also refer to the gears that send power to the rear axle in a predominantly front wheel drive vehicle.

power tools Tools powered by electricity or compressed air.

power train mount A rubber or metal bracket used to secure the engine and transmission into the vehicle. Some vehicles use hydraulic or electrohydraulic power train mounts.

power unit A belt or gear-driven pump that produces hydraulic pressure for use in the steering box or rack.

power winding The current-carrying winding in an alternator or motor.

power-on-demand A feature that shuts down the engine when not needed to save fuel.

power-splitting transmission (PST) A type of hybrid transmission that splits the power flow going to the wheels from one or more electric motors and an internal combustion engine.

prechamber A separate combustion area designed into a diesel cylinder head.

preload The level of pressure placed on bearings that ensures the bearings will be held together.

press-fit pin A description of how a piston pin is placed inside a connecting rod by pressing the pin into the connecting rod.

pressure The force per unit area applied to the surface of an object.

pressure bleeding A bleeding method that uses clean brake fluid under pressure from an auxiliary tool or piece of equipment to force the air and old brake fluid from the hydraulic braking system.

pressure differential valve A valve that monitors any pressure difference between the two separate hydraulic brake circuits; it usually contains a switch to turn on the brake warning light when there is a pressure difference.

pressure plate The assembly that applies and removes the clamping force on the clutch disc.

pressure transducer A device used to measure engine vacuum and display it graphically on a lab scope.

pressure transients Minor fluctuations on the gauges that may indicate a problem.

pressure washer/cleaner A cleaning machine that boosts low-pressure tap water to a high-pressure output.

pressure, or force-feed, lubrication system A lubrication system that has a pump to pressurize the lubricating oil and push it through the engine to moving parts.

prick punch A pinch with a sharp point for accurately marking a point on metal.

primary circuit The low-voltage circuit that turns the coil on and off.

primary cup A seal that holds pressure in the master cylinder when force is applied to the piston.

primary piston A brake piston in the master cylinder moved directly by the pushrod or the power-booster; it generates hydraulic pressure to move the secondary piston.

primary winding The coil of wire in the low voltage circuit that creates the magnetic field in a step-up transformer.

printed circuitry Circuitry that forms the framework for electronic module construction. A printed circuit board holds electronic components that are soldered into place.

probing technique The way in which test probes are connected to a circuit.

procedure A list of the steps required to get the same result each time a task or activity is performed.

progressive rate of deflection The change in deflection rate that occurs as the weight of the vehicle changes. The greater the weight, the lower the rate of deflection due to increased resistance.

proportioning valves Valves used mostly on older vehicles equipped with rear drum brakes to reduce rear wheel hydraulic brake pressure under hard braking or light loads. Located in line with the rear brakes.

propylene-glycol A chemical used as anti-freeze. It is labeled as a nontoxic anti-freeze.

pry bar A high-strength carbon steel rod with offsets for levering and prying.

PT chart A pressure-temperature chart that shows the relationship between air-conditioning pressures and evaporator temperature.

pullers A generic term to describe hand tools that mechanically assist the removal of bearings, gears, pulleys, and other parts.

pulse-width modulation (combustion) The time that the fuel injectors are turned off and on to inject a precise amount of fuel.

punches A generic term to describe a high-strength carbon steel shaft with a blunt point for driving. Center and prick punches are exceptions and have a sharp point for marking or making an indentation.

purge switch A device used to show the computer when purge is occurring. It is used as a feedback device to allow the computer to determine whether flow is happening.

push-on spade terminal A disconnectable type of crimp or solder terminal used to terminate electrical wires.

pushrod A long, thin cylindrical shaft that provides a linkage between the lifters and the rocker arms to control valve opening and closing.

pushrod (braking system) A mechanism used to transmit force from the brake pedal to the master cylinder.

push-type clutch A typical clutch system used in modern vehicles where the clutch fork pushes the release bearing forward to release the friction facing from the pressure plate.

quadrant ratchet The device used in some cable-operated clutches to provide self-adjustment as the clutch disc wears. Some quadrant ratchets adjust if you lift up on the clutch pedal.

quench or squish area The narrow area between the top of the piston at top dead center and the cylinder head. It derives its name from the squishing of the air/fuel mixture into a small "charge."

quenched The state in a combustion chamber in which the flame cannot burn due to cold surfaces or poor distribution of the fuel mixture.

quick take-up master cylinders Cylinders used on disc brake systems that are equipped with low-drag brake calipers to quickly move the brake pads into contact with the brake rotors.

quick take-up valve A valve used to release excess pressure from the larger piston in a quick take-up master cylinder once the brake pads have contacted the brake rotors.

rack A steel rod driven by the pinion with tie-rods on each end or tie-rods connected to the center of the rack.

rack housing The outer shell of the rack-and-pinion steering system that is mounted to the chassis.

rack-and-pinion steering system A steering system composed of a steering wheel, a main shaft, universal joints, and an intermediate shaft. When the steering wheel is turned, movement is transferred by the main shaft and intermediate shaft to the pinion.

radial load The load that is perpendicular to a shaft, usually controlled by bearings or bushings.

radial tire A tire with two or more layers of casing plies and cord loops running radially from bead to bead.

radiation The transfer of heat through the emission of energy in the form of invisible waves.

radiator A device that takes hot coolant and cools it by passing heat energy to the surrounding air.

radiator hoses Rubber hoses that connect the radiator to the engine. Because they are subject to pressure, they are reinforced with a layer of fabric, typically nylon.

radius A straight line extending from the center of a circle to its edge or from the center of a sphere to its surface.

raster The scope pattern where all of the ignition firing sequences are stacked vertically on top of each other.

ratchet A generic term to describe a handle for sockets that allows the user to select direction of rotation. It can turn sockets in restricted areas without the user having to remove the socket from the fastener.

ratcheting box-end wrench A wrench with an inner piece that is able to rotate within the outer housing, allowing it to be repositioned without being removed.

ratcheting screwdriver A screwdriver with a selectable ratchet mechanism built into the handle that allows the screwdriver tip to ratchet as it is being used.

rattle gun A term used describe an air impact wrench based on the noise it makes.

reaction force A force that acts in the opposite direction to another force.

rear-wheel drive (RWD) A drive train layout in which the engine drives the rear wheels.

rebound clip A metal strap that is warped around the leaf spring to prevent excessive flexing of the main leaf during rebound.

receiver filter drier (RFD) The air-conditioning component used on TXV systems to filter and store liquid refrigerant to supply liquid refrigerant to the TXV. It is located between the condenser and the TXV.

reciprocating motion An up-and-down motion within the cylinder.

reciprocating weight The amount of weight that is moving up and down. It is everything from the middle of the connecting rod upward, including the piston, wrist pin, and rings.

reciprocation The back-and-forth movement of the piston assembly inside the cylinder.

recirculating ball steering box A steering box that has worm gear inside a block with a threaded hole in it and gear teeth cut into its outside that engage the sector shaft to move the pitman arm; generally used on trucks and heavy vehicles.

reclaim/recycle machine An air-conditioning machine designed to remove and recycle refrigerant for reuse.

reclaiming The process of removing refrigerant from the air-conditioning system by using an air-conditioning machine; also called recovering.

recovering See ***reclaiming***.

recuperation Process by which brake fluid moves from the reservoir past the edges of the seal into the chamber in front of the piston. This prevents air from being drawn into the hydraulic system caused by low pressure when the brake pedal is released quickly.

reductant A reducing agent.

reduction ratio The ratio between the turn of the steering wheel and the turn of the wheel, both measured in degrees.

reed switch A type of speed sensor that uses a magnetic field to open and close a movable set of contacts. It is used with a rotating magnet to measure rpm of a shaft and send the signal to the PCM.

refrigerant The name given to a chemical compound designed to meet the needs of the refrigeration system.

refrigerant identifiers Devices used to check for impurities in the air-conditioning system.

refrigerant label A label that lists the type and total capacity of refrigerant that is installed in the A/C system.

regenerative braking Technology used in vehicles that allows the vehicle to recapture and store part of the vehicle's kinetic energy in a reusable form when braking. Primarily used in hybrid and electric vehicles.

relay lever A steel rod that transfers movement from the drag link to an idler arm.

release mechanisms Components that operate the clutch. Usually included are the throw-out bearing and the clutch fork. Some manufacturers include the operating system.

reluctor A rotating, toothed wheel that changes the reluctance of a material to conduct magnetic lines of force.

repair order A form used by shops to collect information regarding a vehicle coming in for repair, also referred to as a work order.

required voltage The amount of voltage needed to push current across the electrodes of a spark plug located in the combustion chamber.

residual pressure valve (residual check valve) In drum brake systems, a valve that maintains pressure in the wheel cylinders slightly above atmospheric pressure so that air does not enter the system through the seals in the wheel cylinders.

resistor A component designed to have a fixed resistance.

resistor in series A resistor added to the circuit before or after the load to drop voltage to the load.

respirator Protective gear used to protect the wearer from inhaling harmful dusts or gases. Respirators range from single-use disposable masks to types that have replaceable cartridges. The correct types of cartridge must be used for the type of contaminant encountered.

restriction A blockage that partially stops or slows the flow of a material such as refrigerant.

retarding effect The result of retarding (slowing) the vehicle.

retrofit kit An aftermarket kit that has the fittings and oil to change an R-12 unit over to an R-134a unit.

return springs Springs that retract the brake shoes to their released position.

returnless fuel injection system A type of injection system in which no hot fuel is returned to the tank, thus keeping the fuel in the tank relatively cool and minimizing vaporization.

reverse boost valve A component of the pressure regulator valve that increases line pressure when the vehicle is in reverse.

reverse shift fork A shift fork used to engage the reverse gear.

rheostat An adjustable resistor that varies current flow through a circuit.

rib A design feature created in the metal casting/forging process that places extra metal area on a part for strength and durability, yet keeps the weight of the engine block low.

ribbon cable A type of flat harness in which cables are insulated from each other but joined together side by side.

ridge reamer A tool used to remove the metal lip on top of the cylinder walls caused by engine wear.

rigid non drive axle suspension A type of dead axle suspension system that is non-independent and uses a beam or solid axle.

rigid spring hanger The rigid part typically welded to the body or frame of the vehicle to which the front of the leaf spring is attached.

rigid-axle coil-spring suspension A dead axle that uses a coil spring.

rim The outer circular lip of the metal on which the inside edge of the tire is mounted.

rim flanges The outside edge of the wheel that helps keep the tire from popping off the wheel.

rim width The distance across the rim from one rim flange to the other.

ring gap The distance between the ends of the piston rings when the rings are seated against the inside of the engine cylinder.

ring gear The outer gear of a planetary gear set. The ring gear wraps around the outside of the planetary gears.

ring lands The metal between the ring grooves that supports the rings as the piston moves.

ring tension The built-in force created inside the piston rings due to the fact that the piston rings are made bigger than the cylinder walls to generate a scraping action against the cylinder walls.

rising characteristic A characteristic at a fixed fuel setting where the amount of fuel delivered to the engine will increase as engine speed and pump speed increase.

riveted linings Brake linings riveted to the brake pad backing plate with metal rivets and used on heavier-duty or high-performance vehicles.

rocker arm A lever that actuates a valve by pivoting near the center and pushing on the tip of the valve to open it.

rod A straight piece of steel used to transfer motion within the vehicle's suspension system. It typically has treads cut on one or both ends.

rod beam The area of connecting rod between the big and small ends.

rod bearing A bearing insert located in the big end of the connecting rod.

rod bearing journal A bearing surface that is offset from the centerline of the crankshaft.

rod cap The very bottom part of the connecting rod that retains the rod bearing inserts.

rod journal Also called the crankshaft rod throw, an area machined to a very smooth finish that contains an oil hole to provide oil to lubricate the surfaces of the crankshaft and rod bearing inserts.

roll Movement of a vehicle around its x-axis (the imaginary line down the center of the vehicle from front to back). It is commonly referred to as body roll or lean; when cornering, the body will try to move to the outside of the corner against the suspension.

roll bar Another type of pry bar, with one end used for prying and the other end for aligning larger holes, such as engine motor mounts.

roller bearing A long cylindrical roller held in position by a cage.

rolling code A constantly changing, randomly selected numeric code that is communicated with the engine immobilizer and security system.

rolling resistance Resistance that is present from tires contacting the road and wind resistance against the vehicle while rolling down the highway.

roll-rate sensor A sensor that measures the amount of roll around the vehicle's horizontal axis that a vehicle is experiencing.

room temperature vulcanizing (RTV) silicone A silicone adhesive that sets up or "vulcanizes" at room temperature.

rosin A type of liquid or paste (flux) used to prevent oxidization that is in solid form contained within the solder.

rotary engine An engine that uses a triangular rotor turning in a housing instead of conventional pistons.

rotating assembly The assembly of the crankshaft, connecting rod, and piston that are found inside the engine cylinder block.

rotating weight The amount of weight that is moving in a circular motion, including everything from the center of the connecting rod down to the connecting rod cap and all components of the crankshaft.

rotational force The force created by the rotating wheel when the brakes are applied; it causes the brake components to twist the brake support and ultimately the vehicle in the direction of wheel rotation.

rotational speed The speed at which an object rotates, measured in revolutions per minute (rpm).

rotor (brakes) The main rotating part of a disc brake system.

rotor (engine) A high-voltage rotating switch that transfers voltage from the distributor cap's center terminal to the outer terminals.

rotor arm The portion of the rotor that extends toward, but not touching, the outer distributor cap terminals.

rotor lobes Lobes or rounded edges on rotors that squeeze oil and create pressure.

rotor-type oil pump An oil pump that uses rounded gears to squeeze oil through.

rubber bellows Rubber pieces positioned on each end of the rack to protect the inner joints from dirt and contaminants and retain the grease lubricant inside the rack-and-pinion housing.

rubber-bonded bushing A bushing that has a steel outer housing and inner sleeve with rubber inside; also known as a metalastic bushing.

run-flat technology A tire design that allows the vehicle to keep moving under driver control following a puncture or rapid loss of pressure.

running clearance The amount of space between wheel bearing components while in operation.

Rzeppa joint A type of fixed constant velocity joint that has an inner race, six steel ball bearings, a bearing cage, and an outer race.

SAE J1930 An SAE standard for across-the-board standardization of parts and systems nomenclature.

SAE J2012 An SAE standard for across-the-board identification of generic DTCs.

safe working load (SWL) The maximum safe lifting load for lifting equipment.

safety data sheet (SDS) A sheet that provides information about handling, use, and storage of a material that may be hazardous.

safety-type drop-center rim A rim designed with a slight hump at the inside edge of the bead ledges to hold the tire beads in place during a flat tire.

salvage title Also called a branded title; a record that a vehicle has been severely damaged or deemed a total loss by an insurance company.

sand or bead blasters A cleaning system that uses high-pressure fine particles of glass bead or sand.

sander/polisher A power tool with a rotating disc or head to which polishing or sanding discs can be attached.

scavenge pump A pump used with a dry sump oiling system to pull oil from the dry sump pan and move it to an oil tank outside the engine.

scavenging The process of removing burned gases from the cylinder through the use of moving airflow pulling or extracting the gases out.

scavenging effect A condition caused by moving columns of air, which create a low-pressure area behind them, resulting in a pulling force that is used to pull the remaining burned gases from the combustion chamber. Valve timing affects the amount of scavenging effect an engine has.

Schrader valve A one-way valve used in a valve stem.

scratcher A thin, spring steel wear indicator that is fixed to the backing plate of the brake pad; it emits a high-pitched squeal when the brakes are applied if the brake pads have become too thin.

screw extractor A tool for removing broken screws or bolts.

scrub brakes A brake system that uses leverage to force a friction block against one or more wheels.

scrub radius The distance between two imaginary points on the road surface—the point of center contact between the road surface and the tire, and the intersecting point where the steering axis centerline and the tire centerline contact the road surface.

sealed bearings Wheel bearings that are assembled by the manufacturer with the proper lubrication and sealed for life; cannot normally be disassembled.

secondary circuit The part of an ignition system that operates on higher voltage and delivers the necessary high voltage to the spark plugs.

secondary cup A seal that prevents loss of fluid from the rear of each piston in the master cylinder.

secondary piston A piston that is moved by hydraulic pressure generated by the primary piston in the master cylinder.

secondary winding The high-voltage copper wiring found in an ignition coil.

second-order vibration Vibration that occurs at twice the engine rpm.

sedan A vehicle configuration that has an enclosed body, with a maximum of four doors to allow access to the passenger compartment.

selective catalytic reduction An active emission control system that injects a liquid reductant, or reducing agent, through a special catalyst into the exhaust stream of a diesel engine.

selective thickness shim A shim of a prescribed thickness that is used to control shaft clearances in a transmission.

selector gate The U-shaped cutaway in shift shafts that the shifter lever fits into.

selector shift rail A rod that is attached to the shift fork. These rails move when the shifter lever is moved against them.

self-energizing The property of drum brakes that assists the driver in applying the brakes; when brake shoes come into contact with the moving drum, the friction tends to wedge the shoes against the drum, thus increasing the braking force.

self-leveling A vehicle with automatic load-adjustable shock absorbers.

self-sealing tire A tire constructed with a flexible and malleable lining inside the tire around the inner tubeless membrane. The lining can seal small tread-area punctures instantly and permanently.

semiautomatic climate control system A system that provides automatic function of the heater or cooling only, leaving fan speed and mode selection to the operator.

semiconductor A material used to make microchips, transistors, and diodes.

semi-floating axle An axle that carries the weight of the vehicle; if removed, there is no way to connect the wheel to the vehicle.

sending unit The component in the fuel supply system responsible for sending constant electrical signals to the gas gauge located in the driver information center.

separator PCV system A PCV system that uses a device that uses gravity to allow oil to fall to the bottom of the valve and be returned to the crankcase; the valve prevents liquid from traveling to the intake manifold.

separator plate Sometimes called a spacer plate, a thin sheet metal plate installed between the valve body and the transmission case. Orifices can be installed in the separator plate, and check valves can work with holes in the plate.

series hybrid A hybrid electric vehicle powered by an internal combustion engine, but driven by battery.

series hybrid drive train A type of hybrid transmission in which power flows from the engine through an electric motor. The electric motor supplements the power from the engine to the wheels.

series-parallel circuit A circuit that has both a series and a parallel circuit combined into one circuit.

series-parallel hybrid A hybrid electric vehicle that uses the internal combustion engine and/or the battery pack for propulsion.

series-parallel hybrid drive train A type of hybrid drive train that can function as both a series hybrid and parallel hybrid. That means the gasoline engine can turn a generator that can be used to power an electric motor. The gasoline engine can also drive the vehicle directly through the transmission. And the electric motor can work in parallel with the gasoline engine to drive the vehicle.

service brake A brake system that is operated while the vehicle is moving to slow or stop the vehicle.

service campaign and recall A corrective measure conducted by manufacturers when a safety issue is discovered with a particular vehicle.

service consultant/advisor A service worker who works with both customers and technicians; the first point of contact for customers seeking vehicle repairs.

service history A complete list of all the servicing and repairs that have been performed on a vehicle.

service manager The shop supervisor who is responsible for the management of the service department.

serviceable bearings Wheel bearings that can be disassembled, cleaned, inspected, packed, reinstalled, and adjusted.

servo action A drum brake design where one brake shoe, when activated, applies an increased activating force to the other brake shoe, in proportion to the initial activating force; further enhances the self-energizing feature of some drum brakes.

setback The distance one wheel is set back from the wheel on the opposite side of the axle.

shaft The long, narrow component that carries one or more gears or has gears machined into it.

shielded wiring harness A wiring harness that has shielding built into it to protect it from induced electrical interference.

shift fork A mechanism that moves the synchronizer sleeve to lock the gear to the main shaft.

shift solenoid An electromechanical device used to control oil flow to bands and clutches in an automatic transmission to help shift the transmission.

shift valve A type of spool valve that has multiple fluid inputs and a spring; it is used to direct hydraulic pressure to a clutch or band needed for a shift.

shock absorber A device on a vehicle designed to absorb bumps and jolts caused from driving on irregular surfaces and to dampen body movement.

shop foreman The supervisor in a shop who oversees the work of technicians and staff and communicates with customers and external suppliers.

shop or service manual Manufacturer's or aftermarket information on the repair and service of vehicles.

short Also called a short circuit, the flow of current along an unintended route.

short block An engine assembly that includes the engine block, camshaft, timing set, pistons, rods, and crankshaft installed.

short circuit A condition in which the current flows along an unintended route.

short to power A condition in which current flows from one circuit into another.

short-/long-arm (SLA) suspension A type of control arm suspension system that uses a short control arm on the top and a long control arm on the bottom. This design ensures correct alignment angles when moving through bumps.

shroud A steel or plastic cover placed over the shock rod.

side force The pressure on the wheel that pushes it toward the outside or inside of the rim as the vehicle makes a turn.

side gear A gear that is splined to the axle shaft and meshes with the spider gears and allows the axles to rotate at their own speeds when cornering and turning.

side rail The thin portion of the oil control ring that is used to scrape oil off of the cylinder walls.

signal voltage value Measured voltage in a signal return circuit that is compared to a specified voltage value published by the manufacturer.

sine wave A mathematical function that describes a repetitive waveform such as an alternating current signal.

single flare A sealing system made on the end of metal tubing.

single-piston master cylinder A master cylinder with a single piston that creates hydraulic pressure for all wheel units. If there is a leak in the system, there is a loss of pressure for all wheel units.

single-plate clutch A clutch assembly that uses only one plate to transfer torque from the engine to the transmission. This is the most common type of light vehicle clutch.

single-post hoist A type of vehicle hoist that uses a single central platform to lift a vehicle.

sintering The process of using pressure and heat to bond metal particles.

sintering process A metal hardening process in which the metal is fused together without melting.

slave cylinder The component in a hydraulically operated clutch that converts hydraulic pressure to mechanical movement at the clutch fork.

sledge hammer A heavy hammer, usually with two flat faces, that provides a strong blow.

sliding or floating caliper A type of brake caliper that only has piston(s) on the inboard side of the rotor. The caliper is free to slide or float, thus pulling the outboard brake pad into the rotor when braking force is applied.

sliding spline driveshaft A two-piece driveshaft that is joined in the middle with splines. The driveshaft can slide on itself to increase or decrease in length.

sliding T-handle A handle fitted at 90 degrees to the main body that can be slid from side to side.

slip angle A tire's sideways distortion that makes the vehicle follow a path at an angle to the direction the road wheel is pointing.

slip yoke Part of a two-piece driveshaft that is splined and allows for a change in length of the shaft as the suspension compresses and rebounds.

slow charger A battery charger that charges at low current.

smart charger A battery charger with microprocessor-controlled charging rates and times.

snap ring The spring-steel C-shaped ring that is fitted in a groove and holds gears, bearings, and shafts in place.

snap ring pliers A pair of pliers for installing and removing snap rings or circlips.

sniffer An electronic device used to determine the source of leaks.

socket An enclosed metal tube commonly with 6 or 12 points to remove and install bolts and nuts.

soft plug A thin-walled, metal, cup-shaped disc designed to be pressed into a machined passageway in the block for the purpose of plugging it.

solder A mixture of lead and tin with a low melting point for connecting wires.

soldering irons A heating tool to heat solder and wires to produce a low-resistance joint.

solder-type terminal A terminal that requires soldering to fasten the terminal to the cable or wire.

solenoid An electromagnet with a moving iron core that is used to cause mechanical motion.

solenoid valve An electrically operated valve that when used in brake systems is designed to control the flow of brake fluid in the hydraulic system.

solid axle A single piece of steel that provides a simple means of mounting the hub and wheel units. Also called beam axle or straight axle.

solid rear axle A type of axle that has a one-piece axle housing, so that the action of hitting a bump with one wheel affects the other wheel.

solid rotor A type of brake rotor made of solid metal.

solid valve lifter A non-hydraulic valve lifter.

solid-state relay A relay that performs the function of a mechanical relay but using only electronic components.

solvent tank A tank containing solvents to clean vehicle parts.

spark ignition (SI) engine An engine that relies on an electrical spark to ignite the air and fuel mixture.

spark plug A device that provides a gap for the high-voltage spark to occur in each cylinder.

spark plug reach The length of the spark plug from the seat to the end of the threads.

spark timing The point at which a spark occurs at the spark plug relative to the position of the piston.

specialty springs Springs used to return links and levers on the parking brake system or the self-adjuster mechanism.

speed brace A U-shaped socket wrench that allows high-speed operation. Also called a speeder handle.

speed sensor A sensor responsible for measuring the speed of the vehicle that is read by the speedometer.

speedy sleeve An aftermarket repair kit that consists of a thin metal sleeve that fits tightly over the seal surface of the axle, providing a new, undamaged surface for the seal to ride against.

splash lubrication A lubrication system that relies on oil being splashed onto moving parts by rotating engine parts striking the oil. These systems are typically used in small engines.

spline A ridge or tooth on a driveshaft that meshes with grooves in a mating piece and transfers torque to it, maintaining the angular correspondence between them.

Typically, a shaft and gear that have parallel grooves machined in them so they mate with each other and lock together rotationally.

splined section A flat key made into a shaft to accommodate changes in shaft length due to movement in wheel camber with suspension action.

split diagonally A brake system in which the left front wheel is hydraulically paired with the right rear wheel and the right front wheel is paired with the left rear. This preserves 50% of the braking capability if one of the brake circuits begins to leak.

split front to rear A brake system in which the front brakes operate on one hydraulic circuit and the rear brakes from the other.

spool valve A type of valve commonly used in automatic transmissions that resembles the spool that thread or fishing line comes on.

sport utility vehicle (SUV) A passenger vehicle built on a light-truck chassis; it is usually equipped with four-wheel drive and capable of hauling heavier loads than typical passenger vehicles.

spray wash cabinet A cleaning cabinet that sprays cleaning solution under pressure to clean vehicle parts.

spring A resilient steel part that stores energy when compressed and releases energy when released to its original state; available as a leaf spring, coil spring, or torsion bar.

spring eyes Rolled ends of some springs used to mount springs to the chassis.

spring pressure Pressure exerted by a metal coil usually measured in pounds.

spring shackle bushing A bushing that is positioned in the shackle that the leaf spring mounts to. Bushings allow the spring shackle to move as the leaf spring dimensions change over bumps.

spring-loaded key A part of the synchronizer that helps hold the synchronizer collar in position.

spring-loaded rack guide yoke A spring-containing part that pushes on the back side of the rack to help reduce the play between the rack and the pinion while still allowing for relative movement.

springs and clips Various devices that hold the brake shoes in place or return them to their proper place.

spur gear A type of gear in which the teeth of the gear are cut in a straight line down the axis of the gear.

square cut O-ring An O-ring with a square cross—section that is used to seal the pistons in disc brake calipers.

square file A type of file with a square cross section.

square thread A thread type with square shoulders used to translate rotational to lateral movement.

squib The component inside the airbag inflator that triggers the airbag deployment.

staged governor A governor in which the assembly uses two valves: a primary valve and a secondary valve.

stall test A test that involves raising the engine rpm to wide-open throttle while the brake is firmly applied and the transmission is in gear. The test is used to check torque convertor and transmission operation on some vehicles.

standard torque converter A hydraulic coupling device consisting of an impeller, turbine, stator, and housing; located between the engine and the transmission.

starter teeth Machined teeth located on the ring gear for meshing with the starter drive teeth located in the starter motor.

state of charge The amount of refrigerant in a system compared to how much should be in it.

static imbalance A tire imbalance resulting from a heavy spot on a tire; it will vibrate vertically with the heavy area slapping the road surface with each turn of the wheel.

static toe A setting designed to compensate for slight wear in steering components that may cause the wheels to turn outward or inward while the vehicle is in motion.

station wagon A vehicle configuration with four doors with a roof line that continues into the rear cargo area and a rear door for access.

stator Portion of an electronic ignition system that is mounted to the base of the distributor. It has a circular permanent magnet with a number of projections or teeth corresponding to the number of engine cylinders, and a stationary coil of fine enameled copper wire wound on a plastic reel and positioned inside the magnet.

stator winding A winding in an alternator that creates the current output, or a winding in a motor that creates the needed magnetism for the motor to rotate.

steel hammer A hammer with a head made of hardened steel.

steel rule An accurate measuring ruler made of steel.

steel-disc–type rim A plain steel wheel that is typically covered by a hubcap.

steering angle sensor A sensor that measures the amount of turning a driver desires. This information is used by the ESC system to know the driver's directional intent.

steering arm An arm that extends from the steering knuckle. The tie-rods connect to these arms in order to steer the wheels.

steering axis inclination (SAI) The angle formed by an imaginary line running through the upper and lower steering pivots relative to vertical as viewed from the front.

steering box A device that converts the rotary motion of the steering wheel to the linear motion needed to steer the vehicle.

steering column A column affixed between the steering wheel and the steering box, usually made to collapse during a crash.

steering damper A device used to prevent shocks from irregular roads from being transmitted through the steering linkage and back to the steering wheel.

steering knuckle A device that connects the front wheel to the suspension; pivots on the top and bottom, thus allowing the front wheels to turn.

steering linkage Steel rods that connect the steering box to the steering arms on the steering knuckle.

steering sensor A sensor that can read both torque and rotation from the steering wheel.

steering system A term used to describe all of the components and parts involved in steering a vehicle.

steering wheel position sensor A sensor that signals to the EBCM both the position and speed of the steering wheel.

step-down transformer A transformer used to reduce the voltage, such as to allow a battery charger operated on 120 volts to charge a 12-volt battery.

stepper motor A type of brushless motor with a key difference: It is designed to rotate in fixed steps through a set number of degrees.

step-up transformer A transformer used to increase the voltage from a lower input voltage to a higher output, such as an ignition coil.

stop A rubber part used to control the movement of control arms (suspension arms).

straight edge A measuring device generally made of steel to check how flat a surface is.

straight grinder A powered grinder with the wheel set at 90 degrees to the shaft.

stroke The movement of the piston in the engine from top dead center to bottom dead center, or vice versa. There are four strokes: intake, compression, power, and exhaust.

strut A shock absorber used on a MacPherson strut–type suspension.

stub axle An axle used for one wheel.

stub-axle carrier The body of the stub-axle knuckle.

stud A type of threaded fastener with a thread cut on each end rather than having a bolt head on one end.

subframe A mount attached to the vehicle that is used to support the engine and transaxle assembly.

sulfur dioxide (SO2) A pollutant resulting from sulfur in motor fuel and contributing to acid rain.

sulphuric acid A type of acid that when mixed with pure water forms the basis of battery acid or electrolyte.

sun gear The center gear of a planetary gear set around which the other gears rotate.

sun load (solar) sensor A photodiode that varies voltage based on light. It is used to determine the radiant heat coming from the sun into the passenger cabin and gives an input signal of sunlight load to the ECU.

supercharger A device that pressurizes airflow into the engine, working similar to a turbocharger. The supercharger is driven by the crankshaft through a belt or gears and does require power from the engine.

supplemental restraint system (SRS) A passenger safety system, such as airbags and seat belt pretensioners.

supporting statement A statement that urges the speaker to elaborate on a particular topic.

surface filter A filter that is a simple screen mechanism to catch dirt and other particles in the hydraulic oil as it passes through.

surface roughness average (Ra) A measurement used to classify how rough a particular mating surface is at the microscopic level.

surge protector An electrical protection device for preventing electrical surges.

surge tank A sealed tank that captures coolant coming from the head that has turned to steam and changes the steam back to coolant to be reused by the cooling system.

suspension action Movement of the chassis up and down.

suspension strut A shock absorber designed to reduce spring oscillations.

suspension system A system within a vehicle designed to isolate the vehicle body from road bumps and vibrations.

sway bar A part used in vehicles as a stabilizer, or antiroll bar. It is connected to the chassis in the center, and each end is connected to one side of the suspension system. It is typically installed on the front, and sometimes the rear suspension.

swinging shackle A shackle connected to the rear of the multileaf spring that allows the leaf spring to move downward when a load is placed on the rear of the vehicle.

switch An electrical device with contacts that turns current flow on and off.

symmetric tread pattern A tread pattern with the same tread pattern on both sides of the tire; typically nondirectional.

synchromesh transmission A modern transmission that uses gear synchronizers to match the speeds of gears and shafts during upshifts and downshifts.

synchronizer An assembly that allows for the selection of gears without grinding by matching the speed of the two assemblies.

synchronizer sleeve The sleeve that slides to lock the selected gear to the main shaft. The synchronizer sleeve is part of the synchronizer assembly.

synthetic blend A blend of conventional engine oil and pure synthetic oil.

synthetic oil Synthetic oil that, in its pure form, uses man-made base stocks and is not derived from crude oil. This oil lasts longer and performs better than normal oil. The base stock additives are similar to those in conventional oils.

tandem master cylinder A master cylinder that has two pistons that operate separate braking circuits so that if a leak develops in one circuit, the other circuit can still operate.

tang A part of the bearing insert that helps to lock the bearing insert into the bearing saddles and caps.

tanks Metal or plastic pieces that line the pipes used to connect the tubes together to allow the coolant to continue to flow.

tap A term used to generically describe an internal thread-cutting tool.

tap handle A tool designed to securely hold taps for cutting internal threads.

taper An object that is smaller in diameter at one end.

taper tap A tap with a tapper; it is usually the first of three taps used when cutting internal threads.

tapered roller bearing assembly A type of wheel bearing with races and rollers that are tapered in such a manner that all of the tapered angles meet at a common point, which allows them to roll freely and yet control thrust.

tapered seat A type of lug nut with a tapered end toward the rim that helps center the wheel on the wheel studs.

tappet Another name for a valve lifter. Tappets may be flat or have rollers to ride on the cam lobes.

technical service bulletin (TSB) Information issued by manufacturers to alert technicians of unexpected problems or changes to repair procedures.

temperature grade A standardized grading system that indicates the extent to which heat is generated or dissipated by a tire.

tensile strength A measure of how strong a material is as it is being pulled apart.

terminal A means of providing a low-resistance connection/termination at the end of a wire.

test certificate A certificate issued when lifting equipment has been checked and deemed safe.

tetrafluoroethane (R-134a) An inert colorless gas that can be used as a refrigerant. It is stored in light blue containers.

thermal expansion valve (TXV) system A system with a valve designed to sense evaporator outlet temperature and vary the inlet orifice size accordingly.

thermistor A temperature-controlled variable resistor. As temperature changes, so does resistance.

thermo-control switch A temperature-sensitive switch that is mounted into the radiator or into a coolant passage on the engine to control electric fan operation.

thermostat Located under the thermostat housing, the thermostat regulates the flow of coolant, allowing coolant to flow from the engine to the radiator when the engine is running at its operating temperature.

thixotropy The ability of a semisolid grease to flow when agitated or stressed.

thread file A type of file that cleans clogged or distorted threads on bolts and studs.

thread pitch The coarseness or fineness of a thread as measured by either the threads per inch or the distance from the peak of one thread to the next. Metric fasteners are measured in millimeters.

thread repair A generic term to describe a number of processes that can be used to repair threads.

three-angle grind A process of grinding the valve openings on the cylinder head so that air can pass through them more smoothly and quickly.

three-quarter floating axle An axle on which there is only one wheel bearing which bears the weight of the vehicle, but the axle prevents the wheel from tipping inward or outward.

three-way catalytic converter A converter that changes hydrocarbons, carbon monoxide, and oxides of nitrogen into harmless elements.

threshold limit value (TLV) The maximum allowable concentration of a given material in the surrounding air.

throttle A device used to produce acceleration by controlling the air/fuel mixture.

throttle body The housing on an intake manifold that is used to control the amount of filtered air that enters the cylinders.

throttle body injection (TBI) A fuel injection system that uses one or more fuel injectors mounted above or in the throttle body itself. Also called single-point injection.

throttle position sensor (TPS) A potentiometer that sends an analog signal to the electronic control unit that corresponds to the position of the throttle valve.

throttle valve A type of spool valve that is connected to the throttle on a vehicle. The throttle valve creates a pressure proportional to throttle opening and is used to delay upshifting based on throttle opening.

throttle valve pressure The pressure created by the throttle valve that is proportional to throttle opening.

throw The part of the crankshaft that is offset for the connecting rods to mate with; also called connecting rod journal.

throw-out bearing The part of the clutch release mechanism that imparts clutch pedal force to the rotating pressure plate levers.

thrust angle The angle formed between the centerline of the rear axle in comparison to the centerline of the vehicle.

thrust bearing A main bearing insert that either has integrated flanges or separate flanges that provide bearing surfaces that prevent forward or lateral movement of the crankshaft assembly.

thrust bearing Also called a Torrington bearing, a small roller bearing assembly with the rollers laid flat axially around the centerline of the bearing. The bearing is used to control forward and backward movement of a part in an automatic transmission.

thrust line The imaginary line drawn through the center of the rear axle.

thrust washers Flat, washer-shaped bearings that provide a wear surface between two rotating components that are loaded axially.

thrust-type angular-contact ball bearing A type of bearing that uses a deep groove in the bearing races where the ball bearings ride; this design is for thrust conditions.

tie-rod A steering component that transfers linear motion from the steering box to the steering arms at the front wheels.

tie-rod assembly The part that fits between the rack and the steering arms and transfers the movement of the rack.

timing chain A steel chain connecting the crankshaft assembly to the camshaft assembly.

timing gear A gear that synchronizes the timed events of rotational engine components like camshafts and fuel injection pumps.

tin snips Cutting device for sheet metal, works in a similar fashion to scissors.

tire inflation pressure The level of air in the tire that provides it with load-carrying capacity and affects overall vehicle performance.

tire placard A metal, vinyl, or paper tag permanently affixed to a vehicle that indicates the appropriate tire size and inflation pressure for the vehicle.

tire pressure gauge A gauge used to measure the air pressure within a tire.

tire pressure monitoring system (TPMS) An automatic sensor system in most modern vehicles that alerts drivers of tire pressure problems.

tire valve The valve through which air is inserted into a tire to inflate it.

title history A detailed account of a vehicle's past.

toe-in When the front of the wheels, as seen from above, are closer together than the rear of the wheels.

toe-out on turns The difference in turning angle of the inside tire in comparison to the outside tire. This angle difference allows the tires to roll through the corner rather than the inside tire dragging. Also referred to as Ackermann angle.

toe-out When the rear of the wheels, as seen from above, are closer together than the front of the wheels.

toe-setting Setting of the toe-in or toe-out of the tires to the centerline of the vehicle.

tone wheel The part of the wheel speed sensor that has ribs and valleys used to create an electrical signal inside of the pick-up assembly.

top dead center (TDC) The position of the piston in the cylinder farthest from the crankshaft.

top hat parking brake A drum brake that is located inside a disc brake rotor in order to act as a parking brake.

torque The amount of twisting force applied in a turning application, usually measured in foot-pounds.

torque angle A method of tightening bolts or nuts based on angles of rotation.

torque assist Use of an electric motor to supplement the engine's torque whenever additional torque is needed, allowing for a smaller ICE to be used.

torque converter A device that is turned by the crankshaft and transmits torque to the input shaft of an automatic transmission.

torque converter clutch (TCC) A hydraulically operated clutch located inside the torque converter that applies at predetermined conditions and stops torque converter slippage.

torque multiplication The increase of torque.

torque plate A 2" (51 mm) thick plate that is bolted where the cylinder head is fastened on the engine block.

torque sensor A device used to measure the load on the steering wheel.

torque smoothing A process that uses an electric motor to smooth out engine power pulses when an ICE is operating at low rpm or when the vehicle is using fuel management techniques such as cylinder deactivation.

torque specifications Supplied by manufacturers and describes the amount of twisting force allowable for a fastener or a specification showing the twisting force from an engine crankshaft.

torque steer A condition in which the vehicle pulls to one side during hard acceleration.

torque wrench A tool used to measure the rotational or twisting force applied to fasteners.

torque-to-yield A tightening procedure in which a bolt is designed to be slightly elastic when tightened; the elastic bolt retains an even pressure on the head gasket.

torque-to-yield (TTY) bolts Bolts that are tightened using the torque-to-yield method.

torsion bar A bar made of a steel alloy that is fixed rigidly to the chassis at one end and the suspension control arm at the other to support the weight of a vehicle.

torsion bar A spring-loaded piece of steel connected to the pinion gear at its bottom end and the input shaft at its top. Also, a torsion bar is a type of spring that some vehicles use to hold up a corner of the vehicle.

torsional load A force that is applied by clamping one end of an object to another object that is then twisted.

torsional vibrations The speeding up and slowing down of a shaft, which happen at a relatively high frequency. Crankshafts have torsional vibrations due to the power pulses of the pistons.

toxic dust Any dust that may contain fine particles that could be harmful to humans or the environment.

traction control system (TCS) A computer-controlled system added to ABS to help prevent loss of traction while the vehicle is accelerating.

traction grade A standardized grading system that indicates how well a tire will maintain contact with the road surface when wet.

trailing arm suspension A type of suspension system that uses upper and lower control arms.

trailing shoes Brake shoes installed so that they are applied in the opposite direction to the forward rotation of the brake drum; not self-energizing and less efficient at developing braking force.

transaxle A type of transmission typically used in front-wheel drive vehicles in which the transmission also includes the differential and final drive gear.

transfer case A component that is bolted to the back of the transmission and connects the front and rear axles via the driveshafts.

transformer action The transfer of electrical energy from one coil to another through induction in a transformer.

transmission An assembly that houses a variety of gear sets that allow the vehicle to be driven at a wider range of speeds and terrain conditions than would be possible without a transmission.

transmission control module (TCM) An electronic computer that controls transmission function; it may include adaptive learning capabilities for driver preferences.

transmission input shaft The shaft that brings engine torque into the transmission.

transmission oil temperature (TOT) sensor A type of variable resistor used inside the transmission to monitor oil temperature.

transmission specialist A technician who diagnoses, overhauls, and repairs transmissions.

transmission-mounted parking brake A drum brake that is mounted on the drive shaft just after the transmission to serve as a parking brake.

transverse The orientation of the engine in which the front of the engine is facing the side of the vehicle.

tread wear grade The number imprinted on the sidewall of a tire by the manufacturer as required by the National Highway Traffic Safety Administration (NHTSA) that indicates the tread life of a tire's tread.

triangular file A type of file with three sides so it can get into internal corners.

trim height The amount of ground clearance a vehicle has, measured from a point on the body or frame depending on the manufacturer. Also known as ride height.

trimetal The use of three different types of metals to build up a bearing insert to give it long-lasting wear characteristics.

truck A large heavy vehicle for carrying cargo.

tube flaring tool A tool that makes a sealing flare on the end of metal tubing.

tubes Metal pipes running side to side or up and down that the coolant or refrigerant travels through.

tubing cutter A hand tool for cutting pipe or tubing squarely.

tulip/tripod joint A constant velocity joint that has three equally spaced fingers shaped like a star. This configuration allows in-and-out movement of the shaft while allowing flexing.

turbocharger A device that pressurizes airflow into the engine. The turbocharger works similar to a supercharger, but is driven by the exhaust gases.

turn signal switch A switch that turns the left and right turn signal lights on and off.

turning radius A measure of how small a circle the vehicle can turn around when the steering wheel is turned to the limit.

twin leading shoe drum brake system Brake shoe arrangement in which both brake shoes are self-energizing in the forward direction.

twist drill A hardened steel drill bit for making holes in metals, plastics, and wood.

twisted pair Two conductors that are twisted together to reduce electrical interference.

two-post hoist A type of vehicle hoist that uses two parts (one on each side of vehicle) and four arms to lift the vehicle.

two-stroke engine An engine that uses only two strokes to complete its running cycle.

two-way catalytic converter A converter that changes only hydrocarbons and carbon monoxide into harmless elements.

ultrasonic A method of leak detection that uses a sensitive microphone to hear small refrigerant leaks by amplifying the hissing noise.

umbrella-style valve stem seal A seal that surrounds the top of the valve stem to prevent excessive oil from leaking into the valve stem.

understeer A condition in which a vehicle's front wheels turn sharper than the vehicle's direction when the vehicle is steered around a corner. This vehicle is said to be "loose" in the corners.

unibody design A vehicle design that does not use a rigid frame to support the body. The body panels are designed to provide the strength for the vehicle.

uniform pitch A spring whose pitch (the distance from the center of one coil to the center of the adjacent coil) is the same distance throughout.

Uniform Tire Quality Grading (UTQG) A standardized grading system established by the National Highway Traffic Safety Administration (NHTSA) designed to provide tire buyers with a comparative measure of a tire's tread life, traction, and temperature characteristics.

unitized wheel bearing hub An assembly consisting of the hub, wheel bearing(s), and possibly the wheel flange, which is preassembled and ready to be installed on a vehicle.

universal joint (u-joint) A cross-shaped joint with bearings on each leg where one set of parallel legs is connected to the end of one shaft and the other set of parallel legs is connected to the end of a second shaft. This arrangement allows the shafts to operate at shallow angles to each other.

unsprung mass Any part of the steering and suspension system that is not supported by springs. A large amount of unsprung weight will cause the tire to hop off the ground when hitting bumps, as the weight will overcome dampening of the shock absorbers.

unsprung weight *See* unsprung mass.

urea A chemical reactant specifically designed for use in selective catalytic reduction systems to reduce nitrogen oxides. Also called diesel exhaust fluid.

US Department of Transportation (DOT) A federal agency that regulates transportation safety in the United States, including vehicles' wheels and tires. The DOT requires a code—a series of letters and numbers—to be stamped into the sidewall of every tire made for public use in the United States. These codes contain information such as the date of manufacture and the plant where the tire was manufactured.

V blocks Metal blocks with a V-shaped cutout for holding shafts while working on them. Also referred to as vee blocks.

V engine A term used to describe an engine configuration that uses a single bank of cylinders staggered at a shallow 15-degree V.

vacuum A pressure in an enclosed area that is lower than atmospheric pressure.

vacuum advance unit A mechanism that controls ignition timing advance in relation to engine load and causes the spark at the spark plug to occur sooner based on engine conditions. Its function is to improve fuel economy and, in doing so, reduce exhaust emissions.

vacuum bleeding Bleeding process that uses a vacuum bleeder to pull the air and old brake fluid from the system.

vacuum gauge A device used to measure the amount of vacuum an engine can generate during various operating conditions.

vacuum modulator A device on a hydraulically controlled transmission that converts engine manifold vacuum into an engine load signal called modulator pressure.

vacuum pump A pump used to evacuate the air-conditioning system and put it into a deep vacuum or low pressure to remove moisture.

vacuum servo A vacuum-controlled device that moves the air doors of the air box. It is controlled by the vacuum that comes from the vacuum-type climate control panel.

vacuum tube fluorescent (VTF) A type of lighting used for instrumentation displays on vehicle instrument panel clusters. This type of lighting emits a very bright light with high contrast and can display in various colors. Also called vacuum fluorescent display (VFD).

validating statement A statement that shows common interest in the topic being discussed.

valve A device used to control the flow of air and fuel into the combustion chamber and exhaust gases out of the combustion chamber.

valve body An aluminum or cast iron housing inside the transmission that houses the majority of the valves that control transmission operation.

valve core The one-way spring-loaded valve that screws into the valve stem that allows air to be pumped into a tire and prevents it from flowing out.

valve cover gasket A gasket used to seal the valve cover (also called a rocker arm cover or cylinder head cover) to the cylinder head assembly.

valve face A machined surface on the back of the valve head; this area seals onto the valve seat in the cylinder head.

valve float A condition that occurs when the valves are moving so fast that the spring tension is not great enough to fully seat the valves as designed.

valve guide An insert in the cylinder head through which the valve stem passes and moves.

valve head The portion of the valve that is exposed to the combustion chamber and contains the valve face and margin.

valve keeper A device used to keep the valve spring retainers attached to the valve while in the cylinder head.

valve lifter A device that transfers motion from the cam lobe to a pushrod or directly acts on the valve and spring, depending on if the cam is in the engine block or the cylinder head; sometimes called a tappet.

valve margin The flat surface on the outer edge of the valve head between the valve head and the valve face.

valve overlap The time, usually expressed in degrees of crankshaft rotation, during which both the intake valve and the exhaust valve are open at the same time.

valve seat An integral part of the head, or circular metal rings that are pressed into the cylinder head, that makes up the mating surface where the valve face sits when it is closed.

valve spring A metal coil spring that returns valves to their fully closed positions after being opened.

valve spring retainer A washer-shaped piece of metal positioned near the top of the valve stem that holds the top of the valve spring to keep pressure on the valve while in the cylinder head.

valve stem The shaft that is attached to the valve head and provides the sliding surface for the valve in its guide as it opens and closes.

valve stem (tire) A rubber or steel piece that attaches the tire valve to the rim.

valve stem cap A cap that fits tightly onto the valve stem to prevent debris from clogging it and acts as a secondary seal.

valve tip The end of the valve stem against which the rocker arm, cam follower, or hydraulic bucket-style lifter directly presses to open the valve.

valve train A system encompassing all of the parts used in the opening and closing of the valves.

vapor lock A situation in which vapor forms in the fuel line, and the bubbles of vapor block the flow of fuel and stop the engine.

vaporization The changing of a liquid to a gas through boiling.

variable reluctance sensor A type of wheel speed sensor that uses the principle of magnetic induction to create its signal.

variable resistor A component that has a mechanism for varying resistance.

variable voltage signal A signal that changes based on what the sensor is reading; for example, as temperature varies, so does the voltage signal to the ECU.

variable-diameter pulley (VDP) A type of CVT that uses two pulleys with moveable sheaves, allowing the effective diameter of the pulleys to change, resulting in variable gear ratios.

variable-orifice PVC system A system in which a replaceable, spring-loaded PCV valve regulates gas flow. The position of the PCV valve is controlled by the pressure in the manifold.

vehicle emission control information (VECI) label A label used by technicians to identify engine and emission control information for the vehicle.

vehicle hoist A type of vehicle lifting tool designed to lift the entire vehicle.

vehicle identification number (VIN) A unique serial number that is assigned to each vehicle produced.

vehicle jack A tool for lifting a vehicle.

vehicle safety certification (VSC) label A label certifying that the vehicle meets the Federal Motor Vehicle Safety, Bumper, and Theft Prevention Standards in effect at the time of manufacture.

vehicle speed sensor (VSS) A sensor used by the PCM to measure vehicle speed. It is often located in the transmission extension housing.

vent solenoid A solenoid that allows fresh air to enter the evaporative system during a purge event. Also used for an evaporative system monitoring test.

ventilated rotor A type of brake rotor with passages between the rotor surfaces that are used to improve heat transfer to the atmosphere.

venturi effect The reduction in pressure that results when a fluid or air flows through a constricted section of pipe.

vernier calipers An accurate measuring device for internal, external, and depth measurements that incorporates fixed and adjustable jaws.

viscosity The measurement of the thickness of a liquid.

viscosity index improver An oil additive that resists a change in viscosity over a range of temperatures.

viscosity value A measurement of resistance to diesel fuel flow.

viscous coupler Called a fan clutch, a hub that connects the water pump drive to the cooling fan using a temperature-sensitive viscous fluid to cause the fan to turn faster as the temperature of the air pulled through the radiator increases.

viscous coupling An silicone clutch assembly used in all-wheel drive differentials to provide a slight amount of differential action for control of axle rotational speeds.

volatile organic compound (VOC) The hydrocarbons in petroleum products that contribute to combustion.

volt The unit used to measure potential difference or electrical pressure.

voltage drop The amount of potential difference between two points in a circuit.

volumetric efficiency (VE) A ratio, given as a percentage, of the amount of air actually inducted at a given engine speed at full throttle compared to the internal engine displacement. For a normally aspirated engine (without supercharging or turbocharging), an engine's volumetric efficiency may peak at around 85%. Peak engine torque is developed at peak volumetric efficiency.

VR engine A term used to describe an engine configuration consisting of a single bank of cylinders staggered at a shallow 15-degree V within the bank.

W engine A term used to describe an engine configuration consisting of two VR cylinder banks in a deep V arrangement.

wad punch A type of punch that is hollow for cutting circular shapes in soft materials such as gaskets.

warding file A type of thin, flat file with a tapered end.

warm-up cycle One drive cycle, during which the vehicle starts out cold, warms up, and then cools down after the driving cycle.

warpage A change in the shape of a surface due to distortion or wear.

waste cylinder The cylinder in a waste spark ignition system that receives a spark near the top of its exhaust stroke.

waste spark ignition system An ignition system in which each ignition coil serves two cylinders, with each end of the secondary winding attached by a high-tension lead to a spark plug. The spark is used to ignite the air–fuel mixture in one cylinder and has no effect on the other cylinder.

wastegate A pressure regulator device that allows control of the pressure produced by the turbocharger. The wastegate moves to allow exhaust gases to bypass the turbine wheel of the turbocharger and flow down the exhaust pipe.

water fade Brake fade caused by water-soaked brake linings.

water jacket A passageway for coolant to flow inside the engine block that is formed when the block is cast.

watt The unit for measuring electrical power.

Watt's linkage Another name for a rigid-axle coil-spring suspension that uses two bars similar to a panhard rod and a pivot point on the axle to keep the axle from moving in turns.

web A reinforced area of a metal part formed during the casting process to create strength and durability.

wedge combustion chamber A combustion chamber design where the valves are often directly lined up beside each other in a row and positioned at an angle over the pistons, forming a wedge-shaped combustion chamber.

weight matching The process of matching the tire's lightest point with the rim's heaviest point (generally at the valve stem) for the purpose of reducing the tire's radial imbalance.

weight transfer Weight moving from one set of wheels to the other set of wheels during braking, acceleration, or cornering.

Welch plug A soft, round, metal disc pressed into the engine block to plug a water jacket or oil passageway.

welding helmet Protective gear designed for arc welding; it provides protection against foreign particles entering the eye, and the lens is tinted to reduce the glare of the welding arc.

wet sleeve A replaceable steel cylinder installed into the block that provides a wear surface for the piston and rings. It is in direct contact with coolant on its outside surface.

wheel alignment The practice of aligning the wheels of the vehicle to the centerline of the vehicle and to each other. It ensures that the vehicle will handle correctly and gives best tire wear.

wheel assembly A term used to encompass all components of the wheel and tire.

wheel bearing A component that allows the wheels to rotate freely while supporting the weight of the vehicle, made up of an inner race, outer race, rollers or balls, and a cage.

wheel center The part of the wheel containing the holes for the lug studs.

wheel cylinder A hydraulic cylinder with one or two pistons, seals, dust boots, and a bleeder screw that pushes the brake shoes into contact with the brake drum to slow or stop the vehicle.

wheel cylinder piston clamp A tool that prevents the pistons from being pushed out of the wheel cylinders while the brake shoes are being replaced.

wheel retaining nuts Lug nuts used to hold the wheel on the hub.

wheel rim The part on which the tire is mounted. Also called a "wheel" or "rim."

wheel speed sensor A device that creates an analog or digital signal according to the speed of the wheel.

wheel studs Threaded fasteners that are pressed into the wheel hub flange and used to bolt the wheel onto the vehicle.

wire A conductor usually made of multistranded copper with an external insulated coating.

wire feed welder A welding machine that automatically feeds the filler wire by operating a trigger mechanism on a welding gun.

wiring diagram A schematic drawing and symbol representation of the wiring and components; also called electrical schematic.

wiring harness A collection of wires or cables insulated from each other but bound together.

wiring harness connector A plug that contains multiple terminals with male and female ends.

wishbone control arm Another term for an A-arm.

Woodruff key A half-round, rectangular key that is placed into a half-round, rectangular opening in the nose of the crankshaft or other round shafts found on the engine.

work The process by which one type of energy is transformed into another type of energy.

working pressure The pressure within a hydraulic system while the system is being operated.

worm A gear with a helical, threaded shaft that is attached to the steering column and meshes with a worm wheel that transfers motion from the steering wheel to the steering linkage.

worm gear steering A robust steering system frequently used on heavier vehicles that uses a worm to turn a meshed worm wheel to provide gear reduction, making steering easier for the driver.

worm shaft The protrusion of the worm gear that serves as the point of attachment to the steering column.

wrap leaf A spring containing spring eyes.

wrenches A generic term to describe tools that tighten and loosen fasteners with hexagonal heads.

XH-7 A form of desiccant used with pure R-134a.

XH-9 A form of desiccant used when the refrigerant may not be pure, such as with some imports.

yaw Movement of a vehicle around its z-axis (vertical axis) felt when the vehicle deviates from its straight path, as when skidding sideways and the rear comes around.

yaw sensor A sensor that measures the amount a vehicle is turning around its vertical axis. This information is used by the ESC system to know how much a vehicle is turning.

yield point The point at which a bolt is stretched so hard that it will not return to its original length when loosened; it is measured in pounds per square inch of bolt cross section.

zero camber A tire with no tilt or zero camber angle.

zero offset A condition in which the plane of the hub mounting surface is even with the centerline of the wheel.

zero scrub radius A condition in which the point of center contact between the road surface and the tire and the point where the steering axis centerline contacts the road surface intersect at the road surface.

Zyglo™ A crack detection method used on engine blocks and cylinder heads that uses magnetism and a fluorescent light to find cracks in ferrous metal.

INDEX

Note: Page numbers followed by *f*, or *t* indicate materials in figures, or tables, respectively.

A

B

D

G

H

I

M

S

T

U

V

W

X

Y

Z